The Interlinear HEBREW/GREEK ENGLISH Bible

Volume Three

Psalm 56–Malachi

The Interlinear HEBREW/GREEK ENGLISH Bible

Volume Three

Psalm 56–Malachi

Jay Green,
general editor and translator

ASSOCIATED PUBLISHERS AND AUTHORS, INC.
EVANSVILLE, INDIANA 47713
1978

The Interlinear Hebrew-Greek-English Bible

Published by
ASSOCIATED PUBLISHERS AND AUTHORS, INC.
Evansville, Indiana

Printed in the United States of America

Preface

This third volume of ***The Interlinear Bible*** marks a milestone in the history of Bible study, for it completes the entire Old Testament. And this is of course the first time that this gigantic task has been accomplished. In fact, before this project began, there were only two portions of the Old Testament in interlinear form: ***Genesis*** and ***Exodus***; and, ***The Psalms***. Now, by God's marvelous provision, you have all of it to enrich your souls.

There has been a further application of scholarly minds to the third volume, even more than was possible with the first two. The result, in our opinion, is a still more accurate representation of God's word. You will find in this volume that the accumulation of that wisdom which comes only from experience has brought to this volume the full revelation of God's word that we intended from the start. To assure you of such accuracy, more time and effort were necessary. This explains the 'delay' in publication.

The eagerness of those awaiting this volume is appreciated. For having done without this kind of help for so long, and finding in the first two volumes so much in the way of time saving, accuracy without toil, immediate vocabulary building, etc., owners of the first two volumes 'can't wait' for the rest of the work. More than a thousand letters, and numerous telephone calls, have come to the General Editor, seeking word as to when this third volume would appear. And it is most gratifying to note that this overwhelming response comes from persons in all walks of life. Of course, there is a larger representation of those in scholarly positions, particularly those engaged in the teaching, or learning, of Hebrew. For the first time, we are told, some Hebrew professors have commended an interlinear to their students as a vocabulary builder. But perhaps more remarkable is the interest being shown by those who do not know the Hebrew language at all. And these are not only the preachers and teachers, as one would suppose, but to their considerable ranks is added thousands of 'lay' students of the Bible. These serious students recognize the value of this work. Needless to say, we rejoice in the strong interest evinced by every variety and every level of Bible student.

The fourth volume, which comprises ***The New Testament***, is in progress, God willing, it will be delivered in a few months. In the interim, your prayers are solicited.

JAY GREEN

INVITATION TO PARTICIPATE IN THE NEXT EDITION OF *THE INTERLINEAR BIBLE*

God's people want, and desperately need, the word of God in its most accurate form, not in a paraphrase, much less in a commentary disguised as a Bible. *The Interlinear Bible* demonstrates that word-for-word translation is the only way to achieve such an accurate Bible. In translating into English the original languages, we have attempted within the limitations noted above to give the true sense and meaning of each of God's words to the reader of *The Interlinear Bible*. We recognize, however, that God gives gifts of time, talents, and specialized knowledge to many different individuals. Some of you may very well be able to suggest to us improved renderings of certain portions of the Bible, and your suggestions will be gladly received. Because we do not want to invite a state of confusion in the submission of such suggestions for improvement, we must establish the following rules under which such suggestions are submitted:

A. A clear communication from the word of God is a matter of interest and the responsibility of the whole body of Christ. To sharpen such a communication is the duty of each of you, provided you have abilities in that area.

B. Your suggestions must be for constructive purposes only and must be submitted within the framework and format which is now in use in this Bible.

C. Please observe the following instructions: (1) Suggestions must be brief. There is no staff to read long dissertations on the reasoning behind your suggestion;. (2) Give relative evidence. Particularly cite Biblical usage, because we consider that to be more important than etymology alone; also cite authorities, periodicals, or significant monographs. (3) Your suggestion must be on the basis of a word-on-word translation, rather than "conceptual idea"-on-word. It is not our purpose to re-express the word of God according to our concepts, but to render each word according to its Biblical meaning. (4) All suggestions must be based on the Received Text, either the Masoretic text or the Received Text of Stephens, 1550. No emendations, variant readings, repointing, or editorial interpolation will be used. (5) Place all suggestions on a separate page. Do not include suggestions in the body of a letter regarding other matters. (6) You must realize that you will receive no correspondence in regard to your suggestions. Every suggestion will be carefully considered by our reviewers, but there will be no staff set up for the purpose of carrying on correspondence with those who are interested enough in an accurate rendering of God's word to make suggestions for improvement in *The Interlinear Bible*.

D. Send all suggestions to: Editor, A.P.&A., P.O. Box 5103, Wilmington, Delaware 19808.

HOW TO READ THE ENGLISH LINES UNDER THE HEBREW, OR GREEK

1. Read the English in Hebrew order, that is from right to left.
2. Read the top line first, the line directly under the Hebrew.
3. Read from right to left on the first line, then on the second line.
4. Proceed to the next Hebrew word, reading the top English line first.

In reading the Greek New Testament section, however:

1. You will read in English order, that is from left to right.
2. Since Greek sentence structure is different, words will not be in order.
3. Refer to the English translation on the side to pick up word order.

The Interlinear Hebrew-Greek-English Bible

FOUR VOLUME EDITION

Contents

Hebrew Alphabet

1. The Hebrew is read *from right to left*. The Alphabet consists of 22 letters (and their variations), which are all regarded as *consonants*, being enunciated by the aid of certain "points" or marks, mostly beneath the letters, and which serve as *vowels*. There is no distinction of *capitals*, *italics*, etc.

2. The letters are as follows:

No.	Form.	Name.		Transliteration and Power.
1.	א	'Aleph	*(aw'-lef)*	' unappreciable
2.	ב	Bêyth	*(bayth)*	**b**
3.	ג	Gîymel	*(ghee'-mel)*	**g** hard = γ
4.	ד	Dâleth	*(daw'-leth)*	**d** [cent
5.	ה	Hê'	*(hay)*	**h**, often quies-
6.	ו	Vâv	*(vawv)*	**v**, or **w** quies-
7.	ז	Zayin	*(zah'-yin)*	**z**, as in *zeal* [cent
8.	ח	Chêyth	*(khayth)*	German **ch** = χ [(nearly *kh*)
9.	ט	Têyth	*(tayth)*	**ṭ** = ת [cent
10.	י	Yôwd	*(yode)*	**y**, often quies-
11.	כ, final ך	Kaph	*(caf)*	**k** = ק
12.	ל	Lâmed	*(law'-med)*	**l**
13.	מ, final ם	Mêm	*(mame)*	**m**
14.	נ, final ן	Nûwn	*(noon)*	**n**
15.	ס	Çâmek	*(saw'-mek)*	**ç** = *s* sharp = שׂ
16.	ע	'Ayin	*(ah'-yin)*	' peculiar *
17.	פ, final ף	Phê'	*(fay)*	**ph** = *f* = φ
	פּ	Pê'	*(pay)*	**p**
18.	צ, final ץ	Tsâdêy	*(tsaw-day')*	**ts**
19.	ק	Qôwph	*(cofe)*	**q** = *k* = כ
20.	ר	Rêysh	*(raysh)*	**r**
21.	שׂ	Sîyn	*(seen)*	**s** sharp = ס = σ
	שׁ	Shîyn	*(sheen)*	**sh**
22.	ת	Thâv	*(thawv)*	**th**, as in THin
	תּ	Tâv	*(tawv)*	**t** = ט = τ [= ϑ

* The letter 'Ayin, owing to the difficulty experienced by Occidentals in pronouncing it accurately (it is a deep guttural sound, like that made in *gargling*), is generally neglected (i.e. passed over silently) in reading. We have represented it to the eye (but not exactly to the ear) by the Greek *rough breathing* (for distinctness and typographical convenience, a reversed *apostrophe*) in order to distinguish it from 'Âleph, which is likewise treated as silent, being similarly represented by the Greek *smooth breathing* (the *apostrophe*).

3. The *vowel-points* are the following:

Form.*	Name.		Representation and Power.
(ָ)	Qâmêts	*(caw-mates')*	**â**, as in *All*
(ַ)	Pattach	*('pat'-takh)*	**a**, as in *mAn*, (*fãr*)
(ֲ)	Sheᵉvâ'-Pattach	*(she-vaw' pat'-takh)*	**ă**, as in *hAt*
(ֵ)	Tsêrêy	*(tsay-ray')*	**ê**, as in *thEY* = η
(ֶ)	Çegôwl	*(seg-ole')*	**e**, as in *thEir*; **e**, as in *mEn* = ε
(ֱ)	Sheᵉvâ'-Çegôwl	*(she-vaw' seg-ole')*	**ĕ**, as in *mEt*
(ְ)	Sheᵉvâ' †	*(she-vaw')*	ᵉ obscure, as in [*avErage*; silent, as *e* in *madE*
(ִ)	Chîyriq	*(khee'-rik)*	**î**, as in *machIne* ‡; **i**, as in *supplIant*, [(*misery*, *hIt*)
(ֹ)	Chôwlem §	*(kho'-lem)*	**ô**, as in *no* = ω
(ָ)	Short Qâmêts ‖		**o**, as in *nor* = o
(ֳ)	Sheᵉvâ'-Qâmêts	*(she-vaw' caw-mates')*	**ŏ**, as in *no'*
(וּ)	Shûwrêq *	*(shoo-rake')*	**û**, as in *crUel*
(ֻ)	Qibbûts *	*(kib'-boots)*	**u**, as in *fUll*, *rûde*

4. A point in the bosom of a letter is called *Dâgêsh'*, and is of two kinds, which must be carefully distinguished.

a. Dâgêsh *lenè* occurs only in the letters ב, ג, ד, כ, פ, ת, (technically vocalized *Bᵉgad'-Kᵉphath'*,) when they *begin* a clause or sentence, or are preceded by a consonant *sound;* and simply has the effect of removing their aspiration.†

b. Dâgêsh *fortè* may occur in any letter except א, ה, ח, ע or ר; it is equivalent to *doubling* the letter, and at the same time it removes the aspiration of a Bᵉgad-Kᵉphath letter.‡

5. The *Maqqêph'* (־), like a *hyphen*, unites words only for purposes of pronunciation (by removing the primary accent from all except the last of them), but does not affect their meaning or their grammatical construction.

* The parenthesis-marks ( ) are given here in order to show the place of the vowel-points, whether below, above, or in the middle of the letter.

† *Silent Sheᵉvâ'* is not represented by any mark in our method of transliteration, as it is understood whenever there is no other vowel-point.

‡ *Chîyriq* is thus long only when it is followed by a quiescent *yôwd* (either expressed or implied).

§ *Chôwlem* is written *fully* only over *Vâv*, which is then quiescent (*w*); but when used "defectively" (without the *Vâv*) it may be written either over the left-hand corner of the letter to which it belongs, or over the right-hand corner of the following one.

‖ Short *Qâmêts* is found only in *unaccented syllables ending with a consonant sound.*

* *Shûwrêq* is written only in the bosom of *Vâv*. Sometimes it is said to be "defectively" written (without the *Vâv*), and then takes the form of *Qibbûts*, which in such cases is called *vicarious*.

† In our system of transliteration Dâgêsh *lenè* is represented only in the letters פ and ת, because elsewhere it does not affect the pronunciation (with most Hebraists).

‡ A point in the bosom of ה is called *Mappîyq* (*mappeek'*). It occurs only in the final vowelless letter of a few words, and we have represented it by *hh*. A Dâgêsh *fortè* in the bosom of ו may easily be distinguished from the vowel *Shûwrêq* by noticing that in the former case the letter has a proper vowel-point accompanying it.

It should be noted that both kinds of Dâgêsh are often omitted in writing (being then said to be *implied*), but (in the case at least of Dâgêsh *fortè*) the word is (by most Hebraists) pronounced the same as if it were present.

bring them down to the pit of destruction, men of blood and deceit not will halve their days; but I will trust in You.

תּוֹרִדֵם לִבְאֵר שַׁחַת אַנְשֵׁי דָמִים וּמִרְמָה לֹא־יֶחֱצוּ יְמֵיהֶם

| their | will | not | and | blood | men | de- | the | to | bring | will |
| days | halve | | ,deceit | | of | struction | of pit | down | them |

וַאֲנִי אֶבְטַח־בָּֽךְ׃

| in | will | but |
| .You | trust | I |

PSAL. LVI. נו

PSALM 56

To the chief musician, concerning the silent dove —those far off; of David, a secret treasure —when the Philistines seized him in Gath.

[1] Favor me, O God, for man snuffs me up; all the day fighting oppresses me. [2] My watchers panted for me all the day; for many are proudly fighting over me. [3] The day I am afraid, I will trust in You. [4] In God I will praise His word; in God I have trusted; I will not fear; what will flesh do to me? [5] All the day they pervert my words; all their thoughts (are) against me for evil. [6] They stir up strife; they hide; they mark my footprints as they wait (for) my soul. [7] By iniquity do they escape? In anger the peoples cast down, O God. [8] You have counted my wandering; O put my tears in Your bottle; (are they) not in Your Book? [9] Then my enemies will turn back, in the day I call; this I know, for God (is) for me. [10] In God I will praise the word; in Jehovah I will praise the word. [11] In God I have trusted; I will not fear; what will man do to me? [12] On me, O God, (are) Your vows; I will render to You thank offerings. [13] For You have delivered my soul from death. (Do You) not (keep) my feet from falling, (so that I) may walk before God in the light of the living?

1 לַמְנַצֵּחַ ׀ עַל־יוֹנַת אֵלֶם רְחֹקִים לְדָוִד מִכְתָּם בֶּאֱחֹז אֹתוֹ

| him | in | secret | a | of | those | silent | the concern- | chief the | To |
| | seizing | —treasure | David | ;off far | | dove | ing | | musician |

2 פְלִשְׁתִּים בְּגַת׃ חָנֵּנִי אֱלֹהִים כִּי־שְׁאָפַנִי אֱנוֹשׁ כָּל־הַיּוֹם

| the | all | ;man | snuffs | for | O | Favor | in | the |
| day | | up | me | ,God | ,me | | .Gath | Philistines |

3 לֹחֵם יִלְחָצֵנִי׃ שָׁאֲפוּ שׁוֹרְרַי כָּל־הַיּוֹם כִּי־רַבִּים לֹחֲמִים

| are | many | for | the | all | my | Panted | oppresses | fighting |
| fighting | | ;day | | | watchers | me for | | .me |

4 לִי מָרוֹם׃ יוֹם אִירָא אֲנִי אֵלֶיךָ אֶבְטָח׃
5 בֵּאלֹהִים אֲהַלֵּל

| will | I | God | In | will | in | I | am I | The | .proudly over |
| praise | | | | .trust | You | | | | me |

דְבָרוֹ בֵּאלֹהִים בָּטַחְתִּי לֹא אִירָא מַה־יַּעֲשֶׂה בָשָׂר לִי׃

| to | flesh | will | what | will I | not | have I | in | His |
| ?me | | do | | ;fear | | ;trusted | God | ;word |

6 כָּל־הַיּוֹם דְּבָרַי יְעַצֵּבוּ עָלַי כָּל־מַחְשְׁבֹתָם לָרָע׃
7 יָגוּרוּ ׀

| stir they | for | their | (are) | against | they | my | the | All |
| ;strife up | .evil | thoughts | | me | ;pervert | words | day |

8 יִצְפֹּנוּ הֵמָּה עֲקֵבַי יִשְׁמֹרוּ כַּאֲשֶׁר קִוּוּ נַפְשִׁי׃ עַל־אָוֶן

| iniquity By | (for) | they | as | ,mark | my | they | they |
| | .soul my | wait | | | footprints | | ,hide |

9 פַּלֶּט־לָמוֹ בְּאַף עַמִּים ׀ הוֹרֵד אֱלֹהִים׃ נֹדִי סָפַרְתָּה אָתָּה

| ;You | have | wan-My | O | cast | the | In | for escape |
| | counted | dering | .God | ,down | peoples | anger | ?them is |

10 שִׂימָה דִמְעָתִי בְנֹאדֶךָ הֲלֹא בְּסִפְרָתֶךָ׃ אָז ׀ יָשׁוּבוּ אוֹיְבַי

| my | will | Then | ?Book | Your in | (they are) | Your into | my | O |
| enemies | turn | | | not | | ;bottle | tears | put |

11 אָחוֹר בְּיוֹם אֶקְרָא זֶה־יָדַעְתִּי כִּי־אֱלֹהִים לִי׃ בֵּאלֹהִים

| In | for | God | for | I | this | I | the | in | back |
| God | .me | (is) | | ,know | | ;call | day |

12 אֲהַלֵּל דָּבָר בַּיהוָה אֲהַלֶּל־דָּבָר׃ בֵּאלֹהִים בָּטַחְתִּי לֹא אִירָא

| will I | not | have I | In | the | will I | in | the | will I |
| .fear | ;trusted | God | .word | praise | Jehovah | ;word | praise |

13 מַה־יַּעֲשֶׂה אָדָם לִי׃ עָלַי אֱלֹהִים נְדָרֶיךָ אֲשַׁלֵּם תּוֹדֹת

| thank | will I | Your (are) | O | On | to | man | do will | What |
| offerings | render | ;vows | ,God | ,me | | | ?me |

14 לָךְ׃ כִּי הִצַּלְתָּ נַפְשִׁי מִמָּוֶת הֲלֹא רַגְלַי מִדֶּחִי לְהִתְהַלֵּךְ

| (I that so) | from | my | (You Do) | from | my | have You | For | to |
| walk may | ,falling | feet | (keep) not | .death | soul | delivered | | .You |

לִפְנֵי אֱלֹהִים בְּאוֹר הַחַיִּים׃

| the | the in | God | before |
| ?living | of light | |

PSALM 57

To the Chief Musician. Do not destroy. A Secret Treasure of David, when he fled from Saul in the cave.

[1] Be merciful to me, O God, be merciful to me, for my soul trusts in You; yea, in the shadow of Your wings I will make my hiding-place, until the great destruction passes by. [2] I will cry to God most High, to God who works for me. [3] He shall send from Heaven and save me; He will shame the one who crushes me. Selah. God shall send His mercy and His truth. [4] My soul (is) among lions; I lie (among) those who are set on fire, the sons of men, whose teeth (are) spears and arrows, and their tongue is a sharp sword. [5] Be praised above the heavens, O God; let Your glory (be) over the whole earth.

[6] They have prepared a net for my steps; my soul is bowed down; (they have) dug a pit before me; they have fallen into it. Selah. [7] My heart is fixed, O God, my heart is fixed; I will sing and give praise. [8] Wake up my glory! Wake up, harp and lyre! I will stir the morning-dawn with praise. [9] I will praise You among the peoples, O Lord, I will sing to You among the nations. [10] For Your Mercy (is) great to the heavens, and Your truth to the clouds. [11] Be exalted above the heavens, O God; Your glory over the whole earth.

PSAL. LVII נז

PSALM 57

1 למנצח אל־תשחת לדוד מכתם בברחו מפני־שאול
Saul's from he when secret a of do not chief the To
face fled ,treasure ;David ;destroy ,musician

2 במערה: חנני אלהים | חנני כי בך חסיה נפשי ובצל־
in ,Yea my takes in for merciful be O merciful Be the in
shadow ;soul refuge You ,me to ,God ,me to .cave

3 כנפיך אחסה עד־יעבר הות: אקרא לאלהים עליון
Most God to will I .calamities passes until take I Your
;High call by ,refuge wings'

4 לאל גמר עלי: ישלח משמים | ויושיעני חרף שאפי
who him will He save and from shall He for who to
.me crushes shame ;me Heaven send .me works God

5 סלה ישלח אלהים חסדו ואמתו: נפשי | בתוך לבאם
;lions (is) My His and His God shall .Selah
among soul .truth mercy send

אשכבה להטים בני־אדם שניהם חנית וחצים ולשונם
their and and (are) their ;men the those lie I
tongue ;arrows spears teeth of sons ,fire on (among)

6 חרב חדה: רומה על־השמים אלהים על כל־הארץ
the all over ,God O the above Be .sharp a (is)
earth ,heavens exalted sword

7 כבודך: רשת הכינו לפעמי כפף נפשי כרו לפני שיחה
;pit a before they my bowed is my for they net A Your
me dig ;soul down ,steps prepared .glory

8 נפלו בתוכה סלה: נכון לבי אלהים נכון לבי אשירה
will I my fixed O My is .Selah .it into have they
sing ;heart is ,God ,heart fixed fallen

9 ואזמרה: עורה כבודי עורה הנבל וכנור אעירה שחר:
the will I and harp Wake my Wake give and
.dawn awaken .lyre ,up !glory ,up .praise

10
11 אודך בעמים | אדני אזמרך בלאמים: כי־גדל עד־שמים
the to (is) For the among sing will I O among will I
heavens great .nations You to ,Lord ,peoples the You praise

12 חסדך ועד־שחקים אמתך: רומה על־שמים אלהים על
over O the above Be Your the and Your
,God ,heavens exalted .truth clouds to ,mercy

כל־הארץ כבודך:
Your the all
.glory earth

PSALM 58

To the Chief Musician. Do not destroy. A secret treasure, of David.

[1] Will you indeed speak righteousness in silence? Do you judge uprightly, O sons of men? [2] Yes, in heart you work

PSAL. LVIII נח

PSALM 58

1
2 למנצח אל־תשחת לדוד מכתם: האמנם אלם צדק
righteous- in ,Indeed secret a of do not chief the To
ness silence .treasure ;David ;destroy ;musician

3 תדברון מישרים תשפטו בני אדם: אף־בלב עולת
wicked- in ,Yes ?men O You Do uprightly you will
ness heart of sons ,judge ?speak

violence of your hands in the land. [3] The wicked are estranged from the womb; (they go) astray from the belly, speaking lies. [4] Their poison (is) like the poison of a snake; like the deaf adder, he stops his ear, [5] which will not hear the charmer's voice, a skillful caster of spells. [6] O God, break their teeth in their mouth; break out the big teeth of the young lions, O Jehovah. [7] Let them melt away like waters; they flow off to them; he bends his arrows; (let them be) as though (they were) cut off, [8] as a snail goes (into) melting, a miscarriage of a woman; they do not see the sun. [9] Before your pots can feel the thorns, whether green (or) glowing, He shall sweep it away. [10] The righteous shall rejoice when he sees vengeance; he shall wash his feet in the blood of the wicked. [11] And man will say, Truly, a reward (is) to the righteous; truly, there is a God judging in the earth.

4 תִּפְעָלוּן בָּאָרֶץ חֲמַס יְדֵיכֶם תְּפַלֵּסוּן׃ זֹרוּ רְשָׁעִים מֵרָחֶם

the from the Are you your the the in ;work You
;womb wicked estranged .weigh hands of violence land

5 תָּעוּ מִבֶּטֶן דֹּבְרֵי כָזָב׃ חֲמַת־לָמוֹ כִּדְמוּת חֲמַת־נָחָשׁ כְּמוֹ־

like a the like is to poison lies speakers the from they
;snake of poison them (is) of ,belly stray

6 פֶתֶן חֵרֵשׁ יַאְטֵם אָזְנוֹ׃ אֲשֶׁר לֹא־יִשְׁמַע לְקוֹל מְלַחֲשִׁים

the the will not which his he ,deaf the
,charmers of voice hear ;ear stops adder

7 חוֹבֵר חֲבָרִים מְחֻכָּם׃ אֱלֹהִים הֲרָס־שִׁנֵּימוֹ בְּפִימוֹ מַלְתְּעוֹת

big the their in their break ,God O .skillful spells a
of teeth ;mouth teeth of caster

8 כְּפִירִים נְתֹץ ׀ יְהוָה׃ יִמָּאֲסוּ כְמוֹ־מַיִם יִתְהַלְּכוּ־לָמוֹ

to they ;waters like them Let O break young the
;them off flow away melt .Jehovah ,out lions

9 יִדְרֹךְ חִצָּו כְּמוֹ יִתְמֹלָלוּ׃ כְּמוֹ שַׁבְּלוּל תֶּמֶס יַהֲלֹךְ נֵפֶל

mis- a ,goes (into) snail a as were they as his he
of carriage melting ,off cut though ;arrows bends

10 אֵשֶׁת בַּל־חָזוּ שָׁמֶשׁ׃ בְּטֶרֶם יָבִינוּ סִּירֹתֵיכֶם אָטָד כְּמוֹ־

as the your can Before the they not a
,thorns pots feel .sun see ,woman

11 חַי כְּמוֹ־חָרוֹן יִשְׂעָרֶנּוּ׃ יִשְׂמַח צַדִּיק כִּי־חָזָה נָקָם פְּעָמָיו

his ;vengeance he when The shall sweep shall He glowing as ,green
feet sees righteous rejoice .away it

12 יִרְחַץ בְּדַם הָרָשָׁע׃ וְיֹאמַר אָדָם אַךְ־פְּרִי לַצַּדִּיק אַךְ יֵשׁ־

there truly the to (is) a ,Truly ,man will And the the in shall he
is ;righteous reward say .wicked of blood wash

אֱלֹהִים שֹׁפְטִים בָּאָרֶץ׃

the in judging God a
.earth

PSAL. LIX נט

PSALM 59

PSALM 59

To the Chief Musician. Do not destroy. A Secret Treasure of David, when Saul sent, and they watched the house to kill him.

[1] Deliver me from my enemies, O my God; set me on high from the ones who rise up against me. [2] Deliver me from the workers of evil, and save me from bloody men. [3] For, lo, they lie in wait for my soul; the mighty are gathered against me; not (for) my transgression, and not my sin, O Jehovah. [4] Without (my) fault they run and prepare themselves; awaken to help me, and look. [5] And You, O Jehovah God of hosts, the God of Israel: Awake to visit all the

1 לַמְנַצֵּחַ אַל־תַּשְׁחֵת לְדָוִד מִכְתָּם בִּשְׁלֹחַ שָׁאוּל וַיִּשְׁמְרוּ

they and ,Saul when secret a of do not chief the To
watched sent ,treasure ;David ;destroy ;musician

2 אֶת־הַבַּיִת לַהֲמִיתוֹ׃ הַצִּילֵנִי מֵאֹיְבַי ׀ אֱלֹהָי מִמִּתְקוֹמְמַי

rising those from my O my from Deliver kill to the
me against ;God ,enemies me .him house

3 תְּשַׂגְּבֵנִי׃ הַצִּילֵנִי מִפֹּעֲלֵי אָוֶן וּמֵאַנְשֵׁי דָמִים הוֹשִׁיעֵנִי׃

save ,blood from and ;evil the from Deliver me set
.me of men of workers me .high on

4 כִּי הִנֵּה אָרְבוּ לְנַפְשִׁי יָגוּרוּ עָלַי עַזִּים לֹא־פִשְׁעִי וְלֹא־

and my (for) not mighty against they my for lie they ,lo ,For
not ,transgression —men ,me strive ;soul wait in

5 חַטָּאתִי יְהוָה׃ בְּלִי־עָוֺן יְרוּצוּן וְיִכּוֹנָנוּ עוּרָה לִקְרָאתִי וּרְאֵה׃

and meet to awaken and they (my) Without O my (for)
.see me ;prepare run fault .Jehovah ,sin

6 וְאַתָּה יְהוָה־אֱלֹהִים צְבָאוֹת אֱלֹהֵי יִשְׂרָאֵל הָקִיצָה לִפְקֹד

visit to awake ;Israel the ,hosts God O And
of God (of) Jehovah ,You

nations; be not merciful to any plotting evil. Selah. [6] They return at evening; they howl like a dog, and go around the city. [7] Behold, they bellow with their mouth; swords (are) in their lips; for (they say), Who hears? [8] But You, O Jehovah, shall laugh at them; You will mock at all the nations. [9] O my Strength, to You let me watch; for God (is) my strong tower. [10] The God of my mercy shall meet me; God shall let me see (my desire) on my enemies. [11] Do not kill them, lest my people forget; scatter them by Your power and bring them down, O Jehovah our shield. [12] (For) the sin of their mouth is the word of their lips, and let them be captured in their pride, and for cursing and lying (which) they speak. [13] Consume (them) in (Your) anger; consume, so that they may not be; and they shall know that God (is) ruling in Jacob, to the ends of the earth. Selah.

[14] Yes, they shall return at evening; let them howl like the dog and go around the city; [15] let them wander up and down for food, and growl if they are not satisfied. [16] But I will sing of Your power; yes, I will sing of Your mercy in the morning. For You have been my strong tower, and my hiding-place in the day of my trouble. [17] To You, O my strength, I will sing; for God (is) my strong tower, the God of my mercy.

8 כָּל־הַגּוֹיִם אַל־תָּחֹן כָּל־בֹּגְדֵי אָוֶן סֶלָה׃ יָשׁוּבוּ לָעֶרֶב
at They .Selah .evil slyly any Be not the all
;evening return plotting to merciful .nations

9 יֶהֱמוּ כַכָּלֶב וִיסוֹבְבוּ עִיר׃ הִנֵּה ׀ יַבִּיעוּן בְּפִיהֶם חֲרָבוֹת
swords their with they ,Behold the go and the like they
;mouth bellow .city around ,dog howl

10 בְּשִׂפְתוֹתֵיהֶם כִּי־מִי שֹׁמֵעַ׃ וְאַתָּה יְהוָה תִּשְׂחַק־לָמוֹ
at shall O But ?hears Who for their in (are)
;them laugh ,Jehovah ,You (say they) ;lips

11 12 תִּלְעַג לְכָל־גּוֹיִם׃ עֻזּוֹ אֵלֶיךָ אֶשְׁמֹרָה כִּי־אֱלֹהִים מִשְׂגַּבִּי׃
my (is) God for me let to My nations all at will You
.tower strong ,watch You ;strength mock

אֱלֹהֵי חַסְדּוֹ יְקַדְּמֵנִי אֱלֹהִים יַרְאֵנִי בְשֹׁרְרָי׃ אַל־תַּהַרְגֵם ׀
slay do Not my on me let will God shall my The
,them .foes look ;me meet mercy of God

פֶּן־יִשְׁכְּחוּ עַמִּי הֲנִיעֵמוֹ בְחֵילְךָ וְהוֹרִידֵמוֹ מָגִנֵּנוּ אֲדֹנָי׃
O our bring and Your by scatter my forget lest
.Lord ,shield ,down them strength them ,people

13 חַטַּאת־פִּימוֹ דְּבַר־שְׂפָתֵימוֹ וְיִלָּכְדוּ בִגְאוֹנָם וּמֵאָלָה וּמִכַּחַשׁ
for and for and their in them let and their the (is) their sin The
lying (the) ,cursing ;pride taken be ,lips of word mouth of

14 יְסַפֵּרוּ׃ כַּלֵּה בְחֵמָה כַּלֵּה וְאֵינֵמוֹ וְיֵדְעוּ כִּי־אֱלֹהִים מֹשֵׁל
(is) God that they that they that con- in Consume they
ruling know may ,not be ,sume ;anger (them) .speak

15 בְּיַעֲקֹב לְאַפְסֵי הָאָרֶץ סֶלָה׃ וְיָשֻׁבוּ לָעֶרֶב יֶהֱמוּ כַכָּלֶב
the like shall they at they And .Selah the the to in
dog howl ;evening return shall .earth of ends ,Jacob

16 וִיסוֹבְבוּ עִיר׃ הֵמָּה יְנוּעוּן לֶאֱכֹל אִם־לֹא יִשְׂבְּעוּ וַיָּלִינוּ׃
they then are they not if ;eat to wander they the go and
.growl ,satisfied around ;city around

17 וַאֲנִי ׀ אָשִׁיר עֻזֶּךָ וַאֲרַנֵּן לַבֹּקֶר חַסְדֶּךָ כִּי־הָיִיתָ מִשְׂגָּב לִי
to strong a you for Your the in will I Yes Your will But
,me tower been have ;mercy morning of sing ;strength of sing I

18 וּמָנוֹס בְּיוֹם צַר־לִי׃ עֻזִּי אֵלֶיךָ אֲזַמֵּרָה כִּי־אֱלֹהִים מִשְׂגַּבִּי
my (is) God for will I You to my O to distress the in a and
.tower strong praise sing ,strength .me of day refuge

אֱלֹהֵי חַסְדִּי׃
my the
.mercy of God

PSAL. LX ס

PSALM 60

To the Chief Musician, on the Lily of Testimony. A Secret Treasure of David, to teach; when he struggled with Aram-naharaim, and with Aram of Zobah, when Joab returned, and struck twelve thousand of Edom in the valley of salt.

[1] O God! You who cast us off and broke us,

1 2 לַמְנַצֵּחַ עַל־שׁוּשַׁן עֵדוּת מִכְתָּם לְדָוִד לְלַמֵּד׃ בְּהַצּוֹתוֹ ׀
he when ,teach to of secret a ;Testimony the on chief the To
struggled ;David ;treasure of Lily ;musician

אֶת אֲרַם נַהֲרַיִם וְאֶת־אֲרַם צוֹבָה וַיָּשָׁב יוֹאָב וַיַּךְ אֶת־
and Joab when ,Zobah Aram and naharaim Aram- with
struck returned with

3 אֱדוֹם בְּגֵיא־מֶלַח שְׁנֵים עָשָׂר אָלֶף׃ אֱלֹהִים זְנַחְתָּנוּ פְרַצְתָּנוּ
You cast You O .thousand twelve Salt the in (of)
;us broke ;off us ,God of Valley Edom

You who were angry; now You take us back. [2] You made the earth tremble; You tore it; heal its breaks, for it is shaking. [3] You have shown Your people hard things; You made us drink the wine of trembling. [4] You have given a banner to those who fear You, to lift it up because of the truth. Selah. [5] Save (with) Your right hand and answer me, that Your beloved may be delivered. [6] God has spoken in His holiness, therefore I will rejoice; I will divide Shechem, and measure out the valley of Succoth. [7] Gilead (is) Mine, and Manasseh (is) Mine; Ephraim (is) the strength of My head; Judah (is) My lawgiver; [8] Moab (is) My washpot; over Edom I will cast out My shoe; over me, Philistia, shout in triumph. [9] Who will bring me (into) the strong city? Who will lead me into Edom? [10] Have not You, O God, cast us aside? And will You not go forth with our armies, O God? [11] Give us help against (our) foe, for vain is the deliverance of man. [12] Through God we shall do great things; for He shall tread on our foes.

אָנַפְתָּ תְּשׁוֹבֵב לָנוּ׃ הִרְעַשְׁתָּה אֶרֶץ פְּצַמְתָּהּ רְפָה שְׁבָרֶיהָ 4

its heal tore You the to made You .us take were You
,breaks ;it ;earth tremble back ;angry

כִי־מָטָה׃ הִרְאִיתָ עַמְּךָ קָשָׁה הִשְׁקִיתָנוּ יַיִן תַּרְעֵלָה׃ 5

.trembling the us make You hard- Your have You is it for
of wine drink ;ship people shown .shaking

נָתַתָּה לִּירֵאֶיךָ נֵּס לְהִתְנוֹסֵס מִפְּנֵי קֹשֶׁט סֶלָה׃ לְמַעַן 6 7

That .Selah the because be to a those to have You
.truth of ;displayed banner You fearing given

יֵחָלְצוּן יְדִידֶיךָ הוֹשִׁיעָה יְמִינְךָ וַעֲנֵנוּ׃ אֱלֹהִים דִּבֶּר 8

has God answer and Your save Your be may
spoken .me hand right (with) ,beloved delivered

בְּקָדְשׁוֹ אֶעְלֹזָה אֲחַלְּקָה שְׁכֶם וְעֵמֶק סֻכּוֹת אֲמַדֵּד׃ לִי 9

To measure Succoth the and ,Shechem will I will I His in
Me .out of valley divide ;rejoice ;holiness

גִלְעָד וְלִי מְנַשֶּׁה וְאֶפְרַיִם מָעוֹז רֹאשִׁי יְהוּדָה מְחֹקְקִי׃

My Judah My the Ephraim (is) to and ,Gilead
;lawgiver (is) ;head of strength (is) ;Manasseh Me (is)

מוֹאָב סִיר רַחְצִי עַל־אֱדוֹם אַשְׁלִיךְ נַעֲלִי עָלַי פְּלָשֶׁת 10

,Philistia on My will I Edom over My pot the Moab
me ;shoe out cast ,washing of (is)

הִתְרֹעָעִי׃ מִי יֹבִלֵנִי עִיר מָצוֹר מִי נָחַנִי עַד־אֱדוֹם׃ הֲלֹא־ 11 12

Have ?Edom into will Who ?strong the bring will Who in shout
not me lead city (into) me .triumph

אַתָּה אֱלֹהִים זְנַחְתָּנוּ וְלֹא־תֵצֵא אֱלֹהִים בְּצִבְאוֹתֵינוּ׃ 13 14

our with ,God O You will And us cast ,God O You
?armies ,forth go not ?aside

הָבָה־לָּנוּ עֶזְרָת מִצָּר וְשָׁוְא תְּשׁוּעַת אָדָם׃ בֵּאלֹהִים

Through .man the vain for against help us to Give
God of deliverance (is) ,foe (our)

נַעֲשֶׂה־חָיִל וְהוּא יָבוּס צָרֵינוּ׃

our shall He for great shall we
.foes on tread ,things do

PSAL. LXI   סא

PSALM 61

PSALM 61

To the Chief Musician, on Stringed Instruments. A (Prayer of David.

[1] Hear my cry, O God, and listen to my prayer. [2] From the end of the earth I call to You when my heart faints; O lead me to the Rock (that) is higher than I. [3] For You have been my shelter, a strong tower before the enemy. [4] I will dwell in Your tabernacle forever; I will trust in the shelter of Your wings. Selah. [5] For You, O God, have heard my vows; You appointed the

לַמְנַצֵּחַ עַל־נְגִינַת לְדָוִד׃ שִׁמְעָה אֱלֹהִים רִנָּתִי הַקְשִׁיבָה 1 2

listen and ,cry my ,God O ,Hear .David of stringed on chief the To
to ;instruments ;musician

תְּפִלָּתִי׃ מִקְצֵה הָאָרֶץ אֵלֶיךָ אֶקְרָא בַּעֲטֹף לִבִּי בְּצוּר 3

the in my when will I to the the From my
rock ;heart faints ,call You earth of end .prayer

יָרוּם מִמֶּנִּי תַנְחֵנִי׃ כִּי־הָיִיתָ מַחְסֶה לִי מִגְדַּל־עֹז מִפְּנֵי 4

before strong a for You For lead I than is (that)
tower ,me shelter been have ,me higher

אוֹיֵב׃ אָגוּרָה בְאָהָלְךָ עוֹלָמִים אֶחֱסֶה בְסֵתֶר כְּנָפֶיךָ 5

Your the in me let ;forever Your in me Let the
.wings of shelter hide tent dwell .enemy

סֶלָה׃ כִּי־אַתָּה אֱלֹהִים שָׁמַעְתָּ לִנְדָרָי נָתַתָּ יְרֻשַּׁת יִרְאֵי 6

fearers heritage a You my have O ,You For .Selah
of to gave ;vows heard ,God

inheritance of those who fear Your name. [6] You will add days to the days of the king; his years will be for many generations. [7] He shall sit enthroned forever before God; appoint mercy and truth to preserve Him. [8] Therefore I will sing praise to Your name forever, so that I may pay my vows day (by) day.

7 שְׁמֶךָ׃ יָמִים עַל־יְמֵי־מֶלֶךְ תּוֹסִיף שְׁנוֹתָיו כְּמוֹ־דֹר וָדֹר׃

genera- genera- as his will You the the to Days Your
.tion to tion years ;add king of days .name

8
9 יֵשֵׁב עוֹלָם לִפְנֵי אֱלֹהִים חֶסֶד וֶאֱמֶת מַן יִנְצְרֻהוּ׃ כֵּן

So will they ;appoint and mercy ;God before forever shall He
.him keep truth sit

אֲזַמְּרָה שִׁמְךָ לָעַד לְשַׁלְּמִי נְדָרַי יוֹם ׀ יוֹם׃

(by) day my I that ,forever Your me let
.day vows pay may name praise

PSAL. LXII סב

PSALM 62

To the Chief Musician, to Jeduthun. A Psalm of David.

[1] Only to God is my soul silent; from Him (comes) my salvation. [2] He alone (is) my rock and my salvation, my strong tower; I shall not be greatly moved. [3] How long will you break in against a man? You will shatter him, all of you, like a bowing wall, a tottering fence. [4] Surely, they plotted to cast (him) down from his excellent dignity; they delight in lies; they bless with their mouth, but they curse in their heart. Selah. [5] Only be silent to God, O my soul, for my hope comes from Him. [6] He alone (is) my rock and my salvation, my strong tower; I shall not be shaken. [7] On God (is) my salvation and my glory; my strong rock, my refuge (is) in God. [8] Trust in Him at every time, you people; pour out your heart before Him; God (is) a refuge for us. Selah. [9] Surely the sons of men (are) vanity, the sons of man (are) a lie; they go up in the scales; they (are lighter) than vanity together. [10] Trust not in oppression, and do not be vain in robbery; if riches increase to you, do not set your heart (on them). [11] God has spoken once; twice I have heard this, that power (belongs) to God. [12] Also, O Jehovah, mercy (belongs) to You; for You reward each one according to his work.

1
2 לַמְנַצֵּחַ עַל־יְדוּתוּן מִזְמוֹר לְדָוִד׃ אַךְ אֶל־אֱלֹהִים דּוּמִיָּה

(in) God to Only of psalm a ;Jeduthun to chief the To
silence .David ;musician

3 נַפְשִׁי מִמֶּנּוּ יְשׁוּעָתִי׃ אַךְ־הוּא צוּרִי וִישׁוּעָתִי מִשְׂגַּבִּי לֹא־

not strong my my and my He alone my (comes) from my (is)
;tower ,salvation rock (is) .salvation Him ;soul

4 אֶמּוֹט רַבָּה׃ עַד־אָנָה ׀ תְּהוֹתְתוּ עַל־אִישׁ תְּרָצְּחוּ כֻלְּכֶם

of all will You a against will you when Until .greatly shall I
,you ,him shatter ?man in break shaken be

5 כְּקִיר נָטוּי גָּדֵר הַדְּחוּיָה׃ אַךְ מִשְּׂאֵתוֹ ׀ יָעֲצוּ לְהַדִּיחַ

cast to they his from Surely .tottering fence a ;leaning a like
;down (him) plotted exaltation wall

6 יִרְצוּ כָזָב בְּפִיו יְבָרֵכוּ וּבְקִרְבָּם יְקַלְלוּ־סֶלָה׃ אַךְ לֵאלֹהִים

God to Only .Selah they in but they their with ;lies they
.curse heart their ,bless mouth in joy

7 דּוֹמִּי נַפְשִׁי כִּי־מִמֶּנּוּ תִּקְוָתִי׃ אַךְ־הוּא צוּרִי וִישׁוּעָתִי

my and my He alone my (is) from for my be
,salvation rock (is) .hope Him ,soul ,silent

8 מִשְׂגַּבִּי לֹא אֶמּוֹט׃ עַל־אֱלֹהִים יִשְׁעִי וּכְבוֹדִי צוּר־עֻזִּי

strong my my and my God On shall I not strong my
;rock ;glory salvation (is) .shaken be ;tower

9 מַחְסִי בֵּאלֹהִים׃ בִּטְחוּ בוֹ בְכָל־עֵת ׀ עָם שִׁפְכוּ־לְפָנָיו

before pour (you) ,time in in Trust in (is) my
Him out ;pledge every Him .God refuge

10 לְבַבְכֶם אֱלֹהִים מַחֲסֶה־לָּנוּ סֶלָה׃ אַךְ ׀ הֶבֶל בְּנֵי־אָדָם

.men the vanity Surely .Selah for a God Your
of sons (are) .us refuge (is) ;heart

11 כָּזָב בְּנֵי־אִישׁ בְּמֹאזְנַיִם לַעֲלוֹת הֵמָּה מֵהֶבֶל יָחַד׃ אַל־

not .together (lighter) they ;up go to the in ,man the lie a
vanity than (are) scales of sons (are)

תִּבְטְחוּ בְעֹשֶׁק וּבְגָזֵל אַל־תֶּהְבָּלוּ חַיִל ׀ כִּי־יָנוּב אַל־תָּשִׁיתוּ

set do not be if riches become do not in and in Trust
(on them) increased ;vain ;robbery ,oppression

12 לֵב׃ אַחַת ׀ דִּבֶּר אֱלֹהִים שְׁתַּיִם־זוּ שָׁמַעְתִּי כִּי־עֹז לֵאלֹהִים׃

;God to power that have I thus twice ;God has Once your
(is) ,heard spoken .heart

13 וּלְךָ־אֲדֹנָי חָסֶד כִּי־אַתָּה תְשַׁלֵּם לְאִישׁ כְּמַעֲשֵׂהוּ׃

to according man a reward You for (is) O also
.work his ;mercy ,Lord ,you to

PSAL. LXIII סג

PSALM 63

PSALM 63

A Psalm of David, when he was in the wilderness of Judah.

[1] O God, You (are) my God; I earnestly seek You; my soul thirsts for You; my flesh longs for You, as in a dry and weary land without water. [2] Therefore I have seen you in the holy place, seeing Your power and Your glory. [3] For Your loving-kindness (is) better than life; my lips give praise to You. [4] Therefore I will bless You while I live; I will lift up my hands in Your name. [5] My soul shall be satisfied, as (with) marrow and fatness; and my mouth shall praise (You) with joyful lips, [6] when I remember You upon my bed, I will think on You in the night-watches. [7] For You have been a help to me, and I will rejoice under the shadow of Your wings. [8] My soul is cleaved after You —Your right hand upholds me. [9] And those who seek to destroy my life shall go into the depths of the earth. [10] They shall pour him out by the sword; they shall be a serving for jackals. [11] But the king shall rejoice in God; everyone who swears by Him shall glory, because the mouth of liars shall be stopped.

1 2= מִזְמוֹר לְדָוִד בִּהְיוֹתוֹ בְּמִדְבַּר יְהוּדָה׃ אֱלֹהִים ׀ אֵלִי אַתָּה
You my ,God O .Judah the in he when of psalm A
;(are) God of wilderness was ,David

אֲשַׁחֲרֶךָּ צָמְאָה לְךָ ׀ נַפְשִׁי כָּמַהּ לְךָ בְשָׂרִי בְּאֶרֶץ־צִיָּה
dry a in my for faints my for thirsts earnestly I
land ,flesh You ;soul You ;You seek

3 וְעָיֵף בְּלִי־מָיִם׃ כֵּן בַּקֹּדֶשׁ חֲזִיתִךָ לִרְאוֹת עֻזְּךָ וּכְבוֹדֶךָ׃
Your and Your seeing have I the in So .water without and
.glory power ;You seen place holy weary

4 5 כִּי־טוֹב חַסְדְּךָ מֵחַיִּים שְׂפָתַי יְשַׁבְּחוּנְךָ׃ כֵּן אֲבָרֶכְךָ
will I So .You praise lips my ;life than Your better For
You bless (is) mercy

6= בְחַיָּי בְּשִׁמְךָ אֶשָּׂא כַפָּי׃ כְּמוֹ חֵלֶב וָדֶשֶׁן תִּשְׂבַּע נַפְשִׁי
my be shall and marrow As my will I Your in while
;soul satisfied fatness (with) .hands up lift name ;live I

7 וְשִׂפְתֵי רְנָנוֹת יְהַלֶּל־פִּי׃ אִם־זְכַרְתִּיךָ עַל־יְצוּעָי בְּאַשְׁמֻרוֹת
the in my upon remember I When my shall joy (with) and
watches night ,bed you .mouth praise of lips

8 9 אֶהְגֶּה־בָּךְ׃ כִּי־הָיִיתָ עֶזְרָתָה לִּי וּבְצֵל כְּנָפֶיךָ אֲרַנֵּן׃ דָּבְקָה
is will I Your in and to help a You For on will I
cleaved .shout wings' shadow me been have .You think

10 נַפְשִׁי אַחֲרֶיךָ בִּי תָּמְכָה יְמִינֶךָ׃ וְהֵמָּה לְשׁוֹאָה יְבַקְשׁוּ
seek destroy to And Your upholds me after My
they .hand right ,You soul

11 נַפְשִׁי יָבֹאוּ בְּתַחְתִּיּוֹת הָאָרֶץ׃ יַגִּירֻהוּ עַל־יְדֵי־חָרֶב מְנָת
lot a the hand by shall They the the into shall they my
for ;sword's out him pour .earth of depths come ;life

12 שֻׁעָלִים יִהְיוּ׃ וְהַמֶּלֶךְ יִשְׂמַח בֵּאלֹהִים יִתְהַלֵּל כָּל־
everyone shall ;God in shall the But they jackals
glory. rejoice king .be shall

הַנִּשְׁבָּע בּוֹ כִּי יִסָּכֵר פִּי דוֹבְרֵי־שָׁקֶר׃
.liars the be shall for by who
of mouth shut Him swears

PSAL. LXIV סד

PSALM 64

PSALM 64

To the Chief Musician. A Psalm of David.

[1] O God, hear my voice in my complaint; guard my life from the terror of the enemy. [2] Hide me from the secret plans of plunderers, from the tumult of evildoers, [3] who sharpen their tongue like a sword; they aim their arrows, a bitter word, [4] so that they may shoot at the innocent from a lurking place; suddenly they shoot at him, and fear not. [5] They make themselves strong (in) an

1 2 לַמְנַצֵּחַ מִזְמוֹר לְדָוִד׃ שְׁמַע־אֱלֹהִים קוֹלִי בְשִׂיחִי מִפַּחַד
the from my in my ,God O ,Hear of a chief the To
of dread ;complaint voice .David psalm ;musician

3 אוֹיֵב תִּצֹּר חַיָּי׃ תַּסְתִּירֵנִי מִסּוֹד מְרֵעִים מֵרִגְשַׁת פֹּעֲלֵי
doers the from ;spoilers the from me Hide my guard the
of of tumult of council .life enemy

4 אָוֶן׃ אֲשֶׁר שָׁנְנוּ כַחֶרֶב לְשׁוֹנָם דָּרְכוּ חִצָּם דָּבָר מָר׃
,bitter a their they their a like sharpen who ;evil
word ,arrows aim ;tongues sword

5 6 לִירוֹת בַּמִּסְתָּרִים תָּם פִּתְאֹם יֹרֻהוּ וְלֹא יִירָאוּ׃ יְחַזְּקוּ־
They they and shoot they suddenly the from shoot to
strengthen .fear not ,him at ;perfect ambush

evil plan; they talk of laying snares secretly; they say, Who shall see them? [6] They search thoroughly into wickedness, (saying), We have finished a well-laid plan. And the inward part of man and (the) heart (are) deep! [7] But God shall shoot an arrow at them; their wounds shall suddenly appear. [8] So they shall be confounded; their tongue falls upon themselves; everyone seeing them shall flee. [9] And all men shall fear and shall declare the work of God; yea, they shall in wisdom consider His work. [10] The righteous shall rejoice in Jehovah, and shall trust in Him; and all the upright in heart shall glory.

PSALM 65

To the Chief Musician. A Psalm and Song of David.

[1] To You silence (is) praise, O God, in Zion; and to You is a vow paid. [2] To You who hears prayer, all flesh comes. [3] Things of iniquity are mightier than I; our transgressions, You atone for them. [4] Blessed is (the one) You choose and cause to come near You, he shall dwell (in) Your courts; we shall be satisfied with the goodness of Your house, Your holy temple. [5] You will answer us in righteousness (by) awesome things, O God of our salvation; the Confidence of all the ends of the earth and the sea, of those afar off. [6] By Your strength the mountains are set, banded together with might. [7] (You) still the roaring of the sea, the roar of their waves, and the tumult of the peoples. [8] And the inhabitants of the uttermost parts are afraid of Your signs; You make the outgoings of the morning and the evening to rejoice. [9] You visit the earth and water it; You greatly enrich it; the river of God is full of water — You provide their grain, for in this way You have prepared it. [10] You fill its terraces with water;

לָמוֹ | דָּבָר רָע יְסַפְּרוּ לִטְמוֹן מוֹקְשִׁים אָמְרוּ מִי יִרְאֶה־

see shall Who they ,say ;snares slyly of laying they talk an ;evil (in) thing them- selves

7 לָמוֹ: יַחְפְּשׂוּ־עוֹלֹת תַּמְנוּ חֵפֶשׂ מְחֻפָּשׂ וְקֶרֶב אִישׁ וְלֵב

and heart man's in- And part ward (well) .laid plan a have We finished in- ;justice They investigate ?them

8 9 עָמֹק: וַיֹּרֵם אֱלֹהִים חֵץ פִּתְאוֹם הָיוּ מַכּוֹתָם: וַיַּכְשִׁילֻהוּ

shall they So confounded be their .wounds shall appear ;suddenly an arrow God shoot But them at (are) !deep

10 עָלֵימוֹ לְשׁוֹנָם יִתְנֹדְדוּ כָּל־רֹאֵה בָם: וַיִּירְאוּ כָּל־אָדָם

men all fear And .them seeing every- one shall flee their ;tongue them on (is)

11 וַיַּגִּידוּ פֹּעַל אֱלֹהִים וּמַעֲשֵׂהוּ הִשְׂכִּילוּ: יִשְׂמַח צַדִּיק בַּיהוָה

in Jehovah the righteous Shall rejoice wisely they .consider His ,yea work ;God the of work and declare

וְחָסָה בוֹ וְיִתְהַלְלוּ כָּל־יִשְׁרֵי־לֵב:

.heart the in upright all shall and glory in ;Him take and refuge

PSAL. LXV סה

PSALM 65

1 2 לַמְנַצֵּחַ מִזְמוֹר לְדָוִד שִׁיר: לְךָ דֻמִיָּה תְהִלָּה אֱלֹהִים

God O ,praise silence (is) To You .song a of ;David a psalm chief the To ;musician

3 בְּצִיּוֹן וּלְךָ יְשֻׁלַּם־נֶדֶר: שֹׁמֵעַ תְּפִלָּה עָדֶיךָ כָּל־בָּשָׂר יָבֹאוּ:

.comes flesh all to You ;prayer (You) hear a .vow is paid and You to in ;Zion

4 דִּבְרֵי עֲוֺנֹת גָּבְרוּ מֶנִּי פְשָׁעֵינוּ אַתָּה תְכַפְּרֵם: אַשְׁרֵי |

Blessed is for atone .them You our ,transgressions ;I than are mightier iniquity Things of

5 תִּבְחַר וּתְקָרֵב יִשְׁכֹּן חֲצֵרֶיךָ נִשְׂבְּעָה בְּטוּב בֵּיתֶךָ קְדֹשׁ

holy Your ,house the with of goodness shall we satisfied be Your ;courts shall he in dwell will and ;near bring You (one) choose

6 הֵיכָלֶךָ: נוֹרָאוֹת | בְּצֶדֶק תַּעֲנֵנוּ אֱלֹהֵי יִשְׁעֵנוּ מִבְטַח כָּל־

all con- the of fidence our ;salvation God O of will You ,us answer in righteousness awesome (By) things Your .temple

7 קַצְוֵי־אֶרֶץ וְיָם רְחֹקִים: מֵכִין הָרִים בְּכֹחוֹ נֶאְזָר בִּגְבוּרָה:

;might in is girded Your by ,strength the set are mountains ;off far of and the seas the the ,earth of ends

8 מַשְׁבִּיחַ | שְׁאוֹן יַמִּים שְׁאוֹן גַּלֵּיהֶם וַהֲמוֹן לְאֻמִּים: וַיִּירְאוּ

are And afraid the .peoples the and of tumult their ,waves the of roar the ,seas the of roaring still (You)

9 יֹשְׁבֵי קְצָוֺת מֵאוֹתֹתֶיךָ מוֹצָאֵי בֹקֶר וָעֶרֶב תַּרְנִין: פָּקַדְתָּ

visit You make You .rejoice to and evening the morning out- of goings the Your of ;signs furthest the limits those in living

10 הָאָרֶץ | וַתְּשֹׁקְקֶהָ רַבַּת תַּעְשְׁרֶנָּה פֶּלֶג אֱלֹהִים מָלֵא מָיִם

—water is of full God the of river enrich You ;it greatly water and ;it the earth

11 תָּכִין דְּגָנָם כִּי־כֵן תְּכִינֶהָ: תְּלָמֶיהָ רַוֵּה נַחֵת גְּדוּדֶיהָ

its ;ridges You press fill You ;water with Its furrows have You .it prepared thus for their grain You provide

You deepen its furrows; You make it soft with showers; You bless the sprouting of it. [11] You crown the year of Your goodness, and Your tracks drop with fruitfulness. [12] The pastures of the wilderness drop, and the little hills gird themselves (with) joy. [13] The flocks are outfitted with meadows, the valleys are also covered with grain; they shout for joy and sing.

בִּרְבִיבִים תְּמֹגְגֶנָּה צִמְחָהּ תְּבָרֵךְ׃ עִטַּרְתָּ שְׁנַת טוֹבָתֶךָ 12

Your with the You You its it make You with
,goodness year crown .bless sprouting ;soft showers

וּמַעְגָּלֶיךָ יִרְעֲפוּן דָּשֶׁן׃ יִרְעֲפוּ נְאוֹת מִדְבָּר וְגִיל גְּבָעוֹת 13

the and wilder- the the drip with drop Your and
hills joy (with) ,ness of pastures ;fatness tracks

תַּחְגֹּרְנָה׃ לָבְשׁוּ כָרִים ׀ הַצֹּאן וַעֲמָקִים יַעַטְפוּ־בָר 14

;grain are the also the The fitted are gird
with covered valleys ;flocks meadows with .themselves

יִתְרוֹעֲעוּ אַף־יָשִׁירוּ׃

.sing and shout they
joy for

PSAL. LXVI סו

PSALM 66

To the Chief Musician. A Song. A Psalm.

[1] Make a joyful noise to God, all the earth; [2] Sing out the honor of His name; give glory to His praise. [3] Say to God, How fearful (are) Your works! Through the greatness of Your power, Your enemies pretend obedience to You. [4] All the earth shall worship You; and they sing to You; they praise Your name. Selah. [5] Come and see God's works, who is awesome in His acts toward the sons of men. [6] He turns the sea into dry land; they go through the river on foot; there we will rejoice with Him. [7] He rules by His power forever; His eyes search out the nations; let not the rebels exalt themselves. Selah. [8] Bless our God, O people, and sound out the voice of His praise; [9] who holds our soul in life, and does not allow our foot to slide. [10] For You, O God, have proved us; You have tested us as silver is refined. [11] You have brought us into the net; You laid afflictions on our loins. [12] You have let men ride at our head; we went through fire and through water; but You brought us out to plenty. [13] I will go into Your house with burnt offerings;

לַמְנַצֵּחַ שִׁיר מִזְמוֹר הָרִיעוּ לֵאלֹהִים כָּל־הָאָרֶץ׃ זַמְּרוּ 1 2

Shout the all ,God to a Make a ;song a chief the To
;earth . noise joyful .psalm ;musician

כְבוֹד־שְׁמוֹ שִׂימוּ כָבוֹד תְּהִלָּתוֹ׃ אִמְרוּ לֵאלֹהִים מַה־ 3

How ,God to Say His (to) glory give His the
.praise ;name of honor

נּוֹרָא מַעֲשֶׂיךָ בְּרֹב עֻזְּךָ יְכַחֲשׁוּ לְךָ אֹיְבֶיךָ׃ כָּל־הָאָרֶץ ׀ 4

the All Your to pretend Your the in Your fearful
earth .enemies You obedience ,power of might works (are)

יִשְׁתַּחֲווּ לְךָ וִיזַמְּרוּ־לָךְ יְזַמְּרוּ שִׁמְךָ סֶלָה׃ לְכוּ וּרְאוּ 5

and Come .Selah Your they to they and ;You shall
see .name praise ;you sing worship

מִפְעֲלוֹת אֱלֹהִים נוֹרָא עֲלִילָה עַל־בְּנֵי אָדָם׃ הָפַךְ יָם ׀ 6

the He .men the toward His in is who ,God works the
sea turns of sons acts awesome of

לְיַבָּשָׁה בַּנָּהָר יַעַבְרוּ בְרָגֶל שָׁם נִשְׂמְחָה בּוֹ׃ מֹשֵׁל 7

He in will we there on go they through dry into
rules .Him rejoice ;foot river the ;land

בִּגְבוּרָתוֹ ׀ עוֹלָם עֵינָיו בַּגּוֹיִם תִּצְפֶּינָה הַסּוֹרְרִים ׀ אַל־

not the search the His ;forever His by
rebels ;out nations eyes power

יָרִימוּ לָמוֹ סֶלָה׃ בָּרְכוּ עַמִּים ׀ אֱלֹהֵינוּ וְהַשְׁמִיעוּ קוֹל 8

the sound and our O Bless .Selah them- let
of voice out ,God ,peoples .selves exalt

תְּהִלָּתוֹ׃ הַשָּׂם נַפְשֵׁנוּ בַּחַיִּים וְלֹא־נָתַן לַמּוֹט רַגְלֵנוּ׃ 9

our slip to does and ,life in our who ;praise His
.foot allow not soul places

כִּי־בְחַנְתָּנוּ אֱלֹהִים צְרַפְתָּנוּ כִּצְרָף־כָּסֶף׃ הֲבֵאתָנוּ 10 11

have You .silver one as have You ;God O have You For
us brought refines us refined ,us proved

בַמְּצוּדָה שַׂמְתָּ מוּעָקָה בְמָתְנֵינוּ׃ הִרְכַּבְתָּ אֱנוֹשׁ לְרֹאשֵׁנוּ 12

our at men have You our on afflictions You the into
;head ride let .loins laid ;net

בָּאנוּ בָאֵשׁ וּבַמַּיִם וַתּוֹצִיאֵנוּ לָרְוָיָה׃ אָבוֹא בֵיתְךָ בְעוֹלוֹת 13

burnt with Your will I to You but through and through we
offerings house into go .plenty out us brought ;water fire went

I will pay You my vows,
[14] which my lips have
uttered, and in my trouble
my mouth has spoken.
[15] I will offer burnt sacrifices of fatlings to You,
with the incense of rams; I
will offer bulls with goats.
Selah. [16] Come, hear,
and let me tell, all you who
fear God, what He has done
to my soul. [17] I cried to
Him with my mouth, and
was praises under my
tongue. [18] If I had re-
garded iniquity in my heart,
Jehovah would not have
heard. [19] Surely God has
heard; He has attended to
the voice of my prayer.
[20] Blessed (be) God, who
has not turned away my
prayer, and His mercy from
me!

14 אֲשַׁלֵּם לְךָ נְדָרָי׃ אֲשֶׁר־פָּצוּ שְׂפָתָי וְדִבֶּר־פִּי בַּצַּר־לִי׃

to the in my has and my have which my You will I
.me trouble mouth spoken ,lips uttered ,vows pay

15 עֹלוֹת מֵחִים אַעֲלֶה־לָּךְ עִם־קְטֹרֶת אֵילִים אֶעֱשֶׂה בָקָר

bulls will I ;rams the with to will I fatlings Burnt
offer of incense ,You offer of offerings

16 עִם־עַתּוּדִים סֶלָה׃ לְכוּ־שִׁמְעוּ וַאֲסַפְּרָה כָּל־יִרְאֵי אֱלֹהִים

,God you all let and ,hear ,Come .Selah .he-goats with
fear who ,tell me

17 אֲשֶׁר עָשָׂה לְנַפְשִׁי׃ אֵלָיו פִּי־קָרָאתִי וְרוֹמַם תַּחַת לְשׁוֹנִי׃

my under was and I (with) to my for has He what
.tongue praises ,cried mouth my Him ,soul done

18
19 אָוֶן אִם־רָאִיתִי בְלִבִּי לֹא יִשְׁמַע אֲדֹנָי׃ אָכֵן שָׁמַע אֱלֹהִים

;God has Surely the have would not my in had I If evil
heard .Lord heard ,heart seen

20 הִקְשִׁיב בְּקוֹל תְּפִלָּתִי׃ בָּרוּךְ אֱלֹהִים אֲשֶׁר לֹא־הֵסִיר

has not who ,God Blessed my the to has He
away turned (be) .prayer of voice attended

תְּפִלָּתִי וְחַסְדּוֹ מֵאִתִּי׃

from His and my
.me mercy ,prayer

PSAL. LXVII סז

PSALM 67

To the Chief Musician, for Stringed Instruments. A Psalm. A Song.

[1] May God be merci-
ful to us and bless us, (and)
cause His face to shine
(upon) us. Selah. [2] That
Your way may be known on
earth, Your salvation
among all nations. [3] Let
the peoples thank You, O
God; let all the peoples
thank You. [4] O let the
peoples be glad and sing for
joy; for You shall judge the
peoples righteously and
govern the peoples on earth.
Selah. [5] Let the peoples
give thanks to You, O God;
let all the peoples give
thanks to You. [6] The
earth has given its increase;
God, our own God, shall
bless us. [7] God shall bless
us; and all the ends of the
earth shall fear Him.

1
2 לַמְנַצֵּחַ בִּנְגִינֹת מִזְמוֹר שִׁיר׃ אֱלֹהִים יְחָנֵּנוּ וִיבָרְכֵנוּ יָאֵר

making bless and be May God A A stringed for chief the To
shine ,us us to merciful .song .psalm .instrument ;musician

3 פָּנָיו אִתָּנוּ סֶלָה׃ לָדַעַת בָּאָרֶץ דַּרְכֶּךָ בְּכָל־גּוֹיִם יְשׁוּעָתֶךָ׃

Your nations among Your the in may That .Selah with His
.salvation all ,way earth known be .us face

4 יוֹדוּךָ עַמִּים ׀ אֱלֹהִים יוֹדוּךָ עַמִּים כֻּלָּם׃ יִשְׂמְחוּ וִירַנְּנוּ

sing and let O of all the thank ;God O the Thank
joy for glad be .them ,peoples You ,peoples You

5 לְאֻמִּים כִּי־תִשְׁפֹּט עַמִּים מִישֹׁר וּלְאֻמִּים ׀ בָּאָרֶץ תַּנְחֵם

.guide the on the and ,uprightly the shall You for the
earth peoples peoples judge ;peoples

6
7 סֶלָה׃ יוֹדוּךָ עַמִּים ׀ אֱלֹהִים יוֹדוּךָ עַמִּים כֻּלָּם׃ אֶרֶץ

The of all the let ;God O the Let .Selah
earth .them ,peoples You thank ,peoples You thank

8 נָתְנָה יְבוּלָהּ יְבָרְכֵנוּ אֱלֹהִים אֱלֹהֵינוּ׃ יְבָרְכֵנוּ אֱלֹהִים

,God shall own our ,God shall its has
us bless .God us bless ;increase given

וְיִירְאוּ אוֹתוֹ כָּל־אַפְסֵי־אָרֶץ׃

the the all Him shall and
.earth of ends fear

PSAL. LXVIII . סח

PSALM 68

To the Chief Musician. A Psalm of David. A Song.

[1] God rises up (and)
His enemies are scattered;

1
2 לַמְנַצֵּחַ לְדָוִד מִזְמוֹר שִׁיר׃ יָקוּם אֱלֹהִים יָפוּצוּ אוֹיְבָיו

His are (and) ,God shall A A of chief the To
;enemies scattered arise .song .psalm .David ;musician

and those who hate Him flee from His face. [2] As smoke is driven away, You drive (them) away; as wax melts before the fire, the wicked perish in God's presence. [3] But the righteous are glad; they shout for joy before God; yea, they exult with gladness. [4] Sing to God, sing praise to His name; lift up for Him who rides in the deserts; by Jah, His name; yea, exult in His presence. [5] God in His holy dwelling (is) a father of the fatherless, and a judge of the widows. [6] God causes the lonely to live at home; He brings out those who are bound with chains, while the rebellious dwell in a dry land.

[7] O God, when You marched before Your people, when You walked on through the wilderness. Selah. [8] The earth shook, and the heavens dropped before God, this Sinai before God, the God of Israel. [9] O God, You sent down a shower of plenty, by which You upheld Your inheritance when it was weary: You established it. [10] Your flock lived in it; You, O God, have prepared for the poor in Your goodness. [11] Jehovah gave the word; those who bore it (were) a great army.

[12] Kings of armies fled, they ran away; yea, she who stayed home has divided the spoil. [13] When you lie among the sheepfolds, the wings of a dove are covered with silver, and their feathers with gleaming gold. [14] When the Almighty scatters kings in it, it snows on (mount) Salmon. [15] The mountain of Bashan (is) God's mountain; the Bashan range (is) a mountain of peaks. [16] Why do you gaze in envy, O mountain range, (at the) mountain God chose for His dwelling? Yea, Jehovah will dwell (in it) forever. [17] The chariots of God

3 וְיָנוּסוּ מְשַׂנְאָיו מִפָּנָיו׃ כְּהִנְדֹּף עָשָׁן תִּנְדֹּף כְּהִמֵּס דּוֹנַג
wax as drive You ,smoke is As His from who those and
melts ,away (them) away driven .face Him hate flee

4 מִפְּנֵי־אֵשׁ יֹאבְדוּ רְשָׁעִים מִפְּנֵי אֱלֹהִים׃ וְצַדִּיקִים יִשְׂמְחוּ
be shall the But .God's in the perish the before
;glad righteous presence wicked ,fire

5 יַעַלְצוּ לִפְנֵי אֱלֹהִים וְיָשִׂישׂוּ בְשִׂמְחָה׃ שִׁירוּ ׀ לֵאלֹהִים
.God to Sing with they and ;God before shall they
.gladness exult shall rejoice

זַמְּרוּ שְׁמוֹ סֹלּוּ לָרֹכֵב בָּעֲרָבוֹת בְּיָהּ שְׁמוֹ וְעִלְזוּ לְפָנָיו׃
His in and His by the in Him for up lift His Sing
.presence exult —name Jah ;deserts rides who (song a) ;name to praise

6 אֲבִי יְתוֹמִים וְדַיַּן אַלְמָנוֹת אֱלֹהִים בִּמְעוֹן קָדְשׁוֹ׃
7 אֱלֹהִים ׀
God His in (is) the and the father
.holy dwelling God widows' judge ,orphans'

מוֹשִׁיב יְחִידִים ׀ בַּיְתָה מוֹצִיא אֲסִירִים בַּכּוֹשָׁרוֹת אַךְ־
while with who those He at the makes
,chains bound are out brings ;home lonely dwell

8 סוֹרְרִים שָׁכְנוּ צְחִיחָה׃ אֱלֹהִים בְּצֵאתְךָ לִפְנֵי עַמֶּךָ
Your before Your in God O a in dwell the
,people outgoing .land dry rebellious

9 בְּצַעְדְּךָ בִישִׁימוֹן סֶלָה׃ אֶרֶץ רָעָשָׁה ׀ אַף־שָׁמַיִם נָטְפוּ
dropped the ,yea ;trembled the ;Selah the through Your in
(rain) heavens earth ;wilderness stepping

10 מִפְּנֵי אֱלֹהִים זֶה סִינַי מִפְּנֵי אֱלֹהִים אֱלֹהֵי יִשְׂרָאֵל׃ גֶּשֶׁם
A .Israel the ,God before Sinai this ;God before
of shower of God

11 נְדָבוֹת תָּנִיף אֱלֹהִים נַחֲלָתְךָ וְנִלְאָה אַתָּה כוֹנַנְתָּהּ׃ חַיָּתְךָ
Your established You it (when) Your ;God O shed You plenty
flock .it ,weary was inheritance ,abroad

12 יָשְׁבוּ־בָהּ תָּכִין בְּטוֹבָתְךָ לֶעָנִי אֱלֹהִים׃ אֲדֹנָי יִתֶּן־אֹמֶר
the gave The .God O the for Your in You ;it in dwelt
;word Lord poor goodness provided

13 הַמְבַשְּׂרוֹת צָבָא רָב׃ מַלְכֵי צְבָאוֹת יִדֹּדוּן יִדֹּדוּן וּנְוַת
she and they ,flee armies Kings .great a army bearers the
staying ;flee of (were) it of

14 בֵּית תְּחַלֵּק שָׁלָל׃ אִם־תִּשְׁכְּבוּן בֵּין שְׁפַתָּיִם כַּנְפֵי יוֹנָה
a the the among you If the divided (at)
dove of wings ,sheepfolds down lie .spoil home

15 נֶחְפָּה בַכֶּסֶף וְאֶבְרוֹתֶיהָ בִּירַקְרַק חָרוּץ׃ בְּפָרֵשׂ שַׁדַּי
the When .gold with its and with are
Almighty scatters gleaming feathers ,silver covered

16 מְלָכִים בָּהּ תַּשְׁלֵג בְּצַלְמוֹן׃ הַר־אֱלֹהִים הַר־בָּשָׁן הַר
a ;Bashan the (is) God's mountain (mount) in it ,it in kings
of mount of mountain .Salmon snows

17 גַּבְנֻנִּים הַר־בָּשָׁן׃ לָמָּה ׀ תְּרַצְּדוּן הָרִים גַּבְנֻנִּים הָהָר חָמַד
chose the (at) of O you do Why .Bashan (is) peaks
mountain ,peaks mount ,envy in gaze of mount the

18 אֱלֹהִים לְשִׁבְתּוֹ אַף־יְהוָה יִשְׁכֹּן לָנֶצַח׃ רֶכֶב אֱלֹהִים
God The .forever dwell will Jehovah ,Yea His for God
of chariots (it in) ?dwelling

are myriads, thousands of changes, the Lord among them; (in) Sinai, in the holy place. [18] You have led captivity captive; You have received gifts among men; yea, to dwell (among) the rebellious, O Jehovah God.

[19] Blessed the Lord: day by day He bears burdens for us, the God of our salvation. Selah. [20] Our God (is) the God of salvation; and to Jehovah the Lord the issues of death. [21] Yea, God will crush His enemies' head; the hairy crown of him who walks on in his guilt. [22] The Lord said, I will bring back from Bashan; I will bring back (My people) from the depths of the sea; [23] so that your foot may be dashed in the blood of (your) enemies, the tongue of your dogs in it. [24] They have seen Your processions, O God; the goings of my God, my King, in the holy place. [25] The singers went before, then the players on instruments came; among (them were) the virgins playing the timbrels. [26] O bless God in the congregations, the Lord, from the fountain of Israel. [27] There is little Benjamin their ruler; the leaders of Judah (in) their crowd, (and) the leaders of Zebulun, the leaders of Naphtali.

[28] Your God has ordered your strength; O God, be strong, (in) this You have worked out for us. [29] Because of Your temple over Jerusalem, kings shall bring a present to You. [30] Rebuke the wild beasts of the reeds, the multitude of the bulls, with the calves of the people, each trampling down with pieces of silver; He scatters the people who delight in war. [31] Let be brought bronze out of Egypt; Ethiopia shall stretch her hands to God. [32] Sing to God, kingdoms of the earth; (and) praises to the Lord. Selah. [33] To Him who rides on the heavens of heavens of old; lo, He sends out His

19 רִבֹּתַיִם אַלְפֵי שִׁנְאָן אֲדֹנָי בָם סִינַי בַּקֹּדֶשׁ׃ עָלִיתָ לַמָּרוֹם ׀
;high on have You the in (in) among the ,changes thousands twenty
up gone .place holy ,Sinai ;them Lord of ,thousand

שָׁבִיתָ שֶּׁבִי לָקַחְתָּ מַתָּנוֹת בָּאָדָם וְאַף סוֹרְרִים לִשְׁכֹּן ׀
dwell to the and among gifts have You cap- have You
,(among) rebellious also ;men received ;tivity captive led

20 יָהּ אֱלֹהִים׃ בָּרוּךְ אֲדֹנָי יוֹם ׀ יוֹם יַעֲמָס־לָנוּ הָאֵל יְשׁוּעָתֵנוּ
our the for bears He by day the Blessed .God O
.salvation of God ,us burdens day ;Lord Jah

21 סֶלָה׃ הָאֵל ׀ לָנוּ אֵל לְמוֹשָׁעוֹת וְלֵיהוִה אֲדֹנָי לַמָּוֶת
for the to and of the to God .Selah
death Lord Jehovah ;salvation God us (is)

22 תּוֹצָאוֹת׃ אַךְ־אֱלֹהִים יִמְחַץ רֹאשׁ אֹיְבָיו קָדְקֹד שֵׂעָר
hairy the His the will God ,Yea the
crown ;enemies of head crush .issues

23 מִתְהַלֵּךְ בַּאֲשָׁמָיו׃ אָמַר אֲדֹנָי מִבָּשָׁן אָשִׁיב אָשִׁיב
will I bring will I from the said his in who him of
back bring ;again ,Bashan Lord .guilt on walks

24 מִמְּצֻלוֹת יָם׃ לְמַעַן ׀ תִּמְחַץ רַגְלְךָ בְּדָם לְשׁוֹן כְּלָבֶיךָ
Your the the in Your (may You) so the the from
dogs of tongue blood foot shatter that ;sea of depths

25 מֵאֹיְבִים מִנֵּהוּ׃ רָאוּ הֲלִיכוֹתֶיךָ אֱלֹהִים הֲלִיכוֹת אֵלִי מַלְכִּי
my my goings the ;God O Your They from (Your)
,King ,God of ,processions seen have .it enemies

26 בַקֹּדֶשׁ׃ קִדְּמוּ שָׁרִים אַחַר נֹגְנִים בְּתוֹךְ עֲלָמוֹת תּוֹפֵפוֹת׃
the playing the among the then The went holy the in
.timbrels virgins (were) them ;musicians (came) ,singers before .place

27
28 בְּמַקְהֵלוֹת בָּרְכוּ אֱלֹהִים אֲדֹנָי מִמְּקוֹר יִשְׂרָאֵל׃ שָׁם
There .Israel the from the ,God O the in
is of fountain Lord bless .assemblies

בִּנְיָמִן ׀ צָעִיר רֹדֵם שָׂרֵי יְהוּדָה רִגְמָתָם שָׂרֵי זְבֻלוּן שָׂרֵי
princes Zebu- the their (in) Judah the their little Benja-
lun of princes ;crowd of princes ;ruler min

29 נַפְתָּלִי׃ צִוָּה אֱלֹהֶיךָ עֻזֶּךָ עוּזָּה אֱלֹהִים זוּ פָּעַלְתָּ לָּנוּ׃
for have You this O be your Your has .Naphtali's
.us worked ,God ,strong ;strength God ordered

30
31 מֵהֵיכָלֶךָ עַל־יְרוּשָׁלָםִ לְךָ יוֹבִילוּ מְלָכִים שָׁי׃ גְּעַר חַיַּת
the Rebuke a kings shall to Jerusalem over of Because
of beast .present bring You temple Your

קָנֶה עֲדַת אַבִּירִים ׀ בְּעֶגְלֵי עַמִּים מִתְרַפֵּס בְּרַצֵּי־כָסֶף
;silver with trampling the the with the com- the the
of pieces down peoples of calves ,bulls of pany ,reeds

32 בִּזַּר עַמִּים קְרָבוֹת יֶחְפָּצוּ׃ יֶאֱתָיוּ חַשְׁמַנִּים מִנִּי מִצְרָיִם
;Egypt out bronze be Let who war the He
of brought .in delight peoples scatters

33 כּוּשׁ תָּרִיץ יָדָיו לֵאלֹהִים׃ מַמְלְכוֹת הָאָרֶץ שִׁירוּ לֵאלֹהִים
;God to sing the Kingdoms .God to her shall Ethiopia
earth of hands stretch

34 זַמְּרוּ אֲדֹנָי סֶלָה׃ לָרֹכֵב בִּשְׁמֵי שְׁמֵי־קֶדֶם הֵן יִתֵּן בְּקוֹלוֹ
His He ,lo ;old heavens the on Him To .Selah the praises
,voice gives of of heavens rides who .Lord

voice, a mighty voice. [34] Ascribe strength to God over Israel; His majesty and His strength in the skies. [35] O God, (You are) overwhelming out of Your holy places; the God of Israel (is) He who gives strength and powers to the people. Blessed (be) God!

35 קוֹל עֹז׃ תְּנוּ עֹז לֵאלֹהִים עַל־יִשְׂרָאֵל גַּאֲוָתוֹ וְעֻזּוֹ בַּשְּׁחָקִים׃
the in His and His ;Israel over God to strength As- .mighty a
.skies strength majesty scribe voice

36 נוֹרָא אֱלֹהִים מִמִּקְדָּשֶׁיךָ אֵל יִשְׂרָאֵל הוּא נֹתֵן ׀ עֹז וְתַעֲצֻמוֹת
and strength who He ,Israel the Your of out ;God Awe-
powers gives of God ,places holy (is) some

לָעָם בָּרוּךְ אֱלֹהִים׃
!God Blessed the to
(be) .people

PSALM 69

PSAL. LXIX סט

PSALM 69

To the Chief Musician, Concerning the Lilies. Of David.

[1] Save me, O God, for the waters have come in to (my) soul. [2] I sink in deep mire, and there is no standing; I have come into deep waters where the floods overflow me. [3] I am weary from my crying, my throat is scorched; my eyes fail while I wait for my God. [4] They who hate me without a cause are more than the hairs of my head; they who would destroy me are mighty, my mighty enemies; then I restored what I took not by violence. [5] O God, You know my foolishness; and my sins are not hidden from You. [6] Do not let those who wait on You, O Jehovah God of hosts, be ashamed for my sake; let not the ones who seek You be ashamed for my sake, O God of Israel. [7] Because I suffered reproach for Your sake, shame has covered my face. [8] I have become a stranger to my brothers, and a foreigner to my mother's children. [9] For the zeal of Your house has consumed me; and the reproaches of the ones who reproach You have fallen on me. [10] When I humbled my soul with fasting, it also was to my reproach; [11] I also made sackcloth my clothing, and I became a mockery to them. [12] They who sit in the gate spoke of me; and I (was) the song of drunkards. [13] But (as for) me, my prayer (is) to You, O Jehovah, at a time of favor, O God! In the multitude of Your mercy answer

1
2 לַמְנַצֵּחַ ׀ עַל־שׁוֹשַׁנִּים לְדָוִד׃ הוֹשִׁיעֵנִי אֱלֹהִים כִּי בָאוּ
have for ,God O ,me Save Of the according chief the To
come .David .Lilies to ;musician

3 מַיִם עַד־נָפֶשׁ׃ טָבַעְתִּי ׀ בִּיוֵן מְצוּלָה וְאֵין מָעֳמָד בָּאתִי
have I ;standing and ,deep in sunk I (my) to the
come no is mire .soul waters

4 בְמַעֲמַקֵּי־מַיִם וְשִׁבֹּלֶת שְׁטָפָתְנִי׃ יָגַעְתִּי בְקָרְאִי נִחַר
is my with am I overflowed His and waters into
burnt ,crying weary .me floods deep

5 גְּרוֹנִי כָּלוּ עֵינַי מְיַחֵל לֵאלֹהָי׃ רַבּוּ ׀ מִשַּׂעֲרוֹת רֹאשִׁי
my hairs the More my for while my fail my
head of than .God wait I eyes ;throat

שֹׂנְאַי חִנָּם עָצְמוּ מַצְמִיתַי אֹיְבַי שֶׁקֶר אֲשֶׁר לֹא־גָזַלְתִּי
,stole I not what ;lying my my are without my are
enemies ,destroyers mighty ;cause haters

6 אָז אָשִׁיב׃ אֱלֹהִים אַתָּה יָדַעְתָּ לְאִוַּלְתִּי וְאַשְׁמוֹתַי מִמְּךָ
from my and my know You God O must I then
You sins ;foolishness :restore

7 לֹא־נִכְחָדוּ׃ אַל־יֵבֹשׁוּ בִי ׀ קֹוֶיךָ אֲדֹנָי יְהוִה צְבָאוֹת אַל־
not ;hosts Jehovah O on waiters in let Do not are not
of Lord ,You me ashamed be .hidden

8 יִכָּלְמוּ בִי מְבַקְשֶׁיךָ אֱלֹהֵי יִשְׂרָאֵל׃ כִּי־עָלֶיךָ נָשָׂאתִי חֶרְפָּה
;reproach I for Because .Israel God O seekers in be let
bore sake Your of ,You for me ashamed

9 כִּסְּתָה כְלִמָּה פָנָי׃ מוּזָר הָיִיתִי לְאֶחָי וְנָכְרִי לִבְנֵי אִמִּי׃
my sons to a and my to have I a my shame has
.mother's foreigner ,brothers become stranger .face covered

10 כִּי־קִנְאַת בֵּיתְךָ אֲכָלָתְנִי וְחֶרְפּוֹת חוֹרְפֶיךָ נָפְלוּ עָלָי׃
on have reproachers the and con- has Your the For
.me fallen You of of reproaches ;me sumed house of zeal

11
12 וָאֶבְכֶּה בַצּוֹם נַפְשִׁי וַתְּהִי לַחֲרָפוֹת לִי׃ וָאֶתְּנָה לְבוּשִׁי
my also I to reproach it and my with I And
clothing made .me was ,soul fasting ,wept

13 שָׂק וָאֱהִי לָהֶם לְמָשָׁל׃ יָשִׂיחוּ בִי יֹשְׁבֵי שָׁעַר וּנְגִינוֹת
the and the who They on meditated a to I and sack-
of song ;gate in sit me .proverb them became cloth

14 שׁוֹתֵי שֵׁכָר׃ וַאֲנִי תְפִלָּתִי־לְךָ ׀ יְהוָה עֵת רָצוֹן אֱלֹהִים
!God O ,favor a at O to my (as) But strong drinkers
of time ,Jehovah ,You (is) prayer ,me (for) .drink of

me, in the truth of Your salvation. [14] Deliver me out of the mire, that I may not sink; let me be delivered from those who hate me; and out of the deep waters. [15] Let not the flood-waters overflow me, nor let the deep swallow me up; and let not the pit shut its mouth on me. [16] Hear me, O Jehovah, for Your mercy (is) good; in the multitude of Your tender mercies, turn toward me. [17] And do not hide Your face from Your servant; for I am in trouble; hear me quickly; [18] draw near my soul; redeem it; ransom me because of my enemies. [19] You know my reproach and my shame, and my dishonor; my enemies (are) all before You. [20] Reproach has broken my heart, and I am faint; and I waited for one to show pity, but (there was) no one; and for comforters, but I found none. [21] They also gave me gall in my food; and in my thirst they gave me vinegar to drink. [22] Let their table be a trap before them; and to those at ease a snare. [23] Let their eyes be darkened, that they may not see; and cause their loins (to) be troubled continually. [24] Pour out Your wrath on them; and let the glow of Your anger seize them. [25] Let their home be made desolate; let no one dwell in their tents. [26] For whom You have stricken, they have persecuted; and they gossip to the pain of those You pierced. [27] Put iniquity to their iniquity; and do not let them enter into Your righteousness. [28] Blot them out from the Book of Life; yea, let them not be written with the righteous. [29] But I (am) poor and in pain; O God, Your salvation shall set me on high. [30] I will praise God's name in a song; and I will magnify Him with thanks. [31] And it shall please Jehovah more than bulls, horned (or) hoofed bull. [32] The humble have seen (and) are glad; you who

15 בְּרָב־חַסְדֶּךָ עֲנֵנִי בֶּאֱמֶת יִשְׁעֶךָ׃ הַצִּילֵנִי מִטִּיט וְאַל־
that of out Deliver Your the in answer Your the in
not mire the me .salvation of truth ,me ;mercy of plenty

16 אֶטְבָּעָה אִנָּצְלָה מִשֹּׂנְאַי וּמִמַּעֲמַקֵּי־מָיִם׃ אַל־תִּשְׁטְפֵנִי ׀
overflow let not ;waters of out and my from be me let may I
me deep the ,haters delivered ;sink

שִׁבֹּלֶת מַיִם וְאַל־תִּבְלָעֵנִי מְצוּלָה וְאַל־תֶּאְטַר־עָלַי בְּאֵר
the on let and the swallow let and ;waters the
pit me shut not ;deep up me not of flood

17 פִּיהָ׃ עֲנֵנִי יְהוָה כִּי־טוֹב חַסְדֶּךָ כְּרֹב רַחֲמֶיךָ פְּנֵה אֵלָי׃
toward turn Your the in Your (is) for O Answer its
.me mercies of plenty ;mercy good ,Jehovah ,me .mouth

18
19 וְאַל־תַּסְתֵּר פָּנֶיךָ מֵעַבְדֶּךָ כִּי־צַר־לִי מַהֵר עֲנֵנִי׃ קָרְבָה
draw answer quickly to trouble for Your from Your do And
near ;me ;me (is) ;servant face hide not

20 אֶל־נַפְשִׁי גְאָלָהּ לְמַעַן אֹיְבַי פְּדֵנִי׃ אַתָּה יָדַעְתָּ חֶרְפָּתִי
my know You ransom my because redeem my to
,reproach .me ,enemies of ;it ;soul

21 וּבָשְׁתִּי וּכְלִמָּתִי נֶגְדְּךָ כָּל־צוֹרְרָי׃ חֶרְפָּה ׀ שָׁבְרָה לִבִּי
my has Reproach my all (are) my and my and
,heart broken .enemies You before ;dishonor ,shame

22 וָאָנוּשָׁה וָאֲקַוֶּה לָנוּד וָאַיִן וְלַמְנַחֲמִים וְלֹא מָצָאתִי׃ וַיִּתְּנוּ
they And .found I and for and but for I and am I and
(me) gave none ,comforters ;none ,pity looked ;sick

23 בְּבָרוּתִי רֹאשׁ וְלִצְמָאִי יַשְׁקוּנִי חֹמֶץ׃ יְהִי־שֻׁלְחָנָם לִפְנֵיהֶם
before their Let .vinegar gave they my in and ;gall my in
them table be drink to me thirst food

24 לְפָח וְלִשְׁלוֹמִים לְמוֹקֵשׁ׃ תֶּחְשַׁכְנָה עֵינֵיהֶם מֵרְאוֹת
from their be Let .snare a the to and a for
;seeing ,eyes darkened peace at ones ;trap

25 וּמָתְנֵיהֶם תָּמִיד הַמְעַד׃ שְׁפָךְ־עֲלֵיהֶם זַעְמֶךָ וַחֲרוֹן אַפְּךָ
Your the and Your upon Pour make continually their and
anger of glow ,wrath them out .trouble loins

26 יַשִּׂיגֵם׃ תְּהִי־טִירָתָם נְשַׁמָּה בְּאָהֳלֵיהֶם אַל־יְהִי יֹשֵׁב׃
one let no their in made their be Let seize let
.dwell tents ;desolate home .them

27 כִּי־אַתָּה אֲשֶׁר־הִכִּיתָ רָדָפוּ וְאֶל־מַכְאוֹב חֲלָלֶיךָ יְסַפֵּרוּ׃
they You those the and per- they have whom You For
:gossip ,pierced of pain to ;secuted ,stricken

28
29 תְּנָה־עָוֺן עַל־עֲוֺנָם וְאַל־יָבֹאוּ בְּצִדְקָתֶךָ׃ יִמָּחוּ מִסֵּפֶר חַיִּים
;Life the from Blot Your in let do and their to iniquity put
of Book them .righteousness enter them not ;iniquity

30 וְעִם צַדִּיקִים אַל־יִכָּתֵבוּ׃ וַאֲנִי עָנִי וְכוֹאֵב יְשׁוּעָתְךָ אֱלֹהִים
,God O Your and ,poor But be let not the and
,salvation ;pain in (am) I .written righteous with

31 תְּשַׂגְּבֵנִי׃ אֲהַלְלָה שֵׁם־אֱלֹהִים בְּשִׁיר וַאֲגַדְּלֶנּוּ בְתוֹדָה׃
with will I a in God's name will I set shall
.thanks Him magnify ;song praise .high on me

32
33 וְתִיטַב לַיהוָה מִשּׁוֹר פָּר מַקְרִן מַפְרִיס׃ רָאוּ עֲנָוִים יִשְׂמָחוּ
are (and) The have (and) horned (or) more to shall it And
;glad humble seen .hoofed bull ,bulls than Jehovah good be

34 דרשי אלהים ויחי לבבכם׃ כי־שמע אל־אביונים

the hears For your let ,God who You
needy .heart live seek

35 יהוה ואת־אסיריו לא בזה׃ יהללוהו שמים וארץ ימים

the the and the praise Let does He not His and ,Jehovah
seas ,earth heavens Him .despise prisoners

36 וכל־רמש בם׃ כי אלהים ׀ יושיע ציון ויבנה ערי יהודה

,Judah the He and ;Zion save will God For in moving and
of cities build will .them thing every

37 וישבו שם וירשוה׃ וזרע עבדיו ינחלוה ואהבי שמו

His they and shall His And and there they and
name love who ;it inherit servants' seed .it possess live shall

ישכנו־בה׃

.it in shall
dwell

seek God, your heart shall live. [33] For Jehovah hears the needy, and He does not despise His prisoners. [34] Let the heavens and the earth praise Him, the seas, and everything that moves in them. [35] For God will save Zion; and He will build the cities of Judah, and they shall live there and possess it. [36] And His servants' seed shall inherit it; and they who love His name shall live in it.

PSAL. LXX ע

PSALM 70

1
2 למנצח לדוד להזכיר׃ אלהים להצילני יהוה לעזרתי

help to O deliver to ,God O to bring to of chief the To
,me ,Jehovah !me .remembrance ;David ;musician

3 חושה׃ יבשו ויחפרו מבקשי נפשי יסגו אחור ויכלמו

and backward them let my who those con- and be Let !hurry
,shamed turned be ;soul seek founded ashamed

4 חפצי רעתי׃ ישובו על־עקב בשתם האמרים האח ׀

!Aha who those their a for them Let my who those
,say ,shame of reward back turn .evil desire

5 האח׃ ישישו וישמחו ׀ בך כל־מבקשיך ויאמרו תמיד

,continually let and who those all in be and Let !Aha
say ;You seek You glad ,rejoice

6= יגדל אלהים אהבי ישועתך׃ ואני ׀ עני ואביון אלהים

,God O and poor I But Your lovers ,God be Let
,needy (am) .salvation of magnified

חושה־לי עזרי ומפלטי אתה יהוה אל־תאחר׃

wait do not O You my and my to come
.longer any ;Jehovah ;(are) deliverer help ;me quickly

PSALM 70

To the Chief Musician. A Psalm of David, to bring to remembrance.

[1] O God, deliver me! Hurry, O Jehovah, to help me! [2] Let those who seek after my soul be ashamed and turned pale; let them be turned backward and shamed, those who desire my evil. [3] Let them be turned back for a reward of their shame, those who say, Aha, aha! [4] Let all those who seek You rejoice, and be glad in you; and let those who love Your salvation forever say, Let God be magnified. [5] But I (am) poor and needy, come quickly to me, O God; You (are) my help and my deliverer; O Jehovah, do not wait any longer.

PSAL. LXXI עא

PSALM 71

1
2 בך־יהוה חסיתי אל־אבושה לעולם׃ בצדקתך תצילני

deliver Your in .forever be me let not seek I O In
me righteousness shame to put ;refuge Jehovah You

3 ותפלטני הטה־אלי אזנך והושיעני׃ היה לי ׀ לצור

a for Be save and Your to bow and
of rock me .me ear me down ;me rescue

מעון לבוא תמיד צוית להושיעני כי־סלעי ומצודתי אתה׃

You my and my for save to have You ;always to ,refuge
.(are) fortress rock ;me commanded to come

4
5 אלהי פלטני מיד רשע מכף מעול וחומץ׃ כי־אתה

You For the and the the from the the from deliver my O
(are) .ruthless unjust of palm ,wicked of hand me ,God

PSALM 71

[1] I put my trust in You, O Jehovah, let me not be put to shame forever. [2] In Your righteousness deliver me and rescue me; bow down Your ear to me and save me. [3] Be a rock of strength for me, to which I may always go; You have given a commandment to save me; for You (are) my rock and my fortress. [4] O my God, deliver me out of the hand of the wicked, and out of the palm of the unrighteous, and the ruthless. [5] For You (are) my hope,

O Lord Jehovah, my trust from my youth. [6] I have rested on You from the womb; You are He who took me out of my mother's womb; my praise (shall) always (be) of You. [7] I am like a wonder to many, but You (are) my strong tower. [8] My mouth is filled (with) Your praise, (with) Your glory all the day long. [9] Do not cast me off now at the time of my old age. Do not forsake me when my strength fails. [10] For my enemies speak against me; and those who lurk for my soul plot together. [11] And (they) say, God has forsaken him; pursue him and take him, for there is no one to deliver. [12] O God, do not be far from me; O my God, come quickly to help me. [13] Let them be ashamed; let those who are enemies of my soul be consumed; let them be covered with reproach, and let those seeking evil for me (be) dishonored; [14] and I will always hope, and I will add more on all your praise. [15] My mouth shall proclaim Your righteousness (and) Your salvation all the day; for I do not know the numbers. [16] I will come in the Lord Jehovah's strength; I will speak of Your righteousness, of Yours alone. [17] O God, You have taught me from my youth; and until now I have declared Your wonders. [18] And now that I am old and gray-headed, O God, do not leave me; until I have proclaimed Your strength to the generation. Your might to everyone who is to come. [19] And, O God, Your righteousness (is) very high; for You have done great things; O God, who (is) like You? [20] Who has shown me great and evil troubles; You will turn (me); You make me live; and You will turn from the depths of the earth; You will bring me up. [21] You will multiply my greatness and comfort me on every side. [22] I will also thank You with a harp; Your truth, O my

6 תקותי אדני יהוה מבטחי מנעורי׃ עליך | נסמכתי מבטן

the from ;womb | have I leaned | on You | my from .youth | my trust | ,Jehovah | O Lord | my ,hope

7 ממעי אמי אתה גוזי בך תהלתי תמיד׃ כמופת הייתי

am I | a like wonder | (shall) .(be) always | my praise | in You | who He ;me took | You (are) | my mother's | of out womb

8 לרבים ואתה מחסי־עז׃ ימלא פי תהלתך כל־היום

day the long | all | your (with) ,praise | My mouth | is filled | .strong | my refuge | You but (are) | to ,many

9 תפארתך׃ אל־תשליכני לעת זקנה ככלות כחי אל־

not | my ,strength | when fails | old ;age | the at of time | cast Do off me | not | Your (with) .glory

10 תעזבני׃ כי־אמרו אויבי לי ושמרי נפשי נועצו יחדו׃

,together | plot | my soul | those and watching | against ;me | my enemies | speak | For | forsake do .me

11 12 לאמר אלהים עזבו רדפו ותפשוהו כי־אין מציל׃ אלהים

God O | .deliverer | there for no is | take and ;him | pursue (him) | has ;him forsaken | God | ,saying

13 אל־תרחק ממני אלהי לעזרתי חישה׃ יבשו יכלו שטני

foes the of | be let consumed | them Let ;blush | come .quickly | help to me | my O God | from ;me | be do far | not

14 נפשי יעטו חרפה וכלמה מבקשי רעתי׃ ואני תמיד

continually | and I | for evil ;me | those seeking | and dishonor | reproach | be Let with covered | my .soul

15 איחל והוספתי על־כל־תהלתך׃ פי | יספר צדקתך כל־

all | Your righteousness | shall proclaim | My mouth | Your .praise | all | in | will I and more add | will hope

16 היום תשועתך כי לא ידעתי ספרות׃ אבוא בגברות

strength in | will I come | the .numbers | do I know | not | For | Your .salvation | the ,day

17 אדני יהוה אזכיר צדקתך לבדך׃ אלהים למדתני

have You me taught | ,God O | Yours .alone | Your ,righteousness | will I mention | ;Jehovah's | the Lord

18 מנעורי ועד־הנה אגיד נפלאותיך׃ וגם עד־זקנה | ושיבה

gray- and ,headed | (am I) when old | And even | Your .wonders | have I declared | now and until | my from ;youth

אלהים אל־תעזבני עד־אגיד זרועך לדור לכל־יבוא

is who coming | to everyone | the to ;generation | Your strength | I declare | until | leave do ;me | not | ,God O

19 גבורתך׃ וצדקתך אלהים עד־מרום אשר־עשית גדלות

great ;things | has done | who | the ,heights | (is) to | ,God O | Your And ,righteousness | Your .power

20 אלהים מי כמוך׃ אשר הראיתנו | צרות רבות ורעות

,evil and | great | troubles | shown has me | Who | like ?You | who (is) | ,God O

21 תשוב תחינו ומתהמות הארץ תשוב תעלני׃ תרב |

will You multiply | will You up me bring | will You turn | the earth | from and of depths the | make You ;live me | will You ;(me) turn

22 גדלתי ותסב תנחמני׃ גם־אני | אודך בכלי־נבל אמתך

Your truth | harp a with ;instrument | thank will you | I also | (and) .me comfort | sur- and round | my ,greatness

God I will sing to You with the lyre, O holy one of Israel. [23] My lips shall shout for joy , for I will sing praise to You; also my soul which you have redeemed. [24] And my tongue shall muse on Your righteousness all day; because those seeking my evil are disgraced; they are put to shame.

PSALM 72

Of Solomon.

[1] Give the king Your judgments, O God; and Your righteousness to the king's son. [2] Your people He shall judge in righteousness, and Your poor in justice. [3] The mountains will lift up peace to the people; and the little hills through righteousness. [4] He shall judge the poor of the people; and He shall save the sons of the needy; and He shall crush the oppressor. [5] They shall fear You with the sun; and before the moon in all generations. [6] He shall descend like rain on the mown grass; like showers that water the earth. [7] In His days the righteous shall flourish, and plenty of peace, till (is) not the moon. [8] He shall also rule from sea to sea, and from the River to the ends of the earth. [9] Those dwelling in the desert will bow before Him, and His enemies will lick the dust. [10] The kings of Tarshish and of the isles shall bring presents; the kings of Sheba and Seba shall offer gifts. [11] Yea, all kings shall fall down before Him; all nations shall serve Him. [12] For He shall save the needy who cries, and the poor (with) no helper. [13] He shall have pity on the poor and needy; and He saves the souls of the needy ones. [14] He shall redeem their souls from oppression and violence; and their blood shall be precious in His eyes. [15] And He shall live, and the gold of Sheba shall be given to Him; and prayer shall be made for Him continually; He shall bless Him all the day long. [16] A fullness of grain

23 אֱלֹהָי אֲזַמְּרָה לְךָ בְכִנּוֹר קְדוֹשׁ יִשְׂרָאֵל׃ תְּרַנֵּנָּה שְׂפָתַי כִּי

for My shout shall .Israel Holy O the with to will I my O
,lips joy for of One ,lyre You sing ;God

24 אֲזַמְּרָה־לָּךְ וְנַפְשִׁי אֲשֶׁר פָּדִיתָ׃ גַּם־לְשׁוֹנִי כָּל־הַיּוֹם תֶּהְגֶּה

shall the all my Also You which my also to will I
on muse day tongue .redeemed soul ;You praise sing

צִדְקָתֶךָ כִּי־בֹשׁוּ כִּי־חָפְרוּ מְבַקְשֵׁי רָעָתִי׃

.evil my who those put are for are for righ- Your
seek shame to ,disgraced ;teousness

PSAL. LXXII עב

PSALM 72

1 לִשְׁלֹמֹה ׀ אֱלֹהִים מִשְׁפָּטֶיךָ לְמֶלֶךְ תֵּן וְצִדְקָתְךָ לְבֶן־מֶלֶךְ׃

the to Your and ;give the to Your ,God O (psalm A)
.king's son righteousness king judgments ,Solomon of

2
3 יָדִין עַמְּךָ בְצֶדֶק וַעֲנִיֶּיךָ בְמִשְׁפָּט׃ יִשְׂאוּ הָרִים שָׁלוֹם

peace The lift shall .justice in Your and righ- in Your shall He
mountains up poor teousness people judge

4 לָעָם וּגְבָעוֹת בִּצְדָקָה׃ יִשְׁפֹּט ׀ עֲנִיֵּי־עָם יוֹשִׁיעַ לִבְנֵי אֶבְיוֹן

the the shall He the the shall He through the and the to
,needy of sons save ;people of poor judge .righteousness hills little ;people

5 וִידַכֵּא עוֹשֵׁק׃ יִירָאוּךָ עִם־שָׁמֶשׁ וְלִפְנֵי יָרֵחַ דּוֹר דּוֹרִים׃

genera- genera- the and the with shall They op- the he and
.tions of tion moon before ;sun You fear .pressor crush will

6
7 יֵרֵד כְּמָטָר עַל־גֵּז כִּרְבִיבִים זַרְזִיף אָרֶץ׃ יִפְרַח־בְּיָמָיו

His In shall the that like the on like shall He
days flourish .earth water showers ,grass mown rain descend

8 צַדִּיק וְרֹב שָׁלוֹם עַד־בְּלִי יָרֵחַ׃ וְיֵרְדְּ מִיָּם עַד־יָם וּמִנָּהָר

from and ,sea to from shall He the not (is) till ,peace and The
River the sea rule also ,moon of plenty righteous

9 עַד־אַפְסֵי־אָרֶץ׃ לְפָנָיו יִכְרְעוּ צִיִּים וְאֹיְבָיו עָפָר יְלַחֵכוּ׃

shall the His and desert shall Before the the to
.lick dust enemies ,dwellers bow Him .earth of ends

10 מַלְכֵי תַרְשִׁישׁ וְאִיִּים מִנְחָה יָשִׁיבוּ מַלְכֵי שְׁבָא וּסְבָא

and Sheba kings the shall presents of and Tarshish kings The
Seba of ;bring isles the of

11 אֶשְׁכָּר יַקְרִיבוּ׃ וְיִשְׁתַּחֲווּ־לוֹ כָל־מְלָכִים כָּל־גּוֹיִם

nations all ;kings all before shall ,Yea shall gifts
Him down fall .offer

12
13 יַעַבְדוּהוּ׃ כִּי־יַצִּיל אֶבְיוֹן מְשַׁוֵּעַ וְעָנִי וְאֵין־עֹזֵר לוֹ׃ יָחֹס

shall He to a is and also who the He For serve shall
pity have .him helper not poor the ,cries needy deliver shall .Him

14 עַל־דַּל וְאֶבְיוֹן וְנַפְשׁוֹת אֶבְיוֹנִים יוֹשִׁיעַ׃ מִתּוֹךְ וּמֵחָמָס

from and From He needy the the and and the on
violence oppression . saves ones of souls ;needy poor

15 יִגְאַל נַפְשָׁם וְיֵיקַר דָּמָם בְּעֵינָיו׃ וִיחִי וְיִתֶּן־לוֹ מִזְּהַב

the of be shall and He And His in their shall and their shall He
of gold Him to given ,live shall .sight blood precious be ;souls redeem

16 שְׁבָא וְיִתְפַּלֵּל בַּעֲדוֹ תָמִיד כָּל־הַיּוֹם יְבָרֲכֶנְהוּ׃ יְהִי פִסַּת־

full- a shall shall He the all ;continually for prayer and ;Sheba
of ness be .Him bless long day Him made be shall

shall be in the earth on top of the mountains; its fruit shall shake like Lebanon; and they of the city shall flourish like the grass of the earth. [17] His name shall endure forever; His name shall be proclaimed before the sun; and they shall bless themselves by Him; all nations shall call Him blessed.

[18] Blessed (is) Jehovah God, the God of Israel, who alone does wonderful things. [19] And blessed (is) His glorious name forever; and the whole earth is filled with His glory! Amen and amen!

[20] The prayers of David the son of Jesse have ended.

בַּר בָּאָרֶץ בְּרֹאשׁ הָרִים יִרְעַשׁ כַּלְּבָנוֹן פִּרְיוֹ וְיָצִיצוּ
shall and its like shall the the on the in grain
flourish ;fruit Lebanon shake ;mountains of top earth

17 מֵעִיר כְּעֵשֶׂב הָאָרֶץ׃ יְהִי שְׁמוֹ לְעוֹלָם לִפְנֵי־שֶׁמֶשׁ יִנּוֹן
shall the before ;forever His Shall the the like the of
continue sun name be .earth of grass city

18 שְׁמוֹ וְיִתְבָּרְכוּ בוֹ כָּל־גּוֹיִם יְאַשְּׁרוּהוּ׃ בָּרוּךְ יְהוָה אֱלֹהִים
,God Jehovah Blessed call shall nations all by bless they and His
(is) .blessed Him ;Him themselves ;name

19 אֱלֹהֵי יִשְׂרָאֵל עֹשֵׂה נִפְלָאוֹת לְבַדּוֹ׃ וּבָרוּךְ שֵׁם כְּבוֹדוֹ
His name blessed And .alone wonderful who ,Israel God the
glorious (is) things does of

20 לְעוֹלָם וְיִמָּלֵא כְבוֹדוֹ אֶת־כֹּל הָאָרֶץ אָמֵן וְאָמֵן׃ כָּלּוּ
have and ,Amen the all His is and ;forever
ended !amen .earth glory with filled

תְפִלּוֹת דָּוִד בֶּן־יִשָׁי׃
.Jesse the David The
of son of prayers

PSAL. LXXIII עג

PSALM 73

A Psalm of Asaph.

[1] Truly God (is) good to Israel, to those who are of a pure heart. [2]And (as) (for) me, my feet had almost stumbled; my steps nearly made to slip. [3] For I was jealous of the proud; I looked upon the peace of the wicked. [4] For there are no pangs to their death; but their body (is) fat. [5] They are not in the misery of mortal man; they are not plagued with common men. [6] So pride enchains them; violence covers them (like) a robe. [7] Their eyes swell out with fatness; they have passed the imaginations of the heart. [8] They scoff and speak in malice; from on high they speak cruelty. [9] They set their mouth in the heavens; and their tongue walks through the earth. [10] Because of this His people shall return here; and waters of a full (cup) shall be drained by them. [11] And they say, How does God know? and, Is there knowledge in the Most High? [12] Behold! These (are) the ungodly, who are always at ease; they increase their riches. [13] Surely I have purified my heart in vain; and I have

PSALM 73

1 מִזְמוֹר לְאָסָף אַךְ טוֹב לְיִשְׂרָאֵל אֱלֹהִים לְבָרֵי לֵבָב׃
.heart the to ,God Israel to (is) Truly of A
of pure good .Asaph psalm

2
3 וַאֲנִי כִּמְעַט נָטוּי רַגְלָי כְּאַיִן שֻׁפְּכָה אֲשֻׁרָי׃ כִּי קִנֵּאתִי
was I For my made were nearly my had almost And
jealous .steps slip to ;foot stumbled ,I

4 בַּהוֹלְלִים שְׁלוֹם רְשָׁעִים אֶרְאֶה׃ כִּי אֵין חַרְצֻבּוֹת לְמוֹתָם
their to pangs there For looked I the the the of
;death no are .on wicked of peace ;proud

5 וּבָרִיא אוּלָם׃ בַּעֲמַל אֱנוֹשׁ אֵינֵמוֹ וְעִם־אָדָם לֹא יְנֻגָּעוּ׃
are they not men and are they man the in their is but
.plagued with ;not of trouble ;body fat

6
7 לָכֵן עֲנָקַתְמוֹ גַאֲוָה יַעֲטָף־שִׁית חָמָס לָמוֹ׃ יָצָא מֵחֵלֶב
from swell .them to violence gar- a covers ,pride enchains So
fatness out of ment (like) ,them

8 עֵינֵמוֹ עָבְרוּ מַשְׂכִּיּוֹת לֵבָב׃ יָמִיקוּ וִידַבְּרוּ בְרָע עֹשֶׁק
(of) in and They the imagina- the have they Their
;cruelty malice speak scoff .heart of tions passed ;eyes

9 מִמָּרוֹם יְדַבֵּרוּ׃ שַׁתּוּ בַשָּׁמַיִם פִּיהֶם וּלְשׁוֹנָם תִּהֲלַךְ בָּאָרֶץ׃
through walks their and their the against They they from and
.earth the tongue ;mouth heavens set .speak high on

10
11 לָכֵן יָשִׁיב עַמּוֹ הֲלֹם וּמֵי מָלֵא יִמָּצוּ לָמוֹ׃ וְאָמְרוּ אֵיכָה
How they And by is full a and ;here His shall So
,say .them drained (cup) of waters people return

12 יָדַע־אֵל וְיֵשׁ דֵּעָה בְעֶלְיוֹן׃ הִנֵּה־אֵלֶּה רְשָׁעִים וְשַׁלְוֵי
are who the These !Behold the in knowledge Is ?God does
ease at ,wicked (are) ?High Most there know

13 עוֹלָם הִשְׂגּוּ־חָיִל׃ אַךְ־רִיק זִכִּיתִי לְבָבִי וָאֶרְחַץ בְּנִקָּיוֹן
in I and ;heart my have I in Surely (their) they ;always
innocency washed have cleansed vain .riches increase

washed my hands in innocence. [14] For all the day long I was plagued; and my chastening is at the mornings. [15] If I say, This is the way I will speak; behold, I would deceive a generation of Your children. [16] And (although) I thought, (that I might) understand this, it (was) painful in my eyes, [17] until I went into the sanctuaries of God; now I understood their end. [18] Surely, You will set their feet in slippery places; You will make them fall into ruin. [19] How they are destroyed in a moment, swept away with terrors! [20] Like a dream at the time of awakening, O Jehovah, when You awake, You will despise their image. [21] For my heart was in a ferment, and I was pierced (in my reins.. [22] And I (was) brutish and did not know; I was (like) animals before You. [23] Yet I (was) continually with You; You have taken hold of my right hand. [24] You shall guide me by Your counsel; and at last You will take me (to) glory. [25] Whom have I in Heaven? And I desire no one besides You on earth. [26] My flesh and my heart waste away; God (is) the rock of my heart and my portion forever. [27] For, lo, those who are far from You shall be lost; You have destroyed all who go lusting away from You. [28] (As for) me, (it is) good for me to draw near to God; I have made my refuge in the Lord Jehovah, to declare all Your works.

PSALM 74

A Lesson, of Asaph.

[1] O God, have You cast (us) off forever; will Your anger smoke against the sheep of Your pasture? [2] Remember Your congregation, (which) You purchased in days past, the rod of Your inheritance (which) You have redeemed, this Mount Zion in which You have dwelt. [3] Lift up Your steps to the perpetual desolations; the enemy who

14 15 כַּפָּי׃ וָאֱהִי נָגוּעַ כָּל־הַיּוֹם וְתוֹכַחְתִּי לַבְּקָרִים׃ אִם־אָמַרְתִּי

,say I If the at (is) my and the all plagued For my
.mornings chastening ;day was I .hands

16 אֲסַפְּרָה כְמוֹ הִנֵּה דוֹר בָּנֶיךָ בָגָדְתִּי׃ וָאֲחַשְּׁבָה לָדַעַת

know to I And would I Your gener- a ,behold this in will I
thought .deceive sons of ation ,way speak

17 זֹאת עָמָל הִיא בְעֵינָי׃ עַד־אָבוֹא אֶל־מִקְדְּשֵׁי־אֵל אָבִינָה

dis- I ;God the into went I until my in it painful ,this
cerned of sanctuaries ,eyes (was)

18 לְאַחֲרִיתָם׃ אַךְ בַּחֲלָקוֹת תָּשִׁית לָמוֹ הִפַּלְתָּם לְמַשּׁוּאוֹת׃

.ruins into will You ;them will You slippery in Surely their
fall them make set places .end

19 אֵיךְ הָיוּ לְשַׁמָּה כְרָגַע סָפוּ תַמּוּ מִן־בַּלָּהוֹת׃ כַּחֲלוֹם

a Like !terrors from consumed fin- an in desolation they How
dream ;ished ,instant become have

20 21 מֵהָקִיץ אֲדֹנָי בָּעִיר ׀ צַלְמָם תִּבְזֶה׃ כִּי יִתְחַמֵּץ לְבָבִי

my em- was For will You their In O at
,heart bittered .despise image awaking ,Lord ,awakening

22 וְכִלְיוֹתַי אֶשְׁתּוֹנָן׃ וַאֲנִי־בַעַר וְלֹא אֵדָע בְּהֵמוֹת הָיִיתִי

was I (like) did I and brutish And was I (in) and
animals ;know not (was) I .pierced reins my

23 24 עִמָּךְ׃ וַאֲנִי תָמִיד עִמָּךְ אָחַזְתָּ בְּיַד יְמִינִי׃ בַּעֲצָתְךָ תַנְחֵנִי

shall You Your By .right my have You with continually Yet with
;me guide counsel hand taken ;You (was) I .You

25 וְאַחַר כָּבוֹד תִּקָּחֵנִי׃ מִי־לִי בַשָּׁמָיִם וְעִמְּךָ לֹא־חָפַצְתִּי

do I not And in to Whom shall (to) and
desire You besides ?Heaven me (is) .me take glory afterward

26 בָאָרֶץ׃ כָּלָה שְׁאֵרִי וּלְבָבִי צוּר־לְבָבִי וְחֶלְקִי אֱלֹהִים

God (is) my and my the my and my Waste on
portion heart of rock ;heart flesh away .earth

27 לְעוֹלָם׃ כִּי־הִנֵּה רְחֵקֶיךָ יֹאבֵדוּ הִצְמַתָּה כָּל־זוֹנֶה מִמֶּךָּ׃

from go who all have You shall far those ,lo ,For .forever
.You whoring off cut ;perish You from ,behold

28 וַאֲנִי ׀ קִרֲבַת אֱלֹהִים לִי־טוֹב שַׁתִּי ׀ בַּאדֹנָי יֱהֹוִה מַחְסִי

my Jehovah the in have I (is) to God near- the ,I And
,refuge Lord made ;good me of ness

לְסַפֵּר כָּל־מַלְאֲכוֹתֶיךָ׃

Your all to
.works declare

PSAL. LXXIV עד

PSALM 74

1 מַשְׂכִּיל לְאָסָף לָמָה אֱלֹהִים זָנַחְתָּ לָנֶצַח יֶעְשַׁן אַפְּךָ

Your Will ?forever You have O ,Why .Asaph of ;lesson A
anger smoke off us cast ,God

2 בְּצֹאן מַרְעִיתֶךָ׃ זְכֹר עֲדָתְךָ ׀ קָנִיתָ קֶּדֶם גָּאַלְתָּ שֵׁבֶט

the (as) re- You of You Your Remember Your the against
of rod deemed .old gained assembly ?pasture of sheep

3 נַחֲלָתֶךָ הַר־צִיּוֹן זֶה ׀ שָׁכַנְתָּ בּוֹ׃ הָרִימָה פְעָמֶיךָ לְמַשֻּׁאוֹת

the to Your up Lift in have You ,this Zion Mount Your
.desolations steps .which dwelt ,inheritance

has done evil in the sanctuary. [4] Your adversaries have roared in the middle of Your holy places; they set up their own signs (for) signs. [5] He is known as one bringing axes in on high, against the thick trees. [6] And now they break down its carved work together with axe and hammer [7] They have cast fire in Your sanctuary; they have polluted the place where Your name dwells on earth. [8] They said in their hearts, Let us destroy them together; they have burned up all the meeting-places of God in the land. [9] We did not see our signs; there is no longer any prophet; nor any among us who knows how long. [10] O God, how long shall the enemy speak evil? Shall the enemy blaspheme Your name forever? [11] Why do You withdraw Your hand, even Your right hand? From out of Your bosom, consume (them).

[12] For God (is) my King of old, who works salvation in the midst of the land. [13] You divided the sea by Your strength; You broke the heads of sea-monsters in the waters. [14] You broke the heads of leviathan in pieces; You made him food to the people living in the wilderness. [15] You divided the fountain and the torrent; You dried up mighty rivers. [16] The day (is) Yours, the night (is) also Yours; You have established the light and the sun. [17] You have set all the boundaries of the earth; You have made summer and winter. [18] Remember this: the enemy has blasphemed, O Jehovah; and a foolish people have despised Your name. [19] Do not give the soul of Your turtle-dove to the wild beasts; You will not forever forget the life of Your afflicted ones. [20] Look to (Your) covenant; for the dark places of the earth are full of the houses of violence. [21] O let not the ill-treated ones turn back ashamed; let the poor and needy praise Your

4 נֶצַח כָּל־הֵרַע אוֹיֵב בַּקֹּדֶשׁ׃ שָׁאֲגוּ צֹרְרֶיךָ בְּקֶרֶב מוֹעֲדֶךָ
Your the in Your have ' the in (the) done has per-
;sanctuary of middle enemies roared .sanctuary enemy evil all ,petual

5 שָׂמוּ אוֹתֹתָם אֹתוֹת׃ יִוָּדַע כְּמֵבִיא לְמָעְלָה בִּסְבָךְ־עֵץ
the against high on one as is He (for) their setting
trees thick in bringing known .signs signs up

6 קַרְדֻּמּוֹת׃ וְעַתְּ פִּתּוּחֶיהָ יָּחַד בְּכַשִּׁיל וְכֵילַפּוֹת יַהֲלֹמוּן׃
break they and the in ,together carved its And .axes
.down hammers ax work now

7 8 שִׁלְחוּ בָאֵשׁ מִקְדָּשֶׁךָ לָאָרֶץ חִלְּלוּ מִשְׁכַּן־שְׁמֶךָ׃ אָמְרוּ
They Your place the have they the on Your fire have They
said .name dwells where polluted earth ;sanctuary in cast

9 בְלִבָּם נִינָם יָחַד שָׂרְפוּ כָל־מוֹעֲדֵי־אֵל בָּאָרֶץ׃ אוֹתֹתֵינוּ
signs Our the in God the all have they ;together us Let their in
.land of meeting-places up burned them oppress ,hearts

10 לֹא־רָאִינוּ אֵין־עוֹד נָבִיא וְלֹא־אִתָּנוּ יֹדֵעַ עַד־מָה׃ עַד־
Until .when until (one) with and a longer not we not
knowing us not ;prophet (is) (any) ;see did

11 מָתַי אֱלֹהִים יְחָרֶף צָר יְנָאֵץ אוֹיֵב שִׁמְךָ לָנֶצַח׃ לָמָּה
Why ?forever Your the shall the shall ,God O ,when
name enemy despise,enemy evil speak

12 תָשִׁיב יָדְךָ וִימִינֶךָ מִקֶּרֶב חוֹקְךָ כַלֵּה׃ וֵאלֹהִים מַלְכִּי
my (is) God For consume Your From Your even Your You do
king !(them) ,bosom of out ?hand right ,hand withdraw

13 מִקֶּדֶם פֹּעֵל יְשׁוּעוֹת בְּקֶרֶב הָאָרֶץ׃ אַתָּה פוֹרַרְתָּ בְעָזְּךָ
with divided You the the in salvation who ,old of
might Your .land of midst works

14 יָם שִׁבַּרְתָּ רָאשֵׁי תַנִּינִים עַל־הַמָּיִם׃ אַתָּה רִצַּצְתָּ רָאשֵׁי
the broke You the on sea- the You the
of heads pieces in .waters monsters of heads broke ;sea

15 לִוְיָתָן תִּתְּנֶנּוּ מַאֲכָל לְעָם לְצִיִּים׃ אַתָּה בָקַעְתָּ מַעְיָן וָנָחַל
the and the divided You the of the for food made You levia-
;torrent fountain .wilderness people him ;than

16 אַתָּה הוֹבַשְׁתָּ נַהֲרוֹת אֵיתָן׃ לְךָ יוֹם אַף־לְךָ לָיְלָה אַתָּה
You the to (is) also The to (is) .mighty rivers up dried You
;night You ,day You

17 הֲכִינוֹתָ מָאוֹר וָשָׁמֶשׁ׃ אַתָּה הִצַּבְתָּ כָּל־גְּבוּלוֹת אֶרֶץ קַיִץ
summer the the all have You the and the have
;earth of boundaries fixed .sun light made

18 וָחֹרֶף אַתָּה יְצַרְתָּם׃ זְכָר־זֹאת אוֹיֵב חֵרֵף ׀ יְהוָה וְעַם־
a O has the :thus Remember have You and
people ;Jehovah ,blasphemed enemy .them formed ,winter

19 נָבָל נִאֲצוּ שְׁמֶךָ׃ אַל־תִּתֵּן לְחַיַּת נֶפֶשׁ תּוֹרֶךָ חַיַּת עֲנִיֶּיךָ
Your the Your the the to Do not Your has foolish
afflicted of life ;dove of soul beasts wild give .name despised

20 אַל־תִּשְׁכַּח לָנֶצַח׃ הַבֵּט לַבְּרִית כִּי־מָלְאוּ מַחֲשַׁכֵּי־אֶרֶץ
the dark the full are for the to Look .forever will You not
earth of places of ,covenant forget

21 נְאוֹת חָמָס׃ אַל־יָשֹׁב דַּךְ נִכְלָם עָנִי וְאֶבְיוֹן יְהַלְלוּ שְׁמֶךָ׃
Your praise let the and the ;ashamed the of Let not .violence the
.name needy poor oppressed back turn of abodes

name. [22] Arise, O God, plead Your own cause; remember Your reproach from the fool day by day. [23] Do not forget the voice of Your enemies; the noise of Your foes is going up continually.

22 קוּמָה אֱלֹהִים רִיבָה רִיבֶךָ זְכֹר חֶרְפָּתְךָ מִנִּי־נָבָל כָּל־
all the from Your remember Your plead ,God O ,Arise
fool reproach ;cause own

23 הַיּוֹם׃ אַל־תִּשְׁכַּח קוֹל צֹרְרֶיךָ שְׁאוֹן קָמֶיךָ עֹלֶה תָמִיד׃
.continually is Your the Your the Do not .day the
up going foes of noise ;enemies of voice forget

PSAL. LXXV עה

PSALM 75

To the Chief Musician. Do not destroy. A Psalm of Asaph. A Song.

[1] We have given thanks to You, O God; we have given praise; for Your name is near; Your wonderful works have been told. [2] When I take the appointed time, I shall judge righteously. [3] The earth and all of its inhabitants are melting away; I set firm its pillars. Selah. [4] I said to the proud, Do not be proud; and to the wicked, Do not lift up the horn. [5] Do not lift up your horn on high, do (not) speak with a stiff neck. [6] For exaltations are not from the east, nor from the west, nor from the desert; [7] but God (is) the judge; (He) puts down this (one) and lifts up this (other). [8] For a cup is in the hand of Jehovah; and the wine is foaming, it is fully mixed; and He pours out from it; surely all the wicked of the earth must drain its dregs and drink. [9] But I will witness forever; I will sing praises to the God of Jacob. [10] And I will cut off all the horns of the wicked; (but) the horns of the righteous shall be lifted up.

1 2 לַמְנַצֵּחַ אַל־תַּשְׁחֵת מִזְמוֹר לְאָסָף שִׁיר׃ הוֹדִינוּ לְּךָ ׀
to have We A of psalm A do not chief the To
,You thanks given .song .Asaph .destroy ;musician

3 אֱלֹהִים הוֹדִינוּ וְקָרוֹב שְׁמֶךָ סִפְּרוּ נִפְלְאוֹתֶיךָ׃ כִּי אֶקַּח
take I When Your wonderful have Your is for have we ;God O
.works told been ;name near ;thanks given

4 מוֹעֵד אֲנִי מֵישָׁרִים אֶשְׁפֹּט׃ נְמֹגִים־אֶרֶץ וְכָל־יֹשְׁבֶיהָ
its all and The melting are shall upright- in I set the
;inhabitants of earth away .judge ness ,time

5 אָנֹכִי תִכַּנְתִּי עַמּוּדֶיהָ סֶּלָה׃ אָמַרְתִּי לַהוֹלְלִים אַל־תָּהֹלּוּ
Do not the to say I .Selah its set I
;boast ,boastful .pillars firm

6 וְלָרְשָׁעִים אַל־תָּרִימוּ קָרֶן׃ אַל־תָּרִימוּ לַמָּרוֹם קַרְנְכֶם
,horn your high on lift Do not the lift Do not the to and
up .horn up .wicked

7 תְּדַבְּרוּ בְצַוָּאר עָתָק׃ כִּי לֹא מִמּוֹצָא וּמִמַּעֲרָב וְלֹא
and from nor the from not For .stiff a with do (not)
not ,west the ,east neck speak

8 מִמִּדְבַּר הָרִים׃ כִּי־אֱלֹהִים שֹׁפֵט זֶה יַשְׁפִּיל וְזֶה יָרִים׃
lifts and puts this the (is) God but (are) the from
.up this down ;judge ;exaltations desert

9 כִּי כוֹס בְּיַד־יְהֹוָה וְיַיִן חָמַר ׀ מָלֵא מֶסֶךְ וַיַּגֵּר מִזֶּה אַךְ־
surely from He and is it fully ,foams the and ;Jehovah (is) cup a For
;it out pours ;mixed wine of hand the in

10 שְׁמָרֶיהָ יִמְצוּ יִשְׁתּוּ כֹּל רִשְׁעֵי־אָרֶץ׃ וַאֲנִי אַגִּיד לְעֹלָם
;forever will I But the the all (and) must dregs its
declare .earth of wicked drink drain

11 אֲזַמְּרָה לֵאלֹהֵי יַעֲקֹב׃ וְכָל־קַרְנֵי רְשָׁעִים אֲגַדֵּעַ תְּרוֹמַמְנָה
shall (but) will I the the And .Jacob the to will I
up lifted be ;off cut wicked of horns all of God praises sing

קַרְנוֹת צַדִּיק׃
the horns the
.righteous of

PSAL. LXXVI עו

PSALM 76

To the Chief Musician. For Stringed Instruments. A Psalm of Asaph. A Song of Praise.

[1] God (is) known in Judah; His name (is) great in Israel. [2] And His abode is in Salem; and His dwelling-place in Zion. [3] There He

1 2 לַמְנַצֵּחַ בִּנְגִינֹת מִזְמוֹר לְאָסָף שִׁיר׃ נוֹדָע בִּיהוּדָה אֱלֹהִים
;God Judah in (is) .song A of psalm A with chief the To
known .Asaph .instruments stringed ;musician

3 בְּיִשְׂרָאֵל גָּדוֹל שְׁמוֹ׃ וַיְהִי בְשָׁלֵם סֻכּוֹ וּמְעוֹנָתוֹ בְצִיּוֹן׃
in His and His Salem in is And His (is) Israel in
.Zion dwelling-place ;abode .name great

broke the fiery arrows of the bow, the shield, and the sword, and the battle. Selah. [4] You (are) glorious, (more) excellent than the mountains of prey. [5] The stout-hearted have been stripped; they slept their sleep; and none of the men of might have found their hands. [6] By Your rebuke, O God of Jacob, both the horse and chariot have sunk into a sleep. [7] You are terrifying; and who can stand before You when You are angry? [8] You have caused judgment to be heard from Heaven; the earth feared and was stilled, [9] when God arose to judgment, to save all the meek of the earth. Selah. [10] For the wraths of man thank You; You encircle Yourself (with) the wraths left over. [11] Vow and pray to Jehovah your God; let all that are around Him bring presents to the Fearful One. [12] He shall cut off the spirit in princes; (He is) feared by the kings of the earth.

4 5 שָׁמָּה שִׁבַּר רִשְׁפֵי־קָשֶׁת מָגֵן וְחֶרֶב וּמִלְחָמָה סֶלָה׃ נָאוֹר
glorious .Selah the and the and the the fiery the He There
.battle ,sword ,shield ,bow of arrows broke

6 אַתָּה אַדִּיר מֵהַרְרֵי־טָרֶף׃ אֶשְׁתּוֹלְלוּ ׀ אַבִּירֵי לֵב נָמוּ
they ;heart The been have .prey the than (more) You
slept of stout stripped of mountains excellent ,(are)

7 שְׁנָתָם וְלֹא־מָצְאוּ כָל־אַנְשֵׁי־חַיִל יְדֵיהֶם׃ מִגַּעֲרָתְךָ אֱלֹהֵי
God O Your By their might the any have and their
of ,rebuke .hands of men found not ;sleep

8 יַעֲקֹב נִרְדָּם וְרֶכֶב וָסוּס׃ אַתָּה ׀ נוֹרָא אַתָּה וּמִי־יַעֲמֹד
can and (even) be to are You the and the both sunk ,Jacob
stand who ,You ,feared .horse chariot ,sleep into

9 לְפָנֶיךָ מֵאָז אַפֶּךָ׃ מִשָּׁמַיִם הִשְׁמַעְתָּ דִּין אֶרֶץ יָרְאָה
feared the ;judgment caused You from You when before
earth heard be to Heaven ?angry (are) You

10 וְשָׁקָטָה׃ בְּקוּם־לַמִּשְׁפָּט אֱלֹהִים לְהוֹשִׁיעַ כָּל־עַנְוֵי־אֶרֶץ
the the all save to God judgment to when was and
.earth of humble arose ,still

11 12 סֶלָה׃ כִּי־חֲמַת אָדָם תּוֹדֶךָּ שְׁאֵרִית חֵמֹת תַּחְגֹּר׃ נִדְרוּ
Vow gird You wraths The thank man the For .Selah
.Yourself on of residue ;You of wraths

וְשַׁלְּמוּ לַיהוָה אֱלֹהֵיכֶם כָּל־סְבִיבָיו יֹבִילוּ שַׁי לַמּוֹרָא׃
the to gifts let are who all Your to pay and
.One Fearful bring Him around ;God Jehovah

13 יִבְצֹר רוּחַ נְגִידִים נוֹרָא לְמַלְכֵי־אָרֶץ׃
the the by (is He) ;princes the shall He
.earth of kings feared of spirit off cut

PSAL. LXXVII עז

PSALM 77

PSALM 77

To the Chief Musician on Jeduthun. A Psalm of Asaph.

[1] My voice (is) to God, and I cry; my voice (is) to God, and He listened to me. [2] In the day of my distress I sought the Lord; my hand poured in the night and did not grow numb; my soul refused to be comforted. [3] I remember God and am troubled; I meditate and my spirit faints. Selah. [4] You seized the watches of my eyes; I am troubled, and I cannot speak. [5] I thought upon the days of old, the years of (bygone) ages. [6] I will remember my song in the night; I will speak with my own heart, and my spirit carefully searches. [7] Will the Lord cast off forever; and will He

1 2 לַמְנַצֵּחַ עַל־יְדוּתוּן לְאָסָף מִזְמוֹר׃ קוֹלִי אֶל־אֱלֹהִים
,God to My .psalm A Of .Jeduthun ac- chief the To
(is) voice .Asaph to cording musician

3 וְאֶצְעָקָה קוֹלִי אֶל־אֱלֹהִים וְהַאֲזִין אֵלָי׃ בְּיוֹם צָרָתִי אֲדֹנָי
the my the In to He and ,God to my I and
Lord distress of day .me ear gave (is) voice ;cry

דָּרָשְׁתִּי יָדִי ׀ לַיְלָה נִגְּרָה וְלֹא תָפוּג מֵאֲנָה הִנָּחֵם נַפְשִׁי׃
my be to refused did and was the in my ;sought I
.soul conforted ;numb grow not poured night hand

4 אֶזְכְּרָה אֱלֹהִים וְאֶהֱמָיָה אָשִׂיחָה ׀ וְתִתְעַטֵּף רוּחִי סֶלָה׃
.Selah my and meditate I am and God I
.spirit faints ;troubled remember

5 6 אָחַזְתָּ שְׁמֻרוֹת עֵינָי נִפְעַמְתִּי וְלֹא אֲדַבֵּר׃ חִשַּׁבְתִּי יָמִים
the thought I can I and am I my watches the You
days on .speak not troubled ;eyes of seized

7 מִקֶּדֶם שְׁנוֹת עוֹלָמִים׃ אֶזְכְּרָה נְגִינָתִי בַּלָּיְלָה עִם־לְבָבִי
my with the in my will I .ages the the ,old of
heart own ;night song remember of years

8 אָשִׂיחָה וַיְחַפֵּשׂ רוּחִי׃ הַלְעוֹלָמִים יִזְנַח ׀ אֲדֹנָי וְלֹא־יֹסִיף
will He And the Will forever my and will I
add not ?Lord off cast .spirit searches ,meditate

never be favorable any more? [8] Is His mercy gone forever? Has (His) word failed for all generations? [9] Has God forgotten to be gracious; Has He in anger shut up His tender mercies? Selah.

[10] And I said, This (is) my sickness, the years of the right hand of the Most High. [11] I will remember the works of Jehovah; surely I will remember Your wonders of old. [12] I will also meditate on all Your works and muse of Your doings. [13] O God, Your way (is) in holiness; who (is) a God great like God? [14] You (are) the God who does wonders; You have revealed Your strength among the peoples. [15] You have redeemed Your people with Your power, the sons of Jacob and Joseph. Selah. [16] The waters saw You, O God, the waters saw You; they were afraid; yea, the deeps trembled. [17] The clouds poured out water; the skies uttered a voice; and Your arrows flew out. [18] The voice of Your thunder in the tempest lightnings lit up the world; the earth trembled and quaked! [19] Your way (is) in the sea; and Your path (was) in the great waters; and Your footsteps are not known. [20] You led your people like a flock by the hand of Moses and Aaron.

9 לִרְצוֹת עוֹד׃ הֶאָפֵס לָנֶצַח חַסְדּוֹ גָּמַר אֹמֶר לְדֹר וָדֹר׃

and genera- to (His) Has His forever Has any be to
?generation tion word failed ?mercy ceased ?more pleased

10 11 הֲשָׁכַח חַנּוֹת אֵל אִם־קָפַץ בְּאַף רַחֲמָיו סֶלָה׃ וָאֹמַר

I And .Selah tender His in He has Or ?God be to Has
,said ?mercies anger up shut gracious forgotten

12 חַלּוֹתִי הִיא שְׁנוֹת יְמִין עֶלְיוֹן׃ אֶזְכּוֹר מַעַלְלֵי־יָהּ כִּי־אֶזְכְּרָה

will I Surely :Jah the will I Most the right the the This my
remember of works remember .High of hand of years ,(is) sickness

13 מִקֶּדֶם פִּלְאֶךָ׃ וְהָגִיתִי בְכָל־פָּעֳלֶךָ וּבַעֲלִילוֹתֶיךָ אָשִׂיחָה׃

,muse Your of and Your on I And Your old of
doings works all meditate will .wonders

14 15 אֱלֹהִים בַּקֹּדֶשׁ דַּרְכֶּךָ מִי־אֵל גָּדוֹל כֵּאלֹהִים׃ אַתָּה הָאֵל

the You like great a Who Your holiness in ,God O
God (are) ?God God (is) ;way (is)

16 עֹשֵׂה פֶלֶא הוֹדַעְתָּ בָעַמִּים עֻזֶּךָ׃ גָּאַלְתָּ בִּזְרוֹעַ עַמֶּךָ בְּנֵי־

sons the Your with have You Your the among have You ;wonders who
of ,people arm Your redeemed .strength peoples revealed does

17 יַעֲקֹב וְיוֹסֵף סֶלָה׃ רָאוּךָ מַּיִם | אֱלֹהִים רָאוּךָ מַּיִם יָחִילוּ

were they the saw ,God O The saw .Selah and Jacob
;afraid ;waters You ,waters You .Joseph

18 אַף יִרְגְּזוּ תְהֹמוֹת׃ זֹרְמוּ מַיִם | עָבוֹת קוֹל נָתְנוּ שְׁחָקִים

the gave a The water poured the trembled yea,
;skies voice ,clouds out .deeps

19 אַף־חֲצָצֶיךָ יִתְהַלָּכוּ׃ קוֹל רַעַמְךָ | בַּגַּלְגַּל הֵאִירוּ בְרָקִים

lightnings up lit the in Your The go will Your even
tempest thunder of voice .forth arrows

20 תֵּבֵל רָגְזָה וַתִּרְעַשׁ הָאָרֶץ׃ בַּיָּם דַּרְכֶּךָ וּשְׁבִילֶיךָ בְּמַיִם

in (was) Your and Your (is) In the and trembled the
waters the path ;way sea the !earth quaked ;world

21 רַבִּים וְעִקְּבוֹתֶיךָ לֹא נֹדָעוּ׃ נָחִיתָ כַצֹּאן עַמֶּךָ בְּיַד־

the by Your a like You are not Your and ;great
of hand people flock led .known footsteps

מֹשֶׁה וְאַהֲרֹן׃

and Moses
.Aaron

PSAL. LXXVIII עח

PSALM 78

PSALM 78

A Lesson of Asaph.

[1] O my people, listen to my law; bow your ears to the words of my mouth. [2] I will open my mouth in a parable; I will speak dark sayings of old, [3] which we have heard and known them, and our fathers have told us. [4] We will not hide (them) from their sons; to declare to the coming generation the praises of Jehovah; yea, His strength and His wonderful

1 מַשְׂכִּיל לְאָסָף הַאֲזִינָה עַמִּי תּוֹרָתִי הַטּוּ אָזְנְכֶם לְאִמְרֵי־

the to Your bow my to my O ,ear Give .Asaph of ,lesson A
of words ears ;law ,people

2 3 פִי׃ אֶפְתְּחָה בְמָשָׁל פִּי אַבִּיעָה חִידוֹת מִנִּי־קֶדֶם׃ אֲשֶׁר

which ,old of dark will I my a in will I my
sayings speak ;mouth parable open .mouth

4 שָׁמַעְנוּ וַנֵּדָעֵם וַאֲבוֹתֵינוּ סִפְּרוּ־לָנוּ׃ לֹא נְכַחֵד | מִבְּנֵיהֶם

their from will We not .us to have our and and have we
;sons (them) hide told fathers ,them known heard

לְדוֹר אַחֲרוֹן מְסַפְּרִים תְּהִלּוֹת יְהוָה וֶעֱזוּזוֹ וְנִפְלְאוֹתָיו

won- His and His and ;Jehovah the declaring following the to
,works derful strength of praises generation

works that He has done. [5] For He raised a testimony in Jacob, and set a law in Israel; which He commanded our fathers, to teach them to their sons; [6] so that a coming generation may know; sons shall be born, (and) they shall rise up and tell their sons, [7] so that they might set their hope in God, and not forget the works of God, but keep His commandments. [8] And they shall not be like their fathers, a stubborn and rebellious generation, a generation that prepared not its heart; yea, whose spirit was not faithful with God. [9] The sons of Ephraim (were) armed bowmen; (yet they) turned back in the day of battle. [10] They did not keep the covenant of God, and refused to walk in His law. [11] And they forgot His works, and His wonders which He had shown them. [12] He worked wonders before their fathers in the land of Egypt, the field of Zoan. [13] He divided the sea and passed them through; and He caused the waters to stand in a heap. [14] And He led them by a cloud in the day, and all the night with a light of fire. [15] He split the rocks in the wilderness and made them drink, as (from) great floods. [16] And He brought streams out of the rock, and caused waters to run down like torrents. [17] Yet they sinned still more against Him, to provoke the Most High in the desert. [18] And they tempted God in their heart, by asking food for their souls. [19] And they spoke against God, saying, Shall God be able to set a table in the wilderness? [20] Behold! He struck the rock and the waters gushed out, and the torrents overflowed. Can He also give bread? Will He provide flesh for His people? [21] Therefore Jehovah heard and He was angry; so a fire was kindled against Jacob, and also anger rose up against

5 אֲשֶׁר עָשָׂה׃ וַיָּקֶם עֵדוּת | בְּיַעֲקֹב וְתוֹרָה שָׂם בְּיִשְׂרָאֵל
;Israel in set a and law ,Jacob in a testimony He For raised has He .done which

6 אֲשֶׁר צִוָּה אֶת־אֲבוֹתֵינוּ לְהוֹדִיעָם לִבְנֵיהֶם׃ לְמַעַן יֵדְעוּ |
may know that so their to ;sons them make to known our ,fathers He commanded which

7 דּוֹר אַחֲרוֹן בָּנִים יִוָּלֵדוּ יָקֻמוּ וִיסַפְּרוּ לִבְנֵיהֶם׃ וְיָשִׂימוּ
they that so set may their ,sons tell and up rise shall they (and) be shall born sons ;coming a generation

בֵאלֹהִים כִּסְלָם וְלֹא יִשְׁכְּחוּ מַעַלְלֵי־אֵל וּמִצְוֺתָיו יִנְצֹרוּ׃
.keep His but commands ,God the of works forget and not their ,confidence God in

8 וְלֹא יִהְיוּ | כַּאֲבוֹתָם דּוֹר סוֹרֵר וּמֹרֶה דּוֹר לֹא־הֵכִין לִבּוֹ
its ;heart prepared not gen- eration a and ,rebellious stubborn gen- eration a their like ,fathers they be shall And not

9 וְלֹא־נֶאֶמְנָה אֶת־אֵל רוּחוֹ׃ בְּנֵי־אֶפְרַיִם נוֹשְׁקֵי רוֹמֵי־קָשֶׁת
;bows of shooters were ,armed Ephraim The of sons whose .spirit God with was faithful and not

10 הָפְכוּ בְּיוֹם קְרָב׃ לֹא שָׁמְרוּ בְּרִית אֱלֹהִים וּבְתוֹרָתוֹ
His in and law ,God the of covenant did They keep not .battle the in of day (they yet) turned

11 מֵאֲנוּ לָלֶכֶת׃ וַיִּשְׁכְּחוּ עֲלִילוֹתָיו וְנִפְלְאוֹתָיו אֲשֶׁר הֶרְאָם׃
had He .them shown which His and wonders His ,works they And forgot to .walk they refused

12 נֶגֶד אֲבוֹתָם עָשָׂה פֶלֶא בְּאֶרֶץ מִצְרַיִם שְׂדֵה־צֹעַן׃ בָּקַע
13
He divided .Zoan the of field ,Egypt the in of land wonders He did their fathers Before

14 יָם וַיַּעֲבִירֵם וַיַּצֶּב־מַיִם כְּמוֹ־נֵד׃ וַיַּנְחֵם בֶּעָנָן יוֹמָם וְכָל־
and all by ,day a in cloud He And them led a in as .heap made He and stand waters the passed and ;them through the sea

15 הַלַּיְלָה בְּאוֹר אֵשׁ׃ יְבַקַּע צֻרִים בַּמִּדְבָּר וַיַּשְׁקְ כִּתְהֹמוֹת
(from) as depths made and ,drink them the in wilderness the rocks He split .fire a by of light the night

16 רַבָּה׃ וַיּוֹצִא נוֹזְלִים מִסָּלַע וַיּוֹרֶד כַּנְּהָרוֹת מָיִם׃ וַיּוֹסִיפוּ
17
they And added .waters like torrents made and down run the of ,rock streams he And out brought .great

18 עוֹד לַחֲטֹא־לוֹ לַמְרוֹת עֶלְיוֹן בַּצִּיָּה׃ וַיְנַסּוּ־אֵל בִּלְבָבָם
their in hearts God they And tempted the in .desert Most the High rebel to against against ,Him to sin still

19 לִשְׁאָל־אֹכֶל לְנַפְשָׁם׃ וַיְדַבְּרוּ בֵּאלֹהִים אָמְרוּ הֲיוּכַל
be Shall able ,saying against ,God they And spoke their for .souls food by asking

20 אֵל לַעֲרֹךְ שֻׁלְחָן בַּמִּדְבָּר׃ הֵן הִכָּה־צוּר | וַיָּזוּבוּ מַיִם
the ,waters and out gushed the rock He struck ,Behold the in ?wilderness table a to arrange God

וּנְחָלִים יִשְׁטֹפוּ הֲגַם־לֶחֶם יוּכַל תֵּת אִם־יָכִין שְׁאֵר לְעַמּוֹ׃
His for ?people flesh He provide Will to ?give He is able bread Also were .overflowing the and torrents

21 לָכֵן | שָׁמַע יְהוָה וַיִּתְעַבָּר וְאֵשׁ נִשְּׂקָה בְיַעֲקֹב וְגַם־אַף
anger and also against ,Jacob was kindled a so fire He and ;angry was ,Jehovah heard There- fore

Israel, [22] because they believed not in God, and trusted not in His salvation; [23] and He commanded the fine clouds above; and the doors of the heavens He opened; [24] and He rained on them manna to eat; and He gave the grain of the heavens to them. [25] Man ate the bread of the mighty; He sent them food to the full. He made an east (wind) blow in the heavens; and He led out the south (wind) by His power. [27] And He rained flesh on them like dust, and like the sand of the seas winged birds. [28] And He made them fall amidst His camp, all around to His tents. [29] So they ate and were filled full; for their own lust He brought to them. [30] They were not separated from their lust; their food (was) still in their mouths, [31] and God's wrath came on them and killed the fattest of them; and He struck down the choice ones of Israel.

[32] In all this they sinned still, and believed not in His wonderful works; and He consumed their days in vanity, and their years in sudden terror. [34] When He killed them, then they sought Him; and they turned and searched for God. [35] So they remembered that God (was) their rock, and the Most High God their redeemer. [36] But they flattered Him with their mouth, and with their tongues lied to Him. [37] For their heart was not steadfast with Him; and they were not faithful in His covenant. [38] But He being merciful atoned for iniquity and did not destroy; and He added to turn away His anger, and did not stir up all his wrath [39] For He remembered that they (were) flesh, a breath passing away, and not returning. [40] How often they disobeyed Him in the wilderness, grieving Him in the desert! [41] Yea, they turned back and tempted God, and the Holy

22 עָלָה בְיִשְׂרָאֵל׃ כִּי לֹא הֶאֱמִינוּ בֵּאלֹהִים וְלֹא בָטְחוּ
did trust | and not | ,God in | they did believe | not because | against ;Israel | rose up

23 בִּישׁוּעָתוֹ׃ וַיְצַו שְׁחָקִים מִמָּעַל וְדַלְתֵי שָׁמַיִם פָּתָח׃
He ;opened | the heavens | the and of doors | ;above | fine the clouds | He and commanded | His in ;salvation

24 25 וַיַּמְטֵר עֲלֵיהֶם מָן לֶאֱכֹל וּדְגַן־שָׁמַיִם נָתַן לָמוֹ׃ לֶחֶם
The of bread | to .them | He gave | the heavens | the and of grain | ;eat to | manna | on them | He and rained

26 אַבִּירִים אָכַל אִישׁ צֵידָה שָׁלַח לָהֶם לָשֹׂבַע׃ יַסַּע קָדִים
east an (wind) | made He blow | the to .full | them | He sent | food | ;man | did eat | the mighty

27 בַּשָּׁמָיִם וַיְנַהֵג בְּעֻזּוֹ תֵימָן׃ וַיַּמְטֵר עֲלֵיהֶם כֶּעָפָר שְׁאֵר
,flesh | like dust | them on | He And rained | south the .(wind) | His by power | He and out led | the in ;heavens

28 וּכְחוֹל יַמִּים עוֹף כָּנָף׃ וַיַּפֵּל בְּקֶרֶב מַחֲנֵהוּ סָבִיב
all around | His ,camp | amidst | He And fall them made | .winged | birds | the seas | like and of sand the

29 לְמִשְׁכְּנֹתָיו׃ וַיֹּאכְלוּ וַיִּשְׂבְּעוּ מְאֹד וְתַאֲוָתָם יָבִא לָהֶם׃
to .them | He brought | their for lust own | (the to) ;full | were and filled | they So ate | .tents His to

30 31 לֹא־זָרוּ מִתַּאֲוָתָם עוֹד אָכְלָם בְּפִיהֶם׃ וְאַף אֱלֹהִים ׀ עָלָה
came | God | the and of wrath | their in ,mouths | their food | (was) yet | their from ,lust | They not separated were

32 בָהֶם וַיַּהֲרֹג בְּמִשְׁמַנֵּיהֶם וּבַחוּרֵי יִשְׂרָאֵל הִכְרִיעַ׃ בְּכָל־
all In | struck He .down | Israel | the and of ones choice | fattest the ;them of | and killed | upon them

33 זֹאת חָטְאוּ־עוֹד וְלֹא הֶאֱמִינוּ בְּנִפְלְאוֹתָיו׃ וַיְכַל־בַּהֶבֶל
vanity in | He And consumed | wonderful His in ;works | did believe | and not | still ,more | they sinned | this

34 יְמֵיהֶם וּשְׁנוֹתָם בַּבֶּהָלָה׃ אִם־הֲרָגָם וּדְרָשׁוּהוּ וְשָׁבוּ
they and turned | they then ;Him sought | He ,them killed | When | sudden in .terror | their and years | their ,days

35 וְשִׁחֲרוּ־אֵל׃ וַיִּזְכְּרוּ כִּי־אֱלֹהִים צוּרָם וְאֵל עֶלְיוֹן גֹּאֲלָם׃
their .redeemer | Most High | the and God | their (was) ,rock | God | that | they And remembered | .God searched and for eagerly

36 37 וַיְפַתּוּהוּ בְּפִיהֶם וּבִלְשׁוֹנָם יְכַזְּבוּ־לוֹ׃ וְלִבָּם לֹא־נָכוֹן
was steadfast | not | their For heart | to lied .Him | with and tongues their | their with ,mouth | they But Him deceived

38 עִמּוֹ וְלֹא נֶאֶמְנוּ בִּבְרִיתוֹ׃ וְהוּא רַחוּם ׀ יְכַפֵּר עָוֹן וְלֹא
and not | iniquity | atoned for | being merciful | He But | His in .covenant | were faithful | and they not | with ;Him

39 יַשְׁחִית וְהִרְבָּה לְהָשִׁיב אַפּוֹ וְלֹא־יָעִיר כָּל־חֲמָתוֹ׃ וַיִּזְכֹּר
He For remembered | His .wrath | all up stir | did not | and anger | His away | turn to | He And multiplied | destroy did .(them)

40 כִּי־בָשָׂר הֵמָּה רוּחַ הוֹלֵךְ וְלֹא יָשׁוּב׃ כַּמָּה יַמְרוּהוּ
dis- Him | they obeyed | How often | does .return | and not | passing away | a breath | they ,(were) | flesh | that

41 בַמִּדְבָּר יַעֲצִיבוּהוּ בִּישִׁימוֹן׃ וַיָּשׁוּבוּ וַיְנַסּוּ אֵל וּקְדוֹשׁ
the and of One Holy | ,God | and tempted | they And back turned | the in !desert | grieved Him | the in ,wilderness

One of Israel. [42] They did not remember His hand, on the day He saved them from the enemy; [43] who set His signs in Egypt, and His wonders in the fields of Zoan. [44] He turned their rivers into blood, also their streams (that) they might not drink. [45] He sent swarms of flies against them, and they devoured them; also frogs, and they destroyed them. [46] He also gave their crops to the caterpillar, and their labor to the locust. [47] He killed their vines with hail, and their sycamore trees by sleet. [48] He gave their cattle up to the hail, and their flocks to bolts of fire. [49] He sent the heat of His anger on them, fury and indignation and trouble, a deputation of afflicting angels. [50] He leveled a path for His anger; He did not keep back their soul from death, but gave their life over to the plague. [51] And He struck all the firstborn in Egypt, the first-fruits of strength in the tents of Ham; [52] then He caused His own people to go forth like sheep; and He led them in the wilderness like a flock. [53] And He led them on safely, and they did not fear, but the sea flooded over their enemies.

[54] And He brought them to the border of His holy place; this mountain His right hand had gained. [55] And He cast out the nations before them, and by a line He made fall to them a possession; and He made the tribes of Israel to live in their tents. [56] Yet they tempted and provoked the most high God; and they did not keep His testimonies; [57] but they turned back and were faithless like their fathers; they veered aside like a deceitful bow. [58] For they enraged Him with their high places; and provoked Him to jealousy with their casted images. [59] When God heard, He was angry, and He cast Israel far off; [60] so that He left the tabernacle of Shiloh, He dwelt in the tent among

42 יִשְׂרָאֵל הִתְווּ׃ לֹא־זָכְרוּ אֶת־יָדוֹ יוֹם אֲשֶׁר־פָּדָם מִנִּי־צָר׃

the from He when the His did They not .pained Israel
;enemy them saved day ,hand remember

43
44 אֲשֶׁר־שָׂם בְּמִצְרַיִם אֹתוֹתָיו וּמוֹפְתָיו בִּשְׂדֵה־צֹעַן׃ וַיַּהֲפֹךְ

He .Zoan the in His and His Egypt in set who
turned of field wonders ,signs

45 לְדָם יְאֹרֵיהֶם וְנֹזְלֵיהֶם בַּל־יִשְׁתָּיוּן׃ יְשַׁלַּח בָּהֶם עָרֹב

fly against sent He they (that) not their also their into
,swarms them .drink might ,streams ;rivers blood

46 וַיֹּאכְלֵם וּצְפַרְדֵּעַ וַתַּשְׁחִיתֵם׃ וַיִּתֵּן לֶחָסִיל יְבוּלָם וִיגִיעָם

their and their the to also He they and also they and
labor ,crops caterpillar gave .them destroyed ,frogs ;them devoured

47
48 לָאַרְבֶּה׃ יַהֲרֹג בַּבָּרָד גַּפְנָם וְשִׁקְמוֹתָם בַּחֲנָמַל׃ וַיַּסְגֵּר

He And .sleet by their and their with was He the to
up gave trees sycamore ,vines hail killing .locust

49 לַבָּרָד בְּעִירָם וּמִקְנֵיהֶם לָרְשָׁפִים׃ יְשַׁלַּח־בָּם ׀ חֲרוֹן אַפּוֹ

His the on He the to their and their the to
,anger of heat them sent .bolts flaming flocks ,cattle hail

50 עֶבְרָה וָזַעַם וְצָרָה מִשְׁלַחַת מַלְאֲכֵי רָעִים׃ יְפַלֵּס נָתִיב

path a He .evils angels deputation a and indig- and fury
leveled of of ,trouble nation

51 לְאַפּוֹ לֹא־חָשַׂךְ מִמָּוֶת נַפְשָׁם וְחַיָּתָם לַדֶּבֶר הִסְגִּיר׃ וַיַּךְ

He And gave the to their but their from He not His for
struck .over plague life ,souls death back kept ;anger

52 כָּל־בְּכוֹר בְּמִצְרָיִם רֵאשִׁית אוֹנִים בְּאָהֳלֵי־חָם׃ וַיַּסַּע

He then ;Ham the in strength first- the ;Egypt in the all
forth led of tents of fruits firstborn

53 כַּצֹּאן עַמּוֹ וַיְנַהֲגֵם כַּעֵדֶר בַּמִּדְבָּר׃ וַיַּנְחֵם לָבֶטַח וְלֹא

and ;safely He And the in a like He and own His like
not on them led .wilderness flock them led ,people sheep

54 פָחָדוּ וְאֶת־אוֹיְבֵיהֶם כִּסָּה הַיָּם׃ וַיְבִיאֵם אֶל־גְּבוּל קָדְשׁוֹ

holy His the to He And the covered their but did they
;place of border them brought .sea over enemies ,fear

55 הַר־זֶה קָנְתָה יְמִינוֹ׃ וַיְגָרֶשׁ מִפְּנֵיהֶם ׀ גּוֹיִם וַיַּפִּילֵם בְּחֶבֶל

a by made He and the before He And right His had this
line fall them nations them out cast .hand gained mountain

56 נַחֲלָה וַיַּשְׁכֵּן בְּאָהֳלֵיהֶם שִׁבְטֵי יִשְׂרָאֵל׃ וַיְנַסּוּ וַיַּמְרוּ

and they And .Israel the their in He and pos- a
provoked tested of tribes tents dwell made .session

57 אֶת־אֱלֹהִים עֶלְיוֹן וְעֵדוֹתָיו לֹא שָׁמָרוּ׃ וַיִּסֹּגוּ וַיִּבְגְּדוּ

and they but did they not His and Most God the
betrayed back turned ;keep testimonies ,High

58 כַּאֲבוֹתָם נֶהְפְּכוּ כְּקֶשֶׁת רְמִיָּה׃ וַיַּכְעִיסוּהוּ בְּבָמוֹתָם

their by they For .deceitful a like they their like
;places high Him enraged bow veered ;fathers

59 וּבִפְסִילֵיהֶם יַקְנִיאוּהוּ׃ שָׁמַע אֱלֹהִים וַיִּתְעַבָּר וַיִּמְאַס

He and was and God heard provoked they their with
rejected ;angry jealousy to Him images casted

60 מְאֹד בְּיִשְׂרָאֵל׃ וַיִּטֹּשׁ מִשְׁכַּן שִׁלוֹ אֹהֶל שִׁכֵּן בָּאָדָם׃

among He the ,Shiloh taber- the And .Israel utterly
;men in dwelt tent of nacle left He

men, [61] and delivered His strength into captivity, and His glory into the enemy's hands. [62] He also gave His people to the sword, and was angry with His inheritance. [63] The fire burned up His young men; and His virgins were not praised. [64] His priests fell by the sword; and their widows were not able to weep.

[65] Then the Lord awoke as one asleep; like a mighty man rejoicing (with) wine; [66] and He drove His enemies backward; He put them to a never-ending shame. [67] And He refused the tabernacle of Joseph; and He did not elect the tribe of Ephraim; [68] but chose the tribe of Judah, the mount Zion which He loved. [69] And He built His sanctuary like high places; like the earth He has founded forever. [70] He also chose David His servant, and took him from the sheepfolds; [71] He brought him in from the suckling (ewes); He brought him to feed Jacob His people, and Israel His inheritance. [72] So he fed them in the integrity of his heart, and guided them by his skillful hands.

PSALM 79

A Psalm of Asaph.

[1] O God, the nations have come into Your inheritance; they have defiled Your holy temple; they have laid Jerusalem in heaps. [2] They have given the bodies of Your servants as food for the birds of the sky, the flesh of Your saints to the beast of the earth. [3] They have shed their blood like water all around Jerusalem; and there is no one burying. [4] We have become a shame to our neighbors, a scorn and a mockery to those who are around us. [5] How long, O Jehovah? Will You be angry with us forever? Shall Your jealousy burn like fire? [6] Pour out Your wrath

61
62

וַיִּתֵּן לַשְּׁבִי עֻזּוֹ וְתִפְאַרְתּוֹ בְיַד־צָר : וַיַּסְגֵּר לַחֶרֶב עַמּוֹ

His	the to	He and	the	into	His and	His	into	and
,people	sword	delivered	,enemy's	hands	glory	,strength	captivity	gave

63

וּבְנַחֲלָתוֹ הִתְעַבָּר : בַּחוּרָיו אָכְלָה־אֵשׁ וּבְתוּלֹתָיו לֹא

| not | His and | The | burned | young His | was | His with and |
| | virgins | ;fire | up | men | .angry | inheritance |

64
65

הוּלָּלוּ : כֹּהֲנָיו בַּחֶרֶב נָפָלוּ וְאַלְמְנֹתָיו לֹא תִבְכֶּינָה : וַיִּקַץ

| Then | able were | not | their and | ;fell | the by | His | were |
| awoke | .weep to | | widows | | sword | priests | .praised |

66

כְּיָשֵׁן | אֲדֹנָי כְּגִבּוֹר מִתְרוֹנֵן מִיָּיִן : וַיַּךְ צָרָיו אָחוֹר חֶרְפַּת

| shame a | back- | His He and | (with) | rejoicing | a like | the | one as |
| | ;ward | enemies beat | ;wine | | man mighty | ;Lord | asleep |

67

עוֹלָם נָתַן לָמוֹ : וַיִּמְאַס בְּאֹהֶל יוֹסֵף וּבְשֵׁבֶט אֶפְרַיִם לֹא

| not | Ephraim | the and | ;Joseph | taber- the | He And | them | He | ever- |
| | | of tribe | | of nacle | refused | .to | put | lasting |

68

בָחָר : וַיִּבְחַר אֶת־שֵׁבֶט יְהוּדָה אֶת־הַר צִיּוֹן אֲשֶׁר אָהֵב :

| He | which | Zion | the | ,Judah | the | He But | did He |
| .loved | | | Mount | | of tribe | chose | .elect |

69
70

וַיִּבֶן כְּמוֹ־רָמִים מִקְדָּשׁוֹ כְּאֶרֶץ יְסָדָהּ לְעוֹלָם : וַיִּבְחַר

| also He | .forever | has He | the like | His | high | like | He And |
| chose | | it founded | earth | ;sanctuary | places | | built |

71

בְּדָוִד עַבְדּוֹ וַיִּקָּחֵהוּ מִמִּכְלְאֹת צֹאן : מֵאַחַר עָלוֹת הֱבִיאוֹ

| took He | suck- the | from | ;sheep | the from | took and | His | David |
| ,him | (ewes) ling | after | | of folds | him | ,servant |

72

לִרְעוֹת בְּיַעֲקֹב עַמּוֹ וּבְיִשְׂרָאֵל נַחֲלָתוֹ : וַיִּרְעֵם כְּתֹם לְבָבוֹ

| his | the in | he So | His | and | His | Jacob | feed to |
| ,heart | of integrity | them fed | .inheritance | Israel | ,people |

וּבִתְבוּנוֹת כַּפָּיו יַנְחֵם :

| guided | his | the in and |
| .them | hands | of shield |

PSAL. LXXIX   עט

PSALM 79

1

מִזְמוֹר לְאָסָף אֱלֹהִים בָּאוּ גוֹיִם | בְּנַחֲלָתֶךָ טִמְּאוּ אֶת־

| have they | Your into | the | have | ,God O | psalm A |
| defiled | ;inheritance | nations | come | | .Asaph |

2

הֵיכַל קָדְשֶׁךָ שָׂמוּ אֶת־יְרוּשָׁלַםִ לְעִיִּים : נָתְנוּ אֶת־נִבְלַת

| the | have They | .heaps in | Jerusalem | have they | Your | temple |
| of corpses | given | | | laid | ;holy |

3
4

עֲבָדֶיךָ מַאֲכָל לְעוֹף הַשָּׁמָיִם בְּשַׂר חֲסִידֶיךָ לְחַיְתוֹ־אָרֶץ :

| the | the to | Your | the | ,sky the | the | food as | Your |
| .earth | of beasts | saints | of flesh | | of birds | for | servants |

שָׁפְכוּ דָמָם | כַּמַּיִם סְבִיבוֹת יְרוּשָׁלַםִ וְאֵין קוֹבֵר : הָיִינוּ

| have We | .burying | and | ;Jerusalem | all | like | their have | They |
| been | | is none | | around | water | blood | shed |

5

חֶרְפָּה לִשְׁכֵנֵינוּ לַעַג וָקֶלֶס לִסְבִיבוֹתֵינוּ : עַד־מָה יְהוָה

| O | ,when Until | who those to | a and | a | our to | shame a |
| ?Jehovah | | .us around are | mockery | scorn | ,neighbors |

6

תֶּאֱנַף לָנֶצַח תִּבְעַר כְּמוֹ־אֵשׁ קִנְאָתֶךָ : שְׁפֹךְ חֲמָתְךָ | אֶל־

| to | Your | Pour | Your | fire | like | Shall | ?forever You Will |
| | wrath | out | ?jealousy | | | burn | angry be |

on the nations who have not known You, and on the kingdoms who have not called on Your name. [7] For (they have) eaten up Jacob and laid waste his dwelling-place. [8] O remember not for us the sins of our forefathers; let Your tender mercies meet us speedily, for we have been brought very low. [9] Help us, O God of our salvation, for the matter of the glory of Your name; and deliver us and atone for our sins, for Your name's sake. [10] Why should the nations say, Where (is) their God? Let Him be known among the nations before our eyes, the avenging of the blood of Your servants which has been poured out. [11] Let the groaning of the prisoner come before You; according to the greatness of Your arm, preserve the sons of death. [12] And reward our neighbors sevenfold, their curse into their bosom, with which they have cursed You, O Lord. [13] Then we Your people, and sheep of Your pasture, will give thanks to You forever; we will declare Your praise to all generations.

הַגּוֹיִם אֲשֶׁר לֹא־יְדָעוּךָ וְעַל־מַמְלָכוֹת אֲשֶׁר בְּשִׁמְךָ לֹא
not Your on who the and have not who the
name kingdoms on You known nations

7 8 קָרָאוּ׃ כִּי אָכַל אֶת־יַעֲקֹב וְאֶת־נָוֵהוּ הֵשַׁמּוּ׃ אַל תִּזְכָּר־
O not laid hjs and Jacob they For have
remember .waste place dwelling devoured have .called

לָנוּ עֲוֺנֹת רִאשֹׁנִים מַהֵר יְקַדְּמוּנוּ רַחֲמֶיךָ כִּי דַלּוֹנוּ מְאֹד׃
greatly have we For tender Your let speedily fore- our the for
weakened been .mercies us meet ;fathers of iniquities us

9 עָזְרֵנוּ ׀ אֱלֹהֵי יִשְׁעֵנוּ עַל־דְּבַר כְּבוֹד־שְׁמֶךָ וְהַצִּילֵנוּ וְכַפֵּר
and and Your the the for our God O Help
atone us deliver ;name of glory of matter ,salvation of ,us

10 עַל־חַטֹּאתֵינוּ לְמַעַן שְׁמֶךָ׃ לָמָּה ׀ יֹאמְרוּ הַגּוֹיִם אַיֵּה
Where the should Why Your for our for
(is) ,nations say .name's sake sins

אֱלֹהֵיהֶם יִוָּדַע בַּגּוֹיִם לְעֵינֵינוּ נִקְמַת דַּם־עֲבָדֶיךָ הַשָּׁפוּךְ׃
been has of blood the the our before the in Him Let their
.out poured servants your of avenging ,eyes nations known be ?God

11 תָּבוֹא לְפָנֶיךָ אֶנְקַת אָסִיר כְּגֹדֶל זְרוֹעֲךָ הוֹתֵר בְּנֵי תְמוּתָה׃
.death the preserve Your the by the groan- the before Let
of sons ,arm of greatness ;prisoner of ing You come

12 וְהָשֵׁב לִשְׁכֵנֵינוּ שִׁבְעָתַיִם אֶל־חֵיקָם חֶרְפָּתָם אֲשֶׁר חֵרְפוּךָ
re- they with their their into ,sevenfold our And
.You proached which reproach bosom neighbors return

13 אֲדֹנָי׃ וַאֲנַחְנוּ עַמְּךָ ׀ וְצֹאן מַרְעִיתֶךָ נוֹדֶה לְּךָ לְעוֹלָם
;forever to give will Your the and Your Then O
You thanks pasture of sheep ,people ,we .Lord

לְדֹר וָדֹר נְסַפֵּר תְּהִלָּתֶךָ׃
Your will we gen- and gen- to
.praise declare eration eration

PSAL. LXXX פ

PSALM 80

To the Chief Musician, Concerning the Lilies. A Psalm of Asaph.

[1] O Shepherd of Israel, Hear; You who leads Joseph like a flock; You who dwells (between) the cherubim, shine forth. [2] Stir up Your strength before Ephraim, and Benjamin, and Manasseh, and come to save us. [3] O God, turn us again, and cause Your face to shine; and we shall be saved! [4] O Jehovah God of hosts, how long will You be angry against the prayer of Your people? [5] You fed them with the bread of tears; and You made them drink with tears. [6] You make us a strife for our neighbors; and

1 2 לַמְנַצֵּחַ אֶל־שֹׁשַׁנִּים עֵדוּת לְאָסָף מִזְמוֹר׃ רֹעֵה יִשְׂרָאֵל ׀
,Israel O .psalm A .Asaph of A the concern- chief the To
of Shepherd testimony .lilies ing musician

3 הַאֲזִינָה נֹהֵג כַּצֹּאן יוֹסֵף יֹשֵׁב הַכְּרוּבִים הוֹפִיעָה׃ לִפְנֵי
Before shine the (between) You ;Joseph a like You give
.forth ,cherubim dwell who flock leads who ;ear

אֶפְרַיִם ׀ וּבִנְיָמִן ׀ וּמְנַשֶּׁה עוֹרְרָה אֶת־גְּבוּרָתֶךָ וּלְכָה לִישֻׁעָתָה
save to and Your stir and and Ephraim
come ,might up Manasseh Benjamin

4 5 לָּנוּ׃ אֱלֹהִים הֲשִׁיבֵנוּ וְהָאֵר פָּנֶיךָ וְנִוָּשֵׁעָה׃ יְהוָה
O will we and Your make and us turn ,God O .us
Jehovah !saved be ,face shine again

6 אֱלֹהִים צְבָאוֹת עַד־מָתַי עָשַׁנְתָּ בִּתְפִלַּת עַמֶּךָ׃ הֶאֱכַלְתָּם
made You Your the against be You when until ,hosts of God
eat them ?people of prayer angry will

7 לֶחֶם דִּמְעָה וַתַּשְׁקֵמוֹ בִּדְמָעוֹת שָׁלִישׁ׃ תְּשִׂימֵנוּ מָדוֹן
a make You third a with made You and ;tears the (with)
strife us .time tears drink them of bread

our enemies laugh to themselves. [7] O God of hosts, turn us again, and cause Your face to shine; and we shall be saved.

[8] You have led a vine out of Egypt; You have cast out the nations and have planted it. [9] You cleared before it; You have rooted its roots; and it has filled the land. [10] The hills were covered (with) its shadow; and its boughs (were as) the great cedars. [11] It sent out its boughs to the sea, and its branches to the River. [12] Why have You broken down its hedges, so that all those who pass by the way pluck it? [13] A boar out of the forest wastes it; and the beasts of the field eat it. [14] O God of hosts, we beg You, return! Look down from Heaven and see, and visit this vine, [15] and the vineyard which Your right hand has planted, and the son You made strong for Yourself. [16] (It is) burned with fire, cut down; they perish at the rebuke of Your face. [17] Let Your hand be on the Man of Your right hand; on the Son of man (whom) You have made strong for Yourself. [18] So we will not slide backward from You; make us live, and we will call on Your name. [19] Turn us again, O Jehovah God of hosts; cause Your face to shine, and we shall be saved.

8 לִשְׁכֵנֵינוּ וְאֹיְבֵינוּ יִלְעֲגוּ־לָמוֹ׃ אֱלֹהִים צְבָאוֹת הֲשִׁיבֵנוּ

us turn ,hosts God O to laugh our and our for
again of .themselves enemies ;neighbors

9 וְהָאֵר פָּנֶיךָ וְנִוָּשֵׁעָה׃ גֶּפֶן מִמִּצְרַיִם תַּסִּיעַ תְּגָרֵשׁ גּוֹיִם

the have You have You of out A will we and Your make and
nations out cast ;out led Egypt vine .saved be ;face shine

10 וַתִּטָּעֶהָ׃ פִּנִּיתָ לְפָנֶיהָ וַתַּשְׁרֵשׁ שָׁרָשֶׁיהָ וַתְּמַלֵּא־אָרֶץ׃

the it and its have You and before have You have and
.land filled has ;roots rooted ;it cleared .it planted

11 12 כָּסּוּ הָרִים צִלָּהּ וַעֲנָפֶיהָ אַרְזֵי־אֵל׃ תְּשַׁלַּח קְצִירֶהָ עַד־

to its was It of the (as) its and its (with) The were
boughs sending .God cedars boughs ;shadow hills covered

13 יָם וְאֶל־נָהָר יוֹנְקוֹתֶיהָ׃ לָמָּה פָּרַצְתָּ גְדֵרֶיהָ וְאָרוּהָ כָּל־

by is it that its You have Why its the and the
all plucked ,walls down broken .branches River to ,sea

14 עֹבְרֵי דָרֶךְ׃ יְכַרְסְמֶנָּה חֲזִיר מִיָּעַר וְזִיז שָׂדַי יִרְעֶנָּה׃

feed the and the of out wild A wastes the who
.it on field of movers forest boar it .way by pass

15 אֱלֹהִים צְבָאוֹת שׁוּב נָא הַבֵּט מִשָּׁמַיִם וּרְאֵה וּפְקֹד גֶּפֶן

vine and see and from Look we ,return ,hosts God O
visit Heaven down !You beg of

16 זֹאת׃ וְכַנָּה אֲשֶׁר־נָטְעָה יְמִינֶךָ וְעַל־בֵּן אִמַּצְתָּה לָּךְ׃

for made You the and Your has which and ,this
.Yourself strong son on ,hand right planted shoot the

17 18 שְׂרֻפָה בָאֵשׁ כְּסוּחָה מִגַּעֲרַת פָּנֶיךָ יֹאבֵדוּ׃ תְּהִי־יָדְךָ עַל־

on Your Let they Your the at cut with is It
hand be .perish face of rebuke ;down ,fire burned

19 אִישׁ יְמִינֶךָ עַל־בֶּן־אָדָם אִמַּצְתָּ לָּךְ׃ וְלֹא־נָסוֹג מִמֶּךָּ

from will we So for You man the on Your the
;You backslide not .Yourself ,strengthened of son ,hand right of man

20 תְּחַיֵּנוּ וּבְשִׁמְךָ נִקְרָא׃ יְהוָה אֱלֹהִים צְבָאוֹת הֲשִׁיבֵנוּ

us turn ,hosts of God O will we on and us make
;again Jehovah .call name Your ,live

הָאֵר פָּנֶיךָ וְנִוָּשֵׁעָה׃

will we and Your make
.saved be ,face shine

PSAL. LXXXI פא

PSALM 81

To the Chief Musician on Gittith. Of Asaph.

[1] Sing aloud to God our strength; make a joyful noise to the God of Jacob. [2] Bring a song, and give the timbrel here, the pleasing lyre with the harp. [3] Blow the trumpet in the new moon, at the full moon, on our solemn feast day. [4] For this was a statute for Israel, a law of the God of Jacob. [5] This He ordained a testimony in Joseph, when He went out

PSALM 81

1 2 לַמְנַצֵּחַ עַל־הַגִּתִּית לְאָסָף׃ הַרְנִינוּ לֵאלֹהִים עוּזֵּנוּ הָרִיעוּ

shout our God to Sing .Asaph Of the on chief the To
joy for ;strength aloud .Gittith musician

3 לֵאלֹהֵי יַעֲקֹב׃ שְׂאוּ־זִמְרָה וּתְנוּ־תֹף כִּנּוֹר נָעִים עִם־נָבֶל׃

the with pleasing the the and ,song a Bring .Jacob the to
.harp lyre ,timbrel give of God

4 5 תִּקְעוּ בַחֹדֶשׁ שׁוֹפָר בַּכֶּסֶה לְיוֹם חַגֵּנוּ׃ כִּי חֹק לְיִשְׂרָאֵל

Israel for a For our on the at the the in Blow
statute .feast day moon full ,trumpet moon new

6 הוּא מִשְׁפָּט לֵאלֹהֵי יַעֲקֹב׃ עֵדוּת ׀ בִּיהוֹסֵף שָׂמוֹ בְּצֵאתוֹ

He when He in A .Jacob the of ord- an this
out went ,it set Joseph testimony of God inance ,(was)

over Egypt's land; I heard a language I did not understand; [6] I removed his shoulder from the burden; his hands were delivered from the basket. [7] You called in trouble and I rescued you; I answered you in the secret place of thunder; I tested you at the waters of Meribah. Selah.

[8] O My people, listen, and I will testify to you: O Israel, if you will listen to Me; [9] there shall be no strange god in you; nor shall you worship a foreign god. [10] I (am) Jehovah your God, who brought you out of the land of Egypt; open your mouth wide and I will fill it. [11] But My people would not listen to My voice; and Israel did not consent to Me. [12] So I gave them up to the stubbornness of their own hearts; they walked in their own conceits. [13] O if My people had listened to Me! (If) Israel had walked in My ways, [14] I would soon have subdued their enemies; and I would have turned My hand against their foes — [15] those who hate Jehovah shall cringe to Him; their time (is) forever — [16] yea, He would have fed them with the fat of the wheat; and I would have satisfied you with honey out of the rock.

7 עַל־אֶרֶץ מִצְרָיִם שְׂפַת לֹא־יָדַעְתִּי אֶשְׁמָע׃ הֲסִירוֹתִי מִסֵּבֶל
the from removed I ;heard I did I not a ;Egypt the over
burden understand language of land

8 שִׁכְמוֹ כַּפָּיו מִדּוּד תַּעֲבֹרְנָה׃ בַּצָּרָה קָרָאתָ וָאֲחַלְּצֶךָּ
I and You trouble in were the from his his
;you rescued ,called .freed basket hands ;shoulder

9 אֶעֶנְךָ בְּסֵתֶר רַעַם אֶבְחָנְךָ עַל־מֵי מְרִיבָה סֶלָה׃ שְׁמַע
Listen .Selah .Meribah the at tested I ;thunder the in an- I
of waters you of covert you swered

10 עַמִּי וְאָעִידָה בָּךְ יִשְׂרָאֵל אִם־תִּשְׁמַע־לִי׃ לֹא־יִהְיֶה בְךָ
among There not to will you if ,Israel O against will I and my O
you be shall .Me listen ,you testify ,people

11 אֵל זָר וְלֹא תִשְׁתַּחֲוֶה לְאֵל נֵכָר׃ אָנֹכִי ׀ יְהוָה אֱלֹהֶיךָ
your Jehovah (am) I .foreign a to you shall and ;strange a
God god down bow not god

12 הַמַּעַלְךָ מֵאֶרֶץ מִצְרָיִם הַרְחֶב־פִּיךָ וַאֲמַלְאֵהוּ׃ וְלֹא־שָׁמַע
did But will I and your open ;Egypt the from brought who
listen not .it fill mouth wide of land up you

13 עַמִּי לְקוֹלִי וְיִשְׂרָאֵל לֹא־אָבָה לִי׃ וָאֲשַׁלְּחֵהוּ בִּשְׁרִירוּת
the to gave I So to did not and My to My
of obstinacy ,up him .Me consent Israel ,voice people

14 לִבָּם יֵלְכוּ בְּמוֹעֲצוֹתֵיהֶם׃ לוּ עַמִּי שֹׁמֵעַ לִי יִשְׂרָאֵל
Israel (If) !Me were My if O own their in they their
hearing people .counsels walk ;heart

15 בִּדְרָכַי יְהַלֵּכוּ׃ כִּמְעַט אוֹיְבֵיהֶם אַכְנִיעַ וְעַל־צָרֵיהֶם אָשִׁיב
would I their and would I their soon would My in
turn foes against .subdue enemies ,walk ways

16
17 יָדִי׃ מְשַׂנְאֵי יְהוָה יְכַחֲשׁוּ־לוֹ וִיהִי עִתָּם לְעוֹלָם׃ וַיַּאֲכִילֵהוּ
would He and —forever their and to shall Jehovah who those My
eat him make time is ,Him cringe hate —hand

מֵחֵלֶב חִטָּה וּמִצּוּר דְּבַשׁ אַשְׂבִּיעֶךָ׃
would I (with) of out and the the of
.you satisfy honey rock the ;wheat of fat

PSAL. LXXXII פב

PSALM 82

A Psalm of Asaph.

[1] God stands in the assembly of God; He judges in the midst of the gods. [2] How long will you judge unjustly, and lift up the wicked? Selah. [3] Judge the poor and fatherless; do justice to the afflicted and needy. [4] Deliver the poor and needy; save out of the hand of the wicked. [5] They neither know nor will understand; they walk in darkness; all the foundations of the earth are shaken. [6] I have said, You (are) gods; and, All of you (are) sons of

PSALM 82

1 מִזְמוֹר לְאָסָף אֱלֹהִים נִצָּב בַּעֲדַת־אֵל בְּקֶרֶב אֱלֹהִים
gods the the in God the in stands God .Asaph of psalm A
of midst of company

2 יִשְׁפֹּט׃ עַד־מָתַי תִּשְׁפְּטוּ־עָוֶל וּפְנֵי רְשָׁעִים תִּשְׂאוּ־סֶלָה׃
.Selah ?up lift the and ,unjustly you will when Until He
wicked of faces the judge .judges

3
4 שִׁפְטוּ־דַל וְיָתוֹם עָנִי וָרָשׁ הַצְדִּיקוּ׃ פַּלְּטוּ־דַל וְאֶבְיוֹן מִיַּד
from and the Deliver justice do and af- the the and the Vindicate
hand needy poor .to needy flicted ,orphan poor

5 רְשָׁעִים הַצִּילוּ׃ לֹא יָדְעוּ ׀ וְלֹא יָבִינוּ בַּחֲשֵׁכָה יִתְהַלָּכוּ
they darkness in they and They not .save the
;walk ;understand not ,know wicked's

6 יִמּוֹטוּ כָּל־מוֹסְדֵי אָרֶץ׃ אֲנִי אָמַרְתִּי אֱלֹהִים אַתֶּם וּבְנֵי
and You gods have I the foun- the all are
of sons ;(are) ,said ,earth of dations shaken

the Most High. [7] But you shall die as man, and fall like one of the rulers. [8] Rise, O God, judge the earth; for You shall inherit in all the nations.

7 עֶלְיוֹן כֻּלְּכֶם׃ אָכֵן כְּאָדָם תְּמוּתוּן וּכְאַחַד הַשָּׂרִים תִּפֹּלוּ׃

shall you the like and shall you as But of all Most the
.fall princes of one ,die man .you ,High

8 קוּמָה אֱלֹהִים שָׁפְטָה הָאָרֶץ כִּי־אַתָּה תִנְחַל בְּכָל־הַגּוֹיִם׃

the all in shall You for the judge ,God O ,Rise
.nations inherit ;earth

PSAL. LXXXIII פג

PSALM 83

PSALM 83

A Song. A Psalm of Asaph. [1] O God, do not keep silence to Yourself; do not be speechless; do not be still, O God. [2] For lo, Your enemies are roaring; and those who hate You have lifted up their head. [3] They have taken counsel against Your people; (they) have plotted against Your hidden ones. [4] They have said, Come, let us cut them off from (being a nation; and not will be recalled the name of Israel any more. [5] For they have plotted together with one heart; they have cut a covenant against You; [6] the tents of Edom and of the Ishmaelites; Moab and the Hagarenes; [7] Gebal, and Ammon, and Amalek; Philistia with the dwellers of Tyre. Also Assyria has joined with them; they were an arm to the sons of Lot. Selah. [9] Do to them as (to) Midian, as (to) Sisera, as (to) Jabin at the torrent Kishon. [10] At Endor they perished; they became dung for the ground. [11] Make their nobles like Oreb and Zeeb; and like Zebah and Zalmunna and all their princes [12] who said, Let us take possession, God's pastures for ourselves. [13] O my God, make them as whirling dust, as the stubble before the wind. [14] As the fire burns a forest, and as the flame sets the mountains on fire, [15] so pursue them with your tempest and frighten them with Your storm. [16] Fill their faces with shame, and they will seek Your name, O Jehovah. [17] Let them be

1
2 שִׁיר מִזְמוֹר לְאָסָף׃ אֱלֹהִים אַל־דֳּמִי־לָךְ אַל־תֶּחֱרַשׁ וְאַל־

and be do not silence keep do ,God O .Asaph of psalm a A
not ;speechless ;yourself to not ,song

3 תִּשְׁקֹט אֵל׃ כִּי־הִנֵּה אוֹיְבֶיךָ יֶהֱמָיוּן וּמְשַׂנְאֶיךָ נָשְׂאוּ רֹאשׁ׃

(their) have who those and are Your ,lo For .God O be do
.head up lifted You hate ;roaring enemies ,still

4
5 עַל־עַמְּךָ יַעֲרִימוּ סוֹד וְיִתְיָעֲצוּ עַל־צְפוּנֶיךָ׃ אָמְרוּ לְכוּ

,Come They Your against they and ;counsel They Your against
,said have .ones hidden conspire shrewd take people

6 וְנַכְחִידֵם מִגּוֹי וְלֹא־יִזָּכֵר שֵׁם־יִשְׂרָאֵל עוֹד׃ כִּי נוֹעֲצוּ לֵב,

one con- they For .again Israel name the be will and a from will we and
heart ,spired of recalled not ,nation off them cut

7 יַחְדָּו עָלֶיךָ בְּרִית יִכְרֹתוּ׃ אָהֳלֵי אֱדוֹם וְיִשְׁמְעֵאלִים מוֹאָב

Moab the of and Edom tents the they a against to-
;Ishmaelites of ;cut have covenant You ;gether

8
9 וְהַגְרִים׃ גְּבָל וְעַמּוֹן וַעֲמָלֵק פְּלֶשֶׁת עִם־יֹשְׁבֵי צוֹר׃ גַּם־

Also .Tyre the with Philistia and and ,Gebal the and
of dwellers ;Amalek ,Ammon ;Hagarites

10 אַשּׁוּר נִלְוָה עִמָּם הָיוּ זְרוֹעַ לִבְנֵי־לוֹט סֶלָה׃ עֲשֵׂה־לָהֶם

to Do .Selah .Lot the to an they with has Assyria
them of sons arm were ;them joined

11 כְּמִדְיָן כְּסִיסְרָא כְיָבִין בְּנַחַל קִישׁוֹן׃ נִשְׁמְדוּ בְעֵין־דֹּאר

;dor at were They .Kishon the at (to) as (to) as (to) as
En- destroyed torrent Jabin ,Sisera ,Midian

12 הָיוּ דֹּמֶן לָאֲדָמָה׃ שִׁיתֵמוֹ נְדִיבֵמוֹ כְּעֹרֵב וְכִזְאֵב וּכְזֶבַח

like and and like their Make the for dung they
Zebah ;Zeeb Oreb nobles them .ground became

13 וּכְצַלְמֻנָּע כָּל־נְסִיכֵמוֹ׃ אֲשֶׁר אָמְרוּ נִירְשָׁה־לָּנוּ אֵת נְאוֹת

pastures for take us Let ,said who their all and
ourselves ,possession ;princes Zalmunnah

14
15 אֱלֹהִים׃ אֱלֹהַי שִׁיתֵמוֹ כַגַּלְגַּל כְּקַשׁ לִפְנֵי־רוּחַ׃ כְּאֵשׁ

the As the before the as whirling as make my O .God's
fire .wind stubble ,dust them ,God

16 תִּבְעַר־יַעַר וּכְלֶהָבָה תְּלַהֵט הָרִים׃ כֵּן תִּרְדְּפֵם בְּסַעֲרֶךָ

Your with pursue so the on sets as and the burns
,tempest them ,mountains fire flame the ,forest

17 וּבְסוּפָתְךָ תְבַהֲלֵם׃ מַלֵּא פְנֵיהֶם קָלוֹן וִיבַקְשׁוּ שִׁמְךָ

Your they that ,shame their Fill frighten Your with and
,name seek may faces with .them storm

ashamed and terrified forever; yea, let them be confounded and perish. [18] And let them know – Your name (is) Jehovah – that You alone (are) the Most High over the whole earth.

PSALM 84

To the Chief Musician on Gittith. A Psalm for the Sons of Korah.

[1] How lovely (are) Your tabernacles, O Jehovah of hosts! [2] My soul longs and even faints for the courts of Jehovah; my heart and my flesh cry out for the living God. [3] Even the sparrow has found a house; and the swallow a nest for herself where she may lay her young, (on) Your altars, O Jehovah of hosts, my King and my God. [4] Blessed (are) they who dwell in Your house; they will always be praising You. Selah. [5] Blessed is the man whose strength (is) in You; the highways (are) in their hearts. [6] Passing through the valley of weeping, they will make it a fountain; yea, the rain clothes with blessings. [7] They go from strength to strength, appearing in Zion before God. [8] O Jehovah God of hosts, hear my prayer; listen, O God of Jacob. Selah.

[9] Behold, O God our shield, and look upon the face of Your anointed. [10] For a day in Your courts (is) better than a thousand; I have chosen to stand at the door of the house of my God, than to dwell in the tents of wickedness. [11] For Jehovah God (is) a sun and shield; Jehovah will give grace and glory; nothing good will He withhold from those who walk uprightly. [12] O Jehovah of Hosts, blessed is the man who trusts in You!

18 19 יְהוָה׃ יֵבֹשׁוּ וְיִבָּהֲלוּ עֲדֵי־עַד וְיַחְפְּרוּ וְיֹאבֵדוּ׃ וְיֵדְעוּ כִּי־
that let And and them let and ,forever and them Let Jeho- O
know them .perish pale be terrified ashamed be .vah

אַתָּה שִׁמְךָ יְהוָה לְבַדֶּךָ עֶלְיוֹן עַל־כָּל־הָאָרֶץ׃
the all over the You –Jehovah Your ,You
.earth High Most alone (is) name

PSAL. LXXXIV פד

PSALM 84

1 2 לַמְנַצֵּחַ עַל־הַגִּתִּית לִבְנֵי־קֹרַח מִזְמוֹר׃ מַה־יְּדִידוֹת
lovely How .psalm A Korah the for the on chief the To
(are) of sons .Gittith ,musician

3 מִשְׁכְּנוֹתֶיךָ יְהוָה צְבָאוֹת׃ נִכְסְפָה וְגַם־כָּלְתָה ׀ נַפְשִׁי
My faints and longs .hosts O Your
soul even of Jehovah ,dwellings

4 לְחַצְרוֹת יְהוָה לִבִּי וּבְשָׂרִי יְרַנְּנוּ אֶל אֵל־חָי׃ גַּם־צִפּוֹר ׀
the Even .living the to shout my and my ;Jehovah the for
sparrow God joy for flesh heart of courts

מָצְאָה בַיִת וּדְרוֹר ׀ קֵן לָהּ אֲשֶׁר־שָׁתָה אֶפְרֹחֶיהָ אֶת־
her may she where for the a and a has
,young lay herself swallow nest ;house found

5 מִזְבְּחוֹתֶיךָ יְהוָה צְבָאוֹת מַלְכִּי וֵאלֹהָי׃ אַשְׁרֵי יוֹשְׁבֵי
who they Blessed my and my ,hosts O ,altars Your
in dwell (are) .God king of Jehovah

6 בֵיתֶךָ עוֹד יְהַלְלוּךָ סֶּלָה׃ אַשְׁרֵי אָדָם עוֹז־לוֹ בָךְ מְסִלּוֹת
the in (is) to strength the Blessed .Selah will they always Your
highways ;You him man (is) .You praise ;house

7 בִּלְבָבָם׃ עֹבְרֵי ׀ בְּעֵמֶק הַבָּכָא מַעְיָן יְשִׁיתוּהוּ גַּם־בְּרָכוֹת
(with) even will they a ;weeping the Passing their in (are)
blessings ;it make fountain of valley through .hearts

8 יַעְטֶה מוֹרֶה׃ יֵלְכוּ מֵחַיִל אֶל־חָיִל יֵרָאֶה אֶל־אֱלֹהִים
God before appearing ;strength to from They early the covers
strength go .rain

9 בְּצִיּוֹן׃ יְהוָה אֱלֹהִים צְבָאוֹת שִׁמְעָה תְפִלָּתִי הַאֲזִינָה אֱלֹהֵי
O ear give my hear ,hosts of God O .Zion in
of God ;prayer Jehovah

10 יַעֲקֹב סֶלָה׃ מָגִנֵּנוּ רְאֵה אֱלֹהִים וְהַבֵּט פְּנֵי מְשִׁיחֶךָ׃
Your the look and ,God O ,See our .Selah .Jacob
.anointed of face upon shield

11 כִּי טוֹב־יוֹם בַּחֲצֵרֶיךָ מֵאָלֶף בָּחַרְתִּי הִסְתּוֹפֵף בְּבֵית אֱלֹהַי
my the in at stand to have I a than Your in a (is) For
God of house threshold the chosen ;thousand courts day better

12 מִדּוּר בְּאָהֳלֵי־רֶשַׁע׃ כִּי שֶׁמֶשׁ ׀ וּמָגֵן יְהוָה אֱלֹהִים חֵן
Grace God (is) a and sun a For wicked- the in to than
Jehovah shield .ness of tents dwell

13 וְכָבוֹד יִתֵּן יְהוָה לֹא יִמְנַע־טוֹב לַהֹלְכִים בְּתָמִים׃ יְהוָה
O .integrity in those to with- will He not ;Jehovah will and
of Jehovah walk who good hold give glory

צְבָאוֹת אַשְׁרֵי אָדָם בֹּטֵחַ בָּךְ׃
in who the blessed ,hosts
.You trusts man (is)

PSALM 85

To the Chief Musician, A Psalm for the Sons of Korah.

[1] O Jehovah, You have been gracious to Your land; You have turned back the captivity of Jacob. [2] You have taken away Your people's iniquity; You have covered all of their sins. Selah. [3] You have gathered all of Your wrath; You have turned from the heat of Your anger. [4] O God of our salvation, turn us, and cause Your anger toward us to cease. [5] Will You be angry with us forever? Will you draw out Your anger to all generations? [6] Will You give us life anew, so that Your people may rejoice in You? [7] Show us Your mercy, O Jehovah, and grant us Your salvation. [8] I will hear what Jehovah God will say; for He will speak peace to His people, and to His saints; but let them not turn again to folly. [9] Surely His salvation (is) near to those who fear Him; for glory to dwell in our land. [10] Mercy and truth have met together; righteousness and peace have kissed (each other). [11] Truth shall spring out of the earth; and righteousness looks down from Heaven. [12] Yea, Jehovah shall give good to us; and our land shall yield its increase. [13] Righteousness shall go before Him, and shall make a way for His footsteps.

PSAL. LXXXV פה

PSALM 85

1 2 לַמְנַצֵּחַ לִבְנֵי־קֹרַח מִזְמוֹר׃ רָצִיתָ יְהוָה אַרְצֶךָ שַׁבְתָּ
You Your O have You .psalm A Korah the for chief the To
turned ;land ,Jehovah ,favored of sons .musician

3 שְׁבוּת יַעֲקֹב׃ נָשָׂאתָ עֲוֺן עַמֶּךָ כִּסִּיתָ כָל־חַטָּאתָם סֶלָה׃
.Selah their all You Your iniquity You .Jacob cap- the
.sins covered ;people's away took of tivity

4 5 אָסַפְתָּ כָל־עֶבְרָתֶךָ הֱשִׁיבוֹתָ מֵחֲרוֹן אַפֶּךָ׃ שׁוּבֵנוּ אֱלֹהֵי
God O Turn Your the from You Your all You
of ,us .anger of heat turned ;wrath gathered

6 יִשְׁעֵנוּ וְהָפֵר כַּעַסְךָ עִמָּנוּ׃ הַלְעוֹלָם תֶּאֱנַף־בָּנוּ תִּמְשֹׁךְ
You Will with you Will forever with Your and sal- our
out draw ?us angry be .us anger up break ,vation

7 אַפְּךָ לְדֹר וָדֹר׃ הֲלֹא אַתָּה תָּשׁוּב תְּחַיֵּנוּ וְעַמְּךָ יִשְׂמְחוּ
may Your that You Will Will You not gen- and gen- to Your
rejoice people ,us revive ?turn ?eration eration anger

8 9 בָךְ׃ הַרְאֵנוּ יְהוָה חַסְדֶּךָ וְיֶשְׁעֲךָ תִּתֶּן־לָנוּ׃ אֶשְׁמְעָה מַה
what will I to give Your and Your O Show in
hear .us salvation ,mercy ,Jehovah ,us ?You

יְדַבֵּר הָאֵל יְהוָה כִּי ׀ יְדַבֵּר שָׁלוֹם אֶל־עַמּוֹ וְאֶל־חֲסִידָיו
His and His to peace will He for ;Jehovah God will
;saints to ,people speak say

10 וְאַל־יָשׁוּבוּ לְכִסְלָה׃ אַךְ קָרוֹב לִירֵאָיו יִשְׁעוֹ לִשְׁכֹּן כָּבוֹד
glory to sal- His fearers to (is) Surely .folly to them let but
dwell ,vation Him of near again turn not

11 12 בְּאַרְצֵנוּ׃ חֶסֶד־וֶאֱמֶת נִפְגָּשׁוּ צֶדֶק וְשָׁלוֹם נָשָׁקוּ׃ אֱמֶת
Truth have and righteous- met have and Mercy our in
.kissed peace ness ;together truth .land

13 מֵאֶרֶץ תִּצְמָח וְצֶדֶק מִשָּׁמַיִם נִשְׁקָף׃ גַּם־יְהוָה יִתֵּן
shall Jehovah ,Yea looks from righ- and shall of out
give .down Heaven teousness ;sprout earth the

14 הַטּוֹב וְאַרְצֵנוּ תִּתֵּן יְבוּלָהּ׃ צֶדֶק לְפָנָיו יְהַלֵּךְ וְיָשֵׂם
shall and shall before Righteous- its shall our and ;good
make ,go Him ness .prudence give land

לְדֶרֶךְ פְּעָמָיו׃
His a for
.footsteps way

PSALM 86

A Prayer of David.

[1] O Jehovah, bow down Your ear; answer me, for I (am) poor and needy. [2] Preserve my soul, for I (am) godly; O You my God, save Your servant who trusts in You. [3] Be merciful to Me, O Lord, for I cry

PSAL. LXXXVI פו

PSALM 86

1 תְּפִלָּה לְדָוִד הַטֵּה־יְהוָה אָזְנְךָ עֲנֵנִי כִּי־עָנִי וְאֶבְיוֹן אָנִי׃
I and poor for answer Your O Bow of A
.(am) needy ;me ;ear ,Jehovah ,down .David prayer

2 שָׁמְרָה נַפְשִׁי כִּי־חָסִיד אָנִי הוֹשַׁע עַבְדְּךָ אַתָּה אֱלֹהַי
my You O Your Save ;(am) I godly for my Preserve
,God ,servant ,soul

3 הַבּוֹטֵחַ אֵלֶיךָ׃ חָנֵּנִי אֲדֹנָי כִּי־אֵלֶיךָ אֶקְרָא כָּל־הַיּוֹם׃
the all cry I to for O Favor .You in who
.day You ,Lord ,me trusts

to You daily. [4] Give joy to the soul of Your servant; for to You, O Lord, I lift up my soul. [5] For You, O Lord, (are) good and ready to forgive; and rich in mercy to all who call on You. [6] Give ear, O Lord, to my prayer; listen to my cry of supplication. [7] I will call on You in the day of my trouble, for You will answer me. [8] None among the gods (is) like You, O Lord; nor (any) like Your works. [9] All nations whom You have made shall come and worship before You; yea, Lord, (they) shall glorify Your name. [10] For You (are) great, and do wonderful things; You alone (are) God. [11] Teach me Your way, O Jehovah; I will walk in your truth; unite my heart to fear Your name. [12] With all my heart I will thank You, O Lord my God; and I will glorify Your name forevermore. [13] For Your mercy toward me (is) great; and You have delivered my soul from the lowest Sheol. [14] O God, the proud have risen against me; and the troop of the violent have sought after my life, and have not set You before their eyes. [15] But You, O God, (are) God, full of pity; and gracious, long-suffering and rich in mercy and truth. [16] O turn to me and be gracious to me; give Your strength to Your servant, and save the son of Your handmaid. [17] Show me a token for good, that those who hate me may see and be ashamed, O Jehovah, because You have helped me and You comforted me.

4
5 שַׂמֵּחַ נֶפֶשׁ עַבְדֶּךָ כִּי־אֵלֶיךָ אֲדֹנָי נַפְשִׁי אֶשָּׂא׃ כִּי־אַתָּה
,You For lift I my O to for Your soul the make
up soul ,Lord ,You ,servant of glad

6 אֲדֹנָי טוֹב וְסַלָּח וְרַב־חֶסֶד לְכָל־קֹרְאֶיךָ׃ הַאֲזִינָה יְהוָה
O ear Give call who to mercy and and (are) O
,Jehovah ,to .You on all in rich ,forgiving good ,Lord

7 תְּפִלָּתִי וְהַקְשִׁיבָה בְּקוֹל תַּחֲנוּנוֹתָי׃ בְּיוֹם צָרָתִי אֶקְרָאֶךָּ
call will I my the In sup- my the to and my
,You on trouble of day .plications of voice attend ,prayer

8 כִּי תַעֲנֵנִי׃ אֵין־כָּמוֹךָ בָאֱלֹהִים ׀ אֲדֹנָי וְאֵין כְּמַעֲשֶׂיךָ׃
Your like and ;Lord O among like None will You for
.works are none ,gods the You (is) .me answer

9 כָּל־גּוֹיִם ׀ אֲשֶׁר עָשִׂיתָ יָבוֹאוּ ׀ וְיִשְׁתַּחֲווּ לְפָנֶיךָ אֲדֹנָי וִיכַבְּדוּ
shall and O before and shall have You whom nations All
glorify ,Lord ,You worship come made

10 לִשְׁמֶךָ׃ כִּי־גָדוֹל אַתָּה וְעֹשֵׂה נִפְלָאוֹת אַתָּה אֱלֹהִים לְבַדֶּךָ׃
.alone God You wonderful and You great For Your
(are) ;things do ,(are) .name

11 הוֹרֵנִי יְהוָה ׀ דַּרְכֶּךָ אֲהַלֵּךְ בַּאֲמִתֶּךָ יַחֵד לְבָבִי לְיִרְאָה
fear to my unite Your in will I Your O Teach
heart ;truth walk ;way ,Jehovah ,me

12 שְׁמֶךָ׃ אוֹדְךָ ׀ אֲדֹנָי אֱלֹהַי בְּכָל־לְבָבִי וַאֲכַבְּדָה שִׁמְךָ
Your will I and my with my O will I Your
name glorify ;heart all ,God Lord ,You thank .name

13 לְעוֹלָם׃ כִּי־חַסְדְּךָ גָּדוֹל עָלָי וְהִצַּלְתָּ נַפְשִׁי מִשְּׁאוֹל
the from my You and toward (is) Your For .forever
Sheol soul saved have ;me great mercy

14 תַּחְתִּיָּה׃ אֱלֹהִים ׀ זֵדִים קָמוּ עָלַי וַעֲדַת עָרִיצִים בִּקְשׁוּ
have the the and against have the ,God O .lowest
sought violent of troop ;me risen proud

15 נַפְשִׁי וְלֹא שָׂמוּךָ לְנֶגְדָּם׃ וְאַתָּה אֲדֹנָי אֵל־רַחוּם וְחַנּוּן
and of full (are) O But before have and my
,gracious ,pity ,God ,Lord ,You .themselves You set not ,life

16 אֶרֶךְ אַפַּיִם וְרַב־חֶסֶד וֶאֱמֶת׃ פְּנֵה אֵלַי וְחָנֵּנִי תְּנָה־עֻזְּךָ
Your give and to O and mercy and ,anger long
strength ;me favor ,me turn .truth in rich (before)

17 לְעַבְדֶּךָ וְהוֹשִׁיעָה לְבֶן־אֲמָתֶךָ׃ עֲשֵׂה־עִמִּי אוֹת לְטוֹבָה
for a with Make Your the save and Your to
,good sign me .handmaid of son ;servant

וְיִרְאוּ שֹׂנְאַי וְיֵבֹשׁוּ כִּי־אַתָּה יְהוָה עֲזַרְתַּנִי וְנִחַמְתָּנִי׃
com- and have O ,You for be and my shall and
.me forted me helped ,Jehovah ;ashamed haters see

PSAL. LXXXVII פז

PSALM 87

For the Sons of Korah. A Psalm. A Song.

[1] His foundation (is) in the holy mountains. [2] Jehovah loves the gates of Zion more than all the tents of Jacob. [3] Glorious things (are) spoken of you, O city of God. Selah.

PSALM 87

1
2 לִבְנֵי־קֹרַח מִזְמוֹר שִׁיר יְסוּדָתוֹ בְּהַרְרֵי־קֹדֶשׁ׃ אֹהֵב יְהוָה
Jehovah loves .holiness the in (is) His A A .Korah the For
of mountains foundation .song .psalm of sons

3 שַׁעֲרֵי צִיּוֹן מִכֹּל מִשְׁכְּנוֹת יַעֲקֹב׃ נִכְבָּדוֹת מְדֻבָּר בָּךְ עִיר
O of are Glorious .Jacob tents the more Zion the
of city ,You spoken things of all than of gates

4] I will mention Rahab and Babylon to those who know me; behold, Philistia and Tyre with Ethiopia; this (man) was born there. [5] And it shall be said to Zion, This and that man was born in her; and the Highest Himself shall establish her. [6] Jehovah shall mark down, in recording the nations, this man was born there. Selah. [7] And the singers, the players of the pipe. All my springs (are) in You.

4 הָאֱלֹהִים סֶלָה׃ אַזְכִּיר ׀ רַהַב וּבָבֶל לְיֹדְעָי הִנֵּה פְלֶשֶׁת
Philistia behold those to and Rahab will I .Selah .God
;me knowing Babylon mention

5 וְצוֹר עִם־כּוּשׁ זֶה יֻלַּד־שָׁם׃ וּלְצִיּוֹן ׀ יֵאָמַר אִישׁ וְאִישׁ
a and man A shall it to And .there was This ;Ethiopia with and
man ,said be Zion born (man) Tyre

6 יֻלַּד־בָּהּ וְהוּא יְכוֹנְנֶהָ עֶלְיוֹן׃ יְהוָה יִסְפֹּר בִּכְתוֹב עַמִּים
the re- in shall Jehovah the estab- will and in was
,peoples cording count ,Highest ,her lish He ;her born

7 זֶה יֻלַּד־שָׁם סֶלָה׃ וְשָׁרִים כְּחֹלְלִים כָּל־מַעְיָנַי בָּךְ׃
in (are) my all players the the And .Selah .there was this
.You springs ;pipe the of ,singers born (man)

PSAL. LXXXVIII פח

PSALM 88

A Song. A Psalm for the Sons of Korah, to the Chief Musician on Mahalath, to make humble. A Poem of Heman the Ezrahite.

[1] O Jehovah God of my salvation, I have cried in the day, in the night before You. [2] Let my prayer come before You; bow down Your ear to my cry. [3] For my soul is full of troubles; and my life draws near Sheol. [4] I am counted with those who go down to the pit; I have been like a feeble man, [5] free among the dead, as pierced ones lying in the grave, whom You remember no more; yea, by Your hand they are cut off. [6] You have laid me in the lowest pit, in dark places; in the deeps. [7] Your fury has lain hard upon me, and You afflict (me) with all Your waves. Selah. [8] You have taken my friends away from me; You have made me a hateful thing to them; (I am) shut up, I cannot go out. [9] My eye mourns because of affliction; O Jehovah, I have called on You every day; I have stretched out my hands to You. [10] For will You do wonders to the dead? Shall the dead rise (and) thank You? Selah. [11] Shall Your mercy be declared in the grave; Your faithfulness amidst ruin? [12] Shall Your wonders be known in

1 שִׁיר מִזְמוֹר לִבְנֵי־קֹרַח לַמְנַצֵּחַ עַל־מָחֲלַת לְעַנּוֹת מַשְׂכִּיל
teaching A .Leannoth Mahalath on the To .Korah the for psalm A A
poem musician chief of sons .song

2 לְהֵימָן הָאֶזְרָחִי׃ יְהוָה אֱלֹהֵי יְשׁוּעָתִי יוֹם־צָעַקְתִּי בַלַּיְלָה
in and have I in my of God O the of
night the ,cried day the ,salvation Jehovah .Ezrahite Heman

3
4 נֶגְדֶּךָ׃ תָּבוֹא לְפָנֶיךָ תְּפִלָּתִי הַטֵּה אָזְנְךָ לְרִנָּתִי׃ כִּי־
For my to Your bow my before come Let before
.cry ear down ;prayer You .You

5 שָׂבְעָה בְרָעוֹת נַפְשִׁי וְחַיַּי לִשְׁאוֹל הִגִּיעוּ׃ נֶחְשַׁבְתִּי עִם־
with am I draws Sheol to my and my with full is
counted .near life ;soul evils

6 יוֹרְדֵי בוֹר הָיִיתִי כְּגֶבֶר אֵין־אֱיָל׃ בַּמֵּתִים חָפְשִׁי כְּמוֹ
as ,free the Among without a like have I the go- those
dead .strength man been ;pit to ing

חֲלָלִים ׀ שֹׁכְבֵי קֶבֶר אֲשֶׁר לֹא־זְכַרְתָּם עוֹד וְהֵמָּה מִיָּדְךָ
from they and ;yet You not whom the lying pierced
hand Your remember ,grave in ones

7
8 נִגְזָרוּ׃ שַׁתַּנִי בְּבוֹר תַּחְתִּיּוֹת בְּמַחֲשַׁכִּים בִּמְצֹלוֹת׃ עָלַי
Upon the in dark in ,lowest the in have You are
me .deeps places pit me put .off cut

9 סָמְכָה חֲמָתֶךָ וְכָל־מִשְׁבָּרֶיךָ עִנִּיתָ סֶּלָה׃ הִרְחַקְתָּ מְיֻדָּעַי
my have You .Selah You waves Your and Your has
friends away taken .afflict all with ,fury lain

10 מִמֶּנִּי שַׁתַּנִי תוֹעֵבוֹת לָמוֹ כָּלֻא וְלֹא אֵצֵא׃ עֵינִי דָאֲבָה מִנִּי־
because wastes My will I and (am I) to hateful a have You from
of away eye .out go not up shut ;them thing me made ;me

11 עֹנִי קְרָאתִיךָ יְהוָה בְּכָל־יוֹם שִׁטַּחְתִּי אֵלֶיךָ כַפָּי׃ הֲלַמֵּתִים
to For my to spread I ;day in O called I af-
dead the .hands You out every ,Jehovah ,You on ;fliction

12 תַּעֲשֶׂה־פֶּלֶא אִם־רְפָאִים יָקוּמוּ יוֹדוּךָ סֶּלָה׃ הַיְסֻפַּר
be Shall .Selah (and) rise the Or ?wonders You will
declared ?you thank Rephaim shall do

13 בַּקֶּבֶר חַסְדֶּךָ אֱמוּנָתְךָ בָּאֲבַדּוֹן׃ הֲיִוָּדַע בַּחֹשֶׁךְ פִּלְאֶךָ
Your the in be Shall ?ruin in Your Your the in
,wonders dark known faithfulness ;mercy grave

the dark, and Your righteousness in the land of forgetfulness. [13] But to You I have cried, O Jehovah; and in the morning my prayer shall go before You. [14] O Jehovah, why do you cast off my soul; (why) do You hide Your face from me? [15] I (am) afflicted and dying from childhood; I suffer Your terrors; I am distracted. [16] Your fierce wrath goes over me; Your terrors have cut me off.

[17] They surrounded me like waters all the day long; they have come together around me. [18] You have taken lover and friend far from me; he who knows me, (into) darkness.

PSALM 89

A Poem of Ethan the Ezrahite.

[1] I will sing (of) the mercies of Jehovah forever; I will declare with my mouth Your faithfulness to all generations. [2] For I have said, Mercy shall be built up forever; You shall establish Your faithfulness in the heavens.

[3] I have cut a covenant with My chosen; I have sworn to David My servant, [4] I will establish Your seed forever, and build up Your throne to all generations. Selah.

[5] And the heavens shall thank Your wonders, O Jehovah; also Your faithfulness in the assembly of the saints. [6] For who in the sky shall (one) compare to Jehovah; (who) among the sons of the mighty can be compared to Jehovah? [7] God is greatly to be feared in the congregation of the saints, and to be adored by all around Him. [8] O Jehovah God of hosts, who (is) a mighty Jehovah like You? Your faithfulness (is) all around You. [9] You rule the pride of the sea; when its waves rise high, You still them. [10] You have broken Rahab in pieces, as one that is slain; You have scattered Your enemies with Your

14 וְצִדְקָתְךָ בְּאֶרֶץ נְשִׁיָּה׃ וַאֲנִי ׀ אֵלֶיךָ יְהוָה שִׁוַּעְתִּי
have O ,You to I But forgetful the in Your and
;cried ,Jehovah ?ness of land righteousness

15 וּבַבֹּקֶר תְּפִלָּתִי תְקַדְּמֶךָּ׃ לָמָה יְהוָה תִּזְנַח נַפְשִׁי תַּסְתִּיר
You do my You do O Why go shall my the in and
hide ;soul off cast Jehovah .You before prayer morning

16 פָּנֶיךָ מִמֶּנִּי׃ עָנִי אֲנִי וְגֹוֵעַ מִנֹּעַר נָשָׂאתִי אֵמֶיךָ אָפוּנָה׃
am I Your bear I from and (am) I afflicted from Your
.perplexed ;terrors ;youth (my) dying ?me face

17
18 עָלַי עָבְרוּ חֲרוֹנֶיךָ בִּעוּתֶיךָ צִמְּתוּתֻנִי׃ סַבּוּנִי כַמַּיִם כָּל־
all like en- They cast have Your Your goes Over
waters me circled .off me terrors ;wrath me

19 הַיּוֹם הִקִּיפוּ עָלַי יָחַד׃ הִרְחַקְתָּ מִמֶּנִּי אֹהֵב וָרֵעַ
and lover from have You .together me have they the
;friend me far put around gone ;day

מְיֻדָּעַי מַחְשָׁךְ׃
(into) acquain- my
.darkness tances

PSAL. LXXXIX פט

PSALM 89

1
2 מַשְׂכִּיל לְאֵיתָן הָאֶזְרָחִי׃ חַסְדֵי יְהוָה עוֹלָם אָשִׁירָה לְדֹר
gen- to will I forever Jehovah the the of teaching A
eration ;(of) sing of mercies .Ezrahite Ethan poem

3 וָדֹר ׀ אוֹדִיעַ אֱמוּנָתְךָ בְּפִי׃ כִּי־אָמַרְתִּי עוֹלָם חֶסֶד יִבָּנֶה
be shall Mercy forever have I For my with Your will I gen- and
;up built ,said .mouth faithfulness declare eration

4 שָׁמַיִם ׀ תָּכִן אֱמוּנָתְךָ בָהֶם׃ כָּרַתִּי בְרִית לִבְחִירִי נִשְׁבַּעְתִּי
have I My with a have I in Your will You the
sworn ;chosen covenant cut .them faithfulness set heavens

5 לְדָוִד עַבְדִּי׃ עַד־עוֹלָם אָכִין זַרְעֶךָ וּבָנִיתִי לְדֹר־וָדוֹר
gen- and to build and Your will I forever until My to
eration generation up ,seed establish ;servant David

6 כִּסְאֲךָ סֶלָה׃ וְיוֹדוּ שָׁמַיִם פִּלְאֲךָ יְהוָה אַף־אֱמוּנָתְךָ
Your also O Your the shall And .Selah Your
faithfulness ;Jehovah ,wonders heavens thank .throne

7 בִּקְהַל קְדֹשִׁים׃ כִּי מִי בַשַּׁחַק יַעֲרֹךְ לַיהוָה יִדְמֶה לַיהוָה
to like is to shall the in who For .saints the the in
Jehovah ,Jehovah compare sky of assembly

8 בִּבְנֵי אֵלִים׃ אֵל נַעֲרָץ בְּסוֹד־קְדֹשִׁים רַבָּה וְנוֹרָא עַל־
by be to and ;greatly the the in be to is God the among
feared saints of council feared ?mighty of sons the

9 כָּל־סְבִיבָיו׃ יְהוָה ׀ אֱלֹהֵי צְבָאוֹת מִי־כָמוֹךָ חֲסִין ׀ יָהּ
?Jah a like who ,hosts of God O around all
mighty You (is) Jehovah .him

10 וֶאֱמוּנָתְךָ סְבִיבוֹתֶיךָ׃ אַתָּה מוֹשֵׁל בְּגֵאוּת הַיָּם בְּשׂוֹא
rise when the the rule You around all (is) Your And
high ;sea of pride .You faithfulness

11 גַלָּיו אַתָּה תְשַׁבְּחֵם׃ אַתָּה דִכִּאתָ כֶחָלָל רָהַב בִּזְרוֹעַ
arm with ;Rahab one as have You .them still You its
of slain crushed ,waves

mighty arm. [11] The heavens (are) Yours, and the earth Yours—the world and its fullness—You founded them. [12] You have created the north and the south; Tabor and Herman rejoice in Your name. [13] You have a mighty arm; Your hand is strong, Your right hand is high. [14] Justice and righteousness Your throne's foundation; mercy and truth shall go before Your face. [15] Blessed is the people knowing the joyful sound; O Jehovah, they shall walk in the light of Your face. [16] They shall rejoice in Your name always; and they are exalted in Your righteousness. [17] For You (are) the glory of their strength; and by Your favor You lift up our horn. [18] For Jehovah (is) our shield, and the Holy One of Israel our King.

[19] Then You spoke in a vision to Your holy one; and You said, I have laid help on a mighty one; I have exalted a chosen one from the people. [20] I have found My servant David; I have anointed him with My holy oil. [21] My hand shall be fixed with him; and My arm shall make him strong. [22] An enemy will not exact against him; nor the son of iniquity afflict him. [23] And I will beat down his foes before Him, and plague those hating him. [24] But My faithfulness and My mercy (is) with him; and his horn shall be exalted in My name. [25] And I will set his hand in the sea, and his right hand in the rivers. [26] He shall cry to Me, My father You (are), my God, and the rock of my salvation. [27] And I will make him firstborn; higher than the kings of the earth. [28] I will keep My mercy for him forever; and My covenant shall hold fast with him. [29] And I have established his seed forever, and his throne as the days of the heavens. [30] If his children forsake My law and do not walk in My judgments; [31] if they profane My statutes and do not keep

12 עֻזְּךָ פִּזַּרְתָּ אוֹיְבֶיךָ׃ לְךָ שָׁמַיִם אַף־לְךָ אָרֶץ תֵּבֵל וּמְלֹאָהּ
its and the the to also The to Your have You Your
,fulness world —earth You ,heavens You .enemies scattered might

13 אַתָּה יְסַדְתָּם׃ צָפוֹן וְיָמִין אַתָּה בְרָאתָם תָּבוֹר וְחֶרְמוֹן
and Tabor have You the and The have You
Hermon ;them created south north .them founded

14 בְּשִׁמְךָ יְרַנֵּנוּ׃ לְךָ זְרוֹעַ עִם־גְּבוּרָה תָּעֹז יָדְךָ תָּרוּם יְמִינֶךָ׃
Your high is Your is ;might with an to shout Your at
.hand right ;hand strong arm (is) You ;joy for name

15 צֶדֶק וּמִשְׁפָּט מְכוֹן כִּסְאֶךָ חֶסֶד וֶאֱמֶת יְקַדְּמוּ פָנֶיךָ׃
Your go shall and mercy Your foun- the and Righ-
.face before truth ;throne of dation justice teousness

16 אַשְׁרֵי הָעָם יֹדְעֵי תְרוּעָה יְהוָֹה בְּאוֹר־פָּנֶיךָ יְהַלֵּכוּן׃
shall they Your the in O joyful the who the Blessed
.walk face of light ,Jehovah ;sound know people (is)

17
18 בְּשִׁמְךָ יְגִילוּן כָּל־הַיּוֹם וּבְצִדְקָתְךָ יָרוּמוּ׃ כִּי־תִפְאֶרֶת
the For are they Your in and the all shall They Your in
of glory .exalted righteousness ;day rejoice name

19 עֻזָּמוֹ אָתָּה וּבִרְצֹנְךָ תָּרִים קַרְנֵנוּ׃ כִּי לַיהוָֹה מָגִנֵּנוּ
our Jehovah For our You Your by and You their
,shield (is) .horn up lift favor ,(are) strength

20 וְלִקְדוֹשׁ יִשְׂרָאֵל מַלְכֵּנוּ׃ אָז דִּבַּרְתָּ־בְחָזוֹן לַחֲסִידֶיךָ וַתֹּאמֶר
You and Your to a in You Then .king our Israel the and
,said ;one holy vision spoke of One Holy

21 שִׁוִּיתִי עֵזֶר עַל־גִּבּוֹר הֲרִימוֹתִי בָחוּר מֵעָם׃ מָצָאתִי דָּוִד
David have I the from chosen a have I mighty a on help have I
found .people one exalted ;one laid

22 עַבְדִּי בְּשֶׁמֶן קָדְשִׁי מְשַׁחְתִּיו׃ אֲשֶׁר יָדִי תִּכּוֹן עִמּוֹ אַף־
also with be shall My whom have I My with My
;him fixed hand .him anointed holy oil ;servant

23 זְרוֹעִי תְאַמְּצֶנּוּ׃ לֹא־יַשִּׁא אוֹיֵב בּוֹ וּבֶן־עַוְלָה לֹא יְעַנֶּנּוּ׃
af- shall not iniquity the against An shall not make shall My
.him flict of son ;him enemy exact .strong him arm

24
25 וְכַתּוֹתִי מִפָּנָיו צָרָיו וּמְשַׂנְאָיו אֶגּוֹף׃ וֶאֱמוּנָתִי וְחַסְדִּי עִמּוֹ
with My and My But .plague those and his before will I And
;him (is) mercy faithfulness him hating ,foes face his down beat

26 וּבִשְׁמִי תָּרוּם קַרְנוֹ׃ וְשַׂמְתִּי בַיָּם יָדוֹ וּבַנְּהָרוֹת יְמִינוֹ׃
right his the in and his the in I And his be shall My in and
.hand rivers ,hand sea set will .horn exalted name

27
28 הוּא יִקְרָאֵנִי אָבִי אָתָּה אֵלִי וְצוּר יְשׁוּעָתִי׃ אַף־אָנִי בְּכוֹר
first- I Also my the and my You my cry shall He
born .salvation of rock ,God ,(are) father ,Me to

29 אֶתְּנֵהוּ עֶלְיוֹן לְמַלְכֵי־אָרֶץ׃ לְעוֹלָם אֶשְׁמוֹר־לוֹ חַסְדִּי
My for will I Forever the the than higher make will
;mercy him keep .earth of kings ;him

30 וּבְרִיתִי נֶאֱמֶנֶת לוֹ׃ וְשַׂמְתִּי לָעַד זַרְעוֹ וְכִסְאוֹ כִּימֵי שָׁמָיִם׃
the the as his and his forever I And to (be shall) My and
.heavens of days throne ,seed set have .him confirmed covenant

31
32 אִם־יַעַזְבוּ בָנָיו תּוֹרָתִי וּבְמִשְׁפָּטַי לֹא יֵלֵכוּן׃ אִם־חֻקֹּתַי
My if do not My in and My his forsake If
statutes ,walk judgments ,law children

My commands; [32] then I will visit their wickedness with the rod, and their sins with stripes. [33] But I will not annul My mercy from him, and I will not be false in My faithfulness. [34] I will not profane My covenant, nor change what goes from My lips. [35] Once I have sworn by My holiness; I will not lie to David. [36] His seed shall be forever, and his throne as the sun before Me. [37] Like the moon, it shall be forever; and a faithful witness in the sky. Selah.

[38] But You have cast off and rejected (us); You have been angry with Your anointed. [39] You have turned away from the covenant of Your servant; You have defiled his crown on the ground. [40] You have broken down all his hedges; You have brought his strongholds to ruin. [41] All who pass by the way plunder him; he is a curse to his neighbors. [42] You have set up the right hand of his enemies; You have made all (his) enemies rejoice. [43] And you have blunted the edge of his sword, and have not held him up in battle. [44] You have made his glory to cease and have hurled his throne to the ground. [45] You have shortened the days of his youth; You have covered him (with) shame. Selah. [46] O Jehovah, how long will You hide Yourself? Shall Your wrath burn like fire forever? [47] Remember, I pray, the time of (my) life; for what vanity have you created all the sons of men? [48] What man lives and never sees death? Shall he deliver his soul from the hand of Sheol? Selah. [49] O Lord, where (are) Your former kindnesses, (that) You swore to David in Your faithfulness? [50] Remember, O Lord, the reproach of Your servants; my bearing in my

33 יְחַלְּלוּ וּמִצְוֺתַי לֹא יִשְׁמֹרוּ׃ וּפָקַדְתִּי בְשֵׁבֶט פִּשְׁעָם
trans- their the with will I then ;keep do not My and they
,gressions rod visit commands ,profane

34 וּבִנְגָעִים עֲוֺנָם׃ וְחַסְדִּי לֹא־אָפִיר מֵעִמּוֹ וְלֹא אֲשַׁקֵּר
will I and with from will I not My But their with and
false be not ,him annul mercy .iniquities stripes

35 בֶּאֱמוּנָתִי׃ לֹא־אֲחַלֵּל בְּרִיתִי וּמוֹצָא שְׂפָתַי לֹא אֲשַׁנֶּה׃
will I not My what and My will I not My in
.change lips from goes ,covenant profane .faithfulness

36
37 אַחַת נִשְׁבַּעְתִּי בְקָדְשִׁי אִם־לְדָוִד אֲכַזֵּב׃ זַרְעוֹ לְעוֹלָם
forever His will I to not My by have I Once
seed .lie David ;holiness sworn

38 יִהְיֶה וְכִסְאוֹ כַשֶּׁמֶשׁ נֶגְדִּי׃ כְּיָרֵחַ יִכּוֹן עוֹלָם וְעֵד בַּשַּׁחַק
the in a and ;forever shall it the Like before the as his and shall
sky witness set be moon .Me sun throne ,be

39 נֶאֱמָן סֶלָה׃ וְאַתָּה זָנַחְתָּ וַתִּמְאָס הִתְעַבַּרְתָּ עִם־מְשִׁיחֶךָ׃
Your with have You re- and cast have But .Selah faith-
.anointed angry been (us) jected off You .ful

40
41 נֵאַרְתָּה בְּרִית עַבְדֶּךָ חִלַּלְתָּ לָאָרֶץ נִזְרוֹ׃ פָּרַצְתָּ כָל־
all have You his the to have You Your cove- the have You
down broken .crown ground defiled ;servant of nant spurned

42 גְדֵרֹתָיו שַׂמְתָּ מִבְצָרָיו מְחִתָּה׃ שַׁסֻּהוּ כָּל־עֹבְרֵי דָרֶךְ הָיָה
he the who All plunder (to) his have You his
is ;way by pass him .ruin strongholds set ;walls

43 חֶרְפָּה לִשְׁכֵנָיו׃ הֲרִימוֹתָ יְמִין צָרָיו הִשְׂמַחְתָּ כָּל־אוֹיְבָיו׃
his all have You his right have You his to re- a
.enemies rejoice made ;enemies' hand exalted .neighbors proach

44
45 אַף־תָּשִׁיב צוּר חַרְבּוֹ וְלֹא הֲקֵמֹתוֹ בַּמִּלְחָמָה׃ הִשְׁבַּתָּ
have You .battle in made have and his the have You Also
cease made stand him not ,sword of edge blunted

46 מִטְּהָרוֹ וְכִסְאוֹ לָאָרֶץ מִגַּרְתָּה׃ הִקְצַרְתָּ יְמֵי עֲלוּמָיו
his the have You have the to his and his
;youth of days shortened .hurled ground throne ;lustre

47 הֶעֱטִיתָ עָלָיו בּוּשָׁה סֶלָה׃ עַד־מָה יְהוָה תִּסָּתֵר לָנֶצַח
?forever You will O ,when Until .Selah .shame him on have You
Yourself hide ,Jehovah covered

48 תִּבְעַר כְּמוֹ־אֵשׁ חֲמָתֶךָ׃ זְכָר־אֲנִי מֶה־חָלֶד עַל־מַה־שָּׁוְא
vanity what for time the ,Remember Your fire like Shall
;life of ,please ?wrath burn

49 בָּרָאתָ כָל־בְּנֵי־אָדָם׃ מִי גֶבֶר יִחְיֶה וְלֹא יִרְאֶה־מָּוֶת יְמַלֵּט
he Shall ?death does and lives man What ?men the all You have
deliver see not of sons created

50 נַפְשׁוֹ מִיַּד־שְׁאוֹל סֶלָה׃ אַיֵּה ׀ חֲסָדֶיךָ הָרִאשֹׁנִים ׀ אֲדֹנָי
,Lord O ,former Your Where .Selah ?Sheol the from his
kindnesses (are) of hand soul

51 נִשְׁבַּעְתָּ לְדָוִד בֶּאֱמוּנָתֶךָ׃ זְכֹר אֲדֹנָי חֶרְפַּת עֲבָדֶיךָ שְׂאֵתִי
my Your re- the ,Lord O ,Remember Your in to You (that)
bearing ;servants of proach ?faithfulness David swore

52 בְּחֵיקִי כָּל־רַבִּים עַמִּים׃ אֲשֶׁר חֵרְפוּ אוֹיְבֶיךָ ׀ יְהוָה אֲשֶׁר
(with) O Your re- have (with) ;peoples the all my in
which ;Jehovah ,enemies proached which many bosom

53 חֵרְפוּ עִקְּבוֹת מְשִׁיחֶךָ׃ בָּרוּךְ יְהוָה לְעוֹלָם אָמֵן ׀ וְאָמֵן׃
and amen ;forever Jehovah Blessed Your step the re- they
!amen (be) .anointed of proached

bosom the insults of the many peoples; [51] (with) which Your enemies have cursed, O Jehovah; (with) which they have cursed the footsteps of Your anointed.

[52] Blessed (be) Jehovah forever; amen and amen!

PSAL. XC צ

PSALM 90

1 תְּפִלָּה לְמֹשֶׁה אִישׁ־הָאֱלֹהִים אֲדֹנָי מָעוֹן אַתָּה הָיִיתָ לָּנוּ
us to have You a ,Lord O .God the Moses of A
been habitation of man prayer

2 בְּדֹר וָדֹר׃ בְּטֶרֶם ׀ הָרִים יֻלָּדוּ וַתְּחוֹלֵל אֶרֶץ וְתֵבֵל
the and the You or were the Before gen- and gen- in
;world earth to birth gave ,born mountains .eration eration

3 וּמֵעוֹלָם עַד־עוֹלָם אַתָּה אֵל׃ תָּשֵׁב אֱנוֹשׁ עַד־דַּכָּא וַתֹּאמֶר
,say and ,dust to man You .God You to from even
turn (are) everlasting everlasting

4 שׁוּבוּ בְנֵי־אָדָם׃ כִּי אֶלֶף שָׁנִים בְּעֵינֶיךָ כְּיוֹם אֶתְמוֹל כִּי
when yesterday (are) Your in years a For .men O ,Return
as eyes thousand of sons

5 יַעֲבֹר וְאַשְׁמוּרָה בַלָּיְלָה׃ זְרַמְתָּם שֵׁנָה יִהְיוּ בַּבֹּקֶר
the in they a (as) flooded You the in a (as) and passes it
morning ;are sleep ;away them .night watch by

6 כֶּחָצִיר יַחֲלֹף׃ בַּבֹּקֶר יָצִיץ וְחָלָף לָעֶרֶב יְמוֹלֵל וְיָבֵשׁ׃
and it the in and it the in ;sprouting like
.up dries withers evening ;sprouts blooms morning grass

7
8 כִּי־כָלִינוּ בְאַפֶּךָ וּבַחֲמָתְךָ נִבְהָלְנוּ׃ שַׁתָּ עֲוֺנֹתֵינוּ לְנֶגְדֶּךָ
before our have You are we by and Your by are we For
,You iniquities set .troubled wrath Your .anger consumed

9 עֲלֻמֵנוּ לִמְאוֹר פָּנֶיךָ׃ כִּי כָל־יָמֵינוּ פָּנוּ בְעֶבְרָתֶךָ כִּלִּינוּ
we Your in pass our all For Your the in our
finish ;wrath away days .face of light secret

10 שָׁנֵינוּ כְמוֹ־הֶגֶה׃ יְמֵי־שְׁנוֹתֵינוּ ׀ בָהֶם שִׁבְעִים שָׁנָה וְאִם
and ,years (are) them in ,years our The a like our
if seventy of days .sigh years

בִּגְבוּרֹת שְׁמוֹנִים שָׁנָה וְרָהְבָּם עָמָל וָאָוֶן כִּי־גָז חִישׁ
soon it for and (is) their yet ,years (live) by
passes ;vanity labor pride eighty strength

11
12 וַנָּעֻפָה׃ מִי־יוֹדֵעַ עֹז אַפֶּךָ וּכְיִרְאָתְךָ עֶבְרָתֶךָ׃ לִמְנוֹת
number to Your (so) Your as And Your the knows Who we and
.fury (is) fear ?anger of might .away fly

13 יָמֵינוּ כֵּן הוֹדַע וְנָבִא לְבַב חָכְמָה׃ שׁוּבָה יְהוָה עַד־מָתָי
?when until O ,Return .wisdom heart a we that teach There- our
,Jehovah of bring may ,(us) ,fore days

14 וְהִנָּחֵם עַל־עֲבָדֶיךָ׃ שַׂבְּעֵנוּ בַבֹּקֶר חַסְדֶּךָ וּנְרַנְּנָה וְנִשְׂמְחָה
be and we and Your (with) the in O Your to give and
glad rejoice will ,mercy morning us satisfy .servants pity

15 בְּכָל־יָמֵינוּ׃ שַׂמְּחֵנוּ כִּימוֹת עִנִּיתָנוּ שְׁנוֹת רָאִינוּ רָעָה׃
.evil have we the our to according us Make our all in
seen years ,affliction of days the glad .days

PSALM 90

A Prayer of Moses the Man of God.

[1] O Lord, You have been our dwelling-place in all generations. [2] Before the mountains were brought forth, or ever You had formed the earth and the world; even from everlasting to everlasting You (are) God. [3] You turn man to dust, and say, Return, O sons of men. [4] For a thousand years in Your eyes (are) as yesterday when it passes, and (as) a watch in the night. [5] You flooded them away; they are (as) a sleep; in the morning (they are) like grass growing; [6] in the morning it sprouts and shoots up; in the evening it withers and dries up. [7] For we are burned up by Your anger, and we are troubled by Your wrath. [8] You have set our iniquities before You, our secret (sins) in the light of Your face. [9] For all our days pass away in Your wrath; we finish our years like a murmur. [10] The days of our years (are) seventy; and if (any) by strength (live) eighty years, yet their pride (is) labor and vanity; for it soon passes, and we fly away. [11] Who knows the power of Your anger? And as Your fear (is, so is) Your fury. [12] So teach (us) to number our days, so that we may bring a heart of wisdom. [13] Return, O Jehovah! How long? And give pity to Your servants. [14] O satisfy us in the morning with Your mercy, and we will be glad and rejoice all our days. [15] Make us glad according to the days of our affliction, the years in which we

16 17 יֵרָאֶה אֶל־עֲבָדֶיךָ פָעֳלֶךָ וַהֲדָרְךָ עַל־בְּנֵיהֶם׃ וִיהִי ׀ נֹעַם
the let And their to Your and Your Your to Let
delight be .sons majesty ,work servants appear

אֲדֹנָי אֱלֹהֵינוּ עָלֵינוּ וּמַעֲשֵׂה יָדֵינוּ כּוֹנְנָה עָלֵינוּ וּמַעֲשֵׂה
the and upon establish our the and upon our the
of work ;us hands of work ;us God's Lord

יָדֵינוּ כּוֹנְנֵהוּ׃
establish our
!it ,hands

have seen evil. [16] Let Your work appear to Your servants, and Your majesty to their sons. [17] And let the delight of the Lord our God be upon us; and establish the works of our hands upon us; yea, the work of our hands, establish it!

PSAL. XCI צא

PSALM 91

1 2 יֹשֵׁב בְּסֵתֶר עֶלְיוֹן בְּצֵל שַׁדַּי יִתְלוֹנָן׃ אֹמַר לַיהוָה מַחְסִי
My to will I shall the shade Most the the in who He
refuge :Jehovah say .abide Almighty's High of covert dwells

3 וּמְצוּדָתִי אֱלֹהַי אֶבְטַח־בּוֹ׃ כִּי הוּא יַצִּילְךָ מִפַּח יָקוּשׁ
the from delivers He For in will I my my and
,fowler's trap you .Him trust ,God ,fortress

4 מִדֶּבֶר הַוּוֹת׃ בְּאֶבְרָתוֹ ׀ יָסֶךְ לָךְ וְתַחַת־כְּנָפָיו תֶּחְסֶה
shall you His and ,you shall He His With de- from
;refuge seek wings under cover feathers .structions plague

5 צִנָּה וְסֹחֵרָה אֲמִתּוֹ׃ לֹא תִירָא מִפַּחַד לָיְלָה מֵחֵץ יָעוּף
(that) the of night the shall You not His buckler and a
flies arrow of terror fear .truth (is) shield

6 7 יוֹמָם׃ מִדֶּבֶר בָּאֹפֶל יַהֲלֹךְ מִקֶּטֶב יָשׁוּד צָהֳרָיִם׃ יִפֹּל
shall .noon at (that) the of (that) in the of ;day by
fall waste lays destruction ;walks darkness plague

8 מִצִּדְּךָ ׀ אֶלֶף וּרְבָבָה מִימִינֶךָ אֵלֶיךָ לֹא יִגָּשׁ׃ רַק בְּעֵינֶיךָ
with Only shall it not you your at ten and A your by
eyes your .near come ;hand right thousand ,thousand side

9 תַבִּיט וְשִׁלֻּמַת רְשָׁעִים תִּרְאֶה׃ כִּי־אַתָּה יְהוָה מַחְסִי
my (are) O ,You Because .see wicked the the and shall you
;refuge ,Jehovah of reward ,look

10 עֶלְיוֹן שַׂמְתָּ מְעוֹנֶךָ׃ לֹא־תְאֻנֶּה אֵלֶיךָ רָעָה וְנֶגַע לֹא־יִקְרַב
shall not and ,Evil you shall not habit- your you Most the
near come plague befall .ation make High

11 בְּאָהֳלֶךָ׃ כִּי מַלְאָכָיו יְצַוֶּה־לָּךְ לִשְׁמָרְךָ בְּכָל־דְּרָכֶיךָ׃
your all in keep to for will He His For your
.ways you you order angels .tent

12 13 עַל־כַּפַּיִם יִשָּׂאוּנְךָ פֶּן־תִּגֹּף בָּאֶבֶן רַגְלֶךָ׃ עַל־שַׁחַל וָפֶתֶן
and the On your a on you lest shall They their in
adder lion .foot stone dash .up you bear hands

14 תִּדְרֹךְ תִּרְמֹס כְּפִיר וְתַנִּין׃ כִּי בִי חָשַׁק וַאֲפַלְּטֵהוּ אֲשַׂגְּבֵהוּ
set will I will I has he on Because the and the shall you shall you
.high on him ,him deliver ,love set Me .snake cub lion trample ,tread

15 כִּי־יָדַע שְׁמִי׃ יִקְרָאֵנִי ׀ וְאֶעֱנֵהוּ עִמּוֹ אָנֹכִי בְצָרָה אֲחַלְּצֵהוּ
will I in I with will I and shall He My he for
him rescue ;trouble (be will) him ;him answer ,Me on call .name known has

16 וַאֲכַבְּדֵהוּ׃ אֹרֶךְ יָמִים אַשְׂבִּיעֵהוּ וְאַרְאֵהוּ בִּישׁוּעָתִי׃
My will and will I days (with) honor and
.salvation see him make him satisfy of length .him

[1] He who dwells in the secret place of the Most High shall abide (in) the Almighty's shade. [2] I will say to Jehovah: My refuge and my fortress, my God; I will trust in Him. [3] For He delivers you from the fowler's trap, from destruction's plague. [4] With His feathers He will cover you, and under His wings you shall seek refuge; His truth (is) a shield and buckler. [5] You shall not fear the terror of night, of the arrow (that) flies by day; [6] of the plague (that) walks in darkness; of the destruction laying waste at noonday. [7] A thousand shall fall by your side, and ten thousand at your right hand; it shall not come near you. [8] Only with your eyes you shall look, and see the reward of the wicked. [9] Because You, O Jehovah, (are) my refuge; you make the Most High your habitation. [10] no evil shall befall you, nor shall any plague come near your tent. [11] For He shall give His angels charge over you, to keep you in all your ways. [12] They shall bear you up in their hands lest you dash your foot on a stone. [13] You shall tread on the lion and adder; the young lion and the serpent you shall trample underfoot. [14] Because he has set his love on Me, therefore I will deliver him; I will set him on high, because he has known My name. [15] He shall call on Me and I will answer him; I (will be) with him in trouble; I will deliver him and honor him. [16] I will satisfy him (with) long life and will make him see My salvation.

PSAL. XCII צב

PSALM 92

1= 2 מִזְמוֹר שִׁיר לְיוֹם הַשַּׁבָּת׃ טוֹב לְהֹדוֹת לַיהוָה וּלְזַמֵּר

to and to give to (is It) the for song A .psalm A
praises sing ,Jehovah thanks good .sabbath day

3 לְשִׁמְךָ עֶלְיוֹן׃ לְהַגִּיד בַּבֹּקֶר חַסְדֶּךָ וֶאֱמוּנָתְךָ בַּלֵּילוֹת׃

every Your and Your the in make to Most O Your to
;night faithfulness ,mercy morning known ;High ,name

4 5 עֲלֵי־עָשׂוֹר וַעֲלֵי־נָבֶל עֲלֵי הִגָּיוֹן בְּכִנּוֹר׃ כִּי שִׂמַּחְתַּנִי

have You For the on sounding with the and ten the on
,glad me made .lyre music ,harp on (strings)

6 יְהוָה בְּפָעֳלֶךָ בְּמַעֲשֵׂי יָדֶיךָ אֲרַנֵּן׃ מַה־גָּדְלוּ מַעֲשֶׂיךָ יְהוָה

O Your are How will I Your the in with Jeho- O
,Jehovah ,works great .shout hands of works ;work Your ,vah

7 מְאֹד עָמְקוּ מַחְשְׁבֹתֶיךָ׃ אִישׁ־בַּעַר לֹא יֵדָע וּכְסִיל לֹא־

not fool a does not brutish A Your are very
,know man .thoughts deep

8 יָבִין אֶת־זֹאת׃ בִּפְרֹחַ רְשָׁעִים ׀ כְּמוֹ עֵשֶׂב וַיָּצִיצוּ כָּל־פֹּעֲלֵי

the all and ;grass like the In .this does
of doers blossom wicked flourishing understand

9 10 אָוֶן לְהִשָּׁמְדָם עֲדֵי־עַד׃ וְאַתָּה מָרוֹם לְעֹלָם יְהוָה׃ כִּי הִנֵּה

,lo ,For O ,forever are But .forever (to) them for ;evil
,Jehovah exalted ,You destroyed (be)

אֹיְבֶיךָ ׀ יְהוָה כִּי־הִנֵּה אֹיְבֶיךָ יֹאבֵדוּ יִתְפָּרְדוּ כָּל־פֹּעֲלֵי

the all be shall shall Your ,lo ,for O Your
of doers scattered ;perish enemies ;Jehovah ,enemies

11 12 אָוֶן׃ וַתָּרֶם כִּרְאֵים קַרְנִי בַּלֹּתִי בְּשֶׁמֶן רַעֲנָן׃ וַתַּבֵּט עֵינִי

my shall and .fresh with be will I my the as You But .evil
eye look oil anointed ,horn ox wild up lift will

13 בְּשׁוּרָי בַּקָּמִים עָלַי מְרֵעִים תִּשְׁמַעְנָה אָזְנָי׃ צַדִּיק כַּתָּמָר

the as The my hear shall the against rise who my on
tree palm righteous .ears evildoers me up ;enemies

14 יִפְרָח כְּאֶרֶז בַּלְּבָנוֹן יִשְׂגֶּה׃ שְׁתוּלִים בְּבֵית יְהוָה בְּחַצְרוֹת

the in ,Jehovah the in Those shall he in a like will
of courts of house planted .grow Lebanon cedar ;flourish

15 אֱלֹהֵינוּ יַפְרִיחוּ׃ עוֹד יְנוּבוּן בְּשֵׂיבָה דְּשֵׁנִים וְרַעֲנַנִּים יִהְיוּ׃

they fresh and fat old in shall They still shall ,God ou
;be shall ;age fruit bear .flourish

16 הַגִּיד כִּי־יָשָׁר יְהוָה צוּרִי וְלֹא־עַלְתָה בּוֹ׃

in (is) unrigh- And my ,Jehovah (is) that t
.Him teousness no !rock upright de

PSAL. XCIII צג

PSALM 93

1 לָךְ גֵּאוּת לָבֵשׁ לָבֵשׁ יְהוָה עֹז הִתְאַזָּר אַף־תִּכּוֹן

is ,yea He strength Jeho- clothed is is He majesty ;re
established ;Himself girded vah with ;with clothed

2 3 תִּמּוֹט׃ נָכוֹן כִּסְאֲךָ מֵאָז מֵעוֹלָם אָתָּה׃ נָשְׂאוּ

Have You from from Your (is) shall i
up lifted .(are) everlasting ,then throne established ;shak

PSALM 92

A Psalm, A Song for the Sabbath Day.

[1] (It is) good to give thanks to Jehovah, and to sing praises to Your name, O Most High; [2] to make Your mercy known in the morning, and Your faithfulness every night; [3] on the ten (strings), and on the harp —on the lyre with sounding music. [4] For You have rejoiced me with Your work, O Jehovah; I will shout in the works of Your hands. [5] O Jehovah, Your purposes are very deep. how great are Your works! [6] A brutish man does not know; a fool does not understand this. [7] When the wicked flourish like grass; and all the evildoers blossom; (it is) for them (to be) destroyed forever. [8] But You, O Jehovah, (are) exalted forever. [9] For, lo, Your enemies shall perish; all the evildoers shall be scattered. [10] But You will lift up my horn as the wild ox, and I will be anointed with fresh oil. [11] And my eye shall look on my enemies; my ears shall hear the evildoers who rise up against me. [12] The righteous shall flourish as the palm tree; he shall grow like a cedar in Lebanon. [13] Those planted in the house of Jehovah, in the courts of our God, shall flourish. [14] They shall bear fruit in old age; they shall be fat and fresh; [15] to declare that Jehovah (is) upright, my rock! And in Him (is) no unrighteousness.

PSALM 93

[1] Jehovah reigns; He has clothed Himself with majesty; Jehovah is clothed with strength; He has girded Himself; and (He has) established the world; it shall not be shaken. [2] Your throne (is) established from then; You (are) from everlasting. [3] The floods have lifted

up; O Jehovah, the floods have lifted up their voice; the floods have lifted their roaring waves. [4] Jehovah on high (is) mightier than the noise of many waters, (than) the mighty waves of the sea. [5] Your testimonies are very sure; holiness becomes Your house to length of days, O Jehovah.

נְהָרֹ֑ות ׀ יְהֹוָ֡ה נָשְׂא֣וּ נְהָרֹות֮ קֹולָ֑ם יִשְׂא֖וּ נְהָרֹ֣ות דָּכְיָֽם׃

roar- their | the | have | their | the | have | Jeho- | O | the
waves ing | floods | up lifted | voice | floods | up lifted | vah | | floods

4　מִקֹּלֹ֤ות ׀ מַ֥יִם רַבִּ֗ים אַדִּירִ֣ים מִשְׁבְּרֵי־יָ֑ם אַדִּ֖יר בַּמָּרֹ֣ום

high on | mighty is | the breakers | mighty the | many waters | than more
| | of sea | | of voices the

5　יְהֹוָֽה׃　עֵדֹתֶ֨יךָ ׀ נֶאֶמְנ֬וּ מְאֹ֗ד לְבֵיתְךָ֥ נַֽאֲוָה־קֹ֥דֶשׁ יְהֹוָ֗ה

O | holiness becomes | Your | very | are | Your | Jehovah
Jehovah | | house | | sure | testimonies

לְאֹ֥רֶךְ יָמִֽים׃

days | to
| of length

PSAL. XCIV　צד

PSALM 94

PSALM 94

[1] O Jehovah, God of vengeance; O God of vengeance, shine forth! [2] Lift up Yourself, O judge of the earth; give a just repayment on the proud. [3] O Jehovah, how long (shall) the wicked, how long shall the wicked triumph? [4] They sputter; they speak impudent things; all the workers of evil speak proudly. [5] O Jehovah, they crush Your people and afflict Your inheritance. [6] They kill the widow and the stranger, and murder the orphan. [7] Yet they say, The Lord shall not see, nor shall the God of Jacob observe. [8] Understand, you beastly ones among the people; yea, you fools, when will you be wise? [9] He who planted the ear, shall He not hear? [ ] who formed the eye, [ ] He not see? [10] [ ] chastises the nations, [ ] not punish — He [ ]hes man knowl- [ ]Jehovah knows [ ]ts of man, [ ]are) vain. [ ]the man [ ]ehovah, [ ]Your [ ]rest [ ]til

1　אֵל־נְקָמֹ֥ות יְהֹוָ֑ה אֵ֖ל נְקָמֹ֣ות הֹופִֽיעַ׃ הִ֭נָּשֵׂא שֹׁפֵ֣ט הָאָ֑רֶץ
2

the | judge | O | up Lift | shine | revenges | God | Jehovah | revenges | O
earth | of | yourself | | forth | | of | | | of God

3　הָשֵׁ֥ב גְּמ֝֗וּל עַל־גֵּאִֽים׃ עַד־מָתַ֖י רְשָׁעִ֥ים ׀ יְהֹוָ֑ה עַד־מָתַ֖י

when until | O | the (shall) | when Until | the | on | just a | give
Jehovah | wicked | | proud | repayment

4　רְשָׁעִ֣ים יַעֲלֹֽזוּ׃ יַבִּ֣יעוּ יְדַבְּר֣וּ עָתָ֑ק יִ֝תְאַמְּר֗וּ כָּל־פֹּ֥עֲלֵי אָֽוֶן׃

evil | the | all | speak | impudent | they | They | shall | the
| of workers | | proudly | things | speak | sputter | triumph | wicked

5
6　עַמְּךָ֣ יְהֹוָ֣ה יְדַכְּא֑וּ וְֽנַחֲלָתְךָ֥ יְעַנּֽוּ׃ אַלְמָנָ֣ה וְגֵ֣ר יַהֲרֹ֑גוּ

kill they | and | The | afflict | Your and | they | O | Your
| alien the | widow | | inheritance | crush | Jehovah | people

7　וִיתֹומִ֥ים יְרַצֵּֽחוּ׃ וַ֭יֹּאמְרוּ לֹ֣א יִרְאֶה־יָּ֑הּ וְלֹא־יָ֝בִ֗ין אֱלֹהֵ֥י

the | shall | not | Jehovah | shall | Not | they | Yet | they | the and
of God | perceive | | see | | say | | murder | | orphan

8
9　יַֽעֲקֹֽב׃ בִּ֭ינוּ בֹּעֲרִ֣ים בָּעָ֑ם וּ֝כְסִילִ֗ים מָתַ֥י תַּשְׂכִּֽילוּ׃ הֲנֹ֣טַע

who He | you will | when | you and | among | you | Understand | Jacob
planted | wise be | | fools | people the | brutish

10　אֹ֭זֶן הֲלֹ֣א יִשְׁמָ֑ע אִֽם־יֹ֥צֵֽר עַ֝֗יִן הֲלֹ֣א יַבִּֽיט׃ הֲיֹסֵ֣ר גֹּ֭ויִם הֲלֹ֣א

shall | the | who He | He | shall | the | He | Or | He | shall | the
not | nations chastises | see | not | eye | formed who | hear | not | ear

11　יֹוכִ֑יחַ הַֽמְלַמֵּ֖ד אָדָ֣ם דָּֽעַת׃ יְהֹוָ֗ה יֹ֭דֵעַ מַחְשְׁבֹ֣ות אָדָ֑ם כִּי־

that | man | the | knows | Jehovah | knowl- | man | who He | He
| of thoughts | | | edge | | teaches | rebuke

12　הֵ֣מָּה הָֽבֶל׃ אַשְׁרֵ֤י ׀ הַגֶּ֣בֶר אֲשֶׁר־תְּיַסְּרֶ֣נּוּ יָּ֑הּ וּֽמִתֹּורָתְךָ֥

Your from | O | You | whom | the | Blessed | vain | they
law | Jah | chasten | | man | is | | (are)

13　תְלַמְּדֶֽנּוּ׃ לְהַשְׁקִ֣יט לֹ֖ו מִ֣ימֵי רָ֑ע עַ֤ד יִכָּרֶ֖ה לָרָשָׁ֣ע שָֽׁחַת׃

pit the | the for | dug is | until | evil | from | to | rest give | teach You
wicked | | | | days | him | | | him

14　כִּ֤י ׀ לֹֽא־יִטֹּ֣שׁ יְהֹוָ֣ה עַמֹּ֑ו וְ֝נַחֲלָתֹ֗ו לֹ֣א יַעֲזֹֽב׃ כִּֽי־עַד־צֶ֭דֶק
15

righ- | to | For | He will | not | His and | His | Jehovah | will | not | For
teousness | | | forsake | | inheritance | people | | leave

יָשׁ֣וּב מִשְׁפָּ֑ט וְ֝אַחֲרָ֗יו כָּל־יִשְׁרֵי־לֵֽב׃ מִֽי־יָק֣וּם לִ֤י עִ[ם]

for | will | Who | heart | the | all | it after | judgment | shall
me | up rise | | in upright | | | | | turn

up for Me against the evildoers? Who will stand up for Me against the workers of evil? [17] Unless Jehovah (had been) my help, my soul would almost have dwelt in silence. [18] If I said, My foot was moved, O Jehovah, Your mercy has held me up. [19] In the multitude of my inward thoughts, Your comforts delight my soul. [20] Shall the throne of iniquity have fellowship (with) You, devising perverseness for a statute? [21] They gather themselves together against the soul of the righteous, and condemn the blood of the innocent. [22] But Jehovah is my tower of defense; and my God (is) the rock of my refuge. [23] And He shall turn their own evil upon them; and He shall cut them off in their own wickedness; Jehovah our God shall cut them off!

PSALM 95

[1] O come, let us sing to Jehovah; let us make a joyful noise to the Rock of our salvation. [2] Let us come before His face with praise; let us shout for joy to Him with songs. [3] For Jehovah (is) a great God, and a great King above all gods. [4] The deep places of the earth (are) in His hand; the summits of the mountains also (are) His. [5] The sea (is) His, and He made it; and His hands formed the dry land. [6] O come, let us worship and bow down; let us kneel before Jehovah our Maker. [7] For He (is) our God; and we (are) the people of His pasture, and the sheep of His hand. Today, if you will hear His voice, [8] do not harden your heart as (in) Meribah; as (in) the day of Massah in the wilderness; [9] when your fathers tempted Me, they tested Me and they saw My work. [10] For forty years I was disgusted with this generation; and (I) said, It (is) a people who err in heart;

17 מֵרֵעִים מִי־יִתְיַצֵּב לִי עִם־פֹּעֲלֵי אָוֶן׃ לוּלֵי יְהוָה עֶזְרָתָה
(been had) Jehovah Unless ?evil the against for will Who the
help a of workers Me arise ?evildoers

18 לִּי כִּמְעַט ׀ שָׁכְנָה דוּמָה נַפְשִׁי׃ אִם־אָמַרְתִּי מָטָה רַגְלִי
My was ,say I If my in would almost for
,foot moved .soul silence dwelt have ,me

19 חַסְדְּךָ יְהוָה יִסְעָדֵנִי׃ בְּרֹב שַׂרְעַפַּי בְּקִרְבִּי תַּנְחוּמֶיךָ
Your my in my the In held has O Your
comforts midst ,thoughts of host .up me ,Jehovah ,mercy

20 יְשַׁעַשְׁעוּ נַפְשִׁי׃ הַיְחָבְרְךָ כִּסֵּא הַוּוֹת יֹצֵר עָמָל עֲלֵי־חֹק׃
a for perverse- form- iniquity the allied be Shall my delight
?statute ness ing of throne You to .soul

21
22 יָגוֹדּוּ עַל־נֶפֶשׁ צַדִּיק וְדָם נָקִי יַרְשִׁיעוּ׃ וַיְהִי יְהוָה לִי
to Jehovah But con- they the the and the the against They
me is .demn innocent of blood ,righteous of soul gather

23 לְמִשְׂגָּב וֵאלֹהַי לְצוּר מַחְסִי׃ וַיָּשֶׁב עֲלֵיהֶם ׀ אֶת־אוֹנָם
own their upon He And my the is my and a for
;evil them back turns .refuge of rock God ,stronghold

וּבְרָעָתָם יַצְמִיתֵם יַצְמִיתֵם יְהוָה אֱלֹהֵינוּ׃
our Jehovah cut shall shall He their in and
.God off them ;off them cut wickedness

PSAL. XCV צה

PSALM 95

1
2 לְכוּ נְרַנְּנָה לַיהוָה נָרִיעָה לְצוּר יִשְׁעֵנוּ׃ נְקַדְּמָה פָנָיו
His come us Let our the to us let Jeho- to us let O
face before .salvation of Rock shout ;vah joy for sing ,come

3 בְּתוֹדָה בִּזְמִרוֹת נָרִיעַ לוֹ׃ כִּי אֵל גָּדוֹל יְהוָה וּמֶלֶךְ גָּדוֹל
great a and (is) great God a For to us let with with
king ,Jehovah .Him shout songs ;praise

4 עַל־כָּל־אֱלֹהִים׃ אֲשֶׁר בְּיָדוֹ מֶחְקְרֵי־אָרֶץ וְתוֹעֲפוֹת הָרִים
the the and the deep The in (are) which .gods all above
heights of summits ;earth of places hand His

5
6 לוֹ׃ אֲשֶׁר־לוֹ הַיָּם וְהוּא עָשָׂהוּ וְיַבֶּשֶׁת יָדָיו יָצָרוּ׃ בֹּאוּ
O .formed His the and made and The to which to
,come hands land dry ;it He ,sea (is) Him .Him

7 נִשְׁתַּחֲוֶה וְנִכְרָעָה נִבְרְכָה לִפְנֵי־יְהוָה עֹשֵׂנוּ׃ כִּי־הוּא
He For our Jehovah before us let bow and us let
(is) .Maker kneel ;down worship

לֹהֵינוּ וַאֲנַחְנוּ עַם מַרְעִיתוֹ וְצֹאן יָדוֹ הַיּוֹם אִם־בְּקֹלוֹ
His if Today His the and His the we and ,God
voice .hand of sheep ,pasturing of people (are)

8 עוּ׃ אַל־תַּקְשׁוּ לְבַבְכֶם כִּמְרִיבָה כְּיוֹם מַסָּה
Massah in as (in) as your do not wi
of day the ,Meribah hearts harden

9 ׃ אֲשֶׁר נִסּוּנִי אֲבוֹתֵיכֶם בְּחָנוּנִי גַּם־רָאוּ פָעֳלִי׃
My they and they your tempted when
.work saw Me tried ,fathers .Me

10 שָׁנָה ׀ אָקוּט בְּדוֹר וָאֹמַר עַם תֹּעֵי לֵבָב הֵם
They (their) in who a and the with was I yea
;(are) heart err people ,said ,generation disgusted

and, They do not know My
ways, [11] to whom I
swore in My anger if they
shall enter into My rest.

11 וְהֵם לֹא־יָדְעוּ דְרָכָי׃ אֲשֶׁר־נִשְׁבַּעְתִּי בְאַפִּי אִם־יְבֹאוּן

they If My in swore I to My do not and
enter shall ,anger whom ,ways know they

אֶל־מְנוּחָתִי׃

my into
.rest

PSAL. XCVI צו

PSALM 96

PSALM 96

[1] O sing to Jehovah a
new song; sing to Jehovah,
all the earth. [2] Sing to
Jehovah; bless His name,
bear news of His salvation
day by day. [3] Tell of His
glory among the nations,
His wonders among all
people. [4] For Jehovah
(is) great and greatly to be
praised; He (is) to be feared
above all gods. [5] For all
the gods of the peoples (are)
idols; but Jehovah made the
heavens. [6] Honor and
majesty (are) before Him;
strength and beauty (are) in
His sanctuary. [7] Give to
Jehovah, O families of the
people; give to Jehovah
glory and might. [8] Give
to Jehovah the glory (due)
His name; bring an offering
and come in to His courts.

1
2 שִׁירוּ לַיהוָה שִׁיר חָדָשׁ שִׁירוּ לַיהוָה כָּל־הָאָרֶץ׃ שִׁירוּ

Sing the all to sing ;new song a to sing O
.earth ,Jehovah Jehovah

3 לַיהוָה בָּרְכוּ שְׁמוֹ בַּשְּׂרוּ מִיּוֹם־לְיוֹם יְשׁוּעָתוֹ׃ סַפְּרוּ

Tell His day by day Bear His bless to
.salvation of tidings ;name ,Jehovah

4 בַגּוֹיִם כְּבוֹדוֹ בְּכָל־הָעַמִּים נִפְלְאוֹתָיו׃ כִּי גָדוֹל יְהוָה

Jehovah (is) For His the among His among
great .wonders peoples all ,glory nations the

5 וּמְהֻלָּל מְאֹד נוֹרָא הוּא עַל־כָּל־אֱלֹהִים׃ כִּי ׀ כָּל־אֱלֹהֵי

the all For .gods all above He be to ;greatly be to and
of gods (is) feared praised

6 הָעַמִּים אֱלִילִים וַיהוָה שָׁמַיִם עָשָׂה׃ הוֹד־וְהָדָר לְפָנָיו

before and Honor .made the but (are) the
;Him majesty heavens Jehovah ;idols peoples

7 עֹז וְתִפְאֶרֶת בְּמִקְדָּשׁוֹ׃ הָבוּ לַיהוָה מִשְׁפְּחוֹת עַמִּים הָבוּ

give the families O to Give His in (are) and strength
;peoples of ,Jehovah .sanctuary beauty

8 לַיהוָה כָּבוֹד וָעֹז׃ הָבוּ לַיהוָה כְּבוֹד שְׁמוֹ שְׂאוּ־מִנְחָה

an bring His glory the to Give and glory to
offering ;name (due) Jehovah .might Jehovah

[9] O worship Jehovah in
the beauty of holiness;
tremble before Him, all the
earth. [10] Say among the
nations, Jehovah reigns;
...nd, The world shall be
...blished, it shall not be
...d; He shall judge the
...s in uprightness.
... the heavens be
...et the earth re-
... sea roar, and
... it. [12] Let
...ful, and all
... the trees
... rejoice
... for
... to
...l

9 וּבֹאוּ לְחַצְרוֹתָיו׃ הִשְׁתַּחֲווּ לַיהוָה בְּהַדְרַת־קֹדֶשׁ חִילוּ

tremble ;holiness the in Jehovah worship O His into and
of beauty .courts come

10 מִפָּנָיו כָּל־הָאָרֶץ׃ אִמְרוּ בַגּוֹיִם ׀ יְהוָה מָלָךְ אַף־תִּכּוֹן תֵּבֵל

the be shall ,yea ;reigns Jehovah among Say the all before
,world established ,nations the .earth ,Him

11 בַּל־תִּמּוֹט יָדִין עַמִּים בְּמֵישָׁרִים׃ יִשְׂמְחוּ הַשָּׁמַיִם וְתָגֵל

let and the be Let in the shall He shall it not
rejoice heavens glad .uprightness peoples judge ;moved be

12 הָאָרֶץ יִרְעַם הַיָּם וּמְלֹאוֹ׃ יַעֲלֹז שָׂדַי וְכָל־אֲשֶׁר־בּוֹ אָז

then in that and the be Let its and the Let the
;it (is) all field joyful .fulness sea roar ;earth

13 יְרַנְּנוּ כָּל־עֲצֵי־יָעַר׃ לִפְנֵי יְהוָה ׀ כִּי בָא כִּי בָא לִשְׁפֹּט הָאָרֶץ

the judge to He for He for ;Jehovah Before the the all shall
;earth comes ;comes .forest of trees rejoice

יִשְׁפֹּט־תֵּבֵל בְּצֶדֶק וְעַמִּים בֶּאֱמוּנָתוֹ׃

His with the and with world the shall He
.truth peoples ,righteousness judge

PSAL. XCVII צז

PSALM 97

PSALM 97

[1] Jehovah reigns; let the earth rejoice; let the multitude of islands be glad. [2] Clouds and darkness (are) all around Him; righteousness and judgment (are) the foundation of His throne. [3] A fire goes before Him and burns up His enemies all around. [4] His lightnings lit up the world; the earth saw and trembled. [5] The mountains melted like wax before the face of Jehovah; before the face of Jehovah of the whole earth. [6] The heavens declare His righteousness and all the people see His glory. [7] All who serve graven images are ashamed, those who boast themselves in idols; all gods bow down before Him. [8] Zion heard and was glad; yea, the daughters of Judah rejoiced because of Your judgments, O Jehovah. [9] For You, Jehovah, (are) exalted above all the earth; You are lifted on high far above all gods. [10] You who love Jehovah, hate evil; He keeps the souls of His saints; He delivers them out of the hand of the wicked. [11] Light is sown for the righteous, and gladness for the upright in heart. [12] Be glad in Jehovah, O righteous ones; give thanks to the memory of His holiness.

1
2 יְהוָה מָלָךְ תָּגֵל הָאָרֶץ יִשְׂמְחוּ אִיִּים רַבִּים׃ עָנָן וַעֲרָפֶל
and Clouds the islands be let the let ;reigns Jehovah
darkness .many glad ;earth rejoice

3 סְבִיבָיו צֶדֶק וּמִשְׁפָּט מְכוֹן כִּסְאוֹ׃ אֵשׁ לְפָנָיו תֵּלֵךְ
,goes before fire A His basis the and righteous- all (are)
Him .throne of judgment ness;Him around

4 וּתְלַהֵט סָבִיב צָרָיו׃ הֵאִירוּ בְרָקָיו תֵּבֵל רָאֲתָה וַתָּחֵל
and saw the His up lit His all burns and
trembled ;world lightnings .enemies around up

5 הָאָרֶץ׃ הָרִים כַּדּוֹנַג נָמַסּוּ מִלִּפְנֵי יְהוָה מִלִּפְנֵי אֲדוֹן כָּל־
whole the before ;Jehovah before melted like The the
of Lord wax mountains .earth

6 הָאָרֶץ׃ הִגִּידוּ הַשָּׁמַיִם צִדְקוֹ וְרָאוּ כָל־הָעַמִּים כְּבוֹדוֹ׃
His the all and His the Declare the
.glory peoples see righteousness heavens .earth

7 יֵבֹשׁוּ׀ כָּל־עֹבְדֵי פֶסֶל הַמִּתְהַלְלִים בָּאֱלִילִים הִשְׁתַּחֲווּ־לוֹ
before bow ;idols in boast who those graven who All are
Him down themselves ,images serve ashamed

8 כָּל־אֱלֹהִים׃ שָׁמְעָה וַתִּשְׂמַח׀ צִיּוֹן וַתָּגֵלְנָה בְּנוֹת יְהוּדָה
Judah the rejoiced and ;Zion was and heard .gods all
of daughters glad

9 לְמַעַן מִשְׁפָּטֶיךָ יְהוָה׃ כִּי־אַתָּה׀ יְהוָה עֶלְיוֹן עַל־כָּל־
all above (are) O ,You For O Your because
high ,Jehovah .Jehovah ,judgments of

10 הָאָרֶץ מְאֹד נַעֲלֵיתָ עַל־כָּל־אֱלֹהִים׃ אֹהֲבֵי יְהוָה שִׂנְאוּ
hate ,Jehovah who You .gods all above are You for the
love exalted ;earth

11 רָע שֹׁמֵר נַפְשׁוֹת חֲסִידָיו מִיַּד רְשָׁעִים יַצִּילֵם׃ אוֹר זָרֻעַ
is Light delivers He the of out His souls the He ;evil
sown .them wicked of hand ;saints of keeps

12 לַצַּדִּיק וּלְיִשְׁרֵי־לֵב שִׂמְחָה׃ שִׂמְחוּ צַדִּיקִים בַּיהוָה וְהוֹדוּ
give in righteous O Be .gladness heart for and the for
thanks ;Jehovah ,ones ,glad in upright the ;righteous

לְזֵכֶר קָדְשׁוֹ׃
His the t
.holiness of memo

PSAL. XCVIII צח

PSALM 98

PSALM 98

A Psalm.

[1] O sing to Jehovah a new song; for He has done marvelous things; His right hand and His holy arm have saved for Him the victory. [2] Jehovah has revealed His salvation; He unveiled His righteousness to the eyes of the nations. [3] He has remembered His mercy and His truth to the house of Israel; all the ends of the

1 שִׁירוּ לַיהוָה׀ שִׁיר חָדָשׁ כִּי־נִפְלָאוֹת עָשָׂה הוֹשִׁיעָה־
saved has has He wondrous for ;new song a to sing O
;done things Jehovah

2 וּזְרוֹעַ קָדְשׁוֹ׃ הוֹדִיעַ יְהוָה יְשׁוּעָתוֹ לְעֵינֵי הַגּוֹיִם
the the to His Jehovah made has His and
nations of eyes ;salvation known .holy arm h

3 זָכַר חַסְדּוֹ׀ וֶאֱמוּנָתוֹ לְבֵית יִשְׂרָאֵל רָאוּ
have ;Israel the to His and His has He ri
seen of house truth ,mercy remembered

earth have seen the salvation of our God. [4] Make a joyful noise to Jehovah, all the earth; break out and rejoice and sing praise. [5] Sing praise to Jehovah with the lyre; with the lyre and the voice of a song. [6] With trumpets and the sound of a horn, make a joyful noise before Jehovah the King. [7] Let the sea roar, and the fullness of it; the world, and those who live in it. [8] Let the rivers clap (their) hands; let the heights exult together [9] before Jehovah; for He comes to judge the earth; with righteousness He shall judge the world, and the peoples in uprightness.

4 כָל־אַפְסֵי־אָרֶץ אֵת יְשׁוּעַת אֱלֹהֵינוּ׃ הָרִיעוּ לַיהוָה כָּל־
all to Shout .God our sal- the the the all
Jehovah joyfully of vation earth of ends

5 הָאָרֶץ פִּצְחוּ וְרַנְּנוּ וְזַמֵּרוּ׃ זַמְּרוּ לַיהוָה בְּכִנּוֹר בְּכִנּוֹר
the with the with to Sing sing and and break the
lyre ;lyre Jehovah praise .praise rejoice out ;earth

6 וְקוֹל זִמְרָה׃ בַּחֲצֹצְרוֹת וְקוֹל שׁוֹפָר הָרִיעוּ לִפְנֵי ׀ הַמֶּלֶךְ
king the before shout ,horn a the and With .song a the and
joyfully of sound trumpets of voice

7
8 יְהוָה׃ יִרְעַם הַיָּם וּמְלֹאוֹ תֵּבֵל וְיֹשְׁבֵי בָהּ׃ נְהָרוֹת יִמְחֲאוּ־
clap Let the .it in those and the its and the Let .Jehovah
rivers live who ,world fulness sea roar

9 כָף יַחַד הָרִים יְרַנֵּנוּ׃ לִפְנֵי־יְהוָה כִּי־בָא לִשְׁפֹּט הָאָרֶץ
the judge to He for ,Jehovah before let the to- (their)
;earth comes exult heights ;gether hands

יִשְׁפֹּט־תֵּבֵל בְּצֶדֶק וְעַמִּים בְּמֵישָׁרִים׃
in the and righ- with the shall He
.uprightness peoples teousness world judge

PSAL. XCIX צט

PSALM 99

[1] Jehovah reigns; let the peoples tremble; (He) sits (upon) the cherubim; let the earth quake. [2] Jehovah (is) great in Zion; and He (is) high above all the peoples. [3] They shall thank Your great and fearful name; it (is) holy.

[4] The king's strength also loved judgment; You have established uprightness; You work judgment and righteousness in Jacob. [5] Exalt Jehovah our God
'd worship at His foot-
l; He (is) holy.
'] Moses and Aaron
among His priests;
uel (was) among
called on His
alled to Jeho-
wered them.
hem in the
kept His
w that
You
ah
l

1
2 יְהוָה מָלָךְ יִרְגְּזוּ עַמִּים יֹשֵׁב כְּרוּבִים תָּנוּט הָאָרֶץ׃ יְהוָה
Jehovah the let the (on) (He) the let ;reigns Jehovah
.earth shake ;cherubim sits ;peoples tremble

3 בְּצִיּוֹן גָּדוֹל וְרָם הוּא עַל־כָּל־הָעַמִּים׃ יוֹדוּ שִׁמְךָ גָּדוֹל
great Your They the all above He and (is) Zion in
,name thank shall .peoples (is) high ;great

4 וְנוֹרָא קָדוֹשׁ הוּא׃ וְעֹז מֶלֶךְ מִשְׁפָּט אָהֵב אַתָּה כּוֹנַנְתָּ
have You ;loved judgment the And .(is) it holy and
established king's strength ;fearful

5 מֵישָׁרִים מִשְׁפָּט וּצְדָקָה בְּיַעֲקֹב ׀ אַתָּה עָשִׂיתָ׃ רוֹמְמוּ
Exalt .work You Jacob in and judgment upright-
righteousness ;ness

6 יְהוָה אֱלֹהֵינוּ וְהִשְׁתַּחֲווּ לַהֲדֹם רַגְלָיו קָדוֹשׁ הוּא׃ מֹשֶׁה
Moses .(is) He holy His stool at worship and our Jehovah
;foot- God

וְאַהֲרֹן ׀ בְּכֹהֲנָיו וּשְׁמוּאֵל בְּקֹרְאֵי שְׁמוֹ קֹרְאִים אֶל־יְהוָה
,Jehovah to they His the among and among (were) and
called ;name on callers Samuel ;priests His Aaron

7 וְהוּא יַעֲנֵם׃ בְּעַמּוּד עָנָן יְדַבֵּר אֲלֵיהֶם שָׁמְרוּ עֵדֹתָיו וְחֹק
the and His they ;them to He cloudy the in answered and
law testimonies kept spoke pillar .them He

8 נָתַן־לָמוֹ׃ יְהוָה אֱלֹהֵינוּ אַתָּה עֲנִיתָם אֵל נֹשֵׂא הָיִיתָ לָהֶם
to You who a answered You ,God our O to He
,them were forgives God ;them Jehovah .them gave

וְנֹקֵם עַל־עֲלִילוֹתָם׃ רוֹמְמוּ יְהוָה אֱלֹהֵינוּ וְהִשְׁתַּחֲווּ לְהַר
l at worship and ,God our Jehovah Exalt their on and
.works avenging

קָדְשׁוֹ כִּי־קָדוֹשׁ יְהוָה אֱלֹהֵינוּ׃
.God our Jehovah (is) for His
holy ;holy

PSAL. C ק

PSALM 100

PSALM 100

A Psalm of Thanksgiving.

[1] Shout joyfully to Jehovah, all you lands. [2] Worship Jehovah with gladness; come before His face with joyful singing. [3] Know that Jehovah, He (is) God; He has made us, and not we ourselves — His people and the sheep of His pasture. [4] Enter into His gates with thanksgiving; (into) His courts with praise; be thankful to Him; bless His name. [5] For Jehovah (is) good; His mercy (is) everlasting, and His faithfulness to generation and generation.

1
2 מִזְמוֹר לְתוֹדָה הָרִיעוּ לַיהוָה כָּל־הָאָרֶץ׃ עִבְדוּ אֶת־יְהוָה
Jehovah Serve the all to Shout thanks- of psalm A
.land ,Jehovah joyfully .giving

3 בְּשִׂמְחָה בֹּאוּ לְפָנָיו בִּרְנָנָה׃ דְּעוּ כִּי־יְהוָה הוּא אֱלֹהִים
;God (is) He ,Jehovah that Know with His before come with
.singing face ;gladness

4 הוּא עָשָׂנוּ וְלֹא אֲנַחְנוּ עַמּוֹ וְצֹאן מַרְעִיתוֹ׃ בֹּאוּ שְׁעָרָיו ׀
His Enter His the and His we and made has He
gates into .pasture of sheep people (ourselves) not ,us

5 בְּתוֹדָה חֲצֵרֹתָיו בִּתְהִלָּה הוֹדוּ לוֹ בָּרֲכוּ שְׁמוֹ׃ כִּי־טוֹב
(is) For His bless to be with His (into) with
good .name ,Him thankful ;praise courts ;thanksgiving

יְהוָה לְעוֹלָם חַסְדּוֹ וְעַד־דֹּר וָדֹר אֱמוּנָתוֹ׃
faith- His gen- and genera- and His (is) ;Jehovah
.fulness eration tion unto ;mercy everlasting

PSAL. CI קא

PSALM 101

PSALM 101

A Psalm of David.

[1] I will sing of mercy and judgment; to You, O Jehovah, I will sing praise. [2] I will behave myself wisely in a perfect way; O when will You come to me? I will walk in the integrity of my heart in the midst of my house. [3] I will set no wicked thing before my eyes; I have hated the work of those who turn aside; it shall not fasten upon me. [4] A perverse heart shall depart from me; I will not know evil. [50] (Whoever) secretly slanders his neighbor, I will cut him off; I will not endure him who has a high look and a proud heart. [6] My eyes (shall be) on the faithful of the land, so that they may dwell with me; he who walks in a perfect way shall serve me. [7] He who works falsely shall not live inside my house; he who tells lies shall not be established before my eyes. [8] I will cut off all the wicked of the land; so that I may cut off all the workers of iniquity from the city of Jehovah.

1 לְדָוִד מִזְמוֹר חֶסֶד־וּמִשְׁפָּט אָשִׁירָה לְךָ יְהוָה אֲזַמֵּרָה׃
sing will I O ,You to will I and mercy .psalm A of
praise ,Jehovah ;of sing judgment David

2 אַשְׂכִּילָה ׀ בְּדֶרֶךְ תָּמִים מָתַי תָּבוֹא אֵלָי אֶתְהַלֵּךְ בְּתָם־
in walk will I to will when O ;perfect a in act will I
integrity ?me come You way wisely

3 לְבָבִי בְּקֶרֶב בֵּיתִי׃ לֹא־אָשִׁית ׀ לְנֶגֶד עֵינַי דְּבַר־בְּלִיָּעַל
,worthless a my before will I not my the in my
thing eyes set .house of midst ,heart's

4 עֲשֹׂה־סֵטִים שָׂנֵאתִי לֹא יִדְבַּק בִּי׃ לֵבָב עִקֵּשׁ יָסוּר מִמֶּנִּי
from shall perverse A upon shall it not have I the of doing the
;me depart heart .me fasten ;hated aside turning ones

5 רָע לֹא אֵדָע׃ מְלָושְׁנִי בַסֵּתֶר ׀ רֵעֵהוּ אוֹתוֹ אַצְמִית גְּבַהּ־
(has who) will I him his secretly (Whoever) will I not evil
high a ;off cut ;neighbor slanders .know

6 עֵינַיִם וּרְחַב לֵבָב אֹתוֹ לֹא אוּכָל׃ עֵינַי ׀ בְּנֶאֶמְנֵי־אֶרֶץ
the on (be shall) My will I not him heart a proud and look
,land of faithful the eyes .endure

7 לָשֶׁבֶת עִמָּדִי הֹלֵךְ בְּדֶרֶךְ תָּמִים הוּא יְשָׁרְתֵנִי׃ לֹא־יֵשֵׁב ׀
Shall not minister shall he ,perfect a in who (he) with dwell to
dwell .me to way walks ;me

בְּקֶרֶב בֵּיתִי עֹשֵׂה רְמִיָּה דֹּבֵר שְׁקָרִים לֹא־יִכּוֹן לְנֶגֶד עֵינָי׃
my before shall not ,lies who ,falsely who (he) my inside
.eyes fixed be tells works house

8 לַבְּקָרִים אַצְמִית כָּל־רִשְׁעֵי־אָרֶץ לְהַכְרִית מֵעִיר־יְהוָה
Jehovah the from cut to the the all will I the In
of city off ;land of wicked off cut mornings

כָּל־פֹּעֲלֵי אָוֶן׃
.evil the all
of workers

PSALM 102

A Prayer of the afflicted, when he is faint and pours out his complaint before Jehovah.

[1] Hear my prayer, O Jehovah, and let my cry come to You. [2] Do not hide Your face from me in the day of my trouble; bow down Your ear to me in the day I call; answer me quickly. [3] For my days are finished in smoke, and my bones are burned like a hearth. [4] My heart is stricken and dried like grass, so that I forget to eat my bread. [5] Because of the voice of my sighing, my bones cleave to my flesh. [6] I am like a pelican of the wilderness; I am like an owl of the desert. [7] I watch and am like a sparrow alone on the housetop. [8] My enemies curse me all the day long; those who rave against me have sworn against me. [9] For I have eaten ashes like bread, and have mixed my drink with weeping; [10] because of Your anger and Your wrath; for You have lifted me and cast me down. [11] My days (are) like a shadow stretched out, and I wither like grass.

[12] But You, O Jehovah, shall dwell forever, and Your memory to generation and generation. [13] You shall arise; have mercy on Zion; for the time to pity her, yea, the appointed time has come. [14] For Your servants take pleasure in its stones, and pity its dust. [15] So nations shall fear the name of Jehovah, and all the kings of the earth Your glory. [16] When Jehovah shall build up Zion, He shall appear in His glory. [17] He will turn to the prayer of the destitute, and will not despise their prayer. [18] This shall be written for the generation to come; and people to be created shall praise Jehovah. [19] For He has looked down from the height of His sanctuary;

PSAL. CII קב

PSALM 102

1
2 תְּפִלָּה לְעָנִי כִי־יַעֲטֹף וְלִפְנֵי יְהוָה יִשְׁפֹּךְ שִׂיחוֹ׃ יְהוָה
,Jehovah his pours Jehovah and is he when the of prayer A
.complaint out before ,faint ,afflicted

3 שִׁמְעָה תְפִלָּתִי וְשַׁוְעָתִי אֵלֶיךָ תָבוֹא׃ אַל־תַּסְתֵּר פָּנֶיךָ ׀
Your Do not .come let You to cry my and my hear
face hide ,prayer

מִמֶּנִּי בְּיוֹם צַר־לִי הַטֵּה־אֵלַי אָזְנֶךָ בְּיוֹם אֶקְרָא מַהֵר עֲנֵנִי׃
answer quickly ;call I the in Your me to incline to dis- the in from
.me day ear ;me tress of day me

4
5 כִּי־כָלוּ בְעָשָׁן יָמָי וְעַצְמוֹתַי כְּמוֹקֵד נִחָרוּ׃ הוּכָּה כָעֵשֶׂב
like Is are a like my and my in are For
grass stricken .burned hearth bones ,days smoke finished

6 וַיִּבַשׁ לִבִּי כִּי־שָׁכַחְתִּי מֵאֲכֹל לַחְמִי׃ מִקּוֹל אַנְחָתִי דָּבְקָה
clings my of Because my eat to forget I so my and
,sighing of voice the .bread that ,heart up dried

7 עַצְמִי לִבְשָׂרִי׃ דָּמִיתִי לִקְאַת מִדְבָּר הָיִיתִי כְּכוֹס חֳרָבוֹת׃
.desert the an like am I the pelican a am I my to my
of owl ;wilderness of like .flesh bone

8
9 שָׁקַדְתִּי וָאֶהְיֶה כְּצִפּוֹר בּוֹדֵד עַל־גָּג׃ כָּל־הַיּוֹם חֵרְפוּנִי
reproach the All a on alone a like am and ,watch I
me day .top house bird

10 אוֹיְבָי מְהוֹלָלַי בִּי נִשְׁבָּעוּ׃ כִּי־אֵפֶר כַּלֶּחֶם אָכָלְתִּי וְשִׁקֻּוַי
my and have I like ashes For have against those my
drink ,eaten bread .sworn me raving ;enemies

11 בִּבְכִי מָסָכְתִּי׃ מִפְּנֵי־זַעַמְךָ וְקִצְפֶּךָ כִּי נְשָׂאתַנִי וַתַּשְׁלִיכֵנִי׃
cast and have You for Your and Your because have with
.down me me lifted ;wrath anger of ,mixed weeping

12
13 יָמַי כְּצֵל נָטוּי וַאֲנִי כָּעֵשֶׂב אִיבָשׁ׃ וְאַתָּה יְהוָה לְעוֹלָם
forever O ,You But .wither grass as I and drawn as (are) My
,Jehovah ,out shadow a days

14 תֵּשֵׁב וְזִכְרְךָ לְדֹר וָדֹר׃ אַתָּה תָקוּם תְּרַחֵם צִיּוֹן כִּי־עֵת
the for ;Zion have shall You gen- and gen- to Your and shall
time on mercy ;arise .eration eration memory ;dwell

15 לְחֶנְנָהּ כִּי־בָא מוֹעֵד׃ כִּי־רָצוּ עֲבָדֶיךָ אֶת־אֲבָנֶיהָ וְאֶת־
and ,stones its Your delight For ap- the has for pity to
servants in .time pointed come ,her

16 עֲפָרָהּ יְחֹנֵנוּ׃ וְיִירְאוּ גוֹיִם אֶת־שֵׁם יְהוָה וְכָל־מַלְכֵי הָאָרֶץ
the the and ,Jehovah the nations shall So have its (on)
earth of kings all of name fear .favor dust

17
18 אֶת־כְּבוֹדֶךָ׃ כִּי־בָנָה יְהוָה צִיּוֹן נִרְאָה בִּכְבוֹדוֹ׃ פָּנָה אֶל־
to He His in He ,Zion Jehovah builds When Your
turns .glory appears up .glory

19 תְּפִלַּת הָעַרְעָר וְלֹא בָזָה אֶת־תְּפִלָּתָם׃ תִּכָּתֶב זֹאת לְדוֹר
the for This be shall their despises and the the
generation written .prayer not destitute of prayer

20 אַחֲרוֹן וְעַם נִבְרָא יְהַלֶּל־יָהּ׃ כִּי־הִשְׁקִיף מִמְּרוֹם קָדְשׁוֹ
His the from looked has He For .Jehovah shall be to and ;next
,sanctuary of height down praise created people

Jehovah looked from Heaven to the earth; [20] to hear the groaning of the prisoner, to set free the sons of death; [21] to declare the name of Jehovah in Zion, and His praise in Jerusalem; [22] when the peoples and the kingdoms are gathered together to worship Jehovah.

[23] He diminished my strength in the way; He shortened my days. [24] I said, O my God, do not take me up in the half of my days; Your years (are) through the generation of generations. [25] You have laid the foundation of the earth of old; and the heavens (are) the work of Your hands. [26] They shall perish, but You shall endure; yea, all of them shall become old like a garment; You shall change them like clothing, and they shall be changed. [27] But You (are) He, and Your years shall not be ended. [28] The sons of Your servants shall dwell; and their seed shall be established before You.

PSALM 103

Of David.

[1] Bless Jehovah, O my soul; and all within me His holy name. [2] Bless Jehovah, O my soul, and do not forget all His benefits; [3] who forgives all your iniquities; who heals all your diseases; [4] who redeems your life from ruin; who crowns you (with) kindness and mercies; [5] who satisfies your desire with good; your youth is renewed like the eagle's. [6] Jehovah works righteousness and judgments for all the oppressed. [7] He made known His ways to Moses, His acts to the sons of Israel. [8] Jehovah (is) merciful and gracious, slow to anger and of much mercy. [9] He will not always chasten, nor will He keep His (anger) forever. [10] He has not done to us according to our sins, nor rewarded us according to

---

21 יְהֹוָה מִשָּׁמַיִם ׀ אֶל־אֶרֶץ הִבִּיט׃ לִשְׁמֹעַ אֶנְקַת אָסִיר לְפַתֵּחַ

set to　the　groaning hear to　;looked the　to　from Jehovah
free　,prisoner's　　　　　earth　Heaven

22 בְּנֵי תְמוּתָה׃ לְסַפֵּר בְּצִיּוֹן שֵׁם יְהֹוָה וּתְהִלָּתוֹ בִּירוּשָׁלִָם׃

in　His and ,Jehovah the Zion in　to ;death the
,Jerusalem praise　of name proclaim　of sons

23 24 בְּהִקָּבֵץ עַמִּים יַחְדָּו וּמַמְלָכוֹת לַעֲבֹד אֶת־יְהֹוָה׃ עִנָּה

He .Jehovah serve to　and ,together peoples are When
lessened　　　　kingdoms　　　gathered

25 בַדֶּרֶךְ כֹּחוֹ קִצַּר יָמָי׃ אֹמַר אֵלִי אַל־תַּעֲלֵנִי בַּחֲצִי יָמָי

my the in　take do not my O ,said I　my He　my the in
;days of half　up　,God　.days shortened ;strength way

26 בְּדוֹר דּוֹרִים שְׁנוֹתֶיךָ׃ לְפָנִים הָאָרֶץ יָסַדְתָּ וּמַעֲשֵׂה יָדֶיךָ

Your the and You the　old Of　Your (are) gen- of gen- the in
hands of work ;founded earth　　.years erations eration

27 שָׁמָיִם׃ הֵמָּה ׀ יֹאבֵדוּ וְאַתָּה תַעֲמֹד וְכֻלָּם כַּבֶּגֶד יִבְלוּ

shall　a as　they ,yea shall　You but They　the (are)
;old wax garment all　;stand　,perish　.heavens

28 כַּלְּבוּשׁ תַּחֲלִיפֵם וְיַחֲלֹפוּ׃ וְאַתָּה־הוּא וּשְׁנוֹתֶיךָ לֹא יִתָּמּוּ׃

be shall not Your and (are)　But shall they and shall You　like
.ended　years　,He　You　.changed be ;them change clothing

29 בְּנֵי־עֲבָדֶיךָ יִשְׁכּוֹנוּ וְזַרְעָם לְפָנֶיךָ יִכּוֹן׃

be shall before their and shall Your The
.established You seed ;dwell servants of sons

PSAL. CIII　קג

PSALM 103

1 לְדָוִד ׀ בָּרְכִי נַפְשִׁי אֶת־יְהֹוָה וְכָל־קְרָבַי אֶת־שֵׁם קָדְשׁוֹ׃

His name the within and ;Jehovah my O ,Bless　Of
.holiness of　me　all　,soul　.David

2 3 בָּרְכִי נַפְשִׁי אֶת־יְהֹוָה וְאַל־תִּשְׁכְּחִי כָּל־גְּמוּלָיו׃ הַסֹּלֵחַ

who　His　all　do　and ,Jehovah my O ,Bless
forgives ;benefits forget not　　　,soul

4 לְכָל־עֲוֹנֵכִי הָרֹפֵא לְכָל־תַּחֲלֻאָיְכִי׃ הַגּוֹאֵל מִשַּׁחַת חַיָּיְכִי

your　from　who　your　all who　your all
,life　ruin redeems ;diseases heals ,iniquities

5 הַמְעַטְּרֵכִי חֶסֶד וְרַחֲמִים׃ הַמַּשְׂבִּיעַ בַּטּוֹב עֶדְיֵךְ תִּתְחַדֵּשׁ

re- is　your the with　who　tender and (with) crowns who
newed ;desire good satisfies ;compassion mercy　you

6 כַּנֶּשֶׁר נְעוּרָיְכִי׃ עֹשֵׂה צְדָקוֹת יְהֹוָה וּמִשְׁפָּטִים לְכָל־

all for judgments and ,Jehovah righteous works　your the like
deeds　.youth eagle

7 עֲשׁוּקִים׃ יוֹדִיעַ דְּרָכָיו לְמֹשֶׁה לִבְנֵי יִשְׂרָאֵל עֲלִילוֹתָיו׃

.acts His　Israel the to　to　His made He the
of sons ,Moses ways known .oppressed

8 9 רַחוּם וְחַנּוּן יְהֹוָה אֶרֶךְ אַפַּיִם וְרַב־חָסֶד׃ לֹא־לָנֶצַח יָרִיב

will He always not .mercy and anger slow (is) and compas-
,strive　much　of Jehovah gracious sionate

10 וְלֹא לְעוֹלָם יִטּוֹר׃ לֹא כַחֲטָאֵינוּ עָשָׂה לָנוּ וְלֹא כַעֲוֹנֹתֵינוּ

our to　and .us to has He to according not keep forever nor
iniquities not　done sins our　.(anger)

our iniquities. [11] For as the heavens (are) high above the earth, (so) is His mercy mighty over those who fear Him. [12] As far as the east (is) from the west, (so) far has He removed our transgressions from us. [13] As the pity of a father over his sons, (so) Jehovah pities those who fear Him. [14] For He knows how we are made, remembering that we (are) dust. [15] (As for) man, his days (are) as grass; as the flower of the field, so he flourishes. [16] For the wind passes over it, and it is not; and its place never knows it again. [17] But the mercy of Jehovah (is) from everlasting even to everlasting on those who fear Him; yea, His righteousness to the sons of sons; [18] to those who keep His covenant, and to those who remember His commandments, to do them. [19] Jehovah has prepared His throne in the heavens; and His kingdom rules over all. [20] Bless Jehovah, O angels of His; mighty in strength; doing His word, listening to the voice of His word. [21] Bless Jehovah, all His hosts, ministers of His who do His will. [22] Bless Jehovah, all His works, in all the places of His dominion; bless Jehovah, O my soul.

11 גָּמַל עָלֵינוּ׃ כִּי כִגְבֹהַּ שָׁמַיִם עַל־הָאָרֶץ גָּבַר חַסְדּוֹ עַל־
over His is the above the is as For .us re- has
mercy mighty ,earth heavens high warded

12 יְרֵאָיו׃ כִּרְחֹק מִזְרָח מִמַּעֲרָב הִרְחִיק מִמֶּנּוּ אֶת־פְּשָׁעֵינוּ׃
our from has He the from the far As fearers
.transgressions us far put ,west (is) east (as) .Him of

13
14 כְּרַחֵם אָב עַל־בָּנִים רִחַם יְהוָה עַל־יְרֵאָיו׃ כִּי־הוּא יָדַע
knows He For fearers over Jehovah pities (his) over a the As
.Him of ,sons father of pity

15 יִצְרֵנוּ זָכוּר כִּי־עָפָר אֲנָחְנוּ׃ אֱנוֹשׁ כֶּחָצִיר יָמָיו כְּצִיץ
as his grass as (for As) we dust that remem- our
flower ;days (are) ,man .(are) bering ;form

16 הַשָּׂדֶה כֵּן יָצִיץ׃ כִּי רוּחַ עָבְרָה־בּוֹ וְאֵינֶנּוּ וְלֹא־יַכִּירֶנּוּ
recognizes and it and over passes the For he so ,field the
it not ,not is it wind .flourishes

17 עוֹד מְקוֹמוֹ׃ וְחֶסֶד יְהוָה ׀ מֵעוֹלָם וְעַד־עוֹלָם עַל־יְרֵאָיו
fearers on ever- even from (is) Jehovah the But .place its again
;Him of lasting to ,everlasting of mercy

18 וְצִדְקָתוֹ לִבְנֵי בָנִים׃ לְשֹׁמְרֵי בְרִיתוֹ וּלְזֹכְרֵי פִקֻּדָיו
His remem- and His those to ;sons the to His and
,precepts bering covenant keeping of sons righteousness

19 לַעֲשׂוֹתָם׃ יְהוָה בַּשָּׁמַיִם הֵכִין כִּסְאוֹ וּמַלְכוּתוֹ בַּכֹּל
over His and His has the in Jehovah .them do to
all kingdom ;throne prepared heavens

20 מָשָׁלָה׃ בָּרְכוּ יְהוָה מַלְאָכָיו גִּבֹּרֵי כֹחַ עֹשֵׂי דְבָרוֹ לִשְׁמֹעַ
listen to His doing ;strength mighty His O ,Jehovah Bless .rules
,word of ;angels

21 בְּקוֹל דְּבָרוֹ׃ בָּרְכוּ יְהוָה כָּל־צְבָאָיו מְשָׁרְתָיו עֹשֵׂי רְצוֹנוֹ׃
.will His doing ministers His all ,Jehovah Bless His the to
,His of ,hosts .word of voice

22 בָּרְכוּ יְהוָה ׀ כָּל־מַעֲשָׂיו בְּכָל־מְקֹמוֹת מֶמְשַׁלְתּוֹ בָּרְכִי
bless His the all in His all ,Jehovah Bless
,dominion of places ,works

נַפְשִׁי אֶת־יְהוָה׃
.Jehovah my O
,soul

PSAL. CIV קד

PSALM 104

PSALM 104

[1] Bless Jehovah, O my soul, O Jehovah my God, You are very great; You have put on honor and majesty, [2] covering Yourself (with) light like a cloak, and stretching out the heavens like a curtain; [3] laying like beams of His upper rooms in the waters; setting thick clouds (as) His chariots; walking on the wings of the wind. [4] He makes His angels spirits, His ministers a flaming fire.

1 בָּרְכִי נַפְשִׁי אֶת־יְהוָה יְהוָה אֱלֹהַי גָּדַלְתָּ מְּאֹד הוֹד וְהָדָר
and majesty ;very are You my O .Jehovah my O ,Bless
honor great God Jehovah ,soul

2 לָבָשְׁתָּ׃ עֹטֶה אוֹר כַּשַּׂלְמָה נוֹטֶה שָׁמַיִם כַּיְרִיעָה׃
a like the stretching a like (with) covering have You
;curtain heavens out ;cloak light Yourself ,on put

3 הַמְקָרֶה בַמַּיִם עֲלִיּוֹתָיו הַשָּׂם עָבִים רְכוּבוֹ הַמְהַלֵּךְ עַל־
on who His (as) thick who His (of) the in lays who
marches ;chariot clouds sets ;rooms upper waters beams

4 כַּנְפֵי־רוּחַ׃ עֹשֶׂה מַלְאָכָיו רוּחוֹת מְשָׁרְתָיו אֵשׁ לֹהֵט׃
.flame fire a His ,winds His He the the
of ministers angels makes .wind of wings

[5] He founded the earth on its foundations; it shall not be shaken forever and ever. [6] You have covered the deep as with a robe; the waters stood above the mountains. [7] From Your rebuke, they shall flee; from the sound of Your thunder they hurry away. [8] They go up the mountains; they go down the valleys to the place which You founded for them. [9] You have set a boundary; they may not pass over; they shall not return to cover the earth. [10] (He) sends springs into the valleys; they flow between the hills; [11] they give drink to every animal of the field; wild asses break their thirst; [12] over them the birds of the heavens dwell; they give voice from between the branches. [13] (He) waters the hills from His upper rooms; the earth is satisfied from the fruit of Your works. [14] (He) causes the grass to grow for the cattle, and plants for the service of man; to bring food out of the earth. [15] And wine cheers the heart of man; oil makes (his) face shine; and bread makes man's heart strong. [16] The trees of Jehovah (are) full; the cedars of Lebanon that He planted; [17] there where the birds nest; the fir trees (are) the house of the stork;

[18] high hills (are) for the wild goats; rocks a refuge for the badgers. [19] He made the moon for seasons; the sun knows its going down. [20] You put darkness, and it is night; in it all the forest animals creep. [21] The young lions roar for prey, and to seek their food from God. [22] The sun rises; they are gathered and lie down (in) their dens. [23] Man goes out to his work, and to his labor until

5 6 יסד־ארץ על־מכוניה בל־תמוט עולם ועד׃ תהום
deep The and forever shall it not its on the He
.ever shake ;foundations earth founded

7 כלבוש כסיתו על־הרים יעמדו־מים׃ מן־גערתך ינוסון
they Your From the stand the above You a with as
;flee rebuke .waters mountains ;it covered ,garment

8 מן־קול רעמך יחפזון׃ יעלו הרים ירדו בקעות אל־
to the down go the up go hurry they Your the from
valleys ;mountains —away thunder of sound

9 מקום זה יסדת להם׃ גבול־שמת בל־יעברון בל־ישובון
shall they not shall they not You A for You which the
return .over pass ;set have boundary .them founded place

10 לכסות הארץ׃ המשלח מעינים בנחלים בין הרים
hills the between the into springs sends who ;earth the cover to
;valleys

11 יהלכון׃ ישקו כל־חיתו שדי ישברו פראים צמאם׃
their wild break the animal every give they they
.thirst asses ;field of to drink ;flow

12 עליהם עוף־השמים ישכון מבין עפאים יתנו־קול׃
.voice they branches from ;dwell the the Over
give between heavens of birds them

13 משקה הרים מעליותיו מפרי מעשיך תשבע הארץ׃
—earth the is works Your the from His from the (is He)
satisfied of fruit —rooms upper heights watering

14 מצמיח חציר ׀ לבהמה ועשב לעבדת האדם להוציא
bring to ;man the for and the for grass causing
out of service plants ,cattle grow to

15 לחם מן־הארץ׃ ויין ׀ ישמח לבב־אנוש להצהיל פנים
(his) make to ,men the cheers And the from food
face shine of heart wine .earth

16 משמן ולחם לבב־אנוש יסעד׃ ישבעו עצי יהוה ארזי
cedars ,Jehovah The are .sustains man the and from
of trees satisfied of heart bread ;oil

17 לבנון אשר נטע׃ אשר־שם צפרים יקננו חסידה
,stork the —nest birds there (in) He which Lebanon's
which ;planted

18 ברושים ביתה׃ הרים הגבהים ליעלים סלעים מחסה
refuge a ,rocks the for High mounts her trees fir
;goats wild (are) .house (are)

19 20 לשפנים׃ עשה ירח למועדים שמש ידע מבואו׃ תשת־
put You its knows sun the for the He the for
.down going ;seasons moon made .badgers

21 חשך ויהי לילה בו־תרמש כל־חיתו־יער׃ הכפירים
young The the the all creep it in ;night it and dark-
lions .forest of beasts is ness

22 שאגים לטרף ולבקש מאל אכלם׃ תזרח השמש יאספון
are they ;sun The rises their from to and ,prey for roar
,gathered .food God seek

23 ואל־מעונתם ירבצון׃ יצא אדם לפעלו ולעבדתו עדי־
until to and his to Man goes .down lie their and
service his ,work out dens to

the evening. [24] O Jehovah, how many are Your works! You have made all of them in wisdom; the earth is full of Your riches. [25] This (is) the sea great and wide on both hands; there (are) creeping things even without number; living things, small with great. [26] There the ships go; the great sea-animal You made it to play in it. [27] All of them wait for You, to give (them) their food in due season – [28] You give to them, (and) they gather; You open Your hand, (and) they are filled with good – [29] You hide Your face (and) they are troubled; You gather their breath, (and) they expire and return to their dust. [30] You send out Your Spirit, (and) they are created; and You renew the face of the earth. [31] Jehovah's glory shall be forever; Jehovah shall rejoice in His works. [32] He looks to the earth and it trembles; He touches the hills and they smoke. [33] I will sing to Jehovah during my life; I will sing praise to my God while I exist. [34] My thoughts on Him shall be sweet; I will be glad in Jehovah. [35] Let sinners perish from the earth; and let the wicked be no more; bless Jehovah, O my soul; praise Jehovah!

24 עָֽרֶב׃ מָֽה־רַבּוּ מַעֲשֶׂיךָ ׀ יְהוָה כֻּלָּם בְּחָכְמָה עָשִׂיתָ
have You wisdom in of All O Your many How the
;made them !Jehovah ,works are .evening

25 מָלְאָה הָאָרֶץ קִנְיָנֶךָ׃ זֶה ׀ הַיָּם גָּדוֹל וּרְחַב יָדָיִם שָׁם־
There both and great sea the This Your the full is
(are) ;hands on wide (is) .possessions earth of

26 רֶמֶשׂ וְאֵין מִסְפָּר חַיּוֹת קְטַנּוֹת עִם־גְּדֹלוֹת׃ שָׁם אֳנִיּוֹת
ships There .great with small living ;number even creeping
,things without ,things

27 יְהַלֵּכוּן לִוְיָתָן זֶה־יָצַרְתָּ לְשַׂחֶק־בּוֹ׃ כֻּלָּם אֵלֶיךָ יְשַׂבֵּרוּן
,wait for of All .it in play to You this ,Leviathan ;ply
You them formed

28 לָתֵת אָכְלָם בְּעִתּוֹ׃ תִּתֵּן לָהֶם יִלְקֹטוּן תִּפְתַּח יָדְךָ יִשְׂבְּעוּן
are they Your You they to You its in their give to
satisfied ;hand open ;gather ,them give .time food

29 טוֹב׃ תַּסְתִּיר פָּנֶיךָ יִבָּהֵלוּן תֹּסֵף רוּחָם יִגְוָעוּן וְאֶל־עֲפָרָם
their and they their You are they Your You (with)
dust to expire ,breath gather ;troubled ,face hide .good

30 31 יְשׁוּבוּן׃ תְּשַׁלַּח רוּחֲךָ יִבָּרֵאוּן וּתְחַדֵּשׁ פְּנֵי אֲדָמָה׃ יְהִי
shall the the You and are they Your send You .return
be .ground of face renew ;created ,Spirit out

32 כְבוֹד יְהוָה לְעוֹלָם יִשְׂמַח יְהוָה בְּמַעֲשָׂיו׃ הַמַּבִּיט לָאָרֶץ
the to looks He His in Jehovah shall ;forever Jehovah The
earth .works rejoice of glory

33 וַתִּרְעָד יִגַּע בֶּהָרִים וְיֶעֱשָׁנוּ׃ אָשִׁירָה לַיהוָה בְּחַיָּי אֲזַמְּרָה
will I during to will I they and the He it and
praise ;life my Jehovah sing .smoke heights touches ;trembles

34 לֵאלֹהַי בְּעוֹדִי׃ יֶעֱרַב עָלָיו שִׂיחִי אָנֹכִי אֶשְׂמַח בַּיהוָה׃
in be will I my on be Shall I while my to
.Jehovah glad ;meditation Him sweet .(am) still God

35 יִתַּמּוּ חַטָּאִים ׀ מִן־הָאָרֶץ וּרְשָׁעִים ׀ עוֹד אֵינָם בָּרְכִי נַפְשִׁי
my O ,bless (may) they still the and the from sinners May
,soul ;be not ,wicked ;earth perish

אֶת־יְהוָה הַלְלוּיָהּ׃
praise ;Jehovah
!Jehovah

PSAL. CV קה

PSALM 105

PSALM 105

[1] O give thanks to Jehovah; call on His name; make His deeds known among the peoples. [2] Sing to Him; sing praises to Him; tell of all His wonders. [3] Glory in His holy name; let those who seek Jehovah rejoice. [4] Seek Jehovah and His strength; seek His face without ceasing. [5] Remember His wonders that He has done; His miracles, and the judgments of His mouth.

1 2 הוֹדוּ לַיהוָה קִרְאוּ בִּשְׁמוֹ הוֹדִיעוּ בָעַמִּים עֲלִילוֹתָיו׃ שִׁירוּ־
Sing .deeds His among make His on call to Give
peoples the known ;name ;Jehovah thanks

3 לוֹ זַמְּרוּ־לוֹ שִׂיחוּ בְּכָל־נִפְלְאוֹתָיו׃ הִתְהַלְלוּ בְּשֵׁם קָדְשׁוֹ
His the in Glory His all of tell to Sing to
;holiness of name .wonders ;Him praises ;Him

4 יִשְׂמַח לֵב ׀ מְבַקְשֵׁי יְהוָה׃ דִּרְשׁוּ יְהוָה וְעֻזּוֹ בַּקְּשׁוּ פָנָיו
His seek His and Jehovah Seek .Jehovah those the may
face ;strength seek who of heart rejoice

5 תָּמִיד׃ זִכְרוּ נִפְלְאוֹתָיו אֲשֶׁר־עָשָׂה מֹפְתָיו וּמִשְׁפְּטֵי־פִיו׃
His the and His has He that His Remember .always
.mouth of judgments ;miracles ,done wonders

[6] O seed of His servant Abraham; O sons of Jacob His chosen, [7] He (is) Jehovah our God; His judgments (are) in all the earth; [8] He has remembered His covenant forever; the word He commanded to a thousand generations; [9] which He cut with Abraham, and his oath to Isaac; [10] and he confirmed it to Jacob for a statute, to Israel (for) a perpetual covenant; [11] saying, To you I will give the land of Canaan, the lot of your inheritance; [12] when they were (a few) men of number; very few, and strangers in it; [13] and they went about from nation to nation; from (one) kingdom to another people. [14] He allowed no man to oppress them; yea, He reproved kings for their sakes; [15] (saying), Touch not My anointed, and, Do My prophets no harm. [16] And He called a famine on the land; He broke the whole staff of bread. [17] He sent a man before them — Joseph, (being) sold for a slave; [18] his feet they hurt with chains, into iron came his soul, [19] until the time His word came; the word of Jehovah refined him. [20] The king sent and set him free, the ruler of peoples, and set him free. [21] He made him lord of his house, and ruler over all he owned; [22] to bind his princes at his pleasure, and to teach his elders wisdom.

[23] Israel also came (into) Egypt, and Jacob sojourned in the land of Ham. [24] And He increased His people greatly, and made him stronger than his enemies. [25] He turned their heart to hate His people, to deal craftily with His servants. [26] He sent His servant Moses; Aaron whom He had chosen. [27] They put things of His signs among them, and miracles in the land of Ham. [28] He sent darkness and made it dark;

6
7 זֶרַע אַבְרָהָם עַבְדּוֹ בְּנֵי יַעֲקֹב בְּחִירָיו׃ הוּא יְהוָה אֱלֹהֵינוּ
;God our Jehovah He His ,Jacob sons His Abraham Seed
(is) ;ones chosen of ;servant of

8 בְּכָל־הָאָרֶץ מִשְׁפָּטָיו׃ זָכַר לְעוֹלָם בְּרִיתוֹ דָּבָר צִוָּה
com- He the His forever has He His (are) the all in
manded word ;covenant remembered ;judgments earth

9 לְאֶלֶף דּוֹר׃ אֲשֶׁר כָּרַת אֶת־אַבְרָהָם וּשְׁבוּעָתוֹ לְיִשְׂחָק׃
;Isaac to His and ;Abraham with He which genera- a to
oath cut ,tions thousand

10
111 וַיַּעֲמִידֶהָ לְיַעֲקֹב לְחֹק לְיִשְׂרָאֵל בְּרִית עוֹלָם׃ לֵאמֹר לְךָ
To ,saying ,perpetual a (for) Israel to a for to He and
you covenant ,statute Jacob it confirmed

12 אֶתֵּן אֶת־אֶרֶץ כְּנָעַן חֶבֶל נַחֲלַתְכֶם׃ בִּהְיוֹתָם מְתֵי מִסְפָּר
,number (few a) they when your the ,Canaan the will I
of men were ;inheritance of portion of land give

13 כִּמְעַט וְגָרִים בָּהּ׃ וַיִּתְהַלְּכוּ מִגּוֹי אֶל־גּוֹי מִמַּמְלָכָה אֶל־
to (one) from ;nation to from they and ;it in and very
kingdom nation about went aliens few

14 עַם אַחֵר׃ לֹא־הִנִּיחַ אָדָם לְעָשְׁקָם וַיּוֹכַח עֲלֵיהֶם מְלָכִים׃
;kings their for He ,yea oppress to man did He not .another
sakes reproved ;them allow people

15
16 אַל־תִּגְּעוּ בִמְשִׁיחָי וְלִנְבִיאַי אַל־תָּרֵעוּ׃ וַיִּקְרָא רָעָב עַל־
on a He And do not My to and My touch Do not
famine called .harm prophets ,anointed

17 הָאָרֶץ כָּל־מַטֵּה־לֶחֶם שָׁבָר׃ שָׁלַח לִפְנֵיהֶם אִישׁ לְעֶבֶד
a for a before sent He He bread staff the the
slave ,man them .broke of whole ;land

18
19 נִמְכַּר יוֹסֵף׃ עִנּוּ בַכֶּבֶל רַגְלָיו בַּרְזֶל בָּאָה נַפְשׁוֹ׃ עַד־
until ;soul his came into his with they ;Joseph was
iron ,feet chains hurt sold

20 עֵת בֹּא־דְבָרוֹ אִמְרַת יְהוָה צְרָפָתְהוּ׃ שָׁלַח מֶלֶךְ וַיַּתִּירֵהוּ
loosed and The sent refined Jehovah the His came the
;him king .him of word ;word time

21 מֹשֵׁל עַמִּים וַיְפַתְּחֵהוּ׃ שָׂמוֹ אָדוֹן לְבֵיתוֹ וּמֹשֵׁל בְּכָל־
all over ruler and his of lord made He him set and ,peoples the
,house him .free of ruler

22
23 קִנְיָנוֹ׃ לֶאְסֹר שָׂרָיו בְּנַפְשׁוֹ וּזְקֵנָיו יְחַכֵּם׃ וַיָּבֹא יִשְׂרָאֵל
Israel And teach to his and his at his bind to his
came .wisdom elders ,will princes ,property

24 מִצְרָיִם וְיַעֲקֹב גָּר בְּאֶרֶץ־חָם׃ וַיֶּפֶר אֶת־עַמּוֹ מְאֹד
,greatly His He And .Ham the in so- and ,Egypt (to)
people increased of land journed Jacob

25 וַיַּעֲצִמֵהוּ מִצָּרָיו׃ הָפַךְ לִבָּם לִשְׂנֹא עַמּוֹ לְהִתְנַכֵּל
deal to His hate to their He his than him made and
craftily ,people heart turned .enemies stronger

26
27 בַּעֲבָדָיו׃ שָׁלַח מֹשֶׁה עַבְדּוֹ אַהֲרֹן אֲשֶׁר־בָּחַר־בּוֹ׃ שָׂמוּ
They had He whom Aaron His Moses sent He His with
put .chosen ,servant .servants

28 בָם דִּבְרֵי אֹתוֹתָיו וּמֹפְתִים בְּאֶרֶץ חָם׃ שָׁלַח חֹשֶׁךְ וַיַּחְשִׁךְ
made and dark- sent He .Ham the in and His things among
;dark it ness of land miracles ,signs of them

and they did not rebel against His word. [29] He turned their waters into blood and killed their fish. [30] The land swarmed with frogs in the rooms of their kings. [31] He spoke and swarms of flies came; (and) gnats in all their borders. [32] He gave them hail (for) rain, flaming fire in their land. [33] He struck their vines also, and their fig-trees; and broke the trees of their borders. [34] He spoke and locusts came, and larvae without number, [35] and they ate up all the plants in the land; and ate the fruit of their ground. [36] He also struck all the firstborn in their land, the firstfruit of all their vigor. [37] And He led them out with silver and gold; and not one (was) stumbling among their tribes. [38] Egypt was glad when they departed, for their dread had fallen on them. [39] He spread a cloud for a covering, and fire to give light (in) the night. [40] He asked and He brought quail, and satisfied them (with) the food of Heaven. [41] He opened the rock, and waters gushed out; they went in the dry places (like) a river. [42] For He remembered His holy word, (and) Abraham His servant; [43] and He brought His people out with joy, His chosen with gladness; [44] and He gave to them the lands of the nations; and they inherited the labor of the peoples; [45] so that they might observe His statutes and keep His laws; praise Jehovah!

29 וְלֹא מָרוּ אֶת־דְּבָרוֹ׃ הָפַךְ אֶת־מֵימֵיהֶם לְדָם וַיָּמֶת
and killed / into blood / waters their / He turned / .word His / re- belled against / they and not

30 אֶת־דְּגָתָם׃ שָׁרַץ אַרְצָם צְפַרְדְּעִים בְּחַדְרֵי מַלְכֵיהֶם׃
.kings their / the in of rooms / frogs (with) / Their land / swarmed / .fish their

31
32 אָמַר וַיָּבֹא עָרֹב כִּנִּים בְּכָל־גְּבוּלָם׃ נָתַן גִּשְׁמֵיהֶם בָּרָד
,hail / their rain / He gave / their .border / all in / (and) gnats / fly ,swarms / and came / He spoke

33 אֵשׁ לֶהָבוֹת בְּאַרְצָם׃ וַיַּךְ גַּפְנָם וּתְאֵנָתָם וַיְשַׁבֵּר עֵץ גְּבוּלָם׃
their ,border / the of trees / and broke / their ;trees fig / and / their ,vines / also He struck / their in .land / flames / fire of

34
35 אָמַר וַיָּבֹא אַרְבֶּה וְיֶלֶק וְאֵין מִסְפָּר׃ וַיֹּאכַל כָּל־עֵשֶׂב
the plants / all / they and ate / ;number / without / and larvae / ,locusts / and came / He ,spoke

36 בְּאַרְצָם וַיֹּאכַל פְּרִי אַדְמָתָם׃ וַיַּךְ כָּל־בְּכוֹר בְּאַרְצָם
their in ,land / the firstborn / all / also He struck / their .ground / the of fruit / they and ate / their in ;land

37 רֵאשִׁית לְכָל־אוֹנָם׃ וַיּוֹצִיאֵם בְּכֶסֶף וְזָהָב וְאֵין בִּשְׁבָטָיו
their in tribes / and was none / and ;gold / with silver / led He And out them / their .vigor / all of / first- the fruit

38 כּוֹשֵׁל׃ שָׂמַח מִצְרַיִם בְּצֵאתָם כִּי־נָפַל פַּחְדָּם עֲלֵיהֶם׃
.them on / their dread / had fallen / for / they when ,out went / Egypt / was glad / .stumbling

39
40 פָּרַשׂ עָנָן לְמָסָךְ וְאֵשׁ לְהָאִיר לָיְלָה׃ שָׁאַל וַיָּבֵא שְׂלָו
,quail / He and brought / He ,asked / the (in) .night / give to light / and fire / a for ,covering / a cloud / He spread

41 וְלֶחֶם שָׁמַיִם יַשְׂבִּיעֵם׃ פָּתַח צוּר וַיָּזוּבוּ מַיִם הָלְכוּ בַּצִּיּוֹת
the in deserts / they ,went / ;water / and out gushed / the ,rock / He opened / satisfied .them / heaven / food and of

42 נָהָר׃ כִּי זָכַר אֶת־דְּבַר קָדְשׁוֹ אֶת־אַבְרָהָם עַבְדּוֹ׃
His ;servant / Abraham (and) / His ,holiness / the of word / He remembered / For / a (as) .river

43
44 וַיּוֹצִא עַמּוֹ בְשָׂשׂוֹן בְּרִנָּה אֶת־בְּחִירָיו׃ וַיִּתֵּן לָהֶם אַרְצוֹת
the of lands / to them / He And gave / His .chosen / with gladness / with ;joy / His people / He and out led

45 גּוֹיִם וַעֲמַל לְאֻמִּים יִירָשׁוּ׃ בַּעֲבוּר ׀ יִשְׁמְרוּ חֻקָּיו וְתוֹרֹתָיו
His and laws / His ,statutes / might they observe / that / they ;inherited / peoples the and of labor / ;nations

יִנְצֹרוּ הַלְלוּיָהּ׃
praise !Jehovah / ;keep

PSAL. CVI קו

PSALM 106

[1] Praise Jehovah; give thanks to Jehovah for (He is) good; for His mercy (endures) forever. [2] Who can express the mighty deeds of Jehovah, or make heard all His praise? [3] Blessed are those who keep judgment;

1
2 הַלְלוּיָהּ ׀ הוֹדוּ לַיהוָה כִּי־טוֹב כִּי לְעוֹלָם חַסְדּוֹ׃ מִי
Who / His .mercy / forever / for (is) / (is He) ;good / for / to ,Jehovah / give thanks / Praise ;Jehovah

3 יְמַלֵּל גְּבוּרוֹת יְהוָה יַשְׁמִיעַ כָּל־תְּהִלָּתוֹ׃ אַשְׁרֵי שֹׁמְרֵי
ones the keeping / Blessed (are) / His ?praise / all / make (or) heard / ,Jehovah / mighty the of deeds / can say

he who does righteousness in every season. [4] Remember me, Jehovah, with the favor of Your people; O visit me with Your salvation; [5] to see the good of Your chosen; to rejoice in the joy of Your nation; to glory with Your inheritance.

[6] We have sinned with our fathers; we committed iniquity; we did wrong. [7] Our fathers did not understand Your wonders in Egypt; they did not remember the multitude of Your mercies; and provoked You at the sea, at the Red Sea. [8] But He saved them for His name's sake, to make known His might. [9] And He rebuked the Red Sea, and it dried up; and He made them go through the depths, (as) through the wilderness. [10] And He saved them from the hand of him who hated; yea, redeemed them from the hand of the enemy. [11] And the waters covered their enemies; there was not one of them left. [12] Then they believed His words; they sang His praise. [13] They hurried, they forgot His works; they did not wait for His counsel; [14] and they greedily lusted in the wilderness, and tempted God in the desert. [15] And He gave to them their request, but sent wasting into their soul. [16] And they were jealous of Moses in the camp of Aaron, the saint of Jehovah; [17] the earth opened and swallowed Dathan; and covered Abiram's company. [18] And a fire burned in their company; the flame burned up the wicked. [19] They made a calf in Horeb, and worshiped the casted image; [20] and they changed their Glory into the image of an ox eating grass. [21] They forgot God their deliverer, doing great things in Egypt, [22] wonders in the land of Ham; awesome things by the Red Sea. [23] And He said to destroy them; except Moses His chosen one had stood

4 מִשְׁפָּט עֹשֵׂה צְדָקָה בְכָל־עֵת׃ זָכְרֵנִי יְהוָה בִּרְצוֹן עַמֶּךָ
Your the with ,Jehovah Remember .time in righteousness he ;judgment
;people of favor ,me every does who

5 פָּקְדֵנִי בִּישׁוּעָתֶךָ׃ לִרְאוֹת ׀ בְּטוֹבַת בְּחִירֶיךָ לִשְׂמֹחַ
to Your good the see to Your with me visit
rejoice ;chosen of ;salvation

6 בְּשִׂמְחַת גּוֹיֶךָ לְהִתְהַלֵּל עִם־נַחֲלָתֶךָ׃ חָטָאנוּ עִם־אֲבוֹתֵינוּ
our with have We Your with glory to Your joy the in
;fathers sinned .inheritance ,nation of

7 הֶעֱוִינוּ הִרְשָׁעְנוּ׃ אֲבוֹתֵינוּ בְמִצְרַיִם ׀ לֹא־הִשְׂכִּילוּ נִפְלְאוֹתֶיךָ
Your did not Egypt in Our did we did we
;wonders understand fathers .wrong ;iniquity

8 לֹא זָכְרוּ אֶת־רֹב חֲסָדֶיךָ וַיַּמְרוּ עַל־יָם בְּיַם־סוּף׃ וַיּוֹשִׁיעֵם
He But .Reeds the at the at and Your many they not
them saved of Sea ,sea rebelled ,mercies remembered

9 לְמַעַן שְׁמוֹ לְהוֹדִיעַ אֶת־גְּבוּרָתוֹ׃ וַיִּגְעַר בְּיַם־סוּף וַיֶּחֱרָב
it and ,Reeds the He And His make to His the for
;up dried of Sea rebuked .might known ,name of sake

10 וַיּוֹלִיכֵם בַּתְּהֹמוֹת כַּמִּדְבָּר׃ וַיּוֹשִׁיעֵם מִיַּד שׂוֹנֵא וַיִּגְאָלֵם
ran- and the from He And the in (as) the in He and
them somed ,hater's hand them saved .wilderness ,depths go them made

11 מִיַּד אוֹיֵב׃ וַיְכַסּוּ־מַיִם צָרֵיהֶם אֶחָד מֵהֶם לֹא נוֹתָר׃
was not of one their water and the from
.left them ;enemies covered ;enemy's hand

12
13 וַיַּאֲמִינוּ בִדְבָרָיו יָשִׁירוּ תְּהִלָּתוֹ׃ מִהֲרוּ שָׁכְחוּ מַעֲשָׂיו לֹא־
not His they They His they His they Then
;works forgot ,hurried .praise sang ;words believed

14 חִכּוּ לַעֲצָתוֹ׃ וַיִּתְאַוּוּ תַאֲוָה בַּמִּדְבָּר וַיְנַסּוּ־אֵל בִּישִׁימוֹן׃
the in God and the in lust a they and His for they
.desert tempted ,wilderness lusted ;counsel waited

15
16 וַיִּתֵּן לָהֶם שֶׁאֱלָתָם וַיְשַׁלַּח רָזוֹן בְּנַפְשָׁם׃ וַיְקַנְאוּ לְמֹשֶׁה
of they And their into wasting but their to He And
Moses jealous were .soul sent ,request them gave

17 בַּמַּחֲנֶה לְאַהֲרֹן קְדוֹשׁ יְהוָה׃ תִּפְתַּח־אֶרֶץ וַתִּבְלַע דָּתָן
;Dathan and the opened ;Jehovah holy the ,Aaron of the in
swallowed earth of one camp

18 וַתְּכַס עַל־עֲדַת אֲבִירָם׃ וַתִּבְעַר־אֵשׁ בַּעֲדָתָם לֶהָבָה
the their in a And .Abiram the over and
flame ;company fire burned of company covered

19 תְּלַהֵט רְשָׁעִים׃ יַעֲשׂוּ־עֵגֶל בְּחֹרֵב וַיִּשְׁתַּחֲווּ לְמַסֵּכָה׃
casted the and in calf a They the consumed
;image worshiped ,Horeb made .wicked

20
21 וַיָּמִירוּ אֶת־כְּבוֹדָם בְּתַבְנִית שׁוֹר אֹכֵל עֵשֶׂב׃ שָׁכְחוּ אֵל
God They .grass eating ox an the into their they And
forgot of image Glory changed

22 מוֹשִׁיעָם עֹשֶׂה גְדֹלוֹת בְּמִצְרָיִם׃ נִפְלָאוֹת בְּאֶרֶץ חָם
;Ham the in wonders ,Egypt in great was (who) their
of land things doing ,Deliverer

23 נוֹרָאוֹת עַל־יַם־סוּף׃ וַיֹּאמֶר לְהַשְׁמִידָם לוּלֵי מֹשֶׁה בְּחִירוֹ
His Moses except destroy to He And .Reeds the by awesome
one chosen ,them said of Sea things

before Him in the breach, to turn away His wrath from destroying (them). [24] And they despised the pleasant land; they did not believe His word. [25] And they murmured in their tents, not listening to the voice of Jehovah; [26] and He lifted up His hand to them, to make them fall in the wilderness; [27] to make their seed fall also among the nations, and to scatter them in the lands. [28] They also were joined to Baal-peor, and ate the sacrifices of the dead; [29] and provoked (Him) with their deeds; and a plague broke out among them. [30] Then Phinehas stood and intervened; and the plague was stayed; [31] and it was counted to him for righteousness to generation and generation forever. [32] And they angered (Him) at the waters of Meribah, that it went ill for Moses for their sakes; [33] for they provoked his spirit and he spoke rashly with his lips. [34] They did not destroy the peoples, as Jehovah said to them, [35] but mixed with the nations and learned their works. [36] And they served their idols, and they became a snare to them; [37] yea, they sacrificed their sons and their daughters to the demons; [38] and they shed innocent blood, the blood of their sons and of their daughters, whom they sacrificed to the idols of Canaan; and the land was defiled with the blood. [39] So they were unclean with their works, and went whoring in their acts. [40] And the anger of Jehovah burned against His people; and He abhorred His inheritance. [41] And He gave them into the hand of the nations; and those who hated them ruled them. [42] And their enemies oppressed them; and they were humbled under their hand. [43] Many times He delivered them, but they rebelled in their plans, and sank in their iniquity. [44] And He looked on

24 עָמַד בַּפֶּרֶץ לְפָנָיו לְהָשִׁיב חֲמָתוֹ מֵהַשְׁחִית׃ וַיִּמְאֲסוּ
they And destroying from His turn to before the in stood
despised .(them) wrath away ,Him breach

25 בְּאֶרֶץ חֶמְדָּה לֹא־הֶאֱמִינוּ לִדְבָרוֹ׃ וַיֵּרָגְנוּ בְאָהֳלֵיהֶם לֹא
not their in they And His they not ;pleasant the
;tents murmured .word believed land

26 שָׁמְעוּ בְּקוֹל יְהוָה׃ וַיִּשָּׂא יָדוֹ לָהֶם לְהַפִּיל אוֹתָם בַּמִּדְבָּר׃
the in them cause to to His He and ;Jehovah the to they
,wilderness fall to ,them hand lifted of voice listened

27 28 וּלְהַפִּיל זַרְעָם בַּגּוֹיִם וּלְזָרוֹתָם בָּאֲרָצוֹת׃ וַיִּצָּמְדוּ לְבַעַל
Baal- to they And the in to and the among their cause to and
joined were .lands them scatter ;nations seed fall to

29 פְּעוֹר וַיֹּאכְלוּ זִבְחֵי מֵתִים׃ וַיַּכְעִיסוּ בְּמַעַלְלֵיהֶם וַתִּפְרָץ־
and their with provoked and the the ate and ,peor
out broke ;deeds (Him) ;dead of sacrifices

30 בָּם מַגֵּפָה׃ וַיַּעֲמֹד פִּינְחָס וַיְפַלֵּל וַתֵּעָצַר הַמַּגֵּפָה׃
;plague the was and and Phinehas Then .plague a among
restrained ;intervened stood them

31 32 וַתֵּחָשֶׁב לוֹ לִצְדָקָה לְדֹר וָדֹר עַד־עוֹלָם׃ וַיַּקְצִיפוּ עַל־מֵי
the at they And .forever gen- and gen- to righ- for to was it and
of waters (Him) angered eration eration teousness him reckoned

33 מְרִיבָה וַיֵּרַע לְמֹשֶׁה בַּעֲבוּרָם׃ כִּי־הִמְרוּ אֶת־רוּחוֹ וַיְבַטֵּא
he and spirit his they because their for for it and ,Meribah
rashly spoke provoked ,sakes Moses ill went

34 בִּשְׂפָתָיו׃ לֹא־הִשְׁמִידוּ אֶת־הָעַמִּים אֲשֶׁר אָמַר יְהוָה
Jehovah said as the did They not his with
,peoples destroy .lips

35 36 לָהֶם׃ וַיִּתְעָרְבוּ בַגּוֹיִם וַיִּלְמְדוּ מַעֲשֵׂיהֶם׃ וַיַּעַבְדוּ אֶת־
they And their and the with but to
served .works learned nations mixed ,them

37 עֲצַבֵּיהֶם וַיִּהְיוּ לָהֶם לְמוֹקֵשׁ׃ וַיִּזְבְּחוּ אֶת־בְּנֵיהֶם וְאֶת־
and sons their they ,Yea .snare a them to and their
sacrificed became ;idols

38 בְּנוֹתֵיהֶם לַשֵּׁדִים׃ וַיִּשְׁפְּכוּ דָם נָקִי דַּם־בְּנֵיהֶם וּבְנוֹתֵיהֶם
their and their the inno- blood they and the to their
,daughters sons of blood ,cent shed ,demons daughters

39 אֲשֶׁר זִבְּחוּ לַעֲצַבֵּי כְנָעַן וַתֶּחֱנַף הָאָרֶץ בַּדָּמִים׃ וַיִּטְמְאוּ
they So the with the was and ;Canaan the to they whom
unclean were .blood land defiled of idols sacrificed

40 בְמַעֲשֵׂיהֶם וַיִּזְנוּ בְּמַעַלְלֵיהֶם׃ וַיִּחַר־אַף יְהוָה בְּעַמּוֹ
against Jehovah the And .acts their in went and their by
;people His of anger burned whoring ,works

41 וַיְתָעֵב אֶת־נַחֲלָתוֹ׃ וַיִּתְּנֵם בְּיַד־גּוֹיִם וַיִּמְשְׁלוּ בָהֶם
over ruled and ,nations the into He And His He and
them of hand them gave .inheritance abhorred

42 43 שֹׂנְאֵיהֶם׃ וַיִּלְחָצוּם אוֹיְבֵיהֶם וַיִּכָּנְעוּ תַּחַת יָדָם׃ פְּעָמִים
times their under they and their oppressed And who those
.hand humbled were ,enemies them .them hated

44 רַבּוֹת יַצִּילֵם וְהֵמָּה יַמְרוּ בַעֲצָתָם וַיָּמֹכּוּ בַּעֲוֹנָם׃ וַיַּרְא
He And their in and their in rebelled but He Many
looked .iniquity sank ,counsel they ,them delivered

their affliction when He heard their cry; [45] and He remembered (His) covenant for them, and sighed; according to the multitude of His mercies. [46] And he caused them to be pitied before all their captors.

[47] Save us, O Jehovah our God; and gather us from the nations, to give thanks to Your holy name, to exult in Your praise.

[48] Blessed (is) Jehovah God of Israel from everlasting even to everlasting; and let all the people say, Amen! Praise Jehovah!

45 בַּצַּר לָהֶם בְּשָׁמְעוֹ אֶת־רִנָּתָם׃ וַיִּזְכֹּר לָהֶם בְּרִיתוֹ
His for He and their He when to the on
,covenant them remembered ;cry heard them affliction

46 וַיִּנָּחֵם כְּרֹב חֲסָדָיו׃ וַיִּתֵּן אוֹתָם לְרַחֲמִים לִפְנֵי כָּל־
all before tender to them He And His according and
mercies gave .mercies many to ,sighed

47 שׁוֹבֵיהֶם׃ הוֹשִׁיעֵנוּ ׀ יְהוָה אֱלֹהֵינוּ וְקַבְּצֵנוּ מִן־הַגּוֹיִם
the from and ;God our O ,us Save their
,nations us gather Jehovah .captors

48 לְהוֹדוֹת לְשֵׁם קָדְשֶׁךָ לְהִשְׁתַּבֵּחַ בִּתְהִלָּתֶךָ׃ בָּרוּךְ יְהוָה
Jehovah Blessed Your in boast to Your the to give to
(is) .praise ,holiness of name thanks

אֱלֹהֵי יִשְׂרָאֵל מִן־הָעוֹלָם ׀ וְעַד הָעוֹלָם וְאָמַר כָּל־הָעָם
the all let and ;everlasting even everlast- from ,Israel of God
,people say to ing

אָמֵן הַלְלוּיָהּ׃
Praise !Amen
!Jehovah

PSAL. CVII . קז

PSALM 107

PSALM 107

[1] Give thanks to Jehovah, for (He is) good; for His mercy (is) forever. [2] Let the redeemed of Jehovah say (so); whom He redeemed from the hand of the foe; [3] and gathered them from the lands, from east and from west; from north and from south.

[4] They wandered in the wilderness, in a desert way; they found no city of dwelling; [5] hungry and thirsty, their soul fainted in them; [6] and they cried to Jehovah in the distress; He delivered them from their straits; [7] And He guided them in the right way; to go to a city to live in. [8] Let them thank Jehovah (for) His mercy; and His wonders to the sons of man. [9] For he satisfies the thirsty soul and He fills the hungry soul (with) good

[10] Those who live in the darkness and in the shadow of death, (being) prisoners in affliction and iron — [11] because they rebelled against the words of God and despised the counsel of the Most High, [12] and He humbled their heart by toil; they stumbled and (there was) no helping, [13] then they cried to Jehovah in their distress; He saved them out of their

1
2 הֹדוּ לַיהוָה כִּי־טוֹב כִּי לְעוֹלָם חַסְדּוֹ׃ יֹאמְרוּ גְּאוּלֵי יְהוָה
,Jehovah the say Let His forever for (is He) for to Give
of redeemed (so) .mercy (is) ;good ,Jehovah thanks

3 אֲשֶׁר גְּאָלָם מִיַּד־צָר׃ וּמֵאֲרָצוֹת קִבְּצָם מִמִּזְרָח וּמִמַּעֲרָב
from and from gathered from and the the from He whom
,west ,east ,them lands ,foe of hand redeemed

4 מִצָּפוֹן וּמִיָּם׃ תָּעוּ בַמִּדְבָּר בִּישִׁימוֹן דָּרֶךְ עִיר מוֹשָׁב לֹא
not dwelling a ;way a in the in They from and from
of city desert ,wilderness wandered .south ,north

5
6 מָצָאוּ׃ רְעֵבִים גַּם־צְמֵאִים נַפְשָׁם בָּהֶם תִּתְעַטָּף׃ וַיִּצְעֲקוּ
they and —fainted them in their ,thirsty and hungry they
cried soul —found

7 אֶל־יְהוָה בַּצַּר לָהֶם מִמְּצוּקוֹתֵיהֶם יַצִּילֵם׃ וַיַּדְרִיכֵם
He And delivered He their from to the in Jehovah to
them guided .them straits ;them distress

8 בְּדֶרֶךְ יְשָׁרָה לָלֶכֶת אֶל־עִיר מוֹשָׁב׃ יוֹדוּ לַיהוָה חַסְדּוֹ
His (for) Jehovah them Let .dwelling a to go to ;right the in
;mercy thank of city way

9 וְנִפְלְאוֹתָיו לִבְנֵי אָדָם׃ כִּי־הִשְׂבִּיעַ נֶפֶשׁ שֹׁקֵקָה וְנֶפֶשׁ
the and ,thirsty the He For .man the to His and
soul soul satisfies of sons wonders

10 רְעֵבָה מִלֵּא־טוֹב׃ יֹשְׁבֵי חֹשֶׁךְ וְצַלְמָוֶת אֲסִירֵי עֳנִי וּבַרְזֶל׃
and affliction prison- deep in and dark- Those (with) he hungry
—iron of ers ,shadow ness in living .good fills

11
12 כִּי־הִמְרוּ אִמְרֵי־אֵל וַעֲצַת עֶלְיוֹן נָאָצוּ׃ וַיַּכְנַע בֶּעָמָל לִבָּם
their toil by He And .spurned the the and ,God the they for
;heart subdued High Most of counsel of words at rebelled

13 כָּשְׁלוּ וְאֵין עֹזֵר׃ וַיִּזְעֲקוּ אֶל־יְהוָה בַּצַּר לָהֶם מִמְּצוּקוֹתֵיהֶם
their from to the in Jehovah to they and help- was and they
straits ;them distress cried —ing none stumbled

distresses; [14] He brought them out from darkness and the shadow of death, and He broke apart their bands. [15] Let them thank Jehovah (for) His mercy, and His wonders to the sons of man. [16] For He has broken gates of bronze, and He cut bars of iron in two.

[17] Fools are afflicted from the way of their rebellion and from their iniquities; [18] their soul hates every food; and they draw near the gates of death; [19] then they cry to Jehovah in their distress; He saves them out of their distresses; [20] He sends His word and heals them; and He delivers (them) from all their pitfalls. [21] Let them thank Jehovah (for) His mercy; and His wonders to the sons of men. [22] And let them sacrifice the sacrifices of thanksgiving; and recount His works with rejoicing!

[23] They who go down to the sea in ships, who do business in great waters; [24] these see the works of Jehovah, and His wonders in the deep. [25] For He speaks and raises stormy wind, and makes high its waves; [26] they go up to the heavens, they go down (to) the depths; their soul is melted because in evil; [27] they reel and stagger like a drunken man, and all their wisdom is swallowed up; [28] then they cry to Jehovah in their distress, and He saves them out of their distresses. [29] He settles the storm to be quiet, so that its waves are still; [30] then they are glad, because they are quiet, and he led them to their desired haven. [31] Let them thank Jehovah (for) His mercy, and His wonders to the sons of men; [32] and exalt Him in the congregation of the people; and praise Him in the seat of the elders.

[33] He sets rivers to a wilderness, and water-springs to dry ground; [34] a fruitful land to a salty desert; because of the

14 יוֹשִׁיעֵם׃ יוֹצִיאֵם מֵחֹשֶׁךְ וְצַלְמָוֶת וּמוֹסְרוֹתֵיהֶם יְנַתֵּק׃
broke He .off | their and bands | deep and ,shadow | from darkness | brought He out them | saved He ;them

15 16 יוֹדוּ לַיהוָה חַסְדּוֹ וְנִפְלְאוֹתָיו לִבְנֵי אָדָם׃ כִּי־שִׁבַּר דַּלְתוֹת
of gates | has He For broken | .man | the to of sons | His and wonders | (for) Jehovah ,mercy His | They thank

17 נְחֹשֶׁת וּבְרִיחֵי בַרְזֶל גִּדֵּעַ׃ אֱוִלִים מִדֶּרֶךְ פִּשְׁעָם
their revolt | the from of way | ,Fools | cut He .two in | iron | bars and of | ,bronze

18 וּמֵעֲוֹנֹתֵיהֶם יִתְעַנּוּ׃ כָּל־אֹכֶל תְּתַעֵב נַפְשָׁם וַיַּגִּיעוּ עַד־
to | they and approach | their ;soul | hates | .food every | are ;afflicted | from and ,iniquities their

19 שַׁעֲרֵי מָוֶת׃ וַיִּזְעֲקוּ אֶל־יְהוָה בַּצַּר לָהֶם מִמְּצֻקוֹתֵיהֶם
their from straits | to ;them | the in distress | Jehovah to | they then cry | ;death | the of gates

20 יוֹשִׁיעֵם׃ יִשְׁלַח דְּבָרוֹ וְיִרְפָּאֵם וִימַלֵּט מִשְּׁחִיתוֹתָם׃
their all from .pit-falls | and delivers | heals and ,them | His word | He sends | saves He ;them

21 22 יוֹדוּ לַיהוָה חַסְדּוֹ וְנִפְלְאוֹתָיו לִבְנֵי אָדָם׃ וְיִזְבְּחוּ זִבְחֵי
sacrifices of | And sacrifice they | .man | the to of sons | His and wonders | His (for) Jehovah ,mercy | They thank

23 תוֹדָה וִיסַפְּרוּ מַעֲשָׂיו בְּרִנָּה׃ יוֹרְדֵי הַיָּם בָּאֳנִיּוֹת עֹשֵׂי
who do | in ,ships | the who sea | Those to down go | with !rejoicing | His works | and recount | thanks- ,giving

24 מְלָאכָה בְּמַיִם רַבִּים׃ הֵמָּה רָאוּ מַעֲשֵׂי יְהוָה וְנִפְלְאוֹתָיו
His and wonders | ,Jehovah | the of works | see | these | ,great | in waters | business

25 בִּמְצוּלָה׃ וַיֹּאמֶר וַיַּעֲמֵד רוּחַ סְעָרָה וַתְּרוֹמֵם גַּלָּיו׃
its ;waves | it and high makes | ,storm | wind a of | and raises | He For ,speaks | the in .deep

26 יַעֲלוּ שָׁמַיִם יֵרְדוּ תְהוֹמוֹת נַפְשָׁם בְּרָעָה תִתְמוֹגָג׃
;melted is | evil in | their soul | the (to) ;depths | go they down | (to) ;heaven | they on go

27 28 יָחוֹגּוּ וְיָנוּעוּ כַּשִּׁכּוֹר וְכָל־חָכְמָתָם תִּתְבַּלָּע׃ וַיִּצְעֲקוּ אֶל־
to | they then cry | swallowed is ;up | their wisdom | and all | a like ;drunkard | they stagger | they ;reel

29 יְהוָה בַּצַּר לָהֶם וּמִמְּצוּקֹתֵיהֶם יוֹצִיאֵם׃ יָקֵם סְעָרָה
the storm | He settles | brings He .out them | their from and straits | to ;them | the in distress | Jehovah

30 לִדְמָמָה וַיֶּחֱשׁוּ גַּלֵּיהֶם׃ וַיִּשְׂמְחוּ כִי־יִשְׁתֹּקוּ וַיַּנְחֵם אֶל־
to | He so them led | they for ;quiet are | they then ,glad are | its ;waves | that so still are | a to ,whisper

31 מְחוֹז חֶפְצָם׃ יוֹדוּ לַיהוָה חַסְדּוֹ וְנִפְלְאוֹתָיו לִבְנֵי אָדָם׃
.man | the to of sons | His and wonders | His (for) ,mercy | Jehovah They thank | their .desire | the of haven

32 33 וִירוֹמְמוּהוּ בִּקְהַל עָם וּבְמוֹשַׁב זְקֵנִים יְהַלְלוּהוּ׃ יָשֵׂם
sets He | praise .Him | the elders | the in and of seat | the ;people | the in of assembly | exalt And Him

34 נְהָרוֹת לְמִדְבָּר וּמֹצָאֵי מַיִם לְצִמָּאוֹן׃ אֶרֶץ פְּרִי לִמְלֵחָה
salty to ;desert | fruit | a of land | dry to ;ground | water | and of springs | a to ,wilderness | rivers

wickedness of those who dwell in it. [35] He puts the wilderness into a water-pond; and dry land into water-springs; [36] and He makes the hungry live there, and they may prepare a city of dwelling. [37] And they sow the fields and plant vineyards, and make fruits of produce. [38] He also blesses them, so that they multiply greatly; and He does not allow their cattle to diminish; [39] but they are diminished and humbled, through harshness, affliction and grief; [40] He pours scorn on nobles, and causes them to wander in a desert; there (is) no path. [41] But He raises the poor up from affliction, and He sets families like a flock. [42] The upright shall see and be glad; and all iniquity shuts its mouth. [43] Whoever (is) wise, and will observe these things, they shall understand the mercies of Jehovah.

35 מֵרָעַת יֹשְׁבֵי בָהּ׃ יָשֵׂם מִדְבָּר לַאֲגַם־מַיִם וְאֶרֶץ צִיָּה
dry and ,water a to the puts He .it in who those the from
land of pool wilderness dwell of evil

36 לְמֹצָאֵי מָיִם׃ וַיּוֹשֶׁב שָׁם רְעֵבִים וַיְכוֹנְנוּ עִיר מוֹשָׁב׃
.dwelling a they and hungry there He and ;water to
of city prepare ,ones live makes of springs

37 38 וַיִּזְרְעוּ שָׂדוֹת וַיִּטְּעוּ כְרָמִים וַיַּעֲשׂוּ פְּרִי תְבוּאָה׃ וַיְבָרְכֵם
also He .produce fruit and ,vineyards and fields they And
,them blesses of make plant sow

39 וַיִּרְבּוּ מְאֹד וּבְהֶמְתָּם לֹא יַמְעִיט׃ וַיִּמְעֲטוּ וַיָּשֹׁחוּ מֵעֹצֶר
through put and they but lets He not their and ;greatly and
,coercion ,down diminish ;diminish cattle multiplies

40 רָעָה וְיָגוֹן׃ שֹׁפֵךְ בּוּז עַל־נְדִיבִים וַיַּתְעֵם בְּתֹהוּ לֹא־
not a in makes and ,nobles on scorn (is He) and evil
;waste wander them pouring .grief

41 42 דָרֶךְ׃ וַיְשַׂגֵּב אֶבְיוֹן מֵעוֹנִי וַיָּשֶׂם כַּצֹּאן מִשְׁפָּחוֹת׃ יִרְאוּ
Shall .families a like He and from the set He And a (is)
see flock sets ;affliction needy high on .path

43 יְשָׁרִים וְיִשְׂמָחוּ וְכָל־עַוְלָה קָפְצָה פִּיהָ׃ מִי־חָכָם וְיִשְׁמָר־
will and (is) Who its shuts wickedness and be and the
keep wise .mouth all ;glad upright

אֵלֶּה וְיִתְבּוֹנְנוּ חַסְדֵי יְהוָה׃
.Jehovah the they For these
of mercies discern ?things

PSAL. CVIII קח

PSALM 108

A Song or Psalm of David.

[1] O God, my heart is fixed; I will sing, yea, I will sing songs even with my glory. [2] Awake, harp and lyre! I will awake early; [3] I will thank You, O Jehovah, among the peoples; and I will sing to You among the nations. [4] For Your mercy (is) great above the heavens; and Your truth (reaches) to the clouds. [5] Be lifted up, O God, above the heavens; and Your glory above all the earth; [6] so that Your beloved may be delivered; save (by) Your right hand and answer me. [7] God has spoken in His holiness; I will rejoice; I will portion out Shechem; and I will measure out the valley of Succoth. [8] Gilead (is) Mine (and) Manasseh (is) Mine; and Ephraim is the fort of My head; Judah (is) My lawgiver; [9] Moab (is) My washpot; I will throw My shoe out over Edom; I

1 2 שִׁיר מִזְמוֹר לְדָוִד׃ נָכוֹן לִבִּי אֱלֹהִים אָשִׁירָה וַאֲזַמְּרָה
will I ,yea sing will I ;God O My is .David of psalm A .song A
songs sing ,heart fixed

3 4 אַף־כְּבוֹדִי׃ עוּרָה הַנֵּבֶל וְכִנּוֹר אָעִירָה שָּׁחַר׃ אוֹדְךָ
will I ;early will I ;lyre and harp ,Awake (with) even
You thank awake .glory my

5 בָעַמִּים ׀ יְהוָה וַאֲזַמֶּרְךָ בַּלְאֻמִּים׃ כִּי־גָדוֹל מֵעַל־שָׁמַיִם
the above (is) For the among will I and ;Jehovah the among
heavens great .nations You to sing ,peoples

6 חַסְדֶּךָ וְעַד־שְׁחָקִים אֲמִתֶּךָ׃ רוּמָה עַל־שָׁמַיִם אֱלֹהִים
;God O the above lifted Be Your the even Your
,heavens up .truth (is) clouds to ;mercy

7 וְעַל כָּל־הָאָרֶץ כְּבוֹדֶךָ׃ לְמַעַן יֵחָלְצוּן יְדִידֶיךָ הוֹשִׁיעָה
(by) save Your be may that so Your the all and
;ones beloved delivered ;glory earth above

8 יְמִינְךָ וַעֲנֵנִי׃ אֱלֹהִים ׀ דִּבֶּר בְּקָדְשׁוֹ אֶעְלֹזָה אֲחַלְּקָה שְׁכֶם
;Shechem will I will I His in has God answer and Your
out portion ;rejoice ;holiness spoken .me hand right

9 וְעֵמֶק סֻכּוֹת אֲמַדֵּד׃ לִי גִלְעָד ׀ לִי מְנַשֶּׁה וְאֶפְרַיִם מָעוֹז
the (is) and (is) to (is) To will I Succoth the and
fort Ephraim ,Manasseh Me ;Gilead Me .out measure of valley

10 רֹאשִׁי יְהוּדָה מְחֹקְקִי׃ מוֹאָב ׀ סִיר רַחְצִי עַל־אֱדוֹם
Edom over My pot the Moab My (is) Judah My (of)
;washing of (is) ;lawgiver ;head

will shout in triumph over Philistia. [10] Who will lead me into the fortified city? Who will lead me over Edom? [11] O God, have you not cast us off? And, O God, will You not go out with our armies? [12] Give help to us from distress; for the deliverance of man is vain. [13] In God we shall do mighty things, for He shall trample our foes.

אַשְׁלִיךְ נַעֲלִי עֲלֵי פְּלֶשֶׁת אֶתְרוֹעָע׃ מִי יֹבִלֵנִי עִיר מִבְצָר 11
the city lead will Who shout will I Philistia over My throw will I
;fortified into me .triumph in ;shoe

מִי נָחַנִי עַד־אֱדוֹם׃ הֲלֹא־אֱלֹהִים זְנַחְתָּנוּ וְלֹא־תֵצֵא אֱלֹהִים 12
,God O will You And cast You ,God O Have ?Edom over leads who
,out go not ?off us ,not me

בְּצִבְאֹתֵינוּ׃ הָבָה־לָּנוּ עֶזְרָת מִצָּר וְשָׁוְא תְּשׁוּעַת אָדָם׃ 13
.man the (is) for from help us to Give our with
of deliverance vanity ;distress ?armies

בֵּאלֹהִים נַעֲשֶׂה־חָיִל וְהוּא יָבוּס צָרֵינוּ׃ 14
our shall for mighty shall we God In
.foes trample He ,things do

PSAL. CIX קט

PSALM 109

PSALM 109

To the Chief Musician. A Psalm of David.

[1] O God of my praise, do not be silent; [2] for the mouth of the wicked, and the deceitful mouth are opened against me; they spoke against me (with) a lying tongue. [3] And they hemmed me in (with) words of hatred; and fought against me without a cause. [4] Instead of my love they are my enemies; but I (am in) prayer. [5] And they put on me evil for good; and hatred for my love. [6] Set a wicked man over him; and let an adversary stand at his right hand; [7] when he is judged, let him go out wicked, and let his prayer become sin; [8] let his days be few; and let another take his office; [9] let his sons be orphans, and his wife a widow; [10] and let his sons always beg and wander, and seek (food) out of their ruins; [11] let the money-lender lay a snare for all that (is) his; and let strangers plunder his labor. [12] Let there be none giving mercy to him; nor (any) to have pity on his orphans; [13] let his posterity be cut off; let their name be blotted out in the following generation. [14] Let the iniquity of his fathers be remembered to Jehovah; and let not the sin of his mother be blotted out. [15] Let them be always before Jehovah, so that He may cut off the memory of

לַמְנַצֵּחַ לְדָוִד מִזְמוֹר אֱלֹהֵי תְהִלָּתִי אַל־תֶּחֱרַשׁ׃ כִּי פִי 1 2
the For be do not my God O .psalm A of chief the To
of mouth .silent ,praise of David .musician

רָשָׁע וּפִי־מִרְמָה עָלַי פָּתָחוּ דִּבְּרוּ אִתִּי לְשׁוֹן שָׁקֶר׃ וְדִבְרֵי 3
(with) and false- a (with) against they they against mouth the and the
of words .hood of tongue me spoke ;opened me deceit of ,wicked

שִׂנְאָה סְבָבוּנִי וַיִּלָּחֲמוּנִי חִנָּם׃ תַּחַת־אַהֲבָתִי יִשְׂטְנוּנִי 4
are they ,love my Instead without fought and en- They hatred
;foes my of .cause a me against me circled

וַאֲנִי תְפִלָּה׃ וַיָּשִׂימוּ עָלַי רָעָה תַּחַת טוֹבָה וְשִׂנְאָה תַּחַת 5
for and ;good for evil me on they And (in) I but
hatred put .prayer (am)

אַהֲבָתִי׃ הַפְקֵד עָלָיו רָשָׁע וְשָׂטָן יַעֲמֹד עַל־יְמִינוֹ׃ 6
right his at let a and wicked a over Set .love my
;hand stand foe ,man him

בְּהִשָּׁפְטוֹ יֵצֵא רָשָׁע וּתְפִלָּתוֹ תִּהְיֶה לַחֲטָאָה׃ יִהְיוּ־יָמָיו 7 8
his let ;sin let his and ;wicked him let is he when
days be become prayer forth go ,judged

מְעַטִּים פְּקֻדָּתוֹ יִקַּח אַחֵר׃ יִהְיוּ־בָנָיו יְתוֹמִים וְאִשְׁתּוֹ 9
his and ;orphans his let ;another let his and ;few
wife sons be take office

אַלְמָנָה׃ וְנוֹעַ יָנוּעוּ בָנָיו וְשִׁאֵלוּ וְדָרְשׁוּ מֵחָרְבוֹתֵיהֶם׃ 10
their of out seek and ,beg and his let and ;widow a
;ruins (food) ,sons wander always

יְנַקֵּשׁ נוֹשֶׁה לְכָל־אֲשֶׁר־לוֹ וְיָבֹזּוּ זָרִים יְגִיעוֹ׃ אַל־יְהִי־לוֹ 11 12
to Let not his strangers let and to that for the lay let
him be .labor plunder ;him (is) all exactor snare a

מֹשֵׁךְ חָסֶד וְאַל־יְהִי חוֹנֵן לִיתוֹמָיו׃ יְהִי־אַחֲרִיתוֹ לְהַכְרִית 13
cutting a his Let his on (one) let nor ;mercy giving
;off posterity be .orphans pity having be

בְּדוֹר אַחֵר יִמַּח שְׁמָם׃ יִזָּכֵר ׀ עֲוֹן אֲבֹתָיו אֶל־יְהוָה 14
;Jehovah to his the be Let their be let following the in
fathers of iniquity recalled .name out blotted generation

וְחַטַּאת אִמּוֹ אַל־תִּמָּח׃ יִהְיוּ נֶגֶד־יְהוָה תָּמִיד וְיַכְרֵת 15
He that always Jehovah before Let be let not his the and
off cut may be them .out blotted mother of sin

them from the earth; [16] because he did not remember to do mercy; and persecuted the poor and needy man; and to kill the broken-hearted. [17] Yea, he loved cursing, and it came to him; he also had no pleasure in blessing, and it was far from him. [18] As he clothed himself with cursing, as with a robe, and it came into his bowels like water, and like oil into his bones. [19] Let it be to him as a robe he wraps in, and for a girdle that he always girds on. [20] This (is) the reward of my foes from Jehovah, and (of) those who speak evil against my soul. [21] But You, O Jehovah the Lord, work with me, for Your name's sake; deliver me because Your mercy (is) good. [22] For I (am) poor and needy, and my heart is pierced within me. [23] As a shadow when it stretches out, I am gone; I am shaken off like the locust. [24] My knees stumble from fasting, and my flesh grows lean from fatness. [25] And I have become a reproach to them; they looked at me; they shook their heads. [26] O Jehovah my God, help me; save me according to Your mercy; [27] and they will know that this (is) Your hand; that You, O Jehovah, have done it. [28] They will curse, but You will bless; they rise up and are ashamed; but Your servant will be glad. [29] Let those who accuse me be clothed with shame; and cover themselves in their shame as with a robe. [30] I will greatly thank Jehovah with my mouth; yea, I will praise Him in the midst of the multitude. [31] For He shall stand at the right hand of the poor; to save from those who judge his soul.

16 מֵאֶרֶץ זִכְרָם׃ יַעַן אֲשֶׁר ׀ לֹא־זָכַר עֲשׂוֹת חָסֶד וַיִּרְדֹּף אִישׁ־
the man and persecuted ;mercy do to did he not remember because their ;memory the from earth

17 עָנִי וְאֶבְיוֹן וְנִכְאֵה לֵבָב לְמוֹתֵת׃ וַיֶּאֱהַב קְלָלָה וַתְּבוֹאֵהוּ
came it and .him to ,cursing he And loved .kill to heart the and of broken and ,needy poor

18 וְלֹא־חָפֵץ בִּבְרָכָה וַתִּרְחַק מִמֶּנּוּ׃ וַיִּלְבַּשׁ קְלָלָה כְּמַדּוֹ
his robe as cursing he And on put from .him was it but far in ,blessing had he pleasure And not

19 וַתָּבֹא כַמַּיִם בְּקִרְבּוֹ וְכַשֶּׁמֶן בְּעַצְמוֹתָיו׃ תְּהִי־לוֹ כְּבֶגֶד
a as garment to it Let him be his into .bones as and oil his into ,body as water it and came

20 יַעְטֶה וּלְמֵזַח תָּמִיד יַחְגְּרֶהָ׃ זֹאת ׀ פְּעֻלַּת שֹׂטְנַי מֵאֵת יְהוָה
;Jehovah from my foes the of reward This (is) girds he .on it always for and ;belt a he ,in wraps

21 וְהַדֹּבְרִים רָע עַל־נַפְשִׁי׃ וְאַתָּה ׀ יְהוִה אֲדֹנָי עֲשֵׂה־אִתִּי
with ,me work ,Lord O Jehovah ,You But my against .soul evil those (of) and speak who

22 לְמַעַן שְׁמֶךָ כִּי־טוֹב חַסְדְּךָ הַצִּילֵנִי׃ כִּי־עָנִי וְאֶבְיוֹן אָנֹכִי
,(am) I and needy poor For deliver .me Your ,mercy (is) because good Your for ;name's sake

23 וְלִבִּי חָלַל בְּקִרְבִּי׃ כְּצֵל־כִּנְטוֹתוֹ נֶהֱלָכְתִּי נִנְעַרְתִּי
shaken am I off am I ;gone it when ,out stretches a As shadow within .me (is) pierced my and heart

24 כָּאַרְבֶּה׃ בִּרְכַּי כָּשְׁלוּ מִצּוֹם וּבְשָׂרִי כָּחַשׁ מִשָּׁמֶן׃ וַאֲנִי ׀
25
I And from .fatness grows lean my and flesh from ,fasting stumble My knees the like .locust

26 הָיִיתִי חֶרְפָּה לָהֶם יִרְאוּנִי יְנִיעוּן רֹאשָׁם׃ עָזְרֵנִי יְהוָה
O Jehovah Help ,me their .heads they shook they ;me saw ;them to a reproach have become

27 אֱלֹהָי הוֹשִׁיעֵנִי כְחַסְדֶּךָ׃ וְיֵדְעוּ כִּי־יָדְךָ זֹּאת אַתָּה יְהוָה
O ,Jehovah (that) ,You this ;(is) Your hand that they and know will Your by ;mercy save me my ;God

28 עֲשִׂיתָהּ׃ יְקַלְלוּ־הֵמָּה וְאַתָּה תְבָרֵךְ קָמוּ ׀ וַיֵּבֹשׁוּ וְעַבְדְּךָ
Your servant but are and ;ashamed they ,up rise will I ;bless You but ,They will curse have .it done

29 יִשְׂמָח׃ יִלְבְּשׁוּ שׂוֹטְנַי כְּלִמָּה וְיַעֲטוּ כַמְעִיל בָּשְׁתָּם׃ אוֹדֶה
30
will I thank their in .shame with as robe a wrap and themselves disgrace my foes put Let on be will .glad

31 יְהוָה מְאֹד בְּפִי וּבְתוֹךְ רַבִּים אֲהַלְלֶנּוּ׃ כִּי־יַעֲמֹד לִימִין
right at hand He stand shall For will I .Him praise many the in of midst and my with ;mouth greatly Jeho-vah

אֶבְיוֹן לְהוֹשִׁיעַ מִשֹּׁפְטֵי נַפְשׁוֹ׃
his .soul those from judging save to the ,needy's

PSAL. CX קי

PSALM 110

1 לְדָוִד מִזְמוֹר נְאֻם יְהוָה ׀ לַאדֹנִי שֵׁב לִימִינִי עַד־אָשִׁית
set I until My at ,hand right Sit my to :Lord Jehovah state- of ment A .psalm A of David

PSALM 110

A Psalm of David.

[1] A statement of Jehovah to my Lord, Sit at My right hand, until I set

Your enemies (as) Your footstool. [2] Jehovah shall send the rod of Your strength out of Zion; rule in the midst of Your enemies. [3] Your people (shall be) willing in the day of Your might; in the majesties of holiness from the womb of the dawn, to You (is) the dew of Your youth. [4] Jehovah has sworn and will not repent; You (are) a priest forever after the order of Melchizedek. [5] The Lord at Your right hand shatters kings in the day of His anger. [6] He shall judge among the nations; He shall fill with dead bodies; He shall shatter chiefs over much land. [7] He shall drink out of the brook in the way; therefore He shall lift up the head.

2 אֹיְבֶיךָ הֲדֹם לְרַגְלֶיךָ׃ מַטֵּה עֻזְּךָ יִשְׁלַח יְהוָה מִצִּיּוֹן רְדֵה

rule of out Jehovah shall Your rod The Your for stool a Your
;Zion send strength of .feet enemies

3 בְּקֶרֶב אֹיְבֶיךָ׃ עַמְּךָ נְדָבֹת בְּיוֹם חֵילֶךָ בְּהַדְרֵי־קֹדֶשׁ

;holiness the in Your the in (be shall) Your Your the in
of majesties ;might of day willing people .enemies of midst

4 מֵרֶחֶם מִשְׁחָר לְךָ טַל יַלְדֻתֶיךָ׃ נִשְׁבַּע יְהוָה ׀ וְלֹא יִנָּחֵם

will and Jehovah has Your the to ,dawn the the from
;repent not sworn .youth of dew You of womb

5 אַתָּה־כֹהֵן לְעוֹלָם עַל־דִּבְרָתִי מַלְכִּי־צֶדֶק׃ אֲדֹנָי עַל־

at Lord The .Melchizedek the according forever a You
of order to priest (are)

6 יְמִינְךָ מָחַץ בְּיוֹם־אַפּוֹ מְלָכִים׃ יָדִין בַּגּוֹיִם מָלֵא גְוִיּוֹת

with will He the in shall He .kings His the in shatters Your
;corpses fill ;nations judge anger of day hand right

7 מָחַץ רֹאשׁ עַל־אֶרֶץ רַבָּה׃ מִנַּחַל בַּדֶּרֶךְ יִשְׁתֶּה עַל־כֵּן

therefore shall He the in the From .much land over chiefs will He
;drink way brook shatter

יָרִים רֹאשׁ׃

the shall He
.head up lift

PSAL. CXI קיא

PSALM 111

[1] Praise Jehovah; I will thank Jehovah with all (my) heart; in the secret meeting of the upright, and of the assembly. [2] The works of Jehovah (are) great, sought out by all those desiring them. [3] His work (is) honorable and glorious; and His righteousness endures forever. [4] He has made a memorial for His wonders; Jehovah (is) gracious and full of pity. [5] He has given food to those who fear Him; He will always remember His covenant. [6] He has shown to His people the power of His works, to give to them inheritance of the nations. [7] The works of His hands (are) truth and judgment; all His commandments (are) true, [8] standing firm forever and ever; (they are) done in truth and uprightness. [9] He sent redemption to His people; He has commanded His covenant forever; holy and awesome (is) His name. [10] The fear of Jehovah (is) the beginning of wisdom; all who practice them (have) a good understanding: His praise endures forever!

1 הַלְלוּיָהּ ׀ אוֹדֶה יְהוָה בְּכָל־לֵבָב בְּסוֹד יְשָׁרִים וְעֵדָה׃

the of and the the in the with Jehovah will I Praise
.assembly ,upright of council ;heart all thank ;Jehovah

2
3 גְּדֹלִים מַעֲשֵׂי יְהוָה דְּרוּשִׁים לְכָל־חֶפְצֵיהֶם׃ הוֹד־וְהָדָר

and Honorable desiring those by out sought ,Jehovah the Great
glorious .them all of works (are)

4 פָּעֳלוֹ וְצִדְקָתוֹ עֹמֶדֶת לָעַד׃ זֵכֶר עָשָׂה לְנִפְלְאֹתָיו חַנּוּן

gracious His for has He A .forever endures His and His (is)
;wonders made memorial righteousness ,work

5
6 וְרַחוּם יְהוָה׃ טֶרֶף נָתַן לִירֵאָיו יִזְכֹּר לְעוֹלָם בְּרִיתוֹ׃ כֹּחַ

The His to will He His to He Food (is) full and
of power .covenant forever remember ;fearers gave .Jehovah pity of

7 מַעֲשָׂיו הִגִּיד לְעַמּוֹ לָתֵת לָהֶם נַחֲלַת גּוֹיִם׃ מַעֲשֵׂי יָדָיו

His works The the inheritance to give to His to has He His
hands of .nations of them ,people shown works

8 אֱמֶת וּמִשְׁפָּט נֶאֱמָנִים כָּל־פִּקּוּדָיו׃ סְמוּכִים לָעַד לְעוֹלָם

,ever and forever standing His all (are) true and (are)
firm ,commands ;judgment truth

9 עֲשׂוּיִם בֶּאֱמֶת וְיָשָׁר׃ פְּדוּת ׀ שָׁלַח לְעַמּוֹ צִוָּה לְעוֹלָם

forever has He His to sent He Redemption and truth in being
commanded ;people .uprightness done

10 בְּרִיתוֹ קָדוֹשׁ וְנוֹרָא שְׁמוֹ׃ רֵאשִׁית חָכְמָה ׀ יִרְאַת יְהוָה

;Jehovah the(is) wisdom be- the His (is) and holy His
of fear of ginning .name awesome ;covenant

שֵׂכֶל טוֹב לְכָל־עֹשֵׂיהֶם תְּהִלָּתוֹ עֹמֶדֶת לָעַד׃

!forever is praise His practicing to (is) good under- a
standing ;them all standing

PSAL. CXII קיב

PSALM 112

1 הַלְלוּ־יָהּ ׀ אַשְׁרֵי־אִישׁ יָרֵא אֶת־יְהוָה בְּמִצְוֺתָיו חָפֵץ מְאֹד׃
.greatly he His in ;Jehovah who the Blessed Praise
delights commands fears man (is) !Jehovah

2
3 גִּבּוֹר בָּאָרֶץ יִהְיֶה זַרְעוֹ דּוֹר יְשָׁרִים יְבֹרָךְ׃ הוֹן־וָעֹשֶׁר
and wealth be shall the gen- the his shall the on Mighty
riches ;blessed upright of eration ;seed be earth

4 בְּבֵיתוֹ וְצִדְקָתוֹ עֹמֶדֶת לָעַד׃ זָרַח בַּחֹשֶׁךְ אוֹר לַיְשָׁרִים
the to Light the in rises .forever is his and his in
;upright darkness standing righteousness ;house

5 חַנּוּן וְרַחוּם וְצַדִּיק׃ טוֹב־אִישׁ חוֹנֵן וּמַלְוֶה יְכַלְכֵּל דְּבָרָיו
his will he and showing a Good and full and (is he)
matters nourish ;lending favor man (is) .righteous ,pity of ,gracious

6 בְּמִשְׁפָּט׃ כִּי־לְעוֹלָם לֹא־יִמּוֹט לְזֵכֶר עוֹלָם יִהְיֶה צַדִּיק׃
the be shall forever a for will he not forever For with
.righteous memorial ;shaken be .justice

7
8 מִשְּׁמוּעָה רָעָה לֹא יִירָא נָכוֹן לִבּוֹ בָּטֻחַ בַּיהוָה׃ סָמוּךְ
(is) in trusting his is will he not Bad news
upheld .Jehovah ,heart fixed ,fear

9 לִבּוֹ לֹא יִירָא עַד אֲשֶׁר־יִרְאֶה בְצָרָיו׃ פִּזַּר ׀ נָתַן לָאֶבְיוֹנִים
the to has he has He his upon he until shall he not His
;needy given ;scattered .foes looks fear ;heart

10 צִדְקָתוֹ עֹמֶדֶת לָעַד קַרְנוֹ תָּרוּם בְּכָבוֹד׃ רָשָׁע יִרְאֶה ׀
see shall The .honor with be shall his ;forever is righ- his
wicked exalted horn standing teousness

וְכָעָס שִׁנָּיו יַחֲרֹק וְנָמָס תַּאֲוַת רְשָׁעִים תֹּאבֵד׃
shall wicked the and shall he his be and
.perish ones of desire ;melt ,gnash teeth ;vexed

PSALM 112

[1] Praise Jehovah! Blessed is the man who fears Jehovah, delighting greatly in His commands. [2] His seed shall be mighty on the earth; the generation of the upright shall be blessed; [3] wealth and riches in his house; and his righteousness endures forever. [4] Light rises in the darkness to the upright; (he is) gracious and full of pity and righteousness. [5] Good (is) a man showing favor and lending; he will nourish his matters with equity. [6] For he shall not be shaken forever; the righteous shall be for a memorial forever. [7] He shall not be afraid of evil news; his heart (is) fixed, trusting in Jehovah. [8] His heart (is) upheld; he shall not be afraid, until he looks upon his foes. [9] He has scattered; he has given to the needy; his righteousness endures forever; his horn shall be lifted up with honor. [10] The wicked shall see and be vexed; he shall gnash with his teeth and melt; the desire of the wicked shall perish.

PSAL. CXIII קיג

PSALM 113

1
2 הַלְלוּ־יָהּ ׀ הַלְלוּ עַבְדֵי יְהוָה הַלְלוּ אֶת־שֵׁם יְהוָה׃ יְהִי שֵׁם
the Is .Jehovah the praise ,Jehovah servants ,Praise Praise
of name of name of !Jehovah

3 יְהוָה מְבֹרָךְ מֵעַתָּה וְעַד־עוֹלָם׃ מִמִּזְרַח־שֶׁמֶשׁ עַד־מְבוֹאוֹ
his to sun the the from .forever and from being Jehovah
;going of rising now blessed

4 מְהֻלָּל שֵׁם יְהוָה׃ רָם עַל־כָּל־גּוֹיִם ׀ יְהוָה עַל הַשָּׁמַיִם
the above ,Jehovah nations all above Is .Jehovah the being
heavens high of name praised

5
6 כְּבוֹדוֹ׃ מִי כַּיהוָה אֱלֹהֵינוּ הַמַּגְבִּיהִי לָשָׁבֶת׃ הַמַּשְׁפִּילִי
humbles who ;dwell to sits who our like Who His
himself high on ,God Jehovah (is) .glory

7 לִרְאוֹת בַּשָּׁמַיִם וּבָאָרֶץ׃ מְקִימִי מֵעָפָר דָּל מֵאַשְׁפֹּת יָרִים
lifts He from and the the from raising in and the in see to
dunghill the ;poor dust up ,earth the heavens

PSALM 113

[1] Praise Jehovah! Praise, O servants of Jehovah, praise the name of Jehovah. [2] Blessed is the name of Jehovah from now on and forevermore. [3] From sunrise to his going, Jehovah's name (is) to be praised. [4] Jehovah (is) high above all nations; His glory above the heavens. [5] Who (is) like Jehovah our God, who sits on high to dwell; [6] who humbles Himself to consider (all) in the earth and the heavens! [7] He raises the poor up out of the dust; and He lifts

the needy out of the dunghill, [8] in order to make him sit with nobles, with the nobles of His people. [9] He causes the barren (woman) to live in the house, (as) the joyful mother of sons. Praise Jehovah!

8 9 אֶבְיוֹן׃ לְהוֹשִׁיבִי עִם־נְדִיבִים עִם נְדִיבֵי עַמּוֹ׃ מוֹשִׁיבִי ׀

to causing his the with ;nobles with sit him make to the
dwell ,people of nobles ,needy

עֲקֶרֶת הַבַּיִת אֵם־הַבָּנִים שְׂמֵחָה הַלְלוּ־יָהּ׃

Praise .joyful sons the the (in) the
!Jah of mother ,house barren

PSAL. CXIV קיד

PSALM 114

PSALM 114

[1] When Israel came out of Egypt, the house of Jacob from a people of strange language; [2] Judah became his sanctuary, Israel His kingdom. [3] The sea looked and fled; the Jordan turned back; [4] the mountains skipped like rams; the little hills like lambs! [5] What (ailed) you, O sea, that you flee? O Jordan, that you turn back? [6] O mountains, that you skipped like rams? O little hills, like lambs? [7] Tremble, O earth, from the face of the Lord, from the face of the God of Jacob; [8] who turned the rock (into) a pool of water; the flint into a fountain of waters.

1 2 בְּצֵאת יִשְׂרָאֵל מִמִּצְרָיִם בֵּית יַעֲקֹב מֵעַם לֹעֵז׃ הָיְתָה

became alien a from Jacob the ,Egypt from Israel came When
speech of people of house out

3 יְהוּדָה לְקָדְשׁוֹ יִשְׂרָאֵל מַמְשְׁלוֹתָיו׃ הַיָּם רָאָה וַיָּנֹס הַיַּרְדֵּן

the and saw The His Israel His Judah
Jordan ;fled sea .dominion ,sanctuary

4 יִסֹּב לְאָחוֹר׃ הֶהָרִים רָקְדוּ כְאֵילִים גְּבָעוֹת כִּבְנֵי־צֹאן׃

a like hills the ;rams as skipped the ;back turned
.flock of sons mountains

5 6 מַה־לְּךָ הַיָּם כִּי תָנוּס הַיַּרְדֵּן תִּסֹּב לְאָחוֹר׃ הֶהָרִים

O ?back you that O ?flee you that ,sea O to What
,mountains turn ,Jordan ,you (is)

7 תִּרְקְדוּ כְאֵילִים גְּבָעוֹת כִּבְנֵי־צֹאן׃ מִלִּפְנֵי אָדוֹן חוּלִי

,tremble the From a sons as ,hills O ?rams as you that
Lord before ?flock of skip

8 אָרֶץ מִלִּפְנֵי אֱלוֹהַּ יַעֲקֹב׃ הַהֹפְכִי הַצּוּר אֲגַם־מָיִם חַלָּמִישׁ

flint the ;water (into) the who ,Jacob the from O
of pool a rock turned of God before ,earth

לְמַעְיְנוֹ־מָיִם׃

.water a into
of spring

PSAL. CXV קטו

PSALM 115

PSALM 115

[1] Not to us, O Jehovah, not to us, but to Your name give glory; for Your mercy; because of Your truth. [2] Why do the nations say, Where (is) their God now? [3] But our God (is) in the heavens; He has done all which He has pleased. [4] Their idols (are) silver and gold, the work of man's hands; [5] they (have) mouths, but they do not speak; they (have) eyes, but they do not see; [6] they (have) ears, but they do not hear; they (have) a nose, but they do not smell; [7] their hands, but they do not feel; their feet, but they do not walk; they do not speak through

1 לֹא לָנוּ יְהוָה לֹא־לָנוּ כִּי־לְשִׁמְךָ תֵּן כָּבוֹד עַל־חַסְדְּךָ

Your for ,glory give Your to but to not O to Not
,mercy name ,us ,Jehovah ,us

2 עַל־אֲמִתֶּךָ׃ לָמָּה יֹאמְרוּ הַגּוֹיִם אַיֵּה־נָא אֱלֹהֵיהֶם׃

?God their now Where the say Why Your for
is ,nations .truth

3 4 וֵאלֹהֵינוּ בַשָּׁמָיִם כֹּל אֲשֶׁר־חָפֵץ עָשָׂה׃ עֲצַבֵּיהֶם כֶּסֶף

silver Their has He has He which all the in (is) our But
(are) idols .done pleased ;heavens God

5 וְזָהָב מַעֲשֵׂה יְדֵי אָדָם׃ פֶּה־לָהֶם וְלֹא יְדַבֵּרוּ עֵינַיִם לָהֶם

to eyes they but to mouths ;man the work the and
,them (are) ;speak not ,them (are) of hands of ,gold

6 וְלֹא יִרְאוּ׃ אָזְנַיִם לָהֶם וְלֹא יִשְׁמָעוּ אַף לָהֶם וְלֹא יְרִיחוּן׃

they but to (is) a they but to ears they but
;smell not ,them nose ;hear not ,them (are) ;see not

7 יְדֵיהֶם ׀ וְלֹא יְמִישׁוּן רַגְלֵיהֶם וְלֹא יְהַלֵּכוּ לֹא־יֶהְגּוּ

they not they but their they but their
speak ;march not ,feet ;feel not ,hands

their throat. [8] The ones who make them are like them, everyone trusting in them. [9] O Israel, trust in Jehovah; He (is) their help and their shield. [10] O house of Aaron, trust in Jehovah; He (is) their help and their shield. [11] You who fear Jehovah, trust in Jehovah; He (is) their help and their shield. [12] Jehovah remembers us; He will bless (us); He will bless the house of Israel; He will bless the house of Aaron; [13] He will bless those who fear Jehovah, the small and the great. [14] Jehovah will add (more) upon you, on you and on your sons. [15] You (are) blessed to Jehovah, (who) makes the heavens and the earth. [16] The heavens – the heavens (are) Jehovah's; but He has given the earth to the sons of man. [17] The dead do not praise Jehovah; nor all those who go down into silence; [18] but we will bless Jehovah, from now on and forevermore. Praise Jehovah!

8 בגרונם׃ כמוהם יהיו עשיהם כל אשר־בטח בהם׃
.them in is who every- who those are Like their in
trusting one ;them make them .throat

9 10 ישראל בטח ביהוה עזרם ומגנם הוא׃ בית אהרן
,Aaron O .(is) He their and their in trust ;Israel O
of house shield help ;Jehovah

11 בטחו ביהוה עזרם ומגנם הוא׃ יראי יהוה בטחו ביהוה
in trust ,Jehovah Fearers He their and their in trust
;Jehovah of .(is) shield help ;Jehovah

12 עזרם ומגנם הוא׃ יהוה זכרנו יברך יברך את־בית
the will He will He remembers Jehovah He their and their
of house bless ;bless ;us ;(is) shield help

13 ישראל יברך את־בית אהרן׃ יברך יראי יהוה הקטנים
the ,Jehovah the will He ;Aaron the will He ;Israel
small of fearers bless of house bless

14 עם־הגדלים׃ יסף יהוה עליכם עליכם ועל־בניכם׃
.sons Your and upon upon Jehovah Will .great the and
upon you ,you add

15 16 ברוכים אתם ליהוה עשה שמים וארץ׃ השמים שמים
the The and heavens (who) to you Blessed
heavens ,heavens .earth makes ,Jehovah (are)

17 ליהוה והארץ נתן לבני־אדם׃ לא המתים יהללו־יה
,Jehovah do The not .man the to has He the but to (are)
praise dead of sons given earth ,Jehovah

18 ולא כל־ירדי דומה׃ ואנחנו | נברך יה מעתה ועד־
and from Jehovah will we but ;silence go who all and
for now bless to down not

עולם הללויה׃
Praise .ever
!Jah

PSAL. CXVI קטז

PSALM 116

[1] I love Jehovah because He hears my voice (and) my prayers. [2] Because He has bowed His ear to me, I will also call in my days. [3] The cords of death hemmed me in; and the pains of Sheol found me; I find distress and sorrow; [4] then I call on the name of Jehovah; O Jehovah, I beseech You, deliver My soul! [5] Jehovah (is) gracious and righteous; yes, our God (is) merciful. [6] Jehovah keeps the simple; I was low but He saved me. [7] Return to your rest, O my soul; for Jehovah has blessed you. [8] For You have delivered my soul from death; my eye

1 2 אהבתי כי־ישמע | יהוה את־קולי תחנוני׃ כי־הטה
He Because my ,voice my Jehovah He because love I
inclined .supplication hears

3 אזנו לי ובימי אקרא׃ אפפוני | חבלי־מות ומצרי שאול
Sheol the and ;death The encompassed will I in also to His
of straits of cords me .call days my ;me ears

4= מצאוני צרה ויגון אמצא׃ ובשם־יהוה אקרא אנה יהוה
O pray I :call I Jehovah on then ,find I and distress found
,Jehovah ,You of name the sorrow ;me

5 6 מלטה נפשי׃ חנון יהוה וצדיק ואלהינו מרחם׃ שמר
keeps (is) our and and Jehovah (is) ?soul my deliver
.merciful God ;righteous gracious

7 פתאים יהוה דלותי ולי יהושיע׃ שובי נפשי למנוחיכי
your to my O ,Return He but was I .Jehovah the
,rest ,soul saved me ,low simple

8 כי־יהוה גמל עליכי׃ כי חלצת נפשי ממות את־עיני
eye my from my have You For .you bene- Jeho- for
;death soul rescued fitted vah

from tears (and) my foot from stumbling. [9] I will walk before the face of Jehovah, in the lands of the living. [10] I believed, so I speak; I was greatly afflicted; [11] I said in my alarm, Every man (is) a liar. [12] What shall I return to Jehovah (for) all His benefits to me? [13] I will lift up the cup of salvation and I will call on the name of Jehovah. [14] I will pay my bows to Jehovah now in the presence of all His people. [15] Precious in the eyes of Jehovah (is) the death of His saints. [16] O Jehovah, now I (am) truly Your servant; I (am) Your servant, the son of Your handmaid; You have loosed my bonds. [17] I will sacrifice to You the sacrifice of thanks, and will call on the name of Jehovah. [18] I will pay my vows to Jehovah now in the presence of all His people, [19] in the courts of the house of Jehovah; in your midst, O Jerusalem. Praise Jehovah!

9 מִן־דִּמְעָה אֶת־רַגְלִי מִדֶּחִי: אֶתְהַלֵּךְ לִפְנֵי יְהֹוָה בְּאַרְצוֹת

in	,Jehovah	before	will I		from	foot my	,tears	from
of lands			walk		.stumbling			

10
11 הֶחַיִּים: הֶאֱמַנְתִּי כִּי אֲדַבֵּר אֲנִי עָנִיתִי מְאֹד: אֲנִי אָמַרְתִּי

said	I	;greatly	was	I	;speak I	so	have I	the
			afflicted				;believed	.living

12 בְּחָפְזִי כָּל־הָאָדָם כֹּזֵב: מָה־אָשִׁיב לַיהֹוָה כָּל־תַּגְמוּלוֹהִי

His	for	to	I shall	What	a (is)	man	Every	my in
benefits	all	Jehovah	return		.liar			,alarm

13
14 עָלָי: כּוֹס־יְשׁוּעוֹת אֶשָּׂא וּבְשֵׁם יְהֹוָה אֶקְרָא: נְדָרַי לַיהֹוָה

to	My	will I	Jehovah	on and	will I	salvation The	to
Jehovah	vows	.call		of name the	,up lift	of cup	?me

15 אֲשַׁלֵּם נֶגְדָה־נָּא לְכָל־עַמּוֹ: יָקָר בְּעֵינֵי יְהֹוָה הַמָּוְתָה

the (is)	Jehovah	the in	Precious	His	of	,pray I	the in	will I
death		of eyes		.people	all		,presence	,pay

16 לַחֲסִידָיו: אָנָּה יְהֹוָה כִּי־אֲנִי עַבְדֶּךָ אֲנִי עַבְדְּךָ בֶּן־אֲמָתֶךָ

Your son	the	Your	I	Your	I truly	O	,pray I	His of
	handmaid of	,servant (am)	;servant (am)		.Jehovah			.saints

17 פִּתַּחְתָּ לְמוֹסֵרָי: לְךָ אֶזְבַּח זֶבַח תּוֹדָה וּבְשֵׁם יְהֹוָה אֶקְרָא

.call will	Jehovah	on and	,thanks the	will I	You To	my	have You
	of name the		of sacrifice	sacrifice		.bonds	loosed

18
19 נְדָרַי לַיהֹוָה אֲשַׁלֵּם נֶגְדָה־נָּא לְכָל־עַמּוֹ: בְּחַצְרוֹת ׀ בֵּית

the	the in	His	of	I	the in	will I	to	My
of house	of courts		,people	all	,pray	,presence	pay	Jehovah	vows

יְהֹוָה בְּתוֹכֵכִי יְרוּשָׁלִָם הַלְלוּיָהּ:

Praise		O	your in	,Jehovah
!Jah		.Jerusalem	,midst	

PSAL. CXVII   קיז

PSALM 117

PSALM 117

[1] Praise Jehovah, all nations; praise Him, all peoples. [2] For His mercy is mighty over us; and the truth of Jehovah (is) forever. Praise Jehovah!

1
2 הַלְלוּ אֶת־יְהֹוָה כָּל־גּוֹיִם שַׁבְּחוּהוּ כָּל־הָאֻמִּים: כִּי גָבַר

is	For	.peoples	all	praise	;nations all	,Jehovah	Praise
mighty				,Him			

עָלֵינוּ ׀ חַסְדּוֹ וֶאֱמֶת־יְהֹוָה לְעוֹלָם הַלְלוּיָהּ:

Praise	(is)	Jehovah	the and	His	over
!Jah	.forever		of truth	,mercy	us

PSAL. CXVIII   קיח

PSALM 118

PSALM 118

[1] Give thanks to Jehovah, for (He is) good; because His mercy (endures) forever. [2] Let Israel say now that His mercy (is) forever. [3] Let the house of Aaron say now that His mercy (endures) forever. [4] Let those who fear Jehovah say now that His mercy (endures) forever. [5] I called Jehovah from the distress; He answered me in the large place of Jehovah. [6] Jehovah (is) for me; I will not fear;

1
2 הוֹדוּ לַיהֹוָה כִּי־טוֹב כִּי לְעוֹלָם חַסְדּוֹ: יֹאמַר־נָא יִשְׂרָאֵל

Israel	I	Let	His	(is)	for (is He) for	to	Give
	,pray	,say	.mercy	forever	;good	,Jehovah	thanks

3 כִּי לְעוֹלָם חַסְדּוֹ: יֹאמְרוּ־נָא בֵית־אַהֲרֹן כִּי לְעוֹלָם חַסְדּוֹ:

His	(is)	that	Aaron	the	I	Let	His	(is)	that
.mercy	forever		of house	,pray	,say	.mercy	forever		

4
5 יֹאמְרוּ־נָא יִרְאֵי יְהֹוָה כִּי לְעוֹלָם חַסְדּוֹ: מִן־הַמֵּצַר

the	From	His	(is)	that	Jehovah	who those	I	Let
distress		.mercy	forever			fear	,pray	,say

6 קָרָאתִי יָּהּ עָנָנִי בַמֶּרְחָב יָהּ: יְהֹוָה לִי לֹא אִירָא מַה־

what	will I	not	for	Jehovah	.Jehovah	the in	an- He	;Jehovah	I
	;fear		;me			of place large	me swered		called

what can man do to me? [7] Jehovah is for me among those who help me; and I shall see (my desire) on those who hate me. [8] (It is) better to take refuge in Jehovah than to trust in man; [9] (it is) better to trust in Jehovah than to trust in princes. [10] All the nations surround me; but surely I will destroy them in the name of Jehovah. [11] They surround me; they also surround me; I will surely destroy them in the name of Jehovah. [12] They surround me like bees; they are quenched like the fire of thorns; for surely I will cut them off in the name of Jehovah. [13] Pushing you pushed me to fall; but Jehovah helped me. [14] Jehovah (is) my strength and my song, and He is my salvation. [15] The voice of rejoicing and salvation (is) in the tabernacle of the righteous; the right hand of Jehovah works mightily. [16] The right hand of Jehovah is exalted; the right hand of Jehovah acts mightily. [17] I shall not die, but I shall live and declare the works of Jehovah. [18] Jehovah has grievously chastened me, but He has not given me to death. [19] Open the gates of righteousness to me, I will enter into them; I will thank Jehovah! [20] This (is) the gate of Jehovah; the righteous shall enter into it. [21] I will thank You, for You answered me, and are my salvation. [22] The Stone (which) the builders rejected has become the Head of the corner. [23] This is from Jehovah, it is marvelous in our eyes. [24] This (is) the day Jehovah has made; we will rejoice and be glad in it. [25] O Jehovah, I beseech You, save now; O Jehovah, I beseech You, make prosper now. [26] Blessed (is) he who comes in the name of Jehovah; we blessed you out of the house of Jehovah. [27] Jehovah (is) God, and He gives to us light; tie the sacrifice with cords, to the horns of the altar. [28] You (are) my God,

7 יַּעֲשֶׂה לִי אָדָם׃ יְהֹוָה לִי בְּעֹזְרָי וַאֲנִי אֶרְאֶה בְשֹׂנְאָי׃
those on shall and my among for Jehovah ?man to do can
.me hating look I ;helpers me (is) me

8
9 טוֹב לַחֲסוֹת בַּיהֹוָה מִבְּטֹחַ בָּאָדָם׃ טוֹב לַחֲסוֹת
take to (is It) .man in to than in take to (is It)
refuge better trust Jehovah refuge better

10 בַּיהֹוָה מִבְּטֹחַ בִּנְדִיבִים׃ כָּל־גּוֹיִם סְבָבוּנִי בְּשֵׁם יְהֹוָה
Jehovah the in surround the All .princes in to than in
of name ,me nations trust Jehovah

11 כִּי אֲמִילַם׃ סַבּוּנִי גַם־סְבָבוּנִי בְּשֵׁם יְהֹוָה כִּי אֲמִילַם׃
cut will I surely Jehovah the in they also sur- They cut will I surely
.off them of name ;me surround ,me round .off them

12 סַבּוּנִי כִדְבוֹרִים דֹּעֲכוּ כְּאֵשׁ קוֹצִים בְּשֵׁם יְהֹוָה כִּי אֲמִילַם׃
cut will I surely Jehovah the in ;thorns the like are they like sur- They
.off them of name of fire quenched ;bees me round

13
14 דַּחֹה דְחִיתַנִי לִנְפֹּל וַיהֹוָה עֲזָרָנִי׃ עָזִּי וְזִמְרָת יָהּ וַיְהִי־
He and (is) my and My helped has but ,fall to you Pushing
is ;Jah song strength .me Jehovah me pushed

15 לִי לִישׁוּעָה׃ קוֹל ׀ רִנָּה וִישׁוּעָה בְּאָהֳלֵי צַדִּיקִים יְמִין
right the the in (is) and joyful The .salvation to
hand ;righteous of tents salvation shouting of voice me

16 יְהֹוָה עֹשָׂה חָיִל׃ יְמִין יְהֹוָה רוֹמֵמָה יְמִין יְהֹוָה עֹשָׂה
acts Jehovah right the is Jehovah right The .mightily works Jeho-
of hand ;exalted of hand vah's

17
18 חָיִל׃ לֹא־אָמוּת כִּי־אֶחְיֶה וַאֲסַפֵּר מַעֲשֵׂי יָהּ׃ יַסֹּר
Sorely .Jah the tell and shall I but shall I not .mightily
of works live ,die

19 יִסְּרַנִּי יָּהּ וְלַמָּוֶת לֹא נְתָנָנִי׃ פִּתְחוּ־לִי שַׁעֲרֵי־צֶדֶק אָבֹא־
will I righteous- the to Open has He not to but ,Jah chas-
enter .ness of gates me .me given death me tened

20 בָם אוֹדֶה יָהּ׃ זֶה־הַשַּׁעַר לַיהֹוָה צַדִּיקִים יָבֹאוּ בוֹ׃
into shall the of the This .Jehovah will I into
.it enter righteous ;Jehovah gate (is) thank .them

21
22 אוֹדְךָ כִּי עֲנִיתָנִי וַתְּהִי־לִי לִישׁוּעָה׃ אֶבֶן מָאֲסוּ הַבּוֹנִים
the (which) The .salvation to and an- You for will I
builders rejected stone me are me swered ,You thank

23 הָיְתָה לְרֹאשׁ פִּנָּה׃ מֵאֵת יְהֹוָה הָיְתָה זֹּאת הִיא נִפְלָאת
marvelous it ;this is Jehovah From the the has
(is) .corner of Head become

24 בְּעֵינֵינוּ׃ זֶה־הַיּוֹם עָשָׂה יְהֹוָה נָגִילָה וְנִשְׂמְחָה בוֹ׃
,it in be and will we ;Jehovah has the This our in
glad rejoice made day (is) .eyes

25
26 אָנָּא יְהֹוָה הוֹשִׁיעָה נָּא אָנָּא יְהֹוָה הַצְלִיחָה נָּא׃ בָּרוּךְ
Blessed .now to make O beg I ;now save O beg I
(is) prosper ,Jehovah ,You ,Jehovah ,You

27 הַבָּא בְּשֵׁם יְהֹוָה בֵּרַכְנוּכֶם מִבֵּית יְהֹוָה׃ אֵל ׀ יְהֹוָה
(is) God .Jehovah the from blessed we ;Jehovah the in who he
,Jehovah of house you of name comes

28 וַיָּאֶר לָנוּ אִסְרוּ־חַג בַּעֲבֹתִים עַד־קַרְנוֹת הַמִּזְבֵּחַ׃ אֵלִי
my .altar the the to with the tie ,us to He and
God of horns cords sacrifice light gives

and I will exalt You; My God, I will thank You! [29] O give thanks to Jehovah, for He is good; for His mercy (endures) forever.

29 אתה ואודך אלהי ארוממך׃ הודו ליהוה כי־טוב כי

for (is He) for to give O will I my will I and You
;good Jehovah thanks .You exalt ,God ;You thank ,(are)

לעולם חסדו׃

His forever
!mercy (is)

PSAL. CXIX קיט

PSALM 119

PSALM 119

Aleth

[1] Blessed are the upright in the way, who walk in the law of Jehovah. [2] Blessed (are) those keeping His testimonies, who seek Him with the whole heart. [3] They also do not work injustice; they walk in His ways. [4] You have commanded to carefully keep Your precepts. [5] O that my ways were fixed to keep Your statutes! [6] Then I shall not be ashamed, when I look to all Your commands. [7] I will thank You with integrity of heart, in my learning the judgments of Your righteousness. [8] I will keep Your statutes; do not forsake me utterly.

Beth

[9] By what shall a young man purify his way, to keep (it) according to Your word? [10] I have sought You with my whole heart; do not let me wander from Your commands. [11] I have hidden Your word in my heart, that I might not sin against You. [12] Blessed (are) You, O Jehovah; teach me Your statutes. [13] I have declared all the judgments of Your mouth with my lips; [14] I have rejoiced in the way of Your testimonies as over all riches. [15] I will meditate in Your precepts and I will regard Your ways. [16] I will delight in Your statutes I will not forget Your word.

Gimel

[17] Grant to Your servant (that) I may live, and I will keep Your word. [18] Open my eyes and I will see wonderful things from Your law. [19] I (am) an alien in the earth; hide not Your commandments from me. [20] My soul is breaking

1 2 אשרי תמימי־דרך ההלכים בתורת יהוה׃ אשרי נצרי

those Blessed .Jehovah the in walk who the in the Blessed
keeping (are) of law ,way upright (are)

3 עדתיו בכל־לב ידרשוהו׃ אף לא־פעלו עולה בדרכיו

His in ;injustice they do not Also seek who heart the with His
ways work .Him whole ,testimonies

4 5 הלכו׃ אתה צויתה פקדיך לשמר מאד׃ אחלי יכנו

were that O .carefully be to Your have You they
fixed kept precepts commanded .walk

6 דרכי לשמר חקיך׃ אז לא־אבוש בהביטי אל־כל־

all to I when shall I not Then Your keep to my
look ashamed be !statutes ways

7 מצותיך׃ אודך בישר לבב בלמדי משפטי צדקך׃

righ- Your judg- the my in ,heart with will I Your
.teousness of ments learning of integrity You thank .commands

8 9 את־חקיך אשמר אל־תעזבני עד־מאד׃ במה יזכה־

shall By very till do not will I Your
purify what .much me forsake ;keep statutes

10 נער את־ארחו לשמר כדברך׃ בכל־לבי דרשתיך אל־

not have I my With to according keep To his young a
;You sought heart whole !word Your (it) ?path man

11 תשגני ממצותיך׃ בלבי צפנתי אמרתך למען לא

not that ,word Your have I my In Your from let
hidden heart !commands wander me

12 13 אחטא־לך׃ ברוך אתה יהוה למדני חקיך׃ בשפתי

my With Your teach O ,You Blessed against might I
lips .statutes me ;Jehovah (are) You sin

14 ספרתי כל משפטי־פיך׃ בדרך עדותיך ששתי כעל

as have I Your the in Your judg- the all have I
over rejoiced testimonies of way ;mouth of ments declared

15 16 כל־הון׃ בפקדיך אשיחה ואביטה ארחתיך׃ בחקתיך

Your In Your will I and will I Your In riches all
statutes .ways regard ,meditate precepts

17 אשתעשע לא אשכח דברך׃ גמל על־עבדך אחיה

I (that) Your to Grant Your will I not delight will I
,live may servant .word forget ;myself

18 ואשמרה דברך׃ גל־עיני ואביטה נפלאות מתורתך׃

Your of out wonderful may I that my Open Your keep I and
.law things behold ,eyes .word

19 20 גר אנכי בארץ אל־תסתר ממני מצותיך׃ גרסה נפשי

My is Your from hide do not the in I an
soul crushed .commands me ;earth (am) alien

for the longing to Your judgments in every season. [21] You have rebuked the proud, the cursed ones who wander from Your commands. [22] Remove reproach and scorn from me; for I have kept Your testimonies. [23] Princes also sat, speaking against me; (but) Your servant meditates on Your laws. [24] Your testimonies also (are) my delight, my counselors.

Daleth

[25] My soul clings to the dust; give me life according to Your word [26] I have declared my ways, and You answered me; teach me Your statutes. [27] Make me understand the way of Your precepts, and I will meditate on Your wonders. [28] My soul drops (with) grief; make me strong according to Your word. [29] Remove from me the way of lying, and favor me with Your law. [30] I have chosen the way of truth; I have held Your judgments level; [31] I have clung to Your testimonies; O Jehovah, do not shame me. [32] I will run the way of Your commands, for You shall enlarge my heart.

He

[33] O Jehovah, teach me the way of Your statutes, and I will keep it (to) the end. [34] Make me understand and I will keep Your law, and observe it with the whole heart. [35] Make me walk in the way of Your commands, for in it I delight. [36] Bow my heart to Your testimonies, and not to unjust gain. [37] Turn my eyes from seeing vanity; in Your way give me life. [38] Make Your word sure to Your servant who is (devoted) to Your fear. [39] Turn away my shame which I fear; for Your judgments (are) good [40] Behold, I have longed for Your precepts; give me life in Your righteousness.

Vau

[41] Let Your mercies come to me, O Jehovah, according to Your salvation, by Your word. [42] And I will answer my reprover a word; for I trust in

21 לְתַאֲבָה אֶל־מִשְׁפָּטֶיךָ בְכָל־עֵת׃ גָּעַרְתָּ זֵדִים אֲרוּרִים
cursed the the have You .season in Your to the for
ones ,proud rebuked every judgments longing

22 הַשֹּׁגִים מִמִּצְוֺתֶיךָ׃ גַּל מֵעָלַי חֶרְפָּה וָבוּז כִּי עֵדֹתֶיךָ נָצָרְתִּי׃
have I Your for and reproach from Remove Your from who
.kept testimonies ;scorn me .commands wander

23 גַּם יָשְׁבוּ שָׂרִים בִּי נִדְבָּרוּ עַבְדְּךָ יָשִׂיחַ בְּחֻקֶּיךָ׃ גַּם־
24 Also Your on meditates Your (but) speak- against princes sat Also
.laws servant ;ing me

25 עֵדֹתֶיךָ שַׁעֲשֻׁעָי אַנְשֵׁי עֲצָתִי׃ דָּבְקָה לֶעָפָר נַפְשִׁי
My the to clings my men my (are) Your
;soul dust .counsel of ,delight testimonies

26 חַיֵּנִי כִּדְבָרֶךָ׃ דְּרָכַי סִפַּרְתִּי וַתַּעֲנֵנִי לַמְּדֵנִי חֻקֶּיךָ׃
Your teach You and have I my to according me give
.statutes me ;me answered ,declared ways word Your life

27 דֶּרֶךְ־פִּקּוּדֶיךָ הֲבִינֵנִי וְאָשִׂיחָה בְּנִפְלְאוֹתֶיךָ׃ דָּלְפָה
28 drops Your on will I and me make Your way The
.wonders meditate ;understand precepts of

29 נַפְשִׁי מִתּוּגָה קַיְּמֵנִי כִּדְבָרֶךָ׃ דֶּרֶךְ־שֶׁקֶר הָסֵר מִמֶּנִּי
from Remove lying the to according strengthen (with) My
,me of way .word Your me ;grief soul

30 וְתוֹרָתְךָ חָנֵּנִי׃ דֶּרֶךְ אֱמוּנָה בָחָרְתִּי מִשְׁפָּטֶיךָ שִׁוִּיתִי׃
have I Your have I truth way the favor with and
;level held judgments ;chosen of .me law Your

31 דָּבַקְתִּי בְעֵדְוֺתֶיךָ יְהוָה אַל־תְּבִישֵׁנִי׃ דֶּרֶךְ־מִצְוֺתֶיךָ אָרוּץ
32 will I Your the me put do not O Your to have I
,run commands of way .shame to ,Jehovah ;testimonies clung

33 כִּי תַרְחִיב לִבִּי׃ הוֹרֵנִי יְהוָה דֶּרֶךְ חֻקֶּיךָ וְאֶצְּרֶנָּה
will I and Your the O Teach my shall You for
it keep ,statutes of way ,Jehovah ,me .heart enlarge

34 עֵקֶב׃ הֲבִינֵנִי וְאֶצְּרָה תוֹרָתֶךָ וְאֶשְׁמְרֶנָּה בְכָל־לֵב׃
(my) with observe and Your will I and me Make the (to)
.heart whole it ;law keep understand .end

35 הַדְרִיכֵנִי בִּנְתִיב מִצְוֺתֶיךָ כִּי־בוֹ חָפָצְתִּי׃ הַט־לִבִּי אֶל־
36 to my Bow !delight I in for Your the in to me Cause
heart it ,commands of way walk

37 עֵדְוֺתֶיךָ וְאַל אֶל־בָּצַע׃ הַעֲבֵר עֵינַי מֵרְאוֹת שָׁוְא בִּדְרָכֶךָ
Your in ;vanity from my Turn unjust to and Your
way seeing eyes away .gain not ,testimonies

38 חַיֵּנִי׃ הָקֵם לְעַבְדְּךָ אִמְרָתֶךָ אֲשֶׁר לְיִרְאָתֶךָ׃ הַעֲבֵר
39 Turn to (devoted) who Your Your to Make me give
away .fear Your is ,word servant sure .life

40 חֶרְפָּתִי אֲשֶׁר יָגֹרְתִּי כִּי מִשְׁפָּטֶיךָ טוֹבִים׃ הִנֵּה תָּאַבְתִּי
have I ,Behold (are) Your for ;fear I which my
longed .good judgments reproach

41 לְפִקֻּדֶיךָ בְּצִדְקָתְךָ חַיֵּנִי׃ וִיבֹאֻנִי חֲסָדֶךָ יְהוָה
O Your come Let me give Your in Your for
,Jehovah ,mercies me to .life righteousness ,precepts

42 תְּשׁוּעָתְךָ כְּאִמְרָתֶךָ׃ וְאֶעֱנֶה חֹרְפִי דָבָר כִּי־בָטַחְתִּי
trust I for a my will I And to according Your by
;word reprover answer .word Your ,salvation

Your word. [43] And do not take the word of truth completely out of my mouth; for I have hoped in Your judgments. [44] And I shall keep Your law continually, forever and ever. [45] And I will always walk in the wideness, for I seek Your commands. [46] And I will speak of Your testimonies before kings, and will not be ashamed. [47] And I will delight myself in Your commandments, which I have loved. [48] And I will lift up my hands to Your commandments that I love; and I will meditate on Your statutes.

Zain

[49] Remember the word to Your servant, on which You made me hope. [50] This (is) my comfort in my affliction; for Your word has given me life. [51] The proud have scorned me utterly; I have not veered from Your law. [52] I remembered Your judgments from of old, O Jehovah, and I take comfort. [53] Horror has seized me because of the wicked forsaking Your law. [54] Your statutes have been my songs in the house of my pilgrimages. [55] O Jehovah, I have remembered Your name in the night and have kept Your law. [56] This was done to me, because I kept Your commandments.

Cheth

[57] Jehovah (is) my portion; I have said to keep Your words. [58] I looked for Your favor with all (my) heart; favor me according to Your word. [59] I mused on my ways and turned my feet to Your testimonies. [60] I hurried and delayed not to keep Your commands. [61] The cords of the wicked encircled me; I have not forgotten Your law. [62] At halves of the night I will rise to give thanks to You because of Your righteous judgments. [63] I (am) a companion of all who fear You; yea, of those who keep your precepts. [64] O Jehovah, the

43 בִּדְבָרֶךָ׃ וְאַל־תַּצֵּל מִפִּי דְבַר־אֱמֶת עַד־מְאֹד כִּי לְמִשְׁפָּטֶךָ
Your in for very till truth the my from deliver And Your in
judgments ,much of word mouth not .word

44
45 יִחָלְתִּי׃ וְאֶשְׁמְרָה תוֹרָתְךָ תָמִיד לְעוֹלָם וָעֶד׃ וְאֶתְהַלְּכָה
will I And and forever continually Your I And have I
walk .ever law keep shall .hoped

46 בָרְחָבָה כִּי פִקֻּדֶיךָ דָרָשְׁתִּי׃ וַאֲדַבְּרָה בְעֵדֹתֶיךָ נֶגֶד
before Your of will I .seek I Your for the in
testimonies speak commands ,wideness

47 מְלָכִים וְלֹא אֵבוֹשׁ׃ וְאֶשְׁתַּעֲשַׁע בְּמִצְוֺתֶיךָ אֲשֶׁר אָהָבְתִּי׃
have I which Your in will I And be will and ,kings
.loved commands myself delight .ashamed not

48 וְאֶשָּׂא כַפַּי אֶל־מִצְוֺתֶיךָ אֲשֶׁר אָהָבְתִּי וְאָשִׂיחָה בְחֻקֶּיךָ׃
Your on will I and ;love I which Your to my will I and
.statutes meditate commands hands up lift

49
50 זְכָר־דָּבָר לְעַבְדֶּךָ עַל אֲשֶׁר יִחַלְתָּנִי׃ זֹאת נֶחָמָתִי
my This made You which on Your to the Remember
comfort (is) .hope me ,servant word

51 בְעָנְיִי כִּי אִמְרָתְךָ חִיָּתְנִי׃ זֵדִים הֱלִיצֻנִי עַד־מְאֹד מִתּוֹרָתְךָ
Your from very till have The given has Your for my in
law ;much me scorned proud .life me word ,affliction

52 לֹא נָטִיתִי׃ זָכַרְתִּי מִשְׁפָּטֶיךָ מֵעוֹלָם ׀ יְהוָה וָאֶתְנֶחָם׃
take I and O from Your remem- I have I not
.comfort ,Jehovah ,old of judgments bered .veered

53
54 זַלְעָפָה אֲחָזַתְנִי מֵרְשָׁעִים עֹזְבֵי תּוֹרָתֶךָ׃ זְמִרוֹת הָיוּ־לִי
to have Songs Your forsaking of because has Horror
me been .law wicked the me seized

55 חֻקֶּיךָ בְּבֵית מְגוּרָי׃ זָכַרְתִּי בַלַּיְלָה שִׁמְךָ יְהוָה וָאֶשְׁמְרָה
have and O Your the in have I pilgrim- my the in Your
kept ,Jehovah ,name night remembered .ages of house statutes

56
57 תּוֹרָתֶךָ׃ זֹאת הָיְתָה־לִּי כִּי פִקֻּדֶיךָ נָצָרְתִּי׃ חֶלְקִי
my .kept I Your for to was This .law Your
(is) portion commands ,me done

58 יְהוָה אָמַרְתִּי לִשְׁמֹר דְּבָרֶיךָ׃ חִלִּיתִי פָנֶיךָ בְכָל־לֵב
(my) with Your looked I Your keep to have I ;Jehovah
;heart whole favor for .words said

59 חָנֵּנִי כְּאִמְרָתֶךָ׃ חִשַּׁבְתִּי דְרָכָי וָאָשִׁיבָה רַגְלַי אֶל־
to my and my thought I to according favor
feet turned ways on .word Your me

60
61 עֵדֹתֶיךָ׃ חַשְׁתִּי וְלֹא הִתְמַהְמָהְתִּי לִשְׁמֹר מִצְוֺתֶיךָ׃ חֶבְלֵי
cords The Your keep to delay did and hurried I Your
of .commands not .testimonies

62 רְשָׁעִים עִוְּדֻנִי תּוֹרָתְךָ לֹא שָׁכָחְתִּי׃ חֲצוֹת־לַיְלָה אָקוּם
will I the halves (At) have I not Your hemmed the
rise night of .forgotten law ;in me wicked

63 לְהוֹדוֹת לָךְ עַל מִשְׁפְּטֵי צִדְקֶךָ׃ חָבֵר אָנִי לְכָל־אֲשֶׁר
who of I com- a Your judgments because to give to
all (am) panion .righteous of You thanks

64 יְרֵאוּךָ וּלְשֹׁמְרֵי פִּקּוּדֶיךָ׃ חַסְדְּךָ יְהוָה מָלְאָה הָאָרֶץ
the fills O Your Your of and fear
;earth ,Jehovah ,mercy .precepts keeping those ;You

earth is full of Your mercy; teach me Your statutes.

Teth

[65] You have done good with Your servant, O Jehovah, by Your word. [66] Teach me good judgment and knowledge, for I have believed Your commands. [67] Before I was afflicted I went astray; but now I have kept Your word. [68] You (are) good and do good —teach me Your statutes. [69] The proud have forged a lie against me; I will keep Your precepts with all (my) heart. [70] Their heart is as fat, without feeling; I delight in Your law. [71] For my good I was afflicted, to learn Your statutes. [72] The law of Your mouth (is) better to me than thousands of gold and silver.

Jod

[73] Your hands made me and fixed me; give me discernment that I may learn Your commands. [74] The ones fearing You will see me and rejoice; for I hoped in Your word. [75] I know, O Jehovah, Your judgments (are) right; and in fidelity You afflicted me. [76] Let, please, Your mercy be for my comfort, by Your word to Your servant. [77] Let Your mercies come to me that I may live; for Your law (is) my delight. [78] Let the proud be ashamed, for with lies they perverted me; I will muse on Your precepts. [79] Let fearers of You turn to me, and knowers of Your testimonies. [80] Let my heart be blameless in Your statutes, that I may not be ashamed.

Caph

[81] My soul perishes for Your salvation; I hope in Your word. [82] My eyes fail for Your word, saying, When will You comfort me? [83] For I am like a wineskin in the smoke; I do not forget Your statutes. [84] As what (are) the days of Your servant? When will You pass judgment on my persecutors? [85] The proud have dug pits for me which (are) not according to Your law. [86] All Your

65 חֻקֶּיךָ לַמְּדֵנִי׃ טוֹב עָשִׂיתָ עִם־עַבְדְּךָ יְהוָה כִּדְבָרֶךָ׃
to according O Your with You good teach Your
.word Your ,Jehovah ,servant done have .me statutes

66
67 טוּב טַעַם וָדַעַת לַמְּדֵנִי כִּי בְמִצְוֺתֶיךָ הֶאֱמָנְתִּי׃ טֶרֶם
Before have I Your for teach and judgment Good
.believed commandments ,me knowledge

68 אֶעֱנֶה אֲנִי שֹׁגֵג וְעַתָּה אִמְרָתְךָ שָׁמָרְתִּי׃ טוֹב־אַתָּה
You good have I Your but went I was I
(are) .kept word now ,astray afflicted

69 וּמֵטִיב לַמְּדֵנִי חֻקֶּיךָ׃ טָפְלוּ עָלַי שֶׁקֶר זֵדִים אֲנִי בְּכָל־
with I the lie a against Have Your teach do and
whole ;proud me forged .statutes me ;good

70 לֵב ׀ אֶצֹּר פִּקּוּדֶיךָ׃ טָפַשׁ כַּחֵלֶב לִבָּם אֲנִי תּוֹרָתְךָ
Your (but) Their like without is Your will (my)
law I ;heart fat feeling .precepts keep heart

71
72 שִׁעֲשָׁעְתִּי׃ טוֹב־לִי כִי־עֻנֵּיתִי לְמַעַן אֶלְמַד חֻקֶּיךָ׃ טוֹב־
(is) Your might I that so was I that for (is It) take I
better .statutes learn ,afflicted me good in delight

73 לִי תוֹרַת־פִּיךָ מֵאַלְפֵי זָהָב וָכָסֶף׃ יָדֶיךָ עָשׂוּנִי וַיְכוֹנְנוּנִי
made and have Your and gold thou- than Your The to
;stand me me made hands .silver of sands mouth of law me

74 הֲבִינֵנִי וְאֶלְמְדָה מִצְוֺתֶיךָ׃ יְרֵאֶיךָ יִרְאוּנִי וְיִשְׂמָחוּ כִּי
because and see will who They Your may I that me give
;rejoice me You fear .commands learn understanding

75 לִדְבָרְךָ יִחָלְתִּי׃ יָדַעְתִּי יְהוָה כִּי־צֶדֶק מִשְׁפָּטֶיךָ וֶאֱמוּנָה
in and Your (are) that O ,know I have I Your for
fidelity ;judgments righteous ,Jehovah .hoped word

76
77 עִנִּיתָנִי׃ יְהִי־נָא חַסְדְּךָ לְנַחֲמֵנִי כְּאִמְרָתְךָ לְעַבְדֶּךָ׃ יְבֹאוּנִי
come Let Your to to according my for Your beg I Let have You
me to .servant word Your ,comfort mercy ,You be .me afflicted

78 רַחֲמֶיךָ וְאֶחְיֶה כִּי־תוֹרָתְךָ שַׁעֲשֻׁעָי׃ יֵבֹשׁוּ זֵדִים כִּי־שֶׁקֶר
lies for the be Let my (is) Your for that so Your
with ,proud ashamed .delight law ;live may I mercies

79 עִוְּתוּנִי אֲנִי אָשִׂיחַ בְּפִקּוּדֶיךָ׃ יָשׁוּבוּ לִי יְרֵאֶיךָ וְיֹדְעוּ עֵדֹתֶיךָ׃
Your ones and fearers to Let Your on will I per- they
.testimonies knowing You of me turn .precepts meditate ;me verted

80
81 יְהִי־לִבִּי תָמִים בְּחֻקֶּיךָ לְמַעַן לֹא אֵבוֹשׁ׃ כָּלְתָה
perishes may I not that so Your in blame- my Let
.ashamed be ,statutes less heart be

82 לִתְשׁוּעָתְךָ נַפְשִׁי לִדְבָרְךָ יִחָלְתִּי׃ כָּלוּ עֵינַי לְאִמְרָתֶךָ
Your for My fail .hope I Your in My Your for
,word eyes word ;soul salvation

83 לֵאמֹר מָתַי תְּנַחֲמֵנִי׃ כִּי־הָיִיתִי כְּנֹאד בְּקִיטוֹר חֻקֶּיךָ לֹא
not Your the in a like am I For You will When ,saying
statutes ;smoke wineskin ?me comfort

84 שָׁכָחְתִּי׃ כַּמָּה יְמֵי־עַבְדֶּךָ מָתַי תַּעֲשֶׂה בְרֹדְפַי מִשְׁפָּט׃
?judgment my on You will When Your the (are) As I do
persecutors pass ?servant of days what .forget

85
86 כָּרוּ־לִי זֵדִים שִׁיחוֹת אֲשֶׁר לֹא כְתוֹרָתֶךָ׃ כָּל־מִצְוֺתֶיךָ
Your All according (are) not which pits The for have
commandments .law Your to proud me dug

commands (are) faithful; lying, they persecute me; help me! [87] They had almost finished me on earth; but I forsook not Your precepts. [88] Give me life according to Your mercy; and I will keep the testimonies of Your mouth.

Lamed

[89] Your word is settled in Heaven forever, O Jehovah. [90] Your fidelity (is) to every generation; You founded the earth, and it stands. [91] They stand by Your judgments to this day for all (are) Your servants. [92] Unless Your law (was) my delight, then I had perished in my grief. [93] I will never forget Your precepts; for with them You gave me life. [94] Yours I (am)—save me; for I have sought Your precepts. [95] The wicked waited for me, to destroy me; I will muse on Your testimonies. [96] I have seen an end to all perfection; Your command (is) exceedingly broad.

Mem

[97] O how I love Your law! It is my meditation all day. [98] You make me wiser than my enemies by Your commands; for they (are) forever mine. [99] I have more wisdom than all my teachers; for Your testimonies (are) a meditation to me. [100] I understand more than the aged, for I keep Your precepts. [101] I have kept my feet from every evil way, to keep Your word [102] I turned not from Your judgments; for You have taught me. [103] How sweet are Your words to my palate! More than honey to my mouth! [104] By Your precepts I know; so then I hate every false way.

Nun

[105] Your word (is) a lamp to my feet and a light to my path. [106] I have sworn and I confirm (it), to keep Your righteous judgments. [107] I am greatly afflicted; O Jehovah, give me life according to Your word. [108] Please, O Jehovah, accept the free offering of my mouth, and teach

87 אמונה שקר רדפוני עזרני: כמעט כלוני בארץ ואני
but on hadThey almost help per- they (with) (are)
I ;earth .me finished !me ;me secute lying ;faithful

88 לא־עזבתי פקודיך: כחסדך חיני ואשמרה עדות פיך:
Your testi- the will I and me give Your By Your did not
.mouth of mony keep ;life mercy .precepts forsake

89
90 לעולם יהוה דברך נצב בשמים: לדר ודר אמונתך
Your (is) gen- and gen- to in is Your O ,Forever
;fidelity eration eration .Heaven settled word ,Jehovah

91 כוננת ארץ ותעמד: למשפטיך עמדו היום כי הכל
all for this to They to according it and the You
;day stand judgments Your ,stands still ,earth founded

92
93 עבדיך: לולי תורתך שעשעי אז אבדתי בעניי: לעולם
Forever my in had I then my (was) Your Unless Your (are)
.grief perished ,delight law .servants

94 לא־אשכח פקודיך כי־בם חייתני: לך־אני הושיעני כי
for ,me save I to gave You with for Your will I not
—(am) You .life me them ;precepts forget

95 פקודיך דרשתי: לי קוו רשעים לאבדני עדתיך אתבונן:
will I Your destroy to The me for have I Your
.consider testimonies ;me wicked waited .sought precepts

96
97 לכל־תכלה ראיתי קץ רחבה מצותך מאד: מה
O exceed- Your (is) an have I perfection to
how .ingly commandment broad ;end seen all

98 אהבתי תורתך כל־היום היא שיחתי: מאיבי תחכמני
make You my than medi- my (is) it the all Your love I
wiser me enemies .tation day !law

99 מצותך כי לעולם היא־לי: מכל־מלמדי השכלתי כי
for more have I my than to they forever for Your by
;understanding teachers all .me (are) ;commands

100 עדותיך שיחה לי: מזקנים אתבונן כי פקודיך נצרתי:
.keep I Your because under- I the than to a (are) Your
precepts ,more stand ancients .me meditation testimonies

101 מכל־ארח רע כלאתי רגלי למען אשמר דברך:
Your might I that my had I evil way From
.word keep ,feet kept every

102
103 ממשפטיך לא־סרתי כי־אתה הורתני: מה־נמלצו לחכי
my to sweet How have You for have I not Your From
palate are .me taught ;turned judgments

104 אמרתך מדבש לפי: מפקודיך אתבונן על־כן שנאתי |
hate I therefore get I Your Through my to than More Your
;understanding precepts !mouth honey !words

105 כל־ארח שקר: נר־לרגלי דברך ואור לנתיבתי:
my to a and Your my to A .false way every
.path light ,(is) word feet lamp

106
107 נשבעתי ואקימה לשמר משפטי צדקך: נעניתי עד־
to am I Your judgments to I and have I
afflicted .righteous observe ,(it) confirm sworn

108 מאד יהוה חיני כדברך: נדבות פי רצה־נא יהוה
O ,please accept My free Your by me give O very
,Jehovah ,mouth's offering .word life ,Jehovah ;much

me Your judgments. [109]
My life (is) in my hand continually, yet I do not forget
Your law. [110] The wick-
ed have laid a snare for me;
yet I do not wander from
Your precepts. [111] I have
inherited Your testimonies
forever; for they (are) the
rejoicing of my heart. [112]
I have bowed my heart to
always do Your statutes to
the end.

Samech

[113] I hate doubting
thoughts; but I love Your
law. [114] You (are) my
covert and my shield; I hope
in Your word. [115] De-
part from me, O evildoers,
for I will keep my God's
commands. [116] Uphold
me by Your word, that I
may live; and let me not be
ashamed of my hope. [117]
Hold me up and I will be
saved; and I will always look
to Your statutes. [118] You
have trampled all who go
astray from Your statutes;
for their deceit is falsehood.
[119] (As) dross You have
made all the wicked of the
earth to cease; so I love
Your testimonies. [120] My
flesh has shivered because
of Your fear; and I have
feared Your judgments.

Ain

[121] I have done the
just and right (thing); do
not leave me to my oppressors. [122] Be surety for
Your servant for good; let
not the proud oppress me.
[123] My eyes fail for Your
salvation, and for the word
of Your righteousness.
[124] Deal with Your ser-
vant by Your mercy; and
teach me Your statutes.
[125] I (am) Your servant;
make me consider and I will
know Your testimonies.
[126] (It is) time for Jehovah to work; they have
broken Your law. [127] So
I have loved Your com-
mands, more than gold,
even fine gold. [128] So
I count wholly right all the
precepts; I have hated
every false way.

Pe

[129] Your testimonies
(are) wondrous; so my soul
keeps them. [130] Your
word entering gives light,
instructing the simple ones.

109 וּמִשְׁפָּטֶיךָ לַמְּדֵנִי: נַפְשִׁי בְכַפִּי תָמִיד וְתוֹרָתְךָ לֹא שָׁכָחְתִּי:

do I / not / Your / yet / contin- / in (is) / My / teach / Your and
.forget / law / .ually hand my / life / .me / judgments

110 111 נָתְנוּ רְשָׁעִים פַּח לִי וּמִפִּקּוּדֶיךָ לֹא תָעִיתִי: נָחַלְתִּי עֵדְוֹתֶיךָ

Your / have I / do I / not / Your from / yet for / a / The / have
testimonies inherited / .wander / precepts / ;me snare / wicked / laid

112 לְעוֹלָם כִּי־שְׂשׂוֹן לִבִּי הֵמָּה: נָטִיתִי לִבִּי לַעֲשׂוֹת חֻקֶּיךָ

Your / do to / my / have I / they / my / the / for / ;forever
statutes / heart / bowed / .(are) / heart of rejoicing

113 לְעוֹלָם עֵקֶב: סֵעֲפִים שָׂנֵאתִי וְתוֹרָתְךָ אָהָבְתִּי:

.love I / Your but / ,hate I / doubting / the to / always
law / thoughts / .end

114 115 סִתְרִי וּמָגִנִּי אָתָּה לִדְבָרְךָ יִחָלְתִּי: סוּרוּ מִמֶּנִּי מְרֵעִים

O / from / Depart / .hope I / Your in / You / my and / my
,evildoers / me / word / ;(are) / shield / covert

116 וְאֶצְּרָה מִצְוֹת אֱלֹהָי: סָמְכֵנִי כְאִמְרָתְךָ וְאֶחְיֶה וְאַל־

and / I that / to according / Uphold / my / com- / the / will I for
not / ;live may / word Your / me / .God / of mands / keep

117 תְּבִישֵׁנִי מִשִּׂבְרִי: סָעֲדֵנִי וְאִוָּשֵׁעָה וְאֶשְׁעָה בְחֻקֶּיךָ תָמִיד:

.always / Your to / I and / will I and / me Hold / my of / be me let
statutes / look will / ;saved be / up / .hope / ashamed

118 119 סָלִיתָ כָּל־שׁוֹגִים מֵחֻקֶּיךָ כִּי־שֶׁקֶר תַּרְמִיתָם: סִגִים

(Like) / their / (is) / for / Your from / who / all / have You
,dross / .deceit / falsehood / ;statutes / astray go / trampled

120 הִשְׁבַּתָּ כָל־רִשְׁעֵי־אָרֶץ לָכֵן אָהַבְתִּי עֵדֹתֶיךָ: סָמַר

has / Your / love I / therefore / the / the / all / have You
shivered / .testimonies / ;earth / of wicked / cease made

121 מִפַּחְדְּךָ בְשָׂרִי וּמִמִּשְׁפָּטֶיךָ יָרֵאתִי: עָשִׂיתִי מִשְׁפָּט

(is what) / have I / have I / Your of and / My / of because
just / done / .feared / judgments / ;flesh / fear Your

122 וָצֶדֶק בַּל־תַּנִּיחֵנִי לְעֹשְׁקָי: עֲרֹב עַבְדְּךָ לְטוֹב אַל־יַעַשְׁקֻנִי

let do / not / for / Your for / Be / my to / leave do / not / and
me oppress / ;good / servant surety / .oppressors / me / ;right

123 124 זֵדִים: עֵינַי כָּלוּ לִישׁוּעָתֶךָ וּלְאִמְרַת צִדְקֶךָ: עֲשֵׂה עִם־

with / Deal / Your / the for and / Your for / fail / my / the
.righteousness / of word / ,salvation / eyes / .proud

125 עַבְדְּךָ כְחַסְדֶּךָ וְחֻקֶּיךָ לַמְּדֵנִי: עַבְדְּךָ־אָנִי הֲבִינֵנִי וְאֵדְעָה

I and / me make I / Your / teach / Your and / You by / by
know will / consider ;(am) / servant / .me / statutes / ;mercy / servant

126 127 עֵדֹתֶיךָ: עֵת לַעֲשׂוֹת לַיהוָה הֵפֵרוּ תּוֹרָתֶךָ: עַל־כֵּן

Therefore / Your / have they / for / work to / (is It) / Your
.law / broken / —Jehovah / time / .testimonies

128 אָהַבְתִּי מִצְוֹתֶיךָ מִזָּהָב וּמִפָּז: עַל־כֵּן כָּל־פִּקּוּדֵי כֹל

wholly / the / all / Therefore / fine even / than more / Your / have I
precepts / .gold / ,gold / commands / loved

129 יִשָּׁרְתִּי כָּל־אֹרַח שֶׁקֶר שָׂנֵאתִי: פְּלָאוֹת עֵדְוֹתֶיךָ

Your / (are) / have I / false / way every / count I
;testimonies wonderful / .hated / ;right

130 עַל־כֵּן נְצָרָתַם נַפְשִׁי: פֵּתַח־דְּבָרֶיךָ יָאִיר מֵבִין פְּתָיִם:

the / instruct- / gives / Your / the / my / keeps / therefore
.simple / ing / ,light / word / of entrance / .soul / them

[131] I opened my mouth and panted; for I longed for Your commands. [132] Turn to me and favor me, as is the way of those who love Your name. [133] Fix my steps in Your word; and let no evil rule over me. [134] Redeem me from the oppression of man; and I will keep Your precepts. [135] Make Your face shine on Your servant, and teach me Your statutes. [136] Rivers of waters run down my eyes for they keep not Your law.

Tzaddi

[137] O Jehovah, You (are) righteous, and Your judgments right. [138] You have enjoined righteousness of Your testimonies, and truth exceedingly. [139] My zeal has eaten me up for my enemies have forgotten Your word. [140] Your word (is) pure, and Your servant loves it. [141] I (am) small and despised; I do not forget Your precepts. [142] Your righteousness (is) righteousness forever; and Your law (is) truth. [143] Distress and anguish have found me; Your commands (are) my delight. [144] The righteousness of Your testimonies (is) everlasting; make me know and I will live.

Koph

[145] I creid with (my) whole heart; O Jehovah, answer me; I will keep Your statutes. [146] I cried to You; save me and I will keep Your testimonies. [147] I go before the dawn of day and cry; I hope in Your word. [148] My eyes go before the (night) watches, to meditate on Your word. [149] Hear my voice by Your mercy, O Jehovah; give me life by Your judgment. [150] The pursuers of mischief draw near; they are far from Your law. [151] You (are) near, O Jehovah, and all Your commands (are) truth. [152] Of old I have known from Your testimonies, for You have founded them forever

Resh

[153] Look on my affliction and deliver me, for I do not forget Your law. [154] Plead my cause and

131 132 פִּֽי־פָעַרְתִּי וָאֶשְׁאָפָה כִּי לְמִצְוֺתֶיךָ יָאָבְתִּי׃ פְּנֵה־אֵלַי
to Turn .longed I Your for for and I My
me commands ;panted opened mouth

133 וְחָנֵּנִי כְּמִשְׁפָּט לְאֹהֲבֵי שְׁמֶךָ׃ פְּעָמַי הָכֵן בְּאִמְרָתֶךָ וְאַל־
and Your in Fix my Your those to the is as and
not ;word steps .name love who manner ;me favor

134 תַּשְׁלֶט־בִּי כָל־אָוֶן׃ פְּדֵנִי מֵעֹשֶׁק אָדָם וְאֶשְׁמְרָה פִּקּוּדֶיךָ׃
Your I and ;man the from Redeem .evil any over let do
.precepts keep will of oppression me me rule

135 136 פָּנֶיךָ הָאֵר בְּעַבְדֶּךָ וְלַמְּדֵנִי אֶת־חֻקֶּיךָ׃ פַּלְגֵי־מַיִם יָרְדוּ
run water Rivers Your teach and Your on make Your
down of .statutes me ,servant shine face

137 עֵינָי עַל לֹא־שָׁמְרוּ תוֹרָתֶךָ׃ צַדִּיק אַתָּה יְהוָה וְיָשָׁר
(are) and O You righteous Your do not because my
right ;Jehovah ,(are) .law keep they ,eyes

138 139 מִשְׁפָּטֶיךָ׃ צִוִּיתָ צֶדֶק עֵדֹתֶיךָ וֶאֱמוּנָה מְאֹד׃ צִמְּתַתְנִי
eaten has exceed- and Your righteous- have You Your
up me .ingly truth ,testimonies of ness enjoined .judgments

140 קִנְאָתִי כִּי־שָׁכְחוּ דְבָרֶיךָ צָרָי׃ צְרוּפָה אִמְרָתְךָ מְאֹד
,very Your pure (is) my Your have for My
word .enemies word forgotten ,zeal

141 וְעַבְדְּךָ אֲהֵבָהּ׃ צָעִיר אָנֹכִי וְנִבְזֶה פִּקֻּדֶיךָ לֹא שָׁכָחְתִּי׃
do I not Your and (am) I small loves Your and
.forget precepts ,despised .it servant

142 143 צִדְקָתְךָ צֶדֶק לְעוֹלָם וְתוֹרָתְךָ אֱמֶת׃ צַר־וּמָצוֹק מְצָאוּנִי
have and Distress (is) Your and ;forever righ- (is) righ- Your
;me found anguish .truth law teousness teousness

144 מִצְוֺתֶיךָ שַׁעֲשֻׁעָי׃ צֶדֶק עֵדְוֺתֶיךָ לְעוֹלָם הֲבִינֵנִי וְאֶחְיֶה׃
will I and me make ever- (is) Your right- the my (are) Your
live understand ;lasting testimonies of ness .delight commands

145 146 קָרָאתִי בְכָל־לֵב עֲנֵנִי יְהוָה חֻקֶּיךָ אֶצֹּרָה׃ קְרָאתִיךָ
cried I will I Your O answer (my) with cried I
;You to .keep statutes ;Jehovah ,me ;heart whole

147 הוֹשִׁיעֵנִי וְאֶשְׁמְרָה עֵדֹתֶיךָ׃ קִדַּמְתִּי בַנֶּשֶׁף וָאֲשַׁוֵּעָה
;cry and dawning the go I Your I and me save
day the of before .testimonies keep will

148 לִדְבָרְיךָ יִחָלְתִּי׃ קִדְּמוּ עֵינַי אַשְׁמֻרוֹת לָשִׂיחַ בְּאִמְרָתֶךָ׃
Your in to (night) the My go .hope I Your in
.word meditate ,watches eyes before word

149 150 קוֹלִי שִׁמְעָה כְחַסְדֶּךָ יְהוָה כְּמִשְׁפָּטֶךָ חַיֵּנִי׃ קָרְבוּ רֹדְפֵי
pur- the Draw me give Your by O Your by Hear my
of suers near .life judgment ,Jehovah ,mercy voice

151 זִמָּה מִתּוֹרָתְךָ רָחָקוּ׃ קָרוֹב אַתָּה יְהוָה וְכָל־מִצְוֺתֶיךָ
Your and O You near they Your from mis-
commands all ,Jehovah ,(are) .far are law ;chief

152 אֱמֶת׃ קֶדֶם יָדַעְתִּי מֵעֵדֹתֶיךָ כִּי לְעוֹלָם יְסַדְתָּם׃
have You forever for Your from have I Of (are)
.them founded ;testimonies known old .truth

153 154 רְאֵה־עָנְיִי וְחַלְּצֵנִי כִּי־תוֹרָתְךָ לֹא שָׁכָחְתִּי׃ רִיבָה רִיבִי
my Plead do I not Your for and my Look
cause .forget law ;me deliver affliction on

redeem me; give me life according to Your word. [155] Salvation (is) far from the wicked; for they do not seek Your statutes. [156] O Jehovah, Your tender mercies (are) great; give me life according to Your judgments. [157] My persecutors and enemies (are) many; I do not turn from Your testimonies. [158] I saw the traitors and was grieved, because they did not keep Your word. [159] See how I love Your precepts, O Jehovah; give me life according to Your mercy. [160] The sum of Your word (is) true; every one of Your righteous judgments (endures) forever.

Schin

[161] Princes have persecuted me without cause; but my heart has feared at Your word. [162] I rejoice at Your word, as one who finds great spoil. [163] I hate and despise lying; (but) I love Your law. [164] I praise You seven (times) a day because of Your righteous judgments. [165] Great peace (is) to those who love Your law, and no stumbling-block is to them. [166] O Jehovah, I have hoped for Your salvation, and have done Your precepts. [167] My soul has kept Your testimonies; and I love them greatly. [168] I have kept Your commands and Your testimonies; for all my ways are before You.

Tau

[169] Let my cry come near You, O Jehovah; give me wisdom according to Your word. [170] Let my prayer come before You; deliver me according to Your word. [171] My lips shall utter praise, when You have taught me Your statutes. [172] My tongue shall answer Your word; for all Your commands (are) righteousness. [173] Let Your hand help me; for I have chosen Your precepts. [174] I have longed for

וּגְאָלֵנִי לְאִמְרָתְךָ חַיֵּנִי׃ רָחוֹק מֵרְשָׁעִים יְשׁוּעָה כִּי־חֻקֶּיךָ
Your for ;salvation the from Far (is) me give Your by re- and
statutes wicked ,life word ;me deem

156 157 לֹא דָרָשׁוּ׃ רַחֲמֶיךָ רַבִּים ׀ יְהוָה כְּמִשְׁפָּטֶיךָ חַיֵּנִי׃ רַבִּים
(are) me give to according O (are) Your they do not
many .life judgments Your ;Jehovah ,great mercies .seek

158 רֹדְפַי וְצָרָי מֵעֵדְוֹתֶיךָ לֹא נָטִיתִי׃ רָאִיתִי בֹגְדִים וָאֶתְקוֹטָטָה
was and the saw I do I not Your from my and per- My
;grieved traitors .turn testimonies ;enemies secutors

159 אֲשֶׁר אִמְרָתְךָ לֹא שָׁמָרוּ׃ רְאֵה כִּי־פִקּוּדֶיךָ אָהָבְתִּי
,love I Your how See they not word Your because
precepts .keep did

160 יְהוָה כְּחַסְדְּךָ חַיֵּנִי׃ רֹאשׁ־דְּבָרְךָ אֱמֶת וּלְעוֹלָם כָּל־
every and true (is) Your sum The me give Your by O
of one forever word of .life mercy ;Jehovah

161 מִשְׁפַּט צִדְקֶךָ׃ שָׂרִים רְדָפוּנִי חִנָּם וּמִדְּבָרְיךָ פָּחַד
has Your at but without per- have Princes Your judgments
feared word ;cause me secuted .righteous

162 163 לִבִּי׃ שָׂשׂ אָנֹכִי עַל־אִמְרָתֶךָ כְּמוֹצֵא שָׁלָל רָב׃ שֶׁקֶר
lying .great spoil one as Your at I rejoice my
finds who word .heart

164 שָׂנֵאתִי וַאֲתַעֵבָה תּוֹרָתְךָ אָהָבְתִּי׃ שֶׁבַע בַּיּוֹם הִלַּלְתִּיךָ
praise I a in Seven .love I Your (but) ;despise and hate I
You day (times) law

165 עַל מִשְׁפְּטֵי צִדְקֶךָ׃ שָׁלוֹם רָב לְאֹהֲבֵי תוֹרָתֶךָ וְאֵין לָמוֹ
for and Your those to Great peace Your judgments for
them (is) not ,law love who (is) .righteous

166 167 מִכְשׁוֹל׃ שִׂבַּרְתִּי לִישׁוּעָתְךָ יְהוָה וּמִצְוֹתֶיךָ עָשִׂיתִי׃ שָׁמְרָה
kept has have I Your and O Your for have I an
.done commands ,Jehovah ,salvation hoped .obstacle

168 נַפְשִׁי עֵדֹתֶיךָ וָאֹהֲבֵם מְאֹד׃ שָׁמַרְתִּי פִקּוּדֶיךָ וְעֵדֹתֶיךָ כִּי
for Your and Your have I very I and Your My
;testimonies precepts kept .much them love ;testimonies soul

169 כָל־דְּרָכַי נֶגְדֶּךָ׃ תִּקְרַב רִנָּתִי לְפָנֶיךָ יְהוָה כִּדְבָרְךָ
Your by O You to cry my come Let are my all
word ;Jehovah near .You before ways

170 171 הֲבִינֵנִי׃ תָּבוֹא תְּחִנָּתִי לְפָנֶיךָ כְּאִמְרָתְךָ הַצִּילֵנִי׃ תַּבַּעְנָה
shall deliver to according before my Let me give
utter .me word Your ;You prayer come .wisdom

172 שְׂפָתַי תְּהִלָּה כִּי תְלַמְּדֵנִי חֻקֶּיךָ׃ תַּעַן לְשׁוֹנִי אִמְרָתֶךָ כִּי
for Your My shall Your have You when ,praise My
;word tongue answer .statutes me taught lips

173 כָל־מִצְוֹתֶיךָ צֶּדֶק׃ תְּהִי־יָדְךָ לְעָזְרֵנִי כִּי פִקּוּדֶיךָ בָחָרְתִּי׃
have I Your for help Your Let righ- (are) Your all
.chosen precepts ,me hand .teousness commands

174 תָּאַבְתִּי לִישׁוּעָתְךָ יְהוָה וְתוֹרָתְךָ שַׁעֲשֻׁעָי׃ תְּחִי־נַפְשִׁי
my Let my (is) Your and O Your for have I
soul live .delight law ;Jehovah ,salvation longed

Your salvation, O Jehovah; and Your law (is) my delight. [175] Let my soul live and it will praise You; and let Your judgments help me. [176] I have gone astray like a lost sheep; seek Your servant; for I do not forget Your commandments.

176 וּתְהַלְלֶךָּ וּמִשְׁפָּטֶךָ יַעֲזְרֻנִי׃ תָּעִיתִי כְּשֶׂה אֹבֵד בַּקֵּשׁ
seek ;lost a like have I help Let Your and shall and
sheep astray gone .me judgments ;You praise

עַבְדֶּךָ כִּי מִצְוֺתֶיךָ לֹא שָׁכָחְתִּי׃
do I not Your for Your
.forget commands ;servant

PSAL. CXX קכ

PSALM 120

A Song of Ascents.

[1] In my trouble I cried to Jehovah, and He heard me. [2] O Jehovah, deliver my soul from lying lips, from a deceitful tongue. [3] What shall be given to you; or what shall (one) add to you, O false tongue? [4] Sharp arrows of the mighty, with coals of broom! [5] Woe is me that I sojourn in Mesech; I dwell with the tents of Kedar! [6] My soul has long dwelt to itself, with him who hates peace. [7] I (am for) peace; but when I speak, they (are) for war.

1 2 שִׁיר הַמַּעֲלוֹת אֶל־יְהוָה בַּצָּרָתָה לִּי קָרָאתִי וַיַּעֲנֵנִי׃ יְהוָה
O He and ,cried I me to the in Jehovah To .ascents A
,Jehovah .me heard trouble of song

3 הַצִּילָה נַפְשִׁי מִשְּׂפַת־שֶׁקֶר מִלָּשׁוֹן רְמִיָּה׃ מַה־יִּתֵּן לְךָ
to shall What .deceitful a from ,lying lips from soul my deliver
,you given be tongue

4 וּמַה־יֹּסִיף לָךְ לָשׁוֹן רְמִיָּה׃ חִצֵּי גִבּוֹר שְׁנוּנִים עִם גַּחֲלֵי
coals with ,Sharp the arrows ?false O to (one) shall or
of mighty of tongue ,you add what

5 רְתָמִים׃ אוֹיָה־לִי כִּי־גַרְתִּי מֶשֶׁךְ שָׁכַנְתִּי עִם־אָהֳלֵי קֵדָר׃
!Kedar the with dwell I ;Meshech I that is Woe !broom
of tents in sojourned ,me

6 7 רַבַּת שָׁכְנָה־לָּהּ נַפְשִׁי עִם שׂוֹנֵא שָׁלוֹם׃ אֲנִי־שָׁלוֹם וְכִי
but ,peace I .peace him with my to has Long
when (for am) hates who soul itself dwelt

אֲדַבֵּר הֵמָּה לַמִּלְחָמָה׃
.war for they ,speak I
(are)

PSAL. CXXI קכא

PSALM 121

A Song of Ascents.

[1] I will lift up my eyes to the hills; where shall my help come from? [2] My help (comes) from Jehovah, the Maker of the heavens and earth.

[3] He will not give your foot to slip; He who keeps you will not slumber. [4] Behold, He who keeps Israel shall not slumber nor sleep! [5] Jehovah (is) your keeper; Jehovah (is) your shade on your right hand. [6] The sun shall not strike you by day, nor the moon by night; [7] Jehovah shall keep you from all evil; He shall keep your soul. [8] Jehovah shall keep your going out and your coming in; from now on and till forever.

1 שִׁיר לַמַּעֲלוֹת אֶשָּׂא עֵינַי אֶל־הֶהָרִים מֵאַיִן יָבֹא עֶזְרִי׃
my shall from the to my will I .ascents song A
?help come where ;hills eyes up lift of

2 3 עֶזְרִי מֵעִם יְהוָה עֹשֵׂה שָׁמַיִם וָאָרֶץ׃ אַל־יִתֵּן לַמּוֹט רַגְלֶךָ
your slip to He not the and the the ,Jehovah (comes) My
;foot give will .earth heavens of Maker from help

4 אַל־יָנוּם שֹׁמְרֶךָ׃ הִנֵּה לֹא־יָנוּם וְלֹא יִישָׁן שׁוֹמֵר יִשְׂרָאֵל׃
!Israel who He sleep nor not shall ,Behold who He will not
keeps slumber .you keeps slumber

5 6 יְהוָה שֹׁמְרֶךָ יְהוָה צִלְּךָ עַל־יַד יְמִינֶךָ׃ יוֹמָם הַשֶּׁמֶשׁ
sun The day by your hand on your Jehovah Your Jehovah
.right shade (is) ;keeper (is)

7 לֹא־יַכֶּכָּה וְיָרֵחַ בַּלָּיְלָה׃ יְהוָה יִשְׁמָרְךָ מִכָּל־רָע יִשְׁמֹר
shall He ;evil from shall Jehovah ;night by the nor shall not
keep all you keep moon ,you strike

8 אֶת־נַפְשֶׁךָ׃ יְהוָה יִשְׁמָר־צֵאתְךָ וּבוֹאֶךָ מֵעַתָּה וְעַד־עוֹלָם׃
.forever and from your and your shall Jehovah your
till on now ;in coming out going keep .soul

PSAL. CXXII קכב

PSALM 122

PSALM 122

A Song of Ascents, of David.
[1] I was glad when they said to me, Let us go into the house of Jehovah. [2] Our feet shall stand within your gates, O Jerusalem. [3] Jerusalem is built like a city that (is) joined to itself together; [4] where the tribes go up, the tribes of Jehovah; to the testimony of Israel; to give thanks to the name of Jehovah. [5] For the thrones of judgment were established there, the thrones of the house of David. [6] Pray for the peace of Jerusalem: those who love you shall prosper. [7] Peace be within your walls; prosperity in your towers. [8] Because of my brothers' and companions' sake, I will now say, Peace (be) in you. [9] Because of the house of Jehovah, our God, I will seek your good.

1 שִׁיר הַמַּעֲלוֹת לְדָוִד שָׂמַחְתִּי בְּאֹמְרִים לִי בֵּית יְהוָה נֵלֵךְ׃
us let Jehovah the to they when was I Of .ascents song A
.into go of house me said glad .David of

2 עֹמְדוֹת הָיוּ רַגְלֵינוּ בִּשְׁעָרַיִךְ יְרוּשָׁלָםִ׃
3 יְרוּשָׁלַםִ הַבְּנוּיָה
built is Jerusalem O within Our are standing
.Jerusalem ,gates Your feet

4 כְּעִיר שֶׁחֻבְּרָה־לָּהּ יַחְדָּו׃ שֶׁשָּׁם עָלוּ שְׁבָטִים שִׁבְטֵי־יָהּ
,Jah the the up go where ;together to (is) that a like
of tribes ,tribes itself joined city

5 עֵדוּת לְיִשְׂרָאֵל לְהֹדוֹת לְשֵׁם יְהוָה׃ כִּי שָׁמָּה ׀ יָשְׁבוּ
were there For .Jehovah the to give to ,Israel to testi- a
set of name thanks mony

6 כִסְאוֹת לְמִשְׁפָּט כִּסְאוֹת לְבֵית דָּוִד׃ שַׁאֲלוּ שְׁלוֹם יְרוּשָׁלָםִ
;Jerusalem the Pray .David the the ,judgment the
of peace for of house of thrones thrones

7 יִשְׁלָיוּ אֹהֲבָיִךְ׃ יְהִי־שָׁלוֹם בְּחֵילֵךְ שַׁלְוָה בְּאַרְמְנוֹתָיִךְ׃
your in prosperity within peace May who those shall
.towers ,walls your be .you love prosper

8 לְמַעַן אַחַי וְרֵעָי אֲדַבְּרָה־נָּא שָׁלוֹם בָּךְ׃
9 לְמַעַן בֵּית־יְהוָה
,Jehovah the Because (be) peace ,now will I my and my Because
of house of .you in say ,companions brothers of

אֱלֹהֵינוּ אֲבַקְשָׁה טוֹב לָךְ׃
.your good will I ,God our
seek

PSAL. CXXIII קכג

PSALM 123

PSALM 123

A Song of Ascents.
[1] I will lift up my eyes to You, O Dweller in the heavens. [2] Behold, as the eyes of servants (look) to the hand of their masters; as the eye of a maiden to the hand of her mistress; so our eyes (wait) on Jehovah our God, until He favors us. [3] Favor us, O Jehovah; favor us; for we are exceedingly filled with scorn. [4] Our soul is exceedingly filled for itself (with) the contempt of those at ease, with the scorning of the proud.

1 שִׁיר הַמַּעֲלוֹת אֵלֶיךָ נָשָׂאתִי אֶת־עֵינַי הַיֹּשְׁבִי בַּשָּׁמָיִם׃
the in who You ,eyes my will I You To .ascents A
.heavens dwell up lift of song

2 הִנֵּה כְעֵינֵי עֲבָדִים אֶל־יַד אֲדוֹנֵיהֶם כְּעֵינֵי שִׁפְחָה אֶל־יַד
the to maiden a the as their the (look) servants the as ,Behold
of hand of eyes ;masters of hand to of eyes

3 גְּבִרְתָּהּ כֵּן עֵינֵינוּ אֶל־יְהוָה אֱלֹהֵינוּ עַד שֶׁיְּחָנֵּנוּ׃ חָנֵּנוּ יְהוָה
O Favor He until our Jehovah (wait) our so her
;Jehovah ,us .us favors God on eyes ,mistress

4 חָנֵּנוּ כִּי־רַב שָׂבַעְנוּ בוּז׃ רַבַּת שָׂבְעָה־לָּהּ נַפְשֵׁנוּ הַלַּעַג
the soul Our for is exceedingly .scorn are we exceed- for favor
of contempt itself filled with filled ingly ;us

הַשַּׁאֲנַנִּים הַבּוּז לִגְאֵיוֹנִים׃
the the are who those
.proud of scorn ,ease at

PSAL. CXXIV קכד

PSALM 124

PSALM 124

A Song of Ascents, of David.
[1] Except that had not been Jehovah who was for

1 שִׁיר הַמַּעֲלוֹת לְדָוִד לוּלֵי יְהוָה שֶׁהָיָה לָנוּ יֹאמַר־נָא
O may for who Jehovah Except Of .ascents A
say ,us was that .David of song

us, O may Israel say; [2] except that (it was) Jehovah who was for us when men rose up against us, [3] then they would have swallowed us alive; when their anger burned against us. [4] Then the waters would have flowed over us; the torrent would have covered our soul; [5] then the raging waters would have passed over our soul. [6] Blessed (be) Jehovah who did not give us (as) a prey to their teeth! [7] Our soul has escaped like a bird out of the snare of the fowlers; the snare is broken and we have escaped. [8] Our help (is) in the name of Jehovah, the Maker of the heavens and earth.

2 3 יִשְׂרָאֵל׃ לוּלֵא יְהוָה שֶׁהָיָה לָנוּ בְּקוּם עָלֵינוּ אָדָם׃ אֲזַי

then ,men against us the in of rising for us who was Jehovah Except that ;Israel

4 חַיִּים בְּלָעוּנוּ בַּחֲרוֹת אַפָּם בָּנוּ׃ אֲזַי הַמַּיִם שְׁטָפוּנוּ נַחְלָה

the stream over- ;us flowed had the waters Then against .us their anger being in angry had they ;us swallowed alive

5 עָבַר עַל־נַפְשֵׁנוּ׃ אֲזַי עָבַר עַל־נַפְשֵׁנוּ הַמַּיִם הַזֵּידוֹנִים׃

.raging waters the soul our over had passed then ;soul our over had passed

6 7 בָּרוּךְ יְהוָה שֶׁלֹּא נְתָנָנוּ טֶרֶף לְשִׁנֵּיהֶם׃ נַפְשֵׁנוּ כְּצִפּוֹר

a like bird soul Our their to !teeth a (as) prey give did us who not Jehovah Blessed (be)

8 נִמְלְטָה מִפַּח יוֹקְשִׁים הַפַּח נִשְׁבָּר וַאֲנַחְנוּ נִמְלָטְנוּ׃ עֶזְרֵנוּ

Our help have .escaped we and is broken the snare the ;fowlers the from of snare has escaped

בְּשֵׁם יְהוָה עֹשֵׂה שָׁמַיִם וָאָרֶץ׃

and .earth the heavens the of Maker Jehovah's in (is) name

PSAL. CXXV קכה

PSALM 125

PSALM 125

A Song of Ascents.

[1] They who trust in Jehovah (shall be) like Mount Zion; it is not shaken; it remains forever. [2] The mountains (are) all around Jerusalem, and Jehovah (is) all around His people from this time and forever. [3] For the scepter of the wicked shall not rest on the lot of the righteous; that not the righteous put forth their hands to iniquity. [4] Do good, O Jehovah, to the good; and to the upright in their heart. [5] And those who turn aside to their crooked ways, Jehovah shall lead them with the evildoers. Peace (be) upon Israel.

1 שִׁיר הַמַּעֲלוֹת הַבֹּטְחִים בַּיהוָה כְּהַר־צִיּוֹן לֹא־יִמּוֹט

is it ;shaken not ;Zion (be shall) Mount like in Jehovah who They trust .ascents song A of

2 לְעוֹלָם יֵשֵׁב׃ יְרוּשָׁלִַם הָרִים סָבִיב לָהּ וַיהוָה סָבִיב

all is around and Jehovah to ;her all are around the mountains ,Jerusalem it .remains forever

3 לְעַמּוֹ מֵעַתָּה וְעַד־עוֹלָם׃ כִּי לֹא יָנוּחַ שֵׁבֶט הָרֶשַׁע עַל

on the wicked the of rod shall rest not For .forever and to this from time His people

גּוֹרַל הַצַּדִּיקִים לְמַעַן לֹא־יִשְׁלְחוּ הַצַּדִּיקִים ׀ בְּעַוְלָתָה

iniquity to the righteous put forth not that the ;righteous the of lot

4 יְדֵיהֶם׃ הֵיטִיבָה יְהוָה לַטּוֹבִים וְלִישָׁרִים בְּלִבּוֹתָם׃

their in .hearts the to and upright the to ,good O ,Jehovah ,good Do their .hands

5 וְהַמַּטִּים עֲקַלְקַלּוֹתָם יוֹלִיכֵם יְהוָה אֶת־פֹּעֲלֵי הָאָוֶן שָׁלוֹם

peace ;evil the of workers with Jehovah lead shall them crooked their ,ways those And incline who

עַל־יִשְׂרָאֵל׃

.Israel (be) upon

PSAL. CXXVI

PSALM 126

PSALM 126

A Song of Ascents.

[1] When Jehovah turned back to the captivity of Zion, we were like those who dream. [2] Then our mouth was full of laughter, and our tongue (with) singing; then they said among

1 שִׁיר הַמַּעֲלוֹת בְּשׁוּב יְהוָה אֶת־שִׁיבַת צִיּוֹן הָיִינוּ כְּחֹלְמִים׃

those like .dream who we were ,Zion the of captivity Jehovah the In of turning .ascents song A of

2 אָז יִמָּלֵא שְׂחוֹק פִּינוּ וּלְשׁוֹנֵנוּ רִנָּה אָז יֹאמְרוּ בַגּוֹיִם הִגְדִּיל

great the in nations they said then with ;singing our and tongue our ,mouth laughter was Then of full

the nations, Jehovah (wills) to work with these. [3] Jehovah (did) great with these —Jehovah (did) great to work with us; we are glad, [4] Turn again, O Jehovah, her captivity, like the south streams. [5] Those who sow in tears shall reap with joyful shouting. [6] Surely (he who) walks and weeps bearing a bag of seed shall come again with rejoicing, bringing his sheaves.

3 יְהוָה לַעֲשׂוֹת עִם־אֵלֶּה׃ הִגְדִּיל יְהוָה לַעֲשׂוֹת עִמָּנוּ הָיִינוּ
we with work to Jehovah Great .these with work to Jehovah
are ;us things

4
5 שְׂמֵחִים׃ שׁוּבָה יְהוָה אֶת־שְׁבוּתֵנוּ כַּאֲפִיקִים בַּנֶּגֶב׃
the in the like our O Turn .glad
.south streams ;captivity ,Jehovah ,again

6 הַזֹּרְעִים בְּדִמְעָה בְּרִנָּה יִקְצֹרוּ׃ הָלוֹךְ יֵלֵךְ ׀ וּבָכֹה נֹשֵׂא
bearing and (he) walking shall with ,tears in who Those
,weeps walks ,reap shouting sow

מֶשֶׁךְ־הַזָּרַע בֹּא־יָבֹא בְרִנָּה נֹשֵׂא אֲלֻמֹּתָיו׃
his bearing with come shall the bag a
.sheaves ,rejoicing again seed

PSAL. CXXVII

PSALM 127

PSALM 127

A Song of Ascents for Solomon.

[1] If Jehovah does not build the house, they who build in it labor in vain; if Jehovah does not keep the city, the watchman stays awake in vain. [2] (It is) in vain for you to rise early; to sit up late; to eat the bread of toils; (for) so He gives His beloved sleep. [3] Lo, children (are) the inheritance of Jehovah; the fruit of the womb (is His) reward. [4] As arrows in the hand of a mighty man, so (are) the sons of the young. [5] Blessed is the man who has filled his quiver with them; they shall not be ashamed, for they shall destroy their enemies in the gate.

1 שִׁיר הַמַּעֲלוֹת לִשְׁלֹמֹה אִם־יְהוָה ׀ לֹא־יִבְנֶה בַיִת שָׁוְא
vain in the does not Jehovah If Of .ascents song A
,house build .Solomon of

עָמְלוּ בוֹנָיו בּוֹ אִם־יְהוָה לֹא־יִשְׁמָר־עִיר שָׁוְא ׀ שָׁקַד
stays vain in the does not Jehovah if ;it in its labor
awake ,city keep builders

2 שׁוֹמֵר׃ שָׁוְא לָכֶם ׀ מַשְׁכִּימֵי קוּם מְאַחֲרֵי־שֶׁבֶת אֹכְלֵי לֶחֶם
the to sitting being ,rising being for (is It) the
of bread eat ;up of late of early you vain .keeper

3 הָעֲצָבִים כֵּן יִתֵּן לִידִידוֹ שֵׁנָא׃ הִנֵּה נַחֲלַת יְהוָה בָּנִים
(are) Jehovah the ,Lo .sleep His to He (for) ;toils
;sons of inheritance beloved gives so

4 שָׂכָר פְּרִי הַבָּטֶן׃ כְּחִצִּים בְּיַד־גִּבּוֹר כֵּן בְּנֵי הַנְּעוּרִים׃
the the (so) mighty a in arrows As the the a (is it)
.young of sons (are) ,man's hand .womb of fruit ,reward

5 אַשְׁרֵי הַגֶּבֶר אֲשֶׁר מִלֵּא אֶת־אַשְׁפָּתוֹ מֵהֶם לֹא־יֵבֹשׁוּ כִּי־
for shall they not with his has who the Blessed
,ashamed be ,them quiver filled man (is)

יְדַבְּרוּ אֶת־אוֹיְבִים בַּשָּׁעַר׃
the in their shall they
.gate enemies destroy

PSAL. CXXVIII קכח

PSALM 128

PSALM 128

A Song of Ascents.

[1] Blessed is everyone who fears Jehovah, who walks in His ways. [2] For you shall surely eat the labor of your hands; you (shall be) happy and all (is) good to you. [3] Your wife (shall be) like a fruitful vine by the sides of your house; your sons like olive plants around your table. [4] Behold! So shall the man be blessed who fears Jehovah. [5] Jehovah shall bless you out of Zion; and you shall

1 שִׁיר הַמַּעֲלוֹת אַשְׁרֵי כָּל־יְרֵא יְהוָה הַהֹלֵךְ בִּדְרָכָיו׃
His in who ,Jehovah who every- Blessed .ascents song A
.ways walks fears one (is) of

2
3 יְגִיעַ כַּפֶּיךָ כִּי תֹאכֵל אַשְׁרֶיךָ וְטוֹב לָךְ׃ אֶשְׁתְּךָ ׀ כְּגֶפֶן
like (be) Your to and (shall) you you surely your The
vine a wife .you (is) good happy (be) ;eat shall hands of labor

פֹּרִיָּה בְּיַרְכְּתֵי בֵיתֶךָ בָּנֶיךָ כִּשְׁתִלֵי זֵיתִים סָבִיב לְשֻׁלְחָנֶךָ׃
your around olive like your your the by fruitful
.table plants sons ;house of sides

4 הִנֵּה כִי־כֵן יְבֹרַךְ גָּבֶר יְרֵא יְהוָה׃ יְבָרֶכְךָ יְהוָה מִצִּיּוֹן
of out Jehovah shall .Jehovah who the be shall that so ,Behold
;Zion you bless fears man blessed

see the good of Jerusalem all the days of your life. [6] Yes, you shall see the sons of your sons. Peace (be) upon Israel.

6 וּרְאֵה בְּטוּב יְרוּשָׁלָ͏ִם כֹּל יְמֵי חַיֶּיךָ׃ וּרְאֵה־בָנִים לְבָנֶיךָ

your of the you And your the all Jerusalem the you and
.sons sons see shall .life of days of good see shall

שָׁלוֹם עַל־יִשְׂרָאֵל׃

.Israel upon Peace
(be)

PSAL. CXXIX קכט

PSALM 129

A Song of Ascents.

[1] Many times they have afflicted me from my youth, let Israel now say; [2] they have afflicted me from my youth many times; yet they have not prevailed over me. [3] The plowers plowed on my back; they made their furrows long. [4] Jehovah (is) righteous; He cuts the cords of the wicked in two. [5] Let them all be ashamed and turned back, those who hate Zion; [6] let them be like the grass on the roofs, which dries up before it draws out; [7] with which the reaper does not fill his hand; nor the binder of sheaves his bosom. [8] And those who pass by have never said, The blessing of Jehovah (be) on you; we bless you in the name of Jehovah.

1 שִׁיר הַמַּעֲלוֹת רַבַּת צְרָרוּנִי מִנְּעוּרָי יֹאמַר־נָא יִשְׂרָאֵל׃

;Israel now let my from have they Many .ascents song A
say ,youth me afflicted times of

2
3 רַבַּת צְרָרוּנִי מִנְּעוּרָי גַּם לֹא־יָכְלוּ לִי׃ עַל־גַּבִּי חָרְשׁוּ

plowed my On over they not yet my from have they many
back .me prevailed have ;youth me afflicted times

4 חֹרְשִׁים הֶאֱרִיכוּ לְמַעֲנוֹתָם׃ יְהוָה צַדִּיק קִצֵּץ עֲבוֹת

the cuts He (is) Jehovah their made they the
of cords two in ,righteous .furrows long ;plowers

5
6 רְשָׁעִים׃ יֵבֹשׁוּ וְיִסֹּגוּ אָחוֹר כֹּל שֹׂנְאֵי צִיּוֹן׃ יִהְיוּ כַּחֲצִיר

the like them let ;Zion those all ,back and be Let the
on grass be hate who turned ashamed .wicked

7 גַּגּוֹת שֶׁקַּדְמַת שָׁלַף יָבֵשׁ׃ שֶׁלֹּא מִלֵּא כַפּוֹ קוֹצֵר וְחִצְנוֹ

his nor the his does with dries draws it which the
bosom ;reaper hand fill not which ;up out before ,roofs

8 מְעַמֵּר׃ וְלֹא אָמְרוּ ׀ הָעֹבְרִים בִּרְכַּת־יְהוָה אֲלֵיכֶם בֵּרַכְנוּ

we on (be) Jehovah The who those have And binder the
bless ;you of blessing ;by pass said not .sheaves of

אֶתְכֶם בְּשֵׁם יְהוָה׃

.Jehovah the in you
of name

PSAL. CXXX קל

PSALM 130

A Song of Ascents.

[1] Out of the depths I have called You, O Jehovah. [2] Lord, hear my voice; and let Your ears attend to the voice of my prayers. [3] If You will keep iniquities, O Lord, who shall stand? [4] But forgiveness (is) with You, in order that You may be feared. [5] I wait (for) Jehovah; my soul waits and I hope for His word. [6] My soul (waits) for the Lord more than those who watch for the morning; watching for the morning. [7] Let Israel

1
2 שִׁיר הַמַּעֲלוֹת מִמַּעֲמַקִּים קְרָאתִיךָ יְהוָה׃ אֲדֹנָי שִׁמְעָה

hear ,Lord O have I of Out .ascents song A
.Jehovah ,You called depths the of

3 בְקוֹלִי תִּהְיֶינָה אָזְנֶיךָ קַשֻּׁבוֹת לְקוֹל תַּחֲנוּנָי׃ אִם־עֲוֹנוֹת

iniquities If my the to attentive Your be let my
.prayers of voice ears ,voice

4 תִּשְׁמָר־יָהּ אֲדֹנָי מִי יַעֲמֹד׃ כִּי־עִמְּךָ הַסְּלִיחָה לְמַעַן תִּוָּרֵא׃

may You that (is) with But shall who O O will You
.feared be ,forgiveness You ?stand ,Lord ,Jah ,keep

5
6 קִוִּיתִי יְהוָה קִוְּתָה נַפְשִׁי וְלִדְבָרוֹ הוֹחָלְתִּי׃ נַפְשִׁי לַאדֹנָי

the for soul My .hope I for and my waits ;Jehovah wait I
Lord (waits) word His ,soul (for)

7 מִשֹּׁמְרִים לַבֹּקֶר שֹׁמְרִים לַבֹּקֶר׃ יַחֵל יִשְׂרָאֵל אֶל־יְהוָה

;Jehovah to Israel Let the for watching the for than more
hope .morning ,morning watchers

hope to Jehovah; for with Jehovah (is) mercy; and with Him (is) abundant redemption; [8] and He shall redeem Israel from all his sins.

PSALM 131

A Song of Ascents, of David.

[1] O Jehovah, my heart is not proud; nor have my eyes been lofty; nor have I walked in great things; nor in things too wondrous for me. [2] If not I have set (myself) and have quieted my soul, like one weaned by its mother; my soul on me (is) like one weaned. [3] Let Israel hope in Jehovah from now and till forever.

PSALM 132

A Song of Ascents.

[1] O Jehovah, remember David, (with) all his afflictions; [2] how he swore to Jehovah; he vowed to the Mighty One of Jacob; [3] If I will go into the tent of my house, if I go up on the couch of my bed; [4] if I give sleep to my eyes, slumber to my eyelids; [5] until I search out a place for Jehovah, dwellings for the Mighty One of Jacob. [6] Lo, we have heard of it at Ephratah; we found it in the fields of the forest; [7] we will enter into His tabernacles; we will worship at His footstool. [8] Arise, O Jehovah, into Your rest; You, and the Ark of Your strength; [9] let Your priests be clothed with righteousness; and let Your saints shout for joy. [10] For Your servant David's sake, do not turn away the face of Your anointed. [11] Jehovah has sworn to David (in) truth; He will not turn from it; I will set of the fruit of your

8 כִּֽי־עִם־יְהוָה הַחֶסֶד וְהַרְבֵּה עִמּוֹ פְדוּת׃ וְהוּא יִפְדֶּה אֶת־
will He and ;redemption with and (is) Jehovah with for
redeem Him abundant ;mercy

יִשְׂרָאֵל מִכֹּל עֲוֺנֹתָיו׃
his all from Israel
.iniquities

PSAL. CXXXI קלא

PSALM 131

1 שִׁיר הַֽמַּעֲלוֹת לְדָוִד יְהוָה ׀ לֹא־גָבַהּ לִבִּי וְלֹא־רָמוּ עֵינַי
my been have and my is not O Of .ascents song A
;eyes lofty not ;heart proud ,Jehovah .David of

2 וְלֹא־הִלַּכְתִּי ׀ בִּגְדֹלוֹת וּבְנִפְלָאוֹת מִמֶּנִּי׃ אִם־לֹא שִׁוִּיתִי
have I not If for too things in and great in have I and
set .me wondrous ;things walked not

3 וְדוֹמַמְתִּי נַפְשִׁי כְּגָמֻל עֲלֵי אִמּוֹ כַּגָּמֻל עָלַי נַפְשִׁי׃ יַחֵל
Let my (is) upon the as its by one like my have and
hope .soul me weaned ;mother weaned ,soul quieted

יִשְׂרָאֵל אֶל־יְהוָה מֵעַתָּה וְעַד־עוֹלָם׃
.forever and from Jehovah in Israel
till now

PSAL. CXXXII . קלב

PSALM 132

1 2 שִׁיר הַֽמַּעֲלוֹת זְכוֹר־יְהוָה לְדָוִד אֵת כָּל־עֻנּוֹתוֹ׃ אֲשֶׁר
who his all with for O ,Remember .ascents song A
;afflictions ,David ,Jehovah of

3 נִשְׁבַּע לַיהוָה נָדַר לַאֲבִיר יַעֲקֹב׃ אִם־אָבֹא בְּאֹהֶל בֵּיתִי
my the into will I If .Jacob the to he to swore
,house of tent go of One Mighty vowed ;Jehovah

4 אִם־אֶעֱלֶה עַל־עֶרֶשׂ יְצוּעָי׃ אִם־אֶתֵּן שְׁנָת לְעֵינָי לְעַפְעַפַּי
my to my to sleep give I if ;bed my the on up go I if
eyelids ,eyes of couch

5 תְּנוּמָה׃ עַד־אֶמְצָא מָקוֹם לַיהוָה מִשְׁכָּנוֹת לַאֲבִיר
the for dwellings for place a search I until ;slumber
of One Mighty ,Jehovah out

6 יַעֲקֹב׃ הִנֵּה־שְׁמַעֲנוּהָ בְאֶפְרָתָה מְצָאנוּהָ בִּשְׂדֵי־יָעַר׃
the the in found we at have we ,Lo .Jacob
;forest of fields it ;Ephratah it of heard

7 8 נָבוֹאָה לְמִשְׁכְּנוֹתָיו נִשְׁתַּחֲוֶה לַהֲדֹם רַגְלָיו׃ קוּמָה יְהוָה
O ,Arise his stool at will we His into will we
,Jehovah .foot- worship ;dwellings enter

9 לִמְנוּחָתֶךָ אַתָּה וַאֲרוֹן עֻזֶּךָ׃ כֹּהֲנֶיךָ יִלְבְּשׁוּ־צֶדֶק וַחֲסִידֶיךָ
Your and righ- be let Your Your the and You into Your
saints ;teousness with clothed priests ;strength of Ark ;rest

10 11 יְרַנֵּנוּ׃ בַּעֲבוּר דָּוִד עַבְדֶּךָ אַל־תָּשֵׁב פְּנֵי מְשִׁיחֶךָ׃ נִשְׁבַּע־
has Your the turn do not Your David the For shout
sworn .anointed of face away ,servant of sake .joy for

יְהוָה ׀ לְדָוִד אֱמֶת לֹא־יָשׁוּב מִמֶּנָּה מִפְּרִי בִטְנְךָ אָשִׁית
will I your the Of .it from will He not (in) to Jehovah
set body of fruit turn ;truth David

body on the throne for you. [12] If your sons will keep My covenant and My testimony which I will teach them, their sons shall also sit on your throne till forever. [13] Jehovah has chosen Zion; He has desired (it) for His dwelling-place. [14] This (is) My rest till forever; I will dwell here; for I have desired it. [15] I will surely bless her food; I will satisfy her poor (with) food. [16] And I will clothe her priests (with) salvation; and her saints shall surely shout. [17] I will make the horn of David sprout; I have prepared a lamp for My anointed. [18] I will clothe his enemies (with) shame; but his crown shall shine upon him.

12 לְכִסֵּא־לָךְ׃ אִם־יִשְׁמְרוּ בָנֶיךָ ׀ בְּרִיתִי וְעֵדֹתִי זוֹ אֲלַמְּדֵם

will I which My and My your will If for the on
,them teach testimonies covenant sons keep .you throne

13 גַּם־בְּנֵיהֶם עֲדֵי־עַד יֵשְׁבוּ לְכִסֵּא־לָךְ׃ כִּי־בָחַר יְהוָה

Jehovah has For for the on shall forever till their also
chosen .you throne sit sons

14 בְּצִיּוֹן אִוָּהּ לְמוֹשָׁב לוֹ׃ זֹאת־מְנוּחָתִי עֲדֵי־עַד פֹּה אֵשֵׁב

will I here ;forever till my This to a for has He ;Zion
;dwell rest (is) .Him dwelling (it) desired

15 כִּי אִוִּתִיהָ׃ צֵידָהּ בָּרֵךְ אֲבָרֵךְ אֶבְיוֹנֶיהָ אַשְׂבִּיעַ לָחֶם׃

(with) will I her will I blessing her have I for
.food satisfy poor ;bless food it desired

16 17 וְכֹהֲנֶיהָ אַלְבִּישׁ יֶשַׁע וַחֲסִידֶיהָ רַנֵּן יְרַנֵּנוּ׃ שָׁם ׀ אַצְמִיחַ

make will I There shall shouting her and (with) will I her And
sprout .shout saints ;salvation clothe priests

18 קֶרֶן לְדָוִד עָרַכְתִּי נֵר לִמְשִׁיחִי׃ אוֹיְבָיו אַלְבִּישׁ בֹּשֶׁת

(with) will I his My for lamp a have I of the
;shame clothe enemies .anointed prepared ;David horn

וְעָלָיו יָצִיץ נִזְרוֹ׃

his shall upon but
.crown shine him

PSAL. CXXXIII קלג

PSALM 133

PSALM 133

A Song of Ascents, of David.

[1] See! How good and how pleasant (is) the living of brothers, even in unity! [2] (It is) like the precious oil on the head, that ran down on the beard — Aaron's beard; going down to the mouth of his garments; [3] like the dew of Hermon coming down on the mountains of Zion; for there Jehovah commanded the blessing; life till everlasting.

1 שִׁיר הַמַּעֲלוֹת לְדָוִד הִנֵּה מַה־טּוֹב וּמַה־נָּעִים שֶׁבֶת אַחִים

brothers the (is) pleasant and good How !Behold Of .ascents song A
of living how .David of

2 גַּם־יָחַד׃ כַּשֶּׁמֶן הַטּוֹב ׀ עַל־הָרֹאשׁ יֹרֵד עַל־הַזָּקָן זְקַן

beard the on ran that the on precious like (is It) in even
—beard down ,head oil the !unity

3 אַהֲרֹן שֶׁיֹּרֵד עַל־פִּי מִדּוֹתָיו׃ כְּטַל־חֶרְמוֹן שֶׁיֹּרֵד עַל־הַרְרֵי

the on coming Hermon the like his the to going ,Aaron's
of mountains down of dew ;garments of mouth down

צִיּוֹן כִּי שָׁם ׀ צִוָּה יְהוָה אֶת־הַבְּרָכָה חַיִּים עַד־הָעוֹלָם׃

ever- till life the Jehovah com- there for ;Zion
.lasting ;blessing manded

PSAL. CXXXIV קלד

PSALM 134

PSALM 134

A Song of Ascents.

[1] Behold, bless Jehovah, all servants of Jehovah; who stand in the house of Jehovah at night. [2] Lift up your hands (in) the sanctuary, and bless Jehovah. [3] (May) Jehovah bless you out of Zion, (He) who made the heavens and earth.

1 שִׁיר הַמַּעֲלוֹת הִנֵּה ׀ בָּרְכוּ אֶת־יְהוָה כָּל־עַבְדֵי יְהוָה הָעֹמְדִים

who ;Jehovah servants all ,Jehovah bless ,Behold .ascents song A
stand of of

2 בְּבֵית־יְהוָה בַּלֵּילוֹת׃ שְׂאוּ־יְדֵכֶם קֹדֶשׁ וּבָרְכוּ אֶת־יְהוָה׃

.Jehovah and the (in) your Lift at Jehovah the in
bless ,sanctuary hands up .night of house

3 יְבָרֶכְךָ יְהוָה מִצִּיּוֹן עֹשֵׂה שָׁמַיִם וָאָרֶץ׃

the and the who (He) of out Jehovah Let
.earth heavens made ,Zion you bless

PSAL. CXXXV קלה

PSALM 135

[1] Praise Jehovah! Praise the name of Jehovah; praise, you servants of Jehovah; [2] you who stand in the house of Jehovah, in the courts of the house of our God; [3] praise Jehovah! For Jehovah (is) good! Sing praises to His name, for (it is) delightful. [4] For Jehovah has chosen Jacob to Himself — Israel for His treasure. [5] For I know that Jehovah (is) great, and our Lord (is) above all gods. [6] Every (thing) which Jehovah willed to do, He did, in the heavens and in the earth; and in the seas and all deep places. [7] He causes the vapors to rise from the end of the earth; He makes lightnings for the rain; He brings the wind out of His storehouses; [8] (He) who struck the firstborn of Egypt, from man to animal; [9] (who) sent signs and wonders into your midst, O Egypt, on Pharaoh and on all his servants; [10] who struck great nations, and killed mighty kings; [11] Sihon king of the Amorites; and Og king of Bashan; and all the kingdoms of Canaan. [12] And He gave their land (as) an inheritance, an inheritance to His people Israel. [13] O Jehovah, Your name (endures) forever; O Jehovah, Your memorial (is) from generation and generation. [14] For Jehovah will judge His people; and He will have pity on His servants.

[15] The idols of the nation (are) silver and gold, the work of men's hands; [16] they (have) mouths, but they say nothing; they (have) eyes, but they see nothing; [17] they (have) ears, but they do not hear; yea, there is no breath in their mouths. [18] Those who make them are like them, everyone who is trusting in them. [19] Bless

PSALM 135

1 2 הַלְלוּיָהּ ׀ הַלְלוּ אֶת־שֵׁם יְהוָה הַלְלוּ עַבְדֵי יְהוָה׃ שֶׁעֹמְדִים
who ;Jehovah the Praise ;Jehovah the Praise Praise
stand of servants of name !Jah

3 בְּבֵית יְהוָה בְּחַצְרוֹת בֵּית אֱלֹהֵינוּ׃ הַלְלוּיָהּ כִּי־טוֹב
(is) For praise ;God our the the in ,Jehovah the in
good !Jah of house of courts of house

4 יְהוָה זַמְּרוּ לִשְׁמוֹ כִּי נָעִים׃ כִּי־יַעֲקֹב בָּחַר־לוֹ יָהּ יִשְׂרָאֵל
Israel —Jah for has Jacob For (is it) for His to Sing Jeho-
himself chosen .delightful ,name praises ;vah

5 לִסְגֻלָּתוֹ׃ כִּי אֲנִי יָדַעְתִּי כִּי־גָדוֹל יְהוָה וַאֲדֹנֵינוּ מִכָּל־
above (is) our and ,Jehovah (is) that know I For His for
all Lord great ,treasure

6 אֱלֹהִים׃ כֹּל אֲשֶׁר־חָפֵץ יְהוָה עָשָׂה בַּשָּׁמַיִם וּבָאָרֶץ בַּיַּמִּים
in and in and the in He ,Jehovah willed which Every .gods
;seas the ;earth the heavens ;did do to (thing)

7 וְכָל־תְּהֹמוֹת׃ מַעֲלֶה נְשִׂאִים מִקְצֵה הָאָרֶץ בְּרָקִים לַמָּטָר
the for lightnings the the from the causes He deep and
rain ;earth of end vapors rise to ,places all

8 עָשָׂה מוֹצֵא רוּחַ מֵאוֹצְרוֹתָיו׃ שֶׁהִכָּה בְּכוֹרֵי מִצְרָיִם
,Egypt the who (He) His of out wind (He) He
of firstborn struck ;storehouses brings ;makes

9 מֵאָדָם עַד־בְּהֵמָה׃ שָׁלַח ׀ אוֹתֹת וּמֹפְתִים בְּתוֹכֵכִי מִצְרָיִם
,Egypt O your into and signs (who) ;animal to from
,midst wonders sent man

10 בְּפַרְעֹה וּבְכָל־עֲבָדָיו׃ שֶׁהִכָּה גּוֹיִם רַבִּים וְהָרַג מְלָכִים
kings and great nations who his on and on
killed struck ;servants all Pharaoh

11 עֲצוּמִים׃ לְסִיחוֹן ׀ מֶלֶךְ הָאֱמֹרִי וּלְעוֹג מֶלֶךְ הַבָּשָׁן וּלְכֹל
and ;Bashan king and the king Sihon :mighty
all to of Og ;Amorites of

12 מַמְלְכוֹת כְּנָעַן׃ וְנָתַן אַרְצָם נַחֲלָה נַחֲלָה לְיִשְׂרָאֵל עַמּוֹ׃
His Israel to in- an an (as) their And .Canaan king- the
.people heritance ,inheritance land gave He of doms

13 14 יְהוָה שִׁמְךָ לְעוֹלָם יְהוָה זִכְרְךָ לְדֹר־וָדֹר׃ כִּי־יָדִין יְהוָה
Jehovah will For gen- and gen- from Your O (endures) Your Jeho- O
judge .ation .ation (is) memorial ,Jehovah ;forever name ,vah

15 עַמּוֹ וְעַל־עֲבָדָיו יִתְנֶחָם׃ עֲצַבֵּי הַגּוֹיִם כֶּסֶף וְזָהָב מַעֲשֵׂה
the and (are) the The will He His and His
of work ,gold silver nations of idols .pity have servants on ;people

16 יְדֵי אָדָם׃ פֶּה לָהֶם וְלֹא יְדַבֵּרוּ עֵינַיִם לָהֶם וְלֹא יִרְאוּ׃
they do but to eyes they but they mouths ;men's hands
;see not them (are) ;speak not ,have

17 18 אָזְנַיִם לָהֶם וְלֹא יַאֲזִינוּ אַף אֵין־יֶשׁ־רוּחַ בְּפִיהֶם׃ כְּמוֹהֶם
them Like their in breath there not ,yea do they but to ears
.mouths is ;hear not ,them (are)

19 יִהְיוּ עֹשֵׂיהֶם כֹּל אֲשֶׁר־בֹּטֵחַ בָּהֶם׃ בֵּית יִשְׂרָאֵל בָּרְכוּ
bless ,Israel house O in is who every who are
of .them trusting one ,them make they

Jehovah, O house of Israel; bless Jehovah, O house of Aaron; [20] bless Jehovah, O house of Levi; you who fear Jehovah, bless Jehovah. [21] Blessed (be) Jehovah out of Zion, (He) who dwells at Jerusalem. Praise Jehovah!

אֶת־יְהוָה בֵּית אַהֲרֹן בָּרְכוּ אֶת־יְהוָה׃ בֵּית הַלֵּוִי בָּרְכוּ
bless ,Levi house O ;Jehovah bless Aaron O ,Jehovah
of of house

21 אֶת־יְהוָה יִרְאֵי יְהוָה בָּרְכוּ אֶת־יְהוָה׃ בָּרוּךְ יְהוָה ׀ מִצִּיּוֹן
of out Jehovah Blessed .Jehovah bless ,Jehovah you ,Jehovah
,Zion (be) fear who

שֹׁכֵן יְרוּשָׁלִָם הַלְלוּיָהּ׃
Praise .Jerusalem who
!Jah at dwells

PSAL. CXXXVI קלו

PSALM 136

[1] O give thanks to Jehovah, for (He is) good; for His mercy (endures) forever. [2] O give thanks to the God of gods; for His mercy (endures) forever. [3] O give thanks to the Lord of lords; for His mercy (endures) forever; [4] to Him who alone does great wonders; for His mercy (endures) forever; [5] to Him who by wisdom made the heavens; for His mercy (endures) forever; [6] to Him who spread the earth on the waters; for His mercy (endures) forever; [7] to Him who made great lights; for His mercy (endures) forever; [8] the sun to rule by day; for His mercy (endures) forever; [9] the moon and the stars to rule by night; for His mercy (endures) forever; [10] to Him who struck Egypt in her firstborn; for His mercy (endures) forever; [11] and brought Israel out from among them; for His mercy (endures) forever; [12] with a strong hand and a stretched out arm; for His mercy (endures) forever; [13] who divided the Red Sea into parts; for His mercy (endures) forever; [14] and made Israel go through the middle of it; for His mercy (endures) forever; [15] but shook Pharaoh and his army in the Red Sea; for His mercy (endures) forever; [16] who led His people in the wilderness; for His mercy (endures) forever; [17] to Him

1
2 הוֹדוּ לַיהוָה כִּי־טוֹב כִּי לְעוֹלָם חַסְדּוֹ׃ הוֹדוּ לֵאלֹהֵי
the to give O His (endures) for (is He) for to give O
of God thanks .mercy forever ;good ,Jehovah thanks

3 הָאֱלֹהִים כִּי לְעוֹלָם חַסְדּוֹ׃ הוֹדוּ לַאֲדֹנֵי הָאֲדֹנִים כִּי
for ,Lords the to give O His (endures) for ;Gods
of Lord thanks .mercy forever

4 לְעוֹלָם חַסְדּוֹ׃ לְעֹשֵׂה נִפְלָאוֹת גְּדֹלוֹת לְבַדּוֹ כִּי לְעוֹלָם
(endures) for ;alone great wonders Him To His (endures)
forever does who .mercy forever

5 חַסְדּוֹ׃ לְעֹשֵׂה הַשָּׁמַיִם בִּתְבוּנָה כִּי לְעוֹלָם חַסְדּוֹ׃
His (endures) for by the who Him to His
.mercy forever ,understanding heavens made ;mercy

6
7 לְרֹקַע הָאָרֶץ עַל־הַמָּיִם כִּי לְעוֹלָם חַסְדּוֹ׃ לְעֹשֵׂה אוֹרִים
lights Him to His (endures) for the above the who Him To
made who ;mercy forever ,waters earth spread

8 גְּדֹלִים כִּי לְעוֹלָם חַסְדּוֹ׃ אֶת־הַשֶּׁמֶשׁ לְמֶמְשֶׁלֶת בַּיּוֹם
;day by rule to sun the His (endures) for ;great
;mercy forever

9 כִּי לְעוֹלָם חַסְדּוֹ׃ אֶת־הַיָּרֵחַ וְכוֹכָבִים לְמֶמְשְׁלוֹת בַּלָּיְלָה
;night by rule to the and the His (endures) for
stars moon ;mercy forever

10 כִּי לְעוֹלָם חַסְדּוֹ׃ לְמַכֵּה מִצְרַיִם בִּבְכוֹרֵיהֶם כִּי לְעוֹלָם
(endures) for their in Egypt who Him to His (endures) for
forever ;firstborn struck ;mercy forever

11
12 חַסְדּוֹ׃ וַיּוֹצֵא יִשְׂרָאֵל מִתּוֹכָם כִּי לְעוֹלָם חַסְדּוֹ׃ בְּיָד
a with His (endures) for from Israel and His
hand ;mercy forever ,them among out brought ;mercy

13 חֲזָקָה וּבִזְרוֹעַ נְטוּיָה כִּי לְעוֹלָם חַסְדּוֹ׃ לְגֹזֵר יַם־סוּף
Reeds the Him to His (endures) for stretched a and strong
of Sea divided who ;mercy forever ;out arm

14 לִגְזָרִים כִּי לְעוֹלָם חַסְדּוֹ׃ וְהֶעֱבִיר יִשְׂרָאֵל בְּתוֹכוֹ כִּי
for middle the Israel made and His (endures) for into
;it of through go ;mercy forever ;parts

15 לְעוֹלָם חַסְדּוֹ׃ וְנִעֵר פַּרְעֹה וְחֵילוֹ בְיַם־סוּף כִּי לְעוֹלָם
(endures) for ;Reeds the in and Pharaoh but His (endures
forever of Sea army his shook ;mercy forever

16
17 חַסְדּוֹ׃ לְמוֹלִיךְ עַמּוֹ בַּמִּדְבָּר כִּי לְעוֹלָם חַסְדּוֹ׃ לְמַכֵּה
Him to His (endures) for the in His Him to His
struck who ;mercy forever ;wilderness people led who ;mercy

who struck great kings; for His mercy (endures) forever; [18] and killed majestic kings; for His mercy (endures) forever; [19] Sihon, king of the Amorites; for His mercy (endures) forever; [20] and Og, the king of Bashan; for His mercy (endures) forever; [21] and gave their land for an inheritance; for His mercy (endures) forever; [22] an inheritance to His servant Israel; for His mercy (endures) forever; [23] who remembered us in our low estate; for His mercy (endures) forever; [24] and has rescued us from our enemies; for His mercy (endures) forever; [25] who gives food to all flesh; for His mercy (endures) forever; [26] O give thanks to the God of Heaven; for His mercy (endures) forever.

18 מְלָכִים גְּדֹלִים כִּי לְעוֹלָם חַסְדּוֹ: וַיַּהֲרֹג מְלָכִים אַדִּירִים
majestic kings and His (endures) for great kings
killed ;mercy forever

19 כִּי לְעוֹלָם חַסְדּוֹ: לְסִיחוֹן מֶלֶךְ הָאֱמֹרִי כִּי לְעוֹלָם חַסְדּוֹ:
20 His (endures) for the king ,Sihon His (endures) for
;mercy forever ;Amorites of ;mercy forever

21 וּלְעוֹג מֶלֶךְ הַבָּשָׁן כִּי לְעוֹלָם חַסְדּוֹ: וְנָתַן אַרְצָם לְנַחֲלָה
an for their and His (endures) for ,Bashan the ,Og and
;inheritance land gave ;mercy forever of king

22 כִּי לְעוֹלָם חַסְדּוֹ: נַחֲלָה לְיִשְׂרָאֵל עַבְדּוֹ כִּי לְעוֹלָם
(endures) for His Israel to an His (endures) for
forever ;servant inheritance ;mercy forever

23 חַסְדּוֹ: שֶׁבְּשִׁפְלֵנוּ זָכַר לָנוּ כִּי לְעוֹלָם חַסְדּוֹ: וַיִּפְרְקֵנוּ
24 has and His (endures) for ;us remem- our in who His
us rescued ;mercy forever bered estate low ;mercy

25 מִצָּרֵינוּ כִּי לְעוֹלָם חַסְדּוֹ: נֹתֵן לֶחֶם לְכָל־בָּשָׂר כִּי לְעוֹלָם
(endures) for ;flesh all to food who His (endures) for our from
forever gives ;mercy forever ;enemies

26 חַסְדּוֹ: הוֹדוּ לְאֵל הַשָּׁמַיִם כִּי לְעוֹלָם חַסְדּוֹ:
His (endures) for ;Heaven the to give O His
.mercy forever of God thanks ;mercy

PSAL. CXXXVII — קלז

PSALM 137

[1] We sat down by the rivers of Babylon; also, we wept when we remembered Zion. [2] We hung our lyres on the willows in its midst. [3] For there our captors asked us the words of a song; and our plunderers joy (saying), Sing to us a song of Zion. [4] How shall we sing the song of Jehovah on a foreign soil? [5] If I forget you, O Jerusalem, let my right hand forget; [6] let my tongue cleave to my palate, if I do not remember you — if I do not bring up Jerusalem above the head of my joy. [7] O Jehovah, remember for the sons of Edom the day of Jerusalem; who said, Make it bare! Make it bare, even to its foundation! [8] O daughter of Babylon, O destroyed one! Blessed (is) he who shall repay to you your

1 עַל־נַהֲרוֹת בָּבֶל שָׁם יָשַׁבְנוּ גַּם־בָּכִינוּ בְּזָכְרֵנוּ אֶת־צִיּוֹן:
.Zion we when we ,also we there ,Babylon the By
remembered wept ;down sat of rivers

2 עַל־עֲרָבִים בְּתוֹכָהּ תָּלִינוּ כִּנֹּרוֹתֵינוּ: כִּי שָׁם שְׁאֵלוּנוּ
3 asked there For our we its in the On
us .lyres hung midst willows

שׁוֹבֵינוּ דִּבְרֵי־שִׁיר וְתוֹלָלֵינוּ שִׂמְחָה שִׁירוּ לָנוּ מִשִּׁיר צִיּוֹן:
.Zion song a to Sing ,joy (saying) our and ;song a the our
of us plunderers of words captors

4 אֵיךְ נָשִׁיר אֶת־שִׁיר־יְהוָה עַל אַדְמַת נֵכָר: אִם־אֶשְׁכָּחֵךְ
5 forget I If ?foreign land a on Jehovah the we shall How
.you of song sing

6 יְרוּשָׁלִָם תִּשְׁכַּח יְמִינִי: תִּדְבַּק לְשׁוֹנִי לְחִכִּי אִם־לֹא
not if my to my let right my let O
,palate tongue cleave ;hand forget ,Jerusalem

אֶזְכְּרֵכִי אִם־לֹא אַעֲלֶה אֶת־יְרוּשָׁלִַם עַל רֹאשׁ שִׂמְחָתִי:
.joy my the above Jerusalem not if re- do I
of head bring I —you member

7 זְכֹר יְהוָה לִבְנֵי אֱדוֹם אֵת יוֹם יְרוּשָׁלִָם הָאֹמְרִים עָרוּ
Lay ,said who ;Jerusalem the Edom the for O ,Recall
!bare of day of sons ,Jehovah

8 עָרוּ עַד הַיְסוֹד בָּהּ: בַּת־בָּבֶל הַשְּׁדוּדָה אַשְׁרֵי שֶׁיְּשַׁלֶּם־
shall who he Blessed destroyed O ,Babylon O !its foundation even Lay
repay (is) !one of daughter to ,bare

reward what you did to us. [9] Blessed (is) he who seizes your little ones and dashes (them) against the stone!

9 לָךְ אֶת־גְּמוּלֵךְ שֶׁגָּמַלְתְּ לָנוּ׃ אַשְׁרֵי ׀ שֶׁיֹּאחֵז וְנִפֵּץ אֶת־
and who he Blessed .us to you which your to
dashes seizes (is) reward did reward

עֹלָלַיִךְ אֶל־הַסָּלַע׃
the against your
.stone ones little

PSAL. CXXXVIII קלח

PSALM 138

A Psalm of David.

[1] I will thank You with my whole heart; I will sing praise to You before the gods; [2] I will worship toward Your holy temple; and give thanks to Your name for Your mercy, and for Your truth; for You have magnified Your word above all Your name. [3] You answered me in the day that I cried; You emboldened me in my soul (with) strength. [4] All the kings of the earth shall thank You, O Jehovah; because they have heard the words of Your mouth. [5] Yes, they shall sing in the ways of Jehovah; for the glory of Jehovah (is) great. [6] Though Jehovah (is) high, yet He looks upon the lowly; but the proud He knows from afar. [7] If I walk in the midst of trouble, You give me life; You send out Your hand against the wrath of my enemies; and Your right hand delivers me. [8] Jehovah will perfect (His work) in me; O Jehovah, Your mercy (endures) forever; (You will) not forsake the works of Your hands.

1
2 לְדָוִד ׀ אוֹדְךָ בְכָל־לִבִּי נֶגֶד אֱלֹהִים אֲזַמְּרֶךָּ׃ אֶשְׁתַּחֲוֶה
will I sing will I the before my with will I Of
worship ;You to praise gods ;heart whole You thank .David

אֶל־הֵיכַל קָדְשְׁךָ וְאוֹדֶה אֶת־שְׁמֶךָ עַל־חַסְדְּךָ וְעַל־אֲמִתֶּךָ
Your and Your For Your give and Your temple to-
;truth for ,mercy .name to thanks ;holy ward

3 כִּי־הִגְדַּלְתָּ עַל־כָּל־שִׁמְךָ אִמְרָתֶךָ׃ בְּיוֹם קָרָאתִי וַתַּעֲנֵנִי
an- You ,called I the In Your Your all above have You for
;me swered day .word ,name magnified

4 תַּרְהִבֵנִי בְנַפְשִׁי עֹז׃ יוֹדוּךָ יְהוָה כָּל־מַלְכֵי־אָרֶץ כִּי־שָׁמְעוּ
they because the the All ,Jehovah shall (with) my in made You
heard have ;earth of kings You thank .strength soul bold me

5 אִמְרֵי־פִיךָ׃ וְיָשִׁירוּ בְּדַרְכֵי יְהוָה כִּי גָדוֹל כְּבוֹד יְהוָה׃
.Jehovah the (is) for ;Jehovah the in they And Your the
of glory great of ways sing shall .mouth of words

6
7 כִּי־רָם יְהוָה וְשָׁפָל יִרְאֶה וְגָבֹהַּ מִמֶּרְחָק יְיֵדָע׃ אִם־אֵלֵךְ
walk I If He from the but He the yet Jeho- is Though
.knows afar proud ;upon looks lowly ,vah exalted

בְּקֶרֶב צָרָה תְּחַיֵּנִי עַל אַף אֹיְבַי תִּשְׁלַח יָדֶךָ וְתוֹשִׁיעֵנִי
and Your send You my the against give You ,trouble the in
me delivers ;hand out enemies of wrath ;life me of midst

8 יְמִינֶךָ׃ יְהוָה יִגְמֹר בַּעֲדִי יְהוָה חַסְדְּךָ לְעוֹלָם מַעֲשֵׂי
the (endures) Your O ;me in will Jehovah right Your
of works ;forever mercy ,Jehovah perfect .hand

יָדֶיךָ אַל־תֶּרֶף׃
do not Your
.forsake hands

PSAL. CXXXIX קלט

PSALM 139

To the Chief Musician, A Psalm of David.

[1] O Jehovah, You have searched me and known (me). [2] You know my sitting down, and my rising up; You understand my thought from afar off. [3] You sift my path and my lying down, and are acquainted (with) all my ways. [4] For not a word is on my tongue, but, lo, O Jehovah, You know it all. [5] You have closed me in behind, and in front; and Your hand (is) laid on me.

1
2 לַמְנַצֵּחַ לְדָוִד מִזְמוֹר יְהוָה חֲקַרְתַּנִי וַתֵּדָע׃ אַתָּה יָדַעְתָּ
know You known and have You O .psalm A of chief the To
.(me) me searched ,Jehovah .David ,musician

3 שִׁבְתִּי וְקוּמִי בַּנְתָּה לְרֵעִי מֵרָחוֹק׃ אָרְחִי וְרִבְעִי זֵרִיתָ
You my and My afar from my You my and my
;sift down lying path .off thought understand ;rising sitting

4 וְכָל־דְּרָכַי הִסְכַּנְתָּה׃ כִּי אֵין מִלָּה בִּלְשׁוֹנִי הֵן יְהוָה
O (but) my on word a not For are You my (with) and
,Jehovah ,lo ,tongue is .acquainted ways all

5 יָדַעְתָּ כֻלָּהּ׃ אָחוֹר וָקֶדֶם צַרְתָּנִי וַתָּשֶׁת עָלַי כַּפֶּכָה׃
Your on is and have You in and Behind .all it You
.hand me laid ;in me closed front know

[6] (Such) knowledge (is) too wonderful for me; it is set on high; I am not able to (reach) it. [7] Where shall I go from Your Spirit? Or where shall I flee from Your face? [8] If I go up to Heaven, You (are) there; if I make my bed (in) Sheol, behold, You (are there)! [9] (If) I take the wings of the morning, dwelling in the farthest part of the sea, [10] even there Your hand shall lead me; and Your right hand shall seize me. [11] If I say: Surely the darkness shall cover me; even the night (shall be) light around me. [12] Even the darkness will not be dark from You; but the night shines as the day; as (is) the darkness, so (is) the light. [13] For You have possessed my inward parts; You wove me in the womb of my mother. [14] I will thank You, for with fearful (things) I am wonderful; Your works (are) marvelous, and my soul knows (it) very well. [15] My bones were not hidden from You when I was made in secret; when I was woven in the depths of the earth. [16] Your eyes saw my embryo; and in Your book all (my members) were written; the days they were formed, and none (was) among them. [17] And how precious are Your thoughts to me, O God! How great is the sum of them! [18] (If) I should count them, they are more than the sand; when I awake I am still with You. [19] Surely You will slay the wicked, O God; and bloody men, depart from me. [20] Who will maliciously speak against You; Your enemies are lifted up with vanity. [21] O Jehovah, do not I hate those hating You? And am I (not) detesting those rising against You? [22] I hate them (with) a perfect hatred; they have become my enemies. [23] Search me, O God, and know my heart; try me, and know my thoughts; [24] and see if (any) wicked way (is) in me; and lead me in the way everlasting.

6 7 פְּלִאיָה דַעַת מִמֶּנִּי נִשְׂגְּבָה לֹא־אוּכַל לָהּ׃ אָנָה אֵלֵךְ
shall Where to am I not set is it much too (such) won- (is)
go I .it (reach) able ;high on ;me for knowledge derful

8 מֵרוּחֶךָ וְאָנָה מִפָּנֶיךָ אֶבְרָח׃ אִם־אֶסַּק שָׁמַיִם שָׁם אָתָּה
You there ,Heaven go I If I shall Your from Or Your from
;(are) to up ?flee face where ?Spirit

9 וְאַצִּיעָה שְּׁאוֹל הִנֶּךָּ׃ אֶשָּׂא כַנְפֵי־שָׁחַר אֶשְׁכְּנָה בְּאַחֲרִית
ut- the in I if the the I (If) behold ,Sheol make I if
of part most dwell ,morning of wings take !(there are) You in bed my

10 11 יָם׃ גַּם־שָׁם יָדְךָ תַנְחֵנִי וְתֹאחֲזֵנִי יְמִינֶךָ׃ וָאֹמַר אַךְ־חֹשֶׁךְ
the Surely I If right Your shall and shall Your there even the
darkness ,say .hand me seize ;me lead hand ,sea

12 יְשׁוּפֵנִי וְלַיְלָה אוֹר בַּעֲדֵנִי׃ גַּם־חֹשֶׁךְ לֹא־יַחְשִׁיךְ מִמֶּךָ
from will not the Even around (be shall) the even cover shall
;You dark be darkness .me light night ,me

13 וְלַיְלָה כַּיּוֹם יָאִיר כַּחֲשֵׁיכָה כָּאוֹרָה׃ כִּי־אַתָּה קָנִיתָ
have You For the (is) so the (is) as ;shines the as the but
possessed .light ,darkness day night

14 כִלְיֹתָי תְּסֻכֵּנִי בְּבֶטֶן אִמִּי׃ אוֹדְךָ עַל כִּי נוֹרָאוֹת נִפְלֵיתִי
am I fearful (with) for will I my the in wove You my
.wonderful things ,You thank .mother of womb me ;reins

15 נִפְלָאִים מַעֲשֶׂיךָ וְנַפְשִׁי יֹדַעַת מְאֹד׃ לֹא־נִכְחַד עָצְמִי
My were not very knows my and Your (are)
bones hidden .well (it) soul ,works marvelous

16 מִמֶּךָּ אֲשֶׁר־עֻשֵּׂיתִי בַסֵּתֶר רֻקַּמְתִּי בְּתַחְתִּיּוֹת אָרֶץ׃ גָּלְמִי
My the the in I when in was I when from
embryo .earth of depths woven was ;secret made ,You

רָאוּ עֵינֶיךָ וְעַל־סִפְרְךָ כֻּלָּם יִכָּתֵבוּ יָמִים יֻצָּרוּ וְלֹא אֶחָד
one not and were they the were of all Your and Your saw
(was) formed days ;written them book on ;eyes

17 בָּהֶם׃ וְלִי מַה־יָּקְרוּ רֵעֶיךָ אֵל מֶה עָצְמוּ רָאשֵׁיהֶם׃
sum the great How O Your precious how to And among
!them of is !God ,thoughts are me .them

18 19 אֶסְפְּרֵם מֵחוֹל יִרְבּוּן הֱקִיצֹתִי וְעוֹדִי עִמָּךְ׃ אִם־תִּקְטֹל
will You If with am I I when are they the than should I (If)
,slay .You still ,awake ;more sand , ,them count

20 אֱלוֹהַּ רָשָׁע וְאַנְשֵׁי דָמִים סוּרוּ מֶנִּי׃ אֲשֶׁר יֹמְרוּךָ לִמְזִמָּה
with speak will Who from depart ,blood men and the ,God O
,malice You against .me of ;wicked

21 נָשֻׂא לַשָּׁוְא עָרֶיךָ׃ הֲלוֹא־מְשַׂנְאֶיךָ יְהוָה אֶשְׂנָא וּבִתְקוֹמְמֶיךָ
those with And ?hate I O who those not Do Your with lifted are
,You against rising ,Jehovah ,You hate .enemies vanity up

22 אֶתְקוֹטָט׃ תַּכְלִית שִׂנְאָה שְׂנֵאתִים לְאוֹיְבִים הָיוּ לִי׃
to they enemies hate I a (with) perfect detesting
.me become have ;them hatred ?am I

23 24 חָקְרֵנִי אֵל וְדַע לְבָבִי בְּחָנֵנִי וְדַע שַׂרְעַפָּי׃ וּרְאֵה אִם־
if see and my and me try my and ,God O Search
,thoughts know ;heart know ,me

דֶּרֶךְ־עֹצֶב בִּי וּנְחֵנִי בְּדֶרֶךְ עוֹלָם׃
ever- the in lead and (is) wicked (any)
.lasting way me ;me in way

PSAL. CXL קמ

PSALM 140

PSALM 140

To the Chief Musician, A Psalm of David.

[1] O Jehovah, deliver me from the evil man; keep me from the violent man; [2] who devises evil things in the heart; they stir up wars all the day. [3] They sharpen their tongues like a snake; adders' poison (is) under their lips. Selah. [4] O Jehovah, keep me from the wicked's hands; keep me from the violent man, who plans to trip up my steps. [5] The proud have hidden cords and a trap for me; they have spread a net by the wayside; they have set snares for me. Selah.

[6] I said to Jehovah, You (are) my God; O Jehovah, hear the voice of my prayers. [7] O Jehovah the Lord, the strength of my salvation, You have covered my head in the day of armor. [8] O Jehovah, do not grant the desires of the wicked; do not promote his wicked plan, (lest) they be exalted. Selah. [9] (As for) the leaders of those around me, let the evil of their own lips cover them. [10] Make burning coals fall on them; make them fall into deep pits, so that they do not rise again. [11] Do not let a man of tongue be established in the earth; evil shall hunt the violent man, thrust upon thrust. [12] I know that Jehovah will maintain the cause of the afflicted, the justice of the poor. [13] Surely the righteous shall give thanks to Your name; the upright shall dwell in Your presence.

1 2 לַמְנַצֵּחַ מִזְמוֹר לְדָוִד׃ חַלְּצֵנִי יְהוָה מֵאָדָם רָע מֵאִישׁ
the from ;evil the from O Deliver of psalm A chief the To
man man ,Jehovah ,me .David .musician

3 חֲמָסִים תִּנְצְרֵנִי׃ אֲשֶׁר חָשְׁבוּ רָעוֹת בְּלֵב כָּל־יוֹם יָגוּרוּ
they the all the in evil devises who preserve violent
up stir day ;heart things ;me

4 מִלְחָמוֹת׃ שָׁנְנוּ לְשׁוֹנָם כְּמוֹ־נָחָשׁ חֲמַת עַכְשׁוּב תַּחַת
(is) adders' poison a like their They .wars
under ;snake tongues sharpen

5 שְׂפָתֵימוֹ סֶלָה׃ שָׁמְרֵנִי יְהוָה ׀ מִידֵי רָשָׁע מֵאִישׁ חֲמָסִים
violent the from the from O Keep .Selah their
man ;wicked's hands ,Jehovah ,me .lips

6 תִּנְצְרֵנִי אֲשֶׁר חָשְׁבוּ לִדְחוֹת פְּעָמָי׃ טָמְנוּ־גֵאִים ׀ פַּח לִי
for a The have my trip to plans who preserve
me trap proud hidden .steps up ;me

וַחֲבָלִים פָּרְשׂוּ רֶשֶׁת לְיַד־מַעְגָּל מֹקְשִׁים שָׁתוּ־לִי סֶלָה׃
.Selah for they snares the the by net a have they and
.me set have ;way of side spread ;cords

7 אָמַרְתִּי לַיהוָה אֵלִי אָתָּה הַאֲזִינָה יְהוָה קוֹל תַּחֲנוּנָי׃
my the O ,hear You My to said I
.prayer of voice ,Jehovah ;(are) God ,Jehovah

8 9 יְהוִה אֲדֹנָי עֹז יְשׁוּעָתִי סַכֹּתָה לְרֹאשִׁי בְּיוֹם נָשֶׁק׃ אַל־
not .armor the in my have You my ,strength the O
of day head covered ,salvation's ,Lord Jehovah

10 תִּתֵּן יְהוָה מַאֲוַיֵּי רָשָׁע זְמָמוֹ אַל־תָּפֵק יָרוּמוּ סֶלָה׃ רֹאשׁ
(for As) .Selah they (lest) do his the desires O Do
of head the .exalted be ,promote plan ;wicked's ,Jehovah ,grant

11 מְסִבָּי עֲמַל שְׂפָתֵימוֹ יְכַסֵּמוֹ׃ יִמִּיטוּ עֲלֵיהֶם גֶּחָלִים
coals them on make cover let their evil the those
fall ;them lips of ,me around

12 בָּאֵשׁ יַפִּלֵם בְּמַהֲמֹרוֹת בַּל־יָקוּמוּ׃ אִישׁ לָשׁוֹן בַּל־יִכּוֹן
let do not tongue A that not ;pits into make ;burning
fixed be of man .rise shall they fall them

13 בָּאָרֶץ אִישׁ־חָמָס רָע יְצוּדֶנּוּ לְמַדְחֵפֹת׃ יָדַעְתָּ כִּי־יַעֲשֶׂה
will that know I upon thrust shall evil ,violent the the in
maintain .thrust him hunt man ;earth

14 יְהוָה דִּין עָנִי מִשְׁפַּט אֶבְיֹנִים׃ אַךְ צַדִּיקִים יוֹדוּ לִשְׁמֶךָ
Your to shall righ- the Surely the justice the cause Jeho-
;name thanks give teous .poor's ;afflicted's vah

יֵשְׁבוּ יְשָׁרִים אֶת־פָּנֶיךָ׃
Your the shall
.presence upright in dwell

PSAL. CXLI קמא

PSALM 141

PSALM 141

[1] O Jehovah, I cry to You; hasten to me; hear my voice when I cry to You.

1 מִזְמוֹר לְדָוִד יְהוָה קְרָאתִיךָ חוּשָׁה לִּי הַאֲזִינָה קוֹלִי
my ear give to hasten cry I O .David of psalm A
voice to ;me ;You to ,Jehovah

[2] Let my prayer be established before You (as) incense; the lifting up of my hands (as) the evening sacrifice. [3] O Jehovah, set a guard to my mouth; keep watch on the door of my lips. [4] Do not let my heart turn aside to any evil thing, to practice deeds in wickedness with men who do evil; and do not let me eat of their delicacies. [5] The righteous strike me; (it is) a mercy; and he rebukes me, (it is) oil of the head; let not my head refuse (it); for yet my prayer (shall) also (be) against their evils. [6] Their judges have been dashed against the rock; they shall hear my words; for they are pleasant. [7] As when one ploughs and tears the earth, so our bones are scattered at the mouth of Sheol. [8] But my eyes (are) on You, O Jehovah, my Lord; in You I take refuge; do not make my soul naked. [9] Keep me from the hands of the trap they laid for me; and from the snares of the workers of evil. [10] Let the wicked fall into their own nets at the same time; I even shall pass by.

2 בְּקָרְאִי־לָךְ׃ תִּכּוֹן תְּפִלָּתִי קְטֹרֶת לְפָנֶיךָ מַשְׂאַת כַּפַּי
my lifting the before (as) my be Let to my in
hands of up ;You incense prayer prepared .You calling

3 מִנְחַת־עָרֶב׃ שִׁיתָה יְהוָה שָׁמְרָה לְפִי נִצְּרָה עַל־דַּל
the on keep my to guard a O ,Set .evening the (as)
of door watch ;mouth ,Jehovah sacrifice

4 שְׂפָתָי׃ אַל־תַּט־לִבִּי ׀ לְדָבָר ׀ רָע לְהִתְעוֹלֵל עֲלִלוֹת ׀ בְּרֶשַׁע
wick- in deeds practice to ,evil any- to my let Do not .lips my
edness thing heart aside turn

5 אֶת־אִישִׁים פֹּעֲלֵי־אָוֶן וּבַל־אֶלְחַם בְּמַנְעַמֵּיהֶם׃ יֶהֶלְמֵנִי
strike Let their of let do And .evil who men with
me .delicacies eat me not do

צַדִּיק ׀ חֶסֶד וְיוֹכִיחֵנִי שֶׁמֶן רֹאשׁ אַל־יָנִי רֹאשִׁי כִּי־עוֹד
yet for my let not the (is it) he and a (is it) the
;head refuse ;head of oil ,me rebukes ;mercy ;righteous

6 וּתְפִלָּתִי בְּרָעוֹתֵיהֶם׃ נִשְׁמְטוּ בִידֵי־סֶלַע שֹׁפְטֵיהֶם וְשָׁמְעוּ
shall they their the against been Have against (is) my also
hear ;judges rock down cast .evils their prayer

7 אֲמָרַי כִּי נָעֵמוּ׃ כְּמוֹ פֹלֵחַ וּבֹקֵעַ בָּאָרֶץ נִפְזְרוּ עֲצָמֵינוּ
our are so the rips and one As are they for my
bones scattered ,earth plows when .pleasant ,words

8 לְפִי שְׁאוֹל׃ כִּי אֵלֶיךָ ׀ יְהוִה אֲדֹנָי עֵינָי בְּכָה חָסִיתִי אַל־
not take I in my my O on (are) But .Sheol the at
;refuge You ;eyes ,Lord Jehovah ,You of mouth

9 תְּעַר נַפְשִׁי׃ שָׁמְרֵנִי מִידֵי פַח יָקְשׁוּ לִי וּמֹקְשׁוֹת פֹּעֲלֵי
the the and for they the the from Keep my make do
workers' snares from ,me laid trap of hands me .soul bare

אָוֶן׃ יִפְּלוּ בְמַכְמֹרָיו רְשָׁעִים יַחַד אָנֹכִי עַד־אֶעֱבוֹר׃
shall even I the at the their into Let .evil
.by pass ,time same wicked nets own fall

PSAL. CXLII קמב

PSALM 142

PSALM 142

An Instruction of David, a Prayer when he was in the cave.

[1] I cry to Jehovah with my voice; I pray to Jehovah with my voice. [2] I pour out my musing before Him; I declare my trouble before Him. [3] When my spirit faints within me, then You know my path; they have hidden a snare for me in the path (in) which I walk. [4] I look to the right hand and see, and no one recognizes me; every escape is hidden from me; no one cares for my soul. [5] I cried to You, O Jehovah; I said, You (are) my refuge, my portion in the land of the living

1
2 מַשְׂכִּיל לְדָוִד בִּהְיוֹתוֹ בַמְּעָרָה תְפִלָּה׃ קוֹלִי אֶל־יְהוָה
Jehovah to (with) .prayer A the in his in ,David of An
voice my .cave being instruction

3 אֶזְעָק קוֹלִי אֶל־יְהוָה אֶתְחַנָּן׃ אֶשְׁפֹּךְ לְפָנָיו שִׂיחִי צָרָתִי
my my before pour I I Jehovah to (with) ;cried I
trouble ;musing Him out .prayed voice my

4 לְפָנָיו אַגִּיד׃ בְּהִתְעַטֵּף עָלַי ׀ רוּחִי וְאַתָּה יָדַעְתָּ נְתִיבָתִי
my knew then my within When I before
;path You ,spirit me faints .declare Him

5 בְּאֹרַח־זוּ אֲהַלֵּךְ טָמְנוּ פַח לִי׃ הַבֵּיט יָמִין ׀ וּרְאֵה וְאֵין־
and and the to Look for a have They I (in) the in
none ,see right .me trap hidden .walk which path

6 לִי מַכִּיר אָבַד מָנוֹס מִמֶּנִּי אֵין דּוֹרֵשׁ לְנַפְשִׁי׃ זָעַקְתִּי
cried I my for cares none from escape has is me
.soul ;me perished ;recognizing

אֵלֶיךָ יְהוָה אָמַרְתִּי אַתָּה מַחְסִי חֶלְקִי בְּאֶרֶץ הַחַיִּים׃
the the in my my You ,said I O ;You to
.living of land portion ,refuge (are) ;Jehovah

[6] Attend to my cry; for I am brought very low; deliver me from those who pursue me; for they are stronger than I. [7] Bring my soul out from prison to give thanks to Your name; the righteous shall gather around me; for You shall lay benefits on me.

7 הַקְשִׁיבָה ׀ אֶל־רִנָּתִי כִּי־דַלּוֹתִי מְאֹד הַצִּילֵנִי מֵרֹדְפַי כִּי

for those from deliver ;very am I for my to heed Give
,me pursuing me low brought :cry

8 אָמְצוּ מִמֶּנִּי׃ הוֹצִיאָה מִמַּסְגֵּר ׀ נַפְשִׁי לְהוֹדוֹת אֶת־שְׁמֶךָ

Your give to soul my from out Bring .I than are they
;name to thanks prison stronger

בִּי יַכְתִּרוּ צַדִּיקִים כִּי תִגְמֹל עָלָי׃

.me shall You for the shall me
reward ,righteous surround

PSAL. CXLIII קמג

PSALM 143

PSALM 143

A Psalm of David.

[1] Hear my prayer, O Jehovah; give ear to my supplications; answer me in Your faithfulness, in Your righteousness; [2] and do not enter into judgment with Your servant; for not before You is anyone living just. [3] For the enemy has pursued my soul; he has beaten my life to the ground; he has made me dwell in darkness, like the dead of old. [4] And my spirit within me has fainted; my heart within me is stunned. [5] I remember the days of old; I meditate on all Your works; I muse upon the work of Your hands. [6] I spread out my hands to You; my soul (thirsts) to You like a thirsty land. Selah. [7] O Jehovah, answer me quickly; my spirit is failing; do not hide Your face from me, lest I be like the ones who go down to the pit. [8] Cause me to hear Your mercy in the morning; for I do trust in You; cause me to know the way I should walk; for I lift up my soul to You. [9] O Jehovah, deliver me from my enemies; to You I have hidden. [10] Teach me to do Your will; for You (are) my God; Your Spirit (is) good; lead me into the land of justice. [11] O Jehovah, because of

1 מִזְמוֹר לְדָוִד יְהוָה ׀ שְׁמַע תְּפִלָּתִי הַאֲזִינָה אֶל־תַּחֲנוּנַי

my to ear give my hear O .David of psalm A
;supplications ;prayer ,Jehovah

2 בֶּאֱמֻנָתְךָ עֲנֵנִי בְּצִדְקָתֶךָ׃ וְאַל־תָּבוֹא בְמִשְׁפָּט אֶת־

with into do And Your in answer Your in
judgment enter not .righteousness ,me faithfulness

3 עַבְדֶּךָ כִּי לֹא־יִצְדַּק לְפָנֶיךָ כָל־חָי׃ כִּי רָדַף אוֹיֵב ׀ נַפְשִׁי

my the has For anyone Your in be shall not for Your
;soul enemy pursued .living sight just ;servant

דִּכָּא לָאָרֶץ חַיָּתִי הוֹשִׁיבַנִי בְמַחֲשַׁכִּים כְּמֵתֵי עוֹלָם׃

.old the as ,darkness in made has he my the to has he
of dead dwell me ;life ground crushed

4 וַתִּתְעַטֵּף עָלַי רוּחִי בְּתוֹכִי יִשְׁתּוֹמֵם לִבִּי׃ זָכַרְתִּי יָמִים ׀

5 days the I my stunned is within my within has And
remember ;heart me ;spirit me fainted

6 מִקֶּדֶם הָגִיתִי בְכָל־פָּעֳלֶךָ בְּמַעֲשֵׂה יָדֶיךָ אֲשׂוֹחֵחַ׃ פֵּרַשְׂתִּי

spread I .muse I Your the on Your all on I ;old of
out hands of work ;works meditate

7 יָדַי אֵלֶיךָ נַפְשִׁי ׀ כְּאֶרֶץ־עֲיֵפָה לְךָ סֶלָה׃ מַהֵר עֲנֵנִי ׀ יְהוָה

O Answer quickly .Selah (is) weary a like my ;You to my
,Jehovah ,me .You to land soul hands

כָּלְתָה רוּחִי אַל־תַּסְתֵּר פָּנֶיךָ מִמֶּנִּי וְנִמְשַׁלְתִּי עִם־יֹרְדֵי

who those with be I lest from Your do not my is
to down go like ,me face hide ,spirit failing

8 בוֹר׃ הַשְׁמִיעֵנִי בַבֹּקֶר ׀ חַסְדֶּךָ כִּי־בְךָ בָטָחְתִּי הוֹדִיעֵנִי

me cause do I in for Your the in me Cause the
know to ;trust You ;mercy morning hear to .Pit

9 דֶּרֶךְ־זוּ אֵלֵךְ כִּי־אֵלֶיךָ נָשָׂאתִי נַפְשִׁי׃ הַצִּילֵנִי מֵאֹיְבַי ׀

my from Deliver .soul my up lift I You to for should I way the
,enemies me ;walk which

10 יְהוָה אֵלֶיךָ כִסִּתִי׃ לַמְּדֵנִי ׀ לַעֲשׂוֹת רְצוֹנֶךָ כִּי־אַתָּה אֱלוֹהָי

my You for Your do to me Teach have I to O
;God (are) ,will .hidden You ,Jehovah

11 רוּחֲךָ טוֹבָה תַּנְחֵנִי בְּאֶרֶץ מִישׁוֹר׃ לְמַעַן־שִׁמְךָ יְהוָה

O Your Because .plainness the into lead (is) Your
,Jehovah ,name of of land me ;good Spirit

Your name, make me live; in Your righteousness, bring my soul out of trouble. [12] And in Your mercy cut off my enemies; and destroy all those who afflict my soul; for I (am) Your servant.

PSALM 144

A Psalm of David.

[1] Blessed (be) Jehovah my rock, who teaches my hands for war, my fingers for battle; [2] my mercy and my fortress; my high tower and my deliverer; my shield and in Him I take refuge; (He) who humbles my people under me. [3] O Jehovah, what (is) man that You know him; the son of man, that you esteem him? [4] Man is like to vanity; his days (are) like a shadow that passes. [5] Bow down Your heavens, O Jehovah; and come down; touch the mountains and they shall smoke. [6] Flash out lightning and scatter them; send out Your arrows and confound them. [7] Send Your hand from above; rescue me and deliver me out of great waters, from the hand of the sons of a stranger, [8] whose mouths have spoken vanity; and their right hand (is) a right hand of lies. [9] I will sing a new song to You, O God; I will sing praises to You on a harp of ten strings. [10] (It is You) who gives salvation to kings, who delivers His servant David from the evil sword. [11] Rescue me and deliver me from the hand of strangers, whose mouths have spoken vanity; and their right hand (is) a right hand of lies: [12] so that our sons (may be) like plants grown up in their youth; (and) our daughters like cornerstones hewn like a palace building; [13] (and) our storehouses (may be) full, furnishing kind to kind; our flocks may breed thousands (and) ten thousands in our streets; [14] our oxen (may be) laden; there is no break and

12 תְּחַיֵּנִי בְּצִדְקָתְךָ ׀ תּוֹצִיא מִצָּרָה נַפְשִׁי׃ וּבְחַסְדְּךָ תַּצְמִית

off cut in And .soul my of out bring Your in me make
mercy Your trouble righteousness ;live

אֹיְבָי וְהַאֲבַדְתָּ כָּל־צֹרְרֵי נַפְשִׁי כִּי אֲנִי עַבְדֶּךָ׃

Your I for my those all and my
.servant (am) ;soul afflict who destroy ;enemies

PSAL. CXLIV קמד

PSALM 144

1 לְדָוִד ׀ בָּרוּךְ יְהוָה ׀ צוּרִי הַמְלַמֵּד יָדַי לַקְרָב אֶצְבְּעוֹתַי

fingers my ,war for my who ;rock my Jehovah Blessed (psalm A)
hands teaches (be) .David of

2 לַמִּלְחָמָה׃ חַסְדִּי וּמְצוּדָתִי מִשְׂגַּבִּי וּמְפַלְטִי־לִי מָגִנִּי וּבוֹ

in and my to and high my my and mercy my ;battle for
Him ,shield ;me deliverer tower ;fortress

3 חָסִיתִי הָרוֹדֵד עַמִּי תַחְתָּי׃ יְהוָה מָה־אָדָם וַתֵּדָעֵהוּ בֶּן

the You that man what O under my who He take I
of son ,him know (is) ,Jehovah .me people subdues ;refuge

4 אֱנוֹשׁ וַתְּחַשְּׁבֵהוּ׃ אָדָם לַהֶבֶל דָּמָה יָמָיו כְּצֵל עוֹבֵר׃

that a like his ,like is to Man You that ,man
.passes shadow days vanity ?him esteem

5
6 יְהוָה הַט־שָׁמֶיךָ וְתֵרֵד גַּע בֶּהָרִים וְיֶעֱשָׁנוּ׃ בְּרוֹק בָּרָק

light- Flash they and the touch and Your bow Jeho- O
ning out .smoke shall mountains ;down came heavens down ,vah

7 וּתְפִיצֵם שְׁלַח חִצֶּיךָ וּתְהֻמֵּם׃ שְׁלַח יָדֶיךָ מִמָּרוֹם פְּצֵנִי

rescue from Your Send con- and Your Send scatter and
me ;above hand .them found arrows out ;them

8 וְהַצִּילֵנִי מִמַּיִם רַבִּים מִיַּד בְּנֵי נֵכָר׃ אֲשֶׁר פִּיהֶם דִּבֶּר־

have their whose a sons the the from ,great of out deliver and
spoken mouths ,foreigner of of hand waters me

9 שָׁוְא וִימִינָם יְמִין שָׁקֶר׃ אֱלֹהִים שִׁיר חָדָשׁ אָשִׁירָה לָּךְ

to will I new song a ,God O .lies a (is) their and ;vanity
;You sing of hand right hand right

10 בְּנֵבֶל עָשׂוֹר אֲזַמְּרָה־לָּךְ׃ הַנּוֹתֵן תְּשׁוּעָה לַמְּלָכִים הַפּוֹצֶה

who ,kings to salvation (You is It) to sing will I ten a on
rescues gives who .You praises strings of harp

11 אֶת־דָּוִד עַבְדּוֹ מֵחֶרֶב רָעָה׃ פְּצֵנִי וְהַצִּילֵנִי מִיַּד בְּנֵי־נֵכָר

of sons the from deliver and Rescue .evil the from His David
,foreigners of hand the me me sword servant

12 אֲשֶׁר פִּיהֶם דִּבֶּר־שָׁוְא וִימִינָם יְמִין שָׁקֶר׃ אֲשֶׁר בָּנֵינוּ

our That .lies right a (is) their and ;vanity have their whose
sons of hand hand right spoken mouths

כִּנְטִעִים מְגֻדָּלִים בִּנְעוּרֵיהֶם בְּנוֹתֵינוּ כְזָוִיֹּת מְחֻטָּבוֹת

hewn corner-like our (and) their in up grown like (be may)
pillars daughters ;youths plants

13 תַּבְנִית הֵיכָל׃ מְזָוֵינוּ מְלֵאִים מְפִיקִים מִזַּן אֶל־זַן צֹאונֵנוּ

our ;kind to kind furnishing (be may) our (and) ;palace a the like
flocks ,full storehouses of structure

14 מַאֲלִיפוֹת מְרֻבָּבוֹת בְּחוּצוֹתֵינוּ׃ אַלּוּפֵינוּ מְסֻבָּלִים אֵין

not be may oxen Our our in ten (and) breed may
is ;laden .streets thousands thousands

no going out, and no crying in our streets. [15] Blessed (is) the people that is thus; blessed (is) the people whose God (is) Jehovah!

15 פרץ ואין יוצאת ואין צוחה ברחבתינו: אשרי העם
the people Blessed (are) .streets our in crying and no going out and no a ;break

שככה לו אשרי העם שיהוה אלהיו:
his (is) !God which (to) Jehovah the people Blessed (is) to .it which thus are

PSAL. CXLV קמה

PSALM 145

PSALM 145

A Psalm of Praise, of David.
[1] I will exalt You, my God, O king; and bless Your name forever and ever. [2] I will bless You every day; and I will praise Your name forever and ever. [3] Jehovah (is) great and to be greatly praised; and to His greatness there (is) no finding out. [4] Generation to generation shall praise Your works; and shall declare Your mighty acts. [5] I will muse on the glorious honor of Your majesty, and the things of Your wonderful works. [6] And they shall speak of the might of Your awesome works; and I will declare Your greatness. [7] They shall express the memory of Your great goodness, and they shall sing of Your righteousness. [8] Jehovah (is) gracious and merciful, long to anger and of great mercy; [9] Jehovah (is) good to all; and His tender mercies (are) over all His works. [10] All Your works shall thank You, O Jehovah; and Your saints shall bless You. [11] They shall speak of the glory of Your kingdom, and talk of Your might; [12] to make known His might to the sons of men; yea, the glorious majesty of His kingdom. [13] Your kingdom (is) a kingdom to all eternities; and Your rule in all generation and generation. [14] Jehovah upholds all who fall, and raises up all who are bowed down. [15] The eyes of all hope to You; and You give them their food in due time. [16] (You) open Your hand and satisfy the desire of every living thing. [17] Jehovah (is) righteous in all His ways, and kind in

1 תהלה לדוד ארוממך אלוהי המלך ואברכה שמך לעולם
forever Your name bless and ;King O ,God my will I ,You exalt ,David Of .Praise

2 ועד: בכל־יום אברכך ואהללה שמך לעולם ועד:
and .ever forever Your name praise and will I ;You bless day every In and .ever

3
4 גדול יהוה ומהלל מאד ולגדלתו אין חקר: דור לדור
to Generation generation .search a (is) not His greatness to and ;greatly to and be praised Jehovah Great

5 ישבח מעשיך וגבורתיך יגידו: הדר כבוד הודך ודברי
the and of things Your ,majesty the of glory The of honor shall .declare Your and acts mighty Your ;works shall praise

6 נפלאתיך אשיחה: ועזוז נוראותיך יאמרו וגדלותיך
Your and greatness shall they ;speak awesome Your works the And of might will I .upon muse won- Your works drous

7
8 אספרנה: זכר רב־טובך יביעו וצדקתך ירננו: חנון
Gracious shall they .of sing Your and righteousness shall they ,express Your goodness great The of memory will I .declare

9 ורחום יהוה ארך אפים וגדל־חסד: טוב־יהוה לכל
;all to (is) Jehovah good ;mercy of and great anger long (to) (is) ;Jehovah and merciful

10 ורחמיו על־כל־מעשיו: יודוך יהוה כל־מעשיך וחסידיך
Your and saints Your ;works All O ,Jehovah shall ,You thank His .works all (are) over His and mercies

11
12 יברכוכה: כבוד מלכותך יאמרו וגבורתך ידברו: להודיע
make to known talk ;of Your and might shall They ,of speak Your kingdom the of glory bless shall .You

13 לבני האדם גבורתיו וכבוד הדר מלכותו: מלכותך
Your kingdom His .kingdom the of majesty the and of glory Your ;might men the to of sons

14 מלכות כל־עלמים וממשלתך בכל־דור ודר: סומך
upholds and .generation genera- tion all in Your and rule ;eternities all a (is) of kingdom

15 יהוה לכל־הנפלים וזוקף לכל־הכפופים: עיני כל אליך
to You all The of eyes are who .down bowed all and up raising ;fall who all Jehovah

16 ישברו ואתה נותן־להם את־אכלם בעתו: פותח את־
(You) open due in .time their food them to give and You ;hope

17 ידך ומשביע לכל־חי רצון: צדיק יהוה בכל־דרכיו
His ,ways all in Jehovah (is) righteous the desire living thing of every and satisfy Your hand

all His works. [18] Jehovah (is) near to all who call on Him, to all those who call on Him in truth. [19] He will fulfill the desire of the ones who fear Him; and He will hear their cry and save them. [20] Jehovah preserves all who love Him; but He destroys all the wicked. [21] My mouth shall speak the praise of Jehovah: and all flesh shall bless His holy name forever and ever.

18 וְחָסִיד בְּכָל־מַעֲשָׂיו׃ קָרוֹב יְהוָה לְכָל־קֹרְאָיו לְכֹל אֲשֶׁר
those all to call who to Jehovah (is) His all in and
,Him on all near .works kind

19 יִקְרָאֻהוּ בֶאֱמֶת׃ רְצוֹן־יְרֵאָיו יַעֲשֶׂה וְאֶת־שַׁוְעָתָם יִשְׁמַע
will He their and will He fearers The .truth in call who
,hear cry ,do Him of of desire Him on

20 וְיוֹשִׁיעֵם׃ שׁוֹמֵר יְהוָה אֶת־כָּל־אֹהֲבָיו וְאֵת כָּל־הָרְשָׁעִים
the all but love who all Jehovah preserves save and
wicked ;Him .them

21 יַשְׁמִיד׃ תְּהִלַּת יְהוָה יְדַבֶּר־פִּי וִיבָרֵךְ כָּל־בָּשָׂר שֵׁם
name flesh all bless and My shall Jehovah the He
;mouth speak of praise .destroys

קָדְשׁוֹ לְעוֹלָם וָעֶד׃
and forever His
.ever holy

PSAL. CXLVI קמו

PSALM 146

PSALM 146

[1] Praise Jehovah; praise Jehovah, O my soul. [2] While I live I will praise Jehovah; I will sing praises to my God while I have being. [3] Put not your trust in princes, in a son of man, for there is no salvation in him. [4] His breath will go out, he returns to the earth; his thoughts perish in that day. [5] Blessed (is he) who (has) the God of Jacob in his help; his hope (is) on Jehovah his God; [6] who made the heavens and the earth, the seas and all that (is) in them; who keeps truth forever; [7] who executes judgment for the oppressed; who gives food to the hungry; Jehovah sets free the prisoners; [8] Jehovah opens (the eyes of) the blind; Jehovah raises those bowed down; Jehovah loves the righteous; [9] Jehovah preserves the strangers; He relieves the orphan and the widow; but He warps the way of the wicked. [10] Jehovah shall reign forever; O Zion, your God from generation and generation. Praise Jehovah.

1 2 הַלְלוּ־יָהּ הַלְלִי נַפְשִׁי אֶת־יְהוָה׃ אֲהַלְלָה יְהוָה בְּחַיָּי
I while Jehovah will I !Jehovah my O ,praise Praise
;live praise ,soul ;Jah

3 אֲזַמְּרָה לֵאלֹהַי בְּעוֹדִי׃ אַל־תִּבְטְחוּ בִנְדִיבִים בְּבֶן־אָדָם ׀
;man a in ,princes in trust Do not I while my to sing will I
of son .being have God praises

4 שֶׁאֵין לוֹ תְשׁוּעָה׃ תֵּצֵא רוּחוֹ יָשֻׁב לְאַדְמָתוֹ בַּיּוֹם הַהוּא
that day in the to he His will .salvation to there for
;ground returns ;breath out go him not is

5 אָבְדוּ עֶשְׁתֹּנֹתָיו׃ אַשְׁרֵי שֶׁאֵל יַעֲקֹב בְּעֶזְרוֹ שִׂבְרוֹ עַל־
(is) his his in Jacob (has) who Blessed his perish
on hope ;help of God the (he is) .thoughts

6 יְהוָה אֱלֹהָיו׃ עֹשֶׂה ׀ שָׁמַיִם וָאָרֶץ אֶת־הַיָּם וְאֶת־כָּל־
all and the the and the who his Jehovah
seas ,earth heavens made ;God

7 אֲשֶׁר־בָּם הַשֹּׁמֵר אֱמֶת לְעוֹלָם׃ עֹשֶׂה מִשְׁפָּט ׀ לַעֲשׁוּקִים
the for judgment who ;forever truth who in is that
;oppressed executes keeps ,them

8 נֹתֵן לֶחֶם לָרְעֵבִים יְהוָה מַתִּיר אֲסוּרִים׃ יְהוָה ׀ פֹּקֵחַ
opens Jehovah the sets Jehovah the to food who
(eyes) ;prisoners free ;hungry gives

9 עִוְרִים יְהוָה זֹקֵף כְּפוּפִים יְהוָה אֹהֵב צַדִּיקִים׃ יְהוָה ׀ שֹׁמֵר
keeps Jehovah the loves Jehovah those raises Jehovah the
;righteous ;down bowed ;blind

10 אֶת־גֵּרִים יָתוֹם וְאַלְמָנָה יְעוֹדֵד וְדֶרֶךְ רְשָׁעִים יְעַוֵּת׃ יִמְלֹךְ
shall He the the but He the and the ;aliens the
reign .warps wicked of way ;relieves widow orphan

יְהוָה ׀ לְעוֹלָם אֱלֹהַיִךְ צִיּוֹן לְדֹר וָדֹר הַלְלוּ־יָהּ׃
Praise gen- and from Zion O your ;forever Jehovah
!Jah .eration generation God

PSAL. CXLVII קמז

PSALM 147

PSALM 147

[1] Praise Jehovah; for (it is) good to sing praise to our God; because praise (is) delightful (and) becoming. [2] Jehovah builds up Jerusalem; He gathers the outcasts of Israel. [3] (He) heals the broken-hearted and binds up their sorrows. [4] (He) appoints the number of the stars; He calls to them all by names. [5] Our Lord (is) great and of great might; there is no limit to His understanding. [6] Jehovah relieves the afflicted; He throws the wicked down to the ground. [7] Sing to Jehovah with thanksgiving; sing praise on the lyre to our God, [8] who covers the heavens with clouds; who prepares rain for the earth; who makes grass to grow (on) the mountains. [9] (He) gives the animals their food, to the young ravens that cry. [10] He takes no delight in the strength of the horse; nor any pleasure in the legs of a man. [11] Jehovah takes pleasure in those who fear Him; those who hope in His mercy. [12] Praise Jehovah, O Jerusalem; praise your God, O Zion. [13] For He has made strong the bars of your gates; He has blessed your sons within you. [14] He makes peace (in) your border, He satisfies you (with) the fat of the wheat. [15] He sends His command out (upon) the earth; His word runs very swiftly; [16] He gives snow like wool; He scatters the white frost like ashes; [17] He casts out His ice like crumbs; who can stand before His cold? [18] He sends out His word and melts them; He causes His wind to blow, and the waters flow. [19] He declares His word to Jacob;

1 הַלְלוּיָהּ ׀ כִּי־טוֹב זַמְּרָה אֱלֹהֵינוּ כִּי־נָעִים נָאוָה תְהִלָּה׃
praise (and) de- because our sing to (is it) for Praise
.(is) becoming lightful ;God to praise good ;Jah

2
3 בּוֹנֵה יְרוּשָׁלַםִ יְהוָה נִדְחֵי יִשְׂרָאֵל יְכַנֵּס׃ הָרֹפֵא לִשְׁבוּרֵי
the (He) He Israel the ;Jehovah Jerusalem builds
of broken heals .gathers of outcasts up

4 לֵב וּמְחַבֵּשׁ לְעַצְּבוֹתָם׃ מוֹנֶה מִסְפָּר לַכּוֹכָבִים לְכֻלָּם
them to the of the (He) their and .heart
all ;stars number appoints .sorrows up binds

5 שֵׁמוֹת יִקְרָא׃ גָּדוֹל אֲדוֹנֵינוּ וְרַב־כֹּחַ לִתְבוּנָתוֹ אֵין מִסְפָּר׃
.numbering not His to ;might and Our great (is) He (by)
is understanding of great Lord .calls names

6
7 מְעוֹדֵד עֲנָוִים יְהוָה מַשְׁפִּיל רְשָׁעִים עֲדֵי־אָרֶץ׃ עֱנוּ לַיהוָה
to Sing the to the throws He ;Jehovah the relieves
Jehovah .ground wicked down afflicted

8 בְּתוֹדָה זַמְּרוּ לֵאלֹהֵינוּ בְכִנּוֹר׃ הַמְכַסֶּה שָׁמַיִם ׀ בְּעָבִים
with the (He) the on our to sing with
;clouds heavens covers .lyre God praise ;thanksgiving

9 הַמֵּכִין לָאָרֶץ מָטָר הַמַּצְמִיחַ הָרִים חָצִיר׃ נוֹתֵן לִבְהֵמָה
the to (He) .grass the (on) makes who ;rain the for who
beasts gives mountain grow to earth prepares

10 לַחְמָהּ לִבְנֵי עֹרֵב אֲשֶׁר יִקְרָאוּ׃ לֹא בִגְבוּרַת הַסּוּס יֶחְפָּץ
takes He the the in no .cry that ravens the to their
;delight horse of strength of sons ;food

11 לֹא־בְשׁוֹקֵי הָאִישׁ יִרְצֶה׃ רוֹצֶה יְהוָה אֶת־יְרֵאָיו אֶת־
who those Jehovah takes takes He man a the in not
,Him fear in pleasure .pleasure of legs

12 הַמְיַחֲלִים לְחַסְדּוֹ׃ שַׁבְּחִי יְרוּשָׁלַםִ אֶת־יְהוָה הַלְלִי אֱלֹהַיִךְ
Your praise ;Jehovah O ,Praise His in who those
,God ,Jerusalem .mercy hope

13
14 צִיּוֹן׃ כִּי־חִזַּק בְּרִיחֵי שְׁעָרָיִךְ בֵּרַךְ בָּנַיִךְ בְּקִרְבֵּךְ׃ הַשָּׂם־
He within your has He your the He For .Zion O
makes .you sons blessed ;gates of bars strong made

15 גְּבוּלֵךְ שָׁלוֹם חֵלֶב חִטִּים יַשְׂבִּיעֵךְ׃ הַשֹּׁלֵחַ אִמְרָתוֹ אָרֶץ
the (on) His sends He satisfies He the fat the ,peace your (in)
;earth command out .you wheat of border

16 עַד־מְהֵרָה יָרוּץ דְּבָרוֹ׃ הַנֹּתֵן שֶׁלֶג כַּצָּמֶר כְּפוֹר כָּאֵפֶר
like the like snow (He) His runs very until
ashes frost white ;wool gives .word , swiftly

17
18 יְפַזֵּר׃ מַשְׁלִיךְ קַרְחוֹ כְפִתִּים לִפְנֵי קָרָתוֹ מִי יַעֲמֹד׃ יִשְׁלַח
sends He can who His before like His casts He He
out ?stand cold ;crumbs ice out ;scatters

19 דְּבָרוֹ וְיַמְסֵם יַשֵּׁב רוּחוֹ יִזְּלוּ־מָיִם׃ מַגִּיד דְּבָרָו לְיַעֲקֹב
to His He the and His makes He and His
;Jacob words declares .flow waters ,wind blow ;them melts word

20 חֻקָּיו וּמִשְׁפָּטָיו לְיִשְׂרָאֵל׃ לֹא־עָשָׂה כֵן ׀ לְכָל־גּוֹי וּמִשְׁפָּטִים

(His) and ;nation with so has He not .Israel to His and His
judgments any done judgments statutes

בַּל־יְדָעוּם הַלְלוּיָהּ׃

Praise they have not
!Jah .known

PSALM CXLVIII קמח

PSALM 148

1 הַלְלוּיָהּ ׀ הַלְלוּ אֶת־יְהוָה מִן־הַשָּׁמַיִם הַלְלוּהוּ בַּמְּרוֹמִים׃

the in praise the from Jehovah Praise Praise
.heights Him ;heavens !Jah

2
3 הַלְלוּהוּ כָל־מַלְאָכָיו הַלְלוּהוּ כָּל־צְבָאָו׃ הַלְלוּהוּ שֶׁמֶשׁ

sun Praise His all Praise His all Praise
,Him .hosts ,Him ,angels ,Him

4 וְיָרֵחַ הַלְלוּהוּ כָּל־כּוֹכְבֵי אוֹר׃ הַלְלוּהוּ שְׁמֵי הַשָּׁמָיִם

;heavens O Praise .light stars all praise and
of heaven ,Him of ,Him ;moon

5 וְהַמַּיִם אֲשֶׁר ׀ מֵעַל הַשָּׁמָיִם׃ יְהַלְלוּ אֶת־שֵׁם יְהוָה כִּי

for ;Jehovah the them Let the above that and
of name praise .heavens (are) waters

6 הוּא צִוָּה וְנִבְרָאוּ׃ וַיַּעֲמִידֵם לָעַד לְעוֹלָם חָק־נָתַן וְלֹא

and He a and forever made He And they and com- He
not gave decree ;ever stand them .created were manded

7 יַעֲבוֹר׃ הַלְלוּ אֶת־יְהוָה מִן־הָאָרֶץ תַּנִּינִים וְכָל־תְּהֹמוֹת׃

.deeps and sea- the the from Jehovah Let pass will it
all monsters earth praise .away

8
9 אֵשׁ וּבָרָד שֶׁלֶג וְקִיטוֹר רוּחַ סְעָרָה עֹשָׂה דְבָרוֹ׃ הֶהָרִים

the His fulfilling stormy wind and snow and Fire
mountains ;word ;smoke ;hail

10 וְכָל־גְּבָעוֹת עֵץ פְּרִי וְכָל־אֲרָזִים׃ הַחַיָּה וְכָל־בְּהֵמָה

;cattle and beasts ;cedars and fruit- trees ;hills and
all all all

1 רֶמֶשׂ וְצִפּוֹר כָּנָף׃ מַלְכֵי־אֶרֶץ וְכָל־לְאֻמִּים שָׂרִים וְכָל־

and princes ;peoples and the kings the and creeping
all all earth of ;wing of bird things

2 שֹׁפְטֵי אָרֶץ׃ בַּחוּרִים וְגַם־בְּתוּלוֹת זְקֵנִים עִם־נְעָרִים׃

.youths with old ;virgins and men young the judges
men also ;earth of

3 יְהַלְלוּ ׀ אֶת־שֵׁם יְהוָה כִּי־נִשְׂגָּב שְׁמוֹ לְבַדּוֹ הוֹדוֹ עַל־אֶרֶץ

the (is) His ;alone His is for ;Jehovah the them Let
earth above glory name exalted of name praise

14 וְשָׁמָיִם׃ וַיָּרֶם קֶרֶן ׀ לְעַמּוֹ תְּהִלָּה לְכָל־חֲסִידָיו לִבְנֵי

the of His of the His of the also He and
of sons ,saints all praise ,people horn up lifts .heavens

יִשְׂרָאֵל עַם קְרֹבוֹ הַלְלוּיָהּ׃

Praise to near a ,Israel
!Jah .Him people

His statutes and His judgments to Israel. [20] He has not done so with any nation; and they have not known (His) judgments. Praise Jehovah!

PSALM 148

[1] Praise Jehovah! Praise Jehovah from the heavens; praise Him in the heights. [2] Praise Him, all His angels; praise Him, all His hosts. [3] Praise Him, sun and moon; praise Him, all you stars of light. [4] Praise Him, O heavens of heavens; and O waters that (are) above the heavens. [5] Let them praise the name of Jehovah; for He commanded, and they were created. [6] And He established them forever and ever; He gave a decree that they not pass away. [7] Let the sea-monsters and all deeps praise Jehovah from the earth; [8] fire and hail; snow and smoke; stormy wind fulfilling His word; [9] mountains and all hills; fruitful trees and all cedars; [10] beasts and all cattle; creeping things and birds of the wing; [11] kings of the earth and all people; princes and all judges of the earth; [12] both young men and virgins too; old men with youths. [13] Let them praise the name of Jehovah; for His name alone is exalted; His glory (is) above the earth and heavens. [14] He also lifts up the horn of His people, the praise of all His saints, of the sons of Israel, a people near to Him. Praise Jehovah!

PSALM CXLIX קמט

PSALM 149

[1] Praise Jehovah! Sing to Jehovah a new song, His praise in the assembly of the saints. [2] Let Israel rejoice in Him who made him; let the sons of Zion be joyful in their King. [3] Let them praise His name in the dance; let them sing praise to Him with the timbrel and lyre. [4] For Jehovah takes pleasure in His people; He beautifies the meek with salvation. [5] Let the saints be joyful in glory; let them sing aloud on their beds, [6] (and) the exaltation of God (be) in their throat; and a sword of mouths in their hand, [7] to execute vengeance on the nations, punishment on the peoples; [8] to bind their kings with chains and their nobles with iron bands; [9] to execute on them the judgment written: this (is an) honor for all His saints. Praise Jehovah!

1 הַלְלוּיָהּ ׀ שִׁירוּ לַיהוָה שִׁיר חָדָשׁ תְּהִלָּתוֹ בִּקְהַל חֲסִידִים׃
the the in His ,new song a to Sing Praise
.saints of assembly praise Jehovah !Jah

2 3 יִשְׂמַח יִשְׂרָאֵל בְּעֹשָׂיו בְּנֵי־צִיּוֹן יָגִילוּ בְמַלְכָּם׃ יְהַלְלוּ שְׁמוֹ
His them Let their in be Zion the His in Israel Let
name praise .king joyful of sons ,Maker rejoice

4 בְמָחוֹל בְּתֹף וְכִנּוֹר יְזַמְּרוּ־לוֹ׃ כִּי־רוֹצֶה יְהוָה בְּעַמּוֹ יְפָאֵר
He His in Jehovah takes for to them let and the with the in
adorns ;people pleasure .Him praise sing lyre timbrel ;dance

5 עֲנָוִים בִּישׁוּעָה׃ יַעְלְזוּ חֲסִידִים בְּכָבוֹד יְרַנְּנוּ עַל־מִשְׁכְּבוֹתָם׃
their on them let in the Let with the
,beds aloud sing ;glory saints exult .salvation humble

6 7 רוֹמְמוֹת אֵל בִּגְרוֹנָם וְחֶרֶב פִּיפִיּוֹת בְּיָדָם׃ לַעֲשׂוֹת
execute to their in two- a and their in God the (and)
;hand edged sword ;mouth of exaltation

8 נְקָמָה בַּגּוֹיִם תּוֹכֵחֹת בַּלְאֻמִּים׃ לֶאְסֹר מַלְכֵיהֶם בְּזִקִּים
with their bind to the on punishment the on ven-
chains kings ;peoples ,nations geance

9 וְנִכְבְּדֵיהֶם בְּכַבְלֵי בַרְזֶל׃ לַעֲשׂוֹת בָּהֶם ׀ מִשְׁפָּט כָּתוּב
;written the on execute to ;iron with their and
judgment them of bands nobles

הָדָר הוּא לְכָל־חֲסִידָיו הַלְלוּיָהּ׃
Praise His for this (an)
!Jah .saints all (is) honor

PSALM CL קנ

PSALM 150

[1] Praise Jehovah! Praise God in His holy place; praise Him in the expanse of His might. [2] Praise Him in His mighty acts; praise Him according to His excellent greatness. [3] Praise Him with the sound of the trumpet; praise Him with the harp and lyre. [4] Praise Him with the timbrel and dance; praise Him with stringed instruments and pipes. [5] Praise Him on the sounding cymbals; praise Him with the resounding cymbals. [6] Let everything that breathes praise Jehovah. Praise Jehovah!

1 2 הַלְלוּיָהּ ׀ הַלְלוּ־אֵל בְּקָדְשׁוֹ הַלְלוּהוּ בִּרְקִיעַ עֻזּוֹ׃ הַלְלוּהוּ
Praise His the in praise His in God Praise Praise
Him .might of expanse Him ;place holy !Jah

3 בִגְבוּרֹתָיו הַלְלוּהוּ כְּרֹב גֻּדְלוֹ׃ הַלְלוּהוּ בְּתֵקַע שׁוֹפָר
the the with Praise His according Praise mighty His in
;trumpet of sound Him .greatness excellent to Him ;acts

4 הַלְלוּהוּ בְּנֵבֶל וְכִנּוֹר׃ הַלְלוּהוּ בְתֹף וּמָחוֹל הַלְלוּהוּ
praise and the with Praise and the with Praise
Him ;dance timbrel Him .lyre harp Him

5 בְּמִנִּים וְעוּגָב׃ הַלְלוּהוּ בְצִלְצְלֵי־שָׁמַע הַלְלוּהוּ בְּצִלְצְלֵי
the with praise ;loud the on Praise and with
of cymbals Him cymbals Him .pipes strings

6 תְרוּעָה׃ כֹּל הַנְּשָׁמָה תְּהַלֵּל יָהּ הַלְלוּיָהּ׃
!Jah Praise .Jah Let that every- .resounding
praise breathes thing

מִשְׁלֵי

LIBER PROVERBIORUM

CAPUT. I א

CHAPTER 1

CHAPTER 1

[1] The Proverbs of Solomon, son of David, king of Israel: [2] To know wisdom and instruction; to understand the words of understanding; [3] to receive instruction in prudence, justice, and judgment, and uprightness; [4] to give sense to the youth, knowledge and discretion to the young man [5] — the wise hears and increases learning; and the understanding ones will get wise counsel — [6] to understand a proverb and an allusion; the words of the wise, and their acute sayings.

[7] The fear of Jehovah (is) the beginning of knowledge; fools despise wisdom and instruction. [8] My son, hear your father's instruction; and do not forsake the teaching of your mother; [9] for they (shall be) an ornament of grace to your head, and chains for your neck. [10] My son, if sinners lure you, do not be willing. [11] If they say, Walk with us, let us lie in wait for blood; let us secretly lurk for the innocent without cause; [12] let us swallow them up alive as Sheol; and whole, as those who go down (into) the Pit, [13] we shall find all precious goods; we shall fill our houses (with) spoil; [14] cast in your lot among us; one purse shall be to all of us. [15] My son, do not walk in the way with them! Hold back your foot from their path; [16] for their feet run to evil and they haste to shed blood. [17] For in vain the net is spread in the sight of every bird. [18] And they lie in

1 2 מִשְׁלֵי שְׁלֹמֹה בֶן־דָּוִד מֶלֶךְ יִשְׂרָאֵל׃ לָדַעַת חָכְמָה
wisdom know to :Israel king ,David son ,Solomon The
of of of Proverbs

3 וּמוּסָר לְהָבִין אִמְרֵי בִינָה׃ לָקַחַת מוּסַר הַשְׂכֵּל צֶדֶק
right- pru- instruction to under- the under- to in- and
ness dence in receive ;standing of words stand ;struction

4 וּמִשְׁפָּט וּמֵשָׁרִים׃ לָתֵת לִפְתָאיִם עָרְמָה לְנַעַר דַּעַת
knowledge the to ;prudence the to give to and and
man young simple ;uprightness judgment

5 וּמְזִמָּה׃ יִשְׁמַע חָכָם וְיוֹסֶף לֶקַח וְנָבוֹן תַּחְבֻּלוֹת יִקְנֶה׃
will wise the and ,learning and The hears dis- and
—get counsel understanding increases wise .cretion

6 7 לְהָבִין מָשָׁל וּמְלִיצָה דִּבְרֵי חֲכָמִים וְחִידֹתָם׃ יִרְאַת יְהוָה
Jehovah The their and the the an and a under- to
of fear riddles wise of words enigma proverb stand

8 רֵאשִׁית דָּעַת חָכְמָה וּמוּסָר אֱוִילִים בָּזוּ׃ שְׁמַע בְּנִי
my ,Hear .despise fools and wisdom ;knowledge the (is)
,son instruction of beginning

9 מוּסַר אָבִיךָ וְאַל־תִּטֹּשׁ תּוֹרַת אִמֶּךָ׃ כִּי ׀ לִוְיַת חֵן הֵם
they grace orn- a for your teaching do and your in-
(are) of ament ,mother's forsake not ;father's struction

10 לְרֹאשֶׁךָ וַעֲנָקִים לְגַרְגְּרֹתֶךָ׃ בְּנִי אִם־יְפַתּוּךָ חַטָּאִים אַל־
not ;sinners lure if My your for and your to
you ,son .neck necklaces ,head

11 תֹּבֵא׃ אִם־יֹאמְרוּ לְכָה אִתָּנוּ נֶאֶרְבָה לְדָם נִצְפְּנָה לְנָקִי
the for us let for lie us let with Walk they If be do
innocent lurk ;blood wait in ,us ,say .willing

12 13 חִנָּם׃ נִבְלָעֵם כִּשְׁאוֹל חַיִּים וּתְמִימִים כְּיוֹרְדֵי בוֹר׃ כָּל־
all (into) those as and ;alive Sheol as us let without
.pit the going ,whole them swallow ;cause

14 הוֹן יָקָר נִמְצָא נְמַלֵּא בָתֵּינוּ שָׁלָל׃ גּוֹרָלְךָ תַּפִּיל בְּתוֹכֵנוּ
among Let your (with) our shall we shall We wealth
;us fall lot .spoil houses fill ;find precious

15 כִּיס אֶחָד יִהְיֶה לְכֻלָּנוּ׃ בְּנִי אַל־תֵּלֵךְ בְּדֶרֶךְ אִתָּם מְנַע
Hold with the in do not My all for shall one purse
back !them way walk ,son .us of be

16 רַגְלְךָ מִנְּתִיבָתָם׃ כִּי רַגְלֵיהֶם לָרַע יָרוּצוּ וִימַהֲרוּ לִשְׁפָּךְ־
to they and ,run evil to their for their from your
shed hasten feet ;path foot

17 18 דָּם׃ כִּי־חִנָּם מְזֹרָה הָרָשֶׁת בְּעֵינֵי כָּל־בַּעַל כָּנָף׃ וְהֵם
and the . lord every the in net the is in For .blood
they .wing of of eyes spread vain

wait for their own blood;
they lurk secretly for their
own souls. [19] So are the
ways of everyone who
gets gain; (it) takesaway
its owner's soul.

[20] Wisdom cries
aloud in the plaza; she gives
her voice in the square;
[21] she calls at the head of
gathering places; in the
opening of the gates; in the
city she utters her words:
[22] How long will you
love to be simple, you simple ones? And (how long
will) scorners desire scorning, and fools hate knowledge? [23] Turn back at
my warning; behold, I will
pour out my Spirit to you; I
will make my words known
to you. [24] Because I have
called, and you have re-
fused; I have stretched out
a hand, and none in-
clines; but you have
ignored all my counsel;
you did not want my warn-
ing; [26] I also will laugh in
your calamity, I will mock
when your dread comes;
[27] when your dread
comes like a storm; and
your calamity arrives like a
hurricane when distress and
constraint come on you.
[28] Then they shall call on
me, and I will not answer;
they shall seek me early, but
they shall not find me,
[29] That they hated
knowledge and chose not
the fear of Jehovah.
[30] They did not want my
counsel; they despised all
my reproof; [31] and they
shall eat of the fruit of their
own way, and be filled with
their own lusts. [32] For
the going astray of the
simple kills them; and the
ease of fools destroys them.
[33] But he who listens to
me shall live securely, and
shall be at ease from the
dread of evil.

CHAPTER 2

[1] My son, if you will
receive My words, and hide
My commandments with
you, [2] so that you bow

---

19 לְדָמָם יֶאֱרֹבוּ יִצְפְּנוּ לְנַפְשֹׁתָם: כֵּן אָרְחוֹת כָּל־בֹּצֵעַ

who | every | the are | So | their | for | lurk | they | in lie | their | their for
gets | one | of ways | | souls own | | secretly | | wait; | for | blood own

20 בָּצַע אֶת־נֶפֶשׁ בְּעָלָיו יִקָּח: חָכְמוֹת בַּחוּץ תָּרֹנָּה בָּרְחֹבוֹת

the in | cries | the in | Wisdom | takes he | its | soul the | (unjust)
square - | aloud; | street | | owner | of | | gain

21 תִּתֵּן קוֹלָהּ: בְּרֹאשׁ הֹמִיּוֹת תִּקְרָא בְּפִתְחֵי שְׁעָרִים בָּעִיר

the in | the | the at | she | commotion | head At | her | she
city | gates; | of opening | calls | places | of the | voice. | gives

22 אֲמָרֶיהָ תֹאמֵר: עַד־מָתַי פְּתָיִם תְּאֵהֲבוּ פֶתִי וְלֵצִים

And | sim- | will you | simple | when Until | she | her
scorners | plicity? | love | ones, | | speaks; | words

23 לָצוֹן חָמְדוּ לָהֶם וּכְסִילִים יִשְׂנְאוּ־דָעַת: תָּשׁוּבוּ לְתוֹכַחְתִּי

my at | Turn | ?knowledge | will | And | for | will | scorn
warning; | back | | hate | fools | them? | desire

24 הִנֵּה אַבִּיעָה לָכֶם רוּחִי אוֹדִיעָה דְבָרַי אֶתְכֶם: יַעַן

Because | .you to | my | will I | my | you to | will I | behold,
| | words | known make | spirit | | out pour

25 קָרָאתִי וַתְּמָאֵנוּ נָטִיתִי יָדִי וְאֵין מַקְשִׁיב: וַתִּפְרְעוּ כָל־עֲצָתִי

my | all | you And | .inclines | yet | a | ex- I | you and | have I
advice, | | ignored | | none | hand | tend | refused | called,

26 וְתוֹכַחְתִּי לֹא אֲבִיתֶם: גַּם־אֲנִי בְּאֵידְכֶם אֶשְׂחָק אֶלְעַג

will I | will | your in | I Also | you | not | my and
mock; | laugh; | calamity | .wanted | | | warning

27 בְּבֹא פַחְדְּכֶם: בְּבֹא כְשׁוֹאָה פַּחְדְּכֶם וְאֵידְכֶם כְּסוּפָה

a like | your and | your | a like | when | your | when
tempest | calamity; | dread | storm | comes | dread; | comes

28 יֶאֱתֶה בְּבֹא עֲלֵיכֶם צָרָה וְצוּקָה: אָז יִקְרָאֻנְנִי וְלֹא אֶעֱנֶה

will I | and | shall they | Then | and | distress | upon | when
answer not | | me on call | | constraint | | you | comes; | arrives

29 יְשַׁחֲרֻנְנִי וְלֹא יִמְצָאֻנְנִי: תַּחַת כִּי־שָׂנְאוּ דָעַת וְיִרְאַת יְהֹוָה

Jehovah the and | knowl- | they | That | find shall | but | shall they
of fear | edge, | hated | | me | not early | me seek

30 **31** לֹא בָחָרוּ: לֹא־אָבוּ לַעֲצָתִי נָאֲצוּ כָּל־תּוֹכַחְתִּי: וְיֹאכְלוּ

they and | my | all | they | my | they | Not | .chose | not
eat shall | reproof; | | despised | counsel; | wanted | | | |

32 מִפְּרִי דַרְכָּם וּמִמֹּעֲצֹתֵיהֶם יִשְׂבָּעוּ: כִּי מְשׁוּבַת פְּתָיִם

the | going the | For | be | their with and | own their | the of
simple | of astray | | .filled | devices own | way, | of fruit

33 תַּהַרְגֵם וְשַׁלְוַת כְּסִילִים תְּאַבְּדֵם: וְשֹׁמֵעַ לִי יִשְׁכָּן־בֶּטַח

securely shall | to | one But | destroys | fools | the and | slays
dwell | me listening | | .them | | of ease; | them;

וְשַׁאֲנַן מִפַּחַד רָעָה:

evil | the from | shall and
of fear | ease at be

CAP. II ב

CHAPTER 2

1 **2** בְּנִי אִם־תִּקַּח אֲמָרָי וּמִצְוֹתַי תִּצְפֹּן אִתָּךְ: לְהַקְשִׁיב

you that so | with | hide | my and | my | will you | if | My
bow | you, | | commands | words, | receive | | son,

your ear to wisdom, you shall extend your heart to understanding; [3] for if you cry for discernment, lifting up your voice for understanding; [4] if you seek her as silver, and search for her as hidden treasures; [5] then you shall understand the fear of Jehovah, and find knowledge of God. [6] For Jehovah gives wisdom; out of His mouth (come) knowledge and understanding. [7] He lays up sound wisdom for the upright; (He is) a shield to the ones who walk in integrity, [8] to guard the paths of judgment, and He protects the way of His saints. [9] Then you shall understand righteousness and judgment and honesty; (yea,) every good path. [10] When wisdom enters into your heart; and knowledge is pleasing to your soul; [11] discretion shall keep you; understanding shall watch over you; [12] to deliver you from the evil way; from the man who speaks perverse things; [13] those who leave the paths of uprightness to walk in the ways of darkness; [14] who rejoice to do evil; they delight in the perversities of the wicked; [15] whose paths (are) crooked; yea, they (are) devious in their tracks. [16] (These will) deliver you from the strange woman, from the foreigner who flatters (with) her words; [17] who forsakes the guide of her youth, and forgets the covenant of her God [18] For her house bows down to death, and her tracks to the departed. [19] All going in to her do not return;nor do they reach the paths of life. [20] Then you may walk in the paths of the good, and keep the paths of the righteous. [21] For the upright shall live in the

3 לחכמה אזנך תטה לבך לתבונה: כי אם לבינה תקרא
you under- for if ,for under- to your shall you your to
,cry standing ;standing heart extend ,ear wisdom

4 לתבונה תתן קולך: אם-תבקשנה ככסף וכמטמונים
hidden as and as seek you if your lifting under- for
treasures ,silver her ;voice up standing

5 תחפשנה: אז תבין יראת יהוה ודעת אלהים תמצא:
.find God the and ,Jehovah the shall you then search you
of knowledge of fear know ;her for

6 7 כי-יהוה יתן חכמה מפיו דעת ותבונה: וצפן לישרים
the for He And under- and knowl- His from ,wisdom gives Jehovah For
upright up lays .standing edge (are) mouth

8 תושיה מגן להלכי תם: לנצר ארחות משפט ודרך
the and ;judgment the guard to in those for (is He) sound
of way of paths ,integrity walking ,shield a ;wisdom

9 חסידו ישמר: אז תבין צדק ומשפט ומישרים כל-
every and and righteous- shall you Then He His
,honesty judgment ness understand .guards saints

10 מעגל-טוב: כי-תבוא חכמה בלבך ודעת לנפשך ינעם:
is your to and your into wisdom enters When .good path
;pleasing soul knowledge ;heart

11 12 מזמה תשמר עליך תבונה תנצרכה: להצילך מדרך
the from deliver to watch shall understand- ;you shall dis-
way you you over ing keep cretion

13 רע מאיש מדבר תהפכות: העזבים ארחות ישר ללכת
to upright- paths the ones the perverse speaking the from ;evil
walk ness of leaving ,things man

14 בדרכי-חשך: השמחים לעשות רע יגילו בתהפכות
per- the in they ;evil do to rejoicing ;darkness the in
of versities delight of ways

15 רע: אשר ארחתיהם עקשים ונלוזים במעגלותם:
their in (are) and (are) paths whose the
tracks devious ,crooked ;evil

16 17 להצילך מאשה זרה מנכריה אמריה החליקה: העזבת
who ;flattering her (by) the from ,strange the from will (These)
forsakes words foreigner woman you deliver

18 אלוף נעוריה ואת-ברית אלהיה שכחה: כי שחה אל-
to leads For .forgets her the and her the
down God of covenant ,youth of guide

19 מות ביתה ואל-רפאים מעגלתיה: כל-באיה לא ישובון
;return not going All her the and her death
her to in .tracks dead to ,house

20 ולא ישיגו ארחות חיים: למען תלך בדרך טובים
,good the the in may you order In .life paths the they and
of paths walk that of reach not

21 וארחות צדיקים תשמר: כי-ישרים ישכנו-ארץ
the (in) shall the For .keep may the the and
;land dwell upright righteous of paths

land; and the perfect shall remain in it. [22] But the wicked shall be cut off from the earth; and the transgressors shall be rooted out of it

וּתְמִימִים יִוָּתְרוּ בָהּ׃   וּרְשָׁעִים מֵאֶרֶץ יִכָּרֵתוּ וּבוֹגְדִים 22

| the and | be shall | the | from | the But | .it in | shall | the and |
| treacherous | ;off cut | earth | | wicked | | remain | blameless |

יִסְּחוּ מִמֶּנָּה׃

| from | be shall |
| .it | up rooted |

CAP. III. ג

CHAPTER 3

CHAPTER 3

[1] My son, do not forget my law; but let your heart keep my commands; [2] for they shall add length of days, and long life and peace to you. [3] Mercy and truth will not forsake you; tie them upon your neck; write them on the tablet of your heart; [4] and you shall find favor and good understanding in the sight of God and man. [5] Trust in Jehovah with all your heart; and lean not to your own understanding. [6] In all your ways acknowledge Him, and He shall direct your paths. [7] Do not be wise in your own eyes; fear Jehovah and depart from evil. [8] Healing shall be to your navel and marrow to your bones. [9] Honor Jehovah with your substance, and with the firstfruits of all your increase; [10] and your barns shall be filled (with) plenty; and your presses shall burst (with) new wine. [11] My son, do not despise the chastening of Jehovah; and do not loathe His correction; [12] for whom Jehovah loves He corrects, even as a father the son he loves.

[13] Happy (is) the man who finds wisdom, and the man who gets understanding. [14] For its gain (is) better than the gain from silver; and its produce more than fine gold; [15] she (is) more precious than rubies; and all the things you can desire are not to be compared with her. [16] Length of days (is) in her right hand; riches and honor in her left hand.

בְּנִי תּוֹרָתִי אַל־תִּשְׁכָּח וּמִצְוֹתַי יִצֹּר לִבֶּךָ׃ כִּי אֹרֶךְ יָמִים 1 2

| days | length | for | your | let | my but | do not | My |
| | of | | ;heart | guard | commands | ;forget | teaching ,son |

וּשְׁנוֹת חַיִּים וְשָׁלוֹם יוֹסִיפוּ לָךְ׃ חֶסֶד וֶאֱמֶת אַל־יַעַזְבֻךָ 3

| will | not and | Mercy | .you to | they | and | life | and |
| ,you forsake | truth | | | add shall | peace | | of years |

קָשְׁרֵם עַל־גַּרְגְּרוֹתֶיךָ כָּתְבֵם עַל־לוּחַ לִבֶּךָ׃ וּמְצָא־חֵן 4

| favor and | your | the on | write | your | on | them tie |
| find | ;heart of tablet | them | ;neck | |

וְשֵׂכֶל טוֹב בְּעֵינֵי אֱלֹהִים וְאָדָם׃ בְּטַח אֶל־יְהוָה בְּכָל־ 5

| with | Jehovah | to Trust | and | God | the in | good | and |
| all | | | .man | | of eyes | | wisdom |

לִבֶּךָ וְאֶל־בִּינָתְךָ אַל־תִּשָּׁעֵן׃ בְּכָל־דְּרָכֶיךָ דָעֵהוּ וְהוּא 6

| and acknowledge | your | all In | do | not (own)-your to | and | your |
| He ,Him | ways | | ,lean | understanding | ;heart |

יְיַשֵּׁר אֹרְחֹתֶיךָ׃ אַל־תְּהִי חָכָם בְּעֵינֶיךָ יְרָא אֶת־יְהוָה 7

| Jehovah | fear | your in | wise | be do Not | your | shall |
| | | eyes own | | | .paths | direct |

וְסוּר מֵרָע׃ רִפְאוּת תְּהִי לְשָׁרֶּךָ וְשִׁקּוּי לְעַצְמוֹתֶיךָ׃ כַּבֵּד 8 9

| Honor | your to | and | your to | shall | Healing | from | and |
| | .bones | moisture | navel | be | | .evil | depart |

אֶת־יְהוָה מֵהוֹנֶךָ וּמֵרֵאשִׁית כָּל־תְּבוּאָתֶךָ׃ וְיִמָּלְאוּ אֲסָמֶיךָ 10

| your | shall and | your | all | the from | and | your from | Jehovah |
| barns | filled be | | ;produce | of firstfruits | | substance | |

שָׂבָע וְתִירוֹשׁ יְקָבֶיךָ יִפְרֹצוּ׃ מוּסַר יְהוָה בְּנִי אַל־תִּמְאָס 11

| do | not my | ,Jehovah The | shall | wine your | (with) and | (with) |
| ;despise | ,son | of chastening | .burst | vats | wine new | ;plenty |

וְאַל־תָּקֹץ בְּתוֹכַחְתּוֹ׃ כִּי אֶת אֲשֶׁר־אֱהַב יְהוָה יוֹכִיחַ 12

| He | Jehovah | loves | whom | for | His | do | and |
| ,corrects | | | | | ;correction | loathe | not |

וְכָאָב אֶת־בֵּן יִרְצֶה׃ אַשְׁרֵי אָדָם מָצָא חָכְמָה וְאָדָם 13

| the and | ,wisdom | finding | the | Blessed | is he | the | as even |
| man | | | man | (is) | | son | father a |

יָפִיק תְּבוּנָה׃ כִּי טוֹב סַחְרָהּ מִסְּחַר־כָּסֶף וּמֵחָרוּץ 14

| more and | ;silver | the than | its | better is | For | understanding |
| gold than | | of gain | gain | | | getting |

תְּבוּאָתָהּ׃ יְקָרָה הִיא מִפְּנִינִים וְכָל־חֲפָצֶיךָ לֹא יִשְׁווּ־בָהּ׃ 15

| with | are | not | your all and | than | she | (More) | .produce its |
| her | likened | | delights | ;jewels | | precious | |

אֹרֶךְ יָמִים בִּימִינָהּ בִּשְׂמֹאוֹלָהּ עֹשֶׁר וְכָבוֹד׃ דְּרָכֶיהָ 16 17

| ways Her | and | riches | left her in | her in | days | Length |
| | .honor | | (hand) | (hand)right | (is) | of |

[17] Her ways (are) ways of pleasantness, and all her paths peace. [18] She (is) a tree of life to the ones who lay hold on her; and happy (are) the ones upholding her. [19] Jehovah founded the earth by wisdom; He founded the heavens by understanding; [20] the depths were broken up by His knowledge; and the clouds dropped down the dew. [21] My son, do not let them depart from your eyes; keep sound wisdom and judgment; [22] and they shall be life to your soul, and grace to your neck; [23] then you shall walk in your way safely; and your foot shall not stumble. [24] When you lie down, you shall not dread; yea, you shall lie down and your sleep shall be sweet. [25] Do not be afraid of sudden terror; nor of the destruction of the wicked, when it comes. [26] For Jehovah shall be at your side; and He shall keep your foot from being caught.

[27] Do not withhold good from those to whom it is due, when it is in the power of your hand to do (it). [28] Do not say to your neighbor, Go and come back again; or, Tomorrow I will give; when you have it beside you. [29] Do not plan evil against your neighbor, since he lives trustingly by you. [30] Do not strive with a man without cause, if he has done you no harm. [31] Do not envy the cruel man, and choose not among all his ways. [32] For the perverse one (is) hateful to Jehovah; but His secret (is) with the righteous. [33] The curse of Jehovah (is) in the house of the wicked; but He blesses the abode of the just. [34] Surely He scorns the scorners; but He gives grace to the lowly. [35] The wise shall inherit the honor, but the foolish exalt shame.

18 דַּרְכֵי־נֹעַם וְכָל־נְתִיבוֹתֶיהָ שָׁלוֹם׃ עֵץ־חַיִּים הִיא לַמַּחֲזִיקִים
those for she life tree A are her and pleasant- (are)
hold taking (is) of .peace paths all ,ness of ways

19 בָּהּ וְתֹמְכֶיהָ מְאֻשָּׁר׃ יְהוָה בְּחָכְמָה יָסַד־אָרֶץ כּוֹנֵן
He the founded by Jehovah (are) those and on
fixed ;earth wisdom .blessed her holding ;her

20 שָׁמַיִם בִּתְבוּנָה׃ בְּדַעְתּוֹ תְּהוֹמוֹת נִבְקָעוּ וּשְׁחָקִים יִרְעֲפוּ־
dropped the and were the His By under- by the
down clouds ;up broken depths knowledge .standing heavens

21
22 טָל׃ בְּנִי אַל־יָלֻזוּ מֵעֵינֶיךָ נְצֹר תֻּשִׁיָּה וּמְזִמָּה׃ וְיִהְיוּ
they and and sound keep your from not let My
be shall ;discretion wisdom ;eyes depart them ,son .dew

23 חַיִּים לְנַפְשֶׁךָ וְחֵן לְגַרְגְּרֹתֶיךָ׃ אָז תֵּלֵךְ לָבֶטַח דַּרְכֶּךָ
your (in) with shall you Then your to and your to life
;way safety walk .neck grace ,soul

24 וְרַגְלְךָ לֹא תִגּוֹף׃ אִם־תִּשְׁכַּב לֹא תִפְחָד וְשָׁכַבְתָּ וְעָרְבָה
shall and you and shall you not ,rest you When shall not your and
sweet be lie shall dread .stumble foot

25 שְׁנָתֶךָ׃ אַל־תִּירָא מִפַּחַד פִּתְאֹם וּמִשֹּׁאַת רְשָׁעִים כִּי
for the the of and ,sudden from be do Not your
,wicked of ruin dread afraid .sleep

26
27 תָבֹא׃ כִּי־יְהוָה יִהְיֶה בְכִסְלֶךָ וְשָׁמַר רַגְלְךָ מִלָּכֶד׃ אַל־
Not from your He and your at shall Jehovah For is it
.capture foot keep shall ;loins be .coming

28 תִּמְנַע־טוֹב מִבְּעָלָיו בִּהְיוֹת לְאֵל יָדֶיךָ לַעֲשׂוֹת׃ אַל־תֹּאמַר
do Not do to your the in When its from good do
say .(it) hand of power is it .owners withhold

29 לְרֵעֲךָ לֵךְ וָשׁוּב וּמָחָר אֶתֵּן וְיֵשׁ אִתָּךְ׃ אַל־תַּחֲרֹשׁ עַל־
against do Not with but -will I and and Go your to
plot .you is it ,give tomorrow ,return ,neighbor

30 רֵעֲךָ רָעָה וְהוּא־יוֹשֵׁב לָבֶטַח אִתָּךְ׃ אַל־תָּרוֹב עִם־אָדָם
a with do Not with securely dwells he and evil your
man strive .you neighbor

31 חִנָּם אִם־לֹא גְמָלְךָ רָעָה׃ אַל־תְּקַנֵּא בְּאִישׁ חָמָס וְאַל־
and ,violence against do Not .evil has he not if without
not of man a envy you dealt ,cause

32 תִּבְחַר בְּכָל־דְּרָכָיו׃ כִּי תוֹעֲבַת יְהוָה נָלוֹז וְאֶת־יְשָׁרִים
the with but the (is) Jehovah hateful For his among do
(is) upright devious to .ways all choose

33 סוֹדוֹ׃ מְאֵרַת יְהוָה בְּבֵית רָשָׁע וּנְוֵה צַדִּיקִים יְבָרֵךְ׃
He the the but the on (is) Jehovah The His
.blesses righteous of abode ;wicked's house of curse .council

34
35 אִם־לַלֵּצִים הוּא יָלִיץ וְלַעֲנָיִים יִתֶּן־חֵן׃ כָּבוֹד חֲכָמִים
wise the Honor .grace He to yet ,scorns He the at If
gives lowly the scorners

יִנְחָלוּ וּכְסִילִים מֵרִים קָלוֹן׃
shame (are) the but ,inherit
exalting foolish

CAP. IV ד

CHAPTER 4

[1] Sons, hear the instruction of a father; and listen so as to know understanding. [2] For I give you good teaching; do not forsake my law. [3] For I was my father's son, tender, and an only one in the sight of my mother. [4] He also taught me and said to me, Let your heart cling to my words; keep my commandments and live. [5] Get wisdom, get understanding; do not forsake and do not turn away from the words of my mouth. [6] Do not forsake her, and she will preserve you; love her, and she will keep you. [7] Wisdom (is) the main thing; get wisdom; and with all your getting get understanding. [8] Exalt her, and she will lift you up; she shall bring you to honor when you embrace her. [9] She shall give a wreath of grace to your head; she shall shield you with a crown of glory.

[10] Hear, O my son, and receive my sayings; and the years of your life (shall be) many. [11] I have taught you in the way of wisdom; I have led you in the right tracks; [12] when you go, your tracks shall not be narrowed; and when you run, you shall not stumble. [13] Take fast hold of instruction; do not let her go; keep her, for she (is) your life. [14] Do not enter the path of the wicked; and do not go in the way of evil-doers. [15] Avoid it; do not pass by it; turn from it and pass on. [16] For they do not sleep if they have done no evil; and their sleep is taken away unless they cause (some) to fall. [17] For they eat the bread of wickedness, and drink the wine of violence. [18] But the path of the just (is) as a bright light shining more and more to the perfect day. [19] The way of the wicked (is) as darkness; they do not know at what they stumble.

CHAPTER 4

1 2 שִׁמְעוּ בָנִים מוּסַר אָב וְהַקְשִׁיבוּ לָדַעַת בִּינָה׃ כִּי לֶקַח
teaching For under- to and a teaching ,sons ,Hear
.standing know listen ,father's

3 טוֹב נָתַתִּי לָכֶם תּוֹרָתִי אַל־תַּעֲזֹבוּ׃ כִּי־בֵן הָיִיתִי לְאָבִי
my to was I son For do not law my ,you to give I good
father .forsake

4 רַךְ וְיָחִיד לִפְנֵי אִמִּי׃ וַיֹּרֵנִי וַיֹּאמֶר לִי יִתְמָךְ־דְּבָרַי לִבֶּךָ
your to my May to said and he And my before only and ten-
;heart words cling ,me me taught .mother (son) der

5 שְׁמֹר מִצְוֹתַי וֶחְיֵה׃ קְנֵה חָכְמָה קְנֵה בִינָה אַל־תִּשְׁכַּח
do not under- get ,wisdom Get and my keep
,forget ;standing .live commands

6 וְאַל־תֵּט מֵאִמְרֵי־פִי׃ אַל־תַּעַזְבֶהָ וְתִשְׁמְרֶךָּ אֱהָבֶהָ
love will she and do Not my the from stretch and
her ;you keep her forsake .mouth of words away not

7 וְתִצְּרֶךָּ׃ רֵאשִׁית חָכְמָה קְנֵה חָכְמָה וּבְכָל־קִנְיָנְךָ קְנֵה
get your with and ,wisdom get (is) first The will she and
,getting all ;wisdom thing .you guard

8 9 בִינָה׃ סַלְסְלֶהָ וּתְרוֹמְמֶךָּ תְּכַבֵּדְךָ כִּי תְחַבְּקֶנָּה׃ תִּתֵּן
shall She you when will she will she and Exalt under-
give .her embrace you honor ;up you lift ,her .standing

10 לְרֹאשְׁךָ לִוְיַת־חֵן עֲטֶרֶת תִּפְאֶרֶת תְּמַגְּנֶךָּ׃ שְׁמַע בְּנִי וְקַח
and my ,Hear shall she glory crown a ;grace a your to
receive ,son with you shield of of wreath head

11 אֲמָרָי וְיִרְבּוּ לְךָ שְׁנוֹת חַיִּים׃ בְּדֶרֶךְ חָכְמָה הֹרֵתִיךָ
have I wisdom the In .life the to shall and my
;you taught of way of years you many be ;sayings

12 הִדְרַכְתִּיךָ בְּמַעְגְּלֵי־יֹשֶׁר׃ בְּלֶכְתְּךָ לֹא־יֵצַר צַעֲדֶךָ וְאִם־
and your shall not you When upright- the in made have I
if ,steps narrowed be go .ness of tracks walk you

13 תָּרוּץ לֹא תִכָּשֵׁל׃ הַחֲזֵק בַּמּוּסָר אַל־תֶּרֶף נִצְּרֶהָ כִּי־הִיא
she for keep let do not on Take shall you not you
(is) ,her ;go ;instruction hold .stumble run

14 חַיֶּיךָ׃ בְּאֹרַח רְשָׁעִים אַל־תָּבֹא וְאַל־תְּאַשֵּׁר בְּדֶרֶךְ רָעִים׃
evil the in do and do not the the On your
.ones of way advance not ,enter wicked of path .life

15 16 פְּרָעֵהוּ אַל־תַּעֲבָר־בּוֹ שְׂטֵה מֵעָלָיו וַעֲבוֹר׃ כִּי לֹא יִשְׁנוּ
they do not For and from turn into do not Ignore
sleep .on pass it upon aside ;it pass ;it

17 אִם־לֹא יָרֵעוּ וְנִגְזְלָה שְׁנָתָם אִם־לֹא יַכְשׁוֹלוּ׃ כִּי לָחֲמוּ
they For cause they not if their is and have they not if
eat .stumble to sleep away taken ;evil done

18 לֶחֶם רֶשַׁע וְיֵין חֲמָסִים יִשְׁתּוּ׃ וְאֹרַח צַדִּיקִים כְּאוֹר נֹגַהּ
bright as (is) the the But they violence and wicked- the
light a righteous of path .drink of wine ,ness of bread

19 הוֹלֵךְ וָאוֹר עַד־נְכוֹן הַיּוֹם׃ דֶּרֶךְ רְשָׁעִים כָּאֲפֵלָה לֹא יָדְעוּ
they not as (is) the The the is till and going
know do ;darkness wicked of way .day established shining

[20] My son, listen to my words; bow your ear to what I say; [21] let them not depart from your eyes; keep them in the center of your heart; [22] for they (are) life to those who find them; and healing to all his flesh. [23] Keep your heart with all diligence, for out of it (are) the issues of life. [24] Turn away from you the wicked mouth, and put perverse lips far from you. [25] Let your eyes look straight ahead; and let your eyelids look straight before you. [26] Study the path of your feet; then all your ways (will be) established. [27] Do not turn to the right hand or to the left; turn your foot aside from evil.

20 בַּמֶּה יִכָּשֵׁלוּ׃ בְּנִי לִדְבָרַי הַקְשִׁיבָה לַאֲמָרַי הַט־אָזְנֶךָ׃
your bow what to ;listen my to My they at
;ear say I words ,son .stumble what

21
22 אַל־יַלִּזוּ מֵעֵינֶיךָ שָׁמְרֵם בְּתוֹךְ לְבָבֶךָ׃ כִּי־חַיִּים הֵם
they life for your the in keep your from them let not
(are) ;heart of center them ;eyes depart

23 לְמֹצְאֵיהֶם וּלְכָל־בְּשָׂרוֹ מַרְפֵּא׃ מִכָּל־מִשְׁמָר נְצֹר לִבֶּךָ
your keep diligence With .healing his to and who those to
heart all flesh all them find

24 כִּי מִמֶּנּוּ תּוֹצְאוֹת חַיִּים׃ הָסֵר מִמְּךָ עִקְּשׁוּת פֶּה וּלְזוּת
and ,mouth the from turn .life the (are) of out for
devious crooked you away of issues it

25 שְׂפָתַיִם הַרְחֵק מִמֶּךָּ׃ עֵינֶיךָ לְנֹכַח יַבִּיטוּ וְעַפְעַפֶּיךָ יַיְשִׁרוּ
look let your and let the to Your from put lips
straight eyelids ;look front eyes .you far

26
27 נֶגְדֶּךָ׃ פַּלֵּס מַעְגַּל רַגְלֶךָ וְכָל־דְּרָכֶיךָ יִכֹּנוּ׃ אַל־תֵּט יָמִין
right Do not will your and your the Ponder before
turn .set be ways all ,feet of track .you

וּשְׂמֹאול הָסֵר רַגְלְךָ מֵרָע׃
from your turn ;left or
.evil foot aside

CAP. V ה

CHAPTER 5

[1] My son, listen to my wisdom; bow your ears to my understanding; [2] so that you may keep judgment, and your lips may keep knowledge. [3] For the lips of a strange woman drip honey, and her mouth (is) sweeter than oil; [4] but afterwards, she is bitter as wormwood, sharp as a two-edged sword. [5] Her feet go down to death; her steps take hold on hell. [6] Lest you should meditate on the path of life, her paths are movable — you cannot know (them).

[7] Then hear me now, O children; and depart not from the words of my mouth. [8] Remove your ways far from her; and do not come near to the door of her house; [9] lest you give your honor to others, and your years to the cruel; [10] lest strangers be filled (with) your wealth; and your labors (be) in the house of an alien; [11] and you moan when your end (comes); when your flesh and muscle are eaten

1
2 בְּנִי לְחָכְמָתִי הַקְשִׁיבָה לִתְבוּנָתִי הַט־אָזְנֶךָ׃ לִשְׁמֹר
keep to your bow my to ;listen my to My
;ear understanding wisdom ,son

3 מְזִמּוֹת וְדַעַת שְׂפָתֶיךָ יִנְצֹרוּ׃ כִּי נֹפֶת תִּטֹּפְנָה שִׂפְתֵי
lips the drip honey For may your and discre-
of .guard lips knowledge ,tion

4 זָרָה וְחָלָק מִשֶּׁמֶן חִכָּהּ׃ וְאַחֲרִיתָהּ מָרָה כַלַּעֲנָה חַדָּה
sharp worm- as (as is) after- But her (is) than and strange a
,wood bitter wards she .palate oil smoother ,woman

5 כְּחֶרֶב פִּיּוֹת׃ רַגְלֶיהָ יֹרְדוֹת מָוֶת שְׁאוֹל צְעָדֶיהָ יִתְמֹכוּ׃
take her Sheol (to) down go Her .edges a as
.on hold steps ;death feet of sword

6 אֹרַח חַיִּים פֶּן־תְּפַלֵּס נָעוּ מַעְגְּלֹתֶיהָ לֹא תֵדָע׃
can you not —tracks her are you lest —life The
.(it) know moveable ,ponder of path

7
8 וְעַתָּה בָנִים שִׁמְעוּ־לִי וְאַל־תָּסוּרוּ מֵאִמְרֵי־פִי׃ הַרְחֵק
Remove my the from depart and ;me hear O And
far .mouth of words not do ,sons ,now

9 מֵעָלֶיהָ דַרְכֶּךָ וְאַל־תִּקְרַב אֶל־פֶּתַח בֵּיתָהּ׃ פֶּן־תִּתֵּן
you lest her the to come do and your from
give ,house of door near not ;ways her

10 לַאֲחֵרִים הוֹדֶךָ וּשְׁנֹתֶיךָ לְאַכְזָרִי׃ פֶּן־יִשְׂבְּעוּ זָרִים כֹּחֶךָ
your strangers filled be lest the to your and your others to
;strength (with) ;one cruel years ,vigor

11 וַעֲצָבֶיךָ בְּבֵית נָכְרִי׃ וְנָהַמְתָּ בְאַחֲרִיתֶךָ בִּכְלוֹת בְּשָׂרְךָ
your are when your when you and an house in your and
flesh consumed (comes) end moan alien's toil

away; [12] and say, How I have hated instruction; and my heart despised correction; [13] and I have not bowed to the voice of my teachers; nor bowed my ears to those instructing me. [14] I was almost in all evil in the midst of the congregation and assembly.

[15] Drink waters out of you own cistern, and running waters out of your own well. [16] Should your overflowing springs be scattered outside, like rivers of waters in the streets? [19] Let them be only your own, and not to strangers with you; [18] let your fountains be blessed; and rejoice with the wife of your youth; [19] (she is) a loving deer, a graceful doe; let her breasts satisfy you every time; and always be ravished in her love. [20] And my son, why will you be ravished with a strange woman, and embrace the bosom of a foreigner? [21] For the ways of man (are) before the eyes of Jehovah; and He ponders all his tracks. [22] His own iniquities shall take the wicked himself; and he shall be held with the cords of his sin. [23] He shall die without instruction; and in the greatness of his foolishness, he shall go astray.

12 וּשְׁאֵרֶךָ׃ וְאָמַרְתָּ אֵיךְ שָׂנֵאתִי מוּסָר וְתוֹכַחַת נִאַץ לִבִּי׃

my !heart | despised | And correction | !instruction | have I hated | How | you ,say | and | and .muscle

13 וְלֹא־שָׁמַעְתִּי בְּקוֹל מוֹרָי וְלִמְלַמְּדַי לֹא־הִטִּיתִי אָזְנִי׃

my .ear | turned | not | those to and me teaching | my teachers | the of voice | have I obeyed | and not

14 כִּמְעַט הָיִיתִי בְכָל־רָע בְּתוֹךְ קָהָל וְעֵדָה׃ שְׁתֵה־מַיִם

waters | Drink | con- .gregation | and assembly | the of midst | the in | ,evil | all in | was I | a As little

16 מִבּוֹרֶךָ וְנוֹזְלִים מִתּוֹךְ בְּאֵרֶךָ׃ יָפוּצוּ מַעְיְנֹתֶיךָ חוּצָה

outside | your springs | be Should dispersed | own your .well | the from of midst | flow- and ing | waters | your from cistern own

17 בָּרְחֹבוֹת פַּלְגֵי־מָיִם׃ יִהְיוּ־לְךָ לְבַדֶּךָ וְאֵין לְזָרִים אִתָּךְ׃

with .you | for strangers | and not | you ,alone | for ,you | Let be them | ?waters | (like) of rivers | the in streets

18
19 יְהִי־מְקוֹרְךָ בָרוּךְ וּשְׂמַח מֵאֵשֶׁת נְעוּרֶךָ׃ אַיֶּלֶת אֲהָבִים

,loving | (is She) deer a | Your .youth | the in of wife | and rejoice | ,blessed | your fountain | Let be

וְיַעֲלַת־חֵן דַּדֶּיהָ יְרַוֻּךָ בְכָל־עֵת בְּאַהֲבָתָהּ תִּשְׁגֶּה תָמִיד׃

.always | be ravished | her in love | ,time every | at | let you satisfy | her breasts | grace- ful | a and doe

20
21 וְלָמָּה תִשְׁגֶּה בְנִי בְזָרָה וּתְחַבֵּק חֵק נָכְרִיָּה׃ כִּי נֹכַח ׀

(are) before | For | a .foreigner's | bosom | hug and | alien an ,woman | by | ,son my | you will ,ravished be | And why

22 עֵינֵי יְהוָה דַּרְכֵי־אִישׁ וְכָל־מַעְגְּלֹתָיו מְפַלֵּס׃ עֲווֹנֹתָיו

own His iniquities | is He .pondering | his tracks | and all | a ,man | the of ways | Jehovah | the of eyes

23 יִלְכְּדֻנוֹ אֶת־הָרָשָׁע וּבְחַבְלֵי חַטָּאתוֹ יִתָּמֵךְ׃ הוּא יָמוּת

shall die | He | shall he be seized | his sin | with and of cords the | the ;wicked | cap- will ture ,him

בְּאֵין מוּסָר וּבְרֹב אִוַּלְתּוֹ יִשְׁגֶּה׃

goes he astray | his folly's | in and greatness | instruction | in of absence

CHAPTER 6

[1] My son, if you are surety for your friend, (if) you struck your hand with a stranger, [2] you are snared with the words of your mouth; you are captured with the words of your own mouth. [3] My son, do this then, and deliver yourself when you come into the hand of your friend: go, humble yourself and be bold (to) your friend. [4] Do not give sleep to your eyes, or slumber to your eyelids. [5] Deliver yourself like a gazelle from a hand (of hunter), and as a bird from the fowler's hand.

[6] Go to the ant, lazy man; consider her ways and

CAP. VI ו

CHAPTER 6

1
2 בְּנִי אִם־עָרַבְתָּ לְרֵעֶךָ תָּקַעְתָּ לַזָּר כַּפֶּיךָ׃ נוֹקַשְׁתָּ בְאִמְרֵי־

the with of words | are you snared | your palms | with alien an | you (if) struck | your for ;friend | are you surety | if | My ,son

3 פִיךָ נִלְכַּדְתָּ בְּאִמְרֵי־פִיךָ׃ עֲשֵׂה־זֹאת אֵפוֹא ׀ בְּנִי וְהִנָּצֵל

save and yourself | my ,son | ,then | this | do | your ;mouth | the with of words | are you captured | your ,mouth

4 כִּי בָאתָ בְכַף־רֵעֶךָ לֵךְ הִתְרַפֵּס וּרְהַב רֵעֶיךָ׃ אַל־תִּתֵּן

give do Not | your .friend | be and (to) bold | humble yourself | ,go | your :friend | the into of palm | you come | when

5 שֵׁנָה לְעֵינֶיךָ וּתְנוּמָה לְעַפְעַפֶּיךָ׃ הִנָּצֵל כִּצְבִי מִיָּד וּכְצִפּוֹר

a as bird | and | a from ;hand | a as gazelle | Deliver yourself | your to .eyelids | or slumber | your to eyes | sleep

6 מִיַּד יָקוּשׁ׃ לֵךְ־אֶל־נְמָלָה עָצֵל רְאֵה דְרָכֶיהָ וַחֲכָם׃

be and ;wise | her ways | see | lazy ;man | the ,ant | to Go | the .fowler's | from hand

be wise; [7] who, having no guide, overseer or ruler, [8] provides her bread in the summer; gathers her food in the harvest. [9] How long will you lie down, O lazy man? When will you arise out of your sleep? [10] A little sleep, a little slumber; a little folding of the hands to lie down; [11] so shall your poverty come as one stalking, and your need like an armed man. [12] A worthless person, a wicked man, walks (with) a perverse mouth. [13] He winks with his eyes; he scrapes with his feet; he points with his fingers; [14] perverse things (are) in his heart; he is plotting evil at every time, he sends out strife. [15] Therefore his calamity shall come suddenly; he is quickly broken and there is no healing. [16] These six (things) Jehovah hates; yea, seven are hateful to His soul: [17] a proud look, a lying tongue, and hands that shed innocent blood; [18] a heart that plots of wicked plans; feet hurrying to run to mischief; [19] a false witness who breathes lies; and he who causes strife among brothers.

[20] My son, keep your father's commands; and do not forsake the law of your mother. [21] Tie them to your heart forever; tie them around your neck. [22] When you go, it shall lead you; when you sleep, it shall watch over you; and (when) you awaken, it shall talk (with) you. [23] For the commandment (is) a lamp; and the law a light; and reproofs of instruction (are) a way of life; [24] to keep you from the evil woman, from the flattery of the tongue of the strange woman. [25] Do not lust after her beauty in your heart; and do not let her take you with her eyelids. [26] For on account of a woman, a harlot, (a man comes) to the (last) piece of

7 8 אֲשֶׁר אֵין־לָהּ קָצִין שֹׁטֵר וּמֹשֵׁל׃ תָּכִין בַּקַּיִץ לַחְמָהּ אָגְרָה
gathers her the in provides or over- a to not of
,bread summer ,ruler seer ,leader her is whom

9 בַקָּצִיר מַאֲכָלָהּ׃ עַד־מָתַי עָצֵל ׀ תִּשְׁכָּב מָתַי תָּקוּם
will you When you will lazy O ,when Until her the in
arise ?down lie ,man food harvest

10 מִשְּׁנָתֶךָ׃ מְעַט שֵׁנוֹת מְעַט תְּנוּמוֹת מְעַט ׀ חִבֻּק יָדַיִם
the folding a ,slumber a ,sleep A of out
hands of little little little ?sleep your

11 12 לִשְׁכָּב׃ וּבָא־כִמְהַלֵּךְ רֵאשֶׁךָ וּמַחְסֹרְךָ כְּאִישׁ מָגֵן׃ אָדָם
A a a as your and your one as shall so ;rest to
man .shield of man want ,poverty stalking come

13 בְּלִיַּעַל אִישׁ אָוֶן הוֹלֵךְ עִקְּשׁוּת פֶּה׃ קֹרֵץ בְּעֵינָו מֹלֵל
scraping with winking ,mouth crooked a walks ,evil man a worth-
,eyes his (with) of ,less

14 בְּרַגְלָו מֹרֶה בְּאֶצְבְּעֹתָיו׃ תַּהְפֻּכוֹת ׀ בְּלִבּוֹ חֹרֵשׁ רָע
evil is he his in perverse his with pointing his with
plotting ,heart (are) things ;fingers ;feet

15 בְּכָל־עֵת מִדְנִים יְשַׁלֵּחַ׃ עַל־כֵּן פִּתְאֹם יָבוֹא אֵידוֹ פֶּתַע
quickly his shall suddenly Therefore sends he strife ;time at
,calamity come .out every

16 יִשָּׁבֵר וְאֵין מַרְפֵּא׃ שֶׁשׁ־הֵנָּה שָׂנֵא יְהוָה וְשֶׁבַע תּוֹעֲבוֹת
hateful are and ,Jehovah hates these Six .healing is and is he
to seven (things) not ,broken

17 נַפְשׁוֹ׃ עֵינַיִם רָמוֹת לְשׁוֹן שָׁקֶר וְיָדַיִם שֹׁפְכוֹת דָּם־נָקִי׃
inno- blood shedding and lying a ,high eyes His
;cent hands tongue soul

18 לֵב חֹרֵשׁ מַחְשְׁבוֹת אָוֶן רַגְלַיִם מְמַהֲרוֹת לָרוּץ לָרָעָה׃
,evil to run to hurrying feet ;evil plans that a
plots heart

19 יָפִיחַ כְּזָבִים עֵד שָׁקֶר וּמְשַׁלֵּחַ מְדָנִים בֵּין אַחִים׃
.brothers between strife one and ,lying a ,lies he
out sending witness breathes

20 21 נְצֹר בְּנִי מִצְוַת אָבִיךָ וְאַל־תִּטֹּשׁ תּוֹרַת אִמֶּךָ׃ קָשְׁרֵם
them Tie your the do and your commands my ,Keep
.mother of law forsake not ;father's ,son

22 עַל־לִבְּךָ תָמִיד עָנְדֵם עַל־גַּרְגְּרֹתֶךָ׃ בְּהִתְהַלֶּכְךָ ׀ תַּנְחֶה
shall it you When your on bind con- your on
lead ,go .neck them ,tinually heart

23 אֹתָךְ בְּשָׁכְבְּךָ תִּשְׁמֹר עָלֶיךָ וַהֲקִיצוֹתָ הִיא תְשִׂיחֶךָ׃ כִּי
For talk shall it (when) and over shall it you when ;you
(is) .you (with) ,awaken you ;you watch ,down lie

24 נֵר מִצְוָה וְתוֹרָה אוֹר וְדֶרֶךְ חַיִּים תּוֹכְחוֹת מוּסָר׃ לִשְׁמָרְךָ
keep to ;instruction reproofs life the and a the and com- the a
you of (is) of way ;light law mand lamp

25 מֵאֵשֶׁת רָע מֵחֶלְקַת לָשׁוֹן נָכְרִיָּה׃ אַל־תַּחְמֹד יָפְיָהּ בִּלְבָבֶךָ
your in her do Not strange the tongue the from ,evil the from
;heart beauty after lust .woman of smooth woman

26 וְאַל־תִּקָּחֲךָ בְּעַפְעַפֶּיהָ׃ כִּי בְעַד־אִשָּׁה זוֹנָה עַד־כִּכַּר
(last) the to a of behalf on For her with let do and
of loaf harlot woman a .eyelids you take her not

bread; and (another) man's wife will hunt for the precious soul. [27] Can a man take fire into his bosom and his clothes not be burned? [28] Can a man go on hot coals and his feet not be burned? [29] So (is) he who goes in to his neighbor's wife; everyone touching her shall not be innocent. [30] They do not despise a thief, if he steals to satisfy his soul when he is hungry. [31] But (if) he is found he shall restore sevenfold; he shall give all the goods of his house. [32] He who commits adultery (with) a woman lacks heart; he who does it (is) a destroyer of his own soul. [33] He shall find a wound and dishonor; and his shame shall not be wiped away. [34] For jealousy (is) the rage of a man and he will not spare in the day of vengeance. [35] He will not take every ransom; nor will he consent if you multiply the bribes.

CHAPTER 7

[1] My son, keep my words and store up my commandments within you. [2] Keep my commandments and live; and my law as the pupil of your eye. [3] Tie them on your fingers; write them on the tablet of your heart. [4] Say to wisdom, You (are) my sister; and call understanding (your) kinsman; [5] so that they may keep you from the strange woman, from the alien (with) her flattering words. [6] For I looked through my lattice, at the window of my house, [7] and I saw among the simple ones; I observed among the sons a young man lacking heart; [8] passing through the street near her corner; and he went the way to her house; [9] in the twilight, in the evening; in the black and darkness of night. [10] And, behold, a

27 לֶחֶם וְאֵשֶׁת אִישׁ נֶפֶשׁ יְקָרָה תָצוּד׃ הֲיַחְתֶּה אִישׁ אֵשׁ
fire man a Can hunts precious the (another) and ;bread
take .for soul man's wife

28 בְּחֵיקוֹ וּבְגָדָיו לֹא תִשָּׂרַפְנָה׃ אִם־יְהַלֵּךְ אִישׁ עַל־הַגֶּחָלִים
coals hot on a can Or be not his and his into
man walk ?burned clothes bosom

29 וְרַגְלָיו לֹא תִכָּוֶינָה׃ כֵּן הַבָּא אֶל־אֵשֶׁת רֵעֵהוּ לֹא יִנָּקֶה
be shall not his wife to one So be not his and
innocent ;neighbor's in going (is) ?burned feet

30 כָּל־הַנֹּגֵעַ בָּהּ׃ לֹא־יָבוּזוּ לַגַּנָּב כִּי יִגְנוֹב לְמַלֵּא נַפְשׁוֹ
his satisfy to he when a they not Do .her touch- every-
soul steals ,thief despise ing one

31 כִּי יִרְעָב׃ וְנִמְצָא יְשַׁלֵּם שִׁבְעָתָיִם אֶת־כָּל־הוֹן בֵּיתוֹ יִתֵּן׃
shall he his the all ,sevenfold shall he (if) but is he when
.give house of goods restore found is he ;hungry

32
33 נֹאֵף אִשָּׁה חֲסַר־לֵב מַשְׁחִית נַפְשׁוֹ הוּא יַעֲשֶׂנָּה׃ נֶגַע
A (who) he own his de- a ;heart lacks a (with) doing one
wound .it does (is) soul of stroyer woman adultery

34 וְקָלוֹן יִמְצָא וְחֶרְפָּתוֹ לֹא תִמָּחֶה׃ כִּי־קִנְאָה חֲמַת־גָּבֶר
a the (is) jealousy For be shall not his and shall he and
;man of rage .away wiped reproach ;find dishonor

35 וְלֹא יַחְמוֹל בְּיוֹם נָקָם׃ לֹא־יִשָּׂא פְּנֵי כָל־כֹּפֶר וְלֹא־יֹאבֶה
will he and ;ransom every the will he Not venge- the in will he and
consent not of face lift .ance of day spare not

כִּי תַרְבֶּה־שֹׁחַד׃
the you when
.bribes multiply

CAP. VII ז

CHAPTER 7

1
2 בְּנִי שְׁמֹר אֲמָרָי וּמִצְוֺתַי תִּצְפֹּן אִתָּךְ׃ שְׁמֹר מִצְוֺתַי וֶחְיֵה
and my Keep with treasure my and my keep My
,live commands .you commands ,words ,son

3 וְתוֹרָתִי כְּאִישׁוֹן עֵינֶיךָ׃ קָשְׁרֵם עַל־אֶצְבְּעֹתֶיךָ כָּתְבֵם עַל־
on write your on them Tie your the as my and
them ;fingers .eyes of pupil teaching

4 לוּחַ לִבֶּךָ׃ אֱמֹר לַחָכְמָה אֲחֹתִי אָתְּ וּמֹדָע לַבִּינָה תִקְרָא׃
;call under- to a and you My to Say your tablet
standing kinsman ;(are) sister ,wisdom .heart's

5
6 לִשְׁמָרְךָ מֵאִשָּׁה זָרָה מִנָּכְרִיָּה אֲמָרֶיהָ הֶחֱלִיקָה׃ כִּי
For .smooth her (with) the from ,strange the from keep to
words foreigner woman you

7 בְּחַלּוֹן בֵּיתִי בְּעַד אֶשְׁנַבִּי נִשְׁקָפְתִּי׃ וָאֵרֶא בַפְּתָאיִם אָבִינָה
I the among I and looked I my through my the at
observed ones simple saw ,down lattice house of window

8 בַבָּנִים נַעַר חֲסַר־לֵב׃ עֹבֵר בַּשּׁוּק אֵצֶל פִּנָּהּ וְדֶרֶךְ בֵּיתָהּ
her the and her beside through passing ;heart lacking of among
house to way ;corner street the youth sons the

9
10 יִצְעָד׃ בְּנֶשֶׁף־בְּעֶרֶב יוֹם בְּאִישׁוֹן לַיְלָה וַאֲפֵלָה׃ וְהִנֵּה
And and night the in ,day the at the in he
,behold .darkness of black of evening ,twilight ,walked

woman to meet him, with a harlot's dress, and a guarded heart; [11] she is loud and stubborn; her feet do not stay in her own house; [12] now (she) is outside, now in the streets, and (she) lies in wait at every corner; [13] and she seizes him and kisses him; she hardens her face and says to him, [14] Sacrifices of peace offerings (are) with me; today I have paid my vows; [15] so I came out to meet you, to earnestly seek your face; and I have found you; [16] I have spread my couch with coverings, with striped cloths of Egyptian linen; [17] I have sprinkled my bed with myrrh, aloes and cinnamon; [18] come, let us take our fill of love until the morning; let us delight ourselves with caresses. [19] For my husband (is) not at his house; he is going in the way, far away; [20] he has taken a bag of silver in his hand; at the day of the full moon, he will enter his house. [21] With her many words she caused him to yield; she forced him with the flattering of her lips. [22] He goes after her immediately, as an ox goes to the slaughter; or as one in fetters (goes) to the correction of a fool; [23] until an arrow strikes through his liver; as a bird hastens to the snare, and not knowing that it (is) for his soul.

[24] Now, then, listen to me, O sons; and attend to the words of my mouth: [25] Do not let your heart turn aside to her ways; do not go astray in her paths. [26] For many (are) the wounded she has caused to fall; and numerous all her slain ones. [27] The ways of Sheol (are in) her house, leading down to the rooms of death.

11 אִשָּׁה לִקְרָאתוֹ שִׁית זוֹנָה וּנְצֻרַת לֵב׃ הֹמִיָּה הִיא וְסֹרָרֶת
and she loud ;heart a and har- a (with) meet to a
;stubborn (is) guarded ,lot's dress ,him woman

12 בְּבֵיתָהּ לֹא־יִשְׁכְּנוּ רַגְלֶיהָ׃ פַּעַם ׀ בַּחוּץ פַּעַם בָּרְחֹבוֹת
the in now ,outside now her do not her in
,streets (is she) ;feet dwell house own

13 וְאֵצֶל כָּל־פִּנָּה תֶאֱרֹב׃ וְהֶחֱזִיקָה בּוֹ וְנָשְׁקָה לּוֹ הֵעֵזָה
she ;him and him she and lies she corner every and
hardens kisses seizes .wait in at

14 פָנֶיהָ וַתֹּאמַר לוֹ׃ זִבְחֵי שְׁלָמִים עָלָי הַיּוֹם שִׁלַּמְתִּי נְדָרָי׃
my have I today are peace Sacrifices to says and her
;vows repaid ;me on offerings of ,him face

15
16 עַל־כֵּן יָצָאתִי לִקְרָאתֶךָ לְשַׁחֵר פָּנֶיךָ וָאֶמְצָאֶךָּ׃ מַרְבַדִּים
(with) have I and your seek to meet to came I therefore
coverings you found face early ,you out

17 רָבַדְתִּי עַרְשִׂי חֲטֻבוֹת אֵטוּן מִצְרָיִם׃ נַפְתִּי מִשְׁכָּבִי מֹר
(with) my have I ;Egypt linen striped my have I
,myrrh bed sprinkled of of cloths ,couch spread

18 אֲהָלִים וְקִנָּמוֹן׃ לְכָה נִרְוֶה דֹדִים עַד־הַבֹּקֶר נִתְעַלְּסָה
delight us let the until of us let ,Come and aloes
ourselves ;morning love fill our drink .cinnamon

19 בָּאֳהָבִים׃ כִּי אֵין הָאִישׁ בְּבֵיתוֹ הָלַךְ בְּדֶרֶךְ מֵרָחוֹק׃
far the in is he his in (my) is For with
;off way going ;house husband not .caresses

20
21 צְרוֹר הַכֶּסֶף לָקַח בְּיָדוֹ לְיוֹם הַכֵּסֶא יָבֹא בֵיתוֹ׃ הִטַּתּוּ
turned She his will he full the the at his in has he silver bag a
aside him .house enter moon of day hand taken of

22 בְּרֹב לִקְחָהּ בְּחֵלֶק שְׂפָתֶיהָ תַּדִּיחֶנּוּ׃ הוֹלֵךְ אַחֲרֶיהָ פִּתְאֹם
at after (is He) she lips her the with her the by
,once her going .him forced of flattering ,word of sum

23 כְּשׁוֹר אֶל־טָבַח יָבוֹא וּכְעֶכֶס אֶל־מוּסַר אֱוִיל׃ עַד יְפַלַּח
strikes until a chastise- to one as ;goes the to an as
through ;fool of ment chained slaughter ox

חֵץ כְּבֵדוֹ כְּמַהֵר צִפּוֹר אֶל־פָּח וְלֹא יָדַע כִּי־בְנַפְשׁוֹ הוּא׃
.(is) it his for that knowing and the to a Like his a
soul not ,snare bird's hastening .liver dart

24
25 וְעַתָּה בָנִים שִׁמְעוּ־לִי וְהַקְשִׁיבוּ לְאִמְרֵי־פִי׃ אַל־יֵשְׂטְ
do not my the to and to listen ,sons And
aside turn ;mouth of words incline ,me ,now

26 אֶל־דְּרָכֶיהָ לִבֶּךָ אַל־תֵּתַע בִּנְתִיבוֹתֶיהָ׃ כִּי־רַבִּים חֲלָלִים
the many For her in go do not your her to
wounded (are) .paths astray ,heart ways

27 הִפִּילָה וַעֲצֻמִים כָּל־הֲרֻגֶיהָ׃ דַּרְכֵי שְׁאוֹל בֵּיתָהּ יֹרְדוֹת
going her Sheol The her all and has she
down ,house (are) of ways .ones slain numerous ;fall made

אֶל־חַדְרֵי־מָוֶת׃
.death the to
of rooms

CAP. VIII ח

CHAPTER 8

[1] Does not wisdom call? And does not understanding speak? [2] She stands in the top of high places, by the roadside, between the paths. [3] She cries in the gates; in the entrance to the city; at the coming in of the doors. [4] I call to you, (O) men; and my voice (is) to the sons of men. [5] Understand wisdom, simple ones; and be of an understanding heart, fools! [6] Hear, for I will speak of excellent things; and the opening of my lips (shall be) right things. [7] For my mouth shall speak truth; and wickedness (is) hateful to my lips. [8] All the words of my mouth (are) in righteousness; nothing twisted or perverse (is) in them; [9] they (are) all plain to the understanding one; and right to those who find knowledge. [10] Receive my instruction, and not silver; and knowledge, rather than choice gold. [11] For wisdom (is) better than rubies; and all delights cannot be compared to it. [12] I. wisdom dwell with sense, and search out knowledge of discretion. [13] The fear of Jehovah (is) to hate evil; I hate pride and the love of self, and the evil way, and the perverse mouth. [14] Counsel and sound wisdom are Mine; I (am) understanding; I have strength. [15] By Me kings reign and princes decree righteousness. [16] Princes and nobles rule by Me and all the judges of the earth. [17] I love those who love Me, and those who seek Me early find Me. [18] Riches and honor (are) with Me; enduring riches and righteousness. [19] My fruit (is) better than gold, yea, than fine gold; and My increase (is better than) the best silver. [20] I walk in the path of righteousness, in the midst of the paths of

CHAPTER 8

1 2 הֲלֹא־חָכְמָה תִקְרָא וּתְבוּנָה תִּתֵּן קוֹלָהּ׃ בְּרֹאשׁ־מְרֹמִים

high the on her .gives under- And does wisdom Not
places of head ?voice standing ?call

3 עֲלֵי־דָרֶךְ בֵּית נְתִיבוֹת נִצָּבָה׃ לְיַד־שְׁעָרִים לְפִי־קָרֶת

the before the the At she the between the on
,city ,gates of side !stands paths ,way

4 מְבוֹא פְתָחִים תָּרֹנָּה׃ אֲלֵיכֶם אִישִׁים אֶקְרָא וְקוֹלִי אֶל־

(is) my and ;call I O ,you To she the (at) ,entrance
to voice ,men .cries ,doors

5 בְּנֵי אָדָם׃ הָבִינוּ פְתָאיִם עָרְמָה וּכְסִילִים הָבִינוּ לֵב׃

(in) under- ,fools and ;prudence simple ,Understand .men the
!heart stand ,ones of sons

6 7 שִׁמְעוּ כִּי־נְגִידִים אֲדַבֵּר וּמִפְתַּח שְׂפָתַי מֵישָׁרִים׃ כִּי־אֱמֶת

truth For .things right my the from and will I excellent for ,Hear
lips of opening speak things

8 יֶהְגֶּה חִכִּי וְתוֹעֲבַת שְׂפָתַי רֶשַׁע׃ בְּצֶדֶק כָּל־אִמְרֵי־פִי

my words (are) righ- In wicked- lips my and my shall
;mouth of all teousness .ness (is) to hateful ;palate utter

9 אֵין בָּהֶם נִפְתָּל וְעִקֵּשׁ׃ כֻּלָּם נְכֹחִים לַמֵּבִין וִישָׁרִים

and the to (are) of all and twisted a in is
upright ,discerning straight them ;crooked thing them not

10 לְמֹצְאֵי דָעַת׃ קְחוּ־מוּסָרִי וְאַל־כָּסֶף וְדַעַת מֵחָרוּץ נִבְחָר׃

.choice than rather and ;silver and my Receive knowl- those to
gold knowledge not ,instruction .edge finding

11 כִּי־טוֹבָה חָכְמָה מִפְּנִינִים וְכָל־חֲפָצִים לֹא יִשְׁווּ־בָהּ׃

com- be can not delights and than wisdom better For
.it to pared all ,jewels (is)

12 13 אֲנִי חָכְמָה שָׁכַנְתִּי עָרְמָה וְדַעַת מְזִמּוֹת אֶמְצָא׃ יִרְאַת

The find I discretions knowl- and ;prudence dwell ,wisdom ,I
of fear _ .out of edge (with)

יְהוָה שְׂנֹאת רָע גֵּאָה וְגָאוֹן ׀ וְדֶרֶךְ רָע וּפִי תַהְפֻּכוֹת שָׂנֵאתִי׃

.hate I perverse and ,evil and and pride ;evil to (is) Jehovah
mouth the way the loftiness hate

14 15 לִי־עֵצָה וְתוּשִׁיָּה אֲנִי בִינָה לִי גְבוּרָה׃ בִּי מְלָכִים יִמְלֹכוּ

reign kings By .strength (is) to under- I sound and (is) To
me me ;standing (am) ;wisdom counsel me

16 וְרוֹזְנִים יְחֹקְקוּ צֶדֶק׃ בִּי שָׂרִים יָשֹׂרוּ וּנְדִיבִים כָּל־שֹׁפְטֵי

judges the all and ,rule rulers By right- decree and
of nobles me .eousness princes

17 18 אָרֶץ׃ אֲנִי אֹהֲבַיהָ אֵהָב וּמְשַׁחֲרַי יִמְצָאֻנְנִי׃ עֹשֶׁר־וְכָבוֹד

and Riches find ones and ,love those I the
honor .me me seeking me loving .earth

19 אִתִּי הוֹן עָתֵק וּצְדָקָה׃ טוֹב פִּרְיִי מֵחָרוּץ וּמִפָּז וּתְבוּאָתִי

my and pure and gold than my Better and enduring with
produce ,gold fruit (is) .righteousness wealth ,me

20 מִכֶּסֶף נִבְחָר׃ בְּאֹרַח צְדָקָה אֲהַלֵּךְ בְּתוֹךְ נְתִיבוֹת

the among I righteous- the In .choice than
of paths walk ness of path silver

justice; [21] so that (I) may cause those who love Me to inherit riches; and I will fill up their treasuries.

[22] Jehovah possessed Me in the beginning of His way, before His works from then. [23] I was set up from everlasting; from the beginning, before the earth ever was. [24] When there were no depths, I was spun out; when there were no springs heavy (with) water. [25] Before the mountains were settled; before the hills, I was spun out; [26] before He had made the earth and the fields, or the highest part of the dust of the world. [27] When He prepared the heavens, I was there; when He set a circle on the face of the deep; [28] when He set the clouds above; when He made the strong fountains of the deep; [29] when He gave to the sea its limit, that the waters shouldn't transgress His commands when He decreed the foundations of the earth; [30] then I was at His side, like a master workman; and I was (His) delights daily, rejoicing at every time before Him; [31] rejoicing in the world, His earth; and My delights (were) with the sons of men.

[32] Now, therefore, listen to Me, O children; for blessed (are those who) keep My ways. [33] Hear instruction, and be wise, and do not refuse it. [34] Blessed is the man who hears Me, watching daily at My gates, waiting at the posts of My doors. [35] For whoever finds Me finds life; and he shall obtain favor from Jehovah. [36] But he who sins against Me wrongs his own soul; all who hate Me love death.

21 מִשְׁפָּט׃ לְהַנְחִיל אֹהֲבַי ׀ יֵשׁ וְאֹצְרֹתֵיהֶם אֲמַלֵּא׃
will I their and ;wealth my cause to ,justice
up fill .storehouses lovers inherit to

22
23 יְהוָה קָנָנִי רֵאשִׁית דַּרְכּוֹ קֶדֶם מִפְעָלָיו מֵאָז׃ מֵעוֹלָם
From from his before His the in possessed Jeho-
everlasting then works ,way of beginning me vah

24 נִסַּכְתִּי מֵרֹאשׁ מִקַּדְמֵי־אָרֶץ׃ בְּאֵין־תְּהֹמוֹת חוֹלָלְתִּי בְּאֵין
when I ,depths When the ancient from the from was I
no were ,travailed no were .earth of times ,beginning ;up set

25 מַעְיָנוֹת נִכְבַּדֵּי־מָיִם׃ בְּטֶרֶם הָרִים הָטְבָּעוּ לִפְנֵי גְבָעוֹת
the before were the Before .waters heavy springs
,hills ,sunk mountains with

26 חוֹלָלְתִּי׃ עַד־לֹא עָשָׂה אֶרֶץ וְחוּצוֹת וְרֹאשׁ עַפְרוֹת תֵּבֵל׃
the the the and the and the had He not While I
.world of dust of head ,fields earth made .travailed

27
28 בַּהֲכִינוֹ שָׁמַיִם שָׁם אָנִי בְּחוּקוֹ חוּג עַל־פְּנֵי תְהוֹם׃ בְּאַמְּצוֹ
His in the the on a His in I there the His In
firming ;deep of face circle inscribing ;(was) heavens preparing

29 שְׁחָקִים מִמָּעַל בַּעֲזוֹז עִינוֹת תְּהוֹם׃ בְּשׂוּמוֹ לַיָּם ׀ חֻקּוֹ
its for His in the the making in from the
,limit sea the setting ;deep of springs strong ,above clouds

30 וּמַיִם לֹא יַעַבְרוּ־פִיו בְּחוּקוֹ מוֹסְדֵי אָרֶץ׃ וָאֶהְיֶה אֶצְלוֹ
(at) I and the found- His in pass should not that
,side His was ;earth's ations decreeing ;mouth His over waters the

אָמוֹן וָאֶהְיֶה שַׁעֲשֻׁעִים יוֹם ׀ יוֹם מְשַׂחֶקֶת לְפָנָיו בְּכָל־עֵת׃
.time at before rejoicing (by) day (His) I and work- a
every Him ,day delights was ;man

31 מְשַׂחֶקֶת בְּתֵבֵל אַרְצוֹ וְשַׁעֲשֻׁעַי אֶת־בְּנֵי אָדָם׃
.men the (were) my and His the in rejoicing
of sons with delights earth world

32
33 וְעַתָּה בָנִים שִׁמְעוּ־לִי וְאַשְׁרֵי דְּרָכַי יִשְׁמֹרוּ׃ שִׁמְעוּ מוּסָר
instruc- Hear (who) they My for ;Me to listen (O) And
,tion .keep ways (are) blessed ,sons ,now

34 וַחֲכָמוּ וְאַל־תִּפְרָעוּ׃ אַשְׁרֵי אָדָם שֹׁמֵעַ לִי לִשְׁקֹד עַל־
over to to listening the Blessed do and be and
watch ,me man (is) .ignore not ,wise

35 דַּלְתֹתַי יוֹם ׀ יוֹם לִשְׁמֹר מְזוּזֹת פְּתָחָי׃ כִּי מֹצְאִי מָצָאי*
finds one the For my the guarding (by) day my
me finding .doors of posts ,day doors

36 חַיִּים וַיָּפֶק רָצוֹן מֵיְהוָה׃ וְחֹטְאִי חֹמֵס נַפְשׁוֹ כָּל־מְשַׂנְאַי
hating all own his hurts sin- he But from favor he and ;life
me ;soul Me against ning .Jehovah obtain shall

אָהֲבוּ מָוֶת׃
.death love

CAP. IX ט

CHAPTER 9

[1] Wisdom has built her house; she has carved out her seven pillars; [2] she has slaughtered her

1
2 חָכְמוֹת בָּנְתָה בֵיתָהּ חָצְבָה עַמּוּדֶיהָ שִׁבְעָה׃ טָבְחָה
has She .seven her has she her has Wisdom
slaughtered pillars carved ;house built

slaughter; she has mixed her wine; she has also set her table. [3] She has sent out her maidens; she cries on the highest places of the city: [4] The simple one, let him turn in here; and he lacking heart, she says to him: [5] come eat of my bread, and drink of my wine (which) I have mingled; [6] forsake the foolish and live; and go in the way of understanding.

[7] He who reproves a scorner gets shame to himself; and he who rebukes a wicked man (gets) himself a blot. [8] Do not reprove a scorner, lest he hate you; rebuke a wise man, and he will love you. [9] Give to a wise (man), and he will be still wiser; teach a just (man), and he will increase in learning. [10] The fear of Jehovah (is) the beginning of wisdom; and the knowledge of the holy (is) understanding. [11] For by me your days shall be multiplied; and the years of your life shall be increased. [12] If you are wise, you shall be wise for yourself; but (if) you scorn, you alone shall bear (it).

[13] A foolish woman (is) loud; (she is) thoughtlessness (itself) and knows nothing. [14] For she sits at the door of her house, in a seat in the high places of the city; [15] to call those who pass by; who are going straight (on) their ways: [16] The simple one, let him turn in here; and he lacking heart, she says to him: [17] Stolen waters are sweet, and bread (eaten) in secret is (eaten) in secret is pleasant. [18] But he does not know that the dead (are) there; her guests (are) in the depths of hell.

CHAPTER 10

[1] The proverbs of Solomon: A wise son makes a father rejoice; but a foolish son (is) his mother's sorrow. [2] Treasures of wickedness profit nothing; but righteousness delivers from death. [3] Jehovah will not allow the soul of

3 טָבְחָה מָסְכָה יֵינָהּ אַף עָרְכָה שֻׁלְחָנָהּ׃ שָׁלְחָה נַעֲרֹתֶיהָ
her has She her has she also her has she her
;maidens out sent .table set ;wine mixed ;slaughter

4 תִקְרָא עַל־גַּפֵּי מְרֹמֵי קָרֶת׃ מִי־פֶתִי יָסֻר הֵנָּה חֲסַר־לֵב
,heart One ;here turn (is) Who the heights the on she
lacking aside ,simple :city's of tops calls

5
6 אָמְרָה לּוֹ׃ לְכוּ לַחֲמוּ בְלַחֲמִי וּשְׁתוּ בְּיַיִן מָסָכְתִּי׃ עִזְבוּ
Forsake have I the of and my of eat ,Come to says she
.mixed wine drink ,bread ,him

7 פְתָאיִם וִחְיוּ וְאִשְׁרוּ בְּדֶרֶךְ בִּינָה׃ יֹסֵר ׀ לֵץ לֹקֵחַ לוֹ קָלוֹן
;shame for takes a re- One under- the in and and the
himself scorner buking .standing of way walk ;live simple

8 וּמוֹכִיחַ לְרָשָׁע מוּמוֹ׃ אַל־תּוֹכַח לֵץ פֶּן־יִשְׂנָאֶךָּ הוֹכַח
reprove hate he lest a do Not own his wicked a one and
;you ,scorner reprove .blemish man reproving

9 לְחָכָם וְיֶאֱהָבֶךָּ׃ תֵּן לְחָכָם וְיֶחְכַּם־עוֹד הוֹדַע לְצַדִּיק
just a teach ;more he and a to Give will he and wise a
man wise be will ,one wise .you love ,one

10 וְיוֹסֶף לֶקַח׃ תְּחִלַּת חָכְמָה יִרְאַת יְהוָה וְדַעַת קְדֹשִׁים
Holy the the and ,Jehovah the Wisdom be- The (to) he and
Ones of knowledge of fear (is) of ginning .learning add will

11
12 בִּינָה׃ כִּי־בִי יִרְבּוּ יָמֶיךָ וְיוֹסִיפוּ לְּךָ שְׁנוֹת חַיִּים׃ אִם־
If .life the to shall and your in- shall by For under- (is)
of years you added be ;days crease me .standing

13 חָכַמְתָּ חָכַמְתָּ לָּךְ וְלַצְתָּ לְבַדְּךָ תִשָּׂא׃ אֵשֶׁת כְּסִילוּת
foolishness A bear shall you you if and for are you are you
(is) of woman .(it) alone ,scorn ;yourself wise ,wise

14 הֹמִיָּה פְּתַיּוּת וּבַל־יָדְעָה מָּה׃ וְיָשְׁבָה לְפֶתַח בֵּיתָהּ עַל־
on her the at she And .what she and simple making
,house of door sits knows not ;noise

15 כִּסֵּא מְרֹמֵי קָרֶת׃ לִקְרֹא לְעֹבְרֵי דָרֶךְ הַמְיַשְּׁרִים
going those the in those to call to the the (in) a
straight ,way passing ,city of heights seat

16
17 אֹרְחוֹתָם׃ מִי־פֶתִי יָסֻר הֵנָּה וַחֲסַר־לֵב וְאָמְרָה לּוֹ׃ מַיִם־
waters to says she heart one And !here turn (is) Who their (on)
:him lacking aside ,simple :paths

18 גְּנוּבִים יִמְתָּקוּ וְלֶחֶם סְתָרִים יִנְעָם׃ וְלֹא־יָדַע כִּי־רְפָאִים
the that does he But is (in) and are Stolen
dead know not .pleasant secret bread ,sweet

שָׁם בְּעִמְקֵי שְׁאוֹל קְרֻאֶיהָ׃
her (are) Sheol the in (are)
.guests of depths ,there

CAP. X י

CHAPTER 10

1 מִשְׁלֵי שְׁלֹמֹה בֵּן חָכָם יְשַׂמַּח־אָב וּבֵן כְּסִיל תּוּגַת אִמּוֹ׃
his sorrow foolish a but a makes wise A :Solomon Proverbs
.mother of (is) .son ,father rejoice son of

2
3 לֹא־יוֹעִילוּ אוֹצְרוֹת רֶשַׁע וּצְדָקָה תַּצִּיל מִמָּוֶת׃ לֹא־יַרְעִיב
allows Not from delivers but ;wickedness treasures do Not
hunger to .death righteousness of profit

the righteous to go hungry; but He pushes away the desire of the wicked. [4] He who deals (with) a lazy hand (becomes) poor; but the hand of the hard worker makes wealth. [5] He who gathers in summer (is) a prudent son; he who sleeps in harvest (is) a son who causes shame. [6] Blessings (are) on the head of the just; but violence covers the mouth of the wicked. [7] The memory of the just (is) blessed; but the name of the wicked shall rot. [8] The wise in heart accepts commands; but a babbling fool shall be stumbled. [9] He who walks in integrity walks securely; but he who perverts his way shall be found out. [10] He who winks causes sorrow; but the foolish of lips shall be stumbled. [11] The mouth of the righteous (is) a fountain of life; but violence covers the mouth of the wicked. [12] Hatred stirs up fights; but love covers all sins. [13] Wisdom is found in the lips of him who has understanding; but a rod is (waiting) for him who has no understanding. [14] The wise store up knowledge; but the mouth of the foolish (is) near ruin. [15] The rich man's wealth (is) his strong city; the ruin of the poor (is) their poverty.

[16] The labor of the righteous (is) for life; the gain of the wicked (is) for sin. [17] He who heeds instruction (is) in the way of life; but he who refuses reproof is going astray. [18] He who hides hatred (with) lying lips, and he who speaks a slander (is) foolish. [19] In the abundance of words, transgression does not cease; but he who holds back his lips (is) prudent. [20] The tongue of the just (is) as choice silver; the heart of the wicked (is) as a little thing. [21] The lips of the righteous feed many; but fools die for lack of wisdom. [22] The blessing of Jehovah makes one rich, and He adds no sorrow with it.

4 יְהוָה נֶפֶשׁ צַדִּיק וְהַוַּת רְשָׁעִים יֶהְדֹּף׃ רָאשׁ עֹשֶׂה כַף־
(with) who he (Becomes) pushes He the but the soul the Jehovah
palm a deals poor .away wicked's desire ;righteous of

5 רְמִיָּה וְיַד חָרוּצִים תַּעֲשִׁיר׃ אֹגֵר בַּקַּיִץ בֵּן מַשְׂכִּיל נִרְדָּם
who he ;prudent a (is) in who He makes hard the but ;lazy
sleeps son summer gathers .rich workers' hand

6 בַּקָּצִיר בֵּן מֵבִישׁ׃ בְּרָכוֹת לְרֹאשׁ צַדִּיק וּפִי רְשָׁעִים יְכַסֶּה
covers the but the the to Blessings causing a (is) in
wicked's mouth :just of head (are) .shame son harvest

7
8 חָמָס׃ זֵכֶר צַדִּיק לִבְרָכָה וְשֵׁם רְשָׁעִים יִרְקָב׃ חֲכַם־
The shall the the but a for (is) just the The .violence
of wise :rot wicked of name ,blessing of memory

9 לֵב יִקַּח מִצְוֹת וֶאֱוִיל שְׂפָתַיִם יִלָּבֵט׃ הוֹלֵךְ בַּתֹּם יֵלֶךְ
walks in who He he shall lips the but com- accepts heart
integrity walks .away thrust of foolish ;mands

10 בֶּטַח וּמְעַקֵּשׁ דְּרָכָיו יִוָּדֵעַ׃ קֹרֵץ עַיִן יִתֵּן עַצָּבֶת וֶאֱוִיל
the but ,pain gives the One be shall his who he but ;safely
of foolish eye winking .known ways perverts

11 שְׂפָתַיִם יִלָּבֵט׃ מְקוֹר חַיִּים פִּי צַדִּיק וּפִי רְשָׁעִים יְכַסֶּה
covers the but the mouth life foun- A be shall lips
wicked's mouth ;righteous' (is) of tain .away thrust

12 חָמָס׃ שִׂנְאָה תְּעֹרֵר מְדָנִים וְעַל כָּל־פְּשָׁעִים תְּכַסֶּה
covers trans- all but ,strifes stirs Hatred .violence
gressions over up

13 אַהֲבָה׃ בְּשִׂפְתֵי נָבוֹן תִּמָּצֵא חָכְמָה וְשֵׁבֶט לְגֵו חֲסַר־
one the for a but ;wisdom found is dis- the the On .love
lacking of back (is) rod cerning of lips

14
15 לֵב׃ חֲכָמִים יִצְפְּנוּ־דָעַת וּפִי אֱוִיל מְחִתָּה קְרֹבָה׃ הוֹן
Wealth (is) ruin the but knowl- store The .heart
of .near —fool's mouth ;edge up wise

16 עָשִׁיר קִרְיַת עֻזּוֹ מְחִתַּת דַּלִּים רֵישָׁם׃ פְּעֻלַּת צַדִּיק
the The their (is) the ruin the his the (is) rich the
righteous of work .poverty poor of ;strength of city man

17 לְחַיִּים תְּבוּאַת רָשָׁע לְחַטָּאת׃ אֹרַח לְחַיִּים שׁוֹמֵר מוּסָר
instruc- one life to the (On) for (is) the gain the for (is)
;tion keeping (is) path .sin wicked of ;life

18 וְעוֹזֵב תּוֹכַחַת מַתְעֶה׃ מְכַסֶּה שִׂנְאָה שִׂפְתֵי־שָׁקֶר וּמוֹצִא
one and false- of lips hatred who He going (is) reproof one but
out sending ,hood (has) hides .astray forsaking

19 דִבָּה הוּא כְסִיל׃ בְּרֹב דְּבָרִים לֹא יֶחְדַּל־פָּשַׁע וְחוֹשֵׂךְ
one but trans- ceases not words abun- In .fool a he slander
restraining ;gression of dance (is)

20 שְׂפָתָיו מַשְׂכִּיל׃ כֶּסֶף נִבְחָר לְשׁוֹן צַדִּיק לֵב רְשָׁעִים
the the the the Choice silver prudent (is) lips his
wicked of heart ;just of tongue (is)

21 כִּמְעָט׃ שִׂפְתֵי צַדִּיק יִרְעוּ רַבִּים וֶאֱוִילִים בַּחֲסַר־לֵב
heart lack in but ;many feed the lips The a as (is)
of fools righteous of .little

22 יָמוּתוּ׃ בִּרְכַּת יְהוָה הִיא תַעֲשִׁיר וְלֹא יוֹסִף עֶצֶב עִמָּהּ׃
with pain He and makes it ,Jehovah The .die
.it adds not ;rich of blessing

[23] To work out evil devices (is) as laughter to the foolish; so wisdom (is) to a man of understanding. [24] That which the wicked fears shall come upon him; but the desire of the righteous is granted. [25] As the tornado passes, so the wicked (is) not; but the righteous (is) an everlasting foundation. [26] Like vinegar to the teeth, and like smoke to the eyes, so is the sluggard to those who send him. [27] The fear of Jehovah prolongs days; but the years of the wicked shall be shortened. [28] The expectation of the righteous (is) joyful; but the hope of the wicked shall perish. [29] The way of Jehovah (is) strength to the upright; but ruin (is) to workers of iniquity. [30] The righteous shall never be moved; and the wicked shall not dwell in the land. [31] The mouth of the just flourishes (with) wisdom; but the perverse tongue shall be cut off; [32] The lips of the righteous know what is pleasing; but the mouth of the wicked, (only) perversities.

CHAPTER 11

[1] False balances (are) hateful to Jehovah; but a perfect stone His delight. [2] Pride comes — then shame comes; but with the lowly (is) wisdom. [3] The integrity of the upright guides them; but the perverseness of traitors will devastate them. [4] Riches do not profit in the day of wrath; but righteousness delivers from death. [5] The righteousness of the perfect shall make his way right; but the wicked shall fall by his own wickedness. [6] The righteousness of the upright shall deliver them; but traitors shall be taken in their lust. [7] When a wicked man dies, (his) hope shall perish and the expectation of the unjust shall be lost. [8] The righteous is delivered from distress; and the wicked comes (in) his place. [9] The ungodly is corrupting his neighbor with (his) mouth;

23 24 כִּשְׂחוֹק לִכְסִיל עֲשׂוֹת זִמָּה וְחָכְמָה לְאִישׁ תְּבוּנָה׃ מְגוֹרַת
is What under- the to wis- so evil work to the to laughter As
by feared .standing of man (is) dom ;devices out foolish

25 רָשָׁע הִיא תְבוֹאֶנּוּ וְתַאֲוַת צַדִּיקִים יִתֵּן׃ כַּעֲבוֹר סוּפָה
the passes As is the the but come shall that the
;tempest .given righteous of desire ;him upon ,wicked

26 וְאֵין רָשָׁע וְצַדִּיק יְסוֹד עוֹלָם׃ כַּחֹמֶץ ׀ לַשִּׁנַּיִם וְכֶעָשָׁן
like and the to Like ever- a (is) the but the is so
smoke ,teeth vinegar .lasting foundation righteous ;wicked not

27 לָעֵינַיִם כֵּן הֶעָצֵל לְשֹׁלְחָיו׃ יִרְאַת יְהוָה תּוֹסִיף יָמִים
;days prolongs Jehovah The those to lazy the so the to
of fear .him sending man (is) ,eyes

28 וּשְׁנוֹת רְשָׁעִים תִּקְצֹרְנָה׃ תּוֹחֶלֶת צַדִּיקִים שִׂמְחָה וְתִקְוַת
the but (is) the hope The be shall the the but
of hope ;joy righteous of .shortened wicked of years

29 רְשָׁעִים תֹּאבֵד׃ מָעוֹז לַתֹּם דֶּרֶךְ יְהוָה וּמְחִתָּה לְפֹעֲלֵי
to ruin but ,Jehovah way the the to (Is) shall the
of workers of upright strength .perish wicked

30 אָוֶן׃ צַדִּיק לְעוֹלָם בַּל־יִמּוֹט וּרְשָׁעִים לֹא יִשְׁכְּנוּ־אָרֶץ׃
the shall not the but be shall not forever The .evil
.land in dwell wicked ,shaken righteous

31 32 פִּי־צַדִּיק יָנוּב חָכְמָה וּלְשׁוֹן תַּהְפֻּכוֹת תִּכָּרֵת׃ שִׂפְתֵי צַדִּיק
the lips The be shall perversities the but (with) flour- The mouth
righteous of off cut of tongue ;wisdom ishes righteous'

יֵדְעוּן רָצוֹן וּפִי רְשָׁעִים תַּהְפֻּכוֹת׃
(only) the but is what know
.perversities ,wicked's mouth ;pleasing

CAP. XI יא

CHAPTER 11

1 2 מֹאזְנֵי מִרְמָה תּוֹעֲבַת יְהוָה וְאֶבֶן שְׁלֵמָה רְצוֹנוֹ׃ בָּא
Comes His (is) perfect but ;Jehovah hateful (are) False balances
.delight stone a to

3 זָדוֹן וַיָּבֹא קָלוֹן וְאֶת־צְנוּעִים חָכְמָה׃ תֻּמַּת יְשָׁרִים תַּנְחֵם
guides the The (is) the but ;shame then ,pride
;them upright of integrity .wisdom humble with comes

4 וְסֶלֶף בֹּגְדִים וְשָׁדֵּם׃ לֹא־יוֹעִיל הוֹן בְּיוֹם עֶבְרָה וּצְדָקָה
but ;wrath the in wealth does Not destroys traitors the but
righteousness of day profit them of deceit

5 תַּצִּיל מִמָּוֶת׃ צִדְקַת תָּמִים תְּיַשֵּׁר דַּרְכּוֹ וּבְרִשְׁעָתוֹ יִפֹּל
falls his by but his makes The righteousness from delivers
wickedness ;way straight perfect's .death

6 רָשָׁע׃ צִדְקַת יְשָׁרִים תַּצִּילֵם וּבְהַוַּת בֹּגְדִים יִלָּכֵדוּ׃
be shall traitors in but delivers the righ- The the
.taken lust (their) ;them upright of teousness .wicked

7 בְּמוֹת אָדָם רָשָׁע תֹּאבַד תִּקְוָה וְתוֹחֶלֶת אוֹנִים אָבָדָה׃
be shall wealth the and expect- (his) shall ,wicked a the In
.lost of hope ,ation perish man of death

8 9 צַדִּיק מִצָּרָה נֶחֱלָץ וַיָּבֹא רָשָׁע תַּחְתָּיו׃ בְּפֶה חָנֵף יַשְׁחִת
ruins un- the the With his (in) the and is from righ- The
godly mouth .place wicked enters ;delivered trouble eous

but the just is delivered by knowledge. [10] When the righteous prospers, the city rejoices; and at the wicked's perishing (is) singing. [11] A city is lifted up by the blessing of the upright; but by the wicked's mouth it is overthrown. [12] One despising his friend lacks heart —but an understanding man remains silent. [13] A slanderer is a revealer of secrets; but the faithful of spirit keeps a matter hidden [14] Without guidance the people fall; but safety (is) in a great counselor. [15] One suffers evil when he is surety for a stranger; but one hating strikers of hands is safe. [16] A gracious woman holds to honor; and terrifying men hold to riches. [17] A merciful man does good to his own soul; but the cruel troubles his own flesh. [18] The wicked makes a deceitful wage; but one sowing righteousness (has) a reward of truth. [19] Thus righteousness leads to life; but one pursuing evil, to his death. [20] Hateful to Jehovah (are) the perverse-hearted; but His delight (is) the upright in way. [21] (Though) hand join to hand, the evil shall not be acquitted; but the righteous seed escapes. [22] (As) a ring of gold in a swine's snout, (so is) a beautiful woman yet turning aside discretion. [23] The desire of the righteous (is) only good; the hope of the wicked (is) wrath. [24] There is one who scatters yet increases more; but a withholder of just due (comes) only to poverty. [25] The blessed soul will be made fat; he who waters will also drink fully. [26] One holding back grain, the people curse him; but a blessing to the head of one selling grain. [27] He who early (is) seeking good seeks favor; but one pursuing evil, it shall come to him. [28] One trusting in his riches, he shall fall; but like a green leaf the righteous shall sprout. [29] One troubling his house inherits the wind; and the fool (is) servant to the wise

10 רֵעֵהוּ וּבְדַעַת צַדִּיקִים יֵחָלֵצוּ׃ בְּטוּב צַדִּיקִים תַּעֲלֹץ קִרְיָה

the rejoices the When is the by but his
;city ,righteous prosper .delivered righteous knowledge ,friend

11 וּבַאֲבֹד רְשָׁעִים רִנָּה׃ בְּבִרְכַּת יְשָׁרִים תָּרוּם קָרֶת וּבְפִי

by but ;city a lifted is the the By (is) the the at and
mouth up upright of blessing .singing wicked of perishing

12 רְשָׁעִים תֵּהָרֵס׃ בָּז־לְרֵעֵהוּ חֲסַר־לֵב וְאִישׁ תְּבוּנוֹת

understanding but ;heart lacks his One is it the
of man a friend despising .overthrown wicked's

13 יַחֲרִישׁ׃ הוֹלֵךְ רָכִיל מְגַלֶּה־סּוֹד וְנֶאֱמַן־רוּחַ מְכַסֶּה דָבָר׃

.matter a keeps faith- the but revealer a is (with) One remains
hidden spirit of ful ,secrets of slander going .silent

14
15 בְּאֵין תַּחְבֻּלוֹת יִפָּל־עָם וּתְשׁוּעָה בְּרֹב יוֹעֵץ׃ רַע־יֵרוֹעַ

one Evil .counselor a in but the fall (wise) the In
suffers great (is) safety ;people counsel of absence

16 כִּי־עָרַב זָר וְשֹׂנֵא תֹקְעִים בּוֹטֵחַ׃ אֵשֶׁת־חֵן תִּתְמֹךְ כָּבוֹד

;honor ; holds gracious a (is) strikers one but an is he when
to woman safe (hands of) hating ;alien for surety

17 וְעָרִיצִים יִתְמְכוּ־עֹשֶׁר׃ גֹּמֵל נַפְשׁוֹ אִישׁ חָסֶד וְעֹכֵר שְׁאֵרוֹ

own his but merciful a his (to) Does .riches hold terrify- and
flesh troubles man soul own (well) to (men) ing

18 אַכְזָרִי׃ רָשָׁע עֹשֶׂה פְעֻלַּת־שָׁקֶר וְזֹרֵעַ צְדָקָה שֶׂכֶר אֱמֶת׃

.truth re- a righteous- one but ;falsehood a makes The the
of ward (has) ness sowing of wage wicked .cruel

19
20 כֵּן־צְדָקָה לְחַיִּים וּמְרַדֵּף רָעָה לְמוֹתוֹ׃ תּוֹעֲבַת יְהוָה

Jehovah Hateful his to evil one but (is) righteous- Gen-
(are) to .death own pursuing ;life to ness uine

21 עִקְּשֵׁי־לֵב וּרְצוֹנוֹ תְּמִימֵי דָרֶךְ׃ יָד לְיָד לֹא־יִנָּקֶה רָּע

the be shall not (join) (Though) .way up- the His but ;heart per- the
,one evil acquitted hand to hand in right delight of verse

22 וְזֶרַע צַדִּיקִים נִמְלָט׃ נֶזֶם זָהָב בְּאַף חֲזִיר אִשָּׁה יָפָה

beauti- a (is) a in gold A .escapes the the but
,ful woman ,swine's snout of ring righteous of seed

23 וְסָרַת טָעַם׃ תַּאֲוַת צַדִּיקִים אַךְ־טוֹב תִּקְוַת רְשָׁעִים

the the ;good (is) the The discre- turn- even
wicked of hope only righteous of desire .tion aside ing

24 עֶבְרָה׃ יֵשׁ מְפַזֵּר וְנוֹסָף עוֹד וְחוֹשֵׂךְ מִיֹּשֶׁר אַךְ־לְמַחְסוֹר׃

to (comes) rightness a but ,more in- yet who one There (is)
poverty only of withholder creases scatters is .wrath

25
26 נֶפֶשׁ־בְּרָכָה תְדֻשָּׁן וּמַרְוֶה גַּם־הוּא יוֹרֶא׃ מֹנֵעַ בָּר יִקְּבֻהוּ

curse grain One drink will he also he And be shall blessing The
him back holding ,fully ,watering fat made of soul

27 לְאוֹם וּבְרָכָה לְרֹאשׁ מַשְׁבִּיר׃ שֹׁחֵר טוֹב יְבַקֵּשׁ רָצוֹן

,favor seeks good early One selling one the to a but the
seeking .grain of head blessing ;people

28 וְדֹרֵשׁ רָעָה תְבוֹאֶנּוּ׃ בּוֹטֵחַ בְּעָשְׁרוֹ הוּא יִפֹּל וְכֶעָלֶה

a like but shall he his in one shall it ,evil one but
leaf green ;fall ,riches trusting ;him to come pursuing

29 צַדִּיקִים יִפְרָחוּ׃ עוֹכֵר בֵּיתוֹ יִנְחַל־רוּחַ וְעֶבֶד אֱוִיל לַחֲכַם־

the to the a and the inherits his One shall the
of wise fool (is) servant ;wind house troubling .flourish righteous

of heart. [30] The fruit of the righteous (is) a tree of life; and he who takes souls (is) wise. [31] Behold, the righteous shall be rewarded in the earth; much more the wicked and the sinner.

CHAPTER 12

[1] Whoever loves instruction loves knowledge; but he who hates correction (is) like a brute animal. [2] The good obtain grace from Jehovah; but He will condemn a man of wicked devices. [3] A man shall not be established by wickedness; but the root of the righteous shall not be moved. [4] A woman of virtue (is) a crown to her lord; but one causing shame is like rottenness in his bones. [5] The thoughts of the righteous (are) right; the counsels of the wicked (are) deceit. [6] The words of the wicked ambush (for) blood; but the mouth of the upright shall deliver them. [7] Overthrow the wicked, and they are not; but the house of the righteous stands. [8] A man shall be praised according to his wisdom; but he who is of a crooked heart shall be despised. [9] (He who is) despised, and (has) a servant, (is) better than one being honored and lacking bread. [10] The righteous regards the life of his animal; but the mercies of the wicked (are) cruel. [11] He who tills his land shall be satisfied (with) bread; but he pursuing vanities lacks heart. The wicked desires the net of evils, but the righteous' root gives. [13] In the transgression of the lips (is) the snare of evil, but the righteous will emerge from distress.

[14] A man shall (be) satisfied with good by the fruit of the mouth; and the dealing of a man's hands shall be given back to him. [15] The way of a fool (is) right in his own eyes; but he who listens to advice (is) wise. [16] A fool's wrath is soon known; but one with good sense covers shame. [17] He who speaks truth reveals righteousness; but a

30 31 לֵב׃ פְּרִי־צַדִּיק עֵץ חַיִּים וְלֹקֵחַ נְפָשׁוֹת חָכָם׃ הֵן צַדִּיק
the ,Behold (is) souls one and ;life tree a the fruit The .heart
righteous .wise taking of (is) just of

בָּאָרֶץ יְשֻׁלָּם אַף כִּי־רָשָׁע וְחוֹטֵא׃
the and the in- also be will the in
.sinner wicked deed repaid earth

CAP. XII יב

CHAPTER 12

1 2 אֹהֵב מוּסָר אֹהֵב דָּעַת וְשֹׂנֵא תוֹכַחַת בָּעַר׃ טוֹב יָפִיק
obtains The (is) correction one but ;knowledge (is) instruc- One
good .brutish hating loving tion loving

3 רָצוֹן מֵיְהוָה וְאִישׁ מְזִמּוֹת יַרְשִׁיעַ׃ לֹא־יִכּוֹן אָדָם בְּרֶשַׁע
wick- by a be will Not will He evil a but from favor
;edness man established .condemn plots of man ,Jehovah

4 וְשֹׁרֶשׁ צַדִּיקִים בַּל־יִמּוֹט׃ אֵשֶׁת־חַיִל עֲטֶרֶת בַּעְלָהּ וּכְרָקָב
as but her the (is) virtue A will not the the but
rottennes: ;lord of crown of woman .totter righteous of root

5 בְּעַצְמוֹתָיו מְבִישָׁה׃ מַחְשְׁבוֹת צַדִּיקִים מִשְׁפָּט תַּחְבֻּלוֹת
the (are) the thoughts The one is his in
of counsel ;justice righteous of .shame causing bones

6 רְשָׁעִים מִרְמָה׃ דִּבְרֵי רְשָׁעִים אֱרָב־דָּם וּפִי יְשָׁרִים
the but ,blood am- the words The (is) the
upright's mouth (for) bush wicked of .deceit wicked

7 8 יַצִּילֵם׃ הָפוֹךְ רְשָׁעִים וְאֵינָם וּבֵית צַדִּיקִים יַעֲמֹד׃ לְפִי
the By .stands the the but they and the Overthrow delivers
of mouth righteous of house ,not are ,wicked .them

9 שִׂכְלוֹ יְהֻלַּל־אִישׁ וְנַעֲוֵה־לֵב יִהְיֶה לָבוּז׃ טוֹב נִקְלֶה
despised a Better .despised shall heart the but a be shall his
,one (is) become of perverse ,man praised prudence

10 וְעֶבֶד לוֹ מִמִּתְכַּבֵּד וַחֲסַר־לָחֶם׃ יוֹדֵעַ צַדִּיק נֶפֶשׁ בְּהֶמְתּוֹ
his the the Regards .bread and -honor- one than to a and
,beast of life righteous lacking himself ing him servant

11 וְרַחֲמֵי רְשָׁעִים אַכְזָרִי׃ עֹבֵד אַדְמָתוֹ יִשְׂבַּע־לָחֶם וּמְרַדֵּף
one but (with) be will his who He (are) the the but
pursuing ,bread satisfied land serves .cruel wicked of mercies

12 רֵיקִים חֲסַר־לֵב׃ חָמַד רָשָׁע מְצוֹד רָעִים וְשֹׁרֶשׁ צַדִּיקִים
the a but evils the the Desires .heart lacks vanities
righteous (to) root of net wicked

13 14 יִתֵּן׃ בְּפֶשַׁע שְׂפָתַיִם מוֹקֵשׁ רָע וַיֵּצֵא מִצָּרָה צַדִּיק׃ מִפְּרִי
the From the from will but;evil snare the the the In .gives
of fruit .righteous distress emerge of (is) lips of transgression

15 פִי־אִישׁ יִשְׂבַּע־טוֹב וּגְמוּל יְדֵי־אָדָם יָשׁוּב לוֹ׃ דֶּרֶךְ אֱוִיל
fool a The to will a hands the and (with) is he a mouth
of way .him return man's of dealing ;good satisfied man's

16 יָשָׁר בְּעֵינָיו וְשֹׁמֵעַ לְעֵצָה חָכָם׃ אֱוִיל בַּיּוֹם יִוָּדַע כַּעְסוֹ
vex- his is a in fool A (is) to one but his in is
,ation known day .wise counsel listening eyes own right

17 וְכֹסֶה קָלוֹן עָרוּם׃ יָפִיחַ אֱמוּנָה יַגִּיד צֶדֶק וְעֵד שְׁקָרִים
falsehoods a but right- reveals truth who He the shame but
of witness ,eousness breathes .astute covers

false witness deceit. [18]
There is a rash speaking
like thrusts of a sword; but
the tongue of the wise heals.
[19] The lips of truth are
established forever; but a
lying tongue (is only) while
I wink. [20] Deceit (is) in
the heart of those who plot
evil; but to counselors of
peace (is) joy. [21] No
trouble shall happen to the
just; but the wicked shall be
filled with evil. [22] Lying
lips (are) hateful to Jehovah; but those who deal
truly are His delight.
[23] A wise man conceals
knowledge; but the heart of
fools proclaims their folly.
[24] The hand of the hard
worker shall rule; but the
lazy shall be under service.
[25] Heaviness in a man's
heart makes it droop. but a
good word makes it glad.
[26] The righteous (with)
his friend explores, but the
way of the wicked misleads
them. [27] The lazy does
not start after his game; but
the wealth of a working
man (is) precious. [28] In
the way of righteousness
(is) life; and in that pathway
(is) no death.

18 מרמה: יש בוטה כמדקרות חרב ולשון חכמים מרפא:
(is) the the but a thrusts like rash a There .deceit
.healing wise of tongue ;sword of speaking is

19 20 שפת־אמת תכון לעד ועד־ארגיעה לשון שקר: מרמה
Deceit .falsehood a (is) I (only) but forever are truth The
(is) of tongue wink while established of lips

21 בלב־חרשי־רע וליעצי שלום שמחה: לא־יאנה לצדיק
the to shall Not .joy (is) peace to but ,evil those the in
righteous happen of counselors plotting of heart

22 כל־און ורשעים מלאו רע: תועבת יהוה שפתי־שקר
,falsehood lips Jehovah abomi- An (with) be shall the but every
of to ination .evil filled wicked .trouble

23 ועשי אמונה רצונו: אדם ערום כסה דעת ולב כסילים
fools the but knowl- covers shrewd A His (are) truth those but
of heart ,edge man .delight do who

24 יקרא אולת: יד־חרוצים תמשול ורמיה תהיה למס:
forced will lazi- but shall hard the The .folly calls
.labor become ness ,rule workers of hand out

26 דאגה בלב־איש ישחנה ודבר טוב ישמחנה: יתר
Searches it makes good a but it makes a in Anxiety
out .glad word ,droop man's heart

27 מרעהו צדיק ודרך רשעים תתעם: לא־יחרך רמיה
lazy a does Not misleads the the but the his (with)
one after start .them wicked of way ,righteous friend

28 צידו והון־אדם יקר חרוץ: בארח צדקה חיים ודרך
the and (is) righteousness the In hard a (is) man's but his
of way ,life of path .working precious wealth ;prey

נתיבה אל־מות:
.death (is) (that)
not path

CHAPTER 13

[1] A wise son (hears)
his father's instruction; but
a scorner does not hear
rebuke. [2] From the fruit
of his mouth a man eats
good; but the desire of the
deceiver (is) violence.
[3] He who guards his
mouth keeps his life; he
who opens his lips wide (is)
ruined. [4] The sluggard's
soul is craving, but (is) not
(getting); but the soul of the
hard workers shall be made
fat. [5] The righteous hates
lying; but the wicked is
odious and acts shamefully.
[6] Righteousness keeps
the upright one in the way;
but wickedness overthrows
sin. [7] There are (those)
who act rich, yet (have)
nothing at all; (and
those) who act poor, yet
(have) great wealth. [8]
The ransom of a man's
life (are) his riches

CAP. XIII יג

CHAPTER 13

1 2 בן חכם מוסר אב ולץ לא־שמע גערה: מפרי פי־איש
a mouth the From .rebuke does not a but his instruction wise A
man's of fruit hear scorner ;father's (hears) son

3 יאכל טוב ונפש בגדים חמס: נצר פיו שמר נפשו
his keeps his who He (eats) treach- the the but ,good he
;soul mouth guards violence erous of soul eats

4 פשק שפתיו מחתה־לו: מתאוה ואין נפשו עצל ונפש
the but the soul the not but ,Craving to ruin his who he
of soul ;lazy of (is getting) .him (is) ,lips wide opens

5 חרצים תדשן: דבר־שקר ישנא צדיק ורשע יבאיש
is the but the hates false- A be will hard
odious wicked ;righteous hood of word fat made workers

6 ויחפיר: צדקה תצר תם־דרך ורשעה תסלף חטאת:
.sin over- but ,way the guards Righteousness acts and
throws wickedness of perfect .shamefully

7 8 יש מתעשר ואין כל מתרושש והון רב: כפר נפש־איש
a life The .much but acting one at but acting one There
man's of ransom wealth ,poor ;all not (has) ,rich is

but the poor man does not hear rebuke. [9] The light of the righteous rejoices; but the lamp of the wicked shall be put out. [10] Argument only comes by pride; but wisdom (is) with those who take advice. [11] Wealth from vanity shall be diminished; but he who gathers by labor shall increase. [12] Hope deferred makes the heart sick; but desire fulfilled (is) a tree of life. [13] He who despises the word shall be destroyed; but he who fears the commandment shall be rewarded. [14] The law of the wise (is) a fountain of life, to depart from the snares of death. [15] Good sense gives grace; but the way of transgressors (is) continual. [16] Every prudent one deals with knowledge; but a fool lays open (his) foolishness. [17] A wicked messenger falls into evil; but a faithful ambassador (is) healing. [18] Poverty and shame (shall be to) him who refuses instruction; but he who keeps to correction shall be honored. [19] The desire being (so) is sweet to the soul; but departing from evil (is) hateful to fools. [20] He who walks with the wise shall be wise; but a shepherd of fools shall be broken. [21] Evil pursues sinners; but shall be rewarded (with) good. [22] A good man leaves an inheritance to his son's sons; but the wealth of the sinner (is) laid up for the just. [23] The tilled ground of the poor yields much food; but without justice, it is swept away. [24] He who spares his rod hates his son; but he who loves him seeks him (with) correction. [25] The righteous eats to the satisfying of his soul; but the belly of the wicked shall lack.

9 עָשְׁרוֹ וְרָשׁ לֹא־שָׁמַע גְּעָרָה׃ אוֹר־צַדִּיקִים יִשְׂמָח וְנֵר

but ;rejoices the The .rebuke does not the but his (is)
lamp righteous of light hear poor ,riches

10 רְשָׁעִים יִדְעָךְ׃ רַק־בְּזָדוֹן יִתֵּן מַצָּה וְאֶת־נוֹעָצִים חָכְמָה׃

(is) those with but ,strife comes by Only put is the
,wisdom counsel taking pride .out wicked's

11 הוֹן מֵהֶבֶל יִמְעָט וְקֹבֵץ עַל־יָד יַרְבֶּה׃ תּוֹחֶלֶת מְמֻשָּׁכָה
12

deferred Hope shall hand by one but will from Wealth
.increase gathering ;dwindle vanity

13 מַחֲלָה־לֵב וְעֵץ חַיִּים תַּאֲוָה בָאָה׃ בָּז לְדָבָר יֵחָבֶל לוֹ

him- ruins the One .fulfilled (is) life a but the makes
;self word despising desire of tree ;heart sick

14 וִירֵא מִצְוָה הוּא יְשֻׁלָּם׃ תּוֹרַת חָכָם מְקוֹר חַיִּים לָסוּר

to ,life a (is) the The be shall he the one but
depart of fountain wise of law .rewarded ,command fearing

15 מִמֹּקְשֵׁי מָוֶת׃ שֵׂכֶל־טוֹב יִתֶּן־חֵן וְדֶרֶךְ בֹּגְדִים אֵיתָן׃

con- (is) the but ;grace gives good Pru- .death the from
.tinual traitors of way dence of snares

16 כָּל־עָרוּם יַעֲשֶׂה בְדָעַת וּכְסִיל יִפְרֹשׂ אִוֶּלֶת׃ מַלְאָךְ רָשָׁע
17

wicked mes- A (his) lays a but with deals shrewd Every
senger .folly open fool ,knowledge (one)

18 יִפֹּל בְּרָע וְצִיר אֱמוּנִים מַרְפֵּא׃ רֵישׁ וְקָלוֹן פּוֹרֵעַ מוּסָר

chastise- one shame and Poverty (is) faith- an but into falls
,ment ignoring (for) .healing ful envoy ,evil

19 וְשׁוֹמֵר תּוֹכַחַת יְכֻבָּד׃ תַּאֲוָה נִהְיָה תֶּעֱרַב לְנָפֶשׁ וְתוֹעֲבַת

is it but the to is so keeping The be shall correction one but
to hateful ,soul sweet desire .honored keeping

20 כְּסִילִים סוּר מֵרָע׃ הָלוֹךְ אֶת־חֲכָמִים וַחֲכָם וְרֹעֶה כְסִילִים

fools a but be shall the with who He from to fools
of friend ,wise wise walks .evil depart

21 יֵרוֹעַ׃ חַטָּאִים תְּרַדֵּף רָעָה וְאֶת־צַדִּיקִים יְשַׁלֶּם־טוֹב׃

(with) be shall the but ,evil are Sinners suffers
good rewarded righteous by pursued .evil

22 טוֹב יַנְחִיל בְּנֵי־בָנִים וְצָפוּן לַצַּדִּיק חֵיל חוֹטֵא׃ רָב־אֹכֶל
23

food Much the wealth the for is and (his) sons makes good A
(yields) .sinner's righteous stored ,sons of inherit (man)

24 נִיר רָאשִׁים וְיֵשׁ נִסְפֶּה בְּלֹא מִשְׁפָּט׃ חוֹשֵׂךְ שִׁבְטוֹ שׂוֹנֵא

is his who He .justice when swept but the fallow
hating rod holds back (is) not away is (it) ,poor's land

25 בְנוֹ וְאֹהֲבוֹ שִׁחֲרוֹ מוּסָר׃ צַדִּיק אֹכֵל לְשֹׂבַע נַפְשׁוֹ וּבֶטֶן

the but his satis- to eats The (with) seeks he but his
of belly ,soul's faction righteous .correction him him loving ,son

רְשָׁעִים תֶּחְסָר׃

shall the
.lack wicked

CAP. XIV יד

CHAPTER 14

CHAPTER 14

[1] Wise women build her house, but the foolish pulls it down with her own hands. [2] He who

1 חַכְמוֹת נָשִׁים בָּנְתָה בֵיתָהּ וְאִוֶּלֶת בְּיָדֶיהָ תֶהֶרְסֶנּוּ׃ הוֹלֵךְ
2

One pulls it her with the but her build women Wise
walking .down hands foolish ;house

walks in his uprightness fears Jehovah; but the perverse in his ways despises Him. [3] A rod of pride (is) in the mouth of a fool; but the lips of the wise shall keep them. [4] The stall (is) empty where there (are) no oxen; but much gain (is) by the strength of an ox. [5] A faithful witness will not lie; but a false witness breathes lies. [6] A scorner seeks wisdom but (finds) it not; yet knowledge (is) swift to the discerning. [7] Leave a foolish man, or you will not see the lips of knowledge. [8] The wisdom of the wise (is) to understand his way; but the foolishness of fools (is) deceit. [9] Fools laugh at guilt-offering; but among the righteous (is) favor. [10] The heart knows the bitterness of its soul; and a stranger does not share in its joy. [11] The wicked's house shall be thrown down; but the tent of the upright blessed. [12] There is a way (that seems) right to a man; but the end of it (is) the ways of death. [13] Even in laughter the heart is sorrowful; and the end of that joy (is) heaviness. [14] The backslider in heart shall be filled with his own ways; but a good man from himself. [15] The simple believes everything; but the wise watches his step. [16] The wise fears and departs from evil; but the fool rages and is sure. [17] He who is short of temper acts foolishly; and a man of wicked thoughts is hated. [18] The simple inherit foolishness; but the wise are crowned (with) knowledge. [19] The evil bow before the good; yea, the wicked at the gates of the just. [20] The poor is hated even by his own neighbor; but the rich (has) many friends. [21] He who despises his neighbor sins; but he who has mercy on the poor, O how happy (is) he! [22] Do not those who think evil go astray? But mercy and truth (will be) to those who think

3 בְּיָשְׁרוֹ יְרֵא יְהוָה וּנְלוֹז דְּרָכָיו בּוֹזֵהוּ׃ בְּפִי־אֱוִיל חֹטֶר
a (is) a the In depises his in the but ,Jehovah fears up his in
of rod fool of mouth .Him ways perverse rightness

4 גַּאֲוָה וְשִׂפְתֵי חֲכָמִים תִּשְׁמוּרֵם׃ בְּאֵין אֲלָפִים אֵבוּס בָּר
(is) the ,cattle Where preserve the the but ;pride
;clean manger no (are) .them wise of lips

5 וְרָב־תְּבוּאוֹת בְּכֹחַ שׁוֹר׃ עֵד אֱמוּנִים לֹא יְכַזֵּב וְיָפִיחַ
but will not faithful A .ox an the by increase but
breathes ;lie witness of strength much

6 כְּזָבִים עֵד שָׁקֶר׃ בִּקֶּשׁ־לֵץ חָכְמָה וָאָיִן וְדַעַת לְנָבוֹן נָקָל׃
is the to but it and ,wisdom A seeks .false a lies
.swift discerning ,knowledge ;not is scorner witness

7
8 לֵךְ מִנֶּגֶד לְאִישׁ כְּסִיל וּבַל־יָדַעְתָּ שִׂפְתֵי־דָעַת׃ חָכְמַת
The .knowledge the will you or ,foolish man a from Go
of wisdom of lips know not before

9 עָרוּם הָבִין דַּרְכּוֹ וְאִוֶּלֶת כְּסִילִים מִרְמָה׃ אֱוִלִים יָלִיץ
mock Fools .deceit (is) fools the but his discerns the
of folly ;way astute

10 אָשָׁם וּבֵין יְשָׁרִים רָצוֹן׃ לֵב יוֹדֵעַ מָרַּת נַפְשׁוֹ וּבְשִׂמְחָתוֹ
its in and its bitter- knows The (is) the but at
joy ;soul of ness heart favor righteous among ;guilt

11 לֹא־יִתְעָרַב זָר׃ בֵּית רְשָׁעִים יִשָּׁמֵד וְאֹהֶל יְשָׁרִים יַפְרִיחַ׃
will the the but be will The house a does not
.flourish upright of tent ,wasted wicked's .stranger share

12
13 יֵשׁ דֶּרֶךְ יָשָׁר לִפְנֵי־אִישׁ וְאַחֲרִיתָהּ דַּרְכֵי־מָוֶת׃ גַּם־
Even .death the its but ,man a before (seeming) a There
of ways (is) end upright way is

14 בִּשְׂחֹק יִכְאַב־לֵב וְאַחֲרִיתָהּ שִׂמְחָה תוּגָה׃ מִדְּרָכָיו
his from (is) joy in and the is in
ways own .grief end its ;heart pained laughter

15 יִשְׂבַּע סוּג לֵב וּמֵעָלָיו אִישׁ טוֹב׃ פֶּתִי יַאֲמִין לְכָל־דָּבָר
;word every believes The .good man a from but ;heart The be will
simple himself of backslider filled

16 וְעָרוּם יָבִין לַאֲשֻׁרוֹ׃ חָכָם יָרֵא וְסָר מֵרָע וּכְסִיל מִתְעַבֵּר
passes the but from and fears The .step his watches the but
over foolish ,evil turns wise prudent

17 וּבוֹטֵחַ׃ קְצַר־אַפַּיִם יַעֲשֶׂה אִוֶּלֶת וְאִישׁ מְזִמּוֹת יִשָּׂנֵא׃
is (evil) a and ;foolishly acts (to) who He is and
.hated plots of man anger short (is) .bold

18
19 נָחֲלוּ פְתָאיִם אִוֶּלֶת וַעֲרוּמִים יַכְתִּרוּ דָעַת׃ שַׁחוּ רָעִים
The will (with) are the but foolish- The inherit
evil bow .knowledge circled prudent ;ness simple

20 לִפְנֵי טוֹבִים וּרְשָׁעִים עַל־שַׁעֲרֵי צַדִּיק׃ גַּם־לְרֵעֵהוּ יִשָּׂנֵא
is his by Even the the at the and the before
hated neighbor .just of gates wicked ;good

21 רָשׁ וְאֹהֲבֵי עָשִׁיר רַבִּים׃ בָּז־לְרֵעֵהוּ חוֹטֵא וּמְחוֹנֵן עֲנָיִים
the he but ;sins · his who He (are) rich the but the
,poor favors who neighbor despises .many of lovers ;poor

22 אַשְׁרָיו׃ הֲלוֹא־יִתְעוּ חֹרְשֵׁי רָע וְחֶסֶד וֶאֱמֶת חֹרְשֵׁי טוֹב׃
.good devisers truth and But ?evil devisers go not Do happy
of (follow) mercy of astray !he (is)

of good. [23] In all labor there is profit; but the talk of the lips (tends) only to poverty. [24] The crown of the wise (is) their riches (of wisdom); the foolishness of fools (is) folly. [25] A true witness delivers souls; but a deceitful (witness) speaks lies. [26] In the fear of Jehovah (is) strong trust; and His sons shall have a hiding place. [27] The fear of Jehovah (is) a fountain of life, to turn away from snares of death. [28] In the multitude of people (is) the king's glory; but in the lack of people (is) the ruin of a prince. [29] One slow (to) anger (is) of great understanding; but he who is short of spirit exalts folly. [30] A healthy heart (is) the life of the flesh; but envy (is) the rottenness of the bones. [31] He who oppresses the poor curses his Maker; but he who honors Him has mercy on the needy. [32] The wicked is thrust out in his wickedness; but the righteous (has) hope in his death. [33] Wisdom rests in the heart of the intelligent; and in the midst of fools it is known. [34] Righteousness exalts a nation; but sin (is) a shame to any people. [35] The king's favor (is) toward a servant who acts prudently; but his wrath is (upon) one causing shame.

23 בְּכָל־עֶצֶב יִהְיֶה מוֹתָר וּדְבַר שְׂפָתַיִם אַךְ לְמַחְסוֹר׃
.poverty to only lips the the but ,profit there toil all In
(tends) of word is

24 25 עֲטֶרֶת חֲכָמִים עָשְׁרָם אִוֶּלֶת כְּסִילִים אִוֶּלֶת׃ מַצִּיל נְפָשׁוֹת
souls delivers fool- (is) fools The their is wise the The
ishness of folly .riches of crown

26 עֵד אֱמֶת וְיָפִחַ כְּזָבִים מִרְמָה׃ בְּיִרְאַת יְהוָה מִבְטַח־עֹז
;strong (is) Jehovah the In deceit(ful) a lies but ;true A
trust of fear .(witness) breathes witness

27 וּלְבָנָיו יִהְיֶה מַחְסֶה׃ יִרְאַת יְהוָה מְקוֹר חַיִּים לָסוּר
turn to ;life a (is) Jehovah fear The hiding a shall to and
away of fountain of .place be sons His

28 מִמֹּקְשֵׁי מָוֶת׃ בְּרָב־עָם הַדְרַת־מֶלֶךְ וּבְאֶפֶס לְאֹם
people the in but the (is) people the In .death the from
of lack king's splendor of multitude of snares

29 מְחִתַּת רָזוֹן׃ אֶרֶךְ אַפַּיִם רַב־תְּבוּנָה וּקְצַר־רוּחַ מֵרִים
exalts of one but under- of (is) (to) One a the (is)
spirit short ;standing great anger long prince of ruin

30 אִוֶּלֶת׃ חַיֵּי בְשָׂרִים לֵב מַרְפֵּא וּרְקַב עֲצָמוֹת קִנְאָה׃
(is) bones the the but ;healing A flesh the (is) .folly
jealousy of rottenness of heart (to) life

31 32 עֹשֵׁק דָּל חֵרֵף עֹשֵׂהוּ וּמְכַבְּדוֹ חֹנֵן אֶבְיוֹן׃ בְּרָעָתוֹ יִדָּחֶה
thrust (is) his In the favors one but his curses the op- One
out evildoing .needy Him honoring ,Maker poor pressing

33 רָשָׁע וְחֹסֶה בְמוֹתוֹ צַדִּיק׃ בְּלֵב נָבוֹן תָּנוּחַ חָכְמָה וּבְקֶרֶב
and ;wisdom rests under the In the his in has but the
among standing heart .righteous death refuge ;wicked

34 כְּסִילִים תִּוָּדֵעַ׃ צְדָקָה תְּרוֹמֵם גּוֹי וְחֶסֶד לְאֻמִּים חַטָּאת׃
.sin (is) to a but a exalts Righteousness made is it fools
peoples shame ;nation .known

רְצוֹן־מֶלֶךְ לְעֶבֶד מַשְׂכִּיל וְעֶבְרָתוֹ תִּהְיֶה מֵבִישׁ׃
35 causer a is his but acts who a to (is) The favor
.shame of (upon) wrath ;wisely ,servant king's

CAP. XV טו

CHAPTER 15

[1] A soft answer turns away wrath; but a grievous word stirs up anger. [2] The tongue of the wise uses knowledge rightly; but the mouth of fools pours out foolishness. [3] The eyes of Jehovah (are) in every place, watching the evil and the good. [4] A wholesome tongue (is) a tree of life; but perverseness in it (is) a break of the spirit. [5] A fool despises his father's instruction; but he keeping correction is sensible. [6] In the house of the righteous (is) much treasure; but in the gain of the wicked (is) trouble.

CHAPTER 15

1 2 מַעֲנֶה־רַּךְ יָשִׁיב חֵמָה וּדְבַר־עֶצֶב יַעֲלֶה־אָף׃ לְשׁוֹן
The .anger lifts pain a but ;wrath turns soft answer An
tongue up of word away

3 חֲכָמִים תֵּיטִיב דָּעַת וּפִי כְסִילִים יַבִּיעַ אִוֶּלֶת׃ בְּכָל־מָקוֹם
place In foolish- makes fools' but knowl- makes the
every .ness flow mouth ;ledge good righteous'

4 עֵינֵי יְהוָה צֹפוֹת רָעִים וְטוֹבִים׃ מַרְפֵּא לָשׁוֹן עֵץ חַיִּים
;life a (is) tongue A the and the watching Jehovah the
of tree healing .good evil (are) of eyes

5 וְסֶלֶף בָּהּ שֶׁבֶר בְּרוּחַ׃ אֱוִיל יִנְאַץ מוּסַר אָבִיו וְשֹׁמֵר
one but his instruction despises fool A the in a (is) it in but
keeping father's .spirit breaking perversity

6 תּוֹכַחַת יַעְרִם׃ בֵּית צַדִּיק חֹסֶן רָב וּבִתְבוּאַת רָשָׁע
the the in but ;much (is) the (In) is correction
wicked of increase treasure righteous house astute

[7] The lips of the righteous extend knowledge; but the heart of the fool is not stable. [8] The sacrifice of the wicked (is) a hateful thing to Jehovah; but the prayer of the upright (is) His delight. [9] The way of the wicked (is) hateful to Jehovah; but He loves him who pursues righteousness. [10] Correction (is) grievous to him who forsakes the way; he who hates reproof shall die. [11] Hell and destruction (are) before Jehovah; how much more then the hearts of the sons of men! [12] A scorner does not love one who corrects him; nor will he go to the wise. [13] A joyful heart makes good a face; but by grief of heart the spirit is stricken. [14] The heart of the understanding one seeks knowledge; but the mouth of fools feeds on folly. [15] All the days of the afflicted (are) evil; but gladness of heart is a continual feast. [16] Better (is) a little with the fear of Jehovah than great treasure and tumult with it. [17] Better (is) a dinner of vegetables where love is, than a stalled ox and hatred with it. [18] A furious man stirs up quarreling; but he who is slow to anger calms fighting. [19] The way of the lazy one (is) like a hedge of thorns; but the path of the righteous (is) cast up. [20] A wise son makes a glad father; but a foolish man despises his mother. [21] Foolishness (is) joy to him who lacks understanding; but a man of understanding walks straight. [22] Without counsel, purposes are broken; but by great counselors they rise. [23] A man (has) joy by the answer of his mouth; and how good (is) a word in due season! [24] The path of life (is) upward to the prudent, that he may turn away from Sheol downward. [25] Jehovah will destroy the house of the proud; but He will set up the widow's border. [26] The thoughts of the

7 נֶעְכָּרֶת׃ שִׂפְתֵי חֲכָמִים יְזָרוּ דָעַת וְלֵב כְּסִילִים לֹא־כֵן׃
is not fools the but knowl- scatter the lips The is
.so of heart ;edge wise of .trouble

8 9 זֶבַח רְשָׁעִים תּוֹעֲבַת יְהוָה וּתְפִלַּת יְשָׁרִים רְצוֹנוֹ׃ תּוֹעֲבַת
hateful (is) His (is) the the but ;Jehovah a (is) the sacri-
to .delight upright of prayer to thing hateful wicked's fice

10 יְהוָה דֶּרֶךְ רָשָׁע וּמְרַדֵּף צְדָקָה יֶאֱהָב׃ מוּסָר רָע לְעֹזֵב
one to (is) Instruction He righteous- one but the The Jehovah
forsaking evil .loves ness pursuing ;wicked of way

11 אֹרַח שׂוֹנֵא תוֹכַחַת יָמוּת׃ שְׁאוֹל וַאֲבַדּוֹן נֶגֶד יְהוָה אַף
even ;Jehovah (are) and Sheol .die shall reproof one the
before destruction hating ;path

12 כִּי־לִבּוֹת בְּנֵי־אָדָם׃ לֹא יֶאֱהַב־לֵץ הוֹכֵחַ לוֹ אֶל־חֲכָמִים
the to ;him who one A does not !men sons the the more
wise corrects scorner love of of hearts

13 לֹא יֵלֵךְ׃ לֵב שָׂמֵחַ יֵיטִב פָּנִים וּבְעַצְּבַת־לֵב רוּחַ נְכֵאָה׃
is the heart by but a makes joyful A he will not
.stricken spirit of pain ;face good heart .go

14 15 לֵב נָבוֹן יְבַקֶּשׁ־דָּעַת וּפְנֵי כְסִילִים יִרְעֶה אִוֶּלֶת׃ כָּל־יְמֵי
the All .folly feeds fools the but knowl- seeks the The
of days on of mouth ;edge wise of heart

16 עָנִי רָעִים וְטוֹב־לֵב מִשְׁתֶּה תָמִיד׃ טוֹב־מְעַט בְּיִרְאַת
the with a Better .continual a (is) heart but (are) the
of fear little is feast of goodness ;evil poor

17 יְהוָה מֵאוֹצָר רָב וּמְהוּמָה בוֹ׃ טוֹב אֲרֻחַת יָרָק וְאַהֲבָה־
love and herbs meal a Better with and great than Jehovah
of .it tumult- treasure

18 שָׁם מִשּׁוֹר אָבוּס וְשִׂנְאָה־בוֹ׃ אִישׁ חֵמָה יְגָרֶה מָדוֹן
;strife stirs fury man A with and being than ,there
up of .it hatred stalled oxen

19 וְאֶרֶךְ אַפַּיִם יַשְׁקִיט רִיב׃ דֶּרֶךְ עָצֵל כִּמְשֻׂכַת חָדֶק וְאֹרַח
the but ;thorns like (is) the The .fighting calms anger one but
of path of hedge a lazy of way (to) long

20 יְשָׁרִים סְלֻלָה׃ בֵּן חָכָם יְשַׂמַּח־אָב וּכְסִיל אָדָם בּוֹזֶה
despises a but a makes wise A (is) the
man foolish ;father glad son .up cast righteous

21 אִמּוֹ׃ אִוֶּלֶת שִׂמְחָה לַחֲסַר־לֵב וְאִישׁ תְּבוּנָה יְיַשֶּׁר־לָכֶת׃
.walks straight under- a but ;heart him to (is) Foolishness his
standing of man lacks who joy .mother

22 23 הָפֵר מַחֲשָׁבוֹת בְּאֵין סוֹד וּבְרֹב יוֹעֲצִים תָּקוּם׃ שִׂמְחָה
Joy .rise they counselors by but ;counsel without Purposes frus- are
great trated

24 לָאִישׁ בְּמַעֲנֵה־פִיו וְדָבָר בְּעִתּוֹ מַה־טּוֹב׃ אֹרַח חַיִּים
life The good how its in a and his the by to (is)
of path .(is it) ,time word ;mouth of answer man a

25 לְמַעְלָה לְמַשְׂכִּיל לְמַעַן סוּר מִשְּׁאוֹל מָטָּה׃ בֵּית גֵּאִים
the The .below from may he that the to is
proud of house Sheol turn prudent upward

26 יִסַּח ׀ יְהוָה וְיַצֵּב גְּבוּל אַלְמָנָה׃ תּוֹעֲבַת יְהוָה מַחְשְׁבוֹת
thoughts The Jehovah (are) the border He but ;Jehovah pulls
of (to) hateful .widow's up sets

wicked (are) very hateful to Jehovah; but the words of pleasantness (are) pure. [27] He who is greedy for gain troubles his own house; but he who hates bribes shall live. [28] The heart of the righteous muses (how) to answer; but the mouth of the wicked pours out evil things. [29] Jehovah (is) far from the wicked; but He hears the prayer of the righteous. [30] The light of the eyes rejoices the heart; a good report makes the bones fat. [31] The ear that hears the reproof of life shall remain among the wise. [32] He who refuses instruction despises his own soul; but he who hears reproof gets understanding. [33] The fear of Jehovah (is) instruction in wisdom; and before honor (is) humility.

27 רָע וּטְהֹרִים אִמְרֵי־נֹעַם׃ עֹכֵר בֵּיתוֹ בּוֹצֵעַ בָּצַע וְשׂוֹנֵא
he but unjust who he his Troubles pleasant- the but the
hates who gain gets house ness of words(are) pure ;evil

28 מַתָּנֹת יִחְיֶה׃ לֵב צַדִּיק יֶהְגֶּה לַעֲנוֹת וּפִי רְשָׁעִים יַבִּיעַ
makes the the but to studies the heart The shall bribes
flow wicked of mouth ;answer righteous of .live

29 רָעוֹת׃ רָחוֹק יְהוָה מֵרְשָׁעִים וּתְפִלַּת צַדִּיקִים יִשְׁמָע׃
He the the but the from Jehovah far (is) evil
.hears righteous of prayer ;wicked .things

30 31 מְאוֹר־עֵינַיִם יְשַׂמַּח־לֵב שְׁמוּעָה טוֹבָה תְּדַשֶּׁן־עָצֶם׃ אֹזֶן
The the makes good report a the rejoices the The
ear .bone fat ;heart eyes of light

32 שֹׁמַעַת תּוֹכַחַת חַיִּים בְּקֶרֶב חֲכָמִים תָּלִין׃ פּוֹרֵעַ מוּסָר
correc- who He shall instruc- the in ,life the that
tion ignores .dwell tion of midst of reproof hears

33 מוֹאֵס נַפְשׁוֹ וְשׁוֹמֵעַ תּוֹכַחַת קוֹנֶה לֵּב׃ יִרְאַת יְהוָה מוּסַר
instruc- Jehovah The .heart gets reproof he but own his despises
in tion of fear hears who ;soul

חָכְמָה וְלִפְנֵי כָבוֹד עֲנָוָה׃
(is) honor and ;wisdom
.humility before

CAP. XVI טז

CHAPTER 16

[1] The orderings of the heart (are) for man, and the answer of the tongue from Jehovah. [2] All the ways of a man (are) pure in his own eyes; but Jehovah measures the spirits. [3] Roll your works on Jehovah, and your thoughts shall be blessed. [4] Jehovah has made all for its purpose; yea, even the wicked for the day of evil. [5] Everyone proud in heart (is) hateful (to) Jehovah; (though) hand (join) in hand, he shall not be acquitted. [6] Iniquity is covered by mercy and truth; and in the fear of Jehovah, (men) turn aside from evil. [7] When a man's ways please Jehovah, He makes even his enemies to be at peace with him. [8] Better (is) a little with righteousness than great gains without right. [9] A man's heart plans his way; but Jehovah fixes his steps. [10] An oracle (is) in the lips of the king; his mouth is not traitorous in judgment. [11] A just weight and balance (are) Jehovah's; all the stones of the bag (are)

1 2 לְאָדָם מַעַרְכֵי־לֵב וּמֵיְהוָה מַעֲנֵה לָשׁוֹן׃ כָּל־דַּרְכֵי־אִישׁ
a the All the the from and the The are for
man of ways .tongue of answer Jehovah ,heart of arrays man

3 זַךְ בְּעֵינָיו וְתֹכֵן רוּחוֹת יְהוָה׃ גֹּל אֶל־יְהוָה מַעֲשֶׂיךָ וְיִכֹּנוּ
shall and your Jehovah on Roll .Jehovah the but his in (are)
set be works spirits weighs ;eyes own pure

4 מַחְשְׁבֹתֶיךָ׃ כֹּל פָּעַל יְהוָה לַמַּעֲנֵהוּ וְגַם־רָשָׁע לְיוֹם
the for the and His for Jehovah has all your
of day wicked even ,purpose made .thoughts

5 רָעָה׃ תּוֹעֲבַת יְהוָה כָּל־גְּבַהּ־לֵב יָד לְיָד לֹא יִנָּקֶה׃
.be will he not in hand in proud (is) Jehovah abomi- An .evil
.acquitted hand heart everyone to nation

6 7 בְּחֶסֶד וֶאֱמֶת יְכֻפַּר עָוֺן וּבְיִרְאַת יְהוָה סוּר מֵרָע׃ בִּרְצוֹת
When from (men) Jehovah in and ;iniquity is and By
please .evil turn of fear the covered truth mercy

8 יְהוָה דַּרְכֵי־אִישׁ גַּם־אוֹיְבָיו יַשְׁלִם אִתּוֹ׃ טוֹב מְעַט
a Better with makes He his even a ways Jehovah
little (is) .him peace at enemies ,man's

9 בִּצְדָקָה מֵרֹב תְּבוּאוֹת בְּלֹא מִשְׁפָּט׃ לֵב אָדָם יְחַשֵּׁב
plans A heart .justice without increase than righ- with
man's much teousness

10 דַּרְכּוֹ וַיהוָה יָכִין צַעֲדוֹ׃ קֶסֶם ׀ עַל־שִׂפְתֵי־מֶלֶךְ בְּמִשְׁפָּט
judg- in the the on (is) godly A his fixes but his
ment ;king of lips decision .step Jehovah ,way

11 לֹא יִמְעַל־פִּיו׃ פֶּלֶס ׀ וּמֹאזְנֵי מִשְׁפָּט לַיהוָה מַעֲשֵׂהוּ כָּל־
(is) His to (are) justice and scale A his trait- is not
all work ;Jehovah of balances .mouth orous

His work. [12] (It is) a hateful thing for kings to commit wickedness; for the throne is established by righteousness. [13] Righteous lips (are) the delight of kings; and they love him who speaks uprightly. [14] A king's fury (is) as messengers of death but a wise man will cover over it. [15] In the light of the king's face (is) life ; and his favor (is) like a cloud of the latter rain. [16] How much better to get wisdom than gold! And to get understanding (is) rather to be chosen than silver. [17] The way of the upright (is) to turn away from evil; he who guards his soul watches his way. [18] Pride (goes) before destruction, and a haughty spirit before a fall. [19] It is better (to be) of a lowly spirit with the poor than to divide the spoil with the proud. [20] He who acts prudently shall find good; and he who trusts in Jehovah, O how happy is he! [21] The wise in heart shall be called prudent; and sweetness of lips increases learning. [22] Prudence (is) a fountain of life to those who have it; (but) the teaching of fools (is) folly. [23] The heart of the wise makes his mouth prudent and he adds learning on his lips. [24] Pleasant words (are) an overflowing of honey, sweetness to the soul and healing to the bones. [25] There is a way (that seems) right to a man's face, but the end of it is the ways of death. [26] He who labors works for himself; for his mouth urges him on. [27] A worthless man plots evil; and on his lips (it is) like a burning fire.

[28] A perverse man causes strife; and a whisperer separates close friends. [29] A violent man lures his neighbor, and causes him to go in a way (that is) not good. [30] He who shuts his eyes, to plan perverse things; compressing his lips, he brings evil to pass. [31] The gray head (is) a crown of

אַבְנֵי־כִיס׃ תּוֹעֲבַת מְלָכִים עֲשׂוֹת רֶשַׁע כִּי בִצְדָקָה יִכּוֹן 12
is set | by righteousness | for wickedness | to commit | kings | An abomination for | of stones the bag the

כִּסֵּא׃ רְצוֹן מְלָכִים שִׂפְתֵי־צֶדֶק וְדֹבֵר יְשָׁרִים יֶאֱהָב׃ 13
.loved is | uprightly | he and who speaks | ;Righteous | lips | kings | the (are) of delight | the .throne

חֲמַת־מֶלֶךְ מַלְאֲכֵי־מָוֶת וְאִישׁ חָכָם יְכַפְּרֶנָּה׃ בְּאוֹר־פְּנֵי־ 14 15
face | the In of light | will .it cover | wise man | a but | ;death | (as is) of messengers | A king's | fury

מֶלֶךְ חַיִּים וּרְצוֹנוֹ כְּעָב מַלְקוֹשׁ׃ קְנֹה־חָכְמָה מַה־טּוֹב 16
better | how much | ,wisdom | To get | spring the .rain | a like of cloud | (is) his and favor | (is) ;life | the king's

מֵחָרוּץ וּקְנוֹת בִּינָה נִבְחָר מִכָּסֶף׃ מְסִלַּת יְשָׁרִים סוּר 17
to turn | (is) upright | the highway | The of | above .silver | be to chosen | under- standing | to and get | than !gold

מֵרָע שֹׁמֵר נַפְשׁוֹ נֹצֵר דַּרְכּוֹ׃ לִפְנֵי־שֶׁבֶר גָּאוֹן וְלִפְנֵי 18
and before | Pride ,(goes) | destruction | before | his .way | watches | his soul | who he keeps | from ;evil

כִשָּׁלוֹן גֹּבַהּ רוּחַ׃ טוֹב שְׁפַל־רוּחַ אֶת־עֲנָוִים מֵחַלֵּק שָׁלָל 19
the spoil | to than divide | the with ,poor | of lowness spirit | Better is | .spirit | a haughty | stumbling

אֶת־גֵּאִים׃ מַשְׂכִּיל עַל־דָּבָר יִמְצָא־טוֹב וּבוֹטֵחַ בַּיהוָה 20
in ,Jehovah | he and trusts who | ;good | shall find | a matter | on | who He prudently acts | the .proud | with

אַשְׁרָיו׃ לַחֲכַם־לֵב יִקָּרֵא נָבוֹן וּמֶתֶק שְׂפָתַיִם יֹסִיף לֶקַח׃ 21
persuasion. | increases | lips | sweet- of ness | and | under- standing | be shall called | heart | The in wise | is blessed .he

מְקוֹר חַיִּים שֵׂכֶל בְּעָלָיו וּמוּסַר אֱוִלִים אִוֶּלֶת׃ לֵב חָכָם 22 23
the wise | The of heart | (is) .folly | fools | in- of struction | the but ,owners | its to | pru- dence | life (is) | well A of

יַשְׂכִּיל פִּיהוּ וְעַל־שְׂפָתָיו יֹסִיף לֶקַח׃ צוּף־דְּבַשׁ אִמְרֵי־ 24
(are) words | (with) honey | flow- ing | per- suasion | he adds | his lips | and on | his ,mouth | makes prudent

נֹעַם מָתוֹק לַנֶּפֶשׁ וּמַרְפֵּא לָעָצֶם׃ יֵשׁ דֶּרֶךְ יָשָׁר לִפְנֵי־ 25
before | (seeming) upright | a way | There is | the to .bones | and healing | the to soul | sweet- ness | Pleas- ;ant

אִישׁ וְאַחֲרִיתָהּ דַּרְכֵי־מָוֶת׃ נֶפֶשׁ עָמֵל עָמְלָה לּוֹ כִּי־אָכַף 26
for urges | for ;himself | labors | who labors | The soul | .death of | ways the | its but (is) end | a ,man

עָלָיו פִּיהוּ׃ אִישׁ בְּלִיַּעַל כֹּרֶה רָעָה וְעַל־שְׂפָתָיו כְּאֵשׁ 27
like fire a | his lips | (is it) and on | ;evil | digs up | worth- less | man A | his .mouth | on him

צָרָבֶת׃ אִישׁ תַּהְפֻּכוֹת יְשַׁלַּח מָדוֹן וְנִרְגָּן מַפְרִיד אַלּוּף׃ 28
.friends | separates | a and slanderer | ;strife | sends out | perversities of man | A | .burning

אִישׁ חָמָס יְפַתֶּה רֵעֵהוּ וְהוֹלִיכוֹ בְּדֶרֶךְ לֹא־טוֹב׃ עֹצֶה 29 30
who He shuts | .good | not | a in way | makes and go him | his ,neighbor | lures | violence | A of man

עֵינָיו לַחְשֹׁב תַּהְפֻּכוֹת קֹרֵץ שְׂפָתָיו כִּלָּה רָעָה׃ עֲטֶרֶת 31
crown A of | .evil | brings pass to | his ,lips | com- pressing | perverse things | plan to | his eyes

glory; it is found in the way of righteousness. [32] One slow to anger (is) better than the mighty; and he who rules his spirit than he who takes a city. [33] The lot is cast into the lap, but all ordering of it (is) from Jehovah.

32

תִּפְאֶרֶת שֵׂיבָה בְּדֶרֶךְ צְדָקָה תִּמָּצֵא׃ טוֹב אֶרֶךְ אַפַּיִם

anger	One	(is)	is it	righteous-	the in	gray a	glory
	(to) long	better	.found	ness	of way	head	

33

מִגִּבּוֹר וּמֹשֵׁל בְּרוּחוֹ מִלֹּכֵד עִיר׃ בַּחֵיק יוּטַל אֶת־הַגּוֹרָל

lot The	is	the into	a	one than	his	he and	the than
	cast	bosom	.city	takes who	spirit	rules who	;mighty

וּמֵיהוָה כָּל־מִשְׁפָּטוֹ׃

ordering the	(is) from but
.it of	all Jehovah

CAP. XVII יז

CHAPTER 17

CHAPTER 17

[1] Better (is) a dry piece of bread, and quietness with it, than a house full of sacrifices (with) fighting. [2] A servant who acts prudently shall rule over a son who causes shame; and (he) shall have part of the inheritance among the brothers. [3] The refining pot (is) for silver, and the furnace for gold; but Jehovah tries the hearts. [4] A wicked doer gives heed to false lips; a liar listens to a tongue of evil desire. [5] Whoever scorns the poor reviles his Maker; he who rejoices at calamity shall not be acquitted. [6] Grandsons (are) the crown of old men; and the glory of sons (is) their fathers. [7] A lip of excess is not fitting for a fool; much less are lying lips (for) a prince. [8] A bribe is a stone of grace in the eyes of him who possesses it; wherever he turns, he is prudent. [9] He who covers a transgression seeks love; but he who repeats a matter seperates friends. [10] A reproof enters more into a wise man than a hundred stripes into a fool [11] A rebel seeks evil, so a cruel messenger is sent against him. [12] Let a bear bereaved (of her cubs) meet a man, rather than a fool in his foolishness. [13] Whoever rewards evil for good, evil shall not depart from his house. [14] The beginning of strife (is) like the releasing of water; therefore leave off fighting before it breaks out. [15] He who justifies the wicked, and he who condemns the just,

1
2

טוֹב פַּת חֲרֵבָה וְשַׁלְוָה־בָהּ מִבַּיִת מָלֵא זִבְחֵי־רִיב׃ עֶבֶד

A	(with) sacri-	full	a than	with	and	dry	piece a Better
servant	.strife fices	of	house	,it quietness		bread of	(is)

מַשְׂכִּיל יִמְשֹׁל בְּבֵן־מֵבִישׁ וּבְתוֹךְ אַחִים יַחֲלֹק נַחֲלָה׃

inheri-	the shall he	the	and	causes who	a over	shall	acts who
.tance	share brothers	among		;shame son		rule	prudently

3
4

מַצְרֵף לַכֶּסֶף וְכוּר לַזָּהָב וּבֹחֵן לִבּוֹת יְהוָה׃ מֵרַע מַקְשִׁיב

heeds	evil- An	.Jehovah	the	but	for	the and	for	The
	doer		hearts	tries	;gold	furnace	,silver	crucible

עַל־שְׂפַת־אָוֶן שֶׁקֶר מֵזִין עַל־לְשׁוֹן הַוֹּת׃ לֹעֵג לָרָשׁ חֵרֵף

reviles	the who	He	(evil)	a	to	listens	;false	lips
	poor mocks	.desire of tongue			liar			

6

עֹשֵׂהוּ שָׂמֵחַ לְאֵיד לֹא יִנָּקֶה׃ עֲטֶרֶת זְקֵנִים בְּנֵי בָנִים

,sons	of Sons	old	crown the	be shall	not	at	who he	his
	(is) men		acquitted			calamity	rejoices	;Maker

7

וְתִפְאֶרֶת בָּנִים אֲבוֹתָם׃ לֹא־נָאוָה לְנָבָל שְׂפַת יֶתֶר אַף

much	ex-	lip A	a for	is	not	their	sons	the and
less	cess of		fool	fitting		.fathers		of glory

8

כִּי־לְנָדִיב שְׂפַת־שָׁקֶר׃ אֶבֶן־חֵן הַשֹּׁחַד בְּעֵינֵי בְעָלָיו אֶל־

to	its	the	the in	the	stone a	.lying	lips	for
	,owner	of eyes		bribe (is) grace of			of	noble a

9

כָּל־אֲשֶׁר יִפְנֶה יַשְׂכִּיל׃ מְכַסֶּה־פֶּשַׁע מְבַקֵּשׁ אַהֲבָה וְשֹׁנֶה

one but	,love	seeks	trans-	who He	is he	where every
repeating			gression covers		prudent	turns

10

בְּדָבָר מַפְרִיד אַלּוּף׃ תֵּחַת גְּעָרָה בְמֵבִין מֵהַכּוֹת כְּסִיל

a (into)	than more	an into	A	goes	friends	separates matter a
fool			blows		one astute	rebuke down

11
12

מֵאָה׃ אַךְ־מְרִי יְבַקֶּשׁ־רָע וּמַלְאָךְ אַכְזָרִי יְשֻׁלַּח־בּוֹ׃ פָּגוֹשׁ

Let	against	is	cruel	a so	;evil	seeks	A	only a
meet	.him	sent	messenger			rebel		hundred

13

דֹּב שַׁכּוּל בְּאִישׁ וְאַל־כְּסִיל בְּאִוַּלְתּוֹ׃ מֵשִׁיב רָעָה תַּחַת

instead	evil	who He	his in	fool a	and	,man a	bereaved	a
of		returns	.foolishness		not		(cubs of)	bear

14

טוֹבָה לֹא־תָמִישׁ רָעָה מִבֵּיתוֹ׃ פּוֹטֵר מַיִם רֵאשִׁית מָדוֹן

strife	be- The	water the	(like)	from	evil	shall	not	,good
;(is)	of ginning	of releasing		.house his		depart		

15

וְלִפְנֵי הִתְגַּלַּע הָרִיב נְטוֹשׁ׃ מַצְדִּיק רָשָׁע וּמַרְשִׁיעַ צַדִּיק

the	and	the	who He	for-	striving	breaks it	so
just	condemns	,wicked	justifies	.sake		,out	before

even both of them (are) hateful to Jehovah.

[16] Why (is there) hire in the hand of a fool to get wisdom, and there is not a heart? [17] A friend loves at every time; but a brother is born for the time of trouble. [18] A man lacking heart strikes the palm; he pledges in the presence of his friends. [19] He who loves strife loves rebellion; he who exalts his door seeks ruin. [20] He who has a perverse heart finds no good; and he who has a crooked tongue falls into evil. [21] He who fathers a fool has sorrow for it; yea, the father of a fool has no joy. [22] A cheerful heart makes good healing; but a stricken spirit dries the bone. [23] One takes a bribe out of the bosom of the wicked to stretch the ways of justice. [24] With the face of the wise is wisdom; but the eyes of a fool (are) in the ends of the earth. [25] A foolish son (is) a vexation to his father; and bitterness to her who bore him. [26] And it (is) not good to fine the just; to strike leaders for uprightness. [27] He who restrains his words knows knowledge; a man of understanding (is) cool of spirit. [28] Even a fool who is silent is counted wise, he who shuts his lips (is) counted (as) understanding.

16 תּוֹעֲבַת יְהוָה גַּם־שְׁנֵיהֶם׃ לָמָּה־זֶּה מְחִיר בְּיַד־כְּסִיל

a fool | the in hand of | hire | (is) Why this; | of both .them | even ,Jehovah | (are) to hateful

17 לִקְנוֹת חָכְמָה וְלֶב־אָיִן׃ בְּכָל־עֵת אֹהֵב הָרֵעַ וְאָח לְצָרָה

for trouble | a and brother | the loves ;friend | time | At every | is there ?not | a and heart | wisdom | to obtain

18 יִוָּלֵד׃ אָדָם חֲסַר־לֵב תֹּקֵעַ כָּף עֹרֵב עֲרֻבָּה לִפְנֵי רֵעֵהוּ׃

his .friend | before | a pledge | he pledges | the ;palm | strikes | lacking heart | A man | is .born

19 אֹהֵב פֶּשַׁע אֹהֵב מַצָּה מַגְבִּיהַּ פִּתְחוֹ מְבַקֶּשׁ־שָׁבֶר׃ עִקֶּשׁ־

of One crooked | seeks ,shattering | his door | who he exalts | ;strife | loves | trans- gression | who He loves

21 לֵב לֹא יִמְצָא־טוֹב וְנֶהְפָּךְ בִּלְשׁוֹנוֹ יִפּוֹל בְּרָעָה׃ יֹלֵד

who He fathers | into .evil | falls | his in tongue | one and perverse | ;good | finds | not | heart

22 כְּסִיל לְתוּגָה לוֹ וְלֹא־יִשְׂמַח אֲבִי נָבָל׃ לֵב שָׂמֵחַ יֵיטִב

makes good | joyful | A heart | .fool a | the of father | will rejoice | and not | for ;it | into grief | fool a (falls)

23 גֵּהָה וְרוּחַ נְכֵאָה תְּיַבֶּשׁ־גָּרֶם׃ שֹׁחַד מֵחֵק רָשָׁע יִקָּח

;takes | The wicked | of out bosom the | bribe a | the .bone | dries | stricken | a but spirit | ;healing

24 לְהַטּוֹת אָרְחוֹת מִשְׁפָּט׃ אֶת־פְּנֵי מֵבִין חָכְמָה וְעֵינֵי כְסִיל

fool a | the but of eyes | (is) ;wisdom | the wise | the With of face | .justice | paths of | the | to stretch

25
26 בִּקְצֵה־אָרֶץ׃ כַּעַס לְאָבִיו בֵּן כְּסִיל וּמֶמֶר לְיוֹלַדְתּוֹ׃ גַּם

Also | who her to .him bore | and bitterness | ;foolish | A son | his to father | a (is) vexation | the .earth | the in (are) of ends

27 עֲנוֹשׁ לַצַּדִּיק לֹא־טוֹב לְהַכּוֹת נְדִיבִים עַל־יֹשֶׁר׃ חוֹשֵׂךְ

who He restrains | upright- .ness | for | nobles | strike to | ;good | (is) not | just the | fine to

28 אֲמָרָיו יוֹדֵעַ דָּעַת וְקַר־רוּחַ אִישׁ תְּבוּנָה׃ גַּם אֱוִיל

fool a | Even | under- .standing | a (is) of man | spirit of cool | and | knowl- ;edge | knows | his words

מַחֲרִישׁ חָכָם יֵחָשֵׁב אֹטֵם שְׂפָתָיו נָבוֹן׃

(as) .understanding | lips his | who he shuts | is ;thought | wise | is who silent

CAP. XVIII יח

CHAPTER 18

[1] He that separates himself seeks (his own) desire; he breaks out against all sound wisdom. [2] A fool has no delight in understanding, but only in uncovering his heart. [3] When the wicked comes, scorn comes, too; and with shame (comes) reproach. [4] The words of a man's mouth (are) like deep waters; the fountain of wisdom (like) a flowing brook. [5] To lift up the face of the wicked (is) not good; (nor) to turn

1
2 לְתַאֲוָה יְבַקֵּשׁ נִפְרָד בְּכָל־תּוּשִׁיָּה יִתְגַּלָּע׃ לֹא־יַחְפֹּץ

has delight | not | breaks he .out | sound wisdom | against all | who he ;himself separates | seeks (own his) | To desire

3 כְּסִיל בִּתְבוּנָה כִּי אִם־בְּהִתְגַּלּוֹת לִבּוֹ׃ בְּבוֹא־רָשָׁע בָּא

comes | the ,wicked | When comes | his .heart | uncov- ering | in | only | but | under- ,standing | in | fool A

4 גַּם־בּוּז וְעִם־קָלוֹן חֶרְפָּה׃ מַיִם עֲמֻקִּים דִּבְרֵי פִי־אִישׁ

a ,man's | mouth | the of words | Deep (are) | waters | (comes) .reproach | shame | and with | also ;scorn

5 נַחַל נֹבֵעַ מְקוֹר חָכְמָה׃ שְׂאֵת פְּנֵי־רָשָׁע לֹא־טוֹב לְהַטּוֹת

to (nor) aside turn | (is) not ;good | the wicked | the of face | lift To up | .wisdom | the of fountain | flowing | a is stream

aside the righteous in judgment. [6] A fool's lips enter into argument, yea, his mouth calls for strokes. [7] A fool's mouth (is) his destruction, and his lips (are) the snare of his soul. [8] The words of a talebearer (are) as wounds; yea, they go down into the innermost parts of the heart. [9] And he who is lazy in his work, he is brother one who destroys. [10] The name of Jehovah (is) a tower of strength; the righteous runs into it, and is set on high. [11] The rich man's wealth (is) his strong city; and as a high wall in his imagination. [12] Before destruction a man's heart is haughty; but before honor (goes) humility. [13] If one answers a matter before he hears, it (is) folly and shame to him. [14] The spirit of a man will nourish his sickness; but who can bear a wounded spirit? [15] The heart of the prudent gets knowledge; and the ear of the wise seeks knowledge. [16] A man's bribe makes room for him and brings him before great men. [17] (He who is) first in his cause (seems) just; (but) his neighbor comes and searches him. [18] The lot causes arguments to cease, and divides between the mighty. [19] A brother offended (is worse) than a fortified city; yea, (their) contentions (are) like the bars of a castle. [20] A man's belly shall be satisfied with the fruit of his mouth; he shall be satisfied (with) the produce of his lips. [21] Death and life (are) in the power of the tongue; and those who love it shall eat its fruit. [22] (Whoever) finds a wife finds good, and gets favor from Jehovah. [23] The poor speak with entreaties, but the rich answers fiercely. [24] A man of friends may be broken up; but there is a Lover who sticks closer than a brother.

6 צַדִּיק בַּמִּשְׁפָּט׃ שִׂפְתֵי כְסִיל יָבֹאוּ בְרִיב וּפִיו לְמַהֲלֻמוֹת

for strokes | his and mouth | into ;strife | enter | fool's A | lips | in .judgment | the righteous

7
8 יִקְרָא׃ פִּי־כְסִיל מְחִתָּה־לוֹ וּשְׂפָתָיו מוֹקֵשׁ נַפְשׁוֹ׃ דִּבְרֵי

words The of | his .soul | the (are) of snare | his and lips | to ,him | (is) ruin | A mouth fool's | .calls

9 נִרְגָּן כְּמִתְלַהֲמִים וְהֵם יָרְדוּ חַדְרֵי־בָטֶן׃ גַּם מִתְרַפֶּה

is who he slack | ,Also | the chambers the .belly of | go (into) | and they | like are ;morsels tasty | a slanderer

10 בִמְלַאכְתּוֹ אָח הוּא לְבַעַל מַשְׁחִית׃ מִגְדַּל־עֹז

tower a strength of | destruction | a to of lord | he a | (is) brother | his in ,work

11 שֵׁם יְהוָה בּוֹ־יָרוּץ צַדִּיק וְנִשְׂגָּב׃ הוֹן עָשִׁיר קִרְיַת עֻזּוֹ

his ;strong | are city | The man's rich | riches | is and .exalted | the righteous | run | into Jehovah it ;(is) | The of name

12 וּכְחוֹמָה נִשְׂגָּבָה בְּמַשְׂכִּתוֹ׃ לִפְנֵי־שֶׁבֶר יִגְבַּהּ לֵב־אִישׁ

a ;man's | heart | is haughty | shattering Before | his in .imagination | high | a as and wall

13 וְלִפְנֵי כָבוֹד עֲנָוָה׃ מֵשִׁיב דָּבָר בְּטֶרֶם יִשְׁמַע אִוֶּלֶת הִיא־

(is) it | folly | he ,hears | before | a matter | who He answers | (goes) .humility | honor | but before

14 לוֹ וּכְלִמָּה׃ רוּחַ־אִישׁ יְכַלְכֵּל מַחֲלֵהוּ וְרוּחַ נְכֵאָה מִי

who | stricken | a but spirit | his ;sickness | will endure | a man | The of spirit | and .shame | to him

15 יִשָּׂאֶנָּה׃ לֵב נָבוֹן יִקְנֶה־דָּעַת וְאֹזֶן חֲכָמִים תְּבַקֶּשׁ־דָּעַת׃

.knowledge | seeks | the wise | the and of ear | knowl- ,ledge | gets | the prudent | The of heart | can ? it bear

16
17 מַתָּן אָדָם יַרְחִיב לוֹ וְלִפְנֵי גְדֹלִים יַנְחֶנּוּ׃ צַדִּיק הָרִאשׁוֹן

first The | (seems) just | leads .him | great (men) | and before | for ,him | makes room | a man's | bribe

18 בְּרִיבוֹ יָבֹא רֵעֵהוּ וַחֲקָרוֹ׃ מִדְיָנִים יַשְׁבִּית הַגּוֹרָל וּבֵין

and between | The ,lot | to causes cease | strifes | tests and .him | his neighbor | (but) comes | his in ;cause

19 עֲצוּמִים יַפְרִיד׃ אָח נִפְשָׁע מִקִּרְיַת־עֹז וּמִדְוָנִים כִּבְרִיחַ

the like of bars | and strifes | of city a strength | offended (like is) | A brother | .divides | the mighty

20 אַרְמוֹן׃ מִפְּרִי פִי־אִישׁ תִּשְׂבַּע בִּטְנוֹ תְּבוּאַת שְׂפָתָיו

lips his | the (with) of produce | his ;belly | be shall satisfied | a man's | mouth | the With of fruit | .citadel a

21
22 יִשְׂבָּע׃ מָוֶת וְחַיִּים בְּיַד־לָשׁוֹן וְאֹהֲבֶיהָ יֹאכַל פִּרְיָהּ׃ מָצָא

who He finds | its .fruit | shall eat | those and it loving | hand ,tongue | the in the of | life and (are) | Death | be shall .satisfied be

23 אִשָּׁה מָצָא טוֹב וַיָּפֶק רָצוֹן מֵיְהוָה׃ תַּחֲנוּנִים יְדַבֶּר־רָשׁ

The ,poor | speak | (with) entreaties | from Jehovah | favor | and gets | ,good | finds | wife a

24 וְעָשִׁיר יַעֲנֶה עַזּוֹת׃ אִישׁ רֵעִים לְהִתְרֹעֵעַ וְיֵשׁ אֹהֵב

Lover a | but is there | be may ;up broken | friends | man A of | .roughly | answers | the but rich

דָּבֵק מֵאָח׃

a than .brother | sticks closer | who

CAP. XIX יט

CHAPTER 19

[1] The poor who walks in his integrity (is) better than he who (is) perverse in his lips, who (is) a fool. [2] Also, without knowledge the soul (is) not good; and he who hurries with his feet sins. [3] The foolishness of man overturns his way; and his heart rages against Jehovah. [4] Wealth makes many friends; but the poor is separated from his neighbor. [5] A false witness shall not be acquitted; yea, he who speaks lies shall not escape. [6] Many will beg the favor of a noble; and all are friends to him who gives gifts. [7] All the poor man's brothers hate him; and his friends also surely leave him; he pursues (them) with words, (yet) they are not. [8] He who gets heart loves his own soul; he who keeps understanding finds good. [9] A false witness shall not be acquitted; yea, he who speaks lies shall perish. [10] Luxury is not becoming for a fool; much less for a servant to rule over princes. [11] A man's discretion makes slow his anger; and his glory (is) to pass over a transgression. [12] The king's wrath (is) like a lion's roar; but his favor (is) like dew on the grass. [13] A foolish son (is) calamity to his father; and a wife's quarrelings a never-ending dripping. [14] House and riches (are) the inheritance of fathers; but a prudent wife (is) from Jehovah. [15] Laziness makes one fall into a deep sleep; and an idle soul shall suffer hunger. [16] He who keeps the commandment keeps his own soul; he who despises His ways shall die. [17] He who has pity on the poor lends to Jehovah; and He will reward his dealing to him. [18] Chasten your son, for there is hope; and do not set your soul on making him die. [19] A man great of fury will have

CHAPTER 19

1 2 טוֹב רָשׁ הוֹלֵךְ בְּתֻמּוֹ מֵעִקֵּשׁ שְׂפָתָיו וְהוּא כְסִיל׃ גַּם
,Also .fool a he and ;lips his one than his in who The (is)
(is) (in) crooked integrity walks poor better

3 בְּלֹא־דַעַת נֶפֶשׁ לֹא־טוֹב וְאָץ בְּרַגְלַיִם חוֹטֵא׃ אִוֶּלֶת אָדָם
man The .sins (his) with he and (is) not the knowl- with-
of folly feet rushing ;good soul edge out

4 תְּסַלֵּף דַּרְכּוֹ וְעַל־יְהוָה יִזְעַף לִבּוֹ׃ הוֹן יֹסִיף רֵעִים רַבִּים
;many friends adds Wealth his rages Jehovah and his perverts
.heart against ;way

5 וְדָל מֵרֵעֵהוּ יִפָּרֵד׃ עֵד שְׁקָרִים לֹא יִנָּקֶה וְיָפִיחַ כְּזָבִים
lies a and be shall not falsehoods A is his from the but
of breather ,clean of witness .separated neighbor poor

6 לֹא יִמָּלֵט׃ רַבִּים יְחַלּוּ פְנֵי־נָדִיב וְכָל־הָרֵעַ לְאִישׁ מַתָּן׃
.gifts a to are and a the will Many shall not
of man friends all noble of face beg .escape

7 כָּל אֲחֵי־רָשׁ ׀ שְׂנֵאֻהוּ אַף כִּי מְרֵעֵהוּ רָחֲקוּ מִמֶּנּוּ מְרַדֵּף
pursues he from have his surely also hate poor a the all
(them) ;him far been friends ;him man of brothers

8 אֲמָרִים לֹא־הֵמָּה׃ קֹנֶה־לֵּב אֹהֵב נַפְשׁוֹ שֹׁמֵר תְּבוּנָה
under- who he own his loves heart He they (yet) (with)
standing keeps ;soul gets who .are not ,words

9 לִמְצֹא־טוֹב׃ עֵד שְׁקָרִים לֹא יִנָּקֶה וְיָפִיחַ כְּזָבִים יֹאבֵד׃
shall lies a and be shall not falsehood A .good finds
.perish of breather clean of witness

10 לֹא־נָאוֶה לִכְסִיל תַּעֲנוּג אַף כִּי־לְעֶבֶד ׀ מְשֹׁל בְּשָׂרִים׃
over rule to a for less much ;Luxury a for is not
.rulers servant fool becoming

11 12 שֵׂכֶל אָדָם הֶאֱרִיךְ אַפּוֹ וְתִפְאַרְתּוֹ עֲבֹר עַל־פָּשַׁע׃ נַהַם
roar a over to (it is) and his makes A dis-
.transgression pass glory ;anger slow man's cretion

13 כַּכְּפִיר זַעַף מֶלֶךְ וּכְטַל עַל־עֵשֶׂב רְצוֹנוֹ׃ הַוֺּת לְאָבִיו בֵּן
a (is) his to A his (is) the on as but The rage like (is)
son father ruin .favor grass dew the ;king's lion's a

14 כְּסִיל וְדֶלֶף טֹרֵד מִדְיְנֵי אִשָּׁה׃ בַּיִת וָהוֹן נַחֲלַת אָבוֹת
;fathers the (are) and House .woman a the never a and ,foolish
of legacy riches of strivings ending dropping

15 וּמֵיְהוָה אִשָּׁה מַשְׂכָּלֶת׃ עַצְלָה תַּפִּיל תַּרְדֵּמָה וְנֶפֶשׁ
a and deep (into) one makes Laziness acts who woman a from but
soul ;sleep fall prudently (is) Jehovah

16 רְמִיָּה תִרְעָב׃ שֹׁמֵר מִצְוָה שֹׁמֵר נַפְשׁוֹ בּוֹזֵה דְרָכָיו
His who he own his keeps the who He be shall idle
ways despises ;soul command keeps .hungry

17 18 יוּמָת׃ מַלְוֵה יְהוָה חוֹנֵן דָּל וּגְמֻלוֹ יְשַׁלֶּם־לוֹ׃ יַסֵּר בִּנְךָ
your Chasten to will He his and the one Jehovah Lends shall
,son .him reward dealing poor favoring to .die

19 כִּי־יֵשׁ תִּקְוָה וְאֶל־הֲמִיתוֹ אַל־תִּשָּׂא נַפְשֶׁךָ׃ גְּרָל־חֵמָה
fury great He your lift do not making and ;hope there for
of .soul die him on is

to pay the fine; for if you deliver (him), then you must do it again. [20] Hear advice and receive instruction, that you may be wise in your latter end. [21] Many purposes (are) in a man's heart; but the counsel of Jehovah shall stand. [22] The desire of a man (is) his kindness; and a poor man (is) better than a liar. [23] The fear of Jehovah (tends) to life; he shall rest satisfied; he shall not be visited with evil. [24] A lazy one puts his hand in a dish, and he will not return it to his mouth. [25] Strike a scorner and the simple will become careful; reprove a discerner, and he will discern knowledge. [26] He who assaults (his) father chases (his) mother away; he (is) a son who causes shame and brings reproach. [27] My son, cease to hear the teaching, (and you will) err from the words of knowledge. [28] A worthless witness scorns justice; and the mouth of the wicked devours iniquity. [29] judgments are prepared for scorners, and stripes for the backs of fools.

נֹשֵׂא עֹנֶשׁ כִּי אִם־תַּצִּיל וְעוֹד תּוֹסִף׃ שְׁמַע עֵצָה וְקַבֵּל 20
and counsel Hear must you then you if for a will
accept .add again ,(him) deliver ;fine bear

מוּסָר לְמַעַן תֶּחְכַּם בְּאַחֲרִיתֶךָ׃ רַבּוֹת מַחֲשָׁבוֹת בְּלֶב־ 21
in (are) purposes Many latter your in may you that ,discipline
heart .end wise be

אִישׁ וַעֲצַת יְהוָה הִיא תָקוּם׃ תַּאֲוַת אָדָם חַסְדּוֹ וְטוֹב 22
(is) and his (is) a The shall it ,Jehovah the but a
better ,mercy man of desire .rise of counsel ;man's

רָשׁ מֵאִישׁ כָּזָב׃ יִרְאַת יְהוָה לְחַיִּים וְשָׂבֵעַ יָלִין בַּל־יִפָּקֶד 23
be shall he not he and (tends) Jehovah The .lie a a than (be to)
visited .lodges satisfied ;life to of fear of man poor

רָע׃ טָמַן עָצֵל יָדוֹ בַּצַּלָּחַת גַּם־אֶל־פִּיהוּ לֹא יְשִׁיבֶנָּה׃ 24
will he not his to even a in his lazy A hides (with)
.it return mouth ,dish hand one .evil

לֵץ תַּכֶּה וּפֶתִי יַעְרִם וְהוֹכִיחַ לְנָבוֹן יָבִין דָּעַת׃ מְשַׁדֶּד־ 25
26
who He .knowledge will he dis- a but be will the and Strike a
assaults discern ,cerner reprove ;astute simple scorner

אָב יַבְרִיחַ אֵם בֵּן מֵבִישׁ וּמַחְפִּיר׃ חֲדַל־בְּנִי לִשְׁמֹעַ 27
hear to my ,Cease bringing and causing a (his) chases (his)
,son .reproach shame son ,mother away ,father

מוּסָר לִשְׁגּוֹת מֵאִמְרֵי־דָעַת׃ עֵד בְּלִיַּעַל יָלִיץ מִשְׁפָּט וּפִי 28
and ;justice scorns worthless A .knowledge the from to (only) the
mouth witness of words stray ,discipline

רְשָׁעִים יְבַלַּע־אָוֶן׃ נָכוֹנוּ לַלֵּצִים שְׁפָטִים וּמַהֲלֻמוֹת 29
blows and ,Judgments for are .evil devours the
scorners prepared wicked's

לְגֵו כְּסִילִים׃
.fools the for
of back

CAP. XX כ׳

CHAPTER 20

[1] Wine (is) a mocker; strong drink (is) raging; and all who stay by it are not wise. [2] The fear of a king (is) as the roar of a lion; he who stirs him up to anger wrongs his own soul. [3] For a man to cease from strife (is) an honor; but every fool will be obstinate. [4] The lazy man will not plow because of the cold; he begs at harvest, and nothing is there. [5] Counsel in a man's heart (is) like deep water; but an understanding man will draw it out. [6] Most men will proclaim each his own kindness; but who can find a faithful man? [7] The just one walks in his integrity; blessed (are) his sons after him! [8] A king who sits on

CHAPTER 20

לֵץ הַיַּיִן הֹמֶה שֵׁכָר וְכָל־שֹׁגֶה בּוֹ לֹא יֶחְכָּם׃ נַהַם כַּכְּפִיר 1
2
a like roar A .wise is not by who and strong is ;Wine a
lion it stays each ;drink noisy (is) scorner

אֵימַת מֶלֶךְ מִתְעַבְּרוֹ חוֹטֵא נַפְשׁוֹ׃ כָּבוֹד לָאִישׁ שֶׁבֶת 3
To a for an (is) own his sins stirs who he a the (is)
cease man honor .soul against anger to him ;king of dread

מֵרִיב וְכָל־אֱוִיל יִתְגַּלָּע׃ מֵחֹרֶף עָצֵל לֹא יַחֲרֹשׁ יִשְׁאַל 4
begs he will not The the after reveal fool but from
;plow lazy autumn .himself every ;strife

בַּקָּצִיר וָאָיִן׃ מַיִם עֲמֻקִּים עֵצָה בְלֶב־אִישׁ וְאִישׁ תְּבוּנָה 5
under- a but a in (is) deep Like is but at
standing of man ;man's heart counsel water .nothing ,harvest

יִדְלֶנָּה׃ רָב־אָדָם יִקְרָא אִישׁ חַסְדּוֹ וְאִישׁ אֱמוּנִים מִי 6
who faithful a but own his each will men Many draw will
man ;kindness proclaim .out it

יִמְצָא׃ מִתְהַלֵּךְ בְּתֻמּוֹ צַדִּיק אַשְׁרֵי בָנָיו אַחֲרָיו׃ מֶלֶךְ 7
8
king A after his blessed The his in walks can
!him sons (are) ;just integrity about .find

the throne of judgment scatters away all evil with his eyes. [9] Who can say, I have made my heart clean; I am pure from my sin? [10] A stone and a stone, an ephah and an ephah—both (are) hateful to Jehovah. [11] Even a child is known by his acts, whether his work (is) pure, or upright. [12] The hearing ear and the seeing eye: Jehovah has even made both of them. [13] Do not love sleep, lest you become poor; open your eyes, be satisfied with bread. [14] Bad! Bad! says the buyer; but when (it is) left to him, then he boasts. [15] There is gold and a multitude of gems; but the lips of knowledge (are) a rare jewel. [16] Take the garment of the one who is surety (for) a stranger; and take a pledge from (one who guarantees) for strangers. [17] Bread of deceit (is) sweet to a man; but afterwards his mouth shall be filled (with) gravel. [18] Purposes are established in counsel; and make war with wise guidance. [19] A revealer of secrets walks about as a gossip; so do not associate with him who opens his lips wide. [20] Whoever curses his father or his mother, his lamp shall be put out in deep darkness. [21] An inheritance (may be) gotten quickly in the beginning; but the end of it shall not be blessed. [22] Do not say, I will repay evil; wait on Jehovah and He will save you. [23] A stone and a stone (are) hateful to Jehovah; and a false balance (is) not good. [24] The steps of a man (are) from Jehovah; and what can man discern of his way? [25] (It is) a snare (to) a man to say rashly. A holy thing; and later vowing to pray(about) (it). [26] A wise king scatters the wicked and turns the wheel over them. [27] The spirit of man (is) the lamp of Jehovah, searching all the inward parts of the heart.

9 יוֹשֵׁב עַל־כִּסֵּא־דִין מְזָרֶה בְעֵינָיו כָּל־רָע׃ מִי־יֹאמַר זִכִּיתִי
have I can Who .evil all his with scatters judgment the on who
cleansed ,say eyes of throne sits

10 לִבִּי טָהַרְתִּי מֵחַטָּאתִי׃ אֶבֶן וָאֶבֶן אֵיפָה וְאֵיפָה תּוֹעֲבַת
(are) an and an a and A my from am I my
to hateful —ephah ephah ,stone stone ?sin pure ;heart

11 יְהוָה גַּם־שְׁנֵיהֶם׃ גַּם בְּמַעֲלָלָיו יִתְנַכֶּר־נָעַר אִם־זַךְ וְאִם־
or is whether a himself makes his by Even of both even Jeho-
clean lad known acts .them ,vah

12 יָשָׁר פָּעֳלוֹ׃ אֹזֶן שֹׁמַעַת וְעַיִן רֹאָה יְהוָה עָשָׂה גַם־שְׁנֵיהֶם׃
both even has Jehovah seeing and hearing The his upright
.them of ,made eye the ear .work

13
14 אַל־תֶּאֱהַב שֵׁנָה פֶּן־תִּוָּרֵשׁ פְּקַח עֵינֶיךָ שְׂבַע־לָחֶם׃ רַע
!Evil .bread be your open you lest ,sleep Do not
(with) satisfied eyes dispossessed be love

15 רַע יֹאמַר הַקּוֹנֶה וְאֹזֵל לוֹ אָז יִתְהַלָּל׃ יֵשׁ זָהָב וְרָב־
and gold There he then to when but the says !Evil
many is .boasts ,him left (is it) ;buyer

16 פְּנִינִים וּכְלִי יְקָר שִׂפְתֵי־דָעַת׃ לְקַח־בִּגְדוֹ כִּי־עָרַב זָר
an (for) is he when his Take .knowledge the rare (is) but ;gems
;alien surety garment of lips vessel a

17 וּבְעַד נָכְרִים חַבְלֵהוּ׃ עָרֵב לָאִישׁ לֶחֶם שָׁקֶר וְאַחַר
but ;falsehood Bread a to (is) him bind strangers and
afterwards of man sweet .pledge in for

18 יִמָּלֵא־פִיהוּ חָצָץ׃ מַחֲשָׁבוֹת בְּעֵצָה תִכּוֹן וּבְתַחְבֻּלוֹת
with and are in Purposes (with) his be shall
guidance wise ;established counsel .gravel mouth filled

19 עֲשֵׂה מִלְחָמָה׃ גּוֹלֶה־סּוֹד הוֹלֵךְ רָכִיל וּלְפֹתֶה שְׂפָתָיו
his him to and a as walks secret a A .war make
lips opens who ;gossip about of revealer

20 לֹא תִתְעָרָב׃ מְקַלֵּל אָבִיו וְאִמּוֹ יִדְעַךְ נֵרוֹ בֶּאֱשׁוּן חֹשֶׁךְ׃
.darkness in his be shall his or his who He do not
blackest lamp out put ,mother father curses .associate

21
22 נַחֲלָה מְבֹחֶלֶת בָּרִאשֹׁנָה וְאַחֲרִיתָהּ לֹא תְבֹרָךְ׃ אַל־
not shall not the but the in gotten in- An
.blessed be it of end —beginning hastily heritance

23 תֹּאמַר אֲשַׁלְּמָה־רָע קַוֵּה לַיהוָה וְיֹשַׁע לָךְ׃ תּוֹעֲבַת יְהוָה
Jehovah (are) .you He and on wait ;evil will I ,say Do
to hateful save will Jehovah repay

24 אֶבֶן וָאָבֶן וּמֹאזְנֵי מִרְמָה לֹא־טוֹב׃ מֵיְהוָה מִצְעֲדֵי־גָבֶר
a The from (are) (are) not deceit and a and A
;man of steps Jehovah .good of balances ;stone stone

25 וְאָדָם מַה־יָּבִין דַּרְכּוֹ׃ מוֹקֵשׁ אָדָם יָלַע קֹדֶשׁ וְאַחַר
And holy A say (to) a (to) a (is It) his of can what and
after !thing ,rashly man snare ?way discern he —man

26 נְדָרִים לְבַקֵּר׃ מְזָרֶה רְשָׁעִים מֶלֶךְ חָכָם וַיָּשֶׁב עֲלֵיהֶם
over and ,wise A the scatters inquire to (he)
them turns king wicked vows

27
28 אוֹפָן׃ נֵר יְהוָה נִשְׁמַת אָדָם חֹפֵשׂ כָּל־חַדְרֵי־בָטֶן׃ חֶסֶד
Mercy the the all searching ;man the (is) Jehovah The the
belly of chambers of breath of lamp .wheel

[28] Mercy and truth preserve the king; and his throne is upheld by mercy. [29] The glory of young men (is) their vigor; and the honor of old men (is) the gray head. [30] The stripes of a wound cleanse away evil; and strokes the inward parts of the belly.

29 ואמת יצרו־מלך וסעד בחסד כסאו׃ תפארת בחורים
young glory The his by is and the preserve and
:men of .throne mercy upheld ;king truth

30 כחם והדר זקנים שיבה׃ חברות פצע תמריק ברע
against cleanse a Stripes the old the and their
evil away wound of .head gray :men of honor ;vigor

ומכות חדרי־בטן׃
the the and
.heart of chambers strokes

CHAPTER 21

[1] The king's heart (is) in the hand of Jehovah, (as) streams of waters; He turns it wherever He desires. [2] Every way of a man (is) upright in his own eyes; but Jehovah measures the hearts. [3] To do righteousness and justice is to be chosen for Jehovah more than sacrifice. [4] High eyes, a proud heart, (and) the lamp of the wicked, (is) sin. [5] The thoughts of the diligent (tend) only to plenty; but (those of) every hasty one only to poverty. [6] The getting of treasures by a lying tongue (is) a vapor driven by those who seek death. [7] The violence of the wicked ensnares them, because they refuse to do justice. [8] The way of man (is) perverted and vile; but the pure, his work (is) right. [9] (It is) better to dwell on a corner of a housetop, than (with) a contentious woman, and to share a house. [10] The soul of the wicked desires evil; his neighbor finds no favor in his eyes. [11] The simple is made wise when the scorner is punished; and when the wise is instructed, he receives knowledge. [12] The Righteous One wisely considers the house of the wicked; He overthrows the wicked for his evil. [13] Whoever stops his ears at the cry of the poor, he himself shall also call, and shall not be answered. [14] A gift in secret subdues anger; yea, a bribe in the bosom (quiets) great fury. [15] (It is) joy to the just to do justice; but terror (shall come) to the workers of evil. [16] The man who

CAP. XXI כא

CHAPTER 21

1 פלגי־מים לב־מלך ביד־יהוה על־כל־אשר יחפץ יטנו׃
ex- He He wherever to ;Jehovah in (is) King's the waters (As)
.it tends ,desires of hand the heart of streams

2
3 כל־דרך איש ישר בעיניו ותכן לבות יהוה׃ עשה צדקה
righteous- To .Jehovah the but his in (is) a way Every
ness do hearts weighs ;eyes own right man of

4 ומשפט נבחר ליהוה מזבח׃ רום עינים ורחב־לב נר
the ,heart a and ,eyes Exalted than more for be to is and
of lamp proud .sacrifice Jehovah chosen justice

5 רשעים חטאת׃ מחשבות חרוץ אך־למותר וכל־אץ אך־
only hasty but (tend) only the The .sin (is) the
one every ;plenty to diligent of plans ,wicked

6 למחסור׃ פעל אצרות בלשון שקר הבל נדף מבקשי־
those driven a (is) lying a by treasures The .poverty to
seeking by vapor tongue of getting

7 מות׃ שד־רשעים יגורם כי מאנו לעשות משפט׃
.justice do to they because ensnares the The .death
refuse ,them wicked of violence

8
9 הפכפך דרך איש וזר וזך ישר פעלו׃ טוב לשבת על־
on dwell to (is It) his (is) upright but ;guilty a the Perverted
better .work ,pure the man of way (is)

10 פנת־גג מאשת מדונים ובית חבר׃ נפש רשע אותה־
desires the The to a and strivings a (with) than corner a
wicked of soul .share house of woman roof a of

11 רע לא־יחן בעיניו רעהו׃ בענש־לץ יחכם־פתי ובהשכיל
is when and the made is the is When his his in finds not ;evil
instructed ;simple wise scorner punished .neighbor eyes favor

12 לחכם יקח דעת׃ משכיל צדיק לבית רשע מסלף
over- He the the Righteous The wisely .knowledge he the
turns ;wicked of house One considers receives ,wise

13 רשעים לרע׃ אטם אזנו מזעקת־דל גם־הוא יקרא ולא
and shall he himself also the the at his who He (his) for the
not ,call ,poor of cry ear shuts .evil wicked

14 יענה׃ מתן בסתר יכפה־אף ושחד בחק חמה עזה׃
.strong wrath the in a and ;anger subdues in A be will
,bosom bribe secret gift .heard

15
16 שמחה לצדיק עשות משפט ומחתה לפעלי און׃ אדם
A .evil the to but ;justice do to the to (It)
man of workers ruin righteous joy is

wanders out of the way of prudence shall rest in the congregation of the dead. [17] A man who loves pleasure (shall be) poor; he who loves wine and oil shall not be rich. [18] The wicked (shall be) a ransom for the just; and the treacherous in the place of the upright. [19] (It is) better to live in a land of the wilderness than (with) a contentious woman and vexation. [20] A desirable treasure and oil (are) in the dwelling of the wise; but a foolish man devours it. [21] He who pursues righteousness and mercy finds life, righteousness and honor. [22] A wise one scales the city of the mighty and topples the strength (in which) it trusts. [23] Whoever keeps his mouth and his tongue keeps his soul from distresses. [24] Proud, haughty scorner (is) his name—he who deals in proud wrath. [25] The lust of the lazy man kills him, for his hands have refused to work. [26] He lusts with lust all the day long; but the righteous gives and does not withhold. [27] The sacrifice of the wicked (is) hateful; how much more (when) he brings it with an evil intent! [28] A false witness shall perish; but the man who attends always speaks. [29] A wicked man hardens his face; but the upright fixes his way. [30] (There is) no wisdom nor understanding nor counsel before Jehovah. [31] The horse (is) made ready for the day of battle; but to Jehovah (belongs) deliverance.

17 תּוֹעֶה מִדֶּרֶךְ הַשְׂכֵּל בִּקְהַל רְפָאִים יָנוּחַ׃ אִישׁ מַחְסוֹר
(be shall) poor | A man | shall .rest | the dead | the in of assembly | prudence | the of out of way | who wanders

18 אֹהֵב שִׂמְחָה אֹהֵב יַיִן־וָשֶׁמֶן לֹא יַעֲשִׁיר׃ כֹּפֶר לַצַּדִּיק
the for righteous | (be shall) ransom a | be shall .rich | not | and oil | wine | who he loves | ;pleasure | who loves

19 רָשָׁע וְתַחַת יְשָׁרִים בּוֹגֵד׃ טוֹב שֶׁבֶת בְּאֶרֶץ־מִדְבָּר
wilderness | a in of land | live to | (is It) better | the .treacherous | the upright | in and of place | The ;wicked

20 מֵאֵשֶׁת מִדְוָנִים וָכָעַס׃ אוֹצָר ׀ נֶחְמָד וָשֶׁמֶן בִּנְוֵה חָכָם
the ;wise | in (is) of home the | oil and | desirable | A treasure | and vexation | strivings | a with than of woman

21 וּכְסִיל אָדָם יְבַלְּעֶנּוּ׃ רֹדֵף צְדָקָה וָחָסֶד יִמְצָא חַיִּים
,life | finds | and mercy | righteousness | who He pursues | devours .it | a man | but foolish

22 צְדָקָה וְכָבוֹד׃ עִיר גִּבֹּרִים עָלָה חָכָם וַיֹּרֶד עֹז
the force | and topples | wise A one | scales | the mighty | city the of | and .honor | righteous-ness

23
24 מִבְטֶחָה׃ שֹׁמֵר פִּיו וּלְשׁוֹנוֹ שֹׁמֵר מִצָּרוֹת נַפְשׁוֹ׃ זֵד יָהִיר
arro-gant | ,Proud | his .soul | from distresses | keeps | his and tongue | his mouth | who He keeps | (which in) .trusts it

25 לֵץ שְׁמוֹ עוֹשֶׂה בְּעֶבְרַת זָדוֹן׃ תַּאֲוַת עָצֵל תְּמִיתֶנּוּ כִּי־
for | kills ,him | lazy the man | The of lust | .pride | the in of wrath | who he deals | his —name | ,scoffer

26 מֵאֲנוּ יָדָיו לַעֲשׂוֹת׃ כָּל־הַיּוֹם הִתְאַוָּה תַאֲוָה וְצַדִּיק יִתֵּן
gives | the but righteous | ;lust | lusts he with | the long day | All | .work to | his hands | have refused

27 וְלֹא יַחְשֹׂךְ׃ זֶבַח רְשָׁעִים תּוֹעֵבָה אַף כִּי־בְזִמָּה יְבִיאֶנּוּ׃
brings he !it | an with intent evil | when | much more | (is) ;hateful | the wicked | The of sacrifice | .withholds | and not

28
29 עֵד־כְּזָבִים יֹאבֵד וְאִישׁ שׁוֹמֵעַ לָנֶצַח יְדַבֵּר׃ הֵעֵז אִישׁ
A man | hardens | will .speak | forever | who attends | the but man | shall ;perish | false | A witness

30 רָשָׁע בְּפָנָיו וְיָשָׁר הוּא ׀ יָכִין דַּרְכּוֹ׃ אֵין חָכְמָה וְאֵין
and no | wisdom | There no is | his .way | establishes | he | the but ,upright | his ;face | wicked

31 תְּבוּנָה וְאֵין עֵצָה לְנֶגֶד יְהוָה׃ סוּס מוּכָן לְיוֹם מִלְחָמָה
;battle | the for of day | made is ready | The horse | .Jehovah | before | counsel | and no | under-standing

וְלַיהוָה הַתְּשׁוּעָה׃
(belongs) .deliverance | to but Jehovah

CAP. XXII כב

CHAPTER 22

[1] A (good) name is to be chosen rather than great riches; rather than silver or gold, favor (is) better. [2] The rich and poor meet together; Jehovah (is) the Maker of all of them. [3] A sensible one sees the evil and hides himself; but the

1
2 נִבְחָר שֵׁם מֵעֹשֶׁר רָב מִכֶּסֶף וּמִזָּהָב חֵן טוֹב׃ עָשִׁיר
The rich | (is) better | favor | ,gold or | rather silver than | ;great | than rather riches | A name | be to is chosen

3 וָרָשׁ נִפְגָּשׁוּ עֹשֵׂה כֻלָּם יְהוָה׃ עָרוּם ׀ רָאָה רָעָה וְיִסָּתֵר
hides and ;himself | the evil | sees | sensible A one | .Jehovah | of all them | the is of Maker | meet :together | the and poor

simple go on and are punished. [4] The reward of humility is the fear of Jehovah, riches, and honor, and life. [5] Thorns (and) snares (are) in the way of the perverse; he who keeps his soul shall be far from them. [6] Train up a child in the mouth of his way; even when he is old, he will not depart from it. [7] The rich rules over the poor; and the borrower (is) servant to a man who lends. [8] He who sows injustice will reap evil; and the rod of his wrath shall fail. [9] He who has a good eye, he is blessed; for he gives of his bread to the poor. [10] Throw the scorner out and strife shall go out; yea, quarrels and shame shall cease. [11] He who loves pureness of heart, grace (is on) his lips; the king (shall be) his friend. [12] The eyes of Jehovah keep knowledge; and He overthrows the words of the treacherous. [13] The lazy one says, A lion (is) outside! I will be killed in the streets! [14] The mouth of a strange woman (is) a deep pit; those despised (by) Jehovah shall fall into it. [15] Foolishness (is) bound up in the heart of a child; the rod of correction shall drive it far from him. [16] One oppresses the poor to multiply for himself, another gives to the rich, only (to come) to poverty.

[17] Stretch your ear and hear the words of the wise; and apply your heart to My knowledge; [18] for they are pleasant when you keep them within you; they shall all be fixed together on your lips; [19] so that your trust may be in Jehovah, I caused you to know today, even you. [20] Have I not written to you thirty times with counsels and knowledge; [21] to cause you to know the verity of the words of truth; to return words of truth to those who send you?

[22] Rob not the poor because he (is) poor; and oppress not the afflicted in the gate. [23] For Jehovah

4 וּפְתָיִים עָבְרוּ וְנֶעֱנָשׁוּ׃ עֵקֶב עֲנָוָה יִרְאַת יְהוָה עֹשֶׁר וְכָבוֹד
and ,riches ;Jehovah the (is) humility The are and pass the but
,honor of fear of reward .punished on simple

5 וְחַיִּים׃ צִנִּים פַּחִים בְּדֶרֶךְ עִקֵּשׁ שׁוֹמֵר נַפְשׁוֹ יִרְחַק מֵהֶם׃
from be shall his who he the the in (are) snares ,Thorns and
.them far soul keeps ,crooked of way .life

6 חֲנֹךְ לַנַּעַר עַל־פִּי דַרְכּוֹ גַּם כִּי־יַזְקִין לֹא־יָסוּר מִמֶּנָּה׃
from will he not is he when even his the on a Train
.it aside turn ,old ,way of mouth boy up

7 8 עָשִׁיר בְּרָשִׁים יִמְשׁוֹל וְעֶבֶד לֹוֶה לְאִישׁ מַלְוֶה׃ זוֹרֵעַ
who He who a to the and ;rules over The
sows .lends man borrower (is) servant poor the rich

9 עַוְלָה יִקְצָור־אָוֶן וְשֵׁבֶט עֶבְרָתוֹ יִכְלֶה׃ טוֹב־עַיִן הוּא
He —eye The shall his the and reap shall injustice
of good cease wrath of rod , evil

10 יְבֹרָךְ כִּי־נָתַן מִלַּחְמוֹ לַדָּל׃ גָּרֵשׁ לֵץ וְיֵצֵא מָדוֹן וְיִשְׁבֹּת
shall and ;strife shall and the Drive the to his of he for is
cease out go ,scorner out .poor bread gives ;blessed

11 12 דִּין וְקָלוֹן׃ אֹהֵב טְהָור־לֵב חֵן שְׂפָתָיו רֵעֵהוּ מֶלֶךְ׃ עֵינֵי
The the (be shall) his grace heart pureness who He and quarrels
of eyes .king friend his ;lips (on is) of loves .shame

13 יְהוָה נָצְרוּ דָעַת וַיְסַלֵּף דִּבְרֵי בֹגֵד׃ אָמַר עָצֵל אֲרִי
A lazy The says the the He and ;knowledge keep Jeho-
lion ,one .sly of words overthrows vah

14 בַחוּץ בְּתוֹךְ רְחֹבוֹת אֵרָצֵחַ׃ שׁוּחָה עֲמֻקָּה פִּי זָרוֹת זְעוּם
Those alien mouth the deep pit A be will I the the in (is)
hated women of (is) .killed ,streets of midst outside

יְהוָה יִפָּול־שָׁם׃ אִוֶּלֶת קְשׁוּרָה בְלֶב־נָעַר שֵׁבֶט מוּסָר
discipline rod the a the in bound is Foolish- .there shall (by)
of ;boy of heart up ness fall Jehovah

16 יַרְחִיקֶנָּה מִמֶּנּוּ׃ עֹשֵׁק דָּל לְהַרְבּוֹת לוֹ נֹתֵן לְעָשִׁיר אַךְ
only the to he to multiply to the who He from drive shall
,rich gives ;him poor oppresses .him far it

17 לְמַחְסוֹר׃ הַט אָזְנְךָ וּשְׁמַע דִּבְרֵי חֲכָמִים וְלִבְּךָ תָּשִׁית
apply your and the the and your Stretch (come to)
heart ;wise of words hear ear .poverty to

18 לְדַעְתִּי׃ כִּי־נָעִים כִּי־תִשְׁמְרֵם בְּבִטְנֶךָ יִכֹּנוּ יַחְדָּו עַל־
on together shall they within keep you when (are they) for My to
fixed be ;you them pleasant ;knowledge

19 שְׂפָתֶיךָ׃ לִהְיוֹת בַּיהוָה מִבְטַחֶךָ הוֹדַעְתִּיךָ הַיּוֹם אַף־
even ,today caused I your in that So your
know to you ,trust Jehovah be may .lips

20 21 אָתָּה׃ הֲלֹא כָתַבְתִּי לְךָ שָׁלִשׁוֹם בְּמֹעֵצוֹת וָדָעַת׃ לְהוֹדִיעֲךָ
make to and with thirty to I Have .you
know you ;knowledge counsels times you written not

קֹשְׁטְ אִמְרֵי אֱמֶת לְהָשִׁיב אֲמָרִים אֱמֶת לְשֹׁלְחֶיךָ׃
who him to truth words to ;truth the verity the
you sent of return of words of

22 23 אַל־תִּגְזָל־דָּל כִּי דַל־הוּא וְאַל־תְּדַכֵּא עָנִי בַשָּׁעַר׃ כִּי־
For the in the do and he poor because the Do not
.gate afflicted crush not ;is poor rob

will plead their cause, and will plunder the soul of their plunderers. [24] Do not associate with a possessor of anger; and do not go in with a man of fury, [25] lest you learn his ways and lay a snare for your soul. [26] Do not be of those striking the palm; of those who are for sureties for loans. [27] If you have nothing to repay, why should he take away your bed from under you? [28] Do not move the old landmark which your fathers have set. [29] Do you see a man who is prompt in his business? He shall stand before kings; he shall not stand before obscure (men).

24 יְהוָה יָרִיב רִיבָם וְקָבַע אֶת־קֹבְעֵיהֶם נָפֶשׁ׃ אַל־תִּתְרַע

Do not the (in) plundering those will and their shall Jehovah
associate ,soul them plunder ,cause plead

25 אֶת־בַּעַל אָף וְאֶת־אִישׁ חֵמוֹת לֹא תָבוֹא׃ פֶּן־תֶּאֱלַף

you lest go do not fury a and anger lord a with
learn .in of man with of

26 אֹרְחֹתָו וְלָקַחְתָּ מוֹקֵשׁ לְנַפְשֶׁךָ׃ אַל־תְּהִי בְתֹקְעֵי־כָף

the those of one Do not your for a and his
, palm strike who be .soul snare take paths

27 בַּעֹרְבִים מַשָּׁאוֹת׃ אִם־אֵין־לְךָ לְשַׁלֵּם לָמָּה־יִקַּח מִשְׁכָּבְךָ

your should why to to is If .loans are who
bed take he ,repay you not for sureties

28
29 מִתַּחְתֶּיךָ׃ אַל־תַּסֵּג גְּבוּל עוֹלָם אֲשֶׁר עָשׂוּ אֲבוֹתֶיךָ׃ חָזִיתָ

you Do your have which old the Do not under from
see .fathers set landmark move ?you

אִישׁ ׀ מָהִיר בִּמְלַאכְתּוֹ לִפְנֵי־מְלָכִים יִתְיַצָּב בַּל־יִתְיַצֵּב

shall he not shall He kings before his in is who man a
stand ;stand ?business prompt

לִפְנֵי חֲשֻׁכִּים׃

obscure before
.(men)

CAP. XXIII כג

CHAPTER 23

CHAPTER 23

[1] When you sit down to eat with a ruler, look carefully at what (is) before you; [2] and put a knife to your throat, if you (are) a possessor of soul. [3] Do not desire his delicacies, for it is the bread of lies. [4] Do not labor to be rich; cease from your own understanding. [5] Will your eyes fly on it? And (it) is gone! For surely it makes wings for itself; it flies into the heavens like an eagle. [6] Do not eat the bread of (one having) an evil eye; and do not desire his delicacies; [7] for as he thinks in his heart, so (is) he! He says to you, Eat and drink — but his heart (is) not with you. [8] The morsel you have eaten, you shall vomit up and lose your sweet words. [9] Do not speak in the ears of a fool, for he will trample on the prudence of your words. [10] Do not move the old landmarks;

1 כִּי־תֵשֵׁב לִלְחוֹם אֶת־מוֹשֵׁל בִּין תָּבִין אֶת־אֲשֶׁר לְפָנֶיךָ׃

before (is) what con- care- ruler a with eat to you When
;you sider fully down sit

2
3 וְשַׂמְתָּ שַׂכִּין בְּלֹעֶךָ אִם־בַּעַל נֶפֶשׁ אָתָּה׃ אַל־תִּתְאָו

Do not you a of a if your to a and
desire .(are) soul possesor ,throat knife put

4 לְמַטְעַמּוֹתָיו וְהוּא לֶחֶם כְּזָבִים׃ אַל־תִּיגַע לְהַעֲשִׁיר

be to Do not lies bread it for his
;rich labor of (is) ,delicacies

5 מִבִּינָתְךָ חֲדָל׃ הֲתָעִיף עֵינֶיךָ ׀ בּוֹ וְאֵינֶנּוּ כִּי עָשֹׂה יַעֲשֶׂה־

will it surely For (it) and on your fly Will .cease your from
make !not is ,it eyes understanding

6 לּוֹ כְנָפַיִם כְּנֶשֶׁר וְעוּף הַשָּׁמָיִם׃ אַל־תִּלְחַם אֶת־לֶחֶם

bread the eat Do not the will and an like wings for
of .heavens into fly eagle itself

7 רַע עָיִן וְאַל־תִּתְאָו לְמַטְעַמֹּתָיו׃ כִּי ׀ כְּמוֹ־שָׁעַר בְּנַפְשׁוֹ

his in he as for his do and ;eye an
,soul reckons ;delicacies desire not evil

8 כֶּן־הוּא אֱכוֹל וּשְׁתֵה יֹאמַר לָךְ וְלִבּוֹ בַּל־עִמָּךְ׃ פִּתְּךָ־

Your with (is) not his but to he and Eat (is) so
bit .you heart ;you says ,drink !he

9 אָכַלְתָּ תְקִיאֶנָּה וְשִׁחַתָּ דְּבָרֶיךָ הַנְּעִימִים׃ בְּאָזְנֵי כְסִיל

fool a the In .pleasant your and shall you have you
of ears words spoil ; up vomit ,eaten

10 אַל־תְּדַבֵּר כִּי־יָבוּז לְשֵׂכֶל מִלֶּיךָ׃ אַל־תַּסֵּג גְּבוּל עוֹלָם

old the Do not your the will he for do not
landmark move .words of prudence despise ,speak

and do not enter into the fields of the fatherless; [11] for their Redeemer (is) mighty; He shall plead their cause with you. [12] Bring in your heart to instruction and your ears to the words of knowledge. [13] Do not withhold correction from a child; for (if) you beat him with the rod, he will not die. [14] You shall beat him with the rod and shall deliver his soul from Sheol. [15] My son, if your heart is wise, my heart shall rejoice, even mine. [16] Yes, my reins shall rejoice when your lips speak right things. [17] Do not let your heart envy sinners; but only (be) in the fear of Jehovah all the day long. [18] For surely there is a future; and your hope shall not be cut off. [19] My son, hear and be wise, and advance your heart in the way. [20] Be not among heavy drinkers, among those who eat too much flesh to themselves;

[21] for the drunkard and the glutton are dispossessed; and sleepiness shall clothe (one) with rags. [22] Listen to your father who fathered you; and do not despise your mother when she is old. [23] Obtain the truth and do not sell it; (also) wisdom, and instruction and understanding. [24] The father of the righteous shall greatly rejoice; and he who fathers a wise (child) shall have joy in him. [25] Your father and your mother shall be glad; and she who bore you shall rejoice. [26] My son, give Me your heart; and let your eyes watch My ways: [27] For a harlot (is) a deep pit, and a strange woman (is) a narrow well. [28] Surely she lies in wait, as for prey; and she increases the treacherous among men. [29] Who (has) woe; who sorrow? who (has) contentions; who (has) babbling? Who (has) wounds without cause? Who (has) dullness of eyes? [30] — those who stay long at the wine; those who go to seek mixed wine. [31] Do not look at the wine when it

11 וּבִשְׂדֵי יְתוֹמִים אַל־תָּבֹא׃ כִּי־גֹאֲלָם חָזָק הוּא־יָרִיב אֶת־
shall He is their for do not the into and
plead ;mighty Redeemer ;enter fatherless of fields the

12 רִיבָם אִתָּךְ׃ הָבִיאָה לַמּוּסָר לִבֶּךָ וְאָזְנֶךָ לְאִמְרֵי־דָעַת׃
.knowledge the to your and your for Bring with their
of words ears ,heart instruction in .you cause

13
14 אַל־תִּמְנַע מִנַּעַר מוּסָר כִּי־תַכֶּנּוּ בַשֵּׁבֶט לֹא יָמוּת׃ אַתָּה
You will he not the with you (if) for correc- a from Do not
.die rod him strike ;tion boy withhold

15 בַּשֵּׁבֶט תַּכֶּנּוּ וְנַפְשׁוֹ מִשְּׁאוֹל תַּצִּיל׃ בְּנִי אִם־חָכַם לִבֶּךָ
your is if My shall you from and shall the with
,heart wise ,son .deliver Sheol soul his him beat rod

16 יִשְׂמַח לִבִּי גַם־אָנִי׃ וְתַעְלֹזְנָה כִלְיוֹתָי בְּדַבֵּר שְׂפָתֶיךָ
your when my shall And .I even my shall
lips speak .reins exult ,heart rejoice

17 מֵישָׁרִים׃ אַל־יְקַנֵּא לִבְּךָ בַּחַטָּאִים כִּי אִם־בְּיִרְאַת יְהוָה
Jehovah the in only but against your let Do not right
of fear (be) ;sinners heart envy .things

18
19 כָּל־הַיּוֹם׃ כִּי אִם־יֵשׁ אַחֲרִית וְתִקְוָתְךָ לֹא תִכָּרֵת׃ שְׁמַע־
Hear be shall not your and -here a there surely For the all
.off cut hope after is .day

20 אַתָּה בְנִי וַחֲכָם וְאַשֵּׁר בַּדֶּרֶךְ לִבֶּךָ׃ אַל־תְּהִי בְסֹבְאֵי־יָיִן
;wine heavy with Do not your the in and be and my ,you
of drinkers be .heart way advance ;wise ,son

21 בְּזֹלְלֵי בָשָׂר לָמוֹ׃ כִּי־סֹבֵא וְזוֹלֵל יִוָּרֵשׁ וּקְרָעִים תַּלְבִּישׁ
shall (with) and lose the and the For them- to flesh- with
(one) clothe rags ;all glutton drunkard selves gluttons

22 נוּמָה׃ שְׁמַע לְאָבִיךָ זֶה יְלָדֶךָ וְאַל־תָּבוּז כִּי־זָקְנָה אִמֶּךָ׃
your is she when do and begot this your to Listen .sleepiness
.mother old despise not ;you one :father

23
24 אֱמֶת קְנֵה וְאַל־תִּמְכֹּר חָכְמָה וּמוּסָר וּבִינָה׃ גִּיל יָגִיל
shall greatly under- and and (also) sell do and obtain the
rejoice .standing instruction ,wisdom ;(it) not truth

25 אֲבִי צַדִּיק יוֹלֵד חָכָם וְיִשְׂמַח־בּוֹ׃ יִשְׂמַח־אָבִיךָ וְאִמֶּךָ
your and your be Let in even shall wise a the and right-the The
;mother father glad .him .glad be one of father ;eous of father

26 וְתָגֵל יוֹלַדְתֶּךָ׃ תְּנָה בְנִי לִבְּךָ לִי וְעֵינֶיךָ דְּרָכַי תִּרְצֶנָה׃
let my your and to your my ,Give who she let and
.watch ways eyes ;me heart ,son .you bore rejoice

27
28 כִּי־שׁוּחָה עֲמֻקָּה זוֹנָה וּבְאֵר צָרָה נָכְרִיָּה׃ אַף־הִיא
she surely strange a narrow a and a (is) deep pit a For
;woman well ,harlot

29 כְּחֶתֶף תֶּאֱרֹב וּבוֹגְדִים בְּאָדָם תּוֹסִף׃ לְמִי־אוֹי ׀ לְמִי אֲבוֹי
(is) To (is) To she among the and in lies for as
?sorrow whom ?woe whom .increases men treacherous ;wait prey

לְמִי מִדְוָנִים ׀ לְמִי־שִׂיחַ לְמִי פְּצָעִים חִנָּם לְמִי חַכְלִלוּת
dullness, To without (are) To ?babbling To ;contentions To
of whom ?cause wounds whom whom whom

30
31 עֵינָיִם׃ לַמְאַחֲרִים עַל־הַיָּיִן לַבָּאִים לַחְקֹר מִמְסָךְ׃ אַל־
not mixed seek to those the over who Those ?eyes
.wine in go who ;wine long stay

is red; when it gives its color in the cup; when it goes (down) smoothly — [32] at its last it bites like a snake, and it stings like a basilisk. [33] Your eyes shall look on strange women; and your heart shall speak perverse things. [34] Yes, you shall be as one who lies down in the middle of the sea; or as he who lies on the top of a mast, [35] (saying;) They struck me! I was not sick! They beat me, (yet) I did not know. When I awaken, I will add (to it), I will still seek it.

תֵּרֶא יַיִן כִּי יִתְאַדָּם כִּי־יִתֵּן בַּכִּיס עֵינוֹ יִתְהַלֵּךְ בְּמֵישָׁרִים׃

—smoothly it when its the in it when is it when the look Do
down goes ;eye cup gives ;red (down) wine at

32 33 אַחֲרִיתוֹ כְּנָחָשׁ יִשָּׁךְ וּכְצִפְעֹנִי יַפְרִשׁ׃ עֵינֶיךָ יִרְאוּ זָרוֹת

strange shall Your it like and it a like its at
;women on look eyes stings viper a ;bites snake last

34 וְלִבְּךָ יְדַבֵּר תַּהְפֻּכוֹת׃ וְהָיִיתָ כְּשֹׁכֵב בְּלֶב־יָם וּכְשֹׁכֵב

he as or the the in who one as you And perverse shall your and
lies who ;sea of heart down lies be shall .things speak heart

35 בְּרֹאשׁ חִבֵּל׃ הִכּוּנִי בַל־חָלִיתִי הֲלָמוּנִי בַּל־יָדָעְתִּי מָתַי

When did I not They was I not struck They a the on
.(it) know ;me beat !sick ;me .mast of top

אָקִיץ אוֹסִיף אֲבַקְשֶׁנּוּ עוֹד׃

.still will I will I I will
it seek ,add ,awaken

CAP. XXIV כד

CHAPTER 24

[1] Do not envy evil men, nor desire to be with them. [2] For their heart studies violence, and their lips talk of mischief. [3] Through wisdom a house is built; and it is established by understanding; [4] and by knowledge the rooms shall be filled with all precious and pleasant riches. [5] A wise warrior (is) in strength; yes, a man of knowledge firms up power. . [6] For you shall make war for yourself by wise advice; and safety (is) in the great counselor. [7] Wisdom (is) too high for a fool; he does not open his mouth in the gate. [8] He who plots to do evil shall be called a lord of evil plots. [9] The plot of foolishness (is) sin; and the scorner (is) hateful to men. [10] (If) you faint in the day of distress, your might (is) small. [11] If you hold back (to) deliver those being taken to death, and (those) stumbling for killing; [12] for you say, Behold, we did not know it; does not He who measures the heart consider? And He who keeps your soul, does He (not) know? And He repays to a man according to his work? [13] My son, eat honey because (it is) good; and the honeycomb

CHAPTER 24

1 2 אַל־תְּקַנֵּא בְּאַנְשֵׁי רָעָה וְאַל־תִּתְאָו לִהְיוֹת אִתָּם׃ כִּי־שֹׁד

For with be to do and ,evil men Do not
violence .them desire not of envy

3 יֶהְגֶּה לִבָּם וְעָמָל שִׂפְתֵיהֶם תְּדַבֵּרְנָה׃ בְּחָכְמָה יִבָּנֶה

built is Through .speak lips their and their medi-
wisdom mischief ;heart tates

4 בָּיִת וּבִתְבוּנָה יִתְכּוֹנָן׃ וּבְדַעַת חֲדָרִים יִמָּלְאוּ כָּל־הוֹן

riches all be will the by and is it with and ;house a
with filled rooms knowledge ;established understanding

5 6 יָקָר וְנָעִים׃ גֶּבֶר־חָכָם בַּעוֹז וְאִישׁ־דַּעַת מְאַמֶּץ־כֹּחַ׃ כִּי

For .might up firms know- and in (is) warrior wise A and precious
ledge of man a ;strength .pleasant

בְתַחְבֻּלוֹת תַּעֲשֶׂה־לְּךָ מִלְחָמָה וּתְשׁוּעָה בְּרֹב יוֹעֵץ׃

coun- by (is) and ;war for shall you wise with
.selor great the deliverance yourself make advice

7 8 רָאמוֹת לֶאֱוִיל חָכְמוֹת בַּשַּׁעַר לֹא יִפְתַּח־פִּיהוּ׃ מְחַשֵּׁב

who He his does he not the in ;Wisdom a for too (is)
devises .mouth open gate fool high

9 לְהָרֵעַ לוֹ בַּעַל־מְזִמּוֹת יִקְרָאוּ׃ זִמַּת אִוֶּלֶת חַטָּאת וְתוֹעֲבַת

(is) and (is) foolish- The be shall evil lord a to do to
hateful ;sin ness of plot .called plots of .him ,evil

10 11 לְאָדָם לֵץ׃ הִתְרַפִּיתָ בְּיוֹם צָרָה צַר כֹּחֶכָה׃ הַצֵּל

Deliver your (is) distress the in you (If) the men to
.might narrow of day faint .scorner

12 לְקֻחִים לַמָּוֶת וּמָטִים לַהֶרֶג אִם־תַּחְשׂוֹךְ׃ כִּי־תֹאמַר הֵן

be- you for hold you unless for those and to being those
,hold ,say .back ;killing stumbling ,death taken

לֹא־יָדַעְנוּ זֶה הֲלֹא־תֹכֵן לִבּוֹת הוּא־יָבִין וְנֹצֵר נַפְשְׁךָ הוּא

(Does) your the And consider the He not does ,this did we not
he ,soul of Keeper ?it hearts weighs who know

13 יֵדָע וְהֵשִׁיב לְאָדָם כְּפָעֳלוֹ׃ אֱכָל־בְּנִי דְבַשׁ כִּי־טוֹב וְנֹפֶת

the and (is it) for honey my ,Eat according a to He And
comb ;good ,son ?work his to man repays ?know

(is) sweet to your palate; [14] so (shall) knowledge of wisdom (be) to your soul; when you have found there is a future, and your hope is not cut off. [15] O wicked one, do not lie in ambush against the dwelling of the righteous; do not violate his resting place; [16] for a just one falls seven (times), and rises up again; but the wicked shall stumble into evil. [17] Do not rejoice when your enemy falls; and do not let your heart be glad when he stumbles; [18] lest Jehovah see and it be evil in His eyes; and He turn away His anger from him. [19] Do not burn (in anger) because of evildoers, and do not envy the wicked;[20] for no hereafter shall be to the evil; the lamp of the wicked will be put out. [21] My son, fear Jehovah and the king; do not mix with those who change; [22] for their calamity shall rise suddenly; and who knows the ruin of both of them?

[23] These also are for the wise: to respect persons in judgment (is) not good; [24] he who says to the wicked, You (are) righteous — the people shall curse him; nations shall despise him. [25] But to those who rebuke, it is pleasant; and a good blessing comes to them. [26] He shall kiss the lips that return right words. [27] Prepare your work outside; and make it fit for yourself in the field; and afterwards build your house. [28] Do not be a witness against your neighbor without cause; or deceive with your lips; [29] do not say, I will do to him as he has done to me; I will repay each according to his work. [30] I went over the field of the lazy man, and by the vineyard of the man lacking heart; [31] and, lo, it was all grown up with thistles; nettles had covered its surface and its stone wall was broken down — [32] then I saw — I set my heart on it —

14 מָתוֹק עַל־חִכֶּךָ׃ כֵּן ׀ דְּעֶה חָכְמָה לְנַפְשֶׁךָ אִם־מָצָאתָ
have you when found | to (be) ;soul your | wisdom | knowledge of | so (shall) | your ;palate | ,on | is sweet

15 וְיֵשׁ אַחֲרִית וְתִקְוָתְךָ לֹא תִכָּרֵת׃ אַל־תֶּאֱרֹב רָשָׁע לִנְוֵה
the abode | at | O ,wicked | lie in ,ambush | do | not | cut is .off | not | your and hope | here- after | a there is | that

16 צַדִּיק אַל־תְּשַׁדֵּד רִבְצוֹ׃ כִּי שֶׁבַע ׀ יִפּוֹל צַדִּיק וָקָם
rises and ;again | just a one | falls | seven (times) | for | resting- ;place | his | do violate | not | the ;righteous

17 וּרְשָׁעִים יִכָּשְׁלוּ בְרָעָה׃ בִּנְפֹל אוֹיִבְךָ אַל־תִּשְׂמָח וּבִכָּשְׁלוֹ
when and stumbles he | do ;rejoice | not | your enemy | When falls | into .evil | shall stumble | the but wicked

18 אַל־יָגֵל לִבֶּךָ׃ פֶּן־יִרְאֶה יְהוָה וְרַע בְּעֵינָיו וְהֵשִׁיב מֵעָלָיו
from him | He and away turn | His in ,eyes | (it) and evil (be) | Jehovah | see | lest | your ;heart | let do glad be | not

19 20 אַפּוֹ׃ אַל־תִּתְחַר בַּמְּרֵעִים אַל־תְּקַנֵּא בָּרְשָׁעִים׃ כִּי ׀
for | the ;wicked | do envy | (and) not | of because ,evildoers | glow Do (anger in) | not | His anger

21 לֹא־תִהְיֶה אַחֲרִית לָרָע נֵר רְשָׁעִים יִדְעָךְ׃ יְרָא־אֶת־יְהוָה
,Jehovah | Fear | be shall .out put | the wicked | the of lamp | the to ;evil | here- a after | there be shall | not

22 בְּנִי וָמֶלֶךְ עִם־שׁוֹנִים אַל־תִּתְעָרָב׃ כִּי־פִתְאֹם יָקוּם אֵידָם
their ;woe | shall rise | suddenly | For | do .associate | not | who those with change | the and ;king | my ,son

23 וּפִיד שְׁנֵיהֶם מִי יוֹדֵעַ׃ גַּם־אֵלֶּה לַחֲכָמִים הַכֵּר־פָּנִים
faces | to respect | the for ;wise | these (are) | Also | ?knows who | of both them | the and of ruin

24 בְּמִשְׁפָּט בַּל־טוֹב׃ אֹמֵר לְרָשָׁע צַדִּיק אָתָּה יִקְּבֻהוּ עַמִּים
the ;peoples | shall him curse | you —(are) | righteous | the to —wicked | who He says | (is) .good | not | judgment in

25 יִזְעָמוּהוּ לְאֻמִּים׃ וְלַמּוֹכִיחִים יִנְעָם וַעֲלֵיהֶם תָּבוֹא בִרְכַּת־
blessing a | comes | on and them | is it ;pleasant | those to rebuke who | But | the .nations | abhor shall him

26 27 טוֹב׃ שְׂפָתַיִם יִשָּׁק מֵשִׁיב דְּבָרִים נְכֹחִים׃ הָכֵן בַּחוּץ ׀
outside | Prepare | .straight | words | that return | He kiss shall | lips the | .good

28 מְלַאכְתֶּךָ וְעַתְּדָהּ בַּשָּׂדֶה לָךְ אַחַר וּבָנִיתָ בֵיתֶךָ׃ אַל־תְּהִי
Do be | not | your .house | even build | after- ;wards | for ;you | the in ,field | make and ready it | your ;work

29 עֵד־חִנָּם בְּרֵעֶךָ וַהֲפִתִּיתָ בִּשְׂפָתֶיךָ׃ אַל־תֹּאמַר כַּאֲשֶׁר
As | do ,say | not | your with ;lips | or deceive | a against ,neighbor | witness a causelessly

30 עָשָׂה־לִי כֵּן אֶעֱשֶׂה־לּוֹ אָשִׁיב לָאִישׁ כְּפָעֳלוֹ׃ עַל־שְׂדֵה
the over of field | according .work his to | (each) to man | will I repay | to ;him | will I do | so | to ,me | has he done

31 אִישׁ־עָצֵל עָבַרְתִּי וְעַל־כֶּרֶם אָדָם חֲסַר־לֵב׃ וְהִנֵּה עָלָה
was it ,up grown | and ,lo | ;heartless | the man | the of vineyard | by and | I ,passed | lazy | the man

כֻלּוֹ ׀ קִמְּשֹׂנִים כָּסּוּ פָנָיו חֲרֻלִּים וְגֶדֶר אֲבָנָיו נֶהֱרָסָה׃
broken was .down | its stone | and wall | ;nettles | sur- face | its had covered | with ;thistles | of all it

I looked — I received instruction: [33] A little sleep, a little slumber, a little folding of the hands to sleep; [34] so shall your poverty come stalking; and your want like a man (with) a shield.

32 33 וָאֶחֱזֶה אָנֹכִי אָשִׁית לִבִּי רָאִיתִי לָקַחְתִּי מוּסָר׃ מְעַט שֵׁנוֹת

,sleep A :instruction I looked I my set I I And
little received ;heart ;beheld

34 מְעַט תְּנוּמוֹת מְעַט ׀ חִבֻּק יָדַיִם לִשְׁכָּב׃ וּבָא־מִתְהַלֵּךְ

walking then lie to the folding a ,slumber little a
about comes ;down hands of little

רֵישֶׁךָ וּמַחְסֹרֶיךָ כְּאִישׁ מָגֵן׃

a (with) a like your and your
.shield man want ;poverty

CAP. XXV כה

CHAPTER 25

CHAPTER 25

[1] These (are) the proverbs of Solomon, which the men of Hezekiah king of Judah copied out: [2] The glory of God (is) to conceal a thing; but the glory of kings (is) to search out a matter. [3] The heavens for height; and the earth for depth; but the heart of kings (is) unsearchable. [4] Take away the dross from the silver, and a vessel of the refiner's shall appear. [5] Take away the wicked from before the king; and his throne is established in righteousness [6] Do not honor yourself before a king; and do not stand in the place of the great. [7] For it is better he shall say to you, Come up here ! than that you should be put lower before a noble whom your eyes have seen. [8] Do not hastily go out to fight. What shall you do in the end of it, when your neighbor has put you to shame? [9] Debate your cause with your neighbor; and do not uncover the secret of another; [10] lest he who hears put you to shame; and your slander have no end. [11] A word rightly spoken (is like) apples of gold in settings of silver. [12] (As) a ring of gold, and an ornament of fine gold, (so is) a wise reprover on a hearing ear. [13] Like the cold of snow in harvest-time, (so is) a faithful messenger to those sending him; for he refreshes his master's soul. [14] He who boasts himself of a false gift (is like) clouds and wind,

1 גַּם־אֵלֶּה מִשְׁלֵי שְׁלֹמֹה אֲשֶׁר הֶעְתִּיקוּ אַנְשֵׁי ׀ חִזְקִיָּה

Hezekiah the made which ,Solomon proverbs These also
of men advance of (are)

2 מֶלֶךְ־יְהוּדָה׃ כְּבֹד אֱלֹהִים הַסְתֵּר דָּבָר וּכְבֹד מְלָכִים

kings the but a to God the :Judah king
(is) of glory ;matter conceal (is) of glory of

3 חֲקֹר דָּבָר׃ שָׁמַיִם לָרוּם וָאָרֶץ לָעֹמֶק וְלֵב מְלָכִים אֵין

there kings the but for the and for The a search to
no is of heart ;depth earth ;height heavens .matter out

4 5 חֵקֶר׃ הָגוֹ סִיגִים מִכָּסֶף וַיֵּצֵא לַצֹּרֵף כֶּלִי׃ הָגוֹ רָשָׁע

the Take a the as shall and the from the Take search-
wicked away .vessel refiners out go ,silver dross away .ing

6 לִפְנֵי־מֶלֶךְ וְיִכּוֹן בַּצֶּדֶק כִּסְאוֹ׃ אַל־תִּתְהַדַּר לִפְנֵי־מֶלֶךְ

a before honor Do not his righ- in is and a (from)
;king yourself .throne teousness settled ,king before

7 וּבִמְקוֹם גְּדֹלִים אַל־תַּעֲמֹד׃ כִּי טוֹב אֲמָר־לְךָ עֲלֵה הֵנָּה

!here Come to he is it for do not the the in and
up ,you says better —stand great of place

8 מֵהַשְׁפִּילְךָ לִפְנֵי נָדִיב אֲשֶׁר רָאוּ עֵינֶיךָ׃ אַל־תֵּצֵא לָרִב

to go Do not your have whom a before be you than
fight out .eyes seen noble lower put

מַהֵר פֶּן מַה־תַּעֲשֶׂה בְּאַחֲרִיתָהּ בְּהַכְלִים אֹתְךָ רֵעֶךָ׃

your you has when the in shall what ,lest ;hastily
?neighbor shamed ,it of end do you

9 10 רִיבְךָ רִיב אֶת־רֵעֶךָ וְסוֹד אַחֵר אַל־תְּגָל׃ פֶּן־יְחַסֶּדְךָ

you put lest do not another the and your with Plead your
shame to ;uncover of secret ;neighbor cause

11 שֹׁמֵעַ וְדִבָּתְךָ לֹא תָשׁוּב׃ תַּפּוּחֵי זָהָב בְּמַשְׂכִּיּוֹת כָּסֶף

silver settings in gold (Like) returns not your and who he
of of apples report evil ;hears

12 דָּבָר דָּבֻר עַל־אָפְנָיו׃ נֶזֶם זָהָב וַחֲלִי־כָתֶם מוֹכִיחַ חָכָם

wise a (so) item an and ,golden a As the at spoken a (is)
reprover ,gold of ring .time (right) word

13 עַל־אֹזֶן שֹׁמָעַת׃ כְּצִנַּת־שֶׁלֶג ׀ בְּיוֹם קָצִיר צִיר נֶאֱמָן

faithful a (so) harvest a in snow Like ear an on
messenger of day cold .hearing

14 לְשֹׁלְחָיו וְנֶפֶשׁ אֲדֹנָיו יָשִׁיב׃ נְשִׂיאִים וְרוּחַ וְגֶשֶׁם אַיִן אִישׁ

a (is) (with) but and (Like) makes he his and his to
man ,no rain wind clouds .return master's soul ;senders

and with no rain. [15] A ruler is persuaded by long patience, and a soft tongue breaks the bone. [16] Have you found honey? Eat (only) your fill, lest you be satiated and vomit it out. [17] Withdraw your foot from your neighbor's house; lest he be full of you and hate you. [18] A man who bears false witness against his neighbor (is) a maul, and a sword and a sharp arrow. [19] Confidence in a treacherous man in time of distress (is like) a bad tooth and a slipping foot. [20] (As) he who takes away a garment in cold weather, (and as) vinegar on soda, (so is) he who sings songs to an evil heart. [21] If your enemy is hungry, give him bread to eat; and if he is thirsty, give him water to drink; [22] for you shall heap coals (of fire) on his head; and Jehovah shall reward you. [23] The north wind brings rain; so (does) a secret tongue an angry face. [24] (It is) better to dwell in the corner of the housetop, than to share a house with a contentious woman. [25] (Like) cold waters to a weary soul, so (is) a good report from a far country. [26] The righteous falling down before the wicked (is like) a fouled fountain and a ruined spring. [27] (It is) not good to eat much honey; and to search out their glory (is) glory. [28] He that rules not over his own spirit (is like) a broken-down city, (and) without a wall.

15 מִתְהַלֵּל בְּמַתַּת־שָׁקֶר׃ בְּאֹרֶךְ אַפַּיִם יְפֻתֶּה קָצִין וְלָשׁוֹן

a and tongue | a ,ruler | is persuaded | anger to | length In (before) | false- .hood | gift of | in boasting himself

16 רַכָּה תִּשְׁבָּר־גָּרֶם׃ דְּבַשׁ מָצָאתָ אֱכֹל דַּיֶּךָּ פֶּן־תִּשְׂבָּעֶנּוּ

be you ,satiated | lest | your ,fill | Eat (only) | you Have ?found | honey | the .bone | shatters | soft

17 וַהֲקֵאתוֹ׃ הֹקַר רַגְלְךָ מִבֵּית רֵעֶךָ פֶּן־יִשְׂבָּעֲךָ וּשְׂנֵאֶךָ׃

hate and .you | be he you of full | lest | your ,neighbor's | from house | your foot | make rare | vomit and ,out it

18 19 מֵפִיץ וְחֶרֶב וְחֵץ שָׁנוּן אִישׁ־עֹנֶה בְרֵעֵהוּ עֵד שָׁקֶר׃ שֵׁן

(Like) tooth a | .false witness | against neighbor his | who testifies | (is) man a | a sharp | and arrow | a and ,sword | A ,maul

20 רָעָה וְרֶגֶל מוּעָדֶת מִבְטָח בּוֹגֵד בְּיוֹם צָרָה׃ מַעֲדֶה־בֶּגֶד ׀

a garment | one (As) removing | .distress | a in of day | a traitor | trust (is) in | slipping | a and foot | bad

21 בְּיוֹם קָרָה חֹמֶץ עַל־נָתֶר וְשָׁר בַּשִּׁרִים עַל לֶב־רָע׃ אִם־

If | .evil heart | a | on | with songs | one (so) singing | soda on | (as and) vinegar | ,cold | a in day

22 רָעֵב שֹׂנַאֲךָ הַאֲכִלֵהוּ לָחֶם וְאִם־צָמֵא הַשְׁקֵהוּ מָיִם׃ כִּי

for | ;water | him gave drink to | is he thirsty | and if | ;bread | him give eat to | your ,enemy | is hungry

23 גֶחָלִים אַתָּה חֹתֶה עַל־רֹאשׁוֹ וַיהוָה יְשַׁלֶּם־לָךְ׃ רוּחַ צָפוֹן

north | The wind | .you | shall reward | and Jehovah | his ;head | upon | shall heap | you | coals (fire of)

24 תְּחוֹלֵל גֶּשֶׁם וּפָנִים נִזְעָמִים לְשׁוֹן סָתֶר׃ טוֹב שֶׁבֶת עַל־

on | to dwell | (is It) better | .secret | a (by) tongue | indignant | an and face | ;rain | brings forth

25 פִּנַּת־גָּג מֵאֵשֶׁת מִדְוָנִים וּבֵית חָבֶר׃ מַיִם קָרִים עַל־נֶפֶשׁ

soul a | to | cold | (Like) waters | to .share | a and house | strifes | with than of woman a | roof a corner

26 עֲיֵפָה וּשְׁמוּעָה טוֹבָה מֵאֶרֶץ מֶרְחָק׃ מַעְיָן נִרְפָּשׂ וּמָקוֹר

a and fountain | fouled | (Like) spring a | .far .off | a from country | good | report a (is) | ,weary

27 מָשְׁחָת צַדִּיק מָט לִפְנֵי־רָשָׁע׃ אָכֹל דְּבַשׁ הַרְבּוֹת לֹא־

not | much | honey | eat To | the .wicked | before | tottering | the (are) righteous | ruined

28 טוֹב וְחֵקֶר כְּבֹדָם כָּבוֹד׃ עִיר פְּרוּצָה אֵין חוֹמָה אִישׁ

a (is) man | a wall | without | broken down | (Like) city a | (is) .glory | their glory | to and out search | (is) ;good

אֲשֶׁר ׀ אֵין־מַעְצָר לְרוּחוֹ׃

his to .spirit | control | there not is | (to) whom

CAP. XXVI כו

CHAPTER 26

CHAPTER 26

[1] As snow in summer, and as rain in harvest, so honor (is) not right for a fool. [2] As the wandering bird, as the swallow in its flying, so the causeless curse shall never come. [3] A

1 כַּשֶּׁלֶג ׀ בַּקַּיִץ וְכַמָּטָר בַּקָּצִיר כֵּן לֹא־נָאוֶה לִכְסִיל כָּבוֹד׃

.honor | a for fool | (is) not right | so | in ,harvest | like and rain | in ,summer | Like snow

2 3 כַּצִּפּוֹר לָנוּד כַּדְּרוֹר לָעוּף כֵּן קִלְלַת חִנָּם לֹא תָבֹא׃ שׁוֹט

A whip | shall come | not | causeless | the curse | so | its in ,flying | the as swallow | ,wandering | the As bird

whip for the horse; a bridle for the ass; and a rod for the back of fools. [4] Answer not a fool according to his foolishness, lest you also become like him, even you. [5] Answer a fool according to his foolishness, lest he be wise in his own eyes. [6] He that sends a message by a fool's hand cuts off his own feet (and) drinks injury. [7] (As) the legs of the lame hang limp, (so) a parable in the mouth of fools. [8] As one binding a stone on a sling, so (is) he giving honor to a fool. [9] (As) a thorn going up into the drunkard's hand, so a parable in the mouth of fools. [10] Great is the Former of all things; but ne who hires a fool ; even (is like) he who hires passer-bys [11] As a dog that returns to his own vomit, (so) a fool repeats his foolishness. [12] Do you see a man wise in his own eyes? A fool has (more) hope than he. [13] The lazy one says, A lion (is) in the way; a lion (is) between the streets! [14] (As) the door turns on its hinge, (so) the lazy one on his bed. [15] The lazy one buries his hand in the dish; he is weary to bring it back to his mouth. [16] The lazy one (is) wiser in his own eyes than seven that return a wise answer. [17] the passer-by enrages himself over strife that is not his own, (is like) one who grabs the ears of a dog. [18] As (one) pretending to be feeble, who throws sparks, arrows and death, [19] (so) is the man who deceives his neighbor, saying, Am I not joking? [20] The fire goes out where there is no wood; (so) the strife ceases where (there is) no whisperer. [21] (As) coal to burning embers, and wood to fire; (so) is a contentious man to kindle strife. [22] The words of a whisperer (are) as tasty morsels; and they descend into the chambers of the heart. [23] (As with) silver dross spread over an earthen vessel, (so are)

4	לַסּוּס מֶתֶג לַחֲמוֹר וְשֵׁבֶט לְגֵו כְּסִילִים׃ אַל־תַּעַן כְּסִיל
	fool a　Do not　.fools　the for　a and　the for　a　the for
	answer　　　　　of back　rod　　;ass　bridle　,horse

5	כְּאִוַּלְתּוֹ פֶּן־תִּשְׁוֶה־לּוֹ גַם־אָתָּה׃ עֲנֵה כְּסִיל כְּאִוַּלְתּוֹ פֶּן
	lest　his by　a　Answer　.you even　,him you lest　his by
	,folly　fool　　　　　　　like become　,folly

6	יִהְיֶה חָכָם בְּעֵינָיו׃ מְקַצֶּה רַגְלַיִם חָמָס שֹׁתֶה שֹׁלֵחַ
	who　,drinks　(and)　(own his)　cuts (He)　his in　wise　may he
	sends　violence　feet　off　.eyes own　be

7	דְּבָרִים בְּיַד־כְּסִיל׃ דַּלְיוּ שֹׁקַיִם מִפִּסֵּחַ וּמָשָׁל בְּפִי
	the in　a is so　the　the　Weak　(are)　by　messages
	of mouth　proverb　lame　of legs　.fool's　hand

8	כְּסִילִים׃ כִּצְרוֹר אֶבֶן בְּמַרְגֵּמָה כֵּן־נוֹתֵן לִכְסִיל כָּבוֹד׃
	.honor　a to　he so　a on　a　who he As　.fools
	fool　gives who　,sling　stone　binds

9 10	חוֹחַ עָלָה בְיַד־שִׁכּוֹר וּמָשָׁל בְּפִי כְסִילִים׃ רַב מְחוֹלֵל־
	Former the　Great　.fools　the in　a and　the　into　goes　A
	of　(is)　　of mouth proverb,drunkard's hand　up　thorn

11	כֹּל וְשֹׂכֵר כְּסִיל וְשֹׂכֵר עֹבְרִים׃ כְּכֶלֶב שָׁב עַל־קֵאוֹ כְּסִיל
	fool a　own its to　that　As　those　(like is)　,fool a　he but　all
	,vomit　returns　dog a　.by passing hiring one　hires who ;things

12	שׁוֹנֶה בְאִוַּלְתּוֹ׃ רָאִיתָ אִישׁ חָכָם בְּעֵינָיו תִּקְוָה לִכְסִיל
	a for　(more)　his in　wise　a　you Do　his with　repeats
	fool　hope　?eyes own　man　see　.foolishness

13 14	מִמֶּנּוּ׃ אָמַר עָצֵל שַׁחַל בַּדָּרֶךְ אֲרִי בֵּין הָרְחֹבוֹת׃ הַדֶּלֶת
	the (As)　is a in (is) a　A　The　says　(for) than
	door　　streets! between lion　;way the　lion　,one lazy　.him

15	תִּסּוֹב עַל־צִירָהּ וְעָצֵל עַל־מִטָּתוֹ׃ טָמַן עָצֵל יָדוֹ בַּצַּלָּחַת
	the in　his　The buries　his　on the (so)　its　on　turns
	,dish　hand one lazy　.couch　one lazy　,hinge

16	נִלְאָה לַהֲשִׁיבָהּ אֶל־פִּיו׃ חָכָם עָצֵל בְּעֵינָיו מִשִּׁבְעָה מְשִׁיבֵי
	that　than　his in　The (is)　his　to　bring to　is he
	return　seven　eyes own one lazy　wiser　.mouth　back it　weary

17	טָעַם׃ מַחֲזִיק בְּאָזְנֵי־כָלֶב עֹבֵר מִתְעַבֵּר עַל־רִיב לֹא־לוֹ׃
	to not　strife over enraging　the (is)　a　the one (Like)　wise a
	.him　(is that)　himself　by passer　,dog　of ears　grabs who　.answer

18 19	כְּמִתְלַהְלֵהַּ הַיֹּרֶה זִקִּים חִצִּים וָמָוֶת׃ כֵּן־אִישׁ רִמָּה אֶת־
	who　the so　and　,arrows　,sparks　who　a Like
	deceives　man (is)　,death　throws　madman

20	רֵעֵהוּ וְאָמַר הֲלֹא־מְשַׂחֵק אָנִי׃ בְּאֶפֶס עֵצִים תִּכְבֶּה־אֵשׁ
	the　goes　,wood　where　?I　Am　,says and　his
	;fire　out　no is　joking　not　neighbor

21	וּבְאֵין נִרְגָּן יִשְׁתֹּק מָדוֹן׃ פֶּחָם לְגֶחָלִים וְעֵצִים לְאֵשׁ
	to　and　to burning　(As)　the　grows　whisperer and
	,fire　wood　embers　coal　.strife　silent　no where

22	וְאִישׁ מִדְיָנִים לְחַרְחַר־רִיב׃ דִּבְרֵי נִרְגָּן כְּמִתְלַהֲמִים וְהֵם
	and　like (are)　a　The　.contention　to　strifes　(is) so
	they　,morsels tasty　whisperer of words　kindle　of man a

23	יָרְדוּ חַדְרֵי־בָטֶן׃ כֶּסֶף סִיגִים מְצֻפֶּה עַל־חָרֶשׂ שְׂפָתַיִם
	(are so)　an　over　laid　dross (with As)　the　the　enter
	lips　,vessel earthen　silver　.heart of chambers into

burning lips and a wicked heart. [24] He who hates dissembles with his lips; for he lays up deceit in his inner being; [25] when his voice is gracious, do not believe him, for he (has) seven hateful things in his heart. [26] Hatred is covered by guile; his evil shall be revealed in the assembly. [27] He who digs a pit shall fall into it; and he who rolls a stone shall have it turn back on him. [28] A lying tongue hates tne ones it crushes; and a flattering mouth works stumbling.

24 דְּלֵקִים וְלֶב־רָע׃ בִּשְׂפָתָו יִנָּכֵר שׂוֹנֵא וּבְקִרְבּוֹ יָשִׁית

lays up | his in and being inner | who He dissembles ;hates | with lips his | evil and heart a | burning

25 מִרְמָה׃ כִּי־יְחַנֵּן קוֹלוֹ אַל־תַּאֲמֶן־בּוֹ כִּי שֶׁבַע תּוֹעֵבוֹת

hateful things | seven | for | ,him | do believe | not | his ,voice | is when gracious | ;deceit

26
27 בְּלִבּוֹ׃ תִּכַּסֶּה שִׂנְאָה בְּמַשָּׁאוֹן תִּגָּלֶה רָעָתוֹ בְקָהָל׃ כֹּרֶה

who He digs | the in .assembly | his evil | be shall revealed | by ;guile | Hatred | is covered | in (are) .heart his

28 שַׁחַת בָּהּ יִפֹּל וְגֹלֵל אֶבֶן אֵלָיו תָּשׁוּב׃ לְשׁוֹן־שֶׁקֶר יִשְׂנָא

hates | lying | tongue A | shall it .return | to him | a —stone | he and rolls who | shall ;fall | into it | pit a

דַּכָּיו וּפֶה חָלָק יַעֲשֶׂה מִדְחֶה׃

stumbling | works | flattering mouth | a and | it those crushes

CAP. XXVII כז

CHAPTER 27

[1] Do not boast in the day of tomorrow, for you do not know what a day may bring forth. [2] Let another praise you, and not your own mouth; (let it be) a stranger, and not your own lips. [3] A stone (is) heavy, and sand a burden; but a fool's anger (is) heavier than both. [4] Fury (is) fierce, and anger overflows; but who can stand before jealousy? [5] Better (is) revealed reproof than secret love. [6] Faithful (are) the wounds of a lover; and the kisses of a hated one (are) plentiful. [7] One who is full tramples a honeycomb; but to a hungry soul, every bitter thing (is) sweet. [8] A man wandering from his place (is like) a bird that wanders from the nest. [9] Ointment and perfume give joy to the heart; and one's friend (is) sweet from the counsel of the soul. [10] Do not forsake your friend, nor your father's friend; and do not go into your brother's house in the day of your calamity; (for) a near neighbor (is) better than a brother far away. [11] My son, become wise and give joy to my heart; so that I may return a word to him that taunts me. [12] A sensible man sees the evil and hides himself; the

CHAPTER 27

1
2 אַל־תִּתְהַלֵּל בְּיוֹם מָחָר כִּי לֹא־תֵדַע מַה־יֵּלֶד יוֹם׃ יְהַלֶּלְךָ

praise Let you | a .day | may what bring forth | do you not know | for | to- ,morrow | the in of day | boast | Do | not

3 זָר וְלֹא־פִיךָ נָכְרִי וְאַל־שְׂפָתֶיךָ׃ כֹּבֶד אֶבֶן וְנֵטֶל הַחוֹל

;sand | a and burden | A stone | (is) heavy | own your .lips | and not | one ,foreign | your ;mouth | and not | an- ,alien

4 וְכַעַס אֱוִיל כָּבֵד מִשְּׁנֵיהֶם׃ אַכְזְרִיּוּת חֵמָה וְשֶׁטֶף אָף

;anger | is and overflowing | Fury | fierce (is) | both than .them of | (is) heavier | fool's a | but vexation

5 וּמִי יַעֲמֹד לִפְנֵי קִנְאָה׃ טוֹבָה תּוֹכַחַת מְגֻלָּה מֵאַהֲבָה

love than | revealed | reproof | (is) Better | ?jealousy | before | can stand | but who

6 מְסֻתָּרֶת׃ נֶאֱמָנִים פִּצְעֵי אוֹהֵב וְנַעְתָּרוֹת נְשִׁיקוֹת שׂוֹנֵא׃

hated a ..one | kisses the of | (are) but plentiful | a lover's | wounds | Faithful (are) | .concealed

7 נֶפֶשׁ שְׂבֵעָה תָּבוּס נֹפֶת וְנֶפֶשׁ רְעֵבָה כָּל־מַר מָתוֹק׃

(is) .sweet | bitter thing | every | ,hungry | (to) but soul a | honey-a ;comb | tramples | A sated | soul

8
9 כְּצִפּוֹר נוֹדֶדֶת מִן־קִנָּהּ כֵּן־אִישׁ נוֹדֵד מִמְּקוֹמוֹ׃ שֶׁמֶן

Oil | his from .place | wander- ing | a man | so (is) | its from ,nest | wandering | a Like bird

10 וּקְטֹרֶת יְשַׂמַּח־לֵב וּמֶתֶק רֵעֵהוּ מֵעֲצַת־נָפֶשׁ׃ רֵעֲךָ ׀ וְרֵעַ

nor friend | Your ,friend | the .soul | the from of counsel | one's friend | (is) and sweet | the ;heart | joy give to | and perfume

אָבִיךָ אַל־תַּעֲזֹב וּבֵית אָחִיךָ אַל־תָּבוֹא בְּיוֹם אֵידְךָ טוֹב

(is for) better | your ;calamity | the in of day | go do not into | your brother's | and house | do not ;forsake | your ,father's

11 שָׁכֵן קָרוֹב מֵאָח רָחוֹק׃ חֲכַם בְּנִי וְשַׂמַּח לִבִּי וְאָשִׁיבָה

I that so return may | my ;heart | give and to joy | my ,son | Be ,wise | far .away | a than brother | near | a neighbor

12 חֹרְפִי דָבָר׃ עָרוּם ׀ רָאָה רָעָה נִסְתָּר פְּתָאיִם עָבְרוּ

pass on | the simple | hides and ;himself | the evil | sees | sensible a one | a | my .word reproacher

simple go on (and) are punished. [13] Take the garment of him who is surety for a stranger; and hold him in pledge (who is surety) for a strange woman. [14] He who rises early in the morning and blesses his friend with a loud voice, it is counted as cursing to him. [15] Drops that never cease on a rainy day, and a contentious woman are alike; [16] he who hides her hides the wind and his right hand encounters (slippery) oil. [17] Iron sharpens iron; so a man sharpens his friend's face. [18] The keeper of the fig tree eats its fruit; so he keeping his master is honored. [19] As face (reflects) face (in) the water, so the heart of man (reflects) man. [20] Sheol and destruction are never satisfied; so the eyes of man are never satisfied. [21] The refining pot (tries) silver; and the furnace (tries) gold; and a man (is tried) by the mouth of his praise. [22] If you pound a fool in the mortar with a pestle amidst grain, his foolishness will not turn away from him.

[23] Know well the state of your flock; set your heart on your herds; [24] for riches (are) not forever; nor the crown from generation (to) generation. [25] When the hay is removed, and the tender grass is seen, and the mountain-plants are gathered, [26] the lambs (will be) for your clothing; and the he-goats the price for a field; [27] and there will be goat's milk enough for your food; for the food of your household, and (for) the life of your maidens.

CHAPTER 28

[1] The wicked flee (though) no one (is) pursuing; but the righteous are as bold as a lion. [2] Because of transgression (in) a land, many (are) its rulers; but it is prolonged by a man who has understanding, who knows (right). [3] A poor man that oppresses the weak (is like) a

13 נֶעֱנָשׁוּ׃ קַח־בִּגְדוֹ כִּי־עָרַב זָר וּבְעַד נָכְרִיָּה חַבְלֵהוּ׃
him bind strange a and a is he when his Take are (and)
.pledge in woman for ;stranger for surety garment .punished

14 מְבָרֵךְ רֵעֵהוּ ׀ בְּקוֹל גָּדוֹל בַּבֹּקֶר הַשְׁכֵּים קְלָלָה תֵּחָשֶׁב
be will it cursing rising the in loud a with his who He
as deemed ,early morning voice friend blesses

15 לוֹ׃ דֶּלֶף טוֹרֵד בְּיוֹם סַגְרִיר וְאֵשֶׁת מִדְוָנִים נִשְׁתָּוָה׃
are strivings a and steady a on A dripping to
;alike of woman ;rain of day constant .him

16 17 צֹפְנֶיהָ צָפַן־רוּחַ וְשֶׁמֶן יְמִינוֹ יִקְרָא׃ בַּרְזֶל בְּבַרְזֶל יָחַד
;sharpens iron on Iron .meets his and the hides who he
hand right oil ;wind her hides

18 וְאִישׁ יַחַד פְּנֵי־רֵעֵהוּ׃ נֹצֵר תְּאֵנָה יֹאכַל פִּרְיָהּ וְשֹׁמֵר
he and its eats fig a The his face sharpens a and
keeps who ;fruit tree of keeper .friend's man

19 אֲדֹנָיו יְכֻבָּד׃ כַּמַּיִם הַפָּנִים לַפָּנִים כֵּן לֵב הָאָדָם לָאָדָם׃
(reflects) man a the so (reflects) face (in) As is his
.man the of heart ,face water the .honored master

20 שְׁאוֹל וַאֲבַדֹּה לֹא תִשְׂבַּעְנָה וְעֵינֵי הָאָדָם לֹא תִשְׂבַּעְנָה׃
are not man a the and are not and Sheol
.satisfied of eyes ;satisfied destruction

21 22 מַצְרֵף לַכֶּסֶף וְכוּר לַזָּהָב וְאִישׁ לְפִי מַהֲלָלוֹ׃ אִם־תִּכְתּוֹשׁ
you though his the by a but for the and for refining The
pound praise of mouth man ;gold furnace silver pot

אֶת־הָאֱוִיל ׀ בַּמַּכְתֵּשׁ בְּתוֹךְ הָרִיפוֹת בַּעֱלִי לֹא־תָסוּר מֵעָלָיו
from will not a with grain the amidst the in fool a
him turn ,pestle mortar

23 24 אִוַּלְתּוֹ׃ יָדֹעַ תֵּדַע פְּנֵי צֹאנֶךָ שִׁית לִבְּךָ לַעֲדָרִים׃ כִּי לֹא
(are) for your on your set your face Know well his
not ;herds heart ;flock's .folly

25 לְעוֹלָם חֹסֶן וְאִם־נֵזֶר לְדוֹר דּוֹר׃ גָּלָה חָצִיר וְנִרְאָה־
is and the One gen- (and) genera- to the nor ;riches forever
seen ,grass moves .eration ration crown

26 דֶשֶׁא וְנֶאֶסְפוּ עִשְּׂבוֹת הָרִים׃ כְּבָשִׂים לִלְבוּשֶׁךָ וּמְחִיר
a and for (be will) the the the are and new the
of price ;clothing your lambs mountains of plants gathered ,grass

27 שָׂדֶה עַתּוּדִים׃ וְדֵי ׀ חֲלֵב עִזִּים לְלַחְמְךָ לְלֶחֶם בֵּיתֶךָ
your the for your for goats' milk and the field a
,household of food ,food enough ;goats -he

וְחַיִּים לְנַעֲרוֹתֶיךָ׃
your for and
.maidens of lives the

CAP. XXVIII כח

CHAPTER 28

1 2 נָסוּ וְאֵין־רֹדֵף רָשָׁע וְצַדִּיקִים כִּכְפִיר יִבְטָח׃ בְּפֶשַׁע אֶרֶץ
(in) trans- By are a as the but The pur- and flee
,land a gression .bold lion righteous ;wicked suing none

3 רַבִּים שָׂרֶיהָ וּבְאָדָם מֵבִין יֹדֵעַ כֵּן יַאֲרִיךְ׃ גֶּבֶר רָשׁ וְעֹשֵׁק
who poor A is it thus who dis- a by but rulers many
oppresses man .prolonged ,knows ,cerning man ;(has) it

sweeping rain that (leaves) no food. [4] Those who forsake the law praise the wicked; but those who keep the law strive with them. [5] Evil men do not understand justice; but those seeking Jehovah understand all. [6] Better (is) the poor walking in his integrity than the perverse of two ways, even (if) he (is) rich. [7] He who keeps the law (is) a wise son; but he who is a companion of gluttons shames his father. [8] He who multiplies his wealth by interest and usury, (he shall) gather it for him who pities the weak. [9] Whoever turns aside his ear from hearing the law, even his prayer (is) an abomination. [10] He who causes the upright to go astray in an evil way shall fall into his own pit; and the blameless shall inherit good. [11] A rich man (is) wise in his own eyes; but the discerning weak searches him out. [12] When the righteous rejoice, great (is) the glory; but when the wicked are on the rise, a man will be sought for. [13] He who hides his sins never prospers; but he who confesses and forsakes (them) shall have pity. [14] O the happiness of a man who dreads (God) constantly! But he who hardens his heart falls into evil. [15] The wicked ruler (is) a roaring lion, and a ranging bear, over a weak people. [16] The ruler that lacks understanding even adds oppressions; (but) he who hates unjust gain prolongs his days. [17] Any man oppressed with the blood of a soul shall flee to the pit; let them not uphold him. [18] He who walks uprightly shall be saved; but he who is perverse in his two ways shall fall at once. [19] He who cultivates his ground shall have plenty of bread; but one pursuing vanities shall have much poverty. [20] A faithful man shall (have many blessings; but he rushing to be rich will not be counted innocent. [21] It (is) not good to respect faces; for a man will sin for a piece of bread.

4 דַּלִּים מָטָר סֹחֵף וְאֵין לָחֶם׃ עֹזְבֵי תוֹרָה יְהַלְלוּ רָשָׁע
the praise the Forsakers .food that sweeping a (is) the
;wicked law of no (leaves) rain weak

5 וְשֹׁמְרֵי תוֹרָה יִתְגָּרוּ בָם׃ אַנְשֵׁי־רָע לֹא־יָבִינוּ מִשְׁפָּט
;justice do not Evil men with strive the but
understand .them law of keepers

6 וּמְבַקְשֵׁי יְהוָה יָבִינוּ כֹל׃ טוֹב־רָשׁ הוֹלֵךְ בְּתֻמּוֹ מֵעִקֵּשׁ
the than his in who the Better .all under- Jehovah those but
of crooked integrity walks poor (is) stand seeking

7 דְּרָכַיִם וְהוּא עָשִׁיר׃ נוֹצֵר תּוֹרָה בֵּן מֵבִין וְרֹעֶה זוֹלְלִים
gluttons a but ,wise a (is) the who He .rich (if) even two
of friend son law keeps (is) he ,ways

8 יַכְלִים אָבִיו׃ מַרְבֶּה הוֹנוֹ בְּנֶשֶׁךְ וּבְתַרְבִּית לְחוֹנֵן דַּלִּים
the the for by and by his who He his shames
,weak of pitier usury interest wealth increases .father

9 יִקְבְּצֶנּוּ׃ מֵסִיר אָזְנוֹ מִשְּׁמֹעַ תּוֹרָה גַּם־תְּפִלָּתוֹ תּוֹעֵבָה׃
an (is) his even the from his Who He gathers
.abomination prayer ,law hearing ear aside turns .it

10 מַשְׁגֶּה יְשָׁרִים ׀ בְּדֶרֶךְ רָע בִּשְׁחוּתוֹ הוּא־יִפּוֹל וּתְמִימִים
the and shall he own his into an way in the lead- one
blameless ;fall pit ,evil upright astray ing

11 יִנְחֲלוּ־טוֹב׃ חָכָם בְּעֵינָיו אִישׁ עָשִׁיר וְדַל מֵבִין יַחְקְרֶנּוּ׃
examines dis- the but ;rich A his in (is) .good shall
.him cerning weak man eyes own wise inherit

12 בַּעֲלֹץ צַדִּיקִים רַבָּה תִפְאָרֶת וּבְקוּם רְשָׁעִים יְחֻפַּשׂ אָדָם׃
a be will the when but the great the When
.man sought ,wicked rise ;glory (is) ,righteous rejoice

13
14 מְכַסֶּה פְשָׁעָיו לֹא יַצְלִיחַ וּמוֹדֶה וְעֹזֵב יְרֻחָם׃ אַשְׁרֵי אָדָם
the Blessed has and one but fare will not his who He
man .pity leaving confessing ,well sins hides

15 מְפַחֵד תָּמִיד וּמַקְשֶׁה לִבּוֹ יִפּוֹל בְּרָעָה׃ אֲרִי־נֹהֵם וְדֹב
a and ,roaring A into falls his the but ,always dreading
bear lion .evil heart of hardener (God)

16 שׁוֹקֵק מוֹשֵׁל רָשָׁע עַל עַם־דָּל׃ נָגִיד חֲסַר תְּבוּנוֹת וְרַב
even understand- lacking A .weak a over wicked ruler a charging
adds ing ruler people (is)

17 מַעֲשַׁקּוֹת שֹׂנֵא בֶצַע יַאֲרִיךְ יָמִים׃ אָדָם עָשֻׁק בְּדַם־
the with pressed man A (his) prolongs unjust one oppressions
of blood down .days gain hating

18 נָפֶשׁ עַד־בּוֹר יָנוּס אַל־יִתְמְכוּ־בוֹ׃ הוֹלֵךְ תָּמִים יִוָּשֵׁעַ
be shall blame- who He to them let do shall the to ,soul a
;saved lessly walks him uphold not ;flee pit

19 וְנֶעְקַשׁ דְּרָכַיִם יִפּוֹל בְּאֶחָת׃ עֹבֵד אַדְמָתוֹ יִשְׂבַּע־לָחֶם
(with) have shall his who He at shall two his the but
bread of plenty ground tills .once fall ways in crooked

20 וּמְרַדֵּף רֵיקִים יִשְׂבַּע־רִישׁ׃ אִישׁ אֱמוּנוֹת רַב־בְּרָכוֹת וְאָץ
one but full be shall faithful A sated be shall vanities one but
rushing blessings of man .poverty with pursuing

21 לְהַעֲשִׁיר לֹא יִנָּקֶה׃ הַכֵּר־פָּנִים לֹא־טוֹב וְעַל־פַּת־לֶחֶם
bread a and (is) not faces To be shall not be to
of piece for ;good regard .acquitted rich

[22] A man (with) an evil eye hastens after wealth; but (he) does not know that poverty will come on him. [23] He who reproves a man afterwards finds grace; (more) than he who flatters (with) the tongue. [24] He who robs his father or his mother, and says, (It is) not a transgression — he shall be a companion to a destroyer. [25] The proud in soul stirs up strife; but he who is trusting on Jehovah shall be abundantly satisfied. [26] He who trusts in his own heart is a fool; but he who walks in wisdom shall be delivered. [27] He who gives to the poor shall not lack; but he who hides his eyes shall have plenty of curses. [28] When the wicked rise, a man hides himself; but when they perish, the righteous multiply.

22 יִפְשַׁע־גָּֽבֶר׃ נִבְהָל לַהוֹן אִישׁ רַע עָיִן וְלֹא־יֵדַע כִּי־חֶסֶר
want that (he) but an man A wealth hastens transgress will
knows not eye evil (with) after .man a

23 יְבֹאֶֽנּוּ׃ מוֹכִיחַ אָדָם אַחֲרַי חֵן יִמְצָא מִמַּחֲלִיק לָשֽׁוֹן׃
the (with) he than ;finds (more) after- man a who He come will
.tongue flatters who grace ward reproves him on

24 גּוֹזֵל ׀ אָבִיו וְאִמּוֹ וְאֹמֵר אֵין־פָּשַׁע חָבֵר הוּא לְאִישׁ מַשְׁחִֽית׃
who a to he a a (is it) not and his or his who He
.destroys man (is) partner ;transgression ,says ,mother father robs

25
26 רְחַב־נֶפֶשׁ יְגָרֶה מָדוֹן וּבֹטֵחַ עַל־יְהוָה יְדֻשָּֽׁן׃ בּוֹטֵחַ בְּלִבּוֹ
his in who He be will Jehovah on one but ;strife stirs soul The
heart trusts fat made trusting up of broad

27 הוּא כְסִיל וְהוֹלֵךְ בְּחָכְמָה הוּא יִמָּלֵֽט׃ נוֹתֵן לָרָשׁ אֵין
has the to who He be shall he in he but ;fool a he
no poor gives .delivered ,wisdom walks who (is)

28 מַחְסוֹר וּמַעְלִים עֵינָיו רַב־מְאֵרֽוֹת׃ בְּקוּם רְשָׁעִים יִסָּתֵר
hides the When .curses (have shall) his who he but ;lack
himself ,wicked rise ,many eyes hides

אָדָם וּבְאָבְדָם יִרְבּוּ צַדִּיקִֽים׃
the multiply when but ;man a
.righteous ,perish they

CAP. XXIX כט

CHAPTER 29

CHAPTER 29

[1] A man who hardens the neck after reproofs shall be suddenly broken, and there will be no healing. [2] When the righteous increase, the people rejoice; but the people sigh when the wicked rule. [3] He who loves wisdom gladdens his father; but a friend of harlots wastes wealth. [4] A king establishes a land by justice, but he (who takes) bribes tears it down. [5] a man who flatters his neighbor spreads a net for his feet. [6] There (is) a snare in the sin of an evil man; but the righteous sing and rejoice. [7] The righteous attends to the cause of the weak; (but) the wicked do not discern knowledge. [8] Scornful men puff against a city; but the wise turn away anger. [9] (If) a wise man disputes with a foolish man, even he shakes or laughs, (there will be) no rest. [10] Men of blood hate the blameless; but the upright seek his soul.

1 אִישׁ תּוֹכָחוֹת מַקְשֶׁה־עֹרֶף פֶּתַע יִשָּׁבֵר וְאֵין מַרְפֵּֽא׃
.healing not and be shall suddenly (his) who reproofs A
be will shattered neck hardens of man

2 בִּרְבוֹת צַדִּיקִים יִשְׂמַח הָעָם וּבִמְשֹׁל רָשָׁע יֵאָנַח עָֽם׃
the sigh the when but the rejoice the When
.people wicked rule ;people ,righteous increase

3 אִישׁ־אֹהֵב חָכְמָה יְשַׂמַּח אָבִיו וְרֹעֶה זוֹנוֹת יְאַבֶּד־הֽוֹן׃
.wealth wastes harlots a but his gladdens wisdom who man A
of friend ;father loves

4
5 מֶלֶךְ בְּמִשְׁפָּט יַעֲמִיד אָרֶץ וְאִישׁ תְּרוּמוֹת יֶהֶרְסֶֽנָּה׃ גֶּבֶר
man A it tears (taking) a but a establishes by king A
.down bribes man ,land justice

6 מַחֲלִיק עַל־רֵעֵהוּ רֶשֶׁת פּוֹרֵשׂ עַל־פְּעָמָֽיו׃ בְּפֶשַׁע אִישׁ
a trans- By his for spreads net a his on who
man gression .steps ,neighbor flatters

7 רָע מוֹקֵשׁ וְצַדִּיק יָרוּן וְשָׂמֵֽחַ׃ יֹדֵעַ צַדִּיק דִּין דַּלִּים רָשָׁע
the but the the The knows and sing the but a (is) evil
wicked ;weak of plea righteous .rejoice righteous snare

8 לֹא־יָבִין דָּֽעַת׃ אַנְשֵׁי לָצוֹן יָפִיחוּ קִרְיָה וַחֲכָמִים יָשִׁיבוּ
turn the but ;city a puff scorn Men .knowledge do not
away wise against of discern

9 אָֽף׃ אִישׁ־חָכָם נִשְׁפָּט אֶת־אִישׁ אֱוִיל וְרָגַז וְשָׂחַק וְאֵין
and or he even ,foolish a with disputes wise a (If) .anger
no is laughs shakes man man

10 נָֽחַת׃ אַנְשֵׁי דָמִים יִשְׂנְאוּ־תָם וִישָׁרִים יְבַקְשׁוּ נַפְשֽׁוֹ׃
his seek the but the hate blood Men .rest
.soul upright ;blameless of

[11] A fool speaks all of his mind; but the wise holding back quiets it. [12] (To) a ruler who listens to lying words, all his ministers (are) wicked. [13] The poor and the injurious man meet together; (but) Jehovah enlightens both their eyes. [14] A king that judges the weak truly shall have his throne established forever. [15] The rod and reproof give wisdom; but a youth sent off (is) a shame to his mother. [16] When the wicked are multiplied, transgression increases; but the righteous shall see their fall. [17] Correct your son, and he will make you rest; yea, he shall give delight to your soul. [18] Where there is no vision, the people are let loose; but O the happiness of him who keeps the law! [19] A servant is not corrected by words; though he discerns he will not answer. [20] Do you see a man hasty in his words? More hope for a fool than he! [21] He who pampers his servant from youth shall also afterwards be his successor. [22] An angry man stirs up contention; and a master of fury abounds in transgression. [23] The pride of man brings him low; but the humble in spirit takes hold of honor. [24] He who shares with a thief hates his soul; he hears an oath but does not tell (it). [25] The fear of man brings a snare; but he who trusts Jehovah is set on high. [26] Many seek the face of the ruler; but the judgment of each man is from Jehovah. [27] An unjust man (is) an abomination to the righteous; and the upright of way (are) an abomination to the wicked.

11 12 כל־רוחו יוציא כסיל וחכם באחור ישבחנה׃ משל

ruler A .it quiets holding the but ;fool A brings his all

back wise out spirit of

13 מקשיב על־דבר־שקר כל־משרתיו רשעים׃ רש ואיש

a and The (are) his all ,lying word a to who

of man poor .wicked ministers listens

14 תככים נפגשו מאיר עיני שניהם יהוה׃ מלך שופט

who king A .Jehovah of both the (but) meet injuries

judges them of eyes enlightens ,together

15 באמת דלים כסאו לעד יכון׃ שבט ותוכחת יתן חכמה

;wisdom give and The be shall forever his the with

reproof rod .established throne weak truth

16 ונער משלח מביש אמו׃ ברבות רשעים ירבה־פשע

trans- increases the are When his causes sent a but

;gression ,wicked multiplied .mother to shame off youth

17 וצדיקים במפלתם יראו׃ יסר בנך ויניחך ויתן מעדנים

delight it and you and your Correct shall their the but

give will ,rest get son .see fall righteous

18 לנפשך׃ באין חזון יפרע עם ושמר תורה אשרהו׃

blessed the the And the let are ,vision Where your to

!he is ,law of keeper .people loose no is .soul

19 בדברים לא־יוסר עבד כי־יבין ואין מענה׃ חזית איש

a you Do there he though A is not by

man see .answer no is ,discerns ;servant corrected words

21 אץ בדבריו תקוה לכסיל ממנו׃ מפנק מנער עבדו

his from who He than a for More his in hasty

servant youth pampers !him of fool hope ?words

22 ואחריתו יהיה מנון׃ איש־אף יגרה מדון ובעל חמה

of fury a and conten- stirs anger A (his) he shall his in also

master ,tion up of man .successor be days after

23 רב־פשע׃ גאות אדם תשפילנו ושפל־רוח יתמך כבוד׃

.honor takes spirit the but brings man The trans- abounds

of hold of humble ;low him of pride .gression in

24 25 חולק עם־גנב שונא נפשו אלה ישמע ולא יגיד׃ חרדת

fear The does but he an his hates a with who He

of .(it) tell not ,hears oath ;soul thief shares

26 אדם יתן מוקש ובוטח ביהוה ישגב׃ רבים מבקשים

seeking are Many set is in he but ;snare a brings man

.high on Jehovah trusts who

27 פני־מושל ומיהוה משפט־איש׃ תועבת צדיקים איש

A the hateful (is) each the (is) from but the the

man righteous to .man of judgment Jehovah ruler of face

עול ותועבת רשע ישר־דרך׃

.way the the (is) and ;unjust

upright wicked to hateful

CAP. XXX ל

CHAPTER 30

[1] The words of Agur the son of Jakeh, the burden; the warrior spoke to Ithiel, (even) to Ithiel and

1 דברי אגור בן־יקה המשא נאם הגבר לאיתיאל לאיתיאל

to (even) to the Spoke the Jakeh the Agur The

Ithiel ,Ithiel warrior .burden of son of words

Ucal: [2] Surely I (am more) brutish than anyone; and I do not have the understanding of a man. [3] I have not learned wisdom, but I do know the knowledge of holiness. [4] Who has gone up into Heaven, and has come down? Who has gathered the wind in His fists? Who has bound the waters in (His) garment? Who has made rise all the ends of the earth? What (is) His name, and what (is) His Son's name? Surely you know!

[5] Every word of God (is) tested; He (is) a shield to those who seek refuge in Him. [6] Do not add to His words, lest He reprove you and you be found a liar.

[7] I have asked two (things) from You; do not hold back from me before I die: [8] Remove vanity and the word of a lie far from me; give me not poverty and riches; tear for me my portion of bread; [9] lest I become full and deceive; and say, Who (is) Jehovah? Or lest I become poor and steal, and violate the name of my God.

[10] Do not slander a servant to his master, lest he curse you, and you be found guilty.

[11] A generation curses its father, and does not bless its mother; [12] a generation pure in its own eyes, and yet not washed from its own filth. [13] (There is) a generation, O how lofty (are) its eyes! And its eyelids are lifted up; [14] a generation whose teeth (are like) swords; and its jaw teeth (like) knives, to devour the poor from the earth, and the needy from (among) men. [15] The leech (has) two daughters (crying) Give! Give! Three things (are) not being satisfied; four that never say, Wealth! [16] Sheol, and the barren womb; the earth not filled (with) water; and the fire that never says, Wealth! [17] The eye that makes fun of (his) father, and despises to obey (his) mother — the ravens of the valley shall pick it out; and

2 3 וְאֻכָל׃ כִּי בַעַר אָנֹכִי מֵאִישׁ וְלֹא־בִינַת אָדָם לִי׃ וְלֹא־
not And to (is) a under- the and than (am) I (more) Surely and
me man of standing not man any brutish :Ucal

4 לָמַדְתִּי חָכְמָה וְדַעַת קְדֹשִׁים אֵדָע׃ מִי עָלָה־שָׁמַיִם ׀ וַיֵּרַד
re- and Heaven has Who I do holiness the but ,wisdom have I
?turned (to) up gone .know of knowledge learned

מִי אָסַף־רוּחַ ׀ בְּחָפְנָיו מִי צָרַר־מַיִם ׀ בַּשִּׂמְלָה מִי הֵקִים
made Who the in the has Who His in the has who
rise ?garment waters bound ?fists wind gathered

5 כָּל־אַפְסֵי־אָרֶץ מַה־שְּׁמוֹ וּמַה־שֶּׁם־בְּנוֹ כִּי תֵדָע׃ כָּל־
Every you Surely His name And His What the the all
!know ?Son's (is) what ?name (is) ?earth of ends

6 אִמְרַת אֱלוֹהַּ צְרוּפָה מָגֵן הוּא לַחֹסִים בּוֹ׃ אַל־תּוֹסְףְּ
Do not in seekers to He a is God word
add .Him refuge of (is) shield ;tested of

7 עַל־דְּבָרָיו פֶּן־יוֹכִיחַ בְּךָ וְנִכְזָבְתָּ׃ שְׁתַּיִם שָׁאַלְתִּי
have I Two be you and ,you He lest His to
asked things .liar a found reprove ,words

8 מֵאִתָּךְ אַל־תִּמְנַע מִמֶּנִּי בְּטֶרֶם אָמוּת׃ שָׁוְא ׀ וּדְבַר־כָּזָב
a the and vanity :die I before from hold do not from
lie of word me back ;You

הַרְחֵק מִמֶּנִּי רֵאשׁ וָעֹשֶׁר אַל־תִּתֶּן־לִי הַטְרִיפֵנִי לֶחֶם חֻקִּי׃
my of bread tear to do not and poverty from remove
;portion me for ;me give riches ;me far

9 פֶּן אֶשְׂבַּע ׀ וְכִחַשְׁתִּי וְאָמַרְתִּי מִי יְהוָה וּפֶן־אִוָּרֵשׁ וְגָנַבְתִּי
and become Or ?Jehovah Who and ,deceive and become I lest
,steal poor I lest is ,say ,full

10 וְתָפַשְׂתִּי שֵׁם אֱלֹהָי׃ אַל־תַּלְשֵׁן עֶבֶד אֶל־אֲדֹנָו פֶּן
lest his to a Do not my the and
,master servant slander .God of name violate

11 יְקַלֶּלְךָ וְאָשָׁמְתָּ׃ דּוֹר אָבִיו יְקַלֵּל וְאֶת־אִמּוֹ לֹא יְבָרֵךְ׃
does not its and its genera- A be you and curse he
;bless mother ,curses father tion .guilty held ,you

12 13 דּוֹר טָהוֹר בְּעֵינָיו וּמִצֹּאָתוֹ לֹא רֻחָץ׃ דּוֹר מָה־רָמוּ עֵינָיו
its lofty O genera- A is not from and its in pure genera-
!eyes (are) how tion washed filth its !eyes own tion

14 וְעַפְעַפָּיו יִנָּשֵׂאוּ׃ דּוֹר ׀ חֲרָבוֹת שִׁנָּיו וּמַאֲכָלוֹת מְתַלְּעֹתָיו
jaw its and its swords genera- A lifted are its and
,teeth knives ,teeth (are) tion .up eyelids

15 לֶאֱכֹל עֲנִיִּים מֵאֶרֶץ וְאֶבְיוֹנִים מֵאָדָם׃ לַעֲלוּקָה ׀
leech The To among from the and the from the to
(are) .men needy ,earth poor devour

שְׁתֵּי בָנוֹת הַב ׀ הַב שָׁלוֹשׁ הֵנָּה לֹא תִשְׂבַּעְנָה אַרְבַּע לֹא־
not four ;satisfied not they Three !Give !Give daughters two
(are) (things) (crying)

16 אָמְרוּ הוֹן׃ שְׁאוֹל וְעֹצֶר רָחַם אֶרֶץ לֹא־שָׂבְעָה מַּיִם וְאֵשׁ
the and ;water filled not the the and Sheol !Wealth have
,fire (with) earth ;womb barren ,said

17 לֹא־אָמְרָה הוֹן׃ עַיִן ׀ תִּלְעַג לְאָב וְתָבוּז לִיקְּהַת־אֵם יִקְּרוּהָ
shall (his) to and (his) that The !Wealth has not
it pick ,mother obey despises ,father mocks eye ,said

the sons of the eagle shall eat it.

[18] Three (things) are too wonderful for me; yea, four which I do not know: [19] The way of an eagle in the heavens; the way of a snake on a rock; the way of a ship in the heart of the sea; and the way of a man with a virgin. [20] So (is) the way of an adulterous woman: She eats and wipes her mouth, and says, I have not done any evil.

[21] The earth quakes for three (things); yea, for four (which) it is not able to bear: [22] Under a servant when he reigns; under a fool when he is filled with food; [23] under a hated one when she is married; under a handmaid that is heir to her mistress.

[24] Four (things are) little on the earth, but they (are) the wiser ones of those made wise. [25] The ants (are) a people not strong, yet they prepare their food in summer; [26] the rock-badgers (are) not a powerful people, yet they set their house in the rock; [27] the locusts have no king, yet they go out in a swarm every one; [28] the lizard you can take with the hands; and is in the king's palaces.

[29] There are three (things) that go well in a march; yea, four that go well in walking; [30] a lion is mighty among beasts; and he turns not away from facing all; [31] one girded in loins; and a he-goat; and a king (when his) army is with him.

[32] If you have been foolish in lifting up yourself; or if you have thought evil; (lay your) hand on your mouth! [33] Surely the squeezing of milk brings butter; and the squeezing of the nose brings blood; so the squeezing of wrath brings forth strife.

18 עָרְבֵי־נַחַל וְיֹאכְלוּהָ בְנֵי־נָשֶׁר׃ שְׁלֹשָׁה הֵמָּה נִפְלְאוּ
too they Three .eagle the the shall and the the
wonderful (are) (things) of sons it eat ;valley of ravens

19 מִמֶּנִּי וְאַרְבָּע לֹא יְדַעְתִּים׃ דֶּרֶךְ הַנֶּשֶׁר ׀ בַּשָּׁמַיִם דֶּרֶךְ
the the in an the not four and ,me for
of way ;heavens eagle :of way know I

נָחָשׁ עֲלֵי־צוּר דֶּרֶךְ־אֳנִיָּה בְלֶב־יָם וְדֶרֶךְ גֶּבֶר בְּעַלְמָה׃
a with a the and the the in ship a the a on a
virgin man of way ;sea of heart of way ;rock snake

20 כֵּן ׀ דֶּרֶךְ אִשָּׁה מְנָאָפֶת אָכְלָה וּמָחֲתָה פִיהָ וְאָמְרָה לֹא־
not ,says and her and she woman a the So
mouth wipes eats ;adulterous of way (is)

21 פָעַלְתִּי אָוֶן׃ תַּחַת שָׁלוֹשׁ רָגְזָה אֶרֶץ וְתַחַת אַרְבַּע
four and the quakes three Under (any) have I
under ;earth (things) .evil done

22 לֹא־תוּכַל שְׂאֵת׃ תַּחַת עֶבֶד כִּי יִמְלוֹךְ וְנָבָל כִּי יִשְׂבַּע־
is he when a and he when a :under bear to is it not
with filled fool ;reigns servant up able

23 לָחֶם׃ תַּחַת שְׂנוּאָה כִּי תִבָּעֵל וְשִׁפְחָה כִּי־תִירַשׁ גְּבִרְתָּהּ׃
her is she when a and is she when hated a under ;food
.mistress to heir handmaid ;married one

24 אַרְבָּעָה הֵם קְטַנֵּי־אָרֶץ וְהֵמָּה חֲכָמִים מְחֻכָּמִים׃
those wise the but the little they Four
:wise made of ones (are) they ,earth on (are) (things)

25 26 הַנְּמָלִים עַם לֹא־עָז וַיָּכִינוּ בַקַּיִץ לַחְמָם׃ שְׁפַנִּים עַם לֹא־
not a (are) rock- the their in yet strong not a ants the
people badgers ;food summer prepare they people (are)

27 עָצוּם וַיָּשִׂימוּ בַסֶּלַע בֵּיתָם׃ מֶלֶךְ אֵין לָאַרְבֶּה וַיֵּצֵא חֹצֵץ
a in they yet the to not king a their the in they yet ,mighty
swarm ,out go ,locusts is ;house rock make

28 כֻּלּוֹ׃ שְׂמָמִית בְּיָדַיִם תְּתַפֵּשׂ וְהִיא בְּהֵיכְלֵי מֶלֶךְ׃
the palaces in it and can you the with The of all
king's (is) take hands lizard .them

29 30 שְׁלֹשָׁה הֵמָּה מֵיטִיבֵי צָעַד וְאַרְבָּעָה מֵיטִבֵי לָכֶת׃ לַיִשׁ
lion a in go that four and a in go that They three
(is) ;walking well ,march well (are) (things

31 גִּבּוֹר בַּבְּהֵמָה וְלֹא־יָשׁוּב מִפְּנֵי־כֹל׃ זַרְזִיר מָתְנַיִם אוֹ־תָיִשׁ
the and loins the one ;all from turns he and among mighty
;he goat in girded facing away not ,beasts

32 וּמֶלֶךְ אַלְקוּם עִמּוֹ׃ אִם־נָבַלְתָּ בְהִתְנַשֵּׂא וְאִם־זַמּוֹתָ יָד
(lay) you or lifting in have you If with (is) (his when) a and
hand ;plot if ;yourself foolish been him army king

33 לְפֶה׃ כִּי מִיץ חָלָב יוֹצִיא חֶמְאָה וּמִיץ־אַף יוֹצִיא דָם וּמִיץ
so ;blood out the and ;curds out ,milk squeeze ,For (your) on
squeeze comes nose squeeze comes !mouth

אַפַּיִם יוֹצִיא רִיב׃
.strife brings wrath
forth

CHAPTER 31

[1] The words of king Lemuel, the burden that his mother taught him: [2] What, my son? And what, the son of my womb? And what, the son of my vows? [3] Do not give your strength to women, or your ways to that wiping out kings. [4] (It is) not for kings, O Lemuel; (it is) not for kings to drink wine; nor for princes to lust for strong drink; [5] lest they drink and forget what is decreed, and pervert the judgment of the sons of the afflicted. [6] Give strong drink to him who is perishing; and wine to those who are bitter in soul; [7] let him drink and forget his poverty, and remember his misery no more. [8] Open your mouth for the dumb, in the cause of all the sons of the fatherless. [9] Open your mouth; judge righteously, and defend the poor and needy.

[10] Who can find an able woman? For her value (is) far above jewels. [11] The heart of her husband trusts in her, so that he has no lack (of) gain. [12] She deals with him good and not evil all the days of her life. [13] She seeks wool and flax; and she works delightfully (with) her hands. [14] She is like the merchant-ships; she brings in her food from afar. [15] She also rises while it is still night, and gives game to her household, and a task to her maidens. [16] She has examined a field, and takes it; she plants a vineyard from the fruit of her hands. [17] She has girded her loins with strength, and has strengthened her arms. [18] She tastes whether her gain (is) good; her lamp does not go out by night. [19] She has sent forth her hands on the distaff, and her palms have held the spindle. [20] She stretches out her hand to the poor; yea, she reaches out her hands to the needy.

CAP. XXXI לא

CHAPTER 31

1 2 דִּבְרֵי לְמוּאֵל מֶלֶךְ מַשָּׂא אֲשֶׁר־יִסְּרַתּוּ אִמּוֹ׃ מַה־בְּרִי
my What his taught that the ,King Lemuel The
?son .mother him burden of words

3 וּמַה־בַּר־בִּטְנִי וּמֶה בַּר־נְדָרָי׃ אַל־תִּתֵּן לַנָּשִׁים חֵילֶךָ
your to Do not my the And my the And
,might women give ?vows of son ,what ?womb of son ,what

4 וּדְרָכֶיךָ לַמְחוֹת מְלָכִין׃ אַל לַמְלָכִים ׀ לְמוֹאֵל אַל לַמְלָכִים
for (is it) O for (is It) .kings that to your or
kings not ,Lemuel ,kings not out wiping ways

5 שְׁתוֹ־יָיִן וּלְרוֹזְנִים אֵו שֵׁכָר׃ פֶּן־יִשְׁתֶּה וְיִשְׁכַּח מְחֻקָּק
is what and they lest strong lust to princes nor ,wine to
decreed forget drink ;drink for for drink

6 וִישַׁנֶּה דִּין כָּל־בְּנֵי־עֹנִי׃ תְּנוּ־שֵׁכָר לְאוֹבֵד וְיַיִן לְמָרֵי נָפֶשׁ׃
;soul the to and one to strong Give the sons the the and
of bitter wine perishing drink .afflicted of of right pervert

7 8 יִשְׁתֶּה וְיִשְׁכַּח רִישׁוֹ וַעֲמָלוֹ לֹא יִזְכָּר־עוֹד׃ פְּתַח־פִּיךָ
your Open .more remember not his and his and him let
mouth misery ,poverty forget drink

9 לְאִלֵּם אֶל־דִּין כָּל־בְּנֵי חֲלוֹף׃ פְּתַח־פִּיךָ שְׁפָט־צֶדֶק וְדִין
and righ- judge your Open father- the all the to the for
defend teously ;mouth .less sons of cause ,dumb

10 עָנִי וְאֶבְיוֹן׃ אֵשֶׁת־חַיִל מִי יִמְצָא וְרָחֹק מִפְּנִינִים
above (is) And can who able An and the
gems far ?find woman .needy poor

11 12 מִכְרָהּ׃ בָּטַח בָּהּ לֵב בַּעְלָהּ וְשָׁלָל לֹא יֶחְסָר׃ גְּמָלַתְהוּ
to deals She has he no that so Her heart in trusts her
him .lack gain (of) ,husband's her .value

13 טוֹב וְלֹא־רָע כֹּל יְמֵי חַיֶּיהָ׃ דָּרְשָׁה צֶמֶר וּפִשְׁתִּים וַתַּעַשׂ
she and and wool She her the all ,evil and good
works ;flax seeks .life of days not

14 בְּחֵפֶץ כַּפֶּיהָ׃ הָיְתָה כָּאֳנִיּוֹת סוֹחֵר מִמֶּרְחָק תָּבִיא לַחְמָהּ׃
her she from ;merchant the like She (with) (with)
.food in brings afar . ships is .palms her delight

15 וַתָּקָם ׀ בְּעוֹד לַיְלָה וַתִּתֵּן טֶרֶף לְבֵיתָהּ וְחֹק לְנַעֲרֹתֶיהָ׃
her to a and her to game and ,night while also She
.maidens decree ,household gives still (is it) rises

16 זָמְמָה שָׂדֶה וַתִּקָּחֵהוּ מִפְּרִי כַפֶּיהָ נָטַע כָּרֶם׃
a she her the from and a has She
.vineyard plants palms of fruit ;it takes field examined

17 18 חָגְרָה בְעוֹז מָתְנֶיהָ וַתְּאַמֵּץ זְרוֹעֹתֶיהָ׃ טָעֲמָה כִּי־טוֹב סַחְרָהּ
her whether She her has and her with has She
;gain good (is) tastes .arms strengthened ,loins strength girded

19 לֹא־יִכְבֶּה בַלַּיְלָ נֵרָהּ׃ יָדֶיהָ שִׁלְּחָה בַכִּישׁוֹר וְכַפֶּיהָ
her and the on has She her her by go does not
palms distaff forth sent hands .lamp night out

20 תָּמְכוּ פָלֶךְ׃ כַּפָּהּ פָּרְשָׂה לֶעָנִי וְיָדֶיהָ שִׁלְּחָה לָאֶבְיוֹן׃
the to she her and the to She her the have
.needy reaches hands ;poor spreads palms spindle held

[21] She is not afraid of the snow for her household; for all her household (are) clothed (with) scarlet. [22] She makes herself ornamental coverings; her clothing (is) fine linen and purple. [23] Her husband is known in the gates, when he sits among the elders of the land. [24] She makes fine linen garments, and sells them and she delivers belts to the merchant. [25] Strength and dignity (are) her clothing; and she shall rejoice at the day to come. [26] She opens her mouth in wisdom, and the law of kindness (is) on her tongue. [27] She watches the ways of her household, and does not eat the bread of idleness. [28] Her children rise up and call her blessed; her husband (also), for he praises her. [29] Many (are) the daughters who work ably, but you rise over them all. [30] Favor (is) deceitful, and beauty (is) vain; (but) a woman who fears Jehovah, she shall be praised. [31] Give her of the fruit of her hands; and let her works praise her in the gates.

21 לֹא־תִירָא לְבֵיתָהּ מִשָּׁלֶג כִּי כָל־בֵּיתָהּ לָבֻשׁ שָׁנִים׃

,scarlet clothed are (with) her household all for the of ;snow her for household is She afraid not

22 23 מַרְבַדִּים עָשְׂתָה־לָּהּ שֵׁשׁ וְאַרְגָּמָן לְבוּשָׁהּ׃ נוֹדָע בַּשְּׁעָרִים

the in gates is known clothing (is) her and purple fine linen her to ;self She makes coverings

24 בַּעְלָהּ בְּשִׁבְתּוֹ עִם־זִקְנֵי־אָרֶץ׃ סָדִין עָשְׂתָה וַתִּמְכֹּר וַחֲגוֹר

and belts and ;sells She ,makes linen garments the .land the of elders with he when sits Her ,husband

25 נָתְנָה לַכְּנַעֲנִי׃ עֹז־וְהָדָר לְבוּשָׁהּ וַתִּשְׂחַק לְיוֹם אַחֲרוֹן׃

to .come the at day she and laughs her (are) ;clothing and Strength dignity the to .merchant she gives

26 27 פִּיהָ פָּתְחָה בְחָכְמָה וְתוֹרַת־חֶסֶד עַל־לְשׁוֹנָהּ׃ צוֹפִיָּה

She watches her .tongue (is) on kindness the and of law in ,wisdom She opens her mouth

28 הֲלִיכוֹת בֵּיתָהּ וְלֶחֶם עַצְלוּת לֹא תֹאכֵל׃ קָמוּ בָנֶיהָ

Her children rise up does she .eat not idleness the and of bread her ,household the of ways

29 וַיְאַשְּׁרוּהָ בַּעְלָהּ וַיְהַלְלָהּ׃ רַבּוֹת בָּנוֹת עָשׂוּ חָיִל וְאַתְּ עָלִית

rise but you ,ably who work the daughters Many (are) he for .her praises her ,husband her call and ;blessed

30 עַל־כֻּלָּנָה׃ שֶׁקֶר הַחֵן וְהֶבֶל הַיֹּפִי אִשָּׁה יִרְאַת־יְהוָה הִיא

she ,Jehovah who fears a woman beauty ,(is) and vain Charm deceitful (is) of all them over

31 תִתְהַלָּל׃ תְּנוּ־לָהּ מִפְּרִי יָדֶיהָ וִיהַלְלוּהָ בַשְּׁעָרִים מַעֲשֶׂיהָ׃

her .works the in gates let and her praise her the from ;hands of fruit to Give her be shall .praised

קהלת

LIBER ECCLESIASTAE

CAPUT. I א

CHAPTER 1

CHAPTER 1

[1] The words of the Preacher, the son of David, king in Jerusalem. [2] Vanity of vanities, says the Preacher, vanity of vanities! All (is) vanity! [3] What (is) the profit to a man in all his labor which he labors under the sun? [4] A generation passes away, and (another) generation comes; but the earth stands forever. [5] The sun also arises, and the sun goes (down) and hurries to its place; it arises there (again). [6] The wind goes toward the south, and it turns around to the north; turning (and) turning; and the wind returns on its circuits. [7] All the rivers run into the sea; yet the sea is not full. To the place from where the rivers go, there they return to go (again). [8] All words are wearisome; a man cannot utter (it); the eye is not satisfied to see nor is the ear filled from hearing. [9] That which has been, it is that which shall be. And that which is done is that which shall be done; and (there is) no new (thing) under the sun. [10] Is there (a) thing of which one may say, See, this (is) new? It has already been for the ages, which were before us. [11] (There is) no memory of former (things), and also there is not (any) memory for them of (things) that are to come, with (those) who shall come afterwards.

1 2 דִּבְרֵי קֹהֶלֶת בֶּן־דָּוִד מֶלֶךְ בִּירוּשָׁלִָם׃ הֲבֵל הֲבָלִים

,vanities Vanity in king ,David the the The
of .Jerusalem of son ,Preacher of words

3 אָמַר קֹהֶלֶת הֲבֵל הֲבָלִים הַכֹּל הָבֶל׃ מַה־יִּתְרוֹן לָאָדָם

a to (the) What !vanity All !vanities vanity the says
man profit is) (is) of ,Preacher

4 בְּכָל־עֲמָלוֹ שֶׁיַּעֲמֹל תַּחַת הַשָּׁמֶשׁ׃ דּוֹר הֹלֵךְ וְדוֹר בָּא

comes a and goes A ?sun the under he which his in
generation generation labors labor all

5 וְהָאָרֶץ לְעוֹלָם עֹמָדֶת׃ וְזָרַח הַשֶּׁמֶשׁ וּבָא הַשָּׁמֶשׁ וְאֶל־

and ,sun the and ,sun the And .stands forever the but
to goes arises earth

6 מְקוֹמוֹ שׁוֹאֵף זוֹרֵחַ הוּא שָׁם׃ הוֹלֵךְ אֶל־דָּרוֹם וְסוֹבֵב

turn- and the toward Going there it arises ;panting its
around ing ,south .(again) place

אֶל־צָפוֹן סוֹבֵב ׀ סֹבֵב הוֹלֵךְ הָרוּחַ וְעַל־סְבִיבֹתָיו שָׁב

returns its and the is (and) going the to
circuits on ;wind going ,around around ;north

7 הָרוּחַ׃ כָּל־הַנְּחָלִים הֹלְכִים אֶל־הַיָּם וְהַיָּם אֵינֶנּוּ מָלֵא

.full is it the yet the to are the All the
not sea ;sea going torrents .wind

8 אֶל־מְקוֹם שֶׁהַנְּחָלִים הֹלְכִים שָׁם הֵם שָׁבִים לָלָכֶת׃ כָּל־

All go to returning they there are where the To
.(again) (are) ,going torrents place

הַדְּבָרִים יְגֵעִים לֹא־יוּכַל אִישׁ לְדַבֵּר לֹא־תִשְׂבַּע עַיִן

The is not say to a is not (are) words
eye satisfied .(it) man able ;wearisome

9 לִרְאוֹת וְלֹא־תִמָּלֵא אֹזֶן מִשְּׁמֹעַ׃ מַה־שֶּׁהָיָה הוּא שֶׁיִּהְיֶה

which that it which That from the is and ,see to
;be will (is) ,been has .hearing ear filled not

וּמַה־שֶּׁנַּעֲשָׂה הוּא שֶׁיֵּעָשֶׂה וְאֵין כָּל־חָדָשׁ תַּחַת הַשָּׁמֶשׁ׃

.sun the under new any not So which that it has which and
(thing) is .done be will (is) ,done been that

10 יֵשׁ דָּבָר שֶׁיֹּאמַר רְאֵה־זֶה חָדָשׁ הוּא כְּבָר הָיָה לְעֹלָמִים

the for has it Already it new ,this See one which a Is
ages ,been ?(is) ,say might thing there

11 אֲשֶׁר הָיָה מִלְּפָנֵנוּ׃ אֵין זִכְרוֹן לָרִאשֹׁנִים וְגַם לָאַחֲרֹנִים

after of and former of memory There before were which
(things) also ,(things) no is .us

שֶׁיִּהְיוּ לֹא־יִהְיֶה לָהֶם זִכָּרוֹן עִם שֶׁיִּהְיוּ לָאַחֲרֹנָה׃

after- who those with re- a for be shall not which
.wards be will membrance them ;be will

[12] I the Preacher was king over Israel in Jerusalem. [13] And I gave my heart to seek and search out by wisdom concerning all that is done under the heavens. (It (is) an evil task God has given to the sons of man to be humbled by it. [14] I have seen all the works that are done under the sun: and, behold, all (is) vanity and vexation of spirit! [15] What is crooked cannot be made straight; and (that which is) lacking cannot be numbered. [16] I spoke with my heart, saying, Lo, I have become great and have increased wisdom over all that have been before me over Jerusalem; yea, my heart has seen much wisdom and knowledge. [17] And I gave my heart to know wisdom and to know madness and folly; know that this also is vexation of spirit. [18] For in much wisdom (is) much grief; and he who increases knowledge increases suffering.

12 13 אֲנִי קֹהֶלֶת הָיִיתִי מֶלֶךְ עַל־יִשְׂרָאֵל בִּירוּשָׁלִָם׃ וְנָתַתִּי
I And .Jerusalem in Israel over king was the I
gave Preacher

אֶת־לִבִּי לִדְרוֹשׁ וְלָתוּר בַּחָכְמָה עַל כָּל־אֲשֶׁר נַעֲשָׂה תַּחַת
under done is which all con- by to and seek to my
cerning wisdom investigate heart

הַשָּׁמָיִם הוּא ׀ עִנְיַן רָע נָתַן אֱלֹהִים לִבְנֵי הָאָדָם לַעֲנוֹת
be to men the to God has evil task a it the
afflicted of sons given (is) ;heavens

14 בּוֹ׃ רָאִיתִי אֶת־כָּל־הַמַּעֲשִׂים שֶׁנַּעֲשׂוּ תַּחַת הַשָּׁמֶשׁ וְהִנֵּה
and ,sun the under are which the all have I .it by
,behold done works seen

15 הַכֹּל הֶבֶל וּרְעוּת רוּחַ׃ מְעֻוָּת לֹא־יוּכַל לִתְקֹן וְחֶסְרוֹן
(what) and put be to is not is What (after) and vanity all
lacking ,straight able crooked .wind striving (is)

16 לֹא־יוּכַל לְהִמָּנוֹת׃ דִּבַּרְתִּי אֲנִי עִם־לִבִּי לֵאמֹר אֲנִי הִנֵּה
,behold ,I ,saying my with I spoke be to is not
heart .counted able

הִגְדַּלְתִּי וְהוֹסַפְתִּי חָכְמָה עַל כָּל־אֲשֶׁר־הָיָה לְפָנַי עַל־
over before have who all over wisdom and be- have
me been increased great come

17 יְרוּשָׁלִָם וְלִבִּי רָאָה הַרְבֵּה חָכְמָה וָדָעַת׃ וָאֶתְּנָה לִבִּי
my I And and wisdom abundance has my and ;Jerusalem
heart gave .knowledge of seen heart

לָדַעַת חָכְמָה וְדַעַת הֹלֵלוֹת וְשִׂכְלוּת יָדַעְתִּי שֶׁגַּם־זֶה הוּא
it ,this that know I ;folly and madness to and wisdom know to
(is) also know

18 רַעְיוֹן רוּחַ׃ כִּי בְּרֹב חָכְמָה רַב־כָּעַס וְיוֹסִיף דַּעַת יוֹסִיף
increases knowl- he and ;grief much wisdom in For .wind striving
,edge increases who (is) much (after)

מַכְאוֹב׃
.pain

CAP. II ב

CHAPTER 2

[1] I said in my heart, Come now, I will test you with glee; therefore consider with good. And behold, this also (is) vanity. [2] I said of laughter, (It is) madness; and of glee, What does it do? [3] I sought in my heart (how) to drag my flesh with wine, yet leading my heart with wisdom; and to lay hold on folly, until I might see where the good was for the sons of men, which they should do under the heavens the number of

1 אָמַרְתִּי אֲנִי בְּלִבִּי לְכָה־נָּא אֲנַסְּכָה בְשִׂמְחָה וּרְאֵה בְטוֹב
with And with will I ,now Come my in I said
goodness see .mirth you test ,heart

2 וְהִנֵּה גַם־הוּא הָבֶל׃ לִשְׂחוֹק אָמַרְתִּי מְהוֹלָל וּלְשִׂמְחָה
of and is It ,said I of .vanity this ,also and
,mirth ,madness laughter (is) behold

3 מַה־זֹּה עֹשָׂה׃ תַּרְתִּי בְלִבִּי לִמְשׁוֹךְ בַּיַּיִן אֶת־בְּשָׂרִי וְלִבִּי
my and my with to (how) my with and I does this What
heart flesh wine drag heart explored ?accomplish

נֹהֵג בַּחָכְמָה וְלֶאֱחֹז בְּסִכְלוּת עַד ׀ אֲשֶׁר אֶרְאֶה אֵי־זֶה
where might I until folly on to and in leading
see hold lay wisdom

טוֹב לִבְנֵי הָאָדָם אֲשֶׁר יַעֲשׂוּ תַּחַת הַשָּׁמַיִם מִסְפַּר יְמֵי
days the the under they which ,men the for the
of of number heavens do should of sons good

days of their life. [4] I made great my works; I built houses for myself. I planted vineyards for myself. [5] I made gardens and parks for myself. And I planted trees in them, of every fruit. [6] I made pools of water for myself, to water from them the forest shooting forth trees. [7] I bought slaves and slave-girls. And I had sons of the house; also I had great possessions of a herd and a flock above all that were in Jerusalem before me. [8] I also gathered silver and gold to myself, and the treasure of kings and of the provinces. I provided men singers and women singers for myself, and the delights of the sons of men, a woman and women. [9] So I became great and increased more than all that were before me in Jerusalem; also my wisdom remained with me. [10] And all that my eyes desired, I did not keep from them. I did not withhold my heart from any glee; for my heart rejoiced from all my labor, and this was my part from all my labor. [11] Then I faced on all my works that my hands had done, and on the labor that I had labored to do: and, behold, all (was) vanity and vexation of spirit; and (there was) no profit under the sun.

[12] And I turned to behold wisdom, and madness, and folly. For what (can) the man (do) who comes after the king when they have already done it? [13] Then I saw that there is advantage to wisdom above folly, as far as light (has) advantage above darkness. [14] The wise man's eyes (are) in his head; but the stupid walks in darkness; and I also know that one event happens with all

4 חַיֵּיהֶם׃ הִגְדַּלְתִּי מַעֲשָׂי בָּנִיתִי לִי בָּתִּים נָטַעְתִּי לִי כְּרָמִים׃
.vineyards for I ,houses for built I my made I their
myself planted myself .works great .life

5 עָשִׂיתִי לִי גַּנּוֹת וּפַרְדֵּסִים וְנָטַעְתִּי בָהֶם עֵץ כָּל־פֶּרִי׃
.fruit every a in I and ;parks and gardens for made I
of tree them planted myself

6 עָשִׂיתִי לִי בְּרֵכוֹת מָיִם לְהַשְׁקוֹת מֵהֶם יַעַר צוֹמֵחַ עֵצִים׃
.trees shooting the from water to ,water of pools for made I
forth forest them myself

7 קָנִיתִי עֲבָדִים וּשְׁפָחוֹת וּבְנֵי־בַיִת הָיָה לִי גַּם מִקְנֶה בָקָר
a possession Also to were the and women and men I
herd of .me house of sons slaves slaves bought

8 וָצֹאן הַרְבֵּה הָיָה לִי מִכֹּל שֶׁהָיוּ לְפָנַי בִּירוּשָׁלִָם׃ כָּנַסְתִּי
I in before that above to was great a and
gathered .Jerusalem me were all me flock

לִי גַּם־כֶּסֶף וְזָהָב וּסְגֻלַּת מְלָכִים וְהַמְּדִינוֹת עָשִׂיתִי לִי
for I the and kings the and and silver also for
myself provided .provinces of treasure ,gold myself

9 שָׁרִים וְשָׁרוֹת וְתַעֲנֻגוֹת בְּנֵי הָאָדָם שִׁדָּה וְשִׁדּוֹת׃ וְגָדַלְתִּי
be- I Then con- and con- a ,men the the and women and men
great came .cubines cubine of sons of pleasures ,singers singers

וְהוֹסַפְתִּי מִכֹּל שֶׁהָיָה לְפָנַי בִּירוּשָׁלִָם אַף חָכְמָתִי עָמְדָה
stood my also in before who more and
wisdom ,Jerusalem me were all than increased

10 לִּי׃ וְכֹל אֲשֶׁר שָׁאֲלוּ עֵינַי לֹא אָצַלְתִּי מֵהֶם לֹא־מָנַעְתִּי
did I not from set did I not my asked that And by
withhold .them aside ,eyes all .me

אֶת־לִבִּי מִכָּל־שִׂמְחָה כִּי־לִבִּי שָׂמֵחַ מִכָּל־עֲמָלִי וְזֶה־הָיָה
was and my from rejoiced my for ;mirth from heart my
this ,labor all heart all

11 חֶלְקִי מִכָּל־עֲמָלִי׃ וּפָנִיתִי אֲנִי בְּכָל־מַעֲשַׂי שֶׁעָשׂוּ יָדַי
my which my all on I Then my from my
,hands done had works faced .labor all part

וּבֶעָמָל שֶׁעָמַלְתִּי לַעֲשׂוֹת וְהִנֵּה הַכֹּל הֶבֶל וּרְעוּת רוּחַ
(after) and vanity all and :do to had I that on and
wind striving (was) ,behold labored labor the

12 וְאֵין יִתְרוֹן תַּחַת הַשָּׁמֶשׁ׃ וּפָנִיתִי אֲנִי לִרְאוֹת חָכְמָה
,wisdom to I And .sun the under profit and
see turned is not

וְהוֹלֵלוֹת וְסִכְלוּת כִּי ׀ מֶה הָאָדָם שֶׁיָּבוֹא אַחֲרֵי הַמֶּלֶךְ
,king the after who the what for ,folly and and
comes (do) man (will) ,madness

13 אֵת אֲשֶׁר־כְּבָר עָשׂוּהוּ׃ וְרָאִיתִי אָנִי שֶׁיֵּשׁ יִתְרוֹן לַחָכְמָה
to advantage that I saw Then have they already when
wisdom is there ?it done

14 מִן־הַסִּכְלוּת כִּיתְרוֹן הָאוֹר מִן־הַחֹשֶׁךְ׃ הֶחָכָם עֵינָיו בְּרֹאשׁוֹ
in (are) his wise The .darkness (has) light the as ,folly above
;head his eyes ,man above advantage

וְהַכְּסִיל בַּחֹשֶׁךְ הוֹלֵךְ וְיָדַעְתִּי גַם־אָנִי שֶׁמִּקְרֶה אֶחָד יִקְרֶה
happens one that I also know and ;walks in the but
event darkness fool

of them. [15] Then I said in my heart, As the event of the stupid, even (so) it will happen to me; and why was I then more wise? Then I said in my heart that this also (is) vanity. [16] For there is not a memory of the wise (more than) with the stupid forever, in that already will be forgotten the days to come. And how does the wise die above the stupid? [17] Therefore I hated life; because the work that is done under the sun (is) evil on me; for all (is) vanity and vexation of spirit.

[18] Yes, I hated all my labor that I labored under the sun, because I should leave it to the man who shall be after me. [19] And who knows (whether) the wise man or a fool he will be? Yet he shall rule among all my labor for which I labored and acted wisely under the sun. This (is) also vanity. [20] And I turned about to cause my heart to despair over all the labor which I labored under the sun. [21] When there is a man whose labor (is) with wisdom, and with knowledge, and with success; yet to a man who has not labored with it, he shall give it (for) his share; this also (is) vanity and a great evil. [22] For what is there for man in all his labor, and in strength of his heart which he has labored under the sun? [23] For all his days (are) sufferings and his labor grief; his heart does not even take rest in the night. Even this is also vanity. [24] Is it not good with a man that he should eat and drink, and make his soul see good in his labor. This I also saw, that it (was) from the hand of God. [25] For who can eat, or who can enjoy

15 אֶת־כֻּלָּם׃ וְאָמַרְתִּי אֲנִי בְּלִבִּי כְּמִקְרֵה הַכְּסִיל גַּם־אֲנִי
to even ,fool the the like my in I said Then of all with
me (so) of event heart .them

יִקְרֵנִי וְלָמָּה חָכַמְתִּי אֲנִי אָז יֹתֵר וְדִבַּרְתִּי בְלִבִּי שֶׁגַּם־זֶה
this that my in I Then ?more then I was why And will it
also heart said wise meet

16 הָבֶל׃ כִּי אֵין זִכְרוֹן לֶחָכָם עִם־הַכְּסִיל לְעוֹלָם בְּשֶׁכְּבָר
that in ,forever the (more any) the of a not For (is)
already fool with (than) wise memory is .vanity

הַיָּמִים הַבָּאִים הַכֹּל נִשְׁכָּח וְאֵיךְ יָמוּת הֶחָכָם עִם־הַכְּסִיל׃
!fool the with the does and be will all are which the
wise die how ,forgotten coming days

17 וְשָׂנֵאתִי אֶת־הַחַיִּים כִּי רַע עָלַי הַמַּעֲשֶׂה שֶׁנַּעֲשָׂה תַּחַת
under is that work the me on (is) because ,life Therefore
done evil hated I

18 הַשָּׁמֶשׁ כִּי־הַכֹּל הֶבֶל וּרְעוּת רוּחַ׃ וְשָׂנֵאתִי אֲנִי אֶת־כָּל־
all I Thus (after) and vanity all for ;sun the
hated wind striving (is)

עֲמָלִי שֶׁאֲנִי עָמֵל תַּחַת הַשָּׁמֶשׁ שֶׁאַנִּיחֶנּוּ לָאָדָם שֶׁיִּהְיֶה
will that the to I that ,sun the under had which my
be man it leave must labored I labor

19 אַחֲרָי׃ וּמִי יוֹדֵעַ הֶחָכָם יִהְיֶה אוֹ סָכָל וְיִשְׁלַט בְּכָל־
among he Yet ?fool a or will he wise the knows And after
all rule shall be man (whether) who .me

עֲמָלִי שֶׁעָמַלְתִּי וְשֶׁחָכַמְתִּי תַּחַת הַשָּׁמֶשׁ גַּם־זֶה הָבֶל׃
.vanity this also ;sun the under acted and which (in) my
(is) wisely labored I labor

20 וְסַבּוֹתִי אֲנִי לְיַאֵשׁ אֶת־לִבִּי עַל כָּל־הֶעָמָל שֶׁעָמַלְתִּי תַּחַת
under I which the all over my cause to I And
labored labor heart .despair to turned

21 הַשָּׁמֶשׁ׃ כִּי־יֵשׁ אָדָם שֶׁעֲמָלוֹ בְּחָכְמָה וּבְדַעַת וּבְכִשְׁרוֹן
with and with and with (is) whose man a there When .sun the
;success ,knowledge ,wisdom labor is

וּלְאָדָם שֶׁלֹּא עָמַל־בּוֹ יִתְּנֶנּוּ חֶלְקוֹ גַּם־זֶה הֶבֶל וְרָעָה
evil and vanity this also his shall he with has who to yet
(is) ,share ,it give ,it labored not man a

22 רַבָּה׃ כִּי מֶה־הֹוֶה לָאָדָם בְּכָל־עֲמָלוֹ וּבְרַעְיוֹן לִבּוֹ שֶׁהוּא
which his in and his all in for is what For .great a
he ,heart of striving the ,labor man there

23 עָמֵל תַּחַת הַשָּׁמֶשׁ׃ כִּי כָל־יָמָיו מַכְאֹבִים וָכַעַס עִנְיָנוֹ
his and pains (are) his all For ?sun the under has
;task grief days labored

24 גַּם־בַּלַּיְלָה לֹא־שָׁכַב לִבּוֹ גַּם־זֶה הֶבֶל הוּא׃ אֵין־טוֹב
good Is .(is) it vanity ,this Even his lie does not the in even
not it .heart down night

בָּאָדָם שֶׁיֹּאכַל וְשָׁתָה וְהֶרְאָה אֶת־נַפְשׁוֹ טוֹב בַּעֲמָלוֹ גַּם־
Also his in good soul his cause and and he that a with
?labor see to ,drink eat should man

25 זֹה רָאִיתִי אָנִי כִּי מִיַּד הָאֱלֹהִים הִיא׃ כִּי מִי יֹאכַל וּמִי
or can who For it God the from that I saw this
who eat .(was) of hand

apart from me? [26] For (God) gives wisdom, and knowledge and joy to a man who (is) good in His sight. But to the sinner He gives the task of gathering and collecting, to give to (him who is) good before God. This also (is) vanity and vexation of spirit.

26 יָחוּשׁ חוּץ מִמֶּנִּי׃ כִּי לְאָדָם שֶׁטּוֹב לְפָנָיו נָתַן חָכְמָה וְדַעַת
and knowledge · wisdom · He gives · before Him, · (is) who good · a to man · For · from ?Me · -out side · can enjoy-

וְשִׂמְחָה וְלַחוֹטֶא נָתַן עִנְיָן לֶאֱסוֹף וְלִכְנוֹס לָתֵת לְטוֹב
the to one good · give to · and collecting · of gathering · the task · He gives · the to but sinner · ,joy and

לִפְנֵי הָאֱלֹהִים גַּם־זֶה הֶבֶל וּרְעוּת רוּחַ׃
(after) wind · and striving · vanity · this (is) Also · .God · before

CAP. III ג

CHAPTER 3

[1] To all (there is) a set time, and a time for every matter under the heavens — [2] a time to be born, and a time to die — a time to plant, and a time to pull up what is planted — [3] a time to kill, and a time to heal — a time to tear down, and a time to build up — [4] a time to weep, and a time to laugh — a time to mourn, and a time to dance — [5] a time to throw away stones, and a time to gather stones — a time to embrace, and a time to refrain from embracing — [6] a time to seek, and a time to give up as lost — a time to keep, and a time to throw away — [7] a time to tear, and a time to sew together — a time to keep silence, and a

1 לַכֹּל זְמָן וְעֵת לְכָל־חֵפֶץ תַּחַת הַשָּׁמָיִם׃
the :heavens · under · purpose for every · a and time · set a time · all To (is)

2 עֵת לָלֶדֶת (bear to · a time) — וְעֵת לָמוּת (;die to · a and time)
עֵת לָטַעַת (plant to · a time) — וְעֵת לַעֲקוֹר נָטוּעַ׃ (what ;planted is · uproot to · a and time)

3 עֵת לַהֲרוֹג (kill to · a time) — וְעֵת לִרְפּוֹא (;heal to · a and time)
עֵת לִפְרוֹץ (to down tear · a time) — וְעֵת לִבְנוֹת׃ (build to ;up · a and time)

4 עֵת לִבְכּוֹת (weep to · a time) — וְעֵת לִשְׂחוֹק (;laugh to · a and time)
עֵת סְפוֹד (wail to · a time) — וְעֵת רְקוֹד׃ (;dance to · a and time)

5 עֵת לְהַשְׁלִיךְ אֲבָנִים (stones · throw to away · a time) — וְעֵת כְּנוֹס אֲבָנִים (;stones · gather to · a and time)
עֵת לַחֲבוֹק (to embrace · a time) — וְעֵת לִרְחֹק מֵחַבֵּק׃ (from ;embracing · refrain to · a and time)

6 עֵת לְבַקֵּשׁ (seek to · a time) — וְעֵת לְאַבֵּד (let to perish · a and time)
עֵת לִשְׁמוֹר (keep to · a time) — וְעֵת לְהַשְׁלִיךְ׃ (throw to ;away · a and time)

7 עֵת לִקְרוֹעַ (tear to · a time) — וְעֵת לִתְפּוֹר (sew to ,together · a and time)
עֵת לַחֲשׁוֹת (be to silent · a time) — וְעֵת לְדַבֵּר׃ (;speak to · a and time)

time to speak – [8] a time to love, and a time to hate – a time of war, and a time of peace. [9] What profit (has) he who works have in that in which he labors? [10] I have seen the task which God has given to the sons of men to be humbled by it. [11] He has made everything beautiful in its time; also He has set the eternal in his heart, without which man cannot find out the work that God made from the beginning, even to the end. [12] I know that (there is) no good in them, but for (a man) to rejoice to do good in his life. [13] And also every man that eats and drinks and sees good in his labor, it (is) the gift of God. [14] I know that whatever God does, it shall be forever; nothing is to be added (to it), nor anything is to be taken from it. And God does (it) so that they fear before Him. [15] That which has been, it already is; and that which (is) to be has already been; and God seeks what has been pursued.

[16] And again I saw under the sun the place of justice: wickedness (is) there; and the place of righteousness, iniquity (is) there. [17] I said in my heart, God shall judge the righteous and the wicked; for (there is) a time there for every matter and on every work. [18] I said in my heart concerning the issue of the sons of men, that God might test them, and see that they by themselves (are) beasts. [19] For

8 עֵת לֶאֱהֹב וְעֵת לִשְׂנֹא

;hate to a and time love to a time

עֵת מִלְחָמָה וְעֵת שָׁלוֹם׃

.peace a and of time war a of time

9 10 מַה־יִּתְרוֹן הָעוֹשֶׂה בַּאֲשֶׁר הוּא עָמֵל׃ רָאִיתִי אֶת־הָעִנְיָן

task the have I seen ?labors he that in which who he works advantage (has) What

11 אֲשֶׁר נָתַן אֱלֹהִים לִבְנֵי הָאָדָם לַעֲנוֹת בּוֹ׃ אֶת־הַכֹּל

everything .it by be to humbled ,men the to of sons God has given which

עָשָׂה יָפֶה בְעִתּוֹ גַּם אֶת־הָעֹלָם נָתַן בְּלִבָּם מִבְּלִי אֲשֶׁר

which without their in heart He set has eternity Also its in .time beautiful has He made

לֹא־יִמְצָא הָאָדָם אֶת־הַמַּעֲשֶׂה אֲשֶׁר־עָשָׂה הָאֱלֹהִים מֵרֹאשׁ

the from beginning God makes that the work man can out find not

12 וְעַד־סוֹף׃ יָדַעְתִּי כִּי אֵין טוֹב בָּם כִּי אִם־לִשְׂמוֹחַ וְלַעֲשׂוֹת

do to rejoice to except in them good not is that know I the .end even to

13 טוֹב בְּחַיָּיו׃ וְגַם כָּל־הָאָדָם שֶׁיֹּאכַל וְשָׁתָה וְרָאָה טוֹב

good and sees and ,drinks that eats man every and also his in ,life good

14 בְּכָל־עֲמָלוֹ מַתַּת אֱלֹהִים הִיא׃ יָדַעְתִּי כִּי כָּל־אֲשֶׁר יַעֲשֶׂה

does which all that know I .(is) it God the of gift his ,labor all in

הָאֱלֹהִים הוּא יִהְיֶה לְעוֹלָם עָלָיו אֵין לְהוֹסִיף וּמִמֶּנּוּ אֵין

not is and it from be to ,added not is it to ;forever be shall it ,God

15 לִגְרֹעַ וְהָאֱלֹהִים עָשָׂה שֶׁיִּרְאוּ מִלְּפָנָיו׃ מַה־שֶּׁהָיָה כְּבָר

already which That ,been has before .Him that so fear they does (it) for God to ,diminish

הוּא וַאֲשֶׁר לִהְיוֹת כְּבָר הָיָה וְהָאֱלֹהִים יְבַקֵּשׁ אֶת־נִרְדָּף׃

is what .pursued seeks God for has ,been already ,be will that and which it ,(is)

16 וְעוֹד רָאִיתִי תַּחַת הַשָּׁמֶשׁ מְקוֹם הַמִּשְׁפָּט שָׁמָּה הָרֶשַׁע

wicked- ;ness there (is) justice the of place ;sun the under saw I And again

17 וּמְקוֹם הַצֶּדֶק שָׁמָּה הָרָשַׁע׃ אָמַרְתִּי אֲנִי בְּלִבִּי אֶת־הַצַּדִּיק

The righteous my in .heart I said .wickedness there (is) righteous- ness the and of place

וְאֶת־הָרָשָׁע יִשְׁפֹּט הָאֱלֹהִים כִּי־עֵת לְכָל־חֵפֶץ וְעַל כָּל־

every and for matter for every (is) for time a ;God shall judge the wicked and

18 הַמַּעֲשֶׂה שָׁם׃ אָמַרְתִּי אֲנִי בְּלִבִּי עַל־דִּבְרַת בְּנֵי הָאָדָם

,men the of sons the of matter concern- ing my in heart I said .there work

19 לְבָרָם הָאֱלֹהִים וְלִרְאוֹת שְׁהֶם־בְּהֵמָה הֵמָּה לָהֶם׃ כִּי

For by .themselves they (are) beasts that they in and see to order ,God may that them test that which happens (to) the sons of men and that which happens (to) beasts; even one event to them. As this (one) dies, so dies this; yea, one breath to all; so that there is to the man no advantage over the beast; for all (is) vanity. [20] All go to one place; all are of the dust, and all return to the dust. [21] Who knows the spirit of the sons of man (if) it goes upward, and the spirit of the beast (if) it goes downward to the earth? [22] Therefore I have seen that nothing is better than that the man should rejoice in his works; for that (is) his portion; for who can bring him to see what shall be after him?

מִקְרֶה בְנֵי־הָאָדָם וּמִקְרֶה הַבְּהֵמָה וּמִקְרֶה אֶחָד לָהֶם
to one even ;beasts the and men the the
;them event of event of sons of event

כְּמוֹת זֶה כֵּן מוֹת זֶה וְרוּחַ אֶחָד לַכֹּל וּמוֹתַר הָאָדָם מִן
over man the that so ,all to one even ;this dies so ,this dies as
advantage breath

20 הַבְּהֵמָה אָיִן כִּי הַכֹּל הָבֶל׃ הַכֹּל הוֹלֵךְ אֶל־מָקוֹם אֶחָד
;one place to go All .vanity all for is beast the
(is) ,not

21 הַכֹּל הָיָה מִן־הֶעָפָר וְהַכֹּל שָׁב אֶל־הֶעָפָר׃ מִי יוֹדֵעַ רוּחַ
the knows Who .dust the to return all and ,dust the of are all
of spirit

בְּנֵי הָאָדָם הָעֹלָה הִיא לְמָעְלָה וְרוּחַ הַבְּהֵמָה הַיֹּרֶדֶת
(whether) beast the the and ,upward it (whether) man the
descends of spirit ascends of sons

22 הִיא לְמַטָּה לָאָרֶץ׃ וְרָאִיתִי כִּי אֵין טוֹב מֵאֲשֶׁר יִשְׂמַח
should than better there that Therefore the to downward it
rejoice that nothing is seen have I .earth

הָאָדָם בְּמַעֲשָׂיו כִּי־הוּא חֶלְקוֹ כִּי מִי יְבִיאֶנּוּ לִרְאוֹת בְּמֶה
what see to can who for his that for his in the
him bring ;portion (is) ,works own man

שֶׁיִּהְיֶה אַחֲרָיו׃
after shall
?him be

CAP. IV ד

CHAPTER 4

CHAPTER 4

[1] So I returned and considered all the oppressions that are done under the sun. And behold the tears of those who were oppressed, and they had no comforter! And at the hand of those who oppressed them (there was) power, but they had no comforter. [2] Therefore I commended the dead which are already dead, more than the living which (are) alive till now. [3] Yea, better than both (is he) who has not yet been, who has not seen the evil work that is done under the sun.

[4] And I considered every labor, and every success of the work, that it is the envy of a man against his neighbor; this (is) also vanity and vexation of spirit. [5] The stupid one folds his hands together and

1 וְשַׁבְתִּי אֲנִי וָאֶרְאֶה אֶת־כָּל־הָעֲשֻׁקִים אֲשֶׁר נַעֲשִׂים תַּחַת
under done are that the all saw and I So
oppressions returned

הַשָּׁמֶשׁ וְהִנֵּה ׀ דִּמְעַת הָעֲשֻׁקִים וְאֵין לָהֶם מְנַחֵם וּמִיַּד
at and who one for and who those tears the And .sun the
hand ;comforts them is not oppressed are of ,behold

2 עֹשְׁקֵיהֶם כֹּחַ וְאֵין לָהֶם מְנַחֵם׃ וְשַׁבֵּחַ אֲנִי אֶת־הַמֵּתִים
the I And who one to but (was) their
dead commended .comforts them was not power oppressors'

3 שֶׁכְּבָר מֵתוּ מִן־הַחַיִּים אֲשֶׁר הֵמָּה חַיִּים עֲדֶנָה׃ וְטוֹב
But .still alive they which the more have who
better (are) living than ,died already

מִשְּׁנֵיהֶם אֵת אֲשֶׁר־עֲדֶן לֹא הָיָה אֲשֶׁר לֹא־רָאָה אֶת־
has not who has not to up (that is) ,both than
seen ,been now which them of

4 הַמַּעֲשֶׂה הָרָע אֲשֶׁר נַעֲשָׂה תַּחַת הַשָּׁמֶשׁ׃ וְרָאִיתִי אֲנִי
I saw And .sun the under done is that evil work the

אֶת־כָּל־עָמָל וְאֵת כָּל־כִּשְׁרוֹן הַמַּעֲשֶׂה כִּי הִיא קִנְאַת־אִישׁ
a envy the it that ,work the success every and labor all
man of (is) of

5 מֵרֵעֵהוּ גַּם־זֶה הֶבֶל וּרְעוּת רוּחַ׃ הַכְּסִיל חֹבֵק אֶת־יָדָיו
his folds fool The .wind and vanity this also his against
hands on feeding (is) ;neighbor

eats his own flesh. [6] Better is one handful (with) quietness than both hands full (with) travail and vexation of spirit.

[7] Then I returned and saw vanity under the sun. [8] There is one (alone), and there is not a second; yea, he has neither son nor brother; and there is no end to all his labor; even his eyes are not satisfied with riches; and (he says), For whom do I labor and take good from my soul? This (is) also vanity. Yes, it (is) an evil task.

[9] Two (are) better than one; because they have a good reward for their labor. [10] For if they fall, the one will lift up his fellow. But woe to him, the one that falls, and is not another to lift him up. [11] Also if two lie (together,) then they (have) warmth; but for one, how is he warm? [12] And if one overthrows him, two shall withstand him; and a threefold cord is not with haste torn apart. [13] A poor and a wise child (is) better than the old and stupid king, who does not know to be warned any more. [14] For from the house of the imprisoned he goes forth to reign, although in his kingdom he was born poor. [15] I saw all the living who walk about under the sun, with the second child who shall stand up in his place. [16] (There is) no end to all the people, to all who have been before them; they also who come after shall not rejoice with him. Surely this also (is) vanity and vexation of spirit.

CHAPTER 5

[1] Guard your feet when you go to the house of God, and draw near to hear more than to give a sacrifice (as) stupid ones. For they do not know that they are

6 וְאֹכֵל אֶת־בְּשָׂרוֹ׃ טוֹב מְלֹא כַף נָחַת מִמְּלֹא חָפְנַיִם עָמָל
(with) two than (with) a filled Better own his and
labor fists filled ,rest palm (is) .flesh eats

7 8 וּרְעוּת רוּחַ׃ וְשַׁבְתִּי אֲנִי וָאֶרְאֶה הֶבֶל תַּחַת הַשָּׁמֶשׁ׃ יֵשׁ
There the under vanity saw and I Then (after) and
is .sun returned wind striving

אֶחָד וְאֵין שֵׁנִי גַּם בֵּן וָאָח אֵין־לוֹ וְאֵין קֵץ לְכָל־עֲמָלוֹ גַּם־
even his to an and to not a and a also a and one
;labor all end is not ,him is brother son ,second is not

עֵינָיו לֹא־תִשְׂבַּע עֹשֶׁר וּלְמִי ׀ אֲנִי עָמֵל וּמְחַסֵּר אֶת־נַפְשִׁי
soul my and do I for and ;riches are not his
deprive labor whom with satisfied eyes

9 מִטּוֹבָה גַּם־זֶה הֶבֶל וְעִנְיַן רָע הוּא׃ טוֹבִים הַשְּׁנַיִם מִן
than Two better .(is) it evil a and vanity This also from
(are) task (is) ?good

10 הָאֶחָד אֲשֶׁר יֵשׁ־לָהֶם שָׂכָר טוֹב בַּעֲמָלָם׃ כִּי אִם־יִפֹּלוּ
they if For their with good a to there because ,one
,fall .labor reward them is

הָאֶחָד יָקִים אֶת־חֲבֵרוֹ וְאִילוֹ הָאֶחָד שֶׁיִּפּוֹל וְאֵין שֵׁנִי
a and that one the woe but his cause will the
second is not falls ,him to ;companion rise to one

11 לַהֲקִימוֹ׃ גַּם אִם־יִשְׁכְּבוּ שְׁנַיִם וְחַם לָהֶם וּלְאֶחָד אֵיךְ
how for but to then ,two lie if ,Again make to
.(alone) one ;them warmth together rise him

12 יֵחָם׃ וְאִם־יִתְקְפוֹ הָאֶחָד הַשְּׁנַיִם יַעַמְדוּ נֶגְדּוֹ וְהַחוּט
the And before shall two the ,one over- shall And he is
cord .him stand him power if ?warm

13 הַמְשֻׁלָּשׁ לֹא בִמְהֵרָה יִנָּתֵק׃ טוֹב יֶלֶד מִסְכֵּן וְחָכָם מִמֶּלֶךְ
the than and poor a Better torn is quickly not threefold
king ,wise child (is) .apart

14 זָקֵן וּכְסִיל אֲשֶׁר לֹא־יָדַע לְהִזָּהֵר עוֹד׃ כִּי־מִבֵּית הָסוּרִים
the the from For any to (how) does not who and old
imprisoned of house .more warned be know foolish

15 יָצָא לִמְלֹךְ כִּי גַּם בְּמַלְכוּתוֹ נוֹלַד רָשׁ׃ רָאִיתִי אֶת־כָּל־
all saw I .poor was he his in although be to he
born kingdom ;king goes

הַחַיִּים הַמְהַלְּכִים תַּחַת הַשָּׁמֶשׁ עִם הַיֶּלֶד הַשֵּׁנִי אֲשֶׁר
who second the with ,sun the under walk who the
child living

16 יַעֲמֹד תַּחְתָּיו׃ אֵין־קֵץ לְכָל־הָעָם לְכֹל אֲשֶׁר־הָיָה לִפְנֵיהֶם
before have who all to the to end There of instead stands
;them been ,people all no is .him

גַּם הָאַחֲרוֹנִים לֹא יִשְׂמְחוּ־בוֹ כִּי־גַם־זֶה הֶבֶל וְרַעְיוֹן רוּחַ׃
.wind and vanity this also Surely with shall not later the also
after striving (is) .him rejoice ones

17 שְׁמֹר רַגְלֶיךָ כַּאֲשֶׁר תֵּלֵךְ אֶל־בֵּית הָאֱלֹהִים וְקָרוֹב לִשְׁמֹעַ
,hear to draw and ,God the to you when your Guard
near of house go feet

מִתֵּת הַכְּסִילִים זָבַח כִּי־אֵינָם יוֹדְעִים לַעֲשׂוֹת רָע׃
.evil they that do they for a the (like) than
do know not ,sacrifice fools give to

CAP. V ה

CHAPTER 5

doing evil. [2] Do not be hasty on your mouth, and do not let your heart hurry to bring forth a word before God — for God (is) in Heaven, and you (are) on earth; therefore let your words be few. [3] For the dream comes through the multitude of business; and the stupid one's voice (is known) by the multitude of words. [4] When you vow a vow to God, do not wait to fulfill it. For (He) has no pleasure in the stupid. Fulfill that which you have vowed. [5] (It is) better that you should not vow, than that you should vow and not fulfill it. [6] Do not allow your mouth to cause your flesh to sin; do not say before the angel that it (was) an error. Why should God be angry over your voice and destroy the works of your hands? [7] For in the multitude of dreams even words and vanities abound; but fear God.

[8] If you see the oppression of the poor and removing of justice and righteousness in a province, do not marvel at the matter. For a high one over a high one is observing, and high ones (are) over them. [9] And the advantage of a land is for all; when a king has a field being tilled. [10] He who loves silver shall not be satisfied with silver, nor he who loves plenty (with) increase. This (is) also vanity. [11] When the good multiplies, those who eat them multiply; then what profit (is it) to the owners, except to see (it) with their eyes? [12] The sleep of the one serving (is) sweet, whether he eats little or much; but the abundance of the rich will not allow him to sleep. [13] There is a painful evil

1 אַל־תְּבַהֵל עַל־פִּיךָ וְלִבְּךָ אַל־יְמַהֵר לְהוֹצִיא דָבָר לִפְנֵי
before a bring to do not your and your with be Do not
word forth hurry heart ,mouth hasty

הָאֱלֹהִים כִּי הָאֱלֹהִים בַּשָּׁמַיִם וְאַתָּה עַל־הָאָרֶץ עַל־כֵּן
therefore the (are) and Heaven in God for —God
;earth on you (is)

2 יִהְיוּ דְבָרֶיךָ מְעַטִּים: כִּי בָּא הַחֲלוֹם בְּרֹב עִנְיָן וְקוֹל כְּסִיל
fool's a and ; the the by the comes For .few your let
voice task of greatness dream words be

3 בְּרֹב דְּבָרִים: כַּאֲשֶׁר תִּדֹּר נֶדֶר לֵאלֹהִים אַל־תְּאַחֵר לְשַׁלְּמוֹ
fulfill to do not ,God to vow a you When .words the by
,it delay vow of greatness

4 כִּי אֵין חֵפֶץ בַּכְּסִילִים אֵת אֲשֶׁר־תִּדֹּר שַׁלֵּם: טוֹב אֲשֶׁר
that (is It) fulfill have you that ;fools in pleasure He for
better .(it) ,vowed which no has

5 לֹא־תִדֹּר מִשֶּׁתִּדּוֹר וְלֹא תְשַׁלֵּם: אַל־תִּתֵּן אֶת־פִּיךָ לַחֲטִיא
cause to your Do not fulfill and you that than you not
sin to mouth give .(it) not vow should ,vow should

6 אֶת־בְּשָׂרֶךָ וְאַל־תֹּאמַר לִפְנֵי הַמַּלְאָךְ כִּי שְׁגָגָה הִיא לָמָּה
Why it an that the before do and your
.(was) error angel say not ,flesh

יִקְצֹף הָאֱלֹהִים עַל־קוֹלֶךָ וְחִבֵּל אֶת־מַעֲשֵׂה יָדֶיךָ: כִּי בְרֹב
the in For your the and your at God should
of host ?hands of works destroy voice angry be

7 חֲלֹמוֹת וַהֲבָלִים וּדְבָרִים הַרְבֵּה כִּי אֶת־הָאֱלֹהִים יְרָא:
.fear God but ;abound words and both dreams
vanities

8 אִם־עֹשֶׁק רָשׁ וְגֵזֶל מִשְׁפָּט וָצֶדֶק תִּרְאֶה בַמְּדִינָה אַל־
not the in you and justice the or the op- the If
,province see righteousness of removing poor of pression

תִּתְמַהּ עַל־הַחֵפֶץ כִּי גָבֹהַּ מֵעַל גָּבֹהַּ שֹׁמֵר וּגְבֹהִים עֲלֵיהֶם:
over (are) high and is high a over high a for the at be do
.them ones ,watching one one ,matter amazed

8
9 וְיִתְרוֹן אֶרֶץ בַּכֹּל הִיא מֶלֶךְ לְשָׂדֶה נֶעֱבָד: אֹהֵב כֶּסֶף לֹא־
not silver who He being a has a ;(is) it in ,land a the And
loves .tilled field king all of advantage

יִשְׂבַּע כֶּסֶף וּמִי־אֹהֵב בֶּהָמוֹן לֹא תְבוּאָה גַּם־זֶה הָבֶל:
.vanity this Also (with) not riches he and ,silver be will
(is) ?gain loves who with satisfied

10 בִּרְבוֹת הַטּוֹבָה רַבּוּ אוֹכְלֶיהָ וּמַה־כִּשְׁרוֹן לִבְעָלֶיהָ כִּי
its to profit then who those increase the When
owners (it is) what ;it devour ,thing good increases

11 אִם־רְאוּת עֵינָיו: מְתוּקָה שְׁנַת הָעֹבֵד אִם־מְעַט וְאִם־
or little whether the sleep the (is) his with to except
.man laboring of sweet ?eyes (it) see

12 הַרְבֵּה יֹאכֵל וְהַשָּׂבָע לֶעָשִׁיר אֵינֶנּוּ מַנִּיחַ לוֹ לִישׁוֹן: יֵשׁ
There to him will not the of the but ;eats he much
is .sleep rest rich abundance

(which) I have seen under the sun: riches being kept for their owner to his evil. [14] But those riches perish by an evil use. And he brings forth a son, and nothing (is) in his hand. [15] As he came forth from his mother's womb naked, he turns back to go as he came. And from his labor he may not carry anything which may go in his hand. [16] And this also (is) a painful evil, (that) in all as he came, so shall he go. And what profit (is) to him who has labored for the wind? [17] Also all his days he eats in darkness, and with much sorrow, and his sickness and anger!

[18] See what I have seen: (It is) good (and) right (for one) to eat and to drink, and to see good in all his labor that he labors under the sun the number of the days of his life, which God gives to him — for it (is) his portion. [19] Also every man to whom God has given riches and wealth, and He has given him power to eat of it and to bear his portion, and to rejoice in his labor — this (is) the gift of God. [20] For he shall not much remember the days of his life, because God answers (him) in the joy of his heart.

רָעָה חוֹלָה רָאִיתִי תַּחַת הַשָּׁמֶשׁ עֹשֶׁר שָׁמוּר לִבְעָלָיו
its owner for kept riches ;sun the under I (which) seen have a sickly evil

13 לְרָעָתוֹ׃ וְאָבַד הָעֹשֶׁר הַהוּא בְּעִנְיַן רָע וְהוֹלִיד בֵּן וְאֵין
and is not ,son a he and fathers ,evil an by task those riches But perish his to .evil

14 בְּיָדוֹ מְאוּמָה׃ כַּאֲשֶׁר יָצָא מִבֶּטֶן אִמּוֹ עָרוֹם יָשׁוּב לָלֶכֶת
go to he return shall ,naked his mother's from womb he forth came As .anything his in hand

15 כְּשֶׁבָּא וּמְאוּמָה לֹא־יִשָּׂא בַעֲמָלוֹ שֶׁיֵּלֵךְ בְּיָדוֹ׃ וְגַם־זֹה
this And (is) also his in .hand may that go his in toil may he not carry and anything he as ;came

רָעָה חוֹלָה כָּל־עֻמַּת שֶׁבָּא כֵּן יֵלֵךְ וּמַה־יִּתְרוֹן לוֹ שֶׁיַּעֲמֹל
has who labored to him profit And what shall .go he so he came as (in) all a ,sickly evil

16 לָרוּחַ׃ גַּם כָּל־יָמָיו בַּחֹשֶׁךְ יֹאכֵל וְכַעַס הַרְבֵּה וְחָלְיוֹ
his and sickness ,much with grief he ,eats in darkness his days all Also the for ?wind

17 וָקָצֶף׃ הִנֵּה אֲשֶׁר־רָאִיתִי אָנִי טוֹב אֲשֶׁר־יָפֶה לֶאֱכוֹל
eat to (is it) that beautiful (is It) good .I seen have what Behold and .wrath

וְלִשְׁתּוֹת וְלִרְאוֹת טוֹבָה בְּכָל־עֲמָלוֹ ׀ שֶׁיַּעֲמֹל תַּחַת־הַשֶּׁמֶשׁ
sun the under he that labors his labor in all good to and see to and drink

מִסְפַּר יְמֵי־חַיָּו אֲשֶׁר־נָתַן־לוֹ הָאֱלֹהִים כִּי־הוּא חֶלְקוֹ׃
his .portion it (is) for —God to him gives which his life the of days the of number

18 גַּם כָּל־הָאָדָם אֲשֶׁר נָתַן־לוֹ הָאֱלֹהִים עֹשֶׁר וּנְכָסִים
and ,treasures riches God to him has given whom man every Also

וְהִשְׁלִיטוֹ לֶאֱכֹל מִמֶּנּוּ וְלָשֵׂאת אֶת־חֶלְקוֹ וְלִשְׂמֹחַ בַּעֲמָלוֹ
his in —labor to and rejoice his ,portion to and take it of eat to him gives and power

19 זֹה מַתַּת אֱלֹהִים הִיא׃ כִּי לֹא הַרְבֵּה יִזְכֹּר אֶת־יְמֵי חַיָּיו
his ;life the of days shall he remember much not For It (is) .God the of gift this

כִּי הָאֱלֹהִים מַעֲנֶה בְּשִׂמְחַת לִבּוֹ׃
his .heart the in of joy .to causes respond God for

CAP. VI ו

CHAPTER 6

[1] There is an evil that I have seen under the sun, and it (is) great among men — [2] a man to whom God has given riches, and wealth and honor, so that he lacks nothing for his soul of all that he desires, yet God does not give him

1 יֵשׁ רָעָה אֲשֶׁר רָאִיתִי תַּחַת הַשָּׁמֶשׁ וְרַבָּה הִיא עַל־הָאָדָם׃
—men upon (is) it and great ,sun the under have I seen which an evil There is

2 אִישׁ אֲשֶׁר יִתֶּן־לוֹ הָאֱלֹהִים עֹשֶׁר וּנְכָסִים וְכָבוֹד וְאֵינֶנּוּ
that so nothing and ,honor and treasures ,riches God to him has given whom a man

חָסֵר לְנַפְשׁוֹ ׀ מִכֹּל אֲשֶׁר־יִתְאַוֶּה וְלֹא־יַשְׁלִיטֶנּוּ הָאֱלֹהִים
God give power does yet him not he ,desires that all of his for soul he lacks

לֶאֱכֹל מִמֶּנּוּ כִּי אִישׁ נָכְרִי יֹאכְלֶנּוּ זֶה הֶבֶל וָחֳלִי רָע הוּא׃
.(is) it an and ,vanity this eats foreign a but ,it of eat to
evil disease (is) —it man

3 אִם־יוֹלִיד אִישׁ מֵאָה וְשָׁנִים רַבּוֹת יִחְיֶה וְרַב ׀ שֶׁיִּהְיוּ
that so ,lives many and hundred a a fathers If
are many years (children) man

יְמֵי־שָׁנָיו וְנַפְשׁוֹ לֹא־תִשְׂבַּע מִן־הַטּוֹבָה וְגַם־קְבוּרָה לֹא־
not burial and the from is not his and his the
also ,good satisfied soul ,years of days

4 הָיְתָה לּוֹ אָמַרְתִּי טוֹב מִמֶּנּוּ הַנָּפֶל׃ כִּי־בַהֶבֶל בָּא וּבַחֹשֶׁךְ
in and he with For the than (is) ,say I for is
darkness enters vanity .miscarriage he better ,him

5 יֵלֵךְ וּבַחֹשֶׁךְ שְׁמוֹ יְכֻסֶּה׃ גַּם־שֶׁמֶשׁ לֹא־רָאָה וְלֹא יָדָע
has and has he not sun the Also be shall his in and he
;known not seen .covered name darkness ,goes

6 נַחַת לָזֶה מִזֶּה׃ וְאִלּוּ חָיָה אֶלֶף שָׁנִים פַּעֲמַיִם וְטוֹבָה
good yet ,twice years a he if Even than to more
thousand lives .this this (is) rest

7 לֹא רָאָה הֲלֹא אֶל־מָקוֹם אֶחָד הַכֹּל הוֹלֵךְ׃ כָּל־עֲמַל הָאָדָם
(is) man the All ?go all one place to (do) he not
of labor not —seen has

8 לְפִיהוּ וְגַם־הַנֶּפֶשׁ לֹא תִמָּלֵא׃ כִּי מַה־יּוֹתֵר לֶחָכָם מִן־
more the to advantage what For .filled is not soul the and his for
than wise yet ,mouth

9 הַכְּסִיל מַה־לֶּעָנִי יוֹדֵעַ לַהֲלֹךְ נֶגֶד הַחַיִּים׃ טוֹב מַרְאֵה
the Better the before (how) knowing the to what ;fool the
of sight (is) ?living walk to poor

10 עֵינַיִם מֵהֲלָךְ־נָפֶשׁ גַּם־זֶה הֶבֶל וּרְעוּת רוּחַ׃ מַה־שֶּׁהָיָה
Whatever (after) and vanity this Also the the than eyes the
been has wind striving (is) .soul of wandering

כְּבָר נִקְרָא שְׁמוֹ וְנוֹדָע אֲשֶׁר־הוּא אָדָם וְלֹא־יוּכַל לָדִין
to is he and ;man he that it and its was already
contend able not (is) known is ,name called

11 עִם שֶׁהַתַּקִּיף מִמֶּנּוּ׃ כִּי יֵשׁ־דְּבָרִים הַרְבֵּה מַרְבִּים הָבֶל
,vanity that many things there Since than that Him with
increase are .he stronger is

12 מַה־יֹּתֵר לָאָדָם׃ כִּי מִי־יוֹדֵעַ מַה־טּוֹב לָאָדָם בַּחַיִּים
(this) in man for (is) what knows who For ?man to the what
,life good advantage (is)

מִסְפַּר יְמֵי־חַיֵּי הֶבְלוֹ וְיַעֲשֵׂם כַּצֵּל אֲשֶׁר מִי־יַגִּיד לָאָדָם
man a can who For the as he and his life the the
tell .shadow them does ;vain of days of number

מַה־יִּהְיֶה אַחֲרָיו תַּחַת הַשָּׁמֶשׁ׃
?sun the under after shall what
him be

power to eat of it, but a stranger eats it — this (is) vanity, and it is an evil disease. [3] If a man fathers a hundred (children), and lives many years, and the days of his years are many, and his soul is not filled with the good, and also no burial is for him; I say, an untimely birth (is) better than he. [4] For he comes in with vanity and goes out in darkness, and his name shall be covered in darkness. [5] Also he has not seen nor known the sun; this (one) has more rest than this. [6] Yea, though he lives twice a thousand years, yet he has seen no good. Do not all go to one place? [7] All the labor of man (is) for his mouth, and yet the soul is not filled. [8] For what (is) the advantage to the wise more than the stupid? What (gain) to the poor who knows (how) to walk before the living?

[9] Better (is) the sight of the eyes than the wandering of the soul. This (is) also vanity and vexation of spirit. [10] That which has been is named already, and it is known that he (is) man, and he is not able to contend with Him who prevails over him.

[11] For there are many things that increase vanity, what (is) to man the advantage? [12] For who knows what (is) good for man in (this) life, the number of the days of his vain life; and he spends them as a shadow? For who can tell a man what shall be after him under the sun?

CAP. VII ז

CHAPTER 7

1
2 טוֹב שֵׁם מִשֶּׁמֶן טוֹב וְיוֹם הַמָּוֶת מִיּוֹם הִוָּלְדוֹ׃ טוֹב
(is It) one's the than death the and ,good than (good) a Better
better .birth of day of day oil name (is)

CHAPTER 7

[1] A (good) name (is) better than good ointment, and the day of death than the day of (one's) birth.

[2] (It is) better to go to

the house of mourning than to go to the house of feasting, for it (is) the end of every man, and the living will lay (it) to his heart. [3] Sorrow (is) better than laughter; for by the sadness of the face the heart is made good. [4] The heart of the wise (is) in the house of mourning; but the heart of the stupid (is) in the house of mirth. [5] (It is) better to hear the rebuke of the wise than for a man to hear the song of the stupid one. [6] For as the crackling of thorns under a pot, so (is) the laughter of the fool and this also (is) vanity.

[7] Surely oppression makes a wise man mad; and a bribe destroys the heart. [8] Better (is) the end of a thing than the beginning of it; (and) the patient in spirit (is) better than the proud in spirit. [9] Do not be hasty in your spirit to be vexed; for anger rests in the bosom of the stupid. [10] Do not say, Why was (it) that the former days were better than these? For you do not ask from wisdom in regard to this.

[11] Wisdom (is) good with an inheritance, yea, a gain to those who see the sun. [12] For wisdom (is) in a shadow, (and) money is in a shadow; but the excellency of knowledge is (that) wisdom gives life to those who have it. [13] Consider the work of God; for who can make that straight which He has made crooked? [14] In the day of prosperity be joyful, but in the day of evil take note that God also has made this along with this on the matter that man should not find anything after him. [15] All (things) I have seen in the days of my vanity: there is a just (man) who perishes in his righteousness, and there

לָלֶכֶת אֶל־בֵּית־אֵבֶל מִלֶּכֶת אֶל־בֵּית מִשְׁתֶּה בַּאֲשֶׁר הוּא
that (is) because ,feasting the of house to go to than mourn-ing the of house to go to

3 סוֹף כָּל־הָאָדָם וְהַחַי יִתֵּן אֶל־לִבּוֹ׃ טוֹב כַּעַס מִשְּׂחוֹק
than ,laughter Vexation (is) better his .heart to will (it) lay the and living ;man every the of end

4 כִּי־בְרֹעַ פָּנִים יִיטַב לֵב׃ לֵב חֲכָמִים בְּבֵית אֵבֶל וְלֵב
the but of heart mourn- ,ing the in of house the (is) wise The of heart the .heart made is good the face by for of sadness

5 כְּסִילִים בְּבֵית שִׂמְחָה׃ טוֹב לִשְׁמֹעַ גַּעֲרַת חָכָם מֵאִישׁ
a than man the wise the of rebuke hear to (is It) better .mirth the in of house fools (is)

6 שֹׁמֵעַ שִׁיר כְּסִילִים׃ כִּי כְקוֹל הַסִּירִים תַּחַת הַסִּיר כֵּן
so (is) ,pot a under thorns the like of sound For .fools the of song hearing

7 שְׂחֹק הַכְּסִיל וְגַם־זֶה הָבֶל׃ כִּי הָעֹשֶׁק יְהוֹלֵל חָכָם
wise a ;man makes mad oppression For .vanity this and (is) also the ;fool the of laughter

8 וִיאַבֵּד אֶת־לֵב מַתָּנָה׃ טוֹב אַחֲרִית דָּבָר מֵרֵאשִׁיתוֹ טוֹב
better is its than ;beginning a thing end the of Better (is(.bribe a the heart and destroys

9 אֶרֶךְ־רוּחַ מִגְּבַהּ רוּחַ׃ אַל־תְּבַהֵל בְּרוּחֲךָ לִכְעוֹס כִּי
for be to ,angry your in spirit be do hasty not .spirit the than in proud spirit the of long

10 כַעַס בְּחֵיק כְּסִילִים יָנוּחַ׃ אַל־תֹּאמַר מֶה הָיָה שֶׁהַיָּמִים
the that days was it Why ,say Do not .rests fools the in of bosom vex-ation

הָרִאשֹׁנִים הָיוּ טוֹבִים מֵאֵלֶּה כִּי לֹא מֵחָכְמָה שָׁאַלְתָּ עַל־
to as you do ask from wisdom not For than ?these better were former

11
12 זֶה׃ טוֹבָה חָכְמָה עִם־נַחֲלָה וְיֹתֵר לְרֹאֵי הַשָּׁמֶשׁ׃ כִּי
For .sun the those to see who an and advantage an inheritance with Wisdom (is) good .this

בְּצֵל הַחָכְמָה בְּצֵל הַכָּסֶף וְיִתְרוֹן דַּעַת הַחָכְמָה תְּחַיֶּה
gives to life (that is) wisdom knowledge the but of profit (is) ,silver a in (and) shadow (is) wisdom a in shadow

13 בְעָלֶיהָ׃ רְאֵה אֶת־מַעֲשֵׂה הָאֱלֹהִים כִּי מִי יוּכַל לְתַקֵּן
to straighten able is who For ;God the of work Consider its .possessors

14 אֵת אֲשֶׁר עִוְּתוֹ׃ בְּיוֹם טוֹבָה הֱיֵה בְטוֹב וּבְיוֹם רָעָה רְאֵה
consider evil in but day the good in (.spirit) be good the On day has He ?bent that which

גַּם אֶת־זֶה לְעֻמַּת־זֶה עָשָׂה הָאֱלֹהִים עַל־דִּבְרַת שֶׁלֹּא
that not the upon ,matter God has made this along with this ,also

15 יִמְצָא הָאָדָם אַחֲרָיו מְאוּמָה׃ אֶת־הַכֹּל רָאִיתִי בִּימֵי
the in of days have I seen All (things) .anything after him man should find

הֶבְלִי יֵשׁ צַדִּיק אֹבֵד בְּצִדְקוֹ וְיֵשׁ רָשָׁע מַאֲרִיךְ בְּרָעָתוֹ׃
his in .wickedness pro- (life) longs who man wicked a is there and righ- his in teousness who perishes just a man there is my vanity

is a wicked (man) who prolongs (his life) in his wickedness. [16] Do not be overrighteous, nor make yourself overwise — why should you destroy yourself? [17] Do not be overly wicked, and do not be a fool — why should you die without your time? [18] (It is) good that you should take hold of this; yea, also from this do not let rest your hand. For he who fears God shall come forth with all of them. [19] Wisdom makes the wise stronger, more than ten rulers who are in the city. [20] For (there is) not a just man on the earth that does good and sins not. [21] Also give not your heart to all the words they speak, lest you hear your servant cursing you. [22] For also your own heart knows that you yourself have also cursed others many times. [23] All this I have proved by wisdom: I said, I will be wise; but it (was) far from me. [24] That which is far off and exceeding deep, who can find it out? [25] And I turned my heart about, to know, and to search, and to seek out wisdom, and the reason (of things), and to know the wickedness of folly, even the foolishness of madness: [26] and I found more bitter than death the woman whose heart (is) snares and nets, (and) her hands (like) bonds. He who is good before God shall escape from her, but the sinner shall be taken by her. [27] See, this I have found, says the Preacher, (counting) one to one, to find out the sum — [28] that my soul still is seeking, but I had not found — one man among a thousand I have found, but a woman among all those I have not found. [29] See,

16 אַל־תְּהִי צַדִּיק הַרְבֵּה וְאַל־תִּתְחַכַּם יוֹתֵר לָמָּה תִּשּׁוֹמֵם׃
destroy why ;overly make and much righteous be not
,yourself wise yourself not

17 אַל־תִּרְשַׁע הַרְבֵּה וְאַל־תְּהִי סָכָל לָמָּה תָמוּת בְּלֹא עִתֶּךָ׃
your before should why —fool a be and much be do not
?time die you not wicked

18 טוֹב אֲשֶׁר תֶּאֱחֹז בָּזֶה וְגַם־מִזֶּה אַל־תַּנַּח אֶת־יָדֶךָ כִּי־יְרֵא
who he For your do not from and this you that (is it)
fears .hand rest let this also grasp should good

19 אֱלֹהִים יֵצֵא אֶת־כֻּלָּם׃ הַחָכְמָה תָּעֹז לֶחָכָם מֵעֲשָׂרָה
than the makes Wisdom of all with shall God
ten wise stronger .them forth come

20 שַׁלִּיטִים אֲשֶׁר הָיוּ בָּעִיר׃ כִּי אָדָם אֵין צַדִּיק בָּאָרֶץ אֲשֶׁר
who the on righteous there a For the in are who rulers
earth not is man .city

21 יַעֲשֶׂה־טּוֹב וְלֹא יֶחֱטָא׃ גַּם לְכָל־הַדְּבָרִים אֲשֶׁר יְדַבֵּרוּ
they which the to Also does and good does
speak words all .sin not

22 אַל־תִּתֵּן לִבֶּךָ אֲשֶׁר לֹא־תִשְׁמַע אֶת־עַבְדְּךָ מְקַלְלֶךָ׃ כִּי
For cursing your you not that your do not
.you servant hear may heart give

גַּם־פְּעָמִים רַבּוֹת יָדַע לִבֶּךָ אֲשֶׁר גַּם־אַתְּ* קִלַּלְתָּ אֲחֵרִים׃
.others have you also that your knows many times also
cursed heart

23 כָּל־זֹה נִסִּיתִי בַחָכְמָה אָמַרְתִּי אֶחְכָּמָה וְהִיא רְחוֹקָה
far (was) it but be will I said I :wisdom by have I this All
;wise tested

24 25 מִמֶּנִּי׃ רָחוֹק מַה־שֶּׁהָיָה וְעָמֹק ׀ עָמֹק מִי יִמְצָאֶנּוּ׃ סַבּוֹתִי
turned find can who exceeding and Whatever off far from
about ?it ,deep is .me

אֲנִי וְלִבִּי לָדַעַת וְלָתוּר וּבַקֵּשׁ חָכְמָה וְחֶשְׁבּוֹן וְלָדַעַת
to and the and wisdom to and to and know to my even I
know reckoning seek investigate heart

26 רֶשַׁע כֶּסֶל וְהַסִּכְלוּת הוֹלֵלוֹת׃ וּמוֹצֶא אֲנִי מַר מִמָּוֶת
than more I And .madness the and ,folly wick- the
death bitter found of foolishness of edness

אֶת־הָאִשָּׁה אֲשֶׁר־הִיא מְצוֹדִים וַחֲרָמִים לִבָּהּ אֲסוּרִים
(are and) her (for) nets and snares she of woman the
bonds heart (has) whom

יָדֶיהָ טוֹב לִפְנֵי הָאֱלֹהִים יִמָּלֵט מִמֶּנָּה וְחוֹטֵא יִלָּכֶד בָּהּ׃
.her by be will the but from shall God before good a her
captured sinner ,her escape man .hands

27 רְאֵה זֶה מָצָאתִי אָמְרָה קֹהֶלֶת אַחַת לְאַחַת לִמְצֹא
to one by (adding) the says have I this ,Behold
out find one ,Preacher found

28 חֶשְׁבּוֹן׃ אֲשֶׁר עוֹד־בִּקְשָׁה נַפְשִׁי וְלֹא מָצָאתִי אָדָם אֶחָד
one man have I but ,soul my seeks still that the
:found not ;sum

29 מֵאֶלֶף מָצָאתִי וְאִשָּׁה בְכָל־אֵלֶּה לֹא מָצָאתִי׃ לְבַד רְאֵה
Behold only have I not these among a but have I a among
.found all woman ,found thousand

this only I have found, that God has made man upright, but they have sought out many inventions.

זֶה מָצָאתִי אֲשֶׁר עָשָׂה הָאֱלֹהִים אֶת־הָאָדָם יָשָׁר וְהֵמָּה
they but ,upright man God has that have I this
made ,found
בִקְשׁוּ חִשְּׁבֹנוֹת רַבִּים׃
.many inventions have
out sought

CAP. VIII ח

CHAPTER 8

CHAPTER 8

[1] Who (is) as the wise (man)? And who knows the meaning of a thing? A man's wisdom makes his face shine, and the hardness of his face is changed. [2] I beg you, keep the king's commandment, even on the matter of the oath of God, [3] do not be hasty to go from before him. Do not take a stand in an evil thing; for he does whatever he pleases. [4] Because of the word of a king, (there is) power, and who may say to him, What are you doing? [5] Whoever keeps the commandment shall know no evil thing; a wise man's heart knows both time and judgment. [6] Because to every purpose there is a time and judgment, therefore the evil of man (is) great upon him. [7] For he does not know what shall be; for who can tell him when it shall be? [8] Man is not a ruler over the spirit to restrain the spirit; nor rules in the day of death; and (there is) no discharge in (that) war, nor shall wickedness deliver its possessors. [9] All this I have seen, (and) I gave my heart to every work that is done under the sun: (there is) a time (in) which a man rules over a man for his evil. [10] And so I saw the wicked buried, and they came and went from the place of the holy, and was forgotten in the city, (that) which they had done; this (is) also vanity. [11] Where sentence (on)

1 מִי כְּהֶחָכָם וּמִי יוֹדֵעַ פֵּשֶׁר דָּבָר חָכְמַת אָדָם תָּאִיר פָּנָיו
his makes A wisdom ?thing a inter- the knows or the like Who
,face shine man's of pretation who ,man wise (is)
2 וְעֹז פָּנָיו יְשֻׁנֶּא׃ אֲנִי פִּי־מֶלֶךְ שְׁמֹר וְעַל דִּבְרַת שְׁבוּעַת
the the even ,Keep the mouth I is face his and
of oath of matter on king's ,(say) .changed hardness
3 אֱלֹהִים׃ אַל־תִּבָּהֵל מִפָּנָיו תֵּלֵךְ אַל־תַּעֲמֹד בְּדָבָר רָע
;evil a with do not ;go to his from be Do not .God
matter stand presence hasty
4 כִּי כָל־אֲשֶׁר יַחְפֹּץ יַעֲשֶׂה׃ בַּאֲשֶׁר דְּבַר־מֶלֶךְ שִׁלְטוֹן וּמִי
who which that the the Because .does he he that all for
then ,power has (is) king of word pleases
5 יֹאמַר־לוֹ מַה־תַּעֲשֶׂה׃ שׁוֹמֵר מִצְוָה לֹא יֵדַע דָּבָר רָע וְעֵת
both ;evil a shall not the Whoever you are What to will
time thing know command keeps ?doing ,him say
6 וּמִשְׁפָּט יֵדַע לֵב חָכָם׃ כִּי לְכָל־חֵפֶץ יֵשׁ עֵת וּמִשְׁפָּט
and a there purpose to Because wise a heart knows and
,judgment time is every .man's judgment
7 כִּי־רָעַת הָאָדָם רַבָּה עָלָיו׃ כִּי־אֵינֶנּוּ יֹדֵעַ מַה־שֶּׁיִּהְיֶה כִּי
for shall what does he For upon (is) man the for
,be know not .him great of evil
8 כַּאֲשֶׁר יִהְיֶה מִי יַגִּיד לוֹ׃ אֵין אָדָם שַׁלִּיט בָּרוּחַ לִכְלוֹא
to the over ruler a man Not to can who shall it when
restrain ,spirit is him tell be
אֶת־הָרוּחַ וְאֵין שִׁלְטוֹן בְּיוֹם הַמָּוֶת וְאֵין מִשְׁלַחַת
discharge and ;death the in which that and the
is not of day power has is not ;spirit
9 בַּמִּלְחָמָה וְלֹא־יְמַלֵּט רֶשַׁע אֶת־בְּעָלָיו׃ אֶת־כָּל־זֶה רָאִיתִי
have I this All its wicked- shall and the in
,seen .possessors ness deliver not ;war
וְנָתוֹן אֶת־לִבִּי לְכָל־מַעֲשֶׂה אֲשֶׁר נַעֲשָׂה תַּחַת הַשָּׁמֶשׁ עֵת
(a is) ;sun the under done is that work to my and
time every heart gave
10 אֲשֶׁר שָׁלַט הָאָדָם בְּאָדָם לְרַע לוֹ׃ וּבְכֵן רָאִיתִי רְשָׁעִים
the saw I in And to for man a man rules (in)
wicked this .him evil over which
קְבֻרִים וָבָאוּ וּמִמְּקוֹם קָדוֹשׁ יְהַלֵּכוּ וְיִשְׁתַּכְּחוּ בָעִיר אֲשֶׁר
(these) the in and ,went holy from and they and ,buried
,things ,city forgotten were place the came
11 כֵּן־עָשׂוּ גַּם־זֶה הָבֶל׃ אֲשֶׁר אֵין־נַעֲשָׂה פִתְגָם מַעֲשֵׂה
a (on) a is not Where .vanity this also they thus
work sentence executed (is) —done had

an evil work is not executed speedily, therefore the heart of the sons of men is fully set in them to do evil.

[12] Though a sinner does evil a hundred (times), and (his days) prolonged to him, yet surely I know that it shall be good to those who fear God, who fear before Him. [13] But it shall not be good for the wicked, nor shall he make (his) days longer like a shadow; because he does not fear before God. [14] There is a vanity which is done on the earth: that there are just (men) to whom it happens according to the work of the wicked. And there are wicked men to whom it happens according to the work of the righteous — I said that this also is vanity. [15] Then I praised mirth because nothing is good for man under the sun except to eat, and to drink and to be glad; for that shall go with him in his labor for the days of his life which God gives him under the sun.

[16] When I gave my heart to know wisdom, and to see the business that is done on the earth — for even by day and by night he does not see sleep in his eyes — [17] then I looked at all the work of God, that a man cannot find out the work that is done under the sun; because though a man labors to seek (it) out, yet he shall not find it. And even if the wise (man) speaks of knowing (it), (yet) he shall not be able to find (it).

הָרָעָה מְהֵרָה עַל־כֵּן מָלֵא לֵב בְּנֵי־הָאָדָם בָּהֶם לַעֲשׂוֹת

do to them | in | men | the of sons | the of heart | is filled | therefore | ,speedily | evil

12 רָע׃ אֲשֶׁר חֹטֶא עֹשֶׂה רָע מְאַת וּמַאֲרִיךְ לוֹ כִּי גַּם־יוֹדֵעַ

know also | yet | to ,him | (days) long are | and (times) hundred | a | evil | does | sinner | a Though | .evil

אָנִי אֲשֶׁר יִהְיֶה־טּוֹב לְיִרְאֵי הָאֱלֹהִים אֲשֶׁר יִירְאוּ מִלְּפָנָיו׃

before ,Him | fear | who | ,God | those with fear who | well | will it be | that | I

13 וְטוֹב לֹא־יִהְיֶה לָרָשָׁע וְלֹא־יַאֲרִיךְ יָמִים כַּצֵּל אֲשֶׁר אֵינֶנּוּ

he not | because | a like ;shadow | (his) days | shall he lengthen | and not | the for ,wicked | will it be | not | But well

14 יָרֵא מִלִּפְנֵי אֱלֹהִים׃ יֶשׁ־הֶבֶל אֲשֶׁר נַעֲשָׂה עַל־הָאָרֶץ

the :earth | on | done is | which | a vanity | There is | .God | before | does fear

אֲשֶׁר ׀ יֵשׁ צַדִּיקִים אֲשֶׁר מַגִּיעַ אֲלֵהֶם כְּמַעֲשֵׂה הָרְשָׁעִים

the .wicked's | according works to | it them | whom touches | just men | there are | that

וְיֵשׁ רְשָׁעִים שֶׁמַּגִּיעַ אֲלֵהֶם כְּמַעֲשֵׂה הַצַּדִּיקִים אָמַרְתִּי

said I | the .righteous' | according works to | to them | whom to touches it | wicked men | And are there

15 שֶׁגַּם־זֶה הָבֶל׃ וְשִׁבַּחְתִּי אֲנִי אֶת־הַשִּׂמְחָה אֲשֶׁר אֵין

not is | because | ,mirth | I | Then commended | .vanity | this (is) | that also

טוֹב לָאָדָם תַּחַת הַשֶּׁמֶשׁ כִּי אִם־לֶאֱכֹל וְלִשְׁתּוֹת וְלִשְׂמוֹחַ

to and ,rejoice | to and drink | eat to | except | sun the | under | for man | good

וְהוּא יִלְוֶנּוּ בַעֲמָלוֹ יְמֵי חַיָּיו אֲשֶׁר־נָתַן־לוֹ הָאֱלֹהִים תַּחַת

under | God | to him | gives | which | his life | the of days | his in labor | lodges him with | for that

16 הַשָּׁמֶשׁ׃ כַּאֲשֶׁר נָתַתִּי אֶת־לִבִּי לָדַעַת חָכְמָה וְלִרְאוֹת

to and see | ,wisdom | know to | my heart | gave I | When | .sun the

אֶת־הָעִנְיָן אֲשֶׁר נַעֲשָׂה עַל־הָאָרֶץ כִּי גַם בַּיּוֹם וּבַלַּיְלָה

by and night | by day | even for | the -earth | on | done is | which | the task

17 שֵׁנָה בְּעֵינָיו אֵינֶנּוּ רֹאֶה׃ וְרָאִיתִי אֶת־כָּל־מַעֲשֵׂה הָאֱלֹהִים

,God | the of work | all | I then saw | —sees | he not | his in eyes | sleep

כִּי לֹא יוּכַל הָאָדָם לִמְצוֹא אֶת־הַמַּעֲשֶׂה אֲשֶׁר נַעֲשָׂה

done is | that | work the | find to out | man | able is | not | that

תַּחַת־הַשֶּׁמֶשׁ בְּשֶׁל אֲשֶׁר יַעֲמֹל הָאָדָם לְבַקֵּשׁ וְלֹא יִמְצָא

he will .(it) find | yet not | seek to ,out (it) | man | labors | which | for that | the ,sun | under

וְגַם אִם־יֹאמַר הֶחָכָם לָדַעַת לֹא יוּכַל לִמְצֹא׃

find to .(it) | is he able | (yet) not | of ,(it) knowing | wise the man | speaks | if | And even

CAP. IX ט

CHAPTER 9

[1] For all this I took to heart, even to explain all this, that the righteous and the wise and their works (are) in the hand of God. Whether love or hatred, man does not know all (that is) before them. [2] All (happens) alike to all: (there is) one event to the righteous and to the wicked; to the good and to the clean, and to the unclean; to him who sacrifices and to him who does not sacrifice; as (is) the good (man), so the sinner; (and) he who swears is as (he) who fears an oath. [3] This (is) an evil among all (things) that are done under the sun, that (there is) one event to all. Yea, also the heart of the sons of men is full of evil, and madness (is) in their heart through their lives, and after that (they go) to the dead. [4] For to him who is chosen to all the living there is hope – for a living dog is better than a dead lion. [5] For the living know that they shall die; but the dead do not know anything, nor do they have any more a reward; for their memory is forgotten. [6] Also their love, and their hatred, and their envy has now perished; nor do they any longer have a part forever in all that is done under the sun. [7] Go! Eat your bread with joy and drink your wine with a merry heart, for God now is pleased with your works. [8] Let your garments be white at every time; and let your head lack no ointment. [9] Look (upon) life with the wife whom you

CHAPTER 9

1 כִּי אֶת־כָּל־זֶה נָתַתִּי אֶל־לִבִּי וְלָבוּר אֶת־כָּל־זֶה אֲשֶׁר
that ,this all to even my to took I this all For
explain ,heart

הַצַּדִּיקִים וְהַחֲכָמִים וַעֲבָדֵיהֶם בְּיַד הָאֱלֹהִים גַּם־אַהֲבָה
love Also .God the in their and the and the
of hand (are) works ,wise ,righteous

2 גַּם־שִׂנְאָה אֵין יוֹדֵעַ הָאָדָם הַכֹּל לִפְנֵיהֶם׃ הַכֹּל כַּאֲשֶׁר
that All before all men do not ,hatred also
(happens) .them (is that) know

לַכֹּל מִקְרֶה אֶחָד לַצַּדִּיק וְלָרָשָׁע לַטּוֹב וְלַטָּהוֹר וְלַטָּמֵא
to and to and the to the to and the to one event (is)
,unclean the ,clean the ,good ;wicked ,righteous (is) ;all to

וְלַזֹּבֵחַ וְלַאֲשֶׁר אֵינֶנּוּ זֹבֵחַ כַּטּוֹב כַּחֹטֶא הַנִּשְׁבָּע כַּאֲשֶׁר
as the the so the as sacri- not is to and the to
whom swearer ;sinner good ;ficing him to whom ,sacrificer

3 שְׁבוּעָה יָרֵא׃ זֶה ׀ רָע בְּכֹל אֲשֶׁר־נַעֲשָׂה תַּחַת הַשֶּׁמֶשׁ
,sun the under (is that among an This oath an
done all evil (is) .fears

כִּי־מִקְרֶה אֶחָד לַכֹּל וְגַם לֵב בְּנֵי־הָאָדָם מָלֵא־רָע וְהוֹלֵלוֹת
and ;evil is men the the and to one event that
madness of full of sons of heart also ;all (is)

4 בִּלְבָבָם בְּחַיֵּיהֶם וְאַחֲרָיו אֶל־הַמֵּתִים׃ כִּי־מִי אֲשֶׁר יְבֻחַר
is whoever For the (go they) after and throughout their in
chosen .dead to that ,lives their heart

אֶל כָּל־הַחַיִּים יֵשׁ בִּטָּחוֹן כִּי־לְכֶלֶב חַי הוּא טוֹב מִן
than better it living a for —hope there the all to
(is) dog is ,living

5 הָאַרְיֵה הַמֵּת׃ כִּי הַחַיִּים יוֹדְעִים שֶׁיָּמֻתוּ וְהַמֵּתִים אֵינָם
they the but they that know the For .dead lion a
not ,dead ;die will living

יוֹדְעִים מְאוּמָה וְאֵין־עוֹד לָהֶם שָׂכָר כִּי נִשְׁכַּח זִכְרָם׃
their is for a for any and anything do
.memory forgotten ,reward them more is not know

6 גַּם אַהֲבָתָם גַּם־שִׂנְאָתָם גַּם־קִנְאָתָם כְּבָר אָבָדָה וְחֵלֶק
a and has already their and their and their Also
part ;perished envy hatred love

אֵין־לָהֶם עוֹד לְעוֹלָם בְּכֹל אֲשֶׁר־נַעֲשָׂה תַּחַת הַשָּׁמֶשׁ׃
.sun the under done is that all in forever any for not
more them is

7 לֵךְ אֱכֹל בְּשִׂמְחָה לַחְמֶךָ וּשְׁתֵה בְלֶב־טוֹב יֵינֶךָ כִּי כְבָר
already for your good a with and your with eat ,Go
,wine heart drink ,bread joy

8 רָצָה הָאֱלֹהִים אֶת־מַעֲשֶׂיךָ׃ בְּכָל־עֵת יִהְיוּ בְגָדֶיךָ לְבָנִים
;white your be let time At your with God is
garments every .works pleased

9 וְשֶׁמֶן עַל־רֹאשְׁךָ אַל־יֶחְסָר׃ רְאֵה חַיִּים עִם־אִשָּׁה אֲשֶׁר־
whom the with life Look be let not your upon and
wife (upon) .lacking head oil

love all the days of your life of your vanity, which He gave you under the sun, all the days of your vanity — for that (is) your share in (this) life, and in your labor which you labor under the sun. [10] Whatever your hand finds to do, do (it) with your might: for (there is) no work, or planning, or knowledge, or wisdom in Sheol, there where you go. [11] I returned and saw under the sun that the race (is) not to the swift, or the battle to the mighty, nor even bread to the wise, nor even riches to men of understanding, nor even favor to men of skill — for time and event meets with them all. [12] For man also does not know his time: as the fish that are taken in an evil net, and as the birds that are caught in the trap; like them (are) the sons of men snared in an evil time, when it falls suddenly upon them. [13] This wisdom I saw also under the sun, and it is great to me: [14] (There was) a little city, and few men in it, and a great king came against it and besieged it, and built huge siegeworks against it; [15] and there was found in it a poor wise man, and he by his wisdom delivered the city — yet no man remembered that poor man! [16] And I said, Wisdom (is) better than strength; still the poor man's wisdom is despised and his words are not heard. [17] The words of wise (men) are heard in rest more than the cry of one who rules among the stupid. [18] Wisdom (is) better

אֱהַבְתָּ כָּל־יְמֵי חַיֵּי הֶבְלֶךָ אֲשֶׁר נָתַן־לְךָ תַּחַת הַשֶּׁמֶשׁ כֹּל
all ;sun the under to He which your the the all you
you given has vanity of life of days love

יְמֵי הֶבְלֶךָ כִּי הוּא חֶלְקְךָ בַּחַיִּים וּבַעֲמָלְךָ אֲשֶׁר־אַתָּה עָמֵל
labor you which in and life in your that for your the
labor your share (is) —vanity of days

10 תַּחַת הַשָּׁמֶשׁ׃ כֹּל אֲשֶׁר תִּמְצָא יָדְךָ לַעֲשׂוֹת בְּכֹחֲךָ עֲשֵׂה
;(it) do (all) with ,do to your finds that All .sun the under
might your hand

כִּי אֵין מַעֲשֶׂה וְחֶשְׁבּוֹן וְדַעַת וְחָכְמָה בִּשְׁאוֹל אֲשֶׁר אַתָּה
you where ,Sheol in or or or ,work not for
,wisdom ,knowledge ,planning is

11 הֹלֵךְ שָׁמָּה׃ שַׁבְתִּי וְרָאֹה תַחַת־הַשֶּׁמֶשׁ כִּי לֹא לַקַּלִּים
the to not that sun the under and I .there go
swift saw returned

הַמֵּרוֹץ וְלֹא לַגִּבּוֹרִים הַמִּלְחָמָה וְגַם לֹא לַחֲכָמִים לֶחֶם
(is) the to not and the (is) the to and the (is)
,bread wise even ;battle mighty not ,race

וְגַם לֹא לַנְּבֹנִים עֹשֶׁר וְגַם לֹא לַיֹּדְעִים חֵן כִּי־עֵת וָפֶגַע
oc- and time for ;favor men to not and ,riches astute to not and
currence skill of even men even

12 יִקְרֶה אֶת־כֻּלָּם׃ כִּי גַּם לֹא־יֵדַע הָאָדָם אֶת־עִתּוֹ כַּדָּגִים
the as his man does not also For them to happen
fish ,time know .all

שֶׁנֶּאֱחָזִים בִּמְצוֹדָה רָעָה וְכַצִּפֳּרִים הָאֲחֻזוֹת בַּפָּח כָּהֵם
like the in are that the as and ,evil the in are that
them ;trap seized birds net seized

יוּקָשִׁים בְּנֵי הָאָדָם לְעֵת רָעָה כְּשֶׁתִּפּוֹל עֲלֵיהֶם פִּתְאֹם׃
.suddenly upon it when an time in men the are
them falls ,evil of sons snared

13 גַּם־זֹה רָאִיתִי חָכְמָה תַּחַת הַשָּׁמֶשׁ וּגְדוֹלָה הִיא אֵלָי׃
:me to (is) it great and ,sun the under (as) saw I this Also
wisdom

14 עִיר קְטַנָּה וַאֲנָשִׁים בָּהּ מְעָט וּבָא־אֵלֶיהָ מֶלֶךְ גָּדוֹל וְסָבַב
en- and great a against and ;few it in men and ,little A
circled king it came city

15 אֹתָהּ וּבָנָה עָלֶיהָ מְצוֹדִים גְּדֹלִים׃ וּמָצָא בָהּ אִישׁ מִסְכֵּן
poor a it in was and ;huge siegeworks against and ,it
man found it built

חָכָם וּמִלַּט־הוּא אֶת־הָעִיר בְּחָכְמָתוֹ וְאָדָם לֹא זָכַר אֶת־
remem- not yet his by the he and ;wise
bered man —wisdom city delivered

16 הָאִישׁ הַמִּסְכֵּן הַהוּא׃ וְאָמַרְתִּי אָנִי טוֹבָה חָכְמָה מִגְּבוּרָה
than Wisdom better ,I said And !that poor man
;strength. (is)

17 וְחָכְמַת הַמִּסְכֵּן בְּזוּיָה וּדְבָרָיו אֵינָם נִשְׁמָעִים׃ דִּבְרֵי
The .heard are they his and is poor the but
of words not words ,despised man's wisdom

18 חֲכָמִים בְּנַחַת נִשְׁמָעִים מִזַּעֲקַת מוֹשֵׁל בַּכְּסִילִים׃ טוֹבָה
better among who one than more are quiet in wise
.fools rules of cry the ;heard men

than weapons of conflict; but one sinner destroys much good.

CHAPTER 10

[1] Dead flies cause the ointment of the perfumer to stink (and) ferment; a little foolishness is more rare than wisdom, (and) than honor. [2] The heart of the wise (is) toward his right, but the stupid's heart toward his left. [3] And also, in the way in which a fool walks, his heart fails, and he says to all (that) he is a fool. [4] If the spirit of the ruler rises up against you, do not leave your place; for composure quiets great offenses. [5] There is an evil I have seen under the sun, sins which come from the ruler's presence; [6] folly is set in many high (positions), and many rich men sit in low (places)[7] I have seen slaves on horses, and rulers walking as slaves on the earth. [8] He who digs a pit may fall into it; and one breaking a wall, a snake may bite him. [9] Whoever removes stones may be hurt with them. He who splits wood may be endangered by them. [10] If the iron is blunt, and he does not whet the edges, then he must put more strength to (it); but wisdom (is) an advantage giving success. [11] If the snake will bite without charming, then there (is) no advantage to the owner of the tongue. [12] The words of a wise man's mouth (are) gracious, but the lips of a stupid one swallow him; [13] the beginning of the words of his mouth (is) foolishness; and the end of his mouth (is) evil madness. [14] Yet the fool makes many words; a man knows not what shall be; and what shall be after him, who can tell him? [15] The labor of

חָכְמָה מִכְּלֵי קְרָב וְחוֹטֶא אֶחָד יְאַבֵּד טוֹבָה הַרְבֵּה׃
.much good destroys one but (hostile) than Wisdom
sinner ,conflict of weapons (is)

CAP. X י

CHAPTER 10

1 זְבוּבֵי מָוֶת יַבְאִישׁ יַבִּיעַ שֶׁמֶן רוֹקֵחַ יָקָר מֵחָכְמָה מִכָּבוֹד
than than (more) the ,oil (and) make of Flies
,honor ,wisdom rare ,perfumer's ferment stink death

2 3 סִכְלוּת מְעָט׃ לֵב חָכָם לִימִינוֹ וְלֵב כְּסִיל לִשְׂמֹאלוֹ׃ וְגַם־
And toward fool's a but toward the The .little a folly (is)
also .left his (is) heart right his (is) wise of heart

בַדֶּרֶךְ כְּשֶׁהַסָּכָל הֹלֵךְ לִבּוֹ חָסֵר וְאָמַר לַכֹּל סָכָל הוּא׃
fool a all to he and is his ,walks which in the in
.(is) he that says ;lacking heart fool the way

4 אִם־רוּחַ הַמּוֹשֵׁל תַּעֲלֶה עָלֶיךָ מְקוֹמְךָ אַל־תַּנַּח כִּי מַרְפֵּא
com- for do not your against up rises ruler the the If
posure ,leave place ,you of spirit

5 יַנִּיחַ חֲטָאִים גְּדוֹלִים׃ יֵשׁ רָעָה רָאִיתִי תַּחַת הַשָּׁמֶשׁ
,sun the under have I evil an There .great offenses quiets
seen is

6 כִּשְׁגָגָה שֶׁיֹּצָא מִלִּפְנֵי הַשַּׁלִּיט׃ נִתַּן הַסֶּכֶל בַּמְּרוֹמִים
high in folly Is .ruler's the from which an like
(positions) given presence comes error

7 רַבִּים וַעֲשִׁירִים בַּשֵּׁפֶל יֵשֵׁבוּ׃ רָאִיתִי עֲבָדִים עַל־סוּסִים
,horses on slaves have I .sit humble in rich and ,many
seen (situations) men

8 וְשָׂרִים הֹלְכִים כַּעֲבָדִים עַל־הָאָרֶץ׃ חֹפֵר גּוּמָּץ בּוֹ יִפּוֹל
may into ,pit a who He the on slaves as walking and
;fall it digs .earth rulers

9 וּפֹרֵץ גָּדֵר יִשְּׁכֶנּוּ נָחָשׁ׃ מַסִּיעַ אֲבָנִים יֵעָצֵב בָּהֶם בּוֹקֵעַ
who he by be may stones who He .snake a may ,wall a one and
splits ;them hurt quarries him bite breaking

10 עֵצִים יִסָּכֶן בָּם׃ אִם־קֵהָה הַבַּרְזֶל וְהוּא לֹא־פָנִים קִלְקַל
does the not he and the is If by be may trees
,whet edges ,iron blunt .them endangered

11 וַחֲיָלִים יְגַבֵּר וְיִתְרוֹן הַכְשֵׁיר חָכְמָה׃ אִם־יִשֹּׁךְ הַנָּחָשׁ
the will If (is) giving an but must he more then
snake bite .wisdom success advantage ,exert strength

12 בְּלוֹא־לָחַשׁ וְאֵין יִתְרוֹן לְבַעַל הַלָּשׁוֹן׃ דִּבְרֵי פִי־חָכָם חֵן
grace wise a The the a to advantage then ,charming with-
(are) mouth of words .tongue of master no out

13 וְשִׂפְתוֹת כְּסִיל תְּבַלְּעֶנּוּ׃ תְּחִלַּת דִּבְרֵי־פִיהוּ סִכְלוּת וְאַחֲרִית
the and (is) his the be- the swallow fool a the but
of end ,folly mouth of words of ginning .him of lips

14 פִּיהוּ הוֹלֵלוּת רָעָה׃ וְהַסָּכָל יַרְבֶּה דְבָרִים לֹא־יֵדַע הָאָדָם
man does not ;words makes the Yet .evil (is) his
know many fool madness mouth

15 מַה־שֶּׁיִּהְיֶה וַאֲשֶׁר יִהְיֶה מֵאַחֲרָיו מִי יַגִּיד לוֹ׃ עֲמַל
The to can who after be shall and ;be shall what
of labor ?him tell ,him what

the stupid wearies him, because he does not know (how) to go to the city.

[16] Woe to you, O land, when your king (is) a child and your leaders feast in the morning. [17] Blessed (are) you, O land, when your king (is) the son of nobles and your leaders eat in (due) time, in strength, and not in drinking. [18] The building decays through slothfulness; and through lowering of hands, the house leaks. [19] Food is made for laughter, and wine gladdens life; but money answers all (things). [20] Also do not curse a king in your thought. And do not curse the rich in your bedrooms; for a bird of the heavens shall carry the voice, and that which has wings may tell the matter.

16 הַכְּסִילִים תְּיַגְּעֶנּוּ אֲשֶׁר לֹא־יָדַע לָלֶכֶת אֶל־עִיר׃ אִי־לָךְ
to Woe the to to (how) he not because wearies fools
,you .city go know does him

17 אֶרֶץ שֶׁמַּלְכֵּךְ נָעַר וְשָׂרַיִךְ בַּבֹּקֶר יֹאכֵלוּ׃ אַשְׁרֵיךְ אֶרֶץ
O Blessed .eat the in your and a (is) when O
,land you (are) morning officials lad king your ,land

שֶׁמַּלְכֵּךְ בֶּן־חוֹרִים וְשָׂרַיִךְ בָּעֵת יֹאכֵלוּ בִּגְבוּרָה וְלֹא בַשְּׁתִי׃
for and for ,eat due in your and ,nobles a your when
drinking not ,strength time officials of son (is) king

18 בַּעֲצַלְתַּיִם יִמַּךְ הַמְּקָרֶה וּבְשִׁפְלוּת יָדַיִם יִדְלֹף הַבָּיִת׃
the leaks hands through and the sinks Through
.house of lowering rafter indolence

19 לִשְׂחוֹק עֹשִׂים לֶחֶם וְיַיִן יְשַׂמַּח חַיִּים וְהַכֶּסֶף יַעֲנֶה אֶת־
answers but ,life gladdens and Bread is for
silver wine prepared laughter

20 הַכֹּל׃ גַּם בְּמַדָּעֲךָ מֶלֶךְ אַל־תְּקַלֵּל וּבְחַדְרֵי מִשְׁכָּבְךָ אַל־
not your in and do not king a your in Also all
bed of rooms ;curse thought .(things)

תְּקַלֵּל עָשִׁיר כִּי עוֹף הַשָּׁמַיִם יוֹלִיךְ אֶת־הַקּוֹל וּבַעַל הַכְּנָפַיִם
wings the and the may the a for rich a do
of lord ,voice carry heavens of bird ;man curse

יַגֵּיד דָּבָר׃
the may
.matter tell

CAP. XI יא

CHAPTER 11

CHAPTER 11

[1] Cast your bread on the face of the waters; for you shall find it in many days. [2] Give a share to seven, or even to eight; for you do not know what evil may be on the earth. [3] If the clouds are full of rain, they empty on the earth. And if the tree falls in the south, or in the north, (in the) place where the tree falls, there it shall be. [4] He who watches the wind shall not sow; and he who looks at the clouds shall not reap. [5] As you do not know what (is) the way of the spirit, (as) the bones in the pregnant woman's womb, even so you do not know the works of God who makes all. [6] In the morning sow your seed, and until evening do not rest your hand; for you do not

1 שַׁלַּח לַחְמְךָ עַל־פְּנֵי הַמָּיִם כִּי־בְרֹב הַיָּמִים תִּמְצָאֶנּוּ׃
will you days in for the the on your Send
.it find many ,waters of surface bread out

2 תֶּן־חֵלֶק לְשִׁבְעָה וְגַם לִשְׁמוֹנָה כִּי לֹא תֵדַע מַה־יִּהְיֶה רָעָה
evil may what you not for ;eight to or ;seven to a Give
be know do even share

3 עַל־הָאָרֶץ׃ אִם־יִמָּלְאוּ הֶעָבִים גֶּשֶׁם עַל־הָאָרֶץ יָרִיקוּ
they the on ,rain the full are If the on
;empty earth of clouds .earth

וְאִם־יִפּוֹל עֵץ בַּדָּרוֹם וְאִם בַּצָּפוֹן מְקוֹם שֶׁיִּפּוֹל הָעֵץ שָׁם
there the where (the in) the to or the to the falls and
,tree falls place ,north if ,south tree if

4 יְהוּא׃ שֹׁמֵר רוּחַ לֹא יִזְרָע וְרֹאֶה בֶעָבִים לֹא יִקְצוֹר׃
shall not the at he and shall not the who He shall it
.reap clouds looks who ;sow wind watches .be

5 כַּאֲשֶׁר אֵינְךָ יוֹדֵעַ מַה־דֶּרֶךְ הָרוּחַ כַּעֲצָמִים בְּבֶטֶן הַמְּלֵאָה
pregnant the the in the (as) the the what do you As
,woman of womb bones ,wind of way (is) know not

כָּכָה לֹא תֵדַע אֶת־מַעֲשֵׂה הָאֱלֹהִים אֲשֶׁר יַעֲשֶׂה אֶת־
makes who God the you do not even
of work know so

6 הַכֹּל׃ בַּבֹּקֶר זְרַע אֶת־זַרְעֶךָ וְלָעֶרֶב אַל־תַּנַּח יָדֶךָ כִּי אֵינְךָ
you for your let do not until and your sow the In all
not ;hand rest evening ,seed morning .(things)

know what shall be blessed, this or that — or whether they both (shall be) good as one.

[7] Truly also the light (is) sweet, and (it is) good for the eyes to behold the sun; [8] but if the man lives many years, let him rejoice in them all, and remember the days of darkness; for they shall be many. Whatever may come is vanity.

[9] Rejoice, O young man, in your youth; and let your heart be glad in the days of your youth, and walk in the ways of your heart, and in the sight of your eyes — but know that for all these (things) God will bring you into judgment. [10] Therefore remove vexation from your heart, and put away evil from your flesh; for childhood and prime (of life are) vanity.

יוֹדֵעַ אֵי זֶה יִכְשַׁר הֲזֶה אוֹ־זֶה וְאִם־שְׁנֵיהֶם כְּאֶחָד טוֹבִים׃
(be will) one as they or —this or (either) shall this where do
.good both whether this succeed know

7 8 וּמָתוֹק הָאוֹר וְטוֹב לַעֵינַיִם לִרְאוֹת אֶת־הַשָּׁמֶשׁ׃ כִּי אִם־
if but ;sun the see to the for and the (is) Also
eyes good (is it) light sweet

שָׁנִים הַרְבֵּה יִחְיֶה הָאָדָם בְּכֻלָּם יִשְׂמָח וְיִזְכֹּר אֶת־יְמֵי
the and him let them in ,man the lives many years
of days remember rejoice all

9 הַחֹשֶׁךְ כִּי־הַרְבֵּה יִהְיוּ כָּל־שֶׁבָּא הָבֶל׃ שְׂמַח בָּחוּר
young O ,Rejoice (is) that all they many for ,darkness
man .vanity come may ;be shall

בְּיַלְדוּתֶךָ וִיטִיבְךָ לִבְּךָ בִּימֵי בְחוּרוֹתֶךָ וְהַלֵּךְ בְּדַרְכֵי
the in and your the in your make and your in
of ways walk ,youth of days heart good ,childhood

לִבְּךָ וּבְמַרְאֵי עֵינֶיךָ וְדָע כִּי עַל־כָּל־אֵלֶּה יְבִיאֲךָ הָאֱלֹהִים
God will these all for that but your the in and your
you bring (things) know ;eyes of sight ,heart

10 בַּמִּשְׁפָּט׃ וְהָסֵר כַּעַס מִלִּבֶּךָ וְהַעֲבֵר רָעָה מִבְּשָׂרֶךָ כִּי־
for your from evil make and your from vexa- Therefore into
;flesh pass ,heart tion remove .judgment

הַיַּלְדוּת וְהַשַּׁחֲרוּת הָבֶל׃
(are) prime and childhood
.vanity life of

CAP. XII יב

CHAPTER 12

[1] Remember now your Creator in the days of your youth, while the evil days do not come, or the years draw near when you shall say, I have no pleasure in them; [2] while not (yet) the sun, or the light, or the moon, or the stars, are darkened, or the clouds return after the rain; [3] in the day when the keepers of the house shall tremble, and the strong men are bowed, and the grinders cease because there are few, and those who look out of the windows are darkened, [4] and the doors shall be shut in the streets, when the sound of the mill is low, and one rises up at the voice of a bird, and all the daughters of music are silenced; [5] also they shall be afraid of a high place, and terrors in the way; and the almond tree shall blossom, and the locust becomes burdensome; and desire shall fail

1 וּזְכֹר אֶת־בּוֹרְאֶיךָ בִּימֵי בְּחוּרֹתֶיךָ עַד אֲשֶׁר לֹא־יָבֹאוּ יְמֵי
the do not that So your the in your Remember
of days come long ,youth of days Creator now

2 הָרָעָה וְהִגִּיעוּ שָׁנִים אֲשֶׁר תֹּאמַר אֵין־לִי בָהֶם חֵפֶץ׃ עַד
So .pleasure in for Not you when the and the
long them me is ,say shall years strike ,evil

אֲשֶׁר לֹא־תֶחְשַׁךְ הַשֶּׁמֶשׁ וְהָאוֹר וְהַיָּרֵחַ וְהַכּוֹכָבִים וְשָׁבוּ
or the or the or the or sun the are not that
return ,stars ,moon ,light darkened

3 הֶעָבִים אַחַר הַגָּשֶׁם׃ בַּיּוֹם שֶׁיָּזֻעוּ שֹׁמְרֵי הַבַּיִת וְהִתְעַוְּתוּ
will and the the when the in ;rain the after the
bend ;house of guards trembles day clouds

אַנְשֵׁי הֶחָיִל וּבָטְלוּ הַטֹּחֲנוֹת כִּי מִעֵטוּ וְחָשְׁכוּ הָרֹאוֹת
who they are and they because the will and ;valor men the
out look darkened ;few are grinders idle be of

4 בָּאֲרֻבּוֹת׃ וְסֻגְּרוּ דְלָתַיִם בַּשּׁוּק בִּשְׁפַל קוֹל הַטַּחֲנָה וְיָקוּם
one and ;grinding the is when the in the are and the
arises of sound low ,streets doors shut ;windows

5 לְקוֹל הַצִּפּוֹר וְיִשַּׁחוּ כָּל־בְּנוֹת הַשִּׁיר׃ גַּם מִגָּבֹהַּ יִרָאוּ
are they a of ,Also the the all are and the the at
;afraid place high .song of daughters silenced ;bird of sound

וְחַתְחַתִּים בַּדֶּרֶךְ וְיָנֵאץ הַשָּׁקֵד וְיִסְתַּבֵּל הֶחָגָב וְתָפֵר
and the -him makes and almond the and the along and
fails ;locust burden a self ,tree blooms ;way terrors

— because man goes to his eternal home; and the mourners go about in the street — [6] while not (yet) the silver cord is loosed, or the golden bowl is crushed, or the pitcher is shattered at the fountain, or the wheel broken at the cistern; [7] then the dust shall return to the earth as it was; and the spirit shall return to God who gave it.

[8] Vanity of vanities, says the Preacher; all (is) vanity. [9] And more than that the preacher was wise; he still taught the people knowledge. Yes, he listened, and looked, (and) set in order many proverbs. [10] The Preacher sought to find out pleasing words; and words of truth rightly written. [11] The words of the wise (are) like goads. Yes, as nails driven by the masters of collections, they given from one Shepherd. [12] And more than they, my son, be warned — the making of many books has no end, and much study (is) the weariness of the flesh.

[13] Let us hear the conclusion of the whole matter: Fear God, and keep His commandments — for this applies to every man. [14] For God shall bring every work into judgment, over all that is hidden, whether (it is) good, or whether (it is) evil.

הָאֲבִיּוֹנָה כִּי־הֹלֵךְ הָאָדָם אֶל־בֵּית עוֹלָמוֹ וְסָבְבוּ בַשּׁוּק
the in street | go and about | his ;eternity | house of | the to | man | is because going | ;desire

6 הַסֹּפְדִים׃ עַד אֲשֶׁר לֹא־יֵרָחֵק חֶבֶל הַכֶּסֶף וְתָרֻץ גֻּלַּת
the bowl | is or crushed | the ,silver | cord | is removed | not | Before | the .mourners

הַזָּהָב וְתִשָּׁבֶר כַּד עַל־הַמַּבּוּעַ וְנָרֹץ הַגַּלְגַּל אֶל־הַבּוֹר׃
the .cistern | at | the wheel | is or crushed | the ,spring | at | the pitcher | is or shattered | ,golden

7 וְיָשֹׁב הֶעָפָר עַל־הָאָרֶץ כְּשֶׁהָיָה וְהָרוּחַ תָּשׁוּב אֶל־הָאֱלֹהִים
God | to | shall return | the and spirit | it as ;was | the earth | on | the dust | will Then return

8 אֲשֶׁר נְתָנָהּ׃ הֲבֵל הֲבָלִים אָמַר הַקּוֹהֶלֶת הַכֹּל הָבֶל׃
.vanity | (is) all | the ;Preacher | says | ,vanities | Vanity of | .it gave | who

9 וְיֹתֵר שֶׁהָיָה קֹהֶלֶת חָכָם עוֹד לִמַּד־דַּעַת אֶת־הָעָם וְאִזֵּן
gave and ,ear | the ,people | knowledge | he taught | still more | ;wise | the Preacher | than that | And more

10 וְחִקֵּר תִּקֵּן מְשָׁלִים הַרְבֵּה׃ בִּקֵּשׁ קֹהֶלֶת לִמְצֹא דִּבְרֵי־
words of | find to out | The Preacher | sought | .many | proverbs | set (and) order in | and ;sought

11 חֵפֶץ וְכָתוּב יֹשֶׁר דִּבְרֵי אֱמֶת׃ דִּבְרֵי חֲכָמִים כַּדָּרְבֹנוֹת
like (are) ;ox-goads | wise the | The of words | .truth | words of | upright | and written | ,delight

12 וּכְמַשְׂמְרוֹת נְטוּעִים בַּעֲלֵי אֲסֻפּוֹת נִתְּנוּ מֵרֹעֶה אֶחָד׃ וְיֹתֵר
And more | .one | from Shepherd | are they given | ;collections | the of masters | driven (are) in | nails as and

מֵהֵמָּה בְּנִי הִזָּהֵר עֲשׂוֹת סְפָרִים הַרְבֵּה אֵין קֵץ וְלַהַג
and study | an ;end | has not | many | books | the of making | be warned | my ,son | than ,these

13 הַרְבֵּה יְגִעַת בָּשָׂר׃ סוֹף דָּבָר הַכֹּל נִשְׁמָע אֶת־הָאֱלֹהִים
God | us let .hear | whole | the matter | The of end | .flesh | the weariness of | much (is)

14 יְרָא וְאֶת־מִצְוֹתָיו שְׁמוֹר כִּי־זֶה כָּל־הָאָדָם׃ כִּי אֶת־כָּל־
every | For | .man | every | this for (to applies) | —keep | His and commandments | ,Fear

מַעֲשֶׂה הָאֱלֹהִים יָבִא בְמִשְׁפָּט עַל כָּל־נֶעְלָם אִם־טוֹב
(is it) ,good | whether | that ,hidden is | all | with | into ,judgment | shall bring | God | work

וְאִם־רָע׃
(is it) .evil | or whether

שיר השירים

CANTICUM CANTICORUM

CAPUT. I א

CHAPTER 1

CHAPTER 1

[1] The song of songs, which (is) Solomon's. [2] Let Him kiss me with the kisses of His mouth; for Your loves (are) better than wine. [3] For Your ointments (have) a lovely fragrance; Your name is (as) ointment poured out; therefore the virgins love You. [4] Draw me, we will run after You; the King has brought me (into) His chambers; we will be glad and rejoice in You; we will remember Your loves more than wine; they uprightly love You. [5] I (am) black, but comely, O daughters of Jerusalem, like the tents of Kedar, like the curtains of Solomon. [6] Do not look at me, that I (am) black, that the sun has looked on me. My mother's sons were angry with me; they made me the keeper of the vineyards; (but) my own vineyard I have not kept. [7] Tell me, (You) whom my soul loves, where do You feed, where do You lie down at noon? For why should I be as one who is veiled beside the flocks of Your companions?

[8] If you yourself do not know, most beautiful among women, go in the footsteps of the flock; and feed your kids beside the shepherds' tents. [9] I have compared you, O my love, to my mare in Pharaoh's chariots. [10] Your cheeks (are) lovely with ornaments, your neck with chains (of gold). [11] We will make you ornaments of gold with studs of silver. [12] While the King is in His circle, my spikenard

1
2 שִׁיר הַשִּׁירִים אֲשֶׁר לִשְׁלֹמֹה׃ יִשָּׁקֵנִי מִנְּשִׁיקוֹת פִּיהוּ כִּי־
for His ;mouth | the with of kisses | Him Let me kiss | .Solomon's | which (is) | ,songs | The of song

3 טוֹבִים דֹּדֶיךָ מִיָּיִן׃ לְרֵיחַ שְׁמָנֶיךָ טוֹבִים שֶׁמֶן תּוּרַק שְׁמֶךָ
Your poured ;name (is) out | oint-ment | (are) ;good | Your ointments | a For fragrance | than .wine | Your love | (are) better

4 עַל־כֵּן עֲלָמוֹת אֲהֵבוּךָ׃ מָשְׁכֵנִי אַחֲרֶיךָ נָּרוּצָה הֱבִיאַנִי
brought has me into | will we ;run | after You | Draw ,me | love .You | the virgins | therefore

הַמֶּלֶךְ חֲדָרָיו נָגִילָה וְנִשְׂמְחָה בָּךְ נַזְכִּירָה דֹדֶיךָ מִיַּיִן
above ;wine | Your loves | will we remember | in ;You | rejoice and | will we glad be | His ;chambers | the King

5 מֵישָׁרִים אֲהֵבוּךָ׃ שְׁחוֹרָה אֲנִי וְנָאוָה בְּנוֹת יְרוּשָׁלִָם
,Jerusalem | O of daughters | but comely | ,(am) I | Black | love they .you | the upright

6 כְּאָהֳלֵי קֵדָר כִּירִיעוֹת שְׁלֹמֹה׃ אַל־תִּרְאוּנִי שֶׁאֲנִי שְׁחַרְחֹרֶת
,black | that ,(am) I | look do ,me at | Not | .Solomon | the like of curtains | ,Kedar | the like of tents

שֶׁשֱּׁזָפַתְנִי הַשָּׁמֶשׁ בְּנֵי אִמִּי נִחֲרוּ־בִי שָׂמֻנִי נֹטֵרָה אֶת־
keeper of | they me made | with ;me | were angry | my mother | The of sons | ;sun the | has that me on looked

7 הַכְּרָמִים כַּרְמִי שֶׁלִּי לֹא נָטָרְתִּי׃ הַגִּידָה לִּי שֶׁאָהֲבָה
loves whom | to ,me | Tell | have I .kept | not | which me to is | my (but) vineyard | the ;vineyards

נַפְשִׁי אֵיכָה תִרְעֶה אֵיכָה תַּרְבִּיץ בַּצָּהֳרָיִם שַׁלָּמָה אֶהְיֶה
should be I | For | ?noon at | You do down lie | Where | You do ?feed | where | my ,soul

8 כְּעֹטְיָה עַל עֶדְרֵי חֲבֵרֶיךָ׃ אִם־לֹא תֵדְעִי לָךְ הַיָּפָה בַּנָּשִׁים
among ,women | most beautiful | your-,self | you know | not | If | Your ?companions | the of flocks | beside | one as veiled

צְאִי־לָךְ בְּעִקְבֵי הַצֹּאן וּרְעִי אֶת־גְּדִיֹּתַיִךְ עַל מִשְׁכְּנוֹת
dwellings of | the beside | your kids | and feed | the ,flock | the in of footsteps | your-self | go out

9
10 הָרֹעִים׃ לְסֻסָתִי בְּרִכְבֵי פַרְעֹה דִּמִּיתִיךְ רַעְיָתִי׃ נָאווּ
Lovely (are) | my O .love | have I ,You compared | Pharoah's | among chariots | my mare | To | the .shepherds

11 לְחָיַיִךְ בַּתֹּרִים צַוָּארֵךְ בַּחֲרוּזִים׃ תּוֹרֵי זָהָב נַעֲשֶׂה־לָּךְ
for ,you | will we make | gold | Orna- of ments | strings with (beads of) | your neck | with ,ornaments | your cheeks

12 עִם נְקֻדּוֹת הַכָּסֶף׃ עַד־שֶׁהַמֶּלֶךְ בִּמְסִבּוֹ נִרְדִּי נָתַן רֵיחוֹ׃
its .fragrance | gives | my spikenard | his in ,circle | the (is) King | While | .silver | studs of | with

gives its fragrance. [13] A bundle of myrrh (is) my Beloved to me. (He) shall lodge between my breasts. [14] My Beloved is to me (like) a cluster of henna in the vineyards of Engedi. [15] Behold, you (are) beautiful, my love; behold, you (are) beautiful, your eyes (as) doves' [16] Behold, you (are) beautiful, my Beloved, yea, pleasant. Also our couch (is) green. [17] The beams of our house (are) cedars, (and) our rafters are of firs.

CHAPTER 2

[1] I (am) a rose of Sharon, a lily of the valleys. [2] As a lily among thorns, so (is) My love among the daughters. [3] As the apple among the trees of the forest, so (is) my Beloved among the sons. I delighted in His shadow, and I sat down, and His fruit (was) sweet to my taste. [4] He brought me to the house of wine, and His banner over me (was) love. [5] Feed me with raisin cakes, sustain me with apples — for I (am) sick (with) love. [6] His left hand (is) under my head, and His right hand embraces me. [7] I charge you, O daughters of Jerusalem, by the gazelles, and by the does of the field, that you stirup and that you arouse (my) Love until it pleases.

[8] The voice of my Beloved! Behold, He comes leaping on the mountains, skipping on the hills. [9] My Beloved is like a gazelle or a young deer. Behold, (He) stands behind our wall, looking out of the windows, peering through the lattice. [10] My Beloved answered and said to me, Arouse yourself, My love, My beautiful one, and you come away. [11] For behold, the winter is past; the rain has passed; it (is)

13 14 צְרוֹר הַמֹּר ׀ דּוֹדִי לִי בֵּין שָׁדַי יָלִין׃ אֶשְׁכֹּל הַכֹּפֶר ׀ דּוֹדִי

my henna cluster A shall He my between to my (is) myrrh A
Beloved (is) of .lie breasts ,me Beloved of bundle

15 לִי בְּכַרְמֵי עֵין גֶּדִי׃ הִנָּךְ יָפָה רַעְיָתִי הִנָּךְ יָפָה עֵינַיִךְ יוֹנִים׃

.dove's your are ,behold my are Behold .Engedi the in to
eyes ;beautiful you ;love ,beautiful you of vineyards ,me

16 17 הִנְּךָ יָפֶה דוֹדִי אַף נָעִים אַף־עַרְשֵׂנוּ רַעֲנָנָה׃ קֹרוֹת בָּתֵּינוּ

our The .green is our Also .pleasant ,yea my are ,Behold
houses of beams couch ,Beloved ,beautiful you

אֲרָזִים רַהִיטֵנוּ בְּרוֹתִים׃

.firs of our (and) (are)
rafters ,cedars

CAP. II ב

CHAPTER 2

1 2 אֲנִי חֲבַצֶּלֶת הַשָּׁרוֹן שׁוֹשַׁנַּת הָעֲמָקִים׃ כְּשׁוֹשַׁנָּה בֵּין

among a As the of lily a plain the a I
lily .valleys ,Sharon of of rose (am)

3 הַחוֹחִים כֵּן רַעְיָתִי בֵּין הַבָּנוֹת׃ כְּתַפּוּחַ בַּעֲצֵי הַיַּעַר כֵּן

so the the in the As the among my so ,thorns
(is) ,forest of trees apple .daughters love (is)

דּוֹדִי בֵּין הַבָּנִים בְּצִלּוֹ חִמַּדְתִּי וְיָשַׁבְתִּי וּפִרְיוֹ מָתוֹק לְחִכִּי׃

my to (was) his and I and I his in the among my
.palate sweet fruit ;down sat ,delighted shadow ;sons Beloved

4 5 הֱבִיאַנִי אֶל־בֵּית הַיָּיִן וְדִגְלוֹ עָלַי אַהֲבָה׃ סַמְּכוּנִי בָּאֲשִׁישׁוֹת

with me Feed (was) over His and the house a to He
,raisin-cakes .love me banner ,wine of me brought

רַפְּדוּנִי בַּתַּפּוּחִים כִּי־חוֹלַת אַהֲבָה אָנִי׃ שְׂמֹאלוֹ תַּחַת

(is) left His I love sick for with sustain
under hand .(am) with —apples me

6 7 לְרֹאשִׁי וִימִינוֹ תְּחַבְּקֵנִי׃ הִשְׁבַּעְתִּי אֶתְכֶם בְּנוֹת יְרוּשָׁלִַם

,Jerusalem O ,you charge I embraces his and my
of daughters .me hand right ,head

בִּצְבָאוֹת אוֹ בְּאַיְלוֹת הַשָּׂדֶה אִם־תָּעִירוּ ׀ וְאִם־תְּעוֹרְרוּ

awaken you and you that ,field the the by or the by
not that up stir not of does gazelles

8 אֶת־הָאַהֲבָה עַד שֶׁתֶּחְפָּץ׃ קוֹל דּוֹדִי הִנֵּה־זֶה בָּא מְדַלֵּג

leaping He ,this Be- my The .pleases it until the
comes ,hold !Beloved of voice Beloved

9 עַל־הֶהָרִים מְקַפֵּץ עַל־הַגְּבָעוֹת׃ דּוֹמֶה דוֹדִי לִצְבִי אוֹ

or a to my Is .hills the on skipping the on
gazelle Beloved likened ,mountains

לְעֹפֶר הָאַיָּלִים הִנֵּה־זֶה עוֹמֵד אַחַר כָּתְלֵנוּ מַשְׁגִּיחַ מִן

from looking our behind standing this ,Behold the a to
,wall :one .stag ,deer young

10 הַחַלֹּנוֹת מֵצִיץ מִן־הַחֲרַכִּים׃ עָנָה דוֹדִי וְאָמַר לִי קוּמִי

Rise to said and my Answered the from blooming the
up ,me Beloved .lattice ,windows

11 לָךְ רַעְיָתִי יָפָתִי וּלְכִי־לָךְ׃ כִּי־הִנֵּה הַסְּתָו עָבָר הַגֶּשֶׁם

rain the has the behold ,For your- and beau- My My your-
,passed winter .self come ,one tiful ,love ,self

gone; [12] the flowers appear on the earth; the time of the singing (of) birds has come, and the voice of the turtle-dove is heard in our land; [13] the fig-tree puts forth her green figs, and the vines (with) the blossom give a fragrance. Arise My love; come, My beautiful one, and come yourself. [14] O My dove, in the clefts of the rock, in the secrecy of the steep place, let Me see your form, let Me hear your voice; for your voice (is) sweet and your form (is) beautiful. [15] Take for us the foxes, the little foxes that spoil the vines; and our vineyards (have) blossoms.

[16] My Beloved (is) mine, and I (am) His; He feeds among the lilies. [17] Until when the day breathes, and the shadows flee away, turn, my Beloved, and be like a gazelle or a young one of the stags on the mountains of Bether.

12 חָלַף הָלַךְ לוֹ׃ הַנִּצָּנִים נִרְאוּ בָאָרֶץ עֵת הַזָּמִיר הִגִּיעַ וְקוֹל
the and has the the the on appear The to it has
of voice ;come singing of time ;earth flowers .itself goes ,passed

13 הַתּוֹר נִשְׁמַע בְּאַרְצֵנוּ׃ הַתְּאֵנָה חָנְטָה פַגֶּיהָ וְהַגְּפָנִים
the and unripe her spices fig The our in heard is the
vines ,figs tree .land turtle-dove

14 סְמָדַר נָתְנוּ רֵיחַ קוּמִי לָכִי רַעְיָתִי יָפָתִי וּלְכִי־לָךְ׃ יוֹנָתִי
my O your- and beau- My My ,come ,Arise a give the (by)
,dove .self come one tiful ,love .fragrance blossom

בְּחַגְוֵי הַסֶּלַע בְּסֵתֶר הַמַּדְרֵגָה הַרְאִינִי אֶת־מַרְאַיִךְ
your Me make steep the the in ,rock the the in
.form see place of secrecy of clefts

15 הַשְׁמִיעִנִי אֶת־קוֹלֵךְ כִּי־קוֹלֵךְ עָרֵב וּמַרְאֵיךְ נָאוֶה׃ אֶחֱזוּ
Take (is) your and (is) your for your Me Let
.comely form ,sweet voice ;voice hear

לָנוּ שׁוּעָלִים שֻׁעָלִים קְטַנִּים מְחַבְּלִים כְּרָמִים וּכְרָמֵינוּ
our and the spoiling little foxes the ,foxes the for
vineyards ;vineyards us

16
17 סְמָדַר׃ דּוֹדִי לִי וַאֲנִי לוֹ הָרֹעֶה בַּשּׁוֹשַׁנִּים׃ עַד שֶׁיָּפוּחַ
when Until among He to I and (is) Be- My (have)
blows .lilies the feeds ;him (am) ,me to loved . blossoms

הַיּוֹם וְנָסוּ הַצְּלָלִים סֹב דְּמֵה־לְךָ דוֹדִי לִצְבִי אוֹ לְעֹפֶר
young a or a my to like be ,turn the and the
,deer gazelle ,Beloved ,Yourself ;shadows flee ,day

הָאַיָּלִים עַל־הָרֵי בָתֶר׃
cleft the on ,stag the
mountains

CAP. III ג

CHAPTER 3

[1] By night on my bed I sought (Him) whom my soul loves; I sought Him, but I did not find Him. [2] I will rise now and go about in the city, in the streets and in the broad ways; I will seek (Him) whom my soul loves. I sought Him, but I did not find Him. [3] The watchmen found me going about in the city: (I said,) Have you seen (Him) whom my soul loves? [4] A little while, when I had passed from them, I found (Him) whom my soul loves. I held Him and would not let Him go, until I had brought Him into my mother's house, and into the room of her who conceived me. [5] I charge you, O daughters of

1 עַל־מִשְׁכָּבִי בַּלֵּילוֹת בִּקַּשְׁתִּי אֵת שֶׁאָהֲבָה נַפְשִׁי בִּקַּשְׁתִּיו
sought I my whom (Him) sought I night by my On
;Him ;soul loved bed

2 וְלֹא מְצָאתִיו׃ אָקוּמָה נָּא וַאֲסוֹבְבָה בָעִיר בַּשְּׁוָקִים
the in the in go I and ,now will I did I but
,streets ,city about rise .Him find not

וּבָרְחֹבוֹת אֲבַקְשָׁה אֵת שֶׁאָהֲבָה נַפְשִׁי בִּקַּשְׁתִּיו וְלֹא
but sought I my whom (Him) will I the in and
not ,Him ;soul loves seek ;places broad

3 מְצָאתִיו׃ מְצָאוּנִי הַשֹּׁמְרִים הַסֹּבְבִים בָּעִיר אֵת
the in going (those) The me found find did I
:city about ,watchmen .Him

4 שֶׁאָהֲבָה נַפְשִׁי רְאִיתֶם׃ כִּמְעַט שֶׁעָבַרְתִּי מֵהֶם עַד
until from had I when little A you Have soul my (Him)
,them passed while ?seen loves whom

שֶׁמָּצָאתִי אֵת שֶׁאָהֲבָה נַפְשִׁי אֲחַזְתִּיו וְלֹא אַרְפֶּנּוּ עַד־
until Him let I and seized I my whom (Him) found I
,go not ,Him ;soul loves

5 שֶׁהֲבֵיאתִיו אֶל־בֵּית אִמִּי וְאֶל־חֶדֶר הוֹרָתִי׃ הִשְׁבַּעְתִּי
charge I who her the and my house into brought had I
.me conceived of room into ,mother's Him

Jerusalem, by the gazelles, and by the does of the field, that you do not stir up or awake (my) love til it pleases.
[6] Who (is) this who comes up out of the wilderness like pillars of smoke, perfumed with myrrh and frankincense, from all powders of the merchant? [7] Behold his bed, which (is) Solomon's; sixty strong men (are) around it, of the strong men of Israel. [8] They all hold the sword, instructed in war; each man (has) his sword on his thigh from dread in the night. [9] King Solomon made himself a litter-bed of the woods of Lebanon. [10] He made the poles of it of silver, its back was of gold, its seat was of purple; (and) its middle was fitted (in) love, by the daughters of Jerusalem. [11] Go forth, O daughters of Zion, and see King Solomon with the crown (with) which his mother crowned him in the day of his wedding, and in the day of the gladness of his heart.

אֶתְכֶם בְּנוֹת יְרוּשָׁלַ͏ִם בִּצְבָאוֹת אוֹ בְּאַיְלוֹת הַשָּׂדֶה אִם־
that not ,field the the by of does or the by gazelles ,Jerusalem O of daughters ,you

6 תָּעִירוּ ׀ וְאִם־תְּעוֹרְרוּ אֶת־הָאַהֲבָה עַד־שֶׁתֶּחְפָּץ׃ מִי זֹאת
(is) this Who .pleases it until the Beloved you awaken and not stir you up

עֹלָה מִן־הַמִּדְבָּר כְּתִימְרוֹת עָשָׁן מְקֻטֶּרֶת מוֹר וּלְבוֹנָה מִכֹּל
from all and ,frankincense myrrh perfumed with ,smoke like of pillars the of out wilderness coming up

7 אַבְקַת רוֹכֵל׃ הִנֵּה מִטָּתוֹ שֶׁלִּשְׁלֹמֹה שִׁשִּׁים גִּבֹּרִים סָבִיב
(are) around mighty men sixty is which ;Solomon's his ,bed Behold the ?merchant powders of

8 לָהּ מִגִּבֹּרֵי יִשְׂרָאֵל׃ כֻּלָּם אֲחֻזֵי חֶרֶב מְלֻמְּדֵי מִלְחָמָה
;battle instructed in ,swords hold They all .Israel's mighty of men ,it

9 אִישׁ חַרְבּוֹ עַל־יְרֵכוֹ מִפַּחַד בַּלֵּילוֹת׃ אַפִּרְיוֹן עָשָׂה לוֹ
for him made A palanquin the in .night from dread his thigh on his (has) sword a man

10 הַמֶּלֶךְ שְׁלֹמֹה מֵעֲצֵי הַלְּבָנוֹן׃ עַמּוּדָיו עָשָׂה כֶסֶף רְפִידָתוֹ
its support of ,silver he made poles The it of .Lebanon the of of trees Solomon King

זָהָב מֶרְכָּבוֹ אַרְגָּמָן תּוֹכוֹ רָצוּף אַהֲבָה מִבְּנוֹת יְרוּשָׁלָ͏ִם׃
.Jerusalem the by of daughters ,love was paved its middle (of) ;purple its seat (of) ,gold

11 צְאֶינָה ׀ וּרְאֶינָה בְּנוֹת צִיּוֹן בַּמֶּלֶךְ שְׁלֹמֹה בָּעֲטָרָה שֶׁעִטְּרָה־
which (with) crowned the with crown Solomon King ,Zion O of daughters ,see and out Go

לּוֹ אִמּוֹ בְּיוֹם חֲתֻנָּתוֹ וּבְיוֹם שִׂמְחַת לִבּוֹ׃
his .heart gladness of the on even of day the his ;wedding the on of day his mother him

CAP. IV ד

CHAPTER 4

[1] Behold, you (are) beautiful, My love. Behold, you (are) beautiful; your eyes (as) doves' from behind your veil; your hair (is) like a flock of goats which recline from Mount Gilead. [2] Your teeth (are) like a flock of shorn (sheep), which come up from the washing; of which all of them (are) bearing twins and none barren is among them. [3] Your lips (are) like a cord of scarlet, and your speech (is) becoming; your temples (are) like a piece of pomegranate behind your veil. [4] Your neck (is) like the tower of David, built for an armory; a thousand bucklers hang on it, all the shields of the

1 הִנָּךְ יָפָה רַעְיָתִי הִנָּךְ יָפָה עֵינַיִךְ יוֹנִים מִבַּעַד לְצַמָּתֵךְ
your ;veil from behind doves' Your eyes (are) !beautiful ,Behold you My !love (are) ,beautiful Behold ,you

2 שַׂעְרֵךְ כְּעֵדֶר הָעִזִּים שֶׁגָּלְשׁוּ מֵהַר גִּלְעָד׃ שִׁנַּיִךְ כְּעֵדֶר
a as of flock Your teeth .Gilead from Mount which recline goats like (is) of flock a your hair

הַקְּצוּבוֹת שֶׁעָלוּ מִן־הָרַחְצָה שֶׁכֻּלָּם מַתְאִימוֹת וְשַׁכֻּלָה
barren-ness and bearing ;twins (are) which all they the ;washing-place from come up which shorn (sheep)

3 אֵין בָּהֶם׃ כְּחוּט הַשָּׁנִי שִׂפְתֹתַיִךְ וּמִדְבָּרֵיךְ נָאוֶה כְּפֶלַח
a as of piece (is) comely your and speech your ;lips scarlet a As of cord among ;them not is

4 הָרִמּוֹן רַקָּתֵךְ מִבַּעַד לְצַמָּתֵךְ׃ כְּמִגְדַּל דָּוִיד צַוָּארֵךְ בָּנוּי
built your ,neck (is) David the As of tower your .veil from behind your temples pome- granate a

5 לְתַלְפִּיּוֹת אֶלֶף הַמָּגֵן תָּלוּי עָלָיו כֹּל שִׁלְטֵי הַגִּבּוֹרִים׃
mighty the .men shields of all ;it on hang shields a thousand an for ,armory

mighty men. [5] Your two breasts (are) like two fawns, twins of a gazelle feeding among the lilies. [6] Until when the day breathes, and the shadows flee away, I will go myself to the mountain of myrrh and to the hill of frankincense. [7] You (are) all beautiful, My love; not a blemish (is) in you.

[8] Come with Me from Lebanon, (My) spouse, from Lebanon; look from the top of Amana, from the top of Shenir and Hermon, from the lions' dens, from the mountains of the leopards. [9] You have ravished Me, My sister, (My) spouse; you have ravished Me with one of your eyes, with one chain of your neck. [10] How fair are your loves, My sister, (My) spouse! How (much) better your loves than wine, and the smell of your ointments than all spices! [11] Your lips, (My) spouse, drop (like) the honeycomb; honey and milk (are) under your tongue; and the scents of your garments like the scent of Lebanon. [12] A locked garden (is) My sister, (My) spouse; a heap locked up, a fountain sealed. [13] Your plants (are) an orchard of pomegranates, with pleasant fruits; with henna (and) spikenard, [14] spikenard and saffron; calamus and cinnamon, with all trees of frankincense; myrrh and aloes, with all the chief spices; [15] a fountain of gardens, a well of living waters, and streams from Lebanon. [16] Awake, north (wind), and come, south (wind); blow on my garden, the spices of it flow out. Let my Beloved come into His garden, and eat its pleasant fruits.

5 שְׁנֵי שָׁדַיִךְ כִּשְׁנֵי עֳפָרִים תְּאוֹמֵי צְבִיָּה הָרוֹעִים בַּשּׁוֹשַׁנִּים׃
the among feeding a of twins ,fawns like (are) Your two
.lilies ,gazelle two breasts

6 עַד שֶׁיָּפוּחַ הַיּוֹם וְנָסוּ הַצְּלָלִים אֵלֶךְ לִי אֶל־הַר הַמּוֹר
myrrh the to my- will I the flee and the when Until
of mountain self go ,shadows ,day blows

7 וְאֶל־גִּבְעַת הַלְּבוֹנָה׃ כֻּלָּךְ יָפָה רַעְיָתִי וּמוּם אֵין בָּךְ׃ אִתִּי
8
With on is a and My ,beautiful You .frankincense the and
me .you not blemish ;love all (are) of hills to

מִלְּבָנוֹן כַּלָּה אִתִּי מִלְּבָנוֹן תָּבוֹאִי תָּשׁוּרִי ׀ מֵרֹאשׁ אֲמָנָה
,Amana the from look ;come from with (my) from
of top Lebanon me ,spouse Lebanon

מֵרֹאשׁ שְׂנִיר וְחֶרְמוֹן מִמְּעֹנוֹת אֲרָיוֹת מֵהַרְרֵי נְמֵרִים׃
the the from ,lions' the from and Shenir the from
.leopards of mountains dens ,Hermon of top

9 לִבַּבְתִּנִי אֲחֹתִי כַלָּה לִבַּבְתִּנִי בְּאַחַד מֵעֵינַיִךְ בְּאַחַד עֲנָק
chain with your of with have you (My) My ravished You
one ,eyes one heart my ravished ,spouse ,sister ,heart my

10 מִצַּוְּרֹנָיִךְ׃ מַה־יָּפוּ דֹדַיִךְ אֲחֹתִי כַלָּה מַה־טֹּבוּ דֹדַיִךְ מִיַּיִן
than your better How (my) my your fair How your of
,wine loves (are) much) !spouse ,sister loves (are) .neck

11 וְרֵיחַ שְׁמָנַיִךְ מִכָּל־בְּשָׂמִים׃ נֹפֶת תִּטֹּפְנָה שִׂפְתוֹתַיִךְ כַּלָּה
(my) your (so) the As balsam- than your the and
;spouse ,lips drips honeycomb !spices all ointments of scent

דְּבַשׁ וְחָלָב תַּחַת לְשׁוֹנֵךְ וְרֵיחַ שַׂלְמֹתַיִךְ כְּרֵיחַ לְבָנוֹן׃
.Lebanon the like outer your the and your (are) and honey
of scent garments of scent ;tongue under milk

12 גַּן ׀ נָעוּל אֲחֹתִי כַלָּה גַּל ׀ נָעוּל מַעְיָן חָתוּם׃ שְׁלָחַיִךְ
13
Your .sealed a locked rock a (my) my (is) locked A
(are) plants fountain ;up heap ;spouse ,sister up garden

14 פַּרְדֵּס רִמּוֹנִים עִם פְּרִי מְגָדִים כְּפָרִים עִם־נְרָדִים׃ נֵרְדְּ ׀
spike- ;spikenard with henna ;excellent fruits with pome- orchard an
nard ,granates of

וְכַרְכֹּם קָנֶה וְקִנָּמוֹן עִם כָּל־עֲצֵי לְבוֹנָה מֹר וַאֲהָלוֹת עִם
with and myrrh frankin- trees all with and calamus and
,aloes ;cense of ,cinnamon ;saffron

15 כָּל־רָאשֵׁי בְּשָׂמִים׃ מַעְיַן גַּנִּים בְּאֵר מַיִם חַיִּים וְנֹזְלִים
even ,living waters a ,gardens a balsam the all
flowings of well of fountain spices chief

16 מִן־לְבָנוֹן׃ עוּרִי צָפוֹן וּבוֹאִי תֵימָן הָפִיחִי גַנִּי יִזְּלוּ בְשָׂמָיו
its let my blow south and north ,Awaken from
.spices flow ,garden on ;(wind) ,come ,(wind) .Lebanon

יָבֹא דוֹדִי לְגַנּוֹ וְיֹאכַל פְּרִי מְגָדָיו׃
its fruits eat and His into Be- my Let
.excellent ,garden loved come

CAP. V ה

CHAPTER 5

1 בָּאתִי לְגַנִּי אֲחֹתִי כַלָּה אָרִיתִי מוֹרִי עִם־בְּשָׂמִי אָכַלְתִּי
have I My with My have I (My) My My to have I
eaten ;spice myrrh gathered ,spouse ,sister ,garden come

CHAPTER 5

[1] I have come into My garden, My sister, (My) spouse, I have gathered My myrrh with My spice; I have

eaten My honeycomb with My honey; I have drunk My wine with My milk. Eat, O friends; drink, yea, drink abundantly, beloved ones.

[2] I sleep, but my heart is awake. (It is) the sound of my Beloved that knocks, (saying,) Open to Me, My sister, My love, My dove, My undefiled; for My head is filled with dew, My locks with the drops of the night. [3] I have stripped off my coat; How shall I put it on? I have washed my feet; how shall I defile them? [4] My Beloved put in his hand by the hole (of the door), and my inner being sighed for Him. [5] I rose up to open to my Beloved; and my hands dripped (with) myrrh, and my fingers (with) myrrh, on the handles of the lock. [6] I opened to my Beloved; but my Beloved withdrew, He went on. My soul failed when He spoke; I sought Him, but I could not find Him; I called Him, but He gave me no answer. [7] The watchmen who went about the city found me, (they) struck me, they wounded me; the keepers of the walls lifted my veil from me. [8] I charge you, O daughters of Jerusalem, if you find my Beloved, what do you tell Him? That I (am) sick (with) love.

[9] What (is) your Beloved more than (another) Beloved, most beautiful among women? What (is) your Beloved more than (another) Beloved, that you charge us so? [10] My Beloved (is) white and ruddy; (He) stands out among ten thousand. [11] His head (is like) refined gold, His locks (are) bushy (and) black as a raven. [12] His eyes (are) as (the eyes) of doves on the rivers of waters, washed with milk, sitting on a setting. [13] His cheeks (are) like a bed of spices, a raised bed of aromatic herbs; His lips are (like)

יַעְרִי עִם־דִּבְשִׁי שָׁתִיתִי יֵינִי עִם־חֲלָבִי אִכְלוּ רֵעִים שְׁתוּ
,drink O ,Eat My with My have I My with My
,friends .milk wine drunk ;honey comb

2 וְשִׁכְרוּ דּוֹדִים׃ אֲנִי יְשֵׁנָה וְלִבִּי עֵר קוֹל ׀ דּוֹדִי דוֹפֵק
!knocking my the is my but ,sleeping I beloved drink and
Beloved of sound waking heart (am) .ones .fully

פִּתְחִי־לִי אֲחֹתִי רַעְיָתִי יוֹנָתִי תַמָּתִי שֶׁרֹּאשִׁי נִמְלָא־טָל
,dew filled is My for per- My My My My to Open
with head ;one fect ,dove ,love ,sister ,Me

3 קְוֻצּוֹתַי רְסִיסֵי לָיְלָה׃ פָּשַׁטְתִּי אֶת־כֻּתָּנְתִּי אֵיכָכָה אֶלְבָּשֶׁנָּה
I shall how ;coat My have I the the with My
?on it put off put ,night of drops locks

4 רָחַצְתִּי אֶת־רַגְלַי אֵיכָכָה אֲטַנְּפֵם׃ דּוֹדִי שָׁלַח יָדוֹ מִן
from his sent My I shall how ;feet My have I
hand Beloved ?them soil washed

5 הַחוֹר וּמֵעַי הָמוּ עָלָיו׃ קַמְתִּי אֲנִי לִפְתֹּחַ לְדוֹדִי וְיָדַי
my and my to open to I arose for sighed my and the
hands ;Beloved .Him bowels opening

6 נָטְפוּ־מוֹר וְאֶצְבְּעֹתַי מוֹר עֹבֵר עַל כַּפּוֹת הַמַּנְעוּל׃ פָּתַחְתִּי
opened the the on flowing (with) my and ;myrrh dripped
.bolt of handles myrrh fingers (with)

אֲנִי לְדוֹדִי וְדוֹדִי חָמַק עָבָר נַפְשִׁי יָצְאָה בְדַבְּרוֹ בִּקַּשְׁתִּיהוּ
sought I he when went my went He had my but my to I
him ;spoke out soul ;on ;left Beloved ,Beloved

7 וְלֹא מְצָאתִיהוּ קְרָאתִיו וְלֹא עָנָנִי׃ מְצָאֻנִי הַשֹּׁמְרִים
The found an- he but called I find could I but
watchmen me .me swered not ,him ;him not

הַסֹּבְבִים בָּעִיר הִכּוּנִי פְצָעוּנִי נָשְׂאוּ אֶת־רְדִידִי מֵעָלַי
from veil my they they ,me struck ,city the about going
me lifted ;me wounded

8 שֹׁמְרֵי הַחֹמוֹת׃ הִשְׁבַּעְתִּי אֶתְכֶם בְּנוֹת יְרוּשָׁלִָם אִם־
if ,Jerusalem O ,you charge I .walls the the
of daughters of keepers

9 תִּמְצְאוּ אֶת־דּוֹדִי מַה־תַּגִּידוּ לוֹ שֶׁחוֹלַת אַהֲבָה אָנִי׃ מַה־
What I (with) That to you do what my find you
(is) .am love sick ?Him tell ,Beloved

דּוֹדֵךְ מִדּוֹד הַיָּפָה בַּנָּשִׁים מַה־דּוֹדֵךְ מִדּוֹד שֶׁכָּכָה
that (any) above your What among most (any) above your
thus ,beloved Beloved (is) ?women beautiful ,beloved Beloved

10 הִשְׁבַּעְתָּנוּ׃ דּוֹדִי צַח וְאָדוֹם דָּגוּל מֵרְבָבָה׃ רֹאשׁוֹ כֶּתֶם
11
(like is) His among being and (is) My charge you
gold the head .thousand ten marked ,ruddy bright Beloved ?us

12 פָּז קְוֻצּוֹתָיו תַּלְתַּלִּים שְׁחֹרוֹת כָּעוֹרֵב׃ עֵינָיו כְּיוֹנִים עַל־
on doves as his a as black (are) his re-
eyes ;raven bushy locks ,fined

13 אֲפִיקֵי מָיִם רֹחֲצוֹת בֶּחָלָב יֹשְׁבוֹת עַל־מִלֵּאת׃ לְחָיָו
His .setting a on sitting ,milk with washed ,waters the
cheeks of rivers

כַּעֲרוּגַת הַבֹּשֶׂם מִגְדְּלוֹת מֶרְקָחִים שִׂפְתוֹתָיו שׁוֹשַׁנִּים
(as are) lips His aromatic raised a balsam like (are)
,lilies ;herbs of bed .spices of bed a

lilies dropping flowing myrrh. [14] His hands (are like) gold rings filled with jewels; His body (as) bright ivory overlaid with sapphires; [15] His legs (like) pillars of marble, set on bases of fine gold; His face (is like) Lebanon, excellent as the cedars. [16] His mouth (is) most sweet; and He (is) altogether lovely. This (is) my Beloved, and this (is) my Friend, O daughters of Jerusalem.

14 נֹטְפוֹת מוֹר עֹבֵר׃ יָדָיו גְּלִילֵי זָהָב מְמֻלָּאִים בַּתַּרְשִׁישׁ

with ;jewels | filled | gold | (as are) rods | His hands | .flowing myrrh | dropping

15 מֵעָיו עֶשֶׁת שֵׁן מְעֻלֶּפֶת סַפִּירִים׃ שׁוֹקָיו עַמּוּדֵי שֵׁשׁ

,marble | (as) of pillars | legs His | ;sapphires | overlaid with | ,ivory | fab- a of ric | His body

מְיֻסָּדִים עַל־אַדְנֵי־פָז מַרְאֵהוּ כַּלְּבָנוֹן בָּחוּר כָּאֲרָזִים׃

the as ;cedars | choice | (as) ,Lebanon | face His | fine ;gold | bases of | on | set

16 חִכּוֹ מַמְתַקִּים וְכֻלּוֹ מַחֲמַדִּים זֶה דוֹדִי וְזֶה רֵעִי בְּנוֹת

daugh- O of ters | my ,Friend | and this | my ,Beloved | this (is) | ;desirable | all and Him of | most (is) ;sweet | His mouth

יְרוּשָׁלִָם׃

.Jerusalem

CHAPTER 6

[1] Where has your Beloved gone, most beautiful among women? Where has your Beloved turned? For we seek Him along with you. [2] My Beloved has gone down to His garden, to the terraces of spices, to feed in the gardens and to gather lilies. [3] I (am) my Beloved's, and my Beloved (is) mine; He feeds among the lilies.

[4] O my love, you (are) as beautiful as Tizrah, as lovely as Jerusalem, awesome as bannered (armies). [5] Turn away your eyes from Me, because they overcome Me; your hair (is) like a flock of goats that reclines from Gilead. [6] Your teeth (are) like a flock of sheep of which all of them go up from the washing bearing twins, and (there is) not one barren among them. [7] Your temples behind your veil (are) like a piece of pomegranate. [8] Sixty of them (are) queens, and eighty concubines, and virgins without number. [9] (But) My dove, My undefiled is one (alone). She (is the only) one of her mother. She (is) the choice of her who bore her. The daughters saw her and called her blessed; the queens and the concubines (saw her), and they praised her.

[10] Who (is) she (who) looks down like the morning, fair as the moon, clear

CAP. VI ו

CHAPTER 6

1 אָנָה הָלַךְ דּוֹדֵךְ הַיָּפָה בַּנָּשִׁים אָנָה פָּנָה דוֹדֵךְ וּנְבַקְשֶׁנּוּ

we for Him seek | your ?Beloved | has faced | Where | among ?women | most beautiful | your ,Beloved | gone has Where

2 עִמָּךְ׃ דּוֹדִי יָרַד לְגַנּוֹ לַעֲרֻגוֹת הַבֹּשֶׂם לִרְעוֹת בַּגַּנִּים

the in ,gardens | feed to | balsam-spices | the to of beds | His to ,garden | went down | My Beloved | with .you

3 וְלִלְקֹט שׁוֹשַׁנִּים׃ אֲנִי לְדוֹדִי וְדוֹדִי לִי הָרֹעֶה בַּשּׁוֹשַׁנִּים׃

the among .lilies | He feeds | to (is) ;me | my and Beloved | my to ,Beloved | I (am) | .lilies | to and gather

4 יָפָה אַתְּ רַעְיָתִי כְּתִרְצָה נָאוָה כִּירוּשָׁלִָם אֲיֻמָּה כַּנִּדְגָּלוֹת׃

bannered as .armies | awesome | as Jerusalem | comely | as ,Tirzah | my O ,love | you Beauti- are ful

5 הָסֵבִּי עֵינַיִךְ מִנֶּגְדִּי שֶׁהֵם הִרְהִיבֻנִי שַׂעְרֵךְ כְּעֵדֶר הָעִזִּים

goats | a like of flock | your (is) hair | disturb ;me | because they | from ,me | your eyes | Turn away

6 שֶׁגָּלְשׁוּ מִן־הַגִּלְעָד׃ שִׁנַּיִךְ כְּעֵדֶר הָרְחֵלִים שֶׁעָלוּ מִן

from | which up come | ewes | like (are) of flock a | Your teeth | .Gilead | from | which reclines

7 הָרַחְצָה שֶׁכֻּלָּם מַתְאִימוֹת וְשַׁכֻּלָה אֵין בָּהֶם׃ כְּפֶלַח

a Like of piece | among .them | is not | a and one barren | bearing ,twins | all (are) them of | which | the ;washing

8 הָרִמּוֹן רַקָּתֵךְ מִבַּעַד לְצַמָּתֵךְ׃ שִׁשִּׁים הֵמָּה מְלָכוֹת וּשְׁמֹנִים

and eighty | ,queens | them are | of Sixty | your .veil | from behind | your (are) temples | pome- granate

9 פִּילַגְשִׁים וַעֲלָמוֹת אֵין מִסְפָּר׃ אַחַת הִיא יוֹנָתִי תַמָּתִי

per- my ;one fect | my dove | she ,(is) | ,One (only) | .number | without | and virgins | ,concubines

אַחַת הִיא לְאִמָּהּ בָּרָה הִיא לְיוֹלַדְתָּהּ רָאוּהָ בָנוֹת

the daughters | her saw | one the to ;her bore who | she (is) | the choice | her to ;mother | she (is) | the one

10 וַיְאַשְּׁרוּהָ מְלָכוֹת וּפִילַגְשִׁים וַיְהַלְלוּהָ׃ מִי־זֹאת הַנִּשְׁקָפָה

looks who down | (is) Who ,this | they and .her praised | the and ;concubines | the queens | blessed and ,her

as the sun (and) awesome as bannered (armies)? [11] I went down into the garden of nut-trees, to see the fruits of the ravine, to see whether the vine flowered (and) the pomegranates budded. [12] I did not know, my soul set me on the chariots of my princely people. [13] Return, return, O Shulamite! Return, return, that we may look upon you. What will you see in the Shulamite! As it were the dance of two armies.

כַּמוֹ־שָׁחַר יָפָה כַלְּבָנָה בָּרָה כַּחַמָּה אֲיֻמָּה כַּנִּדְגָּלוֹת׃
bannered as ?(armies) awesome the as ,sun pure the as ,moon fair the as ,dawn

11 אֶל־גִּנַּת אֱגוֹז יָרַדְתִּי לִרְאוֹת בְּאִבֵּי הַנָּחַל לִרְאוֹת הֲפָרְחָה
whether blossomed see to the ,ravine the of fruits see to went I ,down nut trees of the garden To

12 הַגֶּפֶן הֵנֵצוּ הָרִמֹּנִים׃ לֹא יָדַעְתִּי נַפְשִׁי שָׂמַתְנִי מַרְכְּבוֹת
the (on) of chariots set me (but) soul my ,knew I Not the pomegranate (and) budded the vine

עַמִּי נָדִיב׃
.princely My people

CAP. VII ז

CHAPTER 7

[1] How beautiful are your feet in sandals, O prince's daughter! The joints of your thighs (are) like jewels, the work of the hands of a skillful worker [2] Your navel (is like) a round goblet, (which) never lacks mixed wine; your belly (is like) a heap of wheat set about with lilies. [3] Your two breasts (are) like two fawns, twins of a gazelle. [4] Your neck (is like) a tower of ivory; your eyes (like) the fish-pools in Heshbon, by the gate of Bathrabbim; your nose (is like) Lebanon's tower, peering toward the face of Damascus. [5] Your head (is like) Carmel, and the hair of your head like purple; the King (is) held captive in its tresses. [6] How beautiful and how pleasant you are, O love, in delights! [7] This your stature compares to a palm tree, and your breasts to clusters of grapes. [8] I said, I will go up in the palm tree, I will take hold of the stalk of it; now also your breasts shall be like clusters of the vine, and the smell of your face like apples; [9] and the roof of your mouth like the best wine for my Beloved, going down smoothly,

1 שׁוּבִי שׁוּבִי הַשּׁוּלַמִּית שׁוּבִי שׁוּבִי וְנֶחֱזֶה־בָּךְ מַה־תֶּחֱזוּ
will What see you upon we that !you gaze may ,return ,Return O !Shulamite ,return ,Return

2 בַּשּׁוּלַמִּית כִּמְחֹלַת הַמַּחֲנָיִם׃ מַה־יָּפוּ פְעָמַיִךְ בַּנְּעָלִים
,sandals in your footsteps beautiful are How (army) two camps the As of dance the in ?Shulamite

בַּת־נָדִיב חַמּוּקֵי יְרֵכַיִךְ כְּמוֹ חֲלָאִים מַעֲשֵׂה יְדֵי אָמָּן׃
art- ;isan's hands the of work ,jewels (are) like your thighs the of curves ;prince's O daughter

3 שָׁרְרֵךְ אַגַּן הַסַּהַר אַל־יֶחְסַר הַמָּזֶג בִּטְנֵךְ עֲרֵמַת חִטִּים
wheat a (as) of heap your belly mixed ;wine lacks it not ,round a (as) goblet your navel

4 סוּגָה בַּשּׁוֹשַׁנִּים׃ שְׁנֵי שָׁדַיִךְ כִּשְׁנֵי עֳפָרִים תָּאֳמֵי צְבִיָּה׃
;gazelle a twins of ,fawns like two your breasts two with ;lilies hedged about

5 צַוָּארֵךְ כְּמִגְדַּל הַשֵּׁן עֵינַיִךְ בְּרֵכוֹת בְּחֶשְׁבּוֹן עַל־שַׁעַר בַּת־
Bath- the of gate by in ,Heshbon the (as) fish-pools your eyes ;ivory a (as) of tower your neck

6 רַבִּים אַפֵּךְ כְּמִגְדַּל הַלְּבָנוֹן צוֹפֶה פְּנֵי דַמָּשֶׂק׃ רֹאשֵׁךְ
your head ;Damascus the of face peering toward ,Lebanon a (as) of tower your nose ;rabbim

עָלַיִךְ כַּכַּרְמֶל וְדַלַּת רֹאשֵׁךְ כָּאַרְגָּמָן מֶלֶךְ אָסוּר בָּרְהָטִים׃
(its) in .tresses held (is) captive the King like ;purple your head the and of hair (as) ,Carmel on you

7
8 מַה־יָּפִית וּמַה־נָּעַמְתְּ אַהֲבָה בַּתַּעֲנוּגִים׃ זֹאת קוֹמָתֵךְ
your stature This !delights in ,love O pleasant ,you are and how How beautiful

9 דָּמְתָה לְתָמָר וְשָׁדַיִךְ לְאַשְׁכֹּלוֹת׃ אָמַרְתִּי אֶעֱלֶה בְתָמָר
the (in) ;tree palm go will I up ,said I clusters .grapes of to your and breasts palm a to ,tree liken- is ed

אֹחֲזָה בְּסַנְסִנָּיו וְיִהְיוּ־נָא שָׁדַיִךְ כְּאֶשְׁכְּלוֹת הַגֶּפֶן וְרֵיחַ
the and of scent the ,vine like of clusters your breasts please and be let its of ;stalk will I hold take

10 אַפֵּךְ כַּתַּפּוּחִים׃ וְחִכֵּךְ כְּיֵין הַטּוֹב הוֹלֵךְ לְדוֹדִי לְמֵישָׁרִים
,uprightly my for Beloved going down the best like wine your and palate like ;apples your nose

causing the lips of those who are asleep to flow softly.

[10] I (am) my Beloved's, and His desire (is) toward me. [11] Come, my Beloved, let us go forth into the field; let us stay in the villages. [12] Let us get up early into the vineyards; let us see if the vine flowers, (whether) the tender grape appears, (and) the pomegranates bud forth; there I will give You my loves. [13] The love-apples give a smell, and over our gates are all kinds of pleasant fruits, new, also old, (which) I have laid up for You, my Beloved.

11 12 דֹּובֵב שִׂפְתֵי יְשֵׁנִים׃ אֲנִי לְדוֹדִי וְעָלַי תְּשׁוּקָתוֹ׃ לְכָה דוֹדִי
my ,Come desire his and my (am) I sleeping (over) flowing
,Beloved .(is) me toward ,Beloved's .ones' lips softly

13 נֵצֵא הַשָּׂדֶה נָלִינָה בַּכְּפָרִים׃ נַשְׁכִּימָה לַכְּרָמִים נִרְאֶה
us let the to rise us Let the in us let the to us let
see ;vineyards early up .villages lodge ;field out go

אִם־פָּרְחָה הַגֶּפֶן פִּתַּח הַסְּמָדַר הֵנֵצוּ הָרִמּוֹנִים שָׁם אֶתֵּן
will I there pome- the (and) the (whether) the flowers if
give ;granates forth bud ,blossom opens ,vine

14 אֶת־דֹּדַי לָךְ׃ הַדּוּדָאִים נָתְנוּ־רֵיחַ וְעַל־פְּתָחֵינוּ כָּל־מְגָדִים
excellent (are) our and a give love- The to my
;fruits all doors over ,scent apples .you loves

חֲדָשִׁים גַּם־יְשָׁנִים דּוֹדִי צָפַנְתִּי לָךְ׃
for have I my ,old also ,new
.you up laid ,Beloved

CAP. VIII ח

CHAPTER 8

CHAPTER 8

[1] Who can give You as my brother, who sucked the breasts of my mother? (When) I find You outside, I would kiss You; also, they would not despise me. [2] I would lead You, I would bring You into my mother's house; you would instruct me; I would cause You to drink the spiced wine from my pomegranate's juice. [3] His left hand (is) under my head, and His right (hand) would embrace me. [4] I charge you, O daughters of Jerusalem, (that) you do not stir up or awake (my) Love until it pleases. [5] Who (is) this that comes up from the wilderness, leaning on her Beloved! I awakened you under the apple tree; there your mother brought you forth; there she who bore you brought you forth.

[6] Set me as a seal on Your heart, as a seal on Your arm; for love (is) strong as death. Jealousy (is) cruel as Sheol. Its flames (are) coals of fire, a flame of Jehovah. [7] Many waters cannot quench love, nor will the floods drown it. If a man would give all the wealth of his house for love, they surely would despise him.

1 מִי יִתֶּנְךָ כְּאָח לִי יוֹנֵק שְׁדֵי אִמִּי אֶמְצָאֲךָ בַחוּץ אֶשָּׁקְךָ
would I ,outside I (If) my the sucking to as can Who
;you kiss you find !mother of breasts ,me brother you give

2 גַּם לֹא־יָבֻזוּ לִי׃ אֶנְהָגְךָ אֲבִיאֲךָ אֶל־בֵּית אִמִּי תְּלַמְּדֵנִי
would you my house to would I would I .me they not ,also
;me instruct ;mother's you bring ,you lead despise would

3 אַשְׁקְךָ מִיַּיִן הָרֶקַח מֵעֲסִיס רִמֹּנִי׃ שְׂמֹאלוֹ תַּחַת רֹאשִׁי
my (be would) left His pome- my the from the wine would I
,head under hand .granate of juice spiced drink you make

4 וִימִינוֹ תְּחַבְּקֵנִי׃ הִשְׁבַּעְתִּי אֶתְכֶם בְּנוֹת יְרוּשָׁלִָם מַה־תָּעִירוּ
you why ,Jerusalem O ,you charge I embraces his and
up stir should of daughters .me right

5 וּמַה־תְּעֹרְרוּ אֶת־הָאַהֲבָה עַד שֶׁתֶּחְפָּץ׃ מִי זֹאת עֹלָה
coming (is) Who .pleases it until love (my) you should or
up this awaken why

מִן־הַמִּדְבָּר מִתְרַפֶּקֶת עַל־דּוֹדָהּ תַּחַת הַתַּפּוּחַ עוֹרַרְתִּיךָ
awoke I the Under her on leaning the from
;you apple-tree ?Beloved ,wilderness

6 שָׁמָּה חִבְּלַתְךָ אִמֶּךָ שָׁמָּה חִבְּלָה יְלָדַתְךָ׃ שִׂימֵנִי כַחוֹתָם
a as me Set she she there your travailed there
seal .you bore ,travailed ;mother you with

עַל־לִבֶּךָ כַּחוֹתָם עַל־זְרוֹעֶךָ כִּי־עַזָּה כַמָּוֶת אַהֲבָה קָשָׁה
(is) ,love as (is) for your upon a as your upon
cruel death strong ;arm seal ,heart

7 כִשְׁאוֹל קִנְאָה רְשָׁפֶיהָ רִשְׁפֵּי אֵשׁ שַׁלְהֶבֶתְיָה׃ מַיִם רַבִּים
Many waters of flame a ,fire (are) flames its ;jealousy as
.Jehovah of flames Sheol

לֹא יוּכְלוּ לְכַבּוֹת אֶת־הָאַהֲבָה וּנְהָרוֹת לֹא יִשְׁטְפוּהָ אִם־
if over- will I not the and ,love quench to are not
;it flow rivers able

8 יִתֵּן אִישׁ אֶת־כָּל־הוֹן בֵּיתוֹ בָּאַהֲבָה בּוֹז יָבוּזוּ לוֹ׃ אָחוֹת
sister A .him they de- ,love for his the all a would
despise spising house of wealth man give

[8] We have a little sister, and she has no breasts; what shall we do for our sister in the day (in) which she shall be spoken for? [9] If she (is) a wall, we will build on her a turret of silver; and if she (is) a door, we will enclose her with boards of cedar. [10] I (was) a wall, and my breasts like towers; then was I in His eyes as one finding peace.

[11] Solomon had a vineyard in Baal-hamon; he let out the vineyard to keepers; everyone for the fruit of it was to bring a thousand (pieces) of silver. [12] My vineyard, which (is) mine, (is) before me; the thousand (is) to you, O Solomon, and two hundred for the keepers of its fruit. [13] You who dwell in the gardens, the companions listen to your voice; cause me to hear (it). [14] Hurry, my Beloved, and be like a gazelle or a young deer, or the stag on the mountains of spices.

לָנוּ קְטַנָּה וְשָׁדַיִם אֵין לָהּ מַה־נַּעֲשֶׂה לַאֲחֹתֵנוּ בַּיּוֹם

the in day | our for sister | shall do we | what | to ;her | are not | and breasts | ,little | to (is) us

9 שֶׁיְּדֻבַּר־בָּהּ׃ אִם־חוֹמָה הִיא נִבְנֶה עָלֶיהָ טִירַת כָּסֶף

;silver | a turret of | her on | will we build | she ,(is) | wall a | If | for ?her | he spoken | that has

10 וְאִם־דֶּלֶת הִיא נָצוּר עָלֶיהָ לוּחַ אָרֶז׃ אֲנִי חוֹמָה וְשָׁדַי

and breasts my | ,wall a | (was) I | .cedar | boards of | upon her | will we enclose | she ,(is) | a door | and if

11 כַּמִּגְדָּלוֹת אָז הָיִיתִי בְעֵינָיו כְּמוֹצְאֵת שָׁלוֹם׃ כֶּרֶם הָיָה

was | A vineyard | .peace | one as finding | His in eyes | I became | then | ;towers like

לִשְׁלֹמֹה בְּבַעַל הָמוֹן נָתַן אֶת־הַכֶּרֶם לַנֹּטְרִים אִישׁ יָבִא

to was bring | (each) man | to ;keepers | the vineyard | gave he | ;hamor Baal- | at | to Solomon

12 בְּפִרְיוֹ אֶלֶף כָּסֶף׃ כַּרְמִי שֶׁלִּי לְפָנָי הָאֶלֶף לְךָ שְׁלֹמֹה

O ,Solomon | for (is) ,you | the thousand | be- ;me fore | (is) which ,me to (is) | My vineyard | .silver | a thousand | its for fruit

13 וּמָאתַיִם לְנֹטְרִים אֶת־פִּרְיוֹ׃ הַיּוֹשֶׁבֶת בַּגַּנִּים חֲבֵרִים

the companions | the in ,gardens | who You dwell | .fruit its | the for of keepers | two and hundred

14 מַקְשִׁיבִים לְקוֹלֵךְ הַשְׁמִיעִנִי׃ בְּרַח ׀ דּוֹדִי וּדְמֵה־לְךָ לִצְבִי

a gazelle | be and like | my ,Beloved | ,Flee | to me cause (it) hear | your for ;voice | listening (are)

אוֹ לְעֹפֶר הָאַיָּלִים עַל הָרֵי בְשָׂמִים׃

balsam-spices | the of mountains | on | the stag | young a ,deer | or

ישעיה

LIBER JESAIAE

CAPUT. I א

CHAPTER 1

[1] The vision of Isaiah the son of Amoz, which he saw concerning Judah and Jerusalem in the days of Uzziah, Jotham, Ahaz (and) Hezekiah, kings of Judah. [2] Hear, O heavens, and listen, O earth! For Jehovah has spoken: I have nursed and brought up sons, and they have rebelled against Me. [3] The ox knows his owner, and the ass his master's stall, (but) Israel does not know; My people have not understood. [4] Woe, sinful nation, a people heavy (with) iniquity, a seed of evildoers, sons who corrupt! They have forsaken Jehovah; they have rejected the Holy One of Israel; they have gone away backward. [5] Where will you be beaten any more? Will you continue the revolt? The whole head is sick, and the whole heart is faint. [6] From the sole of the foot to the head, no soundness is in it; (only) a wound and a stripe and a fresh blow; they have not been closed, nor bound up, nor was it softened with oil. [7] Your land (is) a desolation; your cities burned with fire; your land before you, strangers devour it; and (it is) a desolation, as overthrown by strangers. [8] And the daughter of Zion is left like a booth in a vineyard, like a hut in a garden, like a besieged city. [9] Except Jehovah of hosts had left for us a survivor, a few, we would be as Sodom, we would become like Gomorrah.

CHAPTER 1

1 חֲזוֹן יְשַׁעְיָהוּ בֶן־אָמוֹץ אֲשֶׁר חָזָה עַל־יְהוּדָה וִירוּשָׁלִָם

and Jerusalem | Judah | concerning | saw he | which | ,Amoz the of son | Isaiah | The of vision

2 בִּימֵי עֻזִּיָּהוּ יוֹתָם אָחָז יְחִזְקִיָּהוּ מַלְכֵי יְהוּדָה׃ שִׁמְעוּ שָׁמַיִם

O ,heavens | ,Hear | .Judah | kings of | (and) ,Hezekiah | ,Ahaz | ,Jotham | ,Uzziah | the in of days

וְהַאֲזִינִי אֶרֶץ כִּי יְהוָה דִּבֵּר בָּנִים גִּדַּלְתִּי וְרוֹמַמְתִּי וְהֵם

but they | brought and ,up | have I reared | sons | has :spoken | Jehovah | For | O !earth | and ,listen

3 פָּשְׁעוּ בִי׃ יָדַע שׁוֹר קֹנֵהוּ וַחֲמוֹר אֵבוּס בְּעָלָיו יִשְׂרָאֵל

(but) Israel | his ,master's | manger | the and ass | his owner | The ox | knows | against .Me | have rebelled

4 לֹא יָדַע עַמִּי לֹא הִתְבּוֹנָן׃ הוֹי ׀ גּוֹי חֹטֵא עַם כֶּבֶד עָוֺן

ini- ;quity | heavy (with) | a people | ,sinful nation | Woe | have .understood | not | My people | does ;know | not

זֶרַע מְרֵעִים בָּנִים מַשְׁחִיתִים עָזְבוּ אֶת־יְהוָה נִאֲצוּ אֶת־

have they spurned | ,Jehovah | have They forsaken | who !corrupt | sons | evil ,doers | seed a of

5 קְדוֹשׁ יִשְׂרָאֵל נָזֹרוּ אָחוֹר׃ עַל־מֶה תֻכּוּ עוֹד תּוֹסִיפוּ סָרָה

the ?revolt | you Will continue | any you will ?more beaten be | Where | back- .ward | they away turned | ,Israel | Holy the of One

6 כָּל־רֹאשׁ לָחֳלִי וְכָל־לֵבָב דַּוָּי׃ מִכַּף־רֶגֶל וְעַד־רֹאשׁ

the head | to | the foot | From of sole | .faint is | heart | and the all | ,sick is | head | All the

אֵין־בּוֹ מְתֹם פֶּצַע וְחַבּוּרָה וּמַכָּה טְרִיָּה לֹא־זֹרוּ וְלֹא

nor | have they not ,closed been | ;fresh a blow and | and stripe a | (only) wound a | sound- ;ness | in it | not is

7 חֻבָּשׁוּ וְלֹא רֻכְּכָה בַּשָּׁמֶן׃ אַרְצְכֶם שְׁמָמָה עָרֵיכֶם שְׂרֻפוֹת

burned with | your cities | a (is) ;desolation | Your land | with .oil | it was softened | nor | bound ,up

אֵשׁ אַדְמַתְכֶם לְנֶגְדְּכֶם זָרִים אֹכְלִים אֹתָהּ וּשְׁמָמָה

(is it) and desolation | ,it | devour | strangers | before ,you | your land | ;fire

8 כְּמַהְפֵּכַת זָרִים׃ וְנוֹתְרָה בַת־צִיּוֹן כְּסֻכָּה בְכָרֶם כִּמְלוּנָה

a like hut | a in ,vineyard | a like booth | Zion the of daughter | left is And | .strangers | over- as by thrown

9 בְמִקְשָׁה כְּעִיר נְצוּרָה׃ לוּלֵי יְהוָה צְבָאוֹת הוֹתִיר לָנוּ

for us | had left | hosts of | Jehovah | Except | .besieged | a like city | a in ,garden

10 שָׂרִיד כִּמְעָט כִּסְדֹם הָיִינוּ לַעֲמֹרָה דָּמִינוּ׃ שִׁמְעוּ

Hear | would we become | as Gomorrah | we ;be would | as Sodom | ,few a | ,survivor

[10] Hear the word of Jehovah, rulers of Sodom; listen to the law of our God, people of Gomorrah! [11] What (good are) the multitude of your sacrifices to Me, says Jehovah? I am full of the burnt offerings of rams and the fat of fed beasts; nor do I delight in the blood of bulls, or of lambs, or of he-goats. [12] When you come to see My face, who has required this at your hand, to trample My courts? [13] Do not add to bringing vain sacrifice; it (is) hateful incense to Me; I cannot endure the new moon and sabbath, the calling of meeting — and the evil assembly! [14] My soul hates your new moons and your yearly feasts. They are a burden to Me; I am weary of bearing them. [15] And when you spread out your hands, I will hide My eyes from you. Yea, when you multiply prayer, I will not hear. Your hands are full of blood. [16] Wash yourselves, make yourselves clean. Put away the evil of your doings from My sight; stop doing evil. [17] Learn to do good; seek justice; reprove the oppressor; judge the orphan; defend the widow.

[18] Come now and let us reason together, says Jehovah: though your sins are as scarlet, they shall be as white as snow; though they are red as the crimson, they shall be like wool! [19] If you are willing and obedient, you shall eat the good of the land. [20] But if you refuse and rebel, you shall be devoured (with) the sword; for the mouth of Jehovah has spoken.

[21] O how the faithful city has become a harlot! She was full of justice; righteousness lodged in it—but now murderers! [22] Your silver has become dross; your wine is diluted with water.

דְבַר־יְהוָה קְצִינֵי סְדֹם הַאֲזִינוּ תּוֹרַת אֱלֹהֵינוּ עַם עֲמֹרָה׃
!Gomorrah O ,God our the listen ;Sodom O ,Jehovah the
of people of law to of rulers of word

11 לָמָּה לִּי רֹב־זִבְחֵיכֶם יֹאמַר יְהוָה שָׂבַעְתִּי עֹלוֹת אֵילִים
,rams burnt am I ?Jehovah says your many to What
of offerings of full ,sacrifices Me (use)

וְחֵלֶב מְרִיאִים וְדַם פָּרִים וּכְבָשִׂים וְעַתּוּדִים לֹא חָפָצְתִּי׃
I do not and and ;bulls the and fattened the and
.in delight he-goats lambs of blood ,cattle of fat

12 כִּי תָבֹאוּ לֵרָאוֹת פָּנָי מִי־בִקֵּשׁ זֹאת מִיֶּדְכֶם רְמֹס חֲצֵרָי׃
My to your from this has who My see to you When
?courts trample ,hand required ,face come

13 לֹא תוֹסִיפוּ הָבִיא מִנְחַת־שָׁוְא קְטֹרֶת תּוֹעֵבָה הִיא לִי
to it abomination incense ;vain sacrifice to do Not
;Me (is) bringing add

14 חֹדֶשׁ וְשַׁבָּת קְרֹא מִקְרָא לֹא־אוּכַל אָוֶן וַעֲצָרָה׃ חָדְשֵׁיכֶם
new Your the and ,evil can I not ;meeting the and new the
moons .assembly endure of calling ,sabbath moon

וּמוֹעֲדֵיכֶם שָׂנְאָה נַפְשִׁי הָיוּ עָלַי לָטֹרַח נִלְאֵיתִי נְשֹׂא׃
bearing am I a upon They My hates your and
.(them) of tired ;burden Me are .soul feasts appointed

15 וּבְפָרִשְׂכֶם כַּפֵּיכֶם אַעְלִים עֵינַי מִכֶּם גַּם כִּי־תַרְבּוּ תְפִלָּה
,prayer you when also from my will I your you when So
multiply ;you eyes hide hands out spread

16 אֵינֶנִּי שֹׁמֵעַ יְדֵיכֶם דָּמִים מָלֵאוּ׃ רַחֲצוּ הִזַּכּוּ הָסִירוּ רֹעַ
the remove purify wash full are blood Your will I
of evil ;yourselves ,yourselves of hands .hear not

17 מַעַלְלֵיכֶם מִנֶּגֶד עֵינָי חִדְלוּ הָרֵעַ׃ לִמְדוּ הֵיטֵב דִּרְשׁוּ
seek do to Learn doing cease My from your
;good .evil ;eyes before doings

מִשְׁפָּט אַשְּׁרוּ חָמוֹץ שִׁפְטוּ יָתוֹם רִיבוּ אַלְמָנָה׃
the plead the judge the reprove ,justice
.widow for ,orphan ;oppressor

18 לְכוּ־נָא וְנִוָּכְחָה יֹאמַר יְהוָה אִם־יִהְיוּ חֲטָאֵיכֶם כַּשָּׁנִים
,scarlet as sins your are though ;Jehovah says us let and ,now Come
,right be

19 כַּשֶּׁלֶג יַלְבִּינוּ אִם־יַאְדִּימוּ כַתּוֹלָע כַּצֶּמֶר יִהְיוּ׃ אִם־תֹּאבוּ
are you If they like the as they though shall they as
willing !be shall wool ,crimson red are ;white be snow

20 וּשְׁמַעְתֶּם טוּב הָאָרֶץ תֹּאכֵלוּ׃ וְאִם־תְּמָאֲנוּ וּמְרִיתֶם
,rebel and you if But shall you the the and
refuse .eat land of good ,hear

21 חֶרֶב תְּאֻכְּלוּ כִּי פִּי יְהוָה דִּבֵּר׃ אֵיכָה הָיְתָה
has How has Jehovah the for be shall you the (by)
become .spoken of mouth devoured sword

לְזוֹנָה קִרְיָה נֶאֱמָנָה מְלֵאֲתִי מִשְׁפָּט צֶדֶק יָלִין בָּהּ וְעַתָּה
but in lodged righ- ;justice (was She) !faithful the harlot a
now —her teousness of full city

22 מְרַצְּחִים׃ כַּסְפֵּךְ הָיָה לְסִיגִים סָבְאֵךְ מָהוּל בַּמָּיִם׃
with is your ;dross has Your !murderers
.water diluted liquor become silver

[23] Your princes (are) rebellious and companions of thieves; every one loves a bribe and is pursuing rewards. They do not judge the orphan, nor does the cause of the widow come to them. [24] Therefore says the Lord, Jehovah of hosts, the mighty One of Israel, Ah, I will ease Myself of My foes and I will avenge Myself of My enemies. [25] And I will return My hand on you and refine as (with) lye your dross, and take away all your alloy. [26] And I will return your judges, as at first, and your advisors, as at the beginning; then you shall be called the city of righteousness, the faithful town. [27] Zion shall be redeemed with justice, and her returning ones with righteousness. [28] And the ruin of the transgressors and of the sinners (shall be) together, and those who forsake Jehovah shall be destroyed. [29] For they shall be ashamed of the trees which you lusted after; and you shall be ashamed of the gardens you have chosen. [30] For you shall be like a tree whose leaf fades, and like a garden that has no water for it. [31] And the strong shall be for tow, and the maker of it for a spark; and they shall both burn together, and no one (is) quenching (them).

23 שָׂרַיִךְ סוֹרְרִים וְחַבְרֵי גַּנָּבִים כֻּלּוֹ אֹהֵב שֹׁחַד וְרֹדֵף
is and bribe a loves every ;thieves com- and are Your
seeking one of panions rebellious rulers

שַׁלְמֹנִים יָתוֹם לֹא יִשְׁפֹּטוּ וְרִיב אַלְמָנָה לֹא־יָבוֹא אֲלֵיהֶם׃
.them to does not the the and do they not the ;gifts
come widow of cause ;judge orphan

24 לָכֵן נְאֻם הָאָדוֹן יְהוָה צְבָאוֹת אֲבִיר יִשְׂרָאֵל הוֹי אֶנָּחֵם
will I ,Alas ,Israel the ,hosts Jehovah the states There-
eased be of One Mighty of ,Lord fore

25 מִצָּרַי וְאִנָּקְמָה מֵאוֹיְבָי׃ וְאָשִׁיבָה יָדִי עָלַיִךְ וְאֶצְרֹף כַּבֹּר
(with) as and upon my I And My of avenge and My of
lye refine you hand return will .enemies Myself ,foes

26 סִיגָיִךְ וְאָסִירָה כָּל־בְּדִילָיִךְ׃ וְאָשִׁיבָה שֹׁפְטַיִךְ כְּבָרִאשֹׁנָה
at as your will I your all take and your
,first the ,judges return .alloy away ,dross

וְיֹעֲצַיִךְ כְּבַתְּחִלָּה אַחֲרֵי־כֵן יִקָּרֵא לָךְ עִיר הַצֶּדֶק קִרְיָה
town a righteous- city a to shall it afterwards the at as your and
,ness of you called be ,beginning advisors

27 28 נֶאֱמָנָה׃ צִיּוֹן בְּמִשְׁפָּט תִּפָּדֶה וְשָׁבֶיהָ בִּצְדָקָה׃ וְשֶׁבֶר
the And with her and be shall with Zion .faithful
of crushing .righteousness returnees redeemed justice

29 פֹּשְׁעִים וְחַטָּאִים יַחְדָּו וְעֹזְבֵי יְהוָה יִכְלוּ׃ כִּי יֵבֹשׁוּ
shall they For be shall Jehovah those and ,together and trans-
ashamed be .destroyed forsake who sinners gressors

מֵאֵילִים אֲשֶׁר חֲמַדְתֶּם וְתַחְפְּרוּ מֵהַגַּנּוֹת אֲשֶׁר בְּחַרְתֶּם׃
have you that the of shall you and you which the of
.chosen gardens ashamed be desired trees

30 כִּי תִהְיוּ כְּאֵלָה נֹבֶלֶת עָלֶהָ וּכְגַנָּה אֲשֶׁר־מַיִם אֵין לָהּ׃
for not water (in) like and whose fades a like you For
.it is which garden a ,leaf tree be shall

31 וְהָיָה הֶחָסֹן לִנְעֹרֶת וּפֹעֲלוֹ לְנִיצוֹץ וּבָעֲרוּ שְׁנֵיהֶם יַחְדָּו
,together both they and a for his and ,tow for the And
burn shall ;spark work strong be will

וְאֵין מְכַבֶּה׃
shall and
.(them) quench none

CAP. II ב

CHAPTER 2

CHAPTER 2

[1] The word that Isaiah the son of Amoz saw concerning Judah and Jerusalem: [2] And it shall come to pass, in the last days, that the mountain of Jehovah's house shall be established in the top of the mountains, and shall be exalted above the hills, and all nations shall flow into it. [3] And many people shall go and say, Come and let us go up to the mount of Jehovah, to the house of the

1 הַדָּבָר אֲשֶׁר חָזָה יְשַׁעְיָהוּ בֶּן־אָמוֹץ עַל־יְהוּדָה וִירוּשָׁלִָם׃
and Judah con- ,Amoz son ,Isaiah saw that The
.Jerusalem cerning of word

2 וְהָיָה ׀ בְּאַחֲרִית הַיָּמִים נָכוֹן יִהְיֶה הַר בֵּית־יְהוָה בְּרֹאשׁ
the in Jehovah's house the be shall estab- ,days the last in it And
of top of mountain lished be will

3 הֶהָרִים וְנִשָּׂא מִגְּבָעוֹת וְנָהֲרוּ אֵלָיו כָּל־הַגּוֹיִם׃ וְהָלְכוּ
will And .nations all it to shall and the above will and the
go flow ;hills exalted be ,mountains

עַמִּים רַבִּים וְאָמְרוּ לְכוּ ׀ וְנַעֲלֶה אֶל־הַר־יְהוָה אֶל־בֵּית
the to Jehovah the to let and ,Come ,say and many peoples
of house of mount up go us

God of Jacob. And He will teach from His ways, and we will walk in His paths. For out of Zion will the Law go forth, and the word of Jehovah from Jerusalem. [4] And He shall judge among the nations and shall rebuke many people. And they shall beat their swords into plowshares, and their spears into pruning-hooks. Nation shall not lift up sword against nation, nor shall they learn war any more. [5] O house of Jacob, come and let us walk in the light of Jehovah. [6] Truly You have forsaken Your people, the house of Jacob, because they are filled from the east, and (are) fortune-tellers like the Philistines; and they please themselves in the sons of foreigners. [7] Also their land is full of silver and gold; there is no end of their treasures, and their land is full of horses; their chariots also are without end. [8] And their land is full of idols; they worship the work of their own hands, that which their own fingers have made. [9] And the lowly one bows down; and the high one lowers himself; therefore You do not forgive them. [10] Enter into the rock and hide in the dust for fear of Jehovah, and from His majesty's glory. [11] The lofty eyes of man shall be humbled, and the pride of men shall be bowed down; and Jehovah alone shall be exalted in that day. [12] For the day of Jehovah of hosts (shall be) on all the proud and lofty ones, and on all that is lifted up, and it will ever be abased; [13] and against all Lebanon's cedars, high and lifted up, and against all the oaks of Bashan, [14] and against all the high mountains, and against all the hills lifted up; [15] and against every tall tower; and against every fortified wall; [16] and against all the ships of Tarshish; and

אֱלֹהֵי יַעֲקֹב וְיֹרֵנוּ מִדְּרָכָיו וְנֵלְכָה בְּאֹרְחֹתָיו כִּי מִצִּיּוֹן

of out Zion | for | His in ,paths | we and walk will | His from ,ways | He and teach will | ,Jacob | the of God

4 תֵּצֵא תוֹרָה וּדְבַר־יְהוָה מִירוּשָׁלִָם׃ וְשָׁפַט בֵּין הַגּוֹיִם

the ,nations | among | He And judge shall | from .Jerusalem | Jehovah's and word | ,law the | go will forth

וְהוֹכִיחַ לְעַמִּים רַבִּים וְכִתְּתוּ חַרְבוֹתָם לְאִתִּים וַחֲנִיתוֹתֵיהֶם

their and spears | into ,plowshares | their swords | they And beat shall | .many | peoples | shall and rebuke

לְמַזְמֵרוֹת לֹא־יִשָּׂא גוֹי אֶל־גּוֹי חֶרֶב וְלֹא־יִלְמְדוּ עוֹד

any more | they shall learn | nor | ,sword | nation against nation | lift shall not up | pruning into ;knives

5
6 מִלְחָמָה׃ בֵּית יַעֲקֹב לְכוּ וְנֵלְכָה בְּאוֹר יְהוָה׃ כִּי

For | .Jehovah | the in of light | let and Come walk us | ,Jacob | O of house | .war

נָטַשְׁתָּה עַמְּךָ בֵּית יַעֲקֹב כִּי מָלְאוּ מִקֶּדֶם וְעֹנְנִים כַּפְּלִשְׁתִּים

the like ;Philistines | (are) and soothsayers | from ,east the | are they filled | for | ,Jacob | the of house | Your ,people | have You forsaken

7 וּבְיַלְדֵי נָכְרִים יַשְׂפִּיקוּ׃ וַתִּמָּלֵא אַרְצוֹ כֶּסֶף וְזָהָב וְאֵין

not and is | and ,gold | (with) silver | his land | is And filled | clap they .(hands their) | foreigners | with and of children

קֵצֶה לְאֹצְרֹתָיו וַתִּמָּלֵא אַרְצוֹ סוּסִים וְאֵין קֵצֶה לְמַרְכְּבֹתָיו׃

his to .chariots | an end | and is not | (with) ,horses | his land | is and filled | his to ,treasures | an end

8 וַתִּמָּלֵא אַרְצוֹ אֱלִילִים לְמַעֲשֵׂה יָדָיו יִשְׁתַּחֲווּ לַאֲשֶׁר עָשׂוּ

have made | that which | he ,worships | his hands | work the of | (with) ;idols | his land | is And filled

9 אֶצְבְּעֹתָיו׃ וַיִּשַּׁח אָדָם וַיִּשְׁפַּל־אִישׁ וְאַל־תִּשָּׂא לָהֶם׃

.them | You forgive | but not | ,man | was and humbled | ,man | was and bowed down | own his .fingers

10 בּוֹא בַצּוּר וְהִטָּמֵן בֶּעָפָר מִפְּנֵי פַּחַד יְהוָה וּמֵהֲדַר גְּאֹנוֹ׃

His ,majesty's | from and glory | ,Jehovah | fear the of | from before | the in dust | and hide | the into rock | Enter

11 עֵינֵי גַּבְהוּת אָדָם שָׁפֵל וְשַׁח רוּם אֲנָשִׁים וְנִשְׂגַּב יְהוָה

Jehovah | will but exalted be | ,men | the of pride | and bowed | be will ,humbled | man's haughtiness | the of eyes

12 לְבַדּוֹ בַּיּוֹם הַהוּא׃ כִּי יוֹם לַיהוָה צְבָאוֹת עַל כָּל־

all | against | hosts (be will) | Jehovah of | the day of | For | .that | day in | He alone

13 גֵּאֶה וָרָם וְעַל כָּל־נִשָּׂא וְשָׁפֵל׃ וְעַל כָּל־אַרְזֵי הַלְּבָנוֹן

,Lebanon | the of cedars | all | and against | ever will it ;abased be | is that lifted | all | and lofty against | and the ;ones proud

14 הָרָמִים וְהַנִּשָּׂאִים וְעַל כָּל־אַלּוֹנֵי הַבָּשָׁן׃ וְעַל כָּל־הֶהָרִים

the mountains | all | and against | ;Bashan | the of oaks | all | and against | lifted and ;up | high

15 הָרָמִים וְעַל כָּל־הַגְּבָעוֹת הַנִּשָּׂאוֹת׃ וְעַל כָּל־מִגְדָּל גָּבֹהַּ

;tall | tower every | and against | ;up lifted | the hills | all | and against | ;high

16 וְעַל כָּל־חוֹמָה בְצוּרָה׃ וְעַל כָּל־אֳנִיּוֹת תַּרְשִׁישׁ וְעַל כָּל־

all | and against | ;Tarshish | the of ships | all | and against | ;fortified | wall every | and against

on all craft of pleasure. [17] And the loftiness of man shall be bowed down, and the pride of men shall be made low; and Jehovah alone shall be exalted in that day. [18] And the idols shall completely pass away. [19] And they shall go into the caves of the rocks, and into the holes of the earth for fear of Jehovah, and from the glory of His majesty; when He arises to quake the earth. [20] In that day a man shall throw his silver idols, and his golden idols, which they made for him to worship, to the moles and to the bats; [21] to go into the crevices of the rocks, and into the clefts of the cliffs, for dread of Jehovah, and from the glory of His majesty; when He arises to quake the earth. [22] Cease from man, whose breath (is) in his nostrils; for in what value is he?

17 שְׂכִיּוֹת הַחֶמְדָּה׃ וְשַׁח גַּבְהוּת הָאָדָם וְשָׁפֵל רוּם אֲנָשִׁים

;men's lofti- ness will and abased be ,man's pride be will And humbled .desirable the craft

18 וְנִשְׂגַּב יְהוָה לְבַדּוֹ בַּיּוֹם הַהוּא׃ וְהָאֱלִילִים כָּלִיל יַחֲלֹף׃

will completely .vanish the And idols .that day in alone Jehovah will and exalted be

19 וּבָאוּ בִּמְעָרוֹת צֻרִים וּבִמְחִלּוֹת עָפָר מִפְּנֵי פַּחַד יְהוָה

Jehovah the of fear from before the dust into and of holes the the ,rocks the into of caves they And go shall

20 וּמֵהֲדַר גְּאוֹנוֹ בְּקוּמוֹ לַעֲרֹץ הָאָרֶץ׃ בַּיּוֹם הַהוּא יַשְׁלִיךְ

shall throw that day In the .earth make to tremble He when arises His ;majesty's from and glory

הָאָדָם אֵת אֱלִילֵי כַסְפּוֹ וְאֵת אֱלִילֵי זְהָבוֹ אֲשֶׁר עָשׂוּ־לוֹ

for they him made which his ,gold idols of and his ,silver of idols man

21 לְהִשְׁתַּחֲוֹת לַחְפֹּר פֵּרוֹת וְלָעֲטַלֵּפִים׃ לָבוֹא בְּנִקְרוֹת

the into of crevices go to to and ,bats the the to moles ,worship to

הַצֻּרִים וּבִסְעִפֵי הַסְּלָעִים מִפְּנֵי פַּחַד יְהוָה וּמֵהֲדַר גְּאוֹנוֹ

His ,majesty's from and glory Jehovah the of dread from before ,cliffs the into and of clefts the the ,rocks

22 בְּקוּמוֹ לַעֲרֹץ הָאָרֶץ׃ חִדְלוּ לָכֶם מִן־הָאָדָם אֲשֶׁר נְשָׁמָה

breath (is) whose man from your- self Cease the .earth make to tremble He when arises

בְּאַפּוֹ כִּי בַמֶּה נֶחְשָׁב הוּא׃

.he be to is esteemed in what for his in ,nostril

CAP. III ג

CHAPTER 3

[1] For behold, the Lord, Jehovah of hosts, takes away the stay and the staff from Jerusalem and Judah; the whole stay of bread and the whole stay of water; [2] the mighty man and the man of war; the judge and the prophet; and the diviner and the elder; [3] the captain of fifty and the accepted of face; the advisor and the artisan; and the expert charmer. [4] And, I will give young boys (to be) their heads, and caprices shall rule over them. [5] And the people shall be crushed, man against man, and a man on his neighbor. The child shall behave insolently against the aged, and the low against the honorable. [6] When a man shall take hold of his brother, (of) the house of his father, (saying, You have) a cloak; come, you be our ruler; let this ruin (be)

1 כִּי הִנֵּה הָאָדוֹן יְהוָה צְבָאוֹת מֵסִיר מִירוּשָׁלִַם וּמִיהוּדָה

from and Judah from Jerusalem is removing ,hosts Jehovah of the Lord ,behold For

2 מַשְׁעֵן וּמַשְׁעֵנָה כֹּל מִשְׁעַן־לֶחֶם וְכֹל מִשְׁעַן־מָיִם׃ גִּבּוֹר

the mighty ;water stay of and whole the bread stay of the whole the and ,staff the stay

3 וְאִישׁ מִלְחָמָה שׁוֹפֵט וְנָבִיא וְקֹסֵם וְזָקֵן׃ שַׂר־חֲמִשִּׁים

,fifty com- of mander the and ;elder the diviner the and ;prophet the judge ;war the and of man

4 וּנְשׂוּא פָנִים וְיוֹעֵץ וַחֲכַם חֲרָשִׁים וּנְבוֹן לָחַשׁ׃ וְנָתַתִּי

I And give will .enchanter the and expert ,craftsmen the and skilled the and counselor of ,face the and exalted

5 נְעָרִים שָׂרֵיהֶם וְתַעֲלוּלִים יִמְשְׁלוּ־בָם׃ וְנִגַּשׂ הָעָם אִישׁ

man the ,people will And oppress over .them shall rule and caprices (be to) rulers their young boys

בְּאִישׁ וְאִישׁ בְּרֵעֵהוּ יִרְהֲבוּ הַנַּעַר בַּזָּקֵן וְהַנִּקְלֶה בַּנִּכְבָּד׃

the against .honorable the and despised against ,elder the the child be will insolent his on ;neighbor and man a against ,man

6 כִּי־יִתְפֹּשׂ אִישׁ בְּאָחִיו בֵּית אָבִיו שִׂמְלָה לְכָה קָצִין

a ruler ,Come !cloak A ,(saying) his ,father's (at) house his of brother a man shall hold When take

under your hand — [7] in that day he shall swear, saying, I will not be a healer; for there is no bread nor a cloak in my house; you shall not make me a ruler of the people. [8] For Jerusalem has stumbled, and Judah has fallen; because their tongue and their deeds toward Jehovah (are) to rebel against the eyes of His glory. [9] The look of their faces witnesses against them; they have declared their sin like Sodom; they do not hide (it). Woe to their soul! For they have dealt evil to themselves. [10] Say to the righteous that (it is) well; for they shall eat of the fruit of their doings. [11] Woe to the wicked! (It shall be) ill; for the reward of his hand is done to him. [12] (As for) My people, children are their oppressors, and women rule over him. O My people, your rulers cause you to go astray, and swallow the way of your paths.

[13] Jehovah stands up to plead His case, and stands up to judge the people. [14] Jehovah will enter into judgment with the elders of His people, and their kings; for you have eaten up the vineyard; the spoil of the poor (is) in your houses. [15] What do you (mean that) you crush My people, and grind the faces of the poor, says the Lord Jehovah of hosts? [16] And Jehovah says, Because the daughters of Zion are proud, and walk with stretched out necks and wanton eyes, walking and mincing as they go, and making a tinkling with their feet; [17] therefore, Jehovah will make the crown of the daughters of Zion scabby; and Jehovah will make their secret parts naked. [18] In that day the Lord will take away the beauty of ankle-bracelets; and the bands of the head, and the crescents, [19] the pendants, and the

7 תְּהְיֶה־לָּנוּ וְהַמַּכְשֵׁלָה הַזֹּאת תַּחַת יָדֶךָ: יִשָּׂא בַיּוֹם
day in will He your under this ruin and for
up lift .hand us be shall

הַהוּא | לֵאמֹר לֹא־אֶהְיֶה חֹבֵשׁ וּבְבֵיתִי אֵין לֶחֶם וְאֵין
and ,bread not in for ;healer a will I not ,saying ,that
not is house my be

8 שִׂמְלָה לֹא תְשִׂימֻנִי קְצִין עָם: כִּי כָשְׁלָה יְרוּשָׁלַם וִיהוּדָה
and ,Jerusalem has For the ruler shall you not ;cloak a
Judah stumbled .people's me appoint

נָפָל כִּי־לְשׁוֹנָם וּמַעַלְלֵיהֶם אֶל־יְהוָה לַמְרוֹת עֵנֵי כְבוֹדוֹ:
His the rebel to Jehovah toward their and their because has
glory of eyes against (are) deeds tongue ,fallen

9 הַכָּרַת פְּנֵיהֶם עָנְתָה בָּם וְחַטָּאתָם כִּסְדֹם הִגִּידוּ לֹא
not have they like their and against witnesses their The
;declared Sodom sin ,them faces of look

10 כִּחֵדוּ אוֹי לְנַפְשָׁם כִּי־גָמְלוּ לָהֶם רָעָה: אִמְרוּ צַדִּיק כִּי־
that the Tell !evil them- to they for their to Woe
righteous selves dealt have ,soul .(it) hide

11 טוֹב כִּי־פְרִי מַעַלְלֵיהֶם יֹאכֵלוּ: אוֹי לְרָשָׁע רָע כִּי־גְמוּל
the for ;evil the to Woe will they their the for (is it)
of doing ,wicked .eat deeds of fruit ,well

12 יָדָיו יֵעָשֶׂה לּוֹ: עַמִּי נֹגְשָׂיו מְעוֹלֵל וְנָשִׁים מָשְׁלוּ בוֹ עַמִּי
My O over rule and (are) their My to be will his
,people .him women ,children oppressors people .him done hand

13 מְאַשְּׁרֶיךָ מַתְעִים וְדֶרֶךְ אֹרְחֹתֶיךָ בִּלֵּעוּ: נִצָּב לָרִיב
to Stands they your the and (you) make your
contend up .swallow paths of way ,stray leaders

14 יְהוָה וְעֹמֵד לָדִין עַמִּים: יְהוָה בְּמִשְׁפָּט יָבוֹא עִם־זִקְנֵי
the with will into Jehovah the to and Jehovah
of elders enter judgment .peoples judge up stands

15 עַמּוֹ וְשָׂרָיו וְאַתֶּם בִּעַרְתֶּם הַכֶּרֶם גְּזֵלַת הֶעָנִי בְּבָתֵּיכֶם:
your in (is) the the the have for their and His
.houses poor of spoil ;vineyard burned you ,rulers people

מַלָּכֶם תְּדַכְּאוּ עַמִּי וּפְנֵי עֲנִיִּים תִּטְחָנוּ נְאֻם־אֲדֹנָי יְהוִה
Jehovah the declares ,grind the the and My You (is) What
of Lord poor of faces ,people crush ?you to

16 צְבָאוֹת: וַיֹּאמֶר יְהוָה יַעַן כִּי גָבְהוּ בְּנוֹת צִיּוֹן
,Zion the proud are Because ,Jehovah said And ?hosts
of daughters

וַתֵּלַכְנָה נְטוּוֹת גָּרוֹן וּמְשַׂקְּרוֹת עֵינָיִם הָלוֹךְ וְטָפֹף תֵּלַכְנָה
they (as) and walking ,eyes with and ,necks with walk and
;go mincing wanton out stretched

17 וּבְרַגְלֵיהֶם תְּעַכַּסְנָה: וְשִׂפַּח אֲדֹנָי קָדְקֹד בְּנוֹת צִיּוֹן וַיהוָה
and ;Zion the crown the the will so a making with and
Jehovah of daughter of Lord scabby make ;tinkling feet their

18 פָּתְהֵן יְעָרֶה: בַּיּוֹם הַהוּא יָסִיר אֲדֹנָי אֵת תִּפְאֶרֶת
the the take will that day In lay will their
of beauty Lord away .bare shame

19 הָעֲכָסִים וְהַשְּׁבִיסִים וְהַשַּׂהֲרֹנִים: הַנְּטִיפוֹת וְהַשֵּׁירוֹת
the and the the and the and the
bracelets ,pendants ,crescents headbands ,anklets

bracelets, and the veils; [20] the head-dresses, and the leg ornaments, and the sashes, and the houses of the soul, and the amulets; [21] the rings and nose jewels; [22] the costly clothing and the outer garments; and the shawls and the purses; [23] the mirrors and the fine linen; and the turbans and the veils. [24] And instead of a perfumed smell, there shall be an odor of decay; and instead of a girdle, a rope; and instead of well-set hair, baldness; and instead of a rich robe, a girding of sackcloth; burning instead of beauty. [25] Your men shall fall by the sword, and your mighty in the war. [26] And her gates shall lament and mourn; and she shal sit deserted on the ground.

20 וְהָרְעָלוֹת׃ הַפְּאֵרִים וְהַצְּעָדוֹת וְהַקִּשֻּׁרִים וּבָתֵּי הַנֶּפֶשׁ

the the and the and ankle the and the the and
,soul of houses sashes bracelets head-dresses ;veils

21
22 וְהַלְּחָשִׁים׃ הַטַּבָּעוֹת וְנִזְמֵי הָאָף׃ הַמַּחֲלָצוֹת וְהַמַּעֲטָפוֹת

outer the and festal the the the and the the and
,garments ,clothing ;nose of rings rings ;amulets

23 וְהַמִּטְפָּחוֹת וְהָחֲרִיטִים׃ הַגִּלְיֹנִים וְהַסְּדִינִים וְהַצְּנִיפוֹת

the and linen the and the the and the and
turbans garments mirrors ;purses mantles

24 וְהָרְדִידִים׃ וְהָיָה תַחַת בֹּשֶׂם מַק יִהְיֶה וְתַחַת חֲגוֹרָה

sash a and shall there smell a per- instead it And the and
of instead ;be decay of fume of be will .veils

נִקְפָּה וְתַחַת מַעֲשֶׂה מִקְשֶׁה קָרְחָה וְתַחַת פְּתִיגִיל מַחֲגֹרֶת

girding a rich a and ;baldness well-set the and ,rope a
of robe of instead ,hair of work of instead

25 שָׂק כִּי־תַחַת יֹפִי׃ מְתַיִךְ בַּחֶרֶב יִפֹּלוּ וּגְבוּרָתֵךְ בַּמִּלְחָמָה׃

the in your and will the by Your .beauty instead a sack-
.battle ones mighty ,fall sword men of scar ;cloth

26 וְאָנוּ וְאָבְלוּ פְּתָחֶיהָ וְנִקָּתָה לָאָרֶץ תֵּשֵׁב׃

shall she the on and her and shall and
.sit ground desolate ;gates mourn lament

CAP. IV ד

CHAPTER 4

CHAPTER 4

[1] And in that day seven women shall take hold of one man, saying, We will eat our own bread and wear our own clothing, only let your name be called on us; collect our shame. [2] In that day will the branch of Jehovah be beautiful and glorious, and the fruit of the earth for pride and for glory for the survivors of Israel. [3] And it shall be, him remaining in Zion, and he who is left in Jerusalem, (He) shall be called holy, every one who is written among the living in Jerusalem; [4] when the Lord shall have washed away the filth of the daughters of Zion, and the blood of Jerusalem shall have been rinsed away from its midst by a spirit of judgment, and by a spirit of burning. [5] And Jehovah will create over all the site of Mount Zion, and on her assemblies, a cloud and smoke by day, and the shining of a flaming fire by

1 וְהֶחֱזִיקוּ שֶׁבַע נָשִׁים בְּאִישׁ אֶחָד בַּיּוֹם הַהוּא לֵאמֹר

,saying ,that day in one man of women seven shall And
of hold take

לַחְמֵנוּ נֹאכֵל וְשִׂמְלָתֵנוּ נִלְבָּשׁ רַק יִקָּרֵא שִׁמְךָ עָלֵינוּ אֱסֹף

collect upon your be let only will we own our and will We own our
;us name called ,wear clothing ,eat bread

2 חֶרְפָּתֵנוּ׃ בַּיּוֹם הַהוּא יִהְיֶה צֶמַח יְהוָה לִצְבִי וּלְכָבוֹד

and beautiful Jehovah the be will . ,that day In our
,glorious of branch .shame

3 וּפְרִי הָאָרֶץ לְגָאוֹן וּלְתִפְאֶרֶת לִפְלֵיטַת יִשְׂרָאֵל׃ וְהָיָה ׀

it And .Israel the for for and for the the and
be shall of survivors glory pride earth of fruit

הַנִּשְׁאָר בְּצִיּוֹן וְהַנּוֹתָר בִּירוּשָׁלִַם קָדוֹשׁ יֵאָמֶר לוֹ כָּל־

every of will it (is He) in he and ,Zion in who him
one —him said be holy ,Jerusalem left is who remains

4 הַכָּתוּב לַחַיִּים בִּירוּשָׁלִָם׃ אִם ׀ רָחַץ אֲדֹנָי אֵת צֹאַת

the the have shall when in the among are who
of filth Lord away washed ;Jerusalem living written

בְּנוֹת־צִיּוֹן וְאֶת־דְּמֵי יְרוּשָׁלִַם יָדִיחַ מִקִּרְבָּהּ בְּרוּחַ מִשְׁפָּט

,judgment a by its from have shall Jerusalem the and ,Zion the
of spirit midst away rinsed of blood of daughters

5 וּבְרוּחַ בָּעֵר׃ וּבָרָא יְהוָה עַל כָּל־מְכוֹן הַר־צִיּוֹן וְעַל־

and ,Zion mount the all over Jehovah Then .burning a by and
over of site create will of spirit

מִקְרָאֶהָ עָנָן ׀ יוֹמָם וְעָשָׁן וְנֹגַהּ אֵשׁ לֶהָבָה לָיְלָה כִּי עַל־

over for by flaming fire a the and and day by a her
;night of shining ,smoke cloud ,assemblies

6 כָּל־כָּבוֹד חֻפָּה׃ וְסֻכָּה תִּהְיֶה לְצֵל־יוֹמָם מֵחֹרֶב וּלְמַחְסֶה
a for and the from by a for there a And canopy a the all
,refuge ,heat day shadow be shall booth .(be will) glory

וּלְמִסְתּוֹר מִזֶּרֶם וּמִמָּטָר׃
.rain and from a for and
storm place hiding

CAP. V ה

CHAPTER 5

1 אָשִׁירָה נָּא לִידִידִי שִׁירַת דּוֹדִי לְכַרְמוֹ כֶּרֶם הָיָה לִידִידִי
my to there a His about my song a my to now will I
Beloved was vineyard ;vineyard Beloved of Beloved sing

2 בְּקֶרֶן בֶּן־שָׁמֶן׃ וַיְעַזְּקֵהוּ וַיְסַקְּלֵהוּ וַיִּטָּעֵהוּ שֹׂרֵק וַיִּבֶן
and choicest the planted and cleared and he And .fatness a a in
built vine (with) it stones of it ,it digged of son horn

מִגְדָּל בְּתוֹכוֹ וְגַם־יֶקֶב חָצֵב בּוֹ וַיְקַו לַעֲשׂוֹת עֲנָבִים וַיַּעַשׂ
it but ,grapes (it for) he And in hewed a and its in a
produced produce to waited .it out vat wine also ,midst tower

3 בְּאֻשִׁים׃ וְעַתָּה יוֹשֵׁב יְרוּשָׁלִַם וְאִישׁ יְהוּדָה שִׁפְטוּ־נָא
ask I judge ,Judah and ,Jerusalem inhab- O And rotten
you of men of itants now .grapes

4 בֵּינִי וּבֵין כַּרְמִי׃ מַה־לַּעֲשׂוֹת עוֹד לְכַרְמִי וְלֹא עָשִׂיתִי בּוֹ
in have I that my to more be could What My and between
?it done not vineyard done .vineyard Me

5 מַדּוּעַ קִוֵּיתִי לַעֲשׂוֹת עֲנָבִים וַיַּעַשׂ בְּאֻשִׁים׃ וְעַתָּה אוֹדִיעָה־
will I now And rotten it but grapes to (it for) I Who
tell ?grapes produced produce waited ?knows

נָּא אֶתְכֶם אֵת אֲשֶׁר־אֲנִי עֹשֶׂה לְכַרְמִי הָסֵר מְשׂוּכָּתוֹ
hedge its will I My to do will I what you now
remove ;vineyard

6 וְהָיָה לְבָעֵר פָּרֹץ גְּדֵרוֹ וְהָיָה לְמִרְמָס׃ וַאֲשִׁיתֵהוּ בָתָה
;waste will I And trampling a will it and its will I ;burned it and
it lay .ground become wall breach be will

לֹא יִזָּמֵר וְלֹא יֵעָדֵר וְעָלָה שָׁמִיר וָשָׁיִת וְעַל הֶעָבִים אֲצַוֶּה
will I the and and briers shall but hoed nor shall it not
command clouds on ;thorns up come pruned be

7 מֵהַמְטִיר עָלָיו מָטָר׃ כִּי כֶרֶם יְהוָה צְבָאוֹת בֵּית יִשְׂרָאֵל
,Israel the hosts Jehovah the For .rain it on from
of house (is) of of vineyard raining

וְאִישׁ יְהוּדָה נְטַע שַׁעֲשׁוּעָיו וַיְקַו לְמִשְׁפָּט וְהִנֵּה מִשְׂפָּח
bloodshed but for He and His plants the Judah the and
,behold justice waited ;delight of (are) of men

8 לִצְדָקָה וְהִנֵּה צְעָקָה׃ הוֹי מַגִּיעֵי בַיִת בְּבַיִת שָׂדֶה
field to house Those Woe !cry a but righ- for
,house touching (to) ,behold teousness

בְשָׂדֶה יַקְרִיבוּ עַד אֶפֶס מָקוֹם וְהוּשַׁבְתֶּם לְבַדְּכֶם בְּקֶרֶב
the in alone are you and ,space the until they field to
of midst dwell to made of end join

9 הָאָרֶץ׃ בְּאָזְנָי יְהוָה צְבָאוֹת אִם־לֹא בָּתִּים רַבִּים לְשַׁמָּה
waste a many houses Surely hosts Jehovah my In the
,(sworn has) of ears !land

night; for on all the glory (shall be) a defense. [6] And there shall be a covering for a shade in the daytime from the heat, and for a place of refuge, and for a hiding place from storm and rain.

CHAPTER 5

[1] Now I will sing to my Beloved a song of my Beloved concerning His vineyard: My Beloved has a vineyard in a very fruitful ~~hill~~. [2] And He dug it, and cleared it of stones, and planted it (with) the choicest vine, and built a tower in its midst, and also made a winepress in it. And He waited (for it) to bring forth grapes but it brought forth wild grapes. [3] And now, O people of Jerusalem, and men of Judah, I ask you, judge between Me and My vineyard. [4] What more could have been done to My vineyard, that I have not done in it? Who knows? I waited (for it) to yield grapes, but it yielded rotten grapes? [5] And now I will tell you what I will do to My vineyard; I will remove its hedge and it shall be eaten up; break down its walls and it shall be a trampling ground. [6] And I will lay it waste; it shall not be pruned nor hoed; but briers and thorns shall spring up; and I will command the clouds that they rain no rain on it. [7] For the vineyard of Jehovah of hosts (is) the house of Israel, and the man of Judah His delightful plant; and He waited for justice, but, lo, bloodshed; for righteousness, but behold, a cry!

[8] Woe (to) those who join house to house, laying field to field until no space is left, and you are made to dwell alone in the middle of the land! [9] Jehovah of hosts (said) in my ears, Truly many houses shall be a waste, big and beautiful,

with no one in them. [10] Yea, ten acres of vineyard shall yield one bath, and the seed of a homer shall yield an ephah. [11] Woe to those who rise early in the morning pursuing fermented drink, tarrying in the twilight, (while) wine inflames them!

[12] And the lyre and the harp; the timbrel and flute, and wine are (at) their feasts; but they do not regard Jehovah's work; yea, they do not see the work of His hands. [13] For this My people have gone into captivity, without knowledge and his glory (is) men of famine; and their multitude is dried up with thirst. [14] For this, Sheol has enlarged itself and opened its mouth without measure. And her glory, and her multitude, and her uproar, and he who exults in her, shall go down (in it). [15] And man is bowed down, and man is humbled, and the eyes of the proud are humbled. [16] But Jehovah of hosts is exalted in judgment, and God the holy One is proven holy in righteousness. [17] Then the lambs shall feed as (in) their pasture, and strangers shall eat the waste places of the fatlings.

[18] (Woe to) those who draw iniquity with cords of vanity, and sin as (with) ropes of a cart; [19] who say, Let Him hurry and hasten His work, so that we may see. And let the purpose of the Holy One of Israel draw near and come, so that we may know. [20] Woe (to) those who say to evil, good; and to good, evil; who put darkness for light, and light for darkness; who put bitter for sweet, and sweet for bitter!

[21] Woe (to) those wise in their own eyes and bright before their faces! [22] Woe (to) those mighty to drink wine, and strong men to mix strong liquor; [23] who justify the

10 יִהְיוּ גְּדֹלִים וְטוֹבִים מֵאֵין יוֹשֵׁב׃ כִּי עֲשֶׂרֶת צִמְדֵּי־כֶרֶם
vineyard acres ten For a without and big shall
of .resident ,beautiful ,become

11 יַעֲשׂוּ בַּת אֶחָת וְזֶרַע חֹמֶר יַעֲשֶׂה אֵיפָה׃ הוֹי
Woe an shall a the and ,one bath shall
(to) .ephah yield homer of seed yield

11 מַשְׁכִּימֵי בַבֹּקֶר שֵׁכָר יִרְדֹּפוּ מְאַחֲרֵי בַנֶּשֶׁף יַיִן יַדְלִיקֵם׃
inflames (while) the in tarrying (to) fermented the in who those
.them wine twilight ;pursue drink morning early rise

12 וְהָיָה כִנּוֹר וָנֶבֶל תֹּף וְחָלִיל וָיַיִן מִשְׁתֵּיהֶם וְאֵת פֹּעַל יְהוָה
Jeho- work but their(at) and and timbrel and lyre And
vah's ,feasts wine flute ,harp are

13 לֹא יַבִּיטוּ וּמַעֲשֵׂה יָדָיו לֹא רָאוּ׃ לָכֵן גָּלָה עַמִּי מִבְּלִי־
without My into go Therefore they not His the and do they not
people exile .see do hands of work ,regard

14 דָעַת וּכְבוֹדוֹ מְתֵי רָעָב וַהֲמוֹנוֹ צִחֵה צָמָא׃ לָכֵן הִרְחִיבָה
has Therefore .thirst is their and ;famine men his and knowl-
enlarged with parched multitude of (is) glory edge

שְׁאוֹל נַפְשָׁהּ וּפָעֲרָה פִיהָ לִבְלִי־חֹק וְיָרַד הֲדָרָהּ וַהֲמוֹנָהּ
her and her will and mea- without its and its Sheol
multitude ,glory descend sure mouth opened appetite

15 וּשְׁאוֹנָהּ וְעָלֵז בָּהּ׃ וַיִּשַּׁח אָדָם וַיִּשְׁפַּל־אִישׁ וְעֵינֵי גְבֹהִים
the the and man is and ,man is And .her in he and her and
proud of eyes humbled down bowed exults who uproar

16 תִּשְׁפַּלְנָה׃ וַיִּגְבַּהּ יְהוָה צְבָאוֹת בַּמִּשְׁפָּט וְהָאֵל הַקָּדוֹשׁ
the and in hosts Jehovah is But are
One Holy God ,judgment of exalted .humbled

17 נִקְדָּשׁ בִּצְדָקָה׃ וְרָעוּ כְבָשִׂים כְּדָבְרָם וְחָרְבוֹת מֵחִים
the waste the and (in) as lambs the Then righteous- in proven is
fatlings of places pasture their feed shall .ness holy

18 גָּרִים יֹאכֵלוּ׃ הוֹי מֹשְׁכֵי הֶעָוֹן בְּחַבְלֵי הַשָּׁוְא
,vanity with iniquity those Woe shall strangers
of cords draw who (to) .eat

19 וְכַעֲבוֹת הָעֲגָלָה חַטָּאָה׃ הָאֹמְרִים יְמַהֵר ׀ יָחִישָׁה מַעֲשֵׂהוּ
His and Him let Who .sin cart a (with) as and
,work hasten hurry say of ropes

לְמַעַן נִרְאֶה וְתִקְרַב וְתָבוֹאָה עֲצַת קְדוֹשׁ יִשְׂרָאֵל וְנֵדָעָה׃
we that so ,Israel holy the the let and let And may we that so
.know may of One of purpose come near draw .(it) see

20 הוֹי הָאֹמְרִים לָרַע טוֹב וְלַטּוֹב רָע שָׂמִים חֹשֶׁךְ
darkness who ;evil to and good ,evil to those Woe
put ,good say who (to)

לְאוֹר וְאוֹר לְחֹשֶׁךְ שָׂמִים מַר לְמָתוֹק וּמָתוֹק לְמָר׃
for sweet and for bitter put who for and for
!bitter sweet ;darkness light light

21 22 הוֹי חֲכָמִים בְּעֵינֵיהֶם וְנֶגֶד פְּנֵיהֶם נְבֹנִים׃ הוֹי גִּבּוֹרִים
those Woe .discerning own their and their in those Woe
mighty (to) faces before eyes own wise (to)

23 לִשְׁתּוֹת יָיִן וְאַנְשֵׁי־חַיִל לִמְסֹךְ שֵׁכָר׃ מַצְדִּיקֵי רָשָׁע עֵקֶב
for the who those fermented mix to valor and ,wine drink to
wicked justify ,drink of men

wicked for a bribe, and turn aside the righteousness of the righteous from him! [24] Therefore, as the tongue of fire devours the stubble, and the flame burns up the chaff; their root shall be like rottenness, and their blossom shall go up like dust, because they have cast away the law of Jehovah of hosts; and despised the word of the Holy One of Israel. [25] Therefore the anger of Jehovah is kindled on His people, and He has stretched out His hand against them and struck them; and the mountains quaked, and their dead bodies were as filth in the midst of the streets. In all this, His anger turns not away, but His hand is stretched out still.

[26] And He will lift up a banner to distant nations and will hiss to them from the ends of the earth; and behold, it shall come with swift speed. [27] None (shall be) weary nor stumble among them; none shall slumber or sleep. Nor shall the girdle of their loins be opened, nor the thong of their sandals broken; [28] whose arrows (are) sharp, and all their bows bent; their horses' hoofs shall appear as flint, and their wheels like a tempest. [29] Their roaring (shall be) like a lion; they shall roar like young lions; yea, they roar and seize the prey and carry (it) away; and no one shall deliver. [30] And in that day they shall roar against them like the roaring of the sea; when one looks to the land, and lo, darkness! distress! And light shall be darkened by its clouds.

24 שֹׁ֑חַד וְצִדְקַ֥ת צַדִּיקִ֖ים יָסִ֥ירוּ מִמֶּֽנּוּ׃ לָכֵ֡ן כֶּאֱכֹל֩ קַ֨שׁ
the as Therefore from turn the the and ,bribe a
stubble devours !him aside righteous of righteousness

לְשׁ֣וֹן אֵ֗שׁ וַחֲשַׁ֤שׁ לֶֽהָבָה֙ יִרְפֶּ֔ה שָׁרְשָׁם֙ כַּמָּ֣ק יִהְיֶ֔ה וּפִרְחָ֖ם
their and shall like their ,falls the (in) dry and ,fire the
blossom ;be rottenness root flame grass of tongue

כָּאָבָ֣ק יַעֲלֶ֑ה כִּ֣י מָאֲס֗וּ אֵ֚ת תּוֹרַת֙ יְהוָ֣ה צְבָא֔וֹת וְאֵ֛ת
and ;hosts Jehovah the have they for shall like
of of law rejected up go dust

25 אִמְרַ֥ת קְדוֹשׁ־יִשְׂרָאֵ֖ל נִאֵֽצוּ׃ עַל־כֵּ֡ן חָרָה֩ אַף־יְהוָ֨ה בְּעַמּ֜וֹ
His on Jehovah the is Therefore .despised Israel Holy the the
,people of anger kindled of One of word

וַיֵּ֨ט יָד֥וֹ עָלָ֛יו וַיַּכֵּ֖הוּ וַיִּרְגְּז֣וּ הֶהָרִ֑ים וַתְּהִ֧י נִבְלָתָ֛ם כַּסּוּחָ֖ה
like their and the and struck and against His He and
offal corpses were ,mountains quaked ;him ;him hand sent

בְּקֶ֣רֶב חוּצ֑וֹת בְּכָל־זֹאת֙ לֹא־שָׁ֣ב אַפּ֔וֹ וְע֖וֹד יָד֥וֹ נְטוּיָֽה׃
stretched is His but His returns not this In the the in
.out hand still ,anger all .streets of midst

26 וְנָֽשָׂא־נֵ֤ס לַגּוֹיִם֙ מֵֽרָח֔וֹק וְשָׁ֥רַק ל֖וֹ מִקְצֵ֣ה הָאָ֑רֶץ וְהִנֵּ֥ה
and the the from for and from the to a He And
behold ;earth of end it whistle ,afar nations banner raise will

27 מְהֵרָ֥ה קַ֖ל יָבֽוֹא׃ אֵין־עָיֵ֤ף וְאֵין־כּוֹשֵׁל֙ בּ֔וֹ לֹ֥א יָנ֖וּם וְלֹ֣א
nor will one not in stumbles and weary None will it quick (with)
slumber ;it none (is) .come speed

יִישָׁ֑ן וְלֹ֤א נִפְתַּח֙ אֵז֣וֹר חֲלָצָ֔יו וְלֹ֥א נִתַּ֖ק שְׂר֥וֹךְ נְעָלָֽיו׃
its thong the be will and its waist- the be shall nor ;sleep
;sandals of broken not ;loins of cloth opened

28 אֲשֶׁ֤ר חִצָּיו֙ שְׁנוּנִ֔ים וְכָל־קַשְּׁתֹתָ֖יו דְּרֻכ֑וֹת פַּרְס֤וֹת סוּסָיו֙
its hooves ;bent bows its and are its of
horses' all ,sharpened arrows which

29 כַּצַּ֣ר נֶחְשָׁ֔בוּ וְגַלְגִּלָּ֖יו כַּסּוּפָֽה׃ שְׁאָגָ֥ה ל֖וֹ כַּלָּבִ֑יא וְשָׁאַ֣ג
it and like (is) Its roaring a like its and ,seem like
roar will ,lion a .windstorm wheels flint

30 כַּכְּפִירִ֗ים וְיִנְהֹם֙ וְיֹאחֵ֥ז טֶ֛רֶף וְיַפְלִ֖יט וְאֵ֥ין מַצִּֽיל׃ וְיִנְהֹ֥ם
it And shall and carries and (its) seizes and it for young like
roar will .deliver none ,away (it) ,prey roars lions

עָלָ֛יו בַּיּ֥וֹם הַה֖וּא כְּנַהֲמַת־יָ֑ם וְנִבַּ֤ט לָאָ֙רֶץ֙ וְהִנֵּה־חֹ֣שֶׁךְ צַ֔ר
dis- ,darkness and the to one when the the like ,that day in over
!tress ,lo ,land looks ;sea of roaring it

וָא֔וֹר חָשַׁ֖ךְ בַּעֲרִיפֶֽיהָ׃
its by is And
.clouds darkened light

CAP. VI ו

CHAPTER 6

[1] In the year that King Uzziah died, then I saw the Lord sitting on a throne, high and lifted up — and His train filled the temple. [2] Above it stood the seraphim. Each one had six

1 בִּשְׁנַת־מוֹת֙ הַמֶּ֣לֶךְ עֻזִּיָּ֔הוּ וָאֶרְאֶ֧ה אֶת־אֲדֹנָ֛י יֹשֵׁ֥ב עַל־כִּסֵּ֖א
a on sitting the I then ,Uzzah King the the In
,throne Lord saw of death of year

2 רָ֣ם וְנִשָּׂ֑א וְשׁוּלָ֖יו מְלֵאִ֥ים אֶת־הַהֵיכָֽל׃ שְׂרָפִ֨ים עֹמְדִ֤ים
stood Seraphim the filled His and and high
.temple train up lifted

wings; with two he covered his face, and with two he covered his feet, and with two he flew. [3] And one cried to another and said, Holy, holy, holy, (is) Jehovah of hosts; the whole earth (is) full of His glory! [4] And the doorposts shook from the voice of the one who cried; and the house was filled with smoke. [5] Then I said, Woe to me! For I am undone; for I (am) a man of unclean lips, and I live amongst a people of unclean lips; for my eyes have seen the King, Jehovah of hosts. [6] Then one of the seraphim flew to me (with) a live coal in his hand, snatched with tongs from the altar. [7] And he touched (it) on my mouth and said, See, this has touched your lips; and your iniquity is taken away, and your sin is covered. [8] And I heard the voice of Jehovah, saying, Whom shall I send, and who will go for Us? Then I said, I (am) here! Send me! [9] And He said, Go and tell this people, Hearing you hear, but do not understand; and seeing you see, but (you) do not know.

[10] Make the heart of this people fat, and make his ears heavy, and shut his eyes; lest he see with his eyes, and hear with his ears, and understand with his heart, and turn, and one heals him. [11] Then I said, Until when, O Lord? And He said, Until (when) cities lie desolate without inhabitant, and the houses without man, and the land is laid waste, a desolation, [12] and Jehovah has sent men far away, and the desolation (is) great in the land. [13] But yet in it (shall be) a tenth, and it shall return

מִמַּעַל לוֹ שֵׁשׁ כְּנָפַיִם שֵׁשׁ כְּנָפַיִם לְאֶחָד בִּשְׁתַּיִם ׀ יְכַסֶּה
he two with each to wings six ,wings six ;Him above
covered one

3 פָנָיו וּבִשְׁתַּיִם יְכַסֶּה רַגְלָיו וּבִשְׁתַּיִם יְעוֹפֵף׃ וְקָרָא זֶה
this And .flew he with and his he with and his
cried two ,feet covered two ,face

אֶל־זֶה וְאָמַר קָדוֹשׁ ׀ קָדוֹשׁ קָדוֹשׁ יְהוָה צְבָאוֹת מְלֹא
(is) ;hosts Jehovah (is) holy ,holy ,Holy ,said and this to
full of

4 כָל־הָאָרֶץ כְּבוֹדוֹ׃ וַיָּנֻעוּ אַמּוֹת הַסִּפִּים מִקּוֹל הַקּוֹרֵא
one the the from the the And His (of) the all
called who of voice threshold of posts shook !glory earth

5 וְהַבַּיִת יִמָּלֵא עָשָׁן׃ וָאֹמַר אוֹי־לִי כִי־נִדְמֵיתִי כִּי אִישׁ טְמֵא־
unclean a for am I for to Woe I Then .smoke was the and
of man ,undone ,me ,said with filled house

שְׂפָתַיִם אָנֹכִי וּבְתוֹךְ עַם־טְמֵא שְׂפָתַיִם אָנֹכִי יֹשֵׁב כִּי אֶת־
for ,live I lips unclean a and ,(am) I lips
of people amongst

6 הַמֶּלֶךְ יְהוָה צְבָאוֹת רָאוּ עֵינָי׃ וַיָּעָף אֵלַי אֶחָד מִן־הַשְּׂרָפִים
the of one to Then my have ,hosts Jehovah the
seraphim me flew .eyes seen of ,King

7 וּבְיָדוֹ רִצְפָּה בְּמֶלְקַחַיִם לָקַח מֵעַל הַמִּזְבֵּחַ׃ וַיַּגַּע עַל־פִּי
my on And the from taken with burning a in and
mouth it touched .altar tongs coal hand his

וַיֹּאמֶר הִנֵּה נָגַע זֶה עַל־שְׂפָתֶיךָ וְסָר עֲוֺנֶךָ וְחַטָּאתְךָ תְּכֻפָּר׃
is your and your is and your on this has ,See ,said and
.covered sin ,iniquity removed ,lips touched

8 וָאֶשְׁמַע אֶת־קוֹל אֲדֹנָי אֹמֵר אֶת־מִי אֶשְׁלַח וּמִי יֵלֶךְ־לָנוּ
for will and I shall Whom ,saying the the I And
?Us go who send ,Lord of voice heard

9 וָאֹמַר הִנְנִי שְׁלָחֵנִי׃ וַיֹּאמֶר לֵךְ וְאָמַרְתָּ לָעָם הַזֶּה שִׁמְעוּ
Hear ,this people tell and Go He And Send Here I Then
,said !me ,I (am) ,said

10 שָׁמוֹעַ וְאַל־תָּבִינוּ וּרְאוּ רָאוֹ וְאַל־תֵּדָעוּ׃ הַשְׁמֵן לֵב־הָעָם
people the Make do but seeing and under- do but hearing
of heart fat .know not see ;stand not

הַזֶּה וְאָזְנָיו הַכְבֵּד וְעֵינָיו הָשַׁע פֶּן־יִרְאֶה בְעֵינָיו וּבְאָזְנָיו
with and with he lest ,shut his and make his and ,this
ears his eyes his see eyes ,heavy ears

11 יִשְׁמָע וּלְבָבוֹ יָבִין וָשָׁב וְרָפָא לוֹ׃ וָאֹמַר עַד־מָתַי אֲדֹנָי
O Until I Then .him one and and under with and ,hear
?Lord ,when ,said heals turn ,stand heart his

וַיֹּאמֶר עַד אֲשֶׁר אִם־שָׁאוּ עָרִים מֵאֵין יוֹשֵׁב וּבָתִּים מֵאֵין
without the even inhabi- without cities lie might that Until He And
houses ,tant desolate ,said

12 אָדָם וְהָאֲדָמָה תִּשָּׁאֶה שְׁמָמָה׃ וְרִחַק יְהוָה אֶת־הָאָדָם
,mankind Jehovah has And a (for) laid the and ,man
away far sent .desolation waste land

13 וְרַבָּה הָעֲזוּבָה בְּקֶרֶב הָאָרֶץ׃ וְעוֹד בָּהּ עֲשִׂירִיָּה וְשָׁבָה
will it and (be will) it in But the the in the great and
return ;tenth a yet .land of midst desolation (is)

and be consumed like the great tree, like the mighty tree, and like the oak that in being felled (yet has) their stump; the holy seed (is) its stump.

CHAPTER 7

[1] And it came to pass, in the days of Ahaz the son of Jotham, the son of Uzziah, king of Judah, that Rezin the king of Syria, and Pekah the son of Remaliah, king of Israel, went up to Jerusalem to a war against it, but were not able to do battle against it. [2] And the house of David was told, saying, Syria is allied with Ephraim. And his heart was shaken, and the heart of his people, as the trees of the forest shake from the wind. [3] Then Jehovah said to Isaiah, Go out to meet Ahaz, you and Shearjashub your son, at the end of the conduit of the upper pool in the highway of the Fuller's Field. [4] And say to him, Be careful and be quiet; do not fear nor be timid of heart because of the two tails of these smoking firebrands, because of the fierce anger of Rezin and Syria, and of the son of Remaliah. [5] Because Syria, Ephraim, and the son of Remaliah have plotted evil aginst you, saying, [6] Let us go up against Judah and make her hated, and break her for ourselves; and set a king in her midst, the son of Tabeel. [7] Thus says the Lord Jehovah, It shall not rise, nor happen. [8] For the head of Syria (is) Damascus, and the head of Damascus (is) Rezin; and within sixty-five years Ephraim shall be broken from (being) a people.

וְהָיְתָה לְבָעֵר כָּאֵלָה וְכָאַלּוֹן אֲשֶׁר בְּשַׁלֶּכֶת מַצֶּבֶת בָּם
of the (have) being in which like and the like burned it and
;them stump felled oak the terebinth be shall

זֶרַע קֹדֶשׁ מַצַּבְתָּהּ׃ *
.stump its holy the
(is) seed

CAP. VII ז

CHAPTER 7

1 וַיְהִי בִּימֵי אָחָז בֶּן־יוֹתָם בֶּן־עֻזִּיָּהוּ מֶלֶךְ יְהוּדָה עָלָה רְצִין
Rezin went ,Judah king Uzziah the ,Jotham the Ahaz the in it And
up of of son of son of days was

מֶלֶךְ־אֲרָם וּפֶקַח בֶּן־רְמַלְיָהוּ מֶלֶךְ־יִשְׂרָאֵל יְרוּשָׁלַםִ
to ,Israel king ,Remaliah the and ,Aram the
Jerusalem of of son Pekah of king

2 לַמִּלְחָמָה עָלֶיהָ וְלֹא יָכֹל לְהִלָּחֵם עָלֶיהָ׃ וַיֻּגַּד לְבֵית דָּוִד
,David the to it And against do to were but against war a to
of house told was .it battle able not ;it

לֵאמֹר נָחָה אֲרָם עַל־אֶפְרָיִם וַיָּנַע לְבָבוֹ וּלְבַב עַמּוֹ כְּנוֹעַ
as his the and his And .Ephraim upon Aram is ,saying
shake ,people of heart ,heart shook resting

3 עֲצֵי־יַעַר מִפְּנֵי־רוּחַ׃ וַיֹּאמֶר יְהוָה אֶל־יְשַׁעְיָהוּ צֵא־
Go ,Isaiah to Jehovan Then the from the the
out said .wind forest of trees

נָא לִקְרַאת אָחָז אַתָּה וּשְׁאָר יָשׁוּב בְּנֶךָ אֶל־קְצֵה תְּעָלַת
the end the to your and you ,Ahaz meet to now
of conduit of ,son jashub Shear-

4 הַבְּרֵכָה הָעֶלְיוֹנָה אֶל־מְסִלַּת שְׂדֵה כוֹבֵס׃ וְאָמַרְתָּ אֵלָיו
to say And .fuller's the the to upper pool the
,him field of highway

הִשָּׁמֵר וְהַשְׁקֵט אַל־תִּירָא וּלְבָבְךָ אַל־יֵרַךְ מִשְּׁנֵי זַנְבוֹת
tails because be let not your and do and be and Be
of two the of timid heart ,fear not ;calm careful

הָאוּדִים הָעֲשֵׁנִים הָאֵלֶּה בָּחֳרִי־אַף רְצִין וַאֲרָם וּבֶן־
the and and Rezin the of because ,these smoking firebrands
of son ,Aram of anger of heat the

5 רְמַלְיָהוּ׃ יַעַן כִּי־יָעַץ עָלֶיךָ אֲרָם רָעָה אֶפְרַיִם וּבֶן־רְמַלְיָהוּ
,Remaliah the and ,Ephraim ,evil Aram against has Because .Remaliah
of son you plotted

6 לֵאמֹר׃ נַעֲלֶה בִיהוּדָה וּנְקִיצֶנָּה וְנַבְקִעֶנָּה אֵלֵינוּ וְנַמְלִיךְ
cause and for break and make and against us Let ,saying
reign to ;ourselves her ,hated her Judah up go

7 מֶלֶךְ בְּתוֹכָהּ אֵת בֶּן־טָבְאַל׃ כֹּה אָמַר אֲדֹנָי יְהוִה
,Jehovah the says Thus .Tabeal the her in king a
Lord of son ,midst

8 לֹא תָקוּם וְלֹא תִהְיֶה׃ כִּי רֹאשׁ אֲרָם דַּמֶּשֶׂק וְרֹאשׁ
the and (is) Aram the For it shall nor will it not
of head Damascus of head .be ,rise

דַּמֶּשֶׂק רְצִין וּבְעוֹד שִׁשִּׁים וְחָמֵשׁ שָׁנָה יֵחַת אֶפְרַיִם מֵעָם׃
from Ephraim be shall years and sixty and (is) Damascus
.people a broken five within ;Rezin

[9] And the head of Ephraim (is) Samaria, and the head of Samaria (is) Remaliah's son. If you will not believe, surely you shall not stand. [10] And Jehovah spoke to Ahaz again, saying, [11] Ask a sign of Jehovah your God; make deep the request, or make (it) high above. [12] But Ahaz said, I will not ask, nor will I tempt Jehovah. [13] And He said, Hear now, O house of David, is it too little that you weary men, but will you weary my God also? [14] Therefore the Lord Himself shall give you a sign, Behold, the virgin shall be with child and shall bring forth a son; and she shall call His name Immanuel. [15] He shall eat curds and honey until He knows to refuse the evil and choose the good. [16] For before the boy shall know to refuse the evil and choose the good, the land that you hate will be forsaken before both her kings. [17] Jehovah shall bring on you and on your people, and on your father's house, days which have not come since the days Ephraim parted from Judah, the king of Assyria.

[18] And it shall come to pass, in that day, Jehovah shall hiss for the fly that (is) in the end of the rivers of Egypt, and for the bee that (is) in the land of Assyria. [19] And they shall come, and they all shall rest in the steep ravines, and in the clefts of the rocks, and in all thorn bushes, and in all pastures. [20] In that day Jehovah shall shave with a razor that is hired, beyond the River, by the king of Assyria, the head and the hair of the feet; and it shall

9 וְרֹאשׁ אֶפְרַיִם שֹׁמְרוֹן וְרֹאשׁ שֹׁמְרוֹן בֶּן־רְמַלְיָהוּ אִם לֹא
not If .Remaliah's (is) Samaria the and (is) Ephraim the And
son of head Samaria of head

10 תַאֲמִינוּ כִּי לֹא תֵאָמֵנוּ׃ וַיּוֹסֶף יְהוָה דַּבֵּר אֶל־אָחָז
,Ahaz to spoke Jehovah And be will you not surely will you
again .established ,believe

11 לֵאמֹר׃ שְׁאַל־לְךָ אוֹת מֵעִם יְהוָה אֱלֹהֶיךָ הַעְמֵק שְׁאָלָה
the make your Jehovah from sign a for Ask ,saying
request deep ;God yourself

12 אוֹ הַגְבֵּהַּ לְמָעְלָה׃ וַיֹּאמֶר אָחָז לֹא־אֶשְׁאַל וְלֹא־אֲנַסֶּה
will I not will I not ,Ahaz said But .above make or
test ,ask high

13 אֶת־יְהוָה׃ וַיֹּאמֶר שִׁמְעוּ־נָא בֵּית דָּוִד הַמְעַט מִכֶּם הַלְאוֹת
weary to for (it Is) ,David O ,now Hear he Then .Jehovah
you little too of house ,said

14 אֲנָשִׁים כִּי תַלְאוּ גַּם אֶת־אֱלֹהָי׃ לָכֵן יִתֵּן אֲדֹנָי הוּא לָכֶם
to Himself the shall Therefore my also will you that ,men
you Lord give ?God weary

אוֹת הִנֵּה הָעַלְמָה הָרָה וְיֹלֶדֶת בֵּן וְקָרָאת שְׁמוֹ עִמָּנוּ אֵל׃
.Immanuel His she and a bear and will the ,behold a
name call will ,son conceive virgin ,sign

15 חֶמְאָה וּדְבַשׁ יֹאכֵל לְדַעְתּוֹ מָאוֹס בָּרָע וּבָחוֹר בַּטּוֹב׃
,good the and the to he when shall He and curds
choose evil refuse knows ,eat honey

16 כִּי בְּטֶרֶם יֵדַע הַנַּעַר מָאֹס בָּרָע וּבָחֹר בַּטּוֹב תֵּעָזֵב
be will ,good the and the to the shall before For
forsaken choose evil reject boy know

17 הָאֲדָמָה אֲשֶׁר־אַתָּה קָץ מִפְּנֵי שְׁנֵי מְלָכֶיהָ׃ יָבִיא יְהוָה
Jehovah shall her both before hate you that the
bring .kings land

עָלֶיךָ וְעַל־עַמְּךָ וְעַל־בֵּית אָבִיךָ יָמִים אֲשֶׁר לֹא־בָאוּ
have not which days your house and your and on
come ,father's on ,people on you

לְמִיּוֹם סוּר־אֶפְרַיִם מֵעַל יְהוּדָה אֵת מֶלֶךְ אַשּׁוּר׃
.Assyria the ,Judah from Ephraim turned the since
of king aside day

18 וְהָיָה בַּיּוֹם הַהוּא יִשְׁרֹק יְהוָה לַזְּבוּב אֲשֶׁר בִּקְצֵה יְאֹרֵי
the the at that the for Jehovah will ,that day in it And
of rivers of end (is) fly whistle be shall

19 מִצְרָיִם וְלַדְּבוֹרָה אֲשֶׁר בְּאֶרֶץ אַשּׁוּר׃ וּבָאוּ וְנָחוּ כֻלָּם
of all and they And .Assyria the in that for and ,Egypt
them rest ,come shall of land (is) bee the

בְּנַחֲלֵי הַבַּתּוֹת וּבִנְקִיקֵי הַסְּלָעִים וּבְכֹל הַנַּעֲצוּצִים וּבְכֹל
and thorn the and the in and ,steep the in
all in bushes all in ,rocks of clefts ravines

20 הַנַּהֲלֹלִים׃ בַּיּוֹם הַהוּא יְגַלַּח אֲדֹנָי בְּתַעַר הַשְּׂכִירָה
is that a with the will that day In the
,hired razor Lord shave .pastures

בְּעֶבְרֵי נָהָר בְּמֶלֶךְ אַשּׁוּר אֶת־הָרֹאשׁ וְשַׂעַר הָרַגְלָיִם וְגַם
and the the and the ,Assyria the by the beyond
also ;feet of hair ,head of king ,River

also sweep away the beard. [21] And it shall come to pass, in that day, that a man shall keep alive a heifer of the herd, and two sheep; [22] and it will be, he shall eat curds from the plenty of milk-making; for everyone who is left in the land shall eat curds. [23] And it will be in that day, that every place where were a thousand vines (worth) a thousand pieces of silver, (it) shall be for briers and thorns. [24] With arrows and bow he shall come there, because all the land shall be briers and thorns. [25] And all the hills which were hoed with the hoe, you shall not come there for fear of briers and thorns; but it shall be for the sending out of the ox, and for trampling of sheep.

21 אֶת־הַזָּקָן תִּסְפֶּה׃ וְהָיָה בַּיּוֹם הַהוּא יְחַיֶּה־אִישׁ עֶגְלַת
heifer of a man shall alive keep ,that day in it And be will shall it .away sweep the beard

22 בָּקָר וּשְׁתֵּי־צֹאן׃ וְהָיָה מֵרֹב עֲשׂוֹת חָלָב יֹאכַל חֶמְאָה
;curds he eat shall milk making the from of of plenty it and ,be will ;sheep and two the ,herd

23 כִּי־חֶמְאָה וּדְבַשׁ יֹאכַל כָּל־הַנּוֹתָר בְּקֶרֶב הָאָרֶץ׃ וְהָיָה
it And be will the .land the in of midst is who left every- one shall eat and honey curds for

בַּיּוֹם הַהוּא יִהְיֶה כָל־מָקוֹם אֲשֶׁר יִהְיֶה־שָּׁם אֶלֶף גֶּפֶן
vines a thousand there is where place every will it ,be ,that day in

24 בְּאֶלֶף כָּסֶף לַשָּׁמִיר וְלַשַּׁיִת יִהְיֶה׃ בַּחִצִּים וּבַקֶּשֶׁת יָבוֹא
shall he come with and bow the the With arrows shall it .be the and thorns the for briars silver a (worth) ,(pieces) thousand

25 שָׁמָּה כִּי־שָׁמִיר וָשַׁיִת תִּהְיֶה כָל־הָאָרֶץ׃ וְכֹל הֶהָרִים
the mountains And all the .land all shall be and thorns briars because ,there

אֲשֶׁר בַּמַּעְדֵּר יֵעָדֵרוּן לֹא־תָבוֹא שָׁמָּה יִרְאַת שָׁמִיר וָשַׁיִת
and ;thorns briars (for) of fear ,there you come shall not were ,hoed the with hoe which

וְהָיָה לְמִשְׁלַח שׁוֹר וּלְמִרְמַס שֶׂה׃
.sheep for and of trampling ,ox the for sending it but be shall

CAP. VIII ח

CHAPTER 8

[1] And Jehovah said to me, Take a big tablet and write in it with a man's pen: Make haste to spoil, hasten to the prey! [2] And I took to myself faithful witnesses to record, Uriah the priest and Zechariah the son of Jeberechiah. [3] And I drew near the prophetess. And she conceived and bore a son. Then Jehovah said to me, call his name, Make haste to spoil, hasten to the prey! [4] For before the child shall know to cry, My father, and, my mother, the riches of Damascus and the spoil of Samaria shall be taken away before the king of Assyria. [5] Jehovah also spoke to me again, saying, [6] Because this people has refused the waters of Shiloah that flow softly, and rejoices in

1 וַיֹּאמֶר יְהוָה אֵלַי קַח־לְךָ גִּלָּיוֹן גָּדוֹל וּכְתֹב עָלָיו בְּחֶרֶט
the with of pen it on and write big a tablet to Take you ,me to Jehovah said And

2 אֱנוֹשׁ לְמַהֵר שָׁלָל חָשׁ בַּז׃ וָאָעִידָה לִּי עֵדִים נֶאֱמָנִים
,faithful witnesses for me took I And record to the !spoil hurry to ;plunder make To (to) haste ;man a

3 אֵת אוּרִיָּה הַכֹּהֵן וְאֶת־זְכַרְיָהוּ בֶּן־יְבֶרֶכְיָהוּ׃ וָאֶקְרַב אֶל־
to I And near drew .Jeberechiah the of son Zechariah and the priest Uriah

הַנְּבִיאָה וַתַּהַר וַתֵּלֶד בֵּן וַיֹּאמֶר יְהוָה אֵלַי קְרָא שְׁמוֹ מַהֵר
Maher- his name Call ,me to Jehovah then said a ;son and bore she conceived and the ,prophetess

4 שָׁלָל חָשׁ בַּז׃ כִּי בְּטֶרֶם יֵדַע הַנַּעַר קְרֹא אָבִי וְאִמִּי יִשָּׂא
be will taken my and ,mother My ,father to ,cry the boy knows before For .baz hash- shalal-

אֶת־חֵיל דַּמֶּשֶׂק וְאֵת שְׁלַל שֹׁמְרוֹן לִפְנֵי מֶלֶךְ אַשּׁוּר׃
.Assyria the of king before Samaria the of plunder and Damascus the of riches

5 6 וַיֹּסֶף יְהוָה דַּבֵּר אֵלַי עוֹד לֵאמֹר׃ יַעַן כִּי מָאַס הָעָם הַזֶּה
this people has rejected Because ,saying ,still me to spoke Jehovah And more

אֵת מֵי הַשִּׁלֹחַ הַהֹלְכִים לְאַט וּמְשׂוֹשׂ אֶת־רְצִין וּבֶן־
the and of son Rezin rejoices and in ,gently which flow Shiloah the of waters

Rezin and Remaliah's son, [7] and, so, behold, the Lord brings on them the waters of the River, mighty and many—the king of Assyria and all his glory. And he shall come up over all its channels and go over all its banks; [8] and he shall pass through Judah; He shall overflow and go over; he shall reach to the neck; and his wings will be stretching out, filling the breadth of your land, O Immanuel. [9] Suffer evil, O peoples, and be broken, and listen, all from the far places of the earth; gird yourselves, and be broken! [10] Counsel a counsel, and it is frustrated; speak a word, and it shall not rise; for God (is) with us.

[11] For Jehovah spoke thus to me with a strong hand, and taught me against walking in the way of this people, saying, [12] Do not say, A conspiracy, to everything of which this people says, A conspiracy! And do not fear its fear, nor dread. [13] Sanctify Jehovah of hosts Himself, and let Him (be) your fear; and let Him (be) your dread. [14] And He shall be for a sanctuary, and for a stone of stumbling and for a rock of falling to both the houses of Israel; for a trap and for a snare to the dweller of Jerusalem. [15] And many among them shall stumble and fall, and be broken and be snared, and be taken. [16] Bind up the testimony, seal the law among My disciples. [17] And I will wait on Jehovah, who hides His face from the house of Jacob; and I will look for Him. [18] Behold! I and the children whom Jehovah has given me (are) for signs and wonders in Israel from Jehovah of hosts, who dwells in Mount

7 רמליהו׃ ולכן הנה אדני מעלה עליהם את־מי הנהר
the the them on brings the ,behold And .Remaliah
,River of waters up Lord ,therefore

העצומים והרבים את־מלך אשור ואת־כל־כבודו ועלה
will it And his all and Assyria king the and powerful
up go .glory of many

8 על־כל־אפיקיו והלך על־כל־גדותיו׃ וחלף ביהודה
through he and its all over go and its all over
;Judah pass shall ;banks channels

שטף ועבר עד־צואר יגיע והיה מטות כנפיו מלא־רחב
the filling his stretching and shall he the to go and shall he
of breadth wings out be will ;reach neck ;over overflow

9 ארצך עמנו אל׃ רעו עמים וחתו והאזינו כל
all and be and O Suffer .Immanuel Your
,listen ,broken ,peoples ,evil ,land

10 מרחקי־ארץ התאזרו וחתו התאזרו וחתו׃ עצו עצה
a Counsel be and gird be and gird the far from
,counsel !broken yourselves ;broken yourselves ;earth of places

11 ותפר דברו דבר ולא יקום כי עמנו אל׃ כי
For (is) with for shall it and ,word a speak is it and
.God us :rise not ;frustrated

כה אמר יהוה אלי בחזקת היד ויסרני מלכת בדרך
the in against taught and the the me to Jehovah spoke thus
of way walking me ,hand of strength

12 העם־הזה לאמר׃ לא־תאמרון קשר לכל אשר־יאמר
says of every- to A ,say Do not ,saying ,this people
which thing conspiracy

העם הזה קשר ואת־מוראו לא־תיראו ולא תעריצו׃
.dread do and ,fear do not fear its And A ,this people
not !conspiracy

13 את־יהוה צבאות אתו תקדישו והוא מוראכם והוא
and fear your and ,sanctify Him ,hosts Jehovah
He ,(be will) He of

14 מעריצכם׃ והיה למקדש ולאבן נגף ולצור מכשול לשני
the to falling a and stumb- a and a He And .dread your
two of rock ling of stone ,sanctuary become shall

15 בתי ישראל לפח ולמוקש ליושב ירושלם׃ וכשלו בם
among shall And .Jerusalem the to a and a for ,Israel houses
them stumble of dweller snare trap of

16 רבים ונפלו ונשברו ונוקשו ונלכדו׃ צור תעודה
the Bind be and be and be and and ,many
,testimony up .taken snared ,broken ,fall

17 חתום תורה בלמדי׃ וחכיתי ליהוה המסתיר פניו מבית
the from His who for will I And my among the seal
of house face hides ,Jehovah wait .disciples law

18 יעקב וקויתי־לו׃ הנה אנכי והילדים אשר נתן־לי יהוה
Jehovah to has whom the and I ,Behold .Him will I and ;Jacob
me given children for look

לאתות ולמופתים בישראל מעם יהוה צבאות השכן
who ,hosts Jehovah from Israel in and for (are)
dwells of wonders signs

Zion. [19] And when they say to you, Seek to those who have familiar spirits, and to wizards who peep and mutter — should not a people seek to its God, (than) for the living to (seek) to the dead? [20] To the law and to the testimony! If they do not speak according to this word, (it is) because there is no dawn to them! [21] And they shall pass through it, hard-pressed and hungry. And it shall be that they shall be hungry; he will rave and curse his king and his God, and face upward. [22] And they shall look to the land, and behold, trouble and darkness, and gloom of anguish; and (to) the darkness are driven; yet not (shall be) gloom for which she (is) in anguish.

19 בְּהַר צִיּוֹן׃ וְכִי־יֹאמְרוּ אֲלֵיכֶם דִּרְשׁוּ אֶל־הָאֹבוֹת וְאֶל־

to and the to Seek ,you to they And .Zion in
mediums say when Mount

הַיִּדְּעֹנִים הַמְצַפְצְפִים וְהַמַּהְגִּים הֲלוֹא־עַם אֶל־אֱלֹהָיו יִדְרֹשׁ

seek God its to a should and who the
people not —mutter peep wizards

20 בְּעַד הַחַיִּים אֶל־הַמֵּתִים׃ לְתוֹרָה וְלִתְעוּדָה אִם־לֹא יֹאמְרוּ

do they not If the to and the To the to the (than)
speak !testimony law ?dead (seek) living for

21 כַּדָּבָר הַזֶּה אֲשֶׁר אֵין־לוֹ שָׁחַר׃ וְעָבַר בָּהּ נִקְשֶׁה וְרָעֵב

and hard through they And .dawn to not then ,this according
.hungry pressed it pass shall them is word to

וְהָיָה כִי־יִרְעַב וְהִתְקַצַּף וְקִלֵּל בְּמַלְכּוֹ וּבֵאלֹהָיו וּפָנָה

and his and his and will he shall they that it And
face ,God king curse rave ,hungry be be shall

22 לְמָעְלָה׃ וְאֶל־אֶרֶץ יַבִּיט וְהִנֵּה צָרָה וַחֲשֵׁכָה מְעוּף צוּקָה

anguish gloom and ,distress ,and they the And .upward
of ,darkness ,behold ;look shall land to

23 וַאֲפֵלָה מְנֻדָּח׃ כִּי לֹא מוּעָף לַאֲשֶׁר מוּצָק לָהּ כָּעֵת

the As .her to anguish for (be shall) not Yet are (they) (to) and
time (was) which gloom .driven darkness

הָרִאשׁוֹן הֵקַל אַרְצָה זְבֻלוּן וְאַרְצָה נַפְתָּלִי וְהָאַחֲרוֹן

after- so ,Naphtali the and Zebulun land the He former the
wards of land of degraded (when)

הִכְבִּיד דֶּרֶךְ הַיָּם עֵבֶר הַיַּרְדֵּן גְּלִיל הַגּוֹיִם׃

the Galilee the beyond the the will He
.nations of ,Jordan ,sea of way glorify

CAP. IX ט

CHAPTER 9

[1] As the former time (when) He degraded the land of Zebulun and the land of Naphtali, so afterwards He will glorify the way of the sea, beyond the Jordan, Galilee of the nations.

[2] The people who walk in darkness have seen a great light; they who dwell in the land of the shadow of death: Light has shone on them. [3] You have multiplied the nation; You have increased the joy. They rejoice before You as in the joy of harvest, as (men) shout when they divide the spoil. [4] For You have broken his burdensome yoke and the staff of his shoulder, the rod of his taskmaster, as (in) the day of Midian. [5] For every boot of the trampler (is) with commotion, and a coat rolled in blood shall be burning fuel for the fire. [6] For to us a Child is born, to us a Son is given; and the princely power shall be on His shoulder; and His name shall be called Wonderful, Counselor, the

1 הָעָם הַהֹלְכִים בַּחֹשֶׁךְ רָאוּ אוֹר גָּדוֹל יֹשְׁבֵי בְּאֶרֶץ צַלְמָוֶת

death- the in who they ;great a have in who The
;shadow of land dwell light seen darkness walk people

2 אוֹר נָגַהּ עֲלֵיהֶם׃ הִרְבִּיתָ הַגּוֹי לֹא הִגְדַּלְתָּ הַשִּׂמְחָה

.joy the have You not the have You on has light
increased ;nation multiplied .them shone

שָׂמְחוּ לְפָנֶיךָ כְּשִׂמְחַת בַּקָּצִיר כַּאֲשֶׁר יָגִילוּ בְּחַלְּקָם שָׁלָל׃

.spoil they when the as as the in they before They
divide rejoicing ;harvest exult ,You rejoice

3 כִּי ׀ אֶת־עֹל סֻבֳּלוֹ וְאֵת מַטֵּה שִׁכְמוֹ שֵׁבֶט הַנֹּגֵשׂ בּוֹ הַחִתֹּתָ

have you ,him him rod the his the and his yoke the For
,broken oppressing of ,shoulder of staff burden of

4 כְּיוֹם מִדְיָן׃ כִּי כָל־סְאוֹן סֹאֵן בְּרַעַשׁ וְשִׂמְלָה מְגוֹלָלָה

rolled a and with (is) the boot every For .Midian the as
coat ,shaking trampler of of day

5 בְּדָמִים וְהָיְתָה לִשְׂרֵפָה מַאֲכֹלֶת אֵשׁ׃ כִּי־יֶלֶד יֻלַּד־לָנוּ

;us to is a For the fuel burning for even shall it in
born child .fire for become blood

בֵּן נִתַּן־לָנוּ וַתְּהִי הַמִּשְׂרָה עַל־שִׁכְמוֹ וַיִּקְרָא שְׁמוֹ פֶּלֶא

wonder- His is and His on the is and to is a
,ful name called ;shoulder government ;us given son

mighty God, the everlasting Father, the Prince of Peace. [7] There is no end to the increase of (His) princely power on the throne of David, and on His kingdom, to order it and to sustain it with justice; and with justice from now on, even forever. The zeal of Jehovah of hosts will do this. [8] The Lord sent a word into Jacob, and it has fallen into Israel. [9] And all the people shall know — Ephraim and the dwellers of Samaria, who say in pride and greatness of heart, [10] Bricks have fallen, but we will build with cut stones; the sycamores are cut down, but we will substitute cedars. [11] And Jehovah will set up Rezin's foes against him, and spur on his enemies (together)— [12] Syria in front, and the Philistines behind—and they shall devour Israel with all the mouth. In all this His anger turns not away, but His hand (is) stretched out still. [13] For the people do not turn to Him who strikes them, and they do not seek Jehovah of hosts. [14] Therefore Jehovah will cut off from Israel head and tail, branch and rush, (in) one day. [15] The elder and the lifted of face, he (is) the head; and the prophet who teaches lies, he (is) the tail. [16] For this people's leaders are led astray, and its guided ones (are) destroyed. [17] For this the Lord shall not rejoice over their young men, nor have pity on their orphans and widows — for everyone (is) a hypocrite and an evildoer, and every mouth speaks foolishness. In all this His anger turns not away, but His hand (is) stretched out still.

[18] For wickedness burns like the fire; it shall devour the briers and thorns and shall kindle the thickets

6 יוֹעֵץ אֵל גִּבּוֹר אֲבִי־עַד שַׂר־שָׁלוֹם׃ לְםַרְבֵּה הַמִּשְׂרָה
the the To .peace Prince Everlasting ,Mighty the Coun-
government of increase of ,Father God ,selor

וּלְשָׁלוֹם אֵין־קֵץ עַל־כִּסֵּא דָוִד וְעַל־מַמְלַכְתּוֹ לְהָכִין אֹתָהּ
it order to His and ,David the on ,end there of and
,kingdom on of throne no is peace

וּלְסַעֲדָהּ בְּמִשְׁפָּט וּבִצְדָקָה מֵעַתָּה וְעַד־עוֹלָם קִנְאַת יְהוָה
Jehovah The .forever and from with and with to and
of of zeal now righteousness justice it sustain

7 צְבָאוֹת תַּעֲשֶׂה־זֹּאת׃ דָּבָר שָׁלַח אֲדֹנָי בְּיַעֲקֹב
,Jacob into the sent word A .this will hosts
Lord do

8 וְנָפַל בְּיִשְׂרָאֵל׃ וְיָדְעוּ הָעָם כֻּלּוֹ אֶפְרַיִם וְיוֹשֵׁב שֹׁמְרוֹן
,Samaria the and Ephraim all the shall And .Israel into it and
of inhabitants ,it of ,people know fallen has

9 בְּגַאֲוָה וּבְגֹדֶל לֵבָב לֵאמֹר׃ לְבֵנִים נָפָלוּ וְגָזִית נִבְנֶה
will we (with) but have Bricks ,saying ,heart and pride in
;build stones cut fallen of greatness

10 שִׁקְמִים גֻּדָּעוּ וַאֲרָזִים נַחֲלִיף׃ וַיְשַׂגֵּב יְהוָה אֶת־צָרֵי רְצִין
Rezin foes the Jehovah has And will we but cut are syca-
of up set .substitute cedars ,down mores

11 עָלָיו וְאֶת־אֹיְבָיו יְסַכְסֵךְ׃ אֲרָם מִקֶּדֶם וּפְלִשְׁתִּים מֵאָחוֹר
—behind the and front in Syria :on spurs his and against
Philistines enemies ,him

וַיֹּאכְלוּ אֶת־יִשְׂרָאֵל בְּכָל־פֶּה בְּכָל־זֹאת לֹא־שָׁב אַפּוֹ וְעוֹד
but His returns not this In the with Israel they and
still ,anger all .mouth all devour

12 יָדוֹ נְטוּיָה׃ וְהָעָם לֹא־שָׁב עַד־הַמַּכֵּהוּ וְאֶת־יְהוָה צְבָאוֹת
hosts Jehovah and who Him to do not the For stretched (is) His
of ,them strikes return people ,out hand

13 לֹא דָרָשׁוּ׃ וַיַּכְרֵת יְהוָה מִיִּשְׂרָאֵל רֹאשׁ וְזָנָב כִּפָּה
branch and head from Jehovah will And do they not
,tail Israel off cut .seek

14 וְאַגְמוֹן יוֹם אֶחָד׃ זָקֵן וּנְשׂוּא־פָנִים הוּא הָרֹאשׁ וְנָבִיא
the and the he ,face and The .one day in and
prophet ;head (is) of lifted elder ,rush

15 מוֹרֶה־שֶּׁקֶר הוּא הַזָּנָב׃ וַיִּהְיוּ מְאַשְּׁרֵי הָעָם־הַזֶּה מַתְעִים
led this people leaders the And the he ,lying teaching
astray of are .tail (is)

16 וּמְאֻשָּׁרָיו מְבֻלָּעִים׃ עַל־כֵּן עַל־בַּחוּרָיו לֹא־יִשְׂמַח ׀ אֲדֹנָי
the shall not their over ,Therefore (are) its and
,Lord rejoice men young .swallowed ones guided

וְאֶת־יְתֹמָיו וְאֶת־אַלְמְנֹתָיו לֹא יְרַחֵם כִּי כֻלּוֹ חָנֵף וּמֵרַע
an and (is) every- for will He not widows their and their and
,evildoer profane one ,pity orphans

וְכָל־פֶּה דֹּבֵר נְבָלָה בְּכָל־זֹאת לֹא־שָׁב אַפּוֹ וְעוֹד יָדוֹ
His but His returns not this all In foolish- speaks mouth and
hand still ,anger .ness every

17 נְטוּיָה׃ כִּי־בָעֲרָה כָאֵשׁ רִשְׁעָה שָׁמִיר וָשַׁיִת תֹּאכֵל וַתִּצַּת
it and shall it and briars wicked- a like burns For out- (is)
kindles devour thorns ;ness fire .stretched

בְּסִבְכֵי הַיַּעַר וַיִּתְאַבְּכוּ גֵּאוּת עָשָׁן׃ בְּעֶבְרַת יְהוָה 18
Jehovah the By .smoke a as they and the thickets the
of of wrath of column ,up roll ,forest of

צְבָאוֹת נֶעְתַּם אָרֶץ וַיְהִי הָעָם כְּמַאֲכֹלֶת אֵשׁ אִישׁ אֶל־
to man the fuel as the and the is hosts
;fire of people is ;land scorched

אָחִיו לֹא יַחְמֹלוּ׃ וַיִּגְזֹר עַל־יָמִין וְרָעֵב וַיֹּאכַל עַל־שְׂמֹאול 19
,left the on he and is and the on he And shall they not his
eats ;hungry ,hand right off cuts .spare ,brother

וְלֹא שָׂבֵעוּ אִישׁ בְּשַׂר־זְרֹעוֹ יֹאכֵלוּ׃ מְנַשֶּׁה אֶת־אֶפְרַיִם 20
;Ephraim ,Manasseh shall own his the each are they but
.eat arm of flesh man ;satisfied not

וְאֶפְרַיִם אֶת־מְנַשֶּׁה יַחְדָּו הֵמָּה עַל־יְהוּדָה בְּכָל־זֹאת לֹא־
not ,this In .Judah against they together ;Manasseh and
all (are) ,Ephraim

שָׁב אַפּוֹ וְעוֹד יָדוֹ נְטוּיָה׃
stretched is His but His returns
.out hand still ,anger

of the forest, and they shall roll upward, like the ascending of smoke. [19] The land is scorched by the wrath of Jehovah of hosts, and the people shall be as the fuel of fire; no man shall spare his brother. [20] And (he shall) cut off on the right hand, yet be hungry; and he shall eat on the left (hand), but not they shall be satisfied; each man shall eat the flesh of his own arm; [21] Manasseh, Ephraim; and Ephraim, Manasseh—together they (are) against Judah. In all this, His anger turns not away, but His hand is stretched out still.

CAP. X י

CHAPTER 10

1
הוֹי הַחֹקְקִים חִקְקֵי־אָוֶן וּמְכַתְּבִים עָמָל כִּתֵּבוּ׃ לְהַטּוֹת 2
keep to (who) toil and in- decrees who those Woe
back ,write writers ,justice of decree to

מִדִּין דַּלִּים וְלִגְזֹל מִשְׁפַּט עֲנִיֵּי עַמִּי לִהְיוֹת אַלְמָנוֹת
widows may that My the from justice to and the from
be ,people of poor away take ,poor judgment

שְׁלָלָם וְאֶת־יְתוֹמִים יָבֹזּוּ׃ וּמַה־תַּעֲשׂוּ לְיוֹם פְּקֻדָּה וּלְשׁוֹאָה 3
of and visita- the in will And they orphans and their
—ruin ,tion of day do you what !plunder ,spoil

מִמֶּרְחָק תָּבוֹא עַל־מִי תָּנוּסוּ לְעֶזְרָה וְאָנָה תַעַזְבוּ כְּבוֹדְכֶם׃
your you will And for you shall whom To it far from
?glory leave where ?help flee ?comes away

בִּלְתִּי כָרַע תַּחַת אַסִּיר וְתַחַת הֲרוּגִים יִפֹּלוּ בְּכָל־זֹאת 4
,this all In they the and the under will he Surely
fall will slain under ,prisoners grovel

לֹא־שָׁב אַפּוֹ וְעוֹד יָדוֹ נְטוּיָה׃ הוֹי אַשּׁוּר שֵׁבֶט 5
the ,Assyria Woe stretched is His but His returns not
of rod to .out hand still ,anger

אַפִּי וּמַטֶּה־הוּא בְיָדָם זַעְמִי׃ בְּגוֹי חָנֵף אֲשַׁלְּחֶנּוּ וְעַל־עַם 6
the on even will I profane Against My their in it the and My
of people ;him send nation a .fury ,hand (is) ,staff ,anger

עֶבְרָתִי אֲצַוֶּנּוּ לִשְׁלֹל שָׁלָל וְלָבֹז בַּז וּלְשׂוּמוֹ מִרְמָס כְּחֹמֶר
the like tram- a to and ,spoil to and ,plunder to will I My
of mud pling them make spoil plunder ,him order wrath

חוּצוֹת׃ וְהוּא לֹא־כֵן יְדַמֶּה וּלְבָבוֹ לֹא־כֵן יַחְשֹׁב כִּי 7
for does so not his and does so not Yet the
;think heart ,intend he .streets

לְהַשְׁמִיד בִּלְבָבוֹ וּלְהַכְרִית גּוֹיִם לֹא מְעָט׃ כִּי יֹאמַר 8
he For .few a not nations to and in (is) to
,says off cut ,heart his destroy

CHAPTER 10

[1] Woe to those who decree decrees of injustice, and writers who write toil; [2] to keep back from judgment the poor, and to steal justice from the poor of My people — that widows may be their prey, that they may rob the orphans! [3] And what will you do in the day of judgment, and of destruction, it shall come from far away? To whom will you run for help? And where will you leave your glory? [4] Surely, he will grovel under the prisoners, and they shall fall under the slain. In all this His anger turns not away, but His hand is stretched out still.

[5] Woe (to) Assyria! The rod of My anger, and the staff in their hand (is) My fury. [6] I will send Him against an ungodly nation, and against the people of My wrath; I will command him to plunder plunder, and to spoil spoil, and to trample them like the mud of the streets. [7] Yet he does not intend so, nor does his heart think so; for it (is) in his heart to destroy and cut off not a few nations. [8] For he

says, Are not my captains all like kings? [9] Is not Calno like Carchemish? Is Hamath not like Arpad? Is Samaria not like Damascus? [10] As my hand has gotten to the kingdoms of the idols — for their graven images (excelled) Jerusalem's and Samaria's — [11] shall I not do to Jerusalem and her idols as I have done to Samaria and her idols? [12] And it will be, when the Lord has broken off all His work on Mount Zion, and on Jerusalem, that I will visit on the fruit of the proud heart of the king of Assyria, and on the glory of his high looks. [13] For he says, I have worked by the strength of my hand and by my wisdom; for I am astute. And I have moved the borders of the nations and have robbed their treasures; and like a mighty one I have subdued the inhabitants. [14] And my hand has found the riches of the people, like a nest; and I have gathered all the earth as forsaken eggs are gathered; and there was none that was moving a wing, nor opening a mouth, nor chirping.

[15] Shall the axe glorify itself over him that chops with it? Or shall the saw magnify itself over him moving it? As (if) a rod (could) wave those who lift it! As (if) a staff (could) raise (what is) not wood! [16] Therefore the Lord, the Lord of hosts, shall send leanness among his fat ones —and under His glory will kindle a burning like the burning of fire. [17] And the light of Israel shall be for a fire, and His Holy One for a flame—and it shall burn and devour his thorns and briers in one day. [18] And He shall consume the glory of his forest and his fruitful field, even from soul to flesh; and it shall be as a sick man melts. [19] And the rest of the

9 הֲלֹא שָׂרַי יַחְדָּו מְלָכִים׃ הֲלֹא כְּכַרְכְּמִישׁ כַּלְנוֹ אִם־לֹא
(is) Or ?Calno like Is ?kings together my Are
not Carchemish not captains not

10 כְּאַרְפַּד חֲמָת אִם־לֹא כְדַמֶּשֶׂק שֹׁמְרוֹן׃ כַּאֲשֶׁר מָצְאָה
found has As ?Samaria like (is) Or ?Hamath like
Damascus not Arpad

יָדִי לְמַמְלְכֹת הָאֱלִיל וּפְסִילֵיהֶם מִירוּשָׁלִַם וּמִשֹּׁמְרוֹן׃
than and than (more were) their and the the to My
,Samaria Jerusalem images carved ,idols of kingdoms hand

11 הֲלֹא כַּאֲשֶׁר עָשִׂיתִי לְשֹׁמְרוֹן וְלֶאֱלִילֶיהָ כֵּן אֶעֱשֶׂה
do I so to and Samaria to have I as should
,idols her done not

12 לִירוּשָׁלִַם וְלַעֲצַבֶּיהָ׃ וְהָיָה כִּי־יְבַצַּע אֲדֹנָי אֶת־כָּל־
all the has when it And her to and to
Lord off broken ,be will ?idols Jerusalem

מַעֲשֵׂהוּ בְּהַר צִיּוֹן וּבִירוּשָׁלִָם אֶפְקֹד עַל־פְּרִי־גֹדֶל לְבַב
heart greatness the on will I on and Zion on His
of of of fruit visit Jerusalem Mount work

13 מֶלֶךְ־אַשּׁוּר וְעַל־תִּפְאֶרֶת רוּם עֵינָיו׃ כִּי אָמַר בְּכֹחַ יָדִי
my By he For his high the and ,Assyria the
hand's might ,says .eyes (of) glory on of king

עָשִׂיתִי וּבְחָכְמָתִי כִּי נְבֻנוֹתִי וְאָסִיר ׀ גְּבֻלֹת עַמִּים וַעֲתִידֹתֵיהֶם
their and ,peoples borders I And am I for my by and have I
treasures of move .astute wisdom ,worked

14 שׁוֹשֵׂתִי וְאוֹרִיד כַּאבִּיר יוֹשְׁבִים׃ וַתִּמְצָא כַקֵּן ׀ יָדִי לְחֵיל
the my a like has And .inhabitants a as I and have
of riches hand nest found one mighty subdue ;robbed

הָעַמִּים וְכֶאֱסֹף בֵּיצִים עֲזֻבוֹת כָּל־הָאָרֶץ אֲנִי אָסָפְתִּי וְלֹא
and have I the all ,forsaken eggs as and the
not ;gathered earth gathers one ;peoples

15 הָיָה נֹדֵד כָּנָף וּפֹצֶה פֶה וּמְצַפְצֵף׃ הֲיִתְפָּאֵר הַגַּרְזֶן עַל
over the glorify Shall one or a or ,wing a one there
axe itself .chirping ,mouth opening moving was

הַחֹצֵב בּוֹ אִם־יִתְגַּדֵּל הַמַּשּׂוֹר עַל־מְנִיפוֹ כְּהָנִיף שֵׁבֶט
rod's a As him over saw the shall Or with him
waving ?it moving itself magnify ?it chopping

16 אֶת־מְרִימָיו כְּהָרִים מַטֶּה לֹא־עֵץ׃ לָכֵן יְשַׁלַּח הָאָדוֹן
the shall Therefore (is) (what) a As who those
,Lord send !wood not staff's raising !it lift

יְהוִה צְבָאוֹת בְּמִשְׁמַנָּיו רָזוֹן וְתַחַת כְּבֹדוֹ יֵקַד יְקֹד כִּיקוֹד
burn- like a will His and ;leanness his among ,hosts Jehovah
of ing ,burning burn glory under ones fat of

17 אֵשׁ׃ וְהָיָה אוֹר־יִשְׂרָאֵל לְאֵשׁ וּקְדוֹשׁוֹ לְלֶהָבָה וּבָעֲרָה
it and a for His and a for Israel the shall And .fire
burn shall ;flame One Holy ,fire of light be

18 וְאָכְלָה שִׁיתוֹ וּשְׁמִירוֹ בְּיוֹם אֶחָד׃ וּכְבוֹד יַעְרוֹ וְכַרְמִלּוֹ
his and his the And .one day in his and his and
,field fruitful forest of glory briars thorns devour

19 מִנֶּפֶשׁ וְעַד־בָּשָׂר יְכַלֶּה וְהָיָה כִּמְסֹס נֹסֵס׃ וּשְׁאָר עֵץ
the the And sick a melts as it and will He flesh even from
of trees of rest .man away be shall ;consume to soul

trees of his forest shall be few, so that a boy might write them.

[20] And it shall come to pass, in that day, that the remnant of Israel, and those who have escaped from the house of Jacob, shall not any more lean on him who struck them; but will truly lean on Jehovah, the Holy One of Israel. [21] The remnant shall return, the remnant of Jacob, to the mighty God. [22] For though Your people Israel is like the sand of the sea, (only) a remnant of it shall return; a decisive end, overflowing (with) righteousness. [23] For the Lord Jehovah of hosts shall make a full end, as ordained, in the midst of all the land. [24] Therefore thus says the Lord Jehovah of Hosts, O My people who dwell (in) Zion, do not fear Assyria! He shall strike you with a rod and shall lift up his staff against you in the way of Egypt. [25] But yet a little while and the fury shall cease, and My anger on their destruction. [26] And Jehovah of hosts shall stir up a whip on him according to the striking of Midian at the rock Oreb; and as His rod (was) on the sea, and he lifted it up in the way of Egypt. [27] And it shall come to pass in that day that his burden shall turn away from on your shoulder, and his yoke from your neck; and the yoke shall be destroyed because of the anointing. [28] He has come to Aiath; he has passed to Migron; he has stored his bag at Michmash. [29] They have crossed the ford; they have bedded down at Geba; Ramah is afraid; Gibeah of Saul has fled. [30] Shriek (with) your voice, daughter of Gallim; bow (your ear) Laishah, afflicted of Anathoth. [31] Madmenah wanders; Gebim's dwellers take refuge. [32] Yet he remains in Nob today; (he)

20 יַעְרוֹ מִסְפָּר יִהְיוּ וְנַעַר יִכְתְּבֵם׃ וְהָיָה ׀ בַּיּוֹם הַהוּא
,that day in it And write could a even shall few his
be will .them boy ;be forest

לֹא־יוֹסִיף עוֹד שְׁאָר יִשְׂרָאֵל וּפְלֵיטַת בֵּית־יַעֲקֹב לְהִשָּׁעֵן
lean to Jacob the the and Israel the more shall not
of house of escaped of remnant add

21 עַל־מַכֵּהוּ וְנִשְׁעַן עַל־יְהוָה קְדוֹשׁ יִשְׂרָאֵל בֶּאֱמֶת׃ שְׁאָר
A .truth in ,Israel Holy the ,Jehovah on will but his on
remnant of One lean ,striker

22 יָשׁוּב שְׁאָר יַעֲקֹב אֶל־אֵל גִּבּוֹר׃ כִּי אִם־יִהְיֶה עַמְּךָ
Your is though For .mighty the to ,Jacob rem- the shall
people God of nant ,return

יִשְׂרָאֵל כְּחוֹל הַיָּם שְׁאָר יָשׁוּב בּוֹ כִּלָּיוֹן חָרוּץ שׁוֹטֵף
over- ,decisive end a of shall a (only) the the like Israel
flowing ;it return remnant ,sea of sand

23 צְדָקָה׃ כִּי כָלָה וְנֶחֱרָצָה אֲדֹנָי יְהוִה צְבָאוֹת עֹשֶׂה
makes hosts Jehovah the and full a For (with)
of Lord ,ordained end .righteousness

24 בְּקֶרֶב כָּל־הָאָרֶץ׃ לָכֵן כֹּה־אָמַר אֲדֹנָי יְהוִה
Jehovah the says thus ,Therefore the all the in
of Lord .land of midst

צְבָאוֹת אַל־תִּירָא עַמִּי יֹשֵׁב צִיּוֹן מֵאַשּׁוּר בַּשֵּׁבֶט יַכֶּכָּה
shall he the With !Assyria ,Zion who my O Do not ,hosts
,you strike rod (in) dwell people ,fear

25 וּמַטֵּהוּ יִשָּׂא־עָלֶיךָ בְּדֶרֶךְ מִצְרָיִם׃ כִּי־עוֹד מְעַט
little a yet But .Egypt the in against shall he his and
of way ,you up lift staff

26 מִזְעָר וְכָלָה זַעַם וְאַפִּי עַל־תַּבְלִיתָם׃ וְעוֹרֵר עָלָיו יְהוָה
Jehovah on shall And their over My and ,fury is and while
of him up stir .destruction ,anger finished

צְבָאוֹת שׁוֹט כְּמַכַּת מִדְיָן בְּצוּר עוֹרֵב וּמַטֵּהוּ עַל־הַיָּם
the (was) (as) and ;Oreb the at Midian the as whip a hosts
;sea on rod His rock of striking

27 וּנְשָׂאוֹ בְּדֶרֶךְ מִצְרָיִם׃ וְהָיָה ׀ בַּיּוֹם הַהוּא יָסוּר סֻבֳּלוֹ
his shall ,that day in shall it And .Egypt the in he and
burden turn be of way it lifted

מֵעַל שִׁכְמֶךָ וְעֻלּוֹ מֵעַל צַוָּארֶךָ וְחֻבַּל עֹל מִפְּנֵי־שָׁמֶן׃
.fatness because the shall and your from his and your from
of yoke destroyed be ;neck on yoke ,shoulder on

28
29 בָּא עַל־עַיַּת עָבַר בְּמִגְרוֹן לְמִכְמָשׂ יַפְקִיד כֵּלָיו׃ עָבְרוּ
They his he at into he ;Aiath on He
crossed .baggage stored Michmash ;Migron passed came

מַעְבָּרָה גֶּבַע מָלוֹן לָנוּ חָרְדָה הָרָמָה גִּבְעַת שָׁאוּל נָסָה׃
has Saul Gibeah ;Ramah is to a Geba the
.fled of terrified ;them lodging (was) ;ford

30
31 צַהֲלִי קוֹלֵךְ בַּת־גַּלִּים הַקְשִׁיבִי לַיְשָׁה עֲנִיָּה עֲנָתוֹת׃ נָדְדָה
wanders .Anathoth af- ;Laishah bow ;Gallim daugh- your Shriek
of flicted (ear your) of ter ,voice with

32 מַדְמֵנָה יֹשְׁבֵי הַגֵּבִים הֵעִיזוּ׃ * עוֹד הַיּוֹם בְּנֹב לַעֲמֹד
(he) in today Yet take Gebim the ;Madmenah
;remains Nob .refuge of dwellers

will shake his hand (against) the mount of the daughter of Zion, the hill of Jerusalem. [33] Behold, the Lord, Jehovah of hosts, shall lop the bough with terror! And the lofty ones shall be cut down, and the proud shall be humbled. [34] And he shall cut down the thickets of the forest with iron, and Lebanon shall fall by a mighty one.

CHAPTER 11

[1] And a Rod proceeds from the stump of Jesse, and a Branch will bear fruit out of his roots. [2] And the Spirit of Jehovah shall rest on Him; the spirit of wisdom and understanding, the spirit of counsel and power; the spirit of knowledge and of the fear of Jehovah; [3] and shall make Him breathe in the fear of Jehovah. But He shall not judge by the seeing of His eyes, nor decide by the hearing of His ears. [4] But He shall judge the poor in righteousness, and shall decide for the meek of the earth rightly. And He shall strike the earth with the rod of His mouth, and He shall slay the wicked with the breath of His lips. [5] And righteousness shall be the encircler of His loins, and faithfulness the encircler of His heart. [6] And the wolf shall live with the lamb; and the leopard shall lie with the kid; and the calf and the young lion and the fatling together; and a little boy shall lead them. [7] The cow and the bear shall feed; their young shall lie together; and the lion shall eat straw like the ox. [8] And the infant shall play on the hole of the asp, and the weaned child shall put his hand on the adder's den. [9] They shall not do evil, nor destroy in all My holy mountain; for the earth shall be full of the knowledge of Jehovah, as the waters cover the sea.

[10] And it shall be in that day that the Root of

33 יְנֹפֵף יָדוֹ הַר בֵּית־צִיּוֹן גִּבְעַת יְרוּשָׁלִָם׃ הִנֵּה הָאָדוֹן

the ,Behold .Jerusalem the ,Zion's daugh- (at) his he
,Lord of hill ter's mount hand shakes

יְהוָה צְבָאוֹת מְסָעֵף פֻּארָה בְּמַעֲרָצָה וְרָמֵי הַקּוֹמָה גְּדֻעִים

be shall high and with the lop shall ,hosts Jehovah
,down cut height of ones ,terror bough off of

34 וְהַגְּבֹהִים יִשְׁפָּלוּ׃ וְנִקַּף סִבְכֵי הַיַּעַר בַּבַּרְזֶל וְהַלְּבָנוֹן

and with the the he And be shall the and
Lebanon ,iron forest of thickets cut shall .lowered ones lofty

בְּאַדִּיר יִפּוֹל׃

shall a by
.fall one mighty

CAP. XI יא

CHAPTER 11

1 2 וְיָצָא חֹטֶר מִגֵּזַע יִשָׁי וְנֵצֶר מִשָּׁרָשָׁיו יִפְרֶה׃ וְנָחָה עָלָיו

on shall And bear will of out a and ,Jesse the from a And
Him rest .fruit roots his branch of stump shoot proceeds

רוּחַ יְהוָה רוּחַ חָכְמָה וּבִינָה רוּחַ עֵצָה וּגְבוּרָה רוּחַ דַּעַת

knowl- the and counsel the and wisdom the ;Jehovah the
edge of spirit ;might of spirit ;understanding of spirit of Spirit

3 וְיִרְאַת יְהוָה׃ וַהֲרִיחוֹ בְּיִרְאַת יְהוָה וְלֹא־לְמַרְאֵה עֵינָיו

His the by But .Jehovah the in is He and Jehovah the and
eyes of seeing not of fear breathe to made of fear

4 יִשְׁפּוֹט וְלֹא־לְמִשְׁמַע אָזְנָיו יוֹכִיחַ׃ וְשָׁפַט בְּצֶדֶק דַּלִּים

poor the righ- in He But .decide His the by and shall He
teousness judge shall ears of hearing not ,judge

וְהוֹכִיחַ בְּמִישׁוֹר לְעַנְוֵי־אָרֶץ וְהִכָּה־אֶרֶץ בְּשֵׁבֶט פִּיו וּבְרוּחַ

with and his with the He And the the for with shall and
breath breath's rod earth strikes earth of meek rightness decide

5 שְׂפָתָיו יָמִית רָשָׁע׃ וְהָיָה צֶדֶק אֵזוֹר מָתְנָיו וְהָאֱמוּנָה

and His the righteous- And the shall He lips His
faithfulness thighs of band ness be shall .wicked kill

6 אֵזוֹר חֲלָצָיו׃ וְגָר זְאֵב עִם־כֶּבֶשׂ וְנָמֵר עִם־גְּדִי יִרְבָּץ וְעֵגֶל

the and shall the with the and the with the And .loins His the
calf ;lie kid leopard ;lamb wolf stay shall of band

7 וּכְפִיר וּמְרִיא יַחְדָּו וְנַעַר קָטֹן נֹהֵג בָּם׃ וּפָרָה וָדֹב תִּרְעֶינָה

shall the and And .them leads little a and ;together the and the and
;feed bear cow the boy fatling cub lion

8 יַחְדָּו יִרְבְּצוּ יַלְדֵיהֶן וְאַרְיֵה כַּבָּקָר יֹאכַל־תֶּבֶן׃ וְשִׁעֲשַׁע

shall And .straw shall the like the and their shall together
play eat ox lion ;young lie

יוֹנֵק עַל־חֻר פָּתֶן וְעַל מְאוּרַת צִפְעוֹנִי גָּמוּל יָדוֹ הָדָה׃ לֹא־

not shall his weaned a the den the and the the over suck- a
.put hand child ,viper of on ;snake of hole ling

9 יָרֵעוּ וְלֹא־יַשְׁחִיתוּ בְּכָל־הַר קָדְשִׁי כִּי־מָלְאָה הָאָרֶץ דֵּעָה

of the be shall for My mountain in they and They
knowing earth full ;holy all destroy not evil do

10 אֶת־יְהוָה כַּמַּיִם לַיָּם מְכַסִּים׃ וְהָיָה בַּיּוֹם הַהוּא

,that day in it And .cover the the as Jehovah
be will sea waters

שרש ישי אשר עמד לנס עמים אליו גוים ידרשו והיתה
shall and be | shall ;seek | nations | to Him | ;peoples | a as of banner | stands | that (is it) | Jesse | the of root
11 מנחתו כבוד׃ והיה ׀ ביום ההוא יוסיף אדני ׀
the Lord | shall add | ,that | day in | it And be shall | .glory | resting His place
שנית ידו לקנות את־שאר עמו אשר־ישאר מאשור
from ,Assyria | remains | that | His ,people | the of remnant | obtain to | His hand | second the time
וממצרים ומפתרוס ומכוש ומעילם ומשנער ומחמת
from and Hamath | from and , Chaldea | from and ,Persia | from and ,Ethiopia | from and ,Pathros | from and ,Egypt
12 ומאיי הים׃ ונשא נס לגוים ואסף נדחי ישראל ונפצות
those and of dispersed | ;Israel | out- of casts | the shall and gather | the for ,nations | a banner | He And lift shall | the .sea | from and of coasts
13 יהודה יקבץ מארבע כנפות הארץ׃ וסרה קנאת אפרים
;Ephraim | the of envy | shall And ,collect | the .earth | wings of | the from four | shall And aside turn | Judah
וצררי יהודה יכרתו אפרים לא־יקנא את־יהודה ויהודה
and Judah | ,Judah | shall envy | not | Ephraim | be shall —off cut | Judah | and of foes
14 לא־יצר את־אפרים׃ ועפו בכתף פלשתים ימה יחדו
together | the to ;west | the (on) Philistines | the onto shoulder | they But fly shall | .Ephraim | shall not trouble
יבזו את־בני־קדם אדום ומואב משלוח ידם ובני עמון
Am- mon | the and of sons | their ,hand | stretch- of ing | the and ,Moab | Edom | the ;east | the of sons | shall they spoil
15 משמעתם׃ והחרים יהוה את לשון ים־מצרים והניף
He and wave shall | ;Egypt | the of sea | the of tongue | Jehovah | shall And destroy utterly | obeying .them
ידו על־הנהר בעים רוחו והכהו לשבעה נחלים והדריך
make and (it) tread | ,torrents (one) | seven into | shall and it strike | His ,wind | the in of heat | the ,river | over | His hand
16 בנעלים׃ והיתה מסלה לשאר עמו אשר ישאר מאשור
from ,Assyria | remains | which | His ,people | the for of remnant | a highway | there And be shall | with .shoes the
כאשר היתה לישראל ביום עלתו מארץ מצרים׃
.Egypt | the from of land | his up going | the in of day | Israel to | was it | as

Jesse shall stand as a banner of the peoples; the nations shall seek to Him, and His rest shall be glory. [11] And it shall be in that day that the Lord shall set His hand the second time to recover the remnant of His people, that remains from Assyria and from Egypt; and from Pathros, and from Ethiopia; and from Persia; and from Shinar; and from Hamath; and from coasts of the sea. [12] And He shall lift up a banner for the nations, and shall gather the outcasts of Israel, and gather those dispersed from Judah, from the four wings of the earth. [13] And the envy of Ephraim shall depart; and Judah's foes shall be cut off – Ephraim shall not envy Judah and Judah shall not trouble Ephraim. [14] But they shall fly onto the shoulder of the Philistines to the west; they shall together spoil those of the east; the stretching of the hand (on) Edom and Moab; and the Ammonites shall obey them. [15] And Jehovah shall utterly destroy the tongue of the Egyptian sea; and with His scorching wind He shall wave His hand over the river, and shall strike it into seven torrents, and make one tread (it) with shoes. [16] And there shall be a highway for the remnant of His people, those left from Assyria, as it was to Israel in the day when he came up out of the land of Egypt.

CAP. XII יב

CHAPTER 12

1 ואמרת ביום ההוא אודך יהוה כי אנפת בי ישב אפך
Your anger | turns away | with ;me | were angry | You though | Jeho- ,vah | will I You thank | ,that | day in | you And say shall
2 ותנחמני׃ הנה אל ישועתי אבטח ולא אפחד כי עזי
my strength | for | be ,afraid | and not | will I trust | my !salvation | God (is) | ,Behold | shall You and .me comfort
3 וזמרת יה יהוה ויהי־לי לישועה׃ ושאבתם־מים
water | you And draw shall | .salvation | to me | He and became | ;Jehovah | Jah | (my) and (is) song

CHAPTER 12

[1] And in that day you shall say, O Jehovah, I will thank You; though You were angry with me, turn away Your anger and You shall comfort me. [2] Behold, God is my salvation! I will trust and not be afraid, for my strength and (my) song (is) Jah Jehovah; yea, He has become my salvation. [3] And you shall with joy draw waters out of

the wells of salvation. [4] And in that day you shall say, Praise Jehovah! Call on His name; declare His doings among the people; make mention that His name is exalted. [5] Sing (to) Jehovah, for He has done majestically; this (is) known in all the earth. [6] Cry and shout, O dweller of Zion! For great (is) the Holy One of Israel in your midst.

4 בְּשָׂשׂוֹן מִמַּעַיְנֵי הַיְשׁוּעָה׃ וַאֲמַרְתֶּם בַּיּוֹם הַהוּא הוֹדוּ
Thank ,that day in you And .salvation the of out with
say shall of wells joy

לַיהוָה קִרְאוּ בִשְׁמוֹ הוֹדִיעוּ בָעַמִּים עֲלִילֹתָיו הַזְכִּירוּ כִּי
that make His the among make His on Call !Jehovah
mention ;doings peoples known ;name

5 נִשְׂגָּב שְׁמוֹ׃ זַמְּרוּ יְהוָה כִּי גֵאוּת עָשָׂה מְיֻדַּעַת זֹאת
this (is) has He majesti- for (to) Sing His is
known ;done cally Jehovah praise .name exalted

6 בְּכָל־הָאָרֶץ׃ צַהֲלִי וָרֹנִּי יוֹשֶׁבֶת צִיּוֹן כִּי־גָדוֹל בְּקִרְבֵּךְ
your in great For !Zion dweller and Cry the in
midst of ,shout .earth all

קְדוֹשׁ יִשְׂרָאֵל׃
.Israel the (is)
of One Holy

CAP. XIII יג

CHAPTER 13

CHAPTER 13

[1] The burden of Babylon, which Isaiah the son of Amoz saw: [2] Lift up a banner on a bare mount; make rise the voice to them; wave the hand, so that they may go into the gates of the nobles. [3] I have commanded My holy ones; I have also called My warriors for My anger, those who rejoice in My highness. [4] The noise of a multitude in the mountains, as of a great people! A tumultuous noise of the kingdoms of nations assembled — Jehovah of hosts is gathering an army for the battle. [5] They come from a distant land, from the end of the heavens; Jehovah and the instruments of His indignation, to destroy the whole land. [6] Howl! For the day of Jehovah (is) at hand; it shall come as a destruction from the Almighty. [7] Therefore all hands shall droop, and every man's heart shall melt; [8] and they shall be afraid. Pangs and sorrows shall take hold of them; they shall be in pain like a woman who travails; they shall be amazed at one another; their faces (shall be) faces of flames. [9] Behold, the day of Jehovah comes, cruel, and (with) wrath and fierce anger, to lay the land waste. And He shall destroy the sinners out

1 2 מַשָּׂא בָּבֶל אֲשֶׁר חָזָה יְשַׁעְיָהוּ בֶּן־אָמוֹץ׃ עַל הַר־נִשְׁפֶּה
bare a on :Amoz the Isaiah saw which ,Babylon The
mountain of son of burden

שְׂאוּ־נֵס הָרִימוּ קוֹל לָהֶם הָנִיפוּ יָד וְיָבֹאוּ פִּתְחֵי נְדִיבִים׃
.nobles the they that the wave to the Make a up Lift
of gates enter may ,hand ;them voice rise .banner

3 אֲנִי צִוֵּיתִי לִמְקֻדָּשָׁי גַּם קָרָאתִי גִבּוֹרַי לְאַפִּי עַלִּיזֵי גַּאֲוָתִי׃
My rejoicers My for My have I also holy My have I
.pride of ,anger warriors called ;ones commanded

4 קוֹל הָמוֹן בֶּהָרִים דְּמוּת עַם־רָב קוֹל שְׁאוֹן מַמְלְכוֹת
kingdoms tumult A !great a like- the the in mul- a The
of of of noise people of ness ;mountains titude of noise

גּוֹיִם נֶאֱסָפִים יְהוָה צְבָאוֹת מְפַקֵּד צְבָא מִלְחָמָה׃
.battle an is hosts Jehovah —assembled nations
of army mustering of

5 בָּאִים מֵאֶרֶץ מֶרְחָק מִקְצֵה הַשָּׁמָיִם יְהוָה וּכְלֵי זַעְמוֹ
His and Jehovah the the from ,distant a from Are
,wrath of weapons ,heavens of end land coming

6 לְחַבֵּל כָּל־הָאָרֶץ׃ הֵילִילוּ כִּי קָרוֹב יוֹם יְהוָה כְּשֹׁד
as ;Jehovah the (is) For !Howl the all to
destruction of day near .land destroy

7 מִשַּׁדַּי יָבוֹא׃ עַל־כֵּן כָּל־יָדַיִם תִּרְפֶּינָה וְכָל־לְבַב אֱנוֹשׁ
man heart and shall hands all ,Therefore shall it the from
of every droop .come Almighty

8 יִמָּס׃ וְנִבְהָלוּ צִירִים וַחֲבָלִים יֹאחֵזוּן כַּיּוֹלֵדָה יְחִילוּן אִישׁ
a shall they woman a as shall and pangs shall they and shall
man ;pain in be travailing ;them seize sorrows ;afraid be ;melt

9 אֶל־רֵעֵהוּ יִתְמָהוּ פְּנֵי לְהָבִים פְּנֵיהֶם׃ הִנֵּה יוֹם־יְהוָה בָּא
,comes Jeho- the ,Behold their flames faces shall they his to
vay of day .faces (be will) of ;amazed be ,neighbor

אַכְזָרִי וְעֶבְרָה וַחֲרוֹן אָף לָשׂוּם הָאָרֶץ לְשַׁמָּה וְחַטָּאֶיהָ
its And .waste the lay to ,anger and and ,cruel
sinners land of heat wrath

of it. [10] For the stars of the sky and their constellations shall not give their light; the sun shall be darkened in its going forth; and the moon shall not reflect its light. [11] And I will visit evil on the world and on the wicked (for) their iniquity. And I will cause the arrogance of the proud to cease; and I will humble the pride of the tyrants.

[12] I will make a man more rare than gold; and a man than the golden wedge of Ophir. [13] So I will shake the heavens, and the earth shall move out of its place, in the wrath of Jehovah of hosts, and in the day of His fierce anger. [14] And it shall be as a gazelle driven away, and as a sheep no one gathers; each man shall look to his own people, and everyone shall flee to his own land. [15] Everyone that is found shall be pierced; and everyone together shall fall by the sword. [16] And their children shall be dashed in pieces before their eyes; their houses shall be robbed and their wives raped. [17] Behold, I will stir up the Medes against them, who shall not value silver; and they shall not delight in gold. [18] And bows shall also smash the young men to pieces; and they shall have no pity on the fruit of the womb; their eye shall not spare sons. [19] And Babylon, the glory of kingdoms, the beauty of the pride of the Chaldeans, shall be as when God overthrew Sodom and Gomorrah. [20] It shall never be inhabited forever, nor shall it be lived in from generation to generation. And the Arabian shall not pitch his tent there, nor shall the shepherds make (flocks) lie there. [21] But the wild beasts of the desert shall lie there; and their houses shall be full of howling creatures; and daughters

10 יַשְׁמִיד מִמֶּנָּה׃ כִּי־כוֹכְבֵי הַשָּׁמַיִם וּכְסִילֵיהֶם לֹא יָהֵלּוּ
shall not their and the the For of out shall He
shine constellations heavens of stars .it destroy

11 אוֹרָם חָשַׁךְ הַשֶּׁמֶשׁ בְּצֵאתוֹ וְיָרֵחַ לֹא־יַגִּיהַ אוֹרוֹ׃ וּפָקַדְתִּי
will I And its shall not the and its in the is their
visit .light reflect moon ;forth going sun dark ;light

עַל־תֵּבֵל רָעָה וְעַל־רְשָׁעִים עֲוֺנָם וְהִשְׁבַּתִּי גְּאוֹן זֵדִים
proud arro- the will I And their the and ,evil the on
,ones of gance cease make .iniquity wicked on world

12 וְגַאֲוַת עָרִיצִים אַשְׁפִּיל׃ אוֹקִיר אֱנוֹשׁ מִפָּז וְאָדָם מִכֶּתֶם
the than a and than man a make will I will I tyrants the and
of gold man ;gold rare more ,low bring of pride

13 אוֹפִיר׃ עַל־כֵּן שָׁמַיִם אַרְגִּיז וְתִרְעַשׁ הָאָרֶץ מִמְּקוֹמָהּ
its of out the shall and will I the ,Therefore .Ophir
,place earth move ,shake heavens

14 בְּעֶבְרַת יְהוָה צְבָאוֹת וּבְיוֹם חֲרוֹן אַפּוֹ׃ וְהָיָה כִּצְבִי
a as it And His the in and ,hosts Jehovah the in
gazelle be shall .anger of heat of day the of of wrath

מֻדָּח וּכְצֹאן וְאֵין מְקַבֵּץ אִישׁ אֶל־עַמּוֹ יִפְנוּ וְאִישׁ
each and they his to each ;gathers and as and ;chased
,one ,look shall people man none sheep a

15 אֶל־אַרְצוֹ יָנוּסוּ׃ כָּל־הַנִּמְצָא יִדָּקֵר וְכָל־הַנִּסְפֶּה יִפּוֹל
shall is who and be shall is who Everyone they his to
fall caught everyone ;pierced found .flee shall land

16 בֶּחָרֶב׃ וְעֹלְלֵיהֶם יְרֻטְּשׁוּ לְעֵינֵיהֶם יִשַּׁסּוּ בָּתֵּיהֶם וּנְשֵׁיהֶם
their and their be shall their before be shall their And the by
wives ;houses robbed ;eyes dashed children .sword

17 תִּשָּׁגַלְנָה׃ הִנְנִי מֵעִיר עֲלֵיהֶם אֶת־מָדַי אֲשֶׁר־כֶּסֶף לֹא
not silver who the against stir ,Behold .raped
,Medes them up I

18 יַחְשֹׁבוּ וְזָהָב לֹא יַחְפְּצוּ־בוֹ׃ וּקְשָׁתוֹת נְעָרִים תְּרַטַּשְׁנָה
dash shall young bows And in shall not and shall
;pieces to men .it delight gold ,reckon

19 וּפְרִי־בֶטֶן לֹא יְרַחֵמוּ עַל־בָּנִים לֹא־תָחוּס עֵינָם׃ וְהָיְתָה
shall And their shall not sons on shall they not the the and
be .eye spare ;pity womb of fruit

בָבֶל צְבִי מַמְלָכוֹת תִּפְאֶרֶת גְּאוֹן כַּשְׂדִּים כְּמַהְפֵּכַת
when as the pride the the ,kingdoms the ,Babylon
overthrew ,Chaldeans of of beauty of glory

20 אֱלֹהִים אֶת־סְדֹם וְאֶת־עֲמֹרָה׃ לֹא־תֵשֵׁב לָנֶצַח וְלֹא תִשְׁכֹּן
be it shall and ,forever shall It not .Gomorrah and Sodom God
in lived not inhabited be

עַד־דּוֹר וָדוֹר וְלֹא־יַהֵל שָׁם עֲרָבִי וְרֹעִים לֹא־יַרְבִּצוּ שָׁם׃
.there make shall not and the there shall And gen- and genera- to
21 lie (flocks) shepherds ,Arabian tent pitch not .eration tion

וְרָבְצוּ־שָׁם צִיִּים וּמָלְאוּ בָתֵּיהֶם אֹחִים וְשָׁכְנוּ שָׁם בְּנוֹת
daughters there and howling of their shall And desert there shall But
of dwell shall ,creatures houses full be .creatures lie

of ostriches shall dwell there; and he-goats shall skip there. [22] And hyenas shall cry, with his widows; and jackals in palaces of delight; and her time to come (is) near, and her days shall not be long.

CHAPTER 14

[1] For Jehovah will have pity (on) Jacob, and will yet choose Israel and set them in their own land. And the stranger shall be joined to them; and they shall cling to the house of Jacob. [2] And the peoples shall take them and bring them to their own place. And the house of Israel shall possess them in the land of Jehovah for slaves and slave-girls. And they shall be captives of their captors, and they shall rule over their oppressors. [3] And it shall be, in the day that Jehovah shall give you rest from your sorrow, and from your trouble, and from the hard bondage in which you were pressed, [4] that you shall take up this song against the king of Babylon and say, O how the oppressor has ceased, the gold-gatherer has ceased! [5] Jehovah has broken the staff of the wicked, the scepter of the rulers [6] who struck the peoples in wrath; who ruled the nations in anger; persecution without restraint. [7] The whole earth is at rest (and) is quiet; they break forth into singing. [8] Yea, the fir trees rejoice over you; the cedars of Lebanon (say), Since you have fallen, no woodcutter has come up against us.

[9] Sheol from below is moved for you, to meet you at your coming; it stirs up the dead for you, all the chief ones of the earth. It has raised all the kings of the nations from their thrones. [10] All of them shall answer and say to you, Are you also made as weak

22 יַעֲנָה וּשְׂעִירִים יְרַקְּדוּ־שָׁם׃ וְעָנָה אִיִּים בְּאַלְמְנוֹתָיו וְתַנִּים
and his with hyenas And .there shall he- and ;ostriches
jackals ,widows cry shall skip goats
בְּהֵיכְלֵי עֹנֶג וְקָרוֹב לָבוֹא עִתָּהּ וְיָמֶיהָ לֹא יִמָּשֵׁכוּ׃
be shall not her and· her (is) to and ,delight in
.prolonged days ,time come near of palaces

CAP. XIV יד

CHAPTER 14

1 כִּי יְרַחֵם יְהוָה אֶת־יַעֲקֹב וּבָחַר עוֹד בְּיִשְׂרָאֵל וְהִנִּיחָם
give and among yet will and ,Jacob on Jehovah have will For
rest them ,Israel choose pity
עַל־אַדְמָתָם וְנִלְוָה הַגֵּר עֲלֵיהֶם וְנִסְפְּחוּ עַל־בֵּית יַעֲקֹב׃
.Jacob the to they and ;them to the shall And their on
of house cling shall alien joined be .land
2 וּלְקָחוּם עַמִּים וֶהֱבִיאוּם אֶל־מְקוֹמָם וְהִתְנַחֲלוּם בֵּית־
the shall And their to bring and peoples shall And
of house them possess .place them them take
יִשְׂרָאֵל עַל אַדְמַת יְהוָה לַעֲבָדִים וְלִשְׁפָחוֹת וְהָיוּ שֹׁבִים
cap- ; they and slave- and for Jehovah land the on Israel
tives be shall , girls slaves of
3 לְשֹׁבֵיהֶם וְרָדוּ בְּנֹגְשֵׂיהֶם׃ וְהָיָה בְּיוֹם הָנִיחַ יְהוָה
Jehovah shall the in it And their over they and their of
rest give day ,be shall .oppressors .rule shall ;captors
לְךָ מֵעָצְבְּךָ וּמֵרָגְזֶךָ וּמִן־הָעֲבֹדָה הַקָּשָׁה אֲשֶׁר עֻבַּד־בָּךְ׃
on was which ,hard the and from and your from to
;you pressed bondage from ,trouble your ,toil you
4 וְנָשָׂאתָ הַמָּשָׁל הַזֶּה עַל־מֶלֶךְ בָּבֶל וְאָמָרְתָּ אֵיךְ שָׁבַת
has How ,say and ,Babylon the against this proverb will you and
ceased of king up take
5 נֹגֵשׂ שָׁבְתָה מַדְהֵבָה׃ שָׁבַר יְהוָה מַטֵּה רְשָׁעִים שֵׁבֶט
staff the the the Jehovah Has gold the has the
of ,wicked of rod broken !gatherer ceased ;exactor
6 מֹשְׁלִים׃ מַכֶּה עַמִּים בְּעֶבְרָה מַכַּת בִּלְתִּי סָרָה רֹדֶה
ruling turning without blow a —wrath in peoples striking ,rulers
;away
7 בָאַף גּוֹיִם מֻרְדָּף בְּלִי חָשָׂךְ׃ נָחָה שָׁקְטָה כָּל־הָאָרֶץ
the All (and) at is .restraint without perse- ;nations in
;earth quiet rest cution anger
8 פָּצְחוּ רִנָּה׃ גַּם־בְּרוֹשִׁים שָׂמְחוּ לְךָ אַרְזֵי לְבָנוֹן מֵאָז
Since Lebanon the over rejoice fir ,Yea .singing break they
,(say) of cedars ;you trees into out
9 שָׁכַבְתָּ לֹא־יַעֲלֶה הַכֹּרֵת עָלֵינוּ׃ שְׁאוֹל מִתַּחַת רָגְזָה לְךָ
for is from Sheol against wood- the will not have you
,you stirred below .us cutter up come ,down lain
לִקְרַאת בּוֹאֶךָ עוֹרֵר לְךָ רְפָאִים כָּל־עַתּוּדֵי אֶרֶץ הֵקִים
has It the he- the all the for it your meet to
raised .earth of goats ,dead you up stirs ;coming
10 מִכִּסְאוֹתָם כֹּל מַלְכֵי גוֹיִם׃ כֻּלָּם יַעֲנוּ וְיֹאמְרוּ אֵלֶיךָ גַּם־
Also to say and shall All the the all their from
,you answer them of .nations of kings thrones

as we? Are you likened to us? [11] Your majesty is lowered into Sheol; the noise of your harps, too. The maggot is spread under you; yea, the worms cover you. [12] O shining star, son of the morning, how you are fallen from the heavens! You who weakens on the nations, you are cut down to the ground. [13] For you have said in your heart, I will go up (to) the heavens; I will raise my throne above the stars of God; and I will sit in mount of the assembly. [14] I will rise over the heights of clouds; I will be likened to the Most High. [15] Yet you shall be brought down to Sheol, to the sides of the Pit. [16] They that see you shall stare and closely watch you: Is this the man who made the earth tremble, that shook the kingdoms, [17] making the world like a wilderness and destroying its cities — he who did not open a house for his prisoners? 18] All the kings of the nations, all of them, lie in glory, each man in his own house. [19] But you are thrown from your grave like a despised branch, (like) the clothing of the slain, those pierced by the sword, those who go down into the stones of the Pit, like a dead body trampled under foot.

[20] You shall not be united with them in burial, because you ruined your land; you have slain your people; the seed of evildoers shall never be called! [21] Prepare for the slaughter of his sons, because of their fathers' iniquity; that they may not rise and possess the land, and fill (with) cities the face of the earth. [22] For I will rise against them, says Jehovah of hosts, and cut off the name and remnant, the son and grandson from Babylon, says Jehovah. [23] I will give it to the hedgehog, and pools of water; and I will sweep it with the

11 אַתָּה חֻלֵּיתָ כָמוֹנוּ אֵלֵינוּ נִמְשָׁלְתָּ׃ הוּרַד שְׁאוֹל גְּאוֹנֶךָ
Your into lowered is are you us To we as made are you
,majesty Sheol !likened !(are) weak

12 הֶמְיַת נְבָלֶיךָ תַּחְתֶּיךָ יֻצַּע רִמָּה וּמְכַסֶּיךָ תּוֹלֵעָה׃ אֵיךְ
How .worms cover and the is Under your noise the
you ,maggot spread you .harps of

נָפַלְתָּ מִשָּׁמַיִם הֵילֵל בֶּן־שָׁחַר נִגְדַּעְתָּ לָאָרֶץ חוֹלֵשׁ עַל־
on who the to are You the son shining O the from have you
weakens ,ground down cut !morning of ,star ,heavens fallen

13 גּוֹיִם׃ וְאַתָּה אָמַרְתָּ בִלְבָבְךָ הַשָּׁמַיִם אֶעֱלֶה מִמַּעַל
above will I the (to) your in have For the
;up go heavens ,heart said you nations

לְכוֹכְבֵי־אֵל אָרִים כִּסְאִי וְאֵשֵׁב בְּהַר־מוֹעֵד בְּיַרְכְּתֵי
the in ,meeting the on I And my will I God the
of sides of mount sit will .throne raise of stars

14
15 צָפוֹן׃ אֶעֱלֶה עַל־בָּמֳתֵי עָב אֶדַּמֶּה לְעֶלְיוֹן׃ אַךְ אֶל־
to Yet the to be will I ;clouds the over will I the
.High Most likened of heights rise .north

16 שְׁאוֹל תּוּרָד אֶל־יַרְכְּתֵי־בוֹר׃ רֹאֶיךָ אֵלֶיךָ יַשְׁגִּיחוּ אֵלֶיךָ
at shall at who They the the to shall you Sheol
you ,stare you you see .Pit of sides ,lowered be

יִתְבּוֹנָנוּ הֲזֶה הָאִישׁ מַרְגִּיז הָאָרֶץ מַרְעִישׁ מַמְלָכוֹת׃
;kingdoms shaking the making the Is shall
,earth tremble man this ,ponder

17 שָׂם תֵּבֵל כַּמִּדְבָּר וְעָרָיו הָרָס אֲסִירָיו לֹא־פָתַח בָּיְתָה׃
a he not his tore its and a like the setting
?house opened prisoners ,down cities ;desert world

18
19 כָּל־מַלְכֵי גוֹיִם כֻּלָּם שָׁכְבוּ בְכָבוֹד אִישׁ בְּבֵיתוֹ׃ וְאַתָּה
you But his in each ,glory in lie all ,nations kings All
.house man them of of

הָשְׁלַכְתָּ מִקִּבְרְךָ כְּנֵצֶר נִתְעָב לְבֻשׁ הֲרֻגִים מְטֹעֲנֵי חָרֶב
the those ,slain the (as) ;despised a like your from are
,sword by pierced of covering branch grave thrown

20 יוֹרְדֵי אֶל־אַבְנֵי־בוֹר כְּפֶגֶר מוּבָס׃ לֹא־תֵחַד אִתָּם בִּקְבוּרָה
;burial in with shall You not .trampled a as ,Pit the the in- who those
them united be corpse of stones to down go

כִּי־אַרְצְךָ שִׁחַתָּ עַמְּךָ הָרַגְתָּ לֹא־יִקָּרֵא לְעוֹלָם זֶרַע
the forever be let not have you your you your because
of seed called ;slain people ;ruined land

21 מְרֵעִים׃ הָכִינוּ לְבָנָיו מַטְבֵּחַ בַּעֲוֹן אֲבוֹתָם בַּל־יָקֻמוּ
them let not their for ,slaughter for Prepare !evildoers
rise ;fathers' iniquity sons his

22 וְיָרְשׁוּ אָרֶץ וּמָלְאוּ פְנֵי־תֵבֵל עָרִים׃ וְקַמְתִּי עֲלֵיהֶם נְאֻם
states against I For (with) the the and the and
,them rise will cities earth of face fill ,land possess

יְהוָה צְבָאוֹת וְהִכְרַתִּי לְבָבֶל שֵׁם וּשְׁאָר וְנִין וָנֶכֶד נְאֻם־
states and son and and name from cut and ,hosts Jehovah
,posterity ,remnant Babylon off of

23 יְהוָה׃ וְשַׂמְתִּיהָ לְמוֹרַשׁ קִפֹּד וְאַגְמֵי־מָיִם וְטֵאטֵאתִיהָ
will I and ;water and the pos- a will I .Jehovah
it sweep of pools ,hedgehog of session it make

broom of ruin, says Jehovah of hosts. [24] Jehovah of hosts has sworn, saying, Surely as I have thought, so it shall be; and as I have purposed, it shall rise; [25] that I will break the Assyrian in My land, and trample him on My mountains. Then his yoke shall depart from them, and his burden shall be taken from his shoulders. [26] This (is) the purpose that is purposed on the whole earth; and this (is) the hand that is stretched out on all the nations. [27] For Jehovah of hosts has purposed and who shall reverse (it)? And His hand is stretched out, who shall pull it back?

[28] This burden was in the year King Ahaz died: [29] Do not rejoice, O Philistia, all of you, that he who struck you has his rod broken; for out of the serpent's root shall come a viper; and his fruit (shall be) a fiery flying serpent. [30] And the firstborn of the poor shall eat; and they who are needy shall lie down in safety; and I will slay your root with famine, and he shall kill your remnant. [31] Howl, O gate! Cry, O city! You, O Philistia, all of you, are melted away — for a smoke shall come from the north, and not one is isolated in his ranks. [32] What then, shall one answer to the messengers of the nation? That Jehovah has founded Zion, and the poor of His people shall trust in it.

בְּמַטְאֲטֵא הַשְׁמֵד נְאֻם יְהוָה צְבָאוֹת׃ 24 נִשְׁבַּע יְהוָה
Jehovah has .hosts Jehovah states ,ruin the with
of sworn of of broom

צְבָאוֹת לֵאמֹר אִם־לֹא כַּאֲשֶׁר דִּמִּיתִי כֵּן הָיָתָה וְכַאֲשֶׁר
as and ,is it so have I as ,Surely ,saying ,hosts
,thought

יָעַצְתִּי הִיא תָקוּם׃ 25 לִשְׁבֹּר אַשּׁוּר בְּאַרְצִי וְעַל־הָרַי
My on and My in Assyria break to shall it have I
mountains ,land ;rise ,purposed

אֲבוּסֶנּוּ וְסָר מֵעֲלֵיהֶם עֻלּוֹ וְסֻבֳּלוֹ מֵעַל שִׁכְמוֹ יָסוּר׃
shall his from his and his from Then trample will I
.go shoulders burden ,yoke them go shall .him

26 זֹאת הָעֵצָה הַיְּעוּצָה עַל־כָּל־הָאָרֶץ וְזֹאת הַיָּד הַנְּטוּיָה
is that the and the all on is that the This
out stretched hand this ;earth purposed purpose (is)

עַל־כָּל־הַגּוֹיִם׃ 27 כִּי־יְהוָה צְבָאוֹת יָעָץ וּמִי יָפֵר וְיָדוֹ
And shall who and ,purposes hosts Jehovah For the all on
hand His ?reverse of .nations

הַנְּטוּיָה וּמִי יְשִׁיבֶנָּה׃ 28 בִּשְׁנַת־מוֹת הַמֶּלֶךְ אָחָז
,Ahaz King the the In turn shall and ex- is
of death of year ?back it who tended

הָיָה הַמַּשָּׂא הַזֶּה׃ 29 אַל־תִּשְׂמְחִי פְלֶשֶׁת כֻּלֵּךְ כִּי נִשְׁבַּר
is for of all O Do not :this burden was
broken ,you ,Philistia ,rejoice

שֵׁבֶט מַכֵּךְ כִּי־מִשֹּׁרֶשׁ נָחָשׁ יֵצֵא צֶפַע וּפִרְיוֹ שָׂרָף
fiery a his and a comes a the from for your the
serpent fruit ;viper forth snake of root ,striking of rod

מְעוֹפֵף׃ 30 וְרָעוּ בְּכוֹרֵי דַלִּים וְאֶבְיוֹנִים לָבֶטַח יִרְבָּצוּ
shall safety in the and the the shall And .flying
;down lie needy ;poor of firstborn feed

וְהֵמַתִּי בָרָעָב שָׁרְשֵׁךְ וּשְׁאֵרִיתֵךְ יַהֲרֹג׃ 31 הֵילִילִי שַׁעַר
O ,Howl shall it your and your with will I and
!gate .kill remnant ,root famine slay

זַעֲקִי־עִיר נָמוֹג פְּלֶשֶׁת כֻּלֵּךְ כִּי מִצָּפוֹן עָשָׁן בָּא וְאֵין בּוֹדֵד
is and ,comes a the from for of all (is) Melted O ,Cry
isolated none smoke north ,you ,Philistia away !city

בְּמוֹעָדָיו׃ 32 וּמַה־יַּעֲנֶה מַלְאֲכֵי־גוֹי כִּי יְהוָה יִסַּד צִיּוֹן וּבָהּ
and ,Zion has Jehovah That the mes- the shall what And his in
it in founded ?nation of sengers answer he .ranks

יֶחֱסוּ עֲנִיֵּי עַמּוֹ׃
His the shall
.people of poor trust

CHAPTER 15

[1] The burden against Moab: Because Ar of Moab is laid waste in a night (and) is silenced; because Kir of Moab is laid waste in a night and (is) silenced — [2] one goes up to the House, even Dibon, the high places to weep. Moab shall

CAP. XV טו

CHAPTER 15

1 מַשָּׂא מוֹאָב כִּי בְּלֵיל שֻׁדַּד עָר מוֹאָב נִדְמָה כִּי בְּלֵיל
a in that is it ,Moab Ar laid is a in that :Moab The
night ;destroyed of waste night of burden

2 שֻׁדַּד קִיר־מוֹאָב נִדְמָה׃ עָלָה הַבַּיִת וְדִיבֹן הַבָּמוֹת לַבֶּכִי
for high the (to) even the to One is it ,Moab Kir laid is
.weeping ,places ,Dibon ,house up goes .destroyed of waste

עַל־נְבוֹ וְעַל מֵידְבָא מוֹאָב יְיֵלִיל בְּכָל־רֹאשָׁיו קָרְחָה כָּל־
every (is) its all on shall Moab Medeba and Nebo over
;baldness heads ,howl over

3 זָקָן גְּרוּעָה׃ בְּחוּצֹתָיו חָגְרוּ שָׂק עַל־גַּגּוֹתֶיהָ וּבִרְחֹבֹתֶיהָ
its in and its on sack- they its In .shorn is beard
squares housetops ;cloth don shall streets

4 כֻּלֹּה יְיֵלִיל יֹרֵד בַּבֶּכִי׃ וַתִּזְעַק חֶשְׁבּוֹן וְאֶלְעָלֵה עַד־יַהַץ
Jahaz as and Heshbon And in going shall every-
as far ;Elealeh cries .weeping down ,howl one

נִשְׁמַע קוֹלָם עַל־כֵּן חֲלֻצֵי מוֹאָב יָרִיעוּ נַפְשׁוֹ יָרְעָה לּוֹ׃
to quivers his shall Moab war- the therefore their is
.him life ;shout of riors ;voice heard

5 לִבִּי לְמוֹאָב יִזְעָק בְּרִיחֶהָ עַד־צֹעַר עֶגְלַת שְׁלִשִׁיָּה כִּי ׀
for years three a ,Zoar (are) her shall Moab to My
;old of heifer to fugitives ;cry heart

מַעֲלֵה הַלּוּחִית בִּבְכִי יַעֲלֶה־בּוֹ כִּי דֶּרֶךְ חוֹרֹנַיִם זַעֲקַת־
cry a Horonaim the (in) for ;it in he with ,Luhith the
of of way up goes weeping of ascent

6 שֶׁבֶר יְעֹעֵרוּ׃ כִּי־מֵי נִמְרִים מְשַׁמּוֹת יִהְיוּ כִּי־יָבֵשׁ חָצִיר
the is for ;are desolations Nimrim the For shall they ruin
;hay up dried of waters .up raise

7 כָּלָה דֶשֶׁא יֶרֶק לֹא הָיָה׃ עַל־כֵּן יִתְרָה עָשָׂה וּפְקֻדָּתָם
their and one the Therefore there not green a the fails
,store ,made remainder .is thing ;grass

8 עַל נַחַל הָעֲרָבִים יִשָּׂאוּם׃ כִּי־הִקִּיפָה הַזְּעָקָה אֶת־גְּבוּל
the cry the gone has For shall they the the over
of border around .them carry willows of brook

9 מוֹאָב עַד־אֶגְלַיִם יִלְלָתָהּ וּבְאֵר אֵילִים יִלְלָתָהּ׃ כִּי מֵי
the For its Elim even and its Eglaim even ,Moab
of waters .howling Beer- to ;howling to

דִימוֹן מָלְאוּ דָם כִּי־אָשִׁית עַל־דִּימוֹן נוֹסָפוֹת לִפְלֵיטַת
the for more Dimon on will I for ;blood are Dimon
of escaped ,(things) bring of full

מוֹאָב אַרְיֵה וְלִשְׁאֵרִית אֲדָמָה׃
the the for and ,lion a ,Moab
.land of remnant

howl over Nebo and over Medeba; all its heads (shall be) bald, (and) every beard shaved. [3] They shall dress with sackcloth in the streets; everyone shall howl on their housetops and in their squares, melting in tears. [4] And Heshbon and Elealeh shall cry; their voice shall be heard as far as Jahaz; so the armed men of Moab shall shout; his soul quivers (within) him. [5] My heart shall be to Moab; her fugitives cry to Zoar, a heifer of three years (old); he goes up the ascent of Luhith, with weeping, for (in) the way of Horonaim they shall raise up a cry of ruin. [6] For Nimrim's waters are desolations; for the hay is dried up; the grass fails; there is not a green thing. [7] Therefore one made the remainder and their store; they shall carry them over the brook of the willows. [8] For the cry has gone around Moab's borders; his howling even to Eglaim; and his howling even to Beer-elim. [9] For Dimon's waters are full of blood; for I will bring more on Dimon, a lion on him who escapes from Moab, and for the remnant of the land.

CAP. XVI טז

CHAPTER 16

1 שִׁלְחוּ־כַר מֹשֵׁל־אֶרֶץ מִסֶּלַע מִדְבָּרָה אֶל־הַר בַּת־צִיּוֹן׃
Zion's the to the (in) from the of the to a Send
.daughter of mount wilderness Sela ,land ruler lamb

2 וְהָיָה כְעוֹף־נוֹדֵד קֵן מְשֻׁלָּח תִּהְיֶינָה בְּנוֹת מוֹאָב מַעְבָּרֹת
the (at) Moab the be shall cast a ,fleeing a as it For
fords of daughters ;out nest bird is

3 לְאַרְנוֹן׃ הָבִיאוּ עֵצָה עֲשׂוּ פְלִילָה שִׁיתִי כַלַּיִל צִלֵּךְ
your the as make ;judgment do ;counsel Take of
shadow night ,Arnon

4 בְּתוֹךְ צָהֳרַיִם סַתְּרִי נִדָּחִים נֹדֵד אַל־תְּגַלִּי׃ יָגוּרוּ בָךְ
with Let do not the the hide ;midday the in
you tarry !uncover fugitive ;outcasts of midst

CHAPTER 16

[1] Send a lamb to the ruler of the land, from the rock of the desert to the mount of the daughter of Zion. [2] For it is as a fleeing bird cast out of the nest — the daughters of Moab shall be (at) the fords of Arnon. [3] Take counsel; do judgment; make your shadow as the night at mid-day; hide the outcasts; uncover not the fugitive! [4] Let My outcasts tarry

with you, Moab; be a hiding-place to them from the face of the destroyer. For the extortioner has ceased; the destroyer has failed; the trampler (is) consumed out of the land. [5] And in mercy the throne shall be established; and (he) shall sit on it in truth in the tabernacle of David, judging and seeking justice, and speeding righteousness.

[6] We have heard of the pride of Moab — very proud — of his pride, his arrogance, and his rage; his babblings shall not (be) so. [7] So Moab shall howl for Moab; everyone shall howl; you shall moan for the raisin-cakes of Kir-hareseth; surely they are smitten! [8] For the fields of Heshbon, the vine of Sibmah droops; the captains of the nations have broken down its choice plants — they have come to Jazer; they wandered in a wilderness; her branches are spread out; they have crossed the sea. [9] Therefore I will bewail the vine of Sibmah with weeping (for) Jazer; I will drench you with my tears, O Heshbon and Elealeh; for the shouting has ceased, for your summer fruits and your harvest have failed. [10] And gladness and joy is gathered up from the fruitful field; and there is no singing and no shouting in the vineyards; the treaders shall tread out no wine in the presses; I have made the exultation to cease; [11] for this reason my bowels shall sound like a harp for Moab, and my inward parts for Kir-haresh. [12] And it shall be, when it is seen that Moab shall be wearied on the high places, then he shall come to his sacred place to pray; but he shall not be able. [13] This (is) the word that Jehovah had spoken to Moab from that time. [14] But now Jehovah has spoken, saying, Within three years, as the years of a hireling, then the glory of Moab shall be disgraced, with all (her) great multitude; and those that are left (shall be) few, small (and) feeble.

נִדָּחַי מוֹאָב הֱוִי־סֵתֶר לָמוֹ מִפְּנֵי שׁוֹדֵד כִּי־אָפֵס הַמֵּץ
ex- the has For the the from to hiding a be ;Moab My
,actor ceased .destroyer of face them place ,outcasts

5 כָּלָה שֹׁד תַּמּוּ רֹמֵס מִן־הָאָרֶץ׃ וְהוּכַן בַּחֶסֶד כִּסֵּא
the in shall And the out the is destruc- has
;throne mercy established be .land of trampler ended ;tion failed

וְיָשַׁב עָלָיו בֶּאֱמֶת בְּאֹהֶל דָּוִד שֹׁפֵט וְדֹרֵשׁ מִשְׁפָּט וּמְהִר
and ,justice and judging ,David the in in it on he and
in swift seeking of tent ,truth sit shall

6 צֶדֶק׃ שָׁמַעְנוּ גְאוֹן־מוֹאָב גֵּא מְאֹד גַּאֲוָתוֹ וּגְאוֹנוֹ וְעֶבְרָתוֹ
his and his and his —very proud —Moab the have We righ-
;rage ,arrogance ,pride of pride of heard .teousness

7 לֹא־כֵן בַּדָּיו׃ לָכֵן יְיֵלִיל מוֹאָב לְמוֹאָב כֻּלֹּה יְיֵלִיל לַאֲשִׁישֵׁי
raisin for shall of all for Moab shall So his so not
cakes ,howl it ;Moab howl .babblings

8 קִיר־חֲרֶשֶׂת תֶּהְגּוּ אַךְ־נְכָאִים׃ כִּי שַׁדְמוֹת חֶשְׁבּוֹן אֻמְלָל
,droop Heshbon the For are they surely shall you hareseth Kir-
of fields !smitten ;moan

גֶּפֶן שִׂבְמָה בַּעֲלֵי גוֹיִם הָלְמוּ שְׂרוּקֶּיהָ עַד־יַעְזֵר נָגָעוּ תָּעוּ
they they Jazer to choice its have nations the ,Sibmah the
wander ;come —plants crushed of masters of vine

9 מִדְבָּר שְׁלֻחוֹתֶיהָ נִטְּשׁוּ עָבְרוּ יָם׃ עַל־כֵּן אֶבְכֶּה בִּבְכִי
the with will Therefore the they are branches her the (in)
of weeping weep .sea crossed ;out spread ;desert

יַעְזֵר גֶּפֶן שִׂבְמָה אֲרַיָּוֶךְ דִּמְעָתִי חֶשְׁבּוֹן וְאֶלְעָלֵה כִּי עַל־
on for and Heshbon my with will I ;Sibmah the Jazer
;Elealeh ,tears you drench of vine

10 קֵיצֵךְ וְעַל־קְצִירֵךְ הֵידָד נָפָל׃ וְנֶאֱסַף שִׂמְחָה וָגִיל מִן־
from and gladness is And has shouting your and your
joy up gathered .fallen harvest on fruit

הַכַּרְמֶל וּבַכְּרָמִים לֹא־יְרֻנָּן לֹא יְרֹעָע יַיִן בַּיְקָבִים לֹא־יִדְרֹךְ
shall not the in wine shout- and singing not the in and fruitful the
out tread presses ;ing not is vineyards ;field

11 הַדֹּרֵךְ הֵידָד הִשְׁבַּתִּי׃ עַל־כֵּן מֵעַי לְמוֹאָב כַּכִּנּוֹר יֶהֱמוּ
shall the like for my Therefore made have I the the
;sound harp Moab belly .cease to shout ;treader

12 וְקִרְבִּי לְקִיר חָרֶשׂ׃ וְהָיָה כִי־נִרְאָה כִּי־נִלְאָה מוֹאָב עַל־
on Moab be shall that is it when it And .haresh Kir- for my and
wearied seen be shall parts inward

13 הַבָּמָה וּבָא אֶל־מִקְדָּשׁוֹ לְהִתְפַּלֵּל וְלֹא יוּכָל׃ זֶה הַדָּבָר
the This shall he but ;pray to sacred his to he then high the
word (is) .able be not place come shall ;place

14 אֲשֶׁר דִּבֶּר יְהוָה אֶל־מוֹאָב מֵאָז׃ וְעַתָּה דִּבֶּר יְהוָה לֵאמֹר
,saying ,Jehovah has But that from Moab to Jehovah had which
spoken now time spoken

בְּשָׁלֹשׁ שָׁנִים כִּשְׁנֵי שָׂכִיר וְנִקְלָה כְּבוֹד מוֹאָב בְּכֹל הֶהָמוֹן
the with ,Moab's glory will then a the as ,years Within
host all abased be ,hireling of years three

הָרָב וּשְׁאָר מְעַט מִזְעָר לוֹא כַבִּיר׃
.mighty not ,small (be shall) the and ;great
;few remnant

CAP. XVII יז

CHAPTER 17

[1] The burden against Damascus: Behold, Damascus is taken away from (being) a city, and it shall be a ruined heap. [2] The cities of Aroer are forsaken; now they are for flocks; they shall lie down and no one terrified (them). [3] And the fortress shall cease from Ephraim; and the kingdom from Damascus and the rest of Syria. As the glory of the sons of Israel, they shall be, says Jehovah of hosts. [4] And it shall be in that day, that Jacob's glory shall be made thin, and the fatness of his flesh shall be made lean. [5] And it shall be as when the harvestman gathers the grain, and his arm reaps the ears; and it shall be as he who gathers ears in the valley of Rephaim. [6] Yet gleaning grapes shall be left in it, as the shaking of an olive tree — two (or) three berries in the top of the uppermost branch; four (or) five in the fruitful branches, says Jehovah God of Israel.

[7] In that day a man shall gaze to his Maker; and his eyes shall look to the Holy One of Israel. [8] And he shall not look to the altars, the work of his hands, and he will not see even the Asherim, and the sun-pillars. [9] In that day his fortified cities shall be as a thing left in the forest, or the branch that they leave, from before the sons of Israel; and it will become a desolation. [10] Because you have forgotten the God of your salvation; and you remembered not the Rock of your strength, so you shall plant pleasing plants and shall graft in a foreign shoot. [11] In the day of your

CHAPTER 17

1 מַשָּׂא דַּמָּשֶׂק הִנֵּה דַמֶּשֶׂק מוּסָר מֵעִיר וְהָיְתָה מְעִי
heap a | it and be shall | (being) city a | from | turned away | is Damascus | ,Behold | Damascus | the of burden

2 מַפָּלָה׃ עֲזֻבוֹת עָרֵי עֲרֹעֵר לַעֲדָרִים תִּהְיֶינָה וְרָבְצוּ וְאֵין
and none | they and down lie | ;are they | for flocks | ;Aroer | The of cities | are forsaken | .ruined

3 מַחֲרִיד׃ וְנִשְׁבַּת מִבְצָר מֵאֶפְרַיִם וּמַמְלָכָה מִדַּמֶּשֶׂק
from Damascus | the and kingdom | from ,Ephraim | the fortress | shall And cease | terrifies .(them)

וּשְׁאָר אֲרָם כִּכְבוֹד בְּנֵי־יִשְׂרָאֵל יִהְיוּ נְאֻם יְהוָה צְבָאוֹת׃
.hosts | Jehovah of | states | they ,be shall | Israel | the of sons | the As of glory | .Syria | the and of rest

4 וְהָיָה בַּיּוֹם הַהוּא יִדַּל כְּבוֹד יַעֲקֹב וּמִשְׁמַן
the and of fatness | ,Jacob | the of glory | be shall weak made | ,that | day in | it And be shall

5 בְּשָׂרוֹ יֵרָזֶה׃ וְהָיָה כֶּאֱסֹף קָצִיר קָמָה וּזְרֹעוֹ שִׁבֳּלִים
ears the | his and arm | the ,grain | the ,harvest | the as of reaping | it And be shall | be shall .lean made | his flesh

6 יִקְצוֹר וְהָיָה כִּמְלַקֵּט שִׁבֳּלִים בְּעֵמֶק רְפָאִים׃ וְנִשְׁאַר־בּוֹ
it in | shall Yet left be | .Rephaim | the in of valley | ears | who he as gathers | it and be shall | ;reaps

עוֹלֵלֹת כְּנֹקֶף זַיִת שְׁנַיִם שְׁלֹשָׁה גַּרְגְּרִים בְּרֹאשׁ אָמִיר
high a ,branch | the in of top | ripe olives | (or) three | two | olive an —tree | the as of shaking | ,gleanings

אַרְבָּעָה חֲמִשָּׁה בִּסְעִפֶיהָ פֹּרִיָּה נְאֻם־יְהוָה אֱלֹהֵי
God of | Jehovah | states | the (of) ,tree fruit | branches in its | five (or) | four

7 יִשְׂרָאֵל׃ בַּיּוֹם הַהוּא יִשְׁעֶה הָאָדָם עַל־עֹשֵׂהוּ וְעֵינָיו אֶל־
to | his and eyes | his ;Maker | on | man a | shall gaze | that | day In | .Israel

8 קְדוֹשׁ יִשְׂרָאֵל תִּרְאֶינָה׃ וְלֹא יִשְׁעֶה אֶל־הַמִּזְבְּחוֹת
the ,altars | to | shall he gaze | And not | shall .look | Israel | Holy the of One

מַעֲשֵׂה יָדָיו וַאֲשֶׁר עָשׂוּ אֶצְבְּעֹתָיו לֹא יִרְאֶה וְהָאֲשֵׁרִים
the Asherim | even | will he ,see | not | his fingers | have made | and what | his ;hands | the of work

9 וְהָחַמָּנִים׃ בַּיּוֹם הַהוּא יִהְיוּ ׀ עָרֵי מָעֻזּוֹ כַּעֲזוּבַת
thing a as in left | his fortified | cities | shall be | that | day In | the and .sun-pillars

הַחֹרֶשׁ וְהָאָמִיר אֲשֶׁר עָזְבוּ מִפְּנֵי בְּנֵי יִשְׂרָאֵל וְהָיְתָה
it and be will | ;Israel | the of sons | from before | they ,leave | that | the or branch | the forest

10 שְׁמָמָה׃ כִּי שָׁכַחַתְּ אֱלֹהֵי יִשְׁעֵךְ וְצוּר מָעֻזֵּךְ לֹא זָכָרְתְּ
did you remember | not | your strength | the and of Rock | your ;salvation | God the of | have you forgotten | Because | deso- a .lation

11 עַל־כֵּן תִּטְּעִי נִטְעֵי נַעֲמָנִים וּזְמֹרַת זָר תִּזְרָעֶנּוּ׃ בְּיוֹם
the In of day | shall you .it sow | foreign- ness | a and of shoot | ,pleasantness | plants of | you plant shall | Therefore

planting you fence it in; and in the morning (that) you make your seed sprout; (your) harvest (is) a heap in that day of grief and incurable pain. [12] Woe (to) the multitude of many peoples; they roar like the roar of seas; and the crash of nations; they crash like the crash of mighty waters! [13] The nations shall crash like the crashing of many waters, but He rebukes it, and it flees far away; and (it) is chased like the chaff of mountains before the wind, and like a rolling thing before a tempest. [14] At eveningtime, behold, terror! Before (it is) morning, it shall not be. This (is) the portion of those who rob us, and the lot of our plunderers.

נִטְעֵךְ תְּשַׂגְשֵׂגִי וּבַבֹּקֶר זַרְעֵךְ תַּפְרִיחִי נֵד קָצִיר בְּיוֹם

the in / the (is) a / make you / your / the in / fence you / your
of day / crop heap / ;sprout / seed / morning / ,in it / planting

12 נַחֲלָה וּכְאֵב אָנוּשׁ׃ הוֹי הֲמוֹן עַמִּים רַבִּים כַּהֲמוֹת

the like / ;many / peoples mul- the / Woe / .incurable / and / sick-
of roar / of titude (to) / pain / ness

יַמִּים יֶהֱמָיוּן וּשְׁאוֹן לְאֻמִּים כִּשְׁאוֹן מַיִם כַּבִּירִים יִשָּׁאוּן׃

they / mighty / waters / the like / ;nations / the and / they / seas
!crash / of crash / of crash / ;roar

13 לְאֻמִּים כִּשְׁאוֹן מַיִם רַבִּים יִשָּׁאוּן וְגָעַר בּוֹ וְנָס מִמֶּרְחָק

far / it and / ,it He but / ;crash / many / waters / the like / Nations
;away / flees / rebukes / of crashing

14 וְרֻדַּף כְּמֹץ הָרִים לִפְנֵי־רוּחַ וּכְגַלְגַּל לִפְנֵי סוּפָה׃ לְעֵת

the At / a / before / a like and / the / before mountains / the like is and
of time / .tempest / thing rolling / ,wind / of chaff chased

עֶרֶב וְהִנֵּה בַלָּהָה בְּטֶרֶם בֹּקֶר אֵינֶנּוּ זֶה חֵלֶק שׁוֹסֵינוּ

our / the / This / shall it / (is it) / Before / !terror / ,and / ,evening
,robbers of portion (is) / .be not ,morning / ,behold

וְגוֹרָל לְבֹזְזֵינוּ׃

our of / the and
.plunderers / lot

CAP. XVIII יח

CHAPTER 18

[1] Woe (to the) land of whirring of wings, which (is) from beyond the rivers of Ethiopia; [2] which sends envoys by the sea, in ships of reeds on the waters: Go, swift messengers, to a nation tall and smooth; to a people terrible from that (time) and onwards, a mighty nation, and (one) trampling down, whose land the rivers have divided! [3] All you dwellers of the world and dwellers of the earth, as one lifts a banner (on the) peaks, you will see; and you will hear as the blowing of a trumpet. [4] For so Jehovah said to me, I will take My rest, and I will watch in My dwelling place; as the glowing heat on light; as the dew-cloud in the heat of harvest. [5] For before the harvest, when the bud is perfect, and the sour grape is ripening in the flower, then he will cut off the sprigs with pruning hooks, and cut down and take away the branches. [6] They shall be left together to the birds of the hills, and to the beasts of the earth. And the birds

1
2 הוֹי אֶרֶץ צִלְצַל כְּנָפָיִם אֲשֶׁר מֵעֵבֶר לְנַהֲרֵי־כוּשׁ׃ הַשֹּׁלֵחַ

which / ,Ethiopia / the / from / which / ,wings / whirring the / Woe
sends / of rivers / beyond / (is) / of / of land / (to)

בַּיָּם צִירִים וּבִכְלֵי־גֹמֶא עַל־פְּנֵי־מַיִם לְכוּ ׀ מַלְאָכִים קַלִּים

,swift / messengers / ,Go / the / the on / papyrus / in even / ,envoys the by
:waters of face / of ships / sea

אֶל־גּוֹי מְמֻשָּׁךְ וּמוֹרָט אֶל־עַם נוֹרָא מִן־הוּא וָהָלְאָה גּוֹי

a / and / ,it from / ,terrible / a / to / and / tall / a / to
nation ,onwards / people / ,smooth / nation

3 קַו־קָו וּמְבוּסָה אֲשֶׁר־בָּזְאוּ נְהָרִים אַרְצוֹ׃ כָּל־יֹשְׁבֵי תֵבֵל

the / inhabitants All / its / the / have / of / tramp- and / mighty
world / of / !land / rivers / divided whom ,down ling

וְשֹׁכְנֵי אָרֶץ כִּנְשֹׂא־נֵס הָרִים תִּרְאוּ וְכִתְקֹעַ שׁוֹפָר תִּשְׁמָעוּ׃

will you / a / the as and / will you (the on) / a / one as / the / and
.hear / ,trumpet of blowing / ;see / peaks / flag / lifts earth of dwellers

4 כִּי כֹה אָמַר יְהוָה אֵלַי אֶשְׁקוֹטָה וְאַבִּיטָה בִמְכוֹנִי

My in / will I and / will I / to / Jehovah / said / so / For
dwelling / watch / rest / ,me

5 כְּחֹם צַח עֲלֵי־אוֹר כְּעָב טַל בְּחֹם קָצִיר׃ כִּי־לִפְנֵי קָצִיר

the / before For / .harvest / the in / dew / the as / ;light upon / glow- / the as
harvest / of heat / of cloud / ing / heat

כְּתָם־פֶּרַח וּבֹסֶר גֹּמֵל יִהְיֶה נִצָּה וְכָרַת הַזַּלְזַלִּים

the / will He then / the (in) / is / ripening / the and / the / is when
sprigs / off cut / ,flower / grape sour / ,bud / perfect

6 בַּמַּזְמֵרוֹת וְאֶת־הַנְּטִישׁוֹת הֵסִיר הֵתַז׃ יֵעָזְבוּ יַחְדָּו לְעֵיט

the to together / They / cut / take / the / and / the with
of birds / left be shall / .down / ,away / branches / ;knives pruning

shall summer on them, and all the beasts of the earth shall winter on them. [7] Then shall be brought to Jehovah of hosts, the present of a people scattered and peeled, and from a nation terrible, from that (time) and onward; a nation mighty and trampling under foot, whose land the rivers have divided, to the place of Jehovah of hosts' name — Mount Zion.

הָרִים וּלְבֶהֱמַת הָאָרֶץ וְקָץ עָלָיו הָעַיִט וְכָל־בֶּהֱמַת הָאָרֶץ
the beast and the on shall and the to and ,mountains
earth of every ,birds them summer ;earth of beasts

7 עָלָיו תֶּחֱרָף׃ בָּעֵת הַהִיא יוּבַל־שַׁי לַיהוָה צְבָאוֹת
hosts Jehovah to a be shall that In shall on
of present brought time .winter them

עַם מְמֻשָּׁךְ וּמוֹרָט וּמֵעַם נוֹרָא מִן־הוּא וָהָלְאָה גּוֹי ׀ קַו־
migh- a and it from ,terrible from and and tall a (from)
nation ;onward people a ,smooth people

קָו וּמְבוּסָה אֲשֶׁר בָּזְאוּ נְהָרִים אַרְצוֹ אֶל־מְקוֹם שֵׁם־יְהוָה
Jehovah the the to its rivers have of and ty
of of name of place ,land divided whom ,trampling

צְבָאוֹת הַר־צִיּוֹן׃
.Zion Mount —hosts

CAP. XIX יט

CHAPTER 19

[1] The burden against Egypt: Behold, Jehovah rides on a flying cloud and is coming into Egypt. And the idols of Egypt shall quake from before Him; and the heart of Egypt shall melt in its midst. [2] And I will set the Egyptians against the Egyptians; and each man shall fight against his brother, and every one against his neighbor; city against city, kingdom against kingdom. [3] And the spirit of Egypt shall fail in its midst, and I will swallow her wisdom. And they shall seek to idols, and to enchanters, and to mediums, and fortune-tellers. [4] And I will deliver the Egyptians into the hand of cruel lords; and a fierce king shall rule them, says the Lord, Jehovah of hosts. [5] And the waters shall fail from the sea, and the river shall fail and dry up. [6] And rivers will be fouled; and the brooks of Egypt will languish and dry up; the reed and the rush shall decay. [7] Bare places at the Nile, by the mouth of the Nile, and everything sown (by) the Nile, shall dry up, driven away, and be no more. [8] The fishermen shall mourn; and all who cast a hook into the Nile shall wail; and those who spread nets on

1 מַשָּׂא מִצְרָיִם הִנֵּה יְהוָה רֹכֵב עַל־עָב קַל וּבָא מִצְרַיִם
.Egypt and ,light a on rides Jehovah ,Behold :Egypt The
enters cloud of burden

וְנָעוּ אֱלִילֵי מִצְרַיִם מִפָּנָיו וּלְבַב מִצְרַיִם יִמַּס בְּקִרְבּוֹ׃
its in shall Egypt the and be- from Egypt the shall And
.midst melt of heart ;Him fore of idols tremble

2 וְסִכְסַכְתִּי מִצְרַיִם בְּמִצְרַיִם וְנִלְחֲמוּ אִישׁ בְּאָחִיו וְאִישׁ
and against each they and against Egypt will I And
each ,brother his man ,fight will ,Egypt up stir

3 בְּרֵעֵהוּ עִיר בְּעִיר מַמְלָכָה בְּמַמְלָכָה׃ וְנָבְקָה רוּחַ־
the will And against kingdom against city his against
of spirit empty be .kingdom ,city ;neighbor

מִצְרַיִם בְּקִרְבּוֹ וַעֲצָתוֹ אֲבַלֵּעַ וְדָרְשׁוּ אֶל־הָאֱלִילִים וְאֶל־
and ,idols the to they And will I its and its in Egypt
to seek shall .swallow counsel ,midst

4 הָאִטִּים וְאֶל־הָאֹבוֹת וְאֶל־הַיִּדְּעֹנִים׃ וְסִכַּרְתִּי אֶת־מִצְרַיִם
Egypt will I And future the and the and the
up shut .tellers to ,mediums to ,enchanters

בְּיַד אֲדֹנִים קָשֶׁה וּמֶלֶךְ עַז יִמְשָׁל־בָּם נְאֻם הָאָדוֹן יְהוָה
Jehovah the states ,them shall fierce a and ;cruel lords the into
of Lord rule king of hand

5
6 צְבָאוֹת׃ וְנִשְּׁתוּ־מַיִם מֵהַיָּם וְנָהָר יֶחֱרַב וְיָבֵשׁ׃ וְהֶאֶזְנִיחוּ
be will And and shall the and from the shall And .hosts
fouled .up dry fail river ,sea the waters up dry

7 נְהָרוֹת דָּלְלוּ וְחָרְבוּ יְאֹרֵי מָצוֹר קָנֶה וָסוּף קָמֵלוּ׃ עָרוֹת
Bare shall and the ;Egypt the and will ;rivers
places .decay rush reed of brooks dry languish

עַל־יְאוֹר עַל־פִּי יְאוֹר וְכֹל מִזְרַע יְאוֹר יִיבַשׁ נִדַּף וְאֵינֶנּוּ׃
be and driven shall the sown every and the mouth by the at
.more no ,away ,up dry Nile (by) thing ,Nile's Nile

8 וְאָנוּ הַדַּיָּגִים וְאָבְלוּ כָּל־מַשְׁלִיכֵי בַיְאוֹר חַכָּה וּפֹרְשֵׂי
those and ;hook a the into who all shall and the shall And
spread who Nile cast wail ;fishermen mourn

the surface of the waters shall droop. [9] And the workers in fine flax, and the weavers of white cloth are ashamed. [10] And her supports shall be broken, and all who make wages sad of soul. [11] Surely the princes of Zoan (are) fools; the advice of the wise ones of Pharaoh has become foolish. How can you say to Pharaoh, I am the son of the wise, the son of ancient kings? [12] Where (are) your wise ones now? Yea, let them tell you; even they know what Jehovah of hosts has planned against Egypt. [13] The princes of Zoan have become fools; the princes of Noph are deceived; they also have caused Egypt to err, the chief of her tribes. [14] Jehovah has mixed a perverse spirit in her midst; and they led astray Egypt in all his work—as a drunkard strays in his vomit. [15] And Egypt shall have no work that the head or tail, the branch or rush may do. [16] In that day Egypt shall be like women; for it shall tremble and fear from before the shaking of the hand of Jehovah of hosts, which He shakes over it. [17] And the land of Judah shall be a terror to Egypt; everyone who mentions it shall fear toward it, from before the purpose of Jehovah of hosts which He has purposed against her. [18] In that day five cities in the land of Egypt shall speak the language of Canaan and swear to Jehovah of hosts. One shall be called, The city of ruin. [19] Then an altar to Jehovah shall be in the midst of the land of Egypt, and a pillar to Jehovah at its

9 מִכְמֹרֶת עַל־פְּנֵי־מַיִם אֻמְלָלוּ׃ וּבֹשׁוּ עֹבְדֵי פִשְׁתִּים
flax the are and shall waters the on nets
in workers ashamed .droop of surface

10 שְׂרִיקוֹת וְאֹרְגִים חוֹרָי׃ וְהָיוּ שָׁתֹתֶיהָ מְדֻכָּאִים כָּל־עֹשֵׂי
who and ,crushed her shall And white and ,combed
make all supports be .cloth of weavers

11 שֶׂכֶר אַגְמֵי־נָפֶשׁ׃ אַךְ־אֱוִלִים שָׂרֵי צֹעַן חַכְמֵי יֹעֲצֵי פַרְעֹה
;Pharaoh's coun- the ,Zoan the (are) Surely .soul sad wages
selors of wise of chiefs fools of

עֵצָה נִבְעָרָה אֵיךְ תֹּאמְרוּ אֶל־פַּרְעֹה בֶּן־חֲכָמִים אֲנִי בֶּן
the I wise the ,Pharaoh to you can How become has (their)
of son ,(am) ones of son say .brutish advice

12 מַלְכֵי־קֶדֶם׃ אַיָּם אֵפוֹא חֲכָמֶיךָ וְיַגִּידוּ נָא לָךְ וְיֵדְעוּ מַה
what they that ;you now let And wise your then Where ?old kings
know may tell them ?ones (are) of

13 יָּעַץ יְהוָה צְבָאוֹת עַל־מִצְרָיִם׃ נוֹאֲלוּ שָׂרֵי צֹעַן נִשְּׁאוּ שָׂרֵי
the are ;Zoan The are .Egypt against hosts Jehovah has
of chiefs deceived of chiefs fools of planned

14 נֹף הִתְעוּ אֶת־מִצְרַיִם פִּנַּת שְׁבָטֶיהָ׃ יְהוָה מָסַךְ בְּקִרְבָּהּ
her in has Jehovah her the ,Egypt have they ;Noph
midst mixed tribes of cornerstone astray led

רוּחַ עִוְעִים וְהִתְעוּ אֶת־מִצְרַיִם בְּכָל־מַעֲשֵׂהוּ כְּהִתָּעוֹת
strays as his all in Egypt they and perverse a
—work astray led spirit

15 שִׁכּוֹר בְּקִיאוֹ׃ וְלֹא־יִהְיֶה לְמִצְרַיִם מַעֲשֶׂה אֲשֶׁר יַעֲשֶׂה
may which ,work Egypt to shall And his in a
do be not .vomit drunkard

16 רֹאשׁ וְזָנָב כִּפָּה וְאַגְמוֹן׃ בַּיּוֹם הַהוּא יִהְיֶה מִצְרַיִם
Egypt shall that day In .rush or branch or head
be ,tail

כַּנָּשִׁים וְחָרַד ׀ וּפָחַד מִפְּנֵי תְּנוּפַת יַד־יְהוָה צְבָאוֹת אֲשֶׁר
which ,hosts Jehovah the the be- from and will it and like
of of hand of shaking fore dread tremble ;women

17 הוּא מֵנִיף עָלָיו׃ וְהָיְתָה אַדְמַת יְהוּדָה לְמִצְרַיִם לְחָגָּא
;terror a Egypt to Judah the shall And .it over shakes He
of land become

כֹּל אֲשֶׁר יַזְכִּיר אֹתָהּ אֵלָיו יִפְחָד מִפְּנֵי עֲצַת יְהוָה
Jehovah the from shall it to it mentions who every
of of purpose before ,dread one

18 צְבָאוֹת אֲשֶׁר־הוּא יוֹעֵץ עָלָיו׃ בַּיּוֹם הַהוּא יִהְיוּ
shall that day In against purposes He which ,hosts
be .it

חָמֵשׁ עָרִים בְּאֶרֶץ מִצְרַיִם מְדַבְּרוֹת שְׂפַת כְּנַעַן וְנִשְׁבָּעוֹת
and Canaan the speaking Egypt the in cities five
swearing of lip of land

19 לַיהוָה צְבָאוֹת עִיר הַהֶרֶס יֵאָמֵר לְאֶחָת׃ בַּיּוֹם
day In .one to be shall it ,ruin city ;hosts to
called of of Jehovah

הַהוּא יִהְיֶה מִזְבֵּחַ לַיהוָה בְּתוֹךְ אֶרֶץ מִצְרַיִם וּמַצֵּבָה אֵצֶל־
beside a and ,Egypt the the in to an shall that
pillar of land of midst Jehovah altar be

20 גְּבוּלָהּ לַיהוָה׃ וְהָיָה לְאוֹת וּלְעֵד לַיהוָה צְבָאוֹת בְּאֶרֶץ

the in hosts to a for and a for it And to its
of land of Jehovah witness ,sign be shall .Jehovah border

מִצְרָיִם כִּי־יִצְעֲקוּ אֶל־יְהוָה מִפְּנֵי לֹחֲצִים וְיִשְׁלַח לָהֶם

to He and ,oppressors because Jeho- to will they for ;Egypt
them send will of vah out cry

21 מוֹשִׁיעַ וָרָב וְהִצִּילָם׃ וְנוֹדַע יְהוָה לְמִצְרַיִם וְיָדְעוּ מִצְרַיִם

Egypt and ,Egypt to Jehovah shall And shall and a and a
know shall known be .them save ,ruler ,savior

אֶת־יְהוָה בַּיּוֹם הַהוּא וְעָבְדוּ זֶבַח וּמִנְחָה וְנָדְרוּ־נֵדֶר לַיהוָה

to a and food and sacrifice and ;that day in Jehovah
Jehovah vow vow ;offering offer shall

22 וְשִׁלֵּמוּ׃ וְנָגַף יְהוָה אֶת־מִצְרַיִם נָגֹף וְרָפוֹא וְשָׁבוּ עַד־יְהוָה

,Jehovah to they and and striking ,Egypt Jehovah shall And re- and
return shall ;healing strike .(it) pay

23 וְנֶעְתַּר לָהֶם וּרְפָאָם׃ בַּיּוֹם הַהוּא תִּהְיֶה מְסִלָּה

a shall that day In shall and them He and
highway be .them heal hear shall

מִמִּצְרַיִם אַשּׁוּרָה וּבָא אַשּׁוּר בְּמִצְרַיִם וּמִצְרַיִם בְּאַשּׁוּר

into and ;Egypt into Assyria shall and to of out
;Assyria Egypt come ;Assyria Egypt

24 וְעָבְדוּ מִצְרַיִם אֶת־אַשּׁוּר׃ בַּיּוֹם הַהוּא יִהְיֶה יִשְׂרָאֵל

Israel be shall that day In .Assyria Egypt shall and
serve

25 שְׁלִישִׁיָּה לְמִצְרַיִם וּלְאַשּׁוּר בְּרָכָה בְּקֶרֶב הָאָרֶץ׃ אֲשֶׁר

whom the the in a with and with third the
,earth of midst blessing ,Assyria Egypt

בֵּרְכוֹ יְהוָה צְבָאוֹת לֵאמֹר בָּרוּךְ עַמִּי מִצְרַיִם וּמַעֲשֵׂה יָדַי

My the and ,Egypt My Blessed ,saying ,hosts Jehovah He
hands of work people (be) of blesses

אַשּׁוּר וְנַחֲלָתִי יִשְׂרָאֵל׃

.Israel My and ,Assyria
inheritance

border. [20] And it shall be for a sign and a witness to Jehovah of hosts in the land of Egypt. For they shall cry to Jehovah because of the oppressors, and He shall send them a deliverer, and a great one; and he shall deliver them.

[21] And Jehovah shall be known to Egypt, and the Egyptians shall know Jehovah in that day and shall offer sacrifice and offering, and vow a vow to Jehovah and repay it. [22] And Jehovah shall strike Egypt. He shall strike and heal. Then they shall return to Jehovah, and He shall hear them and shall heal them. [23] In that day there shall be a highway out of Egypt to Assyria; and the Assyrian shall come into Egypt; and the Egyptian into Assyria; and the Egyptians shall serve the Assyrians. [24] In that day Israel shall be the third with Egypt and with Assyria, a blessing in the midst of the earth; [25] whom Jehovah of hosts shall bless, saying, Blessed (be) My people Egypt, and Assyria, the work of My hands, and Israel My inheritance.

CAP. XX כ

CHAPTER 20

1 בִּשְׁנַת בֹּא תַרְתָּן אַשְׁדּוֹדָה בִּשְׁלֹחַ אֹתוֹ סַרְגוֹן מֶלֶךְ אַשּׁוּר

,Assyria the Sargon him when to Tartan came the In
of king sent ,Ashdod year

2 וַיִּלָּחֶם בְּאַשְׁדּוֹד וַיִּלְכְּדָהּ׃ בָּעֵת הַהִיא דִּבֶּר יְהוָה בְּיַד

the by Jehovah spoke that time at took and against and
of hand ;it ,Ashdod fought

יְשַׁעְיָהוּ בֶן־אָמוֹץ לֵאמֹר לֵךְ וּפִתַּחְתָּ הַשַּׂק מֵעַל מָתְנֶיךָ

your from the and ,Go ,saying ,Amoz the Isaiah
,loins sackcloth loose of son

וְנַעַלְךָ תַחֲלֹץ מֵעַל רַגְלֶךָ וַיַּעַשׂ כֵּן הָלֹךְ עָרוֹם וְיָחֵף׃

and naked walking ,so and your from take your and
.barefoot did he ;foot off shoe

3 וַיֹּאמֶר יְהוָה כַּאֲשֶׁר הָלַךְ עַבְדִּי יְשַׁעְיָהוּ עָרוֹם וְיָחֵף שָׁלֹשׁ

three and naked Isaiah My has Just ,Jehovah And
,barefoot servant walked as said

CHAPTER 20

[1] In the year Tartan came to Ashdod, when Sargon the king of Assyria sent him, and fought against Ashdod and took it; [2] at that time Jehovah spoke by Isaiah the son of Amoz, saying, Go and take the sackcloth from your loins, and take your shoe off your foot. And he did so, walking naked and barefoot. [3] And Jehovah said, Just as My servant Isaiah has walked naked and barefoot

three years — a sign and wonder on Egypt and on Ethiopia — [4] so shall the king of Assyria lead away the Egyptian prisoners, and the Ethiopian captives, young and old — naked and barefoot, and with buttocks uncovered, (to) the shame of Egypt. [5] And they shall be afraid and ashamed of their hope Ethiopia, and of their glory Egypt. [6] And he who lives in this coast shall say in that day, Behold, thus (has become) of our hope (to) which we fled for help there; to be delivered from before the king of Assyria; and, How shall we escape?

4 שָׁנִים אוֹת וּמוֹפֵת עַל־מִצְרַיִם וְעַל־כּוּשׁ׃ כֵּן יִנְהַג מֶלֶךְ־
king the shall so —Ethiopia and Egypt on a and a —years
of away lead on wonder sign

אַשּׁוּר אֶת־שְׁבִי מִצְרַיִם וְאֶת־גָּלוּת כּוּשׁ נְעָרִים וּזְקֵנִים עָרוֹם
naked and young ,Ethiopia exiles and Egypt the Assyria
—old of of captives

5 וְיָחֵף וַחֲשׂוּפַי שֵׁת עֶרְוַת מִצְרָיִם׃ וְחַתּוּ וָבֹשׁוּ מִכּוּשׁ מַבָּטָם
their of be and they And .Egypt the (to) ,but- un- and and
,hope Ethiopia ashamed fear shall of shame ,tocks covered barefoot

6 וּמִן־מִצְרַיִם תִּפְאַרְתָּם׃ וְאָמַר יֹשֵׁב הָאִי הַזֶּה בַּיּוֹם הַהוּא
,that day in this coast that he And their Egypt and
in dwells say shall .glory of

הִנֵּה־כֹה מַבָּטֵנוּ אֲשֶׁר־נַסְנוּ שָׁם לְעֶזְרָה לְהִנָּצֵל מִפְּנֵי מֶלֶךְ
the be- from be to for there we (to) our of thus ,Behold
of king fore delivered ,help fled which hope (become has)

אַשּׁוּר וְאֵיךְ נִמָּלֵט אֲנָחְנוּ׃
?we shall and ;Assyria
escape how

CAP. XXI כא

CHAPTER 21

CHAPTER 21

[1] The burden of the desert of the sea: As whirlwinds in the south pass, it shall come from the desert, from a terrible land. [2] A harsh vision is revealed to me: the deceiver deals deceitfully, and the robber spoils. Go up, O Elam! Besiege, O Media! I have caused all her sighing to cease. [3] Because of this my loins are filled (with) pain; pangs have taken hold on me like the pangs of a woman who travails. From hearing, I am bowed; I am troubled from seeing. [4] My heart wanders; terror overwhelms me; He has turned the twilight of my pleasure into trembling. [5] Prepare the table; watch in the watchtower; eat, drink; arise, princes, (and) anoint the shield. [6] For so the Lord has said to me: Go, set a watchman; he will declare what he sees. [7] And he sees a chariot, a couple of horsemen; a chariot of an ass; a chariot of a camel; then he peers closely, and very closely. [8] And he cried, A lion! My lord, I stand on my

1 מַשָּׂא מִדְבַּר־יָם כְּסוּפוֹת בַּנֶּגֶב לַחֲלֹף מִמִּדְבָּר בָּא מֵאֶרֶץ
a from it the from ,pass the in as the desert the The
land ,comes desert Negev tempests :sea of of burden

2 נוֹרָאָה׃ חָזוּת קָשָׁה הֻגַּד־לִי הַבּוֹגֵד ׀ בּוֹגֵד וְהַשּׁוֹדֵד ׀ שׁוֹדֵד
.spoils the and de- the to is harsh A .terrible
spoiler ,ceives deceiver :me revealed vision

3 עֲלִי עֵילָם צוּרִי מָדַי כָּל־אַנְחָתָה הִשְׁבַּתִּי׃ עַל־כֵּן מָלְאוּ
are There- caused I her All O ,Besiege O Go
filled fore .cease to sighing !Media !Elam ,up

מָתְנַי חַלְחָלָה צִירִים אֲחָזוּנִי כְּצִירֵי יוֹלֵדָה נַעֲוֵיתִי מִשְּׁמֹעַ
from am I travailing a like seized pangs (with) my
;hearing bowed .woman of pangs ,me ;pain loins

4 נִבְהַלְתִּי מֵרְאוֹת׃ תָּעָה לְבָבִי פַּלָּצוּת בִּעֲתָתְנִי אֵת נֶשֶׁף
twi- the overwhelms terror My wanders from am I
of light ;me ;heart .seeing ,troubled

5 חִשְׁקִי שָׂם לִי לַחֲרָדָה׃ עָרֹךְ הַשֻּׁלְחָן צָפֹה הַצָּפִית אָכוֹל
,eat the spread the Prepare into to has He my
;rugs ;table .trembling me turned pleasure

6 שָׁתֹה קוּמוּ הַשָּׂרִים מִשְׁחוּ מָגֵן׃ כִּי כֹה אָמַר אֵלַי
to has so For the (and) ,chiefs ,arise ;drink
me said .shield anoint

7 אֲדֹנָי לֵךְ הַעֲמֵד הַמְצַפֶּה אֲשֶׁר יִרְאֶה יַגִּיד׃ וְרָאָה רֶכֶב
a he And him let he what the station ,Go the
,chariot sees .declare sees ;watchman ,Lord

צֶמֶד פָּרָשִׁים רֶכֶב חֲמוֹר רֶכֶב גָּמָל וְהִקְשִׁיב קֶשֶׁב רַב־
very atten him let a a ,ass an a ,horsemen pair a
tively bow ;camel of chariot of chariot of

8 קָשֶׁב׃ וַיִּקְרָא אַרְיֵה עַל־מִצְפֶּה ׀ אֲדֹנָי אָנֹכִי עֹמֵד תָּמִיד
always stand I my the On a (as) he And atten-
,Lord ,watchtower ,lion ,cried .tively

watchtower continually; and I am stationed at my post all the nights. [9] And, behold, here comes a chariot of a man, a pair of horses. And he answered, and said, Babylon has fallen, has fallen! And He has smashed to the earth all the graven images of her gods. [10] O my threshing, and the grain of my floor! That which I have heard of Jehovah of hosts, the God of Israel, I have told you. [11] The burden against Dumah: (He) calls to me out of Seir, Watchman, what of the night? Watchman, what of the night? [12] The watchman says, The morning comes, and the night, too; if you earnestly inquire, inquire. Come! Return!

[13] The burden of Arabia: You shall stay in the forest of Arabia, O travelers of Dedanites. [14] The people of the land of Tema brought water to him who was thirsty; they went to meet the fugitive with his bread. [15] For they fled from the swords, from the drawn sword, and from the bent bow, and from the hardship of war. [16] For the Lord has said this to me, Within a year, according to the years of a hireling, all the glory of Kedar shall fail; [17] and the rest of the number of archers, those counted mighty of the sons of Kedar, shall be few; for Jehovah God of Israel has spoken.

9 יוֹמָם וְעַל־מִשְׁמַרְתִּי אָנֹכִי נִצָּב כָּל־הַלֵּילוֹת׃ וְהִנֵּה־זֶה בָא
comes ,this ,And behold the night all am I stationed my post and at by ;day

רֶכֶב אִישׁ צֶמֶד פָּרָשִׁים וַיַּעַן וַיֹּאמֶר נָפְלָה נָפְלָה בָּבֶל
!Babylon has fallen Has ,fallen ,said and And answered .horses pair a of a ,man of a chariot

10 וְכָל־פְּסִילֵי אֱלֹהֶיהָ שִׁבַּר לָאָרֶץ׃ מְדֻשָׁתִי וּבֶן־גָּרְנִי אֲשֶׁר
That which my !floor the and of son my O ,threshed the to .earth has he shattered gods her cut the of images And all

שָׁמַעְתִּי מֵאֵת יְהוָה צְבָאוֹת אֱלֹהֵי יִשְׂרָאֵל הִגַּדְתִּי לָכֶם׃
.you to have I told ,Israel the of God ,hosts Jehovah of from have I heard

11 מַשָּׂא דּוּמָה אֵלַי קֹרֵא מִשֵּׂעִיר שֹׁמֵר מַה־מִּלַּיְלָה שֹׁמֵר
Watch- ,man the of ?night what Watch- ,man from ,Seir (He) calls To me ;Dumah The of burden

12 מַה־מִּלֵּיל׃ אָמַר שֹׁמֵר אָתָא בֹקֶר וְגַם־לַיְלָה אִם־תִּבְעָיוּן
would you ,inquire if ;night and also ,Morning comes The ,watchman says the of ?night what

13 בְּעָיוּ שֻׁבוּ אֵתָיוּ׃ מַשָּׂא בַּעְרָב בַּיַּעַר בַּעְרַב תָּלִינוּ
shall you ,stay Arabia the In of forest .Arabia The of burden !Come !Return in- .quire

14 אֹרְחוֹת דְּדָנִים׃ לִקְרַאת צָמֵא הֵתָיוּ מַיִם יֹשְׁבֵי אֶרֶץ תֵּימָא
;Tema the of land the of people water bring the thirsty meet To .Dedanites caravans of

15 בְּלַחְמוֹ קִדְּמוּ נֹדֵד׃ כִּי־מִפְּנֵי חֲרָבוֹת נָדָדוּ מִפְּנֵי ׀ חֶרֶב
the sword from before they ,fled swords from before For the .fugitive meet his with bread

נְטוּשָׁה וּמִפְּנֵי קֶשֶׁת דְּרוּכָה וּמִפְּנֵי כֹּבֶד מִלְחָמָה׃
.battle the of press from and before ,bent the bow from and before ;drawn

16 כִּי־כֹה אָמַר אֲדֹנָי אֵלַי בְּעוֹד שָׁנָה כִּשְׁנֵי שָׂכִיר וְכָלָה כָּל־
all be shall ended a ,hireling the as of years ,year a Within to ,me the Lord has said thus For

17 כְּבוֹד קֵדָר׃ וּשְׁאָר מִסְפַּר־קֶשֶׁת גִּבּוֹרֵי בְנֵי־קֵדָר יִמְעָטוּ
be shall ;few ,Kedar the of sons warriors of the ,archers the of number the and of rest ;Kedar the of glory

כִּי יְהוָה אֱלֹהֵי־יִשְׂרָאֵל דִּבֵּר׃
has .spoken Israel God of Jehovah for

CAP. XXII כב

CHAPTER 22

CHAPTER 22

[1] The burden of the valley of vision: What (ails) you now that you have all gone up to the housetops? [2] Crashings fill the noisy city, the joyous city; your slain ones are not slain by the sword, nor dead in battle. [3] All your rulers fled together from

1 מַשָּׂא גֵּיא חִזָּיוֹן מַה־לָּךְ אֵפוֹא כִּי־עָלִית כֻּלָּךְ לַגַּגּוֹת׃
the to ?housetops all you have gone up that ,now to What you (is) :vision valley the of The of burden

2 תְּשֻׁאוֹת ׀ מְלֵאָה עִיר הוֹמִיָּה קִרְיָה עַלִּיזָה חֲלָלַיִךְ לֹא
not your slain ones ,joyous the city ,noisy fill Crashings the city

3 חַלְלֵי־חֶרֶב וְלֹא מֵתֵי מִלְחָמָה׃ כָּל־קְצִינַיִךְ נָדְדוּ־יָחַד
;together fled your rulers All .battle dead in and not the ,sword slain are by

the bow; all that are found in you were bound, they have been kept prisoner together; they have fled from afar. [4] Therefore I said, Look away from me; I will weep bitterly; do not labor to comfort me over the ruin of the daughters of my people. [5] For it (is) a day of trouble, and of trampling down, and of perplexity by the Lord Jehovah of hosts in the valley of vision; breaking down of a wall, and of crying to the mountains. [6] And Elam carried the quiver with a chariot of a man (and) horsemen; and Kir uncovered the shield. [7] And it was, your choicest valleys were full of chariots, and the horsemen surely set in order at the gate. [8] And he removed Judah's covering; and you looked in that day to the armor of the house of the forest. [9] You have seen also the breaks in the city of David, that they are many; and you gathered the waters of the lower pool. [10] And you have counted Jerusalem's houses; and you have broken down the houses to fortify the wall. [11] And you dug a ditch between the walls for the water of the old pool. But you have not looked to its Maker, nor seen Him who formed it long ago. [12] And in that day the Lord Jehovah of hosts called to weeping and mourning; and to baldness, and to girding with sackcloth. [13] Then, lo, joy and gladness, slaying oxen and killing sheep; eating flesh and drinking wine, (saying), Let us eat and drink, for tomorrow we die! [14] And Jehovah of hosts revealed in my ears, Surely this iniquity shall not be atoned for until you die, says the Lord Jehovah of hosts.

[15] Thus says the Lord Jehovah of hosts, Go! Go to

מִקֶּשֶׁת אֻסָּרוּ כָּל־נִמְצָאַיִךְ אֻסְּרוּ יַחְדָּו מֵרָחוֹק בָּרָחוּ׃
have they from ;together were found all were without
.fled afar bound you in !found bow the

4 עַל־כֵּן אָמַרְתִּי שְׁעוּ מִנִּי אֲמָרֵר בַּבֶּכִי אַל־תָּאִיצוּ לְנַחֲמֵנִי
to hurry do not in will I away Look ,said I Therefore
me comfort ;weeping bitter be ;me from

5 עַל־שֹׁד בַּת־עַמִּי׃ כִּי יוֹם מְהוּמָה וּמְבוּסָה וּמְבוּכָה
and and ,tumult day a For my daugh- the the over
confusion ,trampling of (is it) .people of ter of ruin

לַאדֹנָי יֱהוִה צְבָאוֹת בְּגֵי חִזָּיוֹן מְקַרְקַר קִר וְשׁוֹעַ אֶל־
to and a breaking ,vision the in hosts Jehovah the of
crying ,wall down of valley of Lord

6 הָהָר׃ וְעֵילָם נָשָׂא אַשְׁפָּה בְּרֶכֶב אָדָם פָּרָשִׁים וְקִיר
and (and) a a with the carried And the
Kir ;horsemen man of chariot quiver Elam .mountain

7 עֵרָה מָגֵן׃ וַיְהִי מִבְחַר־עֲמָקַיִךְ מָלְאוּ רָכֶב וְהַפָּרָשִׁים
the and ;chariots were your choicest And the bared
horsemen of full valleys ,was it .shield

8 שֹׁת שָׁתוּ הַשָּׁעְרָה׃ וַיְגַל אֵת מָסַךְ יְהוּדָה וַתַּבֵּט בַּיּוֹם
day in you and ;Judah the he And the at were . set-
looked of covering removed .gate set ting

9 הַהוּא אֶל־נֶשֶׁק בֵּית הַיָּעַר׃ וְאֵת בְּקִיעֵי עִיר־דָּוִד רְאִיתֶם
have you David the the Also the the the to that
,seen of city in breaks .forest of house of armor

10 כִּי־רָבּוּ וַתְּקַבְּצוּ אֶת־מֵי הַבְּרֵכָה הַתַּחְתּוֹנָה׃ וְאֶת־בָּתֵּי
houses And .lower pool the the you and they that
of of waters gathered ;many are

11 יְרוּשָׁלַם סְפַרְתֶּם וַתִּתְצוּ הַבָּתִּים לְבַצֵּר הַחוֹמָה׃ וּמִקְוָה
a And the to the you and you Jerusalem
reservoir .wall fortify houses down broke ;counted

עֲשִׂיתֶם בֵּין הַחֹמֹתַיִם לְמֵי הַבְּרֵכָה הַיְשָׁנָה וְלֹא הִבַּטְתֶּם
have you But .old pool the the for the between you
looked not of water walls made

12 אֶל־עֹשֶׂיהָ וְיֹצְרָהּ מֵרָחוֹק לֹא רְאִיתֶם׃ וַיִּקְרָא אֲדֹנָי יֱהוִה
Jehovah the And .saw you not long from its and its to
of Lord called ago former ;maker

צְבָאוֹת בַּיּוֹם הַהוּא לִבְכִי וּלְמִסְפֵּד וּלְקָרְחָה וְלַחֲגֹר שָׂק׃
sack- to and to and to and to that day in hosts
.cloth with girding ,baldness ;mourning weeping

13 וְהִנֵּה ׀ שָׂשׂוֹן וְשִׂמְחָה הָרֹג ׀ בָּקָר וְשָׁחֹט צֹאן אָכֹל בָּשָׂר
flesh eating ;sheep and oxen slaying and joy ,But
slaughtering ,gladness ,behold

14 וְשָׁתוֹת יָיִן אָכוֹל וְשָׁתוֹ כִּי מָחָר נָמוּת׃ וְנִגְלָה בְאָזְנָי יְהוָה
Jehovah my in And we tomorrow for and ,(saying) ,wine and
of ears revealed !die ,drink Eat drinking

צְבָאוֹת אִם־יְכֻפַּר הֶעָוֹן הַזֶּה לָכֶם עַד־תְּמֻתוּן אָמַר אֲדֹנָי
the says you until ,you to this iniquity be shall Surely ,hosts
Lord ,die for atoned not

15 יֱהוִה צְבָאוֹת׃ כֹּה אָמַר אֲדֹנָי יֱהוִה צְבָאוֹת לֶךְ־בֹּא
come ,Go ,hosts Jehovah the says Thus .hosts Jehovah
of Lord of

this treasurer, to Shebna who (is) over the house, [16] What (is) to you here? And who (is) to you here, that you have carved a tomb for yourself here, (as one) having cut out his tomb on high, having carved out a home for himself in a rock? [17] Behold, Jehovah hurls you (with) a hurling, O man, and grasps you with a grasping. [18] Whirling He will surely whirl you like a ball into a broad land. You shall die there, and there your glorious chariots (shall be) the disgrace of the house of your lord. [19] And I will drive you from your position; and he will pull you from your office. [20] And in that day it shall come to pass, I will call My servant Eliakim the son of Hilkiah. [21] And I will clothe him with your robe, and will fasten on him your girdle; and I will deliver your authority into his hand. And he shall be a father to the inhabitants of Jerusalem and to the house of Judah. [22] And the key of the house of David I will lay on his shoulder; so he shall open, and no one shall shut; and he shall shut, and no one shall open. [23] And I will drive Him (as) a nail in a sure place; and he shall be for a glorious throne to his father's house. [24] And they shall hang on him all the glory of his father's house, the children and the grandchildren, all smaller vessels, from vessels of cups to all the vessels of jars.

[25] In that day, says Jehovah of hosts, the nail that is driven in the sure place shall be removed, and be cut down and fall. And the burden that (was) on it shall be cut off; Jehovah has spoken.

16 אֶל־הַסֹּכֵן הַזֶּה עַל־שֶׁבְנָא אֲשֶׁר עַל־הַבָּיִת׃ מַה־לְּךָ פֹה
?here to What the over who ,Shebna to ,this steward to
you (is) ,house (is)

וּמִי־לְךָ פֹה כִּי־חָצַבְתָּ לְּךָ פֹּה קָבֶר חֹצְבִי מָרוֹם קִבְרוֹ
his on hewing a here for have you that ,here to And
,tomb high ,tomb yourself carved you (is) who

17 חֹקְקִי בַסֶּלַע מִשְׁכָּן לוֹ׃ הִנֵּה יְהוָה מְטַלְטֶלְךָ טַלְטֵלָה
a (with) you hurls Jehovah ,Behold for a the in carving
,hurling ?himself dwelling rock

18 גָּבֶר וְעֹטְךָ עָטֹה׃ צָנוֹף יִצְנָפְךָ צְנֵפָה כַּדּוּר אֶל־אֶרֶץ
a into a like a (with) will He ,Surely a (with) and O
land ball whirling you whirl .grasping you grasps ,man

רַחֲבַת יָדָיִם שָׁמָּה תָמוּת וְשָׁמָּה מַרְכְּבוֹת כְּבוֹדֶךָ קְלוֹן
the your chariots the and you There .hands wide
of shamed ,glory of (are) there ,die shall of

19 בֵּית אֲדֹנֶיךָ׃ וַהֲדַפְתִּיךָ מִמַּצָּבֶךָ וּמִמַּעֲמָדְךָ יֶהֶרְסֶךָ׃
will he from and your from will I And your the
.you pull station your ;position you drive .lord of house

20 וְהָיָה בַּיּוֹם הַהוּא וְקָרָאתִי לְעַבְדִּי לְאֶלְיָקִים בֶּן־חִלְקִיָּהוּ׃
.Hilkiah the Eliakim to My to I that ,that day in it and
of son ,servant call will be shall

21 וְהִלְבַּשְׁתִּיו כֻּתָּנְתֶּךָ וְאַבְנֵטְךָ אֲחַזְּקֶנּוּ וּמֶמְשַׁלְתְּךָ
your and fasten will your and your (with) will I And
authority ;him on sash robe him clothe

אֶתֵּן בְּיָדוֹ וְהָיָה לְאָב לְיוֹשֵׁב יְרוּשָׁלִַם וּלְבֵית יְהוּדָה׃
.Judah to and Jerusalem the to a he And his into will I
of house the of dwellers father be shall .hand give

22 וְנָתַתִּי מַפְתֵּחַ בֵּית־דָּוִד עַל־שִׁכְמוֹ וּפָתַח וְאֵין סֹגֵר וְסָגַר
he and ;shuts and he that his on David the key the I And
,shuts none opens ;shoulder of house of give will

23 וְאֵין פֹּתֵחַ׃ וּתְקַעְתִּיו יָתֵד בְּמָקוֹם נֶאֱמָן וְהָיָה לְכִסֵּא כָבוֹד
glorious a for he and ;sure a in a (as) will I And .opens and
throne be shall place nail him drive none

24 לְבֵית אָבִיו׃ וְתָלוּ עָלָיו כֹּל כְּבוֹד בֵּית־אָבִיו הַצֶּאֱצָאִים
the his house the all on they And his to
offspring ,father's of glory him hang shall .father's house

וְהַצְּפִעוֹת כֹּל כְּלֵי הַקָּטָן מִכְּלֵי הָאַגָּנוֹת וְעַד כָּל־כְּלֵי
vessels all even cups from ,smallness vessels all the and
of to of vessels of ,offshoots

25 הַנְּבָלִים׃ בַּיּוֹם הַהוּא נְאֻם יְהוָה צְבָאוֹת תָּמוּשׁ הַיָּתֵד
the be shall ,hosts Jehovah states ,that day In .jars
nail removed of

הַתְּקוּעָה בְּמָקוֹם נֶאֱמָן וְנִגְדְּעָה וְנָפְלָה וְנִכְרַת הַמַּשָּׂא אֲשֶׁר־
that the shall And and be and ,sure the in is that
burden off cut be .fall ,down cut place driven

עָלֶיהָ כִּי יְהוָה דִּבֵּר׃
has Jehovah for on (was)
.spoken ,it

CAP. XXIII כג

CHAPTER 23

CHAPTER 23

[1] The burden of Tyre: Howl, ships of Tarshish! For it is ruined, without a house, without an entrance. It is revealed to them from the land of Chittim. [2] Be still, O inhabitants of the coast, O merchant of Sidon sailing the sea; they have filled you. [3] And by great waters, the seed of Sihor and the harvest of the river Nile (was) her revenue; and she a mart of nations. [4] Blush, O Sidon, for the sea has spoken, the strength of the sea, saying, I have not travailed nor brought forth, and I have not nourished young men, (nor) raised up virgins. [5] As the report (comes) to Egypt, so they shall be grieved (at) the report of Tyre. [6] Pass over Tarshish; howl, people of the coast! [7] Is this your exulting (city), from days of her old age? Her own feet shall carry it far away to stay. [8] Who has purposed this against Tyre, the crowning (city), whose merchants (are) kings; whose traders (are) the honored of the earth? [9] Jehovah of hosts has purposed it, to stain the pride of all glory, to bring all the honored of the earth into contempt.

[10] Pass through your land as the Nile, O daughter of Tarshish; there is no more strength. [11] He stretched His hand over the sea; He shook the kingdoms; Jehovah has made a decree against the merchant (city), to destroy its forts. [12] And He said, You shall rejoice no more, O crushed one, virgin daughter of Sidon. Arise, go to Chittim; even there you shall have no rest. [13] Behold, the land of the Chaldeans! This people did not exist; the Assyrians founded it for those who live in the desert. They set up its towers; they raised up its palaces. He brought it to

1 מַשָּׂא צֹר הֵילִילוּ ׀ אֳנִיּוֹת תַּרְשִׁישׁ כִּי־שֻׁדַּד מִבַּיִת מִבּוֹא

without without is it For !Tarshish ships ,Howl :Tyre The
.entrance ,house ,ruined of of burden

2 מֵאֶרֶץ כִּתִּים נִגְלָה־לָמוֹ׃ דֹּמּוּ יֹשְׁבֵי אִי סֹחַר צִידוֹן עֹבֵר

cross- ,Sidon Trader the residents Be to is it Kittim the From
ing of ,coast of ,silent .them revealed of land

3 יָם מִלְאוּךְ׃ וּבְמַיִם רַבִּים זֶרַע שִׁחֹר קְצִיר יְאוֹר תְּבוּאָתָהּ

her (was) the the ,Sihor seed ,great by And have they the
;revenue Nile of harvest of waters .you filled ;sea

4 וַתְּהִי סְחַר גּוֹיִם׃ בּוֹשִׁי צִידוֹן כִּי אָמַר־יָם מָעוֹז הַיָּם לֵאמֹר

,saying the the the has for ,Sidon Be .nations the she and
,sea of strength ,sea said ,ashamed of mart was

לֹא־חַלְתִּי וְלֹא־יָלַדְתִּי וְלֹא גִדַּלְתִּי בַחוּרִים רוֹמַמְתִּי

(nor) young have I not brought nor have I not
up raised ,men nourished ;forth travailed

5 בְתוּלוֹת׃ כַּאֲשֶׁר־שֵׁמַע לְמִצְרָיִם יָחִילוּ כְּשֵׁמַע צֹר׃ עִבְרוּ
6

Pass .Tyre the at will they to (comes) the When .virgins
,over of report pained be ,Egypt report

7 תַּרְשִׁישָׁה הֵילִילוּ יֹשְׁבֵי אִי׃ הֲזֹאת לָכֶם עַלִּיזָה מִימֵי־קֶדֶם

old from exult- the to Is the dwellers ,howl ;Tarshish
of days ,(city) ing you this !coast of

8 קַדְמָתָהּ יֹבִלוּהָ רַגְלֶיהָ מֵרָחוֹק לָגוּר׃ מִי יָעַץ זֹאת עַל־צֹר

,Tyre on this has Who to far feet Her carry ?age her
purposed .stay away her

9 הַמַּעֲטִירָה אֲשֶׁר סֹחֲרֶיהָ שָׂרִים כִּנְעָנֶיהָ נִכְבַּדֵּי־אָרֶץ׃ יְהוָה

Jehovah the (are) whose (are) merchants whose crowning the
of ?earth of honored traders ,chiefs ,(city)

צְבָאוֹת יְעָצָהּ לְחַלֵּל גְּאוֹן כָּל־צְבִי לְהָקֵל כָּל־נִכְבַּדֵּי־

the all bring to ,glory all the stain to pur- hosts
of honored contempt into of pride ,it posed

10 אָרֶץ׃ עִבְרִי אַרְצֵךְ כַּיְאֹר בַּת־תַּרְשִׁישׁ אֵין מֵזַח

girdle there ;Tarshish daughter the as your Pass the
no is of ,Nile land through .earth

11 עוֹד׃ יָדוֹ נָטָה עַל־הַיָּם הִרְגִּיז מַמְלָכוֹת יְהוָה צִוָּה אֶל־

against has Jehovah ;kingdoms He the over He His any
decreed shook ;sea stretched hand .more

12 כְּנַעַן לַשְׁמִד מָעֻזְנֶיהָ׃ וַיֹּאמֶר לֹא־תוֹסִיפִי עוֹד לַעֲלוֹז

,rejoice more shall You not he And .forts its to ,Canaan
again ,said destroy

הַמְעֻשָּׁקָה בְּתוּלַת בַּת־צִידוֹן כִּתִּיים קוּמִי עֲבֹרִי גַּם־שָׁם

there even cross ,Arise to .Sidon daughter ,virgin oppressed
;over Kittim of

13 לֹא־יָנוּחַ לָךְ׃ הֵן ׀ אֶרֶץ כַּשְׂדִּים זֶה הָעָם לֹא הָיָה אַשּׁוּר

Assyria did not people This the the ,Behold to is not
;exist !Chaldeans of land .you rest

יְסָדָהּ לְצִיִּים הֵקִימוּ בַחִינָיו עֹרְרוּ אַרְמְנוֹתֶיהָ שָׂמָהּ

they its they siege- their They desert for founded
it made ;palaces stripped ;towers up set !creatures it

ruin. [14] Howl, ships of Tarshish! For your strength is wasted. [15] And it shall come to pass, in that day, that Tyre shall be forgotten seventy years, according to the days of one king. After the end of seventy years, Tyre shall sing like a harlot. [16] Take a harp; go about the city, O harlot who has been forgotten. Do well to play; sing many songs that you may be remembered. [17] And it shall come to pass, after the end of seventy years, that Jehovah will visit Tyre; and she shall turn to her hire and shall commit fornication with all the kingdoms of the earth, on the face of the ground. [18] And her goods and her wages shall be holiness to Jehovah. It shall not be hoarded nor stored, for her goods shall be for those who dwell before Jehovah; to eat enough, and for a choice covering.

14 לְמַפֵּלָה׃ הֵילִילוּ אֳנִיּוֹת תַּרְשִׁישׁ כִּי שֻׁדַּד מָעֻזְּכֶן׃
your is For !Tarshish ships ,Howl a for
.fortress ruined of .ruin

15 וְהָיָה בַּיּוֹם הַהוּא וְנִשְׁכַּחַת צֹר שִׁבְעִים שָׁנָה כִּימֵי מֶלֶךְ
king the as ,years seventy Tyre shall that ,that day in it And
of days forgotten be be shall

16 אֶחָד מִקֵּץ שִׁבְעִים שָׁנָה יִהְיֶה לְצֹר כְּשִׁירַת הַזּוֹנָה׃ קְחִי
Take the the as to will it ,years seventy the At .one
.harlot of song Tyre be of end

כִנּוֹר סֹבִּי עִיר זוֹנָה נִשְׁכָּחָה הֵיטִיבִי נַגֵּן הַרְבִּי־שִׁיר לְמַעַן
that ,songs make to Do !forgotten O the go a
many ;play well harlot ,city about ,harp

17 תִּזָּכֵרִי׃ וְהָיָה מִקֵּץ ׀ שִׁבְעִים שָׁנָה יִפְקֹד יְהוָה אֶת־צֹר
;:Tyre Jehovah will ,years seventy the at it And be may you
visit of end be will .remembered

וְשָׁבָה לְאֶתְנַנָּה וְזָנְתָה אֶת־כָּל־מַמְלְכוֹת הָאָרֶץ עַל־פְּנֵי
the on the the all with will and her to she and
of face ,earth of kingdoms fornicate hire return shall

18 הָאֲדָמָה׃ וְהָיָה סַחְרָהּ וְאֶתְנַנָּהּ קֹדֶשׁ לַיהוָה לֹא יֵאָצֵר
shall It not to holy her and her shall And the
hoarded be .Jehovah wages traffic be .ground

וְלֹא יֵחָסֵן כִּי לַיֹּשְׁבִים לִפְנֵי יְהוָה יִהְיֶה סַחְרָהּ לֶאֱכֹל
eat to traffic her be shall Jehovah before those to for ,stored nor
dwell who

לְשָׂבְעָה וְלִמְכַסֶּה עָתִיק׃
.choice for and to
covering a sufficiency

CAP. XXIV כד

CHAPTER 24

1 הִנֵּה יְהוָה בּוֹקֵק הָאָרֶץ וּבוֹלְקָהּ וְעִוָּה פָנֶיהָ וְהֵפִיץ
and its and makes and the empties Jehovah Be-
scatters ,face distorts waste it ,land ,hold

2 יֹשְׁבֶיהָ׃ וְהָיָה כָעָם כַּכֹּהֵן כַּעֶבֶד כַּאדֹנָיו כַּשִּׁפְחָה כַּגְּבִרְתָּהּ
her so the as his so the as the so the as it And in- its
;mistress ,maid ;master ,servant ;priest ,people is .habitants

כַּקּוֹנֶה כַּמּוֹכֵר כַּמַּלְוֶה כַּלֹּוֶה כַּנֹּשֶׁה כַּאֲשֶׁר נֹשֶׁא בוֹ׃
with the so the as the so the as the so the as
.him debtor ,creditor ;borrower ,lender ;seller ,buyer

3 הִבּוֹק ׀ תִּבּוֹק הָאָרֶץ וְהִבּוֹז ׀ תִּבּוֹז כִּי יְהוָה דִּבֶּר אֶת־
has Jehovah for ;stripped and The be shall com-
spoken utterly ,land emptied pletely

4 הַדָּבָר הַזֶּה׃ אָבְלָה נָבְלָה הָאָרֶץ אֻמְלְלָה נָבְלָה תֵּבֵל
the lan- (and) droops the (and) Mourns .this word
;world guishes ,land languishes

5 אֻמְלָלוּ מְרוֹם עַם־הָאָרֶץ׃ וְהָאָרֶץ חָנְפָה תַּחַת יֹשְׁבֶיהָ
its under is the And the the proud the droop
inhabitants profaned earth .earth of people of

6 כִּי־עָבְרוּ תוֹרֹת חָלְפוּ חֹק הֵפֵרוּ בְּרִית עוֹלָם׃ עַל־כֵּן אָלָה
a Therefore ever- the and a violate ,laws they for
curse .lasting covenant break ,statute transgress

CHAPTER 24

[1] Behold, Jehovah empties the land and makes it bare, changing its face, and scattering its inhabitants. [2] And as (it is) with the people, so with the priest; as with the servant, so with his master; as with the maid, so with her mistress; as with the buyer, so with the seller; as with the creditor, so with the debtor. [3] The land shall be completely emptied and utterly stripped, for Jehovah has spoken this word. [4] The land mourns (and) languishes; the world droops (and) languishes; the proud of the people of the earth droop. [5] And the earth is profaned under its inhabitants, because they transgress laws (and) violate a statute, and break the everlasting covenant. [6] For this the curse

has devoured the land; and
they who live in it are deserted. For this the dwellers
of the land are consumed
and few men are left.
[7] The new wine has
failed; the vine droops; all
the merry-hearted sigh.
[8] The joy of timbrels
ceases; the noise of those
who rejoice ends; the joy
of the harp ceases.
[9] They shall not drink
wine with a song; fermented
drink shall be bitter to those
who drink it. [10] The city
of shame is broken down;
every house is shut, that
none may enter; [11] a
crying over the wine (is) in
the streets; all joy is darkened; the gladness in the
land is exiled. [12] Desolation is remaining in the city
and a ruin; the gate is battered. [13] For it is
thus in the midst of
the land, among the
peoples, (it shall be) as the
shaking of an olive tree, and
as the gleaning of the grapes
when the vintage is done.
[14] They shall lift up their
voice; they shall sing for the
majesty of Jehovah; they
shall cry aloud from the sea.
[15] Therefore glorify Jehovah in the east, the name
of Jehovah God of Israel
in the coasts of the sea.
[16] We have heard songs
from the end of the earth,
the desire of the righteous.
But I said, Leanness to me!
Leanness to me! Woe to me!
The traitors have dealt
treacherously; yes, the
traitors have dealt treacherously. [17] Fear, and the
pit, and the snare (are) on
you, O dweller of the earth.
[18] And it shall happen
that he who flees from the
voice of fear shall fall into
the pit. And he who comes
up out of the middle of the
pit shall be trapped. For the
windows from on high
are opened, and the
earth's foundations quake.
[19] The earth is breaking
(and) breaking! The earth is
crashing (and) crashing!
The earth is tottering, tottering! [20] Like a drunk-
en man, the earth is staggering, staggering! And it rocks
to and fro like a hut. And
its sin is heavy on it; and

אָכְלָה אֶרֶץ וַיֶּאְשְׁמוּ יֹשְׁבֵי בָהּ עַל־כֵּן חָרוּ יֹשְׁבֵי אֶרֶץ
the the are Therefore .it in who they are and the devours
,land of dwellers burned live guilty held ;land

7 וְנִשְׁאַר אֱנוֹשׁ מִזְעָר׃ אָבַל תִּירוֹשׁ אֻמְלְלָה־גָפֶן נֶאֶנְחוּ
sigh the droops new The mourns .few men re- and
,vine ;wine maining

8 כָּל־שִׂמְחֵי־לֵב׃ שָׁבַת מְשׂוֹשׂ תֻּפִּים חָדַל שְׁאוֹן עַלִּיזִים
;revelers the ends the The ceases .heart the all
of noise ,timbrels of joy of merry

9 שָׁבַת מְשׂוֹשׂ כִּנּוֹר׃ בַּשִּׁיר לֹא יִשְׁתּוּ־יָיִן יֵמַר שֵׁכָר לְשֹׁתָיו׃
its to strong is ;wine they not With the the ceases
.drinkers drink bitter drink shall song the .harp of joy

10 11 נִשְׁבְּרָה קִרְיַת־תֹהוּ סֻגַּר כָּל־בַּיִת מִבּוֹא׃ צְוָחָה עַל־הַיַּיִן
the over crying A from house every is ;emptiness the broken Is
wine .entering shut of city down

12 בַּחוּצוֹת עָרְבָה כָּל־שִׂמְחָה גָּלָה מְשׂוֹשׂ הָאָרֶץ׃ נִשְׁאַר
is the the is ;joy all dark- is the in (is)
remaining .land in gladness exiled ened ;streets

13 בָּעִיר שַׁמָּה וּשְׁאִיָּה יֻכַּת־שָׁעַר׃ כִּי־כֹה יִהְיֶה בְּקֶרֶב
the in is it thus For the is a and deso- the in
of midst .gate battered ,ruin ,lation city

הָאָרֶץ בְּתוֹךְ הָעַמִּים כְּנֹקֶף זַיִת כְּעֹלֵלֹת אִם־כָּלָה בָּצִיר׃
grape the is when glean- as an the as the among the
.harvest ended ings ,tree olive of shaking,peoples ,land

14 15 הֵמָּה יִשְׂאוּ קוֹלָם יָרֹנּוּ בִּגְאוֹן יְהוָה צָהֲלוּ מִיָּם׃ עַל־כֵּן
Therefore from cry they Jehovah the for they their lift They
.sea the aloud of majesty ;sing ;voice up

בָּאֻרִים כַּבְּדוּ יְהוָה בְּאִיֵּי הַיָּם שֵׁם יְהוָה אֱלֹהֵי יִשְׂרָאֵל׃
.Israel God Jehovah the the the in ;Jehovah glorify the in
of of name ,sea of coasts east

16 מִכְּנַף הָאָרֶץ זְמִרֹת שָׁמַעְנוּ צְבִי לַצַּדִּיק וָאֹמַר
I But the to Honor have we songs the the From
,said .Righteous ,heard earth of wing

רָזִי־לִי רָזִי־לִי אוֹי לִי בֹּגְדִים בָּגָדוּ וּבֶגֶד בּוֹגְדִים בָּגָדוּ׃
.betray traitors even ,betray Traitors to Woe to Lean- to Lean-
;perfidy !me !me ness !Me ness

17 18 פַּחַד וָפַחַת וָפָח עָלֶיךָ יוֹשֵׁב הָאָרֶץ׃ וְהָיָה הַנָּס מִקּוֹל
the from who he it And the dweller (are) and and Dread
of sound flees be will .earth of ,you on snare pit

הַפַּחַד יִפֹּל אֶל־הַפַּחַת וְהָעוֹלֶה מִתּוֹךְ הַפַּחַת יִלָּכֵד בַּפָּח
the in be shall the of out who he And the into shall dread
.snare taken pit of midst the up comes .pit fall

19 כִּי־אֲרֻבּוֹת מִמָּרוֹם נִפְתָּחוּ וַיִּרְעֲשׁוּ מוֹסְדֵי אָרֶץ׃ רֹעָה
,Breaking the foundations and are on from the For
earth's quake ,opened high windows

הִתְרֹעֲעָה הָאָרֶץ פּוֹר הִתְפּוֹרְרָה אֶרֶץ מוֹט הִתְמוֹטְטָה
is Totter- the is ,Crashing the breaking is
tottering ,ing !earth crashing !earth itself

20 אָרֶץ׃ נוֹעַ תָּנוּעַ אֶרֶץ כַּשִּׁכּוֹר וְהִתְנוֹדְדָה כַּמְּלוּנָה וְכָבֵד
is And a like rocks it And a like the stag- is Stag- the
heavy hut fro and to !drunkard ,earth gering ,gering !earth

it shall fall and not rise again. [21] And it shall come to pass, in that day, Jehovah shall punish the army of the high place on high, and on the kings of the land on the land. [22] And they will be gathered a gathering of prisoners in a dungeon; and they shall be shut up in a prison; and after many days they shall be judged. [23] Then the moon shall blush, and the sun shall be ashamed, when Jehovah of hosts shall reign in Mount Zion, and in Jerusalem, and before His elders (His) glory.

21 עָלֶיהָ פִּשְׁעָהּ וְנָפְלָה וְלֹא־תֹסִיף קוּם׃ וְהָיָה בַּיּוֹם הַהוּא

,that day in it And .rise shall and it and its it on
be shall again not fall shall ;trespass

יִפְקֹד יְהוָה עַל־צְבָא הַמָּרוֹם בַּמָּרוֹם וְעַל־מַלְכֵי הָאֲדָמָה

tne kings the and the in high the the on Jehovah shall
land of on ,place high place of army visit

22 עַל־הָאֲדָמָה׃ וְאֻסְּפוּ אֲסֵפָה אַסִּיר עַל־בּוֹר וְסֻגְּרוּ עַל־

in be will and a in prisoners gather- a will they And the on
up shut ,dungeon of ing gathered be .land

23 מַסְגֵּר וּמֵרֹב יָמִים יִפָּקֵדוּ׃ וְחָפְרָה הַלְּבָנָה וּבוֹשָׁה

be will and the will Then be will they days after and a
ashamed ,moon blush .visited many ;prison

הַחַמָּה כִּי־מָלַךְ יְהוָה צְבָאוֹת בְּהַר צִיּוֹן וּבִירוּשָׁלִַם וְנֶגֶד

and in and ,Zion in hosts Jehovah reigns for ,sun the
before ,Jerusalem Mount of

זְקֵנָיו כָּבוֹד׃

(His is) His
.glory elders

CAP. XXV כה

CHAPTER 25

[1] O Jehovah, You (are) my God! I will exalt You; I will thank Your name, for You have done a wonder: counsels from afar, faithful faithfulness. [2] Because You have made from a city a heap; a walled city a ruin; a palace of foreigners, that it may not (be) a city, that it may never be built. [3] For this the mighty people glorify You, the city of the ruthless nations shall fear You. [4] For You are a fort to the poor; a fort to the needy in his distress, a refuge from the storm, a shadow from the heat, when the breath of the terrible ones (is) like a storm (against) the wall. [5] You shall lay low the noise of foreigners, like the heat in a dry place, the heat with the shadow of cloud; the shouting of the terrible ones shall be laid low. [6] And Jehovah of hosts shall make for all people a feast of fat things in this mountain; a feast of wine on the lees, of fat things full of marrow, on wine on the lees well refined. [7] And He will destroy in this mountain the face of the covering which covers all people, and the

1 יְהוָה אֱלֹהַי אַתָּה אֲרוֹמִמְךָ אוֹדֶה שִׁמְךָ כִּי עָשִׂיתָ פֶּלֶא

a have You for Your will I exalt will I You my ,Jehovah
,wonder done ,name thank .You !(are) God

2 עֵצוֹת מֵרָחוֹק אֱמוּנָה אֹמֶן׃ כִּי שַׂמְתָּ מֵעִיר לַגָּל קִרְיָה

city a a to a from have You For .faithful faithful- from counsels
,heap city made ness ,afar

3 בְצוּרָה לְמַפֵּלָה אַרְמוֹן זָרִים מֵעִיר לְעוֹלָם לֹא יִבָּנֶה׃ עַל־

There may it not to a not for- citadel a ;ruin a into fortified
.built be forever ;city eigners of

4 כֵּן יְכַבְּדוּךָ עַם־עָז קִרְיַת גּוֹיִם עָרִיצִים יִירָאוּךָ׃ כִּי־הָיִיתָ

You For fear shall ruthless nations the ;might peo- glorify fore
are .You of city of ple You

מָעוֹז לַדָּל מָעוֹז לָאֶבְיוֹן בַּצַּר־לוֹ מַחְסֶה מִזֶּרֶם צֵל מֵחֹרֶב

from a from refuge a to the in the to a the to a
,heat shadow ,storm ,him distress ,needy fort ,poor fort

5 כִּי רוּחַ עָרִיצִים כְּזֶרֶם קִיר׃ כְּחֹרֶב בְּצָיוֹן שְׁאוֹן זָרִים

for- the dry a in Like (against) like (is) ruth- the the for
eigners of noise ,place heat .wall a storm a less of breath

6 תַּכְנִיעַ חֹרֶב בְּצֵל עָב זְמִיר עָרִיצִים יַעֲנֶה׃ וְעָשָׂה

shall And be shall the the ,cloud the by (as) shall You
make .humbled ruthless of song of shadow heat ,low lay

יְהוָה צְבָאוֹת לְכָל־הָעַמִּים בָּהָר הַזֶּה מִשְׁתֵּה שְׁמָנִים

fat a this in the for hosts Jehovah
,things of feast mountain peoples all of

7 מִשְׁתֵּה שְׁמָרִים שְׁמָנִים מְמֻחָיִם שְׁמָרִים מְזֻקָּקִים׃ וּבִלַּע

He And .refined on wine of full fat on wine feast a
swallow will lees the ,marrow things ,lees the of

בָּהָר הַזֶּה פְּנֵי־הַלּוֹט ׀ הַלּוֹט עַל־כָּל־הָעַמִּים וְהַמַּסֵּכָה

the and the all over which the the this in
veil ,peoples covers covering of face mountain

veil that is woven over all nations. [8] He will swallow up death in victory! And the Lord Jehovah will wipe away tears from all faces. And He shall remove the reproach of His people from all the earth — for Jehovah has spoken. [9] And one shall say in that day, Lo, this (is) our God; we have waited for Him and He will save us. This (is) Jehovah; we have waited for Him; we will be glad and rejoice in His salvation. [10] For the hand of Jehovah shall rest in this mountain; and Moab shall be trampled under Him, even as straw (is) trampled in the water of a dung pit. [11] And He shall spread His hands in his midst, as he who swims strokes to swim. And He shall lay low his pride with the skill of His hands. [12] And He shall bring down the fortress of the height of your walls; He will lay low; He shall throw down to the ground to the dust.

8 הַנְּסוּכָה עַל־כָּל־הַגּוֹיִם׃ בִּלַּע הַמָּוֶת לָנֶצַח וּמָחָה אֲדֹנָי
the Lord will And wipe away !forever death will He up swallow the .nations all over is that woven

יְהוִה דִּמְעָה מֵעַל כָּל־פָּנִים וְחֶרְפַּת עַמּוֹ יָסִיר מֵעַל כָּל־
all from will He remove His people the And of reproach .faces all from tears Jehovah

9 הָאָרֶץ כִּי יְהוָה דִּבֵּר׃ וְאָמַר בַּיּוֹם הַהוּא הִנֵּה
,Behold ,that day in one And say shall has .spoken Jehovah for the —earth

אֱלֹהֵינוּ זֶה קִוִּינוּ לוֹ וְיוֹשִׁיעֵנוּ זֶה יְהוָה קִוִּינוּ לוֹ נָגִילָה
will we glad be for ;Him have we waited ;Jehovah This (is) He and .us save will for ,Him have we waited this ;(is) our God

10 וְנִשְׂמְחָה בִּישׁוּעָתוֹ׃ כִּי־תָנוּחַ יַד־יְהוָה בָּהָר הַזֶּה וְנָדוֹשׁ
shall and trampled be ;this mountain in Jehovah the of hand shall rest For His in .salvation rejoice and

11 מוֹאָב תַּחְתָּיו כְּהִדּוֹשׁ מַתְבֵּן בְּמֵי מַדְמֵנָה׃ וּפֵרַשׂ יָדָיו
His hands He And spread shall dung a .pit the in of water straw is as trampled under ,Him Moab

בְּקִרְבּוֹ כַּאֲשֶׁר יְפָרֵשׂ הַשֹּׂחֶה לִשְׂחוֹת וְהִשְׁפִּיל גַּאֲוָתוֹ עִם
with his pride He And low lay shall .swim to the swimmer spreads as its in ,midst

12 אָרְבּוֹת יָדָיו׃ וּמִבְצַר מִשְׂגַּב חוֹמֹתֶיךָ הֵשַׁח הִשְׁפִּיל הִגִּיעַ
strike down ,low lay will He ,down bow your walls the of height the And of fortress His .hands the of skill

לָאָרֶץ עַד־עָפָר׃
the .dust even to the to ,earth

CAP. XXVI כו

CHAPTER 26

[1] In that day this song shall be sung in the land of Judah: A strong city (is) ours; He sets up salvation (as our) walls and rampart. [2] Open the gates, and the righteous nation shall come in, preserving faithfulness. [3] You will keep in perfect peace (him whose) mind (is) stayed (on You); because he trusts in You. [4] Trust in Jehovah forever, for in Jah Jehovah (is) everlasting strength. [5] For He bows down those who dwell on high; He lays it low to the ground; He makes it touch even to the dust. [6] The foot shall trample it — the feet of the poor, steps of the weak. [7] The path for the just (is) uprightness; Upright One, level the track of

1 בַּיּוֹם הַהוּא יוּשַׁר הַשִּׁיר־הַזֶּה בְּאֶרֶץ יְהוּדָה עִיר עָז־לָנוּ
(is) strong ;us to A city :Judah the in of land this song be shall sung be that day In

2 יְשׁוּעָה יָשִׁית חוֹמוֹת וָחֵל׃ פִּתְחוּ שְׁעָרִים וְיָבֹא גוֹי־צַדִּיק
,righteous a nation may that come the ,gates Open and .rampart (our as) walls He sets salvation

3 שֹׁמֵר אֱמֻנִים׃ יֵצֶר סָמוּךְ תִּצֹּר שָׁלוֹם ׀ שָׁלוֹם כִּי בְךָ בָּטוּחַ׃
. he .trusts in You for ;peace (in) ,peace will You keep stayed You on the mind faithful- .ness keeping

4 בִּטְחוּ בַיהוָה עֲדֵי־עַד כִּי בְּיָהּ יְהוָה צוּר עוֹלָמִים׃ כִּי
5
For .everlasting Rock a (is) Jehovah in Jah for ,forever in Jehovah Trust

הֵשַׁח יֹשְׁבֵי מָרוֹם קִרְיָה נִשְׂגָּבָה יַשְׁפִּילֶנָּה יַשְׁפִּילָהּ עַד־
to lays He ,low it lays He ,low it lofty the city ;high on the dwellers He bows

6 אֶרֶץ יַגִּיעֶנָּה עַד־עָפָר׃ תִּרְמְסֶנָּה רָגֶל רַגְלֵי עָנִי פַּעֲמֵי
steps of the ,poor feet of The —foot shall it trample the .dust even to makes He touch it the ;ground

דַלִּים׃ אֹרַח לַצַּדִּיק מֵישָׁרִים יָשָׁר מַעְגַּל צַדִּיק תְּפַלֵּס׃
make .level the just the of track Upright ,One (is) ;uprightness the for just The path the .weak

the just. [8] Yes, (in) the path of Your judgments, Jehovah, we awaited You; for Your name and for Your memory (is) the desire of (our) soul. [9] (With) my soul I desire You in the night; yea, (with) my spirit within me I seek You diligently; for when Your judgments (are) in the earth, the dwellers of the world learn righteousness.

[10] The wicked finds favor; he learns not righteousness. In the land of honesty he deals unjustly, and not sees the majesty of Jehovah. [11] Jehovah, Your hand is high; they see not; they see and are ashamed of the zeal of the people. Yea, the fire of Your foes devours them. [12] Jehovah, You will ordain peace for us; for also all our works You have worked for us. [13] Jehovah our God, masters beside You have governed us; only in You we will mention Your name. [14] Dead ones do not live; departed spirits do not rise; because You visited and destroyed them, and caused to perish all memory of them. [15] You have added to the nation, Jehovah; You have added to the nation. You are glorified; You have extended all the ends of the land. Jehovah, in distress they visited You; they poured out a whisper; to them was Your chastening. [17] As a pregnant woman draws near to bear, she writhes, cries in her pangs; so we are before You, Jehovah. [18] We conceived, we writhe; as it were, we gave birth (to) wind. We have not worked salvation (for) the earth, and the world's dwellers have not fallen. [19] Your dead ones shall live, my dead body, they shall arise; awake and sing, dust-dwellers, for the dew of lights (is) your dew; and the earth shall cast out departed spirits. [20] Come, My people, go in your rooms and shut your doors behind you; hide as a little moment til the fury passes.

8 אַף אֹרַח מִשְׁפָּטֶיךָ יְהוָה קִוִּינוּךָ לְשִׁמְךָ וּלְזִכְרְךָ תַּאֲוַת־
the (is) Your for and Your for awaited we ,Jehovah Your the (in) ,Yea
of desire memory name ;You ,judgments of path

9 נָפֶשׁ׃ נַפְשִׁי אִוִּיתִךָ בַּלַּיְלָה אַף־רוּחִי בְקִרְבִּי אֲשַׁחֲרֶךָּ
You seek I within (with) ,yea the in desire I (With) (our)
;diligently me spirit my ;night You soul my .soul

10 כִּי כַּאֲשֶׁר מִשְׁפָּטֶיךָ לָאָרֶץ צֶדֶק לָמְדוּ יֹשְׁבֵי תֵבֵל׃ יֻחַן
finds the inhab- the learn righ- to (are) Your when for
favor .world of itants teousness ,earth the judgments

רָשָׁע בַּל־לָמַד צֶדֶק בְּאֶרֶץ נְכֹחוֹת יְעַוֵּל וּבַל־יִרְאֶה גֵּאוּת
the sees and deals he honesty the In righ- he not The
of majesty not ,unjustly of land .teousness learns ;wicked

11 יְהוָה׃ יְהוָה רָמָה יָדְךָ בַּל־יֶחֱזָיוּן יֶחֱזוּ וְיֵבֹשׁוּ קִנְאַת־
zeal the are and they they not Your is ,Jehovah .Jehovah
of of ashamed see ;see ;hand high

12 עָם אַף־אֵשׁ צָרֶיךָ תֹאכְלֵם׃ יְהוָה תִּשְׁפֹּת שָׁלוֹם
peace will You ,Jehovah devours Your the ,Yea the
ordain .them foes of fire .people

13 לָנוּ כִּי גַּם־כָּל־מַעֲשֵׂינוּ פָּעַלְתָּ לָּנוּ׃ יְהוָה אֱלֹהֵינוּ
Our Jehovah for have You our all also for for
,God .us worked works ;us

14 בְּעָלוּנוּ אֲדֹנִים זוּלָתֶךָ לְבַד־בְּךָ נַזְכִּיר שְׁמֶךָ׃ מֵתִים בַּל־
not Dead Your will we in only beside masters gov- have
ones .name mention You ;You us erned

יִחְיוּ רְפָאִים בַּל־יָקֻמוּ לָכֵן פָּקַדְתָּ וַתַּשְׁמִידֵם וַתְּאַבֵּד כָּל־
all caused and destroyed and You there- do not departed do
perish to them visited fore ,arise spirits ;live

15 זֵכֶר לָמוֹ׃ יָסַפְתָּ לַגּוֹי יְהוָה יָסַפְתָּ לַגּוֹי נִכְבָּדְתָּ רִחַקְתָּ
have You are You the to have You Jeho- the to have You of memory
extended ;glorified ,nation added ;vah ,nation added .them

16 כָּל־קַצְוֵי־אָרֶץ׃ יְהוָה בַּצַּר פְּקָדוּךָ צָקוּן לַחַשׁ
a they visited they in ,Jehovah the the all
;whisper poured ;You distress .land of ends

17 מוּסָרְךָ לָמוֹ׃ כְּמוֹ הָרָה תַּקְרִיב לָלֶדֶת תָּחִיל תִּזְעַק
(and) she give to draws woman a As to (was) Your
cries writhes ,birth near child with .them chastening

18 בַּחֲבָלֶיהָ כֵּן הָיִינוּ מִפָּנֶיךָ יְהוָה׃ הָרִינוּ חַלְנוּ כְּמוֹ יָלַדְנוּ
gave we it as we con- We .Jehovah be- from we so her in
birth ,were ,writhe ,ceived ,You fore are ,pangs

19 רוּחַ יְשׁוּעֹת בַּל־נַעֲשֶׂה אֶרֶץ וּבַל־יִפְּלוּ יֹשְׁבֵי תֵבֵל׃ יִחְיוּ
shall the inhabi- the have and the (for) have we not Salvation (to)
live .world of tants fallen not ,earth worked .wind

מֵתֶיךָ נְבֵלָתִי יְקוּמוּן הָקִיצוּ וְרַנְּנוּ שֹׁכְנֵי עָפָר כִּי טַל אוֹרֹת
lights the for the dwellers and awake shall they dead my Your
(is) of dew ,dust of ,sing ;arise ,body ,ones dead

20 טַלֶּךָ וָאָרֶץ רְפָאִים תַּפִּיל׃ לֵךְ עַמִּי בֹּא בַחֲדָרֶיךָ
your enter My ,Come make shall departed the and your
rooms ,people .fall spirits earth ;dew

וּסְגֹר דְּלָתְךָ בַּעֲדֶךָ חֲבִי כִמְעַט־רֶגַע עַד־יַעֲבָור־זָעַם׃
indigna- passes until ,moment a as hide behind your and
.tion over little ;you doors shut

[21] For, behold, Jehovah comes out of His place to visit on the dweller of the earth his iniquity; the earth shall also reveal her blood, and shall no more cover her dead.

21 כי־הנה יהוה יצא ממקומו לפקד עון ישב־הארץ עליו
on of dweller the in- the visit to His from comes Jehovah be- ,For
;him earth the of iquity place forth ,hold
וגלתה הארץ את־דמיה ולא־תכסה עוד על־הרוגיה:
her over more shall and her the shall also
.slain cover not ,blood earth reveal

CAP. XXVII כז

CHAPTER 27

CHAPTER 27

[1] In that day Jehovah shall visit the sea-monster, the darting serpent, with His great and sharp and strong sword; on the sea-monster, that twisting serpent; and He shall kill the monster that is in the sea. [2] In that day sing to her, A vineyard of red wine; [3] I Jehovah keep it; I will water it (every) moment, lest one punish it; I will keep it night and day. [4] Fury is not in Me. Who will battle Me with briers and thorns? I will step through it; I will burn it at once. [5] Or will he lay hold of My strength that he may make peace with me? Let him make peace with Me. [6] Those who come to Jacob, He shall make take root; Israel shall blossom and bud and fill the world's face (with) fruit. [7] (As) the striking of His striker, He struck him? As the slaying of His slain, he is slain? [8] You will contend with her by driving her away, by sending her away. He shall take away by His biting wind, in the day of His east wind. [9] By this, then shall the iniquity of Jacob be purged; and this is all the fruit to take away his sin; when he makes all the stones of the altar as chalk-stones that are beaten in pieces; Asherim and sun-pillars shall not rise. [10] For the fortified city (shall be) lonely, a pasture forsaken and left like a wilderness. The calf shall feed there, and he shall lie there and eat up its branches. [11] When its branches dry up, they are broken off.

1 ביום ההוא יפקד יהוה בחרבו הקשה והגדולה והחזקה
and and fierce His with Jehovah shall that day In
strong great sword visit
על לויתן נחש ברח ועל לויתן נחש עקלתון והרג את־
He and ;twisting the sea the even ,darting the sea the on
slay shall serpent ,monster on serpent ,monster
2 התנין אשר בים: ביום ההוא כרם חמר ענו־לה:
to sing ,wine vine- a that day In the in which the
;it of yard .sea (is) monster
3 אני יהוה נצרה לרגעים אשקנה פן יפקד עליה לילה
night ,it on one lest water I (every) keep Jehovah I
visit ;it moment ;it
4 ויום אצרנה: חמה אין לי מי־יתנני שמיר שית במלחמה
the in (and) briars will Who to is Fury guard I and
?battle thorns Me give .Me not .it day
5 אפשעה בה אציתנה יחד: או יחזק במעזי יעשה שלום
peace he that My of he will Or at would I through would I
make may strength hold take .once it burn ;it step
6 לי שלום יעשה־לי: הבאים ישרש יעקב יציץ ופרח
and shall ;Jacob take will the (In) with him let Peace with
bud blossom root (days) coming .Me make ;Me
7 ישראל ומלאו פני־תבל תנובה: הכמכת מכהו
His the (As) (with) the the they and Israel
striker of striking .fruit world of face fill will
8 הכהו אם־כהרג הרגיו הרג: בסאסאה בשלחה תריבנה
contend You sending by driving By he is His the as Or He did
.her with away her ,away her ?slain slain of slaying ?him strike
9 הגה ברוחו הקשה ביום קדים: לכן בזאת יכפר עון
in- the be will by Then east the in ,harsh His by shall He
of iquity covered this .wind of day wind remove
יעקב וזה כל־פרי הסר חטאתו בשומו | כל־אבני מזבח
the the all he when his take to the all and ;Jacob
altar of stones makes ;sin away fruit (is) this
10 כאבני־גר מנפצות לא־יקמו אשרים וחמנים: כי עיר
the For sun- and Asherim shall not beaten chalk as
city .pillars rise ,pieces in of stones
בצורה בדד נוה משלח ונעזב כמדבר שם ירעה עגל
the shall There the like for- and left a ,lonely fortified
,calf feed .wilderness saken alone pasture (be will)
11 ושם ירבץ וכלה סעפיה: ביבש קצירה תשברנה
are they its When its eat and shall he and
.off broken ,boughs up dry .branches up lie there

Women shall come and burn them, for it (is) a people without understanding. Therefore, He who made them will not have mercy on them, and He who formed them will show them no favor. [12] And it shall come to pass in that day, that Jehovah shall thresh from the channel of the River to the torrent of Egypt; and you shall be gathered one by one, O children of Israel. [13] And it shall happen in that day, that the great trumpet shall be blown: and those who were perishing in the land of Assyria shall come, and the outcasts in the land of Egypt, and shall worship Jehovah in the holy mountain at Jerusalem.

CHAPTER 28

[1] Woe (to) the crown of pride, of the drunkards of Ephraim, whose glorious beauty is a fading flower which (is) on the head of the fat valley of those who are overcome with wine! [2] Behold, the Lord (is) a mighty and strong one; like a storm of hail, a destroying storm; like a flood of mighty waters overflowing; His hand casts down to the earth. [3] The crown of pride of the drunkards of Ephraim shall be trampled down. [4] And the glorious beauty which is on the head of the fat valley shall be a fading flower; like the firstripe fruit before the summer, which is swallowed by the seeing one who sees it, while it (is) yet in his hand. [5] In that day Jehovah of hosts shall become a crown of glory and a diadem of beauty to the rest of His people; [6] and a spirit of justice to him who sits on the judgment (seat); and strength to those turning the battle back toward the gate. [7] But they also have erred through wine, and have strayed through fermented drink. The priest and the prophet have erred through fermented drink; they have been swallowed by wine; they have strayed through

נָשִׁים בָּאוֹת מְאִירוֹת אוֹתָהּ כִּי לֹא עַם־בִּינוֹת הוּא עַל־כֵּן
There- it discern- a not for ,them (and) come Women
,fore .(is) ment of people burn

12 לֹא־יְרַחֲמֶנּוּ עֹשֵׂהוּ וְיֹצְרוֹ לֹא יְחֻנֶּנּוּ׃ וְהָיָה בַּיּוֹם
day in it And show will not his and his pity shall not
be shall .favor him Former ,Maker him

הַהוּא יַחְבֹּט יְהוָֹה מִשִּׁבֹּלֶת הַנָּהָר עַד־נַחַל מִצְרַיִם וְאַתֶּם
and ;Egypt the to the the from Jehovah shall ,that
you of torrent River of stream thresh

13 תְּלֻקְּטוּ לְאַחַד אֶחָד בְּנֵי יִשְׂרָאֵל׃ וְהָיָה בַּיּוֹם הַהוּא
,that day in it And .Israel sons (by) one be shall
be shall of one gathered

יִתָּקַע בְּשׁוֹפָר גָּדוֹל וּבָאוּ הָאֹבְדִים בְּאֶרֶץ אַשּׁוּר וְהַנִּדָּחִים
the and ,Assyria the in those shall and ,great a be shall
outcasts of land perishing come trumpet blown

בְּאֶרֶץ מִצְרַיִם וְהִשְׁתַּחֲווּ לַיהוָֹה בְּהַר הַקֹּדֶשׁ בִּירוּשָׁלִָם׃
.Jerusalem in holiness the in Jehovah shall and ,Egypt the in
of mountain worship of land

CAP. XXVIII כח

CHAPTER 28

1 הוֹי עֲטֶרֶת גֵּאוּת שִׁכֹּרֵי אֶפְרַיִם וְצִיץ נֹבֵל צְבִי תִפְאַרְתּוֹ
,beauty his the ,fading the and ,Ephraim the pride the Woe
of glory flower of drunkards of of crown (to)

2 אֲשֶׁר עַל־רֹאשׁ גֵּיא־שְׁמָנִים הֲלוּמֵי יָיִן׃ הִנֵּה חָזָק וְאַמִּץ
and might ,Behold !wine those ,fatness the the on which
strength by smitten of valley of head (is)

לַאדֹנָי כְּזֶרֶם בָּרָד שַׂעַר קָטֶב כְּזֶרֶם מַיִם כַּבִּירִים שֹׁטְפִים
over- mighty waters a like destruc- a ,hail a like to (are)
;flowing of storm ;tion of storm of storm ,Lord the

3 הִנִּיחַ לָאָרֶץ בְּיָד׃ בְּרַגְלַיִם תֵּרָמַסְנָה עֲטֶרֶת גְּאוּת שִׁכּוֹרֵי
drunk- the the the be shall feet By with the to sets He
of ards of pride of crown trampled .hand earth down

4 אֶפְרָיִם׃ וְהָיְתָה צִיצַת נֹבֵל צְבִי תִפְאַרְתּוֹ אֲשֶׁר עַל־רֹאשׁ
the on which ,beauty his the ,fading the shall And .Ephraim
of head (is) of glory flower be

גֵּיא שְׁמָנִים כְּבִכּוּרָהּ בְּטֶרֶם קַיִץ אֲשֶׁר יִרְאֶה הָרֹאֶה
one the sees which ,summer before the like ;fatness the
seeing fig early of valley

5 אוֹתָהּ בְּעוֹדָהּ בְּכַפּוֹ יִבְלָעֶנָּה׃ בַּיּוֹם הַהוּא יִהְיֶה
shall that day In swallows he his in yet while :it
become .it hand (is) it

יְהוָֹה צְבָאוֹת לַעֲטֶרֶת צְבִי וְלִצְפִירַת תִּפְאָרָה לִשְׁאָר
the to beauty a for and glory a hosts Jehovah
of rest of diadem of crown of

6 עַמּוֹ׃ וּלְרוּחַ מִשְׁפָּט לַיּוֹשֵׁב עַל־הַמִּשְׁפָּט וְלִגְבוּרָה
might for and the over him to justice a and His
,judgment sits who of spirit ;people

7 מְשִׁיבֵי מִלְחָמָה שָׁעְרָה׃ וְגַם־אֵלֶּה בַּיַּיִן שָׁגוּ וּבַשֵּׁכָר תָּעוּ
stray- by and have by these But toward battle the those to
.ed liquor ,erred wine also .gate the back turning

fermented drink; they err in vision; they stumble in judgment; [8] for all tables are full of vomit (and) filth, without (a clean) place.

[9] Whom shall He teach knowledge? And whom shall He make to understand doctrine? Those weaned from the milk, those drawn from the breasts. [10] For precept (has been) upon precept, precept upon precept; line on line, line on line, here a little, there a little. [11] For with stammering lip and another tongue He will speak to this people; [12] to whom He said, This (is) the rest; cause the weary to rest; and, This (is) the repose. But they were not willing to hear. [13] Yet the word of Jehovah was to them precept on precept, rule on rule, line on line, line on line; here a little, there a little; that they might go, and stumble, and be broken and snared and taken. [14] Therefore hear the word of Jehovah, scornful men, you who rule this people, who (are) in Jerusalem. [15] Because you have said, We have cut a covenant with death; and, We have made a vision with Sheol—when the overwhelming rod passes through, it shall not come to us; for we have made the lie our refuge, and we have hidden in falsehood. [16] Therefore thus says the Lord Jehovah, Behold! I place in Zion a Stone for a foundation, a tried Stone, a precious Cornerstone, a sure Foundation; he who believes shall not make haste. [17] And I will lay justice for a line, and righteousness to the plummet; and the hail shall sweep away the refuge of the lie; and the waters shall overflow the hiding place. [18] And your covenant with death shall be wiped out: and your vision with

כֹּהֵן וְנָבִיא שָׁגוּ בַשֵּׁכָר נִבְלְעוּ מִן־הַיַּיִן תָּעוּ מִן־הַשֵּׁכָר שָׁגוּ
they err ;liquor from they stray ,wine from are they swallowed ;liquor by have erred and prophet Priest

8 בָּרֹאֶה פָּקוּ פְּלִילִיָּה׃ כִּי כָּל־שֻׁלְחָנוֹת מָלְאוּ קִיא צֹאָה
;filth vomit (and) are full of tables all For in .judgment they stumble in ;seeing

9 בְּלִי מָקוֹם׃ אֶת־מִי יוֹרֶה דֵעָה וְאֶת־מִי יָבִין שְׁמוּעָה
the ?message He shall explain whom And knowl- ?edge shall He teach Whom (clean a) .place with- out

10 גְּמוּלֵי מֵחָלָב עַתִּיקֵי מִשָּׁדָיִם׃ כִּי צַו לָצָו צַו לָצָו קַו
line on ;rule rule on ;rule rule (is) For from ?breasts those moving from ,milk Those weaned

11 לָקָו קַו לָקָו זְעֵיר שָׁם זְעֵיר שָׁם׃ כִּי בְּלַעֲגֵי שָׂפָה וּבְלָשׁוֹן
with and tongue ,lip with of stammering For .there a little ,there a little on ;line line on ,line

12 אַחֶרֶת יְדַבֵּר אֶל־הָעָם הַזֶּה׃ אֲשֶׁר ׀ אָמַר אֲלֵיהֶם זֹאת
This (is) to ,them said He (of) whom ;this people to will He speak another

הַמְּנוּחָה הָנִיחוּ לֶעָיֵף וְזֹאת הַמַּרְגֵּעָה וְלֹא אָבוּא שְׁמוֹעַ׃
.hear to they willed But not the .repose this and (is) the ;weary cause rest to the ,rest

13 וְהָיָה לָהֶם דְּבַר־יְהוָה צַו לָצָו צַו לָצָו קַו לָקָו קַו לָקָו
on line ;line on line ;line on rule ;rule on rule ;rule ,Jehovah the of word to them was Yet

זְעֵיר שָׁם זְעֵיר שָׁם לְמַעַן יֵלְכוּ וְכָשְׁלוּ אָחוֹר וְנִשְׁבָּרוּ
be and broken back- ward and stumble they ,go might that ;there a little ;there a little

14 וְנוֹקְשׁוּ וְנִלְכָּדוּ׃ לָכֵן שִׁמְעוּ דְבַר־יְהוָה אַנְשֵׁי לָצוֹן
,scorn men of ,Jehovah the of word hear ,Therefore and .taken and snared

15 מֹשְׁלֵי הָעָם הַזֶּה אֲשֶׁר בִּירוּשָׁלִָם׃ כִּי אֲמַרְתֶּם כָּרַתְנוּ
have We cut have you ,said Because .Jerusalem in who (are) ,this people rulers of

בְרִית אֶת־מָוֶת וְעִם־שְׁאוֹל עָשִׂינוּ חֹזֶה שִׁיט שׁוֹטֵף כִּי־
when over- whelming the whip a ,vision have made Sheol and with ,death with a cove- nant

יַעֲבֹר לֹא יְבוֹאֵנוּ כִּי שַׂמְנוּ כָזָב מַחְסֵנוּ וּבַשֶּׁקֶר נִסְתָּרְנוּ׃
have we .hidden in and falsehood our ,refuge the lie we have made for us to come shall it not passes it ,through

16 לָכֵן כֹּה אָמַר אֲדֹנָי יְהוִה הִנְנִי יִסַּד בְּצִיּוֹן אָבֶן אֶבֶן
a stone a ,stone in Zion lay I Behold ,Jehovah the Lord says thus ,Therefore

17 בֹּחַן פִּנַּת יִקְרַת מוּסָד מוּסָּד הַמַּאֲמִין לֹא יָחִישׁ׃ וְשַׂמְתִּי
I And will put not shall .hurry who he believes ;founded foun- dation a ,precious a cornerstone ,tried

מִשְׁפָּט לְקָו וּצְדָקָה לְמִשְׁקָלֶת וְיָעָה בָרָד מַחְסֵה כָזָב
the ;lie the of refuge hail shall and away sweep a for ;plummet righ- and teousness a for ,line justice

18 וְסֵתֶר מַיִם יִשְׁטֹפוּ׃ וְכֻפַּר בְּרִיתְכֶם אֶת־מָוֶת וְחָזוּתְכֶם
your and vision ;death with your covenant will And be covered shall .overflow waters the and place hiding

Sheol shall not stand. When the overwhelming rod passes through, then you shall be beaten down by it. [19] As often as it passes, it shall take you; for morning by morning it shall pass over. By day and by night, even it shall only be a terror to understand the message. [20] For the bed is shorter than one can stretch himself on; and the cover is narrower than one can wrap himself in. [21] For Jehovah shall rise up, as (He did) at Mount Perazim; He shall be stirred as (in) the valley of Gibeon, to do His work, His strange work; and to perform His act, His strange act. [22] So, then, do not be mockers; lest your bonds be made strong. For I have heard from the Lord Jehovah of hosts that a full end (is) decreed on all the earth.

[23] Listen and hear my voice; pay attention and hear my word: [24] Does the plowman plow all day to sow? Does he open and break the clods of his land? [25] When he has leveled its surface, does he not strew black cummin, and scatter cummin, and place wheat in rows, and place barley, and spelt (in) its border? [26] And He instructs him for the right; his God teaches him. [27] For black cummin is not threshed with the sledge, nor is a cart-wheel turned on cummin, but black cummin is beaten out with the staff, and cummin with the rod. [28] Bread is crushed, but not always threshing one threshes it, and he drives the wheel of his cart; and his horses do not beat it small. [29] This also comes from Jehovah of hosts, doing wonders in counsel, making great sound wisdom.

אֶת־שְׁאוֹל לֹא תָקוּם שׁוֹט שׁוֹטֵף כִּי יַעֲבֹר וִהְיִיתֶם לוֹ
to you then passes When over- the shall not Sheol with
it be shall ,through whelming whip .arise

19 לְמִרְמָס׃ מִדֵּי עָבְרוֹ יִקַּח אֶתְכֶם כִּי־בַבֹּקֶר בַּבֹּקֶר יַעֲבֹר
shall it the in the in for ;you shall it it often As a for
.pass morning ,morning take ,passes as .trampling

20 בַּיּוֹם וּבַלָּיְלָה וְהָיָה רַק־זְוָעָה הָבִין שְׁמוּעָה׃ כִּי־קָצַר
is For the to a only it and in and the In
shorter .message discern terror be shall ,night the day

21 הַמַּצָּע מֵהִשְׂתָּרֵעַ וְהַמַּסֵּכָה צָרָה כְּהִתְכַּנֵּס׃ כִּי כְהַר־
as For oneself than (too) the and oneself than the
Mount .in wrap can narrow cover ,on stretch can bed

פְּרָצִים יָקוּם יְהוָה כְּעֵמֶק בְּגִבְעוֹן יִרְגָּז לַעֲשׂוֹת מַעֲשֵׂהוּ
His do to shall He in the as ;Jehovah shall ,Perazim
;work stirred be ,Gibeon valley up rise

22 זָר מַעֲשֵׂהוּ וְלַעֲבֹד עֲבֹדָתוֹ נָכְרִיָּה עֲבֹדָתוֹ׃ וְעַתָּה אַל־
not And His foreign His to and His strange
now .task (is) ,task perform ;work (is)

תִּתְלוֹצָצוּ פֶּן־יֶחְזְקוּ מוֹסְרֵיכֶם כִּי־כָלָה וְנֶחֱרָצָה שָׁמַעְתִּי
have I (is) even full a For your be lest be do
heard ,decreed end .bonds strengthened ;mockers

23 מֵאֵת אֲדֹנָי יֱהוִה צְבָאוֹת עַל־כָּל־הָאָרֶץ׃ הַאֲזִינוּ
Listen the all on ,hosts Jehovah the from
.earth of Lord

24 וְשִׁמְעוּ קוֹלִי הַקְשִׁיבוּ וְשִׁמְעוּ אִמְרָתִי׃ הֲכֹל הַיּוֹם יַחֲרֹשׁ
plow the Does my hear and pay my hear and
day all :word attention ;voice

25 הַחֹרֵשׁ לִזְרֹעַ יְפַתַּח וִישַׂדֵּד אַדְמָתוֹ׃ הֲלוֹא אִם־שִׁוָּה
has he when Does his break and Does ?sow to the
leveled not ?ground of clods the open he plowman

פָנֶיהָ וְהֵפִיץ קֶצַח וְכַמֹּן יִזְרֹק וְשָׂם חִטָּה שׂוֹרָה וּשְׂעֹרָה
and ,rows in wheat and ,scatter and black then its
barley place cummin ,cummin strew ,surface

26 נִסְמָן וְכֻסֶּמֶת גְּבֻלָתוֹ׃ וְיִסְּרוֹ לַמִּשְׁפָּט אֱלֹהָיו יוֹרֶנּוּ׃
teaches his the for He And its (in) and (its in)
.him God ;right him instructs ?border spelt ,place

27 כִּי לֹא בֶחָרוּץ יוּדַשׁ קֶצַח וְאוֹפַן עֲגָלָה עַל־כַּמֹּן יוּסָּב כִּי
but ,turned is on cart a a nor black is the with not For
cummin of wheel ,cummin threshed sledge

28 בַמַּטֶּה יֵחָבֶט קֶצַח וְכַמֹּן בַּשָּׁבֶט׃ לֶחֶם יוּדָק כִּי לֹא
not but is Bread the with and black beaten is the with
,crushed .rod cummin ,cummin out staff

לָנֶצַח אָדוֹשׁ יְדוּשֶׁנּוּ וְהָמַם גִּלְגַּל עֶגְלָתוֹ וּפָרָשָׁיו לֹא
not his and his wheel the he and one threshing always
horses ,cart of drives ,it threshes

29 יְדֻקֶּנּוּ׃ גַּם־זֹאת מֵעִם יְהוָה צְבָאוֹת יָצָאָה הִפְלִא עֵצָה
,counsel doing comes hosts Jehovah from this Also beat do
in wonders ,forth of small it

הִגְדִּיל תּוּשִׁיָּה׃
sound making
.wisdom great

CAP. XXIX כט

CHAPTER 29

CHAPTER 29

[1] Woe to Ariel, to Ariel, the city (where) David lived! Add year to year; let feasts run their circle. [2] Then I will distress Ariel, and there shall be mourning and sorrow; and it shall be to Me as Ariel. [3] And I will camp as a circle on you, and will besiege on you siege-work; and I will lift up ramparts on you. [4] And you shall be abased, you shall speak from the ground; and your speech shall be bowed; and your voice shall be from the ground, as a spiritist; and your speech shall chirp out of the dust. [5] And the host of your strangers shall be as fine powder, and as chaff passing, the host of terrible ones—and it will be suddenly, instantly; [6] you shall be visited from Jehovah of hosts; with thunder and earthquake, and great noise; tempest and storm, and flame of devouring fire. [7] And the multitude of all the nations who fight against Ariel, even all who attack her and distress her, and her stronghold, shall be like a dream of a night vision. [8] It shall even be as when a hungry one dreams, and, behold, he is eating — but when he awakes, his soul is empty; or, as when a thirsty one dreams, and, behold, he is drinking — but when he awakes, he is faint and his soul is longing. So shall be the multitude of all the nations who fight against Mount Zion.

[9] Wait and wonder! Blind yourselves and be blind! They are drunk, but not with wine! They stagger, but not with fermented drink! [10] For Jehovah has poured out on you the spirit of deep sleep, and has closed your eyes; He has covered the prophets and

1 הוֹי אֲרִיאֵל אֲרִיאֵל קִרְיַת חָנָה דָוִד סְפוּ שָׁנָה עַל־שָׁנָה
;year on year Add !David camped the ,Ariel ,Ariel Woe
(where) city (to)

2 חַגִּים יִנְקֹפוּ׃ וַהֲצִיקוֹתִי לַאֲרִיאֵל וְהָיְתָה תַאֲנִיָּה וַאֲנִיָּה
and mourning there and ,Ariel will I Then run let feasts
;sorrow be shall compress .circle their

3 וְהָיְתָה לִּי כַּאֲרִיאֵל׃ וְחָנִיתִי כַדּוּר עָלַיִךְ וְצַרְתִּי עָלַיִךְ
on will and on a as I And .Ariel as to it and
you besiege ,you circle camp will Me be shall

4 מֻצָּב וַהֲקִמֹתִי עָלַיִךְ מְצֻרֹת׃ וְשָׁפַלְתְּ מֵאֶרֶץ תְּדַבֵּרִי
shall you the from shall you And .ramparts on will I and siege-
,speak ground ;abased be you up lift ;work

וּמֵעָפָר תִּשַּׁח אִמְרָתֵךְ וְהָיָה כְּאוֹב מֵאֶרֶץ קוֹלֵךְ וּמֵעָפָר
from and your the from a as shall And your be shall from and
dust the ;voice ground spiritist be .speech bowed dust the

5 אִמְרָתֵךְ תְּצַפְצֵף׃ וְהָיָה כְּאָבָק דַּק הֲמוֹן זָרַיִךְ וּכְמֹץ
as and your host the fine powder as shall And shall your
chaff ,strangers of be . .chirp speech

6 עֹבֵר הֲמוֹן עָרִיצִים וְהָיָה לְפֶתַע פִּתְאֹם׃ מֵעִם יְהוָה
Jehovah from —instantly ,suddenly it and terrible the ,passing
of be will —ones of host

צְבָאוֹת תִּפָּקֵד בְּרַעַם וּבְרַעַשׁ וְקוֹל גָּדוֹל סוּפָה וּסְעָרָה
and tempest ,great and with and with shall you hosts
storm noise ,earthquake ,thunder :visited be

7 וְלַהַב אֵשׁ אוֹכֵלָה׃ וְהָיָה כַּחֲלוֹם חֲזוֹן לַיְלָה הֲמוֹן כָּל־
all the night a a as shall And .devouring fire and
of multitude of vision ,dream be of flame

הַגּוֹיִם הַצֹּבְאִים עַל־אֲרִיאֵל וְכָל־צֹבֶיהָ וּמְצֹדָתָהּ וְהַמְּצִיקִים
and her and fighting even ,Ariel against who the
compressing ,stronghold her all fight nations

8 לָהּ׃ וְהָיָה כַּאֲשֶׁר יַחֲלֹם הָרָעֵב וְהִנֵּה אוֹכֵל וְהֵקִיץ
he but is he ,and hungry a dreams when as it And .her
awakes —eating ,behold ;one be will

וְרֵיקָה נַפְשׁוֹ וְכַאֲשֶׁר יַחֲלֹם הַצָּמֵא וְהִנֵּה שֹׁתֶה וְהֵקִיץ
he but is he ,and thirsty a dreams as or his is and
awakes —drinking ,behold ;one when ;soul empty

וְהִנֵּה עָיֵף וְנַפְשׁוֹ שׁוֹקֵקָה כֵּן יִהְיֶה הֲמוֹן כָּל־הַגּוֹיִם הַצֹּבְאִים
who the all the shall So is his and is he and
fight nations of host be .longing soul ,faint ,behold

9 עַל־הַר צִיּוֹן׃ הִתְמַהְמְהוּ וּתְמָהוּ הִשְׁתַּעַשְׁעוּ וָשֹׁעוּ
be and Blind and Wait .Zion Mount on
!blind yourselves !wonder

10 שָׁכְרוּ וְלֹא־יַיִן נָעוּ וְלֹא שֵׁכָר׃ כִּי־נָסַךְ עֲלֵיכֶם יְהוָה רוּחַ
a Jehovah you on has For (with) but They (with) but are They
of spirit out poured .liquor not ,slip !wine not ,drunk

תַּרְדֵּמָה וַיְעַצֵּם אֶת־עֵינֵיכֶם אֶת־הַנְּבִיאִים וְאֶת־רָאשֵׁיכֶם
,heads your and the your has and deep
prophets ;eyes closed ,sleep

your rulers, the seers. [11] And the whole vision to you (is) like the words of a sealed book; which they give to one knowing books, saying, Please read this; then he says, I am not able, for it (is) sealed. [12] And the book is given to one who does not know books, saying, Please read this; then he says, I do not know books. [13] And the Lord says, Because this people draws near with its mouth, and with its lips they honor Me; but its heart (is) far from Me; and their fear of Me (is) taught (by) the command (of) men—[14] therefore, behold, I am adding to do wonders with this people; the wonder, even a wonder. For the wisdom of his wise ones shall perish, and the wit of his witty ones shall (also) be hidden. [15] Woe (to) those who go deep to hide their purpose from Jehovah, and their works are in the dark; and they say, Who sees us? and, Who knows us? [16] O your perversity! Shall the former be counted as the clay? For shall the work to its maker say, He did not make me? Or shall the thing formed say to him who formed it, He had no understanding? [17] Is it not yet a little while, and Lebanon shall be turned into a fruitful field; and the fruitful field shall be counted as a forest? [18] And in that day the deaf shall hear the words of the book, and the eyes of the blind shall see out of their gloom and out of darkness. [19] And the humble shall again have joy in Jehovah, and the poor among men shall rejoice in the Holy One of Israel. [20] For the terrible one is brought to nothing; and the scorner is ended; and all that watch for evil are cut off; [21] those who make a man sin by a word, even laying a trap for the judge in the gate; and turn aside the

11 החזים כסה׃ ותהי לכם חזות הכל כדברי הספר
book the | the like of words | the whole | vision | you to | has And been | has He .covered | the ,seers

החתום אשר־יתנו אתו אל־יודע הספר לאמר קרא־נא
,Read ,please | ,saying | ,books | one knowing | to | it | they give | of which | ,sealed

12 זה ואמר לא אוכל כי חתום הוא׃ ונתן הספר על אשר
one who | to | the book | is And given | it .(is) | sealed | for | am I ,able | not | then ;this ,says he

לא־ידע ספר לאמר קרא־נא זה ואמר לא ידעתי ספר׃
.books | do I know | not | he then ,says | ;this | please | Read | ,saying | ,books | does not know

13 ויאמר אדני יען כי נגש העם הזה בפיו ובשפתיו
with and lips its | its with ,mouth | this | people | draws near | Because | the ,Lord | says And

כבדוני ולבו רחק ממני ותהי יראתם אתי מצות אנשים
(by) men | the command | Me | their of fear | and is | from ;Me | (is) far | its but heart | they ,Me honor

14 מלמדה׃ לכן הנני יוסף להפליא את־העם־הזה הפלא
the ,wonder | ,this people | with | do to wonders | am adding | I | ,behold | ,therefore | —taught

ופלא ואבדה חכמת חכמיו ובינת נבניו תסתתר׃
be shall .hidden | his ones witty | the and of wit | wise his ;ones | the of wisdom | shall For perish | a even .wonder

15 הוי המעמיקים מיהוה לסתר עצה והיה במחשך
the in dark | and are | (their) ,counsel | hide to | from Jehovah | who those deep go | Woe (to)

16 מעשיהם ויאמרו מי ראנו ומי ידענו׃ הפככם אם־
Shall | your O !perversity | knows ?us | And who | sees ?us | Who | they and ,say | their ;works

כחמר היצר יחשב כי־יאמר מעשה לעשהו לא עשני
did He ?me make | not | its to ,maker | is what made | shall say | that | be ;counted | the former | the as clay

17 ויצר אמר ליצרו לא הבין׃ הלא־עוד מעט מזער ושב
shall and return | a ,bit | little a of | yet | it Is not | under- He ?stands | not | its to ,former | say | is what Or formed

18 לבנון לכרמל והכרמל ליער יחשב׃ ושמעו ביום
day in | shall And hear | be ?reckoned | the for forest | fruitful the field | fruitful the ,field | the Lebanon

ההוא החרשים דברי־ספר ומאפל ומחשך עיני עורים
blind ones | the of eyes | from and darkness | from and gloom | ,book a | the of words | deaf the | that

19 תראינה׃ ויספו ענוים ביהוה שמחה ואביוני אדם
men | the and of poor | (have) ,joy | in Jehovah | humble ones | shall And again | shall .see

20 בקדוש ישראל יגילו׃ כי־אפס עריץ וכלה לץ ונכרתו
are and off cut | the ;scorner | is and ended | the ruthless | ceases | For | shall .rejoice | Israel | the in of One Holy

21 כל־שקדי און׃ מחטיאי אדם בדבר ולמוכיח בשער
the in gate | for even reprover the | a by ,word | man a | those sin making | ;evil | watching all for

just for a worthless thing.
[22] Therefore, thus says Jehovah, who redeemed Abraham, as to the house of Jacob: Jacob shall not be ashamed now, nor shall his face become pale now.
[23] But when he sees his children in his midst, the work of My hands, they shall sanctify My name; they shall sanctify the Holy One of Jacob and shall fear the God of Israel.
[24] Those who erred in spirit shall come to understanding, and those who murmured shall learn the teaching.

22 יְקֹשׁוּן וַיַּטּוּ בַתֹּהוּ צַדִּיק׃ לָכֵן כֹּה־אָמַר יְהוָה אֶל־
to Jehovah says thus ,Therefore the empty by and they
.righteous (pleas) turn ,ensnare

בֵּית יַעֲקֹב אֲשֶׁר פָּדָה אֶת־אַבְרָהָם לֹא־עַתָּה יֵבוֹשׁ יַעֲקֹב
,Jacob shall now Not :Abraham redeemed (He) ,Jacob the
ashamed be who of house

23 וְלֹא עַתָּה פָּנָיו יֶחֱוָרוּ׃ כִּי בִרְאֹתוֹ יְלָדָיו מַעֲשֵׂה יָדַי
My the his he when Because turn shall his now and
,hands of work ,children sees .pale face not

בְּקִרְבּוֹ יַקְדִּישׁוּ שְׁמִי וְהִקְדִּישׁוּ אֶת־קְדוֹשׁ יַעֲקֹב וְאֶת־
and ,Jacob Holy the will they and My shall they his in
of One sanctify ;name sanctify ,midst

24 אֱלֹהֵי יִשְׂרָאֵל יַעֲרִיצוּ׃ וְיָדְעוּ תֹעֵי־רוּחַ בִּינָה וְרוֹגְנִים
and discern- spirit wan- shall And shall they Israel the
murmurers ,ment of derers know .fear of God

יִלְמְדוּ־לֶקַח׃
.teaching shall
learn

CAP. XXX ל

CHAPTER 30

CHAPTER 30

[1] Woe (to) rebellious sons, says Jehovah, to make counsel, but not from Me; and to weave a web, but not (of) My Spirit, in order to add sin on sin;
[2] who set out to go down (to) Egypt, but have not asked (at) My mouth, to take refuge in the refuge of Pharaoh, and to trust in the shadow of Egypt, [3] and shall become to you the refuge of Pharaoh a shame — and relying on the shadow of Egypt a disgrace.
[4] For were in Zoan his chiefs, and his ambassadors reached (to) Hanes. [5] Every one is ashamed over a people who do not profit them, not for a help, and not for profiting, but for a shame and also for a reproach.

[6] The burden of the beasts of the south: Into the land of trouble and woe, of the lioness and the lion (are) from them, the viper and fiery, flying serpent—they carry their riches on the shoulder of young asses, and their treasures on the hump of camels, to a people who cannot profit, even Egypt; vainly and emtily they help. Therefore I

1 הוֹי בָּנִים סוֹרְרִים נְאֻם־יְהוָה לַעֲשׂוֹת עֵצָה וְלֹא מִנִּי וְלִנְסֹךְ
to and from but ,counsel make to ,Jehovah states ,rebellious sons Woe
weave ;Me not (to)

מַסֵּכָה וְלֹא רוּחִי לְמַעַן סְפוֹת חַטָּאת עַל־חַטָּאת׃
;sin on sin add to order in My (by) but a
,Spirit not ,web

2 הַהֹלְכִים לָרֶדֶת מִצְרַיִם וּפִי לֹא שָׁאָלוּ לָעוֹז בְּמָעוֹז
in take to they not My but (to) go to set who
refuge refuge ,asked mouth ,Egypt down out

3 פַּרְעֹה וְלַחְסוֹת בְּצֵל מִצְרָיִם׃ וְהָיָה לָכֶם מָעוֹז פַּרְעֹה
Pharaoh the you to shall And .Egypt the in to and ,Pharaoh's
of refuge become of shadow trust

4 לְבֹשֶׁת וְהֶחָסוּת בְּצֵל־מִצְרַיִם לִכְלִמָּה׃ כִּי־הָיוּ בְצֹעַן
in were For .disgrace a Egypt the in trust and ,shame a
Zoan of shadow

5 שָׂרָיו וּמַלְאָכָיו חָנֵס יַגִּיעוּ׃ כֹּל הִבְאִישׁ עַל־עַם לֹא־
not a over is Every .reached (to) his and his
people ashamed one Hanes ambassadors ,chiefs

יוֹעִילוּ לָמוֹ לֹא לְעֵזֶר וְלֹא לְהוֹעִיל כִּי לְבֹשֶׁת וְגַם־לְחֶרְפָּה׃
a for and a for but for and a for not ,them do who
.reproach also shame ,profiting not ,help profit

6 מַשָּׂא בַּהֲמוֹת נֶגֶב בְּאֶרֶץ צָרָה וְצוּקָה לָבִיא וָלַיִשׁ
the and the con- and distress the in the beasts the The
lion lioness ;straint of land :Negev of of burden

מֵהֶם אֶפְעֶה וְשָׂרָף מְעוֹפֵף יִשְׂאוּ עַל־כֶּתֶף עֲיָרִים חֵילֵהֶם
their young the on they —flying fiery and viper from (are)
,riches asses of shoulder carry serpent ,them

7 וְעַל־דַּבֶּשֶׁת גְּמַלִּים אוֹצְרֹתָם עַל־עַם לֹא יוֹעִילוּ׃ וּמִצְרַיִם
even can who not a to their camels the and
;Egypt ,profit people ,treasures of hump on

have cried concerning this, Their strength (is) to sit still. [8] Now come, write it before them on a tablet, and note it on a book, so that it may be for the latter day, until forever, [9] that this (is) a rebellious people, lying sons; sons who are not willing to hear the law of Jehovah; [10] who say to the seers, See not; and to visioners, Do not vision for us right things; speak smooth things to us; vision trifles. [11] Turn from the way; stretch from the path; cause the Holy One of Israel to cease from before us. [12] Therefore thus says the Holy One of Israel, Because of your rejection of this word, and your trust in oppression and perversity, even resting on it; [13] therefore this iniquity shall be to you as a broken (section) falling, like the bulging out of a high wall, the breaking of which comes suddenly, in an instant. [14] And its breaking is as the breaking of the potter's vessel, (when) broken in pieces, he has no pity, for in its breaking there shall not be found a sherd to carry fire from the hearth, nor to skim water from a well. [15] For thus says the Lord Jehovah, the Holy One of Israel, In returning and rest you shall be saved; and in quietness and hope shall be your strength. But you were not willing. [16] For you said, No! For we will flee on horse! Therefore, you shall flee. Also, you will ride on the swift! Therefore, those who pursue you shall be swift. [17] One thousand (shall flee) at the rebuke of one; at the rebuke of five, you shall flee, until you are left like a pole on the top of the mountain, and like a sign on a hill.

הֶבֶל וָרִיק יַעְזֹרוּ לָכֵן קָרָאתִי לָזֹאת רַהַב הֵם שָׁבֶת׃
sit to Their strength to have I Therefore they and vainly
.still (is) ,this called .help emptily

8 עַתָּה בּוֹא כָתְבָהּ עַל־לוּחַ אִתָּם וְעַל־סֵפֶר חֻקָּהּ וּתְהִי
it that inscribe a and before a on write ,come ,Now
be may ,it book on ,them tablet it

9 לְיוֹם אַחֲרוֹן לָעַד עַד־עוֹלָם׃ כִּי עַם מְרִי הוּא בָּנִים כֶּחָשִׁים
,lying sons this rebel- a for :forever until ,forever latter the for
,(is) lious people day

10 בָּנִים לֹא־אָבוּ שְׁמוֹעַ תּוֹרַת יְהוָה׃ אֲשֶׁר אָמְרוּ לָרֹאִים
the to say who ,Jehovah the hear to are who not sons
,seers of law willing

לֹא תִרְאוּ וְלַחֹזִים לֹא־תֶחֱזוּ־לָנוּ נְכֹחוֹת דַּבְּרוּ־לָנוּ חֲלָקוֹת
smooth to speak right for have Do not to and ;See not
,things us ;things us vision a ,visioners

11 חֲזוּ מַהֲתַלּוֹת׃ סוּרוּ מִנֵּי־דֶרֶךְ הַטּוּ מִנֵּי־אֹרַח הַשְׁבִּיתוּ
to cause the from stretch the from turn a have trifles
cease ;path ;way aside of vision

12 מִפָּנֵינוּ אֶת־קְדוֹשׁ יִשְׂרָאֵל׃ לָכֵן כֹּה אָמַר קְדוֹשׁ יִשְׂרָאֵל
,Israel Holy the says thus ,Therefore .Israel Holy the from
of One of One us before

יַעַן מָאָסְכֶם בַּדָּבָר הַזֶּה וַתִּבְטְחוּ בְּעֹשֶׁק וְנָלוֹז וַתִּשָּׁעֲנוּ
and and in you and ,this word of your Because
rely ,perversity oppression trust rejection of

13 עָלָיו׃ לָכֵן יִהְיֶה לָכֶם הֶעָוֹן הַזֶּה כְּפֶרֶץ נֹפֵל נִבְעֶה בְּחוֹמָה
a in bulging ,falling a as this iniquity to shall therefore ;it on
wall out breach you be

14 נִשְׂגָּבָה אֲשֶׁר־פִּתְאֹם לְפֶתַע יָבוֹא שִׁבְרָהּ׃ וּשְׁבָרָהּ כְּשֵׁבֶר
(is) as its And its comes an in ,suddenly which made
smashing smashing .smashing ,instant ,high

נֵבֶל יוֹצְרִים כָּתוּת לֹא יַחְמֹל וְלֹא־יִמָּצֵא בִמְכִתָּתוֹ חֶרֶשׂ
a its in there and has he not (when) a vessel's
sherd breaking found is not ;pity ,broken ;potter's

15 לַחְתּוֹת אֵשׁ מִיָּקוּד וְלַחְשֹׂף מַיִם מִגֶּבֶא׃ כִּי כֹה־
thus For from water to or the from fire take to
.pool a skim ,hearth up

אָמַר אֲדֹנָי יְהוִֹה קְדוֹשׁ יִשְׂרָאֵל בְּשׁוּבָה וָנַחַת תִּוָּשֵׁעוּן
shall you and In ,Israel Holy the ,Jehovah the says
;saved be rest returning of One Lord

16 בְּהַשְׁקֵט וּבְבִטְחָה תִּהְיֶה גְּבוּרַתְכֶם וְלֹא אֲבִיתֶם׃ וַתֹּאמְרוּ
you But were you But your shall in and in and
,said .willing not .might be trust quietness

לֹא־כִי עַל־סוּס נָנוּס עַל־כֵּן תְּנוּסוּן וְעַל־קַל נִרְכָּב עַל־כֵּן
Therefore shall we the ,Also you Therefore we horse on For !No
.ride swift on flee shall flee will

17 יִקַּלּוּ רֹדְפֵיכֶם׃ אֶלֶף אֶחָד מִפְּנֵי גַּעֲרַת אֶחָד מִפְּנֵי גַּעֲרַת
the from ;one the (flee shall) One thousand your be shall
of rebuke of rebuke from pursuers swift

חֲמִשָּׁה תָּנֻסוּ עַד אִם־נוֹתַרְתֶּם כַּתֹּרֶן עַל־רֹאשׁ הָהָר וְכַנֵּס
as and the the on the as are you until you five
sign a ,mount of top pole left ,flee shall

[18] And so Jehovah will wait, in order to be gracious to you. For this, then, He will be exalted, to have mercy on you. For Jehovah (is) a God of justice; blessed are all those who wait for Him. [19] For the people shall live in Zion at Jerusalem; you shall surely cry no more. He surely will be gracious to you at the sound of your cry; when He hears, He will answer you. [20] And the Lord gives you the bread of adversity and the water of affliction, yet your teachers shall not be moved any more, but your eyes shall see your teachers. [21] And your ears shall hear a word behind you, saying, This is the way, walk in it; when you go right, or when you go left. [22] And you shall defile the covering of the graven images of your silver, and the covering of your molten images of gold. You shall cast them away like a menstrous cloth; you shall say to it, Get away! [23] Then He shall give rain (for) your seed, with which you sow the ground; and the bread of the produce of the earth even shall be fat and plentiful; in that day, your livestock shall feed in an enlarged pasture. [24] Also the oxen and the young asses that till the ground shall eat seasoned fodder, which has been winnowed with the shovel and with the sieve. [25] And on every high mountain and on every high hill shall be rills, streams of water, in a day of great slaying, when towers fall. [26] And the moonlight shall be like the light of the sun; and the sun's light shall be sevenfold, as the light of seven days, in the day of binding up, Jehovah (binding) the break of His people, and heals the blow of His wound. Behold, the name of Jehovah comes from afar, His anger burning; and

עַל־הַגִּבְעָה׃ וְלָכֵן יְחַכֶּה יְהוָה לַחֲנַנְכֶם וְלָכֵן יָרוּם 18

is He And gracious be to Jehovah waits And .hill the on
high therefore .you to therefore

לְרַחֶמְכֶם כִּי־אֱלֹהֵי מִשְׁפָּט יְהוָה אַשְׁרֵי כָּל־חוֹכֵי לוֹ׃

for who all blessed (is) justice a for mercy have to
.Him wait (are) ;Jehovah of God ,you on

כִּי־עַם בְּצִיּוֹן יֵשֵׁב בִּירוּשָׁלִָם בָּכוֹ לֹא־תִבְכֶּה חָנוֹן 19

Surely you not surely ;Jerusalem in shall Zion in the For
.weep will live people

יָחְנְךָ לְקוֹל זַעֲקֶךָ כְּשָׁמְעָתוֹ עָנָךְ׃ וְנָתַן לָכֶם אֲדֹנָי לֶחֶם 20

bread the you to And will He He when your the at favors He
of Lord gives .you answer ,hears ;cry of sound ,you

צָר וּמַיִם לָחַץ וְלֹא־יִכָּנֵף עוֹד מוֹרֶיךָ וְהָיוּ עֵינֶיךָ רֹאוֹת

to your but your any be shall but oppres- and afflic-
see eyes be shall ,teachers more hidden not ,sion of water tion

אֶת־מוֹרֶיךָ׃ וְאָזְנֶיךָ תִּשְׁמַעְנָה דָבָר מֵאַחֲרֶיךָ לֵאמֹר זֶה 21

This ,saying from word a hear shall your And your
(is) ,you behind ears .teachers

הַדֶּרֶךְ לְכוּ בוֹ כִּי תַאֲמִינוּ וְכִי תַשְׂמְאִילוּ׃ וְטִמֵּאתֶם אֶת־ 22

you And go you or go you when in walk ,way the
defile shall .left when right ;it

צִפּוּי פְּסִילֵי כַסְפֶּךָ וְאֶת־אֲפֻדַּת מַסֵּכַת זְהָבֶךָ תִּזְרֵם כְּמוֹ

like will you your casted the the and your carved the
them strew ;gold of image of case silver of images of case

דָוָה צֵא תֹּאמַר לוֹ׃ וְנָתַן מְטַר זַרְעֲךָ אֲשֶׁר־תִּזְרַע אֶת־ 23

you (with) your rain He Then .it to shall you Go filthy a
sow which ,seed (for) give shall say ,away ;rag

הָאֲדָמָה וְלֶחֶם תְּבוּאַת הָאֲדָמָה וְהָיָה דָשֵׁן וְשָׁמֵן יִרְעֶה

shall and fat shall even the produce the the and the
feed ;fertile be ground of of bread ;ground

מִקְנֶיךָ בַּיּוֹם הַהוּא כַּר נִרְחָב׃ וְהָאֲלָפִים וְהָעֲיָרִים עֹבְדֵי 24

serving the and the Also made a (in) that day in your
asses oxen .wide pasture livestock

הָאֲדָמָה בְּלִיל חָמִיץ יֹאכֵלוּ אֲשֶׁר־זֹרֶה בָרַחַת וּבַמִּזְרֶה׃

with and the with one which shall seasoned fodder the
.fork the shovel winnows ,eat ground

וְהָיָה ׀ עַל־כָּל־הַר גָּבֹהַ וְעַל כָּל־גִּבְעָה נִשָּׂאָה פְּלָגִים 25

,rivulets lifted hill every and high moun- every on And
,up on tain be shall

יִבְלֵי־מָיִם בְּיוֹם הֶרֶג רָב בִּנְפֹל מִגְדָּלִים׃ וְהָיָה אוֹר־ 26

light shall And .towers when ,great slaying a in water streams
be fall of day of

הַלְּבָנָה כְּאוֹר הַחַמָּה וְאוֹר הַחַמָּה יִהְיֶה שִׁבְעָתַיִם כְּאוֹר

the as ,sevenfold be shall —sun s the and ;sun the the like the
of light light of light moon

שִׁבְעַת הַיָּמִים בְּיוֹם חֲבֹשׁ יְהוָה אֶת־שֶׁבֶר עַמּוֹ וּמַחַץ

the and His the Jehovah binding the in ,days seven
of wound ,people of break up of day

מַכָּתוֹ יִרְפָּא׃ הִנֵּה שֵׁם־יְהוָה בָּא מִמֶּרְחָק בֹּעֵר 27

burns from comes Jehovah the ,Behold .heals His
;afar of name blow

and (that which) rises heavy; His lips are full of fury and His tongue like a devouring fire. [28] And like an overflowing torrent, His breath shall divide to the neck, to sift the nations with the sieve of vanity, and a misleading bridle on the jaws of the peoples; [29] the song shall be to you, as the night when the feast is sanctified, and gladness of heart, as one going with the flute, to come into the mount of Jehovah, to the Rock of Israel. [30] And Jehovah shall make the majesty of His voice heard; and He shows the descent of His arm, with raging anger and flame of consuming fire, cloudburst and storm, and stones of hail. [31] For through the voice of Jehovah Assyria shall be crushed, the rod with which He strikes. [32] And every passage of the ordained staff that Jehovah causes to rest on him has been with timbrels and with harps. And in brandishing battles, He will fight with her. [33] For Topheth is ordained from yesterday. Also it (is) prepared for the king; He deepened; He widened; its pyre (with) fire and wood makes great; the breath of Jehovah burns in it like a torrent of brimstone.

אַפּוֹ וְכֹבֶד מַשָּׂאָה שְׂפָתָיו מָלְאוּ זַעַם וּלְשׁוֹנוֹ כְּאֵשׁ אֹכָלֶת׃
.devouring a like His and ,fury full are His (which that) and His
fire tongue of lips ;rises heavy ;anger

28 וְרוּחוֹ כְּנַחַל שׁוֹטֵף עַד־צַוָּאר יֶחֱצֶה לַהֲנָפָה גוֹיִם בְּנָפַת
the in nations sift to shall He the to over- a like His And
of sieve ,divide ,neck flowing torrent breath

-29 שָׁוְא וְרֶסֶן מַתְעֶה עַל לְחָיֵי עַמִּים׃ הַשִּׁיר יִהְיֶה לָכֶם
,you to shall song the ,peoples the on misleading a and ,vanity
be of jaws bridle

כְּלֵיל הִתְקַדֶּשׁ־חָג וְשִׂמְחַת לֵבָב כַּהוֹלֵךְ בֶּחָלִיל לָבוֹא
to come the with one as ,heart glad- and a is night the as
,flute going of ness ,feast sanctified when

30 בְהַר־יְהוָה אֶל־צוּר יִשְׂרָאֵל׃ וְהִשְׁמִיעַ יְהוָה אֶת־הוֹד
the Jehovah shall And .Israel the to ,Jehovah the into
of majesty heard make of Rock of mount

קוֹלוֹ וְנַחַת זְרוֹעוֹ יַרְאֶה בְּזַעַף אַף וְלַהַב אֵשׁ אוֹכֵלָה נֶפֶץ
cloud- con- fire and ,anger with ,shows He His the and His
burst ;suming of flame raging arm of descent ;voice

31 וָזֶרֶם וְאֶבֶן בָּרָד׃ כִּי־מִקּוֹל יְהוָה יֵחַת אַשּׁוּר בַּשֵּׁבֶט יַכֶּה׃
He the with ;Assyria is Jehovah the by For .hail and and
.strikes rod crushed of voice of stones storm

32 וְהָיָה כֹּל מַעֲבַר מַטֵּה מוּסָדָה אֲשֶׁר יָנִיחַ יְהוָה עָלָיו
on Jehovah causes that appoint- the passage every And
him rest to ment of staff of be will

33 בְּתֻפִּים וּבְכִנֹּרוֹת וּבְמִלְחֲמוֹת תְּנוּפָה נִלְחַם־בָּה׃ כִּי־
For with He brandishing in And with and with
.her fights of battles .harps timbrels

עָרוּךְ מֵאֶתְמוּל תָּפְתֶּה גַּם־הוּא לַמֶּלֶךְ הוּכָן הֶעְמִיק הִרְחִב
He He ,prepared the for it ,Also .Topheth from is
;widened ;deepened king (is) yesterday ordained

מְדֻרָתָהּ אֵשׁ וְעֵצִים הַרְבֵּה נִשְׁמַת יְהוָה כְּנַחַל גָּפְרִית
brimstone a like Jehovah The makes wood and (with) pyre its
of torrent of breath !great fire

בֹּעֲרָה בָּהּ׃
.it in burns

CAP. XXXI לא

CHAPTER 31

CHAPTER 31

[1] Woe (to) those who go down to Egypt for help; and lean on horses and trust in chariots, because they are many; and in horsemen, because they are very strong; but they do not look to the Holy One of Israel, nor seek Jehovah. [2] And He also (is) wise and brings evil, and will not nullify His words, but will rise against the house of the evildoers; and against the help of

1 הוֹי הַיֹּרְדִים מִצְרַיִם לְעֶזְרָה וְעַל־סוּסִים יִשָּׁעֵנוּ וַיִּבְטְחוּ עַל־
on trust and they horses and ,help for (to) who those Woe
,lean on Egypt down go (to)

רֶכֶב כִּי רָב וְעַל פָּרָשִׁים כִּי־עָצְמוּ מְאֹד וְלֹא שָׁעוּ עַל־
to they but ;very they because ,horsemen and (is it) for char-
gaze not strong are on ;great ,iotry

2 קְדוֹשׁ יִשְׂרָאֵל וְאֶת־יְהוָה לֹא דָרָשׁוּ׃ וְגַם־הוּא חָכָם וַיָּבֵא
and wise He And .seek not Jehovah and ,Israel Holy the
brings (is) also of One

רָע וְאֶת־דְּבָרָיו לֹא הֵסִיר וְקָם עַל־בֵּית מְרֵעִים וְעַל־עֶזְרַת
help the and evil- the against but turns not His and ,evil
of against doers of house rises ,aside words

3 those who work iniquity.
[3] Now Egypt (is) a man,
and not God. And their
horses (are) flesh, and not
spirit. When Jehovah
stretches out His hand, both
he who helps shall fall, and
he who is helped shall fall;
4 and they shall all fall together. [4] For thus has
said Jehovah to me, As roars
the lion, even the young
lion on his prey, when the
band of shepherds are
gathered against him, he
will not fear their voice nor
humble himself because of
their noise. So Jehovah of
hosts shall come down to
fight for Mount Zion, and
5 on its hill. [5] As birds that
fly, so Jehovah of hosts will
defend Jerusalem; and de-
fending it, He will deliver it;
6 passing over it, He will save
it. [6] Turn back to Him at
whom you have made a
deep revolt, O sons of Israel.
7 [7] For in that day each
shall despise his silver idols
and his gold idols, which
your hands have made for
you—a sin. [8] Then Assyria
shall fall by a sword, not of
(high) man; yea, a sword,
not of (low) man, shall
8 devour him. For he shall
flee for him from the sword,
and his young man shall
become slaves. [9] And his
9 stronghold will pass away
from fear; and his captains
shall tremble at the banner,
says Jehovah — whose fire is
in Zion, and His furnace in
Jerusalem.

פֹּעֲלֵי אָוֶן׃ וּמִצְרַיִם אָדָם וְלֹא־אֵל וְסוּסֵיהֶם בָּשָׂר וְלֹא־
and (are) their And .God and a (is) Now .iniquity workers
not flesh horses not ,man Egypt of

רוּחַ וַיהוָה יַטֶּה יָדוֹ וְכָשַׁל עוֹזֵר וְנָפַל עָזֻר וְיַחְדָּו כֻּלָּם
they and one the will and the will and His stretches And .spirit
all together ;helped fall ,helper stumble ,hand out Jehovah

יִכְלָיוּן׃ כִּי־כֹה אָמַר־יְהוָה ׀ אֵלַי כַּאֲשֶׁר יֶהְגֶּה הָאַרְיֵה
,lion the roars As ,me to Jehovah has thus For will
said .cease

וְהַכְּפִיר עַל־טַרְפּוֹ אֲשֶׁר יִקָּרֵא עָלָיו מְלֹא רֹעִים מִקּוֹלָם
their ,shepherds a against are when his on the even
voice of band him called ,prey lion young

לֹא יֵחָת וּמֵהֲמוֹנָם לֹא יַעֲנֶה כֵּן יֵרֵד יְהוָה צְבָאוֹת לִצְבֹּא
fight to hosts Jehovah shall So frets not at and he not
of descend .himself noise their fears

עַל־הַר־צִיּוֹן וְעַל־גִּבְעָתָהּ׃ כְּצִפֳּרִים עָפוֹת כֵּן יָגֵן יְהוָה
Jehovah will so ,fly birds As .hill its and Zion Mount on
of shield on

צְבָאוֹת עַל־יְרוּשָׁלִָם גָּנוֹן וְהִצִּיל פָּסֹחַ וְהִמְלִיט׃ שׁוּבוּ
Turn He and passing de- and shield- ,Jerusalem over · hosts
back .save will ,over ,livering ing

לַאֲשֶׁר הֶעְמִיקוּ סָרָה בְּנֵי יִשְׂרָאֵל׃ כִּי בַּיּוֹם הַהוּא יִמְאָסוּן
shall that day in For .Israel the a made have (Him) to
reject of sons revolt deep whom (at)

אִישׁ אֱלִילֵי כַסְפּוֹ וֶאֱלִילֵי זְהָבוֹ אֲשֶׁר עָשׂוּ לָכֶם יְדֵיכֶם
your for have which his the and his the each
—hands you made ,gold of idols silver of idols man

חֵטְא׃ וְנָפַל אַשּׁוּר בְּחֶרֶב לֹא־אִישׁ וְחֶרֶב לֹא־אָדָם תֹּאכְלֶנּוּ
de- shall not a and not a by Assyria Then .sin a
.him vour man (of) sword ;man (of) sword fall shall

וְנָס לוֹ מִפְּנֵי־חֶרֶב וּבַחוּרָיו לָמַס יִהְיוּ׃ וְסַלְעוֹ מִמָּגוֹר
from his And shall forced his and the from for he And
fear stronghold .become labor men young ,sword him flee shall

יַעֲבוֹר וְחַתּוּ מִנֵּס שָׂרָיו נְאֻם־יְהוָה אֲשֶׁר־אוּר לוֹ בְּצִיּוֹן
in (is) to fire whose ,Jehovah states his the at shall and pass will
,Zion Him ,chiefs banner tremble ;away

וְתַנּוּר לוֹ בִּירוּשָׁלִָם׃
in to a and
.Jerusalem Him furnace

CAP. XXXII לב

CHAPTER 32

CHAPTER 32

1
2 [1] Behold, a king shall
reign in righteousness, and
princes shall rule in judgment. [2] And a man shall
be as a hiding-place from
the wind; as a shelter from
the tempest; as streams of
water in a dry place; like the
shadow of a great rock in a
3 weary land. [3] And the
eyes of those that see shall
not be dim, and the ears of

הֵן לְצֶדֶק יִמְלָךְ־מֶלֶךְ וּלְשָׂרִים לְמִשְׁפָּט יָשֹׂרוּ׃ וְהָיָה־אִישׁ
a shall And they in for and a shall in ,Behold
man be .rule shall justice ,princes ,king reign righteousness

כְּמַחֲבֵא־רוּחַ וְסֵתֶר זָרֶם כְּפַלְגֵי־מַיִם בְּצָיוֹן כְּצֵל סֶלַע־
rock a the like a in water as ,storm covert and wind hiding a as
of shadow ;place dry of streams from from place

כָּבֵד בְּאֶרֶץ עֲיֵפָה׃ וְלֹא תִשְׁעֶינָה עֵינֵי רֹאִים וְאָזְנֵי שֹׁמְעִים
those the and those the shall And .weary a in heavy
hearing of ears ,seeing of eyes gaze not land

those who hear shall listen. [4] And the heart of the rash shall understand knowledge; and the tongue of those who stutter shall hurry to speak plainly. [5] The fool shall no more be called noble, nor a miser said to be bountiful. [6] For the fool will speak foolishness, and his heart will work iniquity, to do evil, and will utter ungodliness against Jehovah, to make the hungry soul empty; and he causes to fail drink from the thirsty. [7] And the weapons of the miser are evil; he devises wicked plots to destroy the poor with lying words, even the needy when he speaks right. [8] But the noble one counsels noble things; and he shall rise by noble things. [9] O women who are at ease, rise up! Hear my voice, confident daughters, listen to my speech: [10] You shall be shaken days on years, O confident women; for the vintage shall fail; the harvest shall not come. [11] Tremble, you women that are at ease; be shaken, confident women; strip and make yourselves bare, and put (sackcloth) on (your) loins; [12] mourning over the breasts, over the pleasant fields, over the fruitful vine. [13] Thorns (and) briers shall spring up on the land of My people; even over all the houses of joy in the jubilant city. [14] because the palace shall be forsaken; the multitude of the city forsaken; mound and tower are instead caves, until forever, a joy of wild asses; pasture for flocks; [15] until is poured out on us the Spirit from on high, and the wilderness becomes a fruitful field; and the fruitful field is reckoned as a forest. [16] Then justice shall dwell in the wilderness, and righteousness shall dwell in the fruitful field. [17] And the work of righteousness shall be peace; and the service of righteousness shall be quietness and hope forever.

4 תקשבנה׃ ולבב נמהרים יבין לדעת ולשון עלגים תמהר
shall stutterers the and ;knowl- will rash the And shall
hurry of tongue edge discern ones of heart .listen

5 לדבר צחות׃ לא־יקרא עוד לנבל נדיב ולכילי לא
not a and ,noble fool a more shall Not clear speak to
miser called be .things

6 יאמר שוע׃ כי נבל נבלה ידבר ולבו יעשה־און לעשות
do to iniq- works and ,speaks foolish- the For .generous be will
,uity heart his ness fool said

חנף ולדבר אל־יהוה תועה להריק נפש רעב ומשקה
drink and the the make to ,error Jeho- against to and ungod-
of ;hungry of soul empty vah speak liness

7 צמא יחסיר׃ וכלי כליו רעים הוא זמות יעץ לחבל
to ,devises wicked he (are) his the And causes he the
destroy schemes ;evil weapons ,miser .fail to thirsty

8 ענוים באמרי־שקר ובדבר אביון משפט׃ ונדיב נדיבות
noble the But .justice the when even ,lying with af- the
things noble needy speaks of words flicted

9 יעץ והוא על־נדיבות יקום׃ נשים שאננות קמנה
!up rise are who O .rises noble by and de-
,ease at women things he ;vises

10 שמענה קולי בנות בטחות האזנה אמרתי׃ ימים על־
on Days .word my listen ;confident daughters my Hear
to ,voice

שנה תרגזנה בטחות כי כלה בציר אסף בלי יבוא׃
shall not the the fails for confident will you a
,come harvest ;vintage ,women ,quake year

11 חרדו שאננות רגזה בטחות פשטה וערה וחגורה על־
on put and make and strip confident ,quake women ,Tremble
(sackcloth) ,bare you ;women ease at

12 חלצים׃ על־שדים ספדים על־שדי־חמד על־גפן פריה׃
.fruitful the over pleasant- fields over be breasts over (your)
vine ,ness of ,wailing ;loins

13 על אדמת עמי קוץ שמיר תעלה כי על־כל־בתי משוש
,joy houses all over even shall (and) thorns my the On
of ;up go briars people of ground

14 קריה עליזה׃ כי־ארמון נטש המון עיר עזב עפל ובחן
and mound for- is the the is palace the For .jubilant city the
tower ;saken city of crowd ;left

היה בעד מערות עד־עולם משוש פראים מרעה עדרים׃
,flocks pasture wild joy a ,forever till caves instead are
for ;asses of

15 עד־יערה עלינו רוח ממרום והיה מדבר לכרמל וכרמל
the and fruitful a wilder- the and on from the upon poured is until
field fruitful ;field ness becomes ,high Spirit us out

16 ליער יחשב׃ ושכן במדבר משפט וצדקה בכרמל
fruit- the in and ,justice the in shall Then is a as
field ful righteousness wilderness dwell .reckoned forest

17 תשב׃ והיה מעשה הצדקה שלום ועבדת הצדקה השקט
quietness righteous- the and ;peace righteous- the shall And shall
ness of service ness of work be .dwell

[18] And My people shall live in a peaceful home, and in safe dwellings, and in secure resting places. [19] Though it hails when the forest (is) felled, and the city is laid low, [20] blessed (are) you who sow beside all waters, who send out the foot of the ox and the ass.

18 וָבֶטַח עַד־עוֹלָם׃ וְיָשַׁב עַמִּי בִּנְוֵה שָׁלוֹם וּבְמִשְׁכְּנוֹת
in and ,peace a in My shall And .forever till and
of dwellings of home people dwell trust

19 מִבְטַחִים וּבִמְנוּחֹת שַׁאֲנַנּוֹת׃ וּבָרַד בְּרֶדֶת הַיָּעַר וּבַשִּׁפְלָה
the in and the (is) when Though .secure resting and ,safety
place low ,forest felled hails it places in

20 תִּשְׁפַּל הָעִיר׃ אַשְׁרֵיכֶם זֹרְעֵי עַל־כָּל־מָיִם מְשַׁלְּחֵי רֶגֶל־
the send who ,waters all beside who blessed the laid is
of foot out sow you (are) ,city low

הַשּׁוֹר וְהַחֲמוֹר׃
the and the
.ass ox

CAP. XXXIII לג

CHAPTER 33

CHAPTER 33

[1] Woe to you, destroyer, and you who have not been destroyed; traitor, though they have not betrayed you! When you stop plundering, you shall be plundered; when you stop being a traitor, they shall betray you. [2] O Jehovah, be gracious to us; we have hoped in You; be their arm in the mornings, our salvation also in time of distress. [3] At the sound of the tumult, the peoples fled; at Your exaltation, nations scattered. [4] And shall be gathered your prey, as gathers the caterpillar; he runs on it like the running to and fro of locusts. [5] Jehovah is exalted, for (He) lives on high; He has filled Zion (with) justice and righteousness. [6] And He will be the security of your times, strength of salvation, wisdom and knowledge; the fear of Jehovah, it (is) HIs treasure. [7] Behold, their heroes shall cry outside; the envoys of peace shall weep bitterly. [8] The roads are deserted, the path-crosser ceases. He has broken the treaty; he has despised the cities; he respected no man. [9] The land mourns (and) droops; Lebanon is ashamed (and) withers; Sharon is like a wilderness; Bashan and Carmel shaken out. [10] Now I will rise up, says Jehovah; now I will be exalted; now I will be lifted up: [11] You shall conceive chaff; you

1 הוֹי שׁוֹדֵד וְאַתָּה לֹא שָׁדוּד וּבוֹגֵד וְלֹא־בָגְדוּ בָךְ כַּהֲתִמְךָ
you As !you they and and being not you and the Woe
finish betrayed not ,betrayer ;destroyed ,destroyer (to)

2 שׁוֹדֵד תּוּשַּׁד כַּנְּלֹתְךָ לִבְגֹּד יִבְגְּדוּ־בָךְ׃ יְהוָה חָנֵּנוּ
favor O .you they ,betraying you as be will you destroy-
,us ,Jehovah betray shall stop ;destroyed ,ing

לְךָ קִוִּינוּ הֱיֵה זְרֹעָם לַבְּקָרִים אַף־יְשׁוּעָתֵנוּ בְּעֵת צָרָה׃
.distress in our also the in their be have we in
of time salvation ,mornings arm ;hoped You

3 מִקּוֹל הָמוֹן נָדְדוּ עַמִּים מֵרוֹמְמֻתֶךָ נָפְצוּ גּוֹיִם׃ וְאֻסַּף
4
shall And .nations scat- Your at ;peoples fled tumult the At
gathered be tered exaltation of sound

5 שְׁלַלְכֶם אֹסֶף הֶחָסִיל כְּמַשַּׁק גֵּבִים שֹׁקֵק בּוֹ׃ נִשְׂגָּב
is on runs he ,locusts to run as locust the (as) your
exalted .it about fro and ;larvae gathers prey

6 יְהוָה כִּי שֹׁכֵן מָרוֹם מִלֵּא צִיּוֹן מִשְׁפָּט וּצְדָקָה׃ וְהָיָה
He And righ- and (with) Zion has He on (He) for ,Jehovah
be will .teousness justice filled ;high lives

אֱמוּנַת עִתֶּיךָ חֹסֶן יְשׁוּעֹת חָכְמַת וָדָעַת יִרְאַת יְהוָה הִיא
it ,Jehovah the and ,wisdom ,salvation wealth your the
(is) of fear ;knowledge of ,times of security

7 אוֹצָרוֹ׃ הֵן אֶרְאֶלָּם צָעֲקוּ חֻצָה מַלְאֲכֵי שָׁלוֹם
peace the ;outside cry their ,Behold His
of envoys heroes .treasure

8 מַר יִבְכָּיוּן׃ נָשַׁמּוּ מְסִלּוֹת שָׁבַת עֹבֵר אֹרַח הֵפֵר בְּרִית
the has He ;path- the ceases ;highways are shall bitterly
;covenant broken crosser deserted .weep

9 מָאַס עָרִים לֹא חָשַׁב אֱנוֹשׁ׃ אָבַל אֻמְלְלָה אֶרֶץ הֶחְפִּיר
is the (and) Mourns .man he not ;cities has he
ashamed ;land droops respected rejected

לְבָנוֹן קָמַל הָיָה הַשָּׁרוֹן כָּעֲרָבָה וְנֹעֵר בָּשָׁן וְכַרְמֶל׃
and ,Bashan is and a like Sharon Is wither- .Lebanon
.Carmel out shaken ,desert ing

10 עַתָּה אָקוּם יֹאמַר יְהוָה עַתָּה אֵרוֹמָם עַתָּה אֶנָּשֵׂא׃ תַּהֲרוּ
11
shall You be will I now be will I Now ;Jehovah says will I Now
conceive .up lifted ;exalted ,up rise

shall bear stubble — your fiery breath shall devour you. [12] And peoples shall be (as) the burnings of lime; (as) thorns cut away, they shall be burned in fire. [13] Distant ones, hear what I have done; and you (who are) near, acknowledge My might.

[14] The sinners in Zion are afraid; terror has seized the hypocrites: Who of us shall tarry (with) consuming fire? Who of us shall tarry (with) everlasting burnings? [15] He who walks righteously and speaks uprightly; he who despises the gain of oppressions, who shakes his hands free from holding the bribe, who stops his ear from hearing of blood, and shuts his eyes from seeing evil — [16] he shall live on high! his refuge (shall be) the strongholds of rocks, His bread shall be given; his waters are sure. [17] Your eyes shall see the king in his beauty; they shall see a land that is very far off. [18] Your heart shall ponder terror; Where (is) the scribe? Where (is) the weigher? Where is he who counted the towers? [19] You shall not see the fierce people, a people of a difficult lip, or a foreign tongue (that) none can understand. [20] Behold, Zion, the city of our set meetings! Your eyes shall see Jerusalem, a quiet home, a tent that shall not be carried away -- not one of its stakes shall ever be moved, nor shall any of its cords be broken. [21] But there majestic Jehovah (will be) to us a place of rivers and broad streams, in which no ship with oars shall go in it. and a majestic boat shall not pass through it. [22] For Jehovah is our judge; Jehovah is our lawgiver; Jehovah is our king; He will save us. [23] Your ropes are loosened, they could not hold their mast

12 חֲשַׁשׁ תֵּלְדוּ קַשׁ רוּחֲכֶם אֵשׁ תֹּאכַלְכֶם׃ וְהָיוּ עַמִּים
peoples And shall ,fire a your —stubble you ;chaff
be shall .you devour ,breath bear shall

13 מִשְׂרְפוֹת שִׂיד קוֹצִים כְּסוּחִים בָּאֵשׁ יִצַּתּוּ׃ שִׁמְעוּ
,Hear shall they fire in cut thorns ,lime burnings
.burned be ;away of

14 רְחוֹקִים אֲשֶׁר עָשִׂיתִי וּדְעוּ קְרוֹבִים גְּבֻרָתִי׃ פָּחֲדוּ בְצִיּוֹן
in Are My near and have I what distant
Zion afraid .might ,ones know ;done ,ones

חַטָּאִים אָחֲזָה רְעָדָה חֲנֵפִים מִי ׀ יָגוּר לָנוּ אֵשׁ אוֹכֵלָה
?consuming (with) of shall who profane terror has ;sinners
fire us tarry ;ones seized

15 מִי־יָגוּר לָנוּ מוֹקְדֵי עוֹלָם׃ הֹלֵךְ צְדָקוֹת וְדֹבֵר מֵישָׁרִים
right and righteously who He for- (with) of shall Who
,things speaks walks ?ever burnings us tarry

מֹאֵס בְּבֶצַע מַעֲשַׁקּוֹת נֹעֵר כַּפָּיו מִתְּמֹךְ בַּשֹּׁחַד אֹטֵם אָזְנוֹ
his who the from his who ,oppressions gain who he
ear stops ,bribe taking palms shakes of rejects

16 מִשְּׁמֹעַ דָּמִים וְעֹצֵם עֵינָיו מֵרְאוֹת בְּרָע׃ הוּא מְרוֹמִים
high (on) He .evil at from his and ,blood from
places looking eyes shuts of hearing

יִשְׁכֹּן מְצָדוֹת סְלָעִים מִשְׂגַּבּוֹ לַחְמוֹ נִתָּן מֵימָיו נֶאֱמָנִים׃
faith- are his be shall His his rocks Strongholds shall
.ful waters ;given bread .retreat (be will) of !live

17 18 מֶלֶךְ בְּיָפְיוֹ תֶּחֱזֶינָה עֵינֶיךָ תִּרְאֶינָה אֶרֶץ מַרְחַקִּים׃ לִבְּךָ
Your off far a shall they your shall his in The
heart .places of land see ;eyes behold beauty king

יֶהְגֶּה אֵימָה אַיֵּה סֹפֵר אַיֵּה שֹׁקֵל אַיֵּה סֹפֵר אֶת־הַמִּגְדָּלִים׃
the who he Where the Where the Where .terror shall
?towers counted (is) ?weigher (is) ?scribe (is) ponder

19 אֶת־עַם נוֹעָז לֹא תִרְאֶה עַם עִמְקֵי שָׂפָה מִשְּׁמוֹעַ נִלְעַג
foreign from lip difficult a shall you not fierce The
of ;hearing of people ;see people

20 לָשׁוֹן אֵין בִּינָה׃ חֲזֵה צִיּוֹן קִרְיַת מוֹעֲדֵנוּ עֵינֶיךָ תִרְאֶינָה
shall Your set our the ,Zion Be- under- (which) ,tongue
see eyes .meetings of city hold .stands none

יְרוּשָׁלִַם נָוֶה שַׁאֲנָן אֹהֶל בַּל־יִצְעָן בַּל־יִסַּע יְתֵדֹתָיו לָנֶצַח
for- its be shall not be shall not tent a ,quiet a ,Jerusalem
,ever stakes up pulled ,removed home

21 וְכָל־חֲבָלָיו בַּל־יִנָּתֵקוּ׃ כִּי אִם־שָׁם אַדִּיר יְהוָה לָנוּ
for Jehovah ma- there But be shall not its and
us (be will) jestic .off pulled cords all

מְקוֹם־נְהָרִים יְאֹרִים רַחֲבֵי יָדָיִם בַּל־תֵּלֶךְ בּוֹ אֳנִי־שַׁיִט
;oars ship a in shall not both broad (and) ,rivers of place a
with it go ;hands on ,streams

22 וְצִי אַדִּיר לֹא יַעַבְרֶנּוּ׃ כִּי יְהוָה שֹׁפְטֵנוּ יְהוָה מְחֹקְקֵנוּ
our Jehovah our Jehovah For pass shall not majestic and
;lawgiver (is) ;judge (is) .it through boat a

23 יְהוָה מַלְכֵּנוּ הוּא יוֹשִׁיעֵנוּ׃ נִטְּשׁוּ חֲבָלָיִךְ בַּל־יְחַזְּקוּ כֵן
the they not Your are save will He our Jehovah
of base hold ;ropes loosened .us ;king (is)

תָּרְנָם בַּל־פָּרְשׂוּ נֵס אָז חֻלַּק עַד־שָׁלָל מַרְבֶּה פִּסְחִים בָּזְזוּ
spoil the ;much plunder the shall Then the they not their
lame of prey divided sail spread ;mast

24 בַּז׃ וּבַל־יֹאמַר שָׁכֵן חָלִיתִי הָעָם הַיֹּשֵׁב בָּהּ נְשֻׂא עָוֺן׃
ini- taken is in who the am I inhabi- shall And the
.quity away ;it live people ;sick ,tant say not .spoil

CAP. XXXIV לד

CHAPTER 34

1 קִרְבוּ גוֹיִם לִשְׁמֹעַ וּלְאֻמִּים הַקְשִׁיבוּ תִּשְׁמַע הָאָרֶץ וּמְלֹאָהּ
its and the Let !listen and ;hear to nations Come
,fullness ,earth hear ,peoples ,near

2 תֵּבֵל וְכָל־צֶאֱצָאֶיהָ׃ כִּי קֶצֶף לַיהוָה עַל־כָּל־הַגּוֹיִם וְחֵמָה
and the all (is) to wrath For its and the
fury ,nations on Jehovah .offspring all world

3 עַל־כָּל־צְבָאָם הֶחֱרִימָם נְתָנָם לַטָּבַח׃ וְחַלְלֵיהֶם יֻשְׁלָכוּ
be shall their And to gave He de- has He their all on
;out cast slain .slaughter them ;them voted ;army

4 וּפִגְרֵיהֶם יַעֲלֶה בָאְשָׁם וְנָמַסּוּ הָרִים מִדָּמָם׃ וְנָמַקּוּ כָּל־
all shall And their with moun- shall and their shall (from) and
dissolved be .blood tains melt ;stench rise carcases their

צְבָא הַשָּׁמַיִם וְנָגֹלּוּ כַסֵּפֶר הַשָּׁמָיִם וְכָל־צְבָאָם יִבּוֹל כִּנְבֹל
as shall their then the a like shall and the the
droops, ,droop host / all ;heavens scroll rolled be ;heavens of host

5 עָלֶה מִגֶּפֶן וּכִנֹבֶלֶת מִתְּאֵנָה׃ כִּי־רִוְּתָה בַשָּׁמַיִם חַרְבִּי
My the in is For a from the as and the off leaf a
.sword heavens drenched .tree fig drooping ;vine

6 הִנֵּה עַל־אֱדוֹם תֵּרֵד וְעַל־עַם חֶרְמִי לְמִשְׁפָּט׃ חֶרֶב
A for My the and shall it Edom on Be-
sword .judgment ,ban of people on ;descend ,hold

לַיהוָה מָלְאָה דָם הֻדַּשְׁנָה מֵחֵלֶב מִדַּם כָּרִים וְעַתּוּדִים
and lambs the with with is it (with) is it to (is)
,goats of blood ,fatness fat made ;blood filled ;Jehovah

מֵחֵלֶב כִּלְיוֹת אֵילִים כִּי זֶבַח לַיהוָה בְּבָצְרָה וְטֶבַח גָּדוֹל
great a and in to sac- a for —rams the the with
slaughter ,Bozrah Jehovah (is) rifice of kidneys of fat

7 בְּאֶרֶץ אֱדוֹם׃ וְיָרְדוּ רְאֵמִים עִמָּם וּפָרִים עִם־אַבִּירִים
strong with and with wild shall And .Edom the in
,(bulls) bullocks ,them oxen down come of land

8 וְרִוְּתָה אַרְצָם מִדָּם וַעֲפָרָם מֵחֵלֶב יְדֻשָּׁן׃ כִּי יוֹם נָקָם
ven- the For made with their and with their is and
geance of day .fat fatness dust ,blood land drenched

9 לַיהוָה שְׁנַת שִׁלּוּמִים לְרִיב צִיּוֹן׃ וְנֶהֶפְכוּ נְחָלֶיהָ לְזֶפֶת
to its shall And .Zion the for repay- the to (is)
,pitch torrents turned be of cause ments of year ,Jehovah

10 וַעֲפָרָהּ לְגָפְרִית וְהָיְתָה אַרְצָהּ לְזֶפֶת בֹּעֵרָה׃ לַיְלָה וְיוֹמָם
day or Night .burning pitch land its shall and brim- to its and
become ,stone dust

לֹא תִכְבֶּה לְעוֹלָם יַעֲלֶה עֲשָׁנָהּ מִדּוֹר לָדוֹר תֶּחֱרָב לְנֵצַח
forever shall it gen- to From .smoke its shall forever shall it not
;waste lie eration generation arise ;out put be

firm, they could not spread the sail. Then the prey of much plunder will be divided; the lame shall spoil the spoil. [24] And a dweller shall not say, I am sick; the people who live in it, Iniquity is taken away.

CHAPTER 34

[1] Nations, come near to hear; and listen, O peoples! Let the earth hear, and its fullness, the world and all its offspring. [2] For Jehovah's wrath (is) on all the nations, and fury on all their army; He has completely destroyed them; He has delivered them to slaughter. [3] And their slain shall be thrown out; and the stench from their carcases shall rise; and the mountains shall be melted with their blood. [4] And all the host of the heavens shall be dissolved, and shall be rolled together like a scroll the heavens; then all their host shall droop, as a leaf droops off the vine, and as the drooping one from a fig-tree. [5] For My sword is drenched in the heavens. Behold, it shall descend on Edom; and on the people of My curse, for judgment. [6] A sword (is) to Jehovah, it is filled (with) blood; it is made fat with fatness, with the blood of lambs and goats, with the fat of the kidneys of rams — for Jehovah (has) a sacrifice in Bozrah, and a great slaughter in the land of Edom. [7] And wild oxen shall come down with them, and bullocks with strong (ones); and their land is drenched with blood, and their dust made fat with fatness. [8] For the day of vengeance (is) to Jehovah, the year of repayments for Zion's cause. [9] And its torrents shall be turned to pitch, and its dust to brimstone; and its land shall become burning pitch. [10] It shall not be put out night or day; its smoke shall rise forever. From generation to generation, it shall lie waste; no one shall pass

through it forever (and) ever. [11] But the owl and the hedgehog shall possess it; and the eared owl and the raven shall live in it. And He shall stretch out on it the line of shame, and the stones of emptiness. [12] They shall call its nobles (to) a kingdom, but none (shall be) there; and all her chiefs shall be nothing. [13] And thorns shall grow in her palaces, nettles and thistles in its fortresses; and it shall be a home for jackals, a court for daughters of ostriches. [14] The wild beasts of the desert shall also meet with the howling beasts; and the shaggy goat shall cry to his fellow. The screech owl shall also settle there, and find a place of rest for herself. [15] The arrow-snake shall nest there, and shall lay and hatch, and shall gather in her shadow. Vultures shall also be gathered together, each with its mate. [16] Search and read from the book of Jehovah — not one of these fails, each does not miss her mate; for He has commanded my mouth; and His Spirit, He has gathered them. [17] And He has cast a lot for them, and His hand divided it to them by line. They shall possess it till forever, from generation to generation they shall live in it.

11 נְצָחִים אֵין עֹבֵר בָּהּ׃ וִירֵשׁוּהָ קָאַת וְקִפּוֹד וְיַנְשׁוֹף וְעֹרֵב
and eared and and owl shall But through passes no (and)
raven owl ;hedgehog it possess .it one forever

12 יִשְׁכְּנוּ־בָהּ וְנָטָה עָלֶיהָ קַו־תֹהוּ וְאַבְנֵי־בֹהוּ׃ חֹרֶיהָ וְאֵין
even Its .emptiness and shame- the it on He And in shall
none ,nobles of stones ness of line stretch shall .it live

13 שָׁם מְלוּכָה יִקְרָאוּ וְכָל־שָׂרֶיהָ יִהְיוּ אָפֶס׃ וְעָלְתָה אַרְמְנֹתֶיהָ
her (in) shall And .nothing shall her and they a (to) (are)
palaces up go be chiefs all ;call shall kingdom ;there

סִירִים קִמּוֹשׂ וָחוֹחַ בְּמִבְצָרֶיהָ וְהָיְתָה נְוֵה תַנִּים חָצִיר
a ,jackals a it and its in and nettles ,thorns
court for home be shall ;fortresses thistles

14 לִבְנוֹת יַעֲנָה׃ וּפָגְשׁוּ צִיִּים אֶת־אִיִּים וְשָׂעִיר עַל־רֵעֵהוּ
his to the and the with desert shall Also .ostriches for
fellow goat shaggy ;howlers creatures meet of daughters

15 יִקְרָא אַךְ־שָׁם הִרְגִּיעָה לִּילִית וּמָצְאָה לָהּ מָנוֹחַ׃ שָׁמָּה
There place a for and screech the shall there Also shall
.rest of herself find ,owl settle .call

קִנְּנָה קִפּוֹז וַתְּמַלֵּט וּבָקְעָה וְדָגְרָה בְצִלָּהּ אַךְ־שָׁם נִקְבְּצוּ
be shall there Also her in shall and and shall and the shall
assembled .shadow gather ,hatch ,lay ,snake nest

16 דַיּוֹת אִשָּׁה רְעוּתָהּ׃ דִּרְשׁוּ מֵעַל־סֵפֶר יְהוָה וּקְרָאוּ
and Jehovah the from Search her (with) each ,hawks
—read of book .mate

אַחַת מֵהֵנָּה לֹא נֶעְדָּרָה אִשָּׁה רְעוּתָהּ לֹא פָקָדוּ כִּי־פִי
my for lack- not her each does not of one
,mouth ;ing mate -miss these

17 הוּא צִוָּה וְרוּחוֹ הוּא קִבְּצָן׃ וְהוּא־הִפִּיל לָהֶן גּוֹרָל
,lot a for has He And has He His and has He
them cast .them assembled ,Spirit ,commanded

וְיָדוֹ חִלְּקַתָּה לָהֶם בַּקָּו עַד־עוֹלָם יִירָשׁוּהָ לְדוֹר וָדוֹר
gen- and gen- to shall they forever Till a by to divided has His and
eration eration ,it possess .line them it hand

יִשְׁכְּנוּ־בָהּ׃
in shall they
.it live

CAP. XXXV לה

CHAPTER 35

CHAPTER 35

[1] The wilderness and and dry land shall rejoice for them; and the desert shall exult and bloom like the crocus. [2] Blooming it shall bloom and exult, also (with) joy and singing. Lebanon's glory shall be given it, the honor of Carmel and Sharon — they shall see the glory of Jehovah, the majesty of our God. [3] Strengthen the weak hands and firm up the feeble knees. [4] Say to

1 יְשֻׂשׂוּם מִדְבָּר וְצִיָּה וְתָגֵל עֲרָבָה וְתִפְרַח כַּחֲבַצָּלֶת׃
the like and the shall and dry and wilderness joy Shall
.crocus bloom desert exult ;land them for

2 פָּרֹחַ תִּפְרַח וְתָגֵל אַף גִּילַת וְרַנֵּן כְּבוֹד הַלְּבָנוֹן נִתַּן־לָהּ
to shall Lebanon The and (with) also and shall it Surely
,it given be of glory .singing joy ,exult bloom

הֲדַר הַכַּרְמֶל וְהַשָּׁרוֹן הֵמָּה יִרְאוּ כְבוֹד־יְהוָה הֲדַר אֱלֹהֵינוּ׃
.God our the ,Jehovah the shall They and Carmel the
of honor of glory see .Sharon of honor

3
4 חַזְּקוּ יָדַיִם רָפוֹת וּבִרְכַּיִם כֹּשְׁלוֹת אַמֵּצוּ׃ אִמְרוּ
Say firm stumbling the and ,sinking the Stengthen
.up knees hands

those of a hasty heart, Be strong! Fear not! See, your God will come with vengeance; He will come with God's reward and will save you. [5] Then the eyes of the blind shall be opened and the ears of the deaf shall be opened. [6] Then the lame man shall leap like a deer, and the tongue of the dumb shall sing. For waters shall break out in the wilderness, and streams in the desert. [7] And the mirage shall become a pool, and the thirsty land shall become springs of waters; in the home of jackals, in its lair, and a place for the reed and rush. [8] And a highway shall be there, and a way, and it shall be called, The Way of Holiness. The unclean shall not pass over it. And it (is) for them, the wayfaring one; yea, fools shall not go astray. [9] No lion shall be there; no violent one shall go up on it; it shall not be found there. But the redeemed shall walk there. [10] And the ransomed of Jehovah shall return and enter Zion with singing. And they shall attain joy and gladness, everlasting joy on their head. And sorrow and sighing shall flee.

לְנִמְהֲרֵי־לֵב חִזְקוּ אַל־תִּירָאוּ הִנֵּה אֱלֹהֵיכֶם נָקָם יָבוֹא
will (with) your ,Behold !Fear not Be ,heart the to
;come vengeance God !strong of hasty

5 גְּמוּל אֱלֹהִים הוּא יָבוֹא וְיֹשַׁעֲכֶם׃ אָז תִּפָּקַחְנָה עֵינֵי עִוְרִים
the the be shall Then save and will He ,God full the
,blind of eyes opened .you come of dealing

6 וְאָזְנֵי חֵרְשִׁים תִּפָּתַחְנָה׃ אָז יְדַלֵּג כָּאַיָּל פִּסֵּחַ וְתָרֹן לְשׁוֹן
the shall and the a like shall Then be shall deaf the the and
of tongue sing ,lame deer leap .opened of ears

7 אִלֵּם כִּי־נִבְקְעוּ בַמִּדְבָּר מַיִם וּנְחָלִים בָּעֲרָבָה׃ וְהָיָה
shall And the in and ,waters the in shall For the
become .desert torrents wilderness out break .dumb

הַשָּׁרָב לַאֲגַם וְצִמָּאוֹן לְמַבּוּעֵי מָיִם בִּנְוֵה תַנִּים רִבְצָהּ
rest- its ,jackals the in ;water of springs the and ,pool a parched the
;place ing of home land thirsty ground

8 חָצִיר לְקָנֶה וָגֹמֶא׃ וְהָיָה־שָׁם מַסְלוּל וָדֶרֶךְ וְדֶרֶךְ הַקֹּדֶשׁ
Holiness the and a and a there And and ,reed for ,grass
of Way ,way ,highway be shall .rush

יִקָּרֵא לָהּ לֹא־יַעַבְרֶנּוּ טָמֵא וְהוּא־לָמוֹ הֹלֵךְ דֶּרֶךְ וֶאֱוִילִים
fools and the the for And the pass shall Not .it to shall
.way of goer ;them (is) it .unclean .it over called be

9 לֹא יִתְעוּ׃ לֹא־יִהְיֶה שָׁם אַרְיֵה וּפְרִיץ חַיּוֹת בַּל־יַעֲלֶנָּה
go shall not beasts a and ,lion a there shall Not go shall not
;it on up of one violent be .astray

10 לֹא תִמָּצֵא שָׁם וְהָלְכוּ גְּאוּלִים׃ וּפְדוּיֵי יְהוָה יְשֻׁבוּן וּבָאוּ
and shall Jehovah the And redeemed shall But .there shall it not
enter return of ransomed .ones walk found be

צִיּוֹן בְּרִנָּה וְשִׂמְחַת עוֹלָם עַל־רֹאשָׁם שָׂשׂוֹן וְשִׂמְחָה יַשִּׂיגוּ
shall and gladness their on ever- joy and with Zion
reach joy ,head lasting singing
.(them)

וְנָסוּ יָגוֹן וַאֲנָחָה׃
and sorrow And
.sighing flee shall

CAP. XXXVI לו

CHAPTER 36

CHAPTER 36

[1] And it happened, in the fourteenth year of King Hezekiah, that Sennacherib king of Assyria came against all the fortified cities of Judah, and took them. [2] And the king of Assyria sent Rabshakeh from Lachish to Jerusalem to King Hezekiah with a great army. And he stood by the conduit of the upper pool, in the highway of the Fuller's Field. [3] Then Eliakim, Hilkiah's son, who

1 וַיְהִי בְּאַרְבַּע עֶשְׂרֵה שָׁנָה לַמֶּלֶךְ חִזְקִיָּהוּ עָלָה סַנְחֵרִיב
Sennacherib came ,Hezekiah King of year the in it And
up fourteenth ,was

2 מֶלֶךְ־אַשּׁוּר עַל־כָּל־עָרֵי יְהוּדָה הַבְּצֻרוֹת וַיִּתְפְּשֵׂם׃ וַיִּשְׁלַח
sent And took and ,fortified Judah the all against Assyria king
.them of cities of

מֶלֶךְ־אַשּׁוּר ׀ אֶת־רַבְשָׁקֵה מִלָּכִישׁ יְרוּשָׁלַיְמָה אֶל־הַמֶּלֶךְ
King to to from Rabshakeh Assyria the
Jerusalem Lachish of king

חִזְקִיָּהוּ בְּחֵיל כָּבֵד וַיַּעֲמֹד בִּתְעָלַת הַבְּרֵכָה הָעֶלְיוֹנָה
,upper pool the the by he And .massive with Hezekiah
of conduit stood army a

3 בִּמְסִלַּת שְׂדֵה כוֹבֵס׃ וַיֵּצֵא אֵלָיו אֶלְיָקִים בֶּן־חִלְקִיָּהוּ אֲשֶׁר
who ,Hilkiah son ,Eliakim to Then the field the in
(was) of him out came .fuller's of highway

(was) over the house, and Shebna the scribe, and Asaph's son Joah, the recorder, came out to him. [4] And Rabshakeh said to them, Say now to Hezekiah: The great king says this, the king of Assyria, What trust (is) this in which you trust? [5] I say, (Are) only words of the lips counsel and strength for war? Now, in whom have you trusted, that you have rebelled against me? [6] Lo, you trust in the staff of this broken reed, on Egypt—which if a man leans on it, it goes into his palm and pierces it. So (is) Pharaoh king of Egypt to all who trust in him. [7] But if you say to me, We trust in Jehovah our God: Is it not He whose high places and altars Hezekiah has removed? He said to Judah and Jerusalem, You shall worship before this altar! [8] Now, then, exchange pledges with my master the king of Assyria, and I will give you two thousand horses, if you are able to set riders on them. [9] How then will you turn away the face of one captain of the least of my master's servants, and put your trust in Egypt for chariots and horsemen?

[10] And now have I come up against this land to destroy it without Jehovah? Jehovah said to me, Go up to this land and destroy it. [11] Then Eliakim and Shebna and Joah said to Rabshakeh, Please speak to your servants (in) Aramaic, for we hear. But do

4 עַל־הַבָּיִת וְשֶׁבְנָא הַסֹּפֵר וְיוֹאָח בֶּן־אָסָף הַמַּזְכִּיר׃ וַיֹּאמֶר
And said / .recorder the / of Asaph son / Joah and / ,scribe the / Shebna and / ,house the / over

אֲלֵיהֶם רַבְשָׁקֵה אִמְרוּ־נָא אֶל־חִזְקִיָּהוּ כֹּה־אָמַר הַמֶּלֶךְ
king the says Thus ,Hezekiah to now Say ,Rabshakeh them to

הַגָּדוֹל מֶלֶךְ אַשּׁוּר מָה הַבִּטָּחוֹן הַזֶּה אֲשֶׁר בָּטָחְתָּ׃
?trust you which this trust (is) What ,Assyria the of king ,great

5 אָמַרְתִּי אַךְ־דְּבַר־שְׂפָתַיִם עֵצָה וּגְבוּרָה לַמִּלְחָמָה עַתָּה
Now the for ?battle and might counsel ,lips words of (Are) only ,say I

6 עַל־מִי בָטַחְתָּ כִּי מָרַדְתָּ בִּי׃ הִנֵּה בָטַחְתָּ עַל־מִשְׁעֶנֶת
the of staff on you trust ,Behold against ?me have you rebelled that you have trusted whom on

הַקָּנֶה הָרָצוּץ הַזֶּה עַל־מִצְרַיִם אֲשֶׁר יִסָּמֵךְ אִישׁ עָלָיו וּבָא
then comes it ,it on a man (if) leans ,which —Egypt on ,this broken reed

בְכַפּוֹ וּנְקָבָהּ כֵּן פַּרְעֹה מֶלֶךְ־מִצְרַיִם לְכָל־הַבֹּטְחִים עָלָיו׃
on .him who trust all to Egypt king of Pharaoh So (is) and .it pierces his into palm

7 וְכִי־תֹאמַר אֵלַי אֶל־יְהוָה אֱלֹהֵינוּ בָּטָחְנוּ הֲלוֹא הוּא אֲשֶׁר
of whom He it not Is we :trust God our Jehovah in ,me to you say But if

הֵסִיר חִזְקִיָּהוּ אֶת־בָּמֹתָיו וְאֶת־מִזְבְּחֹתָיו וַיֹּאמֶר לִיהוּדָה
Judah to he And said ?altars His and high His places Hezekiah has removed

8 וְלִירוּשָׁלִַם לִפְנֵי הַמִּזְבֵּחַ הַזֶּה תִּשְׁתַּחֲווּ׃ וְעַתָּה הִתְעָרֶב
exchange ,pledges Now ,then shall you !worship this altar Before to and ,Jerusalem

נָא אֶת־אֲדֹנִי הַמֶּלֶךְ אַשּׁוּר וְאֶתְּנָה לְךָ אַלְפַּיִם סוּסִים אִם־
if ,horses two thousand to you I and give will ,Assyria the of king my lord with I ,pray

9 תּוּכַל לָתֶת לְךָ רֹכְבִים עֲלֵיהֶם׃ וְאֵיךְ תָּשִׁיב אֵת פְּנֵי
the of face you will away turn How then .them on riders for you set to are you able

פַּחַת אַחַד עַבְדֵי אֲדֹנִי הַקְּטַנִּים וַתִּבְטַח לְךָ עַל־מִצְרַיִם
Egypt on for you trust and ,least the my master's servants one governor of

10 לְרֶכֶב וּלְפָרָשִׁים׃ וְעַתָּה הֲמִבַּלְעֲדֵי יְהוָה עָלִיתִי עַל־
against I have up come Jehovah without ,now And and ?horsemen for chariotry

הָאָרֶץ הַזֹּאת לְהַשְׁחִיתָהּ יְהוָה אָמַר אֵלַי עֲלֵה אֶל־הָאָרֶץ
land to up Go to ,me said Jehovah destroy to ?it this land

11 הַזֹּאת וְהַשְׁחִיתָהּ׃ וַיֹּאמֶר אֶלְיָקִים וְשֶׁבְנָא וְיוֹאָח אֶל־
to and Joah and Shebna Eliakim Then said destroy and .it this

רַבְשָׁקֵה דַּבֶּר־נָא אֶל־עֲבָדֶיךָ אֲרָמִית כִּי שֹׁמְעִים אֲנָחְנוּ
.we hear for ,Aramaic in your servants to ,please ,Speak Rab- ,shakeh

not speak to us (in) Judean, in the ears of the people on the wall. [12] But Rabshakeh said, Has my master sent me to your master and to you to speak these words? Is it not on the men who sit on the wall, to eat their own dung and to drink their own urine with you? [13] And Rabshakeh stood and cried with a loud voice (in) Judean, and said, Hear the words of the great king, the king of Assyria. [14] Thus says the king, Do not let Hezekiah deceive you, for he will not be able to save you. [15] And let not Hezekiah make you trust in Jehovah, saying, Jehovah will surely save us: This city shall not be delivered into the hand of the king of Assyria. [16] Do not listen to Hezekiah. For the king of Assyria says this: Make peace with me and come out to me; then let each eat of his own fig-tree, and each drink the waters of his own cistern, [17] until I come and move you to a land like your own land, a land of grain and new wine, a land of bread and vineyards.

[18] Lest Hezekiah persuade you, saying, Jehovah will deliver us. Have the gods of the nations delivered a man of his land from the king of Assyria's hand? [19] Where (are) the gods of Hamath, and Arpad? Where the gods of Sepharvaim? And when have they delivered out of my hand? [20] Who among all the gods of these lands has delivered his land out of my

וְאַל־תְּדַבֵּר אֵלֵינוּ יְהוּדִית בְּאָזְנֵי הָעָם אֲשֶׁר עַל־הַחוֹמָה׃
the on who the the in in us to do But
.wall (are) people of ears ,Judean speak not

12 וַיֹּאמֶר רַבְשָׁקֵה הַאֶל אֲדֹנֶיךָ וְאֵלֶיךָ שְׁלָחַנִי אֲדֹנִי לְדַבֵּר
to my sent to and your Has ,Rabshakeh But
speak master me you master to said

אֶת־הַדְּבָרִים הָאֵלֶּה הֲלֹא עַל־הָאֲנָשִׁים הַיֹּשְׁבִים עַל־
on sit who men the on it Is ?these words
not

הַחוֹמָה לֶאֱכֹל אֶת־חֲרָאֵיהֶם וְלִשְׁתּוֹת אֶת־שֵׁינֵיהֶם עִמָּכֶם׃
with their to and own their eat to the
?you urine own drink dung ,wall

13 וַיַּעֲמֹד רַבְשָׁקֵה וַיִּקְרָא בְקוֹל־גָּדוֹל יְהוּדִית וַיֹּאמֶר שִׁמְעוּ
Hear ,said and (in) loud a with and Rabshakeh Then
.Judean voice called stood

14 אֶת־דִּבְרֵי הַמֶּלֶךְ הַגָּדוֹל מֶלֶךְ אַשּׁוּר׃ כֹּה אָמַר הַמֶּלֶךְ
,king the says Thus .Assyria the ,great king the the
of king of words

15 אַל־יַשִּׁא לָכֶם חִזְקִיָּהוּ כִּי לֹא־יוּכַל לְהַצִּיל אֶתְכֶם׃ וְאַל־
And .you save to will He not for ,Hezekiah you let Do not
not able be deceive

יַבְטַח אֶתְכֶם חִזְקִיָּהוּ אֶל־יְהוָה לֵאמֹר הַצֵּל יַצִּילֵנוּ יְהוָה
,Jehovah will Surely ,saying ,Jehovah in Hezekiah you let
us save trust make

16 לֹא תִנָּתֵן הָעִיר הַזֹּאת בְּיַד מֶלֶךְ אַשּׁוּר׃ אַל־תִּשְׁמְעוּ
do Not .Assyria the the into this city be shall not
listen of king of hand delivered

אֶל־חִזְקִיָּהוּ כִּי כֹה אָמַר הַמֶּלֶךְ אַשּׁוּר עֲשׂוּ־אִתִּי בְרָכָה
a with Make ,Assyria the says thus for ;Hezekiah to
,blessing me of king

וּצְאוּ אֵלַי וְאִכְלוּ אִישׁ־גַּפְנוֹ וְאִישׁ תְּאֵנָתוֹ וּשְׁתוּ אִישׁ מֵי־
the each and his (of) and his (of) each let then ;me to and
of waters drink ,tree fig each ,vine man eat out come

17 בוֹרוֹ׃ עַד־בֹּאִי וְלָקַחְתִּי אֶתְכֶם אֶל־אֶרֶץ כְּאַרְצְכֶם אֶרֶץ
a your like a to you take and I until his
of land ,land own land come ,well

18 דָּגָן וְתִירוֹשׁ אֶרֶץ לֶחֶם וּכְרָמִים׃ פֶּן־יַסִּית אֶתְכֶם חִזְקִיָּהוּ
,Hezekiah you persuade Lest and bread land a new and grain
.vineyards of ,wine

לֵאמֹר יְהוָה יַצִּילֵנוּ הַהִצִּילוּ אֱלֹהֵי הַגּוֹיִם אִישׁ אֶת־אַרְצוֹ
his man a the gods the Have deliver will Jehovah ,saying
land of nations of delivered .us

19 מִיַּד מֶלֶךְ אַשּׁוּר׃ אַיֵּה אֱלֹהֵי חֲמָת וְאַרְפָּד אַיֵּה אֱלֹהֵי
the Where and Hamath the Where ?Assyria's the from
of gods (are) ?Arpad of gods (are) of king hand

20 סְפַרְוָיִם וְכִי־הִצִּילוּ אֶת־שֹׁמְרוֹן מִיָּדִי׃ מִי בְּכָל־אֱלֹהֵי
the among Who my from Samaria they have And Shephar-
of gods all (is) ?hand delivered when ?vaim

הָאֲרָצוֹת הָאֵלֶּה אֲשֶׁר־הִצִּילוּ אֶת־אַרְצָם מִיָּדִי כִּי־יַצִּיל
should that from their has that ,these lands
deliver ,hand my land delivered

hand, that Jehovah should keep Jerusalem out of my hand? [21] But they were quiet, and answered him not a word, for this was the king's order, saying, Do not answer him. [22] Then Eliakim the son of Hilkiah, who (was) over the house, and Shebna the scribe, and Asaph's son Joah, the recorder, came with their clothes torn to Hezekiah and reported to him Rabshakeh's words.

21 יְהוָה אֶת־יְרוּשָׁלִַם מִיָּדִי׃ וַיַּחֲרִישׁוּ וְלֹא־עָנוּ אֹתוֹ דָּבָר
a word, him answered and not, they But quiet were, my from ?hand Jerusalem Jehovah

22 כִּי־מִצְוַת הַמֶּלֶךְ הִיא לֵאמֹר לֹא תַעֲנֻהוּ׃ וַיָּבֹא אֶלְיָקִים
Eliakim Then came Answer .him not ,saying it (was) the king's command for

בֶּן־חִלְקִיָּהוּ אֲשֶׁר־עַל־הַבַּיִת וְשֶׁבְנָא הַסֹּפֵר וְיוֹאָח בֶּן
son of and Joah the ,scribe and Shebna the ,house over who (was) ,Hilkiah son of

אָסָף הַמַּזְכִּיר אֶל־חִזְקִיָּהוּ קְרוּעֵי בְגָדִים וַיַּגִּידוּ לוֹ אֵת
to him and reported ,garments (with) torn ,Hezekiah to the ,recorder ,Asaph

דִּבְרֵי רַבְשָׁקֵה׃
.Rabshakeh's words

CAP. XXXVII לז

CHAPTER 37

CHAPTER 37

[1] And it was, when King Hezekiah heard, that he tore his clothes and was covered with sackcloth, and he went into Jehovah's house. [2] And he sent Eliakim, who (was) over the house, and Shebna the scribe, and the elders of the priests covered with sackcloth, to Isaiah the prophet, the son of Amoz. [3] And they said to him, Thus says Hezekiah, This day (is) a day of trouble and reproach blasphemy! For sons have come to the breach, and there is no strength to give birth. [4] It may be Jehovah your God will hear the words of Rabshakeh, whom his master the king of Assyria has sent to reproach the living God, and to rebuke against the words which Jehovah your God has heard, and you shall lift up prayer for the remnant that is found. [5] So the servants of King Hezekiah came to Isaiah. [6] And Isaiah said to them, You shall say this to your master, Thus says Jehovah: Do not fear the words

1 וַיְהִי כִּשְׁמֹעַ הַמֶּלֶךְ חִזְקִיָּהוּ וַיִּקְרַע אֶת־בְּגָדָיו וַיִּתְכַּס בַּשָּׂק
with ,sackcloth was and covered his garments he that tore ,Hezekiah King when heard And ,was it

2 וַיָּבֹא בֵּית יְהוָה׃ וַיִּשְׁלַח אֶת־אֶלְיָקִים אֲשֶׁר־עַל־הַבַּיִת
the ,house over who (was) ,Eliakim he And sent .Jehovah the of house he and entered

וְאֵת ׀ שֶׁבְנָא הַסּוֹפֵר וְאֵת זִקְנֵי הַכֹּהֲנִים מִתְכַּסִּים בַּשַּׂקִּים
with ,sackcloth covered the priests the of elders and the ,scribe Shebna and

3 אֶל־יְשַׁעְיָהוּ בֶן־אָמוֹץ הַנָּבִיא׃ וַיֹּאמְרוּ אֵלָיו כֹּה אָמַר
says Thus ,him to they And said the .prophet ,Amoz the of son Isaiah to

חִזְקִיָּהוּ יוֹם־צָרָה וְתוֹכֵחָה וּנְאָצָה הַיּוֹם הַזֶּה כִּי־בָאוּ בָנִים
sons have For come !this (is) day and ,contempt and reproach trouble A of day ,Hezekiah

4 עַד־מַשְׁבֵּר וְכֹחַ אַיִן לְלֵדָה׃ אוּלַי יִשְׁמַע יְהוָה אֱלֹהֶיךָ
your God Jehovah will hear may it be give to .birth not and is strength the ;breach to

אֵת ׀ דִּבְרֵי רַבְשָׁקֵה אֲשֶׁר שְׁלָחוֹ מֶלֶךְ־אַשּׁוּר ׀ אֲדֹנָיו לְחָרֵף
to reproach his ,master Assyria the of king has ,him sent whom Rabshakeh the of words

אֱלֹהִים חַי וְהוֹכִיחַ בַּדְּבָרִים אֲשֶׁר שָׁמַע יְהוָה אֱלֹהֶיךָ
your ,God Jehovah has heard which the against words and rebuke living the God

5 וְנָשָׂאתָ תְפִלָּה בְּעַד הַשְּׁאֵרִית הַנִּמְצָאָה׃ וַיָּבֹאוּ עַבְדֵי
the of servants So came is that .found the remnant for prayer you and up lift shall

6 הַמֶּלֶךְ חִזְקִיָּהוּ אֶל־יְשַׁעְיָהוּ׃ וַיֹּאמֶר אֲלֵיהֶם יְשַׁעְיָהוּ כֹּה
Thus ,Isaiah them to said And .Isaiah to Hezekiah King

תֹאמְרוּן אֶל־אֲדֹנֵיכֶם כֹּה ׀ אָמַר יְהוָה אַל־תִּירָא מִפְּנֵי
from before Do fear not ,Jehovah says Thus your ,master to shall you say

which you have heard, with which the servants of the king of Assyria have blasphemed Me. [7] Behold, I will send a spirit into him and he shall hear a rumor and return to his own land. And I will cause him to fall by the sword in his own land.

[8] So Rabshakeh returned and found the king of Assyria warring against Libnah; for he had heard that he had set out from Lachish. [9] And he heard about Tirhakah king of Ethiopia, saying, He has come out to fight with you. And he heard and sent messengers to Hezekiah, saying, [10] So you shall say to Hezekiah king of Judah, saying, Do not let your God in whom you trust deceive you, saying, Jerusalem shall not be delivered into the king of Assyria's hand. [11] Lo, you have heard what the kings of Assyria have done to all lands, how they have crushed them; and shall you be saved? [12] Have the gods of the nations saved those whom my fathers have destroyed: Gozan and Haran and Rezeph, and the sons of Eden who (were) in Telassar? [13] Where (is) Hamath's king, and Arpad's king, and the king of the city of Sepharvaim, Hena, and Ivvah?

[14] And Hezekiah received the letter from the hand of the couriers and read it. Then Hezekiah went up to the house of Jehovah and spread it before Jehovah. [15] And Hezekiah prayed to Jehovah, saying, [16] O Jehovah of hosts, God of Israel, who dwells between the cherubim, You (are) He, God, You alone to all the kingdoms of the earth; You have made

הַדְּבָרִים אֲשֶׁר שָׁמַעְתָּ אֲשֶׁר גִּדְּפוּ נַעֲרֵי מֶלֶךְ־אַשּׁוּר אוֹתִי׃
.Me Assyria the the blas- with have you which words the
of king of boys phemed which ,heard

7 הִנְנִי נוֹתֵן בּוֹ רוּחַ וְשָׁמַע שְׁמוּעָה וְשָׁב אֶל־אַרְצוֹ וְהִפַּלְתִּיו
will I And his to and ,report a he and a into give ,Behold
fall him make .land return hear shall ;spirit him I

8 בַחֶרֶב בְּאַרְצוֹ׃ וַיָּשָׁב רַבְשָׁקֵה וַיִּמְצָא אֶת־מֶלֶךְ אַשּׁוּר
Assyria the and Rabshakeh So his in the by
of king found returned .land sword

9 נִלְחָם עַל־לִבְנָה כִּי שָׁמַע כִּי נָסַע מִלָּכִישׁ׃ וַיִּשְׁמַע עַל־
about he And from had he that had he for ;Libnah against fight-
heard .Lachish out set heard ing

תִּרְהָקָה מֶלֶךְ־כּוּשׁ לֵאמֹר יָצָא לְהִלָּחֵם אִתָּךְ וַיִּשְׁמַע וַיִּשְׁלַח
sent and he And with fight to has He ,saying ,Ethiopia king Tirhakah
heard .you out come of

10 מַלְאָכִים אֶל־חִזְקִיָּהוּ לֵאמֹר׃ כֹּה תֹאמְרוּן אֶל־חִזְקִיָּהוּ
Hezekiah to shall you So ,saying ,Hezekiah to messengers
say

מֶלֶךְ־יְהוּדָה לֵאמֹר אַל־יַשִּׁאֲךָ אֱלֹהֶיךָ אֲשֶׁר אַתָּה בּוֹטֵחַ
trust you whom your let Do not ,saying ,Judah King
God you deceive of

11 בּוֹ לֵאמֹר לֹא תִנָּתֵן יְרוּשָׁלַםִ בְּיַד מֶלֶךְ אַשּׁוּר׃ הִנֵּה
,Behold .Assyria's the into Jerusalem be shall Not ,saying in
of king hand delivered ,Him

אַתָּה שָׁמַעְתָּ אֲשֶׁר עָשׂוּ מַלְכֵי אַשּׁוּר לְכָל־הָאֲרָצוֹת
the to Assyria the have what have you
,lands all of kings done heard

12 לְהַחֲרִימָם וְאַתָּה תִּנָּצֵל׃ הַהִצִּילוּ אוֹתָם אֱלֹהֵי הַגּוֹיִם
the the ,them Have shall you and utterly to
nations of gods delivered ?delivered be ;them destroy

אֲשֶׁר־הִשְׁחִיתוּ אֲבוֹתַי אֶת־גּוֹזָן וְאֶת־חָרָן וְרֶצֶף וּבְנֵי־עֶדֶן
Eden and and Haran and Gozan my have whom
of sons the Rezeph :fathers destroyed

13 אֲשֶׁר בִּתְלַשָּׂר׃ אַיֵּה מֶלֶךְ־חֲמָת וּמֶלֶךְ אַרְפָּד וּמֶלֶךְ לָעִיר
the of the and ,Arpad the And ?Hamath the Where in who
of city king of king of king (is) ?Telassar (were)

14 סְפַרְוָיִם הֵנַע וְעִוָּה׃ וַיִּקַּח חִזְקִיָּהוּ אֶת־הַסְּפָרִים מִיַּד
the from the Hezekiah And and ,Hena Shephar-
of hand letters received ?Ivah ,vaim

הַמַּלְאָכִים וַיִּקְרָאֵהוּ וַיַּעַל בֵּית יְהוָה וַיִּפְרְשֵׂהוּ חִזְקִיָּהוּ
Hezekiah spread and ,Jehovah the (to) he And read and the
it of house up went .it ,messengers

15 16 לִפְנֵי יְהוָה׃ וַיִּתְפַּלֵּל חִזְקִיָּהוּ אֶל־יְהוָה לֵאמֹר׃ יְהוָה
Jehovah ,saying ,Jehovah to Hezekiah And .Jehovah before
of prayed

צְבָאוֹת אֱלֹהֵי יִשְׂרָאֵל יֹשֵׁב הַכְּרֻבִים אַתָּה־הוּא הָאֱלֹהִים
,God He You the dwelling ,Israel God ,hosts
(are) ,cherubs (between) of

לְבַדְּךָ לְכֹל מַמְלְכוֹת הָאָרֶץ אַתָּה עָשִׂיתָ אֶת־הַשָּׁמַיִם
the have You the the all to You
heavens made :earth of kingdoms ,alone

the heavens and the earth. [17] Bow down Your ear, O Jehovah, and hear; open Your eye, O Jehovah, and see; and hear all the words of Sennacherib which he has sent to reproach the living God. [18] Truly, O Jehovah, the kings of Assyria have crushed all the lands and their land, [19] and have given their gods into the fire — for they (were) not gods, only the work of men's hands, wood and stone; so they have destroyed them. [20] And now, O Jehovah our God, save us from his hand, so that all the kingdoms of the earth may know that You (are) Jehovah, You alone.

[21] And Isaiah the son of Amoz sent to Hezekiah, saying, Thus says Jehovah God of Israel, Because you have prayed to Me against Sennacherib king of Assyria, [22] this (is) the word Jehovah has spoken about him: The virgin, the daughter of Zion, has despised you, laughing you to scorn; the daughter of Jerusalem has shaken her head at you. [23] Whom have you mocked and blasphemed? And against whom have you lifted your voice, and lifted your eyes on high? Against the Holy One of Israel! [24] You have mocked the Lord and have said, By my many chariots I have come up to the mountain-tops, the sides of Lebanon; and I will cut down its tall cedars, its choice fir trees; and I will go to its greatest height, the forest of its fruitful field.

[25] I have dug and drunk water; and I have dried up all the streams of Egypt with the sole of my feet. [26] Have you not heard it from afar? I made it from days of old, even I formed it? Now I

17 וְאֶת־הָאָרֶץ׃ הַטֵּה יְהוָה ׀ אָזְנְךָ וּשְׁמָע פְּקַח יְהוָה עֵינְךָ
Your O ,open and Your O ,Incline the and
,eye ,Jehovah ;hear ear ,Jehovah .earth

וּרְאֵה וּשְׁמַע אֵת כָּל־דִּבְרֵי סַנְחֵרִיב אֲשֶׁר שָׁלַח לְחָרֵף
to has he which Sennacherib the all and and
reproach sent of words hear ;see

18 אֱלֹהִים חָי׃ אָמְנָם יְהוָה הֶחֱרִיבוּ מַלְכֵי אַשּׁוּר אֶת־כָּל־
all Assyria the laid have O ,Truly .living the
of kings waste ,Jehovah God

19 הָאֲרָצוֹת וְאֶת־אַרְצָם׃ וְנָתֹן אֶת־אֱלֹהֵיהֶם בָּאֵשׁ כִּי לֹא
not for into their have And their and the
—fire the gods given .land ,lands

אֱלֹהִים הֵמָּה כִּי אִם־מַעֲשֵׂה יְדֵי־אָדָם עֵץ וָאֶבֶן וַיְאַבְּדוּם׃
they so and wood ,man the the only but they gods
.them destroyed ;stone of hands of work ,(were)

20 וְעַתָּה יְהוָה אֱלֹהֵינוּ הוֹשִׁיעֵנוּ מִיָּדוֹ וְיֵדְעוּ כָּל־מַמְלְכוֹת
kingdoms the all that so his from save our O And
of know may ,hand us ,God Jehovah ,now

21 הָאָרֶץ כִּי־אַתָּה יְהוָה לְבַדֶּךָ׃ וַיִּשְׁלַח יְשַׁעְיָהוּ בֶן־אָמוֹץ
Amoz the Isaiah sent And You ,Jehovah You that the
of son .alone (are) earth

אֶל־חִזְקִיָּהוּ לֵאמֹר כֹּה־אָמַר יְהוָה אֱלֹהֵי יִשְׂרָאֵל אֲשֶׁר
Because .Israel God Jehovah says Thus ,saying Hezekiah to
of

22 הִתְפַּלַּלְתָּ אֵלַי אֶל־סַנְחֵרִיב מֶלֶךְ אַשּׁוּר׃ זֶה הַדָּבָר אֲשֶׁר־
which the this ,Assyria king Sennacherib about to have you
word (is) of Me prayed

דִּבֶּר יְהוָה עָלָיו בָּזָה לְךָ לָעֲגָה לְךָ בְּתוּלַת בַּת־צִיּוֹן
;Zion the the ,you laughing ,you Has against Jehovah has
of daughter ,virgin scorn to despised :him spoken

23 אַחֲרֶיךָ רֹאשׁ הֵנִיעָה בַּת יְרוּשָׁלִָם׃ אֶת־מִי חֵרַפְתָּ וְגִדַּפְתָּ
and you have Whom .Jerusalem the has (her) behind
?reviled mocked of daughter shaken head you

וְעַל־מִי הֲרִימוֹתָה קּוֹל וַתִּשָּׂא מָרוֹם עֵינֶיךָ אֶל־קְדוֹשׁ
Holy the Against your on and your you have whom And
of One ?eyes high lifted ,voice lifted against

24 יִשְׂרָאֵל׃ בְּיַד עֲבָדֶיךָ חֵרַפְתָּ ׀ אֲדֹנָי וַתֹּאמֶר בְּרֹב רִכְבִּי
my By and the have you your the By !Israel
chariots many ,said Lord mocked servants of hand

אֲנִי עָלִיתִי מְרוֹם הָרִים יַרְכְּתֵי לְבָנוֹן וְאֶכְרֹת קוֹמַת אֲרָזָיו
its tall I and ;Lebanon the ,mountains the (to) have I
,cedars down cut of sides of height up come

25 מִבְחַר בְּרֹשָׁיו וְאָבוֹא מְרוֹם קִצּוֹ יַעַר כַּרְמִלּוֹ׃ אֲנִי
I fruit- its the its the (to) I and fir its choice the
.field ful of forest ,end of height go will ;trees of

קַרְתִּי וְשָׁתִיתִי מָיִם וְאַחְרִב בְּכַף־פְּעָמַי כֹּל יְאֹרֵי מָצוֹר׃
.Egypt the all my the with have and ,water and have
of streams feet of sole up dried drunk dug

26 הֲלוֹא־שָׁמַעְתָּ לְמֵרָחוֹק אוֹתָהּ עָשִׂיתִי מִימֵי קֶדֶם וִיצַרְתִּיהָ
I even old from made I it ?afar from you Have
?it formed of days heard not

have caused it to come, and you are to cause to crash (into) heaps, ruins, fortified cities. [27] And their inhabitants were short of hand, dismayed and ashamed. They were as the field grass and the green herb; like the grass of the housetops, and blasted before it has risen. [28] But I know your sitting down, and your going out, and your coming in, and your raging against Me. [29] Because of your raging against Me, and your complacency has come up to My ears; therefore I will put My hook in your nose, and My bridle in your lips; and I will turn you back by the way you came in.

[30] And this (shall be) the sign to you: You shall eat self-sown grain (this) year; and the second year that which springs up; and in the third year you shall sow and reap, and plant vineyards and eat their fruit. [31] The remnant of the house of Judah that has escaped shall take root downward; and it makes fruit upward. [32] For a remnant shall go out of Jerusalem, and the escaped out of Mount Zion: the zeal of Jehovah of hosts shall do this. [33] Therefore thus says Jehovah to the king of Assyria, He shall not come into this city, nor shoot an arrow there, nor come before it (with) a shield, nor cast a siege-mound on it. [34] He shall return by the same way that he came in, and he shall not come into this city, says, Jehovah. [34] For I will defend over this city to save it, for My own sake and for My servant David's sake.

[36] Then the angel of Jehovah went out and struck a hundred and eighty-five thousand in the camp of the Assyrians. And they rose early in the morning; and behold, they (were) all dead corpses. [37] And Sennacherib king of Assyria

עַתָּה הֲבֵאתִיהָ וּתְהִי לְהַשְׁאוֹת גַּלִּים נִצִּים עָרִים בְּצֻרוֹת׃
.fortified cities ,ruins (into) cause to you and caused have I Now
,heaps crash to are ,come to it

27 וְיֹשְׁבֵיהֶן קִצְרֵי־יָד חַתּוּ וָבֹשׁוּ הָיוּ עֵשֶׂב שָׂדֶה וִירַק דֶּשֶׁא
,herb the and the grass They and were hand of short their So
green field of were .ashamed ,dismayed inhabitants

28 חֲצִיר גַּגּוֹת וּשְׁדֵמָה לִפְנֵי קָמָה׃ וְשִׁבְתְּךָ וְצֵאתְךָ וּבוֹאֲךָ
your and your and your But has it before and house- (like)
,coming going sitting .risen blasted ,tops of grass

29 יָדָעְתִּי וְאֵת הִתְרַגֶּזְךָ אֵלָי׃ יַעַן הִתְרַגֶּזְךָ אֵלַי וְשַׁאֲנַנְךָ
your and against your Because against your and ,know I
complacency ,Me raging of .me raging

עָלָה בְאָזְנָי וְשַׂמְתִּי חַחִי בְּאַפֶּךָ וּמִתְגִּי בִּשְׂפָתֶיךָ וַהֲשִׁיבֹתִיךָ
will I and your in My and your in My therefore My in has
back you turn ;lips bridle nose hook put will I ,ears up come

30 בַּדֶּרֶךְ אֲשֶׁר־בָּאתָ בָּהּ׃ וְזֶה־לְּךָ הָאוֹת אָכוֹל הַשָּׁנָה סָפִיחַ
self-sown (this) eat the to And in you which the by
;grain year :sign you (is) this .it came way

וּבַשָּׁנָה הַשֵּׁנִית שָׁחִים וּבַשָּׁנָה הַשְּׁלִישִׁית זִרְעוּ וְקִצְרוּ
,reap and sow third in and which that second in and
year the ;up springs year the

31 וְנִטְעוּ כְרָמִים וְאִכְלוּ פִרְיָם׃ וְיָסְפָה פְּלֵיטַת בֵּית־יְהוּדָה
Judah the the shall And their eat and vineyards and
of house of escaped add .fruit plant

32 הַנִּשְׁאָרָה שֹׁרֶשׁ לְמָטָּה וְעָשָׂה פְרִי לְמָעְלָה׃ כִּי מִירוּשָׁלִַם
of out For .upward fruit it and down- root that
Jerusalem makes ,ward remains

תֵּצֵא שְׁאֵרִית וּפְלֵיטָה מֵהַר צִיּוֹן קִנְאַת יְהוָה צְבָאוֹת
hosts Jehovah the :Zion of out the and a shall
of of zeal Mount escaped ,remnant out go

33 תַּעֲשֶׂה־זֹּאת׃ לָכֵן כֹּה־אָמַר יְהוָה אֶל־מֶלֶךְ אַשּׁוּר
,Assyria the to Jehovah says thus ,Therefore .this shall
of king do

לֹא יָבוֹא אֶל־הָעִיר הַזֹּאת וְלֹא־יוֹרֶה שָׁם חֵץ וְלֹא־יְקַדְּמֶנָּה
come will and an there shoot and ,this city into shall He not
it before not ,arrow not come

34 מָגֵן וְלֹא־יִשְׁפֹּךְ עָלֶיהָ סֹלְלָה׃ בַּדֶּרֶךְ אֲשֶׁר־בָּא בָּהּ יָשׁוּב
shall He in he that the By seige- a upon will he and a
;return it came way mound it cast not ,shield

35 וְאֶל־הָעִיר הַזֹּאת לֹא יָבוֹא נְאֻם־יְהוָה׃ וְגַנּוֹתִי עַל־הָעִיר
city over I For .Jehovah states shall he not this city and
defend will ,come into

36 הַזֹּאת לְהוֹשִׁיעָהּ לְמַעֲנִי וּלְמַעַן דָּוִד עַבְדִּי׃ וַיֵּצֵא ׀ מַלְאַךְ
the went Then My David for and My for save to ,this
of angel out .servant of sake the sake ,it

יְהוָה וַיַּכֶּה בְּמַחֲנֵה אַשּׁוּר מֵאָה וּשְׁמֹנִים וַחֲמִשָּׁה אָלֶף
.thousand five and and a Assyria the in and Jehovah
eighty hundred .of camp struck

37 וַיַּשְׁכִּימוּ בַבֹּקֶר וְהִנֵּה כֻלָּם פְּגָרִים מֵתִים׃ וַיִּסַּע וַיֵּלֶךְ
and set So .dead (were) they and the in they And
went out corpses all ,behold ,morning early rose

set out, and went and returned, and he lived at Nineveh. [38] And it was, he was worshiping in the house of his god Nisroch, and his sons, Adrammelech and Sharezer, struck him with the sword. And they escaped into the land of Ararat. And his son Esarhaddon reigned in his place.

38 וַיָּשָׁב סַנְחֵרִיב מֶלֶךְ־אַשּׁוּר וַיֵּשֶׁב בְּנִינְוֵה׃ וַיְהִי הוּא

he And in he and ,Assyria the Sennacherib and
,was it .Nineveh lived of king ,returned

מִשְׁתַּחֲוֶה בֵּית ׀ נִסְרֹךְ אֱלֹהָיו וְאַדְרַמֶּלֶךְ וְשַׂרְאֶצֶר בָּנָיו

his and and his Nisroch the (in) was
,sons ,Sharezer Adrammelech ,god of house worshiping

הִכֻּהוּ בַחֶרֶב וְהֵמָּה נִמְלְטוּ אֶרֶץ אֲרָרָט וַיִּמְלֹךְ אֵסַר־חַדֹּן

Esarhaddon And .Ararat the (to) escaped And the with struck
reigned of land they .sword him

בְּנוֹ תַּחְתָּיו׃

his in his
.place son

CAP. XXXVIII לח

CHAPTER 38

CHAPTER 38

[1] In those days Hezekiah was sick to death. And Isaiah the son of Amoz, the prophet, came to him and said to him, Thus says Jehovah, Command your house, for you are dying, and shall not live. [2] Then Hezekiah turned his face to the wall and prayed to Jehovah, [3] and said, I beg You to remember now, O Jehovah, that I have walked before You in truth and with a perfect heart, and have done good in Your eyes. And Hezekiah wept (with) a great weeping. [4] Then the word of Jehovah was to Isaiah, saying, [5] Go and say to Hezekiah: Thus says Jehovah, the God of your father David, I have heard your prayer; I have seen your tears. Behold, I will add fifteen years to your days. [6] And I will deliver you and this city out of the king of Assyria's hand. And I will defend over this city. [7] So this (shall be) the sign to you from Jehovah that Jehovah will do this thing that He has spoken: [8] Behold, I will bring back the shadow of the steps which has gone

1 בַּיָּמִים הָהֵם חָלָה חִזְקִיָּהוּ לָמוּת וַיָּבוֹא אֵלָיו יְשַׁעְיָהוּ

Isaiah to And .death to Hezekiah was those in And
him came sick days

בֶן־אָמוֹץ הַנָּבִיא וַיֹּאמֶר אֵלָיו כֹּה־אָמַר יְהוָה צַו לְבֵיתֶךָ

your Com- ,Jehovah says Thus to he and the ,Amoz the
,house mand ,him said ,prophet of son

2 כִּי מֵת אַתָּה וְלֹא תִחְיֶה׃ וַיַּסֵּב חִזְקִיָּהוּ פָּנָיו אֶל־הַקִּיר

the to his Hezekiah Then shall and ,you are for
,wall face turned .live not dying

3 וַיִּתְפַּלֵּל אֶל־יְהוָה׃ וַיֹּאמַר אָנָּה יְהוָה זְכָר־נָא אֵת אֲשֶׁר

that ,now re- ,Jehovah beg I ,said and ,Jehovah to and
member ,You prayed

הִתְהַלַּכְתִּי לְפָנֶיךָ בֶּאֱמֶת וּבְלֵב שָׁלֵם וְהַטּוֹב בְּעֵינֶיךָ עָשִׂיתִי

have I Your in and ,whole with and truth in before have I
.done eyes good the heart a You about walked

4 וַיֵּבְךְּ חִזְקִיָּהוּ בְּכִי גָדוֹל׃ וַיְהִי דְּבַר־יְהוָה אֶל־יְשַׁעְיָהוּ

,Isaiah to Jehovah the Then .great a Hezekiah And
of word was weeping wept

5 לֵאמֹר׃ הָלוֹךְ וְאָמַרְתָּ אֶל־חִזְקִיָּהוּ כֹּה־אָמַר יְהוָה אֱלֹהֵי

the Jehovah says Thus ,Hezekian to say and Go ,saying
of God

דָּוִד אָבִיךָ שָׁמַעְתִּי אֶת־תְּפִלָּתֶךָ רָאִיתִי אֶת־דִּמְעָתֶךָ הִנְנִי

Behold your have I your have I your David
I .tears seen ;prayer heard ,father

6 יוֹסִף עַל־יָמֶיךָ חֲמֵשׁ עֶשְׂרֵה שָׁנָה׃ וּמִכַּף מֶלֶךְ־אַשּׁוּר

Assyria the from And .years fifteen your to will
of king of hand the days add

7 אַצִּילְךָ וְאֵת הָעִיר הַזֹּאת וְגַנּוֹתִי עַל־הָעִיר הַזֹּאת׃ וְזֶה

this And .this city over I And .this city and will I
(be shall) defend will you deliver

לְּךָ הָאוֹת מֵאֵת יְהוָה אֲשֶׁר יַעֲשֶׂה יְהוָה אֶת־הַדָּבָר הַזֶּה

this thing Jehovah do will that Jehovah from sign the to
you

8 אֲשֶׁר דִּבֵּר׃ הִנְנִי מֵשִׁיב אֶת־צֵל הַמַּעֲלוֹת אֲשֶׁר יָרְדָה

gone has which the the bring ,Behold has He which
down ,steps of shadow back I :spoken

down in the steps of Ahaz with the sun, backward ten steps. So the sun went back up ten steps, by which steps it had gone down!

[9] The writing of Hezekiah king of Judah, when he had been sick and had recovered from his illness: [10] I said in the pause of my days, I shall go to the gates of Sheol; I am deprived of the rest of my years. [11] I said, I shall not see Jah Jehovah in the land of the living; I shall no longer look on man with the inhabitants of the world. [12] My dwelling is plucked up and carried away from me like a shepherd's tent; I have cut off my life like the weaver. He will cut me off from the loom; from day to night You will make an end of me. [13] Like a lion, I set (my time) until morning; so He will break all my bones. From day until night You will make an end of me. [14] Like a swallow (or) a crane, so I chatter; I moan as the dove; my eyes look weakly to the heights. O Jehovah, it presses me down; be surety for me! [15] What shall I say? For He speaks to me, and He has acted. I shall go softly all my years over the bitterness of my soul. [16] O Lord, on them they live, and for all in them (is) the life of my spirit. And you heal me, and make me live. [17] Behold, for peace (was) bitter to me; (yea), bitter; but You loved my soul from the pit of destruction; You have cast all my sins behind Your back. [18] For Sheol cannot thank You; death (cannot) praise You; they going down to the Pit cannot hope for Your truth. [19] The living; the living (is) he thanking You; as I today. The father makes known about Your truth to (his) sons. [20] For Jehovah (is) for my salvation; and we will play my songs all the days of our life, at the house of Jehovah.

[21] For Isaiah had said, Let them take a bunch of

במעלות אחז בשמש אחרנית עשר מעלות ותשב השמש
the went So .steps ten backward the with Ahaz the in
sun back ,sun of steps

9 עשר מעלות במעלות אשר ירדה: מכתב לחזקיהו
of The had it which the by ,steps ten
Hezekiah writing .down gone steps

10 מלך־יהודה בחלתו ויחי מחליו: אני אמרתי בדמי ימי
my the in said I his from had and he when ,Judah king
,days of pause :illness revived sick was of

11 אלכה בשערי שאול פקדתי יתר שנותי: אמרתי לא־
not ,said I my the de- am I ;Sheol the to me Let
.years of rest of prived of gates go

אראה יה יה בארץ החיים לא־אביט אדם עוד עם־יושבי
the with still man shall I not the the in Jehovah Jah shall I
of dwellers on look ;living of land see

12 חדל: דורי נסע ונגלה מני כאהל רעי קפדתי כארג
the like have I ;shepherd's like from and de- is My death- the
weaver off cut tent a ,me removed parted age rest

13 חיי מדלה יבצעני מיום עד־לילה תשלימני: שויתי עד־
until smoothed I an make You night to from cuts He the From my
(soul my) .me of end day ;off me loom .life

בקר כארי כן ישבר כל־עצמותי מיום עד־לילה
night until From my all He so Like .morning
day .bones shatters ,lion a

14 תשלימני: כסוס עגור כן אצפצף אהגה כיונה דלו עיני
my look the as I ;chatter I so a (or) a Like make You
eyes weakly ;dove moan ,crane swallow .me of end

15 למרום יהוה עשקה־לי ערבני: מה־אדבר ואמר־לי
to He For shall What surety be to presses it O the to
,me speaks ?say I .me for ;me down ,Jehovah .heights

16 והוא עשה אדדה כל־שנותי על־מר נפשי: אדני עליהם
them on O my bit- the over my all shall I has and
,Lord .soul of terness years softly go .acted He

17 יחיו ולכל־בהן חיי רוחי ותחלימני והחייני: הנה לשלום
for ,Behold make and You And my the (is) in for and they
peace .live me ,me heal .spirit of life them all ,live

מר־לי מר ואתה חשקת נפשי משחת בלי כי־השלכת
have You for de- the from soul my loved but (yea) to (was)
cast ,struction of pit You ;bitter,me bitter

18 אחרי גוך כל־חטאי: כי־לא שאול תודך מות יהללך
praise (nor) thank can Sheol not For my all Your be-
;You death ,You .sins back hind

19 לא־ישברו יורדי־בור אל־אמתך: חי חי הוא יודך כמוני
I as thanking (is) the The Your for the going they can not
,You he living ,living .truth Pit to down hope

20 היום אב לבנים יודיע אל־אמתך: יהוה להושיעני ונגינותי
therefore my for (is) Jehovah Your about makes (his) to The .today
songs my ;salvation .truth known sons father

21 ננגן כל־ימי חיינו על־בית יהוה: ויאמר ישעיהו ישאו
Let .Isaiah said And .Jehovah the at our the all will we
bear them of house ,life of days play

figs and rub it on the ulcer, and he will live. [22] And Hezekiah said, What (is) the sign that I shall go up to Jehovah's house?

22 דְּבֶלֶת תְּאֵנִים וְיִמְרְחוּ עַל־הַשְּׁחִין וְיֶחִי׃ וַיֹּאמֶר חִזְקִיָּהוּ
,Hezekiah said And he that the on rub and figs cake a
.live may ,boil (it) of

מָה אוֹת כִּי אֶעֱלֶה בֵּית יְהוָה׃
?Jehovah the shall I that the What
of house (to) up go sign (is)

CAP. XXXIX לט

CHAPTER 39

[1] At that time Merodach-baladan, the son of Baladan, king of Babylon, sent letters and a present to Hezekiah — for he had heard that he was ill, and was strengthened. [2] And Hezekiah was glad because of them and let them see the house of his treasure, the silver, and the gold, and the spices, and the good oil, and all his weapons, and all that was found in his treasuries —there was nothing in his house or in all his kingdom that Hezekiah did not make them see. [3] And Isaiah the prophet came to King Hezekiah and said to him, What did these men say? And from where did they come to you? And Hezekiah said, They have come from a distant land to me, from Babylon. [4] Then he said, What have they seen in your house? And Hezekiah said, They have seen all that (is) in my house; there is not a thing among my treasures that I have not made them see. [5] And Isaiah said to Hezekiah, Hear the word of Jehovah of hosts:

[6] Behold, days come when all that (is) in your house, even what your fathers have treasured up until now, shall be carried to Babylon; nothing shall be left, says Jehovah. [7] And they shall take of your sons who shall issue from you, which you shall father; and

1 בָּעֵת הַהִוא שָׁלַח מְרֹאדַךְ בַּלְאֲדָן בֶּן־בַּלְאֲדָן מֶלֶךְ־בָּבֶל
,Babylon king ,Baladan the baladan Merodach- sent that At
of of son time

סְפָרִים וּמִנְחָה אֶל־חִזְקִיָּהוּ וַיִּשְׁמַע כִּי חָלָה וַיֶּחֱזָק׃
was and was he that he for —Hezekiah to a and letters
strong made ill heard had present

2 וַיִּשְׂמַח עֲלֵיהֶם חִזְקִיָּהוּ וַיַּרְאֵם אֶת־בֵּית נְכֹתֹה אֶת־הַכֶּסֶף
,silver the his the let he and .Hezekiah because was And
,treasure of house see them them of glad

וְאֶת־הַזָּהָב וְאֶת־הַבְּשָׂמִים וְאֵת ׀ הַשֶּׁמֶן הַטּוֹב וְאֵת כָּל־
all and ,good oil the and the and the and
,spices ,gold

בֵּית כֵּלָיו וְאֵת כָּל־אֲשֶׁר נִמְצָא בְּאוֹצְרֹתָיו לֹא־הָיָה דָבָר
a there not his in was that all and his the
thing was ;treasuries found weapons of house

3 אֲשֶׁר לֹא־הֶרְאָם חִזְקִיָּהוּ בְּבֵיתוֹ וּבְכָל־מֶמְשַׁלְתּוֹ׃ וַיָּבֹא
Then his in or his in Hezekiah made not which
came .kingdom all house see them

יְשַׁעְיָהוּ הַנָּבִיא אֶל־הַמֶּלֶךְ חִזְקִיָּהוּ וַיֹּאמֶר אֵלָיו מָה־אָמְרוּ ׀
did What to said and ,Hezekiah King to the Isaiah
say ,him prophet

הָאֲנָשִׁים הָאֵלֶּה וּמֵאַיִן יָבֹאוּ אֵלֶיךָ וַיֹּאמֶר חִזְקִיָּהוּ מֵאֶרֶץ
a from ,Hezekiah said And to they did And ?these men
land ?you come where from

4 רְחוֹקָה בָּאוּ אֵלַי מִבָּבֶל׃ וַיֹּאמֶר מָה רָאוּ בְּבֵיתֶךָ וַיֹּאמֶר
And your in have What he Then from to they distant
said ?house seen they ,said .Babylon ,me came

חִזְקִיָּהוּ אֵת כָּל־אֲשֶׁר בְּבֵיתִי רָאוּ לֹא־הָיָה דָבָר אֲשֶׁר
that thing a there not they my in that All ,Hezekiah
is ;seen have house (is)

5 לֹא־הִרְאִיתִם בְּאוֹצְרֹתָי׃ וַיֹּאמֶר יְשַׁעְיָהוּ אֶל־חִזְקִיָּהוּ שְׁמַע
Hear ,Hezekiah to Isaiah Then my among made have I not
said .treasures see them

6 דְּבַר־יְהוָה צְבָאוֹת׃ הִנֵּה יָמִים בָּאִים וְנִשָּׂא ׀ כָּל־אֲשֶׁר
that all shall when ,come days ,Behold :hosts Jehovah the
(is) carried be of of word

בְּבֵיתֶךָ וַאֲשֶׁר אָצְרוּ אֲבֹתֶיךָ עַד־הַיּוֹם הַזֶּה בָּבֶל לֹא־יִוָּתֵר
shall not (to) ,this day until your trea- have even your in
left be ;Babylon fathers up sured what ;house

7 דָּבָר אָמַר יְהוָה׃ וּמִבָּנֶיךָ אֲשֶׁר יֵצְאוּ מִמְּךָ אֲשֶׁר תּוֹלִיד
shall you whom from go shall who your And .Jehovah says a
father ,you forth sons ,thing

they shall be eunuchs in the palace of the king of Babylon. [8] Then Hezekiah said to Isaiah, The word of Jehovah that you have said (is) good. And he said, For there shall be peace and truth in my days.

8 יִקָּחוּ וְהָיוּ סָרִיסִים בְּהֵיכַל מֶלֶךְ בָּבֶל׃ וַיֹּאמֶר חִזְקִיָּהוּ
Hezekiah Then .Babylon the the in eunuchs they and they
said of king of palace be shall ;take shall

אֶל־יְשַׁעְיָהוּ טוֹב דְּבַר־יְהוָה אֲשֶׁר דִּבַּרְתָּ וַיֹּאמֶר כִּי יִהְיֶה
there For he And have you that Jehovah the Good ,Isaiah to
be will ,said .spoken of word (is)

שָׁלוֹם וֶאֱמֶת בְּיָמָי׃
my in and peace
.days truth

CAP. XL מ

CHAPTER 40

[1] Comfort, O comfort My people, says your God. [2] Speak lovingly to the heart of Jerusalem — yea, cry to her that her warfare is done, that her iniquity is pardoned; for she has received of Jehovah's hand double for all her sins. [3] The voice of him who cries in the wilderness: Prepare the way of Jehovah; make straight a highway in the desert for our God. [4] Every valley shall be exalted, and every mountain and hill shall be made low; and the knoll shall be a level place, and the rough places a plain. [5] And the glory of Jehovah shall be revealed, and all flesh shall see (it) together, for the mouth of Jehovah has spoken. [6] A voice said, Cry! And he said, What shall I cry? All flesh is grass, and all its grace as the flower of the field! [7] The grass withers; the flower fades; because the Spirit of Jehovah blows on it. Surely the people (is) grass. [8] The grass withers; the flower fades; but the word of our God shall rise forever. [9] O you who bring good news to Zion, go up for yourself on the high mountain, bringer of tidings to Zion. Lift up your voice with strength, bringer of tidings to Jerusalem. Lift up; do not fear. Say to the cities of Judah, Behold! Your God! [10] Behold, the Lord Jehovah will come with strength, and His arm rules

1
2 נַחֲמוּ נַחֲמוּ עַמִּי יֹאמַר אֱלֹהֵיכֶם׃ דַּבְּרוּ עַל־לֵב יְרוּשָׁלַםִ
,Jerusalem the to Speak .God your says My comfort Com-
of heart ,people ,fort

וְקִרְאוּ אֵלֶיהָ כִּי מָלְאָה צְבָאָהּ כִּי נִרְצָה עֲוֺנָהּ כִּי לָקְחָה
has she for her par- is that her ful- is that ,her to call and
received ;iniquity doned ,warfare filled

3 מִיַּד יְהוָה כִּפְלַיִם בְּכָל־חַטֹּאתֶיהָ׃ קוֹל קוֹרֵא בַּמִּדְבָּר
the in him The .sins her all for double Jehovah's from
,wilderness crying of voice hand

4 פַּנּוּ דֶּרֶךְ יְהוָה יַשְּׁרוּ בָּעֲרָבָה מְסִלָּה לֵאלֹהֵינוּ׃ כָּל־גֶּיא
valley Every our for a the in make ;Jehovah the Pre-
God highway desert straight of way pare

יִנָּשֵׂא וְכָל־הַר וְגִבְעָה יִשְׁפָּלוּ וְהָיָה הֶעָקֹב לְמִישׁוֹר
level a steep the shall and be shall hill and moun- and be shall
,place ground become ;low made tain every ,up lifted

5 וְהָרְכָסִים לְבִקְעָה׃ וְנִגְלָה כְּבוֹד יְהוָה וְרָאוּ כָל־בָּשָׂר
flesh all shall and ,Jehovah the shall And .plain a the and
see of glory revealed be places rough

6 יַחְדָּו כִּי פִּי יְהוָה דִּבֵּר׃ קוֹל אֹמֵר קְרָא וְאָמַר מָה
What he And !Cry ,said A has Jehovah the for to-
,said voice .spoken of mouth ,gether

7 אֶקְרָא כָּל־הַבָּשָׂר חָצִיר וְכָל־חַסְדּוֹ כְּצִיץ הַשָּׂדֶה׃ יָבֵשׁ
Dries the the as its and ,grass flesh All I shall
up !field of flower grace all (is) ?cry

חָצִיר נָבֵל צִיץ כִּי רוּחַ יְהוָה נָשְׁבָה בּוֹ אָכֵן חָצִיר הָעָם׃
the (is) surely on blows Jehovah the for the fades the
.people grass ;it of breath ;flower ,grass

8 יָבֵשׁ חָצִיר נָבֵל צִיץ וּדְבַר אֱלֹהֵינוּ יָקוּם לְעוֹלָם׃
.forever shall God our the but the fades the Dries
rise of word ,flower ;grass up

9 עַל הַר־גָּבֹהַּ עֲלִי־לָךְ מְבַשֶּׂרֶת צִיּוֹן הָרִימִי בַכֹּחַ קוֹלֵךְ
your with Lift .Zion of bringer up Go high the On
,voice strength up to tidings .yourself for mountain

מְבַשֶּׂרֶת יְרוּשָׁלַםִ הָרִימִי אַל־תִּירָאִי אִמְרִי לְעָרֵי יְהוּדָה
,Judah the to Say .fear do not ;up Lift .Jerusalem of bringer
of cities to tidings

10 הִנֵּה אֱלֹהֵיכֶם׃ הִנֵּה אֲדֹנָי יְהוִה בְּחָזָק יָבוֹא וּזְרֹעוֹ מֹשְׁלָה
rules His and will with Jehovah the ,Behold !God your ,Behold
arm ,come strength Lord

11 לו הנה שכרו אתו ופעלתו לפניו׃ כרעה עדרו ירעה

shall He His a Like before His and with (is) His Be- for
;feed flock shepherd .Him wage ,Him reward ,hold .Him

12 בזרעו יקבץ טלאים ובחיקו ישא עלות ינהל׃ מי

Who will He those carry His in and ,lambs shall He His with
.it lead young with ;(them) bosom gather arm

מדד בשעלו מים ושמים בזרת תכן וכל בשלש עפר

the the in en- and meted the by the and the his in has
of dust measure closed ;out span heavens ,waters hand measured

13 הארץ ושקל בפלס הרים וגבעות במאזנים׃ מי־תכן

has Who ?scales in the and the the in and the
out meted hills mounts balance weighed ,earth

14 את־רוח יהוה ואיש עצתו יודיענו׃ את־מי נועץ ויבינהו

who and He took whom With taught His a or ,Jehovah the
Him trained counsel ?Him counsel man of Spirit

וילמדהו בארח משפט וילמדהו דעת ודרך תבונות

discernment the and knowl- taught and ;justice the in taught and
of way ,edge Him of path Him

15 יודיענו׃ הן גוים כמר מדלי וכשחק מאזנים נחשבו הן

,Lo are scales the as and a from a like nations ,Lo known made
.reckoned of dust ,bucket drop (are) ?Him to

16 איים כדק יטול׃ ולבנון אין די בער וחיתו אין די

enough are its and to enough is And takes He a as coasts
(for) not beasts ;burn not Lebanon .up thing little

17 עולה׃ כל־הגוים כאין נגדו מאפס ותהו נחשבו־

are they and than less before as (are) the All burnt a
reckoned emptiness nothing ,Him nothing nations .offering

18
19 לו׃ ואל־מי תדמיון אל ומה־דמות תערכו־לו׃ הפסל

carved The to you will likeness Or ?God you will whom And to
image ?Him array what liken to .Him

נסך חרש וצרף בזהב ירקענו ורתקות כסף צורף׃

he silver chains and overlays the with the and the pours
.casts of ;it gold smelter ;craftsman out

20 המסכן תרומה עץ לא־ירקב יבחר חרש חכם יבקש־

he skilled crafts- a ;chooses that not a (that) (too) He
seeks man rot will tree ,offering for poor

21 לו להכין פסל לא ימוט׃ הלוא תדעו הלוא תשמעו

you Have you Have will that carved a to for
?heard not ?known not .shaken be not ;image prepare ,him

הלוא הגד מראש לכם הלוא הבינותם מוסדות הארץ׃

the the (from) discern you Did ?you to the from it Was
?earth of foundations not beginning told not

22 הישב על־חוג הארץ וישביה כחגבים הנוטה כדק

the like who He like (are) its even the the over who He
curtain stretches ;grasshoppers dwellers ,earth of circle sits

23 שמים וימתחם כאהל לשבת׃ הנותן רוזנים לאין שפטי

judges into poten- who live to a like spreads and the
of ;nothing tates gives ;in tent them ,heavens

24 ארץ כתהו עשה׃ אף בל־נטעו אף בל־זרעו אף בל־

not ,yes they not ,yes shall they not ,Yes He as the
;sown are ;planted be .makes nothing earth

for him. Behold, His reward (is) with Him, and His wage before Him. [11] He shall feed His flock like a shepherd; He shall gather lambs with His arm; and in His bosom carry (them); those with young He will lead it. [12] Who has measured in his hand the waters and the heavens by a span meted out; and enclosed in the measure the dust of the earth, and weighed in the balance the mountains, and the hills in the scales? [13] Who has meted out the Spirit of Jehovah, or a man His counsel taught Him? [14] With whom did He take counsel, and who trained Him and taught Him in the path of justice; and taught Him knowledge, and made known to Him the way of discernment? [15] Lo, nations (are) as a drop from a bucket, and and are reckoned as dust of the scales. Lo, He takes up coasts as a little thing. [16] And Lebanon is not enough to burn, nor are its beasts enough (for) a burnt offering. [17] All the nations (are) as nothing before Him; to Him they are reckoned less than nothing and emptiness.

[18] And to whom will you liken God? Or what likeness will you array to Him? [19] The craftsman pours out, the smelter overlays it with gold; and he casts the chains of silver. [20] He (too) poor for (that) offering chooses a tree that will not rot; he seeks a skilled artisan for him, to prepare a carved image that will not be shaken. [21] Have you not known? Have you not heard? Was it not told from the beginning to you? Did you not discern (from) the foundations of the earth? [22] He who sits on the circle of the earth, even its dwellers (are) like grasshoppers; He who stretches the heavens like a curtain, and spreads them like a tent to live in; [23] who gives potentates into nothing—He makes judges of the earth as nothing. [24] Yes, they shall not be planted; yes, they are not

sown; yes, their stem (is) not taking root in the earth. And He shall also blow on them, and they shall wither, and the tempest shall take them away like stubble. [25] To whom then will you compare Me, or (am) I equaled, says the Holy One? [26] Lift up your eyes on high and look: Who has created these? Who brings out their host by number? By greatness of vigor, and mighty of power, He calls them all by names – not one is lacking. [27] Why will you say, O Jacob; and speak, O Israel; My way is hidden from Jehovah, and my judgment is passed over by my God? [28] Have you not known? Have you not heard? The everlasting God, Jehovah, the Creator of the ends of the earth; He is not faint and does not grow weary; there is no searching to His understanding. [29] (He) gives power to the faint, and to him with no vigor He increases might. [30] Even youths are faint and fatigued; and young men surely shall stumble; but waiters for Jehovah shall renew power; they shall go up (with) wings as the eagles; they shall run and not be weary; they shall walk and not be faint!

שֹׁרֶשׁ בָּאָרֶץ גִּזְעָם וְגַם נָשַׁף בָּהֶם וַיִּבָשׁוּ וּסְעָרָה כַּקַּשׁ
like the and they and on He And their the in taking
stubble tempest ;wither ,them blows also .stem earth root

25 26 תִּשָּׂאֵם׃ וְאֶל־מִי תְדַמְּיוּנִי וְאֶשְׁוֶה יֹאמַר קָדוֹשׁ׃ שְׂאוּ
Lift Holy the says I am or you will whom And take shall
up ?One ,equaled ,Me liken to .away them

מָרוֹם עֵינֵיכֶם וּרְאוּ מִי־בָרָא אֵלֶּה הַמּוֹצִיא בְמִסְפָּר צְבָאָם
their by bringing ,these has who and your on
?host number out created :see eyes high

לְכֻלָּם בְּשֵׁם יִקְרָא מֵרֹב אוֹנִים וְאַמִּיץ כֹּחַ אִישׁ לֹא
not one ;power and vigor great- by He by them to
of mighty of ness ,calls name all

27 נֶעְדָּר׃ לָמָּה תֹאמַר יַעֲקֹב וּתְדַבֵּר יִשְׂרָאֵל נִסְתְּרָה
Is ,Israel O ,speak and O you will Why is
hidden ;Jacob ,say .lacking

28 דַרְכִּי מֵיְהוָה וּמֵאֱלֹהַי מִשְׁפָּטִי יַעֲבוֹר׃ הֲלוֹא יָדַעְתָּ אִם־
Or you Have pass shall my from and from my
?known not ?over judgment God my ,Jehovah way

לֹא שָׁמַעְתָּ אֱלֹהֵי עוֹלָם ׀ יְהוָה בּוֹרֵא קְצוֹת הָאָרֶץ לֹא
not the the the Jehovah ever- The you have not
,earth of ends of Creator ,(is) lasting God ?heard

29 יִיעַף וְלֹא יִיגָע אֵין חֵקֶר לִתְבוּנָתוֹ׃ נֹתֵן לַיָּעֵף כֹּחַ וּלְאֵין
him and ;power the to (He) His to search- not grows and is He
no with faint gives .understanding ing is ,weary not faint

30 אוֹנִים עָצְמָה יַרְבֶּה׃ וְיִעֲפוּ נְעָרִים וְיִגָעוּ וּבַחוּרִים כָּשׁוֹל
surely young and and youths are Even He might ,vigor
men ;fatigued faint .increases

31 יִכָּשֵׁלוּ׃ וְקוֹיֵ יְהוָה יַחֲלִיפוּ כֹחַ יַעֲלוּ אֵבֶר כַּנְּשָׁרִים יָרוּצוּ
they the as (with) they ;power shall Jehovah but shall
run shall ;eagles wings up go shall renew for waiters ;stumble

וְלֹא יִיגָעוּ יֵלְכוּ וְלֹא יִיעָפוּ׃
.faint be and they be and
not walk shall ;weary not

CAP. XLI מא

CHAPTER 41

[1] Be quiet before Me, O coasts; and let peoples renew their power. They come near; then they speak: Let us draw near together for judgment. [2] Who raised up the Righteous from the east? He called Him to His foot; He gives nations before Him and subdues kings; He gives (them) as dust (to) His sword, as driven stubble (to) His bow; [3] He pursues them; He passes on safely; He does not go (by) the way with His feet. [4] Who has planned and done (it), calling forth the genera-

CHAPTER 41

1 הַחֲרִישׁוּ אֵלַי אִיִּים וּלְאֻמִּים יַחֲלִיפוּ כֹחַ יִגְּשׁוּ אָז יְדַבֵּרוּ
they then They .power shall and O before Be
;speak ,near come renew peoples ;coasts ,Me quiet

2 יַחְדָּו לַמִּשְׁפָּט נִקְרָבָה׃ מִי הֵעִיר מִמִּזְרָח צֶדֶק יִקְרָאֵהוּ
called He the the from raised Who us let for to-
Him ?Righteous east up .near draw judgment gether

לְרַגְלוֹ יִתֵּן לְפָנָיו גּוֹיִם וּמְלָכִים יַרְדְּ יִתֵּן כֶּעָפָר חַרְבּוֹ כְּקַשׁ
as His (to) dust as He sub- kings and ,nations before He His to
stubble ,sword gives .dues Him gives ?foot

3 נִדָּף קַשְׁתּוֹ׃ יִרְדְּפֵם יַעֲבוֹר שָׁלוֹם אֹרַח בְּרַגְלָיו לֹא יָבוֹא׃
he not His with (by) ;safely passes He pur- He His to driven
goes feet way the on ;them sues .bow

4 מִי־פָעַל וְעָשָׂה קֹרֵא הַדֹּרוֹת מֵרֹאשׁ אֲנִי יְהוָה רִאשׁוֹן
the Jehovah I the from genera- the calling and has Who
first ?beginning tions forth ,(it) done appointed

and with the last. [5] The coasts have seen and fear; the ends of the earth tremble; they have drawn near; yea, they come. [6] Each man helps his neighbor, and says to his brother, Be strong. [7] So the carver strengthens the refiner; and he smoothing (with) the hammer, him who struck the anvil, saying of the soldering, It (is) good. And he made it strong with nails —it will not totter.

[8] But you, Israel, (are) My servant; Jacob whom I have chosen; the seed of My friend Abraham; [9] whom I have strengthened from the ends of the earth, and from its sides called you; and I said to you, You (are) My servant; I have chosen you, and have not cast you off. [10] Do not fear, for I am with you; do not gaze about, for I (am) your God; I will make you strong; yea, I will help you; yes, I will uphold you with the right hand of My righteousness. [11] Behold, all who were provoked with you shall be ashamed and confounded; they shall be as nothing; and they who fight with you shall perish. [12] You shall seek them and shall not find them; men of your strife shall be as nothing, even men of your battle as ceasing. [13] For I, Jehovah your God am strengthening your right hand; who says to you, Do not fear; I will help you. [14] Fear not, worm of Jacob, men of Israel; I will help you; states Jehovah, and your Redeemer, the Holy One of Israel.

[15] Behold! I have made you a new sharp threshing instrument, a master of mouths; you shall thresh mountains and beat them small, and shall make hills like the chaff. [16] You shall fan them, and the wind will carry them away; and the tempest will scatter them. And you shall rejoice in Jehovah; you shall glory

5 וְאֶת־אַחֲרֹנִים אֲנִי־הוּא׃ רָאוּ אִיִּים וְיִירָאוּ קְצוֹת הָאָרֶץ
the the ;fear and the Have .He I the and
earth of ends coasts seen (am) ,last

6 יֶחֶרְדוּ קָרְבוּ וַיֶּאֱתָיוּן׃ אִישׁ אֶת־רֵעֵהוּ יַעְזֹרוּ וּלְאָחִיו יֹאמַר
,says to and ,helps his Each they and they ;tremble
brother his neighbor man .came ;near drew

7 חֲזָק׃ וַיְחַזֵּק חָרָשׁ אֶת־צֹרֵף מַחֲלִיק פַּטִּישׁ אֶת־הוֹלֶם
who him the smoothing he the the So Be
struck ,hammer (with) ,refiner artisan strengthens .strong

פָּעַם אֹמֵר לַדֶּבֶק טוֹב הוּא וַיְחַזְּקֵהוּ בְמַסְמְרִים לֹא יִמּוֹט׃
will it not with made he And .It good the of saying the
.totter ,nails strong it .(is) ,soldering ,anvil

8 וְאַתָּה יִשְׂרָאֵל עַבְדִּי יַעֲקֹב אֲשֶׁר בְּחַרְתִּיךָ זֶרַע
the have I whom ,Jacob My (are) ,Israel O But
of seed ,chosen ,servant ,you

9 אַבְרָהָם אֹהֲבִי׃ אֲשֶׁר הֶחֱזַקְתִּיךָ מִקְצוֹת הָאָרֶץ וּמֵאֲצִילֶיהָ
from and the the from have I whom My Abraham
sides its ,earth of ends strong made ,friend

קְרָאתִיךָ וָאֹמַר לְךָ עַבְדִּי־אַתָּה בְּחַרְתִּיךָ וְלֹא מְאַסְתִּיךָ׃
cast have and chose I you My to I and called
.off you not ,you .(are) servant ,you said ;you

10 אַל־תִּירָא כִּי־עִמְּךָ אָנִי אַל־תִּשְׁתָּע כִּי־אֲנִי אֱלֹהֶיךָ אִמַּצְתִּיךָ
make I your I for gaze do not I with for do Not
;strong you ;God (am) ,about ;(am) you ,fear

11 אַף־עֲזַרְתִּיךָ אַף־תְּמַכְתִּיךָ בִּימִין צִדְקִי׃ הֵן יֵבֹשׁוּ וְיִכָּלְמוּ
and be shall ,Lo My right with uphold I ,yea help I ,yea
humiliated ashamed .just hand you ;you

כֹּל הַנֶּחֱרִים בָּךְ יִהְיוּ כְאַיִן וְיֹאבְדוּ אַנְשֵׁי רִיבֶךָ׃
con- your men shall and as shall they with are who all
tention of perish ;nothing be ;you provoked

12 תְּבַקְשֵׁם וְלֹא תִמְצָאֵם אַנְשֵׁי מַצֻּתֶךָ יִהְיוּ כְאַיִן וּכְאֶפֶס
as even as shall your men find shall and shall You
ceasing ,nothing be strife of ;them not them seek

13 אַנְשֵׁי מִלְחַמְתֶּךָ׃ כִּי אֲנִי יְהוָה אֱלֹהֶיךָ מַחֲזִיק יְמִינֶךָ
your making am your Jehovah I For your men
,hand right strong God .battle of

14 הָאֹמֵר לְךָ אַל־תִּירָא אֲנִי עֲזַרְתִּיךָ׃ אַל־תִּירְאִי תּוֹלַעַת
worm Do not help will I Do not to who
of ,fear .you ;fear ,you says

יַעֲקֹב מְתֵי יִשְׂרָאֵל אֲנִי עֲזַרְתִּיךְ נְאֻם־יְהוָה וְגֹאֲלֵךְ קְדוֹשׁ
Holy the your and ,Jehovah states help will I ;Israel men ,Jacob
of One ,Redeemer ,you of

15 יִשְׂרָאֵל׃ הִנֵּה שַׂמְתִּיךְ לְמוֹרַג חָרוּץ חָדָשׁ בַּעַל פִּיפִיּוֹת
;mouths a ,new sharp threshing a made I ,Behold .Israel
of master instrument you

16 תָּדוּשׁ הָרִים וְתָדֹק וּגְבָעוֹת כַּמֹּץ תָּשִׂים׃ תִּזְרֵם וְרוּחַ
and shall You shall the as hills and and mountains shall you
wind ,them winnow .make chaff ,crush thresh

תִּשָּׂאֵם וּסְעָרָה תָּפִיץ אוֹתָם וְאַתָּה תָּגִיל בַּיהוָה בִּקְדוֹשׁ
the in in shall And .them will a and carry shall
of One Holy ;Jehovah rejoice you scatter tempest ;away them

in the Holy One of Israel. [17] The poor and the needy seek water, and there is none; their tongue is parched for thirst — I, Jehovah will hear them; the God of Israel will not leave them. [18] I will open rivers in bare places, and fountains in the midst of valleys; I will make the desert for a pool of water, and the dry land springs of water. [19] I will plant cedar in the wilderness, acacia, and myrtle, and the oil-tree; I will set fir, pine and boxwood together in the desert; [20] so that they may see, and know, and consider, and understand together, that the hand of Jehovah has done this; and the Holy One of Israel has created it.

[21] Bring your cause, says Jehovah; let your strong (reasons) come near, says the King of Jacob. [22] Let them draw near and tell us what shall happen; the former things, let them reveal what they (are), that we may set our heart and know their end; or declare to us the coming things. [23] Reveal the coming things hereafter, so that we may know that you (are) gods. Yes, do good, or do evil, that we may gaze and see together. [24] Behold, you (are) of nothing; and your work of nothing; he who chooses you (is) an abomination. [25] I have raised up (one) from the north; and he shall come from the east; he will call on My name. And he shall come (upon) rulers as (on) mortar, and as a potter tramples clay. [26] Who has declared from the beginning, that we may know; and beforetime, that we may say, He is right? Yea, no one declares; yea, no one proclaims; yea, there is no one who hears your words. [27] At first to Zion,

17 ישראל תתהלל׃ העניים והאביונים מבקשים
seek the and The shall you Israel
needy poor .glory

מים ואין לשונם בצמא נשתה אני יהוה אענם אלהי
the answer will Jehovah I is for their and ,water
of God ,them —parched thirst tongue is not

18 ישראל לא אעזבם׃ אפתח על־שפיים נהרות ובתוך
the in and ,rivers bare on will I leave will I not ,Israel
of midst places open .them

בקעות מעינות אשים מדבר לאגם־מים וארץ ציה למוצאי
springs for dry the and ,water a for the will I ,fountains valleys
of land of pool desert make

19 מים׃ אתן במדבר ארז שטה והדס ועץ שמן אשים
will I ;oil and and ,acacia ,cedar the in will I ,water
set of tree ,myrtle wilderness give

20 בערבה ברוש תדהר ותאשור יחדו׃ למען יראו וידעו
and they that ;together box- and ,elm ,fir the in
,know see may wood desert

וישימו וישכילו יחדו כי יד־יהוה עשתה זאת וקדוש
the and ;this has Jehovah the that to- under- and con- and
of One Holy done of hand ,gether stand ,sider

21 ישראל בראה׃ קרבו ריבכם יאמר יהוה הגישו
come let ;Jehovah says your Bring created has Israel
near ,cause near .it

22 עצמותיכם יאמר מלך יעקב׃ יגישו ויגידו לנו את אשר
what us to tell and them Let. Jacob the says strong your
near draw of King .(reasons)

תקרינה הראשנות מה הנה הגידו ונשימה לבנו ונדעה
and our we that them let they what former the shall
know heart set may ,reveal (are) —things ;happen

23 אחריתן או הבאות השמיענו׃ הגידו האתיות לאחור
here- coming the Reveal declare coming the or their
,after things .us to things ;end

ונדעה כי אלהים אתם אף־תיטיבו ותרעו ונשתעה ונרא
and we that do or do ,Yes you gods that we that
see gaze may ,evil ,good .(are) know may

24 יחדו׃ הן־אתם מאין ופעלכם מאפע תועבה יבחר בכם׃
.you who he an (is) of your and of you Be- to-
chooses offense ;nothing work ,nothing (are) hold .gether

25 העירותי מצפון ויאת ממזרח־שמש יקרא בשמי
My on will he the the from he and from (one) have I
.name call ;sun of rising come shall ;north the up raised

26 ויבא סגנים כמו־חמר וכמו יוצר ירמס־טיט׃ מי־הגיד
has Who .clay shall potter a as and mortar as (on) he And
declared trample (on) rulers come shall

מראש ונדעה ומלפנים ונאמר צדיק אף אין־מגיד אף
,yea ;declares not ,Yea (is He) we that before and we that the from
(one) ?right ,say may .time from ;know may ,beginning

27 אין משמיע אף אין־שמע אמריכם׃ ראשון לציון הנה
,Behold . to first At your hears not ,yea ;proclaims not
,Zion .words (one) (one)

(I say), Behold! Behold
them! And I will give to
Jerusalem one bearing tidings. [28] But I saw, and
there was not a man; and
of these, there was not a
counselor, that I may ask
them, and they could
answer a word. [29] Be-
hold, they (are) all evil;
their works (are) nothing;
their images (are) wind
and vanity.

CHAPTER 42

[1] Behold My Servant;
I will uphold Him; My Elect
(in whom) My soul delights!
I have put My spirit on Him;
He shall bring forth justice
to the nations. [2] He
shall not cry or lift up or
cause His voice to be heard
in the street. [3] A bruised
reed He shall not break, and
a smoking wick He shall not
quench; He shall bring forth
justice to truth. [4] He
shall not fail or be discour-
aged until He has set
justice in the earth; and the
coasts shall wait for His law.
[5] Thus says God Je-
hovah, creating the heavens
and stretching them out;
spreading out the earth and
its offspring, giving breath
to the people on it, and
spirit to those walking in it.
[6] I, Jehovah, have called
You in righteousness, and
will hold Your hand, and
will keep You, and give You
for a covenant of the people
for a Light of the nations;
[7] to open blind eyes, to
deliver the prisoner from
the prison; those who sit in
darkness from the prison.
[8] I (am) Jehovah; that is
My name; and I will not give
My glory to another, nor
My praise to engraved
images. [9] Behold, the former things have come to
pass, and I declare new
things — before they hap-
pen, I cause you to hear.

[10] Sing a new song to
Jehovah; His praise from
the end of the earth, you
who go to sea, and all that is

28 הִנֵּם וְלִירוּשָׁלַם מְבַשֵּׂר אֶתֵּן׃ וְאֵרֶא וְאֵין אִישׁ וּמֵאֵלֶּה
of and a and I But will I bearing one to And behold
,these ;man was not ,saw .give tidings Jerusalem !them

29 וְאֵין יוֹעֵץ וְאֶשְׁאָלֵם וְיָשִׁיבוּ דָבָר׃ הֵן כֻּלָּם אָוֶן אֶפֶס
(are) (are) they ,Behold .word a they and may I that coun- a not
nothing ;evil all answer could them ask selor was

מַעֲשֵׂיהֶם רוּחַ וָתֹהוּ נִסְכֵּיהֶם׃
their (are) and wind their
.images casted vanity ;works

CAP. XLII מב

CHAPTER 42

1 הֵן עַבְדִּי אֶתְמָךְ־בּוֹ בְּחִירִי רָצְתָה נַפְשִׁי נָתַתִּי רוּחִי עָלָיו
on My have I My (whom in) My ;Him will I My Behold
;Him Spirit given !soul delights ,elect support ,servant

2 מִשְׁפָּט לַגּוֹיִם יוֹצִיא׃ לֹא יִצְעַק וְלֹא יִשָּׂא וְלֹא־יַשְׁמִיעַ
to cause and lift and shall He not shall He the to justice
heard be not ,up not ,out cry .forth bring nations

3 בַּחוּץ קוֹלוֹ׃ קָנֶה רָצוּץ לֹא יִשְׁבּוֹר וּפִשְׁתָּה כֵהָה לֹא
not growing a and shall He not bruised A His the in
dim wick ,break reed .voice street

4 יְכַבֶּנָּה לֶאֱמֶת יוֹצִיא מִשְׁפָּט׃ לֹא יִכְהֶה וְלֹא יָרוּץ עַד־
until be and shall He not .justice shall He truth to shall He
,crushed not dim grow forth bring ;it quench

5 יָשִׂים בָּאָרֶץ מִשְׁפָּט וּלְתוֹרָתוֹ אִיִּים יְיַחֵילוּ׃ כֹּה־אָמַר
says Thus shall the for and ;justice the in has He
.wait coasts law His earth set

הָאֵל ׀ יְהוָה בּוֹרֵא הַשָּׁמַיִם וְנוֹטֵיהֶם רֹקַע הָאָרֶץ וְצֶאֱצָאֶיהָ
its and the spreading stretch- and the creating Jehovah God
,offspring earth out ,out them ing heavens

6 נֹתֵן נְשָׁמָה לָעָם עָלֶיהָ וְרוּחַ לַהֹלְכִים בָּהּ׃ אֲנִי יְהוָה
Jehovah I .it in those to and ,it on the to breath giving
walk who spirit people

קְרָאתִיךָ בְצֶדֶק וְאַחְזֵק בְּיָדֶךָ וְאֶצָּרְךָ וְאֶתֶּנְךָ לִבְרִית עָם
the cove- a for give and will and Your will and righ- in called have
,people of nant You ,You keep ;hand hold ,teousness You

7 לְאוֹר גּוֹיִם׃ לִפְקֹחַ עֵינַיִם עִוְרוֹת לְהוֹצִיא מִמַּסְגֵּר אַסִּיר
the from deliver to ,blind eyes To .nations a for
;prisoner prison open of light

8 מִבֵּית כֶּלֶא יֹשְׁבֵי חֹשֶׁךְ׃ אֲנִי יְהוָה הוּא שְׁמִי וּכְבוֹדִי
My and My that ;Jehovah I .darkness who those re- the from
glory ;name (is) (am) in sit straint of house

9 לְאַחֵר לֹא־אֶתֵּן וּתְהִלָּתִי לַפְּסִילִים׃ הָרִאשֹׁנוֹת הִנֵּה־בָאוּ
have ,behold former The carved to My and will I not to
,come ,things .images praise ,give another

וַחֲדָשׁוֹת אֲנִי מַגִּיד בְּטֶרֶם תִּצְמַחְנָה אַשְׁמִיעַ אֶתְכֶם׃
.you cause I spring they before declare I new and
hear to ;forth things

10 שִׁירוּ לַיהוָה שִׁיר חָדָשׁ תְּהִלָּתוֹ מִקְצֵה הָאָרֶץ יוֹרְדֵי הַיָּם
the to who the the from His ;new song a to ,Sing
,sea down go ,earth of end praise Jehovah

in it; the coasts and their people. [11] Let the wilderness and its cities lift up, the villages where Kedar lives. Let the dwellers of the rock sing; let them shout from the mountains. [12] They give glory to Jehovah and declare His praise in the islands. [13] Jehovah shall go out as a giant; and He shall stir up His zeal like a warrior; He shall cry, yea, roar on His enemies; He shall act mightily. [14] I have forever kept silence; I have been quiet and refrained Myself; I will cry like a woman in travail; I will pant and gasp at once. [15] I will make mountains and hills become a waste, and dry up all their plants. And I will make the rivers coastlands, and I will dry up pools. [16] And I will lead the blind by a way they knew not; I will lead them in paths they never knew; I will make darkness into light before them, and crooked places a level place —I do these things to them and do not forsake them; [17] They are turned back; they are ashamed (with) shame, those trusting in the carved image, who say to cast images, You (are) our gods. [18] O deaf ones, hear! And O blind see! [19] Who (is) blind but My servant? Or deaf, as My messenger whom I send? Who (is) blind as he who is at peace, and blind as Jehovah's servant? [20] You see many things, but do not observe; (your) ears (are) open, but not any hears. [21] Jehovah is delighted for His righteousness' sake; He will magnify the Law and make (it) honorable.

[22] But this (is) a people robbed and spoiled; they shall all be snared in holes, and prison-houses. They were hidden, they were for spoil, and no one will deliver; a prey, and no one says, Return! [23] Who among you will hear this, will listen and hear for the time to come?

11 וּמְלֹאוֹ אִיִּים וְיֹשְׁבֵיהֶם׃ יִשְׂאוּ מִדְבָּר וְעָרָיו חֲצֵרִים תֵּשֵׁב

(where) the its and the lift Let their and coasts its and
lives villages ,cities wilderness up .inhabitants ,fulness

12 קֵדָר יָרֹנּוּ יֹשְׁבֵי סֶלַע מֵרֹאשׁ הָרִים יִצְוָחוּ׃ יָשִׂימוּ לַיהוָה

to They let the from ;Sela the Let .Kedar
Jehovah give .sing them mountains of top of dwellers sing

13 כָּבוֹד וּתְהִלָּתוֹ בָּאִיִּים יַגִּידוּ׃ יְהוָה כַּגִּבּוֹר יֵצֵא כְּאִישׁ

a as goes a as Jehovah they the in His and ,glory
of man ;out warrior .declare coasts praise

מִלְחָמוֹת יָעִיר קִנְאָה יָרִיעַ אַף־יַצְרִיחַ עַל־אֹיְבָיו יִתְגַּבָּר׃

act will He His on ;roar ,yea will He (His) He battles
.mightily enemies ,shout ;zeal up stirs

14 הֶחֱשֵׁיתִי מֵעוֹלָם אַחֲרִישׁ אֶתְאַפָּק כַּיּוֹלֵדָה אֶפְעֶה אֶשֹּׁם

will I will I woman a like refrained I was I from have I
,pant ,groan travail in ;Myself ,quiet , forever silence kept

15 וְאֶשְׁאַף יָחַד׃ אַחֲרִיב הָרִים וּגְבָעוֹת וְכָל־עֶשְׂבָּם אוֹבִישׁ

dry their and ,hills and mountains will I at will and
.up plants all waste lay .once gasp

16 וְשַׂמְתִּי נְהָרוֹת לָאִיִּים וַאֲגַמִּים אוֹבִישׁ׃ וְהוֹלַכְתִּי עִוְרִים

blind I And will I pools and for rivers I And
ones lead will .up dry , coastlands make will

בְּדֶרֶךְ לֹא יָדָעוּ בִּנְתִיבוֹת לֹא־יָדְעוּ אַדְרִיכֵם אָשִׂים מַחְשָׁךְ

darkness will I will I they not in and they not a by
make ;them lead knew paths ;knew way

לִפְנֵיהֶם לָאוֹר וּמַעֲקַשִּׁים לְמִישׁוֹר אֵלֶּה הַדְּבָרִים עֲשִׂיתִם

to do I things these level a crooked and into before
them —place places ,light them

17 וְלֹא עֲזַבְתִּים׃ נָסֹגוּ אָחוֹר יֵבֹשׁוּ בֹשֶׁת הַבֹּטְחִים בַּפָּסֶל

cut the in those (with) are they ,back are they forsake and
,image trusting ,shame ashamed turned ;them not

18 הָאֹמְרִים לְמַסֵּכָה אַתֶּם אֱלֹהֵינוּ׃ הַחֵרְשִׁים שְׁמָעוּ

!hear deaf O our You cast to say who
,ones .gods (are) , images

19 וְהַעִוְרִים הַבִּיטוּ לִרְאוֹת׃ מִי עִוֵּר כִּי אִם־עַבְדִּי וְחֵרֵשׁ

Or My except (is) Who !see to look O And
,deaf ?servant blind ,ones blind

כְּמַלְאָכִי אֶשְׁלָח מִי עִוֵּר כִּמְשֻׁלָּם וְעִוֵּר כְּעֶבֶד יְהוָה׃

?Jehovah's as and who he as (is) Who (whom) My as
servant blind ,peace at is blind ?send I messenger

20
21 רָאִית רַבּוֹת וְלֹא תִשְׁמֹר פָּקוֹחַ אָזְנַיִם וְלֹא יִשְׁמָע׃ יְהוָה

Jehovah any but (your) open ; ,keep do but many You
.hears not ,ears (are) not ,things see

22 חָפֵץ לְמַעַן צִדְקוֹ יַגְדִּיל תּוֹרָה וְיַאְדִּיר׃ וְהוּא עַם־בָּזוּז

robbed a it But make and the will He righ- His for de- is
people (is) .honorable (it) Law magnify ;teousness' sake lighted

וְשָׁסוּי הָפֵחַ בַּחוּרִים כֻּלָּם וּבְבָתֵּי כְלָאִים הָחְבָּאוּ הָיוּ לָבַז

for They were they re- in and of all ,holes in ensnared and
,spoil were .hidden ;straint of houses ,them ;spoiled

23 וְאֵין מַצִּיל מְשִׁסָּה וְאֵין־אֹמֵר הָשַׁב׃ מִי בָכֶם יַאֲזִין זֹאת

?this will among Who !Return ,says and ,prey a ;delivers and
hear you none none

[24] Who gave Jacob to the plunderer, and Israel to the robbers? Did not Jehovah, against whom we have sinned? For they willed not to walk in His ways, and they did not obey His law. [25] Therefore He has poured on him the fury of His anger, and the strength of battle; and it has set him on fire all around, yet he did not know; and it burned him, yet he did not lay (it) on (his) heart.

24 יקשיב וישמע לאחור׃ מי־נתן למשוסה יעקב וישראל

and Israel ;Jacob the to plunderer gave Who the for .come to time hear and will He (ears) incline

לבזזים הלוא יהוה זו חטאנו לו ולא־אבו בדרכיו הלוך

to walk His in ways they willed For not against ?Him we sinned of whom Jeho- vah Did not to ?robbers

25 ולא שמעו בתורתו׃ וישפך עליו חמה אפו ועזוז

and of force His ,anger fury the of on him He So poured .law His did they obey and not

מלחמה ותלהטהו מסביב ולא ידע ותבער־בו ולא־

but not among ,him it and burned did he ;know yet not all ,around set has it and fire on him ;battle

ישים על־לב׃

(his) on .heart did he (it) lay

CAP. XLIII מג

CHAPTER 43

[1] But now thus says Jehovah who formed you, O Jacob; and He who made you, O Israel: Fear not, for I have redeemed you; I called you by your name; you (are) Mine. [2] When you go through the waters, I will be with you; and through the rivers, they shall not overflow you.

When you walk in the fire, you shall not be burned, nor shall the flame kindle on you. [3] For I am Jehovah your God, the Holy One of Israel, your Savior: I gave Egypt (for) your atonement; Ethiopia and Seba for you. [4] Since you were precious in My eyes, you are honored, and I love you, and I give men for you, and peoples for your soul. [5] Fear not, for I (am) with you; I will bring your seed from the sunrise, and gather you from the sunset. [6] I will say to the north, Give up; and to the south, Do not hold back; bring My sons from afar, and bring My daughters from the ends of the earth; [7] everyone who is called by My name; and I have created him for My glory; I have formed him; yea, I have made him. [8] Bring out the blind people, and the deaf, yet there are eyes, yet ears

1 ועתה כה־אמר יהוה בראך יעקב ויצרך ישראל אל־

not ;Israel who and ,you formed ;Jacob who ,you created Jehovah says thus But ,now

2 תירא כי גאלתיך קראתי בשמך לי־אתה׃ כי־תעבור

you go When .(are) you to Me your by ;name called I (you) re- have I ;you deemed for ,Fear

במים אתך אני ובנהרות לא ישטפוך כי־תלך במו־אש

the ,fire in walk you when shall they ;you overflow not through and ,rivers the I ;(am) with you through ,waters the

3 לא תכוה ולהבה לא תבער־בך׃ כי אני יהוה אלהיך

your ,God Jehovah I (am) For on .you shall kindle not the and flame shall you ;burned be not

קדוש ישראל מושיעך נתתי כפרך מצרים כוש וסבא

and Seba Ethiopia ;Egypt your (for) atonement gave I your ;Savior ,Israel Holy the of One

4 תחתיך׃ מאשר יקרת בעיני נכבדת ואני אהבתיך ואתן

I and give love ,you I and are you ,honored My in ,eyes were you precious Since of instead .you

5 אדם תחתיך ולאמים תחת נפשך׃ אל־תירא כי־אתך

with you for ,Fear not ,soul your instead of and peoples of instead ,you men

6 אני ממזרח אביא זרעך וממערב אקבצך׃ אמר לצפון

the to ,north will I say will I .you gather from and sunset the your ,seed will I bring the from sunrise I ;(am)

תני ולתימן אל־תכלאי הביאי בני מרחוק ובנותי מקצה

the from of end My and daughters from ,afar My sons Bring hold Do !back not to and ,south the Give !up

7 הארץ׃ כל הנקרא בשמי ולכבודי בראתיו יצרתיו אף־

,yea formed I ;him created I ;him for and ,glory My My by ;name is who called everyone the :earth

8 עשיתיו׃ הוציא עם־עור ועינים יש וחרשים ואזנים למו׃

to .him yet (are) ears the and ,deaf there ;are yet eyes ,blind the people Bring out made .him

to him. [9] Let all the nations be assembled, and let the peoples be gathered. Who among them can declare this and cause us to hear former things? Let them give their witnesses, that they may be justified, or let them hear and say, (It is) true. [10] You (are) My witnesses, says Jehovah, and My servant whom I have chosen; that you may know and believe Me, and understand that I am He. Not a god was formed before Me, nor shall any be after Me. [11] I, I (am) Jehovah; and there is no Savior besides Me. [12] I declared, and I saved, and I proclaimed; and there is no strange (god) among you; and you (are) My witnesses, says Jehovah, and I (am) God. [13] Yea, from this day I (am) He, and no one delivers from My hand. I will work, and who shall reverse it?

[14] Thus says Jehovah, your Redeemer, the Holy One of Israel: For your sake I have sent to Babylon and have brought down (as) fugitives all of them, even the Chaldeans, whose cry is in the ships. [15] I (am) Jehovah, your Holy One, the Creator of Israel, your King. [16] Thus says Jehovah, who makes a way in the sea and a path in the stormy waters; [17] who brings out chariot and horse, army and power; they shall lie down together; they shall not rise; they are put out; they are snuffed out like the wick. [18] Do not remember former things, nor consider the things of old. [19] Behold, I will do a new thing; it shall now spring up; shall you not know it? I will even make a way in the wilderness; rivers in the desert. [20] The beast of the field shall honor Me, jackals and daughters of the ostriches; because I give waters in the wilderness, rivers in the desert, to give drink to My people, My chosen. [21] This people (that) I formed for Myself

9 כָּל־הַגּוֹיִם נִקְבְּצוּ יַחְדָּו וְיֵאָסְפוּ לְאֻמִּים מִי בָהֶם יַגִּיד זֹאת
,this can among Who .peoples are and ,together are the All
declare them assembled gathered nations

וְרִאשֹׁנוֹת יַשְׁמִיעֻנוּ יִתְּנוּ עֵדֵיהֶם וְיִצְדָּקוּ וְיִשְׁמְעוּ וְיֹאמְרוּ
,say and let and be and their them Let us cause former and
hear them ;justified ;witnesses give ?hear to things

10 אֱמֶת׃ אַתֶּם עֵדַי נְאֻם־יְהוָה וְעַבְדִּי אֲשֶׁר בָּחָרְתִּי לְמַעַן
that have I whom My and ,Jehovah states My You (is It)
,chosen servant ,witnesses (are) .true

תֵּדְעוּ וְתַאֲמִינוּ לִי וְתָבִינוּ כִּי־אֲנִי הוּא לְפָנַי לֹא־נוֹצַר אֵל
a was not Before .He I that and ,Me and may you
.god formed Me (am) discern believe know

11 וְאַחֲרַי לֹא יִהְיֶה׃ אָנֹכִי אָנֹכִי יְהוָה וְאֵין מִבַּלְעָדַי
besides and ;Jehovah I ,I shall not And
Me is not (am) .be (any) Me after

12 מוֹשִׁיעַ׃ אָנֹכִי הִגַּדְתִּי וְהוֹשַׁעְתִּי וְהִשְׁמַעְתִּי וְאֵין בָּכֶם זָר
an among and pro- I and I and ,declared I .Savior a
alien you is not ;claimed ,saved

13 וְאַתֶּם עֵדַי נְאֻם־יְהוָה וַאֲנִי־אֵל׃ גַּם־מִיּוֹם אֲנִי הוּא וְאֵין
and ,He I from ,Also .God I and ;Jehovah states My you and
none (am) day (this) (am) ,witnesses (are)

14 מִיָּדִי מַצִּיל אֶפְעַל וּמִי יְשִׁיבֶנָּה׃ כֹּה־אָמַר יְהוָה גֹּאַלְכֶם
your Jehovah says Thus reverse will and will I .delivers from
,Redeemer ?it who ,work hand My

קְדוֹשׁ יִשְׂרָאֵל לְמַעַנְכֶם שִׁלַּחְתִּי בָבֶלָה וְהוֹרַדְתִּי בָרִיחִים
(as) brought and to have I your For ,Israel Holy the
fugitives down Babylon sent sake of One

15 כֻּלָּם וְכַשְׂדִּים בָּאֳנִיּוֹת רִנָּתָם׃ אֲנִי יְהוָה קְדוֹשְׁכֶם בּוֹרֵא
the Holy your ,Jehovah I shout their the in even of all
of Creator ,One (am) .joy of of ships Chaldeans ,them

16 יִשְׂרָאֵל מַלְכְּכֶם׃ כֹּה אָמַר יְהוָה הַנּוֹתֵן בַּיָּם דָּרֶךְ
,way a the in who ,Jehovah says Thus .King your ,Israel
sea puts

17 וּבְמַיִם עַזִּים נְתִיבָה׃ הַמּוֹצִיא רֶכֶב־וָסוּס חַיִל וְעִזּוּז יַחְדָּו
to- and force and chariot brings who ,path a mighty in and
gether ;power ,horse out waters

18 יִשְׁכְּבוּ בַּל־יָקוּמוּ דָּעֲכוּ כַּפִּשְׁתָּה כָבוּ׃ אַל־תִּזְכְּרוּ רִאשֹׁנוֹת
former Do not are they the like are they they not shall they
;things remember .out snuffed wick ;quenched ;rise shall ;down lie

19 וְקַדְמֹנִיּוֹת אַל־תִּתְבֹּנָנוּ׃ הִנְנִי עֹשֶׂה חֲדָשָׁה עַתָּה תִצְמָח
shall it now new a do ,Behold ,consider do not things or
;sprout ;thing I ,old of

הֲלוֹא תֵדָעוּהָ אַף אָשִׂים בַּמִּדְבָּר דֶּרֶךְ בִּישִׁמוֹן נְהָרוֹת׃
.rivers the in ;way a the in will I ,Yea know you shall
desert wilderness make ?it not

20 תְּכַבְּדֵנִי חַיַּת הַשָּׂדֶה תַּנִּים וּבְנוֹת יַעֲנָה כִּי־נָתַתִּי בַמִּדְבָּר
the in I because the dau- and jackals the the honor shall
wilderness give ;ostriches of ghters ,field of beast Me

21 מַיִם נְהָרוֹת בִּישִׁימֹן לְהַשְׁקוֹת עַמִּי בְחִירִי׃ עַם־זוּ יָצַרְתִּי
I This My My give to the in rivers ,waters
formed people .chosen ,people drink to ,desert

shall declare My praise.
[22] But you have not
called on Me, Jacob; but
you have been weary of Me,
Israel. [23] You have not
brought Me the lamb of
your burnt offerings;
even your sacrifices have
not honored Me. I
have not caused you to
serve with an offering, nor
wearied you with incense.
[24] You have not bought
sweet cane for Me with
silver, nor have you filled
Me (with) the fat of your
sacrifices; but you bur-
dened Me with your sins;
you wearied Me with your
iniquities. [25] I (am) He
who blots out your sins for
My own sake, and will not
remember your sins.
[26] Cause Me to remem-
ber; let us enter into judgment together; sum up for
yourself, that you may be
justified. [27] Your first
father sinned, and your interpreters transgressed
against Me. [28] And I will
defile the leaders of the
sanctuary, and have given
Jacob to the curse, and
Israel to blasphemies.

22
לִי תְהִלָּתִי יְסַפֵּרוּ: וְלֹא־אֹתִי קָרָאתָ יַעֲקֹב כִּי־יָגַעְתָּ בִּי
of are you for ;Jacob you Me But will they My for
,Me weary ,called not .tell praise ;Me

23
יִשְׂרָאֵל: לֹא־הֵבֵיאתָ לִּי שֵׂה עֹלֹתֶיךָ וּזְבָחֶיךָ לֹא כִבַּדְתָּנִי
honored not your even burnt your lamb, to have you Not .Israel
.Me sacrifices ,offerings of Me brought

24
לֹא הֶעֱבַדְתִּיךָ בְּמִנְחָה וְלֹא הוֹגַעְתִּיךָ בִּלְבוֹנָה: לֹא־קָנִיתָ
You not with wearied and food a with you caused I Not
bought .frankincense you not ,offering serve to

לִי בַכֶּסֶף קָנֶה וְחֵלֶב זְבָחֶיךָ לֹא הִרְוִיתָנִי אַךְ הֶעֱבַדְתַּנִי
made you but filled you not your (with)and cala- with for
serve Me only ;Me sacrifices of fat -mus silver Me

25
בְּחַטֹּאותֶיךָ הוֹגַעְתַּנִי בַּעֲוֹנֹתֶיךָ: אָנֹכִי הוּא מֹחֶה
blotting He I ,I your by wearied you your by
out (am) .iniquities Me ;sins

26
פְשָׁעֶיךָ לְמַעֲנִי וְחַטֹּאותֶיךָ לֹא אֶזְכֹּר: הַזְכִּירֵנִי נִשָּׁפְטָה
us let Remind will I not your and My for your
judge ,Me .remember sins ,sake trespasses

27
יָחַד סַפֵּר אַתָּה לְמַעַן תִּצְדָּק: אָבִיךָ הָרִאשׁוֹן חָטָא
,sinned first Your may you that (for) sum to-
father .justified be ,yourself up ;gether

28
וּמְלִיצֶיךָ פָּשְׁעוּ בִי: וַאֲחַלֵּל שָׂרֵי קֹדֶשׁ וְאֶתְּנָה לַחֵרֶם
the to will and the the will I So against trans- your and
devotion give ,sanctuary of chiefs defile .Me gressed interpreters

יַעֲקֹב וְיִשְׂרָאֵל לְגִדּוּפִים:
to and ,Jacob
.blasphemies Israel

CAP. XLIV מד

CHAPTER 44

CHAPTER 44

[1] Yet now listen, O
Jacob, My servant, and
Israel whom I have chosen:
[2] Thus / says Jehovah,
your maker and your form-
er from the womb, He
helps you. Do not fear,
Jacob My servant; and you,
Jeshurun, I have chosen
him. [3] For I will pour
water on a thirsty place,
and floods on the dry
ground; I will pour My
Spirit on your seed and My
blessing on your offspring.
[4] And they shall spring
up as among grass, as willows by the streams.
[5] One shall say, I (am)
Jehovah's, and another will
call by the name of Jacob;
and this (one) shall write
with his hand, For Jehovah,
and be named by the name
of Israel. [6] Thus says Jehovah, the King of Israel,
and his redeemer, Jehovah

1
2
וְעַתָּה שְׁמַע יַעֲקֹב עַבְדִּי וְיִשְׂרָאֵל בָּחַרְתִּי בוֹ: כֹּה־אָמַר
says Thus :him have I Israel and My Jacob ,listen And
chosen ;servant now

יְהוָה עֹשֶׂךָ וְיֹצֶרְךָ מִבֶּטֶן יַעְזְרֶךָ אַל־תִּירָא עַבְדִּי יַעֲקֹב
;Jacob My and ,fear do not helps He the from your and your Jehovah
servant ,you ,womb Former Maker

3
וִישֻׁרוּן בָּחַרְתִּי בוֹ: כִּי אֶצָּק־מַיִם עַל־צָמֵא וְנֹזְלִים עַל־
on and thirsty a on water will I For .him have I
floods place pour chosen ,Jeshurun

4
יַבָּשָׁה אֶצֹּק רוּחִי עַל־זַרְעֶךָ וּבִרְכָתִי עַל־צֶאֱצָאֶיךָ: וְצָמְחוּ
they And your on My and your on My will I dry
sprout shall .offspring blessing seed spirit pour ;ground

5
בְּבֵין חָצִיר כַּעֲרָבִים עַל־יִבְלֵי־מָיִם: זֶה יֹאמַר לַיהוָה
To shall This .water streams by as ,grass as
Jehovah ,say one of willows among

אֲנִי וְזֶה יִקְרָא בְשֵׁם־יַעֲקֹב וְזֶה יִכְתֹּב יָדוֹ לַיהוָה וּבְשֵׁם
the by and For his shall and ,Jacob the by shall and I
of name ,Jehovah ,hand write this of name call this ;(am)

6
יִשְׂרָאֵל יְכַנֶּה: כֹּה־אָמַר יְהוָה מֶלֶךְ־יִשְׂרָאֵל וְגֹאֲלוֹ
his and ,Israel the Jehovah says Thus be shall Israel
,Redeemer of King .named

of hosts: I (am) the first and I am the last; and no God exists except Me. [7] And who, as I, shall call and shall declare this, and set it in order before Me, since I placed the people of old? And of coming events; yea, which shall come, let them tell for them. [8] Do not fear nor be afraid. Have I not since then made you hear, and declared it? So you (are) My witnesses: Is there a God besides Me? Yea, there is none; I have not known a Rock.

[9] Those who form a carved image are all of them vanity. And their delights do not profit; and they (are) their own witnesses: they do not see or know, that they may be ashamed. [10] Who has formed a god, or melted a graven image, that is worthless? [11] Behold, all his companions shall be ashamed; and the craftsmen (are) of men. They shall gather together, all of them shall stand: they shall dread; they shall be ashamed together. [12] He carves iron with a tool; he works in the coals and forms it with hammers, and works it with his powerful arms; and he shall be hungry, and has no strength; he drinks no water and is weary. [13] He fashions wood, and stretches a line; he marks it with a stylus; he shapes it with the carving tool; and he marks it with a compass. And he makes it according to the figure of a man, as the beauty of a man, to sit in the house. [14] He cuts down cedars and takes cypress and oak, and he strengthens for him in the trees of the forest; he plants a laurel, and rain nourishes. [15] And it shall be for a man to burn; and he takes of them and is warmed; yea, he kindles (it) and bakes bread. Yea, he makes a god and worships; he makes it a carved image and bows to it. [16] He burns half of it in the fire; he eats flesh on half of it – he

יְהוָה צְבָאוֹת אֲנִי רִאשׁוֹן וַאֲנִי אַחֲרוֹן וּמִבַּלְעָדַי אֵין אֱלֹהִים׃
,God there except and the I and the I :hosts Jehovah
no is Me ,last .(am) ,first (am) of

7 וּמִי־כָמוֹנִי יִקְרָא וְיַגִּידֶהָ וְיַעְרְכֶהָ לִי מִשּׂוּמִי עַם־עוֹלָם
.old the I since before it set and and Let ?I as (is) And
of people placed ,Me order in ,it declare call him who

8 וְאֹתִיּוֹת וַאֲשֶׁר תָּבֹאנָה יַגִּידוּ לָמוֹ׃ אַל־תִּפְחֲדוּ וְאַל־
and Do not about them let shall ,yea things And
not ,dread .them declare ,come which ;come to

תִּרְהוּ הֲלֹא מֵאָז הִשְׁמַעְתִּיךָ וְהִגַּדְתִּי וְאַתֶּם עֵדָי הֲיֵשׁ
Is My (are) And and you made I since Have be
there :witnesses you ?declared hear then not .afraid

9 אֱלוֹהַּ מִבַּלְעָדַי וְאֵין צוּר בַּל־יָדָעְתִּי׃ יֹצְרֵי־פֶסֶל כֻּלָּם
of all carved a Those have I not A ,Yea beside God a
them ,image forming .known rock .(is) none ?Me

תֹּהוּ וַחֲמוּדֵיהֶם בַּל־יוֹעִילוּ וְעֵדֵיהֶם הֵמָּה בַּל־יִרְאוּ וּבַל־
and do not they their and do not their And (are)
not ,see witnesses ;profit delights .vanity

10 יֵדְעוּ לְמַעַן יֵבֹשׁוּ׃ מִי־יָצַר אֵל וּפֶסֶל נָסָךְ לְבִלְתִּי הוֹעִיל׃
?profit no to poured an or a has Who may they that do
,out image ,god formed .ashamed be ,know

11 הֵן כָּל־חֲבֵרָיו יֵבֹשׁוּ וְחָרָשִׁים הֵמָּה מֵאָדָם יִתְקַבְּצוּ כֻלָּם
of all them let from they the and be shall his all Be-
them ,assemble ;men (are) ,artisans ,ashamed companions ,hold

12 יַעַמְדוּ יִפְחֲדוּ יֵבֹשׁוּ יָחַד׃ חָרַשׁ בַּרְזֶל מַעֲצָד וּפָעַל
and (with) iron He .together are they they let
works ,tool a engraves ashamed ,dread ;stand

בַּפֶּחָם וּבַמַּקָּבוֹת יִצְּרֵהוּ וַיִּפְעָלֵהוּ בִּזְרוֹעַ כֹּחוֹ גַּם־רָעֵב
is he and his the with and forms with and the in
,hungry ;strength of arm it works ,it hammers the ,coals

13 וְאֵין כֹּחַ לֹא־שָׁתָה מַיִם וַיִּיעָף׃ חָרַשׁ עֵצִים נָטָה קָו
a he ,wood He is and ,water he not ;strength and
;line stretches carves .weary drinks is not

יְתָאֲרֵהוּ בַשֶּׂרֶד יַעֲשֵׂהוּ בַּמַּקְצֻעוֹת וּבַמְּחוּגָה יְתָאֳרֵהוּ
marks he with and carving the with he the with marks he
.it compass a ,tools it makes ;stylus it

וַיַּעֲשֵׂהוּ כְּתַבְנִית אִישׁ כְּתִפְאֶרֶת אָדָם לָשֶׁבֶת בָּיִת׃
(the in) to ,man a the as ,man a the as he And
.house sit of beauty of figure it makes

14 לִכְרָת־לוֹ אֲרָזִים וַיִּקַּח תִּרְזָה וְאַלּוֹן וַיְאַמֶּץ־לוֹ בַּעֲצֵי־יָעַר
the the in for he and and cypress and ,cedars for cuts (He)
;forest of trees him strengthens ;oak takes he him down

15 נָטַע אֹרֶן וְגֶשֶׁם יְגַדֵּל׃ וְהָיָה לְאָדָם לְבָעֵר וַיִּקַּח מֵהֶם
of he and ;burn to a for it And (it) makes and a he
them takes man be shall .grow rain ,laurel plants

וַיָּחָם אַף־יַשִּׂיק וְאָפָה לָחֶם אַף־יִפְעַל־אֵל וַיִּשְׁתָּחוּ עָשָׂהוּ
makes he and god a he ,Yea .bread and he ,yea is and
it ;worships makes bakes ,kindles ;warmed

16 פֶסֶל וַיִּסְגָּד־לָמוֹ׃ חֶצְיוֹ שָׂרַף בְּמוֹ־אֵשׁ עַל־חֶצְיוֹ בָּשָׂר
flesh half on the in he Half .it to and carved a
it of ;fire burns it of bows ,image

roasts roast and is satisfied; yea, he warms himself and says, Ah, I am warm; I have seen the fire. [17] And he makes a god of the rest, his carved image; he bows to it and worships, and prays to it, and says, Deliver me, for you (are) my god. [18] They do not know, nor discern; for he has smeared their eyes from seeing, their hearts from understanding. [19] And not one returns to his heart, nor has knowledge nor discernment to say, I have burned half of it in the fire; and I also have baked bread on its coals; I have roasted flesh and eaten it, and I have made the rest of it into an idol? Shall I bow to a product of a tree? [20] Feeding on ashes, a deceived heart turns him aside, and he does not deliver his soul, nor say, Is there not a lie in my right hand?

[21] Remember these, O Jacob and Israel; for you (are) My servant; I have formed you; you (are) My servant, O Israel; you shall not forget Me. [22] I have blotted out, like a thick cloud, your transgressions; and like a cloud, your sins. Return to Me, for I have redeemed you. [23] Sing, O heavens, for Jehovah has acted. Shout, O lower parts of the earth; burst forth into praise, O mountains, O forest and every tree in it; for Jehovah has redeemed Jacob and glorifies Himself in Israel. [24] Thus says Jehovah, your Redeemer, and He who formed you from the womb, I (am) Jehovah who makes all things; who stretches out the heavens; I alone spreading out the earth; who (was) with Me? [25] (Who) frustrates the signs of the liars, and makes diviners mad; turning sages backward, and making their knowledge foolish? [26] He confirms the word of His servant and completes the counsel of His

יאכל יצלה צלי וישבע אף־יחם ויאמר האח חמותי
am I ,Ah ,says and warms he ,yea is and roast a he he
;warm himself ;satisfied roasts ;eats

17 ראיתי אור׃ ושאריתו לאל עשה לפסלו יסגוד־לו
to he carved his he for the And the have I
it bows ;image ,makes god a it of rest .fire seen

18 וישתחו ויתפלל אליו ויאמר הצילני כי אלי אתה׃ לא
not you my for Deliver ,says and ,it to prays and and
.(are) god ,me it worships

ידעו ולא יבינו כי טח מראות עיניהם מהשכיל לבתם׃
their under- from their from has he for ,discern and They
;hearts standing ,eyes seeing smeared not ,know

19 ולא־ישיב אל־לבו ולא דעת ולא־תבונה לאמר חציו
Half ,say to discernment and (has) and his to one and
it of not knowledge not ,heart returns not

שרפתי במו־אש ואף אפיתי על־גחליו לחם אצלה
have I ;bread its on have I and ,fire the in have I
roasted coals baked also burned

בשר ואכל ויתרו לתועבה אעשה לבול עץ אסגוד׃
I shall a a To have I an for the and and flesh
?bow tree of product !made abomination it of rest ,eaten

20 רעה אפר לב הותל הטהו ולא־יציל את־נפשו ולא
and his he and him turns deceived a ;ashes Feeding
not ,soul delivers not ,aside heart (on)

21 יאמר הלוא־שקר בימיני׃ זכר־אלה יעקב וישראל
and ,Jacob O ,these Remember my in lie a Is ,says he
;Israel ?hand right not

כי עבדי־אתה יצרתיך עבד־לי אתה ישראל לא תנשני׃
shall you not ,Israel O you to a formed I you My for
.Me forget ;(are) Me ,servant ,you ;(are) servant

22 מחיתי כעב פשעיך וכענן חטאותיך שובה אלי כי גאלתיך׃
re- have I for to Return your as and trans- your a as have I
.you deemed ,Me .sins cloud a ;gressions cloud erased

23 רנו שמים כי־עשה יהוה הריעו תחתיות ארץ פצחו
burst the lower O ,Shout .Jehovah has for O ,Sing
;forth ;earth of parts (it) done ,heavens

הרים רנה יער וכל־עץ בו כי־גאל יהוה יעקב ובישראל
in and ,Jacob Jehovah has for in tree and O (into) moun- O
Israel redeemed ,it every ,forest ;praise ,tains

24 יתפאר׃ כה־אמר יהוה גאלך ויצרך מבטן אנכי יהוה
Jehovah I the from your and your Jehovah says Thus glorifies
(am) ,womb Former Redeemer .Himself

25 עשה כל נטה שמים לבדי רקע הארץ מי אתי׃ מפר
Frustra- with who the spreading ;alone I the stretching all who
ting ?me (was) ;earth ,heavens ;things makes

אתות בדים וקסמים יהולל משיב חכמים אחור
back- ones wise turning makes He ,yea ;boasters the
,ward ;mad diviners of signs

26 ודעתם יסכל׃ מקים דבר עבדו ועצת מלאכיו ישלים
He His and His the Confirming making their and
.finishes messengers' counsel ,servant of word .foolish knowledge

messengers. (He) says to Jerusalem, You will be peopled; and to the cities of Judah, You shall be built; and, I will raise up its ruins. [27] (He) says to the deep, Be a waste; and, I will dry up your rivers! [28] (He) says to Cyrus, (You are) My shepherd and all My will he will do, even to say to Jerusalem, You shall be built; and to the temple, You shall be set up.

CHAPTER 45

[1] Thus says Jehovah to His anointed, to Cyrus, whom I have seized by his right hand, to subdue nations before him; yea, I will open the loins of kings, to open before him the two-leaved doors, and the gates shall not be shut. [2] I will go before you and make hills level; I will tear apart the bronze doors and cut the iron bars in two. [3] And I will give you the treasures of darkness, even treasures in secret places, that you may know that I (am) Jehovah, who calls you by your name, the God of Israel. [4] For Jacob My servant's sake, and Israel My elect, even I call you by your name. I name you, but you do not know Me. [5] I (am) Jehovah, and none else (is); there is no God except Me. I will clothe you, though you do not know Me, [6] that they may know from the rising of the sun, and to the sunset, that none besides Me (is); I (am) Jehovah, and none else (is); [7] forming light and creating darkness, making peace and creating evil; I, Jehovah, do all these things.

[8] Drop down, O heavens, from above; and let the cloud pour down righteousness. Let the earth open and let grow salvation,

הָאֹמֵר לִירוּשָׁלַםִ תּוּשָׁב וּלְעָרֵי יְהוּדָה תִּבָּנֶינָה וְחָרְבוֹתֶיהָ
its and shall you ,Judah's to and be will You to Who
wastes ;built be cities ,peopled ,Jerusalem says

27 28 אֲקוֹמֵם׃ הָאֹמֵר לַצּוּלָה חֳרָבִי וְנַהֲרֹתַיִךְ אוֹבִישׁ׃ הָאֹמֵר
Who will I your And a Be the to Who will I
says .up dry rivers !waste ,deep says .up raise

לְכוֹרֶשׁ רֹעִי וְכָל־חֶפְצִי יַשְׁלִם וְלֵאמֹר לִירוּשָׁלַםִ תִּבָּנֶה
be will You to to even shall he My and My ,Cyrus to
;built ,Jerusalem say ,complete pleasure all ,shepherd

וְהֵיכָל תִּוָּסֵד׃
shall You the (to) and
.founded be , temple

CAP. XLV מה

CHAPTER 45

1 כֹּה־אָמַר יְהוָה לִמְשִׁיחוֹ לְכוֹרֶשׁ אֲשֶׁר־הֶחֱזַקְתִּי בִימִינוֹ
his by have I whom ,Cyrus to His to Jehovah says Thus
,hand right seized ,anointed

לְרַד לְפָנָיו גּוֹיִם וּמָתְנֵי מְלָכִים אֲפַתֵּחַ לִפְתֹּחַ לְפָנָיו
before open to will I kings the yea ;nations before to
him ,open of loins him subdue

2 דְּלָתַיִם וּשְׁעָרִים לֹא יִסָּגֵרוּ׃ אֲנִי לְפָנֶיךָ אֵלֵךְ וַהֲדוּרִים
and will before I shall not the and leaved-two
swells ,go you .shut be gates ;doors

3 אוֹשֵׁר דַּלְתוֹת נְחוּשָׁה אֲשַׁבֵּר וּבְרִיחֵי בַרְזֶל אֲגַדֵּעַ׃ וְנָתַתִּי
I And cut iron bars and will I bronze doors make
give .apart of apart break of ;level

לְךָ אוֹצְרוֹת חֹשֶׁךְ וּמַטְמֻנֵי מִסְתָּרִים לְמַעַן תֵּדַע כִּי אֲנִי
I that you that secret riches and ,darkness treasures to
(am) know may ,places of of you

4 יְהוָה הַקּוֹרֵא בְשִׁמְךָ אֱלֹהֵי יִשְׂרָאֵל׃ לְמַעַן עַבְדִּי יַעֲקֹב
,Jacob My the For .Israel the your by who ,Jehovah
servant of sake of God ,name (you) calls

וְיִשְׂרָאֵל בְּחִירִי וָאֶקְרָא לְךָ בִּשְׁמֶךָ אֲכַנְּךָ וְלֹא יְדַעְתָּנִי׃
know you but name I your by you I even My Israel and
.Me not ,you ,name call ,elect

5 אֲנִי יְהוָה וְאֵין עוֹד זוּלָתִי אֵין אֱלֹהִים אֲאַזֶּרְךָ וְלֹא יְדַעְתָּנִי׃
know you though will I .God there except any and ,Jehovah I
,Me not ,you clothe no is Me ,more none (am)

6 לְמַעַן יֵדְעוּ מִמִּזְרַח־שֶׁמֶשׁ וּמִמַּעֲרָבָה כִּי־אֶפֶס בִּלְעָדָי
besides none that the to and the the from may they that
;Me (is) ,sunset sun of rising know

7 אֲנִי יְהוָה וְאֵין עוֹד׃ יוֹצֵר אוֹר וּבוֹרֵא חֹשֶׁךְ עֹשֶׂה שָׁלוֹם
peace making ;darkness and light Forming any and Jeho- I
creating !more none (am)

8 וּבוֹרֵא רָע אֲנִי יְהוָה עֹשֶׂה כָל־אֵלֶּה׃ הַרְעִיפוּ
Drop these all do ,Jehovah ,I ;evil and
,down .things creating

שָׁמַיִם מִמַּעַל וּשְׁחָקִים יִזְּלוּ־צֶדֶק תִּפְתַּח־אֶרֶץ וְיִפְרוּ־יֶשַׁע
salva- let and the let righ- pour let and from O
tion fruit bear ,earth open ;teousness clouds ;above ,heavens

and let righteousness spring
up, together; I Jehovah have
created it. [9] Woe (to) him
who fights with his Former!
A potsherd among the pot-
sherds of the earth! Shall
the clay say to him who
forms it, What are you
making? Or your work, He
has no hands? [10] Woe
(to) him who says to a
father, What are you father-
ing? Or to the woman, What
are you laboring over?
[11] Thus says Jehovah,
the Holy One of Israel, and
his Former. Do you ask Me
the things to come? About
My sons, and about the
work of My hands, do you
ask Me? [12] I have made
the earth and created man
on it; I stretched out the
heavens (with) My hands;
and I have ordered all their
host. [13] I raised him up
in righteousness, and made
straight all his ways. He
shall build My city, and he
will release My captives; not
for price, nor for reward,
says Jehovah of hosts.
[14] Thus says Jehovah,
The labor of Egypt and the
goods of Ethiopia and of
the Sabeans, men of
stature, shall come to you,
and they shall be yours.
They shall come after you,
they shall cross in chains,
and they shall bow to you;
they shall plead. Surely
God (is) in you, and none
else (is), no (other) God.
[15] Truly You (are) a
God who hides Himself, O
God of Israel, the Savior.

[16] They shall be ashamed,
and also are disgraced, all of
them, together they go into
disgrace, carvers of images.
[17] Israel is saved in Jehovah, (with) everlasting salvation. You shall not be
ashamed nor disgraced to
the forevers of eternity.
[18] For thus says Jeho-
vah, Creator of the
heavens; He (is) God, forming the earth and making it;
He has established it; forming it to be inhabited, not

וצדקה תצמיח יחד אני יהוה בראתיו׃ 9 הוי רב
who him Woe strives (to) have .it created Jehovah I ;together make it let sprout righ- and teousness
את־יצרו חרש את־חרשי אדמה היאמר חמר ליצרו
its to ,former clay Shall say the !earth pot- the among of sherds A potsherd his with !Former
מה־תעשה ופעלך אין־ידים לו׃ 10 הוי אמר לאב
a to ,father him says Woe who (to) to ?him hands No (are) your Or ,work you are What ?making
מה־תוליד ולאשה מה־תחילין׃ 11 כה־אמר יהוה קדוש
Holy the of One ,Jehovah says Thus you are ?over laboring What a to Or ,woman you are What ?fathering
ישראל ויצרו האתיות שאלוני על־בני ועל־פעל ידי
My the hands of work and about My ;sons about you Do ?Me ask things the come to his and ,Former Israel
תצוני׃ 12 אנכי עשיתי ארץ ואדם עליה בראתי אני ידי
(with) I hands My ,created it on and man the ,earth have made I you do ?Me ask
נטו שמים וכל־צבאם צויתי׃ 13 אנכי העירתהו בצדק וכל־
and all righ- in ,teousness raised up him I have I .ordered their host and the all ;heavens stretched out
דרכיו אישר הוא־יבנה עירי וגלותי ישלח לא במחיר
for ,price not will he ;release My and captives My ,city shall build He made .straight his ways
ולא בשחד אמר יהוה צבאות׃ 14 כה אמר יהוה
,Jehovah says Thus .hosts Jehovah of says for ,reward and not
יגיע מצרים וסחר־כוש וסבאים אנשי מדה עליך יעברו
shall ,cross to you ,stature of men of and ,Sabeans the Ethiopia the and of goods ,Egypt The of labor
ולך יהיו אחריך ילכו בזקים יעברו ואליך ישתחוו אליך
you to ;bow shall they to and you shall they ;cross in chains shall they ;come after you shall they ;be and you to
יתפללו אך בך אל ואין עוד אפס אלהים׃ 15 אכן אתה אל
a God You (are) Truly .God no (other) any ,more is and not God ;(is) you in ,Surely shall they .plead
מסתתר אלהי ישראל מושיע׃ 16 בושו וגם־נכלמו כלם
of all ;them dis- ,graced are also and ,ashamed are They the .Savior ,Israel the of God hiding ,Himself
יחדו הלכו בכלמה חרשי צירים׃ 17 ישראל נושע ביהוה
in ,Jehovah saved is Israel .images carvers of into ,disgrace go they to- gether
תשועת עולמים לא־תבשו ולא־תכלמו עד־עולמי עד׃
of .eternity for- the evers to be shall disgraced and not shall You not ashamed be .everlasting (with) salvation
18 כי־כה אמר־יהוה בורא השמים הוא האלהים
;God (is) He the ,heavens Creator of ,Jehovah says thus For
יצר הארץ ועשה הוא כוננה לא־תהו בראה לשבת
be to inhabited creating ,it empty not establishes ;it He mak- ;it and ing the earth forming

creating it empty: I (am) Jehovah, and none else (is) [19] I have not spoken in secret, in a dark place of the earth; I did not say to Jacob's seed, Seek Me in vain; I Jehovah speak righteousness; I declaring things that are right. [20] Gather yourselves and come; draw near together, escaped ones of the nations; those who set up the wood of their graven image, and those who pray to a god (who) cannot save — they know nothing. [21] Declare and bring (them) near; yea, let them consult together. Who has revealed this from of old; who has told it from then? Is it not I, Jehovah? And none else (is) a God besides Me, a just God and a Savior; none except Me. [22] Turn to Me and be saved, all the ends of the earth; for I (am) God, and none else (is). [23] I have sworn by Myself, the word has gone out of My mouth (in) righteousness, and shall not return; that to Me every knee shall bow, every tongue shall swear; [24] he shall say, Only in Jehovah do I have righteousness and strength; to Him he comes; and all who are angry with Him shall be ashamed.

[25] In Jehovah all of the seed of Israel shall be justified, and shall glory.

19 יְצָרָהּ אֲנִי יְהוָה וְאֵין עוֹד׃ לֹא בַסֵּתֶר דִּבַּרְתִּי בִּמְקוֹם
a in have I in Not any and Jeho- I forming
of place ,spoken secret .more none ,vah (am) :it

אֶרֶץ חֹשֶׁךְ לֹא אָמַרְתִּי לְזֶרַע יַעֲקֹב תֹּהוּ בַקְּשׁוּנִי אֲנִי יְהוָה
Jehovah I Seek vain in ,Jacob the to did I not ;dark the
;Me of seed say earth

20 דֹּבֵר צֶדֶק מַגִּיד מֵישָׁרִים׃ הִקָּבְצוּ וָבֹאוּ הִתְנַגְּשׁוּ יַחְדָּו
,together draw and Gather right declaring righ- speak
near ,come yourselves .things ,teousness

פְּלִיטֵי הַגּוֹיִם לֹא יָדְעוּ הַנֹּשְׂאִים אֶת־עֵץ פִּסְלָם וּמִתְפַּלְלִים
those and their the who those they not the escaped
pray who ,image of wood up lift know ;nations of ones

21 אֶל־אֵל לֹא יוֹשִׁיעַ׃ הַגִּידוּ וְהַגִּישׁוּ אַף יִוָּעֲצוּ יַחְדָּו מִי
Who to- them let ,yea bring and Declare (who) not a to
.gether consult ;near (it) .saves god

הִשְׁמִיעַ זֹאת מִקֶּדֶם מֵאָז הִגִּידָהּ הֲלוֹא אֲנִי יְהוָה וְאֵין
And ?Jehovah ,I it Is told has from from this has
not not ?it then ,old of revealed

22 עוֹד אֱלֹהִים מִבַּלְעָדַי אֵל־צַדִּיק וּמוֹשִׁיעַ אַיִן זוּלָתִי׃ פְּנוּ־
Turn except none a and just a beside a any
.Me is —Savior God —Me God more

23 אֵלַי וְהִוָּשְׁעוּ כָּל־אַפְסֵי־אָרֶץ כִּי אֲנִי־אֵל וְאֵין עוֹד׃ בִּי
By any and ,God I for the the all be and to
Myself .more none (am) ,earth of ends ,saved Me

נִשְׁבַּעְתִּי יָצָא מִפִּי צְדָקָה דָּבָר וְלֹא יָשׁוּב כִּי־לִי תִּכְרַע
shall to that shall and the righ- (in) My from has have I
bow Me ;return not ,word teousness mouth gone ;sworn

24 כָּל־בֶּרֶךְ תִּשָּׁבַע כָּל־לָשׁוֹן׃ אַךְ בַּיהוָה לִי אָמַר צְדָקוֹת
righ- he (is) in Only .tongue every shall ,knee every
teousness ,says ,me to Jehovah swear

25 וָעֹז עָדָיו יָבוֹא וְיֵבֹשׁוּ כֹּל הַנֶּחֱרִים בּוֹ׃ בַּיהוָה יִצְדְּקוּ
be shall In with are who all they and he to and
justified Jehovah .Him angry ,ashamed are ,comes Him;strength

וְיִתְהַלְלוּ כָּל־זֶרַע יִשְׂרָאֵל׃
.Israel the all shall and
of seed glory

CAP. XLVI מו

CHAPTER 46

CHAPTER 46

[1] Bel has bowed; Nebo stoops; their idols are for the beast, and for the cattle; your things carried are loads; a burden for the weary. [2] They stoop; they bow together; they are not able to deliver the burden; and their soul has gone into captivity. [3] Listen to me, O house of Jacob, and all the remnant of Israel; who are borne from the

1 כָּרַע בֵּל קֹרֵס נְבוֹ הָיוּ עֲצַבֵּיהֶם לַחַיָּה וְלַבְּהֵמָה
for and the for their are ;Nebo stoops ,Bel has
;cattle the beast idols bowed

2 נְשֻׂאֹתֵיכֶם עֲמוּסוֹת מַשָּׂא לַעֲיֵפָה׃ קָרְסוּ כָרְעוּ יַחְדָּו לֹא
not ;together they They the for a (are) things your
bow ,stoop .weary burden ;loads carried

3 יָכְלוּ מַלֵּט מַשָּׂא וְנַפְשָׁם בַּשְּׁבִי הָלָכָה׃ שִׁמְעוּ
Listen has into their and the to are they
.gone captivity soul ;burden rescue able

אֵלַי בֵּית יַעֲקֹב וְכָל־שְׁאֵרִית בֵּית יִשְׂרָאֵל הַעֲמֻסִים מִנִּי־
from are who ,Israel the rem- the and ,Jacob house to
borne of house of nant all of Me

belly, who are carried from the womb: [4] Even to old age I (am) He; and I will bear to gray hair; I made, and I will carry; and I will bear and deliver. [5] To whom will you compare Me and make Me equal; and compare Me, that we may be alike? [6] Those who lavish gold out of the bag, and weigh silver on the measure; they hire a refiner and he makes it a god. They fall down; yea, they worship. [7] They carry it on the shoulder; they bear it and set it in its place, and it stands; it shall not move from its place. Yes, he cries to it, but it does not answer, it does not save him from his distress. [8] Remember this and be a man; take (it), transgressors, from forever. [9] Remember former things of the past, for I am God, and none else (is) God, and none like Me, [10] declaring the end from the beginning, and from the past those things which were not done, saying, My purpose shall rise; and, I will do all My desire;

[11] calling a bird of prey from the sunrise, the man of My counsel from a far off land. Yes, I have spoken; yes, I will bring it; I have formed; yes, I will do it. [12] Listen to Me, mighty ones of heart who are far from righteousness: I bring near My righteousness; it shall not be far off, and My salvation shall not wait; I will place salvation in Zion, My glory for Israel.

4 בֶטֶן הַנְּשֻׂאִים מִנִּי־רָחַם׃ וְעַד־זִקְנָה אֲנִי הוּא וְעַד־שֵׂיבָה
gray and ;He I old Even the from are who the
hair to (am) age to !womb carried ,belly

אֲנִי אֶסְבֹּל אֲנִי עָשִׂיתִי וַאֲנִי אֶשָּׂא וַאֲנִי אֶסְבֹּל וַאֲמַלֵּט׃
and will and will I and ,made I will I
.rescue bear I carry ;bear

5 לְמִי תְדַמְּיוּנִי וְתַשְׁווּ וְתַמְשִׁלוּנִי וְנִדְמֶה׃ הַזָּלִים
Those may we that compare and make and you will To
lavishing ?alike be Me ;equal Me ,Me liken whom

6 זָהָב מִכִּיס וְכֶסֶף בַּקָּנֶה יִשְׁקֹלוּ יִשְׂכְּרוּ צוֹרֵף וְיַעֲשֵׂהוּ
he and re- a they ;weigh the on even of out gold
it makes ,finer hire rod cane silver ,bag a

7 אֵל יִסְגְּדוּ אַף־יִשְׁתַּחֲווּ׃ יִשָּׂאֻהוּ עַל־כָּתֵף יִסְבְּלֻהוּ וְיַנִּיחֻהוּ
rest and bear they the on They they yea they ;god a
it it ;shoulder it carry .worship ;down bow

תַחְתָּיו וְיַעֲמֹד מִמְּקוֹמוֹ לֹא יָמִישׁ אַף־יִצְעַק אֵלָיו וְלֹא
but ,it to he ,Yes shall it not its from it and its in
not cries .depart place ;stands ,place

8 יַעֲנֶה מִצָּרָתוֹ לֹא יוֹשִׁיעֶנּוּ׃ זִכְרוּ־זֹאת וְהִתְאֹשָׁשׁוּ
a be and this Remember saves it not his from it
;man .him distress ,answers

9 הָשִׁיבוּ פוֹשְׁעִים עַל־לֵב׃ זִכְרוּ רִאשֹׁנוֹת מֵעוֹלָם כִּי אָנֹכִי
I for (your) on former Remember from ,transgressors return
(am) .heart things ;forever ,(it)

10 אֵל וְאֵין עוֹד אֱלֹהִים וְאֶפֶס כָּמוֹנִי׃ מַגִּיד מֵרֵאשִׁית
the from declaring ,Me like even ,God any and ;God
beginning none more none

אַחֲרִית וּמִקֶּדֶם אֲשֶׁר לֹא־נַעֲשׂוּ אֹמֵר עֲצָתִי תָקוּם וְכָל־
and shall My ,saying were not things from and the
all ,rise purpose ,done which past the ,end

11 חֶפְצִי אֶעֱשֶׂה׃ קֹרֵא מִמִּזְרָח עַיִט מֵאֶרֶץ מֶרְחָק אִישׁ
the far from bird a the from calling will I My
of man off land a ,prey of sunrise ;do desire

עֲצָתוֹ אַף־דִּבַּרְתִּי אַף־אֲבִיאֶנָּה יָצַרְתִּי אַף־אֶעֱשֶׂנָּה׃
do will I ,yes have I will I ,yes have I ,Yes My
.it ,formed ;it bring ;spoken purpose

12
13 שִׁמְעוּ אֵלַי אַבִּירֵי לֵב הָרְחוֹקִים מִצְּדָקָה׃ קֵרַבְתִּי צִדְקָתִי
righ- My bring I from are who heart mighty to Listen
;teousness near :righteousness far of ones ,Me

לֹא תִרְחָק וּתְשׁוּעָתִי לֹא תְאַחֵר וְנָתַתִּי בְצִיּוֹן תְּשׁוּעָה
,salvation Zion in will I shall not My and shall it not
place ,wait salvation ,off far be

לְיִשְׂרָאֵל תִּפְאַרְתִּי׃
.glory My Israel for

CAP. XLVII מז

CHAPTER 47

[1] Come down and sit down on the dust, O virgin daughter of Babylon; sit on the ground; there is no

1 רְדִי וּשְׁבִי עַל־עָפָר בְּתוּלַת בַּת־בָּבֶל שְׁבִי־לָאָרֶץ אֵין
not the on sit ;Baby- daughter O the on sit and Go
is ;ground lon of virgin ,dust down

throne, O daughter of the Chaldeans; for you shall no more be called tender or delicate. [2] Take millstones and grind meal; push back the veil; draw up the skirt; uncover your leg; pass over rivers. [3] Your nakedness shall be uncovered; yea, your shame shall be seen — I will take vengeance and I will not meet a man; [4] Our Redeemer; Jehovah of hosts (is) His name, the Holy One of Israel. [5] Sit (in) silence, and go into darkness, O daughter of the Chaldeans, for they shall no more call you the mistress of kingdoms.

[6] I was angry with My people; I defiled My inheritance and gave them into your hand. You gave them no mercy; you made very heavy your yoke on the aged. [7] And you said, I shall be a mistress forever; until you did not set these things on your heart, and not did remember its end. [8] Now, then, hear this, O pleasure seeker, who lives carelessly; who says in her heart, I (am), and none else (is); I shall not sit as a widow, nor shall I know the loss of children. [9] But these two things shall suddenly come to you, in one day: loss of children, and widowhood; as complete they come on you, for your many sorceries, for the multitude of your great spells.

[10] For you trusted in your wickedness; you said, No one sees me. Your wisdom and your knowledge, it leads you away, and you said in your heart, I (am) and none else (is). [11] For this evil shall come on you; you shall not know its origin. And mischief shall fall on you; you shall not be able to cover it. And ruin shall come on you suddenly, you shall not know. [12] Stand now among your spells, and with

כִּסֵּא בַּת־כַּשְׂדִּים כִּי לֹא תוֹסִיפִי יִקְרְאוּ־לָךְ רַכָּה וַעֲנֻגָּה׃
and tender you they shall not for the daughter a
.delicate call again ;Chaldeans of ,throne

2 קְחִי רֵחַיִם וְטַחֲנִי קָמַח גַּלִּי צַמָּתֵךְ חֶשְׂפִּי־שֹׁבֶל גַּלִּי־שׁוֹק
the uncover the strip your un- ;meal and mill Take
;leg ;skirt off ;veil cover grind stones

3 עִבְרִי נְהָרוֹת׃ תִּגָּל עֶרְוָתֵךְ גַּם תֵּרָאֶה חֶרְפָּתֵךְ נָקָם אֶקָּח
will I venge- your be shall also Your be shall ,rivers pass
,take ance ;shame seen ;nakedness uncovered over

4 וְלֹא אֶפְגַּע אָדָם׃ גֹּאֲלֵנוּ יְהוָה צְבָאוֹת שְׁמוֹ קְדוֹשׁ
Holy the His (is) hosts Jehovah Our .man a will I and
of One ,name of ,Redeemer meet not

5 יִשְׂרָאֵל׃ שְׁבִי דוּמָם וּבֹאִי בַחֹשֶׁךְ בַּת־כַּשְׂדִּים כִּי לֹא
not for the daughter into go and (in) Sit .Israel
,Chaldeans of ,darkness silence

6 תוֹסִיפִי יִקְרְאוּ־לָךְ גְּבֶרֶת מַמְלָכוֹת׃ קָצַפְתִּי עַל־עַמִּי
My over was I .kingdoms mistress you they shall
;people angry of call again

חִלַּלְתִּי נַחֲלָתִי וָאֶתְּנֵם בְּיָדֵךְ לֹא־שַׂמְתְּ לָהֶם רַחֲמִים עַל־
on compas- to You not your into and inheri- My I
;sion them gave .hand them gave tance defiled

7 זָקֵן הִכְבַּדְתְּ עֻלֵּךְ מְאֹד׃ וַתֹּאמְרִי לְעוֹלָם אֶהְיֶה גְבָרֶת
a shall I forever you And .very your you made the
;mistress be ,said yoke heavy aged

עַד לֹא־שַׂמְתְּ אֵלֶּה עַל־לִבֵּךְ לֹא זָכַרְתְּ אַחֲרִיתָהּ׃
.end its you not your on these you not until
remembered ;heart things set

8 וְעַתָּה שִׁמְעִי־זֹאת עֲדִינָה הַיּוֹשֶׁבֶת לָבֶטַח הָאֹמְרָה בִּלְבָבָהּ
her in says who ;securely who sensual ,this hear No
,heart lives ,one ,then

אֲנִי וְאַפְסִי עוֹד לֹא אֵשֵׁב אַלְמָנָה וְלֹא אֵדַע שְׁכוֹל׃
of loss shall I and a (as) shall I not any is and I
.children know not ,widow sit ;more none (am)

9 וְתָבֹאנָה לָּךְ שְׁתֵּי־אֵלֶּה רֶגַע בְּיוֹם אֶחָד שְׁכוֹל וְאַלְמֹן
and of loss :one day in ,suddenly these two to shall But
;widowhood children things you come

כְּתֻמָּם בָּאוּ עָלַיִךְ בְּרֹב כְּשָׁפַיִךְ בְּעָצְמַת חֲבָרַיִךְ מְאֹד׃
.great your the for your for ,you on they com- as
spells of power ,sorceries many come plete

10 וַתִּבְטְחִי בְרָעָתֵךְ אָמַרְתְּ אֵין רֹאָנִי חָכְמָתֵךְ וְדַעְתֵּךְ הִיא
it your and your sees no you your in you For
,knowledge wisdom me one said ;wickedness trusted

11 שׁוֹבְבָתֶךְ וַתֹּאמְרִי בְלִבֵּךְ אֲנִי וְאַפְסִי עוֹד׃ וּבָא עָלַיִךְ
you on shall But any and I your in you and you leads
come more none (am) ,heart said ;away

רָעָה לֹא תֵדְעִי שַׁחְרָהּ וְתִפֹּל עָלַיִךְ הֹוָה לֹא תוּכְלִי כַּפְּרָהּ
to shall you not mis- you on and its shall you not ;evil
.it cover able be ;chief fall shall ;origin know

12 וְתָבֹא עָלַיִךְ פִּתְאֹם שׁוֹאָה לֹא תֵדָעִי׃ עִמְדִי־נָא בַחֲבָרַיִךְ
among now Stand shall you not ;ruin suddenly on shall And
.spells your .know you come

your many sorceries, in which you have wearied yourself since your youth — perhaps you will be able to profit; perhaps you may cause quaking. [13] You are exhausted by your many plans; let those dividing the heavens stand up now and save you, the gazers into the stars, making known into the new moons what are coming on you. [14] Behold, they are as stubble; the fire burns them; they shall not save their soul from the flame's hand; not is a coal to warm them; nor fire, to sit before it. [15] So they are to you with whom you have labored, your traders from your youth; each one wanders to his own way; no one saves you.

וּבְרֹב כְּשָׁפַיִךְ בַּאֲשֶׁר יָגַעַתְּ מִנְּעוּרָיִךְ אוּלַי תּוּכְלִי הוֹעִיל

to will you perhaps your from you which in your with and
;profit able be ;youth labored ,sorceries many

13 אוּלַי תַּעֲרוֹצִי׃ נִלְאֵית בְּרֹב עֲצָתָיִךְ יַעַמְדוּ־נָא וְיוֹשִׁיעֻךְ

save and. now let your by are You may you perhaps
you up stand ;plans many exhausted quaking cause

הֹבְרוּ שָׁמַיִם הַחֹזִים בַּכּוֹכָבִים מוֹדִיעִים לֶחֳדָשִׁים מֵאֲשֶׁר

from the into making the into the the those
what moons new known ,stars gazers ,heavens dividing

14 יָבֹאוּ עָלָיִךְ׃ הִנֵּה הָיוּ כְקַשׁ אֵשׁ שְׂרָפָתַם לֹא־יַצִּילוּ אֶת־

shall they not burns the as they be- .you on are
save ;them fire ,stubble are hold coming

נַפְשָׁם מִיַּד לֶהָבָה אֵין־גַּחֶלֶת לַחְמָם אוּר לָשֶׁבֶת נֶגְדּוֹ׃

before sit to (nor) warm to coal there the the from their
.it ,fire ,them no is ;flame of hand soul

15 כֵּן הָיוּ־לָךְ אֲשֶׁר יָגָעַתְּ סֹחֲרַיִךְ מִנְּעוּרַיִךְ אִישׁ לְעֶבְרוֹ

his to each your from your you (with) to they So
side own man ;youth traders ,labored whom you are

תָּעוּ אֵין מוֹשִׁיעֵךְ׃

.you saves none they
;wander

CAP. XLVIII מח

CHAPTER 48

[1] Hear this, O house of Jacob, who are called by the name of Israel, and have come out from the waters of Judah, who swear by Jehovah's name and profess by the God of Israel — not in truth or in righteousness. [2] For they are called of the holy city, and rest themselves on the God of Israel; Jehovah of hosts (is) His name. [3] I have foretold the former things from then; and they went out of My mouth; and I made them hear; suddenly I acted, and they came about. [4] Because I knew that you (are) hard, and your neck is a sinew of iron, and your brow brass. [5] And I declared to you from then; before it came I made you hear, lest you should say, My idol did them; and my image and my casted image commanded them. [6] You heard; see it all; and will you not declare? I made you hear new things from now, even hidden things,

1 שִׁמְעוּ־זֹאת בֵּית־יַעֲקֹב הַנִּקְרָאִים בְּשֵׁם יִשְׂרָאֵל וּמִמֵּי

from and ,Israel the by are who ,Jacob house ,this Hear
waters of name called of

יְהוּדָה יָצָאוּ הַנִּשְׁבָּעִים ׀ בְּשֵׁם יְהוָה וּבֵאלֹהֵי יִשְׂרָאֵל

Israel by and ,Jehovah the by swear who have Judah's
of God the of name ;out come

2 יַזְכִּירוּ לֹא בֶאֱמֶת וְלֹא בִצְדָקָה׃ כִּי־מֵעִיר הַקֹּדֶשׁ נִקְרָאוּ

are they the from For righ- in and truth in not —mention
,called holy city .teousness not

וְעַל־אֱלֹהֵי יִשְׂרָאֵל נִסְמָכוּ יְהוָה צְבָאוֹת שְׁמוֹ׃

His (is) hosts Jehovah support Israel the and
.name of ;themselves of God on

3 הָרִאשֹׁנוֹת מֵאָז הִגַּדְתִּי וּמִפִּי יָצְאוּ וְאַשְׁמִיעֵם פִּתְאֹם

suddenly made I and they from and have I from former The
;hear them ;out went mouth my ;foretold then things

4 עָשִׂיתִי וַתָּבֹאנָה׃ מִדַּעְתִּי כִּי קָשֶׁה אָתָּה וְגִיד בַּרְזֶל עָרְפֶּךָ

your (is) iron a and you hard that Because they and ;acted I
.neck of sinew —(are) knew I .about came

5 וּמִצְחֲךָ נְחוּשָׁה׃ וָאַגִּיד לְךָ מֵאָז בְּטֶרֶם תָּבוֹא הִשְׁמַעְתִּיךָ

you made I came it before from to I And .brass your and
hear ;then you declared (is) brow

6 פֶּן־תֹּאמַר עָצְבִּי עָשָׂם וּפִסְלִי וְנִסְכִּי צִוָּם׃ שָׁמַעְתָּ חֲזֵה

be- You commanded my and my and did My you lest
hold ,heard .them image casted image ;them idol ,say should

כֻּלָּהּ וְאַתֶּם הֲלוֹא תַגִּידוּ הִשְׁמַעְתִּיךָ חֲדָשׁוֹת מֵעַתָּה וּנְצֻרוֹת

hidden even from new made I you will You and of all
,things ,now things hear you ?declare not ;it

and you did not know them. [7] They are now created, and not from then; even before today, but you did not hear them; lest you should say, See, I knew them. [8] Yea, you did not hear; yea, you did not know; yea, from then your ear was not opened; for I know you surely will betray and trespass, from the womb it was called to you. [9] For My name's sake I will put off My anger; and for My praise I will hold back for you, so as not to cut you off. [10] Behold, I have refined you, but not with silver; I have chosen you in the furnace of affliction. [11] For My sake, for My sake I will act; for how is it defiled? And I will not give My glory to another.

[12] Listen to Me, O Jacob and Israel, My called: I (am) He; I (am) the first; I surely (am) the last. [13] My hand surely founded earth, and My right hand has stretched out the the heavens; I called, they stood up together. [14] All of you gather and hear: Who among them has declared these things? Jehovah has loved him. He will do His pleasure on Babylon; yea, His arm (shall be on) the Chaldeans. [15] I, I have spoken; yea, I have called him, I brought him, and he causes his way to prosper. [16] Come near to me; hear this: I have not spoken in secret from the beginning. From its being, I (was) there; and now the Lord Jehovah, and His Spirit, has sent Me. [17] Thus says Jehovah, your Redeemer, the Holy One of Israel, I (am) Jehovah your God who teaches you to profit, who leads you in the way you should go. [18] Oh that you had listened to My commands! Then your peace would have been like the river, and your righteousness like the waves of the sea. [19] And your seed would have been like the sand, and your offspring like its grains; his name would not have been cut off

7 ולא ידעתם: עתה נבראו ולא מאז ולפני־יום ולא שמעתם
heard you but ,today even from and are they Now knew you and
;them not before ,then not created .them not

8 פן־תאמר הנה ידעתין: גם לא־שמעת גם לא ידעת גם
,yea did you not ,yea did you not ,Yea knew I ,Behold you lest
;know ;hear .them ,say should

מאז לא־פתחה אזנך כי ידעתי בגוד תבגוד ופשע מבטן
the from and will you surely know I for your was not from
womb trespass betray ;ear opened then

9 קרא לך: למען שמי אאריך אפי ותהלתי אחטם־לך
for will I for and My will I My For to was it
,you back hold praise My ,anger off put name's sake .you called

10 לבלתי הכריתך: הנה צרפתיך ולא בכסף בחרתיך
have I with but have I ,Behold cut to as so
you chosen ;silver not ,you refined .off you not

11 בכור עני: למעני למעני אעשה כי־איך יחל וכבודי לאחר
to My And it is how For will I My for My for affliction the in
another glory ?defiled ,act sake ,sake of furnace

12 לא־אתן: שמע אלי יעקב וישראל מקראי אני־הוא
,He I My Israel and O to Listen will I not
(am) :called ,Jacob ,Me .give

13 אני ראשון אף אני אחרון: אף־ידי יסדה ארץ וימיני
My and the founded My Sure the I surely ;first the I
hand right ;earth hand ,ly .last (am) (am)

14 טפחה שמים קרא אני אליהם יעמדו יחדו: הקבצו כלכם
of all Gather .together they ,them to I called the stretched
you up stood ;heavens out

ושמעו מי בהם הגיד את־אלה יהוה אהבו יעשה חפצו
His will He has Jehovah these has among Who and
pleasure do ;him loved ?things declared them ,hear

15 בבבל וזרעו כשדים: אני אני דברתי אף־קראתיו הביאתיו
brought I have I ,yea have I ,I the (on) His and on
him ;him called ;spoken .Chaldeans arm ;Babylon

16 והצליח דרכו: קרבו אלי שמעו־זאת לא מראש בסתר
in the from not ;this hear to Come .way his makes he and
secret beginning ;me near succeed

דברתי מעת היותה שם אני ועתה אדני יהוה שלחני
sent has Jehovah the and I there ,being its the From have I
,me Lord now ;(was) of time spoken

17 ורוחו: כה־אמר יהוה גאלך קדוש ישראל אני יהוה
Jehovah I ,Israel Holy the your Jehovah says Thus His and
(am) of One ,Redeemer .Spirit

18 אלהיך מלמדך להועיל מדריכך בדרך תלך: לוא
Oh should you the in leading ,profit to teaching your
that .go way you you ,God

הקשבת למצותי ויהי כנהר שלומך וצדקתך כגלי הים:
the the as your and your the like Then My to had you
.sea of waves righteousness ,peace river been had !commands listened

19 ויהי כחול זרעך וצאצאי מעיך כמעותיו לא־יכרת ולא־
and be would not its like your the and your the like And
not ,off cut ;grains belly of offspring ,seed sand been had

יִשָּׁמֵד שְׁמוֹ מִלְּפָנָי׃ צְאוּ מִבָּבֶל בִּרְחוּ מִכַּשְׂדִּים
the from flee from out Go before from his destroyed
.Chaldeans ;Babylon .Me name

בְּקוֹל רִנָּה הַגִּידוּ הַשְׁמִיעוּ זֹאת הוֹצִיאוּהָ עַד־קְצֵה הָאָרֶץ
the the to go it let ,this be let tell rejoicing the with
;earth of end out heard ;(this) of voice

21 אִמְרוּ גָּאַל יְהוָה עַבְדּוֹ יַעֲקֹב׃ וְלֹא צָמְאוּ בָּחֳרָבוֹת הוֹלִיכָם
led He the in they And .Jacob His Jehovah has ,Say
;them deserts ;thirsted not servant redeemed

22 מַיִם מִצּוּר הִזִּיל לָמוֹ וַיִּבְקַע־צוּר וַיָּזֻבוּ מָיִם׃ אֵין שָׁלוֹם
,peace there ;water and ,rock the He And for He from water
no is out gushed split .them flow made rock

אָמַר יְהוָה לָרְשָׁעִים׃
the to ,Jehovah says
.wicked

or destroyed from My presence. [20] Go out of Babylon; flee from the Chaldeans. Tell this with the voice of rejoicing; let this be heard, let it go out to the end of the earth; say, Jehovah has redeemed His servant Jacob. [21] And they did not thirst; He led them in the deserts; He made waters flow out of rock for them. And He cut open the rock and the water gushed out. [22] There is no peace, says Jehovah, to the wicked.

CAP. XLIX מט

CHAPTER 49

1 שִׁמְעוּ אִיִּים אֵלַי וְהַקְשִׁיבוּ לְאֻמִּים מֵרָחוֹק יְהוָה מִבֶּטֶן
the from Jehovah from peoples ,hear and to coasts ,Listen
womb ;afar ,Me

2 קְרָאָנִי מִמְּעֵי אִמִּי הִזְכִּיר שְׁמִי׃ וַיָּשֶׂם פִּי כְּחֶרֶב חַדָּה
;sharp a like My He And My men- He My from called
sword mouth made .name tioned mother's belly ;Me

בְּצֵל יָדוֹ הֶחְבִּיאָנִי וַיְשִׂימֵנִי לְחֵץ בָּרוּר בְּאַשְׁפָּתוֹ הִסְתִּירָנִי׃
hid He His in ;polished a for made and hid He His in
.Me quiver arrow Me ,Me hand's shadow

3
4 וַיֹּאמֶר לִי עַבְדִּי־אָתָּה יִשְׂרָאֵל אֲשֶׁר־בְּךָ אֶתְפָּאָר׃ וַאֲנִי
Then be shall I in whom ,Israel You My to He And
I .glorified You ,(are) servant ,Me said

אָמַרְתִּי לְרִיק יָגַעְתִּי לְתֹהוּ וְהֶבֶל כֹּחִי כִלֵּיתִי אָכֵן מִשְׁפָּטִי
My yet have I My in and for have I for ,said
judgment surely ;spent strength ,vain nothing ;labored nothing

5 אֶת־יְהוָה וּפְעֻלָּתִי אֶת־אֱלֹהָי׃ וְעַתָּה ׀ אָמַר יְהוָה
,Jehovah says And My with My and ,Jehovah (is)
,now .God work with

יֹצְרִי מִבֶּטֶן לְעֶבֶד לוֹ לְשׁוֹבֵב יַעֲקֹב אֵלָיו וְיִשְׂרָאֵל לֹא
not Though to Jacob bring to to (be) to the from My
Israel :Him back ,Him servant ,womb Former

6 יֵאָסֵף וְאֶכָּבֵד בְּעֵינֵי יְהוָה וֵאלֹהַי הָיָה עֻזִּי׃ וַיֹּאמֶר נָקֵל
is It He And My is My and ,Jehovah the in am I yet is
trifling ,said .strength God of eyes honored ,gathered

מִהְיוֹתְךָ לִי עֶבֶד לְהָקִים אֶת־שִׁבְטֵי יַעֲקֹב וּנְצִירֵי יִשְׂרָאֵל
Israel the and ,Jacob the raise to a to You that
of preserved of tribes up ,servant Me be should

לְהָשִׁיב וּנְתַתִּיךָ לְאוֹר גּוֹיִם לִהְיוֹת יְשׁוּעָתִי עַד־קְצֵה
the to My be to ,nations a for also will I .restore to
of end salvation of light You give

7 הָאָרֶץ׃ כֹּה אָמַר־יְהוָה גֹּאֵל יִשְׂרָאֵל קְדוֹשׁוֹ לִבְזֹה־
the to Holy His ,Israel the Jehovah says Thus the
of despised ,One of Redeemer .earth

CHAPTER 49

[1] Coasts, listen to Me; and you people from afar, hear; Jehovah called Me from the womb; He mentioned My name from My mother's belly. [2] And He made My mouth like a sharp sword; He hid Me in the shadow of His hand, and made Me a polished arrow; He hid Me in His quiver; [3] and said to Me, You are My servant, Israel, whom in You I shall be glorified. [4] Then I said, I have labored in vain; I have spent My strength for nothing, and in vain; yet surely My judgment (is) with Jehovah, and My work with My God. [5] And now, says Jehovah who formed Me from the womb to be His servant, to bring Jacob back to Him: Though Israel is not gathered, yet I am honored in the eye of Jehovah, and My God is My strength. [6] And He said, It is (too) little that You should be My servant to raise up the tribes of Jacob, and to restore the preserved ones of Israel; I will also give You for a light of the nations, (that You may) be My salvation to the end of the earth. [7] Thus says Jehovah, the Redeemer of Israel, His Holy One, to the despised of soul, to the

hated of the nation, the servant of rulers, Kings shall see and rise up;(and)chiefs shall worship; because of Jehovah who is faithful, and the Holy One of Israel; and He chose You.

[8] Thus says Jehovah: In a favorable time I have answered You, and in a day of salvation I have helped You. And I will preserve You, and give You for a covenant of the people; to establish the earth, to cause to inherit the desolated inheritances; [9] to say to the prisoners, Go out! To those who are in darkness, Show yourselves! They shall feed in the ways, and their pastures shall be in all high places. [10] They shall not hunger nor thirst; and the heat and sun shall not strike them. For He who has mercy on them shall lead them; and He shall guide them by the springs of water. [11] And I will make all My mountains a way, and My highways shall be set on high. [12] Behold, these shall come from afar; and, lo, these from the north and from the west; and these from the land of Sinim.

[13] Sing, O heavens; and be joyful, O earth; break out into singing, O mountains. For Jehovah has comforted His people and will have pity on His afflicted. [14] But Zion said, Jehovah has forsaken me, and, My Lord has forgotten me. [15] Can a woman forget her suckling child, from pitying the son of her womb? Yes, these may forget, yet I will surely not forget you. [16] Behold, I have carved you on the palms of My hands; your walls (are) always before Me. [17] Your sons hurry; those destroying you and ruining you shall go out from you. [18] Lift up your eyes all around and see! They all gather; they all come to you. (As) I live, says Jehovah, you shall surely wear all of them as an ornament, and bind them on as a bride. [19] For your wastes and your deserted places, and your land of ruins shall even now be too

נפש למתעב גוי לעבד משלים מלכים יראו וקמו שרים
chiefs and shall Kings ,rulers the the the to ,soul
;up rise see of servant , nation of hated

וישתחוו למען יהוה אשר נאמן קדש ישראל ויבחרך׃
He and ,Israel Holy the is who Jehovah because shall
You chose of One ,faithful of ,worship

8 כה אמר יהוה בעת רצון עניתיך וביום ישועה
salvation in and replied I favor- a In ,Jehovah says Thus
of day a ,you to able time

עזרתיך ואצרך ואתנך לברית עם להקים ארץ להנחיל
cause to the estab- to the a for give and will I And helped I
inherit to ,earth lish ,people of covenant You You keep .You

9 נחלות שממות׃ לאמר לאסורים צאו לאשר בחשך
dark- in those to Go the to saying desolated inherit-
.ness ;out ,prisoners ances

10 הגלו על־דרכים ירעו ובכל־שפיים מרעיתם׃ לא ירעבו
shall They not their bare and shall they the By Show
hunger .pastures heights all in ,feed ways !yourselves

ולא יצמאו ולא־יכם שרב ושמש כי־מרחמם ינהגם
lead shall who He For .sun and heat shall and ;thirst and
;them them pities them strike not not

11 ועל־מבועי מים ינהלם׃ ושמתי כל־הרי לדרך ומסלתי
My and ,way a My all I And guide shall water springs and
highways mountains make will .them of by

12 ירמון׃ הנה־אלה מרחוק יבאו והנה־אלה מצפון ומים
from and from these and shall from these ,Behold be shall
;west north ,behold ;come afar .high

13 ואלה מארץ סינים׃ רנו שמים וגילי ארץ יפצחו הרים
O ,break O be and O ,Sing .Sinim the from and
mountains ;earth ,joyful ,heavens of land these

14 רנה כי־נחם יהוה עמו ועניו ירחם׃ ותאמר ציון
,Zion said But will He His and His Jehovah has for (into)
.pity afflicted ,people comforted ;singing

15 עזבני יהוה ואדני שכחני׃ התשכח אשה עולה מרחם
from suckling her a forget Can forgot My and ,Jehovah for-
pitying ,child woman .me Lord me sook

16 בן־בטנה גם־אלה תשכחנה ואנכי לא אשכחך׃ הן על־
on ,Behold will not yet may these ,Yes her the
.you forget I ,forget ?womb of son

17 כפים חקתיך חומתיך נגדי תמיד׃ מהרו בניך מהרסיך
de- those Your hurry .always (are) your have I My
you stroying ;sons Me before walls ;you carved hands

18 ומחריביך ממך יצאו׃ שאי־סביב עיניך וראי כלם
They and your all Lift shall from ruining and
all !see eyes around up .out go you ,you

נקבצו באו־לך חי־אני נאם־יהוה כי כלם כעדי תלבשי
shall you an as them surely ,Jehovah states I As to (and) gather
wear ornament all ,live .you come

19 ותקשרים ככלה׃ כי חרבתיך ושממתיך וארץ הרסתך
de- your and your and your For a as bind and
structions of land ,ruins wastes .bride on them

narrow to live there; and they who swallow you shall be broad. [20] The sons of your bereavement shall yet say in your ears, The place (is) too narrow for me; come near so that I may live. [21] Then you shall say in your heart, Who has borne these to me, for I (am) bereaved and desolate, turned aside and an exile; who then has brought up these? Behold, I was left alone. Where (do) these (come) from? [22] Thus says the Lord Jehovah, Behold, I will lift up My hand to the nations, and will set up My banner to peoples. And they shall bring your sons in the bosom, and your daughters shall be carried on the shoulder. [23] And kings shall be your nursing fathers, and their queens your nurses. They shall bow to you, face (down to) the earth, and lick up the dust of your feet. And you shall know that I (am) Jehovah, by whom they who wait for Me shall not be ashamed. [24] Shall the booty be taken from the mighty, or the lawful captive escape? [25] But thus says Jehovah, Even the captives of the mighty shall be taken away, and the booty of the terrible ones shall be delivered. For I will fight with him who fights with you; and I will save your sons. [26] And those who oppress you, I will feed with their own flesh: and they shall be drunk by their own blood, as with sweet wine. And all flesh shall know that I Jehovah (am) your Savior and your Redeemer, the mighty One of Jacob.

20 כִּי עַתָּה תֵּצְרִי מִיּוֹשֵׁב וְרָחֲקוּ מְבַלְּעָיִךְ׃ עוֹד יֹאמְרוּ בְאָזְנַיִךְ
your in shall Yet who those shall and live to be shall now for
ears say .you swallow wide be ;(there) narrow too
21 בְּנֵי שִׁכֻּלָיִךְ צַר־לִי הַמָּקוֹם גְּשָׁה־לִּי וְאֵשֵׁבָה׃ וְאָמַרְתְּ
you Then I that for come the (is) for Too bereave- your the
say shall .dwell may ,me near ;place me narrow ,ment of sons
בִּלְבָבֵךְ מִי יָלַד־לִי אֶת־אֵלֶּה וַאֲנִי שְׁכוּלָה וְגַלְמוּדָה גֹּלָה ׀
an and bereaved I For ?these to has Who your in
exile ,barren (am) me borne ,heart
וְסוּרָה וְאֵלֶּה מִי גִדֵּל הֵן אֲנִי נִשְׁאַרְתִּי לְבַדִּי אֵלֶּה אֵיפֹה
(from) ,These .alone I ,left was I ,Lo has who and turned and
where ?up brought ,these ;aside
22 הֵם׃ כֹּה־אָמַר אֲדֹנָי יֱהֹוִה הִנֵּה אֶשָּׂא אֶל־גּוֹיִם יָדִי
My the to will I ,Behold ,Jehovah the says Thus (are)
,hand nations up lift Lord ?they
וְאֶל־עַמִּים אָרִים נִסִּי וְהֵבִיאוּ בָנַיִךְ בְּחֹצֶן וּבְנֹתַיִךְ עַל־כָּתֵף
the on your and the in your they And My will peoples and
shoulder daughters ;bosom sons bring shall .banner up set to
23 תִּנָּשֶׂאנָה׃ וְהָיוּ מְלָכִים אֹמְנַיִךְ וְשָׂרוֹתֵיהֶם מֵינִיקֹתַיִךְ אַפַּיִם
faces your their and nursing your kings And be shall
(toward) ;nurses princesses ,fathers be shall .carried
אֶרֶץ יִשְׁתַּחֲווּ־לָךְ וַעֲפַר רַגְלַיִךְ יְלַחֵכוּ וְיָדַעַתְּ כִּי־אֲנִי יְהוָה
,Jehovah I that you And lick your the and to they the
(am) know shall .up feet of dust you bow shall earth
24 אֲשֶׁר לֹא־יֵבֹשׁוּ קֹוָי׃ הֲיֻקַּח מִגִּבּוֹר מַלְקוֹחַ וְאִם־שְׁבִי
the or ,booty a from be Shall waiting those be shall not by
captive warrior taken .Me for ashamed whom
25 צַדִּיק יִמָּלֵט׃ כִּי־כֹה ׀ אָמַר יְהוָה גַּם־שְׁבִי גִבּוֹר יֻקָּח
be shall the captive Even ,Jehovah says thus For ?escape lawful
,taken warrior's
וּמַלְקוֹחַ עָרִיץ יִמָּלֵט וְאֶת־יְרִיבֵךְ אָנֹכִי אָרִיב וְאֶת־בָּנַיִךְ
your and will I your And shall the booty and
sons ;strive striver with .escape tyrant of
26 אָנֹכִי אוֹשִׁיעַ׃ וְהַאֲכַלְתִּי אֶת־מוֹנַיִךְ אֶת־בְּשָׂרָם וְכֶעָסִיס
as and own their who those will I And will I
wine sweet ;flesh you oppress feed .save
דָּמָם יִשְׁכָּרוּן וְיָדְעוּ כָל־בָּשָׂר כִּי אֲנִי יְהוָה מוֹשִׁיעֵךְ וְגֹאֲלֵךְ
your and your Jehovah I that flesh all shall And shall they their
,Redeemer Savior (am) know .drunk be blood
אֲבִיר יַעֲקֹב׃
.Jacob the
One Mighty
of

CAP. L נ

CHAPTER 50

[1] Thus says Jehovah, Where (is) your mother's bill of divorce, whom I have put away? Or to which of My creditors have I sold you? Behold, you were sold for your iniquities, and

1 כֹּה ׀ אָמַר יְהוָה אֵי זֶה סֵפֶר כְּרִיתוּת אִמְּכֶם אֲשֶׁר שִׁלַּחְתִּיהָ
have I whom your divorce scroll the Where Jeho- says Thus
?away put ,mother of of (is) ,vah
אוֹ מִי מִנּוֹשַׁי אֲשֶׁר־מָכַרְתִּי אֶתְכֶם לוֹ הֵן בַּעֲוֺנֹתֵיכֶם
your for ,Behold to you have I that My of who Or
iniquities ?him sold creditors

your mother was put away for your transgressions. [2] Who knows why I have come, and no one (is here)? I called, and none answered. Is My hand surely cut short from ransom? Or is there not power in Me to deliver? Behold, at My rebuke I dry up the sea; I make rivers a wilderness; their fish stink, because of no water, and die in thirst. [3] I clothe the heavens (with) blackness, and make sackcloth their covering.

[4] The Lord Jehovah has given Me the tongue of the learned, to know to help the weary (with) a word; He arouses in the morning; He arouses my ear in the morning, to hear as the learned. [5] The Lord Jehovah has opened My ear and I did not rebel nor turn away. [6] I gave My back to the strikers, and My cheeks to those who plucked; I did not hide My face from shame and spitting. [7] For the Lord Jehovah will help Me; for this reason I was not ashamed. So I have set My face like flint, and I know that I shall not be ashamed. [8] He that justifies Me (is) near; who will contend with Me? Let us stand together; who (is) master of My judgment? Let him come near Me. [9] Behold, the Lord Jehovah will help Me; who (is) he who will condemn Me? Lo, they all shall wear out like a garment; the moth shall eat them.

[10] Who among you fears Jehovah, obeying the voice of His servant, who walks (in) darkness and no light (is) to him? Let him trust in the name of Jehovah and rest on his God. [11] Behold, all you who kindle fire and are surrounded (by) sparks; walk

2 נִמְכַּרְתֶּם וּבְפִשְׁעֵיכֶם שֻׁלְּחָה אִמְּכֶם׃ מַדּוּעַ בָּאתִי וְאֵין
and have knows Who your put was your for and were you
no come why .mother away trespasses ,sold

אִישׁ קָרָאתִי וְאֵין עוֹנֶה הֲקָצוֹר קָצְרָה יָדִי מִפְּדוּת וְאִם־
Or from My cut is Cutting answer- and ,called I one
?ransom ,hand short ,short .ed none ?(here is)

אֵין־בִּי כֹחַ לְהַצִּיל הֵן בְּגַעֲרָתִי אַחֲרִיב יָם אָשִׂים נְהָרוֹת
rivers make I the dry I My at ,Behold ?deliver to power in is
;sea up rebuke Me not

3 מִדְבָּר תִּבְאַשׁ דְּגָתָם מֵאֵין מַיִם וְתָמֹת בַּצָּמָא׃ אַלְבִּישׁ
clothe I .thirst in die and ,water because their stink wil- a
no of fish ;derness

4 שָׁמַיִם קַדְרוּת וְשַׂק אָשִׂים כְּסוּתָם׃ אֲדֹנָי יֱהוִה נָתַן
has Jehovah The their make and black- (with) the
given Lord .covering sackcloth ness heavens

לִי לְשׁוֹן לִמּוּדִים לָדַעַת לָעוּת אֶת־יָעֵף דָּבָר יָעִיר ׀ בַּבֹּקֶר
the in He a (with) the help to ;know to taught the to
,morning arouses ;word weary ,ones of tongue Me

5 בַּבֹּקֶר יָעִיר לִי אֹזֶן לִשְׁמֹעַ כַּלִּמּוּדִים׃ אֲדֹנָי יֱהוִה פָּתַח־
has Jehovah The the as hear to the to He the in
opened Lord taught ,ear Me arouses morning

6 לִי אֹזֶן וְאָנֹכִי לֹא מָרִיתִי אָחוֹר לֹא נְסוּגֹתִי׃ גֵּוִי נָתַתִּי
gave I My turned I not backwards did not I and the to
back away ,rebel ,ear Me

לְמַכִּים וּלְחָיַי לְמֹרְטִים פָּנַי לֹא הִסְתַּרְתִּי מִכְּלִמּוֹת וָרֹק׃
and from did I not My ;pluckers to My and to
.spitting shame hide face cheeks ;strikers

7 וַאדֹנָי יֱהוִה יַעֲזָר־לִי עַל־כֵּן לֹא נִכְלָמְתִּי עַל־כֵּן שַׂמְתִּי
have I therefore was I not therefore ,Me will Jehovah the And
set ;ashamed help Lord

8 פָנַי כַּחַלָּמִישׁ וָאֵדַע כִּי־לֹא אֵבוֹשׁ׃ קָרוֹב מַצְדִּיקִי מִי־
who My Near shall I not that I and like My
;justifier (is) .ashamed be know ,flint face

9 יָרִיב אִתִּי נַעַמְדָה יָּחַד מִי־בַעַל מִשְׁפָּטִי יִגַּשׁ אֵלָי׃ הֵן
,Lo .Me to him Let My master who to- us Let with will
near come ?judgment of (is) ;gether stand ?Me contend

אֲדֹנָי יֱהוִה יַעֲזָר־לִי מִי־הוּא יַרְשִׁיעֵנִי הֵן כֻּלָּם כַּבֶּגֶד יִבְלוּ
shall a like they ,Lo will who He who ;Me will Jehovah the
;out wear garment all ?Me condemn (is) help Lord

10 עָשׁ יֹאכְלֵם׃ מִי בָכֶם יְרֵא יְהוָה שֹׁמֵעַ בְּקוֹל עַבְדּוֹ
His the obeying ,Jehovah fears among Who eat shall the
,servant of voice you .them moth

אֲשֶׁר ׀ הָלַךְ חֲשֵׁכִים וְאֵין נֹגַהּ לוֹ יִבְטַח בְּשֵׁם יְהוָה וְיִשָּׁעֵן
and ,Jehovah the in him Let to light and (in) walks who
lean of name trust ?him (is) no ,darkness

11 בֵּאלֹהָיו׃ הֵן כֻּלְּכֶם קֹדְחֵי אֵשׁ מְאַזְּרֵי זִיקוֹת לְכוּ ׀
walk (by) are who ,fire who of all ,Behold his on
;sparks surrounded kindle you .God

in the light of your fire and in the sparks you are burning. This you shall have from My hand: you shall lie down in torment.

CHAPTER 51

[1] Listen to Me, you who pursue righteousness, seekers of Jehovah: Look to the rock from which you were cut, and to the hole of the pit from which you were dug. [2] Look to your father Abraham, and to Sarah who bore you; for (he being but) one, I called him and blessed and multiplied him. [3] For Jehovah comforts Zion. He comforts all her ruins; yea, He makes her wilderness like Eden and her desert like Jehovah's garden; joy and gladness shall be found in it, thanksgiving and the voice of singing praise.

[4] Listen to Me, My people; and give ear to Me, My nation. For a law shall go out from Me, and I will make rest My justice as light to peoples. [5] My righteousness (is) near; My salvation went out; and My arms shall judge peoples; the coasts shall wait on Me, and they shall hope on My arm. [6] Lift up your eyes to the heavens, and look to the earth from beneath, for the heavens vanish like smoke, and the earth shall wear out like a garment; and those living in it shall die in like manner. But My salvation shall be forever, and My righteousness shall not be broken. [7] Listen to Me, you who know righteousness, the people (who have) My law in their heart. Do not fear the reproach of man, and do not be bowed from their slanders. [8] For the moth shall eat them like a garment, and the worm shall eat them like wool. But My

11 באור אשכם ובזיקות בערתם מידי היתה־זאת לכם

,you to this shall My From are you in and your the in
be hand .burning sparks the ,fire of light

למעצבה תשכבון׃

shall you in
.down lie pain

CAP. LI נא

CHAPTER 51

1 שמעו אלי רדפי צדק מבקשי יהוה הביטו אל־צור

the to Look :Jehovah seekers righ- pursuers ,Me to Listen
rock of ,teousness of

2 חצבתם ואל־מקבת בור נקרתם׃ הביטו אל־אברהם

Abraham to Look which from the the and which from
.dug were you pit of hollow to ,cut were you

אביכם ואל־שרה תחוללכם כי־אחד קראתיו ואברכהו

blessed and called I (being) for bore who Sarah and your
,him ,him one ;you to ,father

3 וארבהו׃ כי־נחם יהוה ציון נחם כל־חרבתיה וישם

He and her all He .Zion Jehovah comforts For in- and
makes ,desolations comforts .him creased

מדברה כעדן וערבתה כגן־יהוה ששון ושמחה ימצא

be shall and joy ;Jehovah's like her and like her
found gladness garden desert ,Eden wilderness

4 בה תודה וקול זמרה׃ הקשיבו אלי עמי ולאומי

My and My ,Me to Listen singing the and thanks- ,it in
,nation ;people .praise of voice giving

אלי האזינו כי תורה מאתי תצא ומשפטי לאור עמים

peoples light as My and shall from law a For give to
to justice ,out go Me .ear Me

5 ארגיע׃ קרוב צדקי יצא ישעי וזרעי עמים ישפטו אלי

on shall peoples My and My went righ- My Near will I
Me ;judge arms ;salvation out ;teousness (is) rest make

6 איים יקוו ואל־זרעי ייחלון׃ שאו לשמים עיניכם

,eyes your the to Lift shall they My and shall coasts
heavens up hope arm on ,wait

והביטו אל־הארץ מתחת כי־שמים כעשן נמלחו והארץ

the and ,vanish like the for from the to look and
earth smoke heavens ;beneath earth

כבגד תבלה וישביה כמו־כן ימותון וישועתי לעולם

forever My But .die shall like in its and shall a like
salvation manner dwellers ;out wear garment

7 תהיה וצדקתי לא תחת׃ שמעו אלי ידעי צדק

righ- knowers to Listen be shall not My and ;be shall
,teousness of ,Me .broken ,righteousness

עם תורתי בלבם אל־תיראו חרפת אנוש ומגדפתם אל־

not their from and ,man the fear Do not their in law My the
blasphemings of reproach .heart of people

8 תחתו׃ כי כבגד יאכלם עש וכצמר יאכלם סס וצדקתי

My But the eat shall like and the eat shall a like For be do
right mothworm them wool ,moth them garment .bowed

righteousness shall be forever, and My salvation to all generations. [9] Awake! Awake! Put on strength, arm of Jehovah. Awake! as days of old, everlasting generations. Was it not You who cut Rahab in pieces, piercing the sea-monster? [10] Was it not You who dried up the sea, the waters of the great deep, who made the depths of the sea a highway for the redeemed to pass? [11] And the ransomed of Jehovah shall return and come with singing (to) Zion. And everlasting joy (shall be) on their head; gladness and joy shall overtake; sorrow and sighing shall flee. [12] I, I (am) He who comforts you. Who (are) you, that you should fear from man? He shall die! And from the son of man? He shall be given (as) grass. [13] And you forget Jehovah your Maker, who has stretched out the heavens and laid the earth's foundations. And you dread continually, every day, from the oppressor's fury, since he was ready to destroy. And where (is) the oppressor's fury? [14] He hurries to be freed, and (that) he not die in the pit, and (that) he does not lack his bread. [15] But I (am) Jehovah your God, stirring the sea, and its waves roar; Jehovah of hosts (is) His name. [16] And I have put My words in your mouth, and I have covered you in the shade of My hand, to plant the heavens and to found the earth, and to say to Zion, You (are) My people.

[17] Awake! Awake! Rise up, O Jerusalem, who drank the cup of His fury from the hand of Jehovah; you drank the bowl of the cup of reeling, you fully drained (them).

[18] No guide (is) for her among all the sons she has borne; and none takes her by the hand, of all the sons she has reared.

9 לְעוֹלָם תִּהְיֶה וִישׁוּעָתִי לְדוֹר דּוֹרִים׃ עוּרִי עוּרִי לִבְשִׁי־
on Put !Awake !Awake gene- to gene- My and shall forever
of ration ration salvation ,be

עֹז זְרוֹעַ יְהוָה עוּרִי כִּימֵי קֶדֶם דֹּרוֹת עוֹלָמִים הֲלוֹא אַתְּ־
You it Was .everlasting genera- ,old days as ,Awake Je- arm
not tions of .hovah's ,strength

10 הִיא הַמַּחְצֶבֶת רַהַב מְחוֹלֶלֶת תַּנִּין׃ הֲלוֹא אַתְּ־הִיא
which ,You it Was sea- the piercing ,Rahab in cutting which
(was) not ?monster pieces (was)

הַמַּחֲרֶבֶת יָם מֵי תְּהוֹם רַבָּה הַשָּׂמָה מַעֲמַקֵּי־יָם דֶּרֶךְ
a the the which ,great the the the one the
way sea of depths made deep of waters ,sea up drying

11 לַעֲבֹר גְּאוּלִים׃ וּפְדוּיֵי יְהוָה יְשׁוּבוּן וּבָאוּ צִיּוֹן בְּרִנָּה
with (to) and shall Jehovah the And the to
,singing Zion come return of ransomed ?redeemed pass

וְשִׂמְחַת עוֹלָם עַל־רֹאשָׁם שָׂשׂוֹן וְשִׂמְחָה יַשִּׂיגוּן נָסוּ יָגוֹן
sor- shall shall joy and gladness their (be shall) ever- joy and
row flee ;overtake ;head on lasting

12 וַאֲנָחָה׃ אָנֹכִי אָנֹכִי הוּא מְנַחֶמְכֶם מִי־אַתְּ וַתִּירְאִי
you that ,you Who comforting ,He (am) I I, and
fear should (are) .you .sighing

13 מֵאֱנוֹשׁ יָמוּת וּמִבֶּן־אָדָם חָצִיר יִנָּתֵן׃ וַתִּשְׁכַּח יְהוָה עֹשֶׂךָ
your Jehovah you And is He (As) ?man from Or He from
,Maker forget .given grass of son the- !die shall ?man

נוֹטֶה שָׁמַיִם וְיֹסֵד אָרֶץ וַתְּפַחֵד תָּמִיד כָּל־הַיּוֹם מִפְּנֵי חֲמַת
the from ,day every ,always you And the and hea- the who
of fury dread .earth founded vens streched

14 הַמֵּצִיק כַּאֲשֶׁר כּוֹנֵן לְהַשְׁחִית וְאַיֵּה חֲמַת הַמֵּצִיק׃ מִהַר
He the the where And to was he since the
hurries ?oppressor of fury (is) .destroy ready ,oppressor

15 צֹעֶה לְהִפָּתֵחַ וְלֹא־יָמוּת לַשַּׁחַת וְלֹא יֶחְסַר לַחְמוֹ׃ וְאָנֹכִי
I But his that and the in he(that) and be to ,bowed
(am) .bread lacks he not ,pit die not ,freed

יְהוָה אֱלֹהֶיךָ רֹגַע הַיָּם וַיֶּהֱמוּ גַּלָּיו יְהוָה צְבָאוֹת שְׁמוֹ׃
His hosts Jehovah its and the stirring your Jehovah
.name (is) of ;waves roar ,sea up ,God

16 וָאָשִׂם דְּבָרַי בְּפִיךָ וּבְצֵל יָדִי כִּסִּיתִיךָ לִנְטֹעַ שָׁמַיִם וְלִיסֹד
and the plant to covered My the in and your in My I And
found heavens ,you hand of shade ,mouth words put have

17 אָרֶץ וְלֵאמֹר לְצִיּוֹן עַמִּי־אָתָּה׃ הִתְעוֹרְרִי הִתְעוֹרְרִי
!Awake !Awake you My to and the
.(are) people ,Zion say to ,earth

קוּמִי יְרוּשָׁלַםִ אֲשֶׁר שָׁתִית מִיַּד יְהוָה אֶת־כּוֹס חֲמָתוֹ
;fury His cup the Jehovah the from drank who O Rise
of of hand ,Jerusalem up

18 אֶת־קֻבַּעַת כּוֹס הַתַּרְעֵלָה שָׁתִית מָצִית׃ אֵין מְנַהֵל לָהּ
for guide No fully you you reeling the the
her (is) .drained ,drank of cup of bowl

מִכָּל־בָּנִים יָלָדָה וְאֵין מַחֲזִיק בְּיָדָהּ מִכָּל־בָּנִים גִּדֵּלָה׃
has she sons the all of by her takes and has she the among
.reared —hand the none ;borne sons all

[19] Those two things happened to you; who shall bewail you? Ruin and shattering and famine, and the sword — who (but) I shall comfort you? [20] Your sons have fainted; they lie at the head of all the streets, like an antelope (in) a net, filled with Jehovah's fury, the rebuke of your God. [21] Now, then, hear this, afflicted and drunken one, but not from wine: [22] Thus says your Lord Jehovah, and your God: He pleads (the cause of) His people. Behold, I have taken the cup of reeling out of your hand, the bowl of the cup of My fury; you shall never drink it again. [23] But I will put it into your oppressor's hand, who have said to your soul, Bow down so that we may go over; and you have laid your back as the ground, and as the street, to those who cross over.

CHAPTER 52

[1] Awake! Awake! Put on your strength, Zion; put on your beautiful robes, O Jerusalem, the holy city, for never again (the) uncircumcised and (the) unclean shall come to you. [2] Shake yourself from the dust; rise up! Sit, Jerusalem! Free yourself from your neckbands, O captive daughter of Zion. [3] For thus says Jehovah: You have sold yourselves for nothing, and you shall not be redeemed with money. [4] For thus says the Lord Jehovah: My people went down into Egypt, to stay there, and Assyria oppressed him without cause. [5] Now, then, what do I have here, says Jehovah? For My people is taken away for nothing. Those who rule them are making him howl, says Jehovah. And My name is despised continually, every day. [6] For this reason My people shall know My name; therefore they shall

19 שְׁתַּיִם הֵנָּה קֹרְאֹתַיִךְ מִי יָנוּד לָךְ הַשֹּׁד וְהַשֶּׁבֶר וְהָרָעָב

and and ,Ruin for shall who came Those two
,famine ,shattering ?you bewail ;you to things

20 וְהַחֶרֶב מִי אֲנַחֲמֵךְ: בָּנַיִךְ עֻלְּפוּ שָׁכְבוּ בְּרֹאשׁ כָּל־חוּצוֹת

the all the at they have Your who (but) the and and
,streets of head of fainted ;sons ?you comfort —sword

21 כְּתוֹא מִכְמָר הַמְּלֵאִים חֲמַת־יְהוָה גַּעֲרַת אֱלֹהָיִךְ: לָכֵן

There- your the ,Jehovah the filled a (in) an like
,fore ,God of rebuke of fury with ,net antelope

22 שִׁמְעִי־נָא זֹאת עֲנִיָּה וּשְׁכֻרַת וְלֹא מִיָּיִן: כֹּה־אָמַר אֲדֹנַיִךְ

your says Thus from but and afflicted ,this now hear
Lord :wine not ,drunken ,one

יְהוָה וֵאלֹהַיִךְ יָרִיב עַמּוֹ הִנֵּה לָקַחְתִּי מִיָּדֵךְ אֶת־כּוֹס

cup the of out have I ,Behold His He your and ,Jehovah
of ,hand your taken .people (for) strives :God

הַתַּרְעֵלָה אֶת־קֻבַּעַת כּוֹס חֲמָתִי לֹא־תוֹסִיפִי לִשְׁתּוֹתָהּ

it drink shall you not My fury the bowl the ,reeling
again of cup of

23 עוֹד: וְשַׂמְתִּיהָ בְּיַד־מוֹגַיִךְ אֲשֶׁר־אָמְרוּ לְנַפְשֵׁךְ שְׁחִי וְנַעֲבֹרָה

we that Bow your to have who your into will I But any
;cross may ,down ,soul said ,oppressor's hand it put .more

וַתָּשִׂימִי כָאָרֶץ גֵּוֵךְ וְכַחוּץ לַעֹבְרִים:

those to as and your the as and
.cross who ,street the ,back ground put

CAP. LII נב

CHAPTER 52

1 עוּרִי עוּרִי לִבְשִׁי עֻזֵּךְ צִיּוֹן לִבְשִׁי ׀ בִּגְדֵי תִפְאַרְתֵּךְ יְרוּשָׁלַ͏ִם

,Jerusalem your robes on put ;Zion your Put !Awake !Awake
,beauty on
of ,strength

2 עִיר הַקֹּדֶשׁ כִּי לֹא יוֹסִיף יָבֹא־בָךְ עוֹד עָרֵל וְטָמֵא: הִתְנַעֲרִי

Shake and uncir- more to come shall not for the city
yourself .unclean cumcised you again ,holy

מֵעָפָר קוּמִי שְּׁבִי יְרוּשָׁלָ͏ִם הִתְפַּתְּחִו מֹסְרֵי צַוָּארֵךְ שְׁבִיָּה

O your the your- Free !Jerusalem ,Sit rise the from
captive ,neck of bands from self !up ;dust

3 בַּת־צִיּוֹן: כִּי־כֹה אָמַר יְהוָה חִנָּם נִמְכַּרְתֶּם וְלֹא

and you were for ;Jehovah says thus For .Zion daugh-
not ,sold nothing of ter

4 בְכֶסֶף תִּגָּאֵלוּ: כִּי כֹה אָמַר אֲדֹנָי יְהוִֹה מִצְרַיִם יָרַד־

went (to) ;Jehovah the says thus For shall you with
down Egypt Lord .redeemed be silver

5 עַמִּי בָרִאשֹׁנָה לָגוּר שָׁם וְאַשּׁוּר בְּאֶפֶס עֲשָׁקוֹ: וְעַתָּה מַה־

what Now oppressed without and ,there to the at My
(is) ,then .him cause Assyria sojourn ,first people

לִּי־פֹה נְאֻם־יְהוָה כִּי־לֻקַּח עַמִּי חִנָּם מֹשְׁלָו יְהֵילִילוּ נְאֻם־

states ,howl His for My taken is For ,Jehovah states ?here to
rulers .nothing people away Me

6 יְהוָה וְתָמִיד כָּל־הַיּוֹם שְׁמִי מִנֹּאָץ: לָכֵן יֵדַע עַמִּי שְׁמִי לָכֵן

there- My My shall There- is My day every And .Jehovah
fore ;name people know ,fore .despised name continually

know in that day, for I (am) He who speaks; behold, I (am) here!

[7] How beautiful on the mountains are the feet of him bringing the gospel, proclaiming peace, bringing good news, proclaiming salvation; saying to Zion, Your God reigns! [8] The voice of your watchmen, they lift the voice together, they sing aloud. For they shall see eye to eye when Jehovah brings back Zion. [9] Break out, sing together, waste places of Jerusalem; for Jehovah comforts His people; He has redeemed Jerusalem. [10] Jehovah has bared His holy arm in the eyes of all the nations; and all the ends of the earth shall see the salvation of our God. [11] Turn! Turn! Leave there! Touch not the unclean! Go out of her midst, purify yourself, bearers of the vessels of Jehovah. [12] For you shall not go out with haste, nor will you go by flight; for Jehovah is going before you, and the God of Israel gathers you.

[13] Behold, My Servant shall rule wisely; He shall be exalted and extolled and be very high. [14] Just as many were astonished over You – so (much was) the disfigurement (of) His appearance away from man, and his form from sons of man-- [15] so He sprinkles from many nations. At Him, kings shall shut their mouths; for they will see that which was told them; and what they had not heard, they will understand.

בַּיּוֹם הַהוּא כִּי־אֲנִי־הוּא הַמְדַבֵּר הִנֵּנִי׃
7 מַה־נָּאווּ עַל־
on beauti- How Behold who He I for ;that day in
are ful !Me ;speaks (am)

הֶהָרִים רַגְלֵי מְבַשֵּׂר מַשְׁמִיעַ שָׁלוֹם מְבַשֵּׂר טוֹב מַשְׁמִיעַ
making of bringing ,peace making bring- him the moun- the
heard ,good tidings heard .tidings ing of feet tains

יְשׁוּעָה אֹמֵר לְצִיּוֹן מָלַךְ אֱלֹהָיִךְ׃
8 קוֹל צֹפַיִךְ נָשְׂאוּ קוֹל
the they your The Your reigns to saying salva-
voice lift ,watchmen of voice !God ,Zion ,tion

יַחְדָּו יְרַנֵּנוּ כִּי עַיִן בְּעַיִן יִרְאוּ בְּשׁוּב יְהוָה צִיּוֹן׃
9 פִּצְחוּ רַנְּנוּ
sing Break .Zion Jehovah when they to eye For sing they to-
,out back brings see shall eye .aloud ,gether

יַחְדָּו חָרְבוֹת יְרוּשָׁלִָם כִּי־נִחַם יְהוָה עַמּוֹ גָּאַל יְרוּשָׁלִָם׃
.Jerusalem has He His Jehovah com- for ;Jerusalem waste to-
redeemed ;people forts of places ,gether

10 חָשַׂף יְהוָה אֶת־זְרוֹעַ קָדְשׁוֹ לְעֵינֵי כָּל־הַגּוֹיִם וְרָאוּ כָּל־
all shall and the all the in His arm the Jehovah has
see ;nations of eyes holiness of bared

אַפְסֵי־אָרֶץ אֵת יְשׁוּעַת אֱלֹהֵינוּ׃
11 סוּרוּ סוּרוּ צְאוּ מִשָּׁם
from Go Turn Turn .God our sal- the the the
!there out !aside !aside of vation earth of ends

טָמֵא אַל־תִּגָּעוּ צְאוּ מִתּוֹכָהּ הִבָּרוּ נֹשְׂאֵי כְּלֵי יְהוָה׃
12 כִּי לֹא
not For .Jehovah the bearers purify her from Go !touch not The
of vessels of yourself ,midst out unclean

בְחִפָּזוֹן תֵּצֵאוּ וּבִמְנוּסָה לֹא תֵלֵכוּן כִּי־הֹלֵךְ לִפְנֵיכֶם יְהוָה
,Jehovah before is for will not in and shall you with
you going ,go you flight ,out go haste

וּמְאַסִּפְכֶם אֱלֹהֵי יִשְׂרָאֵל׃
13 הִנֵּה יַשְׂכִּיל עַבְדִּי יָרוּם
shall He My rule shall ,Behold .Israel the and
exalted be ;servant wisely of God you gathers

וְנִשָּׂא וְגָבַהּ מְאֹד׃
14 כַּאֲשֶׁר שָׁמְמוּ עָלֶיךָ רַבִּים כֵּן־מִשְׁחַת
disfig- the so —many over were as Just .very be and and
urement You astonished high up lifted

מֵאִישׁ מַרְאֵהוּ וְתֹאֲרוֹ מִבְּנֵי אָדָם׃
15 כֵּן יַזֶּה גּוֹיִם רַבִּים עָלָיו
At .many nations He So —man from his and ap- His from away
Him from sprinkles of sons form pearance ,man

יִקְפְּצוּ מְלָכִים פִּיהֶם כִּי אֲשֶׁר לֹא־סֻפַּר לָהֶם רָאוּ וַאֲשֶׁר
and will they to was not that for their kings shall
what ;see them told which ;mouth shut

לֹא־שָׁמְעוּ הִתְבּוֹנָנוּ׃
will they they not
.understand heard

CAP. LIII נג

CHAPTER 53

CHAPTER 53

[1] Who has believed our report? And to whom is the arm of Jehovah revealed? [2] For he comes up before Him as a tender plant, and as a root out of dry ground. He shall have no form nor magnificence

1 מִי הֶאֱמִין לִשְׁמֻעָתֵנוּ וּזְרוֹעַ יְהוָה עַל־מִי נִגְלָתָה׃
2 וַיַּעַל
He For is whom to Jehovah the And our has Who
up comes ?revealed of arm ?report believed

כַּיּוֹנֵק לְפָנָיו וְכַשֹּׁרֶשׁ מֵאֶרֶץ צִיָּה לֹא־תֹאַר לוֹ וְלֹא הָדָר
,majesty and to form a Not .dry of out as and before a as
(is) not ,Him (is) ground root a ,Him shoot

that we should see Him; nor beauty that we should desire Him. [3] (He is) despised and abandoned of men, a man of pains, and acquainted with sickness. And as hiding of faces from Him, being despised and we did not value Him. [4] Surely He has borne our sicknesses, and He carried our pains; yet we esteemed Him plagued, smitten by God, and afflicted. [5] But He was wounded for our transgressions; (He was) bruised for our iniquities; the chastisement of our peace (was) upon Him; and with His wounds we ourselves are healed. [6] All we like sheep have gone astray; we have each one turned to his own way; and Jehovah made meet on Him the iniquity of all of us. [7] He was oppressed, and He was afflicted, but He did not open His mouth. He was led as a lamb to the slaughter; and as an ewe before her shearers is dumb, so He opens not His mouth. [8] He was taken from prison and from justice; and who shall consider His generation? For He was cut off out of the land of the living; He was stricken from the transgression of My people. [9] And He made His grave with the wicked; and with a rich (man) in His death; although He had done no violence, and deceit was not in His mouth. [10] But Jehovah pleased to crush Him, to make Him sick. If He shall put His soul (as) a guilt offering, He shall see (His) seed; He shall prolong (His) days; and the will of Jehovah shall prosper in His hand. [11] He shall see (the fruit) of the travail of His soul; He shall be fully satisfied. By His knowledge shall My righteous Servant justify for many, and He shall bear their iniquities. [12] Because of this I will divide to Him with the great, and with the strong He shall divide the spoil. Because He poured out to death His soul; and He was counted with transgressors; and He bore the sin of many, and made intercession for the transgressors.

3 וְנִרְאֵהוּ וְלֹא־מַרְאֶה וְנֶחְמְדֵהוּ׃ נִבְזֶה וַחֲדַל אִישִׁים אִישׁ
a ,men ab- and despised should we that ap- an not and we that
of man of andoned :him desire pearance ;Him see should

מַכְאֹבוֹת וִידוּעַ חֹלִי וּכְמַסְתֵּר פָּנִים מִמֶּנּוּ נִבְזֶה וְלֹא
and being from faces as And sick- known and
not despised ;Him of hiding nesses of pains

4 חֲשַׁבְנֻהוּ׃ אָכֵן חֳלָיֵנוּ הוּא נָשָׂא וּמַכְאֹבֵינוּ סְבָלָם וַאֲנַחְנוּ
we but carried He our and has He sick- our Surely did we
;them pains ,borne nesses .Him value

5 חֲשַׁבְנֻהוּ נָגוּעַ מֻכֵּה אֱלֹהִים וּמְעֻנֶּה׃ וְהוּא מְחֹלָל מִפְּשָׁעֵנוּ
our for was He But and ,God struck ,plagued esteem-
,transgressions pierced .afflicted by Him ed

מְדֻכָּא מֵעֲוֺנֹתֵינוּ מוּסַר שְׁלוֹמֵנוּ עָלָיו וּבַחֲבֻרָתוֹ נִרְפָּא־
are we with and on (was) our chastise- the our for crushed
healed wounds His ;Him peace of ment ;iniquities

6 לָנוּ׃ כֻּלָּנוּ כַּצֹּאן תָּעִינוּ אִישׁ לְדַרְכּוֹ פָּנִינוּ וַיהוָה הִפְגִּיעַ
made has and have we his to each go like All our-
meet Jehovah ;turned way man ;astray sheep we .selves

7 בּוֹ אֵת עֲוֺן כֻּלָּנוּ׃ נִגַּשׂ וְהוּא נַעֲנֶה וְלֹא יִפְתַּח־פִּיו כַּשֶּׂה
a As His did He but was He and was He .all us the in
lamb .mouth open not ;afflicted ,oppressed of iniquity Him

לַטֶּבַח יוּבָל וּכְרָחֵל לִפְנֵי גֹזְזֶיהָ נֶאֱלָמָה וְלֹא יִפְתַּח פִּיו׃
His He so is her before as and was He the to
.mouth opens not ,dumb shearers ewe an ;led slaughter

8 מֵעֹצֶר וּמִמִּשְׁפָּט לֻקָּח וְאֶת־דּוֹרוֹ מִי יְשׂוֹחֵחַ כִּי נִגְזַר מֵאֶרֶץ
the from was He For shall who His and was He trom and From
of land off cut ?consider generation ;taken justice prison

9 חַיִּים מִפֶּשַׁע עַמִּי נֶגַע לָמוֹ׃ וַיִּתֵּן אֶת־רְשָׁעִים קִבְרוֹ וְאֶת־
and His the with He And to (was) the My tres- the from the
with ,grave wicked put .Him stroke people of pass ;living

10 עָשִׁיר בְּמֹתָיו עַל לֹא־חָמָס עָשָׂה וְלֹא מִרְמָה בְּפִיו׃ וַיהוָה
But His in deceit and had He violence not though His in rich a
Jehovah .mouth (was) not ,done :death (man)

חָפֵץ דַּכְּאוֹ הֶחֱלִי אִם־תָּשִׂים אָשָׁם נַפְשׁוֹ יִרְאֶה זֶרַע יַאֲרִיךְ
shall He ,seed He His guilt a He If make to to pleased
prolong see shall ,soul offering put shall sick Him ,Him crush

11 יָמִים וְחֵפֶץ יְהוָה בְּיָדוֹ יִצְלָח׃ מֵעֲמַל נַפְשׁוֹ יִרְאֶה יִשְׂבָּע
shall He shall He His the Of shall His in Jehovah the and days
.satisfied be ;see soul of travail .prosper hand of pleasure

בְּדַעְתּוֹ יַצְדִּיק צַדִּיק עַבְדִּי לָרַבִּים וַעֲוֺנֹתָם הוּא יִסְבֹּל׃
shall He their and ,many for My righteous shall His By
.bear iniquities servant justify knowledge

12 לָכֵן אֲחַלֶּק־לוֹ בָרַבִּים וְאֶת־עֲצוּמִים יְחַלֵּק שָׁלָל תַּחַת
be- ,spoil shall He the and the with to will I There-
divide strong with ,great Him divide ,fore

אֲשֶׁר הֶעֱרָה לַמָּוֶת נַפְשׁוֹ וְאֶת־פֹּשְׁעִים נִמְנָה וְהוּא חֵטְא־
the He and was trans- and His death to poured He cause
of sin ;counted gressors with ;soul out

רַבִּים נָשָׂא וְלַפֹּשְׁעִים יַפְגִּיעַ׃
made for and ,bore many
.intercession transgressors

CAP. LIV נד

CHAPTER 54

1 רָנִּי עֲקָרָה לֹא יָלָדָה פִּצְחִי רִנָּה וְצַהֲלִי לֹא־חָלָה כִּי־
For who (you)not and song a break that not barren Re-
.travailed ,shout out ;bore ,one ,joice

2 רַבִּים בְּנֵי־שׁוֹמֵמָה מִבְּנֵי בְעוּלָה אָמַר יְהוָה׃ הַרְחִיבִי
Make .Jehovah says the the than the the (are)
larger ,married of sons desolate of sons more

מְקוֹם אָהֳלֵךְ וִירִיעוֹת מִשְׁכְּנוֹתַיִךְ יַטּוּ אַל־תַּחְשֹׂכִי הַאֲרִיכִי
lengthen do not stretch your the and ,tent your the
;spare ;out dwellings of curtains of place

3 מֵיתָרַיִךְ וִיתֵדֹתַיִךְ חַזֵּקִי׃ כִּי־יָמִין וּשְׂמֹאול תִּפְרֹצִי וְזַרְעֵךְ
your And shall you the and the (on) For .strengthen your and your
seed .forth break left right stakes cords

4 גּוֹיִם יִירָשׁ וְעָרִים נְשַׁמּוֹת יוֹשִׁיבוּ׃ אַל־תִּירְאִי כִּי־לֹא
not for Do not indwell will ruined and shall nations
fear .people cities ,possess

תֵבוֹשִׁי וְאַל־תִּכָּלְמִי כִּי־לֹא תַחְפִּירִי כִּי בֹשֶׁת עֲלוּמַיִךְ
your the For shall you not for you shall and be shall you
youth of shame ;wounded be .abashed be not ,ashamed

5 תִּשְׁכָּחִי וְחֶרְפַּת אַלְמְנוּתַיִךְ לֹא תִזְכְּרִי־עוֹד׃ כִּי בֹעֲלַיִךְ
your For any shall you not your the and shall you
husband .more remember widowhood of reproach ,forget

עֹשַׂיִךְ יְהוָה צְבָאוֹת שְׁמוֹ וְגֹאֲלֵךְ קְדוֹשׁ יִשְׂרָאֵל אֱלֹהֵי כָל־
all the ;Israel the (is) your and His Hosts Jehovah your (is)
of God of One Holy Redeemer ;name (is) of ,Maker

6 הָאָרֶץ יִקָּרֵא׃ כִּי־כְאִשָּׁה עֲזוּבָה וַעֲצוּבַת רוּחַ קְרָאָךְ
has spirit grieved and forsaken a as For is He the
you called in woman .called earth

7 יְהוָה וְאֵשֶׁת נְעוּרִים כִּי תִמָּאֵס אָמַר אֱלֹהָיִךְ׃ בְּרֶגַע קָטֹן
little a For your says is she when young a even ,Jehovah
moment .God ,rejected men of wife

8 עֲזַבְתִּיךְ וּבְרַחֲמִים גְּדֹלִים אֲקַבְּצֵךְ׃ בְּשֶׁצֶף קֶצֶף הִסְתַּרְתִּי
hid I wrath a In will I great with but have I
of flood ,you gather compassion ,you left

פָנַי רֶגַע מִמֵּךְ וּבְחֶסֶד עוֹלָם רִחַמְתִּיךְ אָמַר גֹּאֲלֵךְ יְהוָה׃
.Jehovah your says have will I ever- with but from a My
Redeemer ,you on pity lasting mercy ;you moment face

9 כִּי־מֵי נֹחַ זֹאת לִי אֲשֶׁר נִשְׁבַּעְתִּי מֵעֲבֹר מֵי־נֹחַ עוֹד
again Noah the from swore I which to this Noah the For
of waters crossing ,Me (is) of waters

10 עַל־הָאָרֶץ כֵּן נִשְׁבַּעְתִּי מִקְּצֹף עָלַיִךְ וּמִגְּעָר־בָּךְ׃ כִּי הֶהָרִים
the For .you from and with being from have I so the over
mountains rebuking you angry sworn ,earth

יָמוּשׁוּ וְהַגְּבָעוֹת תְּמוּטֶינָה וְחַסְדִּי מֵאִתֵּךְ לֹא־יָמוּשׁ וּבְרִית
the and shall not from My but be the and shall
of covenant ,depart you mercy ,removed hills depart

11 שְׁלוֹמִי לֹא תָמוּט אָמַר מְרַחֲמֵךְ יְהוָה׃ עֲנִיָּה סֹעֲרָה
storm Afflicted .Jehovah pity having says be shall not My
,tossed ,one you on ,removed peace

CHAPTER 54

[1] Rejoice, unfruitful one that never bore; break out a song and shout, you who never travailed. For the sons of the desolate one (are) more than the sons of the married woman, says Jehovah. [2] Make the place of your tent larger, and let them stretch out the curtains of your dwellings. Do not spare, lengthen your cords and strengthen your stakes. [3] For you shall break forth on the right hand and on the left. And your seed shall possess nations, and people will indwell ruined cities. [4] Do not fear, for you shall not be ashamed, nor shall you be disgraced, for you shall not be abashed. For you shall forget the shame of your youth, and shall not remember the reproach of your widowhood any more. [5] For your Maker (is) your husband; Jehovah of hosts (is) His name; and your Redeemer (is) the Holy One of Israel; He is called the God of the whole earth. [6] For Jehovah has called you as a woman forsaken and grieved in spirit, even a wife of young men when she is rejected, says your God. [7] For a little moment I have left you, but I will gather you with great mercies. [8] In a flood of wrath I hid My face from you (for) a moment; but I will have pity on you with everlasting kindness, says Jehovah your Redeemer. [9] For this (is) the waters of Noah to Me; which I swore from passing over the waters of Noah over the earth again, so I have sworn from being angry with you and rebuking you. [10] For the mountains shall depart and the hills be removed, but My mercy shall not depart from you, nor shall the covenant of My peace be removed, says Jehovah who has pity on you.

[11] Afflicted one, storm-tossed, and not

comforted! Behold, I stretch out your stones among antimony, and lay your foundations with sapphires. [12] And I will make your battlements of ruby, and your gates carbuncle stones, and all your borders pleasing stones; [13] and all your sons (with the) taught of Jehovah; and the peace of your sons great. [14] You shall be established in righteousness; (you shall) be far from oppression, for you shall not fear; and from terror, for it shall not come near you. [15] Behold, they shall surely gather, but not from Me. Who has gathered against you? By you he shall fall. [16] Behold, I have created the smith who blows the coal in the fire, and who brings out a weapon for his work; and I have created the destroyer to destroy. [17] Every weapon formed against you shall not prosper, and every tongue that shall rise against you in judgment, you shall condemn. This (is) the inheritance of the servants of Jehovah, and their righteousness is from Me, says Jehovah.

לֹא נֻחָמָה הִנֵּה אָנֹכִי מַרְבִּיץ בַּפּוּךְ אֲבָנַיִךְ וִיסַדְתִּיךְ

your lay and foundations | your ,stones | among antimony | stretch out | I | ,Behold | com- !forted | not

12 בַּסַּפִּירִים׃ וְשַׂמְתִּי כַּדְכֹד שִׁמְשֹׁתַיִךְ וּשְׁעָרַיִךְ לְאַבְנֵי אֶקְדָּח

car- buncle | stones of | your and gates | your ,battlements | ruby of | I And make will | among ,sapphires

13 וְכָל־גְּבוּלֵךְ לְאַבְנֵי־חֵפֶץ׃ וְכָל־בָּנַיִךְ לִמּוּדֵי יְהוָה וְרַב

and great | ;Jehovah | taught of | your sons | and all | ;delight | stones of | your border | and all

14 שְׁלוֹם בָּנָיִךְ׃ בִּצְדָקָה תִּכּוֹנָנִי רַחֲקִי מֵעֹשֶׁק כִּי־לֹא תִירָאִי

shall you ;fear | not | for | from ,oppression | far be | shall you ;set be | righ- teousness | In | your .sons | the (is) of peace

15 וּמִמְּחִתָּה כִּי לֹא־תִקְרַב אֵלָיִךְ׃ הֵן גּוֹר יָגוּר אֶפֶס מֵאוֹתִי

from '.Me | not but | they will ,gather | surely | Be- ,hold | .you to | shall it near come | not | for | from and ,terror

16 מִי־גָר אִתָּךְ עָלַיִךְ יִפּוֹל׃ הֵן אָנֹכִי בָּרָאתִי חָרָשׁ נֹפֵחַ

blow- ing | the ,smith | have created | I | ,Behold | shall he .fall | By you | against ?you | has Who gathered

בְּאֵשׁ פֶּחָם וּמוֹצִיא כְלִי לְמַעֲשֵׂהוּ וְאָנֹכִי בָּרָאתִי מַשְׁחִית

waster | the | have created | I and | his for ;work | a weapon | bring- and out ing | ,coal | the in of fire

17 לְחַבֵּל׃ כָּל־כְּלִי יוּצַר עָלַיִךְ לֹא יִצְלָח וְכָל־לָשׁוֹן תָּקוּם־

shall that arise | tongue | and every | shall ,prosper | not | against you | formed | weapon Every | to .destroy

אִתָּךְ לַמִּשְׁפָּט תַּרְשִׁיעִי זֹאת נַחֲלַת עַבְדֵי יְהוָה וְצִדְקָתָם

their and righteousness | ,Jehovah | the of servants | inheri- of tance | the This (is) | shall you .condemn | in judgment | against you

מֵאִתִּי נְאֻם־יְהוָה׃

.Jehovah | states | from ,Me

CAP. LV נה

CHAPTER 55

[1] Ho, everyone who thirsts, come to the water; and he who (has) no silver, come, buy and eat. Yes, come, buy wine and milk, without silver and without price. [2] Why do you weigh out silver for (that) which is) not bread, and your labor for (that which) never satisfies? Listen carefully to Me and eat that which is good; and let your soul delight itself in fatness. [3] Bend your ear and come to Me; hear, and your soul shall live; and I will cut a covenant everlasting with you, the faithful mercies of David. [4] Behold, I gave Him as a witness to peoples,

CHAPTER 55

1 הוֹי כָּל־צָמֵא לְכוּ לַמַּיִם וַאֲשֶׁר אֵין־לוֹ כֶּסֶף לְכוּ שִׁבְרוּ

,buy grain | ,come | silver (is) | to him not | he and who | the to ;water | come | who every ,thirsts one | ,Ho

וֶאֱכֹלוּ וּלְכוּ שִׁבְרוּ בְּלוֹא־כֶסֶף וּבְלוֹא מְחִיר יַיִן וְחָלָב׃

and .milk | wine | ,price | and without | silver without | buy grain | ,yes come | ;eat and

2 לָמָּה תִשְׁקְלוּ־כֶסֶף בְּלוֹא־לֶחֶם וִיגִיעֲכֶם בְּלוֹא לְשָׂבְעָה

satis- to ?faction | (what) for not (is) | your and labor | ,bread (what) for not (is) | silver | you do out weigh | Why

שִׁמְעוּ שָׁמוֹעַ אֵלַי וְאִכְלוּ־טוֹב וְתִתְעַנַּג בַּדֶּשֶׁן נַפְשְׁכֶם׃

.soul your | fatness in | let and itself delight | the good | eat and | ,Me to | care- fully | Listen

3 הַטּוּ אָזְנְכֶם וּלְכוּ אֵלַי שִׁמְעוּ וּתְחִי נַפְשְׁכֶם וְאֶכְרְתָה

will I and cut | ;soul your | shall and live | ,hear | ;Me to | and come | your ear | Incline

4 לָכֶם בְּרִית עוֹלָם חַסְדֵי דָוִד הַנֶּאֱמָנִים׃ הֵן עֵד לְאוּמִּים

peoples | a (as) to witness | ,Lo | faithful the | David | mercies of | ever- ,lasting | a covenant | with you

a Leader and Commander of peoples. [5] Behold You shall call a nation You do not know; yea, a nation that does not know You shall run to You, because of Jehovah Your God, and for the Holy One of Israel; for He has glorified You.

[6] Seek Jehovah while He may be found; call on Him while He is near. [7] Let the wicked forsake his way and the man of vanity his thoughts; and let him return to Jehovah, and He will have mercy on him — and to our God, for He will abundantly pardon. [8] For My thoughts (are) not your thoughts; nor (are) your ways My ways, says Jehovah. [9] For as the heavens are high from the earth, so My ways are high from your ways, and My thoughts from your thoughts. [10] For as the rain and the snow goes down from the heavens and does not return there, but waters the earth and makes it bring forth and bud, and give seed to the sower and bread to the eater — [11] so shall My word be, which goes out of My mouth; it shall not return to Me void, but it shall accomplish that which I please, and it shall prosper in what I sent it (to do)! [12] For you shall go out with joy and be led out with peace. The mountains and the hills shall break out into song before you, and all the trees of the field shall clap the palm. [13] Instead of the thorn-bush, the fir-tree shall come up; instead of the brier, the myrtle shall come up; and it shall be for a name to Jehovah, for a sign everlasting that shall not be cut off.

5 נְתַתִּיו נָגִיד וּמְצַוֵּה לְאֻמִּים׃ הֵן גּוֹי לֹא־תֵדַע תִּקְרָא וְגוֹי

a and shall You You not a ,Lo .peoples Com- and a gave I
nation ;call know do nation of mander Leader Him

לֹא־יְדָעוּךָ אֵלֶיךָ יָרוּצוּ לְמַעַן יְהוָה אֱלֹהֶיךָ וְלִקְדוֹשׁ יִשְׂרָאֵל

;Israel the for and your Jehovah because shall to that not
of One Holy ,God of ;run You ,You knows

6 כִּי פֵאֲרָךְ׃ • דִּרְשׁוּ יְהוָה בְּהִמָּצְאוֹ קְרָאֻהוּ בִּהְיוֹתוֹ

He while on call He while Jehovah Seek has He for
is Him ;found be may .You glorified

7 קָרוֹב׃ יַעֲזֹב רָשָׁע דַּרְכּוֹ וְאִישׁ אָוֶן מַחְשְׁבֹתָיו וְיָשֹׁב אֶל־

to let and His vanity the and his the Let .near
return him ;thoughts of man ,way wicked forsake

8 יְהוָה וִירַחֲמֵהוּ וְאֶל־אֱלֹהֵינוּ כִּי־יַרְבֶּה לִסְלוֹחַ׃ כִּי לֹא

not For .pardon to will He for our to and may He that Jeho-
(are) multiply ,God ;him pity ,vah

מַחְשְׁבוֹתַי מַחְשְׁבוֹתֵיכֶם וְלֹא דַרְכֵיכֶם דְּרָכָי נְאֻם יְהוָה׃

.Jehovah states My ways your and your My
,ways (are) not ;thoughts thoughts

9 כִּי־גָבְהוּ שָׁמַיִם מֵאָרֶץ כֵּן גָּבְהוּ דְרָכַי מִדַּרְכֵיכֶם

your from My are so the from the are For
,ways ways high ,earth heavens high (as)

10 וּמַחְשְׁבֹתַי מִמַּחְשְׁבֹתֵיכֶם׃ כִּי כַּאֲשֶׁר יֵרֵד הַגֶּשֶׁם וְהַשֶּׁלֶג

and the goes as For your from My and
snow the rain down .thoughts thoughts

מִן־הַשָּׁמַיִם וְשָׁמָּה לֹא יָשׁוּב כִּי אִם־הִרְוָה אֶת־הָאָרֶץ

the it ex- does not to and the from
earth waters cept ,return there ,heavens

11 וְהוֹלִידָהּ וְהִצְמִיחָהּ וְנָתַן זֶרַע לַזֹּרֵעַ וְלֶחֶם לָאֹכֵל׃ כֵּן יִהְיֶה

shall so the to and the to seed and and it makes and
be —eater bread sower give ,sprout forth bring

דְבָרִי אֲשֶׁר יֵצֵא מִפִּי לֹא־יָשׁוּב אֵלַי רֵיקָם כִּי אִם־עָשָׂה

do shall it ex- ,void Me to shall it not My of goes that My
cept return ;mouth out word

12 אֶת־אֲשֶׁר חָפַצְתִּי וְהִצְלִיחַ אֲשֶׁר שְׁלַחְתִּיו׃ כִּי־בְשִׂמְחָה

with For .it sent I what in shall it and ;please I that
joy prosper which

תֵצֵאוּ וּבְשָׁלוֹם תּוּבָלוּן הֶהָרִים וְהַגְּבָעוֹת יִפְצְחוּ לִפְנֵיכֶם

before break shall the and the ;led be with and shall you
you out hills mountains peace ,out go

13 רִנָּה וְכָל־עֲצֵי הַשָּׂדֶה יִמְחֲאוּ־כָף׃ תַּחַת הַנַּעֲצוּץ יַעֲלֶה

shall thorn- the Instead (the) shall the the and (into)
up go bush of palm clap field of trees all ;song

בְרוֹשׁ תַּחַת הַסִּרְפַּד יַעֲלֶה הֲדַס וְהָיָה לַיהוָה לְשֵׁם לְאוֹת

a for a for to it and the shall the instead fir- the
sign ;name Jehovah be shall ;myrtle up go ,brier of ;tree

עוֹלָם לֹא יִכָּרֵת׃

shall that not ever-
off cut be lasting

CAP. LVI נו

CHAPTER 56

CHAPTER 56

[1] Thus says Jehovah: Keep justice and do righteousness, for My salvation (is) near to come, and My righteousness to be revealed. [2] Blessed (is) the man who does this, and the son of man who lays hold on it; keeping sabbath, from defiling it; and keeping his hand from doing every evil. [3] And do not let the son of the foreigner speak, he who joins himself to Jehovah, saying, Jehovah surely separates me from His people; and not do let the eunuch say, Behold, I am a dried tree. [4] For thus says Jehovah to the eunuchs who keep My sabbaths and choose things I am pleased with, and take hold of My covenant, [4] I even will given to them in My house and in My walls a hand and a name better than sons and than daughters; I will give them a name everlasting which shall not be cut off. [6] And the sons of the alien who join themselves on Jehovah to serve Him, and to love Jehovah's name, to be His servants, everyone who keeps from defiling the sabbath, and takes hold of My covenant: [7] even them I will bring to My holy mount and make them joyful in My house of prayer. [8] Their burnt offerings and their sacrifices (shall be) accepted on My altar, for My house shall be called a house of prayer for all the peoples. [8] States the Lord Jehovah, who gathers the outcasts of Israel, I will yet gather beside him his gathered ones. [9] All beasts of the field come to devour, all beasts in the forest! [10] His watchmen (are) blind; they all do not know;

1 כֹּה אָמַר יְהֹוָה שִׁמְרוּ מִשְׁפָּט וַעֲשׂוּ צְדָקָה כִּי־קְרוֹבָה

near for right- do and justice Keep :Jehovah says Thus
(is) eousness

2 יְשׁוּעָתִי לָבוֹא וְצִדְקָתִי לְהִגָּלוֹת׃ אַשְׁרֵי אֱנוֹשׁ יַעֲשֶׂה־

does who man the Blessed be to My and ,come to My
(is) .revealed righteousness ,salvation

זֹּאת וּבֶן־אָדָם יַחֲזִיק בָּהּ שֹׁמֵר שַׁבָּת מֵחַלְּלוֹ וְשֹׁמֵר יָדוֹ

his and from ,sabbath keeping ;it on who man the and ,this
hand keeping ,it defiling holds of son

3 מֵעֲשׂוֹת כָּל־רָע׃ וְאַל־יֹאמַר בֶּן־הַנֵּכָר הַנִּלְוָה אֶל־יְהֹוָה

,Jehovah to who the son let do And .evil every from
himself joins foreigner of speak not doing

לֵאמֹר הַבְדֵּל יַבְדִּילַנִי יְהֹוָה מֵעַל עַמּוֹ וְאַל־יֹאמַר הַסָּרִיס

the let do and His from Jehovah separates Surely ,saying
,eunuch say not ;people me

4 הֵן אֲנִי עֵץ יָבֵשׁ׃ כִּי־כֹה ׀ אָמַר יְהֹוָה לַסָּרִיסִים אֲשֶׁר

who the to Jehovah says thus For dried a I Be-
eunuchs up tree (am) ,hold

יִשְׁמְרוּ אֶת־שַׁבְּתוֹתַי וּבָחֲרוּ בַּאֲשֶׁר חָפָצְתִּי וּמַחֲזִיקִים

take and am I things and My keep
hold ,pleased which with choose sabbaths

5 בִּבְרִיתִי׃ וְנָתַתִּי לָהֶם בְּבֵיתִי וּבְחוֹמֹתַי יָד וָשֵׁם טוֹב

better a and a in and My in them to even I My of
name hand walls My house give will :covenant

מִבָּנִים וּמִבָּנוֹת שֵׁם עוֹלָם אֶתֶּן־לוֹ אֲשֶׁר לֹא יִכָּרֵת׃

be shall not which to will I ever- a than and than
.off cut ,them give lasting name .daughters sons

6 וּבְנֵי הַנֵּכָר הַנִּלְוִים עַל־יְהֹוָה לְשָׁרְתוֹ וּלְאַהֲבָה אֶת־שֵׁם

the to and serve to Jehovah on join who the the And
of name love ,Him themselves alien of sons

יְהֹוָה לִהְיוֹת לוֹ לַעֲבָדִים כָּל־שֹׁמֵר שַׁבָּת מֵחַלְּלוֹ וּמַחֲזִיקִים

takes and from ,sabbath who every ,servants to be- to ,Jehovah
hold ,it defiling keeps one Him come

7 בִּבְרִיתִי׃ וַהֲבִיאוֹתִים אֶל־הַר קָדְשִׁי וְשִׂמַּחְתִּים בְּבֵית

in make and My Mount to will I even My of
of house joyful them ,holy them bring .covenant

תְּפִלָּתִי עוֹלֹתֵיהֶם וְזִבְחֵיהֶם לְרָצוֹן עַל־מִזְבְּחִי כִּי בֵיתִי

My for My on for (are) their and burnt Their My
house ,altar acceptance sacrifices offerings .prayer

8 בֵּית־תְּפִלָּה יִקָּרֵא לְכָל־הָעַמִּים׃ נְאֻם אֲדֹנָי יְהֹוָה מְקַבֵּץ

gather- ,Jehovah the states the all for be shall prayer a
ing Lord .peoples called of house

9 נִדְחֵי יִשְׂרָאֵל עוֹד אֲקַבֵּץ עָלָיו לְנִקְבָּצָיו׃ ▪ כֹּל חַיְתוֹ שָׂדַי

the beasts All his to upon will I yet ,Israel out- the
,field of .ones gathered him gather of casts

10 אֵתָיוּ לֶאֱכֹל כָּל־חַיְתוֹ בַּיָּעַר׃ צֹפָו עִוְרִים כֻּלָּם לֹא

not they (are) His the in beasts all ,eat to come
all ;blind watchmen !forest

they (are) all dumb dogs, they cannot bark, dreaming, lying down, loving to slumber. [11] Yes, dogs (are) greedy of soul; they do not know satisfaction. And they (are) shepherds; they know not discernment; they all look to their own way, each one for his own gain, from his own end, (saying): [12] Come, and let me bring wine, and let us gulp down fermented drink; and tomorrow shall be as this day, great, exceedingly abundant.

יָדְעוּ כֻּלָּם כְּלָבִים אִלְּמִים לֹא יוּכְלוּ לִנְבֹּחַ הֹזִים שֹׁכְבִים

lying ,dreaming ,bark to they not ,dumb dogs (are) they ;know
,down able are all

אֹהֲבֵי לָנוּם׃ וְהַכְּלָבִים עַזֵּי־נֶפֶשׁ לֹא יָדְעוּ שָׂבְעָה וְהֵמָּה 11

And .satisfaction they not ;soul strong dogs And to loving
(are) they know of (are) .slumber

רֹעִים לֹא יָדְעוּ הָבִין כֻּלָּם לְדַרְכָּם פָּנוּ אִישׁ לְבִצְעוֹ

own his for each ,look their to they discern- they not shep-
,gain man way all ;ment know ;herds

מִקָּצֵהוּ׃ אֵתָיוּ אֶקְחָה־יַיִן וְנִסְבְּאָה שֵׁכָר וְהָיָה כָזֶה יוֹם 12

day as shall and fermented let and ,wine me let ,Come his from
this be ;drink gulp us take :end

מָחָר גָּדוֹל יֶתֶר מְאֹד׃

.very abun- ,great to-
dantly ,morrow

CAP. LVII נז

CHAPTER 57

CHAPTER 57

[1] The righteous one perishes, and no one lays (it) to heart; yea, merciful men are gathered, with no one discerning that the righteous is gathered from the face of evil. [2] He shall enter peace; they shall rest on their couches, walking (in) his uprightness. [3] But you, draw near here, sons of the sorceress, seed of the adulterer and the harlot. [4] On whom are you making sport? On whom do you make a wide mouth and draw out the tongue? Are you not children of transgression, a lying seed, [5] being inflamed with idols under every green tree, slaughtering the children in the torrent-beds, under the clefts of the rocks? [6] Your lot (is) in the torrent's smoothnesses; they, they (are) your portion; even to them you have poured a drink offering; you have offered a food offering. Should I be consoled over these? [7] You have set your couch on a lofty and high mountain; yea, you went up there to sacrifice a sacrifice. [8] And you have set up your memorial behind the door and post. For you uncovered yourself from Me and went up; you enlarged your couch; you

הַצַּדִּיק אָבָד וְאֵין אִישׁ שָׂם עַל־לֵב וְאַנְשֵׁי־חֶסֶד נֶאֱסָפִים 1

are mercy and (his) on lays man and ,perishes righ- The
gathered of men ;heart (it) no one teous

בְּאֵין מֵבִין כִּי־מִפְּנֵי הָרָעָה נֶאֱסַף הַצַּדִּיק׃ יָבוֹא שָׁלוֹם 2

shall He the is evil the from that dis- with
;peace enter .righteous gathered of face cerning none

יָנוּחוּ עַל־מִשְׁכְּבוֹתָם הֹלֵךְ נְכֹחוֹ׃ וְאַתֶּם קִרְבוּ־הֵנָּה 3

,here draw But up- his walking their on they
near ,you .rightness (in) ,couches rest shall

בְּנֵי עֹנְנָה זֶרַע מְנָאֵף וַתִּזְנֶה׃ עַל־מִי תִּתְעַנָּגוּ עַל־מִי 4

whom On you are whom On the and the seed the sons
?sport making .harlot adulterer of ,sorceress of

תַּרְחִיבוּ פֶה תַּאֲרִיכוּ לָשׁוֹן הֲלוֹא־אַתֶּם יִלְדֵי־פֶשַׁע זֶרַע

a transgres- children you Are the draw and a make you do
of seed ,sion of not ?tongue out mouth wide

שָׁקֶר׃ הַנֵּחָמִים בָּאֵלִים תַּחַת כָּל־עֵץ רַעֲנָן שֹׁחֲטֵי הַיְלָדִים 5

the slaugh- ,green tree every under with being false-
children tering idols inflamed ,hood

בַּנְּחָלִים תַּחַת סְעִפֵי הַסְּלָעִים׃ בְּחַלְּקֵי־נַחַל חֶלְקֵךְ הֵם 6

,they your (is) torrent's the in ?rocks the the under tor- the in
;portion smoothnesses of clefts ,beds rent

הֵם גּוֹרָלֵךְ גַּם־לָהֶם שָׁפַכְתְּ נֶסֶךְ הֶעֱלִית מִנְחָה הַעַל

Over food a have you drink a have you to even your (are) they
.offering offered ;offering poured them ;lot

אֵלֶּה אֶנָּחֵם׃ עַל הַר־גָּבֹהַּ וְנִשָּׂא שַׂמְתְּ מִשְׁכָּבֵךְ גַּם־ 7

also your have you and high a On be I should these
;couch set lofty mountain ?consoled

שָׁם עָלִית לִזְבֹּחַ זָבַח׃ וְאַחַר הַדֶּלֶת וְהַמְּזוּזָה שַׂמְתְּ 8

have you the and door the And a to went you there
up set post behind .sacrifice sacrifice up

זִכְרוֹנֵךְ כִּי מֵאִתִּי גִּלִּית וַתַּעֲלִי הִרְחַבְתְּ מִשְׁכָּבֵךְ וַתִּכְרָת־

cut you your en- you and you from For your
(covenant) ;couch larged ;up went uncovered Me .memorial

cut a covenant with them; you loved their couch; at a hand you looked. [9] And you went to the king with oil and multiplied your perfume. And you sent your messengers far away, and lowered yourself to Sheol. [10] You were wearied in the length of your way; you did not say, Despair! You found the life of your hand, so you were not sick. [11] And whom have you dreaded, and feared? You have lied and have not remembered Me, not laying (it) on your heart. Have I not been silent, even from forever, and you have not feared Me? [12] I will reveal your righteousness and your works, and they will not benefit you. [13] When you cry, let your gathering deliver you; but the wind shall bear away all of them; vanity takes (them). But he who takes refuge in Me shall inherit the land and possess My holy mountain.

[14] And He shall say, Raise up! Raise up! Clear the way! Make the stumbling block rise from the way of My people. [15] For thus says the high and lofty One who inhabits eternity, and His name is Holy: I dwell in the high and holy place, even with the contrite and humble of spirit; to revive the spirit of the humble and to revive the heart of contrite ones. [16] For I will not contend forever, nor will I always be angry, for the spirit would faint before Me, even the breaths I have made. [17] For I was angry and struck him for the iniquity of his gain; I hid Myself and was angry; yet he went, turning in his heart's way. [18] His ways I have seen, but I will heal him, and will lead him and restore comforting to him and to his mourners. [19] (I) create the fruit of the lips: peace, peace, to the ones far off and near, says Jehovah — and I will heal him. [20] But the wicked are like the troubled sea,

9 לָךְ מֵהֶם אָהַבְתְּ מִשְׁכָּבָם יָד חָזִית׃ וַתָּשֻׁרִי לַמֶּלֶךְ

the to king | you And went | you .looked | a (at) hand | their ;couch | you loved | from ;them | for you

בַּשֶּׁמֶן וַתַּרְבִּי רִקֻּחָיִךְ וַתְּשַׁלְּחִי צִרַיִךְ עַד־מֵרָחֹק וַתַּשְׁפִּילִי

lowered yourself | and far ,away | mes- sengers | your | you And sent | your .perfume | and multiplied | with ,oil

10 עַד־שְׁאוֹל׃ בְּרֹב דַּרְכֵּךְ יָגַעַתְּ לֹא אָמַרְתְּ נוֹאָשׁ חַיַּת

life of | The | ! Despair | you ,said | not | you ;labored | your way | the In of length | .Sheol | to

11 יָדֵךְ מָצָאת עַל־כֵּן לֹא חָלִית׃ וְאֶת־מִי דָּאַגְתְּ וַתִּירְאִי כִּי

For | and ?feared | you have ,dreaded | whom | And | were .sick | you | not | therefore | you ;found | your hand

תְכַזֵּבִי וְאוֹתִי לֹא זָכַרְתְּ לֹא־שַׂמְתְּ עַל־לִבֵּךְ הֲלֹא אֲנִי

Have I | not | your .heart | on | laid (it) | not | have ,remembered | not | Me and | have you ,lied

12 מַחְשֶׁה וּמֵעֹלָם וְאוֹתִי לֹא תִירָאִי׃ אֲנִי אַגִּיד צִדְקָתֵךְ

righ- teousness | your | will reveal | I | have you ?feared | not | Me and | from even forever | been ,silent

13 וְאֶת־מַעֲשַׂיִךְ וְלֹא יוֹעִילוּךְ׃ בְּזַעֲקֵךְ יַצִּילֻךְ קִבּוּצַיִךְ וְאֶת־

but | your ,gathering | let you deliver | When ,cry you | will they .you benefit | and not | your ,works | and

כֻּלָּם יִשָּׂא־רוּחַ יִקַּח־הָבֶל וְהַחוֹסֶה בִי יִנְחַל־אֶרֶץ וְיִירַשׁ

and possess | the land | shall inherit | in Me | who he But refuge takes | .vanity takes (them) | the ;wind | bear shall away | of all them

14 הַר־קָדְשִׁי׃ * וְאָמַר סֹלּוּ־סֹלּוּ פַּנּוּ־דָרֶךְ הָרִימוּ מִכְשׁוֹל

stumb- ling | the block | make rise | the !way | Clear | Raise !up | Raise !up | He And say shall | My .holy | moun- tain

15 מִדֶּרֶךְ עַמִּי׃ כִּי כֹה אָמַר רָם וְנִשָּׂא שֹׁכֵן עַד וְקָדוֹשׁ

and (is) Holy | ,eternity | who inhabits | and One lofty | the high | says | thus | For | My .people | the of way | from

שְׁמוֹ מָרוֹם וְקָדוֹשׁ אֶשְׁכּוֹן וְאֶת־דַּכָּא וּשְׁפַל־רוּחַ לְהַחֲיוֹת

to revive | ;spirit | and of humble | the contrite | even with | dwell I ,in | holy and place | The high | His :name

16 רוּחַ שְׁפָלִים וּלְהַחֲיוֹת לֵב נִדְכָּאִים׃ כִּי לֹא לְעוֹלָם אָרִיב

will I ,contend | forever | not | For | contrite ,ones | the of heart | to and revive | humble ones | the of spirit

וְלֹא לָנֶצַח אֶקְּצוֹף כִּי־רוּחַ מִלְּפָנַי יַעֲטוֹף וּנְשָׁמוֹת אֲנִי

I | the even breaths | be would ,faint | be- fore me | from | the spirit | for | will I ;angry be | always | and not

17 עָשִׂיתִי׃ בַּעֲוֺן בִּצְעוֹ קָצַפְתִּי וְאַכֵּהוּ הַסְתֵּר וְאֶקְצֹף וַיֵּלֶךְ

he yet ,went | was and ;angry | hid I Myself | struck and ;him | was I angry | his gain | the For of iniquity | have .made

18 שׁוֹבָב בְּדֶרֶךְ לִבּוֹ׃ דְּרָכָיו רָאִיתִי וְאֶרְפָּאֵהוּ וְאַנְחֵהוּ וַאֲשַׁלֵּם

and restore | will and him lead | will I but ,him heal | have I seen | His ways | his .heart | the in of way | returning

19 נִחֻמִים לוֹ וְלַאֲבֵלָיו׃ בּוֹרֵא נוֹב שְׂפָתָיִם שָׁלוֹם ׀ שָׁלוֹם

,peace | ,peace | ;lips the | the of fruit | (I) create | his to and .mourners | to him | com- forting

20 לָרָחוֹק וְלַקָּרוֹב אָמַר יְהוָה וּרְפָאתִיו׃ וְהָרְשָׁעִים כַּיָּם

the sea | like | the But (are) wicked | will I and him heal | ,Jehovah | says | the to and ,near | far the to off

which cannot be quiet, and its waves cast up mire and dirt. [21] There is no peace to the wicked, says my God.

21 נִגְרָשׁ כִּי הַשְׁקֵט לֹא יוּכָל וַיִּגְרְשׁוּ מֵימָיו רֶפֶשׁ וָטִיט׃ אֵין
There and mire its cast and is not driven which be
no is .dirt waters up ,able quiet

שָׁלוֹם אָמַר אֱלֹהַי לָרְשָׁעִים׃
the to my says ,peace
.wicked ,God

CAP. LVIII נח

CHAPTER 58

[1] Call out with the throat! Do not spare. Lift up your voice like the trumpet! And show My people their rebellion, and to the house of Jacob their sins. [2] Yet they seek Me day (by) day, and desire to know My ways. As a nation that has done right, and not forsaking the judgment of their God, they ask Me about judgments of righteousness; they desire to draw near to God. [3] (They say), Why have we fasted and You did not see; we have afflicted our soul and You did not notice? Behold, on the day of your fast you find pleasure, and all your toilers you drive hard. [4] Look! You fast for strife and for debate, and to strike with the fist of wickedness. Do not fast as today, to sound your voice in the high place. [5] Is this like the fast I will choose, a day (for) a man to afflict his soul? To bow his head down like a bulrush, and he spreads sackcloth and ashes? Will you call to this a fast, and a day of delight to Jehovah? [6] Is this not the fast I have chosen: to open bands of wickedness, to undo yoke-thongs, and to let the oppressed ones go free, and that you pull off every yoke? [7] Is it not to break your bread to the hungry, that the wandering poor you should bring (to your) house; when you will see the naked and cover him; and you will not hide yourself from your flesh? [8] Then your light shall break as the dawn, and

1 קְרָא בְגָרוֹן אַל־תַּחְשֹׂךְ כַּשּׁוֹפָר הָרֵם קוֹלֶךָ וְהַגֵּד לְעַמִּי
My to And your up lift the like do not the with Call
people show !voice trumpet ;spare ;throat ,out

2 פִּשְׁעָם וּלְבֵית יַעֲקֹב חַטֹּאתָם׃ וְאוֹתִי יוֹם יוֹם יִדְרֹשׁוּן
they day day Yet .sins their Jacob the to and their
,seek (by) me of house ,trespass

וְדַעַת דְּרָכַי יֶחְפָּצוּן כְּגוֹי אֲשֶׁר־צְדָקָה עָשָׂה וּמִשְׁפַּט
the and has right- that a As .desire My knowl- and
of judgment ,done eousness nation ways of edge

אֱלֹהָיו לֹא עָזָב יִשְׁאָלוּנִי מִשְׁפְּטֵי־צֶדֶק קִרְבַת אֱלֹהִים
God draw to righteous- judgments ask they for- not their
to near ;ness of Me of ,sake God

3 יֶחְפָּצוּן׃ לָמָּה צַּמְנוּ וְלֹא רָאִיתָ עִנִּינוּ נַפְשֵׁנוּ וְלֹא תֵדָע
did You and our We did You and we have (say They) they
?notice not soul afflicted ?see not fasted Why .desire

4 הֵן בְּיוֹם צֹמְכֶם תִּמְצְאוּ־חֵפֶץ וְכָל־עַצְּבֵיכֶם תִּנְגֹּשׂוּ׃ הֵן
!Look you your and ;pleasure you your the on Be-
.hard drive toilers all find fast of day ,hold

לְרִיב וּמַצָּה תָּצוּמוּ וּלְהַכּוֹת בְּאֶגְרֹף רֶשַׁע לֹא־תָצוּמוּ
Do not wicked- the with to and you and for
fast .ness of fist strike ,fast debate strife

5 כַיּוֹם לְהַשְׁמִיעַ בַּמָּרוֹם קוֹלְכֶם׃ הֲכָזֶה יִהְיֶה צוֹם אֶבְחָרֵהוּ
will I the is Like your the in make to as
,choose fast this .voice height heard ,today

יוֹם עַנּוֹת אָדָם נַפְשׁוֹ הֲלָכֹף כְּאַגְמֹן רֹאשׁוֹ וְשַׂק וָאֵפֶר
and and ,head his a like bow To his man a to a
ashes sackcloth bulrush down ?soul afflict day

6 יַצִּיעַ הֲלָזֶה תִּקְרָא־צוֹם וְיוֹם רָצוֹן לַיהוָה׃ הֲלוֹא זֶה
this not Is to delight a and fast a you Will this to he
?Jehovah of day call ?spreads

צוֹם אֶבְחָרֵהוּ פַּתֵּחַ חַרְצֻבּוֹת רֶשַׁע הַתֵּר אֲגֻדּוֹת מוֹטָה
the thongs to wicked- bands open to have I the
,yoke of undo ,ness of :chosen fast

7 וְשַׁלַּח רְצוּצִים חָפְשִׁים וְכָל־מוֹטָה תְּנַתֵּקוּ׃ הֲלוֹא פָרֹס
to it Is you that yoke and ,free oppressed to and
break not ?off pull every ones go let

לָרָעֵב לַחְמֶךָ וַעֲנִיִּים מְרוּדִים תָּבִיא בָיִת כִּי־תִרְאֶה עָרֹם
the will you when (your) should you wander- the that your the to
,naked see ;house (to) bring ing poor ,bread hungry

8 וְכִסִּיתוֹ וּמִבְּשָׂרְךָ לֹא תִתְעַלָּם׃ אָז יִבָּקַע כַּשַּׁחַר אוֹרֶךָ
your the as shall Then will you . not from and cover and
,light dawn break ?yourself hide flesh your ,him

your healing shall spring up quickly; and your righteousness shall go before you; Jehovah's glory shall gather you. [9] Then you shall call, and Jehovah will answer; you shall cry, and He will say, Here I (am). If you put the yoke away from your midst, the pointing of the finger and the speaking of vanity; [10] and if you let out your soul to the hungry, and satisfy the afflicted soul, then your light shall rise in the darkness, and your gloom (shall be) as the noonday. [11] And Jehovah shall always guide you and satisfy your soul in dry places, and support your bones. And you shall be like a watered garden, and like a spring of water whose waters do not fail. [12] And those who come of you shall build the old ruins; you shall rear the foundations of many generations; and you shall be called, The repairer of the breach, the restorer of paths to live in.

[13] If you turn your foot away (because) of the Sabbath, (from) doing what you please on My holy day; and call the Sabbath a delight, glorified to the holiness of Jehovah; and shall glorify it, away from doing your own ways, away from finding your own pleasure, or speaking (your) word; [14] then you shall delight yourself in Jehovah. And I will cause you to ride on the heights of the earth, and make you eat (with) the inheritance of your father Jacob — for the mouth of Jehovah has spoken.

וַאֲרֻכָתְךָ מְהֵרָה תִצְמָח וְהָלַךְ לְפָנֶיךָ צִדְקֶךָ כְּבוֹד יְהוָה
Jehovah the righ- your before shall and shall quickly your and
of glory ;teousness you go ;up spring healing

9 יַאַסְפֶךָ׃ אָז תִּקְרָא וַיהוָה יַעֲנֶה תְּשַׁוַּע וְיֹאמַר הִנֵּנִי אִם־
If Here He and shall you shall and shall you Then gather shall
.(am) I .say shall ,cry ;answer Jehovah ,call .you

10 תָּסִיר מִתּוֹכְךָ מוֹטָה שְׁלַח אֶצְבַּע וְדַבֶּר־אָוֶן׃ וְתָפֵק
if and ;vanity the and the the ,yoke the your from turn you
out let you of speaking finger of pointing midst away

לָרָעֵב נַפְשֶׁךָ וְנֶפֶשׁ נַעֲנָה תַּשְׂבִּיעַ וְזָרַח בַּחֹשֶׁךְ אוֹרֶךָ
your the in then ,satisfy afflicted the and your the to
light darkness rise shall soul ,soul hungry

11 וַאֲפֵלָתְךָ כַּצָּהֳרָיִם׃ וְנָחֲךָ יְהוָה תָּמִיד וְהִשְׂבִּיעַ בְּצַחְצָחוֹת
dry in and ,always Jehovah shall And the as your and
places satisfy you guide .noonday gloom

נַפְשֶׁךָ וְעַצְמֹתֶיךָ יַחֲלִיץ וְהָיִיתָ כְּגַן רָוֶה וּכְמוֹצָא מַיִם אֲשֶׁר
which ,water like and ,watered like you And brace your and your
of spring a garden a be shall .up bones ,soul

12 לֹא־יְכַזְּבוּ מֵימָיו׃ וּבָנוּ מִמְּךָ חָרְבוֹת עוֹלָם מוֹסְדֵי דוֹר־
genera- foun- the forever the (those) shall And its prove do not
and tion of dations of wastes you from build .waters false

וָדוֹר תְּקוֹמֵם וְקֹרָא לְךָ גֹּדֵר פֶּרֶץ מְשֹׁבֵב נְתִיבוֹת לָשָׁבֶת׃
live to paths restorer the repair- to one and shall you gene-
.in of ,breach of er ,you call will ;rear ration

13 אִם־תָּשִׁיב מִשַּׁבָּת רַגְלֶךָ עֲשׂוֹת חֲפָצֶךָ בְּיוֹם קָדְשִׁי וְקָרָאתָ
and My day on you what do to your the from turn you If
call ;holy please foot sabbath away

לַשַּׁבָּת עֹנֶג לִקְדוֹשׁ יְהוָה מְכֻבָּד וְכִבַּדְתּוֹ מֵעֲשׂוֹת דְּרָכֶיךָ
own your from away shall and glori- Jehovah the to de- a the
,ways doing it glorify fied of holiness ,light sabbath

14 מִמְּצוֹא חֶפְצְךָ וְדַבֵּר דָּבָר׃ אָז תִּתְעַנַּג עַל־יְהוָה וְהִרְכַּבְתִּיךָ
will I And Jehovah on shall you then (your) or own your from
ride you make yourself delight ;word speaking ,pleasure finding

עַל־בָּמוֹתֵי אָרֶץ וְהַאֲכַלְתִּיךָ נַחֲלַת יַעֲקֹב אָבִיךָ כִּי פִּי
the for your Jacob the (with) make and the high the on
of mouth ,father of inheritance eat you ,earth of places

יְהוָה דִּבֵּר׃
has Jehovah
.spoken

CAP. LIX נט

CHAPTER 59

1 הֵן לֹא־קָצְרָה יַד־יְהוָה מֵהוֹשִׁיעַ וְלֹא־כָבְדָה אָזְנוֹ מִשְּׁמוֹעַ׃
from His is and from Jehovah the is not Be-
.hearing ear heavy not ,saving of hand shortened ,hold

2 כִּי אִם־עֲוֺנֹתֵיכֶם הָיוּ מַבְדִּלִים בֵּינֵכֶם לְבֵין אֱלֹהֵיכֶם
,God your and between separating are your Except
you iniquities

3 וְחַטֹּאותֵיכֶם הִסְתִּירוּ פָנִים מִכֶּם מִשְּׁמוֹעַ׃ כִּי כַפֵּיכֶם
your For from from (His) have your and
hands .hearing ,you face hidden sins

CHAPTER 59

[1] Behold! Jehovah's hand is not shortened from saving, nor is His ear heavy from hearing. [2] But your iniquities are coming between you and your God, and your sins have hidden (His) face from you, from hearing. [3] For your hands are defiled by blood;

yea, your fingers with iniquity. Your lips have spoken falsehood; your tongue murmurs perverseness. [4] No one calls for righteousness; and none pleads with truth; trusting emptiness, and speaking vanity, they conceive mischief and give birth to evil. [5] They hatch adders' eggs and weave the spider's web; he who eats their eggs dies, and that which is crushed hatches out a viper. [6] Their webs shall not become clothing, nor shall they cover themselves with their works; their works (are) works of evil, and the act of violence (is) in their hands. [7] Their feet run to evil, and they hurry to pour out innocent blood; Thoughts of iniquity are their thoughts; wasting and ruin (are) in their tracks. [8] They do not know the way of peace; and no justice is in their tracks. They have made crooked paths for themselves; everyone going in them knows not peace.

[9] Therefore justice is far from us; and righteousness does not overtake us. We wait for light, but behold, dimness; for brightness, but we walk in gloom. [10] We grope (for) the wall like the blind, and we grope as if (we had) no eyes; we stumble at noonday as in the twilight; in deserted places like the dead. [11] We, all of us, roar like bears, and sadly we moan like doves; we look for justice, but none; for salvation, (but) it is far from us. [12] For our trespasses are multiplied before You, and our sins testify against us. For our transgressions (are) with us, and we know our iniquities: [13] transgressing and lying against Jehovah, and departing from our God; speaking oppression and revolt, conceiving

נגאלו בדם ואצבעותיכם בעון שפתותיכם דברו־שקר
false- have lips Your with your and by are
hood spoken .iniquity fingers ;blood defiled

4 לשונכם עולה תהגה׃ אין־קרא בצדק ואין נשפט
pleads and for calls No murmurs perverse- your
none ;righteousness one ness tongue

באמונה בטוח על־תהו ודבר־שוא הרו עמל והוליד און׃
. evil give and mis- they vanity and in trusting with
to birth chief conceive speaking emptiness ;truth

5 ביצי צפעוני בקעו וקורי עכביש יארגו האכל מביציהם
their of who he ;weave the webs and they the Eggs
eggs eats spider of ,hatch adder of

6 ימות והזורה תבקע אפעה׃ קוריהם לא־יהיו לבגד ולא
and ,clothing shall not Their .viper a hatches what and ,dies
not become webs out crushed is

יתכסו במעשיהם מעשיהם מעשי־און ופעל חמס
violence the and ,evil (are) works their their with shall they
of act of works ;works themselves cover

7 בכפיהם׃ רגליהם לרע ירצו וימהרו לשפך דם נקי
inno- blood pour to they and ,run evil to Their their in (is)
,cent out hurry feet .hands

8 מחשבותיהם מחשבות און שד ושבר במסלותם׃ דרך
The their in (are) and wast iniq- (are) thoughts their
of way tracks. ruin ing ;uity of thoughts

שלום לא ידעו ואין משפט במעגלותם נתיבותיהם עקשו
made they paths their their in (is) .justice and they not peace
crooked ;tracks no ;know

9 להם כל דרך בה לא ידע שלום׃ על־כן רחק משפט
justice far is Therefore .peace knows not it in going every- for
one ;them

ממנו ולא תשיגנו צדקה נקוה לאור והנה־חשך לנגהות
bright- for ;darkness but for we righ- overtakes and from
,ness ,behold light wait ;eousness us not ;us

10 באפלות נהלך׃ נגששה כעורים קיר וכאין עינים
eyes as and the (for) the like grope We .walk we in but
no (having) ,wall blind gloom

נגששה כשלנו בצהרים כנשף באשמנים כמתים׃
the as ,fatness in the in as the in we ;grope we
.dead ;twilight noonday stumble

11 נהמה כדבים כלנו וכיונים הגה נהגה נקוה למשפט
for we we sadly like and of all like We
justice wait ,moan doves us ,bears roar

12 ואין לישועה רחקה ממנו׃ כי־רבו פשעינו נגדך וחטאותינו
our and before tres- our multi- For from is it for but
sins ,You passes plied are .us far salvation ;none

13 ענתה בנו כי־פשעינו אתנו ועונתינו ידענום׃ פשע וכחש
and trans- know we our and (are) our For against testify
lying gressing them iniquities ,us with transgressions .us

ביהוה ונסוג מאחר אלהינו דבר־עשק וסרה הרו והגו
and conceiv- and oppression speak- ;God our from and against
uttering ing ,revolt ing after departing ,Jehovah

and speaking words of falsehood from the heart. [14] And justice is driven back; and righteousness stands far off; for truth stumbles in the plaza, and right is not able to enter.

[15] And the truth is lacking; and whoever turns aside from evil is plundered. And Jehovah saw, and it was evil in His eyes, that there was no justice. [16] And He saw that there was no man, and He was astonished that no intercessor was; and His own arm save for Him; and His righteousness sustained Him. [17] For He put on righteousness like armor, and a helmet of salvation on His head. And He put on robes of vengeance (as) clothing; and He put on zeal like a mantle. [18] According to works, so He will repay; fury to His foes, recompense to His enemies—He will repay the coasts. [19] So they shall fear the name of Jehovah from the sunset, and His glory from the sunrise. When the foe comes like a flood, Jehovah's Spirit shall drive on against him. [20] And the Redeemer comes to Zion, and to those in Jacob turning from transgression, says Jehovah. [21] As for Me, this (is) My covenant with them, says Jehovah: My Spirit who is on you, and My words which I have put in your mouth shall not depart out of your mouth, or out of the mouth of your seed, or out of the mouth of your seed's seed, from now on and forever, says Jehovah.

14 מִלֵּב דִּבְרֵי־שָׁקֶר׃ וְהֻסַּג אָחוֹר מִשְׁפָּט וּצְדָקָה מֵרָחוֹק
off far and ;justice back is And .falsehood words from
righteousness driven of heart the

תַּעֲמֹד כִּי־כָשְׁלָה בָרְחוֹב אֱמֶת וּנְכֹחָה לֹא־תוּכַל לָבוֹא׃
.enter to able is not and ,truth the in stumbles for ;stands
right plaza

15 וַתְּהִי הָאֱמֶת נֶעְדֶּרֶת וְסָר מֵרָע מִשְׁתּוֹלֵל וַיַּרְא יְהוָה וַיֵּרַע
it and Jehovah And himself makes from he and ;lacking truth the is And
evil was saw prey a evil turns who

16 בְּעֵינָיו כִּי־אֵין מִשְׁפָּט׃ וַיַּרְא כִּי־אֵין אִישׁ וַיִּשְׁתּוֹמֵם כִּי־
that was He and ,man there that He And .justice there that His in
astonished no was saw no was eyes

17 אֵין מַפְגִּיעַ וַתּוֹשַׁע לוֹ זְרֹעוֹ וְצִדְקָתוֹ הִיא סְמָכָתְהוּ׃ וַיִּלְבַּשׁ
He And sustained it His and His for and inter- an not
on put .Him ,righteousness ;arm Him saved ,cessor was

צְדָקָה כַּשִּׁרְיָן וְכוֹבַע יְשׁוּעָה בְּרֹאשׁוֹ וַיִּלְבַּשׁ בִּגְדֵי נָקָם
ven- of robes He And His on salvation a and like righ-
,geance on put .head of helmet ,armor teousness

18 תִּלְבֹּשֶׁת וַיַּעַט כַּמְעִיל קִנְאָה׃ כְּעַל גְּמֻלוֹת כְּעַל יְשַׁלֵּם
will He so (their) According .zeal a like He and (as)
;repay ,works to mantle on put ;clothing

19 חֵמָה לְצָרָיו גְּמוּל לְאֹיְבָיו לָאִיִּים גְּמוּל יְשַׁלֵּם׃ וְיִירְאוּ
they So will He recom- the to His to recom- His to fury
fear shall .repay pence coasts ;enemies pence ;foes

מִמַּעֲרָב אֶת־שֵׁם יְהוָה וּמִמִּזְרַח־שֶׁמֶשׁ אֶת־כְּבוֹדוֹ כִּי־יָבוֹא
comes When His the from and ,Jehovah the the from
.glory sun of rising the of name sunset

20 כַנָּהָר צָר רוּחַ יְהוָה נֹסְסָה בוֹ׃ וּבָא לְצִיּוֹן גּוֹאֵל וּלְשָׁבֵי
re- to and Re- the Zion to And against drive shall Jeho- the the a like
turnees deemer comes .him on vah of Spirit ,foe flood

21 פֶשַׁע בְּיַעֲקֹב נְאֻם יְהוָה׃ וַאֲנִי זֹאת בְּרִיתִי אוֹתָם אָמַר
says with My this for As .Jehovah states ,Jacob in tres- from
,them covenant (is) ,Me pass

יְהוָה רוּחִי אֲשֶׁר עָלֶיךָ וּדְבָרַי אֲשֶׁר־שַׂמְתִּי בְּפִיךָ לֹא־
not your in have I that My and on who My ;Jehovah
mouth put words ,you (is) Spirit

יָמוּשׁוּ מִפִּיךָ וּמִפִּי זַרְעֲךָ וּמִפִּי זֶרַע זַרְעֲךָ אָמַר יְהוָה
,Jehovah says your seed the or your the or your from shall
,seed's of mouth ,seed of mouth ,mouth depart

מֵעַתָּה וְעַד־עוֹלָם׃
.forever and from
till now

CAP. LX ס

CHAPTER 60

[1] Arise, shine; for your light has come, and the glory of Jehovah has risen on you! [2] For behold, the darkness shall cover the earth, and gross darkness, peoples. But Jehovah shall rise on you, and His glory

1 קוּמִי אוֹרִי כִּי־בָא אוֹרֵךְ וּכְבוֹד יְהוָה עָלַיִךְ זָרָח׃ כִּי־
2 For has on Jehovah the and your has for ;shine ,Arise
.risen you of glory ,light come

הִנֵּה הַחֹשֶׁךְ יְכַסֶּה־אֶרֶץ וַעֲרָפֶל לְאֻמִּים וְעָלַיִךְ יִזְרַח יְהוָה
,Jehovah shall on But .peoples gross and the shall the ,behold
rise you darkness ,earth cover darkness

shall be seen on you. [3] And nations shall walk to your light, and kings to the brightness of your dawning. [4] Lift up your eyes all around and see; they all are assembling, they are coming to you. Your sons shall come from far away, and your daughters shall be supported on the side. [5] Then you shall see and be bright; and your heart shall dread and swell; for the abundance of the sea shall be turned to you; the force of nations shall come to you. [6] A host of camels shall cover you, young camels of Midian and Ephah. All of them shall come from Sheba; they shall carry gold and incense; and they shall proclaim Jehovah's praises. [7] All Kedar's flocks shall be gathered to you; the rams of Nebaioth shall serve you; they shall come up for acceptance (on) My altar; and I will glorify the house of My glory. [8] Who (are) these who fly like a cloud, and with the doves to their windows? [9] For the coasts shall wait for Me, and the ships of Tarshish at the first, to bring your sons from far away, their silver and their gold with them, to the name of Jehovah your God, and to the Holy One of Israel, because He has glorified you

[10] And the sons of the stranger shall build your walls, and their kings shall serve you. For I struck you in My wrath, but I pitied you in My favor. [11] So your gates shall be always open; they shall not be shut day or night, so that men may bring to you the force of nations, and that their kings may be led. [12] For the nations and the kingdom that will not serve you shall perish; yea, the nations shall be utterly destroyed. [13] The glory of Lebanon shall come to you: the juniper, the box-tree and the cypress together, to beautify the place of My sanctuary; yes, I will glorify the

3 וּכְבוֹדוֹ עָלַיִךְ יֵרָאֶה׃ וְהָלְכוּ גוֹיִם לְאוֹרֵךְ וּמְלָכִים לְנֹגַהּ
the to kings and your to nations shall And shall you on His and
of brilliance ,light walk .seen be glory

4 זַרְחֵךְ׃ שְׂאִי סָבִיב עֵינַיִךְ וּרְאִי כֻּלָּם נִקְבְּצוּ בָאוּ־לָךְ
to they are of all ;see and your all Lift your
.you come ,gathered them eyes around up .rising

5 בָּנַיִךְ מֵרָחוֹק יָבֹאוּ וּבְנֹתַיִךְ עַל־צַד תֵּאָמַנָה׃ אָז תִּרְאִי
shall you Then be shall the on your and shall far from Your
see .supported side daughters ,come away sons

וְנָהַרְתְּ וּפָחַד וְרָחַב לְבָבֵךְ כִּי־יֵהָפֵךְ עָלַיִךְ הֲמוֹן יָם חֵיל
the the abun- you to be shall for your and shall and will and
wealth sea's dance turned ;heart swell dread ;bright be

6 גּוֹיִם יָבֹאוּ לָךְ׃ שִׁפְעַת גְּמַלִּים תְּכַסֵּךְ בִּכְרֵי מִדְיָן וְעֵיפָה
and Midian young shall camels mul- A to shall of
.Ephah of camels ,you cover of titude .you come nations

כֻּלָּם מִשְּׁבָא יָבֹאוּ זָהָב וּלְבוֹנָה יִשָּׂאוּ וּתְהִלֹּת יְהוָה
Jehovah the and shall they and gold shall from of All
of praises ;carry incense ;come Sheba them

7 יְבַשֵּׂרוּ׃ כָּל־צֹאן קֵדָר יִקָּבְצוּ לָךְ אֵילֵי נְבָיוֹת יְשָׁרְתוּנֶךְ
minister shall Nebaioth rams to be shall Kedar the All shall they
;you to of ;you gathered of flocks .proclaim

8 יַעֲלוּ עַל־רָצוֹן מִזְבְּחִי וּבֵית תִּפְאַרְתִּי אֲפָאֵר׃ מִי־אֵלֶּה
?these Who will I My the and My (on) for shall they
(are) .beautify beauty of house ,altar acceptance up come

9 כָּעָב תְּעוּפֶינָה וְכַיּוֹנִים אֶל־אֲרֻבֹּתֵיהֶם׃ כִּי־לִי ׀ אִיִּים יְקַוּוּ
shall the for Because their to with and ,fly they a Like
,wait coasts Me .windows doves the cloud

וָאֳנִיּוֹת תַּרְשִׁישׁ בָּרִאשֹׁנָה לְהָבִיא בָנַיִךְ מֵרָחוֹק כַּסְפָּם
their far from your bring to the at Tarshish the and
silver —away sons ,first of ships

וּזְהָבָם אִתָּם לְשֵׁם יְהוָה אֱלֹהַיִךְ וְלִקְדוֹשׁ יִשְׂרָאֵל כִּי
for ;Israel the to and your Jehovah the to with their and
of One Holy ,God of name —them gold

10 פֵאֲרָךְ׃ וּבָנוּ בְנֵי־נֵכָר חֹמֹתַיִךְ וּמַלְכֵיהֶם יְשָׁרְתוּנֶךְ כִּי
For minister shall their and your the the will And beau- He
.you to kings ,walls stranger of sons build .you tified

11 בְקִצְפִּי הִכִּיתִיךְ וּבִרְצוֹנִי רִחַמְתִּיךְ׃ וּפִתְּחוּ שְׁעָרַיִךְ תָּמִיד
;always your shall And pitied I My in but struck I My in
gates open be .you favor you wrath

יוֹמָם וָלַיְלָה לֹא יִסָּגֵרוּ לְהָבִיא אֵלַיִךְ חֵיל גּוֹיִם וּמַלְכֵיהֶם
their and ,nations the you to bring to they not or day
kings of wealth ;shut be shall night

12 נְהוּגִים׃ כִּי־הַגּוֹי וְהַמַּמְלָכָה אֲשֶׁר לֹא־יַעַבְדוּךְ יֹאבֵדוּ
shall they serve will not that the and the For be may
;perish ,you kingdom nation .led

13 וְהַגּוֹיִם חָרֹב יֶחֱרָבוּ׃ כְּבוֹד הַלְּבָנוֹן אֵלַיִךְ יָבוֹא בְּרוֹשׁ
the shall you to Lebanon The be shall utterly the even
juniper ;come of glory .destroyed nations

תִּדְהָר וּתְאַשּׁוּר יַחְדָּו לְפָאֵר מְקוֹם מִקְדָּשִׁי וּמְקוֹם רַגְלַי
My the and My the to ,together the and the
feet of place ;sanctuary of place beautify cypress box-tree

place of My feet. [14] Also the sons of your oppressors shall come to you bowing; and all who despised you shall fall at the soles of your feet. And they shall call you, The City of Jehovah, the Zion of the Holy One of Israel. [15] Instead of your being forsaken and hated, so that no one passes through, I will make you for everlasting majesty, a joy of many generations. [16] You shall also suck the milk of nations, and you shall suck the breast of kings. And you shall know that I Jehovah (am) your Savior and your Redeemer, the mighty One of Jacob. [17] Instead of bronze, I will bring gold; and instead of iron I will bring silver; and instead of timber, bronze; and instead of stones, iron. And I will make your governors peace, and your exactors righteousness. [18] Violence shall not still be heard in your land, or wasting and ruin within your borders; but you shall call your walls, Salvation, and your gates, Praise. [19] The sun shall not still be your light by day, or the brighteness of the moon give you light; but Jehovah shall be for everlasting light to you, and your God for your beauty. [20] Your sun shall not set any more; and your moon shall not withdraw; for Jehovah will become your everlasting light; and the days of your mourning shall end. [21] And your people (shall) all (be) righteous; they shall possess the earth forever, a branch of My planting, a work of My hands, to beautify Myself. [22] A little one shall become a thousand; and a small one a strong nation — I Jehovah will hasten it in its time.

14 אֲכַבֵּד׃ וְהָלְכוּ אֵלַיִךְ שְׁחוֹחַ בְּנֵי מְעַנַּיִךְ וְהִשְׁתַּחֲווּ עַל־
at shall and your the bowing you to shall Also will I
down fall ;oppressors of sons come .glorify

כַּפּוֹת רַגְלַיִךְ כָּל־מְנַאֲצָיִךְ וְקָרְאוּ לָךְ עִיר יְהוָֹה צִיּוֹן קְדוֹשׁ
Holy the the ,Jehovah the ,you they and who all your the
of One of Zion of City call shall ;you despised feet of soles

15 יִשְׂרָאֵל׃ תַּחַת הֱיוֹתֵךְ עֲזוּבָה וּשְׂנוּאָה וְאֵין עוֹבֵר וְשַׂמְתִּיךְ
will I passes and and forsaken your Instead .Israel
you make ,through none ,hated being of

16 לִגְאוֹן עוֹלָם מְשׂוֹשׂ דּוֹר וָדוֹר׃ וְיָנַקְתְּ חֲלֵב גּוֹיִם וְשֹׁד
the and ;nations the you And gen- and gene- joy a ever- for
of breast of milk suck will eration ration of ,lasting majesty

מְלָכִים תִּינָקִי וְיָדַעַתְּ כִּי־אֲנִי יְהוָֹה מוֹשִׁיעֵךְ וְגֹאֲלֵךְ אֲבִיר
mighty the your and your Jehovah I that you And shall you kings
of One ,Redeemer Savior (am) know shall .suck

17 יַעֲקֹב׃ תַּחַת הַנְּחֹשֶׁת אָבִיא זָהָב וְתַחַת הַבַּרְזֶל אָבִיא
will I iron and ;gold will I bronze Instead .Jacob
bring of instead bring of

כֶסֶף וְתַחַת הָעֵצִים נְחֹשֶׁת וְתַחַת הָאֲבָנִים בַּרְזֶל וְשַׂמְתִּי
I And .iron ,stones and ;bronze ,timber and ;silver
make will of instead of instead

18 פְקֻדָּתֵךְ שָׁלוֹם וְנֹגְשַׂיִךְ צְדָקָה׃ לֹא־יִשָּׁמַע עוֹד חָמָס
violence still shall Not .righteousness your and ,peace your
heard be exactors governors

בְּאַרְצֵךְ שֹׁד וָשֶׁבֶר בִּגְבוּלָיִךְ וְקָרָאת יְשׁוּעָה חוֹמֹתַיִךְ
your salvation you but your in ruin or wasting your in
,walls call shall ;borders ,land

19 וּשְׁעָרַיִךְ תְּהִלָּה׃ לֹא־יִהְיֶה־לָּךְ עוֹד הַשֶּׁמֶשׁ לְאוֹר יוֹמָם
by for sun the any to shall Not .Praise your and
,day light more you be .gates

וּלְנֹגַהּ הַיָּרֵחַ לֹא־יָאִיר לָךְ וְהָיָה־לָךְ יְהוָֹה לְאוֹר עוֹלָם
ever- light for Jehovah to But to shall not the bright- the
;lasting you be shall you light give moon of ness

20 וֵאלֹהַיִךְ לְתִפְאַרְתֵּךְ׃ לֹא־יָבוֹא עוֹד שִׁמְשֵׁךְ וִירֵחֵךְ לֹא
not your and your any shall Not your for your and
moon ;sun more set .beauty God

יֵאָסֵף כִּי יְהוָֹה יִהְיֶה־לָּךְ לְאוֹר עוֹלָם וְשָׁלְמוּ יְמֵי אֶבְלֵךְ׃
your the shall and ever- light to will Jehovah for shall
mourning of days end ,lasting you become ;withdraw

21 וְעַמֵּךְ כֻּלָּם צַדִּיקִים לְעוֹלָם יִירְשׁוּ אָרֶץ נֵצֶר מַטָּעַו מַעֲשֵׂה
work a My branch the shall they forever (be shall) of all your And
of ,planting's earth possess ;righteous ,them ,people

22 יָדַי לְהִתְפָּאֵר׃ הַקָּטֹן יִהְיֶה לָאֶלֶף וְהַצָּעִיר לְגוֹי עָצוּם אֲנִי
I —strong a for a and a for shall little A beautify to My
nation one small ;thousand become one .Myself ,hands

יְהוָֹה בְּעִתָּהּ אֲחִישֶׁנָּה׃
hasten will its in Jehovah
.it time

CAP. LXI סא

CHAPTER 61

CHAPTER 61

[1] The Spirit of the Lord Jehovah (is) on Me, because Jehovah has anointed Me to preach the Gospel to the poor. He has sent Me to bind up the broken-hearted, to proclaim liberty to captives, and to the bound ones opening – [2] to proclaim the acceptable year of Jehovah and the day of vengeance of our God; to comfort all who mourn; [3] to appoint to those who mourn in Zion, to give them beauty instead of ashes, the oil of joy instead of mourning, the mantle of praise instead of the spirit of infirmity; so that one calls them trees of righteousness, Jehovah's planting, in order to beautify Himself. [4] And they shall build old ruins; they shall raise up former desolations; and they shall restore the waste cities, ruins of generations and generations. [5] And strangers shall stand and feed your flocks, and the sons of strangers (shall be) your plowmen and your vinedressers. [6] But you shall be called, Priests of Jehovah; Ministers of our God, it will be said of you, You shall eat the riches of the nations, and you shall revel in their glory. [7] Instead of your shame, double; and confusion, they rejoice (in) your portion; for they shall possess a second time in their land; everlasting joy shall be theirs. [8] For I Jehovah love judgment, hating plunder in burnt-offering. And I will give their work in truth; and I will cut an everlasting covenant to them. [9] And their seed shall be known among the nations, and their children among the peoples; all who see them shall acknowledge them, that they (are) the seed Jehovah has blessed. [10] I will greatly rejoice in Jehovah; my soul shall be joyful in

1 רוּחַ אֲדֹנָי יְהוִה עָלָי יַעַן מָשַׁח יְהוָה אֹתִי לְבַשֵּׂר עֲנָוִים
.poor the preach to Me Jehovah has for (is) Jehovah the The
to news good anointed ;Me on Lord of Spirit

שְׁלָחַנִי לַחֲבֹשׁ לְנִשְׁבְּרֵי־לֵב לִקְרֹא לִשְׁבוּיִם דְּרוֹר
,liberty to to ,heart the bind to has He
captives proclaim of broken up Me sent

2 וְלַאֲסוּרִים פְּקַח־קוֹחַ׃ לִקְרֹא שְׁנַת־רָצוֹן לַיהוָה וְיוֹם נָקָם
ven- the and of accept- the pro- to complete the to and
geance of day ,Jehovah ance of year claim ;opening ones bound

3 לֵאלֹהֵינוּ לְנַחֵם כָּל־אֲבֵלִים׃ לָשׂוּם ׀ לַאֲבֵלֵי צִיּוֹן לָתֵת
to ,Zion the to appoint to ;mourners all to our of
give of mourners comfort ;God

לָהֶם פְּאֵר תַּחַת אֵפֶר שֶׁמֶן שָׂשׂוֹן תַּחַת אֵבֶל מַעֲטֵה
the ,mourning instead joy the ,ashes instead beauty to
of mantle of of oil of them

תְהִלָּה תַּחַת רוּחַ כֵּהָה וְקֹרָא לָהֶם אֵילֵי הַצֶּדֶק מַטַּע
plant- righteous- trees ,them (one) that in- the instead praise
of ing ,ness of calls ;firmity of spirit of

4 יְהוָה לְהִתְפָּאֵר׃ וּבָנוּ חָרְבוֹת עוֹלָם שֹׁמְמוֹת רִאשֹׁנִים
former desolations ;forever ruins they And beautify to Jeho-
times of of build shall .Himself ,vah

5 יְקוֹמֵמוּ וְחִדְּשׁוּ עָרֵי חֹרֶב שֹׁמְמוֹת דּוֹר וָדוֹר׃ וְעָמְדוּ
shall And gen- and gene- ruins ,waste cities they and shall they
stand .eration retion of of restore shall ;up raise

6 זָרִים וְרָעוּ צֹאנְכֶם וּבְנֵי נֵכָר אִכָּרֵיכֶם וְכֹרְמֵיכֶם׃ וְאַתֶּם
But your and your (be shall) an and your and strangers
you .vinedressers plowmen alien's sons ;flocks feed

כֹּהֲנֵי יְהוָה תִּקָּרֵאוּ מְשָׁרְתֵי אֱלֹהֵינוּ יֵאָמֵר לָכֶם חֵיל גּוֹיִם
na- Riches .you of will it our Ministers be shall Jehovah Priests
tions of said be God of ;called of

7 תֹּאכֵלוּ וּבִכְבוֹדָם תִּתְיַמָּרוּ׃ תַּחַת בָּשְׁתְּכֶם מִשְׁנֶה וּכְלִמָּה
dis- and ;double your Instead shall you their in and shall you
;grace ,shame of .boast glory ,eat

יָרֹנּוּ חֶלְקָם לָכֵן בְּאַרְצָם מִשְׁנֶה יִירָשׁוּ שִׂמְחַת עוֹלָם תִּהְיֶה
shall forever joy shall they second a their in there- your (in) they
be ;possess time land fore ;portion rejoice

8 לָהֶם׃ כִּי אֲנִי יְהוָה אֹהֵב מִשְׁפָּט שֹׂנֵא גָזֵל בְּעוֹלָה וְנָתַתִּי
I And burnt a in plunder hating ,judg- love Jehovah I For to
give will .offering ,ment .them

9 פְעֻלָּתָם בֶּאֱמֶת וּבְרִית עוֹלָם אֶכְרוֹת לָהֶם׃ וְנוֹדַע בַּגּוֹיִם
the in shall And for will I ever- a and in their
nations known be .them cut lasting covenant ;truth work

זַרְעָם וְצֶאֱצָאֵיהֶם בְּתוֹךְ הָעַמִּים כָּל־רֹאֵיהֶם יַכִּירוּם כִּי
them shall seeing all the the in their and their
that regard them ;peoples of midst offspring ,seed

10 הֵם זֶרַע בֵּרַךְ יְהוָה׃ שׂוֹשׂ אָשִׂישׂ בַּיהוָה תָּגֵל נַפְשִׁי
my let in will I greatly .Jehovah has the they
soul exult ;Jehovah rejoice blessed seed (are)

בֵּאלֹהַי כִּי הִלְבִּישַׁנִי בִּגְדֵי־יֶשַׁע מְעִיל צְדָקָה יְעָטָנִי כֶּחָתָן
my in ;God for me clothed He (with) salva- ;tion of garments the of robe righteous- ness put He ;me on , a as groom.

11 יְכַהֵן פְּאֵר וְכַכַּלָּה תַּעְדֶּה כֵלֶיהָ׃ כִּי כָאָרֶץ תּוֹצִיא צִמְחָהּ
,buds her gives to birth the as earth For her .jewels wears as and bride the (his) adorned ,turban (with) is

וּכְגַנָּה זֵרוּעֶיהָ תַצְמִיחַ כֵּן ׀ אֲדֹנָי יֱהוִֹה יַצְמִיחַ צְדָקָה וּתְהִלָּה
and praise righteous- ness makes grow Jehovah the Lord so makes ,grow which that sown is a as and garden

נֶגֶד כָּל־הַגּוֹיִם׃
the .nations all before

CAP. LXII סב

CHAPTER 62

1 לְמַעַן צִיּוֹן לֹא אֶחֱשֶׁה וּלְמַעַן יְרוּשָׁלִַם לֹא אֶשְׁקוֹט עַד־
until will I ;rest not Jerusalem's for and sake be will I ;silent not Zion's For sake

2 יֵצֵא כַנֹּגַהּ צִדְקָהּ וִישׁוּעָתָהּ כְּלַפִּיד יִבְעָר׃ וְרָאוּ גוֹיִם
nations And see shall .burning a as torch her and salvation righ- her ,teousness as brightness goes forth

צִדְקֵךְ וְכָל־מְלָכִים כְּבוֹדֵךְ וְקֹרָא לָךְ שֵׁם חָדָשׁ אֲשֶׁר פִּי
the of mouth which ,new a name you (one) and calls your ;glory kings all and your ,righteousness

3 יְהוָה יִקֳּבֶנּוּ׃ וְהָיִית עֲטֶרֶת תִּפְאֶרֶת בְּיַד־יְהוָה וּצְנוֹף
a and of diadem ,Jehovah the in of hand beauty crown a of shall You be also shall .designate Jehovah

4 מְלוּכָה בְּכַף־אֱלֹהָיִךְ׃ לֹא־יֵאָמֵר לָךְ עוֹד עֲזוּבָה וּלְאַרְצֵךְ
your and land ;Forsaken any ,more to you be shall Not said your .God the in of hand royalty

לֹא־יֵאָמֵר עוֹד שְׁמָמָה כִּי לָךְ יִקָּרֵא חֶפְצִי־בָהּ וּלְאַרְצֵךְ
your and ,land in (is) ;her My delight be shall ,called you but ;Desolate any ,longer be shall called not

5 בְּעוּלָה כִּי־חָפֵץ יְהוָה בָּךְ וְאַרְצֵךְ תִּבָּעֵל׃ כִּי־יִבְעַל בָּחוּר
young man a marries (as) For be shall .married your and land in ,you Jehovah delights for ;Married

בְּתוּלָה יִבְעָלוּךְ בָּנָיִךְ וּמְשׂוֹשׂ חָתָן עַל־כַּלָּה יָשִׂישׂ עָלַיִךְ
over you shall (so) rejoice the over ,bride bride- groom a as and rejoices your ;sons shall (so) you marry a ,virgin

6 אֱלֹהָיִךְ׃ עַל־חוֹמֹתַיִךְ יְרוּשָׁלִַם הִפְקַדְתִּי שֹׁמְרִים כָּל־הַיּוֹם
the day all ;watchmen have I set O ,Jerusalem your ,walls On your .God

וְכָל־הַלַּיְלָה תָּמִיד לֹא יֶחֱשׁוּ הַמַּזְכִּרִים אֶת־יְהוָה אַל־דֳּמִי
a not let pause be ,Jehovah who you remember shall they not ;silent be ;always the ,night and all

7 לָכֶם׃ וְאַל־תִּתְּנוּ דֳמִי לוֹ עַד־יְכוֹנֵן וְעַד־יָשִׂים אֶת־יְרוּשָׁלִַם
Jerusalem He makes and until He establishes until to him a pause give And not to .you

8 תְּהִלָּה בָּאָרֶץ׃ נִשְׁבַּע יְהוָה בִּימִינוֹ וּבִזְרוֹעַ עֻזּוֹ אִם־אֶתֵּן
I give If will His ;might by and of arm the His by hand right Jehovah has sworn the in .earth praise a

my God; for He clothed me (with) garments of salvation; He put on me the robe of righteousness, as a bridegroom wears (his) turban, and as the bride is adorned (with) her jewels. [11] For as the earth gives birth to her buds, and as a garden causes that which is sown to spring up, so the Lord Jehovah will cause righteousness and praise to spring up before all the nations.

CHAPTER 62

[1] For Zion's sake, I will not be silent; and for Jerusalem's sake, I will not rest; until her righteousness goes forth as brightness, and her salvation as a burning lamp. [2] And nations shall see your righteousness, and all kings your glory; and you shall be called by a new name, which the mouth of Jehovah shall designate. [3] You also shall be a crown of beauty in the hand of Jehovah, and a royal diadem in the hand of your God. [4] You no longer shall be called Forsaken; nor shall your land any longer be called Desolate; but you shall be called, My delight (is) in her; and your land, Married; for Jehovah delights in you, and your land shall be married. [5] For as a young man marries a virgin, (so) shall your sons marry you; and as a bridegroom rejoices over the bride, (so) your God shall rejoice over you.

[6] I have set watchmen on your walls, O Jerusalem; all the day and all the night, they shall not always be silent; you who remember Jehovah, do not let be a pause to you. [7] And give no pause to Him until He sets up and makes Jerusalem a praise in the earth. [8] Jehovah has sworn by His right hand and by the arm of His might: Surely I will no longer give your

grain (as) food for your enemies; and the sons of the stranger shall not drink your new wine for which you have labored. [9] But those who have gathered it shall eat it and praise Jehovah; and they who have collected it shall drink it in My holy courts. [10] Pass! Pass through the gates; prepare the way of the people! Raise up! Raise up the highway; clear (it) from stones; lift up a banner over the peoples. [11] Behold, Jehovah has proclaimed to the end of the earth; Tell the daughter of Zion, Behold, your salvation comes; behold, His reward (is) with Him and His work before Him. [12] And they shall call them, The holy people, the redeemed of Jehovah. And to you it shall be called, Sought out, a city not forsaken.

אֶת־דְּגָנֵךְ עוֹד מַאֲכָל לְאֹיְבַיִךְ וְאִם־יִשְׁתּוּ בְנֵי־נֵכָר תִּירוֹשֵׁךְ
new your a sons shall and your for (as) longer your
wine stranger of drink if ;enemies food grain

9 אֲשֶׁר יָגַעַתְּ בּוֹ׃ כִּי מְאַסְפָיו יֹאכְלֻהוּ וְהִלְלוּ אֶת־יְהוָה
;Jehovah shall and shall its For .for have you which
praise it eat gatherers .it labored

10 וּמְקַבְּצָיו יִשְׁתֻּהוּ בְּחַצְרוֹת קָדְשִׁי׃ עִבְרוּ עִבְרוּ בַּשְּׁעָרִים
through Pass !Pass My courts in shall its and
;gates the .holiness of it drink collectors

פַּנּוּ דֶּרֶךְ הָעָם סֹלּוּ סֹלּוּ הַמְסִלָּה סַקְּלוּ מֵאֶבֶן הָרִימוּ נֵס
a up lift from clear the Raise Raise the the pre-
banner ;stones (it) ;highway up !up !people of way pare

11 עַל־הָעַמִּים׃ הִנֵּה יְהוָה הִשְׁמִיעַ אֶל־קְצֵה הָאָרֶץ אִמְרוּ
say the the to has Jehovah ,Behold the over
;earth of end proclaimed .peoples

לְבַת־צִיּוֹן הִנֵּה יִשְׁעֵךְ בָּא הִנֵּה שְׂכָרוֹ אִתּוֹ וּפְעֻלָּתוֹ לְפָנָיו׃
before His and with (is) His Be- .comes your ,Behold ,Zion the to
.Him work ,Him reward ,hold salvation of daughter

12 וְקָרְאוּ לָהֶם עַם־הַקֹּדֶשׁ גְּאוּלֵי יְהוָה וְלָךְ יִקָּרֵא דְרוּשָׁה
Sought shall it to And .Jehovah the ,holy The people them they And
,out ,called be you of redeemed call shall

עִיר לֹא נֶעֱזָבָה׃
.forsaken not a
city

CAP. LXIII סג

CHAPTER 63

[1] Who (is) this who comes from Edom, with dyed garments from Bozrah, this One adorned in His clothing, inclining in His great power? (It is) I speaking in righteousness, great to save! [2] Why (is) Your clothing red, and Your garments like one who treads in the winepress? [3] I have trodden the winepress, I alone, and no one of the peoples with Me. And I will tread them in My anger and trample them in My fury; and their juice shall be spattered on My garments; and I will pollute all My clothing. [4] For the day of vengeance (is) in My heart, and the year of My redeemed has come. [5] And I looked, and no one (was) helping. And I wondered that no one (was) upholding. Then My own arm saved for Me, and My fury, it upheld Me. [6] And I trod down the people in My anger, and made them drunk in My fury; and I

1 מִי־זֶה ׀ בָּא מֵאֱדוֹם חֲמוּץ בְּגָדִים מִבָּצְרָה זֶה הָדוּר
adorned this from garments (with) from coming this Who
one ,Bozrah dyed ,Edom (is)

בִּלְבוּשׁוֹ צֹעֶה בְּרֹב כֹּחוֹ אֲנִי מְדַבֵּר בִּצְדָקָה רַב לְהוֹשִׁיעַ׃
!save to great righ- in speaking (is It) His in inclining His in
,teousness I ?power great ,clothing

2 3 מַדּוּעַ אָדֹם לִלְבוּשֶׁךָ וּבְגָדֶיךָ כְּדֹרֵךְ בְּגַת׃ פּוּרָה ׀ דָּרַכְתִּי
have I wine- The the in one like your and your (is) knows Who
,trodden press ?winepress treading garments ,clothing red why

לְבַדִּי וּמֵעַמִּים אֵין־אִישׁ אִתִּי וְאֶדְרְכֵם בְּאַפִּי וְאֶרְמְסֵם
trample and My in will I And with man no of and I
them ,anger them tread .Me (was) peoples the ,alone

4 בַּחֲמָתִי וְיֵז נִצְחָם עַל־בְּגָדַי וְכָל־מַלְבּוּשַׁי אֶגְאָלְתִּי׃ כִּי
For will I My and My on their will and My in
.pollute clothes all ;garments juice spatter ;fury

5 יוֹם נָקָם בְּלִבִּי וּשְׁנַת גְּאוּלַי בָּאָה׃ וְאַבִּיט וְאֵין עֹזֵר
help- and I And has My the and in (is) ven- the
!ing none ,looked .come redeemed of year ,heart My geance of day

וְאֶשְׁתּוֹמֵם וְאֵין סוֹמֵךְ וַתּוֹשַׁע לִי זְרֹעִי וַחֲמָתִי הִיא
it My and My for Then uphold- that was I And
,fury ;arm own Me. saved .ing (was) none astonished

6 סְמָכָתְנִי׃ וְאָבוּס עַמִּים בְּאַפִּי וַאֲשַׁכְּרֵם בַּחֲמָתִי וְאוֹרִיד
I and My in made and My in peoples I And upheld
poured ;fury drunk them ,anger trod .Me

poured their juice to the earth.

[7] I will mention the mercies of Jehovah, the praises of Jehovah, according to all that Jehovah has done for us, and the great good to the house of Israel, which He had done to them according to His mercies, and according to the multitude of His lovingkindness. [8] For He said, Surely they (are) My people, sons that do not lie, and He is their Savior. [9] In all their affliction, (He was) not a foe; and the Angel of His face saved them; in His love and in His pity He redeemed them. And He bore them and carried them all the days of old. [10] But they rebelled and provoked His Holy Spirit, so He was turned (to be) their enemy; He fought against them. [11] Then His people remembered the days past, (of) Moses, (saying), Where (is) He who brought up from the sea with the shepherd of His flock? Where (is) He who put His Holy Spirit within him; [12] who led them by Moses' right hand, with His glorious arm, dividing the water before them, to make for Him an everlasting name? [13] (He) led them through the deeps; like the horse in the wilderness, they did not stumble. [14] As the cattle go down into the valley, the Spirit of Jehovah caused him to rest; so did You lead Your people, to make for You a glorious name.

[15] Look down from Heaven, and peer from the place of Your holiness and of Your glory — Where is Your zeal and Your power? The stirring of Your affections and Your mercies toward me, are they held back? [16] For You (are) our Father, though Abraham knows us not, and Israel does not acknowledge us, You, Jehovah, (are) our Father, our Redeemer; Your name (is) from everlasting. [17] O Jehovah, why do You make us wander from Your ways: You harden our heart from

7 לָאָרֶץ נִצְחָם׃ חַסְדֵי יְהוָה ׀ אַזְכִּיר תְּהִלּוֹת יְהוָה
.Jehovah the will I Jehovah The their the to
of praises ,mention of mercies juice earth

כְּעַל כֹּל אֲשֶׁר־גְּמָלָנוּ יְהוָה וְרַב־טוּב לְבֵית יִשְׂרָאֵל אֲשֶׁר־
which ,Israel the to good and ,Jehovah done has that all accord-
of house great the us for to ing

8 גְּמָלָם כְּרַחֲמָיו וּכְרֹב חֲסָדָיו׃ וַיֹּאמֶר אַךְ־עַמִּי הֵמָּה
they My Surely He For loving- His by and His by did He
,(are) people ,said .kindness much mercies them to

9 בָּנִים לֹא יְשַׁקֵּרוּ וַיְהִי לָהֶם לְמוֹשִׁיעַ׃ בְּכָל־צָרָתָם ׀ לֹא
not their all In .Savior a to He and that not sons
(was He) affliction them became ;lie do

צָר וּמַלְאַךְ פָּנָיו הוֹשִׁיעָם בְּאַהֲבָתוֹ וּבְחֶמְלָתוֹ הוּא גְאָלָם
redeemed He His in and His in saved His the and a
.them pity love ;them face of Angel ;foe

10 וַיְנַטְּלֵם וַיְנַשְּׂאֵם כָּל־יְמֵי עוֹלָם׃ וְהֵמָּה מָרוּ וְעִצְּבוּ אֶת־
and rebelled But .forever the all carried and He And
provoked they of days them them bore

11 רוּחַ קָדְשׁוֹ וַיֵּהָפֵךְ לָהֶם לְאוֹיֵב הוּא נִלְחַם־בָּם׃ וַיִּזְכֹּר
Then against fought He (be to) to He so His Spirit
remembered .them ;enemy an them turned was ,Holy

יְמֵי־עוֹלָם מֹשֶׁה עַמּוֹ אַיֵּה ׀ הַמַּעֲלֵם מִיָּם אֵת רֹעֵה צֹאנוֹ
His shep- the with from who He Where His (of) .forever the
?flock of herd sea the up brought (is) :people Moses of days

12 אַיֵּה הַשָּׂם בְּקִרְבּוֹ אֶת־רוּחַ קָדְשׁוֹ׃ מוֹלִיךְ לִימִין מֹשֶׁה
,Moses' by leading His Spirit within who He Where
hand right ;holy him put (is)

זְרוֹעַ תִּפְאַרְתּוֹ בּוֹקֵעַ מַיִם מִפְּנֵיהֶם לַעֲשׂוֹת לוֹ שֵׁם עוֹלָם׃
ever- a for to before the dividing His the
,lasting name Him make ,them water ,beauty of arm

13 14 מוֹלִיכָם בַּתְּהֹמוֹת כַּסּוּס בַּמִּדְבָּר לֹא יִכָּשֵׁלוּ׃ כַּבְּהֵמָה
the As did they not the in the like the through leading
cattle .stumble wilderness horse ,deeps them

בַּבִּקְעָה תֵרֵד רוּחַ יְהוָה תְּנִיחֶנּוּ כֵּן נִהַגְתָּ עַמְּךָ לַעֲשׂוֹת
make to Your You so him caused Jehovah the goes the into
,people lead ,rest to of Spirit .down valley

15 לְךָ שֵׁם תִּפְאָרֶת׃ הַבֵּט מִשָּׁמַיִם וּרְאֵה מִזְּבֻל קָדְשְׁךָ
Your the from see and from Look .beauty a for
holiness of place ,Heaven of name You

וְתִפְאַרְתֶּךָ אַיֵּה קִנְאָתְךָ וּגְבוּרֹתֶיךָ הֲמוֹן מֵעֶיךָ וְרַחֲמֶיךָ
Your and Your The Your and Your where your and
mercies affections of stirring ?might zeal (is) —beauty

16 אֵלַי הִתְאַפָּקוּ׃ כִּי־אַתָּה אָבִינוּ כִּי אַבְרָהָם לֹא יְדָעָנוּ
knows not Abraham though our You For they are toward
us ,Father (are) ?back held ,me

וְיִשְׂרָאֵל לֹא יַכִּירָנוּ אַתָּה יְהוָה אָבִינוּ גֹּאֲלֵנוּ מֵעוֹלָם
ever- from our our Jehovah You acknowledge not Israel and
lasting ;Redeemer ,Father (are) ;us

17 שְׁמֶךָ׃ לָמָּה תַתְעֵנוּ יְהוָה מִדְּרָכֶיךָ תַּקְשִׁיחַ לִבֵּנוּ מִיִּרְאָתֶךָ
from our harden You Your from ,Jehovah You do Why Your (is)
?fear Your heart ;ways ,wander us make .name

Your fear? For Your servants' sake, return the tribes of Your inheritance. [18] For a little people of Your holiness possessed (it); our enemies have trampled Your sanctuary. [19] We are of old; You never ruled over them. Your name was never called on them.

CHAPTER 64

[1] Oh that You would tear the heavens, (and) come down, (that) mountains would flow down from before You. [2] As the brushwood fire burns, fire causes water to boil — to make Your name known to Your foes, (that) nations might tremble before You! [3] When You did terrifying things which we did not look for, You came down; mountains flowed down before You. [4] And from forever they have heard not, they gave not ear; eye has not seen a God except You, who works for him who waits for Him. [5] You met him who rejoices and works righteousness; they recall You in Your ways. Behold, You were angry, for we sinned. In them (is) eternity, we shall be saved. [6] But we are all as the unclean thing, and all our righteousnesses are as a filthy cloth. And we all fade as a leaf, and our iniquities, like the wind, take us away. [7] And there is not one who calls on Your name, who stirs himself up to take hold of You. For You have hidden Your face from us, and have melted us away into our iniquities' hand. [8] But now, Jehovah, You (are) our Father; we (are) the clay and You are our Former; and we all are the work of Your hand. [9] Do not be grievously angry, Jehovah, and do not remember iniquity forever. Behold! Look, please, all of us (are) Your people. [10] Your holy cities are a ruin; Zion is a wilderness; Jerusalem is a desolation.

18 שׁוּב לְמַעַן עֲבָדֶיךָ שִׁבְטֵי נַחֲלָתֶךָ׃ לַמִּצְעָר יָרְשׁוּ עַם־
people possessed a For Your the Your for ,Return
(it) little .inheritance of tribes ,servants' sake

19 קָדְשֶׁךָ צָרֵינוּ בּוֹסְסוּ מִקְדָּשֶׁךָ׃ הָיִינוּ מֵעוֹלָם לֹא־מָשַׁלְתָּ
You not from are We Your have foes our Your
ruled ;forever .sanctuary trampled ;holy

בָּם לֹא־נִקְרָא שִׁמְךָ עֲלֵיהֶם לוּא־קָרַעְתָּ שָׁמַיִם יָרַדְתָּ
come (and) the You O .them on Your was not over
;down heavens tear would that name called ;them

מִפָּנֶיךָ הָרִים נָזֹלּוּ׃
would mountains from
.down flow You before

CAP. LXIV סד

CHAPTER 64

1 כִּקְדֹחַ אֵשׁ הֲמָסִים מַיִם תִּבְעֶה־אֵשׁ לְהוֹדִיעַ שִׁמְךָ לְצָרֶיךָ
Your to Your make to —fire causes water brush- the As
;foes name known boil to ,wood fire burns

2 מִפָּנֶיךָ גּוֹיִם יִרְגָּזוּ׃ בַּעֲשׂוֹתְךָ נוֹרָאוֹת לֹא נְקַוֶּה יָרַדְתָּ
came You we not terrifying You When might nations before
;down expected things did .tremble ,You

3 מִפָּנֶיךָ הָרִים נָזֹלּוּ׃ וּמֵעוֹלָם לֹא־שָׁמְעוּ לֹא הֶאֱזִינוּ עַיִן
eye they not have they not from And flowed mountains before
;ear gave ,heard forever .down You

4 לֹא־רָאָתָה אֱלֹהִים זוּלָתְךָ יַעֲשֶׂה לִמְחַכֵּה־לוֹ׃ פָּגַעְתָּ אֶת־
You for him for who except God a has not·
met .Him waits who works ,You seen

שָׂשׂ וְעֹשֵׂה צֶדֶק בִּדְרָכֶיךָ יִזְכְּרוּךָ הֵן־אַתָּה קָצַפְתָּ וַנֶּחֱטָא
we for were You Be- remem- they Your in righ- and who him
.sinned ,angry ,hold .You ber ways ;teousness works rejoices

5 בָּהֶם עוֹלָם וְנִוָּשֵׁעַ׃ וַנְּהִי כַטָּמֵא כֻּלָּנוּ וּכְבֶגֶד עִדִּים כָּל־
(are) filthy as and of all un- the as we But shall we and (is) In
all garment a us ,thing clean are .saved be ,eternity them

6 צִדְקֹתֵינוּ וַנָּבֶל כֶּעָלֶה כֻּלָּנוּ וַעֲוֺנֵנוּ כָּרוּחַ יִשָּׂאֻנוּ׃ וְאֵין
And us take the like our and all a as we And righ- our
none is .away ,wind ,iniquities us of ,leaf fade teousnesses

קוֹרֵא בְשִׁמְךָ מִתְעוֹרֵר לְהַחֲזִיק בָּךְ כִּי־הִסְתַּרְתָּ פָנֶיךָ מִמֶּנּוּ
from Your have You For of take to stirring Your on calling
,us face hidden .You hold himself up ,name

7 וַתְּמוּגֵנוּ בְּיַד־עֲוֺנֵנוּ׃ וְעַתָּה יְהוָה אָבִינוּ אָתָּה אֲנַחְנוּ הַחֹמֶר
the we You our ,Jehovah But hand the into have and
clay (are) ;(are) Father ,now .iniquities of us melted

8 וְאַתָּה יֹצְרֵנוּ וּמַעֲשֵׂה יָדְךָ כֻּלָּנוּ׃ אַל־תִּקְצֹף יְהוָה עַד־מְאֹד
an to ,Jehovah be Do not all we Your the and our You and
,extreme ,angry .(are) hand of work ;Former (are)

9 וְאַל־לָעַד תִּזְכֹּר עָוֺן הֵן הַבֶּט־נָא עַמְּךָ כֻלָּנוּ׃ עָרֵי קָדְשְׁךָ
Your cities of all Your ,please ,look ,Lo ini- do forever and
holy :(are) us people .quity remember not

10 הָיוּ מִדְבָּר צִיּוֹן מִדְבָּר הָיָתָה יְרוּשָׁלַםִ שְׁמָמָה׃ בֵּית
The deso- a Jerusalem is wilder- a Zion wilder- a are
of house lation ;ness (is) .ness

[11] Our holy and our beautiful house, where our fathers praised You, is burned up with fire; and all our pleasant things have become a ruin. [12] Will You restrain Yourself over these things, Jehovah? Will You be silent and sorely afflict us?

קָדְשֵׁנוּ וְתִפְאַרְתֵּנוּ אֲשֶׁר הִלְלוּךָ אֲבֹתֵינוּ הָיָה לִשְׂרֵפַת
burning a has our praised where our and our
of become ,fathers You ,beauty holiness

11 אֵשׁ וְכָל־מַחֲמַדֵּינוּ הָיָה לְחָרְבָּה׃ הַעַל־אֵלֶּה תִתְאַפַּק
re- You will these Over .ruin a have pleasant our and ;fire
,Yourself strain things become things all

יְהוָה תֶּחֱשֶׁה וּתְעַנֵּנוּ עַד־מְאֹד׃
an to afflict and You Will Jeho-
?extreme us silent be ?vah

CAP. LXV סה

CHAPTER 65

CHAPTER 65

[1] I Myself have been sought, not of those who asked; I have been found, not of those who sought Me. I said, Look upon Me! Look upon Me, to a nation not calling on My name. [2] I have spread out My hands all the day long to a rebellious people who walk (in) the way not good, following their own thoughts; [3] a people who continually provoke Me to My face; who sacrifice in gardens, and burn incense on the bricks; [4] who sit among the graves and lodge in the towers, who eat swine's flesh; and broth of unclean things (in) their pots; [5] who say, Keep to yourself! Do not come near me, for I am holier than you! These (are) a smoke in My nose, a fire burning all the day. [6] Behold! It is written before Me: I will not be silent, except I repay; yea, I will repay to their bosom, [7] your iniquities and the iniquities of your fathers together, says Jehovah; that burned incense on the mountains and have blasphemed Me on the hills. And I will measure their former work upon their bosom.

[8] Thus says Jehovah: As the new wine is found in the cluster, and one says, Do not destroy it, for a blessing (is) in it, so I will do for the sake of My servants, not to destroy the whole. [9] And I will bring forth a

1 נִדְרַשְׁתִּי לְלוֹא שָׁאָלוּ נִמְצֵאתִי לְלֹא בִקְשֻׁנִי אָמַרְתִּי הִנֵּנִי
Behold ,said I who those not have I who those not have I
!Me .Me sought of ,found been ;asked of sought been

2 הִנֵּנִי אֶל־גּוֹי לֹא־קֹרָא בִשְׁמִי׃ פֵּרַשְׂתִּי יָדַי כָּל־הַיּוֹם אֶל־
to the all My have I My on calling not a to Behold
day hands out spread .name nation ,Me

עַם סוֹרֵר הַהֹלְכִים הַדֶּרֶךְ לֹא־טוֹב אַחַר מַחְשְׁבֹתֵיהֶם׃
own their after ,good not the (in) walk who rebellious a
,thoughts way people

3 הָעָם הַמַּכְעִיסִים אוֹתִי עַל־פָּנַי תָּמִיד זֹבְחִים בַּגַּנּוֹת וּמְקַטְּרִים
burning and in sacrificing contin- My to Me who a
incense ,gardens ,ually face provoke people

4 עַל־הַלְּבֵנִים׃ הַיֹּשְׁבִים בַּקְּבָרִים וּבַנְּצוּרִים יָלִינוּ הָאֹכְלִים
eat who they watch in and the among sit who ,bricks the on
,sleep towers ,graves

5 בְּשַׂר הַחֲזִיר וּפְרַק פִּגֻּלִים כְּלֵיהֶם׃ הָאֹמְרִים קְרַב אֵלֶיךָ
to Draw ,say who their (in) unclean broth and ,swine flesh
!yourself near ;pots things of of

אַל־תִּגַּשׁ־בִּי כִּי קְדַשְׁתִּיךָ אֵלֶּה עָשָׁן בְּאַפִּי אֵשׁ יֹקֶדֶת
burning fire a My in a These holier am I for to come not
nose smoke (are) !you than ,me near

6 כָּל־הַיּוֹם׃ הִנֵּה כְתוּבָה לְפָנָי לֹא אֶחֱשֶׁה כִּי אִם־שִׁלַּמְתִּי
;repay I except will I not before is It !Behold the all
,silent be :Me written .day

7 וְשִׁלַּמְתִּי אֶל־חֵיקָם׃ עֲוֺנֹתֵיכֶם וַעֲוֺנֹת אֲבוֹתֵיכֶם יַחְדָּו אָמַר
says ,together your the and your their to I and
fathers of iniquities iniquities ,bosom repay will

יְהוָה אֲשֶׁר קִטְּרוּ עַל־הֶהָרִים וְעַל־הַגְּבָעוֹת חֵרְפוּנִי וּמַדֹּתִי
I And blasphemed the on and the on burned that Jeho-
mete will .Me hills ,mountains incense ,vah

8 פְעֻלָּתָם רִאשֹׁנָה עַל־חֵיקָם׃ כֹּה ׀ אָמַר יְהוָה כַּאֲשֶׁר
As ,Jehovah says Thus their upon former their
.bosom work

יִמָּצֵא הַתִּירוֹשׁ בָּאֶשְׁכּוֹל וְאָמַר אַל־תַּשְׁחִיתֵהוּ כִּי בְרָכָה
a for destroy Do not one and the in new the is
blessing ,it ,says ,cluster wine found

9 בּוֹ כֵּן אֶעֱשֶׂה לְמַעַן עֲבָדַי לְבִלְתִּי הַשְׁחִית הַכֹּל׃ וְהוֹצֵאתִי
will I And the to not in My for will I so (is)
forth bring .whole destroy order,servants sake do ,it in

seed out of Jacob, and out of Judah one to inherit My mountains. And My chosen one shall inherit it, and My servants shall live there. [10] And Sharon shall be a fold of flocks; and the valley of Achor a resting place of herds, for My people who have sought Me. [11] But you (are) those who forsake Jehovah, who forget My holy mountain, who array a table for Fortune, and who fill for Fate mixed wine. [12] And I will number you to the sword, and you shall all bow down to the slaughter, because I called and you did not answer; I spoke and you did not hear; and you did the evil in My eyes, and you chose that in which I had no pleasure. [13] Therefore thus says the Lord Jehovah: Behold, My servants shall eat, but you shall be hungry. Behold, My servants shall drink, but you shall be thirsty. Behold, My servants shall rejoice, but you shall be ashamed. [14] Behold, My servants shall sing for joy of heart, but you shall cry from heartbreak; and howl from breaking of spirit. [15] And you shall leave your name for a curse to My chosen; and the Lord Jehovah shall kill you; and His servants He shall call by another name. [16] (He) who blesses himself in the earth shall bless himself in the God of truth; and he who swears in the earth shall swear by the God of truth; because the former distresses are forgotten, and because they are hidden from My eyes.

[17] For, behold, I create new heavens and new earth; and the things before shall not be recalled, and not shall go up on the heart. [18] However, be glad and rejoice forever in what I create; for, behold, I create

מִיַּעֲקֹב זֶרַע וּמִיהוּדָה יוֹרֵשׁ הָרָי וִירֵשׁוּהָ בְחִירַי וַעֲבָדַי
My and My shall And My to one out and ,seed a of out
servants ,chosen it inherit .mountain inherit Judah of Jacob

10 יִשְׁכְּנוּ־שָׁמָּה׃ וְהָיָה הַשָּׁרוֹן לִנְוֵה־צֹאן וְעֵמֶק עָכוֹר לְרֵבֶץ
resting a Achor the and ;flocks a Sharon shall And .there shall
of place of valley of fold become live

11 בָּקָר לְעַמִּי אֲשֶׁר דְּרָשׁוּנִי׃ וְאַתֶּם עֹזְבֵי יְהוָה הַשְּׁכֵחִים
who ,Jehovah who those you But have who My for ,herds
forget forsake (are) .Me sought people

אֶת־הַר קָדְשִׁי הַעֹרְכִים לַגַּד שֻׁלְחָן וְהַמְמַלְאִים לַמְנִי
for who and ,table a for set who My mountain
Fate fill Fortune order in ,holy

12 מִמְסָךְ׃ וּמָנִיתִי אֶתְכֶם לַחֶרֶב וְכֻלְּכֶם לַטֶּבַח תִּכְרָעוּ
bow shall the to all and the to you will I And mixed
down slaughter you of ,sword number .wine

יַעַן קָרָאתִי וְלֹא עֲנִיתֶם דִּבַּרְתִּי וְלֹא שְׁמַעְתֶּם וַתַּעֲשׂוּ הָרַע
the you and did you and I did you and called I be-
evil did ;hear not spoke ;answer not cause

13 בְּעֵינַי וּבַאֲשֶׁר לֹא־חָפַצְתִּי בְּחַרְתֶּם׃ לָכֵן כֹּה־אָמַר ׀
says thus ,Therefore .chose you had I not that and My in
pleasure which in ;eyes

אֲדֹנָי יְהוִה הִנֵּה עֲבָדַי ׀ יֹאכֵלוּ וְאַתֶּם תִּרְעָבוּ הִנֵּה עֲבָדַי
My ,Behold be shall you but shall My ,Behold ,Jehovah the
servants .hungry ,eat servants Lord

יִשְׁתּוּ וְאַתֶּם תִּצְמָאוּ הִנֵּה עֲבָדַי יִשְׂמָחוּ וְאַתֶּם תֵּבֹשׁוּ׃
be shall but shall My ,Behold be shall but shall
.ashamed you ,rejoice servants .thirsty you ,drink

14 הִנֵּה עֲבָדַי יָרֹנּוּ מִטּוּב לֵב וְאַתֶּם תִּצְעֲקוּ מִכְּאֵב לֵב
;heart from cry shall but ,heart from shall My ,Behold
of pain out you of joy sing servants

15 וּמִשֵּׁבֶר רוּחַ תְּיֵלִילוּ׃ וְהִנַּחְתֶּם שִׁמְכֶם לִשְׁבוּעָה לִבְחִירַי
My to a for your you And shall spirit from and
,chosen curse name leave shall .howl of breaking

16 וֶהֱמִיתְךָ אֲדֹנָי יְהוִה וְלַעֲבָדָיו יִקְרָא שֵׁם אַחֵר׃ אֲשֶׁר
(He) .another name shall He His and ;Jehovah the shall and
who call servants Lord you kill

הַמִּתְבָּרֵךְ בָּאָרֶץ יִתְבָּרֵךְ בֵּאלֹהֵי אָמֵן וְהַנִּשְׁבָּע בָּאָרֶץ
the in he and ;truth the in bless shall the in blesses
earth swears who of God himself earth himself

יִשָּׁבַע בֵּאלֹהֵי אָמֵן כִּי נִשְׁכְּחוּ הַצָּרוֹת הָרִאשֹׁנוֹת וְכִי
and ;former dis- the are for ;truth the by shall
because tresses forgotten of God swear

17 נִסְתְּרוּ מֵעֵינָי׃ כִּי־הִנְנִי בוֹרֵא שָׁמַיִם חֲדָשִׁים וָאָרֶץ חֲדָשָׁה
;new and new heavens create ,behold For from are they
earth I .eyes My hidden

18 וְלֹא תִזָּכַרְנָה הָרִאשֹׁנוֹת וְלֹא תַעֲלֶינָה עַל־לֵב׃ כִּי־אִם־
Except the on shall and things the be shall and
.heart up go not ,before remembered not

שִׂישׂוּ וְגִילוּ עֲדֵי־עַד אֲשֶׁר אֲנִי בוֹרֵא כִּי הִנְנִי בוֹרֵא אֶת־
create ,behold ,for ;create I (in) forever till and be
I what rejoice glad

Jerusalem a rejoicing, and her people a joy. [19] And I will rejoice in Jerusalem, and joy in My people. And the voice of weeping and the voice of crying shall no longer be heard in her. [20] Not shall be there still an infant of days, or an old man that has not filled his days; for the youth shall die the son of a hundred years, but the sinner the son of a hundred years shall be accursed. [21] And they shall build houses and live (in them); and they shall plant vineyards and eat their fruit. [22] They shall not build, and another live (in them); they shall not plant, and another eat. For like the days of the tree (are) the days of My people, and My elect shall grow old (to) the work of their hands. [23] They shall not labor in vain, nor bring forth for terror; for they are the seed of Jehovah's beloved ones, and their offspring with them. [24] And it will be before they call, I will answer; while they are speaking, then I will hear. [25] The wolf and the lamb shall feed as one, and the lion shall eat straw like the ox; and the snake, dust its food. They shall not do evil nor destroy in all My holy mountain, says Jehovah.

19 יְרוּשָׁלַ͏ִם גִּילָה וְעַמָּהּ מָשׂוֹשׂ׃ וְגַלְתִּי בִירוּשָׁלַ͏ִם וְשַׂשְׂתִּי
joy and in I And .joy a her and a Jerusalem
,Jerusalem rejoice will people ,rejoicing

20 בְעַמִּי וְלֹא־יִשָּׁמַע בָּהּ עוֹד קוֹל בְּכִי וְקוֹל זְעָקָה׃ לֹא־
Not crying the and weep- the any her in shall And My in
.out of voice ing of voice more heard be not .people

יִהְיֶה מִשָּׁם עוֹד עוּל יָמִים וְזָקֵן אֲשֶׁר לֹא־יְמַלֵּא אֶת־יָמָיו
;days his has not who an or ,days suck- a any there shall
filled man old of ling more be

כִּי הַנַּעַר בֶּן־מֵאָה שָׁנָה יָמוּת וְהַחוֹטֶא בֶּן־מֵאָה שָׁנָה
years -hun a the the But shall years a the the for
dred of son sinner .die hundred of son boy

21 יְקֻלָּל׃ וּבָנוּ בָתִּים וְיָשָׁבוּ וְנָטְעוּ כְרָמִים וְאָכְלוּ פִּרְיָם׃
their eat and vineyards they and live and houses they And be shall
.fruit plant shall ;(them in) build shall .accursed

22 לֹא יִבְנוּ וְאַחֵר יֵשֵׁב לֹא יִטְּעוּ וְאַחֵר יֹאכֵל כִּי־כִימֵי הָעֵץ
the the like For .eat and shall they not live and they Not
tree of days another plant ;(them in) another build shall

23 יְמֵי עַמִּי וּמַעֲשֵׂה יְדֵיהֶם יְבַלּוּ בְחִירָי׃ לֹא יִיגְעוּ לָרִיק
in they Not .elect My grow shall their the and My the (are)
,vain labor shall (to) old hands of work ;people of days

וְלֹא יֵלְדוּ לַבֶּהָלָה כִּי זֶרַע בְּרוּכֵי יְהוָה הֵמָּה וְצֶאֱצָאֵיהֶם
their and they Jehovah's blessed the for for bring and
offspring ,are ones of seed ;terror forth not

24 אִתָּם׃ וְהָיָה טֶרֶם יִקְרָאוּ וַאֲנִי אֶעֱנֶה עוֹד הֵם מְדַבְּרִים
are they while will I they before it And with
speaking ;answer ,call be will .them

25 וַאֲנִי אֶשְׁמָע׃ זְאֵב וְטָלֶה יִרְעוּ כְאֶחָד וְאַרְיֵה כַּבָּקָר יֹאכַל־
shall the like the and ,one as shall the and The .hear will then
eat ox lion feed lamb wolf I

תֶּבֶן וְנָחָשׁ עָפָר לַחְמוֹ לֹא־יָרֵעוּ וְלֹא־יַשְׁחִיתוּ בְּכָל־הַר
moun- in destroy and they Not .food its dust the and ;straw
tain all not ,evil do shall ,snake

קָדְשִׁי אָמַר יְהוָה׃
.Jehovah says My
,holy

CAP. LXVI סו

CHAPTER 66

[1] Thus says Jehovah: Heaven (is) My throne, and the earth is My footstool. Where then (is) the house that you build for Me? And where then (is) the place (of) My rest? [2] And My hand has made all these things and all these things that exist, says Jehovah. But I will look toward this one, to him who is humble and of a contrite spirit, and who trembles at My word.

[3] He who kills an ox (is as if) he killed a man; he

1 כֹּה אָמַר יְהוָה הַשָּׁמַיִם כִּסְאִי וְהָאָרֶץ הֲדֹם רַגְלָי אֵי־זֶה
then Where My the and My Heaven :Jehovah says Thus
(is) .feet of stool earth ,throne (is)

2 בַיִת אֲשֶׁר תִּבְנוּ־לִי וְאֵי־זֶה מָקוֹם מְנוּחָתִי׃ וְאֶת־כָּל־אֵלֶּה
these all And ?rest My the then And for you that the
things (of) place (is) where ?Me build house

יָדִי עָשָׂתָה וַיִּהְיוּ כָל־אֵלֶּה נְאֻם־יְהוָה וְאֶל־זֶה אַבִּיט אֶל־
to will I this But .Jehovah states these all and has My
,look one to ,things exist ,made hand

3 עָנִי וּנְכֵה־רוּחַ וְחָרֵד עַל־דְּבָרִי׃ שׁוֹחֵט הַשּׁוֹר מַכֵּה־אִישׁ
a he(as is) ,ox the He My at and ,spirit con- and the
;man striking slaughtering .word trembling of trite afflicted

who sacrifices a lamb (is as if) he cuts off a dog's head. He who offers a present, (as if it were) swine's blood; he who marks incense, (as if) he blessed an evil. Yes, they have chosen their way and their soul delights in their abominations. [4] I also will choose their vexations, and I will bring their fears to them; because I called, and no one replied; I spoke, and they did not hear; but they did the evil in My eyes, and chose that in which I had no pleasure.

[5] Hear the word of Jehovah, those who tremble at His word: Your brothers who hate you, who drive you out for My name's sake, have said, Jehovah is glorified! But He shall appear in your joy, and they shall be ashamed. [6] A roaring sound from the city, a sound from the temple, the sound of Jehovah repaying recompense to His enemies!

[7] Before she travailed, she brought forth; before pain came to her, she delivered a male child. [8] Who has heard such a thing? Who has seen such things? Shall the earth be brought forth (in) one day? Shall a nation be born (in) one step? For Zion labored also brought forth her sons. [9] Shall I bring to the birth and not cause to bring forth? says Jehovah. Surely I cause and restrain birth, says your God.

[10] Rejoice with Jerusalem, and be glad with her, all who love her. Rejoice with her a rejoicing, all who mourn for her; [11] that you may suck and be satisfied with her comforting breasts; that you may milk out and delight yourselves with the fullness of her glory. [12] For thus says Jehovah: Behold, I stretch out peace to her like a river, and glory of nations like an overflowing torrent. And you shall suck;

זֹבֵחַ הַשֶּׂה עֹרֵף כֶּלֶב מַעֲלֵה מִנְחָה דַּם־חֲזִיר מַזְכִּיר
he ;swine (as) a he ;dog's a breaking the sacri- he
marking of blood,present offering neck ,lamb ficing

לְבֹנָה מְבָרֵךְ אָוֶן גַּם־הֵמָּה בָּחֲרוּ בְּדַרְכֵיהֶם וּבְשִׁקּוּצֵיהֶם
their in and way their have they ,also an (as) ,incense
abominations chosen — evil blessing

4 נַפְשָׁם חָפֵצָה׃ גַּם־אֲנִי אֶבְחַר בְּתַעֲלֻלֵיהֶם וּמְגוּרֹתָם אָבִיא
will I their and ,vexations their will I Also .delights their
bring fears choose soul

לָהֶם יַעַן קָרָאתִי וְאֵין עוֹנֶה דִּבַּרְתִּי וְלֹא שָׁמֵעוּ וַיַּעֲשׂוּ הָרַע
the they but they and ,spoke I (one) and ,called I because to
evil did ;hear did not ;answered not ,them

5 בְּעֵינַי וּבַאֲשֶׁר לֹא־חָפַצְתִּי בָּחָרוּ׃ שִׁמְעוּ דְּבַר־יְהוָה
,Jehovah the Hear they had I not that and My in
of word .chose in pleasure which ,eyes

הַחֲרֵדִים אֶל־דְּבָרוֹ אָמְרוּ אֲחֵיכֶם שֹׂנְאֵיכֶם מְנַדֵּיכֶם לְמַעַן
for driving hating Your have His at who those
sake out you ,you brothers said :word tremble

6 שְׁמִי יִכְבַּד יְהוָה וְנִרְאֶה בְשִׂמְחַתְכֶם וְהֵם יֵבֹשׁוּ׃ קוֹל
sound A be shall and your in He But !Jehovah is My
of .ashamed they ,joy appear shall glorified ,name's

שָׁאוֹן מֵעִיר קוֹל מֵהֵיכָל קוֹל יְהוָה מְשַׁלֵּם גְּמוּל לְאֹיְבָיו׃
His to recom- repaying Jehovah the the from a from roaring
.enemies pence of sound ,temple sound ,city the

7 בְּטֶרֶם תָּחִיל יָלָדָה בְּטֶרֶם יָבוֹא חֵבֶל לָהּ וְהִמְלִיטָה
she then to pain came before gave she she Before
delivered ,her ;birth ,travailed

8 זָכָר׃ מִי־שָׁמַע כָּזֹאת מִי רָאָה כָּאֵלֶּה הֲיוּחַל אֶרֶץ בְּיוֹם
day in the Shall ?these like has Who like has Who .male a
earth travail. seen ?this heard

אֶחָד אִם־יִוָּלֵד גּוֹי פַּעַם אֶחָת כִּי־חָלָה גַּם־יָלְדָה צִיּוֹן אֶת־
Zion brought also travailed For one (in) a be Shall ?one
forth step nation born

9 בָּנֶיהָ׃ הַאֲנִי אַשְׁבִּיר וְלֹא אוֹלִיד יֹאמַר יְהוָה אִם־אֲנִי
I Sure- .Jehovah says to cause and to bring Shall her
ly ?forth bring not birth the I .sons

10 הַמּוֹלִיד וְעָצַרְתִּי אָמַר אֱלֹהָיִךְ׃ שִׂמְחוּ אֶת־יְרוּשָׁלִַם
,Jerusalem with Rejoice God your says and cause
,restrain ,birth

וְגִילוּ בָהּ כָּל־אֹהֲבֶיהָ שִׂישׂוּ אִתָּהּ מָשׂוֹשׂ כָּל־הַמִּתְאַבְּלִים
who all a with Rejoice who all with be and
mourn ,rejoicing her .her love ,her glad

11 עָלֶיהָ׃ לְמַעַן תִּינְקוּ וּשְׂבַעְתֶּם מִשֹּׁד תַּנְחֻמֶיהָ לְמַעַן תָּמֹצּוּ
may you that her the with be and may you that for
out drain ,comforts of breast satisfied suck ;her

12 וְהִתְעַנַּגְתֶּם מִזִּיז כְּבוֹדָהּ׃ כִּי־כֹה אָמַר יְהוָה הִנְנִי
,Behold Jeho- says thus For her the with delight and
I :vah .glory of fullness yourselves

נֹטֶה־אֵלֶיהָ כְּנָהָר שָׁלוֹם וּכְנַחַל שׁוֹטֵף כְּבוֹד גּוֹיִם וִינַקְתֶּם
you And .nations glory over like and ,peace a like her to hold
;suck shall of flowing torrent a river out

you shall be carried on the side and be dandled on knees. [13] As one whom his mother comforts, so I will comfort you; and you shall be comforted in Jerusalem. [14] And you will see, and your heart shall rejoice, and your bones shall flourish like the grass. And the hand of Jehovah shall be known toward His servants, and He shall be indignant with His enemies.

[15] For, behold, Jehovah will come with fire, and His chariots like the tempest, to return His wrath in fury, and His rebuke in flames of fire. [16] For by fire and by His sword, Jehovah will execute judgment with all flesh; and the slain of Jehovah shall be many. [17] Those who sanctify themselves and purify themselves to the gardens, (each) one in the midst, eaters of swine's flesh, and the hateful thing, and the mouse — (these) shall be cut off together, says Jehovah.

[18] For I (know) their works and their thoughts; it comes to gather all the nations and the tongues, and they shall come and see My glory. [19] And I will set a sign among them, and I will send those who escape from them to the nations of Tarshish, Pul, and Lud, drawers of the bow; to Tubal and Javan, to the far away coasts that have not heard My fame nor seen My glory. And they shall declare My glory among the nations. [20] And they shall bring all your brothers out of all nations, an offering to Jehovah, on horses, and in chariots, and in litters, and on mules, and on camels, to My holy mountain Jerusalem, says Jehovah, as the sons of Israel bring the offering in a clean vessel (to) the house of Jehovah. [21] And I will

13 עַל־צַד תִּנָּשֵׂאוּ וְעַל־בִּרְכַּיִם תְּשָׁעֳשָׁעוּ׃ כְּאִישׁ אֲשֶׁר אִמּוֹ
his whom a As be shall you knees and shall you the on
mother man . dangled on carried be side

14 תְּנַחֲמֶנּוּ כֵּן אָנֹכִי אֲנַחֶמְכֶם וּבִירוּשָׁלַםִ תְּנֻחָמוּ׃ וּרְאִיתֶם
you And shall you in and comfort will I so comforts
,see will .comforted be Jerusalem ;you ,him

וְשָׂשׂ לִבְּכֶם וְעַצְמוֹתֵיכֶם כַּדֶּשֶׁא תִפְרַחְנָה וְנוֹדְעָה יַד־יְהוָה
Jehovah the shall And shall the like your and your shall and
of hand known be .sprout grass bones ,heart rejoice

15 אֶת־עֲבָדָיו וְזָעַם אֶת־אֹיְבָיו׃ כִּי־הִנֵּה יְהוָה בָּאֵשׁ יָבוֹא
will with Jehovah ,behold ,For His (over) He and His toward
,come fire .enemies rage shall ,servants

וְכַסּוּפָה מַרְכְּבֹתָיו לְהָשִׁיב בְּחֵמָה אַפּוֹ וְגַעֲרָתוֹ בְּלַהֲבֵי־
flames in His and His fury in bring to His the like and
of rebuke ,wrath back ,chariots tempest

16 אֵשׁ׃ כִּי בָאֵשׁ יְהוָה נִשְׁפָּט וּבְחַרְבּוֹ אֶת־כָּל־בָּשָׂר וְרַבּוּ
shall and ;flesh all with with and will Jehovah by For .fire
many be sword His ,judge fire

17 חַלְלֵי יְהוָה׃ הַמִּתְקַדְּשִׁים וְהַמִּטַּהֲרִים אֶל־הַגַּנּוֹת אַחַר
behind the to purify and sanctify who Those .Jehovah the
,gardens themselves themselves of slain

אַחַד בַּתָּוֶךְ אֹכְלֵי בְּשַׂר הַחֲזִיר וְהַשֶּׁקֶץ וְהָעַכְבָּר יַחְדָּו
together the and the and ,swine the flesh eaters the in (each)
—mouse ,thing hateful of of , midst one

18 יָסֻפוּ נְאֻם־יְהוָה׃ וְאָנֹכִי מַעֲשֵׂיהֶם וּמַחְשְׁבֹתֵיהֶם בָּאָה
it their and works their For .Jehovah states are they
comes —thoughts (know) I ,off cut

לְקַבֵּץ אֶת־כָּל־הַגּוֹיִם וְהַלְּשֹׁנוֹת וּבָאוּ וְרָאוּ אֶת־כְּבוֹדִי׃
.glory My see and they and the and the all to
come shall ,tongues nations gather

19 וְשַׂמְתִּי בָהֶם אוֹת וְשִׁלַּחְתִּי מֵהֶם ׀ פְּלֵיטִים אֶל־הַגּוֹיִם
the to who those from I and a among I And
:nations escape them send will ,sign them set will

תַּרְשִׁישׁ פּוּל וְלוּד מֹשְׁכֵי קֶשֶׁת תֻּבַל וְיָוָן הָאִיִּים הָרְחֹקִים
far the to and to the drawers and ,Put ,Tarshish
,away coasts ,Javan Tubal ,bow of ,Lud

אֲשֶׁר לֹא־שָׁמְעוּ אֶת־שִׁמְעִי וְלֹא־רָאוּ אֶת־כְּבוֹדִי וְהִגִּידוּ
they And My have and My have not that
declare shall .glory seen not ,fame heard

20 אֶת־כְּבוֹדִי בַּגּוֹיִם׃ וְהֵבִיאוּ אֶת־כָּל־אֲחֵיכֶם ׀ מִכָּל־הַגּוֹיִם ׀
the of out your all they And among My
,nations all brothers bring shall .nations the glory

מִנְחָה ׀ לַיהוָה בַּסּוּסִים וּבָרֶכֶב וּבַצַּבִּים וּבַפְּרָדִים
on and in and in and ,horses on to food— a
,mules ,wagons ,chariots ,Jehovah offering

וּבַכִּרְכָּרוֹת עַל הַר קָדְשִׁי יְרוּשָׁלַםִ אָמַר יְהוָה כַּאֲשֶׁר יָבִיאוּ
bring as ,Jehovah says ,Jerusalem My moun- to on and
holy tain ,dromedaries

21 בְנֵי יִשְׂרָאֵל אֶת־הַמִּנְחָה בִּכְלִי טָהוֹר בֵּית יְהוָה׃ וְגַם־
And .Jehovah the (to) clean a in food— the Israel the
also of house vessel offering of sons

also take some of them for the priests, for the Levites, says Jehovah.

[22] For as the new heavens and the new earth, which I will make, stand before me, says Jehovah, so your seed and your name shall stand. [23] And from new moon to its new moon, and from sabbath to its sabbath, all flesh shall come to worship before Me, says Jehovah. [24] And they shall go out and see the dead bodies of the men who have sinned against Me; for their worm shall not die, nor shall their fire be put out; and they shall be an object of disgust to all flesh.

22 מֵהֶם אֶקַּח לַכֹּהֲנִים לַלְוִיִּם אָמַר יְהוָה׃ כִּי כַאֲשֶׁר הַשָּׁמַיִם
the as For .Jehovah says the for the for will I some
heavens ,Levites ,priests take them of

הַחֲדָשִׁים וְהָאָרֶץ הַחֲדָשָׁה אֲשֶׁר אֲנִי עֹשֶׂה עֹמְדִים לְפָנַי
before stand ,make I which ,new the and new
,Me earth

23 נְאֻם־יְהוָה כֵּן יַעֲמֹד זַרְעֲכֶם וְשִׁמְכֶם׃ וְהָיָה מִדֵּי־חֹדֶשׁ בְּחָדְשׁוֹ
its to new from it And your and your shall so Jeho- states
,moon new moon be will .name seed stand vah

וּמִדֵּי שַׁבָּת בְּשַׁבַּתּוֹ יָבוֹא כָל־בָּשָׂר לְהִשְׁתַּחֲוֺת לְפָנַי אָמַר
says before worship to flesh all shall its to sabbath and
,Me come ,sabbath from

24 יְהוָה׃ וְיָצְאוּ וְרָאוּ בְּפִגְרֵי הָאֲנָשִׁים הַפֹּשְׁעִים בִּי כִּי תוֹלַעְתָּם
their for against have who the dead the and they And Jeho-
worm .Me sinned men of bodies ,see out go shall .vah

לֹא תָמוּת וְאִשָּׁם לֹא תִכְבֶּה וְהָיוּ דֵרָאוֹן לְכָל־בָּשָׂר׃
flesh all to an they and be shall not their and shall not
abhorrence be shall ;out put fire ,die

LIBER JEREMIAE

CAPUT. I א

CHAPTER 1

CHAPTER 1

[1] The words of Jeremiah the son of Hilkiah, (one) of the priests who (were) in Anathoth in the land of Benjamin, [2] (to) whom the word of Jehovah came in the days of Josiah the son of Amon king of Judah, in the thirteenth year of his reign. [3] It also came in the days of Jehoiakim the son of Josiah king of Judah, to the end of the eleventh year of Zedekiah the son of Josiah king of Judah, to the exile of Jerusalem in the fifth month. [4] Then the word of Jehovah came to me, saying, [5] Before I formed you in the belly, I knew you; and before you came out of the womb, I sanctified you. I ordained you a prophet to the nations. [6] Then I said, Ah, Lord Jehovah! Behold, I do not know how to speak; for I (am) a boy.

[7] But Jehovah said to me, Do not say, I (am) a boy; for you shall go to all that I shall send you. And whatever I command you, you shall speak. [8] Do not be afraid of their faces, for I (am) with you to deliver you, says Jehovah. [9] Then Jehovah put out His hand and touched my mouth. And Jehovah said to me, Behold, I have put My words in your mouth. [10] See, I have this day appointed you over the nations and over the kingdoms, to root out, and to

דִּבְרֵי יִרְמְיָהוּ בֶּן־חִלְקִיָּהוּ מִן־הַכֹּהֲנִים אֲשֶׁר בַּעֲנָתוֹת 1

in who the (one) ,Hilkiah the Jeremiah The
Anathoth (were) priests of of son of words

בְּאֶרֶץ בִּנְיָמִן׃ אֲשֶׁר הָיָה דְבַר־יְהוָה אֵלָיו בִּימֵי יֹאשִׁיָּהוּ 2

Josiah the in to Jehovah the came whom ,Benjamin the in
of days him of word of land

בֶן־אָמוֹן מֶלֶךְ יְהוּדָה בִּשְׁלֹשׁ־עֶשְׂרֵה שָׁנָה לְמָלְכוֹ׃ וַיְהִי 3

it Also his of year the in ,Judah king ,Amon the
came .reign thirteenth of of son

בִּימֵי יְהוֹיָקִים בֶּן־יֹאשִׁיָּהוּ מֶלֶךְ יְהוּדָה עַד־תֹּם עַשְׁתֵּי־

eleventh the until ,Judah king ,Judah the Jehoiakim the in
of end of of son of days

עֶשְׂרֵה שָׁנָה לְצִדְקִיָּהוּ בֶן־יֹאשִׁיָּהוּ מֶלֶךְ יְהוּדָה עַד־גְּלוֹת

the to ,Judah king ,Josiah the of the
of exile of of son Zedekiah year

יְרוּשָׁלַםִ בַּחֹדֶשׁ הַחֲמִישִׁי׃ וַיְהִי דְבַר־יְהוָה אֵלַי 4

to Jehovah the Now .fifth the in Jerusalem
,me of word came month

לֵאמֹר׃ בְּטֶרֶם אֶצָּורְךָ בַבֶּטֶן יְדַעְתִּיךָ וּבְטֶרֶם תֵּצֵא 5

you and knew I the in formed I Before :saying
out came before ,you belly ,you

מֵרֶחֶם הִקְדַּשְׁתִּיךָ נָבִיא לַגּוֹיִם נְתַתִּיךָ׃ וָאֹמַר אֲהָהּ 6

,Alas I Then ap- I the to a consecrated I the of
,said .you pointed nations prophet ;you womb

אֲדֹנָי יְהוִה הִנֵּה לֹא־יָדַעְתִּי דַבֵּר כִּי־נַעַר אָנֹכִי׃ וַיֹּאמֶר 7

But .(am) I a for to do I not ,Behold !Jehovah Lord
said boy ,speak how know

יְהוָה אֵלַי אַל־תֹּאמַר נַעַר אָנֹכִי כִּי עַל־כָּל־אֲשֶׁר אֶשְׁלָחֲךָ

send I that all to for ;(am) I a do not to Jehovah
,you boy ,say ,me

תֵּלֵךְ וְאֵת כָּל־אֲשֶׁר אֲצַוְּךָ תְּדַבֵּר׃ אַל־תִּירָא מִפְּנֵיהֶם 8

their of be do Not will you com- I what ever And you
,faces afraid .speak ,you mand .go shall

כִּי־אִתְּךָ אֲנִי לְהַצִּלֶךָ נְאֻם־יְהוָה׃ וַיִּשְׁלַח יְהוָה אֶת־יָדוֹ 9

His Jehovah Then .Jehovah says deliver to I with for
hand forth put ,you ,(am) you

וַיַּגַּע עַל־פִּי וַיֹּאמֶר יְהוָה אֵלַי הִנֵּה נָתַתִּי דְבָרַי בְּפִיךָ׃

your in My have I ,Behold to Jehovah and my on and
.mouth words put ,me said ;mouth touched

רְאֵה הִפְקַדְתִּיךָ ׀ הַיּוֹם הַזֶּה עַל־הַגּוֹיִם וְעַל־הַמַּמְלָכוֹת 10

the and the over this day have I ,See
kingdoms over nations you appointed

tear down, and to destroy, and to throw down; to build, and to plant.

[11] And the word of Jehovah came to me, saying, Jeremiah, what do you see? And I said, I see an almond rod. [12] Then Jehovah said to me, You have seen well; for I will watch over My word to perform it. [13] And the word of Jehovah came to me the second time, saying, What do you see? And I said, I see a boiling pot; and its face (is) from the face of the north. [14] Then Jehovah said to me, Out of the north evil will be set loose on all the inhabitants of the land. [15] For, lo, I will call all the families of the kingdoms of the north, declares Jehovah. And they shall come, and they shall each one set his throne at the entrance of the gates of Jerusalem, and all against its walls all around, and against all the cities of Judah. [16] And I will pronounce My judgments against them regarding all their wickedness, (those) who have forsaken me and have burned incense to other gods, and have worshiped the works of their own hands.

[17] And you must gird up your loins, and arise, and speak to them all that I command you. Do not be dismayed before their faces, lest I prostrate you before them. [18] For, behold, today I have made you a fortified city, and an iron pillar, and bronze walls against the whole land, against the kings of Judah, against her princes, against her priests and to the people of the land. [19] And they shall fight against you; but they shall not overcome you. For I am with you to deliver you, declares Jehovah.

לִנְתוֹשׁ וְלִנְתוֹץ וּלְהַאֲבִיד וְלַהֲרוֹס לִבְנוֹת וְלִנְטוֹעַ׃

to and ,build to to and to and to and to
.plant ,down throw destroy ,down tear ,uproot

11 וַיְהִי דְבַר־יְהוָה אֵלַי לֵאמֹר מָה־אַתָּה רֹאֶה יִרְמְיָהוּ וָאֹמַר

I And ?Jeremiah do you What ,saying to Jehovah the And
,said ,see me of word came

12 מַקֵּל שָׁקֵד אֲנִי רֹאֶה׃ וַיֹּאמֶר יְהוָה אֵלַי הֵיטַבְתָּ לִרְאוֹת

;seen have You to Jehovah Then .see I an rod
well ,me said almond

13 כִּי־שֹׁקֵד אֲנִי עַל־דְּבָרִי לַעֲשֹׂתוֹ׃ וַיְהִי דְבַר־יְהוָה ׀

Jehovah the And perform to My over I will for
of word came .it word watch

אֵלַי שֵׁנִית לֵאמֹר מָה אַתָּה רֹאֶה וָאֹמַר סִיר נָפוּחַ אֲנִי

I boiling pot a I And do you What ,saying second the to
,said ?see (time) me

14 רֹאֶה וּפָנָיו מִפְּנֵי צָפוֹנָה׃ וַיֹּאמֶר יְהוָה אֵלַי מִצָּפוֹן תִּפָּתַח

be will From to Jehovah Then .north the the from its and ,see
loosed north the ,me said of face (is) face

15 הָרָעָה עַל כָּל־יֹשְׁבֵי הָאָרֶץ׃ כִּי ׀ הִנְנִי קֹרֵא לְכָל־

all call will I ,lo For the the all on evil
.land of inhabitants

מִשְׁפְּחוֹת מַמְלְכוֹת צָפוֹנָה נְאֻם־יְהוָה וּבָאוּ וְנָתְנוּ אִישׁ

each will and they and ;Jehovah declares the king- the the
man set come will ,north of doms of families

כִּסְאוֹ פֶּתַח ׀ שַׁעֲרֵי יְרוּשָׁלִַם וְעַל כָּל־חוֹמֹתֶיהָ סָבִיב וְעַל

and around its all and ,Jerusalem the the at his
against walls against of gates of entrance throne

16 כָּל־עָרֵי יְהוּדָה׃ וְדִבַּרְתִּי מִשְׁפָּטַי אוֹתָם עַל כָּל־רָעָתָם

their all re- against My I And .Judah the all
,wickedness garding them judgments utter will of cities

אֲשֶׁר עֲזָבוּנִי וַיְקַטְּרוּ לֵאלֹהִים אֲחֵרִים וַיִּשְׁתַּחֲווּ לְמַעֲשֵׂי

the have and ,other gods to burned and for- have who
of works worshiped incense Me saken

17 יְדֵיהֶם׃ וְאַתָּה תֶּאְזֹר מָתְנֶיךָ וְקַמְתָּ וְדִבַּרְתָּ אֲלֵיהֶם אֵת

them to and and your up gird Now their
speak ,arise ,loins you .hands

כָּל־אֲשֶׁר אָנֹכִי אֲצַוֶּךָּ אַל־תֵּחַת מִפְּנֵיהֶם פֶּן־אֲחִתְּךָ

dismay I lest before be do not command I that all
you ,them dismayed ;you

18 לִפְנֵיהֶם׃ וַאֲנִי הִנֵּה נְתַתִּיךָ הַיּוֹם לְעִיר מִבְצָר וּלְעַמּוּד

and ,fortified city a today have ,behold For before
pillar you made ,I .them

בַּרְזֶל וּלְחֹמוֹת נְחֹשֶׁת עַל־כָּל־הָאָרֶץ לְמַלְכֵי יְהוּדָה לְשָׂרֶיהָ

against ,Judah the against the whole against bronze and an
,rulers her of kings ,land walls ,iron

19 לְכֹהֲנֶיהָ וּלְעַם הָאָרֶץ׃ וְנִלְחֲמוּ אֵלֶיךָ וְלֹא־יוּכְלוּ לָךְ כִּי־

For .you will they but against they And the to and against
overcome not ,you fight will .land's people priests her

אִתְּךָ אֲנִי נְאֻם־יְהוָה לְהַצִּילֶךָ׃

deliver to ,Jehovah declares I with
.you ,(am) you

CAP. II. ב

CHAPTER 2

CHAPTER 2

[1] And the word of Jehovah came to me, saying, [2] Go and cry in the ears of Jerusalem, saying, Thus says Jehovah, I remember you, the kindness of your youth, the love of your espousals, your going after Me in the wilderness, in a land not sown. [3] Israel was holy to Jehovah, the firstfruits of His increase. All that devour him become guilty; evil shall come on them, declares Jehovah. [4] Hear the word of Jehovah, O house of Jacob, and all the families of the house of Israel.

[5] Thus says Jehovah, What iniquity have your fathers found in Me, that they went far from Me and have walked after vanity and have become vain? [6] Nor did they say, Where (is) Jehovah who brought us up out of the land of Egypt, who led us in the wilderness; in a land of deserts and of pits; in a dry land, and death-shade; in a land that no man has passed through, and not a man has lived there? [7] And I brought you into a plentiful country, to eat its fruit and its goodness. But when you entered, you defiled My land and made My inheritance an abomination. [8] The priests did not say, Where (is) Jehovah? And they who handle the law did not know Me. And the shepherds rebelled against Me, and the prophets prophesied by Baal and went after things not profitable.

[9] Therefore I will contend with you, says Jehovah, and with your sons' sons I will contend. [10] For go to the isles of Chittim and see; and send to

1 2 וַיְהִי דְבַר־יְהוָה אֵלַי לֵאמֹר׃ הָלֹךְ וְקָרָאתָ בְאָזְנֵי יְרוּשָׁלִַם

,Jerusalem the in and Go ,saying to Jehovah the And
of ears cry ,me of word came

לֵאמֹר כֹּה אָמַר יְהוָה זָכַרְתִּי לָךְ חֶסֶד נְעוּרַיִךְ אַהֲבַת

the your the ,you re- I ,Jehovah says Thus ,saying
of love ,youth of kindness member

3 כְּלוּלֹתָיִךְ לֶכְתֵּךְ אַחֲרַי בַּמִּדְבָּר בְּאֶרֶץ לֹא זְרוּעָה׃ קֹדֶשׁ

Holy .sown not a in the in after your your
(was) land ,wilderness Me going ,espousals

יִשְׂרָאֵל לַיהוָה רֵאשִׁית תְּבוּאָתֹה כָּל־אֹכְלָיו יֶאְשָׁמוּ רָעָה

evil become that all His first- the to Israel
;guilty it devour ;increase of fruits ,Jehovah

4 תָּבֹא אֲלֵיהֶם נְאֻם־יְהוָה׃ שִׁמְעוּ דְבַר־יְהוָה בֵּית

O ,Jehovah the Hear .Jehovah declares on shall
of house of word ,them come

5 יַעֲקֹב וְכָל־מִשְׁפְּחוֹת בֵּית יִשְׂרָאֵל׃ כֹּה ׀ אָמַר יְהוָה מַה־

What :Jehovah says Thus .Israel the the and ,Jacob
of house of families all

מָּצְאוּ אֲבוֹתֵיכֶם בִּי עָוֶל כִּי רָחֲקוּ מֵעָלָי וַיֵּלְכוּ אַחֲרֵי

after have and from they that in- in your have
walked ,Me far went iquity Me fathers found

6 הַהֶבֶל וַיֶּהְבָּלוּ׃ וְלֹא אָמְרוּ אַיֵּה יְהוָה הַמַּעֲלֶה אֹתָנוּ מֵאֶרֶץ

the from us who Jehovah Where did And have and vanity
of land up brought (is) ,say they not ?vain become

מִצְרָיִם הַמּוֹלִיךְ אֹתָנוּ בַּמִּדְבָּר בְּאֶרֶץ עֲרָבָה וְשׁוּחָה

of and deserts a in the in us who ,Egypt
;pits of land ,wilderness led

בְּאֶרֶץ צִיָּה וְצַלְמָוֶת בְּאֶרֶץ לֹא־עָבַר בָּהּ אִישׁ וְלֹא־יָשַׁב

has and a through has not a in deep and drought a in
lived not ,man it passed land ;darkness of land

7 אָדָם שָׁם׃ וָאָבִיא אֶתְכֶם אֶל־אֶרֶץ הַכַּרְמֶל לֶאֱכֹל פִּרְיָהּ

its eat to plentiful a into you I And ?there a
fruit land brought man

וְטוּבָהּ וַתָּבֹאוּ וַתְּטַמְּאוּ אֶת־אַרְצִי וְנַחֲלָתִי שַׂמְתֶּם לְתוֹעֵבָה׃

an made My and My you and But its and
.abomination inheritance ,land defiled entered you goodness

8 הַכֹּהֲנִים לֹא אָמְרוּ אַיֵּה יְהוָה וְתֹפְשֵׂי הַתּוֹרָה לֹא יְדָעוּנִי

knew not the they And ?Jehovah Where did not The
.Me law handle who (is) ,say priests

וְהָרֹעִים פָּשְׁעוּ בִי וְהַנְּבִיאִים נִבְּאוּ בַבַּעַל וְאַחֲרֵי לֹא־

not things and ,Baal by proph- the and against rebelled the And
after esied prophets ;Me shepherds

9 יוֹעִלוּ הָלָכוּ׃ לָכֵן עֹד אָרִיב אִתְּכֶם נְאֻם־יְהוָה וְאֶת־בְּנֵי

the and ;Jehovah says with will I still Therefore they profit-
of sons with ,you contend .went able

10 בְנֵיכֶם אָרִיב׃ כִּי עִבְרוּ אִיֵּי כִתִּיִּים וּרְאוּ וְקֵדָר שִׁלְחוּ

send and and Kittim the cross For will I your
,to Kedar ,see of coasts to over .contend sons

Kedar; and carefully consider, and see if there is (any) like this. [11] Has a nation changed (its) gods; and they not gods? But My people have changed their Glory without it having profit. [12] Be amazed at this, O heavens, and be horrified; be utterly desolated, declares Jehovah. [13] For My people have committed two evils: they have forsaken Me, the Fountain of living waters, to hew out cisterns for themselves; broken cisterns that can hold no water.

[14] (Is) Israel a servant? Or (is) he a servant of the house? Why has he become a prey? [15] The young lions roared against him; they gave their voice. And they made his land a waste; his cities are ruined without inhabitant. [16] Also the sons of Noph and Tahpanhes have stripped your crown. [17] Have you not done this to yourself, by your forsaking Jehovah your God, when He led you by the way? [18] And now what (is) for you toward the way of Egypt to drink the waters of Sihor? Or what for you toward the way of Assyria, to drink the waters of the River? [19] Your own wickedness shall correct you, and your backslidings shall reprove you; therefore know and see that (is) evil and bitter your forsaking Jehovah your God, and My fear is not in you, declares the Lord Jehovah of hosts.

[20] For long ago you broke your yoke (and) tore up your bands, and you said, I will not serve —when on every high hill and under every green tree you lay down (like) a harlot. [21] Yet I planted you a choice vine, wholly a true seed. How then have you turned into the degenerate shoots of an alien vine to Me? [22] Though you wash yourself with potash, and

והתבוננו מאד וראו הן היתה כזאת׃ ההימיר גוי אלהים
(its) a Has like there if and care- and
,gods nation changed .this (any) is see fully consider

12 והמה לא אלהים ועמי המיר כבודו בלוא יועיל׃ שמו
Be having it without their have My But ?gods (were) and
,amazed .profit Glory changed people not they

13 שמים על־זאת ושערו חרבו מאד נאם־יהוה׃ כי־שתים
two For .Jehovah de- ,utterly be be and ,this at O
clares desolated ;horrified ,heavens

רעות עשה עמי אתי עזבו מקור מים חיים לחצב
to ,living waters foun- the have they Me My have evils
out hew of tain ,forsaken :people committed

להם בארות בארת נשברים אשר לא־יכלו המים׃
.water can not that broken cisterns ;cisterns for
hold themselves

14 העבד ישראל אם־יליד בית הוא מדוע היה לבז׃
a he has Why (is) the a Or ?Israel a (Is)
?prey become ?he house of servant .servant

15 עליו ישאגו כפרים נתנו קולם וישיתו ארצו לשמה עריו
his ;waste a his they and their they young the roared Against
cities land made ;voice gave ;lions him

16 נצתה מבלי ישב׃ גם־בני־נף ותחפנס ירעוך קדקד׃
your have and Noph the Also inhabi- without are
.crown stripped Tahpanhes of sons .tant ruined

17 הלוא־זאת תעשה־לך עזבך את־יהוה אלהיך בעת
the at your Jehovah your by to you Have this not
time God forsaking yourself done

18 מוליכך בדרך׃ ועתה מה־לך לדרך מצרים לשתות
drink to ,Egypt toward for what And the by led He
of way the you (is) ,now ?way you

19 מי שחור ומה־לך לדרך אשור לשתות מי נהר׃ תיסרך
teach will the the drink to ,Assyria toward for Or ?Sihor the
you ?River of waters of way the you what of waters

רעתך ומשבותיך תוכחך ודעי וראי כי־רע ומר עזבך
your and evil that and Therefore re- will your and own Your
forsaking bitter (is) see know .you prove apostasies ,evil

את־יהוה אלהיך ולא פחדתי אליך נאם־אדני יהוה
Jehovah the declares in (is) My and your Jehovah
of Lord ,you fear not ,God

20 צבאות׃ כי מעולם שברתי עלך נתקתי מוסרותיך
your tore (and) your broke you long For .Hosts
;bonds up yoke ago

ותאמרי לא אעבוד כי על־כל־גבעה גבהה ותחת כל־
every and high hill every on for will I not you but
under ;serve ,said

21 עץ רענן את צעה זנה׃ ואנכי נטעתיך שורק כלה זרע
a wholly choice a planted Yet a (like) lay you green tree
seed ,vine you I .harlot down

22 אמת ואיך נהפכת לי סורי הגפן נכריה׃ כי אם־תכבסי
wash you Though ?foreign vine a the for have you How .true
yourself of shoots Me into turned then

multiply soap for yourself, your iniquity is stained before Me, declares the Lord Jehovah. [23] How can you say, I am not defiled; I have not gone after Baalim? See your way in the valley, know what you have done! (You are) a swift camel crossing her ways; [24] a wild ass used to the wilderness, she snuffs up the wind in the desire of her passion; in her occasion, who can turn her away? All those who seek her will not tire themselves; in her month they shall find her. [25] Withhold your foot from (being) bare, and your throat from thirst; but you said, It is hopeless! No! For I love strangers, and after them I will go. [26] As the thief is ashamed when he is found, so is the house of Israel ashamed; they, their kings, their princes, and their priests and their prophets; [27] saying to a log, You (are) my father; and to a stone, You gave me birth. For they turned (their) back to Me, and not (their) face. But in the time of their trouble they will say, Arise and save us! [28] But where (are) your gods that you have made for yourselves? Let them arise, if they can save you in the time of your trouble, for (according to) the number of your cities are your gods, O Judah. [29] Why do you contend with Me? All of you, you have rebelled against Me, says Jehovah. [30] In vain I have stricken your sons; they received no correction. Your own sword has devoured your prophets, like a destroying lion.

[31] O generation, see the word of Jehovah. Have I been a wilderness to Israel or a land of darkness? Why do My people say, We roam; we will come no more to You? [32] Can a virgin forget her ornaments, (or) a bride her attire? Yet My

בַּנֶּתֶר וְתַרְבִּי־לָךְ בֹּרִית נִכְתָּם עֲוֺנֵךְ לְפָנַי נְאֻם אֲדֹנָי
the declares before your (is) ,soap your- for and with
Lord ,Me iniquity stained self multiply ,potash

23 יְהוִה׃ אֵיךְ תֹּאמְרִי לֹא נִטְמֵאתִי אַחֲרֵי הַבְּעָלִים לֹא
not Baals after am I not you can How .Jehovah
;defiled ,say

הָלַכְתִּי רְאִי דַרְכֵּךְ בַּגַּיְא דְּעִי מֶה עָשִׂית בִּכְרָה קַלָּה
swift (are You) have you what Know the in your See have I
camel a !done !valley way ?gone

24 מְשָׂרֶכֶת דְּרָכֶיהָ׃ פֶּרֶא ׀ לִמֻּד מִדְבָּר בְּאַוַּת נַפְשׁוֹ שָׁאֲפָה
she her the in the used wild a her crossing
at sniffs passion of desire ,wilderness to ass ,ways

רוּחַ תַּאֲנָתָהּ מִי יְשִׁיבֶנָּה כָּל־מְבַקְשֶׁיהָ לֹא יִיעָפוּ בְּחָדְשָׁהּ
her in tire will not who those All turn can who her (in) the
month ;themselves her seek ?away her time ;wind

25 יִמְצָאוּנְהָ׃ מִנְעִי רַגְלֵךְ מִיָּחֵף וּגוֹרֹנֵךְ מִצִּמְאָה וַתֹּאמְרִי
you but from your and from your Withhold will they
said ;thirst throat ,bare (being) foot .her find

26 נוֹאָשׁ לוֹא כִּי־אָהַבְתִּי זָרִים וְאַחֲרֵיהֶם אֵלֵךְ׃ כְּבֹשֶׁת גַּנָּב
the is As will I after and ,strangers love I For !No is It
thief ashamed .go them !hopeless

כִּי יִמָּצֵא כֵּן הֹבִישׁוּ בֵּית יִשְׂרָאֵל הֵמָּה מַלְכֵיהֶם שָׂרֵיהֶם
their their ,they ;Israel the is so is he when
,rulers ,kings of house ashamed ,found

27 וְכֹהֲנֵיהֶם וּנְבִיאֵיהֶם׃ אֹמְרִים לָעֵץ אָבִי אַתָּה וְלָאֶבֶן אַתְּ
You to and You my a to say who their and their and
,stone a ;(are) father ,tree ,prophets ,priests

יְלִדְתָּנִי כִּי־פָנוּ אֵלַי עֹרֶף וְלֹא פָנִים וּבְעֵת רָעָתָם יֹאמְרוּ
will they their in But (their) and (their) to they For gave we
,say trouble of time the .face not ,back Me turned .birth

28 קוּמָה וְהוֹשִׁיעֵנוּ׃ וְאַיֵּה אֱלֹהֶיךָ אֲשֶׁר עָשִׂיתָ לָּךְ יָקוּמוּ
them Let for have you that your where But save and Rise
,arise ?you made gods (are) .us up

אִם־יוֹשִׁיעוּךָ בְּעֵת רָעָתֶךָ כִּי מִסְפַּר עָרֶיךָ הָיוּ אֱלֹהֶיךָ יְהוּדָה׃
O your (so) your the (as) for your the in can they if
.Judah ,gods are ,cities of number ;trouble of time you save

29 30 לָמָּה תָרִיבוּ אֵלָי כֻּלְּכֶם פְּשַׁעְתֶּם בִּי נְאֻם־יְהוָה׃ לַשָּׁוְא
In .Jehovah says against have you of All with you do Why
vain ,Me rebelled ,you ?me contend

הִכֵּיתִי אֶת־בְּנֵיכֶם מוּסָר לֹא לָקָחוּ אָכְלָה חַרְבְּכֶם
own Your has they not correction your have I
sword devoured .took ;sons struck

31 נְבִיאֵיכֶם כְּאַרְיֵה מַשְׁחִית׃ הַדּוֹר אַתֶּם רְאוּ דְבַר־יְהוָה
.Jehovah the see you gen- O .destroying a like your
of word ,eration lion ,prophets

הֲמִדְבָּר הָיִיתִי לְיִשְׂרָאֵל אִם־אֶרֶץ מַאְפֵּלְיָה מַדּוּעַ אָמְרוּ
do Why ?darkness a or Israel to Have wilder- a
say of land been I ness

32 עַמִּי רַדְנוּ לוֹא־נָבוֹא עוֹד אֵלֶיךָ׃ הֲתִשְׁכַּח בְּתוּלָה עֶדְיָהּ
her virgin a Can ?You to more we not roam We My
,finery forget come will ;(freely) ,people

people have forgotten Me days without number. [33] What? Do you trim your ways to seek love? Therefore, you have even taught the wicked women your ways. [34] Also on your skirts is found the blood of the souls of the poor innocents; you did not find them breaking in, but on all these. [35] Yet you say, Because I am innocent, surely His anger shall turn from me. Behold, I will judge with you, because you say, I have not sinned. [36] Why do you go about so much to change your way? You also shall be ashamed of Egypt, as you were ashamed of Assyria. [37] Yes, you shall go out from this (place), and your hands on your head. For Jehovah has rejected those in whom you trust, and you will not prosper by them.

33 כַּלָּה קִשֻּׁרֶיהָ וְעַמִּי שְׁכֵחוּנִי יָמִים אֵין מִסְפָּר: מַה־תֵּיטִבִי

you do What .number with- days for- have My Yet her a (or)
trim out Me gotten people ?attire bride

דַּרְכֵּךְ לְבַקֵּשׁ אַהֲבָה לָכֵן גַּם אֶת־הָרָעוֹת לִמַּדְתְּ אֶת־

have you wicked the even There- !love seek to your
taught women fore way

34 דְּרָכָיִךְ: גַּם בִּכְנָפַיִךְ נִמְצְאוּ דַּם נַפְשׁוֹת אֶבְיוֹנִים נְקִיִּים

;innocents poor the lives the the found is your on Also your
of of blood skirts .ways

35 לֹא־בַמַּחְתֶּרֶת מְצָאתִים כִּי עַל־כָּל־אֵלֶּה: וַתֹּאמְרִי כִּי

Be- you Yet .these all on but did you breaking not
cause say ,them find in

נִקֵּיתִי אַךְ שָׁב אַפּוֹ מִמֶּנִּי הִנְנִי נִשְׁפָּט אוֹתָךְ עַל־אָמְרֵךְ

you because with will Behold from His shall surely am I
say ,you judge I .me anger turn ,innocent

36 לֹא חָטָאתִי: מַה־תֵּזְלִי מְאֹד לְשַׁנּוֹת אֶת־דַּרְכֵּךְ גַּם מִמִּצְרַיִם

Egypt of Also your change to so you do Why have I not
?way much about go .sinned

37 תֵּבוֹשִׁי כַּאֲשֶׁר בֹּשְׁתְּ מֵאַשּׁוּר: גַּם מֵאֵת זֶה תֵּצְאִי וְיָדַיִךְ

your and will you this from Even of were you as be will you
hands ,out go (place) .Assyria ashamed ashamed

עַל־רֹאשֵׁךְ כִּי־מָאַס יְהֹוָה בְּמִבְטַחַיִךְ וְלֹא תַצְלִיחִי לָהֶם:

by will you and whom in those Jehovah has for your on
.them prosper not ;trust you rejected ;head

CAP. III ג

CHAPTER 3

CHAPTER 3

[1] (They) say, If a man puts away his wife, and she goes from him and will be for another man, will he return to her again? Would not that land be greatly defiled? But you play the harlot with many lovers; yet (would) you come back to Me? says Jehovah. [2] Lift up your eyes on the high places and see. Where have you not been lain with? By the highways you have sat for them, like an Arab in the wilderness. And you have defiled the land with your fornications and with your wickedness. [3] And the showers are withheld, and there has been no latter rain. And a harlot's forehead was to you; you refused to be ashamed. [4] Have you not just now called to Me, My father, You (are) the friend of my youth? [5] Will He keep His anger forever? Or will He guard (it) to the end? Behold, you have spoken

1 לֵאמֹר הֵן יְשַׁלַּח אִישׁ אֶת־אִשְׁתּוֹ וְהָלְכָה מֵאִתּוֹ וְהָיְתָה

will and from she and his man a go lets if ,Saying
be him goes ,wife

לְאִישׁ־אַחֵר הֲיָשׁוּב אֵלֶיהָ עוֹד הֲלוֹא חָנוֹף תֶּחֱנַף הָאָרֶץ

land be Would greatly not ?again her to he will ,another for
defiled return man

2 הַהִיא וְאַתְּ זָנִית רֵעִים רַבִּים וְשׁוֹב אֵלַי נְאֻם־יְהֹוָה: שְׂאִי

Lift .Jehovah says to you yet ,many com- whore But ?that
up ?Me return panions with you

עֵינַיִךְ עַל־שְׁפָיִם וּרְאִי אֵיפֹה לֹא שֻׁגַּלְתְּ עַל־דְּרָכִים יָשַׁבְתְּ

have you the By you have not Where and bare the on your
sat highways ?with lain been ;see ,heights eyes

לָהֶם כַּעֲרָבִי בַּמִּדְבָּר וַתַּחֲנִיפִי אֶרֶץ בִּזְנוּתַיִךְ וּבְרָעָתֵךְ:

your and your with the you And the in an like for
.wickedness fornications land defiled have .wilderness Arab ,them

3 וַיִּמָּנְעוּ רְבִבִים וּמַלְקוֹשׁ לוֹא הָיָה וּמֵצַח אִשָּׁה זוֹנָה הָיָה

there a And has not the and the the are So
was harlot's forehead .been rain late ,showers withheld

4 לָךְ מֵאַנְתְּ הִכָּלֵם: הֲלוֹא מֵעַתָּה קָרָאתי לִי אָבִי אַלּוּף

the My to you Have just not be to you to
of friend ,father ,Me called now .ashamed refused ;you

5 נְעֻרַי אָתָּה: הֲיִנְטֹר לְעוֹלָם אִם־יִשְׁמֹר לָנֶצַח הִנֵּה דִבַּרְתְּ

have you ,Behold the to He will or ,forever He Will You my
spoken ?end (it) guard anger His keep ?(are) youth

these things and you have done (all) the evil things that you could.

[6] Jehovah also said to me in the days of Josiah the king, Have you seen what the apostate Israel has done? She has gone up on every high hill and under every green tree, and has played the harlot there. [7] And after she had done all these (things), I said, She will return to Me! But she did not return. And her treacherous sister Judah saw (it). [8] And I watched — when for all the causes for which backsliding Israel committed adultery, I put her away and gave her a bill of divorce — yet her treacherous sister Judah did not fear, but went and played the harlot, she also. [9] And it came to pass, from the wantonness of her fornication, she defiled the land and committed adultery with stones and with pieces of wood. [10] And yet for all this her treacherous sister Judah has not turned to Me with her whole heart, but with falsehood, says Jehovah. [11] And Jehovah said to me, The backsliding Israel has justified herself more than treacherous Judah.

[12] Go and cry these words toward the north, and say, Return, O backsliding Israel, says Jehovah; I will not cause My face to fall on you; for I (am) merciful, says Jehovah; I will not keep (anger) forever. [13] Only acknowledge your iniquity, that you have rebelled against Jehovah your God and have scattered your ways to the strangers under every green tree. And you have not obeyed My voice, says Jehovah. [14] Return, O apostate sons, says Jehovah; for I am lord over you. And I

6 וַתַּעֲשִׂי הָרָעוֹת וַתּוּכָל׃ וַיֹּאמֶר יְהוָה אֵלַי בִּימֵי
the in to Jehovah Now you that the (all) you and
of days me said .could things evil done have

יֹאשִׁיָּהוּ הַמֶּלֶךְ הֲרָאִיתָ אֲשֶׁר עָשְׂתָה מְשֻׁבָה יִשְׂרָאֵל
?Israel the done has what you Have ,king the Josiah
apostate seen

הֹלְכָה הִיא עַל־כָּל־הַר גָּבֹהַּ וְאֶל־תַּחַת כָּל־עֵץ רַעֲנָן וַתִּזְנִי־
for- and ,green tree every under and high hill every on She went
nicated up

7 שָׁם׃ וָאֹמַר אַחֲרֵי עֲשׂוֹתָהּ אֶת־כָּל־אֵלֶּה אֵלַי תָּשׁוּב וְלֹא־
but will she to these all has she After I And .there
not ;return Me ,(things) done ,said

8 שָׁבָה וַתִּרְאֶה בָּגוֹדָה אֲחוֹתָהּ יְהוּדָה׃ וָאֵרֶא כִּי עַל־כָּל־
all for When I And .Judah her treacherous and did she
:saw sister (it) saw ,return

אֹדוֹת אֲשֶׁר נִאֲפָה מְשֻׁבָה יִשְׂרָאֵל שִׁלַּחְתִּיהָ וָאֶתֵּן אֶת־
and sent I ,Israel the committed (for) the
gave away her apostate adultery which causes

סֵפֶר כְּרִיתֻתֶיהָ אֵלֶיהָ וְלֹא יָרְאָה בֹּגֵדָה יְהוּדָה אֲחוֹתָהּ
her Judah treacherous did yet ,her to her writ a
,sister fear not divorce of

9 וַתֵּלֶךְ וַתִּזֶן גַּם־הִיא׃ וְהָיָה מִקֹּל זְנוּתָהּ וַתֶּחֱנַף אֶת־הָאָרֶץ
the she her from it And .she also and she but
land defiled harlotry's folly ,was ,whored went

10 וַתִּנְאַף אֶת־הָאֶבֶן וְאֶת־הָעֵץ׃ וְגַם־בְּכָל־זֹאת לֹא־שָׁבָה אֵלַי
to has not this for And .trees and stones with for- and
Me turned all yet with nicated

בָּגוֹדָה אֲחוֹתָהּ יְהוּדָה בְּכָל־לִבָּהּ כִּי אִם־בְּשֶׁקֶר נְאֻם־
says with but her with Judah her treach-
,falsehood ,heart whole sister erous

11 יְהוָה׃ וַיֹּאמֶר יְהוָה אֵלַי צִדְּקָה נַפְשָׁהּ מְשֻׁבָה
the herself Has ,me to Jehovah And .Jehovah
apostate justified said

12 יִשְׂרָאֵל מִבֹּגֵדָה יְהוּדָה׃ הָלֹךְ וְקָרָאתָ אֶת־הַדְּבָרִים הָאֵלֶּה
these words cry and Go .Judah than more Israel
treacherous

צָפוֹנָה וְאָמַרְתָּ שׁוּבָה מְשֻׁבָה יִשְׂרָאֵל נְאֻם־יְהוָה לוֹא־אַפִּיל
will I not ;Jehovah says ,Israel O ,Return ,say and north-
fall make apostate ward

13 פָּנַי בָּכֶם כִּי־חָסִיד אֲנִי נְאֻם־יְהוָה לֹא אֶטּוֹר לְעוֹלָם׃ אַךְ
Only .forever will I not ;Jehovah says I merci- for on My
anger keep (am) full ;you face

דְּעִי עֲוֺנֵךְ כִּי בַּיהוָה אֱלֹהַיִךְ פָּשָׁעַתְּ וַתְּפַזְּרִי אֶת־דְּרָכַיִךְ
your have and have you your against that your know
ways scattered rebelled God Jehovah ,iniquity

לַזָּרִים תַּחַת כָּל־עֵץ רַעֲנָן וּבְקוֹלִי לֹא־שְׁמַעְתֶּם נְאֻם־יְהוָה׃
.Jehovah says have you not My And .green tree every under the to
,obeyed voice strangers

14 שׁוּבוּ בָנִים שׁוֹבָבִים נְאֻם־יְהוָה כִּי אָנֹכִי בָּעַלְתִּי בָכֶם
over lord am I for ;Jehovah says ,apostate sons O Turn
you back

will take you, one from a city, and two from a family, and I will bring you to Zion. [15] And I will give you shepherds according to My heart, who shall feed you (with) knowledge and understanding. [16] And it will come to pass, when you multiply and increase in the land in those days, says Jehovah, they will no longer say, The ark of the covenant of Jehovah! — nor shall it come to the heart, nor shall they remember it; nor shall they miss (it); nor shall it be made any more. [17] At that time they shall call Jerusalem the throne of Jehovah. And all nations shall be gathered to it, to the name of Jehovah, to Jerusalem; and they shall not walk any more after the stubbornness of their evil heart. [18] In those days the house of Judah shall walk with the house of Israel, and they shall come together out of the land of the north to the land that I have given for an inheritance to your fathers. [19] But I said, How (gladly) would I put you among the sons, and give you a pleasant land, a beautiful inheritance (among) the multitudes of nations? And I said, You shall call me, My Father, and shall not turn away from Me.

[20] Surely (as) a wife treacherously departs from her lover, so you have dealt treacherously with Me, O house of Israel, says Jehovah. [21] A voice was heard on the high places, weeping, supplications of the sons of Israel, for they have perverted their way; they have forgotten Jehovah their God. [22] Return, O backsliding sons; I will heal your backslidings! Behold, we come to You; for You (are) Jehovah our God! [23] Truly, for delusion (comes) from the high hills, the tumult on the mountains. Truly in Jehovah our God (is) the salvation of

וְלָקַחְתִּי אֶתְכֶם אֶחָד מֵעִיר וּשְׁנַיִם מִמִּשְׁפָּחָה וְהֵבֵאתִי
I and bring will | a from ,family | two and | a from city | one | ,you | I And take will

אֶתְכֶם צִיּוֹן׃ וְנָתַתִּי לָכֶם רֹעִים כְּלִבִּי וְרָעוּ אֶתְכֶם דֵּעָה 15
(with) knowledge | you | they and feed will | My as ,heart | shepherds | you | I And give will | to .Zion | you

וְהַשְׂכֵּיל׃ וְהָיָה כִּי תִרְבּוּ וּפְרִיתֶם בָּאָרֶץ בַּיָּמִים הָהֵמָּה 16
,those | days in | the in land | are and fruitful | you multiply | when | it And be will | under- and .standing

נְאֻם־יְהוָה לֹא־יֹאמְרוּ עוֹד אֲרוֹן בְּרִית יְהוָה וְלֹא יַעֲלֶה עַל־
to | it will come | and not | ,Jehovah | cove- of nant | the of ark | The | ,still | they say will | not | ,Jehovah says

לֵב וְלֹא יִזְכְּרוּ־בוֹ וְלֹא יִפְקֹדוּ וְלֹא יֵעָשֶׂה עוֹד׃ בָּעֵת הַהִיא 17
that | At time | .again | it will made be | nor | miss (it) | nor | ;it they will remember | nor | the heart

יִקְרְאוּ לִירוּשָׁלַם כִּסֵּא יְהוָה וְנִקְווּ אֵלֶיהָ כָל־הַגּוֹיִם לְשֵׁם
the to of name | ,nations | all | it to | be will And gathered | Jeho- .vah of | the throne | Jerusalem | they call will

יְהוָה לִירוּשָׁלָם וְלֹא־יֵלְכוּ עוֹד אַחֲרֵי שְׁרִרוּת לִבָּם הָרָע׃
.evil | their heart | stub- of bornness | the | after | any more | shall they walk | and not | to ;Jerusalem | ,Jehovah

בַּיָּמִים הָהֵמָּה יֵלְכוּ בֵית־יְהוּדָה עַל־בֵּית יִשְׂרָאֵל וְיָבֹאוּ 18
they and come will | ,Israel | the of house | with | Judah | the of house | shall walk | those | days In

יַחְדָּו מֵאֶרֶץ צָפוֹן עַל־הָאָרֶץ אֲשֶׁר הִנְחַלְתִּי אֶת־
a as to heritage | gave I | that | the land | to | the north | the from of land | to- gether

אֲבוֹתֵיכֶם׃ וְאָנֹכִי אָמַרְתִּי אֵיךְ אֲשִׁיתֵךְ בַּבָּנִים וְאֶתֶּן־לָךְ 19
you | and give | among sons (My) | would I you set | How (gladly) | ,said | I Then | your .fathers

אֶרֶץ חֶמְדָּה נַחֲלַת צְבִי צִבְאוֹת גּוֹיִם וָאֹמַר אָבִי תִּקְרְאוּ
shall You call | My Father | I And ,said | !nations of hosts the | (among) | beautiful | a inheritance | ,pleasant | a land

לִי וּמֵאַחֲרַי לֹא תָשׁוּבוּ׃ אָכֵן בָּגְדָה אִשָּׁה מֵרֵעָהּ כֵּן בְּגַדְתֶּם 20
have you betrayed | so | her from ,companion | a wife | treacherously departs | Surely (as) | turn .away | not | from and Me following | ,Me

בִּי בֵּית יִשְׂרָאֵל נְאֻם־יְהוָה׃ קוֹל עַל־שְׁפָיִים נִשְׁמָע בְּכִי 21
weep- ,ing | was ,heard | bare the heights | on | A voice | .Jehovah | says | ,Israel | O of house | ,Me

תַּחֲנוּנֵי בְּנֵי יִשְׂרָאֵל כִּי הֶעֱווּ אֶת־דַּרְכָּם שָׁכְחוּ אֶת־יְהוָה
Jehovah | have they forgotten | their ,way | have they perverted | for | ,Israel | the of sons | pleadings of

אֱלֹהֵיהֶם׃ שׁוּבוּ בָּנִים שׁוֹבָבִים אֶרְפָּה מְשׁוּבֹתֵיכֶם הִנְנוּ 22
,Behold we | your .apostasies | will I heal | ,apostate | O sons | Return | their .God

אָתָנוּ לָךְ כִּי אַתָּה יְהוָה אֱלֹהֵינוּ׃ אָכֵן לַשֶּׁקֶר מִגְּבָעוֹת
from (comes) ,hills the | for delusion | ,Truly | !God our | Jehovah | You (are) | for | to ;You | come

הָמוֹן הָרִים אָכֵן בַּיהוָה אֱלֹהֵינוּ תְּשׁוּעַת יִשְׂרָאֵל׃ 23
.Israel | the (is) of salvation | God our | in Jehovah | truly | the (on) ;mountains | tumult

Israel. [24] For the shameful thing has eaten up the labor of our fathers from our youth, their flocks and their herds, their sons and their daughters. [25] We lie down in our shame, and our confusion covers us; for we have sinned against Jehovah our God, we and our fathers, from our youth even to this day. And we have not obeyed the voice of Jehovah our God.

24 וְהַבֹּשֶׁת אָכְלָה אֶת־יְגִיעַ אֲבוֹתֵינוּ מִנְּעוּרֵינוּ אֶת־צֹאנָם

their our from our the has the But
flocks ,youth fathers of labor devoured idol

25 וְאֶת־בְּקָרָם אֶת־בְּנֵיהֶם וְאֶת־בְּנוֹתֵיהֶם׃ נִשְׁכְּבָה בְּבָשְׁתֵּנוּ

our in us Let their and their their and
,shame down lie .daughters sons ,herds

וּתְכַסֵּנוּ כְּלִמָּתֵנוּ כִּי לַיהוָה אֱלֹהֵינוּ חָטָאנוּ אֲנַחְנוּ

we have we God our against for our let and
,sinned Jehovah ,disgrace us cover

וַאֲבוֹתֵינוּ מִנְּעוּרֵינוּ וְעַד־הַיּוֹם הַזֶּה וְלֹא שָׁמַעְנוּ בְּקוֹל

the have we And .this day even our from our and
of voice obeyed not to youth ,fathers

יְהוָה אֱלֹהֵינוּ׃

our Jehovah
.God

CAP. IV. ד

CHAPTER 4

[1] If you will return, O Israel, says Jehovah, return to Me. And if you will put away your hateful idols out of My face, then you shall not waver. [2] And you shall swear, (as) Jehovah lives, in truth, in justice and in righteousness; and the nations shall bless themselves in Him, and in Him they shall glory.

[3] For thus says Jehovah to the man of Judah and to Jerusalem, Break up your fallow ground, and do not sow to the thorns. [4] Circumcise yourselves to Jehovah, and take away the foreskin of your heart, O men of Judah and inhabitants of Jerusalem; lest My fury goes forth like fire and burns so that none can put it out; because of the evil of your doings. [5] Declare in Judah, and sound out in Jerusalem; and say, Blow the ram's horn in the land. Cry aloud and say, Assemble yourselves and go into the fortified cities. [6] Lift up a banner toward Zion; flee for safety and do not wait; for I will bring evil from the north, and a great ruin. [7] The lion has come up from his thicket, and a destroyer of nations has set

1 אִם־תָּשׁוּב יִשְׂרָאֵל ׀ נְאֻם־יְהוָה אֵלַי תָּשׁוּב וְאִם־תָּסִיר

will you And .return to ,Jehovah says ,Israel O will you If
remove if Me ,return

2 שִׁקּוּצֶיךָ מִפָּנַי וְלֹא תָנוּד׃ וְנִשְׁבַּעְתָּ חַי־יְהוָה בֶּאֱמֶת

,truth in ,Jehovah (As) you and will and My from hate- your
lives ,swear will ,waver not ,face idols ful

בְּמִשְׁפָּט וּבִצְדָקָה וְהִתְבָּרְכוּ בוֹ גּוֹיִם וּבוֹ יִתְהַלָּלוּ׃

will they in and the in bless will then in and ,justice in
.glory Him ,nations Him themselves ,righteousness

3 כִּי־כֹה ׀ אָמַר יְהוָה לְאִישׁ יְהוּדָה וְלִירוּשָׁלִַם נִירוּ לָכֶם

your Break to and Judah the to Jehovah says thus For
up ,Jerusalem of man

4 נִיר וְאַל־תִּזְרְעוּ אֶל־קֹצִים׃ הִמֹּלוּ לַיהוָה וְהָסִרוּ עָרְלוֹת

fore- the and to Circumcise the to do and fallow
of skin remove ,Jehovah yourselves .thorns sow not ,ground

לְבַבְכֶם אִישׁ יְהוּדָה וְיֹשְׁבֵי יְרוּשָׁלִַם פֶּן־תֵּצֵא כָאֵשׁ

like goes lest ;Jerusalem inhab- and Judah men O your
fire forth of itants of ,heart

5 חֲמָתִי וּבָעֲרָה וְאֵין מְכַבֶּה מִפְּנֵי רֹעַ מַעַלְלֵיכֶם׃ הַגִּידוּ

Declare your the because can that so and My
.doings of evil of ,(it) quench none ,burn wrath

בִּיהוּדָה וּבִירוּשָׁלִַם הַשְׁמִיעוּ וְאִמְרוּ וְתִקְעוּ שׁוֹפָר בָּאָרֶץ

the in ram's the Blow ,say and ,proclaim in and ,Judah in
.land horn Jerusalem

קִרְאוּ מַלְאוּ וְאִמְרוּ הֵאָסְפוּ וְנָבוֹאָה אֶל־עָרֵי הַמִּבְצָר׃

.fortification cities into let and Assemble ,say and aloud Cry
of go us yourselves

6 שְׂאוּ־נֵס צִיּוֹנָה הָעִיזוּ אַל־תַּעֲמֹדוּ כִּי רָעָה אָנֹכִי מֵבִיא

will I evil for do not be toward a lift
bring ;stand ;strong ,Zion banner up

7 מִצָּפוֹן וְשֶׁבֶר גָּדוֹל׃ עָלָה אַרְיֵה מִסֻּבְּכוֹ וּמַשְׁחִית גּוֹיִם

nations a and his from The has .great a even the from
of destroyer ,thicket lion up come smashing ,north

out. He has left his place to make your land a waste. Your cities will fall into ruins without inhabitant. [8] Clothe yourselves with sackcloth for this, wail and howl; for the fierce anger of Jehovah has not turned back from us. [9] And it will be on that day, says Jehovah, the king's heart and the heart of the princes shall fail. And the priests shall be amazed, and the prophets shall be astounded.

[10] Then I said, Ah, Lord Jehovah! Surely You have greatly deceived this people and Jerusalem, saying, You shall have peace; but the sword reaches to the soul. [11] At that time it shall be said to this people and to Jerusalem, A hot wind from the high places in the desert toward the daughter of My people, not to sift nor to cleanse. [12] A wind more full than these shall come for Me. Now also I will utter judgments against them. [13] Behold, he shall come up like clouds, and his chariots like a tempest. His horses are swifter than eagles. Woe to us, for we are plundered! [14] O Jerusalem, wash your heart from wickedness so that you may be saved. How long will your vain thoughts lodge within you? [15] For a voice declares from Dan and proclaims evil from Mount Ephraim. [16] Tell it to the nations: behold, proclaim against Jerusalem. Besiegers are coming from a distant land and will set against the cities of Judah. [17] Like keepers of a field, they are against her all around, because she has rebelled against Me, says Jehovah. [18] Your way and your doings have done these things to you; this is your wickedness, because it is bitter, because it reaches to your heart.

נָסַע יָצָא מִמְּקֹמוֹ לָשׂוּם אַרְצֵךְ לְשַׁמָּה עָרַיִךְ תִּצֶּינָה
in fall will Your .waste a your make to his from has he has
ruins cities land place gone ;out set

8 מֵאֵין יוֹשֵׁב׃ עַל־זֹאת חִגְרוּ שַׂקִּים סִפְדוּ וְהֵילִילוּ כִּי לֹא
not for and wail sack- put this For inhabi- with-
;howl ;cloth on .tant out

9 שָׁב חֲרוֹן אַף־יְהוָה מִמֶּנּוּ׃ וְהָיָה בַיּוֹם־הַהוּא נְאֻם־יְהוָה
,Jehovah says ,that day on it And from Jehovah's anger the has
be will .us of glow turned

יֹאבַד לֵב־הַמֶּלֶךְ וְלֵב הַשָּׂרִים וְנָשַׁמּוּ הַכֹּהֲנִים וְהַנְּבִאִים
the and the be will and the the and the heart shall
prophets ;priests stunned ,officials of heart ,king's fail

10 יִתְמָהוּ׃ וָאֹמַר אֲהָהּ ׀ אֲדֹנָי יְהוִה אָכֵן הַשֵּׁא הִשֵּׁאתָ לָעָם
people have you utterly Surely !Jehovah Lord ,Ah I Then be will
deceived ,said .astounded

הַזֶּה וְלִירוּשָׁלִַם לֵאמֹר שָׁלוֹם יִהְיֶה לָכֶם וְנָגְעָה חֶרֶב עַד־
to the but to shall Peace ;saying and this
sword touches ,you be ,Jerusalem

11 הַנָּפֶשׁ׃ בָּעֵת הַהִיא יֵאָמֵר לָעָם־הַזֶּה וְלִירוּשָׁלִַם רוּחַ צַח
hot A to and this to will it that At the
(from) wind ,Jerusalem people said be time .soul

שְׁפָיִם בַּמִּדְבָּר דֶּרֶךְ בַּת־עַמִּי לוֹא לִזְרוֹת וְלוֹא לְהָבַר׃
to nor to not My the toward the in bare the
!cleanse winnow —people of daughter desert heights

12 רוּחַ מָלֵא מֵאֵלֶּה יָבוֹא לִי עַתָּה גַּם־אֲנִי אֲדַבֵּר מִשְׁפָּטִים
judgments will I also Now for shall than more A
utter .Me come these full wind

13 אוֹתָם׃ הִנֵּה ׀ כַּעֲנָנִים יַעֲלֶה וְכַסּוּפָה מַרְכְּבוֹתָיו קַלּוּ
are his a like and will he like ,Behold against
swifter ;chariots windstorm ,up come clouds .them

14 מִנְּשָׁרִים סוּסָיו אוֹי לָנוּ כִּי שֻׁדָּדְנוּ׃ כַּבְּסִי מֵרָעָה לִבֵּךְ
your from Wash are we for to Woe his than
,heart wickedness !devastated ,us .horses eagles

יְרוּשָׁלִַם לְמַעַן תִּוָּשֵׁעִי עַד־מָתַי תָּלִין בְּקִרְבֵּךְ מַחְשְׁבוֹת
thoughts within will long How may you that so O
of you lodge .saved be ,Jerusalem

15 אוֹנֵךְ׃ כִּי קוֹל מַגִּיד מִדָּן וּמַשְׁמִיעַ אָוֶן מֵהַר אֶפְרָיִם׃
.Ephraim from wicked- and from declares a For your
Mount ness proclaims ,Dan voice ?vanity

16 הַזְכִּירוּ לַגּוֹיִם הִנֵּה הַשְׁמִיעוּ עַל־יְרוּשָׁלִַם נֹצְרִים בָּאִים
are beseigers ,Jerusalem against proclaim ,Behold the to Tell
coming :nations (it)

17 מֵאֶרֶץ הַמֶּרְחָק וַיִּתְּנוּ עַל־עָרֵי יְהוּדָה קוֹלָם׃ כְּשֹׁמְרֵי שָׂדַי
a watch- Like their Judah the against and ,distant from
field of men .voice of cities set will land a

18 הָיוּ עָלֶיהָ מִסָּבִיב כִּי־אֹתִי מָרָתָה נְאֻם־יְהוָה׃ דַּרְכֵּךְ
Your .Jehovah says has she against because all against they
way .rebelled Me ,around her are

וּמַעֲלָלַיִךְ עָשׂוֹ אֵלֶּה לָךְ זֹאת רָעָתֵךְ כִּי מָר כִּי נָגַע עַד־
to it for (is it) for your this to these have your and
reaches ,bitter evil (is) ;you things done doings

19 לִבֵּךְ׃ מֵעַי ׀ מֵעַי אָחוּלָה קִירוֹת לִבִּי הֹמֶה־לִּי
within is My walls O writhe I My My your
me restless !heart of pain in !bowels !bowels .heart

לִבִּי לֹא אַחֲרִשׁ כִּי קוֹל שׁוֹפָר שָׁמַעַתְּ נַפְשִׁי תְּרוּעַת
the my O have I ram's- the the for can I not My
of alarm ,soul .heard horn of sound ,silent be .heart

20 מִלְחָמָה׃ שֶׁבֶר עַל־שֶׁבֶר נִקְרָא כִּי־שֻׁדְּדָה כָּל־הָאָרֶץ
the whole is for has ruin upon Ruin !war
;land devastated ,happened

21 פִּתְאֹם שֻׁדְּדוּ אֹהָלַי רֶגַע יְרִיעֹתָי׃ עַד־מָתַי אֶרְאֶה־נֵּס
the I must long How my a (in) my are suddenly
banner see .curtains moment ,tents devastated

22 אֶשְׁמְעָה קוֹל שׁוֹפָר׃ כִּי ׀ אֱוִיל עַמִּי אוֹתִי לֹא יָדָעוּ
they not Me My (are) For ram's the the (and)
know .people foolish ?horn of sound hear

בָּנִים סְכָלִים הֵמָּה וְלֹא נְבוֹנִים הֵמָּה חֲכָמִים הֵמָּה לְהָרַע
do to they wise ;they have and they stupid children
,evil (are) understanding not ,(are)

23 וּלְהֵיטִיב לֹא יָדָעוּ׃ רָאִיתִי אֶת־הָאָרֶץ וְהִנֵּה־תֹהוּ וָבֹהוּ
and (was it) and the looked I do they not do to but
;void formless ,lo ,earth on .know good

24 וְאֶל־הַשָּׁמַיִם וְאֵין אוֹרָם׃ רָאִיתִי הֶהָרִים וְהִנֵּה רֹעֲשִׁים
they and the looked I their (gave) and the and
,quaked ,lo ,mountains on light none ,heavens to

25 וְכָל־הַגְּבָעוֹת הִתְקַלְקָלוּ׃ רָאִיתִי וְהִנֵּה אֵין הָאָדָם וְכָל־
and ,man there and ,looked I were the and
all no was ,lo .shaken hills all

26 עוֹף הַשָּׁמַיִם נָדָדוּ׃ רָאִיתִי וְהִנֵּה הַכַּרְמֶל הַמִּדְבָּר וְכָל־
and a (was) fruitful the and ,looked I had the the
all ,wilderness land ,lo .fled skies of birds

27 עָרָיו נִתְּצוּ מִפְּנֵי יְהוָה מִפְּנֵי חֲרוֹן אַפּוֹ׃ כִּי־כֹה אָמַר
has thus For His the before Jehovah the at were its
said .anger of glow of presence torn cities

יְהוָה שְׁמָמָה תִהְיֶה כָּל־הָאָרֶץ וְכָלָה לֹא אֶעֱשֶׂה׃
will I not a but the whole shall a ,Jehovah
.make end full ,land be desolation

28 עַל־זֹאת תֶּאֱבַל הָאָרֶץ וְקָדְרוּ הַשָּׁמַיִם מִמָּעַל עַל כִּי־
because ;above the grow and the shall this For
heavens dark ,earth mourn

29 דִּבַּרְתִּי זַמֹּתִי וְלֹא נִחַמְתִּי וְלֹא־אָשׁוּב מִמֶּנָּה׃ מִקּוֹל
the From from I will nor will I and have I have I
of sound .it back turn ,repent not ,purposed ,spoken

פָּרָשׁ וְרֹמֵה קֶשֶׁת בֹּרַחַת כָּל־הָעִיר בָּאוּ בֶּעָבִים וּבַכֵּפִים
among and into They .city every shall the the and horse-
rocks the ,thickets go shall flee bow of shooters men

30 עָלוּ כָּל־הָעִיר עֲזוּבָה וְאֵין־יוֹשֵׁב בָּהֵן אִישׁ׃ וְאַתְּ שָׁדוּד
desolate O And a in shall and is city the All climb
,one you .man them live not ,abandoned .up

מַה־תַּעֲשִׂי כִּי־תִלְבְּשִׁי שָׁנִי כִּי־תַעְדִּי עֲדִי־זָהָב כִּי־תִקְרְעִי
you though gold orna- you though crim- you Though will what
enlarge of ments on put ,son with dress ?do you

[19] My bowels, my bowels! I convulse in pain, O walls of my heart! My heart is restless within me. I cannot be silent, for I have heard. O my soul, the sound of the ram's horn, the alarm of war! [20] Ruin upon ruin has happened; for the whole land is laid waste; suddenly my tents are destroyed; my tents (in) a moment. [21] How long must I see the banner (and) hear the sound of the ram's horn? [22] For My people (are) foolish. They do not know Me. They (are) stupid children and they have no understanding. They (are) wise to do evil, but they do not know to do good. [23] I looked on the earth, and, lo, (it was) without form and void; and to the heavens, and they (had) no light. [24] I looked on the mountains, and, lo, they quaked. And all the hills were shaken. [25] I looked, and, lo, there was no man, and all the birds of the skies had fled. [26] I looked and, lo, the fruitful place (was) a wilderness, and all its cities were broken down at the presence of Jehovah, before His glowing anger. [27] For so Jehovah has said, The whole land shall be a desolation, yet I will not make a full end. [28] The earth shall mourn for this, and the heavens above shall mourn for this, and the heavens above shall grow black; because I have spoken, I have purposed and I will not repent; nor will I turn back from it. [29] Every city shall flee from the noise of the horsemen and bowmen. They shall go into thickets and climb up in the rocks. Every city shall be forsaken, and not a man shall live in them. [30] And you, O stripped one, what will you do? Though you clothe yourself with crimson, though you adorn yourself with ornaments of gold, though you make your eyes

large with paint, you adorn yourself in vain;lovers despise you; they will seek your life. [31] For I have heard a voice like a woman in labor, the anguish as one bearing her first child, the voice of Zion's daughter gasping, and spreading her hands, (saying), Woe (is) to me now; for my soul faints because of murderers.

CHAPTER 5

[1] Roam around in Jerusalem's streets, and see now, and know,and seek in her plazas, if you can find a man, if there is one who does justice, who seeks truth; and I will pardon her. [2] And though they say, (As) Jehovah lives, surely they swear falsely. [3] O Jehovah, are not Your eyes for the truth? You struck them, but they felt no pain; you consumed them; they refused to take correction; they made their faces harder than rock; they have refused to return. Then I said, Surely they (are) poor, they are foolish, for they know not the way of Jehovah, the ordinance of their God. [5] I will go up for myself to the great men and will speak to them. For they have known the way of Jehovah, the judgment of their God. Surely these have joined in breaking the yoke, they have torn off the bonds! [6] Therefore a lion out of the forest shall smite them, a wolf of the deserts shall destroy them, a leopard is watching over their cities. Everyone who goes out from them shall be torn in pieces, because their transgressions are many (and) their backslidings are multiplied.

[7] How shall I pardon you for this? Your sons have forsaken Me and have sworn by (those who are) no gods. When I had fed them to the full, they then committed adultery and gathered themselves by troops in a harlot's house. [8] They were (like) lusty, well-fed stallions in the

בַּפּוּךְ עֵינַיִךְ לַשָּׁוְא תִּתְיַפִּי מָאֲסוּ־בָךְ עֹגְבִים נַפְשֵׁךְ יְבַקֵּשׁוּ׃

will they your ,lovers you. despise adorn you in your with
.seek life ;yourself vain ,eyes paint

31 כִּי קוֹל כְּחוֹלָה שָׁמַעְתִּי צָרָה כְּמַבְכִּירָה קוֹל בַּת־צִיּוֹן

Zion the voice the bearing one as the have I woman a like a For
of daughter of ,child first her anguish ,heard labor in voice

תִּתְיַפֵּחַ תְּפָרֵשׂ כַּפֶּיהָ אוֹי־נָא לִי כִּי־עָיְפָה נַפְשִׁי לְהֹרְגִים׃

of because my faints for to now Woe her and ,gasping
.murderers soul ,me (is) ,hands spreading

CAP. V ה

CHAPTER 5

1 שׁוֹטְטוּ בְּחוּצוֹת יְרוּשָׁלַםִ וּרְאוּ־נָא וּדְעוּ וּבַקְשׁוּ בִרְחוֹבוֹתֶיהָ

open her in and and ,now and ,Jerusalem the in Roam
squares seek ,know see of streets around

אִם־תִּמְצְאוּ אִישׁ אִם־יֵשׁ עֹשֶׂה מִשְׁפָּט מְבַקֵּשׁ אֱמוּנָה

,truth who ,justice who one there if ,man a can you if
seeks does is find

2 וְאֶסְלַח לָהּ׃ וְאִם חַי־יְהוָה יֹאמֵרוּ לָכֵן לַשֶּׁקֶר יִשָּׁבֵעוּ׃

they falsely surely they Jehovah (as) And .her will I and
.swear ,say lives though pardon

3 יְהוָה עֵינֶיךָ הֲלוֹא לֶאֱמוּנָה הִכִּיתָה אֹתָם וְלֹא־חָלוּ כִּלִּיתָם

con- you felt they but them You faith- for (they) are Your O
;them sumed .pain not struck ?fulness not ;eyes ,Jehovah

4 מֵאֲנוּ קַחַת מוּסָר חִזְּקוּ פְנֵיהֶם מִסֶּלַע מֵאֲנוּ לָשׁוּב׃ וַאֲנִי

Then to have they than their made they cor- take to they
I .return refused ;rock faces harder ;rection refused

אָמַרְתִּי אַךְ דַּלִּים הֵם נוֹאֲלוּ כִּי לֹא יָדְעוּ דֶּרֶךְ יְהוָה

,Jehovah the do they not for are they they poor Surely ,said
of way know ,foolish (are)

5 מִשְׁפַּט אֱלֹהֵיהֶם׃ אֵלְכָה־לִּי אֶל־הַגְּדֹלִים וַאֲדַבְּרָה אוֹתָם

them will and great the to for will I their ordi- the
to speak men myself up go .God of nance

כִּי הֵמָּה יָדְעוּ דֶּרֶךְ יְהוָה מִשְׁפַּט אֱלֹהֵיהֶם אַךְ הֵמָּה יַחְדָּו

to- they Surely their ordi- the Jehovah the have they For
gether .God of nance of way known

6 שָׁבְרוּ עֹל נִתְּקוּ מוֹסֵרוֹת׃ עַל־כֵּן הִכָּם אַרְיֵה מִיַּעַר זְאֵב

wolf a from .lion a will Therefore the have they the have
of forest the them smite !bonds burst ;yoke broken

עֲרָבוֹת יְשָׁדְדֵם נָמֵר שֹׁקֵד עַל־עָרֵיהֶם כָּל־הַיּוֹצֵא מֵהֵנָּה

from goes who Every their over is a destroy will the
them out one .cities watching leopard ,them deserts

7 יִטָּרֵף כִּי רַבּוּ פִּשְׁעֵיהֶם עָצְמוּ מְשֻׁבוֹתֵיהֶם׃ אֵי לָזֹאת

for Why their are their are be- be will
this .apostasies numerous ;apostasies many cause torn

אֶסְלוֹחַ־לָךְ בָּנַיִךְ עֲזָבוּנִי וַיִּשָּׁבְעוּ בְּלֹא אֱלֹהִים וָאַשְׂבִּעַ

I When .gods -non by have and for- have Your ?You should I
satiated sworn Me saken sons pardon

8 אוֹתָם וַיִּנְאָפוּ וּבֵית זוֹנָה יִתְגֹּדָדוּ׃ סוּסִים מְיֻזָּנִים מַשְׁכִּים

well-fed lusty stallions they a and they then ;them
.to thronged harlot's house ;adultery did

morning, every one neighing after his neighbor's wife. [9] Shall I not judge for these (things), says Jehovah? And shall not My soul be avenged on such a nation as this?

[10] Go up on her vine-rows and destroy; but do not make a full end. Take away her branches, for they (are) not Jehovah's. [11] For the house of Israel and the house of Judah have dealt very deceitfully against Me, says Jehovah. [12] They have lied against Jehovah and said, (It is) not He; and, No evil shall come on us; and, We shall not see sword or famine. [13] And the prophets shall become wind, and the word (is) not in them; so it shall be done to them. [14] Therefore thus says Jehovah God of hosts: Because you spoke this word, behold, I will make My words in your mouth fire, and this people wood, and it shall consume them. [15] Lo, I will bring a nation on you from far away, O house of Israel, says Jehovah. It (is) a lasting nation, it (is) an ancient nation, a nation whose language you do not know, nor understand what they say. [16] Their quiver (is) as an open grave; they (are) all mighty men. [17] And they shall eat up your sons and your daughters; they shall eat up your flocks and your herds; they shall eat up your vines and your fig-trees. One shall beat down your fortified cities with the sword, those in which you trust. [18] Yet even in those days, says Jehovah, I will not make a full end with you.

[19] And it will be, when you shall say, Why does Jehovah our God do all these (things) to us? Then you shall answer them. Just

9 הָיוּ אִישׁ אֶל־אֵשֶׁת רֵעֵהוּ יִצְהָלוּ׃ הַעַל־אֵלֶּה לוֹא־אֶפְקֹד
I shall not these For .neighing his wife to each they
,punish things neighbor's ;were

נְאֻם־יְהוָה וְאִם־בְּגוֹי אֲשֶׁר כָּזֶה לֹא תִתְנַקֵּם נַפְשִׁי׃
My take will not like that a on And ?Jehovah says
?soul vengeance ,this (is) nation

10 עֲלוּ בְשָׁרוֹתֶיהָ וְשַׁחֵתוּ וְכָלָה אַל־תַּעֲשׂוּ הָסִירוּ נְטִישׁוֹתֶיהָ
her take do not full but and her against Go
,branches away ;make destruction ;destroy vine-rows up

11 כִּי לוֹא לַיהוָה הֵמָּה׃ כִּי בָּגוֹד בָּגְדוּ בִּי בֵּית יִשְׂרָאֵל
Israel the with have they very For they Jehovah's not for
of house me devious been .(are)

12 וּבֵית יְהוּדָה נְאֻם־יְהוָה׃ כִּחֲשׁוּ בַּיהוָה וַיֹּאמְרוּ לוֹא־הוּא
He not ,said and against have They .Jehovah says ,Judah the and
(is) Jehovah lied of house

13 וְלֹא־תָבוֹא עָלֵינוּ רָעָה וְחֶרֶב וְרָעָב לוֹא נִרְאֶה׃ וְהַנְּבִיאִים
the And will we not and and ;evil upon will and
prophets .see famine sword us come not

14 יִהְיוּ לְרוּחַ וְהַדִּבֵּר אֵין בָּהֶם כֹּה יֵעָשֶׂה לָהֶם׃ לָכֵן
Therefore to will it thus in is the and ,wind will
.them done be ;them not word become

כֹּה־אָמַר יְהוָה אֱלֹהֵי צְבָאוֹת יַעַן דַּבֶּרְכֶם אֶת־הַדָּבָר הַזֶּה
,this word you Because :hosts God Jehovah says thus
spoke of

הִנְנִי נֹתֵן דְּבָרַי בְּפִיךָ לְאֵשׁ וְהָעָם הַזֶּה עֵצִים וַאֲכָלָתַם׃
will it and ,wood ,this and ,fire your in My will ,behold
.them devour people mouth words make

15 הִנְנִי מֵבִיא עֲלֵיכֶם גּוֹי מִמֶּרְחָק בֵּית יִשְׂרָאֵל נְאֻם־יְהוָה
.Jehovah says ,Israel O from a you on will ,Lo
of house ,afar nation bring I

גּוֹי ׀ אֵיתָן הוּא גּוֹי מֵעוֹלָם הוּא גּוֹי לֹא־תֵדַע לְשֹׁנוֹ וְלֹא
nor whose do you not a ,(is) it of from a (is) it enduring An
,language know nation old ,nation nation

16 תִשְׁמַע מַה־יְדַבֵּר׃ אַשְׁפָּתוֹ כְּקֶבֶר פָּתוּחַ כֻּלָּם גִּבּוֹרִים׃
mighty (are) of all an like (is) Their they what under-
.men them ;open grave quiver .say stand

17 וְאָכַל קְצִירְךָ וְלַחְמֶךָ יֹאכְלוּ בָּנֶיךָ וּבְנוֹתֶיךָ יֹאכַל צֹאנְךָ
your will they your and your will they your and your they And
flocks devour ;daughters sons devour ;food harvest devour will

וּבְקָרֶךָ יֹאכַל גַּפְנְךָ וּתְאֵנָתֶךָ יְרֹשֵׁשׁ עָרֵי מִבְצָרֶיךָ אֲשֶׁר
which your cities will one your and your will they your and
fortified down beat ;trees fig vines devour ,herds

18 אַתָּה בֹּטֵחַ בָּהֵנָּה בֶּחָרֶב׃ וְגַם בַּיָּמִים הָהֵמָּה נְאֻם־יְהוָה
,Jehovah says ,those days in Yet the with those in trust you
even .sword

19 לֹא־אֶעֱשֶׂה אִתְּכֶם כָּלָה׃ וְהָיָה כִּי תֹאמְרוּ תַּחַת מֶה עָשָׂה
does Why shall you when And com- a you will I not
do ,say ,be will it .end plete make

יְהוָה אֱלֹהֵינוּ לָנוּ אֶת־כָּל־אֵלֶּה וְאָמַרְתָּ אֲלֵיהֶם כַּאֲשֶׁר
as Just ,them to you Then these all us to our Jehovah
say ?(things) God

as you have forsaken Me and served strange gods in your land, so you shall serve strangers in a land (that is) not yours. [20] Declare this in the house of Jacob, and cry it in Judah, saying, [21] Now hear this, O foolish people and without any heart; who have eyes and do not see; who have ears and do not hear: [22] Do you not fear Me? says Jehovah. Will you not tremble from My face, who have placed the sand (for) the boundary for the sea by a never-ending decree, so that it cannot pass it? And though they toss themselves, yet they cannot prevail; though its waves roar, yet they cannot pass over it. [23] But to this people there is a revolting and a rebellious heart; they have turned, and are gone. [24] And they do not say in their heart, Let us now fear Jehovah our God, who gives both the former and the latter rain in its season; He keeps for us the appointed weeks of the harvest.

[25] Your iniquities have turned away these (things), and your sins have withheld good from you. [26] For among My people are found wicked ones; they lie in wait, as he who sets snares; they set a trap; they catch men. [27] Like a cage full of birds, so their houses are full of treachery; therefore they have become great and grown rich. [28] They have become fat, they shine. Yes, they pass over the deeds of the wicked; they do not judge the cause, the cause of the fatherless, that they may prosper; and they do not judge the right of the needy. [29] Shall I not visit for these things? says Jehovah. Shall not My soul be avenged on such a nation as this?

[30] An astounding and horrible thing has happened in the land. [31] The prophets prophesy falsely,

עֲזַבְתֶּם אוֹתִי וַתַּעַבְדוּ אֱלֹהֵי נֵכָר בְּאַרְצְכֶם כֵּן תַּעַבְדוּ
shall you so serve | your in ,land | foreign | gods | and served | Me | have you forsaken

20 זָרִים בְּאֶרֶץ לֹא לָכֶם׃ הַגִּידוּ זֹאת בְּבֵית יַעֲקֹב
,Jacob | the in of house | this | Declare | to .you | not (belonging) | a in land | strangers

21 וְהַשְׁמִיעוּהָ בִיהוּדָה לֵאמֹר׃ שִׁמְעוּ־נָא זֹאת עַם־סָכָל
foolish O people | ,this | now Hear | ,saying | ,Judah in | proclaim it

וְאֵין לֵב עֵינַיִם לָהֶם וְלֹא יִרְאוּ אָזְנַיִם לָהֶם וְלֹא יִשְׁמָעוּ׃
they do .hear | but not | to ,them | ears (are) | they do ;see | but not | to ,them | eyes (are) | ;heart | and without

22 הַאוֹתִי לֹא־תִירָאוּ נְאֻם־יְהוָה אִם מִפָּנַי לֹא תָחִילוּ אֲשֶׁר־
that | you will tremble | not | from face My | Or | .Jehovah | says | you Do ?fear | not | Me

שַׂמְתִּי חוֹל גְּבוּל לַיָּם חָק־עוֹלָם וְלֹא יַעַבְרֶנְהוּ וַיִּתְגָּעֲשׁוּ
they though fall and rise | can it ;it over cross | that so not | eternal an ,decree | the for sea | the (as) boundary | the sand | have I placed

23 וְלֹא יוּכָלוּ וְהָמוּ גַלָּיו וְלֹא יַעַבְרֻנְהוּ׃ וְלָעָם הַזֶּה הָיָה
there is | this | to But people | can they .it over cross | yet not | its waves | Though roar | can they .prevail | yet not

24 לֵב סוֹרֵר וּמוֹרֶה סָרוּ וַיֵּלֵכוּ׃ וְלוֹא־אָמְרוּ בִלְבָבָם נִירָא
us Let fear | their in ,heart | they say do | And not | gone and .away | they turned have | rebel- and ;lious | stubborn | a heart

נָא אֶת־יְהוָה אֱלֹהֵינוּ הַנֹּתֵן גֶּשֶׁם יוֹרֶה וּמַלְקוֹשׁ בְּעִתּוֹ
its in ;time | and latter | both former | the rain | who gives | our ,God | Jehovah | now

25 שְׁבֻעֹת חֻקּוֹת קָצִיר יִשְׁמָר־לָנוּ׃ עֲוֹנוֹתֵיכֶם הִטּוּ־אֵלֶּה
these ,(things) | have away turned | iniquities Your | for .us | He keeps | the harvest | the of appointed | weeks

26 וְחַטֹּאותֵיכֶם מָנְעוּ הַטּוֹב מִכֶּם׃ כִּי־נִמְצְאוּ בְעַמִּי רְשָׁעִים
wicked ;ones | My among people | are found | For | from .you | good | have withheld | your and sins

יָשׁוּר כְּשַׁךְ יְקוּשִׁים הִצִּיבוּ מַשְׁחִית אֲנָשִׁים יִלְכֹּדוּ׃
they .catch | men | ;trap a | set they | ;fowlers | the like of crouching | lie they ,wait in

27 כִּכְלוּב מָלֵא עוֹף כֵּן בָּתֵּיהֶם מְלֵאִים מִרְמָה עַל־כֵּן גָּדְלוּ
have they great become | there- fore | ;treachery | filled are with | their houses | so ,birds | full of | a Like birdcage

28 וַיַּעֲשִׁירוּ׃ שָׁמְנוּ עָשְׁתוּ גַּם עָבְרוּ דִבְרֵי־רָע דִּין לֹא־דָנוּ
they not ,plead do | the cause | the ;wicked | the of deeds | pass they over | Also | they .shine | have they ,fat become | grown and ,rich

29 דִּין יָתוֹם וְיַצְלִיחוּ וּמִשְׁפַּט אֶבְיוֹנִים לֹא שָׁפָטוּ׃ הַעַל־
For | do they .vindicate | not | poor the | the and of right | they that ;prosper may | or- ,phan | the of cause

אֵלֶּה לֹא־אֶפְקֹד נְאֻם־יְהוָה אִם בְּגוֹי אֲשֶׁר־כָּזֶה לֹא תִתְנַקֵּם
be shall avenged | not | like this | that (is) | a on nation | Or | .Jehovah | says | I shall ?punish | not | these things

30 31 נַפְשִׁי׃ שַׁמָּה וְשַׁעֲרוּרָה נִהְיְתָה בָּאָרֶץ׃ הַנְּבִאִים
The prophets | the in .land | has happened | horrible and thing | An appalling | My ?soul

נִבְּאוּ בַשֶּׁקֶר וְהַכֹּהֲנִים יִרְדּוּ עַל־יְדֵיהֶם וְעַמִּי אָהֲבוּ כֵן

.so love (it) My people and ,hands their own according to rule the priests and ,falsely prophesy

וּמַה־תַּעֲשׂוּ לְאַחֲרִיתָהּ׃

the at ?it of end will do they But what

CAP. VI ו

CHAPTER 6

1 הָעִזוּ ׀ בְּנֵי בִנְיָמִן מִקֶּרֶב יְרוּשָׁלִַם וּבִתְקוֹעַ תִּקְעוּ שׁוֹפָר

ram's the horn blow in And Tekoa .Jerusalem the from of midst ,Benjamin O of sons Take ,refuge

וְעַל־בֵּית הַכֶּרֶם שְׂאוּ מַשְׂאֵת כִּי רָעָה נִשְׁקְפָה מִצָּפוֹן

the from ,north looks down evil for ;signal a raise haccerem Beth- and over

2 3 וְשֶׁבֶר גָּדוֹל׃ הַנָּוָה וְהַמְּעֻנָּגָה דָּמִיתִי בַּת־צִיּוֹן׃ אֵלֶיהָ

her To .Zion daugh- of ter the will I ,destroy delicate and one The beautiful .great a even shattering

יָבֹאוּ רֹעִים וְעֶדְרֵיהֶם תָּקְעוּ עָלֶיהָ אֹהָלִים סָבִיב רָעוּ אִישׁ

each man They feed shall all .around tents upon her shall they pitch their with ;flock the shepherds shall come

4 אֶת־יָדוֹ׃ קַדְּשׁוּ עָלֶיהָ מִלְחָמָה קוּמוּ וְנַעֲלֶה בַצָּהֳרָיִם אוֹי

Woe at .noon let and up go us ,arise ;war against her Consecrate his (in) .place

5 לָנוּ כִּי־פָנָה הַיּוֹם כִּי־יִנָּטוּ צִלְלֵי־עָרֶב׃ קוּמוּ וְנַעֲלֶה

let and up go us Arise .evening the of shadows are for out stretched ;day the declines for to ,us

6 בַלַּיְלָה וְנַשְׁחִיתָה אַרְמְנוֹתֶיהָ׃ כִּי כֹה אָמַר יְהוָה

Jehovah of has said thus For .palaces her and destroy by night

צְבָאוֹת כִּרְתוּ עֵצָה וְשִׁפְכוּ עַל־יְרוּשָׁלִַם סֹלְלָה הִיא הָעִיר

the city She (is) siege a ;mound Jerusalem against and cast her trees Cut down ,hosts

7 הָפְקַד כֻּלָּהּ עֹשֶׁק בְּקִרְבָּהּ׃ כְּהָקִיר בּוֹר מֵימֶיהָ כֵּן הֵקֵרָה

keeps she fresh so its ,waters a cistern keeps As fresh her in .midst (is) oppression of all her be to ;punished

רָעָתָהּ חָמָס וָשֹׁד יִשָּׁמַע בָּהּ עַל־פָּנַי תָּמִיד חֳלִי וּמַכָּה׃

and .wounds sickness (are) continually my before face in ;her are heard and Violence destruction her .wickedness

8 הִוָּסְרִי יְרוּשָׁלִַם פֶּן־תֵּקַע נַפְשִׁי מִמֵּךְ פֶּן־אֲשִׂימֵךְ שְׁמָמָה

a desolation make I you lest from ;you My soul be alienated lest O ,Jerusalem Take ,advice

9 אֶרֶץ לוֹא נוֹשָׁבָה׃ כֹּה אָמַר יְהוָה צְבָאוֹת עוֹלֵל

thoroughly ,hosts Jehovah of says Thus .inhabited not a land

יְעוֹלְלוּ כַגֶּפֶן שְׁאֵרִית יִשְׂרָאֵל הָשֵׁב יָדְךָ כְּבוֹצֵר עַל־

over grape a as gatherer your hand bring back ;Israel rem- the of nant a as vine will they glean

10 סַלְסִלּוֹת׃ עַל־מִי אֲדַבְּרָה וְאָעִידָה וְיִשְׁמָעוּ הִנֵּה עֲרֵלָה

un- (is) ,Behold circumcised they that ?hear may give and warning I shall speak whom To the .tendrils

and the priests bear rule by their hands, and my people love (it) so. And what will they do at the end of it?

CHAPTER 6

[1] O sons of Benjamin, take refuge to flee out of the midst of Jerusalem. And blow the ram's horn in Tekoa, and set up a signal over Beth-haccerem; for evil appears out of the north, and great destruction. [2] I will destroy the daughter of Zion, the beautiful and tender one: [3] The shepherds with their flocks shall come to her; they shall pitch tents on her all around. They shall feed each one (in) his place. [4] Consecrate war against her; arise and let us go up at noon. Woe to us! For the day wanes; for the shadows of the evening are stretched out. [5] Arise and let us go up by night, and let us destroy her palaces.

[6] For thus has Jehovah of hosts said, Cut down her trees and cast a mound against Jerusalem! She (is) the city to be visited; all of her (is) oppression in her midst. [7] As a cistern keeps fresh its waters, so she keeps fresh her wickedness. Violence and destruction are heard in her; always before Me (are) grief and wounds. [8] O Jerusalem, take advice, lest my soul be alienated from you; lest I make you a ruin, a land not inhabited.

[9] Thus says Jehovah of hosts, They shall thoroughly glean the remnant of Israel like a vine; bring back your hand as a grape gatherer over the tendrils. [10] To whom shall I speak and give warning that they may hear? Behold, their ear (is) not circumcised and

they cannot listen. Behold, the word of Jehovah is a reproach to them. They have no delight in it. [11] Therefore I am full of the fury of Jehovah; I am weary with holding in. Pour it out on the children in the street, and on the circle of young men together; for even the husband with the wife shall be taken, the elder with fullness of days. [12] And their houses shall be turned to others, fields and wives together; for I will stretch out My hand on the inhabitants of the land, says Jehovah. [13] For everyone from the least of them even to the greatest of them cuts off a profit; and from the prophet even to the priest everyone deals falsely. [14] They have also healed the break of my people slightly, saying, Peace, peace; when there is no peace. [15] Were they ashamed when they had committed idolatry? They were not even at all ashamed, nor did they know to blush. So they shall fall among those who fall. At the time I visit them, they shall be cast down, says Jehovah. [16] Thus says Jehovah, Stand by the ways and see, and ask for the old paths where the good way (is), and walk in it, and you shall find a rest for your souls. But they said, We will not walk. [17] Also I set watchmen over you, (saying), Listen to the sound of the ram's horn. But they said, We will not listen. [18] Therefore hear, O nations, and know, O congregation, that which is (coming) on them. [19] Hear, O earth; behold, I will bring evil on this people, (even) the fruit of their thoughts; because they have not listened to My words, and My law, they also rejected it. [20] To what purpose does there

אָזְנָם וְלֹא יוּכְלוּ לְהַקְשִׁיב הִנֵּה דְבַר־יְהוָה הָיָה לָהֶם
to is Jehovah the ,Behold .listen to are they and their
them of word able not ,ear

11 לְחֶרְפָּה לֹא יַחְפְּצוּ־בוֹ׃ וְאֵת חֲמַת יְהוָה ׀ מָלֵאתִי נִלְאֵיתִי
am I am I Jehovah the Therefore in have they no a
of tired ;full of wrath with .it delight ,reproach

הָכִיל שְׁפֹךְ עַל־עוֹלָל בַּחוּץ וְעַל סוֹד בַּחוּרִים יַחְדָּו כִּי־
for ;together young the the and the in the on Pour holding
men of circle on ,street child out (it) .in (it)

12 גַם־אִישׁ עִם־אִשָּׁה יִלָּכֵדוּ זָקֵן עִם־מְלֵא יָמִים׃ וְנָסַבּוּ
will And .days fullness with the be shall the and the even
turned be of elder ,taken wife husband

בָתֵּיהֶם לַאֲחֵרִים שָׂדוֹת וְנָשִׁים יַחְדָּו כִּי־אַטֶּה אֶת־יָדִי
My will I for ;together and fields ,others to their
hand out stretch wives house

13 עַל־יֹשְׁבֵי הָאָרֶץ נְאֻם־יְהוָה׃ כִּי מִקְּטַנָּם וְעַד־גְּדוֹלָם
their even their from For .Jehovah says the the against
greatest to least ,land of inhabitants

כֻּלּוֹ בּוֹצֵעַ בָּצַע וּמִנָּבִיא וְעַד־כֹּהֵן כֻּלּוֹ עֹשֶׂה שָּׁקֶר׃
.falsely deals every the even from and a cuts every
one priest to prophet the ;profit off one

14 וַיְרַפְּאוּ אֶת־שֶׁבֶר עַמִּי עַל־נְקַלָּה לֵאמֹר שָׁלוֹם ׀ שָׁלוֹם
;peace ,Peace ,saying ,lightly My fracture the they Also
people of healed have

15 וְאֵין שָׁלוֹם׃ הוֹבִשׁוּ כִּי־תוֹעֵבָה עָשׂוּ גַּם־בּוֹשׁ לֹא־יֵבוֹשׁוּ
were They not at even they an when they Were .peace when
;ashamed all ?made abomination ashamed no is there

גַּם־הַכְלִים לֹא יָדָעוּ לָכֵן יִפְּלוּ בַנֹּפְלִים בְּעֵת־פְּקַדְתִּים
punish I the at those among they So they do not blush to also
them time ;fall who fall shall .know

16 יִכָּשְׁלוּ אָמַר יְהוָה׃ כֹּה אָמַר יְהוָה עִמְדוּ עַל־דְּרָכִים
the by Stand ,Jehovah says Thus .Jehovah says be will they
ways ,down cast

וּרְאוּ וְשַׁאֲלוּ ׀ לִנְתִבוֹת עוֹלָם אֵי־זֶה דֶרֶךְ הַטּוֹב וּלְכוּ־בָהּ
in and the way where ,ancient the for ask and and
;it walk ,good (is) paths ,see

17 וּמִצְאוּ מַרְגּוֹעַ לְנַפְשְׁכֶם וַיֹּאמְרוּ לֹא נֵלֵךְ׃ וַהֲקִמֹתִי
I Also will we not they But your for rest a you and
set .(it in) walk ,send .souls find will

עֲלֵיכֶם צֹפִים הַקְשִׁיבוּ לְקוֹל שׁוֹפָר וַיֹּאמְרוּ לֹא נַקְשִׁיב׃
will We not they But ram's the the to ,(saying) watch- over
,listen ,said .horn of sound Listen ,men you

18 19 לָכֵן שִׁמְעוּ הַגּוֹיִם וּדְעִי עֵדָה אֶת־אֲשֶׁר־בָּם׃ שִׁמְעִי הָאָרֶץ
O ,Hear on what con- O and O ,hear there-
;earth .them (coming is) ,gregation ,know ,nations fore

הִנֵּה אָנֹכִי מֵבִיא רָעָה אֶל־הָעָם הַזֶּה פְּרִי מַחְשְׁבוֹתָם כִּי
for their the ,this people on evil will I ,Behold
;thoughts of fruit bring

20 עַל־דְּבָרַי לֹא הִקְשִׁיבוּ וְתוֹרָתִי וַיִּמְאֲסוּ־בָהּ׃ לָמָּה־זֶּה לִי
to this Why .it they also My and have they not My to
Me rejected law ,listened words

come incense to Me from Sheba, and the sweet cane from a far country? Your burnt offerings (are) not for acceptance, nor (are) your sacrifices sweet to Me. [21] Therefore thus says Jehovah, Behold, I am giving stumbling-blocks to this people, and the fathers and the sons together shall stumble on them; neighbor and his friend shall perish. [22] Thus says Jehovah, Behold, a people comes from the north country, and a great nation shall be stirred from the sides of the earth. [23] They shall lay hold on bow and spear; they are cruel and have no mercy. Their voice roars like the sea; and they ride on horses, arrayed like a man for the battle against you, O daughter of Zion. [24] We have heard the rumor of it. Our hands have fallen; anguish has taken hold of us, pain like a woman in travail. [25] Do not go out into the field or walk by the way; for the sword of the enemy, (and) terror from every side.

[26] O daughter of my people, put on sackcloth and roll in ashes. Make mourning for yourself, (as for) an only son, most bitter weeping — for the ravager shall suddenly come on us. [27] I have set you up (as) assayer (and) an examiner among My people, that you may know and examine their way. [28] They are all grievous revolters, walkers of slander; (they are as) bronze and iron — they are all corrupters. [29] The bellows blow; the lead comes whole from the fire; the refiner refines in vain; for the wicked is not separated. [30] Reprobate silver (men) will call them, for Jehovah has rejected them.

לְבוֹנָה מִשְּׁבָא תָבוֹא וְקָנֶה הַטּוֹב מֵאֶרֶץ מֶרְחָק עֹלוֹתֵיכֶם
burnt Your ?far a from good the and does from frankin-
offerings land cane ,come Sheba cense

21 לֹא לְרָצוֹן וְזִבְחֵיכֶם לֹא־עָרְבוּ לִי׃ לָכֵן כֹּה אָמַר יְהוָה
,Jehovah says thus Therefore to are not your and ac- for (are)
.Me pleasing sacrifices ,ceptance not

הִנְנִי נֹתֵן אֶל־הָעָם הַזֶּה מִכְשֹׁלִים וְכָשְׁלוּ בָם אָבוֹת וּבָנִים
and fathers on will and stumbling this people to am ,Behold
sons them stumble ,blocks giving I

22 יַחְדָּו שָׁכֵן וְרֵעוֹ יֹאבֵדוּ׃ כֹּה אָמַר יְהוָה הִנֵּה עַם
a ,Behold ,Jehovah says Thus shall his and neigh- to-
people .perish friend bor ;gether

23 בָּא מֵאֶרֶץ צָפוֹן וְגוֹי גָּדוֹל יֵעוֹר מִיַּרְכְּתֵי־אָרֶץ׃ קֶשֶׁת
Bow the the from be will great a and the from come
.earth of parts remote up stirred nation ,north country

וְכִידוֹן יַחֲזִיקוּ אַכְזָרִי הוּא וְלֹא יְרַחֵמוּ קוֹלָם כַּיָּם יֶהֱמֶה
;roars the like Their have and they cruel will they and
sea voice .mercy no (are) ,on hold lay spear

וְעַל־סוּסִים יִרְכָּבוּ עָרוּךְ כְּאִישׁ לַמִּלְחָמָה עָלַיִךְ בַּת־
daugh- O against the for a as arrayed they horses and
of ter ,you battle man ,ride on

24 צִיּוֹן׃ שָׁמַעְנוּ אֶת־שָׁמְעוֹ רָפוּ יָדֵינוּ צָרָה הֶחֱזִקַתְנוּ חִיל
pain seized has anguish our have ,report its have We !Zion
,us ;hands dropped heard

25 כַּיּוֹלֵדָה׃ אַל־תֵּצְאִי הַשָּׂדֶה וּבַדֶּרֶךְ אַל־תֵּלֵכִי כִּי חֶרֶב
the because do not by or the go do Not tra- a like
sword of ,walk way the ,field into out .woman vailing

26 לְאֹיֵב מָגוֹר מִסָּבִיב׃ בַּת־עַמִּי חִגְרִי־שָׂק וְהִתְפַּלְּשִׁי בָאֵפֶר
the in roll and sack- put my daugh- O all from (and) the of
;ashes cloth on ,people of ter .around terror ,enemy

אֵבֶל יָחִיד עֲשִׂי־לָךְ מִסְפַּד תַּמְרוּרִים כִּי פִתְאֹם יָבֹא
shall suddenly for ,bitterness mourning for make only an the
come of ,yourself (son) of mourning

27 הַשֹּׁדֵד עָלֵינוּ׃ בָּחוֹן נְתַתִּיךָ בְעַמִּי מִבְצָר וְתֵדַע וּבָחַנְתָּ
and you that a (and) My among have I an upon the
test know may ,tester people you set assayer .us destroyer

28 אֶת־דַּרְכָּם׃ כֻּלָּם סָרֵי סוֹרְרִים הֹלְכֵי רָכִיל נְחֹשֶׁת וּבַרְזֶל
iron and Bronze .slander goers rebellious the (are) of All their
(are) of ,ones of revolters them .way

29 כֻּלָּם מַשְׁחִיתִים הֵמָּה׃ נָחַר מַפֻּחַ מֵאֵשְׁתַּם עֹפָרֶת לַשָּׁוְא
in the comes from The blow they corrupters of all
vain ;lead whole fire the ,bellows .(are) ;them

30 צָרַף צָרוֹף וְרָעִים לֹא נִתָּקוּ׃ כֶּסֶף נִמְאָס קָרְאוּ לָהֶם כִּי־
for ,them they Refuse silver is not the for re- he
call separated wicked ,fining refines

מָאַס יְהוָה בָּהֶם׃
.them Jehovah has
rejected

CAP. VII

CHAPTER 7

CHAPTER 7

[1] The word that came to Jeremiah from Jehovah, saying, [2] Stand in the gate of Jehovah's house and declare there this word, and say, Hear the word of Jehovah, all Judah, who enter in at these gates to worship Jehovah. [3] Thus says Jehovah of hosts, the God of Israel, Amend your ways and your doings, and I will let you dwell in this place. [4] Do not trust yourself to lying words, saying, The temple of Jehovah, The temple of Jehovah, The temple of Jehovah, this (is)!

[5] For if you thoroughly amend your ways and your doings; if you truly practice justice between a man and his neighbor; [6] (if) you do not oppress the stranger, the orphan and the widow, and do not shed innocent blood in this place, or walk after other gods to your hurt – [7] then I will let you dwell in this place, in the land that I gave to your fathers, from forever and to forever.

[8] Behold, you trust for yourself on lying words without any gain. [9] Will you steal, murder, and commit adultery, and swear falsely, and burn incense to Baal, and walk after other gods whom you do not know, [10] and (then) come and stand before Me in this house on which is called My name, and say, We are delivered in order to

1 2 הַדָּבָר אֲשֶׁר־הָיָה אֶל־יִרְמְיָהוּ מֵאֵת יְהוָה לֵאמֹר׃ עֲמֹד
Stand ,saying ,Jehovah from Jeremiah to came that The
word

בְּשַׁעַר בֵּית יְהוָה וְקָרָאתָ שָּׁם אֶת־הַדָּבָר הַזֶּה וְאָמַרְתָּ
,say and ,this word there and ,Jehovah's house the in
declare of gate

שִׁמְעוּ דְבַר־יְהוָה כָּל־יְהוּדָה הַבָּאִים בַּשְּׁעָרִים הָאֵלֶּה
these gates at enter who ,Judah all ,Jehovah the Hear
in of word

3 לְהִשְׁתַּחֲוֺת לַיהוָה׃ כֹּה־אָמַר יְהוָה צְבָאוֹת אֱלֹהֵי יִשְׂרָאֵל
,Israel the ,hosts Jehovah says Thus .Jehovah to
of God of worship

הֵיטִיבוּ דַרְכֵיכֶם וּמַעַלְלֵיכֶם וַאֲשַׁכְּנָה אֶתְכֶם בַּמָּקוֹם
place in you will I and your and ways your Amend
dwell let ,doings

4 הַזֶּה׃ אַל־תִּבְטְחוּ לָכֶם אֶל־דִּבְרֵי הַשֶּׁקֶר לֵאמֹר הֵיכַל
The ,saying the words to yourself Do not .this
of temple ,lie of trust

5 יְהוָה הֵיכַל יְהוָה הֵיכַל יְהוָה הֵמָּה׃ כִּי אִם־הֵיטֵיב
thoroughly if For that Jehovah the ,Jehovah the ,Jehovah
.(is) of temple of temple

תֵּיטִיבוּ אֶת־דַּרְכֵיכֶם וְאֶת־מַעַלְלֵיכֶם אִם־עָשׂוֹ תַּעֲשׂוּ
you indeed if your and your you
practice ;doings ways amend

6 מִשְׁפָּט בֵּין אִישׁ וּבֵין רֵעֵהוּ׃ גֵּר יָתוֹם וְאַלְמָנָה לֹא תַעֲשֹׁקוּ
do you not the and the the (if) his and a be- justice
,oppress widow ,orphan ,stranger ;neighbor man tween

וְדָם נָקִי אַל־תִּשְׁפְּכוּ בַּמָּקוֹם הַזֶּה וְאַחֲרֵי אֱלֹהִים אֲחֵרִים
other gods or ,this place in do not inno- and
after shed cent blood

7 לֹא תֵלְכוּ לְרַע לָכֶם׃ וְשִׁכַּנְתִּי אֶתְכֶם בַּמָּקוֹם הַזֶּה
,this place in you will I then –your to do you not
dwell let hurt go

בָּאָרֶץ אֲשֶׁר נָתַתִּי לַאֲבוֹתֵיכֶם לְמִן־עוֹלָם וְעַד־עוֹלָם׃
.forever even forever from your to I , that the in
to ,fathers gave land

8 הִנֵּה אַתֶּם בֹּטְחִים לָכֶם עַל־דִּבְרֵי הַשָּׁקֶר לְבִלְתִּי הוֹעִיל׃
of being without the words upon for are you ,Behold
.use lie of yourself trusting

9 הֲגָנֹב ׀ רָצֹחַ וְנָאֹף וְהִשָּׁבֵעַ לַשֶּׁקֶר וְקַטֵּר לַבַּעַל וְהָלֹךְ
and ,Baal to burn and ,falsely and com- and murder you Will
walk incense swear ,adultery mit ,steal

10 אַחֲרֵי אֱלֹהִים אֲחֵרִים אֲשֶׁר לֹא־יְדַעְתֶּם׃ וּבָאתֶם וַעֲמַדְתֶּם
and then and do you not that other gods after
stand come ,know

לְפָנַי בַּבַּיִת הַזֶּה אֲשֶׁר נִקְרָא־שְׁמִי עָלָיו וַאֲמַרְתֶּם נִצַּלְנוּ
are We ,say and upon My been has which this in before
delivered it name called house Me

do these hateful things? [11] Has this house on which is called My name become a den of robbers in your eyes? Behold, even I have seen, says Jehovah. [12] But go now to My place which (was) in Shiloh, where I made My name dwell at the first, and see what I did to it for the wickedness of My people Israel. [13] And now, because you have done all these works, says Jehovah, and I spoke to you, rising up early and speaking, but you did not hear — and I called you, but you did not answer — [14] therefore I will do to the house on which is called My name, in which you are trusting, and to the place which I gave to you and to your fathers, as I have done to Shiloh. [15] And I will cast you out from My face, as I cast out all your brothers, the whole seed of Ephraim. [16] And you, do not pray for this people; do not lift up cry or prayer for them, nor make intercession with Me, for I will not hear you.

[17] Do you not see what they are doing in the cities of Judah and in the streets of Jerusalem? [18] The sons gather wood, and the fathers kindle the fire, and the women knead dough, to make cakes to the queen of heaven, and to pour out drink offerings to other gods, that they may provoke Me to anger. [19] Do they provoke Me to anger, says Jehovah? Is it

11 לְמַעַן עֲשׂוֹת אֵת כָּל־הַתּוֹעֵבֹת הָאֵלֶּה׃ הַמְעָרַת פָּרִצִים
robbers of den a ?those abominations all do to in
order

הָיָה הַבַּיִת הַזֶּה אֲשֶׁר־נִקְרָא־שְׁמִי עָלָיו בְּעֵינֵיכֶם גַּם אָנֹכִי
I even your in upon My been has which this house Has
?eyes it name called become

12 הִנֵּה רָאִיתִי נְאֻם־יְהוָה׃ כִּי לְכוּ־נָא אֶל־מְקוֹמִי אֲשֶׁר
which My to now go But .Jehovah says have Behold
(was) place ,seen

בְּשִׁילוֹ אֲשֶׁר שִׁכַּנְתִּי שְׁמִי שָׁם בָּרִאשׁוֹנָה וּרְאוּ אֵת אֲשֶׁר־
what and the at there My made I where in
see ,first name dwell ,Shiloh

13 עָשִׂיתִי לוֹ מִפְּנֵי רָעַת עַמִּי יִשְׂרָאֵל׃ וְעַתָּה יַעַן עֲשׂוֹתְכֶם
have you because And .Israel My the because to did I
done ,now people of evil of it

אֶת־כָּל־הַמַּעֲשִׂים הָאֵלֶּה נְאֻם־יְהוָה וָאֲדַבֵּר אֲלֵיכֶם הַשְׁכֵּם
up rising ,you to I and ,Jehovah says ,these works all
early spoke

14 וְדַבֵּר וְלֹא שְׁמַעְתֶּם וָאֶקְרָא אֶתְכֶם וְלֹא עֲנִיתֶם׃ וְעָשִׂיתִי
I therefore did you but ,you I and did you but and
do will —answer not called —hear not ,speaking

לַבַּיִת ׀ אֲשֶׁר נִקְרָא־שְׁמִי עָלָיו אֲשֶׁר אַתֶּם בֹּטְחִים בּוֹ
in are you which upon My been has which the to
,it trusting ,it name called house

וְלַמָּקוֹם אֲשֶׁר־נָתַתִּי לָכֶם וְלַאֲבוֹתֵיכֶם כַּאֲשֶׁר עָשִׂיתִי
have I as your to and you to gave I which the to and
done ,fathers place

15 לְשִׁלוֹ׃ וְהִשְׁלַכְתִּי אֶתְכֶם מֵעַל פָּנָי כַּאֲשֶׁר הִשְׁלַכְתִּי אֶת־
cast I as My from you cast will I And to
away face away .Shiloh

16 כָּל־אֲחֵיכֶם אֵת כָּל־זֶרַע אֶפְרָיִם׃ וְאַתָּה אַל־תִּתְפַּלֵּל ׀
pray do not ,you And .Ephraim seed the your all
of whole ,brothers

בְּעַד־הָעָם הַזֶּה וְאַל־תִּשָּׂא בַעֲדָם רִנָּה וּתְפִלָּה וְאַל־תִּפְגַּע־
do and or cry for lift do and ;this people for
intercede not ,prayer them up not

17 בִּי כִּי־אֵינֶנִּי שֹׁמֵעַ אֹתָךְ׃ הַאֵינְךָ רֹאֶה מָה הֵמָּה עֹשִׂים
are they what Do you .you do I for with
doing see not hear not ,Me

18 בְּעָרֵי יְהוּדָה וּבְחֻצוֹת יְרוּשָׁלִָם׃ הַבָּנִים מְלַקְּטִים עֵצִים
wood gather The ?Jerusalem the in and Judah the in
sons of streets of cities

וְהָאָבוֹת מְבַעֲרִים אֶת־הָאֵשׁ וְהַנָּשִׁים לָשׁוֹת בָּצֵק לַעֲשׂוֹת
to dough knead the and the kindle the and
make women ,fire fathers

כַּוָּנִים לִמְלֶכֶת הַשָּׁמַיִם וְהַסֵּךְ נְסָכִים לֵאלֹהִים אֲחֵרִים
,other gods to drink to and ,heaven the for cakes
offerings out pour of queen

19 לְמַעַן הַכְעִסֵנִי׃ הַאֹתִי הֵם מַכְעִסִים נְאֻם־יְהוָה הֲלוֹא
(it Is) Jehovah says Do they Me may they that
not ,vex .Me vex

not themselves, to the shame of their own faces? [20] Therefore thus says the Lord Jehovah: Behold, My anger and My fury will be poured out on this place—on man and on animal; and on the trees of the field and on the fruit of the ground. And it will burn, and will not be put out.

[21] Thus says Jehovah of hosts, the God of Israel: Add your burnt offerings to your sacrifices and eat flesh. [22] For I did not speak to your fathers, nor command them in the day that I brought them out from the land of Egypt, concerning the matters of burnt offerings or sacrifices. [23] But I commanded them this thing, saying, Obey My voice and I will be your God, and you shall be My people; and, Walk in all the ways that I have commanded you, so that it may be well with you. [24] But they did not listen nor bow their ear, but walked in the plans, in the stubbornness of their evil heart, and went backward and not forward.

[25] Since the day that your fathers came out of the land of Egypt until this day I have even sent to you all My servants the prophets, daily rising up early and sending (them). [26] Yet they did not listen to Me, nor bow their ear, but stiffened their neck. They did worse than their fathers. [27] Therefore you shall speak all these words to them; but they will not listen to you. And you will call to them, but they will not answer you. [28] But you shall say to them, This (is) the nation which does not obey the

20 אֹתָם לְמַעַן בֹּשֶׁת פְּנֵיהֶם׃ לָכֵן כֹּה־אָמַר ׀ אֲדֹנָי
the says thus Therefore own their the to them-
Lord ?faces of shame ,selves

יְהוִה הִנֵּה אַפִּי וַחֲמָתִי נִתֶּכֶת אֶל־הַמָּקוֹם הַזֶּה עַל־הָאָדָם
man on ,this place on be will My and My ,Behold Jeho-
out poured wrath anger

וְעַל־הַבְּהֵמָה וְעַל־עֵץ הַשָּׂדֶה וְעַל־פְּרִי הָאֲדָמָה וּבָעֲרָה
it And the the and the the and ;animal and
burn will .ground of fruit on ;field of trees on on

21 וְלֹא תִכְבֶּה׃ כֹּה אָמַר יְהוָה צְבָאוֹת אֱלֹהֵי יִשְׂרָאֵל
,Israel the hosts Jehovah says Thus be and
of God of .quenched not

22 עֹלוֹתֵיכֶם סְפוּ עַל־זִבְחֵיכֶם וְאִכְלוּ בָשָׂר׃ כִּי לֹא־דִבַּרְתִּי
did I not For .flesh eat and your to Add burnt your
speak sacrifices .offerings

אֶת־אֲבוֹתֵיכֶם וְלֹא צִוִּיתִים בְּיוֹם הוֹצִיאִ אוֹתָם מֵאֶרֶץ
the from them brought I the in command nor your with
of land out day them ,fathers

23 מִצְרָיִם עַל־דִּבְרֵי עוֹלָה וָזָבַח׃ כִּי אִם־אֶת־הַדָּבָר הַזֶּה
this thing But or burnt the about ,Egypt
.sacrifices offering of matters

צִוִּיתִי אוֹתָם לֵאמֹר שִׁמְעוּ בְקוֹלִי וְהָיִיתִי לָכֶם לֵאלֹהִים
,God for to I and My Obey ,saying ,them com- I
you be will voice manded

וְאַתֶּם תִּהְיוּ־לִי לְעָם וַהֲלַכְתֶּם בְּכָל־הַדֶּרֶךְ אֲשֶׁר אֲצַוֶּה
have I that the in ,and a for to will and
commanded way all Walk ,people Me be you

24 אֶתְכֶם לְמַעַן יִיטַב לָכֶם׃ וְלֹא שָׁמְעוּ וְלֹא־הִטּוּ אֶת־אָזְנָם
their incline nor did they But with may it so ,you
,ear listen not .you well be that

וַיֵּלְכוּ בְּמֹעֵצוֹת בִּשְׁרִרוּת לִבָּם הָרָע וַיִּהְיוּ לְאָחוֹר וְלֹא
and back- they and ,evil their the in (their) in but
not ward went heart of stubbornness plans (own) walked

25 לְפָנִים׃ לְמִן־הַיּוֹם אֲשֶׁר יָצְאוּ אֲבוֹתֵיכֶם מֵאֶרֶץ מִצְרַיִם
Egypt the out your came that the Since .forward
of land fathers out day

עַד הַיּוֹם הַזֶּה וָאֶשְׁלַח אֲלֵיכֶם אֶת־כָּל־עֲבָדַי הַנְּבִיאִים
the My all to have I ,this day until
,prophets servants you sent even

26 יוֹם הַשְׁכֵּם וְשָׁלֹחַ׃ וְלוֹא שָׁמְעוּ אֵלַי וְלֹא הִטּוּ אֶת־אָזְנָם
their incline nor to they Yet and up rising daily
,ear ,Me listened not .sending early

27 וַיַּקְשׁוּ אֶת־עָרְפָּם הֵרֵעוּ מֵאֲבוֹתָם׃ וְדִבַּרְתָּ אֲלֵיהֶם אֶת־
them to you So their than they their stif- but
speak shall .fathers worse did ;neck fened

כָּל־הַדְּבָרִים הָאֵלֶּה וְלֹא יִשְׁמְעוּ אֵלֶיךָ וְקָרָאתָ אֲלֵיהֶם
,them to you And to will they but ,these words all
call will .you listen not

28 וְלֹא יַעֲנוּכָה׃ וְאָמַרְתָּ אֲלֵיהֶם זֶה הַגּוֹי אֲשֶׁר לוֹא־שָׁמְעוּ
does not which the This ,them to you But will they but
obey nation (is) say shall .you answer not

voice of Jehovah their God nor receive instruction; truth has perished, and it is cut off from their mouth.

[29] Cut off your hair and throw (it) away, and take up a weeping on the high places. For Jehovah has rejected and forsaken the generation of His wrath. [30] For the sons of Judah have done evil in My eyes, says Jehovah. They have set their idols in the house on which is called My name, in order to defile it. [31] They have built the high places of Tophet, which is in the valley of the son of Hinnom, to burn their sons and their daughters in the fire; which I did not command, nor did it come into My heart. [32] Therefore, behold, the days come, says Jehovah, that it shall no more be called Tophet, or the valley of the son of Hinnom, but the valley of slaughter. For they shall bury in Tophet, from lack of a place. [33] And the bodies of this people shall be food for the birds of the sky, and for the beasts of the earth; and no one shall frighten away. [34] Then I will cause the voice of gladness to cease from the cities of Judah and from the streets of Jerusalem; and the voice of joy, the voice of bridegroom, and the voice of bride. For the land shall become a waste.

בְּקוֹל יְהוָֹה אֱלֹהֵיהוּ וְלֹא לָקְחוּ מוּסָר אָבְדָה הָאֱמוּנָה
truth has ;instruction receive nor their Jehovah the
perished ,God of voice

29 וְנִכְרְתָה מִפִּיהֶם: גָּזִּי נִזְרֵךְ וְהַשְׁלִיכִי וּשְׂאִי עַל־
on and throw and your Cut their from is it and
up take ,away (it) hair off .mouth off cut

30 שְׁפָיִם קִינָה כִּי מָאַס יְהוָֹה וַיִּטֹּשׁ אֶת־דּוֹר עֶבְרָתוֹ: כִּי־
For His gen- the and Jehovah has For a the
.wrath of eration forsaken rejected .dirge heights

עָשׂוּ בְנֵי־יְהוּדָה הָרַע בְּעֵינַי נְאֻם־יְהוָֹה שָׂמוּ שִׁקּוּצֵיהֶם
abomin- their They ;Jehovah says My in evil Judah the have
idols able set have ,eyes of sons done

31 בַּבַּיִת אֲשֶׁר־נִקְרָא־שְׁמִי־עָלָיו לְטַמְּאוֹ: וּבָנוּ בָּמוֹת הַתֹּפֶת
Tophet high the They defile to upon My been has which the in
of places built have .it ,it name called house

אֲשֶׁר בְּגֵיא בֶן־הִנֹּם לִשְׂרֹף אֶת־בְּנֵיהֶם וְאֶת־בְּנֹתֵיהֶם בָּאֵשׁ
the in their and their burn to Hinnom the the in which
;fire daughters sons of son of valley (is)

32 אֲשֶׁר לֹא צִוִּיתִי וְלֹא עָלְתָה עַל־לִבִּי: לָכֵן הִנֵּה יָמִים
the ,behold ,Therefore My into it did nor did I not which
days .heart come ,command

בָּאִים נְאֻם־יְהוָֹה וְלֹא־יֵאָמֵר עוֹד הַתֹּפֶת וְגֵיא בֶן־הִנֹּם
,Hinnom the the or ,Tophet still will it that ,Jehovah says ,come
of son of valley called be not

33 כִּי אִם־גֵּיא הַהֲרֵגָה וְקָבְרוּ בְתֹפֶת מֵאֵין מָקוֹם: וְהָיְתָה
will And .place a from in they for the valley but
be of lack of Tophet bury will ,slaughter of

נִבְלַת הָעָם הַזֶּה לְמַאֲכָל לְעוֹף הַשָּׁמַיִם וּלְבֶהֱמַת הָאָרֶץ
the for and ,sky the the for food this people the
;earth of beasts the of birds of bodies

34 וְאֵין מַחֲרִיד: וְהִשְׁבַּתִּי מֵעָרֵי יְהוּדָה וּמֵחֻצוֹת יְרוּשָׁלִַם
Jerusalem from and Judah the from will I Then frighten will and
of streets the of cities cease make .away none

קוֹל שָׂשׂוֹן וְקוֹל שִׂמְחָה קוֹל חָתָן וְקוֹל כַּלָּה כִּי לְחָרְבָּה
waste a for ,bride the and bride- the ,joy the and glad- the
of voice ,groom of voice of voice of voice ness of voice

תִּהְיֶה הָאָרֶץ:
the will
.land become

CAP. VIII ח

CHAPTER 8

CHAPTER 8

[1] At that time, says Jehovah, they shall bring out the bones of the kings of Judah, and the bones of its princes, and the bones of the priests, and the bones of the prophets, and the bones of the inhabitants of Jerusalem, out of their graves. [2] And they shall spread

1 בָּעֵת הַהִיא נְאֻם־יְהוָֹה וְיוֹצִיאוּ אֶת־עַצְמוֹת מַלְכֵי־יְהוּדָה
,Judah the the shall they ,Jehovah says ,that At
of kings of bones out bring time

וְאֶת־עַצְמוֹת שָׂרָיו וְאֶת־עַצְמוֹת הַכֹּהֲנִים וְאֵת | עַצְמוֹת
the and the the the and
of bones ,priests of bones officials of bones

2 הַנְּבִיאִים וְאֵת עַצְמוֹת יוֹשְׁבֵי־יְרוּשָׁלִָם מִקִּבְרֵיהֶם: וּשְׁטָחוּם
they and their from ,Jerusalem in- the the and the
spread will ;graves of habitants of bones ;prophets

them before the sun, and the moon, and all the host of the heavens, whom they have loved and whom they have served, and after whom they have walked, and whom they have sought, and whom they have worshiped. They shall not be gathered or buried; they shall be dung on the face of the earth. [3] And death shall be chosen rather than life by all the rest of those who remain of this evil family, who remain there in all the places where I have driven them, says Jehovah of hosts.

[4] And you shall say to them, Thus says Jehovah; shall they fall and not arise? Or shall one turn away and not return? [5] Why has this people, Jerusalem, turned back, a never-ending backsliding? They hold fast to deceit; they refuse to return. [6] I listened and heard; they did not speak so; no man repented because of his evil, saying, What have I done? Everyone turned in their own course, as a horse rushes into the battle. [7] Also the stork in the heavens knows her seasons; and the turtle-dove and the swallow and the thrush observe the time of their coming; but My people do not know the judgment of Jehovah.

[8] How do you say, We (are) wise, and the law of Jehovah (is) with us? Lo, certainly the lying pen of the scribes has worked deceit. [9] The wise are ashamed; they are terrified and are captured. Lo, they have rejected the word of Jehovah; and what wisdom is theirs? [10] Therefore I will give their wives to others, their fields to those who shall inherit; for everyone from the least even to the greatest cuts off a

לשמש ולירח ולכל ׀ צבא השמים אשר אהבום ואשר
and have they whom the the to and to and the to
whom ,them loved ,heavens of host all ,moon the ,sun

עבדום ואשר הלכו אחריהם ואשר דרשום ואשר
and have they and after have they and have they
whom ,them sought whom ,them walked whom ,them served

השתחוו להם לא יאספו ולא יקברו לדמן על־פני האדמה
the the on for ;burned nor will They not .them have they
ground of face dung gathered be worshipped

3 יהיו׃ ונבחר מות מחיים לכל השארית הנשארים מן
from who those rem- the all by rather death be will And they
left are of nant life than chosen .be will

המשפחה הרעה הזאת בכל־המקמות הנשארים אשר
where who the all in ,this evil family
remain places

4 הדחתים שם נאם יהוה צבאות׃ ואמרת אליהם כה
Thus ,them to you And .hosts Jehovah says ,there have I
say shall of them driven

5 אמר יהוה היפלו ולא יקומו אם־ישוב ולא ישוב׃ מדוע
Why ?return and one does Or ?arise and they Do ;Jehovah says
not away turn not fall

שובבה העם הזה ירושלם משבה נצחת החזיקו בתרמית
to hold They ?perpetual a ,Jerusalem ,this people turned has
;deceit fast apostasy away

6 מאנו לשוב׃ הקשבתי ואשמע לוא־כן ידברו אין איש
man no did they so not and listened I to they
;speak ;heard .return refuse

נחם על־רעתו לאמר מה עשיתי כלה שב במרצותם
own their in turned Every I have What ,saying his because re-
course one ?done ,evil of pented

7 כסוס שוטף במלחמה׃ גם־חסידה בשמים ידעה
knows the in the Also the into rushes a like
skies stork .battle horse

מועדיה ותר וסוס ועגור שמרו את־עת באנה ועמי
My but their the observe the and the and the and her
people ;coming of time thrush swift turtle-dove ;seasons

8 לא ידעו את משפט יהוה׃ איכה תאמרו חכמים אנחנו
We wise you do How .Jehovah the do not
(are) ,say of judgment know

ותורת יהוה אתנו אכן הנה לשקר עשה עט שקר
the the has deceit ,Lo ;certainly with Jehovah the and
of lie of pen practiced ?us (is) of law

9 ספרים׃ הבשו חכמים חתו וילכדו הנה בדבר־יהוה
Jehovah the ,lo are and are they The put are the
of word ;captured terrified ;wise shame to .scribes

10 מאסו וחכמת־מה להם׃ לכן אתן את־נשיהם לאחרים
,others to their will I There- ?theirs what and have they
wives give fore (is) wisdom ;rejected

שדותיהם ליורשים כי מקטן ועד־גדול כלה בצע בצע
a cuts every the even the from for the to their
;profit off one greatest to least ,possessors fields

profit. From the prophet even to the priest everyone deals falsely. [11] For they have healed the hurt of the daughter of My people slightly, saying, Peace, peace; when there is no peace. [12] Were they ashamed when they had done hateful things? They were not even at all ashamed, nor did they know how to blush; therefore they shall fall among those who fall. In the time of their visitation they shall be made to stumble, says Jehovah.

[13] I will utterly consume them, says Jehovah; no grapes will be on the vine, or figs on the fig-tree, and the leaf withers. And I will give to them those who pass over them. [14] Why do we sit still? Gather yourselves, and let us enter into the fortified cities, and let us perish there. For Jehovah our God has let us perish, and has made us drink water of poison, because we have sinned against Jehovah. [15] We looked for peace, but no good (came); for a time of healing, but behold, terror! [16] The snorting of his horses was heard from Dan; the whole land trembled at the sound of the neighing of his strong ones. For they come and devour the land, and its fullness; the city, and those who live in it. [17] For, behold, I will send serpents among you, vipers (for) which there is no charm; and they shall bite you, says Jehovah.

[18] I suffer from desolation; beyond grief; my heart (is) sick within me. [19] Behold, the voice of the cry of the daughter of My people, from a distant land. Is not Jehovah in Zion? Or is not her king in her? Why have they provoked Me with their graven images, with foreign vanities? [20] Harvest has passed; the summer has ended, and we are not saved. [21] For the breaking of the daughter of My people I am broken; I mourn; horror has seized me. [22] Is there no balm in Gilead? Is there no healer

11 מִנָּבִיא וְעַד־כֹּהֵן כֻּלֹּה עֹשֶׂה שָּׁקֶר׃ וַיְרַפּוּ אֶת־שֶׁבֶר בַּת־
daugh- the the they And .falsely deals every the even the from
of ter of fracture healed have one ,priest to people

12 עַמִּי עַל־נְקַלָּה לֵאמֹר שָׁלוֹם ׀ שָׁלוֹם וְאֵין שָׁלוֹם׃ הֹבִשׁוּ
they Were .peace when ,peace ,Peace ,saying ,slightly My
ashamed no is there people

כִּי תוֹעֵבָה עָשׂוּ גַּם־בּוֹשׁ לֹא־יֵבֹשׁוּ וְהִכָּלֵם לֹא יָדָעוּ לָכֵן
there- did not to how were They not at even they an when
fore ;know they blush ;ashamed all ?made abomination

יִפְּלוּ בַנֹּפְלִים בְּעֵת פְּקֻדָּתָם יִכָּשְׁלוּ אָמַר יְהוָה׃
.Jehovah says will they their the in those among they
,stumble punishment of time ;fall who fall shall

13 אָסֹף אֲסִיפֵם נְאֻם־יְהוָה אֵין עֲנָבִים בַּגֶּפֶן וְאֵין תְּאֵנִים
figs nor the on grapes not ;Jehovah says take will I utterly
vine be will ,away them

14 בַּתְּאֵנָה וְהֶעָלֶה נָבֵל וָאֶתֵּן לָהֶם יַעַבְרוּם׃ עַל־מָה אֲנַחְנוּ
we Why who those to I and ;withers the even the on
.them over pass ,them give will leaf ;tree fig

יֹשְׁבִים הֵאָסְפוּ וְנָבוֹא אֶל־עָרֵי הַמִּבְצָר וְנִדְּמָה־שָּׁם כִּי יְהוָה
Jehovah for ,there let and ,fortified cities into let and Gather sit do
perish us enter us yourselves ?still

15 אֱלֹהֵינוּ הֲדִמָּנוּ וַיַּשְׁקֵנוּ מֵי־רֹאשׁ כִּי חָטָאנוּ לַיהוָה׃ קַוֵּה
We against have we for poison waters made and let has our
waited .Jehovah sinned of drink us ,perish us God

16 לְשָׁלוֹם וְאֵין טוֹב לְעֵת מַרְפֵּה וְהִנֵּה בְעָתָה׃ מִדָּן נִשְׁמַע
has From !terror but ,healing a for ;good but for
heard Dan ,behold of time no (came) peace

נַחְרַת סוּסָיו מִקּוֹל מִצְהֲלוֹת אַבִּירָיו רָעֲשָׁה כָּל־הָאָרֶץ
the all quakes his the the from his snort- the
.land stallions of neighing of sound ;horses of ing

17 וַיָּבוֹאוּ וַיֹּאכְלוּ אֶרֶץ וּמְלוֹאָהּ עִיר וְיֹשְׁבֵי בָהּ׃ כִּי הִנְנִי מְשַׁלֵּחַ
will I ,behold For in those and the its and the and they For
send I .it dwell who ,city fullness land devour come

בָּכֶם נְחָשִׁים צִפְעֹנִים אֲשֶׁר אֵין־לָהֶם לָחַשׁ וְנִשְּׁכוּ אֶתְכֶם
,you they and a for there which vipers ,serpents among
bite will ,charm them not is you

18 19 נְאֻם־יְהוָה׃ מַבְלִיגִיתִי עֲלֵי יָגוֹן עָלַי לִבִּי דַוָּי׃ הִנֵּה־
Behold (is) My within ,grief be- I From .Jehovah says
.sick heart Me yond ,suffer desolation

קוֹל שַׁוְעַת בַּת־עַמִּי מֵאֶרֶץ מַרְחַקִּים הַיהוָה אֵין בְּצִיּוֹן אִם־
Or in Is Jehovah :distant a from My daugh- the the the
?Zion not land people of ter of cry of voice

מַלְכָּהּ אֵין בָּהּ מַדּוּעַ הִכְעִסוּנִי בִּפְסִלֵיהֶם בְּהַבְלֵי נֵכָר׃
?foreign with their with they have Why in is her
vanities ,images graven Me provoked ?her not king

20 21 עָבַר קָצִיר כָּלָה קָיִץ וַאֲנַחְנוּ לוֹא נוֹשָׁעְנוּ׃ עַל־שֶׁבֶר בַּת־
daugh- the the Because are not and the has ,Harvest has
of ter of breaking of .saved ,summer ended by passed

22 עַמִּי הָשְׁבָּרְתִּי קָדַרְתִּי שַׁמָּה הֶחֱזִקָתְנִי׃ הַצֳרִי אֵין בְּגִלְעָד
in Is balm taken has horror ;mourn I am I my
?Gilead no there .me on hold ,broken people

there? Why then has the healing of my people not come?

אִם־רֹפֵא אֵין שָׁם כִּי מַדּוּעַ לֹא עָלְתָה אֲרֻכַת בַּת־עַמִּי׃
My daugh- the the has not Why then ?there is healer Or
?people of ter of healing come no there

CHAPTER 9

[1] Oh, that my head were waters and my eyes a fountain of tears, that I might weep day and night for the slain of the daughter

23 מִי־יִתֵּן רֹאשִׁי מַיִם וְעֵינִי מְקוֹר דִּמְעָה וְאֶבְכֶּה יוֹמָם וָלַיְלָה
and day I that ,tears foun- a and ,waters my that O
night for weep might of tain eyes my head were

אֵת חַלְלֵי בַת־עַמִּי׃
My daugh- the the
.people of ter of slain

CAP. IX ט

CHAPTER 9

of my people! [2] Oh, that I had in the wilderness a lodging place for traveling men, that I might leave my people and go away from them! For they are all adulterers, an assembly of treacherous ones. [3] And they bend their tongues, their bow is a lie. And they are not mighty for the truth on the earth; for they go from evil to evil, they do not know Me, says Jehovah. [4] Let everyone be on guard against his neighbor, and do not trust any brother! For every brother will supplant, and every neighbor will walk as a slanderer. [5] And everyone will deceive his neighbor, and they will not speak the truth. They have taught their tongue to speak lies; they weary themselves to commit iniquity. [6] Your home (is) in the midst of deceit; through deceit they refuse to know Me, says Jehovah. [7] Therefore thus says Jehovah of hosts, Behold, I will refine them and test them; what (else) can I do because of the daughter of My people? [8] Their tongue (is) a murdering arrow; it speaks deceit; (one) speaks peace to his neighbor with his mouth, but in his heart he sets his ambush.

1 מִי־יִתְּנֵנִי בַמִּדְבָּר מְלוֹן אֹרְחִים וְאֶעֶזְבָה אֶת־עַמִּי וְאֵלְכָה
go and my I that ,travelers lodging a the in that O
away people leave might of wilderness had I

2 מֵאִתָּם כִּי כֻלָּם מְנָאֲפִים עֲצֶרֶת בֹּגְדִים׃ וַיַּדְרְכוּ אֶת־
they And treacherous assembly an are of all For from
bend .men of adulterers them !them

לְשׁוֹנָם קַשְׁתָּם שֶׁקֶר וְלֹא לֶאֱמוּנָה גָּבְרוּ בָאָרֶץ כִּי מֵרָעָה
from for the on are they the for and ,lie a their their
evil ;earth mighty truth not (is) bow ,tongues

3 אֶל־רָעָה ׀ יָצָאוּ וְאֹתִי לֹא־יָדָעוּ נְאֻם־יְהוָה׃ אִישׁ
Every .Jehovah says they not and they evil to
man ,know do Me ,go

מֵרֵעֵהוּ הִשָּׁמֵרוּ וְעַל־כָּל־אָח אַל־תִּבְטָחוּ כִּי כָל־אָח עָקוֹב
surely brother every For do not brother any and be Let his against
!trust guarded neighbor

4 יַעְקֹב וְכָל־רֵעַ רָכִיל יַהֲלֹךְ׃ וְאִישׁ בְּרֵעֵהוּ יְהָתֵלּוּ וֶאֱמֶת
the and will his every and goes a neighbor and will
truth ,deceive neighbor man ,as about slanderer every ,supplant

5 לֹא יְדַבֵּרוּ לִמְּדוּ לְשׁוֹנָם דַּבֶּר־שֶׁקֶר הַעֲוֵה נִלְאוּ׃ שִׁבְתְּךָ
Your tired they do to ;lies to their have they will they not
dwelling ,themselves iniquity speak tongue taught ;speak

בְּתוֹךְ מִרְמָה בְּמִרְמָה מֵאֲנוּ דַעַת־אוֹתִי נְאֻם־יְהוָה׃
.Jehovah says ,Me to they through ;deceit the in (is)
know refuse deceit of midst

6 לָכֵן כֹּה אָמַר יְהוָה צְבָאוֹת הִנְנִי צוֹרְפָם וּבְחַנְתִּים כִּי־
for test and refine will ,Behold ,hosts Jehovah says thus There-
,them them I of fore

7 אֵיךְ אֶעֱשֶׂה מִפְּנֵי בַּת־עַמִּי׃ חֵץ שׁוֹחֵט לְשׁוֹנָם מִרְמָה
deceit their slaughtering A My daugh- the for I can what
;tongue (is) arrow ?people of ter do (else)

דִּבֵּר בְּפִיו שָׁלוֹם אֶת־רֵעֵהוּ יְדַבֵּר וּבְקִרְבּוֹ יָשִׂים אָרְבּוֹ׃
his he his in but one his with peace his with it
.ambush sets midst ,speaks neighbor mouth ;speaks

[9] Shall I not visit them for these (things), says Jehovah? Or shall not My soul be avenged on such a nation as this? [10] I will take up a weeping and a wailing for the mountains,

8 הַעַל־אֵלֶּה לֹא־אֶפְקָד־בָּם נְאֻם־יְהוָה אִם־בְּגוֹי אֲשֶׁר כָּזֶה
as such a on Or ?Jehovah says ,them I shall not these For
this nation punish (things)

9 לֹא תִתְנַקֵּם נַפְשִׁי׃ עַל־הֶהָרִים אֶשָּׂא בְכִי וָנֶהִי וְעַל־
and a and a will I the For My be shall not
for .wailing weeping up take mountains ?soul avenged

and a mourning for the pastures of the wilderness; because they are burned up, without a man passing through; and they do not 10 hear the voice of cattle. From the fowl of the skies and to the beast, they have fled; they are gone. [11] And I will make Jerusalem ruins, a den of jackals; and I will make the cities of Judah a desolation, without inhabitant. 11

[12] Who is the wise man that can understand this? And he to whom the mouth of Jehovah has spoken, that he may declare it? Why does the land perish? It is laid waste like the 12 wilderness, so that no one passes through. [13] And Jehovah says, Because they have forsaken My law which I set before them, and have not obeyed My voice, and have not walked in it; [14] but have walked after 13 the stubbornness of their own heart, and after the Baals, which their fathers taught them; [15] therefore thus says Jehovah 14 of hosts, the God of Israel, Behold, I will make this people eat wormwood, and make them drink water of poison. [16] I will also scatter them among the nations, which they nor their fathers 15 have known. And I will send the sword after them until I have consumed them.

[17] Thus says Jehovah 16 of hosts, Think carefully, and call for the wailers, that they may come. And send for the wise women, that they may come. [18] And let them make haste and take up a lament over us, so that our eyes may run down 17 (with) tears, and waters flow (from) our eyelids. [19] For a voice of lament is heard out of Zion. How 18 are we ruined! We are greatly ashamed, because we have forsaken the land, because they have thrown 19 down our dwellings.

נְאוֹת מִדְבָּר קִינָה כִּי נִצְּתוּ מִבְּלִי־אִישׁ עֹבֵר וְלֹא שָׁמְעוּ

they / and passing / a / without / are they for / a / wil- the / pas- the
hear / not ;through / man / devastated ;dirge / derness of / torage

קוֹל מִקְנֶה מֵעוֹף הַשָּׁמַיִם וְעַד־בְּהֵמָה נָדְדוּ הָלָכוּ׃ וְנָתַתִּי 10

I And / are they / have / the / even / the / From .cattle / the
make will .gone ;fled / beast / to / skies / of bird / of voice

אֶת־יְרוּשָׁלַםִ לְגַלִּים מְעוֹן תַּנִּים וְאֶת־עָרֵי יְהוּדָה אֶתֵּן

will I / Judah / the / and ;jackals / a / heap a / Jerusalem
make / of cities / of den ,ruins of

שְׁמָמָה מִבְּלִי יוֹשֵׁב׃ מִי־הָאִישׁ הֶחָכָם וְיָבֵן אֶת־ 11

can that / wise / the / Who / .inhabitant / without / deso- a
understand / man (is) / lation

זֹאת וַאֲשֶׁר דִּבֶּר פִּי־יְהוָה אֵלָיו וְיַגִּדָהּ עַל־מָה אָבְדָה הָאָרֶץ

the / does / Why / he that / to / Jehovah the / has / And ?this
?land / perish / ?it declare may him / of mouth spoken whom

נִצְּתָה כַמִּדְבָּר מִבְּלִי עֹבֵר׃ וַיֹּאמֶר יְהוָה עַל־עָזְבָם 12

have they / Be- Jeho- / And / passes / that so / the like / is It
forsaken cause ,vah / says / .through / none / wilderness waste laid

אֶת־תּוֹרָתִי אֲשֶׁר נָתַתִּי לִפְנֵיהֶם וְלֹא־שָׁמְעוּ בְקוֹלִי וְלֹא־

and / My / have / and / before / set I / which / My
not / ,voice / obeyed not / ,them / law

הָלְכוּ בָהּ׃ וַיֵּלְכוּ אַחֲרֵי שְׁרִרוּת לִבָּם וְאַחֲרֵי הַבְּעָלִים 13

,Baals the / and own their / stub- the / after / have but ;it in / have
after ,heart of bornness / walked / walked

אֲשֶׁר לִמְּדוּם אֲבוֹתָם׃ לָכֵן כֹּה־אָמַר יְהוָה צְבָאוֹת 14

,hosts Jehovah / says thus therefore / their / taught / which
of / ;fathers / them

אֱלֹהֵי יִשְׂרָאֵל הִנְנִי מַאֲכִילָם אֶת־הָעָם הַזֶּה לַעֲנָה

worm- / this / people / make will / ,Behold / ,Israel / the
,wood / eat / I / of God

וְהִשְׁקִיתִים מֵי־רֹאשׁ׃ וַהֲפִצוֹתִים בַּגּוֹיִם אֲשֶׁר לֹא יָדְעוּ 15

have / not / which / among / will I Also / .poison / waters / make and
,known / ,nations the / them scatter / of / drink them

הֵמָּה וַאֲבוֹתָם וְשִׁלַּחְתִּי אַחֲרֵיהֶם אֶת־הַחֶרֶב עַד כַּלּוֹתִי

have I / until / the / after / I And / their nor / they
consumed / ,sword / them / send will / .fathers

אוֹתָם׃ כֹּה אָמַר יְהוָה צְבָאוֹת הִתְבּוֹנְנוּ וְקִרְאוּ 16

and / Consider / ,hosts / Jehovah / says / Thus
call / of / .them

לַמְקוֹנְנוֹת וּתְבוֹאֶינָה וְאֶל־הַחֲכָמוֹת שִׁלְחוּ וְתָבוֹאנָה׃

they that / ,send / wise the / and / they that / the for
.come may / women / to ;come may / ,wailers

וּתְמַהֵרְנָה וְתִשֶּׂנָה עָלֵינוּ נֶהִי וְתֵרַדְנָה עֵינֵינוּ דִּמְעָה 17

(with) / eyes our / that so / a / over / take and / them let And
,tears / down run may lament / us / up / haste make

וְעַפְעַפֵּינוּ יִזְּלוּ־מָיִם׃ כִּי קוֹל נְהִי נִשְׁמַע מִצִּיּוֹן אֵיךְ שֻׁדָּדְנוּ 18

are we / How / from / is lament / a / For .waters / flow / our and
!devastated / ,Zion / heard / of voice / eyelids

בֹּשְׁנוּ מְאֹד כִּי־עָזַבְנוּ אָרֶץ כִּי הִשְׁלִיכוּ מִשְׁכְּנוֹתֵינוּ כִּי־ 19

But / our / have they / for / the / have we for ,greatly are We
.dwellings / down thrown ;land / left / ashamed

[20] Yet hear the word of Jehovah, O women, and let your ear receive the word of His mouth, and teach your daughters a lament, and each one her neighbor a dirge. [21] For death has come into our windows, entering into our citadels, to cut off the children from the street, (the) young men from the plazas. [22] Speak, Thus says Jehovah, Even the bodies of men shall fall as dung on the open field, and as the fallen grain after the reaper, and none shall gather (them).

[23] Thus says Jehovah, Do not let the wise glory in his wisdom, and do not let the mighty glory in his might; do not let the rich glory in his riches — [24] but let him who glories glory in this, that (he) understands and knows Me, that I (am) Jehovah, doing kindness, justice, and righteousness in the earth — for in these I delight, says Jehovah.

[25] Behold, the days come, says Jehovah, that I will punish all the circumcised with foreskin — [26] Egypt, and Judah, and Edom, and the sons of Ammon, and Moab, and all those trimmed on the edges (of their beards), who dwell in the wilderness. For all the nations (are) uncircumcised, and all the house of Israel—those uncircumcised of heart.

שמענה נשים דבר־יהוה ותקח אזנכם דבר־פיו ולמדנה
and teach His mouth the word of your ear let receive and ,Jehovah the word of O ,women ,hear

20 בנתיכם נהי ואשה רעותה קינה׃ כי־עלה מות בחלונינו
our windows through death has come up For .dirge a her neighbor and each a ,lament your daughters

בא בארמנותינו להכרית עולל מחוץ בחורים מרחבות׃
the from .squares open (the and) men young the from ,street the children to cast off our into palaces fortified enter-ing

21 דבר כה נאם־יהוה ונפלה נבלת האדם כדמן על־פני
the on of face dung as men the of bodies will Even fall ,Jehovah says thus ,Speak

22 השדה וכעמיר מאחרי הקוצר ואין מאסף׃ כה | אמר
says Thus gather will .(them) and none the ,reaper after like and the swath the ,field

יהוה אל־יתהלל חכם בחכמתו ואל־יתהלל הגבור
the mighty let do glory and not his in ,wisdom the man wise let Do glory not ,Jehovah

23 בגבורתו אל־יתהלל עשיר בעשרו׃ כי אם־בזאת יתהלל
let glory this in but his in —riches the rich let do glory not his in ,might

המתהלל השכל וידע אותי כי אני יהוה עשה חסד משפט
,justice kind- ,ness doing ,Jehovah I (am) that ,Me and knows he (that) understands who him ,glories

24 וצדקה בארץ כי־באלה חפצתי נאם־יהוה׃ הנה
Behold .Jehovah says I ,delight in these for the in —earth righ- and teousness

25 ימים באים נאם־יהוה ופקדתי על־כל־מול בערלה׃ על־
with —foreskin the circumcised all I that will punish ,Jehovah says ,come the days

מצרים ועל־יהודה ועל־אדום ועל־בני עמון ועל־מואב
,Moab and ,Ammon the and of sons ,Edom and ,Judah and Egypt

ועל כל־קצוצי פאה הישבים במדבר כי כל־הגוים ערלים
uncir- cumcised (are) the nations all for the in ,wilderness who dwell the ,edges those on trimmed all and

וכל־בית ישראל ערלי־לב׃
.heart of uncircumcised those Israel the of house and all

CAP. X

CHAPTER 10

CHAPTER 10

[1] Hear the word which Jehovah speaks to you, O house of Israel. [2] Thus says Jehovah, You shall not be goaded to the way of the nations; and do not be terrified at the signs of the heavens; for the nations are terrified at them. [3] For the customs

1 שמעו את־הדבר אשר דבר יהוה עליכם בית ישראל׃
.Israel O of house ,you to Jehovah speaks which the word Hear

2 כה | אמר יהוה אל־דרך הגוים אל־תלמדו ומאתות
the by and of signs shall you ,goaded be not the ,nations the of way to ,Jehovah says Thus

3 השמים אל־תחתו כי־יחתו הגוים מהמה׃ כי־חקות
the of customs For .them by the nations are terrified for be do ,terrified not the heavens

of the people are vanity; for one cuts a tree out of the forest with the axe, the work of the hands of the craftsman. [4] They adorn it with silver and with gold; they fasten them with nails and hammers, so that it will not fall. [5] They (are) like a rounded post, and they cannot speak; they must surely be carried, because they cannot walk. Do not be afraid of them; for they cannot do evil; and (they can) not do good; it is not with them. [6] There is none like You, O Jehovah; You (are) great, and Your name (is) great in might. [7] Who would not fear You, O King of nations? For for You, it is fitting, because among all the wise of the nations, and in all their kingdoms, there is none like You. [8] But they are at once foolish and animal-like; (their) tree (is) an instruction of vanities.

[9] Silver beaten into plates is brought from Tarshish, and gold from Uphaz, the work of the craftsman, and of the hands of the refiner; violet and purple is their clothing; they (are) all the works of skillful ones. [10] But Jehovah (is) the true God, He (is) the living God, and the everlasting King. At His wrath the earth shall tremble, and the nations shall not be able to stand His fury. [11] Thus you shall say to them, The gods who have not made the heavens and the earth, they shall perish from the earth and from under these heavens. [12] (It is) He who made the earth by His power; who established the world by His wisdom, and who stretched out the heavens by His understanding. [13] When He utters His voice, (there is) a noise of waters in the heavens. He causes the vapors to ascend from the ends of the earth; He makes lightnings for the rain, and brings forth the wind out of His storehouses. [14] Every man is like an animal from (lack

הָעַמִּים הֶבֶל הוּא כִּי־עֵץ מִיַּעַר כְּרָתוֹ מַעֲשֵׂה יְדֵי־חָרָשׁ
of hands the the one the from a for it vanity the
craftsman the of work ,cuts forest tree ,(is) —people

4 בַּמַּעֲצָד׃ בְּכֶסֶף וּבְזָהָב יְיַפֵּהוּ בְּמַסְמְרוֹת וּבְמַקָּבוֹת
with and with They with and with the with
hammers nails ,it adorn gold silver axe

5 יְחַזְּקוּם וְלוֹא יָפִיק׃ כְּתֹמֶר מִקְשָׁה הֵמָּה וְלֹא יְדַבֵּרוּ
can they and they rounded a Like will it that so they
;speak not ,(are) post .wobble not them fasten

נָשׂוֹא יִנָּשׂוּא כִּי־לֹא יִצְעָדוּ אַל־תִּירְאוּ מֵהֶם כִּי־לֹא יָרֵעוּ
can they not for of be Do not can they not for must they surely
evil do ;them afraid .walk ,carried be

6 וְגַם־הֵיטֵיב אֵין אוֹתָם׃ מֵאֵין כָּמוֹךָ יְהוָה גָּדוֹל
great O like There with is it do and
;Jehovah ,You none is .them not ;good not

7 אַתָּה וְגָדוֹל שִׁמְךָ בִּגְבוּרָה׃ מִי לֹא יִרָאֲךָ מֶלֶךְ הַגּוֹיִם
?nations O would not Who .might in Your (is) and You
of King You fear name great ,(are)

כִּי לְךָ יָאָתָה כִּי בְכָל־חַכְמֵי הַגּוֹיִם וּבְכָל־מַלְכוּתָם מֵאֵין
there their in and the wise the among for is it for For
none is ,kingdoms all ,nations of men all ,fitting You

8 כָּמוֹךָ׃ וּבְאַחַת יִבְעֲרוּ וְיִכְסָלוּ מוּסַר הֲבָלִים עֵץ הוּא׃
(is) (their) vanities in- an and are they And like
tree of struction ;foolish stupid altogether .You

9 כֶּסֶף מְרֻקָּע מִתַּרְשִׁישׁ יוּבָא וְזָהָב מֵאוּפָז מַעֲשֵׂה חָרָשׁ
the work the from and is from beaten silver
,craftsman of ,Uphaz gold ,brought Tarshish plates into

וִידֵי צוֹרֵף תְּכֵלֶת וְאַרְגָּמָן לְבוּשָׁם מַעֲשֵׂה חֲכָמִים כֻּלָּם׃
of all skillful the their (is) and violet the the and
.them ones of work ,clothing purple ,goldsmith of hands

10 וַיהוָה אֱלֹהִים אֱמֶת הוּא־אֱלֹהִים חַיִּים וּמֶלֶךְ עוֹלָם מִקִּצְפּוֹ
His At ever- the and ,living the He ;true the (is) But
wrath .lasting king God (is) God Jehovah

11 תִּרְעַשׁ הָאָרֶץ וְלֹא־יָכִלוּ גוֹיִם זַעְמוֹ׃ כִּדְנָה תֵּאמְרוּן
shall you Like His the can and the shall
say .indignation nations endure not ,earth quake

לְהוֹם אֱלָהַיָּא דִּי־שְׁמַיָּא וְאַרְקָא לָא עֲבַדוּ יֵאבַדוּ מֵאַרְעָא
the from shall they have not the and the who The to
earth perish ,made earth heavens gods ,them

12 וּמִן־תְּחוֹת שְׁמַיָּא אֵלֶּה׃ עֹשֵׂה אֶרֶץ בְּכֹחוֹ מֵכִין
es- who His by the He (is It) .these heavens under and
tablished ;power earth made who from

13 תֵּבֵל בְּחָכְמָתוֹ וּבִתְבוּנָתוֹ נָטָה שָׁמָיִם׃ לְקוֹל תִּתּוֹ הֲמוֹן
tumult a His the At .heavens the has His by and His by the
of giving of sound out stretched understanding ,wisdom world

מַיִם בַּשָּׁמַיִם וַיַּעֲלֶה נְשִׂאִים מִקְצֵה אָרֶץ בְּרָקִים לַמָּטָר
the for lightning the the from the causes He the in waters
rain ;earth of end vapors ascend to ;heavens (is)

14 עָשָׂה וַיּוֹצֵא רוּחַ מֵאֹצְרֹתָיו׃ נִבְעַר כָּל־אָדָם מִדַּעַת
(of lack) from man Every is His from the and He
;knowledge stupid .storehouses wind forth brings ,makes

of) knowledge; every refiner is put to shame by the engraved image; for his molten image (is) a lie and no breath (is) in them. [15] They are vanity, the work of delusion; in the time of their judgment they shall perish. [16] The Portion of Jacob (is) not like these; for He (is) the Former of all things; and Israel (is) the tribe of His inheritance; Jehovah of hosts (is) His name.

[17] Gather up your bundle from the ground, you who live under the siege. [18] For thus says Jehovah, Behold, I will sling out the dwellers of the land at this time, and will distress them, so that they may find (Me).

[19] Woe is me for my breaking! My wound is grievous; but I said, Truly this (is) an affliction, and I must bear it. [20] My tent is ravaged, and all My cords are broken; My sons have left Me, and they are not. (There is) no stretching out My tent any more, or setting up My curtains. [21] For the pastors have become like animals, and they have not sought Jehovah; therefore they shall not be blessed, and all their flock shall be scattered. [22] Behold, the noise of a rumor! It comes, and a great commotion out of the north country, to make the cities of Judah a desolation, a den of jackals.

[23] O Jehovah, I know that not to man (belongs) his way; (it is) not to man who walks that he direct his steps. [24] O Jehovah, correct me, but with judgment; not in Your anger, lest You bring me to nothing. [25] Pour out Your fury on the nations who do not know You, and on families who do not call on Your name. For they have eaten up Jacob; and they have devoured him and have destroyed him, and have made his dwelling desolate.

הביש כל־צורף מפסל כי שקר נסכו ולא־רוח בם׃
in (is) breath and his a (is) for the by smith every put is
.them no ,image molten lie ;image graven shame to

15 16 הבל המה מעשה תעתעים בעת פקדתם יאבדו׃ לא־
Not will they their the in ,mockery the They vanity
.perish punishment of time of work ,(are)

כאלה חלק יעקב כי־יוצר הכל הוא וישראל שבט
the (is) Israel and He all the for ,Jacob the these like
of tribe ;(is) of Former of Portion (is)

17 נחלתו יהוה צבאות שמו׃ אספי מארץ כנעתך
your the from Gather His hosts Jehovah in- His
bundle ground up .name (is) of ,heritance

18 יושבתי במצור׃ כי־כה אמר יהוה הנני קולע
will ,Behold ,Jehovah says thus For under who you
out sling I .seige dwell

את־יושבי הארץ בפעם הזאת והצרותי להם למען ימצאו׃
may they so them will and ,this time at the inhab- the
.(Me) find that distress land of itants

19 אוי לי על־שברי נחלה מכתי ואני אמרתי אך
Truly ,said but My is my for to Woe
I ;wound grievous !breaking me

20 זה חלי ואשאנו׃ אהלי שדד וכל־מיתרי נתקו בני יצאני
have my are my and is My must I and a this
,me left sons ;broken cords all ,destroyed tent .it bear sickness (is)

21 ואינם אין־נטה עוד אהלי ומקים יריעותי׃ כי נבערו
be- have For My setting or My any stretch- Not they and
stupid come .curtains up ,tent more out ing is .not are

הרעים ואת־יהוה לא דרשו על־כן לא השכילו וכל־
and will they not therefore have they not Jehovah and the
all ,succeed ;sought ,shepherds

22 מרעיתם נפוצה׃ קול שמועה הנה באה ורעש גדול
great a and it ,Behold !report a The is their
commotion ,comes of sound .scattered flock

מארץ צפון לשום את־ערי יהודה שממה מעון תנים׃
.jackals den a a Judah the make to the the from
of ,desolation of cities ,north of land

23 ידעתי יהוה כי לא לאדם דרכו לא־לאיש הלך והכין
he that who to (is it) ,way his to (belongs) that O ,know I
direct walks man not man not ,Jehovah

24 את־צעדו׃ יסרני יהוה אך במשפט אל־באפך פן
lest Your in not with only O Correct his
,anger ,judgment ,Jehovah ,me .steps

25 תמעטני׃ שפך חמתך על־הגוים אשר לא־ידעוך ועל
and do not who the on Your Pour bring You
on ,You know nations wrath out .nothing to me

משפחות אשר בשמך לא קראו כי־אכלו את־יעקב
;Jacob have they For do not Your on who families
devoured .call name

ואכלהו ויכלהו ואת־נוהו השמו׃
made have his and con- and de- they and
.desolate dwelling him sumed him voured

CAP. XI **יא**

CHAPTER 11

CHAPTER 11

[1] The word that came to Jeremiah from Jehovah, saying, [2] Hear the words of this covenant, and speak to the men of Judah and to the inhabitants of Jerusalem, [3] And say to them, Thus says Jehovah, the God of Israel, Cursed (is) the man who does not obey the words of this covenant, [4] which I commanded your fathers in the day I brought them out of the land of Egypt, from the iron furnace, saying, Obey My voice and do them according to all that I command you, so you shall be My people, and. I will be your God, [5] in order to establish the oath which I swore to your fathers, to give them a land flowing with milk and honey, as (it is) this day. Then I answered and said, Amen, O Jehovah. [6] Then Jehovah said to me, Declare all these words in the cities of Judah, and in the streets of Jerusalem, saying, Hear the words of this covenant and do them. [7] For I solemnly warned your fathers in the day (that) I brought them up out of the land of Egypt, to this day, rising early and warning, saying, Obey My voice. [8] Yet they did not obey nor bow down their ear, but walked each one in the stubbornness of their evil heart. Therefore I will bring on them all the words of this

הַדָּבָר֙ אֲשֶׁ֣ר הָיָ֣ה אֶֽל־יִרְמְיָ֔הוּ מֵאֵ֥ת יְהוָ֖ה לֵאמֹֽר׃ שְׁמְע֗וּ

Hear   ,saying ,Jehovah from   Jeremiah to   came   that   The word

אֶת־דִּבְרֵ֖י הַבְּרִ֣ית הַזֹּ֑את וְדִבַּרְתָּ֞ם אֶל־אִ֣ישׁ יְהוּדָ֗ה וְעַל־

and   Judah   the to   speak and   this   covenant   the

to   of men   of words

יֹשְׁבֵ֣י יְרוּשָׁלָ֑͏ִם וְאָמַרְתָּ֣ אֲלֵיהֶ֔ם כֹּֽה־אָמַ֥ר יְהוָ֖ה אֱלֹהֵ֣י

the   ,Jehovah says Thus   ,them to   say and ;Jerusalem in- the

of God   of habitants

יִשְׂרָאֵ֑ל אָר֣וּר הָאִ֔ישׁ אֲשֶׁר֙ לֹ֣א יִשְׁמַ֔ע אֶת־דִּבְרֵ֖י הַבְּרִ֥ית

covenant   the   does not   who   the   Cursed ,Israel

    of words   obey   man   (is)

הַזֹּֽאת׃ אֲשֶׁ֣ר צִוִּ֣יתִי אֶת־אֲבֽוֹתֵיכֶ֗ם בְּי֨וֹם הוֹצִיאִֽי־אוֹתָ֜ם

them brought I   the in   your   com- I   which   this

    out   day   fathers   manded

מֵאֶֽרֶץ־מִצְרַ֨יִם֙ מִכּ֣וּר הַבַּרְזֶ֜ל לֵאמֹ֗ר שִׁמְע֣וּ בְקוֹלִ֗י וַעֲשִׂיתֶ֤ם

do and   My   Obey   ,saying ,iron the   from   ,Egypt   the from

    voice   furnace   of land

אוֹתָם֙ כְּכֹ֣ל אֲשֶׁר־אֲצַוֶּ֣ה אֶתְכֶ֔ם וִהְיִ֤יתֶם לִי֙ לְעָ֔ם וְאָ֣נֹכִ֔י

I and   a for   to   you So   .you   com- I   that according them

    ,people Me be will   mand   all to

אֶהְיֶ֥ה לָכֶ֖ם לֵֽאלֹהִ֑ים לְמַ֩עַן֩ הָקִ֨ים אֶת־הַשְּׁבוּעָ֜ה אֲשֶׁר־

which   the   to order in   ,God for   to   shall

      oath   establish   you   be

נִשְׁבַּ֣עְתִּי לַאֲבֽוֹתֵיכֶ֗ם לָתֵ֤ת לָהֶם֙ אֶ֛רֶץ זָבַ֥ת חָלָ֖ב וּדְבַ֑שׁ

and   milk   flowing   a   to   give to   your to   swore I

,honey   with   land   them   fathers

כַּיּ֥וֹם הַזֶּ֖ה וָאַ֥עַן וָאֹמַ֖ר אָמֵ֥ן ׀ יְהוָֽה׃ וַיֹּ֤אמֶר יְהוָה֙

Jehovah Then   O   ,Amen ,said and I Then .this (is it) as

     said   .Jehovah   answered   day

אֵלַ֔י קְרָ֨א אֶת־כָּל־הַדְּבָרִ֥ים הָאֵ֖לֶּה בְּעָרֵ֣י יְהוּדָ֑ה וּבְחֻצ֣וֹת

in and   Judah   the in   these   words   all   Proclaim to

of streets the   of cities   ,Me

יְרוּשָׁלַ֖͏ִם לֵאמֹ֑ר שִׁמְע֗וּ אֶת־דִּבְרֵי֙ הַבְּרִ֣ית הַזֹּ֔את וַעֲשִׂיתֶ֖ם

do and   this   covenant   the   Hear   ,saying ,Jerusalem

                  of words

7   אוֹתָֽם׃ כִּי֩ הָעֵ֨ד הַעִדֹ֜תִי בַּאֲבֽוֹתֵיכֶ֗ם בְּי֨וֹם הַעֲלוֹתִ֤י אוֹתָם֙

them brought I   the in   your   I   solemnly For   .them

    up   day   fathers   admonished

מֵאֶ֣רֶץ מִצְרַ֔יִם֙ עַד־הַיּ֥וֹם הַזֶּ֖ה הַשְׁכֵּ֣ם וְהָעֵ֣ד לֵאמֹ֑ר שִׁמְע֖וּ

Obey   ,saying   and   rising   ,this day   to   ,Egypt   of out

        ,admonishing early   of land the

8   בְּקוֹלִֽי׃ וְלֹ֤א שָׁמְעוּ֙ וְלֹֽא־הִטּ֣וּ אֶת־אָזְנָ֔ם וַיֵּ֣לְכ֔וּ אִ֖ישׁ

each   but   their   incline nor   did they   Yet   My

man   walked   ,ear   obey   not   .voice

בִּשְׁרִיר֖וּת לִבָּ֣ם הָרָ֑ע וָאָבִ֨יא עֲלֵיהֶ֜ם אֶֽת־כָּל־דִּבְרֵ֥י הַבְּרִית־

covenant   the   all   them on I So   .evil   their stub- the in

    of words   bring will   heart of bornness

covenant, which I commanded (them) to do; but they did not do. [9] And Jehovah said to me, A plot is found among the men of Judah, and among the inhabitants of Jerusalem. [10] They have turned back to the iniquities of their forefathers, who refused to hear My words. And they went after other gods to serve them. The house of Israel and the house of Judah have broken My covenant which I cut with their fathers.

[11] Therefore thus says Jehovah, Behold, I will bring evil on them, from which they shall not be able to escape; and though they cry to Me, I will not listen to them. [12] Then the cities of Judah and the inhabitants of Jerusalem shall go and cry to the gods to whom they burned incense. But they not at all can save them in the time of their trouble. [13] For (according to) the number of your cities were your gods, O Judah. And (according to) the number of the streets of Jerusalem you have set up altars to (that) shameful thing, altars to burn incense to Baal. [14] And you, do not pray for this people, and do not lift up a cry or prayer for them. For I will not hear in the time they cry to Me for their trouble. [15] What (is to) My beloved in My house, (since) she has committed her many evils? And has the holy flesh removed your evil from you? (How) then do you exult? [16] Jehovah called your name, a green olive tree, fair, (with) desirable fruit. With the noise of a great storm He has set fire to it, and its branches are worthless.

9 הַזֹּאת אֲשֶׁר־צִוִּיתִי לַעֲשׂוֹת וְלֹא עָשׂוּ׃ וַיֹּאמֶר יְהוָה
Jehovah said And they but ;do to com- I which ,this
.do did not manded

10 אֵלָי נִמְצָא־קֶשֶׁר בְּאִישׁ יְהוּדָה וּבְיֹשְׁבֵי יְרוּשָׁלִָם׃ שָׁבוּ
have They .Jerusalem the and ,Judah among plot A is to
returned of inhabitants of men the found ,me

עַל־עֲוֺנֹת אֲבוֹתָם הָרִאשֹׁנִים אֲשֶׁר מֵאֲנוּ לִשְׁמוֹעַ אֶת־
hear to refused who former their the to
fathers of iniquities

דְּבָרַי וְהֵמָּה הָלְכוּ אַחֲרֵי אֱלֹהִים אֲחֵרִים לְעָבְדָם הֵפֵרוּ
have serve to other gods after went and My
broken .them they ,words

בֵית־יִשְׂרָאֵל וּבֵית יְהוּדָה אֶת־בְּרִיתִי אֲשֶׁר כָּרַתִּי אֶת־
with cut I which My Judah the and Israel The
covenant of house of house

11 אֲבוֹתָם׃ לָכֵן כֹּה אָמַר יְהוָה הִנְנִי מֵבִיא אֲלֵיהֶם
them on will Behold ,Jehovah says thus Therefore their
bring I .fathers

רָעָה אֲשֶׁר לֹא־יוּכְלוּ לָצֵאת מִמֶּנָּה וְזָעֲקוּ אֵלַי וְלֹא
not to (if) And from go to will they not which ,evil
,Me cry they ;it forth able be

12 אֶשְׁמַע אֲלֵיהֶם׃ וְהָלְכוּ עָרֵי יְהוּדָה וְיֹשְׁבֵי יְרוּשָׁלִַם
Jerusalem the and Judah the shall Then .them to will I
of inhabitants of cities go listen

וְזָעֲקוּ אֶל־הָאֱלֹהִים אֲשֶׁר הֵם מְקַטְּרִים לָהֶם וְהוֹשֵׁעַ לֹא־
not at But .them to burned they whom the to and
all incense gods cry

13 יוֹשִׁיעוּ לָהֶם בְּעֵת רָעָתָם׃ כִּי מִסְפַּר עָרֶיךָ הָיוּ אֱלֹהֶיךָ
your (so) your the (as) For their the in them can they
,gods were ,cities of number .trouble of time save

יְהוּדָה וּמִסְפַּר חֻצוֹת יְרוּשָׁלִַם שַׂמְתֶּם מִזְבְּחוֹת לַבֹּשֶׁת
the to altars have you ,Jerusalem the the (as) and O
,thing shameful up set of streets of number ;Judah

14 מִזְבְּחוֹת לְקַטֵּר לַבָּעַל׃ וְאַתָּה אַל־תִּתְפַּלֵּל בְּעַד־
for do not ,you And .Baal to burn to altars
pray incense

הָעָם הַזֶּה וְאַל־תִּשָּׂא בַעֲדָם רִנָּה וּתְפִלָּה כִּי ׀ אֵינֶנִּי שֹׁמֵעַ
will I for or cry a for lift do and ,this people
hear not ,prayer them up not

15 בְּעֵת קָרְאָם אֵלַי בְּעַד רָעָתָם׃ מֶה לִידִידִי בְּבֵיתִי
My in My to What their for to they the in
,house beloved (belongs) .trouble Me cry time

עֲשׂוֹתָהּ הַמְזִמָּתָה הָרַבִּים וּבְשַׂר־קֹדֶשׁ יַעַבְרוּ מֵעָלָיִךְ כִּי
but from has holy the And .many her she (since)
you removed flesh evils done has

16 רָעָתֵכִי אָז תַּעֲלֹזִי׃ זַיִת רַעֲנָן יְפֵה פְרִי־תֹאַר קָרָא יְהוָה
Jehovah called ,fine (with) ,fair ,green A you do (How) your
fruit tree olive ;exult then ?evil

שְׁמֵךְ לְקוֹל ׀ הֲמוּלָּה גְדֹלָה הִצִּית אֵשׁ עָלֶיהָ וְרָעוּ דָּלִיּוֹתָיו׃
its are and ,it to fire has He great storm the with your
.branches bad set of sound ;name

[17] And Jehovah of hosts who planted you has spoken evil against you, because of the evil of the house of Israel and of the house of Judah, which they have done to themselves to provoke Me to anger, by burning incense to Baal.

[18] And Jehovah made me know, and I knew. Then You showed me their doings. [19] And I was like a docile lamb being brought to the slaughter; and I did not know that they had plotted schemes against me, (saying), Let us destroy the tree with its fruit, and let us cut him off from the land of the living, so that his name may be remembered no more. [20] But, O Jehovah of hosts who judges with righteousness, who tries the reins and the heart, let me see Your vengeance on them. For to You I have revealed my cause. [21] Therefore thus says Jehovah concerning the men of Anathoth, who seek your life, saying, Do not prophesy in the name of Jehovah, that you do not die by our hand. [22] Therefore thus says Jehovah of hosts, Behold, I will punish them. The young men shall die by the sword; their sons and their daughters shall die by famine; [23] and there shall be no remnant of them. For I will bring evil on the men of Anathoth, (even) the year of their punishment.

17 וַיהוָה צְבָאוֹת הַנּוֹטֵעַ אוֹתָךְ דִּבֶּר עָלַיִךְ רָעָה בִּגְלַל רָעַת
the because ,evil against has you who hosts Jeho- And
of evil of you spoken planted of vah

בֵּית־יִשְׂרָאֵל וּבֵית יְהוּדָה אֲשֶׁר עָשׂוּ לָהֶם לְהַכְעִסֵנִי לְקַטֵּר
burn- by Me vex to them- to they which ,Judah the and Israel the
incense ing ,anger to selves done have of house of house

18 לַבָּעַל׃ וַיהוָה הוֹדִיעַנִי וָאֵדָעָה אָז הִרְאִיתַנִי מַעַלְלֵיהֶם׃
their showed You then I and informed And .Baal to
.doings me ;knew ,me Jehovah

19 וַאֲנִי כְּכֶבֶשׂ אַלּוּף יוּבַל לִטְבוֹחַ וְלֹא־יָדַעְתִּי כִּי־עָלַי
against that did I and the to being docile a like I And
me know not ;slaughter brought lamb (was)

חָשְׁבוּ מַחֲשָׁבוֹת נַשְׁחִיתָה עֵץ בְּלַחְמוֹ וְנִכְרְתֶנּוּ מֵאֶרֶץ
the from us let and its with the us Let schemes had they
of land off him cut ;food tree destroy ,(saying) plotted

20 חַיִּים וּשְׁמוֹ לֹא־יִזָּכֵר עוֹד׃ וַיהוָה צְבָאוֹת שֹׁפֵט
who hosts O ,But .still be may not his that the
with judges of Jehovah remembered name ,living

צֶדֶק בֹּחֵן כְּלָיוֹת וָלֵב אֶרְאֶה נִקְמָתְךָ מֵהֶם כִּי אֵלֶיךָ גִּלִּיתִי
have I to for on Your me let the and the who righ-
revealed you ,them vengeance see ,heart kidneys tries ,teousness

21 אֶת־רִיבִי׃ לָכֵן כֹּה־אָמַר יְהוָה עַל־אַנְשֵׁי עֲנָתוֹת
,Anathoth the about Jehovah says thus Therefore .cause my
of men

הַמְבַקְשִׁים אֶת־נַפְשְׁךָ לֵאמֹר לֹא תִנָּבֵא בְּשֵׁם יְהוָה וְלֹא
that ,Jehovah the in Do not ,saying your who
not of name prophesy ,life seek

22 תָמוּת בְּיָדֵנוּ׃ לָכֵן כֹּה אָמַר יְהוָה צְבָאוֹת הִנְנִי פֹקֵד
will ,Behold ,hosts Jehovah says thus Therefore our by you
punish I of .hand die might

עֲלֵיהֶם הַבַּחוּרִים יָמֻתוּ בַחֶרֶב בְּנֵיהֶם וּבְנוֹתֵיהֶם יָמֻתוּ
shall their and their the by shall young the ,them
die daughters sons ;sword die men

23 בָּרָעָב׃ וּשְׁאֵרִית לֹא תִהְיֶה לָהֶם כִּי־אָבִיא רָעָה אֶל־אַנְשֵׁי
the on evil will I for of will not a and by
of men bring ,them be remnant ;famine

עֲנָתוֹת שְׁנַת פְּקֻדָּתָם׃
their the —Anathoth
.punishment of year

CAP. XII יב

CHAPTER 12

[1] You (are) righteous, O Jehovah, when I complain to You; yet let me speak with You (of Your) judgments. Why does the way of the wicked prosper? (Why) are all (those) at ease who deal treacherously? [2] You planted them; yea, they take root. They grow, they even make fruit. You (are) near in their mouth,

1 צַדִּיק אַתָּה יְהוָה כִּי אָרִיב אֵלֶיךָ אַךְ מִשְׁפָּטִים אֲדַבֵּר
would I (Your about) indeed to might I that O You righteous
speak judgments ;You complain ,Jehovah ,(are)

אוֹתָךְ מַדּוּעַ דֶּרֶךְ רְשָׁעִים צָלֵחָה שָׁלוּ כָּל־בֹּגְדֵי בָגֶד׃
treach- who all are (Why) does the the Why with
.erously deal case at ?prosper wicked of way .You

2 נְטַעְתָּם גַּם־שֹׁרָשׁוּ יֵלְכוּ גַּם־עָשׂוּ פֶרִי קָרוֹב אַתָּה בְּפִיהֶם
their in You near .fruit they even they they also planted You
,mouth (are) make ,grow ;root take ,them

and far from their heart. [3] But, O Jehovah, You know me. You have seen me and tried my heart with You. Pull them out like sheep for the slaughter, and consecrate them for the day of slaughter. [4] How long shall the land mourn, and the grass of every field wither from the wickedness of those who dwell in it? The beasts and the birds are swept away, because they said, He will not see our last end.

[5] If you have run with footmen and they wore you out, then how can you vie with horses? And if in the land of peace, you feel secure, then how will you do in the swelling of Jordan? [6] For even your brothers and the house of your father, even they have dealt treacherously with you; even they have called after you fully. Do not believe them, though they speak good things to you.

[7] I have forsaken My house; I have left My inheritance. I have given the beloved of My soul into the hand of her enemies. [8] My inheritance has become to Me as a lion in the forest; she cried out against Me; therefore I hated it. [9] My inheritance (is) to Me (like) the speckled bird, the birds all around (are) against her. Come, gather all the beasts of the field, bring them to devour. [10] Many shepherds have destroyed My vineyard; they have trampled My portion under foot; they have made My pleasant portion a desolate wilderness. [11] They have made it desolate; it mourns to Me; the whole land is made desolate, but no man lays (it) to heart. [12] The ravagers have come on all high places through the wilderness; for the sword of Jehovah devours from (one) end of the land even to the (other) end of the land; not

3 וְרָחוֹק מִכִּלְיוֹתֵיהֶם׃ וְאַתָּה יְהוָה יְדַעְתָּנִי תִּרְאֵנִי וּבָחַנְתָּ
and have You know O ,you But their from far but
tested me seen ;me ,Jehovah .reins

לִבִּי אִתָּךְ הַתִּקֵם כְּצֹאן לְטִבְחָה וְהַקְדִּשֵׁם לְיוֹם הֲרֵגָה׃
.slaughter the for con- and the for like Separate toward my
of day them secrate ,slaughter sheep them .You heart

4 עַד־מָתַי תֶּאֱבַל הָאָרֶץ וְעֵשֶׂב כָּל־הַשָּׂדֶה יִיבָשׁ
,wither field every the and the shall How
of grass ,land mourn long

מֵרָעַת יֹשְׁבֵי־בָהּ סָפְתָה בְהֵמוֹת וָעוֹף כִּי אָמְרוּ לֹא יִרְאֶה
will He not they for the and The swept are ?it in those the from
see ,said ,birds beasts away dwell who of evil

5 אֶת־אַחֲרִיתֵנוּ׃ כִּי אֶת־רַגְלִים ׀ רַצְתָּה וַיַּלְאוּךָ וְאֵיךְ תְּתַחֲרֶה
you can then they and have you footmen with If last our
compete how ,you wearied ,run .end

אֶת־הַסּוּסִים וּבְאֶרֶץ שָׁלוֹם אַתָּה בוֹטֵחַ וְאֵיךְ תַּעֲשֶׂה
you will then feel you peace in if And ?horses with
do how ,secure of land the

6 בִּגְאוֹן הַיַּרְדֵּן׃ כִּי גַם־אַחֶיךָ וּבֵית־אָבִיךָ גַּם־הֵמָּה בָּגְדוּ
be- have they even your the and your even For the the in
trayed ,father of house brothers ?Jordan of swelling

בָךְ גַּם־הֵמָּה קָרְאוּ אַחֲרֶיךָ מָלֵא אַל־תַּאֲמֵן בָּם כִּי־יְדַבְּרוּ
they though ,them Do not .fully after have they even ,you
speak believe you called

7 אֵלֶיךָ טוֹבוֹת׃ עָזַבְתִּי אֶת־בֵּיתִי נָטַשְׁתִּי אֶת־נַחֲלָתִי
My have I My have I good to
.inheritance left ;house forsaken .things you

8 נָתַתִּי אֶת־יְדִדוּת נַפְשִׁי בְּכַף אֹיְבֶיהָ׃ הָיְתָה־לִּי נַחֲלָתִי
in- My to has her the into My the have I
heritance Me become .enemies of hand soul of beloved given

9 כְּאַרְיֵה בַיָּעַר נָתְנָה עָלַי בְּקוֹלָהּ עַל־כֵּן שְׂנֵאתִיהָ׃ הַעַיִט
the (Like) hated I therefore her against She the in a like
bird .her ;voice Me lifted .forest lion

צָבוּעַ נַחֲלָתִי לִי הַעַיִט סָבִיב עָלֶיהָ לְכוּ אִסְפוּ כָּל־חַיַּת
the all gather ,Go against all (are) the (is) in- My speckled
of beasts .her around birds ;Me to heritance

10 הַשָּׂדֶה הֵתָיוּ לְאָכְלָה׃ רֹעִים רַבִּים שִׁחֲתוּ כַרְמִי בֹּסְסוּ
they My have Many shepherds .devour to bring the
trod ,vineyard destroyed them ,field

אֶת־חֶלְקָתִי נָתְנוּ אֶת־חֶלְקַת חֶמְדָּתִי לְמִדְבַּר שְׁמָמָה׃
.desolate wilder- a My portion have they My
ness pleasant made ;portion

11 שָׂמָהּ לִשְׁמָמָה אָבְלָה עָלַי שְׁמֵמָה נָשַׁמָּה כָּל־הָאָרֶץ כִּי
but the whole is desolate to it deso- a has One
,land made ,Me mourns ,lation it made

12 אֵין אִישׁ שָׂם עַל־לֵב׃ עַל־כָּל־שְׁפָיִם בַּמִּדְבָּר בָּאוּ שֹׁדְדִים
;destroyers have the in the all On .heart to lays man no
come wilderness heights (it)

כִּי חֶרֶב לַיהוָה אֹכְלָה מִקְצֵה אֶרֶץ וְעַד־קְצֵה הָאָרֶץ אֵין
not the the even the (one) from devours of the for
;land of end (other) to land of end Jehovah sword

is peace for any flesh.
[13] They have sown
wheat, but have reaped
thorns. They are worn out;
but they do not profit. And
they shall be ashamed of
your harvests because of
the glow of the anger of
Jehovah.
[14] Thus says Jehovah
against all my wicked neighbors who touch the inheritance which I have caused
My people Israel to inherit:
Behold, I will tear them
from their land, and I will
tear the house of Judah
from among them. [15] And
it shall come to pass, after
I have torn them out, I
will return and have pity
on them, and will bring
them again, each man to his
inheritance and each man to
his land. [16] And it shall
come to pass, if they will
carefully learn the ways of
My people, to swear by My
name, "(As) Jehovah lives";
as they taught My people to
swear by Baal; then they
will be built in the midst of
My people. [17] But if they
will not obey, then I will
tear and destroy that
nation, says Jehovah.

13 שָׁלוֹם לְכָל־בָּשָׂר׃ זָרְעוּ חִטִּים וְקֹצִים קָצָרוּ נֶחְלוּ
are they have but ,wheat They .flesh for peace
exhausted ;reaped thorns sown have any

לֹא יוֹעִלוּ וּבֹשׁוּ מִתְּבוּאֹתֵיכֶם מֵחֲרוֹן אַף־יְהוָה׃
Jeho- anger of because your of are they and they but
.vah's of glow the ,harvests ashamed ;profit not

14 כֹּה ׀ אָמַר יְהוָה עַל־כָּל־שְׁכֵנַי הָרָעִים הַנֹּגְעִים בַּנַּחֲלָה
the who wicked my all against Jeho- says Thus
inheritance touch neighbors vah

אֲשֶׁר־הִנְחַלְתִּי אֶת־עַמִּי אֶת־יִשְׂרָאֵל הִנְנִי נֹתְשָׁם מֵעַל
from will I ,Behold :Israel My have I which
them tear I people inherit to caused

15 אַדְמָתָם וְאֶת־בֵּית יְהוּדָה אֶתּוֹשׁ מִתּוֹכָם׃ וְהָיָה אַחֲרֵי
after it And their from will I Judah the and their
be will .midst tear of house ,land

נָתְשִׁי אוֹתָם אָשׁוּב וְרִחַמְתִּים וַהֲשִׁבֹתִים אִישׁ לְנַחֲלָתוֹ
his to each bring will and pity have and will I ,them have I
inheritance man ,back them them on return out torn

16 וְאִישׁ לְאַרְצוֹ׃ וְהָיָה אִם־לָמֹד יִלְמְדוּ אֶת־דַּרְכֵי עַמִּי לְהִשָּׁבֵעַ
swear to My the will they diligently if it And his to and
,people of ways learn ,be will .land man each

בִּשְׁמִי חַי־יְהוָה כַּאֲשֶׁר לִמְּדוּ אֶת־עַמִּי לְהִשָּׁבֵעַ בַּבַּעַל וְנִבְנוּ
they so ;Baal by to My they as ;Jehovah (as) My by
built be will swear people taught lives ,name

17 בְּתוֹךְ עַמִּי׃ וְאִם לֹא יִשְׁמָעוּ וְנָתַשְׁתִּי אֶת־הַגּוֹי הַהוּא נָתוֹשׁ
cer- that nation I then they not But My the in
,tainly out tear will ,obey will if .people of midst

וְאַבֵּד נְאֻם־יְהוָה׃
.Jehovah says and
,(it) destroy

CAP. XIII יג

CHAPTER 13

[1] Thus says Jehovah
to me, Go and buy for yourself a linen band and put it
on your loins and do not
put it in water. [2] So I
bought a band according to
the word of Jehovah, and
put (it) on my loins.
[3] And the word of Jeho-
vah came to me a second
time, saying, [4] Take the
band that you bought
which (is) on your loins,
and arise; go to Euphrates
and hide it there in the cleft
of the rock. [5] So I went
and hid it by Euphrates, as
Jehovah commanded me.
[6] And it came to pass,

1 כֹּה־אָמַר יְהוָה אֵלַי הָלוֹךְ וְקָנִיתָ לְּךָ אֵזוֹר פִּשְׁתִּים וְשַׂמְתּוֹ
put and linen band a for and Go ,me to Jehovah says Thus
it yourself buy

2 עַל־מָתְנֶיךָ וּבַמַּיִם לֹא תְבִאֵהוּ׃ וָאֶקְנֶה אֶת־הָאֵזוֹר כִּדְבַר
according the I So put do not in and your on
word to band bought .it water ,loins

3 יְהוָה וָאָשִׂם עַל־מָתְנָי׃ וַיְהִי דְבַר־יְהוָה אֵלַי שֵׁנִית
second a to Jehovah the And my on put and Jeho-
,time me of word came .loins (it) vah's

4 לֵאמֹר׃ קַח אֶת־הָאֵזוֹר אֲשֶׁר קָנִיתָ אֲשֶׁר עַל־מָתְנֶיךָ
your on which you which the Take ,saying
,loins (is) bought band

5 וְקוּם לֵךְ פְּרָתָה וְטָמְנֵהוּ שָׁם בִּנְקִיק הַסָּלַע׃ וָאֵלֵךְ
I And .rock the the in there hide and to go and
went of cleft it Euphrates ,arise

6 וָאֶטְמְנֵהוּ בִּפְרָת כַּאֲשֶׁר צִוָּה יְהוָה אוֹתִי׃ וַיְהִי
it And .me Jehovah com- as by hid and
was manded ,Euphrates it

after many days, Jehovah said to me, Arise, go to Euphrates and take the band from there, which I commanded you to hide there. [7] Then I went to Euphrates and dug, and I took the band from the place where I had hidden it there. And behold, the band was ruined; it was not useful for anything. [8] Then the word of Jehovah came to me, saying, [9] Thus says Jehovah, So I will spoil the pride of Judah and the great pride of Jerusalem. [10] This evil people, who refuse to hear My words, who walk in the stubbornness of their heart and walk after other gods to serve them and to worship them, shall even be like this girdle, which is not useful for anything. [11] For as the girdle holds fast to the loins of a man, so I have caused the whole house of Israel and the whole house of Judah to cling to Me, says Jehovah; to be to Me for a people, and for a name, and for praise, and for a glory; but they would not listen.

[12] So you will speak to them this word: Thus says Jehovah God of Israel, Every skin shall be filled with wine. And they shall say to you, Do we not know full well that every skin shall be filled with wine? [13] Then you shall say to them, Thus says Jehovah, Behold, I will fill all the inhabitants of this land, even the kings that sit on David's throne, and the priests, and the prophets, and all the inhabitants of

מִקֵּץ יָמִים רַבִּים וַיֹּאמֶר יְהוָה אֵלַי קוּם לֵךְ פְּרָתָה וְקַח
and to go ,Arise ,me to Jehovah said ,many days after
take Euphrates

7 מִשָּׁם אֶת־הָאֵזוֹר אֲשֶׁר צִוִּיתִיךָ לְטָמְנוֹ־שָׁם׃ וָאֵלֵךְ פְּרָתָה
to I Then .there hide to com- I which the from
Euphrates went you manded band there

וָאֶחְפֹּר וָאֶקַּח אֶת־הָאֵזוֹר מִן־הַמָּקוֹם אֲשֶׁר־טְמַנְתִּיו שָׁמָּה
there had I where the from the I and ,dug and
it hidden place band took

8 וְהִנֵּה נִשְׁחַת הָאֵזוֹר לֹא יִצְלַח לַכֹּל׃ וַיְהִי דְבַר־
the Then any- for was it not the was And
of word came .thing useful band ruined ,behold

9 יְהוָה אֵלַי לֵאמֹר׃ כֹּה אָמַר יְהוָה כָּכָה אַשְׁחִית אֶת־
will I so ,Jehovah says Thus ,saying ,me to Jehovah
ruin

10 גְּאוֹן יְהוּדָה וְאֶת־גְּאוֹן יְרוּשָׁלַםִ הָרָב׃ הָעָם הַזֶּה הָרָע
evil This people .great Jerusalem the and Judah the
of pride of pride

הַמֵּאֲנִים ׀ לִשְׁמוֹעַ אֶת־דְּבָרַי הַהֹלְכִים בִּשְׁרִרוּת לִבָּם
their stub- the in who My hear to who
heart of bornness walk ,words refuse

וַיֵּלְכוּ אַחֲרֵי אֱלֹהִים אֲחֵרִים לְעָבְדָם וּלְהִשְׁתַּחֲוֺת לָהֶם
,them to and serve to other gods after and
worship ,them walk

11 וִיהִי כָּאֵזוֹר הַזֶּה אֲשֶׁר לֹא־יִצְלַח לַכֹּל׃ כִּי כַּאֲשֶׁר יִדְבַּק
clings as For for is not which this like even
.anything useful band be will

הָאֵזוֹר אֶל־מָתְנֵי אִישׁ כֵּן הִדְבַּקְתִּי אֵלַי אֶת־כָּל־בֵּית
house the Me to made I so ,man a the to the
of whole cling of loins band

יִשְׂרָאֵל וְאֶת־כָּל־בֵּית יְהוּדָה נְאֻם־יְהוָה לִהְיוֹת לִי לְעָם
a for to be to ,Jehovah says ,Judah house the and Israel
,people Me of whole

12 וּלְשֵׁם וְלִתְהִלָּה וּלְתִפְאָרֶת וְלֹא שָׁמֵעוּ׃ וְאָמַרְתָּ אֲלֵיהֶם
them to you So would they but for and for and for and
speak will .listen not ;glory ,praise ,name a

אֶת־הַדָּבָר הַזֶּה כֹּה־אָמַר יְהוָה אֱלֹהֵי יִשְׂרָאֵל כָּל־נֵבֶל
skin Every ,Israel God Jehovah says Thus :this word
of

יִמָּלֵא יָיִן וְאָמְרוּ אֵלֶיךָ הֲיָדֹעַ לֹא נֵדַע כִּי כָל־נֵבֶל יִמָּלֵא
be will skin every that we Do not very ,you to they And .wine be will
with filled know well say will with filled

13 יָיִן׃ וְאָמַרְתָּ אֲלֵיהֶם כֹּה־אָמַר יְהוָה הִנְנִי מְמַלֵּא
fill will ,Behold ,Jehovah says thus ,them to you Then ?wine
with I say will

אֶת־כָּל־יֹשְׁבֵי הָאָרֶץ הַזֹּאת וְאֶת־הַמְּלָכִים הַיֹּשְׁבִים לְדָוִד
for that the even ,this the inhab- the all
David sit kings land of itants

עַל־כִּסְאוֹ וְאֶת־הַכֹּהֲנִים וְאֶת־הַנְּבִיאִים וְאֵת כָּל־יֹשְׁבֵי
the all and the and the and his upon
of inhabitants ,prophets ,priests ,throne

Jerusalem, with drunkenness. [14] And I will smash them one against another, even the fathers and the sons together, says Jehovah; I will not pity, nor spare, nor have compassion from their destruction.

[15] Hear and give ear; do not be proud; for Jehovah has spoken. [16] Give glory to Jehovah your God, before He brings darkness, and before your feet stumble on the dark mountains; and, while you look for light, He puts it into death-shade, (and) makes (it) gross darkness. [17] But if you will not hear it, my soul shall weep in secret places for (your) pride. And my eye shall bitterly weep and run down with tears, because Jehovah's flock was captured. [18] Say to the king and to the queen mother, Humble yourselves, sit down; for will come down from your headplaces the crown of your glory. [19] The cities of the south have been shut up, and none are opening. Judah has been carried away captive, all of it; it shall be wholly carried away captive. [20] Lift up your eyes and behold those who come from the north; where (is) the flock (that) was given to you, your beautiful flock? [21] What will you say when He visits you? For you taught them (to be) chiefs over you for a head! Do not pangs seize you like a woman in travail?

[22] And if you say in your heart, Why do these things come upon me? (It is) because of the greatness of your iniquity; your skirts are bared; your heels suffer violence. [23] Can the Ethiopian change his skin, or the leopard his spots? (Then) you also may do good, who are accustomed to doing evil. [24] Therefore I will scatter them as the stubble that passes away to the wilderness wind. [25] This (is) your lot, the share of your measure from Me, says Jehovah; because

14 יְרוּשָׁלִָם שִׁכָּרוֹן׃ וְנִפַּצְתִּים אִישׁ אֶל־אָחִיו וְהָאָבוֹת וְהַבָּנִים
the and the even his against man will I And drunken- ,Jerusalem
sons fathers ,brother them smash .ness

יַחְדָּו נְאֻם־יְהוָה לֹא־אֶחְמוֹל וְלֹא־אָחוּס וְלֹא אֲרַחֵם
have nor ,spare nor will I not ;Jehovah says ,together
,compassion pity

15 מֵהַשְׁחִיתָם׃ שִׁמְעוּ וְהַאֲזִינוּ אַל־תִּגְבָּהוּ כִּי יְהוָה דִּבֵּר׃
has Jehovah for be not give and Hear their from
.spoken ,proud ,ear .destruction

16 תְּנוּ לַיהוָה אֱלֹהֵיכֶם כָּבוֹד בְּטֶרֶם יַחְשִׁךְ וּבְטֶרֶם יִתְנַגְּפוּ
stumble and brings He before glory your to Give
before darkness God Jehovah

רַגְלֵיכֶם עַל־הָרֵי נָשֶׁף וְקִוִּיתֶם לְאוֹר וְשָׂמָהּ לְצַלְמָוֶת
into puts He for while and dark- the on your
,death-shade it ,light wait you ;ness of mountains feet

17 יָשִׁית לַעֲרָפֶל׃ וְאִם לֹא תִשְׁמָעוּהָ בְּמִסְתָּרִים תִּבְכֶּה־
shall secret in will you not But deep (and)
weep places ,it to listen if .gloom up sets

נַפְשִׁי מִפְּנֵי גֵוָה וְדָמֹעַ תִּדְמַע וְתֵרַד עֵינִי דִּמְעָה כִּי נִשְׁבָּה
was for (with) my run and shed and (such) for my
seized ,tears eye down tears bitterly ,pride soul

18 עֵדֶר יְהוָה׃ אֱמֹר לַמֶּלֶךְ וְלַגְּבִירָה הַשְׁפִּילוּ שֵׁבוּ
sit Humble the to and the to Say .Jehovah's flock
;down ,yourselves ,mother queen king

19 כִּי יָרַד מַרְאֲשֹׁתֵיכֶם עֲטֶרֶת תִּפְאַרְתְּכֶם׃ עָרֵי הַנֶּגֶב סֻגְּרוּ
been have the The your the your from will for
,up shut south of cities .glory of crown head-places descend

וְאֵין פֹּתֵחַ הָגְלָת יְהוּדָה כֻּלָּהּ הָגְלָת שְׁלוֹמִים׃
.wholly been has of all ;Judah been has are and
exiled it exiled opening none

20 שְׂאִי עֵינֵיכֶם וּרְאִי הַבָּאִים מִצָּפוֹן אַיֵּה הָעֵדֶר נִתַּן־לָךְ צֹאן
flock to (that) the where the from those and your Lift
,you given was flock (is) ;north come who behold eyes up

21 תִּפְאַרְתֵּךְ׃ מַה־תֹּאמְרִי כִּי־יִפְקֹד עָלַיִךְ וְאַתְּ לִמַּדְתְּ אֹתָם
them taught For ?you He when you will What your
you visits say ?beautiful

עָלַיִךְ אַלֻּפִים לְרֹאשׁ הֲלוֹא חֲבָלִים יֹאחֱזוּךְ כְּמוֹ אֵשֶׁת לֵדָה׃
?bearing a like seize Will birth not a for chieftains (be to)
woman you pangs !head you over

22 וְכִי תֹאמְרִי בִּלְבָבֵךְ מַדּוּעַ קְרָאֻנִי אֵלֶּה בְּרֹב עֲוֹנֵךְ נִגְלוּ
are your Great these hap- have Why your in you And
bared ;iniquity ?things me to pened ,heart say if

23 שׁוּלַיִךְ נֶחְמְסוּ עֲקֵבָיִךְ׃ הֲיַהֲפֹךְ כּוּשִׁי עוֹרוֹ וְנָמֵר חֲבַרְבֻּרֹתָיו
his the or his the Can your suffer your
?spots leopard ,skin Ethiopian change .heels violence ;skirts

24 גַּם־אַתֶּם תּוּכְלוּ לְהֵיטִיב לִמֻּדֵי הָרֵעַ׃ וַאֲפִיצֵם כְּקַשׁ עוֹבֵר
passing the as will I So doing are who do may you (Then)
away stubble them scatter .evil to accustomed ,good also

25 לְרוּחַ מִדְבָּר׃ זֶה גוֹרָלֵךְ מְנָת־מִדַּיִךְ מֵאִתִּי נְאֻם־יְהוָה אֲשֶׁר
because ;Jehovah says from your the your This wilder- the the to
,Me measure of portion ,lot (is) .ness of wind

you have forgotten Me and trusted in falsehood. [26] So I also have stripped off your skirts over your face, that your shame may appear. [27] I have seen your adulteries, and your neighings, the wickedness of your fornication, (and) your abominations, on the hills in the fields. Woe to you, O Jerusalem! Will you not be made clean? How long after (will it) still (be)?

26 שכחת אותי ותבטחי בשקר׃ וגם־אני חשפתי שוליך על־
over your have I also So in and Me have you
skirts off stripped .falsehood trusted forgotten

27 פניך ונראה קלונך׃ נאפיך ומצהלותיך זמת זנותך על־
on your the your and your your may that your
harlotry of evil ;neighings ,adulteries ,shame seen be ,face

גבעות בשדה ראיתי שקוציך אוי לך ירושלם לא תטהרי
you Will not O to Woe your have I the in the
?clean be !Jerusalem you .abominations ,seen field hills

אחרי מתי עד׃
?still how After
long

CAP. XIV יד

CHAPTER 14

CHAPTER 14

[1] That which came, the word of Jehovah to Jeremiah, concerning the matter of droughts. [2] Judah mourns, and her gates droop. They put on mourning for the land, and the cry of Jerusalem has gone up. [3] And their nobles have sent their little ones for water; they came to the cisterns; they found no water. They returned with their vessels empty; they were ashamed and confounded and covered their head. [4] Because the ground was cracked, for there was no rain in the land; the plowmen were ashamed; they covered their head. [5] For even the doe calved in the field and forsook (it), because there was no grass. [6] And the wild asses stood in the high places; they snuffed up the wind like jackals; their eyes failed because (there was) no grass.

[7] O Jehovah, though our iniquities testify against us, act for Your name's sake; for our backslidings are many; we have sinned against You. [8] O Hope of Israel, its Savior in time of trouble, why should You be as a stranger in the land, and as a traveler (who) turns aside to lodge? [9] Why should You be as one who is stunned, as one mighty, who cannot save? Yet You, O Jehovah, (are) in our midst, and Your name is

1 אשר היה דבר־יהוה אל־ירמיהו על־דברי הבצרות׃
:droughts the con- Jeremiah to Jehovah the came That
of matter cerning of word (as) which

2 אבלה יהודה ושעריה אמללו קדרו לארץ וצוחת
the and the for on put They .languish her and Judah mourns
of cry ,land ashes gates

3 ירושלם עלתה׃ ואדיריהם שלחו צעוריהם למים באו
they for little their have their And gone has Jerusalem
came ;water ones sent nobles .up

על־גבים לא־מצאו מים שבו כליהם ריקם בשו והכלמו
and were they ;empty their They .water they no the to
,blushed ashamed vessels ,returned found ;cisterns

4 וחפו ראשם׃ בעבור האדמה חתה כי לא־היה גשם
rain there no for is the Because their and
was ,shattered ground .head covered

5 בארץ בשו אכרים חפו ראשם׃ כי גם־אילת בשדה
the in the even For their they plow- the were the in
field doe .head covered ;men ashamed ;land

6 ילדה ועזוב כי לא־היה דשא׃ ופראים עמדו על־שפים
the on stood the And .grass there no for and gave
;heights asses wild was ,(it) abandoned birth

7 שאפו רוח כתנים כלו עיניהם כי־אין עשב׃ אם־עונינו
our Though .grass there for their failed like the they
iniquities no was eyes ;jackals wind up snuffed

ענו בנו יהוה עשה למען שמך כי־רבו משובתינו לך
against our are for Your for act O against testi-
You ;apostasies many ;name's sake ,Jehovah ,us fy

8 חטאנו׃ מקוה ישראל מושיעו בעת צרה למה תהיה
should why ,distress in its ,Israel O have we
be You of time Savior of Hope .sinned

9 כגר בארץ וכארח נטה ללון׃ למה תהיה כאיש נדהם
,stunned a like should Why to who a as or the in a as
man be You ?lodge in turns traveler ,land stranger

כגבור לא־יוכל להושיע ואתה בקרבנו יהוה ושמך
Your and O our in (are) Yet ?save who not one as
name ,Jehovah ,midst You can ,mighty

called on us. Do not leave us!

[10] Thus says Jehovah to this people; So they have loved to wander; they have not restrained their feet; therefore Jehovah does not accept them. He will now remember their iniquity and punish their sins. [11] Then Jehovah said to me, Do not pray for this people, for good. [12] When they fast, I will not listen to their cry; and when they offer burnt offering, and grain offering, I will not accept them; but I will consume them by the sword, and by famine, and by the plague.

[13] Then I said, Ah, O Lord Jehovah! Behold, the prophets are saying to them, You shall not see the sword, nor shall you have famine; but I will give you true peace in this place. [14] And Jehovah said to me, The prophets prophesy lies in My name. I did not send them and I have not commanded them, nor did I speak to them. They prophesy to you a false vision and a worthless divination, and the deceit of their heart. [15] Therefore thus says Jehovah concerning the prophets who prophesy in My name, and I did not send them; yet they say, Sword and famine shall not be in this land: By sword and famine those prophets shall be consumed. [16] And the people to whom they prophesy shall be cast out in the streets of Jerusalem because of the famine and the sword. And none will bury them, them, their wives, and their sons, and their daughters; for I will pour their wickedness on them.

[17] Therefore you shall speak this word to

10 עָלֵינוּ נִקְרָא אַל־תַּנִּחֵנוּ׃ כֹּה־אָמַר יְהוָה לָעָם הַזֶּה
,this to people Jehovah says Thus leave do .us not is ;called upon us

כֵּן אָהֲבוּ לָנוּעַ רַגְלֵיהֶם לֹא חָשָׂכוּ וַיהוָה לֹא רָצָם עַתָּה
now does ;them accept not therefore Jehovah have they ;restrained not their feet to ;wander have they So loved

11 יִזְכֹּר עֲוֺנָם וְיִפְקֹד חַטֹּאתָם׃ וַיֹּאמֶר יְהוָה אֵלָי
,me to Jehovah Then said .sin their and punish their iniquity will He remember

12 אַל־תִּתְפַּלֵּל בְּעַד־הָעָם הַזֶּה לְטוֹבָה׃ כִּי יָצֻמוּ אֵינֶנִּי שֹׁמֵעַ
will listen I not they When ,fast for .good this people for Do pray not

אֶל־רִנָּתָם וְכִי יַעֲלוּ עֹלָה וּמִנְחָה אֵינֶנִּי רֹצָם כִּי בַּחֶרֶב
the by sword but ;them accept will not I grain and ,offering burnt offering they offer and when their ;cry to

13 וּבָרָעָב וּבַדֶּבֶר אָנֹכִי מְכַלֶּה אוֹתָם׃ וָאֹמַר אֲהָהּ ׀ אֲדֹנָי
O Lord ,Ah I Then ,said .them will consume I by and plague the by and ,famine

יְהוִה הִנֵּה הַנְּבִאִים אֹמְרִים לָהֶם לֹא־תִרְאוּ חֶרֶב וְרָעָב
and famine the ,sword you see shall not ,them to are saying the prophets Behold Jeho- !vah

לֹא־יִהְיֶה לָכֶם כִּי־שְׁלוֹם אֱמֶת אֶתֵּן לָכֶם בַּמָּקוֹם הַזֶּה׃
.this place in you to will I give true peace but for ,you will be not

14 וַיֹּאמֶר יְהוָה אֵלַי שֶׁקֶר הַנְּבִאִים נִבְּאִים בִּשְׁמִי
My in .name prophesy The prophets lies ,me to Jehovah said And

לֹא שְׁלַחְתִּים וְלֹא צִוִּיתִים וְלֹא דִבַּרְתִּי אֲלֵיהֶם חֲזוֹן שֶׁקֶר
,false a vision ;them to I did speak nor have I ,them commanded and not did I them send not

וְקֶסֶם וֶאֱלוּל וְתַרְמוּת לִבָּם הֵמָּה מִתְנַבְּאִים לָכֶם׃
.you to are prophesying they their heart the and of deceit worthless a and divination

15 לָכֵן כֹּה־אָמַר יְהוָה עַל־הַנְּבִאִים הַנִּבְּאִים בִּשְׁמִי וַאֲנִי לֹא־
not and I My in ,name who prophesy the prophets con- cerning Jehovah says thus There- fore

שְׁלַחְתִּים וְהֵמָּה אֹמְרִים חֶרֶב וְרָעָב לֹא יִהְיֶה בָּאָרֶץ הַזֹּאת
:this in land shall be not and famine Sword ,say yet they send did ;them

16 בַּחֶרֶב וּבָרָעָב יִתַּמּוּ הַנְּבִאִים הָהֵמָּה׃ וְהָעָם אֲשֶׁר־הֵמָּה
they whom the And people .those prophets be shall consumed and famine by sword

נִבְּאִים לָהֶם יִהְיוּ מֻשְׁלָכִים בְּחֻצוֹת יְרוּשָׁלִַם מִפְּנֵי ׀ הָרָעָב
the famine because of Jerusalem the into of streets cast out will be to them prophesy

וְהַחֶרֶב וְאֵין מְקַבֵּר לָהֵמָּה הֵמָּה נְשֵׁיהֶם וּבְנֵיהֶם וּבְנֹתֵיהֶם
their and ;daughters their and ,sons their ,wives ,them ,them will bury And none the and .sword

17 וְשָׁפַכְתִּי עֲלֵיהֶם אֶת־רָעָתָם׃ וְאָמַרְתָּ אֲלֵיהֶם אֶת־הַדָּבָר
word them to you So speak shall their .wickedness them on will I for out pour

them: Let my eyes run down with tears night and day, and do not let them cease. For the virgin daughter of my people is broken with a great break, (with) a very grievous blow. [18] If I go out into the field, then I see those killed with the sword! And if I enter into the city, then, behold, diseases of famine! Yes, both the prophet and the priest have gone up into a land that they do not know. [19] Have you completely rejected Judah? or has Your soul hated Zion? Why have You stricken us and (there is) no healing for us? (We) looked for peace, but (came) no good; and for a healing time, but, behold, terror! [20] We acknowledge our wickedness, O Jehovah, the iniquity of our fathers, for we have sinned against You. [21] For Your name's sake, do not spurn; do not dishonor the throne of Your glory. Remember, do not break Your covenant with us. [22] Among the vanities of the nations, are there (any) who make rain fall? Or can the heavens give showers? (Is) it not You, O Jehovah our God? Therefore we will wait for You; for You do all these (things).

הַזֶּה תֵּרַדְנָה עֵינַי דִּמְעָה לַיְלָה וְיוֹמָם וְאַל־תִּדְמֶינָה כִּי
for let do and ,day and night (with) My run Let :this
,cease them not tears eyes down

שֶׁבֶר גָּדוֹל נִשְׁבְּרָה בְּתוּלַת בַּת־עַמִּי מַכָּה נַחְלָה מְאֹד׃
.very grievous a My daughter the is great (with)
blow people of virgin broken break a

אִם־יָצָאתִי הַשָּׂדֶה וְהִנֵּה חַלְלֵי־חֶרֶב וְאִם בָּאתִי הָעִיר
the enter I And the those then ,field the go I If
,city into if !sword with pierced behold in out

18 וְהִנֵּה תַּחֲלוּאֵי רָעָב כִּי גַם־נָבִיא גַם־כֹּהֵן סָחֲרוּ אֶל־אֶרֶץ
a to have the and the both For !famine diseases than
land traveled priest prophet of ,behold

19 וְלֹא יָדָעוּ׃ הֲמָאֹס מָאַסְתָּ אֶת־יְהוּדָה אִם־בְּצִיּוֹן
Zion Or ?Judah You Have utterly do they that
rejected .know not

גָּעֲלָה נַפְשֶׁךָ מַדּוּעַ הִכִּיתָנוּ וְאֵין לָנוּ מַרְפֵּא קַוֵּה לְשָׁלוֹם
for We ?healing for and you have Why Your has
,peace waited us is not us struck ?soul abhorred

20 וְאֵין טוֹב וּלְעֵת מַרְפֵּא וְהִנֵּה בְעָתָה׃ יָדַעְנוּ יְהוָה רִשְׁעֵנוּ
wick- our O We !terror but ,healing a for and good but
,edness ,Jehovah ,know ,behold of time (came) nothing

21 עֲוֺן אֲבוֹתֵינוּ כִּי חָטָאנוּ לָךְ׃ אַל־תִּנְאַץ לְמַעַן שִׁמְךָ
Your for Do not against have we for our ini- the
;name's sake spurn .You sinned ,fathers of quity

אַל־תְּנַבֵּל כִּסֵּא כְבוֹדֶךָ זְכֹר אַל־תָּפֵר בְּרִיתְךָ אִתָּנוּ׃
with Your do not Remem- Your the do not
.us covenant break ,ber .glory of throne dishonor

22 הֲיֵשׁ בְּהַבְלֵי הַגּוֹיִם מַגְשִׁמִים וְאִם־הַשָּׁמַיִם יִתְּנוּ רְבִבִים
?showers can the Or who those the the among Are
grant heavens ?fall rain make nations of vanities there

הֲלֹא אַתָּה־הוּא יְהוָה אֱלֹהֵינוּ וּנְקַוֶּה־לָּךְ כִּי־אַתָּה עָשִׂיתָ
do You for for Therefore our O (Is) You not
;You wait will we ?God Jehovah it

אֶת־כָּל־אֵלֶּה׃
these all
.(things)

CAP. XV טו

CHAPTER 15

[1] Then Jehovah said to me, Though Moses and Samuel stood before Me, My soul (could) not (be) toward this people. Cast (them) out of My face; yea, let them go out. [2] And it will be, if they say to you, Where shall we go? Then you will tell them, Thus says Jehovah: Those who (are) for death, go to death; and those for the sword, to the sword; and those for the famine, to the famine; and

1 וַיֹּאמֶר יְהוָה אֵלַי אִם־יַעֲמֹד מֹשֶׁה וּשְׁמוּאֵל לְפָנַי אֵין
(could) before and Moses stood Though to Jehovah Then
not ,Me Samuel ,me said

2 נַפְשִׁי אֶל־הָעָם הַזֶּה שַׁלַּח מֵעַל־פָּנַי וְיֵצֵאוּ׃ וְהָיָה כִּי־
when it And let and My (them) Send .this people (turn) My
be will .out go them face from away toward soul

יֹאמְרוּ אֵלֶיךָ אָנָה נֵצֵא וְאָמַרְתָּ אֲלֵיהֶם כֹּה־אָמַר יְהוָה
:Jehovah says Thus ,them to you Then shall Where to shall
say will ?go we ,you say

אֲשֶׁר לַמָּוֶת לַמָּוֶת וַאֲשֶׁר לַחֶרֶב לַחֶרֶב וַאֲשֶׁר לָרָעָב
the for and the to the for and to (go) for (are) those
,famine those ,sword ,sword those ;death ,death who

those for the captivity, to the captivity. [3] And I will set over them four kinds, says Jehovah: the sword to kill, and the dogs to drag off, and the birds of the heaven and the beasts of the earth to devour and destroy. [4] And I will cause them to be a terror to all the kingdoms of the earth, because of Manasseh, the son of Hezekiah, king of Judah, for (that) which he did in Jerusalem. [5] For who shall have pity on you, O Jerusalem? Or who shall weep over you? Or who shall go aside to ask your welfare? [6] You have forsaken Me, says Jehovah; you have gone backward; therefore I will stretch out My hand against you and destroy you; I am weary of repenting. [7] And I will sift them with a fork in the gates of the land; I will bereave, I will destroy My people, (since) they do not turn from their ways. [8] Their widows are more numerous about Me than the sand of the seas; I have brought for them a ravager at noonday against the mother of a young man; I caused to fall on her suddenly anguish and terror. [9] She who has borne seven languishes; she has breathed out her life; her sun has gone down while (it was) yet day. She has been ashamed and humiliated; and I will deliver the rest of them to the sword before their enemies, says Jehovah.

[10] Woe to me, my mother, that you have borne me, a man of strife and a man of contention to the whole earth! I have not loaned on usury, nor have men loaned to me on usury; (yet) every one curses me. [11] Jehovah said, Truly I will free you for good. Truly I will cause the enemy to entreat you in the time of

3 לָרָעָב וַאֲשֶׁר לַשְּׁבִי לַשֶּׁבִי׃ וּפָקַדְתִּי עֲלֵיהֶם אַרְבַּע
four over them will I And appoint the to .captivity the for ,captivity and those the to ;famine

מִשְׁפָּחוֹת נְאֻם־יְהוָה אֶת־הַחֶרֶב לַהֲרֹג וְאֶת־הַכְּלָבִים
dogs the and ,kill to sword the :Jehovah says kinds (doom of)

לִסְחֹב וְאֶת־עוֹף הַשָּׁמַיִם וְאֶת־בֶּהֱמַת הָאָרֶץ לֶאֱכֹל
devour to the earth the of beasts and the heavens the of birds and drag to ,off

4 וּלְהַשְׁחִית׃ וּנְתַתִּים לְזַוְעָה לְכֹל מַמְלְכוֹת הָאָרֶץ בִּגְלַל
because of the ,earth king- the of doms all to terror a will I And them make to and .destroy

מְנַשֶּׁה בֶן־יְחִזְקִיָּהוּ מֶלֶךְ יְהוּדָה עַל אֲשֶׁר־עָשָׂה בִּירוּשָׁלִָם׃
in .Jerusalem did he what for ,Judah king of ,Hezekiah the of son Manas- ,seh

5 כִּי מִי־יַחְמֹל עָלַיִךְ יְרוּשָׁלִַם וּמִי יָנוּד לָךְ וּמִי יָסוּר
go will aside Or who for ;you will lament Or who O ?Jerusalem ,you on shall who pity have For

6 לִשְׁאֹל לִשְׁלֹם לָךְ׃ אַתְּ נָטַשְׁתְּ אֹתִי נְאֻם־יְהוָה אָחוֹר
back- ward ;Jehovah says ,Me have forsaken You ?your welfare ask to about

תֵּלֵכִי וָאַט אֶת־יָדִי עָלַיִךְ וָאַשְׁחִיתֵךְ נִלְאֵיתִי הִנָּחֵם׃
.repenting am I of weary and ;you destroy against you My hand will I so extend have you ;gone

7 וָאֶזְרֵם בְּמִזְרֶה בְּשַׁעֲרֵי הָאָרֶץ שִׁכַּלְתִּי אִבַּדְתִּי אֶת־עַמִּי
My ;people will I destroy will I ,bereave the ;land the in of gates a with fork will I And them winnow

8 מִדַּרְכֵיהֶם לוֹא שָׁבוּ׃ עָצְמוּ־לִי אַלְמְנֹתָו מֵחוֹל יַמִּים
the ;seas the than of sand Their widows about Me more are numerous they .turn do not from (for) way their

הֵבֵאתִי לָהֶם עַל־אֵם בָּחוּר שֹׁדֵד בַּצָּהֳרָיִם הִפַּלְתִּי עָלֶיהָ
on her made I fall at ;noonday a destroyer young a ,man of a against mother for ,them have I brought

9 פִּתְאֹם עִיר וּבֶהָלוֹת׃ אֻמְלְלָה יֹלֶדֶת הַשִּׁבְעָה נָפְחָה נַפְשָׁהּ
;life her has she out breathed ,seven who She bore languishes and .terror anguish sud- ,denly

בָּאָה שִׁמְשָׁהּ בְּעֹד יוֹמָם בּוֹשָׁה וְחָפֵרָה וּשְׁאֵרִיתָם לַחֶרֶב
the to sword their and remnant and ;humiliated was she ashamed ;day while yet (was it) her sun has gone

10 אֶתֵּן לִפְנֵי אֹיְבֵיהֶם נְאֻם־יְהוָה׃ אוֹי־לִי אִמִּי כִּי
that my ,mother to Woe ,me .Jehovah says their ,enemies before will I deliver

יְלִדְתִּנִי אִישׁ רִיב וְאִישׁ מָדוֹן לְכָל־הָאָרֶץ לֹא־נָשִׁיתִי וְלֹא־
nor have I ,loaned not the ,land all to con- tention a and of man ,strife a of man have you ,me borne

11 נָשׁוּ־בִי כֻּלֹּה מְקַלְלַונִי׃ אָמַר יְהוָה אִם־לֹא שֵׁרוּתִךָ לְטוֹב
for .good will I you free Truly ,Jehovah Said curses .me (yet) everyone ,me to have they loaned

אִם־לוֹא ׀ הִפְגַּעְתִּי בְךָ בְּעֵת רָעָה וּבְעֵת צָרָה אֶת־הָאֹיֵב׃
the .enemy distress a of time in and evil a of time in you cause will I entreat to Truly

evil and in the time of affliction. [12] Can one break iron, iron or bronze from the north? [13] Your wealth and your treasures I will give for plunder, not for price, but for all your sins, even in all your borders. [14] And I will make (you) pass with your enemies into a land (which) you do not know; for a fire has been kindled in My anger; it shall burn against you.

[15] O Jehovah, You know. Remember me and visit me, and take vengeance for me on those who seek to hurt me. Do not take me away in Your long-suffering; know that for You I bear reproach. [16] Your words were found, and I ate them; and Your word was to me the joy and gladness of my heart; for I am called by Your name, O Jehovah God of hosts. [17] I did not sit on the circle of mockers or rejoice. I sat alone because of Your hand; for You have filled me with wrath. [18] Why has my pain been without end, and my wound uncured, refusing to be healed? Will You surely be to me like a deceitful torrent, (whose) waters fail?

[19] Therefore thus says Jehovah, If you return, then I will bring you again; you shall stand before Me. And if you take the precious from the worthless, you shall be as My mouth. Let them turn back to you, but do not return to them. [20] And I will make you a fortified wall of bronze to this people. And they shall fight against you, but they shall not overcome you; for I (am) with you to save you and to deliver you, says Jehovah. [21] And I will deliver you out of the hand of the wicked, and I will redeem you out of the hand of the ruthless.

12 הֲיָרֹעַ בַּרְזֶל | בַּרְזֶל מִצָּפוֹן וּנְחֹשֶׁת׃ חֵילְךָ וְאוֹצְרוֹתֶיךָ
13 your and Your or the from iron ,iron one Can
treasures wealth ?bronze north break

לָבַז אֶתֵּן לֹא בִמְחִיר וּבְכָל־חַטֹּאותֶיךָ וּבְכָל־גְּבוּלֶיךָ׃
your in even your for but a for not will I for
.borders all ,sins all ,price give prey

14 וְהַעֲבַרְתִּי אֶת־אֹיְבֶיךָ בְּאֶרֶץ לֹא יָדָעְתָּ כִּי־אֵשׁ קָדְחָה
been has a for do you (which) a into your with will I And
kindled fire ;know not land enemies pass (you) make

15 בְאַפִּי עֲלֵיכֶם תּוּקָד׃ אַתָּה יָדַעְתָּ יְהוָה זָכְרֵנִי
Remember O ,know You will it against My in
me .Jehovah .burn you ;anger

וּפָקְדֵנִי וְהִנָּקֶם לִי מֵרֹדְפַי אַל־לְאֶרֶךְ אַפְּךָ תִּקָּחֵנִי דַּע
know take Do Your the for not my on for take and visit
(that) ;away me anger of length .persecutors me vengeance ,me

16 שְׂאֵתִי עָלֶיךָ חֶרְפָּה׃ נִמְצְאוּ דְבָרֶיךָ וָאֹכְלֵם וַיְהִי דְבָרֶיךָ
Your and I and Your were .reproach for bear I
words were ,them ate words found You

לִי לְשָׂשׂוֹן וּלְשִׂמְחַת לְבָבִי כִּי־נִקְרָא שִׁמְךָ עָלַי יְהוָה
O upon Your is for my glad- and the to
,Jehovah me name called ;heart of ness joy me

17 אֱלֹהֵי צְבָאוֹת׃ לֹא־יָשַׁבְתִּי בְסוֹד־מְשַׂחֲקִים וָאֶעְלֹז מִפְּנֵי
because nor merry- the in did I not .hosts God
of ;exult makers of circle sit of

18 יָדְךָ בָּדָד יָשַׁבְתִּי כִּי־זַעַם מִלֵּאתָנִי׃ לָמָּה הָיָה כְאֵבִי נֶצַח
con- my has Why have You indig- for ;sat I alone Your
,tinual pain been .with me filled nation hand

וּמַכָּתִי אֲנוּשָׁה מֵאֲנָה הֵרָפֵא הָיוֹ תִהְיֶה לִי כְּמוֹ אַכְזָב מַיִם
(whose) false a to You Surely be to refusing ,incurable my and
waters ,stream me are ?healed wound

19 לֹא נֶאֱמָנוּ׃ לָכֵן כֹּה־אָמַר יְהוָה אִם־תָּשׁוּב וַאֲשִׁיבְךָ
will I then you if ,Jehovah says thus Therefore be can not
;you restore return .trusted

לְפָנַי תַּעֲמֹד וְאִם־תּוֹצִיא יָקָר מִזּוֹלֵל כְּפִי תִהְיֶה יָשֻׁבוּ הֵמָּה
They may will you My as the from the bring you And will you before
turn .be mouth worthless precious out if .stand Me

20 אֵלֶיךָ וְאַתָּה לֹא־תָשׁוּב אֲלֵיהֶם׃ וּנְתַתִּיךָ לָעָם הַזֶּה לְחוֹמַת
a this to will I And .them to do not but ,you to
of wall people you make turn you

נְחֹשֶׁת בְּצוּרָה וְנִלְחֲמוּ אֵלֶיךָ וְלֹא־יוּכְלוּ לָךְ כִּי־אִתְּךָ אֲנִי
I with for against will but against they And .fortified bronze
,(am) you ,you prevail not ,you fight will

לְהוֹשִׁיעֲךָ וּלְהַצִּילֶךָ נְאֻם־יְהוָה׃ וְהִצַּלְתִּיךָ מִיַּד רָעִים
the the from will I And .Jehovah says to and save to
,wicked of hand you deliver ,you deliver you

וּפְדִתִיךָ מִכַּף עָרִצִים׃
the the from will I and
.ruthless of palm you redeem

CAP. XVI טז

CHAPTER 16

CHAPTER 16

[1] The word of Jehovah came also to me, saying, [2] You shall not take a wife for yourself, nor shall you have sons or daughters in this place. [3] For thus says Jehovah concerning the sons and concerning the daughters who are born in this place, and concerning their mothers who bore them, and concerning their fathers who fathered them in this land; [4] they shall die of deadly diseases; they shall not be mourned, nor shall they be buried; they shall be as dung on the face of the earth. And they shall be destroyed by the sword and by famine; and their bodies shall be food for the birds of the heavens and for the beasts of the earth. [5] For thus says Jehovah, Do not enter into the house of mourning; do not go to weep or moan for them. For I have taken away My peace from this people, says Jehovah, with loving-kindness and compassions. [6] Both the great and the small shall die in this land. They shall not be buried, nor shall (men) mourn for them, nor cut himself, nor make himself bald for them. [7] Nor shall (men) break for them in mourning, to comfort him for the dead. Nor shall (men) give the cup of comfort to drink for one's father or for one's mother.

[8] Also you shall not go into the house of feasting, to sit with them to eat and to drink. [9] For thus says Jehovah of hosts, the God of Israel: Behold, I will cause the voice of mirth to cease out of this place for your eyes, and in your days, and the voice of gladness and

וַיְהִי דְבַר־יְהוָֹה אֵלַי לֵאמֹר: לֹא־תִקַּח לְךָ אִשָּׁה וְלֹא־ 1
nor ,wife a for shall you not ,saying to Jehovah the Also
         yourself take   ,me of word came

יִהְיוּ לְךָ בָּנִים וּבָנוֹת בַּמָּקוֹם הַזֶּה: כִּי־כֹה | אָמַר 2
says thus For .this place in or sons for will
           daughters you be there

יְהוָֹה עַל־הַבָּנִים וְעַל־הַבָּנוֹת הַיִּלּוֹדִים בַּמָּקוֹם הַזֶּה וְעַל־ 3
and ,this place in are who the con- and the con- Jehovah
to as   born daughters cerning sons cerning

אִמֹּתָם הַיֹּלְדוֹת אוֹתָם וְעַל־אֲבוֹתָם הַמּוֹלִדִים אוֹתָם בָּאָרֶץ
in them who their and ;them bore who their
land   fathered fathers concerning   mothers

הַזֹּאת: מְמוֹתֵי תַחֲלֻאִים יָמֻתוּ לֹא יִסָּפְדוּ וְלֹא יִקָּבֵרוּ 4
they will nor be will they not will they diseases from ;this
;buried be mourned ;die of deaths

לְדֹמֶן עַל־פְּנֵי הָאֲדָמָה יִהְיוּ וּבַחֶרֶב וּבָרָעָב יִכְלוּ וְהָיְתָה
will and will they by and the by and they the the on as
be ,perish famine the sword ;be shall earth of face dung

נִבְלָתָם לְמַאֲכָל לְעוֹף הַשָּׁמַיִם וּלְבֶהֱמַת הָאָרֶץ:
the the for and the the for food their
.earth of beasts heavens of birds bodies

כִּי־כֹה | אָמַר יְהוָֹה אַל־תָּבוֹא בֵּית מַרְזֵחַ וְאַל־תֵּלֵךְ 5
do and ;mourning the do not ,Jehovah says thus For
go not of house into enter

לִסְפּוֹד וְאַל־תָּנֹד לָהֶם כִּי־אָסַפְתִּי אֶת־שְׁלוֹמִי מֵאֵת הָעָם
people from My have I for for moan nor to
,peace away taken ,them lament

הַזֶּה נְאֻם־יְהוָֹה אֶת־הַחֶסֶד וְאֶת־הָרַחֲמִים: וּמֵתוּ גְדֹלִים 6
the Both .compassions and loving with ,Jehovah says ,this
great die will kindness

וּקְטַנִּים בָּאָרֶץ הַזֹּאת לֹא יִקָּבֵרוּ וְלֹא־יִסְפְּדוּ לָהֶם וְלֹא
nor for will they nor will they not ;this in the and
,them mourn buried be land small

יִתְגֹּדַד וְלֹא יִקָּרַח לָהֶם: וְלֹא־יִפְרְסוּ לָהֶם עַל־אֵבֶל 7
,mourning in for they will Nor for him- shave nor cut
them (bread) break .them bald self ,himself

לְנַחֲמוֹ עַל־מֵת וְלֹא־יַשְׁקוּ אוֹתָם כּוֹס תַּנְחוּמִים עַל־אָבִיו
one's for consolation the them they will Nor the for com- to
father of cup drink to give .dead him fort

וְעַל־אִמּוֹ: וּבֵית־מִשְׁתֶּה לֹא־תָבוֹא לָשֶׁבֶת אוֹתָם לֶאֱכֹל 8
eat to with sit to will you not feasting the Also one's or
them ,enter of house mother for

וְלִשְׁתּוֹת: כִּי כֹה אָמַר יְהוָֹה צְבָאוֹת אֱלֹהֵי יִשְׂרָאֵל 9
:Israel the ,hosts Jehovah says thus For to and
of God of .drink

הִנְנִי מַשְׁבִּית מִן־הַמָּקוֹם הַזֶּה לְעֵינֵיכֶם וּבִימֵיכֶם קוֹל
the your in and your for this place from cause will ,Behold
of voice days eyes cease to I

the voice of the bridegroom and the voice of the bride.

[10] And it shall come to pass, when you declare to this people all these words, that they will say to you, Why has Jehovah pronounced all this great evil against us? Or what (is) our iniquity, or what (is) our sin that we have committed against Jehovah our God? [11] Then you shall say to them, Because your fathers have forsaken Me, says Jehovah, and have walked after other gods, and have served them, and have worshiped them, and have forsaken Me, and have not kept My law. [12] And you have done more evil than your fathers; for, behold, you walk each one after the stubbornness of his evil heart without listening to Me. [13] Therefore I will cast you out of this land into a land that you do not know, you nor your fathers. And there you shall serve other gods day and night; where I will not grant you favor.

[14] Therefore, behold, the days come, says Jehovah, that it shall no more be said, (As) Jehovah lives, who brought up the children of Israel out of the land of Egypt – [15] but rather (As) Jehovah lives, who brought up the sons of Israel from the land of the north and from all the lands where He had driven them there. And I will bring them again into their land that I gave to their fathers.

[16] Behold, I will send for many fishermen, says Jehovah, and they shall catch them, and after this I will send for many hunters,

10 שָׂשׂוֹן וְקוֹל שִׂמְחָה קוֹל חָתָן וְקוֹל כַּלָּה׃ וְהָיָה כִּי תַגִּיד
you when it And the the and the the (and) glad- the and joy
declare be will .bride of voice bridgroom of voice ness of voice

לָעָם הַזֶּה אֵת כָּל־הַדְּבָרִים הָאֵלֶּה וְאָמְרוּ אֵלֶיךָ עַל־
you to they that ,these words all thus to
say will people

מֶה דִבֶּר יְהוָה עָלֵינוּ אֵת כָּל־הָרָעָה הַגְּדוֹלָה הַזֹּאת וּמֶה
Or ?this great evil all against Jehovah has Why
(is) what us pronounced

11 עֲוֺנֵנוּ וּמֶה חַטָּאתֵנוּ אֲשֶׁר חָטָאנוּ לַיהוָה אֱלֹהֵינוּ׃ וְאָמַרְתָּ
you Then ?God our against have we that sin our what or our
say shall Jehovah sinned (is) ,iniquity

אֲלֵיהֶם עַל אֲשֶׁר־עָזְבוּ אֲבוֹתֵיכֶם אוֹתִי נְאֻם־יְהוָה וַיֵּלְכוּ
have and ,Jehovah says ,Me your have Because ,them to
walked fathers forsaken

אַחֲרֵי אֱלֹהִים אֲחֵרִים וַיַּעַבְדוּם וַיִּשְׁתַּחֲווּ לָהֶם וְאֹתִי עָזָבוּ
have they but ,them have and have and ,other gods after
,forsaken Me worshipped ,them served

12 וְאֶת־תּוֹרָתִי לֹא שָׁמָרוּ׃ וְאַתֶּם הֲרֵעֹתֶם לַעֲשׂוֹת מֵאֲבוֹתֵיכֶם
your than done have And have not My and
,fathers evil more you .kept law

וְהִנְּכֶם הֹלְכִים אִישׁ אַחֲרֵי שְׁרִרוּת לִבּוֹ־הָרָע לְבִלְתִּי
without evil his stub- the after each are be- for
heart of bornness man walking you hold

13 שְׁמֹעַ אֵלָי׃ וְהֵטַלְתִּי אֶתְכֶם מֵעַל הָאָרֶץ הַזֹּאת עַל־
into this land of out you therefore to listening
hurl will I ;Me

הָאָרֶץ אֲשֶׁר לֹא יְדַעְתֶּם אַתֶּם וַאֲבוֹתֵיכֶם וַעֲבַדְתֶּם־שָׁם
there you and your nor you do you not that a
serve will fathers ,know land

אֶת־אֱלֹהִים אֲחֵרִים יוֹמָם וָלַיְלָה אֲשֶׁר לֹא־אֶתֵּן לָכֶם
you will I not where and day other gods
grant ;night

14 חֲנִינָה׃ לָכֵן הִנֵּה־יָמִים בָּאִים נְאֻם־יְהוָה וְלֹא־יֵאָמֵר
will it that ,Jehovah says ,come the ,behold ,Therefore .favor
said be not days

עוֹד חַי־יְהוָה אֲשֶׁר הֶעֱלָה אֶת־בְּנֵי יִשְׂרָאֵל מֵאֶרֶץ מִצְרָיִם׃
Egypt of out Israel the brought who Jeho- (As) ,more
of land the of sons up .vah lives

15 כִּי אִם־חַי־יְהוָה אֲשֶׁר הֶעֱלָה אֶת־בְּנֵי יִשְׂרָאֵל מֵאֶרֶץ צָפוֹן
the the from Israel the brought who ,Jehovah (As) but
,north of land of sons up lives,rather

וּמִכֹּל הָאֲרָצוֹת אֲשֶׁר הִדִּיחָם שָׁמָּה וַהֲשִׁבֹתִים עַל־
into will I And .there had He where the from and
back them bring them banished lands all

16 אַדְמָתָם אֲשֶׁר נָתַתִּי לַאֲבוֹתָם׃ הִנְנִי שֹׁלֵחַ
will ,Behold their to gave I that their
send I .fathers land

לְדַוָּגִים רַבִּים נְאֻם־יְהוָה וְדִיגוּם וְאַחֲרֵי־כֵן אֶשְׁלַח לְרַבִּים
for will I after and they and ,Jehovah says ,many fisher- for
many send this ;them fish will men

and they will hunt them from every mountain, and from every hill, and out of the clefts of the rocks. [17] For My eyes (are) on all their ways; they are not hidden from My face; their iniquity is not hidden from My eyes. [18] And first I will twice repay their iniquity and their sin, because they have defiled My land with the bodies of their hateful things; yea, their hateful idols have filled My inheritance. [19] O Jehovah, my strength and my fortress, and my refuge in the day of affliction, the nations shall come to You from the ends of the earth, and say, Our fathers have inherited only lies, vanity, and no profit is in them. [20] Can a man make gods to himself? But they (are) no gods! [21] Therefore, behold, I will make them know; I will cause them to know My hand and My might; and they shall know that My name (is) Jehovah.

צַיָּדִים וְצָדוּם מֵעַל כָּל־הַר וּמֵעַל כָּל־גִּבְעָה וּמִנְּקִיקֵי
from and ,hill every and moun- every from they and ,hunters
of clefts the from ,tain them hunt will

17 הַסְּלָעִים׃ כִּי עֵינַי עַל־כָּל־דַּרְכֵיהֶם לֹא נִסְתְּרוּ מִלְּפָנָי
My from are they not their all (are) My For the
face hidden ;ways on eyes .rocks

18 וְלֹא־נִצְפַּן עֲוֺנָם מִנֶּגֶד עֵינָי׃ וְשִׁלַּמְתִּי רִאשׁוֹנָה מִשְׁנֵה
double first will I And My from their is not
repay .eyes iniquity hidden

עֲוֺנָם וְחַטָּאתָם עַל חַלְּלָם אֶת־אַרְצִי בְּנִבְלַת שִׁקּוּצֵיהֶם
abomin- their the with My have they for their and their
;idols able of bodies ,land defiled ,sin iniquity

19 וְתוֹעֲבוֹתֵיהֶם מָלְאוּ אֶת־נַחֲלָתִי׃ יְהוָה עֻזִּי וּמָעֻזִּי
my and my Jehovah O My have their ,yea
stronghold strength .inheritance filled abominations

וּמְנוּסִי בְּיוֹם צָרָה אֵלֶיךָ גּוֹיִם יָבֹאוּ מֵאַפְסֵי־אָרֶץ וְיֹאמְרוּ
,say and the the from shall the to ,distress the in my and
,earth of ends come nations You of day refuge

20 אַךְ־שֶׁקֶר נָחֲלוּ אֲבוֹתֵינוּ הֶבֶל וְאֵין־בָּם מוֹעִיל׃ הֲיַעֲשֶׂה־
make Can .profit in and ,vanity our have lies Only
them is not ,fathers inherited

21 לּוֹ אָדָם אֱלֹהִים וְהֵמָּה לֹא אֱלֹהִים׃ לָכֵן הִנְנִי מוֹדִיעָם
make will behold Therefore !gods not they But ?gods man a for
—know them I (are) himself

בַּפַּעַם הַזֹּאת אוֹדִיעֵם אֶת־יָדִי וְאֶת־גְּבוּרָתִי וְיָדְעוּ כִּי־
that they and My and My make will I this time
know will ;might hand know them

שְׁמִי יְהוָה׃
.Jehovah My
(is) name

CAP. XVII יז

CHAPTER 17

CHAPTER 17

[1] The sin of Judah is engraved with a pen of iron; with the point of a diamond (it is) carved on the tablet of their heart, and on the horns of your altars — [2] while their sons remember their altars and their Asherim by the green trees on the high hills. [3] O My mountain in the field, I will give your wealth, all your treasures to the spoil, your high places for sin, throughout all your borders. [4] And you, even through yourself, will let drop from your inheritance which I gave you; and I will cause you to serve your enemies in a land which you do not

1 חַטַּאת יְהוּדָה כְּתוּבָה בְּעֵט בַּרְזֶל בְּצִפֹּרֶן שָׁמִיר חֲרוּשָׁה
is it a the with ;iron an with is Judah The
engraved ;diamond of point stylus written of sin

2 עַל־לוּחַ לִבָּם וּלְקַרְנוֹת מִזְבְּחוֹתֵיכֶם׃ כִּזְכֹּר בְּנֵיהֶם
their while Your the on and their the on
sons remember —altars of horns ,heart of tablet

מִזְבְּחוֹתָם וַאֲשֵׁרֵיהֶם עַל־עֵץ רַעֲנָן עַל גְּבָעוֹת הַגְּבֹהוֹת׃
the hills on green the by their and their
.high trees Asherim altars

3 הֲרָרִי בַּשָּׂדֶה חֵילְךָ כָל־אוֹצְרוֹתֶיךָ לָבַז אֶתֵּן בָּמֹתֶיךָ
high your will I for your all your the in My O
places ,give prey treasures ,wealth ,field mountain

4 בְּחַטָּאת בְּכָל־גְּבוּלֶיךָ׃ וְשָׁמַטְתָּה וּבְךָ מִנַּחֲלָתְךָ אֲשֶׁר
which your from by even will you And your throughout sin for
inheritance yourself drop let .borders all

נָתַתִּי לָךְ וְהַעֲבַדְתִּיךָ אֶת־אֹיְבֶיךָ בָּאָרֶץ אֲשֶׁר לֹא־יָדָעְתָּ
do you not which the in your will I and to gave I
;know land enemies serve you make ;you

know; for you have kindled a fire in My anger; it will burn forever.

[5] Thus says Jehovah, Cursed is the man who trusts in man, and makes flesh his arm, and from Jehovah turns aside his heart. [6] For he shall be like a juniper in the desert, and shall not see when good comes. But he shall live in the parched places in the wilderness, (in) a salt land that is not inhabited. [7] Blessed is the man who trusts in Jehovah, and whose trust is Jehovah. [8] For he shall be like a tree planted by the waters and sends out its roots by the river, and will not fear when the heat comes, but his foliage will be green; and he is not worried in the year of dryness, nor will he cease from yielding fruit.

[9] The heart (is) deceitful above all things, and it is incurable; who can know it? [10] I Jehovah search the heart, I try the reins, even to give to each man according to his ways, according to the fruit of his doings. [11] (As) a partridge broods and does not hatch, (so is) he who makes riches, and not by right; it will leave him in the middle of his days, and in his end he will be a fool.

[12] A glorious high throne from the beginning (is) the place of our sanctuary. [13] O Jehovah, the Hope of Israel, all who forsake You shall be ashamed. Those who depart from Me shall be written in the earth, because they have forsaken Jehovah, the Fountain of living waters. [14] Heal me, O Jehovah, and I shall be healed; save me, and I shall be saved; for You (are) my praise.

[15] Behold, they say to me, Where (is) the word of Jehovah? Let it come now! [16] And I have not hurried away from shepherding after You; nor have I desired the woeful day;

5 כִּי־אֵשׁ קְדַחְתֶּם בְּאַפִּי עַד־עוֹלָם תּוּקָד׃ כֹּה ׀ אָמַר
says Thus will it forever My in have you a for
.burn ;anger kindled fire

יְהוָה אָרוּר הַגֶּבֶר אֲשֶׁר יִבְטַח בָּאָדָם וְשָׂם בָּשָׂר זְרֹעוֹ
his flesh and man in trusts who the Cursed Jeho-
,arm makes man is .vah

6 וּמִן־יְהוָה יָסוּר לִבּוֹ׃ וְהָיָה כְּעַרְעָר בָּעֲרָבָה וְלֹא יִרְאֶה
shall and the in a like he For his turns Jehovah and
see not ,desert juniper be will .heart aside from

כִּי־יָבוֹא טוֹב וְשָׁכַן חֲרֵרִים בַּמִּדְבָּר אֶרֶץ מְלֵחָה וְלֹא
that ,salt a (in) the in dried the will but ,good comes
not land ,wilderness places in live when

7 תֵשֵׁב׃ בָּרוּךְ הַגֶּבֶר אֲשֶׁר יִבְטַח בַּיהוָה וְהָיָה
is and in trusts who the Blessed in- is
,Jehovah man is .habited

8 יְהוָה מִבְטַחוֹ׃ וְהָיָה כְּעֵץ ׀ שָׁתוּל עַל־מַיִם וְעַל־יוּבַל
the and the by planted a like he For his Jehovah
stream by waters tree be will .trust

יְשַׁלַּח שָׁרָשָׁיו וְלֹא יִרְאֶה כִּי־יָבֹא חֹם וְהָיָה עָלֵהוּ רַעֲנָן
—green its will for ,heat comes when will and its sends
foliage be fear not ;roots out

9 וּבִשְׁנַת בַּצֹּרֶת לֹא יִדְאָג וְלֹא יָמִישׁ מֵעֲשׂוֹת פֶּרִי׃ עָקֹב
Deceitful .fruit from he will nor is he not drought the in and
(is) yielding cease ,worried of year

10 הַלֵּב מִכֹּל וְאָנֻשׁ הוּא מִי יֵדָעֶנּוּ׃ אֲנִי יְהוָה חֹקֵר לֵב בֹּחֵן
I the search ,Jehovah I can who ;it is and above the
test ,heart ?it know incurable all heart

11 כְּלָיוֹת וְלָתֵת לְאִישׁ כִּדְרָכָו כִּפְרִי מַעֲלָלָיו׃ קֹרֵא
a (As) .doings his according according each to to even the
partridge of fruit the to ,ways his to man give kidneys

דָגַר וְלֹא יָלָד עֹשֶׂה עֹשֶׁר וְלֹא בְמִשְׁפָּט בַּחֲצִי יָמָו יַעַזְבֶנּוּ
will it his the in with but riches he (is so) does and broods
,him leave days of middle ;justice not makes who ,hatch not

12 וּבְאַחֲרִיתוֹ יִהְיֶה נָבָל׃ כִּסֵּא כָבוֹד מָרוֹם מֵרִאשׁוֹן מְקוֹם
the (is) the from high glorious A .fool a will he at and
of place beginning throne be end his

13 מִקְדָּשֵׁנוּ׃ מִקְוֵה יִשְׂרָאֵל יְהוָה כָּל־עֹזְבֶיךָ יֵבֹשׁוּ יְסוּרַי
leav- Those be will who all O ,Israel the our
Me ing .ashamed You forsake ,Jehovah of hope .sanctuary

בָּאָרֶץ יִכָּתֵבוּ כִּי עָזְבוּ מְקוֹר מַיִם־חַיִּים אֶת־יְהוָה׃
.Jehovah ,living waters the have they for be will the in
of Fountain forsaken ,written earth

14 רְפָאֵנִי יְהוָה וְאֵרָפֵא הוֹשִׁיעֵנִי וְאִוָּשֵׁעָה כִּי תְהִלָּתִי אָתָּה׃
You my for will I and save be will I and O Heal
.(are) praise ;saved be me ;healed ,Jehovah ,me

15
16 הִנֵּה־הֵמָּה אֹמְרִים אֵלָי אַיֵּה דְבַר־יְהוָה יָבוֹא נָא׃ וַאֲנִי
And !now it Let ?Jehovah the Where to say they ,Behold
I come of word (is) ,me

לֹא־אַצְתִּי מֵרֹעֶה אַחֲרֶיךָ וְיוֹם אָנוּשׁ לֹא הִתְאַוֵּיתִי אַתָּה
You I have not woefull the after from have not
;desired day ;You shepherding away hurried

You surely know; the utterance of my lips was before Your face. [17] Do not be a terror to me; You (are) my refuge in the day of evil. [18] Let those who persecute me be ashamed, but do not let me be ashamed; let them be terrified; but do not let me be terrified. Bring on them the day of evil, and destroy them (with) double destruction.

[19] Thus Jehovah said to me: Go and stand in the gate of the sons of the people, by which the kings of Judah come in, and by which they go out, and in all the gates of Jerusalem. [20] And say to them, Hear the word of Jehovah, kings of Judah, and all Judah, and all the residents of Jerusalem who enter in by these gates! [21] Thus says Jehovah, Take heed for the sake of your lives, and do not carry a burden on the Sabbath day, nor bring (it) in by the gates of Jerusalem. [22] And do not carry out a burden from your houses on the Sabbath day, nor do any work, but keep the Sabbath day holy, as I commanded your fathers.

[23] But they did not obey or bow down their ear, but they made their neck stiff, not to hear, nor to receive instruction. [24] And it shall be, if you carefully listen to me, says Jehovah, to bring in no burden through the gates of this city on the Sabbath day, but keep the Sabbath day holy, to do no work in it, [25] then kings and rulers sitting on the throne of David shall enter into the gates of this city, riding in

17 יָדַעְתָּ מוֹצָא שְׂפָתַי נֹכַח פָּנֶיךָ הָיָה׃ אַל־תִּהְיֵה־לִי לִמְחִתָּה

;terror a to Do not .was Your before lips my utter- the know
me be face of ance

18 מַחְסִי־אַתָּה בְּיוֹם רָעָה׃ יֵבֹשׁוּ רֹדְפַי וְאַל־אֵבֹשָׁה אָנִי

;me be let but per- my be Let .evil the in You my
ashamed not secutors ashamed of day (are) refuge

יֵחַתּוּ הֵמָּה וְאַל־אֵחַתָּה אָנִי הָבִיא עֲלֵיהֶם יוֹם רָעָה וּמִשְׁנֶה

(with) and ,evil the on Bring .me be let but ;them be let
double of day them terrified not terrified

19 שִׁבָּרוֹן שָׁבְרֵם׃ כֹּה־אָמַר יְהוָֹה אֵלַי הָלֹךְ וְעָמַדְתָּ

and Go ,me to Jehovah said Thus break breaking
stand .them

בְּשַׁעַר בְּנֵי־עָם אֲשֶׁר יָבֹאוּ בוֹ מַלְכֵי יְהוּדָה וַאֲשֶׁר

and ,Judah the it by enter which the the the in
which of kings ,people of sons of gate

20 יֵצְאוּ בוֹ וּבְכֹל שַׁעֲרֵי יְרוּשָׁלִָם׃ וְאָמַרְתָּ אֲלֵיהֶם שִׁמְעוּ

Hear ,them to say And .Jerusalem the in and by they
of gates all ,it out go

דְבַר־יְהוָֹה מַלְכֵי יְהוּדָה וְכָל־יְהוּדָה וְכֹל יֹשְׁבֵי יְרוּשָׁלִָם

Jerusalem inhab- the and ,Judah and ,Judah kings ,Jehovah the
of itants all all of of word

21 הַבָּאִים בַּשְּׁעָרִים הָאֵלֶּה׃ כֹּה אָמַר יְהוָֹה הִשָּׁמְרוּ

Take ,Jehovah says Thus !these by in who
heed gates enter

בְּנַפְשׁוֹתֵיכֶם וְאַל־תִּשְׂאוּ מַשָּׂא בְּיוֹם הַשַּׁבָּת וַהֲבֵאתֶם

bring nor the day on a do and of sake the for
(them) ,Sabbath burden carry not ,lives your

22 בְּשַׁעֲרֵי יְרוּשָׁלִָם׃ וְלֹא־תוֹצִיאוּ מַשָּׂא מִבָּתֵּיכֶם בְּיוֹם

day on your from a carry do And .Jerusalem the by in
houses burden out not of gates

הַשַּׁבָּת וְכָל־מְלָאכָה לֹא תַעֲשׂוּ וְקִדַּשְׁתֶּם אֶת־יוֹם הַשַּׁבָּת

the day keep but ,do not work and the
,Sabbath holy ,Sabbath

23 כַּאֲשֶׁר צִוִּיתִי אֶת־אֲבוֹתֵיכֶם׃ וְלֹא שָׁמְעוּ וְלֹא הִטּוּ אֶת־

incline nor did they But your I as
obey not .fathers commanded

אָזְנָם וַיַּקְשׁוּ אֶת־עָרְפָּם לְבִלְתִּי שׁוֹמֵעַ וּלְבִלְתִּי קַחַת

receive to nor hear to not their they but their
,neck stiffened ,ear

24 מוּסָר׃ וְהָיָה אִם־שָׁמֹעַ תִּשְׁמְעוּן אֵלַי נְאֻם־יְהוָֹה לְבִלְתִּי ׀

to not ,Jehovah says to you carefully if it And instruc-
,Me listen ,be will .tion

הָבִיא מַשָּׂא בְּשַׁעֲרֵי הָעִיר הַזֹּאת בְּיוֹם הַשַּׁבָּת וּלְקַדֵּשׁ

keep but the day on this city through in a bring
holy ,Sabbath of gates the burden

25 אֶת־יוֹם הַשַּׁבָּת לְבִלְתִּי עֲשׂוֹת־בָּהּ כָּל־מְלָאכָה׃ וּבָאוּ

will then ,work any it in do to not the day
enter Sabbath

בְשַׁעֲרֵי הָעִיר הַזֹּאת מְלָכִים ׀ וְשָׂרִים יֹשְׁבִים עַל־כִּסֵּא

the on sitting and kings this city the into
of throne rulers of gates

chariots and on horses, they, and their rulers, the men of Judah, and the inhabitants of Jerusalem. And this city will be inhabited forever. [26] And they will come from the cities of Judah, and from the places about Jerusalem, and from the land of Benjamin, and from the lowlana, and from the mountains, and from the south, bringing burnt offerings, and sacrifices, and grain offerings, and incense, and bringing sacrifices of thanksgiving to the house of Jehovah. [27] But if you will not listen to Me to keep the Sabbath day holy and not to carry a burden, and enter at the gates of Jerusalem on the Sabbath day — then I will kindle a fire in her gates; and it shall devour the palaces of Jerusalem, and it shall not be put out.

דָּוִד רֹכְבִים ׀ בָּרֶכֶב וּבַסּוּסִים הֵמָּה וְשָׂרֵיהֶם אִישׁ יְהוּדָה
,Judah the their and ,they on and chariots in riding David
of men ,rulers ,horses

26 וְיֹשְׁבֵי יְרוּשָׁלִָם וְיָשְׁבָה הָעִיר־הַזֹּאת לְעוֹלָם׃ וּבָאוּ מֵעָרֵי־
the from they And .forever this city will and ,Jerusalem the and
of cities come will inhabited be of inhabitants

יְהוּדָה וּמִסְּבִיבוֹת יְרוּשָׁלִַם וּמֵאֶרֶץ בִּנְיָמִן וּמִן־הַשְּׁפֵלָה
the and ,Benjamin from and ,Jerusalem the from and ,Judah
Shephelah from of land the around places

וּמִן־הָהָר וּמִן־הַנֶּגֶב מְבִאִים עֹלָה וְזֶבַח וּמִנְחָה וּלְבוֹנָה
frank- and grain and and burnt bringing the and moun- the and
,incense ,offerings sacrifices offerings ,south from ,tains from

27 וּמְבִאֵי תוֹדָה בֵּית יְהוָה׃ וְאִם־לֹא תִשְׁמְעוּ אֵלַי לְקַדֵּשׁ אֶת־
keep to to will you not But .Jehovah's house thank bear- and
holy ,Me listen if offerings to ing

יוֹם הַשַּׁבָּת וּלְבִלְתִּי ׀ שְׂאֵת מַשָּׂא וּבֹא בְּשַׁעֲרֵי יְרוּשָׁלִָם
Jerusalem the at and a carry not and the day
of gates enter ,burden to Sabbath

בְּיוֹם הַשַּׁבָּת וְהִצַּתִּי אֵשׁ בִּשְׁעָרֶיהָ וְאָכְלָה אַרְמְנוֹת יְרוּשָׁלִָם
,Jerusalem the it and her in fire a I then the day on
of palaces devour will ;gates kindle will —Sabbath

וְלֹא תִכְבֶּה׃
be and
.quenched not

CAP. XVIII יח

CHAPTER 18

CHAPTER 18

[1] The word which came to Jeremiah from Jehovah, saying, [2] Arise and go down to the potter's house, and there I will cause you to hear My words. [3] Then I went down to the potter's house, and, behold, he was working a work on the wheel. [4] And the vessel that he made in clay was ruined in the hand of the potter; so he made it again, another vessel, as it seemed good in the eyes of the potter to make (it). [5] Then the word of Jehovah came to me, saying, [6] O house of Israel, can I not do to you as this potter? says Jehovah. Behold, as the clay in the potter's hand, so (are) you in My hand, O house of Israel. [7] The instant I speak concerning a nation,

1
2 הַדָּבָר אֲשֶׁר הָיָה אֶל־יִרְמְיָהוּ מֵאֵת יְהוָה לֵאמֹר׃ קוּם
Arise ,saying ,Jehovah from Jeremiah to came which The
word

3 וְיָרַדְתָּ בֵּית הַיּוֹצֵר וְשָׁמָּה אַשְׁמִיעֲךָ אֶת־דְּבָרָי׃ וָאֵרֵד
went I So My cause will I and the house go and
to down .words hear to you there ,potter's to down

4 בֵּית הַיּוֹצֵר וְהִנֵּהוּ עֹשֶׂה מְלָאכָה עַל־הָאָבְנָיִם׃ וְנִשְׁחַת
was And the on work a was be- and the house
ruined .wheel working he ,hold ;potter's

הַכְּלִי אֲשֶׁר הוּא עֹשֶׂה בַּחֹמֶר בְּיַד הַיּוֹצֵר וְשָׁב וַיַּעֲשֵׂהוּ
made he so the the in clay in made he that the
,it again ;potter of hand vessel

5 כְּלִי אַחֵר כַּאֲשֶׁר יָשַׁר בְּעֵינֵי הַיּוֹצֵר לַעֲשׂוֹת׃ וַיְהִי
Then make to the the in it as ,another vessel
came .(it) potter of eyes good seemed

6 דְבַר־יְהוָה אֵלַי לֵאמוֹר׃ הֲכַיּוֹצֵר הַזֶּה לֹא־אוּכַל לַעֲשׂוֹת
do to I Am not this like ,saying ,me to Jehovah the
able (did) potter of word

לָכֶם בֵּית יִשְׂרָאֵל נְאֻם־יְהוָה הִנֵּה כַחֹמֶר בְּיַד הַיּוֹצֵר
the in the as ,Behold .Jehovah says ?Israel house O to
,potter's hand clay of ,you

7 כֵּן־אַתֶּם בְּיָדִי בֵּית יִשְׂרָאֵל׃ רֶגַע אֲדַבֵּר עַל־גּוֹי
a con- speak I The .Israel house O My in (are) so
,nation cerning instant of ,hand you

8 ועל־ממלכה לנתוש ולנתוץ ולהאביד׃ ושב הגוי ההוא

that nation will if to or put to or uproot to a con- or
turn ;(it) destroy down kingdom cerning

מרעתו אשר דברתי עליו ונחמתי על־הרעה אשר

that the of will I against have I whom its from
evil repent ,it spoken evil

9 חשבתי לעשות לו׃ ורגע אדבר על־גוי ועל־

con- or a concern- speak I the But .it to do to thought I
cerning ,nation ing instant

10 ממלכה לבנות ולנטוע׃ ועשה הרעה בעיני לבלתי

to not My in evil it if to or build to ,kingdom a
,eye does ,(it) plant

שמע בקולי ונחמתי על־הטובה אשר אמרתי להיטיב

do to had I which the of I then My obey
to good said good repent will ,voice

11 אותו׃ ועתה אמר־נא אל־איש־יהודה ועל־יושבי ירושלם

.Jerusalem inhab- the and ,Judah the to please speak Now .it
of itants to of men ,then

לאמר כה אמר יהוה הנה אנכי יוצר עליכם רעה

evil against am I ,Behold ,Jehovah says Thus ,saying
you forming

וחשב עליכם מחשבה שובו נא איש מדרכו הרעה

evil his from each now turn ;plan a against and
way man you devising

12 והיטיבו דרכיכם ומעלליכם׃ ואמרו נואש כי־אחרי

after For is It they But your and ways your make and
!hopeless ,say .doings good

מחשבותינו נלך ואיש שררות לבו־הרע נעשה׃

will we evil his stub- the each and will we own our
.do heart of bornness man ,walk thoughts

13 לכן כה אמר יהוה שאלו־נא בגוים מי שמע כאלה

like has who the among now Ask ,Jehovah says thus There-
?these heard ,nations fore

14 שערורת עשתה מאד בתולת ישראל׃ היעזב מצור שדי

the the from Does .Israel The done has something
field of rock forsake of virgin horrible

15 שלג לבנון אם־ינתשו מים זרים קרים נוזלים׃ כי־

But ?flowing cold foreign the are Or ?Lebanon the
waters uprooted of snow

שכחני עמי לשוא יקטרו ויכשלום בדרכיהם שבולי

the (from) their in made they and burn they vain to My forgot
paths ways stumble them ;incense idols ,people Me

16 עולם ללכת נתיבות דרך לא סלולה׃ לשום ארצם

their make to (the on) not a of (on) walk to ,old
land ;highway way paths

לשמה שרוקת עולם כל עובר עליה ישם ויניד בראשו׃

his will and be will it by who All perpet- a a
.head shake horrified pass ual hissing ,horror

17 כרוח־קדים אפיצם לפני אויב ערף ולא־פנים אראם

will I (My) and (My) the before will I east an Like
.them show face not back ;enemy them scatter wind

and concerning a kingdom, to pluck (it) up and to pull (it) down, and to destroy (it); [8] if that nation, against whom I have spoken, will turn from their evil, I will repent of the evil that I thought to do to it. [9] And the instant I speak concerning a nation, and concerning a kingdom, to build (it) and to plant (it) — [10] if it does evil in My eye, not to obey My voice, then I will repent of the good which I had said to do good to it.

[11] Now, then, please speak to the men of Judah, and to the inhabitants of Jerusalem, saying, Thus Jehovah says, Behold, I am forming evil against you and devising a plan against you. Now each one turn from his evil way and make your ways and your doings good. [12] And they say, It is hopeless! For we will walk after our own thoughts, and we will each one do (according to) the stubbornness of his evil heart. [13] Therefore thus says Jehovah, Ask now among the nations: who has heard like these? The virgin of Israel has done a very horrible thing.

[14] Does the snow of Lebanon cease from the rock of the field? Or the cold flowing waters that come from another place be uprooted? [15] But My people have forgotten Me, they burned incense to vain idols, and they have caused them to stumble in their ways (from) the old paths, to walk (in) bypaths, not (in the) highway; [16] to make their land a desolation, a hissing forever. Everyone who passes by will be amazed and will shake his head. [17] I will scatter them like an east wind before the enemy; I will show them the back, and

not the face, in the day of their calamity.

[18] Then they said, Come and let us plot schemes against Jeremiah. For the law shall not perish from the priest, nor counsel from the wise, nor word from the prophet. Come and let us strike him with the tongue, and let us not listen to any of his words. [19] Attend to me, O Jehovah, and listen to the voice of my adversaries. [20] Should evil be repaid for good? For they have dug a pit for my soul. Remember, I stood before You to speak good concerning them, to turn Your wrath from them. [21] Therefore give their sons to the famine, and give them over to the power of the sword. And let their wives be bereaved, and widows; and let their men be the slain of death, their young men those struck by the sword in battle. [22] Let a cry be heard from their houses, when you bring a troop suddenly on them. For they have dug a pit to seize me, and have hidden snares for my feet. [23] Yet, O Jehovah, You know all their counsel against me to death. Do not atone for their iniquity, nor blot out their sin from Your presence, but let them be those made to stumble before You; deal with them in the time of Your anger.

CHAPTER 19

[1] Thus says Jehovah, Go and buy a potter's earthen jar, and (some) from the elders of the people, and from the elders of the priests. [2] And go out to the valley of the son of Hinnom, which (is) by the entry of Potsherd Gate, and declare there the words that I will speak to you.

18 בְּיוֹם אֵידָם׃ וַיֹּאמְרוּ לְכוּ וְנַחְשְבָה עַל־יִרְמְיָהוּ
.Jeremiah against us let and Come they Then their the in
plot ,said .calamity of day

מַחֲשָׁבוֹת כִּי לֹא־תֹאבַד תּוֹרָה מִכֹּהֵן וְעֵצָה מֵחָכָם וְדָבָר
nor the from nor the from the shall not for ,schemes
word ,wise counsel ,priest law perish

מִנָּבִיא לְכוּ וְנַכֵּהוּ בַלָּשׁוֹן וְאַל־נַקְשִׁיבָה אֶל־כָּל־דְּבָרָיו׃
his any to us let and the with us let and Come the from
.words of listen not ,tongue him strike .prophet

19 20 הַקְשִׁיבָה יְהוָה אֵלַי וּשְׁמַע לְקוֹל יְרִיבָי׃ הַיְשֻׁלַּם תַּחַת־
for be Should adver- my the to and ,me to O Pay
repaid .saries of voice listen ,Jehovah ,attention

טוֹבָה רָעָה כִּי־כָרוּ שׁוּחָה לְנַפְשִׁי זְכֹר ׀ עָמְדִי לְפָנֶיךָ
before stood I ,Remember my for pit a they For ?evil good
You .soul dug have

לְדַבֵּר עֲלֵיהֶם טוֹבָה לְהָשִׁיב אֶת־חֲמָתְךָ מֵהֶם׃
from Your turn to ,good concerning speak to
.them wrath them

21 לָכֵן תֵּן אֶת־בְּנֵיהֶם לָרָעָב וְהַגִּרֵם עַל־יְדֵי־חֶרֶב וְתִהְיֶנָה
let And the the over give and the to their give There-
be .sword of hand to them famine sons ,fore

נְשֵׁיהֶם שַׁכֻּלוֹת וְאַלְמָנוֹת וְאַנְשֵׁיהֶם יִהְיוּ הֲרֻגֵי מָוֶת
;death the be let their and and ,bereaved their
of slain men ;widows wives

22 בַּחוּרֵיהֶם מֻכֵּי־חֶרֶב בַּמִּלְחָמָה׃ תִּשָּׁמַע זְעָקָה מִבָּתֵּיהֶם
their from cry a be Let .battle in the those young their
,houses heard sword by struck men

כִּי־תָבִיא עֲלֵיהֶם גְּדוּד פִּתְאֹם כִּי־כָרוּ שׁיחה לְלָכְדֵנִי
capture to pit a they For .suddenly raiding a them on you when
me dug have party bring

23 וּפַחִים טָמְנוּ לְרַגְלָי׃ וְאַתָּה יְהוָה יָדַעְתָּ אֶת־כָּל־עֲצָתָם
their all know O Yet my for have and
counsel ,Jehovah ,You .feet hidden snares

עָלַי לַמָּוֶת אַל־תְּכַפֵּר עַל־עֲוֹנָם וְחַטָּאתָם מִלְּפָנֶיךָ אַל־
not Your from their or their for do not to against
presence sin ,iniquity atone ;death me

תֶּמְחִי וְהָיוּ מֻכְשָׁלִים לְפָנֶיךָ בְּעֵת אַפְּךָ עֲשֵׂה בָּהֶם׃
with deal Your the in before made those let and blot do
.them anger of time ,You stumble to be them ,out

CAP. XIX יט

CHAPTER 19

1 כֹּה אָמַר יְהוָה הָלֹךְ וְקָנִיתָ בַקְבֻּק יוֹצֵר חָרֶשׂ וּמִזִּקְנֵי הָעָם
the from and ,earthen a jar buy and Go ,Jehovah says Thus
,people of elders the potter's

2 וּמִזִּקְנֵי הַכֹּהֲנִים׃ וְיָצָאתָ אֶל־גֵּיא בֶן־הִנֹּם אֲשֶׁר פֶּתַח שַׁעַר
Gate the by which ,Hinnom the the to go And the from and
of entry (is) of son of valley out .priests of elders the

הַחַרְסוּת וְקָרָאתָ שָּׁם אֶת־הַדְּבָרִים אֲשֶׁר־אֲדַבֵּר אֵלֶיךָ׃
.you to will I that the there and Potsherd
speak words proclaim

[3] And say, Hear the word of Jehovah, O kings of Judah, and inhabitants of Jerusalem. Thus says Jehovah of hosts, the God of Israel, Behold, I will bring evil on this place which all who hear it his ears will tingle. [4] Because they have forsaken Me and have profaned this place, and have burned incense in it to other gods whom neither they nor their fathers have known, nor the kings of Judah; and have filled this place with the blood of innocents. [5] They have also built the high places of Baal, to burn their sons with fire (for) burnt offerings to Baal, which I never commanded nor spoke, nor did (it) come into My heart. [6] Therefore, behold, the days come, says Jehovah, that this place shall no more be called Tophet, or the valley of the son of Hinnom, but, Valley of Slaughter. [7] And I will make the counsel of Judah and Jerusalem come to nothing in this place, and I will cause them to fall by the sword before their enemies, and by the hand of those who seek their life. And I will give their dead bodies for food to the birds of the sky, and for the animals of the earth. [8] And I will make this city a waste and a hissing. Everyone who passes by shall be amazed and shall hiss because of all its plagues. [9] And I will cause them to eat the flesh of their sons and the flesh of their daughters, and they shall each one eat the flesh of his friend in the siege and distress, with which their enemies and those who seek their life shall distress them.

[10] Then you shall break the jar before the eyes of

3 וְאָמַרְתָּ שִׁמְעוּ דְבַר־יְהוָה מַלְכֵי יְהוּדָה וְיֹשְׁבֵי יְרוּשָׁלִָם

.Jerusalem inhab- and Judah kings ,Jehovah the Hear ,say And
of itants of of word

כֹּה־אָמַר יְהוָה צְבָאוֹת אֱלֹהֵי יִשְׂרָאֵל הִנְנִי מֵבִיא רָעָה

evil will ,Behold ,Israel the hosts Jehovah says Thus
bring I of God of

4 עַל־הַמָּקוֹם הַזֶּה אֲשֶׁר כָּל־שֹׁמְעָהּ תִּצַּלְנָה אָזְנָיו׃ יַעַן ׀

Because his tingle will who all which this place on
.ears it hears

אֲשֶׁר עֲזָבֻנִי וַיְנַכְּרוּ אֶת־הַמָּקוֹם הַזֶּה וַיְקַטְּרוּ־בוֹ לֵאלֹהִים

gods to it in have and ,this place have and have they
incense burned profaned Me forsaken

אֲחֵרִים אֲשֶׁר לֹא־יְדָעוּם הֵמָּה וַאֲבוֹתֵיהֶם וּמַלְכֵי יְהוּדָה

;Judah the nor their nor they have neither whom other
of kings ,fathers known

5 וּמָלְאוּ אֶת־הַמָּקוֹם הַזֶּה דַּם נְקִיִּם׃ וּבָנוּ אֶת־בָּמוֹת הַבַּעַל

,Baal high the have They inno- the this place have and
of places built also .cents of blood with filled

לִשְׂרֹף אֶת־בְּנֵיהֶם בָּאֵשׁ עֹלוֹת לַבָּעַל אֲשֶׁר לֹא־צִוִּיתִי

com- I never which ,Baal to burnt (as) with their burn to
manded offerings fire sons

6 וְלֹא דִבַּרְתִּי וְלֹא עָלְתָה עַל־לִבִּי׃ לָכֵן הִנֵּה־יָמִים

the ,behold Therefore My into it did nor ,spoke nor
days .heart up come

בָּאִים נְאֻם־יְהוָה וְלֹא־יִקָּרֵא לַמָּקוֹם הַזֶּה עוֹד הַתֹּפֶת וְגֵיא

the or ,Tophet more this place be will that ,Jehovah says ,come
of valley called not

7 בֶן־הִנֹּם כִּי אִם־גֵּיא הַהֲרֵגָה׃ וּבַקֹּתִי אֶת־עֲצַת יְהוּדָה

Judah counsel the will I And .Slaughter Valley ,but ,Hinnom the
of void make of of son

וִירוּשָׁלִַם בַּמָּקוֹם הַזֶּה וְהִפַּלְתִּים בַּחֶרֶב לִפְנֵי אֹיְבֵיהֶם

their before the by will I and ,this place in and
,enemies sword fall them make Jerusalem

וּבְיַד מְבַקְשֵׁי נַפְשָׁם וְנָתַתִּי אֶת־נִבְלָתָם לְמַאֲכָל לְעוֹף

the to food for dead their I And their who those by and
of birds bodies give will .life seek of hand the

8 הַשָּׁמַיִם וּלְבֶהֱמַת הָאָרֶץ׃ וְשַׂמְתִּי אֶת־הָעִיר הַזֹּאת

this city I And the the to and ,sky the
make will .earth of animals

לְשַׁמָּה וְלִשְׁרֵקָה כֹּל עֹבֵר עָלֶיהָ יִשֹּׁם וְיִשְׁרֹק עַל־כָּל־

all because will and be will it by who All a and horror a
of hiss horrified pass .hissing

9 מַכֹּתֶהָ׃ וְהַאֲכַלְתִּים אֶת־בְּשַׂר בְּנֵיהֶם וְאֵת בְּשַׂר בְּנֹתֵיהֶם

their the and their the will I And its
,daughters of flesh sons of flesh eat them make .plagues

וְאִישׁ בְּשַׂר־רֵעֵהוּ יֹאכֵלוּ בְּמָצוֹר וּבְמָצוֹק אֲשֶׁר יָצִיקוּ

will which the in and the in eat will his the and
oppress distress ,siege friend of flesh each

10 לָהֶם אֹיְבֵיהֶם וּמְבַקְשֵׁי נַפְשָׁם׃ וְשָׁבַרְתָּ הַבַּקְבֻּק לְעֵינֵי

before jar the you Then .life their those and their them
of eyes the break shall seek who enemies

the men who go with you, [11] and shall say to them, Thus says Jehovah of hosts, Even so I will break this people and this city, as (one) breaks the potter's vessel that cannot be made whole again. And they shall bury in Tophet, since no place is (left) to bury. [12] I will do this to this place, says Jehovah, and to its inhabitants, and make this city as Tophet. [13] And the houses of Jerusalem, and the houses of the kings of Judah, shall be defiled as the place of Tophet, because of all the houses on (whose) roofs they have burned incense to all the host of heaven, and have poured out drink offerings to other gods. [14] Then Jeremiah came from Tophet, where Jehovah had sent him there to prophesy. And he stood in the court of Jehovah's house and said to all the people, [15] Thus says Jehovah of hosts, the God of Israel: Behold, I will bring to this city and on all its towns all the evil that I have spoken against it, because they have stiffened their necks in order not to hear My words.

11 האנשים ההלכים אותך׃ ואמרת אליהם כה־אמר
says Thus ,them to shall and say with ,you go who the men

יהוה צבאות ככה אשבר את־העם הזה ואת־העיר הזאת
this city and this people will I break So ,hosts Jehovah of

כאשר ישבר את־כלי היוצר אשר לא־יוכל להרפה
be restored can not that the potter's vessel one breaks as

12 עוד ובתפת יקברו מאין מקום לקבור׃ כן־אעשה
I will do This .bury to place there is since no they bury shall in And Tophet .again

למקום הזה נאם־יהוה וליושביו ולתת את־העיר הזאת
this city and make its to ,inhabitants and ,Jehovah says ,this place to

13 כתפת׃ והיו בתי ירושלם ובתי מלכי יהודה כמקום
the like of place ,Judah the of kings the and of houses ,Jerusalem the of houses And be shall as .Tophet

התפת הטמאים לכל הבתים אשר קטרו על־גגתיהם
their roofs on have they incense burned which the houses because all of ,defiled Tophet

לכל צבא השמים והסך נסכים לאלהים אחרים׃
.other gods to drink offerings have and out poured ;heaven the of host all to

14 ויבא ירמיהו מהתפת אשר שלחו יהוה שם להנבא
to .prophesy there Jehovah had him sent where from ,Tophet Jeremiah Then came

15 ויעמד בחצר בית־יהוה ויאמר אל־כל־העם׃ כה־אמר
says Thus the ,people all to said and Jehovah's house the in of court he And stood

יהוה צבאות אלהי ישראל הנני מבי אל־העיר הזאת
this city to will bring ,Behold :Israel the of God ,hosts Jehovah of

ועל־כל־עריה את כל־הרעה אשר דברתי עליה כי
for against ,it have I spoken that the evil all its towns all and on

הקשו את־ערפם לבלתי שמוע את־דברי׃
My .words hear not to their neck have they stiffened

CAP. XX כ

CHAPTER 20

CHAPTER 20

[1] When Pashur the son of Immer the priest, he also was chief officer in the house of Jehovah, heard that Jeremiah prophesied these things. [2] Then Pashur struck Jeremiah the prophet, and put him in the stocks that (were) in the upper Benjamin Gate,

1 וישמע פשחור בן־אמר הכהן והוא־פקיד נגיד בבית
the in of house chief officer (was) he also the ,priest Immer the of son Pashur When heard

יהוה את־ירמיהו נבא את־הדברים האלה׃ ויכה פשחור
Pashur then struck ,these things prophe- sying Jeremiah Jehovah

2 את ירמיהו הנביא ויתן אתו על־המהפכת אשר בשער
in Gate that (were) the stocks in him and put the ,prophet Jeremiah

which (was) by the house of Jehovah. [3] And it was on the next day that Pashur released Jeremiah from the stocks. Then Jeremiah said to him, Jehovah has not called your name Pashur, but Magor-missabib. [4] For thus says Jehovah, Behold, I will make you a terror to yourself and to all your friends. And they shall fall by the sword of their enemies, and your eyes shall see. And I will give all Judah into the hand of the king of Babylon, and he shall exile them into Babylon, and kill them with the sword. [5] And I will deliver all the wealth of this city, and all its produce; and all its precious things; and all the treasures of the kings of Judah I will give into the hand of their enemies, who will strip them, and take them and carry them to Babylon. [6] And you, Pashur, and all who live in your house, shall go into captivity. And you shall come to Babylon, and you shall die there, and there you shall be buried, you and all your friends to whom you have prophesied lies.

[7] O Jehovah, You have deceived me, and I was deceived. You are stronger than I, and You have prevailed. I am in derision all the day; everyone laughs at me. [8] For whenever I speak, I cry out, I proclaim violence and ruin; for the word of Jehovah has been a reproach and a cause of mocking to me all the day. [9] Then I said, I will not mention Him or speak in His name any more. But (His word) was in my heart like a burning fire shut up in my bones, and I was weary of holding in, and I could not endure (it).

[10] For I heard the evil words of many, Terror is all around! Expose! Yea, let us expose him! Every man of my peace watched for my

---

3

בְּנְיָמִן הָעֶלְיוֹן אֲשֶׁר בְּבֵית יְהֹוָה: וַיְהִי מִמָּחֳרַת וַיֹּצֵא
that　the on　it And　.Jehovah　the by　which　the　Benjamin
released　day next　was　　　　　　of house　(was)　upper

פַּשְׁחוּר אֶת־יִרְמְיָהוּ מִן־הַמַּהְפֶּכֶת וַיֹּאמֶר אֵלָיו יִרְמְיָהוּ
,Jeremiah　him to　Then　the　from　Jeremiah　Pashur
said　.stocks

4

לֹא פַשְׁחוּר קָרָא יְהֹוָה שְׁמֶךָ כִּי אִם־מָגוֹר מִסָּבִיב:
all from　terror　but　your　Jehovah has　Pashur　not
.around　　　　　name　called

כִּי־כֹה אָמַר יְהֹוָה הִנְנִי נֹתֶנְךָ לְמָגוֹר לְךָ וּלְכָל־אֹהֲבֶיךָ
your　to and　to　terror a　will I Behold　,Jehovah　says　thus For
.friends　all　yourself　you make

וְנָפְלוּ בְּחֶרֶב אֹיְבֵיהֶם וְעֵינֶיךָ רֹאוֹת וְאֶת־כָּל־יְהוּדָה אֶתֵּן
will I　Judah　all and　shall　your and　their　the by　they And
give　　　　　　　　;see　eyes　,enemies　of sword　fall will

5

בְּיַד מֶלֶךְ־בָּבֶל וְהִגְלָם בָּבֶלָה וְהִכָּם בֶּחָרֶב: וְנָתַתִּי אֶת־
I And　the with　strike and　into　will he and　,Babylon the　the into
gather will　.sword　them　Babylon　them exile　　　　　of king of hand

כָּל־חֹסֶן הָעִיר הַזֹּאת וְאֶת־כָּל־יְגִיעָהּ וְאֶת־כָּל־יְקָרָהּ וְאֵת
and precious its all and　its　all and　,this　city　the　all
;things　　　　　,produce　　　　　　　of wealth

כָּל־אוֹצְרוֹת מַלְכֵי יְהוּדָה אֶתֵּן בְּיַד אֹיְבֵיהֶם וּבְזָזוּם וּלְקָחוּם
take and　will who　their　into　will I　Judah　the　the　all
them　them strip　,enemies'　hand give　　　　　of king of treasures

6

וֶהֱבִיאוּם בָּבֶלָה: וְאַתָּה פַשְׁחוּר וְכֹל יֹשְׁבֵי בֵיתֶךָ תֵּלְכוּ
shall　your in　who　and　,Pashur　And　　　to　bring and
go　,house　live　all　　　　,you　.Babylon　them

בַּשֶּׁבִי וּבָבֶל תָּבוֹא וְשָׁם תָּמוּת וְשָׁם תִּקָּבֵר אַתָּה וְכָל־
and you　shall you　and　shall you　and　shall you　And　into
all　,buried be　there　,die　there　enter　Babylon　.captivity

7

אֹהֲבֶיךָ אֲשֶׁר־נִבֵּאתָ לָהֶם בַּשָּׁקֶר:
O　have You　　.lies　them to　have you　whom　your
,Jehovah ,me deceived　　　　　　　prophesied　friends

וָאֵפָת חִזַּקְתַּנִי וַתּוּכָל הָיִיתִי לִשְׂחוֹק כָּל־הַיּוֹם כֻּלֹּה לֹעֵג
mocks every　the　all　laughing-a　am I　have and　are You was I and
one　;day　　stock　　　.prevailed　I than stronger .deceived

8

לִי: כִּי־מִדֵּי אֲדַבֵּר אֶזְעָק חָמָס וָשֹׁד אֶקְרָא כִּי־הָיָה
has For　I　　and　violence　cry I　,speak I　when- For　.me
been　.proclaim　ruin　　,out　　　　　　ever

9

דְבַר־יְהֹוָה לִי לְחֶרְפָּה וּלְקֶלֶס כָּל־הַיּוֹם: וְאָמַרְתִּי לֹא
not　I Then　the　all　and　a　to　Jehovah the
,said　　.day　derision　reproach　me　of word

אֶזְכְּרֶנּוּ וְלֹא־אֲדַבֵּר עוֹד בִּשְׁמוֹ וְהָיָה בְלִבִּי כְּאֵשׁ בֹּעֶרֶת
burning　a like　my in　it But　His in　any　speak　or　will I
flame　heart　was　.name　more　　　Him mention

10

עָצֻר בְּעַצְמֹתָי וְנִלְאֵיתִי כַּלְכֵל וְלֹא אוּכָל: כִּי שָׁמַעְתִּי
heard I　For　could I　and　holding　was I and　my in　shut
.(it) endure　not　(it)　of weary　,bones　up

דִּבַּת רַבִּים מָגוֹר מִסָּבִיב הַגִּידוּ וְנַגִּידֶנּוּ כֹּל אֱנוֹשׁ שְׁלֹמִי
my　man　Every us let　,Yea !Expose　all　Terror　,many　the
peace　of　!him expose　　　;around　(is)　　　　of rumor

fall, (saying), Perhaps he will be lured away, and we shall prevail against him, and we shall take our revenge on him. [11] But Jehovah (is) with me like a mighty, awesome one. Therefore my persecutors shall stumble, and they shall not overcome; they shall be greatly ashamed; for they have not acted wisely; an everlasting shame that will not be forgotten. [12] But, O Jehovah of hosts, who tries the righteous (and) sees the reins and the heart, let me see Your vengeance on them; for I have revealed my cause to You. [13] Sing to Jehovah, praise Jehovah; for He has delivered the soul of the poor from the hand of evildoers.

[14] Cursed (is) the day in which I was born; let not the day in which my mother bore me be blessed. [15] Cursed (is) the man who brought news to my father, saying, A man child is born to you; making him very glad. [16] And let that man be as the cities which Jehovah overthrew, and repented not; and let him hear a cry in the morning, and the shouting at noontime; [17] because he did not kill me from the womb; and that my mother would have been my grave, and her womb always great (with me). [18] Why did I come forth from the womb to see toil and sorrow, and my days consumed in shame?

שֹׁמְרֵי צַלְעִי אוּלַי יְפֻתֶּה וְנוּכְלָה לוֹ וְנִקְחָה נִקְמָתֵנוּ מִמֶּנּוּ׃
on our and against we and will he (saying) my watching
.him revenge take him prevail will ,lured Perhaps ,fall for

11 וַיהוָה אוֹתִי כְּגִבּוֹר עָרִיץ עַל־כֵּן רֹדְפַי יִכָּשְׁלוּ וְלֹא יֻכָלוּ
will and will per- my Therefore awesome a like with (is) But
;prevail not ,stumble secutors .one mighty me Jehovah

בֹּשׁוּ מְאֹד כִּי־לֹא הִשְׂכִּילוּ כְּלִמַּת עוֹלָם לֹא תִשָּׁכֵחַ׃
will that not ever- an have they not for ,greatly will they
.forgotten be lasting disgrace ;wisely acted ashamed be

12 וַיהוָה צְבָאוֹת בֹּחֵן צַדִּיק רֹאֶה כְלָיוֹת וָלֵב אֶרְאֶה נִקְמָתְךָ
Your me let the and the (and) the who hosts O But
vengeance see ;heart reins sees righteous tests of Jehovah

13 מֵהֶם כִּי אֵלֶיךָ גִּלִּיתִי אֶת־רִיבִי׃ שִׁירוּ לַיהוָה הַלְלוּ
praise to Sing my have I to for on
,Jehovah .cause revealed You ,them

אֶת־יְהוָה כִּי הִצִּיל אֶת־נֶפֶשׁ אֶבְיוֹן מִיַּד מְרֵעִים׃
.evildoers the from the the has He for ,Jehovah
of hand poor of soul delivered

14 אָרוּר הַיּוֹם אֲשֶׁר יֻלַּדְתִּי בּוֹ יוֹם אֲשֶׁר־יְלָדַתְנִי אִמִּי אַל־
not my bore which the ;it in was I which the Cursed
mother me day born day (is)

15 יְהִי בָרוּךְ׃ אָרוּר הָאִישׁ אֲשֶׁר בִּשַּׂר אֶת־אָבִי לֵאמֹר יֻלַּד־
is ,saying my brought who the Cursed .blessed let
born ,father to news man (is) be

16 לְךָ בֵּן זָכָר שַׂמֵּחַ שִׂמְּחָהוּ׃ וְהָיָה הָאִישׁ הַהוּא כֶּעָרִים
the like that man let And making very ,male a to
cities be .glad him child you

אֲשֶׁר־הָפַךְ יְהוָה וְלֹא נִחָם וְשָׁמַע זְעָקָה בַּבֹּקֶר וּתְרוּעָה
the and the in cry a let and did and ,Jehovah over- which
shouting ,morning hear him ,repent not threw

17 בְּעֵת צָהֳרָיִם׃ אֲשֶׁר לֹא־מוֹתְתַנִי מֵרָחֶם וַתְּהִי־לִי אִמִּי
my for would so the from did he not because ;noon the at
mother me been have ;womb me kill of time

18 קִבְרִי וְרַחְמָהּ הֲרַת עוֹלָם׃ לָמָּה זֶּה מֵרֶחֶם יָצָאתִי לִרְאוֹת
see to did I the from Why .ever great her and my
forth come womb womb ,grave

עָמָל וְיָגוֹן וַיִּכְלוּ בְּבֹשֶׁת יָמָי׃
my in and and toil
?days shame consumed ,torment

CAP. XXI כא

CHAPTER 21

[1] The word which came to Jeremiah from Jehovah, when King Zedekiah sent to him Pashur the son of Melchiah, and Zephaniah the son of Maaseiah the priest, saying, [2] I beg you, inquire of Jehovah for

1 הַדָּבָר אֲשֶׁר־הָיָה אֶל־יִרְמְיָהוּ מֵאֵת יְהוָה בִּשְׁלֹחַ אֵלָיו
to when ,Jehovah from Jeremiah to came which The
him sent word

הַמֶּלֶךְ צִדְקִיָּהוּ אֶת־פַּשְׁחוּר בֶּן־מַלְכִּיָּה וְאֶת־צְפַנְיָה בֶן־
the Zephaniah and ,Melchiah the Pashur Zedekiah King
of son of son

2 מַעֲשֵׂיָה הַכֹּהֵן לֵאמֹר׃ דְּרָשׁ־נָא בַעֲדֵנוּ אֶת־יְהוָה כִּי
for ,Jehovah us for now Inquire ,saying the Maaseiah
of ,priest

us. For Nebuchadnezzar king of Babylon is warring against us. Perhaps Jehovah will deal with us according to all His wonderful works, 3 that he may go up from us.

[3] Then Jeremiah said to them, You shall say this to Zedekiah, [4] Thus says 4 Jehovah the God of Israel: Behold, I will turn back the weapons of war that (are) in your hand, with which you fight against the king of Babylon, and (against) the Chaldeans who besiege you outside the wall. And I will gather them together in the middle of this city. [5] And 5 I Myself will fight against you with an outstretched hand and with a strong arm, even in anger, and in fury, and in great wrath. [6] And 6 I will strike the people of this city, both man and beast; they shall die of a great plague. [7] And afterward, says Jehovah, I will deliver Zedekiah king of 7 Judah, and his servants, and the people, and those who remain in this city, from the plague, from the sword, and from the famine, into the hand of Nebuchadnezzar king of Babylon, and into the hand of their enemies, and into the hand of those who seek their life. And he shall strike them with the edge of the sword; he shall not spare them, nor have pity nor have compassion.

[8] And to this people 8 you shall say, Thus says Jehovah, Behold, I set before you the way of life and the way of death. [9] He 9 who remains in this city shall die by the sword, and by the famine, and by the plague. But he who goes out and falls to the Chaldeans who are besieging you, he shall live, and his life shall

נְבוּכַדְרֶאצַּר מֶלֶךְ־בָּבֶל נִלְחָם עָלֵינוּ אוּלַי יַעֲשֶׂה יְהוָה
Jehovah will Perhaps against is Babylon king Nebuchadnezzar
deal .us warring of

אוֹתָנוּ כְּכָל־נִפְלְאֹתָיו וְיַעֲלֶה מֵעָלֵינוּ: וַיֹּאמֶר יִרְמְיָהוּ
Jeremiah Then from he that wonder- His according with
said .us up go may ,works ful all to us

אֲלֵהֶם כֹּה תֹאמְרֻן אֶל־צִדְקִיָּהוּ: כֹּה־אָמַר יְהוָה אֱלֹהֵי
the Jehovah says Thus ,Zedekiah to shall you Thus to
of God say ,them

יִשְׂרָאֵל הִנְנִי מֵסֵב אֶת־כְּלֵי הַמִּלְחָמָה אֲשֶׁר בְּיֶדְכֶם אֲשֶׁר
which your in that war the turn will ,Behold :Israel
,hand (are) of weapons back I

אַתֶּם נִלְחָמִים בָּם אֶת־מֶלֶךְ בָּבֶל וְאֶת־הַכַּשְׂדִּים הַצָּרִים
who the and ,Babylon the with fight you
besiege Chaldeans of king them against

עֲלֵיכֶם מִחוּץ לַחוֹמָה וְאָסַפְתִּי אוֹתָם אֶל־תּוֹךְ הָעִיר
city the to them will I And the outside you
of midst gather .wall

הַזֹּאת: וְנִלְחַמְתִּי אֲנִי אִתְּכֶם בְּיָד נְטוּיָה וּבִזְרוֹעַ חֲזָקָה
strong with and stretched with against Myself will I And .this
arm a out hand a you fight

וּבְאַף וּבְחֵמָה וּבְקֶצֶף גָּדוֹל: וְהִכֵּיתִי אֶת־יוֹשְׁבֵי הָעִיר
city inhab- the I And .great in and in and in even
of itants strike will rage ,wrath ,anger

הַזֹּאת וְאֶת־הָאָדָם וְאֶת־הַבְּהֵמָה בְּדֶבֶר גָּדוֹל יָמֻתוּ:
will they great a by ;beast and man both ,this
.die plague

וְאַחֲרֵי־כֵן נְאֻם־יְהוָה אֶתֵּן אֶת־צִדְקִיָּהוּ מֶלֶךְ־יְהוּדָה וְאֶת־
and ,Judah king Zedekiah will I ,Jehovah says Then
of deliver .afterwards

עֲבָדָיו וְאֶת־הָעָם וְאֶת־הַנִּשְׁאָרִים בָּעִיר הַזֹּאת מִן־הַדֶּבֶר
the from ,this city in who those and the and his
,plague remain people servants

מִן־הַחֶרֶב וּמִן־הָרָעָב בְּיַד נְבוּכַדְרֶאצַּר מֶלֶךְ־בָּבֶל וּבְיַד
into and ,Babylon king Nebuchadnezzar into the and the from
hand of hand the ,famine from sword

אֹיְבֵיהֶם וּבְיַד מְבַקְשֵׁי נַפְשָׁם וְהִכָּם לְפִי־חֶרֶב לֹא־יָחוּס
will he not the with will he And their who those into and your
spare ;sword's edge them strike .life seek of hand the ,enemies'

עֲלֵיהֶם וְלֹא יַחְמֹל וְלֹא יְרַחֵם: וְאֶל־הָעָם הַזֶּה תֹּאמַר
shall you this people And have nor have nor ,them
,say to .compassion pity

כֹּה אָמַר יְהוָה הִנְנִי נֹתֵן לִפְנֵיכֶם אֶת־דֶּרֶךְ הַחַיִּים וְאֶת־
and life the before set ,Behold ,Jehovah says Thus
of way you I

דֶּרֶךְ הַמָּוֶת: הַיֹּשֵׁב בָּעִיר הַזֹּאת יָמוּת בַּחֶרֶב וּבָרָעָב
by and the by shall this city in who He .death the
,famine the ,sword die dwells of ways

וּבַדָּבֶר וְהַיּוֹצֵא וְנָפַל עַל־הַכַּשְׂדִּים הַצָּרִים עֲלֵיכֶם יְהוָה
shall he ,you are who the to and who he But by and
,live beseiging Chaldeans falls out goes .plague the

be to him for a prize. [10] For I have set My face against this city for evil, and not for good, says Jehovah. It shall be given into the hand of the king of Babylon, and he shall burn it with fire.

[11] And concerning the house of the king of Judah, (say), Hear the word of Jehovah. [12] O house of David, thus says Jehovah: Do justice in the morning, and deliver the plundered ones out of the hand of the oppressor, lest My fury go out like fire, and burn so that none can put (it) out, because of the evil of your doings. [13] Behold, I (am) against you, O dweller of the valley, rock of the plain, says Jehovah; those who say, Who can come down against us? Or who can enter into our homes? [14] But I will punish you according to the fruit of your doings, says Jehovah; and I will kindle a fire in its forest, and it shall devour all things around it.

וְהָיְתָה־לּוֹ נַפְשׁוֹ לְשָׁלָל׃ כִּי־שַׂמְתִּי פָנַי בָּעִיר הַזֹּאת
this against My have I For a for his to and
city face set .prize life him be shall

לְרָעָה וְלֹא לְטוֹבָה נְאֻם־יְהוָה בְּיַד מֶלֶךְ־בָּבֶל תִּנָּתֵן וּשְׂרָפָהּ
will he and will it Babylon the Into .Jehovah says for and for
it burn ,given be of king of hand the ,good not ,evil

11
12 בָּאֵשׁ׃ וּלְבֵית מֶלֶךְ יְהוּדָה שִׁמְעוּ דְּבַר־יְהוָה׃ בֵּית דָּוִד
,David O :Jehovah the ,(say) ,Judah the the to And with
of house of word Hear of king of house .fire

כֹּה אָמַר יְהוָה דִּינוּ לַבֹּקֶר מִשְׁפָּט וְהַצִּילוּ גָזוּל מִיַּד עוֹשֵׁק
op- the from the and ,justice the for Do :Jehovah says thus
,pressor's hand robbed deliver morning

פֶּן־תֵּצֵא כָאֵשׁ חֲמָתִי וּבָעֲרָה וְאֵין מְכַבֶּה מִפְּנֵי רֹעַ
the because can that so and My like go lest
of evil of (it) quench none ,burn wrath fire forth

13 מַעַלְלֵיהֶם׃ הִנְנִי אֵלַיִךְ יֹשֶׁבֶת הָעֵמֶק צוּר הַמִּישֹׁר נְאֻם־
says the rock the dweller O against ,Behold your
,plain of ,valley of ,you (am) I .doings

יְהוָה הָאֹמְרִים מִי־יֵחַת עָלֵינוּ וּמִי יָבוֹא בִּמְעוֹנוֹתֵינוּ׃
our into can Or against can Who who those ,Jehovah
.dwellings enter who ?us down come ,say

14 וּפָקַדְתִּי עֲלֵיכֶם כִּפְרִי מַעַלְלֵיכֶם נְאֻם־יְהוָה וְהִצַּתִּי אֵשׁ
a will I and ;Jehovah says your to according you will I But
fire kindle ,doings of fruit the punish

בְּיַעְרָהּ וְאָכְלָה כָּל־סְבִיבֶיהָ׃
around all may it that its in
.it things devour ,forest

CAP. XXII כב

CHAPTER 22

CHAPTER 22

[1] Thus says Jehovah: Go down to the house of the king of Judah and speak this word there; [2] and say, Hear the word of Jehovah, O king of Judah, who sits on the throne of David, you and your servants, and your people who enter in by these gates. [3] Thus says Jehovah, Do justice and righteousness, and deliver him who is robbed out of the hand of the oppressor. And do no wrong, nor do violence (to) the stranger, the fatherless, or the widow; and do not shed innocent blood in this place. [4] For if you do this thing indeed, then there shall enter in by the gates of this house kings sitting on

1 כֹּה אָמַר יְהוָה רֵד בֵּית־מֶלֶךְ יְהוּדָה וְדִבַּרְתָּ שָּׁם אֶת־
there and ,Judah the the down Go Jeho- says Thus
speak of king of house to ,vah

2 הַדָּבָר הַזֶּה׃ וְאָמַרְתָּ שְׁמַע דְּבַר־יְהוָה מֶלֶךְ יְהוּדָה הַיֹּשֵׁב
who ,Judah O ,Jehovah the Hear ,say and ;this word
sits of king of word

עַל־כִּסֵּא דָוִד אַתָּה וַעֲבָדֶיךָ וְעַמְּךָ הַבָּאִים בַּשְּׁעָרִים
gates by enter who your and your and you ,David the on
in people ,servants of throne

3 הָאֵלֶּה׃ כֹּה ׀ אָמַר יְהוָה עֲשׂוּ מִשְׁפָּט וּצְדָקָה וְהַצִּילוּ
and and justice Do ,Jehovah says Thus .these
deliver ,righteousness

גָזוּל מִיַּד עָשׁוֹק וְגֵר יָתוֹם וְאַלְמָנָה אַל־תֹּנוּ אַל־תַּחְמֹסוּ
do nor do not the or or- the the with op- (his) from the
,violence ,oppress ,widow phan ,stranger ,pressor's hand robbed

4 וְדָם נָקִי אַל־תִּשְׁפְּכוּ בַּמָּקוֹם הַזֶּה׃ כִּי אִם־עָשׂוֹ תַּעֲשׂוּ
you indeed if For .this place in shed do not inno- and
do cent blood

אֶת־הַדָּבָר הַזֶּה וּבָאוּ בְשַׁעֲרֵי הַבַּיִת הַזֶּה מְלָכִים יֹשְׁבִים
sitting kings this house the by will then ,this thing
of gates enter

the throne of David, riding in chariots and on horses, he and his servants and his people. [5] But if you will not hear these words, I swear by Myself, says Jehovah, that this house shall become a ruin. [6] For thus says Jehovah concerning the king of Judah's house, You (are) Gilead to Me, the head of Lebanon; yet surely I will make you a wilderness, cities not inhabited. [7] And I will consecrate destroyers against you, each one with his weapons, and they will cut down your choice cedars and cast into the fire. [8] And many nations shall pass by this city, and they shall say each one to his neighbor, Why has Jehovah done this to this great city? [9] Then they will answer, Because they have forsaken the covenant of Jehovah their God, and worshiped other gods and served them.

[10] Weep not for the dead, nor moan for him; weep bitterly for him who goes away, for he shall return no more, nor see the land of his birth. [11] For thus says Jehovah concerning Shallum the son of Josiah king of Judah, who reigned in the place of his father Josiah, who went forth out of this place; he shall not return there any more. [12] But he shall die there in the place where they have exiled him, and he will see this land no more.

[13] Woe (to) him who builds his house without righteousness, and his upper rooms without justice; his neighbor serves without pay, and he does not give him his wages; [14] who says, I will build myself a

לְדָוִד עַל־כִּסְאוֹ רֹכְבִים בָּרֶכֶב וּבַסּוּסִים הוּא וַעֲבָדָו וְעַמּוֹ׃
his and his and he on and on riding his on of
.people servants ,horses chariots ,throne David

5 וְאִם לֹא תִשְׁמְעוּ אֶת־הַדְּבָרִים הָאֵלֶּה בִּי נִשְׁבַּעְתִּי נְאֻם־
says swear I by ,these words will you not But
Myself obey if

6 יְהוָה כִּי־לְחָרְבָּה יִהְיֶה הַבַּיִת הַזֶּה׃ כִּי־כֹה ׀ אָמַר
says thus For .this house shall ruin a that ,Jehovah
become

יְהוָה עַל־בֵּית מֶלֶךְ יְהוּדָה גִּלְעָד אַתָּה לִי רֹאשׁ הַלְּבָנוֹן
;Lebanon the to You (like) ,Judah the the about Jehovah
of head ,Me (are) Gilead of king of house

7 אִם־לֹא אֲשִׁיתְךָ מִדְבָּר עָרִים לֹא נוֹשָׁבָה׃ וְקִדַּשְׁתִּי עָלֶיךָ
against will I And are not cities wilder- a will I yet
you consecrate .inhabited (which) ,ness you make surely

מַשְׁחִתִים אִישׁ וְכֵלָיו וְכָרְתוּ מִבְחַר אֲרָזֶיךָ וְהִפִּילוּ עַל־
into will and your the will and his with each ,destroyers
cast cedars of best down cut weapons man

8 הָאֵשׁ׃ וְעָבְרוּ גּוֹיִם רַבִּים עַל הָעִיר הַזֹּאת וְאָמְרוּ אִישׁ
each they and ,this city by many nations will And the
man say will pass .fire

אֶל־רֵעֵהוּ עַל־מֶה עָשָׂה יְהוָה כָּכָה לָעִיר הַגְּדוֹלָה הַזֹּאת׃
?this great city to thus ,Jehovah has Why his to
done ,companion

וְאָמְרוּ עַל אֲשֶׁר עָזְבוּ אֶת־בְּרִית יְהוָה אֱלֹהֵיהֶם וַיִּשְׁתַּחֲוּוּ
and their Jehovah the have they Because they Then
worshiped ,God of covenant forsaken ,say will

10 לֵאלֹהִים אֲחֵרִים וַיַּעַבְדוּם׃ אַל־תִּבְכּוּ לְמֵת וְאַל־
nor the for Do not served and other gods
,dead weep .them

תָּנֻדוּ לוֹ בְּכוּ בָכוֹ לַהֹלֵךְ כִּי לֹא יָשׁוּב עוֹד וְרָאָה אֶת־
nor any will he not for him for bitterly weep for lament
see ,more return ,away goes who ;him

11 אֶרֶץ מוֹלַדְתּוֹ׃ כִּי כֹה אָמַר־יְהוָה אֶל־שַׁלֻּם בֶּן־יֹאשִׁיָּהוּ
Josiah the Shallum con- Jehovah says thus For his the
of son cerning .birth of land

מֶלֶךְ יְהוּדָה הַמֹּלֵךְ תַּחַת יֹאשִׁיָּהוּ אָבִיו אֲשֶׁר יָצָא מִן־
from went who his Josiah the in who ,Judah king
forth ,father of place reigned of

12 הַמָּקוֹם הַזֶּה לֹא־יָשׁוּב שָׁם עוֹד׃ כִּי בִּמְקוֹם אֲשֶׁר־הִגְלוּ
have they where the in But any there will he not ;this place
exiled place .more return

אֹתוֹ שָׁם יָמוּת וְאֶת־הָאָרֶץ הַזֹּאת לֹא־יִרְאֶה עוֹד׃
.more will he no this land and will he there ,him
see ,die

13 הוֹי בֹּנֶה בֵיתוֹ בְּלֹא־צֶדֶק וַעֲלִיּוֹתָיו בְּלֹא מִשְׁפָּט בְּרֵעֵהוּ
his ,justice without his and without his who him Woe
neighbor roof-rooms righteousness house builds (to)

14 יַעֲבֹד חִנָּם וּפֹעֲלוֹ לֹא יִתֶּן־לוֹ׃ הָאֹמֵר אֶבְנֶה־לִּי בֵּית
a my- will I ,says who to he not his and without serves
house self build ,him give does wages ,pay

wide house and large upper rooms, and cuts out for it windows; and covered with cedar, and paints with vermilion. [15] Do you reign, because you lust to excel in cedar? Did not your father eat and drink and do justice and righteousness? Then (it was) well for him. [16] He judged the cause of the poor and needy; then (it was) well. Was this not to know me, says Jehovah? [17] But your eyes and your heart (desire) nothing but your unjust gain, and to shed innocent blood, and oppression, and to do violence. [18] Therefore thus says Jehovah concerning Jehoiakim the son of Josiah king of Judah, They shall not mourn for him, (saying), Ah, my brother! or, Ah, sister! They shall not mourn for him, (saying), Ah, lord! or, Ah, his glory! [19] He shall be buried with the burial of an ass, drawn beyond the gates of Jerusalem and thrown out.

[20] Go up to Lebanon and cry. And lift up your voice in Bashan, and cry out from Abarim; for all your lovers are destroyed. [21] I spoke to you in your ease; but you said, I will not hear. This (has been) your way from your youth, for you have not obeyed My voice. [22] The wind shall rule all your shepherds, and your lovers shall go into captivity. Surely then you will be ashamed and will blush for all your wickedness. [23] O dweller in Lebanon, nested in the cedars, how will you be pitied when pangs come to you, the pain as of a woman in labor? [24] (As) I live, says Jehovah, though Coniah the son of Jehoiakim king of Judah were the signet on My right hand, yet I would tear you out of there! [25] And I will give you into the hand

מִדּוֹת וַעֲלִיּוֹת מְרֻוָּחִים וְקָרַע לוֹ חַלּוֹנָי וְסָפוּן בָּאֶרֶז וּמָשׁוֹחַ

and with and its for cut and ,large upper and spacious
paints ,cedar covered windows it out rooms

בַּשָּׁשַׁר׃ הֲתִמְלֹךְ כִּי אַתָּה מְתַחֲרֶה בָאֶרֶז אָבִיךָ הֲלוֹא

nor your in to lust you because you Do with
father ?cedar excel reign .vermilion

16 אָכַל וְשָׁתָה וְעָשָׂה מִשְׁפָּט וּצְדָקָה אָז טוֹב לוֹ׃ דָּן דִּין

cause the He for was it ,Then and justice do and drink and Did
of judged .him well ?righteousness eat

17 עָנִי וְאֶבְיוֹן אָז טוֹב הֲלוֹא־הִיא הַדַּעַת אֹתִי נְאֻם־יְהוָה׃ כִּי

But ?Jehovah says ,Me know to that (Was) (was it) then and the
not .well ;needy poor

אֵין עֵינֶיךָ וְלִבְּךָ כִּי אִם־עַל־בִּצְעֶךָ וְעַל דַּם־הַנָּקִי לִשְׁפּוֹךְ

,shed to inno- blood and your except your and your (want)
cent ,gain unjust heart eyes nothing

18 וְעַל־הָעֹשֶׁק וְעַל־הַמְּרוּצָה לַעֲשׂוֹת׃ לָכֵן כֹּה־אָמַר

says thus Therefore .do to extortion and oppression and

יְהוָה אֶל־יְהוֹיָקִים בֶּן־יֹאשִׁיָּהוּ מֶלֶךְ יְהוּדָה לֹא־יִסְפְּדוּ לוֹ

for will they not ,Judah king Josiah the Jehoiakim con- Jeho-
,him mourn of of son cerning

הוֹי אָחִי וְהוֹי אָחוֹת לֹא־יִסְפְּדוּ לוֹ הוֹי אָדוֹן וְהוֹי הֹדֹה׃

his ,or !lord ,(saying) for They not !sister ,or my ,(saying)
.splendor Alas ,Alas him mourn will ,Alas !brother ,Alas

19 קְבוּרַת חֲמוֹר יִקָּבֵר סָחוֹב וְהַשְׁלֵךְ מֵהָלְאָה לְשַׁעֲרֵי

the beyond thrown and dragged will he ass an the (With)
of gates out off :buried be of burial

20 יְרוּשָׁלִָם׃ עֲלִי הַלְּבָנוֹן וּצְעָקִי וּבַבָּשָׁן תְּנִי קוֹלֵךְ

your lift in and cry and Lebanon Go .Jerusalem
;voice up Bashan ,out to up

21 וְצַעֲקִי מֵעֲבָרִים כִּי נִשְׁבְּרוּ כָּל־מְאַהֲבָיִךְ׃ דִּבַּרְתִּי אֵלַיִךְ

you to spoke I your all are for from cry and
.lovers crushed ,Abarim ,out

בְּשַׁלְוֺתַיִךְ אָמַרְתְּ לֹא אֶשְׁמָע זֶה דַרְכֵּךְ מִנְּעוּרַיִךְ כִּי לֹא־

not for your from your this will I not you (but) your in
,youth way (been has) ;listen ,said ,prosperity

22 שָׁמַעַתְּ בְּקוֹלִי׃ כָּל־רֹעַיִךְ תִּרְעֶה־רוּחַ וּמְאַהֲבַיִךְ בַּשְּׁבִי

into your and the will your All My have you
captivity lovers ,wind rule shepherds .voice obeyed

23 יֵלֵכוּ כִּי אָז תֵּבֹשִׁי וְנִכְלַמְתְּ מִכֹּל רָעָתֵךְ׃ יֹשַׁבְתְּי בַּלְּבָנוֹן

in O your all for and be will you then Surely will
,Lebanon dweller wickedness humiliated ashamed .go

מְקֻנַּנְתִּי בָּאֲרָזִים מַה־נֵּחַנְתְּ בְּבֹא־לָךְ חֲבָלִים חִיל כַּיֹּלֵדָה׃

travail- a as the ,pangs to when will you how the in nested
!woman ing pain you come groan ,cedars

24 חַי־אָנִי נְאֻם־יְהוָה כִּי אִם־יִהְיֶה כָּנְיָהוּ בֶּן־יְהוֹיָקִים מֶלֶךְ

king Jehoiakim the Coniah were though ,Jehovah says ,I (As)
of of son ,live

25 יְהוּדָה חוֹתָם עַל־יַד יְמִינִי כִּי מִשָּׁם אֶתְּקֶנְךָּ׃ וּנְתַתִּיךְ

will I and tear would I from yet My hand on the Judah
you give ;away you there ,right ring signet

of those who seek your life, and into the hand (of those) whose face you fear, even into the hand of Nebuchadnezzar king of Babylon, and into the hand of the Chaldeans. [26] And I will cast you and your mother who bore you into another country where you were not born there, and there you shall die. [27] But concerning the land which they desire with their soul to return there, there they shall not return. [28] Is this man Coniah a despised, broken jar, or a vessel (in which is) no pleasure? Why are they hurled, he and his seed, and are cast into the land which they do not know? [29] O earth, earth, earth! Hear the word of Jehovah! [30] Thus says Jehovah, Write this man childless, a man who shall not prosper in his days. For not one of his seed shall be blessed, sitting on the throne of David and ruling any more in Judah.

בְּיַד מְבַקְשֵׁי נַפְשֶׁךָ וּבְיַד אֲשֶׁר־אַתָּה יָגוֹר מִפְּנֵיהֶם וּבְיַד
even before are you those into and your who those into
hand into ,them dreading whom of hand the ,life seek of hand the
26 נְבוּכַדְרֶאצַּר מֶלֶךְ־בָּבֶל וּבְיַד הַכַּשְׂדִּים׃ וְהֵטַלְתִּי אֹתְךָ
you I And the the into ,Babylon king ..Nebuchad-
hurl,will .Chaldeans' hand of ,nezzar's
וְאֶת־אִמְּךָ אֲשֶׁר יְלָדַתְךָ עַל הָאָרֶץ אַחֶרֶת אֲשֶׁר לֹא־יֻלַּדְתֶּם
were you not where another land into bore who your and
born you mother
27 שָׁם וְשָׁם תָּמוּתוּ׃ וְעַל־הָאָרֶץ אֲשֶׁר הֵם מְנַשְּׂאִים אֶת־
with desire they which the But will you and ,there
land for as .die there
28 נַפְשָׁם לָשׁוּב שָׁם שָׁמָּה לֹא יָשׁוּבוּ׃ הַעֶצֶב נִבְזֶה נָפוּץ
shat- despised a (Is) shall they not ,there ,there return to their
tered jar .return soul
הָאִישׁ הַזֶּה כָּנְיָהוּ אִם־כְּלִי אֵין חֵפֶץ בּוֹ מַדּוּעַ הוּטְלוּ הוּא
he are Why in pleasure not a or ,Coniah this man
hurled ?it is vessel
29 וְזַרְעוֹ וְהֻשְׁלְכוּ עַל־הָאָרֶץ אֲשֶׁר לֹא־יָדָעוּ׃ אֶרֶץ אֶרֶץ אָרֶץ
!earth ,earth O did they not which the into and his and
,earth ?know land thrown ,seed
30 שִׁמְעִי דְּבַר־יְהוָה׃ כֹּה ׀ אָמַר יְהוָה כִּתְבוּ אֶת־הָאִישׁ הַזֶּה
this man Write ,Jehovah says This !Jehovah the Hear
of word
עֲרִירִי גֶּבֶר לֹא־יִצְלַח בְּיָמָיו כִּי לֹא יִצְלַח מִזַּרְעוֹ אִישׁ
a his from will one not For his in will who not man a child-
man ,seed succeed .days prosper ,less
יֹשֵׁב עַל־כִּסֵּא דָוִד וּמֹשֵׁל עוֹד בִּיהוּדָה׃
.Judah in any and David the on sitting
more ruling of throne

CAP. XXIII כג

CHAPTER 23

CHAPTER 23

[1] Woe to the shepherds who destroy and scatter the sheep of My pasture, says Jehovah. [2] Therefore thus says Jehovah the God of Israel against the shepherds who shepherd My people: You have scattered My flock, and have driven them away, and have not tended them. Behold, I will attend upon you the evil of your doings, says Jehovah. [3] And I will gather the remnant of My flock out of all the lands where I have driven them there, and will bring them again to their fold; and they shall be fruitful and multiply. [4] And I will set up

1 הוֹי רֹעִים מְאַבְּדִים וּמְפִצִים אֶת־צֹאן מַרְעִיתִי נְאֻם־יְהוָה׃
.Jehovah says My the and who the Woe
,pasture of sheep scatter destroy shepherds (to)
2 לָכֵן כֹּה־אָמַר יְהוָה אֱלֹהֵי יִשְׂרָאֵל עַל־הָרֹעִים הָרֹעִים
are who the against Israel the Jehovah says thus There-
shepherding shepherds of God fore
אֶת־עַמִּי אַתֶּם הֲפִצֹתֶם אֶת־צֹאנִי וַתַּדִּחוּם וְלֹא פְקַדְתֶּם
at- have and driven and My have You my
to tended not ,away them flock scattered :people
אֹתָם הִנְנִי פֹקֵד עֲלֵיכֶם אֶת־רֹעַ מַעַלְלֵיכֶם נְאֻם־יְהוָה׃
.Jehovah says Your the upon will ,Behold .them
,doings of evil you attend I
3 וַאֲנִי אֲקַבֵּץ אֶת־שְׁאֵרִית צֹאנִי מִכֹּל הָאֲרָצוֹת אֲשֶׁר־הִדַּחְתִּי
have I where the from My the will And
driven lands all flock of remnant gather I
4 אֹתָם שָׁם וַהֲשִׁבֹתִי אֶתְהֶן עַל־נְוֵהֶן וּפָרוּ וְרָבוּ׃ וַהֲקִמֹתִי
will I And and they and their to them will and there them
up set .multiply bear will ;fold back bring

shepherds over them who will tend them. And they will fear no more, nor be terrified; nor will they be missing (anything), says Jehovah.

[5] Behold, the days come, says Jehovah, that I will raise to David a righteous Branch, and a King shall reign and act wisely, and shall do justice and righteousness in the earth. [6] In His days Judah shall be saved, and Israel shall dwell safely. And this is His name (by) which He shall be called, Jehovah our Righteousness. [7] Therefore, behold, the days come, says Jehovah, that they shall no more say, (As) Jehovah lives, who brought the sons of Israel up out of the land of Egypt; [8] but, (As) Jehovah lives, who brought up and led the seed of the house of Israel out of the land of north, and from all the lands where I have driven them there. And they shall dwell on their own land.

[9] My heart within me is broken concerning the prophets; all my bones shake. I am like a drunken man, and like a man overcome by wine, because of Jehovah, and because of the words of His holiness. [10] For the land is full of adulterers. For, the land mourns because of a curse; the pastures of the wilderness are dried up, and their way is evil, and their might (is) not right. [11] For both prophet and priest are ungodly; yes, I have found their wickedness in My house, says Jehovah. [12] Therefore their way shall be to them as slippery places in the darkness; they shall be driven out and fall by it. For I will bring evil on them, (even) the year of their judgment, says Jehovah. [13] And I have seen frivolity among the prophets of Samaria; they

עֲלֵיהֶם רֹעִים וּרְעוּם וְלֹא־יִירְאוּ עוֹד וְלֹא־יֵחַתּוּ וְלֹא יִפָּקֵדוּ
they will not be nor again will they and will who shep- over
,missing be ,terrified fear not ,them tend herds them

5 נְאֻם־יְהוָה׃ הִנֵּה יָמִים בָּאִים נְאֻם־יְהוָה וַהֲקִמֹתִי
will I that ,Jehovah says ,come the ,Behold .Jehovah says
up set days

לְדָוִד צֶמַח צַדִּיק וּמָלַךְ מֶלֶךְ וְהִשְׂכִּיל וְעָשָׂה מִשְׁפָּט
justice will and act and a shall and ,righteous a for
do ,wisely King reign Branch David

6 וּצְדָקָה בָּאָרֶץ׃ בְּיָמָיו תִּוָּשַׁע יְהוּדָה וְיִשְׂרָאֵל יִשְׁכֹּן לָבֶטַח
.safely shall and ,Judah be will His In the in righ- and
dwell Israel saved ,days .earth teousness

7 וְזֶה־שְּׁמוֹ אֲשֶׁר־יִקְרְאוֹ יְהוָה ׀ צִדְקֵנוּ׃ לָכֵן הִנֵּה־יָמִים
the ,behold ,Therefore our Jehovah will He (by) His this And
days .Righteousness :called be which name (is)

בָּאִים נְאֻם־יְהוָה וְלֹא־יֹאמְרוּ עוֹד חַי־יְהוָה אֲשֶׁר הֶעֱלָה
brought who ,Jehovah (As) ,more they that ,Jehovah says ,come
up lives say shall no

8 אֶת־בְּנֵי יִשְׂרָאֵל מֵאֶרֶץ מִצְרָיִם׃ כִּי אִם־חַי־יְהוָה אֲשֶׁר
who ,Jehovah (As) ,but ;Egypt the from Israel the
lives of land of sons

הֶעֱלָה וַאֲשֶׁר הֵבִיא אֶת־זֶרַע בֵּית יִשְׂרָאֵל מֵאֶרֶץ צָפוֹנָה
the the from Israel the the led and brought
,north of land of house of seed up

וּמִכֹּל הָאֲרָצוֹת אֲשֶׁר הִדַּחְתִּים שָׁם וְיָשְׁבוּ עַל־אַדְמָתָם׃
own their upon they And .there have I where the from and
.land dwell will them driven lands all

9 לַנְּבִאִים נִשְׁבַּר לִבִּי בְקִרְבִּי רָחֲפוּ כָּל־עַצְמוֹתַי
my all shake my in my is Concerning
.bones ,midst heart broken ,prophets the

הָיִיתִי כְּאִישׁ שִׁכּוֹר וּכְגֶבֶר עֲבָרוֹ יָיִן מִפְּנֵי יְהוָה וּמִפְּנֵי
and ,Jehovah because ,wine over- like and ,drunken a like am I
of because of by come man a man

10 דִּבְרֵי קָדְשׁוֹ׃ כִּי מְנָאֲפִים מָלְאָה הָאָרֶץ כִּי־מִפְּנֵי אָלָה
a because For the full is adulterers For His the
,curse of .land of .holiness of words

אָבְלָה הָאָרֶץ יָבְשׁוּ נְאוֹת מִדְבָּר וַתְּהִי מְרוּצָתָם רָעָה
,evil their is and wil- the pas- the are the mourns
course ,derness of tures up dried ;land

11 וּגְבוּרָתָם לֹא־כֵן׃ כִּי־גַם־נָבִיא גַם־כֹּהֵן חָנֵפוּ גַּם־בְּבֵיתִי
My in even are priest and prophet both For .right not their and
house ;ungodly (is) might

12 מָצָאתִי רָעָתָם נְאֻם־יְהוָה׃ לָכֵן יִהְיֶה דַרְכָּם לָהֶם
for their shall Therefore .Jehovah says their have I
them way be ,wickedness found

כַּחֲלַקְלַקּוֹת בָּאֲפֵלָה יִדַּחוּ וְנָפְלוּ בָהּ כִּי־אָבִיא עֲלֵיהֶם
on will I For .it by and be will they the in slipperi- like
them bring fall out driven ;darkness ness

13 רָעָה שְׁנַת פְּקֻדָּתָם נְאֻם־יְהוָה׃ וּבִנְבִיאֵי שֹׁמְרוֹן
Samaria among And .Jehovah says their the ,evil
of prophets the ,punishment of year

prophesied by Baal and caused My people Israel to go astray. [14] I have also seen among the prophets of Jerusalem a horrible thing; they commit adultery and walk in falsehood, and they strengthen the hands of evildoers, so that not a man returns from his wickedness. They are all of them like Sodom to Me, and her inhabitants like Gomorrah. [15] Therefore thus says Jehovah of hosts concerning the prophets: Behold, I will feed them wormwood, and make them drink the water of poison; for from the prophets of Jerusalem, ungodliness has gone forth into all the land. [16] Thus says Jehovah of hosts, Do not listen to the words of the prophets who prophesy to you; they make you become vain; they speak a vision of their own heart, not out of the mouth of Jehovah. [17] They say to those who despise Me, Jehovah has said, You shall have peace! And they say to everyone who walks in the stubbornness of his own heart, Evil shall not come on you! [18] For who has stood in the counsel of Jehovah and has seen and heard His word? Who has listened to His word and heard? [19] Behold, the tempest of Jehovah has gone forth in fury, even a whirling tempest; it will whirl on the head of the wicked. [20] The anger of Jehovah shall not turn back until He has executed, and until He has set up the purposes of His heart; in latter days you shall understand it perfectly. [21] I have not sent the prophets, yet they ran; I have not spoken to them, yet they prophesied. [22] But if they had stood in My counsel and had caused My people to hear My words, then they would have

רָאִיתִי תִפְלָה הִנַּבְּאוּ בַבַּעַל וַיַּתְעוּ אֶת־עַמִּי אֶת־יִשְׂרָאֵל׃
.Israel My and Baal by they ,frivolity have I
people mislead prophesied seen

14 וּבִנְבִאֵי יְרוּשָׁלִַם רָאִיתִי שַׁעֲרוּרָה נָאוֹף וְהָלֹךְ
and commit they horrible a have I Jerusalem's among Also
walk adultery :thing seen prophets

בַּשֶּׁקֶר וְחִזְּקוּ יְדֵי מְרֵעִים לְבִלְתִּי־שָׁבוּ אִישׁ מֵרָעָתוֹ הָיוּ־
They his from a does that so evil- the they and false- in
are .wickedness man return not ,doers of hands strengthen ,hood

15 לִי כֻלָּם כִּסְדֹם וְיֹשְׁבֶיהָ כַּעֲמֹרָה׃ לָכֵן כֹּה־אָמַר
says thus Therefore like her and like of all to
.Gomorrah inhabitants Sodom them Me

יְהוָה צְבָאוֹת עַל־הַנְּבִאִים הִנְנִי מַאֲכִיל אוֹתָם לַעֲנָה
worm- them feed will ,Behold the con- hosts Jehovah
,wood I :prophets cerning of

וְהִשְׁקִתִים מֵי־רֹאשׁ כִּי מֵאֵת נְבִיאֵי יְרוּשָׁלִַם יָצְאָה חֲנֻפָּה
ungodli- has Jerusalem the from for ;poison the make and
ness out gone of prophets of water drink them

16 לְכָל־הָאָרֶץ׃ כֹּה־אָמַר יְהוָה צְבָאוֹת אַל־תִּשְׁמְעוּ
Do not ,hosts Jehovah says Thus the into
listen of .land all

עַל־דִּבְרֵי הַנְּבִאִים הַנִּבְּאִים לָכֶם מַהְבִּלִים הֵמָּה אֶתְכֶם
;you they to cause ,you to who the the to
vain become prophesy prophets of words

17 חֲזוֹן לִבָּם יְדַבֵּרוּ לֹא מִפִּי יְהוָה׃ אֹמְרִים אָמוֹר לִמְנַאֲצַי
those to continually They .Jehovah's from not they their a
,Me spurn who say mouth ,speak heart of vision

דִּבֶּר יְהוָה שָׁלוֹם יִהְיֶה לָכֶם וְכֹל הֹלֵךְ בִּשְׁרִרוּת לִבּוֹ
own his stub- the in who And !you to shall Peace ,Jehovah has
,heart of bornness walks everyone be said

18 אָמְרוּ לֹא־תָבוֹא עֲלֵיכֶם רָעָה׃ כִּי מִי עָמַד בְּסוֹד יְהוָה
Jehovah the in has who For !Evil you on will not they
of council stood come ,say

וְיֵרֶא וְיִשְׁמַע אֶת־דְּבָרוֹ מִי־הִקְשִׁיב דְּבָרִי וַיִּשְׁמָע׃
and His has Who His and has and
?heard word to listened ?word heard seen

19 הִנֵּה ׀ סַעֲרַת יְהוָה חֵמָה יָצְאָה וְסַעַר מִתְחוֹלֵל עַל רֹאשׁ
the on ;whirling a even gone has (in) Jehovah the ,Behold
of head tempest forth ,wrath of tempest

20 רְשָׁעִים יָחוּל׃ לֹא יָשׁוּב אַף־יְהוָה עַד־עֲשֹׂתוֹ וְעַד־הֲקִימוֹ
has He and has He until ,Jehovah The will not will it the
out carried until ,executed of anger back turn .whirl wicked

21 מְזִמּוֹת לִבּוֹ בְּאַחֲרִית הַיָּמִים תִּתְבּוֹנְנוּ בָהּ בִּינָה׃ לֹא־
not (with) it will you days in his pur- the
.understanding understand latter ;heart of poses

שָׁלַחְתִּי אֶת־הַנְּבִאִים וְהֵם רָצוּ לֹא־דִבַּרְתִּי אֲלֵיהֶם וְהֵם
yet ,them to have I not ;ran yet the have I
they spoken they ;prophets sent

22 נִבָּאוּ׃ וְאִם־עָמְדוּ בְּסוֹדִי וְיַשְׁמִעוּ דְבָרַי אֶת־עַמִּי וִישִׁבוּם
had they then My My had they then My in had they But prophe-
them turned ,people words hear made counsel stood if .sied

turned them from their evil way and from the evil of their doings. [23] (Am) I a God near by, says Jehovah, and not a God from afar? [24] Or can anyone hide himself in secret places so that I do not see him, says Jehovah? Do I not fill Heaven and earth, says Jehovah? [25] I have heard what the prophets said, who prophesy lies in My name, saying, I have dreamed, I have dreamed. [26] How long is (this) there in the heart of the prophets, the prophets of lies; yea, the prophets of the deceit of their own heart? [27] (They) plot to cause My people to forget My name by their dreams which they tell, each one to his neighbor, as their fathers have forgotten My name for Baal. [28] The prophet who has a dream, let him tell a dream. And he who has My word, let him speak My word faithfully. What (has) the straw to (do) with the grain; says Jehovah? [29] Is not My word thus like fire, says Jehovah, and like a hammer which breaks a rock in pieces? [30] Therefore, Jehovah says, Behold, I (am) against the prophets who steal My words, each one from his neighbor. [31] Jehovah says, Behold, I (am) against the prophets who use their tongues and say, (He) says. [32] Jehovah says, Behold, I (am) against those who prophesy false dreams and tell them, and cause My people to go astray by their lies and by their frivolity. Yet I did not send them nor command them; and they will not profit this people at all, says Jehovah.

[33] And when this people, or the prophet, or a priest, shall ask you, saying, What (is) the burden

23 מִדַּרְכָּם הָרָע וּמֵרֹעַ מַעַלְלֵיהֶם׃ הַאֱלֹהֵי מִקָּרֹב
near by from God a | their .doings | from and of evil the | evil | their from way

24 אֲנִי נְאֻם־יְהוָה וְלֹא אֱלֹהֵי מֵרָחֹק׃ אִם־יִסָּתֵר אִישׁ
a man | hide can himself | Or | from .afar | God a | and not | ,Jehovah says | I ,(am)

בַּמִּסְתָּרִים וַאֲנִי לֹא־אֶרְאֶנּוּ נְאֻם־יְהוָה הֲלוֹא אֶת־הַשָּׁמַיִם
the heavens | not | ?Jehovah says | see do ,him | not I | that so | hiding in places

25 וְאֶת־הָאָרֶץ אֲנִי מָלֵא נְאֻם־יְהוָה׃ שָׁמַעְתִּי אֵת אֲשֶׁר
what | have I heard | ?Jehovah says | ,fill Do | I | the earth | and

אָמְרוּ הַנְּבִאִים הַנִּבְּאִים בִּשְׁמִי שֶׁקֶר לֵאמֹר חָלַמְתִּי
have I ,dreamed | ,saying | ,lies | My in name | who prophesy | the ,prophets | said

26 חָלָמְתִּי׃ עַד־מָתַי הֲיֵשׁ בְּלֵב הַנְּבִאִים נִבְּאֵי הַשָּׁקֶר וּנְבִיאֵי
and of prophets | ,lies | prophets of | the ,prophets | the in of heart | is there | when Until | have I .dreamed

27 תַּרְמִת לִבָּם׃ הַחֹשְׁבִים לְהַשְׁכִּיחַ אֶת־עַמִּי שְׁמִי בַּחֲלוֹמֹתָם
their by dream | My name | My people | make to forget | (They) plan | own their ?heart | the of deceit

אֲשֶׁר יְסַפְּרוּ אִישׁ לְרֵעֵהוּ כַּאֲשֶׁר שָׁכְחוּ אֲבוֹתָם אֶת־שְׁמִי
My name | their fathers | have forgotten | as | his to ;neighbor | each man | they tell | which

28 בַּבָּעַל׃ הַנָּבִיא אֲשֶׁר־אִתּוֹ חֲלוֹם יְסַפֵּר חֲלוֹם וַאֲשֶׁר דְּבָרִי
My word | he but who | (his) ,dream | him let tell | a (has) ,dream | with him | who | The prophet | for !Baal

אִתּוֹ יְדַבֵּר דְּבָרִי אֱמֶת מַה־לַתֶּבֶן אֶת־הַבָּר נְאֻם־יְהוָה׃
?Jehovah says | the ,grain | with | the to straw | What (is) | faith- .fully | My word | him let speak | (has) him with

29 הֲלוֹא כֹה דְבָרִי כָּאֵשׁ נְאֻם־יְהוָה וּכְפַטִּישׁ יְפֹצֵץ סָלַע׃
?rock a | which shatters | a like and hammer | ,Jehovah says | like ,fire | My word | thus | (Is) not

30 לָכֵן הִנְנִי עַל־הַנְּבִאִים נְאֻם־יְהוָה מְגַנְּבֵי דְבָרַי אִישׁ מֵאֵת
from | each man | My ,words | who steal | ,Jehovah says | the ,prophets | against (am) I | ,behold | There- ,fore

31 רֵעֵהוּ׃ הִנְנִי עַל־הַנְּבִאִים נְאֻם־יְהוָה הַלֹּקְחִים לְשׁוֹנָם
their tongue | use who | ,Jehovah says | the ,prophets | against am I | ,behold | his ;neighbor

32 וַיִּנְאֲמוּ נְאֻם׃ הִנְנִי עַל־נִבְּאֵי חֲלֹמוֹת שֶׁקֶר נְאֻם־יְהוָה
,Jehovah says | ,false | dreams | those against prophecy who | ,Behold (am) I | (Jehovah) .says | and ,declare

וַיְסַפְּרוּם וַיַּתְעוּ אֶת־עַמִּי בְּשִׁקְרֵיהֶם וּבְפַחֲזוּתָם וְאָנֹכִי לֹא־
not | yet I | their by and ;frivolity | their by ,lies | My people | lead and astray | tell and ,them

שְׁלַחְתִּים וְלֹא צִוִּיתִים וְהוֹעֵיל לֹא־יוֹעִילוּ לָעָם־הַזֶּה נְאֻם־
says | ,this people | they profit will | not | at and all | command ;them | nor | send did them

33 יְהוָה׃ וְכִי־יִשְׁאָלְךָ הָעָם הַזֶּה אוֹ־הַנָּבִיא אוֹ־כֹהֵן לֵאמֹר
,saying | a ,priest | or | the prophet | or | ,this | people | shall you ask | And when | .Jehovah

of Jehovah? You shall then say to them, What burden? I will even forsake you, says Jehovah. [34] And the prophet, and the priest, and the people, who shall say, The burden of Jehovah, I will even punish that man and his house. [35] So you shall say each one to his neighbor, and each one to his brother, What has Jehovah answered? And what has Jehovah spoken? [36] And you shall mention the burden of Jehovah no more; for each man's word shall be his burden; for you have perverted the words of the living God, of Jehovah of hosts our God. [37] Thus you shall say to the prophet, What has Jehovah answered you? And what has Jehovah spoken? [38] But if you say, The burden of Jehovah; therefore thus says Jehovah, Because you say this word — the burden of Jehovah — and I have sent to you saying, You shall not say, The burden of Jehovah; [39] therefore, behold, I, I will even utterly forget you, and I will cast you off, and the city that I gave to you and to your fathers, qway from My face [40] And I will bring an everlasting reproach on you, and never-ending shame, which shall not be forgotten.

מַה־מַשָּׂא יְהוָה וְאָמַרְתָּ אֲלֵיהֶם אֶת־מַה־מַשָּׂא וְנָטַשְׁתִּי
even will I ?burden What ,them to you Then ?Jehovah the What
abandon say shall of burden (is)

34 אֶתְכֶם נְאֻם־יְהוָה׃ וְהַנָּבִיא וְהַכֹּהֵן וְהָעָם אֲשֶׁר יֹאמַר מַשָּׂא
The ,say shall who the and the and the And .Jehovah declares ,you
of burden people ,priest ,prophet

35 יְהוָה וּפָקַדְתִּי עַל־הָאִישׁ הַהוּא וְעַל־בֵּיתוֹ׃ כֹּה תֹאמְרוּ
shall you So his and that man will I ,Jehovah
say .house punish even

אִישׁ עַל־רֵעֵהוּ וְאִישׁ אֶל־אָחִיו מֶה־עָנָה יְהוָה וּמַה־דִּבֶּר
has And ?Jehovah has What his to each ask his to each
spoken what answered ,brother man ,companion man

36 יְהוָה׃ וּמַשָּׂא יְהוָה לֹא תִזְכְּרוּ־עוֹד כִּי הַמַּשָּׂא יִהְיֶה לְאִישׁ
each for will the for ;again will you not Jehovah the And ?Jehovah
man be burden mention of burden

דְּבָרוֹ וַהֲפַכְתֶּם אֶת־דִּבְרֵי אֱלֹהִים חַיִּים יְהוָה צְבָאוֹת
hosts Jehovah the God the have you for own his
of ,living of words perverted ,word

37 אֱלֹהֵינוּ׃ כֹּה תֹאמַר אֶל־הַנָּבִיא מֶה־עָנָךְ יְהוָה וּמַה־דִּבֶּר
has And ?Jehovah has What the to shall you Thus .God our
spoken what you answered ,prophet say

38 יְהוָה׃ וְאִם־מַשָּׂא יְהוָה תֹּאמֵרוּ לָכֵן כֹּה אָמַר יְהוָה יַעַן
Be- ,Jehovah says thus There- ,say you —Jehovah the And ?Jehovah
cause fore of burden —if

אֲמָרְכֶם אֶת־הַדָּבָר הַזֶּה מַשָּׂא יְהוָה וָאֶשְׁלַח אֲלֵיכֶם
you to I when —Jehovah the —this word say you
sent have of burden

39 לֵאמֹר לֹא תֹאמְרוּ מַשָּׂא יְהוָה׃ לָכֵן הִנְנִי וְנָשִׁיתִי אֶתְכֶם
you even will I ,behold there- ;Jehovah the shall you not ,saying
forget ,I fore of burden —say

נָשֹׁא וְנָטַשְׁתִּי אֶתְכֶם וְאֶת־הָעִיר אֲשֶׁר־נָתַתִּי לָכֶם
you to gave I that the and ,you cast and ,surely
city off

40 וְלַאֲבוֹתֵיכֶם מֵעַל פָּנָי׃ וְנָתַתִּי עֲלֵיכֶם חֶרְפַּת עוֹלָם וּכְלִמּוּת
and ever- an you on I And My away your to and
disgrace ,lasting reproach put will .face from fathers

עוֹלָם אֲשֶׁר לֹא תִשָּׁכֵחַ׃
be will not which per-
.forgotten petual

CAP. XXIV כד

CHAPTER 24

CHAPTER 24

[1] Jehovah showed me, and behold, two baskets of figs set before the temple of Jehovah, after Nebuchadnezzar king of Babylon had carried away captive Jeconiah the son of Jehoiakim king of Judah, and the rulers of Judah, with the craftsmen and the

1 הִרְאַנִי יְהוָה וְהִנֵּה שְׁנֵי דּוּדָאֵי תְאֵנִים מוּעָדִים לִפְנֵי הֵיכַל
the before set figs baskets two and Jehovah showed
of temple of ,behold me

יְהוָה אַחֲרֵי הַגְלוֹת נְבוּכַדְרֶאצַּר מֶלֶךְ־בָּבֶל אֶת־יְכָנְיָהוּ
Jeconiah Babylon king Nebuchadnezzar had after ,Jehovah
of exiled

בֶן־יְהוֹיָקִים מֶלֶךְ יְהוּדָה וְאֶת־שָׂרֵי יְהוּדָה וְאֶת־הֶחָרָשׁ
the with ,Judah the and ,Judah king Jehoiakim the
craftsmen of rulers of of son

smiths, from Jerusalem, and had brought them to Babylon. [2] One basket (had) very good figs, like first-ripe figs. And the other basket (had) very bad figs which could not be eaten, from (their) badness. [3] Then Jehovah said to me, What do you see, Jeremiah? And I said, Figs — the good figs are very good, and the bad are very bad, so that they cannot be eaten, from (their) badness.

[4] Again the word of Jehovah came to me, saying, [5] Thus says Jehovah, the God of Israel: Like these good figs, so I will acknowledge the exiles of Judah, whom I have sent out of this place (into) the land of the Chaldeans for good. [6] For I will set My eyes on them for good, and I will bring them again to this land. And I will build them and not tear down; and I will plant them and not pluck up. [7] And I will give them a heart to know Me, that I (am) Jehovah; and they shall be My people, and I will be their God. For they shall return to Me with their whole heart.

[8] And like the bad figs, which cannot be eaten from badness, for thus says Jehovah, So I will make Zedekiah the king of Judah, and his rulers, and the remnant of Jerusalem who remain in this land, and those who dwell in the land of Egypt — [9] I will even make them a horror among all the kingdoms of the earth for evil, for a reproach and a proverb, a gibe and a curse, in all places where I

2 וְאֶת־הַמַּסְגֵּר מִירוּשָׁלִַם וַיְבִאֵם בָּבֶל׃ הַדּוּד אֶחָד תְּאֵנִים
(had) One basket .Babylon had and from the and
figs to them brought ,Jerusalem smiths

טֹבוֹת מְאֹד כִּתְאֵנֵי הַבַּכֻּרוֹת וְהַדּוּד אֶחָד תְּאֵנִים רָעוֹת
bad (had) other the but ,first-ripe like ,very good
figs basket figs

3 מְאֹד אֲשֶׁר לֹא־תֵאָכַלְנָה מֵרֹעַ׃ וַיֹּאמֶר יְהוָה אֵלַי
to Jehovah Then (their) from be could not which ,very
,me said .badness eaten

מָה־אַתָּה רֹאֶה יִרְמְיָהוּ וָאֹמַר תְּאֵנִים הַתְּאֵנִים הַטֹּבוֹת
good the —figs I And ?Jeremiah ,see do you What
figs ,said

טֹבוֹת מְאֹד וְהָרָעוֹת רָעוֹת מְאֹד אֲשֶׁר לֹא־תֵאָכַלְנָה
can they not that so ,very (are) the but ,very (are)
eaten be bad bad good

4 5 מֵרֹעַ׃ וַיְהִי דְבַר־יְהוָה אֵלַי לֵאמֹר׃ כֹּה־אָמַר
says Thus ,saying to Jehovah the Again from
,me of word came .badness

יְהוָה אֱלֹהֵי יִשְׂרָאֵל כַּתְּאֵנִים הַטֹּבוֹת הָאֵלֶּה כֵּן אַכִּיר אֶת־
will I so ,these good Like :Israel the Jehovah
acknowledge figs of God

גָּלוּת יְהוּדָה אֲשֶׁר שִׁלַּחְתִּי מִן־הַמָּקוֹם הַזֶּה אֶרֶץ כַּשְׂדִּים
the the this place out have I whom ,Judah the
Chaldeans of land (to) of sent of exiles

6 לְטוֹבָה׃ וְשַׂמְתִּי עֵינִי עֲלֵיהֶם לְטוֹבָה וַהֲשִׁבֹתִים עַל־
to will I and ,good for them on My I For ,good for
back them bring eyes set will

הָאָרֶץ הַזֹּאת וּבְנִיתִים וְלֹא אֶהֱרֹס וּנְטַעְתִּים וְלֹא אֶתּוֹשׁ׃
.uproot and will I and tear and will I And .this land
not ,them plant ;down not them build

7 וְנָתַתִּי לָהֶם לֵב לָדַעַת אֹתִי כִּי אֲנִי יְהוָה וְהָיוּ־לִי לְעָם
a for to they and Jeho- I that ,Me know to a them to I And
people Me be will ;vah (am) heart give will

וְאָנֹכִי אֶהְיֶה לָהֶם לֵאלֹהִים כִּי־יָשֻׁבוּ אֵלַי בְּכָל־לִבָּם׃
their with to will they for ;God for them to will I and
.heart whole Me return be

8 וְכַתְּאֵנִים הָרָעוֹת אֲשֶׁר לֹא־תֵאָכַלְנָה מֵרֹעַ כִּי־
for from be can not which bad like And
,badness ,eaten figs the

כֹה ׀ אָמַר יְהוָה כֵּן אֶתֵּן אֶת־צִדְקִיָּהוּ מֶלֶךְ־יְהוּדָה וְאֶת־
and ,Judah the Zedekiah will I So ,Jehovah says thus
of king make

שָׂרָיו וְאֵת ׀ שְׁאֵרִית יְרוּשָׁלִַם הַנִּשְׁאָרִים בָּאָרֶץ הַזֹּאת
,this in are who Jerusalem the and his
land left of remnant rulers

9 וְהַיֹּשְׁבִים בְּאֶרֶץ מִצְרָיִם׃ וּנְתַתִּים לְזַוָעָה לְרָעָה לְכֹל
all to evil for a for even will I —Egypt the in those and
terror them make of land dwell who

מַמְלְכוֹת הָאָרֶץ לְחֶרְפָּה וּלְמָשָׁל לִשְׁנִינָה וְלִקְלָלָה בְּכָל־
all in a and a for a and a for the king- the
,curse gibe ,proverb reproach ,earth of doms

will drive them there. [10] And I will send the sword, the famine, and the plague among them until they are destroyed from on the land that I gave to them and to their fathers.

CHAPTER 25

[1] The word that came to Jeremiah concerning all the people of Judah in the fourth year of Jehoiakim the son of Josiah king of Judah; it (was) the first year of Nebuchadnezzar king of Babylon; [2] which Jeremiah the prophet spoke to all the people of Judah and to all the residents of Jerusalem, saying, [3] From the thirteenth year of Josiah the son of Amon, king of Judah, even to this day, this twenty-three years, the word of Jehovah has come to me, and I have spoken to you, rising up early and speaking, but you have not listened. [4] And Jehovah has sent to you all His servants the prophets, rising early and sending; but you have not listened nor bowed your ear to hear; [5] saying, Now turn each one from his evil way, and from the evil of your doings, and live on the land which Jehovah has given to you and to your fathers from forever even to forever. [6] And do not go after other gods to serve them, and to worship them, and do not provoke Me to anger with the works of your hands; and I will do

10 הַמְּקֹמוֹת אֲשֶׁר־אַדִּיחֵם שָׁם׃ וְשִׁלַּחְתִּי בָם אֶת־הַחֶרֶב
the among I And .there will I where the
,sword them send will them drive places

אֶת־הָרָעָב וְאֶת־הַדָּבֶר עַד־תֻּמָּם מֵעַל הָאֲדָמָה אֲשֶׁר־נָתַתִּי
gave I that the from are they until the and the
land upon destroyed plague ,famine

לָהֶם וְלַאֲבוֹתֵיהֶם׃
to and to
.fathers their them

CAP. XXV כה

CHAPTER 25

1 הַדָּבָר אֲשֶׁר־הָיָה עַל־יִרְמְיָהוּ עַל־כָּל־עַם יְהוּדָה בַּשָּׁנָה
the in Judah the all con- Jeremiah to came that The
year of people cerning word

הָרְבִעִית לִיהוֹיָקִים בֶּן־יֹאשִׁיָּהוּ מֶלֶךְ יְהוּדָה הִיא הַשָּׁנָה
the it ,Judah king Josiah the of fourth
year (was) of of son Jehoiakim

2 הָרִאשֹׁנִית לִנְבוּכַדְרֶאצַּר מֶלֶךְ בָּבֶל׃ אֲשֶׁר דִּבֶּר יִרְמְיָהוּ
Jeremiah spoke which ;Babylon king of first
of Nebuchadnezzar

הַנָּבִיא עַל־כָּל־עַם יְהוּדָה וְאֶל כָּל־יֹשְׁבֵי יְרוּשָׁלַםִ לֵאמֹר׃
,saying ,Jerusalem the all and Judah the all to the
of inhabitants to of people prophet

3 מִן־שְׁלֹשׁ עֶשְׂרֵה שָׁנָה לְיֹאשִׁיָּהוּ בֶן־אָמוֹן מֶלֶךְ יְהוּדָה
,Judah king ,Amon the Josiah of year the thirteenth From
of of son

וְעַד ׀ הַיּוֹם הַזֶּה זֶה שָׁלֹשׁ וְעֶשְׂרִים שָׁנָה הָיָה דְבַר־יְהוָה
Jehovah the has ,years and three this ,this day even
of word come twenty to

4 אֵלַי וָאֲדַבֵּר אֲלֵיכֶם אַשְׁכֵּים וְדַבֵּר וְלֹא שְׁמַעְתֶּם׃ וְשָׁלַח
has And have you but and up rising ,you to have I and to
sent .listened not ,speaking early spoken ,me

יְהוָה אֲלֵיכֶם אֶת־כָּל־עֲבָדָיו הַנְּבִאִים הַשְׁכֵּם וְשָׁלֹחַ וְלֹא
but and rising the His all you to Jehovah
not ;sending early ,prophets servants

5 שְׁמַעְתֶּם וְלֹא־הִטִּיתֶם אֶת־אָזְנְכֶם לִשְׁמֹעַ׃ לֵאמֹר שׁוּבוּ־
turn saying ,hear to ear your inclined nor have you
,listened

נָא אִישׁ מִדַּרְכּוֹ הָרָעָה וּמֵרֹעַ מַעַלְלֵיכֶם וּשְׁבוּ עַל־
upon and your from and ,evil his from each ,now
dwell ,doings of evil the way man

הָאֲדָמָה אֲשֶׁר נָתַן יְהוָה לָכֶם וְלַאֲבוֹתֵיכֶם לְמִן־עוֹלָם
forever from your to and to Jehovah has which the
fathers you given land

6 וְעַד־עוֹלָם׃ וְאַל־תֵּלְכוּ אַחֲרֵי אֱלֹהִים אֲחֵרִים לְעָבְדָם
serve to other gods after go do And .forever even
them not to

וּלְהִשְׁתַּחֲוֹת לָהֶם וְלֹא־תַכְעִיסוּ אוֹתִי בְּמַעֲשֵׂה יְדֵיכֶם וְלֹא
and your the with Me provoke do and ,them to and
not ;hands of works anger to not worship

you no harm. [7] Yet you have not listened to Me, says Jehovah, so that you might provoke Me to anger with the works of your hands; for harm to you.

[8] Therefore thus says Jehovah of hosts, Because you have not obeyed My words, [9] behold, I will send and take all the families of the north, says Jehovah, and Nebuchadnezzar the king of Babylon, My servant; and I will bring them against this land, and against its inhabitants, and against all these nations all around; and I will completely destroy them, and make them a horror, and a hissing, and everlasting ruins. [10] And I will take from them the voice of rejoicing and the voice of gladness, the voice of the bridegroom and the voice of the bride, the sound of the millstones and the light of the lamp. [11] And this whole land shall be a waste and a horror; and these nations shall serve the king of Babylon seventy years.

[12] And, it shall be, when seventy years are fulfilled, I will punish the king of Babylon, and that nation, and the land of the Chaldeans for their iniquity, says Jehovah, and I will make it everlasting ruins. [13] And I will bring on that land all My words which I have spoken against it, all that is written in this book which Jeremiah has prophesied against all the nations. [14] For many nations and great kings will lay service on them, even they. And I will repay them according to their deeds, and according to the work of their own hands.

[15] For thus says Jehovah the God of Israel to me, Take the wine cup of

7 ארע לכם: ולא־שמעתם אלי נאם־יהוה למען הכעסוני
might you that so ,Jehovah says to have you Yet .you to will I
Me provoke ,Me listened not harm do

8 במעשה ידיכם לרע לכם: לכן כה אמר יהוה צבאות
,hosts Jehovah says thus Therefore to for your the with
of .you harm hands of work

9 יען אשר לא־שמעתם את־דברי: הנני שלח ולקחתי
take and will ,behold My have you not Because
send I ,words obeyed

את־כל־משפחות צפון נאם־יהוה ואל־נבוכדראצר מלך
the Nebuchadnezzar even ,Jehovah says the the all
of king to ,north of families

בבל עבדי והבאתים על־הארץ הזאת ועל־ישביה ועל
and inhabi- its and ,this land against will I and My ,Babylon
against ,tants against them bring ;servant

כל־הגוים האלה סביב והחרמתים ושמתים לשמה
horror a make and utterly will I and all these nations all
them them destroy ,around

10 ולשרקה ולחרבות עולם: והאבדתי מהם קול ששון
joy the from will I And ever- ruins and a and
of voice them perish to cause .lasting hissing

וקול שמחה קול חתן וקול כלה קול רחים ואור נר:
the and the sound the and the voice ,gladness the and
.lamp's light ,millstones of ,bride's voice ,bridegroom's of voice

11 והיתה כל־הארץ הזאת לחרבה ולשמה ועבדו הגוים
nations will and a and a this land whole will And
serve ;horror ,waste be

12 האלה את־מלך בבל שבעים שנה: והיה כמלאות
are when it And .years seventy Babylon the these
fulfilled ,be will of king

שבעים שנה אפקד על־מלך־בבל ועל־הגוי ההוא נאם־
says ,that nation and Baby- the will I ,years seventy
,lon of king punish

יהוה את־עונם ועל־ארץ כשדים ושמתי אתו לשממות
ruins it I and the the and their (for) Jeho-
make will ,Chaldeans of land iniquity ,vah

13 עולם: והבאותי על־הארץ ההיא את־כל־דברי אשר־
which My all that land on will I And ever-
words bring .lasting

דברתי עליה את כל־הכתוב בספר הזה אשר־נבא
has which this book in is that all against have I
prophesied written ,it spoken

14 ירמיהו על־כל־הגוים: כי עבדו־בם גם־המה גוים רבים
many nations ,they even will them on For the all against Jere-
service lay .nations miah

ומלכים גדולים ושלמתי להם כפעלם וכמעשה ידיהם:
their according and to according them will I And .great and
.hands of work the to deeds their repay kings

15 כי כה אמר יהוה אלהי ישראל אלי קח את־
Take ,me to Israel the Jehovah says thus For
of God

this wrath from My hand, and cause all the nations to whom I shall send you to drink it. [16] And they shall drink, and reel to and fro, and be maddened, because of the sword that I will send among them. [17] Then I took the cup from Jehovah's hand, and made all the nations drink, to whom Jehovah had sent me: [18] Jerusalem, and the cities of Judah, and their kings, and their princes, to make them a ruin, a horror, a hissing, and a curse, as (it is) this day; [19] Pharaoh king of Egypt, and his servants, and his princes, and all his people; [20] and all the mixed people; and all the kings of the land of Uz; and all the kings of the land of the Philistines, and Ashkelon, and Gaza, and Ekron, and the remnant of Ashdod; [21] Edom; and Moab; and the sons of Ammon; [22] and all the kings of Tyre, and all the kings of Sidon; and the coastal kings which (are) beyond the sea; [23] Dedan and Tema, and Buz, and all who cut the corners (of their beards); [24] and all the kings of Arabia; and all the kings of the mixed people who dwell in the desert; [25] and all the kings of Zimri; and all the kings of Elam; and all the kings of Media; [26] and all the kings of the north, far and near, each one to his brother; and all the kingdoms of the world which (are) on the face of the earth; and the king of

כוס היין החמה הזאת מידי והשקיתה אתו את־כל־
all it cause and drink to from head My this wrath wine the of the of cup

16 הגוים אשר אנכי שלח אותך אליהם׃ ושתו והתגעשו
reel and fro and to they And ,drink shall .them to you shall send I whom the nations

17 והתהללו מפני החרב אשר אנכי שלח ביניתם׃ ואקח
I Then took among .them will send I that the sword because of go and mad

את־הכוס מיד יהוה ואשקה את־כל־הגוים אשר־שלחני
sent had me whom the nations all make and drink to ,Jehovah's hand from the cup

18 יהוה אליהם׃ את־ירושלם ואת־ערי יהודה ואת־מלכיה
her kings and ,Judah the of cities and Jerusalem :them to Jehovah

את־שריה לתת אתם לחרבה לשמה לשרקה ולקללה
a and ,curse ,hissing a horror a waste a them make to her (and) ;rulers

19 כיום הזה׃ את־פרעה מלך־מצרים ואת־עבדיו ואת־
and his servants and ,Egypt king of Pharaoh ;this (is it) as day

20 שריו ואת־כל־עמו׃ ואת כל־הערב ואת כל־מלכי ארץ
the of land kings the of all and mixed the ;people all and his ;people all and his ;rulers

העוץ ואת כל־מלכי ארץ פלשתים ואת־אשקלון ואת־
and ,Ashkelon and the ,Philistines the of land kings the of all and ;Uz

21 עזה ואת־עקרון ואת שארית אשדוד׃ את־אדום ואת־
and ,Edom ;Ashdod the of remnant and ,Ekron and ,Gaza

22 מואב ואת־בני עמון׃ ואת כל־מלכי צר ואת כל־מלכי
the of kings all and ;Tyre the of kings all and ;Ammon the of sons and ;Moab

23 צידון ואת מלכי האי אשר בעבר הים׃ את־דדן ואת־
and Dedan ;sea the beyond which (are) the coasts the of kings and ;Sidon

24 תימא ואת־בוז ואת כל־קצוצי פאה׃ ואת כל־מלכי
the of kings all and the ;edges who trim all and ,Buz and ,Tema

25 ערב ואת כל־מלכי הערב השכנים במדבר׃ ואת ׀ כל־
all and the in ;desert who dwell mixed the people the of kings all and ;Arabia

מלכי זמרי ואת כל־מלכי עילם ואת כל־מלכי מדי׃
;Media the of kings all and ;Elam the of kings all and ;Zimri the of kings

26 ואת ׀ כל־מלכי הצפון הקרבים והרחקים איש אל־
to each man ,for and near the ,north the of kings all and

אחיו ואת כל־הממלכות הארץ אשר על־פני האדמה
the ,earth the on of face which (are) the world kingdoms the of all and his ,brother

Sheshach shall drink after them. [27] So you shall say to them, Thus says Jehovah of hosts, the God of Israel: Drink and be drunk, and vomit, and fall, and do not rise; because of the sword which I will send among you. [28] And it shall be, if they refuse to take the cup from your hand to drink, then you shall say to them, Thus says Jehovah of hosts, You shall certainly drink. [29] For, lo, I begin to bring evil on the city on which is called My name; and shall you be found entirely without guilt? You shall not be without guilt. For I will call for a sword on all the inhabitants of the earth, says Jehovah of hosts. [30] Therefore you prophesy against them all these words, and say to them, Jehovah shall roar from on high, and utter His voice from His holy habitation; He shall mightily roar over His dwelling place; with a shout, He answers, like those who tread out (the grapes), against all the inhabitants of the earth. [31] A roaring will go to the ends of the earth; for Jehovah has a controversy with the nations; He will enter into judgment with all flesh. He will give the wicked to the sword, says Jehovah. [32] Thus says Jehovah of hosts, Behold, evil is going from nation to nation, and a great tempest shall be stirred up from the corners of the earth. [33] And the slain of Jehovah shall be at that day from (one) end of the earth even to the (other) end of the earth; they shall not be mourned, nor gathered, nor buried; they shall be (as) dung on the face of the ground.

[34] Howl, O shepherds, and cry; and roll, O leaders of the flock. For the

27 וּמֶלֶךְ שֵׁשַׁךְ יִשְׁתֶּה אַחֲרֵיהֶם׃ וְאָמַרְתָּ אֲלֵיהֶם כֹּה־אָמַר
says thus ,them to you So after shall Sheshach the and
say will .them drink of king

יְהוָה צְבָאוֹת אֱלֹהֵי יִשְׂרָאֵל שְׁתוּ וְשִׁכְרוּ וּקְיוּ וְנִפְלוּ וְלֹא
and and and be and ,Drink ,Israel the ,hosts Jehovah
not ,fail ,vomit ,drunk of God of

28 תָקוּמוּ מִפְּנֵי הַחֶרֶב אֲשֶׁר אָנֹכִי שֹׁלֵחַ בֵּינֵיכֶם׃ וְהָיָה כִּי
if it And among will – I which the because ;rise
,be will .you send sword of

יְמָאֲנוּ לָקַחַת־הַכּוֹס מִיָּדְךָ לִשְׁתּוֹת וְאָמַרְתָּ אֲלֵיהֶם כֹּה
Thus ,them to you then ,drink to from the take to they
say will hand your cup refuse

29 אָמַר יְהוָה צְבָאוֹת שָׁתוֹ תִשְׁתּוּ׃ כִּי הִנֵּה בָעִיר אֲשֶׁר־
which the in ,lo ,For shall You surely ,hosts Jehovah says
city .drink of

נִקְרָא שְׁמִי עָלֶיהָ אָנֹכִי מֵחֵל לְהָרַע וְאַתֶּם הִנָּקֵה תִנָּקוּ
be shall entirely and bring to begin I upon My been has
?guiltless you ,evil ,it name called

לֹא תִנָּקוּ כִּי חֶרֶב אֲנִי קֹרֵא עַל־כָּל־יֹשְׁבֵי הָאָרֶץ נְאֻם
says the inhabi- the all against am I a for will You not
,earth of tants calling sword ,guiltless be

30 יְהוָה צְבָאוֹת׃ וְאַתָּה תִּנָּבֵא אֲלֵיהֶם אֵת כָּל־הַדְּבָרִים
words all against prophesy Therefore .hosts Jehovah
them you of

הָאֵלֶּה וְאָמַרְתָּ אֲלֵיהֶם יְהוָה מִמָּרוֹם יִשְׁאָג וּמִמְּעוֹן קָדְשׁוֹ
His from and shall from Jehovah ,them to say and ,these
holy habitation ,roar high on

יִתֵּן קוֹלוֹ שָׁאֹג יִשְׁאַג עַל־נָוֵהוּ הֵידָד כְּדֹרְכִים יַעֲנֶה אֶל
against He those like a (with) His over will He mightily His utter
answers tread who shout ;dwelling-place roar ,voice

31 כָּל־יֹשְׁבֵי הָאָרֶץ׃ בָּא שָׁאוֹן עַד־קְצֵה הָאָרֶץ כִּי רִיב
a for the the to A go will the in- the all
quarrel ,earth of end roaring .earth of habitants

לַיהוָה בַּגּוֹיִם נִשְׁפָּט הוּא לְכָל־בָּשָׂר הָרְשָׁעִים נְתָנָם לַחֶרֶב
the to will He The .flesh with He into enter the with (to is)
,sword put wicked all (will) judgment ,nations Jehovah

32 נְאֻם־יְהוָה׃ כֹּה אָמַר יְהוָה צְבָאוֹת הִנֵּה רָעָה יֹצֵאת
going is evil ,Behold ,hosts Jehovah says Thus .Jehovah says
forth of

33 מִגּוֹי אֶל־גּוֹי וְסַעַר גָּדוֹל יֵעוֹר מִיַּרְכְּתֵי־אָרֶץ׃ וְהָיוּ חַלְלֵי
the shall And the the from be will great a and ,nation to from
of slain be .earth of corners stirred tempest nation

יְהוָה בַּיּוֹם הַהוּא מִקְצֵה הָאָרֶץ וְעַד־קְצֵה הָאָרֶץ לֹא
not the (other) the even the (one) from that on Jehovah
;earth of end to earth of end day

יִסָּפְדוּ וְלֹא יֵאָסְפוּ וְלֹא יִקָּבֵרוּ לְדֹמֶן עַל־פְּנֵי הָאֲדָמָה יִהְיוּ׃
they the the on as ;buried nor ,gathered nor will they
.be shall ground of face dung ,mourned be

34 הֵילִילוּ הָרֹעִים וְזַעֲקוּ וְהִתְפַּלְּשׁוּ אַדִּירֵי הַצֹּאן כִּי־מָלְאוּ
are For the leaders O roll and ;cry and shep- O ,Howl
full .flock of ,herds

days of your slaughter and of your scatterings are fulfilled; and you shall fall like a desirable vessel. [35] And refuge has perished from the shepherds, and escape from the leaders of the flock. [36] The sound of the cry of the shepherds, and the howling from the leaders of the flock! For Jehovah is spoiling their pasture. [37] And the peaceful folds are devastated, because of the glow of the anger of Jehovah. [38] Like the lion, He has left His den; for their land is a waste because of the oppressor's anger, and because of His glowing anger.

35 יְמֵיכֶם לִטְב֫וֹחַ וּתְפוֹצוֹתִיכֶם וּנְפַלְתֶּם כִּכְלִי חֶמְדָּה: וְאָבַד

has And .desirable a like you and your and for for
perished vessel fall will ,dispersions ,slaughtering days

36 מָנוֹס מִן־הָרֹעִים וּפְלֵיטָה מֵאַדִּירֵי הַצֹּאן: ק֥וֹל צַעֲקַת

the The the the from and from refuge
of cry of sound .flock of leaders escape ,shepherds

הָרֹעִים וִילְלַת אַדִּירֵי הַצֹּאן כִּי־שֹׁדֵד יְהוָֹה אֶת־מַרְעִיתָם:

their Jehovah is For the the the and shep- the
.pasture destroying !flock of leaders of wailing ,herds

37
38 וְנָדַמּוּ נְאוֹת הַשָּׁלוֹם מִפְּנֵי חֲרוֹן אַף־יְהוָֹה: עָזַב כַּכְּפִיר

the like has He .Jehovah's anger the because the folds are And
lion left of glow of ,peaceful devastated

סֻכּוֹ כִּי־הָיְתָה אַרְצָם לְשַׁמָּה מִפְּנֵי חֲרוֹן הַיּוֹנָה וּמִפְּנֵי

be- and op- the the because waste a their is for his
of cause pressor of anger of land ;den

חֲרוֹן אַפּוֹ:

His the
.anger of glow

CAP. XXVI כו
CHAPTER 26

CHAPTER 26

[1] In the beginning of the reign of Jehoiakim the son of Josiah king of Judah, this word came from Jehovah, saying, [2] Thus says Jehovah: Stand in the court of Jehovah's house and speak to all the cities of Judah which come to worship in the house of Jehovah, all the words that I command you to speak to them — do not keep back a word. [3] It may be that they will listen, and each man turn from his evil way, that I may repent of the evil which I plan to do to them because of the evil of their doings. [4] And you shall say to them, Thus says Jehovah: If you will not listen to Me, to walk in My law which I have set before you, [5] to listen to the words of My servants the prophets whom I am sending to you — even rising up early and sending (them), but you have not listened — [6] then I will make this house like Shiloh and will

1 בְּרֵאשִׁית מַמְלְכוּת יְהוֹיָקִים בֶּן־יֹאשִׁיָּהוּ מֶלֶךְ יְהוּדָה הָיָה

came ,Judah king Josiah the Jehoiakim the the In
of of son of reign of beginning

2 הַדָּבָר הַזֶּה מֵאֵת יְהוָֹה לֵאמֹר: כֹּה ׀ אָמַר יְהוָֹה עֲמֹד

Stand ,Jehovah says Thus ,saying ,Jehovah from this word

בַּחֲצַר בֵּית־יְהוָֹה וְדִבַּרְתָּ עַל־כָּל־עָרֵי יְהוּדָה הַבָּאִים

which Judah the all to speak and ,Jehovah's house the in
come of cities of court

לְהִשְׁתַּחֲוֹת בֵּית־יְהוָֹה אֵת כָּל־הַדְּבָרִים אֲשֶׁר צִוִּיתִךָ לְדַבֵּר

speak to com- I that the all .Jehovah the worship to
you mand words of house at

3 אֲלֵיהֶם אַל־תִּגְרַע דָּבָר: אוּלַי יִשְׁמְעוּ וְיָשֻׁבוּ אִישׁ מִדַּרְכּוֹ

.his from each and will they Perhaps .word a do not to
way man turn listen diminish them

הָרָעָה וְנִחַמְתִּי אֶל־הָרָעָה אֲשֶׁר אָנֹכִי חֹשֵׁב לַעֲשׂוֹת לָהֶם

them to do to am I which the towards may I that ,evil
planning evil repent

4 מִפְּנֵי רֹעַ מַעַלְלֵיהֶם: וְאָמַרְתָּ אֲלֵיהֶם כֹּה אָמַר יְהוָֹה

:Jehovah says Thus ,them to you And their the because
say shall .doings of evil of

5 אִם־לֹא תִשְׁמְעוּ אֵלַי לָלֶכֶת בְּתוֹרָתִי אֲשֶׁר נָתַתִּי לִפְנֵיכֶם:

before have I which My in walk to will you not If
,you set law ,Me listen

לִשְׁמֹעַ עַל־דִּבְרֵי עֲבָדַי הַנְּבִיאִים אֲשֶׁר אָנֹכִי שֹׁלֵחַ אֲלֵיכֶם

,you to am I whom the My the to listen to
sending prophets servants of words

6 וְהַשְׁכֵּם וְשָׁלֹחַ וְלֹא שְׁמַעְתֶּם: וְנָתַתִּי אֶת־הַבַּיִת הַזֶּה

this house I then have you but send- and rising even
make will —listened not (them) ing early up

make this city a curse to all the nations of the earth. [7] So the priests and the prophets and all the people heard Jeremiah speaking these words in the house of Jehovah.

[8] Now it came to pass, when Jeremiah had made an end of speaking all that Jehovah had commanded him to speak to all the people, the priests and the prophets and all the people seized him, saying, You shall surely die! [9] Why have you prophesied in the name of Jehovah, saying, This house shall be like Shiloh, and this city shall be wasted, without inhabitant? And all the people were gathered against Jeremiah in the house of Jehovah.

[10] When the princes of Judah heard these things, then they came up from the king's house to the house of Jehovah and sat down in the entrance of the New Gate of Jehovah. [11] And the priests and the prophets spoke to the princes and to all the people, saying, (Let be) a death sentence for this man, for he has prophesied against this city, as you have heard with your ears.

[12] Then Jeremiah spoke to all the princes and to all the people, saying, Jehovah sent me to prophesy against this house and against this city all the words that you have heard. [13] Therefore, now make good your ways and your doings, and obey the voice of Jehovah your God; and Jehovah will repent toward the evil that He has spoken against you. [14] As for me, behold, I (am) in your hands; do with me as (seems) good and

כְּשִׁלֹה וְאֶת־הָעִיר הַזֹּאתָה אֶתֵּן לִקְלָלָה לְכֹל גּוֹיֵ הָאָרֶץ׃
the the all to curse a will I this city and like
.earth of nations make ,Shiloh

7 וַיִּשְׁמְעוּ הַכֹּהֲנִים וְהַנְּבִאִים וְכָל־הָעָם אֶת־יִרְמְיָהוּ
Jeremiah the and the and the heard And
people all prophets priests

8 מְדַבֵּר אֶת־הַדְּבָרִים הָאֵלֶּה בְּבֵית יְהוָה׃ וַיְהִי ׀ כְּכַלּוֹת
when Now .Jehovah the in these words speaking
finished ,was it of house

יִרְמְיָהוּ לְדַבֵּר אֵת כָּל־אֲשֶׁר־צִוָּה יְהוָה לְדַבֵּר אֶל־כָּל־
all to speak to Jehovah com- had that all speaking Jere-
(him) manded miah

הָעָם וַיִּתְפְּשׂוּ אֹתוֹ הַכֹּהֲנִים וְהַנְּבִיאִים וְכָל־הָעָם לֵאמֹר
,saying the and the and the him seized the
,people all prophets priests ,people

9 מוֹת תָּמוּת׃ מַדּוּעַ נִבֵּיתָ בְשֵׁם־יְהוָה לֵאמֹר כְּשִׁלוֹ יִהְיֶה
shall Like ,saying ,Jehovah the in you have Why shall you Surely
be Shiloh of name prophesied .die

הַבַּיִת הַזֶּה וְהָעִיר הַזֹּאת תֶּחֱרַב מֵאֵין יוֹשֵׁב וַיִּקָּהֵל כָּל־
all were And inhabi- without be will this and ,this house
gathered ?tant desolate city

10 הָעָם אֶל־יִרְמְיָהוּ בְּבֵית יְהוָה׃ וַיִּשְׁמְעוּ ׀ שָׂרֵי יְהוּדָה אֵת
Judah the heard When .Jehovah the in Jeremiah against the
of rulers of house people

הַדְּבָרִים הָאֵלֶּה וַיַּעֲלוּ מִבֵּית־הַמֶּלֶךְ בֵּית יְהוָה וַיֵּשְׁבוּ
sat and Jehovah the (to) the from they then ,these things
of house king's house up came

11 בְּפֶתַח שַׁעַר־יְהוָה הֶחָדָשׁ׃ וַיֹּאמְרוּ הַכֹּהֲנִים וְהַנְּבִאִים
the and priests the spoke And .New (house) the the in
prophets Jehovah's of Gate of entrance

אֶל־הַשָּׂרִים וְאֶל־כָּל־הָעָם לֵאמֹר מִשְׁפַּט־מָוֶת לָאִישׁ הַזֶּה
,this for a (be Let) ,saying the all and the to
man death of sentence ,people to rulers

כִּי נִבָּא אֶל־הָעִיר הַזֹּאת כַּאֲשֶׁר שְׁמַעְתֶּם בְּאָזְנֵיכֶם׃
your with have you as ,this city against has he for
.ears heard prophesied

12 וַיֹּאמֶר יִרְמְיָהוּ אֶל־כָּל־הַשָּׂרִים וְאֶל־כָּל־הָעָם לֵאמֹר יְהוָה
Jehovah ,saying the all and the all to Jeremiah Then
,people to rulers spoke

שְׁלָחַנִי לְהִנָּבֵא אֶל־הַבַּיִת הַזֶּה וְאֶל־הָעִיר הַזֹּאת אֵת כָּל־
all this city and this house against to me sent
against prophesy

13 הַדְּבָרִים אֲשֶׁר שְׁמַעְתֶּם׃ וְעַתָּה הֵיטִיבוּ דַרְכֵיכֶם וּמַעַלְלֵיכֶם
your and your make Therefore have you that the
.doings ways good ,now .heard words

וְשִׁמְעוּ בְּקוֹל יְהוָה אֱלֹהֵיכֶם וְיִנָּחֵם יְהוָה אֶל־הָרָעָה אֲשֶׁר
that the toward Jeho- will and your Jehovah the and
evil vah repent ;God of voice obey

14 דִּבֶּר עֲלֵיכֶם׃ וַאֲנִי הִנְנִי בְיֶדְכֶם עֲשׂוּ־לִי כַּטּוֹב וְכַיָּשָׁר
and (seems) as to do your in ,behold for As against has He
right good me ;hands (am) I ,me You spoken

right to you. [15] But know for certain that if you put me to death you shall surely bring innocent blood on yourselves, and on this city, and on its inhabitants. For truly Jehovah has sent me to you to speak all these words in your ears.

[16] Then the princes and all the people said to the priests and to the prophets, There (is) not a sentence of death for this man; for he has spoken to us in the name of Jehovah our God. [17] Then some of the elders of the land rose up and spoke to all the assembly of the people, saying, [18] Micah the Morasthite prophesied in the days of Hezekiah king of Judah. And he spoke to all the people of Judah, saying, Thus says Jehovah of hosts: Zion shall be plowed (like) a field, and Jerusalem shall become heaps, and the mountain of the house like the high places of a forest. [19] Did Hezekiah king of Judah and all Judah indeed put him to death? Did he not fear Jehovah, and entreat the face of Jehovah; and (did not) Jehovah repent of the evil which He had spoken against them? So we are doing great evil against our souls. [20] And there was also a man who prophesied in the name of Jehovah, Urijah the son of Shemaiah of Kirjath-jearim, who prophesied against this city and against this land according to all the words of Jeremiah. [21] And when Jehoiakim the king, with all his mighty men, and all the princes, heard his words, the king tried to put him to death. But Urijah heard (it), and he was afraid, and fled

15 בְּעֵינֵיכֶם׃ אַךְ ׀ יָדֹעַ תֵּדְעוּ כִּי אִם־מְמִתִים אַתֶּם אֹתִי כִּי־
surely ,me you to put if that know for Only your in
death certain .eyes

דָם נָקִי אַתֶּם נֹתְנִים עֲלֵיכֶם וְאֶל־הָעִיר הַזֹּאת וְאֶל־יֹשְׁבֶיהָ
inhabi- its and ,this city and your- on shall you inno- blood
.tants on on ,selves bring cent

כִּי בֶּאֱמֶת שְׁלָחַנִי יְהוָה עֲלֵיכֶם לְדַבֵּר בְּאָזְנֵיכֶם אֵת כָּל־
all your in speak to you to Jehovah sent has truly For
ears me

16 הַדְּבָרִים הָאֵלֶּה׃ וַיֹּאמְרוּ הַשָּׂרִים וְכָל־הָעָם אֶל־הַכֹּהֲנִים
the to the and the Then .these words
priests people all rulers said

וְאֶל־הַנְּבִיאִים אֵין־לָאִישׁ הַזֶּה מִשְׁפַּט־מָוֶת כִּי בְּשֵׁם יְהוָה
Jehovah the in for ,death sen- a this for Not the and
of name of tence man (is) .prophets to

17 אֱלֹהֵינוּ דִּבֶּר אֵלֵינוּ׃ וַיָּקֻמוּ אֲנָשִׁים מִזִּקְנֵי הָאָרֶץ וַיֹּאמְרוּ
and the the from men Then !us to has he God our
spoke land of elders up rose spoken

18 אֶל־כָּל־קְהַל הָעָם לֵאמֹר׃ מִיכָה הַמּוֹרַשְׁתִּי הָיָה נִבָּא
proph- was the Micah ,saying the the all to
esying Morasthite ,people of assembly

בִּימֵי חִזְקִיָּהוּ מֶלֶךְ־יְהוּדָה וַיֹּאמֶר אֶל־כָּל־עַם יְהוּדָה לֵאמֹר
,saying ,Judah the all to he and ,Judah king Hezekiah the in
of people spoke of of days

כֹּה־אָמַר ׀ יְהוָה צְבָאוֹת צִיּוֹן שָׂדֶה תֵחָרֵשׁ וִירוּשָׁלַיִם עִיִּים
heap a and be will a (like) Zion :hosts Jehovah says Thus
ruins of Jerusalem ,plowed field of

19 תִּהְיֶה וְהַר הַבַּיִת לְבָמוֹת יָעַר׃ הֶהָמֵת הֱמִתֻהוּ חִזְקִיָּהוּ
Hezekiah put Did indeed a high the (as) the the and be- will
death to him .forest of places house of mountain ,come

מֶלֶךְ־יְהוּדָה וְכָל־יְהוּדָה הֲלֹא יָרֵא אֶת־יְהוָה וַיְחַל אֶת־
and Jehovah he Did not ?Judah and Judah king
entreat fear all of

פְּנֵי יְהוָה וַיִּנָּחֶם יְהוָה אֶל־הָרָעָה אֲשֶׁר־דִּבֶּר עֲלֵיהֶם
against had He which the toward Jehovah and ;Jehovah the
?them spoken evil repented of face

20 וַאֲנַחְנוּ עֹשִׂים רָעָה גְדוֹלָה עַל־נַפְשׁוֹתֵינוּ׃ וְגַם־אִישׁ הָיָה
there a And .souls our against great evil are we So
was man also doing

מִתְנַבֵּא בְּשֵׁם יְהוָה אוּרִיָּהוּ בֶּן־שְׁמַעְיָהוּ מִקִּרְיַת הַיְּעָרִים
,jearim Kirjath- at Shemaiah the Urijah ,Jehovah the in proph- who
of son of name esied

וַיִּנָּבֵא עַל־הָעִיר הַזֹּאת וְעַל־הָאָרֶץ הַזֹּאת כְּכֹל דִּבְרֵי
the according this land and ,this city against who
of words all to against prophesied

21 יִרְמְיָהוּ׃ וַיִּשְׁמַע הַמֶּלֶךְ יְהוֹיָקִים וְכָל־גִּבּוֹרָיו וְכָל־הַשָּׂרִים
the and mighty his and ,Jehoiakim the when And .Jeremiah
rulers all ,men all king heard

אֶת־דְּבָרָיו וַיְבַקֵּשׁ הַמֶּלֶךְ הֲמִיתוֹ וַיִּשְׁמַע אוּרִיָּהוּ וַיִּרָא
was and ,Urijah But execute to king the then his
,afraid (it) heard .him sought ,words

and went to Egypt. [22] And Jehoiakim the king sent men to Egypt — Elnathan the son of Achbor, and men with him into Egypt. [23] And they brought Urijah out of Egypt and brought him to Jehoiakim the king, who struck him with the sword and threw his dead body into the graves of the sons of people. [24] However, the hand of Ahikam the son of Shaphan was with Jeremiah, that they should not give him into the hand of the people to put him to death.

22 וַיִּבְרַח וַיָּבֹא מִצְרָיִם׃ וַיִּשְׁלַח הַמֶּלֶךְ יְהוֹיָקִים אֲנָשִׁים
men Jehoiakim King sent And .Egypt went and and
to to fled

מִצְרָיִם אֵת אֶלְנָתָן בֶּן־עַכְבּוֹר וַאֲנָשִׁים אִתּוֹ אֶל־מִצְרָיִם׃
.Egypt into with and ,Achbor the Elnathan —Egypt
him men of son

23 וַיּוֹצִיאוּ אֶת־אוּרִיָּהוּ מִמִּצְרַיִם וַיְבִאֻהוּ אֶל־הַמֶּלֶךְ יְהוֹיָקִים
,Jehoiakim King to brought and from Urijah they And
him Egypt out brought

24 וַיַּכֵּהוּ בֶּחָרֶב וַיַּשְׁלֵךְ אֶת־נִבְלָתוֹ אֶל־קִבְרֵי בְּנֵי הָעָם׃ אַךְ
But the the the into dead his and the with who
.people of sons of graves body threw sword him struck

יַד אֲחִיקָם בֶּן־שָׁפָן הָיְתָה אֶת־יִרְמְיָהוּ לְבִלְתִּי תֶּת־אֹתוֹ
him to not ,Jeremiah with was Shaphan the Ahikam the
give of son of hand

בְיַד־הָעָם לַהֲמִיתוֹ׃
him put to the the into
.death to people of hand

CAP. XXVII כז

CHAPTER 27

CHAPTER 27

[1] In the beginning of the reign of Jehoiakim the son of Josiah king of Judah, this word came to Jeremiah from Jehovah, saying, [2] Thus says Jehovah to me, Make bonds and yokes for yourself and put them on your neck. [3] And send them to the king of Edom, and to the king of Moab, and to the king of the sons of Ammon, and to the king of Tyre, and to the king of Sidon, by the hand of the messengers who came to Jerusalem to Zedekiah king of Judah. [4] And command them to (go to) their masters, saying, Thus says Jehovah of hosts, the God of Israel: Thus you shall say to your masters, [5] I have made the earth (with) man, and the animals that are on the face of the earth, by My great power and by My outstretched arm, and I have given it to whom it seemed right in My eyes. [6] And now I have given all these

1 בְּרֵאשִׁית מַמְלֶכֶת יְהוֹיָקִם בֶּן־יֹאושִׁיָּהוּ מֶלֶךְ יְהוּדָה הָיָה
came ,Judah king Josiah the Jehoiakim reign the the In
of of son of of beginning

2 הַדָּבָר הַזֶּה אֶל־יִרְמְיָה מֵאֵת יְהוָה לֵאמֹר׃ כֹּה־אָמַר
says Thus ,saying ,Jehovah from Jeremiah to this word

יְהוָה אֵלַי עֲשֵׂה לְךָ מוֹסֵרוֹת וּמֹטוֹת וּנְתַתָּם עַל־צַוָּארֶךָ׃
your on put and and bonds for Make to Jehovah
.neck them yokes yourself ,me

3 וְשִׁלַּחְתָּם אֶל־מֶלֶךְ אֱדוֹם וְאֶל־מֶלֶךְ מוֹאָב וְאֶל־מֶלֶךְ בְּנֵי
the king the and ,Moab the and Edom the to And
of sons of to of king to of king them send

עַמּוֹן וְאֶל־מֶלֶךְ צֹר וְאֶל־מֶלֶךְ צִידוֹן בְּיַד מַלְאָכִים הַבָּאִים
who mes- the the by ,Sidon the and ,Tyre the and Am-
to came sengers of hand of king to of king to ,mon

4 יְרוּשָׁלִָם אֶל־צִדְקִיָּהוּ מֶלֶךְ יְהוּדָה׃ וְצִוִּיתָ אֹתָם אֶל־
(go to) them And .Judah king Zedekiah to Jerusalem
to command of

אֲדֹנֵיהֶם לֵאמֹר כֹּה־אָמַר יְהוָה צְבָאוֹת אֱלֹהֵי יִשְׂרָאֵל כֹּה
Thus :Israel the hosts Jehovah says Thus ,saying their
of God of masters

5 תֹאמְרוּ אֶל־אֲדֹנֵיכֶם׃ אָנֹכִי עָשִׂיתִי אֶת־הָאָרֶץ אֶת־הָאָדָם
,man the have I your to shall you
,earth made ,masters say

וְאֶת־הַבְּהֵמָה אֲשֶׁר עַל־פְּנֵי הָאָרֶץ בְּכֹחִי הַגָּדוֹל וּבִזְרוֹעִי
by and ,great My by the the on that the and
arm My power ,earth of face (are) animals

6 הַנְּטוּיָה וּנְתַתִּיהָ לַאֲשֶׁר יָשַׁר בְּעֵינָי׃ וְעַתָּה אָנֹכִי נָתַתִּי
have I And My in seemed it to have and out-
given ,now eyes right whom it given ,stretched

lands into the hand of Nebuchadnezzar the king of Babylon, My servant. And I have also given him the beast of the field to serve him. [7] And all nations shall serve him, and his son, and his son's son, until the time of his own land comes. Also him, and many nations and great kings shall make him a slave. [8] And it shall be, the nation and kingdom which will not serve him, Nebuchadnezzar the king of Babylon, and that will not put its neck in the yoke of the king of Babylon, that nation I will punish, says Jehovah, with the sword and with the famine, and with the plague, until I have destroyed them by his hand. [9] As for you, do not listen to your prophets or to your fortune-tellers, or to your dreamers, or to conjurors, or to your sorcerors, who speak to you, saying, You shall not serve the king of Babylon. [10] For they prophesy a lie to you, to remove you far from your land, that I should drive you out and you should perish. [11] But the nation who will bring its neck into the yoke of the king of Babylon and serve him, I will leave it on its own land, says Jehovah; and it will till it and live in it.

[12] I also spoke to Zedekiah king of Judah according to all these words, saying, Bring your necks into the king of Babylon's yoke and serve him and his people, and live. [13] Why will you die, you and your people, by the sword, by the famine, and by the plague, as Jehovah has spoken against the

אֶת־כָּל־הָאֲרָצוֹת הָאֵלֶּה בְּיַד נְבוּכַדְנֶאצַּר מֶלֶךְ־בָּבֶל
,Babylon the Nebuchadnezzar the into these lands all
of king of hand

7 עַבְדִּי וְגַם אֶת־חַיַּת הַשָּׂדֶה נָתַתִּי לוֹ לְעָבְדוֹ׃ וְעָבְדוּ אֹתוֹ
him shall And serve to to have I the the And My
serve .him him given field of beast also .servant

כָל־הַגּוֹיִם וְאֶת־בְּנוֹ וְאֶת־בֶּן־בְּנוֹ עַד בֹּא־עֵת אַרְצוֹ גַּם־
Also own his the comes until his son and his and ,nations all
.land of time son's ,son

8 הוּא וְעָבְדוּ בוֹ גּוֹיִם רַבִּים וּמְלָכִים גְּדוֹלִים׃ וְהָיָה הַגּוֹי
the it And .great and many nations him will and ,him
nation ,be will kings enslave

וְהַמַּמְלָכָה אֲשֶׁר לֹא־יַעַבְדוּ אֹתוֹ אֶת־נְבוּכַדְנֶאצַּר מֶלֶךְ־
the Nebuchadnezzar ,him will not which the and
of king serve kingdom

בָּבֶל וְאֵת אֲשֶׁר לֹא־יִתֵּן אֶת־צַוָּארוֹ בְּעֹל מֶלֶךְ בָּבֶל
,Babylon the the in its will not that and ,Babylon
of king of yoke neck put

בַּחֶרֶב וּבָרָעָב וּבַדֶּבֶר אֶפְקֹד עַל־הַגּוֹי הַהוּא נְאֻם־יְהוָה
,Jehovah says ,that nation will I with and with and the with
punish plague the famine the sword

9 עַד־תֻּמִּי אֹתָם בְּיָדוֹ׃ וְאַתֶּם אַל־תִּשְׁמְעוּ אֶל־נְבִיאֵיכֶם
your to listen do not for As his by them have I until
,prophets ,you .hand destroyed

וְאֶל־קֹסְמֵיכֶם וְאֶל־חֲלֹמֹתֵיכֶם וְאֶל־עֹנְנֵיכֶם וְאֶל־כַּשָּׁפֵיכֶם
your to or your to or your to or your to or
sorcerers conjurers ,dreamers diviners

אֲשֶׁר־הֵם אֹמְרִים אֲלֵיכֶם לֵאמֹר לֹא תַעַבְדוּ אֶת־מֶלֶךְ
the shall you Not ,saying ,you to speak they who
of king serve

10 בָּבֶל׃ כִּי שֶׁקֶר הֵם נִבְּאִים לָכֶם לְמַעַן הַרְחִיק אֶתְכֶם
you remove order in ,you to prophesy they lie a For .Babylon
far

11 מֵעַל אַדְמַתְכֶם וְהִדַּחְתִּי אֶתְכֶם וַאֲבַדְתֶּם׃ וְהַגּוֹי אֲשֶׁר
that the But will and you will I and your from
nation .perish you out drive ,land

יָבִיא אֶת־צַוָּארוֹ בְּעֹל מֶלֶךְ־בָּבֶל וַעֲבָדוֹ וְהִנַּחְתִּיו עַל־
on will I serve and Babylon the the into neck its will
it leave ,him of king of yoke bring

12 אַדְמָתוֹ נְאֻם־יְהוָה וַעֲבָדָהּ וְיָשַׁב בָּהּ׃ וְאֶל־צִדְקִיָּה מֶלֶךְ־
king Zedekiah Also .it in and will and ;Jehovah says ,land its
of to live it till

יְהוּדָה דִּבַּרְתִּי כְּכָל־הַדְּבָרִים הָאֵלֶּה לֵאמֹר הָבִיאוּ אֶת־
Bring ,saying ,these words according spoke I Judah
all to

13 צַוְּארֵיכֶם בְּעֹל ׀ מֶלֶךְ בָּבֶל וְעִבְדוּ אֹתוֹ וְעַמּוֹ וִחְיוּ׃ לָמָּה
Why and his and him serve and Babylon the the into your
.live ,people of king of yoke necks

תָמוּתוּ אַתָּה וְעַמֶּךָ בַּחֶרֶב בָּרָעָב וּבַדֶּבֶר כַּאֲשֶׁר דִּבֶּר
has as by and the by the by your and you you will
spoken plague the famine ,sword ,people ,die

nation that will not serve the king of Babylon? [14] Therefore do not listen to the words of the prophets who speak to you, saying, You shall not serve the king of Babylon; for they prophesy a lie to you. [15] For I have not sent them, says Jehovah. Yet they prophesy a lie in My name, so that I might drive you out, and that you might perish, you and the prophets who prophesy to you. [16] Also I spoke to the priests and to all this people, saying, Thus says Jehovah, Do not listen to the words of your prophets who prophesy to you, saying, Behold, the vessels of Jehovah's house shall now quickly be brought again from Babylon; for they prophesy a lie to you. [17] Do not listen to them. Serve the king of Babylon and live. Why should this city be a waste? [18] But if they (are) prophets, and if the word of Jehovah is with them, let them now intercede with Jehovah of hosts that the vessels which are left in the house of Jehovah and the house of the king of Judah, and at Jerusalem, may not go to Babylon.

[19] For thus says Jehovah of hosts concerning the pillars, and concerning the sea, and concerning the bases, and concerning the rest of the vessels which remain in this city; [20] which Nebuchadnezzar king of Babylon did not take when he exiled Jeconiah the son of Jehoiakim king of Judah from Jerusalem to Babylon, and all the nobles of Judah and

14 יְהוָה אֶל־הַגּוֹי אֲשֶׁר לֹא־יַעֲבֹד אֶת־מֶלֶךְ בָּבֶל׃ וְאַל־
Therefore Baby- the will not that the against Jeho-
not ?lon of king serve nation vah

תִּשְׁמְעוּ אֶל־דִּבְרֵי הַנְּבִאִים הָאֹמְרִים אֲלֵיכֶם לֵאמֹר לֹא
not ,saying ,you to speak who the the to listen do
prophets of words

15 תַעַבְדוּ אֶת־מֶלֶךְ בָּבֶל כִּי שֶׁקֶר הֵם נִבְּאִים לָכֶם׃ כִּי לֹא
not For .you to prophesy they lie a for ;Babylon the shall You
of king serve

שְׁלַחְתִּים נְאֻם־יְהוָה וְהֵם נִבְּאִים בִּשְׁמִי לַשָּׁקֶר לְמַעַן
so ,lie a My in prophesy Yet .Jehovah says have I
that name they ,them sent

הַדִּיחִי אֶתְכֶם וַאֲבַדְתֶּם אַתֶּם וְהַנְּבִאִים הַנִּבְּאִים לָכֶם׃
.you to who the and you you that and ,you might I
prophesy prophets ,perish may out drive

16 וְאֶל־הַכֹּהֲנִים וְאֶל־כָּל־הָעָם הַזֶּה דִּבַּרְתִּי לֵאמֹר כֹּה אָמַר
says Thus ,saying ,spoke I this people all and the Also
to priests to

יְהוָה אַל־תִּשְׁמְעוּ אֶל־דִּבְרֵי נְבִיאֵיכֶם הַנִּבְּאִים לָכֶם לֵאמֹר
,saying you to who your the to listen do Not Jeho-
prophesy prophets of words ,vah

הִנֵּה כְלֵי בֵית־יְהוָה מוּשָׁבִים מִבָּבֶלָה עַתָּה מְהֵרָה כִּי שֶׁקֶר
lie a for ,quickly now from be will Jehovah the the ,Behold
Babylon back brought of house of vessels

17 הֵמָּה נִבְּאִים לָכֶם׃ אַל־תִּשְׁמְעוּ אֲלֵיהֶם עִבְדוּ אֶת־מֶלֶךְ
the Serve .them to Do not .you to prophesy they
of king listen

18 בָּבֶל וִחְיוּ לָמָּה תִהְיֶה הָעִיר הַזֹּאת חָרְבָּה׃ וְאִם־נְבִאִים
prophets But .waste a this city should Why and Babylon
if be .live

הֵם וְאִם־יֵשׁ דְּבַר־יְהוָה אִתָּם יִפְגְּעוּ־נָא בַּיהוָה צְבָאוֹת
hosts with now them let with Jehovah the is if and they
of Jehovah intercede ,them of word (are)

לְבִלְתִּי־בֹאוּ הַכֵּלִים ׀ הַנּוֹתָרִים בְּבֵית־יְהוָה וּבֵית מֶלֶךְ
the the in and ,Jehovah the in are that the may that
of king of house of house left vessels go not

19 יְהוּדָה וּבִירוּשָׁלִַם בָּבֶלָה׃ כִּי כֹה אָמַר יְהוָה צְבָאוֹת
hosts Jehovah says thus For to at and ,Judah
of .Babylon ,Jerusalem

אֶל־הָעַמֻּדִים וְעַל־הַיָּם וְעַל־הַמְּכֹנוֹת וְעַל יֶתֶר הַכֵּלִים
the the con- and the con- and the con- and the concern-
vessels of rest cerning ,bases cerning ,sea cerning ,pillars ing

20 הַנּוֹתָרִים בָּעִיר הַזֹּאת׃ אֲשֶׁר לֹא־לְקָחָם נְבוּכַדְנֶאצַּר
Nebuchadnezzar did not which ;this city in are which
take left

מֶלֶךְ בָּבֶל בַּגְלוֹתוֹ אֶת־יְכוֹנְיָה בֶן־יְהוֹיָקִים מֶלֶךְ־יְהוּדָה
Judah king Jehoiakim the Jeconiah he when Babylon king
of of son exile into took of

מִירוּשָׁלִַם בָּבֶלָה וְאֵת כָּל־חֹרֵי יְהוּדָה וִירוּשָׁלִָם׃
and Judah the all and to from
.Jerusalem of nobles ,Babylon Jerusalem

Jerusalem. [21] For thus says Jehovah of hosts, the God of Israel, concerning the vessels that remain in the house of Jehovah, and the house of the king of Judah, and Jerusalem: [22] They shall be carried to Babylon, and they shall be there until the day I visit them, says Jehovah. Then I will bring them up and give them back to this place.

21 כִּי כֹה אָמַר יְהוָה צְבָאוֹת אֱלֹהֵי יִשְׂרָאֵל עַל־הַכֵּלִים
the concern- ,Israel the hosts Jehovah says thus For
vessels ing of God of
22 הַנּוֹתָרִים בֵּית יְהוָה וּבֵית מֶלֶךְ־יְהוּדָה וִירוּשָׁלִָם׃ בָּבֶלָה
To and ,Judah the the and Jehovah the are that
Babylon :Jerusalem of king of house of house in left
יוּבָאוּ וְשָׁמָּה יִהְיוּ עַד יוֹם פָּקְדִי אֹתָם נְאֻם־יְהוָה וְהַעֲלִיתִים
will I and ;Jehovah says ,them visit I the until they and be will they
up them bring day be shall there ,brought
וַהֲשִׁבֹתִים אֶל־הַמָּקוֹם הַזֶּה׃
.this place to restore and
them

CAP. XXVIII כח

CHAPTER 28

[1] And it came to pass in that year, in the beginning of the reign of Zedekiah king of Judah, in the fourth year, in the fifth month, Hananiah the son of Azur the prophet, who (was) of Gibeon, spoke to me in the house of Jehovah, for the eyes of the priests and of all the people, saying, [2] Thus speaks Jehovah of hosts, the God of Israel, saying, I have broken the yoke of the king of Babylon. [3] Within two (full) years I will again bring into this place all the vessels of Jehovah's house, which Nebuchadnezzar king of Babylon took away from this place and carried them to Babylon. [4] And I will bring again to this place Jeconiah the son of Jehoiakim king of Judah, with all the exiles of Judah who went into Babylon, says Jehovah. For I will break the yoke of the king of Babylon.

[5] Then the prophet Jeremiah said to the prophet Hananiah for the eyes of the priests, and for the eyes of all the people who stood in the house of Jehovah, [6] even the prophet Jeremiah said, Amen! May Jehovah do

1 וַיְהִי ׀ בַּשָּׁנָה הַהִיא בְּרֵאשִׁית מַמְלֶכֶת צִדְקִיָּה מֶלֶךְ
king Zedekiah the the in that year in it And
of of reign of beginning was
יְהוּדָה בַּשָּׁנַת הָרְבִעִית בַּחֹדֶשׁ הַחֲמִישִׁי אָמַר אֵלַי חֲנַנְיָה
Hananiah to spoke ,fifth the in ,fourth the in ,Judah
me month year
בֶן־עַזּוּר הַנָּבִיא אֲשֶׁר מִגִּבְעוֹן בְּבֵית יְהוָה לְעֵינֵי הַכֹּהֲנִים
the the for ,Jehovah the in from who the Azur the
priests of eyes of house ,Gibeon (was) ,prophet of son
2 וְכָל־הָעָם לֵאמֹר׃ כֹּה־אָמַר יְהוָה צְבָאוֹת אֱלֹהֵי יִשְׂרָאֵל
,Israel the hosts Jehovah says Thus ,saying the and
of God of ,people all
3 לֵאמֹר שָׁבַרְתִּי אֶת־עֹל מֶלֶךְ בָּבֶל׃ בְּעוֹד ׀ שְׁנָתַיִם יָמִים
days two Within .Babylon the the have I ,saying
of years of king of yoke broken
אֲנִי מֵשִׁיב אֶל־הַמָּקוֹם הַזֶּה אֶת־כָּל־כְּלֵי בֵּית יְהוָה אֲשֶׁר
which ,Jehovah the the all this place to bring will I
of house of vessels back
לָקַח נְבוּכַדְנֶאצַּר מֶלֶךְ־בָּבֶל מִן־הַמָּקוֹם הַזֶּה וַיְבִיאֵם
carried and this place from Babylon king Nebuchadnezzar took
to them of away
4 בָּבֶל׃ וְאֶת־יְכָנְיָה בֶן־יְהוֹיָקִים מֶלֶךְ־יְהוּדָה וְאֶת־כָּל־גָּלוּת
the all with ,Judah king Jehoiakim the Jeconiah And .Babylon
of exiles of of son
יְהוּדָה הַבָּאִים בָּבֶלָה אֲנִי מֵשִׁיב אֶל־הַמָּקוֹם הַזֶּה נְאֻם
says ,this place to bring will I to who Judah
back ,Babylon went
5 יְהוָה כִּי אֶשְׁבֹּר אֶת־עֹל מֶלֶךְ בָּבֶל׃ וַיֹּאמֶר יִרְמְיָה
Jeremiah Then .Babylon the the will I For .Jehovah
said of king of yoke break
הַנָּבִיא אֶל־חֲנַנְיָה הַנָּבִיא לְעֵינֵי הַכֹּהֲנִים וּלְעֵינֵי כָל־הָעָם
the all for and the the for the Hananiah to the
people of eyes the priests of eyes prophet prophet
6 הָעֹמְדִים בְּבֵית יְהוָה׃ וַיֹּאמֶר יִרְמְיָה הַנָּבִיא אָמֵן כֵּן
So !Amen the Jeremiah said and ;Jehovah the in who
,prophet of house stood

(so); May Jehovah confirm your words which you have prophesied, to bring again the vessels of Jehovah's house, and all the exiles from Babylon into this place. [7] But hear now this word that I speak in your ears and in the ears of all the people: [8] The prophets who have been before me and before you of old prophesied against many lands and against great kingdoms; of war, and of evil and of plague. [9] (As for) the prophet who prophesies of peace, when the word of the prophet shall come to pass, the prophet shall be known (as one) whom Jehovah has truly sent him.

[10] Then Hananiah the prophet took the yoke from the prophet Jeremiah's neck and broke it. [11] And Hananiah spoke for the eyes of all the people, saying, Thus says Jehovah, Even so I will break the yoke of Nebuchadnezzar king of Babylon from the neck of all nations within the time of two (full) years. And the prophet Jeremiah went his way.

[12] Then the word of Jehovah came to Jeremiah, after Hananiah the prophet had broken the yoke from the neck of the prophet Jeremiah, saying, [13] Go and tell Hananiah, saying, Thus says Jehovah: You have broken yokes of wood, but you shall make instead of them yokes of iron. [14] For thus says Jehovah of hosts, the God of Israel: I have put a yoke of iron on the neck of all these nations to serve Nebuchadnezzar king of Babylon. And they shall serve him. And I have

יַעַשׂ יְהוָה יָקֵם יְהוָה אֶת־דְּבָרֶיךָ אֲשֶׁר נִבֵּאתָ לְהָשִׁיב
bring to back | have you ,prophesied | which | your words | Jehovah | May establish | Jehovah | may do

7 כְּלֵי בֵית־יְהוָה וְכָל־הַגּוֹלָה מִבָּבֶל אֶל־הַמָּקוֹם הַזֶּה׃ אַךְ
But | .this | place | into | from Babylon | the exiles | and all | Jehovah | the of house | the of vessels

שְׁמַע־נָא הַדָּבָר הַזֶּה אֲשֶׁר אָנֹכִי דֹּבֵר בְּאָזְנֶיךָ וּבְאָזְנֵי
in and of ears the | your in ears | speak | I | that | this | word | now | hear

8 כָּל־הָעָם׃ הַנְּבִיאִים אֲשֶׁר הָיוּ לְפָנַי וּלְפָנֶיךָ מִן־הָעוֹלָם
antiquity from | and you before | before me | were | who | the prophets | the ;people | all

וַיִּנָּבְאוּ אֶל־אֲרָצוֹת רַבּוֹת וְעַל־מַמְלָכוֹת גְּדֹלוֹת לְמִלְחָמָה
,war of | ;great | kingdoms | and against | ,many | lands against | prophe- sied

9 וּלְרָעָה וּלְדָבֶר׃ הַנָּבִיא אֲשֶׁר יִנָּבֵא לְשָׁלוֹם בְּבֹא דְּבַר
the of word | comes when pass to | of ,peace | prophesies | who | The prophet | of and .plague | of and ,evil

10 הַנָּבִיא יִוָּדַע הַנָּבִיא אֲשֶׁר־שְׁלָחוֹ יְהוָה בֶּאֱמֶת׃ וַיִּקַּח חֲנַנְיָה
Hana- niah | Then took | .truly | Jehovah | has him sent | (one as) whom | the prophet | be will known | the ,prophet

הַנָּבִיא אֶת־הַמּוֹטָה מֵעַל צַוַּאר יִרְמְיָה הַנָּבִיא וַיִּשְׁבְּרֵהוּ׃
and .it broke | the prophet | Jeremiah's | neck | from | the yoke | the prophet

11 וַיֹּאמֶר חֲנַנְיָה לְעֵינֵי כָּל־הָעָם לֵאמֹר כֹּה אָמַר יְהוָה כָּכָה
Even so | ,Jehovah | says | Thus | ,saying | the ,people | all | the for of eyes | Hananiah | And said

אֶשְׁבֹּר אֶת־עֹל ׀ נְבֻכַדְנֶאצַּר מֶלֶךְ־בָּבֶל בְּעוֹד שְׁנָתַיִם
two of years | within | Babylon | king of | Nebuchadnezzar | the of yoke | will I break

יָמִים מֵעַל צַוַּאר כָּל־הַגּוֹיִם וַיֵּלֶךְ יִרְמְיָה הַנָּבִיא לְדַרְכּוֹ׃
.way his | the prophet | Jeremiah | Then went | .nations | all | the of neck | from | days

12 וַיְהִי דְבַר־יְהוָה אֶל־יִרְמְיָה אַחֲרֵי שְׁבוֹר חֲנַנְיָה
Hana- niah | had broken | after | ,Jeremiah | to | Jehovah | the of word | Then came

הַנָּבִיא אֶת־הַמּוֹטָה מֵעַל צַוַּאר יִרְמְיָה הַנָּבִיא לֵאמֹר׃
,saying | the ,prophet | Jeremiah | the of neck | from | the yoke | the prophet

13 הָלוֹךְ וְאָמַרְתָּ אֶל־חֲנַנְיָה לֵאמֹר כֹּה אָמַר יְהוָה מוֹטֹת עֵץ
wood | yokes of | ,Jehovah | says | Thus | ,saying | ,Hananiah to | say and | Go

14 שָׁבָרְתָּ וְעָשִׂיתָ תַחְתֵּיהֶן מֹטוֹת בַּרְזֶל׃ כִּי כֹה־אָמַר יְהוָה
Jehovah of | says thus For | .iron | yokes of | of instead them | you but make will | have You ,broken

צְבָאוֹת אֱלֹהֵי יִשְׂרָאֵל עֹל בַּרְזֶל נָתַתִּי עַל־צַוַּאר ׀ כָּל־
all | the of neck | on | have I put | iron | a of yoke | ,Israel | the of God | ,hosts

הַגּוֹיִם הָאֵלֶּה לַעֲבֹד אֶת־נְבֻכַדְנֶאצַּר מֶלֶךְ־בָּבֶל וַעֲבָדֻהוּ
they and .him serve will | ;Babylon | king of | Nebuchadnezzar | serve to | ,these | nations

given him the beasts of the field also.

[15] Then the prophet Jeremiah said to Hananiah the prophet, Hear now, Hananiah. Jehovah has not sent you, but you have made this people trust in a lie. [16] Therefore thus says Jehovah, Behold, I am sending you from the face of the earth. You shall die this year, because you have uttered rebellion against Jehovah. [17] So Hananiah the prophet died the same year in the seventh month.

15 וְגַם אֶת־חַיַּת הַשָּׂדֶה נָתַתִּי לוֹ׃ וַיֹּאמֶר יִרְמְיָה הַנָּבִיא
the Jeremiah Then to have I the the And
prophet said .him given field of beasts also

אֶל־חֲנַנְיָה הַנָּבִיא שְׁמַע־נָא חֲנַנְיָה לֹא־שְׁלָחֲךָ יְהוָה וְאַתָּה
but ,Jehovah has not ,Hananiah ,now Hear the Hananiah to
you you sent ,prophet

16 הִבְטַחְתָּ אֶת־הָעָם הַזֶּה עַל־שָׁקֶר׃ לָכֵן כֹּה אָמַר יְהוָה
,Jehovah says this Therefore .lie a in this people made have
trust

הִנְנִי מְשַׁלֵּחֲךָ מֵעַל פְּנֵי הָאֲדָמָה הַשָּׁנָה אַתָּה מֵת כִּי־
for shall you This the the from you send ,Behold
,die year .earth of face away I

17 סָרָה דִבַּרְתָּ אֶל־יְהוָה׃ וַיָּמָת חֲנַנְיָה הַנָּבִיא בַּשָּׁנָה הַהִיא
that year in the Hananiah So .Jehovah against have you apos-
prophet died spoken tasy

בַּחֹדֶשׁ הַשְּׁבִיעִי׃
.seventh the in
month

CAP. XXIX כט

CHAPTER 29

CHAPTER 29

[1] Now these (are) the words of the letter that Jeremiah the prophet sent from Jerusalem to the rest of the elders of the exile, and to the priests, and to the prophets, and to all the people whom Nebuchadnezzar had exiled from Jerusalem to Babylon — [2] after Jeconiah the king, and the queen-mother and the eunuchs, and the princes of Judah and Jerusalem, and the craftsmen, and the smiths had departed from Jerusalem — [3] by the hand of Elasah the son of Shaphan, and Gemariah the son of Hilkiah, whom Zedekiah the king of Judah sent to Babylon to Nebuchadnezzar king of Babylon, saying, [4] Thus says Jehovah of hosts, the God of Israel, to all the exiles whom I have caused to be exiled from Jerusalem to Babylon: [5] Build houses and live; and plant gardens and eat the fruit of them. [6] Take wives, and father sons and daughters. And take wives for your sons,

1 וְאֵלֶּה דִּבְרֵי הַסֵּפֶר אֲשֶׁר שָׁלַח יִרְמְיָה הַנָּבִיא מִירוּשָׁלָיִם
from the Jeremiah sent that letter the words the Now
Jerusalem prophet of (are) these

אֶל־יֶתֶר זִקְנֵי הַגּוֹלָה וְאֶל־הַכֹּהֲנִים וְאֶל־הַנְּבִיאִים וְאֶל־
to and the and the and the the rest the to
,prophets to ,priests to exile of elders of

כָּל־הָעָם אֲשֶׁר הֶגְלָה נְבוּכַדְנֶאצַּר מִירוּשָׁלַיִם בָּבֶלָה׃
to from Nebuchadnezzar had ,whom the all
—Babylon Jerusalem deported people

2 אַחֲרֵי צֵאת יְכָנְיָה־הַמֶּלֶךְ וְהַגְּבִירָה וְהַסָּרִיסִים שָׂרֵי יְהוּדָה
Judah the and the and the and the Jeconiah had after
of leaders eunuchs ,mother queen ,king departed

3 וִירוּשָׁלַיִם וְהֶחָרָשׁ וְהַמַּסְגֵּר מִירוּשָׁלָיִם׃ בְּיַד אֶלְעָשָׂה בֶּן־
the Elasah the by from the and the and and
of son of hand —Jerusalem smiths ,craftsmen ,Jerusalem

שָׁפָן וּגְמַרְיָה בֶּן־חִלְקִיָּה אֲשֶׁר שָׁלַח צִדְקִיָּה מֶלֶךְ־יְהוּדָה
Judah king Zedekiah sent whom ,Hilkiah the and ,Shaphan
of of son Gemariah

4 אֶל־נְבוּכַדְנֶאצַּר מֶלֶךְ בָּבֶל בָּבֶלָה לֵאמֹר׃ כֹּה אָמַר
says Thus ,saying to Babylon king Nebuchadnezzar to
,Babylon of

יְהוָה צְבָאוֹת אֱלֹהֵי יִשְׂרָאֵל לְכָל־הַגּוֹלָה אֲשֶׁר־הִגְלֵיתִי
sent I whom the to ,Israel the ,hosts Jehovah
exile into exiles all of God of

5 מִירוּשָׁלַיִם בָּבֶלָה׃ בְּנוּ בָתִּים וְשֵׁבוּ וְנִטְעוּ גַנּוֹת וְאִכְלוּ
and gardens and ;live and houses Build to from
eat plant :Babylon Jerusalem

6 אֶת־פִּרְיָן׃ קְחוּ נָשִׁים וְהוֹלִידוּ בָּנִים וּבָנוֹת וּקְחוּ לִבְנֵיכֶם
your for And and sons and ,wives Take their
sons take .daughters father .fruit

and give your daughters husbands, that they may bear sons and daughters, and multiply them and not become few. [7] And seek the peace of the city there where I have caused you to be exiled; and pray to Jehovah for it; for in its peace you shall have peace.

[8] For thus says Jehovah of hosts, the God of Israel: Do not let your prophets and your fortune-tellers who (are) in your midst deceive you. And do not listen to your dreams which you dream. [9] For they prophesy falsely to you in My name; I have not sent them, says Jehovah.

[10] For thus says Jehovah, When according to My mouth seventy years have been fulfilled for Babylon, I will visit you and confirm My good word to you, to bring you back to this place. [11] For I know the plans which I am planning for you, says Jehovah; plans of peace and not for evil, to give you a future and a hope. [12] Then you shall call on Me, and you shall go and pray to Me, and I will listen to you. [13] And you shall seek Me and find (Me), when you search for Me with all your heart.

[14] And I will be found by you, says Jehovah. And I will turn away your captivity, and I will gather you from all the nations, and from all the places where I have driven you there, says Jehovah. And I will bring you again into the place

נָשִׁים וְאֶת־בְּנוֹתֵיכֶם תְּנוּ לַאֲנָשִׁים וְתֵלַדְנָה בָּנִים וּבָנוֹת
and ,daughters | sons | they that bear may | husbands to | give | your daughters | and ,wives

7 וּרְבוּ־שָׁם וְאַל־תִּמְעָטוּ׃ וְדִרְשׁוּ אֶת־שְׁלוֹם הָעִיר אֲשֶׁר
where | the city | the of peace | seek And | become .few | and not | ,there | and multiply

הִגְלֵיתִי אֶתְכֶם שָׁמָּה וְהִתְפַּלְלוּ בַעֲדָהּ אֶל־יְהוָה כִּי
for | ,Jehovah | to | it for | and pray | ,there | you | sent have I exile into

8 בִשְׁלוֹמָהּ יִהְיֶה לָכֶם שָׁלוֹם׃ כִּי כֹה אָמַר יְהוָה
Jehovah of | says | thus | For | .peace | for you | there be will | its in peace

צְבָאוֹת אֱלֹהֵי יִשְׂרָאֵל אַל־יַשִּׁיאוּ לָכֶם נְבִיאֵיכֶם אֲשֶׁר־
who (are) | your prophets | you | let Do not deceive | :Israel | the of God | hosts

בְּקִרְבְּכֶם וְקֹסְמֵיכֶם וְאַל־תִּשְׁמְעוּ אֶל־חֲלֹמֹתֵיכֶם אֲשֶׁר
which | your dreams | to | do listen | and not | your and ,diviners | your in midst

9 אַתֶּם מַחְלְמִים׃ כִּי בְשֶׁקֶר הֵם נִבְּאִים לָכֶם בִּשְׁמִי לֹא
not | My in ;name | to you | prophesy | they | falsely | For | .dream | you

10 שְׁלַחְתִּים נְאֻם־יְהוָה׃ כִּי־כֹה אָמַר יְהוָה כִּי לְפִי
My as mouth | When | Jeho- ,vah | says | thus | For | .Jehovah | says | have I them sent

מְלֹאת לְבָבֶל שִׁבְעִים שָׁנָה אֶפְקֹד אֶתְכֶם וַהֲקִמֹתִי עֲלֵיכֶם
for you | and establish | you | will I visit | ,years | seventy | for Babylon | been have fulfilled

11 אֶת־דְּבָרִי הַטּוֹב לְהָשִׁיב אֶתְכֶם אֶל־הַמָּקוֹם הַזֶּה׃ כִּי
For | .this | place | to | you | bring to back | good | word My

אָנֹכִי יָדַעְתִּי אֶת־הַמַּחֲשָׁבֹת אֲשֶׁר אָנֹכִי חֹשֵׁב עֲלֵיכֶם נְאֻם־
says | for ,you | am planning | I | which | the plans | know | I

יְהוָה מַחְשְׁבוֹת שָׁלוֹם וְלֹא לְרָעָה לָתֵת לָכֶם אַחֲרִית
future a | you | give to | ,evil for | and not | peace | plans of | ;Jehovah

12 וְתִקְוָה׃ וּקְרָאתֶם אֹתִי וַהֲלַכְתֶּם וְהִתְפַּלַּלְתֶּם אֵלָי וְשָׁמַעְתִּי
will I and listen | to ,Me | pray and | and come | Me | you Then upon call will | a and .hope

13 אֲלֵיכֶם׃ וּבִקַּשְׁתֶּם אֹתִי וּמְצָאתֶם כִּי תִדְרְשֻׁנִי בְּכָל־
with all | seek you Me | when | find and (Me) | Me | you And seek will | to .you

14 לְבַבְכֶם׃ וְנִמְצֵאתִי לָכֶם נְאֻם־יְהוָה וְשַׁבְתִּי אֶת־שְׁבִיתְכֶם
your ,captivity | I And turn will | .Jehovah | says | by ,you | will I And found be | your .heart

וְקִבַּצְתִּי אֶתְכֶם מִכָּל־הַגּוֹיִם וּמִכָּל־הַמְּקוֹמוֹת אֲשֶׁר הִדַּחְתִּי
have I driven | where | the places | and all from | the ;nations | from all | you | will I and gather

אֶתְכֶם שָׁם נְאֻם־יְהוָה וַהֲשִׁבֹתִי אֶתְכֶם אֶל־הַמָּקוֹם אֲשֶׁר־
which | the place | to | you | will I and back bring | ,Jehovah | says | there | you

from which I sent you into exile from there.

[15] Because you have said, Jehovah has raised up for us prophets in Babylon — [16] for thus says Jehovah to the king who sits on the throne of David, and to all the people who live in this city, your brothers who have not gone out with you into exile — [17] thus says Jehovah of hosts, Behold, I am sending on them the sword, the famine, and the plague, and will make them like vile figs which cannot be eaten from badness. [18] And I will pursue them with the sword, with the famine and with the plague; and I will make them a horror to all the kingdoms of the earth, to be a curse, and a terror, and a hissing, and a reproach among all the nations where I have driven them there. [19] For they have not listened to My words, says Jehovah, which I sent to them by My servants the prophets, rising up early and sending; but you would not hear, says Jehovah.

[20] Therefore you hear the word of Jehovah, all you exiles whom I have sent from Jerusalem to Babylon; [21] thus says Jehovah of hosts, the God of Israel, about Ahab the son of Kolaiah, and about Zedekiah the son of Maaseiah, who prophesy a lie to you in My name: Behold, I will deliver them into the hand of Nebuchadnezzar king of Babylon, and he shall strike them before your eyes. [22] And a curse shall be taken up from them for all the exiles of Judah who (are) in Babylon, saying, May Jehovah make you

15 הִגְלֵיתִי אֶתְכֶם מִשָּׁם׃ כִּי אֲמַרְתֶּם הֵקִים לָנוּ יְהוָה

Jehovah | for us | raised has up | have you ,said | Because | from .there | you | sent I exile into

16 נְבִאִים בָּבֶלָה׃ כִּי־כֹה ׀ אָמַר יְהוָה אֶל־הַמֶּלֶךְ

the king | to | Jehovah | says | thus for | in —Babylon | prophets

הַיּוֹשֵׁב אֶל־כִּסֵּא דָוִד וְאֶל־כָּל־הָעָם הַיּוֹשֵׁב בָּעִיר הַזֹּאת

,this | city in | who dwell | the people | all | and to | ,David | the of throne | on | who sits

17 אֲחֵיכֶם אֲשֶׁר לֹא־יָצְאוּ אִתְּכֶם בַּגּוֹלָה׃ כֹּה אָמַר

says | thus | into —exile | with you | have out gone | not | who | your brothers

יְהוָה צְבָאוֹת הִנְנִי מְשַׁלֵּחַ בָּם אֶת־הַחֶרֶב אֶת־הָרָעָב

the ,famine | the ,sword | on them | am sending | ,Behold I | ,hosts | Jehovah of

וְאֶת־הַדָּבֶר וְנָתַתִּי אוֹתָם כַּתְּאֵנִים הַשֹּׁעָרִים אֲשֶׁר לֹא־

not | which | offensive | figs like | them | will and make | the ,plague | and

18 תֵאָכַלְנָה מֵרֹעַ׃ וְרָדַפְתִּי אַחֲרֵיהֶם בַּחֶרֶב בָּרָעָב וּבַדָּבֶר

with and ,plague the | the with ,famine | the with ,sword | them | will I And pursue | from .badness | be can eaten

וּנְתַתִּים לְזַוְעָה לְכֹל ׀ מַמְלְכוֹת הָאָרֶץ לְאָלָה וּלְשַׁמָּה

a and horror | a for ,curse | the earth | the of kingdoms | all to | a horror | will I and them make

19 וְלִשְׁרֵקָה וּלְחֶרְפָּה בְּכָל־הַגּוֹיִם אֲשֶׁר־הִדַּחְתִּים שָׁם׃ תַּחַת

because | ;there | have I them driven | where | the nations | among all | a and reproach | a and ,hissing

אֲשֶׁר־לֹא־שָׁמְעוּ אֶל־דְּבָרַי נְאֻם־יְהוָה אֲשֶׁר שָׁלַחְתִּי

sent I | which | ,Jehovah | says | My ,words | to | have they listened | not

אֲלֵיהֶם אֶת־עֲבָדַי הַנְּבִאִים הַשְׁכֵּם וְשָׁלֹחַ וְלֹא שְׁמַעְתֶּם

would you listen | but not | and ,sending | up rising early | the ,prophets | My with servants | them to

20 נְאֻם־יְהוָה׃ וְאַתֶּם שִׁמְעוּ דְבַר־יְהוָה כָּל־הַגּוֹלָה אֲשֶׁר

whom | the exiles | all | ,Jehovah | the of word | hear | Therefore you | .Jehovah says

21 שִׁלַּחְתִּי מִירוּשָׁלַםִ בָּבֶלָה׃ כֹּה־אָמַר יְהוָה צְבָאוֹת

hosts | Jehovah of | says | Thus | to ;Babylon | from Jerusalem | have I sent

אֱלֹהֵי יִשְׂרָאֵל אֶל־אַחְאָב בֶּן־קוֹלָיָה וְאֶל־צִדְקִיָּהוּ בֶן־

the of son | Zedekiah | con- and cerning | ,Kolaiah | the of son | Ahab | con- cerning | Israel | the of God

מַעֲשֵׂיָה הַנִּבְּאִים לָכֶם בִּשְׁמִי שָׁקֶר הִנְנִי ׀ נֹתֵן אֹתָם בְּיַד

the into of hand. | them | will deliver | ,Behold I | :lie a | My in name | to you | who prophesy | ,Maaseiah

22 נְבוּכַדְרֶאצַּר מֶלֶךְ־בָּבֶל וְהִכָּם לְעֵינֵיכֶם׃ וְלֻקַּח מֵהֶם

from them | will And taken be | your before .eyes | he and them strike will | ,Babylon | king of | Nebuchadnezzar

קְלָלָה לְכֹל גָּלוּת יְהוּדָה אֲשֶׁר בְּבָבֶל לֵאמֹר יְשִׂמְךָ יְהוָה

Jehovah | May you make | ,saying | in ,Babylon | who (are) | Judah | the of exiles | for all | curse a like Zedekiah and like Ahab, they whom the king of Babylon roasted in the fire, [23] because they have committed folly in Israel, and have committed adultery with their neighbors' wives, and have spoken a lying word in My name, which I have not commanded them; for I (am) He who knows, and a witness, says Jehovah.

[24] You shall also speak to Shemaiah the Nehelamite, saying, [25] Thus speaks Jehovah of hosts, the God of Israel, saying, Because you have sent letters in your name to all the people who (are) in Jerusalem, and to Zephaniah the son of Maaseiah the priest, and to all the priests, saying, [26] Jehovah has made you priest instead of Jehoiada the priest, to be officers (in) the house of Jehovah, over every madman who prophesies, that you should put him into the stocks and into the (torture) collar. [27] Now therefore, why have you not reproved Jeremiah the Anathothite, who prophesies to you? [28] For he therefore sent to us (in) Babylon, saying, This (captivity) is long. Build houses and live, and plant gardens and eat their fruit. [29] And Zephaniah the priest read this letter in the ears of Jeremiah the prophet.

[30] Then the word of Jehovah came to Jeremiah, saying, [31] Send to all the exiles, saying, Thus says Jehovah concerning Shemaiah the Nehelamite: Because Shemaiah has prophesied to you, and I did not send him, and he caused you to trust in a lie, [32] therefore thus says Jehovah, Behold, I will punish Shemaiah the Nehelamite and his seed. There

23 כְּצִדְקִיָּהוּ וּכְאֶחָב אֲשֶׁר־קָלָם מֶלֶךְ־בָּבֶל בָּאֵשׁ׃ יַעַן אֲשֶׁר
because the in Babylon the roasted whom like and like
,fire of king them Ahab Zedekiah

עָשׂוּ נְבָלָה בְּיִשְׂרָאֵל וַיְנַאֲפוּ אֶת־נְשֵׁי רֵעֵיהֶם וַיְדַבְּרוּ דָבָר
a have and their wives with have and ,Israel in disgraceful they
word spoken ,neighbor's adultery committed folly done have

בִּשְׁמִי שֶׁקֶר אֲשֶׁר לוֹא צִוִּיתִם וְאָנֹכִי הַוֹּידֵעַ וָעֵד נְאֻם־
says a and who He I and com- have I not which ,lying My in
,witness ,knows (am) ;them manded name

24 יְהוָה׃ וְאֶל־שְׁמַעְיָהוּ הַנֶּחֱלָמִי תֹּאמַר לֵאמֹר׃ כֹּה־
25 Thus ,saying shall you the Shemaiah Also .Jehovah
,speak Nehelamite to

אָמַר יְהוָה צְבָאוֹת אֱלֹהֵי יִשְׂרָאֵל לֵאמֹר יַעַן אֲשֶׁר אַתָּה
you Because ,saying ,Israel the ,hosts Jehovah says
of God of

שָׁלַחְתָּ בְשִׁמְכָה סְפָרִים אֶל־כָּל־הָעָם אֲשֶׁר בִּירוּשָׁלִַם
in who the all to letters your in have
,Jerusalem (are) people name sent

וְאֶל־צְפַנְיָה בֶן־מַעֲשֵׂיָה הַכֹּהֵן וְאֶל־כָּל־הַכֹּהֲנִים לֵאמֹר׃
,saying the all and the Maaseiah the Zephaniah and
,priests to ,priest of son to

26 יְהוָה נְתָנְךָ כֹהֵן תַּחַת יְהוֹיָדָע הַכֹּהֵן לִהְיוֹת פְּקִדִים בֵּית
the officers be to the Jehoiada instead priest has Jehovah
of house (in) ,priest of you made

יְהוָה לְכָל־אִישׁ מְשֻׁגָּע וּמִתְנַבֵּא וְנָתַתָּה אֹתוֹ אֶל־הַמַּהְפֶּכֶת
the into him you that who madman over ,Jehovah
stocks put ,prophesies every

27 וְאֶל־הַצִּינֹק׃ וְעַתָּה לָמָּה לֹא גָעַרְתָּ בְּיִרְמְיָהוּ הָעֲנְּתֹתִי
the Jeremiah you have not why Now the and
,Anathothite reproved therefore .collar into

28 הַמִּתְנַבֵּא לָכֶם׃ כִּי עַל־כֵּן שָׁלַח אֵלֵינוּ בָּבֶל לֵאמֹר אֲרֻכָּה
long ,saying (in) us to he therefore For to who
Babylon sent ?you prophesies

הִיא בְּנוּ בָתִּים וְשֵׁבוּ וְנִטְעוּ גַנּוֹת וְאִכְלוּ אֶת־פְּרִיהֶן׃
their and gardens and and houses Build It
.fruit eat plant ,dwell .(be will)

29 וַיִּקְרָא צְפַנְיָה הַכֹּהֵן אֶת־הַסֵּפֶר הַזֶּה בְּאָזְנֵי יִרְמְיָהוּ
Jeremiah the in this letter the Zephaniah And
of ears priest read

30 הַנָּבִיא׃ וַיְהִי דְּבַר־יְהוָה אֶל־יִרְמְיָהוּ לֵאמֹר׃
,saying ,Jeremiah to Jehovah the Then the
of word came .prophet

31 שְׁלַח עַל־כָּל־הַגּוֹלָה לֵאמֹר כֹּה אָמַר יְהוָה אֶל־שְׁמַעְיָה
Shemaiah con- Jehovah says Thus ,saying the all to Send
cerning exiles

הַנֶּחֱלָמִי יַעַן אֲשֶׁר נִבָּא לָכֶם שְׁמַעְיָה וַאֲנִי לֹא שְׁלַחְתִּיו
send did not and ,Shemaiah to prophesied Because the
,him I you :Nehelamite

32 וַיַּבְטַח אֶתְכֶם עַל־שָׁקֶר׃ לָכֵן כֹּה־אָמַר יְהוָה הִנְנִי פֹקֵד
will ,Behold ,Jehovah says thus therefore ,lie a in you he and
punish I trust to caused

shall not be to him a man
living among this people;
nor shall he behold the good
which I shall do for My
people, says Jehovah, be-
cause he has uttered re-
bellion against Jehovah.

עַל־שְׁמַעְיָ֥ה הַנֶּחֱלָמִ֖י וְעַל־זַרְע֑וֹ לֹא־יִהְיֶ֨ה ל֥וֹ אִ֛ישׁ ׀ יוֹשֵׁ֣ב

| living | a | to | shall not | his | and | the | the | Shemaiah |
| man | him | be | | ,seed | | | Nehelamite |

בְּתוֹךְ־הָעָ֣ם הַזֶּ֗ה וְלֹֽא־יִרְאֶ֥ה בַטּ֛וֹב אֲשֶׁר־אֲנִ֥י עֹשֶׂה־לְעַמִּ֖י

| My | for | will | I | which | the | he will | nor | ;this | people | the | in |
| people | | do | | | good | see | | | | | of midst |

נְאֻם־יְהוָ֑ה כִּי־סָרָ֥ה דִבֶּ֖ר עַל־יְהוָֽה׃

.Jehovah against he has revolt for ,Jehovah says
                    spoken

CAP. XXX ל

CHAPTER 30

CHAPTER 30

[1] The word that came
to Jeremiah from Jehovah,
saying, [2] Thus speaks
Jehovah God of Israel, saying, Write for yourself all
the words that I have
spoken to you in a book.
[3] For, lo, the days come,
says Jehovah, that I will
turn the captivity of My
people Israel and Judah,
says Jehovah; and I will
cause them to return to the
land that I gave to their
fathers, and they shall
possess it.

[4] And these (are) the
words that Jehovah spoke
concerning Israel and about
Judah. [5] For thus says
Jehovah, We have heard a
sound of trembling, of
dread, and not of peace.
[6] Ask now, and see: if a
man is giving birth? Why do
I see every man (with) his
hands on his loins, like a
woman in travail, and all
faces are turned to pale-
ness? [7] Alas! For that
day (is) great, for none (is)
like it; and it (is) a time of
Jacob's trouble. But he shall
be saved out of it. [8] For it
shall come to pass in that
day, says Jehovah of hosts,
I will break his yoke from
your neck, and I will burst
your bonds. And strangers
shall not again lay service on
him, [9] but they shall
serve Jehovah their God,
and David their king, whom
I will raise up to them.

1
2
הַדָּבָר֙ אֲשֶׁ֣ר הָיָ֣ה אֶֽל־יִרְמְיָ֔הוּ מֵאֵ֥ת יְהוָ֖ה לֵאמֹֽר׃ כֹּֽה־

| Thus | ,saying | ,Jehovah | from | Jeremiah | to | came | that | The |
| | | | | | | | | word |

אָמַ֧ר יְהוָ֛ה אֱלֹהֵ֥י יִשְׂרָאֵ֖ל לֵאמֹ֑ר כְּתָב־לְךָ֗ אֵ֣ת כָּל־הַדְּבָרִ֛ים

| the | all | | for | Write | ,saying | ,Israel | the | Jehovah | says |
| words | | | yourself | | | | of God |

3
אֲשֶׁר־דִּבַּ֥רְתִּי אֵלֶ֖יךָ אֶל־סֵֽפֶר׃ כִּ֠י הִנֵּ֨ה יָמִ֤ים בָּאִים֙ נְאֻם־

| says | ,come | the | ,lo | ,For | .book a | in | you to | have I | that |
| | | days | | | | | | spoken |

יְהוָ֔ה וְשַׁבְתִּ֗י אֶת־שְׁב֛וּת עַמִּ֥י יִשְׂרָאֵ֖ל וִֽיהוּדָ֖ה אָמַ֣ר יְהוָ֑ה

| ,Jehovah says | Judah and | Israel | My | the | I that | ,Jehovah |
| | | | people of | captivity | turn will |

וַהֲשִׁבֹתִ֛ים אֶל־הָאָ֛רֶץ אֲשֶׁר־נָתַ֥תִּי לַאֲבוֹתָ֖ם וִֽירֵשֽׁוּהָ׃

| shall they and | their to | gave I | that | the | to bring will I and |
| .it possess | ,fathers | | | land | back them |

4
וְאֵ֣לֶּה הַדְּבָרִ֗ים אֲשֶׁ֨ר דִּבֶּ֧ר יְהוָ֛ה אֶל־יִשְׂרָאֵ֖ל וְאֶל־יְהוּדָֽה׃

| ,Judah | and | Israel | con- | Jehovah | spoke | that | the | And |
| | | | cerning | | | | words | (are) these |

5
כִּי־כֹה֙ אָמַ֣ר יְהוָ֔ה ק֥וֹל חֲרָדָ֖ה שָׁמָ֑עְנוּ פַּ֖חַד וְאֵ֥ין שָׁלֽוֹם׃

| .peace | and | of | have we | trembling | A | ,Jehovah says | thus for |
| | of not | ,dread | ;heard | | of sound |

6
שַׁאֲלוּ־נָ֣א וּרְא֔וּ אִם־יֹלֵ֖ד זָכָ֑ר מַדּוּעַ֩ רָאִ֨יתִי כָל־גֶּ֜בֶר יָדָ֤יו

| his | man every | I do | Why | a | giving is | if | and | now | Ask |
| hands (with) | | see | | ?male | birth | | ,see |

7
עַל־חֲלָצָיו֙ כַּיּ֣וֹלֵדָ֔ה וְנֶהֶפְכ֥וּ כָל־פָּנִ֖ים לְיֵרָק֑וֹן ה֖וֹי כִּ֥י

| For | !Alas | to | faces | all | have and | woman a | like | his | on |
| | | .paleness | | | turned | bearing | | ,loins |

גָד֥וֹל הַיּ֛וֹם הַה֖וּא מֵאַ֣יִן כָּמֹ֑הוּ וְעֵֽת־צָרָ֥ה הִיא֙ לְיַֽעֲקֹ֔ב וּמִמֶּ֖נָּה

| from but | for | it | distress | a and | like | because | ,that | day | (is) |
| it | ;Jacob | (is) | | of time | ,it | none (is) | | | great |

8
יִוָּשֵֽׁעַ׃ וְהָיָה֩ בַיּ֨וֹם הַה֜וּא נְאֻ֣ם ׀ יְהוָ֣ה צְבָא֗וֹת אֶשְׁבֹּ֤ר

| will I | ,hosts | Jehovah | says | ,that | day in | it And | will he |
| break | of | | | | | be will | saved be |

עֻלּוֹ֙ מֵעַ֣ל צַוָּארֶ֔ךָ וּמוֹסְרוֹתֶ֖יךָ אֲנַתֵּ֑ק וְלֹא־יַֽעַבְדוּ־ב֥וֹ ע֖וֹד

| again | him will | And | will I | your and | your | from | his |
| | enslave not | .up tear | bonds | | ,neck | upon | yoke |

9
זָרִֽים׃ וְעָבְד֕וּ אֵ֖ת יְהוָ֣ה אֱלֹהֵיהֶ֑ם וְאֵת֙ דָּוִ֣ד מַלְכָּ֔ם אֲשֶׁ֥ר

| whom | their | David | and | their | Jehovah | they but | ,strangers |
| | ,king | | | God | | serve shall |

[10] Now you, do not fear, O My servant Jacob, says Jehovah; do not be terrified, O Israel; for, lo, I will save you from afar, and your seed from the land of their captivity. And Jacob shall return and shall be in rest and be quiet, and no one shall make (him) afraid. [11] For I (am) with you, says Jehovah, to save you. Though I make a full end among all nations where I have scattered you, yet I will not make a full end with you; but I will correct you justly, and I will not leave you unpunished. [12] For thus says Jehovah, Your break cannot be cured, your wound is grievous. [13] There is none to plead your cause, for (your) ulcer there is (no) healing medicines for you. [14] All your lovers have forgotten you; they do not seek you. For I have wounded you with the wound of an enemy, with the chastisement of a cruel one, for the greatness of your iniquity; your sins are many. [15] Why do you cry for your affliction? Your sorrow cannot be cured because of the greatness of your iniquity. Your sins are many; (so) I have done these things to you. [16] Therefore all those who devour you shall be devoured; and all your enemies, every one of them, shall go into captivity. And they who rob you shall be (given) to plunder, and I will strip all who strip you. [17] For I will give health back to you, and I will heal you of your wounds, says Jehovah; because they called you, Outcast, (saying), This (is) Zion; no one is seeking for her.

[18] Thus says Jehovah: Behold, I will turn the captivity of Jacob's tents and will have mercy on his dwelling places. And the city shall be built on her ruin-heap, and the palace shall remain on its own place. [19] And out of them shall come thanksgiving, and the voice of those

10 אָקִים לָהֶם׃ וְאַתָּה אַל־תִּירָא עַבְדִּי יַעֲקֹב נְאֻם־יְהוָה
;Jehovah says ,Jacob My O do not Now for will I
servant ,fear ,you them up raise

וְאַל־תֵּחַת יִשְׂרָאֵל כִּי הִנְנִי מוֹשִׁיעֲךָ מֵרָחוֹק וְאֶת־זַרְעֲךָ
your and from save will I ,lo for ;Israel O be do not
seed ,afar you terrified

מֵאֶרֶץ שִׁבְיָם וְשָׁב יַעֲקֹב וְשָׁקַט וְשַׁאֲנַן וְאֵין מַחֲרִיד׃
make will and be and have and Jacob will And their the from
.afraid (him) none untroubled quiet return .captivity of land

11 כִּי־אִתְּךָ אֲנִי נְאֻם־יְהוָה לְהוֹשִׁיעֶךָ כִּי אֶעֱשֶׂה כָלָה בְּכָל־
among a will I for ,you save to ,Jehovah says I with For
all destruction make ,(am) you

הַגּוֹיִם ׀ אֲשֶׁר הֲפִצוֹתִיךָ שָּׁם אַךְ אֹתְךָ לֹא־אֶעֱשֶׂה כָלָה
complete a will I not with only there have I where the
,destruction make you you scattered nations

12 וְיִסַּרְתִּיךָ לַמִּשְׁפָּט וְנַקֵּה לֹא אֲנַקֶּךָּ׃ כִּי כֹה אָמַר
says thus For leave will I not and justly will I but
.unpunished you entirely you chasten

13 יְהוָה אָנוּשׁ לְשִׁבְרֵךְ נַחְלָה מַכָּתֵךְ׃ אֵין־דָּן דִּינֵךְ לְמָזוֹר
(your) for your to There your is Your is Jehovah
ulcer ,cause plead none is .wound grievous ,fracture incurable

14 רְפֻאוֹת תְּעָלָה אֵין לָךְ׃ כָּל־מְאַהֲבַיִךְ שְׁכֵחוּךְ אוֹתָךְ לֹא
not you for- have your All for there healing (no)
;you gotten lovers .you is ,medicines

יִדְרֹשׁוּ כִּי מַכַּת אוֹיֵב הִכִּיתִיךְ מוּסַר אַכְזָרִי עַל רֹב עֲוֺנֵךְ
your great- for foe a chas- the have I an the (with) for do they
;iniquity's ness of tisement ,you struck enemy of wound ,seek

15 עָצְמוּ חַטֹּאתָיִךְ׃ מַה־תִּזְעַק עַל־שִׁבְרֵךְ אָנוּשׁ מַכְאֹבֵךְ
your is your for you do Why your are
pain incurable ,crushing out cry .sins many

16 עַל ׀ רֹב עֲוֺנֵךְ עָצְמוּ חַטֹּאתַיִךְ עָשִׂיתִי אֵלֶּה לָךְ׃ לָכֵן
Therefore to these I (so) your are in- your the for
.you things done have sins many ,iquity of greatness

כָּל־אֹכְלַיִךְ יֵאָכֵלוּ וְכָל־צָרַיִךְ כֻּלָּם בַּשְּׁבִי יֵלֵכוּ וְהָיוּ שֹׁאסַיִךְ
your will And shall into of all your and be will who those all
plunderers be .go captivity ,them ,foes all ;devoured you devour

17 לִמְשִׁסָּה וְכָל־בֹּזְזַיִךְ אֶתֵּן לָבַז׃ כִּי אַעֲלֶה אֲרֻכָה לָךְ
for healing will I For for will I your and for
you up bring .spoil give spoilers all ,plunder

וּמִמַּכּוֹתַיִךְ אֶרְפָּאֵךְ נְאֻם־יְהוָה כִּי נִדָּחָה קָרְאוּ לָךְ צִיּוֹן
Zion you they an for ;Jehovah says will I from and
,(saying) called outcast you heal wounds your

18 הִיא דֹּרֵשׁ אֵין לָהּ׃ כֹּה ׀ אָמַר יְהוָה הִנְנִי־שָׁב
will ,Behold ,Jehovah says Thus .her no is This
turn I one seeking ,(is)

שְׁבוּת אָהֳלֵי יַעֲקוֹב וּמִשְׁכְּנֹתָיו אֲרַחֵם וְנִבְנְתָה עִיר עַל־
on the shall And have will I dwell- his and Jacob's tents cap- the
city built be .on mercy places ing of tivity

19 תִּלָּהּ וְאַרְמוֹן עַל־מִשְׁפָּטוֹ יֵשֵׁב׃ וְיָצָא מֵהֶם תּוֹדָה וְקוֹל
the and thanks- from shall And shall own its on its and its
of voice ,giving them forth go .remain place palace ruin

who are merry. And I will multiply them, and they shall not be few; I will also honor them, and they shall not be small. [20] Also his sons shall be as before, and his assembly shall be established before Me, and I will punish all who oppress them. [21] And his leader shall be from him, and his ruler shall come from among him. And I will cause him to draw near, and he shall approach Me. For who (is) he who pledged his heart to come near to Me, says Jehovah? [22] And you shall be My people, and I will be your God. [23] Behold, the tempest of Jehovah; fury goes forth; a sweeping tempest; it shall swirl on the head of the wicked. [24] The fierce anger of Jehovah shall not turn back until He has finished and until He has fulfilled the intentions of His heart. In latter days you will understand it.

CHAPTER 31

[1] At that time, says Jehovah, I will be the God of all the families of Israel, and they shall be My people. [2] Thus says Jehovah, The people, survivors of the sword, have found grace in the wilderness; Israel, when I go to cause him to rest. [3] Jehovah has appeared to me from far away, (saying), Yes, I have loved you with an everlasting love! Therefore with loving-kindness I have drawn you. [4] Again I will build you, and you shall be built again, O virgin of Israel. You shall again put on your tambourines and go forth in the dance of the merry ones. [5] You shall yet plant vines on the mountains of Samaria; the planters shall plant and shall treat (them) as common. [6] For there shall be a day when the watchmen on Mount Ephraim shall call out, Arise, and let us go up

מְשַׂחֲקִים וְהִרְבִּתִים וְלֹא יִמְעָטוּ וְהִכְבַּדְתִּים וְלֹא יִצְעָרוּ׃
will they and will I also will they and will I And who those
.light be not ,them honor ;few be not ,them multiply .merry are

20 וְהָיוּ בָנָיו כְּקֶדֶם וַעֲדָתוֹ לְפָנַי תִּכּוֹן וּפָקַדְתִּי עַל כָּל־
all will I and be will before his and as his And
punish ,established Me assembly ,before sons be will

21 לֹחֲצָיו׃ וְהָיָה אַדִּירוֹ מִמֶּנּוּ וּמֹשְׁלוֹ מִקִּרְבּוֹ יֵצֵא וְהִקְרַבְתִּיו
will I And come will his from his and from his And his
near him bring .forth midst ruler ,him leader be will .oppressors

וְנִגַּשׁ אֵלָי כִּי מִי הוּא־זֶה עָרַב אֶת־לִבּוֹ לָגֶשֶׁת אֵלַי נְאֻם־
says to come to his gives who he who For .Me he and
,Me near heart pledge in (is) approach will

22 יְהוָה׃ וִהְיִיתֶם לִי לְעָם וְאָנֹכִי אֶהְיֶה לָכֶם לֵאלֹהִים׃
.God for you to be will I and a for to you And ?Jehovah
,people Me be will

23 הִנֵּה ׀ סַעֲרַת יְהוָה חֵמָה יָצְאָה סַעַר מִתְגּוֹרֵר עַל רֹאשׁ
the on ;sweeping a goes wrath ;Jehovah the ,Behold
of head tempest ;forth of tempest

24 רְשָׁעִים יָחוּל׃ לֹא יָשׁוּב חֲרוֹן אַף־יְהוָה עַד־עֲשֹׂתוֹ וְעַד־
and has He until Jeho- anger The turn will not will it the
until ,performed ,vah's of glow back .swirl wicked

25 הֲקִימוֹ מְזִמּוֹת לִבּוֹ בְּאַחֲרִית הַיָּמִים תִּתְבּוֹנְנוּ בָהּ׃ בָּעֵת
At .it will you the in His the has He
time understand days latter ;heart of plans established

הַהִיא נְאֻם־יְהוָה אֶהְיֶה לֵאלֹהִים לְכֹל מִשְׁפְּחוֹת יִשְׂרָאֵל
,Israel the all to God for will I ,Jehovah says that
of families be

וְהֵמָּה יִהְיוּ־לִי לְעָם׃
a for to will and
.people Me be they

CAP. XXXI לא

CHAPTER 31

1 כֹּה אָמַר יְהוָה מָצָא חֵן בַּמִּדְבָּר עַם שְׂרִידֵי חָרֶב הָלוֹךְ
I when the sur- the the the in grace have ,Jehovah says Thus
go will ,sword of vivors ,people wilderness found

2 לְהַרְגִּיעוֹ יִשְׂרָאֵל׃ מֵרָחוֹק יְהוָה נִרְאָה לִי וְאַהֲבַת עוֹלָם
ever- with ;yea to has Jehovah from .Israel give to
lasting love an ,me appeared away far ,rest him

3 אֲהַבְתִּיךְ עַל־כֵּן מְשַׁכְתִּיךְ חָסֶד׃ עוֹד אֶבְנֵךְ וְנִבְנֵית
will you and will I Again loving- drawn have I therefore have I
,rebuilt be ,you build .kindness with you ,you loved

בְּתוּלַת יִשְׂרָאֵל עוֹד תַּעְדִּי תֻפַּיִךְ וְיָצָאת בִּמְחוֹל מְשַׂחֲקִים׃
who those the in go and your will You again .Israel virgin O
.merry make of dance forth tambourines on put of

4 עוֹד תִּטְּעִי כְרָמִים בְּהָרֵי שֹׁמְרוֹן נָטְעוּ נֹטְעִים וְחִלֵּלוּ׃
treat and the will ;Samaria the on vineyards will you again
.common as ,planters plant of mountains plant

5 כִּי יֶשׁ־יוֹם קָרְאוּ נֹצְרִים בְּהַר אֶפְרַיִם קוּמוּ וְנַעֲלֶה צִיּוֹן
Zion let and ,Arise ,Ephraim on the shall (when) a there For
to up go Mount watchmen out call day be will

to Zion to Jehovah our God! [7] For thus says Jehovah, Sing with gladness for Jacob, and shout among the chief of the nations. Cry out, give praise and say, O Jehovah, save Your people, the remnant of Israel. [8] Behold, I will bring them from the north country and gather them from the corners of the earth; among them (are) the blind and the lame, the one with child together (with) the one travailing; a great company shall return here. [9] They shall come with weeping; and with prayers I will lead them; I will cause them to walk by rivers of waters, in a right way; they will not stumble in it; for I am a father to Israel, and Ephraim he (is) My first-born.

[10] Hear the word of Jehovah, O nations, and declare in the coasts from far away. And say, He who scattered Israel will gather him and keep him, as a shepherd his flock. [11] For Jehovah has redeemed Jacob, and ransomed him from the hand of him who was stronger than he. [12] And they shall come and sing in the height of Zion and be glowing over the goodness of Jehovah, for grain and for wine, and for oil, and for the sons of the flock and the herd. And their life shall be as a watered garden; and they shall not pine away any more at all. [13] Then shall the virgin rejoice in the dance, both young men and elders together. For I will turn their mourning into joy, and will comfort them and make them rejoice from their sorrow. [14] And I will fill the soul of the priests with fatness, and My people shall be satisfied with My goodness, says Jehovah.

[15] Thus says Jehovah, A voice was heard in Ramah, wailing (and) bitter weeping; Rachel, weeping for her children, and she

6 אל־יהוה אלהינו׃ כי־כה ׀ אמר יהוה רנו ליעקב
for Sing ,Jehovah says thus For our Jehovah to
Jacob !God

שמחה וצהלו בראש הגוים השמיעו הללו ואמרו הושע
,Save ,say and give ,proclaim the the among and (with)
praise ;nations of chief shout ,gladness

7 יהוה את־עמך את שארית ישראל׃ הנני מביא אותם
them will I ,Behold .Israel the Your O
bring of remnant ,people Jehovah

מארץ צפון וקבצתים מירכתי־ארץ בם עור ופסח הרה
one the the and the among the re- the from gather and north the from
pregnant ,lame blind them ,earth of parts mote them country

8 וילדת יחדו קהל גדול ישובו הנה׃ בבכי יבאו ובתחנונים
with and shall they With .here shall great a along tra- the and
supplications ;come weeping return company ;(with) one vailing

אובילם אוליכם אל־נחלי מים בדרך ישר לא יכשלו
will they not ;right a in ,water streams by make will I will I
stumble way of walk them ;them lead

9 בה כי־הייתי לישראל לאב ואפרים בכרי הוא׃ שמעו
Hear .(is) he My and ,father a Israel to am I for ;it on
firstborn Ephraim

דבר־יהוה גוים והגידו באיים ממרחק ואמרו מזרה
who He ,say And far from the in declare and O ,Jehovah the
scattered .away coasts (it) ,nations of word

10 ישראל יקבצנו ושמרו כרעה עדרו׃ כי־פדה יהוה את־
Jehovah has For his a as keep and gather will Israel
redeemed .flock shepherd ,him him

11 יעקב וגאלו מיד חזק ממנו׃ ובאו ורננו במרום־ציון
Zion the in and they And than one the from saved and Jacob
of height sing come will .he stronger of hand him

ונהרו אל־טוב יהוה על־דגן ועל־תירש ועל־יצהר ועל־
and ,oil and new and grain for ,Jehovah the over be and
for for ,wine for of goodness radiant

בני־צאן ובקר והיתה נפשם כגן רוה ולא־יוסיפו לדאבה
to will they and ;watered as their shall And the and the the
languish continue not garden a life be .herd flock of sons

12 עוד׃ אז תשמח בתולה במחול ובחרים וזקנים יחדו
to- and young both the in the shall Then any
.gether elders men ,dance virgin rejoice .more

והפכתי אבלם לששון ונחמתים ושמחתים מיגונם׃
their from make and will I and ,joy into their will I For
.trouble rejoice them them comfort mourning turn

13 ורויתי נפש הכהנים דשן ועמי את־טובי ישבעו נאם־
says be will My with My and ,fatness the the will I And
,satisfied goodness people priests of soul with fill

14 יהוה׃ כה ׀ אמר יהוה קול ברמה נשמע נהי בכי
and wailing was in A ,Jehovah says Thus .Jehovah
weeping ,heard Ramah voice

תמרורים רחל מבכה על־בניה מאנה להנחם על־בניה
her for be to she her for weeping ,Rachel ;bitter
children comforted refuses ,children

would not be comforted for her children, because they are not. [6] Thus says Jehovah: Hold back your voice from weeping and your eyes from tears. For there will be a reward for your work, says Jehovah; and they shall come again from the land of the enemy. [17] And there is hope for your future, says Jehovah, that (your) sons will come again to their own border.

[18] I have surely heard Ephraim mourning to himself, (saying), You have chastised me, and I was chastised, as a bull not broken in; turn me, and I shall be turned; for You (are) Jehovah my God. [19] For after I had turned away, I repented; and after I was taught, I struck on (my) thigh. I was ashamed, yea, I even blushed, because I bore the disgrace of my youth. [20] Is Ephraim My dear son? Or (is he) a delightful child? For as often as I spoke against him, I earnestly remember him still; therefore My bowels groan for him; I will surely have pity on him, says Jehovah. [21] Set up roadmarks for yourself, make sign posts for yourself. Set your heart toward the highway, (even) the way you went. Turn again, O virgin of Israel, turn again to these your cities.

[22] Until when will you turn to and fro, O backsliding daughter? For Jehovah has created a new thing in the land: a woman shall enclose a man.

[23] Thus says Jehovah of hosts, the God of Israel: Again they will speak this word in the land of Judah and in the cities of it, when I turn again their captivity; Jehovah bless you, O home of righteousness, O mountain of holiness. [24] And Judah and all its cities shall live in it together, the farmers and the shepherds. [25] For I have satisfied the weary soul, and I have

15 כִּי אֵינֶנּוּ׃ כֹּה ׀ אָמַר יְהוָֹה מִנְעִי קוֹלֵךְ מִבֶּכִי וְעֵינַיִךְ
your and from your Hold ,Jehovah says Thus they for
eyes weeping voice back .not are

מִדִּמְעָה כִּי יֵשׁ שָׂכָר לִפְעֻלָּתֵךְ נְאֻם־יְהוָֹה וְשָׁבוּ מֵאֶרֶץ
the from they and ;Jehovah says your for a there For from
of land return will ,work reward be will .tears

16 אוֹיֵב׃ וְיֵשׁ־תִּקְוָה לְאַחֲרִיתֵךְ נְאֻם־יְהוָֹה וְשָׁבוּ בָנִים
(your) will that ,Jehovah says your for hope And the
sons return ,future is there .enemy

17 לִגְבוּלָם׃ שָׁמוֹעַ שָׁמַעְתִּי אֶפְרַיִם מִתְנוֹדֵד יִסַּרְתַּנִי וָאִוָּסֵר
was I and chas- You bemoaning Ephraim have I Surely their to
chastised ,me tened :himself heard .territory

כְּעֵגֶל לֹא לֻמָּד הֲשִׁבֵנִי וְאָשׁוּבָה כִּי אַתָּה יְהוָֹה אֱלֹהָי׃
My Jehovah You for will I and me turn ;trained not a as
.God (are) ;turned be ,back calf bull

18 כִּי־אַחֲרֵי שׁוּבִי נִחַמְתִּי וְאַחֲרֵי הִוָּדְעִי סָפַקְתִּי עַל־יָרֵךְ
(my) on slapped I was I and I turned I after For
.thigh ,instructed after ;repented ,away

19 בֹּשְׁתִּי וְגַם־נִכְלַמְתִּי כִּי נָשָׂאתִי חֶרְפַּת נְעוּרָי׃ הֲבֵן יַקִּיר
dear (Is) my re- the bore I for ,humiliated and was I
son .youth of proach also ,ashamed

לִי אֶפְרַיִם אִם יֶלֶד שַׁעֲשֻׁעִים כִּי־מִדֵּי דַבְּרִי בּוֹ זָכֹר
surely against I as For ?delight child a Or ?Ephraim My
,him spoke as often of (he is)

אֶזְכְּרֶנּוּ עוֹד עַל־כֵּן הָמוּ מֵעַי לוֹ רַחֵם אֲרַחֲמֶנּוּ נְאֻם־
says have will I surely for My groan therefore ;still remem- I
,him on pity ;him bowels him ber

20 יְהוָֹה׃ הַצִּיבִי לָךְ צִיֻּנִים שִׂמִי לָךְ תַּמְרוּרִים שִׁתִי
Set .posts sign for make road- for up Set .Jehovah
yourself ,marks yourself

לִבֵּךְ לַמְסִלָּה דֶּרֶךְ הָלָכְתִּי שׁוּבִי בְּתוּלַת יִשְׂרָאֵל שֻׁבִי
return ,Israel O ,Return you way the the to your
of virgin .went ,highway heart

21 אֶל־עָרַיִךְ אֵלֶּה׃ עַד־מָתַי תִּתְחַמָּקִין הַבַּת הַשּׁוֹבֵבָה כִּי־
For .faithless O turn you will when Until .these your to
daughter ,fro and to cities

בָרָא יְהוָֹה חֲדָשָׁה בָּאָרֶץ נְקֵבָה תְּסוֹבֵב גָּבֶר׃
.man a shall woman a the in new a Jehovah has
encircle ;land thing created

22 כֹּה־אָמַר יְהוָֹה צְבָאוֹת אֱלֹהֵי יִשְׂרָאֵל עוֹד יֹאמְרוּ אֶת־
will they Again :Israel the ,hosts Jehovah says Thus
speak of God of

הַדָּבָר הַזֶּה בְּאֶרֶץ יְהוּדָה וּבְעָרָיו בְּשׁוּבִי אֶת־שְׁבוּתָם
their I when in and Judah the in this word
;captivity turn ,cities its of land

23 יְבָרֶכְךָ יְהוָֹה נְוֵה־צֶדֶק הַר הַקֹּדֶשׁ׃ וְיָשְׁבוּ בָהּ יְהוּדָה
Judah it in Then .holiness mount O of abode O,Jehovah bless
dwell will of righteousness you

24 וְכָל־עָרָיו יַחְדָּו אִכָּרִים וְנָסְעוּ בַּעֵדֶר׃ כִּי הִרְוֵיתִי נֶפֶשׁ
the satisfy I For with they and the ,together its and
soul .flocks travel who farmers cities all

filled every sorrowful soul. [26] Upon this I awoke and looked up; and my sleep was sweet to me.

[27] Behold, the days come, says Jehovah, that I will sow the house of Israel and the house of Judah with the seed of man and the seed of beast. [28] And it shall come to pass, as I have watched over them to pluck up, and to break down, and to throw down, and to destroy, and to afflict; so I will watch over them to build, and to plant, says Jehovah. [29] In those days they shall not say any more, The fathers have eaten sour grapes and the children's teeth are dull. [30] But everyone shall die for his own iniquity. Every man who eats the sour grapes, his teeth shall be dull.

[31] Behold, the days come, says Jehovah, that I will cut a new covenant with the house of Israel, and with the house of Judah, [32] not according to the covenant that I cut with their fathers in the day (that) I took (them) by their hand to bring them out of the land of Egypt — which covenant of Mine they broke, although I was a husband to them, says Jehovah — [33] but this (shall be) the covenant that I will cut with the house of Israel: After those days, says Jehovah, I will put My law in their inward parts and write it on their heart; and I will be their God, and they shall be My people. [34] And they shall no longer each one teach his neighbor and each one his brother, saying, Know Jehovah; for they shall all know Me, from the least of them to the greatest of them, says Jehovah. For I will forgive

25 עֲיֵפָה וְכָל־נֶפֶשׁ דָּאֲבָה מִלֵּאתִי׃ עַל־זֹאת הֱקִיצֹתִי וָאֶרְאֶה
and ,looked ,awoke I this Upon .fill I who languishes soul and every ,weary

26 וּשְׁנָתִי עָרְבָה לִּי׃ הִנֵּה יָמִים בָּאִים נְאֻם־יְהוָה
,Jehovah says ,come the days ,Behold .me to was sweet my and sleep

וְזָרַעְתִּי אֶת־בֵּית יִשְׂרָאֵל וְאֶת־בֵּית יְהוּדָה זֶרַע אָדָם וְזֶרַע
the and of seed man (with) of seed the Judah the and of house Israel the of house I when sow will

27 בְּהֵמָה׃ וְהָיָה כַּאֲשֶׁר שָׁקַדְתִּי עֲלֵיהֶם לִנְתוֹשׁ וְלִנְתוֹץ
to and down tear uproot to over them have I watched as it And be will .beast

וְלַהֲרֹס וּלְהַאֲבִיד וּלְהָרֵעַ כֵּן אֶשְׁקֹד עֲלֵיהֶם לִבְנוֹת וְלִנְטוֹעַ
to and ,plant ,build to over them will I watch so bring to and ;calamity to and ,destroy to and demolish

28 נְאֻם־יְהוָה׃ בַּיָּמִים הָהֵם לֹא־יֹאמְרוּ עוֹד אָבוֹת אָכְלוּ
have eaten the fathers any ,more they say shall not those days In .Jehovah says

29 בֹסֶר וְשִׁנֵּי בָנִים תִּקְהֶינָה׃ כִּי אִם־אִישׁ בַּעֲוֺנוֹ יָמוּת כָּל־
Every will die his in iniquity every man But .dull are the and children's teeth sour grapes

30 הָאָדָם הָאֹכֵל הַבֹּסֶר תִּקְהֶינָה שִׁנָּיו׃ הִנֵּה יָמִים בָּאִים
,come the days ,Behold his .teeth dull be will sour the ,grapes who eats man

נְאֻם־יְהוָה וְכָרַתִּי אֶת־בֵּית יִשְׂרָאֵל וְאֶת־בֵּית יְהוּדָה בְּרִית
a covenant ,Judah the of house and with Israel the of house with I that cut will ,Jehovah says

31 חֲדָשָׁה׃ לֹא כַבְּרִית אֲשֶׁר כָּרַתִּי אֶת־אֲבוֹתָם בְּיוֹם
the in day their fathers with cut I that the like covenant not ,new

הֶחֱזִיקִי בְיָדָם לְהוֹצִיאָם מֵאֶרֶץ מִצְרָיִם אֲשֶׁר־הֵמָּה הֵפֵרוּ
broke they which ,Egypt the from of land bring to out them their by hand took I them

32 אֶת־בְּרִיתִי וְאָנֹכִי בָּעַלְתִּי בָם נְאֻם־יְהוָה׃ כִּי זֹאת הַבְּרִית
the covenant this (is) But .Jehovah says to ,them a was husband although I My ,covenant

אֲשֶׁר אֶכְרֹת אֶת־בֵּית יִשְׂרָאֵל אַחֲרֵי הַיָּמִים הָהֵם נְאֻם־
says ,those days After :Israel the of house with cut will I that

יְהוָה נָתַתִּי אֶת־תּוֹרָתִי בְּקִרְבָּם וְעַל־לִבָּם אֶכְתֲּבֶנָּה וְהָיִיתִי
I and be will will I ;it write their heart and upon their in ,parts inward law My will I put ,Jehovah

33 לָהֶם לֵאלֹהִים וְהֵמָּה יִהְיוּ־לִי לְעָם׃ וְלֹא יְלַמְּדוּ עוֹד אִישׁ
each man again will they teach And not a for .people to Me will be they and ,God for to them

אֶת־רֵעֵהוּ וְאִישׁ אֶת־אָחִיו לֵאמֹר דְּעוּ אֶת־יְהוָה כִּי כוּלָּם
of all them for ;Jehovah Know ,saying his ,brother each and man his neighbor

יֵדְעוּ אוֹתִי לְמִקְּטַנָּם וְעַד־גְּדוֹלָם נְאֻם־יְהוָה כִּי אֶסְלַח
will I forgive For .Jehovah says their greatest even to their from least ,Me shall know

their iniquity, and I will remember their sins no more.

[35] Thus says Jehovah, who gives the sun for a light by day, the ordinances of the moon, and the stars for a light by night; who stirs up the sea so that its waves roar — Jehovah of hosts (is) His name — [36] if these ordinances depart from before Me, says Jehovah, the seed of Israel also shall cease from being a nation before Me forever. [37] Thus says Jehovah, If the heavens above can be measured, and the foundations of the earth below can be searched out, I will also cast off all the seed of Israel for all that they have done, says Jehovah.

[38] Behold, the days come, says Jehovah, that the city shall be built to Jehovah from the Tower of Hananeel to the Corner Gate. [39] And the measuring line shall yet go before it to the hill Gareb, and shall go around to Goath. [40] And the whole valley of the dead bodies, and the ashes, and all the fields to the brook Kidron, to the corner of the Horse Gate east, (shall be) holy to Jehovah. It shall not be torn up nor thrown down any more forever.

34 לַעֲוֺנָם וּלְחַטָּאתָם לֹא אֶזְכָּר־עוֹד׃ כֹּה ׀ אָמַר יְהוָה
,Jehovah says Thus .again will I remember not their sins and their ,iniquity

נֹתֵן שֶׁמֶשׁ לְאוֹר יוֹמָם חֻקֹּת יָרֵחַ וְכוֹכָבִים לְאוֹר לָיְלָה
;night by a for light the stars and the ,moon the of laws day by a for light the sun who gives

35 רֹגַע הַיָּם וַיֶּהֱמוּ גַלָּיו יְהוָה צְבָאוֹת שְׁמוֹ׃ אִם־יָמֻשׁוּ
depart If His .name (is) hosts Jehovah of its —waves that so roar the sea who up stirs

הַחֻקִּים הָאֵלֶּה מִלְּפָנַי נְאֻם־יְהוָה גַּם זֶרַע יִשְׂרָאֵל יִשְׁבְּתוּ
shall cease Israel the of seed also ,Jehovah says from Me before these ordinances

36 מִהְיוֹת גּוֹי לְפָנַי כָּל־הַיָּמִים׃ כֹּה ׀ אָמַר יְהוָה אִם־
If ,Jehovah says Thus .days the all before Me a nation from being

יִמַּדּוּ שָׁמַיִם מִלְמַעְלָה וְיֵחָקְרוּ מוֹסְדֵי־אֶרֶץ לְמָטָּה גַּם־
also ,below the earth foun- of dations the out searched be can and ,above the heavens be can measured

אֲנִי אֶמְאַס בְּכָל־זֶרַע יִשְׂרָאֵל עַל־כָּל־אֲשֶׁר עָשׂוּ נְאֻם־
says have they ,done that all for Israel the of seed all will off cast I

37 יְהוָה׃ הִנֵּה יָמִים נְאֻם־יְהוָה וְנִבְנְתָה הָעִיר
the city will that built be Jehovah says,come the days ,Behold .Jehovah

38 לַיהוָה מִמִּגְדַּל חֲנַנְאֵל עַד־שַׁעַר הַפִּנָּה׃ וְיָצָא עוֹד קָוֵה
line yet will And out go the .Corner Gate to Hananeel the from of Tower to Jehovah

39 הַמִּדָּה נֶגְדּוֹ עַל גִּבְעַת גָּרֵב וְנָסַב גֹּעָתָה׃ וְכָל־הָעֵמֶק
the of valley And whole toward .Goath turn and Gareb hill the to before it the measuring

הַפְּגָרִים ׀ וְהַדֶּשֶׁן וְכָל־הַשְּׁרֵמוֹת עַד־נַחַל קִדְרוֹן עַד־פִּנַּת
the of corner to ,Kidron the brook to the fields and all the and ,ashes dead the ,bodies

שַׁעַר הַסּוּסִים מִזְרָחָה קֹדֶשׁ לַיהוָה לֹא־יִנָּתֵשׁ וְלֹא־יֵהָרֵס
demol- ished nor be will up torn It not to .Jehovah (be will) holy ,east the Horse Gate

עוֹד לְעוֹלָם׃
.forever any more

CAP. XXXII לב

CHAPTER 32

CHAPTER 32

[1] The word that came to Jeremiah from Jehovah in the tenth year of Zedekiah king of Judah, which (was) the eighteenth year of Nebuchadnezzar. [2] For then the king of Babylon's army was besieging Jerusalem. And Jeremiah the

1 הַדָּבָר אֲשֶׁר הָיָה אֶל־יִרְמְיָהוּ מֵאֵת יְהוָה בַּשָּׁנַת הָעֲשִׂרִית
tenth the in year Jehovah from Jeremiah to came that The word

לְצִדְקִיָּהוּ מֶלֶךְ יְהוּדָה הִיא הַשָּׁנָה שְׁמֹנֶה־עֶשְׂרֵה שָׁנָה
year eighteenth ,year the which (was) ,Judah king of of Zedekiah

2 לִנְבוּכַדְרֶאצַּר׃ וְאָז חֵיל מֶלֶךְ בָּבֶל צָרִים עַל־יְרוּשָׁלִָם
.Jerusalem was besieging Babylon the of king the of army For then of .Nebuchadnezzar

prophet was shut up in the court of the guard, which (was) in the king of Judah's house. [3] For Zedekiah king of Judah had shut him up, saying, Why do you prophesy and say, Thus says Jehovah, Behold, I will give this city into the hand of the king of Babylon, and he will take it; [4] and Zedekiah king of Judah shall not escape out of the hand of the Chaldeans, but shall surely be delivered into the hand of the king of Babylon, and he will speak with him mouth to mouth, and with his eyes will see his eyes; [5] and he shall lead Zedekiah into Babylon, and there he shall be until I visit him, says Jehovah – though you fight with the Chaldeans, you shall not succeed.

[6] And Jeremiah said, The word of Jehovah came to me, saying, [7] Behold, Hanameel the son of Shallum your uncle shall come to you, saying, Buy for yourself my field which (is) in Anathoth; for the right to redeem it (is) yours, to buy (it). [8] So Hanameel my uncle's son came to me in the court of the guard, according to the word of Jehovah, and said to me, Please buy my field which (is) in Anathoth, which (is) in the land of Benjamin; for the right of inheritance (is) yours, and the right to redeem (is) yours. Buy (it) for yourself, Then I knew that this (was) the word of Jehovah. [9] And I bought the field that (was) in Anathoth, from my nephew Hanameel, and weighed him the silver, seventeen shekels of silver. [10] And I wrote it in the book, and sealed (it), and called witnesses, and

וירמיהו הנביא היה כלוא בחצר המטרה אשר בית־
the (in) which the the in up shut was the And
of house (was) ,guard of court prophet Jeremiah

3 מלך יהודה׃ אשר כלאו צדקיהו מלך־יהודה לאמר
,saying ,Judah king Zedekiah shut had For .Judah the
of up him of king

מדוע אתה נבא לאמר כה אמר יהוה הנני נתן את־
will ,Behold ,Jehovah says Thus ,saying do you Why
give I ,prophesy

4 העיר הזאת ביד מלך־בבל ולכדה׃ וצדקיהו מלך
king and will he and ,Babylon the the into this city
of Zedekiah ;it take of king of hand

יהודה לא ימלט מיד הכשדים כי־הנתן ינתן ביד מלך־
the the into will surely but the the from shall not Judah
of king of hand given be ,Chaldeans of hand escape

5 בבל ודבר־פיו עם־פיו ועיניו את־עינו תראינה׃ ובבל
into and ;see and his with his and his with his he and ,Babylon
Babylon eyes eyes ,mouth mouth speak will

יולך את־צדקיהו ושם יהיה עד־פקדי אתו נאם־יהוה
;Jehovah says ,him visit I until shall he and ,Zedekiah will he
be there lead

6 כי תלחמו את־הכשדים לא תצליחו׃ ויאמר
said And shall you not the with you though
.suceed Chaldeans fight

7 ירמיהו היה דבר־יהוה אלי לאמר׃ הנה חנמאל בן
the Hanameel ,Behold ,saying ,me to Jehovah The came ,Jeremiah
of son of word

שלם דדך בא אליך לאמר קנה לך את־שדי אשר
which my for Buy ,saying ,you to shall your Shallum
(is) field yourself come uncle

8 בענתות כי לך משפט הגאלה לקנות׃ ויבא אלי חנמאל
Hanameel to So buy to ,redemption the (is) to for in
me came .(it) of right you ;Anathoth

בן־דדי כדבר יהוה אל־חצר המטרה ויאמר אלי קנה
Buy ,me to said and ,guard the the to ,Jehovah's according of Sons
of court word to uncle my

נא את־שדי אשר־בענתות אשר ׀ בארץ בנימין כי לך
to for ,Benjamin the in which in which my please
you of land (is) ,Anathoth (is) field

משפט הירשה ולך הגאלה קנה־לך ואדע כי דבר
the that I Then for Buy right the to and ,possession the (is)
of word knew .yourself (it) .redemption of you of right

9 יהוה הוא׃ ואקנה את־השדה מאת חנמאל בן־דדי
my son Hanameel from the I And that Jehovah
uncle's field bought .(was)

אשר בענתות ואשקלה־לו את־הכסף שבעה שקלים
shekels seven the for and in that
,silver him weighed ,Anathoth (was)

10 ועשרה הכסף׃ ואכתב בספר ואחתם ואעד עדים
,witnesses and sealed and the in I And .silver (of) ten and
called .(it) book (it) wrote

weighed the silver on the scales. [11] So I took the book of the purchase, that which was sealed according to the law and the statutes, and the open copy. [12] And I gave the book of the purchase to Baruch the son of Neriah, the son of Maaseiah, before the eyes of my nephew Hanameel, and before the eyes of the witnesses who wrote in the book of the purchase, before the eyes of all the Jews who sat in the court of the guard.

[13] And I commanded Baruch before their eyes, saying, [14] Thus says Jehovah of hosts, the God of Israel: Take these books, this book of this purchase, both the sealed (book) and the book that is open, and put them in an earthen vessel so that they may last many days. [15] For thus says Jehovah of hosts, the God of Israel: Houses and fields and vineyards will be bought again in this land.

[16] And after I had delivered the book of the purchase to Baruch the son of Neriah, I prayed to Jehovah, saying, [17] Ah, Lord Jehovah! You have made the heavens and the earth by Your great power and Your stretched out arm; there is nothing too hard for You; [18] who exercises loving-kindness to thousands, and repays the iniquity of the fathers into the bosom of their children after them. The great, the mighty God, Jehovah of hosts, (is) His name, [19] great in wisdom and mighty in work; for Your eyes are open on all the ways of the sons of men, to

11 וָאֶשְׁקֹל הַכֶּסֶף בְּמֹאזְנָיִם׃ וָאֶקַּח אֶת־סֵפֶר הַמִּקְנָה אֶת־
the the I So the on the did
,purchase of document took .scales silver weighed

12 הֶחָתוּם הַמִּצְוָה וְהַחֻקִּים וְאֶת־הַגָּלוּי׃ וָאֶתֵּן אֶת־הַסֵּפֶר
the I And open the and the and (containing) which that
of document gave .copy statutes command the sealed was

הַמִּקְנָה אֶל־בָּרוּךְ בֶּן־נֵרִיָּה בֶּן־מַחְסֵיָה לְעֵינֵי חֲנַמְאֵל דֹּדִי
my ,Hanameel before ,Maaseiah the ,Neriah the Baruch to the
(son) uncle's of eyes the of son of son purchase

וּלְעֵינֵי הָעֵדִים הַכֹּתְבִים בְּסֵפֶר הַמִּקְנָה לְעֵינֵי כָּל־הַיְּהוּדִים
the all the before the the in who the before and
Jews of eyes ,purchase of document wrote witnesses of eyes the

13 הַיֹּשְׁבִים בַּחֲצַר הַמַּטָּרָה׃ וָאֲצַוֶּה אֶת־בָּרוּךְ לְעֵינֵיהֶם
before Baruch I And .guard the the in sat who
eyes their commanded of court

14 לֵאמֹר׃ כֹּה־אָמַר יְהוָה צְבָאוֹת אֱלֹהֵי יִשְׂרָאֵל לָקוֹחַ אֶת־
Take :Israel the hosts Jehovah says Thus ,saying
of God of

הַסְּפָרִים הָאֵלֶּה אֵת סֵפֶר הַמִּקְנָה הַזֶּה וְאֵת הֶחָתוּם וְאֵת
and the both ,this purchase the ,these documents
one sealed of document

סֵפֶר הַגָּלוּי הַזֶּה וּנְתַתָּם בִּכְלִי־חָרֶשׂ לְמַעַן יַעַמְדוּ יָמִים
days may they that so an in put and this open docu-
stand earthen vessel them ment

15 רַבִּים׃ כִּי כֹה אָמַר יְהוָה צְבָאוֹת אֱלֹהֵי יִשְׂרָאֵל
:Israel the ,hosts Jehovah says thus For .many
of God of

עוֹד יִקָּנוּ בָתִּים וְשָׂדוֹת וּכְרָמִים בָּאָרֶץ הַזֹּאת׃
.this in and and houses be will Again
land vineyards fields bought

16 וָאֶתְפַּלֵּל אֶל־יְהוָה אַחֲרֵי תִתִּי אֶת־סֵפֶר הַמִּקְנָה אֶל־בָּרוּךְ
Baruch to the the gave I after Jehovah to I And
purchase of document prayed

17 בֶּן־נֵרִיָּה לֵאמֹר׃ אֲהָהּ אֲדֹנָי יְהוִה הִנֵּה ׀ אַתָּה עָשִׂיתָ
have You ,Behold !Jehovah Lord Ah ,saying ,Neriah the
made of son

אֶת־הַשָּׁמַיִם וְאֶת־הָאָרֶץ בְּכֹחֲךָ הַגָּדוֹל וּבִזְרֹעֲךָ הַנְּטוּיָה
stretched Your and great Your by the and the
;out arm power earth heavens

18 לֹא־יִפָּלֵא מִמְּךָ כָּל־דָּבָר׃ עֹשֶׂה חֶסֶד לַאֲלָפִים וּמְשַׁלֵּם
and for loving who ,thing any for too is not
repays ,thousands kindness exercises You difficult

עֲוֺן אָבוֹת אֶל־חֵיק בְּנֵיהֶם אַחֲרֵיהֶם הָאֵל הַגָּדוֹל הַגִּבּוֹר
,mighty ,great the after their the into the ini- the
God ,them children of bosom fathers of quity

19 יְהוָה צְבָאוֹת שְׁמוֹ׃ גְּדֹל הָעֵצָה וְרַב הָעֲלִילִיָּה אֲשֶׁר
for ;deed and ,counsel great His hosts Jehovah
in great in ;name (is) of

עֵינֶיךָ פְּקֻחוֹת עַל־כָּל־דַּרְכֵי בְּנֵי אָדָם לָתֵת לְאִישׁ כִּדְרָכָיו
to according to give to ,men the the all on are Your
ways his man each of sons of ways open eyes

give to each one according to his ways and according to the fruit of his doings. [20] For You have set signs and wonders in the land of Egypt until this day, and in Israel, and among men; and You have made a name for Yourself, as at this day; [21] and have brought Your people Israel out of the land of Egypt with signs, and with wonders, and with a strong hand, and with a stretched out arm, and with great terror. [22] And You have given them this land, which You swore to their fathers to give to them, a land flowing with milk and honey. [23] And they came in and possessed it, but they did not obey Your voice, nor did they walk in Your law. They have not done all that You commanded them to do; therefore You have caused all this evil to come upon them. [24] Behold, the siege mounds have come to the city, to seize it; and the city is given into the hand of the Chaldeans who fight against it, because of the sword, and the famine, and the plague. And what You have spoken has happened; and, behold, You see. [25] And You have said to me, O Lord Jehovah, Buy for yourself the field with silver and call witnesses; for the city is given into the hand of the Chaldeans.

[26] Then the word of Jehovah came to Jeremiah, saying, [27] Behold, I (am) Jehovah, the God of all flesh. Is anything too difficult for Me? [28] Therefore thus says Jehovah: Behold, I will give this city into the hand of the Chaldeans, and into the hand of Nebuchadnezzar king of Babylon, and he shall take it. [29] And the Chaldeans who fight against this city shall enter and set this city

20 וּכִפְרִי מַעֲלָלָיו׃ אֲשֶׁר שַׂמְתָּ אֹתוֹת וּמֹפְתִים בְּאֶרֶץ מִצְרַיִם
Egypt the in and signs have You For his to according
of land wonders set .doings of fruit the

עַד־הַיּוֹם הַזֶּה וּבְיִשְׂרָאֵל וּבָאָדָם וַתַּעֲשֶׂה־לְּךָ שֵׁם כַּיּוֹם
at as ,name a for You and among and in and ,this day until
day Yourself made have ;men Israel

21 הַזֶּה׃ וַתֹּצֵא אֶת־עַמְּךָ אֶת־יִשְׂרָאֵל מֵאֶרֶץ מִצְרַיִם בְּאֹתוֹת
with ,Egypt the from Israel Your have and ,this
,signs of land people out brought

וּבְמוֹפְתִים וּבְיָד חֲזָקָה וּבְאֶזְרוֹעַ נְטוּיָה וּבְמוֹרָא גָּדוֹל׃
.great with and stretched with and ,strong with and with and
terror ,out arm an hand a ,wonders

22 וַתִּתֵּן לָהֶם אֶת־הָאָרֶץ הַזֹּאת אֲשֶׁר־נִשְׁבַּעְתָּ לַאֲבוֹתָם לָתֵת
give to their to You which ,this land to You And
fathers swore them gave

23 לָהֶם אֶרֶץ זָבַת חָלָב וּדְבָשׁ׃ וַיָּבֹאוּ וַיִּרְשׁוּ אֹתָהּ וְלֹא־
but ,it and they And and milk flowing a to
not possessed in came .honey with land ,them

שָׁמְעוּ בְקוֹלֶךָ וּבְתוֹרָתְךָ לֹא־הָלָכוּ אֵת כָּל־אֲשֶׁר צִוִּיתָה
You that all they not Your in and Your did they
commanded ;walk did law ,voice obey

לָהֶם לַעֲשׂוֹת לֹא עָשׂוּ וַתַּקְרֵא אֹתָם אֵת כָּל־הָרָעָה
evil all them You so have they not do to to
on come made ;done them

24 הַזֹּאת׃ הִנֵּה הַסֹּלְלוֹת בָּאוּ הָעִיר לְלָכְדָהּ וְהָעִיר נִתְּנָה
is the and capture to ,city the have siege the ,Behold .this
given city ,it to come mounds

בְּיַד הַכַּשְׂדִּים הַנִּלְחָמִים עָלֶיהָ מִפְּנֵי הַחֶרֶב וְהָרָעָב וְהַדָּבֶר
the and the and the because against who the the into
.plague ,famine sword of ,it fight Chaldeans of hand

25 וַאֲשֶׁר דִּבַּרְתָּ הָיָה וְהִנְּךָ רֹאֶה׃ וְאַתָּה אָמַרְתָּ אֵלַי אֲדֹנָי
O to said have You And see ,lo and has have You And
Lord ,Me .(it) You ,happened spoken what

יְהוִה קְנֵה־לְךָ הַשָּׂדֶה בַּכֶּסֶף וְהָעֵד עֵדִים וְהָעִיר נִתְּנָה
given is the for ,witnesses call and with the for Buy ,Jehovah
city silver field yourself

26 בְּיַד הַכַּשְׂדִּים׃ וַיְהִי דְּבַר־יְהוָה אֶל־יִרְמְיָהוּ לֵאמֹר׃
,saying ,Jeremiah to Jehovah the Then the the into
of word came .Chaldeans of hand

27 הִנֵּה אֲנִי יְהוָה אֱלֹהֵי כָּל־בָּשָׂר הֲמִמֶּנִּי יִפָּלֵא כָּל־דָּבָר׃
?thing any too Is for .flesh all the ,Jehovah I ,Behold
difficult Me of God (am)

28 לָכֵן כֹּה אָמַר יְהוָה הִנְנִי נֹתֵן אֶת־הָעִיר הַזֹּאת בְּיַד
the into this city will ,Behold :Jehovah says thus There-
of hand give I fore

29 הַכַּשְׂדִּים וּבְיַד נְבוּכַדְרֶאצַּר מֶלֶךְ־בָּבֶל וּלְכָדָהּ׃ וּבָאוּ
will And will he and ,Babylon king Nebuchadnezzar into and the
enter .it take will of of hand the ,Chaldeans

הַכַּשְׂדִּים הַנִּלְחָמִים עַל־הָעִיר הַזֹּאת וְהִצִּיתוּ אֶת־הָעִיר
city set and this city against fight who the
Chaldeans

(on) fire, and burn it with the houses on their roofs where they offered incense to Baal, and poured out drink offerings to other gods, to provoke Me to anger. [30] For the sons of Israel and the sons of Judah have only done evil in My eyes from their youth. For the sons of Israel have only provoked Me to anger with the work of their hands, says Jehovah. [31] For this city has been to Me (as) a cause of My anger and My fury from the day that they built it even to this day; that I should remove it from My face [32] because of all the evil of the sons of Israel and of the sons of Judah, which they have done to provoke Me to anger, they, their kings, their princes, their priests, and their prophets, and the men of Judah, and the inhabitants of Jerusalem. [33] And they have turned the back to Me, and not the face; though I taught them, rising up early and teaching, yet they have not listened to receive instruction. [34] But they set their idols in the house on which is called My name, to defile it. [35] And they built the high places of Baal, which (are) in the valley of the son of Hinnom, to cause their sons and their daughters to pass through (the fire) to Molech — which I did not command them, nor did it come into My heart, that they should do this idolatry, to cause Judah to sin.

[36] And now, therefore, thus says Jehovah God of Israel concerning this city, of which you say, It is delivered into the hand of the king of Babylon by the sword, and by the famine, and by the plague: [37] Behold, I will gather them out

הַזֹּאת בָּאֵשׁ וּשְׂרָפוּהָ וְאֵת הַבָּתִּים אֲשֶׁר קִטְּרוּ עַל־גַּגּוֹתֵיהֶם
their on offered they where the with burn and with this
roots incense houses it fire

לַבַּעַל וְהִסִּכוּ נְסָכִים לֵאלֹהִים אֲחֵרִים לְמַעַן הַכְעִסֵנִי׃
Me provoke in ,other gods to drink poured and ,Baal to
.anger to to order offerings out

30 כִּי־הָיוּ בְנֵי־יִשְׂרָאֵל וּבְנֵי יְהוּדָה אַךְ עֹשִׂים הָרַע בְּעֵינַי
My in evil only Judah the and Israel the have For
eyes done of sons of sons

מִנְּעֻרֹתֵיהֶם כִּי בְנֵי־יִשְׂרָאֵל אַךְ מַכְעִסִים אֹתִי בְּמַעֲשֵׂה
the with Me provoked have only Israel the For their from
of work anger to of sons .youth

31 יְדֵיהֶם נְאֻם־יְהוָה׃ כִּי עַל־אַפִּי וְעַל־חֲמָתִי הָיְתָה לִּי
to has My and My (a) For .Jehovah says their
Me been wrath anger (of cause) ,hands

הָעִיר הַזֹּאת לְמִן־הַיּוֹם אֲשֶׁר בָּנוּ אוֹתָהּ וְעַד הַיּוֹם הַזֶּה
;this day to even it they that the from this city
built day

32 לַהֲסִירָהּ מֵעַל פָּנָי׃ עַל כָּל־רָעַת בְּנֵי־יִשְׂרָאֵל וּבְנֵי יְהוּדָה
,Judah the and Israel the the all because My from should I that
of sons of sons of evil of face it remove

אֲשֶׁר עָשׂוּ לְהַכְעִסֵנִי הֵמָּה מַלְכֵיהֶם שָׂרֵיהֶם כֹּהֲנֵיהֶם
their their their ,they provoke to they which
,priests ,rulers ,kings ;anger to Me done have

33 וּנְבִיאֵיהֶם וְאִישׁ יְהוּדָה וְיֹשְׁבֵי יְרוּשָׁלִָם׃ וַיִּפְנוּ אֵלַי עֹרֶף
(their) to they And .Jerusalem the and Judah the and their and
,back Me turned have of inhabitants of men ,prophets

וְלֹא פָנִים וְלַמֵּד אֹתָם הַשְׁכֵּם וְלַמֵּד וְאֵינָם שֹׁמְעִים לָקַחַת
to listened they yet and up rising ,them though the and
receive not have ,teaching early taught I ;face not

34 מוּסָר׃ וַיָּשִׂימוּ שִׁקּוּצֵיהֶם בַּבַּיִת אֲשֶׁר־נִקְרָא־שְׁמִי־עָלָיו
upon My been has which the in abomina- their But .instruction
it name called house idols able set they

35 לְטַמְּאוֹ׃ וַיִּבְנוּ אֶת־בָּמוֹת הַבַּעַל אֲשֶׁר ׀ בְּגֵיא בֶן־הִנֹּם
,Hinnom the the in which ,Baal high the they And defile to
of son of valley (are) of places built .it

לְהַעֲבִיר אֶת־בְּנֵיהֶם וְאֶת־בְּנוֹתֵיהֶם לַמֹּלֶךְ אֲשֶׁר לֹא־
not which to their and their (the) make to
—Molech daughters sons (fire) through pass

צִוִּיתִים וְלֹא עָלְתָה עַל־לִבִּי לַעֲשׂוֹת הַתּוֹעֵבָה הַזֹּאת לְמַעַן
in ,this abomination they that My into it did nor com- did I
to order do should heart come ,them mand

36 הַחֲטִי אֶת־יְהוּדָה׃ וְעַתָּה לָכֵן כֹּה־אָמַר יְהוָה אֱלֹהֵי
the ,Jehovah says thus there- And .Judah cause
of God fore now sin to

יִשְׂרָאֵל אֶל־הָעִיר הַזֹּאת אֲשֶׁר ׀ אַתֶּם אֹמְרִים נִתְּנָה בְּיַד
the into is it ,say you which this city con- Israel
of hand given cerning

37 מֶלֶךְ־בָּבֶל בַּחֶרֶב וּבָרָעָב וּבַדָּבֶר׃ הִנְנִי מְקַבְּצָם מִכָּל־
of out will ,Behold by and by and the by Babylon the
all them gather I :plague the famine sword of king

of all the lands where I have driven them there, in My anger, and in My fury and in great wrath. And I will bring them again to this place, and I will cause them to live in safety. [38] And they shall be My people, and I will be their God. [39] And I will give them one heart and one way, that they may fear Me all the days, to them and to their sons after them.

[40] And I will cut an everlasting covenant with them that I will not turn away from them, to do good to them. But I will put My fear in their heart, that they shall not depart from Me. [41] And I will rejoice over them to do good to them, and I will truly plant them in this land, with all My heart, and with all My soul. [42] For thus says Jehovah: As I have brought all this great evil on this people, so I will bring on them all the good that I am speaking to them.

[43] And fields shall be bought in this land of which you say, It (is) a desolation without man or beast; it has been given into the hand of the Chaldeans. [44] Men shall buy fields for silver, and write it in a book, and seal (it), and call witnesses in the land of Benjamin, and in the places around Jerusalem, and in the cities of Judah, and in the cities of the mountains, and in the cities of the Shephelah, and in the cities of the Negeb. For I will cause their captivity to return, says Jehovah.

הָאֲרָצוֹת אֲשֶׁר הִדַּחְתִּים שָׁם בְּאַפִּי וּבַחֲמָתִי וּבְקֶצֶף גָּדוֹל

great in and in and My in ,there have I where the
     indignation fury My ,anger them driven lands

38 וַהֲשִׁבֹתִים אֶל־הַמָּקוֹם הַזֶּה וְהֹשַׁבְתִּים לָבֶטַח׃ וְהָיוּ לִי

to they And in make and this place to bring will I And
Me be will .safety dwell them back them

39 לְעָם וַאֲנִי אֶהְיֶה לָהֶם לֵאלֹהִים׃ וְנָתַתִּי לָהֶם לֵב אֶחָד

one heart to I And .God for to will and a for
them give will them be I ,people

וְדֶרֶךְ אֶחָד לְיִרְאָה אוֹתִי כָּל־הַיָּמִים לְטוֹב לָהֶם וְלִבְנֵיהֶם

to and to for the all Me they that ,one and
sons their them ,good days fear may way

40 אַחֲרֵיהֶם׃ וְכָרַתִּי לָהֶם בְּרִית עוֹלָם אֲשֶׁר לֹא־אָשׁוּב

will I not that ever- an for I And after
away turn lasting covenant them cut will .them

מֵאַחֲרֵיהֶם לְהֵיטִיבִי אוֹתָם וְאֶת־יִרְאָתִי אֶתֵּן בְּלִבָבָם

their in will I My But .them do to from
heart put fear good them

41 לְבִלְתִּי סוּר מֵעָלָי׃ וְשַׂשְׂתִּי עֲלֵיהֶם לְהֵטִיב אוֹתָם וּנְטַעְתִּים

will I and ,them do to over will I And from shall they that
them plant to good them rejoice .Me depart not

42 בָּאָרֶץ הַזֹּאת בֶּאֱמֶת בְּכָל־לִבִּי וּבְכָל־נַפְשִׁי׃ כִּי־

For My and My with ,truly this in
.soul all with ,heart all land

כֹּה אָמַר יְהוָה כַּאֲשֶׁר הֵבֵאתִי אֶל־הָעָם הַזֶּה אֵת כָּל־

all this people on have I As :Jehovah says thus
brought

הָרָעָה הַגְּדוֹלָה הַזֹּאת כֵּן אָנֹכִי מֵבִיא עֲלֵיהֶם אֶת־כָּל־

all them on will I so ,this great evil
bring

43 הַטּוֹבָה אֲשֶׁר אָנֹכִי דֹּבֵר עֲלֵיהֶם׃ וְנִקְנָה הַשָּׂדֶה בָּאָרֶץ

in fields will And .them to am I that the
land bought be speaking good

הַזֹּאת אֲשֶׁר אַתֶּם אֹמְרִים שְׁמָמָה הִיא מֵאֵין אָדָם וּבְהֵמָה

;beast or man without (is) it A ,say you of ,this
desolation which

44 נִתְּנָה בְּיַד הַכַּשְׂדִּים׃ שָׂדוֹת בַּכֶּסֶף יִקְנוּ וְכָתוֹב בַּסֵּפֶר

a in write and men For fields the into is it
,document (it) ,buy will silver ,Chaldeans' hand given

וְחָתוֹם וְהָעֵד עֵדִים בְּאֶרֶץ בִּנְיָמִן וּבִסְבִיבֵי יְרוּשָׁלִַם וּבְעָרֵי

in and ,Jerusalem the in and ,Benjamin the in witnesses and and
cities around places of land call it seal

יְהוּדָה וּבְעָרֵי הָהָר וּבְעָרֵי הַשְּׁפֵלָה וּבְעָרֵי הַנֶּגֶב כִּי־אָשִׁיב

will I for the in and the in and the in and Judah's
back bring ,Negeb of cities the ,Shephelah cities ,mountain cities

אֶת־שְׁבוּתָם נְאֻם־יְהוָה׃

.Jehovah says their
,captivity

CAP. XXXIII לג

CHAPTER 33

CHAPTER 33

[1] And the word of Jehovah came to Jeremiah the second time, while he was still shut up in the court of the guard, saying, [2] Thus says Jehovah the Maker of it, Jehovah who formed it in order to establish it; Jehovah (is) His name: [3] Call to Me, and I will answer you and tell you great and inscrutable things, you do not know them. [4] For thus says Jehovah, the God of Israel, concerning the houses of this city, and concerning the houses of the kings of Judah, which are torn down (to defend) against the siege mounds, and against the sword: [5] They come to fight with the Chaldeans, and to fill them with the dead bodies of men whom I have struck in My anger and in My fury, and for whom I have hidden My face from this city, because of all their evil. [6] Behold, I will bring to it health and healing, and I will heal them and will show to them the riches of peace and truth. [7] And I will cause the captivity of Judah and the captivity of Israel to return, and will build them, as at the first. [8] And I will cleanse them from all their iniquity which they have sinned against Me; and I will pardon all their iniquities which they have sinned, and which they have transgressed against Me.

[9] And it shall be to Me a name of joy, a praise and a glory to all the nations of the earth, which shall hear all the good that I do to them. And they shall fear and tremble for all the goodness and for all the peace that I do for it. [10] Thus says Jehovah: In

1 וַיְהִי דְבַר־יְהוָה אֶל־יִרְמְיָהוּ שֵׁנִית וְהוּא עֹדֶנּוּ עָצוּר
was still while the Jeremiah to Jehovah the Then
up shut he ,time second of word came

2 בַּחֲצַר הַמַּטָּרָה לֵאמֹר׃ כֹּה־אָמַר יְהוָה עֹשָׂהּ יְהוָה יוֹצֵר
who Jehovah its Jehovah says Thus ,saying guard the the in
formed ,Maker of court

3 אוֹתָהּ לַהֲכִינָהּ יְהוָה ׀ שְׁמוֹ׃ קְרָא אֵלַי וְאֶעֱנֶךָּ וְאַגִּידָה
will and will I and to Call His Jehovah to order in it
tell you answer Me .name (is) ;it establish

4 לְּךָ גְּדֹלוֹת וּבְצֻרוֹת לֹא יְדַעְתָּם׃ כִּי כֹה אָמַר יְהוָה
Jehovah says thus For do you not inscrut- and ,great you
.them know ,things able

אֱלֹהֵי יִשְׂרָאֵל עַל־בָּתֵּי הָעִיר הַזֹּאת וְעַל־בָּתֵּי מַלְכֵי יְהוּדָה
,Judah kings the the and ,this city the con- ,Israel the
of of houses concerning of houses cerning of God

5 הַנְּתֻצִים אֶל־הַסֹּלְלוֹת וְאֶל־הֶחָרֶב׃ בָּאִים לְהִלָּחֵם אֶת־
with fight to They the and siege the against are which
come .sword against ,mounds down torn

הַכַּשְׂדִּים וּלְמַלְאָם אֶת־פִּגְרֵי הָאָדָם אֲשֶׁר הִכֵּיתִי בְאַפִּי
My in have I that men dead the with fill to and the
anger struck of bodies them ,Chaldeans

וּבַחֲמָתִי וַאֲשֶׁר הִסְתַּרְתִּי פָנַי מֵהָעִיר הַזֹּאת עַל כָּל־
all because ,this from My have I and My and
of city face hidden ,wrath

6 רָעָתָם׃ הִנְנִי מַעֲלֶה־לָּהּ אֲרֻכָה וּמַרְפֵּא וּרְפָאתִם וְגִלֵּיתִי
and will I and and health it to will ,Behold their
reveal them heal ,healing up bring I .evil

7 לָהֶם עֲתֶרֶת שָׁלוֹם וֶאֱמֶת׃ וַהֲשִׁבֹתִי אֶת־שְׁבוּת יְהוּדָה
Judah the will I And and peace the them to
of captivity back bring .truth of abundance

8 וְאֵת שְׁבוּת יִשְׂרָאֵל וּבְנִתִים כְּבָרִאשֹׁנָה׃ וְטִהַרְתִּים מִכָּל־
from will I And the at as will and ,Israel the and
them cleanse .first ,them build of captivity

עֲוֺנָם אֲשֶׁר חָטְאוּ־לִי וְסָלַחְתִּי לְכוֹל־עֲוֺנוֹתֵיהֶם אֲשֶׁר
which their all will I and against they which their
iniquities pardon ,Me sinned have iniquity

9 חָטְאוּ־לִי וַאֲשֶׁר פָּשְׁעוּ בִי׃ וְהָיְתָה לִּי לְשֵׁם שָׂשׂוֹן לִתְהִלָּה
praise a ,joy a to it And against have they and against they
of name Me be will .Me rebelled which Me,sinned have

וּלְתִפְאֶרֶת לְכֹל גּוֹיֵי הָאָרֶץ אֲשֶׁר יִשְׁמְעוּ אֶת־כָּל־הַטּוֹבָה
the all shall which the the all to a and
good hear ,earth of nations glory

אֲשֶׁר אָנֹכִי עֹשֶׂה אוֹתָם וּפָחֲדוּ וְרָגְזוּ עַל כָּל־הַטּוֹבָה וְעַל
and the all for and they and ,them for do I that
goodness tremble fear will

10 כָּל־הַשָּׁלוֹם אֲשֶׁר אָנֹכִי עֹשָׂה לָּהּ׃ כֹּה ׀ אָמַר
says Thus .it for do I that peace the all

this place, which you say (shall be) a desert without man and without beast, in the cities of Judah, and in the streets of Jerusalem that are wasted without man, and without inhabitant, and without beast — [11] there shall be heard again the voice of joy and the voice of gladness, the voice of the bridegroom and the voice of the bride, the voice of those saying, Praise Jehovah of hosts, for His mercy (endures) forever; those who shall bring the sacrifice of thanksgiving into the house of Jehovah. For I will bring back the captivity of the land, as at the first, says Jehovah. [12] Thus says Jehovah of hosts: Again in this place,(which is) a waste without man or even beast, and in all its cities (shall be) a home of shepherds causing flocks to lie down. [13] In the cities of the mountains, in the cities of the Shephelah, and in the cities of the Negeb, and in the land of Benjamin, and in the places around Jerusalem, and in the cities of Judah, shall the flocks pass again under the hands of him who tallies, says Jehovah. [14] Behold, the days come, says Jehovah, that I will fulfill the good thing which I have promised to the house of Israel and to the house of Judah.

[15] In those days, and at that time, I will cause a Branch of righteousness to grow up to David. And He shall do judgment and righteousness in the land. [16] In those days Judah shall be saved, and Jerusalem shall dwell in safety; and this is the name that shall be called on her, Jehovah our righteousness.

[17] For thus says Jehovah, David shall not

יְהוָה עוֹד יִשָּׁמַע בַּמָּקוֹם־הַזֶּה אֲשֶׁר אַתֶּם אֹמְרִים חָרֵב
a ,say you which this in will there Again Jeho-
waste place heard be ,vah

הוּא מֵאֵין אָדָם וּמֵאֵין בְּהֵמָה בְּעָרֵי יְהוּדָה וּבְחֻצוֹת
the in and ,Judah the in ,beast and man without it
of streets of cities without (is)

יְרוּשָׁלִַם הַנְשַׁמּוֹת מֵאֵין אָדָם וּמֵאֵין יוֹשֵׁב וּמֵאֵין בְּהֵמָה׃
—beast and inhabi- and ,man without are that Jerusalem
without ,tant without desolate

11 קוֹל שָׂשׂוֹן וְקוֹל שִׂמְחָה קוֹל חָתָן וְקוֹל כַּלָּה קוֹל אֹמְרִים
those the the the and the voice the ,gladness the and joy the
,saying of voice ,bride of voice groom of of voice of voice

הוֹדוּ אֶת־יְהוָה צְבָאוֹת כִּי־טוֹב יְהוָה כִּי־לְעוֹלָם חַסְדּוֹ
His (endures) for Jehovah good for ,hosts Jehovah Praise
,mercy forever ,(is) of

מְבִאִים תּוֹדָה בֵּית יְהוָה כִּי־אָשִׁיב אֶת־שְׁבוּת־הָאָרֶץ
the the will I For Jeho- house sacrifice a who those
land of captivity back bring ,vah's thanksgiving of into bring

12 כְּבָרִאשֹׁנָה אָמַר יְהוָה׃ כֹּה אָמַר יְהוָה צְבָאוֹת
:hosts Jehovah says Thus .Jehovah says the at as
of ,first

עוֹד יִהְיֶה ׀ בַּמָּקוֹם הַזֶּה הֶחָרֵב מֵאֵין־אָדָם וְעַד־בְּהֵמָה
;beast or man with- the ,this place in shall Again
even out waste be

13 וּבְכָל־עָרָיו נְוֵה רֹעִים מַרְבִּצִים צֹאן׃ בְּעָרֵי הָהָר בְּעָרֵי
the in moun- the the In (their) to causing shepherds an its in and
of cities ,tain of cities .flocks down lie of abode cities all

הַשְּׁפֵלָה וּבְעָרֵי הַנֶּגֶב וּבְאֶרֶץ בִּנְיָמִן וּבִסְבִיבֵי יְרוּשָׁלִַם
,Jerusalem the in and ,Benjamin in and the the in and the
around places of land the ,Negeb of cities Shephalah

וּבְעָרֵי יְהוּדָה עֹד תַּעֲבֹרְנָה הַצֹּאן עַל־יְדֵי מוֹנֶה אָמַר
says who him the under the shall again ,Judah the in and
(them) counts of hands flocks pass of cities

14 יְהוָה׃ הִנֵּה יָמִים בָּאִים נְאֻם־יְהוָה וַהֲקִמֹתִי אֶת־
will I that ,Jehovah says ,come the ,Behold .Jehovah
establish days

הַדָּבָר הַטּוֹב אֲשֶׁר דִּבַּרְתִּי אֶל־בֵּית יִשְׂרָאֵל וְעַל־בֵּית
the and Israel the to have I which good the
of house to of house spoken thing

15 יְהוּדָה׃ בַּיָּמִים הָהֵם וּבָעֵת הַהִיא אַצְמִיחַ לְדָוִד צֶמַח
branch a to make will I ,that at and ,those days In .Judah
of David up grow time

16 צְדָקָה וְעָשָׂה מִשְׁפָּט וּצְדָקָה בָּאָרֶץ׃ בַּיָּמִים הָהֵם תִּוָּשַׁע
be will these days In the in righ- and judgment will He and righ-
saved .land teousness execute ,teousness

יְהוּדָה וִירוּשָׁלִַם תִּשְׁכּוֹן לָבֶטַח וְזֶה אֲשֶׁר־יִקְרָא־לָהּ
,her one (name the) and safety in shall and ,Judah
call will which (is) this dwell Jerusalem

17 יְהוָה ׀ צִדְקֵנוּ׃ כִּי־כֹה אָמַר יְהוָה לֹא־יִכָּרֵת לְדָוִד
David to be will Not ,Jehovah says thus For our Jehovah
off cut .righteousness

have cut off a man to sit on the throne of the house of Israel, [18] and for the Levitical priests, they shall not have a man cut off before Me to offer burnt offerings, and to kindle grain offerings, and to do sacrifice continually.

[19] And the word of Jehovah came to Jeremiah, saying, [20] Thus says Jehovah: If you can break My covenant of the day and My covenant of the night, and that should not be day and night in their time; [21] also may My covenant with My servant David be broken, that he should not have a son to reign on his throne, and with the Levitical priests, My ministers. [22] As the host of heaven cannot be numbered, nor the sand of the sea measured, so I will multiply the seed of My servant David and the Levites who minister to Me. [23] And the word of Jehovah came to Jeremiah, saying, [24] Have you not observed what this people have spoken, saying, The two families which Jehovah has chosen, He has also rejected them? And they despise My people, no more to be a nation before them.

[25] Thus says Jehovah: If My covenant (is) not with day and night, I have not appointed the ordinances of Heaven and earth,

[26] then also I will reject the seed of Jacob, and My servant David, (so) not to take of his seed (to be) rulers over the seed of Abraham, Isaac and Jacob. For I will bring back their captivity and have pity on them.

18 אִישׁ יֹשֵׁב עַל־כִּסֵּא בֵית־יִשְׂרָאֵל׃ וְלַכֹּהֲנִים הַלְוִיִּם לֹא־
not Levitical the for and ;Israel the the on sitting man a
priests of house of throne

יִכָּרֵת אִישׁ מִלְּפָנַי מַעֲלֶה עוֹלָה וּמַקְטִיר מִנְחָה וְעֹשֶׂה
and grain make to and burnt offering before man a be will
perform ,offerings smoke ,offerings Me off cut

19 זֶּבַח כָּל־הַיָּמִים׃ וַיְהִי דְּבַר־יְהוָה אֶל־יִרְמְיָהוּ לֵאמוֹר׃
,saying ,Jeremiah to Jehovah the And .days the all sacri-
of word came fice

כֹּה אָמַר יְהוָה אִם־תָּפֵרוּ אֶת־בְּרִיתִי הַיּוֹם וְאֶת־בְּרִיתִי
cove- My and the cove- My can you If :Jehovah says Thus
of nant day of nant break

20
21 הַלָּיְלָה וּלְבִלְתִּי הֱיוֹת יוֹמָם־וָלַיְלָה בְּעִתָּם׃ גַּם־בְּרִיתִי
My (then) their in and day there that the
covenant also ,time night be should not ,night

תֻפַר אֶת־דָּוִד עַבְדִּי מִהְיוֹת־לוֹ בֵן מֹלֵךְ עַל־כִּסְאוֹ וְאֶת־
and his on reigning a to should that My David with be may
with ,throne son him be not ,servant broken

22 הַלְוִיִּם הַכֹּהֲנִים מְשָׁרְתָי׃ אֲשֶׁר לֹא־יִסָּפֵר צְבָא הַשָּׁמַיִם
,heaven the be can not As My the Levitical
of host counted .ministers ,priests

וְלֹא יִמַּד חוֹל הַיָּם כֵּן אַרְבֶּה אֶת־זֶרַע דָּוִד עַבְדִּי וְאֶת־
and My David the will I so the the measured nor
,servant of seed multiply ,sea of sand

23 הַלְוִיִּם מְשָׁרְתֵי אֹתִי׃ וַיְהִי דְּבַר־יְהוָה אֶל־יִרְמְיָהוּ
,Jeremiah to Jehovah the And .Me minister who the
of word came to Levites

24 לֵאמֹר׃ הֲלוֹא רָאִיתָ מָה־הָעָם הַזֶּה דִּבְּרוּ לֵאמֹר שְׁתֵּי
two ,saying have this people what you Have not ,saying
,spoken seen

הַמִּשְׁפָּחוֹת אֲשֶׁר בָּחַר יְהוָה בָּהֶם וַיִּמְאָסֵם וְאֶת־עַמִּי
My And also He has ,them Jehovah has which The
people ?them rejected chosen families

25 יִנְאָצוּן מִהְיוֹת עוֹד גּוֹי לִפְנֵיהֶם׃ כֹּה אָמַר יְהוָה
:Jehovah says Thus before a yet to not they
.them nation be disdain

אִם־לֹא בְרִיתִי יוֹמָם וָלָיְלָה חֻקּוֹת שָׁמַיִם וָאָרֶץ לֹא־
not and heaven ordi- the and (with) My (is) If
earth of nances ,night day covenant not

26 שָׂמְתִּי׃ גַּם־זֶרַע יַעֲקוֹב וְדָוִד עַבְדִּי אֶמְאַס מִקַּחַת מִזַּרְעוֹ
his from not will I My and Jacob the then have I
seed take to ,reject servant David of seed also ,appointed

מֹשְׁלִים אֶל־זֶרַע אַבְרָהָם יִשְׂחָק וְיַעֲקֹב כִּי־אָשׁוּב אֶת־
will I For and ,Isaac ,Abraham the over rulers
back bring .Jacob of seed

שְׁבוּתָם וְרִחַמְתִּים׃
compassion have and their
.them on captivity

CAP. XXXIV לד

CHAPTER 34

CHAPTER 34

[1] The word which came to Jeremiah from Jehovah when Nebuchadnezzar king of Babylon, and all his army, and all the kingdoms of the earth, because his hand rules; and all the people, fought against Jerusalem and against all its cities, saying, [2] Thus says Jehovah, the God of Israel: Go and speak to Zedekiah king of Judah and tell him, Thus says Jehovah, Behold, I will give this city into the hand of the king of Babylon, and he shall burn it with fire. [3] And you shall not escape out of his hand, but shall surely be taken and delivered into his hand. And your eyes shall behold the eyes of the king of Babylon, and he shall speak, his mouth with your mouth; and you shall go to Babylon. [4] Yet hear the word of Jehovah, O Zedekiah king of Judah: Thus says Jehovah about you, You shall not die by the sword. [5] You shall die in peace; and as the burnings of spices (for) your fathers, the former kings which were before you, so they shall burn for you, (Saying), Ah, lord! They will wail for you. For I have spoken the word, says Jehovah.

1 הַדָּבָר אֲשֶׁר־הָיָה אֶל־יִרְמְיָהוּ מֵאֵת יְהוָה וּנְבוּכַדְרֶאצַּר
when Jehovah from Jeremiah to came which The
Nebuchadnezzar word

מֶלֶךְ־בָּבֶל ׀ וְכָל־חֵילוֹ וְכָל־מַמְלְכוֹת אֶרֶץ מֶמְשֶׁלֶת יָדוֹ
his because the the and his and ,Babylon king
,hand rules ,earth of kingdoms all ,army all of

וְכָל־הָעַמִּים נִלְחָמִים עַל־יְרוּשָׁלַםִ וְעַל־כָּל־עָרֶיהָ לֵאמֹר׃
saying its all and Jerusalem against fought the and
,cities against ,peoples all

2 כֹּה־אָמַר יְהוָה אֱלֹהֵי יִשְׂרָאֵל הָלֹךְ וְאָמַרְתָּ אֶל־צִדְקִיָּהוּ
Zedekiah to speak and Go :Israel the Jehovah says Thus
of God

מֶלֶךְ יְהוּדָה וְאָמַרְתָּ אֵלָיו כֹּה אָמַר יְהוָה הִנְנִי נֹתֵן אֶת־
will ,Behold ,Jehovah says Thus to say and Judah king
give I ,him of

3 הָעִיר הַזֹּאת בְּיַד מֶלֶךְ־בָּבֶל וּשְׂרָפָהּ בָּאֵשׁ׃ וְאַתָּה לֹא
not And with will he and ,Babylon the the into this city
you .fire it burn of king of hand

תִמָּלֵט מִיָּדוֹ כִּי תָּפֹשׂ תִּתָּפֵשׂ וּבְיָדוֹ תִּנָּתֵן וְעֵינֶיךָ אֶת־עֵינֵי
the your And .given into and will you surely for his from will
of eyes eyes hand his ,seized be ,hand escape

מֶלֶךְ־בָּבֶל תִּרְאֶינָה וּפִיהוּ אֶת־פִּיךָ יְדַבֵּר וּבָבֶל תָּבוֹא׃
will you and will he your with his and ,see will Babylon the
.to go Babylon ;speak mouth mouth of king

4 אַךְ שְׁמַע דְּבַר־יְהוָה צִדְקִיָּהוּ מֶלֶךְ יְהוּדָה כֹּה־אָמַר יְהוָה
Jehovah says Thus :Judah king O ,Jehovah the hear Yet
of Zedekiah of word

5 עָלֶיךָ לֹא תָמוּת בֶּחָרֶב׃ בְּשָׁלוֹם תָּמוּת וּבְמִשְׂרְפוֹת
the as and shall you peace In the by shall You not of
spices of burnings ;die .sword die .you

אֲבוֹתֶיךָ הַמְּלָכִים הָרִאשֹׁנִים אֲשֶׁר־הָיוּ לְפָנֶיךָ כֵּן יִשְׂרְפוּ־
shall they so before were which former the your (for)
burn ,you kings ,fathers

לָךְ וְהוֹי אָדוֹן יִסְפְּדוּ־לָךְ כִּי־דָבָר אֲנִי־דִבַּרְתִּי נְאֻם־יְהוָה׃
.Jehovah says have I the For for will They ,Ah and for
,spoken word .you lament ,lord (saying) ,you

[6] Then Jeremiah the prophet spoke all these words to Zedekiah king of Judah in Jerusalem, [7] when the king of Babylon's army fought against Jerusalem and against all the cities of Judah that were left, against Lachish, and against Azekah; for these fortified cities remained of the cities of Judah.

6 וַיְדַבֵּר יִרְמְיָהוּ הַנָּבִיא אֶל־צִדְקִיָּהוּ מֶלֶךְ יְהוּדָה
Judah king Zedekiah to the Jeremiah Then
of prophet spoke

7 אֵת כָּל־הַדְּבָרִים הָאֵלֶּה בִּירוּשָׁלָםִ׃ וְחֵיל מֶלֶךְ־בָּבֶל
Babylon the the when in these words all
of king of army ,Jerusalem

נִלְחָמִים עַל־יְרוּשָׁלַםִ וְעַל כָּל־עָרֵי יְהוּדָה הַנּוֹתָרוֹת אֶל־
against were that Judah the all and Jerusalem against fought
;left of cities against

לָכִישׁ וְאֶל־עֲזֵקָה כִּי הֵנָּה נִשְׁאֲרוּ בְּעָרֵי יְהוּדָה עָרֵי
cities Judah among remained those for ;Azekah and ,Lachish
of cities the against

[8] The word that came to Jeremiah from Jehovah, after King Zedekiah had cut a covenant with all the people who were at Jerusalem, to proclaim liberty to them, [9] that each man should let his male slave and each man his slave-girl go free, a Hebrew man and a Hebrew woman, that not should enslave among them a Jew, a man his brother. [10] And all the princes, and all the people who had entered into the covenant, obeyed, each one to let go free his male slave, and each one his slave-girl so that not should enslave among them any more, then they obeyed and let (them) go. [11] But afterward they turned and forced the slaves and the slave-girls whom they had let go free to return! And (they) brought them into service (again) for slaves and for slave-girls. [12] Therefore the word of Jehovah came to Jeremiah from Jehovah, saying, [13] Thus says Jehovah, the God of Israel: I cut a covenant with your fathers in the day I brought them forth out of the land of Egypt, out of the house of slavery, saying,

[14] At the end of seven years each man should let go his brother (who is) a Hebrew, who has been sold to him. When he has served you six years, you shall let him go free from you. But your fathers did not listen to me nor bow down their ear. [15] And you had turned today, and you did right in My eyes, to proclaim liberty each one to his neighbor. And you cut a covenant before Me in the house on which is called My name. [16] But you turned and defiled My name, and

8 מִבְצָר׃ הַדָּבָר אֲשֶׁר־הָיָה אֶל־יִרְמְיָהוּ מֵאֵת יְהוָה
,Jehovah from Jeremiah to came that The word .fortified

אַחֲרֵי כְּרֹת הַמֶּלֶךְ צִדְקִיָּהוּ בְּרִית אֶת־כָּל־הָעָם אֲשֶׁר
who (were) the people all with a covenant Zedekiah King cut had after

9 בִּירוּשָׁלִַם לִקְרֹא לָהֶם דְּרוֹר׃ לְשַׁלַּח אִישׁ אֶת־עַבְדּוֹ
male his slave each man should that go let ,liberty them to to proclaim in ,Jerusalem

וְאִישׁ אֶת־שִׁפְחָתוֹ הָעִבְרִי וְהָעִבְרִיָּה חָפְשִׁים לְבִלְתִּי עֲבָד־
should enslave that not ,free Hebrew a and woman Hebrew a man female his slave each and man

10 בָּם בִּיהוּדִי אָחִיהוּ אִישׁ׃ וַיִּשְׁמְעוּ כָל־הַשָּׂרִים וְכָל־הָעָם
the people and all the rulers all obeyed And .man a his brother Jew a among them

אֲשֶׁר־בָּאוּ בַבְּרִית לְשַׁלַּח אִישׁ אֶת־עַבְדּוֹ וְאִישׁ אֶת־
each and man male his slave man each let to go the into covenant had entered who

שִׁפְחָתוֹ חָפְשִׁים לְבִלְתִּי עֲבָד־בָּם עוֹד וַיִּשְׁמְעוּ וַיְשַׁלֵּחוּ׃
let and .go (them) they and obeyed ,again among them might one enslave so that not ,free female his slave

11 וַיָּשׁוּבוּ אַחֲרֵי־כֵן וַיָּשִׁבוּ אֶת־הָעֲבָדִים וְאֶת־הַשְּׁפָחוֹת
female the slaves and male the slaves made and return afterward they But turned

אֲשֶׁר שִׁלְּחוּ חָפְשִׁים וַיִּכְבִּישׁוּם לַעֲבָדִים וְלִשְׁפָחוֹת׃
for and .slaves female male for slaves they And them subjected .free let they go whom

12 וַיְהִי דְבַר־יְהוָה אֶל־יִרְמְיָהוּ מֵאֵת יְהוָה לֵאמֹר׃ כֹּה־אָמַר
13
says Thus ,saying ,Jehovah from Jeremiah to Jehovah the of word came There- fore

יְהוָה אֱלֹהֵי יִשְׂרָאֵל אָנֹכִי כָּרַתִּי בְרִית אֶת־אֲבוֹתֵיכֶם בְּיוֹם
the in day your fathers with a covenant cut I :Israel the of God ,Jehovah

14 הוֹצִאִי אוֹתָם מֵאֶרֶץ מִצְרַיִם מִבֵּית עֲבָדִים לֵאמֹר׃ מִקֵּץ
the At of end ,saying ,slavery the of house out of ,Egypt the from of land them brought I out

שֶׁבַע שָׁנִים תְּשַׁלְּחוּ אִישׁ אֶת־אָחִיו הָעִבְרִי אֲשֶׁר יִמָּכֵר
been has sold who Hebrew a his brother each man should go let years seven

לְךָ וַעֲבָדְךָ שֵׁשׁ שָׁנִים וְשִׁלַּחְתּוֹ חָפְשִׁי מֵעִמָּךְ וְלֹא־שָׁמְעוּ
did listen But not from .you free shall you then go him let ,years six he When you serves to .him

15 אֲבוֹתֵיכֶם אֵלַי וְלֹא הִטּוּ אֶת־אָזְנָם׃ וַתָּשֻׁבוּ אַתֶּם הַיּוֹם
,today you And turned their .ear incline nor to Me your fathers

וַתַּעֲשׂוּ אֶת־הַיָּשָׁר בְּעֵינַי לִקְרֹא דְרוֹר אִישׁ לְרֵעֵהוּ וַתִּכְרְתוּ
you and cut his to ,neighbor each man liberty to proclaim My in eyes right did and

16 בְרִית לְפָנַי בַּבַּיִת אֲשֶׁר־נִקְרָא שְׁמִי עָלָיו׃ וַתָּשֻׁבוּ וַתְּחַלְּלוּ
and profaned you but turned upon ,it My name been has called which the in house before Me a covenant

each one caused to return his slave, and each his slave-girl, whom you had set free according to their desire. And (you) brought them into service to be slaves and slave-girls to you. [17] Therefore thus says Jehovah: You have not listened to Me, to proclaim liberty, each one to his brother and each one to his neighbor! Behold, I proclaim freedom to you, says Jehovah: to the sword, to the plague and to the famine. And I will cause you to be a horror to all the kingdoms of the earth.

[18] And I will give the men who have transgressed My covenant, who have not done the words of the covenant which they have cut before Me, (when they) cut the calf in two and passed between its parts; [19] the princes of Judah, and the princes of Jerusalem, the eunuchs, and the priests, and all the people of the land who passed between the parts of the calf; [20] I will even give them into the hand of their enemies, and into the hand of those who seek their life. And their dead bodies shall be for food to the birds of the sky and to the beasts of the earth. [21] And I will give Zedekiah king of Judah, and his princes, into the hand of their enemies and into the hand of those who seek their life, and into the hand of the king of Babylon's army that has withdrawn from you. [22] Behold, I will command and cause them to return to this city, says Jehovah. And they shall fight against it, and take it, and burn it with fire. And I will make the cities of Judah a desolation, without a soul to live in it.

אֶת־שְׁמִי וַתָּשִׁבוּ אִישׁ אֶת־עַבְדּוֹ וְאִישׁ אֶת־שִׁפְחָתוֹ אֲשֶׁר־
whom female his each and male his each made and My
slave man ,slave man return ,name

שִׁלַּחְתֶּם חָפְשִׁים לְנַפְשָׁם וַתִּכְבְּשׁוּ אֹתָם לִהְיוֹת לָכֶם
you to be to them .you and to according free had you
subjected ;desire their go let

17 לָכֵן כֹּה־אָמַר יְהוָה אַתֶּם לַעֲבָדִים וְלִשְׁפָחוֹת׃
You ;Jehovah says thus Therefore for and male for
.slave female slaves

לֹא־שְׁמַעְתֶּם אֵלַי לִקְרֹא דְּרוֹר אִישׁ לְאָחִיו וְאִישׁ לְרֵעֵהוּ
his to each and his to each ,liberty to to have not
!neighbor man brother man proclaim Me listened

הִנְנִי קֹרֵא לָכֶם דְּרוֹר נְאֻם־יְהוָה אֶל־הַחֶרֶב אֶל־הַדֶּבֶר
the to the to :Jehovah says ,liberty you to proclaim Be-
,plague ,sword I ,hold

וְאֶל־הָרָעָב וְנָתַתִּי אֶתְכֶם לְזְוָעָה לְכֹל מַמְלְכוֹת הָאָרֶץ׃
the the all to terror a you will I and the and
.earth of kingdoms make ,famine to

18 וְנָתַתִּי אֶת־הָאֲנָשִׁים הָעֹבְרִים אֶת־בְּרִתִי אֲשֶׁר לֹא־הֵקִימוּ
have not who My have who the I And
out carried ,covenant transgressed men give will

אֶת־דִּבְרֵי הַבְּרִית אֲשֶׁר כָּרְתוּ לְפָנָי הָעֵגֶל אֲשֶׁר כָּרְתוּ
they which the before have they which the the
cut calf bull ,Me cut covenant of words

19 לִשְׁנַיִם וַיַּעַבְרוּ בֵּין בְּתָרָיו׃ שָׂרֵי יְהוּדָה וְשָׂרֵי יְרוּשָׁלִַם
,Jerusalem the and ,Judah the its between and into
of rulers of rulers —pieces passed two

הַסָּרִסִים וְהַכֹּהֲנִים וְכֹל עַם הָאָרֶץ הָעֹבְרִים בֵּין בִּתְרֵי
the between who the the and the and the
of pieces passed land of people all ,priests ,eunuchs

20 הָעֵגֶל׃ וְנָתַתִּי אוֹתָם בְּיַד אֹיְבֵיהֶם וּבְיַד מְבַקְשֵׁי נַפְשָׁם
their who those into and their the into them will I bull the
.life seek of hand the ,enemies of hand give even ;calf

וְהָיְתָה נִבְלָתָם לְמַאֲכָל לְעוֹף הַשָּׁמַיִם וּלְבֶהֱמַת הָאָרֶץ׃
the the for and the the for food for their will And
.earth of beasts sky of birds bodies dead be

21 וְאֶת־צִדְקִיָּהוּ מֶלֶךְ־יְהוּדָה וְאֶת־שָׂרָיו אֶתֵּן בְּיַד אֹיְבֵיהֶם
their into will I his and Judah king Zedekiah And
enemies' hand give rulers of

וּבְיַד מְבַקְשֵׁי נַפְשָׁם וּבְיַד חֵיל מֶלֶךְ בָּבֶל הָעֹלִים מֵעֲלֵיכֶם׃
from has that Babylon's the the into and their who those into and
.you withdrawn of king of army of hand ,life seek of hand the

22 הִנְנִי מְצַוֶּה נְאֻם־יְהוָה וַהֲשִׁבֹתִים אֶל־הָעִיר הַזֹּאת וְנִלְחֲמוּ
they And .this city to bring and ,Jehovah says will ,Behold
fight will back them ,command I

עָלֶיהָ וּלְכָדוּהָ וּשְׂרָפֻהָ בָאֵשׁ וְאֶת־עָרֵי יְהוּדָה אֶתֵּן שְׁמָמָה
deso- a will I Judah the And with burn and and against
,lation make of cities .fire it ,it capture ,it

מֵאֵין יֹשֵׁב׃
.inhabitant with-
out

CAP. XXXV לה

CHAPTER 35

[1] The word which came to Jeremiah from Jehovah in the days of Jehoiakim the son of Josiah king of Judah, saying, [2] Go to the house of the Rechabites and speak to them, and bring them into the house of Jehovah, into one of the rooms; and give them wine to drink. [3] Then I took Jaazaniah the son of Jeremiah, the son of Habaziniah, and his brothers, and all his sons, and the whole house of the Rechabites. [4] And I brought them into the house of Jehovah, into the room of the sons of Hanan the son of Igdaliah, a man of God, which (was) near the room of the princes, which (was) above the room of Maaseiah the son of Shallum, the keeper of the door. [5] And I set bowls full of wine and cups before the sons of the house of the Rechabites; and I said to them, Drink wine! [6] But they said, We will not drink wine, for Jonadab the son of Rechab our father commanded us, saying, You shall not drink wine, you nor your sons forever.

[7] And you shall not build a house, nor sow seed, nor plant a vineyard, nor shall there be to you (anything); but all your days you shall live in tents, so that you may live many days on the face of the land where you are staying. [8] So we have obeyed the voice of Jonadab the son of Rechab our father, to all that he commanded us, to drink no wine all our days, we, our wives, our sons, nor our daughters; [9] nor to build

CHAPTER 35

1 הַדָּבָר אֲשֶׁר־הָיָה אֶל־יִרְמְיָהוּ מֵאֵת יְהוָה בִּימֵי יְהוֹיָקִים
Jehoiakim the in Jehovah from Jeremiah to came which The
of days word

2 בֶּן־יֹאשִׁיָּהוּ מֶלֶךְ יְהוּדָה לֵאמֹר׃ הָלוֹךְ אֶל־בֵּית הָרֵכָבִים
the the to Go ,saying ,Judah king Josiah the
Rechabites of house of of son

וְדִבַּרְתָּ אוֹתָם וַהֲבֵאוֹתָם בֵּית יְהוָה אֶל־אַחַת הַלְּשָׁכוֹת
the one into ,Jehovah the bring and them and
;rooms of of house into them to speak

3 וְהִשְׁקִיתָ אוֹתָם יָיִן׃ וָאֶקַּח אֶת־יַאֲזַנְיָה בֶן־יִרְמְיָהוּ בֶּן
the ,Jeremiah the Jaazaniah I Then .wine them give and
of son of son took drink to

חֲבַצִּנְיָה וְאֶת־אֶחָיו וְאֶת־כָּל־בָּנָיו וְאֵת כָּל־בֵּית הָרֵכָבִים׃
the house the and his all and his and Haba-
.Rechabites of whole ,sons ,brothers ,ziniah

4 וָאָבִא אֹתָם בֵּית יְהוָה אֶל־לִשְׁכַּת בְּנֵי חָנָן בֶּן־יִגְדַּלְיָהוּ
,Igdaliah the Hanan the the into ,Jehovah the them I And
of son of sons of room of house into brought

אִישׁ הָאֱלֹהִים אֲשֶׁר־אֵצֶל לִשְׁכַּת הַשָּׂרִים אֲשֶׁר מִמַּעַל
above which the the near which ,God man a
(was) ,rulers of room (was) of

5 לְלִשְׁכַּת מַעֲשֵׂיָהוּ בֶן־שַׁלֻּם שֹׁמֵר הַסַּף׃ וָאֶתֵּן לִפְנֵי ׀ בְּנֵי
the before Then the the ,Shallum the Maaseiah room the
of sons set I .threshold of keeper of son of

בֵית־הָרֵכָבִים גְּבִעִים מְלֵאִים יַיִן וְכֹסוֹת וָאֹמַר אֲלֵיהֶם שְׁתוּ־
Drink ,them to I and and wine of full bowls the the
said ;cups Rechabites of house

6 יָיִן׃ וַיֹּאמְרוּ לֹא נִשְׁתֶּה־יָּיִן כִּי יוֹנָדָב בֶּן־רֵכָב אָבִינוּ צִוָּה
com- father our Rechab the Jonadab for ,wine will We not they But !wine
manded of son drink ,said

7 עָלֵינוּ לֵאמֹר לֹא תִשְׁתּוּ־יַיִן אַתֶּם וּבְנֵיכֶם עַד־עוֹלָם׃ וּבַיִת
a And .forever your nor you ,wine You not ,saying ,us
house sons drink shall

לֹא־תִבְנוּ וְזֶרַע לֹא־תִזְרָעוּ וְכֶרֶם לֹא־תִטָּעוּ וְלֹא יִהְיֶה לָכֶם
you to shall and you not a and shall you not and shall you not
,(anything) be not ,plant shall vineyard ;sow seed ,build

כִּי בָּאֳהָלִים תֵּשְׁבוּ כָּל־יְמֵיכֶם לְמַעַן תִּחְיוּ יָמִים רַבִּים
many days may you so your all shall you tents in but
live that ,days live

8 עַל־פְּנֵי הָאֲדָמָה אֲשֶׁר אַתֶּם גָּרִים שָׁם׃ וַנִּשְׁמַע בְּקוֹל
the have we So .there are you where the the on
of voice obeyed sojourning land of face

יְהוֹנָדָב בֶּן־רֵכָב אָבִינוּ לְכֹל אֲשֶׁר צִוָּנוּ לְבִלְתִּי שְׁתוֹת־
drink to com- he that all to our Rechab the Jonadab
not ,us manded ,father of son

9 יַיִן כָּל־יָמֵינוּ אֲנַחְנוּ נָשֵׁינוּ בָּנֵינוּ וּבְנֹתֵינוּ׃ וּלְבִלְתִּי בְּנוֹת
built to and our and our our ,we our all wine
not ;daughters ,sons ,wives ,days

houses for us for our dwelling; we do not have a vineyard, or field, or seed; [10] but we live in tents, and have obeyed and done according to all that Jonadab our father commanded us. [11] But it came to pass, when Nebuchadnezzar king of Babylon came up against the land, then we said, Come and let us go to Jerusalem because of the army of the Chaldeans, and because of the army of the Syrians. So we are living at Jerusalem.

[12] Then came the word of Jehovah to Jeremiah, saying, [13] Thus says Jehovah of hosts, the God of Israel: Go and tell the men of Judah and the people of Jerusalem, Will you not receive instruction to listen to My words, says Jehovah? [14] The words of Jonadab the son of Rechab, in which he commanded his sons not to drink wine, are done. So to this day they do not drink, but obey their father's commandment. But I have spoken to you, rising early and speaking, but you did not listen to Me. [15] I have also sent to you all My servants the prophets, rising up early and sending, saying, Return now each one from his evil way and amend your doings, and do not go after other gods to serve them, and you shall live in the land which I have given to you and to your fathers. But you have not bowed your ear nor listened to Me. [16] Because the sons of Jonadab the son of Rechab have done the commandment of their father, which He commanded them; but this people has not listened to Me;

[17] therefore thus says Jehovah God of hosts, the

10 בָּתִּים לְשִׁבְתֵּנוּ וְכֶרֶם וְשָׂדֶה וָזֶרַע לֹא יִהְיֶה־לָּנוּ׃ וַנֵּשֶׁב
we And .us to there not ,seed or or a and our for houses
dwell is ,field vineyard ,dwelling

11 בָּאֳהָלִים וַנִּשְׁמַע וַנַּעַשׂ כְּכֹל אֲשֶׁר־צִוָּנוּ יוֹנָדָב אָבִינוּ׃ וַיְהִי
it But our Jonadab com- that according and have and in
,was .father us manded all to done obeyed ,tents

בַּעֲלוֹת נְבוּכַדְרֶאצַּר מֶלֶךְ־בָּבֶל אֶל־הָאָרֶץ וַנֹּאמֶר בֹּאוּ
Come we then the against Babylon king Nebuchadnezzar when
,said ,land of up came

וְנָבוֹא יְרוּשָׁלַםִ מִפְּנֵי חֵיל הַכַּשְׂדִּים וּמִפְּנֵי חֵיל אֲרָם וַנֵּשֶׁב
we so ,Aram the be- and the the because Jerusalem let and
dwell of army of cause ,Chaldeans of army of to go us

12 בִּירוּשָׁלָםִ׃ וַיְהִי דְּבַר־יְהוָה אֶל־יִרְמְיָהוּ לֵאמֹר׃
:saying ,Jeremiah to Jehovah the Then in
of word came .Jerusalem

13 כֹּה־אָמַר יְהוָה צְבָאוֹת אֱלֹהֵי יִשְׂרָאֵל הָלֹךְ וְאָמַרְתָּ לְאִישׁ
the to say and Go :Israel the hosts Jehovah says Thus
of men of God of

יְהוּדָה וּלְיוֹשְׁבֵי יְרוּשָׁלָםִ הֲלוֹא תִקְחוּ מוּסָר לִשְׁמֹעַ אֶל־
to listen to instruc- you Will not :Jerusalem the and Judah
tion receive of inhabitants

14 דְּבָרַי נְאֻם־יְהוָה׃ הוּקַם אֶת־דִּבְרֵי יְהוֹנָדָב בֶּן־רֵכָב אֲשֶׁר־
(in) ,Rechab the Jonadab The carried are ?Jehovah says My
which of son of words out ,words

צִוָּה אֶת־בָּנָיו לְבִלְתִּי שְׁתוֹת־יַיִן וְלֹא שָׁתוּ עַד־הַיּוֹם הַזֶּה
,this day to do they So .wine drink not to his he
drink not sons commanded

כִּי שָׁמְעוּ אֵת מִצְוַת אֲבִיהֶם וְאָנֹכִי דִּבַּרְתִּי אֲלֵיכֶם הַשְׁכֵּם
up rising ,you to have I But their command obey but
early spoken .father's

15 וְדַבֵּר וְלֹא שְׁמַעְתֶּם אֵלָי׃ וָאֶשְׁלַח אֲלֵיכֶם אֶת־כָּל־עֲבָדַי
My all you to I Also .Me to did you but and
servants sent listen not ,speaking

הַנְּבִאִים ׀ הַשְׁכֵּים וְשָׁלֹחַ ׀ לֵאמֹר שֻׁבוּ־נָא אִישׁ מִדַּרְכּוֹ
his from each now Return ,saying and up rising the
way man ,sending early ,prophets

הָרָעָה וְהֵיטִיבוּ מַעַלְלֵיכֶם וְאַל־תֵּלְכוּ אַחֲרֵי אֱלֹהִים
gods after go do and your amend and evil
not ,doings

אֲחֵרִים לְעָבְדָם וּשְׁבוּ אֶל־הָאֲדָמָה אֲשֶׁר־נָתַתִּי לָכֶם
you to have I which the in dwell and serve to other
given land ,them

וְלַאֲבֹתֵיכֶם וְלֹא הִטִּיתֶם אֶת־אָזְנְכֶם וְלֹא שְׁמַעְתֶּם אֵלָי׃
.Me to listened nor ear your have you But your to and
inclined not .fathers

16 כִּי הֵקִימוּ בְּנֵי יְהוֹנָדָב בֶּן־רֵכָב אֶת־מִצְוַת אֲבִיהֶם אֲשֶׁר
which their com- the Rechab the Jonadab the have Because
father of mand of son of sons out carried

17 צִוָּם וְהָעָם הַזֶּה לֹא שָׁמְעוּ אֵלָי׃ לָכֵן כֹּה־אָמַר יְהוָה
Jehovah says thus therefore ;Me to has not this but gave he
listened people ;them

God of Israel: Behold, I will bring on Judah and on all the people of Jerusalem all the evil that I have spoken against them; because I have spoken to them, but they have not heard: and I have called to them, but they did not answer.

[18] And Jeremiah said to the house of the Rechabites, Thus says Jehovah of hosts, the God of Israel: Because you have obeyed the commandment of your father Jonadab, and have kept all his precepts and have done according to all that he has commanded you, [19] so Jehovah of hosts, the God of Israel, says this: Jonadab the son of Rechab shall not have a man cut off to stand before Me all the days.

אֱלֹהֵי צְבָאוֹת אֱלֹהֵי יִשְׂרָאֵל הִנְנִי מֵבִיא אֶל־יְהוּדָה וְאֶל

and on Judah on will bring ,Behold I :Israel the of God ,hosts God of

כָּל־יוֹשְׁבֵי יְרוּשָׁלִַם אֵת כָּל־הָרָעָה אֲשֶׁר דִּבַּרְתִּי עֲלֵיהֶם

against ;them have I spoken that the evil all Jerusalem the of inhabitants all

יַעַן דִּבַּרְתִּי אֲלֵיהֶם וְלֹא שָׁמֵעוּ וָאֶקְרָא לָהֶם וְלֹא עָנוּ׃

did they .answer but not to ,them have I and called they listen did but not ,them to spoke I be- ,cause

18 וּלְבֵית הָרֵכָבִים אָמַר יִרְמְיָהוּ כֹּה־אָמַר יְהוָה צְבָאוֹת

hosts Jehovah of says Thus ,Jeremiah said the Rechabites to And of house the

אֱלֹהֵי יִשְׂרָאֵל יַעַן אֲשֶׁר שְׁמַעְתֶּם עַל־מִצְוַת יְהוֹנָדָב אֲבִיכֶם

your ,father Jonadab the of command have you obeyed Because ,Israel the of God

וַתִּשְׁמְרוּ אֶת־כָּל־מִצְוֺתָיו וַתַּעֲשׂוּ כְּכֹל אֲשֶׁר־צִוָּה אֶתְכֶם׃

;you has he commanded that according all to have and done his commands all have and kept

19 לָכֵן כֹּה אָמַר יְהוָה צְבָאוֹת אֱלֹהֵי יִשְׂרָאֵל לֹא־יִכָּרֵת אִישׁ

man a be shall off cut Not ,Israel the of God ,hosts Jehovah of says thus so

לְיוֹנָדָב בֶּן־רֵכָב עֹמֵד לְפָנַי כָּל־הַיָּמִים׃

.days the all before Me stand ing Rechab the of son to Jonadab

CAP. XXXVI לו

CHAPTER 36

[1] And in the fourth year of Jehoiakim the son of Josiah king of Judah, this word came to Jeremiah from Jehovah, saying, [2] Take for yourself a roll of a book and write in it all the words that I have spoken to you against Israel, and against Judah, and against all the nations, from the day I spoke to you, from the days of Josiah, even to this day. [3] It may be the house of Judah will hear all the evil which I plan to do to them, that they may each man turn from his evil way, and I may forgive their iniquity and their sin. [4] Then Jeremiah called Baruch the son of Neriah. And Baruch

1 וַיְהִי בַּשָּׁנָה הָרְבִיעִת לִיהוֹיָקִים בֶּן־יֹאשִׁיָּהוּ מֶלֶךְ יְהוּדָה

,Judah king of Josiah the of son of Jehoiakim fourth the in year And was it

2 הָיָה הַדָּבָר הַזֶּה אֶל־יִרְמְיָהוּ מֵאֵת יְהוָה לֵאמֹר׃ קַח־לְךָ

for Take yourself ,saying ,Jehovah from Jeremiah to this word came

מְגִלַּת־סֵפֶר וְכָתַבְתָּ אֵלֶיהָ אֵת כָּל־הַדְּבָרִים אֲשֶׁר דִּבַּרְתִּי

have I spoken which the words all it in write and book a a of scroll

אֵלֶיךָ עַל־יִשְׂרָאֵל וְעַל־יְהוּדָה וְעַל־כָּל־הַגּוֹיִם מִיּוֹם דִּבַּרְתִּי

spoke I from day the the ,nations all and against ,Judah and against ,Israel against you to

3 אֵלֶיךָ מִימֵי יֹאשִׁיָּהוּ וְעַד הַיּוֹם הַזֶּה׃ אוּלַי יִשְׁמְעוּ בֵּית

house the of will hear Perhaps .this day to even ,Josiah the from of days you to

יְהוּדָה אֵת כָּל־הָרָעָה אֲשֶׁר אָנֹכִי חֹשֵׁב לַעֲשׂוֹת לָהֶם

,them to do to plan I which evil the all Judah

לְמַעַן יָשׁוּבוּ אִישׁ מִדַּרְכּוֹ הָרָעָה וְסָלַחְתִּי לַעֲוֺנָם

their iniquity will I then forgive ;evil his from way each man may they turn so that

4 וּלְחַטָּאתָם׃ וַיִּקְרָא יִרְמְיָהוּ אֶת־בָּרוּךְ בֶּן־נֵרִיָּה

.Neriah the of son Baruch Jeremiah Then called their and .sin

wrote from the mouth of Jeremiah all the words of Jehovah that He had spoken to him, on a roll of a book. [5] And Jeremiah commanded Baruch, saying, I am shut up; I cannot go to the house of Jehovah; [6] so you go and read in the roll that you have written from my mouth, the words of Jehovah (in) the house of Jehovah, in the ears of the people on the fasting day. And also you shall read them in the ears of all Judah who come out of their cities. [7] It may be their prayer will fall before Jehovah, and each one will turn from his evil way. For great (is) the anger and the wrath that Jehovah has spoken against this people. [8] And Baruch the son of Neriah did according to all that Jeremiah the prophet commanded him, reading in the book of the words of Jehovah (in) the house of Jehovah. [9] And it came to pass, in the fifth year of Jehoiakim the son of Josiah king of Judah, in the ninth month, they called a fast before Jehovah to all the people in Jerusalem, and to all the people who came from the cities of Judah to Jerusalem. [10] Then Baruch read in the book the words of Jeremiah (in) the house of Jehovah, in the room of Gemariah the son of Shaphan the scribe, in the upper court, at the entrance to the New Gate of the house of Jehovah, in the ears of all the people.

[11] When Micaiah the son of Gemariah, the son of Shaphan, had heard all the words of Jehovah out of the book, [12] then he went down into the king's house, into the scribe's room. And, lo, all the rulers were sitting there: Elishama

וַיִּכְתֹּב בָּרוּךְ מִפִּי יִרְמְיָהוּ אֵת כָּל־דִּבְרֵי יְהוָה אֲשֶׁר־דִּבֶּר
had he that Jehovah the all Jeremiah the from Baruch And
spoken of words of mouth wrote

5 אֵלָיו עַל־מְגִלַּת־סֵפֶר׃ וַיְצַוֶּה יִרְמְיָהוּ אֶת־בָּרוּךְ לֵאמֹר
,saying Baruch Jeremiah And .book a the on ,him to
commanded of scroll

6 אֲנִי עָצוּר לֹא אוּכַל לָבוֹא בֵּית יְהוָה׃ וּבָאתָ אַתָּה וְקָרָאתָ
and you go So .Jehovah the go to am I not am I
read of house to able ;up shut

בַמְּגִלָּה אֲשֶׁר־כָּתַבְתָּ מִפִּי אֶת־דִּבְרֵי יְהוָה בְּאָזְנֵי הָעָם
the the in Jehovah the my from have you that the in
people of ears of words ,mouth written scroll

בֵּית יְהוָה בְּיוֹם צוֹם וְגַם בְּאָזְנֵי כָל־יְהוּדָה הַבָּאִים
who Judah all the in And .fasting the on Jehovah's (in)
come of ears also of day house

7 מֵעָרֵיהֶם תִּקְרָאֵם׃ אוּלַי תִּפֹּל תְּחִנָּתָם לִפְנֵי יְהוָה וְיָשֻׁבוּ
will and ,Jehovah before their fall will Perhaps shall you their from
turn supplication .them read cities

אִישׁ מִדַּרְכּוֹ הָרָעָה כִּי־גָדוֹל הָאַף וְהַחֵמָה אֲשֶׁר־דִּבֶּר
has that the and the great For .evil his from each
spoken wrath anger (is) way man

8 יְהוָה אֶל־הָעָם הַזֶּה׃ וַיַּעַשׂ בָּרוּךְ בֶּן־נֵרִיָּה כְּכֹל אֲשֶׁר־
that according Neriah the Baruch did And .this people against Jeho-
all to of son vah

צִוָּהוּ יִרְמְיָהוּ הַנָּבִיא לִקְרֹא בַסֵּפֶר דִּבְרֵי יְהוָה בֵּית
(in) Jehovah the the in read to the Jeremiah com-
house of words book ,prophet him manded

9 יְהוָה׃ וַיְהִי בַשָּׁנָה הַחֲמִשִׁית לִיהוֹיָקִים בֶּן־יֹאשִׁיָּהוּ
Josiah the of fifth the in it And .Jehovah's
of son Jehoiakim year ,was

מֶלֶךְ־יְהוּדָה בַּחֹדֶשׁ הַתְּשִׁעִי קָרְאוּ צוֹם לִפְנֵי יְהוָה כָּל־
all (to) Jehovah before a they ,ninth the in ,Judah king
fast proclaimed month of

הָעָם בִּירוּשָׁלִָם וְכָל־הָעָם הַבָּאִים מֵעָרֵי יְהוּדָה בִּירוּשָׁלִָם׃
.Jerusalem to Judah the from who the and in the
of cities came people all ,Jerusalem people

10 וַיִּקְרָא בָרוּךְ בַּסֵּפֶר אֶת־דִּבְרֵי יִרְמְיָהוּ בֵּית יְהוָה בְּלִשְׁכַּת
the in ,Jehovah's (in) Jeremiah the the in Baruch Then
of room house of words book read

גְּמַרְיָהוּ בֶן־שָׁפָן הַסֹּפֵר בֶּחָצֵר הָעֶלְיוֹן פֶּתַח שַׁעַר בֵּית־
the Gate the the (at) ,upper the in the Shaphan the Gemariah
of house of entrance court scribe of son

11 יְהוָה הֶחָדָשׁ בְּאָזְנֵי כָּל־הָעָם׃ וַיִּשְׁמַע מִכָיְהוּ בֶן־גְּמַרְיָהוּ
.Gemariah the Micaiah When the all the in New Jehovah
of son heard had .people of ears

12 בֶן־שָׁפָן אֶת־כָּל־דִּבְרֵי יְהוָה מֵעַל הַסֵּפֶר׃ וַיֵּרֶד בֵּית־
house he then ,book the from Jehovah the all ,Shaphan the
to down went of words of son

הַמֶּלֶךְ עַל־לִשְׁכַּת הַסֹּפֵר וְהִנֵּה־שָׁם כָּל־הַשָּׂרִים יוֹשְׁבִים
were the all there And the room into the
sitting rulers ,behold .scribe's king's

the scribe, and Delaiah the son of Shemaiah, and Elnathan the son of Achbor, and Gemariah the son of Shaphan, and Zedekiah the son of Hananiah, and all the rulers. [13] Then Micaiah declared to them all the words that he had heard when Baruch read the book in the ears of the people. [14] And all the princes sent Jehudi the son of Nethaniah, the son of Shelemiah, the son of Cushi, to Baruch, saying, Take the roll in your hands, in which you have read in the ears of the people, take it and come. So Baruch the son of Neriah took the roll in his hand and came to them. [15] And they said to him, Sit down now and read it in our ears. So Baruch read in their ears. [16] Now it came to pass, when they had heard all the words, they turned each one to his companion in fear and said to Baruch, We will surely tell to the king of all these words. [17] And they asked Baruch, saying, Tell us now, how did you write all these word? From his mouth? [18] Then Baruch said to them, He spoke all these words to me from his mouth, and I wrote with ink on the book. [19] Then the rulers said to Baruch, Go hide yourselves, you and Jeremiah, and let no man know where you are.

[20] And they went in to the king into the court. But they laid up the roll in the room of Elishama the scribe, and told all the words in the ears of the king. [21] So the king sent

אֱלִישָׁמָע הַסֹּפֵר וּדְלָיָהוּ בֶן־שְׁמַעְיָהוּ וְאֶלְנָתָן בֶּן־עַכְבּוֹר
,Achbor the of son and Elnathan ,Shemaiah the of son and Delaiah the ,scribe Elishama

וּגְמַרְיָהוּ בֶן־שָׁפָן וְצִדְקִיָּהוּ בֶן־חֲנַנְיָהוּ וְכָל־הַשָּׂרִים׃ וַיַּגֵּד 13
Then declared the .rulers and all ,Hananiah the of son and Zedekiah ,Shephan the of son and Gemariah

לָהֶם מִיכָיְהוּ אֵת כָּל־הַדְּבָרִים אֲשֶׁר שָׁמֵעַ בִּקְרֹא בָרוּךְ
Baruch when read had he heard that the words all Micaiah to them

בַּסֵּפֶר בְּאָזְנֵי הָעָם׃ וַיִּשְׁלְחוּ כָל־הַשָּׂרִים אֶל־בָּרוּךְ אֶת־ 14
Baruch to the rulers all sent And the .people the in of ears the book

יְהוּדִי בֶּן־נְתַנְיָהוּ בֶּן־שֶׁלֶמְיָהוּ בֶן־כּוּשִׁי לֵאמֹר הַמְּגִלָּה
scroll the ,saying ,Cushi the of son ,Shelemiah the of son ,Nethaniah the of son Jehudi

אֲשֶׁר קָרָאתָ בָּהּ בְּאָזְנֵי הָעָם קָחֶנָּה בְיָדְךָ וָלֵךְ וַיִּקַּח
So took and .come your in ,hand it take the ,people the in of ears ,it in have you read which

בָּרוּךְ בֶּן־נֵרִיָּהוּ אֶת־הַמְּגִלָּה בְּיָדוֹ וַיָּבֹא אֲלֵיהֶם׃ וַיֹּאמְרוּ 15
they And said .them to and came his in hand scroll the Neriah the of son Baruch

אֵלָיו שֵׁב נָא וּקְרָאֶנָּה בְּאָזְנֵינוּ וַיִּקְרָא בָרוּךְ בְּאָזְנֵיהֶם׃
.ears their in Baruch read So .ears our in and it read now Sit down ,him to

וַיְהִי כְּשָׁמְעָם אֶת־כָּל־הַדְּבָרִים פָּחֲדוּ אִישׁ אֶל־רֵעֵהוּ 16
his companion to each man turned they in fear the ,words all they when had heard it And was

וַיֹּאמְרוּ אֶל־בָּרוּךְ הַגֵּיד נַגִּיד לַמֶּלֶךְ אֵת כָּל־הַדְּבָרִים
words all the to king will We tell surely ,Baruch to said and

הָאֵלֶּה׃ וְאֶת־בָּרוּךְ שָׁאֲלוּ לֵאמֹר הַגֶּד־נָא לָנוּ אֵיךְ כָּתַבְתָּ 17
you did write how to ,us now Tell ,saying they ,asked Baruch And .these

אֶת־כָּל־הַדְּבָרִים הָאֵלֶּה מִפִּיו׃ וַיֹּאמֶר לָהֶם בָּרוּךְ מִפִּיו 18
From mouth his ,Baruch to them Then said From ?mouth his ?these words all

יִקְרָא אֵלַי אֵת כָּל־הַדְּבָרִים הָאֵלֶּה וַאֲנִי כֹּתֵב עַל־הַסֵּפֶר
book the on wrote I and ,these words all me to he read

בַּדְּיוֹ׃ וַיֹּאמְרוּ הַשָּׂרִים אֶל־בָּרוּךְ לֵךְ הִסָּתֵר אַתָּה 19
you hide ,yourself Go ,Baruch to rulers the Then said with .ink

וְיִרְמְיָהוּ וְאִישׁ אַל־יֵדַע אֵיפֹה אַתֶּם׃ וַיָּבֹאוּ אֶל־הַמֶּלֶךְ 20
king the to they And in went you .(are) where let do know not a and man and ,Jeremiah

חָצֵרָה וְאֶת־הַמְּגִלָּה הִפְקִדוּ בְּלִשְׁכַּת אֱלִישָׁמָע הַסֹּפֵר
the ,scribe Elishama the in of room left they the scroll but the into ,court

וַיַּגִּידוּ בְּאָזְנֵי הַמֶּלֶךְ אֵת כָּל־הַדְּבָרִים׃ וַיִּשְׁלַח הַמֶּלֶךְ 21
king the sent So .words the all king the the in of ears they and told

Jehudi to seize the roll. And he took it out of the room of Elishama the scribe. And Jehudi read it in the ears of the king, and in the ears of all the rulers who stood beside the king. [22] Now the king was sitting in the winter house in the ninth month; and with the fire-pan burning before him. [23] And it came to pass, when Jehudi had read three or four leaves, he cut it with the scribe's knife and threw (it) into the fire that (was) in the fire-pan, until all the roll was burned up in the fire that (was) in the fire-pan. [24] Yet the king and all his servants who heard these words were not afraid, not did they tear their garments. [25] But Elnathan and Delaiah and Gemariah had pleaded with the king that he should not burn the roll, but he would not listen to them. [26] And the king commanded Jerahmeel the son of Hammelech, and Seraiah the son of Azriel, and Shelemiah the son of Abdeel, to seize Baruch the scribe and Jeremiah the prophet; but Jehovah hid them.

[27] Then the word of Jehovah came to Jeremiah, after the king had burned the roll, and the words which Baruch wrote from the mouth of Jeremiah, saying, [28] Take for yourself another roll and write on it all the former words that were in the first roll, which Jehoiakim the king of Judah has burned.

את־יהודי לקחת את־המגלה ויקחה מלשכת אלישמע

Elishama | the from of room | he And it took | .scroll the | take to | Jehudi

הספר ויקראה יהודי באזני המלך ובאזני כל־השרים

rulers the | all | the in and of ears | ,king the | the in of ears | Jehudi | read And it | the .scribe

העמדים מעל המלך׃ והמלך יושב בית החרף בחדש 22

the in month | the ,winter | (in) house | was sitting | the Now king | .king the | beside | stood who

התשיעי ואת־האח לפניו מבערת׃ ויהי | כקרוא יהודי 23

Jehudi | had when read | And ,was it | .burning | before him | the brazier | and with | ,ninth

שלש דלתות וארבעה יקרעה בתער הספר והשלך

threw and (it) | the scribe's | with knife | tore he it | ,four or | leaves | three

אל־האש אשר אל־האח עד־תם כל־המגלה על־האש

the fire | in | scroll the | all | was consumed | until | the ,brazier | in | that (was) | the fire | into

אשר על־האח׃ ולא פחדו ולא קרעו את־בגדיהם 24

their garments | they did tear | nor | were ,afraid | Yet not | .brazier the in | that (was)

המלך וכל־עבדיו השמעים את כל־הדברים האלה׃

.these | words | all | heard who | his servants | and all | king the

וגם אלנתן ודליהו וגמריהו הפגעו במלך לבלתי שרף 25

should he burn | that not | the with king | had pleaded | and Gemariah | and Delaiah | Elnathan | But

את־המגלה ולא שמע אליהם׃ ויצוה המלך את־ 26

king the | And commanded | .them to | would he listen | but not | the ,scroll

ירחמאל בן־המלך ואת־שריהו בן־עזריאל ואת־שלמיהו

Shelemiah | and | ,Azriel | the of son | Seraiah | and | king the | the of son | Jerameel

בן־עבדאל לקחת את־ברוך הספר ואת ירמיהו הנביא

the ;prophet | Jeremiah | and | the scribe | Baruch | seize to | Abdeel | the of son

ויסתרם יהוה׃ ויהי דבר־יהוה אל־ירמיהו אחרי | 27

after | ,Jeremiah | to | Jehovah | the of word | Then came | .Jehovah | hid but them

שרף המלך את־המגלה ואת־הדברים אשר כתב

wrote | which | words the | and | ,scroll the | king the | had burned

ברוך מפי ירמיהו לאמר׃ שוב קח־לך מגלה אחרת 28

another | scroll | for Take yourself | again | ,saying | ,Jeremiah's | from mouth | Baruch

וכתב עליה את כל־הדברים הראשנים אשר היו על־

in | were | that | former | words the | all | it upon | and write

המגלה הראשנה אשר שרף יהויקים מלך־יהודה׃

.Judah | the of king | Jehoiakim | has burned | which | ,former | scroll the

[29] And you shall say to Jehoiakim the king of Judah, Thus says Jehovah: You have burned this roll, saying, Why have you written on it, saying, The king of Babylon shall surely come and destroy this land, and shall cause man and beast to cease from there?

29 וְעַל־יְהוֹיָקִים מֶלֶךְ־יְהוּדָה תֹאמַר כֹּה אָמַר יְהוָה אַתָּה
You :Jehovah says Thus shall you Judah the Jehoiakim And
,say of king to

שָׂרַפְתָּ אֶת־הַמְּגִלָּה הַזֹּאת לֵאמֹר מַדּוּעַ כָּתַבְתָּ עָלֶיהָ
it on you have Why ,saying ,this roll have
written burned

לֵאמֹר בֹּא יָבוֹא מֶלֶךְ בָּבֶל וְהִשְׁחִית אֶת־הָאָרֶץ הַזֹּאת
,this land and Babylon The shall surely ,saying
destroy of king come

[30] Therefore thus says Jehovah of Jehoiakim king of Judah: Not shall be (one) to him to sit on the throne of David. And his dead body shall be cast out in the day to the heat, and in the night to the frost. [31] And I will punish him and his seed and his servants for their sin. And I will bring on them, and on the people of Jerusalem, and on the men of Judah, all the evil that I have spoken against them. But they did not listen.

30 וְהִשְׁבִּית מִמֶּנָּה אָדָם וּבְהֵמָה׃ לָכֵן כֹּה־אָמַר יְהוָה
Jehovah says thus Therefore ?beast and man from will and
there cease make

עַל־יְהוֹיָקִים מֶלֶךְ יְהוּדָה לֹא־יִהְיֶה־לּוֹ יוֹשֵׁב עַל־כִּסֵּא
the on sit to to shall Not :Judah king Jehoiakim of
of throne him be (any) of

דָוִד וְנִבְלָתוֹ תִּהְיֶה מֻשְׁלֶכֶת לַחֹרֶב בַּיּוֹם וְלַקֶּרַח בַּלָּיְלָה׃
the in to and the in the to out cast shall His And .David
.night frost the ,day heat be body dead

31 וּפָקַדְתִּי עָלָיו וְעַל־זַרְעוֹ וְעַל־עֲבָדָיו אֶת־עֲוֺנָם וְהֵבֵאתִי
I And their (for) his and seed his and him will I And
bring will .iniquity servants punish

עֲלֵיהֶם וְעַל־יֹשְׁבֵי יְרוּשָׁלִַם וְאֶל־אִישׁ יְהוּדָה אֵת כָּל־
all ,Judah the and ,Jerusalem the and them on
of men on of people on

[32] Then Jeremiah took another roll and gave it to Baruch the scribe, the son of Neriah, who wrote in it from the mouth of Jeremiah all the words of the book which Jehoiakim king of Judah had burned in the fire. And many words like them were added to them.

32 הָרָעָה אֲשֶׁר־דִּבַּרְתִּי אֲלֵיהֶם וְלֹא שָׁמֵעוּ׃ וְיִרְמְיָהוּ
Then did they But against have I that evil the
Jeremiah .listen not .them spoken

לָקַח ׀ מְגִלָּה אַחֶרֶת וַיִּתְּנָהּ אֶל־בָּרוּךְ בֶּן־נֵרִיָּהוּ הַסֹּפֵר
the ,Neriah the ,Baruch to gave and another roll took
,scribe of son it

וַיִּכְתֹּב עָלֶיהָ מִפִּי יִרְמְיָהוּ אֵת כָּל־דִּבְרֵי הַסֵּפֶר אֲשֶׁר
which book the the all Jeremiah from it on who
of words mouth the wrote

שָׂרַף יְהוֹיָקִים מֶלֶךְ־יְהוּדָה בָּאֵשׁ וְעוֹד נוֹסַף עֲלֵיהֶם דְּבָרִים
words them to were And the in Judah king Jehoiakim had
added again .fire of burned

רַבִּים כָּהֵמָּה׃
like many
.them

CAP. XXXVII לז

CHAPTER 37

[1] And King Zedekiah the son of Josiah reigned instead of Coniah the son of Jehoiakim, whom Nebuchadnezzar king of Babylon made king in the land of Judah. [2] But not he, nor his servants, nor the people of the land, listened to the words of Jehovah which He

1 וַיִּמְלָךְ־מֶלֶךְ צִדְקִיָּהוּ בֶּן־יֹאשִׁיָּהוּ תַּחַת כָּנְיָהוּ בֶּן־יְהוֹיָקִים
,Jehoiakim the Coniah instead Josiah the Zedekiah King And
of son of of son reigned

2 אֲשֶׁר הִמְלִיךְ נְבוּכַדְרֶאצַּר מֶלֶךְ־בָּבֶל בְּאֶרֶץ יְהוּדָה׃ וְלֹא
But .Judah the in Babylon king Nebuchadnezzar made whom
not of land of king

שָׁמַע הוּא וַעֲבָדָיו וְעַם הָאָרֶץ אֶל־דִּבְרֵי יְהוָה אֲשֶׁר
which Jehovah the to the the nor his nor he listened
of words land of people servants

spoke by the prophet Jeremiah. [3] And Zedekiah the king sent Jehucal the son of Shelemiah and Zephaniah the son of Maaseiah the priest to the prophet Jeremiah, saying, Pray now to Jehovah our God for us. [4] Now Jeremiah came in and went out among the people, for they had not put him into prison. [5] Then Pharaoh's army had come forth out of Egypt. And when the Chaldeans who besieged Jerusalem heard news of them, they departed from Jerusalem.

[6] Then the word of Jehovah came to the prophet Jeremiah, saying, [7] Thus says Jehovah, the God of Israel: You shall say this to the king of Judah, who sent you to Me to inquire of Me: Behold, Pharaoh's army, which has come out to help you, shall return to Egypt into their own land. [8] And the Chaldeans shall come again and fight against this city, and take it, and burn it with fire. [9] Thus says Jehovah: Do not deceive yourselves, saying, The Chaldeans will surely leave us; for they shall not leave. [10] For though you had stricken the whole army of the Chaldeans who fight against you, and there remained (only) wounded men among them, (yet) they would rise up, each man in his tent, and burn this city with fire.

[11] And it came to pass, when the army of Chaldeans departed from Jerusalem, because of Pharaoh's army, [12] then Jeremiah went out of Jerusalem to go into the land of Benjamin, to receive a portion

3 דִּבֶּר בְּיַד יִרְמְיָהוּ הַנָּבִיא׃ וַיִּשְׁלַח הַמֶּלֶךְ צִדְקִיָּהוּ אֶת־
Zedekiah King the And the Jeremiah the by He
sent .prophet of hand spoke

יְהוּכַל בֶּן־שֶׁלֶמְיָה וְאֶת־צְפַנְיָהוּ בֶן־מַעֲשֵׂיָה הַכֹּהֵן אֶל־
to the Maaseiah the Zephaniah and ,Shelemiah the Jehucal
priest of son of son

יִרְמְיָהוּ הַנָּבִיא לֵאמֹר הִתְפַּלֶּל־נָא בַעֲדֵנוּ אֶל־יְהוָה
Jehovah to us for now Pray ,saying the Jeremiah
,prophet

4 אֱלֹהֵינוּ׃ וְיִרְמְיָהוּ בָּא וְיֹצֵא בְּתוֹךְ הָעָם וְלֹא־נָתְנוּ אֹתוֹ
him they for the among went and came Now .God our
put had not ,people out in Jeremiah

5 בֵּית הַכְּלִיא׃ וְחֵיל פַּרְעֹה יָצָא מִמִּצְרָיִם וַיִּשְׁמְעוּ
when And .Egypt of had Pharaoh's Then .prison a in
heard out come army of house

הַכַּשְׂדִּים הַצָּרִים עַל־יְרוּשָׁלִַם אֶת־שִׁמְעָם וַיֵּעָלוּ מֵעַל
from they of news Jerusalem who the
departed ,them besieged Chaldeans

6 יְרוּשָׁלִָם׃ וַיְהִי דְּבַר־יְהוָה אֶל־יִרְמְיָהוּ הַנָּבִיא
the Jeremiah to Jehovah the Then .Jerusalem
,prophet of word came

7 לֵאמֹר׃ כֹּה־אָמַר יְהוָה אֱלֹהֵי יִשְׂרָאֵל כֹּה תֹאמְרוּ אֶל־
to shall you This :Israel the ,Jehovah says Thus ,saying
say of God

מֶלֶךְ יְהוּדָה הַשֹּׁלֵחַ אֶתְכֶם אֵלַי לְדָרְשֵׁנִי הִנֵּה ׀ חֵיל
army ,Behold inquire to Me to you sent who ,Judah the
:Me of of king

8 פַּרְעֹה הַיֹּצֵא לָכֶם לְעֶזְרָה שָׁב לְאַרְצוֹ מִצְרָיִם׃ וְשָׁבוּ
shall And of his to shall ,help to you to which Pharaoh's
return .Egypt land own return out came

הַכַּשְׂדִּים וְנִלְחֲמוּ עַל־הָעִיר הַזֹּאת וּלְכָדֻהָ וּשְׂרָפֻהָ בָאֵשׁ׃
with burn and take and ,this city against and the
.fire it ,it fight Chaldeans

9 כֹּה אָמַר יְהוָה אַל־תַּשִּׁאוּ נַפְשֹׁתֵיכֶם לֵאמֹר הָלֹךְ
Surely ,saying ,yourselves Do not ,Jehovah says Thus
deceive

10 יֵלְכוּ מֵעָלֵינוּ הַכַּשְׂדִּים כִּי לֹא יֵלֵכוּ׃ כִּי אִם־הִכִּיתֶם כָּל־
the had you though For shall they not for the from will
whole struck .leave ;Chaldeans us leave

חֵיל כַּשְׂדִּים הַנִּלְחָמִים אִתְּכֶם וְנִשְׁאֲרוּ־בָם אֲנָשִׁים
men among there and against fight who the army
them remained ,you Chaldeans of

מְדֻקָּרִים אִישׁ בְּאָהֳלוֹ יָקוּמוּ וְשָׂרְפוּ אֶת־הָעִיר הַזֹּאת
this city burn and would they his in each ,wounded
up rise ,tent man

11 בָּאֵשׁ׃ וְהָיָה בְּהֵעָלוֹת חֵיל הַכַּשְׂדִּים מֵעַל יְרוּשָׁלִַם מִפְּנֵי
because ,Jerusalem from Chaldeans the left when it And with
of of army ,was .fire

12 חֵיל פַּרְעֹה׃ וַיֵּצֵא יִרְמְיָהוּ מִירוּשָׁלִַם לָלֶכֶת אֶרֶץ
the go to of Jeremiah Then .Pharaoh's army
of land (into) Jerusalem out went

from there in the midst of the people. [13] And it happened, (when) he (was) in the gate of Benjamin, a captain of the guard (was) there, whose name was Irijah, the son of Shelemiah, the son of Hananiah. And he took Jeremiah the prophet, saying, You are falling to the Chaldeans. [14] Then Jeremiah said, A lie! I am not falling to the Chaldeans. But he did not listen to him; so Irijah took Jeremiah and brought him to the princes. [15] And the princes were angry with Jeremiah and struck him and put him in the house of prison, the house of Jonathan the scribe. For they had made it into a house of prison.

[16] When Jeremiah had entered into the house of the pit, and into the cells, then Jeremiah remained there many days. [17] And Zedekiah the king sent and took him out. And the king asked him secretly in his house and said, Is there word from Jehovah? And Jeremiah said, There is. For, He said, You shall be delivered into the hand of the king of Babylon. [18] And Jeremiah said to King Zedekiah, What have I sinned against you, or against your servants, or against this people, that you have put me in the house of prison? [19] Where now (are) your prophets who prophesied to you, saying, The king of Babylon shall not come against you or against this land? [20] Therefore hear now, I beg you, O my lord the king; I beseech you, let my plea fall before you, that you do not make me return to the house of Jonathan the scribe, lest I die there. [21] Then Zedekiah the king commanded and they committed Jeremiah

בִּנְיָמִן לַחֲלִק מִשָּׁם בְּתוֹךְ הָעָם׃ וַיְהִי־הוּא בְּשַׁעַר בִּנְיָמִן 13

,Benjamin the in (as) it And the the in from receive to Benja-
of gate (was) he ,was .people of midst there portion a ,min

וְשָׁם בַּעַל פְּקִדֻת וּשְׁמוֹ יִרְאִיָּיה בֶּן־שֶׁלֶמְיָה בֶּן־חֲנַנְיָה

,Hananiah the ,Shelemiah the Irijah his and the cap- a and
of son of son name ,guard of tain there

וַיִּתְפֹּשׂ אֶת־יִרְמְיָהוּ הַנָּבִיא לֵאמֹר אֶל־הַכַּשְׂדִּים אַתָּה

You the to ,saying the Jeremiah he And
Chaldeans ,prophet seized

נֹפֵל׃ וַיֹּאמֶר יִרְמְיָהוּ שֶׁקֶר אֵינֶנִּי נֹפֵל עַל־הַכַּשְׂדִּים וְלֹא 14

But the to am I not !lie A ,Jeremiah Then are
not .Chaldeans falling said .falling

שָׁמַע אֵלָיו וַיִּתְפֹּשׂ יִרְאִיָּיה בְּיִרְמְיָהוּ וַיְבִאֵהוּ אֶל־הַשָּׂרִים׃

the to brought and Jeremiah Irijah seized so to did he
.rulers him ;him listen

וַיִּקְצְפוּ הַשָּׂרִים עַל־יִרְמְיָהוּ וְהִכּוּ אֹתוֹ וְנָתְנוּ אוֹתוֹ בֵּית 15

the (in) him put and ,him and Jeremiah with the were And
of house struck rulers angry

הָאֵסוּר בֵּית יְהוֹנָתָן הַסֹּפֵר כִּי־אֹתוֹ עָשׂוּ לְבֵית הַכֶּלֶא׃

.prison a into they it For the Jonathan the (in) prison
of house made had .scribe of house

כִּי בָא יִרְמְיָהוּ אֶל־בֵּית הַבּוֹר וְאֶל־הַחֲנֻיוֹת וַיֵּשֶׁב־שָׁם 16

there then the and pit the the into Jeremiah had When
remained ,cells into of house entered

יִרְמְיָהוּ יָמִים רַבִּים׃ וַיִּשְׁלַח הַמֶּלֶךְ צִדְקִיָּהוּ וַיִּקָּחֵהוּ 17

took and Zedekiah king the sent And .many days Jeremiah
.out him

וַיִּשְׁאָלֵהוּ הַמֶּלֶךְ בְּבֵיתוֹ בַּסֵּתֶר וַיֹּאמֶר הֲיֵשׁ דָּבָר מֵאֵת

from word Is ,said and secretly his in king the asked And
there house him

יְהוָה וַיֹּאמֶר יִרְמְיָהוּ יֵשׁ וַיֹּאמֶר בְּיַד־מֶלֶךְ בָּבֶל תִּנָּתֵן׃

shall you Baby- the Into He For There ,Jeremiah said And Jeho-
.given be lon's of king hand ,said .is ?vah

וַיֹּאמֶר יִרְמְיָהוּ אֶל־הַמֶּלֶךְ צִדְקִיָּהוּ מֶה חָטָאתִי לְךָ 18

against have I What ,Zedekiah King to Jeremiah said And
,you sinned

וְלַעֲבָדֶיךָ וְלָעָם הַזֶּה כִּי־נְתַתֶּם אוֹתִי אֶל־בֵּית הַכֶּלֶא׃

?prison the in me you that ,this against or against or
of house put have people ,servants Your

וְאַיֵּו נְבִיאֵיכֶם אֲשֶׁר־נִבְּאוּ לָכֶם לֵאמֹר לֹא־יָבֹא מֶלֶךְ־ 19

The shall not ,saying ,you to prophesied who your Where
of king come prophets (are) now

בָּבֶל עֲלֵיכֶם וְעַל הָאָרֶץ הַזֹּאת׃ וְעַתָּה שְׁמַע־נָא אֲדֹנִי 20

my O beg I ,hear Therefore ?this land or against Baby-
lord ,you now against you lon

הַמֶּלֶךְ תִּפָּל־נָא תְחִנָּתִי לְפָנֶיךָ וְאַל־תְּשִׁבֵנִי בֵּית יְהוֹנָתָן

Jonathan the me make do and before plea my please let ,king the
of house to return not ,you fall

הַסֹּפֵר וְלֹא אָמוּת שָׁם׃ וַיְצַוֶּה הַמֶּלֶךְ צִדְקִיָּהוּ וַיַּפְקִדוּ 21

they and ,Zedekiah the Then .there die I lest the
committed king commanded ,scribe

into the court of the guard-house, and that they should give him a piece of bread out of the bakers' street daily, until all the bread of the city was gone. And Jeremiah remained in the court of the guard-house.

אֶת־יִרְמְיָהוּ בַּחֲצַר הַמַּטָּרָה וְנָתֹן לוֹ כִכַּר־לֶחֶם לַיּוֹם
daily bread a to they and guard- the the into Jeremiah
of piece him gave ,house of court

מִחוּץ הָאֹפִים עַד־תֹּם כָּל־הַלֶּחֶם מִן־הָעִיר וַיֵּשֶׁב יִרְמְיָהוּ
Jeremiah And .city the of the all was until the of out
remained bread gone ,bakers' street

בַּחֲצַר הַמַּטָּרָה׃
guard- the the in
.house of court

CAP. XXXVIII לח

CHAPTER 38

[1] And Shephatiah the son of Mattan, and Gedaliah the son of Pashur, and Jucal the son of Shelemiah, and Pashur the son of Malchiah, heard the words that Jeremiah had spoken to all the people, saying, [2] Thus says Jehovah, He who remains in this city shall die by the sword, by the famine, and by the plague. But he who goes forth to the Chaldeans shall live; and shall be to him his life as a prize, and he shall live. [3] Thus says Jehovah: This city shall surely be given into the hand of the king of Babylon's army, and he shall take it. [4] Therefore the rulers said to the king, We beg you, let this man be put to death. For in this way he weakens the hands of the men of war who remain in this city, and the hands of all the people, in speaking these words to them; for this man does not seek the good of this people, but the evil.

[5] Then Zedekiah the king said, Behold, he (is) in your hand. For the king can not do anything against you. [6] Then they took Jeremiah and threw him into the pit of Malchiah the son of the king, which (was) in the court of the guard-house. And they let Jeremiah down with ropes; and

1 וַיִּשְׁמַע שְׁפַטְיָה בֶן מַתָּן וּגְדַלְיָהוּ בֶּן־פַּשְׁחוּר וְיוּכַל בֶּן
the and ,Pashhur the and ,Mattan the Shephatiah And
of son Jucal of son Gedaliah of son heard

שֶׁלֶמְיָהוּ וּפַשְׁחוּר בֶּן־מַלְכִּיָּה אֶת־הַדְּבָרִים אֲשֶׁר יִרְמְיָהוּ
Jeremiah that the Malchiah the and ,Shelemiah
words of son Pashhur

2 מְדַבֵּר אֶל־כָּל־הָעָם לֵאמֹר׃ כֹּה אָמַר יְהוָה הַיֹּשֵׁב בָּעִיר
city in who He ,Jehovah says Thus ,saying the all to had
remains ,people spoken

הַזֹּאת יָמוּת בַּחֶרֶב בָּרָעָב וּבַדָּבֶר וְהַיֹּצֵא אֶל־הַכַּשְׂדִּים
the to he But the by and the by the by shall this
Chaldeans out going .plague ,famine ,sword die

3 יְחְיֶה וְהָיְתָה־לּוֹ נַפְשׁוֹ לְשָׁלָל וָחָי׃ כֹּה אָמַר יְהוָה
:Jehovah says Thus he and a as his to shall and shall
.live shall ,prize life him be ;live

הִנָּתֹן תִּנָּתֵן הָעִיר הַזֹּאת בְּיַד חֵיל מֶלֶךְ־בָּבֶל וּלְכָדָהּ׃
he and Babylon's the army the into this city shall Surely
.it take shall of king of hand given be

4 וַיֹּאמְרוּ הַשָּׂרִים אֶל־הַמֶּלֶךְ יוּמַת נָא אֶת־הָאִישׁ הַזֶּה כִּי
For .this man Please be let ,king the to rulers the Therefore
executed said

עַל־כֵּן הוּא מְרַפֵּא אֶת־יְדֵי אַנְשֵׁי הַמִּלְחָמָה הַנִּשְׁאָרִים ׀
who war the men the weakens he this in
remain of of hands way

בָּעִיר הַזֹּאת וְאֵת יְדֵי כָל־הָעָם לְדַבֵּר אֲלֵיהֶם כַּדְּבָרִים
words them to in the all the and ,this city in
speaking ,people of hands

הָאֵלֶּה כִּי ׀ הָאִישׁ הַזֶּה אֵינֶנּוּ דֹרֵשׁ לְשָׁלוֹם לָעָם הַזֶּה כִּי
but ,this of the seek does this man for ;these
people good not

5 אִם־לְרָעָה׃ וַיֹּאמֶר הַמֶּלֶךְ צִדְקִיָּהוּ הִנֵּה־הוּא בְּיֶדְכֶם כִּי־
For your in he ,Behold ,Zedekiah ,king the Then .evil the
.hand (is) said

6 אֵין הַמֶּלֶךְ יוּכַל אֶתְכֶם דָּבָר׃ וַיִּקְחוּ אֶת־יִרְמְיָהוּ וַיַּשְׁלִכוּ
and Jeremiah Then (any) against able is king the not
threw took they .thing you do to

אֹתוֹ אֶל־הַבּוֹר ׀ מַלְכִּיָּהוּ בֶן־הַמֶּלֶךְ אֲשֶׁר בַּחֲצַר הַמַּטָּרָה
guard- the the in which the the Malchiah the into him
house of court (was) ,king of son of pit

no water was in the pit, only mud. So Jeremiah sank into the mud.

[7] Now Ebed-melech, the Ethiopian man of the eunuchs which was in the king's house, heard that they had put Jeremiah into the pit – the king then sitting in the gate of Benjamin – [8] Ebed-melech went out of the king's house and spoke to the king, saying, [9] My lord the king, these men have done evil in all that they have done to Jeremiah the prophet, whom they have thrown into the pit. And he has died because of the famine in the place where he is, for (there is) no more food in the city. [10] Then the king commanded Ebed-melech the Ethiopian, saying, Take in your hand thirty men from here and lift Jeremiah the prophet up out of the pit before he dies. [11] So Ebed-melech took the men in his hand and went into the king's house, to under the treasury. And he took worn out clothes and worn out rags from there and let them down by ropes into the pit to Jeremiah.

[12] And Ebed-melech the Ethiopian said to Jeremiah, Now put (these) old worn out clothes and rags under the armpits of your hands, under the ropes. And Jeremiah did so. [13] So they drew up Jeremiah with ropes and took him out of the pit. And Jeremiah lived in the court of the guard-house.

[14] Then Zedekiah the king sent and took Jeremiah

וַיְשַׁלְּחוּ אֶת־יִרְמְיָהוּ בַּחֲבָלִים וּבַבּוֹר אֵין־מַיִם כִּי אִם־
only ,water not in and with Jeremiah they And
was pit the ,ropes down let

7 טִיט וַיִּטְבַּע יִרְמְיָהוּ בַּטִּיט׃ וַיִּשְׁמַע עֶבֶד־מֶלֶךְ הַכּוּשִׁי
the ,melechEbed- And the into Jeremiah sank So .mud
Ethiopian heard .mud

אִישׁ סָרִיס וְהוּא בְּבֵית הַמֶּלֶךְ כִּי־נָתְנוּ אֶת־יִרְמְיָהוּ אֶל־
into Jeremiah they that the in which the man
put had ,king's house (was) eunuchs of

8 הַבּוֹר וְהַמֶּלֶךְ יוֹשֵׁב בְּשַׁעַר בִּנְיָמִן׃ וַיֵּצֵא עֶבֶד־מֶלֶךְ מִבֵּית
of melech Ebed- and ;Benjamin the in sitting the and ;pit the
house out went of gate king

9 הַמֶּלֶךְ וַיְדַבֵּר אֶל־הַמֶּלֶךְ לֵאמֹר׃ אֲדֹנִי הַמֶּלֶךְ הֵרֵעוּ
done have the My ,saying ,king the to and the
evil ,king lord spoke king's

הָאֲנָשִׁים הָאֵלֶּה אֵת כָּל־אֲשֶׁר עָשׂוּ לְיִרְמְיָהוּ הַנָּבִיא
the to have they that in these men
,prophet Jeremiah done all

אֵת אֲשֶׁר־הִשְׁלִיכוּ אֶל־הַבּוֹר וַיָּמָת תַּחְתָּיו מִפְּנֵי הָרָעָב
the because his in he And the into have they whom
,famine of place died has .pit thrown

10 כִּי אֵין הַלֶּחֶם עוֹד בָּעִיר׃ וַיְצַוֶּה הַמֶּלֶךְ אֵת עֶבֶד־מֶלֶךְ
melech Ebed- king the Then the in more food there for
commanded .city no is

הַכּוּשִׁי לֵאמֹר קַח בְּיָדְךָ מִזֶּה שְׁלֹשִׁים אֲנָשִׁים וְהַעֲלִיתָ
lift and ,men thirty from your in Take ,saying the
up here hand ,Ethiopian

11 אֶת־יִרְמְיָהוּ הַנָּבִיא מִן־הַבּוֹר בְּטֶרֶם יָמוּת׃ וַיִּקַּח | עֶבֶד־
Ebed- So .dies he before the out the Jeremiah
took pit of prophet

מֶלֶךְ אֶת־הָאֲנָשִׁים בְּיָדוֹ וַיָּבֹא בֵית־הַמֶּלֶךְ אֶל־תַּחַת
under to the house went and his in the melech
king's into hand men

הָאוֹצָר וַיִּקַּח מִשָּׁם בְּלוֹיֵ הסחבות וּבְלוֹיֵ מְלָחִים
rags and clothes worn from he And the
out worn out there took .treasury

12 וַיְשַׁלְּחֵם אֶל־יִרְמְיָהוּ אֶל־הַבּוֹר בַּחֲבָלִים׃ וַיֹּאמֶר עֶבֶד־
Ebed- said And .ropes by the into Jeremiah to let and
pit down them

מֶלֶךְ הַכּוּשִׁי אֶל־יִרְמְיָהוּ שִׂים נָא בְּלוֹאֵי הַסְּחָבוֹת
clothes (these) now Put .Jeremiah to the melech
out worn Ethiopian

וְהַמְּלָחִים תַּחַת אַצִּלוֹת יָדֶיךָ מִתַּחַת לַחֲבָלִים וַיַּעַשׂ
And the under your arm- the under rags and
did .ropes ,hands of pits

13 יִרְמְיָהוּ כֵּן׃ וַיִּמְשְׁכוּ אֶת־יִרְמְיָהוּ בַּחֲבָלִים וַיַּעֲלוּ אֹתוֹ
him took and with Jeremiah they So .so Jeremiah
out ropes up drew

14 מִן־הַבּוֹר וַיֵּשֶׁב יִרְמְיָהוּ בַּחֲצַר הַמַּטָּרָה׃ וַיִּשְׁלַח הַמֶּלֶךְ
the Then guard- the the in Jeremiah And the of
king sent .house of court dwelt .pit

the prophet to him into the third entrance that is in the house of Jehovah. And the king said to Jeremiah, I will ask you a thing; do not hide a thing from me. [15] Then Jeremiah said to Zedekiah, If I declare (it) to you, will you not surely put me to death? And if I counsel you, you will not listen to me. [16] And Zedekiah the king swore secretly to Jeremiah, saying, (As) Jehovah lives, who made us this soul, I will not put you to death, nor will I give you into the hand of these men who seek your life. [17] Then Jeremiah said to Zedekiah, Thus says Jehovah, the God of hosts, the God of Israel: If you will surely go out to the king of Babylon's princes, then your soul shall live, and this city shall not be burned with fire. And you and your house shall live.

[18] But if you will not go out to the king of Babylon's princes, then this city shall be given into the hands of the Chaldeans, and they shall burn it with fire, and you shall not escape out of their hand. [19] And Zedekiah the king said to Jeremiah, I am afraid of the Jews who have fallen to the Chaldeans, and they deliver me into their hand, and they abuse me. [20] But Jeremiah said, They shall not deliver (you). I beseech you, obey the voice of Jehovah which I speak to you; and it will be well to you, and your soul will live. [21] But if you refuse to go out, this (is) the word Jehovah has shown to me:

צִדְקִיָּהוּ וַיִּקַּח אֶת־יִרְמְיָהוּ הַנָּבִיא אֵלָיו אֶל־מָבוֹא הַשְּׁלִישִׁי
the third entrance into to him the prophet Jeremiah and took Zedekiah

אֲשֶׁר בְּבֵית יְהוָה וַיֹּאמֶר הַמֶּלֶךְ אֶל־יִרְמְיָהוּ שֹׁאֵל אֲנִי
I will ask ,Jeremiah to king the said And .Jehovah the in of house that (is)

15 אֹתְךָ דָּבָר אַל־תְּכַחֵד מִמֶּנִּי דָּבָר׃ וַיֹּאמֶר יִרְמְיָהוּ אֶל־
to Jeremiah said Then (any) .thing from me hide do not (one) ;thing you

צִדְקִיָּהוּ כִּי אַגִּיד לְךָ הֲלוֹא הָמֵת תְּמִיתֵנִי וְכִי אִיעָצְךָ
counsel I ,you And if you will ?me execute surely not to ,you declare I (it) If ,Zedekiah

16 לֹא תִשְׁמַע אֵלָי׃ וַיִּשָּׁבַע הַמֶּלֶךְ צִדְקִיָּהוּ אֶל־יִרְמְיָהוּ
Jeremiah to Zedekiah king the And swore .me to will you listen not

בַּסֵּתֶר לֵאמֹר חַי־יְהוָה אֵת אֲשֶׁר עָשָׂה־לָנוּ אֶת־הַנֶּפֶשׁ
soul for us made who ,Jehovah (As) lives ,saying ,secretly

הַזֹּאת אִם־אֲמִיתֶךָ וְאִם־אֶתֶּנְךָ בְּיַד הָאֲנָשִׁים הָאֵלֶּה אֲשֶׁר
who these men the into of hand will I you give not and ,you execute will I not ,this

17 מְבַקְשִׁים אֶת־נַפְשֶׁךָ׃ וַיֹּאמֶר יִרְמְיָהוּ אֶל־צִדְקִיָּהוּ
,Zedekiah to Jeremiah said Then .life your seek

כֹּה־אָמַר יְהוָה אֱלֹהֵי צְבָאוֹת אֱלֹהֵי יִשְׂרָאֵל אִם־יָצֹא תֵצֵא
will you surely out go If :Israel the of God ,hosts the of God ,Jehovah says Thus

אֶל־שָׂרֵי מֶלֶךְ־בָּבֶל וְחָיְתָה נַפְשֶׁךָ וְהָעִיר הַזֹּאת לֹא תִשָּׂרֵף
shall burned be not this city and your ,soul shall then live Baby- ,lon's the of king princes to

18 בָּאֵשׁ וְחָיִתָה אַתָּה וּבֵיתֶךָ׃ וְאִם לֹא־תֵצֵא אֶל־שָׂרֵי מֶלֶךְ
the of king princes to will you out go not But if your and .house you shall and live with ;fire

בָּבֶל וְנִתְּנָה הָעִיר הַזֹּאת בְּיַד הַכַּשְׂדִּים וּשְׂרָפוּהָ בָּאֵשׁ
with ,fire they and it burn shall the ,Chaldeans the into of hands this city shall then given be Baby- ,lon's

19 וְאַתָּה לֹא־תִמָּלֵט מִיָּדָם׃ וַיֹּאמֶר הַמֶּלֶךְ צִדְקִיָּהוּ
Zedekiah king the said And of out .hand their shall escape not you and

אֶל־יִרְמְיָהוּ אֲנִי דֹאֵג אֶת־הַיְּהוּדִים אֲשֶׁר נָפְלוּ אֶל־
to have fallen who the Jews am of afraid I ,Jeremiah to

20 הַכַּשְׂדִּים פֶּן־יִתְּנוּ אֹתִי בְּיָדָם וְהִתְעַלְּלוּ־בִי׃ וַיֹּאמֶר
said But .me they and abuse their into ,hand me they lest deliver the ,Chaldeans

יִרְמְיָהוּ לֹא יִתֵּנוּ שְׁמַע־נָא ׀ בְּקוֹל יְהוָה לַאֲשֶׁר אֲנִי דֹּבֵר
am speaking I which Jehovah the of voice please obey They ; give shall not Jere- ,miah

21 אֵלֶיךָ וְיִיטַב לְךָ וּתְחִי נַפְשֶׁךָ׃ וְאִם־מָאֵן אַתָּה לָצֵאת זֶה
this (is) go to ,out you refuse But if your .soul will and live with it and ,you well be will ;you to

[22] And, behold, all the women who are left in the king of Judah's house shall be brought forth to the king of Babylon's princes, and they will say, Your friends have seduced you and have prevailed against you. Your feet have sunk in the mire, (and) they have turned back. [23] And they shall bring out all your wives and your sons to the Chaldeans. And you shall not escape out of their hand, but shall be taken by the hand of the king of Babylon. And you shall cause this city to be burned with fire.

[24] Then Zedekiah said to Jeremiah, Let no man know of these words, and you shall not die. [25] But if the rulers hear that I have talked with you, and they come to you and say to you, Tell us now what you said to the king; do not hide it from us, and we will not put you to death; also what the king said to you; [26] then you shall say to them, I presented my cry before the king, that he would not cause me to return to Jonathan's house, to die there. [27] Then all the rulers came to Jeremiah and asked him. And he told them according to all these words that the king had commanded. And they were silent with him; for the matter was not heard. [28] So Jeremiah stayed in the court of the guard-house until the day Jerusalem was captured; and he was (present) when Jerusalem was captured.

22 הדבר אשר הראני יהוה: והנה כל־הנשים אשר נשארו

left are who the all And :Jehovah has which the
women ;behold me shown word

בבית מלך־יהודה מוצאות אל־שרי מלך בבל והנה

and ,Babylon's the princes to be shall Judah's the in
they of king out brought of king house

אמרות הסיתוך ויכלו לך אנשי שלמך הטבעו בבץ רגלך

Your the in have your The against have and have shall
feet mire sunk ;peace of men you prevailed seduced ,say

23 נסגו אחור: ואת־כל־נשיך ואת־בניך מוצאים אל־

to shall they your and your all And .back they and
out bring sons wives turned

הכשדים ואתה לא־תמלט מידם כי ביד מלך־בבל

Babylon the the by but of out shall not And the
of king of hand hand their escape you .Chaldeans

24 תתפש ואת־העיר הזאת תשרף באש: ויאמר

Then with be shall this city And be shall
said .fire burned seized

צדקיהו אל־ירמיהו איש אל־ידע בדברים־האלה ולא

and ,these of Let not a ,Jeremiah to Zedekiah
not words know man

25 תמות: וכי־ישמעו השרים כי־דברתי אתך ובאו אליך

to they and with have I that the hear But shall you
you come ,you talked rulers if .die

ואמרו אליך הגידה־נא לנו מה־דברת אל־המלך אל־

not the to you what us now Tell ,you to say and
;king said

26 תכחד ממנו ולא נמיתך ומה־דבר אליך המלך: ואמרת

you then the you to said also will we and from hide do
say shall ;king what ;kill you not ,us (it)

אליהם מפיל־אני תחנתי לפני המלך לבלתי השיבני

would he not that ,king the before my I was ,them to
to me return plea presenting

27 בית יהונתן למות שם: ויבאו כל־השרים אל־

to the all Then .there die to Jonathan's house
rulers came

ירמיהו וישאלו אתו ויגד להם ככל־הדברים האלה אשר

that these words according them he And .him and Jeremiah
all to told asked

28 צוה המלך ויחרשו ממנו כי לא־נשמע הדבר: וישב

So the was not for with they And the had
lived .matter heard ;him quiet were .king ordered

ירמיהו בחצר המטרה עד־יום אשר־נלכדה ירושלם •

;Jerusalem was the until guard- the the in Jeremiah
captured day house of court

והיה כאשר נלכדה ירושלם:

.Jerusalem was when he and
captured (present) was

CAP. XXXIX לט

CHAPTER 39

CHAPTER 39

[1] In the ninth year of Zedekiah king of Judah, in the tenth month, Nebuchadnezzar king of Babylon, and all his army, came against Jerusalem, and they besieged it. [2] In the eleventh year of Zedekiah, in the fourth month, the ninth of the month, the city was breached. [3] And all the rulers of the king of Babylon came in and sat in the middle gate: Nergal-sharezer, Samgar-nebo, Sarsechim, chief of the eunuchs, Nergal-sharezer, Rabmag, and all the rest of the rulers of the king of Babylon.

[4] And it came to pass, when Zedekiah the king of Judah and all the men of war saw them, then they fled, and went out from the city by night, by the way of the king's garden, by the gate between the two walls. And he went by the way of the Arabah. [5] But the Chaldeans' army pursued after them and overtook Zedekiah in the Arabah of Jericho. And they took him and brought him up to Nebuchadnezzar king of Babylon, (to) Riblah in the land of Hamath, where he spoke judgment on him. [6] Then the king of Babylon killed the sons of Zedekiah before his eyes at Riblah. Also the king of Babylon killed all the rulers of Judah. [7] He also put out Zedekiah's eyes and put him in bronze fetters, to carry him to Babylon.

[8] And the Chaldeans burned the king's house and the houses of the people with fire and broke down the walls of Jerusalem.

1 בַּשָּׁנָה הַתְּשִׁעִית לְצִדְקִיָּהוּ מֶלֶךְ־יְהוּדָה בַּחֹדֶשׁ הָעֲשִׂרִי
,tenth the in ,Judah king Zedekiah of ninth the In
month of year

בָּא נְבוּכַדְרֶאצַּר מֶלֶךְ־בָּבֶל וְכָל־חֵילוֹ אֶל־יְרוּשָׁלִַם וַיָּצֻרוּ
they and Jeru- against his and Babylon king Nebuchadnezzar came
besieged ,salem army all of

2 עָלֶיהָ׃ בְּעַשְׁתֵּי־עֶשְׂרֵה שָׁנָה לְצִדְקִיָּהוּ בַּחֹדֶשׁ הָרְבִיעִי
,fourth the in of year the In .it
month ,Zedekiah eleventh

3 בְּתִשְׁעָה לַחֹדֶשׁ הָבְקְעָה הָעִיר׃ וַיָּבֹאוּ כֹּל שָׂרֵי
the all And .city the was the of the
of rulers in came breached ,month ninth

מֶלֶךְ־בָּבֶל וַיֵּשְׁבוּ בְּשַׁעַר הַתָּוֶךְ נֵרְגַל שַׂרְאֶצֶר סַמְגַּר־נְבוּ
nebo Samgar- ,sharezer Nergal- the gate in and Babylon the
:middle sat of king

שַׂר־סְכִים רַב־סָרִיס נֵרְגַל שַׂרְאֶצֶר רַב־מָג וְכָל־שְׁאֵרִית
the and mag Rab- ,sharezer Nergal- the chief ,Sarsechim
of rest all ,eunuchs of

4 שָׂרֵי מֶלֶךְ־בָּבֶל׃ וַיְהִי כַּאֲשֶׁר רָאָם צִדְקִיָּהוּ מֶלֶךְ־יְהוּדָה
Judah king Zedekiah saw when it And .Babylon the the
of them ,was of king of rulers

וְכֹל אַנְשֵׁי הַמִּלְחָמָה וַיִּבְרְחוּ וַיֵּצְאוּ לַיְלָה מִן־הָעִיר דֶּרֶךְ
the (by) the from by went and they the men and
of way ,city night out ,fled ,war of all

גַּן הַמֶּלֶךְ בְּשַׁעַר בֵּין הַחֹמֹתַיִם וַיֵּצֵא דֶּרֶךְ הָעֲרָבָה׃
the the (by) And two the between the by the garden
.Arabah of way went he .walls gate ,king's

5 וַיִּרְדְּפוּ חֵיל־כַּשְׂדִּים אַחֲרֵיהֶם וַיַּשִּׂגוּ אֶת־צִדְקִיָּהוּ בְּעַרְבוֹת
the in Zedekiah and after the the But
of Arabah took them Chaldeans of army pursued

יְרֵחוֹ וַיִּקְחוּ אֹתוֹ וַיַּעֲלֻהוּ אֶל־נְבוּכַדְרֶאצַּר מֶלֶךְ־בָּבֶל
,Babylon king Nebuchadnezzar to brought and ,him they And Jeri-
of up him took .cho

6 רִבְלָתָה בְּאֶרֶץ חֲמָת וַיְדַבֵּר אִתּוֹ מִשְׁפָּטִים׃ וַיִּשְׁחַט
Then .judgment him on he where ,Hamath the in (to)
killed spoke of land Riblah

מֶלֶךְ בָּבֶל אֶת־בְּנֵי צִדְקִיָּהוּ בְּרִבְלָה לְעֵינָיו וְאֵת כָּל־חֹרֵי
the all Also before Riblah at Zedekiah the Babylon the
of rulers .eyes his of sons of king

7 יְהוּדָה שָׁחַט מֶלֶךְ בָּבֶל׃ וְאֶת־עֵינֵי צִדְקִיָּהוּ עִוֵּר וַיַּאַסְרֵהוּ
bound and he Zedekiah the And .Babylon the killed Judah
him ,blinded of eyes of king

8 בַּנְחֻשְׁתַּיִם לָבִיא אֹתוֹ בָּבֶלָה׃ וְאֶת־בֵּית הַמֶּלֶךְ וְאֶת־בֵּית
the and the house And to him carry to bronze in
of houses king's .Babylon ,fetters

הָעָם שָׂרְפוּ הַכַּשְׂדִּים בָּאֵשׁ וְאֶת־חוֹמוֹת יְרוּשָׁלִַם נָתָצוּ׃
broke Jerusalem the and with the burned the
.down of walls ,fire Chaldeans people

[9] Then Nebuzar-adan the captain of the guard deported (to) Babylon the rest of the people who remained in the city, and those who fell away, who fell to him with the rest of the people that remained. [10] But Nebuzar-adan the captain of the guard left (some) of the poor people, who was not a thing to them, in the land of Judah, and gave to them vineyards and fields on that day.

[11] Now Nebuchadnezzar king of Babylon gave an order concerning Jeremiah to Nebuzar-adan the captain of the guard, saying [12] Take him and set your eyes on him, and do not do any evil to him. But do with him even as he shall say to you. [13] So Nebuzar-adan the captain of the guard sent, and Nebushasban, chief of the eunuchs, and Nergal-sharezer, Rabmag, and all the king of Babylon's leaders, [14] even they sent and took Jeremiah out of the court of the guard-house. And they gave him to Gedaliah the son of Ahikam the son of Shaphan, to take him to the house. So he lived among the people.

[15] And the word of Jehovah came to Jeremiah, while he was shut up in the court of the guard-house, saying, [16] Go and speak to Ebed-melech the Ethiopian, saying, Thus says Jehovah of hosts, the God of Israel: Behold, I am bringing My words on this city for evil, and not for good; and they shall be before you in that day. [17] But I will deliver you in that day, says Jehovah. And you shall not be given into the hand of the men, of them whom you fear. [18] For I will surely

9 וְאֵת יֶתֶר הָעָם הַנִּשְׁאָרִים בָּעִיר וְאֶת־הַנֹּפְלִים אֲשֶׁר נָפְלוּ
fell who who those and the in who the the Then
,away fell ,city remained people of rest

עָלָיו וְאֵת יֶתֶר הָעָם הַנִּשְׁאָרִים הֶגְלָה נְבוּזַרְאֲדָן רַב־טַבָּחִים
the cap- the Nebuzaradan deported who the the and to
guard of tain remained people of rest ,him

10 בָּבֶל׃ וּמִן הָעָם הַדַּלִּים אֲשֶׁר אֵין־לָהֶם מְאוּמָה הִשְׁאִיר
left ,thing a to was who ,poor the But (to)
them not people of .Babylon

נְבוּזַרְאֲדָן רַב־טַבָּחִים בְּאֶרֶץ יְהוּדָה וַיִּתֵּן לָהֶם כְּרָמִים
vineyards to and ,Judah the in the cap- the Nebuzar-
them gave of land ,guard of tain adan

11 וִיגֵבִים בַּיּוֹם הַהוּא׃ וַיְצַו נְבוּכַדְרֶאצַּר מֶלֶךְ־בָּבֶל עַל־
con- Babylon king Nebuchadnezzar gave And that day on and
cerning of order an fields

12 יִרְמְיָהוּ בְּיַד נְבוּזַרְאֲדָן רַב־טַבָּחִים לֵאמֹר׃ קָחֶנּוּ וְעֵינֶיךָ
your and Take ,saying the cap- the Nebuzar- the by Jeremiah
eyes him ,guard of tain adan of hand

שִׂים עָלָיו וְאַל־תַּעַשׂ לוֹ מְאוּמָה רָע כִּי אִם כַּאֲשֶׁר יְדַבֵּר
shall he as even But .evil anything to do and on set
say him not ,him

13 אֵלֶיךָ כֵּן עֲשֵׂה עִמּוֹ׃ וַיִּשְׁלַח נְבוּזַרְאֲדָן רַב־טַבָּחִים
the cap- the Nebuzar- sent And with do thus ,you to
,guard of tain adan .him

וּנְבוּשַׁזְבָּן רַב־סָרִיס וְנֵרְגַל שַׂרְאֶצֶר רַב־מָג וְכֹל רַבֵּי מֶלֶךְ־
the leaders and mag Rab- ,sharezer and the chief Nebu- and
of king of all Nergal ,eunuchs of shasban

14 בָּבֶל׃ וַיִּשְׁלְחוּ וַיִּקְחוּ אֶת־יִרְמְיָהוּ מֵחֲצַר הַמַּטָּרָה וַיִּתְּנוּ
they And guard- the of out Jeremiah took and they and ,Babylon
gave .house of court the sent

אֹתוֹ אֶל־גְּדַלְיָהוּ בֶּן־אֲחִיקָם בֶּן־שָׁפָן לְהוֹצִאֵהוּ אֶל־הַבָּיִת
the to take to ,Shaphan the ,Ahikam the Gedaliah to him
.house him of son of son

15 וַיֵּשֶׁב בְּתוֹךְ הָעָם׃ וְאֶל־יִרְמְיָהוּ הָיָה דְבַר־יְהוָה
,Jehovah the came Jeremiah to And the among he So
of word .people lived

16 בִּהְיֹתוֹ עָצוּר בַּחֲצַר הַמַּטָּרָה לֵאמֹר׃ הָלוֹךְ וְאָמַרְתָּ לְעֶבֶד־
Ebed- to and Go ,saying guard- the the in shut while
speak house of court up was he

מֶלֶךְ הַכּוּשִׁי לֵאמֹר כֹּה־אָמַר יְהוָה צְבָאוֹת אֱלֹהֵי יִשְׂרָאֵל
:Israel the ,hosts Jehovah says Thus ,saying the melech
of God of ,Ethiopian

הִנְנִי מֵבִי אֶת־דְּבָרַי אֶל־הָעִיר הַזֹּאת לְרָעָה וְלֹא לְטוֹבָה
for and for this city on My am ,Behold
;good not ,evil words bringing I

17 וְהָיוּ לְפָנֶיךָ בַּיּוֹם הַהוּא׃ וְהִצַּלְתִּיךָ בַיּוֹם־הַהוּא נְאֻם־יְהוָה
.Jehovah says ,that day in will I But .that in before they and
you deliver day you be shall

18 וְלֹא תִנָּתֵן בְּיַד הָאֲנָשִׁים אֲשֶׁר־אַתָּה יָגוֹר מִפְּנֵיהֶם׃ כִּי
For .them of fear you whom ,men the the into shall you And
of hand given be not

deliver you, and you shall not fall by the sword, but your life shall be as a prize to you, because you have put your trust in Me, says Jehovah.

מַלֵּט אֲמַלֶּטְךָ וּבַחֶרֶב לֹא תִפֹּל וְהָיְתָה לְךָ נַפְשְׁךָ לְשָׁלָל
a as your to shall but you not by and will I surely
,prize life you be ,fall shall sword the ,you deliver

כִּי־בָטַחְתָּ בִּי נְאֻם־יְהוָה׃
.Jehovah says in have you be-
,Me trusted cause

Cap. XL. מ

CHAPTER 40

CHAPTER 40

[1] This is the word that came to Jeremiah from Jehovah, after Nebuzar-adan the captain of the guard had sent him from Ramah, when he had taken him, and he was bound in chains, among all the captives of Jerusalem and Judah, who were being exiled to Babylon. [2] And the captain of the guard took Jeremiah and said to him, Jehovah your God has spoken this evil against this place. [3] Now Jehovah has brought (it), and has done according as He has said; because you have sinned against Jehovah and have not obeyed His voice, therefore this thing has come upon you. [4] And now, behold, I set you free today from the chains which (were) on your hand. If it (is) good in your eyes to come with me into Babylon, come. And I will set my eye on you. But if it (is) evil in your eyes to come with me into Babylon, stay. Behold, all the land (is) before you. To good and to the right in your eyes to go, go there — [5] and while he had not yet returned — Or go back to Gedaliah the son of Ahikam the son of Shaphan, whom the king of Babylon has appointed over the cities of Judah, and live with him among the people. Or to all (that is) right in your eyes to go, go. So the captain of the guard gave him food and a reward, and

1 הַדָּבָר אֲשֶׁר הָיָה אֶל־יִרְמְיָהוּ מֵאֵת יְהוָה אַחַר ׀ שַׁלַּח
had after ,Jehovah from Jeremiah to came which The
sent word

אֹתוֹ נְבוּזַרְאֲדָן רַב־טַבָּחִים מִן־הָרָמָה בְּקַחְתּוֹ אֹתוֹ וְהוּא־
and ;him he when ,Ramah from the the Nebuzar-adan him
he taken had guard of captain

אָסוּר בָּאזִקִּים בְּתוֹךְ כָּל־גָּלוּת יְרוּשָׁלִַם וִיהוּדָה הַמֻּגְלִים
were who and Jerusalem the all among ,chains in was
exiled being Judah of captives bound

2 בָּבֶלָה׃ וַיִּקַּח רַב־טַבָּחִים לְיִרְמְיָהוּ וַיֹּאמֶר אֵלָיו יְהוָה
Jehovah to said and Jeremiah the cap- the And to
,him guard of tain took .Babylon

3 אֱלֹהֶיךָ דִּבֶּר אֶת־הָרָעָה הַזֹּאת אֶל־הַמָּקוֹם הַזֶּה׃ וַיָּבֵא
has And .this place against this evil has your
,(it) brought spoken God

וַיַּעַשׂ יְהוָה כַּאֲשֶׁר דִּבֵּר כִּי־חֲטָאתֶם לַיהוָה וְלֹא־שְׁמַעְתֶּם
have and against have you be- has He according Jeho- has and
obeyed not ,Jehovah sinned cause ;said as vah done

4 בְּקוֹלוֹ וְהָיָה לָכֶם דְּבַר הַזֶּה׃ וְעַתָּה הִנֵּה פִתַּחְתִּיךָ הַיּוֹם
today you set I ,behold And .this thing you on therefore His
free now come has ,voice

מִן־הָאזִקִּים אֲשֶׁר עַל־יָדֶךָ אִם־טוֹב בְּעֵינֶיךָ לָבוֹא אִתִּי
with to your in good If your on which the from
me come eyes .hands (were) chains

בָבֶל בֹּא וְאָשִׂים אֶת־עֵינִי עָלֶיךָ וְאִם־רַע בְּעֵינֶיךָ לָבוֹא־
go to your in evil But .you on eye my I And .come into
eyes if set will ,Babylon

אִתִּי בָבֶל חֲדָל רְאֵה כָּל־הָאָרֶץ לְפָנֶיךָ אֶל־טוֹב וְאֶל־
and good to before (is) the all ,Behold .stay into with
to .you land ,Babylon me

5 הַיָּשָׁר בְּעֵינֶיךָ לָלֶכֶת שָׁמָּה לֵךְ׃ וְעוֹדֶנּוּ לֹא־יָשׁוּב וְשֻׁבָה
go Or had he not while and —go there ,go to your in the
back —returned yet eyes right

אֶל־גְּדַלְיָה בֶן־אֲחִיקָם בֶּן־שָׁפָן אֲשֶׁר הִפְקִיד מֶלֶךְ־בָּבֶל
Babylon the has whom ,Shaphan the Ahikam the Gedaliah to
of king appointed of son of son

בְּעָרֵי יְהוּדָה וְשֵׁב אִתּוֹ בְּתוֹךְ הָעָם אוֹ אֶל־כָּל־הַיָּשָׁר
(is that) all to Or the among with and ,Judah the over
right .people him live of cities

בְּעֵינֶיךָ לָלֶכֶת לֵךְ וַיִּתֶּן־לוֹ רַב־טַבָּחִים אֲרֻחָה וּמַשְׂאֵת
a and ration the cap- the to So .go ,go to your in
,reward guard of tain him gave eyes

sent him away. [6] Then Jeremiah went to Gedaliah the son of Ahikam at Mizpah, and lived with him among the people who were left in the land.

[7] Now when all the rulers of the army who (were) in the field, they and their men, heard that the king of Babylon had appointed Gedaliah the son of Ahikam over the land, and had appointed with him men, and women, and children, and (many) of the poor of the land, of those who were not exiled to Babylon, [8] then they came to Gedaliah to Mizpah, even Ishmael the son of Nethaniah, and Johanan and Jonathan the sons of Kareah, and Seraiah the son of Tanhumeth, and the sons of Ephai of Netopha, and Jezaniah the son of the Maachathite, they and their men. [9] And Gedaliah the son of Ahikam the son of Shaphan swore to them and to their men, saying, Do not fear to serve the Chaldeans. Live in the land and serve the king of Babylon and it shall be well with you. [10] (As for) me, behold, I will live at Mizpah to serve before the Chaldeans, who have come to us. But you go gather wine, and the harvest, and oil, and fill your vessels, and live in your cities that you have taken.

[11] Also when all the Jews that (were) in Moab and among the sons of Ammon, and in Edom, and who (were) in all the lands, heard that the king of Babylon had left a remnant of Judah and that he had set over them Gedaliah the son of Ahikam, the son of Shaphan — [12] even all the Jews returned out of all places where they were driven, and came to the land

6 וַיְשַׁלְּחֵהוּ׃ וַיָּבֹא יִרְמְיָהוּ אֶל־גְּדַלְיָה בֶן־אֲחִיקָם הַמִּצְפָּתָה
of Ahikam the Gedaliah to Jeremiah Then sent and
,Mizpah of son went .away him

7 וַיֵּשֶׁב אִתּוֹ בְּתוֹךְ הָעָם הַנִּשְׁאָרִים בָּאָרֶץ׃ וַיִּשְׁמְעוּ
when And the in were who the among with and
heard .land left people him lived

כָל־שָׂרֵי הַחֲיָלִים אֲשֶׁר בַּשָּׂדֶה הֵמָּה וְאַנְשֵׁיהֶם כִּי־הִפְקִיד
had that their and they the in who the the all
appointed ,men ,field (were) armies of rulers

מֶלֶךְ־בָּבֶל אֶת־גְּדַלְיָהוּ בֶן־אֲחִיקָם בָּאָרֶץ וְכִי ׀ הִפְקִיד
had and the over Ahikam the Gedaliah Babylon the
appointed land of son of king

אִתּוֹ אֲנָשִׁים וְנָשִׁים וָטָף וּמִדַּלַּת הָאָרֶץ מֵאֲשֶׁר לֹא־הָגְלוּ
were not those of the of and and and ,men with
exiled who land poor the children women him

8 בָּבֶלָה׃ וַיָּבֹאוּ אֶל־גְּדַלְיָה הַמִּצְפָּתָה וְיִשְׁמָעֵאל בֶּן־נְתַנְיָהוּ
,Nethaniah the even ,Mispah to Gedaliah to they to
of son Ishmael came ;Babylon

וְיוֹחָנָן וְיוֹנָתָן בְּנֵי־קָרֵחַ וּשְׂרָיָה בֶן־תַּנְחֻמֶת וּבְנֵי ׀ עוֹפַי
Ephai the and ,Tanhumeth the and ,Kareah the and and
of sons of son Seriaiah of sons Jonathan ,Johanan

9 הַנְּטֹפָתִי וִיזַנְיָהוּ בֶּן־הַמַּעֲכָתִי הֵמָּה וְאַנְשֵׁיהֶם׃ וַיִּשָּׁבַע
And their and they the the and of
swore .men ,Maachathite of son Jezaniah ,Netopha

לָהֶם גְּדַלְיָהוּ בֶן־אֲחִיקָם בֶּן־שָׁפָן וּלְאַנְשֵׁיהֶם לֵאמֹר אַל־
not ,saying to and Shaphan the Ahikam the Gedaliah to
,men their of son of son them

תִּירְאוּ מֵעֲבוֹד הַכַּשְׂדִּים שְׁבוּ בָאָרֶץ וְעִבְדוּ אֶת־מֶלֶךְ
king the and the in Live the serve to fear Do
of serve land .Chaldeans

10 בָּבֶל וְיִיטַב לָכֶם׃ וַאֲנִי הִנְנִי יֹשֵׁב בַּמִּצְפָּה לַעֲמֹד
serve to Mizpah at will ,behold (for As) with will it and Baby-
live I ,me .you well be ,lon

לִפְנֵי הַכַּשְׂדִּים אֲשֶׁר יָבֹאוּ אֵלֵינוּ וְאַתֶּם אִסְפוּ יַיִן וְקַיִץ
the and wine (go) you But .us to have who the before
,harvest gather come ,Chaldeans

11 וְשֶׁמֶן וְשִׂמוּ בִּכְלֵיכֶם וּשְׁבוּ בְּעָרֵיכֶם אֲשֶׁר־תְּפַשְׂתֶּם׃ וְגַם
Also have you that your in live and your and and
when .seized cities ,vessels fill ,oil

כָּל־הַיְּהוּדִים אֲשֶׁר־בְּמוֹאָב ׀ וּבִבְנֵי־עַמּוֹן וּבֶאֱדוֹם וַאֲשֶׁר
who and in and sons the and in that the all
(were) ;Edom Ammon of Moab (were) Jews

בְּכָל־הָאֲרָצוֹת שָׁמְעוּ כִּי־נָתַן ׀ מֶלֶךְ־בָּבֶל שְׁאֵרִית לִיהוּדָה
of a Babylon the had that heard the all in
,Judah remnant of king left lands

וְכִי הִפְקִיד עֲלֵיהֶם אֶת־גְּדַלְיָהוּ בֶּן־אֲחִיקָם בֶּן־שָׁפָן׃
—Shaphan the Ahikam the Gedaliah over had he and
of son of son them appointed that

12 וַיָּשֻׁבוּ כָל־הַיְּהוּדִים מִכָּל־הַמְּקֹמוֹת אֲשֶׁר נִדְּחוּ־שָׁם וַיָּבֹאוּ
and there had they where places out the all even
to came ,driven been all of Jews returned

of Judah, to Gedaliah, to Mizpah, and gathered wine and the harvest (in) great abundance.

[13] And Johanan the son of Kareah, and all the captains of the army that (were) in the field, came to Gedaliah to Mizpah. [14] And (they) said to him, You certainly know that Baalis the king of the Ammonites has sent Ishmael the son of Nethaniah to strike your soul. But Gedaliah the son of Ahikam did not believe them. [15] Then Johanan the son of Kareah spoke to Gedaliah in Mizpah secretly, saying, Please let me go. And I will strike Ishmael the son of Nethaniah, and a man shall not know. Why should he strike your soul, and all the Jews who are gathered to you be scattered, and the remnant in Judah perish? [16] But Gedaliah the son of Ahikam said to Johanan the son of Kareah, You shall not do this thing. For you speak falsely concerning Ishmael.

אֶרֶץ־יְהוּדָה אֶל־גְּדַלְיָהוּ הַמִּצְפָּתָה וַיַּאַסְפוּ יַיִן וָקַיִץ
the and harvest | wine | and gathered | ,Mizpah to | ,Gedaliah | to | ,Judah | the of land

13 הַרְבֵּה מְאֹד׃ וְיוֹחָנָן בֶּן־קָרֵחַ וְכָל־שָׂרֵי הַחֲיָלִים אֲשֶׁר
that (were) | army the | the of captains | and all | Kareah the of son | And Johanan | .great | (in) abundance

14 בַּשָּׂדֶה בָּאוּ אֶל־גְּדַלְיָהוּ הַמִּצְפָּתָה׃ וַיֹּאמְרוּ אֵלָיו הֲיָדֹעַ
Certainly | to ,him | they And said | .Mizpah to | Gedaliah | to | came | the in field

תֵּדַע כִּי בַּעֲלִיס ׀ מֶלֶךְ בְּנֵי־עַמּוֹן שָׁלַח אֶת־יִשְׁמָעֵאל בֶּן
the of son | Ishmael | has sent | Ammon the of sons | king the of | Baalis | that | you know

נְתַנְיָה לְהַכֹּתְךָ נָפֶשׁ וְלֹא־הֶאֱמִין לָהֶם גְּדַלְיָהוּ בֶּן־אֲחִיקָם׃
.Ahikam | the of son | Gedaliah | them | did believe | But not | .soul | strike to your | Nethaniah

15 וְיוֹחָנָן בֶּן־קָרֵחַ אָמַר אֶל־גְּדַלְיָהוּ בַסֵּתֶר בַּמִּצְפָּה לֵאמֹר
,saying | ,Mizpah in | secretly | Gedaliah | to | spoke | Kareah the of son | Then Johanan

אֵלְכָה נָּא וְאַכֶּה אֶת־יִשְׁמָעֵאל בֶּן־נְתַנְיָה וְאִישׁ לֹא יֵדָע
shall not .know | a and man | ,Nethaniah the of son | Ishmael | I And will strike | .Please | me let go

לָמָּה יַכֶּכָּה נֶּפֶשׁ וְנָפֹצוּ כָּל־יְהוּדָה הַנִּקְבָּצִים אֵלֶיךָ וְאָבְדָה
and perish | ,you to | are who gathered | the Jews | all should and be scattered | soul your | he strike | Why does

16 שְׁאֵרִית יְהוּדָה׃ וַיֹּאמֶר גְּדַלְיָהוּ בֶן־אֲחִיקָם אֶל־יוֹחָנָן
Johanan | to | Ahikam | the of son | Gedliah | said But | ?Judah | rem- the of nant

בֶּן־קָרֵחַ אַל־תַּעַשׂ אֶת־הַדָּבָר הַזֶּה כִּי־שֶׁקֶר אַתָּה דֹבֵר
speak | you | falsely | for | ,this | thing | shall you not do | ,Kareah the of son

אֶל־יִשְׁמָעֵאל׃
.Ishmael | con- cerning

CAP. XLI. מא

CHAPTER 41

CHAPTER 41

[1] Now it came to pass, in the seventh month, Ishmael the son of Nethaniah the son of Elishama, of the royal seed, and of the rulers of the king, and ten men with him, came to Gedaliah the son of Ahikam to Mizpah. And there they ate bread together in Mizpah. [2] Then Ishmael the son of Nethaniah arose, and the ten men who were with him, and struck Gedaliah the son of Ahikam the son of Shaphan with the sword.

1 וַיְהִי ׀ בַּחֹדֶשׁ הַשְּׁבִיעִי בָּא יִשְׁמָעֵאל בֶּן־נְתַנְיָה בֶן־אֱלִישָׁמָע
Elishama | the of son | Nethaniah the of son | Ishmael | came | ,seventh | the in month | it And was

מִזֶּרַע הַמְּלוּכָה וְרַבֵּי הַמֶּלֶךְ וַעֲשָׂרָה אֲנָשִׁים אִתּוֹ אֶל־
to | with ,him | men | ten and | the ,king | the of and of rulers | ,royal | the of seed

גְּדַלְיָהוּ בֶן־אֲחִיקָם הַמִּצְפָּתָה וַיֹּאכְלוּ שָׁם לֶחֶם יַחְדָּו
to- gether | food | there | they And ate | .Mizpah to | ,Ahikam | the of son | Gedaliah

2 בַּמִּצְפָּה׃ וַיָּקָם יִשְׁמָעֵאל בֶּן־נְתַנְיָה וַעֲשֶׂרֶת הָאֲנָשִׁים ׀
men the | ten and | ,Nethaniah the of son | Ishamel | Then arose | .Mizpah in

אֲשֶׁר־הָיוּ אִתּוֹ וַיַּכּוּ אֶת־גְּדַלְיָהוּ בֶן־אֲחִיקָם בֶּן־שָׁפָן בַּחֶרֶב
the with .sword | Shaphan the of son | Ahikam the of son | Gedaliah | and struck | with ,him | were | who

And they killed him whom the king of Babylon had appointed over the land. [3] Ishmael also struck all the Jews who were with him, with Gedaliah, at Mizpah, and the Chaldeans who were found there, the men of war. [4] And it came to pass, the second day after he had killed Gedaliah — and no one knew — [5] men from Shechem came from Shiloh, and from Samaria, eighty men, (with) (their) beards shaved, and their clothes torn, and having cut themselves, with offerings, and incense in their hand, to bring (them) to the house of Jehovah. [6] And Ishmael the son of Nethaniah went forth from Mizpah to meet them, walking as he walked, and weeping. And it came to pass, as he met them, he said to them, Come to Gedaliah the son of Ahikam. [7] And when they came into the middle of the city, Ishmael the son of Nethaniah killed them, he and the men who (were) with him, (throwing them) into the middle of the pit. [8] But ten men were found among them who said to Ishmael, Do not kill us, for we have treasures in the field, (of) wheat, and barley, and oil, and honey. So he held back, not killing them with their brothers.

[9] And the pit there, (in) which Ishmael had thrown all the dead bodies of the men, whom he had struck because of Gedaliah, (was) the one which Asa the king had made for fear of Baasha king of Israel; Ishmael the son of Nethaniah filled it with the slain. [10] Then Ishmael took captive all the rest of the people who (were) in Mizpah, the king's daughters and all the

3 וַיָּמֶת אֹתוֹ אֲשֶׁר־הִפְקִיד מֶלֶךְ־בָּבֶל בָּאָרֶץ׃ וְאֵת כָּל־
all Also the over Babylon the ap- had whom him they And
.land of king pointed killed

הַיְּהוּדִים אֲשֶׁר־הָיוּ אִתּוֹ אֶת־גְּדַלְיָהוּ בַּמִּצְפָּה וְאֶת־
and ,Mizpah at Gedaliah with with were who the
,him Jews

הַכַּשְׂדִּים אֲשֶׁר נִמְצְאוּ־שָׁם אֵת אַנְשֵׁי הַמִּלְחָמָה הִכָּה
struck the of men ,there were who the
,war found Chaldeans

4 יִשְׁמָעֵאל׃ וַיְהִי בַּיּוֹם הַשֵּׁנִי לְהָמִית אֶת־גְּדַלְיָהוּ וְאִישׁ לֹא
not and ,Gedaliah he after second the on And .Ishmael
man a killed had day ,was it

5 יָדָע׃ וַיָּבֹאוּ אֲנָשִׁים מִשְּׁכֶם מִשִּׁלוֹ וּמִשֹּׁמְרוֹן שְׁמֹנִים אִישׁ
,men eighty from and from from men came —knew
,Samaria ,Shiloh Shechem

מְגֻלְּחֵי זָקָן וּקְרֻעֵי בְגָדִים וּמִתְגֹּדְדִים וּמִנְחָה וּלְבוֹנָה בְּיָדָם
their in and (with) and having and (their) and (their) (with)
,hand incense offerings ,themselves cut ,clothes torn ,beards shaved

6 לְהָבִיא בֵּית יְהוָה׃ וַיֵּצֵא יִשְׁמָעֵאל בֶּן־נְתַנְיָה לִקְרָאתָם
meet to Nethaniah the Ishmael went And .Jehovah the bring to
them of son forth of house to (them)

מִן־הַמִּצְפָּה הֹלֵךְ הָלֹךְ וּבֹכֶה וַיְהִי כִּפְגֹשׁ אֹתָם וַיֹּאמֶר
said he ,them he as it And and he as walking ,Mizpah from
met ,was .weeping walked

7 אֲלֵיהֶם בֹּאוּ אֶל־גְּדַלְיָהוּ בֶּן־אֲחִיקָם׃ וַיְהִי כְּבוֹאָם אֶל־
into they when And .Ahikam the Gedaliah to Come ,them to
came of son

תּוֹךְ הָעִיר וַיִּשְׁחָטֵם יִשְׁמָעֵאל בֶּן־נְתַנְיָה אֶל־תּוֹךְ הַבּוֹר
,pit the the into ;Nethaniah the Ishmael killed ,city the the
of middle of son them of middle

8 הוּא וְהָאֲנָשִׁים אֲשֶׁר־אִתּוֹ׃ וַעֲשָׂרָה אֲנָשִׁים נִמְצְאוּ־בָם
among were men ten But with who the and he
;them found .him (were) men

וַיֹּאמְרוּ אֶל־יִשְׁמָעֵאל אַל־תְּמִתֵנוּ כִּי־יֶשׁ־לָנוּ מַטְמֹנִים
treasures us to there for kill Do not ,Ishmael to they and
is ,us said

בַּשָּׂדֶה חִטִּים וּשְׂעֹרִים וְשֶׁמֶן וּדְבָשׁ וַיֶּחְדַּל וְלֹא הֱמִיתָם
kill did and he So and ,oil and and (of) the in
them not ,back held .honey ,barley ,wheat ,field

9 בְּתוֹךְ אֲחֵיהֶם׃ וְהַבּוֹר אֲשֶׁר הִשְׁלִיךְ שָׁם יִשְׁמָעֵאל אֵת ׀
Ishmael there had where the And their with
thrown pit .brothers

כָּל־פִּגְרֵי הָאֲנָשִׁים אֲשֶׁר הִכָּה בְּיַד־גְּדַלְיָהוּ הוּא אֲשֶׁר
which (was) ,Gedaliah because had he whom men the dead the all
one the of struck of bodies

עָשָׂה הַמֶּלֶךְ אָסָא מִפְּנֵי בַּעְשָׁא מֶלֶךְ־יִשְׂרָאֵל אֹתוֹ מִלֵּא
filled it ;Israel king Baasha for Asa the had
with of of fear king made

10 יִשְׁמָעֵאל בֶּן־נְתַנְיָהוּ חֲלָלִים׃ וַיִּשְׁבְּ ׀ יִשְׁמָעֵאל אֶת־כָּל־
all Ishmael took Then .slain the Nethaniah the Ishmael
captive of son

people who stayed in Mizpah, whom Nebuzar-adan the captain of the guard had entrusted to Gedaliah the son of Ahikam. And Ishmael the son of Nethaniah carried them away captive and went to go over to the Ammonites.

[11] But when Johanan the son of Kareah, and all the captains of the army who (were) with him, heard of all the evil that Ishmael the son of Nethaniah had done, [12] then they took all the men and went to fight with Ishmael the son of Nethaniah. And they found him by the great waters that (are) in Gibeon.

[13] Now when all the people who (were) with Ishmael saw Johanan the son of Kareah, and all the captains of the army who (were) with him, then they were glad. [14] So all the people that Ishmael had taken captive from Mizpah turned around and came back, and went to Johanan the son of Kareah. [15] But Ishmael the son of Nethaniah escaped from Johanan with eight men, and went to the Ammonites. [16] Then Johanan the son of Kareah and all the captains of the army that (were) with him took all the remnant of the people whom he had recovered from Ishmael the son of Nethaniah, from Mizpah — after he had killed Gedaliah the son of Ahikam — mighty men of war, and the women, and the children, and the eunuchs, whom he had brought again from Gibeon. [17] And they departed and lived in the inn of Chimham, which is by Bethlehem, to go to enter

שְׁאֵרִית הָעָם אֲשֶׁר בַּמִּצְפָּה אֶת־בְּנוֹת הַמֶּלֶךְ וְאֶת־כָּל־

all and the daughters ,Mizpah in who the rest the
,king's (were) people of

הָעָם הַנִּשְׁאָרִים בַּמִּצְפָּה אֲשֶׁר הִפְקִיד נְבוּזַרְאֲדָן רַב־

the Nebuzar-adan com- had whom ,Mizpah in were who the
of captain to mitted left people

טַבָּחִים אֶת־גְּדַלְיָהוּ בֶּן־אֲחִיקָם וַיִּשְׁבֵּם יִשְׁמָעֵאל בֶּן־

the Ishmael took And .Ahikam the Gedaliah the
of son captive of son guard

11 נְתַנְיָה וַיֵּלֶךְ לַעֲבֹר אֶל־בְּנֵי עַמּוֹן׃ וַיִּשְׁמַע יוֹחָנָן בֶּן־קָרֵחַ

Kareah the Johanan when But ,Ammon the to go to and Nethaniah
of son heard of sons over went

וְכָל־שָׂרֵי הַחֲיָלִים אֲשֶׁר אִתּוֹ אֵת כָּל־הָרָעָה אֲשֶׁר עָשָׂה

had that the all of with who the cap- the and
done evil ,him (were) army of tains all

12 יִשְׁמָעֵאל בֶּן־נְתַנְיָה׃ וַיִּקְחוּ אֶת־כָּל־הָאֲנָשִׁים וַיֵּלְכוּ לְהִלָּחֵם

fight to and the all then ,Nethaniah the Ishmael
went men took they of son

עִם־יִשְׁמָעֵאל בֶּן־נְתַנְיָה וַיִּמְצְאוּ אֹתוֹ אֶל־מַיִם רַבִּים אֲשֶׁר

that great the by him they And .Nethaniah the Ishmael with
(are) waters found of son

13 בְּגִבְעוֹן׃ וַיְהִי כִּרְאוֹת כָּל־הָעָם אֲשֶׁר אֶת־יִשְׁמָעֵאל אֶת־

Ishmael with who the all when Now in
(were) people saw .Gibeon

יוֹחָנָן בֶּן־קָרֵחַ וְאֵת כָּל־שָׂרֵי הַחֲיָלִים אֲשֶׁר אִתּוֹ וַיִּשְׂמָחוּ׃

they then with who the the all and ,Kareah the Johanan
.glad were ,him (were) army of captains of son

14 וַיָּסֹבּוּ כָּל־הָעָם אֲשֶׁר־שָׁבָה יִשְׁמָעֵאל מִן־הַמִּצְפָּה וַיָּשֻׁבוּ

and Mizpah from Ishmael taken had that the all turned And
back came captive people around

15 וַיֵּלְכוּ אֶל־יוֹחָנָן בֶּן־קָרֵחַ׃ וְיִשְׁמָעֵאל בֶּן־נְתַנְיָה נִמְלַט

escaped Nethaniah the But .Kareah the Johanan to and
of son Ishmael of son went

16 בִּשְׁמֹנָה אֲנָשִׁים מִפְּנֵי יוֹחָנָן וַיֵּלֶךְ אֶל־בְּנֵי עַמּוֹן׃ וַיִּקַּח

Then .Ammon the to and ,Johanan from ,men with
took of sons went eight

יוֹחָנָן בֶּן־קָרֵחַ וְכָל־שָׂרֵי הַחֲיָלִים אֲשֶׁר־אִתּוֹ אֵת כָּל־

all with that the cap- the and Kareah the Johanan
him (were) army of tains all of son

שְׁאֵרִית הָעָם אֲשֶׁר הֵשִׁיב מֵאֵת יִשְׁמָעֵאל בֶּן־נְתַנְיָה מִן־

from ,Nethaniah the Ishmael from had he whom the rem- the
of son recovered people of nant

הַמִּצְפָּה אַחַר הִכָּה אֶת־גְּדַלְיָה בֶּן־אֲחִיקָם גְּבָרִים אַנְשֵׁי

men mighty ,Ahikam the Gedaliah had he after —Mizpah
of of son struck

הַמִּלְחָמָה וְנָשִׁים וָטַף וְסָרִסִים אֲשֶׁר הֵשִׁיב מִגִּבְעוֹן׃

from had he whom the and the and the and ,war
.Gibeon again brought ,eunuchs ,children ,women

17 וַיֵּלְכוּ וַיֵּשְׁבוּ בְּגֵרוּת כִּמְוֹהָם אֲשֶׁר־אֵצֶל בֵּית לָחֶם לָלֶכֶת

go to ,Bethlehem by which ,Chimham the in and they And
(is) of inn lived left

Egypt, [18] because of the Chaldeans. For they were afraid of them, because Ishmael the son of Nethaniah had struck Gedaliah the son of Ahikam, whom the king of Babylon had appointed in the land.

18 לָבוֹא מִצְרָיִם׃ מִפְּנֵי הַכַּשְׂדִּים כִּי יָרְאוּ מִפְּנֵיהֶם כִּי־הִכָּה

had because of were they For the because ,Egypt to
struck ,them afraid .Chaldeans of enter

יִשְׁמָעֵאל בֶּן־נְתַנְיָה אֶת־גְּדַלְיָהוּ בֶּן־אֲחִיקָם אֲשֶׁר־הִפְקִיד

had whom ,Ahikam the Gedaliah Nethaniah the Ishmael
appointed of son of son

מֶלֶךְ־בָּבֶל בָּאָרֶץ׃

the in Babylon the
.land of king

CAP. XLII. מב

CHAPTER 42

[1] Then all the captains of the army and Johanan the son of Kareah, and Jezaniah the son of Hoshaiah, and all the people from the least even to the greatest, came near, [2] and said to Jeremiah the prophet, We beg you, let fall our plea before you and pray for us to Jehovah your God, for all this remnant, for we are left (but) a few of many, as your eyes see us. [3] that Jehovah your God may show us the way in which we may walk, and the thing that we may do. [4] Then Jeremiah the prophet said to them, I have heard (you). Behold, I will pray to Jehovah your God according to your words; and it shall be, all the word Jehovah shall answer, I will declare (it) to you; I will not keep a thing back from you. [5] Then they said to Jeremiah, Let Jehovah be a true and faithful witness between us if we do not do according to all things which Jehovah your God shall send you to us, so we will do. [6] Whether (it is) good, or whether (it is) evil, we will obey the voice of Jehovah your God, to whom we send you; so that it may be well with us when we obey the voice of Jehovah our God.

1 וַיִּגְּשׁוּ כָּל־שָׂרֵי הַחֲיָלִים וְיוֹחָנָן בֶּן־קָרֵחַ וִיזַנְיָה בֶּן־הוֹשַׁעְיָה

,Hoshaiah the and ,Kareah the and ,army the the all Then
of son Jezaniah of son Johanan of captains near came

2 וְכָל־הָעָם מִקָּטֹן וְעַד־גָּדוֹל׃ וַיֹּאמְרוּ אֶל־יִרְמְיָהוּ הַנָּבִיא

the Jeremiah to said and the even the from the and
,prophet ;greatest to least people all

תִּפָּל־נָא תְחִנָּתֵנוּ לְפָנֶיךָ וְהִתְפַּלֵּל בַּעֲדֵנוּ אֶל־יְהוָה אֱלֹהֶיךָ

your Jehovah to us for pray and before our now Let
,God you plea fall

בְּעַד כָּל־הַשְּׁאֵרִית הַזֹּאת כִּי־נִשְׁאַרְנוּ מְעַט מֵהַרְבֵּה כַּאֲשֶׁר

as ,many of (but) are we for ,this remnant all for
few a left

3 עֵינֶיךָ רֹאוֹת אֹתָנוּ׃ וְיַגֶּד־לָנוּ יְהוָה אֱלֹהֶיךָ אֶת־הַדֶּרֶךְ

the your Jehovah to may that ,us see your
way God us show eyes

4 אֲשֶׁר נֵלֶךְ־בָּהּ וְאֶת־הַדָּבָר אֲשֶׁר נַעֲשֶׂה׃ וַיֹּאמֶר אֲלֵיהֶם

them to said Then .do may we that thing the and ,in may we which
walk

יִרְמְיָהוּ הַנָּבִיא שָׁמַעְתִּי הִנְנִי מִתְפַּלֵּל אֶל־יְהוָה אֱלֹהֵיכֶם

your Jehovah to pray will ,Behold have I the Jeremiah
God I .heard ,prophet

כְּדִבְרֵיכֶם וְהָיָה כָּל־הַדָּבָר אֲשֶׁר־יַעֲנֶה יְהוָה אֶתְכֶם אַגִּיד

will I ,you Jehovah shall which the all it and to according
declare answer word ,be shall ,words your

5 לָכֶם לֹא־אֶמְנַע מִכֶּם דָּבָר׃ וְהֵמָּה אָמְרוּ אֶל־יִרְמְיָהוּ יְהִי

Let ,Jeremiah to said Then a from will I not to
be they .thing you back keep ;you

יְהוָה בָּנוּ לְעֵד אֱמֶת וְנֶאֱמָן אִם־לֹא כְּכָל־הַדָּבָר אֲשֶׁר

which things according not if and true a between Jeho-
all to ,faithful witness us vah

6 יִשְׁלָחֲךָ יְהוָה אֱלֹהֶיךָ אֵלֵינוּ כֵּן נַעֲשֶׂה׃ אִם־טוֹב וְאִם־

or (is it) Whether shall we so ,us to your Jehovah shall
whether ,good .do God you send

רָע בְּקוֹל ׀ יְהוָה אֱלֹהֵינוּ אֲשֶׁר אֲנוּ שֹׁלְחִים אֹתְךָ אֵלָיו

to you send we whom ,God our Jehovah the (is it)
Him of voice ,evil

נִשְׁמָע לְמַעַן אֲשֶׁר יִיטַב־לָנוּ כִּי נִשְׁמַע בְּקוֹל יְהוָה

Jehovah the obey we when with may it that so will we
of voice us well be ;obey

[7] And it happened, at the end of ten days the word of Jehovah came to Jeremiah. [8] Then he called Johanan the son of Kareah, and all the captains of the army that were with him, and all the people from the least even to the greatest. [9] And (he) said to them, Thus says Jehovah, the God of Israel, to whom you sent me to present your petition before Him: [10] If you will still remain in this land, then I will build you up and will not pull down; and I will plant you and will not pluck up. For I repent of the evil that I have done to you. [11] Do not be afraid of the king of Babylon, of whom you are afraid. Do not be afraid of him, says Jehovah; for I (am) with you to save you and to deliver you from his hand. [12] And I will show mercies to you, so that he may have pity on you and cause you to return to your own land.

[13] But if you say, We will not live in this land, or obey the voice of Jehovah your God, [14] saying, No, but we will go into the land of Egypt, where we shall see no war or hear the sound of the trumpet, and not we will hunger for bread; and there we will live; [15] then now hear the word of Jehovah, O remnant of Judah, Thus says Jehovah of hosts, the God of Israel: If you surely set your faces to go into Egypt, and go to live there, [16] then it shall come to pass, the sword

7 אֱלֹהֵֽינוּ׃ וַיְהִי מִקֵּץ עֲשֶׂרֶת יָמִים וַיְהִי דְבַר־יְהוָה
Jehovah the came days ten the at it And .God our
of word of end ,was

8 אֶל־יִרְמְיָהוּ׃ וַיִּקְרָא אֶל־יוֹחָנָן בֶּן־קָרֵחַ וְאֶל כָּל־שָׂרֵי
the all to and ,Kareah the Johanan to he Then .Jeremiah to
of captains of son called

9 הַחֲיָלִים אֲשֶׁר אִתּוֹ וּלְכָל־הָעָם לְמִקָּטֹן וְעַד־גָּדוֹל׃ וַיֹּאמֶר
he And the even the from the and with that the
said .greatest to least people all ,him (were) army

אֲלֵיהֶם כֹּה־אָמַר יְהוָה אֱלֹהֵי יִשְׂרָאֵל אֲשֶׁר שְׁלַחְתֶּם אֹתִי
me you whom ,Israel the ,Jehovah says Thus ,them to
sent of God

10 אֵלָיו לְהַפִּיל תְּחִנַּתְכֶם לְפָנָיו׃ אִם־שׁוֹב תֵּשְׁבוּ בָּאָרֶץ
in will you still If before your present to to
land remain :Him petition Him

הַזֹּאת וּבָנִיתִי אֶתְכֶם וְלֹא אֶהֱרֹס וְנָטַעְתִּי אֶתְכֶם וְלֹא
and you will I and tear and you will I then ,this
not plant ;down not up build

11 אֶתּוֹשׁ כִּי נִחַמְתִּי אֶל־הָרָעָה אֲשֶׁר עָשִׂיתִי לָכֶם׃ אַל־
not .you to have I that evil the to repent I For pluck
done .up

תִּירְאוּ מִפְּנֵי מֶלֶךְ בָּבֶל אֲשֶׁר־אַתֶּם יְרֵאִים מִפָּנָיו אַל־
not of are you whom ,Babylon the of be Do
.him afraid of king afraid

תִּירְאוּ מִמֶּנּוּ נְאֻם־יְהוָה כִּי־אִתְּכֶם אֲנִי לְהוֹשִׁיעַ אֶתְכֶם
you save to (am) I with for ;Jehovah says ,him of be Do
you afraid

12 וּלְהַצִּיל אֶתְכֶם מִיָּדוֹ׃ וְאֶתֵּן לָכֶם רַחֲמִים וְרִחַם אֶתְכֶם
you he and mercies you on I And his from you to and
pity will show will .hand deliver

13 וְהֵשִׁיב אֶתְכֶם אֶל־אַדְמַתְכֶם׃ וְאִם־אֹמְרִים אַתֶּם לֹא נֵשֵׁב
will we not ,you say if But own your to you cause and
live .land return to

14 בָּאָרֶץ הַזֹּאת לְבִלְתִּי שְׁמֹעַ בְּקוֹל יְהוָה אֱלֹהֵיכֶם׃ לֵאמֹר
,saying ,God our Jehovah the obey or ,this in
of voice land

לֹא כִּי אֶרֶץ מִצְרַיִם נָבוֹא אֲשֶׁר לֹא־נִרְאֶה מִלְחָמָה וְקוֹל
the and war will we not where will we Egypt the but ,No
of sound see ,into go of land

15 שׁוֹפָר לֹא נִשְׁמָע וְלַלֶּחֶם לֹא־נִרְעָב וְשָׁם נֵשֵׁב׃ וְעַתָּה
And will we and will we for and will we not the
now .live there ;hunger not bread ;hear trumpet

לָכֵן שִׁמְעוּ דְבַר־יְהוָה שְׁאֵרִית יְהוּדָה כֹּה־אָמַר יְהוָה
Jehovah says Thus ,Judah O ,Jehovah the hear there-
of of remnant of word fore

צְבָאוֹת אֱלֹהֵי יִשְׂרָאֵל אִם־אַתֶּם שׂוֹם תְּשִׂמוּן פְּנֵיכֶם לָבֹא
go to your set surely you If :Israel the ,hosts
into faces of God

16 מִצְרַיִם וּבָאתֶם לָגוּר שָׁם׃ וְהָיְתָה הַחֶרֶב אֲשֶׁר אַתֶּם
you which the it then ,there and you and ,Egypt
sword ,be will sojourn go

which you feared shall overtake you there in the land of Egypt; and the famine which you were anxious about shall cling to you there in Egypt, and you shall die there. [17] So (it) shall be to all the men who have set their faces to go into Egypt in order to live there. They shall die by the sword, by the famine, and by the plague. And none of them shall remain or escape from the evil that I will bring on them. [18] For thus says Jehovah of hosts, the God of Israel: As My anger and My fury has been poured out on the people of Jerusalem, so shall My fury be poured out on you when you shall enter Egypt. And you shall be a curse, and a horror, and a shame, and a reproach; and you shall not see this place any more.

[19] Jehovah has spoken about you, O remnant of Judah. Do not go into Egypt. Know that I have surely testified against you today. [20] For you used deceit against your souls when you sent me to Jehovah your God, saying, Pray for us to Jehovah our God; and according to all that Jehovah our God shall say, so declare to us, and we will do (it). [21] And I have declared (it) to you this day; but you have not obeyed the voice of Jehovah your God, or anything for which He has sent me to you. [22] Now therefore know certainly that you shall die by the sword, by the famine, and by the plague, in the place where you desire to go to sojourn.

יְרֵאִים מִמֶּנָּה שָׁם תַּשִּׂיג אֶתְכֶם בְּאֶרֶץ מִצְרָיִם וְהָרָעָב
the and famine ;Egypt the in of land you shall overtake there from feared

אֲשֶׁר־אַתֶּם ׀ דֹּאֲגִים מִמֶּנּוּ שָׁם יִדְבַּק אַחֲרֵיכֶם מִצְרַיִם
,Egypt (in) you to shall cling there about were anxious you which

17 וְשָׁם תָּמֻתוּ׃ וְיִהְיוּ כָל־הָאֲנָשִׁים אֲשֶׁר־שָׂמוּ אֶת־פְּנֵיהֶם
their faces have set who the men all it And ,be will shall you .die and there

לָבוֹא מִצְרַיִם לָגוּר שָׁם יָמוּתוּ בַּחֶרֶב בָּרָעָב וּבַדֶּבֶר וְלֹא־
and none the by and ;plague the by ,famine the by ,sword they die shall ,there to sojourn Egypt go to into

יִהְיֶה לָהֶם שָׂרִיד וּפָלִיט מִפְּנֵי הָרָעָה אֲשֶׁר אֲנִי מֵבִיא
will bring I that evil the from or escape remain of them shall

18 עֲלֵיהֶם׃ כִּי כֹה אָמַר יְהוָה צְבָאוֹת אֱלֹהֵי יִשְׂרָאֵל כַּאֲשֶׁר
As :Israel the of God ,hosts Jehovah of says thus For .them on

נִתַּךְ אַפִּי וַחֲמָתִי עַל־יֹשְׁבֵי יְרוּשָׁלִַם כֵּן תִּתַּךְ חֲמָתִי
My fury shall flow so ,Jerusalem the of people on My and fury My anger has flowed

עֲלֵיכֶם בְּבֹאֲכֶם מִצְרָיִם וִהְיִיתֶם לְאָלָה וּלְשַׁמָּה וְלִקְלָלָה
a and ,shame a and ,horror ,curse a you And become shall .Egypt you when enter you on

19 וּלְחֶרְפָּה וְלֹא־תִרְאוּ עוֹד אֶת־הַמָּקוֹם הַזֶּה׃ דִּבֶּר יְהוָה
Jehovah has spoken .this place again you see shall and not a and ;reproach

עֲלֵיכֶם שְׁאֵרִית יְהוּדָה אַל־תָּבֹאוּ מִצְרָיִם יָדֹעַ תֵּדְעוּ כִּי־
that know Surely .Egypt go Do into not .Judah O of remnant about ,you

20 הַעִידֹתִי בָכֶם הַיּוֹם׃ כִּי הִתְעֵתֶים בְּנַפְשׁוֹתֵיכֶם כִּי־אַתֶּם
you when against souls your used you deceit For .today against you have I testified

שְׁלַחְתֶּם אֹתִי אֶל־יְהוָה אֱלֹהֵיכֶם לֵאמֹר הִתְפַּלֵּל בַּעֲדֵנוּ
us for Pray ,saying ,God your Jehovah to me sent

אֶל־יְהוָה אֱלֹהֵינוּ וּכְכֹל אֲשֶׁר יֹאמַר יְהוָה אֱלֹהֵינוּ כֵּן
so ,God our Jehovah say shall that accord- and all to ing ;God our Jehovah to

21 הַגֶּד־לָנוּ וְעָשִׂינוּ׃ וָאַגִּד לָכֶם הַיּוֹם וְלֹא שְׁמַעְתֶּם בְּקוֹל
the of voice have you obeyed but not this ;day to you have I And declared we and .(it) do will to declare ,us

22 יְהוָה אֱלֹהֵיכֶם וּלְכֹל אֲשֶׁר־שְׁלָחַנִי אֲלֵיכֶם׃ וְעַתָּה יָדֹעַ
surely Now therefore .you to has He me sent (for) which or anything ,God your Jehovah

תֵּדְעוּ כִּי בַּחֶרֶב בָּרָעָב וּבַדֶּבֶר תָּמוּתוּ בַּמָּקוֹם אֲשֶׁר
where the in place shall you die the by and plague the by ,famine the by ,sword that know

חֲפַצְתֶּם לָבוֹא לָגוּר שָׁם׃
.there to sojourn go to desire you

CAP. XLIII מג

CHAPTER 43

CHAPTER 43

[1] And it came to pass, when Jeremiah had finished speaking to all the people all the words of Jehovah their God, for which Jehovah their God had sent him to them — all these words — [12] Azariah the son of Hoshaiah and Johanan the son of Kareah, and all the proud men then spoke, saying to Jeremiah, You speak falsely! Jehovah our God has not sent you to say, Do not go to Egypt to sojourn. there. [3] But Baruch the son of Neriah sets you against us, to deliver us into the hand of the Chaldeans, that they might put us to death and exile us to Babylon. [4] So Johanan the son of Kareah, and all the captains of the army, and all the people, did not obey the voice of Jehovah, to live in the land of Judah. [5] But Johanan the son of Kareah, and all the captains of the army, took all the remnant of Judah who had returned from all the nations, where they had been driven, to dwell in the land of Judah — [6] men, and women, and children, and the king's daughters, and every person that Nebuzar-adan the captain of the guard had left with Gedaliah the son of Ahikam the son of Shaphan, and Jeremiah, the prophet, and Baruch the son of Neriah; [7] and they came into the land of Egypt, for they did not obey the voice of Jehovah. And they came to Tahpanhes.

[8] Then the word of Jehovah came to Jeremiah

1 וַיְהִי כְּכַלּוֹת יִרְמְיָהוּ לְדַבֵּר אֶל־כָּל־הָעָם אֶת־כָּל־דִּבְרֵי
the all the all to speaking Jeremiah had when it And
of words people finished ,was

יְהוָה אֱלֹהֵיהֶם אֲשֶׁר שְׁלָחוֹ יְהוָה אֱלֹהֵיהֶם אֲלֵיהֶם אֵת
—them to their Jehovah had (for) their Jehovah
God him sent which ,God

2 כָּל־הַדְּבָרִים הָאֵלֶּה׃ וַיֹּאמֶר עֲזַרְיָה בֶן־הוֹשַׁעְיָה
Hoshaiah the Azariah spoke —these words all
of son

וְיוֹחָנָן בֶּן־קָרֵחַ וְכָל־הָאֲנָשִׁים הַזֵּדִים אֹמְרִים אֶל־יִרְמְיָהוּ
,Jeremiah to saying ,proud men the all and ,Kareah the and
of son Johanan

שֶׁקֶר אַתָּה מְדַבֵּר לֹא שְׁלָחֲךָ יְהוָה אֱלֹהֵינוּ לֵאמֹר לֹא־
not ,say to God our Jehovah sent has not !speak You falsely
you

3 תָבֹאוּ מִצְרַיִם לָגוּר שָׁם׃ כִּי בָּרוּךְ בֶּן־נֵרִיָּה מַסִּית אֹתְךָ
you is Neriah the Baruch But .there to Egypt Do
inciting of son sojourn go to

בָּנוּ לְמַעַן תֵּת אֹתָנוּ בְיַד־הַכַּשְׂדִּים לְהָמִית אֹתָנוּ וּלְהַגְלוֹת
to and us put to the the into us deliver to against
exile death to ,Chaldeans of hand ,us

4 אֹתָנוּ בָּבֶל׃ וְלֹא־שָׁמַע יוֹחָנָן בֶּן־קָרֵחַ וְכָל־שָׂרֵי הַחֲיָלִים
the cap- the and Kareah the Johanan did So to us
,army of tains all of son obey not .Babylon

5 וְכָל־הָעָם בְּקוֹל יְהוָה לָשֶׁבֶת בְּאֶרֶץ יְהוּדָה׃ וַיִּקַּח יוֹחָנָן
Johanan But .Judah the in live to ,Jehovah the the and
took of land of voice people all

בֶּן־קָרֵחַ וְכָל־שָׂרֵי הַחֲיָלִים אֵת כָּל־שְׁאֵרִית יְהוּדָה אֲשֶׁר־
who Judah the all army the cap- the and ,Kareah the
of remnant of tains all of son

שָׁבוּ מִכָּל־הַגּוֹיִם אֲשֶׁר נִדְּחוּ־שָׁם לָגוּר בְּאֶרֶץ יְהוּדָה׃
—Judah the in to there had they where the from re- had
of land driven been nations all turned

6 אֶת־הַגְּבָרִים וְאֶת־הַנָּשִׁים וְאֶת־הַטַּף וְאֶת־בְּנוֹת הַמֶּלֶךְ
the daughters and ,children and ,women and ,men
,king's

וְאֵת כָּל־הַנֶּפֶשׁ אֲשֶׁר הִנִּיחַ נְבוּזַרְאֲדָן רַב־טַבָּחִים אֶת־
with the the Nebuzar-adan left had that person every and
guard of captain

גְּדַלְיָהוּ בֶּן־אֲחִיקָם בֶּן־שָׁפָן וְאֵת יִרְמְיָהוּ הַנָּבִיא וְאֶת־
and the Jeremiah and ,Shaphan the Ahikam the Gedaliah
,prophet of son of son

7 בָּרוּךְ בֶּן־נֵרִיָּהוּ׃ וַיָּבֹאוּ אֶרֶץ מִצְרַיִם כִּי לֹא שָׁמְעוּ בְּקוֹל
the they not for ,Egypt the they And .Neriah the Baruch
of voice obey did of land into came of son

8 יְהוָה וַיָּבֹאוּ עַד־תַּחְפַּנְחֵס׃ וַיְהִי דְבַר־יְהוָה אֶל־
to Jehovah the Then .Tahpanhes to they And Jeho-
of word came came .vah

in Tahpanhes, saying, [9] Take great stones to your hand, and hide them in the mortar in the brickwork which (is) at the entrance to Pharaoh's house in Tahpanhes, in the sight of the men of Judah. [10] And say to them, Thus says Jehovah of hosts, the God of Israel: Behold, I will send and take Nebuchadnezzar the king of Babylon, My servant, and will set his throne on these stones that I have hidden. And he shall spread his royal pavilion over them. [11] And when he comes, he shall strike the land of Egypt. And whoever (is) for death (shall go) to death, and whoever (is) for captivity (shall go) into captivity, and whoever (is) for the sword, to the sword. [12] And I will kindle a fire in the houses of the gods of Egypt. And he shall burn them and take them captive. And he shall adorn himself with the land of Egypt, as a shepherd covers himself with his robe; and he shall go forth from there in peace. [13] He shall also break the obelisks of The House of the Sun which (is) in the land of Egypt; and he shall burn with fire the houses of the gods of the Egyptians.

9 ירמיהו בתחפנחס לאמר: קח בידך אבנים גדלות
,great | stones | your in hand | Take | ,saying | in Tahpanhes | Jeremiah

וטמנתם במלט במלבן אשר בפתח בית־פרעה
Pharaoh's | house | the at to entrance | which (is) | the in brickwork | the in mortar | hide and them

10 בתחפנחס לעיני אנשים יהודים: ואמרת אליהם כה־
Thus | ,them to | say And | .Judah of | men the | the in of sight | in ,Tahpanhes

אמר יהוה צבאות אלהי ישראל הנני שלח ולקחתי את־
take and | will send | Behold I | ,Israel | the of God | hosts | Jehovah of | says

נבוכדראצר מלך־בבל עבדי ושמתי כסאו ממעל
on | his throne | will and set | My ,servant | ,Babylon | king of | Nebuchadnezzar

לאבנים האלה אשר טמנתי ונטה את־שפרורו עליהם:
over .them | his pavillion | he And spread shall | have I .hidden | that | these | stones

11 ובאה והכה את־ארץ מצרים אשר למות למות ואשר
and whoever | (go shall) ,death to | for death | Whoever (is) | :Egypt | the of land | shall He strike | when And comes he

12 לשבי לשבי ואשר לחרב לחרב: והצתי אש בבתי
the in of houses | fire a | I And kindle will | the to .sword | the for ,sword | and whoever | into ;captivity | cap- for tivity

אלהי מצרים ושרפם ושבם ועטה את־ארץ מצרים
,Egypt | the of land | will he and cleanse | seize and ,them | will he and ,them burn | ,Egypt | the of gods

13 כאשר־יעטה הרעה את־בגדו ויצא משם בשלום: ושבר
shall He break also | .peace in | from there | he and go shall | his with ;robe | shep- a herd | covers himself | as

את־מצבות בית שמש אשר בארץ מצרים ואת־בתי
the of houses | and | ;Egypt | the in of land | which (is) | sun the | the of house | the of obelisks

אלהי מצרים ישרף באש:
with .fire | shall he burn | the Egyptians | the of gods

CAP. XLIV. מד

CHAPTER 44

[1] The word that came to Jeremiah concerning all the Jews who were living in the land of Egypt at Migdol, and at Tahpanhes, and at Noph, and in the land of Pathros, saying, [2] Thus says Jehovah of hosts, the God of Israel: You have seen all the evil that I have brought on Jerusalem, and

1 הדבר אשר־היה אל־ירמיהו אל כל־היהודים הישבים
were who living | the Jews | all | con- cerning | Jeremiah to | came | that | The word

בארץ מצרים הישבים במגדל ובתחפנחס ובנף ובארץ
the in and of land | at and ,Noph | at and ,Tahpanhes | ,Migdel at | those living | ,Egypt | the in of land

2 פתרוס לאמר: כה־אמר יהוה צבאות אלהי ישראל
:Israel | God the of | ,hosts | Jehovah of | says Thus | ,saying | ,Pathros

אתם ראיתם את כל־הרעה אשר הבאתי על־ירושלם
,Jerusalem | on | have I brought | that | evil the | all | have seen | You

on all the cities of Judah. And, look! This day (they are) a ruin, and no man lives in them; [3] because of the evil which they have done, by provoking Me to anger, by going to burn incense, by serving other gods that they did not know – they, you, nor your fathers. [4] However, I sent to you all My servants the prophets, rising early and sending, saying, Oh do not commit this idolatry which I hate! [5] But they did not listen nor bow their ear to turn from their wickedness, not to burn incense to other gods. [6] Therefore My fury and My anger was poured out and was kindled in the cities of Judah and in the streets of Jerusalem. And they are wasted (and) deserted, as this day. [7] And now thus says Jehovah, the God of hosts, the God of Israel: Why do you commit great evil against your souls, to cut off from you man and woman, child and infant out of Judah, not leaving to yourselves a remnant;

[8] to provoke Me to wrath with the works of your hands, burning incense to other gods in the land of Egypt where you have gone to live there, that I might cut you off, and that you might be a curse and a reproach among all the nations of the earth? [9] Have you forgotten the wickedness of your fathers, and the wickedness of the kings of Judah, and the wickedness of his wives, and your own wickedness, and the wickedness of your wives, which they have committed in the land of Judah and in

וְעַל כָּל־עָרֵי יְהוּדָה וְהִנָּם חָרְבָּה הַיּוֹם הַזֶּה וְאֵין בָּהֶם

them in no and ,This day ruin a And .Judah the all and
one !behold of cities on

3 יוֹשֵׁב׃ מִפְּנֵי רָעָתָם אֲשֶׁר עָשׂוּ לְהַכְעִסֵנִי לָלֶכֶת לְקַטֵּר

burn to by provoking by they which evil the because ;lives
,incense going ,anger to Me ,done have of

לַעֲבֹד לֵאלֹהִים אֲחֵרִים אֲשֶׁר לֹא יְדָעוּם הֵמָּה אַתֶּם

,you ,they did they not that other gods by
—know serving

4 וַאֲבֹתֵיכֶם׃ וָאֶשְׁלַח אֲלֵיכֶם אֶת־כָּל־עֲבָדַי הַנְּבִיאִים הַשְׁכֵּים

rising the My all you to However your nor
early ,prophets servants sent I .fathers

וְשָׁלֹחַ לֵאמֹר אַל־נָא תַעֲשׂוּ אֵת דְּבַר־הַתֹּעֵבָה הַזֹּאת אֲשֶׁר

which this abominable thing do Oh not ,saying and
commit ,sending

5 שָׂנֵאתִי׃ וְלֹא שָׁמְעוּ וְלֹא־הִטּוּ אֶת־אָזְנָם לָשׁוּב מֵרָעָתָם

their from turn to their bow nor did they But !hate I
,wickedness ear ,listen not

6 לְבִלְתִּי קַטֵּר לֵאלֹהִים אֲחֵרִים׃ וַתִּתַּךְ חֲמָתִי וְאַפִּי וַתִּבְעַר

was and My and My was So .other gods to burn to not
kindled ,anger fury out poured incense

בְּעָרֵי יְהוּדָה וּבְחֻצוֹת יְרוּשָׁלִַם וַתִּהְיֶינָה לְחָרְבָּה לִשְׁמָמָה

(and) wasted they And .Jerusalem in and Judah the in
deserted are of streets the of cities

7 כַּיּוֹם הַזֶּה׃ וְעַתָּה כֹּה־אָמַר יְהוָה אֱלֹהֵי צְבָאוֹת

,hosts the Jehovah says thus And .this day as
of God now

אֱלֹהֵי יִשְׂרָאֵל לָמָה אַתֶּם עֹשִׂים רָעָה גְדוֹלָה אֶל־

against great evil do you Why :Israel the
commit of God

נַפְשֹׁתֵכֶם לְהַכְרִית לָכֶם אִישׁ־וְאִשָּׁה עוֹלֵל וְיוֹנֵק מִתּוֹךְ

out and child and man from cut to your
of ,infant ,woman you off ,souls

8 יְהוּדָה לְבִלְתִּי הוֹתִיר לָכֶם שְׁאֵרִית׃ לְהַכְעִסֵנִי בְּמַעֲשֵׂי

the with provoke to a your- to leaving not ,Judah
of works wrath to Me ;remnant selves

יְדֵיכֶם לְקַטֵּר לֵאלֹהִים אֲחֵרִים בְּאֶרֶץ מִצְרַיִם אֲשֶׁר־אַתֶּם

you where Egypt the in other gods to burn to your
of land incense ,hands

בָּאִים לָגוּר שָׁם לְמַעַן הַכְרִית לָכֶם וּלְמַעַן הֱיוֹתְכֶם

might you and ,you might I that ,there to have
be that off cut sojourn gone

9 לִקְלָלָה וּלְחֶרְפָּה בְּכֹל גּוֹיֵי הָאָרֶץ׃ הֲשְׁכַחְתֶּם אֶת־רָעוֹת

wicked- the you Have the the among a and curse a
of ness forgotten ?earth of nations all reproach

אֲבוֹתֵיכֶם וְאֶת־רָעוֹת ׀ מַלְכֵי יְהוּדָה וְאֵת רָעוֹת נָשָׁיו

his wick- the and ,Judah the the and your
,wives of edness of kings of wickedness ,fathers

וְאֵת רָעֹתֵיכֶם וְאֵת רָעֹת נְשֵׁיכֶם אֲשֶׁר עָשׂוּ בְּאֶרֶץ יְהוּדָה

Judah the in they which your the and own your and
of land done have ,wives of wickedness ,wickedness

the streets of Jerusalem?
[10] They are not humbled
to this day, nor have they
feared, nor walked in My
law, nor in My statutes
which I have set before you
and before your fathers.
[11] Therefore thus
says Jehovah of hosts, the
God of Israel: Behold, I will
set My face against you for
evil, and to cut off all
Judah. [12] And I will take
the remnant of Judah who
have set their faces to go
into the land of Egypt to
live there; and they shall all
be consumed (and) fall in
the land of Egypt. They
shall be consumed by the
sword, by the famine. They
shall die, from the least even
to the greatest, by the
sword and by the famine;
and they shall be a curse, a
horror, and a shame, and a
reproach. [13] For I will
punish those who dwell in
the land of Egypt, as I have
punished Jerusalem, by the
sword, by the famine, and
by the plague, [14] so that
none of the remnant of
Judah, which has gone into
the land of Egypt to
sojourn there, will be an
escaped one, a survivor, or
return to the land of Judah
(to) which they are lifting
up their soul, to return to
live there. For none shall
return except those who
escape.

[15] Then all the men
who knew that their wives
had burned incense to other
gods, and all the women
who stood by, a great
assembly, even all the
people who lived in the land
of Egypt, in Pathros, an-
swered Jeremiah, saying,
[16] (As for) the word that
you have spoken to us in the
name of Jehovah, we will
not listen to you. [17] But

10 וּבְחֻצוֹת יְרוּשָׁלָ‍ִם׃ לֹא דֻכְּאוּ עַד הַיּוֹם הַזֶּה וְלֹא יָרְאוּ

have they and this day to are They not ?Jerusalem the in and
,feared not humbled of streets

וְלֹא־הָלְכוּ בְתוֹרָתִי וּבְחֻקֹּתַי אֲשֶׁר־נָתַתִּי לִפְנֵיכֶם וְלִפְנֵי

and before set I which my in and My in walked and
before you statutes not ,law not

11 אֲבוֹתֵיכֶם׃ לָכֵן כֹּה־אָמַר יְהוָה צְבָאוֹת אֱלֹהֵי

the ,hosts Jehovah says thus Therefore your
of God of .fathers

יִשְׂרָאֵל הִנְנִי שָׂם פָּנַי בָּכֶם לְרָעָה וּלְהַכְרִית אֶת־כָּל־יְהוּדָה׃

.Judah all to and for against My will ,Behold ,Israel
off cut ,evil you face set I

12 וְלָקַחְתִּי אֶת־שְׁאֵרִית יְהוּדָה אֲשֶׁר־שָׂמוּ פְנֵיהֶם לָבוֹא

go to their have who Judah the I And
into faces set of remnant take will

אֶרֶץ־מִצְרַיִם לָגוּר שָׁם וְתַמּוּ כֹל בְּאֶרֶץ מִצְרַיִם יִפֹּלוּ

they ,Egypt the in all they and ,there to Egypt the
fall shall of land cease will sojourn of land

בַּחֶרֶב בָּרָעָב יִתַּמּוּ מִקָּטֹן וְעַד־גָּדוֹל בַּחֶרֶב וּבָרָעָב יָמֻתוּ

they by and the by the even the from will and the by the by
;die shall famine the sword ,greatest to least ,cease famine ,sword

13 וְהָיוּ לְאָלָה לְשַׁמָּה וְלִקְלָלָה וּלְחֶרְפָּה׃ וּפָקַדְתִּי עַל־

will I For a and a and ,horror a ,curse a they And
punish .reproach ,shame be shall

הַיּוֹשְׁבִים בְּאֶרֶץ מִצְרַיִם כַּאֲשֶׁר פָּקַדְתִּי עַל־יְרוּשָׁלָ‍ִם

Jerusalem have I as ,Egypt the in who those
punished of land live

14 בַּחֶרֶב בָּרָעָב וּבַדָּבֶר׃ וְלֹא יִהְיֶה פָּלִיט וְשָׂרִיד לִשְׁאֵרִית

the for a or es- an be will and the by and the by the by
of remnant survivor ,one caped not ;plague ,famine ,sword

יְהוּדָה הַבָּאִים לָגוּר־שָׁם בְּאֶרֶץ מִצְרַיִם וְלָשׁוּב ׀ אֶרֶץ

the return or Egypt the in there to has which ,Judah
of land to of land sojourn ,gone

יְהוּדָה אֲשֶׁר־הֵמָּה מְנַשְּׂאִים אֶת־נַפְשָׁם לָשׁוּב לָשֶׁבֶת שָׁם

.there to to their are they (to) Judah
dwell return ,soul up lifting which

15 כִּי לֹא־יָשׁוּבוּ כִּי אִם־פְּלֵטִים׃ וַיַּעֲנוּ אֶת־יִרְמְיָהוּ

,Jeremiah Then who those except shall none For
answered .escape return

כָּל־הָאֲנָשִׁים הַיֹּדְעִים כִּי־מְקַטְּרוֹת נְשֵׁיהֶם לֵאלֹהִים

gods to their burned had that knew who men the all
wives incense

אֲחֵרִים וְכָל־הַנָּשִׁים הָעֹמְדוֹת קָהָל גָּדוֹל וְכָל־הָעָם

the even ,great a stood who the and ,other
people all assembly ,by women all

16 הַיֹּשְׁבִים בְּאֶרֶץ־מִצְרַיִם בְּפַתְרוֹס לֵאמֹר׃ הַדָּבָר אֲשֶׁר

which (to As) ,saying in Egypt the in who
word the ,Pathros of land lived

17 דִּבַּרְתָּ אֵלֵינוּ בְּשֵׁם יְהוָה אֵינֶנּוּ שֹׁמְעִים אֵלֶיךָ׃ כִּי עָשֹׂה

cer- But .you to listen will we ,Jehovah the in us to have you
tainly not of name spoken

we will certainly do whatever thing goes out of our own mouth, to burn incense to the queen of heaven, and to pour out drink offerings to her, as we have done, we, and our fathers, our kings, and our princes, in the cities of Judah, and in the streets of Jerusalem. And we had plenty of food, and were well, and saw no evil. [18] But since we stopped burning incense to the queen of heaven, and pouring out drink offerings to her, we have lacked all (things) and have been devoured by the sword and by the famine. [19] And when we burned incense to the queen of heaven and poured out drink offerings to her, did we make her cakes to worship her and pour out drink offerings to her without our men?

[20] Then Jeremiah said to all the people — to the men and to the women, and to all the people who were giving him answer, [21] The incense that you burned in the cities of Judah, and in the streets of Jerusalem, you, and your father, your kings, and your princes, and the people of the land, did not Jehovah remember them? Yea, it came into His heart. [22] And Jehovah could no longer hold back because of the evil of your doings, because of the hateful things which you have committed. Therefore your land is a waste, and a horror, and a curse, without inhabitant, as this day. [23] Because you have burned incense, and because you have sinned against Jehovah, and have not obeyed the voice of Jehovah, in His law, or in His statutes, and you did not walk in His testimonies; therefore this evil has happened to you, as (at) this

נַעֲשֶׂה אֶת־כָּל־הַדָּבָר ׀ אֲשֶׁר־יָצָא מִפִּינוּ לְקַטֵּר לִמְלֶכֶת
the to burn to our of goes that thing every will we
of queen incense ,mouth out do

הַשָּׁמַיִם וְהַסֵּיךְ־לָהּ נְסָכִים כַּאֲשֶׁר עָשִׂינוּ אֲנַחְנוּ וַאֲבֹתֵינוּ
our and ,we have we as drink to to and ,heaven
,fathers ,done ,offerings her out pour

מְלָכֵינוּ וְשָׂרֵינוּ בְּעָרֵי יְהוּדָה וּבְחֻצוֹת יְרוּשָׁלִָם וַנִּשְׂבַּע
had we and ;Jerusalem the in and ,Judah the in our and our
of plenty of streets of cities princes ,kings

18 לֶחֶם וַנִּהְיֶה טוֹבִים וְרָעָה לֹא רָאִינוּ׃ וּמִן־אָז חָדַלְנוּ
we then And .see did not evil and ,well and ,bread
stopped from were

לְקַטֵּר לִמְלֶכֶת הַשָּׁמַיִם וְהַסֵּךְ־לָהּ נְסָכִים חָסַרְנוּ כֹל
all have we drink her to and ,heaven the to burning
;(things) lacked ,offerings out poured of queen incense

19 וּבַחֶרֶב וּבָרָעָב תָּמְנוּ׃ וְכִי־אֲנַחְנוּ מְקַטְּרִים לִמְלֶכֶת
the to burned we And been have by and by and
of queen incense when .devoured famine the ,sword the

הַשָּׁמַיִם וּלְהַסֵּךְ לָהּ נְסָכִים הֲמִבַּלְעֲדֵי אֲנָשֵׁינוּ עָשִׂינוּ לָהּ
to we did our without drink to poured and heaven
her make men ,offerings her out

20 כַּוָּנִים לְהַעֲצִבָה וְהַסֵּךְ לָהּ נְסָכִים׃ וַיֹּאמֶר יִרְמְיָהוּ
Jeremiah said Then drink her to and make to cakes
?offerings out pour image an

אֶל־כָּל־הָעָם עַל־הַגְּבָרִים וְעַל־הַנָּשִׁים וְעַל־כָּל־הָעָם הָעֹנִים
were who the all and the and the to the all to
giving people to ,women to men —people

21 אֹתוֹ דָּבָר לֵאמֹר׃ הֲלוֹא אֶת־הַקִּטֵּר אֲשֶׁר קִטַּרְתֶּם בְּעָרֵי
the in you that the Did ,saying ,answer him
of cities burned incense not

יְהוּדָה וּבְחֻצוֹת יְרוּשָׁלִַם אַתֶּם וַאֲבוֹתֵיכֶם מַלְכֵיכֶם וְשָׂרֵיכֶם
your and your your and ,you ,Jerusalem the in and Judah
,princes ,kings ,fathers of streets

22 וְעַם הָאָרֶץ אֹתָם זָכַר יְהוָה וַתַּעֲלֶה עַל־לִבּוֹ׃ וְלֹא־יוּכַל
could And His into it And ?Jehovah re- them the the and
not .heart came membered ,land of people

יְהוָה עוֹד לָשֵׂאת מִפְּנֵי רֹעַ מַעַלְלֵיכֶם מִפְּנֵי הַתּוֹעֵבֹת אֲשֶׁר
which the because your the because hold still Jehovah
abominations of ,doings of evil of back

עֲשִׂיתֶם וַתְּהִי אַרְצְכֶם לְחָרְבָּה וּלְשַׁמָּה וְלִקְלָלָה מֵאֵין
without a and a and ,waste a your Therefore have you
,curse ,horror land is .done

23 יוֹשֵׁב כְּהַיּוֹם הַזֶּה׃ מִפְּנֵי אֲשֶׁר קִטַּרְתֶּם וַאֲשֶׁר חֲטָאתֶם
have you and have you Because .this day as inhabi-
sinned because ,incense burned ,tant

לַיהוָה וְלֹא שְׁמַעְתֶּם בְּקוֹל יְהוָה וּבְתֹרָתוֹ וּבְחֻקֹּתָיו
His in or His in ,Jehovah the have and against
,statutes ,law of voice obeyed not ,Jehovah

וּבְעֵדְוֹתָיו לֹא הֲלַכְתֶּם עַל־כֵּן קָרָאת אֶתְכֶם הָרָעָה הַזֹּאת
,this evil you hap- has therefore you not His in and
to pened ,walked testimonies

day. [24] Jeremiah also said to all the people, and to all the women, Hear the word of Jehovah, all Judah who (are) in the land of Egypt, thus says Jehovah of hosts, the God of Israel, saying: [25] You and your wives have both spoken with your mouths and fulfilled with your hands, saying, We will surely fulfill our vows that we have vowed, to burn incense to the queen of heaven, and to pour out drink offerings to her. You certainly do perform your vows and certainly establish your vows. [26] Therefore hear the word of Jehovah, all Judah that lives in the land of Egypt. Behold, I have sworn by My great name, says Jehovah, that My name will no more be named in the mouth of any man of Judah in all the land of Egypt, saying, The Lord Jehovah lives. [27] Behold, I will watch over them for evil, and not for good; and all the men of Judah who (are) in the land of Egypt shall be destroyed by the sword and by the famine, until they come to an end. [28] And he who escapes the sword shall return out of the land of Egypt to the land of Judah, few in number; and all the remnant of Judah who have gone into the land of Egypt to live there shall know whose word shall stand, Mine or theirs.

[29] And this (shall be) a sign to you, says Jehovah, that I will punish you in this place so that you may know that My words shall surely stand against you for evil. [30] Thus says Jehovah, Behold, I am giving Pharaoh-hophra king of

24 כַּיּוֹם הַזֶּה׃ וַיֹּאמֶר יִרְמְיָהוּ אֶל־כָּל־הָעָם וְאֶל כָּל־
all and the all to Jeremiah Also .this (at) as
to people said day

הַנָּשִׁים שִׁמְעוּ דְּבַר־יְהוָה כָּל־יְהוּדָה אֲשֶׁר בְּאֶרֶץ מִצְרָיִם׃
,Egypt the in who Judah all ,Jehovah the Hear the
of land (are) of word ,women

25 כֹּה־אָמַר יְהוָה־צְבָאוֹת אֱלֹהֵי יִשְׂרָאֵל לֵאמֹר אַתֶּם
You :saying ,Israel the hosts Jehovah says Thus
of God of

וּנְשֵׁיכֶם וַתְּדַבֵּרְנָה בְּפִיכֶם וּבִידֵיכֶם מִלֵּאתֶם ׀ לֵאמֹר עָשֹׂה
Surely ,saying ,fulfilled with and your with both have your and
hands your mouths spoken wives

נַעֲשֶׂה אֶת־נְדָרֵינוּ אֲשֶׁר נָדַרְנוּ לְקַטֵּר לִמְלֶכֶת הַשָּׁמַיִם
,heaven the to burn to have we that our will we
of queen incense ,vowed vows fulfill

וּלְהַסֵּךְ לָהּ נְסָכִים הָקֵים תָּקִימְנָה אֶת־נִדְרֵיכֶם וְעָשֹׂה
and your you Surely drink her to to and
surely vows establish .offerings out pour

26 תַּעֲשֶׂינָה אֶת־נִדְרֵיכֶם׃ לָכֵן שִׁמְעוּ דְבַר־יְהוָה כָּל־יְהוּדָה
Judah all ,Jehovah the hear ,Therefore your perform
of word .vows

הַיֹּשְׁבִים בְּאֶרֶץ מִצְרַיִם הִנְנִי נִשְׁבַּעְתִּי בִּשְׁמִי הַגָּדוֹל אָמַר
says ,great My by have ,Behold ;Egypt the in who
name sworn I of land sojourns

יְהוָה אִם־יִהְיֶה עוֹד שְׁמִי נִקְרָא ׀ בְּפִי ׀ כָּל־אִישׁ יְהוּדָה
,Judah man any the in named My more will (that) Jeho-
of of mouth name be no ,vah

27 אֹמֵר חַי־אֲדֹנָי יְהוִה בְּכָל־אֶרֶץ מִצְרָיִם׃ הִנְנִי שֹׁקֵד עֲלֵיהֶם
over am ,Behold .Egypt the in ,Jehovah The lives ,saying
them watching I of land all Lord

לְרָעָה וְלֹא לְטוֹבָה וְתַמּוּ כָל־אִישׁ יְהוּדָה אֲשֶׁר בְּאֶרֶץ
the in who Judah the all will and for and for
of land (are) of men cease ;good not ,evil

28 מִצְרַיִם בַּחֶרֶב וּבָרָעָב עַד־כְּלוֹתָם׃ וּפְלִיטֵי חֶרֶב יְשֻׁבוּן
shall the who he And come they until the by and the by ,Egypt
return sword escapes .end an to ,famine sword

מִן־אֶרֶץ מִצְרַיִם אֶרֶץ יְהוּדָה מְתֵי מִסְפָּר וְיָדְעוּ כָּל־שְׁאֵרִית
the all shall And .number men ,Judah the to Egypt the of out
of remnant know of of land of land

יְהוּדָה הַבָּאִים לְאֶרֶץ־מִצְרַיִם לָגוּר שָׁם דְּבַר־מִי יָקוּם
shall word whose there to Egypt the into have who Judah
,stand sojourn of land gone

29 מִמֶּנִּי וּמֵהֶם׃ וְזֹאת לָכֶם הָאוֹת נְאֻם־יְהוָה כִּי־פֹקֵד אֲנִי
am I that ,Jehovah states the you to this And or Mine
punishing ,sign (be shall) .theirs

עֲלֵיכֶם בַּמָּקוֹם הַזֶּה לְמַעַן תֵּדְעוּ כִּי קוֹם יָקוּמוּ דְבָרַי
My shall surely that may you so ,this place in you
words stand know that

30 עֲלֵיכֶם לְרָעָה׃ כֹּה ׀ אָמַר יְהוָה הִנְנִי נֹתֵן אֶת־פַּרְעֹה
Pharaoh- am Behold ,Jehovah says Thus .evil for against
giving I you

Egypt into the hand of his enemies, and into the hand of those who seek his soul, as I gave Zedekiah king of Judah into the hand of Nebuchadnezzar king of Babylon, his enemy that sought his soul.

חָפְרַע מֶלֶךְ־מִצְרַיִם בְּיַד אֹיְבָיו וּבְיַד מְבַקְשֵׁי נַפְשׁוֹ כַּאֲשֶׁר

as	,soul his	seekers	into and	his	the into	Egypt	king	Hophra
		of	of hand	the	,enemies of hand			

נָתַתִּי אֶת־צִדְקִיָּהוּ מֶלֶךְ־יְהוּדָה בְּיַד נְבוּכַדְרֶאצַּר מֶלֶךְ־

king	Nebuchadnezzar	the into	Judah	king	Zedekiah	gave I
of		of hand		of		

בָּבֶל אֹיְבוֹ וּמְבַקֵּשׁ נַפְשׁוֹ׃

his	that	his ,Babylon
.soul	sought	enemy

CAP. XLV מה

CHAPTER 45

CHAPTER 45

[1] The word that Jeremiah the prophet spoke to Baruch the son of Neriah, when he had written these words in a book from the mouth of Jeremiah, in the fourth year of Jehoiakim the son of Josiah king of Judah, saying, [2] Thus says Jehovah, the God of Israel, to you, O Baruch: [3] You said, Woe is me now, for Jehovah has added grief to my pain; I fainted in my sighing, and I find no rest.

[4] So you shall say to him, Jehovah says this: Behold, (that) which I have built I am tearing down, and that which I have planted I am pulling up, even all the land to Me itself. [5] And do you seek great things for yourself? Do not seek (them); for behold, I will bring evil on all flesh, says Jehovah. But I will give your soul to you as a prize, on all the places where you go there.

1 הַדָּבָר אֲשֶׁר דִּבֶּר יִרְמְיָהוּ הַנָּבִיא אֶל־בָּרוּךְ בֶּן־נֵרִיָּה

,Neriah	the	Baruch	to	the	Jeremiah	spoke	that	The
of son				prophet				word

בְּכָתְבוֹ אֶת־הַדְּבָרִים הָאֵלֶּה עַל־סֵפֶר מִפִּי יִרְמְיָהוּ בַּשָּׁנָה

the in	,Jeremiah	the from	a	in	these	words	he when
year		of mouth	book				written had

2 הָרְבִעִית לִיהוֹיָקִים בֶּן־יֹאשִׁיָּהוּ מֶלֶךְ יְהוּדָה לֵאמֹר׃ כֹּה

Thus	,saying	Judah	of king	Josiah	the	of	fourth
				of son	Jehoiakim		

3 אָמַר יְהוָה אֱלֹהֵי יִשְׂרָאֵל עָלַיִךְ בָּרוּךְ׃ אָמַרְתָּ אוֹי־נָא לִי

to	now Woe	You	O	,you to	Israel	the	Jehovah	says
,me	(is) ,said	:Baruch				of God		

כִּי־יָסַף יְהוָה יָגוֹן עַל־מַכְאֹבִי יָגַעְתִּי בְּאַנְחָתִי וּמְנוּחָה לֹא

not	rest and	my in	fainted I	my	to grief	Jehovah has for
		;groaning		pain		added

4 מָצָאתִי׃ כֹּה תֹּאמַר אֵלָיו כֹּה אָמַר יְהוָה הִנֵּה אֲשֶׁר־

that	,Behold	,Jehovah	says	Thus	to	shall you	So	.find I
which					,him	say		

בָּנִיתִי אֲנִי הֹרֵס וְאֵת אֲשֶׁר־נָטַעְתִּי אֲנִי נֹתֵשׁ וְאֶת־כָּל־הָאָרֶץ

the	all	even	am I	have I	that and	and	tear- am I	have I
land				;up pulling	,planted which		;down ing	built

5 לִי־הִיא׃ וְאַתָּה תְּבַקֶּשׁ־לְךָ גְדֹלוֹת אַל־תְּבַקֵּשׁ כִּי הִנְנִי מֵבִיא

am ,behold for	seek Do	not	great	for seek do	And	.itself to
bringing I	;(them)		?things yourself	you		Me

רָעָה עַל־כָּל־בָּשָׂר נְאֻם־יְהוָה וְנָתַתִּי לְךָ אֶת־נַפְשְׁךָ לְשָׁלָל

a as	your	to	I But	.Jehovah states	,flesh	all	on	evil
,prize	soul		you give will					

עַל כָּל־הַמְּקֹמוֹת אֲשֶׁר תֵּלֶךְ־שָׁם׃

.there	you	where	the	all	on
go			places		

CAP. XLVI מו

CHAPTER 46

CHAPTER 46

[1] The word of Jehovah which came to Jeremiah the prophet against the nations; [2] against Egypt, against the army of Pharaoh-necho king of Egypt, which was by the river

1 אֲשֶׁר הָיָה דְבַר־יְהוָה אֶל־יִרְמְיָהוּ הַנָּבִיא עַל־הַגּוֹיִם׃

the	against	the	Jeremiah	to	Jehovah	The	came	which
;nations		prophet			of word			

2 לְמִצְרַיִם עַל־חֵיל פַּרְעֹה נְכוֹ מֶלֶךְ מִצְרַיִם אֲשֶׁר־הָיָה עַל־

by	was	which	Egypt	king Necho	Pharaoh-	the	against	against
				of	of army		,Egypt	

Euphrates in Carchemish, which Nebuchadnezzar king of Babylon struck, in the fourth year of Jehoiakim the son of Josiah king of Judah: [3] Set in order the buckler and shield and draw near to battle. [4] Harness the horses and get up, O horsemen; yea, stand with helmets, polish the spears, put on coats of mail. [5] Why have I seen? They (are) afraid (and) turned backward. And their mighty ones are beaten down, and have fled (for) refuge, and do not look back. Terror (is) all around, says Jehovah. [6] Do not let the swift flee away, nor the mighty man escape. They stumbled and fell to the north, by the side of the river Euphrates. [7] Who is this rising up like the Nile, whose waters surge about like the rivers? [8] Egypt rises up like the Nile, and (his) waters surge about like the rivers. And he says, I will go up (and) will cover the earth; I will destroy the city and its people. [9] Come up, horses; and rage, chariots! And let the mighty men come forth — the Ethiopians and the Libyans who handle the shield, and the Lydians who handle (and) bend the bow. [10] For this (is) the day of the Lord Jehovah of hosts, a day of vengeance, that He may avenge Himself of His foes. And the sword shall devour, and be sated and made drunk with their blood, for a sacrifice (is) to the Lord Jehovah of hosts in the north country by the river Euphrates. [11] Go up into Gilead and take balm, O virgin, the daughter of Egypt; in vain shall you use many remedies; healing is not for you. [12] The nations have heard of your shame, and your cry has filled the land. For the mighty man has stumbled against the mighty; they have fallen together, both of them.

[13] The word that Jehovah spoke to Jeremiah

נְהַר־פְּרָת בְּכַרְכְּמִשׁ אֲשֶׁר הִכָּה נְבוּכַדְרֶאצַּר מֶלֶךְ בָּבֶל
,Babylon king Nebuchadnezzar struck which in Euphrates the
of ,Carchemish river

3 בִּשְׁנַת הָרְבִיעִית לִיהוֹיָקִים בֶּן־יֹאשִׁיָּהוּ מֶלֶךְ יְהוּדָה׃ עִרְכוּ
in Set :Judah king Josiah the of the year in
order of of son Jehoiakim fourth

4 מָגֵן וְצִנָּה וּגְשׁוּ לַמִּלְחָמָה׃ אִסְרוּ הַסּוּסִים וַעֲלוּ הַפָּרָשִׁים
O get and the Harness .battle for draw and and the
;horsemen ,up horses near ,shield buckler

5 וְהִתְיַצְּבוּ בְּכוֹבָעִים מִרְקוּ הָרְמָחִים לִבְשׁוּ הַסִּרְיֹנֹת׃ מַדּוּעַ
Why of coats on put ;spears the polish with stand and
.mail ;helmets

רָאִיתִי הֵמָּה חַתִּים נְסֹגִים אָחוֹר וְגִבּוֹרֵיהֶם יֻכַּתּוּ וּמָנוֹס
(for) and are their And back- (and) afraid they I have
refuge crushed ones mighty ?ward turned (are) ,seen

6 נָסוּ וְלֹא הִפְנוּ מָגוֹר מִסָּבִיב נְאֻם־יְהוָה׃ אַל־יָנוּס הַקַּל
the let Do not .Jehovah states all terror look do and have
,swift flee ,around (is) ;back not ,fled

וְאַל־יִמָּלֵט הַגִּבּוֹר צָפוֹנָה עַל־יַד נְהַר־פְּרָת כָּשְׁלוּ וְנָפָלוּ׃
.fell and they Euphrates the the by the to the let do and
stumbled river of side north ;mighty escape not

7
8 מִי־זֶה כַּיְאֹר יַעֲלֶה כַּנְּהָרוֹת יִתְגָּעֲשׁוּ מֵימָיו׃ מִצְרַיִם כַּיְאֹר
like Egypt whose surge the like rising the like this Who
Nile the ?waters about rivers ;up Nile (is)

יַעֲלֶה וְכַנְּהָרוֹת יִתְגֹּעֲשׁוּ מָיִם וַיֹּאמֶר אַעֲלֶה אֲכַסֶּה־אֶרֶץ
the (and) will I he and (his) surge like and rises
;earth cover up go says ;waters about rivers the ;up

9 אֹבִידָה עִיר וְיֹשְׁבֵי בָהּ׃ עֲלוּ הַסּוּסִים וְהִתְהֹלְלוּ הָרֶכֶב
!chariots ,rage and ;horses Come .it in the and the will I
,up dwellers city destroy

וְיֵצְאוּ הַגִּבּוֹרִים כּוּשׁ וּפוּט תֹּפְשֵׂי מָגֵן וְלוּדִים תֹּפְשֵׂי דֹּרְכֵי
(and) who the and the who and the mighty the let And
bend handle Lydians ,shield handle Libyans Ethiopians men out come

10 קָשֶׁת׃ וְהַיּוֹם הַהוּא לַאדֹנָי יְהוִה צְבָאוֹת יוֹם נְקָמָה לְהִנָּקֵם
avenge to venge- day a ;hosts Jehovah to (is) that day For .bow the
Himself ,ance of of Lord the

מִצָּרָיו וְאָכְלָה חֶרֶב וְשָׂבְעָה וְרָוְתָה מִדָּמָם כִּי זֶבַח לַאדֹנָי
the to sac- a for their with made and be and the shall And His of
Lord (is) rifice ,blood drunk sated ,sword devour .foes

11 יְהוִה צְבָאוֹת בְּאֶרֶץ צָפוֹן אֶל־נְהַר־פְּרָת׃ עֲלִי גִלְעָד וּקְחִי
and (into) up Go .Euphrates the by north the in hosts Jehovah
take Gilead river land of

צֳרִי בְּתוּלַת בַּת־מִצְרָיִם לַשָּׁוְא הִרְבֵּיתִי רְפֻאוֹת תְּעָלָה אֵין
not healing ;remedies you shall vain in ;Egypt daughter virgin O ,balm
many use of

12 לָךְ׃ שָׁמְעוּ גוֹיִם קְלוֹנֵךְ וְצִוְחָתֵךְ מָלְאָה הָאָרֶץ כִּי־גִבּוֹר
the For the has your and your (of) The have for
mighty .land filled cry ,shame nations heard .you

13 בְּגִבּוֹר כָּשָׁלוּ יַחְדָּו נָפְלוּ שְׁנֵיהֶם׃ הַדָּבָר אֲשֶׁר דִּבֶּר
spoke that The of both they together has the against
word .them ;fallen have ;stumbled mighty

the prophet, of the coming of Nebuchadnezzar king of Babylon to strike the land of Egypt. [14] Declare (it) in Egypt, and make it heard in Migdol, and make it heard in Noph and in Tahpanhes: Say, Stand fast and get yourself ready, for the sword shall devour all around you. [15] Why is your mighty one swept away? He did not stand, because Jehovah thrust him down. [16] He made many stumble; yea, one fell on his neighbor. And they said, Arise, and let us go again to our own people and to the land of our birth, away from the oppressing sword. [17] They cried there, Pharaoh king of Egypt (is) a noise; he has passed the chosen time. [18] (As) I live, says the King whose name (is) Jehovah of hosts, Surely as Tabor (is) among the mountains, and as Carmel is by the sea, he shall come. [19] O daughter dwelling in Egypt, get ready to go into captivity. For Noph shall be a waste, and a ruin without inhabitant. [20] Egypt (is) a beautiful heifer, but a stinger comes out of the north. [21] Also her hired ones (are) in the midst of her like calves of the stall; for they also have turned back, fleeing together. They did not stand, because the day of their calamity had come on them, the time of their visitation. [22] Its sound (is) like a serpent's going, for they shall go in force and come against her with axes like woodcutters. [23] They have cut down her forest, says Jehovah, though it cannot be searched — because they are more than the locusts and there is no number to them. [24] The daughter of Egypt shall be ashamed. She shall be delivered into the hand of the people of the north. [25] Jehovah of hosts, the God of Israel, says: Behold, I am punishing the multitudes of No,

יְהוָה אֶל־יִרְמְיָהוּ הַנָּבִיא לָבוֹא נְבוּכַדְרֶאצַּר מֶלֶךְ בָּבֶל
Babylon king Nebuchadnezzar the of the Jeremiah to Jehovah
of of coming ,prophet

14 לְהַכּוֹת אֶת־אֶרֶץ מִצְרָיִם׃ הַגִּידוּ בְמִצְרַיִם וְהַשְׁמִיעוּ
make and ,Egypt in Proclaim .Egypt the strike to
heard it (it) of land

בְמִגְדּוֹל וְהַשְׁמִיעוּ בְנֹף וּבְתַחְפַּנְחֵס אִמְרוּ הִתְיַצֵּב וְהָכֵן
pre- and Stand ,say in and in make and ;Migdol in
pare fast ;Tahpanhes Noph heard (it)

15 לָךְ כִּי־אָכְלָה חֶרֶב סְבִיבֶיךָ׃ מַדּוּעַ נִסְחַף אַבִּירֶיךָ לֹא
not your swept is Why around all the shall for your-
?one mighty away you sword devour ,self

עָמַד כִּי יְהוָה הֲדָפוֹ׃ הִרְבָּה כּוֹשֵׁל גַּם־נָפַל אִישׁ אֶל־רֵעֵהוּ
his on one fell ,yea ,stumble made He thrust Jehovah be- He
.neighbor many .down him cause ,stood

16 וַיֹּאמְרוּ קוּמָה ׀ וְנָשֻׁבָה אֶל־עַמֵּנוּ וְאֶל־אֶרֶץ מוֹלַדְתֵּנוּ מִפְּנֵי
away our the and our to let and ,Arise they And
from ,birth of land to ,people return us ,said

17 חֶרֶב הַיּוֹנָה׃ קָרְאוּ שָׁם פַּרְעֹה מֶלֶךְ־מִצְרַיִם שָׁאוֹן הֶעֱבִיר
has he a (is) Egypt king Pharaoh ,there They the sword
passed ;noise of cried .oppressing

18 הַמּוֹעֵד׃ חַי־אָנִי נְאֻם־הַמֶּלֶךְ יְהוָה צְבָאוֹת שְׁמוֹ כִּי כְּתָבוֹר
as Surely whose hosts Jehovah the states I (As) chosen the
Tabor (is) name of ,king , ,live .time

19 בֶּהָרִים וּכְכַרְמֶל בַּיָּם יָבוֹא׃ כְּלֵי גוֹלָה עֲשִׂי לָךְ יוֹשֶׁבֶת
dwelling for Prepare exile vessels shall he by (is) as and the in (is)
in ,yourself of .come ,sea the Carmel ,mountains

בַּת־מִצְרָיִם כִּי־נֹף לְשַׁמָּה תִהְיֶה וְנִצְּתָה מֵאֵין יוֹשֵׁב׃
a without a and shall waste a Noph for ,Egypt O
.dweller ruin become daughter

20
21 עֶגְלָה יְפֵה־פִיָּה מִצְרָיִם קֶרֶץ מִצָּפוֹן בָּא בָא׃ גַּם־שְׂכִרֶיהָ
her Also .comes surely the from a (but) Egypt a heifer
mercenaries north stinger ,(is) beautiful

בְקִרְבָּהּ כְּעֶגְלֵי מַרְבֵּק כִּי־גַם־הֵמָּה הִפְנוּ נָסוּ יַחְדָּיו לֹא
not ;together fleeing have they also for ;stall the like her in
,turned of calves midst

22 עָמָדוּ כִּי יוֹם אֵידָם בָּא עֲלֵיהֶם עֵת פְּקֻדָּתָם׃ קוֹלָהּ כַּנָּחָשׁ
a like Its their the upon has their the because they
snake's sound .punishment of time ,them come calamity of day ,stood

יֵלֵךְ כִּי־בְחַיִל יֵלֵכוּ וּבְקַרְדֻּמּוֹת בָּאוּ לָהּ כְּחֹטְבֵי עֵצִים׃
.wood like against come with and shall they in for ;going
of cutters her axes ;go force

23 כָּרְתוּ יַעְרָהּ נְאֻם־יְהוָה כִּי לֹא יֵחָקֵר כִּי רַבּוּ מֵאַרְבֶּה
the than are they be- be can it not though ,Jehovah states her cut They
locusts more cause —searched ,forests down

24 וְאֵין לָהֶם מִסְפָּר׃ הֹבִישָׁה בַּת־מִצְרָיִם נִתְּנָה בְּיַד עַם־
people the into shall She ;Egypt The be shall (a by) them to and
of hand given be of daughter ashamed .number not is

צָפוֹן׃ אָמַר יְהוָה צְבָאוֹת אֱלֹהֵי יִשְׂרָאֵל הִנְנִי פוֹקֵד אֶל־
to pun- am ,Behold :Israel the ,hosts Jehovah says the
ishing I of God of .north

and Pharaoh, and Egypt, with her gods and her kings, even Pharaoh and those who trust in him; [26] and I will deliver them into the hand of those who seek their lives, and into the hand of Nebuchadnezzar king of Babylon, and into the hand of his servants. And afterward it will be inhabited, as in the days of old, states Jehovah.

[27] But you, do not fear, O My servant Jacob, and be not afraid, O Israel. For, behold, I am saving you from afar off, and your seed from the land of their exile. And Jacob shall return and be in rest and at ease, and none shall make (him) afraid. [28] You shall not fear, O Jacob My servant, says Jehovah, for I (am) with you. For I will make a full end of all the nations where I have driven you there. But I will not make a full end (of) you, but correct you justly and by no means I will not leave you unpunished.

אמון מנא ועל־פרעה ועל־מצרים ועל־אלהיה ועל־מלכיה
her and her with ,Egypt and Pharaoh and ,No mul- the
,kings gods of titude

26 ועל־פרעה ועל הבטחים בו׃ ונתתים ביד מבקשי נפשם
their seekers the into will I and in who those and Pharaoh even
,lives of of hand them give ;him trust

וביד נבוכדראצר מלך־בבל וביד עבדיו ואחרי־כן תשכן
be will it And his into and ,Babylon king ,Nebuchadnezzar's and
peopled afterward .servant's hand of hand into

27 כימי־קדם נאם־יהוה׃ ואתה אל־תירא עבדי יעקב
,Jacob My O do not ,you But .Jehovah states ,old the as
servant ,fear of days

ואל־תחת ישראל כי הנני מושעך מרחוק ואת־זרעך
your and afar from saving am ,behold For .Israel O be and
seed ,off you I ,afraid not

28 מארץ שבים ושב יעקוב ושקט ושאנן ואין מחריד׃ אתה
You make shall and at and be and Jacob shall and their the from
,afraid not ,ease rest in return ;exile of land

אל־תירא עבדי יעקב נאם־יהוה כי אתך אני כי אעשה
will I for I with for ,Jehovah states ,Jacob My O shall not
make ;(am) you servant ,fear

כלה בכל־הגוים ׀ אשר הדחתיך שמה ואתך לא־אעשה
will I not (of) But .there have I where the of full a
make you you driven nations all end

כלה ויסרתיך למשפט ונקה לא אנקך׃
leave I will not by and justly correct but full a
.unpunished you means no you ;end

CAP. XLVII מז

CHAPTER 47

[1] The word of Jehovah that came to Jeremiah the prophet against the Philistines, before Pharaoh struck Gaza. [2] Thus says Jehovah: Behold, waters rise up out of the north, and shall be an overflowing torrent, and shall overflow the land and all its fullness; the city and those who dwell in it. Then the men shall cry, and all the people of the land shall wail. [3] At the noise of the stamping of the hoofs of his strong (horses), at the rushing of his chariots, the rumbling of his wheels, the fathers shall not look back to (their) sons, because of feebleness of hands; [4] because of the day that comes to destroy all the Philistines; to cut off from Tyre and Sidon, every survivor who helps. For

CHAPTER 47

1 אשר היה דבר־יהוה אל־ירמיהו הנביא אל־פלשתים
the against the Jeremiah to Jehovah The came which
,Philistines prophet of word

2 בטרם יכה פרעה את־עזה׃ כה ׀ אמר יהוה הנה־מים
waters Behold Jeho- says Thus .Gaza Pharaoh struck before
,vah

עלים מצפון והיו לנחל שוטף וישטפו ארץ ומלואה עיר
the its and the shall and over- an a and of out rise
,city ;fulness land overflow ,flowing torrent become north the up

3 וישבי בה וזעקו האדם והילל כל יושב הארץ׃ מקול
the At the inhabi- all shall and the Then .it in and
of noise .land's tants wail ,men cry shall dwellers

שעטת פרסות אביריו מרעש לרכבו המון גלגליו לא־
not his rumb- the his of the at strong his hoofs the stamp- the
;wheels of ling ,chariots rushing ;ones of of ing

4 הפנו אבות אל־בנים מרפיון ידים׃ על־היום הבא לשדוד
to that the because ;hands from (their) to the shall
destroy comes day of of despair ,sons fathers back look

את־כל־פלשתים להכרית לצר ולצידון כל שריד עזר
who survivor every and from cut to the all
.helps Sidon Tyre off ;Philistines

Jehovah will plunder the Philistines, the rest of the coast of Caphtor. [5] Baldness has come on Gaza. Ashkelon is ruined. O remnant of their valley, until when will you cut yourself? [6] O sword of Jehovah, until when will it you not be quiet? Put yourself into your sheath; rest and be still. [7] How can you be quiet, since Jehovah has given it a command? Against Ashkelon and against the seashore, there He has set it.

כִּי־שֹׁדֵד יְהוָה אֶת־פְּלִשְׁתִּים שְׁאֵרִית אִי כַפְתּוֹר׃ בָּאָה
has .Caphtor the rem- the the Jehovah is For
come of coast of nant ,Philistines destroying

קָרְחָה אֶל־עַזָּה נִדְמְתָה אַשְׁקְלוֹן שְׁאֵרִית עִמְקָם עַד־מָתַי
when until their remnant O Ashkelon is ;Gaza on Baldness
,valley of ruined

6 תִּתְגּוֹדָדִי׃ הוֹי חֶרֶב לַיהוָה עַד־אָנָה לֹא תִשְׁקֹטִי הֵאָסְפִי
Put you will not when until of sword O cut you will
yourself ?quiet be ,Jehovah ?yourself

7 אֶל־תַּעְרֵךְ הֵרָגְעִי וָדֹמִּי׃ אֵיךְ תִּשְׁקֹטִי וַיהוָה צִוָּה־לָהּ אֶל־
Against com- has since you can How be and rest Your into
?it manded Jehovah ,quiet be .still ;sheath

אַשְׁקְלוֹן וְאֶל־חוֹף הַיָּם שָׁם יְעָדָהּ׃
has He there the shore and Ashkelon
.it set ,sea against

CAP. XLVIII מח

CHAPTER 48

[1] Thus says Jehovah of hosts, the God of Israel, against Moab: Woe to Nebo, for it is ravaged; Kiriathaim is put to shame is put to shame and razed. [2] Not shall be praise of Moab still. In Heshbon they have plotted evil against it, (saying), Come and let us cut it off as a nation. And you shall be silenced, O madmen; a sword will go after you. [3] A voice of crying from horonaim, plundering and great ruin! [4] Moab is destroyed, her little ones have caused a cry to be heard. [5] For in the ascent to Luhith, with weeping they shall go up weeping; for in the descent to Horonaim, the enemies have heard a cry of ruin. [6] Flee! Save your lives, and be like a naked thing in the wilderness.

[7] For because you have trusted in your works and in your treasures, you shall also be seized. And Chemosh shall go into exile; both his priests and his princes. [8] And a plunderer shall come on every city, and no city shall escape. Also the valley shall perish, and the plain shall be destroyed, as Jehovah has spoken. [9] Give wings to

1 לְמוֹאָב כֹּה־אָמַר יְהוָה צְבָאוֹת אֱלֹהֵי יִשְׂרָאֵל הוֹי אֶל־נְבוֹ
,Nebo to Woe :Israel the hosts Jehovah says thus Against
of God of ,Moab

כִּי שֻׁדָּדָה הֹבִישָׁה נִלְכְּדָה קִרְיָתָיִם הֹבִישָׁה הַמִּשְׂגָּב
the to put is ;Kiriathaim (and) to put is is it for
fortress shame seized shame ;ravaged

2 וָחָתָּה׃ אֵין עוֹד תְּהִלַּת מוֹאָב בְּחֶשְׁבּוֹן חָשְׁבוּ עָלֶיהָ רָעָה
,evil against have they in ;Moab praise more There and
it plotted Heshbon of no be shall .razed

לְכוּ וְנַכְרִיתֶנָּה מִגּוֹי גַּם־מַדְמֵן תִּדֹּמִּי אַחֲרַיִךְ תֵּלֶךְ חָרֶב׃
.sword a will after be shall you O And a as us let and (saying)
go you ;silenced ,Madmen .nation off it cut Come

3 4 קוֹל צְעָקָה מֵחֹרֹנָיִם שֹׁד וָשֶׁבֶר גָּדוֹל׃ נִשְׁבְּרָה מוֹאָב
;Moab is !great and plunder- from crying A
destroyed ruin ing ,Horonaim of voice

5 הִשְׁמִיעוּ זְּעָקָה צְעוֹרֶיהָ׃ כִּי מַעֲלֵה הַלֻּחוֹת בִּבְכִי יַעֲלֶה־
shall they with Luhith the (in) For little her cry a caused have
up go weeping to ascent .ones heard be to

6 בֶּכִי כִּי בְּמוֹרַד חוֹרֹנַיִם צָרֵי צַעֲקַת־שֶׁבֶר שָׁמֵעוּ׃ נֻסוּ
!Flee have ruin a the ,Horonaim the in for weep-
.heard of cry enemies to descent ;ing

7 מַלְּטוּ נַפְשְׁכֶם וְתִהְיֶינָה כַּעֲרוֹעֵר בַּמִּדְבָּר׃ כִּי יַעַן בִּטְחֵךְ
you be- For the in a like be and your Save
trust cause .wilderness thing naked ,lives

בְּמַעֲשַׂיִךְ וּבְאוֹצְרוֹתַיִךְ גַּם־אַתְּ תִּלָּכֵדִי וְיָצָא כְמִישׁ בַּגּוֹלָה
into Chemosh And be shall you also your in and your in
;exile go shall .seized ,treasures works

8 כֹּהֲנָיו וְשָׂרָיו יַחְדָּו׃ וְיָבֹא שֹׁדֵד אֶל־כָּל־עִיר וְעִיר לֹא תִמָּלֵט
shall no and ,city every to a shall And .together and his
.escape city spoiler come rulers his priests

9 וְאָבַד הָעֵמֶק וְנִשְׁמַד הַמִּישֹׁר אֲשֶׁר אָמַר יְהוָה׃ תְּנוּ־צִיץ
wings Give .Jehovah has as the be shall and the shall Also
spoken ,plain destroyed ,valley perish

Moab, for it will fly away; and its cities shall be a desert, without an inhabitant in them. [10] Cursed (is) he who does the work of Jehovah deceitfully, and cursed (is) he who keeps back his sword from blood.

[11] Moab has been at ease from his youth, and he has settled on his lees and has not been emptied from vessel to vessel; he has not gone into captivity. So his taste remains in him, and his scent is not changed. [12] Therefore behold, the days come, says Jehovah, that I will send pourers to him who shall pour him off, and shall empty his vessels and break their jars in pieces. [13] And Moab shall be ashamed of Chemosh, as the house of Israel was ashamed of their confidence Bethel.

[14] How do you say, We (are) mighty and strong men for the war? [15] Moab is plundered and her cities have come up. And his chosen young men have gone down to the slaughter, says the King, whose name (is) Jehovah of hosts. [16] The calamity of Moab is near to come, and his affliction hurries fast. [17] All you who are around him, mourn for him. And all who know his name, say, How the strong staff is broken, the beautiful rod! [18] O dweller, daughter of Dibon, come down from glory and sit in thirst. For a plunderer of Moab shall come upon you; he has ruined your strongholds. [19] O dweller of Aroer, stand by the way and watch. Ask him who flees and her who escapes; say, What has happened? [20] Moab is put to shame, for it is razed. Wail and cry! Tell it in Arnon that Moab is stripped. [21] And judgment has come to the plain country: on Holon, and on Jahazah, and on Mephaath, [22] and on Dibon, and on

לְמוֹאָב כִּי נָצֹא תֵּצֵא וְעָרֶיהָ לְשַׁמָּה תִהְיֶינָה מֵאֵין יוֹשֵׁב
a without shall desert a its And .away will it for to
dweller ,become cities fly Moab

10 בָּהֵן׃ אָרוּר עֹשֶׂה מְלֶאכֶת יְהוָה רְמִיָּה וְאָרוּר מֹנֵעַ חַרְבּוֹ
his who he and deceit Jehovah the who he Cursed in
sword keeps (is) cursed ;fully of work does (is) .them

11 מִדָּם׃ שַׁאֲנַן מוֹאָב מִנְּעוּרָיו וְשֹׁקֵט הוּא אֶל־שְׁמָרָיו וְלֹא־
and his on he has and his from Moab been has from
not ,lees settled ,youth ease at .blood

הוּרַק מִכְּלִי אֶל־כֶּלִי וּבַגּוֹלָה לֹא הָלָךְ עַל־כֵּן עָמַד טַעְמוֹ
his remains So has he not into and ;vessel to from been has
taste .gone exile vessel emptied

12 בּוֹ וְרֵיחוֹ לֹא נָמָר׃ לָכֵן הִנֵּה־יָמִים בָּאִים נְאֻם־יְהוָה
,Jehovah states ,come the behold Therefore is not his and in
days .changed scent ,him

וְשִׁלַּחְתִּי־לוֹ צֹעִים וְצֵעֻהוּ וְכֵלָיו יָרִיקוּ וְנִבְלֵיהֶם יְנַפֵּצוּ׃
break their and shall his and will who pourers to will I that
.pieces in jars ;empty vessels ,off him pour him send

13 וּבֹשׁ מוֹאָב מִכְּמוֹשׁ כַּאֲשֶׁר־בֹּשׁוּ בֵּית יִשְׂרָאֵל מִבֵּית אֵל
of Israel the was as of Moab will And
Bethel of house ashamed ,Chemosh ashamed be

14 מִבְטֶחָם׃ אֵיךְ תֹּאמְרוּ גִּבּוֹרִים אֲנָחְנוּ וְאַנְשֵׁי־חַיִל לַמִּלְחָמָה׃
the for strong and We mighty you do How their
?war men (are) ,say .confidence

15 שֻׁדַּד מוֹאָב וְעָרֶיהָ עָלָה וּמִבְחַר בַּחוּרָיו יָרְדוּ לַטָּבַח נְאֻם־
states the to have young his And have her and ,Moab is
,slaughter gone men chosen .up come cities spoiled

16 הַמֶּלֶךְ יְהוָה צְבָאוֹת שְׁמוֹ׃ קָרוֹב אֵיד־מוֹאָב לָבוֹא וְרָעָתוֹ
his and to Moab The (is) whose hosts Jehovah the
affliction ,come of calamity near .(is) name of ,king

17 מִהֲרָה מְאֹד׃ נֻדוּ לוֹ כָּל־סְבִיבָיו וְכֹל יֹדְעֵי שְׁמוֹ אִמְרוּ
,say his who And are who all for Mourn .fast hurries
,name know all .him around ,him

18 אֵיכָה נִשְׁבַּר מַטֵּה־עֹז מַקֵּל תִּפְאָרָה׃ רְדִי מִכָּבוֹד *יֹשְׁבִי
and from Come !beautiful the ,strong the is How
sit glory down rod staff broken

בַצָּמָא יֹשֶׁבֶת בַּת־דִּיבוֹן כִּי־שֹׁדֵד מוֹאָב עָלָה בָךְ שִׁחֵת
has he upon shall Moab plun- a For .Dibon daughter O ,thirst in
ruined ;you come of derer of ,dweller

19 מִבְצָרָיִךְ׃ אֶל־דֶּרֶךְ עִמְדִי וְצַפִּי יוֹשֶׁבֶת עֲרוֹעֵר שַׁאֲלִי־נָס
him Ask .Aroer dweller O and Stand the by strong- your
flees who of ,watch way .holds

20 וְנִמְלָטָה אִמְרִי מַה־נִּהְיָתָה׃ הֹבִישׁ מוֹאָב כִּי־חַתָּה הֵילִילִי
Wail is it for ,Moab to put is has What ,say her and
.razed shame ?happened ;escapes who

21 *וְזַעֲקִי הַגִּידוּ בְאַרְנוֹן כִּי שֻׁדַּד מוֹאָב׃ וּמִשְׁפָּט בָּא אֶל־
to has And .Moab is that in Tell and
come judgment stripped Arnon (it) !cry

22 אֶרֶץ הַמִּישֹׁר אֶל־חֹלוֹן וְאֶל־יַהְצָה וְעַל־*מוֹפָעַת׃ וְעַל־
on and ;Mephaath and ;Jahazah and Holon to the country
on to ;plain

Nebo, and on Beth-diblathaim, [23] and on Kiriathaim, and on Beth-gamul, and on Bethmeon, [24] and Kerioth, and on Bozrah, and on all the cities of the land of Moab, far and near. [25] The horn of Moab is cut off, and his arm is broken, says Jehovah.

[26] Make him drunk, for he boasted against Jehovah. Moab also shall wallow in his vomit, and he also shall be a mockery. [27] For was not Israel a mockery to you? Was he found among thieves? For ever since you spoke of him, you skipped for joy. [28] O you who dwell in Moab, leave the cities and live in the rock, and be like the dove who makes her nest in the sides of the mouth of the pit. [29] We have heard the pride of Moab; he is exceeding proud. His loftiness, and his pride, and his arrogance, and his elevated heart, [30] I have known, states Jehovah. His wrath and (it is) not so; his boast, they have not done so. [31] Therefore I will wail for Moab, and I will cry out for all Moab; (he) shall mourn for the men of Kirheres. [32] O vine of Sibmah, I will weep for you more than the weeping of Jazer. Your plants have gone over the sea; they reach to the sea of Jazer. A spoiler has fallen on your harvest and on your grape crop. [33] And joy and gladness is taken from the plentiful field, and from the land of Moab. And I have caused wine to cease from the winepresses; none shall tread (the grapes) with shouting; (their) shouting (shall be) no shouting. [34] From the city of Heshbon to Elealeh, to Jahaz, they have given their voice, from Zoar to Horonaim, (like) a heifer three years old; for the waters of Nimrim also shall be desolate. [35] Also I will cause him who offers in the high places to cease in Moab, says Jehovah, and

23 דִּיבוֹן וְעַל־נְבוֹ וְעַל־בֵּית דִּבְלָתָיִם׃ וְעַל קִרְיָתַיִם וְעַל־בֵּית
Beth- and ;Kiriathaim and ;diblathaim Beth- and ;Nebo and ;Dibon
on on on on

24 גָּמוּל וְעַל־בֵּית מְעוֹן׃ וְעַל־קְרִיּוֹת וְעַל־בָּצְרָה וְעַל כָּל־
all and ;Bozrah and ;Kerioth and ;meon Beth- and ;gamul
on on on on

25 עָרֵי אֶרֶץ מוֹאָב הָרְחֹקוֹת וְהַקְּרֹבוֹת׃ נִגְדְּעָה קֶרֶן מוֹאָב
,Moab The off cut is .near and far ,Moab the cities the
of horn of land of

26 וּזְרֹעוֹ נִשְׁבָּרָה נְאֻם יְהוָה׃ הַשְׁכִּירֻהוּ כִּי עַל־יְהוָה הִגְדִּיל
he Jehovah against for him Make .Jehovah states is his and
.boasted ,drunk ,broken arm

27 וְסָפַק מוֹאָב בְּקִיאוֹ וְהָיָה לִשְׂחֹק גַּם־הוּא׃ וְאִם ׀ לוֹא
not For .he also a shall and his in Moab also shall
mockery be ,vomit wallow

הַשְּׂחֹק הָיָה לְךָ יִשְׂרָאֵל אִם־בְּגַנָּבִים נִמְצָאָה כִּי־מִדֵּי
ever For he Was among ?Israel to was a
since ?found thieves you mockery

28 דְבָרֶיךָ בּוֹ תִּתְנוֹדָד׃ עִזְבוּ עָרִים וְשִׁכְנוּ בַּסֶּלַע יֹשְׁבֵי מוֹאָב
;Moab dwellers the in and the Leave skipped you of spoke you
of ,rock dwell cities .joy for ,him

29 וִהְיוּ כְיוֹנָה תְּקַנֵּן בְּעֶבְרֵי פִי־פָחַת׃ שָׁמַעְנוּ גְאוֹן־מוֹאָב
;Moab the have We .pit the the the in making the like and
of pride heard of mouth of sides nest her dove be

30 גֵּאֶה מְאֹד גָּבְהוֹ וּגְאוֹנוֹ וְגַאֲוָתוֹ וְרֻם לִבּוֹ׃ אֲנִי יָדַעְתִּי נְאֻם־
states have I his and his and his and His exceed- proud
,known .heart high arrogance pride ,loftiness .ing

31 יְהוָה עֶבְרָתוֹ וְלֹא־כֵן בַּדָּיו לֹא־כֵן עָשׂוּ׃ עַל־כֵּן עַל־מוֹאָב
Moab for Therefore they so not his (is it) and wrath his Jeho-
.done have ,boast ;so not vah

אֲיֵלִיל וּלְמוֹאָב כֻּלֹּה אֶזְעָק אֶל־אַנְשֵׁי קִיר־חֶרֶשׂ יֶהְגֶּה׃
shall he Kirheres the (and) will I all for and will I
.mourn of men for ,out cry Moab ,wail

32 מִבְּכִי יַעְזֵר אֶבְכֶּה־לָּךְ הַגֶּפֶן שִׂבְמָה נְטִישֹׁתַיִךְ עָבְרוּ יָם
the have your ;Sibmah O for will I ,Jazer's weep-
;sea crossed plants of vine ,you weep ing

33 עַד יָם יַעְזֵר נָגָעוּ עַל־קֵיצֵךְ וְעַל־בְּצִירֵךְ שֹׁדֵד נָפָל׃ וְנֶאֶסְפָה
is And has a your and your on they Jazer the to
taken .fallen spoiler crop grape on harvest .reach of sea

שִׂמְחָה וָגִיל מִכַּרְמֶל וּמֵאֶרֶץ מוֹאָב וְיַיִן מִיקָבִים הִשְׁבַּתִּי
made I the from And .Moab from and the from glad- and joy
;cease to winepresses wine of land the field fruitful ness

34 לֹא־יִדְרֹךְ הֵידָד הֵידָד לֹא הֵידָד׃ מִזַּעֲקַת חֶשְׁבּוֹן עַד־
to Heshbon the From .shouting not shout- the with shall not
of cry (be shall) ing ;shouting tread

אֶלְעָלֵה עַד־יַהַץ נָתְנוּ קוֹלָם מִצֹּעַר עַד־חֹרֹנַיִם עֶגְלַת
a ,Horonaim to from their have they ,Jahaz to ,Elealeh
heifer Zoar ;voice given

35 שְׁלִשִׁיָּה כִּי גַּם־מֵי נִמְרִים לִמְשַׁמּוֹת יִהְיוּ׃ וְהִשְׁבַּתִּי לְמוֹאָב
Moab will I And shall desolate Nimrim the also for years three
cease make .become of waters ;old

him who burns incense to his gods. [36] Therefore my heart shall sound for Moab like flutes, and my heart shall sound like flutes for the men of Kirheres, because the riches that he has gotten have perished. [37] For every head (shall be) bald, and every beard clipped. On all the hands (shall be) cuttings, and on the loins sackcloth. [38] On all the housetops of Moab, and in its streets, (there is) weeping for all. For I have broken Moab like a vessel; in it is no pleasure, says Jehovah. [39] They shall howl, (saying), How it is broken down! How has Moab turned (his) back (in) shame! So Moab shall be a mockery, and a terror to all those around him. [40] For thus says Jehovah: Behold, he shall fly like an eagle and shall spread his wings toward Moab. [41] Kerioth is captured, and the strongholds are seized; and the mighty men's hearts in Moab shall be at that day like the heart of a woman in (her) pangs. [42] And Moab shall be destroyed from (being) a people, because he has magnified against Jehovah.[43] Fear and the pit, and the snare, (shall be) on you, O Moabite, states Jehovah. [44] He who flees from the terror shall fall into the pit; and he who gets up out of the pit shall be taken in the snare. For I will bring on it, on Moab, the year of their punishment, states Jehovah. [45] Those who fled stood powerless in the shadow of Heshbon, for a fire shall come out of Heshbon, and a flame out of the midst of Sihon, and shall devour the temples of Moab and the crown of the head of the sons of tumult. [46] Woe to you, Moab! The people of Chemosh have perished; for your sons are taken away into exile, and your daughters into exile.

36 נְאֻם־יְהוָה מַעֲלֶה בָמָה וּמַקְטִיר לֵאלֹהָיו׃ עַל־כֵּן לִבִּי
my Therefore his to who he and the (in) who he ,Jehovah states
heart .gods incense burns ,places high offers

לְמוֹאָב כַּחֲלִלִים יֶהֱמֶה וְלִבִּי אֶל־אַנְשֵׁי קִיר־חֶרֶשׂ
Kirheres the for my and shall like for
of men heart ,sound flutes Moab

37 כַּחֲלִילִים יֶהֱמֶה עַל־כֵּן יִתְרַת עָשָׂה אָבָדוּ׃ כִּי כָל־רֹאשׁ
head every For have has he the because shall like
.perished gotten riches ,sound flutes

קָרְחָה וְכָל־זָקָן גְּרֻעָה עַל כָּל־יָדַיִם גְּדֻדֹת וְעַל־מָתְנַיִם
the and (be shall) the all On .clipped beard and (be shall)
loins on ,gashes hands every bald

38 שָׂק׃ עַל כָּל־גַּגּוֹת מוֹאָב וּבִרְחֹבֹתֶיהָ כֻּלֹּה מִסְפֵּד כִּי־
For (is there) (for) its in and ,Moab the all On sack-
.weeping all ,streets of housetops .cloth

39= שָׁבַרְתִּי אֶת־מוֹאָב כִּכְלִי אֵין־חֵפֶץ בּוֹ נְאֻם־יְהוָה׃ אֵיךְ
How .Jehovah states in pleasure there a like Moab have I
,it no is ;vessel broken

חַתָּה הֵילִילוּ אֵיךְ הִפְנָה־עֹרֶף מוֹאָב בּוֹשׁ וְהָיָה מוֹאָב
Moab shall So (in) Moab (his) has How shall they is it
become .shame back turned !howl !dismayed

40 לִשְׂחֹק וְלִמְחִתָּה לְכָל־סְבִיבָיו׃ כִּי־כֹה אָמַר יְהוָה
:Jehovah says thus For those all to a and a
.him around terror ,mockery

41 הִנֵּה כַנֶּשֶׁר יִדְאֶה וּפָרַשׂ כְּנָפָיו אֶל־מוֹאָב׃ נִלְכְּדָה הַקְּרִיּוֹת
,Kerioth is .Moab toward his and shall he an like Be-
captured wings spread fly eagle hold

וְהַמְּצָדוֹת נִתְפָּשָׂה וְהָיָה לֵב גִּבּוֹרֵי מוֹאָב בַּיּוֹם הַהוּא כְּלֵב
the like that of Moab the hearts and are the and
of heart day of mighty of be shall ;seized strongholds

42 אִשָּׁה מְצֵרָה׃ וְנִשְׁמַד מוֹאָב מֵעָם כִּי עַל־יְהוָה הִגְדִּיל׃
has he Jehovah against be- from Moab be shall And (her) woman a
.magnified cause people a destroyed .pangs in

43
44 פַּחַד וָפַחַת וָפָח עָלֶיךָ יוֹשֵׁב מוֹאָב נְאֻם־יְהוָה׃ הַנִּיס מִפְּנֵי
from who He .Jehovah states ,Moab O (be shall) and the and ,Fear
flees of dweller ,you on snare the ,pit

הַפַּחַד יִפֹּל אֶל־הַפַּחַת וְהָעֹלֶה מִן־הַפַּחַת יִלָּכֵד בַּפָּח
the in be shall the out who he and the into shall the
;snare taken pit of up gets ;pit fall terror

45 כִּי־אָבִיא אֵלֶיהָ אֶל־מוֹאָב שְׁנַת פְּקֻדָּתָם נְאֻם־יְהוָה׃ בְּצֵל
the In .Jehovah states their year the ,Moab on ,it on will I for
of shadow ,punishment of bring

חֶשְׁבּוֹן עָמְדוּ מִכֹּחַ נָסִים כִּי־אֵשׁ יָצָא מֵחֶשְׁבּוֹן וְלֶהָבָה מִבֵּין
from a and of shall fire a for those power- stood Heshbon
midst flame ,Heshbon out come ;fled who less

46 סִיחֹן וַתֹּאכַל פְּאַת מוֹאָב וְקָדְקֹד בְּנֵי שָׁאוֹן׃ אוֹי־לְךָ מוֹאָב
!Moab to Woe .tumult the the and Moab the shall and ;Sihon's
,you of sons of crown of temples devour

אָבַד עַם־כְּמוֹשׁ כִּי־לֻקְּחוּ בָנֶיךָ בַּשֶּׁבִי וּבְנֹתֶיךָ בַּשִּׁבְיָה׃
into your and into your taken are for ;Chemosh The have
.exile daughters ,exile sons away of people perished

[47] But I will restore the prisoners of Moab in the end of the days, says Jehovah. Thus far (is) the judgment of Moab.

CHAPTER 49

[1] Thus says Jehovah to the sons of Ammon: Has Israel no sons? Has he no heir? Why does their king inherit Gad, and his people dwell in its cities? [2] Therefore, behold, the days come, says Jehovah, that I will cause a shout of war to be heard in Rabbah of the sons of Ammon; and it shall be a heap, a ruin; and her towns shall be burned with fire. Then shall Israel inherit his inheritance, says Jehovah. [3] Wail, O Heshbon, for Ai is spoiled! Cry, daughters of Rabbah; gird yourselves with sackcloth, mourn, and run to and fro in the walls! For their king shall go into exile, his priests and his princes together. [4] Why do you glory in your valleys, your flowing valley, O backsliding daughter? She trusted in her treasures, (saying), Who shall come to me? [5] Behold, I will bring a dread on you, says the Lord Jehovah of hosts, from all those who are around you. And you shall be driven out, each man before him; and there shall be none to gather up the runaways. [6] And after this I will bring again the prisoners of the sons of Ammon, says Jehovah.

[7] Thus says Jehovah of hosts concerning Edom: Is wisdom no more in Teman? Has counsel perished from the prudent? Has their wisdom vanished? [8] Flee, turn back, go deep to dwell,

47 וְשַׁבְתִּי שְׁבוּת־מוֹאָב בְּאַחֲרִית הַיָּמִים נְאֻם־יְהוָה עַד־הֵנָּה
thus far ;Jehovah states the the in Moab pri- the I But
,days of end of soners restore will
מִשְׁפַּט מוֹאָב׃
.Moab the (is)
of judgment

CAP. XLIX מט

CHAPTER 49

1 לִבְנֵי עַמּוֹן כֹּה אָמַר יְהוָה הֲבָנִים אֵין לְיִשְׂרָאֵל אִם־
Or ?Israel to Are sons ,Jehovah says Thus :Ammon the To
no there of sons
יוֹרֵשׁ אֵין לוֹ מַדּוּעַ יָרַשׁ מַלְכָּם אֶת־גָּד וְעַמּוֹ בְּעָרָיו יָשָׁב׃
?dwell its in his and ,Gad their does Why to not heir
cities people king inherit ?him is
2 לָכֵן הִנֵּה יָמִים בָּאִים נְאֻם־יְהוָה וְהִשְׁמַעְתִּי אֶל־רַבַּת
Rabbah against will I that ,Jehovah states ,come the ,behold There-
of heard make days ,fore
בְּנֵי־עַמּוֹן תְּרוּעַת מִלְחָמָה וְהָיְתָה לְתֵל שְׁמָמָה וּבְנֹתֶיהָ
her and ;ruin a ,heap a shall it and ;war shout a Ammon the
towns become of of sons
בָּאֵשׁ תִּצַּתְנָה וְיָרַשׁ יִשְׂרָאֵל אֶת־יֹרְשָׁיו אָמַר יְהוָה׃
.Jehovah says his Israel will and be shall with
,inheritance inherit ,burned fire
3 הֵילִילִי חֶשְׁבּוֹן כִּי שֻׁדְּדָה־עַי צְעַקְנָה בְּנוֹת רַבָּה חֲגֹרְנָה
on gird ;Rabbah daughters ,Cry !Ai is for O ,Wail
of spoiled ,Heshbon
שַׂקִּים סְפֹדְנָה וְהִתְשׁוֹטַטְנָה בַּגְּדֵרוֹת כִּי מַלְכָּם בַּגּוֹלָה
into their for the in to run and ,mourn sack-
exile king ;walls fro and ;cloth
4 יֵלֵךְ כֹּהֲנָיו וְשָׂרָיו יַחְדָּיו׃ מַה־תִּתְהַלְלִי בָּעֲמָקִים זָב
flow- in you do Why .together his and his shall
ing ,valleys glory princes priests ,go
עִמְקֵךְ הַבַּת הַשּׁוֹבֵבָה הַבֹּטְחָה בְּאֹצְרֹתֶיהָ מִי יָבוֹא אֵלָי׃
to shall Who her in She .backsliding O your
?me come ,treasures trusted daughter ,valley
5 הִנְנִי מֵבִיא עָלַיִךְ פַּחַד נְאֻם־אֲדֹנָי יְהוִה צְבָאוֹת מִכָּל־
from ,hosts Jehovah the states a on will ,Behold
all of Lord dread you bring I
6 סְבִיבָיִךְ וְנִדַּחְתֶּם אִישׁ לְפָנָיו וְאֵין מְקַבֵּץ לַנֹּדֵד׃ וְאַחֲרֵי־
And the gather to and before each will you And around
after .runaways is not ,him one out driven be .you
7 כֵן אָשִׁיב אֶת־שְׁבוּת בְּנֵי־עַמּוֹן נְאֻם־יְהוָה׃ לֶאֱדוֹם
Concerning .Jehovah states ,Ammon the the will I this
,Edom of sons of prisoners restore
כֹּה אָמַר יְהוָה צְבָאוֹת הַאֵין עוֹד חָכְמָה בְּתֵימָן אָבְדָה
Has ?Teman in wisdom more no Is :hosts Jehovah says thus
perished of
8 עֵצָה מִבָּנִים נִסְרְחָה חָכְמָתָם׃ נֻסוּ הָפְנוּ הֶעְמִיקוּ לָשֶׁבֶת
,dwell to deep go turn ,Flee their Has the from counsel
,back ?wisdom vanished ?prudent

O people of Dedan. For I will bring the calamity of Esau on him (in) the time I will visit him. [9] If the gatherers of grapes come to you, would they not leave gleanings? If thieves (come) by night, will they destroy their sufficiency? [10] But I have stripped Esau; I have uncovered his secret places, and he shall not be able to hide himself. His seed is spoiled, also his brothers and his neighbors; and he is not. [11] Leave your orphans; I will keep (them) alive; and let your widows trust in Me. [12] For thus says Jehovah: Behold, those whose judgment was not to drink of the cup have surely drunk. And are you (to) go altogether unpunished? You shall not go unpunished, but you shall surely drink. [13] For I have sworn by Myself, says Jehovah, that Bozrah shall become a ruin, a reproach, a waste, and a curse. And all its cities shall be wastes forever. [14] I have heard a message from Jehovah, and a herald is sent to the nations: Gather together and come against her, and rise up to the battle. [15] For lo, I will make you small among the nations, despised among men. [16] Your fearfulness has deceived you, the pride of your heart, O you who dwell in the clefts of the rock, who hold the height of the hill. Though you should make your nest as high as the eagle, I will bring you down from there, says Jehovah. [17] And Edom shall be a ruin; everyone who goes by it shall be amazed and shall hiss at all the plagues of it. [18] As in the overthrow of Sodom and Gomorrah and its neighbor, states Jehovah, no man shall remain there; a son of man shall not live in it. [19] Behold, he shall come up like a lion from the pride of Jordan against the

9 יֹשְׁבֵי דְּדָן כִּי אֵיד עֵשָׂו הֵבֵאתִי עָלָיו עֵת פְּקַדְתִּיו׃ אִם־
If punish I the (in) on will I Esau the for ,Dedan resi-
.him time him bring of calamity of dents

בֹּצְרִים בָּאוּ לָךְ לֹא יַשְׁאִרוּ עוֹלֵלוֹת אִם־גַּנָּבִים בַּלַּיְלָה
by (come) thieves If ?gleanings would not to come grape- the
,night leave they ,you gatherers

10 הִשְׁחִיתוּ דַיָּם׃ כִּי־אֲנִי חָשַׂפְתִּי אֶת־עֵשָׂו גִּלֵּיתִי אֶת־
have I ;Esau have I But their will they
uncovered stripped .sufficiency destroy

מִסְתָּרָיו וְנֶחְבָּה לֹא יוּכָל שֻׁדַּד זַרְעוֹ וְאֶחָיו וּשְׁכֵנָיו
his and his also His is shall he not to and secret his
;neighbors brothers ,seed spoiled .able be himself hide ,places

11 וְאֵינֶנּוּ׃ עָזְבָה יְתֹמֶיךָ אֲנִי אֲחַיֶּה וְאַלְמְנוֹתֶיךָ עָלַי תִּבְטָחוּ׃
.trust let on your and keep will I your Leave is he and
Me widows ;alive ,orphans .not

12 כִּי־כֹה ׀ אָמַר יְהוָה הִנֵּה אֲשֶׁר־אֵין מִשְׁפָּטָם
judgment was whose ,Behold ,Jehovah says thus For
not

לִשְׁתּוֹת הַכּוֹס שָׁתוֹ יִשְׁתּוּ וְאַתָּה הוּא נָקֹה תִּנָּקֶה לֹא
not be to entirely are And they surely ,cup the drink to
?acquitted you .drank

13 תִנָּקֶה כִּי שָׁתֹה תִּשְׁתֶּה׃ כִּי בִי נִשְׁבַּעְתִּי נְאֻם־יְהוָה כִּי־
that ,Jehovah states have I by For shall you surely but shall you
,sworn Myself .drink ,acquitted be

לְשַׁמָּה לְחֶרְפָּה לְחֹרֶב וְלִקְלָלָה תִּהְיֶה בָצְרָה וְכָל־עָרֶיהָ
its And .Bozrah shall a and ,waste a a ,horror a
cities all become curse ,reproach

14 תִּהְיֶינָה לְחָרְבוֹת עוֹלָם׃ שְׁמוּעָה שָׁמַעְתִּי מֵאֵת יְהוָה
,Jehovah from have I message a .forever wastes become shall
heard

וְצִיר בַּגּוֹיִם שָׁלוּחַ הִתְקַבְּצוּ וּבֹאוּ עָלֶיהָ וְקוּמוּ לַמִּלְחָמָה׃
the for and against and Gather ;sent is the to a and
.battle up rise ,her come together nations herald

15
16 כִּי־הִנֵּה קָטֹן נְתַתִּיךָ בַּגּוֹיִם בָּזוּי בָּאָדָם׃ תִּפְלַצְתְּךָ הִשִּׁיא
has Your among despised among made I small ,lo For
deceived dreadfulness .men ,nations the you

אֹתָךְ זְדוֹן לִבֶּךָ שֹׁכְנִי בְּחַגְוֵי הַסֶּלַע תֹּפְשִׂי מְרוֹם גִּבְעָה
the the hold who ,rock the the in who you your the ,you
.hill of height of clefts live ,heart of pride

17 כִּי־תַגְבִּיהַּ כַּנֶּשֶׁר קִנֶּךָ מִשָּׁם אוֹרִידְךָ נְאֻם־יְהוָה׃ וְהָיְתָה
And .Jehovah states bring will I from your the as you Though
be shall ,down you there ,nest eagle high make

אֱדוֹם לְשַׁמָּה כֹּל עֹבֵר עָלֶיהָ יִשֹּׁם וְיִשְׁרֹק עַל־כָּל־מַכּוֹתֶהָ׃
its all at shall and be shall by who every ;horror a Edom
.plagues hiss amazed it passes one

18 כְּמַהְפֵּכַת סְדֹם וַעֲמֹרָה וּשְׁכֵנֶיהָ אָמַר יְהוָה לֹא־יֵשֵׁב שָׁם
there shall not ,Jehovah says its and and Sodom over- the As
dwell ,neighbor Gomorrah of throw

19 אִישׁ וְלֹא־יָגוּר בָּהּ בֶּן־אָדָם׃ הִנֵּה כְּאַרְיֵה יַעֲלֶה מִגְּאוֹן
the from shall he a like Behold .man a it in shall not ;man
of pride up come lion of son sojourn

home of the strong. But I will suddenly make him run away from her. And who is (the) chosen (one) I may appoint over her? For who is like Me? And who will summon Me? And who (is) that shepherd who will stand before Me? [20] Therefore hear the counsel of Jehovah which He has planned against Edom, and His purposes which He has purposed against the inhabitants of Teman: Surely they shall drag them, the least of the flock. Surely He shall make their pastures a ruin over them. [21] The earth is moved at the noise of their fall; when (they) cried, the noise of it was heard in the Red Sea. [22] Behold, he shall come up and fly like the eagle, and spread his wings over Bozrah. And at that day the heart of the mighty men of Edom shall be like the heart of a woman in her pangs.

[23] Concerning Damascus: Hamath and Arpad are put to shame, for they have heard bad news; they are melted; (there is) anxiety in the sea; it cannot be quiet. [24] Damascus has become feeble; she has turned to flee, and panic has seized (her); anguish and sorrows have taken her like a woman in labor. [25] How is the city of praise forsaken, the city of my joy! [26] Therefore her young men shall fall in her streets, and all the men of war shall be silenced in that day, says Jehovah of hosts. [27] And I will kindle a fire in the wall of Damascus, and it shall burn up the palaces of Ben-hadad.

[28] Thus says Jehovah concerning Kedar, and concerning the kingdoms of Hazor, which Nebuchadnezzar king of Babylon struck: Arise, go up to Kedar, and strip the men of

הַיַּרְדֵּן אֶל־נְוֵה אֵיתָן כִּי־אַרְגִּיעָה אֲרִיצֶנּוּ מֵעָלֶיהָ וּמִי
And from away him make will I but the the against Jordan
(is) who .it run suddenly ;strong of pasture

בָחוּר אֵלֶיהָ אֶפְקֹד כִּי מִי כָמוֹנִי וּמִי יוֹעִדֶנִּי וּמִי־זֶה רֹעֶה
a then And sum- will And like who For shall I over chosen
shepherd (is) who ?Me mon who ?Me (is) .appoint it

20 אֲשֶׁר יַעֲמֹד לְפָנָי׃ לָכֵן שִׁמְעוּ עֲצַת־יְהוָה אֲשֶׁר יָעַץ אֶל־
against has He which Jehovah the hear Therefore before shall who
planned of counsel ?Me stand

אֱדוֹם וּמַחְשְׁבוֹתָיו אֲשֶׁר חָשַׁב אֶל־יֹשְׁבֵי תֵימָן אִם־לֹא
Surely :Teman the against has He which His and ;Edom
of dwellers purposed purposes

יִסְחָבוּם צְעִירֵי הַצֹּאן אִם־לֹא יַשִּׁים עֲלֵיהֶם נְוֵהֶם׃
their over shall He Surely the least the shall they
.pastures them desolate make .flock of ;them drag

21 מִקּוֹל נִפְלָם רָעֲשָׁה הָאָרֶץ צְעָקָה בְּיַם־סוּף נִשְׁמַע
was Reeds the in they (when) the moved is their the at
heard of Sea cried ;earth fall of noise

22 קוֹלָהּ׃ הִנֵּה כַנֶּשֶׁר יַעֲלֶה וְיִדְאֶה וְיִפְרֹשׂ כְּנָפָיו עַל־
over his and ,fly and shall he the like ,Behold its
wings spread up come eagle .noise

בָּצְרָה וְהָיָה לֵב גִּבּוֹרֵי אֱדוֹם בַּיּוֹם הַהוּא כְּלֵב אִשָּׁה
a the like that day at Edom mighty the the And .Bozrah
woman of heart of men of heart be shall

23 מְצֵרָה׃ לְדַמֶּשֶׂק בּוֹשָׁה חֲמָת וְאַרְפָּד כִּי־שְׁמֻעָה
news for and Hamath put are Concerning her in
,Arpad shame to :Damascus .pangs

24 רָעָה שָׁמְעוּ נָמֹגוּ בַּיָּם דְּאָגָה הַשְׁקֵט לֹא יוּכָל׃ רָפְתָה
become has is it not be to (is there) the in are they they bad
feeble able quiet ;anxiety ,sea ;melted ;heard have

דַמֶּשֶׂק הִפְנְתָה לָנוּס וְרֶטֶט הֶחֱזִיקָה צָרָה וַחֲבָלִים
pangs and distress has panic and ,flee to has she ;Damascus
:(her) seized turned

25 אֲחָזַתָּה כַּיּוֹלֵדָה׃ אֵיךְ לֹא־עֻזְּבָה עִיר תְּהִלָּה קִרְיַת
the ,praise the is not How woman a as taken have
of town of city forsaken .labor in her

26 מְשׂוֹשִׂי׃ לָכֵן יִפְּלוּ בַחוּרֶיהָ בִּרְחֹבֹתֶיהָ וְכָל־אַנְשֵׁי
men and her in young her shall Therefore !joy my
of all ,streets men fall

27 הַמִּלְחָמָה יִדַּמּוּ בַּיּוֹם הַהוּא נְאֻם יְהוָה צְבָאוֹת׃ וְהִצַּתִּי
will I And .hosts Jehovah states ,that day in be shall the
kindle of silenced war

אֵשׁ בְּחוֹמַת דַּמֶּשֶׂק וְאָכְלָה אַרְמְנוֹת בֶּן־הֲדָד׃
.hadad Ben- the shall it and ,Damascus the in fire a
of palaces up burn of wall

28 לְקֵדָר ׀ וּלְמַמְלְכוֹת חָצוֹר אֲשֶׁר הִכָּה נְבוּכַדְרֶאצּוֹר מֶלֶךְ־
king Nebuchadnezzar struck which Hazor concerning and Concerning
of of kingdoms the ,Kedar

בָּבֶל כֹּה אָמַר יְהוָה קוּמוּ עֲלוּ אֶל־קֵדָר וְשָׁדְדוּ אֶת־בְּנֵי־
the and ,Kedar to up Go ,Arise :Jehovah says Thus Baby-
of men strip .lon

29 קֶדֶם׃ אָהֳלֵיהֶם וְצֹאנָם יִקָּחוּ יְרִיעוֹתֵיהֶם וְכָל־כְּלֵיהֶם

their and their They their and their the
,vessels all ,curtains ;take shall flocks tents .east

30 וּגְמַלֵּיהֶם יִשְׂאוּ לָהֶם וְקָרְאוּ עֲלֵיהֶם מָגוֹר מִסָּבִיב׃ נֻסוּ

,Flee all Fear ,them to they And them- to they their and
!around (is) cry shall .selves take shall camels

נֻּדוּ מְאֹד הֶעְמִיקוּ לָשֶׁבֶת יֹשְׁבֵי חָצוֹר נְאֻם־יְהוָה כִּי־

For .Jehovah states ,Hazor O ,dwell to deep go ,far go
of dwellers away

יָעַץ עֲלֵיכֶם נְבוּכַדְרֶאצַּר מֶלֶךְ־בָּבֶל עֵצָה וְחָשַׁב עֲלֵיהֶם

against has and counsel Babylon king Nebuchadnezzar against has
you plotted of you planned

31 מַחֲשָׁבָה׃ קוּמוּ עֲלוּ אֶל־גּוֹי שְׁלֵיו יוֹשֵׁב לָבֶטַח נְאֻם־יְהוָה

,Jehovah states ,securely who at the to up go ,Arise .scheme a
dwells ease nation

32 לֹא־דְלָתַיִם וְלֹא־בְרִיחַ לוֹ בָּדָד יִשְׁכֹּנוּ׃ וְהָיוּ גְמַלֵּיהֶם

their shall And they alone (are) bars nor gates not
camels become .dwell ;it to

לָבַז וַהֲמוֹן מִקְנֵיהֶם לְשָׁלָל וְזֵרִתִים לְכָל־רוּחַ קְצוּצֵי פֵאָה

the those ,winds to will I And .spoil a their mul- the and a
.corners cut who all them scatter cattle of titude ,prize

33 וּמִכָּל־עֲבָרָיו אָבִיא אֶת־אֵידָם נְאֻם־יְהוָה׃ וְהָיְתָה חָצוֹר

Hazor And .Jehovah states their will I sides from And
be shall ,calamity bring it of all

לִמְעוֹן תַּנִּים שְׁמָמָה עַד־עוֹלָם לֹא־יֵשֵׁב שָׁם אִישׁ וְלֹא־

nor ,man A there shall not .forever until ruin a ,jackals dwell- a
live for ing

34 יָגוּר בָּהּ בֶּן־אָדָם׃ אֲשֶׁר הָיָה דְבַר־יְהוָה אֶל־

to Jehovah The came which .man (any) it in so-
of word of son journ

יִרְמְיָהוּ הַנָּבִיא אֶל־עֵילָם בְּרֵאשִׁית מַלְכוּת צִדְקִיָּה מֶלֶךְ־

king Zedekiah the the in Elam against the Jeremiah
of of reign of beginning prophet

35 יְהוּדָה לֵאמֹר׃ כֹּה אָמַר יְהוָה צְבָאוֹת הִנְנִי שֹׁבֵר אֶת־

am ,Behold :hosts Jehovah says Thus ,saying ,Judah
breaking I of

36 קֶשֶׁת עֵילָם רֵאשִׁית גְּבוּרָתָם׃ וְהֵבֵאתִי אֶל־עֵילָם אַרְבַּע

the Elam on will I And their the ,Elam the
four bring .might of first of bow

רוּחוֹת מֵאַרְבַּע קְצוֹת הַשָּׁמַיִם וְזֵרִתִים לְכֹל הָרֻחוֹת

winds toward will and the of ends the from winds
all them scatter ,heavens four

הָאֵלֶּה וְלֹא־יִהְיֶה הַגּוֹי אֲשֶׁר לֹא־יָבוֹא שָׁם נִדְּחֵי עוֹלָם׃

.Elam out- the there shall not where a shall And .these
of casts come nation be not

37 וְהַחְתַּתִּי אֶת־עֵילָם לִפְנֵי אֹיְבֵיהֶם וְלִפְנֵי ׀ מְבַקְשֵׁי נַפְשָׁם

their those and their before Elam I And
.life seek who before enemies terrify will

וְהֵבֵאתִי עֲלֵיהֶם ׀ רָעָה אֶת־חֲרוֹן אַפִּי נְאֻם־יְהוָה וְשִׁלַּחְתִּי

will I And .Jehovah states My the ,evil them on I And
send ,anger of burning bring will

the east. [29] They shall take their tents and their flocks. They shall take their curtains, and all their vessels, and their camels to themselves. And they shall cry to them, Fear (is) all around!

[30] Flee, go far away, go deep to dwell, O dwellers of Hazor, says Jehovah, for Nebuchadnezzar king of Babylon has taken counsel against you and has plotted a scheme against you. [31] Arise, go up to the nation at ease, says Jehovah, who dwells securely; neither gates nor bars (are) to it; and they dwell alone. [32] And their camels shall be a prize, and the multitude of their cattle a prey. And I will scatter them to all winds, those who cut the corners. And I will bring their calamity from all sides of it, says Jehovah. [33] And Hazor shall be a dwelling for jackals, a ruin forever. No man shall live there, nor (any) son of man sojourn in it.

[34] The word of Jehovah that came to Jeremiah the prophet against Elam in the beginning of the reign of Zedekiah king of Judah, saying, [35] Thus says Jehovah of hosts: Behold, I will break the bow of Elam, the chief of their might. [36] And I will bring the four winds from the four ends of the heavens on Elam, and will scatter them toward all those winds. And there shall be no nation where the outcasts of Elam shall not come. [37] For I will cause Elam to be afraid before their enemies and before those who seek their life. And I will bring evil on them, the burning of My anger, says Jehovah. And I will send the sword after

them until I have destroyed them; [38] and I will set My throne in Elam and will destroy the king and the princes from there, says Jehovah.

[39] But it shall come to pass, in the latter days, I will bring again the prisoners of Elam, says Jehovah.

CHAPTER 50

[1] The word that Jehovah spoke against Babylon, against the land of the Chaldeans, by Jeremiah the prophet: [2] Declare among the nations, and cause them to hear, and lift up a banner. Cause them to hear, do not hide it; say, Babylon is captured; Bel is put to shame; Merodach is broken in pieces; her images are put to shame, her idols are broken in pieces. [3] For a nation comes up against her from the north, which shall make her land a desert; yea, no one shall dwell in it. They shall flee; they shall depart; both man and animal.

[4] Then, in those days, and at that time, states Jehovah, the sons of Israel shall come, they and the sons of Judah together; going and weeping, they shall go, and shall seek Jehovah their God. [5] They shall ask the way (to) Zion, there with their faces, (saying), Come and let us join ourselves to Jehovah (in) an everlasting covenant not (to) be forgotten. [6] My people are lost sheep; their shepherds have caused them to go astray; they turned them away (on) the mountains; they have gone from mountain to hill; they have forgotten their resting place. [7] All who have found them have devoured them. And their enemies said, We are not guilty, whereas they have sinned against Jehovah, the habitations of righteousness, and their fathers' hope, Jehovah —[8] Flee from Babylon's midst and go out of the land

38 אחריהם את־החרב עד כלותי אותם׃ ושמתי כסאי

My will I And .them have I until the after
throne set consumed sword them

39 בעילם והאבדתי משם מלך ושרים נאם־יהוה׃ והיה ׀

it And .Jehovah states the and the from will and Elam in
,be will ,rulers king there destroy

באחרית הימים אשוב את־שבית עילם נאם־יהוה׃

.Jehovah states ,Elam the will I ,days the latter in
of prisoners restore

CAP. L נ

CHAPTER 50

1 הדבר אשר דבר יהוה אל־בבל אל־ארץ כשדים ביד

the by the the against ,Babylon against Jeho- spoke that The
of hand ,Chaldeans of land vah word

2 ירמיהו הנביא׃ הגידו בגוים והשמיעו ושאו־נס השמיעו

(them) make a lift and make and the in Declare the Jeremiah
;hear ,banner up ;hear (them) nations :prophet

אל־תכחדו אמרו נלכדה בבל הביש בל חת מרדך

;Mero- broken is ;Bel put is ;Babylon is ,say hide do not
;dach pieces in shame to seized ;it

3 הבישו עצביה חתו גלוליה׃ כי עלה עליה גוי מצפון

the from a against comes For .idols her broken and her put and
,north nation her up pieces in ;images shame to

הוא־ישית את־ארצה לשמה ולא־יהיה יושב בה מאדם

both ;it in dwell shall no and ;horror a her shall which
man one land make

4 ועד־בהמה נדו הלכו׃ בימים ההמה ובעת ההיא נאם־

states that at and ,these days In will they will ,animal and
time .depart ,flee

יהוה יבאו בני־ישראל המה ובני־יהודה יחדו הלוך ובכו

and going to- Judah the and they ,Israel the shall ,Jehovah
weeping ;gether of sons of sons come

5 ילכו ואת־יהוה אלהיהם יבקשו׃ ציון ישאלו דרך הנה

there the shall They (to) shall they their Jehovah and they
way of ask Zion .seek God ,go shall

פניהם באו ונלוו אל־יהוה ברית עולם לא תשכח׃

(be to) not ever- an (in) Jehovah to let and (saying) (with)
.forgotten lasting covenant join us ,Come ,faces their

6 צאן אבדות היה עמי רעיהם התעום הרים שובבים מהר

from turned they the (on) them led have their My are Lost sheep
mountain ;away them mountain ;astray shepherds ;people

7 אל־גבעה הלכו שכחו רבצם׃ כל־מצאיהם אכלום

de- have have who All resting their have they they hill to
;them voured them found .place forgotten ,gone have

וצריהם אמרו לא נאשם תחת אשר חטאו ליהוה נוה־

hab- the against have they whereas are We not ,said their and
of itations Jehovah sinned ;guilty enemies

8 צדק ומקוה אבותיהם יהוה׃ נדו מתוך בבל ומארץ

the from ,Baby- from Flee .Jehovah their hope and righ-
of land ,lon's midst ,fathers' ,teousness

of the Chaldeans, and be as the he-goats before the flocks.

[9] For, lo, I am stirring up a company of great nations from a northern land, against Babylon. And they shall set themselves in order against her. She shall be captured from there; their arrows (shall be) as (those) of a mighty skillful man; they shall not return empty. [10] And Chaldea shall be a prize; all who plunder her shall be satisfied, says Jehovah. [11] Because you rejoice, because you exult, O destroyers of My inheritance; because you are fat like the heifer (in) grass, and neigh like strong ones; [12] your mother shall be deeply ashamed; she who bore you shall turn pale. Behold, the last of the nations (shall be) a wilderness, a dry land, and a desert. [13] Because of the wrath of Jehovah it shall not be inhabited, but it shall be wholly a waste; everyone who goes by Babylon shall be amazed and hiss at all her plagues. [14] Put yourselves in order against Babylon all around; all you who tread the bow, shoot at her. Do not spare arrows, for she has sinned against Jehovah. [15] Shout against her all around. She has given her hand; her foundations have fallen, her walls have been thrown down; for it (is) the vengeance of Jehovah. Take vengeance on her. As she has done, do to her. [16] Cut off the sower from Babylon, and the one who handles the sickle in the time of harvest. From before a sword of the oppressor they shall turn, each one to his people. And they shall flee, each one to his own land.

[17] Israel is a scattered sheep, (by) lions driven away. First, the king of Assyria devoured him; and last, this Nebuchadnezzar king of Babylon has broken his bones. [18] Therefore thus says Jehovah of hosts, the God of Israel: Behold, I

9 כַּשְׂדִּים יֵצֵאוּ וִהְיוּ כְּעַתּוּדִים לִפְנֵי־צֹאן׃ כִּי הִנֵּה אָנֹכִי

I ,lo For the before the as and go the
.flocks he-goats be ,forth Chaldeans

מֵעִיר וּמַעֲלֶה עַל־בָּבֶל קְהַל־גּוֹיִם גְּדֹלִים מֵאֶרֶץ צָפוֹן

a from great nations a Baby- against bring and am
,northern land of company lon up arousing

וְעָרְכוּ לָהּ מִשָּׁם תִּלָּכֵד חִצָּיו כְּגִבּוֹר מַשְׂכִּיל לֹא יָשׁוּב

will they not skillful a as their shall She from against they and
return man mighty arrows;captured be there .her array will

10 רֵיקָם׃ וְהָיְתָה כַשְׂדִּים לְשָׁלָל כָּל־שֹׁלְלֶיהָ יִשְׂבָּעוּ נְאֻם

states be shall who all ;prize a Chaldea shall And .empty
,satisfied her plunder become

11 יְהוָה׃ כִּי תִשְׂמְחוּ כִּי תַעַלְזוּ שֹׁסֵי נַחֲלָתִי כִּי תָפוּשׁוּ

are you because My spoilers you because you Because .Jehovah
fat ;inheritance of ,exult ,rejoice

12 כְּעֶגְלָה דָשָׁה וְתִצְהֲלוּ כָּאַבִּרִים׃ בּוֹשָׁה אִמְּכֶם מְאֹד

;greatly your be shall strong like neigh and (in) the like
mother ashamed ,ones ,grass heifer

חָפְרָה יוֹלַדְתְּכֶם הִנֵּה אַחֲרִית גּוֹיִם מִדְבָּר צִיָּה וַעֲרָבָה׃

a and dry a (be shall) the last the ,Behold who she turn shall
.desert land ,desert a nations of .bore you pale

13 מִקֶּצֶף יְהוָה לֹא תֵשֵׁב וְהָיְתָה שְׁמָמָה כֻּלָּהּ כֹּל עֹבֵר עַל־

by who every of all ,waste a it but will it not Jehovah's Because
passes one ;it be will in lived be wrath of

14 בָּבֶל יִשֹּׁם וְיִשְׁרֹק עַל־כָּל־מַכּוֹתֶיהָ׃ עִרְכוּ עַל־בָּבֶל ׀

Baby- against Array her all at shall and be shall Babylon yourselves .plagues hiss ,amazed lon

סָבִיב כָּל־דֹּרְכֵי קֶשֶׁת יְדוּ אֵלֶיהָ אַל־תַּחְמְלוּ אֶל־חֵץ כִּי

for ;arrows do not ;her at shout ;bow a you all all
spare tread who ,around

15 לַיהוָה חָטָאָה׃ הָרִיעוּ עָלֶיהָ סָבִיב נָתְנָה יָדָהּ נָפְלוּ

have her has She all against Shout has she against
fallen ;hand given ,around her .sinned Jehovah

אָשְׁיוֹתֶיהָ נֶהֶרְסוּ חוֹמוֹתֶיהָ כִּי נִקְמַת יְהוָה הִיא הִנָּקְמוּ

Take it Jehovah the for her been have her
vengeance .(is) of vengeance ;walls down thrown ;pillars

16 בָהּ כַּאֲשֶׁר עָשְׂתָה עֲשׂוּ־לָהּ׃ כִּרְתוּ זוֹרֵעַ מִבָּבֶל וְתֹפֵשׂ

him and from the off Cut .her to do has she As on
using Babylon sower ,done .her

מַגָּל בְּעֵת קָצִיר מִפְּנֵי חֶרֶב הַיּוֹנָה אִישׁ אֶל־עַמּוֹ יִפְנוּ

shall they his to each the sword a from .harvest the in the
;turn people one ,oppressor of before of time sickle

17 וְאִישׁ לְאַרְצוֹ יָנֻסוּ׃ שֶׂה פְזוּרָה יִשְׂרָאֵל אֲרָיוֹת הִדִּיחוּ

driven lions (by) Israel scattered a shall his to each and
.away ,(is) sheep :flee land one

הָרִאשׁוֹן אֲכָלוֹ מֶלֶךְ אַשּׁוּר וְזֶה הָאַחֲרוֹן עִצְּמוֹ נְבוּכַדְרֶאצַּר

Nebuchadnezzar (has) last and ;Assyria the devoured The
bones his(broken) this of king ,first

18 מֶלֶךְ בָּבֶל׃ לָכֵן כֹּה־אָמַר יְהוָה צְבָאוֹת אֱלֹהֵי

the ,hosts Jehovah says thus Therefore .Babylon king
of God of of

am punishing the king of Babylon and his land, as I have punished the king of Assyria. [19] And I will again bring Israel to his home, and he shall feed on Carmel and Bashan, and his soul shall be satisfied on Mount Ephraim and Gilead. [20] In those days, and at that time, says Jehovah, the iniquity of Israel shall be sought for, and it is not; and the sins of Judah, and they shall not be found; for I will pardon those whom I leave as a remnant.

[21] Go up against the land of Merathaim, against it and against the people of Pekod. Waste and destroy after them, says Jehovah, and do according to all that I have commanded you. [22] A sound of battle (is) in the land, and of great ruin. [23] How the hammer of the whole earth is cut in two and broken! How Babylon has become a ruin among the nations! [24] I have laid a trap for you, and you are also captured, O Babylon, and you did not know. You were found and also caught, because you have fought against Jehovah. [25] Jehovah has opened His armory and has brought out the weapons of His indignation. For this (is) a work of Jehovah God of hosts in the land of the Chaldeans. [26] Come against her from the end; open her granaries; pile her up as heaps, and destroy her completely. Let not a remnant be left. [27] Put to the sword all her bulls; let them go down to the slaughter. Woe to them! For their day has come, the time of their punishment. [28] The voice of those who flee and escape out of the land of Babylon, to declare in Zion the vengeance of Jehovah our God, the vengeance of

יִשְׂרָאֵל הִנְנִי פֹקֵד אֶל־מֶלֶךְ בָּבֶל וְאֶל־אַרְצוֹ כַּאֲשֶׁר
as his and Babylon the am ,Behold :Israel
;land of king punishing I

19 פָּקַדְתִּי אֶל־מֶלֶךְ אַשּׁוּר׃ וְשֹׁבַבְתִּי אֶת־יִשְׂרָאֵל אֶל־נָוֵהוּ
his to Israel will I And .Assyria the I
,pasture again bring of king punished

וְרָעָה הַכַּרְמֶל וְהַבָּשָׁן וּבְהַר אֶפְרַיִם וְהַגִּלְעָד תִּשְׂבַּע
be shall and Ephraim on and and Carmel will he and
satisfied Gilead Mount ,Bashan on feed

20 נַפְשׁוֹ׃ בַּיָּמִים הָהֵם וּבָעֵת הַהִיא נְאֻם־יְהוָה יְבֻקַּשׁ אֶת־
be shall ,Jehovah states ,that at and ,those days In his
for sought time .soul

עֲוֹן יִשְׂרָאֵל וְאֵינֶנּוּ וְאֶת־חַטֹּאת יְהוּדָה וְלֹא תִמָּצֶאינָה כִּי
for shall they and ,Judah the and it and Israel's ini-
;found be not of sins ;not is quity

21 אֶסְלַח לַאֲשֶׁר אַשְׁאִיר׃ עַל־הָאָרֶץ מְרָתַיִם עֲלֵה
up go ,Merathaim the Against as leave I those will I
of land .remnant a whom pardon

עָלֶיהָ וְאֶל־יוֹשְׁבֵי פְּקוֹד חֲרֹב וְהַחֲרֵם אַחֲרֵיהֶם נְאֻם־יְהוָה
;Jehovah states after and waste ;Pekod the and against
,them destroy of dwellers against ;it

22 וַעֲשֵׂה כְּכֹל אֲשֶׁר צִוִּיתִיךָ׃ קוֹל מִלְחָמָה בָּאָרֶץ וְשֶׁבֶר
a and in (is) battle A com- have I that according do and
ruin ,land the of sound .you manded all to

23 גָּדוֹל׃ אֵיךְ נִגְדַּע וַיִּשָּׁבֵר פַּטִּישׁ כָּל־הָאָרֶץ אֵיךְ הָיְתָה
has How the all the and cut is How .great
become !earth of hammer broken off

24 לְשַׁמָּה בָּבֶל בַּגּוֹיִם׃ יָקֹשְׁתִּי לָךְ וְגַם־נִלְכַּדְתְּ בָּבֶל וְאַתְּ
and ;Babylon are you and for have I the among Babylon horror a
you ,captured also ,you trap a laid !nations

לֹא יָדָעַתְּ נִמְצֵאת וְגַם־נִתְפַּשְׂתְּ כִּי בַיהוָה הִתְגָּרִית׃
you against because ,caught and were you did not
.fought Jehovah also found ;know

25 פָּתַח יְהוָה אֶת־אוֹצָרוֹ וַיּוֹצֵא אֶת־כְּלֵי זַעְמוֹ כִּי־מְלָאכָה
work a For His the has and his Jehovah has
.fury of weapons out brought armory opened

26 הִיא לַאדֹנָי יְהוִה צְבָאוֹת בְּאֶרֶץ כַּשְׂדִּים׃ בֹּאוּ־לָהּ מִקֵּץ
from against Come the the in hosts Jehovah the of this
;end the her .Chaldeans of land of Lord (is)

פִּתְחוּ מַאֲבֻסֶיהָ סָלּוּהָ כְמוֹ־עֲרֵמִים וְהַחֲרִימוּהָ אַל־תְּהִי־
be Let not completely and ,heaps like pile her open
.her destroy up her ;granaries

27 לָהּ שְׁאֵרִית׃ חִרְבוּ כָּל־פָּרֶיהָ יֵרְדוּ לַטָּבַח הוֹי עֲלֵיהֶם
!them to Woe the to them let her all to Put a to
.slaughter down go ;bulls sword the .remnant her

28 כִּי־בָא יוֹמָם עֵת פְּקֻדָּתָם׃ קוֹל נָסִים וּפְלֵטִים מֵאֶרֶץ
the from and those The their time the their has For
of land escape flee who of voice .punishment of ,day come

בָּבֶל לְהַגִּיד בְּצִיּוֹן אֶת־נִקְמַת יְהוָה אֱלֹהֵינוּ נִקְמַת הֵיכָלוֹ׃
His venge- the our Jehovah venge- the in to ,Babylon
.temple of ance ,God of ance Zion declare

His temple. [29] Call the archers together against Babylon. All you who tread the bow, camp against it all around; let none of them escape. Repay her according to her work; according to all that she has done, do to her. For she has been proud against Jehovah, against the Holy One of Israel. [30] Therefore her young men shall fall in the streets, and all her men of war shall be silenced in that day, says Jehovah. [31] Behold, I (am) against you, O proud ones, says the Lord Jehovah of hosts; for your day has come, the time I will punish you. [32] And the proud one shall stumble and fall, and none shall raise him up. And I will kindle a fire in his cities, and it shall burn up everything all around him.

[33] Thus says Jehovah of hosts: The sons of Israel and the sons of Judah are oppressed together; yea, all who captured them held them fast; they refused to let them go. [34] Their Redeemer (is) strong; Jehovah of hosts (is) His name. He shall surely plead their cause, so that he may give rest to the land, and give turmoil to the inhabitants of Babylon.

[35] A sword (is) on the Chaldeans, states Jehovah, and on the residents of Babylon, and on her princes, and on her wise men. [36] A sword is on the liars, and they shall become fools; a sword (is) on her mighty men, and they shall be broken down. [37] A sword (is) on his horses and to his chariots, and to all the mixed people who (are) in her midst; and they shall become women; a sword (is) to her treasuries, and they shall be robbed. [38] A drought (is) on her waters; and they shall be dried up. For it (is) the land of idols, and they boast themselves in idols. [39] Therefore the beasts of the desert shall dwell

29 הַשְׁמִיעוּ אֶל־בָּבֶל ׀ רַבִּים כָּל־דֹּרְכֵי קֶשֶׁת חֲנוּ עָלֶיהָ
against camp ,bow a who you All the Baby- against Call
it tread .archers lon together
סָבִיב אַל־יְהִי־ פְּלֵיטָה שַׁלְּמוּ־לָהּ כְּפָעֳלָהּ כְּכֹל אֲשֶׁר
that according according her Repay .escape of let not all
all to ;work her to them (any) ;around
עָשְׂתָה עֲשׂוּ־לָהּ כִּי אֶל־יְהוָה זָדָה אֶל־קְדוֹשׁ יִשְׂרָאֵל׃
.Israel the against has she Jehovah against For to do has she
of One Holy ,proud been .her done
30 לָכֵן יִפְּלוּ בַחוּרֶיהָ בִּרְחֹבֹתֶיהָ וְכָל־אַנְשֵׁי מִלְחַמְתָּהּ יִדַּמּוּ
be shall war her men and the in young her shall There-
silenced of all ,streets men fall fore
31 בַּיּוֹם הַהוּא נְאֻם־יְהוָה׃ הִנְנִי אֵלֶיךָ זָדוֹן נְאֻם־אֲדֹנָי
the proud O against ,Behold .Jehovah states ,that day in
Lord ,one ,you (am) I
32 יְהוִה צְבָאוֹת כִּי בָּא יוֹמְךָ עֵת פְּקַדְתִּיךָ׃ וְכָשַׁל זָדוֹן
the shall And punish will I the your has for ,hosts Jehovah
one proud stumble .you time ,day come of
וְנָפַל וְאֵין לוֹ מֵקִים וְהִצַּתִּי אֵשׁ בְּעָרָיו וְאָכְלָה כָּל־
every- shall his in fire a will I And shall him and and
thing devour ,cities kindle .up lift none ,fall
33 סְבִיבֹתָיו׃ כֹּה אָמַר יְהוָה צְבָאוֹת עֲשׁוּקִים בְּנֵי־
The are :hosts Jehovah says Thus around all
of sons oppressed of .him
יִשְׂרָאֵל וּבְנֵי־יְהוּדָה יַחְדָּו וְכָל־שֹׁבֵיהֶם הֶחֱזִיקוּ בָם מֵאֲנוּ
they ;them held cap- who all and to- Judah the and ,Israel
refused fast them tured ;gether of sons
34 שַׁלְּחָם׃ גֹּאֲלָם ׀ חָזָק יְהוָה צְבָאוֹת שְׁמוֹ רִיב יָרִיב אֶת־
will He surely His (is) hosts Jehovah (is) Their let to
plead ;name of ,strong Redeemer .go them
35 רִיבָם לְמַעַן הִרְגִּיעַ אֶת־הָאָרֶץ וְהִרְגִּיז לְיֹשְׁבֵי בָבֶל׃ חֶרֶב
A .Babylon the to give and the give may He so their
sword of residents turmoil ,land to rest that ,cause
עַל־כַּשְׂדִּים נְאֻם־יְהוָה וְאֶל־יֹשְׁבֵי בָבֶל וְאֶל־שָׂרֶיהָ וְאֶל־
and her and ,Babylon resi- the and ,Jehovah states the (is)
to ,,rulers to of dents to ,Chaldeans on
36 חֲכָמֶיהָ׃ חֶרֶב אֶל־הַבַּדִּים וְנֹאָלוּ חֶרֶב אֶל־גִּבּוֹרֶיהָ וָחָתּוּ׃
they and mighty her (is) a they and the (is) A wise her
.broken are ,men to sword ;fools be will ,liars to sword .men
37 חֶרֶב אֶל־סוּסָיו וְאֶל־רִכְבּוֹ וְאֶל־כָּל־הָעֶרֶב אֲשֶׁר בְּתוֹכָהּ
her in who mixed the all and his and his (is) A
;midst (are) people to ,chariots to horses to sword
38 וְהָיוּ לְנָשִׁים חֶרֶב אֶל־אוֹצְרֹתֶיהָ וּבֻזָּזוּ׃ חֹרֶב אֶל־מֵימֶיהָ
her (is) A shall they and her (is) sword a ;women they and
;waters to drought .robbed be ,treasuries to become shall
39 וְיָבֵשׁוּ כִּי אֶרֶץ פְּסִלִים הִיא וּבָאֵימִים יִתְהֹלָלוּ׃ לָכֵן יֵשְׁבוּ
shall Therefore boast they in and ,(is) it idols the For they and
dwell .themselves idols of land .up dry will
צִיִּים אֶת־אִיִּים וְיָשְׁבוּ בָהּ בְּנוֹת יַעֲנָה וְלֹא־תֵשֵׁב עוֹד
again shall And the daugh- the in shall and ;jackals with desert
dwell not .ostrich of ters her dwell creatures

(there) with the jackals; and the daughters of the ostrich shall dwell in her. And it shall not again have anyone (in it) forever; it shall not be lived in until generation and generation. [40] As God overthrew Sodom and Gomorrah and their neighbors, says Jehovah, (so) no man shall live there; nor shall a son of man live in it. [41] Behold, a people shall come from the north, and a great nation, and many kings shall be stirred up from the farthest parts of the earth. [42] They lay hold of a bow and spear; they (shall be) cruel and will show no mercy; their voice shall roar like the sea; and arrayed like a man for the battle, they shall ride against you, O daughter of Babylon. [43] The king of Babylon has heard their report, and his hands became feeble; anguish took hold of him, pangs like (those) of a woman in labor. [44] Behold, he shall come up like a lion, from the swelling of Jordan, to the pasture of the strong. But I will make them suddenly run away from it; and who is a chosen (one) I will appoint over it. For who is like Me? And who will summon Me? And who (is) that shepherd who will stand before Me? [45] Therefore hear the counsel of Jehovah that He has planned against Babylon; and His purposes which He has purposed against the land of the Chaldeans; surely shall drag them the least of the flock; surely He shall make (their) pasture desolate over them. [46] At the sound of the capture of Babylon the earth shall tremble, and a cry is heard among the nations.

40 לָנֶצַח וְלֹא תִשְׁכּוֹן עַד־דּוֹר וָדוֹר׃ כְּמַהְפֵּכַת אֱלֹהִים אֶת־
God As gene- and genera- until shall it and ;forever
overthrew .ration tion in lived be not

סְדֹם וְאֶת־עֲמֹרָה וְאֶת־שְׁכֵנֶיהָ נְאֻם־יְהוָה לֹא־יֵשֵׁב שָׁם
there shall not ,Jehovah states their and Gomorrah and Sodom
dwell ,neighbors

41 אִישׁ וְלֹא־יָגוּר בָּהּ בֶּן־אָדָם׃ הִנֵּה עַם בָּא מִצָּפוֹן וְגוֹי
a and the from is a ,Behold .man son a it in shall and ;man a
nation ,north coming people of sojourn not

42 גָּדוֹל וּמְלָכִים רַבִּים יֵעֹרוּ מִיַּרְכְּתֵי־אָרֶץ׃ קֶשֶׁת וְכִידֹן
and bow a the the from be shall many and ,great
spear .earth of parts far aroused kings

יַחֲזִיקוּ אַכְזָרִי הֵמָּה וְלֹא יְרַחֵמוּ קוֹלָם כַּיָּם יֶהֱמֶה וְעַל־
and shall the like their show shall and they cruel lay They
on ,roar sea voice ;mercy not (be shall) ;of hold

סוּסִים יִרְכָּבוּ עָרוּךְ כְּאִישׁ לַמִּלְחָמָה עָלַיִךְ בַּת־בָּבֶל׃
.Babylon O against the for a like arrayed shall they horses
of daughter ,you battle man ,ride

43 שָׁמַע מֶלֶךְ־בָּבֶל אֶת־שִׁמְעָם וְרָפוּ יָדָיו צָרָה הֶחֱזִיקַתְהוּ
hold took anguish his hang their Babylon The has
,him of ;hands limp ,report of king heard

44 חִיל כַּיּוֹלֵדָה׃ הִנֵּה כְּאַרְיֵה יַעֲלֶה מִגְּאוֹן הַיַּרְדֵּן אֶל־נְוֵה
the to ,Jordan the from shall he a like ,Behold woman a as pangs
of pasture of pride ,up come lion .labor in

אֵיתָן כִּי־אַרְגִּעָה אֲרוּצֵם מֵעָלֶיהָ וּמִי בָחוּר אֵלֶיהָ אֶפְקֹד
will I over chosen a and away them make will I For the
.appoint it one who ;it from run suddenly .strong

כִּי מִי כָמוֹנִי וּמִי יוֹעִדֶנִּי וּמִי־זֶה רֹעֶה אֲשֶׁר יַעֲמֹד לְפָנָי׃
before will who shepherd this And sum- will And like who For
?Me stand (is) who ?Me mon who ?Me (is)

45 לָכֵן שִׁמְעוּ עֲצַת־יְהוָה אֲשֶׁר יָעַץ אֶל־בָּבֶל וּמַחְשְׁבוֹתָיו
His and ,Babylon against has He that Jehovah the hear There-
purposes planned of counsel fore

אֲשֶׁר חָשַׁב אֶל־אֶרֶץ כַּשְׂדִּים אִם־לֹא יִסְחָבוּם צְעִירֵי
the drag shall ,surely the the against has He which
of least ,them ;Chaldeans of land purposed

46 הַצֹּאן אִם־לֹא יַשִּׁים עֲלֵיהֶם נָוֶה׃ מִקּוֹל נִתְפְּשָׂה בָבֶל
,Babylon the of the At (their) over will He surely the
of capture sound .pasture them desolate make ;flock

נִרְעֲשָׁה הָאָרֶץ וּזְעָקָה בַּגּוֹיִם נִשְׁמָע׃
is the among a and the shall
.heard nations cry ,earth tremble

CAP. LI נא

CHAPTER 51

[1] Thus says Jehovah: Behold, I am raising up a destroying wind against Babylon, and against those who dwell in the midst of those who rise up against Me. [2] And I will send winnowers to Babylon, who

1 כֹּה אָמַר יְהוָה הִנְנִי מֵעִיר עַל־בָּבֶל וְאֶל־יֹשְׁבֵי לֵב קָמָי
my in those and Babylon against am ,Behold ,Jehovah says Thus
foes of heart living against arousing I

2 רוּחַ מַשְׁחִית׃ וְשִׁלַּחְתִּי לְבָבֶל ׀ זָרִים וְזֵרוּהָ וּבֹקְקוּ אֶת־
will and will who sifters to I And .destroying a
empty her sift Babylon send will wind

shall winnow her and shall empty her land. For in the day of evil, they shall be against her all around. [3] Let not fully tread the treader his bow, nor lift himself up in his armor. And do not spare her young men; utterly destroy all her army. [4] Thus the slain shall fall in the land of the Chaldeans, yea, thrust through in her streets. [5] For neither Israel nor Judah has been forsaken by his God, by Jehovah of hosts, though their land was filled with guilt against the Holy One of Israel. [6] Flee out of the middle of Babylon; yea, each man deliver his soul. Do not be silenced in her iniquity, for it (is) the time of Jehovah's vengeance; He will give to her a just reward. [7] Babylon (was) a golden cup in the hand of Jehovah, making all the earth drunk. The nations have drunk of her wine; therefore the nations are insane. [8] Suddenly Babylon has fallen; and it is broken. Wail for her; take balm for her pain, if perhaps she may be healed. [9] We would have healed Babylon, but she is not healed. Forsake her and let us go, each one into his own country; for her judgment reaches to the heavens and is lifted up to the skies. [10] Jehovah has brought forth our righteousness; come and let us declare in Zion the work of Jehovah our God.

[11] Sharpen the arrows; fill the shields; Jehovah has raised up the spirit of the kings of the Medes. For His plan (is) against Babylon, to destroy (it); because it (is) the vengeance of Jehovah, the vengeance of His temple. [12] Set up the banner to the walls of Babylon; make the watch strong; set up the watches; prepare the ambushes. For Jehovah has both planned and done that

3 אַרְצָהּ כִּי־הָיוּ עָלֶיהָ מִסָּבִיב בְּיוֹם רָעָה׃ אֶל־יִדְרֹךְ יִדְרֹךְ
tread fully Not .evil the in all against they For her
let of day around her be shall .land

הַדֹּרֵךְ קַשְׁתּוֹ וְאֶל־יִתְעַל בְּסִרְיֹנוֹ וְאַל־תַּחְמְלוּ אֶל־בַּחֻרֶיהָ
young her do And his in him- lift nor his the
;men spare not .armor up self ,bow treader

4 הַחֲרִימוּ כָּל־צְבָאָהּ׃ וְנָפְלוּ חֲלָלִים בְּאֶרֶץ כַּשְׂדִּים וּמְדֻקָּרִים
pierced and the the in the Thus her all utterly
through Chaldeans of land slain fall shall .hosts destroy

5 בְּחוּצוֹתֶיהָ׃ כִּי לֹא־אַלְמָן יִשְׂרָאֵל וִיהוּדָה מֵאֱלֹהָיו
his by Judah or Israel been has not For her in
,God widowed .streets

מֵיְהוָה צְבָאוֹת כִּי אַרְצָם מָלְאָה אָשָׁם מִקְּדוֹשׁ יִשְׂרָאֵל׃
.Israel the against guilt filled was their though ,hosts Jeho- by
of One Holy with land of vah

6 נֻסוּ ׀ מִתּוֹךְ בָּבֶל וּמַלְּטוּ אִישׁ נַפְשׁוֹ אַל־תִּדַּמּוּ בַּעֲוֺנָהּ כִּי
for her in be do not his each and ,Babylon the from Flee
;iniquity silenced ;soul man deliver of midst

7 עֵת נְקָמָה הִיא לַיהוָה גְּמוּל הוּא מְשַׁלֵּם לָהּ׃ כּוֹס־זָהָב
golden A .her to will He just a Jehovah's it vengeance the
cup render reward (is) of time

בָּבֶל בְּיַד־יְהוָה מְשַׁכֶּרֶת כָּל־הָאָרֶץ מִיֵּינָהּ שָׁתוּ גוֹיִם עַל־
The have her of the all making ,Jehovah the in (was).
;nations drunk wine .earth drunk of hand Babylon

8 כֵּן יִתְהֹלְלוּ גוֹיִם׃ פִּתְאֹם נָפְלָה בָבֶל וַתִּשָּׁבֵר הֵילִילוּ
Wail is it and ,Babylon has Suddenly the are there-
.broken fallen .nations insane fore

9 עָלֶיהָ קְחוּ צֳרִי לְמַכְאוֹבָהּ אוּלַי תֵּרָפֵא׃ רִפִּאנוּ אֶת־בָּבֶל
,Babylon would We may she if her for balm take for
healed have .healed be perhaps ;pain ;her

וְלֹא נִרְפָּתָה עִזְבוּהָ וְנֵלֵךְ אִישׁ לְאַרְצוֹ כִּי־נָגַע אֶל־הַשָּׁמַיִם
the to reaches for his into each let and Forsake is she but
heavens ;country own one ,go us her .healed not

10 מִשְׁפָּטָהּ וְנִשָּׂא עַד־שְׁחָקִים׃ הוֹצִיא יְהוָה אֶת־צִדְקֹתֵינוּ
our Jehovah brought has the to is and her
;righteousness forth .skies up lifted ,judgment

11 בֹּאוּ וּנְסַפְּרָה בְצִיּוֹן אֶת־מַעֲשֵׂה יְהוָה אֱלֹהֵינוּ׃ הָבֵרוּ
Sharpen .God our Jehovah the Zion in let and come
of work declare us

הַחִצִּים מִלְאוּ הַשְּׁלָטִים הֵעִיר יְהוָה אֶת־רוּחַ מַלְכֵי מָדַי
the the spirit the Jehovah has the fill the
.Medes of kings of aroused ;shields ;arrows

כִּי־עַל־בָּבֶל מְזִמָּתוֹ לְהַשְׁחִיתָהּ כִּי־נִקְמַת יְהוָה הִיא נִקְמַת
ven- the ,(is) it Jehovah the because destroy to His Baby- against For
of geance of vengeance ;(it) plan lon (is)

12 הֵיכָלוֹ׃ אֶל־חוֹמֹת בָּבֶל שְׂאוּ־נֵס הַחֲזִיקוּ הַמִּשְׁמָר הָקִימוּ
up set the make the Set Babylon the to His
.watch strong ;banner up of walk .temple

שֹׁמְרִים הָכִינוּ הָאֹרְבִים כִּי גַם־זָמַם יְהוָה גַּם־עָשָׂה אֵת
done and Jehovah has both For the prepare the
planned .ambushes ;watches

which He spoke against the people of Babylon. [13] O you who live on many waters, rich in treasures, your end has come, the measure of your unjust gain. [14] Jehovah of hosts has sworn by Himself, (saying), Surely I will fill you with men as with locusts; and they shall lift up a shout against you. [15] He has made the earth by His power; He has established the world by His wisdom, and stretched out the heavens by His understanding. [16] When He gives (His) voice, a multitude of waters is in the heavens; and he causes the mists to ascend from the end of the earth; He makes lightnings for rain, and brings forth the wind out of His treasuries. [17] Every man is brutish in knowledge; every refiner is put to shame by idols. For his molded image (is) a lie, and (there is) no breath in them. [18] They (are) vanity, the work of errors; in the time of their punishment they shall perish. [19] The Portion of Jacob (is) not like them; for He (is) the Former of all things, and the rod of His inheritance; Jehovah of hosts (is) His name. [20] You (are) My war club (and) weapons of war; for with you I will shatter nations, and with you I will destroy kingdoms. [21] And with you I will shatter the horse and his rider; and with you I will shatter the chariot and his charioteer. [22] And I will with you shatter man and woman; and with you I will shatter old and young; and with you I will shatter the young man and the girl. [23] And I will shatter the shepherd and his flock with you. And I will shatter with you the farmer and his team; and with you I will shatter heads and rulers. [24] And I will give to Babylon and to all the people of Chaldea all the evil that they have done in Zion before your eyes, states Jehovah. [25] Behold, I (am) against you, O destroying mountain, says Jehovah, who destroy all

13 אֲשֶׁר־דִּבֶּר אֶל־יֹשְׁבֵי בָבֶל: שֹׁכַנְתְּי עַל־מַיִם רַבִּים רַבַּת

rich ,many waters by you O .Babylon in-the against He that
in live who of habitants spoke which

14 אוֹצָרֹת בָּא קִצֵּךְ אַמַּת בִּצְעֵךְ: נִשְׁבַּע יְהוָה צְבָאוֹת בְּנַפְשׁוֹ

by hosts Jehovah Has unjust your the your has ,treasures
,Himself of sworn .gain of measure ,end come

15 כִּי אִם־מִלֵּאתִיךְ אָדָם כַּיֶּלֶק וְעָנוּ עָלַיִךְ הֵידָד: עֹשֶׂה

has He .shout a against they and with as men fill will I Surely
made you lift will locusts with you

אֶרֶץ בְּכֹחוֹ מֵכִין תֵּבֵל בְּחָכְמָתוֹ וּבִתְבוּנָתוֹ נָטָה שָׁמָיִם:

the stretched His by and His by the He His by the
.heavens out understanding ,wisdom world established ;power earth

16 לְקוֹל תִּתּוֹ הֲמוֹן מַיִם בַּשָּׁמַיִם וַיַּעַל נְשִׂאִים מִקְצֵה־אָרֶץ

the the from the He and the in waters mul- a He (His) When
;earth of end mists up go makes ,heavens (is) of titude ,gives voice

17 בְּרָקִים לַמָּטָר עָשָׂה וַיּוֹצֵא רוּחַ מֵאֹצְרֹתָיו: נִבְעַר כָּל־

Every is His of out the brings and He rain for lightnings
brutish .treasuries wind forth ,makes

אָדָם מִדַּעַת הֹבִישׁ כָּל־צֹרֵף מִפָּסֶל כִּי שֶׁקֶר נִסְכּוֹ וְלֹא

and molded his a (is) for ;idols by refiner every put is in man
is not ,image lie shame to ;knowledge

18 רוּחַ בָּם: הֶבֶל הֵמָּה מַעֲשֵׂה תַּעְתֻּעִים בְּעֵת פְּקֻדָּתָם יֹאבֵדוּ:

shall they their the in ;errors work a They vanity in breath
.perish punishment of time of (are) .them

19 לֹא־כְאֵלֶּה חֵלֶק יַעֲקֹב כִּי־יוֹצֵר הַכֹּל הוּא וְשֵׁבֶט נַחֲלָתוֹ

in- His the and He all the for ;Jacob The like not
;heritance of rod ,(is) things of Former of portion them

20 יְהוָה צְבָאוֹת שְׁמוֹ: מַפֵּץ־אַתָּה לִי כְּלֵי מִלְחָמָה

;war (and) Me to You a His (is) hosts Jehovah
of weapons (are) war-club .name of

21 וְנִפַּצְתִּי בְךָ גּוֹיִם וְהִשְׁחַתִּי בְךָ מַמְלָכוֹת: וְנִפַּצְתִּי בְךָ

with will I And ..kingdoms with will I and ,nations with will I for
you shatter you destroy you shatter

22 סוּס וְרֹכְבוֹ וְנִפַּצְתִּי בְךָ רֶכֶב וְרֹכְבוֹ: וְנִפַּצְתִּי בְךָ אִישׁ

man with will I And his and the with will I and his and the
you shatter .charioteer chariot you shatter ;rider horse

וְאִשָּׁה וְנִפַּצְתִּי בְךָ זָקֵן וָנָעַר וְנִפַּצְתִּי בְךָ בָּחוּר וּבְתוּלָה:

the and young the with will I and and old with will I and
.girl man you shatter ;young you shatter ;woman

23 וְנִפַּצְתִּי בְךָ רֹעֶה וְעֶדְרוֹ וְנִפַּצְתִּי בְךָ אִכָּר וְצִמְדּוֹ וְנִפַּצְתִּי

will I and his and the with will I And his and the with will I And
shatter ;team farmer you shatter ;flock shepherd you shatter

24 בְךָ פַּחוֹת וּסְגָנִים: וְשִׁלַּמְתִּי לְבָבֶל וּלְכֹל יוֹשְׁבֵי כַשְׂדִּים

Chaldea the to and to will I And and governors with
of dwellers all Babylon repay .rulers you

אֵת כָּל־רָעָתָם אֲשֶׁר־עָשׂוּ בְצִיּוֹן לְעֵינֵיכֶם נְאֻם יְהוָה:

.Jehovah states before Zion in they that their all
,eyes your done have evil

25 הִנְנִי אֵלֶיךָ הַר הַמַּשְׁחִית נְאֻם־יְהוָה הַמַּשְׁחִית

destroy who .Jehovah states ,destroying O against ,Behold
mountain ,you (am) I

the earth. And I will stretch out My hand on you and roll you down from the rocks, and I will make you a burned mountain. [26] And they shall not take a stone from you for a corner, or a stone for foundations; but you shall be a waste forever, says Jehovah. [27] Set up a banner in the land; blow a trumpet among the nations; consecrate nations against her. Call the kingdoms of Ararat, Minni, and Ashkenaz together against her; set a captain against her. Cause the horses to come up as the rough locusts. [28] Consecrate against her nations with the kings of the Medes, their captains, and all their rulers, and all the land of his kingdom. [29] And the land shall tremble and writhe in pain. For every purpose of Jehovah shall be done against Babylon, to make the land of Babylon a desert without inhabitant. [30] The mighty men of Babylon have stopped fighting; they have dwelt in strongholds; their might has withered; they became women; they have burned her houses; her bars are broken. [31] A runner shall run to meet a runner, and a herald to meet a herald, to announce to the king of Babylon that his city is captured from end (to end); [32] and that the fords are seized. And they have burned the reeds with fire, and the men of war are terrified. [33] For thus says Jehovah of hosts, the God of Israel: The daughter of Babylon (is) like a threshing floor; (it is) time to thresh her. Yet a little while, and the time of her harvest shall come.

[34] Nebuchadnezzar the king of Babylon has devoured us. He has crushed us. He has made us an empty vessel. He has swallowed us up like a jackal; he has filled his belly with my good things; he has thrown

אֶת־כָּל־הָאָרֶץ וְנָטִיתִי אֶת־יָדִי עָלֶיךָ וְגִלְגַּלְתִּיךָ מִן־הַסְּלָעִים
the from roll and on My will I And the all
;rocks down you you hand out stretch .earth

26 וּנְתַתִּיךָ לְהַר שְׂרֵפָה׃ וְלֹא־יִקְחוּ מִמְּךָ אֶבֶן לְפִנָּה וְאֶבֶן
a or a for a from they And .burned a will I and
stone corner stone you take shall not mountain you make

27 לְמוֹסָדוֹת כִּי־שִׁמְמוֹת עוֹלָם תִּהְיֶה נְאֻם־יְהוָה׃ שְׂאוּ־נֵס
a up Set .Jehovah states you forever waste a but for
banner ,be shall ;foundations

בָּאָרֶץ תִּקְעוּ שׁוֹפָר בַּגּוֹיִם קַדְּשׁוּ עָלֶיהָ גּוֹיִם הַשְׁמִיעוּ
Call .nations against consecrate among a blow the in
her ;nations the trumpet ;land

עָלֶיהָ מַמְלְכוֹת אֲרָרַט מִנִּי וְאַשְׁכְּנָז פִּקְדוּ עָלֶיהָ טִפְסָר
a against appoint and ,Minni ,Ararat king- the against
;marshal her ;Ashkenaz of doms her

28 הַעֲלוּ־סוּס כְּיֶלֶק סָמָר׃ קַדְּשׁוּ עָלֶיהָ גוֹיִם אֶת־מַלְכֵי מָדַי
the the with nations against Consecrate .rough as the to cause
,Medes of kings her locusts horses up come

אֶת־פַּחוֹתֶיהָ וְאֶת־כָּל־סְגָנֶיהָ וְאֵת כָּל־אֶרֶץ מֶמְשַׁלְתּוֹ׃
his the all and her all and her
.dominion of land ,rulers governors

29 וַתִּרְעַשׁ הָאָרֶץ וַתָּחֹל כִּי קָמָה עַל־בָּבֶל מַחְשְׁבוֹת יְהוָה
,Jehovah the Baby- against shall for and the shall And
of purposes lon stand ,writhes land tremble

30 לָשׂוּם אֶת־אֶרֶץ בָּבֶל לְשַׁמָּה מֵאֵין יוֹשֵׁב׃ חָדְלוּ גִבּוֹרֵי
mighty The have a without a Babylon the to
of men stopped .dweller desert of land make

בָבֶל לְהִלָּחֵם יָשְׁבוּ בַּמְּצָדוֹת נָשְׁתָה גְבוּרָתָם הָיוּ לְנָשִׁים
;women they their has ,strong in have they ,fighting Baby-
became ;might withered ,holds dwelt lon

31 הִצִּיתוּ מִשְׁכְּנֹתֶיהָ נִשְׁבְּרוּ בְרִיחֶיהָ׃ רָץ לִקְרַאת־רָץ יָרוּץ
shall a meet to A her are her are
,run runner runner .bars broken ;dwellings burned

וּמַגִּיד לִקְרַאת מַגִּיד לְהַגִּיד לְמֶלֶךְ בָּבֶל כִּי־נִלְכְּדָה עִירוֹ
his is that Babylon the to to a meet to a and
city captured of king announce herald herald

32 מִקָּצֶה׃ וְהַמַּעְבָּרוֹת נִתְפָּשׂוּ וְאֶת־הָאֲגַמִּים שָׂרְפוּ בָאֵשׁ
with have they the and are the that and end from
;fire burned reeds ;seized fords .(end) to

33 וְאַנְשֵׁי הַמִּלְחָמָה נִבְהָלוּ׃ כִּי כֹה אָמַר יְהוָה צְבָאוֹת
hosts Jehovah says thus For are war the and
of .terrified of men

אֱלֹהֵי יִשְׂרָאֵל בַּת־בָּבֶל כְּגֹרֶן עֵת הִדְרִיכָהּ עוֹד מְעַט וּבָאָה
shall and little a Yet thresh to time a as (is) Babylon the :Israel the
come ,while .her ;grain-floor of daughter of God

34 עֵת־הַקָּצִיר לָהּ׃ אֲכָלַנוּ הֲמָמַנוּ נְבוּכַדְרֶאצַּר מֶלֶךְ בָּבֶל
.Babylon king Nebuchadnezzar has devoured Has to the a
of ,us crushed ,us .her harvest of time

הִצִּיגָנוּ כְּלִי רִיק בְּלָעָנוּ כַּתַּנִּין מִלָּא כְרֵשׂוֹ מֵעֲדָנָי הֱדִיחָנוּ׃
cast has he with his has he a like has He an vessel has He
.out me ;delicacies belly filled ;jackal us swallowed .empty us set

me out; [35] the violence done to me and to my flesh (is) on Babylon, the dweller in Zion shall say; and Jerusalem shall say, My blood shall be on the inhabitants of Chaldea. [36] Therefore thus says Jehovah: Behold, I will plead your cause and take vengeance for you; and I will dry up her sea and make her well dry. [37] And Babylon shall become heaps, a home for jackals, a horror and a hissing, without an inhabitant. [38] They shall roar together like lions. They shall growl like lions' cubs. [39] In their heat I will make their feasts, and I will make them drunk so that they rejoice and sleep a never-ending sleep, and never awaken, says Jehovah. [40] I will bring them down like lambs to the slaughter, like rams with he-goats. [41] How Sheshach is captured! And how the praise of the whole earth is seized! How Babylon has become a ruin among the nations! [42] The sea has come up over Babylon; she is covered with the multitude of its waves. [43] Her cities have become a ruin, a dry land and a wilderness, a land in which no man dwells, neither does (any) son of man pass by it. [44] And I will punish Bel in Babylon, and I will bring forth out of his mouth that which he has swallowed up. And the nations shall not flow together any more to him; yea, the wall of Babylon shall fall.

[45] My people, go out of her midst; and each man deliver his soul from the fierce anger of Jehovah. [46] And lest your heart faint and you fear the report that shall be heard in the land; the report shall come in a year, and after that the report shall come in (another) year; and there shall be violence in the land, ruler against ruler.

35 חֲמָסִי וּשְׁאֵרִי עַל־בָּבֶל תֹּאמַר יֹשֶׁבֶת צִיּוֹן וְדָמִי אֶל־יֹשְׁבֵי
resi- (is) my and ;Zion the say shall —Babylon (is) to that My
dents to blood in dweller on flesh my ,wrong

36 כַשְׂדִּים תֹּאמַר יְרוּשָׁלִָם׃ לָכֵן כֹּה אָמַר יְהוָה
,Jehovah says thus Therefore .Jerusalem say shall ,Chaldea's

הִנְנִי־רָב אֶת־רִיבֵךְ וְנִקַּמְתִּי אֶת־נִקְמָתֵךְ וְהַחֲרַבְתִּי אֶת־
will I and ;you for take and your plead ,Behold
up dry vengeance case I

37 יַמָּהּ וְהֹבַשְׁתִּי אֶת־מְקוֹרָהּ׃ וְהָיְתָה בָבֶל ׀ לְגַלִּים ׀ מְעוֹן
haunt a ,heaps Babylon shall And .well her make and her
for become dry sea

38 תַּנִּים שַׁמָּה וּשְׁרֵקָה מֵאֵין יוֹשֵׁב׃ יַחְדָּו כַּכְּפִרִים יִשְׁאָגוּ
shall They like together a without a and horror a ,jackals
;roar lions .dweller ,hissing

39 נָעֲרוּ כְּגוֹרֵי אֲרָיוֹת׃ בְּחֻמָּם אָשִׁית אֶת־מִשְׁתֵּיהֶם
their will I their In .lions' like shall they
.feasts make heat cubs growl

וְהִשְׁכַּרְתִּים לְמַעַן יַעֲלֹזוּ וְיָשְׁנוּ שְׁנַת־עוֹלָם וְלֹא יָקִיצוּ נְאֻם
states ,awaken and never- a and they that so make will I And
not ,ending sleep sleep rejoice drunk them

40 יְהוָה׃ אוֹרִידֵם כְּכָרִים לִטְבוֹחַ כְּאֵילִים עִם־עַתּוּדִים׃
.he-goats with like the for like bring will I .Jehovah
rams ,slaughter lambs down them

41 אֵיךְ נִלְכְּדָה שֵׁשַׁךְ וַתִּתָּפֵשׂ תְּהִלַּת כָּל־הָאָרֶץ אֵיךְ הָיְתָה
has How the all the how And !Sheshach cap- is How
become !earth of praise seized is tured

42 לְשַׁמָּה בָּבֶל בַּגּוֹיִם׃ עָלָה עַל־בָּבֶל הַיָּם בַּהֲמוֹן גַּלָּיו
its the with the Babylon over Has the among Babylon ruin a
waves of host ;sea up come !nations

43 נִכְסָתָה׃ הָיוּ עָרֶיהָ לְשַׁמָּה אֶרֶץ צִיָּה וַעֲרָבָה אֶרֶץ לֹא־
not land a a and ,dry land a ,ruin a Her have is she
,desert cities become .covered

44 יֵשֵׁב בָּהֵן כָּל־אִישׁ וְלֹא־יַעֲבֹר בָּהֵן בֶּן־אָדָם׃ וּפָקַדְתִּי
will I And .man (any) it by does and ;man any in dwells
punish of son pass not which

עַל־בֵּל בְּבָבֶל וְהֹצֵאתִי אֶת־בִּלְעוֹ מִפִּיו וְלֹא־יִנְהֲרוּ אֵלָיו
to shall And his from has he (what) will I and in Bel
him flow not .mouth swallowed out bring ,Babylon

45 עוֹד גּוֹיִם גַּם־חוֹמַת בָּבֶל נָפָלָה׃ צְאוּ מִתּוֹכָהּ עַמִּי וּמַלְּטוּ
and My her of out Go shall Babylon the even the still
deliver ;people ,midst .fall of wall ,nations

46 אִישׁ אֶת־נַפְשׁוֹ מֵחֲרוֹן אַף־יְהוָה׃ וּפֶן־יֵרַךְ לְבַבְכֶם
your faint And .Jehovah anger the from his each
heart lest of burning soul man

וְתִירְאוּ בַּשְּׁמוּעָה הַנִּשְׁמַעַת בָּאָרֶץ וּבָא בַשָּׁנָה הַשְּׁמוּעָה
the a in and the in shall that the you and
,report year come ;land heard be report fear

וְאַחֲרָיו בַּשָּׁנָה הַשְּׁמוּעָה וְחָמָס בָּאָרֶץ מֹשֵׁל עַל־מֹשֵׁל׃
.ruler against ruler the in and the a in after and
,land violence ;report year that

[47] Therefore, behold, the days come that I will punish on the idols of Babylon. And her whole land shall be put to shame, and all her slain shall fall in her midst. [48] Then the heavens and the earth, and all that (is) in them, shall shout for Babylon; for the spoilers shall come to her from the north, says Jehovah. [49] As Babylon is to fall for the slain of Israel, so for Babylon the slain of all the earth shall fall. [50] You who have escaped the sword, go away. Do not stand still. Remember Jehovah afar off, and let Jerusalem come into your heart. [51] We have turned pale because we have heard reproach; dishonor has covered our faces, for foreigners have come into the holy places of Jehovah's house. [52] Therefore, behold, the days are coming, says Jehovah, that I will punish on her idols; and through all her land the wounded shall groan. [53] Though Babylon should mount up to the heavens, and though she should fortify the height of her strength, (yet) spoilers shall come to her from Me, says Jehovah. [54] A sound of a cry (comes) from Babylon, and great ruin from the land of the Chaldeans, [55] because Jehovah is stripping Babylon and will perish the great voice out of her. And her waves will roar like many waters; the noise of their voice is given. [56] Because the ravager is coming on her, on Babylon, and her mighty men will be captured. Every one of their bows is broken, for Jehovah the God of vengeance shall surely repay. [57] And I will make her princes drunk, and her wise ones, her captains, and her rulers, and her mighty men. And they shall sleep a never-ending sleep and not awaken, says the King whose name is Jehovah of hosts. [58] Thus says Jehovah of hosts: The broad

47 לָכֵן הִנֵּה יָמִים בָּאִים וּפָקַדְתִּי עַל־פְּסִילֵי בָבֶל וְכָל־אַרְצָהּ
her And .Babylon the on will I that come the ,behold There-
land all of idols punish days fore

48 תֵּבוֹשׁ וְכָל־חֲלָלֶיהָ יִפְּלוּ בְתוֹכָהּ׃ וְרִנְּנוּ עַל־בָּבֶל שָׁמַיִם
the Babylon over will And her in shall her and be shall
heavens shout .midst fall slain all ,shamed

וָאָרֶץ וְכֹל אֲשֶׁר בָּהֶם כִּי מִצָּפוֹן יָבוֹא־לָהּ הַשּׁוֹדְדִים
the to shall the from for in that and the and
,plunderers her come north ;them (is) all ,earth

49 נְאֻם־יְהוָה׃ גַּם־בָּבֶל לִנְפֹּל חַלְלֵי יִשְׂרָאֵל גַּם־לְבָבֶל
for so ,Israel the (for) to is Babylon As .Jehovah states
Babylon of slain fall

50 נָפְלוּ חַלְלֵי כָל־הָאָרֶץ׃ פְּלֵטִים מֵחֶרֶב הִלְכוּ אַל־תַּעֲמֹדוּ
stand do not go the who You the all the shall
.still ,away ,sword escaped have .earth of slain fall

זִכְרוּ מֵרָחוֹק אֶת־יְהוָה וִירוּשָׁלַםִ תַּעֲלֶה עַל־לְבַבְכֶם׃
your into let and ,Jehovah afar Remember
.heart come Jerusalem off

51 בֹּשְׁנוּ כִּי־שָׁמַעְנוּ חֶרְפָּה כִּסְּתָה כְלִמָּה פָּנֵינוּ כִּי בָּאוּ זָרִים
aliens have for our dishonor has ;reproach have we be- We
come ;faces covered heard cause blush

52 עַל־מִקְדְּשֵׁי בֵּית יְהוָה׃ לָכֵן הִנֵּה־יָמִים בָּאִים נְאֻם־
states are the ,behold Therefore .Jehovah's house holy the into
,coming days of places

53 יְהוָה וּפָקַדְתִּי עַל־פְּסִילֶיהָ וּבְכָל־אַרְצָהּ יֶאֱנֹק חָלָל׃ כִּי־
Though the shall her and ,idols on will I that Jeho-
.wounded groan land all through punish ,vah

תַעֲלֶה בָבֶל הַשָּׁמַיִם וְכִי תְבַצֵּר מְרוֹם עֻזָּהּ מֵאִתִּי יָבֹאוּ
shall from her height should she and the Babylon should
come Me ,strong fortify though ,heavens to ascend

54 שֹׁדְדִים לָהּ נְאֻם־יְהוָה׃ קוֹל זְעָקָה מִבָּבֶל וְשֶׁבֶר גָּדוֹל
great and from cry a A .Jehovah states to spoilers
ruin ,Babylon of sound ,her

55 מֵאֶרֶץ כַּשְׂדִּים׃ כִּי־שֹׁדֵד יְהוָה אֶת־בָּבֶל וְאִבַּד מִמֶּנָּה
from will and Babylon Jehovah is because the the from
her perish stripping ,Chaldeans of land

קוֹל גָּדוֹל וְהָמוּ גַלֵּיהֶם כְּמַיִם רַבִּים נִתַּן שְׁאוֹן קוֹלָם׃
their the is ,many like their will And .great the
.voice of noise given waters waves roar voice

56 כִּי בָא עָלֶיהָ עַל־בָּבֶל שׁוֹדֵד וְנִלְכְּדוּ גִּבּוֹרֶיהָ חִתְּתָה
are mighty her is the ,Babylon on ,her on has Be-
shattered ;men destroying ravager come cause

57 קַשְּׁתוֹתָם כִּי אֵל גְּמֻלוֹת יְהוָה שַׁלֵּם יְשַׁלֵּם׃ וְהִשְׁכַּרְתִּי
will I And will surely ,Jehovah ,vengeance the for their
drunk make .repay of God ,bows

שָׂרֶיהָ וַחֲכָמֶיהָ פַּחוֹתֶיהָ וּסְגָנֶיהָ וְגִבּוֹרֶיהָ וְיָשְׁנוּ שְׁנַת־עוֹלָם
never- a they And her and her and her wise her and her
ending sleep sleep shall .men mighty ,rulers governors ,ones ,princes

58 וְלֹא יָקִיצוּ נְאֻם־הַמֶּלֶךְ יְהוָה צְבָאוֹת שְׁמוֹ׃ כֹּה־
Thus whose hosts Jehovah the states awaken and
.(is) name of ,King not

walls of Babylon shall be utterly laid bare, and her high gates shall be burned with fire; and the peoples shall labor as for vanity; and the peoples as for fire; and they shall be weary.

[59] The word which Jeremiah the prophet commanded Seraiah the son of Neriah, the son of Maaseiah, when he went with Zedekiah the king of Judah into Babylon in the fourth year of his reign. And Seraiah (was) quarter-master. [60] So Jeremiah wrote in a book all the evil that should come on Babylon, all these words that are written against Babylon. [61] And Jeremiah said to Seraiah, When you come to Babylon and shall see and shall read all these words,

אָמַר יְהוָה צְבָאוֹת חֹמוֹת בָּבֶל הָרְחָבָה עַרְעֵר תִּתְעַרְעָר
be shall completely broad Babylon the ;hosts Jehovah says
,bare laid of walls of

וּשְׁעָרֶיהָ הַגְּבֹהִים בָּאֵשׁ יִצַּתּוּ וְיָגְעוּ עַמִּים בְּדֵי־רִיק וּלְאֻמִּים
the and ,vanity as the shall and shall with high her and
peoples for peoples labor ;burned be fire gates

59 בְּדֵי־אֵשׁ וְיָעֵפוּ׃ הַדָּבָר אֲשֶׁר־צִוָּה ׀ יִרְמְיָהוּ הַנָּבִיא
the Jeremiah com- which The they and ,fire as
prophet manded word .weary be shall for

אֶת־שְׂרָיָה בֶן־נֵרִיָּה בֶּן־מַחְסֵיָה בְּלֶכְתּוֹ אֶת־צִדְקִיָּהוּ
Zedekiah with he when ,Maasaiah the Neriah the Seraiah
went of son of son

מֶלֶךְ־יְהוּדָה בָּבֶל בִּשְׁנַת הָרְבִעִית לְמָלְכוֹ וּשְׂרָיָה שַׂר
(was) And his of the year in (into) Judah king
quarter- Seraiah .reign fourth Babylon of

60 מְנוּחָה׃ וַיִּכְתֹּב יִרְמְיָהוּ אֵת כָּל־הָרָעָה אֲשֶׁר־תָּבוֹא אֶל־
to should that the all Jeremiah So .master
come evil wrote

בָּבֶל אֶל־סֵפֶר אֶחָד אֵת כָּל־הַדְּבָרִים הָאֵלֶּה הַכְּתֻבִים
are that these words all ;one book in Baby-
written lon

61 אֶל־בָּבֶל׃ וַיֹּאמֶר יִרְמְיָהוּ אֶל־שְׂרָיָה כְּבֹאֲךָ בָבֶל וְרָאִיתָ
shall and Baby- you When ,Seraiah to Jeremiah said And Baby- against
see to come .lon

[62] then you shall say, O Jehovah, You have spoken against this place to cut it off, so that shall not be in it a dweller, from man to animal, but it shall be a ruin forever. [63] And it shall be, when you have finished reading this book, you shall tie a stone to it and throw it into the middle of the Euphrates. [64] And you shall say, In this way shall Babylon sink, and shall not rise from the evil that I am bringing on her. And they shall be weary. Thus far are the words of Jeremiah.

62 וְקָרָאתָ אֵת כָּל־הַדְּבָרִים הָאֵלֶּה׃ וְאָמַרְתָּ יְהוָה אַתָּה
You O you then ,these words all shall and
,Jehovah ,say shall read

דִבַּרְתָּ אֶל־הַמָּקוֹם הַזֶּה לְהַכְרִיתוֹ לְבִלְתִּי הֱיוֹת־בּוֹ יוֹשֵׁב
a it in shall that so cut to ,this place about have
,dweller be not ,off it spoken

63 לְמֵאָדָם וְעַד־בְּהֵמָה כִּי־שִׁמְמוֹת עוֹלָם תִּהְיֶה׃ וְהָיָה
it And shall it forever ruin a but ,beast to even from
be will .be man

כְּכַלֹּתְךָ לִקְרֹא אֶת־הַסֵּפֶר הַזֶּה תִּקְשֹׁר עָלָיו אֶבֶן
a it to shall you ,this book reading you when
stone tie finish

64 וְהִשְׁלַכְתּוֹ אֶל־תּוֹךְ פְּרָת׃ וְאָמַרְתָּ כָּכָה תִּשְׁקַע בָּבֶל וְלֹא־
and ,Babylon shall this In you And the the into throw and
not sink way ,say shall .Euphrates of middle it

תָקוּם מִפְּנֵי הָרָעָה אֲשֶׁר אָנֹכִי מֵבִיא עָלֶיהָ וְיָעֵפוּ עַד־הֵנָּה
far thus they And .it on am I that the from shall
(are) .weary be shall bringing evil rise

דִּבְרֵי יִרְמְיָהוּ׃
.Jeremiah the
of words

CAP. LII נב

CHAPTER 52

CHAPTER 52

[1] Zedekiah (was) twenty-one years old when he began to reign, and he

1 בֶּן־עֶשְׂרִים וְאַחַת שָׁנָה צִדְקִיָּהוּ בְּמָלְכוֹ וְאַחַת עֶשְׂרֵה
and he when ,Zedekiah ,years one twenty A
eleven ,king became of son

reigned eleven years in Jerusalem. And his mother's name was Hamutal the daughter of Jeremiah of Libnah. [2] And he did evil in the eyes of Jehovah according to all that Jehoiakim had done. [3] For because of the anger of Jehovah it was in Jerusalem and Judah — until He had cast them out from His face — that Zedekiah rebelled against the king of Babylon.

[4] And in the ninth year of his reign, in the tenth month, in the tenth (day) of the month, Nebuchadnezzar king of Babylon came, he and all his army, against Jerusalem, and pitched against it and built a siege-wall against it all around. [5] So the city came under attack until the eleventh year of King Zedekiah. [6] And in the fourth month, in the ninth of the month, the famine was severe in the city, so that there was no food for the people of the land. [7] Then the city was breached, and all the men of war fled and went out of the city by night by the way of the gate between the two walls, which was by the king's garden — now the Chaldeans lay all around the city — and they went by the way of the Arabah.

[8] But the army of the Chaldeans pursued after the king and overtook Zedekiah in the Arabah of Jericho. And all his army was scattered from him. [9] Then they took the king and carried him up to the king of Babylon, to Riblah in the land of Hamath, where he gave judgments against him [10] And the king of Babylon killed the sons of Zedekiah before his eyes. He also killed all the leaders of Judah in Riblah. [11] Then

שָׁנָה מָלַךְ בִּירוּשָׁלִָם וְשֵׁם אִמּוֹ חֲמִיטַל בַּת־יִרְמְיָהוּ
Jeremiah the Hamutal his name And in he years
of daughter (was) mother's .Jerusalem reigned

2 מִלִּבְנָה׃ וַיַּעַשׂ הָרַע בְּעֵינֵי יְהוָה כְּכֹל אֲשֶׁר־עָשָׂה יְהוֹיָקִים׃
.Jehoiakim had that accord- Jehovah the in evil he And of
done all to ing of eyes did .Libnah

3 כִּי ׀ עַל־אַף יְהוָה הָיְתָה בִּירוּשָׁלִַם וִיהוּדָה עַד־הִשְׁלִיכוֹ
had He until and in was it ,Jehovah's anger be- For
cast —Judah Jerusalem of cause

4 אוֹתָם מֵעַל פָּנָיו וַיִּמְרֹד צִדְקִיָּהוּ בְּמֶלֶךְ בָּבֶל׃ וַיְהִי
it And .Babylon against Zedekiah And His of out them
was of king the rebelled .presence

בַּשָּׁנָה הַתְּשִׁעִית לְמָלְכוֹ בַּחֹדֶשׁ הָעֲשִׂירִי בֶּעָשׂוֹר לַחֹדֶשׁ
the of the in ,tenth the in his of ninth the in
,month (day) tenth month ,reign year

בָּא נְבוּכַדְרֶאצַּר מֶלֶךְ־בָּבֶל הוּא וְכָל־חֵילוֹ עַל־יְרוּשָׁלִַם
.Jerusalem against his and he ,Babylon king Nebuchadnezzar .came
,army all of

5 וַיַּחֲנוּ עָלֶיהָ וַיִּבְנוּ עָלֶיהָ דָּיֵק סָבִיב׃ וַתָּבֹא הָעִיר בַּמָּצוֹר
under city the So all siege- a against and against and
attack came .around wall it built ,it pitched

6 עַד עַשְׁתֵּי־עֶשְׂרֵה שָׁנָה לַמֶּלֶךְ צִדְקִיָּהוּ׃ בַּחֹדֶשׁ הָרְבִיעִי
,fourth in And .Zedekiah King of year the until
month the eleventh

בְּתִשְׁעָה לַחֹדֶשׁ וַיֶּחֱזַק הָרָעָב בָּעִיר וְלֹא־הָיָה לֶחֶם לְעַם
the for food there and the in the was the of the in
of people was not ,city famine severe ,month ninth

7 הָאָרֶץ׃ וַתִּבָּקַע הָעִיר וְכָל־אַנְשֵׁי הַמִּלְחָמָה יִבְרְחוּ וַיֵּצְאוּ
and fled war the men and the was Then the
out went of all ,city breached .land

מֵהָעִיר לַיְלָה דֶּרֶךְ שַׁעַר בֵּין־הַחֹמֹתַיִם אֲשֶׁר עַל־גַּן הַמֶּלֶךְ
the garden by which two the between the the by by the of
.king's (was) ,walls gate of way night city

8 וְכַשְׂדִּים עַל־הָעִיר סָבִיב וַיֵּלְכוּ דֶּרֶךְ הָעֲרָבָה׃ וַיִּרְדְּפוּ
But the the by they and all the around the Now
pursued .Arabah of way went ,around city (lay) Chaldeans

חֵיל־כַּשְׂדִּים אַחֲרֵי הַמֶּלֶךְ וַיַּשִּׂיגוּ אֶת־צִדְקִיָּהוּ בְּעַרְבֹת
the in Zedekiah and king the after the the
of Arabah overtook Chaldeans of army

9 יְרֵחוֹ וְכָל־חֵילוֹ נָפֹצוּ מֵעָלָיו׃ וַיִּתְפְּשׂוּ אֶת־הַמֶּלֶךְ וַיַּעֲלוּ
and the they Then from was his And .Jericho
bore king seized .him scattered army all

אֹתוֹ אֶל־מֶלֶךְ בָּבֶל רִבְלָתָה בְּאֶרֶץ חֲמָת וַיְדַבֵּר אִתּוֹ
against he where ,Hamath the in to ,Babylon the to him
him spoke of land Riblah of king

10 מִשְׁפָּטִים׃ וַיִּשְׁחַט מֶלֶךְ־בָּבֶל אֶת־בְּנֵי צִדְקִיָּהוּ לְעֵינָיו וְגַם
And before Zedekiah the Babylon the slew And .judgments
also .eyes his of sons of king

11 אֶת־כָּל־שָׂרֵי יְהוּדָה שָׁחַט בְּרִבְלָתָה׃ וְאֶת־עֵינֵי צִדְקִיָּהוּ
Zedekiah the Then .Riblah in slew he Judah the all
of eyes of rulers

he put out the eyes of Zedekiah. And the king of Babylon bound him in bronze fetters and carried him to Babylon. And he put him in prison till the day of his death.

[12] Now in the fifth month, in the tenth of the month, which (was) the nineteenth year of Nebuchadnezzar king of Babylon, Nebuzar-adan, captain of the guard, who stood before the king of Babylon, came into Jerusalem. [13] And (he) burned the house of Jehovah, and the king's house. And he burned with fire all the houses of Jerusalem, and all the houses of the great ones. [14] And all the army of the Chaldeans who (were) with the captain of the guard broke down all the walls of Jereusalem all around. [15] Then Nebuzar-adan the captain of the guard exiled (some) of the poor of the people, and the rest of the people who remained in the city, and those who fell away, who fell to the king of Babylon, and the rest of the multitude. [16] But Nebuzar-adan the captain of the guard left (some) of the poor of the land for vinedressers and for farmers. [17] Also the Chaldeans broke the pillars of bronze that (were) in the house of Jehovah, and the bases, and the bronze sea that (was) in Jehovah's house, and carried all the bronze from them to Babylon. [18] They also took away the pots, and the shovels, and the snuffers, and the bowls, and the spoons, and all the vessels of bronze with which they served. [19] And the captain of the guard took away the basins, and the firepans, and the bowls, and the pots, and the lampstands, and the spoons,

עִוֵּר וַיַּאַסְרֵהוּ בַנְחֻשְׁתַּיִם וַיְבִאֵהוּ מֶלֶךְ־בָּבֶל בָּבֶלָה
to Babylon the carried and bronze with bound And put he
.Babylon of king him fetters him .out

12 וַיִּתְּנֵהוּ בְבֵית־הַפְּקֻדֹּת עַד־יוֹם מוֹתוֹ׃ וּבַחֹדֶשׁ הַחֲמִישִׁי
,fifth in And his the till prison a in he And
month the .death of day of house him put

בֶּעָשׂוֹר לַחֹדֶשׁ הִיא שְׁנַת תְּשַׁע־עֶשְׂרֵה שָׁנָה לַמֶּלֶךְ
King of year nineteenth the which the of the in
year (was) ,month tenth

נְבוּכַדְרֶאצַּר מֶלֶךְ־בָּבֶל בָּא נְבוּזַרְאֲדָן רַב־טַבָּחִים עָמַד
who the captain Nebuzar- came ,Babylon king Nebuchadnezzar
stood guard of adan of

13 לִפְנֵי מֶלֶךְ־בָּבֶל בִּירוּשָׁלָםִ׃ וַיִּשְׂרֹף אֶת־בֵּית־יְהוָה וְאֶת־
and ,Jehovah the he And into Babylon the before
of house burned .Jerusalem of king

בֵּית הַמֶּלֶךְ וְאֵת כָּל־בָּתֵּי יְרוּשָׁלַםִ וְאֶת־כָּל־בֵּית הַגָּדוֹל
great the the all and Jerusalem the all And the house
ones of houses of houses .king's

14 שָׂרַף בָּאֵשׁ׃ וְאֶת־כָּל־חֹמוֹת יְרוּשָׁלַםִ סָבִיב נִתְּצוּ כָּל־חֵיל
the all broke all Jerusalem the all And with he
of army down around of walls .fire burned

15 כַּשְׂדִּים אֲשֶׁר אֶת־רַב־טַבָּחִים׃ וּמִדַּלּוֹת הָעָם וְאֶת־יֶתֶר
the and the the of And the the with who the
of rest people of poor .guard of captain (were) Chaldeans

הָעָם | הַנִּשְׁאָרִים בָּעִיר וְאֶת־הַנֹּפְלִים אֲשֶׁר נָפְלוּ אֶל־מֶלֶךְ
the to fell who who those and the in who the
of king ,away fell ,city remained people

בָּבֶל וְאֵת יֶתֶר הָאָמוֹן הֶגְלָה נְבוּזַרְאֲדָן רַב־טַבָּחִים׃
the the Nebuzar-adan exiled the rest the and ;Babylon
.guard of captain multitude of

16 וּמִדַּלּוֹת הָאָרֶץ הִשְׁאִיר נְבוּזַרְאֲדָן רַב־טַבָּחִים לְכֹרְמִים
for the cap- the Nebuzar-adan left the the of But
vinedressers guard of tain land of poor

וּלְיֹגְבִים׃ וְאֶת־עַמּוּדֵי הַנְּחֹשֶׁת אֲשֶׁר לְבֵית־יְהוָה וְאֶת־
and ,Jehovah the in that bronze the Also for and
of house (were) of pillars .farmers

17 הַמְּכֹנוֹת וְאֶת־יָם הַנְּחֹשֶׁת אֲשֶׁר בְּבֵית־יְהוָה שִׁבְּרוּ כַשְׂדִּים
the broke ,Jehovah's in that the sea and the
,Chaldeans house (were) bronze ,stands

וַיִּשְׂאוּ אֶת־כָּל־נְחֻשְׁתָּם בָּבֶלָה׃ וְאֶת־הַסִּרוֹת וְאֶת־הַיָּעִים
the and the Also to their all and
,shovels pots .Babylon bronze carried

18 וְאֶת־הַמְזַמְּרוֹת וְאֶת־הַמִּזְרָקֹת וְאֶת־הַכַּפּוֹת וְאֵת כָּל־כְּלֵי
vessels all and the and the and the and
of ,spoons ,bowls ,snuffers

הַנְּחֹשֶׁת אֲשֶׁר־יְשָׁרְתוּ בָהֶם לָקָחוּ׃ וְאֶת־הַסִּפִּים וְאֶת־
and the And they with they which bronze
,basins .took ,them served

19 הַמַּחְתּוֹת וְאֶת־הַמִּזְרָקוֹת וְאֶת־הַסִּירוֹת וְאֶת־הַמְּנֹרוֹת וְאֶת־
and the and the and the and the
,lampstands ,pots ,bowls ;firepans

and the cups; the golden ones (in) gold and the silver ones (in) silver; [20] the two pillars, one sea, and twelve bronze bulls that (were) under the bases, which King Solomon had made in the house of Jehovah; the weight of the bronze of all these vessels was not (known). [21] And the pillars, the height of one pillar (was) eighteen cubits. And a line of twelve cubits went around it, and its thickness (was) four fingers. (It was) hollow. [22] And a capital of bronze (was) on it. And the height of one capital (was) five cubits, with network and pomegranates on the capitals all around, all of bronze. And like these (was) the second pillar, and the pomegranates. [23] And there were ninety-six pomegranates on a side; all the pomegranates on the network (were) a hundred all around.

[24] And the captain of the guard took Seraiah the chief priest, and Zephaniah the second priest, and the three doorkeepers. [25] He also took out of the city one eunuch who was in charge of the men of war; and seven men who saw the king's face, who were found in the city; and the scribe of the commander of the army, who mustered the people of the land; and sixty men of the people of the land who were found in the middle of the city. [26] And Nebuzar-adan the captain of the guard took them and brought them to the king of Babylon to Riblah. [27] And the king of Babylon struck

הַכַּפּוֹת וְאֶת־הַמְּנַקִּיּוֹת אֲשֶׁר זָהָב זָהָב וַאֲשֶׁר־כֶּסֶף כָּסֶף
(in) silver and (in) gold what the and the
;silver (was) what ;gold (was) ;cups ,spoons

20 לָקַח רַב טַבָּחִים׃ הָעַמּוּדִים ׀ שְׁנַיִם הַיָּם אֶחָד וְהַבָּקָר
and ,one sea ,two pillars the the cap- the took
bulls ;guard of tain away

שְׁנֵים־עָשָׂר נְחֹשֶׁת אֲשֶׁר־תַּחַת הַמְּכֹנוֹת אֲשֶׁר עָשָׂה הַמֶּלֶךְ
King the had which the under that bronze twelve
made ,stands (were)

שְׁלֹמֹה לְבֵית יְהוָה לֹא־הָיָה מִשְׁקָל לִנְחֻשְׁתָּם כָּל־הַכֵּלִים
vessels all bronze the the was not ;Jehovah the for Solomon
of of weight (known) of house

21 הָאֵלֶּה׃ וְהָעַמּוּדִים שְׁמֹנֶה עֶשְׂרֵה אַמָּה קוֹמָה הָעַמֻּד
the the (was) cubits eighteen (to as) And .these
pillar of height ,pillars the

הָאֶחָד וְחוּט שְׁתֵּים־עֶשְׂרֵה אַמָּה יְסֻבֶּנּוּ וְעָבְיוֹ אַרְבַּע
four its and went cubits twelve a And .one
thickness ,it around of line

22 אֶצְבָּעוֹת נָבוּב׃ וְכֹתֶרֶת עָלָיו נְחֹשֶׁת וְקוֹמַת הַכֹּתֶרֶת
capital the And (of) (was) a And (was it) ;fingers
of height .bronze it on capital .hollow

הָאַחַת חָמֵשׁ אַמּוֹת וּשְׂבָכָה וְרִמּוֹנִים עַל־הַכּוֹתֶרֶת סָבִיב
all the on pome- and with ,cubits (was) one
;around capital granates network five

23 הַכֹּל נְחֹשֶׁת וְכָאֵלֶּה לָעַמּוּד הַשֵּׁנִי וְרִמּוֹנִים׃ וַיִּהְיוּ הָרִמֹּנִים
pome- there And the and second the (was) And .bronze of all
granates were .pomegranates pillar these like

תִּשְׁעִים וְשִׁשָּׁה רוּחָה כָּל־הָרִמּוֹנִים מֵאָה עַל־הַשְּׂבָכָה
the on a (were) the all a on six ninety-
network hundred pomegranates ,side

24 סָבִיב׃ וַיִּקַּח רַב־טַבָּחִים אֶת־שְׂרָיָה כֹּהֵן הָרֹאשׁ וְאֶת־
and the priest Seraiah the cap- the And all
,chief guard of tain took .around

25 צְפַנְיָה כֹּהֵן הַמִּשְׁנֶה וְאֶת־שְׁלֹשֶׁת שֹׁמְרֵי הַסַּף׃ וּמִן־הָעִיר
the Also the keepers three and the priest Zepha-
city of out .door of ,second niah

לָקַח סָרִיס אֶחָד אֲשֶׁר־הָיָה פָקִיד ׀ עַל־אַנְשֵׁי הַמִּלְחָמָה
;war the men of in was who one eunuch he
of charge took

וְשִׁבְעָה אֲנָשִׁים מֵרֹאֵי פְנֵי־הַמֶּלֶךְ אֲשֶׁר־נִמְצְאוּ בָעִיר וְאֵת
and the in were who the the who men and
;city found ,king of face saw seven

סֹפֵר שַׂר הַצָּבָא הַמַּצְבִּא אֶת־עַם הָאָרֶץ וְשִׁשִּׁים אִישׁ
men and the the who the the scribe
sixty ;land of people mustered ,army of chief of

26 מֵעַם הָאָרֶץ הַנִּמְצְאִים בְּתוֹךְ הָעִיר׃ וַיִּקַּח אוֹתָם נְבוּזַרְאֲדָן
Nebuzar adan them And the the in were who the the of
took .city of middle found land of people

27 רַב־טַבָּחִים וַיֹּלֶךְ אוֹתָם אֶל־מֶלֶךְ בָּבֶל רִבְלָתָה׃ וַיַּכֶּה
And .Riblah to Babylon the to them and the the
struck of king brought ,guard of chief

them and slew them in Riblah in the land of Hamath; and Judah was exiled from off his land.

[28] This is the people whom Nebuchadnezzar exiled: in the seventh year, three thousand and twenty-three Jews; [29] in the eighteenth year of Nebuchadnezzar, eight hundred thirty-two souls; [30] in the twenty-third year of Nebhucadnezzar Nebuzar-adam the chief executioner exiled seven hundred forty-five souls of the Jews; all the souls (were) four thousand and six hundred.

[31] And it was, in the thirty-seventh year of the exile of Jehoichim king of Judah, in the twelfth month, in the twenty-fifth of the month, Evil-Merodach king of Babylon in the year of his reign lifted up the head of Jehoichin king of Judah, and brought him from the prison-house. [31] And he spoke kindly to him and set his throne above the throne of the kings who (were) with him in Babylon. [33] And he changed his prison garments, and he ate bread before his face continually all the days of his life. [34] And his allowance in continual allowance was given to him from the king of Babylon, the matter of a day in its day, until the day of his death, all the days of his life.

אֹתָם מֶלֶךְ בָּבֶל וַיְמִתֵם בְּרִבְלָה בְּאֶרֶץ חֲמָת וַיִּגֶל יְהוּדָה

Judah was exiled and Ha-math of land the in Riblah in slew them and Babylon the of king them

28 מֵעַל אַדְמָתוֹ׃ זֶה הָעָם אֲשֶׁר הֶגְלָה נְבוּכַדְרֶאצַּר בִּשְׁנַת־

the in year :Nebuchadnezzar exiled whom the people This (is) his .land from off

29 שֶׁבַע יְהוּדִים שְׁלֹשֶׁת אֲלָפִים וְעֶשְׂרִים וּשְׁלֹשָׁה׃ בִּשְׁנַת

the in year ;three and twenty- thousand three Jews ,seventh

שְׁמוֹנֶה עֶשְׂרֵה לִנְבוּכַדְרֶאצַּר מִירוּשָׁלִַם נֶפֶשׁ שְׁמֹנֶה מֵאוֹת

hundred eight souls from Jerusalem of Nebuchadnezzar teenth eigh-

30 שְׁלֹשִׁים וּשְׁנָיִם׃ בִּשְׁנַת שָׁלֹשׁ וְעֶשְׂרִים לִנְבוּכַדְרֶאצַּר

of Nebuchadnezzar and twentieth three the in year ;two thirty-

הֶגְלָה נְבוּזַרְאֲדָן רַב־טַבָּחִים יְהוּדִים נֶפֶשׁ שֶׁבַע מֵאוֹת

hundred seven souls the Jews chief the executioner Nebuzar- adan exiled

אַרְבָּעִים וַחֲמִשָּׁה כָּל־נֶפֶשׁ אַרְבַּעַת אֲלָפִים וְשֵׁשׁ מֵאוֹת׃

.hundred and six thousand four souls (were) all the ;five forty-

31 וַיְהִי בִשְׁלֹשִׁים וְשֶׁבַע שָׁנָה לְגָלוּת יְהוֹיָכִן מֶלֶךְ־

king Jehoichim the of of exile year seventh the in thirty- And ,was it

יְהוּדָה בִּשְׁנֵים עָשָׂר חֹדֶשׁ בְּעֶשְׂרִים וַחֲמִשָּׁה לַחֹדֶשׁ נָשָׂא

lifted up the of month fifth the in twenty- ,month the in twelfth of Judah

אֱוִיל מְרֹדַךְ מֶלֶךְ בָּבֶל בִּשְׁנַת מַלְכֻתוֹ אֶת־רֹאשׁ יְהוֹיָכִין

Jehoiachin head the of his of reign the in year Babylon king of Merodach Evil-

32 מֶלֶךְ־יְהוּדָה וַיֹּצֵא אֹתוֹ מִבֵּית הַכְּלִיא׃ וַיְדַבֵּר אִתּוֹ טֹבוֹת

kindly to him he And spoke .prison- the from house him and brought Judah king of

וַיִּתֵּן אֶת־כִּסְאוֹ מִמַּעַל לְכִסֵּא מְלָכִים אֲשֶׁר אִתּוֹ בְּבָבֶל׃

in .Babylon with him who (were) the of kings the throne above his throne and set

33 וְשִׁנָּה אֵת בִּגְדֵי כִלְאוֹ וְאָכַל לֶחֶם לְפָנָיו תָּמִיד כָּל־יְמֵי

the days all continually before face his bread he and ate prison gar-his ments he And changed

34 חַיָּו׃ וַאֲרֻחָתוֹ אֲרֻחַת תָּמִיד נִתְּנָה־לּוֹ מֵאֵת מֶלֶךְ־בָּבֶל

of Babylon the king from to him was given continual an allowance his And allowance his of .life

דְּבַר־יוֹם בְּיוֹמוֹ עַד־יוֹם מוֹתוֹ כֹּל יְמֵי חַיָּיו׃

his of .life the days all his of death the until day its in day day a the of matter

איכה

LIBER THRENORUM

CAPUT. I א

CHAPTER 1

[1] How alone sits the city. (that was) full of people! Like a widow she has become, (one) great among the nations; a noblewoman among the provinces, has become a tribute-payer. [2] She bitterly weeps in the night, and her tears (are) on her cheeks; among all her lovers, she has no comforter. All her friends dealt deceitfully with her; they became to her enemies. [3] Judah has went captive from affliction and from great slavery. She dwells among the nations; she finds no rest; all her pursuers have overtaken her between the straits. [4] The roads of Zion (are) in mourning without (any) going to the appointed (feasts). All her gates are deserted; her priests sigh; her virgins are afflicted, and she (is in) bitterness. [5] Her foes have become chief; her enemies are at ease; for Jehovah has afflicted her for the multitude of her trespasses. Her children have gone (as) captive before the foe. [6] And from the daughter of Zion all her splendor has departed; her princes have become like bucks; they find no pasture, and they have gone without strength before the pursuer. [7] Jerusalem remembers all her desirable things which were (in) the days of old. (in) the days of her affliction and of her wanderings, when her people fell into the hand of the foe and was not (any) ally to her. The adversaries saw her; they laughed at her cessations. [8] Jerusalem has grievously sinned; therefore she has become defiled;

CHAPTER 1

1 אֵיכָה ׀ יָשְׁבָה בָדָד הָעִיר רַבָּתִי עָם הָיְתָה כְּאַלְמָנָה

a like has She !people full the alone sits How
;widow become of city

2 רַבָּתִי בַגּוֹיִם שָׂרָתִי בַּמְּדִינוֹת הָיְתָה לָמַס׃ בָּכוֹ תִבְכֶּה

she bitterly tribute a has the among noble- a the among (one)
weeps ;payer become ,provinces woman nations great

בַּלַּיְלָה וְדִמְעָתָהּ עַל לֶחֱיָהּ אֵין־לָהּ מְנַחֵם מִכָּל־אֹהֲבֶיהָ

her of out com- a to not her (are) her and the in
;lovers all forter her is ;cheeks on tears ,night

3 כָּל־רֵעֶיהָ בָּגְדוּ בָהּ הָיוּ לָהּ לְאֹיְבִים׃ גָּלְתָה יְהוּדָה מֵעֹנִי

from Judah went .haters to they with dealt her all
affliction captive her became ;her deceit in friends

וּמֵרֹב עֲבֹדָה הִיא יָשְׁבָה בַגּוֹיִם לֹא מָצְאָה מָנוֹחַ כָּל־

all ;rest she not the among dwells she ;slavery from and
finds ,nations great

4 רֹדְפֶיהָ הִשִּׂיגוּהָ בֵּין הַמְּצָרִים׃ דַּרְכֵי צִיּוֹן אֲבֵלוֹת מִבְּלִי

with- in (are) Zion The .straits the be- over- have pur- her
out mourning of roads tween her taken suers

בָּאֵי מוֹעֵד כָּל־שְׁעָרֶיהָ שׁוֹמֵמִין כֹּהֲנֶיהָ נֶאֱנָחִים בְּתוּלֹתֶיהָ

her are her (are) her all set (any)
virgins ;groaning priests ;desolate gates ;(feasts) to going

5 נּוּגוֹת וְהִיא מַר־לָהּ׃ הָיוּ צָרֶיהָ לְרֹאשׁ אֹיְבֶיהָ שָׁלוּ כִּי־

for are her ;chief as Her have (in is) and (are)
,ease at haters foes become .bitterness she ,afflicted

יְהוָה הוֹגָהּ עַל־רֹב פְּשָׁעֶיהָ עוֹלָלֶיהָ הָלְכוּ שְׁבִי לִפְנֵי־צָר׃

the before captive have her tres- her the for has Jehovah
.foe gone children ;passes of many her afflicted

6 וַיֵּצֵא מִן־בַּת־צִיּוֹן כָּל־הֲדָרָהּ הָיוּ שָׂרֶיהָ כְּאַיָּלִים לֹא־מָצְאוּ

they not like her have her all Zion the from has And
find ;bucks rulers become ,splendor of daughter out gone

7 מִרְעֶה וַיֵּלְכוּ בְלֹא־כֹחַ לִפְנֵי רוֹדֵף׃ זָכְרָה יְרוּשָׁלִַם יְמֵי

(in) Jerusalem remem- the before strength with- and ,pasture
of days bers ,pursuer out go they

עָנְיָהּ וּמְרוּדֶיהָ כֹּל מַחֲמֻדֶיהָ אֲשֶׁר הָיוּ מִימֵי קֶדֶם בִּנְפֹל

the in previous from were which desirable her all her and af- her
of falling days things ,wanderings fliction

עַמָּהּ בְּיַד־צָר וְאֵין עוֹזֵר לָהּ רָאוּהָ צָרִים שָׂחֲקוּ עַל־

at .they ;foes the saw for (any) is and foes's into her
laughed her her ally not ;hand the people

8 מִשְׁבַּתֶּהָ׃ חֵטְא חָטְאָה יְרוּשָׁלִַם עַל־כֵּן לְנִידָה הָיָתָה כָּל־

all has one as therefore ,Jerusalem has utterly her
;become defiled sinned .cessations

ones who honored her despised her because they have seen her nakedness; yea, she sighs and turns backward. [9] Her uncleanness (is) in her skirts; she did not remember her end, and has gone down astoundingly; she had no comforter. O Jehovah, behold my affliction, for the enemy has magnified (himself). [10] The enemy has spread out his hand on all her desirable things; indeed she has seen the nations enter into her holy place, whom You commanded (that) they not enter into Your congregation. [11] All her people sigh, from seeking bread. They gave their desirable things for food to revive the soul. See, O Jehovah, and look on (me), for I have become vile.

[12] (Is it) nothing to you, all you who pass by? Behold and see if there is any sorrow like my sorrow, which is done to me, with which Jehovah has afflicted (me) in the day of His burning anger. [13] From on high He has sent fire into my bones, and subdued it. He spread a net for my feet; He has turned me back; He gave me desolation; all the days (I) faint. [14] The yoke of my transgressions is bound by His hand; they intertwine; they rise on my neck. He caused my strength to falter; the Lord gave me into (their) hands; I am not able to rise up. [15] The Lord has trampled all my mighty ones in my midst; He called a gathering against me to crush my young men. (As) a winepress, the Lord trod the virgin daughter of Judah. [16] For these (things) I weep; my eye, my eye runs down (with) water, because far from me is a comforter reviving my soul. My sons are desolate because the enemy prevails. [17] Zion spreads forth her hands, there is not (one) comforting to her; Jehovah has commanded concerning Jacob (that) his enemies

מִכְּבָדֶיהָ הִזִּילוּהָ כִּי־רָאוּ עֶרְוָתָהּ גַּם־הִיא נֶאֶנְחָה וַתָּשָׁב
turns and groans she also her they for despise knowing ones
;nakedness saw ,her her

9 אָחוֹר: טֻמְאָתָהּ בְּשׁוּלֶיהָ לֹא זָכְרָה אַחֲרִיתָהּ וַתֵּרֶד
has and ,end her did she not her in (is) un- Her .backward
down gone remember ;skirts cleanness

פְּלָאִים אֵין מְנַחֵם לָהּ רְאֵה יְהוָה אֶת־עָנְיִי כִּי הִגְדִּיל אוֹיֵב:
the magnified for my O ,See for comforter is astound-
.hater affliction Jehovah .her no ;ingly

10 יָדוֹ פָּרַשׂ צָר עַל כָּל־מַחֲמַדֶּיהָ כִּי־רָאֲתָה גוֹיִם בָּאוּ מִקְדָּשָׁהּ
holy her enter the has she in- desirable her all on The spread his
,place nations seen deed ;things foe out hand

11 אֲשֶׁר צִוִּיתָה לֹא־יָבֹאוּ בַקָּהָל לָךְ: כָּל־עַמָּהּ נֶאֱנָחִים
,groan her All of the in they not You which
people .You assembly enter commanded

מְבַקְשִׁים לֶחֶם נָתְנוּ מַחֲמַדֵּיהֶם בְּאֹכֶל לְהָשִׁיב נָפֶשׁ
the for for desirable their they bread seeking from
.soul reviving food things gave

12 רְאֵה יְהוָה וְהַבִּיטָה כִּי הָיִיתִי זוֹלֵלָה: לוֹא אֲלֵיכֶם כָּל־
all ,you to (it Is) .vile have I for ,look and O ,See
nothing become Jehovah

עֹבְרֵי דֶרֶךְ הַבִּיטוּ וּרְאוּ אִם־יֵשׁ מַכְאוֹב כְּמַכְאֹבִי אֲשֶׁר
which my like sorrow there if and Look the passing
,sorrow is see ?way by

13 עוֹלַל לִי אֲשֶׁר הוֹגָה יְהוָה בְּיוֹם חֲרוֹן אַפּוֹ: מִמָּרוֹם
on From His burning the in Jehovah has which to is
high .anger of day afflicted ,me done

שָׁלַח־אֵשׁ בְּעַצְמֹתַי וַיִּרְדֶּנָּה פָּרַשׂ רֶשֶׁת לְרַגְלַי הֱשִׁיבַנִי
has He my for net a He subdued and my into fire He
me turned ,feet spread ;it ,bones sent

14 אָחוֹר נְתָנַנִי שֹׁמֵמָה כָּל־הַיּוֹם דָּוָה: נִשְׂקַד עַל פְּשָׁעַי
tres- my The is .faint the all ,desolation He ,back
passes of yoke bound days me gave

בְּיָדוֹ יִשְׂתָּרְגוּ עָלוּ עַל־צַוָּארִי הִכְשִׁיל כֹּחִי נְתָנַנִי אֲדֹנָי
the gave my made He my on they inter- they His by
Lord me strength falter ,neck rise ;twine ;hand

15 בִּידֵי לֹא־אוּכַל קוּם: סִלָּה כָל־אַבִּירַי אֲדֹנָי בְּקִרְבִּי קָרָא
He my in the mighty my all Has .rise to am I not into
called ;midst Lord ones trampled able ;hands

עָלַי מוֹעֵד לִשְׁבֹּר בַּחוּרָי גַּת דָּרַךְ אֲדֹנָי לִבְתוּלַת בַּת־
daughter the the trod a (as) my crush to meet-a against
of virgin Lord ;winepress ;men young ing me

16 יְהוּדָה: עַל־אֵלֶּה אֲנִי בוֹכִיָּה עֵינִי עֵינִי יֹרְדָה מַּיִם כִּי־
for (with) runs my my ;weep I these On .Judah
water down eye ,eye of account

רָחַק מִמֶּנִּי מְנַחֵם מֵשִׁיב נַפְשִׁי הָיוּ בָנַי שׁוֹמֵמִים כִּי נָבָר
pre- for ,desolated my are my reviving a from is
vails sons ;soul comforter me far

17 פֵּרְשָׂה צִיּוֹן בְּיָדֶיהָ אֵין מְנַחֵם לָהּ צִוָּה יְהוָה לְיַעֲקֹב
about Jehovah or- to com- (one) is her Zion spreads the
Jacob dered ;me forting not hands .hater

(should be) all around him; Jersalem has become among them as an impure thing.

[18] Jehovah is righteous, for I have rebelled against His commandment. I beseech you, all people, hear and behold my sorrow. My virgins and my young men have gone into captivity. [19] I called for my lovers; (but) they deceived me; my priests and my elders expired in the city while they sought food for them to bring back their life. [20] Behold, O Jehovah, for I am distressed; my inward parts ferment; my heart is overturned within me, for I have grievously rebelled. On the outside the sword bereaves; in the house (it is) as death. [21] They hear that I sigh; (there is) not a comforter to me. All my enemies have heard my evil; they are glad that You have done (it). You will bring the day (that) You have called, and they shall be like me. [22] Let all their wickedness come before You; and do to them as You have done to me for all my transgressions. For my sighs are many, and my heart (is) faint.

CHAPTER 2

[1] How the Lord has clouded over the daughter of Zion in His anger, (and) cast the beauty of Israel down from Heaven to the earth, and remembered not His footstool in the day of His anger! [2] The Lord has swallowed up all the homes of Jacob and has not pitied. In His rage He has thrown down the strongholds of the daughter of Judah; He has brought (them) down to the ground; He has defiled the kingdom and its rulers. [3] He has cut off all the horn of Israel in fierce anger; He has drawn back His right hand from the face of the enemy, and He burned against Jacob like a flaming fire; He devours all around. [4] He has trod His

18 סְבִיבָיו צָרָיו הָיְתָה יְרוּשָׁלַ͏ִם לְנִדָּה בֵּינֵיהֶם׃ צַדִּיק הוּא

(is) Righteous among an Jerusalem has ;foes his around
.them impurity become him

יְהוָה כִּי־פִיהוּ מָרִיתִי שִׁמְעוּ־נָא כָל־עַמִּים וּרְאוּ מַכְאֹבִי

my and peoples all ,please ,hear rebelled I His for ,Jehovah
.sorrow see ;against mouth

19 בְּתוּלֹתַי וּבַחוּרַי הָלְכוּ בַשֶּׁבִי׃ קָרָאתִי לַמְאַהֲבַי הֵמָּה

they my to called I into went my and virgins My
,lovers .exile men young

רִמּוּנִי כֹּהֲנַי וּזְקֵנַי בָּעִיר גָּוָעוּ כִּי־בִקְשׁוּ אֹכֶל לָמוֹ וְיָשִׁיבוּ

they that for food they for ex- the in my and my deceived
back bring them sought ;pired city elders priests ;me

20 אֶת־נַפְשָׁם׃ רְאֵה יְהוָה כִּי־צַר־לִי מֵעַי חֳמַרְמָרוּ נֶהְפַּךְ

turned is ,ferment My to distress for O ,See their
over innards ;me ,Jehovah .soul

לִבִּי בְּקִרְבִּי כִּי מָרוֹ מָרִיתִי מִחוּץ שִׁכְּלָה־חֶרֶב בַּבַּיִת

the in the bereaves outside ;rebelled I for within my
house ,sword utterly ,me heart

21 כַּמָּוֶת׃ שָׁמְעוּ כִּי נֶאֱנָחָה אָנִי אֵין מְנַחֵם לִי כָּל־אֹיְבַי

my all for com- a not ;I groan for They as (is it)
haters ,me forter is ,hear .death

שָׁמְעוּ רָעָתִי שָׂשׂוּ כִּי אַתָּה עָשִׂיתָ הֵבֵאתָ יוֹם־קָרָאתָ וְיִהְיוּ

they and have You the will You have You that they ,evil my have
be shall ,called day bring ;(this) done rejoice heard

22 כָמוֹנִי׃ תָּבֹא כָל־רָעָתָם לְפָנֶיךָ וְעוֹלֵל לָמוֹ כַּאֲשֶׁר עוֹלַלְתָּ

have You as to do and before their all Let like
done them ,You evil come .me

לִי עַל כָּל־פְּשָׁעַי כִּי־רַבּוֹת אַנְחֹתַי וְלִבִּי דַוָּי׃

.faint my and my are for my all for to
heart groans many ;trespasses me

CAP. II ב

CHAPTER 2

1 אֵיכָה יָעִיב בְּאַפּוֹ ׀ אֲדֹנָי אֶת־בַּת־צִיּוֹן הִשְׁלִיךְ מִשָּׁמַיִם

the from cast He !Zion the the His in has How
heavens of daughter Lord anger clouded

אֶרֶץ תִּפְאֶרֶת יִשְׂרָאֵל וְלֹא־זָכַר הֲדֹם־רַגְלָיו בְּיוֹם אַפּוֹ׃

His the in His the remem- and ,Israel the (the to)
.anger of day foot of stool bered not of beauty earth

2 בִּלַּע אֲדֹנָי *לֹא חָמַל אֵת כָּל־נְאוֹת יַעֲקֹב הָרַס בְּעֶבְרָתוֹ

His in He ;Jacob the all pitied not The swallowed
anger destroyed of abodes ,Lord up

מִבְצְרֵי בַת־יְהוּדָה הִגִּיעַ לָאָרֶץ חִלֵּל מַמְלָכָה וְשָׂרֶיהָ׃

its and the has He the to made He ;Judah the strong- the
;rulers kingdom defiled ;earth touch of daughter of holds

3 גָּדַע בָּחֳרִי־אַף כֹּל קֶרֶן יִשְׂרָאֵל הֵשִׁיב אָחוֹר יְמִינוֹ מִפְּנֵי

the from His back has He ;Israel the all anger in cut He
of face hand right turned of horn of heat off

4 אוֹיֵב וַיִּבְעַר בְּיַעֲקֹב כְּאֵשׁ לֶהָבָה אָכְלָה סָבִיב׃ דָּרַךְ

He all con- it ;flame a as Jacob in He and the
trod .around sumes of fire burned ;haters

bow like an enemy, set His right hand like an adversary and killed all (who were) desirable to the eye in the tent of the daughter of Zion. He poured out His fury like fire. [5] The Lord was like an enemy; He swallowed up Israel; He swallowed up all her palaces, destroyed his strongholds; and He increased mourning and weeping in the daughter of Judah. [6] And He violated His booth like a garden; destroying His meeting places. Jehovah has made to forget meeting places and sabbaths in Zion; and He rejected king and priest in His anger's fury. [7] The Lord cast off His altar; He rejected His holy place; He has delivered the walls of her palaces into the hater's hand; they gave a noise in Jehovah's house, as a day of meeting. [8] Jehovah purposed to destroy the wall of the daughter of Zion; He has stretched out a line; He has not withdrawn His hand from swallowing; and He made rampart and wall to lament; they droop together. [9] Her gates have sunk in the ground; He has dispersed and shattered her bars; her kings and her rulers (are) among the nations; the law is not; also her prophets have not found a vision from Jehovah; [10] On the ground they sit; the elders of Zion's daughters are silent; they send up dust on their head; they gird on sackcloths; the virgins of Jerusalem let their heads hang to the ground. [11] And at an end with tears (are) my eyes; my innards ferment; my liver is poured on the ground, for the ruin of the daughter of my people; in the fainting of children and babies in the plazas of the city. [12] They say to their mothers, Where (are) grain and wine? In their fainting like the wounded in the plazas of the city, in their pouring out their lives to their mothers' bosom. [13] What can I testify for you? What will I liken to you, daughter

---

כִּשְׁחִתוּ כְּאוֹיֵב נִצָּב יְמִינוֹ כְּצָר וַיַּהֲרֹג כֹּל מַחֲמַדֵּי־עָיִן בְּאֹהֶל

the in   the   desirable   all   and   like   right His   set   a like   His
of tent   eye   (these)   killed   ,foe   a hand   ,hater   bow

5   בַּת־צִיּוֹן שָׁפַךְ כָּאֵשׁ חֲמָתוֹ: הָיָה אֲדֹנָי ׀ כְּאוֹיֵב בִּלַּע

He   a like   The   was   His   a like   He   ;Zion the
swallowed ,hater   Lord   .fury   fire   out poured   of daughter

יִשְׂרָאֵל בִּלַּע כָּל־אַרְמְנוֹתֶיהָ שִׁחֵת מִבְצָרָיו וַיֶּרֶב בְּבַת־

in   He and   strong- his   destroyed   ,palaces his   all   He   ,Israel
daughter   increased   ;holds   swallowed

6   יְהוּדָה תַּאֲנִיָּה וַאֲנִיָּה: וַיַּחְמֹס כַּגַּן שֻׂכּוֹ שִׁחֵת מֹעֲדוֹ שִׁכַּח

made   His   destroyed   His   a like   He And   and   mourning   Judah's
forget   ;meetings   ,booth   garden   violated   weeping

יְהוָה ׀ בְּצִיּוֹן מוֹעֵד וְשַׁבָּת וַיִּנְאַץ בְּזַעַם־אַפּוֹ מֶלֶךְ וְכֹהֵן:

and   king   His   the in   He and   and   meeting   in   Jehovah
.priest   anger of fury   rejected   ,sabbaths   places   Zion

7   זָנַח אֲדֹנָי ׀ מִזְבְּחוֹ נִאֵר מִקְדָּשׁוֹ הִסְגִּיר בְּיַד־אוֹיֵב חוֹמֹת

walls the   the   into   has He   holy His   re- He   His   The   has
of   hater's   hand   delivered   ,place   jected   ,altar   Lord   off cast

8   אַרְמְנוֹתֶיהָ קוֹל נָתְנוּ בְּבֵית־יְהוָה כְּיוֹם מוֹעֵד: חָשַׁב

Deter-   .meeting   a as   Jehovah   the in   they   a   ;palaces her
mined   of day   of house   gave   noise

יְהוָה ׀ לְהַשְׁחִית חוֹמַת בַּת־צִיּוֹן נָטָה קָו לֹא־הֵשִׁיב יָדוֹ

His   has He   not   a   He   ;Zion's daugh-   the   destroy to   Jehovah
hand   returned   ,line   stretched   ter   of wall

9   מִבַּלֵּעַ וַיַּאֲבֶל־חֵל וְחוֹמָה יַחְדָּו אֻמְלָלוּ: טָבְעוּ בָאָרֶץ

the in   Have   they   together   and   ram- made He   and from
earth   sunk   .languish   ,wall   part   lament ;swallowing

שְׁעָרֶיהָ אִבַּד וְשִׁבַּר בְּרִיחֶיהָ מַלְכָּהּ וְשָׂרֶיהָ בַגּוֹיִם אֵין

is the   among   her and   her   ;bars her   and   dis- He   her
not :nations   (are) rulers   kings   shattered   persed   ;gates

10   תּוֹרָה גַּם־נְבִיאֶיהָ לֹא־מָצְאוּ חָזוֹן מֵיְהוָה: יֵשְׁבוּ לָאָרֶץ

the on   They   from   a   have   not   her   also   the
,ground   sit   .Jehovah   vision   found   prophets   ;law

יִדְּמוּ זִקְנֵי בַת־צִיּוֹן הֶעֱלוּ עָפָר עַל־רֹאשָׁם חָגְרוּ שַׂקִּים

sack-   they   their   on   dust   on   ;Zion's daugh-   the   are
;cloths   on gird   ,head   up send   ter of elders   silent

11   הוֹרִידוּ לָאָרֶץ רֹאשָׁן בְּתוּלֹת יְרוּשָׁלָםִ: כָּלוּ בַדְּמָעוֹת

tears with   And   at   .Jerusalem   virgins the   their   the to   let
   end an   of   heads   ground   hang

עֵינַי חֳמַרְמְרוּ מֵעַי נִשְׁפַּךְ לָאָרֶץ כְּבֵדִי עַל־שֶׁבֶר בַּת־

daughter   the   for   my   the on   is   my   ferment   my
of ruin   ,liver   ground   poured   ,innards   ,eyes

12   עַמִּי בֵּעָטֵף עוֹלֵל וְיוֹנֵק בִּרְחֹבוֹת קִרְיָה: לְאִמֹּתָם יֹאמְרוּ

they   their To   the   the in   and   children   the in   my
,say   mothers   .city   of plazas   babies   of fainting   ;people's

אַיֵּה דָּגָן וָיָיִן בְּהִתְעַטְּפָם כֶּחָלָל בִּרְחֹבוֹת עִיר בְּהִשְׁתַּפֵּךְ

their in   the   the in   the like   their In   and grain   Where
out pouring   ,city   of plazas   wounded   fainting   ?wine   (are)

13   נַפְשָׁם אֶל־חֵיק אִמֹּתָם: מָה־אֲעִידֵךְ מָה אֲדַמֶּה־לָּךְ הַבַּת

O   to   I shall   What   I can   What   their   the to   their
daughter   ,you compare   ?you for   testify   .mothers   of bosom   lives

of Jerusalem? What shall I equate to you, so that I may comfort you, O virgin daughter of Zion? For great like the sea (is) your crushing; who can heal you? [14] Your prophets have seen false and foolish things for you, and they have not disclosed about your iniquity, to turn away your captivity; but have seen false oracles and seductions for you. [15] All who pass by clap (their) hands at you. They hiss and wag their head at the daughter of Jerusalem, (saying), (Is) this the city which they called the perfection of beauty, the joy of the whole earth? [16] All your enemies have opened their mouth against you; they hiss and gnash the teeth; they say, We have swallowed (her) up. Certainly this is the day that we looked for; we have found, we have seen. [17] Jehovah has done (that) which He has purposed; He fulfilled His word which He commanded from days of old. He has thrown down and has not pitied; and He has caused the enemy to rejoice over you; He set up the horn of your foes. [18] Their heart cried to the Lord, O wall of the daughter of Zion, let tears run down like a torrent by day and night; give yourself no relief; let not the daughter of your eye rest. [19] Arise, cry out in the night, at the beginning of the watches, pour out your heart like water before the face of Jehovah. Lift up your hands toward Him for the eye of your young children, who faint with hunger in the head of every street.

[20] Behold, O Jehovah, and consider to whom You have done this. Shall women eat their fruit, children of tender care? Should priest and prophet be killed in the holy place of the Lord? [21] Young and old lie on the ground of streets; my virgins and my young men have fallen by the sword. You have killed (them) in the day of Your

יְרוּשָׁלִַם מָה אַשְׁוֶה־לָּךְ וַאֲנַחֲמֵךְ בְּתוּלַת בַּת־צִיּוֹן כִּי־גָדוֹל
great For ?Zion daugh- virgin O may I that to I shall What ?Jerusalem's
of ter ,you comfort ,you equate

14 כַּיָּם שִׁבְרֵךְ מִי יִרְפָּא־לָךְ׃ נְבִיאַיִךְ חָזוּ לָךְ שָׁוְא וְתָפֵל
and false- for visioned Your ?you can who your (is) like
,folly hood you prophets heal ;crushing sea the

וְלֹא־גִלּוּ עַל־עֲוֺנֵךְ לְהָשִׁיב שְׁבִיתֵךְ וַיֶּחֱזוּ לָךְ מַשְׂאוֹת שָׁוְא
false- burdens for they and your turn to your about dis- and
hood of you visioned ;captivity back ,iniquity closed not

15 וּמַדּוּחִים׃ סָפְקוּ עָלַיִךְ כַּפַּיִם כָּל־עֹבְרֵי דֶרֶךְ שָׁרְקוּ וַיָּנִעוּ
and they the passing all their you at Clap and
wag hiss ,way by hands .seductions

רֹאשָׁם עַל־בַּת יְרוּשָׁלִָם הֲזֹאת הָעִיר שֶׁיֹּאמְרוּ כְּלִילַת יֹפִי
,beauty per- the they which the (Is) :Jerusalem the at their
of fection called city this of daughter head

16 מָשׂוֹשׂ לְכָל־הָאָרֶץ׃ פָּצוּ עָלַיִךְ פִּיהֶם כָּל־אֹיְבַיִךְ שָׁרְקוּ
they your all their against Have ?earth the of joy the
hiss ,haters mouth you opened all

וַיַּחַרְקוּ־שֵׁן אָמְרוּ בִּלָּעְנוּ אַךְ זֶה הַיּוֹם שֶׁקִּוִּינֻהוּ מָצָאנוּ
have we which for the this Surely have We ,say they the and
,found ;waited we day (is) !up swallowed ;teeth gnash

17 רָאִינוּ׃ עָשָׂה יְהוָה אֲשֶׁר זָמָם בִּצַּע אֶמְרָתוֹ אֲשֶׁר צִוָּה
He which word His He He (that) Jehovah has have we
commanded fulfilled ,planned which done .(it) seen

מִימֵי־קֶדֶם הָרַס וְלֹא חָמָל וַיְשַׂמַּח עָלַיִךְ אוֹיֵב הֵרִים קֶרֶן
the He the over He and ;pitied and has He .antiquity from
of horn raised ,hater you glad made not dashed of days

18 צָרָיִךְ׃ צָעַק לִבָּם אֶל־אֲדֹנָי חוֹמַת בַּת־צִיּוֹן הוֹרִידִי כַנַּחַל
a like send let ,Zion's daugh- O the to Their cried your
torrent down ter of wall ;Lord heart .foes

דִּמְעָה יוֹמָם וָלַיְלָה אַל־תִּתְּנִי פוּגַת לָךְ אַל־תִּדֹּם בַּת־
the rest let not to relief give do not and day by tears
of daughter ,yourself ,night

19 עֵינֵךְ׃ קוּמִי ׀ רֹנִּי בַלַּיִל* לְרֹאשׁ אַשְׁמֻרוֹת שִׁפְכִי כַמַּיִם
like out pour ;watches the the at the in cry ,Arise your
waters of head night out .eye

לִבֵּךְ נֹכַח פְּנֵי אֲדֹנָי שְׂאִי אֵלָיו כַּפַּיִךְ עַל־נֶפֶשׁ עוֹלָלַיִךְ
your the for your to lift the the before your
children of life hands Him up ;Lord of face heart

20 הָעֲטוּפִים בְּרָעָב בְּרֹאשׁ כָּל־חוּצוֹת׃ רְאֵה יְהוָה וְהַבִּיטָה
!look and O ,See open every the at with (are who)
,Jehovah .place of head hunger faint

לְמִי עוֹלַלְתָּ כֹּה אִם־תֹּאכַלְנָה נָשִׁים פִּרְיָם עֹלְלֵי טִפֻּחִים
tender children their women Should ?thus You have To
?care of ,fruit eat done whom

21 אִם־יֵהָרֵג בְּמִקְדַּשׁ אֲדֹנָי כֹּהֵן וְנָבִיא׃ שָׁכְבוּ לָאָרֶץ חוּצוֹת
open the the on Lie and priest the the in be Should
places of ground down ?prophet Lord of place holy killed

נַעַר וְזָקֵן בְּתוּלֹתַי וּבַחוּרַי נָפְלוּ בֶחָרֶב הָרַגְתָּ בְּיוֹם אַפֶּךָ
Your the in have You the by have my and my and young
,anger of day killed ;sword fallen youth choice virgins ;old

anger; You have killed, You have not pitied. [22] You have called as in a day of appointed meeting my terrors all around, so that in the day of Jehovah's anger none escaped or remained. Those whom I have swaddled and brought up, my enemy has consumed (them).

CHAPTER 3

[1] I the man have seen affliction by the rod of His wrath. [2] He led me and made (me) go in darkness, and not light. [3] Surely He has turned against me; He turns His hand (against me) all the day. [4] He has wasted my flesh and my skin; He has broken my bones. [5] He has built against me and has put around (me) bitterness and pain. [6] He has made me live in dark places, like the dead of old. [7] He walled around me, and I cannot go out; He has made my bronze (chain) heavy. [8] Also when I cry out and call for help, He shuts out my prayer. [9] He has walled up my ways with cut stone; He has made my paths crooked. [10] He (was) to me (like) a bear lying in wait; a lion in secret places. [11] He has turned my ways aside and torn me to pieces. He made me desolate. [12] He has trod His bow and set me up as a mark for the arrow. [13] He caused the sons of His quiver to enter into my inward parts. [14] I was a mockery to all my people; their song all the day. [15] He has filled me with bitterness; (He) made me drunk (with) wormwood. [16] And He broke my teeth with gravel stones; He has trampled me in the ashes. [17] And You have cast off my soul from peace; I forgot blessedness. [18] And I said, My strength and my hope from Jehovah is gone. [19] Remember my affliction and my wandering (as) wormwood and bitterness. [20] My soul vividly remembers and bows down

22 טָבַחְתָּ לֹא חָמָלְתָּ׃ תִּקְרָא כְיוֹם מוֹעֵד מְגוּרַי מִסָּבִיב וְלֹא

and ,around all my appointed in as have You have You not have You
not terrors meeting of day a called !pitied ,killed

הָיָה בְּיוֹם אַף־יְהוָה פָּלִיט וְשָׂרִיד אֲשֶׁר־טִפַּחְתִּי וְרִבִּיתִי

and have I Whom a or an Jehovah the the in was
,up brought nursed ;survivor escapee of anger of day

אֹיְבִי כִלָּם׃

con- has my
!(them) sumed enemy

CAP. III ג

CHAPTER 3

1
2 אֲנִי הַגֶּבֶר רָאָה עֳנִי בְּשֵׁבֶט עֶבְרָתוֹ׃ אוֹתִי נָהַג וַיֹּלַךְ

made and He me His of the by afflic- have man the I
go (me) led .wrath rod tion seen

3 חֹשֶׁךְ וְלֹא־אוֹר׃ אַךְ בִּי יָשֻׁב יַהֲפֹךְ יָדוֹ כָּל־הַיּוֹם׃

the all His He He against Surely .light and in
.day hand turns ;turned me not darkness

4
5 בִּלָּה בְשָׂרִי וְעוֹרִי שִׁבַּר עַצְמוֹתָי׃ בָּנָה עָלַי וַיַּקַּף רֹאשׁ

bitter- put has and against He .bones my has He my and flesh my has He
ness (me) around me built shattered ;skin wasted

6
7 וּתְלָאָה׃ בְּמַחֲשַׁכִּים הוֹשִׁיבַנִי כְּמֵתֵי עוֹלָם׃ גָּדַר

He .old the like made has He places dark In and
walled of dead live me .hardship

8 בַּעֲדִי וְלֹא אֵצֵא הִכְבִּיד נְחָשְׁתִּי׃ גַּם כִּי אֶזְעַק וַאֲשַׁוֵּעַ

shout and cry I when Also bronze my has He can I and around
,help for out .(chain) heavy made ;out go not ,me

9
10 שָׂתַם תְּפִלָּתִי׃ גָּדַר דְּרָכַי בְּגָזִית נְתִיבֹתַי עִוָּה׃ דֹּב

bear A .crooked paths my cut with ways my has He my shuts He
(are) ,stone up walled .prayer out

11 אֹרֵב הוּא לִי אֲרִיה בְּמִסְתָּרִים׃ דְּרָכַי סוֹרֵר וַיְפַשְּׁחֵנִי

me torn and has He ways My secret in lion a to He lying
,pieces to deflected .places ,me (was) wait in

12 שָׂמַנִי שֹׁמֵם׃ דָּרַךְ קַשְׁתּוֹ וַיַּצִּיבֵנִי כַּמַּטָּרָא לַחֵץ׃

the for mark a as set and bow His has He .desolate He
.arrow up me trod me made

13
14 הֵבִיא בְּכִלְיוֹתָי בְּנֵי אַשְׁפָּתוֹ׃ הָיִיתִי שְּׂחֹק לְכָל־עַמִּי

my all to a was I .quiver His the my into made He
,people mockery of sons parts inward enter

15 נְגִינָתָם כָּל־הַיּוֹם׃ הִשְׂבִּיעַנִי בַמְּרוֹרִים הִרְוַנִי לַעֲנָה׃

worm- (with) made (He) bit- with has He the all their
.wood drunk me ,terness me filled .day song

16
17 וַיַּגְרֵס בֶּחָצָץ שִׁנָּי הִכְפִּישַׁנִי בָּאֵפֶר׃ וַתִּזְנַח מִשָּׁלוֹם נַפְשִׁי

my from You And the in has He my with He And
;soul peace off cast .ashes me trampled teeth gravel broke

18 נָשִׁיתִי טוֹבָה׃ וָאֹמַר אָבַד נִצְחִי וְתוֹחַלְתִּי מֵיְהוָה׃

from my and my is Gone I And .goodness have I
.Jehovah hope strength ,said forgotten

19
20 זְכָר־עָנְיִי וּמְרוּדִי לַעֲנָה וָרֹאשׁ׃ זָכוֹר תִּזְכּוֹר וְתָשִׁיחַ עָלַי

upon bows and remembers Vividly and wormwood my and my Remem-
me down .bitterness ,roaming affliction ber

upon me. [21] I recall this to my heart; therefore I hope.

[22] (It is by) Jehovah's kindness that we are not destroyed, for His mercies never fail. [23] (They are) new every morning; great (is) Your faithfulness. [24] Jehovah (is) my portion, says my soul; therefore I will hope in Him. [25] Jehovah (is) good to those who wait for Him; to the soul (who) seeks Him. [26] (It is) good that (a man) hopes even (in) silence for the salvation of Jehovah. [27] (It is) good for a man that he bear the yoke in his youth. [28] He sits alone and is silent, because He laid (it) on him. [29] He puts his mouth in the dust, if perhaps there is hope. [30] He gives (his) cheek to Him who strikes him; he is filled with reproach. [31] For the Lord will not cast off forever; [32] for though He causes grief, He will have pity according to the multitude of His kindnesses. [33] For He does not afflict from His heart, nor does He grieve the sons of men. [34] To crush all the prisoners of earth under his feet; [35] to turn aside the judgment of a man before the face of the Most High; [36] to wrong a man in his cause; (this) the Lord does not see.

[37] Who (is) this (who) speaks, and it comes to pass, (when) the Lord does not command (it)? [38] The evil and the good do not come out of the mouth of the Most High? [39] What? Should mankind complain, a living man, because of his sins? [40] Let us search and try our ways and turn again to Jehovah. [41] Let us lift up our hearts (and) hands to God in Heaven. [42] We have trespassed and have rebelled;You, You have not forgiven. [43] You have wrapped yourself with anger and pursued us; You have slain; You have not pitied. [44] You have wrapped Yourself with a cloud, (so that any) prayer should not pass through. [45] You have made us (as)

21 22 נַפְשִׁי׃ זֹאת אָשִׁיב אֶל־לִבִּי עַל־כֵּן אוֹחִיל׃ חַסְדֵי
kind- (By) .hope I therefore my to bring I This my
nesses ,heart back .soul

23 יְהוָה כִּי לֹא־תָמְנוּ כִּי לֹא־כָלוּ רַחֲמָיו׃ חֲדָשִׁים לַבְּקָרִים
by new His are not for are we not that Jeho-
;mornings (they are) ;mercies ended ,consumed (is it) vah's

24 רַבָּה אֱמוּנָתֶךָ׃ חֶלְקִי יְהוָה אָמְרָה נַפְשִׁי עַל־כֵּן אוֹחִיל
shall I therefore my says ,Jehovah My faith- Your great
hope ,soul (is) portion .fulness (is)

25 26 לוֹ׃ טוֹב יְהוָה לְקוָֹו לְנֶפֶשׁ תִּדְרְשֶׁנּוּ׃ טוֹב וְיָחִיל
he that (is It) seeks (that) the to those to Jehovah Good for
hopes good .Him soul ,Him anointing (is) .Him

27 וְדוּמָם לִתְשׁוּעַת יְהוָה׃ טוֹב לַגֶּבֶר כִּי־יִשָּׂא עֹל בִּנְעוּרָיו׃
his in a he that a for (is It) .Jehovah the for (in) even
.youth yoke bear man good of salvation silence

28 29 יֵשֵׁב בָּדָד וְיִדֹּם כִּי נָטַל עָלָיו׃ יִתֵּן בֶּעָפָר פִּיהוּ אוּלַי
perhaps his the in He upon He for is and alone He
,mouth dust puts :him (it) laid ,silent sits

30 31 יֵשׁ תִּקְוָה׃ יִתֵּן לְמַכֵּהוּ לֶחִי יִשְׂבַּע בְּחֶרְפָּה׃ כִּי לֹא
not For with is He his his to He .hope there
.reproach filled ,cheek smiter gives is

32 33 יִזְנַח לְעוֹלָם אֲדֹנָי׃ כִּי אִם־הוֹגָה וְרִחַם כְּרֹב חֲסָדָו׃ כִּי
For kind- His the as will He causes He if For the forever will
.nesses of many pity have ,grief .Lord off cast

34 לֹא עִנָּה מִלִּבּוֹ וַיַּגֶּה בְּנֵי־אִישׁ׃ לְדַכֵּא תַּחַת רַגְלָיו
His under To .man the nor His from He not
feet crush of sons grieves ,heart afflicts

35 כֹּל אֲסִירֵי אָרֶץ׃ לְהַטּוֹת מִשְׁפַּט־גָּבֶר נֶגֶד פְּנֵי עֶלְיוֹן׃
Most the the before man a the turn to ;earth the all
,High of face of justice aside of prisoners

36 37 לְעַוֵּת אָדָם בְּרִיבוֹ אֲדֹנָי לֹא רָאָה׃ מִי זֶה אָמַר
(who) this Who does not the his in a to
,speaks (is) .see Lord :cause man wrong

38 וַתֶּהִי אֲדֹנָי לֹא צִוָּה׃ מִפִּי עֶלְיוֹן לֹא תֵצֵא הָרָעוֹת וְהַטּוֹב׃
the and evil the goes not Most the From com- not the it and
?good out High's mouth ?manding Lord ,occurs

39 40 מַה־יִּתְאוֹנֵן אָדָם חָי גֶּבֶר עַל־חֲטָאָו׃ נַחְפְּשָׂה
us Let his because ,man living man- Should ?What
search ?sins of ,kind complain

41 דְרָכֵינוּ וְנַחְקֹרָה וְנָשׁוּבָה עַד־יְהוָה׃ נִשָּׂא לְבָבֵנוּ אֶל־
(and) hearts our Let .Jehovah to return and examine and our
lift us ,(them) ways

42 כַּפָּיִם אֶל־אֵל בַּשָּׁמָיִם׃ נַחְנוּ פָשַׁעְנוּ וּמָרִינוּ אַתָּה לֹא
not ,You and have We :Heaven in God to hands
,rebelled transgressed

43 סָלָחְתָּ׃ סַכֹּתָה בָאַף וַתִּרְדְּפֵנוּ הָרַגְתָּ לֹא חָמָלְתָּ׃
have You not have You pur- and with have You have You
.pitied ,slain ;us sued anger Yourself wrapped .forgiven

44 45 סַכֹּתָה בֶעָנָן לָךְ מֵעֲבוֹר תְּפִלָּה׃ סְחִי וּמָאוֹס תְּשִׂימֵנוּ
have You and Sweepings (any) passing from for a with have You
,us made garbage .prayer through ,You cloud covered

the sweepings and garbage in the midst of the peoples. [46] All our enemies have opened their mouth against us. [47] Dread and a pit have come to us, shame and ruin. [48] Streams of water run down my eye, for the ruin of the daughter of my people. [49] My eye flows out and does not cease, without stopping, [50] until Jehovah shall look down and see from Heaven. [51] My eye pains my soul from all the daughters of my city. [52] My enemies have hunted me, like a bird, undeservedly. [53] They have cut off my life in the pit and threw stones at me. [54] Waters flowed over my head; I said, I am cut off.

[55] I called on Your name, O Jehovah, out of the lowest pit. [56] You have heard my voice; do not hide Your ear at my relief, at my cry for help. [57] You drew near in the day I called on You. You said, Fear not. [58] O Lord, You spoke for the causes of my soul; You redeemed my life. [59] Jehovah, You have seen my wrong; judge my cause. [60] You have seen all their vengeance, all their plots against me. [61] You have heard their reproach, O Jehovah; all their plots against me, [62] the lips of those rising against me, and their scheming against me all the day. [63] Behold their sitting down and their rising up; I (am) their song. [64] You will return to them a reward, O Jehovah, according to the work of their hands. [65] You will give them dullness of heart, Your curse on them. [66] Pursue and destroy them in anger from under the heavens of Jehovah.

46
47 בְּקֶרֶב הָעַמִּים׃ פָּצוּ עָלֵינוּ פִּיהֶם כָּל־אֹיְבֵינוּ׃ פַּחַד
Dread our all their against Have the the in
.enemies mouth us opened .peoples of midst

48 וָפַחַת הָיָה לָנוּ הַשֵּׁאת וְהַשָּׁבֶר׃ פַּלְגֵי־מַיִם תֵּרַד עֵינִי
my run waters Streams. .ruin and devas- ,us to is a and
eye down of tation pit

49 עַל־שֶׁבֶר בַּת־עַמִּי׃ עֵינִי נִגְּרָה וְלֹא תִדְמֶה מֵאֵין
from ,ceases and flows My my daugh- the the for
being not not out eye .people of ter of ruin

50
51 הֲפֻגוֹת׃ עַד־יַשְׁקִיף וְיֵרֶא יְהוָה מִשָּׁמָיִם׃ עֵינִי עוֹלְלָה
treats My the from Jehovah and shall until (any)
severely eye .heavens see down look ,stopping

52 לְנַפְשִׁי מִכֹּל בְּנוֹת עִירִי׃ צוֹד צָדוּנִי כַּצִּפּוֹר אֹיְבַי
my a like have Surely my daugh- the from my to
haters bird me hunted .city of ters all ,soul

53
54 חִנָּם׃ צָמְתוּ בַבּוֹר חַיָּי וַיַּדּוּ־אֶבֶן בִּי׃ צָפוּ־מַיִם עַל־
upon Waters over- .me at threw and my the in have They unde-
flowed stones life pit off cut .servedly

55 רֹאשִׁי אָמַרְתִּי נִגְזָרְתִּי׃ קָרָאתִי שִׁמְךָ יְהוָה מִבּוֹר
the from O Your called I am I ,said I my
pit ,Jehovah ,name .off cut ;head

56 תַּחְתִּיּוֹת׃ קוֹלִי שָׁמָעְתָּ אַל־תַּעְלֵם אָזְנְךָ לְרַוְחָתִי לְשַׁוְעָתִי׃
cry my at my at Your do not have You My .lowest
.help for ,relief ear hide ;heard voice

57
58 קָרַבְתָּ בְּיוֹם אֶקְרָאֶךָּ אָמַרְתָּ אַל־תִּירָא׃ רַבְתָּ אֲדֹנָי
O spoke You !Fear not You called I the in came You
,Lord for ,said ;You day near

59 רִיבֵי נַפְשִׁי גָּאַלְתָּ חַיָּי׃ רָאִיתָה יְהוָה עַוָּתָתִי שָׁפְטָה
judge my O have You my You my causes the
;wrong ,Jehovah ,seen .life redeemed ,soul of

60 מִשְׁפָּטִי׃ רָאִיתָה כָּל־נִקְמָתָם כָּל־מַחְשְׁבֹתָם לִי׃
against plots their all their all have You my
.me ,vengeance seen .cause

61
62 שָׁמַעְתָּ חֶרְפָּתָם יְהוָה כָּל־מַחְשְׁבֹתָם עָלָי׃ שִׂפְתֵי קָמַי
my Lips against plots their all O their have You
uprisers' .me ,Jehovah ,reproach heard

63 וְהֶגְיוֹנָם עָלַי כָּל־הַיּוֹם׃ שִׁבְתָּם וְקִימָתָם הַבִּיטָה אֲנִי
I ;at look their and Their the all against their and
(am) rising sitting .day me scheming

64 מַנְגִּינָתָם׃ תָּשִׁיב לָהֶם גְּמוּל יְהוָה כְּמַעֲשֵׂה יְדֵיהֶם׃
their the to as O a to will You .song their
;hands of work ,Jehovah ,reward them return

65
66 תִּתֵּן לָהֶם מְגִנַּת־לֵב תַּאֲלָתְךָ לָהֶם׃ תִּרְדֹּף בְּאַף וְתַשְׁמִידֵם
destroy and in Pursue to your ,heart insolence to will You
them anger .them curse of them give

מִתַּחַת שְׁמֵי יְהוָה׃
.Jehovah the from
of heavens under

CAP. IV ד

CHAPTER 4

CHAPTER 4

[1] How the gold dims, the pure gold is changed! The stones of the sanctuary are poured out in the top of every street. [2] The precious sons of Zion are weighed against pure gold: How they are counted as earthen pitchers, the work of the potter's hand! [3] Even the jackals drew out the breast; they suckle their young ones; the daughter of my people (is) as cruel as the ostriches in the wilderness. [4] The tongue of the nursling clings to the roof of his mouth because of thirst; the young children ask bread; no (one) is breaking to them. [5] Those who ate delicacies are desolate in the streets; those who were brought up in scarlet embrace dunghills. [6] And the iniquity of the daughter of my people is greater than the sin of Sodom, (which was) overthrown as in a moment, and no hands were whirled on her. [7] Her Nazarites were purer than snow; whiter than milk; they were more ruddy (of) bone than corals; their cutting lapis lazuli: [8] Their appearance is blacker than soot; they are not recognized in the streets; their skin has shriveled on their bones; it is dried up; it has become like a stick. [9] Better are ones killed by the sword than ones stricken by hunger; for these flow away, pierced because of the fruits of my fields. [10] The hands of the pitying women have boiled their own children; they became food to them in the ruin of the daughter of my people. [11] Jehovah has fulfilled His fury; He has poured out the glow of His anger and has kindled a fire in Zion, and it has devoured its foundations. [12] The kings of the earth, and all the inhabitants of the world, would not have believed that the foe and the enemy would go in the gates of Jerusalem. [13] Because of the sins of

1 אֵיכָה יוּעַם זָהָב יִשְׁנֶא הַכֶּתֶם הַטּוֹב תִּשְׁתַּפֵּכְנָה אַבְנֵי־
the of stones poured Are out !good gold the is the changed ,gold dims How

2 קֹדֶשׁ בְּרֹאשׁ כָּל־חוּצוֹת׃ בְּנֵי צִיּוֹן הַיְקָרִים הַמְסֻלָּאִים
are weighed precious Zion The of sons .street every the at the of head sanctuary

3 בַּפָּז אֵיכָה נֶחְשְׁבוּ לְנִבְלֵי־חֶרֶשׂ מַעֲשֵׂה יְדֵי יוֹצֵר׃ גַּם־
Even !potter a the of hands work the of earthen as vessels are they reckoned How against :gold pure

תַּנִּין חָלְצוּ שַׁד הֵינִיקוּ גּוּרֵיהֶן בַּת־עַמִּי לְאַכְזָר כִּי עֵנִים
the like ostriches (become has) ,cruel my daugh- people's ter their ;young they suckle the ,breast drew out jackals

4 בַּמִּדְבָּר׃ דָּבַק לְשׁוֹן יוֹנֵק אֶל־חִכּוֹ בַּצָּמָא עוֹלָלִים שָׁאֲלוּ
ask young the children in ;thirst his palate to the tongue the nursling of Clings the in .wilderness

5 לֶחֶם פֹּרֵשׂ אֵין לָהֶם׃ הָאֹכְלִים לְמַעֲדַנִּים נָשַׁמּוּ בַּחוּצוֹת
the in ;streets are desolate delicacies ones The eating for .them not is breaking ;bread

6 הָאֱמֻנִים עֲלֵי תוֹלָע חִבְּקוּ אַשְׁפַּתּוֹת׃ וַיִּגְדַּל עֲוֺן בַּת־עַמִּי
my daugh- people's ter ini- quity is And greater .dunghills embrace scarlet on ones the raised

מֵחַטַּאת סְדֹם הַהֲפוּכָה כְמוֹ־רָגַע וְלֹא־חָלוּ בָהּ יָדָיִם׃
.hands on her were spun and not a (in) as ,moment (was which) overthrown ,Sodom the than of sin

7 זַכּוּ נְזִירֶיהָ מִשֶּׁלֶג צַחוּ מֵחָלָב אָדְמוּ עֶצֶם מִפְּנִינִים סַפִּיר
lapis lazuli than ,corals (of) bone were they redder than ;milk whiter than ,snow Her Nazarites were purer

8 גִּזְרָתָם׃ חָשַׁךְ מִשְּׁחוֹר תָּאֳרָם לֹא נִכְּרוּ בַּחוּצוֹת צָפַד
has shriveled the in ;streets are they not recognized their ;appearance soot than Is darker their .cutting

9 עוֹרָם עַל־עַצְמָם יָבֵשׁ הָיָה כָעֵץ׃ טוֹבִים הָיוּ חַלְלֵי־חֶרֶב
the sword ones by killed are Better like .wood has it become is it ,up dried their bones on their skin

10 מֵחַלְלֵי רָעָב שֶׁהֵם יָזוּבוּ מְדֻקָּרִים מִתְּנוּבֹת שָׂדָי׃ יְדֵי
The hands my .fields of because of produce the pierced flew ,(away) who ,hunger ones than by killed

נָשִׁים רַחֲמָנִיּוֹת בִּשְּׁלוּ יַלְדֵיהֶן הָיוּ לְבָרוֹת לָמוֹ בְּשֶׁבֶר
the in of ruin to them food they become own their ;children have boiled com- passionate women's

11 בַּת־עַמִּי׃ כִּלָּה יְהוָה אֶת־חֲמָתוֹ שָׁפַךְ חֲרוֹן אַפּוֹ וַיַּצֶּת־
has and kindled His ;anger fierce has He out poured His ,fury Jehovah has completed my daughter .people's

12 אֵשׁ בְּצִיּוֹן וַתֹּאכַל יְסוֹדֹתֶיהָ׃ לֹא הֶאֱמִינוּ מַלְכֵי־אֶרֶץ וְכֹל
and all the earth the of kings have would Not believed its .foundations has it and consumed in ,Zion a fire

13 יֹשְׁבֵי תֵבֵל כִּי יָבֹא צַר וְאוֹיֵב בְּשַׁעֲרֵי יְרוּשָׁלִַם׃ מֵחַטֹּאת
of Because of sins the .Jerusalem the in of gates the and enemy the foe would that go the world the of dwellers

her prophets (and) the iniquities of her priests, shedding the blood of the just in her midst; [14] they reeled blind in the streets; they are defiled with blood, so that not (any) are able to touch their clothes. [15] They cried to them, Depart! Unclean! Depart, depart! Touch not! Indeed they fled and reeled; they said among the nations, They will not continue to sojourn. [16] The face of Jehovah has apportioned them; He will no longer look on them; they did not lift up the faces of the priests; they did not favor the elders. [17] While we are, our eyes fail for our help (for) nothing; in our watching we have watched for a nation; it does not save. [18] They hunted our steps from going in our streets; our end is near, our days were fulfilled, for our end had come. [19] Our pursuers were swifter than the eagles of the heavens; they hotly pursued us on the mountains, they lay in wait for us in the wilderness. [20] The breath of our nostrils, the anointed of Jehovah, was captured in their pits; (of) whom we said, In his shadow we shall live among the nations.

[21] Rejoice and be glad, O daughter of Edom, living in the land of Uz; the cup also shall pass through to you; you shall be drunken and shall make yourself naked.

[22] The punishment of your iniquity (is) fulfilled, O daughter of Zion; He will no more exile you; He will visit your iniquity, O daughter of Edom; He will uncover your sins.

14 נְבִיאֶיהָ עֲוֺנֹת כֹּהֲנֶיהָ הַשֹּׁפְכִים בְּקִרְבָּהּ דַּם צַדִּיקִים׃ נָעוּ
they reeled the righteous blood of her in midst shedding her ,priests ini- quities the her ,prophets

עִוְרִים בַּחוּצוֹת נְגֹאֲלוּ בַּדָּם בְּלֹא יוּכְלוּ יִגְּעוּ בִּלְבֻשֵׁיהֶם׃
their .clothing touch (any) are so to able not with ,blood are they defiled the in ;streets blind

15 סוּרוּ טָמֵא קָרְאוּ לָמוֹ סוּרוּ סוּרוּ אַל־תִּגָּעוּ כִּי נָצוּ גַם־
and fled they In- deed !Touch not !Depart !Depart to ,them they called !Unclean De- !part

16 נָעוּ אָמְרוּ בַּגּוֹיִם לֹא יוֹסִפוּ לָגוּר׃ פְּנֵי יְהוָה חִלְּקָם לֹא
not ;them appor- tioned has Jeho- vah The of face live to .there will they continue Not among ,nations they said ;reeled

יוֹסִיף לְהַבִּיטָם פְּנֵי כֹהֲנִים לֹא נָשָׂאוּ זְקֵנִים לֹא חָנָנוּ׃
they .favored not the elders they ,rejected not the priests the of face regard to ;them will He continue

17 עוֹדֵינָה תִּכְלֶינָה עֵינֵינוּ אֶל־עֶזְרָתֵנוּ הָבֶל בְּצִפִּיָּתֵנוּ צִפִּינוּ
have we watched our in watching ;vain help our for our eyes fail While ,are we

18 אֶל־גּוֹי לֹא יוֹשִׁעַ׃ צָדוּ צְעָדֵינוּ מִלֶּכֶת בִּרְחֹבֹתֵינוּ קָרַב
came near open our ;places in from going our steps They hunted .saves it not a for —nation

19 קִצֵּנוּ מָלְאוּ יָמֵינוּ כִּי־בָא קִצֵּנוּ׃ קַלִּים הָיוּ רֹדְפֵינוּ מִנִּשְׁרֵי
the than of eagles our pursuers were Swifter our .end had for come our ,days were fulfilled our ,end

20 שָׁמַיִם עַל־הֶהָרִים דְּלָקֻנוּ בַּמִּדְבָּר אָרְבוּ לָנוּ׃ רוּחַ אַפֵּינוּ
our ,nostrils The of breath .us for lay they wait in the in wilderness hotly they ,us pursued the mountains on the ;heavens

מְשִׁיחַ יְהוָה נִלְכַּד בִּשְׁחִיתוֹתָם אֲשֶׁר אָמַרְנוּ בְּצִלּוֹ נִחְיֶה
shall we live his In shadow ,said we (of) whom their ,pits in was captured ,Jehovah the of anointed

21 בַגּוֹיִם׃ שִׂישִׂי וְשִׂמְחִי בַּת־אֱדוֹם יוֹשַׁבְתִּי בְּאֶרֶץ עוּץ
;Uz the in of land living ,Edom daughter of be and ,glad Rejoice the among .nations

22 גַּם־עָלַיִךְ תַּעֲבָר־כּוֹס תִּשְׁכְּרִי וְתִתְעָרִי׃ תַּם־עֲוֺנֵךְ בַּת־
daughter of your Complete ,punishment make and .naked yourself shall you drunken be ;cup the shall pass to you also

צִיּוֹן לֹא יוֹסִיף לְהַגְלוֹתֵךְ פָּקַד עֲוֺנֵךְ בַּת־אֱדוֹם גִּלָּה עַל־
will He expose ,Edom daughter of your ,iniquity will He visit ;exile to you shall He continue not ,Zion

חַטֹּאתָיִךְ׃
.sins your

CAP. V ה

CHAPTER 5

CHAPTER 5

[1] Remember, O Jehovah, what has come upon us; look down and see our shame. [2] Our inheritance has been turned to strangers, our houses to foreigners. [3] We are orphans, there is

1 זְכֹר יְהוָה מֶה־הָיָה לָנוּ הַבִּיט וּרְאֵה אֶת־חֶרְפָּתֵנוּ׃
.shame our see and regard ,us to has become what ,Jehovah O Remem ,ber

2
3 נַחֲלָתֵנוּ נֶהֶפְכָה לְזָרִים בָּתֵּינוּ לְנָכְרִים׃ יְתוֹמִים הָיִינוּ
,are We orphans to .foreigners our houses to ,strangers been has turned Our in- heritance

no father; our mothers (are) as widows.[4] We drank our water for silver; our wood comes to us at a price. [5] On our necks we (are) pursued; we grow weary and no rest is given to us. [6] We have given the hand to Egypt, (to) Assyria, to be satisfied with bread. [7] Our fathers have sinned, and they are not; we have borne their iniquities. [8] Servants rule over us; there is no rescuer from their hand. [9] We bring in our bread with our souls, because of the sword of the wilderness. [10] Our skin is hot like an oven because of the fever heat of famine. [11] They raped the women in Zion, virgins in the cities of Judah. [12] Princes were hanged by their hand; the faces of the elders were not honored. [13] They took the young men to grind, and the youths stumbled at the wood. [14] The elders have ceased from the gate, the young men from their music. [15] The joy of our heart has ceased; our dance has turned into mourning. [16] The crown has fallen from our head; woe now to us! For we have sinned. [17] Our heart is faint for this; our eyes are dim for these (things). [18] On the mountain of Zion, which (is) laid waste, the foxes walk about on it. [19] You, O Jehovah, remain forever; Your throne to generation and generation. [20] Why do You forget us forever (and) forsake us for length of days? [21] Return us to You, O Jehovah, and we shall turn; renew our days as of old, [22] unless You have utterly rejected us; You are very angry against us.

4 אֵין אָב אִמֹּתֵינוּ כְּאַלְמָנוֹת׃ מֵימֵינוּ בְּכֶסֶף שָׁתִינוּ עֵצֵינוּ

our have we for Our like (are) our a not
wood ,drunk silver water .widows mothers' ;father is

5 בִּמְחִיר יָבֹאוּ׃ עַל צַוָּארֵנוּ נִרְדָּפְנוּ יָגַעְנוּ לֹא הוּנַח־לָנוּ׃

to rest is not grow we are we our On .comes a for
.us given ,weary ;pursued necks price

6
7 מִצְרַיִם נָתַנּוּ יָד אַשּׁוּר לִשְׂבֹּעַ לָחֶם׃ אֲבֹתֵינוּ חָטְאוּ

have our (with) be to the to the have we the (To)
,sinned fathers ,bread satisfied Assyrian ,hand given Egyptians

8 אֵינָם *אֲנַחְנוּ עֲוֺנֹתֵיהֶם סָבָלְנוּ׃ עֲבָדִים מָשְׁלוּ בָנוּ פֹּרֵק

rescuer over rule Servants have their we they and
,us .borne iniquities ;not are

9 אֵין מִיָּדָם׃ בְּנַפְשֵׁנוּ נָבִיא לַחְמֵנוּ מִפְּנֵי חֶרֶב הַמִּדְבָּר׃

the the the from our bring we our With their from not
.wilderness of sword of face bread in souls .hand is

10
11 עוֹרֵנוּ כְּתַנּוּר נִכְמָרוּ מִפְּנֵי זַלְעֲפוֹת רָעָב׃ נָשִׁים בְּצִיּוֹן

Zion in The .famine fever the because burned is like Our
women of heat of ,black oven an skin

12 עִנּוּ בְּתֻלֹת בְּעָרֵי יְהוּדָה׃ שָׂרִים בְּיָדָם נִתְלוּ פְּנֵי זְקֵנִים

the the were their by Rulers .Judah the in virgins they
elders of faces ,hanged hand of cities ,raped

13 לֹא נֶהְדָּרוּ׃ בַּחוּרִים טְחוֹן נָשָׂאוּ וּנְעָרִים בָּעֵץ כָּשָׁלוּ׃

.stumbled the at the and ,lifted hand the young The were not
wood youths mill men .honored

14
15 זְקֵנִים מִשַּׁעַר שָׁבָתוּ בַּחוּרִים מִנְּגִינָתָם׃ שָׁבַת מְשׂוֹשׂ

The has their from young the have the from The
of joy ceased .music men ,ceased gate elders

16 לִבֵּנוּ נֶהְפַּךְ לְאֵבֶל מְחֹלֵנוּ׃ נָפְלָה עֲטֶרֶת רֹאשֵׁנוּ אוֹי־

woe ;head our The has .dance our to has our
crown from fallen mourning turned ,heart

17 נָא לָנוּ כִּי חָטָאנוּ׃ עַל־זֶה הָיָה דָוֶה לִבֵּנוּ עַל־אֵלֶּה חָשְׁכוּ

dim these for our faint is this For have we For to now
(things) ,heart .sinned !us

18
19 עֵינֵינוּ׃ עַל הַר־צִיּוֹן שֶׁשָּׁמֵם שׁוּעָלִים הִלְּכוּ־בוֹ׃ אַתָּה

,You on walk foxes laid ,Zion the On our
.it about ,waste of mount .eyes

20 יְהוָה לְעוֹלָם תֵּשֵׁב כִּסְאֲךָ לְדֹר וָדוֹר׃ לָמָּה לָנֶצַח

for Why gen- and gen- to Your ,remain forever O
ever .eration eration throne Jehovah

21 תִּשְׁכָּחֵנוּ תַּעַזְבֵנוּ לְאֹרֶךְ יָמִים׃ הֲשִׁיבֵנוּ יְהוָה ׀ אֵלֶיךָ

,You to O ,us Return ?days the forsake You do
Jehovah of length us ,us forget

22 וְנָשׁוּבָ חַדֵּשׁ יָמֵינוּ כְּקֶדֶם׃ כִּי אִם־מָאֹס מְאַסְתָּנוּ קָצַפְתָּ

are You have You utterly unless of as our renew we and
angry ,us rejected ,old days ;return shall

עָלֵינוּ עַד־מְאֹד׃

very to against
.much us

יחזקאל

LIBER EZECHIELIS

CAPUT. I א

CHAPTER 1

CHAPTER 1

[1] And it was, in the thirtieth year, in the fourth (month), in the first of the month, I (was) among the captives by the river Chebar —the heavens were opened and I saw visions of God. [2] On the fifth of the month, the fifth year of the captivity of Jehoichim the king; the word of Jehovah certainly became (known) to Ezekiel, the son of Buzi the priest in the land of the Chaldeans, by the river Chebar. And there the hand of Jehovah was on him.

[4] And I looked, and behold, a windstorm came out of the north, a great cloud, and a fire flashing itself, and a brightness to it all around and out of its midst; like the color of polished bronze out of the midst of the fire. [5] Also from its midst (came) the likeness of four living creatures. And this (was) how they looked; they (had) the likeness of a man: [6] and four faces (were) to each, and four wings to each of them; [7] and their feet (were) straight feet; and the sole of their feet like the sole of a calf's foot; and they sparkled like the color of burnished copper. [8] And the hands of a man (extended) from under their wings on their four sides; and their faces and their wings (were) to the four of them, [9] joining each one to the other (by) their wings. They did not turn in their going; each one went toward the front of their face. [10] And the likeness of their faces: the face of a man; and the face of a lion,

1 וַיְהִי׀ בִּשְׁלֹשִׁים שָׁנָה בָּרְבִיעִי בַּחֲמִשָּׁה לַחֹדֶשׁ וַאֲנִי בְתוֹךְ־

among I as the of fifth the in the in ,year the in Now
(was) ,month (day) ,(month) fourth thirtieth ,was it

הַגּוֹלָה עַל־נְהַר־כְּבָר נִפְתְּחוּ הַשָּׁמַיִם וָאֶרְאֶה מַרְאוֹת

visions saw I and the were ,Chebar river the by the
heavens opened captives

2 אֱלֹהִים׃ בַּחֲמִשָּׁה לַחֹדֶשׁ הִיא הַשָּׁנָה הַחֲמִישִׁית לְגָלוּת

the of fifth the year the it the of the On .God of
of captivity (was) ,month fifth

3 הַמֶּלֶךְ יוֹיָכִין׃ הָיֹה הָיָה דְבַר־יְהוָה אֶל־יְחֶזְקֵאל בֶּן־בּוּזִי

,Buzi the ,Ezekiel to Jehovah the became becoming Jehoia- the
of son of word ,chim king

הַכֹּהֵן בְּאֶרֶץ כַּשְׂדִּים עַל־נְהַר־כְּבָר וַתְּהִי עָלָיו שָׁם יַד־

the there upon And .Chebar river the by the the in the
of hand him was Chaldeans of land priest

4 יְהוָה׃ וָאֵרֶא וְהִנֵּה רוּחַ סְעָרָה בָּאָה מִן־הַצָּפוֹן עָנָן גָּדוֹל

,great a the out came storm wind a and I And .Jehovah
cloud ,north of of ,behold ,looked

וְאֵשׁ מִתְלַקַּחַת וְנֹגַהּ לוֹ סָבִיב וּמִתּוֹכָהּ כְּעֵין הַחַשְׁמַל

polished the like of out and all to a and flashing a and
bronze of color ,midst its ,around it brightness ,itself fire

5 מִתּוֹךְ הָאֵשׁ׃ וּמִתּוֹכָהּ דְּמוּת אַרְבַּע חַיּוֹת וְזֶה מַרְאֵיהֶן

how (was) And living four the its from Also the the of out
;looked they this .creatures of likeness (came) midst .fire of middle

6 דְּמוּת אָדָם לָהֵנָּה׃ וְאַרְבָּעָה פָנִים לְאֶחָת וְאַרְבַּע כְּנָפַיִם

wings four and ,each to faces four and to (was) man a the
;them of likeness

7 לְאַחַת לָהֶם׃ וְרַגְלֵיהֶם רֶגֶל יְשָׁרָה וְכַף רַגְלֵיהֶם כְּכַף

the like their the and straight- feet their and ;them of each to
of sole (was) feet of sole ;ness of (were) feet

8 רֶגֶל עֵגֶל וְנֹצְצִים כְּעֵין נְחֹשֶׁת קָלָל׃ וִידֵו אָדָם מִתַּחַת

from a the And .burnished of the like they and a the
under man of hands copper of color sparkled ;calf of foot

כַּנְפֵיהֶם עַל אַרְבַּעַת רִבְעֵיהֶם וּפְנֵיהֶם וְכַנְפֵיהֶם לְאַרְבַּעְתָּם׃

the to (were) their and their and their four the on wings their
,them of four wings faces ;sides of

9 חֹבְרֹת אִשָּׁה אֶל־אֲחוֹתָהּ כַּנְפֵיהֶם לֹא־יִסַּבּוּ בְלֶכְתָּן

their in did they Not their other the to each joining
;going turn .wings one

10 אִישׁ אֶל־עֵבֶר פָּנָיו יֵלֵכוּ׃ וּדְמוּת פְּנֵיהֶם פְּנֵי אָדָם וּפְנֵי

the and a face the their the And they their the toward each
of face ,man of ,faces of likeness .went face of front one

on the right (side) to the four of them; and the face of an ox on the left (side) to the four of them; and the face of an eagle to the four of them. [11] So their faces (were). And their wings were spread upward; to each, the two (wings of) each one were joined; and two (wings) covering their bodies. [12] And each went toward the front of their faces. To where the spirit was to go, there they went; they did not turn in their going. [13] And the likeness of the living creatures: they appeared like coals of burning fire; like the appearance of torches. It (was) continually circling among the living creatures. And the fire (was) bright, and out of the fire went forth lightning. [14] And the living creatures kept running and returning, like the appearance of a flash of lightning.

[15] And I looked at the living creatures, and behold, one wheel (was) on the earth beside the living creatures, with the four of its faces. [16] The appearance of the wheels, and their workmanship (was) like the color of beryl; and the one likeness (was) to the four of them. And their appearance and their workmanship was like the wheel in the middle of the wheel. [17] On the four of their sides, in their going they went; they did not turn in their going. [18] And their rims, they (were) even high, even awesome they (were); and their rims (were) full of eyes all around the four of them. [19] And in the going of the living creatures the wheels went beside them; and in the lifting up of the living creatures from on the earth, the wheels were lifted up; [20] Where on the spirit was to go, they went there; there the spirit (was) to go; and the wheels were lifted up along with them. For the spirit of the living creature (was) in the wheels. [21] In their going, these went; and in

אַרְיֵה אֶל־הַיָּמִין לְאַרְבַּעְתָּם וּפְנֵי־שׁוֹר מֵהַשְּׂמֹאול
left the on | an | the and | of four the to | right the on | ,lion a
(side) | ox | of face | ;them | (side)

11 לְאַרְבַּעְתָּן וּפְנֵי־נֶשֶׁר לְאַרְבַּעְתָּן׃ וּפְנֵיהֶם וְכַנְפֵיהֶם פְּרֻדוֹת
were | their And | their so | of four the to | an the and | of four the to
spread | wings | .(were) faces | .them | eagle of face | ;them

מִלְמָעְלָה לְאִישׁ שְׁתַּיִם חֹבְרוֹת אִישׁ וּשְׁתַּיִם מְכַסּוֹת אֵת
covering | two and | (of) | joined were | two the | each to | ;upward
(wings) | ,one each | (wings)

12 גְּוִיֹּתֵיהֶנָה׃ וְאִישׁ אֶל־עֵבֶר פָּנָיו יֵלֵכוּ אֶל אֲשֶׁר יִהְיֶה־
was | where To | .went | their | the toward | each And | .bodies their
faces | of front

13 שָׁמָּה הָרוּחַ לָלֶכֶת יֵלֵכוּ לֹא יִסַּבּוּ בְּלֶכְתָּן׃ וּדְמוּת הַחַיּוֹת
living the the And | their in | did they | not | they | ,go to | the | there
,creatures of likeness | .going | turn | ;went | spirit

מַרְאֵיהֶם כְּגַחֲלֵי־אֵשׁ בֹּעֲרוֹת כְּמַרְאֵה הַלַּפִּדִים הִיא
It | .torches | the like (and) | ,burning | fire | like | they
(was) | of appearance | of coals | appeared

מִתְהַלֶּכֶת בֵּין הַחַיּוֹת וְנֹגַהּ לָאֵשׁ וּמִן־הָאֵשׁ יוֹצֵא בָרָק׃
.lightning | went | the | and | fire the | And | living the among | continually
forth | fire | of out | (was) | bright | .creatures | circling

14 וְהַחַיּוֹת רָצוֹא וָשׁוֹב כְּמַרְאֵה הַבָּזָק׃
15 וָאֵרֶא הַחַיּוֹת וְהִנֵּה
and | living the | I And | of flash a | ap- the like | re- and | kept | living the And
,behold | ,creatures | at looked | .lightning | of pearance | ,turning | running | creatures

16 אוֹפַן אֶחָד בָּאָרֶץ אֵצֶל הַחַיּוֹת לְאַרְבַּעַת פָּנָיו׃ מַרְאֵה
ap- the | its | the with | living the | beside | the on | one | wheel
of pearance | .faces | of four | ,creatures | earth | (was)

הָאוֹפַנִּים וּמַעֲשֵׂיהֶם כְּעֵין תַּרְשִׁישׁ וּדְמוּת אֶחָד לְאַרְבַּעְתָּן
four the to | one | the and | ,beryl | the like | their and | wheels The
.them of | (was) | likeness | of color | workmanship

וּמַרְאֵיהֶם וּמַעֲשֵׂיהֶם כַּאֲשֶׁר יִהְיֶה הָאוֹפַן בְּתוֹךְ הָאוֹפָן׃
.wheel the | the in | wheel the | was | like | their and | their And
of middle | workmanship | appearance

17 עַל־אַרְבַּעַת רִבְעֵיהֶן בְּלֶכְתָּם יֵלֵכוּ לֹא יִסַּבּוּ בְּלֶכְתָּן׃
their in | did they | not | they | their In | their | of four the | On
.going | turn | ;went | going | .sides

18 וְגַבֵּיהֶן וְגֹבַהּ לָהֶם וְיִרְאָה לָהֶם וְגַבֹּתָם מְלֵאֹת עֵינַיִם
eyes | (were) | their and | to | even | to | even | their And
of full | rims | ;them | awesome | them | high | ,rims

19 סָבִיב לְאַרְבַּעְתָּן׃ וּבְלֶכֶת הַחַיּוֹת יֵלְכוּ הָאוֹפַנִּים אֶצְלָם
beside | wheels the | went | living the | in And | four the | all
;them | ,creatures of going the | .them of | around

20 וּבְהִנָּשֵׂא הַחַיּוֹת מֵעַל הָאָרֶץ יִנָּשְׂאוּ הָאוֹפַנִּים׃ עַל אֲשֶׁר
upon | where- | ;wheels the | were | the | from | living the | the in and
up lifted | ,earth | upon | creatures | of up lifting

יִהְיוּ־שָׁם הָרוּחַ לָלֶכֶת יֵלֵכוּ שָׁמָּה הָרוּחַ לָלֶכֶת וְהָאוֹפַנִּים
the and | ;go to | (their) | there they | ,go to | the | there | was
wheels | spirit | ;went | spirit

21 יִנָּשְׂאוּ לְעֻמָּתָם כִּי רוּחַ הַחַיָּה בָּאוֹפַנִּים׃ בְּלֶכְתָּם יֵלֵכוּ
these | their In | in (was) | living the | the | For | with along | were
;went | going | .wheels the | creature | of spirit | .them | up lifted

their standing still, these stood still. And in their being lifted from on the earth, the wheels were lifted up along with them. For the spirit of the living creature (was) in the wheels.

[22] And a likeness (was) over the heads of the living creature, an expanse, like the color of awesome crystal, stretched out over their heads from above. [23] And under the expanse their wings (were) straight; the one toward the other; to each, two (wings) covering all this side and to each two covering on that (side of) their bodies. [24] And I heard the sound of their wings, like the sound of great waters; like the voice of the Almighty. In their going (was) the sound of tumult, like the sound of an army. In their standing still, they let down their wings. [25] And there was a voice from the expanse that (was) over their heads. In their standing still, they let down their wings. [26] And from above the expanse that (was) over their heads (was) an appearance like a sapphire stone, the likeness of a throne. And on the likeness of the throne (was) a likeness in appearance like a man on it from above. [27] And I saw (Him), like the color of polished bronze, looking like fire within it all around. From the likeness of His loins and upward, and from the likeness of His loins and downward, I saw (Him), looking like fire, and brightness to it all around. [28] As the appearance of the bow that is in the cloud in the day of the rain, so appeared the brightness all around. This (was) the appearance of the likeness of the glory of Jehovah. And I saw; and I fell on my face; and I heard a voice of One speaking.

וּבְעָמְדָם יַעֲמֹדוּ וּבְהִנָּשְׂאָם מֵעַל הָאָרֶץ יִנָּשְׂאוּ הָאוֹפַנִּים

wheels the were ,earth the from their in And these their in and
up lifted upon lifted being .still stood ,still standing

22 לְעֻמָּתָם כִּי רוּחַ הַחַיָּה בָּאוֹפַנִּים׃ וּדְמוּת עַל־רָאשֵׁי

the over a And the in (was) living the the For with along
of heads (was) likeness .wheels creature of spirit .them

הַחַיָּה רָקִיעַ כְּעֵין הַקֶּרַח הַנּוֹרָא נָטוּי עַל־רָאשֵׁיהֶם

heads their over stretched ,awesome crystal the like an living the
out of color ,expanse creature

23 מִלְמָעְלָה׃ וְתַחַת הָרָקִיעַ כַּנְפֵיהֶם יְשָׁרוֹת אִשָּׁה אֶל־

toward one the (were) wings their the And .above from
,straight expanse under

אֲחוֹתָהּ לְאִישׁ שְׁתַּיִם מְכַסּוֹת לָהֵנָּה וּלְאִישׁ שְׁתַּיִם מְכַסּוֹת

covering two to and this all covering two each to .other the
(wings) each ,(side) (wings)

24 לָהֵנָּה אֵת גְּוִיֹּתֵיהֶם׃ וָאֶשְׁמַע אֶת־קוֹל כַּנְפֵיהֶם כְּקוֹל

the like their sound the I And .bodies their (of) that on
of sound ,wings of heard (side)

מַיִם רַבִּים כְּקוֹל־שַׁדַּי בְּלֶכְתָּם קוֹל הֲמֻלָּה כְּקוֹל מַחֲנֶה

an the like tumult the their In the the like ;great waters
.army of sound of sound going .Almighty of voice

25 בְּעָמְדָם תְּרַפֶּינָה כַנְפֵיהֶן׃ וַיְהִי־קוֹל מֵעַל לָרָקִיעַ אֲשֶׁר

that the from a there And their let they their In
(was) expanse upon voice was .wings down ,still standing

26 עַל־רֹאשָׁם בְּעָמְדָם תְּרַפֶּינָה כַנְפֵיהֶן׃ וּמִמַּעַל לָרָקִיעַ

the from And .wings their they (and) their In their over
expanse above down let still standing ,heads

אֲשֶׁר עַל־רֹאשָׁם כְּמַרְאֵה אֶבֶן־סַפִּיר דְּמוּת כִּסֵּא וְעַל

And a like- the ,sapphire a looking their over that
on .throne of ness (was) of stone like heads (was)

27 דְּמוּת הַכִּסֵּא דְּמוּת כְּמַרְאֵה אָדָם עָלָיו מִלְמָעְלָה׃ וָאֵרֶא ׀

I And .above from it on man a appear- in a (was) the like- the
,(Him) saw like ance likeness throne of ness

כְּעֵין חַשְׁמַל כְּמַרְאֵה־אֵשׁ בֵּית־לָהּ סָבִיב מִמַּרְאֵה מָתְנָיו

His the From all it within fire looking polished the like
loins of likeness .around like bronze of color

וּלְמָעְלָה וּמִמַּרְאֵה מָתְנָיו וּלְמַטָּה רָאִיתִי כְּמַרְאֵה־אֵשׁ וְנֹגַהּ

and ,fire looking saw I and His the from and and
brightness like ,(Him) ,downward loins of likeness ,upward

28 לוֹ סָבִיב׃ כְּמַרְאֵה הַקֶּשֶׁת אֲשֶׁר יִהְיֶה בֶעָנָן בְּיוֹם הַגֶּשֶׁם

,rain the the in the in is that bow the ap- the As all to
of day cloud of pearance .around it

כֵּן מַרְאֵה הַנֹּגַהּ סָבִיב הוּא מַרְאֵה דְּמוּת כְּבוֹד־יְהוָה

.Jehovah the like- the ap- the This all the appeared so
of glory of ness of pearance (was) .around brightness

וָאֶרְאֶה וָאֶפֹּל עַל־פָּנַי וָאֶשְׁמַע קוֹל מְדַבֵּר׃

One a I and my on I even (when) And
.speaking of voice heard ,face fell ,saw I

CAP. II ב

CHAPTER 2

[1] And He said to me, Son of man, stand on your feet and I will speak to you. [2] And the Spirit entered into me as He spoke to me; and He set me on my feet; and I heard Him speaking to me. [3] And He said to me, Son of man, I am sending you to the sons of Israel, to the nations, the rebelling ones who have rebelled against Me; they and their fathers have sinned against Me, to this day. [4] And the sons (are) stiff of face and hard of heart; I am sending you to them. And you shall say to them, Thus says the Lord Jehovah: [5] And they—whether they will hear, or whether they will forbear; for they are a rebellious house —yea, they shall know that a prophet has been among them.

[6] And you, son of man, do not be afraid of them and of their words. Do not be afraid, though briers and thorns (are) with you, and (though) you are living among scorpions. Do not be afraid of their words; and do not be frightened by their faces, though they (are) a house of rebellion. [7] And you shall speak My words to them, whether they will hear, or whether they will forbear; for they (are) rebellious.

[8] But you, son of man, hear what I am saying to you. Do not be like (that) rebellious house of rebellion; open your mouth and eat what I am giving to you. [9] And I looked; and behold, a hand was extended to me; and behold, a roll of a book (was) in it. [10] And He spread it

CHAPTER 2

1
2 וַיֹּאמֶר אֵלָי בֶּן־אָדָם עֲמֹד עַל־רַגְלֶיךָ וַאֲדַבֵּר אֹתָךְ׃ וַתָּבֹא
And .you to I and your on stand of Son ,me to He And
entered speak will feet ,man said
בִי רוּחַ כַּאֲשֶׁר דִּבֶּר אֵלַי וַתַּעֲמִדֵנִי עַל־רַגְלָי וָאֶשְׁמַע אֵת
I and my on set He and to He as the into
heard ,feet me ,me spoke Spirit me
3 מִדַּבֵּר אֵלָי׃ וַיֹּאמֶר אֵלַי בֶּן־אָדָם שׁוֹלֵחַ אֲנִי אוֹתְךָ
you I am ,man of Son to He And .me to Him
sending ,me said speaking
אֶל־בְּנֵי יִשְׂרָאֵל אֶל־גּוֹיִם הַמּוֹרְדִים אֲשֶׁר מָרְדוּ־בִי הֵמָּה
they against have who rebelling the the to ,Israel the to
;Me rebelled ones ,nations of sons
4 וַאֲבוֹתָם פָּשְׁעוּ בִי עַד־עֶצֶם הַיּוֹם הַזֶּה׃ וְהַבָּנִים קְשֵׁי פָנִים
of (are) the And .this day the to against have their and
face stiff sons ,Me sinned fathers
וְחִזְקֵי־לֵב אֲנִי שׁוֹלֵחַ אוֹתְךָ אֲלֵיהֶם וְאָמַרְתָּ אֲלֵיהֶם כֹּה
Thus ,them to you And .them to you am I ;heart and
say shall sending of hard
5 אָמַר אֲדֹנָי יְהוִה׃ וְהֵמָּה אִם־יִשְׁמְעוּ וְאִם־יֶחְדָּלוּ כִּי בֵּית
a for will they or they whether And .Jehovah the says
of house —stop whether hear will ,they Lord
6 מְרִי הֵמָּה וְיָדְעוּ כִּי־נָבִיא הָיָה בְתוֹכָם׃ וְאַתָּה בֶן־אָדָם
,man Son ,you And among has a that they but they rebel-
of .them been prophet know shall (are) lion
אַל־תִּירָא מֵהֶם וּמִדִּבְרֵיהֶם אַל־תִּירָא כִּי סָרָבִים וְסַלּוֹנִים
thorns and briers though be do Not their of and of be do not
,afraid .words them afraid
אוֹתָךְ וְאֶל־עַקְרַבִּים אַתָּה יוֹשֵׁב מִדִּבְרֵיהֶם אַל־תִּירָא
be do Not their of are you scorpions and with (are)
;afraid words .living among ,you
7 וּמִפְּנֵיהֶם אַל־תֵּחָת כִּי בֵּית מְרִי הֵמָּה׃ וְדִבַּרְתָּ אֶת־דְּבָרַי
words My you And they of a though be do not their by even
speak shall .(are) rebellion house frightened .faces
אֲלֵיהֶם אִם־יִשְׁמְעוּ וְאִם־יֶחְדָּלוּ כִּי מְרִי הֵמָּה׃
they rebellious for will they or will they whether to
.(are) ;stop whether hear ,them
8 וְאַתָּה בֶן־אָדָם שְׁמַע אֵת אֲשֶׁר־אֲנִי מְדַבֵּר אֵלֶיךָ אַל־תְּהִי־
be do Not .you to am I what hear of son But
saying ,man ,you
מֶרִי כְּבֵית הַמֶּרִי פְּצֵה פִיךָ וֶאֱכֹל אֵת אֲשֶׁר־אֲנִי נֹתֵן אֵלֶיךָ׃
.you to am I what eat and your open ;rebellion like rebellious
giving mouth of house (that)
9
10 וָאֶרְאֶה וְהִנֵּה־יָד שְׁלוּחָה אֵלָי וְהִנֵּה־בוֹ מְגִלַּת־סֵפֶר׃ וַיִּפְרֹשׂ
He And a a (was) in and to was a and I And
spread .book of roll it ,behold ;me extended hand ,behold ;looked

before me; and it was written on the face and the back; and written on it (were) weepings, and mourning and woe.

CHAPTER 3

[1] And He said to me, Son of man, eat what you find. Eat this roll, and go speak to the house of Israel. [2] So I opened my mouth and He made me eat that roll. [3] And He said to me, Son of man, make your belly eat, and fill your bowels with the roll, this that I give to you. And I ate; and it was in my mouth like honey for sweetness.

[4] And He said to me, Son of man, Go! Come to the house of Israel and speak with My words to them. [5] For you are not sent to a people of deep lip and hardness of tongue, (but) to the house of Israel;

[6] not to many peoples deep of lip and of a hard tongue, whose words you cannot hear. If rather I had sent you to them, they would have listened to you. [7] But the house of Israel is not willing to listen to you, for they are not willing to listen to Me; for all the house of Israel, they (are) strong of forehead and hard of heart. [8] Behold, I have made your face strong over against their faces, and your forehead strong over against their foreheads; I have made your forehead as an adamant harder than flint. Do not fear them; and do not be frightened by

אוֹתָהּ לְפָנַי וְהִיא כְתוּבָה פָּנִים וְאָחוֹר וְכָתוּב אֵלֶיהָ קִנִים
(were) it on and the and the on was it and before it
,weepings written ,back face written ;me

וָהֶגֶה וָהִי׃
and and
.woe mourning

CAP. III. ג

CHAPTER 3

1 וַיֹּאמֶר אֵלַי בֶּן־אָדָם אֵת אֲשֶׁר־תִּמְצָא אֱכוֹל אֱכוֹל אֶת־
Eat .eat find you what ,man Son ,me to He And
of said

2 הַמְּגִלָּה הַזֹּאת וְלֵךְ דַּבֵּר אֶל־בֵּית יִשְׂרָאֵל׃ וָאֶפְתַּח אֶת־
I So .Israel the to speak and ,this roll the
opened of house ,go

3 פִּי וַיַּאֲכִלֵנִי אֵת הַמְּגִלָּה הַזֹּאת׃ וַיֹּאמֶר אֵלַי בֶּן־אָדָם
,man Son ,me to He And .that roll the He and my
of said eat me made mouth

בִּטְנְךָ תַאֲכֵל וּמֵעֶיךָ תְמַלֵּא אֵת הַמְּגִלָּה הַזֹּאת אֲשֶׁר אֲנִי
I that this ,roll the with fill your and cause your
bowels ,eat to belly

4 נֹתֵן אֵלֶיךָ וָאֹכְלָה וַתְּהִי בְּפִי כִּדְבַשׁ לְמָתוֹק׃ וַיֹּאמֶר
He And for like my in it and I And to give
said .sweetness honey mouth was ;ate .you

אֵלַי בֶּן־אָדָם לֶךְ־בֹּא אֶל־בֵּית יִשְׂרָאֵל וְדִבַּרְתָּ בִדְבָרַי
My with speak and Israel the to !Go ,man Son ,me to
words of house Come of

5 אֲלֵיהֶם׃ כִּי לֹא אֶל־עַם עִמְקֵי שָׂפָה וְכִבְדֵי לָשׁוֹן אַתָּה
you tongue hard- and lip deep a to not For .them to
of ness of people

6 שָׁלוּחַ אֶל־בֵּית יִשְׂרָאֵל׃ לֹא ׀ אֶל־עַמִּים רַבִּים עִמְקֵי שָׂפָה
lip of deep many peoples to not ;Israel the (but) are
of house to ,sent

וְכִבְדֵי לָשׁוֹן אֲשֶׁר לֹא־תִשְׁמַע דִּבְרֵיהֶם אִם־לֹא אֲלֵיהֶם
them to rather If .words can you not that tongue of and
hear hard a

7 שְׁלַחְתִּיךָ הֵמָּה יִשְׁמְעוּ אֵלֶיךָ׃ וּבֵית יִשְׂרָאֵל לֹא יֹאבוּ
is not Israel the But to have would they had I
willing of house .you listened ,you sent

לִשְׁמֹעַ אֵלֶיךָ כִּי־אֵינָם אֹבִים לִשְׁמֹעַ אֵלַי כִּי כָּל־בֵּית יִשְׂרָאֵל
,Israel the all for to to are not for to listen to
of house ;Me listen willing they ,you

8 חִזְקֵי־מֵצַח וּקְשֵׁי־לֵב הֵמָּה׃ הִנֵּה נָתַתִּי אֶת־פָּנֶיךָ חֲזָקִים
strong your have I ,Behold they heart and fore- strong
face made .(are) of hard —head of

9 לְעֻמַּת פְּנֵיהֶם וְאֶת־מִצְחֲךָ חָזָק לְעֻמַּת מִצְחָם׃ כְּשָׁמִיר
an as their over strong your and their over
adamant ;foreheads against forehead faces against

חָזָק מִצֹּר נָתַתִּי מִצְחֶךָ לֹא־תִירָא אוֹתָם וְלֹא־תֵחַת
be do And .them fear do Not your have I than harder
frightened not .forehead made flint

by their faces, though they (are) a house of rebellion. [10] And He said to me, Son of man, all My words which I speak to you, receive into your heart, and hear with your ears. [11] And go! Come to the exiles, to the sons of your people, and speak to them and say to them, Thus says the Lord Jehovah—whether they will hear, or whether they will stop. [12] And the Spirit lifted me, and I heard behind me a sound of a great tumult, (saying), Blessed (be) the glory of Jehovah from His place; [13] and the sound of the wings of the living creatures touching each one to the other; and the sound of the wheels along with them; and the sound of a great tumult. [14] So the Spirit lifted me and took me, and I went bitterly in the heat of my spirit; but the hand of Jehovah was strong on me.

[15] Then I came to the exiles, at Tel-aviv, those dwelling by the river Chebar. And I sat there (where) they were sitting; I also sat there seven days, being stunned among them. [16] And it was, at the end of the seven days; and it was, the word of Jehovah to me, saying, [17] Son of man, I have made you a watchman for the house of Israel. And hear the word of My mouth, and warn them from Me. [18] In My saying to the wicked, Surely you shall die—and you do not warn him, and you do not speak to warn the wicked from his wicked way, to save his life—he, the wicked, shall die in his iniquity; but I will require his blood at your hand. [19] And you, because you have warned the wicked, and he does not turn from his wickedness or from his way, he, the

10 מִפְּנֵיהֶם כִּי בֵּית מְרִי הֵמָּה׃ וַיֹּאמֶר אֵלַי בֶּן־אָדָם
,man Son ,me to He And they rebellion a though their by
of said .(are) of house faces

אֶת־כָּל־דְּבָרַי אֲשֶׁר אֲדַבֵּר אֵלֶיךָ קַח בִּלְבָבְךָ וּבְאָזְנֶיךָ
with and your into receive to speak I which My all
ears your ,heart you words

11 שְׁמָע׃ וְלֵךְ בֹּא אֶל־הַגּוֹלָה אֶל־בְּנֵי עַמֶּךָ וְדִבַּרְתָּ אֲלֵיהֶם
,them to speak and your the to the to Come And .hear
,people of sons ,exiles !go

וְאָמַרְתָּ אֲלֵיהֶם כֹּה אָמַר אֲדֹנָי יֱהֹוִה אִם־יִשְׁמְעוּ וְאִם־
or they whether —Jehovah the says Thus ,them to say and
whether hear will Lord

12 יֶחְדָּלוּ׃ וַתִּשָּׂאֵנִי רוּחַ וָאֶשְׁמַע אַחֲרַי קוֹל רַעַשׁ גָּדוֹל
,great tumult a a behind I and the lifted And will they
of sound me heard ,Spirit me .stop

13 בָּרוּךְ כְּבוֹד־יְהוָה מִמְּקוֹמוֹ׃ וְקוֹל ׀ כַּנְפֵי הַחַיּוֹת מַשִּׁיקוֹת
touching living the the the and His from Jehovah the (saying)
creatures of wings of sound ;place of glory (be) Blessed

אִשָּׁה אֶל־אֲחוֹתָהּ וְקוֹל הָאוֹפַנִּים לְעֻמָּתָם וְקוֹל רַעַשׁ
a the and with along wheels the the and the to each
tumult of sound ,them of sound other one

14 גָּדוֹל׃ וְרוּחַ נְשָׂאַתְנִי וַתִּקָּחֵנִי וָאֵלֵךְ מַר בַּחֲמַת רוּחִי
my the in bitterly I and took and me lifted the So .great
;spirit of heat went ,me Spirit

15 וְיַד־יְהוָה עָלַי חָזָקָה׃ וָאָבוֹא אֶל־הַגּוֹלָה תֵּל אָבִיב
,aviv Tel- at the to I Then was on Jehovah the but
,exiles came .strong me of hand

הַיֹּשְׁבִים אֶל־נְהַר־כְּבָר וָאֲשֶׁר הֵמָּה יוֹשְׁבִים שָׁם וָאֵשֵׁב
also I ;there were they I And .Chebar the by those
dwelt dwelling sat river dwelling

16 שָׁם שִׁבְעַת יָמִים מַשְׁמִים בְּתוֹכָם׃ וַיְהִי מִקְצֵה
the at it And among being days seven there
of end ,was .them appalled

17 שִׁבְעַת יָמִים וַיְהִי דְבַר־יְהוָה אֵלַי לֵאמֹר׃ בֶּן
Son ,saying ,me to Jehovah the and ;days seven the
of of word ,was it

אָדָם צֹפֶה נְתַתִּיךָ לְבֵית יִשְׂרָאֵל וְשָׁמַעְתָּ מִפִּי דָּבָר
the My of hear And .Israel the for have I a ,man
word mouth of house you made watchman

18 וְהִזְהַרְתָּ אוֹתָם מִמֶּנִּי׃ בְּאָמְרִי לָרָשָׁע מוֹת תָּמוּת וְלֹא
and shall you Surely the to My In from them warn and
not —die ,wicked saying .Me

הִזְהַרְתּוֹ וְלֹא דִבַּרְתָּ לְהַזְהִיר רָשָׁע מִדַּרְכּוֹ הָרְשָׁעָה
,wicked the his from the warn to you and warn you
(way) ,way wicked speak not ;him

19 לְחַיֹּתוֹ הוּא רָשָׁע בַּעֲוֺנוֹ יָמוּת וְדָמוֹ מִיָּדְךָ אֲבַקֵּשׁ׃ וְאַתָּה
,you And will I your at his but shall his in the he save to
.require hand blood ;die iniquity wicked —life his

כִּי־הִזְהַרְתָּ רָשָׁע וְלֹא־שָׁב מֵרִשְׁעוֹ וּמִדַּרְכּוֹ הָרְשָׁעָה הוּא
he wicked the from or his from he and the have you be-
,way his wickedness turns not ,wicked warned cause

shall die in his iniquity; but you have delivered your soul. [20] And when the righteous turns from his righteousness and does injustice, and I lay a stumbling-block before him, he shall die. Since you have not warned him, he shall die in his sin, and his righteousness which he has done shall not be remembered; but I will require his blood at your hand. [21] But you, because you warned him, the righteous, so that the righteous should not sin—and he does not sin—living he shall live, because he is warned; and you have delivered your soul.

[22] And the hand of Jehovah was on me there. And He said to me, Arise, go forth into the plain, and there I will speak with you. [23] And I arose and went forth into the plain; and behold, there the glory of Jehovah was standing, like the glory which I saw by the river Chebar. And I fell on my face. [24] And the Spirit entered into me and stood me on my feet, and spoke with me. And He said to me, Come, shut yourself within your house! [25] But you, son of man, behold, they shall put on you cords and shall bind you with them; and you shall not go out among them. [26] And I will make your tongue cling to your palate, and you shall be dumb; and there shall not be to them a mediating man; for they (are) a rebellious house. [27] But in My speaking with you I will open your mouth, and you shall say to them, Thus says the Lord Jehovah: He who hears, let him hear; and he who stops, let him stop; for they (are) a rebellious house.

20 בַּעֲוֺנוֹ יָמוּת וְאַתָּה אֶת־נַפְשְׁךָ הִצַּלְתָּ׃ וּבְשׁוּב צַדִּיק
the righteous when turns And have .delivered soul your you but shall ;die his in iniquity

מִצִּדְקוֹ וְעָשָׂה עָוֶל וְנָתַתִּי מִכְשׁוֹל לְפָנָיו הוּא יָמוּת כִּי
Since shall .die he before ,him stumbling-a block I and lay in- justice and does his from righteousness

לֹא הִזְהַרְתּוֹ בְּחַטָּאתוֹ יָמוּת וְלֹא תִזָּכַרְןָ צִדְקָתוֹ אֲשֶׁר
which his righteousness be shall remembered and not shall he ,die his in sin have you ,him warned not

21 עָשָׂה וְדָמוֹ מִיָּדְךָ אֲבַקֵּשׁ׃ וְאַתָּה כִּי הִזְהַרְתּוֹ צַדִּיק לְבִלְתִּי
that so not the ,righteous warned you ,him because But ,you will I .require your at ,hand his but blood has he ;done

חֲטֹא צַדִּיק וְהוּא לֹא־חָטָא חָיוֹ יִחְיֶה כִּי נִזְהָר וְאַתָּה
you and is he ,warned because shall he .live living does ,sin not he and the ,righteous should sin

22 אֶת־נַפְשְׁךָ הִצַּלְתָּ׃ וַתְּהִי עָלַי שָׁם יַד־יְהוָה וַיֹּאמֶר
He And said .Jehovah the of hand there on me And was have .delivered soul your

23 אֵלַי קוּם צֵא אֶל־הַבִּקְעָה וְשָׁם אֲדַבֵּר אוֹתָךְ׃ וָאָקוּם
I And arose with .you will I speak and there plain the into go forth Arise to ,me

וָאֵצֵא אֶל־הַבִּקְעָה וְהִנֵּה־שָׁם כְּבוֹד־יְהוָה עֹמֵד כַּכָּבוֹד
the like glory was standing Jehovah the of glory there and ,behold the ;plain into went and forth

24 אֲשֶׁר רָאִיתִי עַל־נְהַר־כְּבָר וָאֶפֹּל עַל־פָּנָי׃ וַתָּבֹא־בִי רוּחַ
the Spirit into me And entered my on .face I And fell .Chebar the river by saw I which

וַתַּעֲמִדֵנִי עַל־רַגְלָי וַיְדַבֵּר אֹתִי וַיֹּאמֶר אֵלַי בֹּא הִסָּגֵר
shut yourself ,Come ,me to He And said with .me and spoke my feet on stood and me

25 בְּתוֹךְ בֵּיתֶךָ׃ וְאַתָּה בֶן־אָדָם הִנֵּה נָתְנוּ עָלֶיךָ עֲבוֹתִים
cords upon you they put shall ,behold ,man son of But ,you your !house within

26 וַאֲסָרוּךָ בָּהֶם וְלֹא תֵצֵא בְּתוֹכָם׃ וּלְשׁוֹנְךָ אַדְבִּיק אֶל־
to make will I cling your And tongue among .them shall you out go and not with ,them shall and you bind

חִכֶּךָ וְנֶאֱלַמְתָּ וְלֹא־תִהְיֶה לָהֶם לְאִישׁ מוֹכִיחַ כִּי בֵּית מְרִי
rebel- lious a house for medi- ating man a them to shall be and shall not you and ;dumb be your ,palate

27 הֵמָּה׃ וּבְדַבְּרִי אוֹתְךָ אֶפְתַּח אֶת־פִּיךָ וְאָמַרְתָּ אֲלֵיהֶם
,them to you and say shall your ,mouth will I open with ,you My in But speaking they .(are)

כֹּה אָמַר אֲדֹנָי יְהוִה הַשֹּׁמֵעַ ׀ יִשְׁמָע וְהֶחָדֵל ׀ יֶחְדָּל כִּי
for him let ;stop he and stops who him let ;hear who He ,hears :Jehovah the Lord says Thus

בֵּית מְרִי הֵמָּה׃
they .(are) rebellion of a house

CHAPTER 4

[1] And you, son of man, take to yourself a brick, and lay it before you, and engrave on it a city—Jerusalem. [2] And lay on it a siege, and build on it a fort, and cast up on it a ramp. And place on it a camp, and set on it battering rams all around. [3] And you, take to yourself a griddle of iron, and place it (as) a wall of iron between you and the city. And place your face against it; and it shall be under siege; and thrust upon it. It is a sign to the house of Israel.

[4] And you, lie down on your side, the left, and lay the iniquity of the house of Israel on it; the number of the days that you shall lie down on it, you shall bear their iniquity. [5] For I have laid on you the years of their iniquity, by the number of days: three hundred and ninety days. And you shall bear the house of Israel's iniquity. [6] And when you complete them, even lie on your side, the right, the second; and you shall bear the house of Judah's iniquity—forty days, a day for a year; a day for a year I have set it for you. [7] And you shall set your face toward the siege of Jerusalem, and your arm bared; and you shall prophesy on it. [8] And behold, I will put cords on you, and you cannot turn from your side to your (other) side, until you have completed the days of your siege. [9] And you, take to yourself wheat, and barley, and beans, and lentils, and millet, and spelt,

CAP. IV. ד

CHAPTER 4

1 וְאַתָּה בֶן־אָדָם קַח־לְךָ לְבֵנָה וְנָתַתָּה אוֹתָהּ לְפָנֶיךָ וְחַקּוֹתָ
and before it lay and a to take ,man son And
engrave ,you brick yourself of ,you

2 עָלֶיהָ עִיר אֶת־יְרוּשָׁלִָם׃ וְנָתַתָּה עָלֶיהָ מָצוֹר וּבָנִיתָ
and ,siege a upon lay And .Jerusalem a upon
build it ,city it

עָלֶיהָ דָּיֵק וְשָׁפַכְתָּ עָלֶיהָ סֹלְלָה וְנָתַתָּה עָלֶיהָ מַחֲנוֹת
,camp a upon Also .ramp a upon cast and ,fort a upon
it place it up it

3 וְשִׂים־עָלֶיהָ כָּרִים סָבִיב׃ וְאַתָּה קַח־לְךָ מַחֲבַת בַּרְזֶל
iron griddle a to take ,you And all battering upon set and
of yourself .around rams it

וְנָתַתָּה אוֹתָהּ קִיר בַּרְזֶל בֵּינְךָ וּבֵין הָעִיר וַהֲכִינֹתָה אֶת־
place And the and between iron (as) it place and
.city between you of wall a

פָּנֶיךָ אֵלֶיהָ וְהָיְתָה בַמָּצוֹר וְצַרְתָּ עָלֶיהָ אוֹת הִיא לְבֵית
the to It sign a upon and under it and against your
of house (is) .it thrust siege be shall ,it face

4 יִשְׂרָאֵל׃ וְאַתָּה שְׁכַב עַל־צִדְּךָ הַשְּׂמָאלִי וְשַׂמְתָּ אֶת־
lay and ,left the your on lie And .Israel
,side down ,you

עֲוֺן בֵּית־יִשְׂרָאֵל עָלָיו מִסְפַּר הַיָּמִים אֲשֶׁר תִּשְׁכַּב עָלָיו
,it on shall you that days the the ;it on Israel house the the
down lie of number of of iniquity

5 תִּשָּׂא אֶת־עֲוֺנָם׃ וַאֲנִי נָתַתִּי לְךָ אֶת־שְׁנֵי עֲוֺנָם לְמִסְפַּר
the by their the on have For their shall you
of number ,iniquity of years you laid I .iniquity bear

יָמִים שְׁלֹשׁ־מֵאוֹת וְתִשְׁעִים יוֹם וְנָשָׂאתָ עֲוֺן בֵּית־יִשְׂרָאֵל׃
.Israel's the iniquity you So .days and hundred three ,days
of house bear shall ninety

6 וְכִלִּיתָ אֶת־אֵלֶּה וְשָׁכַבְתָּ עַל־צִדְּךָ הַיְמָנִי שֵׁנִית וְנָשָׂאתָ
you and the right the your on lie ,them when And
bear shall ;second side even complete you

אֶת־עֲוֺן בֵּית־יְהוּדָה אַרְבָּעִים יוֹם יוֹם לַשָּׁנָה יוֹם לַשָּׁנָה
a for a a for a —days forty Judah's the iniquity
,year day —year day of house

7 נְתַתִּיו לָךְ׃ וְאֶל־מְצוֹר יְרוּשָׁלִַם תָּכִין פָּנֶיךָ וּזְרֹעֲךָ חֲשׂוּפָה
,bared your and your shall you Jerusalem the And for have I
arm ,face set of siege toward .you it set

8 וְנִבֵּאתָ עָלֶיהָ׃ וְהִנֵּה נָתַתִּי עָלֶיךָ עֲבוֹתִים וְלֹא־תֵהָפֵךְ
can you and ,cords upon will I ,And upon you and
turn not you place ,behold .it prophesy shall

9 מִצִּדְּךָ אֶל־צִדֶּךָ עַד־כַּלּוֹתְךָ יְמֵי מְצוּרֶךָ׃ וְאַתָּה קַח־לְךָ
for take And your the have you until your to your from
yourself ,you .siege of days completed side (other) side

חִטִּין וּשְׂעֹרִים וּפוֹל וַעֲדָשִׁים וְדֹחַן וְכֻסְּמִים וְנָתַתָּה אוֹתָם
them place and spelt and and ,lentils and and and ,wheat
,millet ,beans ,barley

בִּכְלִי אֶחָד וְעָשִׂיתָ אוֹתָם לְךָ לְלָחֶם מִסְפַּר הַיָּמִים אֲשֶׁר־
that days the (to) into for them and single a in
of number ;bread yourself prepare vessel

אַתָּה ׀ שׁוֹכֵב עַל־צִדְּךָ שְׁלֹשׁ־מֵאוֹת וְתִשְׁעִים יוֹם תֹּאכְלֶנּוּ׃
shall you ,days ninety and hundred three your on are you
.it eat ,side lying

10 וּמַאֲכָלְךָ אֲשֶׁר תֹּאכְלֶנּוּ בְּמִשְׁקוֹל עֶשְׂרִים שֶׁקֶל לַיּוֹם מֵעֵת
from ;day a shekels twenty weight by shall you which your And
time (be shall) it eat food

11 עַד־עֵת תֹּאכְלֶנּוּ׃ וּמַיִם בִּמְשׂוּרָה תִשְׁתֶּה שִׁשִּׁית הַהִין
;hin a sixth the shall you measure by And shall you time to
of part ,drink water .it eat

12 מֵעֵת עַד־עֵת תִּשְׁתֶּה׃ וְעֻגַת שְׂעֹרִים תֹּאכְלֶנָּה וְהִיא בְּגֶלְלֵי
with it and shall you ,barley a And shall you time to from
of dung ,it eat of cake .drink time

13 צֵאַת הָאָדָם תְּעֻגֶנָה לְעֵינֵיהֶם׃ וַיֹּאמֶר יְהוָה כָּכָה
Even ,Jehovah said And their in shall you man ex- the
so .sight ,it bake of crement

יֹאכְלוּ בְנֵי־יִשְׂרָאֵל אֶת־לַחְמָם טָמֵא בַּגּוֹיִם אֲשֶׁר אַדִּיחֵם
will I where among defiled their Israel the shall
them drive nations the bread of sons eat

14 שָׁם׃ וָאֹמַר אֲהָהּ אֲדֹנָי יְהוִה הִנֵּה נַפְשִׁי לֹא מְטֻמָּאָה
been has not my ,Behold !Jehovah Lord ,Ah I Then .there
.defiled soul ,said

וּנְבֵלָה וּטְרֵפָה לֹא־אָכַלְתִּי מִנְּעוּרַי וְעַד־עַתָּה וְלֹא־בָא
has And .now even my from have I not torn a on a Even
come not until ,youth eaten animal carcase

15 בְּפִי בְּשַׂר פִּגּוּל׃ וַיֹּאמֶר אֵלַי רְאֵה נָתַתִּי לְךָ אֶת־
to have I ,See to He Then .unclean flesh my into
you given ,me said mouth

צְפוּעֵי הַבָּקָר תַּחַת גֶּלְלֵי הָאָדָם וְעָשִׂיתָ אֶת־לַחְמְךָ עֲלֵיהֶם׃
over your you and ;man dung the in cattle dung the
.it bread prepare shall of of place of

16 וַיֹּאמֶר אֵלַי בֶּן־אָדָם הִנְנִי שֹׁבֵר מַטֵּה־לֶחֶם בִּירוּשָׁלִָם
.Jerusalem in bread the am Behold man Son ,me to He And
of staff breaking I of said

וְאָכְלוּ־לֶחֶם בְּמִשְׁקָל וּבִדְאָגָה וּמַיִם בִּמְשׂוּרָה וּבְשִׁמָּמוֹן
in and ,measure by And with and weight by bread they And
horror water .anxiety eat shall

17 יִשְׁתּוּ׃ לְמַעַן יַחְסְרוּ לֶחֶם וָמָיִם וְנָשַׁמּוּ אִישׁ וְאָחִיו
his with each be and and bread will they because shall they
,brother one appalled ,water lack ,drink

וְנָמַקּוּ בַּעֲוֹנָם׃
their in will and
.iniquity away waste

CAP. V ה

CHAPTER 5

1 וְאַתָּה בֶן־אָדָם קַח־לְךָ ׀ חֶרֶב חַדָּה תַּעַר הַגַּלָּבִים תִּקָּחֶנָּה
it take ;barber a the ,sharp sword a to take ,man son ,you And
of razor yourself of

and place them in a single vessel, and prepare them for yourself into bread; (to) the number of days that you are lying on your side—three hundred and ninety days—you shall eat it. [10] And your food which you shall eat it (shall be) by weight, twenty shekels a day; from time to time you shall eat it. [11] And you shall drink water by measure, the sixth part of a hin; from time to time you shall drink. [12] And a cake of barley, you shall eat it; and you shall bake it with dung of the excrement of man, in their sight. [13] And Jehovah said, Even so the sons of Israel shall eat their defiled bread among the nations where I will drive them there. [14] Then I said, Ah, Lord Jehovah! Behold, my soul has not been defiled. I have not even eaten a carcase on a torn animal from my youth, even until now. And unclean flesh has not come into my mouth. [15] Then He said to me, See, I have given to you the dung of cattle in place of the dung of man; and you shall prepare your bread over it.

[16] And He said to me, Son of man, behold, I am breaking the staff of bread in Jerusalem. And they shall eat bread by weight and with anxiety. And they shall drink water by measure and in horror; because they will lack bread and water, and each one be appalled with his brother; and (they) will waste away in their iniquity.

CHAPTER 5

[1] And you, son of man, take to yourself a sharp sword, the razor of

a barber; take it to yourself, and make it pass over your head and over your beard. And take to yourself scales to weigh, and to divide them out; [2] you shall burn a third part in the fire, in the midst of the city, when the days of the siege are fulfilled; you shall take the third part (and) beat with a sword all around it; and you shall scatter the third part into the wind; and I will draw out a sword after them. [3] Also you shall take from there a few in number, and bind them in your skirts. [4] And take from them again and throw them into the middle of the fire, and burn them in the fire; (for) from it shall come forth a fire into all the house of Israel.

[5] Thus says the Lord Jehovah: This (is) Jerusalem; I have set her in the midst of the nations; and all around her (are) the lands. [6] And she has defiled My judgments; and wickedness more than the nations; and My laws more than the lands that (are) all around her; for they have rejected My judgments and My laws; they have not walked in them. [7] Therefore thus says the Lord Jehovah: Because you rebelled more than the nations that (are) all around you, (and) have not walked in My laws, and have not performed My judgments; and according to the judgments of the nations that (are) all around you, you have not done; [8] therefore thus says the Lord Jehovah: Behold, I, even I (am) against you, and will execute in your midst judgments in the sight of the nations. [9] And I will do in you that which I have not done, and which I will not do the like again, for all your abominations. [10] Therefore, the fathers

לְךָ וְהַעֲבַרְתָּ עַל־רֹאשְׁךָ וְעַל־זְקָנֶךָ וְלָקַחְתָּ לְךָ מֹאזְנֵי
scales to take And your and your over make and to
yourself .beard over head pass it yourself

2 מִשְׁקָל וְחִלַּקְתָּם׃ שְׁלִשִׁית בָּאוּר תַּבְעִיר בְּתוֹךְ הָעִיר
the the in shall you ,the in third a divide and weigh to
,city of midst ,burn fire part ,out them

כִּמְלֹאת יְמֵי הַמָּצוֹר וְלָקַחְתָּ אֶת־הַשְּׁלִשִׁית תַּכֶּה בַחֶרֶב
a with beat third the you and the the are when
sword (and) part take shall ;siege of days fulfilled

סְבִיבוֹתֶיהָ וְהַשְּׁלִשִׁית תִּזְרֶה לָרוּחַ וְחֶרֶב אָרִיק אַחֲרֵיהֶם׃
.them after will I a and the into shall you the and around all
out draw sword ,wind scatter part third ;it

3
4 וְלָקַחְתָּ מִשָּׁם מְעַט בְּמִסְפָּר וְצַרְתָּ אוֹתָם בִּכְנָפֶיךָ׃ וּמֵהֶם
of And your in them bind and ,number in few a from you Also
them .skirts there take shall

עוֹד תִּקָּח וְהִשְׁלַכְתָּ אוֹתָם אֶל־תּוֹךְ הָאֵשׁ וְשָׂרַפְתָּ אֹתָם
them burn and the the into them throw and ,take again
,fire of middle

5 בָּאֵשׁ מִמֶּנּוּ תֵצֵא־אֵשׁ אֶל־כָּל־בֵּית יִשְׂרָאֵל׃ כֹּה אָמַר
says Thus .Israel the all into a come shall (for) the in
of house fire forth it from ;fire

אֲדֹנָי יְהוִה זֹאת יְרוּשָׁלִַם בתוך הגוים שמתיה וסביבותיה
around all and have I the the in .Jerusalem This :Jehovah the
her her set nations of middle (is) Lord

6 אֲרָצוֹת׃ וַתֶּמֶר אֶת־מִשְׁפָּטַי לְרִשְׁעָה מִן־הַגּוֹיִם וְאֶת־
and the more for My she And the
,nations than wickedness judgments defiled has .lands

חֻקּוֹתַי מִן־הָאֲרָצוֹת אֲשֶׁר סְבִיבוֹתֶיהָ כִּי בְמִשְׁפָּטַי מָאָסוּ
have they My for around all that the more My
rejected judgments ;her (are) lands than laws

7 וְחֻקּוֹתַי לֹא־הָלְכוּ בָהֶם׃ לָכֵן כֹּה־אָמַר ׀ אֲדֹנָי יְהוִה
:Jehovah the says thus Therefore in have they not My and
Lord .them walked ;laws

יַעַן הֲמָנְכֶם מִן־הַגּוֹיִם אֲשֶׁר סְבִיבוֹתֵיכֶם בְּחֻקּוֹתַי לֹא
not in (and) around all that the more you Because
laws My ,you (are) nations than rebelled

הֲלַכְתֶּם וְאֶת־מִשְׁפָּטַי לֹא עֲשִׂיתֶם וּכְמִשְׁפְּטֵי הַגּוֹיִם אֲשֶׁר
that the the as and have not My and have
(are) nations of judgments ,performed judgments ,walked

8 סְבִיבוֹתֵיכֶם לֹא עֲשִׂיתֶם׃ לָכֵן כֹּה אָמַר אֲדֹנָי יְהוִה
,Jehovah the says thus ,therefore have you not around all
Lord ;done you

הִנְנִי עָלַיִךְ גַּם־אָנִי וְעָשִׂיתִי בְתוֹכֵךְ מִשְׁפָּטִים לְעֵינֵי הַגּוֹיִם׃
the the in judgments your in will and ,I even (am) ,Behold
.nations of sight midst execute ,you against ,I

9 וְעָשִׂיתִי בָךְ אֵת אֲשֶׁר לֹא־עָשִׂיתִי וְאֵת אֲשֶׁר־לֹא־אֶעֱשֶׂה
will I not which and have I not that in I I And
do ,done which you do will

כָּמֹהוּ עוֹד יַעַן כָּל־תּוֹעֲבֹתָיִךְ׃ 10 לָכֵן אָבוֹת יֹאכְלוּ
shall the ,Therefore your all for ,again like the
eat fathers .abominations it of

shall eat the sons in your midst, and the sons shall eat their fathers. And I will execute judgments against you, and I will scatter the whole remnant of you into every wind. [11] Therefore, (as) I live, says the Lord Jehovah, Surely because you have defiled My sanctuary with all your idolatries and with all your abominations, so I also will withdraw. And My eye shall not spare, and I will not have pity.

[12] A third part of you shall die by the plague, and shall be consumed by the famine in your midst. And a third part shall fall by the sword all around you; and a third part I will scatter into every wind; and I will draw out a sword after them. [13] And My anger shall be spent, and I will make My fury rest on them, and I will be eased. And they shall know that I, Jehovah, have spoken in my zeal, in My fulfilling My fury on them. [14] And I will make you into a waste and a reproach among the nations that (are) around you; in the eyes of all who pass by. [15] And it shall be a reproach and a taunt, an example and a wonder, to the nations which (are) all around you, when I shall execute against you judgments in anger and in fury and in rebukes (among) them. I, Jehovah, have spoken. [16] When I shall send the arrows of evil famine against them, which shall be for ruin, for which I will send them to destroy you; and I will increase the famine on you, and break to you the staff of bread; [17] yea, I will send on you famine and evil beasts, and you will be bereaved; and pestilence and blood shall pass among you; and I shall bring a sword on you. I, Jehovah, have spoken.

בָנִים בְּתוֹכֵךְ וּבָנִים יֹאכְלוּ אֲבוֹתָם וְעָשִׂיתִי בָךְ שְׁפָטִים

,judgments against you | I And do will | their .fathers | shall eat | the and sons | your in ,midst | the sons

11 וְזֵרִיתִי אֶת־כָּל־שְׁאֵרִיתֵךְ לְכָל־רוּחַ׃ לָכֵן חַי־אָנִי נְאֻם

says | (as) ,live I | ,Therefore | .wind | into every | of remnant you | the whole | I and scatter will

אֲדֹנָי יֱהֹוִה אִם־לֹא יַעַן אֶת־מִקְדָּשִׁי טִמֵּאת בְּכָל־שִׁקּוּצַיִךְ

your idolatries | with all | have you defiled | My sanctuary | because | Surely | ,Jehovah | the Lord

וּבְכָל־תּוֹעֲבֹתַיִךְ וְגַם־אֲנִי אֶגְרַע וְלֹא־תָחוֹס עֵינִי וְגַם־אֲנִי

I and | My ,eye | shall (you) spare | And not | with- .draw | will I | also so | your ,abominations | with and all

12 לֹא אֶחְמוֹל׃ שְׁלִשִׁתַיִךְ בַּדֶּבֶר יָמוּתוּ וּבָרָעָב יִכְלוּ

be shall consumed | by and famine | shall ,die | the by plague | third A you of part | have will .pity | not

בְתוֹכֵךְ וְהַשְּׁלִשִׁית בַּחֶרֶב יִפְּלוּ סְבִיבוֹתַיִךְ וְהַשְּׁלִישִׁית

third a and part | around all ;you | shall fall | the by sword | third a And part | your in .midst

13 לְכָל־רוּחַ אֱזָרֶה וְחֶרֶב אָרִיק אַחֲרֵיהֶם׃ וְכָלָה אַפִּי וַהֲנִחוֹתִי

will I and rest make | My ,anger | shall So spent be | after .them | will I out draw | a and sword | will I ,scatter | wind | into every

חֲמָתִי בָּם וְהִנֶּחָמְתִּי וְיָדְעוּ כִּי־אֲנִי יְהוָה דִּבַּרְתִּי בְּקִנְאָתִי

My in ,zeal | have spoken | Jehovah | I that | they And know shall | will I and .eased be | on ,them | My fury

14 בְּכַלּוֹתִי חֲמָתִי בָּם׃ וְאֶתְּנֵךְ לְחָרְבָּה וּלְחֶרְפָּה בַּגּוֹיִם

the among nations | a and reproach | a into waste | will I And you make | on .them | My fury | My in fulfilling

15 אֲשֶׁר סְבִיבוֹתַיִךְ לְעֵינֵי כָּל־עוֹבֵר׃ וְהָיְתָה חֶרְפָּה וּגְדוּפָה

a and taunt | a reproach | it So be shall | who .by pass | all | the in of eyes | around all ,you | that (are)

מוּסָר וּמְשַׁמָּה לַגּוֹיִם אֲשֶׁר סְבִיבוֹתַיִךְ בַּעֲשׂוֹתִי בָךְ

against you | shall I when execute | around all ,you | which (are) | the to nations | a and wonder | an example

שְׁפָטִים בְּאַף וּבְחֵמָה וּבְתֹכְחוֹת חֵמָה אֲנִי יְהוָה דִּבַּרְתִּי׃

have .(it) spoken | Jehovah | I | (among) .them | in and rebukes | in and fury | in anger | judgments

16 בְּשַׁלְּחִי אֶת־חִצֵּי הָרָעָב הָרָעִים בָּהֶם אֲשֶׁר־הָיוּ לְמַשְׁחִית

,ruin for | shall which be | against ,them | evil | famine | arrows the of | I When send shall

אֲשֶׁר־אֲשַׁלַּח אוֹתָם לְשַׁחֶתְכֶם וְרָעָב אֹסֵף עֲלֵיכֶם

,you upon | will I increase | the and famine | destroy to ;you | them | will I send | for which

17 וְשָׁבַרְתִּי לָכֶם מַטֵּה־לָחֶם׃ וְשִׁלַּחְתִּי עֲלֵיכֶם רָעָב וְחַיָּה

and beasts | famine | you on | I ,yea send will | ;bread | the of staff | you to | break and

רָעָה וְשִׁכְּלֻךְ וְדֶבֶר וָדָם יַעֲבָר־בָּךְ וְחֶרֶב אָבִיא עָלַיִךְ אֲנִי

I | upon .you | shall I bring | a and sword | among ;you | shall pass | and blood | and pestilence | will you and ;bereft be | ,evil

יְהוָה דִּבַּרְתִּי׃

have .spoken | Jehovah

CAP. VI ו

CHAPTER 6

CHAPTER 6

[1] And it (was) the word of Jehovah to me, saying, [2] Son of man, set your face towards the mountains of Israel, and prophesy against them. [3] And say, Mountains of Israel, hear the word of the Lord Jehovah: Thus says the Lord Jehovah to the mountains, and to the hills, to the ravines and to the valleys: Behold, I will bring on you a sword, and I will destroy your high places. [4] And your altars shall be ruined, and your pillars shall be broken. And I will throw down your slain before your idols. [5] And I will put the dead bodies of the sons of Israel before their idols; and I will scatter your bones around your altars. [6] In all your dwelling-places the cities shall be laid waste, and the high places shall be deserted; so that your altars may be laid waste and become guilty; and (that) your idols may be broken and brought to an end; and (that) your pillars may be cut down and your works wiped out. [7] And the slain shall fall in your midst; and you shall know that I (am) Jehovah.

[8] Yet I will leave an excess, so that may be to you those who escape the sword among the nations, in your scattering among the lands. [9] And those who escape shall remember Me among the nations where they will be made captive, because I was broken (by) their heart whoring, which has turned away from Me, and by their whoring eyes, which go after their idols. And they shall loathe against their faces for the evils which they have done in all their abominations. [10] And they shall know that I (am) Jehovah; I have not said in vain to do this evil to them.

1
2 וַיְהִי דְבַר־יְהוָה אֵלַי לֵאמֹר׃ בֶּן־אָדָם שִׂים פָּנֶיךָ אֶל־הָרֵי

the towards your set ,man Son ,saying ,me to Jehovah the it And
of mountains face of of word (was)

3 יִשְׂרָאֵל וְהִנָּבֵא אֲלֵיהֶם׃ וְאָמַרְתָּ הָרֵי יִשְׂרָאֵל שִׁמְעוּ דְּבַר־

word the hear ,Israel Mountains ,say And against and ,Israel
of of .them prophesy

אֲדֹנָי יְהוִה כֹּה־אָמַר אֲדֹנָי יְהוִה לֶהָרִים וְלַגְּבָעוֹת לָאֲפִיקִים

the to the to and the to Jehovah the says Thus :Jehovah the
ravines ,hills ,mountains Lord Lord

וְלַגֵּאָיוֹת הִנְנִי אֲנִי מֵבִיא עֲלֵיכֶם חֶרֶב וְאִבַּדְתִּי בָּמוֹתֵיכֶם׃

high your I and a you upon will I ,Behold to and
.places destroy will ,sword bring :valleys the

4 וְנָשַׁמּוּ מִזְבְּחוֹתֵיכֶם וְנִשְׁבְּרוּ חַמָּנֵיכֶם וְהִפַּלְתִּי חַלְלֵיכֶם

slain your will I And your shall and ,altars your shall And
down throw .pillars broken be ruined be

5 לִפְנֵי גִּלּוּלֵיכֶם׃ וְנָתַתִּי אֶת־פִּגְרֵי בְּנֵי יִשְׂרָאֵל לִפְנֵי גִּלּוּלֵיהֶם

their before Israel the dead the I And .idols your before
;idols of sons of bodies put will

6 וְזֵרִיתִי אֶת־עַצְמוֹתֵיכֶם סְבִיבוֹת מִזְבְּחוֹתֵיכֶם׃ בְּכֹל

all In .altars your around bones your I and
scatter will

מוֹשְׁבוֹתֵיכֶם הֶעָרִים תֶּחֱרַבְנָה וְהַבָּמוֹת תִּישָׁמְנָה לְמַעַן

that so be shall the and be shall cities the dwelling- your
,deserted places high ,waste laid places

יֶחֶרְבוּ וְיֶאְשְׁמוּ מִזְבְּחוֹתֵיכֶם וְנִשְׁבְּרוּ וְנִשְׁבְּתוּ גִּלּוּלֵיכֶם

,idols your brought and be may and ,altars your become and be may
end an to broken guilty waste laid

7 וְנִגְדְּעוּ חַמָּנֵיכֶם וְנִמְחוּ מַעֲשֵׂיכֶם׃ וְנָפַל חָלָל בְּתוֹכְכֶם

your in the And .works your and pillars your may and
,midst slain fall shall out wiped down cut be

8 וִידַעְתֶּם כִּי־אֲנִי יְהוָה׃ וְהוֹתַרְתִּי בִּהְיוֹת לָכֶם פְּלִיטֵי חֶרֶב

the escapees you to that so will I Yet .Jehovah I that you and
sword of be may excess an leave (am) know shall

9 בַּגּוֹיִם בְּהִזָּרוֹתֵיכֶם בָּאֲרָצוֹת׃ וְזָכְרוּ פְלִיטֵיכֶם אוֹתִי בַּגּוֹיִם

among Me your shall And the among your in the among
nations the escapees remember .lands scattering ,nations

אֲשֶׁר נִשְׁבּוּ־שָׁם אֲשֶׁר נִשְׁבַּרְתִּי אֶת־לִבָּם הַזּוֹנֶה אֲשֶׁר־

which whoring their (by) was I because be will they where
heart broken ,captive made

סָר מֵעָלַי וְאֵת עֵינֵיהֶם הַזֹּנוֹת אַחֲרֵי גִּלּוּלֵיהֶם וְנָקֹטּוּ

they And their after go which their and from has
loathe shall .idols whoring eyes by ,Me turned

10 בִּפְנֵיהֶם אֶל־הָרָעוֹת אֲשֶׁר עָשׂוּ לְכֹל תּוֹעֲבֹתֵיהֶם׃ וְיָדְעוּ

they And their all in they which the for their against
know shall .abominations done have evils faces

כִּי־אֲנִי יְהוָה לֹא אֶל־חִנָּם דִּבַּרְתִּי לַעֲשׂוֹת לָהֶם הָרָעָה

evil to do to have I vain in not ;Jehovah I that
them said (am)

[11] Thus says the Lord Jehovah: Strike with your hand, and stamp with your foot, and say, Alas for all the evil abominations of the house of Israel! For they shall fall by the sword, by the famine, and by the plague. [12] He who is far off shall die by the plague; and he who is near shall fall by the sword; and he who remains and is besieged shall die by the famine. So I will fulfill My fury on them. [13] And you shall know that I (am) Jehovah, when their slain shall be in the midst of their idols all around their altars, on every high hill, in all the tops of the mountains, and under every green tree, and under every leafy oak; the place where they offered there a soothing aroma to all their idols. [14] And I will stretch out My hand on them and make the land a desolation, even more desolate than the desert toward Diblath, in all their dwelling-places. And they shall know that I (am) Jehovah.

11 הַזֹּאת׃ כֹּה־אָמַר אֲדֹנָי יְהוִה הַכֵּה בְכַפְּךָ וּרְקַע
and with Strike :Jehovah the says Thus .this
stamp hand your Lord

בְּרַגְלְךָ וֶאֱמָר־אָח אֶל כָּל־תּוֹעֲבוֹת רָעוֹת בֵּית יִשְׂרָאֵל
!Israel the evil the abomina- all for Alas ,say and your with
of house of tions ,foot

12 אֲשֶׁר בַּחֶרֶב בָּרָעָב וּבַדֶּבֶר יִפֹּלוּ׃ הָרָחוֹק בַּדֶּבֶר יָמוּת
shall the by who He shall they by and the by the by For
;die plague off far is .fall ,plague the famine ,sword

וְהַקָּרוֹב בַּחֶרֶב יִפּוֹל וְהַנִּשְׁאָר וְהַנָּצוּר בָּרָעָב יָמוּת וְכִלֵּיתִי
will I So shall the by is and he and shall the by who he and
fulfill .die famine besieged remains who ;fall sword near is

13 חֲמָתִי בָּם׃ וִידַעְתֶּם כִּי־אֲנִי יְהוָה בִּהְיוֹת חַלְלֵיהֶם בְּתוֹךְ
the in their shall when ,Jehovah I that you And on My
of midst slain be (am) know shall .them fury

גִּלּוּלֵיהֶם סְבִיבוֹת מִזְבְּחוֹתֵיהֶם אֶל כָּל־גִּבְעָה רָמָה בְּכֹל
all in ,high hill every on ,altars their around all idols their

רָאשֵׁי הֶהָרִים וְתַחַת כָּל־עֵץ רַעֲנָן וְתַחַת כָּל־אֵלָה עֲבֻתָּה
,leafy oak every and ,green tree every and the the
under under ,mountains of tops

14 מְקוֹם אֲשֶׁר נָתְנוּ־שָׁם רֵיחַ נִיחֹחַ לְכֹל גִּלּוּלֵיהֶם׃ וְנָטִיתִי
will I So .idols their all to soothing an there they where the
out stretch aroma offered place

אֶת־יָדִי עֲלֵיהֶם וְנָתַתִּי אֶת־הָאָרֶץ שְׁמָמָה וּמְשַׁמָּה מִמִּדְבַּר
the than more even a the and them upon My
desert desolate ,desolation land make hand

דִּבְלָתָה בְּכֹל מוֹשְׁבוֹתֵיהֶם וְיָדְעוּ כִּי־אֲנִי יְהוָה׃
.Jehovah I that they And dwelling- their all in toward
(am) know shall .places ,Diblath

CAP. VII ז

CHAPTER 7

CHAPTER 7

[1] And it was the word of Jehovah to me, saying, [2] And you, son of man, thus says the Lord Jehovah to the land of Israel: An end! The end has come on the four corners of the land. [3] Now (is) the end on you, and I will send My anger on you and will judge you according to your ways, and will lay on you all your abominations. [4] And My eye shall not spare you, and I will not have pity. But I will lay your ways upon you, and your abominations shall be in your midst; and you shall know that I (am) Jehovah.

1
2 וַיְהִי דְבַר־יְהוָה אֵלַי לֵאמֹר׃ וְאַתָּה בֶן־אָדָם כֹּה־אָמַר
says thus ,man son ,you And ,saying ,me to Jehovah the it And
of of word ,was

אֲדֹנָי יְהוִה לְאַדְמַת יִשְׂרָאֵל קֵץ בָּא הַקֵּץ עַל־אַרְבַּעַת
four the on The has An :Israel the to Jehovah the
end come !end of land Lord

3 כַּנְפוֹת הָאָרֶץ׃ עַתָּה הַקֵּץ עָלַיִךְ וְשִׁלַּחְתִּי אַפִּי בָךְ
on My I and on the Now the corners
you anger send will ,you (is) end .land of

4 וּשְׁפַטְתִּיךְ כִּדְרָכָיִךְ וְנָתַתִּי עָלַיִךְ אֵת כָּל־תּוֹעֲבוֹתָיִךְ׃ וְלֹא־
And your all upon will and to according will and
not .abominations you lay ways your you judge

תָחוֹס עֵינִי עָלַיִךְ וְלֹא אֶחְמוֹל כִּי דְרָכַיִךְ עָלַיִךְ אֶתֵּן
will I upon your But will I and ,you upon My shall
,lay you ways .pity have not eye spare

וְתוֹעֲבוֹתַיִךְ בְּתוֹכֵךְ תִּהְיֶין וִידַעְתֶּם כִּי־אֲנִי יְהוָה׃
.Jehovah I that you and shall your in your and
(am) know shall ;be midst abominations

[5] Thus says the Lord Jehovah: An evil! An only evil! Behold, it has come! [6] An end has come; the end has come! It has awakened against you; behold, it has come! [7] The encirclement has come to you, O dwellers of the land. The time has come; the day of tumult is near, and not a shout of the hills. [8] Now I will soon pour out My fury on you, and fulfill My anger on you. And I will judge you according to your ways, and will put on you all your abominations. [9] And My eye shall not spare, and I will not have pity; I will put on you according to your ways, and your abominations that are in your midst. And you shall know that I (am) Jehovah who strikes. [10] Behold the day! Behold, it has come; the encirclement has gone out; the rod has blossomed; pride has budded. [11] Violence has risen for a rod of wickedness. None of them (shall remain;) and none of their multitude, and none of their riches, and none eminent among them. [12] The time has come; the day has arrived. Let not the buyer rejoice, and let not the sellers mourn; for wrath (is) on all her multitude. [13] For the seller shall not return to that which is sold, although they still are among the living—for the vision (is) to all her multitude; and a man shall not return in his iniquity; his life shall not be held strong. [14] They have blown the trumpet, even to make all ready; but none goes to the battle; for My wrath (is) on all her multitude. [15] The sword (is) outside, and the plague and the famine (are) inside. He who (is) in the field shall die with the sword; and he who (is) in the city, (the) famine and plague shall devour him.

[16] But (if) their fugitives shall escape, then (they) shall be on the mountains like doves of the valleys, all of them

5 6 כֹּה אָמַר אֲדֹנָי יְהוִה רָעָה אַחַת רָעָה הִנֵּה בָאָה׃ קֵץ
An has it ,Behold !evil an An :Jehovah the says Thus
end !come only :evil Lord

7 בָּא בָּא הַקֵּץ הֵקִיץ אֵלָיִךְ הִנֵּה בָּאָה׃ בָּאָה הַצְּפִירָה
encircle- the Has has it ,behold against has It the has has
ment come .come ,you awakened .end come ,come

אֵלֶיךָ יוֹשֵׁב הָאָרֶץ בָּא הָעֵת קָרוֹב הַיּוֹם מְהוּמָה וְלֹא־הֵד
a and tumult day the is the Has the O ,you to
of shout not of near ,time come .land of dwellers

8 הָרִים׃ עַתָּה מִקָּרוֹב אֶשְׁפּוֹךְ חֲמָתִי עָלַיִךְ וְכִלֵּיתִי אַפִּי בָּךְ
on My and ,you on My will I soon Now the
.you anger fulfill fury out pour .hills

9 וּשְׁפַטְתִּיךְ כִּדְרָכָיִךְ וְנָתַתִּי עָלַיִךְ אֵת כָּל־תּוֹעֲבוֹתָיִךְ׃ וְלֹא־
And your all you on and to according will I And
not .abominations put will ways your you judge

תָחוֹס עֵינִי וְלֹא אֶחְמוֹל כִּדְרָכַיִךְ עָלַיִךְ אֶתֵּן וְתוֹעֲבוֹתַיִךְ
your and will I you on to according will I and My shall
abominations ,put ways your ;pity have not ,eye spare

10 בְּתוֹכֵךְ תִּהְיֶיןָ וִידַעְתֶּם כִּי אֲנִי יְהוָה מַכֶּה׃ הִנֵּה הַיּוֹם
the Behold who Jehovah I that you And that your in
!day .strikes (am) know shall .are midst

11 הִנֵּה בָאָה יָצְאָה הַצְּפִרָה צָץ הַמַּטֶּה פָּרַח הַזָּדוֹן׃ הֶחָמָס
Violence .pride has ;rod the has the gone has has it ,Behold
budded blossomed ;circling out ;come

קָם לְמַטֵּה־רֶשַׁע לֹא־מֵהֶם וְלֹא מֵהֲמוֹנָם וְלֹא מֶהֱמֵהֶם
their of and their of and them of None wicked- a for has
riches none ;multitude none (;remain shall) .ness of rod risen

12 וְלֹא־נֹהַּ בָּהֶם׃ בָּא הָעֵת הִגִּיעַ הַיּוֹם הַקּוֹנֶה אַל־יִשְׂמָח
Let not the the has The has among none and
,rejoice buyer .day arrived ;time come .them eminent

13 וְהַמּוֹכֵר אַל־יִתְאַבָּל כִּי חָרוֹן אֶל־כָּל־הֲמוֹנָהּ׃ כִּי הַמּוֹכֵר
the For her all on wrath for let not the and
seller .multitude (is) ;mourn sellers

אֶל־הַמִּמְכָּר לֹא יָשׁוּב וְעוֹד בַּחַיִּים חַיָּתָם כִּי־חָזוֹן אֶל־כָּל־
all to the for they among although shall not which that to
vision living the still ,return sold is

14 הֲמוֹנָהּ לֹא יָשׁוּב וְאִישׁ בַּעֲוֹנוֹ חַיָּתוֹ לֹא־יִתְחַזָּקוּ׃ תָּקְעוּ
have They hold shall not his his in a and shall not her
blown .strong life iniquity man return multitude

בַתָּקוֹעַ וְהָכִין הַכֹּל וְאֵין הֹלֵךְ לַמִּלְחָמָה כִּי חֲרוֹנִי אֶל־
on My for ,battle the to goes but ;all to even the
(is) wrath none ready make ,trumpet

15 כָּל־הֲמוֹנָהּ׃ הַחֶרֶב בַּחוּץ וְהַדֶּבֶר וְהָרָעָב מִבָּיִת אֲשֶׁר
He (are) the and the and (is) The her all
(is) who .inside famine plague ,outside sword .multitude

בַּשָּׂדֶה בַּחֶרֶב יָמוּת וַאֲשֶׁר בָּעִיר רָעָב וָדֶבֶר יֹאכְלֶנּוּ׃
devour shall and (the) the in he and shall the with the in
.him plague famine city (is) who ;die sword field

16 וּפָלְטוּ פְּלִיטֵיהֶם וְהָיוּ אֶל־הֶהָרִים כְּיוֹנֵי הַגֵּאָיוֹת כֻּלָּם הֹמוֹת
,mourning of all the like the on then their (if) But
them ,valleys of doves mountains be shall fugitives escape

mourning, each for his iniquity. [17] All hands shall be feeble, and all knees shall go (as) water. [18] They shall also gird (on) sackcloth, and trembling shall cover them; and shame (shall be) on all faces, and baldness on all their heads. [19] They shall throw their silver in the streets, and their gold shall be an impure thing. Their silver and their gold shall not be able to deliver them in the day of the wrath of Jehovah. They shall not satisfy their soul, and they shall not fill their bowels; for their iniquity has become for a stumbling-block. [20] And the beauty of his ornament He has set it in majesty. But they made with it the images of their abominations, and of their hateful things; therefore I have put it to them as an impure thing. [21] And I will also give it into the hand of the strangers for a prize; and to the wicked of the earth for a spoil; and they shall defile it. [22] I also will turn My face from them, and they shall defile My hidden (place); and robbers shall enter into it and defile it.

[23] Make the chain; for the land is full of bloody judgments, and the city is full of violence. [24] And I will bring the worst of the nations, and they shall possess their houses. And I will make cease the pomp of the strong; and their holy places shall be defiled. [25] Anguish comes! And they shall seek peace, but none (shall be). [26] Disaster on disaster shall come, and rumor to rumor shall be. And they shall seek a vision from the prophet; but the law shall perish from the priest, and counsel from the elders. [27] The king shall mourn, and the prince shall be clothed with despair; and the hands of the people of the land shall be terrified, according to their way I will do to them; and according to their judgments I will judge them; and they shall know that I (am) Jehovah.

17 אִישׁ בַּעֲוֺנוֹ׃ כָּל־הַיָּדַיִם תִּרְפֶּינָה וְכָל־בִּרְכַּיִם תֵּלַכְנָה מָּיִם׃
.water shall knees and be shall hands All his for each
(as) go all feeble .iniquity

18 וְחָגְרוּ שַׂקִּים וְכִסְּתָה אוֹתָם פַּלָּצוּת וְאֶל כָּל־פָּנִים בּוּשָׁה
shame faces all and ;trembling them shall and sack- also They
(be shall) on cover ,cloth gird shall

19 וּבְכָל־רָאשֵׁיהֶם קָרְחָה׃ כַּסְפָּם בַּחוּצוֹת יַשְׁלִיכוּ וּזְהָבָם
their and shall They the in their .baldness their on and
gold ,throw streets silver heads all

לְנִדָּה יִהְיֶה כַּסְפָּם וּזְהָבָם לֹא־יוּכַל לְהַצִּילָם בְּיוֹם עֶבְרַת
the the in deliver to be shall not their and Their shall impure an
of wrath of day them able gold silver .be thing

יְהוָה נַפְשָׁם לֹא יְשַׂבֵּעוּ וּמֵעֵיהֶם לֹא יְמַלֵּאוּ כִּי־מִכְשׁוֹל
stum- a for shall they not their and shall They not their .Jehovah
block bling ,fill bowels satisfy soul

20 עֲוֺנָם הָיָה׃ וּצְבִי עֶדְיוֹ לְגָאוֹן שָׂמָהוּ וְצַלְמֵי תוֹעֲבֹתָם
their the But set He in his the And has in- their
abominations of images .it majesty ,ornament of beauty .become quity

21 שִׁקּוּצֵיהֶם עָשׂוּ בוֹ עַל־כֵּן נְתַתִּיו לָהֶם לְנִדָּה׃ וּנְתַתִּיו
will I And an as to have I therefore with they their of and
it give .thing impure them it put ;it made things hateful

22 בְּיַד־הַזָּרִים לָבַז וּלְרִשְׁעֵי הָאָרֶץ לְשָׁלָל וְחִלְּלוּהָ׃ וַהֲסִבּוֹתִי
will I shall they and a for the the to and a for the the into
turn also .it defile ,spoil earth of wicked ,prize strangers of hand

פָנַי מֵהֶם וְחִלְּלוּ אֶת־צְפוּנִי וּבָאוּ־בָהּ פָּרִיצִים וְחִלְּלוּהָ׃
defile and robbers into shall and hidden My they and from My
.it it enter ;(place) defile shall ,them face

23 עֲשֵׂה הָרַתּוֹק כִּי הָאָרֶץ מָלְאָה מִשְׁפַּט דָּמִים וְהָעִיר מָלְאָה
full is the and ,bloody of full is the for the Make
city judgments land ;chain

24 חָמָס׃ וְהֵבֵאתִי רָעֵי גוֹיִם וְיָרְשׁוּ אֶת־בָּתֵּיהֶם וְהִשְׁבַּתִּי
will I And their they and the the will I So of
cease make .houses possess shall ,nations of worst bring .violence

25 גְּאוֹן עַזִּים וְנִחֲלוּ מְקַדְשֵׁיהֶם׃ קְפָדָה־בָא וּבִקְשׁוּ שָׁלוֹם
,peace they and ;comes Anguish holy their be shall and the the
seek shall .places defiled ;strong of pomp

26 וָאָיִן׃ הֹוָה עַל־הֹוָה תָּבוֹא וּשְׁמֻעָה אֶל־שְׁמוּעָה תִּהְיֶה
.be shall rumor to rumor and shall disaster upon Disaster but
,come .none

וּבִקְשׁוּ חָזוֹן מִנָּבִיא וְתוֹרָה תֹּאבַד מִכֹּהֵן וְעֵצָה מִזְּקֵנִים׃
the from and the from shall the but the from a they And
.elders counsel ,priest perish law ;prophet vision seek shall

27 הַמֶּלֶךְ יִתְאַבָּל וְנָשִׂיא יִלְבַּשׁ שְׁמָמָה וִידֵי עַם־הָאָרֶץ
land the the the and with be shall the and shall king The
of people of hands ,despair clothed prince ,mourn

תִּבָּהַלְנָה מִדַּרְכָּם אֶעֱשֶׂה אוֹתָם וּבְמִשְׁפְּטֵיהֶם אֶשְׁפְּטֵם
will I to according and ,them to will I to according be shall
;them judge judgments their do way their .terrified

וְיָדְעוּ כִּי־אֲנִי יְהוָה׃
.Jehovah I that they and
(am) know shall

CHAPTER 8

[1] And it was in the sixth year, on the fifth of the month, I was sitting in my house; and the elders of Judah were sitting before me; and the hand of the Lord Jehovah fell on me there. [2] And I looked, and behold, a likeness as the look of fire; from the appearance of His loins and downward, (like) fire; and from His loins and upward, as the look of brightness, like the color of polished metal. [3] And He put forth the form of a hand, and took me by the lock of my head. And the Spirit lifted me between the earth and the heavens, and brought me to Jerusalem—in the visions of God—to the opening of the inner gate facing north, where there (was) the seat of the image of jealousy, which causes jealousy. [4] And, behold, the glory of the God of Israel (was) there; like the appearance which I saw in the plain.

[5] And He said to me, Son of man, lift up now your eyes (to) the way northward. So I lifted up my eyes (to) the way northward; and behold, from the north, at the gate of the altar, this (was the) image of jealousy at the entrance. [6] And He said to me, Son of man, do you see what they are doing, the great abominations which the house of Israel is doing here; that I should be far from My sanctuary? But you turn again; you shall see greater abominations!

[7] And He brought me to the opening of the court; and I looked; and behold, a single hole in the wall. Then He said to me, Son of man, dig now in the wall. And I dug in the wall; and, behold,

CAP. VIII ח

CHAPTER 8

1 וַיְהִי ׀ בַּשָּׁנָה הַשִּׁשִּׁית בַּשִּׁשִּׁי בַּחֲמִשָּׁה לַחֹדֶשׁ אֲנִי יוֹשֵׁב
was sitting | I | the of ,month | the on fifth | the in ,(month) sixth | the ,sixth | year in | it And was

בְּבֵיתִי וְזִקְנֵי יְהוּדָה יוֹשְׁבִים לְפָנַי וַתִּפֹּל עָלַי שָׁם יַד
the of hand | there | on me | fell and | before ,me | were sitting | Judah | the and of elders | my in ;house

2 אֲדֹנָי יְהוִה׃ וָאֶרְאֶה וְהִנֵּה דְמוּת כְּמַרְאֵה־אֵשׁ מִמַּרְאֵה
ap- the from of pearance | ,fire | the as of look | a likeness | and ,behold | I Then ,looked | .Jehovah | the Lord

מָתְנָיו וּלְמַטָּה אֵשׁ וּמִמָּתְנָיו וּלְמַעְלָה כְּמַרְאֵה־זֹהַר כְּעֵין
the like of color | bright- ,ness | the as of look | and ,upward | from and loins His | (like) ;fire | and downward | His loins

3 הַחַשְׁמַלָה׃ וַיִּשְׁלַח תַּבְנִית יָד וַיִּקָּחֵנִי בְּצִיצִת רֹאשִׁי וַתִּשָּׂא
And up lifted | my .head | a by of lock | took and me | a ,hand | the of form | He And forth put | polished .metal

אֹתִי רוּחַ ׀ בֵּין־הָאָרֶץ וּבֵין הַשָּׁמַיִם וַתָּבֵא אֹתִי יְרוּשָׁלַמָה
to Jerusalem | me | and brought | the ,heavens | and between | the between earth | the Spirit | me

בְּמַרְאוֹת אֱלֹהִים אֶל־פֶּתַח שַׁעַר הַפְּנִימִית הַפּוֹנָה צָפוֹנָה
,north | facing | inner the | gate | the of opening | to | ,God | the in of visions

4 אֲשֶׁר־שָׁם מוֹשַׁב סֵמֶל הַקִּנְאָה הַמַּקְנֶה׃ וְהִנֵּה־שָׁם כְּבוֹד
the of glory | (was) there | ,And ,behold | causes .jealousy | which jealousy | the of image | seat the of | there (was) | where

5 אֱלֹהֵי יִשְׂרָאֵל כַּמַּרְאֶה אֲשֶׁר רָאִיתִי בַּבִּקְעָה׃ וַיֹּאמֶר אֵלַי
to ,me | He Then said | the in .plain | saw I | which | the as appearance | ,Israel | the of God

בֶּן־אָדָם שָׂא־נָא עֵינֶיךָ דֶּרֶךְ צָפוֹנָה וָאֶשָּׂא עֵינַי דֶּרֶךְ
the (to) way | my eyes | I So up lifted | .northward | the (to) way | your eyes | now | lift up | ,man | Son of

צָפוֹנָה וְהִנֵּה מִצָּפוֹן לְשַׁעַר הַמִּזְבֵּחַ סֵמֶל הַקִּנְאָה הַזֶּה
this (was) | jealousy | image of | ,altar the | the at of gate | the from north | and ,behold | ,northward

6 בַּבִּאָה׃ וַיֹּאמֶר אֵלַי בֶּן־אָדָם הֲרֹאֶה אַתָּה מָהֵם עֹשִׂים
are ,doing | what they | you | do see | ,man | Son of | to ,me | He And said | the at .entrance

תּוֹעֵבוֹת גְּדֹלוֹת אֲשֶׁר בֵּית־יִשְׂרָאֵל ׀ עֹשִׂים פֹּה לְרָחֳקָה
I that far be should | ,here | is doing | Israel | the of house | which | the great | abominations

7 מֵעַל מִקְדָּשִׁי וְעוֹד תָּשׁוּב תִּרְאֶה תּוֹעֵבוֹת גְּדֹלוֹת׃ וַיָּבֵא
He And brought | !greater abominations | shall you see | you ;return | But still | My ?sanctuary | from

אֹתִי אֶל־פֶּתַח הֶחָצֵר וָאֶרְאֶה וְהִנֵּה חֹר־אֶחָד בַּקִּיר׃
the in .wall | single | a hole | and ,behold | I and ,looked | the ;court | the of opening | to | me

8 וַיֹּאמֶר אֵלַי בֶּן־אָדָם חֲתָר־נָא בַקִּיר וָאֶחְתֹּר בַּקִּיר וְהִנֵּה
and ,behold | the in wall | I And dug | the in .wall | now dig | ,man | Son of | to ,me | He Then said

an opening! [9] And He said to me, Go in and see the wicked abominations that they are doing here. [10] And I went in and saw. And behold, every form of creeping thing, and hateful beast, and all the idols of the house of Israel, were carved on the wall round (and) round. [11] And seventy men of the elders of the house of Israel, and Jaazaniah, the son of Shaphan, standing among them—(they) were standing before them, and each man (had) his censer in his hand; and the odor of the cloud of incense (was) rising. [12] And He said to me, Son of man, have you seen what the elders of the house of Israel are doing in the dark, each man in the rooms of his image? For they are saying, Jehovah does not see us; Jehovah has forsaken the earth.

[13] And He said to me, You turn again, you shall see greater abominations which they are doing. [14] And He brought me to the opening of the gate of the house of Jehovah, which (was) toward the north. And behold, women were sitting there, weeping for Tammuz. [15] And He said to me, Have you seen, son of man? You turn again; you shall see greater abominations than these. [16] And He brought me into the court of the house of Jehovah, the inner (court); and behold, at the opening of the temple of Jehovah, between the porch and the altar (were) about twenty five men (with) their backs to the temple of Jehovah, and their faces eastward; and they bowed themselves eastward to the sun. [17] And He said to me, Have you seen, son of man? Is it nothing to the house of

9= פתח אחד׃ ויאמר אלי בא וראה את־התועבות הרעות
the wicked abominations see and in Go ,me to He And said .an opening

10 אשר הם עשים פה׃ ואבוא ואראה והנה כל־תבנית
form of every And ,behold .saw and I So in went .here are doing they that

רמש ובהמה שקץ וכל־גלולי בית ישראל מחקה על־
on were carved ,Israel the of house the of idols and all ,hateful beast and creeping .thing

11 הקיר סביב ׀ סביב׃ ושבעים איש מזקני בית־ישראל
,Israel the of house the of elders men And seventy (and) .round round the wall

ויאזניהו בן־שפן עמד בתוכם עמדים לפניהם ואיש
each and man before ,them were standing among —them standing ,Shaphan the of son and —Jaazaniah

12 מקטרתו בידו ועתר ענן־הקטרת עלה׃ ויאמר אלי
,me to He Then said .rising incense the of cloud the and of odor his in ;hand censer his

הראית בן־אדם אשר זקני בית־ישראל עשים בחשך
the in ,dark are doing Israel the of house the of elders what ,man Son of you have ,seen

איש בחדרי משכיתו כי אמרים אין יהוה ראה אתנו
;us see Jehovah does not are they ,saying For ?image his the in of rooms each man

13 עזב יהוה את־הארץ׃ ויאמר אלי עוד תשוב תראה
shall you see you ;return Still ,me to He And said the .earth Jehovah has forsaken

14 תועבות גדלות אשר־המה עשים׃ ויבא אתי אל־פתח
the of opening to me He And brought are .doing they which greater abomina- tions

שער בית־יהוה אשר על־הצפונה והנה־שם הנשים
women there ,And ,behold the .north toward which (was) .Jehovah the of house the of gate

15 ישבות מבכות את־התמוז׃ ויאמר אלי הראית בן־אדם
?man son of you Have ,seen to ,me He And said for .Tammuz weeping were ,sitting

16 עוד תשוב תראה תועבות גדלות מאלה׃ ויבא אתי אל־
into me He And brought than .these greater abominations \you see shall you ,return Still

חצר בית־יהוה הפנימית והנה־פתח היכל יהוה בין
be- tween ,Jehovah the of temple the at of opening and ,behold ,inner the Jehovah's house the of court

האולם ובין המזבח כעשרים וחמשה איש אחריהם
their backs men (with) five and about (were) twenty the ,altar and between the porch

אל־היכל יהוה ופניהם קדמה והמה משתחויתם קדמה
eastward bowed themselves and they ;eastward their faces and Jehovah the of temple to

17 לשמש׃ ויאמר אלי הראית בן־אדם הנקל לבית יהודה
Judah the to of house it Is nothing ?man son of you Have ,seen ,me to He And said the to .sun

Judah from doing the abominations which they do here? For they have filled the land (with) violence, and have returned to provoke Me to anger. And behold, they are putting the branch to their nose! [18] And I also will deal with fury; My eye shall not spare, and I will not have pity. And though they cry in My ears (with) a loud voice, I will not hear them.

מֵעֲשׂוֹת אֶת־הַתּוֹעֵבוֹת אֲשֶׁר עָשׂוּ־פֹה כִּי־מָלְאוּ אֶת־הָאָרֶץ
the land | have they filled | For ?here they do | which | the abominations | from doing

חָמָס וַיָּשֻׁבוּ לְהַכְעִיסֵנִי וְהִנָּם שֹׁלְחִים אֶת־הַזְּמוֹרָה אֶל־
to | branch the | are they putting | And ,behold | provoke to .anger to Me | have and returned | (with) violence

18 אַפָּם׃ וְגַם־אֲנִי אֶעֱשֶׂה בְחֵמָה לֹא־תָחוֹס עֵינִי וְלֹא אֶחְמוֹל
will I .pity have | And not | My .eye | shall spare | not | with ;fury | will deal | I So also | their .nose

וְקָרְאוּ בְאָזְנַי קוֹל גָּדוֹל וְלֹא אֶשְׁמַע אוֹתָם׃
.them | will I hear | not then | ,loud | (with) voice a | My ears | in though | And cry they

CAP. IX ט

CHAPTER 9

[1] And He cried in my ears (with) a loud voice, saying, Let the overseers of the city draw near, even each (with) his destroying weapon in his hand. [2] And behold, six men were coming from the way of the Upper Gate, which faces north; and each (had) his shattering weapon in his hand. And one man among them was clothed in linen, and an ink horn of a scribe at his loins. And they went in and stood beside the bronze altar. [3] And the glory of the God of Israel had gone on from upon the cherub, on which it was, to the threshold of the house. And He called to the man clothed in linen, who (had) the ink horn of a scribe at his loins. [4] And Jehovah said to him, Pass through in the midst of the city, in the midst of Jerusalem, and mark a mark on the foreheads of the men who are groaning and are mourning over all the abominations that are done in her midst. [5] And to those He said in my hearing, Pass over in the city after him, and strike. Let not your eye spare, and do not have pity. [6] Slay old, choice men, and virgins, and children, and

1 וַיִּקְרָא בְאָזְנַי קוֹל גָּדוֹל לֵאמֹר קָרְבוּ פְּקֻדּוֹת הָעִיר וְאִישׁ
even each | the ,city | over- of seers | the Let near draw | ,saying | ,loud | (with) voice a | my ears | in | He And cried

2 כְּלִי מַשְׁחֵתוֹ בְּיָדוֹ׃ וְהִנֵּה שִׁשָּׁה אֲנָשִׁים בָּאִים ׀ מִדֶּרֶךְ
the from of way | were coming | men | six | And ,behold | his in .hand | his destroying | weapon

שַׁעַר הָעֶלְיוֹן אֲשֶׁר ׀ מָפְנֶה צָפוֹנָה וְאִישׁ כְּלִי מַפָּצוֹ בְּיָדוֹ
his in .hand | his shattering | weapon | and each | ,north | faces | which | the Upper | Gate

וְאִישׁ־אֶחָד בְּתוֹכָם לָבֻשׁ בַּדִּים וְקֶסֶת הַסֹּפֵר בְּמָתְנָיו
his at .loins | a scribe's | an and ink horn | in ,linen | was clothed | among them | one | And man

3 וַיָּבֹאוּ וַיַּעַמְדוּ אֵצֶל מִזְבַּח הַנְּחֹשֶׁת׃ וּכְבוֹד ׀ אֱלֹהֵי יִשְׂרָאֵל
Israel | God the of | the And of glory | .bronze | the altar | beside | and stood | they And in went

נַעֲלָה מֵעַל הַכְּרוּב אֲשֶׁר הָיָה עָלָיו אֶל מִפְתַּן הַבָּיִת
the .house's | threshold | to | upon ,it | was it | where | the cherub | from upon | had on gone

וַיִּקְרָא אֶל־הָאִישׁ הַלָּבֻשׁ הַבַּדִּים אֲשֶׁר קֶסֶת הַסֹּפֵר
scribe's | the inkhorn | who (had) | ,linen in | clothed | the man | to | He And called

4 בְּמָתְנָיו׃ וַיֹּאמֶר יְהוָה אֵלָו עֲבֹר בְּתוֹךְ הָעִיר בְּתוֹךְ
the in of midst | the ,city | the in of midst | Pass through | to ,him | Jehovah | said And | his at .loins

יְרוּשָׁלָם וְהִתְוִיתָ תָּו עַל־מִצְחוֹת הָאֲנָשִׁים הַנֶּאֱנָחִים
are who groaning | men the | the of foreheads | on | a mark | mark and | ,Jerusalem

5 וְהַנֶּאֱנָקִים עַל כָּל־הַתּוֹעֵבוֹת הַנַּעֲשׂוֹת בְּתוֹכָהּ׃ וּלְאֵלֶּה
to And those | her in .midst | are that done | the abominations | all of | over | are and mourning

אָמַר בְּאָזְנַי עִבְרוּ בָעִיר אַחֲרָיו וְהַכּוּ עַל־תָּחֹס עֵינֵיכֶם
eye your | Let not spare | and .strike | after him | the in city | Pass over | my in hearing | He said

6 וְאַל־תַּחְמֹלוּ׃ זָקֵן בָּחוּר וּבְתוּלָה וְטַף וְנָשִׁים תַּהַרְגוּ
slay | and ;women | and ,children | ,virgins and | choice ,men | Old | have do .pity | and not

women; to destruction. But to every man who has on him the mark, do not come near. And begin from My sanctuary. And they began with the old men who (were) before the house. [7] And He said to them, Defile the house and fill the courts (with) the slain. Go forth! And they went out and killed in the city.

[8] And it was, as they struck, and I remained; (even) I; then I fell on my face and I cried and said, Ah, Lord Jehovah! Will You destroy all the remnant of Israel in Your pouring out Your fury on Jerusalem? [9] And He said to me, The iniquity of the house of Israel is very, very great; and the land is filled (with) blood, and the city is full of perversity. For they say, Jehovah has forsaken the land, and, Jehovah does not see. [10] And even I, My eye does not spare, and I will not have pity; I will put their way on their head. [11] And behold, the man clothed with linen, who (had) the ink horn at his loins, reported the matter, saying, I have done as You commanded me.

לְמַשְׁחִית וְעַל־כָּל־אִישׁ אֲשֶׁר־עָלָיו הַתָּו אַל־תִּגַּשׁוּ
come do not the on who man every But to
.near mark him has to .destruction
וּמִמִּקְדָּשִׁי תָּחֵלּוּ וַיָּחֵלּוּ בָּאֲנָשִׁים הַזְּקֵנִים אֲשֶׁר לִפְנֵי הַבָּיִת׃
the before who old the with they And .begin from And
.house (were) men began sanctuary My
77 וַיֹּאמֶר אֲלֵיהֶם טַמְּאוּ אֶת־הַבַּיִת וּמַלְאוּ אֶת־הַחֲצֵרוֹת
courts the fill and ,house the Defile ,them to He And
said
8 חֲלָלִים צֵאוּ וְיָצְאוּ וְהִכּוּ בָעִיר׃ וַיְהִי כְּהַכּוֹתָם וְנֵאשֲׁאַר
I and they as And the in and they And Go the (with)
;remained struck ,was it .city killed out went !forth .slain
אָנִי וָאֶפְּלָה עַל־פָּנַי וָאֶזְעַק וָאֹמַר אֲהָהּ אֲדֹנָי יֱהוִֹה הֲמַשְׁחִית
destroy Will !Jehovah Lord ,Ah and I and my on I and ;I
,said ,cried face fell
אַתָּה אֵת כָּל־שְׁאֵרִית יִשְׂרָאֵל בְּשָׁפְכְּךָ אֶת־חֲמָתְךָ עַל־
on Your Your in Israel the all You
fury out pouring of remnant
9 יְרוּשָׁלִָם׃ וַיֹּאמֶר אֵלַי עֲוֺן בֵּית־יִשְׂרָאֵל וִיהוּדָה גָּדוֹל
(is) and Israel's The iniquity to He And ?Jerusalem
great Judah's of house ,me said
בִּמְאֹד מְאֹד וַתִּמָּלֵא הָאָרֶץ דָּמִים וְהָעִיר מָלְאָה מֻטֶּה כִּי
For per- full is the and (with) the is and ,much very in
.versity of city blood land filled
10 אָמְרוּ עָזַב יְהוָה אֶת־הָאָרֶץ וְאֵין יְהוָה רֹאֶה׃ וְגַם אֲנִי
,I And does Jehovah and the Jehovah has they
even see not ,land forsaken ,say
11 לֹא־תָחוֹס עֵינִי וְלֹא אֶחְמֹל דַּרְכָּם בְּרֹאשָׁם נָתָתִּי׃ וְהִנֵּה
And will I their on their I will and My does not
,behold .put head way ;pity have not ,eye spare
הָאִישׁ ׀ לְבֻשׁ הַבַּדִּים אֲשֶׁר הַקֶּסֶת בְּמָתְנָיו מֵשִׁיב דָּבָר
the reported his at the who ,linen clothed the
,matter ,loins inkhorn (had) with man
לֵאמֹר עָשִׂיתִי כַּאֲשֶׁר צִוִּיתָנִי׃
have You as have I ,saying
.me commanded done

CAP. X י

CHAPTER 10

[1] And I looked, and behold, in the expanse that (was) over the head of the cherubim, like a sapphire stone, like the look of the form of a throne, appeared above them. [2] And He spoke to the man clothed (with) linen, and said, Go in among the wheels, under the cherub, and fill your hands with coals of fire

1 וָאֶרְאֶה וְהִנֵּה אֶל־הָרָקִיעַ אֲשֶׁר עַל־רֹאשׁ הַכְּרֻבִים כְּאֶבֶן
a like the the over that the in and I And
stone ,cherubim of head (was) expanse ,behold ,looked
2 סַפִּיר כְּמַרְאֵה דְּמוּת כִּסֵּא נִרְאָה עֲלֵיהֶם׃ וַיֹּאמֶר אֶל־
to He And above appeared a the the as sapphire
spoke .them ,throne of form of look
הָאִישׁ ׀ לְבֻשׁ הַבַּדִּים וַיֹּאמֶר בֹּא אֶל־בֵּינוֹת לַגַּלְגַּל
the among to Go ,said and ,linen clothed man the
,wheels in (with)
אֶל־תַּחַת לַכְּרוּב וּמַלֵּא חָפְנֶיךָ גַחֲלֵי־אֵשׁ מִבֵּינוֹת
from fire coals hands your fill and the under to
between of with ,cherub

from between the cherubim, and sprinkle on the city. And he went in before me. [3] And the cherubim were standing on the right side of the house when he, the man, went in; and the cloud filled the inner court. [4] And the glory of Jehovah arose from the cherub, over the threshold of the house. And the house was filled with the cloud; and the court was full of the radiance of the glory of Jehovah. [5] And the sound of cherubim wings was heard to the outer court, as the voice of God Almighty when He speaks. [6] And when He had commanded the man clothed with linen, saying, Take fire from between the wheels, from between the cherubim; then he went and stood beside the wheel. [7] And he stretched out his hand, (one) cherub, from between the cherubim, to the fire that (was) between the cherubim. And he lifted and put (it) into the hands of the one clothed with linen. And he took (it) and went out.

[8] And the form of a man's hand was seen under their wings. [9] And I looked, and behold, the four wheels beside the cherubim; one wheel beside one cherub; and the look of the wheels like the color of a stone of Tarshish. [10] And their appearance (was) like one, the four of them; as if the wheel were in the midst of the wheel. [11] In their going on their four sides they went. They did not turn in their going; for (to) the place where the head faces, after it they went. They did not turn in their going. [12] And all

3 לַכְּרֻבִים וּזְרֹק עַל־הָעִיר וַיָּבֹא לְעֵינָי׃ וְהַכְּרֻבִים עֹמְדִים
were the And before he And the upon and the
standing cherubim .me in went .city sprinkle ,cherubim

מִימִין לַבַּיִת בְּבֹאוֹ הָאִישׁ וְהֶעָנָן מָלֵא אֶת־הֶחָצֵר
the filled the and the he when the right the on
court cloud ;man ,in went house of side

4 הַפְּנִימִית׃ וַיָּרָם כְּבוֹד־יְהוָה מֵעַל הַכְּרוּב עַל מִפְתַּן
thres- the over the from Jehovah the And .inner
of hold ,cherub upon of glory arose

הַבָּיִת וַיִּמָּלֵא הַבַּיִת אֶת־הֶעָנָן וְהֶחָצֵר מָלְאָה אֶת־נֹגַהּ
the with full was the and the with the was And the
of radiance of court ,cloud house filled .house

5 כְּבוֹד יְהוָה׃ וְקוֹל כַּנְפֵי הַכְּרוּבִים נִשְׁמַע עַד הֶחָצֵר
the to was cherubim wings the And .Jehovah's glory
court heard of sound

6 הַחִיצֹנָה כְּקוֹל אֵל־שַׁדַּי בְּדַבְּרוֹ׃ וַיְהִי בְּצַוֺּתוֹ אֶת־הָאִישׁ
the had He when And He when Almighty God as outer
man commanded .speaks of voice the

לְבֻשׁ־הַבַּדִּים לֵאמֹר קַח אֵשׁ מִבֵּינוֹת לַגַּלְגַּל מִבֵּינוֹת
from the from fire Take ,saying ,linen clothed
between ,wheels between with

7 לַכְּרוּבִים וַיָּבֹא וַיַּעֲמֹד אֵצֶל הָאוֹפָן׃ וַיִּשְׁלַח הַכְּרוּב אֶת־
(one) And the beside and he then the
cherub out stretched .wheel stood went ,cherubim

יָדוֹ מִבֵּינוֹת לַכְּרוּבִים אֶל־הָאֵשׁ אֲשֶׁר בֵּינוֹת הַכְּרֻבִים
the between that the to the from his
.cherubim (was) fire cherubim between hand

8 וַיִּשָּׂא וַיִּתֵּן אֶל־חָפְנֵי לְבֻשׁ הַבַּדִּים וַיִּקַּח וַיֵּצֵא׃ וַיֵּרָא
was And went and He And .linen one the the into and he And
seen .out (it) took with clothed of hands (it) put lifted

9 לַכְּרֻבִים תַּבְנִית יַד־אָדָם תַּחַת כַּנְפֵיהֶם׃ וָאֶרְאֶה וְהִנֵּה
and I And their under man's a the the in
,behold ,looked .wings hand of form cherubim

אַרְבָּעָה אוֹפַנִּים אֵצֶל הַכְּרוּבִים אוֹפַן אֶחָד אֵצֶל הַכְּרוּב
cherub beside one wheel the beside wheels four the
(was) ,cherubim

אֶחָד וְאוֹפַן אֶחָד אֵצֶל הַכְּרוּב אֶחָד וּמַרְאֵה הָאוֹפַנִּים
the the and ;one cherub beside one and ,one
wheels of look wheel

10 כְּעֵין אֶבֶן תַּרְשִׁישׁ׃ וּמַרְאֵיהֶם דְּמוּת אֶחָד לְאַרְבַּעְתָּם
four the one (was) their And Tarshish stone a the like
,them of like appearance of of color

11 כַּאֲשֶׁר יִהְיֶה הָאוֹפַן בְּתוֹךְ הָאוֹפָן׃ בְּלֶכְתָּם אֶל־אַרְבַּעַת
four on their In the the in the were if as
going .wheel of midst wheel

רִבְעֵיהֶם יֵלֵכוּ לֹא יִסַּבּוּ בְּלֶכְתָּם כִּי הַמָּקוֹם אֲשֶׁר־יִפְנֶה
faces where the (to) for their in they Not they their
place ;going turn did .went sides

12 הָרֹאשׁ אַחֲרָיו יֵלֵכוּ לֹא יִסַּבּוּ בְּלֶכְתָּם׃ וְכָל־בְּשָׂרָם
their And their in they Not they after the
flesh all .going turn did .went it ,head

their flesh, and their backs, and their hands, and their wings, and the wheels, were full of eyes all around; (even) their wheels which the four of them had. [13] As for the wheels it was cried to them in my hearing, Whirling wheel! [14] And four faces (were) to each. The first face (was) the face of a cherub; and the second face the face of a man; and the third a face of a lion; and the fourth the face of an eagle. [15] And the cherubim arose. This (is) the living creature that I saw by the river Chebar.

[16] And in the cherubim's going, the wheels went beside them; and when the cherubim lifted their wings to soar from the earth, the wheels did not turn, also they from beside them. [17] When they stood still, (these) stood still; and when they rose, (these also) lifted up. For the spirit of the living creature (was) in them. [18] And the glory of Jehovah went from the threshold of the house and stood over the cherubim. [19] And the cherubim lifted their wings and rose from the earth in my sight. When they went out, the wheels also (were) with them; and he stood at the door of the gate of the house of Jehovah, the eastern. And the glory of the God of Israel (was) over them from above. [20] This (is) the living creature that I saw under the God of Israel by the river Chebar; and I knew that they (were) cherubim. Four, (even) four faces (are) to each; and four wings to each. And the form of a man's hands (was) under their wings. [22] And the form of their faces, they (are) the faces

וְגַבֵּהֶם וִידֵיהֶם וְכַנְפֵיהֶם וְהָאוֹפַנִּים מְלֵאִים עֵינַיִם סָבִיב
all eyes were the and their and their and their and
,around of full wheels ,wings ,hands ,backs

13 לְאַרְבַּעְתָּם אוֹפַנֵּיהֶם׃ לָאוֹפַנִּים לָהֶם קוֹרָא הַגַּלְגַּל בְּאָזְנָי׃
my in whirling was it to for As their four the which
.hearing ,wheel ,cried them wheels the .wheels had them of

14 וְאַרְבָּעָה פָנִים לְאֶחָד פְּנֵי הָאֶחָד פְּנֵי הַכְּרוּב וּפְנֵי הַשֵּׁנִי
the and ,cherub's the The face to faces four And
second face face (was) first .each (were)

15 פְּנֵי אָדָם וְהַשְּׁלִישִׁי פְּנֵי אַרְיֵה וְהָרְבִיעִי פְּנֵי־נָשֶׁר׃ וַיֵּרֹמּוּ
And .eagle's an the and ,lion's a the and a (was)
arose face (was) fourth face (was) third ,man's face

16 הַכְּרוּבִים הִיא הַחַיָּה אֲשֶׁר רָאִיתִי בִּנְהַר־כְּבָר׃ וּבְלֶכֶת
in And .Chebar the by saw I that living the This the
going river creature (is) .cherubim

הַכְּרוּבִים יֵלְכוּ הָאוֹפַנִּים אֶצְלָם וּבִשְׂאֵת הַכְּרוּבִים אֶת־
the when and beside the went the
cherubim lifted ;them wheels ,cherubim

כַּנְפֵיהֶם לָרוּם מֵעַל הָאָרֶץ לֹא־יִסַּבּוּ הָאוֹפַנִּים גַּם־הֵם
also the did not the from soar to their
they ,wheels turn ,earth upon wings

17 מֵאֶצְלָם׃ בְּעָמְדָם יַעֲמֹדוּ וּבְרוֹמָם יֵרוֹמּוּ אוֹתָם כִּי רוּחַ
the For themselves (these) when and stood they When beside from
of spirit .(also) lifted rose they ,still ,still stood .them

18 הַחַיָּה בָּהֶם׃ וַיֵּצֵא כְּבוֹד יְהוָה מֵעַל מִפְתַּן הַבָּיִת וַיַּעֲמֹד
and the thres- the from Jehovah the And in (was) living the
stood house of hold upon of glory went .them creature

19 עַל־הַכְּרוּבִים׃ וַיִּשְׂאוּ הַכְּרוּבִים אֶת־כַּנְפֵיהֶם וַיֵּרוֹמּוּ
and their the And the over
rose wings cherubim lifted .cherubim

מִן־הָאָרֶץ לְעֵינַי בְּצֵאתָם וְהָאוֹפַנִּים לְעֻמָּתָם וַיַּעֲמֹד
he and with wheels the they When my in the from
stood ,them (were) also ,out went .sight earth

פֶּתַח שַׁעַר בֵּית־יְהוָה הַקַּדְמוֹנִי וּכְבוֹד אֱלֹהֵי־יִשְׂרָאֵל
Israel the the And the Jehovah's house the the at
(was) of God of glory .eastern of gate of door

20 עֲלֵיהֶם מִלְמָעְלָה׃ הִיא הַחַיָּה אֲשֶׁר רָאִיתִי תַּחַת אֱלֹהֵי־
God the under saw I that living the This from over
of creature (is) .above them

21 יִשְׂרָאֵל בִּנְהַר כְּבָר וָאֵדַע כִּי כְרוּבִים הֵמָּה׃ אַרְבָּעָה
Four they cherubim that I and ,Chebar the by Israel
.(were) knew river

אַרְבָּעָה פָנִים לְאֶחָד וְאַרְבַּע כְּנָפַיִם לְאֶחָד וּדְמוּת יְדֵי
hands the And to wings four and ,each to faces four (even)
of form .each (are)

22 אָדָם תַּחַת כַּנְפֵיהֶם׃ וּדְמוּת פְּנֵיהֶם הֵמָּה הַפָּנִים אֲשֶׁר
that the they their the And their (was) a
faces (are) ,faces of form .wings under man's

רָאִיתִי עַל־נְהַר־כְּבָר מַרְאֵיהֶם וְאוֹתָם אִישׁ אֶל־עֵבֶר
straight each even their ,Chebar the by saw I
;theirs appearances river

פָּנָיו יֵלֵכוּ׃
they forward
.went

CAP. XI יא

CHAPTER 11

1 וַתִּשָּׂא אֹתִי רוּחַ וַתָּבֵא אֹתִי אֶל־שַׁעַר בֵּית־יְהוָה הַקַּדְמוֹנִי
the Jehovah's house the to me and the me And
,eastern of gate brought Spirit lifted

הַפּוֹנֶה קָדִימָה וְהִנֵּה בְּפֶתַח הַשַּׁעַר עֶשְׂרִים וַחֲמִשָּׁה אִישׁ
—men five and twenty the the at And .eastward which
gate of opening ,behold faces

וָאֶרְאֶה בְתוֹכָם אֶת־יַאֲזַנְיָה בֶן־עַזֻּר וְאֶת־פְּלַטְיָהוּ בֶן־
the Pelatiah and Azzur the Jaazaniah among I And
of son of son them saw

2 בְּנָיָהוּ שָׂרֵי הָעָם׃ וַיֹּאמֶר אֵלַי בֶּן־אָדָם אֵלֶּה
these ,man Son ,me to he And the chiefs ,Benaiah
(are) of said .people of

הָאֲנָשִׁים הַחֹשְׁבִים אָוֶן וְהַיֹּעֲצִים עֲצַת־רָע בָּעִיר הַזֹּאת׃
,this in wicked advice and evil plot who men the
city advise

3 הָאֹמְרִים לֹא בְקָרוֹב בְּנוֹת בָּתִּים הִיא הַסִּיר וַאֲנַחְנוּ
we and the She houses us let is it Not ,say who
(are) ,pot (is) build ;near

4
5 הַבָּשָׂר׃ לָכֵן הִנָּבֵא עֲלֵיהֶם הִנָּבֵא בֶּן־אָדָם׃ וַתִּפֹּל עָלַי
on And !man son ,prophesy against prophesy There- the
me fell of ;them fore flesh

רוּחַ יְהוָה וַיֹּאמֶר אֵלַי אֱמֹר כֹּה־אָמַר יְהוָה כֵּן אֲמַרְתֶּם
have you Thus ,Jehovah says Thus :Speak to said and Jehovah the
,said ,me of Spirit

6 בֵּית יִשְׂרָאֵל וּמַעֲלוֹת רוּחֲכֶם אֲנִי יְדַעְתִּיהָ׃ הִרְבֵּיתֶם
have You .it know I your the for ;Israel house
multiplied myself spirit of steps of

7 חַלְלֵיכֶם בָּעִיר הַזֹּאת וּמִלֵּאתֶם חוּצֹתֶיהָ חָלָל׃ לָכֵן כֹּה־
thus There- the (with) her you and ,this city in your
fore .slain streets filled have slain

אָמַר אֲדֹנָי יְהוִה חַלְלֵיכֶם אֲשֶׁר שַׂמְתֶּם בְּתוֹכָהּ הֵמָּה
They her in have you whom Your :Jehovah the says
(are) ,midst laid slain Lord

8 הַבָּשָׂר וְהִיא הַסִּיר וְאֶתְכֶם הוֹצִיא מִתּוֹכָהּ׃ חֶרֶב יְרֵאתֶם
have You the of out will I you But the and the
,feared sword .midst her forth bring .pot (is) she ,flesh

9 וְחֶרֶב אָבִיא עֲלֵיכֶם נְאֻם אֲדֹנָי יְהוִה׃ וְהוֹצֵאתִי אֶתְכֶם
you I And .Jehovah the says upon will I a But
bring will Lord ,you bring sword

מִתּוֹכָהּ וְנָתַתִּי אֶתְכֶם בְּיַד־זָרִים וְעָשִׂיתִי בָכֶם שְׁפָטִים׃
.judgments against I and ,strangers' into you and of out
you make will hand give midst her

that I saw by the river Chebar, their appearances, even theirs; each straight forward they went.

CHAPTER 11

[1] And the Spirit lifted me and brought me to the gate of the house of Jehovah, the eastern which faces eastward. And behold, at the opening of the gate (were) twenty-five men. And I saw among them Jaazaniah the son of Azzur, and Pelatiah the son of Benaiah, chiefs of the people. [2] And he said to me, Son of man, these (are) the men who plot evil and advise wicked advice in this city; [3] who say, It is not near; let us build houses; she (is) the pot; and we (are) the flesh. [4] Therefore prophesy against them; prophesy, son of man! [5] And the Spirit of Jehovah fell on me and said to me, Speak: Thus says Jehovah, Thus you have said, house of Israel; for I Myself know the steps of your spirit. [6] You have multiplied your slain in this city, and you have filled her streets (with) the slain. [7] Therefore thus says the Lord Jehovah: You slain whom you have laid in her midst, they (are) the flesh, and she (is) the pot. But I will bring you forth out of her midst. [8] You have feared the sword; but I will bring a sword on you, says the Lord Jehovah. [9] And I will bring you out of her midst and give you into the hand of strangers; and I will execute judgments against you.

[10] You shall fall by the sword. I will judge you to the border of Israel, and you shall know that I (am) Jehovah. [11] This (city) shall not be for a pot to you, nor shall you be in its midst for flesh. [12] I will judge you to the border of Israel, and you shall know that I (am) Jehovah —in whose statutes you have not walked, and My judgments you have not done; yea, as the judgments of the nations who are all around you, you have done.

[13] And it was, when I prophesied, Pelatiah the son of Benaiah died. Then I fell on my face and cried with a loud voice, and said, Ah Lord Jehovah! Will You make an end (of) the remnant of Israel? [14] And the word of Jehovah was to me, saying, [14] Son of man, your brothers, your brothers the men of your redemption, and all the house of Israel, all of whom have (heard) the inhabitants of Jerusalem saying to them, Go far away from Jehovah; this land is given to us for a possession. [16] Therefore say, Thus says the Lord Jehovah: Though I have sent them far off among the nations, and though I scattered them among the lands; yet I was to them as a little sanctuary in the countries where they had gone there. [17] Therefore say, Thus says the Lord Jehovah: I shall gather you from the peoples and assemble you out of the lands where you were scattered in them; and I shall give to you the land of Israel. [18] And they will come there, and they will remove all its hateful things and all its abominations from it. [19] And I shall give to

10 בַּחֶרֶב תִּפֹּלוּ עַל־גְּבוּל יִשְׂרָאֵל אֶשְׁפּוֹט אֶתְכֶם וִידַעְתֶּם
you and ,you will I Israel the to shall you the by
know shall judge of border .fall sword

11 כִּי־אֲנִי יְהוָה׃ הִיא לֹא־תִהְיֶה לָכֶם לְסִיר וְאַתֶּם תִּהְיוּ
be shall nor a for you to be shall not This .Jehovah I that
you ,pot (city) (am)

12 בְּתוֹכָהּ לְבָשָׂר אֶל־גְּבוּל יִשְׂרָאֵל אֶשְׁפֹּט אֶתְכֶם׃ וִידַעְתֶּם
you and ,you will I Israel the To for its in
know shall judge of border .flesh midst

כִּי־אֲנִי יְהוָה אֲשֶׁר בְּחֻקַּי לֹא הֲלַכְתֶּם וּמִשְׁפָּטַי לֹא
not My and have you not My in of —Jehovah I that
judgments ,walked statutes whom (am)

13 עֲשִׂיתֶם וּכְמִשְׁפְּטֵי הַגּוֹיִם אֲשֶׁר סְבִיבוֹתֵיכֶם עֲשִׂיתֶם׃ וַיְהִי
And have you around are who the the as and have you
was it .done ,you all nations of judgments ,done

כְּהִנָּבְאִי וּפְלַטְיָהוּ בֶן־בְּנָיָה מֵת וָאֶפֹּל עַל־פָּנַי וָאֶזְעַק קוֹל
a with and my on I Then .died Benaiah the he Pelatiah I when
voice cried face fell of son (was) ,prophesied

גָּדוֹל וָאֹמַר אֲהָהּ אֲדֹנָי יְהוִה כָּלָה אַתָּה עֹשֶׂה אֵת שְׁאֵרִית
the (of) Will You an !Jehovah Lord Ah ,said and ,loud
of remnant make end

14 15 יִשְׂרָאֵל׃ וַיְהִי דְבַר־יְהוָה אֵלַי לֵאמֹר׃ בֶּן־אָדָם
,man Son ,saying to Jehovah the And ?Israel
of ,me of word was

אַחֶיךָ אַחֶיךָ אַנְשֵׁי גְאֻלָּתֶךָ וְכָל־בֵּית יִשְׂרָאֵל כֻּלֹּה אֲשֶׁר
whom of all Israel the and your men the your your
of house all redemption of ,brothers ,brothers

אָמְרוּ לָהֶם יֹשְׁבֵי יְרוּשָׁלַםִ רַחֲקוּ מֵעַל יְהוָה לָנוּ הִיא
this us to Jehovah from far Go ,Jerusalem the to have
away of dwellers them said

16 נִתְּנָה הָאָרֶץ לְמוֹרָשָׁה׃ לָכֵן אֱמֹר כֹּה אָמַר אֲדֹנָי
the says Thus ,say Therefore a for land is
Lord .possession given

יְהוִה כִּי הִרְחַקְתִּים בַּגּוֹיִם וְכִי הֲפִיצוֹתִים בָּאֲרָצוֹת וָאֱהִי
I yet the among scattered I and among sent have I Though Jeho-
was ;lands them though ,nations the off far them :vah

17 לָהֶם לְמִקְדָּשׁ מְעַט בָּאֲרָצוֹת אֲשֶׁר־בָּאוּ שָׁם׃ לָכֵן
Therefore .there they where the in little a as to
gone had countries sanctuary them

אֱמֹר כֹּה־אָמַר אֲדֹנָי יְהוִה וְקִבַּצְתִּי אֶתְכֶם מִן־הָעַמִּים
the from you shall I :Jehovah the says Thus ,say
peoples gather Lord

וְאָסַפְתִּי אֶתְכֶם מִן־הָאֲרָצוֹת אֲשֶׁר נְפֹצוֹתֶם בָּהֶם וְנָתַתִּי
I and in were you where the out you and
give shall ,them scattered lands of assemble

18 לָכֶם אֶת־אַדְמַת יִשְׂרָאֵל׃ וּבָאוּ־שָׁמָּה וְהֵסִירוּ אֶת־
they and ,there they And .Israel the you to
remove will come will of land

19 כָּל־שִׁקּוּצֶיהָ וְאֶת־כָּל־תּוֹעֲבוֹתֶיהָ מִמֶּנָּה׃ וְנָתַתִּי לָהֶם
to I And .it from its all and hateful its all
them give shall abominations things

them one heart, and I will put a new spirit within you. And I will remove the stony heart out of their flesh, and will give them a heart of flesh, [20] so that they may walk in My statutes and keep My judgments, and do them. And they shall be to Me for a people, and I will be to them for God. [21] And (as) to (those whose) heart is going to the heart of their hateful things, and (after) their abominations, I will give their way on their heads, declares the Lord Jehovah.

[22] Then the cherubim lifted up their wings, and the wheels (were) beside them. And the glory of the God of Israel (was) over them from above. [23] And the glory of Jehovah went up from the midst of the city and stood on the mountain which (is) on the east of the city.

[24] And the spirit lifted me and brought me into Chaldea, to the exiles, in a vision by the Spirit of God. And the vision that I had seen went up from me. [25] And I spoke to the exiles all the things which Jehovah had shown me.

לֵב אֶחָד וְרוּחַ חֲדָשָׁה אֶתֵּן בְּקִרְבְּכֶם וַהֲסִרֹתִי לֵב הָאֶבֶן
stony the shall I And within will I new a and ,one heart
heart remove .you put spirit

20 מִבְּשָׂרָם וְנָתַתִּי לָהֶם לֵב בָּשָׂר׃ לְמַעַן בְּחֻקֹּתַי יֵלֵכוּ וְאֶת־
and they My in that so ,flesh a them will and of out
walk may statutes of heart give ,flesh their

מִשְׁפָּטַי יִשְׁמְרוּ וְעָשׂוּ אֹתָם וְהָיוּ־לִי לְעָם וַאֲנִי אֶהְיֶה לָהֶם
to be will I and a for to And .them do and ,keep judg- My
them ,people Me be shall they ments

21 לֵאלֹהִים׃ וְאֶל־לֵב שִׁקּוּצֵיהֶם וְתוֹעֲבוֹתֵיהֶם לִבָּם הֹלֵךְ
is their their (after) and hateful their the to And .God for
;going heart abominations ;things of heart

22 דַּרְכָּם בְּרֹאשָׁם נָתַתִּי נְאֻם אֲדֹנָי יְהוִה׃ וַיִּשְׂאוּ הַכְּרוּבִים
the Then .Jehovah the states will I their on their
cherubim up lifted Lord ,give heads way

אֶת־כַּנְפֵיהֶם וְהָאוֹפַנִּים לְעֻמָּתָם וּכְבוֹד אֱלֹהֵי יִשְׂרָאֵל
Israel the the And beside the and their
(was) of God of glory .them wheels wings

23 עֲלֵיהֶם מִלְמָעְלָה׃ וַיַּעַל כְּבוֹד יְהוָה מֵעַל תּוֹךְ הָעִיר וַיַּעֲמֹד
and the the from Jehovah the And .above from over
stood city of midst of glory up went them

24 עַל־הָהָר אֲשֶׁר מִקֶּדֶם לָעִיר׃ וְרוּחַ נְשָׂאַתְנִי וַתְּבִאֵנִי
brought and me lifted the And the of the on which the on
me spirit .city east (is) mountain

כַּשְׂדִּימָה אֶל־הַגּוֹלָה בַּמַּרְאֶה בְּרוּחַ אֱלֹהִים וַיַּעַל מֵעָלַי
from So .God the by a in the to ,Chaldea into
me up went of Spirit vision ,exiles

25 הַמַּרְאֶה אֲשֶׁר רָאִיתִי׃ וָאֲדַבֵּר אֶל־הַגּוֹלָה אֵת כָּל־דִּבְרֵי
the all the to I And had I that the
of things exiles spoke .seen vision

יְהוָה אֲשֶׁר הֶרְאָנִי׃
had He which Jehovah
.me shown

CAP. XII יב

CHAPTER 12

CHAPTER 12

[1] And the word of Jehovah was to me, saying, [2] Son of man, you dwell in the midst of a rebellious house, who have eyes to see, and they do not see; they have ears to hear, and they do not hear; for they (are) a rebellious house. [3] And you, son of man, prepare for yourself vessels for exile, and go into exile by day in their sight. And you shall be exiled from your place to another place in their sight. Perhaps they will see that they (are) a

1
2 וַיְהִי דְבַר־יְהוָה אֵלַי לֵאמֹר׃ בֶּן־אָדָם בְּתוֹךְ בֵּית־הַמֶּרִי
a house the in ,man Son ,saying to Jehovah the And
rebellious of midst of ,me of word was

אַתָּה יֹשֵׁב אֲשֶׁר עֵינַיִם לָהֶם לִרְאוֹת וְלֹא רָאוּ אָזְנַיִם לָהֶם
to ears they and see to to eyes who ,dwell you
them (are) ;see not them (are)

3 לִשְׁמֹעַ וְלֹא שָׁמֵעוּ כִּי בֵּית מְרִי הֵם׃ וְאַתָּה בֶן
son ,you And they a house for they and ,hear to
of .(are) rebellious ,hear not

אָדָם עֲשֵׂה לְךָ כְּלֵי גוֹלָה וּגְלֵה יוֹמָם לְעֵינֵיהֶם וְגָלִיתָ
you And their in by go and ,exile vessels for prepare ,man
exiled be shall .sight day exile into for yourself

מִמְּקוֹמְךָ אֶל־מָקוֹם אַחֵר לְעֵינֵיהֶם אוּלַי יִרְאוּ כִּי בֵּית
house that they Perhaps their in another place to your from
,see will .sight place

house. [4] And you shall bring forth your vessels, as vessels for exile, by day in their sight. And you shall go forth at evening in their sight, as those going into exile. [5] In their sight dig for yourself through the wall, and carry out through it. [6] In their sight you shall carry on the shoulder; in the dark carry (it) out. You shall cover your face, so that you do not see the ground; for I have set you as a wonder to the house of Israel. [7] And I did so, as I was commanded. I brought forth my vessel, as vessels for exile, by day; and in the evening I dug for myself through the wall by hand; I brought (it) out in the dark; I carried (it) on (my) shoulder in their sight.

[8] And in the morning the word of Jehovah was to me, saying, [9] Son of man, Has not the house of Israel said to you, What are you doing? [10] Say to them, Thus says the Lord Jehovah: This burden (is to) the prince in Jerusalem, and to all the house of Israel who (are) among them. [11] Say, I (am) your wonder. As I have done, so it shall be done to them. They shall go into exile, into captivity. [12] And the prince who (is) among them shall carry on (his) shoulder in the dark, and go forth through the wall. They shall dig to bring out by it. He shall cover his face so that he does not look with the eye (on) the earth. [13] And I will spread My net on him, and he shall be taken in My snare. And I will bring him to Babylon, the land of the Chaldeans. Yet he will not see it; and he shall die there. [14] And all who (are) around him, his help, and all his bands, I will

4 מְרִי הֵמָּה׃ וְהוֹצֵאתָ כֵלֶיךָ כִּכְלֵי גוֹלָה יוֹמָם לְעֵינֵיהֶם

their in | day by | ,exile | as | your | shall you | Then | they re- a
.sight | | | for vessels | ,vessels | forth bring | | .(are) bellious

5 וְאַתָּה תֵּצֵא בָעֶרֶב לְעֵינֵיהֶם כְּמוֹצָאֵי גּוֹלָה׃ לְעֵינֵיהֶם

their In | .exile | those as | their in | at | go shall | you And
sight | | | ,sight | evening | forth

6 חֲתָר־לְךָ בַקִּיר וְהוֹצֵאתָ בּוֹ׃ לְעֵינֵיהֶם עַל־כָּתֵף תִּשָּׂא

shall you | the on | their In | through | carry and | through | for | Dig
;carry | shoulder | sight | .it | out | ,wall the | you

בַּעֲלָטָה תוֹצִיא פָּנֶיךָ תְכַסֶּה וְלֹא תִרְאֶה אֶת־הָאָרֶץ כִּי־

for | ,ground the | see you | so | shall you | Your | carry | the in
| | not that | cover | | face | .out (it) | dark

7 מוֹפֵת נְתַתִּיךָ לְבֵית יִשְׂרָאֵל׃ וָאַעַשׂ כֵּן כַּאֲשֶׁר צֻוֵּיתִי כְּלִי

My | was I | as | ,so | I And | .Israel | the to | have I | a as
vessel | .commanded | did | | | | of house | you set | wonder

הוֹצֵאתִי כִּכְלֵי גוֹלָה יוֹמָם וּבָעֶרֶב חָתַרְתִּי־לִי בַקִּיר בְּיָד

by | through | for | dug I | the in and | by | ,exile | vessels as | brought I
.hand | wall the | me | . | evening | ;day | | for | ,forth

8 בַּעֲלָטָה הוֹצֵאתִי עַל־כָּתֵף נָשָׂאתִי לְעֵינֵיהֶם׃ וַיְהִי

And | their in | carried I | (my) on | brought I | the in
was | .sight | (it) | shoulder | .out (it) | dark

9 דְבַר־יְהוָה אֵלַי בַּבֹּקֶר לֵאמֹר׃ בֶּן־אָדָם הֲלֹא אָמְרוּ אֵלֶיךָ

to | said | Has | ,man | Son | ,saying | the in | to | Jehovah | the
you | | not | of | | | ,morning | me | | of word

10 בֵּית יִשְׂרָאֵל מָה אַתָּה עֹשֶׂה׃ אֱמֹר אֲלֵיהֶם

,them to | Say | are | you | What | ,rebellious the | ,Israel | the
| | ?doing | | | house | | of house

כֹּה אָמַר אֲדֹנָי יְהוָה הַנָּשִׂיא הַמַּשָּׂא הַזֶּה בִּירוּשָׁלַ͏ִם

in | This | burden | the | :Jehovah | the | says | Thus
Jerusalem | (to is) | | prince | | Lord

11 וְכָל־בֵּית יִשְׂרָאֵל אֲשֶׁר־הֵמָּה בְתוֹכָם׃ אֱמֹר אֲנִי מוֹפֶתְכֶם

your | I. | ,Say | among | they | who | Israel | the and
.wonder | (am) | | .them | (are) | | | of house all

כַּאֲשֶׁר עָשִׂיתִי כֵּן יֵעָשֶׂה לָהֶם בַּגּוֹלָה בַשְּׁבִי יֵלֵכוּ׃

They | into | into | to | shall it | so | have I | As
.go shall | ,captivity | ,exile | .them | done be | | ,done

12 וְהַנָּשִׂיא אֲשֶׁר־בְּתוֹכָם אֶל־כָּתֵף יִשָּׂא בַּעֲלָטָה וְיֵצֵא בַקִּיר

through | go and | the in | shall | (his) on | among | who | the And
wall the | forth | ,dark | carry | shoulder | them | (is) | prince

יַחְתְּרוּ לְהוֹצִיא בּוֹ פָּנָיו יְכַסֶּה יַעַן אֲשֶׁר לֹא־יִרְאֶה לָעַיִן

the with | does | not | so shall | He | his | by | bring to | They
eye | look | | that | cover | face | .it | out | dig shall

13 הוּא אֶת־הָאָרֶץ׃ וּפָרַשְׂתִּי אֶת־רִשְׁתִּי עָלָיו וְנִתְפַּשׂ

he and | ,him on | net My | will I | the | (on) | (is) he
taken be shall | | | spread also | .earth

בִּמְצוּדָתִי וְהֵבֵאתִי אֹתוֹ בָבֶלָה אֶרֶץ כַּשְׂדִּים וְאוֹתָהּ לֹא־

not | it Yet | the | the | to | him | I And | My in
.Chaldeans of land | ,Babylon | | bring will | .snare

14 יִרְאֶה וְשָׁם יָמוּת׃ וְכֹל אֲשֶׁר סְבִיבֹתָיו עֶזְרֹה וְכָל־אֲגַפָּיו

his | and | his | around | who | And | shall he | and | will he
,bands | all | ,help | him | (are) | all | .die | there | ,see

scatter to every wind; and I will draw out a sword after them. [15] And they shall know that I (am) Jehovah, when I shall scatter them among the nations, and scatter them in the lands. [16] But I will leave a few men of them from the sword, from the famine, and from the plague, so that they may declare all their abominations among the nations, there where they go. And they shall know that I (am) Jehovah.

[17] And the word of Jehovah was to me, saying, [18] Son of man, eat your bread with quaking, and drink your water with trembling and with anxiety. [19] And say to the people of the land: Thus says the Lord Jehovah to the dwellers of Jerusalem, to the land of Israel: They shall eat their bread with anxiety, and drink their water with horror, so that her land may be desolated of her fulness, because of the violence of all those who live in her. [20 And the cities that have people shall be laid waste, and the land shall be desolate. And they shall know that I (am) Jehovah.

[21] And the word of Jehovah was to me, saying, [22] Son of man, what (is) this proverb to you on the land of Israel, saying, The days are long, and every vision shall perish? [23] Therefore tell them, Thus says the Lord Jehovah: I will make this proverb to cease, and they shall not again use it in Israel; however, say to them, The days draw near, and the matter of every vision. [24] For there shall not again be every vain vision nor slippery divination within the house of Israel.

15 אֱזָרֶה לְכָל־רוּחַ וְחֶרֶב אָרִיק אַחֲרֵיהֶם׃ וְיָדְעוּ כִּי־אֲנִי
I that they And .them after will I a and ;wind to will I
(am) know shall out draw sword every scatter

יְהוָה בַּהֲפִיצִי אוֹתָם בַּגּוֹיִם וְזֵרִיתִי אוֹתָם בָּאֲרָצוֹת׃
the in them and the among them I when ,Jehovah
.lands scatter nations scatter shall

16 וְהוֹתַרְתִּי מֵהֶם אַנְשֵׁי מִסְפָּר מֵחֶרֶב מֵרָעָב וּמִדָּבֶר לְמַעַן
so from and the from the from few a men of will I But
that ,plague the ,famine ,sword them leave

יְסַפְּרוּ אֶת־כָּל־תּוֹעֲבוֹתֵיהֶם בַּגּוֹיִם אֲשֶׁר־בָּאוּ שָׁם וְיָדְעוּ
they And .there they where the among their all may they
know shall go nations abominations declare

17
18 כִּי־אֲנִי יְהוָה׃ וַיְהִי דְבַר־יְהוָה אֵלַי לֵאמֹר׃ בֶּן
Son ,saying ,me to Jehovah the And .Jehovah I that
of of word was (am)

אָדָם לַחְמְךָ בְּרַעַשׁ תֹּאכֵל וּמֵימֶיךָ בְּרָגְזָה וּבִדְאָגָה תִּשְׁתֶּה׃
.drink with and with your and eat with your ,man
anxiety trembling water quaking bread

19 וְאָמַרְתָּ אֶל־עַם־הָאָרֶץ כֹּה־אָמַר אֲדֹנָי יֱהוִה לְיוֹשְׁבֵי
the to Jehovah the says Thus the the to say And
of dwellers Lord :land of people

יְרוּשָׁלִַם אֶל־אַדְמַת יִשְׂרָאֵל לַחְמָם בִּדְאָגָה יֹאכֵלוּ
They with their :Israel the to ,Jerusalem
eat shall anxiety bread of land

וּמֵימֵיהֶם בְּשִׁמָּמוֹן יִשְׁתּוּ לְמַעַן תֵּשַׁם אַרְצָהּ מִמְּלֹאָהּ
her of her be may that so ,drink with their and
fulness land desolated horror water

20 מֵחֲמַס כָּל־הַיֹּשְׁבִים בָּהּ׃ וְהֶעָרִים הַנּוֹשָׁבוֹת תֶּחֱרַבְנָה
be shall have that the And in who those all of because
,waste laid people cities .her live of violence the

21 וְהָאָרֶץ שְׁמָמָה תִהְיֶה וִידַעְתֶּם כִּי־אֲנִי יְהוָה׃ וַיְהִי
And .Jehovah I that you And shall desolate the and
was (am) know shall .be land

22 דְבַר־יְהוָה אֵלַי לֵאמֹר׃ בֶּן־אָדָם מָה־הַמָּשָׁל הַזֶּה לָכֶם
you to this proverb what ,man Son ,saying to Jehovah the
(is) of ,me of word

עַל־אַדְמַת יִשְׂרָאֵל לֵאמֹר יַאַרְכוּ הַיָּמִים וְאָבַד כָּל־חָזוֹן׃
?vision every and days The are ,saying ,Israel the on
perish shall long of land

23 לָכֵן אֱמֹר אֲלֵיהֶם כֹּה־אָמַר אֲדֹנָי יֱהוִה הִשְׁבַּתִּי אֶת־
make will I :Jehovah the says Thus ,them tell There-
cease to Lord fore

הַמָּשָׁל הַזֶּה וְלֹא־יִמְשְׁלוּ אֹתוֹ עוֹד בְּיִשְׂרָאֵל כִּי אִם־דַּבֵּר
say ,however ;Israel in still it shall they and ,this proverb
use not

24 אֲלֵיהֶם קָרְבוּ הַיָּמִים וּדְבַר כָּל־חָזוֹן׃ כִּי לֹא יִהְיֶה עוֹד
still shall there not For .vision every the and The draw ,them to
be of matter ,days near

25 כָּל־חֲזוֹן שָׁוְא וּמִקְסַם חָלָק בְּתוֹךְ בֵּית יִשְׂרָאֵל׃ כִּי אֲנִי
,I For .Israel the within slippery nor vain vision every
of house divination

[25] For I, Jehovah, will speak; the thing which I shall speak shall be done. It shall not be delayed again; for in your days, O house of rebellion, I will say the word and will do it, declares the Lord Jehovah.

[26] And the word of Jehovah was to me, saying, [27] Son of man, behold, the house of Israel (is) saying, The vision that he is seeing (is) for many days, and he prophesies for times far off. [28] Therefore say to them, Thus says the Lord Jehovah: Not any of My words will be delayed any longer; what I have spoken, (that) word shall be done, declares the Lord Jehovah.

יְהֹוָה אֲדַבֵּר אֵת אֲשֶׁר אֲדַבֵּר דָּבָר וְיֵעָשֶׂה לֹא תִמָּשֵׁךְ

shall It   not   be shall   the   shall I   (and)   will   .Jehovah,
delayed be   .done   thing   speak   what   ,speak

עוֹד כִּי בִימֵיכֶם בֵּית הַמֶּרִי אֲדַבֵּר דָּבָר וַעֲשִׂיתִיו נְאֻם

states   will and   the   will I   ,rebellious O   your in   for ;still
    ,it do   word   say   house   ,days

26
27
אֲדֹנָי יְהֹוָה: וַיְהִי דְבַר־יְהֹוָה אֵלַי לֵאמֹר: בֶּן־אָדָם

,man Son   ,saying   to Jehovah the   And   .Jehovah   the
of   ,me   of word   was   Lord

הִנֵּה בֵית־יִשְׂרָאֵל אֹמְרִים הֶחָזוֹן אֲשֶׁר־הוּא חֹזֶה לְיָמִים

for (is)   is   he   that   The   ,saying ;Israel the   ,behold
days   seeing   vision   of house

28
רַבִּים וּלְעִתִּים רְחוֹקוֹת הוּא נִבָּא: לָכֵן אֱמֹר אֲלֵיהֶם כֹּה

Thus   to   say Therefore proph-   he   off   far   for and   ,many
,them   esies   times

אָמַר אֲדֹנָי יְהֹוָה לֹא־תִמָּשֵׁךְ עוֹד כָּל־דְּבָרַי אֲשֶׁר אֲדַבֵּר

have I   what   My   any   any   be will   Not :Jehovah the   says
,spoken   ;words of   longer delayed   Lord

דָּבָר וְיֵעָשֶׂה נְאֻם אֲדֹנָי יְהֹוָה:

.Jehovah the   states   shall   (that)
Lord   ,done be   word

CAP. XIII. יג.
CHAPTER 13

CHAPTER 13

[1] And the word of Jehovah was to me, saying, [2] Son of man, prophesy against the prophets of Israel who prophesy. And say to those who prophesy out of their own heart, Hear the word of Jehovah: [3] Thus says the Lord Jehovah, Woe to the foolish prophets who walk after their own spirit, and have seen nothing! [4] O Israel, your prophets are like foxes in the deserts. [5] You have not gone up into the breaks, nor built a wall around the house of Israel, that it might stand in the battle, in the day of Jehovah. [6] They have seen vanity and lying divination, saying, Jehovah declares. And Jehovah has not sent them; but they hoped to confirm (their) word. [7] Did you not see a vain vision and speak a lying divination; yet (you) say, Jehovah declares—though I have not spoken?

1
2
וַיְהִי דְבַר־יְהֹוָה אֵלַי לֵאמֹר: בֶּן־אָדָם הִנָּבֵא אֶל־נְבִיאֵי

the against prophesy ,man Son   ,saying ,me to Jehovah the   And
of prophets   of   of word   was

יִשְׂרָאֵל הַנִּבָּאִים וְאָמַרְתָּ לִנְבִיאֵי מִלִּבָּם שִׁמְעוּ דְּבַר־

the   Hear   their of out   those to   say And   who   Israel
of word   ,heart own   prophesy who   .prophesy

3
יְהֹוָה: כֹּה אָמַר אֲדֹנָי יְהֹוָה הוֹי עַל־הַנְּבִיאִים הַנְּבָלִים

foolish the   prophets   to   Woe ,Jehovah the   says   Thus :Jehovah
                      Lord

4
אֲשֶׁר הֹלְכִים אַחַר רוּחָם וּלְבִלְתִּי רָאוּ: כְּשֻׁעָלִים בׇּחֳרָבוֹת

the in   foxes like   have   and   own their after   walk   who
deserts   !seen   nothing   spirit

5
נְבִיאֶיךָ יִשְׂרָאֵל הָיוּ: לֹא עֲלִיתֶם בַּפְּרָצוֹת וַתִּגְדְּרוּ גָדֵר

wall a built nor   the into   have You not   .are ,Israel O   your
          ,breaks   up gone   prophets

6
עַל־בֵּית יִשְׂרָאֵל לַעֲמֹד בַּמִּלְחָמָה בְּיוֹם יְהֹוָה: חָזוּ שָׁוְא

vanity They   .Jehovah the in   the in   it that   ,Israel   the around
seen have   of day   battle stand might   of house

וְקֶסֶם כָּזָב הָאֹמְרִים נְאֻם־יְהֹוָה וַיהֹוָה לֹא שְׁלָחָם וְיִחֲלוּ

they but sent has   not   And   .Jehovah states ,saying   ,lying and
hoped   ;them   Jehovah   divination

7
לְקַיֵּם דָּבָר: הֲלוֹא מַחֲזֵה־שָׁוְא חֲזִיתֶם וּמִקְסַם כָּזָב

lying   a and   see you   vain vision a   Did   (their)   to
   divination   not   .word   confirm

אֲמַרְתֶּם וְאֹמְרִים נְאֻם־יְהֹוָה וַאֲנִי לֹא דִבַּרְתִּי:

have   not though ,Jehovah states (you) yet   speak
?spoken   I   ,say

[8] Therefore thus says the Lord Jehovah: Because you have spoken vanity and have seen a lie, therefore, behold, I (am) against you, declares the Lord Jehovah. [9] And My hand shall be against the prophets who see vanity and who divine a lie! They shall not be in the council of My people, and they shall not be written in the writing of the house of Israel; and they shall not enter into the land of Israel. And you shall know that I (am) the Lord Jehovah.

[10] Because, even because they made My people stray, saying, Peace—and there was no peace—and he builds a wall, and behold, (others) daubed it (with) lime. [11] Say to those daubing (with) lime, Yea, it will fall; a flooding rain will be; and you, O hailstones, shall fall; and a raging wind shall break. [12] And lo, the wall having fallen, it shall not be said to you, Where (is) the daubing with which you have daubed?

[13] Therefore, thus says the Lord Jehovah: I will even break (with) a raging wind in My fury. And there shall be a flooding rain in My anger; and hailstones in (My) fury, to consume it. [14] And I will break down the wall that you have daubed (with) lime, and bring it down to the ground; and I will bare its base. And it shall fall, and you will be consumed in its midst; and you shall know that I (am) Jehovah. [15] And I will fulfill My wrath in the wall and in those who daubed it (with) lime; and I will say to you, The wall is not; and, Those who daubed it (are) not [16]—the prophets of Israel who prophesy (as) to Jerusalem, and who see for her visions of peace —and there is no peace—declares the Lord Jehovah.

[17] And you, son of

8 לָכֵן כֹּה אָמַר אֲדֹנָי יְהוִה יַעַן דַּבֶּרְכֶם שָׁוְא וַחֲזִיתֶם כָּזָב
,lie a and vanity have you Be- :Jehovah the says thus There-
seen spoken cause Lord fore

9 לָכֵן הִנְנִי אֲלֵיכֶם נְאֻם אֲדֹנָי יֱהוִה׃ וְהָיְתָה יָדִי אֶל־
against My And .Jehovah the states against behold there-
hand be shall Lord ,you (am) I fore

הַנְּבִיאִים הַחֹזִים שָׁוְא וְהַקֹּסְמִים כָּזָב בְּסוֹד עַמִּי לֹא־יִהְיוּ
they not My the In !lie a who and vanity see who the
,be shall people of council divine prophets

וּבִכְתָב בֵּית־יִשְׂרָאֵל לֹא יִכָּתֵבוּ וְאֶל־אַדְמַת יִשְׂרָאֵל לֹא
not Israel the and shall they not Israel the the in and
of land into ,written be of house of writing

10 יָבֹאוּ וִידַעְתֶּם כִּי־אֲנִי אֲדֹנָי יֱהוִה׃ יַעַן וּבְיַעַן הִטְעוּ אֶת־
stray they even ,Because .Jehovah the I that you And shall
made because Lord (am) know shall .enter they

עַמִּי לֵאמֹר שָׁלוֹם וְאֵין שָׁלוֹם וְהוּא בֹּנֶה חַיִץ וְהִנָּם טָחִים
(others) and wall a builds and —peace and —Peace ,saying My
daubed ,behold he no was there ,people

11 אֹתוֹ תָּפֵל׃ אֱמֹר אֶל־טָחֵי תָפֵל וְיִפֹּל הָיָה ׀ גֶּשֶׁם שׁוֹטֵף
a rain be will it ,Yea (with) those to Say (with) it
;flooding ;fall will ,lime daubing .lime

וְאַתֵּנָה אַבְנֵי אֶלְגָּבִישׁ תִּפֹּלְנָה וְרוּחַ סְעָרוֹת תְּבַקֵּעַ׃
shall raging a and shall ,hail O ,you and
.break wind ;fall of stones

12 וְהִנֵּה נָפַל הַקִּיר הֲלוֹא יֵאָמֵר אֲלֵיכֶם אַיֵּה הַטִּיחַ אֲשֶׁר
with the Where ,you to said be it shall the having ,And
which daubing (is) not wall fallen ,lo

13 טַחְתֶּם׃ לָכֵן כֹּה אָמַר אֲדֹנָי יֱהוִה וּבִקַּעְתִּי רוּחַ־
a (with) will I :Jehovah the says thus Therefore have you
wind break even Lord ?daubed

סְעָרוֹת בַּחֲמָתִי וְגֶשֶׁם שֹׁטֵף בְּאַפִּי יִהְיֶה וְאַבְנֵי אֶלְגָּבִישׁ
hail and there My in a a And My in raging
of stones ;be shall anger flooding rain fury

14 בְּחֵמָה לְכָלָה׃ וְהָרַסְתִּי אֶת־הַקִּיר אֲשֶׁר־טַחְתֶּם תָּפֵל
(with) have you that the will I So con- to (My) in
,lime daubed wall down break .it sume fury

וְהִגַּעְתִּיהוּ אֶל־הָאָרֶץ וְנִגְלָה יְסֹדוֹ וְנָפְלָה וּכְלִיתֶם בְּתוֹכָהּ
its in will you and it And its I and the to bring and
;midst consumed be fall shall .base bare will ;ground down it

15 וִידַעְתֶּם כִּי־אֲנִי יְהוָה׃ וְכִלֵּיתִי אֶת־חֲמָתִי בַּקִּיר וּבַטָּחִים
those in and the in My I So .Jehovah I that you and
daubed who wall wrath fulfill will (am) know shall

16 אֹתוֹ תָּפֵל וְאֹמַר לָכֶם אֵין הַקִּיר וְאֵין הַטָּחִים אֹתוֹ׃ נְבִיאֵי
the —it who those and the Is ,you to will and (with) it
of prophets daubed (are) not ,wall not say ;lime

יִשְׂרָאֵל הַנִּבְּאִים אֶל־יְרוּשָׁלִַם וְהַחֹזִים לָהּ חֲזוֹן שָׁלֹם
,peace visions for who and ,Jerusalem (as) who Israel
of her see to prophesy

17 וְאֵין שָׁלֹם נְאֻם אֲדֹנָי יֱהוִה׃ וְאַתָּה בֶן־אָדָם שִׂים
set ,man son ,you And .Jehovah the states ,peace and
of Lord no is there

man, set your face against the daughters of your people, who prophesy out of their heart; and prophesy against them, [18] and say, Thus says the Lord Jehovah: Woe to those sewing bands to all joints of my hands, and make long veils for the head of every (man of) stature, to hunt souls! Will you hunt the souls of My people; and will you save alive the souls for yourselves? [19] And you will profane Me among My people for handfuls of barley, and for bits of bread, to put to death the souls that should not die, and to save alive the souls that should not live; by your lying to My people, who listen to lies.

[20] Therefore, thus says the Lord Jehovah: Behold, I (am) against your bands with which you are hunting there the souls, to make (them) fly. And I will tear them from your arms and will send out the souls, souls which you are hunting, to make (them) fly. [21] Also I will tear your long veils and deliver My people out of your hand, and they shall not again be in your hand to be hunted. And you shall know that I (am) Jehovah. [22] Because you have saddened the heart of the righteous (with) lies, and I have not made him sad; and have strengthened the hands of the wicked, so that he should not turn from his evil way, to keep him alive. [23] Therefore you shall not see vanity; and you shall not divine any divination. And I will deliver My people out of your hand; and you shall know that I (am) Jehovah.

פָּנַיִךְ אֶל־בְּנוֹת עַמְּךָ הַמִּתְנַבְּאוֹת מִלִּבְּהֶן וְהִנָּבֵא עֲלֵיהֶן׃

against and of out prophesy who your the against your
,them prophesy ;heart their ,people of daughters face

18 וְאָמַרְתָּ כֹּה־אָמַר ׀ אֲדֹנָי יְהוִֹה הוֹי לִמְתַפְּרוֹת כְּסָתוֹת

bands those to Woe :Jehovah the says Thus ,say and
sewing Lord

עַל ׀ כָּל־אַצִּילֵי יָדַי וְעֹשׂוֹת הַמִּסְפָּחוֹת עַל־רֹאשׁ כָּל־

every the for veils long and my joints all to
of head make ,hands of

קוֹמָה לְצוֹדֵד נְפָשׁוֹת הַנְּפָשׁוֹת תְּצוֹדֵדְנָה לְעַמִּי וּנְפָשׁוֹת

the and My of you will The !souls hunt to (of man)
souls ,people hunt souls ,stature

19 לָכֶנָה תְחַיֶּינָה׃ וַתְּחַלֶּלְנָה אֹתִי אֶל־עַמִּי בְּשַׁעֲלֵי שְׂעֹרִים

barley hand- for My among Me will you And you will your- for
of fuls people profane ?alive save selves

וּבִפְתוֹתֵי לֶחֶם לְהָמִית נְפָשׁוֹת אֲשֶׁר לֹא־תְמוּתֶנָה וּלְחַיּוֹת

to and ,die should not that souls the put to ,bread for and
alive save death to of bits

נְפָשׁוֹת אֲשֶׁר לֹא־תִחְיֶינָה בְּכַזֶּבְכֶם לְעַמִּי שֹׁמְעֵי כָזָב׃

.lies who My to your by should not that souls the
to listen people lying ,live

20 לָכֵן כֹּה־אָמַר ׀ אֲדֹנָי יְהוִֹה הִנְנִי אֶל־כִּסְּתוֹתֵיכֶנָה

your against ,Behold :Jehovah the says thus Therefore
bands (am) I Lord

אֲשֶׁר אַתֵּנָה מְצֹדְדוֹת שָׁם אֶת־הַנְּפָשׁוֹת לְפֹרְחוֹת וְקָרַעְתִּי

I And make to souls the there are you with
tear will .fly (them) hunting which

אֹתָם מֵעַל זְרוֹעֹתֵיכֶם וְשִׁלַּחְתִּי אֶת־הַנְּפָשׁוֹת אֲשֶׁר אַתֶּם

you which ,souls the will and arms your from them
out send

21 מְצֹדְדוֹת אֶת־נְפָשִׁים לְפֹרְחֹת׃ וְקָרַעְתִּי אֶת־מִסְפְּחֹתֵיכֶם

veils long your I Also make to souls are
tear will .fly hunting

וְהִצַּלְתִּי אֶת־עַמִּי מִיֶּדְכֶן וְלֹא־יִהְיוּ עוֹד בְּיֶדְכֶן לִמְצוּדָה

be to your in yet they and of out My and
.hunted hand be shall not ,hand your people deliver

22 וִידַעְתֶּן כִּי־אֲנִי יְהוָה׃ יַעַן הַכְאוֹת לֵב־צַדִּיק שֶׁקֶר וַאֲנִי לֹא

not and (with) the the have you Be- .Jehovah I that you And
,lies righteous of heart saddened cause (am) know shall

הִכְאַבְתִּיו וּלְחַזֵּק יְדֵי רָשָׁע לְבִלְתִּי־שׁוּב מִדַּרְכּוֹ הָרָע

, evil his from he that so the the have and made have I
way turn should not ,wicked of hands .strong made ;sad him

23 לְהַחֲיֹתוֹ׃ לָכֵן שָׁוְא לֹא תֶחֱזֶינָה וְקֶסֶם לֹא־תִקְסַמְנָה עוֹד

.any shall you not and shall you not vanity Therefore keep to
divine divination ,see .alive him

וְהִצַּלְתִּי אֶת־עַמִּי מִיֶּדְכֶן וִידַעְתֶּן כִּי־אֲנִי יְהוָה׃

.Jehovah I that you and of out My will I And
(am) know shall ;hand your people deliver

CAP. XIV יד

CHAPTER 14

CHAPTER 14

[1] And was to me men of the elders of Israel, and sat before me. [2] And came the word of Jehovah to me, saying, [3] Son of man, these men have set up their idols in their hearts, and have put the stumbling-block of their iniquity before their faces. Should I at all be sought by them?

[4] Therefore speak to them and say to them, Thus says the Lord Jehovah: Every man of the house of Israel who sets up his idols in his heart, and puts the stumblingblock of his iniquity before his face, and comes to the prophet; I, Jehovah, will answer him in it by the host of his idols; [5] so that I may capture the house of Israel in their own heart, who are estranged from Me by their idols, all of them.

[6] Therefore, say to the house of Israel, Thus says the Lord Jehovah: Turn, and be turned from your idols, and from all your abominations turn away your faces. [7] For every man of the house of Israel, or of the alien who sojourns in Israel, who is separated from after Me, and sets up his idols in his heart, and puts the stumblingblock of iniquity before his face, and comes to the prophet to inquire of him concerning Me; I, Jehovah, will answer him Myself. [8] And I will set My face against that man, and I will make him for a sign and for proverbs; and I will cut him off from the midst of My people; and you shall know that I (am) Jehovah.

1 וַיָּבוֹא אֵלַי אֲנָשִׁים מִזִּקְנֵי יִשְׂרָאֵל וַיֵּשְׁבוּ לְפָנָי׃
2 וַיְהִי

And came | before .me | sat and | Israel | the of of elders | men | to me | Then was

3 דְבַר־יְהֹוָה אֵלַי לֵאמֹר׃ בֶּן־אָדָם הָאֲנָשִׁים הָאֵלֶּה הֶעֱלוּ

have up set | these | men | ,man Son of | ,saying | ,me to Jehovah | the of word

גִלּוּלֵיהֶם עַל־לִבָּם וּמִכְשׁוֹל עֲוֹנָם נָתְנוּ נֹכַח פְּנֵיהֶם הַאִדָּרֹשׁ

all At | their .faces | before | put | their iniquity | the and of stumblingblock | ,hearts their in | idols their

4 אִדָּרֵשׁ לָהֶם׃ לָכֵן דַּבֵּר־אוֹתָם וְאָמַרְתָּ אֲלֵיהֶם

,them to | say and | them | speak to | Therefore | by ?them | I should sought be

כֹּה־אָמַר ׀ אֲדֹנָי יֱהֹוִה אִישׁ אִישׁ מִבֵּית יִשְׂרָאֵל אֲשֶׁר

who | Israel | the of of house | man | Every | :Jehovah | the Lord | says Thus

יַעֲלֶה אֶת־גִּלּוּלָיו אֶל־לִבּוֹ וּמִכְשׁוֹל עֲוֹנוֹ יָשִׂים נֹכַח פָּנָיו

his ,face | before | puts | his iniquity | stum- the and of blingblock | his heart | in | idols his | up sets

וּבָא אֶל־הַנָּבִיא אֲנִי יְהֹוָה נַעֲנֵיתִי לוֹ בָהּ בְּרֹב גִּלּוּלָיו׃

;idols his | the by of host | it in | him | will answer | Jehovah | I | the ;prophet | to | and comes

5 לְמַעַן תְּפֹשׂ אֶת־בֵּית־יִשְׂרָאֵל בְּלִבָּם אֲשֶׁר נָזֹרוּ מֵעָלַי

from Me | are estranged | who | their in heart own | Israel | the of house | may I capture | that so

6 בְּגִלּוּלֵיהֶם כֻּלָּם׃ לָכֵן אֱמֹר ׀ אֶל־בֵּית יִשְׂרָאֵל

,Israel | the of house | to | say | Therefore | of all .them | their by idols

כֹּה אָמַר אֲדֹנָי יֱהֹוִה שׁוּבוּ וְהָשִׁיבוּ מֵעַל גִּלּוּלֵיכֶם וּמֵעַל

and from | ,idols your | from | be and turned | ,Turn | :Jehovah | the Lord | says | Thus

7 כָּל־תּוֹעֲבֹתֵיכֶם הָשִׁיבוּ פְנֵיכֶם׃ כִּי אִישׁ אִישׁ מִבֵּית

the of of house | man | every | For | .faces your | away turn | your abominations | all

יִשְׂרָאֵל וּמֵהַגֵּר אֲשֶׁר־יָגוּר בְּיִשְׂרָאֵל וְיִנָּזֵר מֵאַחֲרַי וְיַעַל

sets and up | after from ;Me | is who separated | ,Israel in | sojourns who | of or alien the | ,Israel

גִּלּוּלָיו אֶל־לִבּוֹ וּמִכְשׁוֹל עֲוֹנוֹ יָשִׂים נֹכַח פָּנָיו וּבָא אֶל

to | and comes | his ,face | before | puts | his iniquity | stum- the and of blingblock | his ,heart | in | idols his

8 הַנָּבִיא לִדְרָשׁ־לוֹ בִי אֲנִי־יְהֹוָה נַעֲנֶה־לּוֹ בִּי׃ וְנָתַתִּי פָנַי

My face | I And set will | My- .self | him | will answer | ,Jehovah | ,I | of ;Me | him | seek to | the prophet

בָּאִישׁ הַהוּא וַהֲשִׂמֹתִיהוּ לְאוֹת וְלִמְשָׁלִים וְהִכְרַתִּיו

will I and off him cut | for and ,proverbs | a for sign | will I and him make | that | against man

9 מִתּוֹךְ עַמִּי וִידַעְתֶּם כִּי־אֲנִי יְהֹוָה׃ וְהַנָּבִיא כִי־יְפֻתֶּה

is he if deceived | the And prophet | .Jehovah | I that (am) | you and know shall | My ;people | the from of midst

[9] And the prophet, if he is deceived and he speaks a word, I, Jehovah, have deceived that prophet; and I will stretch out My hand on him and will destroy him from the midst of My people Israel. [10] And they shall bear their iniquity; as the iniquity of the inquirer, so the iniquity of the prophet shall be. [11] So that the house of Israel may not stray any more from after Me, and not be defiled again with all their transgressions—but they are to Me for a people, and I will be to them for God, declares the Lord Jehovah.

[12] And the word of Jehovah was to me, saying, [13] Son of man, a land, when it sins aginst Me by traitorous betraying, then I will stretch out My hand on it and will shatter to it the staff of bread, and will send on it famine. And I will cut off from it man and beast. [14] And were these three men in its midst: Noah, Daniel, and Job; they by their righteousness should deliver (only) their souls, declares the Lord Jehovah. [15] If I make evil beasts go through the land, and they bereave it, and it is desolate, so that no one would go through because of the beasts; [16] (even if) these three men (were in its midst, (as I live, declares the Lord Jehovah, they would deliver neither sons nor daughters; they would deliver only themselves; but the land would be desolate. [17] Or (if) I bring a sword on that land and say, Let a sword go through the land, and I will cut off man and beast from it; [18] even (if) these three men (were) in its midst, (as) I live, declares the Lord Jehovah, they should not deliver sons or daughters, but they only would deliver themselves. [19] Or (if)

וְדִבֶּר דָּבָר אֲנִי יְהוָה פִּתֵּיתִי אֵת הַנָּבִיא הַהוּא וְנָטִיתִי אֶת־

I and ,that prophet have Jehovah ,I a he and
out stretch will deceived ,word speaks

10 יָדִי עָלָיו וְהִשְׁמַדְתִּיו מִתּוֹךְ עַמִּי יִשְׂרָאֵל׃ וְנָשְׂאוּ עֲוֹנָם

their they And .Israel My the from will and on My
;iniquity bear shall people of midst him destroy him hand

11 כַּעֲוֺן הַדֹּרֵשׁ כַּעֲוֺן הַנָּבִיא יִהְיֶה׃ לְמַעַן לֹא־יִתְעוּ עוֹד בֵּית־

the any may not that So shall the in- the so in- the the as
of house more stray .be prophet of quity ,quirer of iniquity

יִשְׂרָאֵל מֵאַחֲרַי וְלֹא־יִטַּמְּאוּ עוֹד בְּכָל־פִּשְׁעֵיהֶם וְהָיוּ־לִי

to but their with again be and from Israel
Me are they ,transgressions all defiled not ,Me after

לְעָם וַאֲנִי אֶהְיֶה לָהֶם לֵאלֹהִים נְאֻם אֲדֹנָי יְהוִה׃

.Jehovah the states ,God for to will and a for
Lord them be I ,people

12 וַיְהִי דְבַר־יְהוָה אֵלַי לֵאמֹר׃
13 בֶּן־אָדָם אֶרֶץ כִּי תֶחֱטָא־לִי

against it when a ,man Son ,saying to Jehovah the And
Me sins ,land of ,me of word was

לִמְעָל־מַעַל וְנָטִיתִי יָדִי עָלֶיהָ וְשָׁבַרְתִּי לָהּ מַטֵּה־לָחֶם

bread the it to will and it on My will I then traitorous by
of staff shatter hand out stretch ,betraying

14 וְהִשְׁלַחְתִּי־בָהּ רָעָב וְהִכְרַתִּי מִמֶּנָּה אָדָם וּבְהֵמָה׃ וְהָיוּ

And .beast and man from will I And .famine on will and
were it off cut it send

שְׁלֹשֶׁת הָאֲנָשִׁים הָאֵלֶּה בְּתוֹכָהּ נֹחַ דָּנִאֵל וְאִיּוֹב הֵמָּה

they ,Job and Daniel ,Noah its in these men three
,midst

15 בְצִדְקָתָם יְנַצְּלוּ נַפְשָׁם נְאֻם אֲדֹנָי יְהוִה׃ לוּ־חַיָּה רָעָה

evil beasts If .Jehovah the states their (only) should their by
Lord ,souls deliver righteousness

אַעֲבִיר בָּאָרֶץ וְשִׁכְּלָתָּה וְהָיְתָה שְׁמָמָה מִבְּלִי עוֹבֵר מִפְּנֵי

because go would that so ,desolate is it and they and the go make I
of through one no ,it bereave ,land through

16 הַחַיָּה׃ שְׁלֹשֶׁת הָאֲנָשִׁים הָאֵלֶּה בְּתוֹכָהּ חַי־אָנִי נְאֻם אֲדֹנָי

the states ,I (as) its in these ,men (if even) the
Lord live ,midst (were) three ;beasts

יְהוִה אִם־בָּנִים וְאִם־בָּנוֹת יַצִּילוּ הֵמָּה לְבַדָּם יִנָּצֵלוּ וְהָאָרֶץ

the but would only they would they daugh- nor sons neither Jeho-
land ,deliver themselves ;deliver ters ,vah

17 תִּהְיֶה שְׁמָמָה׃ אוֹ חֶרֶב אָבִיא עַל־הָאָרֶץ הַהִיא וְאָמַרְתִּי

,say and that land on bring I sword a Or .desolate would
(if) be

18 חֶרֶב תַּעֲבֹר בָּאָרֶץ וְהִכְרַתִּי מִמֶּנָּה אָדָם וּבְהֵמָה׃ וּשְׁלֹשֶׁת

(if) even ;beast and man from will I and the go Let a
three it off cut ,land through sword

הָאֲנָשִׁים הָאֵלֶּה בְּתוֹכָהּ חַי־אָנִי נְאֻם אֲדֹנָי יְהוִה לֹא יַצִּילוּ

they not ,Jehovah the states I (as) its in these men
deliver should Lord live ,midst (were)

19 בָּנִים וּבָנוֹת כִּי הֵם לְבַדָּם יִנָּצֵלוּ׃ אוֹ דֶּבֶר אֲשַׁלַּח אֶל־

into send I a Or would only they but or sons
plague (if) .deliver themselves ,daughters

I send a plague into that land and pour out My fury on it in blood, to cut off from it man and beast; [20] even (if) Noah, Daniel, and Job (were) in its midst, (as) I live, declares the Lord Jehovah, they would deliver neither son nor daughter; they by their righteousness would deliver (only) their souls.

[21] For thus says the Lord Jehovah, How much more when the four of My evil judgments: sword, and famine, and evil beast, and plague, I send on Jerusalem, to cut off from it man and beast! [22] Yet, behold, there shall be left in it escaping ones that shall be led out, sons and daughters. Behold, they shall come out to you, and you shall see their way and their doings; and you will be comforted for the evil which I have brought against Jerusalam, (for) all which I have brought upon it. [23] And they will comfort you when you see their way and their doings; and you will know that not in vain I have done all that I did in it, declares the Lord Jehovah.

הָאָרֶץ הַהִיא וְשָׁפַכְתִּי חֲמָתִי עָלֶיהָ בְּדָם לְהַכְרִית מִמֶּנָּה
from it | cut to off | in ,blood | it on | My fury | pour and out | that | land

20 אָדָם וּבְהֵמָה׃ וְנֹחַ דָּנִאֵל וְאִיּוֹב בְּתוֹכָהּ חַי־אָנִי נְאֻם
states | I (as) live | in (were) ,midst its | Job and | Daniel | (if) even ,Noah | ;beast and | man

אֲדֹנָי יְהוִה אִם־בֵּן אִם־בַּת יַצִּילוּ הֵמָּה בְּצִדְקָתָם יַצִּילוּ
would deliver | their by righteousness | they | would ;deliver | they daughter | nor | son | neither | Jehovah, | the Lord

21 נַפְשָׁם׃ כִּי כֹה אָמַר אֲדֹנָי יְהוִה אַף כִּי־אַרְבַּעַת
of four | the | when | How more much | ,Jehovah | the Lord | says | thus | For | their (only) .souls

שְׁפָטַי ׀ הָרָעִים חֶרֶב וְרָעָב וְחַיָּה רָעָה וָדֶבֶר שִׁלַּחְתִּי
send I | and ,plague | ,evil | and beast | and ,famine | ,sword | :evil | My judgments

22 אֶל־יְרוּשָׁלִָם לְהַכְרִית מִמֶּנָּה אָדָם וּבְהֵמָה׃ וְהִנֵּה
Yet ,behold | !beast and | man | from it | cut to off | ,Jerusalem | on

נוֹתְרָה־בָּהּ פְּלֵטָה הַמּוּצָאִים בָּנִים וּבָנוֹת הִנָּם יוֹצְאִים
come shall out | ,Behold they | and daughters | sons | shall that ,out led be | escaping ones | in it | shall there left be

אֲלֵיכֶם וּרְאִיתֶם אֶת־דַּרְכָּם וְאֶת־עֲלִילוֹתָם וְנִחַמְתֶּם עַל־
for | will you and comforted be | their ;doings | and | way their | you and see shall | ,you to

הָרָעָה אֲשֶׁר הֵבֵאתִי עַל־יְרוּשָׁלִַם אֵת כָּל־אֲשֶׁר הֵבֵאתִי
have I brought | which | all | (for) | ,Jerusalem against | have I brought | which | the evil

23 עָלֶיהָ׃ וְנִחֲמוּ אֶתְכֶם כִּי־תִרְאוּ אֶת־דַּרְכָּם וְאֶת־עֲלִילוֹתָם
their ,doings | and | their way | you when see | you | they And comfort will | upon .it

וִידַעְתֶּם כִּי לֹא חִנָּם עָשִׂיתִי אֵת כָּל־אֲשֶׁר־עָשִׂיתִי בָּהּ נְאֻם
states | in ,it | did I | that | all | have I done | in vain | not | that | you and know will

אֲדֹנָי יְהוִה׃
.Jehovah | the Lord

CAP. XV טו

CHAPTER 15

[1] And the word of Jehovah was to me, saying, [2] Son of man, How is the vine tree more than any (other) tree, (or than) a branch that is among the trees of the forest? [3] Shall wood be taken from it to do work? Or will (men) take from it a peg to hang every vessel on it? [4] Behold, it is put in the fire for fuel. Both its ends

1
2 וַיְהִי דְבַר־יְהוָה אֵלַי לֵאמֹר׃ בֶּן־אָדָם מַה־יִּהְיֶה עֵץ
the tree | is | How | ,man Son of | ,saying | ,me to | Jehovah | the And of word was

3 הַגֶּפֶן מִכָּל־עֵץ הַזְּמוֹרָה אֲשֶׁר הָיָה בַּעֲצֵי הַיָּעַר׃ הֲיֻקַּח
be Shall taken | the ?forest | the among of trees | is | that | (than or) branch a | ,tree more any than | vine

מִמֶּנּוּ עֵץ לַעֲשׂוֹת לִמְלָאכָה אִם־יִקְחוּ מִמֶּנּוּ יָתֵד לִתְלוֹת
hang to | peg a | it from | will Or take (men) | ?work | do to | wood from it

4 עָלָיו כָּל־כֶּלִי׃ הִנֵּה לָאֵשׁ נִתַּן לְאָכְלָה אֵת שְׁנֵי קְצוֹתָיו
ends its | Both | .fuel for | is it put | the in fire | ,Behold | ?vessel every | it on

the fire devours, and its middle is charred. Is it fit for work? [5] Behold, when it was whole, it was not made for work. How much less when the fire has devoured it, and it is charred! Shall it yet be made to work?

[6] Therefore thus says the Lord Jehovah: As the vine tree in the trees of the forest, which I have given it to the fire for fuel, so I will give the dwellers of Jerusalem. [7] And I will place My face against them. They shall go out from the fire, and the fire shall devour them. And you shall know that I (am) Jehovah, when I set My face against them. [8] And I will give the land (to be) desolate, because they have done a sly act, declares the Lord Jehovah.

5 אָכְלָה הָאֵשׁ וְתוֹכוֹ נָחָר הֲיִצְלַח לִמְלָאכָה׃ הִנֵּה בִּהְיוֹתוֹ

| when was it | Behold | ?work for | it Is | is | its and | The | devours |
| | | fit | | .charred | middle | ,fire | |

תָמִים לֹא יֵעָשֶׂה לִמְלָאכָה אַף כִּי־אֵשׁ אֲכָלַתְהוּ וַיֵּחָר

| is it and | de- has | the when | How | .work for | was it | not | ,whole |
| !charred | ,it voured | fire | less much | | made | | |

6 וְנַעֲשָׂה עוֹד לִמְלָאכָה׃ לָכֵן כֹּה אָמַר אֲדֹנָי יְהוִה׃

| ,Jehovah the | says thus Therefore | ?work for | any | it Shall |
| Lord | | | longer made be |

כַּאֲשֶׁר עֵץ־הַגֶּפֶן בְּעֵץ הַיַּעַר אֲשֶׁר־נְתַתִּיו לָאֵשׁ לְאָכְלָה

| ,fuel for | the to | have I which | the | the in | vine | the | As |
| | fire | it given | ,forest | of trees | tree | |

7 כֵּן נָתַתִּי אֶת־יֹשְׁבֵי יְרוּשָׁלִָם׃ וְנָתַתִּי אֶת־פָּנַי בָּהֶם מֵהָאֵשׁ

| the From | against | My | I And | .Jerusalem | the | will I | so |
| fire | .them | face | place will | | of dwellers | give | |

יָצָאוּ וְהָאֵשׁ תֹּאכְלֵם וִידַעְתֶּם כִּי־אֲנִי יְהוָה בְּשׂוּמִי אֶת־

| I when | Jehovah | I that | you And | devour shall | the and | they |
| set | | (am) | know shall | .them | fire | ,out go shall |

8 פָּנַי בָּהֶם׃ וְנָתַתִּי אֶת־הָאָרֶץ שְׁמָמָה יַעַן מָעֲלוּ מַעַל נְאֻם

| states | sly a | have they | be- | (be to) | the | I And | against My |
| ,act | done | cause | ,desolate | land | give will | .them face |

אֲדֹנָי יְהוִה׃

| | | .Jehovah the |
| | | Lord |

CAP. XVI טז
CHAPTER 16

CHAPTER 16

[1] And the word of Jehovah was to me, saying, [2] Son of man, cause Jerusalem to know her abominations; [3] and say, Thus says the Lord Jehovah to Jerusalem: Your origin and your birth (are) of the land of Canaan. Your father (was) an Amorite, and your mother a Hittite. [4] As for your birth, in the day you were born, your navel was not cut, and you were not washed with water to cleanse (you); and you were not at all salted; and you were not at all swaddled. [5] An eye did not have pity on you, to do to you one of these, to have compassion on you. But you were thrown into the face of the field; for your person was loathed in the day you were born. [6] And (when) I passed by you and saw you trampled in your

1 2 וַיְהִי דְבַר־יְהוָה אֵלַי לֵאמֹר׃ בֶּן־אָדָם הוֹדַע אֶת־יְרוּשָׁלִָם

| Jerusalem | cause | ,man Son | ,saying | ,me to | Jehovah the | And |
| | know to | of | | | of word | was |

3 אֶת־תּוֹעֲבֹתֶיהָ׃ וְאָמַרְתָּ כֹּה־אָמַר אֲדֹנָי יְהוִה לִירוּשָׁלִַם

| :Jerusalem to | Jehovah the | says Thus | ,say and |
| | Lord | | .abominations |

מְכֹרֹתַיִךְ וּמֹלְדֹתַיִךְ מֵאֶרֶץ הַכְּנַעֲנִי אָבִיךְ הָאֱמֹרִי וְאִמֵּךְ

| your and | an (was) | Your | .Canaan | of (are) | your and | Your |
| mother | Amorite | father | | of land | birth | origin |

4 הַחִתִּית׃ וּמוֹלְדוֹתַיִךְ בְּיוֹם הוּלֶּדֶת אוֹתָךְ לֹא־כָרַּת שָׁרֵּךְ

| your | was | not | ,you | were | the in | your | for As | a |
| navel | cut | | | born | day | ,birth | | .Hittite |

וּבְמַיִם לֹא־רֻחַצְתְּ לְמִשְׁעִי וְהָמְלֵחַ לֹא הֻמְלַחַתְּ וְהָחְתֵּל

| all at and | were you | not | all at and | cleanse to | were you not | with and |
| ,salted | | washed | | | ;(you) | water |

5 לֹא חֻתָּלְתְּ׃ לֹא־חָסָה עָלַיִךְ עַיִן לַעֲשׂוֹת לָךְ אַחַת מֵאֵלֶּה

| ,these of | one | to | do to | an | you on | did Not | were you not |
| | | you | | ,eye | | pity have | .swaddled |

לְחֻמְלָה עָלָיִךְ וַתֻּשְׁלְכִי אֶל־פְּנֵי הַשָּׂדֶה בְּגֹעַל נַפְשֵׁךְ בְּיוֹם

| the in | your | was for | the | the into | you | But | .you on | have to |
| day | person | loathed | ,field | of face | thrown were | | compassion |

6 הֻלֶּדֶת אֹתָךְ׃ וָאֶעֱבֹר עָלַיִךְ וָאֶרְאֵךְ מִתְבּוֹסֶסֶת בְּדָמָיִךְ

| your in | trampled | saw and | by | (when) And | .you | were |
| ,blood | | you | you | passed I | | born |

blood, I said to you in your blood, Live! Yea, I said to you in your blood, Live!
[7] As a myriad, as the field shoot I have made you and you are grown and are great, and you come in the finest ornaments. Breasts are formed, and your hair is grown; and you (were) naked and bare. [8] And I passed by you and I looked on you; and behold, your time (was) the time of love. And I spread My skirt over you and covered your nakedness. And I swore to you and entered into a covenant with you, declares the Lord Jehovah; and you became Mine. [9] And I washed you with water. I washed away your blood from you, and I anointed you with oil. [10] And I dressed you (with) broidered work, and I shod you (with) dugong. And I wrapped you (in) fine linen, and I covered you (in) silk. [11] I also adorned you (with) ornaments, and I put bracelets on your hands, and a chain on your neck. [12] And I put a ring on your nose, and earrings on your ears, and a crown of beauty on your head. [13] And you were adorned with gold and silver. And your clothing (was) fine linen and silk and embroidered work. Fine flour and honey and oil you ate. And you were very, very beautiful; and you advanced to regal estate. [14] And your name went out among the nations, because of your beauty; for it (was) perfect, by My splendor which I had set on you, declares the Lord Jehovah.
[15] But you trusted in your beauty, and played the harlot because of your name, and poured out your fornications on all who passed by—it was to him! [16] And you took from your clothes and made for you high places of various colors, and whored on them. (Such) not have come, and shall not be. [17] And you have taken things of beauty, of My gold and of my silver, which I had given you, and made

7 וָאֹמַר לָךְ בְּדָמַיִךְ חֲיִי וָאֹמַר לָךְ בְּדָמַיִךְ חֲיִי׃ רְבָבָה כְּצֶמַח
the as a As .Live your in to I ,Yea !Live your in to said I
of shoot ,myriad .blood you said ,blood you

הַשָּׂדֶה נְתַתִּיךְ וַתִּרְבִּי וַתִּגְדְּלִי וַתָּבֹאִי בַּעֲדִי עֲדָיִים שָׁדַיִם
Breasts .ornaments the you and are and you and have I the
finest ,come ,great ,grown are ,you made field

8 נָכֹנוּ וּשְׂעָרֵךְ צִמֵּחַ וְאַתְּ עֵרֹם וְעֶרְיָה׃ וָאֶעֱבֹר עָלַיִךְ וָאֶרְאֵךְ
looked and by I And and (were) and is your and are
,you on you passed .bare naked you ;grown hair ,formed

וְהִנֵּה עִתֵּךְ עֵת דֹּדִים וָאֶפְרֹשׂ כְּנָפִי עָלַיִךְ וָאֲכַסֶּה עֶרְוָתֵךְ
your and you over My I And .love (was) your and
.nakedness covered skirt spread of time the time ,behold

וָאֶשָּׁבַע לָךְ וָאָבוֹא בִבְרִית אֹתָךְ נְאֻם אֲדֹנָי יְהוִה וַתִּהְיִי
you and ,Jehovah the states with a into and to I And
became Lord ,you covenant entered you swore

9 לִי׃ וָאֶרְחָצֵךְ בַּמַּיִם וָאֶשְׁטֹף דָּמַיִךְ מֵעָלָיִךְ וָאֲסֻכֵךְ בַּשָּׁמֶן׃
.oil with I and from your washed I with I And .Mine
you anointed ,you blood away .water you washed

10 וָאַלְבִּישֵׁךְ רִקְמָה וָאֶנְעֲלֵךְ תָּחַשׁ וָאֶחְבְּשֵׁךְ בַּשֵּׁשׁ וַאֲכַסֵּךְ
I and fine (in) I And (with) I and em- (with) clothed I And
you covered ,linen you wrapped ,dugong you shod work broidered you

11 מֶשִׁי׃ וָאֶעְדֵּךְ עֶדִי וָאֶתְּנָה צְמִידִים עַל־יָדַיִךְ וְרָבִיד עַל־
on a and your on bracelets I and (with) also I (with)
chain ,hands put ornaments you adorned .silk

12 גְּרוֹנֵךְ׃ וָאֶתֵּן נֶזֶם עַל־אַפֵּךְ וַעֲגִילִים עַל־אָזְנָיִךְ וַעֲטֶרֶת
a and your on and your on ring a I And your
crown ,ears earrings ,nose put .neck

13 תִּפְאֶרֶת בְּרֹאשֵׁךְ׃ וַתַּעְדִּי זָהָב וָכֶסֶף וּמַלְבּוּשֵׁךְ שֵׁשִׁי וָמֶשִׁי
and fine your And and with you And your on beauty of
silk linen (was) clothing .silver gold adorned were .head

וְרִקְמָה סֹלֶת וּדְבַשׁ וָשֶׁמֶן אָכָלְתִּי וַתִּיפִי בִּמְאֹד מְאֹד
,very very you And .ate you oil and and Fine em- and
beautiful were honey flour .work broidered

14 וַתִּצְלְחִי לִמְלוּכָה׃ וַיֵּצֵא לָךְ שֵׁם בַּגּוֹיִם בְּיָפְיֵךְ כִּי כָּלִיל
(was) for of because among name your And regal to you and
perfect ;beauty your ,nations the out went .estate advanced

הוּא בַּהֲדָרִי אֲשֶׁר־שַׂמְתִּי עָלַיִךְ נְאֻם אֲדֹנָי יְהוִה׃
.Jehovah the states ,you on set had I which My by it
Lord splendor

15 וַתִּבְטְחִי בְיָפְיֵךְ וַתִּזְנִי עַל־שְׁמֵךְ וַתִּשְׁפְּכִי אֶת־תַּזְנוּתַיִךְ
your poured and your because played and your in you But
fornications out ,name of harlot the beauty trusted

16 עַל־כָּל־עוֹבֵר לוֹ־יֶהִי׃ וַתִּקְחִי מִבְּגָדַיִךְ וַתַּעֲשִׂי־לָךְ בָּמוֹת
high for and your from you And it to passed all on
places you made clothes took .was him —by who

17 טְלֻאוֹת וַתִּזְנִי עֲלֵיהֶם לֹא בָאוֹת וְלֹא יִהְיֶה׃ וַתִּקְחִי כְּלֵי
things have You shall and (Such) not .them on played and vari- of
of taken also .be not come have harlot the ,colors ous

תִפְאַרְתֵּךְ מִזְּהָבִי וּמִכַּסְפִּי אֲשֶׁר נָתַתִּי לָךְ וַתַּעֲשִׂי־לָךְ
to and ,you had I which of and My of ,beauty
yourself made given ,silver My gold

images of males and whored with them, and took your embroidered clothes and covered them, and My oil and My incense you have given to their face. [19] Also My food which I gave you, fine flour and oil and honey which I fed you, you have given it to their face for a soothing aroma. And it was, declares the Lord Jehovah. [20] And you have taken your sons and your daughters, whom you have borne to Me, and you gave these to them for food. Are your fornications small? [21] You have slaughtered My sons, and gave them, to cause these to pass through (the fire) for them.

[22] And (in) all your abominations and your fornications, you have not remembered the days of your youth, when you were naked and bare; you were squirming in your blood. [23] And it was, after all your evil—woe, woe to you! says the Lord Jehovah [24] You have also built yourself a mound, and you have made yourself a high place in every open place. [25] At every head of the highway you have built your high place and have made your beauty despised, and have parted your feet to all who passed by, and have multiplied your fornications. [26] You have whored with the sons of Egypt, your neighbors, great of flesh, and have multiplied your fornication to provoke Me to anger. [27] Behold, I have stretched out My hand over you, and I drew back your portion, and I gave you to the will of those who hate you, the Philistines' daughters, who are ashamed of your wicked way. [28] You have (also) whored with the sons of Assyria without being satisfied; yea, you whored and yet you were not satisfied. [29] And you have multiplied your fornication in the land of Canaan, (to the) Chaldean, and yet you were not satisfied with this.

18 צַלְמֵי זָכָר וַתִּזְנִי־בָם׃ וַתִּקְחִי אֶת־בִּגְדֵי רִקְמָתֵךְ וַתְּכַסִּים
covered and / your / clothes / took and / with / and males / images
,them / embroidered / them / whored / of

19 וְשַׁמְנִי וּקְטָרְתִּי נָתַתְּ לִפְנֵיהֶם׃ וְלַחְמִי אֲשֶׁר־נָתַתִּי לָךְ
,you / I / which / My Also / their to / have you / My and / My and
gave / food / .face / given / incense / oil

סֹלֶת וָשֶׁמֶן וּדְבַשׁ הֶאֱכַלְתִּיךְ וּנְתַתִּיהוּ לִפְנֵיהֶם לְרֵיחַ
an for / their to / have you / ,you fed I / honey and / and / fine
aroma / face / it given / which / oil / flour

20 נִיחֹחַ וַיֶּהִי נְאֻם אֲדֹנָי יְהוִה׃ וַתִּקְחִי אֶת־בָּנַיִךְ וְאֶת־בְּנוֹתַיִךְ
your / and / sons your / you And .Jehovah / the / states it And sooth-
,daughters / taken have / Lord / ,was / .ing

אֲשֶׁר יָלַדְתְּ לִי וַתִּזְבָּחִים לָהֶם לֶאֱכוֹל הַמְעַט מִתַּזְנוּתָךְ׃
your / Are / .food for / to / you and / to / have you whom
?fornications / small / them / these gave / Me / borne

21 וַתִּשְׁחֲטִי אֶת־בָּנַי וַתִּתְּנִים בְּהַעֲבִיר אוֹתָם לָהֶם׃ וְאֵת
22
And / for / these / to cause to / gave and / sons My / have You
(in) / .them / through pass / ,them / slaughtered

כָּל־תּוֹעֲבֹתַיִךְ וְתַזְנֻתַיִךְ לֹא זָכַרְתִּי אֶת־יְמֵי נְעוּרַיִךְ בִּהְיוֹתֵךְ
you when / your / the / have you / not / your and / your / all
were / ,youth / of days / remembered / fornications / abominations

23 עֵרֹם וְעֶרְיָה מִתְבּוֹסֶסֶת בְּדָמֵךְ הָיִית׃ וַיְהִי אַחֲרֵי כָּל־
all / after / And / you / your in / squirming (and) / and / naked
,was it / .were / blood / bare

24 רָעָתֵךְ אוֹי־אוֹי לָךְ נְאֻם אֲדֹנָי יְהוִה׃ וַתִּבְנִי־לָךְ גֶּב וַתַּעֲשִׂי־
you and / a / your- / have you / !Jehovah / the / says / to woe ,woe / your
made have / mound / self / built also / Lord / ,you / —evil

25 לָךְ רָמָה בְּכָל־רְחוֹב׃ אֶל־כָּל־רֹאשׁ דֶּרֶךְ בָּנִית רָמָתֵךְ
high your / You / the / head every / At / open / in / high a / your-
place / built have / highway / of / place / every / place / self

וַתְּתַעֲבִי אֶת־יָפְיֵךְ וַתְּפַשְּׂקִי אֶת־רַגְלַיִךְ לְכָל־עוֹבֵר וַתַּרְבִּי
have and / who / all to / your / have and / your / have and
multiplied / ,by passed / feet / parted / ,beauty / despised made

26 אֶת־תַּזְנוּתָךְ׃ וַתִּזְנִי אֶל־בְּנֵי־מִצְרַיִם שְׁכֵנַיִךְ גִּדְלֵי בָשָׂר
,flesh / great / your / ,Egypt / the with / have You / your
of / ,neighbors / of sons / whored / .fornications

27 וַתַּרְבִּי אֶת־תַּזְנֻתֵךְ לְהַכְעִיסֵנִי׃ וְהִנֵּה נָטִיתִי יָדִי עָלַיִךְ
over / My / have I / —Behold / provoke to / your / have and
you / hand / out stretched / .anger to Me / fornication / multiplied

וָאֶגְרַע חֻקֵּךְ וָאֶתְּנֵךְ בְּנֶפֶשׁ שֹׂנְאוֹתַיִךְ בְּנוֹת פְּלִשְׁתִּים
the / daugh- / the / who those / the to / I and / your / I and
,Philistines / of ters / ,you hate / of will / you gave / share / back drew

28 הַנִּכְלָמוֹת מִדַּרְכֵּךְ זִמָּה׃ וַתִּזְנִי אֶל־בְּנֵי אַשּׁוּר מִבִּלְתִּי
without / Assyria / the / with / have You / .wicked / way your / are who
of sons / whored / of ashamed

29 שָׂבְעָתֵךְ וַתִּזְנִים וְגַם לֹא שָׂבָעַתְּ׃ וַתַּרְבִּי אֶת־תַּזְנוּתֵךְ אֶל־
in / forni- / your / you And / were you / not / and / you ,Yea / being your
cation / multiplied have / .satisfied / yet / whored / .satisfied

30 אֶרֶץ כְּנַעַן כַּשְׂדִּימָה וְגַם־בְּזֹאת לֹא שָׂבָעַתְּ׃ מָה אֲמֻלָה
weak / How / were you / not / with / and / (to) / Canaan / the
(is) / .satisfied / ,this / yet / ,Chaldean / of land

[30] How weak (is) your heart, states the Lord Jehovah, since you do all these (things), the work of a woman, an overbearing harlot; [31] in that you built your mound in the head of every highway, and you make your high place in every open place, yet you have not been as a harlot, (even) to scorn wages. [32] The adulterous wife: instead of her husband, she takes strangers! [33] They give a gift to all harlots, but you give your gifts to all your lovers, and bribe them to come to you from all around, for your fornication. [34] And in you was the opposite from (those) women, in your fornications, for that none whores after you, and in you giving wages, and hire is not given to you; thus you are opposite.

[35] Therefore, O harlot, hear the word of Jehovah—[36] Thus says the Lord Jehovah: Because your lewdness was poured out, and your nakedness was bared, in your fornications with your lovers and with the idols of your abominations, and by the blood of your sons whom you gave to them; [37] therefore, behold, I will gather all your lovers with whom you have been pleased, even all whom you have loved—with all whom you have hated—I will even gather them against you from all around, and will uncover your nakedness to them, and they will see all your nakedness. [38] And I will judge you with judgments of adulteresses, and shedders of blood. And I will give you blood of fury and jealousy. [39] And I will give you into their hand, and they will raze your mound, and will demolish your high places. They shall also strip you of your clothes, and shall take your beautiful things, and leave you naked and bare. [40] And they will raise against you a company, and they shall stone you

לבתך נאם אדני יהוה בעשותך את־כל־אלה מעשה
the these all you since ,Jehovah the states your
of work ,(things) do Lord ,heart

31 אשה זונה שלטת׃ בבנותיך גבך בראש כל־דרך ורמתך
your and high- every the in your you that in an harlot a
place high ,way of head mound built —overbearing ,woman

32 עשיתי בכל־רחוב ולא־הייתי כזונה לקלס אתנן׃ האשה
The .wages scorn to a as have you yet open in you
wife ,harlot been not ,place every make

33 המנאפת תחת אישה תקח את־זרים׃ לכל־זנות יתנו
they harlots To !strangers she her instead ,adulterous
give all takes husband of

נדה ואת נתת את־נדניך לכל־מאהביך ותשחדי אותם
them bribe and your all to gifts your give but a
lovers you ,gift

34 לבוא אליך מסביב בתזנותיך׃ ויהי־בך הפך מן־הנשים
(those) from the in And your for all from to to
women opposite you was .fornication around you come

בתזנותיך ואחריך לא זונה ובתתך אתנן ואתנן לא־נתן
is not and ,wages in and whores none that for your in
given wages giving you you after ,fornications

35 לך ותהי להפך׃ לכן זונה שמעי דבר־יהוה׃ כה
36
Thus .Jehovah the hear O There- .opposite thus to
of word ,harlot ,fore are you ;you

אמר אדני יהוה יען השפך נחשתך ותגלה ערותך
naked- your was and your poured was Be- :Jehovah the says
,ness bared lewdness out cause Lord

בתזנותיך על־מאהביך ועל כל־גלולי תועבותיך וכדמי
the by and your the all and your with your in
of blood ,abominations of idols with lovers fornications

37 בניך אשר נתת להם׃ לכן הנני מקבץ את־כל־מאהביך
your all will ,behold there- to you whom your
,lovers gather I fore ;them gave sons

אשר ערבת עליהם ואת כל־אשר אהבת על כל־אשר
whom all with have you whom all even ,them with have you whom
,loved pleased been

שנאת וקבצתי אתם עליך מסביב וגליתי ערותך אלהם
them to your will and all from against them even will I have you
nakedness uncover around you gather —hated

38 וראו את־כל־ערותך׃ ושפטתיך משפטי נאפות ושפכת
and adulteresses judg- with will I And your all they and
of shedders of ments you judge .nakedness see will

39 דם ונתתיך דם חמה וקנאה׃ ונתתי אתך בידם והרסו
they and their into you will I And and fury blood I And .blood
raise-will hand give .jealousy of you give will

גבך ונתצו רמתיך והפשיטו אותך בגדיך ולקחו כלי
things shall and your of you shall They high your will and your
take ,clothes strip also .places demolish mound

40 תפארתך והניחוך עירם ועריה׃ והעלו עליך קהל ורגמו
they and a against they And and naked leave and your
stone shall ,company you raise will .bare you beautiful

with stones, and cut you with their swords. [41] And they shall burn your houses with fire, and make judgments against you in the sight of many women; and I will make you stop whoring; and also, you shall not give hire again. [42] So I will make My fury to rest against you, and My jealousy shall depart from you, and I will be quiet and will not be angry any more. [43] Because you have not remembered the days of your youth, but have troubled Me in all these; so, behold, I also will give (back) your way on (your) head, declares the Lord Jehovah. And you shall not commit the wickedness above all your abominations.

[44] Behold, all who use proverbs shall use (this) proverb against you, saying, As the mother, (so is) the daughter. [45] You (are) your mother's daughter, who despises her husband and her sons. And you (are) the sister of your sisters, who despise their husbands and their sons. Your mother (was) a Hittite, and your father)was) an Amorite. [46] And your older sister (is) Samaria; she and her daughters who are dwelling on your left—and your younger sister from you, who dwells on the right, (is) Sodom, and her daughters. [47] Yet you have not walked in their ways, nor have done by their abominations; as (if) only a little (thing), you were even more ruined than they in all your ways. [48] As I live, declares the Lord Jehovah, your sister Sodom, she nor her daughters, have done as you and your daughters have done. [49] Behold, this was the iniquity of your sister Sodom: pride, fulness of bread, and abundance of idleness was in her and her daughters; and she did not strengthen the poor and needy's hand. [50] And they were (also) haughty, and did abomination before My face.

41 אוֹתָךְ בָּאָבֶן וּבִתְּקוּךְ בְּחַרְבוֹתָם׃ וְשָׂרְפוּ בָתַּיִךְ בָּאֵשׁ
with your they And their with cut and with you
.fire houses burn shall .swords you stones

וְעָשׂוּ־בָךְ שְׁפָטִים לְעֵינֵי נָשִׁים רַבּוֹת וְהִשְׁבַּתִּיךְ מִזּוֹנָה
;whoring will I and ,many women the in judgments against and
stop you make of sight you make

42 וְגַם־אֶתְנַן לֹא תִתְּנִי־עוֹד׃ וַהֲנִחֹתִי חֲמָתִי בָּךְ וְסָרָה קִנְאָתִי
My shall and against My will I So .again shall you not wages and
jealousy depart ,you fury rest to make give also

43 מִמֵּךְ וְשָׁקַטְתִּי וְלֹא אֶכְעַס עוֹד׃ יַעַן אֲשֶׁר לֹא־זָכַרְתִּי
have you not Because .still be will and will I and from
remembered angry not quiet be ,you

אֶת־יְמֵי נְעוּרַיִךְ וַתִּרְגְּזִי־לִי בְּכָל־אֵלֶּה וְגַם־אֲנִי הֵא דַּרְכֵּךְ ׀
your ,behold also so ;these all in Me have but your the
way ,I troubled ,youth of days

בְּרֹאשׁ נָתַתִּי נְאֻם אֲדֹנָי יְהוִה וְלֹא עָשִׂיתִי אֶת־הַזִּמָּה עַל
above the shall you And .Jehovah the states give will (your) on
wickedness commit not Lord (back) head

44 כָּל־תּוֹעֲבֹתָיִךְ׃ הִנֵּה כָּל־הַמֹּשֵׁל עָלַיִךְ יִמְשֹׁל לֵאמֹר כְּאִמָּה
the As ,saying use shall against use who all Behold your all
,mother ,proverb (this) you proverbs .abominations

45 בִּתָּהּ׃ בַּת־אִמֵּךְ אַתְּ גֹּעֶלֶת אִישָׁהּ וּבָנֶיהָ וַאֲחוֹת אֲחוֹתֵךְ
your the And her and her who You your daughter her (so)
sisters of sister .sons husband despises ,(are) mother's .daughter

אַתְּ אֲשֶׁר גָּעֲלוּ אַנְשֵׁיהֶן וּבְנֵיהֶן אִמְּכֶן חִתִּית וַאֲבִיכֶן אֱמֹרִי׃
an your and a Your their and their despise who you
.Amorite father ,Hittite mother .sons ,husbands ,(are)

46 וַאֲחוֹתֵךְ הַגְּדוֹלָה שֹׁמְרוֹן הִיא וּבְנוֹתֶיהָ הַיּוֹשֶׁבֶת עַל־
on are who her and she (is) older your And
dwelling daughters ,Samaria sister

שְׂמֹאולֵךְ וַאֲחוֹתֵךְ הַקְּטַנָּה מִמֵּךְ הַיּוֹשֶׁבֶת מִימִינֵךְ סְדֹם
(is) ,right your dwells who from younger your and ;left your
Sodom on ,you sister

47 וּבְנוֹתֶיהָ׃ וְלֹא בְדַרְכֵיהֶן הָלַכְתְּ וּבְתוֹעֲבוֹתֵיהֶן עָשִׂיתי
have their by nor have you their in Yet her and
.done abominations ,walked ways not .daughters

48 כִּמְעַט קָט וַתַּשְׁחִתִי מֵהֶן בְּכָל־דְּרָכָיִךְ׃ חַי־אָנִי נְאֻם
states I As .ways your all in more were You only (if) as
live they than ruined even (thing) little

אֲדֹנָי יְהוִה אִם־עָשְׂתָה סְדֹם אֲחוֹתֵךְ הִיא וּבְנוֹתֶיהָ כַּאֲשֶׁר
as her nor she your Sodom has not ,Jehovah the
,daughters ,sister done Lord

49 עָשִׂית אַתְּ וּבְנוֹתָיִךְ׃ הִנֵּה־זֶה הָיָה עֲוֹן סְדֹם אֲחוֹתֵךְ גָּאוֹן
,pride your Sodom the was ,this ,Behold your and you have you
,sister of iniquity .daughters ,done

שִׂבְעַת־לֶחֶם וְשַׁלְוַת הַשְׁקֵט הָיָה לָהּ וְלִבְנוֹתֶיהָ וְיַד־עָנִי
the and her and in was idleness and bread fulness
poor hand ;daughters her of abundance of

50 וְאֶבְיוֹן לֹא הֶחֱזִיקָה׃ וַתִּגְבְּהֶינָה וַתַּעֲשֶׂינָה תוֹעֵבָה לְפָנָי
before abomination did and they And did she not the and
.Me haughty were .strengthen needy's

And I turned them away as I saw (fit). [51] And Samaria has not sinned as (much as) half your sins; but you have multiplied your abominations which you have done. [52] Also you bear your shame in that you have pleaded for your sisters, by your sins which you did abominably more than they. They are more righteous than you. And also you be ashamed and bear your shame, since you have justified your sisters. [53] When I shall return their captivity, the captivity of Sodom and her daughters, and the captivity of Samaria and her daughters, then (also) the captivity of your captivity in their midst. [54] So that you may bear your shame and may blesh from all that you have done, since you are a comfort to them. [55] When your sisters, Sodom and her daughters, shall return to their former state, and Samaria and her daughters shall return to their former state, then you and your daughters shall return to your former state. [56] For your sister Sodom was not to be heard from your mouth in the day of your pride, before your evil was uncovered, as at the time of the reproach of the daughters of Syria, and all those around her; the Philistines' daughters who hated you from all around. [58] You are bearing your wickedness and your abominations, declares Jehovah. [59] For thus says the Lord Jehovah: I will even deal with you as you have done, who have despised the oath in breaking the covenant.

[60] But I will remember My covenant with you in the days of your youth, and I will raise up to you an everlasting covenant. [61] Then you shall remember your ways and be

51 וָאָסִיר אֶתְהֶן כַּאֲשֶׁר רָאִיתִי׃ וְשֹׁמְרוֹן כַּחֲצִי חַטֹּאתַיִךְ לֹא
not sins your half as of Samaria And saw I .(fit) as them I And away turned

חָטָאָה וַתַּרְבִּי אֶת־תּוֹעֲבוֹתַיִךְ מֵהֵנָּה וַתְּצַדְּקִי אֶת־אֲחוֹתֵךְ
sisters your have and justified more ,they than your abominations have you but multiplied has ,sinned

52 בְּכָל־תּוֹעֲבֹתַיִךְ אֲשֶׁר עָשִׂיתִי׃ גַּם־אַתְּ ׀ שְׂאִי כְלִמָּתֵךְ אֲשֶׁר
in that your shame bear you Also have you .done which your abominations by all

פִּלַּלְתְּ לַאֲחוֹתֵךְ בְּחַטֹּאתַיִךְ אֲשֶׁר־הִתְעַבְתְּ מֵהֵן תִּצְדַּקְנָה
more are They more righteous .they than did you abominably which your by sins your for ,sisters have you pleaded

מִמֵּךְ וְגַם־אַתְּ בּוֹשִׁי וּשְׂאִי כְלִמָּתֵךְ בְּצַדֶּקְתֵּךְ אַחְיוֹתֵךְ׃
your .sisters have you since justified your ,shame bear and be ashamed you And also than .you

53 וְשַׁבְתִּי אֶת־שְׁבִיתְהֶן אֶת־שְׁבִית סְדֹם וּבְנוֹתֶיהָ וְאֶת־שְׁבִית
the of captivity and her and ,daughters Sodom the of captivity their ,captivity I When return shall

54 שֹׁמְרוֹן וּבְנוֹתֶיהָ וּשְׁבִית שְׁבִיתַיִךְ בְּתוֹכְהֵנָה׃ לְמַעַן תִּשְׂאִי
may you bear So that their in .midst cap- your tivity the then of captivity her and ,daughters Samaria

55 כְלִמָּתֵךְ וְנִכְלַמְתְּ מִכֹּל אֲשֶׁר עָשִׂית בְּנַחֲמֵךְ אֹתָן׃ וַאֲחוֹתַיִךְ
your When ,sisters to .them comfort a are you since have you ,done that from all may and blush your shame

סְדֹם וּבְנוֹתֶיהָ תָּשֹׁבְןָ לְקַדְמָתָן וְשֹׁמְרוֹן וּבְנוֹתֶיהָ תָּשֹׁבְןָ
shall return her and daughters and Samaria their to ,state former shall return her and ,daughters Sodom

56 לְקַדְמָתָן וְאַתְּ וּבְנוֹתַיִךְ תְּשֻׁבֶינָה לְקַדְמַתְכֶן׃ וְלוֹא הָיְתָה
was For not former your to .state shall return your and daughters then you their to ,state former

57 סְדֹם אֲחוֹתֵךְ לִשְׁמוּעָה בְּפִיךְ בְּיוֹם גְּאוֹנָיִךְ׃ בְּטֶרֶם תִּגָּלֶה
was uncovered before ,pride your the in of day from mouth your be to heard your sister Sodom

רָעָתֵךְ כְּמוֹ עֵת חֶרְפַּת בְּנוֹת־אֲרָם וְכָל־סְבִיבוֹתֶיהָ בְּנוֹת
daugh- ters those ;her around of and all ,Syria of daughters the reproach of the the of time at as your ,evil

58 פְּלִשְׁתִּים הַשָּׁאטוֹת אוֹתָךְ מִסָּבִיב׃ אֶת־זִמָּתֵךְ וְאֶת־
and your wickedness all from .around you hated who the ,Philistines

59 תּוֹעֲבוֹתַיִךְ אַתְּ נְשָׂאתִים נְאֻם יְהוָה׃ כִּי כֹה אָמַר
says thus For .Jehovah states are ,bearing You your abominations

אֲדֹנָי יְהוִה וְעָשִׂית אוֹתָךְ כַּאֲשֶׁר עָשִׂית אֲשֶׁר־בָּזִית אָלָה
the oath have despised who have you ,done as with you will I deal even :Jehovah the Lord

60 לְהָפֵר בְּרִית׃ וְזָכַרְתִּי אֲנִי אֶת־בְּרִיתִי אוֹתָךְ בִּימֵי נְעוּרָיִךְ
your ,youth the in of days with you My covenant I will But remember the .covenant in breaking

61 וַהֲקִימוֹתִי לָךְ בְּרִית עוֹלָם׃ וְזָכַרְתְּ אֶת־דְּרָכַיִךְ וְנִכְלַמְתְּ
be and ,ashamed ways your you Then remember shall ever- .lasting a covenant to you will I and up raise

ashamed, when you shall receive your sisters, the older than you, to the younger than you. And I will give them to you for daughters, but not by your covenant. [62] And I will raise up, (even) I, My covenant with you. And you shall know that I (am) Jehovah; [63] so that you may remember and be ashamed, and will not any more open to you the mouth, because of your shame—when I am covered for you for all that you have done, declares the Lord Jehovah.

CHAPTER 17

[1] And the word of Jehovah was to me, saying: [2] Son of man, put forth a riddle and speak a parable to the house of Israel. [3] And say, Thus says the Lord Jehovah: A great eagle (with) great wings, long of pinion (and) full of feathers, which was to him different colors, came to Lebanon and took the top of the cedar. [4] He plucked off the first of its young twigs and brought it into a land of traders! He set it n a city of merchants. [5] He also took of the seed of the land and planted it in a field of seed. He took (it) by great waters; he set it (as) a willow. [6] And it sprouted and became a spreading vine, low (of stature), (and it) turned its branches to face toward him; and its roots were under him. So it became a vine and made branches and sent out boughs. [7] Also there was another great eagle (with) great wings and many feathers. And, behold, this vine bent its roots toward him, and sent out its branches to him, to water it,

בְּקַחְתֵּךְ אֶת־אֲחוֹתַיִךְ הַגְּדֹלוֹת מִמֵּךְ אֶל־הַקְּטַנּוֹת מִמֵּךְ

than .you | younger the | to | than you | ,older the | ,sisters your | you when receive shall

62 וְנָתַתִּי אֶתְהֶן לָךְ לְבָנוֹת וְלֹא מִבְּרִיתֵךְ׃ וַהֲקִימוֹתִי אֲנִי

I | will I And up raise | your by .covenant | but not | for ,daughters | to you | them | I And give will

63 אֶת־בְּרִיתִי אִתָּךְ וְיָדַעַתְּ כִּי־אֲנִי יְהוָה׃ לְמַעַן תִּזְכְּרִי וָבֹשְׁתְּ

be and ,ashamed | may you remember | so that | ;Jehovah | I that (am) | you And know shall | with .you | My covenant

וְלֹא יִהְיֶה־לָּךְ עוֹד פִּתְחוֹן פֶּה מִפְּנֵי כְּלִמָּתֵךְ בְּכַפְּרִי־לָךְ

for you | am I when covered | your ,shame | because of | (your) mouth | to open | ,still | to you | will be | and not

לְכָל־אֲשֶׁר עָשִׂית נְאֻם אֲדֹנָי יְהוִה׃

.Jehovah | the Lord | states | you ,done have | that | all for

CAP. XVII יז

CHAPTER 17

1 וַיְהִי דְבַר־יְהוָה אֵלַי לֵאמֹר׃ בֶּן־אָדָם חוּד חִידָה וּמְשֹׁל
2
and speak | riddle a | put forth | ,man | Son of | ,saying | to ,me | Jehovah | the of word | And was

3 מְשֹׁל מָשָׁל אֶל־בֵּית יִשְׂרָאֵל׃ וְאָמַרְתָּ כֹּה־אָמַר ׀ אֲדֹנָי יְהוִה

:Jehovah | the Lord | says Thus | ,say And | .Israel | the of house | to | a parable

הַנֶּשֶׁר הַגָּדוֹל גְּדוֹל הַכְּנָפַיִם אֶרֶךְ הָאֵבֶר מָלֵא הַנּוֹצָה

,feathers | (and) of full | pinion | long of | ,wings | (with) great | great | An eagle

אֲשֶׁר־לוֹ הָרִקְמָה בָּא אֶל־הַלְּבָנוֹן וַיִּקַּח אֶת־צַמֶּרֶת הָאָרֶז׃

the .cedar | of top the | and took | Lebanon | to | came | different ,colors | to him | which was

4 אֵת רֹאשׁ יְנִיקוֹתָיו קָטָף וַיְבִיאֵהוּ אֶל־אֶרֶץ כְּנַעַן בְּעִיר

a In of city | of !traders | a land | into | brought and it | He off plucked | young its twigs | the of chief

5 רֹכְלִים שָׂמוֹ׃ וַיִּקַּח מִזֶּרַע הָאָרֶץ וַיִּתְּנֵהוּ בִּשְׂדֵה־זָרַע

.seed | a in of field | planted and it | the land | the of of seed | also He took | He .it set | merchants

6 קָח עַל־מַיִם רַבִּים צַפְצָפָה שָׂמוֹ׃ וַיִּצְמַח וַיְהִי לְגֶפֶן

a vine | and became | if And sprouted | set he .it | a (as) willow | ;great | waters by | He (it) took

סֹרַחַת שִׁפְלַת קוֹמָה לִפְנוֹת דָּלִיּוֹתָיו אֵלָיו וְשָׁרָשָׁיו תַּחְתָּיו

under him | its and roots | toward ,him | its branches | to face | (and) turned | (of) low ,(stature) | spread- ,ing

7 יִהְיוּ וַתְּהִי לְגֶפֶן וַתַּעַשׂ בַּדִּים וַתְּשַׁלַּח פֹּארוֹת׃ וַיְהִי נֶשֶׁר־

eagle | Also was | .boughs | sent and out | branches | and made | a vine | it So became | .were

אֶחָד גָּדוֹל גְּדוֹל כְּנָפַיִם וְרַב נוֹצָה וְהִנֵּה הַגֶּפֶן הַזֹּאת

this | vine | And behold | .feathers | and many | wings | (with) great | great | another

כָּפְנָה שָׁרָשֶׁיהָ עָלָיו וְדָלִיּוֹתָיו שִׁלְחָה־לּוֹ לְהַשְׁקוֹת אוֹתָהּ

,it | water to | to ,him | sent out | its and branches | toward him | roots its | bent

away from the beds of its planting. [8] It was planted in a good field by great waters, to make branches, and to bear fruit; to be a splendid vine. [9] Say, Thus says the Lord Jehovah: Shall it prosper? Shall he not pull up its roots and cut off its fruit, and wither it? All the leaves of its sprouting shall wither, and not with great power, nor by many people, (can) (any) raise it by its roots. [10] And, behold, being planted, shall it prosper? Shall it not utterly wither when the east wind touches it? It shall wither in the beds (where) it sprouted.

[11] And the word of Jehovah came to me, saying, [12] Say not to the rebellious house: Do you not know what these (mean)? Speak: Behold, the king of Babylon has come to Jerusalem and has taken its king and its rulers and brought them to himself at Babylon. [13] And he took of the royal seed, and has cut with him a covenant, and made him enter into an oath. And he took the mighty of the land, so that the kingdom might be low; that it might not lift itself up; to keep its covenant, that it might stand. [15] But he rebelled against him, in sending his messengers to Egypt, to give horses and many people to him. Shall he prosper? Shall he who does these (things) escape? Or shall he break the covenant and be delivered? [16] (As) I live, declares the Lord Jehovah, Surely, in the place of the king who made him king, whose oath he despised and whose covenant he broke; with him he shall die in the midst of Babylon. [17] And not with (a) great army and (a)

8 מֵעֲרֻגוֹת מַטָּעָהּ׃ אֶל־שָׂדֶה טּוֹב אֶל־מַיִם רַבִּים הִיא
it great waters by good field a In its from away
.planting of beds the

שְׁתוּלָה לַעֲשׂוֹת עָנָף וְלָשֵׂאת פֶּרִי לִהְיוֹת לְגֶפֶן אַדָּרֶת׃
.splendid vine a be to ,fruit to and ,branches to was
bear make ,planted

9 אֱמֹר כֹּה אָמַר אֲדֹנָי יְהוִה תִּצְלָח הֲלוֹא אֶת־שָׁרָשֶׁיהָ
roots its Shall it Shall :Jehovah the says Thus ,Say
not he ?prosper Lord

יְנַתֵּק וְאֶת־פִּרְיָהּ ׀ יְקוֹסֵס וְיָבֵשׁ כָּל־טַרְפֵּי צִמְחָהּ תִּיבָשׁ
shall its the all and ,off cut fruit its and up pull
,wither sprouting of leaves it wither

וְלֹא־בִזְרֹעַ גְּדוֹלָה וּבְעַם רָב לְמַשְׂאוֹת אוֹתָהּ מִשָּׁרָשֶׁיהָ׃
.roots its by it raise to ,many by nor ,great with and
people power not

10 וְהִנֵּה שְׁתוּלָה הֲתִצְלָח הֲלֹא כְּגַעַת בָּהּ רוּחַ הַקָּדִים תִּיבַשׁ
wither east the it when Shall it shall being And
wind touches not it ?prosper ,planted ,behold

11 יָבֹשׁ עַל־עֲרֻגֹת צִמְחָהּ תִּיבָשׁ׃ וַיְהִי דְבַר־יְהוָה
Jehovah the And shall it it (where) the In ?utterly
of word came .wither sprouted beds

12 אֵלַי לֵאמֹר׃ אֱמָר־נָא לְבֵית הַמֶּרִי הֲלֹא יְדַעְתֶּם מָה־
what know you Do :rebellious the to now Say ,saying ,me to
not house

אֵלֶּה אֱמֹר הִנֵּה־בָא מֶלֶךְ־בָּבֶל יְרוּשָׁלִַם וַיִּקַּח אֶת־מַלְכָּהּ
king its has and to Babylon the has ,Behold :Speak these
taken Jerusalem of king come ?(mean)

13 וְאֶת־שָׂרֶיהָ וַיָּבֵא אוֹתָם אֵלָיו בָּבֶלָה׃ וַיִּקַּח מִזֶּרַע הַמְּלוּכָה
royal the of he And at to them and its and
seed took .Babylon himself brought rulers

וַיִּכְרֹת אִתּוֹ בְּרִית וַיָּבֵא אֹתוֹ בְּאָלָה וְאֶת־אֵילֵי הָאָרֶץ לָקָח׃
took he the the And an into him made and a with has and
land of mighty .oath enter covenant him cut

14 לִהְיוֹת מַמְלָכָה שְׁפָלָה לְבִלְתִּי הִתְנַשֵּׂא לִשְׁמֹר אֶת־
keep to might it not ,low the that so
;itself lift that kingdom be might

15 בְּרִיתוֹ לְעָמְדָהּ׃ וַיִּמְרָד־בּוֹ לִשְׁלֹחַ מַלְאָכָיו מִצְרַיִם
,Egypt to his in against he But might it that its
messengers sending him rebelled .stand ,covenant

לָתֶת־לוֹ סוּסִים וְעַם־רָב הֲיִצְלָח הֲיִמָּלֵט הָעֹשֵׂה אֵלֶּה
these who he Shall he Shall .many and horses to to
?(things) does escape ?prosper people him give

16 וְהֵפֵר בְּרִית וְנִמְלָט׃ חַי־אָנִי נְאֻם אֲדֹנָי יְהוִה אִם־לֹא
Surely ,Jehovah the states (As) be and the shall Or
Lord I live ?delivered covenant break he

בִּמְקוֹם הַמֶּלֶךְ הַמַּמְלִיךְ אֹתוֹ אֲשֶׁר בָּזָה אֶת־אָלָתוֹ וַאֲשֶׁר
of and his he of ,him made who king the the in
whom oath despised whom king of place

17 הֵפֵר אֶת־בְּרִיתוֹ אִתּוֹ בְתוֹךְ־בָּבֶל יָמוּת׃ וְלֹא בְחַיִל גָּדוֹל
great with And shall he Babylon the in with his he
army not .die of midst him ;covenant broke

great company shall Pharaoh work for him in the war by casting up mounds and building siege walls to cut off many souls. [18] And he has despised the oath by breaking the covenant, and, behold, he had given his hand, and he has done all these (things)—he shall not escape.

[19] Therefore, thus says the Lord Jehovah: (As) I live, surely My oath that he has despised, and My covenant that he has broken, I will even give it on his head. [20] And I will spread My net on him, and he shall be taken in My snare, and I will bring him to Babylon; and I will judge him there with his treason which he has betrayed against Me. [21] And all his fugitives shall fall by the sword, with all his bands; and those who remain shall be scattered to every wind. And you shall know that I, Jehovah, have spoken. [22] Thus says the Lord Jehovah: I will also take, (even) I, of the top of the highest cedar, and will place (it); I will crop off a tender one from the first of its young twigs; and I will plant (it), (even) I, on a high and lofty mountain.. [23] I will plant it in a high mountain of Israel. And it will bear boughs and produce fruit, and will become a majestic cedar. And every bird of every wing shall dwell under it; they shall dwell in the shadow of its branches. [24] And all the trees of the field shall know that I, Jehovah, have brought down the high tree (and) have exalted the low tree; have dried up the green tree, and have made the dry tree flourish. I, Jehovah, have spoken and have acted.

וּבְקָהָל רָב יַעֲשֶׂה אוֹתוֹ פַרְעֹה בַמִּלְחָמָה בִּשְׁפֹּךְ סֹלְלָה
and company | great | shall work | for him | Pharaoh | the in ,war | casting by up | mounds

וּבִבְנוֹת דָּיֵק לְהַכְרִית נְפָשׁוֹת רַבּוֹת׃ וּבָזָה אָלָה לְהָפֵר
18
and building | siege walls | to cut off | souls | .many | he And has despised | the oath | by breaking

בְּרִית וְהִנֵּה נָתַן יָדוֹ וְכָל־אֵלֶּה עָשָׂה לֹא יִמָּלֵט׃
the covenant, | and behold, | he had given | his hand, | and all | these | he has done, | not | he shall escape.

19 לָכֵן כֹּה־אָמַר אֲדֹנָי יְהוִה חַי־אָנִי אִם־לֹא אָלָתִי אֲשֶׁר בָּזָה
There-fore | thus says | the Lord | Jehovah: | (As) I live | surely | My oath | that | he has despised,

20 וּבְרִיתִי אֲשֶׁר הֵפִיר וּנְתַתִּיו בְּרֹאשׁוֹ׃ וּפָרַשְׂתִּי עָלָיו רִשְׁתִּי
and My covenant | that | he has broken, | even I will give it | on his head. | And I will spread | on him | My net,

וְנִתְפַּשׂ בִּמְצוּדָתִי וַהֲבִיאוֹתִיהוּ בָבֶלָה וְנִשְׁפַּטְתִּי אִתּוֹ שָׁם
and he shall be taken | in My snare, | and I will bring him | to Babylon, | and I will judge | him | there

21 מַעֲלוֹ אֲשֶׁר מָעַל־בִּי׃ וְאֵת כָּל־מִבְרָחָו בְּכָל־אֲגַפָּיו
with his treason | which | he has betrayed against Me. | And | all | his fugitives | with all | his bands

בַּחֶרֶב יִפֹּלוּ וְהַנִּשְׁאָרִים לְכָל־רוּחַ יִפָּרֵשׂוּ וִידַעְתֶּם כִּי אֲנִי
by the sword | shall fall, | and those who remain | to every | wind | shall be scattered. | And you shall know | that | I,

22 יְהוָה דִּבַּרְתִּי׃ כֹּה אָמַר אֲדֹנָי יְהוִה וְלָקַחְתִּי אָנִי
Jehovah, | have spoken. | Thus | says | the Lord | Jehovah: | I will also take, | I,

מִצַּמֶּרֶת הָאֶרֶז הָרָמָה וְנָתָתִּי מֵרֹאשׁ יֹנְקוֹתָיו רַךְ אֶקְטֹף
of the top of | the cedar | highest | and will set (it); | from the chief of | its young twigs | a tender one | I will crop off,

23 וְשָׁתַלְתִּי אָנִי עַל הַר־גָּבֹהַּ וְתָלוּל׃ בְּהַר מְרוֹם יִשְׂרָאֵל
and will plant (it) | I | on | a mountain | high | and lofty. | in a mountain of | high, | Israel

אֶשְׁתֳּלֶנּוּ וְנָשָׂא עָנָף וְעָשָׂה פֶרִי וְהָיָה לְאֶרֶז אַדִּיר וְשָׁכְנוּ
I will plant it. | And it will bear | boughs | and produce | fruit, | and become | a cedar | majestic. | And shall dwell

24 תַחְתָּיו כֹּל צִפּוֹר כָּל־כָּנָף בְּצֵל דָּלִיּוֹתָיו תִּשְׁכֹּנָּה׃ וְיָדְעוּ
under it | every | bird of | every wing; | in the shadow of | its branches | they shall dwell. | And shall know

כָּל־עֲצֵי הַשָּׂדֶה כִּי אֲנִי יְהוָה הִשְׁפַּלְתִּי עֵץ גָּבֹהַּ הִגְבַּהְתִּי
all | the trees of | the field | that | I, | Jehovah, | have brought down | the tree | high, | have exalted

עֵץ שָׁפָל הוֹבַשְׁתִּי עֵץ לָח וְהִפְרַחְתִּי עֵץ יָבֵשׁ אֲנִי יְהוָה
the tree | low, | have dried up | the tree | green, | and have made flourish | the tree | dry. | I | Jehovah,

דִּבַּרְתִּי וְעָשִׂיתִי׃
have spoken | and have acted.

CAP. XVIII יח

CHAPTER 18

1 2 וַיְהִי דְבַר־יְהוָה אֵלַי לֵאמֹר׃ מַה־לָּכֶם אַתֶּם מֹשְׁלִים אֶת־

use you to What ,saying ,me to Jehovah the And
that you (it is) of word was

הַמָּשָׁל הַזֶּה עַל־אַדְמַת יִשְׂרָאֵל לֵאמֹר אָבוֹת יֹאכְלוּ בֹסֶר

sour have The ,saying ,Israel the con- this proverb
grapes eaten fathers of land cerning

3 וְשִׁנֵּי הַבָּנִים תִּקְהֶינָה׃ חַי־אָנִי נְאֻם אֲדֹנָי יֱהֹוִה אִם־יִהְיֶה

there not ,Jehovah the states As ?dull are the the and
is Lord I live sons of teeth

4 לָכֶם עוֹד מְשֹׁל הַמָּשָׁל הַזֶּה בְּיִשְׂרָאֵל׃ הֵן כָּל־הַנְּפָשׁוֹת

the all ,Behold .Israel in this proverb use to any to
souls longer you

לִי הֵנָּה כְּנֶפֶשׁ הָאָב וּכְנֶפֶשׁ הַבֵּן לִי־הֵנָּה הַנֶּפֶשׁ הַחֹטֵאת

,sins that the they to the the also the the As they to
soul ;(are) me son of soul ,father of soul .(are) Me

5 הִיא תָמוּת׃ וְאִישׁ כִּי־יִהְיֶה צַדִּיק וְעָשָׂה מִשְׁפָּט וּצְדָקָה׃

and which that and righteous is that a But shall it
;right just is does man .die

6 אֶל־הֶהָרִים לֹא אָכָל וְעֵינָיו לֹא נָשָׂא אֶל־גִּלּוּלֵי בֵּית

the idols the to has not his and has not the on
of house of up lifted eyes eaten mountains

יִשְׂרָאֵל וְאֶת־אֵשֶׁת רֵעֵהוּ לֹא טִמֵּא וְאֶל־אִשָּׁה נִדָּה לֹא

not men- woman a and has not his wife and ;Israel
struating to ;defiled neighbor's

7 יִקְרָב׃ וְאִישׁ לֹא יוֹנֶה חֲבֹלָתוֹ חוֹב יָשִׁיב גְּזֵלָה לֹא יִגְזֹל

has not by re- he the (to) his (but) has not a and come has
,robbed robbery ;turns debtor pledge ,pressed man ;near

8 לַחְמוֹ לְרָעֵב יִתֵּן וְעֵירֹם יְכַסֶּה־בָּגֶד׃ בַּנֶּשֶׁךְ לֹא־יִתֵּן

has he not on (with) has he the and has the to his (but)
lent interest ;clothing covered naked given hungry bread

וְתַרְבִּית לֹא יִקָּח מֵעָוֶל יָשִׁיב יָדוֹ מִשְׁפַּט אֱמֶת יַעֲשֶׂה

has true justice his has he from has he not and
done ;hand kept injustice ;taken increase

9 בֵּין אִישׁ לְאִישׁ׃ בְּחֻקּוֹתַי יְהַלֵּךְ וּמִשְׁפָּטַי שָׁמַר לַעֲשׂוֹת

deal to has My and has My in and man be-
kept judgments walked statutes ;man tween

10 אֱמֶת צַדִּיק הוּא חָיֹה יִחְיֶה נְאֻם אֲדֹנָי יֱהֹוִה׃ וְהוֹלִיד בֵּן־

a if And .Jehovah the states he surely he righteous —truly
son fathers he Lord live shall ,(is)

11 פָּרִיץ שֹׁפֵךְ דָּם וְעָשָׂה אָח מֵאַחַד מֵאֵלֶּה׃ וְהוּא אֶת־

(if) even ;these of from a does and ,blood who is who
he one ,brother (to) sheds ,violent

כָּל־אֵלֶּה לֹא עָשָׂה כִּי גַם אֶל־הֶהָרִים אָכַל וְאֶת־אֵשֶׁת

wife and has he the on also that does not these any
;eaten mountains ;(himself) of

12 רֵעֵהוּ טִמֵּא׃ עָנִי וְאֶבְיוֹן הוֹנָה גְּזֵלוֹת גָּזָל חֲבֹל לֹא יָשִׁיב

has not the he Thieving has he the and the has his
;returned pledge ;stole .pressed needy poor defiled neighbor's

CHAPTER 18

[1] And the word of Jehovah was to me, saying, [2] What (is it) to you that you use this proverb concerning the land of Israel, saying, The fathers have eaten sour grapes, and the teeth of the sons are dull? [3] (As) I live, declares the Lord Jehovah, there is not to you any longer (occasion) to use this proverb in Israel. [4] Behold, they (are) all My souls. As the soul of the father, also the soul of the son—they (are) Mine—the soul that sins, it shall die!

[5] But a man that is righteouse and does that which is just and right: [6] has not eaten on the mountains, and his eyes (has) not lifted up to the idols of the house of Israel; and his neighbor's wife has not defiled; and has not come near to a menstruating woman; [7] and has not oppressed a man, (but) he returns his pledge (to) the debtor; (and) has not robbed by robbery, (but) has given his bread to the hungry, and he has covered the naked (with) clothing; [8] he has not lent on interest, and he has not taken increase; he has kept his hand from injustice, having done true justice between man and man; [9] he has walked in My statutes and has kept My judgments to deal truly—he (is) righteous—surely he shall live, declares the Lord Jehovah.

[10] And if he fathers a son who is violent, who sheds blood, and does to a brother (any) one of these [11]—even he does not any of these—that also he has eaten on the mountains and has defiled his neighbor's wife; [12] he has oppressed the poor and needy—thieving he stole; (he) has not returned the pledge;

and has lifted up his eyes to the idols; he has committed abomination; [13] (he) has lent on interest and has taken increase—shall he also live? He shall not live—he has done all these abominations; he shall surely die; his blood shall be on him!

[14] Now, behold, (if) he fathers a son who sees all his father's sins which he has done, and sees, and does not do like them—[15] (he) has not eaten on the mountains; and has not lifted up his eyes to the idols of the house of Israel; has not defiled his neighbor's wife; [16] and has not oppressed a man; has not withheld the pledge; and has not robbed by robbery—he has given his bread to the hungry, and he has covered the naked (with) clothes; [17] has withdrawn his hand from the poor, and has not received interest and increase; (he) has done My judgments, has walked in My statutes—he shall not die for the iniquity of his father; he shall surely live! [18] His father, because he did extortion, robbed (his) brother by robbery, and did what is not good among his people, behold, even he shall die in his iniquity.

[19] Yet you say, Why? Does not the son bear the iniquity of the father? When the son has done justice and righteousness: he has kept all My statutes and has done them; surely he shall live, [20] the soul that sins, it shall die. A son shall not bear the iniquity of the father, and a father shall not bear the iniquity of the son. The rightness of the righteous shall be upon him, and the wickedness of the wicked shall be on him.

[21] But the wicked, if he will turn from all his sins which he has done, and keep all My statutes, and do justice and righteousness, surely he shall live—he shall not die.

13 ואל־הגלולים נשא עיניו תועבה עשה: בנשך נתן
has on has he abomination his has idols the and
lent interest ;committed ,eyes up lifted to
ותרבית לקח וחי לא יחיה את כל־התועבות האלה
these abominations all shall He not he shall has and
!live ?live also ,taken increase
14 עשה מות יומת דמיו בו יהיה: והנה הוליד בן וירא
who a he (if) Now shall on his shall he surely has he
sees son fathers ,behold !be him blood ,die ;done
את־כל־חטאת אביו אשר עשה וירא* ולא יעשה כהן:
like does and and has he which his sins all
;them do not ,sees ,done father's
15 על־ההרים לא אכל ועיניו לא נשא אל־גלולי בית
the the to has not his and has not the on
of house of idols up lifted eyes ;eaten mountains
16 ישראל את־אשת רעהו לא טמא: ואיש לא הונה חבל
the has not a and has not his wife ;Israel
pledge ;pressed man ;defiled neighbor's
לא חבל וגזלה לא גזל לחמו לרעב נתן ועירום כסה־
has he the and has he the to his has not by and has not
covered naked given hungry bread ;robbed robbery ;withheld
17 בגד: מעני השיב ידו נשך ותרבית לא לקח משפטי
My has not and interest his has the from (with)
judgments ;received increase ;hand withdrawn poor ;dress
עשה בחקותי הלך הוא לא ימות בעון אביו חיה יחיה:
shall he surely his the for shall not he has My in has
!live ,father of iniquity die ;walked statutes ;done
18 אביו כי־עשק עשק גזל גזל אח ואשר לא־טוב עשה
did is not and (his) by robbed ex- he because His
good what ,brother robbery ,tortion did ,father
19 בתוך עמיו והנה־מת בעונו: ואמרתם מדע לא־נשא
bear Does you Yet his in he ,behold his among
not ?Why ,say .iniquity die shall even ,people
הבן בעון האב והבן משפט וצדקה עשה את כל־חקותי
My all has and justice When the ini- the the
statutes ,done righteousness son the ?father of quity son
20 שמר ויעשה אתם חיה יחיה: הנפש החטאת היא תמות
shall it ,sins that The shall he surely ,them has and has he
.die soul .live done kept
בן לא־ישא ׀ בעון האב ואב לא ישא בעון הבן צדקת
right-The the the shall not a and the the shall not A
of ness .son of iniquity bear father father of iniquity bear son
הצדיק עליו תהיה ורשעת רשע עליו תהיה:
shall on the the and ,be shall on the
.be him wicked of wickedness him righteous
21 והרשע כי ישוב מכל־חטאתו אשר עשה ושמר את־
and has he which sins his from will he if the But
keep ,done all turn ,wicked
כל־חקותי ועשה משפט וצדקה חיה יחיה לא ימות:
shall he not shall he surely and justice do and My all
.die ;live ,righteousness ,statutes

[22] All his transgressions that he has done, they shall not be mentioned to him; in his righteousness that he has done he shall live. [23] Do I actually desire the death of the wicked? declares the Lord Jehovah: Is it not that he should turn from his ways and live? [24] But when the righteous turns from his righteousness and does injustice; by all the abominations that the wicked do, he does; shall he live? All his righteousness that he has done shall not be remembered in his treason that he has betrayed, and in his sin that he has sinned —in them he shall die.

[25] Yet you say, The way of the Lord is not fair. Hear now, O house of Israel, is not My way fair? Are not your ways unfair? [26] When a righteous one turns from his righteousness and does injustice, and dies in them—he shall die for his injustice that he has done. [27] And when the wicked turns from his wickedness that he has done, and does justice and righteousness, he shall keep his soul alive. [28] Because he considers and turns from all his transgressions that he has done, surely he shall live; he shall not die. [29] Yet the house of Israel says, The way of the Lord is not fair. Are not My ways fair, O house of Israel? Is it not your ways that are not fair? [30] Therefore, each man by his ways, I will judge you, O house of Israel, declares the Lord Jehovah. Turn and be made to turn from all your transgressions, and iniquity shall not be a stumbling-block to you. [31] Cast away from you all your transgressions by which you have transgressed in them; and make for yourselves a new heart and a new spirit, for why will

22 כָּל־פְּשָׁעָיו אֲשֶׁר עָשָׂה לֹא יִזָּכְרוּ לוֹ בְּצִדְקָתוֹ אֲשֶׁר־עָשָׂה
has he that his in to shall they not has he that his All
done righteousness ;him mentioned be done transgressions

23 יִחְיֶה׃ הֶחָפֹץ אֶחְפֹּץ מוֹת רָשָׁע נְאֻם אֲדֹנָי יְהֹוָה הֲלוֹא
it Is :Jehovah the states the the desire I Do shall he
not Lord ?wicked of death actually .live

24 בְּשׁוּבוֹ מִדְּרָכָיו וְחָיָה׃ וּבְשׁוּב צַדִּיק מִצִּדְקָתוֹ
his from the when But ?live and his from he that
righteousness righteous turns ways turn should

וְעָשָׂה עָוֶל כְּכֹל הַתּוֹעֵבוֹת אֲשֶׁר־עָשָׂה הָרָשָׁע יַעֲשֶׂה וָחָי
shall he the do that the all by in- does and
?live he ,does wicked abominations ;justice

כָּל־צִדְקֹתָו אֲשֶׁר־עָשָׂה לֹא תִזָּכַרְנָה בְּמַעֲלוֹ אֲשֶׁר־מָעַל
has he that his in be shall not has he that his All
,betrayed treason remembered done righteousness

25 וּבְחַטָּאתוֹ אֲשֶׁר־חָטָא בָּם יָמוּת׃ וַאֲמַרְתֶּם לֹא יִתָּכֵן דֶּרֶךְ
The fair is not you Yet he in has he that his in and
of way ,say .die shall them ,sinned sin

אֲדֹנָי שִׁמְעוּ־נָא בֵּית יִשְׂרָאֵל הֲדַרְכִּי לֹא יִתָּכֵן הֲלֹא
Are ?fair not My Is ,Israel O ,now Hear the
not way of house .Lord

26 דַּרְכֵיכֶם לֹא יִתָּכֵנוּ׃ בְּשׁוּב־צַדִּיק מִצִּדְקָתוֹ וְעָשָׂה עָוֶל
in- does and his from righteous a When ?fair not ways your
justice righteousness one turns

27 וּמֵת עֲלֵיהֶם בְּעַוְלוֹ אֲשֶׁר־עָשָׂה יָמוּת׃ וּבְשׁוּב רָשָׁע
the when And shall he nas he that his for them in and
wicked turns .die ,done injustice dies

מֵרִשְׁעָתוֹ אֲשֶׁר עָשָׂה וַיַּעַשׂ מִשְׁפָּט וּצְדָקָה הוּא אֶת־נַפְשׁוֹ
soul his he and justice does and has he that his from
,righteousness done wickedness

28 יְחַיֶּה׃ וַיִּרְאֶה וַיָּשׁוֹב מִכָּל־פְּשָׁעָיו אֲשֶׁר עָשָׂה חָיוֹ יִחְיֶה
shall he surely has he that his from turns and Because keep shall
;live ,done transgressions all considers he .alive

29 לֹא יָמוּת׃ וְאָמְרוּ בֵּית יִשְׂרָאֵל לֹא יִתָּכֵן דֶּרֶךְ אֲדֹנָי
the The is not ,Israel the says Yet shall he not
.Lord of way fair of house .die

הַדְּרָכַי לֹא יִתָּכְנוּ בֵּית יִשְׂרָאֵל הֲלֹא דַרְכֵיכֶם לֹא יִתָּכֵן׃
are that not ways your it Is ?Israel O Are not My
?fair not of house ,fair ways

30 לָכֵן אִישׁ כִּדְרָכָיו אֶשְׁפֹּט אֶתְכֶם בֵּית יִשְׂרָאֵל נְאֻם אֲדֹנָי
the states ,Israel O ,you will I his by each There-
Lord of house judge ,ways man ,fore

יְהֹוָה שׁוּבוּ וְהָשִׁיבוּ מִכָּל־פִּשְׁעֵיכֶם וְלֹא־יִהְיֶה לָכֶם
you to shall and your from made be and Turn .Jehovah
be not transgressions all turn to

31 לְמִכְשׁוֹל עָוֹן׃ הַשְׁלִיכוּ מֵעֲלֵיכֶם אֶת־כָּל־פִּשְׁעֵיכֶם אֲשֶׁר
by your all you from away Cast .iniquity block a for
which transgressions stumbling of

פְּשַׁעְתֶּם בָּם וַעֲשׂוּ לָכֶם לֵב חָדָשׁ וְרוּחַ חֲדָשָׁה וְלָמָּה
why for ,new a and new heart a for And in have you
spirit yourselves make them transgressed

you die, O house of Israel? [32] For I do not have pleasure in the death of him who dies, declares the Lord Jehovah. So turn and live.

32 תָמֻתוּ בֵּית יִשְׂרָאֵל׃ כִּי לֹא אֶחְפֹּץ בְּמוֹת הַמֵּת נְאֻם אֲדֹנָי

the states who him the in have I do not For ?Israel O you will
Lord ,dies of death pleasure of house ,die

יְהוִה וְהָשִׁיבוּ וִחְיוּ׃

.live and So .Jehovah
turn

CAP. XIX יט

CHAPTER 19

CHAPTER 19

[1] And you take up a lament for the rulers of Israel, [2] and say, What (is) your mother? A lioness—she lay down among young lions; she reared her cubs. [3] And she raised one of her cubs; he became a young lion and learned to tear the prey; he ate men. [4] Also the nations heard of him. He was taken in their pit, and they brought him in chains to the land of Egypt. [5] And when she saw that she had waited (and) her hope had been lost, then she took another of her cubs (and) made him a young lion. [6] And he went about among the lions. He became a young lion and learned to catch the prey; he ate men. [7] And he knew his widows, and he laid waste their cities; and the land and its fulness were desolated from the sound of his roaring. [8] Then the nations set against him on every side from the provinces, and spread their net over him; he was taken in their pit. [9] And they put him in a cage in chains, and brought him to the king of Babylon. They brought him into hunting nets; so that his voice should not any longer be heard on the mountains of Israel.

[10] Your mother (is) like a vine in your blood, planted by the waters. She was fruitful and full of branches because of many waters. [11] And rods (were) to her, strong for the scepters of rulers; and its stature was exalted among the thick branches. And it was seen in her height, with the multitude

1 2 וְאַתָּה שָׂא קִינָה אֶל־נְשִׂיאֵי יִשְׂרָאֵל׃ וְאָמַרְתָּ מָה אִמְּךָ

your What ,say and ,Israel the for a take And
?mother (is) of rulers lament up you

לְבִיָּא בֵּין אֲרָיוֹת רָבָצָה בְּתוֹךְ כְּפִרִים רִבְּתָה גוּרֶיהָ׃

her reared she young among She lions among A
.cubs lions ;down lay .lioness

3 וַתַּעַל אֶחָד מִגֻּרֶיהָ כְּפִיר הָיָה וַיִּלְמַד לִטְרָף־טֶרֶף אָדָם

men the tear to and he young a her of one she And
;prey learned became lion ;cubs raised

4 אָכָל׃ וַיִּשְׁמְעוּ אֵלָיו גּוֹיִם בְּשַׁחְתָּם נִתְפָּשׂ וַיְבִאֻהוּ בַחַחִים

in they and was He their In the of heard Also he
chains him brought ,taken pit .nations him .ate

5 אֶל־אֶרֶץ מִצְרָיִם׃ וַתֵּרֶא כִּי נוֹחֲלָה אָבְדָה תִּקְוָתָהּ וַתִּקַּח

she then her had (and) had she that when And .Egypt the to
took ,hope lost been waited saw she of land

6 אֶחָד מִגֻּרֶיהָ כְּפִיר שָׂמָתְהוּ׃ וַיִּתְהַלֵּךְ בְּתוֹךְ־אֲרָיוֹת כְּפִיר

young a the among he And .him made a (and) her of another
lion .lions about walked lion young cubs

7 הָיָה וַיִּלְמַד לִטְרָף־טֶרֶף אָדָם אָכָל׃ וַיֵּדַע אַלְמְנוֹתָיו

,widows his he And .ate he men ;prey the to and be- he
knew catch learned came

8 וְעָרֵיהֶם הֶחֱרִיב וַתֵּשַׁם אֶרֶץ וּמְלֹאָהּ מִקּוֹל שַׁאֲגָתוֹ׃ וַיִּתְּנוּ

Then his the from its and the were and laid he their and
set .roaring of sound fulness land desolated ,waste cities

עָלָיו גּוֹיִם סָבִיב מִמְּדִינוֹת וַיִּפְרְשׂוּ עָלָיו רִשְׁתָּם בְּשַׁחְתָּם

their in ;net their over and the from every on the against
pit him spread ,provinces side nations him

9 נִתְפָּשׂ׃ וַיִּתְּנֻהוּ בַסּוּגַר בַּחַחִים וַיְבִאֻהוּ אֶל־מֶלֶךְ בָּבֶל

.Babylon the to brought and in a in they And was he
of king him chains cage him put .taken

יְבִאֻהוּ בַּמְּצֹדוֹת לְמַעַן לֹא־יִשָּׁמַע קוֹלוֹ עוֹד אֶל־הָרֵי

the on any his be should not so hunting into They
of mountains longer voice heard that nets him brought

10 יִשְׂרָאֵל׃ אִמְּךָ כַגֶּפֶן בְּדָמְךָ עַל־מַיִם שְׁתוּלָה פֹּרִיָּה

was She .planted the by your in a like Your .Israel
fruitful waters ,blood vine (is) mother

11 וַעֲנֵפָה הָיְתָה מִמַּיִם רַבִּים׃ וַיִּהְיוּ־לָהּ מַטּוֹת עֹז אֶל־שִׁבְטֵי

the for strong ,rods her to And .many because was full and
of scepters was waters of branches of

מֹשְׁלִים וַתִּגְבַּהּ קוֹמָתוֹ עַל־בֵּין עֲבֹתִים וַיֵּרָא בְגָבְהוֹ בְּרֹב

the with her in it And thick the among its was and ;rulers
of many height seen was .branches stature exalted

of its branches. [12] But she was plucked in fury. She was thrown to the ground, and the east wind dried up her fruit. Her strong rods were torn away and withered; the fire burned it. [13] And now she is planted in the wilderness, in a dry and thirsty ground. [14] And fire has gone out from a rod of her branches; it consumed her fruit, and there is not in her a strong rod (to be) a scepter to rule. It (is) a lament, and has become a lament.

12 דָּלִיּוֹתָיו׃ וַתֻּתַּשׁ בְּחֵמָה לָאָרֶץ הֻשְׁלָכָה וְרוּחַ הַקָּדִים הוֹבִישׁ

dried up | east | the and wind | was She ,thrown | the to ground | .fury in | she But plucked was | its .branches

13 פִּרְיָהּ הִתְפָּרְקוּ וְיָבֵשׁוּ מַטֵּה עֻזָּהּ אֵשׁ אֲכָלָתְהוּ׃ וְעַתָּה

And now | .it burned | the fire | Her ;strong | rods | and withered | torn were away | her .fruit

14 שְׁתוּלָה בַמִּדְבָּר בְּאֶרֶץ צִיָּה וְצָמָא׃ וַתֵּצֵא אֵשׁ מִמַּטֵּה

a from of rod | fire | has And out gone | and .thirsty | dry a | in ground | the in ,wilderness | is she planted

בַדֶּיהָ פִּרְיָהּ אָכָלָה וְלֹא־הָיָה בָהּ מַטֵּה עֹז שֵׁבֶט לִמְשׁוֹל

.rule to | a (be to) scepter | strong | rod a | in her | is | and not | it consumed | her fruit | her ,branches

קִינָה הִיא וַתְּהִי לְקִינָה׃

.lament a | has and become | It ,(is) | a lament

CAP. XX כ

CHAPTER 20

CHAPTER 20

[1] And it was in the seventh year, in the fifth (month), the tenth of the month, men came from the elders of Israel to inquire (of) Jehovah, and sat before me. [2] Then the word of Jehovah was to me saying, [3] Son of man, speak to the elders of Israel and say to them, Thus says the Lord Jehovah: Have you come to inquire (of) Me? (As) I live, says the Lord Jehovah, I will not be inquired of by you, declares the Lord Jehovah. [4] Will you judge them; will you judge, son of man? Cause them to know the abominations of their fathers. [5] And say to them, Thus says the Lord Jehovah: In the day I chose Israel and lifted My hand to the seed of the house of Jacob—and I was made known to them in the land of Egypt—when I lifted up My hand to them, saying, I (am) Jehovah your God; [6] in that day I lifted up My hand to them to bring them out from the land of Egypt into a land that I had searched out for them, flowing (with) milk and (with) honey, the glory

1 וַיְהִי ׀ בַּשָּׁנָה הַשְּׁבִיעִית בַּחֲמִשִׁי בֶּעָשׂוֹר לַחֹדֶשׁ בָּאוּ

came | the of ,month | tenth the | the in ,(month) fifth | ,seventh | the in year | And was it

אֲנָשִׁים מִזִּקְנֵי יִשְׂרָאֵל לִדְרֹשׁ אֶת־יְהוָה וַיֵּשְׁבוּ לְפָנָי׃

before .me | sat and | (of) Jehovah | inquire to | Israel | from of elders the | men

2 וַיְהִי דְבַר־יְהוָה אֵלַי לֵאמֹר׃ בֶּן־אָדָם דַּבֵּר אֶת־זִקְנֵי
3

the of elders | speak to | ,man | Son of | ,saying | to ,me | Jehovah | the of word | Then was

יִשְׂרָאֵל וְאָמַרְתָּ אֲלֵהֶם כֹּה אָמַר אֲדֹנָי יְהוִה הֲלִדְרֹשׁ

to Have inquire | :Jehovah | the Lord | says | Thus | ,them to | say and | Israel

אֹתִי אַתֶּם בָּאִים חַי־אָנִי אִם־אִדָּרֵשׁ לָכֶם נְאֻם אֲדֹנָי

the Lord | states | by ,you | be will I of inquired | not | (As) ,I live | ?come | You | (of) Me

4 יְהוִה׃ הֲתִשְׁפֹּט אֹתָם הֲתִשְׁפּוֹט בֶּן־אָדָם אֶת־תּוֹעֲבוֹת

abomi- the of nations | ?man | son of | you will ,judge | ,them | you Will judge | .Jehovah

5 אֲבוֹתָם הוֹדִיעֵם׃ וְאָמַרְתָּ אֲלֵיהֶם כֹּה־אָמַר אֲדֹנָי יְהוִה

:Jehovah | the Lord | says | Thus | ,them to | say And | them cause .know to | their fathers

בְּיוֹם בָּחֳרִי בְיִשְׂרָאֵל וָאֶשָּׂא יָדִי לְזֶרַע בֵּית יַעֲקֹב וָאִוָּדַע

was I and known made | ,Jacob | the of house | the to of seed | My hand | and lifted | Israel | I that chose | the In day

לָהֶם בְּאֶרֶץ מִצְרָיִם וָאֶשָּׂא יָדִי לָהֶם לֵאמֹר אֲנִי יְהוָה

Jehovah | I (am) | ,saying | ,them to | My hand | I when up lifted | ;Egypt | the in of land | to them

6 אֱלֹהֵיכֶם׃ בַּיּוֹם הַהוּא נָשָׂאתִי יָדִי לָהֶם לְהוֹצִיאָם מֵאֶרֶץ

the from of land | bring to out them | to them | My hand | lifted I up | that | day in | ;God your

מִצְרָיִם אֶל־אֶרֶץ אֲשֶׁר־תַּרְתִּי לָהֶם זָבַת חָלָב וּדְבַשׁ צְבִי

the glory | and ,honey | (with) milk | flowing | for ,them | had I out searched | that | a land | into | Egypt

it (is) to all lands; [7] then I said to them, Let each man cast away the filthy idols of his eyes, and do not defile yourselves with the idols of Egypt. I (am) Jehovah your God. [8] But they rebelled against Me, and would not listen to Me. They did not each man throw away the filthy idols of their eyes, and they did not forsake the idols of Egypt. Then I said, I will pour out My fury against them, to fulfill My anger against them in the midst of the land of Egypt. [9] But I worked for My name's sake, that it should not be profaned before the nations, of whom they (were) among them, of whom I made Myself known to them in their sight, by bringing them out of the land of Egypt.

[10] So I made them leave from the land of Egypt and brought them into the wilderness. [11] And I gave them My statutes, and My judgments I made them know, which (if) a man does them he will even live by them. [12] And I also gave them My sabbaths to be a sign between Me and them, that (they) might know that I (am) Jehovah, who sets them apart. [13] But the house of Israel rebelled against Me in the wilderness; they did not walk in My statutes, and they despised My judgments; which (if) a man does them he will even live by them. And they greatly profaned My sabbaths. Then I said, (I) will pour out My fury on them in the wilderness, to destroy them. [14] But I worked for My name's sake, that it should not be profaned before the nations, of whom I brought them out in their sight. [15] And I also lifted up My hand to them in the wilderness, that (I) would not bring them into the land which I had given,

7 הִיא לְכָל־הָאֲרָצוֹת׃ וָאֹמַר אֲלֵהֶם אִישׁ שִׁקּוּצֵי עֵינָיו
his eyes | filthy the of idols | each man | ,them to | I then said | ,lands | to all | (is) it

הַשְׁלִיכוּ וּבְגִלּוּלֵי מִצְרַיִם אַל־תִּטַּמָּאוּ אֲנִי יְהוָה אֱלֹהֵיכֶם׃
.God your | Jehovah | I (am) | defile do .yourselves | not | Egypt | with and of idols the | cast Let ,away

8 וַיַּמְרוּ־בִי וְלֹא אָבוּ לִשְׁמֹעַ אֵלַי אִישׁ אֶת־שִׁקּוּצֵי עֵינֵיהֶם
their eyes | filthy the of idols | each man | .Me to | listen to | would not | and against ,Me | they But rebelled

לֹא הִשְׁלִיכוּ וְאֶת־גִּלּוּלֵי מִצְרַיִם לֹא עָזָבוּ וָאֹמַר לִשְׁפֹּךְ
will (I) out pour | I Then ,said | they .forsake did | not | Egypt | the of idols | and | did They ,away throw | not

חֲמָתִי עֲלֵיהֶם לְכַלּוֹת אַפִּי בָּהֶם בְּתוֹךְ אֶרֶץ מִצְרָיִם׃
.Egypt | the of land | the in of middle | against them | My anger | fulfill to | against them | My fury

9 וָאַעַשׂ לְמַעַן שְׁמִי לְבִלְתִּי הֵחֵל לְעֵינֵי הַגּוֹיִם אֲשֶׁר־הֵמָּה
they (were) | of whom | the nations | before | be should it profaned | that not | My name | the for of sake | I But worked

בְתוֹכָם אֲשֶׁר נוֹדַעְתִּי אֲלֵיהֶם לְעֵינֵיהֶם לְהוֹצִיאָם מֵאֶרֶץ
the of of land | bringing by out them | their in ,sight | them to | made I known Myself | whom of | among ,them

10 מִצְרָיִם׃ וָאוֹצִיאֵם מֵאֶרֶץ מִצְרָיִם וָאֲבִאֵם אֶל־הַמִּדְבָּר׃
the .wilderness | into | brought and them | Egypt | the from of land | made I So leave them | .Egypt

11 וָאֶתֵּן לָהֶם אֶת־חֻקּוֹתַי וְאֶת־מִשְׁפָּטַי הוֹדַעְתִּי אוֹתָם אֲשֶׁר
which | ,them | made I know | My judgments | and | My ,statutes | them | I And gave

12 יַעֲשֶׂה אוֹתָם הָאָדָם וָחַי בָּהֶם׃ וְגַם אֶת־שַׁבְּתוֹתַי נָתַתִּי
gave I | My sabbaths | And also | .them by | will he live even | ,man | them | (if) does

לָהֶם לִהְיוֹת לְאוֹת בֵּינִי וּבֵינֵיהֶם לָדַעַת כִּי אֲנִי יְהוָה
Jehovah | I (am) | that (they) know might | that | and ,them | between Me | sign a | be to | to them

13 מְקַדְּשָׁם׃ וַיַּמְרוּ־בִי בֵית־יִשְׂרָאֵל בַּמִּדְבָּר בְּחֻקּוֹתַי לֹא־
not | My in statutes | the in ;wilderness | Israel | the of house | against Me | But rebelled | sets who .apart them

הָלָכוּ וְאֶת־מִשְׁפָּטַי מָאָסוּ אֲשֶׁר יַעֲשֶׂה אֹתָם הָאָדָם וָחַי
will he live even | ,man a | them | (if) does | which | they —despised | My judgments | and | did they walk

בָּהֶם וְאֶת־שַׁבְּתֹתַי חִלְּלוּ מְאֹד וָאֹמַר לִשְׁפֹּךְ חֲמָתִי עֲלֵיהֶם
them on | My fury | will (I) out pour | I Then ,said | .greatly | they profaned | My sabbaths | And | by .them

14 בַּמִּדְבָּר לְכַלּוֹתָם׃ וָאֶעֱשֶׂה לְמַעַן שְׁמִי לְבִלְתִּי הֵחֵל לְעֵינֵי
before | be should it profaned | that not | My ,name | the for of sake | I But worked | destroy to .them | the in ,wilderness

15 הַגּוֹיִם אֲשֶׁר הוֹצֵאתִים לְעֵינֵיהֶם׃ וְגַם־אֲנִי נָשָׂאתִי יָדִי
My hand | lifted up | I And also | their in .sight | brought I out them | of whom | the nations

לָהֶם בַּמִּדְבָּר לְבִלְתִּי הָבִיא אוֹתָם אֶל־הָאָרֶץ אֲשֶׁר־נָתַתִּי
had I ,(them) given | which | the land | into | them | would (I) bring | that not | the in ,wilderness | to them

flowing (with) milk and honey; it (is) the glory to all the lands; [16] because they despised My judgments, and they did not walk in My statutes, and they profaned My sabbaths; for their heart went after their idols. [17] And My eye spared them, from destroying them; and I did not make of them an end in the wilderness. [18] But I said to their sons in the wilderness, Do not walk in the statutes of your fathers and do not keep their judgments; and do not defile yourselves with their idols. [19] I (am) Jehovah your God. Walk in My statutes, and keep My judgments, and do them; [20] and keep My sabbaths holy; and they shall be a sign between you and Me, that (you) may know that I (am) Jehovah your God. [21] But the sons rebelled against Me; they did not walk in My statutes, and they did not keep My judgments, to do them; which, (if) a man does them, he shall live by them —to fulfill My anger against them in the wilderness. [22] But I withdrew My hand and acted for My name's sake, that it should not be profaned in the sight of the nations, from whom I brought them out in their sight. [23] Also I lifted up My hand to them in the wilderness, to scatter them among the nations and sow them among the lands, [24] because they had not done My judgments, and had despised My statutes, and had profaned My sabbaths; and their eyes were after their fathers' idols. [25] Therefore I gave them statutes not good,

16 זָבַת חָלָב וּדְבַשׁ צְבִי הִיא לְכָל־הָאֲרָצוֹת׃ יַעַן בְּמִשְׁפָּטַי
My judgments because the ;lands all to (is) it the glory and ,honey (with) flowing milk

מָאָסוּ וְאֶת־חֻקּוֹתַי לֹא־הָלְכוּ בָהֶם וְאֶת־שַׁבְּתוֹתַי חִלֵּלוּ כִּי
for they ,profaned My sabbaths and in ,them walked not My statutes and they despised

17 אַחֲרֵי גִלּוּלֵיהֶם לִבָּם הֹלֵךְ׃ וַתָּחָס עֵינִי עֲלֵיהֶם מִשַּׁחֲתָם
destroy-;them from ing them My eye And spared .went their heart their idols after

18 וְלֹא־עָשִׂיתִי אוֹתָם כָּלָה בַּמִּדְבָּר׃ וָאֹמַר אֶל־בְּנֵיהֶם
their sons to I But said the in .wilderness end an of them did I make and not

בַּמִּדְבָּר בְּחוּקֵּי אֲבוֹתֵיכֶם אַל־תֵּלֵכוּ וְאֶת־מִשְׁפְּטֵיהֶם
their judgments and Do ;walk not your fathers the in of statutes the in ,wilderness

19 אַל־תִּשְׁמֹרוּ וּבְגִלּוּלֵיהֶם אַל־תִּטַּמָּאוּ׃ אֲנִי יְהוָה אֱלֹהֵיכֶם
.God your Jehovah I (am) defile do .yourselves not with and idols their ;keep do not

20 בְּחֻקּוֹתַי לֵכוּ וְאֶת־מִשְׁפָּטַי שִׁמְרוּ וַעֲשׂוּ אוֹתָם׃ וְאֶת־
and ,them do and ,keep My judgments and Walk My in statutes

שַׁבְּתוֹתַי קַדֵּשׁוּ וְהָיוּ לְאוֹת בֵּינִי וּבֵינֵיכֶם לָדַעַת כִּי אֲנִי
I (am) that (you) that know may ,you and between Me sign a they and be shall keep ;holy My sabbaths

21 יְהוָה אֱלֹהֵיכֶם׃ וַיַּמְרוּ־בִי הַבָּנִים בְּחֻקּוֹתַי לֹא־הָלָכוּ וְאֶת־
and They ,walk did not My in statutes the .sons against Me But rebelled .God your Jehovah

מִשְׁפָּטַי לֹא־שָׁמְרוּ לַעֲשׂוֹת אוֹתָם אֲשֶׁר יַעֲשֶׂה אוֹתָם
them (if) does ,which —them do to they ,keep did not My judgments

הָאָדָם וָחַי בָּהֶם אֶת־שַׁבְּתוֹתַי חִלֵּלוּ וָאֹמַר לִשְׁפֹּךְ חֲמָתִי
My fury would (I) out pour I Then said they .profaned My sabbaths by ,them shall he live ,man a

22 עֲלֵיהֶם לְכַלּוֹת אַפִּי בָּם בַּמִּדְבָּר׃ וַהֲשִׁבֹתִי אֶת־יָדִי וָאַעַשׂ
and acted My hand I But withdrew the in .wilderness against them My anger fulfill to on ,them

לְמַעַן שְׁמִי לְבִלְתִּי הֵחֵל לְעֵינֵי הַגּוֹיִם אֲשֶׁר־הוֹצֵאתִי
brought I out from whom the nations the in of sight be should it profaned that not My name the for of sake

23 אוֹתָם לְעֵינֵיהֶם׃ וְגַם־אֲנִי נָשָׂאתִי אֶת־יָדִי לָהֶם בַּמִּדְבָּר
the in wilderness them to My hand lifted up I Also their in .sight them

24 לְהָפִיץ אֹתָם בַּגּוֹיִם וּלְזָרוֹת אוֹתָם בָּאֲרָצוֹת׃ יַעַן מִשְׁפָּטַי
My judgments because the among ,lands them and sow among nations the them to scatter

לֹא־עָשׂוּ וְחֻקּוֹתַי מָאָסוּ וְאֶת־שַׁבְּתוֹתַי חִלֵּלוּ וְאַחֲרֵי גִּלּוּלֵי
idols and after had ,profaned My sabbaths and had ,despised My and statutes they not ,done had

25 אֲבוֹתָם הָיוּ עֵינֵיהֶם׃ וְגַם־אֲנִי נָתַתִּי לָהֶם חֻקִּים לֹא
not statutes them gave I Therefore their .eyes were their fathers'

and judgments by (which) they could not live. [26] And I defiled them by their own gifts, by making all that open the womb to cross (the fire), so that I might waste them; to the end that they might know that I (am) Jehovah.

[27] Therefore speak to the house of Israel, son of man, and say to them, Thus says the Lord Jehovah: Yet in this your fathers have blasphemed Me, by betraying a betrayal against Me. [28] When I had brought them into the land (for) which I lifted up My hand, to give it to them, then they saw every high hill, and every leafy tree! And they offered their sacrifices there. And they gave their provoking offering there. They also made there their soothing aroma, and poured out there their drink offerings. [29] Then I said to them, What (is) the high place to which you go there? And its name is called High Place to this day. [30] Therefore say to the house of Israel, Thus says the Lord Jehovah: Are you being defiled in the way of your fathers? And do you go whoring after their filthy idols? [31] For when you lift up your gifts, when you pass your sons through the fire, you defile yourselves with all your idols, even to (this) day. And shall I be inquired of by you, O house of Israel? (As) I live, declares the Lord Jehovah, I will not be inquired of by you. [32] And what comes up on your spirit surely shall not occur, that you say, We will be like the nations (and) like the families of the lands, to serve wood and stone. [33] (As) I live, says the Lord Jehovah, Surely with a mighty

---

26　טוֹבִים וּמִשְׁפָּטִים לֹא יִחְיוּ בָּהֶם׃ וָאֲטַמֵּא אוֹתָם בְּמַתְּנוֹתָם

| | their by | them | have I And | by | they not | and | ,good |
| | ,gifts own | | defiled | .them live could | judgments |

בְּהַעֲבִיר כָּל־פֶּטֶר רֶחֶם לְמַעַן אֲשִׁמֵּם לְמַעַן אֲשֶׁר יֵדְעוּ

| they | that | the | might I | that so | the | that | all | to making by |
| .know | | end | ,them waste | | womb | open | (fire the) cross |

27　אֲשֶׁר אֲנִי יְהוָה׃ לָכֵן דַּבֵּר אֶל־בֵּית יִשְׂרָאֵל בֶּן־אָדָם

| ,man | son | ,Israel | the | to | speak Therefore | ,Jehovah I | that |
| of | | | of house | | | (am) |

וְאָמַרְתָּ אֲלֵיהֶם כֹּה אָמַר אֲדֹנָי יְהוִה עוֹד זֹאת גִּדְּפוּ אוֹתִי

| Me | have | this in | Yet | :Jehovah | the | says | Thus | ,them to | say and |
| | blasphemed | | | | Lord |

28　אֲבוֹתֵיכֶם בְּמַעֲלָם בִּי מָעַל׃ וָאֲבִיאֵם אֶל־הָאָרֶץ אֲשֶׁר

| (for) | the | into | had I | When | a | against | doing by | fathers your |
| which | land | | them brought | .betrayal | Me |

נָשָׂאתִי אֶת־יָדִי לָתֵת אוֹתָהּ לָהֶם וַיִּרְאוּ כָל־גִּבְעָה רָמָה

| ,high | hill | every | then | ,them to | it | give to | My | lifted I |
| | | | saw they | | | hand | up |

וְכָל־עֵץ עָבֹת וַיִּזְבְּחוּ־שָׁם אֶת־זִבְחֵיהֶם וַיִּתְּנוּ־שָׁם כַּעַס

| pro- | there they And | their | there they And | !leafy | tree and |
| voking | gave | .sacrifices | offered | | every |

קָרְבָּנָם וַיָּשִׂימוּ שָׁם רֵיחַ נִיחוֹחֵיהֶם וַיַּסִּיכוּ שָׁם אֶת־נִסְכֵּיהֶם׃

| drink their | there | and | their | aroma | there also | They | their |
| .offerings | | out poured | soothing | | | | made .offering |

29　וָאֹמַר אֲלֵהֶם מָה הַבָּמָה אֲשֶׁר־אַתֶּם הַבָּאִים שָׁם וַיִּקָּרֵא

| is And | ?there | go | you | to | high the | What | ,them to | I Then |
| called | | | | which | place | (is) | | said |

30　שְׁמָהּ בָּמָה עַד הַיּוֹם הַזֶּה׃ לָכֵן אֱמֹר אֶל־בֵּית

| the to | say Therefore | .this | day | to | High | its |
| of house | | | | | Place name |

יִשְׂרָאֵל כֹּה אָמַר אֲדֹנָי יְהוִה הַבְּדֶרֶךְ אֲבוֹתֵיכֶם אַתֶּם

| are | your | the In | :Jehovah | the | says | Thus | ,Israel |
| you | fathers | of way | | Lord |

31　נִטְמָאִים וְאַחֲרֵי שִׁקּוּצֵיהֶם אַתֶּם זֹנִים׃ וּבִשְׂאֵת מַתְּנֹתֵיכֶם

| ,gifts your | when For | go | you do | filthy | their | And |
| | up lift you | ?whoring | | idols | | after | ?defiled |

בְּהַעֲבִיר בְּנֵיכֶם בָּאֵשׁ אַתֶּם נִטְמָאִים לְכָל־גִּלּוּלֵיכֶם עַד־

| even | your | with | defile | you | the | your make you when |
| to | idols | all | yourselves | ,fire | sons | through pass |

הַיּוֹם וַאֲנִי אִדָּרֵשׁ לָכֶם בֵּית יִשְׂרָאֵל חַי־אָנִי נְאֻם אֲדֹנָי

| the | states | (As) | ?Israel | O | by | be shall | And | (this) |
| Lord | .I live | | | of house | ,you | of inquired | I | .day |

32　יְהוִה אִם־אִדָּרֵשׁ לָכֶם׃ וְהָעֹלָה עַל־רוּחֲכֶם הָיוֹ לֹא

| not surely | your | on | what And | .you by | be will I | not | ,Jehovah |
| | spirit | | up comes | | of inquired |

תִהְיֶה אֲשֶׁר אַתֶּם אֹמְרִים נִהְיֶה כַגּוֹיִם כְּמִשְׁפְּחוֹת

| the like | the like | We | ,say | you | that | ,be shall |
| of families | ,nations | be will |

33　הָאֲרָצוֹת לְשָׁרֵת עֵץ וָאָבֶן׃ חַי־אָנִי נְאֻם אֲדֹנָי יְהוִה אִם־

| sure | ,Jehovah | the | says | (As) | and | wood | serve to | the |
| | | Lord | | ,I live | .stone | | | ,lands |

hand, and with an arm stretched out, and with fury poured out, I will reign over you. [34] And I will bring you out from the peoples, and gather you from the lands in which you are scattered among them; with a mighty hand, and with an arm stretched out, and with fury poured out. [35] And I will bring you into the wilderness of the peoples; and I will be judging with you there face to face. [36] Just as I was judging your fathers in the wilderness of the land of Egypt, so I will be judging you, declares the Lord Jehovah. [37] And I will cause to pass you under the rod, and I will bring you into the bond of the covenant. [38] And I will purge from among you the rebels and the transgressors against Me; I will bring them out of the land where they sojourn. And they shall not enter to the land of Israel. And they shall know that I (am) Jehovah.

[39] And you, O house of Israel, thus says the Lord Jehovah: (Every) man go serve his idols, and (do so) hereafter, if you will not listen to Me. But you will not still profane My holy name with your gifts and with your idols. [40] For in My holy mountain, in the mountain height (of) Israel, declares the Lord Jehovah, all the house of Israel shall serve Me there, all of him in the land. There I will accept them, and there I will seek your heave offerings, and the firstfruits of your offerings with all your holy things. [41] I will accept you with a soothing aroma, when I bring you from the peoples and gather you from the

לֹא בְּיָד חֲזָקָה וּבִזְרוֹעַ נְטוּיָה וּבְחֵמָה שְׁפוּכָה אֶמְלוֹךְ
will I reign | poured ,out | with and fury | stretched out | with and arm an | mighty | a with hand | ly

34 עֲלֵיכֶם׃ וְהוֹצֵאתִי אֶתְכֶם מִן־הָעַמִּים וְקִבַּצְתִּי אֶתְכֶם מִן
from | you | gather and | the peoples | from | you | will I And out bring | over .you

הָאֲרָצוֹת אֲשֶׁר נְפוֹצֹתֶם בָּם בְּיָד חֲזָקָה וּבִזְרוֹעַ נְטוּיָה
stretched out | with and arm an | mighty | a with hand | among ,them | are you scattered | which in | the lands

35 וּבְחֵמָה שְׁפוּכָה׃ וְהֵבֵאתִי אֶתְכֶם אֶל־מִדְבַּר הָעַמִּים
the ,peoples | the of wilderness | into | you | I And bring will | poured .out | with and fury

36 וְנִשְׁפַּטְתִּי אִתְּכֶם שָׁם פָּנִים אֶל־פָּנִים׃ כַּאֲשֶׁר נִשְׁפַּטְתִּי
was I judging | as Just | .face to | face | there | you with | will I and judging be

אֶת־אֲבוֹתֵיכֶם בְּמִדְבַּר אֶרֶץ מִצְרַיִם כֵּן אִשָּׁפֵט אִתְּכֶם
,you | be will I judging | so | ,Egypt | the of land | the in of wilderness | your fathers

37 נְאֻם אֲדֹנָי יְהוִה׃ וְהַעֲבַרְתִּי אֶתְכֶם תַּחַת הַשָּׁבֶט וְהֵבֵאתִי
will I and bring | ,rod the | under | you | will I And pass to cause | .Jehovah | the Lord | states

38 אֶתְכֶם בְּמָסֹרֶת הַבְּרִית׃ וּבָרוֹתִי מִכֶּם הַמֹּרְדִים וְהַפּוֹשְׁעִים
the and transgressors | ;rebels the | from you among | I And purge will | the .covenant | the into of bond | you

בִּי מֵאֶרֶץ מְגוּרֵיהֶם אוֹצִיא אוֹתָם וְאֶל־אַדְמַת יִשְׂרָאֵל
Israel | the of land | And to | .them | will I bring | they where sojourn | of out land the | against ;Me

39 לֹא יָבוֹא וִידַעְתֶּם כִּי־אֲנִי יְהוָה׃ וְאַתֶּם בֵּית־יִשְׂרָאֵל כֹּה־
Thus | ,Israel | O of house | And ,you | .Jehovah | I that (am) | you And know shall | they .enter shall | not

אָמַר אֲדֹנָי יְהוִה אִישׁ גִּלּוּלָיו לְכוּ עִבְדוּ וְאַחַר אִם־אֵינְכֶם
will you not | if | and hereafter | (and) ,serve | go | his idols | (Every) man | :Jehovah | the Lord | says

שֹׁמְעִים אֵלַי וְאֶת־שֵׁם קָדְשִׁי לֹא תְחַלְּלוּ־עוֹד בְּמַתְּנוֹתֵיכֶם
your with gifts | still will you profane | not | My holy | name | But | .Me to | listen

40 וּבְגִלּוּלֵיכֶם׃ כִּי בְהַר־קָדְשִׁי בְּהַר ׀ מְרוֹם יִשְׂרָאֵל נְאֻם
states | ,Israel | height (of) | the in mountain | My ,holy | in mountain | For | with and .idols your

אֲדֹנָי יְהוִה שָׁם יַעַבְדֻנִי כָּל־בֵּית יִשְׂרָאֵל כֻּלֹּה בָּאָרֶץ שָׁם
There | the in .land | of all him | ,Israel | the of house | all | shall Me serve | there | ,Jehovah | the Lord

אֶרְצֵם וְשָׁם אֶדְרוֹשׁ אֶת־תְּרוּמֹתֵיכֶם וְאֶת־רֵאשִׁית
the of firstfruits | and | your offerings heave | will I seek | and there | ac- will I ,them cept

41 מַשְׂאוֹתֵיכֶם בְּכָל־קָדְשֵׁיכֶם׃ בְּרֵיחַ נִיחֹחַ אֶרְצֶה
will I accept | soothing | an with aroma | holy your .things | with all | your offerings

אֶתְכֶם בְּהוֹצִיאִי אֶתְכֶם מִן־הָעַמִּים וְקִבַּצְתִּי אֶתְכֶם מִן
from | you | gather and | the peoples | from | you | I when out bring | ,you

lands where you have been scattered in them. And I will be sanctified among you in the eyes of the nations. [42] And you shall know that I (am) Jehovah, when I bring you into the land of Israel, to the land (for) which I lifted up My hand to give it to your fathers. [43] And you shall remember there your ways and all your deeds by which you have been defiled in them. And you will hate yourselves to your faces for all your evils which you have done. [44] And you shall know that I (am) Jehovah, when I have worked with you for My name's sake; (and) not by your evil ways, nor by your corrupt deeds, O house of Israel, declares the Lord Jehovah.

הָאֲרָצוֹת אֲשֶׁר נְפֹצֹתֶם בָּם וְנִקְדַּשְׁתִּי בָכֶם לְעֵינֵי הַגּוֹיִם׃
the the in among will I And in have you where the
.nations of eyes you sanctified be .them scattered been lands

42 וִידַעְתֶּם כִּי־אֲנִי יְהוָה בַּהֲבִיאִי אֶתְכֶם אֶל־אַדְמַת יִשְׂרָאֵל
,Israel the into you I when ,Jehovah I that you And
of land bring (am) know shall

אֶל־הָאָרֶץ אֲשֶׁר נָשָׂאתִי אֶת־יָדִי לָתֵת אוֹתָהּ לַאֲבוֹתֵיכֶם׃
your to it give to My lifted I (for) the to
.fathers hand up which land

43 וּזְכַרְתֶּם־שָׁם אֶת־דַּרְכֵיכֶם וְאֵת כָּל־עֲלִילוֹתֵיכֶם אֲשֶׁר
by deeds your all and ways your there you And
which remember shall

נִטְמֵאתֶם בָּם וּנְקֹטֹתֶם בִּפְנֵיכֶם בְּכָל־רָעוֹתֵיכֶם אֲשֶׁר
which your for your to will you And in been have you
evils all faces yourselves hate ,them defiled

44 עֲשִׂיתֶם׃ וִידַעְתֶּם כִּי־אֲנִי יְהוָה בַּעֲשׂוֹתִי אִתְּכֶם לְמַעַן
the for with I when Jehovah I that you And have you
of sake you worked have (am) know shall .done

שְׁמִי לֹא כְדַרְכֵיכֶם הָרָעִים וְכַעֲלִילוֹתֵיכֶם הַנִּשְׁחָתוֹת בֵּית
O ,corrupt your by nor ,evil your by not My
of house deeds ways ,name

יִשְׂרָאֵל נְאֻם אֲדֹנָי יְהוִה׃
.Jehovah the states ,Israel
Lord

CAP. XXI כא

CHAPTER 21

CHAPTER 21

[1] And the word of Jehovah was to me, saying, [2] Son of man, set your face the way of the south, and drop (a word) to the south, and prophesy against the forest of the field of the Negev. [3] And say to the forest of the Negev, Hear the word of Jehovah; thus says the Lord Jehovah: Behold, I will kindle in you a fire, and it will eat up among you every moist tree and every dry tree. The glowing of the flame shall not be put out; and by it shall be scorched all the faces from the Negev to the north. [4] And all flesh shall see that I, Jehovah, have kindled it; it shall not be put out. [5] Then I said, Ah, Lord Jehovah! They are saying of me, Does he not speak in parables?

[6] And the word of Jehovah was to me, saying,

1
2 וַיְהִי דְבַר־יְהוָה אֵלַי לֵאמֹר׃ בֶּן־אָדָם שִׂים פָּנֶיךָ דֶּרֶךְ
the your set ,man Son ,saying to Jehovah the And
of way face of ,me of word was

תֵּימָנָה וְהַטֵּף אֶל־דָּרוֹם וְהִנָּבֵא אֶל־יַעַר הַשָּׂדֶה נֶגֶב׃
the field the the against and the to drop and the
.Negev of of forest prophesy ,south (word a) south

3 וְאָמַרְתָּ לְיַעַר הַנֶּגֶב שְׁמַע דְּבַר־יְהוָה כֹּה־אָמַר אֲדֹנָי יְהוִה
:Jehovah the says Thus .Jehovah the Hear the the to say And
Lord of word ,Negev of forest

הִנְנִי מַצִּית־בְּךָ ׀ אֵשׁ וְאָכְלָה בְךָ כָל־עֵץ־לַח וְכָל־עֵץ יָבֵשׁ
.dry tree and moist tree every among it and ,fire a in will ,Behold
every you up eat will you kindle I

לֹא־תִכְבֶּה לַהֶבֶת שַׁלְהֶבֶת וְנִצְרְבוּ־בָהּ כָּל־פָּנִים מִנֶּגֶב
the from the all it by be shall and the the be shall Not
Negev faces scorched ;flame of glowing out put

4 צָפוֹנָה׃ וְרָאוּ כָּל־בָּשָׂר כִּי אֲנִי יְהוָה בִּעַרְתִּיהָ לֹא תִּכְבֶּה׃
be shall It not have ,Jehovah ,I that flesh all And the to
.out put .it kindled see shall .north

5 וָאֹמַר אֲהָהּ אֲדֹנָי יְהוִה הֵמָּה אֹמְרִים לִי הֲלֹא מְמַשֵּׁל
speak Does of are They !Jehovah Lord ,Ah I Then
not ,me saying ,said

6
7 מְשָׁלִים הוּא׃ וַיְהִי דְבַר־יְהוָה אֵלַי לֵאמֹר׃ בֶּן־
Son ,saying to Jehovah the And ?he in
of ,me of word was parables

[7] Son of man, set your face against Jerusalem and drop (a word) toward the holy places, and prophesy against the land of Israel. [8] And say to the land of Israel, Thus says Jehovah: Behold, I (am) against you and will draw out My sword from its sheath, and (I) will cut off from you the righteous and the wicked. [9] Therefore, My sword shall be drawn from its sheath against all flesh, from the Negev to the north. [10] And all flesh shall know that I, Jehovah, have drawn out My sword from its sheath. It shall not return any more. [11] And you, son of man, groan with the breaking of your loins; and groan with bitterness before their eyes. [12] And it will be, when they say to you, For what do you groan? Then you shall say, Because of the news that is coming; and every heart will melt, and all hands become feeble; and every spirit will faint; and all knees will flow (as) water. Behold, it comes; and it shall be, declares the Lord Jehovah.

[13] And the word of Jehovah was to me, saying, [14] Son of man, prophesy and say, Thus says the Lord; say, A sword! A sword is sharpened, and also is polished! So as to slaughter; (for) a slaughter it is sharpened; so that it may be there (as) a flash, it is polished. Or shall we rejoice? You are despising the rod of My son, every tree! [16] And He has given it to be polished, to be taken by the hand. It is sharpened, the sword; and it is polished, to give it into the hand of the slayer. [17] Cry out and howl, son of man. For it shall be on My people. It (shall be)

אָדָם שִׂים פָּנֶיךָ אֶל־יְרוּשָׁלִַם וְהַטֵּף אֶל־מִקְדָּשִׁים וְהִנָּבֵא
and prophesy | holy the places | toward | drop and (word a) | Jerusalem | against | your face | set | ,man

8 אֶל־אַדְמַת יִשְׂרָאֵל׃ וְאָמַרְתָּ לְאַדְמַת יִשְׂרָאֵל כֹּה אָמַר
says | Thus | ,Israel | the to of land | say And | .Israel | the of land | against

יְהוָה הִנְנִי אֵלַיִךְ וְהוֹצֵאתִי חַרְבִּי מִתַּעְרָהּ וְהִכְרַתִּי מִמֵּךְ
from you | will and off cut | its from sheath | My sword | will and out draw | against you | ,Behold (am) I | Jeho- :vah

9 צַדִּיק וְרָשָׁע׃ יַעַן אֲשֶׁר־הִכְרַתִּי מִמֵּךְ צַדִּיק וְרָשָׁע לָכֵן
there- fore | the and ,wicked | the righteous | from you | will I off cut | Since that | the and .wicked | the righteous

10 תֵּצֵא חַרְבִּי מִתַּעְרָהּ אֶל־כָּל־בָּשָׂר מִנֶּגֶב צָפוֹן׃ וְיָדְעוּ
will and know | the to ,north | the from Negev | flesh | all against | its from sheath | My sword | be shall drawn

כָּל־בָּשָׂר כִּי אֲנִי יְהוָה הוֹצֵאתִי חַרְבִּי מִתַּעְרָהּ לֹא תָשׁוּב
shall It return | not | its from .sheath | My sword | have out drawn | ,Jehovah | ,I | that | flesh | all

11 עוֹד׃ וְאַתָּה בֶן־אָדָם הֵאָנַח בְּשִׁבְרוֹן מָתְנַיִם
(your) ;loins | the with of breaking | groan | ,man son of | ,you And | any .more

12 וּבִמְרִירוּת תֵּאָנַח לְעֵינֵיהֶם׃ וְהָיָה כִּי־יֹאמְרוּ אֵלֶיךָ עַל־
For | ,you to | they say | when | it And ,be will | their before .eyes | groan | with and bitterness

מָה אַתָּה נֶאֱנָח וְאָמַרְתָּ אֶל־שְׁמוּעָה כִי־בָאָה וְנָמֵס כָּל־
every | will and melt | is that ;coming | the news | Because of | You Then ,say shall | do ?groan | you | what

לֵב וְרָפוּ כָל־יָדַיִם וְכִהֲתָה כָל־רוּחַ וְכָל־בִּרְכַּיִם תֵּלַכְנָה
will flow | knees | and all | ,spirit every | will and faint | ,hands | all will and feeble be | ,heart

13 מַּיִם הִנֵּה בָאָה וְנִהְיָתָה נְאֻם אֲדֹנָי יְהוִה׃ וַיְהִי
And was | .Jehovah | the Lord | states | it and ,be shall | it ,comes | ,Behold | (as) .water

14 דְבַר־יְהוָה אֵלַי לֵאמֹר׃ בֶּן־אָדָם הִנָּבֵא וְאָמַרְתָּ כֹּה אָמַר
says | Thus | ,say and | prophesy | ,man Son of | ,saying | to ,me | Jehovah | the of word

15 אֲדֹנָי אֱמֹר חֶרֶב חֶרֶב הוּחַדָּה וְגַם־מְרוּטָה׃ לְמַעַן טְבֹחַ
to ;slaughter | as So | !polished | and also | is sharpened | A sword | A !sword | ,Say | the .Lord

טֶבַח הוּחַדָּה לְמַעַן הֱיֵה־לָהּ בָּרָק מֹרָטָּה אוֹ נָשִׂישׂ שֵׁבֶט
The of rod | we shall ?rejoice | Or | is it .polished | flash a | to it | there be may | that so | is it ;sharpened | a (for) slaughter

16 בְּנִי מֹאֶסֶת כָּל־עֵץ׃ וַיִּתֵּן אֹתָהּ לְמָרְטָה לִתְפֹּשׂ בַּכָּף
the by .hand | be to taken | be to polished | it | He And given has | !tree every | are you ,despising | My son

הִיא הוּחַדָּה חֶרֶב וְהִיא מֹרָטָּה לָתֵת אוֹתָהּ בְּיַד־הוֹרֵג׃
the .slayer | the into of hand | it | give to | . is ,polished | it and | The ,sword | is ,sharpened | it

17 זְעַק וְהֵילֵל בֶּן־אָדָם כִּי־הִיא הָיְתָה בְעַמִּי הִיא בְּכָל־
all | on | It (be shall) | My on .people | be shall | it | For | .man son of | ,howl and | Cry out

on all the rulers of Israel, they are thrown to the sword with My people; therefore, slap your thigh. [18] Because (it is) a test; and what if even the despising rod shall not be? declares the Lord Jehovah. [19] And you, son of man, prophesy and strike (your) palm to palm. And let be doubled the sword the third time, the sword of the slain. It (is) the sword of the slain, the great one that surrounds them; [20] so that (their) heart may melt and many stumble at all their gates. I have given the threatening sword. Ah! It is made like lightning; it is wrapped for a slaughter.

[21] Sharpen yourself on the right! Set yourself on the left, wherever your face is appointed. [22] And also I, I will strike My palm to My palm, and I will cause My fury to rest. I, Jehovah, have spoken. [23] And the word of Jehovah was to me, saying, [24] And you, son of man, set for yourself two ways, that the sword of the king of Babylon may come. Both of them shall come out from one land. And create a hand at the head of the way to the city; create it. [25] You shall set a way that the sword may enter (into) Rabbah of the sons of Ammon, and (into) Judah, into fortified Jerusalem. [26] For the king of Babylon shall stand at the parting of the way, at the head of the two ways to practice divination. He shall shake arrows; he shall ask household idols; he shall look at the liver. [27] At his right shall be the divining (for) Jerusalem, to set battering rams, to open the mouth in the slaughter, to lift up the voice with shouting; to set battering rams against the gates; to cast up

---

נְשִׂיאֵי יִשְׂרָאֵל מְגוּרֵי אֶל־חֶרֶב הָיוּ אֶת־עַמִּי לָכֵן סְפֹק

slap therefore My with They the to thrown .Israel the
,people are sword of rulers

18 אֵלֶיךָ: כִּי בֹחַן וּמָה אִם־גַּם־שֵׁבֶט מֹאֶסֶת לֹא יִהְיֶה

,be shall not despising the even if and (is it) Because your
rod what ;test a .thigh

19 נְאֻם אֲדֹנָי יְהֹוִה: וְאַתָּה בֶן־אָדָם הִנָּבֵא וְהַךְ כַּף

(your) and prophesy ,man son ,you And ?Jehovah the states
palm strike of Lord

אֶל־כָּף וְתִכָּפֵל חֶרֶב שְׁלִישִׁתָה חֶרֶב חֲלָלִים הִיא חֶרֶב

the It .slain the the third the the be let And .palm to
of sword (is) of sword time sword doubled

20 הֶחָלָל הַגָּדוֹל הַחֹדֶרֶת לָהֶם: לְמַעַן לָמוּג לֵב וְהַרְבֵּה

many and (their) may that so ,them which great the the
,heart melt surrounds one ,slain

הַמִּכְשֹׁלִים עַל כָּל־שַׁעֲרֵיהֶם נָתַתִּי אִבְחַת־חֶרֶב אָח

!Ah .sword the have I their all at stumble
threatening given .gates

21 עֲשׂוּיָה לְבָרָק מְעֻטָּה לְטָבַח: הִתְאַחֲדִי הֵימִנִי הַשִׂימִי

Set the on Sharpen a for is it like is It
yourself !right yourself .slaughter wrapped ,lightning made

22 הַשְׂמִילִי אָנָה פָּנַיִךְ מֻעָדוֹת: וְגַם־אֲנִי אַכֶּה כַפִּי אֶל־כַּפִּי

My to My will I also And is your where- on
,palm palm strike I .appointed face ever ,left The

23 וַהֲנִחֹתִי חֲמָתִי אֲנִי יְהוָה דִּבַּרְתִּי: וַיְהִי דְבַר־יְהוָה

Jehovah the And have Jehovah I My will I and
of word was spoken .fury rest to cause

24 אֵלַי לֵאמֹר: וְאַתָּה בֶן־אָדָם שִׂים־לְךָ שְׁנַיִם דְּרָכִים

ways two for set ,man son ,you And ,saying ,me to
yourself of

לָבוֹא חֶרֶב מֶלֶךְ־בָּבֶל מֵאֶרֶץ אֶחָד יֵצְאוּ שְׁנֵיהֶם וְיָד בָּרֵא

create a And of Both shall one from .Babylon the the may that
hand .them out come land of king of sword come

25 בְּרֹאשׁ־דֶּרֶךְ עִיר בָּרֵא: הֶרֶךְ תָּשִׂים לָבוֹא חֶרֶב אֶת

(into) the may that shall You a create the the the at
sword enter set way .it ,city of way of head

26 רַבַּת בְּנֵי־עַמּוֹן וְאֶת־יְהוּדָה בִירוּשָׁלִַם בְּצוּרָה: כִּי־עָמַד

shall For .fortified into and Ammon the Rabbah
stand Jerusalem ,Judah of sons of

מֶלֶךְ־בָּבֶל אֶל־אֵם הַדֶּרֶךְ בְּרֹאשׁ שְׁנֵי הַדְּרָכִים לִקְסָם־

to ways the the at the the at Babylon the
practice two of head way of mother of king

27 קֶסֶם קִלְקַל בַּחִצִּים שָׁאַל בַּתְּרָפִים רָאָה בַכָּבֵד: בִּימִינוֹ

his At the at shall he household shall he ;arrows shall He divina-
right .liver look ;idols ask shake .tion

הָיָה הַקֶּסֶם יְרוּשָׁלִַם לָשׂוּם כָּרִים לִפְתֹּחַ פֶּה בְּרֶצַח

the in the open to battering set to (for) the shall
,slaughter mouth ,rams ,Jerusalem divining be

לְהָרִים קוֹל בִּתְרוּעָה לָשׂוּם כָּרִים עַל־שְׁעָרִים לִשְׁפֹּךְ

cast to the against battering set to with the lift to
up ,gates rams ,shouting voice up

a mound, and to build a siege wall. [28] And it shall be to them an empty divining in their sight, those who have sworn oaths to them. But he will remember iniquity, that they may be taken. [29] Therefore thus says the Lord Jehovah: Because you made remembrance of your iniquity, in that your transgressions are uncovered, so that your sins are seen in all your deeds—because you have been remembered, you shall be taken with the palm. [30] And you, O slain, wicked prince of Israel, of whom has come his day in the time of iniquity of the end. [31] Thus says the Lord Jehovah: Remove the diadem and lift off the crown. This (shall) not (be) (as) this (was). Lift up the low one, and make the high one low. [32] Ruin, ruin, ruin, I will appoint it! Also this shall not be until the coming of Him to whom is the right; and I will give it.

[33] And you, son of man, prophesy and say, Thus says the Lord Jehovah concerning the sons of Ammon, and as to their shame; even say: The sword, the sword is drawn, (it is) polished for slaughter to make an end, so that (it may be) like lightning; [34] while they see vain visions for you; while they divine a lie to you, to put you on the necks of the slain of the wicked, (of) whom their day has come, in the time of iniquity (it) (shall have) an end. [35] Return it to its sheath. In the place where you were created, in the land of your origin, I will judge you. [36] And I will pour out on you My disgust—with the fire of My wrath I will blow against you, and give you into the hand

28 סֹלְלָה לִבְנוֹת דָּיֵק׃ וְהָיָה לָהֶם כִּקְסָום־שָׁוְא בְּעֵינֵיהֶם

their in empty an them to it And siege a to and mound a
,sight divining be shall .wall build

שְׁבֻעֵי שְׁבֻעוֹת לָהֶם וְהוּא־מַזְכִּיר עָוֺן לְהִתָּפֵשׂ׃

may they that ,iniquity will But .them to oaths who those
.taken be remember he sworn have

29 לָכֵן כֹּה־אָמַר אֲדֹנָי יְהוִה יַעַן הַזְכַּרְכֶם עֲוֺנְכֶם בְּהִגָּלוֹת

are that in your made you Because Jeho- the says thus There-
uncovered ,iniquity of remembrance :vah Lord fore

פִּשְׁעֵיכֶם לְהֵרָאוֹת חַטֹּאותֵיכֶם בְּכֹל עֲלִילוֹתֵיכֶם יַעַן

be- ,deeds your all in sins your that so trans- your
cause seen are tressions

30 הִזָּכֶרְכֶם בַּכַּף תִּתָּפֵשׂוּ׃ וְאַתָּה חָלָל רָשָׁע נְשִׂיא

prince wicked O ,you And be shall the with have you
of ,slain .taken palm recalled been

31 יִשְׂרָאֵל אֲשֶׁר־בָּא יוֹמוֹ בְּעֵת עֲוֺן קֵץ׃ כֹּה אָמַר

says Thus the ini- the in his has of ,Israel
.end of quity of time day come whom

אֲדֹנָי יְהוִה הָסִיר הַמִּצְנֶפֶת וְהָרִים הָעֲטָרָה זֹאת לֹא־זֹאת

this (as) not This the lift and the Remove :Jehovah the
(was) (be shall) .crown off diadem Lord

32 הַשָּׁפָלָה הַגְבֵּהַ וְהַגָּבֹהַּ הַשְׁפִּיל׃ עַוָּה עַוָּה עַוָּה אֲשִׂימֶנָּה

set will I ruin ,ruin ,Ruin make the and up Lift low the
!it .low one high one

גַּם־זֹאת לֹא הָיָה עַד־בֹּא אֲשֶׁר־לוֹ הַמִּשְׁפָּט וּנְתַתִּיו׃

will I and the is Him to the until shall not this Also
.it give ;right whom of coming be

33 וְאַתָּה בֶן־אָדָם הִנָּבֵא וְאָמַרְתָּ כֹּה אָמַר אֲדֹנָי יְהוִה אֶל־

concern- Jehovah the says Thus ,say and prophesy ,man son And
ing Lord of ,you

בְּנֵי עַמּוֹן וְאֶל־חֶרְפָּתָם וְאָמַרְתָּ חֶרֶב חֶרֶב פְּתוּחָה לְטֶבַח

for ;drawn is the The even their as and Ammon the
slaughter sword ,sword :say ,shame to of sons

34 מְרוּטָה לְהָכִיל לְמַעַן בָּרָק׃ בַּחֲזוֹת לָךְ שָׁוְא בִּקְסָם־

they while ,vain for they while (be may it) that so make to (is it)
divine you visions see lightning (like) end an polished

לָךְ כָּזָב לָתֵת אוֹתָךְ אֶל־צַוְּארֵי חַלְלֵי רְשָׁעִים אֲשֶׁר־בָּא

has whom the slain the the on you place to ,lie a to
come wicked of of necks you

35 יוֹמָם בְּעֵת עֲוֺן קֵץ׃ הָשַׁב אֶל־תַּעְרָהּ בִּמְקוֹם אֲשֶׁר־

where the In its to Return .end an iniquity the in their
place .sheath (it) (have shall) of time day

36 נִבְרֵאת בְּאֶרֶץ מְכֻרוֹתַיִךְ אֶשְׁפֹּט אֹתָךְ׃ וְשָׁפַכְתִּי עָלַיִךְ

you on will I And .you will I your the in were you
out pour judge origin of land ,created

זַעְמִי בְּאֵשׁ עֶבְרָתִי אָפִיחַ עָלַיִךְ וּנְתַתִּיךְ בְּיַד אֲנָשִׁים

men the into give and against will I My the with My
of hand you ,you blow wrath of fire ;disgust

of beastly men, skilled in destruction. [37] You shall be to the fire for food. Your blood shall be in the midst of the land. You shall not be remembered. For I, Jehovah, have spoken.

CHAPTER 22

[1] And the word of Jehovah was to me, saying, [2] And you, son of man, will you judge; will you judge the bloody city? Then cause her to know all her abominations. [3] Then you shall say, Thus says the Lord Jehovah: The city sheds blood in her midst, that her time may come; and makes idols against herself, to defile (herself). [4] By your blood which you have shed, you are guilty; and by your idols which you have made, you are defiled. And your days (are) brought near, and have come to your years. Therefore I have made you a reproach to the nations, and a mocking to all the lands. [5] Those who are near, and those who are far from you, shall mock against you, O defiled of name, abounding in tumult. [6] Behold, the rulers of Israel, each man by his might, has been in you to enter in (and) shed blood.. [7] In you they have despised father and mother. In your midst they have dealt with the alien by oppression. In you they oppressed the widow and the orphan. [8] You have despised My holy things, and have profaned My sabbaths. [9] In you are men of slander, in order to shed blood; and in you they eat on the mountains; in your midst they commit fornication. [10] In you he has uncovered the nakedness of the father; in you they humbled the defiled (by her) impurity. [11] And a man has done abomination with his neighbor's wife; and a man has defiled his daughter-in-law in fornication; and a man

37 בערים חרשי משחית׃ לאש תהיה לאכלה דמך יהיה
shall Your for shall You the to .destruction skilled ,beastly
be blood .food be fire in

בתוך הארץ לא תזכרי כי אני יהוה דברתי׃
have Jehovah I For shall You not the the in
.spoken remembered be .land of midst

CAP. XXII כב

CHAPTER 22

1
2 ויהי דבר־יהוה אלי לאמר׃ ואתה בן־אדם התשפט
you will ,man son ,you And ,saying ,me to Jehovah the And
,judge of of word was

התשפט את־עיר הדמים והודעתה את כל־תועבותיה׃
her all cause Then ?bloody the you will
.abominations know to her city judge

3 ואמרת כה אמר אדני יהוה עיר שפכת דם בתוכה
her in blood sheds The :Jehovah the says Thus you Then
,midst city Lord ,say shall

4 לבוא עתה ועשתה גלולים עליה לטמאה׃ בדמך אשר־
which your By defile to against idols and her may that
blood .(herself) herself makes ,time come

שפכת אשמת ובגלוליך אשר־עשית טמאת ותקריבי
brought And are you have you which by and are you have you
near .defiled made idols your ;guilty shed

ימיך ותבוא עד־שנותיך על־כן נתתיך חרפה לגוים
the to a have I Therefore your to have and your
nations reproach you made .years come ,days

5 וקלסה לכל־הארצות׃ הקרבות והרחקות ממך יתקלסו־
shall from those and who Those the all to a and
mock ,you far are who ,near are .lands mocking

6 בך טמאת השם רבת המהומה׃ הנה נשיאי ישראל
,Israel the ,Behold .tumult abounding ,name de- O against
of rulers in of filed ,you

7 איש לזרעו היו בך למען שפך־דם׃ אב ואם הקלו בך
In have they and father .blood shed enter to in has his by each
.you despised mother in you been ,might man

8 לגר עשו בעשק בתוכך יתום ואלמנה הונו בך׃ קדשי
holy My In op- they the and the your In by have they with
things .you pressed ,widow orphan .midst oppression dealt alien the

9 בזית ואת־שבתתי חללת׃ אנשי רכיל היו בך למען
order in In are slander of men have My and have you
to you .profaned sabbaths despised

10 שפך־דם ואל־ההרים אכלו בך זמה עשו בתוכך׃ ערות־
naked- the your in they forni- in they the and ;blood shed
of ness .midst do cation ;you eat mountains on

11 אב גלה־בך טמאת הנדה ענו־בך׃ ואיש ׀ את־אשת
wife with a And in they (her) defiled the In un- has he the
man .you humbled impurity (by) ;you covered father

רעהו עשה תועבה ואיש את־כלתו טמא בזמה ואיש
a and forni- in has daughter- his a and abomina- has his
man ;cation defiled in-law man ;tion done neighbor's

has humbled within you his sister, his father's daughter. [12] In you they have taken bribes, in order to shed blood. You have taken interest and increase; and you have gained by extortion (of) your neighbor; and you have forgotten Me, declares the Lord Jehovah

[13] And behold, I have struck My palm against your gain which you have made, and at your blood which has been in your midst. [14] Can your heart stand, or can your hands be strong, in the days that I shall deal with you? I, Jehovah, have spoken, and (I) will act. [15] And I will scatter you among the nations, and sow you in the lands, and (I) will destroy your uncleanness out of you. [16] And you will be profaned in you in the sight of the nations, and you shall know that I (am) Jehovah.

[17] And the word of Jehovah was to me, saying, [18] Son of man, the house of Israel has become dross to Me. All of them (are) bronze and tin, and iron and lead, in the middle of the furnace; they are the dross of silver. [19] Therefore thus says the Lord Jehovah: Because all of you have become for dross, therefore, behold, I will gather you into the midst of Jerusalem. [20] (As they) gather silver, and bronze, and iron, and lead, and tin, into the middle of the furnace, to blow the fire on it to melt (it); so I will gather (you) in My anger and in My fury; and I will leave (you) and melt you. [21] And I will collect you and blow on you in the fire of My wrath; and you shall be melted in its midst. [22] And you shall know that I, Jehovah, have poured out My fury on you.

[23] And the word of Jehovah was to me, saying,

12 אֶת־אֲחֹתוֹ בַת־אָבִיו עִנָּה־בָךְ׃ שֹׁחַד לָֽקְחוּ־בָךְ לְמַעַן
order in In have they bribes in has his daughter his
to you taken .you humbled father's ,sister

שְׁפָךְ־דָּם נֶשֶׁךְ וְתַרְבִּית לָקַחַתְּ וַתְּבַצְּעִי רֵעַיִךְ בַּעֹשֶׁק וְאֹתִי
and by your (of) you and have You and interest .blood shed
Me ,extortion neighbor gained have ,taken increase

13 שָׁכַחַתְּ נְאֻם אֲדֹנָי יְהוִה׃ וְהִנֵּה הִכֵּיתִי כַפִּי אֶל־בִּצְעֵךְ
your against My have I And .Jehovah the states have you
gain unjust palm struck ,behold Lord ,forgotten

14 אֲשֶׁר עָשִׂית וְעַל־דָּמֵךְ אֲשֶׁר הָיוּ בְּתוֹכֵךְ׃ הֲיַעֲמֹד לִבֵּךְ
your Can your in has which your and have you which
,heart stand .midst been blood at ,made

אִם־תֶּחֱזַקְנָה יָדַיִךְ לַיָּמִים אֲשֶׁר אֲנִי עֹשֶׂה אוֹתָךְ אֲנִי
I with shall I that the in your be can or
?you deal days ,hands strong

15 יְהוָה דִּבַּרְתִּי וְעָשִׂיתִי׃ וַהֲפִיצוֹתִי אוֹתָךְ בַּגּוֹיִם וְזֵרִיתִיךְ
sow and the among you will I And will and have Jehovah
you nations scatter .act spoken

16 בָּאֲרָצוֹת וַהֲתִמֹּתִי טֻמְאָתֵךְ מִמֵּךְ׃ וְנִחַלְתְּ בָּךְ לְעֵינֵי גוֹיִם
the the in in will you And of out your will and the in
,nations of sight you profaned be .you uncleanness destroy ,lands

17 וְיָדַעַתְּ כִּי־אֲנִי יְהוָה׃ וַיְהִי דְבַר־יְהוָה אֵלַי לֵאמֹר׃
,saying to Jehovah the And .Jehovah I that you and
,me of word was (am) know shall

18 בֶּן־אָדָם הָיוּ־לִי בֵית־יִשְׂרָאֵל לְסוּג כֻּלָּם נְחֹשֶׁת וּבְדִיל
,tin and (are) All for Israel the to has ,man Son
,bronze them of .dross of house Me become of

19 וּבַרְזֶל וְעוֹפֶרֶת בְּתוֹךְ כּוּר סִגִים כֶּסֶף הָיוּ׃ לָכֵן כֹּה
thus There- they silver the the the in ,lead and and
,fore are of dross ;furnace of middle ,iron

אָמַר אֲדֹנָי יְהוִה יַעַן הֱיוֹת כֻּלְּכֶם לְסִגִים לָכֵן הִנְנִי קֹבֵץ
will ,behold there- for all you have Be- :Jehovah the says
gather I ,fore ,dross become cause Lord

20 אֶתְכֶם אֶל־תּוֹךְ יְרוּשָׁלִָם׃ קְבֻצַת כֶּסֶף וּנְחֹשֶׁת וּבַרְזֶל
,iron and and ,silver (they As) .Jerusalem the into you
bronze gather of midst

וְעוֹפֶרֶת וּבְדִיל אֶל־תּוֹךְ כּוּר לָפַחַת־עָלָיו אֵשׁ לְהַנְתִּיךְ
;melt to the it on blow to the the into tin and ,lead and
,(it) fire ,furnace of midst

21 כֵּן אֶקְבֹּץ בְּאַפִּי וּבַחֲמָתִי וְהִנַּחְתִּי וְהִתַּכְתִּי אֶתְכֶם׃ וְכִנַּסְתִּי
will I And .you melt and will I and in and My in will I so
collect (you) leave ,fury My anger (you) gather

אֶתְכֶם וְנָפַחְתִּי עֲלֵיכֶם בְּאֵשׁ עֶבְרָתִי וְנִתַּכְתֶּם בְּתוֹכָהּ׃
the in shall you and My the in you on blow and you
.it of midst melted be ,wrath of fire

22 כְּהִתּוּךְ כֶּסֶף בְּתוֹךְ כּוּר כֵּן תֻּתְּכוּ בְתוֹכָהּ וִידַעְתֶּם כִּי־
that you And its in shall you so the the in silver is As
know shall .midst melted be ,furnace of midst melted

23 אֲנִי יְהוָה שָׁפַכְתִּי חֲמָתִי עֲלֵיכֶם׃ וַיְהִי דְבַר־יְהוָה
Jehovah the And .you on My have Jehovah I
of word was fury out poured

[24] Son of man, speak to her: You (are) a land, she (is) not being cleansed; you are not rained on in the day of disgust. [25] A plot (by) her prophets (is) in her midst, like a roaring lion tearing prey. They have devoured souls; and they have taken the riches and gems; they multiplied her widows in her midst. [26] Her priests have violated My law and have profaned My holy things; they have not divided between the holy and the common; and between the unclean and the clean they have not taught; and they have hidden their eyes from My sabbaths; and I am profaned among them. [27] Her rulers in her midst (are) like wolves tearing prey, to shed blood, to destroy souls, in order to gain unjust gain. [28] And her prophets have daubed themselves (with) slime, seeing empty visions, and divining to them lies, saying, Thus says the Lord Jehovah, when Jehovah has not spoken. [29] The people of the land have used oppression and practiced robbery; and they troubled the poor and the needy; and (they) have oppressed without justice. [30] And I sought among them a man to wall up a wall, and stand in the breach before Me for the land, that I should not destroy it; but I found not. [31] Thus I have poured out on them My disgust, with the fire of My wrath I consumed them; I have given their way on their heads; states the Lord Jehovah.

24 אֵלַי לֵאמֹר׃ בֶּן־אָדָם אֱמָר־לָהּ אַתְּ אֶרֶץ לֹא מְטֹהָרָה
being not a You to say ,man Son ,saying to
cleansed land (are) :her of ,me

25 הִיא לֹא גֻשְּׁמָהּ בְּיוֹם זָעַם׃ קֶשֶׁר נְבִיאֶיהָ בְּתוֹכָהּ כַּאֲרִי
a like her in (is) her (by) .plot A .disgust the in are you not she
lion ,midst prophets of day on rained ,(is)

שׁוֹאֵג טֹרֵף טָרֶף נֶפֶשׁ אָכָלוּ חֹסֶן וִיקָר יִקָּחוּ אַלְמְנוֹתֶיהָ
widows her have they and the have They souls .prey tearing roaring
;taken gems riches ;devoured

26 הִרְבּוּ בְתוֹכָהּ׃ כֹּהֲנֶיהָ חָמְסוּ תוֹרָתִי וַיְחַלְּלוּ קָדָשַׁי בֵּין
be- holy My have and law My have Her her in they
tween ;things profaned violated priests .midst multiplied

קֹדֶשׁ לְחֹל לֹא הִבְדִּילוּ וּבֵין־הַטָּמֵא לְטָהוֹר לֹא הוֹדִיעוּ
have they not the and the and have they not the and the
;taught clean unclean between ,divided common holy

27 וּמִשַּׁבְּתוֹתַי הֶעְלִימוּ עֵינֵיהֶם וָאֵחַל בְּתוֹכָם׃ שָׂרֶיהָ בְקִרְבָּהּ
her in Her among am I and their have they My from and
midst rulers .them profaned ,eyes hidden sabbaths

כִּזְאֵבִים טֹרְפֵי טָרֶף לִשְׁפָּךְ־דָּם לְאַבֵּד נְפָשׁוֹת לְמַעַן
in ,souls to ,blood to ,prey tearing like (are)
to order destroy shed wolves

28 בְּצֹעַ בָּצַע׃ וּנְבִיאֶיהָ טָחוּ לָהֶם תָּפֵל חֹזִים שָׁוְא וְקֹסְמִים
and empty seeing (with) them- have her And unjust gain
divining visions ,slime selves daubed prophets .gain

לָהֶם כָּזָב אֹמְרִים כֹּה אָמַר אֲדֹנָי יֱהֹוִה וַיהֹוָה לֹא דִבֵּר׃
has not when ,Jehovah the says Thus ,saying ,lies to
.spoken Jehovah Lord them

29 עַם הָאָרֶץ עָשְׁקוּ עֹשֶׁק וְגָזְלוּ גָּזֵל וְעָנִי וְאֶבְיוֹן הוֹנוּ וְאֶת־
and they the and and ;robbery and oppression have the The
;troubled needy poor the practiced used land of people

30 הַגֵּר עָשְׁקוּ בְּלֹא מִשְׁפָּט׃ וָאֲבַקֵּשׁ מֵהֶם אִישׁ גֹּדֵר־גָּדֵר
wall a to a among I And .justice without have the
wall man them sought oppressed alien

וְעֹמֵד בַּפֶּרֶץ לְפָנַי בְּעַד הָאָרֶץ לְבִלְתִּי שַׁחֲתָהּ וְלֹא מָצָאתִי׃
.found I but should I not that the for before the in and
not ;it destroy ,land Me breach stand

31 וָאֶשְׁפֹּךְ עֲלֵיהֶם זַעְמִי בְּאֵשׁ עֶבְרָתִי כִּלִּיתִים דַּרְכָּם בְּרֹאשָׁם
their on their con- I My the with My on have I Thus
heads way ;them sumed wrath of fire ,disgust them out poured

נָתַתִּי נְאֻם אֲדֹנָי יֱהֹוִה׃
.Jehovah the states have I
Lord ,given

CAP. XXIII כג

CHAPTER 23

[1] And the word of Jehovah was to me, saying, [2] Son of man, two women, daughters of one mother, there were. And they whored in Egypt; in their youth they whored

1
2 וַיְהִי דְבַר־יְהֹוָה אֵלַי לֵאמֹר׃ בֶּן־אָדָם שְׁתַּיִם נָשִׁים בְּנוֹת
daughters ,women two ,man Son ,saying to Jehovah the And
of of ,me of word was

3 אֵם־אַחַת הָיוּ׃ וַתִּזְנֶינָה בְמִצְרַיִם בִּנְעוּרֵיהֶן זָנוּ שָׁמָּה
there they their in ;Egypt in they And there ,one mother
,whored youth whored .were

there their breasts were handled, and there their virgin nipples were squeezed. [4] And their names (were) Oholah, the oldest; and Oholibah, her sister. And they were Mine, and they bore sons and daughters. And their names: Samaria (is) Oholah, and Jerusalem (is) Oholibah. [5] And Oholah whored under Me. And she lusted after her lovers, to neighboring Assyria, [6] clothed with purple, governors and rulers, all of them desirable young men; horsemen riding horses. [7] And she gave her harlotries on them, the choice sons of Assyria; (with) all of them, and with all whom she lusted after; she defiled herself with all their idols. [8] And she did not leave her fornications from Egypt; for they lay with her in her youth, and they squeezed her virgin nipples, and poured their fornications on her. [9] Therefore I have given her into the hand of her lovers, into the hand of the sons of Assyria whom she lusted on them. [10] They uncovered her nakedness. They took her sons and her daughters. And they killed her with the sword. And she became famous among women; and they executed judgments on her.

[11] And her sister Oholibah saw; and she was more corrupt in her lust than she; and her fornications were greater than her sister's. [12] She lusted to the sons of Assyria, neighboring governors and rulers clothed most perfectly; horsemen riding horses, all of them desirable young men. [13] Then I saw that she was defiled; one way (was) to both of them. [14] And she added to her fornications. And she saw men carved on the wall—images of the Chaldeans

4 מֹעֲכוּ שְׁדֵיהֶן וְשָׁם עִשּׂוּ דַּדֵּי בְּתוּלֵיהֶן׃ וּשְׁמוֹתָן אָהֳלָה
,Oholah their And their nipples were and their were
(were) names .virgin squeezed there ,breasts handled

הַגְּדוֹלָה וְאָהֳלִיבָה אֲחוֹתָהּ וַתִּהְיֶינָה לִי וַתֵּלַדְנָה בָּנִים
sons they and ,Mine they And .sister her and the
bore were ,Oholibah ;oldest

5 וּבָנוֹת וּשְׁמוֹתָן שֹׁמְרוֹן אָהֳלָה וִירוּשָׁלַםִ אָהֳלִיבָה׃ וַתִּזֶן
And .Oholibah (is) and ,Oholah Samaria their And and
whored Jerusalem (is) :names .daughters

אָהֳלָה תַּחְתָּי וַתַּעְגַּב עַל־מְאַהֲבֶיהָ אֶל־אַשּׁוּר קְרוֹבִים׃
,neighboring Assyria to her after she And under Oholah
,lovers lusted .Me

6 לְבֻשֵׁי תְכֵלֶת פַּחוֹת וּסְגָנִים בַּחוּרֵי חֶמֶד כֻּלָּם פָּרָשִׁים
horsemen of all desirable young and governors ,purple clothed
,them men ,rulers with

7 רֹכְבֵי סוּסִים׃ וַתִּתֵּן תַּזְנוּתֶיהָ עֲלֵיהֶם מִבְחַר בְּנֵי־אַשּׁוּר
,Assyria sons the ,them on her she And .horses riding
of choice harlotries gave

8 כֻּלָּם וּבְכֹל אֲשֶׁר־עָגְבָה בְּכָל־גִּלּוּלֵיהֶם נִטְמָאָה׃ וְאֶת־
And defiled she their with she whom with and all (with)
.herself idols all lusted all them of

תַּזְנוּתֶיהָ מִמִּצְרַיִם לֹא עָזָבָה כִּי אוֹתָהּ שָׁכְבוּ בִנְעוּרֶיהָ
her in they with for did she not from forni- her
,youth lay her ;leave Egypt catnions

9 וְהֵמָּה עִשּׂוּ דַּדֵּי בְתוּלֶיהָ וַיִּשְׁפְּכוּ תַזְנוּתָם עָלֶיהָ׃ לָכֵן
Therefore on their poured and her nipples squeezed and
.her fornications ,virgin they

נְתַתִּיהָ בְּיַד־מְאַהֲבֶיהָ בְּיַד בְּנֵי אַשּׁוּר אֲשֶׁר עָגְבָה עֲלֵיהֶם׃
.them on she whom Assyria the the into her the into have I
lusted of sons of hand ,lovers of hand her given

10 הֵמָּה גִּלּוּ עֶרְוָתָהּ בָּנֶיהָ וּבְנוֹתֶיהָ לָקָחוּ וְאוֹתָהּ בַּחֶרֶב
the with her and They her and her her uncovered They
sword ,took daughters sons .nakedness

11 הָרָגוּ וַתְּהִי־שֵׁם לַנָּשִׁים וּשְׁפוּטִים עָשׂוּ בָהּ׃ וַתֵּרֶא אֲחוֹתָהּ
her saw And on they and among famous she And they
sister .her executed judgments ,women became .killed

אָהֳלִיבָה וַתַּשְׁחֵת עַגְבָתָהּ מִמֶּנָּה וְאֶת־תַּזְנוּתֶיהָ מִזְּנוּנֵי
were fornications her and than her in was she and ,Oholibah
than greater ,she lust corrupt more

12 אֲחוֹתָהּ׃ אֶל־בְּנֵי אַשּׁוּר עָגָבָה פַּחוֹת וּסְגָנִים קְרֹבִים
,neighboring and governors she Assyria the To her
rulers ,lusted of sons .sister's

לְבֻשֵׁי מִכְלוֹל פָּרָשִׁים רֹכְבֵי סוּסִים בַּחוּרֵי חֶמֶד כֻּלָּם׃
of all desirable young ,horses riding horsemen most clothed
.them men ,perfectly

13
14 וָאֵרֶא כִּי נִטְמָאָה דֶּרֶךְ אֶחָד לִשְׁתֵּיהֶן׃ וַתּוֹסֶף אֶל־תַּזְנוּתֶיהָ
her to she And of both to one way was she that I Then
.fornications added .them (was) ;defiled saw

וַתֵּרֶא אַנְשֵׁי מְחֻקֶּה עַל־הַקִּיר צַלְמֵי כַשְׂדִּיים חֲקֻקִים
engraved the images the on carved men she And
Chaldeans of —wall saw

engraved with red color; [15] girded with girdles on their loins; with overflowing turbans on their heads, the look of rulers, all of them, like the sons of Babylon (in) Chaldea, the land of their birth— [16] and she lusted after them, to the look of their eyes, and sent messengers to them into Chaldea. [17] And the sons of Babylon came to her, to the bed of love; and they defiled her with their fornications. And she was defiled with them, and her soul was alienated from them. [18] And she uncovered her fornications and uncovered her nakedness. Then My soul was alienated from her, just as My soul was alienated from her sister. [19] And she multiplied her fornications to recall the days of her youth, in which she had whored in the land of Egypt. [20] And she lusted on their lovers of whom the flesh of asses resembles their flesh; and (as) the issue of horses their issue. [21] So you longed for the wickedness of your youth, when (they) squeezed your nipples from Egypt, for the sake of the breasts of your youth.

[22] Therefore, O Oholibah, thus says the Lord Jehovah: Behold, I will arouse your lovers against you from all around; [23] the sons of Babylon, and all the Chaldeans, Pekod, and Shoa, and Koa, all the sons of Assyria with them— desirable young men, governors and rulers, all of them; third heads and called ones; all of them riding horses. [24] And they shall come against you (with) weapons, chariots, and wheels, and with a group of peoples; buckler and shield and helmet shall set against you all around. And I will give before them

15 בַּשָּׁשַׁר׃ חֲגוֹרֵי אֵזוֹר בְּמָתְנֵיהֶם סְרוּחֵי טְבוּלִים בְּרָאשֵׁיהֶם
their on turbans over- with their on with girded red with
,heads flowing ,loins girdles ;color

מַרְאֵה שָׁלִשִׁים כֻּלָּם דְּמוּת בְּנֵי־בָבֶל כַּשְׂדִּים אֶרֶץ
the ,Chaldea Babylon the like of all ,rulers look the
of land (in) of sons ,them of

16 מוֹלַדְתָּם׃ וַתַּעְגַּב עֲלֵיהֶם לְמַרְאֵה עֵינֶיהָ וַתִּשְׁלַח מַלְאָכִים
messengers sent and her the to after she and their
eyes of look ,them lusted —birth

17 אֲלֵיהֶם כַּשְׂדִּימָה׃ וַיָּבֹאוּ אֵלֶיהָ בְנֵי־בָבֶל לְמִשְׁכַּב דֹּדִים
,love (her) to Babylon the her to And into them to
of bed of sons came .Chaldea

וַיְטַמְּאוּ אוֹתָהּ בְּתַזְנוּתָם וַתִּטְמָא־בָם וַתֵּקַע נַפְשָׁהּ מֵהֶם׃
from her was and with she And their with her they and
.them soul alienated ,them defiled was .fornications defiled

18 וַתְּגַל תַּזְנוּתֶיהָ וַתְּגַל אֶת־עֶרְוָתָהּ וַתֵּקַע נַפְשִׁי מֵעָלֶיהָ
on from My was Then her and forni- her she And
her soul alienated .nakedness uncovered cations uncovered

19 כַּאֲשֶׁר נָקְעָה נַפְשִׁי מֵעַל אֲחוֹתָהּ׃ וַתַּרְבֶּה אֶת־תַּזְנוּתֶיהָ
her she And her from My was as just
fornications multiplied .sister upon soul alienated

20 לִזְכֹּר אֶת־יְמֵי נְעוּרֶיהָ אֲשֶׁר זָנְתָה בְּאֶרֶץ מִצְרָיִם׃ וַתַּעְגְּבָה
she And .Egypt the in had she in her the to
lusted of land whored which youth of days recall

עַל פִּלַגְשֵׁיהֶם אֲשֶׁר בְּשַׂר חֲמוֹרִים בְּשָׂרָם וְזִרְמַת סוּסִים
horses (as) and their asses flesh the of their on
of issue the ;flesh resembles of whom ,lovers

21 זִרְמָתָם׃ וַתִּפְקְדִי אֵת זִמַּת נְעוּרָיִךְ בַּעְשׂוֹת מִמִּצְרַיִם
from (they) when your wicked- the you So their
Egypt squeezed ,youth of ness for longed .issue

22 דַּדַּיִךְ לְמַעַן שְׁדֵי נְעוּרָיִךְ׃ לָכֵן אָהֳלִיבָה כֹּה־אָמַר
says thus O ,Therefore your the the for your
,Oholibah .youth of breasts of sake nipples

אֲדֹנָי יֱהוִֹה הִנְנִי מֵעִיר אֶת־מְאַהֲבַיִךְ עָלַיִךְ אֵת אֲשֶׁר־נָקְעָה
is of against your will ,Behold :Jehovah the
alienated whom you lovers arouse I Lord

23 נַפְשֵׁךְ מֵהֶם וַהֲבֵאתִים עָלַיִךְ מִסָּבִיב׃ בְּנֵי בָבֶל וְכָל־
and ,Babylon the all from against will I And from your
all of sons ,around you them bring .them soul

כַּשְׂדִּים פְּקוֹד וְשׁוֹעַ וְקוֹעַ כָּל־בְּנֵי אַשּׁוּר אוֹתָם בַּחוּרֵי
young with Assyria the all and and ,Pekod the
men —them of sons ,Koa ,Shoa ,Chaldeans

חֶמֶד פַּחוֹת וּסְגָנִים כֻּלָּם שָׁלִשִׁים וּקְרוּאִים רֹכְבֵי סוּסִים
horses riding called and third of all and governors de-
,ones heads ,them ,rulers ,sirable

24 כֻּלָּם׃ וּבָאוּ עָלַיִךְ הֹצֶן רֶכֶב וְגַלְגַּל וּבִקְהַל עַמִּים צִנָּה
buck- ;peoples with and and ,chariots (with) against they And of all
ler of group a wheels ,weapons you come shall .them

וּמָגֵן וְקוֹבַע יָשִׂימוּ עָלַיִךְ סָבִיב וְנָתַתִּי לִפְנֵיהֶם מִשְׁפָּט
,judgment before I And all against shall and and
them give will .around you set helmet shield

judgment, and they will judge you by their judgments. [25] And I will give My jealousy against you, and they will deal with you in fury. Your nose and your ears they will take, and the rest of you shall fall by the sword. They will take your sons and your daughters, and the rest of you shall be devoured by the fire. [26] And they will strip you (of) your clothes, and take the means of your beauty. [27] And I will make cease your wickedness from you, and your fornication from the land of Egypt; and you shall not lift up your eyes to them; and Egypt shall not be remembered by you any more.

[28] For thus says the Lord Jehovah: Behold, I will give you in the hand of those whom you hate, in the hand of whom your soul was alienated from them. [29] And they shall deal with you in hatred, and take all your wealth, and shall leave you naked and bare. And the nudity of your adulteries will be bared, even your lewdness and your fornications. [30] These things will be done to you because you have whored after the nations, because that you are defiled with their idols. [31] You have walked in the way of your sister, and I will give her cup into your hand. [32] Thus says the Lord Jehovah: You shall drink your sister's cup deep and wide; you shall be laughed at and mocked; for it holds much. [33] (In) drunkenness and sorrow you are filled, the cup of horror and ruin, the cup of your sister Samaria. [34] And you shall drink it and drain (it). And you break its fragments, and tear off your breasts. For I have spoken, declares the Lord Jehovah. [35] Therefore thus says the Lord Jehovah: Because you have forgotten Me and cast Me behind your back, thus also you bear your wickedness

---

25 וְשָׁפְט֖וּךְ בְּמִשְׁפְּטֵיהֶ֑ם ׃ וְנָתַתִּ֤י קִנְאָתִי֙ בָּ֔ךְ וְעָשׂ֥וּ אוֹתָ֖ךְ
you · they and against · My · I And · their · by · will they and
with deal will, you · jealousy · give will .judgments · you judge

בְּחֵמָ֔ה אַפֵּ֥ךְ וְאָזְנַ֖יִךְ יָס֑וּרוּ וְאַחֲרִיתֵ֖ךְ בַּחֶ֥רֶב תִּפּֽוֹל ׃ הֵ֖מָּה
They · shall · the by · rest the and will they · your and · Your .fury in
.fall · sword · you of, take · ears · nose

26 בָנַ֥יִךְ וּבְנוֹתַ֖יִךְ יִקָּ֑חוּ וְאַחֲרִיתֵ֖ךְ תֵּאָכֵ֣ל בָּאֵ֑שׁ ׃ וְהִפְשִׁיט֖וּךְ
will they And · the by · be shall · rest the and · will · your and · your and
you strip · .fire · devoured · you of, take · daughters · sons

27 אֶת־בְּגָדַ֑יִךְ וְלָקְח֖וּ כְּלֵ֣י תִפְאַרְתֵּֽךְ ׃ וְהִשְׁבַּתִּ֤י זִמָּתֵךְ֙ מִמֵּ֔ךְ
from · your · will I And · your · the · take and · your (of)
,you · wickedness cease make .beauty · of means · clothes

וְאֶת־זְנוּתֵ֖ךְ מֵאֶ֣רֶץ מִצְרָ֑יִם וְלֹא־תִשְׂאִ֤י עֵינַ֙יִךְ֙ אֲלֵיהֶ֔ם
them to · your · you shall · and, Egypt · the from · your and
· eyes · up lift · not · of land · fornication

28 וּמִצְרַ֖יִם לֹ֥א תִזְכְּרִי־עֽוֹד ׃ כִּ֣י כֹ֤ה אָמַר֙ אֲדֹנָ֣י יְהוִ֔ה
:Jehovah the · says · thus For · any · shall you not · and
Lord · .more remember · Egypt

הִנְנִ֤י נֹֽתְנֵךְ֙ בְּיַ֣ד אֲשֶׁ֣ר שָׂנֵ֔את בְּיַ֖ד אֲשֶׁר־נָקְעָ֥ה נַפְשֵׁ֖ךְ מֵהֶֽם ׃
from · your · of · the in · those the in · will ,Behold
.them · soul alienated whom · hand, hate · whom of hand · you give I

29 וְעָשׂ֨וּ אֹתָ֜ךְ בְּשִׂנְאָ֗ה וְלָקְחוּ֙ כָּל־יְגִיעֵ֔ךְ וַעֲזָב֖וּךְ עֵרֹ֣ם
naked · shall and · your · all · shall and · hatred in · with · they And
you leave, wealth · take · you deal shall

30 וְעֶרְיָ֑ה וְנִגְלָה֙ עֶרְוַ֣ת זְנוּנַ֔יִךְ וְזִמָּתֵ֖ךְ וְתַזְנוּתָֽיִךְ ׃ עָשֹׂ֥ה אֵ֖לֶּה
These · be will · your and · your · even · adul- your · the · will And · and
things · done · .fornications · lewdness, teries · of nudity · bared be .bare

לָ֖ךְ בִּזְנוֹתֵ֣ךְ אַחֲרֵ֣י גוֹיִ֑ם עַ֥ל אֲשֶׁר־נִטְמֵ֖את בְּגִלּוּלֵיהֶֽם ׃
their with · are you · that · because the · after · you because to
.idols · defiled, nations · whored have you

31
32 בְּדֶ֥רֶךְ אֲחוֹתֵ֖ךְ הָלָ֑כְתְּ וְנָתַתִּ֥י כוֹסָ֖הּ בְּיָדֵֽךְ ׃ כֹּ֤ה אָמַר֙
says · Thus · your into · her · I and · have You · your · the in
.hand · cup · give will, walked · sister · of way

אֲדֹנָ֣י יְהוִ֔ה כּ֤וֹס אֲחוֹתֵךְ֙ תִּשְׁתִּ֔י הָעֲמֻקָּ֖ה וְהָרְחָבָ֑ה תִּהְיֶ֣ה
shall you ;wide and · deep · shall You · your · cup :Jehovah the
be · drink · sister's · Lord

33 לִצְחֹ֣ק וּלְלַ֔עַג מִרְבָּ֖ה לְהָכִ֑יל ׃ שִׁכָּר֥וֹן וְיָג֖וֹן תִּמָּלֵ֑אִי כּ֚וֹס
the · are you · and · (With) · it for · much · and · laughed
of cup · filled, sorrow · drunkenness .holds · at ;mocked

34 שַׁמָּ֣ה וּשְׁמָמָ֔ה כּ֖וֹס אֲחוֹתֵ֣ךְ שֹׁמְר֑וֹן ׃ וְשָׁתִ֤ית אוֹתָהּ֙ וּמָצִ֔ית
drain and · it · you And .Samaria · your · cup the, ruin and · horror
.(it) · drink shall · sister · of

וְאֶת־חֲרָשֶׂ֖יהָ תְּגָרֵ֑מִי וְשָׁדַ֖יִךְ תְּנַתֵּ֑קִי כִּ֚י אֲנִ֣י דִבַּ֔רְתִּי נְאֻ֖ם
states · have · I · For .off tear · your and · shall you · its · And
,spoken · breasts, break · fragments

אֲדֹנָ֥י יְהוִֽה ׃

35 לָכֵ֗ן כֹּ֤ה אָמַר֙ אֲדֹנָ֣י יְהוִ֔ה יַ֚עַן שָׁכַ֣חַתְּ
have you · Be- :Jehovah the · says · thus · Therefore .Jehovah the
forgotten · cause · Lord · Lord

אֹתִ֔י וַתַּשְׁלִ֥יכִי אוֹתִ֖י אַחֲרֵ֣י גַוֵּ֑ךְ וְגַם־אַ֛תְּ שְׂאִ֥י זִמָּתֵ֖ךְ וְאֶת־
and · your · bear · you · thus · your behind · Me · cast and · Me
wickedness · also, back

and your adulteries.

[36] And Jehovah said to me, Son of man, will you judge Oholah and Oholibah? Then declare to them their abominations. [37] For they did adultery and blood (is) on their hands. And they did adultery with their idols, and even their sons whom they bore to Me they make pass to them, to be devoured. [38] Even still they have done this to Me: They have defiled My sanctuary in that day, and have profaned My sabbaths. [39] And when they had slain their sons to their idols, then they came into My sanctuary in that day to profane it. And, lo, this they have done in the midst of My house. [40] Furthermore, they have sent for men to come from a distance, of whom a messenger was sent to them. And behold, they came, for whom you washed, painted your eyes, and were adorned (with) gems; [41] and you sat on a glorious bed, and a table prepared before it, and My incense and My oil you set on it. [42] And the sound of a crowd at ease (was) with her; and with the men of the host mankind were brought, drunkards from the wilderness; and they put bracelets on their hands, and crowns of beauty on their heads. [43] Then I said about the one worn (in) adulteries, Will they now whore with her, and she (with them)? [44] And they went in to her, as (they) go in to a woman of harlotry, so they went in to Oholah and to Oholibah the wicked women.

[45] And (as) righteous men they shall judge them (with) the judgment of adulteresses, and the judgment of women who shed blood; because they (are) adulteresses, and blood (is) in their hands. [46] For

36 תַּזְנוּתָיִךְ׃ וַיֹּאמֶר יְהוָה אֵלַי בֶּן־אָדָם הֲתִשְׁפּוֹט אֶת־
you will ,man Son to Jehovah said And your
judge of ,me .adulteries

37 אָהֳלָה וְאֶת־אָהֳלִיבָה וְהַגֵּד לָהֶן אֵת תּוֹעֲבוֹתֵיהֶן׃ כִּי
For their to Then ?Oholibah and Oholah
.abominations them declare

נִאֵפוּ וְדָם בִּידֵיהֶן וְאֶת־גִּלּוּלֵיהֶן נִאֵפוּ וְגַם אֶת־בְּנֵיהֶן אֲשֶׁר
whom their and did they their And their in and did they
,sons even adultery idols with .hands (is) blood adultery

38 יָלְדוּ־לִי הֶעֱבִירוּ לָהֶם לְאָכְלָה׃ עוֹד זֹאת עָשׂוּ לִי טִמְּאוּ
have They to they this Even be to to make they to they
defiled :Me done have still .devoured them pass ,Me bore

39 אֶת־מִקְדָּשִׁי בַּיּוֹם הַהוּא וְאֶת־שַׁבְּתוֹתַי חִלֵּלוּ׃ וּבְשַׁחֲטָם
they when And have My and that day in My
slain had ,profaned sabbaths sanctuary

אֶת־בְּנֵיהֶם לְגִלּוּלֵיהֶם וַיָּבֹאוּ אֶל־מִקְדָּשִׁי בַּיּוֹם הַהוּא
that day in My into they then their to their
sanctuary came ,idols sons

40 לְחַלְּלוֹ וְהִנֵּה־כֹה עָשׂוּ בְּתוֹךְ בֵּיתִי׃ וְאַף כִּי תִשְׁלַחְנָה
have they ,Furthermore My the in they this And pro- to
sent .house of midst done have ,lo .it fane

לַאֲנָשִׁים בָּאִים מִמֶּרְחָק אֲשֶׁר מַלְאָךְ שָׁלוּחַ אֲלֵיהֶם
.them to sent was a of a from come to men for
messenger whom ,distance

41 וְהִנֵּה־בָאוּ לַאֲשֶׁר רָחַצְתְּ כָּחַלְתְּ עֵינַיִךְ וְעָדִית עֶדִי׃ וְיָשַׁבְתְּ
you and (with) were and your painted you for they And
sat ;gems adorned eyes ,washed whom ,came ,behold

עַל־מִטָּה כְבוּדָּה וְשֻׁלְחָן עָרוּךְ לְפָנֶיהָ וּקְטָרְתִּי וְשַׁמְנִי
My and My and before prepared a and ,glorious a bed on
oil incense ,it table

42 שַׂמְתְּ עָלֶיהָ׃ וְקוֹל הָמוֹן שָׁלֵו בָהּ וְאֶל־אֲנָשִׁים מֵרֹב
the of the and (was) ease at a the And .it on set you
of host men with ;her with crowd of sound

אָדָם מוּבָאִים סוֹבָאִים מִמִּדְבָּר וַיִּתְּנוּ צְמִידִים אֶל־יְדֵיהֶן
their on bracelets they and the from drunkards were man-
hands put ,wilderness brought kind

43 וַעֲטֶרֶת תִּפְאֶרֶת עַל־רָאשֵׁיהֶן׃ וָאֹמַר לַבָּלָה נִאוּפִים עַתְּ
now (in) the about I Then their on beauty and
,adulteries worn one said .heads of crowns

44 יִזְנֶה תַזְנוּתֶהָ וָהִיא׃ וַיָּבוֹא אֵלֶיהָ כְּבוֹא אֶל־אִשָּׁה זוֹנָה
;harlotry a to (they) as ,her to they And she and whore will
of woman in go in went ?(them with) her with they

45 כֵּן בָּאוּ אֶל־אָהֳלָה וְאֶל־אָהֳלִיבָה אִשֹּׁת הַזִּמָּה׃ וַאֲנָשִׁים
(as) And .wicked the ,Oholibah and Oholah to they so
men women to in went

צַדִּיקִם הֵמָּה יִשְׁפְּטוּ אוֹתְהֶם מִשְׁפַּט נֹאֲפוֹת וּמִשְׁפַּט
the and ,adulteresses the (with) them shall they ,righteous
of judgment of judgment judge

46 שֹׁפְכוֹת דָּם כִּי נֹאֲפֹת הֵנָּה וְדָם בִּידֵיהֶן׃ כִּי כֹה אָמַר
says thus For their in and they adulteresses be- ;blood women
.hands (is) blood ,(are) cause shed who

אֲדֹנָי יֱהוִה הַעֲלֵה עֲלֵיהֶם קָהָל וְנָתֹן אֶתְהֶן לַזַעֲוָה וְלָבַז׃
to and terror to them and an them on Bring :Jehovah the
.plunder give assembly up Lord

47 וְרָגְמוּ עֲלֵיהֶן אֶבֶן קָהָל וּבָרֵא אוֹתְהֶן בְּחַרְבוֹתָם בְּנֵיהֶם
their their with them cut and the (with) them shall And
sons .swords down assembly stones stone

48 וּבְנוֹתֵיהֶם יַהֲרֹגוּ וּבָתֵּיהֶן בָּאֵשׁ יִשְׂרֹפוּ׃ וְהִשְׁבַּתִּי זִמָּה מִן
out wicked- will I So shall they with their and They their and
of ness cease make .burn fire houses ,slay shall daughters

49 הָאָרֶץ וְנִוַּסְּרוּ כָּל־הַנָּשִׁים וְלֹא תַעֲשֶׂינָה כְּזִמַּתְכֶנָה׃ וְנָתְנוּ
they And to according do to and the all may that the
put shall .wickedness your not women taught be ,land

זִמַּתְכֶנָה עֲלֵיכֶן וַחֲטָאֵי גִלּוּלֵיכֶן תִּשֶּׂאינָה וִידַעְתֶּם כִּי אֲנִי
I that you And shall you your the and on your
(am) know shall .bear idols of sins ,you wickedness

אֲדֹנָי יֱהוִה׃
.Jehovah the
Lord

CAP. XXIV כד

CHAPTER 24

1 וַיְהִי דְבַר־יְהוָה אֵלַי בַּשָּׁנָה הַתְּשִׁיעִית בַּחֹדֶשׁ הָעֲשִׂירִי
,tenth the in ,ninth the in to Jehovah the And
month year me of word was

2 בֶּעָשׂוֹר לַחֹדֶשׁ לֵאמֹר׃ בֶּן־אָדָם כְּתוֹב־לְךָ אֶת־שֵׁם הַיּוֹם
the the for write ,man Son ,saying the of the in
;day of name yourself of ,month (day) tenth

אֶת־עֶצֶם הַיּוֹם הַזֶּה סָמַךְ מֶלֶךְ־בָּבֶל אֶל־יְרוּשָׁלִַם בְּעֶצֶם
very in Jerusalem to- Babylon the has :this day very
ward of king leaned

3 הַיּוֹם הַזֶּה׃ וּמְשֹׁל אֶל־בֵּית־הַמֶּרִי מָשָׁל וְאָמַרְתָּ אֲלֵיהֶם
,them to say and a rebellious the to speak And .this day
parable house

כֹּה אָמַר אֲדֹנָי יְהוִה שְׁפֹת הַסִּיר שְׁפֹת וְגַם־יְצֹק בּוֹ מָיִם׃
.water in pour and Set the Set :Jehovah the says Thus
it also ,on (it) .pot on Lord

4 אֱסֹף נְתָחֶיהָ אֵלֶיהָ כָּל־נֵתַח טוֹב יָרֵךְ וְכָתֵף מִבְחַר עֲצָמִים
bones the the and the ,good piece every ,it into its Gather
choice .shoulder thigh pieces

5 מַלֵּא׃ מִבְחַר הַצֹּאן לָקוֹחַ וְגַם דּוּר הָעֲצָמִים תַּחְתֶּיהָ
;it under bones the pile and Take the the Fill
also flock of choice .(with it)

6 רַתַּח רְתָחֶיהָ גַּם־בָּשְׁלוּ עֲצָמֶיהָ בְּתוֹכָהּ׃ לָכֵן כֹּה
thus Therefore .it in bones its them let also it make boiling
seethe ,boil

אָמַר ׀ אֲדֹנָי יְהוִה אוֹי עִיר הַדָּמִים סִיר אֲשֶׁר חֶלְאָתָה בָהּ
,it in rust whose the to the city Woe :Jehovah the says
(is) pot ,bloody to Lord

וְחֶלְאָתָה לֹא יָצְאָה מִמֶּנָּה לִנְתָחֶיהָ לִנְתָחֶיהָ הוֹצִיאָהּ
Bring piece by piece !it of has not its and
,out it out gone rust

thus says the Lord Jehovah: Bring up on them an assembly, and give them to terror and plunder. [47] And the assembly shall stone them (with) stones, and cut them down with their swords. They shall slay their sons and their daughters, and they shall burn their houses with fire. [48] So I will make cease wickedness out of the land, that all the women may be taught , and not to do according to your wickedness. [49] And they shall put your wickedness on you, and you shall bear the sins of your idols. And you shall know that I (am) the Lord Jehovah.

CHAPTER 24

[1] And the word of Jehovah was to me, in the ninth year, in the tenth month, in the tenth (day) of the month, saying, [2] Son of man, write for yourself the name of the day; this very day; the king of Babylon has leaned toward Jerusalem in this very day. [3] And speak to the rebellious house a parable, and say to them, Thus says the Lord Jehovah: Set on the pot. Set (it) on, and also pour water in it. [4] Gather its pieces into it, every good piece, the thigh and the shoulder. Fill (it) (with) choice bones, the choice of the flock. [5] Take and also pile the bones under it; boiling make it boil; also let them seethe its bones in it.

[6] Therefore thus says the Lord Jehovah: Woe to the bloody city, to the pot whose rust (is) in it, and its rust has not gone out of it! Bring it out piece by piece.

Let not a lot fall on it. [7] For her blood is in her midst; she set it on a shining rock. She did not pour it on the ground, to cover it (with) dust. [8] to cause fury to come up to take vengeance. I have put her blood on a shining rock, that it should not be covered. [9] Therefore thus says the Lord Jehovah: Woe to the bloody city! I also shall make great the pile. [10] And kindle the fire on the wood, complete the flesh, and mix in the spice; and let the bones be burned. [11] Then make it stand on its coals empty, so that it may be hot, and its bronze may glow, and its defilement be melted in its midst, (that) its rust may be consumed. [12] She is wearied with toil, and the increase of her rust did not go out; her rust (will be) in the fire. [13] In your defilement (is) wickedness. Because I have cleaned you, yet you are not clean; you shall not be cleansed from your defilement any more until I have made cease My fury on you. [14] I, Jehovah, have spoken. It shall come, and I will do (it). I will not let go, and I will not spare; I will not pity. By your ways and by your doings they shall judge you, declares the Lord Jehovah.

[15] And the word of Jehovah was to me, saying, [16] Son of man, behold, I am taking from you the desire of your eyes with a blow. Yet you shall not wail, and not weep, and your tears shall not come. [17] Groan, (but) be silent; do not make a mourning (for) the dead. Bind your turban on you, and put your shoes on your feet, and do not cover over the mustache; and do not eat the bread of men.

7 לֹא־נָפַל עָלֶיהָ גּוֹרָל׃ כִּי דָמָהּ בְּתוֹכָהּ הָיָה עַל־צְחִיחַ

a shining | on | ;is | her in midst | her blood | For | .lot a | it on | let fall | not

סֶלַע שָׂמָתְהוּ לֹא שְׁפָכַתְהוּ עַל־הָאָרֶץ לְכַסּוֹת עָלָיו עָפָר׃

(with) dust | it | cover to | the ,ground | on | did She it pour | not | set she .it | rock

8 לְהַעֲלוֹת חֵמָה לִנְקֹם נָקָם נָתַתִּי אֶת־דָּמָהּ עַל־צְחִיחַ סָלַע

,rock | a shining | on | her blood | have I put | ven- ,geance | take to | fury | cause to up come to

9 לְבִלְתִּי הִכָּסוֹת׃ לָכֵן כֹּה אָמַר אֲדֹנָי יְהוִה אוֹי עִיר

city | Woe to | :Jehovah | the Lord | says | thus | Therefore | be should it .covered | not that

10 הַדָּמִים גַּם־אֲנִי אַגְדִּיל הַמְּדוּרָה׃ הַרְבֵּה הָעֵצִים הַדְלֵק

kindle | ,wood the | on And | .pile the | make shall great | I | also | the !bloody

הָאֵשׁ הָתֵם הַבָּשָׂר וְהַרְקַח הַמֶּרְקָחָה וְהָעֲצָמוֹת יֵחָרוּ׃

be let .burned | the and bones | ;spice the | mix and in | the ,flesh | complete | the ,fire

11 וְהַעֲמִידֶהָ עַל־גֶּחָלֶיהָ רֵקָה לְמַעַן תֵּחַם וְחָרָה נְחֻשְׁתָּהּ

,bronze its | may and glow | may it ,hot be | so that | ,empty | its coals | on | make Then stand it

12 וְנִתְּכָה בְתוֹכָהּ טֻמְאָתָהּ תִּתֹּם חֶלְאָתָהּ׃ תְּאֻנִים הֶלְאָת

is She ,wearied | with toil | .rust its | may (that) consumed be | defile- ;ment its | its in midst | may and melted be

13 וְלֹא־תֵצֵא מִמֶּנָּה רַבַּת חֶלְאָתָהּ בְּאֵשׁ חֶלְאָתָהּ׃ בְּטֻמְאָתֵךְ

your In (is) defilement | rust her .(be will) | the in fire | ;rust her | in- the crease | from her | go did out | and not

זִמָּה יַעַן טִהַרְתִּיךְ וְלֹא טָהַרְתְּ מִטֻּמְאָתֵךְ לֹא תִטְהֲרִי־עוֹד

any more | shall you cleansed be | not | your from defilement | you are ,clean | yet not | have I ,you cleaned | Be- cause | wicked- .ness

14 עַד־הֲנִיחִי אֶת־חֲמָתִי בָּךְ׃ אֲנִי יְהוָה דִּבַּרְתִּי בָּאָה וְעָשִׂיתִי

will I .(it) do | and shall It ,come | have .spoken | Jehovah | I | on .you | My fury | have I cease made | until

לֹא־אֶפְרַע וְלֹא־אָחוּס וְלֹא אֶנָּחֵם כִּדְרָכַיִךְ וְכַעֲלִילוֹתַיִךְ

your by and ,doings | your By ways | will I .pity | not | will I ;spare | and not | will I go let | not

15 שְׁפָטוּךְ נְאֻם אֲדֹנָי יְהוִה׃ וַיְהִי דְבַר־יְהוָה אֵלַי לֵאמֹר׃

,saying | to ,me | Jehovah | the of word | And was | .Jehovah | the Lord | states | shall they you judge

16 בֶּן־אָדָם הִנְנִי לֹקֵחַ מִמְּךָ אֶת־מַחְמַד עֵינֶיךָ בְּמַגֵּפָה וְלֹא

Yet not | a with .blow | your eyes | the of desire | from you | am taking | ,behold I | ,man Son of

17 תִסְפֹּד וְלֹא תִבְכֶּה וְלוֹא תָבוֹא דִּמְעָתֶךָ׃ הֵאָנֵק ׀ דֹּם

Be .silent | Groan ,(silently) | .tears your | shall come | and not | ,weep | and not | shall you ,wail

מֵתִים אֵבֶל לֹא־תַעֲשֶׂה פְּאֵרְךָ חֲבוֹשׁ עָלֶיךָ וּנְעָלֶיךָ תָּשִׂים

put | your and shoes | on ,you | Bind | your turban | make do .(them for) | not | a mourning | the (for) dead

בְּרַגְלֶיךָ וְלֹא תַעְטֶה עַל־שָׂפָם וְלֶחֶם אֲנָשִׁים לֹא תֹאכֵל׃

.eat do | not | men | the and of bread | the ,mustache | over | do cover | and not | your on ,feet

[18] So I spoke to the people in the morning. And my wife died in the evening. And I did in the morning as I was commanded. [19] And the people said to me, Will you not tell us what these things (are) to us, that you are doing? [20] Then I said to them, the word of Jehovah was to me, saying, [21] Speak to the house of Israel, Thus says the Lord Jehovah: Behold, I will profane My sanctuary, the pride of your strength, the desire of your eyes, and that which your soul pities. And your sons and your daughters, whom you have forsaken, shall fall by the sword. [22] And you shall do as I have done. You shall not cover over the mustache, and you shall not eat the bread of man. [23] And your turbans (shall be) on your heads, and your shoes on your feet. You shall not wail, and not shall weep; but you shall rot away in your iniquities, and each man groan to his brother. [24] So Ezekiel is for a sign to you. As all that he has done, you shall do. And when it comes, then you shall know that I (am) the Lord Jehovah.

[25] And you, son of man, will (it) not (be) on the day (when) I take from them their strength, the joy of their beauty, the desire of their eyes, and the lifting up of their soul —their sons and their daughters? [26] He will come in day, he who escaped to you, to cause (you) to hear (with your) ears. [27] In that day your mouth shall be opened to the escaped one, and you shall speak and not be dumb any longer. And you shall be to them a sign, and they shall know that I (am) Jehovah.

18 וָאֲדַבֵּר אֶל־הָעָם בַּבֹּקֶר וַתָּמָת אִשְׁתִּי בָּעָרֶב וָאַעַשׂ

I and did | the in ,evening | wife my | died And | the in .morning | the people | to | I So spoke

19 בַבֹּקֶר כַּאֲשֶׁר צֻוֵּיתִי׃ וַיֹּאמְרוּ אֵלַי הָעָם הֲלֹא־תַגִּיד לָנוּ

us | you tell | Will not | the ,people | to me | said And | was I .commanded | as | the in morning

20 מָה־אֵלֶּה לָּנוּ כִּי אַתָּה עֹשֶׂה׃ וָאֹמַר אֲלֵיהֶם דְּבַר־יְהוָה

Jehovah | the of word | ,them to | I Then said | are ?doing | you that | to us (are) | these things | what

21 הָיָה אֵלַי לֵאמֹר׃ אֱמֹר ׀ לְבֵית יִשְׂרָאֵל כֹּה־אָמַר אֲדֹנָי

the Lord | says Thus | ,Israel | the to of house | Speak | ,saying | ,me to | was

יְהוִה הִנְנִי מְחַלֵּל אֶת־מִקְדָּשִׁי גְּאוֹן עֻזְּכֶם מַחְמַד עֵינֵיכֶם

,eyes your | desire the of | your ,strength | the of pride | My sanctuary | will profane | ,Behold I | Jeho- :vah

וּמַחְמַל נַפְשְׁכֶם וּבְנֵיכֶם וּבְנוֹתֵיכֶם אֲשֶׁר עֲזַבְתֶּם בַּחֶרֶב

the by sword | have you forsaken | whom | your and daughters | your And sons | .soul your | that and pities which

22 יִפֹּלוּ׃ וַעֲשִׂיתֶם כַּאֲשֶׁר עָשִׂיתִי עַל־שָׂפָם לֹא תַעְטוּ וְלֶחֶם

the and of bread | shall you not ,cover | the mustache | On | have I .done | as | you And do shall | shall .fall

23 אֲנָשִׁים לֹא תֹאכֵלוּ׃ וּפְאֵרֵכֶם עַל־רָאשֵׁיכֶם וְנַעֲלֵיכֶם

your and shoes | your heads | on | your And (be shall) turbans | shall you .eat | not | men

בְּרַגְלֵיכֶם לֹא תִסְפְּדוּ וְלֹא תִבְכּוּ וּנְמַקֹּתֶם בַּעֲוֺנֹתֵיכֶם

your in iniquities | shall you but away rot | ;weep | and not | shall You wail | not | your on .feet

2
24 וּנְהַמְתֶּם אִישׁ אֶל־אָחִיו׃ וְהָיָה יְחֶזְקֵאל לָכֶם לְמוֹפֵת

a for .sign | you to | Ezekiel | is So | his .brother | to | each man | groan and

כְּכֹל אֲשֶׁר־עָשָׂה תַּעֲשׂוּ בְּבֹאָהּ וִידַעְתֶּם כִּי אֲנִי אֲדֹנָי

the Lord | I (am) | that | you then know shall | when And ;comes it | shall you .do | has he ,done | that | all As

25 יְהוִה׃ וְאַתָּה בֶן־אָדָם הֲלוֹא בְּיוֹם קַחְתִּי מֵהֶם אֶת־

from them | (when) take I | the on day | (it) will (be) not | ,man | son of | ,you And | .Jehovah

מָעֻזָּם מְשׂוֹשׂ תִּפְאַרְתָּם אֶת־מַחְמַד עֵינֵיהֶם וְאֶת־מַשָּׂא

the of up lifting | and | ,eyes their | the of desire | ,beauty their | joy the of | their ,strength

26 נַפְשָׁם בְּנֵיהֶם וּבְנוֹתֵיהֶם׃ בַּיּוֹם הַהוּא יָבוֹא הַפָּלִיט אֵלֶיךָ

to ,you | who he escaped | will come | he | day In | their and ?daughters | their sons | their ,soul

27 לְהַשְׁמָעוּת אָזְנָיִם׃ בַּיּוֹם הַהוּא יִפָּתַח פִּיךָ אֶת־הַפָּלִיט

the to ,one escaped | your mouth | be shall opened | that | day In | (your with) .ears | cause to hear to (you)

וּתְדַבֵּר וְלֹא תֵאָלֵם עוֹד וְהָיִיתָ לָהֶם לְמוֹפֵת וְיָדְעוּ כִּי־

that | they and know shall | ,sign a | them to | you And be shall | any .longer | be dumb | and not | you speak shall

אֲנִי יְהוָה׃

.Jehovah | I (am)

CAP. XXV כה

CHAPTER 25

[1] And the word of Jehovah was to me, saying, [2] Son of man, set your face aganst the sons of Ammon and prophesy against them. [3] And say to the sons of Ammon, Hear the word of the Lord Jehovah. Thus says the Lord Jehovah: Because you have said, Aha, against My sanctuary, when it was profaned, and against the land of Israel when it was ruined, and against the house of Judah when they went into exile; [4] therefore, behold, I will give you to the sons of the east for a possession. And they shall set their camp sites among you, and put among you their dwellings. [5] They shall eat your fruit, and they shall drink your milk. And I will give Rabbah for a pasture (for) camels, and the sons of Ammon for a resting place (for) flocks. And you shall know that I (am) Jehovah. [6] For thus says the Lord Jehovah: Because you have clapped the hand, and you stamped the foot, and rejoiced with all your spite in (your) soul against the land of Israel; [7] therefore, behold, I will stretch out My hand on you and will give you as a prize to the nations. And I will cut you off from the peoples, and I will make you perish from the lands. I will destroy you. And you shall know that I (am) Jehovah.

[8] Thus says the Lord Jehovah: Because Moab and Seir say, Behold, the house of Judah (is) like all the nations; [9] therefore, behold, I will open the side of Moab from the cities, from his cities, from his borders, the glory of the land: Beth-jeshimoth, Baal-meon, and Kiriathaim; to

CHAPTER 25

1 2 וַיְהִי דְבַר־יְהוָה אֵלַי לֵאמֹר׃ בֶּן־אָדָם שִׂים פָּנֶיךָ אֶל־בְּנֵי
the against your set ,man Son ,saying to Jehovah the And
of sons face of ,me of word was

3 עַמּוֹן וְהִנָּבֵא עֲלֵיהֶם׃ וְאָמַרְתָּ לִבְנֵי עַמּוֹן שִׁמְעוּ דְּבַר־
the Hear ,Ammon the to say And against and Ammon
of word of sons .them prophesy

אֲדֹנָי יְהוִה כֹּה־אָמַר אֲדֹנָי יְהוִה יַעַן אָמְרֵךְ הֶאָח אֶל־
against ,Aha have you Be- :Jehovah the says Thus .Jehovah the
,said cause Lord Lord

מִקְדָּשִׁי כִּי־נִחָל וְאֶל־אַדְמַת יִשְׂרָאֵל כִּי נָשַׁמָּה וְאֶל־בֵּית
the and was it when Israel the and was it when My
of house against ,ruined of land against ,profaned sanctuary

4 יְהוּדָה כִּי הָלְכוּ בַּגּוֹלָה׃ לָכֵן הִנְנִי נֹתְנָךְ לִבְנֵי־קֶדֶם
the the to will ,behold ,therefore into they when Judah
east of sons you give I ;exile went

לְמוֹרָשָׁה וְיִשְּׁבוּ טִירוֹתֵיהֶם בָּךְ וְנָתְנוּ בָךְ מִשְׁכְּנֵיהֶם
their among and among their they And a for
.dwellings you put you sites camp set shall .possession

5 הֵמָּה יֹאכְלוּ פִרְיֵךְ וְהֵמָּה יִשְׁתּוּ חֲלָבֵךְ׃ וְנָתַתִּי אֶת־רַבָּה
Rabbah I And your shall and your shall They
give will .milk drink they ,fruit eat

לִנְוֵה גְמַלִּים וְאֶת־בְּנֵי עַמּוֹן לְמִרְבַּץ־צֹאן וִידַעְתֶּם כִּי־אֲנִי
I that you And (for) resting a for Ammon the and (for) a for
(am) know shall .flocks place of sons ,camels pasture

6 יְהוָה׃ כִּי כֹה אָמַר אֲדֹנָי יְהוִה יַעַן מַחְאֲךָ יָד
(your) have you Be- :Jehovah the says thus For .Jehovah
hand clapped cause Lord

וְרַקְעֲךָ בְּרָגֶל וַתִּשְׂמַח בְּכָל־שָׁאטְךָ בְּנֶפֶשׁ אֶל־אַדְמַת
the against (your) in your with and (your) you and
of land soul spite all rejoiced ,foot stamped

7 יִשְׂרָאֵל׃ לָכֵן הִנְנִי נָטִיתִי אֶת־יָדִי עָלֶיךָ וּנְתַתִּיךָ לְבַג
a as will and on My will ,Behold ,therefore ;Israel
prize you give you hand out stretch I

לַגּוֹיִם וְהִכְרַתִּיךָ מִן־הָעַמִּים וְהַאֲבַדְתִּיךָ מִן־הָאֲרָצוֹת
the from will I and the from will I And the to
.lands perish you make peoples off you cut .nations

8 אַשְׁמִידְךָ וְיָדַעְתָּ כִּי־אֲנִי יְהוָה׃ כֹּה אָמַר אֲדֹנָי
the says Thus .Jehovah I that you and will I
Lord (am) know shall ,you destroy

יְהוִה יַעַן אֱמֹר מוֹאָב וְשֵׂעִיר הִנֵּה כְּכָל־הַגּוֹיִם בֵּית
the (is) the like ,Behold ,Seir and Moab say Be- :Jehovah
of house nations all cause

9 יְהוּדָה׃ לָכֵן הִנְנִי פֹתֵחַ אֶת־כֶּתֶף מוֹאָב מֵהֶעָרִים מֵעָרָיו
his from the from Moab the will ,behold there- ;Judah
cities ,cities of side open I ,fore

מִקָּצֵהוּ צְבִי אֶרֶץ בֵּית הַיְשִׁימֹת בַּעַל מְעוֹן וְקִרְיָתָמָה׃
and meon Baal- ,jeshimoth Beth- the the his from
,Kiriathaim ;land of glory ,borders

to the sons of the east, with the sons of Ammon. [10] And I will give it for a possession so that not may be recalled the sons of Ammon among the nations. [11] And I will execute on Moab judgments. And they shall know that I (am) Jehovah.

[12] Thus says the Lord Jehovah: Because Edom has acted by taking vengeance against the house of Judah, and they are very guilty, and are avenged on them; [13] therefore, thus says the Lord Jehovah; I will stretch My hand on Edom and will cut off from it man and beast; and I will lay it waste, from Teman even to Dedan they shall fall by the sword. [14] And I will put My vengeance on Edom by the hand of My people Israel. And they shall do in Edom as (is) My anger, and as (is) My fury. And they shall know My vengeance, declares the Lord Jehovah.

[15] Thus says the Lord Jehovah: Because the Philistines have acted in vengeance, and have taken vengeance with spite in (their) soul, to destroy (with) perpetual enmity; [16] therefore, thus says the Lord Jehovah: Behold, I will stretch My hand on the Philistines, and I will cut off the Cherethim, and will destroy the rest of the coast of the sea. [17] And I will execute on them great vengeances, with rebukes of fury. And they will know that I (am) Jehovah,

10 לבני־קדם על־בני עמון ונתתיה למורשה למען לא־
not that so a possession for will I it give And .Ammon the of sons with the east the to of sons

11 תזכר בני־עמון בגוים׃ ובמואב אעשה שפטים וידעו
they And shall know .judgments will I execute on And Moab the among .nations Ammon the of sons be may recalled

12 כי־אני יהוה׃ כה אמר אדני יהוה יען עשות אדום
Edom has acted Be- cause :Jehovah the Lord says Thus .Jehovah I (am) that

בנקם נקם לבית יהודה ויאשמו אשום ונקמו בהם׃
;them on are and avenged very they and guilty are ,Judah the against of house ven- geance by taking

13 לכן כה אמר אדני יהוה ונטתי ידי על־אדום והכרתי
will and off cut Edom on My hand will I stretch :Jehovah the Lord says thus ,there- fore

ממנה אדם ובהמה ונתתיה חרבה מתימן ודדנה בחרב
the by sword to even Dedan from Teman ,waste will I and it lay ;beast and man from it

14 יפלו׃ ונתתי את־נקמתי באדום ביד עמי ישראל ועשו
they And do shall .Israel , My people the by of hand Edom on ven- geance My I And put will shall they .fall

באדום כאפי וכחמתי וידעו את־נקמתי נאם אדני יהוה׃
.Jehovah the Lord states ven- ,geance My they And know shall (is) as and .fury My My (is) as anger in Edom

15 כה אמר אדני יהוה יען עשות פלשתים בנקמה
in ;vengeance the Philistines have acted Be- cause :Jehovah the Lord says Thus

16 וינקמו נקם בשאט בנפש למשחית איבת עולם׃ לכן
therefore per- ,petual enmity destroy to (with) (their) in soul with spite vengeance have and taken

כה אמר אדני יהוה הנני נוטה ידי על־פלשתים והכרתי
will I and off cut the Philistines on My hand will ,Behold stretch I :Jehovah the Lord says thus

17 את־כרתים והאבדתי את־שארית חוף הים׃ ועשיתי בם
on them will I And execute the .sea coast the of the of rest will and destroy the ,Cherethim

נקמות גדלות בתוכחות חמה וידעו כי־אני יהוה בתתי
I when put ,Jehovah I (am) that they And know will .fury with of rebukes great ven- geances

את־נקמתי בם׃
on .them My vengeance

CAP. XXVI כו

CHAPTER 26

[1] And it was, in the eleventh year, in the first of the month, the word of Jehovah was to me, saying, Son of man, because that Tyre has spoken against

1 ויהי בעשתי־עשרה שנה באחד לחדש היה דבר־יהוה
Jehovah the of word was the of ,month the in first ,year eleventh the in it And ,was

2 אלי לאמר׃ בן־אדם יען אשר־אמרה צר על־ירושלם
,Jerusalem against Tyre has said that because ,man Son of ,saying to ,me

Jerusalem, Aha! She is shattered, the doors of the peoples; she has turned to me; I shall be filled; she is laid waste. [3] Therefore, thus says the Lord Jehovah: Behold, I (am) against you, O Tyre. And I will bring up against you many nations, as the sea brings its waves. [4] And they shall destroy the walls of Tyre, and break down her towers. I will also scrape her dust from her, and make her like a shining rock. [5] It shall be a spreading place for nets in the midst of the sea. For I have spoken, declares the Lord Jehovah. And she shall be a spoil to the nations. [6] And her daughters who (are) in the field shall be killed by the sword; and they shall know that I (am) Jehovah.

[7] For thus says the Lord Jehovah: Behold, I will bring on Tyre Nebuchadnezzar, king of Babylon, from the north, a king of kings, with horses, and with chariots, and with a company of horsemen, even many people. [8] He shall kill your daughters in the field with the sword. And he shall make siege walls against you, and cast against you a mound; and raise a buckler against you. [9] And he will set the blow of his ram against your walls; and he shall break down your towers with his axes. [10] From the multitude of his horses, their dust shall cover you. From the sound of the horsemen, and the wheels , and chariots, your walls shall shake; when he enters your gates, as (men) enter a city that is breached. [11] With the hoofs of his horses he will trample all your streets. He shall kill your people by the sword, and the pillars of your strength shall go down to the ground. [12] And they shall plunder your wealth, and rob your merchandise. And they shall raze your walls, and destroy your desirable houses. And your stones and your timbers, and your dust in the midst of the

הֶאָח נִשְׁבְּרָה דַּלְתוֹת הָעַמִּים נָסֵבָּה אֵלָי אִמָּלְאָה הָחֳרָבָה׃
is she shall I to has she the the is she !Aha
.waste laid ;filled be ;me turned ;peoples of doors ,shattered

3 לָכֵן כֹּה אָמַר אֲדֹנָי יְהוִה הִנְנִי עָלַיִךְ צֹר וְהַעֲלֵיתִי עָלַיִךְ
against will I And O against ,Behold :Jehovah the says thus There-
you up bring Tyre ,you (am) I Lord fore

4 גּוֹיִם רַבִּים כְּהַעֲלוֹת הַיָּם לְגַלָּיו׃ וְשִׁחֲתוּ חֹמוֹת צֹר
Tyre the they And .waves its the brings as ,many nations
of walls destroy shall sea

וְהָרְסוּ מִגְדָּלֶיהָ וְסִחֵיתִי עֲפָרָהּ מִמֶּנָּה וְנָתַתִּי אוֹתָהּ לִצְחִיחַ
a like her make and from her will I her break and
shining her dust scrape also .towers down

5 סָלַע׃ מִשְׁטַח חֲרָמִים תִּהְיֶה בְּתוֹךְ הַיָּם כִּי אֲנִי דִבַּרְתִּי
have I For the the in shall It nets spreading a .rock
,spoken .sea of midst be for place

6 נְאֻם אֲדֹנָי יְהוִה וְהָיְתָה לְבַז לַגּוֹיִם׃ וּבְנוֹתֶיהָ אֲשֶׁר בַּשָּׂדֶה
the in who her And the to spoil a she And .Jehovah the states
field (are) daughters .nations be shall Lord

7 בַּחֶרֶב תֵּהָרַגְנָה וְיָדְעוּ כִּי־אֲנִי יְהוָה׃ כִּי כֹה אָמַר
says thus For .Jehovah I that they and be shall the by
(am) know shall ;killed sword

אֲדֹנָי יְהוִה הִנְנִי מֵבִיא אֶל־צֹר נְבוּכַדְרֶאצַּר מֶלֶךְ־בָּבֶל
,Babylon king Nebuchadnezzar Tyre on will ,Behold :Jehovah the
of bring I Lord

מִצָּפוֹן מֶלֶךְ מְלָכִים בְּסוּס וּבְרֶכֶב וּבְפָרָשִׁים וְקָהָל וְעַם־
even a with and with and with ,kings king a the from
people ,company horsemen ,chariots ,horses of north

8 רָב׃ בְּנוֹתַיִךְ בַּשָּׂדֶה בַּחֶרֶב יַהֲרֹג וְנָתַן עָלַיִךְ דָּיֵק וְשָׁפַךְ
and siege against he And shall He the with the in your .many
cast ,walls you make shall .kill sword field daughters

9 עָלַיִךְ סֹלְלָה וְהֵקִים עָלַיִךְ צִנָּה׃ וּמְחִי קָבָלּוֹ יִתֵּן בְּחֹמוֹתָיִךְ
your against will he his the And a against and ,mound a against
,walls set ram of blow .buckler you raise you

10 וּמִגְדְּלֹתַיִךְ יִתֹּץ בְּחַרְבוֹתָיו׃ מִשִּׁפְעַת סוּסָיו יְכַסֵּךְ אֲבָקָם
their shall his the From his with shall he your and
.dust you cover ,horses of plenty .axes down break towers

מִקּוֹל פָּרַשׁ וְגַלְגַּל וָרֶכֶב תִּרְעַשְׁנָה חוֹמוֹתַיִךְ בְּבֹאוֹ
he when ,walls your shake shall and the and the the From
enters ,chariots ,wheels ,horsemen of sound

11 בִּשְׁעָרַיִךְ כִּמְבוֹאֵי עִיר מְבֻקָּעָה׃ בְּפַרְסוֹת סוּסָיו יִרְמֹס
will he his the With is that a (men) as your
trample horses of hoofs .breached city enter ,gates

אֶת־כָּל־חוּצוֹתָיִךְ עַמֵּךְ בַּחֶרֶב יַהֲרֹג וּמַצְּבוֹת עֻזֵּךְ לָאָרֶץ
the to your the and shall He the by Your your all
ground strength of pillars ,kill sword people .streets

12 תֵּרֵד׃ וְשָׁלְלוּ חֵילֵךְ וּבָזְזוּ רְכֻלָּתֵךְ וְהָרְסוּ חוֹמוֹתַיִךְ
,walls your they And your and your they And go shall
raze shall .merchandise plunder ,wealth spoil shall .down

וּבָתֵּי חֶמְדָּתֵךְ יִתֹּצוּ וַאֲבָנַיִךְ וְעֵצַיִךְ וַעֲפָרֵךְ בְּתוֹךְ מַיִם
the the in your and your and your And .destroy your and
water of midst dust timbers stones desirable houses

water they shall set. [13] And I will make cease the noise of your songs; and the sound of your harps shall not be heard any more. [14] And I will make you like a shining rock. You shall be a spreading place for nets; you shall not be built any more; for I, Jehovah, have spoken, declares the Lord Jehovah.

[15] Thus says the Lord Jehovah to Tyre: Shall not the coastlands shake at the sound of your fall, when the slain groan, when the slaughter occurs in your midst? [16] Then shall come down from their thrones all the rulers of the sea and lay aside their robes, and strip off their embroidered garments. They shall be clothed; they shall sit on the ground, and shall tremble at (every) moment, and be appalled at you. [17] And they shall take up a lament for you, and say to you, How you are perished, who lived by the seas, the city well-praised, which was strong in the sea, she and her inhabitants, who put their terror on all her inhabitants! [18] Now the coasts shall tremble (in) the day of your fall. And the coasts that (are) by the sea shall be troubled at your going. [19] For thus says the Lord Jehovah: When I shall make you a ruined city, like the cities that do not have inhabitants; when I shall bring up the deep on you, and shall cover you with great waters; [20] and I shall bring you down with those who go into the Pit, with the people of old time; and I shall set you in the earth's lowest parts, in places ruined from days of old, with ones who go to the Pit, so that you have no inhabitants; but I gave glory in the land of the living—

13 יָשִׂימוּ׃ וְהִשְׁבַּתִּי הֲמוֹן שִׁירָיִךְ וְקוֹל כִּנּוֹרַיִךְ לֹא יִשָּׁמַע
be shall not your the and your the will I And shall they
heard harps of sound ;songs of noise cease make .set

14 עוֹד׃ וּנְתַתִּיךְ לִצְחִיחַ סֶלַע מִשְׁטַח חֲרָמִים תִּהְיֶה לֹא
not you nets spreading A .rock a like will I And any
;be shall of place shining you make .more

תִבָּנֶה עוֹד כִּי אֲנִי יְהוָה דִּבַּרְתִּי נְאֻם אֲדֹנָי יְהוִה׃
.Jehovah the states have Jehovah I for any shall you
Lord ,spoken ;more built be

15 כֹּה אָמַר אֲדֹנָי יְהוִה לְצוֹר הֲלֹא ׀ מִקּוֹל מַפַּלְתֵּךְ בֶּאֱנֹק
when ,fall your the at Shall to Jehovah the says Thus
groan of sound not :Tyre Lord

16 חָלָל בֵּהָרֵג הֶרֶג בְּתוֹכֵךְ יִרְעֲשׁוּ הָאִיִּים׃ וְיָרְדוּ מֵעַל
from shall Then the shake your in the when the
down come ?coastlands ,midst slaughter occurs slain

כִּסְאוֹתָם כֹּל נְשִׂיאֵי הַיָּם וְהֵסִירוּ אֶת־מְעִילֵיהֶם וְאֶת־בִּגְדֵי
garments and ,robes their lay and the the all their
aside sea of rulers thrones

רִקְמָתָם יִפְשֹׁטוּ חֲרָדוֹת ׀ יִלְבָּשׁוּ עַל־הָאָרֶץ יֵשֵׁבוּ וְחָרְדוּ
shall and they the on shall They (with) .off strip their
tremble ,sit shall ground ,clothed be tremblings embroidered

17 לִרְגָעִים וְשָׁמְמוּ עָלָיִךְ׃ וְנָשְׂאוּ עָלַיִךְ קִינָה וְאָמְרוּ לָךְ אֵיךְ
How to say and a for they And .you at be and (every) at
,you ,lament you up take shall appalled ,moment

אָבַדְתְּ נוֹשֶׁבֶת מִיַּמִּים הָעִיר הַהֻלָּלָה אֲשֶׁר הָיְתָה חֲזָקָה
strong was which well- city the the by who are you
,praised ,seas lived ,perished

18 בַיָּם הִיא וְיֹשְׁבֶיהָ אֲשֶׁר־נָתְנוּ חִתִּיתָם לְכָל־יוֹשְׁבֶיהָ׃ עַתָּה
Now her on their put who her and she the in
.dwellers all terror ,dwellers ,sea

יֶחֶרְדוּ הָאִיִּן יוֹם מַפַּלְתֵּךְ וְנִבְהֲלוּ הָאִיִּים אֲשֶׁר־בַּיָּם
the by that the shall And .fall your the (in) the shall
sea (are) coasts troubled be of day coasts tremble

19 מִצֵּאתֵךְ׃ כִּי כֹה אָמַר אֲדֹנָי יְהוִה בְּתִתִּי אֹתָךְ עִיר
a you I When :Jehovah the says thus For your at
city make shall Lord .going

נֶחֱרֶבֶת כֶּעָרִים אֲשֶׁר לֹא־נוֹשָׁבוּ בְּהַעֲלוֹת עָלַיִךְ אֶת־תְּהוֹם
,deep the on shall I when have not that the like ,ruined
you up bring ;dwellers cities

20 וְכִסּוּךְ הַמַּיִם הָרַבִּים׃ וְהוֹרַדְתִּיךְ אֶת־יוֹרְדֵי בוֹר אֶל־עַם
the with the who those with shall I and ;great waters shall and
of people ,pit into go down you bring you cover

עוֹלָם וְהוֹשַׁבְתִּיךְ בְּאֶרֶץ תַּחְתִּיּוֹת כָּחֳרָבוֹת מֵעוֹלָם אֶת־
with days from places in lowest the in shall I and old
,old of ruined ,parts earth's you set ,time

יוֹרְדֵי בוֹר לְמַעַן לֹא תֵשֵׁבִי וְנָתַתִּי צְבִי בְּאֶרֶץ חַיִּים׃
the the in glory I but have you not so the who ones
—living of land gave dwellers that ,pit to go

[21] I will give you terrors; and you will not be. Though you are sought, yet you shall not be found any more forever, declares the Lord Jehovah.

21 בַּלָּהוֹת אֶתְּנֵךְ וְאֵינֵךְ וּתְבֻקְשִׁי וְלֹא־תִמָּצְאִי עוֹד לְעוֹלָם
,forever any shall you yet you Though you and will I terrors
more found be not ,sought are .be not will ;you give

נְאֻם אֲדֹנָי יְהוִה׃
.Jehovah the states
Lord

CAP. XXVII כז

CHAPTER 27

[1] And the word of Jehovah was to me, saying, [2] And you, son of man, take up a lament for Tyre. [3] And say to Tyre, O you who dwell at the entrances of the sea, a merchant of the peoples for many coastlands, thus says the Lord Jehovah: O Tyre, you have said, I (am) perfect of beauty. [4] In the heart of the seas are your borders; your builders have perfected your beauty. [5] They have made for you all your planks of fir-trees of Senir; they have taken a cedar from Lebanon to make a mast for you. [6] They have made your oars (of) the oaks of Bashan; they made your deck (with) ivory from the coasts of Chittim, daughter of Assyria. [7] Of fine linen, with embroidered work from Egypt, was what you spread out to be an ensign for you; purple and violet from the coasts of Elishah was your covering. [8] The residents of Sidon and Arvad were rowers to you. Your wise ones, O Tyre, were in you; they (were) your sailors. [9] The elders of Gebal and her wise men were with you, reinforcing your seams. All the ships of the sea and their seamen were with you, to exchange your merchandise. [10] Persia and Lud and Lydia were in your army, men of war (to) you; they hung the shield and the helmet in you; they gave your splendor. [11] The sons of Arvad and your army (were) on your walls all around; and warriors were

CHAPTER 27

1
2 וַיְהִי דְבַר־יְהוָה אֵלַי לֵאמֹר׃ וְאַתָּה בֶן־אָדָם שָׂא עַל־צֹר
Tyre for take ,man son ,you And ,saying ,me to Jehovah the And
up of of word was

3 קִינָה׃ וְאָמַרְתָּ לְצוֹר הַיֹּשֶׁבְתִּי עַל־מְבוֹאֹת יָם רֹכֶלֶת
mer- a the the at you O ,Tyre to say And a
of chant ,sea of entrances dwell who .lament

הָעַמִּים אֶל־אִיִּים רַבִּים כֹּה אָמַר אֲדֹנָי יְהוִה צוֹר אַתְּ
you O :Jehovah the says thus ,many coast- for the
,Tyre Lord lands peoples

4 אָמַרְתְּ אֲנִי כְּלִילַת יֹפִי׃ בְּלֵב יַמִּים גְּבוּלָיִךְ בֹּנַיִךְ כָּלְלוּ
have your your are the the in ,beauty perfect I have
perfected builders ;borders seas of heart of (am) ,said

5 יָפְיֵךְ׃ בְּרוֹשִׁים מִשְּׂנִיר בָּנוּ לָךְ אֵת כָּל־לֻחֹתָיִם אֶרֶז
a your all for They Senir of of your
cedar ;planks you made have fir-trees .beauty

6 מִלְּבָנוֹן לָקָחוּ לַעֲשׂוֹת תֹּרֶן עָלָיִךְ׃ אַלּוֹנִים מִבָּשָׁן עָשׂוּ
They Bashan of the (of) for mast a make to have they from
made have oaks .you taken Lebanon

7 מִשּׁוֹטָיִךְ קַרְשֵׁךְ עָשׂוּ־שֵׁן בַּת־אֲשֻׁרִים מֵאִיֵּי כִּתִּים׃ שֵׁשׁ
fine Of .Chittim the from of daughter (with) they your your
linen of coasts ,Assyria ,ivory made deck ;oars

בְּרִקְמָה מִמִּצְרַיִם הָיָה מִפְרָשֵׂךְ לִהְיוֹת לָךְ לְנֵס תְּכֵלֶת
purple a for be to you what was from em- with
;ensign you out spread Egypt work broidered

8 וְאַרְגָּמָן מֵאִיֵּי אֱלִישָׁה הָיָה מְכַסֵּךְ׃ יֹשְׁבֵי צִידוֹן וְאַרְוַד הָיוּ
were and Sidon resi- The your was Elishah the from and
Arvad of dents ,covering of coasts violet

9 שָׁטִים לָךְ חֲכָמַיִךְ צוֹר הָיוּ בָךְ הֵמָּה חֹבְלָיִךְ׃ זִקְנֵי גְבַל
Gebal The your they in were O wise Your to rowers
of elders .sailors (were) ,you ,Tyre ,ones .you

וַחֲכָמֶיהָ הָיוּ בָךְ מַחֲזִיקֵי בִּדְקֵךְ כָּל־אֳנִיּוֹת הַיָּם וּמַלָּחֵיהֶם
their and the the All your rein- with were her and
seamen sea of ships .seams forcing you men wise

10 הָיוּ בָךְ לַעֲרֹב מַעֲרָבֵךְ׃ פָּרַס וְלוּד וּפוּט הָיוּ בְחֵילֵךְ
your in were and and Persia your to with were
,army Lydia Lud .merchandise exchange you

אַנְשֵׁי מִלְחַמְתֵּךְ מָגֵן וְכוֹבַע תִּלּוּ־בָךְ הֵמָּה נָתְנוּ הֲדָרֵךְ׃
your gave they in they the and the war men
.splendor ;you hung helmet shield ;you (to) of

11 בְּנֵי אַרְוַד וְחֵילֵךְ עַל־חוֹמוֹתַיִךְ סָבִיב וְגַמָּדִים בְּמִגְדְּלוֹתַיִךְ
your in towers and all walls your on your and Arvad The
warriors ,around (were) army of sons

in your towers. They hung their weapons on your walls all around; they have perfected your beauty. [12] Tarshish (was) your trader, from the multitude of (your) wealth; with silver, iron, tin, and lead, they gave for your wares. [13] Javan, Tubal, and Meshech, they (were) your merchants; they gave the souls of men and vessels of bronze for your goods. [14] From the house of Togarmah they gave horses and war-horses and mules for your wares. [15] The sons of Dedan (were) your merchants; many coastlands (were) the traffic of your hand. Tusks of ivory and ebony they brought as your gift. [16] Syria (was) your trader, from the multitude of your works, with emeralds, violet, and embroidered work, and fine linen, and coral, and rubies they gave for your wares. [17] Judah and the land of Israel, they (were) your merchants; with wheat (from) Minnith and Pannag, and honey and oil and balm they gave for your goods. [18] Damascus (was) your trader in the multitude of your works, from the multitude of all (your) wealth; in the wine of Helbon, and white wool. [19] And Dan and Javan going about gave for your wares; smooth iron, cassia, and cane were among your goods. [20] Dedan (was) your merchant in loose cloths for riding. [21] Arabia and all the princes of Kedar, they (were) traders of your hand, in lambs and rams and goats; in them (was) your trade. [22] The merchants of Sheba and Raamah, they (were) your merchants; with the chief of all the spices, and with every precious stone, and gold, they gave for your wares. [23] Haran, and Canneh, and Eden, the merchants of Sheba, Asshur, Chilmad (were) your merchants; they (were) your merchants in perfect things, in purple

הָיוּ שִׁלְטֵיהֶם תִּלּוּ עַל־חוֹמוֹתַיִךְ סָבִיב הֵמָּה כָּלְלוּ יָפְיֵךְ׃

your have they all walls your on They their .were
.beauty perfected ;around hung weapons

12 תַּרְשִׁישׁ סֹחַרְתֵּךְ מֵרֹב כָּל־הוֹן בְּכֶסֶף בַּרְזֶל בְּדִיל וְעוֹפֶרֶת

,lead and ,tin ,iron with (your) the from your Tarshish
,silver ;wealth of plenty trader (was)

13 נָתְנוּ עִזְבוֹנָיִךְ׃ יָוָן תֻּבַל וָמֶשֶׁךְ הֵמָּה רֹכְלָיִךְ בְּנֶפֶשׁ אָדָם

men the your they and Tubal ,Javan your they
of souls ;merchants (were) Meshech .wares for gave

14 וּכְלֵי נְחֹשֶׁת נָתְנוּ מַעֲרָבֵךְ׃ מִבֵּית תּוֹגַרְמָה סוּסִים

horses Togarmah the From your for they bronze and
of house .goods gave of vessels

15 וּפָרָשִׁים וּפְרָדִים נָתְנוּ עִזְבוֹנָיִךְ׃ בְּנֵי דְדָן רֹכְלַיִךְ אִיִּים

coast- your Dedan The your they mules and war- and
lands ;merchants (were) of sons .wares for gave horses

רַבִּים סְחֹרַת יָדֵךְ קַרְנוֹת שֵׁן וְהָובְנִים הֵשִׁיבוּ אֶשְׁכָּרֵךְ׃

your as they ebony and ivory Tusks your the many
.gift brought of .hand of traffic (were)

16 אֲרָם סֹחַרְתֵּךְ מֵרֹב מַעֲשָׂיִךְ בְּנֹפֶךְ אַרְגָּמָן וְרִקְמָה וּבוּץ

fine and em- and violet with your the from your Syria
,linen ,work broidered ,emeralds .works of plenty trader (was)

17 וְרָאמֹת וְכַדְכֹּד נָתְנוּ בְּעִזְבוֹנָיִךְ׃ יְהוּדָה וְאֶרֶץ יִשְׂרָאֵל

Israel the and Judah your for They and ,coral and
of land .wares gave rubies

הֵמָּה רֹכְלָיִךְ בְּחִטֵּי מִנִּית וּפַנַּג וּדְבַשׁ וָשֶׁמֶן וָצֹרִי נָתְנוּ

they and oil and and and (from) With your they
gave balm honey ,Pannag Minnith wheat .merchants (were)

18 מַעֲרָבֵךְ׃ דַּמֶּשֶׂק סֹחַרְתֵּךְ בְּרֹב מַעֲשַׂיִךְ מֵרֹב כָּל־הוֹן

(your) all the from your the in your Damascus your for
,wealth of plenty ,works of plenty trader (was) .goods

19 בְּיֵין חֶלְבּוֹן וְצֶמֶר צָחַר׃ וְדָן וְיָוָן מְאוּזָּל בְּעִזְבוֹנַיִךְ נָתָנוּ

;gave your for going and And .white and Helbon the in
wares about Javan Dan wool of wine

20 בַּרְזֶל עָשׁוֹת קִדָּה וְקָנֶה בְּמַעֲרָבֵךְ הָיָה׃ דְּדָן רֹכַלְתֵּךְ

your Dedan .were your among and ,cassia ,smooth iron
merchant (was) goods cane

21 בְּבִגְדֵי־חֹפֶשׁ לְרִכְבָּה׃ עֲרַב וְכָל־נְשִׂיאֵי קֵדָר הֵמָּה סֹחֲרֵי

traders they ,Kedar the and ,Arabia .riding for loose in
of (were) of princes all cloths

22 יָדֵךְ בְּכָרִים וְאֵילִם וְעַתּוּדִים בָּם סֹחֲרָיִךְ׃ רֹכְלֵי שְׁבָא

Sheba The your (was) in ,goats and rams and lambs in your
of merchants .trade them ,hand

וְרַעְמָה הֵמָּה רֹכְלָיִךְ בְּרֹאשׁ כָּל־בֹּשֶׂם וּבְכָל־אֶבֶן יְקָרָה

precious stone with and the all the with your they and
every spices of chief ;merchants (were) ,Raamah

23 וְזָהָב נָתְנוּ עִזְבוֹנָיִךְ׃ חָרָן וְכַנֵּה וָעֶדֶן רֹכְלֵי שְׁבָא אַשּׁוּר

Asshur ,Sheba the and and ,Haran your for they and
of merchants Eden Canneh .wares gave ,gold

24 כִּלְמַד רֹכַלְתֵּךְ׃ הֵמָּה רֹכְלַיִךְ בְמַכְלֻלִים בִּגְלוֹמֵי תְּכֵלֶת

purple cloth in perfect in your they your Chilmad
of ,things merchants (were) ;merchants (were)

cloths, and embroidered work, and in carpets of many colors, with tightly bound cords, and cedars among your merchandise. [25] The ships of Tarshish (were) the travelers of your goods. And you were filled and made very glorious in the heart of the seas. [26] Your rowers brought you into great waters; the east wind has broken you in the heart of the seas. [27] Your wealth and your wares, your goods, your seamen, and your sailors reinforcing your seams, and the traders of your goods, and all men of war to you, who (are) in you, and all your assembly which (is) in your midst, shall fall into the heart of the seas, in the day of your ruin. [28] The pasture lands will shake at the sound of the cry of your sailors. [29] And all who handle the oar shall come down from their ships, the seamen, all the sailors of the sea; on the land they shall stand, [30] and will make heard their voice against you, and shall cry bitterly, and shall throw dust on their heads; they shall wallow in the ashes. [31] And they shall be bald for you, and gird with sackcloth; and they shall weep for you with bitterness of soul, (with) a bitter wailing. [32] And they shall take up for you a lament (in) their mourning, and lament over you. Who (is) like Tyre, as her who is quiet in the midst of the sea? [33] When your wares went out from the seas, you satisfied many peoples. With the plenty of your riches and your goods, you enriched the kings of the earth. [34] At (this time) you are broken from the seas, by the depths of the waters; your goods and all your assembly in your midst have fallen. [35] All the residents of the coasts are appalled at you;

וְרִקְמָה וּבְגִנְזֵי בְּרֹמִים בַּחֲבָלִים חֲבֻשִׁים וַאֲרֻזִים

cedars and | tightly ,bound | cords with | ,colors many | in and of carpets | embroi- and work dered

25 בְּמַרְכֻלְתֵּךְ׃ אֳנִיּוֹת תַּרְשִׁישׁ שָׁרוֹתַיִךְ מַעֲרָבֵךְ וַתִּמָּלְאִי

you And filled were | .goods your | the (were) of travelers | Tarshish | The of ships | your among .merchandise

26 וַתִּכְבְּדִי מְאֹד בְּלֵב יַמִּים׃ בְּמַיִם רַבִּים הֱבִאוּךְ הַשָּׁטִים

rowers | brought have you | great | into waters | the .seas | the in of heart | very | made and glorious

27 אֹתָךְ רוּחַ הַקָּדִים שְׁבָרֵךְ בְּלֵב יַמִּים׃ הוֹנֵךְ וְעִזְבוֹנַיִךְ

your and ,wares | Your wealth | the .seas | the in of heart | has you broken | east | the wind | ;Your

מַעֲרָבֵךְ מַלָּחַיִךְ וְחֹבְלַיִךְ מַחֲזִיקֵי בִדְקֵךְ וְעֹרְבֵי מַעֲרָבֵךְ

your ,goods | the and of traders | your ,seams | rein- forcing | your and sailors | your ,seamen | your ,goods

וְכָל־אַנְשֵׁי מִלְחַמְתֵּךְ אֲשֶׁר־בָּךְ וּבְכָל־קְהָלֵךְ אֲשֶׁר בְּתוֹכֵךְ

your in ,midst | which (is) | your assembly | and all | in ,you | who (are) | war you to | men of | and all

28 יִפְּלוּ בְּלֵב יַמִּים בְּיוֹם מַפַּלְתֵּךְ׃ לְקוֹל זַעֲקַת חֹבְלָיִךְ

your sailors | the of cry | the at of sound | your .ruin | the in of day | the seas | the into of heart | shall fall

29 יִרְעֲשׁוּ מִגְרֹשׁוֹת׃ וְיָרְדוּ מֵאֳנִיּוֹתֵיהֶם כֹּל תֹּפְשֵׂי מָשׁוֹט

,oar the | who handle | all | their from ships | shall And come down | pasture The .lands | will shake

30 מַלָּחִים כֹּל חֹבְלֵי הַיָּם אֶל־הָאָרֶץ יַעֲמֹדוּ׃ וְהִשְׁמִיעוּ עָלַיִךְ

against you | will and make heard | shall they stand | the land | on | the ;sea | the of sailors | all | the seamen

בְּקוֹלָם וְיִזְעֲקוּ מָרָה וְיַעֲלוּ עָפָר עַל־רָאשֵׁיהֶם בָּאֵפֶר

the in ashes | their ;heads | on | dust | shall and throw | ,bitterly | shall and cry | their ,voice

31 יִתְפַּלָּשׁוּ׃ וְהִקְרִיחוּ אֵלַיִךְ קָרְחָה וְחָגְרוּ שַׂקִּים וּבָכוּ אֵלַיִךְ

for you | they and weep shall | with ;sackcloth | and gird | bald | you for | they And be shall | shall they .wallow

32 בְּמַר־נֶפֶשׁ מִסְפֵּד מָר׃ וְנָשְׂאוּ אֵלַיִךְ בְּנִיהֶם קִינָה וְקוֹנְנוּ

and lament | a lament | their (in) mourning | for you | they And up take shall | .bitter | a (with) wailing | soul | with of bitterness

33 עָלַיִךְ מִי כְצוֹר כְּדֻמָה בְּתוֹךְ הַיָּם׃ בְּצֵאת עִזְבוֹנַיִךְ מִיַּמִּים

from ,seas the | your wares | went When out | the ?sea | the in of midst | her as quiet is who | like ,Tyre (is) | Who :you | over

הִשְׂבַּעַתְּ עַמִּים רַבִּים בְּרֹב הוֹנַיִךְ וּמַעֲרָבַיִךְ הֶעֱשַׁרְתְּ מַלְכֵי־

kings the of | you enriched | your and ;goods | your riches | the With of plenty | .many peoples | you satisfied

34 אָרֶץ׃ עֵת נִשְׁבֶּרֶת מִיַּמִּים בְּמַעֲמַקֵּי־מָיִם מַעֲרָבֵךְ וְכָל־

all and | your goods | the ;waters | the by of depths | the from ,seas | are you broken | At (time this) | the .earth

35 קְהָלֵךְ בְּתוֹכֵךְ נָפָלוּ׃ כֹּל יֹשְׁבֵי הָאִיִּים שָׁמְמוּ עָלַיִךְ

,you at | are appalled | the coasts | resi- the of dents | All | have .fallen | your in midst | your assembly

and their kings are horribly terrified; (their) faces tremble. [36] The traders among the peoples hiss over you; you have become terrors. And you shall not be forever.

CHAPTER 28

[1] And the word of Jehovah was to me, saying, [2] Son of man, say to the ruler of Tyre, Thus says the Lord Jehovah, Because your heart is lifted up, and you have said, I (am) a god; I sit in the seat of gods, in the heart of the seas—yet you (are) a man, and not God, though you give your heart as the heart of gods— [3] Behold, you (are) wiser than Daniel; every (one of the) secret (things) are not hidden (to) you. [4] With your wisdom and with your understanding you have made riches for yourself, and have put gold and silvver into your treasuries. [5] By your great wisdom, by your trade you have multiplied your riches, and your heart is lifted up because of your riches. [6] Therefore, thus says the Lord Jehovah: Because you have given your heart as the heart of gods, [7] therefore, behold, I will bring on you awesome strangers (of) the nations. And they shall draw their swords against the beauty of your wisdom, and will profane your splendor. [8] They shall bring you to the Pit, and you shall die the deaths of the slain in the heart of the seas. [9] Will you still say, I (am) gods, before him who kills you? But you (are) a man, and not God, in the hand of him who kills you. [10] You shall die the deaths of the uncircumcised, by the hand of strangers. For I have spoken, says the Lord Jehovah.

[11] And the word of Jehovah was to me, saying, [12] Son of man, take up a lament over the king of Tyre, and say to him, Thus

36 וּמַלְכֵיהֶם שָׂעֲרוּ שַׂעַר רָעֲמוּ פָּנִים׃ סֹחֲרִים בָּעַמִּים שָׁרְקוּ
hiss the among The (their) tremble ;horribly are their and
peoples traders .faces terrified kings
עָלַיִךְ בַּלָּהוֹת הָיִית וְאֵינֵךְ עַד־עוֹלָם׃
.forever you And have you terrors over
be not shall .become ;you

CAP. XXVIII כח

CHAPTER 28

1
2 וַיְהִי דְבַר־יְהוָה אֵלַי לֵאמֹר׃ בֶּן־אָדָם אֱמֹר לִנְגִיד צֹר כֹּה
Thus ,Tyre the to say ,man Son ,saying ,me to Jehovah the And
of ruler of of word was
אָמַר ׀ אֲדֹנָי יֱהוִה יַעַן גָּבַהּ לִבְּךָ וַתֹּאמֶר אֵל אָנִי מוֹשַׁב
the in I a you and your is Because :Jehovah the says
of seat ,(am) god ,said have heart up lifted Lord
אֱלֹהִים יָשַׁבְתִּי בְּלֵב יַמִּים וְאַתָּה אָדָם וְלֹא־אֵל וַתִּתֵּן לִבְּךָ
your though ,God and a (are) you yet the the in sit I gods
heart give you not man —seas of heart
3 כְּלֵב אֱלֹהִים׃ הִנֵּה חָכָם אַתָּה מִדָּנִאֵל כָּל־סָתוּם לֹא
not secret every than you wiser ,Behold —gods the as
(things) (of one) ;Daniel (are) of heart
4 עֲמָמוּךָ׃ בְּחָכְמָתְךָ וּבִתְבוּנָתְךָ עָשִׂיתָ לְּךָ חָיִל וַתַּעַשׂ זָהָב
gold have and ,riches for have you your with and your With hidden are
put yourself made understanding wisdom .you (to)
5 וָכֶסֶף בְּאוֹצְרוֹתֶיךָ׃ בְּרֹב חָכְמָתְךָ בִּרְכֻלָּתְךָ הִרְבִּיתָ חֵילֶךָ
your have you your by your By your into and
,riches multiplied trade ,wisdom great .treasuries silver
6 וַיִּגְבַּהּ לְבָבְךָ בְּחֵילֶךָ׃ לָכֵן כֹּה אָמַר אֲדֹנָי יֱהוִה
:Jehovah the says thus Therefore of because your is and
Lord —riches your heart up lifted
7 יַעַן תִּתְּךָ אֶת־לְבָבְךָ כְּלֵב אֱלֹהִים׃ לָכֵן הִנְנִי מֵבִיא עָלֶיךָ
on will behold ,therefore ,gods the as your have you Be-
you bring I of heart heart given cause
זָרִים עָרִיצֵי גּוֹיִם וְהֵרִיקוּ חַרְבוֹתָם עַל־יְפִי חָכְמָתֶךָ וְחִלְּלוּ
will and your the against their they And the awe- strangers
profane ,wisdom of beauty swords draw shall .nations some
8 יִפְעָתֶךָ׃ לַשַּׁחַת יוֹרִדוּךָ וָמַתָּה מְמוֹתֵי חָלָל בְּלֵב יַמִּים׃
the the in the the you and shall They the to your
.seas of heart slain of deaths die shall ,you bring Pit .splendor
9 הֶאָמֹר תֹּאמַר אֱלֹהִים אָנִי לִפְנֵי הֹרְגֶךָ וְאַתָּה אָדָם וְלֹא־
and man a But who him before I gods ,say you Will
not (are) you ?you kills ,(am) still
10 אֵל בְּיַד מְחַלְלֶיךָ׃ מוֹתֵי עֲרֵלִים תָּמוּת בְּיַד־זָרִים כִּי אֲנִי
I For strangers' by shall You uncir- the the who him the in God
hand ,die cumcised of deaths .you kills of hand
11 דִבַּרְתִּי נְאֻם אֲדֹנָי יֱהוִה׃ וַיְהִי דְבַר־יְהוָה אֵלַי
to Jehovah the And .Jehovah the says have
,me of word was Lord ,spoken
12 לֵאמֹר׃ בֶּן־אָדָם שָׂא קִינָה עַל־מֶלֶךְ צוֹר וְאָמַרְתָּ לּוֹ כֹּה
Thus to say and Tyre the over a take ,man Son ,saying
,him of king lament up of

says the Lord Jehovah: You seal the measure, full of wisdom and perfect in beauty. [13] You have been in the garden of Eden; every precious stone (was) your covering, the ruby, the topaz, and the diamond, the beryl, the onyx, and the jaspers; the sapphire, the turquoise, and the emerald, and gold. The workmanship of your tabrets and of your pipes in you—in the day you were created, then were prepared. [14] You (were) the anointed cherub that covers, and I had put you in the holy height of God, (where) you were. You walked up and down in the midst of the stones of fire. [15] You were perfect in your ways from the day you were created, until iniquity was found in you. [16] By the multitude of your trade they filled your midst (with) violence, and you sinned. So I cast you profaned from the height of God, and I destroyed you, O covering cherub, from among the stones of fire. [17] Your heart was lifted up because of your beauty; you corrupted your wisdom because of your splendor. I have cast you to the ground. I will put you before kings, that they may see you. [18] By the host of your iniquities, by the iniquity of your trade, you have profaned your holy places; thus I brought a fire from your midst; it shall devour you, and I will give you for ashes on the earth, in the sight of all who see you. [19] All who know you among the peoples shall be appalled at you; you shall be terrors, and you will not be forever.

[20] And the word of Jehovah was to me, saying, [21] Son of man, set your face against Sidon and prophesy against her, [22] And say, Thus says the Lord Jehovah, Behold, I (am) against you, O Sidon, and I will be glorified in your midst. And they shall know that I (am) Jehovah, when I have done judgments in her, and shall be sanctified by her.

אָמַר אֲדֹנָי יְהוִה אַתָּה חוֹתֵם תָּכְנִית מָלֵא חָכְמָה וּכְלִיל
and wisdom full the seal You :Jehovah the says
in perfect of ,measure Lord

13 יֹפִי׃ בְּעֵדֶן גַּן־אֱלֹהִים הָיִיתָ כָּל־אֶבֶן יְקָרָה מְסֻכָתֶךָ אֹדֶם
the your precious stone every have You God the Eden in .beauty
,ruby ,covering (was) ;been of garden

פִּטְדָה וְיָהֲלֹם תַּרְשִׁישׁ שֹׁהַם וְיָשְׁפֵה סַפִּיר נֹפֶךְ וּבָרְקַת
the and tur- the the the and the the the and the
emerald ,quoise ,sapphire ,jaspers onyx ,beryl ,diamond ,topaz

וְזָהָב מְלֶאכֶת תֻּפֶּיךָ וּנְקָבֶיךָ בָּךְ בְּיוֹם הִבָּרַאֲךָ כּוֹנָנוּ׃
were then were you the in in of and your work- The and
.prepared created day —you pipes your tabrets of manship .gold

14 אַתְּ־כְּרוּב מִמְשַׁח הַסּוֹכֵךְ וּנְתַתִּיךָ בְּהַר קֹדֶשׁ אֱלֹהִים הָיִיתָ
(where) God holy the in I and that anointed the You
.were you of height you put had ,covers cherub (were)

15 בְּתוֹךְ אַבְנֵי־אֵשׁ הִתְהַלָּכְתָּ׃ תָּמִים אַתָּה בִּדְרָכֶיךָ מִיּוֹם
the from your in You were walked You fire the the in
day ways perfect .down and up of stones of midst

16 הִבָּרְאָךְ עַד־נִמְצָא עַוְלָתָה בָּךְ׃ בְּרֹב רְכֻלָּתְךָ מָלוּ תוֹכְךָ
your they your the By in iniquity was until were you
midst filled trade of plenty .you found ,created

חָמָס וַתֶּחֱטָא וָאֲחַלֶּלְךָ מֵהַר אֱלֹהִים וָאַבֶּדְךָ כְּרוּב הַסֹּכֵךְ
,covering O I and ,God the from cast I So you and (with)
cherub ,you destroyed of height profaned you .sinned ,violence

17 מִתּוֹךְ אַבְנֵי־אֵשׁ׃ גָּבַהּ לִבְּךָ בְּיָפְיֶךָ שִׁחַתָּ חָכְמָתְךָ עַל־
because your cor- you your for Your was .fire the from
of wisdom rupted ;beauty heart up lifted of stones among

יִפְעָתֶךָ עַל־אֶרֶץ הִשְׁלַכְתִּיךָ לִפְנֵי מְלָכִים נְתַתִּיךָ לְרַאֲוָה
they that will I kings before have I the to your
see may ,you put .you cast ground .splendor

18 בָךְ׃ מֵרֹב עֲוֹנֶיךָ בְּעֶוֶל רְכֻלָּתְךָ חִלַּלְתָּ מִקְדָּשֶׁיךָ וָאוֹצִא־
I thus holy your have you your the by your the By .you
brought ;places profaned ,trade of iniquity ,iniquities of host

אֵשׁ מִתּוֹכְךָ הִיא אֲכָלַתְךָ וָאֶתֶּנְךָ לְאֵפֶר עַל־הָאָרֶץ לְעֵינֵי
the in the on for will I and shall it your from a
of sight earth ashes you give ,you devour ;midst fire

19 כָּל־רֹאֶיךָ׃ כָּל־יוֹדְעֶיךָ בָּעַמִּים שָׁמְמוּ עָלֶיךָ בַּלָּהוֹת הָיִיתָ
shall you terrors at be shall the among who All see who all
,be ;you appalled peoples you know .you

20 וְאֵינְךָ עַד־עוֹלָם׃ וַיְהִי דְבַר־יְהוָה אֵלַי לֵאמֹר׃
,saying ,me to Jehovah the And .forever you and
of word was be will not

21 22 בֶּן־אָדָם שִׂים פָּנֶיךָ אֶל־צִידוֹן וְהִנָּבֵא עָלֶיהָ׃ וְאָמַרְתָּ כֹּה
Thus ,say And against and Sidon against your set ,man Son
.her prophesy face of

אָמַר אֲדֹנָי יְהוִה הִנְנִי עָלַיִךְ צִידוֹן וְנִכְבַּדְתִּי בְּתוֹכֵךְ וְיָדְעוּ
they And your in will I and O against ,Behold :Jehovah the says
know shall .midst glorified be ,Sidon ,you (am) I Lord

23 כִּי־אֲנִי יְהוָה בַּעֲשׂוֹתִי בָהּ שְׁפָטִים וְנִקְדַּשְׁתִּי בָהּ׃ וְשִׁלַּחְתִּי־
will I And by be shall and judgments in I when ,Jehovah I that
send .her sanctified her done have (am)

[23] And I will send a plague into her, and blood into her streets. And the slain will fall in her midst by the sword, on her from all around. And they shall know that I (am) Jehovah.

[24] And there will not be a pricking brier or a painful thorn to the house of Israel any more, from all who surround them, who hate them. And they shall know that I (am) the Lord Jehovah. [25] Thus says the Lord Jehovah: When I have gathered the house of Israel from the peoples of whom they are dispersed among them, and have been sanctified in them in the sight of the nations, then they shall dwell on their land which I have given to My servant Jacob. [26] And they shall dwell in it securely, and shall build houses and plant vineyards. Yes, they shall dwell securely, when I have done judgments on all those who hate them round about them. And they shall know that I (am) Jehovah their God.

בָּהּ דֶּבֶר וָדָם בְּחוּצוֹתֶיהָ וְנִפְלַל חָלָל בְּתוֹכָהּ בְּחֶרֶב
the by her in the will And her into and a into
sword midst slain fall .streets blood ,plague her

24 עָלֶיהָ מִסָּבִיב וְיָדְעוּ כִּי־אֲנִי יְהוָה׃ וְלֹא־יִהְיֶה עוֹד לְבֵית
the to any will And .Jehovah I that they And all from on
of house more be not (am) know shall .around her

יִשְׂרָאֵל סִלּוֹן מַמְאִיר וְקוֹץ מַכְאִב מִכֹּל סְבִיבֹתָם הַשָּׁאטִים
hate who surround who from painful a or pricking brier a Israel
,them all thorn

25 אוֹתָם וְיָדְעוּ כִּי אֲנִי אֲדֹנָי יְהוִה׃ כֹּה־אָמַר אֲדֹנָי
the says Thus .Jehovah the I that they And .them
Lord Lord (am) know shall

יְהוִה בְּקַבְּצִי ׀ אֶת־בֵּית יִשְׂרָאֵל מִן־הָעַמִּים אֲשֶׁר נָפֹצוּ
are they of the from Israel the have I When Jeho-
dispersed whom peoples of house gathered :vah

בָם וְנִקְדַּשְׁתִּי בָם לְעֵינֵי הַגּוֹיִם וְיָשְׁבוּ עַל־אַדְמָתָם אֲשֶׁר
which their on they then the the in in have and among
land dwell shall ,nations of sight them sanctified been ,them

26 נָתַתִּי לְעַבְדִּי לְיַעֲקֹב׃ וְיָשְׁבוּ עָלֶיהָ לָבֶטַח וּבָנוּ בָתִּים
houses shall and securely it in they And .Jacob My to have I
build dwell shall servant given

וְנָטְעוּ כְרָמִים וְיָשְׁבוּ לָבֶטַח בַּעֲשׂוֹתִי שְׁפָטִים בְּכֹל הַשָּׁאטִים
who those on judgments I when securely they ,Yes .vineyards and
hate all done have ,dwell shall plant

אֹתָם מִסְּבִיבוֹתָם וְיָדְעוּ כִּי אֲנִי יְהוָה אֱלֹהֵיהֶם׃
their Jehovah I that they And about round them
.God (am) know shall .them

CAP. XXIX כט

CHAPTER 29

CHAPTER 29

[1] In the tenth year, in the tenth (month), in the twelfth of the month, the word of Jehovah was to me, saying, [2] Son of man, set your face against Pharaoh king of Egypt, and prophesy against him and against Egypt, all of it. [3] Speak and say, Thus says the Lord Jehovah: Behold, I (am) against you, Pharaoh king of Egypt, great monster who lies in the midst of his rivers, who has said, My river (is) mine, and I have made it. [4] But I will put hooks in your jaws, and I will cause to stick to your scales the fish of your rivers; and I will bring you up from amidst your rivers, and all the

1 בַּשָּׁנָה הָעֲשִׂרִית בָּעֲשִׂרִי בִּשְׁנֵים עָשָׂר לַחֹדֶשׁ הָיָה דְבַר־
the was the of (day) the in the in ,tenth the year In
of word ,month twelfth ,(month) tenth

2 יְהוָה אֵלַי לֵאמֹר׃ בֶּן־אָדָם שִׂים פָּנֶיךָ עַל־פַּרְעֹה מֶלֶךְ
king Pharaoh against your set ,man Son ,saying to Jehovah
of face of ,me

3 מִצְרַיִם וְהִנָּבֵא עָלָיו וְעַל־מִצְרַיִם כֻּלָּהּ׃ דַּבֵּר וְאָמַרְתָּ
,say and Speak .it of all ,Egypt and against and ,Egypt
against him prophesy

כֹּה־אָמַר ׀ אֲדֹנָי יְהוִה הִנְנִי עָלֶיךָ פַּרְעֹה מֶלֶךְ־מִצְרַיִם
,Egypt king Pharaoh against ,Behold :Jehovah the says Thus
of ,you (am) I Lord

הַתַּנִּים הַגָּדוֹל הָרֹבֵץ בְּתוֹךְ יְאֹרָיו אֲשֶׁר אָמַר לִי יְאֹרִי
My mine has who his the in who great monster
river (is) ,said ,rivers of midst lies

4 וַאֲנִי עֲשִׂיתִנִי׃ וְנָתַתִּי חַחִיים בִּלְחָיֶיךָ וְהִדְבַּקְתִּי דְגַת־
the will I and your in hooks I But made have and
of fish stick to cause ,jaws put will .it I

יְאֹרֶיךָ בְּקַשְׂקְשֹׂתֶיךָ וְהַעֲלִיתִיךָ מִתּוֹךְ יְאֹרֶיךָ וְאֵת כָּל־
all and your from will I and your to your
,rivers amidst up you bring ,scales rivers

fish of your rivers shall stick to your scales. [5] And I will leave you (to) the wilderness, you and all the fish of your rivers; you shall fall on the open field; you shall not be removed or gathered. I have given you to the beasts of the field and to the birds of the heavens for food. [6] And all the inhabitants of Egypt shall know that I (am) Jehovah, because they have been a staff of reed to the house of Israel. [7] When they seized you by your hand, you broke and tore off all their shoulder. And when they leaned on you, you shattered and made all their loins stand.

[8] Therefore thus says the Lord Jehovah: Behold, I will bring on you a sword and will cut off from you man and beast. And the land of Egypt shall become for a desolation and a waste; and they shall know that I (am) Jehovah, because he has said, The River is mine, and I have made it. [10] Therefore, behold, I (am) against you and against your rivers; and I will give the land of Egypt for an utter waste (and) a desolation, from Migdol (to) Syene, even to the border of Ethiopia. [11] The foot of man shall not pass through it; and the foot of beast shall not pass through it; and you shall not dwell forty years. [12] And I will make the land of Egypt a desolation in the midst of the lands that are desolate; and her cities shall be desolate among the wasted cities forty years. And I will disperse Egypt among the nations, and sow them among the lands.

[13] For thus says the Lord Jehovah: At the end of forty years I will gather Egypt from the peoples

5 דְּגַת יְאֹרֶיךָ בְּקַשְׂקְשֹׂתֶיךָ תִּדְבָּק׃ וּנְטַשְׁתִּיךָ הַמִּדְבָּרָה
the will I And .stick shall your to your the
,wilderness (to) you leave scales rivers of fish

אוֹתְךָ וְאֵת כָּל־דְּגַת יְאֹרֶיךָ עַל־פְּנֵי הַשָּׂדֶה תִּפּוֹל לֹא
not shall you field the on your the all and you
.fall open ;rivers of fish

תֵאָסֵף וְלֹא תִקָּבֵץ לְחַיַּת הָאָרֶץ וּלְעוֹף הַשָּׁמַיִם נְתַתִּיךָ
have I the the to and the the to .gathered or shall You
you given heavens of birds field of beasts removed be

6 לְאָכְלָה׃ וְיָדְעוּ כָּל־יֹשְׁבֵי מִצְרַיִם כִּי אֲנִי יְהוָה יַעַן הֱיוֹתָם
have they be- ,Jehovah I that Egypt the all shall And for
been cause (am) of dwellers know .food

7 מִשְׁעֶנֶת קָנֶה לְבֵית יִשְׂרָאֵל׃ בְּתָפְשָׂם בְּךָ בַכַּפְּךָ תֵּרוֹץ
you your by you they When .Israel the to reed staff a
broke ,hand seized of house of

וּבָקַעְתָּ לָהֶם כָּל־כָּתֵף וּבְהִשָּׁעֲנָם עָלֶיךָ תִּשָּׁבֵר וְהַעֲמַדְתָּ
made and shat- you on they when And the all to tore and
stand tered ,you leaned .shoulder them off

8 לָהֶם כָּל־מָתְנָיִם׃ לָכֵן כֹּה אָמַר אֲדֹנָי יְהוִה הִנְנִי
,Behold :Jehovah the says thus Therefore .loins the all to
I Lord them

9 מֵבִיא עָלַיִךְ חֶרֶב וְהִכְרַתִּי מִמֵּךְ אָדָם וּבְהֵמָה׃ וְהָיְתָה
shall And and man from cut and sword a on will
become .beast you off you bring

אֶרֶץ־מִצְרַיִם לִשְׁמָמָה וְחָרְבָּה וְיָדְעוּ כִּי־אֲנִי יְהוָה יַעַן
be- ,Jehovah I that they and a and a for Egypt the
cause (am) know shall ;waste desolation of land

10 אָמַר יְאֹר לִי וַאֲנִי עֲשִׂיתִי׃ לָכֵן הִנְנִי אֵלֶיךָ וְאֶל־יְאֹרֶיךָ
your and against ,Behold There- made have and mine The has he
,rivers against you (am) I ,fore .(it) I (is) River ,said

וְנָתַתִּי אֶת־אֶרֶץ מִצְרַיִם לְחָרְבוֹת חֹרֶב שְׁמָמָה מִמִּגְדֹּל
from a (and) utter an for Egypt the I and
Migdol ,desolation waste of land give will

11 סְוֵנֵה וְעַד־גְּבוּל כּוּשׁ׃ לֹא תַעֲבָר־בָּהּ רֶגֶל אָדָם וְרֶגֶל
the and ;man the it pass shall Not .Ethiopia the even (to)
of foot of foot through of border to ,Syene

12 בְּהֵמָה לֹא תַעֲבָר־בָּהּ וְלֹא תֵשֵׁב אַרְבָּעִים שָׁנָה׃ וְנָתַתִּי
I And .years forty shall you and ;it pass shall not beast
make will dwell not through

אֶת־אֶרֶץ מִצְרַיִם שְׁמָמָה בְּתוֹךְ ׀ אֲרָצוֹת נְשַׁמּוֹת וְעָרֶיהָ
her and are that the the in a Egypt the
cities ;desolate lands of midst desolation of land

בְּתוֹךְ עָרִים מָחֳרָבוֹת תִּהְיֶיןָ שְׁמָמָה אַרְבָּעִים שָׁנָה וַהֲפִצֹתִי
will I And .years forty desolate be shall wasted the among
disperse cities

13 אֶת־מִצְרַיִם בַּגּוֹיִם וְזֵרִיתִים בָּאֲרָצוֹת׃ כִּי כֹה אָמַר
says thus For the among sow and the among Egypt
.lands them nations

אֲדֹנָי יְהוִה מִקֵּץ אַרְבָּעִים שָׁנָה אֲקַבֵּץ אֶת־מִצְרַיִם מִן
from Egypt will I years forty the At :Jehovah the
gather of end Lord

where they are scattered there. [14] And I will return the captivity of Egypt and will make them return (to) the land of Pathros, to the land of their origin. And they shall be a lowly kingdom there. [15] It shall be the lowest of the kingdoms, and shall not lift itself any more above the nations. And I will diminish them so that they will not rule over the nations. [16] And it shall not be any more as confidence for the house of Israel, recalling the iniquity of their turning after them. And they shall know that I (am) Jehovah.

[17] And it was, in the twenty-seventh year, in the first (month), in the first of the month, the word of Jehovah was to me, saying, [18] Son of man, Nebuchchadnezzar king of Babylon caused his army to serve a great service against Tyre. Every head was made bald, and every shoulder was rubbed bare. Yet there was no hire to him or to his army from Tyre, for the service that he had served against it. [19] Therefore, thus says the Lord Jehovah: Behold, I will give to Nebuchadnezzar king of Babylon the land of Egypt. And he shall carry her host and spoil her spoil, and seize her plunder. And it shall be hire for his army. [20] For his labor which he served against it, I have given him the land of Egypt, because they worked for Me, declares the Lord Jehovah.

[21] In that day I will make bud a horn to the house of Israel, and I will give to you the opening of the mouth in their midst. And they shall know that I (am) Jehovah.

14 העמים אשר־נפצו שמה׃ ושבתי את־שבות מצרים
,Egypt the will I And .there were they where the
of captivity return scattered peoples

והשבתי אתם ארץ פתרוס על־ארץ מכורתם והיו שם
there they And their the to ,Pathros the (to) them will and
be shall .origin of land of land return make

15 ממלכה שפלה׃ מן־הממלכות תהיה שפלה ולא־
and the shall It the of .lowly a
not lowest be kingdoms kingdom

תתנשא עוד על־הגוים והמעטתים לבלתי רדות בגוים׃
the over will they that so will I And the above any lift shall
.nations rule not them lessen nations more itself

16 ולא יהיה־עוד לבית ישראל למבטח מזכיר עון בפנותם
turning their the recalling as Israel the for any shall it And
of iniquity ,confidence of house more be not

17 אחריהם וידעו כי אני אדני יהוה׃ ויהי בעשרים
the in it And .Jehovah the I that they And after
twenty- ,was Lord (am) know shall .them

ושבע שנה בראשון באחד לחדש היה דבר־יהוה אלי
to Jehovah the was the of the in the in ,year seventh
,me of word ,month first ,(month) first

18 לאמר׃ בן־אדם נבוכדראצר מלך־בבל העביד את־חילו
his caused Babylon king Nebuchadnezzar ,man Son ,saying
army serve to of of

עבדה גדולה אל־צר כל־ראש מקרח וכל־כתף מרוטה
rubbed was shoulder and was head Every .Tyre against great a
.bare every ,bald made service

ושכר לא־היה לו ולחילו מצר על־העבדה אשר־עבד
had he that the for from to or to there not Yet
served service ,Tyre army his him was wages

19 עליה׃ לכן כה אמר אדני יהוה הנני נתן לנבוכדראצר
Nebuchadnezzar to will ,Behold Jeho- the says thus Therefore against
give I :vah Lord .it

מלך־בבל את־ארץ מצרים ונשא המנה ושלל שללה
her and her he And .Egypt the Babylon king
,spoil spoil host carry shall of land of

20 ובזז בזה והיתה שכר לחילו׃ פעלתו אשר־עבד בה נתתי
have I against he which his For his for wages it And plun- her and
given ,it served labor .army be shall .der seize

לו את־ארץ מצרים אשר עשו לי נאם אדני יהוה׃ ביום
In .Jehovah the states for they because ,Egypt the him
day Lord ,Me worked of land

21 ההוא אצמיח קרן לבית ישראל ולך אתן פתחון־פה
the the will I to and ,Israel the to horn a will I that
mouth of opening give you of house bud make

בתוכם וידעו כי־אני יהוה׃
.Jehovah I that they And their in
(am) know shall .midst

CHAPTER 30

[1] And the word of Jehovah was to me, saying, [2] Son of man, prophesy and say, Thus says the Lord Jehovah: Howl, Alas for the day! [3] For the day (is) near, even the day of Jehovah (is) near, a day of clouds; it shall be the time of the nation. [4] And the sword shall come on Egypt, and anguish shall be in Ethiopia, when the slain shall fall in Egypt, and they shall take her host; and her foundations shall be razed. [5] Ethiopia, and Lydia, and Lud, and all the mixed people; and Chub, and the sons of the land of the covenant with them, shall fall by the sword.

[6] Thus says Jehovah: Even those leaning on Egypt shall fall, and the pride of her power go down. From Migdol to Syene they shall fall with her by the sword, declares the Lord Jehovah. [7] And they will be ruined amidst the wasted lands; and his cities shall be in the midst of the desolated cities. [8] And they shall know that I (am) Jehovah, when I set a fire in Egypt, and all her helpers shall be crushed. [9] In that day messengers shall go out from before Me in ships, to terrify the confident Ethiopia, and anguish shall be on them, as in the day of Egypt; for behold it is coming.

[10] Thus says the Lord Jehovah: I will make the multitude of Egypt cease by the hand of Nebuchadnezzar king of Babylon. [11] He and his people with him, awesome of the nations, shall be brought to corrupt the land. And they shall draw their swords against Egypt and fill the land (with) the slain. [12] And I will make the rivers dry land, and sell

CAP. XXX ל

CHAPTER 30

1 2 וַיְהִי דְבַר־יְהוָה אֵלַי לֵאמֹר׃ בֶּן־אָדָם הִנָּבֵא וְאָמַרְתָּ כֹּה
Thus ,say and prophesy ,man Son ,saying to Jehovah the And
of ,me of word was

3 אָמַר אֲדֹנָי יֱהוִה הֵילִילוּ הָהּ לַיּוֹם׃ כִּי־קָרוֹב יוֹם וְקָרוֹב
(is) even the (is) For the Alas ,Howl :Jehovah the says
near ,day near !day (for) Lord

4 יוֹם לַיהוָה יוֹם עָנָן עֵת גּוֹיִם יִהְיֶה׃ וּבָאָה חֶרֶב בְּמִצְרַיִם
,Egypt on the shall And shall it the the ;clouds a of the
sword come .be nation of time of day Jehovah day

וְהָיְתָה חַלְחָלָה בְּכוּשׁ בִּנְפֹל חָלָל בְּמִצְרָיִם וְלָקְחוּ הֲמוֹנָהּ
her they and ,Egypt in the when in anguish shall and
;host take shall slain fall shall ,Ethiopia be

5 וְנֶהֶרְסוּ יְסוֹדוֹתֶיהָ׃ כּוּשׁ וּפוּט וְלוּד וְכָל־הָעֶרֶב וְכוּב וּבְנֵי
the and and mixed the and and and ,Ethiopia foun- her shall and
of sons ,Chub ,people all ,Lud ,Lydia .dations razed be

6 אֶרֶץ הַבְּרִית אִתָּם בַּחֶרֶב יִפֹּלוּ׃ כֹּה אָמַר יְהוָה
:Jehovah says Thus shall the by with the the
.fall sword them covenant of land

וְנָפְלוּ סֹמְכֵי מִצְרַיִם וְיָרַד גְּאוֹן עֻזָּהּ מִמִּגְדֹּל סְוֵנֵה בַּחֶרֶב
the by to Migdol From her the go and ,Egypt those shall Even
sword Syene .power of pride down on leaning fall

7 יִפְּלוּ־בָהּ נְאֻם אֲדֹנָי יֱהוִה׃ וְנָשַׁמּוּ בְּתוֹךְ אֲרָצוֹת נְשַׁמּוֹת
the lands amidst they And .Jehovah the states with they
,wasted ruined be will Lord her fall shall

8 וְעָרָיו בְּתוֹךְ־עָרִים נַחֲרָבוֹת תִּהְיֶינָה׃ וְיָדְעוּ כִּי־אֲנִי יְהוָה
,Jehovah I that they And .be shall the cities the in his and
(am) know shall desolated of midst cities

9 בְּתִתִּי־אֵשׁ בְּמִצְרַיִם וְנִשְׁבְּרוּ כָּל־עֹזְרֶיהָ׃ בַּיּוֹם הַהוּא
that day In her all shall and ,Egypt in a I when
.helpers crushed be fire set

יֵצְאוּ מַלְאָכִים מִלְּפָנַי בַּצִּים לְהַחֲרִיד אֶת־כּוּשׁ בֶּטַח
con- the terrify to in before from messengers go shall
fident Ethiopia ships Me out

וְהָיְתָה חַלְחָלָה בָהֶם כְּיוֹם מִצְרַיִם כִּי הִנֵּה בָּאָה׃
is it ,behold for ;Egypt in as on anguish shall and
.coming of day the ,them be

10 כֹּה אָמַר אֲדֹנָי יֱהוִה וְהִשְׁבַּתִּי אֶת־הֲמוֹן מִצְרַיִם. בְּיַד
by Egypt multi- the will I :Jehovah the says Thus
hand of tude cease make Lord

11 נְבוּכַדְרֶאצַּר מֶלֶךְ־בָּבֶל׃ הוּא וְעַמּוֹ אִתּוֹ עָרִיצֵי גוֹיִם
the awe- with his and He .Babylon king ,Nebuchadnezzar's
,nations of some ,him people of

מוּבָאִים לְשַׁחֵת הָאָרֶץ וְהֵרִיקוּ חַרְבוֹתָם עַל־מִצְרַיִם
Egypt against their they And the corrupt to be shall
swords draw shall .land brought

12 וּמָלְאוּ אֶת־הָאָרֶץ חָלָל׃ וְנָתַתִּי יְאֹרִים חָרָבָה וּמָכַרְתִּי
sell and dry the I And (with) the fill and
,land rivers make will .slain the land

the land into the hand of evil ones. And I will waste the land, and her fullness, by the hand of strangers. I Jehovah have spoken.

[13] Thus says the Lord Jehovah: I will also destroy the idols, and I will make vanities cease from Noph. And there shall not any longer be a prince of the land of Egypt. And I will put fear in the land of Egypt. [14] And I will make Pathros desolate, and will set a fire in Zoan, and will do judgments in Thebes. [15] And I will pour my fury on Sin, the strength of Egypt. And I will cut off the multitude of Thebes. [16] And I will set a fire in Egypt; Sin shall greatly anguish; and Thebes shall be broken through; and Noph (shall have) daily woes; the young men of Aven and Pibeseth shall fall by the sword; and they shall go into captivity. [18] At Tehaphnehes the day will be held back, when I shatter there the yokes of Egypt. And the pride of her strength shall cease in her; a cloud shall cover her; and her daughters shall go into captivity. [19] And I will do judgments in Egypt. And they shall know that I (am) Jehovah.

[20] And it was, in the eleventh year, in the first (month) in the seventh of the month, the word of Jehovah was to me, saying, [21] Son of man, I have shattered the arm of Pharaoh king of Egypt. And behold, it shall not be bound up to give healing, to set a bandage to bind it, to make it strong to handle the sword. [22] Therefore, thus says the Lord Jehovah: Behold, I (am) against Pharaoh king of Egypt, and I will shatter his arms, the strong one, and the shattered one. And I will cause the sword to fall

אֶת־הָאָרֶץ בְּיַד־רָעִים וַהֲשִׁמֹּתִי אֶרֶץ וּמְלֹאָהּ בְּיַד־זָרִים
.strangers the by hand | her and fullness | the ,land | will I And waste | evil .ones | the into of hand | the land

13 אֲנִי יְהוָה דִּבַּרְתִּי׃ כֹּה־אָמַר אֲדֹנָי יְהוִה וְהַאֲבַדְתִּי
also will I destroy | :Jehovah | the Lord | says Thus | have .spoken | Jehovah | I

גִלּוּלִים וְהִשְׁבַּתִּי אֱלִילִים מִנֹּף וְנָשִׂיא מֵאֶרֶץ־מִצְרַיִם לֹא
not | Egypt | the of of land | a And prince | from .Noph | vanities | will I and cease make | the idols

14 יִהְיֶה־עוֹד וְנָתַתִּי יִרְאָה בְּאֶרֶץ מִצְרָיִם׃ וַהֲשִׁמֹּתִי אֶת־
will I And desolate make | .Egypt | the in of land | fear | I And put will | any be shall .longer

15 פַּתְרוֹס וְנָתַתִּי אֵשׁ בְּצֹעַן וְעָשִׂיתִי שְׁפָטִים בְּנֹא׃ וְשָׁפַכְתִּי
will I And pour | in .Thebes | judgments | will and do | ,Zoan in | a fire | will and set | ,Pathros

16 חֲמָתִי עַל־סִין מָעוֹז מִצְרָיִם וְהִכְרַתִּי אֶת־הֲמוֹן נֹא׃ וְנָתַתִּי
I And set will | .Thebes | the of multitude | will I And off cut | .Egypt | the of strength | ,Sin | on | My fury

אֵשׁ בְּמִצְרַיִם חוּל תָּחִיל סִין וְנֹא תִּהְיֶה לְהִבָּקֵעַ וְנֹף צָרֵי
woes and Noph | broken ,through | be shall | and Thebes | Sin | shall anguish | greatly | :Egypt in | a fire

17 יוֹמָם׃ בַּחוּרֵי אָוֶן וּפִי־בֶסֶת בַּחֶרֶב יִפֹּלוּ וְהֵנָּה בַּשְּׁבִי תֵלַכְנָה׃
.go shall | into captivity | and they | shall ;fall | the by sword | and Pibeseth | Aven | young the of men | .daily

18 וּבִתְחַפְנְחֵס חָשַׂךְ הַיּוֹם בְּשִׁבְרִי־שָׁם אֶת־מֹטוֹת מִצְרַיִם
.Egypt | the of yokes | there | I when shatter | the ,day | be will back held | At Tehaphnehes

וְנִשְׁבַּת־בָּהּ גְּאוֹן עֻזָּהּ הִיא עָנָן יְכַסֶּנָּה וּבְנוֹתֶיהָ בַּשְּׁבִי
into captivity | her and daughters | shall ,cover | a cloud | her | her ;strength | the of pride | in her | shall And cease

19 תֵּלַכְנָה׃ וְעָשִׂיתִי שְׁפָטִים בְּמִצְרָיִם וְיָדְעוּ כִּי־אֲנִי יְהוָה׃
.Jehovah | I (am) | that | they And know shall | .Egypt in | judgments | I And do will | .go shall

20 וַיְהִי בְּאַחַת עֶשְׂרֵה שָׁנָה בָּרִאשׁוֹן בְּשִׁבְעָה לַחֹדֶשׁ הָיָה
was | the of ,month | the in seventh | the in ,(month) first | year | the in eleventh | And ,was it

21 דְבַר־יְהוָה אֵלַי לֵאמֹר׃ בֶּן־אָדָם אֶת־זְרוֹעַ פַּרְעֹה מֶלֶךְ־
king of | Pharaoh | the of arm | ,man Son of | ,saying | ,me to | Jehovah | the of word

מִצְרַיִם שָׁבַרְתִּי וְהִנֵּה לֹא־חֻבְּשָׁה לָתֵת רְפֻאוֹת לָשׂוּם
set to | ,healing | give to | shall it not bound be | And ,behold | have I .shattered | Egypt

22 חִתּוּל לְחָבְשָׁהּ לְחָזְקָהּ לִתְפֹּשׂ בֶּחָרֶב׃ לָכֵן כֹּה־אָמַר
says thus Therefore | the .sword | to handle | make to strong it | bind to ,it | a bandage

אֲדֹנָי יְהוִה הִנְנִי אֶל־פַּרְעֹה מֶלֶךְ־מִצְרַיִם וְשִׁבַּרְתִּי אֶת־
will I and shatter | ,Egypt | king of | Pharaoh against | Be- (am) I ,hold | :Jehovah | the Lord

זְרֹעֹתָיו אֶת־הַחֲזָקָה וְאֶת־הַנִּשְׁבָּרֶת וְהִפַּלְתִּי אֶת־הַחֶרֶב
the sword | will I And fall to cause | the .one shattered | and | strong the one | his ,arms

out of his hand. [23] And I will scatter Egypt among the nations, and will sow them through the lands. [24] And I will strengthen the arms of the king of Babylon, and put My sword in his hand. But I will shatter the arms of Pharaoh, and he will groan with the groanings of the slain before him. [25] But I will strengthen the arms of the king of Babylon, and the arms of Pharaoh shall fall; and they shall know that I (am) Jehovah, when I put My sword into the king of Babylon's hand —and he will stretch it against the land of Egypt. [26] And I will scatter Egypt among the nations, and sow them among the lands. And they shall know that I (am) Jehovah.

23 מִיָּדוֹ׃ וַהֲפִצוֹתִי אֶת־מִצְרַיִם בַּגּוֹיִם וְזֵרִיתִים בָּאֲרָצוֹת׃
the through ;lands | will and them sow | the among nations | Egypt | will I And scatter | of out .hand his

24 וְחִזַּקְתִּי אֶת־זְרֹעוֹת מֶלֶךְ בָּבֶל וְנָתַתִּי אֶת־חַרְבִּי בְּיָדוֹ
his in .hand | My sword | put and | ,Babylon | the of king | the of arms | will I And strengthen

וְשָׁבַרְתִּי אֶת־זְרֹעוֹת פַּרְעֹה וְנָאַק נַאֲקוֹת חָלָל לְפָנָיו׃
before .him | the slain | the with of groanings | he and groan will | Pharaoh | arms the of | will I But shatter

25 וְהַחֲזַקְתִּי אֶת־זְרֹעוֹת מֶלֶךְ בָּבֶל וּזְרֹעוֹת פַּרְעֹה תִּפֹּלְנָה
;fall shall | Pharaoh | the and of arms | ,Babylon | the of king | the of arms | will I But strengthen

וְיָדְעוּ כִּי־אֲנִי יְהוָה בְּתִתִּי חַרְבִּי בְּיַד מֶלֶךְ־בָּבֶל וְנָטָה
he and stretch will | ,Babylon's the of king | into hand | My sword | I when put | ,Jehovah | I (am) | that they and know shall

26 אוֹתָהּ אֶל־אֶרֶץ מִצְרָיִם׃ וַהֲפִצוֹתִי אֶת־מִצְרַיִם בַּגּוֹיִם
the among ,nations | Egypt | will I And scatter | .Egypt | the against of land | it

וְזֵרִיתִי אוֹתָם בָּאֲרָצוֹת וְיָדְעוּ כִּי־אֲנִי יְהוָה׃
.Jehovah | I (am) | that they And know shall | the among .lands | them | and sow

CAP. XXXI. לא

CHAPTER 31

[1] And it was, in the eleventh year, in the third (month), on the first of the month, the word of Jehovah was to me, saying, [2] Son of man, speak to Pharaoh king of Egypt and to his host: To whom are you like in your greatness? [3] Behold, Assyria (was) a cedar in Lebanon, (with) fair branches and forest shade, and exalted in height; and among the thick boughs was his top. [4] The waters made him great; the deep made him high with her rivers; (it) was going all around her planting, and she sent out her channels to all the trees of the field. [5] Therefore his height was lifted up above all the trees of the field, and his boughs were multiplied, and his branches became long, because of the many waters, in his sending. [6] All the birds of the heavens nested in his boughs, and under his

1 וַיְהִי בְּאַחַת עֶשְׂרֵה שָׁנָה בַּשְּׁלִישִׁי בְּאֶחָד לַחֹדֶשׁ הָיָה
was | the of ,month | the on first | the in ,(month) third | ,year | the in eleventh | it And was

2 דְבַר־יְהוָה אֵלַי לֵאמֹר׃ בֶּן־אָדָם אֱמֹר אֶל־פַּרְעֹה מֶלֶךְ־
king of | Pharaoh | to | speak | ,man Son of | ,saying | ,me to | Jehovah | the of word

3 מִצְרַיִם וְאֶל־הֲמוֹנוֹ אֶל־מִי דָּמִיתָ בְגָדְלֶךָ׃ הִנֵּה אַשּׁוּר
Assyria ,Behold (was) | your in ?greatness | you are whom To like · | his ;host | and to | Egypt

אֶרֶז בַּלְּבָנוֹן יְפֵה עָנָף וְחֹרֶשׁ מֵצַל וּגְבַהּ קוֹמָה וּבֵין עֲבֹתִים
thick the and boughs among | ;height in | and exalted | shade forest | and branches fair | (with) | in ,Lebanon | a cedar

4 הָיְתָה צַמַּרְתּוֹ׃ מַיִם גִּדְּלוּהוּ תְּהוֹם רֹמְמָתְהוּ אֶת־
with | him made high | deep the | him made ;great | The waters | .top his | was

נַהֲרֹתֶיהָ הֹלֵךְ סְבִיבוֹת מַטָּעָהּ וְאֶת־תְּעָלֹתֶיהָ שִׁלְחָה אֶל
to | sent she out | her channels | and | her ,planting | all around | was (it) going | her rivers

5 כָּל־עֲצֵי הַשָּׂדֶה׃ עַל־כֵּן גָּבְהָא קֹמָתוֹ מִכֹּל עֲצֵי הַשָּׂדֶה
the ,field | the of trees | above all | his height | was up lifted | Therefore | the .field | the of trees | all

וַתִּרְבֶּינָה סַרְעַפֹּתָיו וַתֶּאֱרַכְנָה פֹּארֹתָו מִמַּיִם רַבִּים
,many | of because waters the | his branches | became and long | his ,boughs | were and multiplied

6 בְּשַׁלְּחוֹ׃ בִּסְעַפֹּתָיו קִנְנוּ כָּל־עוֹף הַשָּׁמַיִם וְתַחַת פֹּארֹתָיו
his branches | and under | the ,heavens | the of birds | All | nested | his in boughs | his in .sending

7 יָלְדוּ כֹּל חַיַּת הַשָּׂדֶה וּבְצִלּוֹ יֵשְׁבוּ כֹּל גּוֹיִם רַבִּים׃ וַיְּיִף
he And .great nations all dwelt in and the the all gave
fair was shadow his ,field of beasts birth

בְּגָדְלוֹ בְּאֹרֶךְ דָּלִיּוֹתָיו כִּי־הָיָה שָׁרְשׁוֹ אֶל־מַיִם רַבִּים׃
.many waters to root his was For his the in his in
.branches of length ,greatness

8 אֲרָזִים לֹא־עֲמָמֻהוּ בְּגַן־אֱלֹהִים בְּרוֹשִׁים לֹא דָמוּ אֶל־
to were not fir the ;God the in over- not The
like trees of garden him shadow cedars

סְעַפֹּתָיו וְעַרְמֹנִים לֹא־הָיוּ כְּפֹארֹתָיו כָּל־עֵץ בְּגַן־אֱלֹהִים
God the in tree Every his like were not the and his
of garden .branches trees plane ,boughs

9 לֹא־דָמָה אֵלָיו בְּיָפְיוֹ׃ יָפֶה עֲשִׂיתִיו בְּרֹב דָּלִיּוֹתָיו וַיְקַנְאֻהוּ
envied and his by have I beautiful his in to was not
him ,branches many him made .beauty him like

10 כָּל־עֲצֵי־עֵדֶן אֲשֶׁר בְּגַן הָאֱלֹהִים׃ לָכֵן כֹּה אָמַר
says thus Therefore .God the in that Eden the all
of garden (were) of trees

אֲדֹנָי יֱהֹוִה יַעַן אֲשֶׁר גָּבַהְתָּ בְּקוֹמָה וַיִּתֵּן צַמַּרְתּוֹ אֶל־
to top his he and ,height in were you that Be- :Jehovah the
set has exalted cause Lord

11 בֵּין עֲבוֹתִים וְרָם לְבָבוֹ בְּגָבְהוֹ׃ וְאֶתְּנֵהוּ בְּיַד אֵל גּוֹיִם
the the hand in have I so his in his is and thick the among
.nations of mighty him given ;height heart up lifted ,boughs

12 עָשׂוֹ יַעֲשֶׂה לוֹ כְּרִשְׁעוֹ גֵּרַשְׁתִּהוּ׃ וַיִּכְרְתֻהוּ זָרִים עָרִיצֵי
fear- the ,strangers have And have I his for with shall He surely
of ful off him cut .him expelled evil ;him deal

גוֹיִם וַיִּטְּשֻׁהוּ אֶל־הֶהָרִים וּבְכָל־גֵּאָיוֹת נָפְלוּ דָלִיּוֹתָיו
his have the in and the On have and the
,branches fallen valleys all mountains .him left ,nations

וַתִּשָּׁבַרְנָה פֹארֹתָיו בְּכָל־אֲפִיקֵי הָאָרֶץ וַיֵּרְדוּ מִצִּלּוֹ כָּל־
all his from have And the the all in his have and
shadow gone .land of ravines boughs broken been

13 עַמֵּי הָאָרֶץ וַיִּטְּשֻׁהוּ׃ עַל־מַפַּלְתּוֹ יִשְׁכְּנוּ כָּל־עוֹף הַשָּׁמָיִם
the the all shall his On have and the the
,heavens of birds dwell fall .him left ,land of people

14 וְאֶל־פֹּארֹתָיו הָיוּ כֹּל חַיַּת הַשָּׂדֶה׃ לְמַעַן אֲשֶׁר לֹא־יִגְבְּהוּ
be may not that order in the the all shall his and
exalted ,field of beasts be branches on

בְקוֹמָתָם כָּל־עֲצֵי־מַיִם וְלֹא־יִתְּנוּ אֶת־צַמַּרְתָּם אֶל־בֵּין
among top their give and the (by) the all their in
not ,waters trees height

עֲבֹתִים וְלֹא־יַעַמְדוּ אֵלֵיהֶם בְּגָבְהָם כָּל־שֹׁתֵי מַיִם כִּי כֻלָּם
of all For .waters drink- all their in their stand and thick the
them ing ,exaltation mighty up not ;boughs

נִתְּנוּ לַמָּוֶת אֶל־אֶרֶץ תַּחְתִּית בְּתוֹךְ בְּנֵי אָדָם אֶל־יוֹרְדֵי
those with ,men the the in ,parts lowest the to ,death to are
down going of sons of midst earth's given

15 בוֹר׃ כֹּה־אָמַר אֲדֹנָי יֱהֹוִה בְּיוֹם רִדְתּוֹ שְׁאֹלָה הֶאֱבַלְתִּי
a caused I ,Sheol to went he the In :Jehovah the says Thus the (into)
.mourning down day Lord .Pit

branches all the beasts of the field gave birth; and in his shadow dwell all great nations. [7] And he was fair in his greatness, in the length of his branches. For his root was to many waters. [8] The cedars did not overshadow him in the garden of God; the fir-trees were not like his boughs; and the plane trees were not like his branches. Every tree in the garden of God was not like unto him in his beauty. [9] I have made him beautiful by his many branches, and all the trees of Eden that (were) in the garden of God envied him.

[10] Therefore thus says the Lord Jehovah: Because you were exalted in height, and he has set his top among the thick boughs, and his heart is lifted up in his height; [11] so I have given him in the mighty hand of the nations. He shall surely deal with him; I have expelled him for his evil. [12] And strangers have cut him off, the fearful of the nations, and have left him. His branches have fallen on the mountains and in all the valleys, and his boughs have been broken in all the ravines of the land. And all the people of the land have gone from his shadow, and have left him. [13] On his fall shall dwell all the birds of the heavens, and on his branches shall be all the beasts of the field, [14] in order that all the trees (by) the waters may not be exalted in their height, and do not give their top among the thick boughs; and do not stand up in their mighty exaltation; all drinking waters. For all of them are given to death, to the earth's lowest parts, in the midst of the sons of men, with those going down (into) the Pit. [15] Thus says the Lord Jehovah: In the day he went down to Sheol. I

caused a mourning. I covered over him the deep, and I held back her rivers; and many waters were confined. [16] And I darkened Lebanon on him, and all the trees of the field wilted away because of him. I made the nations shake at the sound of his fall, when I cast him down to Sheol with those going down (in) the Pit. And all the trees of Eden shall be cheered in the earth's lowest parts, the choice and best of Lebanon, all that drink waters. [17] They also went down with him into Sheol, to the slain of the sword, even his arm, who dwelt in his shadow in the midst of the nations.

[18] To whom are you like in glory and greatness among Eden's trees? Yet you shall go down with the trees of Eden to the earth's lowest parts. You shall lie amidst the uncircumcised, with the slain of the sword. He is Pharaoh and all (his) host, declares the Lord Jehovah.

כִּסֵּתִי עָלָיו אֶת־תְּהוֹם וָאֶמְנַע נַהֲרוֹתֶיהָ וַיִּכָּלְאוּ מַיִם רַבִּים
.many waters were and her held I and the over I
confined ,rivers back held ,deep him covered

16 וָאַקְדִּר עָלָיו לְבָנוֹן וְכָל־עֲצֵי הַשָּׂדֶה עָלָיו עֻלְפֶּה׃ מִקּוֹל
the at wilted because the the and ;Lebanon on I And
of sound .away him of field of trees all him darkened

מַפַּלְתּוֹ הִרְעַשְׁתִּי גוֹיִם בְּהוֹרִדִי אֹתוֹ שְׁאֹלָה אֶת־יוֹרְדֵי בוֹר
the (in) those with Sheol to him I when the made I fall his
.Pit down going down cast ,nations shake

וַיִּנָּחֲמוּ בְּאֶרֶץ תַּחְתִּית כָּל־עֲצֵי־עֵדֶן מִבְחַר וְטוֹב־לְבָנוֹן
,Lebanon and the ,Eden the all parts lowest the in shall And
of best choice of trees earth's cheered be

17 כָּל־שֹׁתֵי מָיִם׃ גַּם הֵם אִתּוֹ יָרְדוּ שְׁאֹלָה אֶל־חַלְלֵי־חָרֶב
the the to Sheol went with They also .waters that all
,sword of slain into down him drink

18 וּזְרֹעוֹ יָשְׁבוּ בְצִלּוֹ בְּתוֹךְ גּוֹיִם׃ אֶל־מִי דָמִיתָ כָּכָה בְּכָבוֹד
glory in like you are whom To the the in his in who his even
.nations of midst shadow dwelt ,arm

וּבְגֹדֶל בַּעֲצֵי־עֵדֶן וְהוּרַדְתָּ אֶת־עֲצֵי־עֵדֶן אֶל־אֶרֶץ תַּחְתִּית
.parts lowest the to Eden's with you Yet ?Eden's among great- and
earth's trees down go shall trees ness

בְּתוֹךְ עֲרֵלִים תִּשְׁכַּב אֶת־חַלְלֵי־חֶרֶב הוּא פַרְעֹה וְכָל־
all and Pharaoh He the the with shall you uncir- the Amidst
(is) .sword of slain lie cumcised

הֲמוֹנֹה נְאֻם אֲדֹנָי יְהוִה׃
.Jehovah the states (his)
Lord ,host

CAP. XXXII לב

CHAPTER 32

[1] And it was, in the twelfth year, in the twelfth month, on the first of the month, the word of Jehovah was to me, saying, [2] Son of man, take up a lament over Pharaoh king of Egypt, and say to him, You were like a young lion of the nations, but you (are) like the monster in the seas. And you gushed in your rivers, and stirred up the waters with your feet, and fouled their rivers. [3] Thus says the Lord Jehovah: Thus I will spread out My net over you, with an assembly of many peoples; and they will lift you up in My net. [4] Then I will leave you on the land; on the face of the field I will hurl you, and will make dwell on

1 וַיְהִי בִּשְׁתֵּי עֶשְׂרֵה שָׁנָה בִּשְׁנֵי־עָשָׂר חֹדֶשׁ בְּאֶחָד לַחֹדֶשׁ
the of the on ,month the in ,year the in it And
,month first twelfth twelfth ,was

2 הָיָה דְבַר־יְהוָה אֵלַי לֵאמֹר׃ בֶּן־אָדָם שָׂא קִינָה עַל־
over a take ,man Son ,saying to Jehovah the was
lament up of ,me of word

פַּרְעֹה מֶלֶךְ־מִצְרַיִם וְאָמַרְתָּ אֵלָיו כְּפִיר גּוֹיִם נִדְמֵיתָ
were you the young A .him to say and ,Egypt king Pharaoh
;like nations of lion of

וְאַתָּה כַּתַּנִּים בַּיַּמִּים וַתָּגַח בְּנַהֲרוֹתֶיךָ וַתִּדְלַח־מַיִם
the stirred and your in you And the in the like but
waters up ,rivers gushed .seas monster (are) you

3 בְּרַגְלֶיךָ וַתִּרְפֹּס נַהֲרוֹתָם׃ כֹּה אָמַר אֲדֹנָי יְהוִה
:Jehovah the says Thus their fouled and your with
Lord .rivers ,feet

וּפָרַשְׂתִּי עָלֶיךָ אֶת־רִשְׁתִּי בִּקְהַל עַמִּים רַבִּים וְהֶעֱלוּךָ
will they and ;many peoples an with ,net My over will I Thus
up you lift of assembly you out spread

4 בְּחֶרְמִי׃ וּנְטַשְׁתִּיךָ בָאָרֶץ עַל־פְּנֵי הַשָּׂדֶה אֲטִילֶךָ וְהִשְׁכַּנְתִּי
will and will I the the on the on will I Then My in
dwell make ,you hurl field of face ;land you leave .net

you all the birds of the heavens, and I will fill from you the beasts of all the earth. [5] And I will put your flesh on the mountains and fill the valleys (with) your height. [6] And I will also make the land drink your discharge of your blood, to the mountains, and the ravines shall be full of you. [7] And I will cover when (I) quench you the heavens, and darken their stars; I will cover the sun with a cloud, and the moon shall not give its light. [8] I will darken all the shining of lights in the heavens over you, and will give darkness on your land, declares the Lord Jehovah. [9] I will also vex the heart of many peoples, when I bring your breaking among the nations, to the lands which you have not known. [10] And I will make many peoples appalled at you, and their kings will be horribly afraid at you, when I brandish My sword before their faces. And they shall quake at (every) moment, (each) man for his own life, in the day of your fall.

[11] For thus says the Lord Jehovah: The sword of the king of Babylon shall come on you. [12] By the swords of the mighty I will make your host fall, the fearful of the nations, all of them. And they shall spoil the pride of Egypt, and all its multitude shall be destroyed. [13] I will also destroy all her beasts from on the great waters; and the foot of man shall not stir them any longer; and the hoofs of beasts shall not stir them up. [14] Then I will make their waters settle, and cause their rivers to run as oil, says the Lord Jehovah. [15] When I shall make the land of Egypt a ruin, and the land shall be stripped of its fullness; when I shall strike all those who dwell in it;

עָלֶיךָ כָּל־עוֹף הַשָּׁמַיִם וְהִשְׂבַּעְתִּי מִמְּךָ חַיַּת כָּל־הָאָרֶץ׃
the all the from will I and the the all on
.earth of beasts you fill ,heavens of birds you

5 וְנָתַתִּי אֶת־בְּשָׂרְךָ עַל־הֶהָרִים וּמִלֵּאתִי הַגֵּאָיוֹת רָמוּתֶךָ׃
your valleys the fill and the on your I And
.height (with) mountains flesh put will

6 וְהִשְׁקֵיתִי אֶרֶץ צָפָתְךָ מִדָּמְךָ אֶל־הֶהָרִים וַאֲפִקִים יִמָּלְאוּן
be shall the and the to your dis- your the also will I
full ravines ;mountains ,blood of charge land drink make

7 מִמֶּךָּ׃ וְכִסֵּיתִי בְכַבּוֹתְךָ שָׁמַיִם וְהִקְדַּרְתִּי אֶת־כֹּכְבֵיהֶם
;stars their darken and the (I) when I And .you of
,heavens you quench cover will

8 שֶׁמֶשׁ בֶּעָנָן אֲכַסֶּנּוּ וְיָרֵחַ לֹא־יָאִיר אוֹרוֹ׃ כָּל־מְאוֹרֵי אוֹר
lights the All .light its shall not the and will I a with the
of shining give moon ,cover cloud sun

בַּשָּׁמַיִם אַקְדִּירֵם עָלֶיךָ וְנָתַתִּי חֹשֶׁךְ עַל־אַרְצְךָ נְאֻם אֲדֹנָי
the states your on darkness will and over will I the in
Lord ,land give you darken heavens

9 יְהוִה׃ וְהִכְעַסְתִּי לֵב עַמִּים רַבִּים בַּהֲבִיאִי שִׁבְרְךָ בַּגּוֹיִם
the among your I when ,many peoples the also will I .Jehovah
,nations breaking bring of heart vex

10 עַל־אֲרָצוֹת אֲשֶׁר לֹא־יְדַעְתָּם׃ וַהֲשִׁמּוֹתִי עָלֶיךָ עַמִּים
peoples you at will I And have you not which the to
appalled make .known lands

רַבִּים וּמַלְכֵיהֶם יִשְׂעֲרוּ עָלֶיךָ שַׂעַר בְּעוֹפְפִי חַרְבִּי עַל־
before My I when ,horribly you at be will their and ,many
sword brandish afraid kings

פְּנֵיהֶם וְחָרְדוּ לִרְגָעִים אִישׁ לְנַפְשׁוֹ בְּיוֹם מַפַּלְתֶּךָ׃
.fall your the in his for (each) (every) at they And their
of day ,life own man ,moment quake shall .faces

11 כִּי כֹה אָמַר אֲדֹנָי יְהוִה חֶרֶב מֶלֶךְ־בָּבֶל תְּבוֹאֶךָ׃ בְּחַרְבוֹת
12
the By come shall Babylon the The :Jehovah the says thus For
of swords .you on of king of sword Lord

גִּבּוֹרִים אַפִּיל הֲמוֹנֶךָ עָרִיצֵי גוֹיִם כֻּלָּם וְשָׁדְדוּ אֶת־גְּאוֹן
pride the they And of all the fear- the your will I the
of spoil shall .them ,nations of ful ,host fall make mighty

13 מִצְרַיִם וְנִשְׁמַד כָּל־הֲמוֹנָהּ׃ וְהַאֲבַדְתִּי אֶת־כָּל־בְּהֶמְתָּהּ
beasts her all also will I the all shall and ,Egypt
destroy .it of multitude destroyed be

מֵעַל מַיִם רַבִּים וְלֹא תִדְלָחֵם רֶגֶל־אָדָם עוֹד וּפַרְסוֹת
the and any man the stir shall and the the from
of hoofs ;longer of foot up them not ;great waters on

14 בְּהֵמָה לֹא תִדְלָחֵם׃ אָז אַשְׁקִיעַ מֵימֵיהֶם וְנַהֲרוֹתָם כַּשֶּׁמֶן
oil as their and their will I Then stir shall not beasts
rivers ,waters settle make .up them

15 אוֹלִיךְ נְאֻם אֲדֹנָי יְהוִה׃ בְּתִתִּי אֶת־אֶרֶץ מִצְרַיִם שְׁמָמָה
,ruin a Egypt the I When .Jehovah the says to cause
of land make shall Lord ,run

וּנְשַׁמָּה אֶרֶץ מִמְּלֹאָהּ בְּהַכּוֹתִי אֶת־כָּל־יֹשְׁבֵי בָהּ וְיָדְעוּ
they then in those all I when its of the shall and
know shall ;it dwell who strike shall ;fulness land stripped be

then they shall know that I (am) Jehovah. [16] This is the lament, and they shall lament her; the daughters of the nations shall lament her. Over Egypt and over all her multitude, they shall lament her, declares the Lord Jehovah. [17] And it was, in the twelfth year, in the fifteenth of the month, the word of Jehovah was to me, saying, [18] Son of man, wail over the host of Egypt, and bring him down, her and the daughters of the majestic nations, to the earth's lowest parts, with those going down (to) the Pit. [19] Than whom are you more lovely? Go down and be laid with the uncircumcised. [20] They shall fall in the midst of the slain of the sword. She is given to the sword; they draw her and all her multitudes. [21] The strong of the mighty shall speak to him from the midst of Sheol; they went with his helpers; they lie, the uncircumcised, slain by the sword. [22] There (is) Assyria and all her assembly —all around him (are) his graves; all of them (are) slain, fallen by the sword; [23] of whom are given her graves in the recesses of the Pit; and her assembly is all around her grave; all of them (are) slain, fallen by the sword, because they gave terror in the land of the living. [24] There (is) Elam and all her multitude around her grave; all of them (are) slain, fallen by the sword, who went down uncircumcised into the earth's lowest parts; who gave their terror in the land of the living. Yet they bore their shame with those going down (to) the Pit. [25] In the midst of the slain they have put a bed for her, with all her multitude; her graves (are) all around him; all of them uncircumcised, slain by the sword; though their terror was given in the

16 כִּי־אֲנִי יְהוָה׃ קִינָה הִיא וְקוֹנְנוּהָ בְּנוֹת הַגּוֹיִם תְּקוֹנֵנָּה
shall lament the nations' daughters they and shall her lament This (is) the lament .Jehovah I (am) that

אוֹתָהּ עַל־מִצְרַיִם וְעַל־כָּל־הֲמוֹנָהּ תְּקוֹנֵנָּה אוֹתָהּ נְאֻם
states ,her shall they lament her ,multitude all and over Egypt Over .her

17 אֲדֹנָי יְהוִה׃ וַיְהִי בִּשְׁתֵּי עֶשְׂרֵה שָׁנָה בַּחֲמִשָּׁה עָשָׂר
the in fifteenth ,year the twelfth in it And ,was .Jehovah the Lord

18 לַחֹדֶשׁ הָיָה דְבַר־יְהוָה אֵלַי לֵאמֹר׃ בֶּן־אָדָם נְהֵה עַל־
over wail ,man Son of ,saying ,me to Jehovah the of word was the of ,month

הֲמוֹן מִצְרַיִם וְהוֹרִדֵהוּ אוֹתָהּ וּבְנוֹת גּוֹיִם אַדִּרִם אֶל־אֶרֶץ
the earth's to the majestic nations the and of daughters her bring and ,down him Egypt the of host

19 תַּחְתִּיּוֹת אֶת־יוֹרְדֵי בוֹר׃ מִמִּי נָעָמְתְּ רְדָה וְהָשְׁכְּבָה
be and laid Go down you are ?lovely Than whom the (to) Pit those with down going lowest ,parts

20 אֶת־עֲרֵלִים׃ בְּתוֹךְ חַלְלֵי־חֶרֶב יִפֹּלוּ חֶרֶב נִתָּנָה מָשְׁכוּ
they draw is She ;given the to sword They .fall shall ,,sword the the of slain the In of midst the .uncircumcised with

21 אוֹתָהּ וְכָל־הֲמוֹנֶיהָ׃ יְדַבְּרוּ־לוֹ אֵלֵי גִבּוֹרִים מִתּוֹךְ שְׁאוֹל
;Sheol the from of midst the mighty The of strong to him shall speak her .multitudes and all her

22 אֶת־עֹזְרָיו יָרְדוּ שָׁכְבוּ הָעֲרֵלִים חַלְלֵי חָרֶב׃ שָׁם אַשּׁוּר
Assyria There the .sword slain by uncircum- ,cised the they ,lie they ;went his helpers with

וְכָל־קְהָלָהּ סְבִיבוֹתָיו קִבְרֹתָיו כֻּלָּם חֲלָלִים הַנֹּפְלִים
fallen (are) ,slain of all them his ;graves around all (are) him her ;assembly and all

23 בֶּחָרֶב׃ אֲשֶׁר נִתְּנוּ קִבְרֹתֶיהָ בְּיַרְכְּתֵי־בוֹר וַיְהִי קְהָלָהּ
her assembly and is the ,Pit the in of recesses graves her are given of whom the by ;sword

סְבִיבוֹת קְבֻרָתָהּ כֻּלָּם חֲלָלִים נֹפְלִים בַּחֶרֶב אֲשֶׁר־נָתְנוּ
they gave because the by ,sword fallen (are) ,slain of all them her ;grave all around

24 חִתִּית בְּאֶרֶץ חַיִּים׃ שָׁם עֵילָם וְכָל־הֲמוֹנָהּ סְבִיבוֹת קְבֻרָתָהּ
her ;grave around her multitude and all Elam There (is) the .living the in of land terror

כֻּלָּם חֲלָלִים הַנֹּפְלִים בַּחֶרֶב אֲשֶׁר־יָרְדוּ עֲרֵלִים ׀ אֶל־אֶרֶץ
the earth's into uncircum- cised went who .down the by ,sword fallen (are) ,slain of all them

תַּחְתִּיּוֹת אֲשֶׁר נָתְנוּ חִתִּיתָם בְּאֶרֶץ חַיִּים וַיִּשְׂאוּ כְלִמָּתָם
their shame they Yet bore the .living the in of land their terror gave who lowest ;parts

25 אֶת־יוֹרְדֵי בוֹר׃ בְּתוֹךְ חֲלָלִים נָתְנוּ מִשְׁכָּב לָהּ בְּכָל־הֲמוֹנָהּ
her .multitude with all for ,her bed a They put have the slain the In of midst the (to) .Pit those with down going

סְבִיבוֹתָיו קִבְרֹתֶהָ כֻּלָּם עֲרֵלִים חַלְלֵי־חֶרֶב כִּי נִתַּן חִתִּיתָם
their terror was given though the ;sword slain by uncircum- ,cised of all them Her ,graves around all (are) him

land of the living, yet they have become their shame with those going down (to) the Pit; in the midst of the slain he is put. [26] There (is) Meshech, Tubal and all her multitude, all around him (are) her graves. All of them (are) uncircumcised, slain by the sword; though they gave their terror in the land of the living; [27] and they shall not lie with the mighty who are fallen, of the uncircumcised, who have gone down (to) Sheol with their weapons of war. And they have put their swords under their heads, but their iniquities shall be on their bones, though the terror of the mighty (was) in the land of the living. [28] And you shall be broken in the midst of the uncircumcised, and shall lie with the slain by the sword. [29] There (is) Edom, her kings and all her rulers, who are placed in their might with the slain of the sword; they shall lie with the uncircumcised, and with those going down (to) the Pit. [30] These (are) the princes of the north, all of them, and all the Sidonians, who have gone down with the slain in their terror. They are ashamed of their might. And they lie uncircumcised with those slain by the sword, and bear their shame with those going down (to) the Pit. [31] Pharaoh shall see them and be cheered over all his multitude, those slain by the sword, Pharaoh and all the army, declares the Lord Jehovah. [32] For I had put his terror in the land of the living. But he will be laid amidst the uncircumcised with those slain by the sword, Pharaoh and all his multitude, declares the Lord Jehovah.

CHAPTER 33

[1] And the word of Jehovah was to me, saying, [2] Son of man, speak to the sons of your people

בְּאֶרֶץ חַיִּים וַיִּשְׂאוּ כְלִמָּתָם אֶת־יוֹרְדֵי בוֹר בְּתוֹךְ חֲלָלִים
the the in the (to) those with their they yet the the in
slain of midst ;Pit down going shame become have ,living of land

26 נִתָּן׃ שָׁם מֶשֶׁךְ תֻּבַל וְכָל־הֲמוֹנָהּ סְבִיבוֹתָיו קִבְרוֹתֶיהָ
.graves her around all her and Tubal ,Meshech There is he
(are) him ;multitude all (is) .put

כֻּלָּם עֲרֵלִים מְחֻלְלֵי חֶרֶב כִּי־נָתְנוּ חִתִּיתָם בְּאֶרֶץ חַיִּים׃
the the in their they though the slain uncircum- of All
;living of land terror gave ;sword by ,cised (are) them

27 וְלֹא יִשְׁכְּבוּ אֶת־גִּבּוֹרִים נֹפְלִים מֵעֲרֵלִים אֲשֶׁר יָרְדוּ־שְׁאוֹל
Sheol gone have who the of are who the with shall they and
(to) down ,uncircumcised ,fallen mighty lie not

בִּכְלֵי־מִלְחַמְתָּם וַיִּתְּנוּ אֶת־חַרְבוֹתָם תַּחַת רָאשֵׁיהֶם וַתְּהִי
but their under their they And their with
be shall ,heads swords put have .war of weapons

28 עֲוֺנֹתָם עַל־עַצְמוֹתָם כִּי־חִתִּית גִּבּוֹרִים בְּאֶרֶץ חַיִּים׃ וְאַתָּה
And the the in mighty the the though their on their
you .living of land (was) of terror ,bones iniquities

29 בְּתוֹךְ עֲרֵלִים תִּשָּׁבַר וְתִשְׁכַּב אֶת־חַלְלֵי־חָרֶב׃ שָׁמָּה אֱדוֹם
,Edom There the the with shall and be shall uncir- the the in
(is) .sword by slain lie ,broken cumcised of midst

מְלָכֶיהָ וְכָל־נְשִׂיאֶיהָ אֲשֶׁר־נִתְּנוּ בִגְבוּרָתָם אֶת־חַלְלֵי־חָרֶב
the the with their in put are who her and her
;sword of slain might ,rulers all kings

30 הֵמָּה אֶת־עֲרֵלִים יִשְׁכָּבוּ וְאֶת־יֹרְדֵי בוֹר׃ שָׁמָּה נְסִיכֵי צָפוֹן
the the These the (to) those with and ,lie shall uncir- the with they
,north of princes (are) .Pit down going cumcised

כֻּלָּם וְכָל־צִדֹנִי אֲשֶׁר־יָרְדוּ אֶת־חֲלָלִים בְּחִתִּיתָם מִגְּבוּרָתָם
their from their in the with gone have who the and of all
might .terror slain down ,Sidonians all ,them

בּוֹשִׁים וַיִּשְׁכְּבוּ עֲרֵלִים אֶת־חַלְלֵי־חֶרֶב וַיִּשְׂאוּ כְלִמָּתָם
their bear and the those with uncircum- they And are They
shame ,sword by slain cised lie .ashamed

31 אֶת־יוֹרְדֵי בוֹר׃ אוֹתָם יִרְאֶה פַרְעֹה וְנִחַם עַל־כָּל־הֲמוֹנֹה
his all over be and Pharaoh shall them the (to) those with
31 ;multitude cheered see .Pit down going

32 חַלְלֵי־חֶרֶב פַּרְעֹה וְכָל־חֵילוֹ נְאֻם אֲדֹנָי יְהוִה׃ כִּי־נָתַתִּי
had I For .Jehovah the states the and Pharaoh the slain
put Lord ,army all sword by

אֶת־חִתִּיתוֹ בְּאֶרֶץ חַיִּים וְהֻשְׁכַּב בְּתוֹךְ עֲרֵלִים אֶת־חַלְלֵי־
those with uncir- the amidst will he But the the in terror his
by slain cumcised laid be ,living of land

חֶרֶב פַּרְעֹה וְכָל־הֲמוֹנֹה נְאֻם אֲדֹנָי יְהוִה׃
.Jehovah the states his and Pharaoh the
Lord ,multitude all ,sword

CAP. XXXIII לג

CHAPTER 33

1
2 וַיְהִי דְבַר־יְהוָה אֵלַי לֵאמֹר׃ בֶּן־אָדָם דַּבֵּר אֶל־בְּנֵי־עַמְּךָ
your the to speak ,man Son ,saying ,me to Jehovah the And
people of sons of of word was

and say to them: When I bring the sword on it, on a land, and take the people of the land, one man from their borders, and set him to them for a watchman; [3] and (when) he sees the sword coming on the land, and he blows the trumpet and warns the people, and the hearer hears the sound of the trumpet, [4] and does not take warning; and the sword comes and takes him: his blood shall be on his own head. [5] He heard the trumpet's sound and did not take warning; his blood shall be on himself. But he who took warning, he shall deliver his soul. [6] But the watchman, if he sees the sword coming, and does not blow the trumpet, and the people are not warned; and the sword comes and takes from them a soul, he is taken in his iniquity. But I will require his blood from the watchman's hand.

[7] And you, son of man, I have set you (as) a watchman to the house of Israel. And you shall hear the word from Me, and warn them from Me. [8] When I say to the wicked, O wicked, surely you shall die; and you do not speak to warn the wicked from his way, that wicked one shall die in his iniquity, but I will require his blood from your hand. [9] But you, if you warn the wicked from his way, to turn from it; and he does not turn from his way, he shall die in his iniquity. But you have delivered your soul. [10] And you, son of man, say to the house of Israel, Thus you have spoken, saying, Surely our transgressions and our sins (are) on us, and we are rotting in them; and then shall we live? [11] Say to them: (As) declares

וְאָמַרְתָּ אֲלֵיהֶם אֶרֶץ כִּי־אָבִיא עָלֶיהָ חָרֶב וְלָקְחוּ עַם־
the take and the it on I When a (on) :them to say and
of people ,sword bring land

הָאָרֶץ אִישׁ אֶחָד מִקְצֵיהֶם וְנָתְנוּ אֹתוֹ לָהֶם לְצֹפֶה׃
a for them to him set and their from one man the
;watchman ,borders ,land

3 וְרָאָה אֶת־הַחֶרֶב בָּאָה עַל־הָאָרֶץ וְתָקַע בַּשּׁוֹפָר וְהִזְהִיר
warns and the he and the on coming the (when) and
trumpet blows ,land sword sees he

4 אֶת־הָעָם׃ וְשָׁמַע הַשֹּׁמֵעַ אֶת־קוֹל הַשּׁוֹפָר וְלֹא נִזְהָר
takes and trumpet's the hearer the hears and the
,warning not sound ;people

5 וַתָּבוֹא חֶרֶב וַתִּקָּחֵהוּ דָּמוֹ בְרֹאשׁוֹ יִהְיֶה׃ אֵת קוֹל
The .be shall his on his takes and the and
sound head own blood ;him sword comes

הַשּׁוֹפָר שָׁמַע וְלֹא נִזְהָר דָּמוֹ בּוֹ יִהְיֶה וְהוּא נִזְהָר נַפְשׁוֹ
his took who But shall on his took and he trumpet's
soul ,warning he .be himself blood ;warning not ,heard

6 מִלֵּט׃ וְהַצֹּפֶה כִּי־יִרְאֶה אֶת־הַחֶרֶב בָּאָה וְלֹא־תָקַע
does and coming the sees he if the But shall he
blow not sword ,watchman .deliver

בַּשּׁוֹפָר וְהָעָם לֹא־נִזְהָר וַתָּבוֹא חֶרֶב וַתִּקַּח מֵהֶם נָפֶשׁ
,soul a from and the and are not the and the
them takes sword comes ;warned people ,trumpet

הוּא בַּעֲוֺנוֹ נִלְקָח וְדָמוֹ מִיַּד־הַצֹּפֶה אֶדְרֹשׁ׃ וְאַתָּה
,you And will I watch- the from his But is his in he
.require man's hand blood .taken iniquity

7 בֶן־אָדָם צֹפֶה נְתַתִּיךָ לְבֵית יִשְׂרָאֵל וְשָׁמַעְתָּ מִפִּי
from you And .Israel the to have I a ,man son
Me hear shall of house you set watchman of

8 דָּבָר וְהִזְהַרְתָּ אֹתָם מִמֶּנִּי׃ בְּאָמְרִי לָרָשָׁע רָשָׁע מוֹת
surely O the to I When from them warn and the
,wicked ,wicked say .Me ,word

תָּמוּת וְלֹא דִבַּרְתָּ לְהַזְהִיר רָשָׁע מִדַּרְכּוֹ הוּא רָשָׁע בַּעֲוֺנוֹ
his in wicked that his from the warn to do you and shall you
iniquity one ,way wicked speak not ;die

9 יָמוּת וְדָמוֹ מִיָּדְךָ אֲבַקֵּשׁ׃ וְאַתָּה כִּי־הִזְהַרְתָּ רָשָׁע מִדַּרְכּוֹ
his from the you if But will I from his but shall
,way wicked warn ,you .require hand your blood ;die

לָשׁוּב מִמֶּנָּה וְלֹא־שָׁב מִדַּרְכּוֹ הוּא בַּעֲוֺנוֹ יָמוּת וְאַתָּה
you But shall his in he his from he and from turn to
.die iniquity ,way turns not ;it

10 נַפְשְׁךָ הִצַּלְתָּ׃ וְאַתָּה בֶן־אָדָם אֱמֹר אֶל־בֵּית יִשְׂרָאֵל
,Israel the to say ,man son ,you And have your
of house of .delivered soul

כֵּן אֲמַרְתֶּם לֵאמֹר כִּי־פְשָׁעֵינוּ וְחַטֹּאתֵינוּ עָלֵינוּ וּבָם
in and on (are) our and our Surely ,saying have you Thus
them ,us sins transgressions ,spoken

11 אֲנַחְנוּ נְמַקִּים וְאֵיךְ נִחְיֶה׃ אֱמֹר אֲלֵיהֶם חַי־אָנִי ׀ נְאֻם ׀
states (As) :them to Say we shall and are we
?live then ;rotting

the Lord Jehovah, I do not have pleasure in the death of the wicked, except in the turning of the wicked from his way, and live. Turn! Turn from your evil ways! For why will you die, O house of Israel?

[12] And you, son of man, say to the sons of your people, The righteousness of the righteous shall not deliver him in the day of his trespass. And the evil of the evil, he shall not fall by it, in the day he turns from his wickedness. And the righteous shall not be able to live by it, in the day he sins. [13] Though I say to the righteous: he shall surely live—and he trusts in his own righteousness and commits iniquity, all his righteousness shall not be remembered—but for his iniquity which he has done, for it he shall die. [14] And though I say to the wicked: You shall surely die—if he turns from his sin and does justice and righteousness: [15] the wicked returns the pledge; he repays the thing stolen; he walks in the statutes of life, not doing iniquity—he shall surely live; he shall not die. [16] All his sins which he has sinned shall not be remembered to him; he has done justice and righteousness; he shall surely live. [17] Yet the sons of your people say, The way of the Lord is not fair. But they (and) their way is not fair. [18] When the righteous turns from his righteousness, and does iniquity, he shall even die by them. [19] But if the wicked turns from his wickedness, and does justice and righteousness, he shall live by them. [20] Yet you say, The way of the Lord is not fair. Each man by his ways I will judge you, O house of Israel.

[21] And it was, in the twelfth year, in the tenth (month), on the fifth of the

אדני יהוה אם־אחפץ במות הרשע כי אם־בשוב רשע
the the in except the the in have I not ,Jehovah the
wicked of turning ,wicked of death pleasure Lord

מדרכו וחיה שובו שובו מדרכיכם הרעים ולמה תמותו
you will why for ;evil your from turn ,Turn and his from
,die ways .live way

12 בית ישראל: ואתה בן־אדם אמר אל־בני־עמך
your the to say ,man son ,you And ?Israel O
people of sons of of house

צדקת הצדיק לא תצילנו ביום פשעו ורשעת הרשע לא־
not the the And his the in deliver shall not the righteous- The
,evil of evil .trespass of day him righteous of ness

יכשל בה ביום שובו מרשעו וצדיק לא יוכל לחיות בה
by live to shall not the And his from he the in ,it by shall he
it able be righteous .wickedness turns day fall

13 ביום חטאתו: באמרי לצדיק חיה יחיה והוא־בטח
trusts and shall he surely the to I Though .sins he the in
he —live ,righteous say day

על־צדקתו ועשה עול כל־צדקתו לא תזכרנה ובעולו
his for but be shall not his all ,iniquity and own his in
iniquity —remembered righteousness commits righteousness

14 אשר־עשה בו ימות: ובאמרי לרשע מות תמות ושב
he if shall You surely the to though And shall he for has he that
turns —die ,wicked say I .die it ,done

15 מחטאתו ועשה משפט וצדקה: חבל ישיב רשע גזלה
thing the the returns the righ- and justice and his from
robbed ,wicked pledge ;teousness does sin

ישלם בחקות החיים הלך לבלתי עשות עול חיו יחיה
shall he surely ;iniquity doing not ,walks he life the in he
;live of statutes ,repays

16 לא ימות: כל־חטאתו אשר חטא לא תזכרנה לו משפט
justice to be shall not has he which his All shall he not
;him remembered sinned sins .die

17 וצדקה עשה חיו יחיה: ואמרו בני עמך לא יתכן דרך
The fair is not your the say Yet shall he surely has he righ- and
of way ,people of sons .live ;done teousness

18 אדני והמה דרכם לא־יתכן: בשוב־צדיק מצדקתו
his from the When .fair is not their (and) But the
righteousness righteous turns way they .Lord

19 ועשה עול ומת בהם: ובשוב רשע מרשעתו ועשה
does and his from the if But .them by shall he ,iniquity and
wickedness wicked turns die even does

20 משפט וצדקה עליהם הוא יחיה: ואמרתם לא יתכן
fair is not you Yet shall he them by and justice
,say .live ,righteousness

דרך אדני איש כדרכיו אשפוט אתכם בית ישראל:
.Israel O ,you will I his by Each the the
of house judge ,ways man .Lord of way

21 ויהי בשתי עשרה שנה בעשרי בחמשה לחדש
the of the on tenth the in ,year the in And
month fifth ,(month) twelfth was it

month of our exile, one who escaped out of Jerusalem came to me, saying, The city has been stricken. [22] And the hand of Jehovah was on me in the evening, before the escaped one came. And He had opened my mouth until he came to me in the morning. And my mouth was opened, and I was not dumb any longer. [23] Then the word of Jehovah was to me, saying, [24] Son of man, the inhabitants of ruins are speaking, these in the land of Israel, saying, Abraham was one, and he possessed the land; but we (are) many; the land is given to us for a possession. [25] Therefore say to them, Thus says the Lord Jehovah: You eat on the blood, and you lift your eyes up to your idols, and you shed blood! And shall you possess the land? [26] You stand on your sword, and you each do abominations, defiling his neighbor's wife. And shall you possess the land? [27] Thus say to them, Thus says the Lord Jehovah: (As) I live, surely those in the ruins shall fall by the sword, and he who (is) in the face of the field I will give him to the beasts to be eaten; and those in the forts and in the caves shall die by the plague. [28] For I have made the land desolate and a waste, and the pride of her strength has ceased. And the heights of Israel shall be a waste, that none will go through. [29] Then they shall know that I (am) Jehovah, when I have made the land desolate and a waste, because of all their abominations which they have done.

[30] And you, son of man, the sons of your people are talking about you beside the walls, and

לְגָלוּתֵנוּ בָּא־אֵלַי הַפָּלִיט מִירוּשָׁלַםִ לֵאמֹר הֻכְּתָה
been has ,saying of out who one to came our of
stricken ,Jerusalem escaped me ,exile

22 הָעִיר׃ וְיַד־יְהוָה הָיְתָה אֵלַי בָּעֶרֶב לִפְנֵי בּוֹא הַפָּלִיט
escaped the came before the in me on was Jehovah And The
.one ,evening of hand the .city

וַיִּפְתַּח אֶת־פִּי עַד־בּוֹא אֵלַי בַּבֹּקֶר וַיִּפָּתַח פִּי וְלֹא נֶאֱלַמְתִּי
was I and my was And the in me to he until my had He And
dumb not mouth opened .morning came mouth opened

23 24 עוֹד׃ וַיְהִי דְבַר־יְהוָה אֵלַי לֵאמֹר׃ בֶּן־אָדָם יֹשְׁבֵי
resi- the ,man Son ,saying ,me to Jehovah the And any
of dents of of word was .longer

הֶחֳרָבוֹת הָאֵלֶּה עַל־אַדְמַת יִשְׂרָאֵל אֹמְרִים לֵאמֹר אֶחָד
one ,saying are Israel the in these ,ruins
,speaking of land

הָיָה אַבְרָהָם וַיִּירַשׁ אֶת־הָאָרֶץ וַאֲנַחְנוּ רַבִּים לָנוּ נִתְּנָה
given is us to ;many we but the he and ,Abraham was
(are) ;land possessed

25 הָאָרֶץ לְמוֹרָשָׁה׃ לָכֵן אֱמֹר אֲלֵיהֶם כֹּה־אָמַר ׀ אֲדֹנָי
the says Thus ,them to say Therefore a for the
Lord .possession land

יְהוִה עַל־הַדָּם ׀ תֹּאכֵלוּ וְעֵינֵכֶם תִּשְׂאוּ אֶל־גִּלּוּלֵיכֶם וְדָם
and your to lift you your and ,eat You the on :Jehovah
blood ,idols up eyes blood

26 תִּשְׁפֹּכוּ וְהָאָרֶץ תִּירָשׁוּ׃ עֲמַדְתֶּם עַל־חַרְבְּכֶם עֲשִׂיתֶן
do you your on stand You shall you the and ;shed you
,sword ?possess land

תּוֹעֵבָה וְאִישׁ אֶת־אֵשֶׁת רֵעֵהוּ טִמֵּאתֶם וְהָאָרֶץ תִּירָשׁוּ׃
shall you the and ;defiles his wife and abomina-
?possess land neighbor's each tions

27 כֹּה־תֹאמַר אֲלֵהֶם כֹּה־אָמַר אֲדֹנָי יְהוִה חַי־אָנִי אִם־לֹא
surely (As) :Jehovah the says Thus ,them to say Thus
,I live Lord

אֲשֶׁר בֶּחֳרָבוֹת בַּחֶרֶב יִפֹּלוּ וַאֲשֶׁר עַל־פְּנֵי הַשָּׂדֶה לַחַיָּה
the to field the the in he and shall the by the in those
beasts of face (is) who ,fall sword ruins

נְתַתִּיו לְאָכְלוֹ וַאֲשֶׁר בַּמְּצָדוֹת וּבַמְּעָרוֹת בַּדֶּבֶר יָמוּתוּ׃
shall the by in and the in and be to will I
.die plague caves the forts those ,eaten him give

28 וְנָתַתִּי אֶת־הָאָרֶץ שְׁמָמָה וּמְשַׁמָּה וְנִשְׁבַּת גְּאוֹן עֻזָּהּ וְשָׁמְמוּ
be shall And her the has and a and desolate the I For
waste a .strength of pride ceased ,waste land made have

29 הָרֵי יִשְׂרָאֵל מֵאֵין עוֹבֵר׃ וְיָדְעוּ כִּי־אֲנִי יְהוָה בְּתִתִּי אֶת־
I when ,Jehovah I that they Then go will that ,Israel the
made have (am) know shall .through none of heights

הָאָרֶץ שְׁמָמָה וּמְשַׁמָּה עַל כָּל־תּוֹעֲבֹתָם אֲשֶׁר עָשׂוּ׃
have they which their all because a and desolate the
.done abominations of waste land

30 וְאַתָּה בֶן־אָדָם בְּנֵי עַמְּךָ הַנִּדְבָּרִים בְּךָ אֵצֶל הַקִּירוֹת
walls the beside about talking are your the ,man son And
you people of sons of ,you

in the doors of the houses, and one speaks to one, each man with his brother, saying, Come now and hear what the word (is), which comes from Jehovah. [31] And they come to you as people come, and they sit before you (as) My people; and they hear your words; but they will not do them. For they produce much love with their mouth, (but) their heart goes after their unjust gain. [32] And lo, you (are) to them as a singer of love songs: a beautiful voice, and playing well on an instrument—for they hear your words, but they are not doing them. [33] So when it comes, behold, it is coming—then they will know that a prophet has been in their midst.

וּבְפִתְחֵי הַבָּתִּים וְדִבֶּר־חַד אֶת־אַחַד אִישׁ אֶת־אָחִיו לֵאמֹר

| the in and of doors | the the houses, | speaks and | one one to | each man | his with brother, | saying, |

31 בֹּאוּ־נָא וְשִׁמְעוּ מָה הַדָּבָר הַיּוֹצֵא מֵאֵת יְהֹוָה: וַיָּבוֹאוּ

| now Come | hear | what the | which comes | from | Jehovah. | And they come |

אֵלֶיךָ כְּמָבוֹא־עָם וְיֵשְׁבוּ לְפָנֶיךָ עַמִּי וְשָׁמְעוּ אֶת־דְּבָרֶיךָ

| as you to come | as people people, | they and sit you before | My (as) people | they and hear | your words; |

וְאוֹתָם לֹא יַעֲשׂוּ כִּי־עֲגָבִים בְּפִיהֶם הֵמָּה עֹשִׂים וְאַחֲרֵי

| them but | not will do. | For | their with mouth | they | produce, | (but) after |

32 בִּצְעָם לִבָּם הֹלֵךְ: וְהִנְּךָ לָהֶם כְּשִׁיר עֲגָבִים יְפֵה קוֹל

| their un-gain just | their heart | goes. | And lo, you | to (are) them | of singer songs, | love | beautiful, | a voice |

33 וּמֵטִב נַגֵּן וְשָׁמְעוּ אֶת־דְּבָרֶיךָ וְעֹשִׂים אֵינָם אוֹתָם: וּבְבֹאָהּ

| well play | an (on) instrument, | they and hear | your words, | are but doing | not them | they. | So when it comes, |

הִנֵּה בָאָה וְיָדְעוּ כִּי נָבִיא הָיָה בְתוֹכָם:

| behold, is it | coming— | know will they then | that | a prophet | has been | their in midst. |

CAP. XXXIV לד

CHAPTER 34

CHAPTER 34

[1] And the word of Jehovah was to me, saying, [2] Son of man, prophesy against the shepherds of Israel. Prophesy and say to them, to the shepherds, Thus says the Lord Jehovah: Woe to the shepherds of Israel who are feeding themselves! Should not the shepherds feed the flock? [3] You eat the fat, and clothe yourselves with the wool; you sacrifice the fat ones; you do not feed the flock. [4] You have not made the weak strong, and you have not healed the sick; and you have not bound up the broken. And the banished have not been brought back, and you have not sought the lost; but you rule them with force and harshness. [5] And they were scattered for the lack of a shepherd; and they became for food to all the beasts of the field, when they were

1
2 וַיְהִי דְבַר־יְהֹוָה אֵלַי לֵאמֹר: בֶּן־אָדָם הִנָּבֵא עַל־רוֹעֵי

| the And of word was | Jehovah | me to | saying, | Son of man | prophesy, | the against of shepherds |

יִשְׂרָאֵל הִנָּבֵא וְאָמַרְתָּ אֲלֵיהֶם לָרֹעִים כֹּה אָמַר | אֲדֹנָי

| Israel. | Prophesy | say and | them, to | the to shepherds, | Thus says | the Lord |

יְהֹוָה הוֹי רֹעֵי יִשְׂרָאֵל אֲשֶׁר הָיוּ רֹעִים אוֹתָם הֲלוֹא

| Jeho- to vah: | Woe | Israel's shepherds | who | are | feeding | themselves! | Should not |

3 הַצֹּאן יִרְעוּ הָרֹעִים: אֶת־הַחֵלֶב תֹּאכֵלוּ וְאֶת־הַצֶּמֶר

| the flock | feed | the shepherds? | the fat | You eat | the with and wool |

4 תִּלְבָּשׁוּ הַבְּרִיאָה תִּזְבָּחוּ הַצֹּאן לֹא תִרְעוּ: אֶת־הַנַּחְלוֹת

| clothe yourselves; | fat the ones; | sacrifice | the flock | not you feed. | The weak |

לֹא חִזַּקְתֶּם וְאֶת־הַחוֹלָה לֹא־רִפֵּאתֶם וְלַנִּשְׁבֶּרֶת לֹא

| not have you strengthened, | the and sick | not have you healed; | the and broken | not |

חֲבַשְׁתֶּם וְאֶת־הַנִּדַּחַת לֹא הֲשֵׁבֹתֶם וְאֶת־הָאֹבֶדֶת לֹא

| have you up bound. | the And banished | not | have and brought back, | the and lost | not |

5 בִקַּשְׁתֶּם וּבְחָזְקָה רְדִיתֶם אֹתָם וּבְפָרֶךְ: וַתְּפוּצֶינָה מִבְּלִי

| have you sought; | with but force | you rule | them | with and harshness. | And they were scattered | for of lack |

רֹעֶה וַתִּהְיֶינָה לְאָכְלָה לְכָל־חַיַּת הַשָּׂדֶה וַתְּפוּצֶינָה:

| a shepherd; | they and became | food for | all to of beasts | the the field, | when they were scattered. |

scattered. [6] My sheep strayed through all the mountains and on every high hill. And My sheep were scattered on all the face of the earth; and none searched, and none sought (for them). [7] Therefore, shepherds, hear the word of Jehovah, [8] (As) I live, declares the Lord Jehovah, surely because My sheep became a prey, and My sheep became food for all the beasts of the field, from not having (a) shepherd—and My shepherds did not search (for) My sheep, but the shepherds fed themselves, and did not feed My flock—[9] therefore, O shepherds, hear the word of Jehovah: [10] Thus says the Lord Jehovah: Behold, I (am) against the shepherds, and I will require My sheep from their hand, and cause them to cease from pastoring the sheep. And the shepherds shall not feed themselves any longer, for I will deliver My sheep from their mouth, and they will not be food to devour.

[11] For thus says the Lord Jehovah: Behold, I Myself will search for My sheep and seek them out. [12] As a shepherd seeks his flock in the day that he is among his scattered sheep, so I will seek out My sheep, and will deliver them from all the places where they were scattered, in a day of cloud and thick cloud. [13] And I will bring them out from the peoples, and gather them from the lands, and will bring them to their land and feed them on the mountains of Israel by the ravines, and in all the dwellings of the land. [14] I will feed them in a good pasture, and on the high mountains of Israel shall be their fold; they shall lie there in a good fold, and (in a) fat pasture they

6 יִשְׁגּוּ צֹאנִי בְּכָל־הֶהָרִים וְעַל כָּל־גִּבְעָה רָמָה וְעַל כָּל־
all And .high hill every and the through My strayed
on on mountains all sheep

7 פְּנֵי הָאָרֶץ נָפֹצוּ צֹאנִי וְאֵין דּוֹרֵשׁ וְאֵין מְבַקֵּשׁ׃ לָכֵן
There- sought and searched and My were the the
,fore .(them for) none none ,sheep scattered earth of face

8 רֹעִים שִׁמְעוּ אֶת־דְּבַר יְהוָה׃ חַי־אָנִי נְאֻם ׀ אֲדֹנָי יֱהוִה
,Jehovah the states (As) :Jehovah the hear shep-
Lord ,I live of word ,herds

אִם־לֹא יַעַן הֱיוֹת־צֹאנִי ׀ לָבַז וַתִּהְיֶינָה צֹאנִי לְאָכְלָה לְכָל־
all for food for My and a for My because be- surely
sheep became ,prey sheep came

חַיַּת הַשָּׂדֶה מֵאֵין רֹעֶה וְלֹא־דָרְשׁוּ רֹעַי אֶת־צֹאנִי וַיִּרְעוּ
but My (for) My did And .shepherd from the the
fed ,sheep shepherds search not no having ,field of beasts

9 הָרֹעִים אוֹתָם וְאֶת־צֹאנִי לֹא רָעוּ׃ לָכֵן הָרֹעִים שִׁמְעוּ
hear O There- did not My and them- the
,shepherds ,fore .feed flock selves shepherds

10 דְּבַר־יְהוָה׃ כֹּה־אָמַר אֲדֹנָי יֱהוִה הִנְנִי אֶל־הָרֹעִים
the against ,Behold ,Jehovah the says Thus :Jehovah the
shepherds (am) I Lord of word

וְדָרַשְׁתִּי אֶת־צֹאנִי מִיָּדָם וְהִשְׁבַּתִּים מֵרְעוֹת צֹאן וְלֹא־
And the from them cause and their from My will I and
not .sheep pastoring cease to hand sheep require

יִרְעוּ עוֹד הָרֹעִים אוֹתָם וְהִצַּלְתִּי צֹאנִי מִפִּיהֶם וְלֹא־תִהְיֶיןָ
will they and their from My will I for them- the any shall
be not ,mouth sheep deliver ,selves shepherds longer feed

11 לָהֶם לְאָכְלָה׃ כִּי כֹּה אָמַר אֲדֹנָי יֱהוִה הִנְנִי־אָנִי
My- ,Behold :Jehovah the says thus For .devour to food
self I Lord

12 וְדָרַשְׁתִּי אֶת־צֹאנִי וּבִקַּרְתִּים׃ כְּבַקָּרַת רֹעֶה עֶדְרוֹ בְּיוֹם
the in his a seeks As seek and sheep My search will
day flock shepherd .out them for

הֱיוֹתוֹ בְתוֹךְ־צֹאנוֹ נִפְרָשׁוֹת כֵּן אֲבַקֵּר אֶת־צֹאנִי וְהִצַּלְתִּי
will and My will I so ,scattered his among he that
deliver sheep out seek sheep is

אֶתְהֶם מִכָּל־הַמְּקוֹמֹת אֲשֶׁר נָפֹצוּ שָׁם בְּיוֹם עָנָן וַעֲרָפֶל׃
thick and cloud a in there were they where the from them
.cloud of day scattered places all

13 וְהוֹצֵאתִים מִן־הָעַמִּים וְקִבַּצְתִּים מִן־הָאֲרָצוֹת וַהֲבִיאוֹתִים
will and the from gather and the from will I And
them bring ,lands them ,peoples out them bring

אֶל־אַדְמָתָם וּרְעִיתִים אֶל־הָרֵי יִשְׂרָאֵל בָּאֲפִיקִים וּבְכֹל
in and the by Israel the on feed and their to
all ,ravines of mountains them land

14 מוֹשְׁבֵי הָאָרֶץ׃ בְּמִרְעֶה־טּוֹב אֶרְעֶה אֹתָם וּבְהָרֵי מְרוֹם־
high the on and ,them will I good a in the dwell- the
mountains feed pasture .land of ings

יִשְׂרָאֵל יִהְיֶה נְוֵהֶם שָׁם תִּרְבַּצְנָה בְּנָוֶה טּוֹב וּמִרְעֶה שָׁמֵן
fat (a in) and ,good a in shall they there their shall Israel of
pasture fold lie ;fold be

they shall feed, all the mountains of Israel. [15] I will feed My sheep, and I will make them lie down, declares the Lord Jehovah. [16] I will seek the lost, and I will return the banished. And I will bind up the broken, and I will make the weak strong. But I will destroy the fat and the strong; I will feed them with judgment. [17] And you, My flock, thus says the Lord Jehovah: Behold, I judge between lamb and lamb, (between) rams and he-goats. [18] Is it a small thing to you to have fed on the good pasture, but the rest of your pastures you must trample with your feet? And have you drunk of the clear waters, but the rest you must foul with your feet? [19] And My sheep, (what) your feet have trampled, they must feed on; and what is fouled (with) your feet, they must drink. [20] Therefore thus says the Lord Jehovah to them: Behold, I Myself will even judge between the fat lamb and the lean lamb. [21] Because you have thrust with side and with shoulder, and with your horns have pushed all the weak, until that you have scattered them to the outside; [22] but I will save My sheep, and they shall not any longer be for a prey; and I will judge between lamb and lamb. [23] And I will raise up over them one shepherd. And He shall feed them; My servant David, He shall feed them; and He shall be to them for a shepherd. [24] And I Jehovah will be their God; and My servant David a ruler among them; I Jehovah have spoken. [25] And I will cut a covenant of peace with them, and make evil beasts cease out of the land. And they shall live in the wilderness

תִּרְעֶינָה אֶל־הָרֵי יִשְׂרָאֵל׃ 15 אֲנִי אֶרְעֶה צֹאנִי וַאֲנִי אַרְבִּיצֵם
them make will and My feed will I .Israel the all shall they
,down lie I ,sheep of mountains feed

נְאֻם אֲדֹנָי יְהוִה׃ 16 אֶת־הָאֹבֶדֶת אֲבַקֵּשׁ וְאֶת־הַנִּדַּחַת אָשִׁיב
will I the and will I lost the .Jehovah the states
.return banished seek Lord

וְלַנִּשְׁבֶּרֶת אֶחֱבֹשׁ וְאֶת־הַחוֹלָה אֲחַזֵּק וְאֶת־הַשְּׁמֵנָה וְאֶת־
and the But will I the and will I the And
fat .strengthen weak ,up bind broken

הַחֲזָקָה אַשְׁמִיד אֶרְעֶנָּה בְמִשְׁפָּט׃ 17 וְאַתֵּנָה צֹאנִי כֹּה אָמַר
says thus My ,you And with will I will I strong the
,flock .judgment them feed .destroy

אֲדֹנָי יְהוִה הִנְנִי שֹׁפֵט בֵּין־שֶׂה לָשֶׂה לָאֵילִים וְלָעַתּוּדִים׃
.he-goats and (between) and lamb be- judge ,Behold :Jehovah the
rams ,lamb tween I Lord

18 הַמְעַט מִכֶּם הַמִּרְעֶה הַטּוֹב תִּרְעוּ וְיֶתֶר מִרְעֵיכֶם תִּרְמְסוּ
must you your the but have to good the to a it Is
trample pastures of rest ,on fed pasture you thing small

בְּרַגְלֵיכֶם וּמִשְׁקַע־מַיִם תִּשְׁתּוּ וְאֵת הַנּוֹתָרִים בְּרַגְלֵיכֶם
your with rest the but have you waters of And your with
feet ,drunk clear the ?feet

תִּרְפֹּשׂוּן׃ 19 וְצֹאנִי מִרְמַס רַגְלֵיכֶם תִּרְעֶינָה וּמִרְפַּשׂ רַגְלֵיכֶם
your (with) what and must they your have (what) My And must you
,feet fouled is ,on feed feet trampled ,sheep .foul

תִּשְׁתֶּינָה׃ 20 לָכֵן כֹּה אָמַר אֲדֹנָי יְהוִה אֲלֵיהֶם הִנְנִי־
,Behold :them to Jehovah the says thus Therefore (must) they
I Lord .drink

אָנִי וְשָׁפַטְתִּי בֵּין־שֶׂה בִרְיָה וּבֵין שֶׂה רָזָה׃ 21 יַעַן בְּצַד
with Because the lamb and fat the lamb between even will My-
side .lean judge self

וּבְכָתֵף תֶּהְדֹּפוּ וּבְקַרְנֵיכֶם תְּנַגְּחוּ כָּל־הַנַּחְלוֹת עַד אֲשֶׁר
that until the all have with and have you with and
,weak pushed horns your ,thrust shoulder

הֲפִיצוֹתֶם אוֹתָנָה אֶל־הַחוּצָה׃ 22 וְהוֹשַׁעְתִּי לְצֹאנִי וְלֹא־
and My will I but the to them have you
not ,sheep save ;outside scattered

תִהְיֶינָה עוֹד לָבַז וְשָׁפַטְתִּי בֵּין שֶׂה לָשֶׂה׃ 23 וַהֲקִמֹתִי עֲלֵיהֶם
over will I And and lamb be- will I and a for any shall they
them up raise .lamb tween judge ;prey longer be

רֹעֶה אֶחָד וְרָעָה אֶתְהֶן אֵת עַבְדִּי דָוִיד הוּא יִרְעֶה אֹתָם
,them shall He David My ,them He And .one shepherd
feed servant feed shall

וְהוּא יִהְיֶה לָהֶן לְרֹעֶה׃ 24 וַאֲנִי יְהוָה אֶהְיֶה לָהֶם לֵאלֹהִים
,God to be will Jehovah And a for to shall He and
them I .shepherd them be

וְעַבְדִּי דָוִד נָשִׂיא בְתוֹכָם אֲנִי יְהוָה דִּבַּרְתִּי׃ 25 וְכָרַתִּי לָהֶם
with I And have Jehovah I among ruler a David My and
them cut will .spoken ;them servant

בְּרִית שָׁלוֹם וְהִשְׁבַּתִּי חַיָּה־רָעָה מִן־הָאָרֶץ וְיָשְׁבוּ בַמִּדְבָּר
the in they And the out evil beasts make and ,peace cove- a
wilderness live shall .land of cease of nant

securely, and sleep in the forests. [26] And I will make them and the places around My hill a blessing. And I will bring down the shower in its season; there shall be showers of blessing. [27] And the tree of the field shall yield its fruit, and the earth shall yield its increase. And they shall be on their land securely; and they shall know that I (am) Jehovah, when I have broken the staffs of their yoke, and have rescued them from the hand of their slavers. [28] And they shall not any more be a prey to the nations; and the beast of the land shall not eat them; but they shall live securely, and no one shall terrify. [29] And I will raise up for them a planting place of name; and they shall not any more (be of) those gathered of famine in the land, and shall not any more bear the shame of the nations. [30] And they shall know that I Jehovah their God (am) with them; and they (are) My people, the house of Israel, declares the Lord Jehovah. [31] And you, My sheep, the sheep of My pasture, you (are) men, (and) I (am) your God, declares the Lord Jehovah.

26 לָבֶטַח וְיָשְׁנוּ בַּיְּעוֹרִים׃ וְנָתַתִּי אוֹתָם וּסְבִיבוֹת גִּבְעָתִי
hill My · the and · them · I And · the in · sleep and · securely
around places · make will · .forests

27 בְּרָכָה וְהוֹרַדְתִּי הַגֶּשֶׁם בְּעִתּוֹ גִּשְׁמֵי בְרָכָה יִהְיוּ׃ וְנָתַן
shall And · there · blessing · showers · its in · the · will I And · a
yield · .be shall · of · ;season · shower · down bring · .blessing

עֵץ הַשָּׂדֶה אֶת־פִּרְיוֹ וְהָאָרֶץ תִּתֵּן יְבוּלָהּ וְהָיוּ עַל־אַדְמָתָם
their · on · they And · its · shall · the and · ,fruit its · the · the
land · be shall · .increase · yield · earth · field · of tree

לָבֶטַח וְיָדְעוּ כִּי־אֲנִי יְהוָה בְּשִׁבְרִי אֶת־מַטּוֹת עֻלָּם
their · the · have I when · ,Jehovah · I · that · they and · ;securely
yoke · of staffs · broken · (am) · know shall

28 וְהִצַּלְתִּים מִיַּד הָעֹבְדִים בָּהֶם׃ וְלֹא־יִהְיוּ עוֹד בַּז לַגּוֹיִם
the to · a · any · they And · .their · slavers' · from · have and
,nations · prey · more · be shall not · hand · them rescued

וְחַיַּת הָאָרֶץ לֹא תֹאכְלֵם וְיָשְׁבוּ לָבֶטַח וְאֵין מַחֲרִיד׃
shall · and · ,securely · they but · eat shall · not · the · the and
.terrify · none · live shall · .them · land · of beast

29 וַהֲקִמֹתִי לָהֶם מַטָּע לְשֵׁם וְלֹא־יִהְיוּ עוֹד אֲסֻפֵי רָעָב
famine · those · any · they · and · ;name of · planting a · for · will I And
of gathered · more · shall · not · place · them · up raise

30 בָּאָרֶץ וְלֹא־יִשְׂאוּ עוֹד כְּלִמַּת הַגּוֹיִם׃ וְיָדְעוּ כִּי־אֲנִי יְהוָה
Jehovah · I · that · they And · the · the · any · shall · and · the in
know shall · .nations · of shame · more · bear · not · ,land

אֱלֹהֵיהֶם אִתָּם וְהֵמָּה עַמִּי בֵּית יִשְׂרָאֵל נְאֻם אֲדֹנָי יְהוִה׃
.Jehovah · the · states · ,Israel · the · My (are) · and with (am) · their
Lord · of house · ,people · they · ;them · God

31 וְאַתֵּן צֹאנִי צֹאן מַרְעִיתִי אָדָם אַתֶּם אֲנִי אֱלֹהֵיכֶם נְאֻם
states · ,God your · (and) · you · men · My · the · My · And
(am) I · ,(are) · ,pasture · of sheep · ,sheep · ,you

אֲדֹנָי יְהוִה׃
.Jehovah · the
Lord

CAP. XXXV לה
CHAPTER 35

CHAPTER 35

[1] And the word of Jehovah was to me, saying, [2] Son of man, set your face against Mount Seir and prophesy against it. [3] And say to it, Thus says the Lord Jehovah: Behold, I (am) against you, Mount Seir; and I will stretch My hand against you; and I will make you a ruin and a waste; [4] I will lay your cities waste, and you shall be a ruin; and you shall know that I (am) Jehovah. [5] Because there was to you everlasting enmity, and you poured out the

1 2 וַיְהִי דְבַר־יְהוָה אֵלַי לֵאמֹר׃ בֶּן־אָדָם שִׂים פָּנֶיךָ עַל־הַר
Mount · against · your · set · ,man · Son · ,saying · ,me to · Jehovah · the · And
face · of · of word · was

3 שֵׂעִיר וְהִנָּבֵא עָלָיו׃ וְאָמַרְתָּ לּוֹ כֹּה אָמַר אֲדֹנָי יְהוִה
:Jehovah · the · says · Thus · ,it to · say And · against · and · Seir
Lord · .it · prophesy

הִנְנִי אֵלֶיךָ הַר־שֵׂעִיר וְנָטִיתִי יָדִי עָלֶיךָ וּנְתַתִּיךָ שְׁמָמָה
ruin a · will I and · against · My · will I and · ,Seir Mount · against · ,Behold
you make · ,you · hand · stretch · ,you · (am) I

4 וּמְשַׁמָּה׃ עָרֶיךָ חָרְבָּה אָשִׂים וְאַתָּה שְׁמָמָה תִהְיֶה וְיָדַעְתָּ
you and · shall · ruin a · you and · will I · waste · your · a and
know shall · ;be · lay, · cities · .waste

5 כִּי־אֲנִי יְהוָה׃ יַעַן הֱיוֹת לְךָ אֵיבַת עוֹלָם וַתַּגֵּר אֶת־בְּנֵי־
the · you and · ever- · enmity · to · there · Because · .Jehovah · I that
of sons · poured · ,lasting · you · was · (am)

sons of Israel to the hands of the sword in the time of their calamity, in the time of (the) iniquity of the end. [6] Therefore, (As) I live, declares the Lord Jehovah, surely for blood I appoint you, and blood shall pursue you. Since you have not hated blood, so blood shall pursue you. [7] And I will make Mount Seir a ruin and a waste, and cut off from it the one passing through, and the one returning. [8] And I will fill his mountains (with) his slain. (In) your hills and (in) your valleys, and (in) all your torrent, the slain by the sword shall fall in them. [9] I will make you forever those ruins, and your cities shall not be inhabited. And you shall know that I (am) Jehovah. [10] Because you have said, These two nations and these two lands will be mine, and we shall possess it — Jehovah was there— [11] therefore, (As) I live, declares the Lord Jehovah, I will act by your anger and by envy which you have done out of your hatred against them; and I will be known among them when I have judged you. [12] And you shall know that I (am) Jehovah. I have heard all your revilings which you have spoken against the mountains of Israel, saying, Desolation! They are given to us for food! [13] And you magnified with your mouth against Me, and have multiplied your words against Me; I have heard. [14] Thus says the Lord Jehovah: As all the earth rejoices, I will make you a ruin. [15] As you rejoiced at the inheritance of the house of Israel, because that (was a) ruin, so I will do to you. You shall be a ruin, O Mount Seir and all Edom, all of it. And they shall know that I (am) Jehovah.

6 יִשְׂרָאֵל עַל־יְדֵי־חָרֶב בְּעֵת אֵידָם בְּעֵת עֲוֺן קֵץ׃ לָכֵן חַי־
(As) there- the iniquity the in their the in the the to Israel
live ,fore ;end's of time ,calamity of time sword of hands

אָנִי נְאֻם אֲדֹנָי יֱהוִה כִּי־לְדָם אֶעֶשְׂךָ וְדָם יִרְדְּפֶךָ אִם־לֹא
not Since pur- shall and do I for surely ,Jehovah the states ,I
.you sue blood ,you make blood Lord

7 דָם שָׂנֵאתָ וְדָם יִרְדְּפֶךָּ׃ וְנָתַתִּי אֶת־הַר שֵׂעִיר לְשִׁמְמָה
a for Seir Mount I And pur- shall so have you blood
ruin make will .you sue blood ,hated

8 וּשְׁמָמָה וְהִכְרַתִּי מִמֶּנּוּ עֹבֵר וָשָׁב׃ וּמִלֵּאתִי אֶת־הָרָיו
his will I And the and passer- the from cut and a and
mountains fill returnee through it off ,waste

חֲלָלָיו גִּבְעוֹתֶיךָ וְגֵאוֹתֶיךָ וְכָל־אֲפִיקֶיךָ חַלְלֵי־חֶרֶב יִפְּלוּ
shall the the your (in) and (in) and your (In) his (with)
fall sword by slain ,torrent all ,valleys your hills .slain

9 בָהֶם׃ שִׁמְמוֹת עוֹלָם אֶתֶּנְךָ וְעָרֶיךָ לֹא תִישַׁבְנָה וִידַעְתֶּם
you And be shall not your and will I forever Those .them in
know shall .inhabited cities ,you make ruins

10 כִּי־אֲנִי יְהוָה׃ יַעַן אֲמָרְךָ אֶת־שְׁנֵי הַגּוֹיִם וְאֶת־שְׁתֵּי
these and nations These have you Because .Jehovah I that
two two ,said (am)

11 הָאֲרָצוֹת לִי תִהְיֶינָה וִירַשְׁנוּהָ וַיהוָה שָׁם הָיָה׃ לָכֵן חַי־אָנִי
I (As) there- —was there Jeho- Yet we and be will mine lands
live fore vah —it possess shall

נְאֻם אֲדֹנָי יֱהוִה וְעָשִׂיתִי כְּאַפְּךָ וּכְקִנְאָתְךָ אֲשֶׁר עָשִׂיתָה
have you which by and your by will I ,Jehovah the states
done envy anger act Lord

12 מִשִּׂנְאָתֶיךָ בָּם וְנוֹדַעְתִּי בָם כַּאֲשֶׁר אֶשְׁפְּטֶךָ׃ וְיָדַעְתָּ כִּי־
that you And have I when among will I and against of out
know shall .you judged them known be ;them hatred your

אֲנִי יְהוָה שָׁמַעְתִּי ׀ אֶת־כָּל־נָאָצוֹתֶיךָ אֲשֶׁר אָמַרְתָּ עַל־
against have you which your all have I .Jehovah I
spoken revilings heard (am)

13 הָרֵי יִשְׂרָאֵל לֵאמֹר ׀ שָׁמֵמָה לָנוּ נִתְּנוּ לְאָכְלָה׃ וַתַּגְדִּילוּ
you And .food for are they To !Desolation ,saying ,Israel the
magnified given us of mountains

עָלַי בְּפִיכֶם וְהַעְתַּרְתֶּם עָלַי דִּבְרֵיכֶם אֲנִי שָׁמָעְתִּי׃
have I your against have and your with against
.heard ;words Me multiplied ,mouth Me

14 כֹּה אָמַר אֲדֹנָי יֱהוִה כִּשְׂמֹחַ כָּל־הָאָרֶץ שְׁמָמָה אֶעֱשֶׂה־
will I ruin a ;earth the all rejoices As :Jehovah the says Thus
make Lord

15 לָּךְ׃ כְּשִׂמְחָתְךָ לְנַחֲלַת בֵּית־יִשְׂרָאֵל עַל אֲשֶׁר־שָׁמֵמָה
(a was) that because Israel the the at you As .you
,ruin of house of inheritance rejoiced

כֵּן אֶעֱשֶׂה־לָּךְ שְׁמָמָה תִהְיֶה הַר־שֵׂעִיר וְכָל־אֱדוֹם כֻּלָּהּ
of all ,Edom and Seir O shall you ruin A to will I so
.it all Mount ,be .you do

וְיָדְעוּ כִּי־אֲנִי יְהוָה׃
.Jehovah I that they And
(am) know shall

CAP. XXXVI לו

CHAPTER 36

CHAPTER 36

[1] And you, son of man, prophesy to Israel's mountains and say, O heights of Israel, hear the word of Jehovah. [2] Thus says the Lord Jehovah: Because the enemy has said against you, Aha! Everlasting heights have become a possession to us. [3] Therefore prophesy and say, Thus says the Lord Jehovah: Because, yea, because of the wasting and crushing of you from all around, that you might be a possession to the rest of the nations, and you were lifted on the lip of the tongue, and the talking of the people; therefore, mountains of Israel, hear the word of the Lord Jehovah: Thus says the Lord Jehovah to the mountains and to the hills, to the ravines and to the valleys, to the wastes of desolation and to the forsaken cities, which became a prey and a mocking to the rest of the nations that (are) all around; [5] therefore thus says the Lord Jehovah: Surely I have spoken in the fire of My jealousy against the rest of the nations, and against Edom, all of her who have given My land to themselves for a possession with all joy of heart, with scorning of soul, to drive it out for a prey. [6] Therefore prophesy concerning the land of Israel, and say to the mountains and to the hills, to the ravines and to the valleys, Thus says the Lord Jehovah: Behold, I have spoken in My jealousy and in My fury, because you have borne the shame of the nations. [7] Therefore thus says the Lord Jehovah: I have lifted up My hand; surely

1 וְאַתָּה בֶן־אָדָם הִנָּבֵא אֶל־הָרֵי יִשְׂרָאֵל וְאָמַרְתָּ הָרֵי יִשְׂרָאֵל
,Israel O ,say and Israel the to prophesy ,man son And
of heights of mountains of ,you

2 שִׁמְעוּ דְּבַר־יְהוָה׃ כֹּה אָמַר אֲדֹנָי יְהוִה יַעַן אָמַר הָאוֹיֵב
the has Be- :Jehovah the says Thus .Jehovah the hear
enemy said cause Lord of word

3 עֲלֵיכֶם הֶאָח וּבָמוֹת עוֹלָם לְמוֹרָשָׁה הָיְתָה לָּנוּ׃ לָכֵן
There- .us to have a For ever- heights !Aha against
fore become possession lasting ,you

הִנָּבֵא וְאָמַרְתָּ כֹּה אָמַר אֲדֹנָי יְהוִה יַעַן בְּיַעַן שַׁמּוֹת וְשָׁאֹף
and the be- yea Be- :Jehovah the says Thus ,say and prophesy
crushing wasting cause ,cause Lord

אֶתְכֶם מִסָּבִיב לִהְיוֹתְכֶם מוֹרָשָׁה לִשְׁאֵרִית הַגּוֹיִם וַתַּעֲלוּ
you and the the to a you that all from you of
lifted were ,nations of rest possession be might around

4 עַל־שְׂפַת לָשׁוֹן וְדִבַּת־עָם׃ לָכֵן הָרֵי יִשְׂרָאֵל שִׁמְעוּ
hear ,Israel mountains There- the the and the the on
of ,fore .people's talking tongue of lip

דְּבַר־אֲדֹנָי יְהוִה כֹּה־אָמַר אֲדֹנָי יְהוִה לֶהָרִים וְלַגְּבָעוֹת
to and the to Jehovah the says Thus :Jehovah the the
,hills the mountains Lord Lord of word

לָאֲפִיקִים וְלַגֵּאָיוֹת וְלֶחֳרָבוֹת הַשֹּׁמְמוֹת וְלֶעָרִים הַנֶּעֱזָבוֹת
,forsaken to and ,desolation the to to and the to
cities the of wastes ,valleys the ravines

5 אֲשֶׁר הָיוּ לְבַז וּלְלַעַג לִשְׁאֵרִית הַגּוֹיִם אֲשֶׁר מִסָּבִיב׃ לָכֵן
there- all that the the to a and a be- which
,fore ;around (are) nations of rest mocking prey came

כֹּה־אָמַר אֲדֹנָי יְהוִה אִם־לֹא בְּאֵשׁ קִנְאָתִי דִבַּרְתִּי עַל־
against have I My the in Surely :Jehovah the says thus
spoken jealousy of fire Lord

שְׁאֵרִית הַגּוֹיִם וְעַל־אֱדוֹם כֻּלָּא אֲשֶׁר נָתְנוּ־אֶת־אַרְצִי ׀
My have who all ,Edom and the rest the
land given her of against ,nations of

לָהֶם לְמוֹרָשָׁה בְּשִׂמְחַת כָּל־לֵבָב בִּשְׁאָט נֶפֶשׁ לְמַעַן
to soul scorn- with the all joy with a for them- to
of ing ,heart of possession selves

6 מִגְרָשָׁהּ לָבַז׃ לָכֵן הִנָּבֵא עַל־אַדְמַת יִשְׂרָאֵל וְאָמַרְתָּ
say and Israel the concerning prophesy There- a for it drive
of land fore .prey out

לֶהָרִים וְלַגְּבָעוֹת לָאֲפִיקִים וְלַגֵּאָיוֹת כֹּה־אָמַר ׀ אֲדֹנָי יְהוִה
:Jehovah the says Thus to and the to to and the to
Lord ,valleys the ,ravines ,hills the mountains

הִנְנִי בְקִנְאָתִי וּבַחֲמָתִי דִּבַּרְתִּי יַעַן כְּלִמַּת גּוֹיִם נְשָׂאתֶם׃
have you the the because have My in and My in ,Behold
.borne nations of shame ,spoken fury jealousy I

7 לָכֵן כֹּה אָמַר אֲדֹנָי יְהוִה אֲנִי נָשָׂאתִי אֶת־יָדִי אִם־
sure- ;hand My have I :Jehovah the says thus Therefore
up lifted Lord

the nations that surround you, they shall bear their shame. [8] But you, O mountains of Israel, you shall put out your branches and your fruit you shall bear for My people Israel. For they are drawing near to come. [9] For behold, I (am) for you. and I will turn to you, and you shall be tilled and sown. [10] And I will multiply men on you, all the house of Israel; all of it. And the cities shall be inhabited, and the wastes shall be built. [11] And I will multiply men on you, and beast, and they will grow and be fruitful; and I will make you dwell as you formerly (were); and I will do better than at your beginnings. And you shall know that I (am) Jehovah. [12] I will cause men to walk on you, My people Israel; and they will possess you, and you will be an inheritance to them, and not will increase any more their bereavement.

[13] Thus says the Lord Jehovah: Because they said to you, You (are) a devourer of men; and you have bereaved your nations; [14] therefore you shall not devour men any longer, and you shall not make your nations fall any more, declares the Lord Jehovah. [15] And I will not let you hear the shame of the nations any longer; and you shall not bear the disgrace of the peoples any more; and you shall not cause your nations to fall any more, declares the Lord Jehovah.

[16] And the word of Jehovah was to me, saying, [17] Son of man, (when) the house of Israel dwelt on their land, they even defiled it by their ways and by their doings—as the defilement of woman's impurity, their way was before Me. [18] Thus I poured out My fury on them, because of the blood that they had poured out on the land, and for their idols they defiled it.

8 לֹא הַגּוֹיִם אֲשֶׁר־לָכֶם מִסָּבִיב הֵמָּה כְּלִמָּתָם יִשָּׂאוּ׃ וְאַתֶּם
But shall their they ,surround you that the ly
,you .bear shame nations

הָרֵי יִשְׂרָאֵל עַנְפְּכֶם תִּתֵּנוּ וּפֶרְיְכֶם תִּשְׂאוּ לְעַמִּי יִשְׂרָאֵל
.Israel My for shall you your and shall you your ,Israel moun- O
people bear fruit out put branches of tains

9 כִּי קֵרְבוּ לָבוֹא׃ כִּי הִנְנִי אֲלֵיכֶם וּפָנִיתִי אֲלֵיכֶם וְנֶעֱבַדְתֶּם
shall you and ,you to I and ,you for ,behold for ;come to they For
tilled be turn will (am) I near draw

10 וְנִזְרַעְתֶּם׃ וְהִרְבֵּיתִי עֲלֵיכֶם אָדָם כָּל־בֵּית יִשְׂרָאֵל כֻּלֹּה
of all ,Israel the all ,men you on will I And .sown and
.it of house multiply

11 וְנוֹשְׁבוּ הֶעָרִים וְהֶחֳרָבוֹת תִּבָּנֶינָה׃ וְהִרְבֵּיתִי עֲלֵיכֶם אָדָם
man you on will I And be shall the and the shall And
multiply .built wastes ,cities in dwelt be

וּבְהֵמָה וְרָבוּ וּפָרוּ וְהוֹשַׁבְתִּי אֶתְכֶם כְּקַדְמוֹתֵיכֶם וְהֵטִבֹתִי
will I and ;(were) you as you will I and be and will and and
better do formerly dwell make ,fruitful grow ,beast

12 מֵרִאשֹׁתֵיכֶם וִידַעְתֶּם כִּי־אֲנִי יְהוָה׃ וְהוֹלַכְתִּי עֲלֵיכֶם
you on cause will I .Jehovah I that you And your at than
walk to (am) know shall .beginnings

אָדָם אֶת־עַמִּי יִשְׂרָאֵל וִירֵשׁוּךָ וְהָיִיתָ לָהֶם לְנַחֲלָה וְלֹא־
and an to you and they and ;Israel My ,men
not ,inheritance them be will ,you possess will people

13 תוֹסִף עוֹד לְשַׁכְּלָם׃ כֹּה אָמַר אֲדֹנָי יְהוִה יַעַן אֹמְרִים
they Be- :Jehovah the says Thus their to any add
said cause Lord .bereavement longer

14 לָכֶם אֹכֶלֶת אָדָם אָתְּ וּמְשַׁכֶּלֶת גּוֹיַךְ הָיִית׃ לָכֵן אָדָם
men there- ;have you your bereaved and You men de- a ,you to
fore nations ;(are) of vourer

לֹא־תֹאכְלִי עוֹד וְגוֹיַךְ לֹא תְכַשְּׁלִי־עוֹד נְאֻם אֲדֹנָי יְהוִה׃
.Jehovah the states any shall you not your and any shall you not
Lord ;more fall make nations ,longer devour

15 וְלֹא־אַשְׁמִיעַ אֵלַיִךְ עוֹד כְּלִמַּת הַגּוֹיִם וְחֶרְפַּת עַמִּים לֹא
not the the and the the any you will I And
peoples of disgrace ;nations of shame longer hear let not

תִשְׂאִי־עוֹד וְגוֹיַךְ לֹא־תַכְשִׁלִי עוֹד נְאֻם אֲדֹנָי יְהוִה׃
.Jehovah the states any shall you not your and any shall you
Lord more fall to cause nations ;longer bear

16 17 וַיְהִי דְבַר־יְהוָה אֵלַי לֵאמֹר׃ בֶּן־אָדָם בֵּית יִשְׂרָאֵל
Israel the (when) ,man Son ,saying ,me to Jehovah the And
of house of of word was

יֹשְׁבִים עַל־אַדְמָתָם וַיְטַמְּאוּ אוֹתָהּ בְּדַרְכָּם וּבַעֲלִילוֹתָם
their by and their by it even they their on dwelt
.doings ways defiled ,land

18 כְּטֻמְאַת הַנִּדָּה הָיְתָה דַרְכָּם לְפָנָי׃ וָאֶשְׁפֹּךְ חֲמָתִי עֲלֵיהֶם
them on My I Thus before their was woman's a de- the as
fury poured .Me way impurity of filement

עַל־הַדָּם אֲשֶׁר־שָׁפְכוּ עַל־הָאָרֶץ וּבְגִלּוּלֵיהֶם טִמְּאוּהָ׃
they their for and the on they that the because
.it defiled (which by) idols ,land out poured had blood of

And I scattered them among the nations, and they were sown among the lands; I judged them by their way and by their doings. [20] And (when) they entered into the nations where they went there, they even profaned My holy name, by saying to them, These (are) the people of Jehovah, and they are gone out of His land. [21] But I had pity for My holy name which the house of Israel had profaned among the nations, there where they went.

[22] Therefore say to the house of Israel, Thus says the Lord Jehovah: I do not do (this) for your sake, O house of Israel, but only for My holy name, which you profaned among the nations, there where you went. [23] And I will sanctify My great name which was profaned among the nations, which you profaned amidst them. And the nations shall know that I (am) Jehovah, declares the Lord Jehovah, when I am sanctified in you in their eyes. [24] For I will take you from the nations, and gather you out of all the lands, and bring you into your land. [25] Then I will sprinkle clean waters on you, and you shall be clean. I will cleanse you from all your defilement and from all your idols. [26] I will also give you a new heart; and I will put a new spirit within you. And I will take away the stony heart out of your flesh, and I will give to you a heart of flesh. [27] And I will put My Spirit within you, and make (it) that you will walk in My statutes; and you shall keep My judgments, and do them. [28] And you shall dwell in the land that I gave to your fathers. And you shall be to Me a people,

19 וָאָפִיץ אֹתָם בַּגּוֹיִם וַיִּזָּרוּ בָּאֲרָצוֹת כְּדַרְכָּם וְכַעֲלִילוֹתָם
their by and their by the among they and among them I And
doings way ;lands sown were ,nations the scattered

20 שְׁפַטְתִּים׃ וַיָּבוֹא אֶל־הַגּוֹיִם אֲשֶׁר־בָּאוּ שָׁם וַיְחַלְּלוּ אֶת־
even they ,there they where the into (when) And judged I
profaned went nations entered they .them

שֵׁם קָדְשִׁי בֶּאֱמֹר לָהֶם עַם־יְהוָה אֵלֶּה וּמֵאַרְצוֹ יָצָאוּ׃
are they of out and These Jehovah the ,them to saying by My name
.gone land His ,(are) of people ,holy

21 וָאֶחְמֹל עַל־שֵׁם קָדְשִׁי אֲשֶׁר חִלְּלֻהוּ בֵּית יִשְׂרָאֵל בַּגּוֹיִם
the among Israel the had which My name for I But
nations of house profaned ,holy pity had

22 אֲשֶׁר־בָּאוּ שָׁמָּה׃ לָכֵן אֱמֹר לְבֵית־יִשְׂרָאֵל כֹּה
Thus ,Israel the to say Therefore .there they where
of house went

אָמַר אֲדֹנָי יֱהוִה לֹא לְמַעַנְכֶם אֲנִי עֹשֶׂה בֵּית יִשְׂרָאֵל כִּי
but ,Israel O do I your for Not :Jehovah the says
of house ,(this) sake Lord

אִם־לְשֵׁם־קָדְשִׁי אֲשֶׁר חִלַּלְתֶּם בַּגּוֹיִם אֲשֶׁר־בָּאתֶם שָׁם׃
.there went you where the among you which My for only
nations profaned holy name

23 וְקִדַּשְׁתִּי אֶת־שְׁמִי הַגָּדוֹל הַמְחֻלָּל בַּגּוֹיִם אֲשֶׁר חִלַּלְתֶּם
you which the among was which great name My will I And
profaned ,nations profaned sanctify

בְּתוֹכָם וְיָדְעוּ הַגּוֹיִם כִּי־אֲנִי יְהוָה נְאֻם אֲדֹנָי יֱהוִה בְּהִקָּדְשִׁי
am I when ,Jehovah the states ,Jehovah I that the shall And amidst
sanctified Lord (am) nations know .them

24 בָכֶם לְעֵינֵיהֶם׃ וְלָקַחְתִּי אֶתְכֶם מִן־הַגּוֹיִם וְקִבַּצְתִּי אֶתְכֶם
you gather and the from you I For their in you in
,nations take will .eyes

25 מִכָּל־הָאֲרָצוֹת וְהֵבֵאתִי אֶתְכֶם אֶל־אַדְמַתְכֶם׃ וְזָרַקְתִּי
will I Then your into you bring and the of out
sprinkle .land ,lands all

עֲלֵיכֶם מַיִם טְהוֹרִים וּטְהַרְתֶּם מִכֹּל טֻמְאוֹתֵיכֶם וּמִכָּל־
from and your From shall you and ,clean waters you on
all ;defilement all .clean be

26 גִּלּוּלֵיכֶם אֲטַהֵר אֶתְכֶם׃ וְנָתַתִּי לָכֶם לֵב חָדָשׁ וְרוּחַ
a and ;new heart a you will I .you will I idols your
spirit give also cleanse

חֲדָשָׁה אֶתֵּן בְּקִרְבְּכֶם וַהֲסִרֹתִי אֶת־לֵב הָאֶבֶן מִבְּשַׂרְכֶם
your of out stony heart the will I And within will I new
,flesh away take .you put

27 וְנָתַתִּי לָכֶם לֵב בָּשָׂר׃ וְאֶת־רוּחִי אֶתֵּן בְּקִרְבְּכֶם וְעָשִׂיתִי
and within will I My And .flesh heart a you to I and
make you put Spirit of give will

28 אֵת אֲשֶׁר־בְּחֻקַּי תֵּלֵכוּ וּמִשְׁפָּטַי תִּשְׁמְרוּ וַעֲשִׂיתֶם׃ וִישַׁבְתֶּם
you And do and shall you My and you (for) My in that
dwell shall .them keep judgments ;walk (to) statutes (is) which

בָּאָרֶץ אֲשֶׁר נָתַתִּי לַאֲבֹתֵיכֶם וִהְיִיתֶם לִי לְעָם וְאָנֹכִי
I and a to you And your to gave I that the in
,people Me be shall .fathers land

and I will be God to you. [29] I will also save you from all your defilements, and I will call for grain and increase it; and I will not put on you a famine. [30] And I will multiply the fruit of the tree, and the produce of the field, in order that you will not any more receive the disgrace of famine among the nations. [31] Then you shall remember your evil ways and your doings that were not good; and you will despise yourselves in your own eyes for your iniquities and for your abominations. [32] I am not doing (this) for your sake, declares the Lord Jehovah; let it be known to you. Be ashamed and confounded for your ways, O house of Israel.

[33] Thus says the Lord Jehovah: In the day I cleanse you from all your iniquities, I will cause (to) (be) inhabited the cities, and the wastes shall be built. [34] And the desolated land shall be cultivated, rather than being a ruin in the sight of all who also pass by. [35] And they shall say, This land that was desolated has become like the Garden of Eden. And the wasted and desolated and razed cities are fortified (and) indwelt. [36] And the nations shall know, (they) that are left all around you, that I, Jehovah, built the razed (places), (and) planted that which was desolated. I, Jehovah, have spoken, and will do (it).

[37] Thus says the Lord Jehovah: Yet this I will be sought (unto) by the house of Israel, to act for them, (that) I will increase them lika a flock, (with) men. [38] As a holy flock, as the flock of

29 אֶהְיֶה לָכֶם לֵאלֹהִים׃ וְהוֹשַׁעְתִּי אֶתְכֶם מִכֹּל טֻמְאוֹתֵיכֶם
your from you will I .God you to be will
,defilements all save also

וְקָרָאתִי אֶל־הַדָּגָן וְהִרְבֵּיתִי אֹתוֹ וְלֹא־אֶתֵּן עֲלֵיכֶם רָעָב׃
a you on will I and ,it and grain for will I and
.famine put not increase call

30 וְהִרְבֵּיתִי אֶת־פְּרִי הָעֵץ וּתְנוּבַת הַשָּׂדֶה לְמַעַן אֲשֶׁר לֹא־
not that order in the the and tree the the will I And
,field of produce of fruit multiply

31 תִקְחוּ עוֹד חֶרְפַּת רָעָב בַּגּוֹיִם׃ וּזְכַרְתֶּם אֶת־דַּרְכֵיכֶם
ways your shall you Then among famine the any will you
remember .nations the of disgrace more receive

הָרָעִים וּמַעַלְלֵיכֶם אֲשֶׁר לֹא־טוֹבִים וּנְקֹטֹתֶם בִּפְנֵיכֶם עַל
for own your in will you and were not that your and evil
eyes yourselves despise ,good doings

32 עֲוֺנֹתֵיכֶם וְעַל תּוֹעֲבֹתֵיכֶם׃ לֹא לְמַעַנְכֶם אֲנִי־עֹשֶׂה נְאֻם
states am I your for not your and your
,(this) doing sake .abominations for iniquities

אֲדֹנָי יְהוִה יִוָּדַע לָכֶם בּוֹשׁוּ וְהִכָּלְמוּ מִדַּרְכֵיכֶם בֵּית
house O your for con- and Be .you to it let ;Jehovah the
of ,ways founded ashamed known be Lord

33 יִשְׂרָאֵל׃ כֹּה אָמַר אֲדֹנָי יְהוִה בְּיוֹם טַהֲרִי אֶתְכֶם מִכֹּל
from you cleanse I the In :Jehovah the says Thus .Israel
all day Lord

34 עֲוֺנוֹתֵיכֶם וְהוֹשַׁבְתִּי אֶת־הֶעָרִים וְנִבְנוּ הֶחֳרָבוֹת׃ וְהָאָרֶץ
the And the shall and the make will I your
land .wastes built be ,cities inhabited ,iniquities

הַנְּשַׁמָּה תֵּעָבֵד תַּחַת אֲשֶׁר הָיְתָה שְׁמָמָה לְעֵינֵי כָּל־עוֹבֵר׃
also all the in ruin a being rather be shall desolated
.by pass of sight than cultivated

35 וְאָמְרוּ הָאָרֶץ הַלֵּזוּ הַנְּשַׁמָּה הָיְתָה כְּגַן־עֵדֶן וְהֶעָרִים הֶחֳרֵבוֹת
wasted the And .Eden like has was that This land they And
cities of garden the become desolated ,say shall

36 וְהַנְשַׁמּוֹת וְהַנֶּהֱרָסוֹת בְּצוּרוֹת יָשָׁבוּ׃ וְיָדְעוּ הַגּוֹיִם אֲשֶׁר
that the shall And (and) fortified are razed and and
nations know .inhabited desolated

יִשָּׁאֲרוּ סְבִיבוֹתֵיכֶם כִּי ׀ אֲנִי יְהוָה בָּנִיתִי הַנֶּהֱרָסוֹת
razed the built Jehovah I that around all are
.(places) you left

37 נָטַעְתִּי הַנְּשַׁמָּה אֲנִי יְהוָה דִּבַּרְתִּי וְעָשִׂיתִי׃ כֹּה
Thus will and have Jehovah I which that (and)
.(it) do ,spoken ;desolated was planted

אָמַר אֲדֹנָי יְהוִה עוֹד זֹאת אִדָּרֵשׁ לְבֵית־יִשְׂרָאֵל לַעֲשׂוֹת
act to Israel the by will I this Yet :Jehovah the says
of house sought be Lord

38 לָהֶם אַרְבֶּה אֹתָם כַּצֹּאן אָדָם׃ כְּצֹאן קָדָשִׁים כְּצֹאן
the as ,holy a As (with) a like them will I for
of flock flock .men flock increase .them

Jerusalem in her appointed (feasts), so the wasted cities shall be filled (with) flocks of men; and they shall know that I (am) Jehovah.

CHAPTER 37

[1] The hand of Jehovah was on me, and brought me by the Spirit of Jehovah, and made me rest in the midst of a valley; and it was full of bones; [2] and He made me pass among them all around. And behold, very many (were) on the face of the valley. And, behold! (They were) very dry. [3] And He said to me, Son of man, can these bones live? And I said, O Lord Jehovah, You know. [4] And He said to me, Prophesy to these bones and say to them, O dry bones, hear the word of Jehovah!

[5] Thus says the Lord Jehovah to these bones: Behold, I will make breath enter into you, and you shall live. [6] And I will put sinews on you, and will bring flesh on you, and spread skin over you, and put breath in you, and you shall live. And you shall know that I (am) Jehovah. [7] So I prophesied as I was commanded. And as I prophesied, there was a noise. And, behold, a shaking! And the bones draw near, a bone to its bones. [8] And I watched, and, behold! The sinews and the flesh came up on them, and the skin spread over them from above. But there (was) no breath in them. [9] Then He said to me, Prophesy to the breath; prophesy, son of man, and say to the breath, Thus says

יְרוּשָׁלַ͏ִם בְּמוֹעֲדֶיהָ כֵּן תִּהְיֶינָה הֶעָרִים הֶחֳרֵבוֹת מְלֵאוֹת
filled wasted the cities be shall so her in ,Jerusalem ,(feasts) appointed

צֹאן אָדָם וְיָדְעוּ כִּי־אֲנִי יְהוָה׃
.Jehovah I that (am) they and know shall ;men (with) of flocks

CAP. XXXVII לז

CHAPTER 37

1 הָיְתָה עָלַי יַד־יְהוָה וַיּוֹצִאֵנִי בְרוּחַ יְהוָה וַיְנִיחֵנִי בְּתוֹךְ
the in of midst made and rest me Jehovah the by of Spirit brought and me ,Jehovah The of hand on me was

2 הַבִּקְעָה וְהִיא מְלֵאָה עֲצָמוֹת׃ וְהֶעֱבִירַנִי עֲלֵיהֶם סָבִיב ׀
all among them made He and pass me ,bones was of full it and ;valley a

סָבִיב וְהִנֵּה רַבּוֹת מְאֹד עַל־פְּנֵי הַבִּקְעָה וְהִנֵּה יְבֵשׁוֹת
(were They) dry ,And !behold .valley the the on of face very (were) many And ,behold .around

3 מְאֹד׃ וַיֹּאמֶר אֵלַי בֶּן־אָדָם הֲתִחְיֶינָה הָעֲצָמוֹת הָאֵלֶּה
?these bones live can ,man Son of ,me to He And said .very

4 וָאֹמַר אֲדֹנָי יְהוִה אַתָּה יָדָעְתָּ׃ וַיֹּאמֶר אֵלַי הִנָּבֵא עַל־
to Prophesy ,me to He And said .know You ,Jehovah O Lord I And ,said

הָעֲצָמוֹת הָאֵלֶּה וְאָמַרְתָּ אֲלֵיהֶם הָעֲצָמוֹת הַיְבֵשׁוֹת שִׁמְעוּ
hear ,dry bones O ,them to say and these bones

5 דְּבַר־יְהוָה׃ כֹּה אָמַר אֲדֹנָי יְהוִה לָעֲצָמוֹת הָאֵלֶּה
:these bones to Jehovah the Lord says Thus .Jehovah the of word

6 הִנֵּה אֲנִי מֵבִיא בָכֶם רוּחַ וִחְיִיתֶם׃ וְנָתַתִּי עֲלֵיכֶם גִּידִים
,sinews you on will I And put you and .live shall ,breath into you make will enter I ,Behold

וְהַעֲלֵתִי עֲלֵיכֶם בָּשָׂר וְקָרַמְתִּי עֲלֵיכֶם עוֹר וְנָתַתִּי בָכֶם
you in put and ,skin you spread and over ,flesh you on will and up bring

7 רוּחַ וִחְיִיתֶם וִידַעְתֶּם כִּי־אֲנִי יְהוָה׃ וְנִבֵּאתִי כַּאֲשֶׁר צֻוֵּיתִי
was I .commanded as I So prophesied .Jehovah I that (am) you And know shall you and .live shall ,breath

וַיְהִי־קוֹל כְּהִנָּבְאִי וְהִנֵּה־רַעַשׁ וַתִּקְרְבוּ עֲצָמוֹת עֶצֶם אֶל־
to bone a ,bones the draw And near a !shaking And ,behold I as .prophesied a noise And was

8 עַצְמוֹ׃ וְרָאִיתִי וְהִנֵּה עֲלֵיהֶם גִּדִים וּבָשָׂר עָלָה וַיִּקְרַם
spread and over came ,up the and flesh The sinews them on and !behold I And ,watched .bones its

9 עֲלֵיהֶם עוֹר מִלְמָעְלָה וְרוּחַ אֵין בָּהֶם׃ וַיֹּאמֶר אֵלַי הִנָּבֵא
Prophesy to ,me He Then said .them in not But (was) breath .above from the skin them

אֶל־הָרוּחַ הִנָּבֵא בֶן־אָדָם וְאָמַרְתָּ אֶל־הָרוּחַ כֹּה־אָמַר ׀
says Thus the ,breath to say and ,man son of ,prophesy the ;breath to

the Lord Jehovah: Come from the four winds, O Spirit, and breathe on these slain ones, that they may live. [10] So I prophesied as He commanded me, and the breath came into them. And they lived, and stood on their feet, a very, very great army. [11] Then He said to me, Son of man, these bones, they (are) all the house of Israel. Behold, they say, Our bones are dried, and our hope is perished—we are cut off to ourselves. [12] Therefore prophesy and say to them, Thus says the Lord Jehovah: Behold, I will open your graves, and cause you to come up out of your graves, O My people, and will bring you to the land of Israel. [13] And you shall know that I (am) Jehovah, when I have opened your graves, and have brought you up out of your graves, O My people. [14] And I shall put My Spirit in you, and you shall live; and I will put you on your own land. And you shall know that I Jehovah have spoken and done (it), says Jehovah.

[15] And the word of Jehovah was to me, saying, [16] And you, son of man, take one stick to yourself and write on it, For Judah and for the sons of Israel, his companions. Then take one stick and write on it, For Joseph, the stick of Ephraim and all the house of Israel, his companions. [17] And draw them one to one for yourself, into one stick; and they shall become for oneness in your hand. [18] And when the sons of your people shall speak to you, saying, Will you not declare to us what (these) mean to you?

אֲדֹנָי יְהוִה מֵאַרְבַּע רוּחוֹת בֹּאִי הָרוּחַ וּפְחִי בַּהֲרוּגִים

slain on and ,Spirit O ,Come ,winds the from :Jehovah the
ones breathe four Lord

הָאֵלֶּה וְיִחְיוּ: וְהִנַּבֵּאתִי כַּאֲשֶׁר צִוָּנִי וַתָּבוֹא בָהֶם הָרוּחַ 10

the into and com- He as I So they that ,these
,breath them came ,me manded prophesied .live may

וַיִּחְיוּ וַיַּעַמְדוּ עַל־רַגְלֵיהֶם חַיִל גָּדוֹל מְאֹד מְאֹד: וַיֹּאמֶר 11

He Then .very ,very great army a their on and they and
said ,feet stood lived

אֵלַי בֶּן־אָדָם הָעֲצָמוֹת הָאֵלֶּה כָּל־בֵּית יִשְׂרָאֵל הֵמָּה הִנֵּה

,Behold they Israel the all ,these bones ,man Son ,me to
(are) of house of

אֹמְרִים יָבְשׁוּ עַצְמוֹתֵינוּ וְאָבְדָה תִקְוָתֵנוּ נִגְזַרְנוּ לָנוּ:

to are we —hope our is and ,bones Our dried are ,say they
,ourselves off cut perished

לָכֵן הִנָּבֵא וְאָמַרְתָּ אֲלֵיהֶם כֹּה־אָמַר אֲדֹנָי יְהוִה הִנֵּה 12

,Behold :Jehovah the says Thus ,them to say and prophesy There-
Lord fore

אֲנִי פֹתֵחַ אֶת־קִבְרוֹתֵיכֶם וְהַעֲלֵיתִי אֶתְכֶם מִקִּבְרוֹתֵיכֶם

your of out you to cause and your will I
,graves up come ,graves open

עַמִּי וְהֵבֵאתִי אֶתְכֶם אֶל־אַדְמַת יִשְׂרָאֵל: וִידַעְתֶּם כִּי־אֲנִי 13

I that you And .Israel the to you will and My O
(am) know shall of land bring ,people

יְהוָה בְּפִתְחִי אֶת־קִבְרוֹתֵיכֶם וּבְהַעֲלוֹתִי אֶתְכֶם

you have and ,graves your have I when ,Jehovah
up brought opened

מִקִּבְרוֹתֵיכֶם עַמִּי: וְנָתַתִּי רוּחִי בָכֶם וִחְיִיתֶם וְהִנַּחְתִּי 14

will I and you and ,you in My I And My O your of out
put ,live shall Spirit put shall .people ,graves

אֶתְכֶם עַל־אַדְמַתְכֶם וִידַעְתֶּם כִּי אֲנִי יְהוָה דִּבַּרְתִּי וְעָשִׂיתִי

have and have Jehovah I that you And own your on you
(it) done spoken know shall .land

נְאֻם־יְהוָה:

.Jehovah says

וַיְהִי דְבַר־יְהוָה אֵלַי לֵאמֹר: וְאַתָּה 16 15

And ,saying ,me to Jehovah the And
,you of word was

בֶן־אָדָם קַח־לְךָ עֵץ אֶחָד וּכְתֹב עָלָיו לִיהוּדָה וְלִבְנֵי

for and Judah For ,it on and one stick to take ,man son
of sons the write yourself of

יִשְׂרָאֵל חֲבֵרָו וּלְקַח עֵץ אֶחָד וּכְתוֹב עָלָיו לְיוֹסֵף עֵץ

the For ,it on write and (another) stick Then his ,Israel
of stick ,Joseph one take .companions

אֶפְרַיִם וְכָל־בֵּית יִשְׂרָאֵל חֲבֵרָו: וְקָרַב אֹתָם אֶחָד אֶל־ 17

to one them And his ,Israel the and ,Ephraim
draw .companions of house all

אֶחָד לְךָ לְעֵץ אֶחָד וְהָיוּ לַאֲחָדִים בְּיָדֶךָ: וְכַאֲשֶׁר יֹאמְרוּ 18

shall when And your in one- for they and ;one into for (another)
speak .hand ness become shall stick yourself one

אֵלֶיךָ בְּנֵי עַמְּךָ לֵאמֹר הֲלוֹא־תַגִּיד לָנוּ מָה־אֵלֶּה לָּךְ:

to these what us to you Will ,saying your the you to
?you (mean) declare not ,people of sons

Say to them, Thus says the Lord Jehovah: Behold, I will take the stick of Joseph which (is) in the hand of Ephrain, and the tribes of Israel, his companions; and I will put them with him, with the stick of Judah, and will make them one stick; and they shall be one in My hand.

[20] And the sticks shall be in your hand, (on) which you write on them, before their eyes. [21] And say to them, Thus says the Lord Jehovah: Behold, I will take the sons of Israel from among the nations, there where they have gone, and will gather them from all around, and will bring them into their own land. [22] And I will make them one nation in the land, on the mountains of Israel; and one king shall be to them all for a king. And they shall not be still two nations; and they will not be split into two kingdoms any more. [23] And they will not still be defiled with their idols; and with their filthy idols; nor with all of their transgressions. But I will save them out of all their dwelling-places where they have sinned in them; and I will cleanse them. So they shall be to Me for a people, and I will be to them for God. [24] And My servant David (shall) be king over them. And there shall be one shepherd to all of them. And they shall walk in My judgments, and keep My statutes, and do them. [25] And they shall dwell on the land that I have given to My servant, to Jacob, (there) where your fathers dwelt in it. And they shall dwell on it, they and their sons, and the sons of their sons forever. And My servant David (shall be) a ruler to them forever. [26] And I will cut with them a covenant

19 דַּבֵּר אֲלֵהֶם כֹּה־אָמַר אֲדֹנָי יֱהוִה הִנֵּה אֲנִי לֹקֵחַ אֶת־עֵץ
the will I ,Behold :Jehovah the says Thus ,them to Say
of stick take Lord

יוֹסֵף אֲשֶׁר בְּיַד־אֶפְרַיִם וְשִׁבְטֵי יִשְׂרָאֵל חֲבֵרָו וְנָתַתִּי אוֹתָם
them I and his ,Israel the and ,Ephraim the in which ,Joseph
put will ,companions of tribes of hand (is)

עָלָיו אֶת־עֵץ יְהוּדָה וַעֲשִׂיתִם לְעֵץ אֶחָד וְהָיוּ אֶחָד בְּיָדִי׃
My in one they and ,one stick will and ,Judah the with with
.hand be shall them make of stick ,him

20 21 וְהָיוּ הָעֵצִים אֲשֶׁר־תִּכְתֹּב עֲלֵיהֶם בְּיָדְךָ לְעֵינֵיהֶם׃ וְדַבֵּר
And their before your in them on write you which the And
say .eyes hand sticks be shall

אֲלֵיהֶם כֹּה־אָמַר אֲדֹנָי יֱהוִה הִנֵּה אֲנִי לֹקֵחַ אֶת־בְּנֵי
the will I ,Behold :Jehovah the says Thus ,them to
of sons take Lord

יִשְׂרָאֵל מִבֵּין הַגּוֹיִם אֲשֶׁר הָלְכוּ־שָׁם וְקִבַּצְתִּי אֹתָם
them will and ,there have they where the from Israel
gather gone nations among

22 מִסָּבִיב וְהֵבֵאתִי אוֹתָם אֶל־אַדְמָתָם׃ וְעָשִׂיתִי אֹתָם לְגוֹי
nation them will I And own their into them will and all from
make .land bring around

אֶחָד בָּאָרֶץ בְּהָרֵי יִשְׂרָאֵל וּמֶלֶךְ אֶחָד יִהְיֶה לְכֻלָּם לְמֶלֶךְ
a for them to shall one king and ,Israel the on the in one
.king all be of mountains ,land

וְלֹא יִהְיֶה־עוֹד לִשְׁנֵי גוֹיִם וְלֹא יֵחָצוּ עוֹד לִשְׁתֵּי מַמְלָכוֹת
kingdoms into still will they and ,nations two still they And
two split be not be shall not

23 עוֹד׃ וְלֹא יִטַּמְּאוּ עוֹד בְּגִלּוּלֵיהֶם וּבְשִׁקּוּצֵיהֶם וּבְכֹל
with nor their with and their with still will they And any
of all ;idols filthy ;idols defiled be not .more

פִּשְׁעֵיהֶם וְהוֹשַׁעְתִּי אֹתָם מִכֹּל מוֹשְׁבֹתֵיהֶם אֲשֶׁר חָטְאוּ
have they where dwelling their of out them will I But trans- their
sinned places all save .gressions

בָהֶם וְטִהַרְתִּי אוֹתָם וְהָיוּ־לִי לְעָם וַאֲנִי אֶהְיֶה לָהֶם
to be will and a for to they So .them will I and in
them I ,people Me be shall cleanse ,them

24 לֵאלֹהִים׃ וְעַבְדִּי דָוִד מֶלֶךְ עֲלֵיהֶם וְרוֹעֶה אֶחָד יִהְיֶה
there one And over (be shall) David My And .God for
be shall shepherd .them king servant

25 לְכֻלָּם וּבְמִשְׁפָּטַי יֵלֵכוּ וְחֻקֹּתַי יִשְׁמְרוּ וְעָשׂוּ אוֹתָם׃ וְיָשְׁבוּ
they And .them and ,keep My and shall they My in And all to
dwell shall do ,statutes ,walk judgments .them of

עַל־הָאָרֶץ אֲשֶׁר נָתַתִּי לְעַבְדִּי לְיַעֲקֹב אֲשֶׁר יָשְׁבוּ־בָהּ
in dwelt where ,Jacob to My to have I that the on
it ,servant given land

אֲבוֹתֵיכֶם וְיָשְׁבוּ עָלֶיהָ הֵמָּה וּבְנֵיהֶם וּבְנֵי בְנֵיהֶם עַד־
for their the and their and they ;it on they And your
sons of sons ,sons dwell shall .fathers

26 עוֹלָם וְדָוִד עַבְדִּי נָשִׂיא לָהֶם לְעוֹלָם׃ וְכָרַתִּי לָהֶם בְּרִית
cove- a with I And .forever them to ruler a servant My And .ever
of nant them cut will (be shall) David

שָׁלוֹם בְּרִית עוֹלָם יִהְיֶה אוֹתָם וּנְתַתִּים וְהִרְבֵּיתִי אוֹתָם

,them and will I And with shall It ever- an .peace
multiply them place .them be lasting covenant

27 וְנָתַתִּי אֶת־מִקְדָּשִׁי בְּתוֹכָם לְעוֹלָם׃ וְהָיָה מִשְׁכָּנִי עֲלֵיהֶם

with My shall And .forever their in My I and
.them tabernacle be midst sanctuary put will

28 וְהָיִיתִי לָהֶם לֵאלֹהִים וְהֵמָּה יִהְיוּ־לִי לְעָם׃ וְיָדְעוּ הַגּוֹיִם

the shall And a for to shall they and ,God for them to I And
nations know .people Me be be will

כִּי אֲנִי יְהוָה מְקַדֵּשׁ אֶת־יִשְׂרָאֵל בִּהְיוֹת מִקְדָּשִׁי בְּתוֹכָם

their in My when ,Israel sanctify Jehovah I that
midst sanctuary be shall

לְעוֹלָם׃ *

.forever

CAP. XXXVIII לח

CHAPTER 38

1
2 וַיְהִי דְבַר־יְהוָה אֵלַי לֵאמֹר׃ בֶּן־אָדָם שִׂים פָּנֶיךָ אֶל־גּוֹג

,Gog against your set ,man Son ,saying ,me to Jehovah the And
face of of word was

3 אֶרֶץ הַמָּגוֹג נְשִׂיא רֹאשׁ מֶשֶׁךְ וְתֻבָל וְהִנָּבֵא עָלָיו׃ וְאָמַרְתָּ

,say And against and and Meshech Rosh the Magog the
.him prophesy ,Tubal of prince of land

כֹּה אָמַר אֲדֹנָי יְהוִה הִנְנִי אֵלֶיךָ גּוֹג נְשִׂיא רֹאשׁ מֶשֶׁךְ

Meshech ,Rosh the O against ,Behold :Jehovah the says Thus
of prince ,Gog ,you (am) I Lord

4 וְתֻבָל׃ וְשׁוֹבַבְתִּיךָ וְנָתַתִּי חַחִים בִּלְחָיֶיךָ וְהוֹצֵאתִי אוֹתְךָ

you will I and your into hooks put and will I And and
out bring ,jaws back you turn .Tubal

וְאֶת־כָּל־חֵילֶךָ סוּסִים וּפָרָשִׁים לְבֻשֵׁי מִכְלוֹל כֻּלָּם קָהָל

a of all most clothed and horses your all and
assembly ,them perfectly ,horsemen ,army

5 רָב צִנָּה וּמָגֵן תֹּפְשֵׂי חֲרָבוֹת כֻּלָּם׃ פָּרַס כּוּשׁ וּפוּט

and Ethiopia ;Persia of all ,sword handlers and (with) great
Libya :them of ,shield buckler

6 אִתָּם כֻּלָּם מָגֵן וְכוֹבָע׃ גֹּמֶר וְכָל־אֲגַפֶּיהָ בֵּית תּוֹגַרְמָה

Togarmah the her and Gomer and (with) of all with
of house ;bands all ;helmet shield them ,them

7 יַרְכְּתֵי צָפוֹן וְאֶת־כָּל־אֲגַפָּיו עַמִּים רַבִּים אִתָּךְ׃ הִכֹּן

Be with many peoples his all and the the (from)
,prepared .you ;bands ,north of recesses

וְהָכֵן לְךָ אַתָּה וְכָל־קְהָלֶךָ הַנִּקְהָלִים עָלֶיךָ וְהָיִיתָ לָהֶם

to be and ,you to are that your and you for pre- and
them assembled assembly all ,yourself pared

8 לְמִשְׁמָר׃ מִיָּמִים רַבִּים תִּפָּקֵד בְּאַחֲרִית הַשָּׁנִים תָּבוֹא ׀

shall you years the In shall you many After a for
come after .visited be days .guard

אֶל־אֶרֶץ ׀ מְשׁוֹבֶבֶת מֵחֶרֶב מְקֻבֶּצֶת מֵעַמִּים רַבִּים עַל

on ,many of out gathered the from turned the into
peoples ,sword back land

of peace, an everlasting covenant it shall be with them. And I will place them and multiply; and I will put My sanctuary in their midst forever. [27] And My tabernacle shall be with them. And I will be their God, and they shall be My people. [28] And the nations shall know that I, Jehovah, sanctify Israel, when My sanctuary shall be in their midst forever.

CHAPTER 38

[1] And the word of Jehovah was to me, saying, [2] Son of man, set your face against Gog, the land of Magog the prince of Rosh, Meshech and Tubal, and prophesy against him. [3] And say, Thus says the Lord Jehovah: Behold, I (am) against you, O Gog, the prince of Rosh, Meshech and Tubal. [4] And I will turn you back and put hooks into your jaws; and I will bring out you and all your army, horses and horsemen, clothed most perfectly, all of them, a great assembly (with) buckler and shield, all of them sword-handlers: [5] Persia, Ethiopia, and Libya with them; all of them (with) shield and helmet; [6] Gomer and all her bands; the house of Togarmah (from) the recesses of the north, and all his bands; many peoples with you. [7] Be prepared; yea, prepared for yourself, and all your assembly that are assembled to you; and be a guard to them. [8] After many days you shall be visited. In the after years you shall come into the land turned back from the sword, gathered out of many peoples, on the

mountains of Israel which have been for a continual waste, but he has been brought out of the peoples; and they shall dwell securely, all of them. [9] And you shall go up; you shall come like a storm; you shall be like a cloud to cover the land, you and all your bands, and many peoples with you.

[10] Thus says the Lord Jehovah: And it shall be in that day words shall come up into your heart, and you shall devise an evil plan. [11] And you shall say, I will go up to the land of open spaces; I will go (to) those at ease, who live securely, all of them living with no walls; and there are no bars and gates to them; [12] in order to spoil a spoil, and to steal a prize; to turn your hand on the inhabited waste places; and on the people gathered out of the nations, who have gotten livestock and goods; who dwell in the center of the earth. [13] Sheba and Dedan and the merchants of Tarshish, and all its young lions, shall say to you, Have you come to spoil a spoil? Have you gathered your assembly to steal a prize, to carry away silver and gold, to take away livestock and goods; to spoil a great spoil? [14] Therefore prophesy, son of man, and say to Gog: Thus says the Lord Jehovah: Shall you not know in that day when My people Israel dwells securely? [15] And you shall come from your place out of the recesses of the north, you and many peoples with you, all of them riding on horses, a great assembly, and a mighty army. [16] And you shall come up on My people Israel like a cloud, to cover the land; it shall be in the after days; and I will bring you against My land, so that the

הָרֵי יִשְׂרָאֵל אֲשֶׁר־הָיוּ לְחָרְבָּה תָּמִיד וְהִיא מֵעַמִּים

the | of | out | he but | con- | a for | have which | Israel | the
peoples | | | | tinual, | waste | been | | of mountains

9 הוּצָאָה וְיָשְׁבוּ לָבֶטַח כֻּלָּם: וְעָלִיתָ כַּשֹּׁאָה תָבוֹא כֶּעָנָן

a like | shall you | a like | you And | of all | ,securely | they and | been has
cloud | ;come | storm | ;up go shall | .them | | dwell shall | ;out brought

לְכַסּוֹת הָאָרֶץ תִּהְיֶה אַתָּה וְכָל־אֲגַפֶּיךָ וְעַמִּים רַבִּים אוֹתָךְ:

with | many | and | your | and | you shall you | the | cover to
.you | | peoples | ,bands | all | | be | land

10= כֹּה אָמַר אֲדֹנָי יְהוִה וְהָיָה בַּיּוֹם הַהוּא יַעֲלוּ

shall | that | day in | it And | :Jehovah | the | says | Thus
up go | | | be shall | | Lord

11 דְבָרִים עַל־לְבָבֶךָ וְחָשַׁבְתָּ מַחֲשֶׁבֶת רָעָה: וְאָמַרְתָּ אֶעֱלֶה

will I | you And | .evil | plan an | you and | your | into | words
up go | say shall | | devise shall | ,heart | |

עַל־אֶרֶץ פְּרָזוֹת אָבוֹא הַשֹּׁקְטִים יֹשְׁבֵי לָבֶטַח כֻּלָּם יֹשְׁבִים

living | of all | ,securely | who | those | will I | open | the | to
| them | | live | ,ease at | (to) go | ;spaces of | land

12 בְּאֵין חוֹמָה וּבְרִיחַ וּדְלָתַיִם אֵין לָהֶם: לִשְׁלֹל שָׁלָל וְלָבֹז

to and | a | spoil to | ;them to | there | bars and | ,walls | with
steal | ,spoil | | | not are | gates | | no

בַּז לְהָשִׁיב יָדְךָ עַל־חֳרָבוֹת נוֹשָׁבֹת וְאֶל־עַם מְאֻסָּף מִגּוֹיִם

of out | gathered | the and | ;in dwelt | waste | the | on | your | turn to | a
,nations the | | people | | places | | | hand | | ;prize

13 עֹשֶׂה מִקְנֶה וְקִנְיָן יֹשְׁבֵי עַל־טַבּוּר הָאָרֶץ: שְׁבָא וּדְדָן

and | Sheba | .earth the | the | in | who | and livestock | have who
,Dedan | | of center | dwell | ;goods | | gotten

וְסֹחֲרֵי תַרְשִׁישׁ וְכָל־כְּפִירֶיהָ יֹאמְרוּ לְךָ הֲלִשְׁלֹל שָׁלָל

spoil a | to Have | ,you to | shall | young its | and | ,Tarshish | the and
| spoil | | say | ,lions | all | | of merchants

אַתָּה בָּא הֲלִקְבֹּץ בָּא הִקְהַלְתָּ קָהָלֶךָ לָשֵׂאת | כֶּסֶף וְזָהָב

and | silver | carry to | you | a | Have ?come | you
;gold | | away | ;assembly | gathered | prize | steal to

14 לָקַחַת מִקְנֶה וְקִנְיָן לִשְׁלֹל שָׁלָל גָּדוֹל: לָכֵן הִנָּבֵא בֶן־

son ,prophesy | There- | ?great | spoil a | spoil to | and livestock | take to
of | ,fore | | | | ;goods | away

אָדָם וְאָמַרְתָּ לְגוֹג כֹּה אָמַר אֲדֹנָי יְהוִה | הֲלוֹא בַּיּוֹם

day in | Shall | :Jehovah | the | says | Thus | ,Gog to | say and | ,man
| not | | Lord

15 הַהוּא בְּשֶׁבֶת עַמִּי יִשְׂרָאֵל לָבֶטַח תֵּדָע: וּבָאתָ מִמְּקוֹמְךָ

your from | you And | you | securely | Israel | My | when | that
place | come shall | ?know | | | people | dwells

מִיַּרְכְּתֵי צָפוֹן אַתָּה וְעַמִּים רַבִּים אִתָּךְ רֹכְבֵי סוּסִים כֻּלָּם

of all | horses | riding | with | many | and | you | the | the of out
,them | | on | ,you | | peoples | | ,north | of recesses

16 קָהָל גָּדוֹל וְחַיִל רָב: וְעָלִיתָ עַל־עַמִּי יִשְׂרָאֵל כֶּעָנָן לְכַסּוֹת

cover to | a like | Israel | My | on | you And | .mighty | and ,great | as- a
| ,cloud | | people | | up come shall | | army | sembly

הָאָרֶץ בְּאַחֲרִית הַיָּמִים תִּהְיֶה וַהֲבִאוֹתִיךָ עַל־אַרְצִי לְמַעַן

so | My | against | will I and | shall It | days | the in | the
that | ,land | | you bring | ,be | | after | .land

nations may know Me, when I shall be sanctified in you before their eyes, O Gog. [17] Thus says the Lord Jehovah: Are you he of whom I have spoken in former days, by the hand of My servants, the prophets of Israel, who prophesied in those days (and) years, to bring you against them? [18] And it shall be on that day, when Gog comes against the land of Israel—declares the Lord Jehovah—My fury shall come up in My face. [19] And in My jealousy, in the fire of My wrath, I have spoken. Surely, in that day there shall be a great quaking in the land of Israel. [20] And the fish of the sea, and the birds of the heavens, and the beasts of the field, and all creeping things that creep on the earth, and all men who (are) on the face of the earth, shall quake at My face. And the mountains shall be thrown down and the steep places shall fall, and every wall shall fall to the ground. [21] And I shall call a sword against him on all My mountains, declares the Lord Jehovah. (Each) man's sword shall be against his brother. [22] And I will judge him with a plague and with blood, and an overflowing shower, and hailstones; I will rain fire and brimstone on him, and on his bands, and on the many peoples who (are) with him. [23] And I will magnify Myself and sanctify Myself. And I will be known in the eyes of the many nations; and they shall know that I (am) Jehovah.

17 כֹּה־ דַּעַת הַגּוֹיִם אֹתִי בְּהִקָּדְשִׁי בְךָ לְעֵינֵיהֶם גּוֹג׃

Thus O their before in shall I when Me the may
,Gog ,eyes you sanctified be nations know

אָמַר אֲדֹנָי יְהוִה הַאַתָּה־הוּא אֲשֶׁר־דִּבַּרְתִּי בְּיָמִים קַדְמוֹנִים

former days in have I of he Are :Jehovah the says
spoken whom you Lord

בְּיַד עֲבָדַי נְבִיאֵי יִשְׂרָאֵל הַנִּבְּאִים בַּיָּמִים הָהֵם שָׁנִים לְהָבִיא

bring to (many) those days in who ,Israel the ser- My the by
years prophesied of prophets vants of hand

18 עַל־ אֹתְךָ עֲלֵיהֶם׃ וְהָיָה בַּיּוֹם הַהוּא בְּיוֹם בּוֹא גוֹג

against Gog comes when ,that day on it And against you
be shall ?them

אַדְמַת יִשְׂרָאֵל נְאֻם אֲדֹנָי יְהוִה תַּעֲלֶה חֲמָתִי בְּאַפִּי׃

My in My come shall ,Jehovah the states ,Israel the
.face fury up Lord of land

19 וּבְקִנְאָתִי בְאֵשׁ־עֶבְרָתִי דִּבַּרְתִּי אִם־לֹא בַּיּוֹם הַהוּא יִהְיֶה

there that day in Surely have I My the in My in And
be shall .spoken ,wrath of fire ,jealousy

20 רַעַשׁ גָּדוֹל עַל אַדְמַת יִשְׂרָאֵל׃ וְרָעֲשׁוּ מִפָּנַי דְּגֵי הַיָּם וְעוֹף

the and the the My at shall And ,Israel the in great a
of birds ,sea of fish face shake of land shaking

הַשָּׁמַיִם וְחַיַּת הַשָּׂדֶה וְכָל־הָרֶמֶשׂ הָרֹמֵשׂ עַל־הָאֲדָמָה וְכֹל

and the on that creeping and the the and the
all ,earth creep things all ,field of beasts ,heavens

הָאָדָם אֲשֶׁר עַל־פְּנֵי הָאֲדָמָה וְנֶהֶרְסוּ הֶהָרִים וְנָפְלוּ

shall and the be shall And the the on who men
fall ,mountains down cast .earth of face (are)

21 הַמַּדְרֵגוֹת וְכָל־חוֹמָה לָאָרֶץ תִּפּוֹל׃ וְקָרָאתִי עָלָיו לְכָל־

on against will I And shall the to wall and steep the
all him call .fall ground every ,places

הָרַי חֶרֶב נְאֻם אֲדֹנָי יְהוִה חֶרֶב אִישׁ בְּאָחִיו תִּהְיֶה׃

.be shall his against (Each) sword .Jehovah the states ,sword a My
brother man's Lord mountains

22 וְנִשְׁפַּטְתִּי אִתּוֹ בְּדֶבֶר וּבְדָם וְגֶשֶׁם שׁוֹטֵף וְאַבְנֵי אֶלְגָּבִישׁ

;hail and over- a and with and a with him will I And
of stones ,flowing shower .blood plague judge

אֵשׁ וְגָפְרִית אַמְטִיר עָלָיו וְעַל־אֲגַפָּיו וְעַל־עַמִּים רַבִּים אֲשֶׁר

who many the and his and on will I and fire
(are) peoples on ,bands on ,him rain brimstone

23 אִתּוֹ׃ וְהִתְגַּדִּלְתִּי וְהִתְקַדִּשְׁתִּי וְנוֹדַעְתִּי לְעֵינֵי גּוֹיִם רַבִּים

,many ,nations the in will I And sanctify and will I And with
of eyes known be .Myself Myself magnify .him

וְיָדְעוּ כִּי־אֲנִי יְהוָה׃

.Jehovah I that they and
(am) know shall

CAP. XXXIX לט

CHAPTER 39

1 וְאַתָּה בֶן־אָדָם הִנָּבֵא עַל־גּוֹג וְאָמַרְתָּ כֹּה אָמַר אֲדֹנָי יְהוִה

:Jehovah the says Thus ,say and ;Gog against proph- ,man son And
Lord esy of ,you

CHAPTER 39

[1] And you, son of man, prophesy against Gog and say, Thus says the Lord Jehovah: Behold, I

2 הִנְנִי אֵלֶיךָ גּוֹג נְשִׂיא רֹאשׁ מֶשֶׁךְ וְתֻבָל׃ וְשֹׁבַבְתִּיךָ
will I And and Meshech ,Rosh the O against ,Behold
back you turn .Tubal of prince ,Gog ,you (am) I

וְשִׁשֵּׁאתִיךָ וְהַעֲלִיתִיךָ מִיַּרְכְּתֵי צָפוֹן וַהֲבֵאוֹתִךָ עַל־הָרֵי
the on bring will and the the from will I And lead and
of mountains you ,north of recesses up you bring .on you

33 יִשְׂרָאֵל׃ וְהִכֵּיתִי קַשְׁתְּךָ מִיַּד שְׂמֹאולְךָ וְחִצֶּיךָ מִיַּד יְמִינְךָ
your of out your and your of out your will I And .Israel
right hand arrows ,left hand bow strike

4 אַפִּיל׃ עַל־הָרֵי יִשְׂרָאֵל תִּפּוֹל אַתָּה וְכָל־אֲגַפֶּיךָ וְעַמִּים
the and your and ,you you Israel the On cause will
peoples ,bands all ,fall shall of mountains .fall to

אֲשֶׁר אִתָּךְ לְעֵיט צִפּוֹר כָּל־כָּנָף וְחַיַּת הַשָּׂדֶה נְתַתִּיךָ
will I the the and ,wing every bird a birds the to with who
you give field of beasts of ,prey of .you (are)

5 לְאָכְלָה׃ עַל־פְּנֵי הַשָּׂדֶה תִּפּוֹל כִּי אֲנִי דִבַּרְתִּי נְאֻם אֲדֹנָי
the states have I for shall you the the On .food for
Lord ,spoken ,fall field of face

6 יְהוִה׃ וְשִׁלַּחְתִּי־אֵשׁ בְּמָגוֹג וּבְיֹשְׁבֵי הָאִיִּים לָבֶטַח וְיָדְעוּ
they And .securely the the on and on a will I And .Jehovah
know shall coasts of dwellers ,Magog fire send

7 כִּי־אֲנִי יְהוָה׃ וְאֶת־שֵׁם קָדְשִׁי אוֹדִיעַ בְּתוֹךְ עַמִּי יִשְׂרָאֵל
.Israel My the in will I My name And .Jehovah I that
people of midst known make holy (am)

וְלֹא־אַחֵל אֶת־שֵׁם־קָדְשִׁי עוֹד וְיָדְעוּ הַגּוֹיִם כִּי־אֲנִי יְהוָה
,Jehovah I that the shall And any My name let will I And
(am) nations know more holy profaned be not

8 קָדוֹשׁ בְּיִשְׂרָאֵל׃ הִנֵּה בָאָה וְנִהְיָתָה נְאֻם אֲדֹנָי יְהוִה
.Jehovah the states is it and has it ,Behold .Israel in Holy the
Lord ,done come One

9 הוּא הַיּוֹם אֲשֶׁר דִּבַּרְתִּי׃ וְיָצְאוּ יֹשְׁבֵי ׀ עָרֵי יִשְׂרָאֵל וּבִעֲרוּ
shall and ,Israel the resi- the shall And have I of the That
afire set of cities of dents out go .spoken which day (is)

וְהִשִּׂיקוּ בְּנֶשֶׁק וּמָגֵן וְצִנָּה בְּקֶשֶׁת וּבְחִצִּים וּבְמַקֵּל יָד
the the and the and the the and the and the burn and
,hand of staff ,arrows bow ,buckler ,shield :weapons

10 וּבְרֹמַח וּבִעֲרוּ בָהֶם אֵשׁ שֶׁבַע שָׁנִים׃ וְלֹא־יִשְׂאוּ עֵצִים מִן
out wood they And .years seven (with) them they And the and
of take shall not fire burn shall .spears

הַשָּׂדֶה וְלֹא יַחְטְבוּ מִן־הַיְּעָרִים כִּי בַנֶּשֶׁק יְבַעֲרוּ־אֵשׁ
(with) shall they the for the out cut and the
.fire burn weapons ;forest of down not ,field

וְשָׁלְלוּ אֶת־שֹׁלְלֵיהֶם וּבָזְזוּ אֶת־בֹּזְזֵיהֶם נְאֻם אֲדֹנָי יְהוִה׃
.Jehovah the states who those and who those they And
Lord ,them robbed rob them spoiled spoil shall

11 וְהָיָה בַיּוֹם הַהוּא אֶתֵּן לְגוֹג ׀ מְקוֹם־שָׁם קֶבֶר בְּיִשְׂרָאֵל
,Israel in grave a ,there place a to will I that day on it And
Gog give be will

גֵּי הָעֹבְרִים קִדְמַת הַיָּם וְחֹסֶמֶת הִיא אֶת־הָעֹבְרִים וְקָבְרוּ
they And who those it shall And the east who those the
bury shall .by pass up stop .sea of by pass of valley

(am) against you, O Gog, the prince of Rosh, Meshech and Tubal. [2] And I will turn you back, and lead you on. And I will bring you up from the recesses of the north, and will bring you on the mountains of Israel. [3] And I will strike your bow out of your left hand, and your arrows out of your right hand (I) will cause to fall. [4] You shall fall on the mountains of Israel, you and all your bands, and the people who (are) with you. I will give you for food to the birds of prey, a bird of every wing, and (to) the beasts of the field. [5] You shall fall on the face of the field, for I have spoken, declares the Lord Jehovah. [6] And I will send a fire on Magog, and on the secure inhabitants of the coasts. And they shall know that I (am) Jehovah. [7] And I will make My holy name known in the midst of My people Israel. And I will not let My holy name be profaned any more. And the nations shall know that I (am) Jehovah, the Holy One of Israel. [8] Behold! It has come, and it is done, declares the Lord Jehovah. That (is) the day of which I have spoken. [9] And the inhabitants of the cities of Isreal shall go out, and shall set afire and burn the weapons; even the shield and the bucker, the bow and the arrows, and the hand-staff, and the spears. And they shall burn them (with) fire seven years. [10] And they shall not take wood out of the field, and shall not cut down out of the forest; for they shall burn the weapons (with) fire. And they shall spoil those who spoiled them, and rob those who robbed them, declares the Lord Jehovah.

[11] And it will be on that day I will give to Gog a place there, a grave in Israel, the valley of those who pass by, east of the sea. And those who pass by shall stop it up. And they

shall bury Gog there, and all his multitude, and shall call (it) The Valley of the Multitude of Gog. [12] And the house of Israel shall bury them, in order to cleanse the land, seven months. [13] And the people of the land shall bury. And it shall be for a name to them, the day when I (am) glorified, declares the Lord Jehovah. [14] And they shall separate men who continually pass through the land, burying those who passed through, who remain on the face of the earth, to cleanse it; at the end of seven months they shall make a search. [15] And (as) they pass, those who pass through the land, and (any) man sees a bone, then he shall build beside it a post, until the buriers have buried it in The Valley of the Multitude of Gog. [16] And also the name of the city (is) The Multitude. And they shall cleanse the land.

[17] And you, son of man, Thus says the Lord Jehovah: Say to the bird of every wing, and to every beast of the field: Gather yourselves and come; collect yourselves from all around to My sacrifice which I sacrifice for you, a great sacrifice on the mountains of Israel, so that you may eat flesh and drink blood. [18] You shall eat the flesh of the mighty, and drink the blood of the princes of the earth; (of) rams, lambs, goats, (and) bulls, all of them fatlings of Bashan. [19] And you shall eat fat until satiated; and drink blood until drunkenness, of My sacrifice which I have sacrificed for you. [20] And you shall be satiated at My table, (with) horses and chariots, and all mighty men of war, declares the Lord Jehovah. [21] And I will put My glory among the nations, and all the nations shall see My judgments which I have

12 שם את־גוג ואת־כל־המונה וקראו גיא המון גוג׃ וקברום
shall And .Gog Mul- the The shall and his all and Gog there
them bury of titude of Valley ,(it) call ,multitude

בית ישראל למען טהר את־הארץ שבעה חדשים׃
.months seven the cleanse to in ,Israel the
,land order of house

13 וקברו כל־עם הארץ והיה להם לשם יום הכבדי נאם
states I when the a for to it And the the shall And
,glorified am day name them be shall .land of people (them) bury

14 אדני יהוה׃ ואנשי תמיד יבדילו עברים בארץ מקברים
burying the pass who shall they contin- And .Jehovah the
,land through separate ually men Lord

את־העברים את־הנותרים על־פני הארץ לטהרה מקצה
the at cleanse to the the on remain who who those
of end ;it ,earth of face ,through passed

15 שבעה־חדשים יחקרו׃ ועברו העברים בארץ וראה
(any) and the who those (as) And shall they months seven
sees ,land through pass ,pass they .search a make

עצם אדם ובנה אצלו ציון עד קברו אתו המקברים
buriers the it have until a beside he then ,man a
buried ,post it build shall bone

16 אל־גיא המון גוג׃ וגם שם־עיר המונה וטהרו הארץ׃
the they And The (is) the the And .Gog Mul- the The in
.land cleanse shall .Multitude city of name also of titude of Valley

17 ואתה בן־אדם כה־אמר אדני יהוה אמר לצפור כל־
every the to Say :Jehovah the says Thus ,man son And
of bird Lord of ,you

כנף ולכל חית השדה הקבצו ובאו האספו מסביב על־
to all from your- collect and Gather the beast to and wing
around selves ;come yourselves :field of every

זבחי אשר אני זבח לכם זבח גדול על הרי ישראל
,Israel the on great a for sacrifice I which My
of mountains sacrifice ,you sacrifice

18 ואכלתם בשר ושתיתם דם׃ בשר גבורים תאכלו ודם־
the and shall You the the .blood drink and flesh you that so
of blood ,eat mighty of flesh eat may

נשיאי הארץ תשתו אילים כרים ועתודים פרים מריאי
fatlings (of) (of) and (of) (of) ,drink the the
of ,bulls ,goats ,lambs ,rams earth of princes

19 בשן כלם׃ ואכלתם־חלב לשבעה ושתיתם דם לשכרון
until blood drink and until fat you And of all Bashan
,drunkenness ,satiated eat shall .them

20 מזבחי אשר־זבחתי לכם׃ ושבעתם על־שלחני סוס
(with) My at shall you So for have I which My of
horses table satiated be .you sacrificed sacrifice

21 ורכב גבור וכל־איש מלחמה נאם אדני יהוה׃ ונתתי
I And .Jehovah the states ,war the and mighty (with) and
put will Lord of men all men ,chariots

את־כבודי בגוים וראו כל־הגוים את־משפטי אשר עשיתי
have I which My the all shall and among My
,done judgments nations see ,nations the glory

done, and My hand that I have laid on them. [22] So the house of Israel shall know that I (am) Jehovah their God, from that day and onward. [23] And the nations shall know that the house of Israel was exiled for their iniquity. Because they betrayed Me, thus I hid My face from them and gave them into the hand of their enemies. And they fell by the sword, all of them. [24] According to their uncleanness and according to their sins, I have done to them, and have hidden My face from them. [25] Therefore thus says the Lord Jehovah: Now I will return the captivity of Jacob, and will have mercy on all the house of Israel, and (I) will be jealous for My holy name; [26] and they shall have borne their shame and all their treachery which they have done against Me, when they dwell on their land securely, and no one terrifies (them). [27] When I have returned them from the peoples, and gathered them out of the hand of their enemies, and am sanctified in them in the sight of many nations; [28] then they shall know that I (am) Jehovah their God, who exiles them among the nations. But I have gathered them to their own land, and have not left any of them there. [29] And I will not any more hide My face from them, for I have poured out My Spirit on the house of Israel, declares the Lord Jehovah.

22 וְאֶת־יָדִי אֲשֶׁר־שַׂמְתִּי בָהֶם׃ וְיָדְעוּ בֵּית יִשְׂרָאֵל כִּי אֲנִי
I that Israel the shall So on have I that My and
(am) of house know .them laid hand

23 יְהוָה אֱלֹהֵיהֶם מִן־הַיּוֹם הַהוּא וָהָלְאָה׃ וְיָדְעוּ הַגּוֹיִם כִּי
that the shall And and that day from their Jehovah
nations know .onward God

בַעֲוֹנָם גָּלוּ בֵית־יִשְׂרָאֵל עַל אֲשֶׁר מָעֲלוּ־בִי וָאַסְתִּר פָּנַי
My I thus ,Me they that Be- .Israel the was their for
face hid betrayed cause of house exiled iniquity

24 מֵהֶם וָאֶתְּנֵם בְּיַד צָרֵיהֶם וַיִּפְּלוּ בַחֶרֶב כֻּלָּם׃ כְּטֻמְאָתָם
their to As of all the by they And their the into gave and from
uncleanness .them ,sword fell .enemies of hand them them

25 וּכְפִשְׁעֵיהֶם עָשִׂיתִי אֹתָם וָאַסְתִּר פָּנַי מֵהֶם׃ לָכֵן כֹּה אָמַר
says thus There- from My have and ,them have I according and
fore .them face hidden to done sins their

אֲדֹנָי יֱהוִה עַתָּה אָשִׁיב אֶת־שְׁבִית יַעֲקֹב וְרִחַמְתִּי כָּל־
all have will and ,Jacob the will I Now :Jehovah the
the on mercy of captivity return Lord

26 בֵּית יִשְׂרָאֵל וְקִנֵּאתִי לְשֵׁם קָדְשִׁי׃ וְנָשׂוּ אֶת־כְּלִמָּתָם וְאֶת־
and their they (after) My name for will and ,Israel house
shame also borne have ;holy jealous be of

כָּל־מַעֲלָם אֲשֶׁר מָעֲלוּ־בִי בְּשִׁבְתָּם עַל־אַדְמָתָם לָבֶטַח
securely their on they when against they which their all
land dwell ,Me done have treachery

27 וְאֵין מַחֲרִיד׃ בְּשׁוֹבְבִי אוֹתָם מִן־הָעַמִּים וְקִבַּצְתִּי אֹתָם
them and the from them have I When .terrifies no and
gathered peoples returned have one

28 מֵאַרְצוֹת אֹיְבֵיהֶם וְנִקְדַּשְׁתִּי בָם לְעֵינֵי הַגּוֹיִם רַבִּים׃ וְיָדְעוּ
they then ;many nations the in in am and their of out
know shall of sight them sanctified ,enemies' lands

כִּי אֲנִי יְהוָה אֱלֹהֵיהֶם בְּהַגְלוֹתִי אֹתָם אֶל־הַגּוֹיִם וְכִנַּסְתִּים
have I But the among them exiles who their Jehovah I that
them gathered .nations ,God (am)

29 אֶל־אַדְמָתָם וְלֹא־אוֹתִיר עוֹד מֵהֶם שָׁם׃ וְלֹא־אַסְתִּיר עוֹד
any will I And .there of any have and own their to
more hide not them left not ,land

פָּנַי מֵהֶם אֲשֶׁר שָׁפַכְתִּי אֶת־רוּחִי עַל־בֵּית יִשְׂרָאֵל נְאֻם
states ,Israel the on My have I for from My
of house Spirit out poured ,them face

אֲדֹנָי יֱהוִה׃
.Jehovah the
Lord

CAP. XL מ

CHAPTER 40

[1] In the twenty-fifth year of our exile, in the beginning of the year, in the tenth of the month, in the fourteenth year after the city was struck,

1 בְּעֶשְׂרִים וְחָמֵשׁ שָׁנָה לְגָלוּתֵנוּ בְּרֹאשׁ הַשָּׁנָה בֶּעָשׂוֹר
the in the the in our of year fifth the In
tenth ,year of beginning ,exile twenty-

לַחֹדֶשׁ בְּאַרְבַּע עֶשְׂרֵה שָׁנָה אַחַר אֲשֶׁר הֻכְּתָה הָעִיר
the was after year the in the of
,city struck fourteenth ,month

on that same day the hand of Jehovah was on me, and brought me there. [2] In the visions of God, He brought me into the land of Israel, and made me rest on a very high mountain; and it was as the structure of a city on the south. [3] And He brought me there; and Behold, a man whose appearance (was) as the appearance of bronze, and a line of flax in his hand, and a measuring reed; and he stood in the gate. [4] And the man said to me, Son of man, look with your eyes, and hear with your ears, and set your heart on all that I shall show you. For in order to show you, you are brought here. Declare to the house of Israel all that you see.

[5] And, behold, a wall on the outside of the house all around; and in the man's hand a measuring reed (of) six cubits, with a cubit and a span! So he measured the breadth of the building one reed; and the height, one reed. [6] Then he came to the gate which faced eastward, and went up its steps and measured the threshold of the gate, one reed wide; even the one threshold, one reed wide. [7] And a room, one reed long and one reed wide. And between the rooms (were) five cubits. And the threshold of the gate from beside the porch of the gate, from the house, (was) one reed.

[8] He also measured the porch of the gate from the house, one reed. [9] Then he measured the porch of the gate, eight cubits. And its pillars, two cubits. And the porch of the gate from the house.

בְּעֶצֶם ׀ הַיּוֹם הַזֶּה הָיְתָה עָלַי יַד־יְהוָה וַיָּבֵא אֹתִי שָׁמָּה׃
.there me and Jehovah the on was that day same on
brought of hand me

2 בְּמַרְאוֹת אֱלֹהִים הֱבִיאַנִי אֶל־אֶרֶץ יִשְׂרָאֵל וַיְנִיחֵנִי אֶל־
on made and Israel the into brought He God the In
rest me of land me of visions

3 הַר גָּבֹהַּ מְאֹד וְעָלָיו כְּמִבְנֵה־עִיר מִנֶּגֶב׃ וַיָּבֵיא אוֹתִי
me He And the on city a the as on and ;very high a
brought .south of structure ,was it mountain

שָׁמָּה וְהִנֵּה־אִישׁ מַרְאֵהוּ כְּמַרְאֵה נְחֹשֶׁת וּפְתִיל־פִּשְׁתִּים
flax a and ,bronze the as (was) whose man a and ;there
of line of appearance appearance ,behold

4 בְּיָדוֹ וּקְנֵה הַמִּדָּה וְהוּא עֹמֵד בַּשָּׁעַר׃ וַיְדַבֵּר אֵלַי הָאִישׁ
the me to said And the in stood And measur- a and his in
,man .gate he !ing reed ,hand

בֶּן־אָדָם רְאֵה בְעֵינֶיךָ וּבְאָזְנֶיךָ שְּׁמָע וְשִׂים לִבְּךָ לְכֹל
all on your set and ,hear with and your with look ,man Son
heart ears your eyes of

אֲשֶׁר־אֲנִי מַרְאֶה אוֹתָךְ כִּי לְמַעַן הַרְאוֹתְכָה הֻבָאתָה
are you you show to in For .you shall I that
brought order show

5 הֵנָּה הַגֵּד אֶת־כָּל־אֲשֶׁר־אַתָּה רֹאֶה לְבֵית יִשְׂרָאֵל׃ וְהִנֵּה
,And .Israel the to see you that all Declare .here
,behold of house

חוֹמָה מִחוּץ לַבַּיִת סָבִיב ׀ סָבִיב וּבְיַד הָאִישׁ קְנֵה הַמִּדָּה
measuring a the in and ,around all the of the on wall a
reed man's hand house outside

שֵׁשׁ־אַמּוֹת בָּאַמָּה וָטֹפַח וַיָּמָד אֶת־רֹחַב הַבִּנְיָן קָנֶה אֶחָד
;one reed the breadth the he So a and a with ,cubits (of)
,building of measured !span cubit six

6 וְקוֹמָה קָנֶה אֶחָד׃ וַיָּבוֹא אֶל־שַׁעַר אֲשֶׁר פָּנָיו דֶּרֶךְ
the faced which the to he Then .one reed the and
way gate came ,height

הַקָּדִימָה וַיַּעַל בְּמַעֲלוֹתָו וַיָּמָד ׀ אֶת־סַף הַשַּׁעַר קָנֶה אֶחָד
one reed ,gate the the and steps its and east
of threshold measured up went

7 רֹחַב וְאֵת סַף אֶחָד קָנֶה אֶחָד רֹחַב׃ וְהַתָּא קָנֶה אֶחָד
one reed a And .wide one reed ,one the even ;wide
room threshold

אֹרֶךְ וְקָנֶה אֶחָד רֹחַב וּבֵין הַתָּאִים חָמֵשׁ אַמּוֹת וְסַף
the And .cubits (were) the And .wide one and long
of threshold five rooms between reed

8 הַשַּׁעַר מֵאֵצֶל אֻלָם הַשַּׁעַר מֵהַבַּיִת קָנֶה אֶחָד׃ וַיָּמָד אֶת־
also He .one (was) the from the the from the
measured reed house gate of porch beside gate

9 אֻלָם הַשַּׁעַר מֵהַבָּיִת קָנֶה אֶחָד׃ וַיָּמָד אֶת־אֻלָם הַשַּׁעַר
the the he Then .one reed the from the the
,gate of porch measured ,house gate of porch

שְׁמֹנֶה אַמּוֹת וְאֵילָו שְׁתַּיִם אַמּוֹת וְאֻלָם הַשַּׁעַר מֵהַבָּיִת׃
the from the the And .cubits two its And .cubits eight
.house gate of porch pillars

[10] And the gaterooms eastward (were) three from here, and three from there; one measure to the three of them; and one measure (was) to the pillars, from here and from there. [11] And he measured the breadth of the gate-opening, ten cubits; the length of the gate (was) thirteen cubits. [12] And the border in front of the rooms (was) one cubit; and the border from here, one cubit. And the room (was) six cubits from here, and six cubits from there. [13] And he measured the gate of the room from roof to roof, twenty-five cubits wide, door to door. [14] He also made the pillars, sixty cubits, even to the court-pillar, (from) the gate round (and) round. [15] And on the face of the entrance gate, to the face of the porch of the inner gate (was) fifty cubits; [16] and windows, lattices, (were) to the rooms, and to their pillars inside the gate round (and) round; and thus for the porches; and windows (were) round (and) round inside; and to a pillar (were) palm trees. [17] And he brought me into the outer court. And behold, chambers, and a pavement made for the court round (and) round. Thirty chambers (were) on the pavement. [18] And the pavement by the side of the gates to equal the length of the gates (was) the lower pavement. [19] Then he measured the breadth from the face of the lower gate to the face of the inner court, on the outside, a hundred cubits eastward and northward. [20] And the gate which faces the way of the north

10 וְתָאֵי הַשַּׁעַר דֶּרֶךְ הַקָּדִים שְׁלֹשָׁה מִפֹּה וּשְׁלֹשָׁה מִפֹּה

from and from three east the on the the And
,there three here (were) way gate of rooms

מִדָּה אַחַת לִשְׁלָשְׁתָּם וּמִדָּה אַחַת לָאֵלִם מִפֹּה וּמִפּוֹ׃

from and from the to one and three the to one measure
.there here pillars (was) measure - ;them of (was)

11 וַיָּמָד אֶת־רֹחַב פֶּתַח־הַשַּׁעַר עֶשֶׂר אַמּוֹת אֹרֶךְ הַשַּׁעַר

the The .cubits ten the the the he And
gate of length ,gate of opening of breadth measured

12 שְׁלוֹשׁ עֶשְׂרֵה אַמּוֹת׃ וּגְבוּל לִפְנֵי הַתָּאוֹת אַמָּה אֶחָת

,one (was) the front in the And .cubits thirteen (was)
cubit rooms of border

וְאַמָּה־אַחַת גְּבוּל מִפֹּה וְהַתָּא שֵׁשׁ־אַמּוֹת מִפֹּו וְשֵׁשׁ

and from cubits six the And from the one and
six ,here (was) room here border cubit

13 אַמּוֹת מִפֹּו׃ וַיָּמָד אֶת־הַשַּׁעַר מִגַּג הַתָּא לְגַגּוֹ רֹחַב עֶשְׂרִים

(was it) wide to the the from the he And from cubits
twenty- ;roof room of roof gate measured .there

14 וְחָמֵשׁ אַמּוֹת פֶּתַח נֶגֶד פָּתַח׃ וַיַּעַשׂ אֶת־אֵילִים שִׁשִּׁים

sixty the also He .door to door ,cubits five
:pillars made

15 אַמָּה וְאֶל־אֵיל הֶחָצֵר הַשַּׁעַר סָבִיב ׀ סָבִיב׃ וְעַל־פְּנֵי

the And (and) round the (from) the the even ,cubits
of face on .round gate court of pillar to

הַשַּׁעַר הַיְאתוֹן עַל־לִפְנֵי אֻלָם הַשַּׁעַר הַפְּנִימִי חֲמִשִּׁים

fifty (was) inner gate the the the to the the
of porch of face entrance of gate

16 אַמָּה׃ וְחַלֹּנוֹת אֲטֻמוֹת אֶל־הַתָּאִים וְאֶל אֵלֵיהֵמָה

their to and the to latices and —cubits
pillars rooms windows

לִפְנִימָה לַשַּׁעַר סָבִיב ׀ סָבִיב וְכֵן לָאֵלַמּוֹת וְחַלּוֹנוֹת

windows and the for and (and) round the inside
(were) ;porches thus round gate

17 סָבִיב ׀ סָבִיב לִפְנִימָה וְאֶל־אַיִל תִּמֹרִים׃ וַיְבִיאֵנִי אֶל־

into he And palm (were) (each) and ;inside (and) round
me brought .trees pillar to round

הֶחָצֵר הַחִיצוֹנָה וְהִנֵּה לְשָׁכוֹת וְרִצְפָה עָשׂוּי לֶחָצֵר סָבִיב ׀

round the for made a and chambers And .outer the
court pavement ,behold court

18 סָבִיב שְׁלֹשִׁים לְשָׁכוֹת אֶל־הָרִצְפָה׃ וְהָרִצְפָה אֶל־כֶּתֶף

the by the And the on chambers Thirty (and)
of side pavement .pavement (were) !round

19 הַשְּׁעָרִים לְעֻמַּת אֹרֶךְ הַשְּׁעָרִים הָרִצְפָה הַתַּחְתּוֹנָה׃ וַיָּמָד

he Then .lower the (was) the the equal to gates the
measured pavement gates of length

רֹחַב מִלִּפְנֵי הַשַּׁעַר הַתַּחְתּוֹנָה לִפְנֵי הֶחָצֵר הַפְּנִימִי מִחוּץ

the on inner the the to lower the the from the
,outside court of face gate of face breadth

20 מֵאָה אַמָּה הַקָּדִימָה וְהַצָּפוֹן׃ וְהַשַּׁעַר אֲשֶׁר פָּנָיו דֶּרֶךְ

the faces which the And and eastward cubits a
of way gate .northward hundred

of the outer court, he measured its length and its breadth. [21] And its rooms (were) three from here, and three from there; and its pillars and its porches were as the first measure—its length fifty cubits, and its breadth twenty-five cubits. [22] And its windows, and its porches and its palm trees (were) as the measure of the gate that faces eastward. And they went up to it by seven steps; and its porches (were) before them. [23] And the gate of the inner court (was) across from the gate toward the north and toward the east. And he measured from gate to gate, a hundred cubits. [24] And he led me southward; and behold, a gate southward! And he measured its pillars and its porches according to these measures. [25] And windows (were) in it, and its porches round (and) round like these windows. Fifty cubits (was) the length, and twenty-five cubits the breadth. [26] And seven steps (were) going up to it, and its porches before them. And palm trees (were) to it, one from here and one from there, to its pillars. [27] And a gate (was) to the inner court southward. And he measured from gate to gate southward, a hundred cubits.

[28] And he brought me to the inner court by the south gate. And he measured the south gate by these measures. [29] And its rooms and its pillars and its porches (were) as these measures. And windows (were) to it, and its porches round (and) round. (It was) fifty cubits long, and twenty-five cubits wide. [30] And the porches round (and)

21 הַצָּפוֹן לֶחָצֵר הַחִיצוֹנָה מָדַד אָרְכּוֹ וְרָחְבּוֹ׃ וְתָאָו
its And | its and | its | he | ,outer | the of | the
rooms | .breadth | length | measured | | court | north

שְׁלוֹשָׁה מִפּוֹ וּשְׁלֹשָׁה מִפּוֹ וְאֵילָו וְאֵלַמָּו הָיָה כְּמִדַּת
the as | were | its and | its And | from | and | from | (were)
of measure | | porches | pillars | .there | three | here | three

הַשַּׁעַר הָרִאשׁוֹן חֲמִשִּׁים אַמָּה אָרְכּוֹ וְרֹחַב חָמֵשׁ וְעֶשְׂרִים
twenty-five | the and | Its | cubits | (was) | .first | the
| breadth | ,length | | fifty

22 בָּאַמָּה׃ וְחַלּוֹנוֹ וְאֵילַמָּו וְתִימֹרָו כְּמִדַּת הַשַּׁעַר אֲשֶׁר פָּנָיו
faces | that | gate the | as (were) | its and | its and | its And | .cubits
| | | of measure the | trees palm | ,porches | ,windows

דֶּרֶךְ הַקָּדִים וּבְמַעֲלוֹת שֶׁבַע יַעֲלוּ־בוֹ וְאֵילַמָּו לִפְנֵיהֶם׃
(were) | its and | to | they | seven | by And | the | the
.them before | porches | ;it up went | | | steps | .east | of way

23 וְשַׁעַר לֶחָצֵר הַפְּנִימִי נֶגֶד הַשַּׁעַר לַצָּפוֹן וְלַקָּדִים וַיָּמָד
he And | toward and | the toward | the | across | inner | the | the And
measured | .east the | north | gate | from | (was) | court | of gate

24 מִשַּׁעַר אֶל־שַׁעַר מֵאָה אַמָּה׃ וַיּוֹלִכֵנִי דֶּרֶךְ הַדָּרוֹם וְהִנֵּה־
and | the | the | he And | .cubits | a | gate | to | from
behold | ,south | of way | me led | | hundred | | | gate

שַׁעַר דֶּרֶךְ הַדָּרוֹם וּמָדַד אֵילָו וְאֵילַמָּו כַּמִּדּוֹת הָאֵלֶּה׃
.these | according | its and | its | he And | the | the | gate a
| measures to | porches | pillars | measured | .south | of way

25 וְחַלּוֹנִים לוֹ וּלְאֵילַמָּו סָבִיב ׀ סָבִיב כְּהַחַלֹּנוֹת הָאֵלֶּה
.these | windows like | (and) | round | its and | ,it in | win- And
| | round | | porches | | (were) dows

26 חֲמִשִּׁים אַמָּה אֹרֶךְ וְרֹחַב חָמֵשׁ וְעֶשְׂרִים אַמָּה׃ וּמַעֲלוֹת
steps And | .cubits | twenty-five | the and | The | cubits | (was)
| | | breadth | ,length | | fifty

שִׁבְעָה עֹלוֹתָו וְאֵילַמָּו לִפְנֵיהֶם וְתִמֹרִים לוֹ אֶחָד מִפּוֹ
from | one | ,it to | palm And | before | its and | going | seven
here | | | (were) trees | .them | porches | ,it to up | (were)

27 וְאֶחָד מִפּוֹ אֶל־אֵילָו׃ וְשַׁעַר לֶחָצֵר הַפְּנִימִי דֶּרֶךְ הַדָּרוֹם
the | the | inner | the to | a And | its | to | from | one and
.south | of way | | court | (was) gate | .pillars | | there

28 וַיָּמָד מִשַּׁעַר אֶל־הַשַּׁעַר דֶּרֶךְ הַדָּרוֹם מֵאָה אַמּוֹת׃ וַיְבִיאֵנִי
he And | .cubits | a | the | the | gate | to | from | he And
me brought | | hundred | south | of way | | | gate measured

אֶל־חָצֵר הַפְּנִימִי בְּשַׁעַר הַדָּרוֹם וַיָּמָד אֶת־הַשַּׁעַר הַדָּרוֹם
south | the | he And | the | gate by | inner | the | to
| gate | measured | .south | | | court

29 כַּמִּדּוֹת הָאֵלֶּה׃ וְתָאָו וְאֵלָו וְאֵלַמָּו כַּמִּדּוֹת הָאֵלֶּה
.these | as (were) | its and | its and | its And | .these | by
| measures | porches | pillars | rooms | | measures

וְחַלּוֹנוֹת לוֹ וּלְאֵלַמָּו סָבִיב ׀ סָבִיב חֲמִשִּׁים אַמָּה אֹרֶךְ
long | cubits | (was It) | (and) | round | its and | to | win- And
| | fifty | .round | | porches | ,it | (were) dows

30 וְרֹחַב עֶשְׂרִים וְחָמֵשׁ אַמּוֹת׃ וְאֵלַמּוֹת סָבִיב ׀ סָבִיב אֹרֶךְ
long | (and) | round | the And | .cubits | five | twenty- | and
| round | | porches | | | | wide

(and) round (were) twenty-five cubits long and five cubits wide. [31] And its porches (were) toward the outer court; and palm trees on its pillars. And its stairway (had) eight steps.

[32] And he brought me into the inner court eastward. And he measured the gate by these measures. [33] And its rooms, and its pillars, and its porches (were) as these measures. And windows (were) to it, and to its porches round (and) round. (It was) fifty cubits long and twenty-five cuibts wide. [34] And its porches (were) toward the outer court. And palm trees (were) on its pillars from here and from there. And its stairway (had) eight steps.

[35] And he brought me to the north gate and measured by these measures; [36] its rooms, its posts, and its porches; and windows (were) to it round (and) round. (It was) fifty cubits long and twenty-five cubits wide. [37] And its pillars (were) toward the outer court. And palm trees (were) on its pillars, from here and from there; and its stairway (had) eight steps. [38] And the chamber and its door (was) by the pillars of the gates; they wasned the burnt offering there. [39] And in the porch of the gate (were) two tables from here, and two tables from there, to slaughter on them the burnt offering, and the sin offering, and the guilt offering. [40] And to the side outside, as one goes up to the door of the gate northward, (were) two tables. [41] Four tables (were) from here, and four tables from there, by the

31 חָמֵשׁ וְעֶשְׂרִים אַמָּה וְרֹחַב חָמֵשׁ אַמּוֹת׃ וְאֵלַמָּו אֶל־

toward its And .cubits five wide and cubits twenty- five
(were) porches

הֶחָצֵר הַחִיצוֹנָה וְתִמֹרִים אֶל־אֵילָו וּמַעֲלוֹת שְׁמוֹנֶה מַעֲלוֹ׃

its eight steps And its on palm And .outer the
.stairway (had) .pillars (were) trees court

32 וַיְבִיאֵנִי אֶל־הֶחָצֵר הַפְּנִימִי דֶּרֶךְ הַקָּדִים וַיָּמָד אֶת־הַשַּׁעַר

the he And the the inner the into he And
gate measured .east of way court me brought

33 כַּמִּדּוֹת הָאֵלֶּה׃ וְתָאָו וְאֵלָו וְאֵלַמָּו כַּמִּדּוֹת הָאֵלֶּה

.these as its and its and its And .these by
measures (were) porches pillars rooms measures

וְחַלּוֹנוֹת לוֹ וּלְאֵלַמָּו סָבִיב ׀ סָבִיב אֹרֶךְ חֲמִשִּׁים אַמָּה

cubits fifty (was It) (and) round its to and ,it to win- And
long .round porches (were) dows

34 וְרֹחַב חָמֵשׁ וְעֶשְׂרִים אַמָּה׃ וְאֵלַמָּו לֶחָצֵר הַחִיצוֹנָה

.outer the toward its And .cubits twenty- five and
court (were) porches wide

וְתִמֹרִים אֶל־אֵלָו מִפּוֹ וּמִפּוֹ וּשְׁמֹנֶה מַעֲלוֹת מַעֲלוֹ׃

its steps eight And from and from its on palm And
.stairway (had) there here pillars (were) trees

35
36 וַיְבִיאֵנִי אֶל־שַׁעַר הַצָּפוֹן וּמָדַד כַּמִּדּוֹת הָאֵלֶּה׃ תָּאָו

its ;these by and north the to he And
,rooms measures measured gate me brought

אֵלָו וְאֵלַמָּו וְחַלּוֹנוֹת לוֹ סָבִיב ׀ סָבִיב אֹרֶךְ חֲמִשִּׁים אַמָּה

cubits fifty (was It) (and) round it to win- and its and its
long .round (were) dows ;porches posts

37 וְרֹחַב חָמֵשׁ וְעֶשְׂרִים אַמָּה׃ וְאֵילָו לֶחָצֵר הַחִיצוֹנָה

.outer the toward its And .cubits twenty- five and
court (were) pillars wide

וְתִמֹרִים אֶל־אֵילָו מִפּוֹ וּמִפּוֹ וּשְׁמֹנֶה מַעֲלוֹת מַעֲלוֹ׃

its steps eight And from and from its on palm And
.stairway (had) there here ,pillars (were) trees

38 וְלִשְׁכָּה וּפִתְחָהּ בְּאֵילִים הַשְּׁעָרִים שָׁם יָדִיחוּ אֶת־הָעֹלָה׃

burnt the they there ,gates the the by its and the And
.offering washed of pillars (was) door chamber

39 וּבְאֻלָם הַשַּׁעַר שְׁנַיִם שֻׁלְחָנוֹת מִפּוֹ וּשְׁנַיִם שֻׁלְחָנוֹת מִפֹּה

from tables two and from tables (were) the the in And
,there here two gate of porch

40 לִשְׁחוֹט אֲלֵיהֶם הָעוֹלָה וְהַחַטָּאת וְהָאָשָׁם׃ וְאֶל־הַכָּתֵף

the And guilt the and sin the and burnt the them on to
side to .offering offering offering slaughter

מִחוּצָה לָעוֹלֶה לְפֶתַח הַשַּׁעַר הַצָּפוֹנָה שְׁנַיִם שֻׁלְחָנוֹת

.tables (were) ,northward the the to one as ,outside
two gate of door up goes

וְאֶל־הַכָּתֵף הָאַחֶרֶת אֲשֶׁר לְאֻלָם הַשַּׁעַר שְׁנַיִם שֻׁלְחָנוֹת׃

.tables (were) the the at which ,other the And
two ,gate of porch (was) side on

41 אַרְבָּעָה שֻׁלְחָנוֹת מִפֹּה וְאַרְבָּעָה שֻׁלְחָנוֹת מִפֹּה לְכֶתֶף

the by from tables four and from tables Four
of side ,there (were) ,here (were)

side of the gate, eight tables; they slaughter on them. [42] And the four tables for burnt offering (were) cut stone, one cubit and a half long, and one cubit and a half wide, and one cubit high. They also rested on them the instruments with which they slaughtered, by them the burnt offering and the sacrifice. [43] And the double hooks, one span, were fastened in the house round (and) round. And on the tables (was) the flesh of the offering. [44] And from the outside to the inner gate (were) the chambers of the singers in the inner court, which (was) at the side of the north gate. And their face (was) southward; one at the side of the east gate looked northward. [45] And he said to me, This chamber facing southward (is) for the priests, the keepers of the charge of the house. [46] And the chamber facing northward (is) for the priests, the keepers of the charge of the altar. They (are) the sons of Zadok who come near to Jehovah, of the sons of Levi, to serve Him. [47] So he measured the court: a hundred cubits long and a hundred cubits wide, a square; and the altar (was) before the house.

[48] And he brought me to the porch of the house, and measured (each) pillar of the porch, five cubits from here, and five cubits from there. And the gate (was three cubits wide from here, and three cubits from there. [49] The length of the porch (was) twenty cubits, and eleven cubits

42 השער שמונה שלחנות אליהם ישחטו: וארבעה שלחנות

tables the And four they .slaughter them on ;tables eight the ;gate

לעולה אבני גזית ארך אמה אחת וחצי ורחב אמה

cubit and wide a and ,half one cubit long ,cut (were) stone burnt for offering

אחת וחצי וגבה אמה אחת אליהם ויניחו את־הכלים

the instruments also they rested them On .one cubit and high a and ,half one

43 אשר ישחטו את־העולה בם והזבח: והשפתים טפח

span the And ,hooks double the and .sacrifice by them burnt the offering they slaughtered with which

אחד מוכנים בבית סביב | סביב ואל־השלחנות בשר

the (was) of flesh the tables And on (and) .round round the in house were fastened ,one

44 הקרבן: ומחוצה לשער הפנימי לשכות שרים בחצר

the in court the singers the of chambers inner (were) the to gate the from And outside the .offering

הפנימי אשר אל־כתף שער הצפון ופניהם דרך הדרום

the ;south the of way their And (was) face .north the gate the of side at which (was) ,inner

45 אחד אל־כתף שער הקדים פני דרך הצפן: וידבר

he And said the .north the of way looked east the gate the of side at one

אלי זה הלשכה אשר פניה דרך הדרום לכהנים שמרי

the of keepers the for (is) ,priests the ,south the of way whose (is) face ,chamber This to ,me

46 משמרת הבית: והלשכה אשר פניה דרך הצפון לכהנים

the for (is) ,priests the north the of way whose (is) face the And chamber the .house the of charge

שמרי משמרת המזבח המה בני־צדוק הקרבים מבני־

the of of sons come who ,near Zadok the of sons They (are) the .altar charge the of the of keepers

47 לוי אל־יהוה לשרתו: וימד את־החצר ארך | מאה אמה

cubits a hundred long the :court he So measured serve to .Him ,Jehovah to ,Levi

48 ורחב מאה אמה מרבעת והמזבח לפני הבית: ויבאני

he And me brought the .house before the and (was) altar ,square a ,cubits a hundred and wide

אל־אלם הבית וימד אל אלם חמש אמות מפה וחמש

five and from here cubits five the ,porch (each) of pillar and measured the house the of porch to

אמות מפה ורחב השער שלש אמות מפו ושלש אמות

cubits and three from here cubits three gate the And (was) wide from .there cubits

49 מפו: ארך האלם עשרים אמה ורחב עשתי עשרה אמה

,cubits eleven and wide ,cubits (was) twenty the porch The of length from .there

wide, even with the steps by which they went up to it. And columns (were) by the pillars, one from here, and one from there.

CHAPTER 41

[1] Then he brought me to the temple and measured the pillars, six cubits wide from here, and six cubits broad from there —the width of the tent. [2] And the door (was) ten cubits wide. And the sides of the door (were) five cubits from here, and five cubits from there. And he measured its length, forty cubits; and twenty cubits wide. [3] And he went inside and measured the pillars of the door, two cubits; and the door (was) six cubits; and the width of the door, seven cubits. [4] And he measured its length, twenty cubits; and the width, twenty cubits, to the face of the temple. And he said to me, This (is) the holy of holies.

[5] And he measured the wall of the house, six cubits; and the width of (each) side chamber, four cubits, round (and) round the house all around. [6] And the side chambers (were) a side chamber over a side chamber, three (stories), and thirty times. And (they) entered the wall which (was) of the house for the side chambers round (and) round, that they may be fastened; but they were not fastened in the wall of the house. [7] And a widening and a winding upwards (and) upwards for the side chambers—for the winding around of the house (went) upward (and) upward, round (and) round the house. Therefore the width of the house (went) up,

וּבַֽמַּעֲלוֹת אֲשֶׁר יַעֲלוּ אֵלָיו וְעַמֻּדִים אֶל־הָאֵלִים אֶחָד
one the ,pillars by (were) And columns .it to they up went which by the steps with even

מִפֹּה וְאֶחָד מִפֹּה׃
from .there and one from ,here

CAP. XLI מא

CHAPTER 41

1 וַיְבִאֵנִי אֶל־הַהֵיכָל וַיָּמָד אֶת־הָאֵלִים שֵׁשׁ־אַמּוֹת רֹחַב
wide cubits six ,pillars the and measured the temple to me he Then brought

2 מִפּוֹ וְשֵׁשׁ־אַמּוֹת רֹחַב־מִפּוֹ רֹחַב הָאֹהֶל׃ וְרֹחַב הַפֶּתַח
door the (was) And wide .tent the the of width from ,there broad cubits and six from ,here

עֶשֶׂר אַמּוֹת וְכִתְפוֹת הַפֶּתַח חָמֵשׁ אַמּוֹת מִפּוֹ וְחָמֵשׁ
five and from ,here cubits five door the (were) the And of sides .cubits ten

אַמּוֹת מִפּוֹ וַיָּמָד אָרְכּוֹ אַרְבָּעִים אַמָּה וְרֹחַב עֶשְׂרִים
twenty wide and ,cubits forty its ,length he And measured from .there cubits

3 אַמָּה׃ וּבָא לִפְנִימָה וַיָּמָד אֵיל־הַפֶּתַח שְׁתַּיִם אַמּוֹת
;cubits two the ,door pillars the of and measured inside he Then went .cubits

4 וְהַפֶּתַח שֵׁשׁ אַמּוֹת וְרֹחַב הַפֶּתַח שֶׁבַע אַמּוֹת׃ וַיָּמָד אֶת־
he So measured .cubits seven ,door the the and of width ,cubits six the and (was) door

אָרְכּוֹ עֶשְׂרִים אַמָּה וְרֹחַב עֶשְׂרִים אַמָּה אֶל־פְּנֵי הַהֵיכָל
the .temple the to of face ,cubits twenty the and ,width ;cubits twenty its ,length

5 וַיֹּאמֶר אֵלַי זֶה קֹדֶשׁ הַקֳּדָשִׁים׃ וַיָּמָד קִיר־הַבַּיִת שֵׁשׁ
six the ,house the of wall he And measured .holies the of holy This (is) to ,me he And said

אַמּוֹת וְרֹחַב הַצֵּלָע אַרְבַּע אַמּוֹת סָבִיב ׀ סָבִיב לַבַּיִת
the house (and) round round ,cubits (was) four side (each) chamber the and of width ;cubits

6 סָבִיב׃ וְהַצְּלָעוֹת צֵלָע אֶל־צֵלָע שָׁלוֹשׁ וּשְׁלֹשִׁים פְּעָמִים
.times thirty and three (stories) side a over ,chamber side a chamber the And (were) side chambers all .around

וּבָאוֹת בַּקִּיר אֲשֶׁר־לַבַּיִת לַצְּלָעוֹת סָבִיב ׀ סָבִיב לִהְיוֹת
they that be may (and) ,round round side the for chambers the of house which (was) the wall (they) And entered

7 אֲחוּזִים וְלֹא־יִהְיוּ אֲחוּזִים בְּקִיר הַבָּיִת׃ וְרָחֲבָה וְנָסְבָה
a and winding a And widening .house the the in of wall fastened they were but not ,fastened

לְמַעְלָה לְמַעְלָה לַצְּלָעוֹת כִּי מוּסַב־הַבַּיִת לְמַעְלָה
(went) upward the house the winding of around For side the for .chambers upwards upwards (and)

לְמַעְלָה סָבִיב ׀ סָבִיב לַבַּיִת עַל־כֵּן רֹחַב־לַבַּיִת לְמָעְלָה
(went) ,upward the of house the width Therefore the .house (and) round round (and) ,upward

8 וְכֵן הַתַּחְתּוֹנָה יַעֲלֶה עַל־הָעֶלְיוֹנָה לַתִּיכוֹנָה׃ וְרָאִיתִי לַבַּיִת
the of also I the by the to went it the (from) and
house saw .(story) middle highest up lowest so

גֹּבַהּ סָבִיב ׀ סָבִיב מְיֻסְּדוֹת הַצְּלָעוֹת מְלוֹ הַקָּנֶה שֵׁשׁ
(of) reed (were) side the foun- the (and) round the
six full a chambers of dations ,round height

9 אַמּוֹת אַצִּילָה׃ רֹחַב הַקִּיר אֲשֶׁר־לַצֵּלָע אֶל־הַחוּץ חָמֵשׁ
five outside to the for which ,wall the The .joining cubits
(was) the side chamber (was) of width by

10 אַמּוֹת וַאֲשֶׁר מֻנָּח בֵּית צְלָעוֹת אֲשֶׁר לַבָּיִת׃ וּבֵין הַלְּשָׁכוֹת
the And the of that side the be- (was) what and, cubits
chambers between .house (were) chambers tween left

11 רֹחַב עֶשְׂרִים אַמָּה סָבִיב לַבַּיִת סָבִיב ׀ סָבִיב׃ וּפֶתַח
the And (and) round the circling cubits twenty the (was)
of door .round house of width

הַצֵּלָע לַמֻּנָּח פֶּתַח אֶחָד דֶּרֶךְ הַצָּפוֹן וּפֶתַח אֶחָד לַדָּרוֹם
the toward one door and the the one door the to side the
.south ,north of way ,space open chamber

12 וְרֹחַב מְקוֹם הַמֻּנָּח חָמֵשׁ אַמּוֹת סָבִיב ׀ סָבִיב׃ וְהַבִּנְיָן
the And (and) round cubits (was) open the the the And
building .round five space of place of width

אֲשֶׁר אֶל־פְּנֵי הַגִּזְרָה פְּאַת דֶּרֶךְ־הַיָּם רֹחַב שִׁבְעִים אַמָּה
.cubits (was) wide the the the at sep- the before that
seventy west of way end area arate (was)

וְקִיר הַבִּנְיָן חָמֵשׁ־אַמּוֹת רֹחַב סָבִיב ׀ סָבִיב וְאָרְכּוֹ תִּשְׁעִים
(was) its and (and) round wide cubits (was) the the And
ninety length ,round five building of wall

13 אַמָּה׃ וּמָדַד אֶת־הַבַּיִת אֹרֶךְ מֵאָה אַמָּה וְהַגִּזְרָה וְהַבִּנְיָה
the and the And .cubits a long ,house the he So .cubits
building ,area separate hundred measured

14 וְקִירוֹתֶיהָ אֹרֶךְ מֵאָה אַמָּה׃ וְרֹחַב פְּנֵי הַבַּיִת וְהַגִּזְרָה
the and house the the the And .cubits a long its and
area separate of face of width hundred (were) wall

15 לַקָּדִים מֵאָה אַמָּה׃ וּמָדַד אֹרֶךְ־הַבִּנְיָן אֶל־פְּנֵי הַגִּזְרָה
separate the the to the the he And .cubits a the toward
area of face building of length measured hundred east

אֲשֶׁר עַל־אַחֲרֶיהָ וְאַתּוּקֶיהָא מִפּוֹ וּמִפּוֹ מֵאָה אַמָּה וְהַהֵיכָל
the and ,cubits a from and from its and its on which
temple hundred there here gallery ;rear (was)

16 הַפְּנִימִי וְאֻלַמֵּי הֶחָצֵר׃ הַסִּפִּים וְהַחַלּוֹנִים הָאֲטֻמוֹת
,laticed the and the ,court the the and inner
windows ,thresholds of porches

וְהָאַתִּיקִים ׀ סָבִיב לִשְׁלָשְׁתָּם נֶגֶד הַסַּף שְׂחִיף עֵץ סָבִיב ׀
round (with) were the opposite three their all the and
wood panelled ,threshold ,(stories) around galleries

17 סָבִיב וְהָאָרֶץ עַד־הַחַלֹּנוֹת וְהַחַלֹּנוֹת מְכֻסּוֹת׃ עַל־מֵעַל
above to were the and the to up (from) and (and)
that ;covered windows ,windows ground the ;round

הַפֶּתַח וְעַד־הַבַּיִת הַפְּנִימִי וְלַחוּץ וְאֶל־כָּל־הַקִּיר סָבִיב ׀
round the all and and ,inner the even the
wall to ,outside house to ,door

and so (from) the lowest it went up to the highest, by the middle (story). [8] I also saw the height of the house round (and) round, the foundations of the side chambers (were) a full reed (of) six cubits by joining. [9] The width of the wall which (was) for the side chamber to the outside was five cubits, [10] and that which (was) left between the side chambers that (were) of the house. And between the chambers (was) the width of twenty cubits circling the house round (and) round. [11] And the door of the side chamber (was) toward the open space, one door northward, and one door southward. And the width of the place of the open space (was) five cuibts round (and) round. [12] And the building that (was) before the separate area at the end of the way of the west (was) seventy cubits wide, and the wall of the building (was) five cubits wide round (and) round; and its length, ninety cubits.

[13] And he measured the house, a hundred cubits long. And the separate area, and the building and its wall (were) a hundred cubits long. [14] And the width of the face of the house, and the separate area toward the east, a hundred cubits. [15] And he measured the length of the building to the face of the separate area which (was) on its rear; and its gallery from here and from there, a hundred cubits; and the inner temple, and the porches of the court, [16] the thresholds, and the laticed windows, and the galleries all around, their three (stories) opposite the threshold, were panelled (with) wood round (and) round; and (from) the ground up to the windows; and the windows were covered; to that above the door, even to the inner house, and outside, and to all the wall round (and)

round inside and outside by measure. [18] And it was made (with) cherubs and palm trees; and a palm tree (was) between cherub and cherub. [19] And two faces (were) to a cherub, the face of a man toward the palm tree from here, and a young lion's face toward the palm tree from there. It was made to all the house round (and) round. [20] From the ground to above the door cherubs and palm trees (were) made, and (on) the wall of the temple. [21] The temple doorposts (were) squared, and the face of the sanctuary, the appearance as (its) appearance. [22] The altar of wood (was) three cubits high, and its length two cubits. And its corners (are) to it, and its length, and its walls, (were) wood. And he said to me, This (is) the table that (is) before Jehovah. [23] And two doors (were) to the temple and the sanctuary. [24] And two doors (are) to (each) of the doors, two turning doors—two for the one door, and two for the other door. [25] And cherubs and palm trees were made on them, on the doors of the temple, like those made on the walls; and thick wood on the face of the porch outside. [26] And laticed windows, and palm trees, (were) from here and from there, on the sides of the porch, and the side chambers of the house, and thick (planks).

18 סָבִיב בַּפְּנִימִי וּבַחִיצוֹן מִדּוֹת׃ וְעָשׂוּי כְּרוּבִים וְתִמֹּרִים

palm and (with) it And by and inside (and)
,trees cherubs made was .measure outside round

19 וְתִמֹּרָה בֵּין־כְּרוּב לִכְרוּב וּשְׁנַיִם פָּנִים לַכְּרוּב׃ וּפְנֵי אָדָם

man a the to (were) faces two And and cherub (was) a and
of face ,cherub a .cherub between tree palm

אֶל־הַתִּמֹּרָה מִפּוֹ וּפְנֵי־כְפִיר אֶל־הַתִּמֹּרָה מִפּוֹ עָשׂוּי אֶל־

to was It from palm the toward young a and from palm the toward
made ;there tree lion's face ,here tree

20 כָּל־הַבַּיִת סָבִיב ׀ סָבִיב׃ מֵהָאָרֶץ עַד־מֵעַל הַפֶּתַח

the above to the From (and) round the all
door ground .round house

21 הַכְּרוּבִים וְהַתִּמֹּרִים עֲשׂוּיִם וְקִיר הַהֵיכָל׃ הַהֵיכָל מְזוּזַת

door- The the (on) and ,made palm and (were)
posts temple .temple of wall the trees cherubs

22 רְבֻעָה וּפְנֵי הַקֹּדֶשׁ הַמַּרְאֶה כַּמַּרְאֶה׃ הַמִּזְבֵּחַ עֵץ שָׁלוֹשׁ

(was) wood altar The (its) as ap- the the the and (were)
three of .appearance pearance ,sanctuary of face ,squared

אַמּוֹת גָּבֹהַּ וְאָרְכּוֹ שְׁתַּיִם אַמּוֹת וּמִקְצֻעוֹתָיו לוֹ וְאָרְכּוֹ

its and to its And .cubits (was) its and ,high cubits
,length ,it (are) corners two length

וְקִירֹתָיו עֵץ וַיְדַבֵּר אֵלַי זֶה הַשֻּׁלְחָן אֲשֶׁר לִפְנֵי יְהוָה׃

.Jehovah before that the This to he And .wood its and
(is) table (is) ,me said (were) walls

23
24 וּשְׁתַּיִם דְּלָתוֹת לַהֵיכָל וְלַקֹּדֶשׁ׃ וּשְׁתַּיִם דְּלָתוֹת לַדְּלָתוֹת

(each) to (are) doors two And the and the to doors two And
doors the of .sanctuary temple (were)

שְׁתַּיִם מוּסַבּוֹת דְּלָתוֹת שְׁתַּיִם לְדֶלֶת אֶחָת וּשְׁתֵּי דְלָתוֹת

the for and ,one the for two —doors turning two
door two door

25 לָאַחֶרֶת׃ וַעֲשׂוּיָה אֲלֵיהֶן אֶל־דַּלְתוֹת הַהֵיכָל כְּרוּבִים

cherubs the doors the on ,them on were And .other
temple of made

וְתִמֹּרִים כַּאֲשֶׁר עֲשׂוּיִם לַקִּירוֹת וְעָב עֵץ אֶל־פְּנֵי הָאוּלָם

porch the the on wood and the on those like palm and
of face thick ;walls made trees

26 מֵהַחוּץ׃ וְחַלּוֹנִים אֲטֻמוֹת וְתִמֹּרִים מִפּוֹ וּמִפּוֹ אֶל־כִּתְפוֹת

sides the on from and from palm and laticed windows And .outside
of ,there here trees

הָאוּלָם וְצַלְעוֹת הַבַּיִת וְהָעֻבִּים׃

thick and the side the and the
.(planks) ,house of chambers porch

CAP. XLII מב

CHAPTER 42

[1] And he brought me out into the outer court, northward. And he brought me into the chamber that (was) across from the separate area, which (was) in front of the building to

1 וַיּוֹצִאֵנִי אֶל־הֶחָצֵר הַחִיצוֹנָה הַדֶּרֶךְ דֶּרֶךְ הַצָּפוֹן וַיְבִאֵנִי

he And the toward way the ,outer the into he Then
me brought .north court out me brought

אֶל־הַלִּשְׁכָּה אֲשֶׁר נֶגֶד הַגִּזְרָה וַאֲשֶׁר־נֶגֶד הַבִּנְיָן אֶל־

to the front in and separate the across that the into
building of (was) which area from (was) chamber

the north. [2] To the face of (its) length (was) a hundred cubits, the north door, and fifty cubits wide. [3] Across from the twenty (cubits) which (were) to the inner court, and opposite the pavement which (was) to the outer court, gallery on the face of gallery, in three (stories). [4] And before the chambers (was) a walk ten cubits wide, to the inside, a way of one cubit. And their doors (were) toward the north. [5] And the upper chambers (were) shorter, for the galleries consumed more than them, than from the lower and middle ones in the building. [6] For they (were) in three (stories), and there (were) no columns to them like the columns of the courts. So (the third) was made narrower than the lower and middle (stories), from the ground.

[7] And the wall that (was) outside near the chambers the way of the outer court, on the face of the chambers, its length (was) fifty cubits. [8] For the length of the chambers that (was) in the outer court (was) fifty cubits. And behold, in the face of the temple (was) a hundred cubits. [9] And under these chambers (was) the entrance on the east side as one goes into them from the outer court. [10] In the wall of the court eastward, to the face of the separate area, and to the face of the building, (were) chambers. [11] And the way before them looked like the chambers which (were) northward; as their length, so their width. And all their exits (were) as their patterns, and as their doors. [12] And as the doors of the chambers that (were) southward. there

2 הַצָּפוֹן׃ אֶל־פְּנֵי אֹרֶךְ אַמּוֹת הַמֵּאָה פֶּתַח הַצָּפוֹן וְהָרֹחַב

wide and ,north the a (was) (its) the To the
door ,hundred cubits length of face .north

3 חֲמִשִּׁים אַמּוֹת׃ נֶגֶד הָעֶשְׂרִים אֲשֶׁר לֶחָצֵר הַפְּנִימִי וְנֶגֶד

and the court for which the Across .cubits fifty
opposite ,inner (were) twenty from

רִצְפָה אֲשֶׁר לֶחָצֵר הַחִיצוֹנָה אַתִּיק אֶל־פְּנֵי־אַתִּיק

,gallery the on gallery the court to which the
of face ,outer (was) pavement

4 בַּשְּׁלִשִׁים׃ וְלִפְנֵי הַלְּשָׁכוֹת מַהֲלַךְ עֶשֶׂר אַמּוֹת רֹחַב אֶל־

to ,wide cubits ten a (was) the And three in
walk chambers before .(stories)

5 הַפְּנִימִית דֶּרֶךְ אַמָּה אֶחָת וּפִתְחֵיהֶם לַצָּפוֹן׃ וְהַלְּשָׁכוֹת

the And the toward their And .one cubit a the
chambers .north (were) doors of way ,inside

הָעֶלְיוֹנֹת קְצֻרוֹת כִּי־יוֹכְלוּ אַתִּיקִים מֵהֵנָּה מֵהַתַּחְתֹּנוֹת

the from than than the consumed for (were) upper
lower ,them galleries more ,shorter

6 וּמֵהַתִּיכֹנוֹת בִּנְיָן׃ כִּי מְשֻׁלָּשׁוֹת הֵנָּה וְאֵין לָהֶן עַמּוּדִים

(were) to and they three in For the in middle and
columns them not ,(were) (stories) .building ones

כְּעַמּוּדֵי הַחֲצֵרוֹת עַל־כֵּן נֶאֱצַל מֵהַתַּחְתֹּנוֹת וּמֵהַתִּיכֹנוֹת

middle the and the than made was So .courts the the like
(stories) lower narrower (third the) of columns

7 מֵהָאָרֶץ׃ וְגָדֵר אֲשֶׁר־לַחוּץ לְעֻמַּת הַלְּשָׁכוֹת דֶּרֶךְ הֶחָצֵר

the the the near outside that the And the from
court of way chambers (was) wall .ground

8 הַחִצוֹנָה אֶל־פְּנֵי הַלְּשָׁכוֹת אָרְכּוֹ חֲמִשִּׁים אַמָּה׃ כִּי־

For .cubits (was) length its ,chambers the the on outer
fifty of face

אֹרֶךְ הַלְּשָׁכוֹת אֲשֶׁר לֶחָצֵר הַחִצוֹנָה חֲמִשִּׁים אַמָּה וְהִנֵּה

And .cubits (was) outer the in that the the
,behold fifty court (was) chambers of length

9 עַל־פְּנֵי הַהֵיכָל מֵאָה אַמָּה׃ וּמִתַּחְתָּה הַלְּשָׁכוֹת הָאֵלֶּה

these chambers under And .cubits a (was) the the in
(was) hundred temple of face

10 הַמֵּבוֹא מֵהַקָּדִים בְּבֹאוֹ לָהֵנָּה מֵהֶחָצֵר הַחִצֹנָה׃ בְּרֹחַב

the in .outer the from into one as the on the
of width court them goes ,side east entrance

גֶּדֶר הֶחָצֵר דֶּרֶךְ הַקָּדִים אֶל־פְּנֵי הַגִּזְרָה וְאֶל־פְּנֵי הַבִּנְיָן

the the to and separate the the to the the the the
,building of face ,area of face ,east of way court of wall

11 לְשָׁכוֹת׃ וְדֶרֶךְ לִפְנֵיהֶם כְּמַרְאֵה הַלְּשָׁכוֹת אֲשֶׁר דֶּרֶךְ

the which the looked before the And (were there)
of way (were) chambers like them way .chambers

הַצָּפוֹן כְּאָרְכָּן כֵּן רָחְבָּן וְכֹל מוֹצָאֵיהֶן וּכְמִשְׁפְּטֵיהֶן

their as their And their so their as the
,patterns exits all .width (was) ,length ;north

12 וּכְפִתְחֵיהֶן׃ וּכְפִתְחֵי הַלְּשָׁכוֹת אֲשֶׁר דֶּרֶךְ הַדָּרוֹם פֶּתַח

(there) south the the that the the as And their as and
door a (was) of way (were) chambers of doors .doors

(was) a door in the head of the way, the way directly in the face of the wall, the way of the east, as one enters them.

[13] And he said to me, The north chambers, the south chambers which (are) to the face of the separate area, they (are) holy chambers, there where the priests shall eat, who approach to Jehovah, the holiest of holy (things). There they shall lay the holiest of holy (things), even the food offering, and the sin offering, and the guilt offering. For the place (is) holy. [14] When the priests enter, then they shall not go out of the sanctuary into the outer court, but they shall lay their clothes there by which they minister by them; for they (are) holy; they shall put on other clothes and shall approach to that (which is) for the people. [15] And he finished measuring the inner house, and he brought me forth the way of the gate whose face (is) eastward, and measured round (and) round. [16] He measured the east side with the measuring reed, five hundred reeds with the measuring reed, all around. [17] He measured the north side, five hundred reeds with the measuring reed, all around. [18] He measured the south side, five hundred reeds with the measuring reed. [19] He turned to the west side, measuring five hundred reeds with the measuring reed. [20] By the four sides he measured it. It had a wall round (and) round, five hundred (reeds) long and five hundred wide, to separate between the holy and the common.

בְּרֹאשׁ דֶּרֶךְ דֶּרֶךְ בִּפְנֵי הַגְּדֶרֶת הֲגִינָה דֶּרֶךְ הַקָּדִים

,east the of way | the directly | wall the | the of face | the way | the ,way | the in of head

13 בְּבוֹאָן׃ וַיֹּאמֶר אֵלַי לִשְׁכוֹת הַצָּפוֹן לִשְׁכוֹת הַדָּרוֹם אֲשֶׁר

which (are) | south | the chambers | ,north | the chambers | to ,me | he Then said | one as .them enters

אֶל־פְּנֵי הַגִּזְרָה הֵנָּה ׀ לִשְׁכוֹת הַקֹּדֶשׁ אֲשֶׁר יֹאכְלוּ־שָׁם

there | shall eat | where | ,holy | chambers | they (are) | sep- ,area arate | the | the to of face

הַכֹּהֲנִים אֲשֶׁר־קְרוֹבִים לַיהוָה קָדְשֵׁי הַקֳּדָשִׁים שָׁם יַנִּיחוּ ׀

shall they lay | There | holy .(things) | the of holiest | to Jehovah | approach | who | the priests

קָדְשֵׁי הַקֳּדָשִׁים וְהַמִּנְחָה וְהַחַטָּאת וְהָאָשָׁם כִּי הַמָּקוֹם

the (is) place | For | the and .offering guilt | sin the and ,offering | the even ,offering food | holy ,(things) | the of holiest

14 קָדֹשׁ׃ בְּבֹאָם הַכֹּהֲנִים וְלֹא־יֵצְאוּ מֵהַקֹּדֶשׁ אֶל־הֶחָצֵר

the court | into | the of sanctuary | shall they then out go not | ,priests the | When enter | .holy

הַחִיצוֹנָה וְשָׁם יַנִּיחוּ בִגְדֵיהֶם אֲשֶׁר־יְשָׁרְתוּ בָהֶן כִּי־קֹדֶשׁ

holy | for | by ;them | they minister | by which | their clothes | shall they lay | but there | ,outer

15 הֵנָּה יִלְבְּשׁוּ בְּגָדִים אֲחֵרִים וְקָרְבוּ אֶל־אֲשֶׁר לָעָם׃ וְכִלָּה

he And ended | the for .people | that (is which) | to | shall and approach | other | clothes | shall they on put | they ;(are)

אֶת־מִדּוֹת הַבַּיִת הַפְּנִימִי וְהוֹצִיאַנִי דֶּרֶךְ הַשַּׁעַר אֲשֶׁר

whose | the gate | the of way | brought he and forth me | inner | the house | measuring

16 פָּנָיו דֶּרֶךְ הַקָּדִים וּמְדָדוֹ סָבִיב ׀ סָבִיב׃ מָדַד רוּחַ הַקָּדִים

east | the side | He measured | (and) . round | round | meas- and it ured | the ,east | the of way | face (is)

בִּקְנֵה הַמִּדָּה חֲמֵשׁ־אֵמוֹת קָנִים בִּקְנֵה הַמִּדָּה סָבִיב׃

all .around | the ,measuring | with reed | reeds | hundred five | ,measuring the with reed

17 מָדַד רוּחַ הַצָּפוֹן חֲמֵשׁ־מֵאוֹת קָנִים בִּקְנֵה הַמִּדָּה סָבִיב׃

all .around | the ,measuring | with reed | reeds | hundred five | ,north | side the | He measured

18 אֵת רוּחַ הַדָּרוֹם מָדָד חֲמֵשׁ־מֵאוֹת קָנִים בִּקְנֵה הַמִּדָּה׃

the .measuring | with reed | reeds | hundred five | He ,measured | south | side the

19 סָבַב אֶל־רוּחַ הַיָּם מָדַד חֲמֵשׁ־מֵאוֹת קָנִים בִּקְנֵה הַמִּדָּה׃

the .measuring | with reed | reeds | hundred five | measuring | ,west side the to | He turned

20 לְאַרְבַּע רוּחוֹת מְדָדוֹ חוֹמָה לוֹ סָבִיב ׀ סָבִיב אֹרֶךְ חֲמֵשׁ

five | long | (and) ,round | round | It had | a wall | meas- He .it ured | sides | the by four

מֵאוֹת וְרֹחַב חֲמֵשׁ מֵאוֹת לְהַבְדִּיל בֵּין הַקֹּדֶשׁ לְחֹל׃

the and .common | the holy | between | to separate | ,hundred | five | and wide | hundred ,(reeds)

CAP. XLIII מג

CHAPTER 43

CHAPTER 43

[1] And he led me to the gate, the gate that faces eastward. [2] And behold, the glory of the God of Israel came from the way of the east. And His voice (was) like the voice of many waters. And the earth shone from His glory. [3] And as the appearance of the vision which I saw, as the appearance which I saw when I came to destroy the city; and the appearances as that I saw by the river Chebar. And I fell on my face. [4] And the glory of Jehovah came into the house, the way of the gate of which its face (is) eastward. [5] And the Spirit took me up and brought me into the inner court. And, behold, the glory of Jehovah filled the house!

[6] And I heard (one) speaking to me from the house; and a Man was standing beside me. And He said to me, Son of man, the place of My throne and the place of the soles of My feet, there where I will dwell among the sons of Israel forever, even the house of Israel shall not defile My holy name any more; they nor their kings, by their fornication, nor by the corpses of their kings in their high places. [8] In their giving of their threshold (by) My threshold, and their door post beside My door post, and the wall between Me and them; even they have defiled My holy name by their abominations that they have done. And I consumed them in My anger. [9] Now (let) them put away their fornication, and the corpses of their kings, from Me, and I will dwell in their midst forever.

[10] You, son of man, declare to the house of

1 2 וַיֹּלִכֵנִי אֶל־הַשָּׁעַר שַׁעַר אֲשֶׁר פֹּנֶה דֶּרֶךְ הַקָּדִים׃ וְהִנֵּה
,And .east the the faces that the ,gate the to he And
,behold of way gate me led

כְּבוֹד אֱלֹהֵי יִשְׂרָאֵל בָּא מִדֶּרֶךְ הַקָּדִים וְקוֹלוֹ כְּקוֹל מַיִם
waters the like His And the the from came Israel the glory the
of voice voice .east of way of God of

3 רַבִּים וְהָאָרֶץ הֵאִירָה מִכְּבֹדוֹ׃ וּכְמַרְאֵה הַמַּרְאֶה אֲשֶׁר
which the the as And His from shone the And .many
vision of appearance .glory earth

רָאִיתִי כַּמַּרְאֶה אֲשֶׁר־רָאִיתִי בְּבֹאִי לְשַׁחֵת אֶת־הָעִיר
.city the to I when saw I which the as ,saw I
destroy came appearance

וּמַרְאוֹת כַּמַּרְאֶה אֲשֶׁר רָאִיתִי אֶל־נְהַר כְּבָר וָאֶפֹּל אֶל־
on I And .Chebar the by saw I that the as the And
fell river appearance appearances

4 פָּנָי׃ וּכְבוֹד יְהוָה בָּא אֶל־הַבָּיִת דֶּרֶךְ שַׁעַר אֲשֶׁר פָּנָיו
its of the the the into came Jehovah the And my
face which gate of way ,house of glory .face

5 דֶּרֶךְ הַקָּדִים׃ וַתִּשָּׂאֵנִי רוּחַ וַתְּבִאֵנִי אֶל־הֶחָצֵר הַפְּנִימִי
.inner the into brought and the took So .east the the (is)
court me Spirit up me of way

6 וְהִנֵּה מָלֵא כְבוֹד־יְהוָה הַבָּיִת׃ וָאֶשְׁמַע מִדַּבֵּר אֵלַי מֵהַבָּיִת
the from to (one) I And the Jehovah the filled ,And
;house me speaking heard !house of glory ,behold

7 וְאִישׁ הָיָה עֹמֵד אֶצְלִי׃ וַיֹּאמֶר אֵלַי בֶּן־אָדָם אֶת־מְקוֹם
the ,man Son to He And beside standing was a and
of place of ,me said .me Man

כִּסְאִי וְאֶת־מְקוֹם כַּפּוֹת רַגְלַי אֲשֶׁר אֶשְׁכָּן־שָׁם בְּתוֹךְ בְּנֵי־
the among there will I where My the the and My
of sons dwell ,feet of soles of place throne

יִשְׂרָאֵל לְעוֹלָם וְלֹא יְטַמְּאוּ עוֹד בֵּית־יִשְׂרָאֵל שֵׁם קָדְשִׁי
My name Israel the still shall even .forever Israel
,holy of house defile not

8 הֵמָּה וּמַלְכֵיהֶם בִּזְנוּתָם וּבְפִגְרֵי מַלְכֵיהֶם בָּמוֹתָם׃ בְּתִתָּם
their In their in kings their by nor their by their nor they
of giving .places high of corpses the ,fornication ,kings

סִפָּם אֶת־סִפִּי וּמְזוּזָתָם אֵצֶל מְזוּזָתִי וְהַקִּיר בֵּינִי וּבֵינֵיהֶם
;them and between the and door My beside their and My (by) their
Me wall ,post post door ,threshold threshold

וְטִמְּאוּ אֶת־שֵׁם קָדְשִׁי בְּתוֹעֲבוֹתָם אֲשֶׁר עָשׂוּ וָאֲכַל אֹתָם
them I Thus have they that their by My name they even
consumed .done abominations holy defiled have

9 בְּאַפִּי׃ עַתָּה יְרַחֲקוּ אֶת־זְנוּתָם וּפִגְרֵי מַלְכֵיהֶם מִמֶּנִּי
from their the and their them (let) Now My in
,Me ,kings of corpses ,fornication away put .anger

10 וְשָׁכַנְתִּי בְתוֹכָם לְעוֹלָם׃ אַתָּה בֶן־אָדָם הַגֵּד אֶת־
declare ,man son ,You .forever their in will I and
of midst dwell

Isreal the (temple) house, and they will blush from their iniquities. And let them measure its size. [11] And if they are ashamed of all that they have done, the form of the house, and its arrangement, and its exits, and its entrances, and all its forms, and all its statutes, and all its forms, and all its laws, make known to them. And write in their sight, so that they may observe all its form, and all its statutes, and do them. [12] This (is) the law of the house: On the top of the mountain (is) all its border, round (and) round (being) most holy. Behold, this (is) the law of the house.

[13] And these (are) the measures of the altar by the cubit—the cubit (is) a cubit and a span—even the base (shall be) a cubit, and the width a cubit, and its border on its edge all around (shall be) one span. And this (is) the upper part of the altar. [14] And from the base (on) the ground to the lower ledge (shall be) two cubits, and the width one cubit. And from the smaller ledge to the greater ledge (shall be) four cubits, and the width a cubit. [15] And the altar hearth (shall be) four cubits, and from the altar hearth and upward (shall) (be) four horns. [16] And the altar hearth (shall be) twelve (cubits) long, and twelve wide, square in its four sides. [17] And the ledge (shall be) fourteen long (and) fourteen wide in its four sides. And the border around it (shall be) a half cubit, and the base for it a cubit all around. And its steps face the east.

[18] And He said to me, Son of man, thus says

בֵּית־יִשְׂרָאֵל אֶת־הַבַּיִת וְיִכָּלְמוּ מֵעֲוֺנוֹתֵיהֶם וּמָדְדוּ אֶת־
them let And their from they and (temple) the Israel the (to)
measure .iniquities blush will house of house

11 תָּכְנִית׃ וְאִם־נִכְלְמוּ מִכֹּל אֲשֶׁר־עָשׂוּ צוּרַת הַבַּיִת וּתְכוּנָתוֹ
its and the the have they that of are they And (its)
arrangement ,house of form ,done all ashamed if .size

וּמוֹצָאָיו וּמוֹבָאָיו וְכָל־צוּרֹתָו וְאֵת כָּל־חֻקֹּתָיו וְכָל־צוּרֹתָו
its and its all and its and its and its and
,forms all ,statutes ,forms all ,entrances exits

וְכָל־תּוֹרֹתָו הוֹדַע אוֹתָם וּכְתֹב לְעֵינֵיהֶם וְיִשְׁמְרוּ אֶת־כָּל־
all they that so their in And to make its and
observe may ,sight (it) write them known ,laws all

12 צוּרָתוֹ וְאֶת־כָּל־חֻקֹּתָיו וְעָשׂוּ אוֹתָם׃ זֹאת תּוֹרַת הַבָּיִת
the the This .them do and its all and its
:house of law (is) ,statutes ,form

עַל־רֹאשׁ הָהָר כָּל־גְּבֻלוֹ סָבִיב ׀ סָבִיב קֹדֶשׁ קָדָשִׁים הִנֵּה־
,Behold .holy (being) (and) round its all (is) the the On
most ,round ,border mountain of top

13 זֹאת תּוֹרַת הַבָּיִת׃ וְאֵלֶּה מִדּוֹת הַמִּזְבֵּחַ בָּאַמּוֹת אַמָּה
the the by the meas- the And the law the this
(is) cubit —cubit altar of ures (are) these !house of (is)

אַמָּה וָטֹפַח וְחֵיק הָאַמָּה וְאַמָּה־רֹחַב וּגְבוּלָהּ אֶל־שְׂפָתָהּ
edge its on its and the a and (be shall) even a and a
border ,width cubit ,cubit a base the —span cubit

14 סָבִיב זֶרֶת הָאֶחָד וְזֶה גַּב הַמִּזְבֵּחַ׃ וּמֵחֵיק הָאָרֶץ עַד־
to the (on) from And .altar's the height And .one (be shall) all
ground base the (is) this span around

הָעֲזָרָה הַתַּחְתּוֹנָה שְׁתַּיִם אַמּוֹת וְרֹחַב אַמָּה אֶחָת
.one cubit the and ,cubits (be shall) lower the
width two ledge

וּמֵהָעֲזָרָה הַקְּטַנָּה עַד־הָעֲזָרָה הַגְּדוֹלָה אַרְבַּע אַמּוֹת
,cubits (be shall) greater ledge the to smaller the from And
four ledge

15 וְרֹחַב הָאַמָּה׃ וְהַהַרְאֵל אַרְבַּע אַמּוֹת וּמֵהָאֲרִאֵיל וּלְמַעְלָה
and the from and ,cubits (be shall) the And (one) the and
upward hearth altar four hearth altar .cubit width

16 הַקְּרָנוֹת אַרְבַּע׃ וְהָאֲרִאֵיל שְׁתֵּים עֶשְׂרֵה אֹרֶךְ בִּשְׁתֵּים
two ,long (cubits) (be shall) the And .four (be shall)
twelve hearth altar horns

17 עֶשְׂרֵה רֹחַב רָבוּעַ אֶל אַרְבַּעַת רְבָעָיו׃ וְהָעֲזָרָה אַרְבַּע
(be shall) the And .sides its four the in square wide (and)
four- ledge of ten

עֶשְׂרֵה אֹרֶךְ בְּאַרְבַּע עֶשְׂרֵה רֹחַב אֶל־אַרְבַּעַת רְבָעֶיהָ
.sides its four the in wide (and) four ,long ten (and)
of ten (cubits)

וְהַגְּבוּל סָבִיב אוֹתָהּ חֲצִי הָאַמָּה וְהַחֵיק־לָהּ אַמָּה סָבִיב
all (be shall) for the and ,cubit a half it around the And
.around cubit a it base (be shall) border

18 וּמַעֲלֹתֵהוּ פְּנוֹת קָדִים׃ וַיֹּאמֶר אֵלַי בֶּן־אָדָם כֹּה אָמַר
says thus .man Son ,me to He And .east the face its And
of said steps

the Lord Jehovah: These (are) the statutes of the altar in the day of its being made to offer on it burnt offerings, and to sprinkle on it blood. [19] And you shall give to the priests of the Levites, they who (are) from the seed of Zadok, who approach to Me, declares the Lord Jehovah, to serve Me, a bull, a son of the herd, for a sin offering. [20] And you shall take of its blood and put (it) on its four horns, and on the four corners of the ledge, and on the border all around. And you shall cleanse it and atone for it. [21] And you shall take the bull of the sin offering, and he shall burn (it) at the appointed (place) of the house outside the sanctuary. [22] And on the second day you shall bring a buck of the goats, perfect, for a sin offering. And they shall cleanse the altar , as they cleansed (it) with the bull. [23] When you have finished cleansing (it), you shall bring a bull, a son of the herd, perfect; and a ram out of the flock, perfect. [24] And you shall bring them before Jehovah, and the priests shall cast on them salt, and they shall offer them (for) a burnt offering to Jehovah. [25] (For) seven days you shall prepare a he-goat (for) a sin offering daily. And they shall prepare a bull, a son of the herd, and a ram out of the flock, perfect. [26] They shall atone seven days (for) the altar, and cleanse it, and fill his hands. [27] And when the days are completed, it shall be (that) on the eighth day and forward, the priests shall make your burnt offerings and your peace offerings on the altar. And I will accept you, declares the Lord Jehovah.

אֲדֹנָי יֱהוִה אֵלֶּה חֻקּוֹת הַמִּזְבֵּחַ בְּיוֹם הֵעָשׂוֹתוֹ לְהַעֲלוֹת
offer to being its made the in of day altar the the of statutes These (are) :Jehovah the Lord

19 עָלָיו עוֹלָה וְלִזְרֹק עָלָיו דָּם׃ וְנָתַתָּה אֶל־הַכֹּהֲנִים הַלְוִיִּם
the Levites priests the of to you And give shall .blood on it to and sprinkle burnt ,offerings it on

אֲשֶׁר הֵם מִזֶּרַע צָדוֹק הַקְּרֹבִים אֵלַי נְאֻם אֲדֹנָי יֱהוִה
,Jehovah the Lord states ,Me to who approach ,Zadok the from of seed they (are) of whom

20 לְשָׁרְתֵנִי פַּר בֶּן־בָּקָר לְחַטָּאת׃ וְלָקַחְתָּ מִדָּמוֹ וְנָתַתָּה עַל־
on put and (it) its of blood you And take shall sin a for .offering the son a herd of a ,bull serve to ,Me

אַרְבַּע קַרְנֹתָיו וְאֶל־אַרְבַּע פִּנּוֹת הָעֲזָרָה וְאֶל־הַגְּבוּל
the border and on ,ledge the corners of the four and on ,horns its four

21 סָבִיב וְחִטֵּאתָ אוֹתוֹ וְכִפַּרְתָּהוּ׃ וְלָקַחְתָּ אֵת הַפָּר הַחַטָּאת
sin the ,offering the of bull you And take shall atone and .it for it you So cleanse shall all .around

22 וּשְׂרָפוֹ בְּמִפְקַד הַבַּיִת מִחוּץ לַמִּקְדָּשׁ׃ וּבַיּוֹם הַשֵּׁנִי תַּקְרִיב
shall you bring the second on And day the .sanctuary outside the house of set the at (place) shall he and burn

שְׂעִיר־עִזִּים תָּמִים לְחַטָּאת וְחִטְּאוּ אֶת־הַמִּזְבֵּחַ כַּאֲשֶׁר
as altar the they And cleanse shall sin a for .offering perfect the ,goats buck a of

23 חִטְּאוּ בַּפָּר׃ בְּכַלּוֹתְךָ מֵחַטֵּא תַּקְרִיב פַּר בֶּן־בָּקָר תָּמִים
,perfect the a ,herd of son a ,bull shall you bring cleansing (it), have you When finished the with .bull (it) they cleansed

24 וְאַיִל מִן־הַצֹּאן תָּמִים׃ וְהִקְרַבְתָּם לִפְנֵי יְהוָה וְהִשְׁלִיכוּ
shall and cast ,Jehovah before shall you And them bring .perfect the flock out of a and ram

25 הַכֹּהֲנִים עֲלֵיהֶם מֶלַח וְהֶעֱלוּ אוֹתָם עֹלָה לַיהוָה׃ שִׁבְעַת
(For) seven to .Jehovah burnt a offering them (for) they and offer shall ,salt them on priests the

יָמִים תַּעֲשֶׂה שְׂעִיר־חַטָּאת לַיּוֹם וּפַר בֶּן־בָּקָר וְאַיִל מִן
out of a and ram the ,herd a of son a And ,bull .daily sin a (for) offering he- a goat shall you prepare days

26 הַצֹּאן תְּמִימִים יַעֲשׂוּ׃ שִׁבְעַת יָמִים יְכַפְּרוּ אֶת־הַמִּזְבֵּחַ
the (for) ,altar shall they atone days Seven shall they .prepare perfect the flock

27 וְטִהֲרוּ אֹתוֹ וּמִלְאוּ יָדוֹ׃ וִיכַלּוּ אֶת־הַיָּמִים וְהָיָה בַיּוֹם
the on day shall it (that) be ,days the when And completed are his .hands fill and ,it and cleanse

הַשְּׁמִינִי וָהָלְאָה יַעֲשׂוּ הַכֹּהֲנִים עַל־הַמִּזְבֵּחַ אֶת־עוֹלוֹתֵיכֶם
burnt your ,offerings altar the on priests the shall make and ,forward eighth

וְאֶת־שַׁלְמֵיכֶם וְרָצֵאתִי אֶתְכֶם נְאֻם אֲדֹנָי יֱהוִה׃
.Jehovah the Lord states ,you will I And accept peace your .offerings and

CAP. XLIV מד

CHAPTER 44

CHAPTER 44

[1] And he brought me back the way of the gate of the outer sanctuary, facing east. And it was shut. [2] And Jehovah said to me, This gate shall be shut; it will not be opened; and a man shall not enter by it; because Jehovah, the God of Israel, has entered by it; thus it shall be shut. [3] (As for) the prince, he shall sit in it to eat bread before Jehovah. He shall enter by the way of the porch of the gate, and by his way shall go out.

[4] And he brought me by the way of the north gate, to the face of the house. And I looked, and behold! The glory of Jehovah! And I fell on my face. [5] And Jehovah said to me, Son of man, set your heart and see with your eyes, and hear with your ears all that I say to you of all the statutes of the house of Jehovah, and of all its laws. And set your heart to the entrance of the house, with all the exits of the sanctuary. [6] And you shall say to the rebellious, to the house of Israel, Thus says the Lord Jehovah: Enough to you, of all your abominations, O house of Israel, [7] when you brought in the sons of aliens, uncircumcised of heart and uncircumcised of flesh, to be in My sanctuary, to profane it—(even) My house, when you bring near My bread, the fat and the blood. And they have broken My covenant by all your abominations. [8] And you have not kept the charge of My holy things, but you have set (them) as keepers of My charge in My sanctuary for themselves. [9] Thus says the

1 וַיָּשֶׁב אֹתִי דֶּרֶךְ שַׁעַר הַמִּקְדָּשׁ הַחִיצוֹן הַפֹּנֶה קָדִים וְהוּא
it And .east facing outer the the the me he Then
sanctuary of gate of way back brought
2 סָגוּר׃ וַיֹּאמֶר אֵלַי יְהוָה הַשַּׁעַר הַזֶּה סָגוּר יִהְיֶה לֹא
not ;be shall shut This gate ,Jehovah me to said Then was
.shut
יִפָּתֵחַ וְאִישׁ לֹא־יָבֹא בוֹ כִּי יְהוָה אֱלֹהֵי־יִשְׂרָאֵל בָּא בוֹ
by has ,Israel the ,Jehovah Be- by shall not a and be will it
,it entered of God cause .it enter man ;opened
3 וְהָיָה סָגוּר׃ אֶת־הַנָּשִׂיא נָשִׂיא־הוּא יֵשֶׁב־בּוֹ לֶאֱכוֹל־לֶחֶם
bread eat to in shall he (as) ,prince the (As) .shut it thus
it sit prince (for be shall
לִפְנֵי יְהוָה מִדֶּרֶךְ אוּלָם הַשַּׁעַר יָבוֹא וּמִדַּרְכּוֹ יֵצֵא׃
go shall by and shall He gate the the the by .Jehovah before
.out way his ,enter of porch of way
4 וַיְבִיאֵנִי דֶּרֶךְ־שַׁעַר־הַצָּפוֹן אֶל־פְּנֵי הַבַּיִת וָאֵרֶא וְהִנֵּה מָלֵא
filled and I And the the to north the the he Then
!behold ,looked .house of face gate of way me brought
5 כְבוֹד־יְהוָה אֶת־בֵּית יְהוָה וָאֶפֹּל אֶל־פָּנָי׃ וַיֹּאמֶר אֵלַי
me to said And my on I And !Jehovah the Jehovah The
.face fell of house of glory
יְהוָה בֶּן־אָדָם שִׂים לִבְּךָ וּרְאֵה בְעֵינֶיךָ וּבְאָזְנֶיךָ שְׁמָע אֵת
hear with and your with and your set ,man Son ,Jehovah
ears your ,eyes see heart of
כָּל־אֲשֶׁר אֲנִי מְדַבֵּר אֹתָךְ לְכָל־חֻקּוֹת בֵּית־יְהוָה וּלְכָל־
of and ,Jehovah the the of you to say I that all
all of house of statutes all
תּוֹרֹתָו וְשַׂמְתָּ לִבְּךָ לִמְבוֹא הַבַּיִת בְּכֹל מוֹצָאֵי הַמִּקְדָּשׁ׃
the exits the with the the to your set And its
.sanctuary of all ,house of entrance heart .laws
6 וְאָמַרְתָּ אֶל־מֶרִי אֶל־בֵּית יִשְׂרָאֵל כֹּה אָמַר אֲדֹנָי יְהוִה
:Jehovah the says Thus ,Israel the to the to you And
Lord of house ,rebellious say shall
7 רַב־לָכֶם מִכָּל־תּוֹעֲבוֹתֵיכֶם בֵּית יִשְׂרָאֵל׃ בַּהֲבִיאֲכֶם בְּנֵי־
the you when ,Israel O your of to Enough
of sons in brought of house ,abominations all ,you
נֵכָר עַרְלֵי־לֵב וְעַרְלֵי בָשָׂר לִהְיוֹת בְּמִקְדָּשִׁי לְחַלְּלוֹ אֶת־
to My in be to ,flesh uncir- and heart uncir- ,aliens
—it profane ,sanctuary of cumcised of cumcised
בֵּיתִי בְּהַקְרִיבְכֶם אֶת־לַחְמִי חֵלֶב וָדָם וַיָּפֵרוּ אֶת־בְּרִיתִי
My they And the and the My you when My (even)
covenant broken have .blood fat ,bread near bring ,house
8 אֶל כָּל־תּוֹעֲבוֹתֵיכֶם׃ וְלֹא שְׁמַרְתֶּם מִשְׁמֶרֶת קָדָשָׁי
holy My the have you And your all by
,things of charge kept not .abominations
9 וַתְּשִׂימוּן לְשֹׁמְרֵי מִשְׁמַרְתִּי בְּמִקְדָּשִׁי לָכֶם׃ כֹּה־אָמַר
says Thus them- for My in charge My keepers as have you but
.selves sanctuary of (them) set

Lord Jehovah: All sons of an alien, uncircumcised of heart and uncircumcised of flesh, shall not enter into My sanctuary, or any son of an alien who (is) among the sons of Israel. [10] But the Levites who have gone far from Me, when Israel went astray, who went astray from Me, after their idols—and they shall bear their iniquity. [11] Yet they shall be ministers in My sanctuary, overseers at the gates of the house, and ministering (in) the house. They shall slaughter the burnt offering and the sacrifice for the people; and they shall stand to minister to them. [12] Because that they ministered to them before their idols, and became to the house of Israel a stumbling-block of iniquity; therefore I have lifted up My hand against them, declares the Lord Jehovah; and they shall bear their iniquity. [13] And they shall not come near to Me to serve as priest to Me, nor to come near to any of My holy things, to the holiest of the holy things; but they shall bear their shame and their abominations which they have done. But I will give them (to be) keepers of the charge of the house for all its service, and for all that shall be done in it.

[15] But the priests, the Levites, the sons of Zadok, who kept the charge of My sanctuary when the sons of Israel went astray from Me, they shall come near Me to serve Me. And they shall stand before Me, to bring near to Me the fat and the blood, declares the Lord Jehovah. [16] They shall enter into My sanctuary, and they shall come near to My table, to serve Me; and they shall keep My charge. [17] And it shall be, when they enter in the gates of the inner court,

אֲדֹנָי יְהוִה כָּל־בֶּן־נֵכָר עֶרֶל לֵב וְעֶרֶל בָּשָׂר לֹא יָבוֹא

shall not ,flesh uncir- and heart uncir- an sons :Jehovah the
enter   of cumcised   of cumcised   alien of   Lord

10 אֶל־מִקְדָּשִׁי לְכָל־בֶּן־נֵכָר אֲשֶׁר בְּתוֹךְ בְּנֵי יִשְׂרָאֵל: כִּי

.Israel   the   among   who   an   son   or   My   into
        of sons   (is)   alien of any   ,sanctuary

אִם־הַלְוִיִּם אֲשֶׁר רָחֲקוּ מֵעָלַי בִּתְעוֹת יִשְׂרָאֵל אֲשֶׁר תָּעוּ

went who ,Israel   went   when from gone have who   the   But
astray   astray ,Me   far   Levites

11 מֵעָלַי אַחֲרֵי גִּלּוּלֵיהֶם וְנָשְׂאוּ עֲוֹנָם: וְהָיוּ בְמִקְדָּשִׁי מְשָׁרְתִים

,ministers My   in they Yet their and their   after   from
        sanctuary be shall .iniquity bear shall —idols   Me

פְּקֻדּוֹת אֶל־שַׁעֲרֵי הַבַּיִת וּמְשָׁרְתִים אֶת־הַבָּיִת הֵמָּה

They the (in)   and   the   the   at   overseers
                .house ministering house of gates

יִשְׁחֲטוּ אֶת־הָעֹלָה וְאֶת־הַזֶּבַח לָעָם וְהֵמָּה יַעַמְדוּ לִפְנֵיהֶם

before shall and   the for   the   and   the burnt the   shall
them   stand they ,people sacrifice offering   slaughter

12 לְשָׁרְתָם: יַעַן אֲשֶׁר יְשָׁרְתוּ אוֹתָם לִפְנֵי גִלּוּלֵיהֶם וְהָיוּ

and ,idols their before them   they   that Because minister to
became   to ministered   .them to

לְבֵית־יִשְׂרָאֵל לְמִכְשׁוֹל עָוֹן עַל־כֵּן נָשָׂאתִי יָדִי עֲלֵיהֶם

against My   have I   therefore ;iniquity stumbling-a Israel the to
,them hand   up lifted   of block   of house

13 נְאֻם אֲדֹנָי יְהוִה וְנָשְׂאוּ עֲוֹנָם: וְלֹא־יִגְּשׁוּ אֵלַי לְכַהֵן לִי

to serve to to   shall they And their they and ;Jehovah the states
,Me priest as Me   near come not .iniquity bear shall   Lord

וְלָגֶשֶׁת עַל־כָּל־קָדָשַׁי אֶל־קָדְשֵׁי הַקֳּדָשִׁים וְנָשְׂאוּ כְּלִמָּתָם

their they but   holy the the   to holy My   any to come to nor
shame bear shall ;things of holiest ,things   of   near

14 וְתוֹעֲבוֹתָם אֲשֶׁר עָשׂוּ: וְנָתַתִּי אוֹתָם שֹׁמְרֵי מִשְׁמֶרֶת

the   keepers   them   I But have they which   their and
of charge   of (be to) give will .done   abominations

הַבַּיִת לְכֹל עֲבֹדָתוֹ וּלְכֹל אֲשֶׁר יֵעָשֶׂה בּוֹ:

the But   .it in be shall that for and   its   for   the
,priests   done   all ,service all   house

15 הַלְוִיִּם בְּנֵי צָדוֹק אֲשֶׁר שָׁמְרוּ אֶת־מִשְׁמֶרֶת מִקְדָּשִׁי בִּתְעוֹת

went when My charge the   kept who ,Zadok the   the
astray sanctuary of   of sons ,Levites

בְּנֵי־יִשְׂרָאֵל מֵעָלַי הֵמָּה יִקְרְבוּ אֵלַי לְשָׁרְתֵנִי וְעָמְדוּ לְפָנַי

before they And serve to Me   shall they   from Israel
Me stand shall .Me approach   near   ,Me   of sons

16 לְהַקְרִיב לִי חֵלֶב וָדָם נְאֻם אֲדֹנָי יְהוִה: הֵמָּה יָבֹאוּ אֶל־

into shall They .Jehovah the states the and the   to bring to
enter   Lord   ,blood fat Me   near

מִקְדָּשִׁי וְהֵמָּה יִקְרְבוּ אֶל־שֻׁלְחָנִי לְשָׁרְתֵנִי וְשָׁמְרוּ אֶת־

they and serve to   My   to come shall and   My
keep shall ,Me ,table near   they   ,sanctuary

17 מִשְׁמַרְתִּי: וְהָיָה בְּבוֹאָם אֶל־שַׁעֲרֵי הֶחָצֵר הַפְּנִימִית בִּגְדֵי

gar- with ,inner the   the   in they When it And .charge My
ments   court of gates   enter   ,be shall

with linen garments they shall be clothed. And wool shall not come up on them while they minister in the gates of the inner court, and in the house. [18] Turbans of linen shall be on their heads, and linen undergarments shall be on their loins. They shall not gird with sweat. [19] And when they go out into the outer court, to the outer court to the people, they shall put off their garments by which they ministered in them, and lay them in the holy chambers. And they shall put on other garments, and they shall not sanctify the people with their own garments. [20] And they shall not shave their heads, and they shall not send forth long hair; trimming they shall trim their heads. [21] And every priest shall not drink wine when they enter into the inner court. [22] And they shall not take a widow, or a divorcee, for themselves for wives; but they shall take only virgins of the seed of the house of Israel, or a widow who is the widow of a priest.

[23] And they shall teach My people between the holy and the common, and between the clean and the unclean, to make them known. [24] And in a dispute, they shall stand to judge; they shall judge it by My judgments. And they shall observe My laws and My statutes in My set (feasts); and they shall sanctify My sabbaths. [25] And he shall not come to a dead man, to defile (himself); but for father, or for mother, or for a son, or for a daughter, for a brother, or for a sister who has not had a husband, they may defile themselves. [26] And after he is cleansed, they shall count seven days for him. [27] And in the day he goes into the sanctuary

פשתים ילבשו ולא־יעלה עליהם צמר בשרתם בשערי
the in they while wool them on shall And be shall they linen
of gates minister up come not .clothed

18 החצר הפנימית וביתה: פארי פשתים יהיו על־ראשם
their on shall linen Turbans in and ,inner the
heads be of .house the court

ומכנסי פשתים יהיו על־מתניהם לא יחגרו ביזע:
with shall They not .loins their on shall linen under- and
.sweat gird be of garments

19 ובצאתם אל־החצר החיצונה אל־החצר החיצונה אל־
to outer the to ,outer the into when And
court court out go they

העם יפשטו את־בגדיהם אשר־המה משרתם בם
in ministered they by their shall they the
,them which garments off put ,people

והניחו אותם בלשכת הקדש ולבשו בגדים אחרים ולא־
and ,other garments they And .holy the in them lay and
not on put shall chambers

20 יקדשו את־העם בבגדיהם: וראשם לא יגלחו ופרע
long and they not their And own their with the shall they
hair ,shave shall heads .garments people sanctify

21 לא ישלחו כסום יכסמו את־ראשיהם: ויין לא־ישתו
shall not And .heads their shall they trimming shall they not
drink wine trim ;forth send

22 כל־כהן בבואם אל־החצר הפנימית: ואלמנה וגרושה
a or a And .inner the into they when priest every
divorcee widow court enter

לא־יקחו להם לנשים כי אם־בתולת מזרע בית ישראל
,Israel the the of virgins But for for shall they not
of house of seed only .wives themselves take

23 והאלמנה אשר־תהיה אלמנה מכהן יקחו: ואת־עמי
My And shall they priest a the is who a and
people .take of widow widow

24 יורו בין קדש לחל ובין־טמא לטהור יודעם: ועל־ריב
a And make to the and un- the and the and the between they
dispute in .known them ,clean clean between ,common holy teach shall

המה יעמדו לשפט במשפטי ושפטהו ואת־תורתי
My And shall they My by —judge to shall they
laws .it judge judgments stand

ואת־חקתי בכל־מועדי ישמרו ואת־שבתותי יקדשו:
shall they My and shall they appointed My in My and
.sanctify sabbaths ;observe (feasts) statutes

25 ואל־מת אדם לא יבוא לטמאה כי אם־לאב ולאם ולבן
for or for or for but defile to shall he not man a And
,son a ,mother ,father ;(himself) ;come dead to

26 ולבת לאח ולאחות אשר־לא־היתה לאיש יטמאו: ואחרי
And de- may they a has not who a for or a for a for or
after .themselves file ,husband had sister ,brother ,daughter

27 טהרתו שבעת ימים יספרו־לו: וביום באו אל־הקדש
the into he in And for shall they days seven is he
,sanctuary goes day the .him count ,cleansed

to the inner court, to minister in the sanctury, he shall bring his sin offering, declares the Lord Jehovah. [28] And it shall be to them for an inheritance—I (am) their inheritance; and you shall not give them possession in Israel—I (am) their possession. [29] They shall eat the food offering and the sin offering and the guilt offering; and every devoted thing in Israel shall be to them. [30] And the first of all the firstfruits of all, and every (one of the) heave offerings of all, of all your heave-offerings, shall be for the priests. And the first of your dough you shall give to the priest, to cause a blessing to rest on your house. [31] Every corpse and torn thing, or birds, or of beasts, the priests shall not eat.

אֶל־הֶחָצֵר הַפְּנִימִית לְשָׁרֵת בַּקֹּדֶשׁ יַקְרִיב חַטָּאתוֹ נְאֻם
states sin his shall he the in minister to ,inner the to
,offering bring ,sanctuary court

28 אֲדֹנָי יְהוִה׃ וְהָיְתָה לָהֶם לְנַחֲלָה אֲנִי נַחֲלָתָם וַאֲחֻזָּה
pos- and their (am) I an for them to it And .Jehovah the
session ;inheritance .inheritance be shall Lord

29 לֹא־תִתְּנוּ לָהֶם בְּיִשְׂרָאֵל אֲנִי אֲחֻזָּתָם׃ הַמִּנְחָה וְהַחַטָּאת
sin the and food the their I ;Israel in them shall you not
offering offering .possession (am) give

וְהָאָשָׁם הֵמָּה יֹאכְלוּם וְכָל־חֵרֶם בְּיִשְׂרָאֵל לָהֶם יִהְיֶה׃
shall to Israel in devoted and ;eat shall They the and
.be them thing every offering guilt

30 וְרֵאשִׁית כָּל־בִּכּוּרֵי כֹל וְכָל־תְּרוּמַת כֹּל מִכֹּל תְּרוּמוֹתֵיכֶם
heave- your of ,all heave and ,all the all the And
,offerings all of offerings every of firstfruits of first

לַכֹּהֲנִים יִהְיֶה וְרֵאשִׁית עֲרִיסוֹתֵיכֶם תִּתְּנוּ לַכֹּהֵן לְהָנִיחַ
cause to the to shall you dough your the And shall the for
rest to priest give of first .be priests

31 בְּרָכָה אֶל־בֵּיתֶךָ׃ כָּל־נְבֵלָה וּטְרֵפָה מִן־הָעוֹף וּמִן־
of or birds or torn and corpse Every your on a
thing .house blessing

הַבְּהֵמָה לֹא יֹאכְלוּ הַכֹּהֲנִים׃
.priests the shall not ,beasts
eat

CAP. XLV מה

CHAPTER 45

[1] And when you shall divide the land by lot for an inheritance, you shall offer a heave-offering to Jehovah, a holy (portion) of the land. The length shall be twenty-five thousand (cubits) long, and the width ten thousand. It (shall be) holy in all its borders all around. [2] Of this there shall be for the sanctuary five hundred by five hundred (cubits), square all around; and fifty cubits of open space (shall) (be) to it all around. [3] And from this measure you shall measure the length, twenty-five thousand (cubits), and the width, ten thousand. And in it shall be the sanctuary, the holiest of the holy. [4] It is the holy (portion) of the land for the priests, the ministers of the sanctuary it shall be, who come near to minister to Jehovah.

1 וּבְהַפִּילְכֶם אֶת־הָאָרֶץ בְּנַחֲלָה תָּרִימוּ תְרוּמָה לַיהוָה ׀
to heave- a shall you an for the you when And
,Jehovah offering offer ,inheritance land lot by divide shall

קֹדֶשׁ מִן־הָאָרֶץ אֹרֶךְ חֲמִשָּׁה וְעֶשְׂרִים אֶלֶף אֹרֶךְ וְרֹחַב
the and ,long thousand twenty- (be shall) The the of holy a
width (cubits) five length .land (portion)

2 עֲשָׂרָה אָלֶף קֹדֶשׁ־הוּא בְכָל־גְּבוּלָהּ סָבִיב׃ יִהְיֶה מִזֶּה
this Of there all its in It holy ,thousand ten
be shall .around borders all (be shall)

אֶל־הַקֹּדֶשׁ חֲמֵשׁ מֵאוֹת בַּחֲמֵשׁ מֵאוֹת מְרֻבָּע סָבִיב
all square hundred five by hundred five the for
.around (cubits) sanctuary

3 וַחֲמִשִּׁים אַמָּה מִגְרָשׁ לוֹ סָבִיב׃ וּמִן־הַמִּדָּה הַזֹּאת תָּמוֹד
shall you this measure And all to open of cubits And
measure from .around it space fifty

אֹרֶךְ חֲמֵשׁ וְעֶשְׂרִים אֶלֶף וְרֹחַב עֲשֶׂרֶת אֲלָפִים וּבוֹ־יִהְיֶה
shall And thousand ten the and thousand twenty- five the
be it in .(cubits) width ,(cubits) length

4 הַמִּקְדָּשׁ קֹדֶשׁ קָדָשִׁים׃ קֹדֶשׁ מִן־הָאָרֶץ הוּא לַכֹּהֲנִים
the for it the of holy The holy the holiest the the
,priests (is) land (portion) .(places) of ,sanctuary

מְשָׁרְתֵי הַמִּקְדָּשׁ יִהְיֶה הַקְּרֵבִים לְשָׁרֵת אֶת־יְהוָה וְהָיָה
it And .Jehovah to come who shall it the the
be shall to minister near ,be sanctuary of ministers

And it shall be for them a place for their houses, and a holy place for the sanctuary. [5] And twenty-five (cubits in) length, and ten thousand (cubits in) width shall be for the Levites, the ministers of the house, for them, for a possession, twenty chambers.

[6] And you shall give the possession of the city, five thousand (cubits) wide and twenty-five thousand long, beside the heave-offering of the holy (lot) —it shall be for the whole house of Israel. [7] And for the prince, from here, and from there, for the heave-offering of the holy (place), and of the possession of the city, from the side west westward, and from the side east eastward —and the length (shall be) alongside one of the portions, from the west border to the east border—[8] it shall be to him fo a possession in Israel, and My princes shall not oppress My people any more. And they shall give the land to the house of Israel according to their tribes.

[9] Thus says the Lord Jehovah, Enough for you, O princes of Israel! Violence and oppression turn away; and do justice and righteousness. Take away your acts of violence from My people, declares the Lord Jehovah. [10] Just balances and a just ephah, and a just bath, let there be to you. [11] The ephah and the bath shall be one measure, that the bath may contain the tenth of the homer; and the tenth of the homer the ephah. Its measure shall be to the homer. [12] And the shekel (shall be) twenty gerahs: twenty-five shekels, (and fifteen shekels is

5 לָהֶם מְקוֹם לְבָתִּים וּמִקְדָּשׁ לַמִּקְדָּשׁ׃ וַחֲמִשָּׁה וְעֶשְׂרִים
twenty- five And the for .sanctuary a and place holy their for houses a place for them

אֶלֶף אֹרֶךְ וַעֲשֶׂרֶת אֲלָפִים רֹחַב יִהְיֶה לַלְוִיִּם מְשָׁרְתֵי
the of ministers the for ,Levites be shall (in) ,width thousand (cubits) ten and (in) thousand ,length (cubits)

6 הַבַּיִת לָהֶם לַאֲחֻזָּה עֶשְׂרִים לְשָׁכֹת׃ וַאֲחֻזַּת הָעִיר תִּתְּנוּ
shall you give the city the And of possession .chambers twenty a for —possession for —them the ,house

חֲמֵשֶׁת אֲלָפִים רֹחַב וְאֹרֶךְ חֲמִשָּׁה וְעֶשְׂרִים אֶלֶף לְעֻמַּת
beside ,thousand (cubits) twenty- five long and wide thousand (cubits) five

7 תְּרוּמַת הַקֹּדֶשׁ לְכָל־בֵּית יִשְׂרָאֵל יִהְיֶה׃ וְלַנָּשִׂיא מִזֶּה
from here for And prince the shall It .be Israel house of the for whole holy the (lot) heave- the of offering

וּמִזֶּה לִתְרוּמַת הַקֹּדֶשׁ וְלַאֲחֻזַּת הָעִיר אֶל־פְּנֵי תְרוּמַת
heave- the offering the to of face the ;city the of and of possession holy the ,(lot's) heave- for offering from and there

הַקֹּדֶשׁ וְאֶל־פְּנֵי אֲחֻזַּת הָעִיר מִפְּאַת־יָם יָמָּה וּמִפְּאַת
from and side the west- ,ward west the from side ,city the the of possession the to and of face holy the (lot's)

קֵדְמָה קָדִימָה וְאֹרֶךְ לְעֻמּוֹת אַחַד הַחֲלָקִים מִגְּבוּל יָם
west the from border the ,portions of one (be shall) alongside the And length .eastward east

8 אֶל־גְּבוּל קָדִימָה׃ לָאָרֶץ יִהְיֶה־לּוֹ לַאֲחֻזָּה בְּיִשְׂרָאֵל וְלֹא־
and not ,Israel in a for possession to him shall It be a for land .east the border to

יוֹנוּ עוֹד נְשִׂיאַי אֶת־עַמִּי וְהָאָרֶץ יִתְּנוּ לְבֵית־יִשְׂרָאֵל
Israel the to of house shall they give the And land My .people My princes still shall oppress

9 לְשִׁבְטֵיהֶם׃ כֹּה־אָמַר אֲדֹנָי יְהוִה רַב־לָכֶם נְשִׂיאֵי
O of princes for Enough ,you ,Jehovah the Lord says Thus to according .tribes their

יִשְׂרָאֵל חָמָס וָשֹׁד הָסִירוּ וּמִשְׁפָּט וּצְדָקָה עֲשׂוּ הָרִימוּ
Take away .do and righteousness justice and turn ,away op- and pression Violence !Israel

10 גְּרֻשֹׁתֵיכֶם מֵעַל עַמִּי נְאֻם אֲדֹנָי יְהוִה׃ מֹאזְנֵי־צֶדֶק וְאֵיפַת־
a and ephah ,Just balances .Jehovah the Lord states My ,people from of acts your violence

11 צֶדֶק וּבַת־צֶדֶק יְהִי לָכֶם׃ הָאֵיפָה וְהַבַּת תֹּכֶן אֶחָד יִהְיֶה
shall ,be one measure the and bath The ephah .you to let be there ,just a and bath ,just

לָשֵׂאת מַעְשַׂר הַחֹמֶר הַבָּת וַעֲשִׂירִת הַחֹמֶר הָאֵיפָה אֶל־
to the .ephah the homer the and of tenth the ,bath the homer the of tenth may that contain

12 הַחֹמֶר יִהְיֶה מַתְכֻּנְתּוֹ׃ וְהַשֶּׁקֶל עֶשְׂרִים גֵּרָה עֶשְׂרִים
Twenty .gerahs (be shall) twenty the And shekel .measure Its be shall the homer

שְׁקָלִים חֲמִשָּׁה וְעֶשְׂרִים שְׁקָלִים עֲשָׂרָה וַחֲמִשָּׁה שֶׁקֶל
,shekels fifteen (and) ,shekels twenty- five ,shekels

a maneh shall be to you. [13] This (is) the heave-offering that you shall offer: the sixth of an ephah of a homer of wheat, and the sixth of an ephah of a homer of barley. [14] And the statute of oil, the bath of oil, the tenth of the bath out of the cor—(of) ten baths, homer; for ten baths (are) a homer; [15] and one lamb out of the flock, out of two hundred, out of the watered (land) of Israel; for a food offering, and for a burnt offering, and for peace offerings, to atone for them, declares the Lord Jehovah. [16] All the people of the land shall be at this heave-offering for the prince in Israel. [17] And burnt offerings shall be on the prince, and a food offering, and drink offerings, in the feasts, and on the new moons, and on the sabbaths, in all the appointed feasts of the house of Israel. He shall prepare the sin offering, and the food offering, and the burnt offering, and the peace offerings, to atone for the house of Israel.

[18] Thus says the Lord Jehovah: In the first (month), on the first of the month, you shall take a bull, a son of the herd, perfect, and cleanse the sanctuary. [19] And the priest shall take of the blood of the sin offering and put (it) on the door posts of the house, and on the four corners of the ledge of the altar, and on the gateposts of the inner court. [20] And so you shall do on the seventh of the month for each man who goes astray, and for the simple. And you shall atone for the house. [21] In the first (month, in the fourteenth day of the month, the Passover shall be to you, a feast of seven

13 הַמָּנֶה יִהְיֶה לָכֶם׃ זֹאת הַתְּרוּמָה אֲשֶׁר תָּרִימוּ שִׁשִּׁית
the shall you that heave- the This .you to be shall maneh a
of sixth :offer offering (is)

הָאֵיפָה מֵחֹמֶר הַחִטִּים וְשִׁשִּׁיתֶם הָאֵיפָה מֵחֹמֶר הַשְּׂעֹרִים׃
.barley a of an the and wheat a of an
of homer ephah of sixth of homer ephah

14 וְחֹק הַשֶּׁמֶן הַבַּת הַשֶּׁמֶן מַעְשַׂר הַבַּת מִן־הַכֹּר עֲשֶׂרֶת
ten (of) the out the the ,oil the ,oil the And
—cor of bath of tenth of bath of statute

15 הַבַּתִּים חֹמֶר כִּי־עֲשֶׂרֶת הַבַּתִּים חֹמֶר׃ וְשֶׂה־אַחַת מִן
out one and a baths ten for a baths
of lamb ;homer (are) ,homer

הַצֹּאן מִן־הַמָּאתַיִם מִמַּשְׁקֵה יִשְׂרָאֵל לְמִנְחָה וּלְעוֹלָה
burnt a for and a for ;Israel the of out two out the
,offering ,offering food of (land) watered ,hundred of ,flock

16 וְלִשְׁלָמִים לְכַפֵּר עֲלֵיהֶם נְאֻם אֲדֹנָי יְהוִה׃ כֹּל הָעָם
the All .Jehovah the states for to peace for and
of people Lord ,them atone ,offerings

17 הָאָרֶץ יִהְיוּ אֶל־הַתְּרוּמָה הַזֹּאת לַנָּשִׂיא בְּיִשְׂרָאֵל׃ וְעַל־
And .Israel in the for this heave- to shall the
on prince offering be land

הַנָּשִׂיא יִהְיֶה הָעוֹלוֹת וְהַמִּנְחָה וְהַנֵּסֶךְ בַּחַגִּים וּבֶחֳדָשִׁים
the on and the in drink and food a and burnt shall the
,moons new ,feasts ,offerings offering ,offerings be prince

וּבַשַּׁבָּתוֹת בְּכָל־מוֹעֲדֵי בֵּית יִשְׂרָאֵל הוּא־יַעֲשֶׂה אֶת־
shall He .Israel the appointed the all in the on and
prepare of house of feasts ,sabbaths

הַחַטָּאת וְאֶת־הַמִּנְחָה וְאֶת־הָעוֹלָה וְאֶת־הַשְּׁלָמִים לְכַפֵּר
to peace the and burnt the and food the and sin the
atone ,offerings ,offering ,offering .offering

18 בְּעַד בֵּית־יִשְׂרָאֵל׃ כֹּה־אָמַר אֲדֹנָי יְהוִה בָּרִאשׁוֹן
the In :Jehovah the says Thus Israel the for
.(month) first Lord of house

בְּאֶחָד לַחֹדֶשׁ תִּקַּח פַּר־בֶּן־בָּקָר תָּמִים וְחִטֵּאתָ אֶת־
and ,perfect the son a a shall you the of the on
cleanse ,herd of ,bull take ,month first

19 הַמִּקְדָּשׁ׃ וְלָקַח הַכֹּהֵן מִדַּם הַחַטָּאת וְנָתַן אֶל־מְזוּזַת
door the on put and sin the the of the shall And the
of posts (it) offering of blood priest take .sanctuary

הַבַּיִת וְאֶל־אַרְבַּע פִּנּוֹת הָעֲזָרָה לַמִּזְבֵּחַ וְעַל־מְזוּזַת שַׁעַר
the the and the of the corners the and the
of gate of posts on ,altar ledge of four on ,house

20 הֶחָצֵר הַפְּנִימִית׃ וְכֵן תַּעֲשֶׂה בְּשִׁבְעָה בַחֹדֶשׁ מֵאִישׁ
each for the of the on shall you And .inner the
man month (day) seventh do so court

21 שֹׁגֶה וּמִפֶּתִי וְכִפַּרְתֶּם אֶת־הַבָּיִת׃ בָּרִאשׁוֹן בְּאַרְבָּעָה
the in first the In the shall you And for and goes who
four- ,(month) .house for atone .simple the astray

עָשָׂר יוֹם לַחֹדֶשׁ יִהְיֶה לָכֶם הַפָּסַח חָג שְׁבֻעוֹת יָמִים
;days seven a the you to there the of day (and)
of feast ,Passover be shall ,month tenth

days; unleavened bread is
eaten. [22] And the prince
shall prepare on that day
for himself and for the
people of the land a bull
(for) a sin offering.
[23] And seven days of
the feast he shall prepare a
burnt offering to Jehovah,
seven bulls and seven rams,
perfect, daily (for) the sev-
en days, and (for) a sin offering a kid of the goats
daily. [24] And a food offering of an ephah for a
bull, and an ephah for a
ram, he shall prepare; and
of oil a hin for an ephah.
[25] In the seventh
(month), in the fifteenth
day of the month, at the
feast, he shall prepare like
these seven days as the sin
offering, as the burnt offering, as the food offering,
and as the oil.

22 מַצּוֹת יֵאָכֵל׃ וְעָשָׂה הַנָּשִׂיא בַּיּוֹם הַהוּא בַּעֲדוֹ וּבְעַד כָּל־
all and for that on the shall And is unleavened
for himself day prince prepare .eaten bread

23 עַם הָאָרֶץ פַּר חַטָּאת׃ וְשִׁבְעַת יְמֵי־הֶחָג יַעֲשֶׂה עוֹלָה
burnt a shall he the days And sin a (for) a the the
offering prepare feast of seven .offering bull land of people

לַיהוָה שִׁבְעַת פָּרִים וְשִׁבְעַת אֵילִים תְּמִימִם לַיּוֹם שִׁבְעַת
the daily perfect rams seven and bulls seven to
seven (for) ,Jehovah

24 הַיָּמִים וְחַטָּאת שְׂעִיר עִזִּים לַיּוֹם׃ וּמִנְחָה אֵיפָה לַפָּר
a for an food a And .daily the a a (for) and ,days
,bull ephah of offering goats of kid offering sin

25 וְאֵיפָה לָאַיִל יַעֲשֶׂה וְשֶׁמֶן הִין לָאֵיפָה׃ בַּשְּׁבִיעִי בַּחֲמִשָּׁה
the in the In an for a of and shall he a for an and
five ,(month) seventh .ephah hin oil ,prepare ,ram ephah

26 עָשָׂר יוֹם לַחֹדֶשׁ בֶּחָג יַעֲשֶׂה כָאֵלֶּה שִׁבְעַת הַיָּמִים כַּחַטָּאת
sin the as days seven like shall he the at the of day (and)
,offering these prepare ,feast ,month tenth

כָּעֹלָה וְכַמִּנְחָה וְכַשָּׁמֶן׃
as and food the as the as
.oil the offering ,offering burnt

CAP. XLVI מו

CHAPTER 46

CHAPTER 46

[1] Thus says the
Lord Jehovah: The gate of
the inner court that faces
east shall be shut the six
working days. But on the
Sabbath day it shall be
opened, and in the day of
the new moon it shall be
opened. [2] And the prince
shall enter by way of the
porch of the gate from outside, and shall stand by the
gatepost, and shall prepare
the priests his burnt offering and his peace offerings;
and he shall worship at the
threshold of the gate. Then
he shall go out, but the
gate shall not be shut until
the evening. [3] And the
people of the land shall
worship (at) the door of
that gate, on the Sabbaths,
and on the new moons, be-
fore Jehovah. [4] And the
burnt offering that the
prince shall bring to Jehovah on the Sabbath day
(shall be) six lambs, perfect,
and a ram, perfect. [5] And
the food offering (shall be)
an ephah for a ram, and a
food offering for the lambs,
a gift of his hand, and a hin
of oil to an ephah.

1 כֹּה־אָמַר אֲדֹנָי יְהוִה שַׁעַר הֶחָצֵר הַפְּנִימִית הַפֹּנֶה קָדִים
east faces that inner court the The :Jehovah the says Thus
of gate Lord

יִהְיֶה סָגוּר שֵׁשֶׁת יְמֵי הַמַּעֲשֶׂה וּבְיוֹם הַשַּׁבָּת יִפָּתֵחַ וּבְיוֹם
in and be shall it the on But .working days the shut shall
of day the ,opened Sabbath day six be

2 הַחֹדֶשׁ יִפָּתֵחַ׃ וּבָא הַנָּשִׂיא דֶּרֶךְ אוּלָם הַשַּׁעַר מִחוּץ וְעָמַד
shall and from the the way by the shall And be shall it new the
stand ,outside gate of porch of prince enter .opened moon

עַל־מְזוּזַת הַשַּׁעַר וְעָשׂוּ הַכֹּהֲנִים אֶת־עוֹלָתוֹ וְאֶת־שְׁלָמָיו
peace his and burnt his the shall and the the by
,offerings offering priests prepare ,gate of post

וְהִשְׁתַּחֲוָה עַל־מִפְתַּן הַשַּׁעַר וְיָצָא וְהַשַּׁעַר לֹא־יִסָּגֵר עַד־
until be shall not the but he Then .gate the the at shall he and
shut gate ,out go shall of threshold worship

3 הָעָרֶב׃ וְהִשְׁתַּחֲווּ עַם־הָאָרֶץ פֶּתַח הַשַּׁעַר הַהוּא בַּשַּׁבָּתוֹת
the on ,that gate the (at) the the shall And the
Sabbaths of door land of people worship .evening

4 וּבֶחֳדָשִׁים לִפְנֵי יְהוָה׃ וְהָעֹלָה אֲשֶׁר־יַקְרִב הַנָּשִׂיא לַיהוָה
to the shall that burnt the And Jeho- before the on and
Jehovah prince bring offering .vah ,moons new

5 בְּיוֹם הַשַּׁבָּת שִׁשָּׁה כְבָשִׂים תְּמִימִם וְאַיִל תָּמִים׃ וּמִנְחָה
food the And .perfect a and ,perfect lambs (be shall) the on
offering ram six Sabbath day

אֵיפָה לָאַיִל וְלַכְּבָשִׂים מִנְחָה מַתַּת יָדוֹ וְשֶׁמֶן הִין לָאֵיפָה׃
an to a oil and his gift a food a for and a for (be shall)
.ephah hin of ,hand of ,offering lambs the ,ram ephah an

[6] And in the day of the new moon: a bull , a son of the herd, perfect; and six lambs, and a ram, they shall be perfect. [7] And an ephah for a bull, and an ephah for a ram, he shall prepare a food offering; and for the lambs as his hand can reach; and a hin of oil to an ephah. [8] And when the prince shall enter, he shall enter by way of the gate porch, and by its way he shall leave.[9] But when the people of the land come before Jehovah at the appointed feasts, he who enters by way of the north gate to worship shall leave by way of the south gate. And he who enters by way of the south gate shall leave by way of the north gate; he shall not return by way of the gate by which he came in, but shall leave opposite it. [10] And the prince shall go in in their midst when they go in, and when they leave he shall leave. [11] And in the feasts, and in the appointed feasts, the food offering shall be an ephah to a bull, and an ephah to a ram, and to the lambs a gift of his hand; and a hin of oil to an ephah. [12] And when the prince prepares a free offering, a burnt offering or peace offerings (as) free offering to Jehovah, then one shall open to him the gate facing east. And he shall prepare his burnt offering and his peace offerings as he does on the Sabbath day. And he shall leave; and the gate is shut after he leaves. [13] And a lamb, a son of a year, perfect, you shall prepare a burnt offering daily to Jehovah; from dawn to dawn you shall prepare it. [14] And you shall prepare a food offering for it from dawn to dawn, a sixth of an ephah, and a third of a hin of oil to wet the fine flour; a food offering to Jehovah —perfect statutes forever. [15] Thus they shall prepare the lamb, and the food

6 וּבְיוֹם הַחֹדֶשׁ פַּר בֶּן־בָּקָר תְּמִימִם וְשֵׁשֶׁת כְּבָשִׂים וָאָיִל
a and lambs six and perfect the son a a new the in And
;ram herd of ,bull moon of day

7 תְּמִימִם יִהְיוּ׃ וְאֵיפָה לַפָּר וְאֵיפָה לָאַיִל יַעֲשֶׂה מִנְחָה
food a shall he a for an and a for an And shall they perfect
,offering prepare ,ram ephah ,bull ephah .be

8 וְלַכְּבָשִׂים כַּאֲשֶׁר תַּשִּׂיג יָדוֹ וְשֶׁמֶן הִין לָאֵיפָה׃ וּבְבוֹא
when And an to a of and his can as the for and
enter shall .ephah hin oil ,hand reach (as much) lambs

9 הַנָּשִׂיא דֶּרֶךְ אוּלָם הַשַּׁעַר יָבוֹא וּבְדַרְכּוֹ יֵצֵא׃ וּבְבוֹא עַם־
the when But shall he by and shall he gate the the way by the
of people come .out go way its ,enter of porch of ,prince

הָאָרֶץ לִפְנֵי יְהוָה בַּמּוֹעֲדִים הַבָּא דֶּרֶךְ שַׁעַר צָפוֹן
north the way by who he appoint- the at Jehovah before the
gate of enters ,feasts ed land

לְהִשְׁתַּחֲוֹת יֵצֵא דֶּרֶךְ־שַׁעַר נֶגֶב וְהַבָּא דֶּרֶךְ־שַׁעַר נֶגֶב יֵצֵא
shall south the way by he And .south the way by shall worship to
leave gate of enters who gate of leave

דֶּרֶךְ־שַׁעַר צָפוֹנָה לֹא יָשׁוּב דֶּרֶךְ הַשַּׁעַר אֲשֶׁר־בָּא בוֹ כִּי
but ,in he by the by shall he not ;north the way by
came which gate of way return gate of

10 נִכְחוֹ יֵצֵאוּ׃ וְהַנָּשִׂיא בְּתוֹכָם בְּבוֹאָם יָבוֹא וּבְצֵאתָם יֵצֵאוּ׃
shall he when and go shall they when their in the And shall opposite
.leave leave they ,in in go midst prince .leave it

11 וּבַחַגִּים וּבַמּוֹעֲדִים תִּהְיֶה הַמִּנְחָה אֵיפָה לַפָּר וְאֵיפָה לָאַיִל
a to an and a to an food the shall the in and the in And
,ram ephah ,bull ephah offering be feasts appointed feasts

12 וְלַכְּבָשִׂים מַתַּת יָדוֹ וְשֶׁמֶן הִין לָאֵיפָה׃ וְכִי־יַעֲשֶׂה הַנָּשִׂיא
the prepares And an to a of and his gift a the to and
prince when .ephah hin oil ,hand of lambs

נְדָבָה עוֹלָה אוֹ־שְׁלָמִים נְדָבָה לַיהוָה וּפָתַח לוֹ אֶת־הַשַּׁעַר
the to one then to free (as) peace or burnt a free a
gate him open shall ,Jehovah offering offerings offering ,offering

הַפֹּנֶה קָדִים וְעָשָׂה אֶת־עֹלָתוֹ וְאֶת־שְׁלָמָיו כַּאֲשֶׁר יַעֲשֶׂה
does he as peace his and burnt his he And .east facing
offerings offering prepare shall

13 בְּיוֹם הַשַּׁבָּת וְיָצָא וְסָגַר אֶת־הַשַּׁעַר אַחֲרֵי צֵאתוֹ׃ וְכֶבֶשׂ
a And he after gate the is and he And the on
,lamb .leaves shut ;leave shall .Sabbath day

בֶּן־שְׁנָתוֹ תָּמִים תַּעֲשֶׂה עוֹלָה לַיּוֹם לַיהוָה בַּבֹּקֶר בַּבֹּקֶר
dawn to from to daily burnt a shall you ,perfect a son a
dawn ;Jehovah offering ,prepare ,year of

14 תַּעֲשֶׂה אֹתוֹ׃ וּמִנְחָה תַעֲשֶׂה עָלָיו בַּבֹּקֶר בַּבֹּקֶר שִׁשִּׁית
sixth a dawn to from for shall you a And .it shall you
of dawn it prepare offering food prepare

הָאֵיפָה וְשֶׁמֶן שְׁלִישִׁית הַהִין לָרֹס אֶת־הַסֹּלֶת מִנְחָה לַיהוָה
to food a fine the to ,hin a third a oil and an
,Jehovah offering ;flour moisten of ,ephah

15 חֻקּוֹת עוֹלָם תָּמִיד׃ וְעָשׂוּ אֶת־הַכֶּבֶשׂ וְאֶת־הַמִּנְחָה וְאֶת־
and food the and ,lamb the they Thus .perfect forever statutes
.offering prepare shall

offering, and the oil, from
dawn to dawn a burnt
offering continually
[16] Thus says the
Lord Jehvoah: If the prince
gives a gift to (any) man
(of) his inheritance, it
shall be to his sons; it (is)
their possession by inheritance. [17] But if he
gives it of his inheritance
to one of his servants, then
it shall be his until the year
of liberty; then it shall return to the prince; his inheritance (is) only his sons';
it shall be to them. [18]
And the prince shall not
take of the people's inheritance, oppressing them
from their possession; from
his possession he shall bequeath (to) his sons, so
that My people not shall be
dispersed, each man from
his possession.
[19] And he brought
me through the entry
which (was) at the side of
the gate, into the holy
chambers for the priests,
facing north. And behold,
there (was) a place on the
two sides westward. [20]
And he said to me, This
(is) the place where the
priests shall boil there the
guilt offering and the sin
offering, where they shall
bake the food offering; so
as not to bring (them) out
to the outer court to sanctify the people. [21] And
(he led) me out to the outer
court, and he made me pass
by the four corners of the
court. And behold, a court
in (each) corner of the
enclosed courts: forty long
and thirty wide—one mea-
sure to the four of them,
being made in corners. [23]
And a row around in them,
around the four of them,

16 הַשֶּׁמֶן בַּבֹּקֶר בַּבֹּקֶר עוֹלַת תָּמִיד׃ כֹּה־אָמַר אֲדֹנָי
the oil from dawn to dawn burnt a continually. Thus says the
Lord offering

יְהוִה כִּי־יִתֵּן הַנָּשִׂיא מַתָּנָה לְאִישׁ מִבָּנָיו נַחֲלָתוֹ הִיא לְבָנָיו
Jeho- If gives the gift a to (any) man (of) his it his to
vah: prince inheritance sons

17 תִּהְיֶה אֲחֻזָּתָם הִיא בְּנַחֲלָה׃ וְכִי־יִתֵּן מַתָּנָה מִנַּחֲלָתוֹ לְאַחַד
shall be; their it (is) by But if he a gift of his to one
possession inheritance. gives it inheritance

מֵעֲבָדָיו וְהָיְתָה לּוֹ עַד־שְׁנַת הַדְּרוֹר וְשָׁבַת לַנָּשִׂיא אַךְ
of his then it to until the liberty; then it to the only
servants, shall be him year of shall return prince,

18 נַחֲלָתוֹ בָּנָיו לָהֶם תִּהְיֶה׃ וְלֹא־יִקַּח הַנָּשִׂיא מִנַּחֲלַת הָעָם
his in- his (is) to it shall And shall the of the
heritance sons', them be. not take prince inheritance people's,

לְהוֹנֹתָם מֵאֲחֻזָּתָם מֵאֲחֻזָּתוֹ יַנְחִל אֶת־בָּנָיו לְמַעַן אֲשֶׁר לֹא־
oppressing from their from his he shall his (to) so that not
them possession; possession bequeath sons,

19 יָפֻצוּ עַמִּי אִישׁ מֵאֲחֻזָּתוֹ׃ וַיְבִיאֵנִי בַמָּבוֹא אֲשֶׁר עַל־כֶּתֶף
be dis- My each from his And he through the which at the
persed people, man possession. brought me entry (was) side of

הַשַּׁעַר אֶל־הַלְּשָׁכוֹת הַקֹּדֶשׁ אֶל־הַכֹּהֲנִים הַפֹּנוֹת צָפוֹנָה
the into the holy for the priests, facing north.
gate, chambers

20 וְהִנֵּה־שָׁם מָקוֹם בַּיַּרְכָתָם יָמָּה׃ וַיֹּאמֶר אֵלַי זֶה הַמָּקוֹם
And there a place on the two west- And he to me, This the
behold, (was) sides ward. said (is) place

אֲשֶׁר יְבַשְּׁלוּ־שָׁם הַכֹּהֲנִים אֶת־הָאָשָׁם וְאֶת־הַחַטָּאת אֲשֶׁר
where shall there the priests the guilt and the sin where
boil offering offering,

יֹאפוּ אֶת־הַמִּנְחָה לְבִלְתִּי הוֹצִיא אֶל־הֶחָצֵר הַחִיצוֹנָה
they shall the food so that not to bring to the outer
bake offering; out (them) court

21 לְקַדֵּשׁ אֶת־הָעָם׃ וַיּוֹצִיאֵנִי אֶל־הֶחָצֵר הַחִיצֹנָה וַיַּעֲבִירֵנִי
to the And (he led) to the outer, and he made
sanctify people. me out court me pass

אֶל־אַרְבַּעַת מִקְצוֹעֵי הֶחָצֵר וְהִנֵּה חָצֵר בְּמִקְצֹעַ הֶחָצֵר חָצֵר
by the four corners the And, a court in (each) the a
of court. behold! corner of court, court

22 בְּמִקְצֹעַ הֶחָצֵר׃ בְּאַרְבַּעַת מִקְצֹעוֹת הֶחָצֵר חֲצֵרוֹת קְטֻרוֹת
in (each) the In the corners the (were) enclosed:
corner of court. four of court courts

אַרְבָּעִים אֹרֶךְ וּשְׁלֹשִׁים רֹחַב מִדָּה אַחַת לְאַרְבַּעְתָּם
forty long and thirty wide, measure one to the four
(cubits) (was) of them

23 מְהֻקְצָעוֹת׃ וְטוּר סָבִיב בָּהֶם סָבִיב לְאַרְבַּעְתָּם וּמְבַשְּׁלוֹת
being made And a in them (was) around of the four and boiling
in corners. row around, them, places

and boiling places were 24
made under the rows
round about. [24] And he
said to me, These (are) the
houses of those who boil,
where the ministers of the
house shall boil there the
sacrifice of the people.

עָשׂוּי מִתַּחַת הַטִּירוֹת סָבִיב׃ וַיֹּאמֶר אֵלַי אֵלֶּה בֵּית

| the | These | ,me to | he Then | round | rows the | under | were |
| of houses | (are) | | said | .about | | | made |

הַמְבַשְׁלִים אֲשֶׁר יְבַשְׁלוּ־שָׁם מְשָׁרְתֵי הַבַּיִת אֶת־זֶבַח הָעָם׃

| the | the sacri- | the | the | the | there | shall | where | who | those |
| .people | of fice | house | of ministers | | | boil | | ,boil |

CAP. XLVII מז

CHAPTER 47

CHAPTER 47

[1] And he returned to 1
the door of the house. And
behold, water came out
from under the threshold
of the house eastward. For
the face of the house (is)
east, and the water came
down from under the right
side of the house, at the 2
south from the altar. [2]
And he led me out by way
of the north gate, and led
me the way outside to the
outer gate, by the way facing east. And behold, water
was trickling out of the
right side.

[3] When the man 3
went out eastward, and the
line in his hand, he measured a thousand cubits; and
he passed me through the
water, water (to) the
ankles. [4] And he measur- 4
ed a thousand, and passed
me through the water,
water (to) the knees. And
he measure a thousand,
and passed me through 5
water (to) the loins. [5]
And he measured a thou-
sand, a torrent which I was
not able to pass; for the 6
water had risen, water to
swim (in)—a torrent that
could not be passed. [6]
And he said to me, Have 7
you seen, son of man? And
he led me and made me re-
turn to the lip of the torrent. [7] When I returned, 8
then behold, on the lip of
the torrent (were) many
trees on this side and on
(that) side. [8] And he
said to me, These waters go
out toward the eastern cir-
cuit, and go down into the
Arabah and enter the sea; 9
they are brought out into
the sea and the waters shall
be healed. [9] And it will
be, every soul that lives,
which swarms in every
(place) where the two torrents go there, shall live.

וַיְשִׁבֵנִי אֶל־פֶּתַח הַבַּיִת וְהִנֵּה־מַיִם יֹצְאִים מִתַּחַת מִפְתַּן

| thres- the | from | came | water | ,And | .house the | the | the | to | he And |
| of hold | under | out | | ,behold | | of door | | | returned |

הַבַּיִת קָדִימָה כִּי־פְנֵי הַבַּיִת קָדִים וְהַמַּיִם יֹרְדִים מִתַּחַת

| from | came | the | and | ,east | the | the | For | .eastward | the |
| under | down | water | | | (is) house | of face | | | house |

מִכֶּתֶף הַבַּיִת הַיְמָנִית מִנֶּגֶב לַמִּזְבֵּחַ׃ וַיּוֹצִאֵנִי דֶּרֶךְ־שַׁעַר

| the | way | by | led he Then | the | from | the | at | ,right | the | the |
| gate | of | | out me | .altar | south | | | | house | of side |

צָפוֹנָה וַיְסִבֵּנִי דֶּרֶךְ חוּץ אֶל־שַׁעַר הַחוּץ דֶּרֶךְ הַפּוֹנֶה קָדִים

| .east | facing | the | by | ,outer | the | to | outside | the | led and | ,north |
| | | way | | | gate | | | way | | me |

וְהִנֵּה־מַיִם מְפַכִּים מִן־הַכָּתֵף הַיְמָנִית׃ בְּצֵאת־הָאִישׁ קָדִים 3

| east- | the | went When | .right | the | the | out | was | water | ,And |
| ward | man | out | | side of | | | trickling | | ,behold |

בְּקָו בְּיָדוֹ וַיָּמָד אֶלֶף בָּאַמָּה וַיַּעֲבִרֵנִי בַמַּיִם מֵי אָפְסָיִם׃

| the | water | the | through | he and | ,cubits | thou- a | he | his in | the and |
| .ankles | (to) | | ,water | me passed | | sand | measured | ,hand | line |

וַיָּמָד אֶלֶף וַיַּעֲבִרֵנִי בַמַּיִם מַיִם בִּרְכָּיִם וַיָּמָד אֶלֶף וַיַּעֲבִרֵנִי 4

| passed | and | thou- a | he | And | the | water | through | pass- | and | thou- a | he | And |
| through | me | sand | measured | .knees | (to) | | water | ed me | | sand | measured | |

מֵי מָתְנָיִם׃ וַיָּמָד אֶלֶף נַחַל אֲשֶׁר לֹא־אוּכַל לַעֲבֹר כִּי־גָאוּ 5

| had | for | ;pass to | was I | not | which | a | thou- a | he And | the | water |
| risen | | | able | | | | torrent | ,said | measured | .loins (to) |

הַמַּיִם מֵי שָׂחוּ נַחַל אֲשֶׁר לֹא־יֵעָבֵר׃ וַיֹּאמֶר אֵלַי הֲרָאִיתָ 6

| you Have | ,me to | he And | be could | not | that | a | | to water | the |
| ,seen | | said | .passed | | | torrent | ,(in) swim | ,water |

בֶן־אָדָם וַיּוֹלִכֵנִי וַיְשִׁבֵנִי עַל־שְׂפַת הַנָּחַל׃ בְּשׁוּבֵנִי וְהִנֵּה 7

| then | I When | the | lip the | to | made and | he Then | ?man | son |
| ,behold | ,returned | .torrent | of | | return me | me led | | of |

אֶל־שְׂפַת הַנַּחַל עֵץ רַב מְאֹד מִזֶּה וּמִזֶּה׃ וַיֹּאמֶר אֵלַי הַמַּיִם 8

| waters | to | he And | on and | this on | very | many | trees | the | lip the | on |
| | ,me | said | .side (that) | side | | | | torrent of | |

הָאֵלֶּה יוֹצְאִים אֶל־הַגְּלִילָה הַקַּדְמוֹנָה וְיָרְדוּ עַל־הָעֲרָבָה

| the | into | go and | ,eastern | the | toward | out go | These |
| Arabah | | down | | circuit | | |

וּבָאוּ הַיָּמָּה אֶל־הַיָּמָּה הַמּוּצָאִים וְנִרְפְּאוּ הַמָּיִם׃ וְהָיָה כָל־ 9

| every | it And | the | shall and | are they | the | into | ;sea the and |
| ,be will | | .waters | healed be | out brought | | sea | enter |

נֶפֶשׁ חַיָּה אֲשֶׁר־יִשְׁרֹץ אֶל כָּל־אֲשֶׁר יָבוֹא שָׁם נַחְלַיִם יִחְיֶה

| shall | two the | there | go | ,where | every | in | swarms | which | that | soul |
| .live | torrents | | | | (place) | | | | | ,lives |

And there shall be very many fish, because these waters shall come there. And they shall be healed. And all shall live there where the torrent goes. [10] And it will be, the fisherman shall stand on it; from Engedi even to Eneglaim, a spreading place for nets there shall be; their fish shall be by its kind, like the fish of the Great Sea, very many; its swamps and its marshes even shall be healed; for they shall be given salt. [12] And by the torrent shall go up on its lip all trees (for) food, on this and on that (side); its leaf shall not fade, and its fruit shall not fail; by its months it will bear, because its waters come out from the sanctuary. And its fruit shall be for food, and its leaf for healing.

[13] Thus says the Lord Jehovah: This (shall be) the border by which you shall inherit the land, by the twelve tribes of Israel: Joseph (shall have) (two) portions. [14] And you shall inherit it, each man like his brother, that I lifted up My hand to give it to your fathers; and this land shall fall to you for an inheritance. [15] And this the border of the land to the north side, from the Great Sea, the way of Hethlon, to entrance of Zedad, [16] Hamath, Berothah, Sibraim, which (is) between the border of Damascus and the border of Hamath; Hazer-hatticon, which (is) by the border of Hauran. [17] And the border shall be from the sea (to) Hazar-enon, (at) the border of Damascus, and the north northward, even the border of Hamath. And (this is) the north side. [18] And the east side from between Hauran, and Damascus, and Gilead, and the land of Israel (shall be)

וְהָיָה הַדָּגָה רַבָּה מְאֹד כִּי בָאוּ שָׁמָּה הַמַּיִם הָאֵלֶּה וְיֵרָפְאוּ
shall they And .these waters there shall be- ,very many fish there And
be shall
.healed be come cause

10 וָחָי כֹּל אֲשֶׁר־יָבוֹא שָׁמָּה הַנָּחַל׃ וְהָיָה יַעַמְדוּ עָלָיו דַּוָּגִים
fish- the it on shall it And the there goes where all And
;erman stand ,be will .torrent live shall

מֵעֵין גֶּדִי וְעַד־עֵין עֶגְלַיִם מִשְׁטוֹחַ לַחֲרָמִים יִהְיוּ לְמִינָה תִּהְיֶה
shall its by there for spreading a ,Eneglaim even from
be kind ;be shall nets place to Engedi

11 דְגָתָם כִּדְגַת הַיָּם הַגָּדוֹל רַבָּה מְאֹד׃ בִּצֹּאתוֹ וּגְבָאָיו וְלֹא
even its and its ,very many ,Great the the like their
marshes swamps Sea of fish ,fish

12 יֵרָפְאוּ לְמֶלַח נִתָּנוּ׃ וְעַל־הַנַּחַל יַעֲלֶה עַל־שְׂפָתוֹ מִזֶּה ׀
this on lip its on go shall the And shall they for be shall
(side) up torrent by .given be salt ;healed

וּמִזֶּה ׀ כָּל־עֵץ־מַאֲכָל לֹא־יִבּוֹל עָלֵהוּ וְלֹא־יִתֹּם פִּרְיוֹ לָחֳדָשָׁיו
its by its shall and its shall not (for) trees all on and
months .fruit fail not ,leaf fade ,food (side) that

יְבַכֵּר כִּי מֵימָיו מִן־הַמִּקְדָּשׁ הֵמָּה יוֹצְאִים וְהָיוּ פִרְיוֹ
its And .out come they the from its because will It
fruit be shall sanctuary ,waters ,bear

13 לְמַאֲכָל וְעָלֵהוּ לִתְרוּפָה׃ כֹּה אָמַר אֲדֹנָי יְהוִה גֵּה
This :Jehovah the says Thus .healing for its and ,food for
(be shall) Lord leaf

גְּבוּל אֲשֶׁר תִּתְנַחֲלוּ אֶת־הָאָרֶץ לִשְׁנֵי עָשָׂר שִׁבְטֵי יִשְׂרָאֵל
.Israel tribes the by the shall you by the
of twelve land inherit which border

14 יוֹסֵף חֲבָלִים׃ וּנְחַלְתֶּם אוֹתָהּ אִישׁ כְּאָחִיו אֲשֶׁר נָשָׂאתִי
lifted I which his like each ,it shall you And (two) Joseph
up ,brother man inherit .portions (have shall)

אֶת־יָדִי לְתִתָּהּ לַאֲבֹתֵיכֶם וְנָפְלָה הָאָרֶץ הַזֹּאת לָכֶם
you to this land shall and your to it give to hand My
fall ;fathers

15 בְּנַחֲלָה׃ וְזֶה גְּבוּל הָאָרֶץ לִפְאַת צָפוֹנָה מִן־הַיָּם הַגָּדוֹל
,Great the from ,north the to the bor- the And in- an for
Sea side land of der this .heritance

16 הַדֶּרֶךְ חֶתְלֹן לְבוֹא צְדָדָה׃ חֲמָת ׀ בֵּרוֹתָה סִבְרַיִם אֲשֶׁר
which ,Sibraim ,Berothah ,Hamath ,Zedad the to .Hethlon way the
(is) of entrance of

בֵּין־גְּבוּל דַּמֶּשֶׂק וּבֵין גְּבוּל חֲמָת חָצֵר הַתִּיכוֹן אֲשֶׁר אֶל־
by which ,hatticon Hazer- ;Hamath the and Damascus the between
(is) of border of border

17 גְּבוּל חַוְרָן׃ וְהָיָה גְבוּל מִן־הַיָּם חֲצַר עֵינוֹן גְּבוּל דַּמֶּשֶׂק
Damascus the (at) ,enon Hazar- the from the shall And .Hauran the
of border (to) sea border be of border

18 וְצָפוֹן ׀ צָפוֹנָה וּגְבוּל חֲמָת וְאֵת פְּאַת צָפוֹן׃ וּפְאַת קָדִים
east the And .north (is this) And .Hamath the even north- the and
side side the of border ,ward north

מִבֵּין חַוְרָן וּמִבֵּין־דַּמֶּשֶׂק וּמִבֵּין הַגִּלְעָד וּמִבֵּין אֶרֶץ יִשְׂרָאֵל
Israel the and ,Gilead and ,Damascus and ,Hauran from
of land between

the Jordan, from the border to the Eastern Sea you shall measure. And (this is) the east side. [19] And the Negev side southward from Tamar, to the waters of Meriboth-kadesh, the torrent to the Great Sea. And (this is) the south side to the Negev. [20] And the west side (is) the Great Sea from the border until beside the entrance of Hamath. This (is) the west side. [21] And you shall divide this land for yourselves by the tribes of Israel. [22] And it will be, you shall divide by lot for an inheritance to yourselves, and to the aliens who sojourn among you, who shall father sons among you. And they shall be to you as native-born among the sons of Israel. They shall be allotted an inheritance among the tribes of Israel. [23] And it shall be, in the tribe in which the alien stays, there you shall give his inheritance, declares the Lord Jehovah.

הַיַּרְדֵּן מִגְּבוּל עַל־הַיָּם הַקַּדְמוֹנִי תָּמֹדּוּ וְאֵת פְּאַת קָדִימָה׃

.east (is this) And shall you ,Eastern the to the from (be shall)
side the .measure Sea border ,Jordan the

19 וּפְאַת נֶגֶב תֵּימָנָה מִתָּמָר עַד־מֵי מְרִיבוֹת קָדֵשׁ נַחֲלָה אֶל־

to the ,kadesh Meriboth- the to from south- Negev the And
torrent of waters ,Tamar ward side

20 הַיָּם הַגָּדוֹל וְאֵת פְּאַת־תֵּימָנָה נֶגְבָּה׃ וּפְאַת־יָם הַיָּם הַגָּדוֹל

Great the west the And the to south (is this) and ,Great the
Sea (is) side .Negev side the Sea

21 מִגְּבוּל עַד־נֹכַח לְבוֹא חֲמָת זֹאת פְּאַת־יָם׃ וְחִלַּקְתֶּם אֶת־

shall you And .west the This .Hamath the until the from
divide side (is) of entrance beside border

22 הָאָרֶץ הַזֹּאת לָכֶם לְשִׁבְטֵי יִשְׂרָאֵל׃ וְהָיָה תַּפִּלוּ אוֹתָהּ

it shall you it And .Israel the by for this land
lot by divide ,be will of tribes yourselves

בְּנַחֲלָה לָכֶם וּלְהַגֵּרִים הַגָּרִים בְּתוֹכְכֶם אֲשֶׁר־הוֹלִדוּ בָנִים

sons shall who among who the to and your- to an for
father ,you sojourn aliens ,selves inheritance

בְּתוֹכְכֶם וְהָיוּ לָכֶם כְּאֶזְרָח בִּבְנֵי יִשְׂרָאֵל אִתְּכֶם יִפְּלוּ

shall They with .Israel the among native- as to they And among
allotted be you of sons the born you be shall .you

23 בְנַחֲלָה בְּתוֹךְ שִׁבְטֵי יִשְׂרָאֵל׃ וְהָיָה בַשֵּׁבֶט אֲשֶׁר־גָּר הַגֵּר

stays the which the in it And .Israel the among in- an
alien tribe ,be shall of tribes heritance

אִתּוֹ שָׁם תִּתְּנוּ נַחֲלָתוֹ נְאֻם אֲדֹנָי יְהוִה׃

.Jehovah the states in- his shall you there in
Lord ,heritance give ,it

CAP. XLVIII מח

CHAPTER 48

CHAPTER 48

[1] And these (are) the names of the tribes: From the north end, at the hand of the way of Hethlon (to) the entrance of Hamath, Hazar-enon, the border of Damascus northward at the hand of Hamath; and there shall be to it an east side (and a) west—Dan, one (part). [2] And by the border of Dan, from the east side to the west side, Asher, one (part). [3] And by the border of Asher, from the east side even to the west side, Napthtali, one (part). [4] And by the border of Naphtali, from the east side to the west side, Manasseh, one (part). [5] And by the border of Manasseh from the east side to the west side, Ephraim, one (part). [6] And by the

1 וְאֵלֶּה שְׁמוֹת הַשְּׁבָטִים מִקְצֵה צָפוֹנָה אֶל־יַד דֶּרֶךְ־חֶתְלֹן

,Hethlon the the at north the From the the these And
of way of hand end :tribes of names (are)

לְבוֹא־חֲמָת חֲצַר עֵינָן גְּבוּל דַּמֶּשֶׂק צָפוֹנָה אֶל־יַד חֲמָת

-Hamath the at north- Damascus the ,enon Hazar- ,Hamath the (to)
of hand ward of border of entrance

2 וְהָיוּ־לוֹ פְאַת־קָדִים הַיָּם דָּן אֶחָד׃ וְעַל ׀ גְּבוּל דָּן מִפְּאַת

the from ,Dan the by And one .Dan (and) east side a to there and
side of border .(part) ,west it be shall

3 קָדִים עַד־פְּאַת יָמָּה אָשֵׁר אֶחָד׃ וְעַל ׀ גְּבוּל אָשֵׁר מִפְּאַת

the from ,Asher the And one Asher ,west the to east
side of border by .(part) side

4 קָדִימָה וְעַד־פְּאַת־יָמָּה נַפְתָּלִי אֶחָד׃ וְעַל ׀ גְּבוּל נַפְתָּלִי

,Naphtali the And one Naphtali ,west the even east
of border by .(part) side to

5 מִפְּאַת קָדִמָה עַד־פְּאַת יָמָּה מְנַשֶּׁה אֶחָד׃ וְעַל ׀ גְּבוּל

the And one Manasseh ,west the to east the from
of border by .(part) side side

6 מְנַשֶּׁה מִפְּאַת קָדִמָה עַד־פְּאַת יָמָּה אֶפְרַיִם אֶחָד׃ וְעַל ׀

And one Ephraim ,west the to east the from Manasseh
by .(part) side side

גְּבוּל אֶפְרַיִם מִפְּאַת קָדִים וְעַד־פְּאַת־יָמָּה רְאוּבֵן אֶחָד:								
one	Reuben	,west	the	even	east	the from	Ephraim	the
.(part)			side		side	side		of border

וְעַל גְּבוּל רְאוּבֵן מִפְּאַת קָדִים עַד־פְּאַת יָמָּה יְהוּדָה אֶחָד:								
one	Judah	,west	the	to	east	the from	Reuben	the And
.(part)			side		side	side		of border by

וְעַל גְּבוּל יְהוּדָה מִפְּאַת קָדִים עַד־פְּאַת יָמָּה תִהְיֶה								
be shall	,west	the	to	east	the from	Judah	the	And
		side		side	side		of border	by

הַתְּרוּמָה אֲשֶׁר־תָּרִימוּ חֲמִשָּׁה וְעֶשְׂרִים אֶלֶף רֹחַב וְאֹרֶךְ								
and	wide	thousand	twenty-	five	shall you	which	heave- the	
,long		(cubits)			,offer		offering	

כְּאַחַד הַחֲלָקִים מִפְּאַת קָדִימָה עַד־פְּאַת־יָמָּה וְהָיָה							
shall And	.west	the	to	east	the from	,parts the	one as
be		side			side		of

הַמִּקְדָּשׁ בְּתוֹכוֹ: הַתְּרוּמָה אֲשֶׁר תָּרִימוּ לַיהוָה אֹרֶךְ							
long	to	shall you	that	heave- The	its in	the	
	Jehovah	offer		offering	.midst	sanctuary	

חֲמִשָּׁה וְעֶשְׂרִים אֶלֶף וְרֹחַב עֲשֶׂרֶת אֲלָפִים: וְלָאֵלֶּה							
for And	thousand	ten	wide and	thousand	twenty-	(be shall)	
these	(cubits)			,(cubits)		five	

תִּהְיֶה תְרוּמַת־הַקֹּדֶשׁ לַכֹּהֲנִים צָפוֹנָה חֲמִשָּׁה וְעֶשְׂרִים						
twenty-	five	northward	the for	holy	heave- the	shall
			:priests		offering	be

אֶלֶף וְיָמָּה רֹחַב עֲשֶׂרֶת אֲלָפִים וְקָדִימָה רֹחַב עֲשֶׂרֶת							
ten	wide	and	thousand	ten	wide	and	thou-
		eastward	,(cubits)			westward	,sand

אֲלָפִים וְנֶגְבָּה אֹרֶךְ חֲמִשָּׁה וְעֶשְׂרִים אֶלֶף וְהָיָה מִקְדַּשׁ־						
the	shall And	thousand	twenty-	five	long	and	thousand
of sanctuary	be	.(cubits)				southward	(cubits)

יְהוָה בְּתוֹכוֹ: לַכֹּהֲנִים הַמְקֻדָּשׁ מִבְּנֵי צָדוֹק אֲשֶׁר שָׁמְרוּ						
have	who	,Zadok	the of	are who	the for	its in	Jehovah
kept			of sons	,sanctified	priests	;midst	

מִשְׁמַרְתִּי אֲשֶׁר לֹא־תָעוּ בִּתְעוֹת בְּנֵי יִשְׂרָאֵל כַּאֲשֶׁר תָּעוּ							
went	as	,Israel	the	went when	go did not	who	My
astray			of sons	astray	astray		,charge

הַלְוִיִּם: וְהָיְתָה לָהֶם תְּרוּמִיָּה מִתְּרוּמַת הָאָרֶץ קֹדֶשׁ							
the	land the	heave- the from	heave- the	,them to	shall And	the	
of holiest		of offering	offering		be	Levites	

קֳדָשִׁים אֶל־גְּבוּל הַלְוִיִּם: וְהַלְוִיִּם לְעֻמַּת גְּבוּל הַכֹּהֲנִים							
the	the	along-	the And	the	the	by	holy the
,priests	of border	side	,Levites	.Levites	of border		places

חֲמִשָּׁה וְעֶשְׂרִים אֶלֶף אֹרֶךְ וְרֹחַב עֲשֶׂרֶת אֲלָפִים כָּל־אֹרֶךְ							
the	All	thousand	ten	wide and	long	thousand	twenty-	(have shall)
length	.(cubits)					(cubits)		five

חֲמִשָּׁה וְעֶשְׂרִים אֶלֶף וְרֹחַב עֲשֶׂרֶת אֲלָפִים: וְלֹא־יִמְכְּרוּ							
shall they	And	thousand	ten	the and	thousand	twenty-	(be shall)
sell	not	.(cubits)		width	,(cubits)		five

מִמֶּנּוּ וְלֹא יָמֵר וְלֹא יַעֲבֹר רֵאשִׁית הָאָרֶץ כִּי־קֹדֶשׁ לַיהוָה:							
to	(is it) For	the	first- the	to cause	and	shall and	of (any)
.Jehovah	holy		.land	of fruits	away pass not	,trade not	,it

---

border of Ephraim, from the east side even to the west side, Reuben, one (part). [7] And by the border of Reuben, from the east side to the west side, Judah, one (part). [8] And by the border of Judah, from the east side to the west side, shall be the heave-offering which you shall offer—twenty-five thousand (cubits) wide and long, as one of the parts, from the east side to the west side. And the sanctuary shall be in its midst. [9] The heave-offering that you shall offer to Jehovah (shall be) twenty-five thousand (cubits) long and ten thousand (cubits) wide. [10] And for these shall be the holy heave-offering for the priests: northward twenty-five thousand, and westward ten thousand (cubits); and eastward ten thousand wide, and southward twenty-five thousand (cubits) long. And the sanctuary of Jehovah shall be in its midst; [11] for the priests who are sanctified, of the sons of Zadok, who have kept My charge, who did not go astray when the sons of Israel went astray, as the Levites went astray. [12] And the heave-offering shall be to them, from the heave-offering of the land, the holiest of the holy places, by the border of the Levites.

[13] And the Levites, alongside the border of the priests, (shall have) twenty-five thousand (cubits) long and ten thousand wide. All the length (shall be) twenty-five thousand, and the width ten thousand. [14] And they shall not sell (any) of it, and shall not trade, and shall not cause to pass away the first-fruits of the land. For (it is) holy to Jehovah.

And the five thousand that are left in the width in front of the twenty-five thousand, it (is) common for the city, for dwelling, and for open land. Ana the city shall be in its midst. [16] And these (shall ba) its measures: the north side, four thousand and five hundred; and the south side five, (even) four thousand and five hundred (cubits); and the east side, four thousand and five hundred; and the west side, four thousand and five hundred (cubits). [17] And the open land shall be of the city northward, two hundred and fifty; and southward, two hundred and fifty; and eastward, two hundred and fifty; and westward, two hundred and fifty (cubits). [18] And the remainder in length alongside the heave-offering of the holy (parts) (shall be) ten thousand eastward, and ten thousand westward. And it shall be alongside the heave-offering of the holy (part). and its produce shall be for bread to those who serve the city. [19] And he who serves the city shall serve it out of all the tribes of Israel. [20] All the heave-offering (shall be) twenty-five thousand by twenty-five thousand; four-square. You shall offer the holy heave-offering, to the possession of the city. [21] And the remainder (is) for the prince, on this (side) and on that, of the holy heave-offering, and of the possession of the city, in the face of the twenty-five thousand of the heave-offering to the east border, and westward in the face of the twenty-five thousand to the west border; alongside the parts of the prince. And it shall be a holy heave-offering; and

15 וַחֲמֵשֶׁת אֲלָפִים הַנּוֹתָר בָּרֹחַב עַל־פְּנֵי חֲמִשָּׁה וְעֶשְׂרִים
twenty- five the front in of the in width are that left .thousand the And five
אֶלֶף חֹל־הוּא לָעִיר לְמוֹשָׁב וּלְמִגְרָשׁ וְהָיְתָה הָעִיר בְּתוֹכֹה׃
its in .midst the city shall And be for and .land open for ,dwelling the for ,city it com- (is) mon thousand
16 וְאֵלֶּה מִדּוֹתֶיהָ פְּאַת צָפוֹן חֲמֵשׁ מֵאוֹת וְאַרְבַּעַת אֲלָפִים
thousand ;(cubits) four and hundred five north the side its :measures these And (be shall)
וּפְאַת־נֶגֶב חֲמֵשׁ חֲמֵשׁ מֵאוֹת וְאַרְבַּעַת אֲלָפִים וּמִפְּאַת
the and side thousand ;(cubits) four and hundred (even) five ,five south the and side
קָדִים חֲמֵשׁ מֵאוֹת וְאַרְבַּעַת אֲלָפִים וּפְאַת־יָמָּה חֲמֵשׁ
five ,west the and side thousand ;(cubits) four and hundred five ,east
17 מֵאוֹת וְאַרְבַּעַת אֲלָפִים׃ וְהָיָה מִגְרָשׁ לָעִיר צָפוֹנָה
,northward the of city open the land And be shall thousand .(cubits) four and hundred
חֲמִשִּׁים וּמָאתַיִם וְנֶגְבָּה חֲמִשִּׁים וּמָאתַיִם וְקָדִימָה חֲמִשִּׁים
fifty east- ward and two and ;hundred fifty south- ward and two and ;hundred fifty
18 וּמָאתַיִם וְיָמָּה חֲמִשִּׁים וּמָאתָיִם׃ וְהַנּוֹתָר בָּאֹרֶךְ לְעֻמַּת ׀
alongside in length the And remainder two and .hundred fifty west- ward and two and ;hundred
תְּרוּמַת הַקֹּדֶשׁ עֲשֶׂרֶת אֲלָפִים קָדִימָה וַעֲשֶׂרֶת אֲלָפִים
thousand (cubits) ten and eastward thousand (cubits) (be shall) ten holy the (parts) heave- the of offering
יָמָּה וְהָיָה לְעֻמַּת תְּרוּמַת הַקֹּדֶשׁ וְהָיְתָה תְבוּאָתֹה לְלֶחֶם
for bread its produce shall And be holy the .(part) heave- the of offering alongside it And be shall west- .ward
19 לְעֹבְדֵי הָעִיר׃ וְהָעֹבֵד הָעִיר יַעַבְדוּהוּ מִכֹּל שִׁבְטֵי יִשְׂרָאֵל׃
.Israel the of tribes of out all serve shall it the city he And serves who the .city those to serve who
20 כָּל־הַתְּרוּמָה חֲמִשָּׁה וְעֶשְׂרִים אֶלֶף בַּחֲמִשָּׁה וְעֶשְׂרִים
twenty- five by thousand twenty- (be shall) five heave- the offering All
אֶלֶף רְבִיעִית תָּרִימוּ אֶת־תְּרוּמַת הַקֹּדֶשׁ אֶל־אֲחֻזַּת הָעִיר׃
.city the the of possession to ,holy heave- the offering shall You offer four ,square ;thousand
21 וְהַנּוֹתָר לַנָּשִׂיא מִזֶּה ׀ וּמִזֶּה ׀ לִתְרוּמַת־הַקֹּדֶשׁ וְלַאֲחֻזַּת
the of and of possession ,holy heave- the of offering on and that this on (side) for (is) prince the the And remainder
הָעִיר אֶל־פְּנֵי חֲמִשָּׁה וְעֶשְׂרִים אֶלֶף ׀ תְּרוּמָה עַד־גְּבוּל
the border to heave- the offering thousand of twenty- five the front in of the ,city
קָדִימָה וְיָמָּה עַל־פְּנֵי חֲמִשָּׁה וְעֶשְׂרִים אֶלֶף עַל־גְּבוּל יָמָּה
;west the border to thousand twenty- five the front in of and westward ,east
לְעֻמַּת חֲלָקִים לַנָּשִׂיא וְהָיְתָה תְּרוּמַת הַקֹּדֶשׁ וּמִקְדַּשׁ
the and of sanctuary ;holy heave- a offering it And be shall the of .prince parts the alongside

the sanctuary of the house in its midst. [22] And to the prince shall be from the possession of the Levites, and from the city's possession, amidst (that) which is for the prince—between the border of Judah and the border of Benjamin. [23] And the rest of the tribes, from the east side to the west side, Benjamin one (part). [24] And by the border of Benjamin, from the east side to the west side, Simeon one (part). [25] And by the border of Simeon, from the east side to the west side, Issachar one (part). [26] And by the border of Issachar, from the east side to the west side, Zebulun one (part). [27] And by the border of Zebulun, from the east side to the west side, Gad one (part). [28] And by the border of Gad to the south side southward even shall be the border from Tamar to the waters of Meribath Kadesh, to the torrent to the Great Sea. [29] This (is) the land which you shall divide by lot for an inheritance to the tribes of Israel, and these their parts, declares the Lord Jehovah.

[30] And these (are) the exits of the city on the north side, four thousand and five hundred measures. [31] And the gates of the city (shall be) by the names of the tribes of Israel: three gates northward: the gate of Reuben, one; the gate of Judah, one; the gate of Levi, one. [32] And at the east side four thousand five hundred—and three gates: even the gate of Joseph, one; the gate of Benjamin, one; the gate of Dan, one.[32] And the south side four thousand and five hundred measures;

22 הַבַּיִת בְּתוֹכֹה׃ וּמֵאֲחֻזַּת הַלְוִיִּם וּמֵאֲחֻזַּת הָעִיר בְּתוֹךְ אֲשֶׁר
(that) which amidst the city's from and possession the Levites the from possession of And its in .midst the house

לַנָּשִׂיא יִהְיֶה בֵּין ׀ גְּבוּל יְהוּדָה וּבֵין גְּבוּל בִּנְיָמִן לַנָּשִׂיא
the to prince —Benjamin the of border and Judah the of border between —is the for prince

23 יִהְיֶה׃ וְיֶתֶר הַשְּׁבָטִים מִפְּאַת קָדִימָה עַד־פְּאַת־יָמָּה בִּנְיָמִן
Benjamin ,west the side to east the from side the ,tribes the And of rest shall .be

24 אֶחָד׃ וְעַל ׀ גְּבוּל בִּנְיָמִן מִפְּאַת קָדִימָה עַד־פְּאַת־יָמָּה
,west the side to east the from side ,Benjamin the of border And by one .(part)

25 שִׁמְעוֹן אֶחָד׃ וְעַל ׀ גְּבוּל שִׁמְעוֹן מִפְּאַת קָדִימָה עַד־פְּאַת־
the side to east the from side ,Simeon the of border And by one .(part) Simeon

26 יָמָּה יִשָּׂשכָר אֶחָד׃ וְעַל ׀ גְּבוּל יִשָּׂשכָר מִפְּאַת קָדִימָה
east the from side Issachar the of border by And .part one Issachar ,west

27 עַד־פְּאַת־יָמָּה זְבוּלֻן אֶחָד׃ וְעַל ׀ גְּבוּל זְבוּלֻן מִפְּאַת קָדִימָה
east the from side ,Zebulun the of border And by one .(part) Zebulun ,west the side to

28 עַד־פְּאַת־יָמָּה גָּד אֶחָד׃ וְעַל גְּבוּל גָּד אֶל־פְּאַת נֶגֶב תֵּימָנָה
south- ,ward Negev the side to Gad the of border by And one .(part) Gad ,west the side to

וְהָיָה גְבוּל מִתָּמָר מֵי מְרִיבַת קָדֵשׁ נַחֲלָה עַל־הַיָּם הַגָּדוֹל׃
.Great the Sea to the to torrent ,Kadesh Meribath- the of waters to Tamar from the border even be shall

29 זֹאת הָאָרֶץ אֲשֶׁר־תַּפִּילוּ מִנַּחֲלָה לְשִׁבְטֵי יִשְׂרָאֵל וְאֵלֶּה
and these ,Israel the to of tribes an for inheritance shall you which lot by divide the land This (is)

30 מַחְלְקוֹתָם נְאֻם אֲדֹנָי יְהוִה׃ וְאֵלֶּה תּוֹצְאֹת הָעִיר
the city the of exits these And (are) .Jehovah the Lord states ,parts their

31 מִפְּאַת צָפוֹן חֲמֵשׁ מֵאוֹת וְאַרְבַּעַת אֲלָפִים מִדָּה׃ וְשַׁעֲרֵי
the And of gates .measures thousand four and hundred five ,north the on side

הָעִיר עַל־שְׁמוֹת שִׁבְטֵי יִשְׂרָאֵל שְׁעָרִים שְׁלוֹשָׁה צָפוֹנָה
north- ;ward three gates :Israel the of tribes the of names (be shall) by the city

32 שַׁעַר רְאוּבֵן אֶחָד שַׁעַר יְהוּדָה אֶחָד שַׁעַר לֵוִי אֶחָד׃ וְאֶל־
at And .one ,Levi the of gate ;one ,Judah the of gate ;one ,Reuben the of gate

פְּאַת קָדִימָה חֲמֵשׁ מֵאוֹת וְאַרְבַּעַת אֲלָפִים וּשְׁעָרִים
gates and thousand ;(cubits) four and hundred five ,east side the

שְׁלֹשָׁה וְשַׁעַר יוֹסֵף אֶחָד שַׁעַר בִּנְיָמִן אֶחָד שַׁעַר דָּן אֶחָד׃
.one ,Dan the of gate ;one ,Benjamin the of gate ;one ,Joseph the even of gate :three

33 פְּאַת־נֶגְבָּה חֲמֵשׁ מֵאוֹת וְאַרְבַּעַת אֲלָפִים מִדָּה וּשְׁעָרִים
gates and ;measures thousand four and hundred five south side the And

and three gates: the gate of Simeon, one; the gate of Issachar, one; the gate of Zebulun, one. [34] The west side four thousand and five hundred; their gates three: the gate of Gad, one; the gate of Asher, one; the gate of Naphtali, one. All around (it shall be) eighteen thousand (cubits). And the name of the city from (that) day: Jehovah (is) there.

שְׁלֹשָׁה שַׁעַר שִׁמְעוֹן אֶחָד שַׁעַר יִשָּׂשכָר אֶחָד שַׁעַר זְבוּלֻן

,Zebulun the of gate ;one ,Issachar the of gate ;one ,Simeon the of gate :three

34 אֶחָד׃ פְּאַת־יָמָּה חֲמֵשׁ מֵאוֹת וְאַרְבַּעַת אֲלָפִים שַׁעֲרֵיהֶם

their gates thousand ;(cubits) four and hundred five west The side .one

שְׁלֹשָׁה שַׁעַר גָּד אֶחָד שַׁעַר אָשֵׁר אֶחָד שַׁעַר נַפְתָּלִי אֶחָד׃

.one ,Naphtali the of gate ;one Asher the of gate ;one ,Gad the of gate :three

סָבִיב שְׁמֹנָה עָשָׂר אָלֶף וְשֵׁם־הָעִיר מִיּוֹם יְהוָה ׀ שָׁמָּה׃

(is) .there Jehovah (that) :day from the city the of name And .(cubits) thousand eighteen (be shall it) All around

LIBER DANIELIS

CAPUT. I א

CHAPTER 1

CHAPTER 1

[1] In the third year of the reign of Jehoiakim king of Judah, Nebuchadnezzar king of Babylon came to Jerusalem and circled it. [2] And the Lord gave Jehoiakim king of Judah into his hand, with part of the vessels of the house of God, which he carried into the land of Shinar to the house of his god. And he brought the vessels into the treasure house of his god.

[3] And the king spoke to Ashpenaz the chief of his eunuchs, that he should bring (some) of the sons of Israel, and of the king's seed, and of the nobles; [4] young men (in) whom was no blemish, but who were good of appearance and skillful in all wisdom, having knowledge and understanding learning, even those (with) strength in them to stand in the king's palace, and to them they might teach the learning and the language of the Chaldeans. [5] And the king set them the portion of a day in its day from the king's food, and of the wine which he drank so as to bring them up three years, so that at the end of them they might stand before the king. [6] And there were among them of the sons of Judah: Daniel, Hananiah, Mishael and Azariah, [7] to whom the chief of the eunuchs gave names. For he called Daniel Belteshazzar; and Hananiah, Shadrach; and Mishael, Meshach; and Azariah, Abednego.

1 בִּשְׁנַת שָׁלוֹשׁ לְמַלְכוּת יְהוֹיָקִים מֶלֶךְ־יְהוּדָה בָּא

came ,Judah king of Jehoiakim the of of reign third the In year

2 נְבוּכַדְנֶאצַּר מֶלֶךְ־בָּבֶל יְרוּשָׁלַםִ וַיָּצַר עָלֶיהָ׃ וַיִּתֵּן אֲדֹנָי

the Lord And gave .it and beseiged (to) Jerusalem Babylon king of Nebuchadnezzar

בְּיָדוֹ אֶת־יְהוֹיָקִים מֶלֶךְ־יְהוּדָה וּמִקְצָת כְּלֵי בֵית־הָאֱלֹהִים

,God the of house the of vessels part with of Judah king of Jehoiakim his hand

וַיְבִיאֵם אֶרֶץ־שִׁנְעָר בֵּית אֱלֹהָיו וְאֶת־הַכֵּלִים הֵבִיא בֵּית

the house took he into the vessels And his .god the (to) of house Shinar the of land bore he and to them

3 אוֹצַר אֱלֹהָיו׃ וַיֹּאמֶר הַמֶּלֶךְ לְאַשְׁפְּנַז רַב סָרִיסָיו לְהָבִיא

bring to his eunuchs chief of the to ,Ashpenaz the king said And his .god treasure of

4 מִבְּנֵי יִשְׂרָאֵל וּמִזֶּרַע הַמְּלוּכָה וּמִן־הַפַּרְתְּמִים׃ יְלָדִים

young men ,nobles the and of ,royal of and seed the ,Israel the of of sons

אֲשֶׁר אֵין־בָּהֶם כָּל־מאוּם וְטוֹבֵי מַרְאֶה וּמַשְׂכִּילִים בְּכָל־

all in having and understanding look but of good ,blemish any in them not was (in) whom

חָכְמָה וְיֹדְעֵי דַעַת וּמְבִינֵי מַדָּע וַאֲשֶׁר כֹּחַ בָּהֶם לַעֲמֹד

to stand in them (with) strength even those ,learning and understanding knowledge having ,wisdom

5 בְּהֵיכַל הַמֶּלֶךְ וּלְלַמְּדָם סֵפֶר וּלְשׁוֹן כַּשְׂדִּים׃ וַיְמַן לָהֶם

to them And set the .Chaldeans the and of tongue the writing teach to and them the ,king's in palace

הַמֶּלֶךְ דְּבַר־יוֹם בְּיוֹמוֹ מִפַּת־בַּג הַמֶּלֶךְ וּמִיֵּין מִשְׁתָּיו

his ,drinking the and of wine the king's food from its in day a day of portion the king

6 וּלְגַדְּלָם שָׁנִים שָׁלוֹשׁ וּמִקְצָתָם יַעַמְדוּ לִפְנֵי הַמֶּלֶךְ׃ וַיְהִי

And were .king the before they stand may at that so end their three years to and them rear

7 בָהֶם מִבְּנֵי יְהוּדָה דָּנִיֵּאל חֲנַנְיָה מִישָׁאֵל וַעֲזַרְיָה׃ וַיָּשֶׂם

and assigned and ,Azariah Mishael ,Hananiah ,Daniel :Judah the of of sons among them

לָהֶם שַׂר הַסָּרִיסִים שֵׁמוֹת וַיָּשֶׂם לְדָנִיֵּאל בֵּלְטְשַׁאצַּר

;Belteshazzar for ,Daniel he and assigned ;names the eunuchs the of chief for ,them

וְלַחֲנַנְיָה שַׁדְרַךְ וּלְמִישָׁאֵל מֵישַׁךְ וְלַעֲזַרְיָה עֲבֵד נְגוֹ׃

.Abednego for and ,Azariah ;Meshach for and ,Mishael ;Shadrach for and ,Hananiah

[8] But Daniel laid on his heart that he would not defile himself with the king's food, or with the wine which he drank. So he asked of the chief of the eunuchs that he might not defile himself. [9] Now God had given Daniel kindness and compassion before the chief of the eunuchs. [10] And the chief of the eunuchs said to Daniel, I fear my lord the king, who has chosen your food and your drink. For why should he see your faces worse looking than the boys who (are) of your age? Then you would forfeit my head to the king. [11] Then Daniel said to Melzar, whom the chief of the eunuchs had set over Daniel, Hananiah, Mishael and Azariah, [12] I beg you, test your servants ten days. And let be given to us vegetables that we may eat, and water that we may drink. [13] Then let our faces be looked on before you, our look and the look of the boys who eat of the king's food. And as you see, deal so with your servants. [14] So he listened to them in this matter and tested them for ten days. [15] And at the end of ten days their faces looked better and fatter of flesh than all the boys who were eating the king's food. [16] So Melzar took away their food and the wine that they were to drink, and he gave them vegetables.

[17] As for these four boys, God gave them knowledge and skill in all writing and wisdom. And Daniel had understanding in

8 וַיָּשֶׂם דָּנִיֵּאל עַל־לִבּוֹ אֲשֶׁר לֹא־יִתְגָּאַל בְּפַתְבַּג הַמֶּלֶךְ
the food with would he not that his upon Daniel But
,king's himself defile heart laid

וּבְיֵין מִשְׁתָּיו וַיְבַקֵּשׁ מִשַּׂר הַסָּרִיסִים אֲשֶׁר לֹא יִתְגָּאָל׃
might he not that the the of he So his the or
.himself defile eunuchs of chief sought .drinking of wine

9 וַיִּתֵּן הָאֱלֹהִים אֶת־דָּנִיֵּאל לְחֶסֶד וּלְרַחֲמִים לִפְנֵי שַׂר
the before and kindness Daniel God had Now
of chief compassion given

10 הַסָּרִיסִים׃ וַיֹּאמֶר שַׂר הַסָּרִיסִים לְדָנִיֵּאל יָרֵא אֲנִי אֶת־
I fear Daniel to the the said And the
eunuchs of chief .eunuchs

אֲדֹנִי הַמֶּלֶךְ אֲשֶׁר מִנָּה אֶת־מַאֲכַלְכֶם וְאֶת־מִשְׁתֵּיכֶם
;drink your and food your has who the my
appointed ,king lord

אֲשֶׁר לָמָּה יִרְאֶה אֶת־פְּנֵיכֶם זֹעֲפִים מִן־הַיְלָדִים אֲשֶׁר
who boys the than worse faces your he should why for
(are) looking see

11 כְּגִילְכֶם וְחִיַּבְתֶּם אֶת־רֹאשִׁי לַמֶּלֶךְ׃ וַיֹּאמֶר דָּנִיֵּאל אֶל־
to Daniel Then the to my would you Then your as
said .king head forfeit ?age

הַמֶּלְצַר אֲשֶׁר מִנָּה שַׂר הַסָּרִיסִים עַל־דָּנִיֵּאל חֲנַנְיָה
,Hananiah Daniel over the chief the had he whom the
eunuchs of appointed ,overseer

12 מִישָׁאֵל וַעֲזַרְיָה׃ נַס־נָא אֶת־עֲבָדֶיךָ יָמִים עֲשָׂרָה וְיִתְּנוּ־
let and ,ten days your Please test and ,Mishael
given be servants ,Azariah

13 לָנוּ מִן־הַזֵּרֹעִים וְנֹאכְלָה וּמַיִם וְנִשְׁתֶּה׃ וְיֵרָאוּ לְפָנֶיךָ
before let Then we that and we that the (some) to
you seen be .drink may water ,eat may vegetables of us

מַרְאֵינוּ וּמַרְאֵה הַיְלָדִים הָאֹכְלִים אֵת פַּתְבַּג הַמֶּלֶךְ
the food eat who boys the the and our
;king's of look look

14 וְכַאֲשֶׁר תִּרְאֵה עֲשֵׂה עִם־עֲבָדֶיךָ׃ וַיִּשְׁמַע לָהֶם לַדָּבָר הַזֶּה
,this to to he So your with deal you as And
matter them listened .servants ,see

15 וַיְנַסֵּם יָמִים עֲשָׂרָה׃ וּמִקְצָת יָמִים עֲשָׂרָה נִרְאָה מַרְאֵיהֶם
their looked ,ten days the at And .ten days and
appearance of end them tested

טוֹב וּבְרִיאֵי בָּשָׂר מִן־כָּל־הַיְלָדִים הָאֹכְלִים אֵת פַּתְבַּג
food were who the all than flesh and better
eating boys of fatter

16 הַמֶּלֶךְ׃ וַיְהִי הַמֶּלְצַר נֹשֵׂא אֶת־פַּתְבָּגָם וְיֵין מִשְׁתֵּיהֶם
their the and their took the So the
,drinks of wine food away overseer .king's

17 וְנֹתֵן לָהֶם זֵרְעֹנִים׃ וְהַיְלָדִים הָאֵלֶּה אַרְבַּעְתָּם נָתַן לָהֶם
to gave ,four these for as And .vegetables to he and
them boys them gave

הָאֱלֹהִים מַדָּע וְהַשְׂכֵּל בְּכָל־סֵפֶר וְחָכְמָה וְדָנִיֵּאל הֵבִין
had but and writing in and knowledge God
skill Daniel ;wisdom all insight

all visions and dreams. [18] Now at the end of the days that the king had said to bring them in, the chief of the eunuchs brought them in before Nebuchadnezzar. [19] And the king talked with them. And among them all was found none like Daniel, Hananiah, Mishael and Azariah. So they stood before the king. [20] And (in) any matter of wisdom (and) understanding that the king asked from them, he found them ten times better than all the horoscopists (and) the conjurers who (were) in all his kingdom. [21] And Daniel continued to the first year of King Cyrus.

18 בְּכָל־חָזוֹן וַחֲלֹמוֹת׃ וּלְמִקְצָת הַיָּמִים אֲשֶׁר־אָמַר הַמֶּלֶךְ
the had when the the at Now and visions in
king said ,days of end .dreams all

19 לַהֲבִיאָם וַיְבִיאֵם שַׂר הַסָּרִיסִים לִפְנֵי נְבֻכַדְנֶצַּר׃ וַיְדַבֵּר
And .Nebuchadnezzar before the chief the then bring to
spoke eunuchs of them brought ,in them

אִתָּם הַמֶּלֶךְ וְלֹא נִמְצָא מִכֻּלָּם כְּדָנִיֵּאל חֲנַנְיָה מִישָׁאֵל
Mishael ,Hananiah like all among was but the with
Daniel them found none ,king them

20 וַעֲזַרְיָה וַיַּעַמְדוּ לִפְנֵי הַמֶּלֶךְ׃ וְכֹל דְּבַר חָכְמַת בִּינָה אֲשֶׁר־
that under- wisdom matter And the before they so and
standing (or) of any .king stood ,Azariah

בִּקֵּשׁ מֵהֶם הַמֶּלֶךְ וַיִּמְצָאֵם עֶשֶׂר יָדוֹת עַל־כָּל־הַחַרְטֻמִּים
horoscopists the all better times ten found he the from sought
than them ,king them

21 הָאַשָּׁפִים אֲשֶׁר בְּכָל־מַלְכוּתוֹ׃ וַיְהִי דָּנִיֵּאל עַד־שְׁנַת אַחַת
first the until Daniel And his in who the (and)
year continued .kingdom all (were) conjurers

לְכוֹרֶשׁ הַמֶּלֶךְ׃
the Cyrus of
.king

CAP. II ב

CHAPTER 2

CHAPTER 2

[1] And in the second year of Nebuchadnezzar's reign, Nebuchadnezzar was dreaming dreams, and his spirit was troubled, and his sleep was finished on him. [2] Then the king said to call to the horoscopists, and to the conjurers, and to the sorcerers, and to the Chaldeans, to tell to the king his dreams. So they came and stood before the king. [3] And the king said to them, I have dreamed a dream and my spirit was troubled to know the dream. [4] Then the Chaldeans spoke to the king (in) Aramaic, O king, live forever! Tell your servants the dream and we will reveal the meaning. [5] The king answered and said to the Chaldeans, The word (is) assured from me, If you will not make known to me the dream and its meaning, (from your) limbs you will be taken, and your houses shall be made an outhouse. [6] But if you show the dream and its meaning, you shall receive gifts and a present and great honor from me. Therefore reveal the dream and the meaning

1 וּבִשְׁנַת שְׁתַּיִם לְמַלְכוּת נְבֻכַדְנֶצַּר חָלַם נְבֻכַדְנֶצַּר חֲלֹמוֹת
,dreams Nebuchad- dreamed Nebuchad- the of second in And
nezzar ,nezzar of reign year the

2 וַתִּתְפָּעֶם רוּחוֹ וּשְׁנָתוֹ נִהְיְתָה עָלָיו׃ וַיֹּאמֶר הַמֶּלֶךְ לִקְרֹא
call to king the said Then .him on was his and his was and
finished sleep ,spirit troubled

לַחַרְטֻמִּים וְלָאַשָּׁפִים וְלַמְכַשְּׁפִים וְלַכַּשְׂדִּים לְהַגִּיד לַמֶּלֶךְ
the to tell to the to and the to and the to and the to
king ,Chaldeans ,sorcerers ,conjurers ,horoscopists

3 חֲלֹמֹתָיו וַיָּבֹאוּ וַיַּעַמְדוּ לִפְנֵי הַמֶּלֶךְ׃ וַיֹּאמֶר לָהֶם הַמֶּלֶךְ
,king the to said And .king the before and they So his
them stood came .dreams

4 חֲלוֹם חָלַמְתִּי וַתִּפָּעֶם רוּחִי לָדַעַת אֶת־הַחֲלוֹם׃ וַיְדַבְּרוּ
Then .dream the know to my was and have I a
spoke spirit troubled ,dreamed dream

הַכַּשְׂדִּים לַמֶּלֶךְ אֲרָמִית מַלְכָּא לְעָלְמִין חֱיִי אֱמַר חֶלְמָא
the Tell !live forever ,king O —Aramaic the to the
dream —king Chaldeans

5 לְעַבְדָיךְ וּפִשְׁרָא נְחַוֵּא׃ עָנֵה מַלְכָּא וְאָמַר לְכַשְׂדָּיֵא מִלְּתָה
The the to said and The answered will we the and your to
word ,Chaldeans king .reveal meaning ,servants

מִנִּי אַזְדָּא הֵן לָא תְהוֹדְעוּנַּנִי חֶלְמָא וּפִשְׁרֵהּ הַדָּמִין
(your from) its and the make will you not If (is) from
limbs ,meaning dream me to known .assured me

6 תִּתְעַבְדוּן וּבָתֵּיכוֹן נְוָלִי יִתְּשָׂמוּן׃ וְהֵן חֶלְמָא וּפִשְׁרֵהּ
its and the But be shall out- an your and be will you
meaning dream if .made house houses ,taken

of it to me. [7] They answered again and said, Let the king tell his servants the dream and we will reveal its meaning. [8] The king answered and said, I know that you surely want to gain time, because you see the thing (is) assured from me. [9] But if you will not make the dream known to me, (there is) one law for you. For you have agreed upon lying and deceiving words to speak before me, until the time has changed. Therefore tell me the dream; then I shall know that you can reveal its meaning to me.

[10] The Chaldeans answered before the king and said, There is not a man on the earth who can reveal the king's matter because not any king, lord or ruler has asked such a thing from any horoscopist or conjurer or Chaldeans, [11] for rare (is) the thing that the king asks. And there is no other who may reveal it before the king, except the gods, whose dwelling is not with flesh. [12] Thereupon the king was enraged and angered. And he commanded all the wise men of Babylon to be destroyed. [13] And the law went out that the wise men should be killed. And they looked for Daniel and his friends to be killed.

[14] Then Daniel answered (with) counsel and insight to Arioch the captain of the king's guard, who had gone out to kill the wise men of Babylon.

תְּהַחֲוֺן מַתְּנָן וּנְבִזְבָּה וִיקָר שַׂגִּיא תְּקַבְּלוּן מִקֳּדָמַי לָהֵן
There- before from shall you great and a and ,gifts make you
fore .me receive honor ,present ,known

7 חֶלְמָא וּפִשְׁרֵהּ הַחֲוֺנִי׃ עֲנוֹ תִנְיָנוּת וְאָמְרִין מַלְכָּא חֶלְמָא
the king the ,said and again They reveal its and the
dream replied .me to meaning dream

8 יֵאמַר לְעַבְדוֹהִי וּפִשְׁרָה נְהַחֲוֵה׃ עָנֵה מַלְכָּא וְאָמַר מִן־
For ,said and The answered will we the and his to Let
king .reveal meaning ,servants tell

יַצִּיב יָדַע אֲנָה דִּי עִדָּנָא אַנְתּוּן זָבְנִין כָּל־קֳבֵל דִּי חֲזֵיתוֹן
see you because ,buy you time that I know certain

9 דִּי־אַזְדָּא מִנִּי מִלְּתָא׃ דִּי הֵן־חֶלְמָא לָא תְהוֹדְעֻנַּנִי חֲדָה
one reveal will you not the if But the from (is) that
,me to dream .word me assured

הִיא דָתְכוֹן וּמִלָּה כִדְבָה וּשְׁחִיתָה הִזְדְּמִנְתּוּן לְמֵאמַר
speak to have you corrupt and lying for your (is)
upon agreed words ,law

קֳדָמַי עַד דִּי עִדָּנָא יִשְׁתַּנֵּא לָהֵן חֶלְמָא אֱמַרוּ לִי וְאִנְדַּע
I and to tell the There- is the until before
know shall me dream fore .changed time ,me

10 דִּי פִשְׁרֵהּ תְּהַחֲוֺנַּנִי׃ עֲנוֹ כַשְׂדָּיֵא קֳדָם־מַלְכָּא וְאָמְרִין
,said and king the before the answered can you its that
Chaldeans .me to reveal meaning

לָא־אִיתַי אֱנָשׁ עַל־יַבֶּשְׁתָּא דִּי מִלַּת מַלְכָּא יוּכַל לְהַחֲוָיָה
make to able is the matter who the on a There not
,known king's earth man is

כָּל־קֳבֵל דִּי כָּל־מֶלֶךְ רַב וְשַׁלִּיט מִלָּה כִדְנָה לָא שְׁאֵל
has not like thing a or ,chief ,king any because
asked this lord

11 לְכָל־חַרְטֹּם וְאָשַׁף וְכַשְׂדָּי׃ וּמִלְּתָא דִי־מַלְכָּא שָׁאֵל יַקִּירָה
(is) asks the that the And or or horoscopist any
.rare king thing ,Chaldean ,conjurer

וְאָחֳרָן לָא אִיתַי דִּי יְחַוִּנַּהּ קֳדָם מַלְכָּא לָהֵן אֱלָהִין דִּי
(the) except ,king the before may who there no And
,gods it reveal is other

12 מְדָרְהוֹן עִם־בִּשְׂרָא לָא אִיתוֹהִי׃ כָּל־קֳבֵל דְּנָה מַלְכָּא
king the ,Thereupon .is not flesh with whose
was dwelling

בְּנַס וּקְצַף שַׂגִּיא וַאֲמַר לְהוֹבָדָה לְכֹל חַכִּימֵי בָבֶל׃
.Babylon wise the all destroy to he And .very and very
of men commanded angered enraged

13 וְדָתָא נֶפְקַת וְחַכִּימַיָּא מִתְקַטְּלִין וּבְעוֹ דָּנִיֵּאל וְחַבְרוֹהִי
his and Daniel they And be should the that went the And
companions sought .killed men wise out law

14 לְהִתְקְטָלָה׃ בֵּאדַיִן דָּנִיֵּאל הֲתִיב עֵטָא וּטְעֵם
and (with) answered Daniel Then .killed be to
insight counsel

לְאַרְיוֹךְ רַב־טַבָּחַיָּא דִּי מַלְכָּא דִּי נְפַק לְקַטָּלָה לְחַכִּימֵי
wise the kill to had who the body-guard the to
of men out gone king's of chief Arioch

[15] He answered and said to Arioch the king's captain, Why (is) the decree so hasty from before the king? Then Arioch made the thing known to Daniel. [16] Then Daniel went in and asked of the king that he would give him time, and he would show the king the meaning. [17] Then Daniel went to his house and declared the thing to Hananiah, Mishael, and Azariah, his companions, [18] that they might pray for the mercies of God in Heaven about this secret, that Daniel and his companions should not perish with the rest of the wise men of Babylon.

[19] Then the secret was revealed to Daniel in a night vision, and Daniel blessed the God of Heaven. [20] Daniel answered and said, Blessed be the name of God forever and ever, for wisdom and might (are) His. [21] And He changes the times and the seasons. He removes kings and sets up kings. He gives wisdom to the wise and knowledge to those who have understanding. [22] He reveals the deep and secret things. He knows what (is) in the darkness, and the light dwells with Him. [23] I thank You and praise You, O God of my fathers, who has given me wisdom and might and has made me know what we ask of You. For You have revealed to us the king's matter.

[24] Thereupon Daniel went in to Arioch, whom the king had chosen to destroy the wise men of Babylon; he went and said

15 בָּבֶֽל׃ עָנֵה וְאָמַר לְאַרְיוֹךְ שַׁלִּיטָא דִּי־מַלְכָּא עַל־מָה

Why (is) ,king's the captain Arioch to said and He answered .Babylon

דָתָא מְהַחְצְפָה מִן־קֳדָם מַלְכָּא אֱדַיִן מִלְּתָא הוֹדַע אַרְיוֹךְ

Arioch made known the matter Then ?king the before from urgent so the decree

16 לְדָנִיֵּאל׃ וְדָנִיֵּאל עַל וּבְעָא מִן־מַלְכָּא דִּי זְמָן יִנְתֵּן־לֵהּ

him he give would time that the king from and asked went in Then Daniel .Daniel to

17 וּפִשְׁרָא לְהַחֲוָיָה לְמַלְכָּא׃ אֱדַיִן דָּנִיֵּאל לְבַיְתֵהּ

his to house Daniel Then the to .king would he known make the meaning

אֲזַל וְלַחֲנַנְיָה מִישָׁאֵל וַעֲזַרְיָה חַבְרוֹהִי מִלְּתָא הוֹדַע׃

made ;known the matter his ,companions and ,Azariah ,Mishael to and ,Hananiah ,went

18 וְרַחֲמִין לְמִבְעֵא מִן־קֳדָם אֱלָהּ שְׁמַיָּא עַל־רָזָה דְּנָה דִּי

that ,this about secret Heaven the of God before from they that ask might for mercies

לָא יְהֹבְדוּן דָּנִיֵּאל וְחַבְרוֹהִי עִם־שְׁאָר חַכִּימֵי בָבֶל׃

.Babylon wise the of men the with of rest his and companions Daniel perish should not

19 אֱדַיִן לְדָנִיֵּאל בְּחֶזְוָא דִּי־לֵילְיָא רָזָא גֲלִי אֱדַיִן דָּנִיֵּאל בָּרִךְ

blessed Daniel Then was .revealed the secret the of night a in vision Daniel to Then

20 לֶאֱלָהּ שְׁמַיָּא׃ עָנֵה דָנִיֵּאל וְאָמַר לֶהֱוֵא שְׁמֵהּ דִּי־אֱלָהָא

God of the name Be ,said and Daniel answered .Heaven the of God

מְבָרַךְ מִן־עָלְמָא וְעַד־עָלְמָא דִּי חָכְמְתָא וּגְבוּרְתָא דִּי־

(are) the and power the wisdom for ,ever and forever blessed

21 לֵהּ הִיא׃ וְהוּא מְהַשְׁנֵא עִדָּנַיָּא וְזִמְנַיָּא מְהַעְדֵּה מַלְכִין

kings He removes the and ;seasons the times changes He And to .Him

וּמְהָקֵים מַלְכִין יָהֵב חָכְמְתָא לְחַכִּימִין וּמַנְדְּעָא לְיָדְעֵי

those to have who and knowledge the to ,men wise the wisdom He gives .kings sets and up

22 בִינָה׃ הוּא גָּלֵא עַמִּיקָתָא וּמְסַתְּרָתָא יָדַע מָה בַחֲשׁוֹכָא

the in ,darkness what (is) He knows secret and .things the deep reveals He under- .standing

23 וּנְהוֹרָא עִמֵּהּ שְׁרֵא׃ לָךְ ׀ אֱלָהּ אֲבָהָתִי מְהוֹדֵא וּמְשַׁבַּח

praise and thank my ,fathers O of God To ,You .dwells with Him the and light

אֲנָה דִּי חָכְמְתָא וּגְבוּרְתָא יְהַבְתְּ לִי וּכְעַן הוֹדַעְתַּנִי דִּי־

what made has know me and now to ;me has given the and power the wisdom who ,I

24 בְּעֵינָא מִנָּךְ דִּי־מִלַּת מַלְכָּא הוֹדַעְתֶּנָא׃ כָּל־קֳבֵל דְּנָה

,Thereupon made have You .us to known the king's matter For from .You we asked

דָּנִיֵּאל עַל עַל־אַרְיוֹךְ דִּי מַנִּי מַלְכָּא לְהוֹבָדָה לְחַכִּימֵי בָּבֶל

Baby- ;lon wise the of men destroy to the king had whom appointed ,Arioch to went in Daniel

this to him, Do not destroy the wise men of Babylon. Bring me in before the king, and I will show the meaning to the king. [25] Then Arioch quickly brought Daniel in before the king and spoke thus to him, I have found a man of the captives of Judah who will make the meaning known to the king. [26] The king answered and said to Daniel, whose name (was) Belteshazzar, Are you able to reveal to me the dream which I have seen and its meaning? [27] Daniel answered before the king and said, The secret which the king has demanded cannot be shown to the king by the wise men, the conjurers, the horoscopists, the fortune-tellers. [28] But there is a God in Heaven who reveals secrets and makes known to King Nebuchadnezzar what shall be in the latter days. Your dream, and the visions of your head on your bed, (was) this: [29] As for you, O king, your thoughts came on your bed, what should happen after this. And He who reveals secrets makes known to you what shall come to pass. [30] But as for me, this secret is not revealed to me for (any) wisdom that I have more than any living man, but so that the meaning might be made known to the king, and that you might know the thoughts of your heart.

[31] You, O king, were seeing, and behold a certain great image! That great image stood before you with a brilliant brightness; and its form (was) dreadful. [32] This image's head

אֱזַל ׀ וְכֵן אֲמַר־לֵהּ לְחַכִּימֵי בָבֶל אַל־תְּהוֹבֵד הַעֵלְנִי
me Bring in | Do .destroy | not | Babylon | wise the of men | to ,him | he said | and thus | he went

25 קֳדָם מַלְכָּא וּפִשְׁרָא לְמַלְכָּא אֲחַוֵּא׃ אֱדַיִן אַרְיוֹךְ
Arioch | Then | will I .declare | the to king | the and meaning | the ,king | before

בְּהִתְבְּהָלָה הַנְעֵל לְדָנִיֵּאל קֳדָם מַלְכָּא וְכֵן אֲמַר־לֵהּ דִּי־
to ,him | he spoke | and thus | the ,king | before | Daniel | brought in | hurriedly

הַשְׁכַּחַת גְּבַר מִן־בְּנֵי גָלוּתָא דִּי יְהוּד דִּי פִשְׁרָא לְמַלְכָּא
the to king | the meaning | who | Judah | of | exiles | the of | man a | have I found

26 יְהוֹדַע׃ עָנֵה מַלְכָּא וְאָמַר לְדָנִיֵּאל דִּי שְׁמֵהּ בֵּלְטְשַׁאצַּר
,Belteshazzar | name whose (was) | ,Daniel to | said and | The king | answered | make will .known

27 הַאִיתָךְ כָּהֵל לְהוֹדָעֻתַנִי חֶלְמָא דִּי־חֲזֵית וּפִשְׁרֵהּ׃ עָנֵה
answered | its and ?meaning | have I seen | which | the dream | make to me to known | able | you Are

דָנִיֵּאל קֳדָם מַלְכָּא וְאָמַר רָזָא דִּי־מַלְכָּא שָׁאֵל לָא
not | has ,asked | the king | which | The secret | ,said and | the king | before | Daniel

חַכִּימִין אָשְׁפִין חַרְטֻמִּין גָּזְרִין יָכְלִין לְהַחֲוָיָה לְמַלְכָּא׃
the to .king | declare to | are able | astrologers | horo- ,scopists | ,conjurers | wise the ,men

28 בְּרַם אִיתַי אֱלָהּ בִּשְׁמַיָּא גָּלֵא רָזִין וְהוֹדַע לְמַלְכָּא
King to | makes and known | secrets | who reveals | Heaven in | God a | there is | But

נְבוּכַדְנֶצַּר מָה דִּי לֶהֱוֵא בְּאַחֲרִית יוֹמַיָּא חֶלְמָךְ וְחֶזְוֵי
the and of visions | Your dream | .days | the in latter | be shall | what | Nebuchad-nezzar

29 רֵאשָׁךְ עַל־מִשְׁכְּבָךְ דְּנָה הוּא׃ אַנְתְּה מַלְכָּא
,king O | for As ,you | ;(was) | this | bed your | on | your head

רַעְיוֹנָךְ עַל־מִשְׁכְּבָךְ סְלִקוּ מָה דִּי לֶהֱוֵא אַחֲרֵי דְנָה וְגָלֵא
the And of Revealer | .this | after | should happen | what | came up | your bed | on | your thoughts

30 רָזַיָּא הוֹדְעָךְ מָה־דִי לֶהֱוֵא׃ וַאֲנָה לָא בְחָכְמָה דִּי־אִיתַי
there is | that | of because wisdom | not | as And ,me for | come shall .pass to | what | reveals you to | secrets

בִּי מִן־כָּל־חַיַּיָּא רָזָא דְנָה גֱּלִי לִי לָהֵן עַל־דִּבְרַת דִּי
that | order in | but | to ,me | is revealed | this | secret | living any man | more than | with me

פִשְׁרָא לְמַלְכָּא יְהוֹדְעוּן וְרַעְיוֹנֵי לִבְבָךְ תִּנְדַּע׃
might you .know | your heart | the that of thoughts | making ,known | the to king | the meaning

31 אַנְתְּ מַלְכָּא חָזֵה הֲוַיְתָ וַאֲלוּ צְלֵם חַד שַׂגִּיא צַלְמָא דִּכֵּן
That | image | !great | certain | image | and behold | ,were | seeing | ,king O | ,You

32 רַב וְזִיוֵהּ יַתִּיר קָאֵם לְקָבְלָךְ וְרֵוֵהּ דְּחִיל׃ הוּא צַלְמָא
image's | That | (was) .terrifying | its and appearance | ,you before | stood | extra- ordinary | an with brightness | great

(was) of fine gold; its breasts and its arms (were) of silver; its belly and its thighs (were) of bronze; [33] its legs (were) of iron; its feet (were) partly of iron and partly of clay. [34] You continued until a stone was cut out without hands, which struck the image on its feet of iron and clay and broke them to pieces. [35] Then the iron, the clay, the bronze, the silver and the gold were broken to pieces together; and became like the chaff of the summer threshing floors. And the wind carried them away, so that no trace was found for them. And the stone that struck the image became a great mountain and filled the whole earth.

[36] This (is) the dream; and we will tell the meaning of it before the king. [37] You, O king, (are) the king of kings. For the God of Heaven has given you the kingdom, the power, and the strength, and the honor. [38] And wherever the sons of men, the animals of the field and the birds of the sky live, He has given into your hand and has made you ruler over them all. You (are) the head of gold. [39] And in your place shall arise another kingdom lower than yours, and another third kingdom of bronze, which shall rule in all the earth. [40] And the fourth kingdom shall be (as) strong as iron. Since iron crushes and smashes all thing, and as the iron that shatters all these, it will crush and shatter. [41] And as to that (which) you saw, the feet and the toes, partly of potters' clay and partly of iron, (the) kingdom shall be divided. But there shall be in it the strength of the iron because you saw the iron mixed with clay of the potter [42] And (as) the toes of the feet (were) partly of iron and partly of clay, (so)

רֵאשֵׁהּ דִּי־דְהַב טָב חֲדוֹהִי וּדְרָעוֹהִי דִּי כְסַף מְעוֹהִי

its ;silver (were) its and its ,fine gold of head
belly of arms breast (was)

33 וְיַרְכָתֵהּ דִּי נְחָשׁ׃ שָׁקוֹהִי דִּי פַרְזֶל רַגְלוֹהִי מִנְּהוֹן דִּי

of partly feet its ;iron of legs its ;bronze of its and
(were) (were) thighs

34 פַרְזֶל וּמִנְּהוֹן דִּי חֲסַף׃ חָזֵה הֲוַיְתָ עַד דִּי הִתְגְּזֶרֶת אֶבֶן

a cut was until You seeing .clay of and iron
stone out continued partly

דִּי־לָא בִידַיִן וּמְחָת לְצַלְמָא עַל־רַגְלוֹהִי דִּי פַרְזְלָא וְחַסְפָּא

clay and iron of feet its on the which ,hands without
image struck

35 וְהַדֵּקֶת הִמּוֹן׃ בֵּאדַיִן דָּקוּ כַחֲדָה פַּרְזְלָא חַסְפָּא נְחָשָׁא

the the the together were Then .them and
bronze ,clay ,iron crushed crushed

כַּסְפָּא וְדַהֲבָא וַהֲווֹ כְּעוּר מִן־אִדְּרֵי־קַיִט וּנְשָׂא הִמּוֹן רוּחָא

the them And .summer the of the like and the and the
,wind away took floors threshing chaff became ;gold ,silver

וְכָל־אֲתַר לָא־הִשְׁתְּכַח לְהוֹן וְאַבְנָא ׀ דִּי־מְחָת לְצַלְמָא

the struck that the But for found was not trace so
image stone .them any that

36 הֲוָת לְטוּר רַב וּמְלָאת כָּל־אַרְעָא׃ דְּנָה חֶלְמָא וּפִשְׁרֵהּ

its and the This the whole filled and great a became
meaning ;dream (is) .earth mountain

37 נֵאמַר קֳדָם־מַלְכָּא׃ אַנְתְּה מַלְכָּא מֶלֶךְ מַלְכַיָּא דִּי אֱלָהּ

the for ,kings the the ,king O ,You .king the before will we
of God of king (are) tell

38 שְׁמַיָּא מַלְכוּתָא חִסְנָא וְתָקְפָּא וִיקָרָא יְהַב־לָךְ׃ וּבְכָל־

where- And .you to has the and the and the the Heaven
given honor strength ,power ,kingdom

דִּי דָאְרִין בְּנֵי־אֲנָשָׁא חֵיוַת בָּרָא וְעוֹף־שְׁמַיָּא יְהַב בִּידָךְ

your into He the the or the the ,men the dwells ever
,hand given has ,sky of birds ,field of animals of sons

39 וְהַשְׁלְטָךְ בְּכָלְּהוֹן אַנְתְּה הוּא רֵאשָׁה דִּי דַהֲבָא׃ וּבָתְרָךְ

in And .gold of head that You of all over has and
place your (are) .them rule you made

תְּקוּם מַלְכוּ אָחֳרִי אֲרַע מִנָּךְ וּמַלְכוּ תְלִיתָאָה אָחֳרִי דִּי

of another third and than lower another kingdom shall
kingdom ,yours arise

40 נְחָשָׁא דִּי תִשְׁלַט בְּכָל־אַרְעָא׃ וּמַלְכוּ רְבִיעָאָה תֶּהֱוֵא

be shall the And the in rule shall which ,bronze
fourth kingdom .earth all

תַקִּיפָה כְּפַרְזְלָא כָּל־קֳבֵל דִּי פַרְזְלָא מְהַדֵּק וְחָשֵׁל כֹּלָּא

all and crushes iron much as in ,iron as strong (as)
;things smashes (as)

41 וּכְפַרְזְלָא דִּי־מְרָעַע כָּל־אִלֵּין תַּדִּק וְתֵרֹעַ׃ וְדִי־חֲזַיְתָה

you as And and will it ,these all shatters that like and
,saw that .shatter crush iron the

רַגְלַיָּא וְאֶצְבְּעָתָא מִנְּהֵן חֲסַף דִּי־פֶחָר וּמִנְּהֵן פַּרְזֶל

,iron and (the) of clay partly the and the
of partly potter of toes feet

the kingdom shall be partly strong and partly fragile. [43] And as you saw the iron mixed with the clay of the clay, they shall be mixed with the seed of men. But they shall not adhere to one another, even as iron does not mix with clay. [44] And in the days of these kings, the God of Heaven shall set up a kingdom which shall never be destroyed. And the kingdom shall not be left to other people. It shall break in pieces and destroy all these kingdoms, and it shall stand forever. [45] Because you saw that the stone was cut out of the mountain without hands, and that it broke in pieces the iron, the bronze, the clay, the silver and the gold — the great God has made known to the king what shall happen after this. And the dream (is) certain, and the meaning of it is trustworthy.

[46] Then King Nebuchadnezzar fell on his face and worshiped Daniel. And he commanded to offer an offering and incense to him. [47] The king answered Daniel and said, Your God truly (is) a God of gods and a Lord of kings, and a Revealer of secrets, since you could reveal this secret. [48] Then the king made Daniel great and gave him many great gifts. And he

מַלְכוּ פְלִיגָה תֶּהֱוֵה וּמִן־נִצְבְּתָא דִי־פַרְזְלָא לֶהֱוֵא־בַהּ
in shall there the of the But .be shall divided (the)
,it be iron strength of kingdom

42 כָּל־קֳבֵל דִּי חֲזַיְתָה פַּרְזְלָא מְעָרַב בַּחֲסַף טִינָא׃ וְאֶצְבְּעָת
the (as) And the with mixed iron the saw you because
of toes .clay of clay

רַגְלַיָּא מִנְהֵין פַּרְזֶל וּמִנְהֵין חֲסַף מִן־קְצָת מַלְכוּתָא תֶּהֱוֵה
be shall the partly (so) ,clay and iron partly feet the
kingdom of partly of (were)

43 תַקִּיפָא וּמִנַּהּ תֶּהֱוֵא תְבִירָה׃ דִּי חֲזַיְתָ פַּרְזְלָא מְעָרַב
mixed iron the saw you And .fragile shall it and strong
as .be partly

בַּחֲסַף טִינָא מִתְעָרְבִין לֶהֱוֺן בִּזְרַע אֲנָשָׁא וְלָא־לֶהֱוֺן דָּבְקִין
shall they But .men the with be shall they the with
adhere not of seed mixed ,clay of clay

דְּנָה עִם־דְּנָה הֵא־כְדִי פַרְזְלָא לָא מִתְעָרַב עִם־חַסְפָּא׃
the with mix does not iron the as even ,another to one
.clay

44 וּבְיוֹמֵיהוֹן דִּי מַלְכַיָּא אִנּוּן יְקִים אֱלָהּ שְׁמַיָּא מַלְכוּ דִּי
which a Heaven the shall ,these kings of the in And
kingdom of God up set days

לְעָלְמִין לָא תִתְחַבַּל וּמַלְכוּתָה לְעַם אָחֳרָן לָא תִשְׁתְּבִק
be shall not another to the And be shall not forever
.left kingdom .destroyed

תַּדִּק וְתָסֵף כָּל־אִלֵּין מַלְכְוָתָא וְהִיא תְּקוּם לְעָלְמַיָּא׃
forever shall and ,kingdoms these all make and will It
stand it of end an crush

45 כָּל־קֳבֵל דִּי־חֲזַיְתָ דִּי מִטּוּרָא אִתְגְּזֶרֶת אֶבֶן דִּי־לָא בִידַיִן
,hands without (the) cut was the of out that you Because
stone mountain saw

וְהַדֶּקֶת פַּרְזְלָא נְחָשָׁא חַסְפָּא כַּסְפָּא וְדַהֲבָא אֱלָהּ רַב
great (the) the and the the the the it that and
God —gold ,silver ,clay ,bronze ,iron crushed

הוֹדַע לְמַלְכָּא מָה דִּי לֶהֱוֵא אַחֲרֵי דְנָה וְיַצִּיב חֶלְמָא
the cer- And .this after shall what the to made has
dream (is) tain happen king known

46 וּמְהֵימַן פִּשְׁרֵהּ׃ בֵּאדַיִן מַלְכָּא נְבוּכַדְנֶצַּר נְפַל
fell Nebuchadnezzar King Then its trust- and
.meaning worthy

עַל־אַנְפּוֹהִי וּלְדָנִיֵּאל סְגִד וּמִנְחָה וְנִיחֹחִין אֲמַר לְנַסָּכָה
offer to he and an and ,worshiped Daniel and his on
commanded incense ,offering face

47 לֵהּ׃ עָנֵה מַלְכָּא לְדָנִיֵּאל וְאָמַר מִן־קְשֹׁט דִּי אֱלָהֲכוֹן
,God your truth Of ,said and Daniel The answered to
king .him

הוּא אֱלָהּ אֱלָהִין וּמָרֵא מַלְכִין וְגָלֵה רָזִין דִּי יְכֵלְתָּ לְמִגְלֵא
to you since ,secrets a and ,kings Lord and gods a He
reveal able were of Revealer of of God (is)

48 רָזָא דְנָה׃ אֱדַיִן מַלְכָּא לְדָנִיֵּאל רַבִּי וּמַתְּנָן רַבְרְבָן
great gifts and made Daniel king the Then .this secret
,great

made him ruler over all the province of Babylon and chief of the prefects over all the wise men of Babylon. [49] Then Daniel asked of the king, and he set Shadrach, Meshach and Abednego over the affairs of the province of Babylon, But Daniel (sat) in the gate of the king.

שַׂגִּיאָן יְהַב־לֵהּ וְהַשְׁלְטֵהּ עַל כָּל־מְדִינַת בָּבֶל וְרַב־סִגְנִין

and Chief-Prefect Babylon of province the all over made he And ruler him to .him gave many

עַל כָּל־חַכִּימֵי בָּבֶל׃ וְדָנִיֵּאל בְּעָא מִן־מַלְכָּא וּמַנִּי עַל

49 over he and appointed the ,king of asked Then Daniel .Babylon wise the of men all over

עֲבִידְתָּא דִּי מְדִינַת בָּבֶל לְשַׁדְרַךְ מֵישַׁךְ וַעֲבֵד נְגוֹ וְדָנִיֵּאל

Daniel But (sat) and .Abednego Meshach ,Shadrach ,Babylon the of province of the business

בִּתְרַע מַלְכָּא׃

the .king the in of gate

CAP. III ג

CHAPTER 3

CHAPTER 3

[1] Nebuchadnezzar the king made an image of gold, whose height (was) sixty cubits; its breadth, six cubits. He set it up in the plain of Dura, in the province of Babylon. [2] Then Nebuchadnezzar the king sent to gather together the satraps, the prefects, the governors, the counselors, the treasurers, the judges, the justices; and all the officials of the provinces were gathered together to the dedication of the image that Nebuchadnezzar the king had set up. [3] Then were gathered the satraps, the prefects, the governors, the counselors, the treasurers, the judges, the justices, and all the officials of the provinces were gathered together to the dedication of the image that Nebuchadnezzar the king had set up. And they stood before the image that Nebuchadnezzar had set up. [4] Then the herald cried with strength, To you it is commanded, O peoples, nations and languages; [5] at the time you hear the sound of the horn, the pipe, zither, the lyre, the harp, bagpipes, and all kinds of music, you shall fall down and worship the golden image that Nebuchadnezzar

1 נְבוּכַדְנֶצַּר מַלְכָּא עֲבַד צְלֵם דִּי־דְהַב רוּמֵהּ אַמִּין שִׁתִּין

,sixty (was) cubits its height ,gold of an image made king the Nebuchadnezzar

פְּתָיֵהּ אַמִּין שִׁת אֲקִימֵהּ בְּבִקְעַת דּוּרָא בִּמְדִינַת בָּבֶל׃

.Babylon the in of province ,Dura the in of plain set He up it .six cubits its breadth

2 וּנְבוּכַדְנֶצַּר מַלְכָּא שְׁלַח לְמִכְנַשׁ ׀ לַאֲחַשְׁדַּרְפְּנַיָּא סִגְנַיָּא

the ,prefects the ,satraps gather to together sent the king Nebuchadnezzar

וּפַחֲוָתָא אֲדַרְגָּזְרַיָּא גְדָבְרַיָּא דְּתָבְרַיָּא תִּפְתָּיֵא וְכֹל שִׁלְטֹנֵי

officials the and of all the ,magistrates the ,judges the ,treasurers the ,counselors the and ;governors

מְדִינָתָא לְמֵתֵא לַחֲנֻכַּת צַלְמָא דִּי הֲקֵים נְבוּכַדְנֶצַּר

Nebuchadnezzar set had up that the image the to of dedication come to the ,provinces

3 מַלְכָּא׃ בֵּאדַיִן מִתְכַּנְּשִׁין אֲחַשְׁדַּרְפְּנַיָּא סִגְנַיָּא וּפַחֲוָתָא

the governors the ,prefects the ,satraps were gathered Then .king the

אֲדַרְגָּזְרַיָּא גְדָבְרַיָּא דְּתָבְרַיָּא תִּפְתָּיֵא וְכֹל שִׁלְטֹנֵי מְדִינָתָא

the provinces of officials and all the ,magistrates the ,judges the ,treasurers the ,counselors

לַחֲנֻכַּת צַלְמָא דִּי הֲקֵים נְבוּכַדְנֶצַּר מַלְכָּא וְקָאְמִין לָקֳבֵל

before they and stood ;king the Nebuchadnezzar had up set that the image's to dedi- cation

4 צַלְמָא דִּי הֲקֵים נְבוּכַדְנֶצַּר׃ וְכָרוֹזָא קָרֵא בְחָיִל לְכוֹן

To you with ,strength shouted the Then herald .Nebuchadnezzar had up set that the image

5 אָמְרִין עַמְמַיָּא אֻמַּיָּא וְלִשָּׁנַיָּא׃ בְּעִדָּנָא דִּי־תִשְׁמְעוּן קָל ׀

sound- ing hear you that the at time and ;languages nations O ,peoples is it com- manded

קַרְנָא מַשְׁרוֹקִיתָא קַיתְרֹס סַבְּכָא פְסַנְתֵּרִין סוּמְפֹּנְיָה

,bagpipe ,harp the ,lyre ,zither ,pipe the the is ,horn

וְכֹל זְנֵי זְמָרָא תִּפְּלוּן וְתִסְגְּדוּן לְצֶלֶם דַּהֲבָא דִּי הֲקֵים

set has up that golden the image worship and shall you down fall ,music kinds of and all

the king has set up. [6] And whoever does not fall down and worship, at the moment they will be thrown into the middle of a burning fiery furnace. [7] Thereupon at that time, when all the peoples heard the sound of the horn, the pipe, zither, the lyre, harp, and all kinds of music, all the peoples, the nations and the languages fell down, worshiping the golden image that Nebuchadnezzar the king had set up.

[8] Therefore at that time men, Chaldeans, came near and accused the Jews. [9] They spoke and said to King Nebuchadnezzar, O king, live forever. [10] You, O king, have made a decree that every man who shall hear the sound of the horn, the pipe, zither, the lyre, harp and the bagpipe, and all kinds of music, shall fall down and worship the golden image. [11] And whoever does not fall down and worship, he should be thrown into the middle of a burning fiery furnace. [12] There are men, Jews, whom you have set over the business of the province of Babylon: Shadrach, Meshach and Abednego. These men, O king, do not pay attention to you. They do not serve your gods or worship the golden image which you have set up.

[13] Then Nebuchadnezzar in anger and wrath commanded to bring Shadrach, Meshach, and Abednego. Then they brought these men before the king. [14] Nebuchadnezzar

6 נְבוּכַדְנֶצַּר מַלְכָּא׃ וּמַן־דִּי־לָא יִפֵּל וְיִסְגֻּד בַּהּ־שַׁעֲתָא
moment At and does not who- And .king the Nebuchadnezzar
that ,worship down fall ever

7 יִתְרְמֵא לְגוֹא־אַתּוּן נוּרָא יָקִדְתָּא׃ כָּל־קֳבֵל דְּנָה בֵּהּ
at ,Thereupon .burning fire a amidst will be
that of furnace cast

זִמְנָא כְּדִי שָׁמְעִין כָּל־עַמְמַיָּא קָל קַרְנָא מַשְׁרוֹקִיתָא
pipe the the the the all heard when ,time
horn of sound peoples

קִיתָרֹס שַׂבְּכָא פְּסַנְטֵרִין וְכֹל זְנֵי זְמָרָא נָפְלִין כָּל־עַמְמַיָּא
the all fell ,music kinds and ,harp the ,zither
,peoples down of all ,lyre

אֻמַיָּא וְלִשָּׁנַיָּא סָגְדִין לְצֶלֶם דַּהֲבָא דִּי הֲקֵים נְבוּכַדְנֶצַּר
Nebuchad- had that golden the worshiping the and the
nezzar up set image languages ,nations

8 מַלְכָּא׃ כָּל־קֳבֵל דְּנָה בֵּהּ־זִמְנָא קְרִבוּ גֻּבְרִין כַּשְׂדָּאִין
,Chaldeans ,men came time at ,Thereupon the
near that .king

9 וַאֲכַלוּ קַרְצֵיהוֹן דִּי יְהוּדָיֵא׃ עֲנוֹ וְאָמְרִין לִנְבוּכַדְנֶצַּר
Nebuchad- to said and They .Jews the of bits the and
nezzar answered chewed

10 מַלְכָּא מַלְכָּא לְעָלְמִין חֱיִי׃ אַנְתָּה מַלְכָּא שָׂמְתָּ טְּעֵם
a have ,king O ,You !live forever ,king O the
decree made ,King

דִּי־כָל־אֱנָשׁ דִּי יִשְׁמַע קָל קַרְנָא מַשְׁרֹקִיתָא קַיתְרֹס
zither ,pipe the the the shall who man every that
,horn of sound hear

שַׂבְּכָא פְּסַנְתֵּרִין וְסִיפֹּנְיָא וְכֹל זְנֵי זְמָרָא יִפֵּל וְיִסְגֻּד לְצֶלֶם
the and fall shall ,music kinds and the and ,harp ,lyre the
image worship down of all ,bagpipe

11 דַּהֲבָא׃ וּמַן־דִּי־לָא יִפֵּל וְיִסְגֻּד יִתְרְמֵא לְגוֹא־אַתּוּן נוּרָא
fire a amidst be shall he and fall does not who- And .golden
of furnace thrown ,worship down ever

12 יָקִדְתָּא׃ אִיתַי גֻּבְרִין יְהוּדָאיִן דִּי־מַנִּיתָ יָתְהוֹן עַל־עֲבִידַת
the over them you whom ,Jewish ,men There .burning
of business set have are

מְדִינַת בָּבֶל שַׁדְרַךְ מֵישַׁךְ וַעֲבֵד נְגוֹ גֻּבְרַיָּא אִלֵּךְ לָא־
not Those men and Meshach ,Shadrach :Babylon pro- the
.Abednego of vince

שָׂמוּ עֲלָךְ מַלְכָּא טְעֵם לֵאלָהָךְ לָא פָלְחִין וּלְצֶלֶם
the and do they not your ;attention ,king O ,you to do
image ,serve gods pay

13 דַּהֲבָא דִּי הֲקֵימְתָּ לָא סָגְדִין׃ בֵּאדַיִן נְבוּכַדְנֶצַּר
,Nebuchadnezzar Then do they not have you which golden
.worship up set

בִּרְגַז וַחֲמָא אֲמַר לְהַיְתָיָה לְשַׁדְרַךְ מֵישַׁךְ וַעֲבֵד נְגוֹ בֵּאדַיִן
Then .Abednego ,Meshach ,Shadrach bring to com- and in
manded wrath anger

14 גֻּבְרַיָּא אִלֵּךְ הֵיתָיוּ קֳדָם מַלְכָּא׃ עָנֵה נְבוּכַדְנֶצַּר וְאָמַר
and Nebuchadnezzar an- .king the before they those men
swered brought

spoke and said to them, (Is it) true, O Shadrach, Meshach and Abednego? Do you not serve my gods nor worship the golden image which I have set up? [15] Now if you are ready, at the time you hear the sound of the horn, the pipe, zither, the lyre, harp and bagpipe, and all kinds of music, fall down and worship the image which I have made. But if you do not worship, in that moment you shall be thrown into the middle of a burning fiery furnace. And who (is) that god who shall deliver you out of my hand? [16] Shadrach, Meshach and Abednego answered and said to the king, O Nebuchadnezzar, we have no need to answer you on this matter. [17] Lo, if it is (so), our God whom we serve is able to deliver us from the burning fiery furnace, then He will deliver (us) out of your hand, O king. [18] And, if not, let it be known to you, O king, that we will not serve your gods or worship the golden image which you have set up.

[19] Then Nebuchadnezzar was filled with wrath, and the form of his face was changed against Shadrach, Meshach and Abednego. He spoke and commanded to heat the furnace seven times more than it was usual to heat it. [20] And he commanded mighty men of valor, who (were) in his army, to tie up Shadrach, Meshach and Abednego, to throw (them) into the burning fiery furnace. [21] Then these men were tied up in their

לְהוֹן הַצְדָּא שַׁדְרַךְ מֵישַׁךְ וַעֲבֵד נְגוֹ לֵאלָהַי לָא אִיתֵיכוֹן
are you not gods my and Abednego ,Meshach O ,Shadrach it Is ,true to ,them

15 פָּלְחִין וּלְצֶלֶם דַּהֲבָא דִּי הֲקֵימֶת לָא־סָגְדִין׃ כְּעַן הֵן
if Now are you not ?worshiping have I set up which golden the and image ,serving

אִיתֵיכוֹן עֲתִידִין דִּי בְעִדָּנָא דִּי־תִשְׁמְעוּן קָל קַרְנָא
,horn the the of sound hear you that the at time ,ready are you

מַשְׁרוֹקִיתָא קִיתָרֹס שַׂבְּכָא פְּסַנְתֵּרִין וְסוּמְפֹּנְיָה וְכֹל ׀ זְנֵי
kinds of and all and ,bagpipe ,harp ,lyre the ,zither pipe the

זְמָרָא תִּפְּלוּן וְתִסְגְּדוּן לְצַלְמָא דִּי־עַבְדֵת וְהֵן לָא תִסְגְּדוּן
do you ,worship not But if have I .made which the image and worship fall down ,music

בַּהּ־שַׁעֲתָה תִתְרְמוֹן לְגוֹא־אַתּוּן נוּרָא יָקִדְתָּא וּמַן־הוּא
(is) that And who .burning fire a of furnace amidst shall you cast be moment in that

16 אֱלָהּ דִּי־יְשֵׁיזְבִנְכוֹן מִן־יְדָי׃ עֲנוֹ שַׁדְרַךְ מֵישַׁךְ וַעֲבֵד נְגוֹ
and Abednego Meshach ,Shadrach answered my ?hand out of deliver shall you who god

וְאָמְרִין לְמַלְכָּא נְבוּכַדְנֶצַּר לָא־חַשְׁחִין אֲנַחְנָה עַל־דְּנָה
this ,matter on we (have) need not Nebuchad- ,nezzar O the to ,king said and

17 פִּתְגָם לַהֲתָבוּתָךְ׃ הֵן אִיתַי אֱלָהַנָא דִּי־אֲנַחְנָא פָלְחִין
serve we whom God our is it (that) If return to .you to word a

יָכִל לְשֵׁיזָבוּתַנָא מִן־אַתּוּן נוּרָא יָקִדְתָּא וּמִן־יְדָךְ מַלְכָּא
,king O from then ,hand your burning fire the from of furnace us deliver to is able

18 יְשֵׁיזִב׃ וְהֵן לָא יְדִיעַ לֶהֱוֵא־לָךְ מַלְכָּא דִּי לֵאלָהָיךְ לָא־
not gods your that ,king O to ,you be it let known ,not But if will He (us) deliver

אִיתַנָא פָלְחִין וּלְצֶלֶם דַּהֲבָא דִּי הֲקֵימְתָּ לָא נִסְגֻּד׃
will we .worship not have you up set which golden the and image ,serve will we

19 בֵּאדַיִן נְבוּכַדְנֶצַּר הִתְמְלִי חֱמָא וּצְלֵם אַנְפּוֹהִי
face his the and of expression ,wrath was filled with Nebuchadnezzar Then

אֶשְׁתַּנִּו עַל־שַׁדְרַךְ מֵישַׁךְ וַעֲבֵד נְגוֹ עָנֵה וְאָמַר לְמֵזֵא
heat to and directed He answered and .Abednego Meshach ,Shadrach against was changed

20 לְאַתּוּנָא חַד־שִׁבְעָה עַל דִּי חֲזֵה לְמֵזְיֵהּ׃ וּלְגֻבְרִין גִּבָּרֵי־
mighty men of And heat to .it was it usual than more seven times the furnace

חַיִל דִּי בְחַיְלֵהּ אֲמַר לְכַפָּתָה לְשַׁדְרַךְ מֵישַׁךְ וַעֲבֵד נְגוֹ
and Abednego Meshach ,Shadrach bind to he ordered his in ,army who (were) valor

21 לְמִרְמֵא לְאַתּוּן נוּרָא יָקִדְתָּא׃ בֵּאדַיִן גֻּבְרַיָּא אִלֵּךְ כְּפִתוּ
were bound those men Then .burning fire the into of furnace throw to (them)

tunics, their mantles and their turbans, and their (other) clothes, and were thrown into the middle of the burning fiery furnace. [22] Thereupon, because the king's commandment was urgent, and the furnace exceedingly hot, the flame of the fire killed those men who took up Shadrach, Meshach and Abednego. [23] And these three men, Shadrach, Meshach and Abednego, fell down bound into the middle of the burning fiery furnace. [24] Then Nebuchadnezzar the king was amazed. And he rose up in haste; he spoke and said to his royal officials, Did we not throw three men bound into the middle of the fire? They replied, and said to the king, True, O king. [25] He answered and said, Lo, I see four men loose, walking in the middle of the fire, and there is not an injury among them. And the form of the fourth is like a son of (the) gods. [26] Then Nebuchadnezzar came near to the door of the burning fiery furnace; he answered and said, Shadrach, Meshach and Abednego, servants of the most high God, come forth and come (here). Then Shadrach, Meshach and Abednego came out of the middle of the fire.

[27] And the satraps, prefects, the governors, and the king's officials, gathered together, (and) saw these men (on whose) bodies the fire had no power and the hair of their head was not scorched, nor were their mantles changed, nor had the smell of fire clung on

בְּסַרְבָּלֵיהוֹן פַּטְּשֵׁיהוֹן וְכַרְבְּלָתְהוֹן וּלְבֻשֵׁיהוֹן וּרְמִיו
were and thrown | their and clothes (other), | their and turbans, | their tunics | their in mantles,

22 לְגוֹא־אַתּוּן נוּרָא יָקִדְתָּא׃ כָּל־קֳבֵל דְּנָה מִן־דִּי מִלַּת
word | because | ,Thereupon | .burning | fire | the of furnace | amidst

מַלְכָּא מַחְצְפָה וְאַתּוּנָא אֵזֵה יַתִּירָה גֻּבְרַיָּא אִלֵּךְ דִּי
who | those | men | ,exceedingly | was heated | the and furnace | ,urgent was | the king's

הַסִּקוּ לְשַׁדְרַךְ מֵישַׁךְ וַעֲבֵד נְגוֹ קַטִּל הִמּוֹן שְׁבִיבָא דִּי
of | flame the | them | killed | and Abednego | Meshach | ,Shadrach | up took

23 נוּרָא׃ וְגֻבְרַיָּא אִלֵּךְ תְּלָתֵּהוֹן שַׁדְרַךְ מֵישַׁךְ וַעֲבֵד נְגוֹ
and ,Abednego | Meshach | ,Shadrach | three the ,them of | ,those | men But | .fire the

24 נְפַלוּ לְגוֹא־אַתּוּן־נוּרָא יָקִדְתָּא מְכַפְּתִין׃ אֱדַיִן
Then | .bound | burning | fire | the of furnace | amidst | fell down

נְבוּכַדְנֶצַּר מַלְכָּא תְּוַהּ וְקָם בְּהִתְבְּהָלָה עָנֵה וְאָמַר
said and | he answered | ;haste in | he and up rose | was ;amazed | king the | Nebuchad- nezzar

לְהַדָּבְרוֹהִי הֲלָא גֻבְרִין תְּלָתָה רְמֵינָא לְגוֹא־נוּרָא מְכַפְּתִין
?bound | the fire | the into of midst | we did throw | three | men | Not | royal his to ,officials

25 עָנַיִן וְאָמְרִין לְמַלְכָּא יַצִּיבָא מַלְכָּא׃ עָנֵה וְאָמַר הָא־אֲנָה
I | ,Behold | ,said and | He answered | .king O | ,Certainly | the to ,king | said and | They answered

חָזֵה גֻּבְרִין אַרְבְּעָה שְׁרַיִן מַהְלְכִין בְּגוֹא־נוּרָא וַחֲבָל לָא־
not | and injury | the ,fire | the in of midst | walking | loose | four | men | see

אִיתַי בְּהוֹן וְרֵוֵהּ דִּי רְבִיעָאָה דָּמֵה לְבַר־אֱלָהִין׃
.gods (the) | a of son | like is | the fourth | of | the and look | among ;them | there is

26 בֵּאדַיִן קְרֵב נְבוּכַדְנֶצַּר לִתְרַע אַתּוּן נוּרָא יָקִדְתָּא עָנֵה
an- swered | he ;burning | fire | fur- of nace | the | the to of door | Nebuchadnezzar | drew near | Then

וְאָמַר שַׁדְרַךְ מֵישַׁךְ וַעֲבֵד־נְגוֹ עַבְדוֹהִי דִּי־אֱלָהָא עִלָּאָה
most ,high | God the | of | servants | and ,Abednego | ,Meshach | ,Shadrach | and ,said

פֻּקוּ וֶאֱתוֹ בֵּאדַיִן נָפְקִין שַׁדְרַךְ מֵישַׁךְ וַעֲבֵד נְגוֹ מִן־גּוֹא
from amidst | and Abednego | Meshach | ,Shadrach | came out | Then | and .come | come out

27 נוּרָא׃ וּמִתְכַּנְּשִׁין אֲחַשְׁדַּרְפְּנַיָּא סִגְנַיָּא וּפַחֲוָתָא וְהַדָּבְרֵי
royal and officials | the ,governors | the ,prefects | the ,satraps | Then gathered | the .fire

מַלְכָּא חָזַיִן לְגֻבְרַיָּא אִלֵּךְ דִּי לָא־שְׁלֵט נוּרָא בְּגֶשְׁמְהוֹן
their over ,body | the fire | had power | not | those | men | saw | the ,king's

וּשְׂעַר רֵאשְׁהוֹן לָא הִתְחָרַךְ וְסַרְבָּלֵיהוֹן לָא שְׁנוֹ וְרֵיחַ
the and of smell | were ,changed | not | their and mantles | was ,scorched | not | their head | the and of hair

them. [28] Nebuchadnezzar spoke and said, Blessed (be) the God of Shadrach, Meshach and Abednego who has sent His Angel and has delivered His servants who trusted in Him, and have changed the king's words and have given their bodies that they might not serve nor worship any god except their own God. [29] Therefore I make a decree, that every people, nation and language who speak anything amiss about the God of Shadrach, Meshach and Abednego, (from their) limbs they will be taken, and their houses shall be made an outhouse. Because there is no other God who can deliver like this. [30] Then the king made prosper Shadrach, Meshach and Abednego in the province of Babylon.

CHAPTER 4

[1] Nebuchadnezzar the king, to all peoples, nations and the languages that live in all the earth: Peace be multiplied to you. [2] It seemed good before me to declare the signs and wonders that the most high God has done with me. [3] How great (are) His signs! And how mighty (are) His wonders? His kingdom (is) an everlasting kingdom, and His rule (is) from generation to generation.

[4] I, Nebuchadnezzar, was at ease in my house and flourishing in my palace. [5] I saw a dream and it terrified me, and (the) thoughts on my bed and the visions of my head troubled

28 נוּר לָא עֲדָת בְּהוֹן׃ עָנֵה נְבוּכַדְנֶצַּר וְאָמַר בְּרִיךְ אֱלָהֲהוֹן
God the Blessed be ,said and Nebuchad- nezzar answered on ,them did cling not fire

דִּי־שַׁדְרַךְ מֵישַׁךְ וַעֲבֵד נְגוֹ דִּי־שְׁלַח מַלְאֲכֵהּ וְשֵׁיזִב
has and delivered His angel has sent who and ,Abednego Meshach ,Shadrach of

לְעַבְדוֹהִי דִּי הִתְרְחִצוּ עֲלוֹהִי וּמִלַּת מַלְכָּא שַׁנִּיו וִיהַבוּ
have and given have changed the king's and word ,Him in trusted who His servants

גֶשְׁמֵיהוֹן דִּי לָא־יִפְלְחוּן וְלָא־יִסְגְּדוּן לְכָל־אֱלָהּ לָהֵן
except god any might they worship and not they serve might not that their bodies

29 לֵאלָהֲהוֹן׃ וּמִנִּי שִׂים טְעֵם דִּי כָל־עַם אֻמָּה וְלִשָּׁן דִּי־
who and language nation peo- ,ple every that a ,decree is given by And me own their .God

יֵאמַר שָׁלָה עַל־אֱלָהֲהוֹן דִּי־שַׁדְרַךְ מֵישַׁךְ וַעֲבֵד נְגוֹא
and ,Abednego Meshach ,Shadrach of the God about anything amiss speaks .told I

הַדָּמִין יִתְעֲבֵד וּבַיְתֵהּ נְוָלִי יִשְׁתַּוֵּה כָּל־קֳבֵל דִּי לָא אִיתַי
there is not since be will ,made out- an house his and house will he ,taken be (from) limbs

30 אֱלָהּ אָחֳרָן דִּי־יִכֻּל לְהַצָּלָה כִּדְנָה׃ בֵּאדַיִן מַלְכָּא
king the Then .this like deliver to able is who another God

הַצְלַח לְשַׁדְרַךְ מֵישַׁךְ וַעֲבֵד נְגוֹ בִּמְדִינַת בָּבֶל׃
.Babylon the in of province and Abednego Meshach ,Shadrach made prosper

31 נְבוּכַדְנֶצַּר מַלְכָּא לְכָל־עַמְמַיָּא אֻמַיָּא וְלִשָּׁנַיָּא דִּי־דָארִין
dwell that the and languages the nations the ,peoples all to ,king the Nebuchad- nezzar

32 בְּכָל־אַרְעָא שְׁלָמְכוֹן יִשְׂגֵּא׃ אָתַיָּא וְתִמְהַיָּא דִּי עֲבַד עִמִּי
with me has done that the and wonders The signs be .increased Your peace the :earth in all

33 אֱלָהָא עִלָּיאָ שְׁפַר קָדָמַי לְהַחֲוָיָה׃ אָתוֹהִי כְּמָה רַבְרְבִין
great !(are) How His signs .declare to before seemed it me good most high the God

וְתִמְהוֹהִי כְּמָה תַקִּיפִין מַלְכוּתֵהּ מַלְכוּת עָלַם וְשָׁלְטָנֵהּ
His and (is) dominion ever- ,lashing an kingdom king- His (is) dom mighty !(are) how His And wonders

עִם־דָּר וְדָר׃
to .generation gen- eration from

CAP. IV ד

CHAPTER 4

1
2 אֲנָה נְבוּכַדְנֶצַּר שְׁלֵה הֲוֵית בְּבֵיתִי וְרַעְנַן בְּהֵיכְלִי׃ חֵלֶם
a dream .palace my in flourish- ing my in ,house was ease at Nebuchadnezzar ,I

חֲזֵית וִידַחֲלִנַּנִי וְהַרְהֹרִין עַל־מִשְׁכְּבִי וְחֶזְוֵי רֵאשִׁי יְבַהֲלֻנַּנִי׃
troubled .me my head the and of visions bed my on (the) and conceptions it and ,me terrified saw I

me. [6] So I made a decree to bring in all the wise men of Babylon before me, that they might make known to me the meaning of the dream. [7] Then the horoscopists, the conjurers, the Chaldeans, and the fortune-tellers came in. And I told the dream before them, but they did not make the meaning of it known to me.

[8] But at the last Daniel came in before me, whose name (was) Belteshazzar, according to the name of my god, and in whom (is) the spirit of the holy gods. And I told the dream before him: [9] O Belteshazzar, master of the horoscopists, because I know that the spirit of the holy gods (is) in you, and no secret troubles you, tell me the visions of my dream that I have seen, and its meaning. [10] As to the visions of my head on my bed: I was looking, and behold, a tree in the middle of the earth. And its height (was) great. [11] The tree became great and strong, and its height reached to the sky; and its appearance to the end of all the earth. [12] The leaves of it (were) beautiful, and its fruit plentiful, and food for all (was) in it. The animals of the field sought shade under it, and the birds of the sky lived in its boughs, and all flesh was fed by it. [13] I was looking in the visions of my head on my bed: and, behold, a watcher, even a holy one, came down from Heaven. [14] He cried aloud and said this, Cut down the tree and cut off its branches. Shake off its leaves and scatter its fruit. Let the animals flee from under it and the birds (leave) its branches. [15] But leave the stump of its roots in the earth, even with a fetter of iron and bronze, in the grass of the field. And let it be wet with the dew of the heavens, and

3 וּמִנִּי שִׂים טְעֵם לְהַנְעָלָה קֳדָמַי לְכֹל חַכִּימֵי בָבֶל דִּי־פְשַׁר

mean- that Babylon wise the all before bring to a was by So
ing of men me in decree made me

4 חֶלְמָא יְהוֹדְעֻנַּנִי׃ בֵּאדַיִן עָלִּלִין חַרְטֻמַיָּא אָשְׁפַיָּא כַּשְׂדָּיֵא

the the horo- the came Then might they the
,Chaldeans ,conjurers ,scopists in .me to reveal dream's

וְגָזְרַיָּא וְחֶלְמָא אָמַר אֲנָה קֳדָמֵיהוֹן וּפִשְׁרֵהּ לָא־מְהוֹדְעִין

did they not its but before I told the and the and
known make meaning :them dream ,gazers

5 לִי׃ וְעַד אָחֳרֵין עַל קָדָמַי דָּנִיֵּאל דִּי־שְׁמֵהּ בֵּלְטְשַׁאצַּר

,Belteshazzar name whose ,Daniel before came last But to
(was) me in at .me

כְּשֻׁם אֱלָהִי וְדִי רוּחַ־אֱלָהִין קַדִּישִׁין בֵּהּ וְחֶלְמָא קָדָמוֹהִי

him before the and in holy the the and and my by
dream ;him (is) gods of spirit ,god's name

6 אַמְרֵת׃ בֵּלְטְשַׁאצַּר רַב חַרְטֻמַיָּא דִּי | אֲנָה יִדְעֵת דִּי רוּחַ

the that knew I because horo- the chief ,Belteshazzar O :hid I
of spirit ,scopists of

אֱלָהִין קַדִּישִׁין בָּךְ וְכָל־רָז לָא־אָנֵס לָךְ חֶזְוֵי חֶלְמִי דִי־

that my the .you does not secret any in holy the
dream of visions baffle ,you (is) gods

7 חֲזֵית וּפִשְׁרֵהּ אֱמַר׃ וְחֶזְוֵי רֵאשִׁי עַל־מִשְׁכְּבִי חָזֵה הֲוֵית

,was I looking ,bed my on my the to As tell its and have I
head of visions .(me) meaning seen

8 וַאֲלוּ אִילָן בְּגוֹא אַרְעָא וְרוּמֵהּ שַׂגִּיא׃ רְבָה אִילָנָא וּתְקִף

and The became (was) its and the the in a and
,strong tree great .great height ,earth of middle tree ,behold

9 וְרוּמֵהּ יִמְטֵא לִשְׁמַיָּא וַחֲזוֹתֵהּ לְסוֹף כָּל־אַרְעָא׃ עָפְיֵהּ

Its the all the to its and the to reached its and
foliage .earth of end appearance ,sky height

שַׁפִּיר וְאִנְבֵּהּ שַׂגִּיא וּמָזוֹן לְכֹלָּא־בֵהּ תְּחֹתוֹהִי תַּטְלֵל |

sought it under in all For and ,abundant its and (was)
shade .it (was) .food fruit ,lovely

חֵיוַת בָּרָא וּבְעַנְפוֹהִי יְדוּרָן צִפֲּרֵי שְׁמַיָּא וּמִנֵּהּ יִתְּזִין כָּל־

all was from and the birds the dwelt its in and the ani- The
fed it ,sky of branches ,field of mals

10 בִּשְׂרָא׃ חָזֵה הֲוֵית בְּחֶזְוֵי רֵאשִׁי עַל־מִשְׁכְּבִי וַאֲלוּ עִיר

a ,lo and ,bed my on my the in was I looking .flesh
,watcher head of visions

11 וְקַדִּישׁ מִן־שְׁמַיָּא נָחִת׃ קָרֵא בְחַיִל וְכֵן אָמַר גֹּדּוּ אִילָנָא

the Cut he and ,aloud He came Heaven from a even
tree down ,said thus cried .down one holy

וְקַצִּצוּ עַנְפוֹהִי אַתַּרוּ עָפְיֵהּ וּבַדַּרוּ אִנְבֵּהּ תְּנֻד חֵיוְתָא מִן־

from the Let its and its shake its cut and
animals flee .fruit scatter ,foliage off ,branches off

12 תְּחֹתוֹהִי וְצִפְּרַיָּא מִן־עַנְפוֹהִי׃ בְּרַם עִקַּר שָׁרְשׁוֹהִי בְּאַרְעָא

the in its the But its from the and ,it under
earth roots of stump .branches birds

שְׁבֻקוּ וּבֶאֱסוּר דִּי־פַרְזֶל וּנְחָשׁ בְּדִתְאָא דִּי בָרָא וּבְטַל

with and the of the in and iron of with even ,leave
of dew the ,field grass ,bronze fetter a

his portion (be) with the animals in the grass of the earth. [16] Let his heart be changed from man's, and let the heart of an animal be given to him. And let seven times pass over him. [17] This matter (is) by the decree of the watchers, and the command by the word of the holy ones — so that the living may know that the most High rules in the kingdom of men, and gives it to whomever He will; and sets up over it the lowest of men. [18] I, King Nebuchadnezzar, have seen this dream. Now you, O Belteshazzar, declare its meaning, since all the wise men of my kingdom are not able to reveal the meaning to me. But you (are) able, for the spirit of the holy gods (is) in you.

[19] Then Daniel, whose name (was) Belteshazzar, was stunned for one hour, and his thoughts troubled him. The king spoke and said, Belteshazzar, do not let the dream or the meaning of it trouble you. Belteshazzar answered and said, My lord, the dream (is) to those who hate you and its meaning (is) to your foes. [20] The tree that you saw, which became great and strong, whose height reached to the heavens, and the sight of it to all the earth. [21] And its leaves (were) beautiful and its fruit plentiful, and in it (was) food for all; under which the animals of the field lived, and in its branches the birds of the sky had their home; [22] it (is) you, O king, for you have become great and strong. For your greatness has grown and reaches to the heavens, and your rule to the end of the earth.

13 שְׁמַיָּא יִצְטַבַּע וְעִם־חֵיוְתָא חֲלָקֵהּ בַּעֲשַׂב אַרְעָא׃ לִבְבֵהּ
his the the in (be let) the and him let the
heart .earth of grass lot his animals with ,wet be heavens

מִן־אֲנָשָׁא יְשַׁנּוֹן וּלְבַב חֵיוָא יִתְיְהִב לֵהּ וְשִׁבְעָה עִדָּנִין
times seven And to be let the the and be Let man's the from
.him given beast of heart ,changed (heart)

14 יַחְלְפוּן עֲלוֹהִי׃ בִּגְזֵרַת עִירִין פִּתְגָמָא וּמֵאמַר קַדִּישִׁין
holy the (the) and the the the By .him over pass let
(is) ones of command ,matter (is) watchers of decree

שְׁאֵלְתָא עַד־דִּבְרַת דִּי־יִנְדְּעוּן חַיַּיָּא דִּי־שַׁלִּיט עִלָּיָא
Most the (is) that the may that so ,affair the
High Master living know

בְּמַלְכוּת אֲנָשָׁא וּלְמַן־דִּי יִצְבֵּא יִתְּנִנַּהּ וּשְׁפַל אֲנָשִׁים יְקִים
sets He men the and gives He He to and ;men king- the in
up of lowliest ,it ,wishes whomever of dom

15 עֲלַיהּ׃ דְּנָה חֶלְמָא חֲזֵית אֲנָה מַלְכָּא נְבוּכַדְנֶצַּר וְאַנְתָּה
Now .Nebuchadnezzar King ,I have the This .it over
you seen dream (is)

בֵּלְטְשַׁאצַּר פִּשְׁרֵא ׀ אֱמַר כָּל־קֳבֵל דִּי ׀ כָּל־חַכִּימֵי
wise the all much as in ,tell its ,Belteshazzar O
of men as meaning

מַלְכוּתִי לָא־יָכְלִין פִּשְׁרָא לְהוֹדָעוּתַנִי וְאַנְתָּה כָּהֵל דִּי
for are you But known make to the are not my
,able .me to meaning able kingdom

16 רוּחַ־אֱלָהִין קַדִּישִׁין בָּךְ׃ אֱדַיִן דָּנִיֵּאל דִּי־שְׁמֵהּ בֵּלְטְשַׁאצַּר
,Belteshazzar name whose ,Daniel Then in holy the the
(was) .you (is) gods of spirit

אֶשְׁתּוֹמַם כְּשָׁעָה חֲדָה וְרַעְיֹנֹהִי יְבַהֲלֻנֵּהּ עָנֵה מַלְכָּא וְאָמַר
and The answered troubled his and ,a for was
,said king .him thoughts moment stunned

בֵּלְטְשַׁאצַּר חֶלְמָא וּפִשְׁרֵא אַל־יְבַהֲלָךְ עָנֵה בֵלְטְשַׁאצַּר
Belteshazzar answered let do not its and the ,Belteshazzar
.you trouble ;meaning dream

17 וְאָמַר מָרִאי חֶלְמָא לְשָׂנְאָךְ וּפִשְׁרֵהּ לְעָרָךְ׃ אִילָנָא
tree The your to its and your to the My ,said and
.adversaries meaning haters (be) dream ,lord

דִּי חֲזַיְתָ דִּי רְבָה וּתְקִף וְרוּמֵהּ יִמְטֵא לִשְׁמַיָּא וַחֲזוֹתֵהּ
its and the to reached whose and became which you that
appearance sky height ,strong great ,saw

18 לְכָל־אַרְעָא׃ וְעָפְיֵהּ שַׁפִּיר וְאִנְבֵּהּ שַׂגִּיא וּמָזוֹן לְכֹלָּא־
all for and (was) its and (was) its And the all to
(was) food ,abundant fruit ,lovely foliage .earth

בֵהּ תְּחֹתוֹהִי תְּדוּר חֵיוַת בָּרָא וּבְעַנְפוֹהִי יִשְׁכְּנָן צִפְּרֵי
the dwelt its in and the the dwelled under ;it in
of birds branches ,field of animals which

19 שְׁמַיָּא׃ אַנְתָּה־הוּא מַלְכָּא דִּי רְבַית וּתְקֵפְתְּ וּרְבוּתָךְ
your for and have you for ,king O it You .sky the
greatness ,strong great became ,(is)

20 רְבָת וּמְטָת לִשְׁמַיָּא וְשָׁלְטָנָךְ לְסוֹף אַרְעָא׃ וְדִי חֲזָא
saw And the the to your and the to and has
as .earth of end dominion ,sky reached grown

[23] And as the king saw a watcher and a holy one coming down from Heaven, and saying, Cut the tree down and destroy it. Yet leave the stump of its roots in the earth, even with a fetter of iron and bronze in the grass of the field. And let him be wet with the dew of the heavens and his portion (be) with the animals of the field, until seven times pass over him; [24] this (is) the meaning, O king, and this the decree of the Most High, which has come on my lord the king. [25] And you shall be driven from men, and your dwelling shall be with the animals of the field, and they shall make you eat grass like oxen. And they shall wet you with the dew of the heavens, and seven times shall pass over you, until you have realized that the Most High rules in the kingdom of men, and that He gives it to whomever He desires. [26] And they that commanded to leave the stump of the tree roots: your kingdom (shall be) sure to you after you have realized that Heaven rules. [27] Therefore, O king, let my advice be pleasing to you, and break off your sins by righteousness, and your iniquities by showing mercy to the poor; if there will be duration to your prosperity.

[28] All this came on the king, Nebuchadnezzar. [29] At the end of twelve months he walked in the palace of the kingdom of Babylon. [30] The king spoke and said, (Is) this not great Babylon that I have built for the house of the kingdom, by the might of my power and for the honor of my majesty? [31] The word (was) still in the king's mouth, a voice came down from Heaven, (saying), O

מַלְכָּא עִיר וְקַדִּישׁ נָחִת ׀ מִן־שְׁמַיָּא וְאָמַר גֹּדּוּ אִילָנָא
tree the Cut and ,Heaven from coming a and a king the
down ,saying down ,one holy ,watcher

וְחַבְּלוּהִי בְּרַם עִקַּר שָׁרְשׁוֹהִי בְּאַרְעָא שְׁבֻקוּ וּבֶאֱסוּר
a with even leave the in roots its the But destroy and
band earth of stump .it

דִּי־פַרְזֶל וּנְחָשׁ בְּדִתְאָה דִּי בָרָא וּבְטַל שְׁמַיָּא יִצְטַבַּע
him let the the with and the of the in and iron of
;wet be heavens of dew field grass tender ,bronze

וְעִם־חֵיוַת בָּרָא חֲלָקֵהּ עַד דִּי־שִׁבְעָה עִדָּנִין יַחְלְפוּן עֲלוֹהִי׃
over by pass times seven until (be let) the ani- the and
:him lot his field of mals with

21 דְּנָה פִשְׁרָא מַלְכָּא וּגְזֵרַת עִלָּיָא הִיא דִּי מְטָת עַל־מָרִאי
my on has which this Most the the and ;king O the this
lord come (is) High of decree ,meaning (is)

22 מַלְכָּא׃ וְלָךְ טָרְדִין מִן־אֲנָשָׁא וְעִם־חֵיוַת בָּרָא לֶהֱוֵה
shall the ani- the and ,men from be shall And :king the
be field of mals with driven you

מְדֹרָךְ וְעִשְׂבָּא כְתוֹרִין ׀ לָךְ יְטַעֲמוּן וּמִטַּל שְׁמַיָּא לָךְ
you the the of And be shall you like with and your
,heavens of dew .fed oxen grass the ;abode

מְצַבְּעִין וְשִׁבְעָה עִדָּנִין יַחְלְפוּן עֲלָךְ עַד ׀ דִּי־תִנְדַּע דִּי־
that you until over shall times seven and be shall
know ,you by pass ,wet

שַׁלִּיט עִלָּיָא בְּמַלְכוּת אֲנָשָׁא וּלְמַן־דִּי יִצְבֵּא יִתְּנִנַּהּ׃
gives He He to and ;men the for Most the (is)
.it ,wishes whomever of kingdom High Ruler

23 וְדִי אֲמַרוּ לְמִשְׁבַּק עִקַּר שָׁרְשׁוֹהִי דִּי אִילָנָא מַלְכוּתָךְ
your the of roots the the leave to they in And
kingdom :tree of stump commanded that

24 לָךְ קַיָּמָא מִן־דִּי תִנְדַּע דִּי שַׁלִּטִן שְׁמַיָּא׃ לָהֵן מַלְכָּא
,king O ,Therefore .Heaven rules that have you after (be shall) for
realized enduring you

מִלְכִּי יִשְׁפַּר עֲלָךְ וַחֲטָיָךְ בְּצִדְקָה פְרֻק וַעֲוָיָתָךְ בְּמִחַן
by your and break righ- by your and ,you to be let my
pitying iniquities ,off teousness sins pleasing counsel

25 עֲנָיִן הֵן תֶּהֱוֵא אַרְכָא לִשְׁלֵוְתָךְ׃ כֹּלָּא מְטָא עַל־נְבוּכַדְנֶצַּר
Nebuchad- on came All your to duration there if the
nezzar (this) .prosperity be will ;poor

26 מַלְכָּא׃ לִקְצָת יַרְחִין תְּרֵי־עֲשַׂר עַל־הֵיכַל מַלְכוּתָא
the the in ,twelve months the at ,king the
kingdom of palace of end

27 דִּי בָבֶל מְהַלֵּךְ הֲוָה׃ עָנֵה מַלְכָּא וְאָמַר הֲלָא דָא־הִיא
this (Is) and The answered he walking Babylon of
not ,said king .was

בָּבֶל רַבְּתָא דִּי־אֲנָה בֱנַיְתַהּ לְבֵית מַלְכוּ בִּתְקַף חִסְנִי
my the by ,royal the for have I that the Babylon
power of might palace it built ,great

28 וְלִיקָר הַדְרִי׃ עוֹד מִלְּתָא בְּפֻם מַלְכָּא קָל מִן־שְׁמַיָּא
Heaven from a ,king's the in The still my the for
voice mouth (was) word ?majesty of house

King Nebuchadnezzar, to you it is declared. The kingdom has been taken from you! [32] And you shall be driven from men, and your dwelling (shall be) with the animals of the field. They shall make you eat grass like oxen, and seven times shall pass over you, until you know that the Most High rules in the kingdom of men, and that He gives it to whomever He will. [33] The same hour the thing was fulfilled on Nebuchadnezzar. And he was driven from men and he ate grass like oxen, and his body was wet with the dew of the heavens, until his hair had grown like eagle's (feathers) and his nails like birds' (claws). [34] And at the end of the days, I Nebuchadnezzar lifted up my eyes to Heaven, and my understanding returned to me, and I blessed the Most High. And I praised and honored Him who lives forever, whose kingdom (is) an everlasting kingdom, and His rule from generation to generation. [35] And all the inhabitants of the earth are counted as nothing. And He does according to His will among the army of Heaven and in the inhabitants of the earth. And no one can strike with His hand, or say to Him, What are You doing? [36] At that time my reason returned to me, and the glory of my kingdom, my honor and my brightness returned to me. And my advisors and my nobles sought to me. And I was re-established in my kingdom, and excellent majesty was added to me. [37] Now I, Nebuchadnezzar, praise and exalt and honor the King of Heaven, all whose works (are) truth, and His ways justice. And those who walk in pride He is able to humble.

נְפַל לָךְ אָמְרִין נְבוּכַדְנֶצַּר מַלְכָּא מַלְכוּתָה עֲדָת מִנָּךְ׃
from been has the ,king O Nebuchadnezzar is it To :fell
!you taken kingdom ,declared you

29 וּמִן־אֲנָשָׁא לָךְ טָרְדִין וְעִם־חֵיוַת בָּרָא מְדֹרָךְ עִשְׂבָּא
the ;abode your the ani- the and be shall you men And
grass field of mals with ,driven from

כְתוֹרִין לָךְ יְטַעֲמוּן וְשִׁבְעָה עִדָּנִין יַחְלְפוּן עֲלָךְ עַד ׀ דִּי־
until over pass shall times seven and be shall you oxen like
you by ,fed

תִנְדַּע דִּי־שַׁלִּיט עִלָּאָה בְּמַלְכוּת אֲנָשָׁא וּלְמַן דִּי־יִצְבֵּא
He that and ,men the in Most the (is) that you
,wishes whomever to of kingdom High Ruler know

30 יִתְּנִנַּהּ׃ בַּהּ־שַׁעֲתָא מִלְּתָא סָפַת עַל־נְבוּכַדְנֶצַּר וּמִן־אֲנָשָׁא
men and Nebuchad- on was the ,moment In gives He
from :nezzar fulfilled thing its .it

טְרִיד וְעִשְׂבָּא כְתוֹרִין יֵאכֻל וּמִטַּל שְׁמַיָּא גִּשְׁמֵהּ יִצְטַבַּע
wet was his the from and ,ate he oxen like the and was he
body ,heavens of dew the grass ,driven

31 עַד דִּי שַׂעְרֵהּ כְּנִשְׁרִין רְבָה וְטִפְרוֹהִי כְצִפְּרִין׃ וְלִקְצָת
the at And birds' like his and had eagles' like his until
of end .(claws) nails ,grown (feathers) hair

יוֹמַיָּה אֲנָה נְבוּכַדְנֶצַּר עַיְנַי ׀ לִשְׁמַיָּא נִטְלֵת וּמַנְדְּעִי עֲלַי
to my and lifted Heaven to my ,Nebuchadnezzar ,I the
me understanding ,up eyes .days

יְתוּב וּלְעִלָּאָה בָּרְכֵת וּלְחַי עָלְמָא שַׁבְּחֵת וְהַדְּרֵת דִּי שָׁלְטָנֵהּ
whose ;honored and I who Him and ,blessed I the and re-
(is) dominion praised forever lives High Most ,turned

32 שָׁלְטָן עָלַם וּמַלְכוּתֵהּ עִם־דָּר וְדָר׃ וְכָל־דָּאֲרֵי אַרְעָא כְּלָה
as the the all And gen- to gen- from His and ever- an
nothing earth of dwellers .eration eration kingdom ,lasting dominion

חֲשִׁיבִין וּכְמִצְבְּיֵהּ עָבֵד בְּחֵיל שְׁמַיָּא וְדָאֲרֵי אַרְעָא וְלָא
And the the (in) and Heaven the in He according And are
none .earth of dwellers of army does will His to .counted

33 אִיתַי דִּי־יְמַחֵא בִידֵהּ וְיֵאמַר לֵהּ מָה עֲבַדְתְּ׃ בֵּהּ־זִמְנָא
time At You are What to say or his with can who there
that ?doing ,Him ,hand strike is

מַנְדְּעִי ׀ יְתוּב עֲלַי וְלִיקַר מַלְכוּתִי הַדְרִי וְזִוִי יְתוּב עֲלַי
to returned my and my my the and to returned my
.me luster majesty ,kingdom of glory ,me reason

וְלִי הַדָּבְרַי וְרַבְרְבָנַי יְבַעוֹן וְעַל־מַלְכוּתִי הָתְקְנַת וּרְבוּ
and re- was I my and ,sought my and my And
greatness ,settled kingdom over nobles advisers me to

34 יַתִּירָה הוּסְפַת־לִי׃ כְּעַן אֲנָה נְבוּכַדְנֶצַּר מְשַׁבַּח וּמְרוֹמֵם
exalt and praise ,Nebuchadnezzar ,I Now .me to was exceed-
added ing

וּמְהַדַּר לְמֶלֶךְ שְׁמַיָּא דִּי כָל־מַעֲבָדוֹהִי קְשֹׁט וְאֹרְחָתֵהּ
His and truth His all for ,Heaven the and
ways (are) works of King glorify

דִּין וְדִי מַהְלְכִין בְּגֵוָה יָכִל לְהַשְׁפָּלָה׃
.humble to is He in walking And jus-
able pride those .tice

CAP. V ה
CHAPTER 5

CHAPTER 5

[1] Belshazzar the king made a great feast to a thousand of his nobles. And he drank wine before the thousand. [2] Belshazzar, while he tasted the wine, commanded the golden and silver vessels brought, those his father Nebuchadnezzar had taken out of the temple which was at Jerusalem, that the king and his princes, his wives and his concubines, might drink from them. [3] Then they brought the golden vessels that were taken out of the temple of the house of God which was at Jerusalem. And the king, and his nobles, his wives and his concubines, drank with them; [4] they drank wine and praised the gods of gold, and of silver, and of bronze, of iron, of wood and of stone.

[5] At that moment fingers of a man's hand came out and wrote on the plaster of the wall of the king's palace across from the lampstand. And the king saw the part of the hand that wrote. [6] Then the king's color was changed, and his thoughts troubled him, so that the joints of his loins shook, and his knees knocked against one another. [7] The king cried aloud to bring in the conjurers, the Chaldeans and the fortune-tellers. The king spoke and said to the wise men of Babylon, Any man who can read this writing and reveal its meaning shall be clothed with purple and (have) a chain of gold around his neck. And he shall rule third

1 בֵּלְשַׁאצַּר מַלְכָּא עֲבַד לְחֶם רַב לְרַבְרְבָנֹוהִי אֲלַף וְלָקֳבֵל

the in and a his for great a made king the Belshazzar
of presence ,thousand ,nobles   feast

2 אַלְפָּא חַמְרָא שָׁתֵה: בֵּלְשַׁאצַּר אֲמַר ׀ בִּטְעֵם חַמְרָא

,wine the when com- Belshazzar he wine the
tasting manded .drank thousand

לְהַיְתָיָה לְמָאנֵי דַּהֲבָא וְכַסְפָּא דִּי הַנְפֵּק נְבוּכַדְנֶצַּר

Nebuchadnezzar had those and gold the bring to
taken ,silver of vessels

אֲבוּהִי מִן־הֵיכְלָא דִּי בִירוּשְׁלֶם וְיִשְׁתֹּון בְּהֹון מַלְכָּא

,king the with might that in which the out his
them drink ,Jerusalem (was) temple of father

3 וְרַבְרְבָנֹוהִי שֵׁגְלָתֵהּ וּלְחֵנָתֵהּ: בֵּאדַיִן הַיְתִיו מָאנֵי דַהֲבָא

gold the they Then his and wives his his and
of vessels brought .concubines ,nobles

דִּי הַנְפִּקוּ מִן־הֵיכְלָא דִּי־בֵית אֱלָהָא דִּי בִירוּשְׁלֶם וְאִשְׁתִּיו

And in which God the of the out been had that
drank .Jerusalem (was) of house temple of taken

4 בְּהֹון מַלְכָּא וְרַבְרְבָנֹוהִי שֵׁגְלָתֵהּ וּלְחֵנָתֵהּ: אִשְׁתִּיו חַמְרָא

wine they his and ,wives his his and the with
drank ;concubines ,nobles king them

וְשַׁבַּחוּ לֵאלָהֵי דַּהֲבָא וְכַסְפָּא נְחָשָׁא פַרְזְלָא אָעָא

,wood ,iron ,bronze ,silver and ,gold gods the and
of praised

5 וְאַבְנָא: בַּה־שַׁעֲתָא נְפַקוּ אֶצְבְּעָן דִּי יַד־אֱנָשׁ וְכָתְבָן לָקֳבֵל

opposite and a hand of fingers came moment At and
wrote ,man's out that .stone

נֶבְרַשְׁתָּא עַל־גִּירָא דִּי־כְתַל הֵיכְלָא דִּי מַלְכָּא וּמַלְכָּא

the And the of the wall the of the the on lamp- the
king .king palace of plaster stand

6 חֲזֵה פַּס יְדָא דִּי כָתְבָא: אֱדַיִן מַלְכָּא זִיוֹהִי שְׁנוֹהִי

was his king the Then .wrote that the the saw
,changed color hand the the of palm

וְרַעְיֹנֹהִי יְבַהֲלוּנֵּהּ וְקִטְרֵי חַרְצֵהּ מִשְׁתָּרַיִן וְאַרְכֻבָּתֵהּ דָּא

one his and ,shook his the and troubled his and
knees loins of joints ,him thoughts

7 לְדָא נָקְשָׁן: קָרֵא מַלְכָּא בְּחַיִל לְהֶעָלָה לְאָשְׁפַיָּא כַּשְׂדָּיֵא*

the the bring to aloud The cried .knocked against
,Chaldeans ,conjurers in king this

וְגָזְרַיָּא עָנֵה מַלְכָּא וְאָמַר ׀ לְחַכִּימֵי בָבֶל דִּי כָל־אֱנָשׁ

man Any ,Babylon wise the to said and The answered the and
of men king .gazers

דִּי־יִקְרֵה כְּתָבָה דְנָה וּפִשְׁרֵהּ יְחַוִּנַּנִי אַרְגְּוָנָא יִלְבַּשׁ

be shall purple declare its and this writing can who
with clothed me to meaning read

וְהַמְנִיכָא דִי־דַהֲבָא עַל־צַוְּארֵהּ וְתַלְתִּי בְמַלְכוּתָא יִשְׁלַט:

shall he the in And his around gold of the and
.rule kingdom third .neck (be shall) necklace

in the kingdom. [8] Then all the king's wise men came in. But they could not read the writing or make the meaning known to the king. [9] Then King Belshazzar was greatly troubled, and his face was changing on him, and his nobles were puzzled.

[10] The queen came into the banquet house because of the words of the king and his nobles. The queen spoke and said, O king, live forever. Do not let your thoughts trouble you or let your face be changed. [11] There is a man in your kingdom in whom (is) the spirit of the holy gods. And in the days of your father light and understanding and wisdom was found in him, like the wisdom of the gods. The King Nebuchadnezzar, your father, the king, made him master of the horoscopists, conjurers, Chaldeans (and) fortune-tellers, [12] because an excellent spirit, and knowledge, and understanding, explaining of dreams and revealing of hard sentences, and the melting away of doubts were found in this Daniel, whom the king named Belteshazzar. Now let Daniel be called. And he will reveal the meaning. [13] Then Daniel was brought in before the king. The king spoke and said to Daniel, Are you that Daniel who (is) of the sons of the captivity of Judah, whom the king my father brought out of Judah? [14] I have even heard of you, that the spirit of the gods (is) in you, and light and excellent wisdom and understanding are found in you. [15] And now the wise men and the conjurers have been brought

8 אֱדַיִן עָלְּלִין כֹּל חַכִּימֵי מַלְכָּא וְלָא־כָהֲלִין כְּתָבָא לְמִקְרֵא

read to the were they But the wise all came Then
writing able not .king's men in

9 וּפִשְׁרָא לְהוֹדָעָה לְמַלְכָּא׃ אֱדַיִן מַלְכָּא בֵּלְשַׁאצַּר

Belshazzar King Then the to make to the or
.king known meaning

שַׂגִּיא מִתְבָּהַל וְזִיוֹהִי שָׁנַיִן עֲלוֹהִי וְרַבְרְבָנוֹהִי מִשְׁתַּבְּשִׁין׃

were his and on was his and was greatly
.perplexed nobles ,him changing face ,terrified

10 מַלְכְּתָא לָקֳבֵל מִלֵּי מַלְכָּא וְרַבְרְבָנוֹהִי לְבֵית מִשְׁתְּיָא

the to his and the words the because ,queen The
banquet- house ,nobles king of of

עַלַּלַת עֲנָת מַלְכְּתָא וַאֲמֶרֶת מַלְכָּא לְעָלְמִין חֱיִי אַל־

not !live forever ,king O ,said and queen the answered ;came

11 יְבַהֲלוּךְ רַעְיוֹנָךְ וְזִיוָיךְ אַל־יִשְׁתַּנּוֹ׃ אִיתַי גְּבַר בְּמַלְכוּתָךְ

your in a There be let not your and your let Do
kingdom man is .changed face ,thoughts alarm

דִּי רוּחַ אֱלָהִין קַדִּישִׁין בֵּהּ וּבְיוֹמֵי אֲבוּךְ נַהִירוּ וְשָׂכְלְתָנוּ

and ,light your the in And in holy gods the the
,insight father of days .(is) whom of spirit

וְחָכְמָה כְּחָכְמַת־אֱלָהִין הִשְׁתְּכַחַת בֵּהּ וּמַלְכָּא נְבֻכַדְנֶצַּר

Nebuchad- King And in found was ,gods (the) the like and
nezzar .him of wisdom wisdom

אֲבוּךְ רַב חַרְטֻמִּין אָשְׁפִין כַּשְׂדָּאִין גָּזְרִין הֲקִימֵהּ אֲבוּךְ

your appointed star- ,Chaldeans ,conjurers horo- the master your
father ;him gazers (and) ,scopists of ,father

12 מַלְכָּא׃ כָּל־קֳבֵל דִּי רוּחַ יַתִּירָא וּמַנְדַּע וְשָׂכְלְתָנוּ

and and ,extraordinary an (was this) ;king the
(in) insight ,knowledge spirit because

מְפַשַּׁר חֶלְמִין וְאַחֲוָיַת אֲחִידָן וּמְשָׁרֵא קִטְרִין הִשְׁתְּכַחַת

found were ,problems and ,riddles and ,dreams inter-
solving of showing preting

בֵּהּ בְּדָנִיֵּאל דִּי־מַלְכָּא שָׂם־שְׁמֵהּ בֵּלְטְשַׁאצַּר כְּעַן דָּנִיֵּאל

Daniel Now .Belteshazzar his gave the whom ,Daniel in
name king this

13 יִתְקְרֵי וּפִשְׁרָה יְהַחֲוֵה׃ בֵּאדַיִן דָּנִיֵּאל הֻעַל קֳדָם

before was Daniel Then will he the and be let
in brought .declare meaning ,called

מַלְכָּא עָנֵה מַלְכָּא וְאָמַר לְדָנִיֵּאל אַנְתְּה־הוּא דָנִיֵּאל דִּי־

who Daniel (Are) you ,Daniel to said and The answered the
(is) that king .king

מִן־בְּנֵי גָלוּתָא דִּי יְהוּד דִּי הַיְתִי מַלְכָּא אַבִי מִן־יְהוּד׃

?Judah out my the brought whom ,Judah of the the of
of father king removed sons

14 שִׁמְעֵת עֲלָיךְ דִּי רוּחַ אֱלָהִין בָּךְ וְנַהִירוּ וְשָׂכְלְתָנוּ וְחָכְמָה

and and and in (the) the that ,you of I Even
wisdom ,insight ,light ,you (is) gods of spirit heard have

15 יַתִּירָה הִשְׁתְּכַחַת בָּךְ׃ וּכְעַן הֻעַלּוּ קֳדָמַי חַכִּימַיָּא אָשְׁפַיָּא

the wise the before been have And in found are extra-
,conjurers ,men me in brought now .you ordinary

in before me, so that they might read this writing and make the meaning known to me. But they could not show the meaning of the thing. [16] And I have heard of you that you can tell meanings and melt away doubts. Now if you can read the writing and reveal its meaning to me, you shall be clothed with purple and (have) a golden chain around your neck, and you will rule third in the kingdom.

[17] Then Daniel answered and said before the king, Let your gifts be to yourself, and give your rewards to another. Yet I will read the writing to the king and make the meaning known to him. [18] O king, the most high God gave Nebuchadnezzar your father a kingdom, and majesty and glory and honor. [19] And for the majesty that He gave him, all peoples, nations and languages trembled and feared before him. He killed whom he desired, and whom he desired, he kept alive. And whom he would, he set up, and whom he desired, he put down. [20] But when his heart was lifted up and his mind hardened in pride, he was put down from the throne of his kingdom, and they took his glory from him. [21] And he was driven from the sons of men. And his heart was made like the animals, and his home (was) with the wild asses. They fed him with grass like oxen, and his body was wet with the dew of the heavens, until he knew that the most high God rules in the kingdom of men and that He appoints over it whomever He will.

דִּי־כְתָבָה דְנָה יִקְרוֹן וּפִשְׁרֵהּ לְהוֹדָעֻתַנִי וְלָא־כָהֲלִין

were they But known make its and might they this writing so
able not .me to meaning ,read that

16 פְּשַׁר־מִלְּתָא לְהַחֲוָיָה׃ וַאֲנָה שִׁמְעֵת עֲלָךְ דִּי־תִוכֻל

are you that ,you of have I And .declare to meaning the
able heard thing the of

פִּשְׁרִין לְמִפְשַׁר וְקִטְרִין לְמִשְׁרֵא כְּעַן הֵן תִּוכֻל כְּתָבָא

the are you if Now .solve to and to meanings
writing able problems ,interpret

לְמִקְרֵא וּפִשְׁרֵהּ לְהוֹדָעֻתַנִי אַרְגְּוָנָא תִלְבַּשׁ וְהַמְנוּכָא דִי־

of the and will you purple reveal to its and ,read to
necklace ,with clothed be ,me to meaning

דַהֲבָא עַל־צַוְּארָךְ וְתַלְתָּא בְמַלְכוּתָא תִּשְׁלַט׃

will you the in third and your around gold
.rule kingdom ,neck (be shall)

17 בֵּאדַיִן עָנֵה דָנִיֵּאל וְאָמַר קֳדָם מַלְכָּא מַתְּנָתָךְ לָךְ לֶהֶוְיָן

,be let to Your the before said and Daniel answered Then
yourself gifts ,king

וּנְבָזְבְּיָתָךְ לְאָחֳרָן הַב בְּרַם כְּתָבָא אֶקְרֵא לְמַלְכָּא וּפִשְׁרָא

the and the to will I the Yet .give to your and
meaning ,king read writing another presents

18 אֲהוֹדְעִנֵּהּ׃ אַנְתָּה מַלְכָּא אֱלָהָא עִלָּאָה מַלְכוּתָא וּרְבוּתָא

and the Most the ,king O (for As) make will I
,greatness ,kingdom High God ,you .him to known

19 וִיקָרָא וְהַדְרָה יְהַב לִנְבֻכַדְנֶצַּר אֲבוּךְ׃ וּמִן־רְבוּתָא דִּי

that the And your Nebuchadnezzar gave and and
greatness from .father splendor ,majesty

יְהַב־לֵהּ כֹּל עַמְמַיָּא אֻמַּיָּא וְלִשָּׁנַיָּא הֲווֹ זָאֲעִין וְדָחֲלִין מִן־

from and shaking were the and the the all to He
fearing languages ,nations ,peoples ,him gave

קֳדָמוֹהִי דִּי־הֲוָא צָבֵא הֲוָה קָטֵל וְדִי־הֲוָה צָבֵא הֲוָה מַחֵא

kept he ,wished he and ;killed he ,wished he Whom before
.alive whom .him

וְדִי־הֲוָה צָבֵא הֲוָה מָרִים וְדִי־הֲוָא צָבֵא הֲוָא מַשְׁפִּל׃

.humbled he wished he and ;exalted he ,wished he And
whom whom

20 וּכְדִי רִם לִבְבֵהּ וְרוּחֵהּ תִּקְפַת לַהֲזָדָה הָנְחַת מִן־כָּרְסֵא

the from was he act to grew his and his was But
of throne deposed ,insolently hard spirit ,heart lifted when

21 מַלְכוּתֵהּ וִיקָרֵהּ הֶעְדִּיו מִנֵּהּ׃ וּמִן־בְּנֵי אֲנָשָׁא טְרִיד

was he men the And from taken was (his) and his
,driven of sons from .him away majesty ,kingdom

וְלִבְבֵהּ ׀ עִם־חֵיוְתָא שַׁוִּי וְעִם־עֲרָדַיָּא מְדוֹרֵהּ עִשְׂבָּא כְתוֹרִין

oxen like grass his (was) wild the and was the like his and
;dwelling asses with ;made animals heart

יְטַעֲמוּנֵּהּ וּמִטַּל שְׁמַיָּא גִּשְׁמֵהּ יִצְטַבַּע עַד דִּי־יְדַע דִּי־

that he until ;wet was body his the (with) and fed they
knew heavens of dew the ,him

שַׁלִּיט אֱלָהָא עִלָּאָה בְּמַלְכוּת אֲנָשָׁא וּלְמַן־דִּי יִצְבֵּא יְהָקֵים

He He that and ;men the in Most the (is)
appoints ,wishes whomever of kingdom High God Ruler

[22] And you his son, O Belshazzar, have not bowed your heart, though you knew all this. [23] But you have lifted up yourself against the Lord of Heaven. And they have brought the vessels of His house before you. And you and your nobles, your wives and your concubines, have drunk wine from them. And you have praised the gods of silver, and gold, of bronze, iron, wood and stone, which do not see nor hear, nor know. And you have not glorified the God in whose hand your breath (is), and to whom belong all your ways. [24] Then was the part of the hand sent from Him. And this writing was written.

[25] And this is the writing that was written, MENE, MENE, TEKEL, and UPHARSIN. [26] This (is) the meaning of the thing: MENE, God has numbered your kingdom and finished it. [27] TEKEL, You are weighed in the balances and found lacking. [28] PERES, Your kingdom is divided and given to the Medes and Persians. [29] Then Belshazzar commanded, and they clothed Daniel with purple and a chain of gold around his neck. And they made a proclamation concerning him, that he should be the third ruler in the kingdom.

[30] In that night Belshazzar the king of the Chaldeans was killed.

22 עֲלוֹהִי: וְאַנְתְּה בְּרֵהּ בֵּלְשַׁאצַּר לָא הַשְׁפֵּלְתְּ לִבְבָךְ כָּל־
even your have not ,Belshazzar O ,son his you And .it over
,heart humbled

23 קֳבֵל דִּי כָל־דְּנָה יְדַעְתָּ: וְעַל־מָרֵא שְׁמַיָּא ׀ הִתְרוֹמַמְתָּ
have you Heaven the But you this all though
,yourself exalted of Lord against .knew

וּלְמָאנַיָּא דִּי־בַיְתֵהּ הַיְתִיו קָדָמָךְ וְאַנְתְּה וְרַבְרְבָנָךְ
your and ,you and before have they His of the and
,nobles ;you brought house vessels

שֵׁגְלָתָךְ וּלְחֵנָתָךְ חַמְרָא שָׁתַיִן בְּהוֹן וְלֵאלָהֵי כַסְפָּא וְדַהֲבָא
,gold and silver the And with have wine your and your
of gods .them drunk ,concubines wives

נְחָשָׁא פַרְזְלָא אָעָא וְאַבְנָא דִּי לָא־חָזַיִן וְלָא־שָׁמְעִין וְלָא
and do and do not which and wood ,iron (of)
not ,hear not ,see ,stone ,bronze

יָדְעִין שַׁבַּחְתָּ וְלֵאלָהָא דִּי־נִשְׁמְתָךְ בִּידֵהּ וְכָל־אֹרְחָתָךְ
,ways your and whose in your (is) the But have you do
all hand life-breath God .praised ,know

24 לֵהּ לָא הַדַּרְתָּ: בֵּאדַיִן מִן־קֳדָמוֹהִי שְׁלִיחַ פַּסָּא דִי־יְדָא
the of the was before from Then have you not Him
.hand palm sent Him .glorified

25 וּכְתָבָא דְנָה רְשִׁים: וּדְנָה כְתָבָא דִּי רְשִׁים מְנֵא מְנֵא
,MENE ,MENE was that the this And was this And
,written writing (is) .written writing

26 תְּקֵל וּפַרְסִין: דְּנָה פְּשַׁר מִלְּתָא מְנֵא מְנָה־אֱלָהָא
God has ,MENE the meaning This and ,TEKEL
numbered :thing's (is) .UPHARSIN

27 מַלְכוּתָךְ וְהַשְׁלְמַהּ: תְּקֵל תְּקִלְתָּה בְמֹאזַנְיָא וְהִשְׁתְּכַחַתְּ
found and the on are You ,TEKEL finished and your
,scales weighed .it kingdom

28 חַסִּיר: פְּרֵס פְּרִיסַת מַלְכוּתָךְ וִיהִיבַת לְמָדַי וּפָרָס:
and (the) to given and Your divided is ,PERES .lacking
.Persians Medes kingdom

29 בֵּאדַיִן ׀ אֲמַר בֵּלְשַׁאצַּר וְהַלְבִּשׁוּ לְדָנִיֵּאל אַרְגְּוָנָא
(with) Daniel they and ,Belshazzar commanded Then
;purple clothed

וְהַמְוּנְכָא דִּי־דַהֲבָא עַל־צַוְּארֵהּ וְהַכְרִזוּ עֲלוֹהִי דִּי־לֶהֱוֵא
he that about they And .neck his around gold of the and
was ,him proclaimed necklace

30 שַׁלִּיט תַּלְתָּא בְּמַלְכוּתָא: בֵּהּ בְּלֵילְיָא קְטִיל בֵּלְשַׁאצַּר
Belshazzar was night In the in third the ruler
killed that .kingdom

מַלְכָּא כַשְׂדָּיָא:
the king the
.Chaldeans of

CAP. VI ו

CHAPTER 6

[31] And Darius the Mede took the kingdom, when a son of sixty-two years.

1 וְדָרְיָוֶשׁ מָדָיָא קַבֵּל מַלְכוּתָא כְּבַר שְׁנִין שִׁתִּין וְתַרְתֵּין:
.two and sixty years a when the took the And
of son kingdom over Mede Darius

CHAPTER 6

[1] It pleased Darius to set over the kingdom a hundred and twenty satraps, that they might be over the whole kingdom. [2] And over them (were) three presidents; Daniel (was) one of them; so that these satraps might give account to them and the king should have no loss. [3] Then this Daniel was distinguishing himself above the presidents and satraps, because an excellent spirit (was) in him. And the king was planning to set him over all the kingdom.

[4] Then the presidents and satraps sought to find occasion against Daniel concerning the kingdom. But they could find no occasion or fault, because he (was) faithful. There was no error or fault found in him. [5] Then these men said, We shall not find any occasion against this Daniel unless we find (it) against him concerning the law of his God. [6] Then these presidents and satraps gathered together to the king and said this to him, King Darius, live forever. [7] All the presidents of the kingdom, the prefects, and the satraps, the officials and the governors have planned together to establish a royal law, and to make a strong ban, that whoever shall ask a petition of any god or man for thirty days, except from you, O king, he shall be thrown into the den of lions. [8] Now, O king, establish the ban and sign

2 שְׁפַר קֳדָם דָּרְיָוֶשׁ וַהֲקִים עַל־מַלְכוּתָא לַאֲחַשְׁדַּרְפְּנַיָּא
satraps the over set to Darius before It
kingdom good seemed

3 מְאָה וְעֶשְׂרִין דִּי לֶהֱוֺן בְּכָל־מַלְכוּתָא׃ וְעֵלָּא מִנְּהוֹן
them over and ,kingdom the over they that and a
whole be might ,twenty hundred

סָרְכִין תְּלָתָה דִּי דָנִיֵּאל חַד מִנְּהוֹן דִּי־לֶהֱוֺן אֲחַשְׁדַּרְפְּנַיָּא
satraps might so of one Daniel —three presi-
that —them (was) dents

4 אִלֵּין יָהֲבִין לְהוֹן טַעְמָא וּמַלְכָּא לָא־לֶהֱוֵא נָזִק׃ אֱדַיִן
Then suffer would not the and ,account to give these
.loss king them

דָּנִיֵּאל דְּנָה הֲוָא מִתְנַצַּח עַל־סָרְכַיָּא וַאֲחַשְׁדַּרְפְּנַיָּא כָּל־
satraps the and the above distinguishing was this Daniel
presidents himself

קֳבֵל דִּי רוּחַ יַתִּירָא בֵּהּ וּמַלְכָּא עֲשִׁית לַהֲקָמוּתֵהּ עַל־
over appoint to was the And in superb a because
him planning king .him (was) spirit

5 כָּל־מַלְכוּתָא׃ אֱדַיִן סָרְכַיָּא וַאֲחַשְׁדַּרְפְּנַיָּא הֲווֹ בָעַיִן עִלָּה
pretext seek- were the and the Then the all
ing satraps presidents .kingdom

לְהַשְׁכָּחָה לְדָנִיֵּאל מִצַּד מַלְכוּתָא וְכָל־עִלָּה וּשְׁחִיתָה
fault or pretext But .kingdom the concern- against find to
any ing Daniel

לָא־יָכְלִין לְהַשְׁכָּחָה כָּל־קֳבֵל דִּי־מְהֵימַן הוּא וְכָל־שָׁלוּ
error And he trust- because ,find to they not
any .(was) worthy able were

6 וּשְׁחִיתָה לָא הִשְׁתְּכַחַת עֲלוֹהִי׃ אֱדַיִן גֻּבְרַיָּא אִלֵּךְ אָמְרִין
,said these men Then .him in found was not fault or

דִּי לָא נְהַשְׁכַּח לְדָנִיֵּאל דְּנָה כָּל־עִלָּא לָהֵן הַשְׁכַּחְנָא
(it) find we unless pretext any this against shall we Not
Daniel find

7 עֲלוֹהִי בְּדָת אֱלָהֵהּ׃ אֱדַיִן סָרְכַיָּא וַאֲחַשְׁדַּרְפְּנַיָּא אִלֵּן
these the and the Then .God his the in against
satraps presidents of law him

הַרְגִּשׁוּ עַל־מַלְכָּא וְכֵן אָמְרִין לֵהּ דָּרְיָוֶשׁ מַלְכָּא לְעָלְמִין
forever ,King Darius O to they and ,king the to gathered
,him said thus together

חֱיִי׃ אִתְיָעַטוּ כֹּל ׀ סָרְכֵי מַלְכוּתָא סִגְנַיָּא וַאֲחַשְׁדַּרְפְּנַיָּא
satraps the and the the presi- the All counsel took !live
,prefects ,kingdom of dents together

הַדָּבְרַיָּא וּפַחֲוָתָא לְקַיָּמָה קְיָם מַלְכָּא וּלְתַקָּפָה אֱסָר דִּי
that ban make to and ,royal a to the and royal the
strong statute establish governors ,officials

כָל־דִּי־יִבְעֵא בָעוּ מִן־כָּל־אֱלָהּ וֶאֱנָשׁ עַד־יוֹמִין תְּלָתִין לָהֵן
except ,thirty days for man or god any of a shall who-
petition ask ever

8 מִנָּךְ מַלְכָּא יִתְרְמֵא לְגֹב אַרְיָוָתָא׃ כְּעַן מַלְכָּא תְּקִים
establish ,king O ,Now .lions the into shall he ,king O from
of pit thrown be you

the document, so that it may not be changed according to the law of the Medes and Persians, which does not pass away. [9] So King Darius signed the document and the ban.

[10] And Daniel, when he had learned that the document was signed, went to his house. And his windows (were) open in his roof-room toward Jerusalem. He knelt on his knees three times in the day and prayed and praised before his God, as he did from before. [11] Then these men met together and found Daniel praying and confessing before his God. [12] Then they came near and spoke before the king concerning the king's ban, Have you not signed a ban that every man who shall ask of any god or man within thirty days, except of you, O king, shall be thrown into the lions' den? The king answered and said, The thing (is) certain, according to the law of the Medes and Persians, which does not pass away.

[13] Then they answered and said before the king, Daniel, who (is) of the sons of the captivity of Judah, has not respected you, O king, or the ban that you have signed, but he makes his prayer three times in the day. [14] Then the king, when he heard the word, was very much displeased with himself. And he set the heart on Daniel, to deliver him. And he labored until sundown to deliver him. [15] Then these men met before the king and said to

אֱסָרָא וְתִרְשֻׁם כְּתָבָא דִּי לָא לְהַשְׁנָיָה כְּדָת־מָדַי וּפָרַס
and the the as be may it not so the sign and ban the
,Persians Medes of law changed that document

10 דִּי־לָא תֶעְדֵּא׃ כָּל־קֳבֵל דְּנָה מַלְכָּא דָּרְיָוֶשׁ רְשַׁם כְּתָבָא
the signed Darius King ,Consequently pass does not which
document .away

11 וֶאֱסָרָא׃ וְדָנִיֵּאל כְּדִי יְדַע דִּי־רְשִׁים כְּתָבָא עַל לְבַיְתֵהּ
his to he the was that he when And the and
.house went ,document signed knew ,Daniel .ban

וְכַוִּין פְּתִיחָן לֵהּ בְּעִלִּיתֵהּ נֶגֶד יְרוּשְׁלֶם וְזִמְנִין תְּלָתָה
three And .Jerusalem toward his in to open And
times roof-chamber him (were) windows

בְיוֹמָא הוּא ׀ בָּרֵךְ עַל־בִּרְכוֹהִי וּמְצַלֵּא וּמוֹדֵא קֳדָם
before and prayed and his on knelt he the in
praised knees ,day

12 אֱלָהֵהּ כָּל־קֳבֵל דִּי־הֲוָא עָבֵד מִקַּדְמַת דְּנָה׃ אֱדַיִן
Then .this before from doing he as ,God his
was

גֻּבְרַיָּא אִלֵּךְ הַרְגִּשׁוּ וְהַשְׁכַּחוּ לְדָנִיֵּאל בָּעֵה וּמִתְחַנַּן קֳדָם
before seeking and praying Daniel found and assembled those men
mercy

13 אֱלָהֵהּ׃ בֵּאדַיִן קְרִבוּ וְאָמְרִין קֳדָם־מַלְכָּא עַל־אֱסָר
ban con- king the before spoke and they Then .God his
cerning near came

מַלְכָּא הֲלָא אֱסָר רְשַׁמְתָּ דִּי כָל־אֱנָשׁ דִּי־יִבְעֵא מִן־כָּל־
any of shall who man any that you Have a not the
ask signed ban ;king's

אֱלָהּ וֶאֱנָשׁ עַד־יוֹמִין תְּלָתִין לָהֵן מִנָּךְ מַלְכָּא יִתְרְמֵא לְגֹוב
the into be shall ,king O from except ,thirty days for man or god
of pit thrown ,you

אַרְיָוָתָא עָנֵה מַלְכָּא וְאָמַר יַצִּיבָא מִלְּתָא כְּדָת־מָדַי וּפָרַס
and the the by thing The certain ,said and The answered ?lions
,Persians Medes of law ,(is) king

14 דִּי־לָא תֶעְדֵּא׃ בֵּאדַיִן עֲנוֹ וְאָמְרִין קֳדָם מַלְכָּא דִּי דָנִיֵּאל
,Daniel ,king the before said and they Then pass does not which
answered .away

דִּי מִבְּנֵי גָלוּתָא דִּי יְהוּד לָא־שָׂם עֲלָיךְ מַלְכָּא טְעֵם
attention ,king O ,you to has not ,Judah of the the of who
paid exile of sons (is)

וְעַל־אֱסָרָא דִּי רְשַׁמְתָּ וְזִמְנִין תְּלָתָה בְּיוֹמָא בָּעֵא בָּעוּתֵהּ׃
his asks he the in three but have you that the to or
.petition day times ,signed ban

15 אֱדַיִן מַלְכָּא כְּדִי מִלְּתָא שְׁמַע שַׂגִּיא בְּאֵשׁ עֲלוֹהִי וְעַל
And with was he very he the when the Then
on .himself displeased ,heard word ,king

דָּנִיֵּאל שָׂם בָּל לְשֵׁיזָבוּתֵהּ וְעַד מֶעָלֵי שִׁמְשָׁא הֲוָא מִשְׁתַּדַּר
striving was he the the And deliver to (his) he Daniel
sun of going until .him heart set

16 לְהַצָּלוּתֵהּ׃ בֵּאדַיִן גֻּבְרַיָּא אִלֵּךְ הַרְגִּשׁוּ עַל־מַלְכָּא וְאָמְרִין
said and the before assembled those men Then deliver to
king .him

the king, O king, know that the law of the Medes and Persians (is) that every ban or law which the king enacts may not be changed. [16] And the king commanded. And they brought Daniel and threw (him) into the lions' den. The king spoke and said to Daniel, Your God, whom you always serve, will deliver you. [17] And a stone was brought and laid on the mouth of the den. And the king sealed it with his own signet, and with the signet of his nobles, that the affair might not be changed concerning Daniel.

[18] Then the king went to his palace and spent the night fasting. And diversions were not brought before him; and his sleep fled from him. [19] Then the king arose in the dawn, in the daylight, and hurried to the lions' den. [20] And when he came to the den, he cried with a grieved voice to Daniel. The king spoke and said to Daniel, O Daniel, servant of the living God, is your God whom you always serve able to deliver you from the lions? [21] Then Daniel said to the king, O king, live forever. [22] My God has sent His Angel, and He has shut the lions' mouths. And they have not hurt me, because in His sight purity was found in me. And also before you, O king, I have done no harm. [23] Then the king was exceedingly happy for him. And (he) commanded that they should take Daniel up out of the den. So Daniel was taken up out of the den, and no kind of hurt was

לְמַלְכָּא דַּע מַלְכָּא דִּי־דָת לְמָדַי וּפָרַס דִּי־כָל־אֱסָר וּקְיָם
and ban every (is) and (the) of the that ,king O ,Know the to
statute that Persians Medes law ,king

17 דִּי־מַלְכָּא יְהָקֵים לָא לְהַשְׁנָיָה׃ בֵּאדַיִן מַלְכָּא אֲמַר
,ordered the Then be may not establishes the which
king .changed king

וְהַיְתִיו לְדָנִיֵּאל וּרְמוֹ לְגֻבָּא דִּי אַרְיָוָתָא עָנֵה מַלְכָּא
The answered .lions the of the into threw and Daniel they And
king pit (him) brought

וְאָמַר לְדָנִיֵּאל אֱלָהָךְ דִּי אַנְתְּה פָּלַח־לֵהּ בִּתְדִירָא הוּא
He ,constantly serve you whom Your ,Daniel to and
,God said

18 יְשֵׁיזְבִנָּךְ׃ וְהֵיתָיִת אֶבֶן חֲדָה וְשֻׂמַת עַל־פֻּם גֻּבָּא וְחַתְמַהּ
sealed And the the on laid and a stone was And deliver will
it .pit of mouth brought .you

מַלְכָּא בְּעִזְקְתֵהּ וּבְעִזְקָת רַבְרְבָנוֹהִי דִּי לָא־תִשְׁנֵא צְבוּ
the might not that his the with and his with king the
affair change ,nobles of signet ,signet

19 בְּדָנִיֵּאל׃ אֱדַיִן אֲזַל מַלְכָּא לְהֵיכְלֵהּ וּבָת טְוָת וְדַחֲוָן לָא־
not and ;fasting and his to king the went Then concerning
diversions night the spent palace .Daniel

20 הַנְעֵל קָדָמוֹהִי וְשִׁנְתֵּהּ נַדַּת עֲלוֹהִי׃ בֵּאדַיִן מַלְכָּא
king the Then from fled his and before were
.him sleep ;him brought

בִּשְׁפַּרְפָּרָא יְקוּם בְּנָגְהָא וּבְהִתְבְּהָלָה לְגֻבָּא דִּי־אַרְיָוָתָא
the of the to haste and the in arose the in
lions pit in ,daylight dawn

21 אֲזַל׃ וּכְמִקְרְבֵהּ לְגֻבָּא לְדָנִיֵּאל בְּקָל עֲצִיב זְעִק עָנֵה
an- he sorrowful a with Daniel to the to when And .went
swered ;cried voice ,pit near drew he

מַלְכָּא וְאָמַר לְדָנִיֵּאל דָּנִיֵּאל עֲבֵד אֱלָהָא חַיָּא אֱלָהָךְ דִּי
whom your ,living the servant O ,Daniel to said and king the
God God of ,Daniel

אַנְתָּה פָּלַח־לֵהּ בִּתְדִירָא הֲיִכִל לְשֵׁיזָבוּתָךְ מִן־אַרְיָוָתָא׃
?lions the from deliver to He is ,constantly serve you
you able

22
23 אֱדַיִן דָּנִיֵּאל עִם־מַלְכָּא מַלִּל מַלְכָּא לְעָלְמִין חֱיִי׃ אֱלָהִי
God My .live forever ,king O ,spoke king the with Daniel Then

שְׁלַח מַלְאֲכֵהּ וּסֲגַר פֻּם אַרְיָוָתָא וְלָא חַבְּלוּנִי כָּל־קֳבֵל
because have they And the mouths He and His has
me harmed not .lions' shut has ,angel sent

דִּי קָדָמוֹהִי זָכוּ הִשְׁתְּכַחַת לִי וְאַף קֳדָמָיךְ מַלְכָּא חֲבוּלָה
harm ,king O before And in found was inno- before
,you also .me cence Him

24 לָא עַבְדֵת׃ בֵּאדַיִן מַלְכָּא שַׂגִּיא טְאֵב עֲלוֹהִי וּלְדָנִיֵּאל
Daniel And for glad greatly king the Then have I not
.him was .done

אֲמַר לְהַנְסָקָה מִן־גֻּבָּא וְהֻסַּק דָּנִיֵּאל מִן־גֻּבָּא וְכָל־חֲבָל
harm and ,pit the out Daniel was and the from bring to he
any of brought ;pit up said

found on him, because he trusted in his God.

[24] And the king commanded, and they brought those men who had accused Daniel. And they threw (them) into the lions' den; them, their sons and their wives. And the lions overpowered them and crushed all their bones in pieces before they came to the lower part of the den.

[25] Then King Darius wrote to all the peoples, the nations and the languages who were living in all the earth: Peace be multiplied to you. [26] I make a decree that in all my kingdom's domain men shall tremble and fear before the God of Daniel. For He (is) the living God and endures forever, and His kingdom (is) the one which shall not be destroyed. And His rule (shall be) to the end. [27] He delivers and rescues, and He works signs and wonders in the heavens and in earth, He who has delivered Daniel from the power of the lions.

[28] So this Daniel was blessed in the reign of Darius, and in the reign of Cyrus the Persian.

25 לָא־הִשְׁתְּכַח בֵּהּ דִּי הֵימִן בֵּאלָהֵהּ׃ וַאֲמַר מַלְכָּא וְהַיְתִיו

they and ,king the And his in he because on found was not
brought ordered .God trusted ,him

גֻּבְרַיָּא אִלֵּךְ דִּי־אֲכַלוּ קַרְצוֹהִי דִּי דָנִיֵּאל וּלְגֹב אַרְיָוָתָא

lions the into And .Daniel of bits the had who those men
of pit the chewed

רְמוֹ אִנּוּן בְּנֵיהוֹן וּנְשֵׁיהוֹן וְלָא־מְטוֹ לְאַרְעִית גֻּבָּא עַד דִּי־

before the the to did they And their and their ,them they
pit of bottom reach not .wives sons cast

26 שְׁלִטוּ בְהוֹן אַרְיָוָתָא וְכָל־גַּרְמֵיהוֹן הַדִּקוּ׃ בֵּאדַיִן דָּרְיָוֶשׁ

Darius Then they their and ;lions the them over-
.crushed bones all powered

מַלְכָּא כְּתַב לְכָל־עַמְמַיָּא אֻמַיָּא וְלִשָּׁנַיָּא דִּי־דָאְרִין בְּכָל־

all in were who the and the the to wrote King
living languages ,nations ,peoples all

27 אַרְעָא שְׁלָמְכוֹן יִשְׂגֵּא׃ מִן־קֳדָמַי שִׂים טְעֵם דִּי ׀ בְּכָל־

all in that a was before from be Your the
,decree given me ;increased peace :earth

שָׁלְטָן מַלְכוּתִי לֶהֱוֺן זָאְעִין וְדָחֲלִין מִן־קֳדָם אֱלָהֵהּ דִּי־

of God the before fear and tremble (men) my domain
shall ,kingdom's

דָנִיֵּאל דִּי־הוּא ׀ אֱלָהָא חַיָּא וְקַיָּם לְעָלְמִין וּמַלְכוּתֵהּ

His and ,forever and living God the He For .Daniel
kingdom enduring (is)

28 דִּי־לָא תִתְחַבַּל וְשָׁלְטָנֵהּ עַד־סוֹפָא׃ מְשֵׁיזִב וּמַצִּל וְעָבֵד

He and and He the (be shall) His and be shall not the (is)
works ,rescues delivers .end to dominion ,destroyed which one

אָתִין וְתִמְהִין בִּשְׁמַיָּא וּבְאַרְעָא דִּי שֵׁיזִיב לְדָנִיֵּאל מִן־יַד

the from Daniel has who the in and the in and signs
of hand delivered ;earth heavens wonders

29 אַרְיָוָתָא׃ וְדָנִיֵּאל דְּנָה הַצְלַח בְּמַלְכוּת דָּרְיָוֶשׁ וּבְמַלְכוּת

the in and ,Darius the in made was this Daniel So .lions the
of reign of reign prosper to

כּוֹרֶשׁ פָּרְסָאָ׃

.Persian the Cyrus

CAP. VII ז

CHAPTER 7

CHAPTER 7

[1] In the first year of Belshazzar king of Babylon, Daniel saw a dream and visions of his head on his bed. Then he wrote the dream, giving the sum of the matters. [2] Daniel spoke and said, In my vision by night I was looking. And, behold! The four winds of the heavens were stirring up the Great Sea. [3] And four great beasts came up from

1 בִּשְׁנַת חֲדָה לְבֵלְאשַׁצַּר מֶלֶךְ בָּבֶל דָּנִיֵּאל חֵלֶם חֲזָה וְחֶזְוֵי

and saw a Daniel ,Babylon king of first the In
of visions dream of Belshazzar year

רֵאשֵׁהּ עַל־מִשְׁכְּבֵהּ בֵּאדַיִן חֶלְמָא כְתַב רֵאשׁ מִלִּין אֲמַר׃

he the sum the he the Then .bed his on his
.related matters of ;wrote dream head

2 עָנֵה דָנִיֵּאל וְאָמַר חָזֵה הֲוֵית בְּחֶזְוִי עִם־לֵילְיָא וַאֲרוּ

And .night by my in was I looking ,said and Daniel an-
!behold vision swered

3 אַרְבַּע רוּחֵי שְׁמַיָּא מְגִיחָן לְיַמָּא רַבָּא׃ וְאַרְבַּע חֵיוָן

beasts four And .great sea the were the The four
stirring heavens of winds

the sea, different from one another. [4] The first (was) like a lion and had eagle's wings. I watched until its wings were torn off. And it was lifted up from the earth and made to stand on two feet like a man; and a man's heart was given to it. [5] And, behold, another beast, a second, like a bear. And it raised itself up on one side, and three ribs were in its mouth between its teeth. And they said this to it: Arise, eat up much flesh. [6] After this I watched, and, lo, another like a leopard, which had four wings of a bird on its back! For also to the beast (were) four heads. And rulership was given to it. [7] And after this I looked in the night visions; and, behold, the fourth beast, fearful and terrifying, and very strong! And it (had) great iron teeth. It devoured and broke in pieces, and stamped what was left with its feet. And it (was) different from all the beasts that (were) before it; and it had ten horns. [8] I was thinking about the horns; and, behold, another little horn came up among them, before whom three of the first horns were pulled up by the roots. And, behold, in this horn (were) eyes like the eyes of man, and a mouth speaking great things.

[9] I watched until the thrones were set up, and the Ancient of Days sat, whose robe (was) white as snow, and the hair of His head like the pure wool; His throne (was like) flames of fire, its wheels burning fire. [10] A stream of fire went out and

4 רְבַרְבָן סָלְקָן מִדַּיְמָא שָׁנֵין דָא מִדָּא: קַדְמָיְתָא כְאַרְיֵה

a like   The   from this different the from came great
,lion (was) first .this   ,sea   up

וְגַפִּין דִּי־נְשַׁר לַהּ חָזֵה הֲוֵית עַד דִּי־מְּרִיטוּ גַפַּיהּ וּנְטִילַת

was it And the   torn were   until was I looking .it to an of and and
up lifted .wings off   (were) eagle wings

מִן־אַרְעָא וְעַל־רַגְלַיִן כֶּאֱנָשׁ הָקִימַת וּלְבַב אֱנָשׁ יְהִיב לַהּ:

.it to was man's a and to made a like two and the from
     given heart   ;stand man feet on earth

5 וַאֲרוּ חֵיוָה אָחֳרִי תִנְיָנָה דָּמְיָה לְדֹב וְלִשְׂטַר־חַד הֳקִמַת

was it one on And .bear a like ,second a ,another beast And
up raised side   ,behold

וּתְלָת עִלְעִין בְּפֻמַּהּ בֵּין שִׁנַּיהּ וְכֵן אָמְרִין לַהּ קוּמִי אֲכֻלִי

devour ,Arise :it to said they And its between its in ribs and
                                    .teeth mouth   (were) three

6 בְּשַׂר שַׂגִּיא: בָּאתַר דְּנָה חָזֵה הֲוֵית וַאֲרוּ אָחֳרִי כִּנְמַר

a like another ,and was I looking this After .much flesh
,leopard ,behold

וְלַהּ גַּפִּין אַרְבַּע דִּי־עוֹף עַל־גַּבַּיהּ וְאַרְבְּעָה רֵאשִׁין לְחֵיוְתָא

the to heads four also its on a of four wings and
;beast (were)   side bird   it to

7 וְשָׁלְטָן יְהִיב לַהּ: בָּאתַר דְּנָה חָזֵה הֲוֵית בְּחֶזְוֵי לֵילְיָא

the in was I looking this After .it to was and
;night of visions   given dominion

וַאֲרוּ חֵיוָה רְבִיעָאָה דְּחִילָה וְאֵימְתָנִי וְתַקִּיפָא יַתִּירָה וְשִׁנַּיִן

And .exceedingly strong and and frightful the beast ,and
teeth ,terrifying ,fourth ,behold

דִּי־פַרְזֶל לַהּ רַבְרְבָן אָכְלָה וּמַדֱּקָה וּשְׁאָרָא בְּרַגְלַיהּ

feet its with what and and It .great it to iron of
left was ,crushed devoured (were)

רָפְסָה וְהִיא מְשַׁנְּיָה מִן־כָּל־חֵיוָתָא דִּי קָדָמַיהּ וְקַרְנַיִן

horns and before that the all from was it And ;it
(were) beasts different .trampled

8 עֲשַׂר לַהּ: מִשְׂתַּכַּל הֲוֵית בְּקַרְנַיָּא וַאֲלוּ קֶרֶן אָחֳרִי זְעֵירָה

little another horn and the was I considering .it to ten
,behold ,horns (were)

סִלְקָת בֵּינֵיהֵן וּתְלָת מִן־קַרְנַיָּא קַדְמָיְתָא אֶתְעֲקַרוּ מִן־

from were first the of and among came
uprooted horns three ;them up

קָדָמַהּ וַאֲלוּ עַיְנִין כְּעַיְנֵי אֲנָשָׁא בְּקַרְנָא־דָא וּפֻם מְמַלִּל

speaking a and ,this (were) the the like eyes And before
mouth horn on man of eyes ,behold .it

9 רַבְרְבָן: חָזֵה הֲוֵית עַד דִּי כָרְסָוָן רְמִיו וְעַתִּיק יוֹמִין יְתִב

,sat Days the and were thrones until was I looking great
of Ancient ,up set .things

לְבוּשֵׁהּ כִּתְלַג חִוָּר וּשְׂעַר רֵאשֵׁהּ כַּעֲמַר נְקֵא כָּרְסְיֵהּ

His .pure like His the and ,white snow as whose
throne wool head of hair (was) robe

10 שְׁבִיבִין דִּי־נוּר גַּלְגִּלּוֹהִי נוּר דָּלִק: נְהַר דִּי־נוּר נָגֵד וְנָפֵק

and ,ran fire of A .burning (were) its ;fire of (like was)
issued river fire wheels flames

came out from before Him. A thousand thousands served Him, and a myriad myriad stood before Him —the court was set, and the books were opened. [11] I then watched because of the voice of the great words which the horn spoke. I watched until the beast was killed and his body was destroyed and given to the burning flame. [12] And the rest of the beasts, they had their dominion taken away. Yet length of life was given them for a season and time. [13] I saw in the night visions, and, behold, (one) like the Son of man came with the clouds of the heavens, and He came to the Ancient of Days. And they brought Him near before Him. [14] And there was given to Him dominion and glory, and a kingdom, that all peoples, nations and languages should serve Him. His dominion (is) an everlasting dominion which shall not pass away, and His kingdom that which shall not be destroyed.

[15] I, Daniel, was distressed in my spirit in its sheath, and the visions of my head troubled me. [16] And I came near one of those who stood by and asked him the truth of all this. So he told me and made me know the meaning of the things. [17] These great beasts, which are four, (are) four kings; they shall arise out of the earth. [18] But the saints of the Most High shall receive the kingdom and possess the kingdom forever, even forever and ever. [19] Then I wanted to know the truth of the fourth beast, which was different from all of them, very frightening, whose teeth (were) iron and

מִן־קֳדָמוֹהִי אֶלֶף אַלְפִים יְשַׁמְּשׁוּנֵּהּ וְרִבּוֹ רִבְוָן קֳדָמוֹהִי
before Him myriads myriad a and served ,Him thousands a thousand before ;Him from

11 יְקוּמוּן דִּינָא יְתִב וְסִפְרִין פְּתִיחוּ׃ חָזֵה הֲוֵית בֵּאדַיִן
then ,was I looking were .opened books and ,sat The court .stood

מִן־קָל מִלַּיָּא רַבְרְבָתָא דִּי קַרְנָא מְמַלֱּלָה חָזֵה הֲוֵית עַד
until was I looking ,spoke the horn which great the words the for of sound

דִּי קְטִילַת חֵיוְתָא וְהוּבַד גִּשְׁמַהּ וִיהִיבַת לִיקֵדַת אֶשָּׁא׃
.fire the the to of burning and given his body was and destroyed the ,beast was killed

12 וּשְׁאָר חֵיוָתָא הֶעְדִּיו שָׁלְטָנְהוֹן וְאַרְכָה בְחַיִּין יְהִיבַת לְהוֹן
to them was given life of Yet length their .dominion taken was away the ;beasts the And of rest

13 עַד־זְמַן וְעִדָּן׃ חָזֵה הֲוֵית בְּחֶזְוֵי לֵילְיָא וַאֲרוּ עִם־עֲנָנֵי
the of clouds with and ,behold ,night the in of visions was I looking a and .season a for time

שְׁמַיָּא כְּבַר אֱנָשׁ אָתֵה הֲוָא וְעַד־עַתִּיק יוֹמַיָּא מְטָה
He .came Days the of Ancient to and ,was coming man like (one) of Son the the heavens

14 וּקְדָמוֹהִי הַקְרְבוּהִי׃ וְלֵהּ יְהִב שָׁלְטָן וִיקָר וּמַלְכוּ וְכֹל
that all a and ,kingdom and ,glory ,dominion was given to And Him brought they .near Him before And Him

עַמְמַיָּא אֻמַיָּא וְלִשָּׁנַיָּא לֵהּ יִפְלְחוּן שָׁלְטָנֵהּ שָׁלְטָן עָלַם
ever- lasting an dominion His (is) dominion shall .serve Him the and languages the ,nations the ,peoples

15 דִּי־לָא יֶעְדֵּה וּמַלְכוּתֵהּ דִּי־לָא תִתְחַבַּל׃ אֶתְכְּרִיַּת
was distressed be shall .destroyed not that which His and kingdom pass shall not ,away which

16 רוּחִי אֲנָה דָנִיֵּאל בְּגוֹא נִדְנֶה וְחֶזְוֵי רֵאשִׁי יְבַהֲלֻנַּנִי׃ קִרְבֵת
came I near alarmed .me my head the and of visions its amidst ,sheath ,Daniel ,I My ,spirit

עַל־חַד מִן־קָאֲמַיָּא וְיַצִּיבָא אֶבְעֵא־מִנֵּהּ עַל־כָּל־דְּנָה
.this all of from him asked the and truth who those of ,by stood one to

17 וַאֲמַר־לִי וּפְשַׁר מִלַּיָּא יְהוֹדְעִנַּנִי׃ אִלֵּין חֵיוָתָא רַבְרְבָתָא
,great beasts These known made .me to the things the and of meaning ,me he And told

18 דִּי אִנִּין אַרְבַּע אַרְבְּעָה מַלְכִין יְקוּמוּן מִן־אַרְעָא׃ וִיקַבְּלוּן
shall But receive the out .earth of shall they arise ;kings four (are) ,four which (are)

מַלְכוּתָא קַדִּישֵׁי עֶלְיוֹנִין וְיַחְסְנוּן מַלְכוּתָא עַד־עָלְמָא וְעַד
even ,forever the kingdom and possess Most the High holy the of ones the kingdom

19 עָלַם עָלְמַיָּא׃ אֱדַיִן צְבִית לְיַצָּבָא עַל־חֵיוְתָא רְבִיעָיְתָא
,fourth the beast of know to truth the I desired Then (and) .ever forever

דִּי־הֲוָת שָׁנְיָה מִן־כָּלְּהוֹן דְּחִילָה יַתִּירָה שִׁנַּהּ דִּי־פַרְזֶל
,iron of (were) its teeth ,very frightening of all from ,them different was which

its nails bronze, (who) devoured, broke in pieces, and stamped the rest with his feet; [20] and of the ten horns that were in his head, and the other which came up and before whom three fell; even that horn that (had) eyes, and a mouth speaking great things, and its look (was) greater than his fellows. [21] I watched, and that horn made war with the saints and overcame them [22] until the Ancient of Days came, and judgment was given to the saints of the Most High. And the time came that the saints possessed the kingdom. [23] So he said, The fourth beast shall be the fourth kingdom on earth, which shall be different from all kingdoms and shall devour all the earth and shall trample it down and break it in pieces. [24] And the ten horns out of this kingdom (are) ten kings; they shall rise; and another shall rise after them. And he shall be different from the first, and he shall humble three kings. [25] And he shall speak words against the Most High and shall wear out the saints of the Most High, and he intends to change times and law. And they shall be given into his hand until a time and times and one-half time. [26] But the judgment shall sit, and they shall take away his rulership, to cut off and to destroy until the end. [27] And the kingdom and rulership and the greatness of the kingdom under all the heavens shall be given to the people of the saints of the Most High, whose kingdom is an everlasting kingdom. And all kingdoms shall serve and obey Him. [28] Here (is) the end of the matter. As for me,

וְטִפְרַיהּ דִּי־נְחָשׁ אָכְלָה מַדֱּקָה וּשְׁאָרָא בְּרַגְלַיהּ רָפְסָה׃
,trampled feet its with what and left was ,crushed (and) ate (who) ,up ,bronze of its and nails

20 וְעַל־קַרְנַיָּא עֲשַׂר דִּי בְרֵאשַׁהּ וְאָחֳרִי דִּי סִלְקַת וּנְפַלוּ
fell and came up which the and other its ,head on that (were) ten the and horns of

מִן־קֳדָמַיהּ תְּלָת וְקַרְנָא דִכֵּן וְעַיְנִין לַהּ וּפֻם מְמַלִּל
speaking a and mouth ,it to eyes and (were) that even horn ,three before from him

21 רַבְרְבָן וְחֶזְוַהּ רַב מִן־חַבְרָתַהּ׃ חָזֵה הֲוֵית וְקַרְנָא דִכֵּן
that and horn ,was I looking its .fellows than (was) greater its and look great ;things

22 עָבְדָא קְרָב עִם־קַדִּישִׁין וְיָכְלָה לְהוֹן׃ עַד דִּי־אֲתָה עַתִּיק
the of Ancient came until ;them over- and powered holy (His) ,ones with war made

יוֹמַיָּא וְדִינָא יְהִב לְקַדִּישֵׁי עֶלְיוֹנִין וְזִמְנָא מְטָה וּמַלְכוּתָא
the kingdom that came the And time Most the .High the for of saints was given the and judgment ,Days

23 הֶחֱסִנוּ קַדִּישִׁין׃ כֵּן אֲמַר חֵיוְתָא רְבִיעָיְתָא מַלְכוּ רְבִיעָיָא
the fourth kingdom fourth The beast ,said he So holy (His) .ones pos- sessed

תֶּהֱוֵא בְּאַרְעָא דִּי תִשְׁנֵא מִן־כָּל־מַלְכְוָתָא וְתֵאכֻל כָּל־
all shall and devour king- the doms all from be shall different which the on ;earth shall be

24 אַרְעָא וּתְדוּשִׁנַּהּ וְתַדְּקִנַּהּ׃ וְקַרְנַיָּא עֲשַׂר מִנַּהּ מַלְכוּתָה
kingdom (are) of out this ten the And horns crush and .it trample and ,it the ;earth

עַשְׂרָה מַלְכִין יְקֻמוּן וְאָחֳרָן יְקוּם אַחֲרֵיהוֹן וְהוּא יִשְׁנֵא
be shall different And he after .them shall rise and another shall they ;rise ;kings ten

25 מִן־קַדְמָיֵא וּתְלָתָה מַלְכִין יְהַשְׁפִּל׃ וּמִלִּין לְצַד עִלָּיָא
the High Most against And words shall he .humble kings three and the ones previous from

יְמַלִּל וּלְקַדִּישֵׁי עֶלְיוֹנִין יְבַלֵּא וְיִסְבַּר לְהַשְׁנָיָה זִמְנִין וְדָת
and .law times change to he and intends wear shall ,out Most the High the and of ones holy shall he ,speak

26 וְיִתְיַהֲבוּן בִּידֵהּ עַד־עִדָּן וְעִדָּנִין וּפְלַג עִדָּן׃ וְדִינָא יִתִּב
will sit the But court .time one and half and ,times a time until his into hand they And given be shall

27 וְשָׁלְטָנֵהּ יְהַעְדּוֹן לְהַשְׁמָדָה וּלְהוֹבָדָה עַד־סוֹפָא׃ וּמַלְכוּתָא
the And ,kingdom the .end until to and destroy to exterminate shall they ,away take his and dominion

וְשָׁלְטָנָא וּרְבוּתָא דִּי מַלְכְוָת תְּחוֹת כָּל־שְׁמַיָּא יְהִיבַת
be shall given the ,heavens all under the kingdoms of the and greatness the and ,dominion

לְעַם קַדִּישֵׁי עֶלְיוֹנִין מַלְכוּתֵהּ מַלְכוּת עָלַם וְכֹל שָׁלְטָנַיָּא
the dominion And all ever- .lasting an kingdom whose (is) kingdom Most the ,High the holy of ones the to of people

28 לֵהּ יִפְלְחוּן וְיִשְׁתַּמְּעוּן׃ עַד־כָּה סוֹפָא דִּי־מִלְּתָא אֲנָה
As ,me for the .matter of end the Here (is) .obey and shall serve Him

Daniel, my thoughts troubled me much, and my face changed on me. But I kept the matter in my heart.

דָנִיֵּאל שַׂגִּיא ׀ רַעְיוֹנַי יְבַהֲלֻנַּנִי וְזִיוַי יִשְׁתַּנּוֹן עֲלַי וּמִלְּתָא
the But .me on changed my and alarmed my greatly ,Daniel
matter color ,me thoughts

בְּלִבִּי נִטְרֵת׃
.kept I my in
heart

CAP. VIII ח

CHAPTER 8

CHAPTER 8

[1] In the third year of the reign of King Belshazzar, a vision appeared to me, Daniel, after that which appeared to me at the first. [2] And I looked in a vision. And it came to pass, when I looked, I (was) at Shushan the citadel, which (is) in the province of Elam. And in a vision I looked, and I was by the river of Ulai. [3] Then I lifted up my eyes and looked. And, behold, a ram was standing before the river, having two horns. And the two horns (were) high, but one (was) higher than the other, and the higher one came up last. [4] I saw the ram pushing westward and northward and southward, so that no beasts could stand before him, nor (any) who could deliver out of his hand. But he did according to his will and became great. [5] And I was watching, and behold, a he-goat came from the west, over the face of all the earth, and did not touch the ground. And the goat (had) an outstanding horn between his eyes. [6] And he came to the ram with two horns, which I had seen standing before the river, and (he) ran to him in the fury of his power. [7] And I saw him come close to the ram. And he was moved with anger against him, and struck the ram and broke his two horns. And there was no power in the ram to stand before him. But he threw him down to the

1 בִּשְׁנַת שָׁלוֹשׁ לְמַלְכוּת בֵּלְאשַׁצַּר הַמֶּלֶךְ חָזוֹן נִרְאָה אֵלַי
to appeared a ,king the Belshazzar the of third the In
;me vision of reign year

2 אֲנִי דָנִיֵּאל אַחֲרֵי הַנִּרְאָה אֵלַי בַּתְּחִלָּה׃ וָאֶרְאֶה בֶּחָזוֹן
the in I And the at me to which that after ,Daniel (to)
,vision looked .beginning appeared ,me

וַיְהִי בִּרְאֹתִי וַאֲנִי בְּשׁוּשַׁן הַבִּירָה אֲשֶׁר בְּעֵילָם הַמְּדִינָה
the Elam in which the at I I when it and
(is) citadel Shushan (was) ,looked ,was
.province

3 וָאֶרְאֶה בֶּחָזוֹן וַאֲנִי הָיִיתִי עַל־אוּבַל אוּלָי׃ וָאֶשָּׂא עֵינַי
my I Then .Ulai the by was I and the in I And
eyes up lifted of Canal ,vision looked

וָאֶרְאֶה וְהִנֵּה ׀ אַיִל אֶחָד עֹמֵד לִפְנֵי הָאֻבָל וְלוֹ קְרָנָיִם
two to and the before was a ram and and
.horns it ,canal standing ,behold ,looked

וְהַקְּרָנַיִם גְּבֹהוֹת וְהָאַחַת גְּבֹהָה מִן־הַשֵּׁנִית וְהַגְּבֹהָה
the and the than higher one but (were) two the And
one higher ,other (was) ,high horns

4 עֹלָה בָּאַחֲרֹנָה׃ רָאִיתִי אֶת־הָאַיִל מְנַגֵּחַ יָמָּה וְצָפוֹנָה
north- and west- butting ram the saw I .last came
ward ward up

וָנֶגְבָּה וְכָל־חַיּוֹת לֹא־יַעַמְדוּ לְפָנָיו וְאֵין מַצִּיל מִיָּדוֹ וְעָשָׂה
he And from could and before might not beasts that so and
did .hand his deliver none ,him stand all ,southward

5 כִרְצֹנוֹ וְהִגְדִּיל׃ וַאֲנִי ׀ הָיִיתִי מֵבִין וְהִנֵּה צְפִיר־הָעִזִּים בָּא
came the a and ,considering was I And became and his by
goats of male ,behold .great ,will

מִן־הַמַּעֲרָב עַל־פְּנֵי כָל־הָאָרֶץ וְאֵין נוֹגֵעַ בָּאָרֶץ וְהַצָּפִיר
he- the And the touch did and the all the over ,west the from
(had) goat .ground not ,earth of face

6 קֶרֶן חָזוּת בֵּין עֵינָיו׃ וַיָּבֹא עַד־הָאַיִל בַּעַל הַקְּרָנַיִם אֲשֶׁר
which two the with the to he And his between con- an
horns ram came .eyes spicuous horn

7 רָאִיתִי עֹמֵד לִפְנֵי הָאֻבָל וַיָּרָץ אֵלָיו בַּחֲמַת כֹּחוֹ׃ וּרְאִיתִיו
saw I And his the in it to he and the before standing had I
him .power of fury ran ,canal seen

מַגִּיעַ ׀ אֵצֶל הָאַיִל וַיִּתְמַרְמַר אֵלָיו וַיַּךְ אֶת־הָאַיִל וַיְשַׁבֵּר
and the and against became he And the beside came
shattered ram struck ,him furious .ram close

אֶת־שְׁתֵּי קְרָנָיו וְלֹא־הָיָה כֹחַ בָּאַיִל לַעֲמֹד לְפָנָיו וַיַּשְׁלִיכֵהוּ
threw he But before to the in power there And its two
down him .him stand ram was not .horns

ground and stamped on him. And there was no one able to deliver the ram from his power. [8] Then the he-goat became very great. And when he was strong, the great horn was broken. And in its place came up four outstanding (ones) toward the four winds of the heavens. [9] And out of one of them came a little horn, which became very great, toward the south and toward the east and toward the bountiful (land). [10] And it became great, (even) to the host of the heavens. And it cast down (some) of the host and of the stars to the ground and stamped on them. [11] Yes, he magnified himself even to the leader of the host; and the daily (sacrifice) was taken away by him, and the place of his sanctuary was cast down. [12] And a host was given with the daily (sacrifice) because of transgressions. And it threw the truth down to the ground; and it worked and succeeded. [13] Then I heard a certain holy one speaking, and another holy one said to that one who spoke, Until when (is) the vision, the regular (sacrifice) and the desolating trespass, to give both the sanctuary and the host to be trampled? [14] And he said to me, For two thousand, three hundred evenings, mornings; and will be vindicated the sanctuary.

[15] And it was, when I Daniel had seen the vision, then I sought meaning; and behold, the form of a man stood before me. [16] And I heard a man's voice between Ulai's (banks), and he called and said, Gabriel, make this one discern the vision. [17] So he came beside my place. And when he came, I feared and fell on my face. But he said to me, Discern, O son of man, for the vision (is) for the time of the end. [18] And while he was speaking with me, I was stunned

8 ארצה וירמסהו ולא־היה מציל לאיל מידו׃ וצפיר
the Then his from the deliver could and trampled and the to
of male .hand ram none ,him ground

העזים הגדיל עד־מאד וכעצמו נשברה הקרן הגדולה
.great horn the was when And .very became the
broken ,mighty was he great goats

ותעלנה חזות ארבע תחתיה לארבע רוחות השמים׃
the winds the toward ,place its in four con- came And
.heavens of four spicuous up

9 ומן־האחת מהם יצא קרן־אחת מצעירה ותגדל־יתר
,very be- and ,little a horn came of one And
great came them of out

10 אל־הנגב ואל־המזרח ואל־הצבי׃ ותגדל עד־צבא
the to (even) it And boun- the and ,east the and the toward
of host ,great became .(land) tiful toward toward south

השמים ותפל ארצה מן־הצבא ומן־הכוכבים ותרמסם׃
trampled and ,stars the and host the of the to it And the
.them of ground down cast .heavens

11 ועד שר־הצבא הגדיל וממנו הרים התמיד והשלך
was and regular the was by and magnified he the ruler to Even
down cast ,(sacrifice) removed him ,himself host of the

12 מכון מקדשו׃ וצבא תנתן על־התמיד בפשע ותשלך
it and through regular the with was a And His place the
down cast ;trespass (sacrifice) given host .sanctuary of

13 אמת ארצה ועשתה והצליחה׃ ואשמעה אחד־קדוש
holy a I Then and it and the to truth
one certain heard .prospered worked ;ground

מדבר ויאמר אחד קדוש לפלמוני המדבר עד־מתי
when Until ,spoke who that to holy another said and ,speaking
(is) one one

החזון התמיד והפשע שמם תת וקדש וצבא מרמס׃
be to the and the both to ,desolating the and regular the the
?trampled host sanctuary give trespass (sacrifice) ,vision

14 ויאמר אלי עד ערב בקר אלפים ושלש מאות ונצדק
be will then hun- and two mornings evenings For ,me to he And
vindicated ;dred three thousand (and) said

15 קדש׃ ויהי בראתי אני דניאל את־החזון ואבקשה בינה
;meaning I then the Daniel I when it And (the)
sought ,vision seen had ,was .sanctuary

16 והנה עמד לנגדי כמראה גבר׃ ואשמע קול־אדם בין
be- man's a voice I And .man a the like before there then
tween heard of appearance me stood ,behold

אולי ויקרא ויאמר גבריאל הבן להלז את־המראה׃
the this make ,Gabriel ,said and he and ,Ulai
.vision (man) discern called

17 ויבא אצל עמדי ובבאו נבעתי ואפלה על־פני ויאמר
he But .face my on fell and was I when And my beside he So
said afraid ,came he .place came

18 אלי הבן בן־אדם כי לעת־קץ החזון׃ ובדברו עמי
with he as And the the the for for ,man O ,Discern ,me to
,me speaking was .vision end of time (is) of son

on my face toward the ground. But he touched me and set me upright. [19] And he said, Behold, I will make you know what shall happen in the last end of the indignation. For (it is) for the time appointed (the) end (shall come). [20] The ram which you saw with two horns (is) the kings of Media and Persia. [21] And the shaggy goat (is) the king of Greece. And the great horn that (is) between his eyes is the first king. [22] And as for that which is broken, and four stood up in its place — four kingdoms shall stand up out of the nation, but not in its power. [23] And in the latter time of their kingdom, when the transgressors have come to the full, a king, strong of face, and skilled at intrigues, shall stand up. [24] And his power shall be mighty, but not by his own power. And marvelously he shall destroy, and he shall prosper, and work, and destroy the mighty and the holy people. [25] And also through his understanding, he shall cause deceit to succeed in his hand. And he shall magnify himself in his own heart and shall destroy many at ease. He shall also stand up against the Ruler of rulers, but he shall be broken without (a) hand. [26] And the morning and evening vision that was told (is) true. But you shut up the vision; for it (shall be) for many days. [27] And I, Daniel, was faint. And I was sick (for) days. Afterwards, I got up and did the king's business. And I was amazed at the vision. But there was no understanding.

נִרְדַּמְתִּי עַל־פָּנַי אָרְצָה וַיִּגַּע־בִּי וַיַּעֲמִידֵנִי עַל־עָמְדִי׃

.place my on me set and he But the to my on lay I
upright me touched .ground face stunned

19 וַיֹּאמֶר הִנְנִי מוֹדִיעֲךָ אֵת אֲשֶׁר־יִהְיֶה בְּאַחֲרִית הַזָּעַם כִּי

For in- the last the in shall what make will ,Behold he And
(is it) .dignation of end happen know you I ,said

20 לְמוֹעֵד קֵץ׃ הָאַיִל אֲשֶׁר־רָאִיתָ בַּעַל הַקְּרָנָיִם מַלְכֵי מָדַי

Media the :horns two with you which The (the) the for
of kings saw ram .end of time set

21 וּפָרָס׃ וְהַצָּפִיר הַשָּׂעִיר מֶלֶךְ יָוָן וְהַקֶּרֶן הַגְּדוֹלָה אֲשֶׁר־

that great the And .Greece the ,shaggy the And and
(is) horn of king he-goat .Persia

22 בֵּין־עֵינָיו הוּא הַמֶּלֶךְ הָרִאשׁוֹן׃ וְהַנִּשְׁבֶּרֶת וַתַּעֲמֹדְנָה

stood and that for as And .first king the (is) its between
up ,broken was which eyes

אַרְבַּע תַּחְתֶּיהָ אַרְבַּע מַלְכֻיוֹת מִגּוֹי יַעֲמֹדְנָה וְלֹא בְכֹחוֹ׃

its with but stand shall of out kingdoms four its in four
.power not ,up nation the ,place

23 וּבְאַחֲרִית מַלְכוּתָם כְּהָתֵם הַפֹּשְׁעִים יַעֲמֹד מֶלֶךְ עַז־פָּנִים

,face strong king a shall trans- the have when their the in And
of up stand ,gressors finished ,kingdom of time latter

24 וּמֵבִין חִידוֹת׃ וְעָצַם כֹּחוֹ וְלֹא בְכֹחוֹ וְנִפְלָאוֹת יַשְׁחִית

shall he And his by but his mighty and ;intrigues and
,destroy marvelously .power own not ,power at skilled

25 וְהִצְלִיחַ וְעָשָׂה וְהִשְׁחִית עֲצוּמִים וְעַם־קְדֹשִׁים׃ וְעַל־

And .holy the and mighty the destroy and and shall he and
through people ,accomplish ,prosper

שִׂכְלוֹ וְהִצְלִיחַ מִרְמָה בְּיָדוֹ וּבִלְבָבוֹ יַגְדִּיל וּבְשַׁלְוָה יַשְׁחִית

shall he be and will he his in And his in deceit make will he his
destroy ;ease at himself lift heart own .hand succeed skill

26 רַבִּים וְעַל שַׂר־שָׂרִים יַעֲמֹד וּבְאֶפֶס יָד יִשָּׁבֵר׃ וּמַרְאֵה

the And be shall he a with- but shall he rulers the Also .many
of vision .broken hand out ,up stand of Ruler against

הָעֶרֶב וְהַבֹּקֶר אֲשֶׁר נֶאֱמַר אֱמֶת הוּא וְאַתָּה סְתֹם הֶחָזוֹן

the Shut But .(is) it true ,told was that the and the
,vision up !you morning evening

27 כִּי לְיָמִים רַבִּים׃ וַאֲנִי דָנִיֵּאל נִהְיֵיתִי וְנֶחֱלֵיתִי יָמִים

.days was I And .faint was Daniel ,I And .many for for
(for) sick days (is it)

וָאָקוּם וָאֶעֱשֶׂה אֶת־מְלֶאכֶת הַמֶּלֶךְ וָאֶשְׁתּוֹמֵם עַל־הַמַּרְאֶה

,vision the at was I And the business did and I Then
amazed .king's arose

וְאֵין מֵבִין׃

under- not but
.standing was

CAP. IX ט

CHAPTER 9

CHAPTER 9

[1] In the first year of Darius the son of Ahasuerus, of the seed of the Medes, who was made king

1 בִּשְׁנַת אַחַת לְדָרְיָוֶשׁ בֶּן־אֲחַשְׁוֵרוֹשׁ מִזֶּרַע מָדָי אֲשֶׁר

who the the of ,Ahasuerus the Darius of first the In
,Medes of seed of son year

over the realm of the Chaldeans, [2] in the first year of his reign, I, Daniel, understood the number of the years by books, which came as the word of Jehovah to Jeremiah the prophet, that He would accomplish seventy years in the desolations of Jerusalem.

[3] And I set my face toward the Lord God, to seek by prayer and holy desires, with fasting and sackcloth and ashes. [4] And I prayed to Jehovah my God, and made my confession, saying, O Lord, the great and awesome God, keeping the covenant and mercy to those who love Him, and to those who keep His commandments; [5] we have sinned and have committed iniquity, and have done wickedly, and have rebelled, even by departing from Your commandments and from Your judgments. [6] And we have not listened to Your servants the prophets, who spoke in Your name to our kings, our princes and our fathers, and to all the people of the land. [7] O Lord, righteousness (belongs) to You, but to us the shame of our faces, as (it) is today; to the men of Judah and to the residents of Jerusalem, and to all Israel, both near and at a distance, through all the lands where You have scattered them, because of their sin which they have sinned against You. [8] O Lord, shamefacedness (belongs) to us, to our kings, to our rulers, and to our fathers, because we have sinned against You. [9] To the Lord our God (belong) mercies and pardons, for we have rebelled against Him. [10] We have not obeyed the voice of the Lord our God, to walk in His laws which He set before us by His servants the prophets. [11] Yes, all Israel has transgressed Your law, and

2 הָמְלַךְ עַל מַלְכוּת כַּשְׂדִּים׃ בִּשְׁנַת אַחַת לְמָלְכוֹ אֲנִי
,I his of first the In the king- the over made was
,reign year ,Chaldeans of dom king

דָּנִיֵּאל בִּינֹתִי בַּסְּפָרִים מִסְפַּר הַשָּׁנִים אֲשֶׁר הָיָה דְבַר־
word the came which years the the the by understood ,Daniel
of (as) of number ,books

יְהוָה אֶל־יִרְמִיָה הַנָּבִיא לְמַלֹּאות לְחָרְבוֹת יְרוּשָׁלִַם שִׁבְעִים
seventy —Jerusalem the for would He that the Jeremiah to Jehovah
of desolations accomplish ,prophet

3 שָׁנָה׃ וָאֶתְּנָה אֶת־פָּנַי אֶל־אֲדֹנָי הָאֱלֹהִים לְבַקֵּשׁ תְּפִלָּה
by seek to ,God the toward face my set I And .years
prayer Lord

4 וְתַחֲנוּנִים בְּצוֹם וְשַׂק וָאֵפֶר׃ וָאֶתְפַּלְלָה לַיהוָה אֱלֹהַי
,God my to prayed I And .dust and and with sup- and
Jehovah sackcloth fasting ,plications

וָאֶתְוַדֶּה וָאֹמְרָה אָנָּא אֲדֹנָי הָאֵל הַגָּדוֹל וְהַנּוֹרָא שֹׁמֵר
who and great God the O ,pray I ,said and and
keeps ,awesome ,Lord confessed

5 הַבְּרִית וְהַחֶסֶד לְאֹהֲבָיו וּלְשֹׁמְרֵי מִצְוֹתָיו׃ חָטָאנוּ וְעָוִינוּ
did and have we com- His those to and who those to and cove- the
,iniquity sinned ;mands keep who ,Him love lovingkindness nant

6 וְהִרְשַׁעְנוּ וּמָרָדְנוּ וְסוֹר מִמִּצְוֹתֶךָ וּמִמִּשְׁפָּטֶיךָ׃ וְלֹא
And Your from and Your from and have and done have and
not .judgments commands turned ,rebelled ,wickedly

שָׁמַעְנוּ אֶל־עֲבָדֶיךָ הַנְּבִיאִים אֲשֶׁר דִּבְּרוּ בְּשִׁמְךָ אֶל־
to Your in spoke who the Your to have we
name ,prophets servants listened

7 מְלָכֵינוּ שָׂרֵינוּ וַאֲבֹתֵינוּ וְאֶל כָּל־עַם הָאָרֶץ׃ לְךָ אֲדֹנָי
O (belongs) the the all and our and our our
,Lord ,You to .land of people to ,fathers ,leaders ,kings

הַצְּדָקָה וְלָנוּ בֹּשֶׁת הַפָּנִים כַּיּוֹם הַזֶּה לְאִישׁ יְהוּדָה וּלְיוֹשְׁבֵי
res- to and Judah the to ;this (at) as (our) the to but righ-
of idents of men day ,faces of shame us teousness

יְרוּשָׁלִַם וּלְכָל־יִשְׂרָאֵל הַקְּרֹבִים וְהָרְחֹקִים בְּכָל־הָאֲרָצוֹת
lands the through who and are who ,Israel to and ,Jerusalem
all ,afar are near all

8 אֲשֶׁר הִדַּחְתָּם שָׁם בְּמַעֲלָם אֲשֶׁר מָעֲלוּ־בָךְ׃ אֲדֹנָי לָנוּ
us to O against have they which their for ,there have You where
(is) ,Lord .You done unfaithfulness them sown

בֹּשֶׁת הַפָּנִים לִמְלָכֵינוּ לְשָׂרֵינוּ וְלַאֲבֹתֵינוּ אֲשֶׁר חָטָאנוּ
have we because our to and our to our to ,faces shame
sinned ,fathers ,rulers ,kings of

9 לָךְ׃ לַאדֹנָי אֱלֹהֵינוּ הָרַחֲמִים וְהַסְּלִחוֹת כִּי מָרַדְנוּ בּוֹ׃
against have we for ,pardons and mercies our Lord the To against
.Him rebelled God (belong) .You

10 וְלֹא שָׁמַעְנוּ בְּקוֹל יְהוָה אֱלֹהֵינוּ לָלֶכֶת בְּתוֹרֹתָיו אֲשֶׁר־
which His in walk to ,God our Jehovah the have we And
laws of voice obeyed not

11 נָתַן לְפָנֵינוּ בְּיַד עֲבָדָיו הַנְּבִיאִים׃ וְכָל־יִשְׂרָאֵל עָבְרוּ אֶת־
has Israel And .prophets the His by before He
transgressed all servants us set

turned aside, that they might not obey Your voice. Therefore the curse has poured out on us, and the oath that is written in the law of Moses the servant of God, because we have sinned against Him. [12] And He has confirmed His words which He spoke against us and against our judges who judge us, by bringing on us a great evil. For under the whole heavens (it) has not been done as (it) has been done to Jerusalem. [13] As it is written in the law of Moses, all this evil has come on us. Yet we did not make our prayer before Jehovah our God, that we might turn from our iniquities and understand Your truth. [14] Therefore Jehovah has watched over the evil and has brought it on us. For Jehovah our God (is) righteous in all His works which He does. For we did not obey His voice. [15] And now, O Lord our God, who has brought Your people out of the land of Egypt with a mighty hand, and has made for Himself a name, as it is today, we have sinned, we have done wickedly.

[16] O Lord, I pray to You, according to all Your righteousness, let Your anger and Your fury be turned away from Your city Jerusalem, Your holy mountain. Because for our sins, and for the iniquities of our fathers, Jerusalem and Your people (have become) a curse to all around us. [17] Now, therefore, O our God, hear the prayer of Your servant and his holy desires, and cause Your face to shine on Your sanctuary that (is) desolate, for the Lord's sake. [18] O my God, bow down Your ear and hear. Open Your eyes and see our ruins, and the city which is called by Your

תּוֹרָתֶךָ וְסוֹר לְבִלְתִּי שְׁמוֹעַ בְּקֹלֶךָ וַתִּתַּךְ עָלֵינוּ הָאָלָה
the curse, us on has And poured out Your voice. obeying not and veered, Your law
וְהַשְּׁבֻעָה אֲשֶׁר כְּתוּבָה בְּתוֹרַת מֹשֶׁה עֶבֶד־הָאֱלֹהִים כִּי
because, God the servant of Moses the in law of written is that oath the and
12 חָטָאנוּ לוֹ׃ וַיָּקֶם אֶת־דְּבָרָיו ׀ אֲשֶׁר־דִּבֶּר עָלֵינוּ וְעַל־
and against us against He spoke which words His has He And confirmed against Him. have we sinned
שֹׁפְטֵינוּ אֲשֶׁר שְׁפָטוּנוּ לְהָבִיא עָלֵינוּ רָעָה גְדֹלָה אֲשֶׁר
which great, evil a us on by bringing us judged, who our judges
לֹא־נֶעֶשְׂתָה תַּחַת כָּל־הַשָּׁמַיִם כַּאֲשֶׁר נֶעֶשְׂתָה בִּירוּשָׁלִָם׃
Jerusalem. to has it been done as the heavens whole under been has done not
13 כַּאֲשֶׁר כָּתוּב בְּתוֹרַת מֹשֶׁה אֵת כָּל־הָרָעָה הַזֹּאת בָּאָה
has come this evil all Moses, the in of law is it written As
עָלֵינוּ וְלֹא־חִלִּינוּ אֶת־פְּנֵי ׀ יְהוָה אֱלֹהֵינוּ לָשׁוּב מֵעֲוֺנֵנוּ
our from iniquities we that turn might God, our Jehovah the before of face made we prayer our Yet not us. on
14 וּלְהַשְׂכִּיל בַּאֲמִתֶּךָ׃ וַיִּשְׁקֹד יְהוָה עַל־הָרָעָה וַיְבִיאֶהָ
has and it brought evil, the over Jehovah has And watched truth. Your under- and stand
עָלֵינוּ כִּי־צַדִּיק יְהוָה אֱלֹהֵינוּ עַל־כָּל־מַעֲשָׂיו אֲשֶׁר עָשָׂה
does. He which His works all in God our Jehovah righteous (is) For us. on
15 וְלֹא שָׁמַעְנוּ בְּקֹלוֹ׃ וְעַתָּה ׀ אֲדֹנָי אֱלֹהֵינוּ אֲשֶׁר הוֹצֵאתָ
brought has who God, our Lord O now, And His voice. did we obey And not
אֶת־עַמְּךָ מֵאֶרֶץ מִצְרַיִם בְּיָד חֲזָקָה וַתַּעַשׂ־לְךָ שֵׁם כַּיּוֹם
(it is) as day a name for Yourself has and made mighty, a with hand Egypt the of out of land Your people
16 הַזֶּה חָטָאנוּ רָשָׁעְנוּ׃ אֲדֹנָי כְּכָל־צִדְקֹתֶךָ יָשָׁב־נָא אַפְּךָ
Your anger please away let turn righ- teousness, Your according all to O Lord, have we evilly done. have we sinned, this;
וַחֲמָתְךָ מֵעִירְךָ יְרוּשָׁלִַם הַר־קָדְשֶׁךָ כִּי בַחֲטָאֵינוּ וּבַעֲוֺנוֹת
and of iniquities of because sins our For Your mountain holy. Jerusalem, Your from city Your and fury
17 אֲבֹתֵינוּ יְרוּשָׁלִַם וְעַמְּךָ לְחֶרְפָּה לְכָל־סְבִיבֹתֵינוּ׃ וְעַתָּה ׀
And now those us around all to (become have) reproach a Your and people Jerusalem our fathers,
שְׁמַע אֱלֹהֵינוּ אֶל־תְּפִלַּת עַבְדְּךָ וְאֶל־תַּחֲנוּנָיו וְהָאֵר פָּנֶיךָ
Your face make and shine his supplications, and to Your servant prayer the of to our O God, listen,
18 עַל־מִקְדָּשְׁךָ הַשָּׁמֵם לְמַעַן אֲדֹנָי׃ הַטֵּה אֱלֹהַי ׀ אָזְנְךָ
Your ear my O God, Incline, the Lord's. for sake (is) that desolate, Your sanctuary on
וּשְׁמָע פְּקַחָה עֵינֶיךָ וּרְאֵה שֹׁמְמֹתֵינוּ וְהָעִיר אֲשֶׁר־נִקְרָא
called is which the and city our desolations, see and Your eyes Open and hear.

name. For we do not present our prayers before You on account of our righteousnesses, but because of Your great mercies. [19] O Lord, hear! O Lord, forgive! O Lord, listen and act! Do not delay, for Your own sake, O my God, for Your name is called on Your city and on Your people.

[20] And while I was speaking and praying and confessing my sin and the sin of my people Israel, and lifting my cry before Jehovah my God for the holy mountain of my God, [21] yes, while I was causing to fall my prayers, then that one, Gabriel, whom I had seen in the vision at the beginning, in my exhaustion touched me, being caused to fly, about the time of the evening sacrifice. [22] And he illumined me, and talked with me, and said, O Daniel, I have now come out to give you skill in understanding. [23] At the beginning of your prayers the commandment came forth, and I have come to reveal. For you (are) greatly beloved. Then understand the matter and pay attention to the vision. [24] Seventy weeks are decreed as to your people and as to your holy city to finish the transgression and to make an end of sins, and to make atonement for iniquity, and to bring in everlasting righteousness, and to seal up the vision and prophecy, and to anoint the Most Holy. [25] Know, then, and understand, (that) from the going out of the commandment to restore and to build Jerusalem to Messiah (the) Prince (shall be) seven weeks and sixty-two weeks. The street shall be built again, and the wall, even in times of affliction. [26] And after sixty-two weeks, Messiah shall be cut

שִׁמְךָ עָלֶיהָ כִּי ׀ לֹא עַל־צִדְקֹתֵינוּ אֲנַחְנוּ מַפִּילִים תַּחֲנוּנֵינוּ
our supplication do present we righ- our teousnesses on account of not For .it on Your name

19 לְפָנֶיךָ כִּי עַל־רַחֲמֶיךָ הָרַבִּים׃ אֲדֹנָי ׀ שְׁמָעָה אֲדֹנָי ׀ סְלָחָה
!forgive ,Lord O !hear ,Lord O .great Your mercies because of but before ,You

אֲדֹנָי הַקֲשִׁיבָה וַעֲשֵׂה אַל־תְּאַחַר לְמַעַנְךָ אֱלֹהַי כִּי־שִׁמְךָ
Your name for my O ,God Your for sake own Do ,delay not !act and listen ,Lord O

20 נִקְרָא עַל־עִירְךָ וְעַל־עַמֶּךָ׃ וְעוֹד אֲנִי מְדַבֵּר וּמִתְפַּלֵּל
praying and was speaking I And while Your .people and on Your city on called is

וּמִתְוַדֶּה חַטָּאתִי וְחַטַּאת עַמִּי יִשְׂרָאֵל וּמַפִּיל תְּחִנָּתִי
sup- my plication causing and fall to ,Israel my people the and of sin ,sin my con- and fessing

21 לִפְנֵי יְהוָה אֱלֹהַי עַל הַר־קֹדֶשׁ אֱלֹהָי׃ וְעוֹד אֲנִי מְדַבֵּר
was speaking I and while ;God my holy the of mountain for God my Jehovah before

בַּתְּפִלָּה וְהָאִישׁ גַּבְרִיאֵל אֲשֶׁר רָאִיתִי בֶחָזוֹן בַּתְּחִלָּה
the at ,beginning the in vision had I seen whom ,Gabriel the then man ,prayer in

22 מֻעָף בִּיעָף נֹגֵעַ אֵלַי כְּעֵת מִנְחַת־עָרֶב׃ וַיָּבֶן וַיְדַבֵּר עִמִּי
with talked and ,me he And illumined evening the .sacrifice about of time the ,me touched (my) in weariness was flown

23 וַיֹּאמַר דָּנִיֵּאל עַתָּה יָצָאתִי לְהַשְׂכִּילְךָ בִינָה׃ בִּתְחִלַּת
be- the At of ginning under- .standing you give to in skill have I come now O ,Daniel ,said and

תַּחֲנוּנֶיךָ יָצָא דָבָר וַאֲנִי בָּאתִי לְהַגִּיד כִּי חֲמוּדוֹת אָתָּה
;you greatly are beloved for to .declare have come and com- I ,mand the came forth your supplications

24 וּבִין בַּדָּבָר וְהָבֵן בַּמַּרְאֶה׃ שָׁבֻעִים שִׁבְעִים נֶחְתַּךְ עַל־
to as are decreed Seventy weeks the .vision and understand matter the so heed

עַמְּךָ ׀ וְעַל־עִיר קָדְשֶׁךָ לְכַלֵּא הַפֶּשַׁע וּלְחָתֵם חַטָּאוֹת
,sins make to and of end an trans- the gression finish to ,holy your city as and to Your people

וּלְכַפֵּר עָוֺן וּלְהָבִיא צֶדֶק עֹלָמִים וְלַחְתֹּם חָזוֹן וְנָבִיא
and prophecy vision seal to and up ,everlasting righteous- ness to and in bring ,iniquity to and for atone

25 וְלִמְשֹׁחַ קֹדֶשׁ קָדָשִׁים׃ וְתֵדַע וְתַשְׂכֵּל מִן־מֹצָא דָבָר
an order the from of issuing under- and ,stand Then ,know .Most Holy the to and anoint

לְהָשִׁיב וְלִבְנוֹת יְרוּשָׁלִַם עַד־מָשִׁיחַ נָגִיד שָׁבֻעִים שִׁבְעָה
seven (be shall) weeks (the) Prince Messiah to ,Jerusalem to and rebuild to restore

וְשָׁבֻעִים שִׁשִּׁים וּשְׁנַיִם תָּשׁוּב וְנִבְנְתָה רְחוֹב וְחָרוּץ
ditch and (with) plaza be shall it built Again .two and sixty weeks and

26 וּבְצוֹק הָעִתִּים׃ וְאַחֲרֵי הַשָּׁבֻעִים שִׁשִּׁים וּשְׁנַיִם יִכָּרֵת
be shall off cut ,two and sixty weeks the And after .times the in even of affliction

off, but nothing is His. And the people of a coming prince shall destroy the city and the sanctuary. And the end of it (shall be) with the flood, and ruins are determined, to the end (shall) (be) war.

[27] And he shall confirm a covenant with the many (for) one week. And in the middle of the week he shall cause the sacrifice and the offering to cease, and on wings as a desolator, abominations, even until the end. And that which was decreed shall be poured on the desolator.

CHAPTER 10

[1] In the third year of Cyrus king of Persia a thing was revealed to Daniel, whose name was called Belteshazzar. And the thing (was) true, and a great conflict. And he understood the thing and (had) understanding of the vision. [2] In those days I, Daniel, was mourning three weeks of days. [3] I ate no food for delight, and no flesh or wine came into my mouth. I did not anoint myself at all until three weeks of days were fulfilled. [4] And in the twenty-fourth day of the first month, as I was by the side of the great river, which (is) Tigris, [5] then I lifted up my eyes and looked: And, behold, a certain man was clothed in linen, whose loins were wrapped in fine gold from Uphaz. [6] His body also (was) like the beryl, and his face looked like lightning. And his eyes (were) like torches of fire, and his arms and his feet in color like polished bronze, and the sound of his words as the noise of a multitude. [7] And I, Daniel, alone

מָשִׁיחַ וְאֵין לוֹ וְהָעִיר וְהַקֹּדֶשׁ יַשְׁחִית עַם נָגִיד הַבָּא

.coming a the destroy shall the and the And to and ,Messiah
prince of people sanctuary city .Him is not

27 וְקִצּוֹ בַשֶּׁטֶף וְעַד קֵץ מִלְחָמָה נֶחֱרֶצֶת שֹׁמֵמוֹת׃ וְהִגְבִּיר

he And .desolations are (be shall) (the) and (be shall) its And
confirm shall determined ;war end until ,flood the with end

בְּרִית לָרַבִּים שָׁבוּעַ אֶחָד וַחֲצִי הַשָּׁבוּעַ יַשְׁבִּית ׀ זֶבַח

sacrifice shall he week the in And .one (for) the with a
cease make of half the week many covenant

וּמִנְחָה וְעַל כְּנַף שִׁקּוּצִים מְשֹׁמֵם וְעַד־כָּלָה וְנֶחֱרָצָה תִּתַּךְ

shall which that And (the) even a abominations wing a and and
out pour decreed was .end until ,desolator as upon ,offering

עַל־שֹׁמֵם׃

the on
.desolator

CAP. X י

CHAPTER 10

1 בִּשְׁנַת שָׁלוֹשׁ לְכוֹרֶשׁ מֶלֶךְ פָּרַס דָּבָר נִגְלָה לְדָנִיֵּאל

,Daniel to was a ,Persia king Cyrus third the In
revealed thing of year

אֲשֶׁר־נִקְרָא שְׁמוֹ בֵּלְטְשַׁאצַּר וֶאֱמֶת הַדָּבָר וְצָבָא גָדוֹל

.great a and ,thing the And .Belteshazzar whose was
conflict (was) true name called

2 וּבִין אֶת־הַדָּבָר וּבִינָה לוֹ בַּמַּרְאֶה׃ בַּיָּמִים הָהֵם אֲנִי

,I those days In the in to under- and the he And
.vision him (was) standing word understood

3 דָנִיֵּאל הָיִיתִי מִתְאַבֵּל שְׁלֹשָׁה שָׁבֻעִים יָמִים׃ לֶחֶם חֲמֻדוֹת

desirable food .days weeks three mourning was ,Daniel
of

לֹא אָכַלְתִּי וּבָשָׂר וָיַיִן לֹא־בָא אֶל־פִּי וְסוֹךְ לֹא־סָכְתִּי עַד־

until did I not at and my to did not and and ,ate I not
myself anoint all ,mouth come wine flesh

4 מְלֹאת שְׁלֹשֶׁת שָׁבֻעִים יָמִים׃ וּבְיוֹם עֶשְׂרִים וְאַרְבָּעָה

fourth and twenty the in And .days of weeks three were
day fulfilled

לַחֹדֶשׁ הָרִאשׁוֹן וַאֲנִי הָיִיתִי עַל־יַד הַנָּהָר הַגָּדוֹל הוּא

which ,great the the by was I as ,first the of
(is) river of side month

5 חִדָּקֶל׃ וָאֶשָּׂא אֶת־עֵינַי וָאֵרֶא וְהִנֵּה אִישׁ־אֶחָד לָבוּשׁ

was certain a and and my I then ,Tigris
in clothed man ,behold :looked eyes up lifted

6 בַּדִּים וּמָתְנָיו חֲגֻרִים בְּכֶתֶם אוּפָז׃ וּגְוִיָּתוֹ כְתַרְשִׁישׁ וּפָנָיו

his and the like his also Uphaz fine in were his and ,linen
face ,beryl (was) body from gold girded loins

כְּמַרְאֵה בָרָק וְעֵינָיו כְּלַפִּידֵי אֵשׁ וּזְרֹעֹתָיו וּמַרְגְּלֹתָיו כְּעֵין

the as his and his and ,fire torches like his and ;lightning the like
of eyes feet arms of eyes of appearance

7 נְחֹשֶׁת קָלָל וְקוֹל דְּבָרָיו כְּקוֹל הָמוֹן׃ וְרָאִיתִי אֲנִי דָנִיֵּאל

,Daniel ,I saw And mul- a the as his the and ,polished bronze
.titude of noise words of sound

saw the vision. For the men who were with me did not see the vision. But a great quaking fell on them, so that they fled to hide themselves. [8] Then I was left alone and saw this great vision, and there remained no strength in me. For my color was turned within me to corruption, and I kept no strength. [9] Yet I heard the sound of his words. And when I heard the sound of his words, then I was stunned on my face, and my face (was) toward the ground.

[10] And, behold, a hand touched me and set me tottering on my knees and the palms of my hands. [11] And he said to me, O Daniel, a man greatly beloved, understand the words that I speak to you and stand up. For to you I am now sent. And when he had spoken this word to me, I stood trembling. [12] Then he said to me, Do not fear, Daniel. For from the first day that you set your heart to understand and to humble yourself before your God, your words were heard. And I have come because of your words. [13] But the king of the kingdom of Persia withstood me twenty-one days. But, lo, Michael, one of the first rulers, came to help me. And I stayed there with the kings of Persia. [14] Now I have come to make you understand what shall happen to your people in the latter days. For the vision (is) yet for (many) days. [15] And when he had spoken such words to me, I set my face to the ground and I became speechless. [16] And, behold, (one) looking like the

לְבַדִּי אֶת־הַמַּרְאָה וְהָאֲנָשִׁים אֲשֶׁר־הָיוּ עִמִּי לֹא־רָאוּ אֶת־

did see not with me were who the men while ,vision the alone

הַמַּרְאָה אֲבָל חֲרָדָה גְדֹלָה נָפְלָה עֲלֵיהֶם וַיִּבְרְחוּ בְּהֵחָבֵא׃

hide to .themselves they fled and ,them on fell great a trembling But .vision the

8 וַאֲנִי נִשְׁאַרְתִּי לְבַדִּי וָאֶרְאֶה אֶת־הַמַּרְאָה הַגְּדֹלָה הַזֹּאת

,this great vision saw and alone left was I Then

וְלֹא־נִשְׁאַר־בִּי כֹּחַ וְהוֹדִי נֶהְפַּךְ עָלַי לְמַשְׁחִית וְלֹא עָצַרְתִּי

kept I not and ,corruption to within me was turned my For color .strength in me there remained and not

9 כֹּחַ׃ וָאֶשְׁמַע אֶת־קוֹל דְּבָרָיו וּכְשָׁמְעִי אֶת־קוֹל דְּבָרָיו

his ,words the of sound I when And heard his .words the of sound heard I Yet .strength

10 וַאֲנִי הָיִיתִי נִרְדָּם עַל־פָּנַי וּפָנַי אָרְצָה׃ וְהִנֵּה־יָד נָגְעָה

touched a hand And ,behold the toward .ground my and (was) face my on ,face lying stunned was I then

11 בִּי וַתְּנִיעֵנִי עַל־בִּרְכַּי וְכַפּוֹת יָדָי׃ וַיֹּאמֶר אֵלַי דָּנִיֵּאל אִישׁ־

man a O ,Daniel ,me to he And said my .hands the and of palms my knees on me set and ,me shaking

חֲמֻדוֹת הָבֵן בַּדְּבָרִים אֲשֶׁר אָנֹכִי דֹּבֵר אֵלֶיךָ וַעֲמֹד עַל־

in and stand you to speak I that words the under- stand greatly ,beloved

עָמְדֶךָ כִּי עַתָּה שֻׁלַּחְתִּי אֵלֶיךָ וּבְדַבְּרוֹ עִמִּי אֶת־הַדָּבָר

word with me he when And had spoken .you to sent I am now For your .place

12 הַזֶּה עָמַדְתִּי מַרְעִיד׃ וַיֹּאמֶר אֵלַי אַל־תִּירָא דָנִיֵּאל כִּי

for ,Daniel Do ,fear not ,me to he Then said .trembling stood I ,this

מִן־הַיּוֹם הָרִאשׁוֹן אֲשֶׁר נָתַתָּ אֶת־לִבְּךָ לְהָבִין וּלְהִתְעַנּוֹת

humbling and yourself to understand your heart set you that first the from day

13 לִפְנֵי אֱלֹהֶיךָ נִשְׁמְעוּ דְבָרֶיךָ וַאֲנִי־בָאתִי בִּדְבָרֶיךָ׃ וְשַׂר

the But of leader your for .words have I And come your .words were heard your ,God before

מַלְכוּת פָּרַס עֹמֵד לְנֶגְדִּי עֶשְׂרִים וְאֶחָד יוֹם וְהִנֵּה מִיכָאֵל

,Michael But ,lo .days and one twenty against stood me Persia king- the of dom

אַחַד הַשָּׂרִים הָרִאשֹׁנִים בָּא לְעָזְרֵנִי וַאֲנִי נוֹתַרְתִּי שָׁם

there stayed I And help to .me came ,first rulers the of one

14 אֵצֶל מַלְכֵי פָרָס׃ וּבָאתִי לַהֲבִינְךָ אֵת אֲשֶׁר־יִקְרָה

shall happen what make to understand you I Now come have .Persia kings the of with

15 לְעַמְּךָ בְּאַחֲרִית הַיָּמִים כִּי־עוֹד חָזוֹן לַיָּמִים׃ וּבְדַבְּרוֹ עִמִּי

with me he when And had spoken .days for the vision yet For (is) .days latter the in your to people

16 כַּדְּבָרִים הָאֵלֶּה נָתַתִּי פָנַי אַרְצָה וְנֶאֱלָמְתִּי׃ וְהִנֵּה כִּדְמוּת

in as (one) form And ,behold became I and .speechless the to ground my face set I ,tnese according words to

sons of men touched my lips. Then I opened my mouth and spoke and said to him who stood before me, O Lord, my pangs have come over me, because of the vision, and I have no strength left. [17] For how can the servant of my lord speak with my lord? For as for me, there is no power left in me; yea, there is no breath left in me. [18] Then again (one) looking like a man came and touched me, and he made me strong; [19] and he said, O man greatly loved, do not fear. Peace to you. Be strong. Yes, be strong. And when he had spoken to me, I was made strong. And (I) said, Speak, my lord, for you have made me strong. [20] Then he said, Do you know why I have come to you? And now I will return to fight with the ruler of Persia. And when I have gone out, lo, the ruler of Greece shall come. [21] But I will tell you that which is written in the Scripture of Truth. And no one shows himself courageous with me in these things except Michael your ruler.

בְּנֵי אָדָם נֹגֵעַ עַל־שְׂפָתָי וָאֶפְתַּח־פִּי וָאֲדַבְּרָה וָאֹמְרָה

said and spoke and my I Then .lips my touched men the
mouth opened of sons

אֶל־הָעֹמֵד לְנֶגְדִּי אֲדֹנִי בַּמַּרְאָה נֶהֶפְכוּ צִירַי עָלַי וְלֹא

and over my have of because ,lord O before who him to
not ,me pangs come ,visions the ,me stood

17 עָצַרְתִּי כֹּחַ׃ וְהֵיךְ יוּכַל עֶבֶד אֲדֹנִי זֶה לְדַבֵּר עִם־אֲדֹנִי

my with speak this my the can how For .strength have I
lord lord of servant left

זֶה וַאֲנִי מֵעַתָּה לֹא־יַעֲמָד־בִּי כֹחַ וּנְשָׁמָה לֹא נִשְׁאֲרָה־בִי׃

.me in is there not ,yea ;power in is not hence- as For ?this
left breath me left forth ,me for

18 19 וַיֹּסֶף וַיִּגַּע־בִּי כְּמַרְאֵה אָדָם וַיְחַזְּקֵנִי׃ וַיֹּאמֶר אַל־תִּירָא

,fear do not he And make and ,man a in (one) me touched Then
,said .strong me as form again

אִישׁ־חֲמֻדוֹת שָׁלוֹם לָךְ חֲזַק וַחֲזָק וּכְדַבְּרוֹ עִמִּי הִתְחַזַּקְתִּי

made was I to he when And be ,yea be to Peace greatly O
.stronger ,me spoken had .strong ;strong ;you ,loved man

20 וָאֹמְרָה יְדַבֵּר אֲדֹנִי כִּי חִזַּקְתָּנִי׃ וַיֹּאמֶר הֲיָדַעְתָּ לָמָּה־

why you Do he And made you for my Let I And
know ,said .strong me ,lord speak ,said

בָּאתִי אֵלֶיךָ וְעַתָּה אָשׁוּב לְהִלָּחֵם עִם־שַׂר פָּרָס וַאֲנִי

And .Persia the with fight to will I now And ?you to have I
I when of ruler return come

21 יוֹצֵא וְהִנֵּה שַׂר־יָוָן בָּא׃ אֲבָל אַגִּיד לְךָ אֶת־הָרָשׁוּם בִּכְתָב

the in is what you will I But shall Greece the then have
of writing inscribed tell .come of ruler ,lo ,out gone

אֱמֶת וְאֵין אֶחָד מִתְחַזֵּק עִמִּי עַל־אֵלֶּה כִּי אִם־מִיכָאֵל

Michael except these in with himself shows one And .truth
things me courageous not

שַׂרְכֶם׃

your
.ruler

CAP. XI יא

CHAPTER 11

CHAPTER 11

[1] And I, in the first year of Darius the Mede, I was standing for a supporter and a fortress for him. [2] And now I will tell you the truth. Behold, three kings shall yet stand up in Persia. And the fourth shall be far richer than all. And by his strength, through his riches, he shall stir up all against the kingdom of Greece. [3] And a mighty king shall stand up who shall rule with great authority and do according to his will. [4] And when he shall stand up, his kingdom shall be broken and

1 וַאֲנִי בִּשְׁנַת אַחַת לְדָרְיָוֶשׁ הַמָּדִי עָמְדִי לְמַחֲזִיק וּלְמָעוֹז

a for and a for my ,Mede the Darius of first the in And
fortress supporter standing year ,I

2 לוֹ׃ וְעַתָּה אֱמֶת אַגִּיד לָךְ הִנֵּה־עוֹד שְׁלֹשָׁה מְלָכִים

kings three yet ,Behold .you to will I the now And for
tell truth .him

עֹמְדִים לְפָרַס וְהָרְבִיעִי יַעֲשִׁיר עֹשֶׁר־גָּדוֹל מִכֹּל וּכְחֶזְקָתוֹ

he when And than far richer be shall the and ;Persia in shall
strong is .all fourth up stand

3 בְעָשְׁרוֹ יָעִיר הַכֹּל אֵת מַלְכוּת יָוָן׃ וְעָמַד מֶלֶךְ גִּבּוֹר

,mighty king a shall And .Greece the all shall he his by
up stand of kingdom up stir ,rulers

4 וּמָשַׁל מִמְשָׁל רַב וְעָשָׂה כִּרְצוֹנוֹ׃ וּכְעָמְדוֹ תִּשָּׁבֵר מַלְכוּתוֹ

his be shall when And to according do and great with shall and
kingdom broken ,up stands he .will his authority rule

and to others besides these.
And the king of the south shall be strong. And (one) of his rulers, even he shall overcome him and he will rule; his rule (will be) a great rule. And at the end of years, they shall join together, and the daughter of the king of the south shall come to the king of the north to make a treaty. But she shall not keep the power of the arm. And he will not stand, nor his arm. But she will be given up, and those who brought her, and her begetter, and her supporter in (the) times. [7] But the shoots of her roots will rise (in) his place, and he shall come to the army and will enter into the king of the north's fortress. And he will act against them and will show power; [8] and he will also bring their gods with their casted images, with vessels of their possessions, silver and gold, into exile (to) Egypt. And he shall stand from the king of the north. [9] And the king of the south will come into (his) kingdom, and will return to his own land. [10] But his sons shall be stirred up and will gather a host of great forces. And (one) will certainly come and overflow and pass through. And he will return and be stirred up, to his fortress. [11] And the king of the south will be furious and will go out and fight with him, with the king of the north. And he will raise a great host. But the host will be given into his hand. [12] And capturing the host, his heart will be lifted up. And he will make myriads fall, but he will not prevail. [13] For the king of the north will return and will raise a host greater than the former; and at the end of the times, years, he will certainly come with a great army and with much equipment. [14] And in those times

וְתֵחָץ לְאַרְבַּע רוּחוֹת הַשָּׁמָיִם וְלֹא לְאַחֲרִיתוֹ וְלֹא כְמָשְׁלוֹ

to according nor his to and ,heavens the winds the to be shall and
authority his ,posterity not of four divided

אֲשֶׁר מָשָׁל כִּי תִנָּתֵשׁ מַלְכוּתוֹ וְלַאֲחֵרִים מִלְּבַד־אֵלֶּה׃

.these besides (given) and his be shall For he with
others to ,kingdom up pulled .ruled which

5 וְיֶחֱזַק מֶלֶךְ־הַנֶּגֶב וּמִן־שָׂרָיו וְיֶחֱזַק עָלָיו וּמָשָׁל מִמְשָׁל

rule A he and on will he and his And .south the the shall And
.rule will ,him strong be ,rulers of (one) of king strong be

6 רַב מֶמְשַׁלְתּוֹ׃ וּלְקֵץ שָׁנִים יִתְחַבָּרוּ וּבַת מֶלֶךְ־הַנֶּגֶב

the of king the and join shall they ,years the at And (be shall) great
south's daughter ,together of end .rule his

תָּבֹא אֶל־מֶלֶךְ הַצָּפוֹן לַעֲשׂוֹת מֵישָׁרִים וְלֹא־תַעְצֹר כּוֹחַ

the shall she But an make to the king the to shall
of power keep not .agreement north of come

הַזְּרוֹעַ וְלֹא יַעֲמֹד וּזְרֹעוֹ וְתִנָּתֵן הִיא וּמְבִיאֶיהָ וְהַיֹּלְדָהּ

her and who those and she be shall But his nor shall he And the
,begetter ,her brought up given .arm ,stand not .arm

7 וּמַחֲזִקָהּ בָּעִתִּים׃ וְעָמַד מִנֵּצֶר שָׁרָשֶׁיהָ כַּנּוֹ וְיָבֹא אֶל־

to he and (in) ,roots her the of will But (those) in her and
come shall ,place his of shoots stand .times supporter

הַחַיִל וְיָבֹא בְּמָעוֹז מֶלֶךְ הַצָּפוֹן וְעָשָׂה בָהֶם וְהֶחֱזִיק׃

shall and against he And the king the the into shall and the
.power show them act shall .north of of fortress enter army

8 וְגַם אֱלֹהֵיהֶם עִם־נְסִכֵיהֶם עִם־כְּלֵי חֶמְדָּתָם כֶּסֶף וְזָהָב

and silver their vessels with their with their And
gold possessions of images molten gods also

בַּשְּׁבִי יָבִא מִצְרָיִם וְהוּא שָׁנִים יַעֲמֹד מִמֶּלֶךְ הַצָּפוֹן׃

.north the the from shall years he And (to) will he into
of king stand .Egypt bring exile

9 וּבָא בְּמַלְכוּת מֶלֶךְ הַנֶּגֶב וְשָׁב אֶל־אַדְמָתוֹ׃ וּבָנָו יִתְגָּרוּ
10

be shall his But own his to will and the king the (his) into and
up stirred sons .land return ,south of kingdom come will

וְאָסְפוּ הֲמוֹן חֲיָלִים רַבִּים וּבָא בוֹא וְשָׁטַף וְעָבָר וְיָשֹׁב

he Then pass and over- and cer- (one) And .great forces mul- a shall and
return shall .through flow tainly come shall of titude gather

11 וְיִתְגָּרוּ עַד־מָעֻזֹּה׃ וְיִתְמַרְמַר מֶלֶךְ הַנֶּגֶב וְיָצָא וְנִלְחַם עִמּוֹ

with and will and the king the shall And his to be and
,him fight out go south of furious become .fortress ,up stirred

עִם־מֶלֶךְ הַצָּפוֹן וְהֶעֱמִיד הָמוֹן רָב וְנִתַּן הֶהָמוֹן בְּיָדוֹ׃

his into the shall But .great host a he And .north the the with
.hand host given be raise shall of king

12 וְנִשָּׂא הֶהָמוֹן יָרוּם לְבָבוֹ וְהִפִּיל רִבֹּאוֹת וְלֹא יָעוֹז׃ וְשָׁב
13

shall For shall he but ,myriads will he And his be shall the cap- And
return .prevail not fall make .heart up lifted ,host turing

מֶלֶךְ הַצָּפוֹן וְהֶעֱמִיד הָמוֹן רַב מִן־הָרִאשׁוֹן וּלְקֵץ הָעִתִּים

the at and ;former the than greater a shall and the the
,times of end the host raise ,north of king

14 שָׁנִים יָבוֹא בוֹא בְּחַיִל גָּדוֹל וּבִרְכוּשׁ רָב׃ וּבָעִתִּים הָהֵם

those in And .much with and great a with cer- shall he ,years
times equipment army tainly come

many shall stand up against
the king of the south. And
the sons of the violent ones
of your people shall lift up
to establish (the) vision; but
they shall stumble. [15] So
the king of the north shall
come and heap up a siege-
mound and seize a fortified
city. And the south's arms
shall not stand, nor people
of his choice; for there will
be no strength to stand.
[16] But he who comes will
do as he wills, and none
shall stand before him; and
he shall stand in the glorious land, and destruction
in his hand. [17] And he
shall set his face to go in
with the strength of his
whole kingdom, and upright
ones with him; so he shall
do. And he shall give the
daughter of women to him,
to destroy it. But she will
not stand, nor be for him.
[18] And he shall turn
his face to the coasts and
shall capture many. But a
ruler shall make his re-
proach cease for him, but
his reproach shall return to
him. [19] Then he shall
turn his face toward the
fortresses of his own land,
but he will stumble and fall
and shall not be found.
[20] Then shall stand in his
place one who sends a tax-
exactor, (for) the glory of
(the) kingdom. But within
a few days he will be broken
but not in anger and not in
battle. [21] And one de-
spised shall stand up in his
place, and they shall not
give to him the king's honor
—but he shall come in while
at ease and take (the) kingdom by intrigues. [22] And
the forces of the overflow
shall be swept from before
him, and they will be brok-
en, and also the ruler of a
covenant. [23] And after
they join themselves to him,
he shall practice deceit. For
he shall come and be strong
with a few people. [24] He
will enter safely, even into
the rich places of (the) province. And he shall do what
his fathers have not done,
nor his fathers' fathers. He
shall plunder and spoil, and
scatter goods among them.
And he shall devise his plots

רַבִּים יַעַמְדוּ עַל־מֶלֶךְ הַנֶּגֶב וּבְנֵי ׀ פָּרִיצֵי עַמְּךָ יִנַּשְּׂאוּ
lift shall your violent the the And the the against stand shall many
up people of ones of sons .south of king up

15 לְהַעֲמִיד חָזוֹן וְנִכְשָׁלוּ׃ וְיָבֹא מֶלֶךְ הַצָּפוֹן וְיִשְׁפֹּךְ סוֹלְלָה
siege a heap and the the shall So shall they but (the) establish to
mound up north of king come .stumble ;vision

וְלָכַד עִיר מִבְצָרוֹת וּזְרֹעוֹת הַנֶּגֶב לֹא יַעֲמֹדוּ וְעַם מִבְחָרָיו
his of nor shall not the the And .fortified city a and
,choice people ,stand south of arms seize

16 וְאֵין כֹּחַ לַעֲמֹד׃ וְיַעַשׂ הַבָּא אֵלָיו כִּרְצוֹנוֹ וְאֵין עוֹמֵד
shall and he as against who he will But .stand to strength for
stand none ,wills him comes do be will not

17 לְפָנָיו וְיַעֲמֹד בְּאֶרֶץ־הַצְּבִי וְכָלָה בְיָדוֹ׃ וְיָשֵׂם ׀ פָּנָיו לָבוֹא
go to his He Also his in and ,glorious the in he And before
in face set shall .hand destruction land stand shall .him

בְּתֹקֶף כָּל־מַלְכוּתוֹ וִישָׁרִים עִמּוֹ וְעָשָׂה וּבַת הַנָּשִׁים יִתֶּן־
shall he women the And he so with upright and his whole the with
give of daughter .do shall him ones ,kingdom of strength

18 לוֹ לְהַשְׁחִיתָהּ וְלֹא תַעֲמֹד וְלֹא־לוֹ תִהְיֶה׃ וְיָשֵׁב ׀ פָּנָיו
his he And .be for nor shall she But destroy to to
face turn shall him ,stand not .it him

לְאִיִּים וְלָכַד רַבִּים וְהִשְׁבִּית קָצִין חֶרְפָּתוֹ לוֹ בִּלְתִּי חֶרְפָּתוֹ
his but for his ruler a shall But .many shall and the to
reproach ,him reproach cease make capture coasts

19 יָשִׁיב לוֹ׃ וְיָשֵׁב פָּנָיו לְמָעוּזֵּי אַרְצוֹ וְנִכְשַׁל וְנָפַל וְלֹא
and fall and will he but own his the toward his he Then to shall
not stumble ,land of fortresses face turn shall .him return

20 יִמָּצֵא׃ וְעָמַד עַל־כַּנּוֹ מַעֲבִיר נוֹגֵשׂ הֶדֶר מַלְכוּת וּבְיָמִים
within But (the) the (for) an who one his in shall Then be shall
days .kingdom of glory exactor sends place stand .found

21 אֲחָדִים יִשָּׁבֵר וְלֹא בְאַפַּיִם וְלֹא בְמִלְחָמָה׃ וְעָמַד עַל־
in shall And .battle in and anger in but will he few a
up stand not not ,broken be

כַּנּוֹ נִבְזֶה וְלֹא־נָתְנוּ עָלָיו הוֹד מַלְכוּת וּבָא בְשַׁלְוָה וְהֶחֱזִיק
take and while he But .king's the honor to they and des- one his
ease at enter will him give shall not ,pised place

22 מַלְכוּת בַּחֲלַקְלַקּוֹת׃ וּזְרֹעוֹת הַשֶּׁטֶף יִשָּׁטְפוּ מִלְּפָנָיו
before from shall the the And .intrigues by (the)
him swept be overflow of forces kingdom

23 וְיִשָּׁבֵרוּ וְגַם נְגִיד בְּרִית׃ וּמִן־הִתְחַבְּרוּת אֵלָיו יַעֲשֶׂה
shall he to join they And a ruler the and will they and
practice ,him themselves after .covenant of also ,broken be

24 מִרְמָה וְעָלָה וְעָצַם בִּמְעַט־גּוֹי׃ בְּשַׁלְוָה וּבְמִשְׁמַנֵּי מְדִינָה
(the) the into even ,Safely .people a with shall and he For .deceit
,province of places rich few strong be come shall

יָבוֹא וְעָשָׂה אֲשֶׁר לֹא־עָשׂוּ אֲבֹתָיו וַאֲבוֹת אֲבֹתָיו בִּזָּה
Plunder his nor his have not what he And will he
.fathers' fathers ,fathers done do shall .enter

וּשְׁלָל וּרְכוּשׁ לָהֶם יִבְזוֹר וְעַל מִבְצָרִים יְחַשֵּׁב מַחְשְׁבֹתָיו
plots his shall he the And shall he among and and
devise ,strongholds against .scatter them goods ,spoil

against the forts, even for a time. [25] And he will stir up his power and his heart against the king of the south with a great army. And the king of the south will be stirred to battle with a great and very mighty army. But he shall not stand, for they shall devise plots against him. [26] Yes, those who eat his food shall destroy him, and his army shall overflow. And many will fall down slain. [27] And both of these kings, their hearts (seek) to do evil, and they will speak false at one table. But it shall not prosper, for (the) end (comes) at the set time. [28] And he will return to his land with great wealth. And his heart (will) (be) against (the) holy covenant; and he will act, and he will return to his land. [29] At the set time he will return and come against the south, but it will not be as the former or the latter.

[30] For Kittim's ships will come against him; then he will be grieved and turn back and be furious against (the) holy covenant. And he shall act and will return and heed those forsaking (the) holy covenant. [31] And forces will stand from him, and they will profane the sanctuary, the fortress; and shall remove the set (sacrifice); and they will put the desolating abomination. [32] And he will ruin evildoers against (the) covenant by flatteries. But the people knowing their God will be strong and will work. [33] And the understanders in the people will teach many —yet they will stumble by the sword and flame; by exile and spoil, (for) days. [34] And stumbling they will be helped with a little help. But many will join them, with hypocrisy. [35] And of the understanders shall stumble, to refine and to purge them, and make white, to the time of (the) end. For (it is) still for the set time. [36] And the king will do according to his will and he will exalt and magnify above every god; even speaking wondrous things against the God of gods and

25 וְעַד־עֵת׃ וְיָעֵר כֹּחוֹ וּלְבָבוֹ עַל־מֶלֶךְ הַנֶּגֶב בְּחַיִל גָּדוֹל

.great a with the the against his and his he And a even
army south of king heart power stir will .time for

וּמֶלֶךְ הַנֶּגֶב יִתְגָּרֶה לַמִּלְחָמָה בְּחַיִל־גָּדוֹל וְעָצוּם עַד־מְאֹד

.very and great a with battle to be shall the the And
mighty army up stirred south of king

26 וְלֹא יַעֲמֹד כִּי־יַחְשְׁבוּ עָלָיו מַחֲשָׁבוֹת׃ וְאֹכְלֵי פַתְבָּגוֹ

food his those Even .plots against shall they for shall he But
eat who him devise ,stand not

27 יִשְׁבְּרוּהוּ וְחֵילוֹ יִשְׁטוֹף וְנָפְלוּ חֲלָלִים רַבִּים׃ וּשְׁנֵיהֶם

both And .many slain shall And over- shall his and destroy shall
,them of down fall .flow army ,him

הַמְּלָכִים לְבָבָם לְמֵרָע וְעַל־שֻׁלְחָן אֶחָד כָּזָב יְדַבֵּרוּ וְלֹא

But shall they lie(s) one table and do to hearts their ,kings the
not .speak at ,evil (be shall)

28 תִצְלָח כִּי־עוֹד קֵץ לַמּוֹעֵד׃ וְיָשֹׁב אַרְצוֹ בִּרְכוּשׁ גָּדוֹל

.great wealth with his he And set the at (the) still for shall it
land to return will .time end ,prosper

29 וּלְבָבוֹ עַל־בְּרִית קֹדֶשׁ וְעָשָׂה וְשָׁב לְאַרְצוֹ׃ לַמּוֹעֵד יָשׁוּב

will he the At .land his he and he and ;holy (the) against his And
return time set to return shall ,do shall covenant heart

30 וּבָא בַנֶּגֶב וְלֹא־תִהְיֶה כָרִאשֹׁנָה וְכָאַחֲרֹנָה׃ וּבָאוּ בוֹ

against will For the as or former the as shall it But against and
him come .latter be not .south the come

צִיִּים כִּתִּים וְנִכְאָה וְשָׁב וְזָעַם עַל־בְּרִית־קוֹדֶשׁ וְעָשָׂה

he And .holy (the) against be and turn and shall he Then .Kittim ships
,work shall covenant furious back grieved be of

31 וְשָׁב וְיָבֵן עַל־עֹזְבֵי בְּרִית קֹדֶשׁ׃ וּזְרֹעִים מִמֶּנּוּ יַעֲמֹדוּ

shall from And .holy (the) for- the and he and
,stand him forces covenant of sakers heed return will

וְחִלְּלוּ הַמִּקְדָּשׁ הַמָּעוֹז וְהֵסִירוּ הַתָּמִיד וְנָתְנוּ הַשִּׁקּוּץ

the they and regular the shall and the ,sanctuary the they and
abomination put shall ,(sacrifice) remove ;fortress profane will

32 מְשֹׁמֵם׃ וּמַרְשִׁיעֵי בְרִית יַחֲנִיף בַּחֲלַקּוֹת וְעַם יֹדְעֵי אֱלֹהָיו

their who the But by shall he (the) evildoers And that
God know people .flatteries ruin ,covenant against .desolates

33 יַחֲזִקוּ וְעָשׂוּ׃ וּמַשְׂכִּילֵי עָם יָבִינוּ לָרַבִּים וְנִכְשְׁלוּ בְּחֶרֶב

the by will they Yet .many will (the) who those And will and be will
sword stumble instruct people among understand .work ,strong

34 וּבְלֶהָבָה בִּשְׁבִי וּבְבִזָּה יָמִים׃ וּבְהִכָּשְׁלָם יֵעָזְרוּ עֵזֶר מְעָט

a help shall they they when And (for) by and by by and
.little with helped be ,stumble shall .days ,spoil ,exile flame

35 וְנִלְווּ עֲלֵיהֶם רַבִּים בַּחֲלַקְלַקּוֹת׃ וּמִן־הַמַּשְׂכִּילִים יִכָּשְׁלוּ

shall who those And .hypocrisy with many them to shall But
,stumble understand of join

לִצְרוֹף בָּהֶם וּלְבָרֵר וְלַלְבֵּן עַד־עֵת קֵץ כִּי־עוֹד לַמּוֹעֵד׃

the for (is it) For (the) the to make and to and them to
.time set still .end of time ,white ,purge refine

36 וְעָשָׂה כִרְצוֹנוֹ הַמֶּלֶךְ וְיִתְרוֹמֵם וְיִתְגַּדֵּל עַל־כָּל־אֵל וְעַל

even ;god every above and shall he And .king the according will And
against magnify himself exalt will his to do

shall succeed until the fury is fulfilled. For that which is decreed shall be done. [37] He shall not regard the God of his fathers, nor the desire of women, nor love any god. For he shall magnify himself above all. [38] But in his place he shall honor the god of forces; and he shall honor a god whom his fathers did not know, with gold and silver and with precious stones and desirable things. [39] So he shall do in the strongholds of the fortresses with a foreign god, whom he shall acknowledge. He shall multiply in glory; and he shall cause them to rule over many and shall divide the land for a price. [40] And at the time of (the) end, the king of the south shall push at him. And the king of the north shall come against him like a tempest, with chariots and with horsemen and with many ships. And he shall go into the lands and shall overflow and pass over. [41] He shall also enter into the glorious land and many shall be stumbled. But these shall escape out of his hand: Edom and Moab and the chief of the sons of Ammon. [42] He shall also stretch out his hand on the lands; and the land of Egypt shall not escape. [43] But he shall have power over the treasures of gold and silver, and over all the precious things of Egypt. And the Libyans and the Ethiopians (shall be) at his steps. [44] But news from the east and from the north shall trouble him. Then he shall go out with great fury to destroy and to cut off many. [45] And he shall plant his palace tents between (the) seas in the glorious holy mountain. Yet he shall come to his end, and no helper shall come to help him.

אֵל אֵלִים יְדַבֵּר נִפְלָאוֹת וְהִצְלִיחַ עַד־כָּלָה זַעַם כִּי־נֶחֱרָצָה

is	which	that	For the	is	until	shall	and	marvelous	shall	gods	the
decreed			.fury	fulfilled		succeed	,things	speak	of God

37 נַעֲשָׂתָה: וְעַל־אֱלֹהֵי אֲבֹתָיו לֹא יָבִין וְעַל־חֶמְדַּת נָשִׁים

| ,women | desire the | and | will he | not | his | | God the | And | be shall |
| | of | not | ,regard | brothers | of | | .done |

38 וְעַל־כָּל־אֱלוֹהַּ לֹא יָבִין כִּי עַל־כֹּל יִתְגַּדָּל: וְלֶאֱלֹהַּ מָעֻזִּים

| fortresses the | But | shall he | all above | For | will he not | god | any | and |
| of god | .regard | | himself magnify | | .regard |

עַל־כַּנּוֹ יְכַבֵּד וְלֶאֱלֹהַּ אֲשֶׁר לֹא־יְדָעֻהוּ אֲבֹתָיו יְכַבֵּד

| shall he | his | did | not | which | the and | shall he | his in |
| honor | ,fathers | know | | god | ;honor | place |

39 בְּזָהָב וּבְכֶסֶף וּבְאֶבֶן יְקָרָה וּבַחֲמֻדוֹת: וְעָשָׂה לְמִבְצְרֵי

| fort-the | in | he And | | with and | ,precious | with and | with and | with |
| of tresses | do shall | | .things desirable | | stones | | silver | gold |

מָעֻזִּים עִם־אֱלוֹהַּ נֵכָר אֲשֶׁר הִכִּיר יַרְבֶּה כָבוֹד וְהִמְשִׁילָם

| will he and | | ;glory | shall He | shall he | whom | ,alien | god an | with | (the) |
| rule them make | | | increase | .acknowledge | | | | | fortresses |

40 בָּרַבִּים וַאֲדָמָה יְחַלֵּק בִּמְחִיר: וּבְעֵת קֵץ יִתְנַגַּח עִמּוֹ

| with | engage shall | (the) | the at | And | a for | divide shall | the and | ,many over |
| him | butting in | | end | of time | .price | | land |

מֶלֶךְ הַנֶּגֶב וְיִשְׂתָּעֵר עָלָיו מֶלֶךְ הַצָּפוֹן בְּרֶכֶב וּבְפָרָשִׁים

| horse-with | and | with | ,north the | the | against | come will And | the | king |
| ,men | | ,chariots | | | of king | | him | tempest a as | .south of |

41 וּבָאֳנִיּוֹת רַבּוֹת וּבָא בַאֲרָצוֹת וְשָׁטַף וְעָבָר: וּבָא בְּאֶרֶץ

| the into | shall He | pass and | shall and | the into | he And | .many | with and |
| land | enter also | .over | overflow | lands | come shall | | ships |

הַצְּבִי וְרַבּוֹת יִכָּשֵׁלוּ וְאֵלֶּה יִמָּלְטוּ מִיָּדוֹ אֱדוֹם וּמוֹאָב

| and | ,Edom | of out | escape shall | these But | be will | many and | ,glorious |
| Moab | | :hand his | | .stumbled |

42 וְרֵאשִׁית בְּנֵי עַמּוֹן: וְיִשְׁלַח יָדוֹ בַּאֲרָצוֹת וְאֶרֶץ מִצְרַיִם

| Egypt | the and | the against | his | will also and | ;Ammon the | the and |
| | of land | ;lands | hand out stretch | | of sons | of chief |

43 לֹא תִהְיֶה לִפְלֵיטָה: וּמָשַׁל בְּמִכְמַנֵּי הַזָּהָב וְהַכֶּסֶף וּבְכֹל

| over and | and | gold | the over | he But | .escape | shall | not |
| all | ,silver | | of treasures | rule will |

44 חֲמֻדוֹת מִצְרַיִם וְלֻבִים וְכֻשִׁים בְּמִצְעָדָיו: וּשְׁמֻעוֹת יְבַהֲלֻהוּ

| trouble shall | news But | His in | the and | the And | .Egypt's | desirable |
| him | | .steps | Ethiopians | Libyans | | things |

מִמִּזְרָח וּמִצָּפוֹן וְיָצָא בְּחֵמָא גְדֹלָה לְהַשְׁמִיד וּלְהַחֲרִים

| devote to | and | destroy to | great | fury with | he Then | from and | the from |
| destruction to | out go will | | .north the | east |

45 רַבִּים: וְיִטַּע אָהֳלֵי אַפַּדְנוֹ בֵּין יַמִּים לְהַר־צְבִי־קֹדֶשׁ וּבָא

| he Yet | .holy | glorious the | in | (the) | between | his | tents | he And | .many |
| come shall | | mountain | ,seas | | | palace | | plant shall |

עַד־קִצּוֹ וְאֵין עוֹזֵר לוֹ:

| for | a not | and | his | to |
| .him | helper | is | ,end |

CAP. XII יב

CHAPTER 12

[1] And at that time Michael shall stand up, the great ruler who stands for the sons of your people. And there shall be a time of trouble, such as never was from the existence of a nation, until that time. And at that time, your people shall be delivered, everyone that shall be found written in the Book. [2] And many of those who sleep in the dust of the earth shall awake, some to everlasting life and some to reproaches, (and) to everlasting contempt. [3] And those who are wise shall shine as the brightness of the firmament; and those who turn many to righteousness as the stars forever and ever. [4] But you, O Daniel, shut up the words and seal the book to the end time. Many shall run to and fro, and knowledge shall be increased.

[5] Then I, Daniel, looked. And, behold, another two stood there, the one on this (side) of the river bank and one on that (side) of the river back [6] And (one) said to the man clothed in linen, who (was) on the waters of the river, How long until the end of these wonders? [7] And I heard the man clothed in linen, who (was) on the waters of the river, when he held up his right and his left (hand) to Heaven and swore by Him who lives forever that it (shall be) for a time, times and a half. And when they have made an end of scattering the power of the holy people, all these (things) shall be finished. [8] And I heard, but I did not understand. Then I said, O my Lord, what (shall be) the end of these (things)? [9] And He said, Go, Daniel! For the words (are) closed up and sealed until

CHAPTER 12

1 וּבָעֵת הַהִיא יַעֲמֹד מִיכָאֵל הַשַּׂר הַגָּדוֹל הָעֹמֵד עַל־בְּנֵי
the for of sons who stands great the ruler ,Michael shall up stand that at And time

עַמֶּךָ וְהָיְתָה עֵת צָרָה אֲשֶׁר לֹא־נִהְיְתָה מִהְיוֹת גּוֹי עַד
until a nation the from of existence has been not such as ,distress a of time there And be shall your .people

הָעֵת הַהִיא וּבָעֵת הַהִיא יִמָּלֵט עַמְּךָ כָּל־הַנִּמְצָא כָּתוּב
written shall that found be every- one your ,people be shall delivered ,that at And time .that time

2 בַּסֵּפֶר׃ וְרַבִּים מִיְּשֵׁנֵי אַדְמַת־עָפָר יָקִיצוּ אֵלֶּה לְחַיֵּי
life to some shall ,awake dust of ground the in sleep who those of many And the in .Book

3 עוֹלָם וְאֵלֶּה לַחֲרָפוֹת לְדִרְאוֹן עוֹלָם׃ וְהַמַּשְׂכִּלִים יַזְהִרוּ
shall shine are who wise those And ever- .lasting to (and) abhorrence to reproaches and some ever- lasting

כְּזֹהַר הָרָקִיעַ וּמַצְדִּיקֵי הָרַבִּים כַּכּוֹכָבִים לְעוֹלָם וָעֶד׃
and .ever forever stars the as many turn- righteousness to those and ing firm- ament the the as of shine

4 וְאַתָּה דָנִיֵּאל סְתֹם הַדְּבָרִים וַחֲתֹם הַסֵּפֶר עַד־עֵת קֵץ
(the) .end the to of time book the seal and words the shut up O ,Daniel ,you But

5 יְשֹׁטְטוּ רַבִּים וְתִרְבֶּה הַדָּעַת׃ וְרָאִיתִי אֲנִי דָנִיֵּאל וְהִנֵּה
and ,behold ,Daniel ,I looked Then .knowledge shall and increased be ,Many roam shall around

שְׁנַיִם אֲחֵרִים עֹמְדִים אֶחָד הֵנָּה לִשְׂפַת הַיְאֹר וְאֶחָד הֵנָּה
that on and (side) one the ,river the of of lip this on (side) one were ,standing other two

6 לִשְׂפַת הַיְאֹר׃ וַיֹּאמֶר לָאִישׁ לְבוּשׁ הַבַּדִּים אֲשֶׁר מִמַּעַל
on who (was) ,linen clothed in the to man (one) And said the .river the of of lip

7 לְמֵימֵי הַיְאֹר עַד־מָתַי קֵץ הַפְּלָאוֹת׃ וָאֶשְׁמַע אֶת־הָאִישׁ
man the I And heard the ?wonders of the when Until end (is) the ,river waters the of

לְבוּשׁ הַבַּדִּים אֲשֶׁר מִמַּעַל לְמֵימֵי הַיְאֹר וַיָּרֶם יְמִינוֹ
his right he when up held the ,river the of waters on who (was) ,linen clothed in

וּשְׂמֹאלוֹ אֶל־הַשָּׁמַיִם וַיִּשָּׁבַע בְּחֵי הָעוֹלָם כִּי לְמוֹעֵד
a for ,time that (is it) ,forever Him by lives who swore and the heavens to left his and (hand)

מוֹעֲדִים וָחֵצִי וּכְכַלּוֹת נַפֵּץ יַד־עַם־קֹדֶשׁ תִּכְלֶינָה כָל־
all be shall finished ,holy people's power the break- ing when And finish they a and .half times

8 אֵלֶּה׃ וַאֲנִי שָׁמַעְתִּי וְלֹא אָבִין וָאֹמְרָה אֲדֹנִי מָה אַחֲרִית
end the of what (be shall) my O ,lord I And ,said did I .understand not but ,heard And I these .(things)

9 אֵלֶּה׃ וַיֹּאמֶר לֵךְ דָּנִיֵּאל כִּי־סְתֻמִים וַחֲתֻמִים הַדְּבָרִים
words the sealed and closed (are) up For !Daniel ,Go he And ,said these ?(things)

the end-time. [10] Many
shall be purified and made
white and tested. But the
wicked shall do wickedly.
And none of the wicked
shall understand, but the
wise shall understand.
[11] And from the time the
daily (sacrifice) shall be
taken away, and the abom-
ination that makes desolate
set up, (shall be) a thousand,
two hundred and ninety
days. [12] Blessed is he
who waits and comes to the
thousand, three hundred
and thirty-five days.
[13] But you go on to the
end; for you shall rest and
stand in your lot at the end
of the days.

10 עַד־עֵת קֵץ׃ יִתְבָּרֲרוּ וְיִתְלַבְּנוּ וְיִצָּרְפוּ רַבִּים וְהִרְשִׁיעוּ

do shall But .Many and made and be shall (the) the until
wickedly refined white purified .end of time

11 רְשָׁעִים וְלֹא יָבִינוּ כָּל־רְשָׁעִים וְהַמַּשְׂכִּלִים יָבִינוּ׃ וּמֵעֵת

from And will wise the but the all will and the
time .discern ;wicked of discern not ;wicked

הוּסַר הַתָּמִיד וְלָתֵת שִׁקּוּץ שֹׁמֵם יָמִים אֶלֶף מָאתָיִם

two a (be shall) that abomi- the set and regular the be shall
hundred thousand days desolates nation up (sacrifice) abolished

12 וְתִשְׁעִים׃ אַשְׁרֵי הַמְחַכֶּה וְיַגִּיעַ לְיָמִים אֶלֶף שְׁלֹשׁ מֵאוֹת

hundred three (the) days to and who he Blessed .ninety and
thousand comes waits (is)

13 שְׁלֹשִׁים וַחֲמִשָּׁה׃ וְאַתָּה לֵךְ לַקֵּץ וְתָנוּחַ וְתַעֲמֹד לְגֹרָלְךָ

your for and you and the to go But .five and thirty
lot stand rest shall ;end on you

לְקֵץ הַיָּמִין׃

the the at
.days of end

הושע

LIBER HOSEAE

CAPUT. I א

CHAPTER 1

[1] The word of Jehovah that came to Hosea, the son of Beeri, in the days of Uzziah, Jotham, Ahaz (and) Hezekiah, kings of Judah; and in the days of Jeroboam the son of Joash, king of Israel. [2] The beginning of the speaking of Jehovah of Hosea. And Jehovah said to Hosea, Go, take to yourself a wife of harlotry and children of harlotry. For the land has utterly gone lusting away from Jehovah. [3] So he went and took Gomer the daughter of Diblaim, who conceived and bore him a son. [4] And Jehovah said to him, Call his name Jezreel. For still (in) a little I will visit the blood of Jezreel on the house of Jehu, and will cause the kingdom of the house of Israel to cease. [5] And it shall be in that day I will break the bow of Israel in the valley of Jezreel.

[6] And she conceived again and bore a daughter. And He said to him, Call her name Loruhamah, for I will not again have mercy (on) the house of Israel still; but I will completely take them away. [7] But I will have mercy on the house of Judah, and will save them by Jehovah their God. And I will not save them by bow or by sword, or by battle, by horses, or by horsemen.

[8] Now when she had weaned Loruhamah, and

CHAPTER 1

1 דְּבַר־יְהוָה ׀ אֲשֶׁר הָיָה אֶל־הוֹשֵׁעַ בֶּן־בְּאֵרִי בִּימֵי עֻזִּיָּה
,Uzziah the in ,Beeri the Hosea to was that Jehovah The
of days of son of word

יוֹתָם אָחָז יְחִזְקִיָּה מַלְכֵי יְהוּדָה וּבִימֵי יָרָבְעָם בֶּן־יוֹאָשׁ
,Joash the Jeroboam in and ;Judah kings ,Hezekiah ,Ahaz ,Jotham
of son of days the of

2 מֶלֶךְ יִשְׂרָאֵל׃ תְּחִלַּת דִּבֶּר־יְהוָה בְּהוֹשֵׁעַ וַיֹּאמֶר יְהוָה אֶל־
to Jehovah And by Jehovah the be- The .Israel king
said :Hosea of speaking of ginning of

הוֹשֵׁעַ לֵךְ קַח־לְךָ אֵשֶׁת זְנוּנִים וְיַלְדֵי זְנוּנִים כִּי־זָנֹה תִזְנֶה
goes surely For .harlotry and harlotry wife a to take ,Go ,Hosea
whoring of children of yourself

3 הָאָרֶץ מֵאַחֲרֵי יְהוָה׃ וַיֵּלֶךְ וַיִּקַּח אֶת־גֹּמֶר בַּת־דִּבְלָיִם
,Diblaim the Gomer took and he So .Jehovah away land the
of daughter went from

4 וַתַּהַר וַתֵּלֶד לוֹ בֵּן׃ וַיֹּאמֶר יְהוָה אֵלָיו קְרָא שְׁמוֹ יִזְרְעֶאל
.Jezreel his Call to Jehovah said And a to bore and she and
name ,him .son him conceived

כִּי־עוֹד מְעַט וּפָקַדְתִּי אֶת־דְּמֵי יִזְרְעֶאל עַל־בֵּית יֵהוּא
,Jehu the on Jezreel the will I and little a yet For
of house of blood visit ,(while)

5 וְהִשְׁבַּתִּי מַמְלְכוּת בֵּית יִשְׂרָאֵל׃ וְהָיָה בַּיּוֹם הַהוּא וְשָׁבַרְתִּי
will I that ,that day in it And .Jezreel the kingdom the will and
break be shall of house of cease make

6 אֶת־קֶשֶׁת יִשְׂרָאֵל בְּעֵמֶק יִזְרְעֶאל׃ וַתַּהַר עוֹד וַתֵּלֶד בַּת
a bore and again she And .Jezreel the in Israel the
.daughter conceived of valley of bow

וַיֹּאמֶר לוֹ קְרָא שְׁמָהּ לֹא רֻחָמָה כִּי לֹא אוֹסִיף עוֹד אֲרַחֵם
have will more I not for ,ruhama Lo- her Call to He And
mercy again name ,him said

7 אֶת־בֵּית יִשְׂרָאֵל כִּי־נָשֹׂא אֶשָּׂא לָהֶם׃ וְאֶת־בֵּית יְהוּדָה
Judah the But .them take will I com- but ;Israel the
of house away pletely of house

אֲרַחֵם וְהוֹשַׁעְתִּים בַּיהוָה אֱלֹהֵיהֶם וְלֹא אוֹשִׁיעֵם בְּקֶשֶׁת
bow by save will I But .God their Jeho- by save will and have will I
them not vah them ,on mercy

8 וּבְחֶרֶב וּבְמִלְחָמָה בְּסוּסִים וּבְפָרָשִׁים׃ וַתִּגְמֹל אֶת־לֹא
Lo- she And .horsemen by and ,horses by ,battle by and by and
weaned had ,sword

she conceived and bore a son. [9] Then He said, Call his name Loammi; for you (are) not My people, and I will not be for you.

[10] Yet the number of the sons of Israel shall be as the sea-sand, which is not measured nor numbered. And in the place where it is said to them, You (are) not My people; it shall be said to them, Sons of the Living God. [11] And the sons of Judah and the sons of Israel shall be gathered together and shall set over themselves one head. And they shall go up out of the land; for great (shall be) the day of Jezreel.

CHAPTER 2

[1] Say to your brothers, Ammi, and to your sisters, Ruhamah. [2] Strive! With your mother, strive; for she (is) not my wife, and I (am) not her husband. Let her therefore put away her harlotry from her face, and her adulteries from between her breasts, [3] lest I strip her naked and set her out as in the day that she was born, and make her as the wilderness, and place her like a dry land, and kill her with thirst. [4] And I will not have pity for her sons, for they (are) the sons of harlotry. [5] For their mother is a harlot. She who conceived them has acted shamefully. For she said, I will go after my lovers who give my bread and my water, my wool and my flax, my oil and my drink.

[6] Therefore, behold, I will hedge your way with thorns and I will wall up her wall; that she shall not find her paths; [7] and she shall follow after her lovers, but she shall not overtake them. And she shall look for them, but she shall not find (them). Then she shall say, I

9 רֻחָמָה וַתַּהַר וַתֵּלֶד בֵּן׃ וַיֹּאמֶר קְרָא שְׁמוֹ לֹא עַמִּי כִּי אַתֶּם
you for ;ammi Lo- his Call He Then .son a and she and ,ruhamah
(are) name ,said bore conceived

לֹא עַמִּי וְאָנֹכִי לֹא־אֶהְיֶה לָכֶם׃
for be will not I and My not
you people

CAP. II ב

CHAPTER 2

1 וְהָיָה מִסְפַּר בְּנֵי־יִשְׂרָאֵל כְּחוֹל הַיָּם אֲשֶׁר לֹא־יִמַּד וְלֹא
and is not which the the as Israel the number the Yet
not ,measured ,sea of sand of sons of be shall

יִסָּפֵר וְהָיָה בִּמְקוֹם אֲשֶׁר־יֵאָמֵר לָהֶם לֹא־עַמִּי אַתֶּם
you My Not ,them to said is it which the in it And num-
;(are) people of place ,be shall .bered

2 יֵאָמֵר לָהֶם בְּנֵי אֵל־חָי׃ וְנִקְבְּצוּ בְּנֵי־יְהוּדָה וּבְנֵי־יִשְׂרָאֵל
Israel the and Judah the be shall And .living the Sons to shall it
of sons of sons gathered God of ,them said be

יַחְדָּו וְשָׂמוּ לָהֶם רֹאשׁ אֶחָד וְעָלוּ מִן־הָאָרֶץ כִּי גָדוֹל יוֹם
the great for ;land the out they And .one head for shall and to-
of day (be shall) of up go shall themselves set gether

3 יִזְרְעֶאל׃ אִמְרוּ לַאֲחֵיכֶם עַמִּי וְלַאֲחוֹתֵיכֶם רֻחָמָה׃ רִיבוּ
;Strive ,Ruhamah your to and ,Ammi your to Say .Jezreel
,sisters ,brothers

4 בְאִמְּכֶם רִיבוּ כִּי־הִיא לֹא אִשְׁתִּי וְאָנֹכִי לֹא אִישָׁהּ וְתָסֵר
let And hus- her not I and My not she for ;strive your with
turn her .band (am) wife (is) mother

5 זְנוּנֶיהָ מִפָּנֶיהָ וְנַאֲפוּפֶיהָ מִבֵּין שָׁדֶיהָ׃ פֶּן־אַפְשִׁיטֶנָּה
her strip I lest ,breasts her from her and her from her
between adultery ,face harlotry

עֲרֻמָּה וְהִצַּגְתִּיהָ כְּיוֹם הִוָּלְדָהּ וְשַׂמְתִּיהָ כַמִּדְבָּר וְשַׁתִּהָ
place and the as set and being her the as her set and naked
her ,wilderness her ,born of day out

6 כְּאֶרֶץ צִיָּה וַהֲמִתִּיהָ בַּצָּמָא׃ וְאֶת־בָּנֶיהָ לֹא אֲרַחֵם כִּי־
for will I not her And .thirst with kill and ,drought a like
,pity sons her of land

7 בְנֵי זְנוּנִים הֵמָּה׃ כִּי זָנְתָה אִמָּם הֹבִישָׁה הוֹרָתָם כִּי
For con- who she acted has their a is For they harlotry the
.them ceived shamefully ;mother harlot .(are) of sons

אָמְרָה אֵלְכָה אַחֲרֵי מְאַהֲבַי נֹתְנֵי לַחְמִי וּמֵימַי צַמְרִי
wool my my and my the ,lovers my after go me Let ,said she
,water bread of givers

8 וּפִשְׁתִּי שַׁמְנִי וְשִׁקּוּיָי׃ לָכֵן הִנְנִי־שָׂךְ אֶת־דַּרְכֵּךְ בַּסִּירִים
,thorns with way your hedge be- There- my and ,oil my my and
I ,hold ,fore .drink ,flax

9 וְגָדַרְתִּי אֶת־גְּדֵרָהּ וּנְתִיבוֹתֶיהָ לֹא תִמְצָא׃ וְרִדְּפָה אֶת־
shall she And shall she not paths her and her I and
pursue .find ,wall up wall

מְאַהֲבֶיהָ וְלֹא־תַשִּׂיג אֹתָם וּבִקְשָׁתַם וְלֹא תִמְצָא וְאָמְרָה
she Then shall she but shall she And .them shall she but ,lovers her
,say shall .find not ,them for search overtake not

will go and return to my first husband, for then (it was) better with me than now. [8] For she did not know that I gave her grain and wine and oil, and I multiplied her silver and the gold they prepared for the Baal. [9] Therefore I will return and take My grain in its time, and My wine in its season. And I will take back My wool and My flax to cover her nakedness. [10] And now I will uncover her shamefulness to the eyes of her lovers, and a man shall not deliver her out of My hand. [11] I will also cause all her joy to cease, her feast days, her new moons, and her sabbaths, and all her solemn feasts. [12] And I will destroy her vines and her fig tree, of which she has said, They (are) my rewards that my lovers have given me. And I will set them for a forest, and the beasts of the field shall eat them. [13] And I will visit on her the days of the Baals, (in) which she burned incense to them, and she adorned herself with her noserings and her jewels, and she went after her lovers and forgot Me, says Jehovah.

[14] Therefore, behold, I will lure her and bring her to the wilderness and speak to her heart. [15] And I will give her her vineyards from there, and the valley of Achor for a door of hope. And she shall answer there, as in the days of her youth, and as in the day when she came up out of the land of Egypt. [16] And at that day, says Jehovah, you shall call Me, My husband, and shall no more call Me, my Baal. [17] For I will take away the names of the Baals out of her mouth. And they shall no more be remembered by their name. [18] And in that day I will cut a covenant for them

אֵלְכָה וְאָשׁוּבָה אֶל־אִישִׁי הָרִאשׁוֹן כִּי טוֹב לִי אָז מֵעָתָּה׃

than then for (was it) for ,first my to might I that me Let
.now Me better husband return go

10 וְהִיא לֹא יָדְעָה כִּי אָנֹכִי נָתַתִּי לָהּ הַדָּגָן וְהַתִּירוֹשׁ

new and grain her to gave I that did not she For
wine know

11 וְהַיִּצְהָר וְכֶסֶף הִרְבֵּיתִי לָהּ וְזָהָב עָשׂוּ לַבָּעַל׃ לָכֵן אָשׁוּב

will I There- the for they and to multi- I silver and olive and
return fore .Baal made gold her plied ;oil

וְלָקַחְתִּי דְגָנִי בְּעִתּוֹ וְתִירוֹשִׁי בְּמוֹעֲדוֹ וְהִצַּלְתִּי צַמְרִי

wool My will I And its in My and its in My take and
recover .season wine new ,time grain

12 וּפִשְׁתִּי לְכַסּוֹת אֶת־עֶרְוָתָהּ׃ וְעַתָּה אֲגַלֶּה אֶת־נַבְלֻתָהּ

her will I now And her cover to My and
lewdness uncover .nakedness flax

13 לְעֵינֵי מְאַהֲבֶיהָ וְאִישׁ לֹא־יַצִּילֶנָּה מִיָּדִי׃ וְהִשְׁבַּתִּי כָּל־

all will I And My from shall not a and ,lovers her the to
cease make .hand her deliver man of eyes

14 מְשׂוֹשָׂהּ חַגָּהּ חָדְשָׁהּ וְשַׁבַּתָּהּ וְכֹל מוֹעֲדָהּ׃ וַהֲשִׁמֹּתִי

will I And solemn her and her and new her her ,joy her
destroy .feasts all ,sabbaths ,moons ,feasts

גַּפְנָהּ וּתְאֵנָתָהּ אֲשֶׁר אָמְרָה אֶתְנָה הֵמָּה לִי אֲשֶׁר נָתְנוּ־

have that ,me to they Rewards has she of her and her
given (are) ,said which ,tree fig vines

15 לִי מְאַהֲבָי וְשַׂמְתִּים לְיַעַר וַאֲכָלָתַם חַיַּת הַשָּׂדֶה׃ וּפָקַדְתִּי

will I And .field the the eat shall and a for will I And .lovers My to
visit of beasts them forest them set me

עָלֶיהָ אֶת־יְמֵי הַבְּעָלִים אֲשֶׁר תַּקְטִיר לָהֶם וַתַּעַד נִזְמָהּ

nose her decks and to brings she whom ,Baals the the her on
rings (with) herself ,them incense of days

וְחֶלְיָתָהּ וַתֵּלֶךְ אַחֲרֵי מְאַהֲבֶיהָ וְאֹתִי שָׁכְחָה נְאֻם־יְהוָה׃

.Jehovah says ,forgets Me but ,lovers her after goes and her and
,jewels

16 לָכֵן הִנֵּה אָנֹכִי מְפַתֶּיהָ וְהֹלַכְתִּיהָ הַמִּדְבָּר וְדִבַּרְתִּי עַל־

to speak and the (to) her bring and her lure I ,behold There-
wilderness ,fore

17 לִבָּהּ׃ וְנָתַתִּי לָהּ אֶת־כְּרָמֶיהָ מִשָּׁם וְאֶת־עֵמֶק עָכוֹר לְפֶתַח

an for Achor the and from her her to I And her
of entrance of valley ,there vineyards give will .heart

תִּקְוָה וְעָנְתָה שָּׁמָּה כִּימֵי נְעוּרֶיהָ וּכְיוֹם עֲלוֹתָהּ מֵאֶרֶץ־

the from went she as and ,youth her the as ,there she And .hope
of land up when day the of days answer shall

18 מִצְרָיִם׃ וְהָיָה בַיּוֹם־הַהוּא נְאֻם־יְהוָה תִּקְרְאִי אִישִׁי

hus- My shall you ,Jehovah says ,that day in it And .Egypt
,band ,call ,be shall

19 וְלֹא־תִקְרְאִי־לִי עוֹד בַּעְלִי׃ וַהֲסִרֹתִי אֶת־שְׁמוֹת הַבְּעָלִים

Baals the names the will I For .Baal My ,more Me call shall and
of away take not

20 מִפִּיהָ וְלֹא־יִזָּכְרוּ עוֹד בִּשְׁמָם׃ וְכָרַתִּי לָהֶם בְּרִית בַּיּוֹם

day in a for will I And their by more shall they And her from
covenant them cut .name remembered be not .mouth

with the beasts of the field, and with the birds of the sky and the creeping things of the ground. And I will break the bow and the sword and the battle out of the earth, and I will make them to lie down safely. [19] And I will betroth you to Me forever. Yes, I will betroth you to Me in righteousness, and in judgment, and in mercy and in compassions. [20] I will even betroth you to Me in faithfulness. And you shall know Jehovah. [21] And it shall be in that day I will answer, says Jehovah. I will answer the heavens and they shall answer the earth; [22] and the earth shall hear the grain and the wine and the oil; and they shall hear Jezreel. [23] And I will sow her to Me in the earth. And I will have mercy on her who had not had mercy. And I will say to (those) not My people, You (are) My people! And he shall say, My God!

הַהוּא עִם־חַיַּת הַשָּׂדֶה וְעִם־עוֹף הַשָּׁמַיִם וְרֶמֶשׂ הָאֲדָמָה
.ground the the and sky the the and ,field the the with that
of things creeping of birds with of beasts

וְקֶשֶׁת וְחֶרֶב וּמִלְחָמָה אֶשְׁבּוֹר מִן־הָאָרֶץ וְהִשְׁכַּבְתִּים
make will I and ,earth the out will I battle and and bow And
down lie them of break sword

21 לָבֶטַח׃ וְאֵרַשְׂתִּיךְ לִי לְעוֹלָם וְאֵרַשְׂתִּיךְ לִי בְּצֶדֶק
righ- in Me to will I ,Yes .forever Me to will I And .securely
,teousness you betroth you betroth

22 וּבְמִשְׁפָּט וּבְחֶסֶד וּבְרַחֲמִים׃ וְאֵרַשְׂתִּיךְ לִי בֶּאֱמוּנָה וְיָדַעַתְּ
you And faith- in to will I And in and in and in and
know shall .fulness Me you betroth .compassions ,mercy ,judgment

23 אֶת־יְהוָה׃ וְהָיָה ׀ בַּיּוֹם הַהוּא אֶעֱנֶה נְאֻם־יְהוָה אֶעֱנֶה
will I .Jehovah says will I that day in it And .Jehovah
answer ,answer ,be shall

24 אֶת־הַשָּׁמָיִם וְהֵם יַעֲנוּ אֶת־הָאָרֶץ׃ וְהָאָרֶץ תַּעֲנֶה אֶת־
shall the and the shall and ,heavens the
answer earth ;earth answer they

הַדָּגָן וְאֶת־הַתִּירוֹשׁ וְאֶת־הַיִּצְהָר וְהֵם יַעֲנוּ אֶת־יִזְרְעֶאל׃
,Jezreel shall and olive the and new the and the
answer they ;oil wine grain

25 וּזְרַעְתִּיהָ לִּי בָּאָרֶץ וְרִחַמְתִּי אֶת־לֹא רֻחָמָה וְאָמַרְתִּי לְלֹא־
Lo- to will I And .ruhama Lo- will I And the in to will I And
say on mercy have .earth Me her sow

עַמִּי עַמִּי־אַתָּה וְהוּא יֹאמַר אֱלֹהָי׃
!God My shall And you My ,ammi
,say he !(are) people

CAP. III ג

CHAPTER 3

[1] Then Jehovah said to me, Go again. Love a woman loved by a friend, yet an adulteress, according to the love of Jehovah toward the sons of Israel, who look to other gods and love raisin-cakes of grapes. [2] So I bought her for myself with fifteen (pieces of) silver, and (for) a homer of barley, and a half of barley. [3] And I said to her, You shall stay with me many days. You shall not be a harlot. nor be to a man; so I also (will be) for you. [4] For the sons of Israel shall stay many days (with) no king, and no prince, and (with) no sacrifice, and no pillars, and no ephod or teraphim. [5] Afterward

1 וַיֹּאמֶר יְהוָה אֵלַי עוֹד לֵךְ אֱהַב־אִשָּׁה אֲהֻבַת רֵעַ וּמְנָאָפֶת
an yet a loved a love ,Go ,again to Jehovah said Then
,adulteress ,friend by woman ,me

כְּאַהֲבַת יְהוָה אֶת־בְּנֵי יִשְׂרָאֵל וְהֵם פֹּנִים אֶל־אֱלֹהִים
gods to turn they and ,Israel the (toward) Jeho- to according
of sons vah of love the

2 אֲחֵרִים וְאֹהֲבֵי אֲשִׁישֵׁי עֲנָבִים׃ וָאֶכְּרֶהָ לִּי בַּחֲמִשָּׁה עָשָׂר
fifteen with for I So .grapes raisin love and other
,me her bought of cakes

3 כָּסֶף וְחֹמֶר שְׂעֹרִים וְלֶתֶךְ שְׂעֹרִים׃ וָאֹמַר אֵלֶיהָ יָמִים
days ,her to I And .barley a and ,barley a and (of pieces)
said of half of homer ,silver

רַבִּים תֵּשְׁבִי לִי לֹא תִזְנִי וְלֹא תִהְיִי לְאִישׁ וְגַם־אֲנִי אֵלָיִךְ׃
.you to I so a to be nor shall You not with shall you Many
(be will) also ;man ,harlot .a be .me stay

4 כִּי ׀ יָמִים רַבִּים יֵשְׁבוּ בְּנֵי יִשְׂרָאֵל אֵין מֶלֶךְ וְאֵין שָׂר
,prince and king no ,Israel the shall many days For
no (with) of sons stay

5 וְאֵין זֶבַח וְאֵין מַצֵּבָה וְאֵין אֵפוֹד וּתְרָפִים׃ אַחַר יָשֻׁבוּ
shall Afterward .teraphim or ephod no and ,pillar and sacri- and
return no ,fice no

the sons of Israel shall return and seek Jehovah their God and David their king. And they shall fear Jehovah and His goodness in the end of the days.

CHAPTER 4

[1] Sons of Israel, hear Jehovah's word, for Jehovah (has) a quarrel with the land's residents; for no truth and no mercy and no knowledge of God in the land. [2] Lying and swearing; and killing and stealing; and doing adultery increase, and blood touches against blood. [3] Therefore the land shall mourn, and every one living in it shall droop, with the beasts of the field and the birds of the heavens —yes, also the fish of the sea shall be removed. [4] Yet let not a man strive with nor reprove a man. For your people (are) as a priest striven with. [5] So you shall stumble (in) the day, and the prophet also shall stumble with you (at) night, and I destroy your mother.

[6] My people are destroyed for lack of knowledge. Because you rejected the knowledge, I also rejected you from being priest to Me. Since you have forgotten the law of your God, I will forget your sons; even I. [7] As they were increased, so they sinned against Me. I will change their glory into shame. [8] They eat up the sin of My people, and they lift their heart to their iniquity. [9] And it will be, Like people, like priest. And I will visit their ways on them, and repay them for their doings. [10] For they shall eat and not have enough. They shall fornicate and not increase; because they have stopped listening to Jehovah. [11] Fornication and wine and new wine take away the heart.

[12] My people seek advice by their wood (idols), and their rod declares to them. For the

בְּנֵי יִשְׂרָאֵל וּבִקְשׁוּ אֶת־יְהוָה אֱלֹהֵיהֶם וְאֵת דָּוִד מַלְכָּם
.king their David and God their Jehovah shall and Israel the
seek of sons
וּפָחֲדוּ אֶל־יְהוָה וְאֶל־טוּבוֹ בְּאַחֲרִית הַיָּמִים׃
.days the the in good- His and Jehovah they And
of ends ness fear shall

CAP. IV. ד

CHAPTER 4

1 שִׁמְעוּ דְבַר־יְהוָה בְּנֵי יִשְׂרָאֵל כִּי רִיב לַיהוָה עִם־יוֹשְׁבֵי
in- the with to quarrel a For .Israel sons ,Jehovah the Hear
of habitants Jehovah (is) of of word
הָאָרֶץ כִּי אֵין־אֱמֶת וְאֵין־חֶסֶד וְאֵין־דַּעַת אֱלֹהִים בָּאָרֶץ׃
the in God knowl- and ,mercy and ,truth no for the
;land of edge no no is ,land
2 אָלֹה וְכַחֵשׁ וְרָצֹחַ וְגָנֹב וְנָאֹף פָּרָצוּ וְדָמִים בְּדָמִים נָגָעוּ׃
.touches against blood and ;increase doing and and and and ;swearing
blood ,adultery stealing killing ,lying
3 עַל־כֵּן תֶּאֱבַל הָאָרֶץ וְאֻמְלַל כָּל־יוֹשֵׁב בָּהּ בְּחַיַּת הַשָּׂדֶה
field the the with ,it in who every- shall and the shall There-
of beasts lives one droop ,land mourn fore
4 וּבְעוֹף הַשָּׁמַיִם וְגַם־דְּגֵי הַיָּם יֵאָסֵפוּ׃ אַךְ אִישׁ אַל־יָרֵב
let not man a Yet be shall the the ,Yes .heavens the with and
with strive .removed sea of fish also of birds the
5 וְאַל־יוֹכַח אִישׁ וְעַמְּךָ כִּמְרִיבֵי כֹהֵן׃ וְכָשַׁלְתָּ הַיּוֹם וְכָשַׁל
shall and the (in) you So a as (are) your For a reprove and
stumble ,day stumble shall .priest with striven people .man not
6 גַּם־נָבִיא עִמְּךָ לָיְלָה וְדָמִיתִי אִמֶּךָ׃ נִדְמוּ עַמִּי מִבְּלִי
lack for My de- are your will I and (at) with the also
of people stroyed .mother destroy ,night you prophet
הַדָּעַת כִּי אַתָּה הַדַּעַת מָאַסְתָּ וְאֶמְאָסְאךָ מִכַּהֵן לִי
to being from rejected I also ,rejected the you Because knowl-
.Me priest you knowledge .edge
7 וַתִּשְׁכַּח תּוֹרַת אֱלֹהֶיךָ אֶשְׁכַּח בָּנֶיךָ גַּם־אָנִי׃ כְּרֻבָּם כֵּן
so were they As .I even your will I ,God your law the you Since
,increased ;sons forget of forgotten have
8 חָטְאוּ־לִי כְּבוֹדָם בְּקָלוֹן אָמִיר׃ חַטַּאת עַמִּי יֹאכֵלוּ וְאֶל־
to and they My sin The will I shame into Their glory against they
,up eat people of .change .Me sinned
9 עֲוֺנָם יִשְׂאוּ נַפְשׁוֹ׃ וְהָיָה כָעָם כַּכֹּהֵן וּפָקַדְתִּי עָלָיו דְּרָכָיו
their on will I And like, like it And their they their
;ways them visit .priest ,people ;be will .heart lift iniquity
10 וּמַעֲלָלָיו אָשִׁיב לוֹ׃ וְאָכְלוּ וְלֹא יִשְׂבָּעוּ הִזְנוּ וְלֹא יִפְרֹצוּ
;increase and shall They have and they For to will I their and
not ,fornicate .enough not eat shall .them return doings
11 כִּי־אֶת־יְהוָה עָזְבוּ לִשְׁמֹר׃ זְנוּת וְיַיִן וְתִירוֹשׁ יִקַּח־לֵב׃
the take new and and Fornica- .hear to have they Jehovah because
.heart wine wine tion ceased
12 עַמִּי בְּעֵצוֹ יִשְׁאָל וּמַקְלוֹ יַגִּיד לוֹ כִּי רוּחַ זְנוּנִים הִתְעָה
led has harlotry the For to declares their and seek their by My
.astray of spirit .them rod ,advice wood people

spirit of fornications has caused (them) to go astray. And they fornicated from under their God. [13] They sacrifice on the tops of the mountains and burn incense on the hills, under oak and poplar and terebinth, because its shade is good. Therefore your daughters shall be whores, and your brides shall commit adultery. [14] I will not punish your daughters when they fornicate, nor your brides when they commit adultery. For the (men) themselves go aside with harlots; and they sacrifice with temple prostitutes; the people (who) do not understand are thrust down.

[15] Though you, Israel, do harlotry, do not let Judah become guilty. And do not come (to) Gilgal, nor go up to Beth-aven, nor swear, (As) Jehovah lives. [16] For Israel is stubborn like a stubborn heifer. Now Jehovah will feed them as a lamb in a roomy place. [17] Ephraim (is) joined to idols. Let him alone. [18] Their drink is sour. They are fornicating continually. Her shields dearly love shame. [19] The wind has bound her up in her wings; and they shall be ashamed because of their sacrifices.

13 וַיִּזְנוּ מִתַּחַת אֱלֹהֵיהֶם׃ עַל־רָאשֵׁי הֶהָרִים יְזַבֵּחוּ וְעַל־
on and sac- they the tops the On their from they And
,rifice mountains of .God under fornicated

הַגְּבָעוֹת יְקַטֵּרוּ תַּחַת אַלּוֹן וְלִבְנֶה וְאֵלָה כִּי־טוֹב צִלָּהּ
(is) good for and and oak under in- burn hills the
.shade its ,terebinth poplar ,cense

14 עַל־כֵּן תִּזְנֶינָה בְּנוֹתֵיכֶם וְכַלּוֹתֵיכֶם תְּנָאַפְנָה׃ לֹא־אֶפְקוֹד
will I not commit shall your and your be shall Therefore
punish .adultery brides ,daughters harlots

עַל־בְּנוֹתֵיכֶם כִּי תִזְנֶינָה וְעַל־כַּלּוֹתֵיכֶם כִּי תְנָאַפְנָה כִּי־הֵם
they For com- they when your not they when your on
.adultery mit brides ,fornicate ,daughters

עִם־הַזֹּנוֹת יְפָרֵדוּ וְעִם־הַקְּדֵשׁוֹת יְזַבֵּחוּ וְעָם לֹא־יָבִין
under- do not the and they temple and go harlots with
stand (who) people ;sacrifice prostitutes with ;apart

15 יִלָּבֵט׃ אִם־זֹנֶה אַתָּה יִשְׂרָאֵל אַל־יֶאְשַׁם יְהוּדָה וְאַל־
not And .Judah be let not ,Israel you do Though thrust are
guilty harlotry .down

תָּבֹאוּ הַגִּלְגָּל וְאַל־תַּעֲלוּ בֵּית אָוֶן וְאַל־תִּשָּׁבְעוּ חַי־יְהוָה׃
.Jehovah (As) ,swear nor ,aven to go nor (to) do
lives Beth- to up ,Gilgal come

16 כִּי כְּפָרָה סֹרֵרָה סָרַר יִשְׂרָאֵל עַתָּה יִרְעֵם יְהוָה כְּכֶבֶשׂ
a like Jehovah feed will Now .Israel is ,stubborn a as For
lamb them stubborn heifer

17 בַּמֶּרְחָב׃ חֲבוּר עֲצַבִּים אֶפְרָיִם הַנַּח־לוֹ׃ סָר סָבְאָם
18
their turned Has .him Let (is) idols Joined a in
.drink aside alone .Ephraim to .place roomy

19 הַזְנֵה הִזְנוּ אָהֲבוּ הֵבוּ קָלוֹן מָגִנֶּיהָ׃ צָרַר רוּחַ אוֹתָהּ
her The binds her shame dearly love they. Contin-
wind up .shields ;fornicate ually

בִּכְנָפֶיהָ וְיֵבֹשׁוּ מִזִּבְחוֹתָם׃
their of because they and her in
.sacrifices ashamed be shall ;wings

CAP. V. ה

CHAPTER 5

CHAPTER 5

[1] Hear this, O priests, and listen, house of Israel! And give ear, house of the king! For the judgment (is) toward you, because you have been a snare to Mizpah and a net spread on Tabor. [2] And revolters have gone deep (in) slaughtering; and I chasten them all. [3] I know Ephraim, and Israel has not hidden from me. For now, O Ephraim, you have fornicated; Israel is defiled. [4] Their doings will not allow them to turn

1 שִׁמְעוּ־זֹאת הַכֹּהֲנִים וְהַקְשִׁיבוּ ׀ בֵּית יִשְׂרָאֵל וּבֵית הַמֶּלֶךְ
,king the And !Israel house ,listen and ;priests O ,this Hear
of house of

הַאֲזִינוּ כִּי לָכֶם הַמִּשְׁפָּט כִּי־פַח הֱיִיתֶם לְמִצְפָּה וְרֶשֶׁת
net a and ,Mizpah to have you a for the (is) toward For !ear give
been snare ,judgment you

2 פְּרוּשָׂה עַל־תָּבוֹר׃ וְשַׁחֲטָה שֵׂטִים הֶעְמִיקוּ וַאֲנִי מוּסָר
chasten I and gone have revolters (in) And .Tabor on spread
,deep slaughtering

3 לְכֻלָּם׃ אֲנִי יָדַעְתִּי אֶפְרַיִם וְיִשְׂרָאֵל לֹא־נִכְחַד מִמֶּנִּי כִּי
For from has not Israel and ,Ephraim know I .all them
.Me hidden

4 עַתָּה הִזְנֵיתָ אֶפְרַיִם נִטְמָא יִשְׂרָאֵל׃ לֹא יִתְּנוּ מַעַלְלֵיהֶם
Their will not .Israel defiled is O have you ,now
deeds (them) allow ;Ephraim ,fornicated

to their God. For the spirit of fornication is in their midst, and they know not Jehovah. [5] And the pride of Israel answers to his face. So Israel and Ephraim shall stumble in their iniquity. Judah shall also stumble with them. [6] They shall go with their flocks and with their herds to seek Jehovah, but they shall not find; He has withdrawn Himself from them. [7] They have acted treacherously against Jehovah, for they have brought forth strange sons. Now a new moon shall devour them with their portions. [8] Blow a horn in Gibeah, a trumpet in Ramah. Cry aloud, Beth-aven; after you, O Benjamin. [9] Ephraim shall be desolate in the day of correction. Among the tribes of Israel, I have made known that which is sure. [10] The chiefs of Judah (were) like those who remove a border; I will pour out My wrath on them like water. [11] Ephraim is oppressed, crushed in judgment; because he was pleased, he walked after the command. [12] Therefore I to Ephraim (am) as a moth, and to the house of Judah as rottenness. [13] When Ephraim saw his sickness and Judah his wound, then Ephraim went to Assyria, and sent to King Jareb. Yet he could not heal you nor did he cure you of your wound. [14] For I (am) to Ephraim as the lion, and as the young lion to the house of Judah; I, (even) I, tear and go away; I take away, and no one rescues.

[15] I will go; I will return to My place until they confess their guilt and seek My face. In their affliction, they will seek Me diligently.

לָשׁוּב אֶל־אֱלֹהֵיהֶם כִּי רוּחַ זְנוּנִים בְּקִרְבָּם וְאֶת־יְהוָה לֹא
not Jehovah and their in (is) forni- the For their to to
,midst cation of spirit .God return

5 יָדָעוּ׃ וְעָנָה גְאוֹן־יִשְׂרָאֵל בְּפָנָיו וְיִשְׂרָאֵל וְאֶפְרַיִם יִכָּשְׁלוּ
shall and Israel So his to Israel the shall So they
stumble Ephraim .face of pride answer .know

6 בַּעֲוֺנָם כָּשַׁל גַּם־יְהוּדָה עִמָּם׃ בְּצֹאנָם וּבִבְקָרָם יֵלְכוּ
They with and their with with Judah also stumbles their in
go shall herds their flocks .them .iniquity

7 לְבַקֵּשׁ אֶת־יְהוָה וְלֹא יִמְצָאוּ חָלַץ מֵהֶם׃ בַּיהוָה בָּגָדוּ
did They against from has He shall they but ,Jehovah seek to
,deceit Jehovah .them withdrawn ;find not

כִּי־בָנִים זָרִים יָלָדוּ עַתָּה יֹאכְלֵם חֹדֶשׁ אֶת־חֶלְקֵיהֶם׃
.portions their with new a de- shall Now have they strange sons for
moon them vour .borne

8 תִּקְעוּ שׁוֹפָר בַּגִּבְעָה חֲצֹצְרָה בָּרָמָה הָרִיעוּ בֵּית
Beth- Cry ;Ramah in a in a Blow
,aloud trumpet ,Gibeah horn

9 אָוֶן אַחֲרֶיךָ בִּנְיָמִין׃ אֶפְרַיִם לְשַׁמָּה תִהְיֶה בְּיוֹם תּוֹכֵחָה
.correction the in shall waste a Ephraim O after ;aven
of day become .Benjamin ,you

10 בְּשִׁבְטֵי יִשְׂרָאֵל הוֹדַעְתִּי נֶאֱמָנָה׃ הָיוּ שָׂרֵי יְהוּדָה
Judah The were is what made have I ,Israel the Among
of chiefs .confirmed known of tribes

11 כְּמַסִּיגֵי גְּבוּל עֲלֵיהֶם אֶשְׁפּוֹךְ כַּמַּיִם עֶבְרָתִי׃ עָשׁוּק
oppressed My the like will I them on a removers as
.wrath water out pour ;border of

12 אֶפְרַיִם רְצוּץ מִשְׁפָּט כִּי הוֹאִיל הָלַךְ אַחֲרֵי־צָו׃ וַאֲנִי
I And the after he was he for ,judgment crushed (is)
(am) .command walked ,pleased in ,Ephraim

13 כָעָשׁ לְאֶפְרַיִם וְכָרָקָב לְבֵית יְהוּדָה׃ וַיַּרְא אֶפְרַיִם אֶת־
Ephraim When .Judah the to as and Ephraim to a as
saw of house rottenness moth

חָלְיוֹ וִיהוּדָה אֶת־מְזֹרוֹ וַיֵּלֶךְ אֶפְרַיִם אֶל־אַשּׁוּר וַיִּשְׁלַח
sent and Assyria to Ephraim then his Judah and his
went ,wound sickness

אֶל־מֶלֶךְ יָרֵב וְהוּא לֹא יוּכַל לִרְפֹּא לָכֶם וְלֹא־יִגְהֶה מִכֶּם
you he and you heal to was not he Yet .Jareb King to
cured not able

14 מָזוֹר׃ כִּי אָנֹכִי כַשַּׁחַל לְאֶפְרַיִם וְכַכְּפִיר לְבֵית יְהוּדָה
;Judah the to the as and ,Ephraim to the as I For (the of)
of house lion young lion (am) .wound

15 אֲנִי אֲנִי אֶטְרֹף וְאֵלֵךְ אֶשָּׂא וְאֵין מַצִּיל׃ אֵלֵךְ אָשׁוּבָה
Me let will I .rescues no and take I ;go and tear (even) ,I
return ;go one ,away ,I

אֶל־מְקוֹמִי עַד אֲשֶׁר־יֶאְשְׁמוּ וּבִקְשׁוּ פָנָי בַּצַּר לָהֶם
to the In My and confess they until place My to
,them distress .face seek guilt their

יְשַׁחֲרֻנְנִי׃
seek will they
.diligently me

CHAPTER 6

[1] Come and let us return to Jehovah. For He has torn, and He will heal us. He has stricken, and He will bind us up. [2] After two days He will bring us to life. In the third day He will raise us up, and we shall live before Him. [3] Then we shall know, we who follow on to know Jehovah. His going forth is established as the dawn; and He shall come to us as the rain, as the latter (and) former rain to the earth.

[4] O Ephraim, what shall I do to you? O Judah, what shall I do to you? For your goodness is like a morning cloud, and it goes away like the early dew. [5] So I have hewn by the prophets; I have slain them by the words of My mouth; and My judgments (are like) the light (that) goes forth. [6] For I desired mercy and not sacrifice, and the knowledge of God more than burnt offerings. [7] But, like Adam, they have broken the covenant; they have acted like traitors against Me there. [8] Gilead (is) a city of those who work iniquity, slippery with bloodmarks. [9] And as troops of robbers wait for a man, the company of priests murder (in) the way to Shechem; for they have done wickedness. [10] I have seen a horrible thing in the house of Israel: the fornication of Ephraim (is) there; Israel is defiled. [11] Also, O Judah, a harvest is appointed to you, when I return the captivity of My people.

CHAPTER 7

[1] When I would have healed Israel, then the iniquity of Ephraim was uncovered, and the wickedness of Samaria. For they have worked falsehood. And a thief comes inside; the troop of robbers plunders outside. [2] And they do not think within their

CAP. VI ו

CHAPTER 6

1 לְכוּ וְנָשׁוּבָה אֶל־יְהוָה כִּי הוּא טָרָף וְיִרְפָּאֵנוּ יַךְ
He will He but has He For .Jehovah to let and Come
,struck .us heal ,torn return us
2 וְיַחְבְּשֵׁנוּ׃ יְחַיֵּנוּ מִיֹּמָיִם בַּיּוֹם הַשְּׁלִישִׁי יְקִמֵנוּ וְנִחְיֶה
shall we and will He third the In two after will He will He but
live ,up us lift day .days us revive .up us bind
3 לְפָנָיו׃ וְנֵדְעָה נִרְדְּפָה לָדַעַת אֶת־יְהוָה כְּשַׁחַר נָכוֹן
is the As .Jehovah know to us let let Then before
sure ,dawn pursue ,know us .Him
4 מֹצָאוֹ וְיָבוֹא כַגֶּשֶׁם לָנוּ כְּמַלְקוֹשׁ יוֹרֶה אָרֶץ׃ מָה אֶעֱשֶׂה
do I shall What the (to) former the as ,us to the as He and going His
.earth rain rain latter rain come shall ;forth
לְּךָ אֶפְרַיִם מָה אֶעֱשֶׂה־לְּךָ יְהוּדָה וְחַסְדְּכֶם כַּעֲנַן־בֹּקֶר
,morning a like your For ?Judah O to I shall What ?Ephraim O to
of cloud (is) faithfulness ,you do ,you
5 וְכַטַּל מַשְׁכִּים הֹלֵךְ׃ עַל־כֵּן חָצַבְתִּי בַּנְּבִיאִים הֲרַגְתִּים
slain have I the by have I So (and) rising like and
them ;prophets hewn .going ,early ;dew the
6 בְּאִמְרֵי־פִי וּמִשְׁפָּטֶיךָ אוֹר יֵצֵא׃ כִּי חֶסֶד חָפַצְתִּי וְלֹא־
and ,desired I faith- For (that) the (as) your and My the by
not fulness .forth goes light ,judgments ,mouth of words
7 זָבַח וְדַעַת אֱלֹהִים מֵעֹלוֹת׃ וְהֵמָּה כְּאָדָם עָבְרוּ בְרִית
;covenant have like ,they But than more God the and sacri-
transgressed ,Adam .offerings burnt of knowledge ;fice
8 שָׁם בָּגְדוּ בִי׃ גִּלְעָד קִרְיַת פֹּעֲלֵי אָוֶן עֲקֻבָּה מִדָּם׃
from slippery ,trouble those city a Gilead against did they there
.blood work who of (is) .Me deceit
9 וּכְחַכֵּי אִישׁ גְּדוּדִים חֶבֶר כֹּהֲנִים דֶּרֶךְ יְרַצְּחוּ שֶׁכְמָה כִּי
for to murder the (in) priests com- the of troops a as And
;Shechem way of pany ,robbers man for wait
10 זִמָּה עָשׂוּ׃ בְּבֵית יִשְׂרָאֵל רָאִיתִי שַׁעֲרִירִיָּה שָׁם זְנוּת
har- the there horrible a have I Israel the In have they wicked-
of lotry :thing seen of house .done ness
11 לְאֶפְרַיִם נִטְמָא יִשְׂרָאֵל׃ גַּם־יְהוּדָה שָׁת קָצִיר לָךְ בְּשׁוּבִי
I when for a set is O ,Also .Israel is Ephraim
return ,you harvest ,Judah defiled ;(is)
שְׁבוּת עַמִּי׃
My cap- the
.people of tivity

CAP. VII ז

CHAPTER 7

1 כְּרָפְאִי לְיִשְׂרָאֵל וְנִגְלָה עֲוֹן אֶפְרַיִם וְרָעוֹת שֹׁמְרוֹן כִּי
For .Samaria the and ,Ephraim the was then ,Israel would I When
of wickedness of iniquity uncovered healed have
2 פָעֲלוּ שָׁקֶר וְגַנָּב יָבוֹא פָּשַׁט גְּדוּד בַּחוּץ׃ וּבַל־יֹאמְרוּ
do they And .outside troop a plunders ;comes a And false- have they
say not robbers of thief .hood worked

hearts (that) I remember all their wickedness. Now their own doings have hemmed them in. They are before My face. [3] They make the king glad with their wickedness, and the rulers with their lies. [4] They (are) all adulterers, like an oven heated by the baker: he ceases from stirring, from kneading the dough, while it is leavened. [5] (In) the day of our king the rulers have sickened themselves (with) the heat of wine. He stretches out his hand with scorners. [6] For they have brought near their heart like an oven, while they lie in wait. Their baker sleeps all night. In the morning, it burns like a flaming fire. [7] They are all hot as an oven and devour their judges. All their kings have fallen. Not one among them calls to Me. [8] Ephraim, he mixed himself among the peoples. Ephraim is a cake not turned. [9] Strangers have eaten up his strength, yet he does not know (it). Yea, gray hairs are here and there on him, yet he does not know (it). [10] And the pride of Israel testifies to his face. And they do not return to Jehovah their God, nor seek Him on all this.

[11] Ephraim also is like a silly dove without heart. They call (to) Egypt. They go to Assyria. [12] When they go, I will spread My net on them. I will bring them down like the birds of the heavens. I will chastise them, as a report to their assembly. [13] Woe to them! For they have fled from Me. Ruin to them! For they have transgressed against Me. Though I would redeem them, yet they have spoken lies against Me. [14] And they have not cried to Me with their heart, when they howled on their beds. They gather themselves for grain and wine; they turn against Me. [15] Though I bound, I

לִלְבָבָם כָּל־רָעָתָם זָכָרְתִּי עַתָּה סְבָבוּם מַעַלְלֵיהֶם נֶגֶד
Before own their hemmed have Now re- I their all their in
.doings in them .member wilderness (that) hearts

3 פָּנַי הָיוּ׃ בְּרָעָתָם יְשַׂמְּחוּ־מֶלֶךְ וּבְכַחֲשֵׁיהֶם שָׂרִים׃
.rulers the their with and the made they their With they My
lies ,king glad wickedness .are face

4 כֻּלָּם מְנָאֲפִים כְּמוֹ תַנּוּר בֹּעֵרָה מֵאֹפֶה יִשְׁבּוֹת מֵעִיר
from he the by heated an like ,adulterers They
,stirring ceases :baker oven all (are)

5 מִלּוּשׁ בָּצֵק עַד־חֻמְצָתוֹ׃ יוֹם מַלְכֵּנוּ הֶחֱלוּ שָׂרִים חֲמַת
the (with) the sickened our the (In) is it while the from
of heat rulers themselves king of day .leavened ,dough kneading

6 מִיָּיִן מָשַׁךְ יָדוֹ אֶת־לֹצְצִים׃ כִּי־קֵרְבוּ כַתַּנּוּר לִבָּם בְּאָרְבָּם
lie they while their the like they For .scorners with his put He .wine
.wait in ,heart oven near brought hand out

כָּל־הַלַּיְלָה יָשֵׁן אֹפֵהֶם בֹּקֶר הוּא בֹעֵר כְּאֵשׁ לֶהָבָה׃
.flame a as burns it the In their sleeps the All
of fire ,morning ,baker night

7 כֻּלָּם יֵחַמּוּ כַּתַּנּוּר וְאָכְלוּ אֶת־שֹׁפְטֵיהֶם כָּל־מַלְכֵיהֶם נָפָלוּ
have kings their All .judges their and the as are They
.fallen devour oven hot all

8 אֵין־קֹרֵא בָהֶם אֵלָי׃ אֶפְרַיִם בָּעַמִּים הוּא יִתְבּוֹלָל אֶפְרַיִם
Ephraim mixes he the among Ephraim to among calls Not
.himself peoples (is) .Me them one

9 הָיָה עֻגָה בְּלִי הֲפוּכָה׃ אָכְלוּ זָרִים כֹּחוֹ וְהוּא לֹא יָדָע
does not he yet his Strangers have .turned not a is
.(it) know ,strength eaten cake

10 גַּם־שֵׂיבָה זָרְקָה בּוֹ וְהוּא לֹא יָדָע׃ וְעָנָה גְאוֹן־יִשְׂרָאֵל
Israel the And know does not he yet on here are gray ,Yea
of pride testifies .(it) ,him there and hairs

בְּפָנָיו וְלֹא־שָׁבוּ אֶל־יְהוָה אֱלֹהֵיהֶם וְלֹא בִקְשֻׁהוּ בְּכָל־
all in Him seek nor ,God their Jehovah to do they But his to
return not .face

11 זֹאת׃ וַיְהִי אֶפְרַיִם כְּיוֹנָה פוֹתָה אֵין לֵב מִצְרַיִם קָרָאוּ
They Egypt (To) .heart with- silly a as Ephraim Also .this
.call out dove is

12 אַשּׁוּר הָלָכוּ׃ כַּאֲשֶׁר יֵלֵכוּ אֶפְרוֹשׂ עֲלֵיהֶם רִשְׁתִּי כְּעוֹף
like ;net My them on will I they when .go they (To)
of birds spread ,go Assyria

13 הַשָּׁמַיִם אוֹרִידֵם אַיְסִרֵם כְּשֵׁמַע לַעֲדָתָם׃ אוֹי לָהֶם כִּי־
For to Woe their to a as chastise will I bring will I the
!them .congregation report ,them .down them heavens

נָדְדוּ מִמֶּנִּי שֹׁד לָהֶם כִּי־פָשְׁעוּ בִי וְאָנֹכִי אֶפְדֵּם וְהֵמָּה
they yet re- would Though against have they For to Ruin from have they
,them deem I .Me trespassed !them .Me fled

14 דִּבְּרוּ עָלַי כְּזָבִים׃ וְלֹא־זָעֲקוּ אֵלַי בְּלִבָּם כִּי יְיֵלִילוּ עַל־
on they when their with to they And .lies against have
howled ,heart Me cried have not Me spoken

15 מִשְׁכְּבוֹתָם עַל־דָּגָן וְתִירוֹשׁ יִתְגּוֹרָרוּ יָסוּרוּ בִי׃ וַאֲנִי
Though against they gather They new and grain for .beds their
I .Me turn :themselves wine

strengthened their arms, yet they think evil against Me. [16] They return, (but) not to the (Most) High. They are like a treacherous bow. Their rulers shall fall by the sword, from the rage of the tongue. This (shall be) their scorn in the land of Egypt.

16   יִסַּרְתִּי חִזַּקְתִּי זְרוֹעֹתָם וְאֵלַי יְחַשְּׁבוּ־רָע׃ יָשׁוּבוּ ׀ לֹא עַל

the to	not	re- They	.evil	they	yet	;arms their	strengthen I	,bound
.High	(but)	,turn		think		Me against		

הָיוּ כְּקֶשֶׁת רְמִיָּה יִפְּלוּ בַחֶרֶב שָׂרֵיהֶם מִזַּעַם לְשׁוֹנָם זוֹ

This	their	the	from	Their	the by	shall	.treachery	a as	They
(is)	.tongue	of rage		,rulers	sword	fall		of bow	are

לַעְגָּם בְּאֶרֶץ מִצְרָיִם׃

.Egypt	the in	their
	of land	scorn

CAP. VIII   ח

CHAPTER 8

CHAPTER 8

[1] (Put) a horn to your mouth. (He comes) like an eagle against the house of Jehovah, because they have broken My covenant and have sinned against My law. [2] Israel shall cry to Me, My God, we know You. [3] Israel has thrown off good; the enemy shall pursue him. [4] They have set up kings, but not by Me. They have made princes, but I did not know (it). They have made themselves idols (with) their silver and their gold, so that they may be cut off.

[5] Your calf, O Samaria, has cast (you) off. My anger is kindled against them. Until when will they not attain purity? [6] For from Israel it (came) also. The workman made it, and it (is) not God. But the calf of Samaria shall be fragments. [7] For they sow the wind, and they shall reap the tempest. He has no stalk; the bud shall yield no flour. If it does yield, the strangers shall swallow it up. [8] Israel is swallowed up. Now they are among the nations as a vessel in which is no pleasure. [9] For they have gone up to Assyria, a wild ass alone by himself. Ephraim has hired lovers,

[10] Yes, though they have hired among the nations, now I will gather them. And they began to be few, from the burden of the king of princes. [11] Because Ephraim has made many altars to sin, altars are sin to him. [12] I will write to him the great things of My law; they were counted as a

1   אֶל־חִכְּךָ שֹׁפָר כַּנֶּשֶׁר עַל־בֵּית יְהֹוָה יַעַן עָבְרוּ בְרִיתִי

My	have they	for	,Jehovah	the against	(comes He)	a	your	(Put)
,covenant	overpassed			of house	eagle an as	:horn	mouth	to

2 3   וְעַל־תּוֹרָתִי פָּשָׁעוּ׃ לִי יִזְעָקוּ אֱלֹהַי יְדַעֲנוּךָ יִשְׂרָאֵל׃ זָנַח

has	.Israel	know we	My	shall	To	have	law My	and
off cast		,You	God	,cry	Me	.trespassed		against

4   יִשְׂרָאֵל טוֹב אוֹיֵב יִרְדְּפוֹ׃ הֵם הִמְלִיכוּ וְלֹא מִמֶּנִּי הֵשִׂירוּ

made They	by	but	set have	They	shall	the	;good	Israel
,princes	Me	not	kings up			.him pursue	enemy	

וְלֹא יָדַעְתִּי כַּסְפָּם וּזְהָבָם עָשׂוּ לָהֶם עֲצַבִּים לְמַעַן יִכָּרֵת׃

may they that so	,idols	for	They	their and	their (with)	I	but
.off cut be		them	made	gold	silver	.(it) knew	not

5   זָנַח עֶגְלֵךְ שֹׁמְרוֹן חָרָה אַפִּי בָּם עַד־מָתַי לֹא יוּכְלוּ נִקָּיֹן׃

?purity they will not	when Until	against My	is	.Samaria	Your cast has
attain		.them	anger kindled		,calf off (you)

6   כִּי מִיִּשְׂרָאֵל וְהוּא חָרָשׁ עָשָׂהוּ וְלֹא אֱלֹהִים דִּיָּא כִּי־

For	.(is)	God	and	,it made	The	it also	Israel from	For
			not		artisan	.(came)		

7   שְׁבָבִים יִהְיֶה עֵגֶל שֹׁמְרוֹן׃ כִּי רוּחַ יִזְרָעוּ וְסוּפָתָה יִקְצֹרוּ

shall they	the and	they	the	For	.Samaria	the	shall	splinters
.reap	tempest	sow	wind			of calf	be	

קָמָה אֵין־לוֹ צֶמַח בְּלִי יַעֲשֶׂה־קֶּמַח אוּלַי יַעֲשֶׂה זָרִים

strangers does it	If	.flour	shall	not	bud the	to is	A
make			make			;him not	stalk

8   יִבְלָעֻהוּ׃ נִבְלַע יִשְׂרָאֵל עַתָּה הָיוּ בַגּוֹיִם כִּכְלִי אֵין־חֵפֶץ

pleasure is	a as	the among	they	Now	.Israel	swallowed is	swallow shall
no	vessel	nations	are			up	.up it

9   כִּי־הֵמָּה עָלוּ אַשּׁוּר פֶּרֶא בּוֹדֵד לוֹ אֶפְרַיִם הִתְנוּ

has	Ephraim	by	alone	wild a	to	have	they	For	in
hired		,himself		ass	,Assyria	up gone		.which	

10   אֲהָבִים׃ גַּם כִּי־יִתְנוּ בַגּוֹיִם עַתָּה אֲקַבְּצֵם וַיָּחֵלּוּ מְעָט

,few	they And	will I	now	the among	they though	,Yes	.lovers
(be to)	began	.them	gather	,nations	hired have		

11   מִמַּשָּׂא מֶלֶךְ שָׂרִים׃ כִּי־הִרְבָּה אֶפְרַיִם מִזְבְּחוֹת לַחֲטֹא

—sin to	altars	Ephraim	made has	For	.rulers	king the	the from
			many			of	of burden

12   הָיוּ־לוֹ מִזְבְּחוֹת לַחֲטֹא׃ אֶכְתָּוב־לוֹ רֻבֵּי תּוֹרָתִי כְּמוֹ־זָר

a as	My	great the	for	will I	—sin to	altars	to they
stranger	;law	of things	him	write			him are

stranger. [13] They sacrifice flesh (for) the sacrifices of My offerings, and they eat. Jehovah did not accept them. Now He will remember their iniquity and punish their sins. They shall return (to) Egypt. [14] For Israel has forgotten his Maker, and builds temples. And Judah has multiplied fortified cities; but I will send a fire on his cities, and it shall burn up her citadels.

CHAPTER 9

[1] O Israel, do not rejoice for joy, like the peoples. For you have gone lusting away from your God. You have loved a reward on all threshing floors of grain. [2] The floor and the winepress shall not feed them, and the new wine shall fail in her. [3] They shall not live in Jehovah's land. But Ephraim shall return to Egypt; and they shall eat unclean things in Assyria. [4] They shall not offer wine to Jehovah. They shall not be pleasing to Him. Their sacrifices (shall be) like the bread of trouble to them; all who eat it shall be defiled; for their bread for their person shall not come into the house of Jehovah. [5] What will you do in the day of meeting, and in the day of the feast of Jehovah? [6] For, lo, they have gone from destruction. Egypt shall gather them; Memphis shall bury them. Nettles shall possess the desirable things of their silver; thorns (shall be) in their tents. [7] The days of her visitation have come. The days of vengeance have come. Israel shall know. The prophet (is) a fool. The spiritual man (is) insane, because of the greatness of your iniquity and your great hatred. [8] Ephraim (is) a watchman with my God. The prophet (is) a snare of a fowler in all his ways; hatred (is) in the house of his God. [9] They have deeply corrupted, as in the

13 נֶחְשָֽׁבוּ׃ זִבְחֵי הַבְהָבַי יִזְבְּחוּ בָשָׂר וַיֹּאכֵלוּ יְהוָה לֹא רָצָם
ac- did not Jehovah they and flesh they My the For were they
.them cept .eat sacrifice ,gifts of sacrifices .counted
עַתָּה יִזְכֹּר עֲוֺנָם וְיִפְקֹד חַטֹּאותָם הֵמָּה מִצְרַיִם יָשׁוּבוּ׃
shall Egypt (to) They .sins their and their will He Now
.return visit iniquity remember
14 וַיִּשְׁכַּח יִשְׂרָאֵל אֶת־עֹשֵׂהוּ וַיִּבֶן הֵיכָלוֹת וִיהוּדָה הִרְבָּה
has Judah And .temples and his Israel has For
multiplied builds ,Maker forgotten
עָרִים בְּצֻרוֹת וְשִׁלַּחְתִּי אֵשׁ בְּעָרָיו וְאָכְלָה אַרְמְנֹתֶיהָ׃
her shall it and his on a will I but inacces- cities
.citadels consume ,cities fire send :sible

CAP. IX ט

CHAPTER 9

1 אַל־תִּשְׂמַח יִשְׂרָאֵל׀ אֶל־גִּיל כָּעַמִּים כִּי זָנִיתָ מֵעַל אֱלֹהֶיךָ
your away have you For the as ,joy for ,Israel O do not
.God from fornicated .peoples rejoice
2 אָהַבְתָּ אֶתְנָן עַל כָּל־גָּרְנוֹת דָּגָן׃ גֹּרֶן וָיֶקֶב לֹא יִרְעֵם
feed shall not the and The .grain grain all on harlot's a have You
,them winepress floor of floors hire loved
3 וְתִירוֹשׁ יְכַחֶשׁ בָּהּ׃ לֹא יֵשְׁבוּ בְּאֶרֶץ יְהוָה וְשָׁב אֶפְרַיִם
Ephraim But .Jehovah the in They not .her in shall new and
return shall of land live shall fail wine
4 מִצְרַיִם וּבְאַשּׁוּר טָמֵא יֹאכֵלוּ׃ לֹא־יִסְּכוּ לַיהוָה׀ יַיִן וְלֹא
And .wine to They not shall they unclean in and ;Egypt to
not Jehovah pour shall .eat things Assyria
יֶעֶרְבוּ־לוֹ זִבְחֵיהֶם כְּלֶחֶם אוֹנִים לָהֶם כָּל־אֹכְלָיו יִטַּמָּאוּ
be shall eat who all to trouble the as (are) Their to shall they
;defiled it ;them of bread sacrifices .Him pleasing be
5 כִּי־לַחְמָם לְנַפְשָׁם לֹא יָבוֹא בֵּית יְהוָה׃ מַה־תַּעֲשׂוּ לְיוֹם
the in you will What .Jehovah the into shall it not their for their for
of day do of house come ;person (is) bread
6 מוֹעֵד וּלְיוֹם חַג־יְהוָה׃ כִּי־הִנֵּה הָלְכוּ מִשֹּׁד מִצְרַיִם
Egypt from have they ,behold ,For ?Jehovah the in and meet-
.destruction gone of feast of day the ,ing
תְּקַבְּצֵם מֹף תְּקַבְּרֵם מַחְמַד לְכַסְפָּם קִמּוֹשׂ יִירָשֵׁם חוֹחַ
thorns shall nettles their of Desirable bury shall Memphis shall
;possess ,silver things .them ;them gather
7 בְּאָהֳלֵיהֶם׃ בָּאוּ׀ יְמֵי הַפְּקֻדָּה בָּאוּ יְמֵי הַשִּׁלֻּם יֵדְעוּ
shall .vengeance the have her The have (be shall)
know of days come ,visitation of days come .tents their in
יִשְׂרָאֵל אֱוִיל הַנָּבִיא מְשֻׁגָּע אִישׁ הָרוּחַ עַל רֹב עֲוֺנְךָ וְרַבָּה
and your great for the The (is) the a (is) ,Israel
great iniquity ,spirit man of insane .prophet fool
8 מַשְׂטֵמָה׃ צֹפֶה אֶפְרַיִם עִם־אֱלֹהָי נָבִיא פַּח יָקוֹשׁ עַל־
on a snare The my with Ephraim a (your)
fowler's (is) prophet .God (is) watchman .hatred
9 כָּל־דְּרָכָיו מַשְׂטֵמָה בְּבֵית אֱלֹהָיו׃ הֶעְמִיקוּ שִׁחֵתוּ כִּימֵי
(in) as cor- have They .God his the in hatred ;ways his all
of days the rupted deeply of house (is)

days of Gibeah. He will remember their iniquity; He will punish their sins. [10] I found Israel like grapes in the wilderness. I saw your fathers as the firstfruit in the fig tree at her first time. They came (to) Baal-peor and set themselves apart to a shameful thing. And they became hateful like that which they loved. [11] Ephraim is like a bird; their glory shall fly away from birth, and from the womb, and from conception. [12] Though they nourish their sons, yet I will make them childless, without a man. Yes, woe also to them when I turn from them! [13] Ephraim, as when I looked toward Tyre, was planted in a pleasant place. But Ephraim shall bring forth his sons to the slayer. [14] Give them, O Jehovah; what will You give? Give them a miscarrying womb and dry breasts. [15] All their wickedness (is) in Gilgal, for there I hated them. I will drive them out of My house for the wickedness of their doings; I will not love them again; all their rulers (are) revolters. [16] Ephraim is stricken; their root is dried up; they shall bear no fruit. Yes, though they bear, yet I will kill the beloved of their womb. [17] My God shall cast them away because they did not listen to Him; and they shall be wanderers among the nations.

10 הַגִּבְעָה יִזְכּוֹר עֲוֺנָם יִפְקוֹד חַטֹּאותָם׃ כַּעֲנָבִים בַּמִּדְבָּר

the in grapes Like .sons their will He their recall Gibeah
wilderness visit ;iniquity

מָצָאתִי יִשְׂרָאֵל כְּבִכּוּרָה בִתְאֵנָה בְּרֵאשִׁיתָהּ רָאִיתִי

saw I its at the in the As .Israel found I
beginning tree fig firstfruit

אֲבוֹתֵיכֶם הֵמָּה בָּאוּ בַעַל־פְּעוֹר וַיִּנָּזְרוּ לַבֹּשֶׁת וַיִּהְיוּ

they And to and peor Baal- (to) came They .fathers your
became .shame separated

11 שִׁקּוּצִים כְּאָהֳבָם׃ אֶפְרַיִם כָּעוֹף יִתְעוֹפֵף כְּבוֹדָם מִלֵּדָה

from ,glory their fly shall a like for As which that like hateful
,birth away bird ,Ephraim .loved they ,things

12 וּמִבֶּטֶן וּמֵהֵרָיוֹן׃ כִּי אִם־יְגַדְּלוּ אֶת־בְּנֵיהֶם וְשִׁכַּלְתִּים

make will I yet their they Though from and from and
,childless them ,sons nourish .conception ,womb the

13 מֵאָדָם כִּי־גַם־אוֹי לָהֶם בְּשׂוּרִי מֵהֶם׃ אֶפְרַיִם כַּאֲשֶׁר־

when as ,Ephraim from I when to woe also ,Yes without
!them turn them .man a

רָאִיתִי לְצוֹר שְׁתוּלָה בְנָוֶה וְאֶפְרַיִם לְהוֹצִיא אֶל־הֹרֵג

the to bring (shall) But a in planted was toward looked I
slayer forth Ephraim .meadow ,Tyre

14 בָּנָיו׃ תֶּן־לָהֶם יְהוָה מַה־תִּתֵּן תֶּן־לָהֶם רֶחֶם מַשְׁכִּיל

miscarrying a to Give will what ;Jehovah to Give his
womb them ?give You ,them .sons

15 וְשָׁדַיִם צֹמְקִים׃ כָּל־רָעָתָם בַּגִּלְגָּל כִּי־שָׁם שְׂנֵאתִים עַל

for hated I there for ,Gilgal in (is) their All .dry and
;them evil breasts

רֹעַ מַעַלְלֵיהֶם מִבֵּיתִי אֲגָרְשֵׁם לֹא אוֹסֵף אַהֲבָתָם כָּל־

all ;them love will I not will I of out doings their the
again ;them drive house My of evil

16 שָׂרֵיהֶם סֹרְרִים׃ הֻכָּה אֶפְרַיִם שָׁרְשָׁם יָבֵשׁ פְּרִי בְלִי־

not fruit is their ;Ephraim is .revolters rulers their
;up dried root stricken (are)

17 יַעֲשׂוּן גַּם כִּי יֵלֵדוּן וְהֵמַתִּי מַחֲמַדֵּי בִטְנָם׃ יִמְאָסֵם אֱלֹהַי

My cast shall their beloved the I yet they though ,Yes they
,God away them .womb of ones kill will ,bear .make shall

כִּי לֹא שָׁמְעוּ לוֹ וְיִהְיוּ נֹדְדִים בַּגּוֹיִם׃

among wanderers they and to did they not be-
.nations the be shall ;Him listen cause

CHAPTER 10

[1] Israel (is) a luxuriant vine. He bears fruit for himself. According to the multitude of his fruit, he has increased the altars. They have made beautiful images according to the goodness of his land. [2] Their heart is divided. Now they shall be found guilty; He shall break down their altars; He shall spoil their images. [3] For now

CAP. X י

CHAPTER 10

1 גֶּפֶן בּוֹקֵק יִשְׂרָאֵל פְּרִי יְשַׁוֶּה־לּוֹ כְּרֹב לְפִרְיוֹ הִרְבָּה

has he his of the As for He fruit Israel luxuriant A
increased ,fruit plenty .himself bears .(is) wine

2 לַמִּזְבְּחוֹת כְּטוֹב לְאַרְצוֹ הֵיטִיבוּ מַצֵּבוֹת׃ חָלַק לִבָּם עַתָּה

Now their is .pillars have they his of the As .altars the
.heart divided decorated land goodness

3 יֶאְשָׁמוּ הוּא יַעֲרֹף מִזְבְּחוֹתָם יְשֹׁדֵד מַצֵּבוֹתָם׃ כִּי עַתָּה

now For .pillars their shall He their shall He shall they
despoil ;altars down break ;guilty be

they shall say, We have no king because we did not fear Jehovah. What then should a king do for us? [4] They have spoken words, swearing falsely to cut a covenant. So judgment springs up like hemlock in the furrows of the field. [5] The people of Samaria shall dread because of the calves of Beth-aven. For its people shall mourn over it; and its priests (who) rejoiced on it for its glory (shall mourn) because it has departed from it. [6] It shall also be carried to Assyria, a present to King Jareb. Ephraim shall receive shame, and Israel shall be ashamed of his own counsel. [7] Samaria is cut off; her king is as a bough on the face of the water. [8] Also the high places of Aven, the sin of Israel, shall be destroyed. The thorn and the thistle shall come up on their altars. And they shall say to the mountains, Cover us; and to the hills, Fall on us. [9] O Israel, you have sinned from the days of Gibeah. There they stood; the battle against the sons of iniquity did not overtake them in Gibeah. [10] When I desire, I shall bind them. And the peoples shall be gathered against them, when they shall bind themselves to their two furrows. [11] And Ephraim (is) a trained heifer, loving to tread out. But I passed over on the goodness of her neck; I will make Ephraim to ride; Judah shall plow; Jacob shall break clods to him. [12] Sow to yourselves in righteousness, reap as mercy. Break up your plowed ground. For (it is) time to seek Jehovah, until He comes and rains righteousness on you. [13] You have plowed wickedness, you have reaped iniquity. You have eaten the fruit of lies because you trusted in your way, in the multitude of your mighty men. [14] Therefore an uproar shall arise among the peoples. And all your

יֹאמְרוּ אֵין מֶלֶךְ לָנוּ כִּי לֹא יָרֵאנוּ אֶת־יְהוָה וְהַמֶּלֶךְ מַה־
What the then .Jehovah did we not be- ,us to king No shall they
king fear cause (is) ,say

4 יַּעֲשֶׂה־לָּנוּ׃ דִּבְּרוּ דְבָרִים אָלוֹת שָׁוְא כָּרֹת בְּרִית וּפָרַח
So cove- a cut to empti- swearing ,words have They for should
up springs .nant ness spoken ?us do

5 כָּרֹאשׁ מִשְׁפָּט עַל תַּלְמֵי שָׂדָי׃ לְעֶגְלוֹת בֵּית אָוֶן יָגוּרוּ
shall aven Beth- of Because the fur- the on judgment as
dread of calves the .field of rows hemlock

שְׁכַן שֹׁמְרוֹן כִּי־אָבַל עָלָיו עַמּוֹ וּכְמָרָיו עָלָיו יָגִילוּ עַל־
for re- (who) it on its and its over shall For .Samaria's people
joiced ,priests ;people it mourn

6 כְּבוֹדוֹ כִּי־גָלָה מִמֶּנּוּ׃ גַּם־אוֹתוֹ לְאַשּׁוּר יוּבָל מִנְחָה לְמֶלֶךְ
king to a be shall Assyria to it Also .it from has it be- its
present ,carried departed cause ,glory

7 יָרֵב בָּשְׁנָה אֶפְרַיִם יִקָּח וְיֵבוֹשׁ יִשְׂרָאֵל מֵעֲצָתוֹ׃ נִדְמֶה
cut is own his from Israel shall and shall Ephraim shame .Jareb
off .counsel ashamed be ,receive

8 שֹׁמְרוֹן מַלְכָּהּ כְּקֶצֶף עַל־פְּנֵי־מָיִם׃ וְנִשְׁמְדוּ בָּמוֹת אָוֶן
,Aven high the be shall Also the the on a as ,king her ,Samaria
of places destroyed .waters of face bough

חַטַּאת יִשְׂרָאֵל קוֹץ וְדַרְדַּר יַעֲלֶה עַל־מִזְבְּחוֹתָם וְאָמְרוּ
they And .altars their on come shall the and The .Israel sin the
say shall up thistle thorn of

9 לֶהָרִים כַּסּוּנוּ וְלַגְּבָעוֹת נִפְלוּ עָלֵינוּ׃ מִימֵי הַגִּבְעָה
Gibeah the From .us on Fall the to and Cover the to
of days ,hills ;us ,mountains

חָטָאתָ יִשְׂרָאֵל שָׁם עָמָדוּ לֹא־תַשִּׂיגֵם בַּגִּבְעָה מִלְחָמָה
battle the Gibeah in over- not they There .Israel O have you
them takes ;stood ,sinned

10 עַל־בְּנֵי עַלְוָה׃ בְּאַוָּתִי וְאֶסֳּרֵם וְאֻסְּפוּ עֲלֵיהֶם עַמִּים בְּאָסְרָם
they when ,peoples against shall And will I then I When.injustice the against
themselves bind them gathered be them bind desire of sons

11 לִשְׁתֵּי עֹנֹתָם׃ וְאֶפְרַיִם עֶגְלָה מְלֻמָּדָה אֹהַבְתִּי לָדוּשׁ וַאֲנִי
I But tread to love I ;trained heifer a (is) And their to
.out Ephraim .iniquities two

עָבַרְתִּי עַל־טוּב צַוָּארָהּ אַרְכִּיב אֶפְרַיִם יַחֲרוֹשׁ יְהוּדָה
;Judah shall ;Ephraim make will I ;neck her the on passed
plow ride to of goodness over

12 יְשַׂדֶּד־לוֹ יַעֲקֹב׃ זִרְעוּ לָכֶם לִצְדָקָה קִצְרוּ לְפִי־חֶסֶד נִירוּ
Break .mercy as reap righ- in your- to Sow .Jacob for shall
up ,teousness selves him harrow

לָכֶם נִיר וְעֵת לִדְרוֹשׁ אֶת־יְהוָה עַד־יָבוֹא וְיֹרֶה צֶדֶק לָכֶם׃
to righ- rains and He until ,Jehovah seek to For plowed to
.you teousness comes time .ground you

13 חֲרַשְׁתֶּם־רֶשַׁע עַוְלָתָה קְצַרְתֶּם אֲכַלְתֶּם פְּרִי־כָחַשׁ כִּי־
because ,lies the have You have you iniquity wicked- have You
of fruit eaten .reaped ;ness plowed

14 בָטַחְתָּ בְדַרְכְּךָ בְּרֹב גִּבּוֹרֶיךָ׃ וְקָאם שָׁאוֹן בְּעַמֶּךָ וְכָל־
And your among an shall And your in your in you
all .peoples uproar arise .warriors many ,way trusted

strongholds shall be spoiled, as Shalman spoiled Beth-arbel in the day of battle. The mother was dashed in pieces on (her) sons. [15] So He does to you, Bethel, because of your great wickedness. In the dawn the king of Israel shall be completely cut off.

CHAPTER 11

[1] When Israel (was) a child, then I loved him, and I called My son out of Egypt. [2] (As) they called to them, so they went from their face. They sacrifice to the Baals, and burn incense to graven images. [3] I also taught Ephraim to go; he took them on their arms. But they did not know that I healed them. [4] I drew them with cords of a man, with bands of love. And I was to them as those who take off the yoke on their jaws. And gently I give food to him.

[5] He shall not return to the land of Egypt, but Assyria, he (shall be) his king, because they refused to return. [6] And the sword shall whirl in his cities and shall destroy his bars, and devour, because of their own counsels. [7] And My people are bent to backsliding from Me. And they call him to the Most High, no one at all would exalt (Him). [8] How shall I give you up, Ephraim? (How) shall I deliver you, Israel? How shall I make you like Admah? Shall I set you as Zeboim? My heart has turned within Me; My compassions are kindled together. [9] I will not carry out the heat of My anger; I will not return to destroy Ephraim. For I (am) God and not a man, the Holy One in your midst. And I will not enter into the city. [10] They shall walk after Jehovah. He shall roar like a lion. When He roars, then sons shall tremble from the west. [11] They shall tremble like a bird out of Egypt,

מִבְצָרֶיךָ יוּשַּׁד כְּשֹׁד שַׁלְמַן בֵּית אַרְבֵאל בְּיוֹם מִלְחָמָה

.battle the in arbel (of) by the as be shall strong- your
of day Beth- Shalman ruin ,despoiled holds

15 אֵם עַל־בָּנִים רֻטָּשָׁה׃ כָּכָה עָשָׂה לָכֶם בֵּית־אֵל מִפְּנֵי רָעַת

great because ,el Beth- to He So dashed was (her) on The
of ,you does .pieces in sons mother

רָעַתְכֶם בַּשַּׁחַר נִדְמֹה נִדְמָה מֶלֶךְ יִשְׂרָאֵל׃

.Israel king the be shall completely the In your
of off cut dawn .wickedness

CAP. XI יא

CHAPTER 11

1
2 כִּי נַעַר יִשְׂרָאֵל וָאֹהֲבֵהוּ וּמִמִּצְרַיִם קָרָאתִי לִבְנִי׃ קָרְאוּ

they (As) .son My called I of out and loved I then Israel a When
called Egypt ,him ,(was) child

לָהֶם כֵּן הָלְכוּ מִפְּנֵיהֶם לַבְּעָלִים יְזַבֵּחוּ וְלַפְּסִלִים יְקַטֵּרוּן׃

burn to and they the to their from they so to
.incense images carved sacrifice Baals ;face went ,them

3 וְאָנֹכִי תִרְגַּלְתִּי לְאֶפְרַיִם קָחָם עַל־זְרוֹעֹתָיו וְלֹא יָדְעוּ כִּי

that did they But His on took He ;Ephraim to taught I Also
know not .arms them walk

4 רְפָאתִים׃ בְּחַבְלֵי אָדָם אֶמְשְׁכֵם בַּעֲבֹתוֹת אַהֲבָה וָאֶהְיֶה

I And .love bands with drew I a With healed I
was of ;them man of cords .them

5 לָהֶם כִּמְרִימֵי עֹל עַל לְחֵיהֶם וְאַט אֵלָיו אוֹכִיל׃ לֹא יָשׁוּב

shall He not give I to And their on the those as to
return .food him gently .jaws yoke off taking them

6 אֶל־אֶרֶץ מִצְרַיִם וְאַשּׁוּר הוּא מַלְכּוֹ כִּי מֵאֲנוּ לָשׁוּב׃ וְחָלָה

shall And to re- they for his he but ,Egypt the to
whirl .return fused ,king (be shall) ,Assyria of land

7 חֶרֶב בְּעָרָיו וְכִלְּתָה בַדָּיו וְאָכָלָה מִמֹּעֲצוֹתֵיהֶם׃ וְעַמִּי

My And their of because shall and his shall and his in the
people .counsels own consume bars destroy cities sword

8 תְלוּאִים לִמְשׁוּבָתִי וְאֶל־עַל יִקְרָאֻהוּ יַחַד לֹא יְרוֹמֵם׃ אֵיךְ

How exalt would not at call they to And backsliding to bent are
.(Him) all ,him High Most the .Me from

אֶתֶּנְךָ אֶפְרַיִם אֲמַגֶּנְךָ יִשְׂרָאֵל אֵיךְ אֶתֶּנְךָ כְאַדְמָה אֲשִׂימְךָ

I Shall ?Admah like I shall How ?Israel shall (How) ?Ephraim I shall
you set you make ,you deliver I ,up you give

9 כִּצְבֹאיִם נֶהְפַּךְ עָלַי לִבִּי יַחַד נִכְמְרוּ נִחוּמָי׃ לֹא אֶעֱשֶׂה

will I not com- My are together My within has ?Zeboim as
out carry .passions kindled ;heart Me turned

חֲרוֹן אַפִּי לֹא אָשׁוּב לְשַׁחֵת אֶפְרָיִם כִּי אֵל אָנֹכִי וְלֹא־

and I God For .Ephraim destroy to will I not My the
not (am) return ;anger of heat

10 אִישׁ בְּקִרְבְּךָ קָדוֹשׁ וְלֹא אָבוֹא בְּעִיר׃ אַחֲרֵי יְהוָה יֵלְכוּ

they Jehovah After the into will I And Holy the your in a
.walk shall .city enter not .One midst ,man

11 כְּאַרְיֵה יִשְׁאָג כִּי־הוּא יִשְׁאַג וְיֶחֶרְדוּ בָנִים מִיָּם׃ יֶחֶרְדוּ

did They the from sons shall then ,roars He When shall He a As
tremble .west tremble .roar lion

and like a dove out of the land of Assyria. And I will make them live in their houses, says Jehovah. [12] Ephraim circles around Me with lies; and the house of Israel (circles) with deceit; but Judah still rules with God and is faithful with the saints.

CHAPTER 12

[1] Ephraim feeds on wind and follows after the east wind; all the day multiplies lies and ruin. And they cut a covenant with Assyria. And oil is carried into Egypt. [2] Jehovah also has a quarrel with Judah and will punish Jacob according to his ways; He will repay him according to his acts.

[3] He took his brother by the heel in the womb, and by his strength he contended with God. [4] Yes, he wept and pleaded to Him, and he contended with the Angel and overcame. He finds us (at) Bethel, and there He speaks with us, [5] even Jehovah the God of hosts. Jehovah (is) his memorial. [6] Therefore you turn to your God, keep mercy and judgment and wait on your God continually.

[7] (He is) a merchant; the scales of deceit (are) in his hand; he loves to oppress. [8] And Ephraim said, Yet I am rich; I have found much wealth for myself. (In) all my labors they shall find in me no iniquity that (is) sin. [9] And I (am) Jehovah, your God from the land of Egypt, yet I will make you live in tents, as in the days of meeting. [10] I have also spoken by the prophets, and I have multiplied visions; and the prophets use parables. [11] (Is) Gilead iniquity? Surely they have been vanity. They sacrificed bulls in Gilgal. Yes, their altars

כְּצִפּוֹר מִמִּצְרַיִם וּכְיוֹנָה מֵאֶרֶץ אַשּׁוּר וְהוֹשַׁבְתִּים עַל־
in will I And .Assyria the from as and from a as
live them make of land dove a ,Egypt bird

בָּתֵּיהֶם נְאֻם־יְהוָה׃
.Jehovah says their
,houses

CAP. XII יב

CHAPTER 12

12 סְבָבֻנִי בְכַחַשׁ אֶפְרַיִם וּבְמִרְמָה בֵּית יִשְׂרָאֵל וִיהוּדָה עֹד
still but ;Israel the with and ;Ephraim with surrounds
Judah of house deceit lying Me

2 רָד עִם־אֵל וְעִם־קְדוֹשִׁים נֶאֱמָן׃ אֶפְרַיִם רֹעֶה רוּחַ וְרֹדֵף
and wind feeds Ephraim is holy the and ,God with rules
pursues on .faithful ones with

קָדִים כָּל־הַיּוֹם כָּזָב וָשֹׁד יַרְבֶּה וּבְרִית עִם־אַשּׁוּר יִכְרֹתוּ
,cut they Assyria with a And mul- he and lies the All east the
covenant .tiplies ruin day .wind

3 וְשֶׁמֶן לְמִצְרַיִם יוּבָל׃ וְרִיב לַיהוָה עִם־יְהוּדָה וְלִפְקֹד עַל־
to even ,Judah with to (is) a And is Egypt into and
visit Jehovah quarrel .carried oil

4 יַעֲקֹב כִּדְרָכָיו כְּמַעֲלָלָיו יָשִׁיב לוֹ׃ בַּבֶּטֶן עָקַב אֶת־אָחִיו
his took he the In to will He to according to according Jacob
,brother heel the by womb .him repay acts his ;ways his

5 וּבְאוֹנוֹ שָׂרָה אֶת־אֱלֹהִים׃ וַיָּשַׂר אֶל־מַלְאָךְ וַיֻּכָל בָּכָה
wept he and Angel the with he ,Yes .God with con- he by and
;overcame contended tended strength his

6 וַיִּתְחַנֶּן־לוֹ בֵּית־אֵל יִמְצָאֶנּוּ וְשָׁם יְדַבֵּר עִמָּנוּ׃ וַיהוָה
even ,us with He and finds He el (At) to and
Jehovah speaks there ,us Beth- Him pleaded

7 אֱלֹהֵי הַצְּבָאוֹת יְהוָה זִכְרוֹ׃ וְאַתָּה בֵּאלֹהֶיךָ תָשׁוּב חֶסֶד
mercy ;return your to Therefore his Jehovah .hosts the
God you .memorial (is) of God

8 וּמִשְׁפָּט שְׁמֹר וְקַוֵּה אֶל־אֱלֹהֶיךָ תָּמִיד׃ כְּנַעַן בְּיָדוֹ מֹאזְנֵי
scales his in a (is He) .always God your on and ,keep and
of (are) hand ;merchant wait judgment

9 מִרְמָה לַעֲשֹׁק אָהֵב׃ וַיֹּאמֶר אֶפְרַיִם אַךְ עָשַׁרְתִּי מָצָאתִי
have I am I yet ,Ephraim said And he to ;deceit
found ;rich .loves oppress

10 אוֹן לִי כָּל־יְגִיעַי לֹא יִמְצְאוּ־לִי עָוֹן אֲשֶׁר־חֵטְא׃ וְאָנֹכִי
I And .sin that iniquity in shall they not my (in) for wealth
(am) (is) me find labors all ;me

יְהוָה אֱלֹהֶיךָ מֵאֶרֶץ מִצְרָיִם עֹד אוֹשִׁיבְךָ בְאָהָלִים כִּימֵי
the as ,tents in make will I yet ,Egypt the from your Jehovah
of days live you of land ,God

11 מוֹעֵד׃ וְדִבַּרְתִּי עַל־הַנְּבִיאִים וְאָנֹכִי חָזוֹן הִרְבֵּיתִי וּבְיַד
the by and have visions I and ,prophets the by have I Also .meeting
of hand ,multiplied spoken

12 הַנְּבִיאִים אֲדַמֶּה׃ אִם־גִּלְעָד אָוֶן אַךְ־שָׁוְא הָיוּ בַּגִּלְגָּל
Gilgal In they vanity Surely ?evil Gilead (Is) use prophets the
.been have .parables

(are) as heaps in the furrows of the fields. [12] And Jacob fled into the field of Syria, and Israel served for a wife; and he shepherded for a wife. [13] And by a prophet Jehovah brought up Israel out of Egypt, and by a prophet he was kept safe. [14] Ephraim has provoked (Me) to anger most bitterly. Therefore he shall leave his blood to him, and his Lord shall turn his reproach on him.

13 שְׁוָרִים זִבֵּחוּ גַּם מִזְבְּחוֹתָם כְּגַלִּים עַל תַּלְמֵי שָׂדָי׃ וַיִּבְרַח
fled And the fur- the on as altars their ,Yes they bullocks
.field of rows heaps (are) .sacrificed
יַעֲקֹב שְׂדֵה אֲרָם וַיַּעֲבֹד יִשְׂרָאֵל בְּאִשָּׁה וּבְאִשָּׁה שָׁמָר׃
kept he a for and a for Israel and ,Syria the into Jacob
.watch wife ;wife served of field
14 וּבְנָבִיא הֶעֱלָה יְהוָה אֶת־יִשְׂרָאֵל מִמִּצְרָיִם וּבְנָבִיא נִשְׁמָר׃
was he a by and ,Egypt from Israel Jehovah brought a by And
.guarded prophet up prophet
15 הִכְעִיס אֶפְרַיִם תַּמְרוּרִים וְדָמָיו עָלָיו יִטּוֹשׁ וְחֶרְפָּתוֹ יָשִׁיב
shall his and shall He on Therefore most Ephraim made has
turn reproach ,leave him blood his .bitterly angry (Me)
לוֹ אֲדֹנָיו׃
.Lord his to
him

CAP. XIII יג

CHAPTER 13

[1] When Ephraim spoke trembling, he was lifted up in Israel; but he offended in Baal, and he died. [2] And now they sin more and more, and have made themselves a casted image of their silver, idols according to their own understanding, all of it the work of the craftsmen. They say of them, Let they who sacrifice, men, kiss calves. [3] Therefore they shall be as the morning cloud and as the early dew that passes away; as chaff storm-driven from the threshing floor, and as the smoke out of the chimney. [4] Yet I (am) Jehovah your God from the land of Egypt, and you shall know no God but Me. For there is no Savior besides Me.

[5] I knew you in the wilderness, in the land of great dryness. [6] According to their pasture, so were they filled. They were filled and their heart was lifted up; therefore they have forgotten Me. [7] Therefore I am as a lion to them; I will watch by the way like a leopard. [8] I will meet them like a bear whose cubs are taken away, and will tear the lining of their heart. And there I will devour them like a lion; the wild beast shall tear them.

[9] O Israel, you are destroyed, but your help (is) in Me. [10] Where (is)

1 כְּדַבֵּר אֶפְרַיִם רְתֵת נָשָׂא הוּא בְּיִשְׂרָאֵל וַיֶּאְשַׁם בַּבַּעַל
,Baal in he but ;Israel in he up lifted ,trembling Ephraim When
offended (himself) spoke
2 וַיָּמֹת׃ וְעַתָּה ׀ יוֹסִפוּ לַחֲטֹא וַיַּעֲשׂוּ לָהֶם מַסֵּכָה מִכַּסְפָּם
their of casted a them- have and ,sin more they now And he and
,silver image selves made more and .died
כִּתְבוּנָם עֲצַבִּים מַעֲשֵׂה חָרָשִׁים כֻּלֹּה לָהֶם הֵם אֹמְרִים
,say they Of of all craftsmen work ,idols their by
them .it of skill
3 זֹבְחֵי אָדָם עֲגָלִים יִשָּׁקוּן׃ לָכֵן יִהְיוּ כַּעֲנַן־בֹּקֶר וְכַטַּל
as and morning a as they Therefore let calves ,men who They
dew the of cloud be shall .kiss them ,sacrifice
4 מַשְׁכִּים הֹלֵךְ כְּמֹץ יְסֹעֵר מִגֹּרֶן וּכְעָשָׁן מֵאֲרֻבָּה׃ וְאָנֹכִי
I Yet the of out as and the from storm as ,go to rising
,(am) .chimney smoke ;floor driven chaff early
יְהוָה אֱלֹהֶיךָ מֵאֶרֶץ מִצְרָיִם וֵאלֹהִים זוּלָתִי לֹא תֵדָע
shall you not other gods and ,Egypt the from God your Jehovah
.know Me than of land
5 וּמוֹשִׁיעַ אַיִן בִּלְתִּי׃ אֲנִי יְדַעְתִּיךָ בַּמִּדְבָּר בְּאֶרֶץ תַּלְאֻבוֹת׃
.drought the in the in known have I besides not a For
of land ,wilderness you .Me is Savior
6 כְּמַרְעִיתָם וַיִּשְׂבָּעוּ שָׂבְעוּ וַיָּרָם לִבָּם עַל־כֵּן שְׁכֵחוּנִי׃
for- have they therefore their he and were They were so to According
.Me gotten ;heart up lifted filled .filled they ,pasture their
7
8 וָאֱהִי לָהֶם כְּמוֹ־שָׁחַל כְּנָמֵר עַל־דֶּרֶךְ אָשׁוּר׃ אֶפְגְּשֵׁם
meet will I will I the by a as ;lion a as to Now
them .watch way leopard them am I
כְּדֹב שַׁכּוּל וְאֶקְרַע סְגוֹר לִבָּם וְאֹכְלֵם שָׁם כְּלָבִיא חַיַּת
the a as there will I And their the will and ,bereaved a as
of beast ;lion them devour .heart of lining tear bear
9
10 הַשָּׂדֶה תְּבַקְּעֵם׃ שִׁחֶתְךָ יִשְׂרָאֵל כִּי־בִי בְעֶזְרֶךָ׃ אֱהִי
Where .help your in but ,Israel O are You tear shall the
(is) (is) Me ,destroyed .them field

your king? Where is any other who may save you in all your cities? And your judges of whom you said, Give me a king and princes? [11] I give to you a king in My anger, and take (him) away in My fury. 12] The iniquity of Ephraim (is) bound up; his sin (is) hidden. [13] The pains of a woman in travail shall come on him; he (is) not a wise son, for he cannot stand still in the time of the breaking forth of sons. [14] I will ransom them from the power of Sheol. I will redeem them from death. O death, where (are) your plagues? O Sheol, where (is) your ruin. Repentance shall be hidden from My eyes.

[15] Though he is fruitful among brothers, an east wind shall come. The wind of Jehovah shall come up from the wilderness and his spring shall become dry, and his fountain shall be dried up. He shall plunder the treasure of all desirable vessels. [16] Samaria shall be desolate, for she has rebelled against her God. They shall fall by the sword. Their infants shall be dashed in pieces, and their women with child shall be ripped up.

CHAPTER 14

[1] O Israel, return to Jehovah your God, for you have fallen by your sin. [2] Take with you words and turn to Jehovah. Say to Him, Take away all iniquity and receive (us) graciously, and we will give the calves of our lips. [3] Assyria shall not save us. We will not ride on horses. We shall not say any more to the work of our hands, Our gods! For in You the fatherless find mercy.

[4] I will heal their backslidings; I will love them freely; for My anger has turned away from him. [5] I will be as the dew to Israel; he shall blossom as the lily and cast out his roots like Lebanon. [6] His branches shall go and his beauty shall be like the olive tree, and his smell like

מַלְכְּךָ אֵפוֹא וְיוֹשִׁיעֲךָ בְּכָל־עָרֶיךָ וְשֹׁפְטֶיךָ אֲשֶׁר אָמַרְתָּ
,said you of your and your in may he that ,now king your
whom judges ;cities all you save

11 תְּנָה־לִּי מֶלֶךְ וְשָׂרִים׃ אֶתֶּן־לְךָ מֶלֶךְ בְּאַפִּי וְאֶקַּח בְּעֶבְרָתִי׃
My in take and My in a to I and a to Give
.fury away ,anger king you give ?rulers king me

12
13 צָרוּר עֲוֹן אֶפְרָיִם צְפוּנָה חַטָּאתוֹ׃ חֶבְלֵי יוֹלֵדָה יָבֹאוּ
shall woman a The .sin his hidden ;Ephraim The bound is
come travail in of pains (is) of iniquity .up

לוֹ הוּא־בֵן לֹא חָכָם כִּי־עֵת לֹא־יַעֲמֹד בְּמִשְׁבַּר בָּנִים׃
.sons of time the in does he not (in) for ,wise not a he to
of out breaking stand time the son (is) ;him

14 מִיַּד שְׁאוֹל אֶפְדֵּם מִמָּוֶת אֶגְאָלֵם אֱהִי דְבָרֶיךָ מָוֶת אֱהִי
where O your Where re- will I From will I Sheol's from
(is) ;death ,plagues (are) .them deem death .them ransom grave

15 קָטָבְךָ שְׁאוֹל נֹחַם יִסָּתֵר מֵעֵינָי׃ כִּי הוּא בֵּין אַחִים יַפְרִיא
is brothers among he Though My from is Repent- O your
,fruitful .eyes hid ance ?Sheol ,ruin

יָבוֹא קָדִים רוּחַ יְהוָה מִמִּדְבָּר עֹלֶה וְיֵבוֹשׁ מְקוֹרוֹ וְיֶחֱרַב
shall and his shall and comes the from Jehovah The east an shall
up dried be ,spring dry become ,up wilderness of wind .wind come

מַעְיָנוֹ הוּא יִשְׁסֶה אוֹצַר כָּל־כְּלִי חֶמְדָּה׃
.desire vessels all trea- the shall He his
of of sure plunder ,fountain

CAP. XIV יד

CHAPTER 14

1 תֶּאְשַׁם שֹׁמְרוֹן כִּי מָרְתָה בֵּאלֹהֶיהָ בַּחֶרֶב יִפְּלוּ עֹלְלֵיהֶם
infants Their they the By her against has she for ,Samaria be shall
.fall shall sword .God rebelled desolate

2 יְרֻטָּשׁוּ וְהָרִיּוֹתָיו יְבֻקָּעוּ׃ שׁוּבָה יִשְׂרָאֵל עַד יְהוָה
Jehovah to ,Israel O ,Return ripped preg- their and be shall
.up women nant ,dashed

3 אֱלֹהֶיךָ כִּי כָשַׁלְתָּ בַּעֲוֹנֶךָ׃ קְחוּ עִמָּכֶם דְּבָרִים וְשׁוּבוּ אֶל־
to and words you with Take your by have you for ,God your
return .iniquity fallen

יְהוָה אִמְרוּ אֵלָיו כָּל־תִּשָּׂא עָוֹן וְקַח־טוֹב וּנְשַׁלְּמָה פָרִים
the we that receive and ini- Take all ,Him to Say .Jehovah
of calves give may well (us) ,quity away

4 שְׂפָתֵינוּ׃ אַשּׁוּר ׀ לֹא יוֹשִׁיעֵנוּ עַל־סוּס לֹא נִרְכָּב וְלֹא־
And will we not a on save shall not Assyria .lips our
not .ride horse .us

נֹאמַר עוֹד אֱלֹהֵינוּ לְמַעֲשֵׂה יָדֵינוּ אֲשֶׁר־בְּךָ יְרֻחַם יָתוֹם׃
the finds in For our the to !gods Our any shall we
.orphan mercy You .hands of work ,more say

5
6 אֶרְפָּא מְשׁוּבָתָם אֹהֲבֵם נְדָבָה כִּי שָׁב אַפִּי מִמֶּנּוּ׃ אֶהְיֶה
will I from away My has for ;freely will I back- their will I
be .him anger turned them love ;sliding heal

7 כַטַּל לְיִשְׂרָאֵל יִפְרַח כַּשּׁוֹשַׁנָּה וְיַךְ שָׁרָשָׁיו כַּלְּבָנוֹן׃ יֵלְכוּ
shall like his and the as shall he ;Israel to the as
go .Lebanon roots out cast ,lily blossom dew

Lebanon. [7] They who live under his shadow shall return; they shall live (like) the grain, and blossom like the vine; their scent (shall be) as the wine of Lebanon. [8] Ephraim (shall say), What (is) to me any more with idols? I have watched; and I made sing. I (am) like a green cypress tree. Your fruit is found from Me. [9] Who (is) wise and discerns these things? (Who is) discerning and knows them? For the ways of Jehovah are right, and the saints shall walk in them. But transgressors shall fall in them.

8 יֹנְקוֹתָיו וִיהִי כַזַּיִת הוֹדוֹ וְרֵיחַ לוֹ כַּלְּבָנוֹן׃ יָשֻׁבוּ יֹשְׁבֵי

who They shall as (is) to and his in the as he and His
live return .Lebanon him smell beauty tree olive be shall ,branches

9 בְצִלּוֹ יְחַיּוּ דָגָן וְיִפְרְחוּ כַגָּפֶן זִכְרוֹ כְּיֵין לְבָנוֹן׃ אֶפְרַיִם

Ephraim .Lebanon the as their the as and the shall they his in
,(say shall) of wine scent ,vine blossom ,grain (as) live ;shadow

מַה־לִּי עוֹד לָעֲצַבִּים אֲנִי עָנִיתִי וַאֲשׁוּרֶנּוּ אֲנִי כִּבְרוֹשׁ רַעֲנָן

.green a as I made I and ;answered I ?idols with any to What
cypress (am) .sing him more me (is)

10 מִמֶּנִּי פֶּרְיְךָ נִמְצָא׃ מִי חָכָם וְיָבֵן אֵלֶּה נָבוֹן וְיֵדָעֵם כִּי־

For knows and Dis- these and wise Who .found is Your From
?them ,cerning ?things discerns (is) fruit Me

יְשָׁרִים דַּרְכֵי יְהוָה וְצַדִּקִים יֵלְכוּ בָם וּפֹשְׁעִים יִכָּשְׁלוּ בָם׃

in shall trans- But in shall holy and ,Jehovah the (are)
.them stumble gressors .them walk ones of ways right

יואל

LIBER JOELIS

CAPUT. I. א

CHAPTER 1

[1] The word of Jehovah that was to Joel the son of Pethuel. [2] Hear this, you old men; and give ear, all you people of the land. Has this been in your days or even in the days of your fathers? [3] Tell your sons of it, and your sons their sons, and their sons to another generation. [4] That which the cutting locust has left, the swarming locust has eaten. And that which the swarming locust has left, the young locust has eaten. And that which the young locust has left, the stripping locust has eaten. [5] Awake, drunkards, and weep. And wail, all you drinkers of wine, over the grape juice; for it is cut off from your mouth. [6] For a nation has come up on my land, strong and without number; its teeth (are) the teeth of a lion, and it has the jaw teeth of a lioness. [7] He has laid my vine waste and fragmented my fig tree. He has made it completely bare and cast away; its branches grow white.

[8] Wail like a virgin clothed with sackcloth over the husband of her youth. [9] The food offering and the drink offering have been cut off from the house of Jehovah — the priests, Jehovah's ministers, mourn. [10] The field is wasted; the land mourns, for the grain is wasted. The new wine is dried up. The oil (tree) droops. [11] Be ashamed, farmers; howl, vinedressers; for the wheat and for the barley, because the harvest of the field has perished. [12] The vine is dried up, and the fig-tree

CHAPTER 1

1
2 דְּבַר־יְהוָה אֲשֶׁר הָיָה אֶל־יוֹאֵל בֶּן־פְּתוּאֵל׃ שִׁמְעוּ־
Hear of son the Joel to was that of word The
.Pethuel Jehovah

זֹאת הַזְּקֵנִים וְהַאֲזִינוּ כֹּל יוֹשְׁבֵי הָאָרֶץ הֲהָיְתָה זֹּאת
this Has the dwellers all give and old you ,this
been :land of ,ear ;men

3 בִּימֵיכֶם וְאִם בִּימֵי אֲבֹתֵיכֶם׃ עָלֶיהָ לִבְנֵיכֶם סַפֵּרוּ וּבְנֵיכֶם
your and ,Recount your to about your the in or your in
sons sons it ?fathers of day even ,days

4 לִבְנֵיהֶם וּבְנֵיהֶם לְדוֹר אַחֵר׃ יֶתֶר הַגָּזָם אָכַל הָאַרְבֶּה
swarming the ate the was What .another gen- to their and their to
;locust ,cutter by left eration sons sons

וְיֶתֶר הָאַרְבֶּה אָכַל הַיָּלֶק וְיֶתֶר הַיֶּלֶק אָכַל הֶחָסִיל׃
strip- the ate locust the and locust the ate swarming the and
.locust ping ,larvae of left ;larvae ,locust of left

5 הָקִיצוּ שִׁכּוֹרִים וּבְכוּ וְהֵילִלוּ כָּל־שֹׁתֵי יָיִן עַל־עָסִיס כִּי
for the over wine all wail and and ,drunkards ,Awake
,must grape of drinkers ;weep

6 נִכְרַת מִפִּיכֶם׃ כִּי־גוֹי עָלָה עַל־אַרְצִי עָצוּם וְאֵין מִסְפָּר
(with) and strong my on has a For your from is it
;number not ,land up come nation .mouth off cut

7 שִׁנָּיו שִׁנֵּי אַרְיֵה וּמְתַלְּעוֹת לָבִיא לוֹ׃ שָׂם גַּפְנִי לְשַׁמָּה
,waste my has It .has it a of the and a teeth its
vine laid lioness teeth jaw ,lion's teeth

וּתְאֵנָתִי לִקְצָפָה חָשֹׂף חֲשָׂפָהּ וְהִשְׁלִיךְ הִלְבִּינוּ שָׂרִיגֶיהָ׃
its grow threw and stripped it com- ,fragmented my and
branches white ;away (it) it pletely tree fig

8
9 אֵלִי כִּבְתוּלָה חֲגֻרַת־שַׂק עַל־בַּעַל נְעוּרֶיהָ׃ הָכְרַת מִנְחָה
food The been have her the over with girded a like Wail
offering off cut .youth of husband ,sackcloth virgin

10 וָנֶסֶךְ מִבֵּית יְהוָה אָבְלוּ הַכֹּהֲנִים מְשָׁרְתֵי יְהוָה׃ שֻׁדַּד
are .Jehovah ministers the mourn :Jehovah the from the and
wasted of ,priests of house libation

שָׂדֶה אָבְלָה אֲדָמָה כִּי שֻׁדַּד דָּגָן הוֹבִישׁ תִּירוֹשׁ אֻמְלַל
droops new the is the is for the mourns The
;wine up dried ,grain wasted ,land ,fields

11 יִצְהָר׃ הֹבִישׁוּ אִכָּרִים הֵילִילוּ כֹּרְמִים עַל־חִטָּה וְעַל־
and the over vine- ,howl ;farmers Be oil the
over wheat ,dressers ,ashamed .tree

12 שְׂעֹרָה כִּי אָבַד קְצִיר שָׂדֶה׃ הַגֶּפֶן הוֹבִישָׁה וְהַתְּאֵנָה
the and dried is The the har- the has for the
,tree fig ;up vine .field of vest perished ;barley

droops; (the) pomegranate and the palm tree and the apple tree, all the trees of the field are dried up, because joy has dried up from the sons of men. [13] Clothe yourselves and lament, priests. Howl, ministers of the altar. Come, spend the night in sackcloth, ministers of my God. For the food offering and the drink offering are held back from the house of your God.

[14] Set apart a fast. Call a solemn assembly; gather the elders, all the inhabitants of the land, (into) the house of Jehovah your God. And cry to Jehovah. [15] Alas for the day! For the day of Jehovah is at hand. And it shall come as a destruction from the Almighty. [16] Is not the food cut off before you eyes, joy and gladness from the house of our God? [17] The seed shrivels under their clods; the storage bins are laid waste; the granaries are broken down, for the grain has dried up. [18] How the beasts groan! The herds of cattle are perplexed because they have no pasture. Yes, the flocks of sheep are destroyed. [19] O Jehovah, to You I will cry, for the fire has burned up the pastures of the wilderness, and the flame has burned all the trees of the field. [20] The beasts of the field also cry to You, for the rivers of water are dried up and the fire has burned up the pastures of the wilderness.

אֻמְלָלָה רִמּוֹן גַּם־תָּמָר וְתַפּוּחַ כָּל־עֲצֵי הַשָּׂדֶה יָבֵשׁוּ כִּי־

for are the the all the and the and pome- ;droops
,dried field of trees ,apple palm granate

13 הֹבִישׁ שָׂשׂוֹן מִן־בְּנֵי אָדָם׃ חִגְרוּ וְסִפְדוּ הַכֹּהֲנִים

;priests and Gird .men the from joy has
,lament of sons up dried

הֵילִילוּ מְשָׁרְתֵי מִזְבֵּחַ בֹּאוּ לִינוּ בַשַּׂקִּים מְשָׁרְתֵי אֱלֹהָי

my ministers in lodge ,come the ministers howl
.God of ,sackcloth ;altar of

14 כִּי נִמְנַע מִבֵּית אֱלֹהֵיכֶם מִנְחָה וָנָסֶךְ׃ קַדְּשׁוּ־צוֹם

;fast a Set the and food the God your the from with- is For
apart .libation offering of house held

קִרְאוּ עֲצָרָה אִסְפוּ זְקֵנִים כֹּל יֹשְׁבֵי הָאָרֶץ בֵּית יְהוָה

Jehovah the (in) the inhabi- the all the gather solemn a call
of house land of tants ,elders ;assembly

15 אֱלֹהֵיכֶם וְזַעֲקוּ אֶל־יְהוָה׃ אֲהָהּ לַיּוֹם כִּי קָרוֹב יוֹם

day the at For the for Alas .Jehovah to cry and ;God your
of (is) hand !day out

16 יְהוָה וּכְשֹׁד מִשַּׁדַּי יָבוֹא׃ הֲלוֹא נֶגֶד עֵינֵינוּ אֹכֶל נִכְרָת

cut the our before (Is) will it the from as ,yea Jeho-
off food eyes not .come Almighty ruin a ;vah

17 מִבֵּית אֱלֹהֵינוּ שִׂמְחָה וָגִיל׃ עָבְשׁוּ פְרֻדוֹת תַּחַת

under The shrivels and joy ,God our the from
seed ?gladness of house

מֶגְרְפֹתֵיהֶם נָשַׁמּוּ אֹצָרוֹת נֶהֶרְסוּ מַמְּגֻרוֹת כִּי הֹבִישׁ דָּגָן׃

the has for the torn are store- the laid are ;clods their
.grain up dried ;granaries down ;houses waste

18 מַה־נֶּאֶנְחָה בְהֵמָה נָבֹכוּ עֶדְרֵי בָקָר כִּי אֵין מִרְעֶה לָהֶם

for pasture not for live- The are the groan How
.them (is) ;stock of herds vexed !beasts

19 גַּם־עֶדְרֵי הַצֹּאן נֶאְשָׁמוּ׃ אֵלֶיךָ יְהוָה אֶקְרָא כִּי־אֵשׁ אָכְלָה

has the for will I O To are sheep the Even
burned fire ;call ,Jehovah ,you .perishing of flocks

20 נְאוֹת מִדְבָּר וְלֶהָבָה לִהֲטָה כָּל־עֲצֵי הַשָּׂדֶה׃ גַּם־בַּהֲמוֹת

the Also the the all has the and the pas- the
of beasts .field of trees burned flame ;plains of tures

שָׂדֶה תַּעֲרוֹג אֵלֶיךָ כִּי יָבְשׁוּ אֲפִיקֵי מָיִם וְאֵשׁ אָכְלָה

has the and ,water rivers the have for for long the
burned fire of up dried ;You field

נְאוֹת הַמִּדְבָּר׃

the of pas- the
wilderness of tures

CAP II ב

CHAPTER 2

CHAPTER 2

[1] Blow a trumpet in Zion and shout an alarm in My holy mountain. Let all the inhabitants of the land tremble. For the day of Jehovah approaches, for (it is) near; [2] a day of darkness and of gloominess, a

1 תִּקְעוּ שׁוֹפָר בְּצִיּוֹן וְהָרִיעוּ בְּהַר קָדְשִׁי יִרְגְּזוּ כֹּל יֹשְׁבֵי

inhab- all Let .holy My in shout and in a Blow
itants tremble mount alarm an ,Zion trumpet

2 הָאָרֶץ כִּי־בָא יוֹם־יְהוָה כִּי קָרוֹב׃ יוֹם חֹשֶׁךְ וַאֲפֵלָה יוֹם

a gloom- and dark- day a (is it) for ,Jehovah the for the
of day ;iness ness of ;near of day comes ;land's

day of clouds and of thick darkness, as the morning spread on the mountains — a great and a strong people, there has never been the like, nor shall there ever be again to the years of many generations; [3] a fire devours before it, and behind it a flame burns; the land (is) as the garden of Eden before them, and behind them a desolate wilderness; yes, and there is no escape to them. [4] They look like horses; and like war horses so they run. [5] They shall leap like the noise of chariots on the tops of the mountains, like the noise of flames of fire that devours the stubble, like a strong people set in battle order. [6] Before their face, the people shall be much pained; all faces shall collect heat. [7] They shall run like a mighty one; they shall go up the wall as men of war; andthey each go on his way; and they do not change their paths. [8] And each does not press his brother. They (each) go in his paths. And (if) they fall behind their weapons, they shall not be cut off. [9] They shall rush on the city; they shall run on the wall; they shall climb up on the houses; they shall enter in by the windows like a thief. [10] The earth shall quake before them; the heavens shall shake. The sun and moon shall grow dark, and the stars shall gather in their light. [11] And Jehovah shall give His voice before His army. For His camp (is) very great. For strong (is) he who does His word. For the day of Jehovah (is) very great and terrifying. And who can endure it?

[12] Yet even now, states Jehovah, turn to Me with all your heart, and with fasting, and with weeping and with mourning. [13] Yes, tear your heart and not your robes, and turn to Jehovah your God:

עָנָן וַעֲרָפֶל כְּשַׁחַר פָּרֻשׂ עַל־הֶהָרִים עַם רַב וְעָצוּם כָּמֹהוּ
it like and great a the on spread the as and clouds
;strong people ;mountains out dawn gloom

לֹא נִהְיָה מִן־הָעוֹלָם וְאַחֲרָיו לֹא יוֹסֵף עַד־שְׁנֵי דּוֹר וָדוֹר׃
gen- and gen- the to (be will) and ,it after the from has not
eration eration of years again not past been

3 לְפָנָיו אָכְלָה אֵשׁ וְאַחֲרָיו תְּלַהֵט לֶהָבָה כְּגַן־עֵדֶן הָאָרֶץ
the garden the as a burns and ,fire devours Before
land Eden of ;flame it behind it

לְפָנָיו וְאַחֲרָיו מִדְבַּר שְׁמָמָה וְגַם־פְּלֵיטָה לֹא־הָיְתָה לּוֹ׃
to is not escape ,yes ;desolation wilder- a and before
.them and of ness it behind

4 5 כְּמַרְאֵה סוּסִים מַרְאֵהוּ וּכְפָרָשִׁים כֵּן יְרוּצוּן׃ כְּקוֹל
the As they so as and ap- its horses ap- the As
of noise .run ;horses war pearance (is) of pearance

מַרְכָּבוֹת עַל־רָאשֵׁי הֶהָרִים יְרַקֵּדוּן כְּקוֹל לַהַב אֵשׁ אֹכְלָה
that fire the the as they the the on chariots
devours of flames of noise ;leap mountains of heads

6 קַשׁ כְּעַם עָצוּם עֱרוּךְ מִלְחָמָה׃ מִפָּנָיו יָחִילוּ עַמִּים כָּל־
all the are Before .battle in set strong a as the
;peoples pained them for order people ,chaff

7 פָּנִים קִבְּצוּ פָארוּר׃ כְּגִבּוֹרִים יְרֻצוּן כְּאַנְשֵׁי מִלְחָמָה
battle men as shall they a As .heat collect faces
of ;run one mighty

יַעֲלוּ חוֹמָה וְאִישׁ בִּדְרָכָיו יֵלֵכוּן וְלֹא יְעַבְּטוּן אֹרְחוֹתָם׃
their they and they his on and the they
.paths change not ,go way each ;wall up go

8 וְאִישׁ אָחִיו לֹא יִדְחָקוּן גֶּבֶר בִּמְסִלָּתוֹ יֵלֵכוּן וּבְעַד הַשֶּׁלַח
their And they his in (each) ;presses not his And
weapons behind .go paths man brother each

9 יִפֹּלוּ לֹא יִבְצָעוּ׃ בָּעִיר יָשֹׁקּוּ בַּחוֹמָה יְרֻצוּן בַּבָּתִּים יַעֲלוּ
they the on they the on they the On are they not they
;up go houses ;run wall ;rush city .off cut ,fall

10 בְּעַד הַחַלּוֹנִים יָבֹאוּ כַּגַּנָּב׃ לְפָנָיו רָגְזָה אֶרֶץ רָעֲשׁוּ שָׁמָיִם
the shake the quakes Before a like they the by
,heavens ,earth them .thief enter windows

11 שֶׁמֶשׁ וְיָרֵחַ קָדָרוּ וְכוֹכָבִים אָסְפוּ נָגְהָם׃ וַיהוָה נָתַן קוֹלוֹ
His gives And their gather the and grow and the
voice Jehovah .light in stars ,dark moon sun

לִפְנֵי חֵילוֹ כִּי רַב מְאֹד מַחֲנֵהוּ כִּי עָצוּם עֹשֵׂה דְבָרוֹ כִּי־
For His who he strong for His very great for His before
.word does (is) ,camp (is) ;army

12 גָדוֹל יוֹם־יְהוָה וְנוֹרָא מְאֹד וּמִי יְכִילֶנּוּ׃ וְגַם־עַתָּה נְאֻם־
states even Yet can and ;very and Jehovah the great
,now ?it endure who fearful of day

יְהוָה שֻׁבוּ עָדַי בְּכָל־לְבַבְכֶם וּבְצוֹם וּבִבְכִי וּבְמִסְפֵּד׃
with and with and with and your with to turn ,Jehovah
.wailing ,weeping ,fasting heart all Me

13 וְקִרְעוּ לְבַבְכֶם וְאַל־בִּגְדֵיכֶם וְשׁוּבוּ אֶל־יְהוָה אֱלֹהֵיכֶם
.God your Jehovah to and your and your And
return ,clothes not heart tear

For He (is) gracious and merciful, slow to anger and of great kindness, and He repents concerning the evil. [14] Who knows (if) He will return and repent and leave a blessing behind Him, a food offering and a drink offering for Jehovah your God?

[15] Blow a trumpet in Zion, sanctify a fast, call a solemn gathering. [16] Gather the people, sanctify the congregation, gather the elders, gather the children and those who suck the breasts; let the bridegroom go out of his room and the bride out of her bridal room. [17] Let the priests, ministers of Jehovah, weep between the porch and the altar, and let them say, Have pity on Your people, O Jehovah, and do not give Your inheritance to shame, for a proverb among those of the nations. Why should they say among the peoples, Where (is) their God?

[18] Then Jehovah will be jealous for His land and have pity on His people. [19] Yes, Jehovah will answer and say to His people, Behold, I will send you grain, and wine, and oil, and you shall be satisfied with it. And I will no more make you a curse among the nations. [20] But I will remove the northern (army) far from you, and will drive him into a dry and deserted land, with his face toward the eastern sea and his rear toward the western sea. And his stink shall come up, and his ill odor shall come up, because he (was) doing great things.

[21] Fear not, O land. Be glad and rejoice; for Jehovah is doing great things. [22] Fear not, beasts of the field, for the pastures of the wilderness grow green; for the tree bears her fruit; the fig-tree and the vine give their strength. [23] Be glad then, sons of Zion, and rejoice in Jehovah your God. For He

כי־חנון ורחום הוא ארך אפים ורב־חסד ונחם על־
about He and great and anger slow He and For
repents ,kindness of (to) (is) merciful gracious

14 הרעה׃ מי יודע ישוב ונחם והשאיר אחריו ברכה
a behind and and will He knows Who .evil
,blessing Him leave repent return (if)

15 מנחה ונסך ליהוה אלהיכם׃ תקעו שופר בציון
,Zion in a Blow ?God your for a and food a
trumpet Jehovah libation offering

16 קדשו־צום קראו עצרה׃ אספו־עם קדשו קהל קבצו
gather the sanctify Gather solemn a call sanctify
;assembly ,people the .assembly ,fast a

זקנים אספו עוללים ויונקי שדים יצא חתן מחדרו וכלה
the and his from the go let the suck- and the gather the
bride room groom out ;breast of lings children elders

17 מחפתה׃ בין האולם ולמזבח יבכו הכהנים משרתי
ministers the let the and the Between her from
of ,priests weep ,altar porch .room bridal

יהוה ויאמרו חוסה יהוה על־עמך ואל־תתן נחלתך
in- Your do and Your on O Have let and Jehovah
heritance give not ,people ,Jehovah ,pity ,say them

לחרפה למשל־בם גוים למה יאמרו בעמים איה
Where the among should Why the among a for shame to
(is) ,peoples say they nations of those proverb

18
19 אלהיהם׃ ויקנא יהוה לארצו ויחמל על־עמו׃ ויען יהוה
Jehovah And His on have and His for Jehovah will Then ?God their
answer let .people pity land jealous be

ויאמר לעמו הנני שלח לכם את־הדגן והתירוש והיצהר
,oil and ,wine and ,grain to (am) ,Behold His to say and
you sending I ,people

20 ושבעתם אתו ולא־אתן אתכם עוד חרפה בגוים׃ ואת־
But the among a any you will I And with will you and
.nations shame more make not .it satisfied be

הצפוני ארחיק מעליכם והדחתיו אל־ארץ ציה ושממה
and dryness a into will and ,you from re- will I the
;desolation of land him drive far move northener

את־פניו אל־הים הקדמני וספו אל־הים האחרון ועלה
shall And .western the toward his and eastern the toward his with
up come sea rear sea face

21 באשו ותעל צחנתו כי הגדיל לעשות׃ אל־תיראי אדמה
,land Fear not (was) great he for his shall and his
.doing things ,stench up come ,stink

22 גילי ושמחי כי־הגדיל יהוה לעשות׃ אל־תיראו בהמות
beasts be Do not (is) Jehovah great for be and rejoice
of ,afraid .doing things ,glad

שדי כי דשאו נאות מדבר כי־עץ נשא פריו תאנה וגפן
the and fig the its bears the For wil- the pas- the grow for the
vine tree fruit tree .derness of tures green ;field

23 נתנו חילם׃ ובני ציון גילו ושמחו ביהוה אלהיכם כי־
For .God your in be and rejoice ,Zion's And their give
Jehovah glad sons .strength

has given you the former rain according to righteousness, and He will cause the rain to come down for you, the former rain and the latter rain in the first (month). [24] And the floors shall be full with grain, and the wine-vats shall overflow with wine, and oil. [25] And I will restore to you the years which the swarming locust has eaten, the locust larvae, and the stripping locust, and the cutting locust, My great army which I sent among you. [26] And you shall eat fully and be satisfied, and you will raise the name of Jehovah your God, who has dealt with you wondrously. And My people shall not be ashamed forever. [27] And you shall know that I (am) in Israel's midst, and that I (am) Jehovah your God, and none else: and my people shall not be ashamed forever.

נָתַן לָכֶם אֶת־הַמּוֹרֶה לִצְדָקָה וַיּוֹרֶד לָכֶם גֶּשֶׁם מוֹרֶה
early the the to made and to according early the to has He
rain ,rain you down come ,righteousness rain you given

24 וּמַלְקוֹשׁ בָּרִאשׁוֹן׃ וּמָלְאוּ הַגֳּרָנוֹת בָּר וְהֵשִׁיקוּ הַיְקָבִים
wine the will and (with) grain the will And the at the and
vats overflow grain floors full be .first rain latter

25 תִּירוֹשׁ וְיִצְהָר׃ וְשִׁלַּמְתִּי לָכֶם אֶת־הַשָּׁנִים אֲשֶׁר אָכַל
has which years the to will I And and new (with)
eaten you restore .oil wine

הָאַרְבֶּה הַיֶּלֶק וְהֶחָסִיל וְהַגָּזָם חֵילִי הַגָּדוֹל אֲשֶׁר שִׁלַּחְתִּי
sent I which great My cut- the and strip- the and the swarm- the
army,locust ting ,locust ping ,larvae ,locust ing

26 בָּכֶם׃ וַאֲכַלְתֶּם אָכוֹל וְשָׂבוֹעַ וְהִלַּלְתֶּם אֶת־שֵׁם יְהוָה
Jehovah the will you and be and fully you And among
of name praise ;satisfied eat shall .you

אֱלֹהֵיכֶם אֲשֶׁר־עָשָׂה עִמָּכֶם לְהַפְלִיא וְלֹא־יֵבֹשׁוּ עַמִּי
My be will And .wondrously with has who ,God your
people ashamed not you done

27 לְעוֹלָם׃ וִידַעְתֶּם כִּי בְקֶרֶב יִשְׂרָאֵל אָנִי וַאֲנִי יְהוָה
Jehovah I and I Israel the in that you And .forever
(am) ,(am) of midst know shall

אֱלֹהֵיכֶם וְאֵין עוֹד וְלֹא־יֵבֹשׁוּ עַמִּי לְעוֹלָם׃
.forever My be will and any and ,God your
people ashamed not ,other (is) not

CAP. III ג

CHAPTER 3

[28] And it shall be afterward, I will pour out My Spirit on all flesh. And your sons and your daughters shall prophesy your old men shall dream dreams, your young men shall see visions. [29] And also I will pour out My Spirit on the slaves and on the slave-girls in those days. [30] And I will give signs in the heavens, and in the earth: blood and fire and columns of smoke. [31] The sun shall be turned to darkness and the moon to blood, before the coming of the great and awesome day of Jehovah. [32] For it shall be, (that) all who shall call on the name of Jehovah shall be saved. For salvation shall be in Mount Zion and in Jerusalem, as Jehovah has said,

1 וְהָיָה אַחֲרֵי־כֵן אֶשְׁפּוֹךְ אֶת־רוּחִי עַל־כָּל־בָּשָׂר וְנִבְּאוּ
will And .flesh all on Spirit My will I ,afterward it And
prophesy out pour be will

בְּנֵיכֶם וּבְנוֹתֵיכֶם זִקְנֵיכֶם חֲלֹמוֹת יַחֲלֹמוּן בַּחוּרֵיכֶם
young your will dreams old your your and your
men ,dream men ;daughters sons

2 חֶזְיֹנוֹת יִרְאוּ׃ וְגַם עַל־הָעֲבָדִים וְעַל־הַשְּׁפָחוֹת בַּיָּמִים
days in the and slaves the on and ;see will visions
slave-girls on also

3 הָהֵמָּה אֶשְׁפּוֹךְ אֶת־רוּחִי׃ וְנָתַתִּי מוֹפְתִים בַּשָּׁמַיִם
the in signs I And .Spirit My will I those
heavens give will out pour

4 וּבָאָרֶץ דָּם וָאֵשׁ וְתִימֲרוֹת עָשָׁן׃ הַשֶּׁמֶשׁ יֵהָפֵךְ לְחֹשֶׁךְ
dark- to be will sun the ;smoke columns and and blood on and
ness turned of fire ;earth the

5 וְהַיָּרֵחַ לְדָם לִפְנֵי בּוֹא יוֹם יְהוָה הַגָּדוֹל וְהַנּוֹרָא׃ וְהָיָה
it For and great Jehovah the the before to the and
be will .awesome of day of coming ,blood moon

כֹּל אֲשֶׁר־יִקְרָא בְּשֵׁם יְהוָה יִמָּלֵט כִּי בְּהַר־צִיּוֹן וּבִירוּשָׁלַםִ
Jerusalem and Mount in for be will ,Jehovah the on shall who (that)
in Zion ,saved of name call all

and among the saved whom Jehovah shall call.

תִּהְיֶה פְלֵיטָה כַּאֲשֶׁר אָמַר יְהוָה וּבַשְּׂרִידִים אֲשֶׁר

whom the and ,Jehovah has as ,salvation shall
saved among said be

יְהוָה קֹרֵא׃

shall Jehovah
.call

CHAPTER 3

[1] For, behold, in those days and in that time, (when) I will bring again the exiles of Judah and Jerusalem, [2] I will also gather all nations and will bring them down into the valley of Jehoshaphat. And I will enter into judgment with them there for My people and My inheritance Israel, whom they have scattered among the nations and shared out My land. [3] And they have cast lots for My people. And (they) have given a boy for a harlot, and sold a girl for wine, and they drank. [4] And also what (are) you to Me, Tyre and Sidon, and all the regions of Philistia??(Are) you rendering repayment to Me? And if you (are) repaying Me, swiftly, speedily I will turn your reward on your own head, [5] (in) that you have taken My silver and My gold and have carried My desirable things into Your temples. [6] You have also sold the sons of Judah and the sons of Jerusalem to the sons of the Greeks, that you might remove them far from their border. [7] Behold, I (am) arousing them from the place where you have sold them and will return your reward on your own head. [8] And I will sell your sons and your daughters into the hand of the sons of Judah, and they shall sell them to the Sabeans, to a nation far off; for Jehovah has spoken it.

[9] Proclaim this among the nations: Sanctify a war, wake up the

CAP. IV ד

CHAPTER 4

1 כִּי הִנֵּה בַּיָּמִים הָהֵמָּה וּבָעֵת הַהִיא אֲשֶׁר אָשׁוּב אֶת־

will I (in) ,that in and those days in ,behold For
return which time

2 שְׁבוּת יְהוּדָה וִירוּשָׁלִָם׃ וְקִבַּצְתִּי אֶת־כָּל־הַגּוֹיִם וְהוֹרַדְתִּים

bring will and the all will I and and Judah the
down them ,nations gather ;Jerusalem of exiles

אֶל־עֵמֶק יְהוֹשָׁפָט וְנִשְׁפַּטְתִּי עִמָּם שָׁם עַל־עַמִּי וְנַחֲלָתִי

in- my and My for there with will I And Jehosh- the to
heritance people them judgment enter .aphat of valley

3 יִשְׂרָאֵל אֲשֶׁר פִּזְּרוּ בַגּוֹיִם וְאֶת־אַרְצִי חִלֵּקוּ׃ וְאֶל־עַמִּי

My for And they My and the in they whom ,Israel
people .out shared land ,nations scattered

יַדּוּ גוֹרָל וַיִּתְּנוּ הַיֶּלֶד בַּזּוֹנָה וְהַיַּלְדָּה מָכְרוּ בַיַּיִן וַיִּשְׁתּוּ׃

they and for was a and a for boy a they and ;lots they
.drank ,wine sold girl ,harlot gave cast

4 וְגַם מָה־אַתֶּם לִי צֹר וְצִידוֹן וְכֹל גְּלִילוֹת פְּלָשֶׁת הַגְּמוּל

Repay- ?Philistia the and and Tyre to you what And
ment of regions all ,Sidon ,Me (are) also

אַתֶּם מְשַׁלְּמִים עָלָי וְאִם־גֹּמְלִים אַתֶּם עָלַי קַל מְהֵרָה

speedily swiftly (to) you repaying And (to) (are) you
(and) ,Me (are) if ?Me restoring

5 אָשִׁיב גְּמֻלְכֶם בְּרֹאשְׁכֶם׃ אֲשֶׁר־כַּסְפִּי וּזְהָבִי לְקַחְתֶּם

have you My and My (in) your on re- your will I
taken gold silver that ;head own payment return

6 וּמַחֲמַדַּי הַטֹּבִים הֲבֵאתֶם לְהֵיכְלֵיכֶם׃ וּבְנֵי יְהוּדָה וּבְנֵי

the and Judah the And your to have you good My and
of sons of sons .temples brought treasures

יְרוּשָׁלִַם מְכַרְתֶּם לִבְנֵי הַיְּוָנִים לְמַעַן הַרְחִיקָם מֵעַל

from re- might you that the the to have you Jerusalem
them move ,Javanites of sons sold

7 גְּבוּלָם׃ הִנְנִי מְעִירָם מִן־הַמָּקוֹם אֲשֶׁר־מְכַרְתֶּם אֹתָם

them have you the from arousing ,Behold their
sold place them (am) I .border

8 שָׁמָּה וַהֲשִׁבֹתִי גְמֻלְכֶם בְּרֹאשְׁכֶם׃ וּמָכַרְתִּי אֶת־בְּנֵיכֶם

sons your I And your on re- your will I and to
sell will .head own payment return ,there

וְאֶת־בְּנוֹתֵיכֶם בְּיַד בְּנֵי יְהוּדָה וּמְכָרוּם לִשְׁבָאיִם אֶל־גּוֹי

a to the to will they and ,Judah the the into your and
nation ,Sabeans them sell of sons of hand daughters

9 רָחוֹק כִּי יְהוָה דִּבֵּר׃ קִרְאוּ־זֹאת בַּגּוֹיִם קַדְּשׁוּ

Sanctify among this Call has Jehovah for ;off far
:nations the spoken

mighty men, let all men of war draw near; let them come up. [10] Beat your plowshares into swords, and your pruning hooks into spears. Let the weak say, I (am) strong. [11] Gather yourselves and come, all you nations, and gather yourselves together all around. Cause Your mighty ones to come down, O Jehovah. [12] Let the nations be awakened and come up to the valley of Jehoshaphat. For there I will sit to judge all the nations all around. [13] Put in the sickle, for the harvest is ripe. Come, go down, for the press is full; the vats overflow, for their wickedness is great. [14] Multitudes, multitudes in the valley of decision! For the day of Jehovah (is) near in the valley of decision. [15] The sun and the moon shall be darkened, and the stars shall gather in their light. [16] Jehovah shall also roar out of Zion and give His voice from Jerusalem. And the heavens and the earth shall shake. But Jehovah (is) a refuge for His people and the stronghold to the sons of Israel. [17] And you shall know that I (am) Jehovah your God dwelling in Zion, My holy mountain. And Jerusalem shall be a holy thing, and strangers shall not pass through her any more.

[18] And it shall be in that day, the mountains shall drop down new wine, and the hills shall flow (with) milk, and all the streams of Judah shall flow (with) waters. And a fountain shall come forth from the house of Jehovah and shall water the valley of Shittim. [19] Egypt shall be a ruin and Edom shall be a deserted wilderness, because of violence to the sons of Judah, whose innocent blood they shed in their land. [20] But Judah shall

מִלְחָמָה הָעִירוּ הַגִּבּוֹרִים יִגְּשׁוּ יַעֲלוּ כָּל אַנְשֵׁי הַמִּלְחָמָה׃
war   the   all   let draw   let   Mighty the   awaken   ;war a
                     of men   up come ,near   ;man

10 כַּתּוּ אִתֵּיכֶם לַחֲרָבוֹת וּמַזְמְרֹתֵיכֶם לִרְמָחִים הַחַלָּשׁ יֹאמַר
let   weak the   ;spears to   your and   swords to   your   Beat
,say   hooks pruning.   plowshares

11 גִּבּוֹר אָנִי׃ עוּשׁוּ וָבֹאוּ כָל־הַגּוֹיִם מִסָּבִיב וְנִקְבָּצוּ שָׁמָּה
to   gather and   all   nations all   and Hasten   !(am) I mighty
.there   yourselves   around   (you)   come

12 הַנְחַת יְהוָה גִּבּוֹרֶיךָ׃ יֵעוֹרוּ וְיַעֲלוּ הַגּוֹיִם אֶל־עֵמֶק
the   to   the   come and   be Let   Your   O   Bring
of valley   nations   up   aroused   .ones mighty   Jehovah   down

יְהוֹשָׁפָט כִּי שָׁם אֵשֵׁב לִשְׁפֹּט אֶת־כָּל־הַגּוֹיִם מִסָּבִיב׃
all   the   all   judge to   will I   there For   Jehosh-
.around   nations   sit   .aphat

13 שִׁלְחוּ מַגָּל כִּי בָשַׁל קָצִיר בֹּאוּ רְדוּ כִּי־מָלְאָה גַת הֵשִׁיקוּ
overflow   the   full is for   go   ;Come   the   ripe is for   the   Send
;press   down   .harvest   sickle

14 הַיְקָבִים כִּי רַבָּה רָעָתָם׃ הֲמוֹנִים הֲמוֹנִים בְּעֵמֶק הֶחָרוּץ
!decision   the in   multitudes ,Multitudes   .evil their   (is) for   wine the
of valley   great   ,vats

15 כִּי קָרוֹב יוֹם יְהוָה בְּעֵמֶק הֶחָרוּץ׃ שֶׁמֶשׁ וְיָרֵחַ קָדָרוּ
grow   the and   The   .decision   the in   Jehovah   the   (is)   For
,dark   moon   sun   of valley   of day   near

16 וְכוֹכָבִים אָסְפוּ נָגְהָם׃ וַיהוָה מִצִּיּוֹן יִשְׁאָג וּמִירוּשָׁלִַם יִתֵּן
give   from and   ,roars   from   and   their   gather   the and
Jerusalem   Zion Jehovah   ,light   in   stars

קוֹלוֹ וְרָעֲשׁוּ שָׁמַיִם וָאָרֶץ וַיהוָה מַחֲסֶה לְעַמּוֹ וּמָעוֹז לִבְנֵי
the   to   a and   His for   a (is)   But   the and   the   and   His
of sons   fort   people   refuge   Jehovah   .earth   heavens   quake   ,voice

17 יִשְׂרָאֵל׃ וִידַעְתֶּם כִּי אֲנִי יְהוָה אֱלֹהֵיכֶם שֹׁכֵן בְּצִיּוֹן הַר־
moun-   in   dwelling   God your   Jehovah   I   that   you And   .Israel
tain   Zion   (am)   know shall

קָדְשִׁי וְהָיְתָה יְרוּשָׁלִַם קֹדֶשׁ וְזָרִים לֹא־יַעַבְרוּ־בָהּ עוֹד׃
any   through   will not   and   holy a   Jerusalem   shall And   My
.more   her   pass   aliens   ,thing   be   .holy

18 וְהָיָה בַיּוֹם הַהוּא יִטְּפוּ הֶהָרִים עָסִיס וְהַגְּבָעוֹת
the and   new   the   will   ,that   day in   it And
hills   ,wine   mountains   drop   be will

תֵּלַכְנָה חָלָב וְכָל־אֲפִיקֵי יְהוּדָה יֵלְכוּ מָיִם וּמַעְיָן מִבֵּית
the from a And   (with)   will   of   the   and   (with)   will
of house   spring   .waters   flow   Judah   streams   all   ,milk   flow

19 יְהוָה יֵצֵא וְהִשְׁקָה אֶת־נַחַל הַשִּׁטִּים׃ מִצְרַיִם לִשְׁמָמָה
a   .Egypt   .Shittim   torrent the   will and   will Jehovah
desolation   of valley   water   out go

תִהְיֶה וֶאֱדוֹם לְמִדְבַּר שְׁמָמָה תִהְיֶה מֵחֲמַס בְּנֵי יְהוּדָה
,Judah   the   vio- from   will   desolate   wilder-   a   and   will
of sons   to lence   become   ness   Edom   become

20 אֲשֶׁר־שָׁפְכוּ דַם־נָקִיא בְּאַרְצָם׃ וִיהוּדָה לְעוֹלָם תֵּשֵׁב
will   forever   But   their in   innocent   they   whose
,dwell   Judah   .land   blood   shed

וִירוּשָׁלַם לְדוֹר וָדוֹר׃ וְנִקֵּיתִי דָּמָם לֹא־נִקֵּיתִי וַיהוָה 21

and Jerusalem | to generation | and generation. | And I will cleanse | their blood | (which) I not cleansed, | and Jehovah

שֹׁכֵן בְּצִיּוֹן׃

(is) dwelling | in Zion.

dwell forever, and Jerusalem to generation and generation. [21] And I will cleanse their blood (which) I have not cleansed; and Jehovah (is) dwelling in Zion.

עמוס

LIBER AMOS

CAPUT. I א

CHAPTER 1

CHAPTER 1

[1] The words of Amos — who was among the herdsmen of Tekoa — which he saw concerning Israel in the days of Uzziah king of Judah, and in the days of Jeroboam the son of Joash king of Israel, two years before the earthquake. [2] And he said, Jehovah will roar from Zion and utter His voice from Jerusalem. And the pastures of the shepherds shall mourn, and the top of Carmel shall dry up. [3] Thus says Jehovah: For three transgressions of Damascus, and for four, I will not turn back (from) it; for they have threshed Gilead with threshing instruments of iron. [4] But I will send a fire against the house of Hazael, and it shall devour the palaces of Benhadad. [5] I will also break the bar of Damascus, and cut off the dweller from the Valley of Aven and him who holds the scepter from Beth-Eden. And the people of Syria shall go captive to Kir, says Jehovah.

[6] Thus says Jehovah: For three transgressions of Gaza, and for four, I will not turn back (from) it; for they departed (as) exiles to deliver up a complete (population) to Edom. [7] But I will send a fire against the wall of Gaza, and it shall devour its palaces. [8] And I will cut off Ashdod's dwellers and him who holds the scepter from Ashkelon, and I will turn My hand against Ekron; and the remnant of the Philistines shall perish, says the Lord Jehovah.

1 דִּבְרֵי עָמוֹס אֲשֶׁר־הָיָה בַנֹּקְדִים מִתְּקוֹעַ אֲשֶׁר חָזָה עַל־
con- he which from the among was who —Amos The
cerning saw ,Tekoa shepherds of words

יִשְׂרָאֵל בִּימֵי ׀ עֻזִּיָּה מֶלֶךְ־יְהוּדָה וּבִימֵי יָרָבְעָם בֶּן־יוֹאָשׁ
Joash the Jeroboam the in and ,Judah king Uzziah the in Israel
of son of days of of days

2 מֶלֶךְ יִשְׂרָאֵל שְׁנָתַיִם לִפְנֵי הָרָעַשׁ׃ וַיֹּאמַר ׀ יְהוָה מִצִּיּוֹן
from Jehovah he And the before years two ,Israel king
Zion ,said .earthquake of

יִשְׁאָג וּמִירוּשָׁלִַם יִתֵּן קוֹלוֹ וְאָבְלוּ נְאוֹת הָרֹעִים וְיָבֵשׁ
shall and the pas- the shall And His will from and will
dry be ,shepherds of tures mourn .voice give Jerusalem roar

3 רֹאשׁ הַכַּרְמֶל׃ כֹּה אָמַר יְהוָה עַל־שְׁלֹשָׁה פִּשְׁעֵי
trans- three For :Jehovah says Thus .Carmel the
of gressions of top

דַמֶּשֶׂק וְעַל־אַרְבָּעָה לֹא אֲשִׁיבֶנּוּ עַל־דּוּשָׁם בַּחֲרֻצוֹת
threshing with they for will I not ,four and ,Damascus
of sledges threshed ;it withdraw for

4 הַבַּרְזֶל אֶת־הַגִּלְעָד׃ וְשִׁלַּחְתִּי אֵשׁ בְּבֵית חֲזָאֵל וְאָכְלָה
it and ,Hazael the against a will I But .Gilead iron
devour shall of house fire send

5 אַרְמְנוֹת בֶּן־הֲדָד׃ וְשָׁבַרְתִּי בְּרִיחַ דַּמֶּשֶׂק וְהִכְרַתִּי יוֹשֵׁב
the cut and ,Damascus the will I And .Hadad Ben- the
inhabitant off of bar down break of palaces

מִבִּקְעַת־אָוֶן וְתוֹמֵךְ שֵׁבֶט מִבֵּית עֶדֶן וְגָלוּ עַם־אֲרָם קִירָה
,Kir to Aram the shall And .Eden from the him and Aven the from
of people captive go Beth- scepter holds who of Valley

6 אָמַר יְהוָה׃ כֹּה אָמַר יְהוָה עַל־שְׁלֹשָׁה פִּשְׁעֵי עַזָּה
Gaza trans- three For :Jehovah says Thus .Jehovah says
of gressions

וְעַל־אַרְבָּעָה לֹא אֲשִׁיבֶנּוּ עַל־הַגְלוֹתָם גָּלוּת שְׁלֵמָה
complete a (as) they for will I not ,four and
(population) exiles deported ;it withdraw for

7 לְהַסְגִּיר לֶאֱדוֹם׃ וְשִׁלַּחְתִּי אֵשׁ בְּחוֹמַת עַזָּה וְאָכְלָה
it and ,Gaza the against fire a will I But .Edom to deliver to
devour shall of wall send up

8 אַרְמְנֹתֶיהָ׃ וְהִכְרַתִּי יוֹשֵׁב מֵאַשְׁדּוֹד וְתוֹמֵךְ שֵׁבֶט מֵאַשְׁקְלוֹן
;Ashkelon from the him and Ashdod from the also will I .palaces its
scepter holds who inhabitant off cut

וַהֲשִׁיבוֹתִי יָדִי עַל־עֶקְרוֹן וְאָבְדוּ שְׁאֵרִית פְּלִשְׁתִּים אָמַר
says ,Philistines the the shall and ;Ekron against My will I and
of remnant perish hand turn

[9] Thus says Jehovah: For three transgressions of Tyre, and for four, I will not turn it back; for they delivered up (as) exiles a whole (population) to Edom and did not remember the brotherly covenant. [10] But I will send a fire against the wall of Tyre, and it shall devour its palaces.

[11] Thus says Jehovah: For three transgressions of Edom, and for four, I will not turn it back; for he pursued his brother with the sword, and corrupted his companions, and his anger tore continually, and he kept it, his wrath forever. [12] But I will send a fire against Teman, and it shall devour the palaces of Bozrah.

[13] Thus says Jehovah: For three transgressions of the sons of Ammon, and for four, I will not turn it back; for they have ripped open the women of Gilead (who were) with child, to make their border larger. [14] But I will kindle a fire against the wall of Rabbah, and it shall devour its palaces, with a war-cry in the day of battle, with a storm in the day of the tempest. [15] And their king shall go into captivity, he and his princes together, says Jehovah.

9 אֲדֹנָי יְהוִה׃ כֹּה אָמַר יְהוָה עַל־שְׁלֹשָׁה פִּשְׁעֵי־צֹר
,Tyre trans- three For :Jehovah ,says Thus .Jehovah the
of gressions Lord

וְעַל־אַרְבָּעָה לֹא אֲשִׁיבֶנּוּ עַל־הַסְגִּירָם גָּלוּת שְׁלֵמָה
complete a (as) they for will I not ,four and
(population) exiles up delivered ;it withdraw for

10 לֶאֱדוֹם וְלֹא זָכְרוּ בְּרִית אַחִים׃ וְשִׁלַּחְתִּי אֵשׁ בְּחוֹמַת צֹר
,Tyre the against a will I But .brothers cove- the re- did and ,Edom to
of wall fire send of nant member not

11 וְאָכְלָה אַרְמְנֹתֶיהָ׃ כֹּה אָמַר יְהוָה עַל־שְׁלֹשָׁה
three For :Jehovah says Thus .palaces its shall it and
devour

פִּשְׁעֵי אֱדוֹם וְעַל־אַרְבָּעָה לֹא אֲשִׁיבֶנּוּ עַל־רָדְפוֹ בַחֶרֶב
the with he for will I not ,four and ,Edom trans-
sword pursued ;it withdraw for of gressions

אָחִיו וְשִׁחֵת רַחֲמָיו וַיִּטְרֹף לָעַד אַפּוֹ וְעֶבְרָתוֹ שְׁמָרָה נֶצַח׃
.forever kept he his and his con- and his cor- and his
it wrath ,anger tinually tore compassions rupted ,brother

12 וְשִׁלַּחְתִּי אֵשׁ בְּתֵימָן וְאָכְלָה אַרְמְנוֹת בָּצְרָה׃
.Bozrah palaces the shall it and against fire a will I So
of devour ,Teman send

13 כֹּה אָמַר יְהוָה עַל־שְׁלֹשָׁה פִּשְׁעֵי בְנֵי־עַמּוֹן וְעַל־אַרְבָּעָה
,four and ,Ammon the trans- three For :Jehovah says Thus
for of sons of gressions

לֹא אֲשִׁיבֶנּוּ עַל־בִּקְעָם הָרוֹת הַגִּלְעָד לְמַעַן הַרְחִיב אֶת־
enlarge order in ,Gilead preg- the ripped they for will I not
to of women nant open ;it withdraw

14 גְּבוּלָם׃ וְהִצַּתִּי אֵשׁ בְּחוֹמַת רַבָּה וְאָכְלָה אַרְמְנוֹתֶיהָ
,palaces its shall it and ,Rabbah the against a will I So their
devour of wall fire kindle .border

15 בִּתְרוּעָה בְּיוֹם מִלְחָמָה בְּסַעַר בְּיוֹם סוּפָה׃ וְהָלַךְ מַלְכָּם
their shall And the the in a with ,battle the in a with
king go .windstorm of day tempest of day war-cry

בַּגּוֹלָה הוּא וְשָׂרָיו יַחְדָּו אָמַר יְהוָה׃
.Jehovah says ,together his and he into
rulers .exile

CAP. II ב

CHAPTER 2

CHAPTER 2

[1] Thus says Jehovah: For three transgressions of Moab, and for four, I will not turn it back; for he burned the bones of the king of Edom into lime. [2] But I will send a fire against Moab, and it shall devour the palaces of Kerioth. And Moab shall die with uproar, with a war-cry, with the sound of the ram's horn. [3] And I will cut off the judge from its midst and will kill all its princes with

1 כֹּה אָמַר יְהוָה עַל־שְׁלֹשָׁה פִּשְׁעֵי מוֹאָב וְעַל־אַרְבָּעָה לֹא
not ,four and ,Moab trans- three For :Jehovah says Thus
for of gressions

2 אֲשִׁיבֶנּוּ עַל־שָׂרְפוֹ עַצְמוֹת מֶלֶךְ־אֱדוֹם לַשִּׂיד׃ וְשִׁלַּחְתִּי־
will I But into Edom the bones the he for will I
send .lime of king of burned ;it withdraw

אֵשׁ בְּמוֹאָב וְאָכְלָה אַרְמְנוֹת הַקְּרִיּוֹת וּמֵת בְּשָׁאוֹן מוֹאָב
Moab with And .Kerioth palaces the shall it and against a
uproar die shall of devour ,Moab fire

3 בִּתְרוּעָה בְּקוֹל שׁוֹפָר׃ וְהִכְרַתִּי שׁוֹפֵט מִקִּרְבָּהּ וְכָל־שָׂרֶיהָ
its and its from who he will I And ram's the with (and) a with
rulers all ,midst judges off cut .horn of sound the ,war-cry

him, says Jehovah.

[4] Thus says Jehovah: For three transgressions of Judah, and for four, I will not turn it back; for they despised the law of Jehovah and they have not kept His statutes. Their lies after which their fathers walked have caused them to go astray. [5] But I shall send a fire against Judah, and it shall devour the palaces of Jerusalem.

[6] Thus says Jehovah: For three transgressions of Israel, and for four, I will not turn it back; for they sold the righteous for silver, and the poor for a pair of sandals. [7] Those who trample on the dust of the earth on the head of the helpless, and turn aside the way of the meek. And a man and his father will go (in) to the (same) girl to profane My holy name. [8] And they will stretch out down beside every altar on clothes taken in pledge, and they will drink the wine of those being fined (in) the house of their God.

[9] Yet I destroyed the Amorite from before them, (whose) height (was) like the height of the cedars; and he (was) strong as the great trees. And I destroyed his fruit from above and his roots from below. [10] Also I brought you up from the land of Egypt and led you in the wilderness forty years, to possess the land of the Amorite. [11] And I raised up from your sons for prophets, and for Nazarites from your young men. (Is this) not even so, O sons of Israel, states Jehovah? [12] But you gave the Nazarites wine to drink, and you commanded the prophets, saying, Do not prophesy. [13] Behold, I am pressed

אֶהֱרוֹג עִמּוֹ אָמַר יְהוָה׃ 4 כֹּה אָמַר יְהוָה עַל־שְׁלֹשָׁה
three For :Jehovah says Thus .Jehovah says with will I
,him slay

פִּשְׁעֵי יְהוּדָה וְעַל־אַרְבָּעָה לֹא אֲשִׁיבֶנּוּ עַל־מָאֳסָם אֶת־
they for will I not ,four and ,Judah trans-
rejected ;it withdraw for of gressions [

תּוֹרַת יְהוָה וְחֻקָּיו לֹא שָׁמָרוּ וַיַּתְעוּם כִּזְבֵיהֶם אֲשֶׁר־
which their led And have they not his and ,Jehovah law the
lies astray them .kept statutes of

הָלְכוּ אֲבוֹתָם אַחֲרֵיהֶם׃ 5 וְשִׁלַּחְתִּי אֵשׁ בִּיהוּדָה וְאָכְלָה
shall it and against fire a shall I But after their walked
devour ,Judah send .them fathers

אַרְמְנוֹת יְרוּשָׁלִָם׃ 6 כֹּה אָמַר יְהוָה עַל־שְׁלֹשָׁה
three For :Jehovah says Thus .Jerusalem palaces the
of

פִּשְׁעֵי יִשְׂרָאֵל וְעַל־אַרְבָּעָה לֹא אֲשִׁיבֶנּוּ עַל־מִכְרָם בַּכֶּסֶף
for they for will I not ,four and ,Israel trans-
silver sold ;it withdraw for of gressions

צַדִּיק וְאֶבְיוֹן בַּעֲבוּר נַעֲלָיִם׃ 7 הַשֹּׁאֲפִים עַל־עֲפַר־אֶרֶץ
the the upon who Those pair a for the and the
earth of dust trample ,sandals of poor ,righteous

בְּרֹאשׁ דַּלִּים וְדֶרֶךְ עֲנָוִים יַטּוּ וְאִישׁ וְאָבִיו יֵלְכוּ אֶל־
to will his and a And they the the and the the on
go father man .divert humble of way ,helpers of head

הַנַּעֲרָה לְמַעַן חַלֵּל אֶת־שֵׁם קָדְשִׁי׃ 8 וְעַל־בְּגָדִים חֲבֻלִים
in taken garments And My the profane order in (same) the
pledge on .holiness of name to ,girl

יַטּוּ אֵצֶל כָּל־מִזְבֵּחַ וְיֵין עֲנוּשִׁים יִשְׁתּוּ בֵּית אֱלֹהֵיהֶם׃
their the (in) will they being those and ,altar every beside they
.God of house drink fined of wine the out stretch

9 וְאָנֹכִי הִשְׁמַדְתִּי אֶת־הָאֱמֹרִי מִפְּנֵיהֶם אֲשֶׁר כְּגֹבַהּ אֲרָזִים
the the like who before from Amorite the destroyed I Yet
cedars of height ,them

גָּבְהוֹ וְחָסֹן הוּא כָּאַלּוֹנִים וָאַשְׁמִיד פִּרְיוֹ מִמַּעַל וְשָׁרָשָׁיו
his and from his I And the like he and his (was)
roots above fruit destroyed .trees great (was) strong ;height

מִתָּחַת׃ 10 וְאָנֹכִי הֶעֱלֵיתִי אֶתְכֶם מֵאֶרֶץ מִצְרַיִם וָאוֹלֵךְ
led and Egypt the from you up brought I Also from
of land .below

אֶתְכֶם בַּמִּדְבָּר אַרְבָּעִים שָׁנָה לָרֶשֶׁת אֶת־אֶרֶץ הָאֱמֹרִי׃
the land the to ,years forty the in you
.Amorite of possess wilderness

11 וָאָקִים מִבְּנֵיכֶם לִנְבִיאִים וּמִבַּחוּרֵיכֶם לִנְזִרִים הַאַף אֵין־
not (it Is) for (some) your from and for (some) your from I And
even .Nazarites men young prophets sons up raised

זֹאת בְּנֵי יִשְׂרָאֵל נְאֻם־יְהוָה׃ 12 וַתַּשְׁקוּ אֶת־הַנְּזִרִים יָיִן
,wine the give you But ?Jehovah declares ,Israel sons O ,this
Nazarites drink to of

וְעַל־הַנְּבִיאִים צִוִּיתֶם לֵאמֹר לֹא תִּנָּבְאוּ׃ 13 הִנֵּה אָנֹכִי מֵעִיק
totter I ,Behold Do not ,saying you prophets the and
.prophesy ,commanded to

under you, as a cart full of cut grain is pressed. [14] And refuge shall perish from the swift, and the strong shall not strengthen his power, nor shall the mighty deliver his life; [15] and he who handles the bow shall not stand. And he swift-footed will not save; and the horse-rider shall not save his life. [16] And the stout-hearted among the mighty shall run away naked in that day, states Jehovah.

14 תַּחְתֵּיכֶם כַּאֲשֶׁר תָּעִיק הָעֲגָלָה הַמְלֵאָה לָהּ עָמִיר׃ וְאָבַד
shall And cut (of) of full the cart the totters as under
perish .grain it produce (with) ,you

מָנוֹס מִקָּל וְחָזָק לֹא־יְאַמֵּץ כֹּחוֹ וְגִבּוֹר לֹא־יְמַלֵּט נַפְשׁוֹ׃
his will not the and his shall not the and the from refuge
.life save mighty ,power strengthen strong ,swift

15 וְתֹפֵשׂ הַקֶּשֶׁת לֹא יַעֲמֹד וְקַל בְּרַגְלָיו לֹא יְמַלֵּט וְרֹכֵב
he and save will not his with the And shall not bow the he And
rides who ,(himself) feet swift .stand handles who

16 הַסּוּס לֹא יְמַלֵּט נַפְשׁוֹ׃ וְאַמִּיץ לִבּוֹ בַּגִּבּוֹרִים עָרוֹם יָנוּס
shall naked the among his the And his shall not the
flee mighty heart in one stout .life save horse

בַּיּוֹם־הַהוּא נְאֻם־יְהוָה׃
.Jehovah declares ,that day in

CAP. III ג

CHAPTER 3

[1] Hear this word that Jehovah has spoken against you, sons of Israel, against all the family which I brought up from the land of Egypt, saying, [2] You only have I known of all the families of the earth. Therefore I will punish you (for) all your iniquities. [3] Will two walk together unless they have met by appointment? [4] Will a lion roar in the forest when there is no prey for him? Will a young lion cry out of his den unless he has caught? [5] Will a bird fall in a trap on the earth where no bait is for it? Will a trap spring up from the earth and nothing at all be caught? [6] If a ram's horn be blown in a city, will the people not also be afraid? If there is calamity in a city, has Jehovah not even done (it)? [7] For the Lord Jehovah will do nothing unless He reveals His secret to His servants the prophets. [8] A lion has roared; who will not fear? The Lord Jehovah has spoken; who will not prophesy?

[9] Cry out at the

CHAPTER 3

1 שִׁמְעוּ אֶת־הַדָּבָר הַזֶּה אֲשֶׁר דִּבֶּר יְהוָה עֲלֵיכֶם בְּנֵי יִשְׂרָאֵל
,Israel sons against Jehovah has which this word Hear
of ,you spoken

עַל כָּל־הַמִּשְׁפָּחָה אֲשֶׁר הֶעֱלֵיתִי מֵאֶרֶץ מִצְרַיִם לֵאמֹר׃
,saying ,Egypt the from brought I which family the all against
of land up

2 רַק אֶתְכֶם יָדַעְתִּי מִכֹּל מִשְׁפְּחוֹת הָאֲדָמָה עַל־כֵּן אֶפְקֹד
will I Therefore .earth the families the all of have I you Only
visit of known

3 עֲלֵיכֶם אֵת כָּל־עֲוֹנֹתֵיכֶם׃ הֲיֵלְכוּ שְׁנַיִם יַחְדָּו בִּלְתִּי אִם־
unless ,together two walk Will your all you upon
.iniquities

4 נוֹעָדוּ׃ הֲיִשְׁאַג אַרְיֵה בַּיַּעַר וְטֶרֶף אֵין לוֹ הֲיִתֵּן כְּפִיר
young a Will for is there when the in lion a roar Will are they
lion give ?him no prey forest ?agreed

5 קוֹלוֹ מִמְּעֹנָתוֹ בִּלְתִּי אִם־לָכָד׃ הֲתִפֹּל צִפּוֹר עַל־פַּח
trap a into bird a fall Will has he unless his from his
?caught ,den voice

הָאָרֶץ וּמוֹקֵשׁ אֵין לָהּ הֲיַעֲלֶה־פַּח מִן־הָאֲדָמָה וְלָכוֹד לֹא
nothing at and the from trap a Will for there bait and the (on)
all ,ground up spring ?it not is ground

6 יִלְכּוֹד׃ אִם־יִתָּקַע שׁוֹפָר בְּעִיר וְעָם לֹא יֶחֱרָדוּ אִם־תִּהְיֶה
there If will not the ,city a in ram's a blown is If it
is ?tremble also people horn ?captures

7 רָעָה בְּעִיר וַיהוָה לֹא עָשָׂה׃ כִּי לֹא יַעֲשֶׂה אֲדֹנָי יְהוִה
Jehovah the do will not For has not even a in calamity
Lord ?(it) done Jehovah ,city

8 דָּבָר כִּי אִם־גָּלָה סוֹדוֹ אֶל־עֲבָדָיו הַנְּבִיאִים׃ אַרְיֵה שָׁאָג
has lion A the His to secret His He unless thing a
!roared .prophets servants counsel reveals

9 מִי לֹא יִירָא אֲדֹנָי יְהוִה דִּבֶּר מִי לֹא יִנָּבֵא׃ הַשְׁמִיעוּ
Proclaim will not Who has Jehovah The will not Who
(it) ?prophesy !spoken Lord ?fear

עַל־אַרְמְנוֹת בְּאַשְׁדּוֹד וְעַל־אַרְמְנוֹת בְּאֶרֶץ מִצְרַיִם וְאִמְרוּ

,say and ,Egypt the in palaces the and Ashdod in palaces the at
of land at

הֵאָסְפוּ עַל־הָרֵי שֹׁמְרוֹן וּרְאוּ מְהוּמֹת רַבּוֹת בְּתוֹכָהּ

its in many panics see and ,Samaria the on Gather
,midst of mountains yourselves

10 וַעֲשׁוּקִים בְּקִרְבָּהּ׃ וְלֹא־יָדְעוּ עֲשׂוֹת־נְכֹחָה נְאֻם־יְהוָה

,Jehovah declares ,right to (how) do they For its in and
do know not .midst oppressions

11 הָאֹצְרִים חָמָס וָשֹׁד בְּאַרְמְנוֹתֵיהֶם׃ לָכֵן כֹּה אָמַר

says thus Therefore .palaces their in and violence those
destruction up storing

אֲדֹנָי יְהוִה צַר וּסְבִיב הָאָרֶץ וְהוֹרִד מִמֵּךְ עֻזֵּךְ וְנָבֹזּוּ

will and your from will he And the all even An :Jehovah the
robbed be fortress you lower !land around enemy Lord

12 אַרְמְנוֹתָיִךְ׃ כֹּה אָמַר יְהוָה כַּאֲשֶׁר יַצִּיל הָרֹעֶה מִפִּי

the from the snatches As :Jehovah says Thus .palaces your
of mouth shepherd

הָאֲרִי שְׁתֵּי כְרָעַיִם אוֹ בְדַל־אֹזֶן כֵּן יִנָּצְלוּ בְּנֵי יִשְׂרָאֵל

,Israel the be shall so an a or ,legs two the
of sons snatched ,ear of piece lion

13 הַיֹּשְׁבִים בְּשֹׁמְרוֹן בִּפְאַת מִטָּה וּבִדְמֶשֶׁק עָרֶשׂ׃ שִׁמְעוּ

Hear a (on) in and ,bed a ·a in Samaria in those
.couch Damascus of corner dwelling

14 וְהָעִידוּ בְּבֵית יַעֲקֹב נְאֻם־אֲדֹנָי יְהוִה אֱלֹהֵי הַצְּבָאוֹת׃ כִּי

For .hosts God the ,Jehovah the declares ,Jacob the in and
of Lord of house testify

בְּיוֹם פָּקְדִי פִשְׁעֵי־יִשְׂרָאֵל עָלָיו וּפָקַדְתִּי עַל־מִזְבְּחוֹת בֵּית־

Beth- altars the upon will I upon Israel trans- the I the in
of visit also ,him of gressions visit day

15 אֵל וְנִגְדְּעוּ קַרְנוֹת הַמִּזְבֵּחַ וְנָפְלוּ לָאָרֶץ׃ וְהִכֵּיתִי בֵית־

house will I And the to and the horns the be will And .el
strike .ground fall shall ,altar of broken

הַחֹרֶף עַל־בֵּית הַקַּיִץ וְאָבְדוּ בָּתֵּי הַשֵּׁן וְסָפוּ בָּתִּים רַבִּים

,great the and ;ivory the shall and the house with the
houses away swept of houses perish ,summer winter

נְאֻם־יְהוָה׃

.Jehovah declares

palaces in Ashdod, and at the palaces in the land of Egypt, and say, Gather yourselves on the mountains of Samaria, and see many uproars in its midst, and oppressions in its midst.
[10] For they do not know to do right, states Jehovah, those who store up violence and robbery in their palaces.
[11] Therefore thus says the Lord Jehovah: An enemy! and (he shall be) all around the land; and he shall bring down from you your fortress, and your palaces shall be plundered.
[12] Thus says Jehovah: As the shepherd takes two legs out of the mouth of the lion, or a piece of an ear, so shall the sons of Israel be taken out, those who dwell in Samaria in a corner of a bed, and in Damascus (on) a couch.
[13] Hear and testify in the house of Jacob, states the Lord Jehovah, the God of hosts.
[14] For in the day I visit the transgressions of Israel on him, I will also visit on the altars of Bethel. And the horns of the altar shall be broken and shall fall to the ground.
[15] And I will strike the winter house with the summer house, and the houses of ivory shall perish; and the great houses shall be swept away, states Jehovah.

CAP. IV ד

CHAPTER 4

1 שִׁמְעוּ הַדָּבָר הַזֶּה פָּרוֹת הַבָּשָׁן אֲשֶׁר בְּהַר שֹׁמְרוֹן הָעֹשְׁקוֹת

those ,Samaria the in who ,Bashan cows ,this word Hear
oppressing of mountain (are) of

דַּלִּים הָרֹצְצוֹת אֶבְיוֹנִים הָאֹמְרוֹת לַאֲדֹנֵיהֶם הָבִיאָה

Bring their to those ,poor the those the
,husbands saying crushing ,helpless

2 וְנִשְׁתֶּה׃ נִשְׁבַּע אֲדֹנָי יְהוִה בְּקָדְשׁוֹ כִּי הִנֵּה יָמִים בָּאִים

are the ,behold that His by Jehovah the Has we that
coming days holiness Lord sworn .drink may

CHAPTER 4

[1] Hear this word, cows of Bashan who (are) in the mountain of Samaria, who press down the helpless, who crush the poor; who say to their masters, Bring in, and we shall drink.
[2] The Lord Jehovah has sworn by His holiness, that the days shall come on you

that He will lift you up with the hooks, and your children with fishhooks. [3] And you shall go out (at) the breaches, each woman before her. And you shall throw down the high place, states Jehovah.

[4] Come into Bethel and transgress; (at) Gilgal multiply transgressing. And bring your sacrifices for the morning, your tithes for three days; [5] and offer a sacrifice of thanksgiving from that which is leavened; and cry out, publish (the) free offerings! For so you love (to do), sons of Israel, states the Lord Jehovah.

[6] And I also have given you cleanness of teeth in all your cities, and lack of bread in all your places; and you have not returned to Me, states Jehovah. [7] And I have also withheld the rain from you, when (it was) yet three months to the harvest. And I caused rain to fall on one city, and caused it not to rain on another city. One piece was rained on, and the piece where it did not rain dried up. [8] So two or three cities staggered to one city in order to drink water, but they were not satisfied; and you have not returned to Me, states Jehovah. [9] I have struck you with blasting and mildew. The multitude of your gardens, and your vineyards, and your figs, and your olives, the creeping locust devoured; and you have not returned to Me, states Jehovah. [10] I have sent a plague among you in the way of Egypt. I have killed your young men with the sword and your horses with the captivity; and I have made the stench of your camps to come up even into your nostrils; and you have not returned to Me, states Jehovah. [11] I have overthrown among you, as God

עֲלֵיכֶם וְנִשָּׂא אֶתְכֶם בְּצִנּוֹת וְאַחֲרִיתְכֶן בְּסִירוֹת דּוּגָה׃
.fishing with the and with you He and upon
for hooks you of last ,hooks meat up lift will ,you

3 וּפְרָצִים תֵּצֶאנָה אִשָּׁה נֶגְדָּהּ וְהִשְׁלַכְתֶּנָה הַהַרְמוֹנָה נְאֻם־
declares high the shall you And before each shall you the (at) And
,place down throw .her woman ,out go breaches

4 יְהוָה׃ בֹּאוּ בֵית־אֵל וּפִשְׁעוּ הַגִּלְגָּל הַרְבּוּ לִפְשֹׁעַ וְהָבִיאוּ
And trans- increase (At) and ,el Beth- Enter .Jehovah
bring .gressing Gilgal !rebel

5 לַבֹּקֶר זִבְחֵיכֶם לִשְׁלֹשֶׁת יָמִים מַעְשְׂרֹתֵיכֶם׃ וְקַטֵּר
and ;tithes your days for your the for
burn three ,sacrifices morning

מֵחָמֵץ תּוֹדָה וְקִרְאוּ נְדָבוֹת הַשְׁמִיעוּ כִּי כֵן אֲהַבְתֶּם בְּנֵי
sons love you so For announce voluntary and thank a that from
of ,(do to) .(them) ,offerings proclaim ,offering leavened

6 יִשְׂרָאֵל נְאֻם אֲדֹנָי יְהוִה׃ וְגַם אֲנִי נָתַתִּי לָכֶם נִקְיוֹן
cleanness to have I And .Jehovah the declares ,Israel
of you given also Lord

שִׁנַּיִם בְּכָל־עָרֵיכֶם וְחֹסֶר לֶחֶם בְּכֹל מְקוֹמֹתֵיכֶם וְלֹא־
and ;places your all in bread and your in teeth
not of lack ,cities all

7 שַׁבְתֶּם עָדַי נְאֻם־יְהוָה׃ וְגַם אָנֹכִי מָנַעְתִּי מִכֶּם אֶת־הַגֶּשֶׁם
the from have I And .Jehovah declares to have you
,rain you withheld also ,Me returned

בְּעוֹד שְׁלֹשָׁה חֳדָשִׁים לַקָּצִיר וְהִמְטַרְתִּי עַל־עִיר אֶחָת
one city on made I And the to months three yet when
fall rain .harvest (was it)

וְעַל־עִיר אַחַת לֹא אַמְטִיר חֶלְקָה אַחַת תִּמָּטֵר וְחֶלְקָה
a but rained was one portion made I not another city and
portion ,upon ;fall rain on

8 אֲשֶׁר־לֹא־תַמְטִיר עָלֶיהָ תִּיבָשׁ׃ וְנָעוּ שְׁתַּיִם שָׁלֹשׁ עָרִים
cities (or) two And .up dried it on did it not where
three staggered rain

אֶל־עִיר אַחַת לִשְׁתּוֹת מַיִם וְלֹא יִשְׂבָּעוּ וְלֹא־שַׁבְתֶּם עָדַי
to have you and were they but ,water drink to one city to
,Me returned not ;satisfied not

9 נְאֻם־יְהוָה׃ הִכֵּיתִי אֶתְכֶם בַּשִּׁדָּפוֹן וּבַיֵּרָקוֹן הַרְבּוֹת גַּנּוֹתֵיכֶם
your mul- the with and with you have I .Jehovah de-
gardens of titude ,mildew scorching struck clares

וְכַרְמֵיכֶם וּתְאֵנֵיכֶם וְזֵיתֵיכֶם יֹאכַל הַגָּזָם וְלֹא־שַׁבְתֶּם עָדַי
to have you and the was your and your and your and
,Me returned not ;locust devouring ,olives figs vinegards

10 נְאֻם־יְהוָה׃ שִׁלַּחְתִּי בָכֶם דֶּבֶר בְּדֶרֶךְ מִצְרַיִם הָרַגְתִּי
have I .Egypt the in plague a among have I .Jehovah declares
killed of way you sent

בַחֶרֶב בַּחוּרֵיכֶם עִם שְׁבִי סוּסֵיכֶם וָאַעֲלֶה בְּאֹשׁ מַחֲנֵיכֶם
your stench the made I and your the with young your the with
camps of up come to ;horses of captivity ,men sword

11 וּבְאַפְּכֶם וְלֹא־שַׁבְתֶּם עָדַי נְאֻם־יְהוָה׃ הָפַכְתִּי בָכֶם
among have I .Jehovah declares to have you and into even
you overthrown ,Me returned not ;noses your

overthrew Sodom and Gomorrah, and you were like a firebrand plucked out of the burning; and you have not returned to Me, states Jehovah. [12] Therefore I will do this to you, O Israel: because of this I will do to you; prepare to meet your God, O Israel. [13] For lo, He who forms mountains and creates the wind, and declares to man what His thought (is); He who makes the dawn darkness, and treads on the high places of the earth; Jehovah, the God of hosts, (is) His name.

כְּמַהְפֵּכַת אֱלֹהִים אֶת־סְדֹם וְאֶת־עֲמֹרָה וַתִּהְיוּ כְּאוּד מֻצָּל
snatched a like you and ,Gomorrah and Sodom (of) God's like
firebrand were overthrow

12 מִשְּׂרֵפָה וְלֹא־שַׁבְתֶּם עָדַי נְאֻם־יְהוָה׃ לָכֵן כֹּה אֶעֱשֶׂה־
will I thus Therefore .Jehovah declares unto have you and the from
do ,Me returned not ,burning

לְּךָ יִשְׂרָאֵל עֵקֶב כִּי־זֹאת אֶעֱשֶׂה־לָּךְ הִכּוֹן לִקְרַאת־אֱלֹהֶיךָ
,God your meet to prepare to will I this because :Israel O to
;you do of ,you

13 יִשְׂרָאֵל׃ כִּי הִנֵּה יוֹצֵר הָרִים וּבֹרֵא רוּחַ וּמַגִּיד לְאָדָם מַה־
what to and the and mountains He ,behold For .Israel O
(is) man declares wind creates forms who

שֵּׂחוֹ עֹשֵׂה שַׁחַר עֵיפָה וְדֹרֵךְ עַל־בָּמֳתֵי אָרֶץ יְהוָה אֱלֹהֵי־
God the ,Jehovah the high the upon and ,darkness (into) who He His
of ,earth of places treads dawn makes ;thought

צְבָאוֹת שְׁמוֹ׃
His hosts
.name (is)

CHAPTER 5

[1] Hear this word which I am lifting against you, a weeping, O house of Israel. [2] The virgin of Israel has fallen, and not will rise again; she lies forsaken on her land; there is no one raising her up. [3] For thus says the Lord Jehovah: The city that goes out (by) a thousand shall have a hundred left. And that which goes out (by) a hundred shall have ten left to the house of Israel.

[4] For thus says Jehovah to the house of Israel: Seek Me, and live. [5] But do not seek Bethel, nor enter Gilgal, and do not cross to Beer-sheba; for Gilgal shall surely go into captivity, and Bethel shall come to nothing. [6] Seek Jehovah, and live; lest He break out like a fire (on) the house of Joseph and devour, and no one is quenching (it) for Bethel. [7] He abandoned those who turn justice to wormwood, and leave off righteousness in the earth. [8] He who created the Pleiades and Orion, and who turns the shadow of

CAP. V ה

CHAPTER 5

1 שִׁמְעוּ אֶת־הַדָּבָר הַזֶּה אֲשֶׁר אָנֹכִי נֹשֵׂא עֲלֵיכֶם קִינָה בֵּית
O ,dirge a against am I which this word Hear
of house ,you lifting

2 יִשְׂרָאֵל׃ נָפְלָה לֹא־תוֹסִיף קוּם בְּתוּלַת יִשְׂרָאֵל נִטְּשָׁה
lies she ;Israel virgin the arise will and has She .Israel
unattended of again not ,fallen

3 עַל־אַדְמָתָהּ אֵין מְקִימָהּ׃ כִּי כֹה אָמַר אֲדֹנָי יְהוִה
:Jehovah the says thus For raising is there her on
Lord .up her none ;land

הָעִיר הַיֹּצֵאת אֶלֶף תַּשְׁאִיר מֵאָה וְהַיּוֹצֵאת מֵאָה תַּשְׁאִיר
have will hundred a that and ,hundred a have will thou- a goes that The
left (strong) forth goes which left (strong) sand forth city

4 עֲשָׂרָה לְבֵית יִשְׂרָאֵל׃ כִּי כֹה אָמַר יְהוָה לְבֵית
the to Jehovah says thus For .Israel the to ten
of house of house

5 יִשְׂרָאֵל דִּרְשׁוּנִי וִחְיוּ׃ וְאַל־תִּדְרְשׁוּ בֵּית־אֵל וְהַגִּלְגָּל לֹא
not and ,el Beth- seek do But .live and ,Me Seek :Israel
Gilgal not

תָבֹאוּ וּבְאֵר שֶׁבַע לֹא תַעֲבֹרוּ כִּי הַגִּלְגָּל גָּלֹה יִגְלֶה וּבֵית
and go will surely Gilgal for cross do not sheba and do
Beth- ,exile into ;to over Beer- ;enter

6 אֵל יִהְיֶה לְאָוֶן׃ דִּרְשׁוּ אֶת־יְהוָה וִחְיוּ פֶּן־יִצְלַח כָּאֵשׁ
a like He lest and ,Jehovah Seek for shall el
fire rush ;live .nothing be

7 בֵּית יוֹסֵף וְאָכְלָה וְאֵין־מְכַבֶּה לְבֵית־אֵל׃ הַהֹפְכִים לְלַעֲנָה
into who Those .el for quench- there and and Joseph the (on)
wormwood turn Beth- (it) ing none is ,devour of house

8 מִשְׁפָּט וּצְדָקָה לָאָרֶץ הִנִּיחוּ׃ עֹשֵׂה כִימָה וּכְסִיל וְהֹפֵךְ
and and the who He he the in righ- and ,justice
turns ,Orion Pleiades made ;abandoned earth teousness

death into the morning, and made the day dark (with) night; who calls for the waters of the sea and pours them out on the face of the earth; Jehovah (is) His name; [9] who causes destruction to flash out against the strong, and destruction comes against the fortress. [10] They hate him who rebukes in the gate, and they despise him who speaks uprightly. [11] Therefore, because of your trampling on the poor, and you take tribute of grain from him; you have built houses of hewn stone, but you shall not live in them. You have planted desirable vineyards, but you shall not drink wine from them. [12] For I know your many transgressions and your many sins: afflicting the just; taking of a bribe; and turning aside the poor in the gate. [13] Therefore the understanding ones shall keep silent in that time; for it (is) an evil time. [14] Seek good, and not evil, that you may live; and so Jehovah, the God of hosts, (shall be) with you, as you have spoken. [15] Hate evil, and love good, and establish justice in the gate. It may be that Jehovah the God of hosts will be gracious (to) the remnant of Joseph. [16] So thus says Jehovah, the God of hosts, the Master: Wailing (shall be) in all streets; and they shall say in all the highways, Alas! Alas! And they shall call the farmer to the mourning, and those knowing wailing to lamentation. And wailing (will be) in all vineyards, for I will pass among you, says Jehovah. [18] Woe to those desiring the day of Jehovah! To what end (is) it for you? The day of Jehovah (is) darkness and not light, [19] as (if) a man fled from before a lion, and the bear met him; or he goes into the

לַבֹּקֶר צַלְמָוֶת וְיוֹם לַיְלָה הֶחְשִׁיךְ הַקּוֹרֵא לְמֵי־הַיָּם

the sea | the for of waters | who calls | He ;darkened | (into) night | the and day | deep the ,darkness | the into morning

9 וַיִּשְׁפְּכֵם עַל־פְּנֵי הָאָרֶץ יְהוָה שְׁמוֹ׃ הַמַּבְלִיג שֹׁד עַל־עָז

the strong | on | destruction | flashes He with forth | His .name | Jehovah (is) | the ;earth | the of face | on | pours and out them

10 וְשֹׁד עַל־מִבְצָר יָבוֹא׃ שָׂנְאוּ בַשַּׁעַר מוֹכִיחַ וְדֹבֵר תָּמִים

uprightly | him and speak who | who him ,reproves | the in gate | They hate | .comes | the fortress | on | and destruction

11 יְתָעֵבוּ׃ לָכֵן יַעַן בּוֹשַׁסְכֶם עַל־דָּל וּמַשְׂאַת־בַּר תִּקְחוּ מִמֶּנּוּ

from ;him | you take | grain | and of tribute | the ,poor | on | your trampling | because of | There- ,fore | they .abhor

בָּתֵּי גָזִית בְּנִיתֶם וְלֹא־תֵשְׁבוּ בָם כַּרְמֵי־חֶמֶד נְטַעְתֶּם וְלֹא

but not | have you ,planted | beauty | Vine- of yards | in .them | shall you dwell | but not | have you ,built | hewn stones | houses of

12 תִשְׁתּוּ אֶת־יֵינָם׃ כִּי יָדַעְתִּי רַבִּים פִּשְׁעֵיכֶם וַעֲצֻמִים

and numerous | your (are) ,transgressions | many | know I | For | their .wine | shall you drink

חַטֹּאתֵיכֶם צֹרְרֵי צַדִּיק לֹקְחֵי כֹפֶר וְאֶבְיוֹנִים בַּשַּׁעַר הִטּוּ׃

they .aside turn | the in gate | the and poor | ,bribe a | taking of | the ,righteous | oppressing of | your (are) :sins

13 לָכֵן הַמַּשְׂכִּיל בָּעֵת הַהִיא יִדֹּם כִּי עֵת רָעָה הִיא׃

.(is) it | evil | an time | for | keep will ;silent | that | in time | who he prudent is | Therefore

14 דִּרְשׁוּ־טוֹב וְאַל־רָע לְמַעַן תִּחְיוּ וִיהִי־כֵן יְהוָה אֱלֹהֵי־

God the of | ,Jehovah | ,so | may and be it | may you ;live | so that | ,evil | and not | good | Seek

15 צְבָאוֹת אִתְּכֶם כַּאֲשֶׁר אֲמַרְתֶּם׃ שִׂנְאוּ־רָע וְאֶהֱבוּ טוֹב

,good | love and | evil | Hate | have you .spoken | as | with ,you | hosts (is)

וְהַצִּיגוּ בַשַּׁעַר מִשְׁפָּט אוּלַי יֶחֱנַן יְהוָה אֱלֹהֵי־צְבָאוֹת

hosts | God the of | Jehovah | be will gracious | Perhaps | .justice | the in gate | and establish

16 שְׁאֵרִית יוֹסֵף׃ לָכֵן כֹּה־אָמַר יְהוָה אֱלֹהֵי צְבָאוֹת

hosts | God the of | ,Jehovah | says | thus | ,Therefore | .Joseph | the (to) of remnant

אֲדֹנָי בְּכָל־רְחֹבוֹת מִסְפֵּד וּבְכָל־חוּצוֹת יֹאמְרוּ הוֹ־הוֹ

!Alas !Alas | shall they ,say | the streets | in and all | ;wailing | squares open (be will) | in all | the :Lord

17 וְקָרְאוּ אִכָּר אֶל־אֵבֶל וּמִסְפֵּד אֶל־יוֹדְעֵי נֶהִי׃ וּבְכָל־כְּרָמִים

vineyards | in And all | lamen- .tation | those knowing | to | and wailing | the ,mourning | to | the farmer | they And call shall

18 מִסְפֵּד כִּי־אֶעֱבֹר בְּקִרְבְּךָ אָמַר יְהוָה׃ הוֹי הַמִּתְאַוִּים

those desiring | Woe to | .Jehovah | says | your in ,midst | will I pass | for | (be will) ,wailing

אֶת־יוֹם יְהוָה לָמָּה־זֶּה לָכֶם יוֹם יְהוָה הוּא־חֹשֶׁךְ וְלֹא־

and not | darkness | it (is) | Jehovah | The of day | for ?you | this | What | !Jehovah (is) | day the of

19 אוֹר׃ כַּאֲשֶׁר יָנוּס אִישׁ מִפְּנֵי הָאֲרִי וּפְגָעוֹ הַדֹּב וּבָא

he or enters | the ;bear | met and him | the ,lion | from before | a man | fled | (if) as | ,light

house and leans his hand on the wall, and a snake bites him. [20] (Shall) not the day of Jehovah (be) darkness and not light? Even very dark, and no brightness in it?

[21] I hate, I despise your feast days, and I will not delight in your solemn assemblies. [22] Though you offer Me burnt offerings and your grain offerings, I will not be pleased; nor will I regard the peace offerings of your fat animals. [23] Take the noise of your songs away from Me; and I will not hear the melody of your stringed instruments. [24] But let justice roll down like waters, and righteousness like an ever-flowing stream. [25] Have you offered sacrifices and offerings to Me forty years in the wilderness, O house of Israel? [26] Yea, you have carried the booth of your king and Kiyyun, your images, the star of your gods which you made for yourselves. [27] Therefore I will cause you to go into captivity beyond Damascus, says Jehovah, the God of hosts (is) His name.

20 הַבַּיִת וְסָמַךְ יָדוֹ עַל־הַקִּיר וּנְשָׁכוֹ הַנָּחָשׁ׃ הֲלֹא־חֹשֶׁךְ
darkness (Is) the bites and the against his and the
not .snake him ,wall hand leans house

21 יוֹם יְהוָה וְלֹא־אוֹר וְאָפֵל וְלֹא־נֹגַהּ לוֹ׃ שָׂנֵאתִי מָאַסְתִּי
reject I ,hate I ?it in bright- and even ,light and ,Jehovah the
ness no gloomy not of day

22 חַגֵּיכֶם וְלֹא אָרִיחַ בְּעַצְּרֹתֵיכֶם׃ כִּי אִם־תַּעֲלוּ־לִי עֹלוֹת
burnt to offer you if For festive your in will I and feast your
,offerings Me up .assemblies delight not ,days

23 וּמִנְחֹתֵיכֶם לֹא אֶרְצֶה וְשֶׁלֶם מְרִיאֵיכֶם לֹא אַבִּיט׃ הָסֵר
Take will I not fattened your peace and will I not grain your and
away .upon look animals of offerings ;pleased be ,offerings

24 מֵעָלַי הֲמוֹן שִׁרֶיךָ וְזִמְרַת נְבָלֶיךָ לֹא אֶשְׁמָע׃ וְיִגַּל כַּמַּיִם
like let But will I not your the and your the from
waters down roll .hear harps of melody ;songs of sound Me

25 מִשְׁפָּט וּצְדָקָה כְּנַחַל אֵיתָן׃ הַזְּבָחִים וּמִנְחָה הִגַּשְׁתֶּם־
you Did grain and the ever- an like righ- and ,justice
present offerings sacrifices .flowing stream teousness

26 לִי בַמִּדְבָּר אַרְבָּעִים שָׁנָה בֵּית יִשְׂרָאֵל׃ וּנְשָׂאתֶם אֵת
you, Yea ?Israel house O ,years forty the in to
bore of wilderness Me

סִכּוּת מַלְכְּכֶם וְאֵת כִּיּוּן צַלְמֵיכֶם כּוֹכַב אֱלֹהֵיכֶם אֲשֶׁר
which your star the your ,Kiyyun and your the
gods of ,images king of booth

27 עֲשִׂיתֶם לָכֶם׃ וְהִגְלֵיתִי אֶתְכֶם מֵהָלְאָה לְדַמָּשֶׂק אָמַר
says ,Damascus beyond you I ,Therefore your- for you
exile into take will ?selves made

יְהוָה אֱלֹהֵי־צְבָאוֹת שְׁמוֹ׃
His hosts the ,Jehovah
.name (is) of God

CAP. VI ו

CHAPTER 6

[1] Woe (to) those at ease in Zion, and those trusting in the mountain of Samaria, those noted (as) chief of the nations; to them the house of Israel came! [2] Cross to Calneh and see; and from there go to Hamath the great. Then go down to Gath of the Philistines. (Are they) better than these kingdoms, or their border than your border? [3] You who put the evil day far away and cause the seat of violence to come near; [4] who lie on beds of ivory and stretch themselves on their couches, and eat the lambs out of the flock, and the calves out of the midst of the stall; [5] who chant to

1 הוֹי הַשַּׁאֲנַנִּים בְּצִיּוֹן וְהַבֹּטְחִים בְּהַר שֹׁמְרוֹן נְקֻבֵי רֵאשִׁית
the those ,Samaria the in those and ,Zion in at those Woe
of chief (as) noted of mountain trusting ease (to)

2 הַגּוֹיִם וּבָאוּ לָהֶם בֵּית יִשְׂרָאֵל׃ עִבְרוּ כַלְנֵה וּרְאוּ וּלְכוּ
and and to Cross !Israel house the to and the
go ;see Calneh over of them came ,nations

מִשָּׁם חֲמַת רַבָּה וּרְדוּ גַת־פְּלִשְׁתִּים הֲטוֹבִים מִן־הַמַּמְלָכוֹת
kingdoms than (they Are) .Philistines the (to) go And the (to) from
better of Gath down .great Hamath there

3 הָאֵלֶּה אִם־רַב גְּבוּלָם מִגְּבֻלְכֶם׃ הַמְנַדִּים לְיוֹם רָע וַתַּגִּישׁוּן
they but ,evil the who Those your than their greater or ,these
near bring day off thrust ?territory territory

4 שֶׁבֶת חָמָס׃ הַשֹּׁכְבִים עַל־מִטּוֹת שֵׁן וּסְרֻחִים עַל־עַרְשׂוֹתָם
their on those and ,ivory beds on who those ;violence the
,couches sprawled of lie of seat

5 וְאֹכְלִים כָּרִים מִצֹּאן וַעֲגָלִים מִתּוֹךְ מַרְבֵּק׃ הַפֹּרְטִים עַ
to those the the from bull and the from lambs those and
improvising ;stall of midst calves flock eating

the sound of the harp, inventing instruments of music for themselves, like David; [6] who drink bowls of wine, and anoint with the chief oils; but they are not grieved for the breaking of Joseph!

[7] Therefore now they shall go into exile with the first of the exiles, and the feast of those who stretch themselves shall cease. [8] The Lord Jehovah has sworn by Himself, states Jehovah, the God of hosts: I abhor the pride of Jacob and hate his palaces; and I will deliver up the city and its fullness. [9] And it shall come to pass, if remain ten men in one house, then they shall die. [10] And his uncle shall lift him up, and he who burns him, to bring out the bones from the house, and shall say to that (one) in the recesses of the house, Are (any) still with you? And he shall say, No. Then he shall say, Hush! For not one shall mention the name of Jehovah. [11] For, behold, Jehovah commands, and He will strike the great house into pieces, and the little house (into) breaches.

[12] Shall horses run on the rock? Or will one plow with oxen (there)? For you have turned justice into poison, and the fruit of righteousness into wormwood; [13] those rejoicing for nothing; those saying, Have we not taken horns to ourselves by our own strength? [14] For behold, I will raise a nation up against you, O house of Israel, states Jehovah, the God of hosts. And they shall oppress you from the entrance of Hamath to the torrent of the Arabah.

6 פִּי הַנָּבֶל כְּדָוִיד חָשְׁבוּ לָהֶם כְּלֵי־שִׁיר׃ הַשֹּׁתִים בְּמִזְרְקֵי
bowls from those ,song instru- for they like ;harp the the
of drinking of ments themselves invent David of sound

יַיִן וְרֵאשִׁית שְׁמָנִים יִמְשָׁחוּ וְלֹא נֶחְלוּ עַל־שֵׁבֶר יוֹסֵף׃
!Joseph the for do they but anoint they oils the with ,wine
of breaking grieve not ;(themselves) of best

7 לָכֵן עַתָּה יִגְלוּ בְּרֹאשׁ גֹּלִים וְסָר מִרְזַח סְרוּחִים׃
the feast the will and the the with will they now There-
.sprawlers of cease ,exiles of first exile into go fore

8 נִשְׁבַּע אֲדֹנָי יֱהוִה בְּנַפְשׁוֹ נְאֻם־יְהוָה אֱלֹהֵי צְבָאוֹת מְתָאֵב
abhor :hosts God the ,Jehovah de- by Jehovah The has
of clares ,Himself Lord sworn

אָנֹכִי אֶת־גְּאוֹן יַעֲקֹב וְאַרְמְנֹתָיו שָׂנֵאתִי וְהִסְגַּרְתִּי עִיר
the I and ;hate I palaces his and ,Jacob the I
city deliver will of pride

9 וּמְלֹאָהּ׃ וְהָיָה אִם־יִוָּתְרוּ עֲשָׂרָה אֲנָשִׁים בְּבַיִת אֶחָד וָמֵתוּ׃
they then ,one in men ten are if it And its and
.die will house left ,be will .fullness

10 וּנְשָׂאוֹ דּוֹדוֹ וּמְסָרְפוֹ לְהוֹצִיא עֲצָמִים מִן־הַבַּיִת וְאָמַר לַאֲשֶׁר
that to shall and the from the bring to his and his will And
(left one) say ,house bones out burner uncle up him lift

בְּיַרְכְּתֵי הַבַּיִת הַעוֹד עִמָּךְ וְאָמַר אָפֶס וְאָמַר הָס כִּי לֹא
not For !Hush he Then .None he And with (any) Are the the in
say will ,say shall ?you still ,house of recesses

11 לְהַזְכִּיר בְּשֵׁם יְהוָה׃ כִּי־הִנֵּה יְהוָה מְצַוֶּה וְהִכָּה
He and com- is Jehovah, behold ,For .Jehovah the must one
strike will ,manding of name mention

12 הַבַּיִת הַגָּדוֹל רְסִיסִים וְהַבַּיִת הַקָּטֹן בְּקִעִים׃ הַיְרֻצוּן בַּסֶּלַע
the on run Do (into) little the and pieces (into) great the
rock .breaches house rubble of house

סוּסִים אִם־יַחֲרוֹשׁ בַּבְּקָרִים כִּי־הֲפַכְתֶּם לְרֹאשׁ מִשְׁפָּט
justice into have you For with (there) one will Or ?horses
poison turned ?oxen plow

13 וּפְרִי צְדָקָה לְלַעֲנָה׃ הַשְּׂמֵחִים לְלֹא דָבָר הָאֹמְרִים הֲלוֹא
not those ,thing for those into righteous- the and
,saying no rejoicing ,wormwood ness of fruit

14 בְחָזְקֵנוּ לָקַחְנוּ לָנוּ קַרְנָיִם׃ כִּי הִנְנִי מֵקִים עֲלֵיכֶם בֵּית
house O against am ,behold For .horns our- to we Have own our by
of ,you up rising I selves taken strength

יִשְׂרָאֵל נְאֻם־יְהוָה אֱלֹהֵי הַצְּבָאוֹת גּוֹי וְלָחֲצוּ אֶתְכֶם מִלְּבוֹא
the from you they And a hosts God the ,Jehovah declares ;Israel
of entrance oppress will nation of

חֲמָת עַד־נַחַל הָעֲרָבָה׃
.Arabah the the to Hamath
of torrent

CAP. VII ז

CHAPTER 7

[1] Thus the Lord Jehovah showed me; and, behold, He is forming locusts in the beginning of the shooting up of the latter

1 כֹּה הִרְאַנִי אֲדֹנָי יֱהוִה וְהִנֵּה יוֹצֵר גֹּבַי בִּתְחִלַּת עֲלוֹת
coming the the at locusts is He and ;Jehovah the showed Thus
of up of beginning forming ,behold Lord me

growth; and, behold, the latter growth after the king's mowings. [2] And it came to pass, when it had made an end of eating the grass of the land, then I said, Lord Jehovah, please forgive. How shall Jacob stand? For he (is) small. [3] Jehovah repented concerning this: It shall not be, says Jehovah.

[4] Thus the Lord Jehovah caused me to see: And, behold, the Lord Jehovah was calling to contend by fire. And it consumed the great deep, and devouring part of it. [5] Then I said, O Lord Jehovah, please stop! How shall Jacob stand? For he (is) small. [6] Jehovah repented concerning this: It shall not be, says the Lord Jehovah.

[7] Thus He showed me. And, behold, the Lord was standing by the wall (made) by a plumb-line, and a plumb-line in His hand. [8] And Jehovah said to me, Amos, what do you see? And I said, A plumbline. And the Lord said, Behold, I will set a plumbline in the midst of My people Israel. I will not again pass over him any more. [9] And the high places of Isaac shall be desolated; and the holy places of Israel shall be laid waste; and I will rise against the house of Jeroboam with the sword.

[10] Then Amaziah the priest of Bethel sent to Jeroboam the king of Israel, saying, Amos has plotted against you in the midst of the house of Israel. The land is not able to endure all his words. [11] For thus Amos says: Jeroboam shall die by the sword, and Israel shall surely go into exile out of his land. [12] And Amaziah said to Amos, Seer, go, flee for yourself into the land of Judah, and eat bread and prophesy there.

2 הַלֶּקֶשׁ וְהִנֵּה־לֶקֶשׁ אַחַר גִּזֵּי הַמֶּלֶךְ׃ וְהָיָה אִם־כִּלָּה
it when it And the the after late the and late the
finished ,was .king of mowings grass behold ,grass

לֶאֱכוֹל אֶת־עֵשֶׂב הָאָרֶץ וָאֹמַר אֲדֹנָי יְהוִה סְלַח־נָא מִי
How .Please for- ,Jehovah Lord I then the vege- the eating
give said ,land of tation

3 יָקוּם יַעֲקֹב כִּי קָטֹן הוּא׃ נִחַם יְהוָה עַל־זֹאת לֹא תִהְיֶה
shall it not ;this con- Jehovah re- ?(is) he small for ,Jacob can
,be cerning pented stand

4 אָמַר יְהוָה׃ כֹּה הִרְאַנִי אֲדֹנָי יְהוִה וְהִנֵּה קֹרֵא לָרִב
to was And :Jehovah the showed Thus .Jehovah says
contend calling ,behold Lord me

בָּאֵשׁ אֲדֹנָי יְהוִה וַתֹּאכַל אֶת־תְּהוֹם רַבָּה וְאָכְלָה אֶת־
and ,great the was it And .Jehovah the by
devouring deep consuming Lord fire

5 הַחֵלֶק׃ וָאֹמַר אֲדֹנָי יְהוִה חֲדַל־נָא מִי יָקוּם יַעֲקֹב כִּי קָטֹן
small for ,Jacob can How !Please stop ,Jehovah Lord I Then the
stand ,said .portion

6 הוּא׃ נִחַם יְהוָה עַל־זֹאת גַּם־הִיא לֹא תִהְיֶה אָמַר אֲדֹנָי
the says ,be shall not it Also :this con- Jehovah repented he
Lord cerning ?(is)

7 יְהוִה׃ כֹּה הִרְאַנִי וְהִנֵּה אֲדֹנָי נִצָּב עַל־חוֹמַת אֲנָךְ
plumb- a the by was the And showed He Thus .Jehovah
line of wall standing Lord ,behold ,me

8 וּבְיָדוֹ אֲנָךְ׃ וַיֹּאמֶר יְהוָה אֵלַי מָה־אַתָּה רֹאֶה עָמוֹס וָאֹמַר
I And ?Amos are you What ,me to Jehovah said And a in and
,said ,seeing .plumbline hand His

אֲנָךְ וַיֹּאמֶר אֲדֹנָי הִנְנִי שָׂם אֲנָךְ בְּקֶרֶב עַמִּי יִשְׂרָאֵל לֹא־
Not .Israel my the in plumb- a am Behold the said And a
people of midst line setting I ,Lord .plumbline

9 אוֹסִיף עוֹד עֲבוֹר לוֹ׃ וְנָשַׁמּוּ בָּמוֹת יִשְׂחָק וּמִקְדְּשֵׁי יִשְׂרָאֵל
Israel the and ,Isaac high the be will And .him pass any will I
of places holy of places desolated over more again

10 יֶחֱרָבוּ וְקַמְתִּי עַל־בֵּית יָרָבְעָם בֶּחָרֶב׃ וַיִּשְׁלַח אֲמַצְיָה
Amaziah sent Then the with Jeroboam the against will I Then be will
.sword of house up rise .waste laid

כֹּהֵן בֵּית־אֵל אֶל־יָרָבְעָם מֶלֶךְ־יִשְׂרָאֵל לֵאמֹר קָשַׁר עָלֶיךָ
against has ,saying ,Israel king the Jeroboam to el Beth- the
you conspired of of priest

עָמוֹס בְּקֶרֶב בֵּית יִשְׂרָאֵל לֹא־תוּכַל הָאָרֶץ לְהָכִיל אֶת־
to the is Not .Israel the the in Amos
endure land able of house of midst

11 כָּל־דְּבָרָיו׃ כִּי־כֹה אָמַר עָמוֹס בַּחֶרֶב יָמוּת יָרָבְעָם וְיִשְׂרָאֵל
and ,Jeroboam shall the By ,Amos says thus For his all
Israel die sword .words

12 גָּלֹה יִגְלֶה מֵעַל אַדְמָתוֹ׃ וַיֹּאמֶר אֲמַצְיָה אֶל־עָמוֹס
,Amos to Amaziah said And .land his from go will surely
exile into

חֹזֶה לֵךְ בְּרַח־לְךָ אֶל־אֶרֶץ יְהוּדָה וֶאֱכָל־שָׁם לֶחֶם וְשָׁם
and bread there and ,Judah the to for flee ,go ,Seer O
there eat of land yourself

[13] But do not add to prophesying any more at Bethel; for it (is) the king's holy place, and it (is) the royal house.

[14] Then Amos answered and said to Amaziah: I (was) not a prophet, nor (was) I a prophet's son. But I (was) a herdsman and a gatherer (from) sycamore trees. [15] And Jehovah took me from behind the flock, and Jehovah said to me, Go, prophesy to My people Israel.

[16] Now, then, hear the word of Jehovah: You say, Do not prophesy against Israel and do not drop (words) against the house of Isaac. [17] Therefore thus says Jehovah: Your wife shall be a harlot in the city, and your sons and your daughters shall fall by the sword, and your land shall be divided by a line. And you shall die in a defiled land. And Israel shall surely go into captivity out of his land.

תִּנָּבֵא׃ וּבֵית אֵל לֹֽא־תוֹסִיף עוֹד לְהִנָּבֵא כִּי מִקְדַּשׁ־מֶלֶךְ 13

the holy the king of place for ;prophesy any more do again not el (at) But Beth- .prophesy

הוּא וּבֵית מַמְלָכָה הֽוּא׃ וַיַּעַן עָמוֹס וַיֹּאמֶר אֶל־אֲמַצְיָה 14

:Amaziah to said and Amos Then answered .(is) it royal the and house ,(is) it

לֹֽא־נָבִיא אָנֹכִי וְלֹא בֶן־נָבִיא אָנֹכִי כִּֽי־בוֹקֵר אָנֹכִי וּבוֹלֵס

a and gatherer ,I (was) a herdsman For .I (was) a prophet of the son and not ,I (was) a prophet not

שִׁקְמִֽים׃ וַיִּקָּחֵנִי יְהוָה מֵאַחֲרֵי הַצֹּאן וַיֹּאמֶר אֵלַי יְהוָה לֵךְ 15

,Go ,Jehovah to me said and the ,flock from behind Jehovah took me And syc- (from) .trees amore

הִנָּבֵא אֶל־עַמִּי יִשְׂרָאֵֽל׃ וְעַתָּה שְׁמַע דְּבַר־יְהוָה אַתָּה אֹמֵר 16

are ,saying You :Jehovah the of word hear ,now And .Israel my people to prophesy

לֹא תִנָּבֵא עַל־יִשְׂרָאֵל וְלֹא תַטִּיף עַל־בֵּית יִשְׂחָֽק׃ לָכֵן כֹּה־ 17

thus There- fore .Isaac the against of house Do drip ,and not ,Israel against Do prophesy not

אָמַר יְהוָה אִשְׁתְּךָ בָּעִיר תִּזְנֶה וּבָנֶיךָ וּבְנֹתֶיךָ בַּחֶרֶב יִפֹּלוּ

will ,fall the by sword your daughters and your sons and be- ,harlot a come will the in city Your wife :Jehovah says

וְאַדְמָתְךָ בַּחֶבֶל תְּחֻלָּק וְאַתָּה עַל־אֲדָמָה טְמֵאָה תָּמוּת

will you .die defiled land a upon ,you And be shall .divided a by line your and land

וְיִשְׂרָאֵל גָּלֹה יִגְלֶה מֵעַל אַדְמָתֽוֹ׃

.land his from go will exile into surely And Israel

CAP. VIII ח

CHAPTER 8

[1] Thus the Lord Jehovah showed me; and, behold, a basket of summer fruit! [2] And He said, Amos, what do you see? And I said, A basket of summer fruit. And Jehovah said to me, The end has come on My people Israel; I will not again pass by him any more. [3] And the songs of the temple they shall howl in that day, states the Lord Jehovah. The dead bodies (shall be) many; in every place one shall throw (them) out with silence.

[4] Hear this, you who swallow up the poor, even to make the humble of the land to cease, [5] saying, When will the new moon have passed, so that we may buy grain; and the sabbath, that we may open the wheat, making the ephah small and the shekel great, and perverting the balances

כֹּה הִרְאַנִי אֲדֹנָי יְהוִה וְהִנֵּה כְּלוּב קָֽיִץ׃ וַיֹּאמֶר מָֽה־אַתָּה 1 2

you What He And ,said summer .fruit basket a of and ,behold ;Jehovah the Lord showed me Thus

רֹאֶה עָמוֹס וָאֹמַר כְּלוּב קָיִץ וַיֹּאמֶר יְהוָה אֵלַי בָּא הַקֵּץ

the end Has come to ,me Jehovah said And summer .fruit basket A of I And ,said ?Amos are ,seeing

אֶל־עַמִּי יִשְׂרָאֵל לֹֽא־אוֹסִיף עוֹד עֲבוֹר לֽוֹ׃ וְהֵילִילוּ שִׁירוֹת 3

songs the of they And howl will .him pass over any more will I again not ;Israel My people to

הֵיכָל בַּיּוֹם הַהוּא נְאֻם אֲדֹנָי יְהוִה רַב הַפֶּגֶר בְּכָל־מָקוֹם

place every in the ;corpses Many (be will) .Jehovah the Lord declares ,that day in the temple

הִשְׁלִיךְ הָֽס׃ שִׁמְעוּ־זֹאת הַשֹּׁאֲפִים אֶבְיוֹן וְלַשְׁבִּית 4

to and cease make the poor who you trample ,this Hear (saying) throws one !Hush ,out (them)

עֲנִוֵּי־אָֽרֶץ׃ לֵאמֹר מָתַי יַעֲבֹר הַחֹדֶשׁ וְנַשְׁבִּירָה שֶּׁבֶר 5

?grain we that so buy may new the ,moon have will When passed ,saying the ,earth of the humble

וְהַשַּׁבָּת וְנִפְתְּחָה־בָּר לְהַקְטִין אֵיפָה וּלְהַגְדִּיל שֶׁקֶל וּלְעַוֵּת

to and falsify the ,shekel to and enlarge the ephah to diminish the ,wheat we that so open may the Or ,sabbath

of deceit; [6] in order to
buy the helpless with silver,
and the poor for a pair of
sandals; and sell the chaff of
the wheat? [7] Jehovah has
sworn by the pride of
Jacob, Surely I will not
forget forever all their
works. [8] Shall not the
land tremble for this and all
who dwell in it mourn? And
all of it shall rise up like the
Nile. And it shall overflow
and sink like the Nile of
Egypt. [9] And it shall
come to pass in that day,
states the Lord Jehovah,
that I will cause the sun to
go down at noon, and I will
darken the earth in the day
of light. [10] And I will
turn your feasts to mourning, and all your songs into a
weeping; and I will bring up
sackcloth on all loins, and
baldness on every head.
And I will make it like the
mourning for an only one;
and the end of it like a bitter
day.

[11] Behold, the days
are coming, states the Lord
Jehovah, that I will send a
famine into the land — not a
famine for bread nor a thirst
for water, but rather to
hearing the words of Jehovah. [12] And they shall
wander from sea to sea, and
from the north even to the
east; they shall roam about
to seek the word of Jeho-
vah, and they shall not find
(it). [13] In that day the
beautiful virgins and the
young men shall faint with
thirst. [14] They who
swear by the guilt of
Samaria and say, (As) your
God lives, O Dan! And, (as)
the way of Beer-sheba lives!
Even they shall fall and not
rise up again.

CHAPTER 9

[1] I saw the Lord
standing by the altar. And
He said, Strike the capital of

---

6 מֹאזְנֵי מִרְמָה: לִקְנוֹת בַּכֶּסֶף דַּלִּים וְאֶבְיוֹן בַּעֲבוּר נַעֲלָיִם
of pair a | for | the and | the | with | buy | to | ;deceit | the
,sandals | | poor | ,helpless | silver | | | | of balances

7 וּמַפַּל בַּר נַשְׁבִּיר: נִשְׁבַּע יְהוָה בִּגְאוֹן יַעֲקֹב אִם־אֶשְׁכַּח
will I | Not | ,Jacob | the by | Jehovah | Has | may we | the the that
forget | | | of pride | | sworn | .sell | wheat of chaff

8 לָנֶצַח כָּל־מַעֲשֵׂיהֶם: הַעַל זֹאת לֹא־תִרְגַּז הָאָרֶץ וְאָבַל
and | the | will | not | this | Because | their | all | for
mourn | ,land | quake | | | of | .works | | ever

כָּל־יוֹשֵׁב בָּהּ וְעָלְתָה כָאֹר כֻּלָּהּ וְנִגְרְשָׁה וְנִשְׁקָה כִּיאוֹר
the like | sinks and | it and | of all | the like | will And | ?it in | who | all
of Nile | down | overflows | ;it | Nile | up rise | | dwell

9 מִצְרָיִם: וְהָיָה בַּיּוֹם הַהוּא נְאֻם אֲדֹנָי יְהוִה וְהֵבֵאתִי
will I that | ,Jehovah | the declares | ,that | day in | it And | .Egypt
set make | | Lord | | | be shall |

10 הַשֶּׁמֶשׁ בַּצָּהֳרָיִם וְהַחֲשַׁכְתִּי לָאָרֶץ בְּיוֹם אוֹר: וְהָפַכְתִּי
will I And | .light | the in | the | will I and | ,noon at | sun the
turn | | of day | earth | dark make | |

חַגֵּיכֶם לְאֵבֶל וְכָל־שִׁירֵיכֶם לְקִינָה וְהַעֲלֵיתִי עַל־כָּל־מָתְנַיִם
loins | all | on | will I and | a into | your | and to | your
| | | up bring | ;dirge | songs | all | ,mourning feasts

שָׂק וְעַל־כָּל־רֹאשׁ קָרְחָה וְשַׂמְתִּיהָ כְּאֵבֶל יָחִיד וְאַחֲרִיתָהּ
it after and | only an | the like | will I And | .baldness | head | every and | and sack-
;son for mourning | | | it make | | | | on | cloth

11 כְּיוֹם מָר: הִנֵּה יָמִים בָּאִים נְאֻם אֲדֹנָי יְהוִה וְהִשְׁלַחְתִּי
will I that | ,Jehovah | the declares | are | the | ,Behold | bitter- a like
send | | Lord | ,coming | days | | .ness of day

רָעָב בָּאָרֶץ לֹא־רָעָב לַלֶּחֶם וְלֹא־צָמָא לַמַּיִם כִּי אִם־
but | for | a | and | for | a | not | the into | a
rather | ,water | thirst | not | ,bread | famine | | —land | famine

12 לִשְׁמֹעַ אֵת דִּבְרֵי יְהוָה: וְנָעוּ מִיָּם עַד־יָם וּמִצָּפוֹן וְעַד־
even | from and | ,sea to | from | they And | .Jehovah | the | hear to
to | north | | sea | stagger will | | of words

13 מִזְרָח יְשׁוֹטְטוּ לְבַקֵּשׁ אֶת־דְּבַר־יְהוָה וְלֹא יִמְצָאוּ: בַּיּוֹם
day In | will they and | Jehovah | the | seek to | will they | the
.(it) find | not | of word | | about roam | ;east

הַהוּא תִּתְעַלַּפְנָה הַבְּתוּלֹת הַיָּפוֹת וְהַבַּחוּרִים בַּצָּמָא:
with | the and | beautiful | virgins the | faint | will | that
.thirst | men young |

14 הַנִּשְׁבָּעִים בְּאַשְׁמַת שֹׁמְרוֹן וְאָמְרוּ חֵי אֱלֹהֶיךָ דָּן וְחֵי דֶּרֶךְ
the (as) And | O | your | (As) | ,say and | Samaria | the by | swearing Those
of way | lives | !Dan | ,God | lives | | of guilt |

בְּאֵר־שֶׁבַע וְנָפְלוּ וְלֹא־יָקוּמוּ עוֹד:
.again | rise | and they | so | ,sheba | Beer-
| up | not | fall will |

CAP. IX ט

CHAPTER 9

1 רָאִיתִי אֶת־אֲדֹנָי נִצָּב עַל־הַמִּזְבֵּחַ וַיֹּאמֶר הַךְ הַכַּפְתּוֹר
the | Strike | He And | .altar the | by standing | the | saw I
capital | | ,said | | | Lord |

the door, and the thresholds will shake; and break them on the head of all of them. And I will kill the rest of them with the sword. Not one of them fleeing shall flee, and not a fugitive of them shall escape.
[2] And if they dig into Sheol, from there My hand shall take them. And if they go up to the heavens, I will bring them down from there. [3] And if they hide themselves in the top of Carmel, I will search and take them out from there. And if they hide from My eyes in the bottom of the sea, from there I will command the serpent and he shall bite them. [4] And if they go into captivity before their enemies, from there I will command the sword, and it shall kill them; and I will set My eyes on them for evil, and not for good. [5] And the Lord Jehovah of hosts (is) He who touches the earth so that it melts; and all dwelling in it shall mourn. And all of it will rise up like the Nile, and sink down like the Nile of Egypt. [6] (It is) He who builds His staircase in the heavens, and He has founded His firmament on the earth; He who calls for the sea-waters and pours them out on the earth's face—Jehovah His name. [7] Are you not like the sons of the Ethiopians to Me, O sons of Israel, states Jehovah? Have I not brought Israel up out of the land of Egypt, and the Philistines from Caphtor, and the Syrians from Kir? [8] Behold, the eyes of the Lord Jehovah (are) on the sinful kingdom, and I will destroy it from the face of the earth; only that I will not completely destroy the house of Jacob, states Jehovah. [9] For, behold, I will command, and I will shake the house of

וירעשו הספים ובצעם בראש כלם ואחריתם בחרב
the with sword | rest the And them of | of all .them | the on of head | break and them | the ;thresholds | will and shake

2 אהרג לא־ינוס להם נס ולא־ימלט להם פליט׃ אם־
If | a .fugitive | of them | will escape | and not | one ,fleeing | of them | will Not flee | will I .kill

יחתרו בשאול משם ידי תקחם ואם־יעלו השמים משם
from there | the ,heavens | go they to up | And if | shall .them take | My hand | from there | into ,Sheol | dig they though

3 אורידם׃ ואם־יחבאו בראש הכרמל משם אחפש
will I search | from there | ,Carmel | the in of top | hide they themselves | And if | bring will I .down them

ולקחתים ואם־יסתרו מנגד עיני בקרקע הים משם אצוה
will I command | from there | the ,sea | the in of bottom | My eye | from before | they hide | And if | take will I and .them

4 את־הנחש ונשכם׃ ואם־ילכו בשבי לפני איביהם משם
from there | their ,enemies | before | into captivity | they go | And if | will it and .them bite | the serpent

אצוה את־החרב והרגתם ושמתי עיני עליהם לרעה
,evil for | them on | My eye | I and set will | will it and ;them kill | the ,sword | will I command

5 ולא לטובה׃ ואדני יהוה הצבאות הנוגע בארץ ותמוג
that so ,melts it | the earth | who He touches | hosts (is) | Jehovah of | the And Lord | .good for | and not

ואבלו כל־יושבי בה ועלתה כיאר כלה ושקעה כיאר
the like of Nile | sink and down | of all it | the like Nile | will And up rise | .it in | who dwell | all | shall and mourn

6 מצרים׃ הבונה בשמים מעלותו ואגדתו על־ארץ יסדה
has He ;it founded | the earth | over | His and ,firmament | His ;staircase | the in heavens | who He builds | .Egypt

הקרא למי־הים וישפכם על־פני הארץ יהוה שמו׃
His .name | Jehovah (is) | the —earth | the on of face | pours and out them | the the for sea of waters | who He calls

7 הלוא כבני כשיים אתם לי בני־ישראל נאם־יהוה
?Jehovah de-clares | ,Israel | sons O of | to ,me | you | the Ethiopians | the like of sons | Are not

הלוא את־ישראל העליתי מארץ מצרים ופלשתיים
the and Philistines | ,Egypt | the from of land | I Have up brought | Israel | not

8 מכפתור וארם מקיר׃ הנה עיני ׀ אדני יהוה בממלכה
the on kingdom | Jehovah (are) | the Lord | the ,Behold of eyes | from ?Kir | and Aram | from ,Caphtor

החטאה והשמדתי אתה מעל פני האדמה אפס כי לא
not | that only | the ;earth | the from of face | it | will I and destroy | ,sinful

9 השמיד אשמיד את־בית יעקב נאם־יהוה׃ כי־הנה אנכי
I | ,behold For | .Jehovah de-clares | ,Jacob | house the of | will I destroy | fully

מצוה והנעותי בכל־הגוים את־בית ישראל כאשר ינוע
one shakes | as | ,Israel | house the of | the nations | among all | will I and shake | com-am ,manding

Israel among all the nations,
as one shakes with a sieve,
yet not a grain shall fall (to)
the ground. [10] All the
sinners of My people shall
die by the sword, (those)
who say, The evil shall not
come near or go before us.
[11] In that day I will
raise up the booth of David
that has fallen, and will wall
up its breaks. And I will
raise up its ruins, and I will
build it as the days of old;
[12] so that they may
possess the remnant of
Edom and all the nations
(on) whom My name is
called, states Jehovah who
is doing this. [13] Behold,
the days are coming, states
Jehovah, that the plowman
shall overtake the reaper,
and the treader of grapes
him who sows seed. And the
mountains shall drop new
wine, and all the hills will be
dissolved. [14] And I will
again bring the captivity of
My people Israel, and they
shall build the waste cities
and live in (them); and they
shall plant vineyards and
drink the wine of them.
They shall also make gar-
dens and eat the fruit of
them. [15] And I will plant
them on their land, and
they shall no more be pulled
up out of their land which I
have given to them, says
Jehovah your God.

10 בִּכְבָרָה וְלֹא־יִפּוֹל צְרוֹר אָרֶץ׃ בַּחֶרֶב יָמוּתוּ כֹּל חַטָּאֵי
the all die shall the By the (to) a shall yet a with
of sinners sword .ground pebble fall not ,sieve

11 עַמִּי הָאֹמְרִים לֹא־תַגִּישׁ וְתַקְדִּים בַּעֲדֵינוּ הָרָעָה׃ בַּיּוֹם
day In the us about come or will not saying those My
.calamity front in near draw ,people

הַהוּא אָקִים אֶת־סֻכַּת דָּוִיד הַנֹּפֶלֶת וְגָדַרְתִּי אֶת־פִּרְצֵיהֶן
.breaches its wall and has that David booth the will I that
up fallen of up raise

12 וַהֲרִסֹתָיו אָקִים וּבְנִיתִיהָ כִּימֵי עוֹלָם׃ לְמַעַן יִירְשׁוּ אֶת־
may they so ;old the as will I and will I its And
possess that of days it rebuild ,up raise ruins

שְׁאֵרִית אֱדוֹם וְכָל־הַגּוֹיִם אֲשֶׁר־נִקְרָא שְׁמִי עֲלֵיהֶם נְאֻם־
declares upon My called is whom the and Edom rem- the
,them name nations all of nant

13 יְהוָה עֹשֶׂה זֹּאת׃ הִנֵּה יָמִים בָּאִים נְאֻם־יְהוָה וְנִגַּשׁ
shall and ,Jehovah de- are the ,Behold .this is who Jeho-
near draw clares coming days doing vah

חוֹרֵשׁ בַּקֹּצֵר וְדֹרֵךְ עֲנָבִים בְּמֹשֵׁךְ הַזָּרַע וְהִטִּיפוּ הֶהָרִים
the will And the the grapes he and the the
mountains drip .seed of sower treads who ,reaper plowman

14 עָסִיס וְכָל־הַגְּבָעוֹת תִּתְמוֹגַגְנָה׃ וְשַׁבְתִּי אֶת־שְׁבוּת עַמִּי
My cap- the I And be will hills the and ,must
people of tivity turn will .dissolved all

יִשְׂרָאֵל וּבָנוּ עָרִים נְשַׁמּוֹת וְיָשָׁבוּ וְנָטְעוּ כְרָמִים וְשָׁתוּ אֶת־
and ,vineyards they and they and are which the they and ,Israel
drink plant shall ,dwell shall ,desolate cities build shall

15 יֵינָם וְעָשׂוּ גַנּוֹת וְאָכְלוּ אֶת־פְּרִיהֶם׃ וּנְטַעְתִּים עַל־אַדְמָתָם
their on will I And their and gardens they And their
,land them plant .fruit eat make shall .wine

וְלֹא יִנָּתְשׁוּ עוֹד מֵעַל אַדְמָתָם אֲשֶׁר־נָתַתִּי לָהֶם אָמַר
says to have I which their from again will they and
,them given land uprooted be not

יְהוָה אֱלֹהֶיךָ׃
your Jehovah
.God

CHAPTER 1

[1] The vision of Obadiah: Thus says the Lord Jehovah concerning Edom, We have heard a message from Jehovah, and a messenger is sent among the nations; arise, and let us rise up against her for battle. [2] Behold, I have given you small among the nations; you are greatly despised.

[3] The pride of your heart has deceived you, dwelling in the clefts of the rock, his dwelling (is) high; who says in his heart, Who shall bring me down to the ground? [4] Though you rise high as the eagle, and though (you) set your nest between the stars, I will bring you down from there, states Jehovah. [5] If thieves came to you, if destroyers by night — how you have been like them! Would they not have stolen until they had enough? If the grape-gatherers came to you, would they not leave gleanings? [6] How Esau is searched out! His hidden things are sought out! [7] All the men of your covenant have dismissed you to the border; the men who were at peace with you have deceived you (and) have prevailed over you. They are setting your bread a snare under you; no understanding (is) in him. [8] Shall I not in that day even destroy the wise out of Edom and understanding out of the mount of Esau, states Jehovah? [9] And your mighty ones, Teman, shall be afraid, so that each man from the mount of Esau may be cut off by slaughter.

[10] Shame shall cover you from the violence against your brother Jacob, and you shall be cut off forever. [11] On the day of your standing opposite, on

ע ב ד י ה

LIBER OBADIAE

CAPUT. I א

CHAPTER 1

1 חֲזוֹן עֹבַדְיָה כֹּה־אָמַר אֲדֹנָי יְהוִה לֶאֱדוֹם שְׁמוּעָה שָׁמַעְנוּ

have we heard | message a | concerning ,Edom | Jehovah | the Lord | says Thus | :Obadiah | The vision of

מֵאֵת יְהוָה וְצִיר בַּגּוֹיִם שֻׁלָּח קוּמוּ וְנָקוּמָה עָלֶיהָ

against her | us let and up rise | Rise ,up | ;sent is | the among nations | a and messenger | ,Jehovah | from

2 לַמִּלְחָמָה׃ הִנֵּה קָטֹן נְתַתִּיךָ בַּגּוֹיִם בָּזוּי אַתָּה מְאֹד׃

.greatly | you (are) | being despised | the among ;nations | have I you given | small | ,Behold | .battle for

3 זְדוֹן לִבְּךָ הִשִּׁיאֶךָ שֹׁכְנִי בְחַגְוֵי־סֶלַע מְרוֹם שִׁבְתּוֹ אֹמֵר

saying | his ;dwelling | lofty (is) | the ,rock | the in of clefts | dwelling | deceived has ,you | your heart of | The pride

4 בְּלִבּוֹ מִי יוֹרִדֵנִי אָרֶץ׃ אִם־תַּגְבִּיהַּ כַּנֶּשֶׁר וְאִם־בֵּין כּוֹכָבִים

the stars | between | and though | the as ,eagle | rise you high | Though | the (to) ?ground | bring shall down me | Who | his in ,heart

5 שִׂים קִנֶּךָ מִשָּׁם אוֹרִידְךָ נְאֻם־יְהוָה׃ אִם־גַּנָּבִים בָּאוּ־לְךָ

to ,you | came | thieves | If | .Jehovah declares | will I ,down you bring | from there | your ,nest | set to

אִם־שׁוֹדְדֵי לַיְלָה אֵיךְ נִדְמֵיתָה הֲלוֹא יִגְנְבוּ דַּיָּם אִם־

If | their ?sufficiency | have they stolen | Would not | been have you !(them) like | how | by —night | those destroying | if

6 בֹּצְרִים בָּאוּ לָךְ הֲלוֹא יַשְׁאִירוּ עֹלֵלוֹת׃ אֵיךְ נֶחְפְּשׂוּ עֵשָׂו

!Esau | searched is out | How | ?gleanings | they leave | would not | to ,you | came | pick- those grapes ing

7 נִבְעוּ מַצְפֻּנָיו׃ עַד־הַגְּבוּל שִׁלְּחוּךָ כֹּל אַנְשֵׁי בְרִיתֶךָ

your ;covenant | men the of | all | have they ,you dismissed | the border | To | hidden his !things | are sought

הִשִּׁיאוּךָ יָכְלוּ לְךָ אַנְשֵׁי שְׁלֹמֶךָ לַחְמְךָ יָשִׂימוּ מָזוֹר תַּחְתֶּיךָ

under ;you | a (as) snare | are they setting | Your bread | your .peace | men the of | over have (and) you prevailed | de- they you luded

8 אֵין תְּבוּנָה בּוֹ׃ הֲלוֹא בַּיּוֹם הַהוּא נְאֻם־יְהוָה וְהַאֲבַדְתִּי

I even destroy | ,Jehovah declares | ,that | the in day | Shall not | in .him | under standing | there no is

9 חֲכָמִים מֵאֱדוֹם וּתְבוּנָה מֵהַר עֵשָׂו׃ וְחַתּוּ גִבּוֹרֶיךָ תֵּימָן

Teman | your ,ones mighty | shall And afraid be | ?Esau | the from of mountain | under- and standing | Edom from | wise the ones

10 לְמַעַן יִכָּרֶת־אִישׁ מֵהַר עֵשָׂו מִקָּטֶל׃ מֵחֲמַס אָחִיךָ יַעֲקֹב

Jacob | your brother | the from against violence | slaugh- by ;ter | Esau | the from of mountain | each man | be may off cut | so that

11 תְּכַסְּךָ בוּשָׁה וְנִכְרַתָּ לְעוֹלָם׃ בְּיוֹם עֲמָדְךָ מִנֶּגֶד בְּיוֹם

the on of day | ,opposite | your standing | the On of day | .forever | shall you and off cut be | ,shame | shall you cover

the day that the strangers took captive his force, and foreigners entered his gates and cast lots for Jerusalem, even you (were) like one of them. [12] But you should not have looked on your brother's day, on the day of his estrangement; nor should you have rejoiced over the sons of Judah in the day of their ruin; nor should you have enlarged your mouth in the day of distress. [13] You should not have entered into My people's gate on the day of his calamity, nor should you have sent out against his force in the day of his calamity. [14] Nor should you have stood on the crossways to cut off his escapees; nor should you have shut up his survivors in the day of distress. [15] For Jehovah's day (is) near on all the nations; as you have done, it shall be done to you; your reward shall return on your head. [16] For as you have drunk on My holy mount, (so) all the nations shall drink always. Yea, they shall drink, and shall swallow; and they will be as (if) they had not been.

[17] But the escapees shall be on Mount Zion, and it shall be holy; and the house of Jacob shall possess their own possessions. [18] And the house of Jacob shall be a fire, and the house of Joseph a flame, and the house of Esau for straw. And they shall burn among them and consume them And no survivor shall be to the house of Esau, for Jehovah has spoken. [19] And Negev shall possess Esau's mountain, and the Philistines' low country; and they shall possess Ephraim's fields and Samaria's fields; and Benjamin (and) Gilead. [20] And the exiles of this force to the sons of Israel (shall) possess (that of) the Canaanites, to Zarephath; and the exiles of Jerusalem, who (are) in Sepharad, the cities of the Negev. [21] And deliverers shall

שְׁבוֹת זָרִים חֵילוֹ וְנָכְרִים בָּאוּ שְׁעָרָו וְעַל־יְרוּשָׁלִַם יַדּוּ
cast Jerusalem and his entered and his the taking
for gates foreigners ,force strangers captive

12 גוֹרָל גַּם־אַתָּה כְּאַחַד מֵהֶם׃ וְאַל־תֵּרֶא בְיוֹם־אָחִיךָ בְּיוֹם
the on your the on should you But of like you even ,lots
of day brother of day looked have not .them one (were)

נָכְרוֹ וְאַל־תִּשְׂמַח לִבְנֵי־יְהוּדָה בְּיוֹם אָבְדָם וְאַל־תַּגְדֵּל
should you and their the in Judah the over should you and es- his
enlarged have not ;destruction of day of sons rejoiced have not ;trangement

13 פִּיךָ בְּיוֹם צָרָה׃ אַל־תָּבוֹא בְשַׁעַר־עַמִּי בְּיוֹם אֵידָם אַל־
not their the on My the into should You not .distress the in your
;calamity of day people of gate entered have of day mouth

תֵּרֶא גַם־אַתָּה בְּרָעָתוֹ בְּיוֹם אֵידוֹ וְאַל־תִּשְׁלַחְנָה בְחֵילוֹ
his against should you and his the on his on you even should
force out sent have not ,calamity of day evil looked have

14 בְּיוֹם אֵידוֹ׃ וְאַל־תַּעֲמֹד עַל־הַפֶּרֶק לְהַכְרִית אֶת־פְּלִיטָיו
his off cut to the upon should you And his the in
;escapees ,crossways stood have not .calamity of day

15 וְאַל־תַּסְגֵּר שְׂרִידָיו בְּיוֹם צָרָה׃ כִּי־קָרוֹב יוֹם־יְהוָה עַל־
upon Jehovah the near For .distress the in sur- his should you and
of day (is) of day vivors up shut have not

כָּל־הַגּוֹיִם כַּאֲשֶׁר עָשִׂיתָ יֵעָשֶׂה לָּךְ גְּמֻלְךָ יָשׁוּב בְּרֹאשֶׁךָ׃
your on shall your to shall it have you as the all
.head return reward ;you done be ,done ;nations

16 כִּי כַּאֲשֶׁר שְׁתִיתֶם עַל־הַר קָדְשִׁי יִשְׁתּוּ כָל־הַגּוֹיִם תָּמִיד
con- the all shall holi- My the upon have you as For
.tinually nations drink ,ness of mountain drunk

17 וְשָׁתוּ וְלָעוּ וְהָיוּ כְּלוֹא הָיוּ׃ וּבְהַר צִיּוֹן תִּהְיֶה פְלֵיטָה
who those shall Zion the on But had they not as and swal- and they And
,escaped have be of mountain .been be will lowed ,drank

18 וְהָיָה קֹדֶשׁ וְיָרְשׁוּ בֵּית יַעֲקֹב אֵת מוֹרָשֵׁיהֶם׃ וְהָיָה בֵית־
the shall And own their Jacob the shall and ;holy it and
of house be .possessions of house possess be shall

יַעֲקֹב אֵשׁ וּבֵית יוֹסֵף לֶהָבָה וּבֵית עֵשָׂו לְקַשׁ וְדָלְקוּ בָהֶם
among they And for Esau the and a Joseph the and a Jacob
them burn shall .straw of house ,flame of house ,fire

וַאֲכָלוּם וְלֹא־יִהְיֶה שָׂרִיד לְבֵית עֵשָׂו כִּי יְהוָה דִּבֵּר׃
has Jehovah for ,Esau the to sur- a shall there And con- and
.spoken of house vivor be not .them sume

19 וְיָרְשׁוּ הַנֶּגֶב אֶת־הַר עֵשָׂו וְהַשְּׁפֵלָה אֶת־פְּלִשְׁתִּים וְיָרְשׁוּ
they and ;Philistines the low the and ,Esau the (of those) shall And
possess shall of country of mountain Negev possess

אֶת־שְׂדֵה אֶפְרַיִם וְאֵת שְׂדֵה שֹׁמְרוֹן וּבִנְיָמִן אֶת־הַגִּלְעָד׃
.Gilead (with) and ;Samaria the and Ephraim fields the
Benjamin of fields of

20 וְגָלֻת הַחֵל־הַזֶּה לִבְנֵי יִשְׂרָאֵל אֲשֶׁר־כְּנַעֲנִים עַד־צָרְפַת
;Zarephath (is) the who Israel the to this the And
to Canaanites (are) of sons force of exiles

21 וְגָלֻת יְרוּשָׁלִַם אֲשֶׁר בִּסְפָרַד יִרְשׁוּ אֵת עָרֵי הַנֶּגֶב׃ וְעָלוּ
shall And the the shall they ;Sepharad in who Jerusalem the and
up go .south of cities possess (are) of exile

come into the mountain of Zion to judge the mountain of Esau; and the kingdom shall be to Jehovah.

מוֹשִׁעִים בְּהַר צִיּוֹן לִשְׁפֹּט אֶת־הַר עֵשָׂו וְהָיְתָה לַיהוָה

to Jehovah | shall be | and | ;Esau | the mountain of | judge | to | Zion | the mountain of | into | those delivering

הַמְּלוּכָה׃ ׃

.Kingdom the

י ו נ ה

LIBER JONAE

CAPUT. I א

CHAPTER 1

CHAPTER 1

[1] And the word of Jehovah was to Jonah the son of Amittai, saying, [2] Arise, go to Nineveh, the great city, and cry out against it; for their wickedness has come up before Me. [3] But Jonah rose up to flee to Tarshish from before Jehovah; and went down to Joppa. And he found a ship going to Tarshish; and he gave its fare, and went down into it, in order to go with them to Tarshish, from before Jehovah.

[4] But Jehovah hurled a great wind into the sea, and there was a mighty storm in the sea, so that the ship was near to be broken. [5] Then the seamen were afraid, and each man cried to his gods, and they threw out the goods that (were) in the ship into the sea in order to lighten (it) from upon them. But Jonah had gone down into the hold of the ship; and he lay down, and was sound asleep. [6] And the chief of the seamen came near to him and said to him, What is it to you, O sound sleeper? Arise, cry out to your god! It may be our god will notice us, and we will not perish. [7] And they said, each one to his fellow, Come and let us cast lots, so that we may know on whose account this evil (has come) to us. So they cast lots, and the lot fell on Jonah. [8] Then they said to him, Please tell us, on whose account (is) this evil to us? What (is) your business? And where do you

1 2 וַיְהִי דְּבַר־יְהוָֹה אֶל־יוֹנָה בֶן־אֲמִתַּי לֵאמֹר׃ קוּם לֵךְ
go ,Arise ,saying ,Amittai the Jonah to Jehovah the And
of son of word was

אֶל־נִינְוֵה הָעִיר הַגְּדוֹלָה וּקְרָא עָלֶיהָ כִּי־עָלְתָה רָעָתָם
their come has for against cry and ,great the ,Nineveh to
evil up ;it out city

3 לְפָנָי׃ וַיָּקָם יוֹנָה לִבְרֹחַ תַּרְשִׁישָׁה מִלִּפְנֵי יְהוָֹה וַיֵּרֶד
went and Jeho- from Tarshish to flee to Jonah rose But before
to down ;vah before up .Me

יָפוֹ וַיִּמְצָא אֳנִיָּה ׀ בָּאָה תַרְשִׁישׁ וַיִּתֵּן שְׂכָרָהּ וַיֵּרֶד בָּהּ
into went and its he and ;Tarshish to going ship a he And .Joppa
,it down ,fare gave found

4 לָבוֹא עִמָּהֶם תַּרְשִׁישָׁה מִלִּפְנֵי יְהוָֹה׃ וַיהוָֹה הֵטִיל רוּחַ־
a hurled But .Jehovah from ,Tarshish to with go to
wind Jehovah before them

גְּדוֹלָה אֶל־הַיָּם וַיְהִי סַעַר־גָּדוֹל בַּיָּם וְהָאֳנִיָּה חִשְּׁבָה
near was the and the in great a there and the into great
ship ,sea storm was ,sea

5 לְהִשָּׁבֵר׃ וַיִּירְאוּ הַמַּלָּחִים וַיִּזְעֲקוּ אִישׁ אֶל־אֱלֹהָיו וַיָּטִלוּ
they and his to each and the were And be to
hurled ,gods man cried ,sailors afraid .broken

אֶת־הַכֵּלִים אֲשֶׁר בָּאֳנִיָּה אֶל־הַיָּם לְהָקֵל מֵעֲלֵיהֶם וְיוֹנָה
And upon from lighten to the into the in which utensils the
Jonah .them (it) sea ship (were)

6 יָרַד אֶל־יַרְכְּתֵי הַסְּפִינָה וַיִּשְׁכַּב וַיֵּרָדַם׃ וַיִּקְרַב אֵלָיו רַב
the him to came And was and he and ,ship the re- the into had
of chief near .asleep sound ,down laid of cesses down gone

הַחֹבֵל וַיֹּאמֶר לוֹ מַה־לְּךָ נִרְדָּם קוּם קְרָא אֶל־אֱלֹהֶיךָ
your to cry ,Arise sound O to What to said and the
!God out ?sleeper ,you (it is) ,him ,seamen

7 אוּלַי יִתְעַשֵּׁת הָאֱלֹהִים לָנוּ וְלֹא נֹאבֵד׃ וַיֹּאמְרוּ אִישׁ אֶל־
to each they And will we and ,us of the take will Per-
man ,said .perish not god notice haps

רֵעֵהוּ לְכוּ וְנַפִּילָה גוֹרָלוֹת וְנֵדְעָה בְּשֶׁלְּמִי הָרָעָה הַזֹּאת
this evil whose on may we that ,lots us let and ,Go com- his
(happened) account know cast ,panion

8 לָנוּ וַיַּפִּלוּ גּוֹרָלוֹת וַיִּפֹּל הַגּוֹרָל עַל־יוֹנָה׃ וַיֹּאמְרוּ אֵלָיו
,him to they And .Jonah on lot the fell and ,lots they And to
said cast .us

הַגִּידָה־נָּא לָנוּ בַּאֲשֶׁר לְמִי־הָרָעָה הַזֹּאת לָנוּ מַה־מְּלַאכְתְּךָ
your What to this evil whom account on to Please tell
?occupation (is) ?us (is) of us

come from? What (is) your country, and of what people (are) you? [9] And he said to them, I (am) a Hebrew. And I fear Jehovah, the God of Heaven, who has made the sea and the dry land. [10] Then the men were afraid (with) a great fear. And (they) said to him, What is this (that) you have done? For the men knew that he was fleeing from before Jehovah, because he had told them. [11] Then they said to him, What shall we do to you, that the sea may be calm from on us? For the sea was going on and being stormy. [12] And he said to them, Take me up and throw me out into the sea. And the sea shall be calm from on you. For I know that this great storm is on you for my sake. [13] But the men rowed to return to the dry land. But they were not able, for the sea was going on and being stormy against them. [14] And they cried out to Jehovah and said, We beseech You, O Jehovah, we beseech You, let us not perish for this man's life, and do not lay on us innocent blood. For You, O Jehovah, have done as You desired. [15] And they lifted Jonah up and threw him into the sea; and the sea ceased from its raging. [16] Then the men feared Jehovah (with) a great fear and offered a sacrifice to Jehovah, and vowed vows.

9 וּמֵאַיִן תָּבוֹא מָה אַרְצֶךָ וְאֵי־מִזֶּה עַם אָתָּה׃ וַיֹּאמֶר
he said And | (are) ?you | people | from And what | your ?country | What (is) | you do ?come | from And where

אֲלֵיהֶם עִבְרִי אָנֹכִי וְאֶת־יְהוָה אֱלֹהֵי הַשָּׁמַיִם אֲנִי יָרֵא
,fear | I | heavens the | God the of | Jehovah And | I .(am) | a Hebrew | ,them to

10 אֲשֶׁר־עָשָׂה אֶת־הַיָּם וְאֶת־הַיַּבָּשָׁה׃ וַיִּירְאוּ הָאֲנָשִׁים יִרְאָה
(with) fear | men the | were And afraid | dry the .land | and | the sea | has made | who

גְדוֹלָה וַיֹּאמְרוּ אֵלָיו מַה־זֹּאת עָשִׂיתָ כִּי־יָדְעוּ הָאֲנָשִׁים כִּי־
that | the men | knew | For | have you ?done | this What (is) | to ,him | they And said | .great

11 מִלִּפְנֵי יְהוָה הוּא בֹרֵחַ כִּי הִגִּיד לָהֶם׃ וַיֹּאמְרוּ אֵלָיו
to him | they And said | to .them | had he (it) told | for | was ,fleeing | he | Jehovah | from before

מַה־נַּעֲשֶׂה לָּךְ וְיִשְׁתֹּק הַיָּם מֵעָלֵינוּ כִּי הַיָּם הוֹלֵךְ וְסֹעֵר׃
being and .stormy | was on going | the sea | For | upon from ?us | the sea | may that calm become | to you | we shall What do

12 וַיֹּאמֶר אֲלֵיהֶם שָׂאוּנִי וַהֲטִילֻנִי אֶל־הַיָּם וְיִשְׁתֹּק הַיָּם
the sea | will Then calmed be | the .sea | into | hurl and me | me Lift up | ,them to | he And said

מֵעֲלֵיכֶם כִּי יוֹדֵעַ אָנִי כִּי בְשֶׁלִּי הַסַּעַר הַגָּדוֹל הַזֶּה עֲלֵיכֶם׃
upon .you | this (is) | great | storm | account on me of | that | I | know | For | upon from .you

13 וַיַּחְתְּרוּ הָאֲנָשִׁים לְהָשִׁיב אֶל־הַיַּבָּשָׁה וְלֹא יָכֹלוּ כִּי הַיָּם
the sea | for | were they ,able | but not | the ,land dry | to | bring to back | the men | But rowed

14 הוֹלֵךְ וְסֹעֵר עֲלֵיהֶם׃ וַיִּקְרְאוּ אֶל־יְהוָה וַיֹּאמְרוּ אָנָּה יְהוָה
O ,Jehovah | ,Please | ,said and | Jehovah | to | they And out cried | against .them | being and stormy | was on going

אַל־נָא נֹאבְדָה בְּנֶפֶשׁ הָאִישׁ הַזֶּה וְאַל־תִּתֵּן עָלֵינוּ דָּם
blood | upon us | lay do | and not | ,this | man's | because life of | us let perish | please not

15 נָקִיא כִּי־אַתָּה יְהוָה כַּאֲשֶׁר חָפַצְתָּ עָשִׂיתָ׃ וַיִּשְׂאוּ
they And up lifted | You (so) .done have | You ,desired | as | O ,Jehovah | ,You | For | inno- .cent

16 אֶת־יוֹנָה וַיְטִלֻהוּ אֶל־הַיָּם וַיַּעֲמֹד הַיָּם מִזַּעְפּוֹ׃ וַיִּירְאוּ
And feared | its .raging | from | the sea | stood and (still) | the ;sea | into | hurled and him | Jonah

הָאֲנָשִׁים יִרְאָה גְדוֹלָה אֶת־יְהוָה וַיִּזְבְּחוּ־זֶבַח לַיהוָה
to ,Jehovah | sac- rifice | a | they and offered | ,Jehovah | great | a (with) fear | the men

וַיִּדְּרוּ נְדָרִים׃
.vows | and vowed

CAP. II ב

CHAPTER 2

[17] Now Jehovah had ordained a great fish to swallow Jonah. And Jonah

1 וַיְמַן יְהוָה דָּג גָּדוֹל לִבְלֹעַ אֶת־יוֹנָה וַיְהִי יוֹנָה בִּמְעֵי
the in | Jonah | And | .Jonah | to | great fish | a | Jeho- vah | had appointed Now

was in the belly of the fish three days and three nights.

CHAPTER 2

[1] Then Jonah prayed to Jehovah his God out of the fish's belly, [2] and said, I cried out from my distress to Jehovah, and He answered me. Out of the belly of Sheol I cried for help. You heard my voice. [3] For You cast me (into the) deep, into the heart of the seas, and the current encircled me. All Your breakers and Your waves passed over me. [4] Then I said, I am cast out from before Your eyes; yet I will look again toward Your holy temple. [5] Waters encompassed me, (even) to (my) soul. The depth closed around me; seaweed was clinging to my head. [6] I went down to the bottoms of the mountains; the earth with her bars (was) about me forever. But You brought up my life from the pit, O Jehovah my God. [7] When my soul fainted within me, I remembered Jehovah; and my prayer came to You, to Your holy temple. [8] Those who revere vain idols forsake their faithfulness; [9] but I will sacrifice to You with the voice of thanksgiving; I will fulfill that which I have vowed. Salvation (belongs) to Jehovah!

[10] And Jehovah spoke to the fish, and it vomited Jonah out onto the dry land.

2 הַדָּ֔ג שְׁלֹשָׁ֥ה יָמִ֖ים וּשְׁלֹשָׁ֥ה לֵילֽוֹת׃ וַיִּתְפַּלֵּ֣ל יוֹנָ֔ה אֶל־
to Jonah Then .nights three and days three the
prayed fish

3 יְהוָ֖ה אֱלֹהָ֑יו מִמְּעֵ֖י הַדָּגָֽה׃ וַיֹּ֗אמֶר קָ֠רָאתִי מִצָּ֥רָה לִ֛י
to the from cried I ,said and ,fish the the from his Jehovah
me distress out of stomach God

אֶל־יְהוָ֖ה וַֽיַּעֲנֵ֑נִי מִבֶּ֧טֶן שְׁא֛וֹל שִׁוַּ֖עְתִּי שָׁמַ֥עְתָּ קוֹלִֽי׃
my You (and) cried I Sheol the From He and Jehovah to
.voice heard help for of belly .me answered

4 וַתַּשְׁלִיכֵ֤נִי מְצוּלָה֙ בִּלְבַ֣ב יַמִּ֔ים וְנָהָ֖ר יְסֹבְבֵ֑נִי כָּל־מִשְׁבָּרֶ֥יךָ
Your All surrounded the and waters the into (the into) You For
breakers .me current of heart ,depths me threw

5 וְגַלֶּ֖יךָ עָלַ֥י עָבָֽרוּ׃ וַאֲנִ֣י אָמַ֔רְתִּי נִגְרַ֖שְׁתִּי מִנֶּ֣גֶד עֵינֶ֑יךָ אַ֚ךְ
Only Your from am I ,said I And .passed over Your and
.eyes before off cast me waves

6 אוֹסִ֣יף לְהַבִּ֔יט אֶל־הֵיכַ֖ל קָדְשֶֽׁךָ׃ אֲפָפ֤וּנִי מַ֙יִם֙ עַד־נֶ֔פֶשׁ
the to Waters encompassed Your temple to look will I
.soul me .holy again

7 תְּה֖וֹם יְסֹבְבֵ֑נִי ס֖וּף חָב֥וּשׁ לְרֹאשִֽׁי׃ לְקִצְבֵ֤י הָרִים֙ יָרַ֔דְתִּי
went I the the to my to was seaweed surrounded The
;down mountains of bases .head clinging ;me deep

הָאָ֛רֶץ בְּרִחֶ֥יהָ בַעֲדִ֖י לְעוֹלָ֑ם וַתַּ֧עַל מִשַּׁ֛חַת חַיַּ֖י יְהוָ֥ה
O my the from You But .forever (was) her with the
Jehovah ,life pit up brought me about bars earth

8 אֱלֹהָֽי׃ בְּהִתְעַטֵּ֤ף עָלַי֙ נַפְשִׁ֔י אֶת־יְהוָ֖ה זָכָ֑רְתִּי וַתָּב֤וֹא
came and I Jehovah my within fainted When my
;remembered ,soul me .God

9 אֵלֶ֙יךָ֙ תְּפִלָּתִ֔י אֶל־הֵיכַ֖ל קָדְשֶֽׁךָ׃ מְשַׁמְּרִ֖ים הַבְלֵי־שָׁ֑וְא
vanity vanities who Those Your temple to my to
of revere .holy ,prayer You

10 חַסְדָּ֖ם יַעֲזֹֽבוּ׃ וַאֲנִ֗י בְּק֤וֹל תּוֹדָה֙ אֶזְבְּחָה־לָּ֔ךְ אֲשֶׁ֥ר נָדַ֖רְתִּי
have I that to will thanks- the with but ;forsake their
vowed which ;You sacrifice giving of voice I faithfulness

11 אֲשַׁלֵּ֑מָה יְשׁוּעָ֖תָה לַיהוָֽה׃ וַיֹּ֥אמֶר יְהוָ֖ה לַדָּ֑ג וַיָּקֵ֥א אֶת־
it and the to Jehovah And .Jehovah to salvation will I
vomited ,fish spoke (belongs) fulfill

יוֹנָ֖ה אֶל־הַיַּבָּשָֽׁה׃
dry the on to Jonah
.land

CAP. III ג

CHAPTER 3

[1] And the word of Jehovah came to Jonah the second time, saying, [2] Arise, go to Nineveh, the great city, and proclaim to it the proclamation that I am declaring to you. [3] And Jonah arose and went to Nineveh, according to the word of Jehovah.

1
2 וַיְהִ֧י דְבַר־יְהוָ֛ה אֶל־יוֹנָ֖ה שֵׁנִ֥ית לֵאמֹֽר׃ ק֛וּם לֵ֥ךְ אֶל־נִֽינְוֵ֖ה
,Nineveh to go ,Arise ,saying second the Jonah to Jehovah the And
,time of word came

הָעִ֣יר הַגְּדוֹלָ֑ה וּקְרָ֤א אֵלֶ֙יהָ֙ אֶת־הַקְּרִיאָ֔ה אֲשֶׁ֥ר אָנֹכִ֖י
I that proclamation the it to cry and great the
out city

3 דֹּבֵ֥ר אֵלֶֽיךָ׃ וַיָּ֣קָם יוֹנָ֗ה וַיֵּ֛לֶךְ אֶל־נִֽינְוֶ֖ה כִּדְבַ֣ר יְהוָ֑ה
.Jehovah's according ,Nineveh to and ,Jonah rose And to de- am
word to went up .you claring

Now Nineveh was a great city to God of three days' journey. [4] And Jonah began to enter into the city a day's journey. And he cried out and said, Yet forty days and Nineveh shall be overthrown!

[5] So the men of Nineveh believed in God; and they called a fast and put on sackclothes; from the greatest of them even to the least of them. [6] And the word touched even to the king of Nineveh, and he arose from his throne. And he took his robe from him and covered himself (with) sackcloth, and sat on the ashes. [7] And he proclaimed and said in Nineveh by the decree of the king and his great ones, saying, Let not the man or the animal, the herd or the flock, taste anything. Let them not feed nor drink water. [8] But let man and animal be covered (with) sackcloth. And let them call with strength to God. And let them each one turn from his evil way, and from the violence that (is) in their hands. [9] Who knows? He may turn, and God may repent and turn away from His anger's glow, that we do not perish.

[10] And God saw their works, that they turned from their evil way. And God repented over the evil that He had declared to do to them, and He did not do (it).

וְנִינְוֵה הָיְתָה עִיר־גְּדוֹלָה לֵאלֹהִים מַהֲלַךְ שְׁלֹשֶׁת יָמִים׃
.days three a ,God to great city a was Now
journey Nineveh

4 וַיָּחֶל יוֹנָה לָבוֹא בָעִיר מַהֲלַךְ יוֹם אֶחָד וַיִּקְרָא וַיֹּאמַר
,said and he And .one day journey a the into to Jonah And
out cried of city enter began

5 עוֹד אַרְבָּעִים יוֹם וְנִינְוֵה נֶהְפָּכֶת׃ וַיַּאֲמִינוּ אַנְשֵׁי נִינְוֵה
Nineveh men the And be shall Nineveh and days forty Yet
of believed !overthrown

בֵּאלֹהִים וַיִּקְרְאוּ־צוֹם וַיִּלְבְּשׁוּ שַׂקִּים מִגְּדוֹלָם וְעַד־קְטַנָּם׃
their even their from sack- put and a they and ;God in
.least to greatest ;clothes on fast proclaimed

6 וַיִּגַּע הַדָּבָר אֶל־מֶלֶךְ נִינְוֵה וַיָּקָם מִכִּסְאוֹ וַיַּעֲבֵר אַדַּרְתּוֹ
robe his he and his from he and ,Nineveh the even the And
off took ,throne arose of king to word touched

7 מֵעָלָיו וַיְכַס שַׂק וַיֵּשֶׁב עַל־הָאֵפֶר׃ וַיַּזְעֵק וַיֹּאמֶר בְּנִינְוֵה
in said and he And the on sat and (with) and him from
Nineveh proclaimed .ashes ,sackcloth covered

מִטַּעַם הַמֶּלֶךְ וּגְדֹלָיו לֵאמֹר הָאָדָם וְהַבְּהֵמָה הַבָּקָר
the ,beast the and The ,saying his and the the by
herd man ,ones great king's decree

וְהַצֹּאן אַל־יִטְעֲמוּ מְאוּמָה אַל־יִרְעוּ וּמַיִם אַל־יִשְׁתּוּ׃
them let not and them let not ;anything taste let not the and
.drink water ,feed ,flock

8 וְיִתְכַּסּוּ שַׂקִּים הָאָדָם וְהַבְּהֵמָה וְיִקְרְאוּ אֶל־אֱלֹהִים
God to let And .beast and man (with) let But
call them sackcloth covered be

בְּחָזְקָה וְיָשֻׁבוּ אִישׁ מִדַּרְכּוֹ הָרָעָה וּמִן־הֶחָמָס אֲשֶׁר
that the and ,evil his from each let And with
(is) violence from way man turn .strength

9 בְּכַפֵּיהֶם׃ מִי־יוֹדֵעַ יָשׁוּב וְנִחַם הָאֱלֹהִים וְשָׁב מֵחֲרוֹן אַפּוֹ
His the from and God may and may He ,knows Who their in
,anger of glow turn repent ;turn .palms

10 וְלֹא נֹאבֵד׃ וַיַּרְא הָאֱלֹהִים אֶת־מַעֲשֵׂיהֶם כִּי־שָׁבוּ מִדַּרְכָּם
their from they that their God saw And will we that
way turned ,deeds .perish not

הָרָעָה וַיִּנָּחֶם הָאֱלֹהִים עַל־הָרָעָה אֲשֶׁר־דִּבֶּר לַעֲשׂוֹת־
do to had He that the over God And .evil
declared evil repented

לָהֶם וְלֹא עָשָׂה׃
did He and to
.(it) do not ,them

CAP. IV ד

CHAPTER 4

[1] But it was displeasing to Jonah and he became angry. [2] And he prayed to Jehovah and said, O Jehovah, was this not my saying while I was still on my land? Therefore I fled

1 2 וַיֵּרַע אֶל־יוֹנָה רָעָה גְדוֹלָה וַיִּחַר לוֹ׃ וַיִּתְפַּלֵּל אֶל־יְהוָה
Jehovah to he And for was it and ,great cal- a Jonah's to it But
prayed .him kindled lamity eye

וַיֹּאמַר אָנָּה יְהוָה הֲלוֹא־זֶה דְבָרִי עַד־הֱיוֹתִי עַל־אַדְמָתִי
own my on I while my this (Was) O ,Please ,said and
?land was word not ,Jehovah

before to Tarshish, for I knew that You (are) a gracious God, and merciful, slow to anger, and of great grace; and One who repents over calamity. [3] And now, O Jehovah, I beg You, take my life from Me. For better (is) my death than my life.

[4] And Jehovah said, Is anger kindled to you rightly? [5] And Jonah went out from the city and sat on the east of the city. And he made for himself a booth there, and sat under it in the shade until he should see what would happen in the city. [6] And Jehovah God ordained a plant, and it came up over Jonah to be shade over his head, in order to deliver him from his misery. And Jonah rejoiced with great joy over the plant. [7] But God ordained a worm when the dawn rose on the morrow; and it struck the plant and it withered. [8] And it came to pass, when the sun shone, that God ordained a scorching east wind; and the sun struck the head of Jonah, so that he fainted and he asked for his life to die. And he said, Better (is) my death then my life. [9] And God said to Jonah, Is your anger kindled rightly over the plant? And he said, My anger is kindled rightly, (even) to death. [10] Then Jehovah said, You have had pity on the plant, for which you had not labored nor made it grow — which was the son of a night, and perished the son of a night — [11] and should I not spare Nineveh, the great city, in which are more than

עַל־כֵּן קִדַּמְתִּי לִבְרֹחַ תַּרְשִׁישָׁה כִּי יָדַעְתִּי כִּי אַתָּה אֵל־
a You that know I for to flee did I Therefore
God (are) ,Tarshish first at

3 חַנּוּן וְרַחוּם אֶרֶךְ אַפַּיִם וְרַב־חֶסֶד וְנִחָם עַל־הָרָעָה׃ וְעַתָּה
And .calamity over One and ,grace and ,anger slow and ,gracious
,now repents who of great to ,compassionate

4 יְהוָה קַח־נָא אֶת־נַפְשִׁי מִמֶּנִּי כִּי טוֹב מוֹתִי מֵחַיָּי׃ וַיֹּאמֶר
said And my than my better For from life my please take O
.life death (is) .me ,Jehovah

5 יְהוָה הַהֵיטֵב חָרָה לָךְ׃ וַיֵּצֵא יוֹנָה מִן־הָעִיר וַיֵּשֶׁב
sat and the from Jonah Then to anger Is rightly ,Jehovah
city out went ?you kindled

מִקֶּדֶם לָעִיר וַיַּעַשׂ לוֹ שָׁם סֻכָּה וַיֵּשֶׁב תַּחְתֶּיהָ בַּצֵּל עַד
until the in it under sat and a there for he And the of the on
shade ,booth himself made .city east

6 אֲשֶׁר יִרְאֶה מַה־יִּהְיֶה בָּעִיר׃ וַיְמַן יְהוָה־אֱלֹהִים קִיקָיוֹן
,plant a God Jehovah And the in would what should he
appointed .city happen see

וַיַּעַל ׀ מֵעַל לְיוֹנָה לִהְיוֹת צֵל עַל־רֹאשׁוֹ לְהַצִּיל לוֹ מֵרָעָתוֹ
his from him to his over shade be to Jonah over it and
.misery deliver ,head up came

7 וַיִּשְׂמַח יוֹנָה עַל־הַקִּיקָיוֹן שִׂמְחָה גְדוֹלָה׃ וַיְמַן הָאֱלֹהִים
God But .great joy (with) plant the over Jonah And
appointed rejoiced

תּוֹלַעַת בַּעֲלוֹת הַשַּׁחַר לַמָּחֳרָת וַתַּךְ אֶת־הַקִּיקָיוֹן וַיִּיבָשׁ׃
it and ,plant the it and the of the the in worm a
.up dried struck ;morrow dawn of rising

8 וַיְהִי ׀ כִּזְרֹחַ הַשֶּׁמֶשׁ וַיְמַן אֱלֹהִים רוּחַ קָדִים חֲרִישִׁית
scorching east an God had that the when it And
wind appointed ,sun shone ,was

וַתַּךְ הַשֶּׁמֶשׁ עַל־רֹאשׁ יוֹנָה וַיִּתְעַלָּף וַיִּשְׁאַל אֶת־נַפְשׁוֹ
life his he And he that so ,Jonah the on sun the And
for asked .fainted of head struck

9 לָמוּת וַיֹּאמֶר טוֹב מוֹתִי מֵחַיָּי׃ וַיֹּאמֶר אֱלֹהִים אֶל־יוֹנָה
,Jonah to God said And my than my Better he And .die to
.life death (is) ,said

הַהֵיטֵב חָרָה־לְךָ עַל־הַקִּיקָיוֹן וַיֹּאמֶר הֵיטֵב חָרָה־לִי עַד־
(even) to Anger rightly he And ?plant the over to anger Is rightly
to me kindled is ,said you kindled

10 מָוֶת׃ וַיֹּאמֶר יְהוָה אַתָּה חַסְתָּ עַל־הַקִּיקָיוֹן אֲשֶׁר לֹא־
not which plant the on had You ,Jehovah said And .death
compassion

עָמַלְתָּ בּוֹ וְלֹא גִדַּלְתּוֹ שֶׁבִּן־לַיְלָה הָיָה וּבִן־לַיְלָה אָבָד׃
it night a the and was a the which made you and with did you
.perished of son night of son ,grow it not ,it labor

11 וַאֲנִי לֹא אָחוּס עַל־נִינְוֵה הָעִיר הַגְּדוֹלָה אֲשֶׁר יֶשׁ־בָּהּ
it in there which great city the Nineveh on have should not And
is compassion I

a hundred and twenty thousand persons who do not know between his right hand and his left hand, and many cattle?

הַרְבֵּה מִשְׁתֵּים־עֶשְׂרֵה רִבּוֹ אָדָם אֲשֶׁר לֹא־יָדַע בֵּין־יְמִינוֹ
his between right | do not know | who | men | ten thousand | twelve | than | more

לִשְׂמֹאלוֹ וּבְהֵמָה רַבָּה׃
?many | cattle and | his to ,left

מ י כ ה

LIBER MICHAE

CAPUT. I א

CHAPTER 1

CHAPTER 1

[1] The word of Jehovah that came to Micah the Morashthite in the days of Jotham, Ahaz (and) Hezekiah, kings of Judah, which he saw upon Samaria and Jerusalem. [2] Let the peoples hear, all of them. Attend, O earth, and its fullness. And let the Lord Jehovah be a witness against you, the Lord from His holy temple. [3] For, behold, Jehovah (is) coming out of His place, and will come down and walk on the high places of the earth. [4] And the mountains shall melt under Him, and the valleys shall cleave themselves, as wax before the fire, as waters poured out on a steep place. [5] All this (is) against the transgression of Jacob, and against the sins of the house of Israel. What (is) the transgression of Jacob? Is it not Samaria? And what (are) the high places of Judah? Are they not Jerusalem? [6] And I will make Samaria into ruins of the field, planting places for a vineyard. And I will pour down her stones into the valley, and I will uncover her foundations. [7] And all her graven images shall be beaten to pieces, and all her gifts shall be burned with fire, and I will make a desolation all her idols. For she gathered (it) from the reward of a harlot, and they shall return to the reward of a harlot. [8] Because of this I will wail and howl; I will go stripped and naked; I will make a wailing like the jackals; yea, mourn like the daughters of the ostrich. [9] For her wounds (are) incurable; for it has come to

1 דְּבַר־יְהוָה ׀ אֲשֶׁר הָיָה אֶל־מִיכָה הַמֹּרַשְׁתִּי בִּימֵי יוֹתָם
,Jotham the in of days the Morashthite Micah to was that Jehovah The of word

אָחָז יְחִזְקִיָּה מַלְכֵי יְהוּדָה אֲשֶׁר־חָזָה עַל־שֹׁמְרוֹן וִירוּשָׁלִָם׃
and .Jerusalem Samaria upon he saw which ,Judah kings of ,Hezekiah Ahaz (and)

2 שִׁמְעוּ עַמִּים כֻּלָּם הַקְשִׁיבִי אֶרֶץ וּמְלֹאָהּ וִיהִי אֲדֹנָי יֱהוִה
Jehovah the Lord let and be its and fulness O earth Pay ,attention of all .them the ,peoples hear Let

3 בָּכֶם לְעֵד אֲדֹנָי מֵהֵיכַל קָדְשׁוֹ׃ כִּי־הִנֵּה יְהוָה יֹצֵא
com- ing out (is) Jehovah ,behold ,For His .holiness the from of temple the Lord a for ,witness against you

4 מִמְּקוֹמוֹ וְיָרַד וְדָרַךְ עַל־בָּמוֹתֵי־אָרֶץ׃ וְנָמַסּוּ הֶהָרִים
the mountains shall And melt the .earth high the upon of places and tread will and come down His from ,place

תַּחְתָּיו וְהָעֲמָקִים יִתְבַּקָּעוּ כַּדּוֹנַג מִפְּנֵי הָאֵשׁ כְּמַיִם מֻגָּרִים
poured out as waters the ,fire before as wax cleave shall ,themselves the and valleys under ,Him

5 בְּמוֹרָד׃ בְּפֶשַׁע יַעֲקֹב כָּל־זֹאת וּבְחַטֹּאות בֵּית יִשְׂרָאֵל
.Israel the of house the against and of sins ,this all Jacob the Against (is) of transgression a on .slope

מִי־פֶשַׁע יַעֲקֹב הֲלוֹא שֹׁמְרוֹן וּמִי בָּמוֹת יְהוּדָה הֲלוֹא
(they Are) not ?Judah high the of places (are) And what ?Samaria (it Is) not ?Jacob the What of transgression (is)

6 יְרוּשָׁלִָם׃ וְשַׂמְתִּי שֹׁמְרוֹן לְעִי הַשָּׂדֶה לְמַטָּעֵי כָרֶם
vine- a .yard plantings ,field the into of ruins Samaria will I And make ?Jerusalem

7 וְהִגַּרְתִּי לַגַּי אֲבָנֶיהָ וִיסֹדֶיהָ אֲגַלֶּה׃ וְכָל־פְּסִילֶיהָ יֻכַּתּוּ
be shall ,smashed graven her images And all will I .bare lay her and foundations her ,stones the into valley will I And down pour

וְכָל־אֶתְנַנֶּיהָ יִשָּׂרְפוּ בָאֵשׁ וְכָל־עֲצַבֶּיהָ אָשִׂים שְׁמָמָה כִּי
For a .desolation will I make her idols and all with ,fire be shall burned her hires and all

8 מֵאֶתְנַן זוֹנָה קִבָּצָה וְעַד־אֶתְנַן זוֹנָה יָשׁוּבוּ׃ עַל־זֹאת
this Because of shall they .return a harlot the of hire to and gath- she ered (them) a harlot the from of hire

אֶסְפְּדָה וְאֵילִילָה אֵילְכָה שֵׁילָל וְעָרוֹם אֶעֱשֶׂה מִסְפֵּד
wailing a will I make and ;naked stripped will I go ;howl and will I wail

9 כַּתַּנִּים וְאֵבֶל כִּבְנוֹת יַעֲנָה׃ כִּי אֲנוּשָׁה מַכּוֹתֶיהָ כִּי־בָאָה
has it come for her ;wounds incurable For (are) the .ostrich the like of daughters and mourn the like ;jackals

Judah; it has reached to the gate of my people, to Jerusalem.

[10] Do not declare (it) in Gath; weeping do not weep; in the house of Leaphrah wallow (in) dust. [11] Pass over to them, O dweller of Shaphir, in nakedness of shame. The dweller of Zaanan has not gone out; the mourning of Beth-ezel shall take from you its place of standing. [12] For the inhabitant of Maroth wait for good; for evil came down from Jehovah to the gate of Jerusalem. [13] Inhabitant of Lachish, tie the chariot to the stallion; she (is) the beginning of sin to the daughter of Zion, for the transgressions of Israel were found in you. [14] Therefore you shall give parting gifts to Moresheth-gath. The houses of Achzib (are) for a lying thing to the kings of Israel. [15] I will bring again an heir to you, O dweller of Mareshah. The glory of Israel shall come to Adullam. [16] Make yourself bald, and cut off (your hair) for the sons of your delight. Make your baldness increase like the eagle; for they go into exile from you.

10 עַד־יְהוּדָה נָגַע עַד־שַׁעַר עַמִּי עַד־יְרוּשָׁלִָם׃ בְּגַת אַל־
not In .Jerusalem to my the to has it ;Judah to
Gath ,people of gate reached

תַּגִּידוּ בָּכוֹ אַל־תִּבְכּוּ בְּבֵית לְעַפְרָה עָפָר הִתְפַּלָּשְׁתִּי׃
.wallow dust (in) Leaphrah the in ;weep do not weeping do
of house ;(it) declare

11 עִבְרִי לָכֶם יוֹשֶׁבֶת שָׁפִיר עֶרְיָה־בֹשֶׁת לֹא יָצְאָה יוֹשֶׁבֶת
in- the gone has Not .shame in ,Shaphir inhab- O to Cross
of habitant out of nakedness of itant ,them over

12 צַאֲנָן מִסְפַּד בֵּית הָאֵצֶל יִקַּח מִכֶּם עֶמְדָּתוֹ׃ כִּי־חָלָה
wait For standing its from shall Haezel Beth- the ;Zaanon
.place you take of wailing

לְטוֹב יוֹשֶׁבֶת מָרוֹת כִּי־יָרַד רָע מֵאֵת יְהוָה לְשַׁעַר
the to Jehovah from evil came for ;Maroth inhabi- the for
of gate down of tant good

13 יְרוּשָׁלִָם׃ רְתֹם הַמֶּרְכָּבָה לָרֶכֶשׁ יוֹשֶׁבֶת לָכִישׁ רֵאשִׁית
be- the ;Lachish inhabitant the to chariot the Tie .Jerusalem
of ginning of ,stallion

14 חַטָּאת הִיא לְבַת־צִיּוֹן כִּי־בָךְ נִמְצְאוּ פִּשְׁעֵי יִשְׂרָאֵל׃ לָכֵן
There- .Israel trans- the were in for ,Zion the to she sin
fore of gressions found you of daughter (is)

תִּתְּנִי שִׁלּוּחִים עַל מוֹרֶשֶׁת גַּת בָּתֵּי אַכְזִיב לְאַכְזָב לְמַלְכֵי
the to a for (are) Achzib The .Gath Moresheth to parting shall you
of kings deception of houses gifts give

15 יִשְׂרָאֵל׃ עֹד הַיֹּרֵשׁ אָבִי לָךְ יוֹשֶׁבֶת מָרֵשָׁה עַד־עֲדֻלָּם
Adullam To .Mareshah inhabitant to will I the Again .Israel
of ,you bring inheritor

16 יָבוֹא כְּבוֹד יִשְׂרָאֵל׃ קָרְחִי וָגֹזִּי עַל־בְּנֵי תַּעֲנוּגָיִךְ הַרְחִבִי
Increase your the for and your- Make .Israel glory the shall
.delight of sons shear bald self of come

קָרְחָתֵךְ כַּנֶּשֶׁר כִּי־גָלוּ מִמֵּךְ׃
from go they for the like your
.you exile into ;eagle baldness

CAP. II ב

CHAPTER 2

[1] Woe to those plotting wickedness and working evil on their beds! In the light of the morning they practice it, because it is in the power of their hand. [2] And they covet fields and seize (them); and houses, and carry (them) away. So they oppress a man and his household, even a man and his inheritance. [3] Therefore thus says Jehovah: Behold, against this family I (am) planning an evil, which you shall not remove your necks from there; nor shall you go proudly, for it (is) an evil time.

1 הוֹי חֹשְׁבֵי־אָוֶן וּפֹעֲלֵי רָע עַל־מִשְׁכְּבוֹתָם בְּאוֹר הַבֹּקֶר
the the In !beds their on evil pre- and wick- those Woe
morning of light paring edness plotting (to)

2 יַעֲשׂוּהָ כִּי יֶשׁ־לְאֵל יָדָם׃ וְחָמְדוּ שָׂדוֹת וְגָזָלוּ וּבָתִּים
and seize and fields they And their the in it for do they
houses ,(them) covet .hand of power is ,it

3 וְנָשָׂאוּ וְעָשְׁקוּ גֶּבֶר וּבֵיתוֹ וְאִישׁ וְנַחֲלָתוֹ׃ לָכֵן כֹּה
thus Therefore his and a even his and man a they And carry and
.inheritance man ,household oppress .off (them)

אָמַר יְהוָה הִנְנִי חֹשֵׁב עַל־הַמִּשְׁפָּחָה הַזֹּאת רָעָה אֲשֶׁר
which ,evil an this family against (am) ,Behold :Jehovah says
plotting I

לֹא־תָמִישׁוּ מִשָּׁם צַוְּארֹתֵיכֶם וְלֹא תֵלְכוּ רוֹמָה כִּי עֵת
time for ,exalted you shall and your from shall you not
go not ;necks there remove

[4] In that day one shall lift up a parable against you and lament a lament of lamenting; he says, We shall be completely stripped; He has exchanged the share of my people. How He has removed (it) for me! To the apostate He has divided our fields. [5] Therefore there shall not be one casting a line by lot in the congregation of Jehovah. [6] Do not drop (words as) they drop! They shall not drop (words) about these; they shall not draw reproaches back.

[7] House of Jacob, (it is) said, The Spirit of Jehovah is limited, if these (are) His doings? Do not My words do good with the one walking upright? [8] Even yesterday, My people has risen up (like) an enemy. You strip off an inner robe from before an outer garment, from those who pass by trustfully, those returning (from) war. [9] You have thrown the wives of My people out from the house of her delight; from her children you have taken away My majesty forever. [10] Arise and depart! For this (is) not (your) rest; because of uncleanness (which) destroys, even a grievous destruction. [11] If a man walks (with) wind, and (in) deceit he lies, (saying), I will drop (words) to you for wine and for fermented drink, he shall even be the (word) dropper for this people.

[12] I will surely gather all of you, Jacob; I will surely gather the remnant of Israel. I will set him together like the sheep of Bozrah, like a flock in the midst of its fold. They shall make a commotion because of men. [13] The breaker has come up before them; they have broken up and have passed through the gate and have gone out by it. And their king shall pass through before them, and Jehovah at the head of them.

4 רָעָה הִיא׃ בַּיּוֹם הַהוּא יִשָּׂא עֲלֵיכֶם מָשָׁל וְנָהָה נְהִי
a lament and a against shall one that day In it evil an
of lament ,parable you up lift .(is)

נִהְיָה אָמַר שָׁדוֹד נְשַׁדֻּנוּ חֵלֶק עַמִּי יָמִיר אֵיךְ יָמִישׁ לִי
for has He How has He my portion The be shall we Destroy- he lament-
!me (it) removed .exchanged people of .destroyed ing ,says ;ing

5 לְשׁוֹבֵב שָׂדֵינוּ יְחַלֵּק׃ לָכֵן לֹא־יִהְיֶה לְךָ מַשְׁלִיךְ חֶבֶל
mea- a one for shall there not There- has He our the To
line suring casting you be fore .divided fields apostate

6 בְּגוֹרָל בִּקְהַל יְהוָה׃ אַל־תַּטִּפוּ יַטִּיפוּן לֹא־יַטִּפוּ לָאֵלֶּה
about shall they Not they (as) do Not .Jehovah the in by
;these (words) drop .drop (words) drop of assembly lot

7 לֹא יִסַּג כְּלִמּוֹת׃ הֶאָמוּר בֵּית־יַעֲקֹב הֲקָצַר רוּחַ יְהוָה
,Jehovah the Is ,Jacob house (it Is) .reproaches shall not
of Spirit limited of ,said back draw

אִם־אֵלֶּה מַעֲלָלָיו הֲלוֹא דְבָרַי יֵיטִיבוּ עִם הַיָּשָׁר הוֹלֵךְ׃
?walking up- the with doing My (Are) His these if
one right good words not ?doings (are)

8 וְאֶתְמוּל עַמִּי לְאוֹיֵב יְקוֹמֵם מִמּוּל שַׂלְמָה אֶדֶר תַּפְשִׁטוּן
strip you a a From risen have an as My Even
,off cloak garment before .up enemy people ,yesterday

9 מֵעֹבְרִים בֶּטַח שׁוּבֵי מִלְחָמָה׃ נְשֵׁי עַמִּי תְּגָרְשׁוּן מִבֵּית
the from have you My The .war (from) those confi- those from
of house out driven people of wives returning ,dently by passing

10 תַּעֲנֻגֶיהָ מֵעַל עֹלָלֶיהָ תִּקְחוּ הֲדָרִי לְעוֹלָם׃ קוּמוּ וּלְכוּ כִּי
For and Arise .forever My have you her from her
!go majesty taken children upon ;delight

11 לֹא־זֹאת הַמְּנוּחָה בַּעֲבוּר טָמְאָה תְּחַבֵּל וְחֶבֶל נִמְרָץ׃ לוּ־
If !painful a even (which) unclean- because ;rest this not
destruction ,destroys ness of (is)

אִישׁ הֹלֵךְ רוּחַ וָשֶׁקֶר כִּזֵּב אַטִּף לְךָ לַיַּיִן וְלַשֵּׁכָר וְהָיָה
he even fer- and for for will I he (in) and (with) walks man a
be shall ,drink mented wine you drop ;lies deceit wind

12 מַטִּיף הָעָם הַזֶּה׃ אָסֹף אֶאֱסֹף יַעֲקֹב כֻּלָּךְ קַבֵּץ אֲקַבֵּץ
will I surely of all ,Jacob will I Surely .this people (word) a
gather ;you of gather for dropper

שְׁאֵרִית יִשְׂרָאֵל יַחַד אֲשִׂימֶנּוּ כְּצֹאן בָּצְרָה כְּעֵדֶר בְּתוֹךְ
the in a like ;Bozrah the like will I together ;Israel rem- the
of midst flock of sheep him set of nant

13 הַדָּבְרוֹ תְּהִימֶנָה מֵאָדָם׃ עָלָה הַפֹּרֵץ לִפְנֵיהֶם פָּרְצוּ
have they ;them before one the come Has because be will they its
breached through breaking up .men of commotion in ,pasture

וַיַּעֲבֹרוּ שַׁעַר וַיֵּצְאוּ בוֹ וַיַּעֲבֹר מַלְכָּם לִפְנֵיהֶם וַיהוָה
and ,them before their shall And by have and the have and
Jehovah king through pass .it out gone ,gate through passed

בְּרֹאשָׁם׃
their at
.head

CAP. III ג

CHAPTER 3

[1] And I said, I beg you, hear, heads of Jacob and magistrates of the house of Israel. (Is it) not for you to know justice? [2] Those hating good and loving evil; who pull their skin off them, and their flesh from their bones; [3] who also eat the flesh of My people, and cause their skin to come off from them; and they break their bones and shatter as that in the pot, and as flesh in the midst of the kettle. [4] Then they shall cry out to Jehovah, but He will not answer them. He will even hide His face from them in that time, as they have done evil in their doings.

[5] Thus says Jehovah concerning the prophets who make My people err, who bite with their teeth and call out, Peace! And whoever does not give for their mouth, they even sanctify a war against him. [6] Therefore you (shall have) a night (without) vision. And (you shall have) darkness (without) divination. And the sun shall go down on the prophets, and the day shall be dark over them. [7] And the seers shall be ashamed, and the diviners shall blush; all of them, yes, they shall cover over their lips, for there is no answer (from) God.

[8] But I am full of power (by) the Spirit of Jehovah, and justice and might, to declare to Jacob his transgression, and to Israel his sin. [9] I beseech you, hear this, heads of the house of Jacob, and magistrates of the house of Israel, who abhor justice and pervert all equity; [10] those building up Zion with blood, and Jerusalem with

CHAPTER 3

1 וָאֹמַר שִׁמְעוּ־נָא רָאשֵׁי יַעֲקֹב וּקְצִינֵי בֵּית יִשְׂרָאֵל הֲלוֹא

(it Is) not .Israel house the of and of magistrates Jacob of heads ,please ,Hear I And ,said

2 לָכֶם לָדַעַת אֶת־הַמִּשְׁפָּט׃ שֹׂנְאֵי טוֹב וְאֹהֲבֵי רָעָה גֹּזְלֵי

those ;evil stripping and loving good Those hating ?justice know to for you

3 עוֹרָם מֵעֲלֵיהֶם וּשְׁאֵרָם מֵעַל עַצְמוֹתָם׃ וַאֲשֶׁר אָכְלוּ

eat who and ;bones their from upon their and flesh upon from ,them their skin

שְׁאֵר עַמִּי וְעוֹרָם מֵעֲלֵיהֶם הִפְשִׁיטוּ וְאֶת־עַצְמֹתֵיהֶם

bones their and to cause ;off come upon from them their and skin My ,people flesh the of

פִּצֵּחוּ וּפָרְשׂוּ כַּאֲשֶׁר בַּסִּיר וּכְבָשָׂר בְּתוֹךְ קַלָּחַת׃ אָז יִזְעֲקוּ

shall they Then out cry a .kettle the in of midst as and flesh the in ,pot that as and shatter they break

אֶל־יְהוָה וְלֹא יַעֲנֶה אוֹתָם וְיַסְתֵּר פָּנָיו מֵהֶם בָּעֵת הַהִיא

,that time in from them His face He And hide will .them will He answer but not ,Jehovah to

5 כַּאֲשֶׁר הֵרֵעוּ מַעַלְלֵיהֶם׃ כֹּה אָמַר יְהוָה עַל־

con- cerning Jehovah says Thus their (in) .doings have they evil done as just

הַנְּבִיאִים הַמַּתְעִים אֶת־עַמִּי הַנֹּשְׁכִים בְּשִׁנֵּיהֶם וְקָרְאוּ

they and ,out call their with teeth biting those My ,people causing those err to the prophets

שָׁלוֹם וַאֲשֶׁר לֹא־יִתֵּן עַל־פִּיהֶם וְקִדְּשׁוּ עָלָיו מִלְחָמָה׃

.war a against him they even sanctify their for ,mouth does not give And who(ever) !Peace

6 לָכֵן לַיְלָה לָכֶם מֵחָזוֹן וְחָשְׁכָה לָכֶם מִקְּסֹם וּבָאָה הַשֶּׁמֶשׁ

sun the shall And set from (apart) .divining for you and darkness from (apart) ,vision for you a Therefore night (be shall)

7 עַל־הַנְּבִיאִים וְקָדַר עֲלֵיהֶם הַיּוֹם׃ וּבֹשׁוּ הַחֹזִים וְחָפְרוּ

shall and blush the ,seers shall And ashamed be the .day upon them shall and black be the ,prophets on

הַקֹּסְמִים וְעָטוּ עַל־שָׂפָם כֻּלָּם כִּי אֵין מַעֲנֵה אֱלֹהִים׃

.God answer (from) there for no is of all ,them their lip over they and cover shall those ;divining

8 וְאוּלָם אָנֹכִי מָלֵאתִי כֹחַ אֶת־רוּחַ יְהוָה וּמִשְׁפָּט וּגְבוּרָה

,might and and justice ,Jehovah the of Spirit ,power am of full I But

9 לְהַגִּיד לְיַעֲקֹב פִּשְׁעוֹ וּלְיִשְׂרָאֵל חַטָּאתוֹ׃ שִׁמְעוּ־נָא

,please ,Hear .sin his to and Israel his ,transgression to Jacob to declare

זֹאת רָאשֵׁי בֵּית יַעֲקֹב וּקְצִינֵי בֵּית יִשְׂרָאֵל הַמְתַעֲבִים

abhorring those ,Israel the of house magis- and of trates Jacob the of house heads of ,this

10 מִשְׁפָּט וְאֵת כָּל־הַיְשָׁרָה יְעַקֵּשׁוּ׃ בֹּנֶה צִיּוֹן בְּדָמִים

with ,bloodshed Zion those building (who) ;pervert uprightness all and ,justice

iniquity. [11] The heads of her judge for a bribe, and her priests teach for pay, and her prophets divine for silver, yet they will lean on Jehovah; saying, (Is) not Jehovah among us? No evil shall come on us!
[12] Therefore, on account of you, Zion shall be plowed (as) a field, and Jerusalem shall become heaps, and the mountain of the house into high places of the forest.

11 וִירוּשָׁלִַם בְּעַוְלָה׃ רָאשֶׁיהָ ׀ בְּשֹׁחַד יִשְׁפֹּטוּ וְכֹהֲנֶיהָ
her and ,judge a for heads Her with and
priests bribe .iniquity Jerusalem

בִּמְחִיר יוֹרוּ וּנְבִיאֶיהָ בְּכֶסֶף יִקְסֹמוּ וְעַל־יְהוָה יִשָּׁעֵנוּ
will they Jehovah yet ;divine for her and ,instruct a for
,lean upon silver prophets price

12 לֵאמֹר הֲלוֹא יְהוָה בְּקִרְבֵּנוּ לֹא־תָבוֹא עָלֵינוּ רָעָה׃ לָכֵן
There- !evil upon shall Not our in Jehovah not (Is) ,saying
,fore us come ?midst

בִּגְלַלְכֶם צִיּוֹן שָׂדֶה תֵחָרֵשׁ וִירוּשָׁלִַם עִיִּין תִּהְיֶה וְהַר
the and shall ruins Jerusalem and be shall a (as) Zion of because
of mount ,be ,plowed field ,you

הַבַּיִת לְבָמוֹת יָעַר׃
the the into the
.forest of places high house

CAP. IV. ד

CHAPTER 4

[1] But it shall come to pass in the end of the days, the mountain of the house of Jehovah shall be established on the top of the mountains, and it shall be lifted up from the hills; and peoples shall flow on it. [2] And many nations shall come and say, Come, and let us go up to the mountain of Jehovah and to the house of the God of Jacob. And He will teach us from His ways, and we will walk in His paths. For the law shall go forth out of Zion, and the word of Jehovah from Jerusalem.

[3] And He shall judge between many peoples, and will decide for strong nations afar off. And they shall beat their swords into plowshares, and their spears into pruning hooks. Nation shall not lift up a sword against nation, nor shall they learn war (any) more. [4] But they shall each one sit under his vine and under his fig-tree; and there shall not be trembling. For the mouth of Jehovah of hosts has spoken. [5] For all the peoples walk, (each) one in the name of his god; but we will walk in the name of Jehovah our God forever and ever. [6] In that day, states Jehovah, I will gather

1 וְהָיָה ׀ בְּאַחֲרִית הַיָּמִים יִהְיֶה הַר בֵּית־יְהוָה נָכוֹן בְּרֹאשׁ
the on founded Jeho- house the the be shall the end the in it And
of head vah of of mountain ,days of be shall

2 הֶהָרִים וְנִשָּׂא הוּא מִגְּבָעוֹת וְנָהֲרוּ עָלָיו עַמִּים׃ וְהָלְכוּ
shall And .peoples upon shall and the from it be shall and the
come it flow ;hills lifted ,mountains

גּוֹיִם רַבִּים וְאָמְרוּ לְכוּ ׀ וְנַעֲלֶה אֶל־הַר־יְהוָה וְאֶל־בֵּית
house the and Jehovah the to let and ,Come ,say and many nations
of to of mountain up go us

אֱלֹהֵי יַעֲקֹב וְיוֹרֵנוּ מִדְּרָכָיו וְנֵלְכָה בְּאֹרְחֹתָיו כִּי מִצִּיּוֹן
from For His in will we and His from will He And .Jacob the
Zion .paths walk ,ways us instruct of God

3 תֵּצֵא תוֹרָה וּדְבַר יְהוָה מִירוּשָׁלִָם׃ וְשָׁפַט בֵּין עַמִּים
peoples between He And from Jehovah the and the go shall
judge shall .Jerusalem of word ,law forth

רַבִּים וְהוֹכִיחַ לְגוֹיִם עֲצֻמִים עַד־רָחוֹק וְכִתְּתוּ חַרְבֹתֵיהֶם
their they And far strong for will and many
swords hammer shall .distant nations decide

לְאִתִּים וַחֲנִיתֹתֵיהֶם לְמַזְמֵרוֹת לֹא־יִשְׂאוּ גּוֹי אֶל־גּוֹי חֶרֶב
a a against a shall Not pruning into their and into
,sword nation nation up lift .knives spears ,plowshares

4 וְלֹא־יִלְמְדוּן עוֹד מִלְחָמָה׃ וְיָשְׁבוּ אִישׁ תַּחַת גַּפְנוֹ וְתַחַת
and his under (each) they But .war (any) shall they and
under vine man sit shall more learn not

5 תְּאֵנָתוֹ וְאֵין מַחֲרִיד כִּי־פִי יְהוָה צְבָאוֹת דִּבֵּר׃ כִּי כָּל־
all For has hosts Jehovah the For .trembling not and his
.spoken of of mouth be will ;tree fig

הָעַמִּים יֵלְכוּ אִישׁ בְּשֵׁם אֱלֹהָיו וַאֲנַחְנוּ נֵלֵךְ בְּשֵׁם־יְהוָה
Jehovah the in will we but his the in (each) ,walk the
of name walk ,god of name man peoples

6 אֱלֹהֵינוּ לְעוֹלָם וָעֶד׃ בַּיּוֹם הַהוּא נְאֻם־יְהוָה אֹסְפָה
will I ,Jehovah states ,that day In and forever God our
gather .ever

the lame, and I will gather the banished, and her whom I have afflicted. [7] And I will make the lame into a remnant, and her who was cast off into a strong nation; and Jehovah shall reign over them in Mount Zion from now on, and to forever.

[8] And you, tower of the flock, the hill of the daughter of Zion, to you it shall come, and the rulers, the chiefs; the kingdom of the daughter of Jerusalem. [9] Now why do you cry aloud an outcry? Is there no king in you? Has your counselor perished? For pangs have seized you like a woman in labor. [10] Be in pain and deliver, daughter of Zion, like a woman in travail. For now you shall go out from the city, and you shall live in the field. And you shall come to Babylon. There you shall be delivered. There Jehovah shall redeem you from the hand of your enemies.

[11] Now also many nations are gathered against you, saying, Let her be defiled, and let our eyes look on Zion. [12] But they do not know the plans of Jehovah, nor do they understand His counsel. For He has gathered them like the sheaf to the threshing floor. [13] Arise and thresh, O daughter of Zion; for I will make your horn iron, and I will make your hoofs bronze. And you shall beat many people into pieces. And I will devote their gain to Jehovah, and their wealth to the Lord of all the earth.

CHAPTER 5

[1] Now gather yourself together, daughter of a troop; one sets a siege against us. They shall strike the judge of Israel with a rod on the cheek. [2] And

7 הַצֹּלֵעָה וְהַנִּדָּחָה אֲקַבֵּצָה וַאֲשֶׁר הֲרֵעֹתִי׃ וְשַׂמְתִּי אֶת־

will I And have I and will I the and the
make .(to) evil done who(ever) ,gather banished ,lame

הַצֹּלֵעָה לִשְׁאֵרִית וְהַנַּהֲלָאָה לְגוֹי עָצוּם וּמָלַךְ יְהוָה עֲלֵיהֶם

over Jehovah shall and ;strong a into having she and a into the
them reign nation removed been ,remnant lame

8 בְּהַר צִיּוֹן מֵעַתָּה וְעַד־עוֹלָם׃ וְאַתָּה מִגְדַּל־עֵדֶר

the tower ,you And .forever to and from Zion the in
,flock of now of mountain

עֹפֶל בַּת־צִיּוֹן עָדֶיךָ תֵּאתֶה וּבָאָה הַמֶּמְשָׁלָה הָרִאשֹׁנָה

chief the ,rulers the shall and shall it you to ,Zion the of hill
;(ones) come ,happen of daughter

9 מַמְלֶכֶת לְבַת־יְרוּשָׁלִָם׃ עַתָּה לָמָּה תָרִיעִי רֵעַ הֲמֶלֶךְ

king A an cry you do why Now .Jerusalem the kingdom the
?outcry aloud of daughter of

10 אֵין־בָּךְ אִם־יוֹעֲצֵךְ אָבָד כִּי־הֶחֱזִיקֵךְ חִיל כַּיּוֹלֵדָה׃ חוּלִי

in Be one like pain seized has For has your Or among is
pain .birth giving you ?perished adviser ?you not

וָגֹחִי בַּת־צִיּוֹן כַּיּוֹלֵדָה כִּי עַתָּה תֵצְאִי מִקִּרְיָה וְשָׁכַנְתְּ בַּשָּׂדֶה

the in you and the from shall you now For one like ,Zion daugh- and
,field abide ,city out go .birth giving of ter ,deliver

וּבָאת עַד־בָּבֶל שָׁם תִּנָּצֵלִי שָׁם יִגְאָלֵךְ יְהוָה מִכַּף אֹיְבָיִךְ׃

your the from Jehovah shall there shall you There .Babylon to you and
.enemies of palm you redeem ;delivered be come shall

11 וְעַתָּה נֶאֶסְפוּ עָלַיִךְ גּוֹיִם רַבִּים הָאֹמְרִים תֶּחֱנָף וְתַחַז בְּצִיּוֹן

against let and her Let ,saying ,many nations against are And
Zion look ,defiled be you gathered now

12 עֵינֵינוּ׃ וְהֵמָּה לֹא יָדְעוּ מַחְשְׁבוֹת יְהוָה וְלֹא הֵבִינוּ עֲצָתוֹ

His they do and ,Jehovah of plans the do not they But our
.counsel understand not know .eyes

13 כִּי קִבְּצָם כֶּעָמִיר גֹּרְנָה׃ קוּמִי וָדוֹשִׁי בַת־צִיּוֹן כִּי קַרְנֵךְ

your for ,Zion daugh- and Arise the to the like has He For
horn of ter ,thresh .floor threshing sheaf them gathered

אָשִׂים בַּרְזֶל וּפַרְסֹתַיִךְ אָשִׂים נְחוּשָׁה וַהֲדִקּוֹת עַמִּים רַבִּים

.many peoples you and ;bronze will I your and ,iron will I
crush shall make hoofs make

14 וְהַחֲרַמְתִּי לַיהוָה בִּצְעָם וְחֵילָם לַאֲדוֹן כָּל־הָאָרֶץ׃ עַתָּה

Now the all the to their and their to will I And
.earth of Lord wealth ,gain unjust Jehovah consecrate

תִּתְגֹּדְדִי בַת־גְּדוּד מָצוֹר שָׂם עָלֵינוּ בַּשֵּׁבֶט יַכּוּ עַל־הַלְּחִי

the upon shall they a With against one a ;troop a daugh band
cheek strike rod .us sets siege of ter ,together

אֵת שֹׁפֵט יִשְׂרָאֵל׃

.Israel one the
judging

CAP. V ה

CHAPTER 5

you, Bethlehem Ephratah, you who are little among the thousands of Judah, out

1 וְאַתָּה בֵּית־לֶחֶם אֶפְרָתָה צָעִיר לִהְיוֹת בְּאַלְפֵי יְהוּדָה

,Judah the among being least ,Ephratha Bethlehem ,you And
of thousands

of you He shall come forth to Me to be ruler in Israel, and His goings forth (have been) from of old, from the days of eternity. [3] Therefore He will give them over until the time that she who labors has brought forth; then the rest of His brothers shall return to the sons of Israel.

[4] And He shall stand and feed in the strength of Jehovah, in the majesty of the name of Jehovah His God; and they shall sit, for now He is great to the ends of the earth. [5] And this (One) shall be peace. When Assyria shall come into our land; and when he shall walk in our palaces, then we shall raise against him seven shepherds and eight anointed ones of man. [6] And they shall mar the land of Assyria with the sword, and the land of Nimrod at her entrances. So He shall deliver (us) from Assyria, when he comes into our land and when he walks within our border. [7] And the remnant of Jacob shall be in the midst of many peoples as dew from Jehovah, as showers on a blade of grass, which does not wait for man, nor delay for the sons of men.

[8] And the remnant of Jacob shall be among the nations, in the midst of many peoples, like a lion among the beasts of the forest, like a young lion among the flocks of sheep; who both tramples down and tears in pieces if he goes through — and there is no one to deliver. [9] Your hands shall be high above your foes, and all your enemies shall be cut off. [10] And it shall come to pass in that day, states Jehovah, I will cut off your horses out of your midst, and I will destroy your chariots. [11] And I will cut off the cities of your land, and pull down all your strongholds. [12] And I will cut off sorceries out of your hand, and you shall have no fortune-tellers. [13] I will also cut off your graven images, and your pillars from your midst.

מִמְּךָ לִי יֵצֵא לִהְיוֹת מוֹשֵׁל בְּיִשְׂרָאֵל וּמוֹצָאֹתָיו מִקֶּדֶם
(been have) His and ,Israel in one be- to shall He to of out
,old of from forth comings ruling come forth come Me you

2 מִימֵי עוֹלָם׃ לָכֵן יִתְּנֵם עַד־עֵת יוֹלֵדָה יָלָדָה וְיֶתֶר אֶחָיו
His the then given has one the the until will He There- .eternity the from
brothers of rest ;birth birth giving time (over) them give fore of days

3 יְשׁוּבוּן עַל־בְּנֵי יִשְׂרָאֵל׃ וְעָמַד וְרָעָה בְּעֹז יְהוָה בִּגְאוֹן
the in ,Jehovah the in pas- and He And .Israel the to shall
of majesty of strength (us) ture stand shall of sons return

שֵׁם יְהוָה אֱלֹהָיו וְיָשָׁבוּ כִּי־עַתָּה יִגְדַּל עַד־אַפְסֵי־אָרֶץ׃
the the to is He now for they and His Jehovah the
.earth of ends great ,sit shall ;God of name

4 וְהָיָה זֶה שָׁלוֹם אַשּׁוּר ׀ כִּי־יָבוֹא בְאַרְצֵנוּ וְכִי יִדְרֹךְ
shall he and our into shall he when Assyria ,peace this shall And
tread when ;land come be

בְּאַרְמְנֹתֵינוּ וַהֲקֵמֹנוּ עָלָיו שִׁבְעָה רֹעִים וּשְׁמֹנָה נְסִיכֵי
anointed and shepherds seven against shall we then ,palaces our in
of ones eight him up raise

5 אָדָם׃ וְרָעוּ אֶת־אֶרֶץ אַשּׁוּר בַּחֶרֶב וְאֶת־אֶרֶץ נִמְרֹד
Nimrod the and the with Assyria the shall they And .man
of land ,sword of land depasture

בִּפְתָחֶיהָ וְהִצִּיל מֵאַשּׁוּר כִּי־יָבוֹא בְאַרְצֵנוּ וְכִי־יִדְרֹךְ
shall he and our into shall he when from shall He And her at
tread when land come ,Assyria (us) deliver .entrances

6 בִּגְבוּלֵנוּ׃ וְהָיָה ׀ שְׁאֵרִית יַעֲקֹב בְּקֶרֶב עַמִּים רַבִּים
many peoples the in Jacob remnant the shall And our within
of midst of be .border

כְּטַל מֵאֵת יְהוָה כִּרְבִיבִים עֲלֵי־עֵשֶׂב אֲשֶׁר לֹא־יְקַוֶּה לְאִישׁ
for does not which ,grass blade a as ,Jehovah from dew as
man wait of (on) showers

7 וְלֹא יְיַחֵל לִבְנֵי אָדָם׃ וְהָיָה שְׁאֵרִית יַעֲקֹב בַּגּוֹיִם בְּקֶרֶב
the in the among Jacob remnant the And .man the for does and
of midst ,nations of be shall of sons delay not

עַמִּים רַבִּים כְּאַרְיֵה בְּבַהֲמוֹת יַעַר כִּכְפִיר בְּעֶדְרֵי־צֹאן
;sheep the among a like the the among a like ,many peoples
of flocks lion young ,forest of beasts lion

8 אֲשֶׁר אִם־עָבַר וְרָמַס וְטָרַף וְאֵין מַצִּיל׃ תָּרֹם יָדְךָ עַל־
above Your be shall .delivering there and and both passes he if ,which
hand high none is —tears tramples through

9 צָרֶיךָ וְכָל־אֹיְבֶיךָ יִכָּרֵתוּ׃ וְהָיָה בַיּוֹם־הַהוּא נְאֻם־
states ,that day in it And be shall your and your
be shall .off cut enemies all ,foes

10 יְהוָה וְהִכְרַתִּי סוּסֶיךָ מִקִּרְבֶּךָ וְהַאֲבַדְתִּי מַרְכְּבֹתֶיךָ׃ וְהִכְרַתִּי
will I And your will I and your from your will I that Jeho-
off cut .chariots destroy ,midst horses off cut ,vah

11 עָרֵי אַרְצֶךָ וְהָרַסְתִּי כָּל־מִבְצָרֶיךָ׃ וְהִכְרַתִּי כְשָׁפִים מִיָּדֶךָ
your from sorceries will I And your all pull and your the
hand off cut .fortresses down ,land of cities

12 וּמְעוֹנְנִים לֹא יִהְיוּ־לָךְ׃ וְהִכְרַתִּי פְסִילֶיךָ וּמַצֵּבוֹתֶיךָ מִקִּרְבֶּךָ
your from your and graven your will I And for there not and
;midst pillars ,images off cut .you be shall sorcerers

And you shall not any more worship the work of your hands. [14] And I will pluck your shrines out of your midst; and I will destroy your cities. [15] And I will execute vengeance in anger and in fury (on) the nations, such as they have not heard.

CHAPTER 6

[1] Hear now what Jehovah says: Arise, contend with the mountains and let the hills hear your voice. [2] Mountains, hear Jehovah's case, also you enduring foundations of the earth; for Jehovah has a quarrel with His people, and He will plead His case with Israel. [3] My people, what have I done to you? And how have I made you weary? Answer against Me! [4] For I brought you up out of the land of Egypt, and redeemed you out of the house of bondage; and I sent Moses, Aaron and Miriam before you. [5] O My people, remember now what Balak king of Moab planned, and what Balaam the son of Beor answered him from Shittim to Gilgal, so that you may know the righteousnesses of Jehovah.

[6] With what shall I come before Jehovah, bow myself before God the Most High? Shall I come before Him with burnt offerings, with calves the sons of a year? [7] Will Jehovah be pleased with thousands of rams, with ten thousands of torrents of oil? Shall I give my firstborn (for) my transgression, the fruit of my body (for) the sin of my soul? [8] He has declared to you, man, what (is) good; and what Jehovah requires from you, but to do justice and to love grace and to walk humbly with your God? [9] Jehovah's voice

13 וְלֹא־תִשְׁתַּחֲוֶה עוֹד לְמַעֲשֵׂה יָדֶיךָ׃ וְנָתַשְׁתִּי אֲשֵׁירֶיךָ מִקִּרְבֶּךָ
your from your will I And your the to (any) shall you and
,midst shrines up pluck .hands of work more down bow not

14 וְהִשְׁמַדְתִּי עָרֶיךָ׃ וְעָשִׂיתִי בְּאַף וּבְחֵמָה נָקָם אֶת־הַגּוֹיִם
the (on) vengeance in and in will I And your will I and
,nations fury anger perform .cities destroy

אֲשֶׁר לֹא שָׁמֵעוּ׃
have they not such
.heard as

CAP. VI ו

CHAPTER 6

1 שִׁמְעוּ־נָא אֵת אֲשֶׁר־יְהוָה אֹמֵר קוּם רִיב אֶת־הֶהָרִים
,mountains the contend ,Arise (is) Jehovah what please Hear
with :saying

2 וְתִשְׁמַעְנָה הַגְּבָעוֹת קוֹלֶךָ׃ שִׁמְעוּ הָרִים אֶת־רִיב יְהוָה
,Jehovah the ,mountains ,Hear your hills the hear let and
of contention .voice

וְהָאֵתָנִים מֹסְדֵי אָרֶץ כִּי רִיב לַיהוָה עִם־עַמּוֹ וְעִם־יִשְׂרָאֵל
Israel with and His with has con- a for the foundations the and
,people Jehovah tention ;earth of constant

3 יִתְוַכָּח׃ עַמִּי מֶה־עָשִׂיתִי לְךָ וּמָה הֶלְאֵתִיךָ עֲנֵה בִי׃
against Answer I have And to I have what My will He
!Me ?you wearied how ?you done ,people .dispute

4 כִּי הֶעֱלִתִיךָ מֵאֶרֶץ מִצְרַיִם וּמִבֵּית עֲבָדִים פְּדִיתִיךָ וָאֶשְׁלַח
I and redeemed I servants from and ,Egypt the from brought I For
sent ;you of house the of land up you

5 לְפָנֶיךָ אֶת־מֹשֶׁה אַהֲרֹן וּמִרְיָם׃ עַמִּי זְכָר־נָא מַה־יָּעַץ
planned what please re- My and ,Aaron ,Moses before
member ,people .Miriam

בָּלָק מֶלֶךְ מוֹאָב וּמֶה־עָנָה אֹתוֹ בִּלְעָם בֶּן־בְּעוֹר מִן־הַשִּׁטִּים
Shittim from ,Beor the Balaam him an- and ,Moab king Balak
of son swered what of

6 עַד־הַגִּלְגָּל לְמַעַן דַּעַת צִדְקוֹת יְהוָה׃ בַּמָּה אֲקַדֵּם יְהוָה
,Jehovah I shall With .Jehovah righ- the may you so ,Gilgal to
before come what of teousness know that

אִכַּף לֵאלֹהֵי מָרוֹם הַאֲקַדְּמֶנּוּ בְעוֹלוֹת בַּעֲגָלִים בְּנֵי שָׁנָה׃
?year a of sons with burnt with come I Shall lofti- the to bow
of ,calves ,offerings Him before nesses of God down

7 הֲיִרְצֶה יְהוָה בְּאַלְפֵי אֵילִים בְּרִבְבוֹת נַחֲלֵי־שָׁמֶן הַאֶתֵּן
I Shall ?oil torrents myriads with ,rams with Jehovah be Will
give of of of thousands pleased

8 בְּכוֹרִי פִּשְׁעִי פְּרִי בִטְנִי חַטַּאת נַפְשִׁי׃ הִגִּיד לְךָ אָדָם
,man to has He ?soul my the (for) my fruit the my (for) my
,you declared of sin womb of ,transgression firstborn

מַה־טּוֹב וּמָה יְהוָה דּוֹרֵשׁ מִמְּךָ כִּי אִם־עֲשׂוֹת מִשְׁפָּט
,justice do to except from (is) Jehovah and ;good what
you seeking what (is)

9 וְאַהֲבַת חֶסֶד וְהַצְנֵעַ לֶכֶת עִם־אֱלֹהֶיךָ׃ קוֹל יְהוָה
Jehovah The your with walk to to and ,grace to and
of voice ?God humble be love

cries to the city; and sound wisdom one will see Your name; hear the rod and (Him) who appointed it.

[10] Is there yet the house of the wicked in the treasures of wickedness, and cursed ephah of leanness? [11] Shall I (declare) wicked balances to be pure, and a bag of deceitful weights? [12] (For) her rich (men) are full of violence, and her inhabitants speak lies, and their tongue (is) deceit in their mouth. [13] So I also have made (you) sick to strike you, laying (you) waste because of your sins. [14] You shall eat, but not be satisfied; and your hunger (shall be) in your midst. And you shall draw back, but shall not save; and that which you save I will give up to the sword. [15] You shall sow, but you shall not reap. You shall tread the olive, but you shall not anoint (yourself) with oil; and new wine, but shall not drink wine.

[16] And (one) has kept himself (as to) the statutes of Omri, and all the works of the house of Ahab, and you walk in their counsels, so that I may give you for a horror, and her inhabitants for a hissing. And you shall bear the shame of My people.

לָעִיר יִקְרָא וְתוּשִׁיָּה יִרְאֶה שְׁמֶךָ שִׁמְעוּ מַטֶּה וּמִי יְעָדָהּ׃
appointed and the ,Hear Your will one sound and calls the to
?it who rod ;name see wisdom ;out city

10 עוֹד הַאִשׁ בֵּית רָשָׁע אֹצְרוֹת רֶשַׁע וְאֵיפַת רָזוֹן זְעוּמָה׃
?cursed leanness an and wicked- the the the in is Yet
of ephah ,ness of treasures wicked of house there

11 12 הַאֶזְכֶּה בְּמֹאזְנֵי רֶשַׁע וּבְכִיס אַבְנֵי מִרְמָה׃ אֲשֶׁר
Which ?fraud weights a and wickedness of scales I Shall
of of bag pure (declare)

עֲשִׁירֶיהָ מָלְאוּ חָמָס וְיֹשְׁבֶיהָ דִּבְּרוּ־שָׁקֶר וּלְשׁוֹנָם רְמִיָּה
(is) their and ,lie a speak her and ,violence are rich her
deceit tongue inhabitants of full ,ones

13 בְּפִיהֶם׃ וְגַם־אֲנִי הֶחֱלֵיתִי הַכּוֹתֶךָ הַשְׁמֵם עַל־חַטֹּאתֶךָ׃
your because desolate to strike to made have I So their in
.sins of (you) ,you sick (you) also .mouth

14 אַתָּה תֹאכַל וְלֹא תִשְׂבָּע וְיֶשְׁחֲךָ בְּקִרְבֶּךָ וְתַסֵּג וְלֹא
but will you And in be will your and be but shall You
not ,back draw .midst your hunger ;satisfied not eat

15 תַפְלִיט וַאֲשֶׁר תְּפַלֵּט לַחֶרֶב אֶתֵּן׃ אַתָּה תִזְרַע וְלֹא תִקְצוֹר
shall you but shall You will I the to you what and keep shall
.reap not ,sow .give sword ,save ;safe

אַתָּה תִדְרֹךְ־זַיִת וְלֹא־תָסוּךְ שֶׁמֶן וְתִירוֹשׁ וְלֹא תִשְׁתֶּה־יָּיִן׃
.wine shall you but new and (with) shall you but the shall You
drink not ,wine ;oil anoint not ,olive tread

16 וְיִשְׁתַּמֵּר חֻקּוֹת עָמְרִי וְכֹל מַעֲשֵׂה בֵית־אַחְאָב וַתֵּלְכוּ
you and ,Ahab the work the and ,Omri the (to as) has (one) And
walk of house of all of statutes himself kept

בְּמֹעֲצוֹתָם לְמַעַן תִּתִּי אֹתְךָ לְשַׁמָּה וְיֹשְׁבֶיהָ לִשְׁרֵקָה
a for her and a for you may I that so their in
;hissing inhabitants ,horror give ,counsels

וְחֶרְפַּת עַמִּי תִּשָּׂאוּ׃
shall you My the And
.bear people of disgrace

CAP. VII ז

CHAPTER 7

[1] Woe to me! For I am like the gatherings of the summer fruits, like the grape-gleanings of the vintage. There is no cluster to eat; my soul desires the first-ripe fruit. [2] The pious has perished from the earth, and the upright is not among men. All of them lie in wait for blood; each one hunts his brother (with) a net. [3] Both hands (are) on evil, to do (it) well. The prince asks for a bribe, the judge also; and the great (man) speaks the lust of his soul; he (does), and they weave it together. [4] The best of them (is) like a brier;

1 אַלְלַי לִי כִּי הָיִיתִי כְּאָסְפֵּי־קַיִץ כְּעֹלְלֹת בָּצִיר אֵין־אֶשְׁכּוֹל
cluster a There the the like ripe the like I For to Woe
(grapes of) not is .vintage of gleanings ,fruit of gatherings am !me

2 לֶאֱכוֹל בִּכּוּרָה אִוְּתָה נַפְשִׁי׃ אָבַד חָסִיד מִן־הָאָרֶץ וְיָשָׁר
the and the from the Has my craves early the ;eat to
upright ,earth pious perished .soul fig

בָּאָדָם אַיִן כֻּלָּם לְדָמִים יֶאֱרֹבוּ אִישׁ אֶת־אָחִיהוּ יָצוּדוּ
hunts his (each) in lie for of All not among
brother, man ;wait bloodshed them .is man

3 חֵרֶם׃ עַל־הָרַע כַּפַּיִם לְהֵיטִיב הַשַּׂר שֹׁאֵל וְהַשֹּׁפֵט
the also (is) The do to both evil Upon a (with)
,judge ,asking ruler .well (it) ,palms (are) .net

4 בַּשִּׁלּוּם וְהַגָּדוֹל דֹּבֵר הַוַּת נַפְשׁוֹ הוּא וַיְעַבְּתוּהָ׃ טוֹבָם
Their they and he his the speaks the and a for
best .it interweave ,(does) ;soul of lust (man) great ,bribe

the upright (is sharper) than a hedge of thorns. The day of your watchmen, your visitation comes; now their shame shall come.

[5] Put no faith in a companion; put no trust in a friend; keep the door of your mouth from her who lies (in) your bosom; [6] for son despises father; a daughter rises up against her mother; the bride against her mother-in-law; a man's enemies (are) the men of his own house. [7] But I will look to Jehovah. I will wait for the God of my salvation; my God will hear me!

[8] Rejoice not against me, my enemy; for (if) I fall I shall arise. For (if) I sit in darkness, Jehovah is a light to me. [9] I will bear the fury of Jehovah because I have sinned against Him, until He pleads my cause and brings forth justice for me. He will bring me out to the light; I shall see His righteousness. [10] And my enemy shall see; and shame shall cover her, the one saying to me, Where (is) He, Jehovah your God? My eyes shall look on her; now she shall be for a trampling like the mud of the streets. [11] A day of building your walls, that day the limit shall be far removed; [12] that day he shall come even to you from Assyria, and (from) the besieged cities, and from the siege even to the River, and from sea to sea, and (from) mountain (to) mountain. [13] But the land shall become a waste because of those who dwell in it, from the fruit of their doings.

[14] Feed your people with Your rod, the flock of Your inheritance, who dwell alone (in) the woods, in the midst of Carmel. Let them feed in Bashan and Gilead, as (in) the days of old. [15] According to the days of your coming out of the land of Egypt, I will cause him to see wonderful things.

[16] The nation shall see and be ashamed from all their might; they shall set (their) hand on (their)

כְּחֵדֶק יָשָׁר מִמְּסוּכָה יוֹם מְצַפֶּיךָ פְּקֻדָּתְךָ בָאָה עַתָּה
now is your your The a than more the like (is)
;coming visitation ,watchers of day .thorn-hedge upright ;thorn a

5 תִהְיֶה מְבוּכָתָם׃ אַל־תַּאֲמִינוּ בְרֵעַ אַל־תִּבְטְחוּ בְּאַלּוּף
a in put do not a in put do Not their be shall
;friend trust ;companion faith .confusion

6 מִשֹּׁכֶבֶת חֵיקֶךָ שְׁמֹר פִּתְחֵי־פִיךָ׃ כִּי־בֵן מְנַבֵּל אָב בַּת
a ;father is son For your the guard your (in) her from
daughter despising .mouth of opening bosom reclining

7 קָמָה בְאִמָּהּ כַּלָּה בַּחֲמֹתָהּ אֹיְבֵי אִישׁ אַנְשֵׁי בֵיתוֹ׃ וַאֲנִי
But own his the (are) a ene- the her against the her against rises
I .house of men man of mies ;law-in-mother bride ,mother up

8 בַּיהוָה אֲצַפֶּה אוֹחִילָה לֵאלֹהֵי יִשְׁעִי יִשְׁמָעֵנִי אֱלֹהָי׃ אַל־
Not my hear will my the for will I will to
!God me ;salvation of God wait .look Jehovah

תִּשְׂמְחִי אֹיַבְתִּי לִי כִּי נָפַלְתִּי קָמְתִּי כִּי־אֵשֵׁב בַּחֹשֶׁךְ יְהוָה
Jehovah in sit I for shall I ,fall I for over my ,rejoice do
,darkness (if) ;arise (if) ;me ,enemy

9 אוֹר לִי׃ זַעַף יְהוָה אֶשָּׂא כִּי חָטָאתִי לוֹ עַד אֲשֶׁר
(when) until against have I because will I Jehovah The for a (is)
,Him sinned ,bear of rage .me light

יָרִיב רִיבִי וְעָשָׂה מִשְׁפָּטִי יוֹצִיאֵנִי לָאוֹר אֶרְאֶה בְּצִדְקָתוֹ׃
His shall I the to will He my and my He
.righteousness see ;light out me bring .justice makes case contends

10 וְתֵרֶא אֹיַבְתִּי וּתְכַסֶּהָ בוּשָׁה הָאֹמְרָה אֵלַי אַיּוֹ יְהוָה
Jehovah Where ,me to one the ,shame shall and my shall And
He (is) saying her cover ;enemy see

אֱלֹהָיִךְ עֵינַי תִּרְאֶינָּה בָּהּ עַתָּה תִּהְיֶה לְמִרְמָס כְּטִיט
the like a for shall she now on will My your
of mud trampling become ;her look eyes ?God

11 12 חוּצוֹת׃ יוֹם לִבְנוֹת גְּדֵרָיִךְ יוֹם הַהוּא יִרְחַק־חֹק׃ יוֹם
(in) the be shall that (in) your building day A the
day ;limit remote day ;walls (stone) of .streets

הוּא וְעָדֶיךָ יָבוֹא לְמִנִּי אַשּׁוּר וְעָרֵי מָצוֹר וּלְמִנִּי מָצוֹר
the from and ,siege the and ,Assyria from shall he to even that
siege of cities come you

13 וְעַד־נָהָר וְיָם מִיָּם וְהַר הָהָר׃ וְהָיְתָה הָאָרֶץ לִשְׁמָמָה
a the shall And the (to) and from and the even
desolation land become .mountain mountain ,sea sea ,River to

14 עַל־יֹשְׁבֶיהָ מִפְּרִי מַעַלְלֵיהֶם׃ רְעֵה עַמְּךָ בְשִׁבְטֶךָ
Your with Your Pasture their the from those because
,rod people .doings of fruit ,it in dwelling of

צֹאן נַחֲלָתֶךָ שֹׁכְנִי לְבָדָד יַעַר בְּתוֹךְ כַּרְמֶל יִרְעוּ בָשָׁן
(in) them Let .Carmel the in the (in) alone dwelling Your flock the
Bashan pasture of midst ,thicket ,possession of

15 וְגִלְעָד כִּימֵי עוֹלָם׃ כִּימֵי צֵאתְךָ מֵאֶרֶץ מִצְרָיִם אַרְאֶנּוּ
cause will I ,Egypt the from your the As .old (in) as and
see to him of land out coming of days of days the ,Gilead

16 נִפְלָאוֹת׃ יִרְאוּ גוֹיִם וְיֵבֹשׁוּ מִכֹּל גְּבוּרָתָם יָשִׂימוּ יָד עַל־
over the shall they their from be and the Shall extraordinary
hand set ;might all ashamed nations see .things

mouth; their ears shall be deaf. [17] They shall lick the dust like a snake; they shall tremble out of their holes like crawlers of the earth; they shall dread Jehovah our God; they shall fear from You. [18] Who (is) a God like You, forgiving iniquity and passing by the transgression of the remnant of His inheritance? He does not make strong His anger forever, because He delights (in) grace. [19] He will turn, He will show us mercy; He will trample our iniquities; and You will cast all their sins into the depths of the sea. [20] You will give faithfulness to Jacob; grace to Abraham, which You have sworn to our fathers from the days of old.

17 פֶּה אָזְנֵיהֶם תֶּחֱרַשְׁנָה׃ יְלַחֲכוּ עָפָר כַּנָּחָשׁ כְּזֹחֲלֵי אֶרֶץ
the like the like the shall They be shall their the
;earth of crawlers ,snake dust lick .deaf ears ;mouth

יִרְגְּזוּ מִמִּסְגְּרֹתֵיהֶם אֶל־יְהוָה אֱלֹהֵינוּ יִפְחָדוּ וְיִרְאוּ מִמֶּךָּ׃
(from) shall they shall they our Jehovah to their of out shall they
.You fear ;dread God ;fastnesses tremble

18 מִי־אֵל כָּמוֹךָ נֹשֵׂא עָוֹן וְעֹבֵר עַל־פֶּשַׁע לִשְׁאֵרִית נַחֲלָתוֹ
His remnant the the over and ,iniquity lifting like a Who
?possession of of transgression passing off ,You God (is)

19 לֹא־הֶחֱזִיק לָעַד אַפּוֹ כִּי־חָפֵץ חֶסֶד הוּא׃ יָשׁוּב יְרַחֲמֵנוּ
show (to) will He .He grace desires for His for He does not
;mercy us ,turn ,anger ever strong make

יִכְבֹּשׁ עֲוֹנֹתֵינוּ וְתַשְׁלִיךְ בִּמְצֻלוֹת יָם כָּל־חַטֹּאותָם׃
.sins their all the the into will You and our will He
sea of depths cast ;iniquities trample

20 תִּתֵּן אֱמֶת לְיַעֲקֹב חֶסֶד לְאַבְרָהָם אֲשֶׁר־נִשְׁבַּעְתָּ לַאֲבֹתֵינוּ
our to have You which ,Abraham to grace ,Jacob to faith- will You
fathers sworn fulness give

מִימֵי קֶדֶם׃
.old the from
of days

נחום

LIBER NAHUM

CAPUT. I א

CHAPTER 1

CHAPTER 1

[1] The burden of Nineveh: The book of the vision of Nahum the Elkoshite. [2] God (is) jealous, and Jehovah revenges; Jehovah revenges and is a possessor of wrath. Jehovah takes vengeance against His foes, and He keeps (wrath) against His enemies. [3] Jehovah (is) slow (to) anger, and great of power, and will not at all clear (the guilty). Jehovah (has) His way in the tempest and in the storm, and the clouds (are) the dust of His feet. [4] He rebukes the sea and makes it dry, and dries up all the rivers. Bashan and Carmel wither; and the flower of Lebanon withers. [5] The mountains quake from Him, and the hills melt, and the earth is lifted up from before Him, even the world and all who dwell in it. [6] Who can stand before His fury? And who can rise against the heat of His anger? His wrath is poured out like fire, and the rocks are broken down from Him. [7] Jehovah (is) good, for a stronghold in the day of distress, and He knows those who trust in Him. [8] But with a flood passing through He will make a complete end of its place, and darkness shall pursue His enemies. [9] What are you plotting against Jehovah? He will make an utter end; distress shall not rise up a second time. [10] For as long as thorns are interwoven, so with their drink they are drunken; they shall be devoured like stubble fully dried. [11] One who devises evil against Jehovah has come out of you, one counseling worthlessness. [12] Thus says Jehovah: Though in full strength, and so many, yet then they shall

1 מַשָּׂא נִֽינְוֵה סֵפֶר חֲזוֹן נַחוּם הָאֶלְקֹשִׁי׃ אֵל קַנּוֹא וְנֹקֵם
2
is and ,jealous God .Elkoshite the Nahum the book the :Nineveh The
avenging (is) of vision of of burden

יְהוָה נֹקֵם יְהוָה וּבַעַל חֵמָה נֹקֵם יְהוָה לְצָרָיו וְנוֹטֵר הוּא
He keeps and against Jehovah takes .wrath a and Jehovah is ;Jehovah
(wrath) ,foes His vengeance of possessor avenging

3 לְאֹיְבָיו׃ יְהוָה אֶרֶךְ אַפַּיִם וּגְדָול־כֹּחַ וְנַקֵּה לֹא יְנַקֶּה
does He not by and power and ,anger long Jehovah His against
,acquit means any of great (before) (is) .enemies

4 יְהוָה בְּסוּפָה וּבִשְׂעָרָה דַּרְכּוֹ וְעָנָן אֲבַק רַגְלָיו׃ גּוֹעֵר
He His the (are) the and His the in and the in Jehovah
rebukes .feet of dust clouds ,way storm tempest (is)

בַּיָּם וַיַּבְּשֵׁהוּ וְכָל־הַנְּהָרוֹת הֶחֱרִיב אֻמְלַל בָּשָׁן וְכַרְמֶל
and Bashan withers dries He rivers the and makes and the
;Carmel .up all ,dry it ,sea

5 וּפֶרַח לְבָנוֹן אֻמְלָל׃ הָרִים רָעֲשׁוּ מִמֶּנּוּ וְהַגְּבָעוֹת הִתְמֹגָגוּ
melt hills the and because quake The .withers Lebanon the and
,Him of mountains of flower

6 וַתִּשָּׂא הָאָרֶץ מִפָּנָיו וְתֵבֵל וְכָל־יֹשְׁבֵי בָהּ׃ לִפְנֵי זַעְמוֹ
His Before .it in the and the even be- from the is and
fury inhabitants all world ,Him fore earth up lifted

מִי יַעֲמוֹד וּמִי יָקוּם בַּחֲרוֹן אַפּוֹ חֲמָתוֹ נִתְּכָה כָאֵשׁ וְהַצֻּרִים
the and like poured is His His the against can And can who
rocks ,fire out wrath ?anger of heat rise who ?stand

7 נִתְּצוּ מִמֶּנּוּ׃ טוֹב יְהוָה לְמָעוֹז בְּיוֹם צָרָה וְיֹדֵעַ חֹסֵי בוֹ׃
in who those He and dis- the in (a for) Jehovah good because broken are
.Him trust knows ,tress of day stronghold .Him of down

8 וּבְשֶׁטֶף עֹבֵר כָּלָה יַעֲשֶׂה מְקוֹמָהּ וְאֹיְבָיו יִרְדָּף־חֹשֶׁךְ׃
.darkness will His and its of will He complete a passing with But
pursue enemies ,place make destruction through flood a

9 מַה־תְּחַשְּׁבוּן אֶל־יְהוָה כָּלָה הוּא עֹשֶׂה לֹא־תָקוּם
shall not will He complete a ?Jehovah against you are What
up rise .make destruction plotting

10 פַּעֲמַיִם צָרָה׃ כִּי עַד־סִירִים סְבֻכִים וּכְסָבְאָם סְבוּאִים
are who their like and are thorns as For .Distress second a
,drunken drunkards ;interwoven as long time

11 אֻכְּלוּ כְּקַשׁ יָבֵשׁ מָלֵא׃ מִמֵּךְ יָצָא חֹשֵׁב עַל־יְהוָה רָעָה
,evil Jehovah against one come has Out .fully dried like shall they
plotting forth you of straw devoured be

12 יֹעֵץ בְּלִיָּעַל׃ כֹּה ׀ אָמַר יְהוָה אִם־שְׁלֵמִים וְכֵן
and ,complete Though ,Jehovah says Thus .worthlessness one
so counseling

be cut off, and shall pass away. And though I have afflicted you, I will not afflict you any more. [13] And now I will break his yoke from on you, and will tear away your bonds. [14] And Jehovah has commanded concerning you, not (one) of your name shall be sown any more; I will cut off the graven image and the molten image out of the house of your gods; I will appoint your grave, for you are despised.

[15] Behold! The feet of Him bearing good news, proclaiming, Peace! O Judah, celebrate your feasts; fulfill your vows; for the worthless will not continue to pass through among you; he is completely cut off.

CHAPTER 2

[1] He who breaks into pieces is coming up against your face. Guard the ramparts, watch the way, make (your) loins strong, fortify (your) power exceedingly. [2] For Jehovah has turned the glory of Jacob, as the glory of Israel. For the plunderers have plundered them, and have destroyed their vine branches. [3] The shield of his mighty ones has become red; the mighty men (are) clothed in scarlet; the chariots will flame like iron (torches) in the day of preparation; and the cypress trees shall be shaken. [4] The chariots shall race madly in the streets. They shall run to and fro in the broad ways. Their appearance (is) like torches. They dart about like the lightnings. [5] He shall remember his nobles. They shall stumble in their walking. They shall hurry to its wall, and the covering shall be prepared. [6] The gates of the rivers shall be opened, and the palace shall be melted. [7] And the captive train is uncovered (and) shall be led away captive; and her maids are moaning like the sound of doves, beating on their breast. [8] But Nineveh (is) like a pool of water throughout her days; yet

13 רַבִּים וְכֵן נָגֹזּוּ וְעָבָר וְעִנִּתִךְ לֹא אֲעַנֵּךְ עוֹד׃ וְעַתָּה
now And any will I not I Though and be will they yet ,many
.more you afflict ,you afflicted .vanish off cut therefore

14 אֶשְׁבֹּר מֹטֵהוּ מֵעָלָיִךְ וּמוֹסְרֹתַיִךְ אֲנַתֵּק׃ וְצִוָּה עָלֶיךָ יְהוָה
,Jehovah about has And will I your and upon from his will I
you commanded .away tear bonds ,you yoke break

לֹא־יִזָּרַע מִשִּׁמְךָ עוֹד מִבֵּית אֱלֹהֶיךָ אַכְרִית פֶּסֶל וּמַסֵּכָה
the and graven the will I your of Out any your from be shall not
;image cast image off cut gods of house the .more name sown (one)

אָשִׂים קִבְרֶךָ כִּי קַלּוֹתָ׃
are you for your will I
.despised ,grave appoint

CAP. II ב

CHAPTER 2

1 הִנֵּה עַל־הֶהָרִים רַגְלֵי מְבַשֵּׂר מַשְׁמִיעַ שָׁלוֹם חָגִּי יְהוּדָה
O Celebrate !Peace are bearing Him feet the the Upon ,Behold
,Judah proclaiming ,news good of mountains

חַגַּיִךְ שַׁלְּמִי נְדָרָיִךְ כִּי לֹא יוֹסִיף עוֹד לַעֲבוֹר־בָּךְ בְּלִיַּעַל
the among pass to any will not for your fulfill your
;worthless you through more continue ;vows ;feasts

2 כֻּלֹּה נִכְרָת׃ עָלָה מֵפִיץ עַל־פָּנַיִךְ נָצוֹר מְצוּרָה צַפֵּה־
watch the Guard your against one the com- Is is he com-
,rampart .face scattering up ing .off cut pletely

3 דֶרֶךְ חַזֵּק מָתְנַיִם אַמֵּץ כֹּחַ מְאֹד׃ כִּי שָׁב יְהוָה אֶת־גְּאוֹן
the Jehovah has For exceed- the firm the strengthen the
of glory turned .ingly power up ,loins ,way

יַעֲקֹב כִּגְאוֹן יִשְׂרָאֵל כִּי בְקָקוּם בֹּקְקִים וּזְמֹרֵיהֶם שִׁחֵתוּ׃
have they their and those emptied have For .Israel the like ,Jacob
.destroyed branches vine ,emptying them of glory

4 מָגֵן גִּבֹּרֵיהוּ מְאָדָּם אַנְשֵׁי־חַיִל מְתֻלָּעִים בְּאֵשׁ־פְּלָדֹת
iron the with in clothed valor the become has mighty his The
(be shall) of fire ;scarlet (are) of men ;red ones of shield

5 הָרֶכֶב בְּיוֹם הֲכִינוֹ וְהַבְּרֹשִׁים הָרְעָלוּ׃ בַּחוּצוֹת יִתְהוֹלְלוּ
as run the In made are the and pre- his the in the
mad if streets .quiver to cypresses ;paration of day chariotry

הָרֶכֶב יִשְׁתַּקְשְׁקוּן בָּרְחֹבוֹת מַרְאֵיהֶן כַּלַּפִּידִם כַּבְּרָקִים
the Like .torches like ap- Their open the in rush shall They the
lightnings (is) pearance .squares fro and to .chariots

6 יְרוֹצֵצוּ׃ יִזְכֹּר אַדִּירָיו יִכָּשְׁלוּ בַּהֲלִיכוֹתָם יְמַהֲרוּ חוֹמָתָהּ
,wall its shall They their in shall They its shall He dart they
to hurry .walking stumble .nobles remember .about

7 וְהֻכַן הַסֹּכֵךְ׃ שַׁעֲרֵי הַנְּהָרוֹת נִפְתָּחוּ וְהַהֵיכָל נָמוֹג׃
be shall the and be shall rivers the gates The the shall and
.melted palace ,opened of .covering up set

8 וְהֻצַּב גֻּלְּתָה הֹעֲלָתָה וְאַמְהֹתֶיהָ מְנַהֲגוֹת כְּקוֹל יוֹנִים
,doves the like are her and carried and un- is the And
of sound moaning handmaids ,away covered train captive

9 מְתֹפְפֹת עַל־לִבְבֵהֶן׃ וְנִינְוֵה כִבְרֵכַת־מַיִם מִימֵי הִיא
;her the from water a like (is) But their on beating
of days of pool Nineveh .breast

they shall flee away. Halt! Halt! (they cry), but no one turns himself. [9] Seize the silver, seize the gold! for there is no end to the treasure, wealth from all precious vessels. [10] She is empty and void and waste. And the heart melts, and the knees knock together, and trembling (is) in all the loins, and all their faces collect heat. [11] Where (is) the end of the lions, and the feeding place for the young lions, where the lion (and) the lioness walked there, the lion's cub, and no one frightens (them)? [12] The lion tears in pieces enough for his cubs, and strangles for his lionesses, and has filled his holes (with) prey and his dens (with) torn prey. [13] Behold, I (am) against you, states Jehovah of hosts, and I will burn her chariots in the smoke, and the sword shall devour your young lions. And I will cut off your prey from the earth, and the voice of your messengers shall not be heard any more.

וְהֵמָּה נָסִים עִמְדוּ עֲמֹדוּ וְאֵין מַפְנֶה׃ בֹּזּוּ כֶסֶף בֹּזּוּ 10

Plunder the Plunder turns who there but !Stand !Stand are Now
!silver .himself none is ,(cry they) .fleeing they

זָהָב וְאֵין קֵצֶה לַתְּכוּנָה כָּבֹד מִכֹּל כְּלִי חֶמְדָּה׃ בּוּקָה 11

(is She) .precious objects from riches the to end there For the
,empty all treasure no is !gold

וּמְבוּקָה וּמְבֻלָּקָה וְלֵב נָמֵס וּפַק בִּרְכַּיִם וְחַלְחָלָה בְּכָל־

all in trembling and ,knees the and is the And and even
(is) of knocking ,melted heart .devastated waste

מָתְנַיִם וּפְנֵי כֻלָּם קִבְּצוּ פָארוּר׃ אַיֵּה מְעוֹן אֲרָיוֹת 12

,lions the den the Where .heat collect of all the and ,loins the
of (is) them of faces

וּמִרְעֶה הוּא לַכְּפִרִים אֲשֶׁר הָלַךְ אַרְיֵה לָבִיא שָׁם גּוּר

the ,there the lion walked where the for the and
of cub lioness ,lions young place feeding

אַרְיֵה וְאֵין מַחֲרִיד׃ אַרְיֵה טֹרֵף בְּדֵי גֹרוֹתָיו וּמְחַנֵּק 13

and ,cubs his enough in tears lion The terrify shall and ;lion a
strangles for pieces .(them) none

לְלִבְאֹתָיו וַיְמַלֵּא־טֶרֶף חֹרָיו וּמְעֹנֹתָיו טְרֵפָה׃ הִנְנִי אֵלַיִךְ 14

against Behold torn (with) his even his (with) has and his for
,you (am) I .prey lairs ,holes prey filled ,lionesses

נְאֻם יְהוָה צְבָאוֹת וְהִבְעַרְתִּי בֶעָשָׁן רִכְבָּהּ וּכְפִירַיִךְ

your and her the in will I and ,hosts Jehovah declares
lions young ,chariots smoke burn of

תֹּאכַל חָרֶב וְהִכְרַתִּי מֵאֶרֶץ טַרְפֵּךְ וְלֹא־יִשָּׁמַע עוֹד

any be shall and your the from will I And the shall
more heard not ,prey earth off cut .sword devour

קוֹל מַלְאָכֵכֵה׃

your the
.messengers of voice

CAP. III. ג

CHAPTER 3

[1] Woe to the bloody city! All of it (is) a lie, full of plunder; the prey is not withdrawn. [2] The sound of a whip, and the sound of rattling of a wheel, and a galloping horse, and of a bounding chariot. [3] The horseman lifts up both the gleam of the sword and the lightning of the spear; and many (are) slain, and a mass of dead bodies and no end of corpses; they stumble on their dead bodies; [4] because of the many fornications of the well-favored harlot, the mistress of magic, who sells nations through her fornications, and families through her magic acts. [5] Behold, I (am) against you, says Jehovah of hosts, and I will lift up your skirts over your

הוֹי עִיר דָּמִים כֻּלָּהּ כַּחַשׁ פֶּרֶק מְלֵאָה לֹא יָמִישׁ טָרֶף׃ 1

the is not ;of full plunder ,lie a of All !blood the Woe
.prey withdrawn (is) it of city (to)

קוֹל שׁוֹט וְקוֹל רַעַשׁ אוֹפָן וְסוּס דֹּהֵר וּמֶרְכָּבָה מְרַקֵּדָה׃ 2

.bounding a and ,galloping a and a the the and ,whip a The
chariot horse ,wheel of clatter of sound of sound

פָּרָשׁ מַעֲלֶה וְלַהַב חֶרֶב וּבְרַק חֲנִית וְרֹב חָלָל וְכֹבֶד פָּגֶר 3

corpses a and (are) and the the and the the and mount- is The
of mass ,slain many ;spear of lightning ,sword of gleam ,ing horseman

וְאֵין קֵצֶה לַגְּוִיָּה יִכְשְׁלוּ בִּגְוִיָּתָם׃ מֵרֹב זְנוּנֵי זוֹנָה טוֹבַת 4

well the harlotries Because their on they the to an not and
harlot of many of .corpses stumble ;bodies end is

חֵן בַּעֲלַת כְּשָׁפִים הַמֹּכֶרֶת גּוֹיִם בִּזְנוּנֶיהָ וּמִשְׁפָּחוֹת

families and her by nations sells who sorceries the ,favored
,harlotries of mistress

בִּכְשָׁפֶיהָ׃ הִנְנִי אֵלַיִךְ נְאֻם יְהוָה צְבָאוֹת וְגִלֵּיתִי שׁוּלַיִךְ 5

your will I and ,hosts Jehovah declares against ,Behold her by
skirts up lift of ,you (am) I .sorceries

face. And I will make the nations see your nakedness, and the kingdoms your shame. [6] And I will cast filth on you and will disgrace you. And I will set you as a spectacle. [7] And it shall be, that all those who look on you shall flee from you, and shall say, Nineveh is laid waste; who will weep for her? From where shall I seek comforters for you? [8] Are you better than No-Amon, who dwelt among the Nile branches, (with) waters surrounding her, whose rampart (was) the sea, the waters her wall? [9] Ethiopia and Egypt (were) her strength; yea, without end; Put and Lubim were among your helpers; [10] yet she went into exile; she went into captivity; her children were also broken in pieces at the head of all the streets; and they cast lots for her honored ones, and all her great ones were bound in chains. [11] You also shall be drunken; you shall be hidden, you also shall seek a stronghold from the enemy. [12] All your strongholds (shall be like) fig-trees with the firstfruits; if they are shaken, they shall even fall on the mouth of the eater. [13] Behold, your people in your midst (are) women; the gates of your land shall surely be opened to your enemies; the fire shall devour your bars. [14] Draw water of the siege; fortify your strongholds; go into the clay and tread in the mortar; make the brick mold strong. [15] There fire shall devour you; the sword shall cut you off; it shall eat you up like the locust larvae. Make yourself as many as the locust larvae, multiply like the locusts. [16] You have increased your merchants above the stars of the heavens; the locust larvae shall strip off and fly away. [17] Your crowned ones (are) like the locusts, and your officers like a swarm of locusts that camp in the hedges in the cold day; the sun rises, and they flee away, and the place where they (are) is not

6 על־פניך והראיתי גוים מערך וממלכות קלונך: והשלכתי
will I And cast | your .shame | the and kingdoms | your nakedness | the nations | cause will I and see to | your over ,face

7 עליך שקצים ונבלתיך ושמתיך כראי: והיה כל־ראיך
seeing all you | it And ,be shall | a as .spectacle | will I And you set | will and ,you disdain | filth | you on

ידוד ממך ואמר שדדה נינוה מי ינוד לה מאין אבקש
I shall seek | From where | for ?her | will who lament | ;Nineveh | laid is waste | shall and ,say | from you away | shall flee

8 מנחמים לך: התיטבי מנא אמון הישבה ביארים מים
waters | the among ,branches Nile | that dwell | ,Amon | than -No | you Are better | for ?you | comforters

9 סביב לה אשר־חיל ים מים חומתה: כוש עצמה ומצרים
;Egypt and | (her) ,might | Ethiopia (was) | her ?wall | the waters | the ,sea (was) | whose rampart | ,her | sur- rounding

10 ואין קצה פוט ולובים היו בעזרתך: גם־היא לגלה
into ,exile | she (went) | Yet | your among .helpers | were | Lubim and | Put | ;end | even without

הלכה בשבי גם עלליה ירטשו בראש כל־חוצות ועל־
and for | ;streets the | all | the at of head | dashed were pieces to | her children | also | into ,captivity | she went

11 נכבדיה ידו גורל וכל־גדוליה רתקו בזקים: גם־את
you Also | .chains in | were bound | her ones great | and all | ,lots | they cast | her ones honored

12 תשכרי תהי נעלמה גם־את תבקשי מעוז מאויב: כל־
All | the from .enemy | a fortress | seek shall | you also | ;hidden | shall you be | be shall ;drunken

מבצריך תאנים עם־בכורים אם־ינועו ונפלו על־פי
the upon of mouth | they then fall shall | are they if ,shaken | first- the ;fruits | with | fig (are) trees | your fortresses

13 אוכל: הנה עמך נשים בקרבך לאיביך פתוח נפתחו
be shall opened | wide | your to enemies | your in ;midst | (are) women | your people | Behold | the .eater

14 שערי ארצך אכלה אש בריחיך: מי מצור שאבי־לך
for !yourself | draw | the siege | Water of | gate your .bars | the fire | shall devour | your ;land | gates the of

חזקי מבצריך באי בטיט ורמסי בחמר החזיקי מלבן:
the .mold | make strong | the in ;mortar | and tread | the clay | into go | your ;fortifications | Strengthen

15 שם תאכלך אש תכריתך חרב תאכלך כילק התכבד
Multiply yourself | the as .larvae | shall it you devour | the ;sword | cut shall off you | ,fire devour will There you

16 כילק התכבדי כארבה: הרבית רכליך מכוכבי השמים
the ;heavens | the than more of stars | your merchants | have You increased | the like .locusts | multiply yourself | the as ,larvae

17 ילק פשט ויעף: מנזריך כארבה וטפסריך כגוב גובי
locusts a (are) of swarm | your and officials | the like ,locusts | nobles Your (are) | fly and .away | shall off strip | the larvae

החונים בגדרות ביום קרה שמש זרחה ונודד ולא־נודע
is known | and not | they and ,flee | ,rises | sun the | ;cold | the in of day | the in hedges | that camp

known. [18] Your shepherds slumber, O king of Assyria. Your nobles are lying down. Your people are scattered on the mountains, and no one gathers. [19] There is no healing for your fracture. Your wound (is) severe. All who hear of your report shall clap the hand over you; for on whom has your wickedness not passed continually?

מְקוֹמוֹ אַיָּם׃ נָמוּ רֹעֶיךָ מֶלֶךְ אַשּׁוּר יִשְׁכְּנוּ אַדִּירֶיךָ נָפֹשׁוּ 18

are scattered | your .nobles | lying down | Are | .Assyria | king of | O | Your ,shepherds | slumber | where | (are) they. | their place.

עַמְּךָ עַל־הֶהָרִים וְאֵין מְקַבֵּץ׃ אֵין־כֵּהָה לְשִׁבְרֶךָ נַחְלָה 19

(is) severe | your ;fracture | for | healing | Not is | any .collecting | and is not | the ,mountains | on | Your people

מַכָּתֶךָ כֹּל ׀ שֹׁמְעֵי שִׁמְעֲךָ תָּקְעוּ כַף עָלֶיךָ כִּי עַל־מִי לֹא־

not | whom | on | for | over ;you | the hand | shall clap | your report | those of hearing | All | your .wound

עָבְרָה רָעָתְךָ תָּמִיד׃

?continually | your evil | has passed

חבקוק

LIBER HABAKKUK

CAPUT. I א

CHAPTER 1

CHAPTER 1

[1] The burden which Habakkuk the prophet saw: [2] O Jehovah, until when shall I cry for help and You will not hear? I cry out to You, Violence! But you do not save! [3] Why do You show me iniquity, and You look upon toil? For destruction and violence (are) before me; and there is strife, and contention rises up. [4] Therefore the law has become void, and justice does not go forth continually. For the wicked hems in the righteous; therefore perverted justice goes forth. [5] Look among the nations and see, and wonder marvelously. For will work a work in your days (which) you will not believe, (even) if it is told. [6] For, lo, I raise up the Chaldeans, the bitter and hasty nation, which is going into the broad spaces of the land to possess tents not his own. [7] He (is) terrible and fearful; his judgment and his glory comes from himself. [8] His horses also are swifter than leopards, and are fiercer than the evening wolves. And their horsemen spread themselves, and their horsemen come from afar; they shall fly like the eagle, rushing to eat. [9] All of him comes for violence; the troop of their faces (are) eastward, and they gather captives like the sand. [10] And he scoffs at the kings, and the officers (are) a scorn to him. He laughs at every stronghold, and he heaps up dirt and captures it. [11] Then he sweeps on (as) the wind, and he transgresses, and is guilty;

1 הַמַּשָּׂא אֲשֶׁר חָזָה חֲבַקּוּק הַנָּבִיא׃ עַד־אָנָה יְהוָה שִׁוַּעְתִּי
2 I shall Jehovah ,when Until the Habakkuk saw which The
,aid for call .prophet burden
3 וְלֹא תִשְׁמָע אֶזְעַק אֵלֶיךָ חָמָס וְלֹא תוֹשִׁיעַ׃ לָמָּה תַרְאֵנִי
You do Why You But !Violence to cry I will You and
me show !save not ,You out ?hear not
אָוֶן וְעָמָל תַּבִּיט וְשֹׁד וְחָמָס לְנֶגְדִּי וַיְהִי רִיב וּמָדוֹן יִשָּׂא׃
rises and ,strife and (are) and And You toil and ,evil
.up contention is ;me before violence ruin ?behold
4 עַל־כֵּן תָּפוּג תּוֹרָה וְלֹא־יֵצֵא לָנֶצַח מִשְׁפָּט כִּי רָשָׁע
the For .justice continually goes and the become has Therefore
wicked forth not ,law helpless
5 מַכְתִּיר אֶת־הַצַּדִּיק עַל־כֵּן יֵצֵא מִשְׁפָּט מְעֻקָּל׃ רְאוּ
See being justice goes therefore the entraps
.perverted forth ;righteous
בַגּוֹיִם וְהַבִּיטוּ וְהִתַּמְּהוּ תְּמָהוּ כִּי־פֹעַל פֹּעֵל בִּימֵיכֶם לֹא
(which) your in is a For be be and and the among
not ,days working work !amazed ,amazed ,behold nations
6 תַאֲמִינוּ כִּי יְסֻפָּר׃ כִּי־הִנְנִי מֵקִים אֶת־הַכַּשְׂדִּים הַגּוֹי
the ,Chaldeans the am ,behold ,For be it though will you
nation up raising I .you told ,believe
הַמַּר וְהַנִּמְהָר הַהוֹלֵךְ לְמֶרְחֲבֵי־אֶרֶץ לָרֶשֶׁת מִשְׁכָּנוֹת
dwellings to the broad the into is that and bitter
possess land of spaces going ,impetuous
7 לֹּא־לוֹ׃ אָיֹם וְנוֹרָא הוּא מִמֶּנּוּ מִשְׁפָּטוֹ וּשְׂאֵתוֹ יֵצֵא׃
came his and his from ;(is) he and Terrible to not
.forth majesty judgment himself fearful .him
8 וְקַלּוּ מִנְּמֵרִים סוּסָיו וְחַדּוּ מִזְּאֵבֵי עֶרֶב וּפָשׁוּ פָּרָשָׁיו
Their out spread the the than are and his than are And
,horsemen .evening of wolves fiercer ,horses leopards swifter
9 וּפָרָשָׁיו מֵרָחוֹק יָבֹאוּ יָעֻפוּ כְּנֶשֶׁר חָשׁ לֶאֱכוֹל׃ כֻּלֹּה
of All .eat to hurrying the as shall they shall from their and
him ,eagle fly ;come afar horsemen
לְחָמָס יָבוֹא מְגַמַּת פְּנֵיהֶם קָדִימָה וַיֶּאֱסֹף כַּחוֹל שֶׁבִי׃
.captives the like they and (are) their troop the shall for
sand gather ,eastward faces of ;come violence
10 וְהוּא בַּמְּלָכִים יִתְקַלָּס וְרֹזְנִים מִשְׂחָק לוֹ הוּא לְכָל־מִבְצָר
fortress to he to (be shall) and shall the against And
every ,him scorn a officials ,scoff kings he
11 יִשְׂחָק וַיִּצְבֹּר עָפָר וַיִּלְכְּדָהּ׃ אָז חָלַף רוּחַ וַיַּעֲבֹר וְאָשֵׁם
is and he and (as) he Then capture and dirt shall he and shall
,guilty transgress wind on sweeps .it up heap ,scorn

(crediting) his power (in) this to his god.

[12] Are You from of old, Jehovah my God, my Holy One? We shall not die, Jehovah, You have ordained him for judgment. And, (O) Rock, You have established him for correction. [13] (You are) of purer eyes than to behold evil, and to look on vexation are not able; why do You look on those who deal deceitfully? Will You be silent when the wicked swallows (one) more righteous than he? [14] For You make man like the fish of the sea, like creeping things with no ruler over him. [15] He takes up all of him with the hook; he drags him with his net and gathers him with his seine; therefore he rejoices and exults. [16] So he sacrifices to his net and burns incense to his seine; because by them his portion (is) fat and his food is rich. [17] Shall he therefore empty his net, and spare not to slay the nations continually?

12 זוּ כֹחוֹ לֵאלֹהוֹ׃ הֲלוֹא אַתָּה מִקֶּדֶם יְהוָה אֱלֹהַי קְדֹשִׁי

my my Jehovah from You Are his to his this
?One Holy ,God ,old of not .god power

לֹא נָמוּת יְהוָה לְמִשְׁפָּט שַׂמְתּוֹ וְצוּר לְהוֹכִיחַ יְסַדְתּוֹ׃

estab- you to ,And have You For ;Jehovah shall we Not
.him lished correct ,Rock .him set judgment ,die

13 טְהוֹר עֵינַיִם מֵרְאוֹת רָע וְהַבִּיט אֶל־עָמָל לֹא תוּכָל לָמָּה

why are You not vexa- upon to and ,evil to than eyes Purer
;able tion look view (are You) of

14 תַּבִּיט בּוֹגְדִים תַּחֲרִישׁ בְּבַלַּע רָשָׁע צַדִּיק מִמֶּנּוּ׃ וַתַּעֲשֶׂה

You For than more (one) the when You Will dealing those You do
make ?he righteous wicked swallows silent be ?deceitfully watch

15 אָדָם כִּדְגֵי הַיָּם כְּרֶמֶשׂ לֹא־מֹשֵׁל בּוֹ׃ כֻּלֹּה בְּחַכָּה הֵעֲלָה

takes he a with Everyone over one not creep- like the the like man
;up hook him of . .him ruling (is) ,things ing ,sea of fish

יְגֹרֵהוּ בְחֶרְמוֹ וְיַאַסְפֵהוּ בְּמִכְמַרְתּוֹ עַל־כֵּן יִשְׂמַח וְיָגִיל׃

and he therefore his with gathers and his with drags he
.exults rejoices ;fishnet him ,net him

16 עַל־כֵּן יְזַבֵּחַ לְחֶרְמוֹ וִיקַטֵּר לְמִכְמַרְתּוֹ כִּי בָהֵמָּה שָׁמֵן

grows them by be- his to burns and his to he Therefore
fat cause ;fishnet incense net sacrifices

17 חֶלְקוֹ וּמַאֲכָלוֹ בְּרִאָה׃ הַעַל כֵּן יָרִיק חֶרְמוֹ וְתָמִיד לַהֲרֹג

slay to and ,net his he ,Therefore .rich is his and his
continually empty shall food ,portion

גּוֹיִם לֹא יַחְמוֹל׃

he shall not nations
?spare

CAP. II ב

CHAPTER 2

CHAPTER 2

[1] I will stand on my guard, and set myself on the tower, and watch to see what He will say against me, and what I shall answer on my rebuke. [2] And Jehovah answered me and said, Write the vision, and engrave (it) on the tablets, that he who reads it may run. [3] For the vision (is) still for the set time, but it pants to the end, and does not lie. Though it lingers, wait for it; because it will surely come; it will not tarry. [4] Behold, the soul of him (who) is lifted up is not upright in him; but the just shall live by his faith.

[5] And also indeed wine betrays a proud man, and he is not content; who enlarges his soul as Sheol, and (is) like death, and is

1 עַל־מִשְׁמַרְתִּי אֶעֱמֹדָה וְאֶתְיַצְּבָה עַל־מָצוֹר וַאֲצַפֶּה לִרְאוֹת

see to and the on set and will I guard my On
watch bulwark myself ,stand

2 מַה־יְדַבֶּר־בִּי וּמָה אָשִׁיב עַל־תּוֹכַחְתִּי׃ וַיַּעֲנֵנִי יְהוָה

Jehovah an- And my upon shall I and against will He what
me swered .rebuke return what ,me say

וַיֹּאמֶר כְּתֹב חָזוֹן וּבָאֵר עַל־הַלֻּחוֹת לְמַעַן יָרוּץ קוֹרֵא בוֹ׃

.it is who may he so the on en- and the Write ,said and
reading run that ,tablets (it) grave ,vision

3 כִּי עוֹד חָזוֹן לַמּוֹעֵד וְיָפֵחַ לַקֵּץ וְלֹא יְכַזֵּב אִם־יִתְמַהְמָהּ

,delays it Though does and the to it but the for the still For
.lie not ,end pants ,time set (is) vision

4 חַכֵּה־לוֹ כִּי־בֹא יָבֹא לֹא יְאַחֵר׃ הִנֵּה עֻפְּלָה לֹא־יָשְׁרָה

,upright is not puffed is ,Behold will it not will it surely for for wait
,up .tarry ;come ;it

5 נַפְשׁוֹ בּוֹ וְצַדִּיק בֶּאֱמוּנָתוֹ יִחְיֶה׃ וְאַף כִּי־הַיַּיִן בֹּגֵד גֶּבֶר

a betrays the ,indeed And shall his by the but in his
man wine also .live faith just ,him soul

יָהִיר וְלֹא יִנְוֶה אֲשֶׁר הִרְחִיב כִּשְׁאוֹל נַפְשׁוֹ וְהוּא כַמָּוֶת

like he and his Sheol like widens who is he and ,proud
,death (is) ,soul ;content not

not satisfied, but gathers all nations to himself, and heaps to himself all the peoples; shall not these, all of them, lift up a parable against him, and a mocking riddle to him, and say, Woe to him who increases (what is) not his! How long, then, shall he load on himself heavy pledges? [7] Shall not those who strike you rise up suddenly, and (those) who shake you awake; yea, you shall be a prize to him? [8] Because you have stripped many nations, all the rest of the peoples shall strip you; from the blood of man, and the violence of the land, and the city, and all who live in it.

[9] Woe (to) him who robs evil booty for his house to set his nest on high, to be delivered from the hand of evil! [10] You have advised shame for your house to make an end of many peoples, and are sinning (in) your soul. [11] For the stone shall cry out from the wall, and the beam shall answer it from the wood.

[12] Woe to him who builds a town with blood, and establishes a city by iniquity! [13] Behold, is it not from Jehovah of hosts that the peoples labor only for fire; yea, nations weary themselves only for vanity? [14] For the earth shall be filled with the knowledge of the glory of Jehovah, as the waters cover the sea.

[15] Woe to him who causes his friend to drink, pouring out your wineskin and also making (him) drunk, in order to look on their nakedness! [16] You are filled with shame instead of glory; you drink also, and be seen (as) uncircumcised. The cup of Jehovah's right hand shall be turned on you, and shame (shall be) on your glory. [17] For the violence of Lebanon shall cover you, and the ruin of beasts shall terrify them because of man's blood, and the violence of the land, the city, and all who live in it.

[18] What does an image profit, for its maker

וְלֹא יִשְׂבָּע וַיֶּאֱסֹף אֵלָיו כָּל־הַגּוֹיִם וַיִּקְבֹּץ אֵלָיו כָּל־הָעַמִּים׃
the all to and the all to but sat- is and
;peoples himself collects ,nations himself gathers ,isfied not

6 הֲלוֹא־אֵלֶּה כֻלָּם עָלָיו מָשָׁל יִשָּׂאוּ וּמְלִיצָה חִידוֹת לוֹ
to riddle a and ,up lift a against of all ,these shall
,him mocking parable him ,them not

וְיֹאמַר הוֹי הַמַּרְבֶּה לֹא־לוֹ עַד־מָתַי וּמַכְבִּיד עָלָיו עַבְטִיט׃
the upon he even when Until to (is what) one the Woe and
?pledges himself loading (is) !him not increasing (to) ,say

7 הֲלוֹא פֶתַע יָקוּמוּ נֹשְׁכֶיךָ וְיִקְצוּ מְזַעְזְעֶיךָ וְהָיִיתָ לִמְשִׁסּוֹת
prize a you and who those be and who those rise suddenly Shall
become ,you shake aroused you strike up not

8 לָמוֹ׃ כִּי־אַתָּה שַׁלּוֹתָ גּוֹיִם רַבִּים יְשָׁלּוּךָ כָּל־יֶתֶר עַמִּים
the the all shall ,many nations have you Because to
,peoples of rest you plunder plundered ?him

9 מִדְּמֵי אָדָם וַחֲמַס־אֶרֶץ קִרְיָה וְכָל־יֹשְׁבֵי בָהּ׃ הוֹי
Woe .it in those and the and the the and ,man from
(to) dwelling all city land of violence of blood the

בֹּצֵעַ בֶּצַע רָע לְבֵיתוֹ לָשׂוּם בַּמָּרוֹם קִנּוֹ לְהִנָּצֵל מִכַּף־רָע׃
!evil the from be to his the in set to his for evil booty the him
of hand delivered ,nest height ,house of robbing

10 יָעַצְתָּ בֹּשֶׁת לְבֵיתֶךָ קְצוֹת־עַמִּים רַבִּים וְחוֹטֵא נַפְשֶׁךָ׃
your (in) are and ,many peoples make to your for shame have You
.soul sinning of end an house counselled

11 כִּי־אֶבֶן מִקִּיר תִּזְעָק וְכָפִיס מֵעֵץ יַעֲנֶנָּה׃
12 הוֹי בֹּנֶה
him (to) Woe shall the from the and cry shall from the For
building .it answer wood beam ,out wall the stone

13 עִיר בְּדָמִים וְכוֹנֵן קִרְיָה בְּעַוְלָה׃ הֲלוֹא הִנֵּה מֵאֵת יְהוָה
Jehovah from ,behold it Is by city a and with a
of ,not !iniquity establishing ,blood town

צְבָאוֹת וְיִיגְעוּ עַמִּים בְּדֵי־אֵשׁ וּלְאֻמִּים בְּדֵי־רִיק יִעָפוּ׃
grow emptiness only and ;fire only peoples that ,hosts
.weary for nations for toil

14 כִּי תִּמָּלֵא הָאָרֶץ לָדַעַת אֶת־כְּבוֹד יְהוָה כַּמַּיִם יְכַסּוּ
cover the as ,Jehovah glory the the with the be shall For
waters of of knowledge earth filled

15 עַל־יָם׃ הוֹי מַשְׁקֵה רֵעֵהוּ מְסַפֵּחַ חֲמָתְךָ וְאַף שַׁכֵּר
making and your pouring his causing him Woe the over
,drunk also ,wineskin out ,friend drink to (to) .sea

16 לְמַעַן הַבִּיט עַל־מְעוֹרֵיהֶם׃ שָׂבַעְתָּ קָלוֹן מִכָּבוֹד שְׁתֵה
drink from (with) are You their upon look order in
;glory shame satiated !nakedness to

גַם־אַתָּה וְהֵעָרֵל תִּסּוֹב עָלֶיךָ כּוֹס יְמִין יְהוָה וְקִיקָלוֹן עַל־
on disgrace ,Jehovah right the the upon Shall seen be and you also
of hand of cup you turn !uncircumcised

17 כְּבוֹדֶךָ׃ כִּי־חֲמַס לְבָנוֹן יְכַסֶּךָּ וְשֹׁד בְּהֵמוֹת יְחִיתַן מִדְּמֵי
the from shall beasts the and shall Lebanon the For your
of blood them terrify of ruin ,you cover of violence .glory

18 אָדָם וַחֲמַס־אֶרֶץ קִרְיָה וְכָל־יֹשְׁבֵי בָהּ׃ מָה־הוֹעִיל פֶּסֶל
an does What .it in those and the the the and ,man
,image profit dwelling all ,city ,land of violence

has carved it; a molten image, and a teacher of a lie; for the maker trusts his work on it, to make mute idols? [19] Woe to him who says to the wood, Awake! to a mute stone, Arise, it shall teach! Behold, it (is) overlaid (with) gold and silver, but any breath is not in its midst. [20] But Jehovah (is) in His holy temple; let all the earth be silent before Him.

כִּי פָסְלוֹ יֹצְרוֹ מַסֵּכָה וּמוֹרֶה שָּׁקֶר כִּי־בָטַח יֹצֵר יִצְרוֹ
his the trusts For false- an and casted a its carved has for
work maker ?hood of instructor image ;maker it

19 עָלָיו לַעֲשׂוֹת אֱלִילִים אִלְּמִים׃ הוֹי אֹמֵר לָעֵץ הָקִיצָה
!Awake the to one the Woe ?mute idols make to upon
,wood saying (to) ,it

עוּרִי לְאֶבֶן דּוּמָם הוּא יוֹרֶה הִנֵּה־הוּא תָּפוּשׂ זָהָב וָכֶסֶף
and (with) is it ,Behold shall it ;silent a to !Arise
,silver gold overlaid !instruct stone

20 וְכָל־רוּחַ אֵין בְּקִרְבּוֹ׃ וַיהוָה בְּהֵיכַל קָדְשׁוֹ הַס מִפָּנָיו
before be His the in (is) But its in not breath and
,Him silent ;holiness of temple Jehovah .midst is any

כָּל־הָאָרֶץ׃
.earth the all

CAP. III ג

CHAPTER 3

CHAPTER 3

[1] A prayer of Habakkuk the prophet concerning erring ones. [2] Jehovah, I have heard Your report. I am afraid, Jehovah; give new life (to) Your work in the midst of years; in the midst of years make known; in wrath remember mercy. [3] God comes from Teman, and the Holy One from Mount Paran. Selah. His majesty covers the heavens, and His praise fills the earth. [4] And (His) brightness is as the light; rays from His hand (are) to Him, and there (was) a hiding of His strength. [5] A plague goes before Him, and lightning went forth at His feet. [6] He stood and measured the earth; He looked and shook nations; and the ancient mountains were shattered, the eternal hills bowed down; the goings of eternity are His. [7] I saw the tents of Cushan under calamity; the curtains of the land of Midian trembled. [8] Did Jehovah burn against rivers? Or (was) Your anger against the rivers? Or Your fury against the sea? For You ride on Your horses, Your chariots of salvation. [9] You bare Your bow naked; (according) to the oaths of the rod of Your

1
2 תְּפִלָּה לַחֲבַקּוּק הַנָּבִיא עַל שִׁגְיֹנוֹת׃ יְהוָה שָׁמַעְתִּי שִׁמְעֲךָ
Your have I ,Jehovah .Shigionoth on the Habakkuk of A
;report heard ,prophet prayer

יָרֵאתִי יְהוָה פָּעָלְךָ בְּקֶרֶב שָׁנִים חַיֵּיהוּ בְּקֶרֶב שָׁנִים
years the in it give ,years the in Your (to) Jeho- am I
of midst ;life of midst work ,vah ;afraid

3 תּוֹדִיעַ בְּרֹגֶז רַחֵם תִּזְכּוֹר׃ אֱלוֹהַּ מִתֵּימָן יָבוֹא וְקָדוֹשׁ
the and ,comes from God .remember com- anger in make
One Holy Teman passion ;known

מֵהַר־פָּארָן סֶלָה כִּסָּה שָׁמַיִם הוֹדוֹ וּתְהִלָּתוֹ מָלְאָה
fills His and His the covers .Selah .Paran the from
praise ,majesty heavens of mountain

4 הָאָרֶץ׃ וְנֹגַהּ כָּאוֹר תִּהְיֶה קַרְנַיִם מִיָּדוֹ לוֹ וְשָׁם חֶבְיוֹן
a (was) and to (are) from rays ;is the as (His) And the
of covering there , His hand His light brightness .earth

5
6 עֻזֹּה׃ לְפָנָיו יֵלֶךְ דָּבֶר וְיֵצֵא רֶשֶׁף לְרַגְלָיו׃ עָמַד ׀ וַיְמֹדֶד
and He His at lightning and ,plague a goes Before His
measured stood .feet forth went Him .strength

אֶרֶץ רָאָה וַיַּתֵּר גּוֹיִם וַיִּתְפֹּצְצוּ הַרְרֵי־עַד שַׁחוּ גִּבְעוֹת
the bowed ;ancient the were and ;nations and He the
of hills down mountains shattered shook looked ;earth

7 עוֹלָם הֲלִיכוֹת עוֹלָם לוֹ׃ תַּחַת אָוֶן רָאִיתִי אָהֳלֵי כוּשָׁן
;Cushan tents the saw I calamity Under to eternity goings the ;eternity
of .Him (are) of

8 יִרְגְּזוּן יְרִיעוֹת אֶרֶץ מִדְיָן׃ הֲבִנְהָרִים חָרָה יְהוָה אִם
Or ?Jehovah burn against Did Midian the the trembled
(was) rivers of land of curtains

בַּנְּהָרִים אַפֶּךָ אִם־בַּיָּם עֶבְרָתֶךָ כִּי תִרְכַּב עַל־סוּסֶיךָ
Your on You (For) Your against Or Your the against
,horses ride ?fury sea the ?anger rivers

9 מַרְכְּבֹתֶיךָ יְשׁוּעָה׃ עֶרְיָה תֵעוֹר קַשְׁתֶּךָ שְׁבֻעוֹת מַטּוֹת
rods the (to according) Your You Naked .salvation Your
of of oaths the ;bow bare of chariots

word. Selah. You cut through the earth (with) rivers. [10] They saw You; mountains trembled. The storm of water passed over; the deep gave its voice (and) lifted up its hands on high. [11] The sun (and) moon stood still in their dwelling. At the light of Your arrows they go, at the shining of Your gleaming spear. [12] You march into the land in fury. You thresh nations in anger. [13] You went forth for the salvation of Your people, for the salvation of Your anointed. You struck the head from the house of the wicked, to bare the foundation to the neck. Selah. [14] You pierced the head of his warriors with his shafts; they rush to scatter me; their rejoicing (is) to devour the meek in a secret place. [15] You trod in the sea with Your horses, the foaming of many waters. [16] I heard and my belly trembled; my lips quivered at the sound. Rottenness entered into my bones, and I trembled within myself that I might rest for the day of distress; to come up against the people he invades him.

[17] Though the fig-tree shall not blossom; and fruit is not on the vines; the work of the olive fails; and the fields make no food; the flock is cut off from the fold; and no herd (is) in the stalls; [18] yet I will exult in Jehovah, I will rejoice in the God of my salvation. [19] Jehovah the Lord (is) my might, and He sets my feet like hinds' (feet), and He will make me to walk on my high places.

To the chief singer, on my stringed instruments.

10 אֹמֶר סֶלָה נְהָרוֹת תְּבַקַּע־אָרֶץ׃ רָאוּךָ יָחִילוּ הָרִים זֶרֶם

The .mountains tremble They the have You (with) .Selah (Your)
of storm ;You saw .earth split rivers .word

11 מַיִם עָבָר נָתַן תְּהוֹם קוֹלוֹ רוֹם יָדֵיהוּ נָשָׂא׃ שֶׁמֶשׁ יָרֵחַ

the (and) The lifted it its high its the gave passed water
moon sun .up hands ;voice deep ;over

12 עָמַד זְבֻלָה לְאוֹר חִצֶּיךָ יְהַלֵּכוּ לְנֹגַהּ בְּרַק חֲנִיתֶךָ׃ בְּזַעַם

fury In Your light- the the at they Your the At (their) in stood
.spear of ning of splendor ,march arrows of light .dwelling

13 תִּצְעַד־אָרֶץ בְּאַף תָּדוּשׁ גּוֹיִם׃ יָצָאתָ לְיֵשַׁע עַמֶּךָ לְיֵשַׁע

the for Your the for went You .nations You In the march You
of saving people of salvation forth thresh anger .land into

אֶת־מְשִׁיחֶךָ מָחַצְתָּ רֹּאשׁ מִבֵּית רָשָׁע עָרוֹת יְסוֹד עַד־

to foun- the bare to the the from the You Your
dation ,wicked of house head struck .anointed

14 צַוָּאר סֶלָה׃ נָקַבְתָּ בְמַטָּיו רֹאשׁ פְּרָזָו יִסְעֲרוּ לַהֲפִיצֵנִי

scatter to rush they his head the his with You .Selah the
;me ;warriors of shafts pierced .neck

15 עֲלִיצֻתָם כְּמוֹ־לֶאֱכֹל עָנִי בַּמִּסְתָּר׃ דָּרַכְתָּ בַיָּם סוּסֶיךָ חֹמֶר

foam- the Your the (in) You the to the to (is) their
of ing ,horses sea trod .place secret meek devour as rejoicing

16 מַיִם רַבִּים׃ שָׁמַעְתִּי ׀ וַתִּרְגַּז בִּטְנִי לְקוֹל צָלֲלוּ שְׂפָתַי יָבוֹא

Enters my quivered the at my and heard I .many waters
.lips sound ;belly trembled

רָקָב בַּעֲצָמַי וְתַחְתַּי אֶרְגָּז אֲשֶׁר אָנוּחַ לְיוֹם צָרָה לַעֲלוֹת

come to ;distress the for might I that I within and my into rotten-
up of day rest ,trembled myself ,bones ness

17 לְעַם יְגוּדֶנּוּ׃ כִּי־תְאֵנָה לֹא־תִפְרָח וְאֵין יְבוּל בַּגְּפָנִים כִּחֵשׁ

(and) the on produce and does not fig the Though in- he against
fails ,vines is not ,bud tree .him vades people the

מַעֲשֵׂה־זַיִת וּשְׁדֵמוֹת לֹא־עָשָׂה אֹכֶל גָּזַר מִמִּכְלָה צֹאן וְאֵין

and the the from (is) and ,food make not the and the the
is not ,flock fold off cut fields ,olive of work

18 בָּקָר בָּרְפָתִים׃ וַאֲנִי בַּיהוָה אֶעְלוֹזָה אָגִילָה בֵּאלֹהֵי יִשְׁעִי׃

sal- my the in will I ,exult will in I yet the in herd
.vation of God rejoice Jehovah ,stalls

19 יְהוִה אֲדֹנָי חֵילִי וַיָּשֶׂם רַגְלַי כָּאַיָּלוֹת וְעַל־בָּמוֹתַי יַדְרִכֵנִי

will He high my and the like my He and my (is) the Jehovah
.walk me make places on ,hinds' feet set ,might Lord

לַמְנַצֵּחַ בִּנְגִינוֹתָי׃

stringed my on chief the To
.instruments ,musician

צ פ נ י ה

LIBER ZEPHANIAE

CAPUT. I א

CHAPTER 1

CHAPTER 1

[1] The word of Jehovah which was to Zephaniah the son of Cushi, the son of Gedaliah, the son of Amariah, the son of Hezekiah, in the days of Josiah the son of Amon, king of Judah. [2] I will completely snatch away all from on the face of the ground, states Jehovah. [3] I will snatch away man and beast. I will snatch away the birds of the heavens and the fish of the sea, and the stumbling-blocks, (even) the wicked. And I will cut off man from the face of the ground, states Jehovah. [4] I will also stretch out My hand on Judah, and on all the inhabitants of Jerusalem. And I will cut off the remnant of Baal from this place, the name of the idol-worshipers, with the priests;

[5] and those bowing to the host of the heavens on the housetops; and those bowing, swearing to Jehovah yet swearing by Malcham; [6] and those drawing back from after Jehovah, and (those) who have not sought Jehovah, nor asked of Him. [7] Be silent before the face of the Lord Jehovah, for the day of Jehovah (is) near! For Jehovah has appointed a sacrifice; He has consecrated His called ones. [8] And it shall be, in the day of Jehovah's sacrifice, that I will punish the rulers and the king's sons, and all who are clothed (in) foreign clothing. [9] Also in that day I

1 דְּבַר־יְהוָה ׀ אֲשֶׁר־הָיָה אֶל־צְפַנְיָה בֶּן־כּוּשִׁי בֶן־גְּדַלְיָה
,Gedaliah the ,Cushi the Zephaniah to was which Jehovah The
of son of son of word
בֶּן־אֲמַרְיָה בֶּן־חִזְקִיָּה בִּימֵי יֹאשִׁיָּהוּ בֶן־אָמוֹן מֶלֶךְ יְהוּדָה׃
.Judah king ,Amon the ,Josiah the in ,Hezekiah the ,Amariah the
of of son of days of son of son
2 אָסֹף אָסֵף כֹּל מֵעַל פְּנֵי הָאֲדָמָה נְאֻם־יְהוָה׃
3 אָסֵף
will I .Jehovah statement the the from all will I com-
snatch of ,ground of face on away snatch pletely
אָדָם וּבְהֵמָה אָסֵף עוֹף־הַשָּׁמַיִם וּדְגֵי הַיָּם וְהַמַּכְשֵׁלוֹת
stumbling the and the the and the the will I and man
,blocks ,sea of fish heavens of birds snatch ,beast
אֶת־הָרְשָׁעִים וְהִכְרַתִּי אֶת־הָאָדָם מֵעַל פְּנֵי הָאֲדָמָה
the the from man will I And .wicked the (even)
,ground of face on off cut
4 נְאֻם־יְהוָה׃ וְנָטִיתִי יָדִי עַל־יְהוּדָה וְעַל כָּל־יוֹשְׁבֵי יְרוּשָׁלִָם
.Jerusalem those all and Judah against My will I And Jehovah state-
in dwelling against hand out stretch of ment
וְהִכְרַתִּי מִן־הַמָּקוֹם הַזֶּה אֶת־שְׁאָר הַבַּעַל אֶת־שֵׁם
the ,Baal remnant the this place from will I And
of name of off cut
5 הַכְּמָרִים עִם־הַכֹּהֲנִים׃ וְאֶת־הַמִּשְׁתַּחֲוִים עַל־הַגַּגּוֹת
the on those and ;priests the with the
roofs bowing idolators
לִצְבָא הַשָּׁמָיִם וְאֶת־הַמִּשְׁתַּחֲוִים הַנִּשְׁבָּעִים לַיהוָה
to swearing those and the the to
,Jehovah ,bowing ;heavens of host
6 וְהַנִּשְׁבָּעִים בְּמַלְכָּם׃ וְאֶת־הַנְּסוֹגִים מֵאַחֲרֵי יְהוָה וַאֲשֶׁר
and ,Jehovah from drawing those and by swearing yet
who after back ;Malcham
7 לֹא־בִקְשׁוּ אֶת־יְהוָה וְלֹא־דְרָשֻׁהוּ׃ הַס מִפְּנֵי אֲדֹנָי יְהוִה
,Jehovah the before Be asked have and ,Jehovah have not
Lord silent .Him of not sought
כִּי קָרוֹב יוֹם יְהוָה כִּי־הֵכִין יְהוָה זֶבַח הִקְדִּישׁ קְרֻאָיו׃
called His has He a Jehovah has For !Jehovah the (is) for
.ones consecrated ;sacrifice appointed of day near
8 וְהָיָה בְּיוֹם זֶבַח יְהוָה וּפָקַדְתִּי עַל־הַשָּׂרִים וְעַל־
and the upon will I that ,Jehovah the the in it And
upon rulers visit of sacrifice of day ,be shall
9 בְּנֵי הַמֶּלֶךְ וְעַל כָּל־הַלֹּבְשִׁים מַלְבּוּשׁ נָכְרִי׃ וּפָקַדְתִּי
will I And .foreign (in) those all and the the
visit clothing clothed upon ,king of sons

will punish all those who leap on the threshold, who fill their masters' houses (with) violence and deceit. [10] And it shall be in that day, states Jehovah, the sound of a cry from the Fish Gate, and a howling from the Second, and a great breaking from the hills. [11] Howl, dwellers of Maktesh, for all the people of Canaan are cut down; all those who carry silver are cut off. [12] And it shall be in that time, I will search Jerusalem with lamps, and punish the men being settled on their lees; who say in their heart, Jehovah will not do good, nor will He do evil. [13] And their goods shall become a prize and their houses a waste. They shall also build houses, but not live (there); and they shall plant vineyards, but not drink their wine. [14] The great day of Jehovah (is) near. (It is) near and rushing greatly, the sound of the day of Jehovah. The mighty man shall cry out there bitterly. [15] That day (is) a day of wrath, a day of adversity and distress, a day of waste and ruin, a day of darkness and gloom, a day of clouds and thick darkness, [16] a day of the ram's horn and alarm against the fortified cities and against the high towers. [17] And I will bring distress to man, and they shall walk like the blind, because they have sinned against Jehovah. And their blood shall be poured out as dust, and their flesh like dung. [18] Their silver and their gold shall not be able to deliver them in the day of the wrath of Jehovah. But

עַל כָּל־הַדּוֹלֵג עַל־הַמִּפְתָּן בַּיּוֹם הַהוּא הַמְמַלְאִים בֵּית
house the of | those filling | ,that | day in | the threshold | on | those leaping | all upon

10 אֲדֹנֵיהֶם חָמָס וּמִרְמָה׃ וְהָיָה בַיּוֹם הַהוּא נְאֻם־
statement of | ,that | day in | it And be shall | and .deceit | (with) violence | their masters

יְהוָה קוֹל צְעָקָה מִשַּׁעַר הַדָּגִים וִילָלָה מִן־הַמִּשְׁנֶה וְשֶׁבֶר
a and breaking | the ,Second | from | a and howling | the ,Fish | from Gate | cry a | the of sound | ,Jehovah

11 גָּדוֹל מֵהַגְּבָעוֹת׃ הֵילִילוּ יֹשְׁבֵי הַמַּכְתֵּשׁ כִּי נִדְמָה כָּל־
all | have perished | for | ,Maktesh | dwellers of | ,Howl | the from .hills | great

12 עַם כְּנַעַן נִכְרְתוּ כָּל־נְטִילֵי כָסֶף׃ וְהָיָה בָּעֵת
time in | it And be shall | .silver | those carrying | all | cut are off | ;Canaan the of people

הַהִיא אֲחַפֵּשׂ אֶת־יְרוּשָׁלִַם בַּנֵּרוֹת וּפָקַדְתִּי עַל־הָאֲנָשִׁים
men the | upon | visit and | ,lamps with | Jerusalem | will I out search | ,that

הַקֹּפְאִים עַל־שִׁמְרֵיהֶם הָאֹמְרִים בִּלְבָבָם לֹא־יֵיטִיב יְהוָה
,Jehovah | do will Not good | their in ,heart | those saying | their ;lees | on | being settled

13 וְלֹא יָרֵעַ׃ וְהָיָה חֵילָם לִמְשִׁסָּה וּבָתֵּיהֶם לִשְׁמָמָה וּבָנוּ
they And build shall | a .desolation | their and houses | ,prize a | their wealth | shall And become | will He .evil do | and not

14 בָתִּים וְלֹא יֵשֵׁבוּ וְנָטְעוּ כְרָמִים וְלֹא יִשְׁתּוּ אֶת־יֵינָם׃ קָרוֹב
near (Is) | .wine their | drink | but not | ,vineyards | they and plant shall | dwell ,(there) | but not | ,houses

יוֹם־יְהוָה הַגָּדוֹל קָרוֹב וּמַהֵר מְאֹד קוֹל יוֹם יְהוָה מַר
Bit- terly | .Jehovah | the of day | the of sound | ,greatly | and hurrying | (is It) near | the .great | Jehovah day of

15 צֹרֵחַ שָׁם גִּבּוֹר׃ יוֹם עֶבְרָה הַיּוֹם הַהוּא יוֹם צָרָה
adversity | day of | ,that | (is) day | wrath | day A of | the .man mighty | there | shall out cry

וּמְצוּקָה יוֹם שֹׁאָה וּמְשׁוֹאָה יוֹם חֹשֶׁךְ וַאֲפֵלָה יוֹם עָנָן
clouds | a of day | and ,gloom | darkness | a of day | ,ruin and | waste | a of day | and ,distress

16 וַעֲרָפֶל׃ יוֹם שׁוֹפָר וּתְרוּעָה עַל הֶעָרִים הַבְּצֻרוֹת וְעַל
and against | ,fortified | the cities | against | and alarm | ram's the horn | a of day | thick and ,darkness

17 הַפִּנּוֹת הַגְּבֹהוֹת׃ וַהֲצֵרֹתִי לָאָדָם וְהָלְכוּ כַּעִוְרִים כִּי
be- cause | blind like ,men | they and walk shall | ,man to | will I And distress bring | .high | the towers

18 לַיהוָה חָטָאוּ וְשֻׁפַּךְ דָּמָם כֶּעָפָר וּלְחֻמָם כַּגְּלָלִים׃ גַּם־
Also | .dung like | their and flesh | like ,dust | their blood | be shall And out poured | they .sinned | against Jehovah

כַּסְפָּם גַּם־זְהָבָם לֹא־יוּכַל לְהַצִּילָם בְּיוֹם עֶבְרַת יְהוָה
.Jehovah | the of wrath | the in of day | deliver to them | be shall able | not | their gold | and | their silver

all the earth shall be consumed by the fire of His jealousy. For He shall make a full, yea, a speedy end of all the dwellers in the land.

CHAPTER 2

[1] Gather yourselves together; even gather, O nation not ashamed; [2] before the birth of the decree, the day shall pass like the chaff, yet not before the hot anger of Jehovah comes on you, yet not before the day of Jehovah's anger comes on you. [3] Seek Jehovah, all the meek of the earth who have done His justice; seek righteousness, seek meekness. It may be you shall be hidden in the day of the anger of Jehovah.

[4] For Gaza shall be forsaken, and Ashkelon a ruin. They shall drive Ashdod out at the noonday, and Ekron shall be rooted up. [5] Woe (to) the inhabitants of the seacoast, the nation of the Cherethites! The word of Jehovah (is) against you, Canaan, the land of the Philistines; I will destroy you so as not to be an inhabitant. [6] And the seacoast shall be pastures, shepherds' meadows, and folds for the flock. [7] And the coast shall be for the remnant of the house of Judah; they shall feed on them. In the houses of Ashkelon, they shall lie down in the evening, for Jehovah their God shall visit them and return their captivity.

[8] I have heard the reproach of Moab and the curses of the sons of Ammon, with which they have cursed My people and have magnified (themselves) on their border. [9] Therefore, (as) I live, states Jehovah of hosts, the God of Israel, surely Moab shall be as Sodom, and the sons of Ammon like Gomorrah; a place possessed by nettles and a salt

וּבְאֵשׁ קִנְאָתוֹ תֵּאָכֵל כָּל־הָאָרֶץ כִּי כָלָה אַךְ־נִבְהָלָה יַעֲשֶׂה

shall He make | speedy a end | ,yea | ,full a | For | the .earth | all | be shall consumed | His jealousy | the by But of fire

אֵת כָּל־יֹשְׁבֵי הָאָרֶץ׃

the .earth | in- of habitants | the all | (of)

CAP. II ב

CHAPTER 2

1 הִתְקוֹשְׁשׁוּ וָקוֹשּׁוּ הַגּוֹי לֹא נִכְסָף׃

2 בְּטֶרֶם לֶדֶת חֹק כְּמֹץ

the like chaff | the birth ,decree | the of | before | ;ashamed | not | O nation | even ,gather | Gather ;yourselves

עָבַר יוֹם בְּטֶרֶם ׀ לֹא־יָבוֹא עֲלֵיכֶם חֲרוֹן אַף־יְהוָה בְּטֶרֶם

before yet | ,Jehovah | the heat of anger | the of | on you | comes | not | yet before | the ,day | shall pass

3 לֹא־יָבוֹא עֲלֵיכֶם יוֹם אַף־יְהוָה׃ בַּקְּשׁוּ אֶת־יְהוָה כָּל־עַנְוֵי

the of meek | all | ,Jehovah | Seek | .Jehovah | the of anger | the of day | you on | comes | not

הָאָרֶץ אֲשֶׁר מִשְׁפָּטוֹ פָּעָלוּ בַּקְּשׁוּ־צֶדֶק בַּקְּשׁוּ עֲנָוָה אוּלַי

Perhaps | meek- .ness | seek | righteous- ,ness | seek | have ;done | His justice | who | the ,earth

4 תִּסָּתְרוּ בְּיוֹם אַף־יְהוָה׃ כִּי עַזָּה עֲזוּבָה תִהְיֶה וְאַשְׁקְלוֹן

Ashkelon and | shall ,be | abandoned | Gaza | For | .Jehovah | the of anger | the in of day | shall you hidden be

לִשְׁמָמָה אַשְׁדּוֹד בַּצָּהֳרַיִם יְגָרְשׁוּהָ וְעֶקְרוֹן תֵּעָקֵר׃

be shall .uprooted | Ekron and | shall they ,out her drive | the in noonday | —Ashdod | deso- a ;lation

5 הוֹי יֹשְׁבֵי חֶבֶל הַיָּם גּוֹי כְּרֵתִים דְּבַר־יְהוָה עֲלֵיכֶם כְּנַעַן

,Canaan | against ,you | Jehovah (is) | The of word | Chere- !thites | the of nation | the ,sea | the coast of | those on dwelling | Woe (to)

6 אֶרֶץ פְּלִשְׁתִּים וְהַאֲבַדְתִּיךְ מֵאֵין יוֹשֵׁב׃ וְהָיְתָה חֶבֶל הַיָּם

the sea | the of coast | shall And be | in- an .habitant | be so not | will I and you destroy | the ,Philistines | the of land

7 נְוֹת כְּרֹת רֹעִים וְגִדְרוֹת צֹאן׃ וְהָיָה חֶבֶל לִשְׁאֵרִית בֵּית

the of house | rem- of nant | the for | the coast | shall And be | the .flock | folds and for | ,shepherds mea- (for)dows | pas- ,tures

יְהוּדָה עֲלֵיהֶם יִרְעוּן בְּבָתֵּי אַשְׁקְלוֹן בָּעֶרֶב יִרְבָּצוּן כִּי

for | shall they ,down lie | the in evening | ,Ashkelon | the in of houses | shall they :pasture | upon them | ;Judah

8 יִפְקְדֵם יְהוָה אֱלֹהֵיהֶם וְשָׁב שְׁבוּתָם׃ שָׁמַעְתִּי חֶרְפַּת

con- the of tempt | have I heard | their .captivity | and return | their God | Jehovah | visit shall them

מוֹאָב וְגִדּוּפֵי בְּנֵי עַמּוֹן אֲשֶׁר חֵרְפוּ אֶת־עַמִּי וַיַּגְדִּילוּ עַל־

upon | have and great become | My people | have they cursed | (with) which | ,Ammon | the of sons | the and of reproaches | Moab

9 גְּבוּלָם׃ לָכֵן חַי־אָנִי נְאֻם יְהוָה צְבָאוֹת אֱלֹהֵי יִשְׂרָאֵל כִּי

surely | ,Israel | God the of | ,hosts | Jehovah of | ,declares | ,I live | (as) | There- ,fore | their .border

מוֹאָב כִּסְדֹם תִּהְיֶה וּבְנֵי עַמּוֹן כַּעֲמֹרָה מִמְשַׁק חָרוּל

nettles | pos- a of session | :Gomorrah like | Ammon and of sons the | ,be shall | like Sodom | Moab pit, and a ruin forever. The remnant of My people shall spoil them, and the rest of the nation shall possess them. [10] They shall have this for their pride, because they have cursed and magnified (themselves) against the people of Jehovah of hosts. [11] Jehovah (will be) frightening to them; for He will (make) lean all the gods of the earth, and will worship Him, (each) man from his place, and all the coasts of the nations.

[12] And you, O Ethiopians, pierced by My sword they (shall be). [13] And He will stretch out His hand against the north and destroy Assyria, and will make Nineveh a desolation, dry like the desert. [14] And flocks shall lie down in her midst, all the beasts of a nation: both the pelican and the bittern shall lodge in its pillar capitals. A voice shall sing at the window; ruin (shall be) at the doorsill, for the cedar-work He will bare. [15] This (is) the rejoicing city dwelling confidently, who says in her heart, I (am) and there is none (other) still. How a ruin she has become, a place for beasts to lie down! Everyone who passes near her shall hiss; he shall shake his fist!

ומכרה־מלח ושממה עד־עולם שארית עמי יבזום ויתר
the and shall My remnant The .forever to a and ,salt a and
of rest ,them spoil people of desolation of pit

10 גוי ינחלום׃ זאת להם תחת גאונם כי חרפו ויגדלו על־
against have and have they for their instead to This inherit shall the
great become cursed ,pride of them (be shall) .them nations

11 עם יהוה צבאות׃ נורא יהוה עליהם כי רזה את כל־
all will He for to Jehovah (be Will) .hosts Jehovah
lean (make) ;them frightening of people

אלהי הארץ וישתחוו־לו איש ממקומו כל איי הגוים׃
the the all his from (each) to will and the gods the
nations of islands ,place man ,Him bow ,earth of

12
13 גם־אתם כושים חללי חרבי המה׃ ויט ידו על־צפון
the against His He And they My pierced O ,you Also
north hand extends (are) sword by ,Ethiopians

ויאבד את־אשור וישם את־נינוה לשממה ציה כמדבר׃
the like dry a Nineveh will and ,Assyria and
.desert ,desolation make destroys

14 ורבצו בתוכה עדרים כל־חיתו־גוי גם־קאת גם־קפד
the and the both a ani- His all ,flocks her in shall And
bittern pelican ;nation of mals midst down lie

בכפתריה ילינו קול ישורר בחלון חרב בסף כי ארזה
cedar- the for the on ruin the at shall A shall pillar its in
work ,doorsill (be will) ;window sing voice .lodge capitals

15 ערה׃ זאת העיר העליזה היושבת לבטח האמרה
one the ,confidently dwelling joyful the city This will He
saying (is) .bare lay

בלבבה אני ואפסי עוד איך ׀ היתה לשמה מרבץ לחיה
for resting a a has she How (other) and I her in
!animals place ,desolation become .still is none (am) ,heart

כל עובר עליה ישרק יניע ידו׃
his shall he shall near passing Every-
!hand shake ;hiss her one

CAP. III ג

CHAPTER 3

[1] Woe (to) her rebelling and being defiled, (to) the oppressing city! [2] She did not listen to the voice; she did not receive correction; she trusted not in Jehovah; she did not draw near to her God. [3] Her rulers within her (are) roaring lions; her judges evening wolves; they do not gnaw the bones for the morning. [4] Her prophets (are) proud, men of deceit; her priests have profaned the sanctuary; they have done violence (to) the Law. [5] The righteous Jehovah (is) in her midst; He will not do iniquity. Every morning He

1
2 הוי מראה ונגאלה העיר היונה׃ לא שמעה בקול לא
not the to did she Not !oppressing the being and her Woe
;voice listen city ,defiled rebelling (to)

לקחה מוסר ביהוה לא בטחה אל־אלהיה לא קרבה׃
did she not her to did she not Jehovah in correc- did she
.near draw God ;trust ;tion receive

3 שריה בקרבה אריות שאגים שפטיה זאבי ערב לא
not the (are) her ;roaring (are) her in Her
(even) ;evening of wolves judges lions midst rulers

4 גרמו לבקר׃ נביאיה פחזים אנשי בגדות כהניה חללו־
have her ;deceit of men (are) Her the for they do
profaned priests ,proud prophets ,morning bones gnaw

5 קדש חמסו תורה׃ יהוה צדיק בקרבה לא יעשה עולה
;iniquity will He not her in the Jehovah the they holy the
do ;midst (is) righteous .law violated ;place

gives His justice to the light; He does not fail, but the unjust knows no shame. [6] I have cut off nations; their towers are ruined. I made their streets waste, so that none passes by. Their cities are destroyed, without a man, without inhabitant. [7] I said, Surely you will fear Me; you will receive instruction; then her dwelling shall not be cut off, all that I appointed for her. But they rose early, they corrupted all their doings.

[8] Therefore wait for Me, states Jehovah, for the day I rise up to the prey. For My judgment (is) to gather the nations, for Me to gather the kingdoms, to pour on them My fury, all My hot anger. For all the earth shall be burned up with the fire of My jealousy. [9] For then I will change to the peoples a clear speech, to call all of them by the name of Jehovah, to serve Him (with) one shoulder. [10] From beyond the rivers of Ethiopia My worshipers, the daughter of My scattered ones, shall bring My food offering. [11] In that day you shall not be ashamed from all your doings (in) which you have transgressed against Me. For then I will take away those who rejoice in your pride out of your midst, and you shall not again be proud any more in My holy mountain. [12] I will also leave in the midst of you a poor and weak people, and they shall trust in the name of Jehovah. [13] The remnant of Israel shall not do iniquity nor speak lies; and a deceitful tongue shall not be found in their mouth. For they shall feed and lie down, and no one shall frighten (them).

[14] Shout for joy, daughter of Zion; shout, Israel; be glad and rejoice with all the heart, daughter of Jerusalem. [15] Jehovah has taken away your judgments; He has cast out your

בַּבֹּקֶר בַּבֹּקֶר מִשְׁפָּטוֹ יִתֵּן לָאוֹר לֹא נֶעְדָּר וְלֹא־יוֹדֵעַ עַוָּל
the knows but He does not the to He His by morning
unjust not ;fail ;light gives justice morning

6 בֹּשֶׁת׃ הִכְרַתִּי גוֹיִם נָשַׁמּוּ פִּנּוֹתָם הֶחֱרַבְתִּי חוּצוֹתָם
their have I their are ;nations have I ,shame
streets waste laid .towers desolated off cut

7 מִבְּלִי עוֹבֵר נִצְדּוּ עָרֵיהֶם מִבְּלִי־אִישׁ מֵאֵין יוֹשֵׁב׃ אָמַרְתִּי
,said I inhab- an there from a that their laid Are passing that so
.itant being not ,man is not cities waste .by (is) none

אַךְ־תִּירְאִי אוֹתִי תִּקְחִי מוּסָר וְלֹא־יִכָּרֵת מְעוֹנָהּ כֹּל אֲשֶׁר־
that all her be shall and correc- will you ;Me will you Surely
,dwelling off cut not ,tion receive fear

8 פָּקַדְתִּי עָלֶיהָ אָכֵן הִשְׁכִּימוּ הִשְׁחִיתוּ כֹּל עֲלִילוֹתָם׃ לָכֵן
There- their all they rose they But for I
fore .doings corrupted ;early .her appointed

חַכּוּ־לִי נְאֻם־יְהוָה לְיוֹם קוּמִי לְעַד כִּי מִשְׁפָּטִי לֶאֱסֹף
to justice My For the to rise I the for ;Jehovah declares for wait
gather (is) .prey up day ,Me

גּוֹיִם לְקָבְצִי מַמְלָכוֹת לִשְׁפֹּךְ עֲלֵיהֶם זַעְמִי כֹּל חֲרוֹן אַפִּי
My heat the all My on pour to the Me for the
.anger of ,fury them out ,kingdoms collect to ,nations

9 כִּי בְּאֵשׁ קִנְאָתִי תֵּאָכֵל כָּל־הָאָרֶץ׃ כִּי־אָז אֶהְפֹּךְ אֶל־עַמִּים
the to will I then For the all be shall My the with For
peoples change .earth consumed jealousy of fire

שָׂפָה בְרוּרָה לִקְרֹא כֻלָּם בְּשֵׁם יְהוָה לְעָבְדוֹ שְׁכֶם אֶחָד׃
.one (with) serve to ,Jehovah the by all call to ,clear lip a
shoulder Him of name them of

10 מֵעֵבֶר לְנַהֲרֵי־כוּשׁ עֲתָרַי בַּת־פּוּצַי יוֹבִלוּן מִנְחָתִי׃
11 בַּיּוֹם
day In food My shall of daughter the wor- My Ethiopia the From
.offering bring ones scattered My ,shipers of rivers across

הַהוּא לֹא תֵבוֹשִׁי מִכֹּל עֲלִילֹתַיִךְ אֲשֶׁר פָּשַׁעַתְּ בִּי כִּי־אָז
then For against have you (in) your from shall you not that
.Me transgressed which doings all ashamed be

אָסִיר מִקִּרְבֵּךְ עַלִּיזֵי גַּאֲוָתֵךְ וְלֹא־תוֹסִפִי לְגָבְהָה עוֹד בְּהַר
the in still be shall you and your (in) those your from will I
of hill high again not ,majesty rejoicing midst withdraw

12 קָדְשִׁי׃ וְהִשְׁאַרְתִּי בְקִרְבֵּךְ עַם עָנִי וָדָל וְחָסוּ בְּשֵׁם יְהוָה׃
.Jehovah the in they and and poor a your in will I And My
of name trust shall ;weak people midst leave .holiness

13 שְׁאֵרִית יִשְׂרָאֵל לֹא־יַעֲשׂוּ עַוְלָה וְלֹא־יְדַבְּרוּ כָזָב וְלֹא־
and ;lies speak and ,iniquity shall not Israel rem- The
not not do of nant

יִמָּצֵא בְּפִיהֶם לְשׁוֹן תַּרְמִית כִּי־הֵמָּה יִרְעוּ וְרָבְצוּ וְאֵין
and lie and shall they For .deceit a their in be shall
is none ,down pasture of tongue mouth found

14 מַחֲרִיד׃ רָנִּי בַּת־צִיּוֹן הָרִיעוּ יִשְׂרָאֵל שִׂמְחִי וְעָלְזִי
and glad be ;Israel ,shout ;Zion daugh- Shout frightening
rejoice of ter ,joy for .(them)

15 בְּכָל־לֵב בַּת יְרוּשָׁלָםִ׃ הֵסִיר יְהוָה מִשְׁפָּטַיִךְ פִּנָּה אֹיְבֵךְ
your has He your Jehovah turned Has .Jerusalem daughter the with
.enemy removed ,judgments away of ,heart all

enemy. The King of Israel, Jehovah, (is) in your midst; you shall not fear evil any more. [16] In that day it shall be said to Jerusalem, Fear not! Zion, do not let your hands droop. [17] Jehovah your God (is) mighty in your midst; He will save. He will rejoice over you with joy. He is silent in His love. He rejoices over you with a joyful shout. [18] I will gather the afflicted ones from the appointed place; they were from you, a lifting up (of) reproach over her. [19] Behold, at that time I will deal with all those who afflict you. And I will save her who is lame, and gather her who was thrust out. And I will give them for a praise and for a name in all the land of their shame. [20] In that time I will bring you, even in the time I gather you. For I will give you for a name and for a praise among all the peoples of the earth, when I turn back your captivity before your eyes, says Jehovah.

16 מֶלֶךְ יִשְׂרָאֵל ׀ יְהוָה בְּקִרְבֵּךְ לֹא־תִירְאִי רָע עוֹד׃ בַּיּוֹם
day In (any) evil shall you not your in (is) Jehovah ,Israel The
.more fear ;midst of King

הַהוּא יֵאָמֵר לִירוּשָׁלִַם אַל־תִּירָאִי צִיּוֹן אַל־יִרְפּוּ יָדָיִךְ׃
your let do Not !Zion ,fear do Not ,Jerusalem to shall it that
!hands droop said be

17 יְהוָה אֱלֹהַיִךְ בְּקִרְבֵּךְ גִּבּוֹר יוֹשִׁיעַ יָשִׂישׂ עָלַיִךְ בְּשִׂמְחָה
.joy with over will He will He (is) your in your Jehovah
you rejoice .save ;mighty midst God

18 יַחֲרִישׁ בְּאַהֲבָתוֹ יָגִיל עָלַיִךְ בְּרִנָּה׃ נוּגֵי מִמּוֹעֵד אָסַפְתִּי
will I the from Those shout a with over He His in is He
;gather place appointed afflicted .joy of you rejoices ;love silent

19 מִמֵּךְ הָיוּ מַשְׂאֵת עָלֶיהָ חֶרְפָּה׃ הִנְנִי עֹשֶׂה אֶת־כָּל־
all will ,Behold (of) over lifting a they from
with deal I .reproach her up ,were you

מְעַנַּיִךְ בָּעֵת הַהִיא וְהוֹשַׁעְתִּי אֶת־הַצֹּלֵעָה וְהַנִּדָּחָה אֲקַבֵּץ
will I being her and being her will I And .that at afflicting
.gather out thrust ,lame save time you

20 וְשַׂמְתִּים לִתְהִלָּה וּלְשֵׁם בְּכָל־הָאָרֶץ בָּשְׁתָּם׃ בָּעֵת הַהִיא
that In their the in for and a for will I And
time .shame of land all name a praise them give

אָבִיא אֶתְכֶם וּבָעֵת קַבְּצִי אֶתְכֶם כִּי־אֶתֵּן אֶתְכֶם לְשֵׁם
a for you will I For .you My in even ,you will I
name give gathering of time the bring

וְלִתְהִלָּה בְּכֹל עַמֵּי הָאָרֶץ בְּשׁוּבִי אֶת־שְׁבוּתֵיכֶם לְעֵינֵיכֶם
your before your I when the the among for and
,eyes captivity return ,earth of peoples all praise a

אָמַר יְהוָה׃
.Jehovah says

חגי

LIBER HAGGAI

CAPUT. I א

CHAPTER 1

CHAPTER 1

[1] In the second year of Darius the king, in the sixth month, in the first day of the month, the word of Jehovah came by Haggai the prophet to Zerubbabel the son of Shealtiel, governor of Judah, and to Joshua the son of Jehozadak, the high priest, saying, [2] Thus speaks Jehovah of hosts, saying, This people says, The time is not come, the time for Jehovah's house to be built. [3] Then came the word of Jehovah by Haggai the prophet, saying, [4] Is it time for you yourselves to live in your finished houses, and this house to lie waste? [5] And now thus says Jehovah of hosts: Set your heart on your ways; [6] you have sown much and bring in little; (you) eat, but not to be satisfied; (you) drink, but not to be filled with drink; you dress, but warmth is not to one; and he who hires himself is selling himself for a bag full of holes.

[7] Thus says Jehovah of hosts: Set your heart on your ways. [8] Go up the mountain and bring wood and build the house. And I will be pleased with it, and I will be glorified, says Jehovah. [9] (You) looked for much, and behold, little! And when you brought (it) home, then I blew on it. Why, states Jehovah of hosts? Because of My house that (is) ruined, and you,

1 בִּשְׁנַת שְׁתַּיִם לְדָרְיָוֶשׁ הַמֶּלֶךְ בַּחֹדֶשׁ הַשִּׁשִּׁי בְּיוֹם אֶחָד
the day in the in ,king the Darius of the year In
first ,sixth month second

לַחֹדֶשׁ הָיָה דְבַר־יְהוָה בְּיַד־חַגַּי הַנָּבִיא אֶל־זְרֻבָּבֶל בֶּן
son ,Zerubbabel to the Haggai by Jehovah the came the of
of prophet of word ,month

שְׁאַלְתִּיאֵל פַּחַת יְהוּדָה וְאֶל־יְהוֹשֻׁעַ בֶּן־יְהוֹצָדָק הַכֹּהֵן
priest ,Jehosadak son ,Joshua and ,Judah governor ,Shealtiel
of to of

2 הַגָּדוֹל לֵאמֹר׃ כֹּה אָמַר יְהוָה צְבָאוֹת לֵאמֹר הָעָם הַזֶּה
This people ,saying ,hosts Jehovah says Thus ,saying ,high the
of

3 אָמְרוּ לֹא עֶת־בֹּא עֶת־בֵּית יְהוָה לְהִבָּנוֹת׃ וַיְהִי דְּבַר
the Then .built be to Jehovah's for the is The not ,says
of word came house time ,come time

4 יְהוָה בְּיַד־חַגַּי הַנָּבִיא לֵאמֹר׃ הַעֵת לָכֶם אַתֶּם לָשֶׁבֶת
live to your- for is It ,saying the Haggai by Jehovah
selves you time ,prophet

5 בְּבָתֵּיכֶם סְפוּנִים וְהַבַּיִת הַזֶּה חָרֵב׃ וְעַתָּה כֹּה אָמַר יְהוָה
Jehovah says thus And lie to this and ,finished your in
of now ?waste house houses

6 צְבָאוֹת שִׂימוּ לְבַבְכֶם עַל־דַּרְכֵיכֶם׃ זְרַעְתֶּם הַרְבֵּה וְהָבֵא
and much have you ;ways your on your Set :hosts
in bring sown heart

מְעָט אָכוֹל וְאֵין־לְשָׂבְעָה שָׁתוֹ וְאֵין־לְשָׁכְרָה לָבוֹשׁ וְאֵין
but (you) be to but (you) be to but (you) ;little
is not ,dress ;filled not ,drink ;satisfied not eat

7 לְחֹם לוֹ וְהַמִּשְׂתַּכֵּר מִשְׂתַּכֵּר אֶל־צְרוֹר נָקוּב׃ כֹּה
Thus .holes a for sells who he and to warmth
of bag himself himself hires ;one

8 אָמַר יְהוָה צְבָאוֹת שִׂימוּ לְבַבְכֶם עַל־דַּרְכֵיכֶם׃ עֲלוּ
Go your on your Set :hosts Jehovah says
up .ways heart of

הָהָר וַהֲבֵאתֶם עֵץ וּבְנוּ הַבָּיִת וְאֶרְצֶה־בּוֹ וְאֶכָּבְדָ אָמַר
says will I and with will I And the and wood bring and the
,glorified be ,it pleased be .house build mountain

9 יְהוָה׃ פָּנֹה אֶל־הַרְבֵּה וְהִנֵּה לִמְעָט וַהֲבֵאתֶם הַבַּיִת וְנָפַחְתִּי
I then ,home when And !little and much for (You) Jeho-
blew (it) brought you behold looked .vah

בוֹ יַעַן מֶה נְאֻם יְהוָה צְבָאוֹת יַעַן בֵּיתִי אֲשֶׁר־הוּא חָרֵב
,ruined is that My Because ?hosts Jehovah says ,Why on
house of of .it

(each) man, run to his house. [10] Therefore the heavens above you have held back from dew, and the earth is held back (from) her produce. [11] And I called for a drought on the land, and on the mountains, and on the grain, and on the new wine, and on the oil, and on that which the ground produces, and on man, and on cattle, and on all the labor of your hands.

[12] Then Zerubbabel the son of Shealtiel, and Joshua the son of Jehozadak, the high priest, and all the remnant of the people, obeyed the voice of Jehovah their God, and the words of Haggai the prophet, as Jehovah their God had sent him. And the people feared before Jehovah. [13] Then Haggai, Jehovah's messenger, spoke Jehovah's message to the people, saying, I (am) with you, says Jehovah. [14] And Jehovah stirred up the spirit of Zerubbabel the son of Shealtiel, governor of Judah, and the spirit of Joshua the son of Jehozadak, the high priest, and the spirit of all the remnant of the people. And they came and worked on the house of Jehovah of hosts, their God, [15] in the twenty-fourth day of the sixth month, in the second year of Darius the king.

10 וְאַתֶּם רָצִים אִישׁ לְבֵיתוֹ׃ עַל־כֵּן עֲלֵיכֶם כָּלְאוּ שָׁמַיִם
the heavens held back have above you Therefore his to .house (each) man run and you

11 מִטָּל וְהָאָרֶץ כָּלְאָה יְבוּלָהּ׃ וָאֶקְרָא חֹרֶב עַל־הָאָרֶץ וְעַל־
and on the ,land on a drought I And for called her (from) .produce held is back the and earth from ,dew

הֶהָרִים וְעַל־הַדָּגָן וְעַל־הַתִּירוֹשׁ וְעַל־הַיִּצְהָר וְעַל אֲשֶׁר
that which and on the ,oil and on new the ,wine and on the ,grain and on the ,mountains

תּוֹצִיא הָאֲדָמָה וְעַל־הָאָדָם וְעַל־הַבְּהֵמָה וְעַל כָּל־יְגִיעַ
the of labor all and on ,cattle and on ,man and on the ,ground brings forth

12 כַּפָּיִם׃ וַיִּשְׁמַע זְרֻבָּבֶל ׀ בֶּן־שַׁלְתִּיאֵל וִיהוֹשֻׁעַ בֶּן
the of son and Joshua ,Shealtiel the of son Zerubbabel Then obeyed your .hands

יְהוֹצָדָק הַכֹּהֵן הַגָּדוֹל וְכֹל ׀ שְׁאֵרִית הָעָם בְּקוֹל יְהוָה
Jehovah the of voice the ,people the of remnant and all the ,high priest ,Jehosadak

אֱלֹהֵיהֶם וְעַל־דִּבְרֵי חַגַּי הַנָּבִיא כַּאֲשֶׁר שְׁלָחוֹ יְהוָה
Jehovah sent had him as the ,prophet Haggai the of words and their ,God

13 אֱלֹהֵיהֶם וַיִּירְאוּ הָעָם מִפְּנֵי יְהוָה׃ וַיֹּאמֶר חַגַּי מַלְאַךְ
the of messenger Haggai Then spoke .Jehovah before the people And feared their .God

יְהוָה בְּמַלְאֲכוּת יְהוָה לָעָם לֵאמֹר אֲנִי אִתְּכֶם נְאֻם־יְהוָה׃
.Jehovah says with ,you I (am) ,saying the to ,people Jehovah's message .Jehovah

14 וַיָּעַר יְהוָה אֶת־רוּחַ זְרֻבָּבֶל בֶּן־שַׁלְתִּיאֵל פַּחַת יְהוּדָה וְאֶת־
and ,Judah governor of ,Shealtiel the of son Zerubbabel the of spirit Jehovah And stirred

רוּחַ יְהוֹשֻׁעַ בֶּן־יְהוֹצָדָק הַכֹּהֵן הַגָּדוֹל וְאֶת־רוּחַ כֹּל שְׁאֵרִית
rem- of nant the all the of spirit and the ,high priest , Jehosadak son of Joshua the of spirit

הָעָם וַיָּבֹאוּ וַיַּעֲשׂוּ מְלָאכָה בְּבֵית־יְהוָה צְבָאוֹת אֱלֹהֵיהֶם׃
,God their hosts Jehovah of the on of house work and they did And came the .people

15 בְּיוֹם עֶשְׂרִים וְאַרְבָּעָה לַחֹדֶשׁ בַּשִּׁשִּׁי בִּשְׁנַת שְׁתַּיִם
the second year in the ,sixth month of fourth twenty- the in day

לְדָרְיָוֶשׁ הַמֶּלֶךְ׃
.king the Darius of

CAP. II ב

CHAPTER 2

[1] In the seventh (month), on the twenty-first of the month, the word of Jehovah came by the prophet Haggai, saying, [2] Now speak to Zerubbabel the son of Shealtiel, governor of Judah, and to

1 בַּשְּׁבִיעִי בְּעֶשְׂרִים וְאֶחָד לַחֹדֶשׁ הָיָה דְּבַר־יְהוָה בְּיַד־חַגַּי
Haggai by Jehovah the of word came the of ,month first the on twenty- the In ,(month) seventh

2 הַנָּבִיא לֵאמֹר׃ אֱמָר־נָא אֶל־זְרֻבָּבֶל בֶּן־שַׁלְתִּיאֵל פַּחַת
governor of ,Shealtiel son of Zerubbabel to Now speak ,saying the ,prophet

Joshua the son of Jehozadak, the high priest, and to the remnant of the people, saying, [3] Who is left among you who saw this house in her former glory? And how do you see it now? When compared to it, (is it) not as nothing in your eyes? [4] Yet now be strong, O Zerubbabel, says Jehovah. And be strong, O Joshua, son of Jehozadak, the high priest. And be strong, all people of the land, says Jehovah, and work. For I (am) with you, states Jehovah of hosts. [5] The word that I covenanted with you when you came out of Egypt, so My Spirit abides among you; do not fear. [6] For thus says Jehovah of hosts: Yet once, it (is) a little while, and I will shake the heavens and the earth and the sea and the dry land. [7] And I will shake all the nations; and the desire of all nations shall come. And I will fill this house (with) glory, says Jehovah of hosts. [8] The silver (is) Mine, and the gold Mine, says Jehovah of hosts. [9] The glory of this latter house shall be greater than that of the former, says Jehovah of hosts. And in this place I will give peace, says Jehovah of hosts.

[10] In the twenty-fourth of the ninth (month), in the second year of Darius, the word of Jehovah came by Haggai the prophet, saying, [11] Thus says Jehovah of hosts: Now

יְהוּדָה וְאֶל־יְהוֹשֻׁעַ בֶּן־יְהוֹצָדָק הַכֹּהֵן הַגָּדוֹל וְאֶל־שְׁאֵרִית
rem- the and ,high the priest Jehosadak son ,Joshua and ,Judah
of nant to of to

3 הָעָם לֵאמֹר׃ מִי בָכֶם הַנִּשְׁאָר אֲשֶׁר רָאָה אֶת־הַבַּיִת
house saw who left is among Who ,saying the
you ,people

הַזֶּה בִּכְבוֹדוֹ הָרִאשׁוֹן וּמָה אַתֶּם רֹאִים אֹתוֹ עַתָּה הֲלוֹא
(it Is) ?now it see you do And ?former its in this
,not how glory

4 כָמֹהוּ כְּאַיִן בְּעֵינֵיכֶם׃ וְעַתָּה חֲזַק זְרֻבָּבֶל ׀ נְאֻם־יְהוָה
.Jehovah says O be now Yet your in as like
,Zerubbabel ,strong ?eyes nothing it

וַחֲזַק יְהוֹשֻׁעַ בֶּן־יְהוֹצָדָק הַכֹּהֵן הַגָּדוֹל וַחֲזַק כָּל־עַם
people all be And the priest Jehosadak son O be And
of ,strong .high of ,Joshua ,strong

הָאָרֶץ נְאֻם־יְהוָה וַעֲשׂוּ כִּי־אֲנִי אִתְּכֶם נְאֻם יְהוָה צְבָאוֹת׃
.hosts Jehovah says with I For and ,Jehovah says the
of ,you (am) .work ,land

5 אֶת־הַדָּבָר אֲשֶׁר כָּרַתִּי אִתְּכֶם בְּצֵאתְכֶם מִמִּצְרַיִם וְרוּחִי
My so of out you when with cut I which The
Spirit ,Egypt came you word

6 עֹמֶדֶת בְּתוֹכְכֶם אַל־תִּירָאוּ׃ כִּי כֹה אָמַר יְהוָה
Jehovah says thus For .fear do not among abides
of ;you

צְבָאוֹת עוֹד אַחַת מְעַט הִיא וַאֲנִי מַרְעִישׁ אֶת־הַשָּׁמַיִם
the shake will I and it little a ,once Yet :hosts
heavens ,(is) while

7 וְאֶת־הָאָרֶץ וְאֶת־הַיָּם וְאֶת־הֶחָרָבָה׃ וְהִרְעַשְׁתִּי אֶת־כָּל־
all will I And dry the and the and the and
shake .ground sea earth

הַגּוֹיִם וּבָאוּ חֶמְדַּת כָּל־הַגּוֹיִם וּמִלֵּאתִי אֶת־הַבַּיִת הַזֶּה
this house will I And the all the shall and the
fill .nations of desire come ,nations

8 כָּבוֹד אָמַר יְהוָה צְבָאוֹת׃ לִי הַכֶּסֶף וְלִי הַזָּהָב נְאֻם
says the and The (is) .hosts Jehovah says (with)
,gold Me to ,silver Me to of ,glory

9 יְהוָה צְבָאוֹת׃ גָּדוֹל יִהְיֶה כְּבוֹד הַבַּיִת הַזֶּה הָאַחֲרוֹן
latter this house The be will greater .hosts Jehovah
of glory of

מִן־הָרִאשׁוֹן אָמַר יְהוָה צְבָאוֹת וּבַמָּקוֹם הַזֶּה אֶתֵּן שָׁלוֹם
,peace will I this in And .hosts Jehovah says the than
give place of ,former

10 נְאֻם יְהוָה צְבָאוֹת׃ בְּעֶשְׂרִים וְאַרְבָּעָה לַתְּשִׁיעִי
the of fourth the In .hosts Jehovah says
,(month) ninth twenty- of

בִּשְׁנַת שְׁתַּיִם לְדָרְיָוֶשׁ הָיָה דְבַר־יְהוָה בְּיַד־חַגַּי הַנָּבִיא
the Haggai by Jehovah the came ,Darius of the year in
,prophet of word second

11 לֵאמֹר׃ כֹּה אָמַר יְהוָה צְבָאוֹת שְׁאַל־נָא אֶת־הַכֹּהֲנִים
the Now ask :hosts Jehovah says Thus ,saying
priests of

ask the priests the law, saying, [12] Behold, one carries holy flesh in one wing of his wing and touches his wing to the bread, or pottage, or wine, or oil, or any food, with his wing, shall it become holy? And the priest answered and said, No. [13] And Haggai said, If the unclean of body touches these, is it unclean? And the priests answered and said, It shall be unclean. [14] Then Haggai answered and said, So (is) this people, and so (is) this nation before Me, states Jehovah. And so (is) every work of their hands, and that which they offer there (is) unclean. [15] And now, I ask you, set your heart on it: From this day and onward, before a stone was laid on a stone in the temple of Jehovah; [16] from then onward, (one) came to a heap of twenty (measures), and there were (but) ten; when (one) came to the wine vat in order to draw out fifty from the press, and there were twenty. [17] I struck you with blight, and with mildew, and with hail, in all the labors of your hands; yet you did not (turn) to Me, says Jehovah. [18] Now set your heart from this day and forward, from the twenty-fourth day of the ninth (month), from the day that Jehovah's temple was established; set your heart: [19] (Is) the seed still in the barn? Yes, as yet the vine, and the fig-tree, and the pomegranate, and the olive-tree have not brought forth; from this day I will bless.

[20] And a second time the word of Jehovah came to Haggai in the twenty-fourth of the month, saying, [21] Speak to Zerubbabel the governor of

12 תּוֹרָה לֵאמֹר׃ הֵן יִשָּׂא־אִישׁ בְּשַׂר־קֹדֶשׁ בִּכְנַף בִּגְדוֹ וְנָגַע
and his the in holy flesh man a carried Be- ,saying ,law the
touches garment of wing ,hold

בִּכְנָפוֹ אֶל־הַלֶּחֶם וְאֶל־הַנָּזִיד וְאֶל־הַיַּיִן וְאֶל־שֶׁמֶן וְאֶל־
or ,oil or ,wine or boiled or the to his
food ,bread wing

13 כָּל־מַאֲכָל הֲיִקְדָּשׁ וַיַּעֲנוּ הַכֹּהֲנִים וַיֹּאמְרוּ לֹא׃ וַיֹּאמֶר
said And .No ,said and priests the And it will ,food any
answered ?holy become

חַגַּי אִם־יִגַּע טְמֵא־נֶפֶשׁ בְּכָל־אֵלֶּה הֲיִטְמָא וַיַּעֲנוּ הַכֹּהֲנִים
priests the And it is ,these any body the touches If Hag-
answered ?unclean of of unclean ,gai

14 וַיֹּאמְרוּ יִטְמָא׃ וַיַּעַן חַגַּי וַיֹּאמֶר כֵּן הָעָם־הַזֶּה וְכֵן־הַגּוֹי
nation and ,this people So ,said and Haggai And be shall It ,said and
(is) so (is) answered .unclean

הַזֶּה לְפָנַי נְאֻם־יְהוָה וְכֵן כָּל־מַעֲשֵׂה יְדֵיהֶם וַאֲשֶׁר
that and their work every And .Jehovah states before this
which ,hands (of) (is) so ,Me

15 יַקְרִיבוּ שָׁם טָמֵא הוּא׃ וְעַתָּה שִׂימוּ־נָא לְבַבְכֶם מִן־הַיּוֹם
day from your now set ,now And .is unclean there they
heart offer

הַזֶּה וָמָעְלָה מִטֶּרֶם שׂוּם־אֶבֶן אֶל־אֶבֶן בְּהֵיכַל יְהוָה׃
;Jehovah the in a on stone a the Before and this
of temple stone of placing :onward

16 מִהְיוֹתָם בָּא אֶל־עֲרֵמַת עֶשְׂרִים וְהָיְתָה עֲשָׂרָה בָּא אֶל־
to (one) (but) there and twenty heap a to (one) then from
came ;ten were ,(measures) of came ,on

17 הַיֶּקֶב לַחְשֹׂף חֲמִשִּׁים פּוּרָה וְהָיְתָה עֶשְׂרִים׃ הִכֵּיתִי
struck I (but) there and the from fifty draw to wine the
.twenty were ,trough wine of out vat

אֶתְכֶם בַּשִּׁדָּפוֹן וּבַיֵּרָקוֹן וּבַבָּרָד אֵת כָּל־מַעֲשֵׂה יְדֵיכֶם
your the (in) with and with and with you
;hands (of) work all ,hail ,mildew ,blight

18 וְאֵין־אֶתְכֶם אֵלַי נְאֻם־יְהוָה׃ שִׂימוּ־נָא לְבַבְכֶם מִן־הַיּוֹם
day from your Now set .Jehovah says to did you yet
heart ,Me (turn) not

הַזֶּה וָמָעְלָה מִיּוֹם עֶשְׂרִים וְאַרְבָּעָה לַתְּשִׁיעִי לְמִן־הַיּוֹם
the from the of fourth the from and this
day ,(month) ninth twenty- day ,onward

19 אֲשֶׁר־יֻסַּד הֵיכַל־יְהוָה שִׂימוּ לְבַבְכֶם׃ הַעוֹד הַזֶּרַע
the still (is) ;heart your set ;Jehovah's temple was that
seed established

בַּמְּגוּרָה וְעַד־הַגֶּפֶן וְהַתְּאֵנָה וְהָרִמּוֹן וְעֵץ הַזַּיִת לֹא נָשָׂא
have not the and the and the and the Even the in
;borne olive tree ,pomegranate ,tree fig vine ?barn

20 מִן־הַיּוֹם הַזֶּה אֲבָרֵךְ׃ וַיְהִי דְבַר־יְהוָה ׀ שֵׁנִית אֶל־
to second a Jehovah the And will I this day from
time of word came .bless

21 חַגַּי בְּעֶשְׂרִים וְאַרְבָּעָה לַחֹדֶשׁ לֵאמֹר׃ אֱמֹר אֶל־זְרֻבָּבֶל
Zerubbabel to Speak ,saying the of fourth the in Haggai
,month twenty-

Judah, saying, I will shake
the heavens and the earth.
[22] And I will overthrow
the throne of the kingdoms,
and I will destroy the
strength of the kingdoms of
the nations. And I will overthrow the chariots and
those who ride in them; and
the horses and their riders
shall come down, each one
by the sword of his brother.
[23] In that day, says
Jehovah of hosts, I will take
you, O Zerubbabel, My servant, the son of Shealtiel,
says Jehovah, and will make
you like a signet (ring); for I
have chosen you, says Jehovah of hosts.

פַּחַת־יְהוּדָה לֵאמֹר אֲנִי מַרְעִישׁ אֶת־הַשָּׁמַיִם וְאֶת־הָאָרֶץ׃

the .earth | and | the heavens | shake will | I | ,saying | ,Judah | gov- the of ernor

22 וְהָפַכְתִּי כִּסֵּא מַמְלָכוֹת וְהִשְׁמַדְתִּי חֹזֶק מַמְלְכוֹת הַגּוֹיִם

the .nations | kingdom of | the of strength | the | will I and destroy | the ,kingdoms' | the throne | will I And overthrow

וְהָפַכְתִּי מֶרְכָּבָה וְרֹכְבֶיהָ וְיָרְדוּ סוּסִים וְרֹכְבֵיהֶם אִישׁ

(each) man | their and ,riders | the horses | will and down come | their and ;riders | the chariots | will I And overthrow

23 בְּחֶרֶב אָחִיו׃ בַּיּוֹם הַהוּא נְאֻם־יְהוָה צְבָאוֹת אֶקָּחֲךָ

will I ,you take | ,hosts of | Jehovah states | ,that | day In | his .brother | the by of sword

זְרֻבָּבֶל בֶּן־שְׁאַלְתִּיאֵל עַבְדִּי נְאֻם־יְהוָה וְשַׂמְתִּיךָ כַּחוֹתָם

a like ;(ring) signet | will and you make | ,Jehovah states | My ,servant | Shealtiel | son of | Zerub- O babel

כִּי־בְךָ בָחַרְתִּי נְאֻם יְהוָה צְבָאוֹת׃

.hosts | Jehovah of | states | have I ,chosen | you for

זכריה

LIBER ZACHARIAE

CAPUT. I א

CHAPTER 1

CHAPTER 1

[1] In the eighth month, in the second year of Darius, the word of Jehovah came to Zechariah, the son of Berechiah, the son of Iddo the prophet, saying, [2] Jehovah has been very angry with your fathers. [3] Therefore you say to them, Thus says Jehovah of hosts: Turn to Me, says Jehovah of hosts, and I will turn to you, says Jehovah of hosts. [4] Do not be as your fathers, to whom the former prophets have proclaimed to them, saying, Thus says Jehovah of hosts: Turn now from your evil ways and your evil doings; but they did not hear or give heed to Me, says Jehovah. [5] Your fathers, where (are) they? And the prophets, do they live forever? [6] But My words and My statutes which I commanded My servants the prophets, did they not overtake your fathers? And they returned and said, As Jehovah of hosts planned to do to us, according to our ways and according to our doings, so He has done with us.

[7] On the twenty-fourth day of the eleventh month, it (is) the month Shebat, in the second year of Darius, the word of Jehovah came to Zechariah, the son of Berechiah, the son of Iddo the prophet, saying, [8] I saw at night;

1 בַּחֹדֶשׁ הַשְּׁמִינִי בִּשְׁנַת שְׁתַּיִם לְדָרְיָוֶשׁ הָיָה דְבַר־יְהוָה
Jehovah the was ,Darius of the year in the In
of word second ,eighth month

2 אֶל־זְכַרְיָה בֶּן־בֶּרֶכְיָה בֶּן־עִדּוֹ הַנָּבִיא לֵאמֹר׃ קָצַף יְהוָה
Jehovah was ,saying the Iddo son ,Berechiah son Zechariah to
angry ,prophet of of

3 עַל־אֲבוֹתֵיכֶם קָצֶף׃ וְאָמַרְתָּ אֲלֵהֶם כֹּה אָמַר יְהוָה
Jehovah says Thus ,them to Therefore .anger your with
of say you -fathers

צְבָאוֹת שׁוּבוּ אֵלַי נְאֻם יְהוָה צְבָאוֹת וְאָשׁוּב אֲלֵיכֶם
,you to I and ,hosts Jehovah says to Turn :hosts
turn will of ,Me

4 אָמַר יְהוָה צְבָאוֹת׃ אַל־תִּהְיוּ כַאֲבֹתֵיכֶם אֲשֶׁר קָרְאוּ־
pro- have to your as be Do not .hosts Jehovah says
claimed whom ,fathers of

אֲלֵיהֶם הַנְּבִיאִים הָרִאשֹׁנִים לֵאמֹר כֹּה אָמַר יְהוָה צְבָאוֹת
:hosts Jehovah says Thus ,saying ,former the prophets them to
of

שׁוּבוּ נָא מִדַּרְכֵיכֶם הָרָעִים וּמַעַלְלֵיכֶם הָרָעִים וְלֹא שָׁמְעוּ
did they but ;evil from and evil your from now Turn
listen not doings your ways

5 וְלֹא־הִקְשִׁיבוּ אֵלַי נְאֻם־יְהוָה׃ אֲבוֹתֵיכֶם אַיֵּה־הֵם וְהַנְּבִאִים
the And ?they where Your .Jehovah says to give did and
,prophets (are) ,fathers ,Me heed not

6 הַלְעוֹלָם יִחְיוּ׃ אַךְ ׀ דְּבָרַי וְחֻקַּי אֲשֶׁר צִוִּיתִי אֶת־עֲבָדַי
My com- I which My and My But they do forever
servants manded statutes words ?live

הַנְּבִיאִים הֲלוֹא הִשִּׂיגוּ אֲבֹתֵיכֶם וַיָּשׁוּבוּ וַיֹּאמְרוּ כַּאֲשֶׁר זָמַם
pur- As ,said and they And your they did not the
poses returned ?fathers overtake ,prophets

יְהוָה צְבָאוֹת לַעֲשׂוֹת לָנוּ כִּדְרָכֵינוּ וּכְמַעֲלָלֵינוּ כֵּן עָשָׂה
has He so according and to according ,us to do to hosts Jehovah
done ,deeds our to ways our of

7 אִתָּנוּ׃ בְּיוֹם עֶשְׂרִים וְאַרְבָּעָה לְעַשְׁתֵּי־עָשָׂר חֹדֶשׁ הוּא־
(is) it, ,month the of and the day On with
eleventh fourth twenty- .us

חֹדֶשׁ שְׁבָט בִּשְׁנַת שְׁתַּיִם לְדָרְיָוֶשׁ הָיָה דְבַר־יְהוָה אֶל־
to Jehovah the came ,Darius of the year in ,Shebat the
. of word second month

8 זְכַרְיָה בֶּן־בֶּרֶכְיָהוּ בֶּן־עִדּוֹא הַנָּבִיא לֵאמֹר׃ רָאִיתִי ׀ הַלַּיְלָה
,night saw I ,saying the Iddo son ,Berechiah son Zecha-
at ,prophet of of ,riah

and, behold! A Man riding on a red horse. And He stood among the myrtle trees that (were) in the ravine. And behind Him (were) red, sorrel and white horses. [9] Then I said, My lord, what (are) these? And the angel who was speaking with me said to me, I will show you what these (are). [10] And the Man who stood among the myrtle trees answered and said, These (are) those whom Jehovah has sent to walk to and fro through the earth. [11] And they answered the Angel of Jehovah who stood among the myrtle trees and said, We have walked to and fro through the earth, and behold, all the earth sits still and is at rest.

[12] Then the Angel of Jehovah answered and said, O Jehovah of hosts, until when will You not have pity on Jerusalem and on the cities of Judah, against which You have cursed these seventy years? [13] And Jehovah answered the angel who was talking with me (with) good words (and) comforting words. [14] So the angel who was talking with me said to me, Cry out, saying, Thus says Jehovah of hosts: I am jealous for Jerusalem and for Zion with a great jealousy. [15] And I am very, very angry at the nations at ease; (in) that I was but a little angry, and they gave help for evil. [16] Therefore thus says Jehovah: I have returned to Jerusalem with compassions; My house shall be built in it, says Jehovah of hosts; and a line shall be stretched over Jerusalem. [17] Cry out again, saying, Thus says Jehovah of hosts:

וְהִנֵּה־אִישׁ רֹכֵב עַל־סוּס אָדֹם וְהוּא עֹמֵד בֵּין הַהֲדַסִּים
myrtle trees the among stood he And red a .horse on riding a man and ,behold

אֲשֶׁר בַּמְּצֻלָה וְאַחֲרָיו סוּסִים אֲדֻמִּים שְׂרֻקִּים וּלְבָנִים׃
and .white ,sorrel ,red horses behind And (were) Him the in .ravine that (were)

9 וָאֹמַר מָה־אֵלֶּה אֲדֹנִי וַיֹּאמֶר אֵלַי הַמַּלְאָךְ הַדֹּבֵר בִּי אֲנִי
I with ,me was who speaking the angel me to said And My ?Lord ,these What (are) I Then ,said

10 אַרְאֶךָּ מָה־הֵמָּה אֵלֶּה׃ וַיַּעַן הָאִישׁ הָעֹמֵד בֵּין־הַהֲדַסִּים
the trees myrtle among who stood man the And answered .these (are) what will you show

11 וַיֹּאמַר אֵלֶּה אֲשֶׁר שָׁלַח יְהוָה לְהִתְהַלֵּךְ בָּאָרֶץ׃ וַיַּעֲנוּ
they And answered the in .earth walk to about Jehovah has sent those whom These (are) ,said and

אֶת־מַלְאַךְ יְהוָה הָעֹמֵד בֵּין הַהֲדַסִּים וַיֹּאמְרוּ הִתְהַלַּכְנוּ
have We about walked ,said and myrtle the trees among who stood Jehovah the of Angel

12 בָאָרֶץ וְהִנֵּה כָל־הָאָרֶץ יֹשֶׁבֶת וְשֹׁקָטֶת׃ וַיַּעַן מַלְאַךְ יְהוָה
Jeho- vah Angel the of Then answered at is and .peace sits the earth all and ,behold the in ,earth

וַיֹּאמַר יְהוָה צְבָאוֹת עַד־מָתַי אַתָּה לֹא־תְרַחֵם אֶת־
have will on compassion not You when Until ,hosts O of Jehovah ,said and

יְרוּשָׁלִַם וְאֵת עָרֵי יְהוּדָה אֲשֶׁר זָעַמְתָּה זֶה שִׁבְעִים שָׁנָה׃
?years seventy these have You cursed which ,Judah the of cities and Jerusalem

13 וַיַּעַן יְהוָה אֶת־הַמַּלְאָךְ הַדֹּבֵר בִּי דְּבָרִים טוֹבִים דְּבָרִים
(and) words (with) ,good words with me was who speaking the Angel Jehovah And answered

14 נִחֻמִים׃ וַיֹּאמֶר אֵלַי הַמַּלְאָךְ הַדֹּבֵר בִּי קְרָא לֵאמֹר כֹּה
Thus ,saying Cry ,out with ,me was who speaking the Angel me to said So .comforting

אָמַר יְהוָה צְבָאוֹת קִנֵּאתִי לִירוּשָׁלִַם וּלְצִיּוֹן קִנְאָה גְדוֹלָה׃
great a (with) jealousy for and Zion for Jerusalem am I jealous :hosts Jehovah of says

15 וְקֶצֶף גָּדוֹל אֲנִי קֹצֵף עַל־הַגּוֹיִם הַשַּׁאֲנַנִּים אֲשֶׁר אֲנִי קָצַפְתִּי
was angry I (in) that ;ease at the nations at am angry I great with And anger

16 מְעָט וְהֵמָּה עָזְרוּ לְרָעָה׃ לָכֵן כֹּה־אָמַר יְהוָה שַׁבְתִּי
have I returned :Jehovah says thus Therefore .evil for helped then they a ,little

לִירוּשָׁלִַם בְּרַחֲמִים בֵּיתִי יִבָּנֶה בָּהּ נְאֻם יְהוָה צְבָאוֹת
;hosts Jehovah of says ,it in be shall built My house with ;compassions to Jerusalem

17 וְקָוֶה יִנָּטֶה עַל־יְרוּשָׁלִָם׃ עוֹד ׀ קְרָא לֵאמֹר כֹּה אָמַר
says Thus ,saying ,out Cry again .Jerusalem over be will stretched a and line

clothes, and he stood before the Angel. [4] And He answered and spoke to those who stood before Him, saying, Take away the filthy clothes from him. And to him He said, Behold, I have caused your iniquity to pass from you, and I will clothe you with costly robes. [5] And I said, Let them set a clean turban on his head. So they set a clean turban on his head and clothed him with clothing. And the Angel of Jehovah stood by. [6] And the Angel of Jehovah admonished Joshua, saying, [7] Thus says Jehovah of hosts: If you will walk in My ways, and if you will keep My charge, then you shall also judge My house and shall also keep My courts, and I will give you room to walk among these who stand by.

[8] Hear now, O Joshua the high priest, you and your fellows who sit before you; for they (are) men of symbol. For, behold, I will bring forth My Servant the Branch. [9] For behold the stone that I have set before Joshua; on one stone (are) seven eyes; behold, I will engrave its engraving, says Jehovah of hosts, and I will remove the iniquity of that land in one day. [10] In that day, says Jehovah of hosts, you shall invite (each) man to his neighbor to (sit) under the vine and under the fig-tree.

4 צוֹאִים וְעֹמֵד לִפְנֵי הַמַּלְאָךְ׃ וַיַּעַן וַיֹּאמֶר אֶל־הָעֹמְדִים

who those standing were / to / and spoke / He And answered / the .Angel / before / he and stood / ,filthy

לְפָנָיו לֵאמֹר הָסִירוּ הַבְּגָדִים הַצֹּאִים מֵעָלָיו וַיֹּאמֶר אֵלָיו

to ,him / He And said / from .him / filthy / the garments / Remove / ,saying / before ,Him

5 רְאֵה הֶעֱבַרְתִּי מֵעָלֶיךָ עֲוֺנֶךָ וְהַלְבֵּשׁ אֹתְךָ מַחֲלָצוֹת׃ וָאֹמַר

I And ,said / festal .garments / with you / will I and clothe / your ,iniquity / from you / have I pass to caused / ,See

יָשִׂימוּ צָנִיף טָהוֹר עַל־רֹאשׁוֹ וַיָּשִׂימוּ הַצָּנִיף הַטָּהוֹר עַל־

on / clean / turban a / they So sat / his .head / on / clean / a turban / them Let set

6 רֹאשׁוֹ וַיַּלְבִּשֻׁהוּ בְּגָדִים וּמַלְאַךְ יְהוָה עֹמֵד׃ וַיָּעַד מַלְאַךְ

the of Angel / And charged / .stood / Jehovah / the and of Angel / with ,clothes / clothed and him / his head

7 יְהוָה בִּיהוֹשֻׁעַ לֵאמֹר׃ כֹּה־אָמַר יְהוָה צְבָאוֹת אִם־בִּדְרָכַי

My ways / in / If / :hosts of / Jehovah / says Thus / ,saying / ,Joshua / Jehovah

תֵּלֵךְ וְאִם אֶת־מִשְׁמַרְתִּי תִשְׁמֹר וְגַם־אַתָּה תָּדִין אֶת־בֵּיתִי

My house / shall judge / you / then also / will you ,keep / My service / if and / you ,walk will

וְגַם תִּשְׁמֹר אֶת־חֲצֵרַי וְנָתַתִּי לְךָ מַהְלְכִים בֵּין הָעֹמְדִים

are who by standing / among / goings / to you / I and give will / My ,courts / shall keep / and also

8 הָאֵלֶּה׃ שְׁמַע־נָא יְהוֹשֻׁעַ ׀ הַכֹּהֵן הַגָּדוֹל אַתָּה וְרֵעֶיךָ

your and friends / you / ,high / the priest / O Joshua / ,now Hear / .these

הַיֹּשְׁבִים לְפָנֶיךָ כִּי־אַנְשֵׁי מוֹפֵת הֵמָּה כִּי־הִנְנִי מֵבִיא אֶת־

will forth bring / ,behold I / ,For / they .(are) / symbol / men of / for / before ;you / are who sitting

9 עַבְדִּי צֶמַח׃ כִּי ׀ הִנֵּה הָאֶבֶן אֲשֶׁר נָתַתִּי לִפְנֵי יְהוֹשֻׁעַ

;Joshua / before / have I set / which / the stone / behold / For / the .Branch / My Servant

עַל־אֶבֶן אַחַת שִׁבְעָה עֵינַיִם הִנְנִי מְפַתֵּחַ פִּתֻּחָהּ נְאֻם יְהוָה

Jehovah of / says / its ,engraving / will engrave / ,behold I / ;eyes / seven / one (are) / stone / on

10 צְבָאוֹת וּמַשְׁתִּי אֶת־עֲוֺן הָאָרֶץ־הַהִיא בְּיוֹם אֶחָד׃ בַּיּוֹם

day In / .one / day in / that / land / iniquity the of / I and remove will / ,hosts

הַהוּא נְאֻם יְהוָה צְבָאוֹת תִּקְרְאוּ אִישׁ לְרֵעֵהוּ אֶל־תַּחַת

under / to (sit) / his to neighbor / (each) man / shall you invite / ,hosts / Jehovah of / says / ,that

גֶּפֶן וְאֶל־תַּחַת תְּאֵנָה׃

the .tree fig / under / and / the vine

CAP. IV ד

CHAPTER 4

[1] And the angel who was talking with me came again and awakened me, as a man that is awakened out of

CHAPTER 4

1 וַיָּשָׁב הַמַּלְאָךְ הַדֹּבֵר בִּי וַיְעִירֵנִי כְּאִישׁ אֲשֶׁר־יֵעוֹר מִשְּׁנָתוֹ׃

his from ,sleep / is awakened / who / a as man / awoke and ,me / with me / was who speaking / the angel / And returned his sleep, [2] and said to me, What do you see? And I said, I see, and behold, a lampstand all of it gold, and a bowl on the top of it. And its seven lamps (are) on it, and seven spouts each to the seven lamps which (are) on its top; [3] and two olive trees beside it; one on the right of the bowl and one on its left. [4] So I answered and spoke to the angel who was talking with me, saying, What (are) these, my lord? [5] Then the angel who was talking with me answered and said to me, Do you know what these (are)? And I said, No, my lord. [6] Then he answered and spoke to me, saying, This (is) the word of Jehovah to Zerubbabel, saying, Not by might, nor by power, but by My Spirit, says Jehovah of hosts. [7] Who (are) you, O great mountain? Before Zerubbabel (you shall become) a plain. And he shall bring forth the top-stone (with) shoutings, Grace! Grace to it! [8] And the word of Jehovah was to me, saying, [9] The hands of Zerubbabel have laid the foundation of this house; his hands shall also finish (it); and you shall know that Jehovah of hosts has sent me to you. [10] For who has despised the day of small things? For they shall rejoice and shall see the plummet stone in the hand of Zerubbabel; these seven (are) the eyes of Jehovah; they run to and fro through all the earth.

[11] Then I answered and said to him, What (are) these two olive trees on the right of the lampstand and on the left of it? [12] And I answered a second time and said to him, What are the two olive branches which (are) beside the two pipes which empty the golden

2 וַיֹּאמֶר אֵלַי מָה אַתָּה רֹאֶה וָאֹמַר רָאִיתִי וְהִנֵּה מְנוֹרַת
lamp- a and see I I And do you What ,me to and
of stand ,behold ,said ?see said

זָהָב כֻּלָּהּ וְגֻלָּהּ עַל־רֹאשָׁהּ וְשִׁבְעָה נֵרֹתֶיהָ עָלֶיהָ שִׁבְעָה
seven on (are) its And .top its on a and of all ,gold
,it lamps seven bowl ,it

3 וְשִׁבְעָה מוּצָקוֹת לַנֵּרוֹת אֲשֶׁר עַל־רֹאשָׁהּ׃ וּשְׁנַיִם זֵיתִים
olive two and ;top its on which the to lips and
trees (are) lamps seven

4 עָלֶיהָ אֶחָד מִימִין הַגֻּלָּה וְאֶחָד עַל־שְׂמֹאלָהּ׃ וָאַעַן וָאֹמַר
and I So .lefts its on one and the the on one beside
said answered ,bowl of right ,it

5 אֶל־הַמַּלְאָךְ הַדֹּבֵר בִּי לֵאמֹר מָה אֵלֶּה אֲדֹנִי׃ וַיַּעַן הַמַּלְאָךְ
the Then my these What ,saying with was who the to
angel answered ?lord (are) ,me speaking angel

הַדֹּבֵר בִּי וַיֹּאמֶר אֵלַי הֲלוֹא יָדַעְתָּ מָה־הֵמָּה אֵלֶּה וָאֹמַר
I And ?these (are) what you Do not ,me to said and with was who
,said know me speaking

6 לֹא אֲדֹנִי׃ וַיַּעַן וַיֹּאמֶר אֵלַי לֵאמֹר זֶה דְּבַר־יְהוָה אֶל־
to Jehovah the This ,saying ,me to said and he Then my ,No
of word (is) answered .lord

זְרֻבָּבֶל לֵאמֹר לֹא בְחַיִל וְלֹא בְכֹחַ כִּי אִם־בְּרוּחִי אָמַר
says My by but by nor by Not ,saying Zerub-
.Spirit ,power ,might babel

7 יְהוָה צְבָאוֹת׃ מִי־אַתָּה הַר־הַגָּדוֹל לִפְנֵי זְרֻבָּבֶל לְמִישֹׁר
!plain a Zerubbabel Before ?great O ,you Who .hosts Jehovah
(become) mountain (are) of

וְהוֹצִיא אֶת־הָאֶבֶן הָרֹאשָׁה תְּשֻׁאוֹת חֵן ׀ חֵן לָהּ׃
to Grace !Grace (with) top stone the he And
!it ,shouts out bring shall

8
9 וַיְהִי דְבַר־יְהוָה אֵלַי לֵאמֹר׃ יְדֵי זְרֻבָּבֶל יִסְּדוּ הַבַּיִת הַזֶּה
;this house have Zerubbabel The ,saying ,me to Jehovah the And
founded of hands of word was

וְיָדָיו תְּבַצַּעְנָה וְיָדַעְתָּ כִּי־יְהוָה צְבָאוֹת שְׁלָחַנִי אֲלֵיכֶם׃
.you to sent has hosts Jehovah that you and shall his and
Me of know shall ;(it) finish hands

10 כִּי מִי בַז לְיוֹם קְטַנּוֹת וְשָׂמְחוּ וְרָאוּ אֶת־הָאֶבֶן הַבְּדִיל בְּיַד
in plummet stone the shall and they For small the has who For
hand see rejoice shall ?things of day despised

זְרֻבָּבֶל שִׁבְעָה־אֵלֶּה עֵינֵי יְהוָה הֵמָּה מְשׁוֹטְטִים בְּכָל־
all in roam they ,Jehovah the these seven Zerub-
around of eyes (are) —babel's

11 הָאָרֶץ׃ וָאַעַן וָאֹמַר אֵלָיו מַה־שְּׁנֵי הַזֵּיתִים הָאֵלֶּה עַל־
on these olive two What to said and I Then the
trees (are) ,him answered .earth

12 יְמִין הַמְּנוֹרָה וְעַל־שְׂמֹאולָהּ׃ וָאַעַן שֵׁנִית וָאֹמַר אֵלָיו
to said and second a I And left its and lamp- the the
,him time answered on stand of right

מַה־שְׁתֵּי שִׁבֲּלֵי הַזֵּיתִים אֲשֶׁר בְּיַד שְׁנֵי צַנְתְּרוֹת הַזָּהָב
,gold of pipes the beside which olives clusters the What
two (are) of two (are)

(oil) out of themselves?
[13] And he spoke to me,
saying, Do you not know
what these (are)? And I
said, No, my lord.
[14] Then he said, These
(are) the two sons of fresh
oil who stand by the Lord
of the whole earth.

13 הַמְרִיקִים מֵעֲלֵיהֶם הַזָּהָב׃ וַיֹּאמֶר אֵלַי לֵאמֹר הֲלוֹא
not ,saying ,me to he And golden the from are which
spoke ?(oil) themselves emptying

14 יָדַעְתָּ מָה־אֵלֶּה וָאֹמַר לֹא אֲדֹנִי׃ וַיֹּאמֶר אֵלֶּה שְׁנֵי בְנֵי־
sons the These he Then my No I And these what you Do
of two (are) ,said .lord ,said ?(are) know

הַיִּצְהָר הָעֹמְדִים עַל־אֲדוֹן כָּל־הָאָרֶץ׃
the all the by are who fresh
.earth of Lord standing oil

CAP. V ה

CHAPTER 5

[1] Then I turned and
lifted up my eyes and
looked. And, behold, a flying scroll! [2] And he said
to me, What do you see?
And I answered, I see a
flying scroll; its length (is)
twenty cubits and its width
ten cubits. [3] And he said
to me, This (is) the curse
that goes forth over the face
of the whole earth. For
everyone who henceforth
steals shall be cut off according to it; and everyone
who swears henceforth shall
be cut off according to it.
[4] I will bring it forth, says
Jehovah of hosts. And I
shall enter into the house of
the thief and into the house
of him who swears falsely
by My name. And it shall
remain in the midst of his
house, and shall destroy it,
and its timber and its
stones.
[5] Then the angel who
was talking with me went
out and said to me, Now lift
up your eyes and see what
this (is) that goes forth.
[6] And I said, What (is) it?
And he said, This is the
ephah that goes forth. And
he said, This (is) their form
in all the earth. [7] And,
behold, there was lifted up a
lead cover; and this (is) a
woman who sits in the
midst of the ephah.
[8] And he said, This (is)
wickedness. And he cast
her into the midst of the
ephah; and he cast the
lead stone on its mouth.
[9] Then I lifted up my
eyes and looked, And, be-
hold, two women came

CHAPTER 5

1
2 וָאָשׁוּב וָאֶשָּׂא עֵינַי וָאֶרְאֶה וְהִנֵּה מְגִלָּה עָפָה׃ וַיֹּאמֶר
he And .flying scroll a and and my lifted I And
said ,behold ;looked eyes up again

אֵלַי מָה אַתָּה רֹאֶה וָאֹמַר אֲנִי רֹאֶה מְגִלָּה עָפָה אָרְכָּהּ
lengths its ;flying scroll a see I I And ?see do you What to
(is) ,said ,me

3 עֶשְׂרִים בָּאַמָּה וְרָחְבָּהּ עֶשֶׂר בָּאַמָּה׃ וַיֹּאמֶר אֵלַי זֹאת
This ,me to he And .cubits ten its and cubits twenty
(is) said width

הָאָלָה הַיּוֹצֵאת עַל־פְּנֵי כָל־הָאָרֶץ כִּי כָל־הַגֹּנֵב מִזֶּה
hence- who all For the whole the over goes that the
forth steal .earth of face forth curse

4 כָּמוֹהָ נִקָּה וְכָל־הַנִּשְׁבָּע מִזֶּה כָּמוֹהָ נִקָּה׃ הוֹצֵאתִיהָ נְאֻם
says will I be will according hence- who and be will accord-
,out it bring off cut it to forth swear all ;off cut it to ing

יְהוָה צְבָאוֹת וּבָאָה אֶל־בֵּית הַגַּנָּב וְאֶל־בֵּית הַנִּשְׁבָּע בִּשְׁמִי
My by who him the and the the into it And .hosts Jehovah
name swears of house into thief of house go shall of

לַשָּׁקֶר וְלָנָה בְּתוֹךְ בֵּיתוֹ וְכִלַּתּוּ וְאֶת־עֵצָיו וְאֶת־אֲבָנָיו׃
its and its and shall and his within it And .falsely
.stones timber it destroy ,house remain shall

5 וַיֵּצֵא הַמַּלְאָךְ הַדֹּבֵר בִּי וַיֹּאמֶר אֵלַי שָׂא נָא עֵינֶיךָ וּרְאֵה
see and your now Lift ,me to said and with was who the went Then
eyes up me speaking angel forth

6 מָה הַיּוֹצֵאת הַזֹּאת׃ וָאֹמַר מַה־הִיא וַיֹּאמֶר זֹאת הָאֵיפָה
the This he And ?it What I And .(is) this goes that what
ephah (is) ,said (is) ,said forth

7 הַיּוֹצֵאת וַיֹּאמֶר זֹאת עֵינָם בְּכָל־הָאָרֶץ׃ וְהִנֵּה כִּכַּר עֹפֶרֶת
lead a cover And the all in their This he And goes that
,behold .earth appearance (is) ,said .forth

8 נִשֵּׂאת וְזֹאת אִשָּׁה אַחַת יוֹשֶׁבֶת בְּתוֹךְ הָאֵיפָה׃ וַיֹּאמֶר
he And the the in sitting a woman and lifted was
,said .ephah of midst (is) this ;up

זֹאת הָרִשְׁעָה וַיַּשְׁלֵךְ אֹתָהּ אֶל־תּוֹךְ הָאֵיפָה וַיַּשְׁלֵךְ אֶת־
he and the the into her he And .wickedness This
cast ;ephah of midst cast (is)

9 אֶבֶן הָעֹפֶרֶת אֶל־פִּיהָ׃ וָאֶשָּׂא עֵינַי וָאֵרֶא וְהִנֵּה שְׁתַּיִם
two and and my I Then its on lead the
,behold ,looked eyes up lifted .opening stone

out. And the wind (was) in their wings; for they had wings like the wings of the stork. And they lifted up the ephah between the earth and the heavens. [10] Then I said to the angel who was talking with me, Where are they going with the ephah? [11] And he said to me, To build a house for it in the land of Shinar; and it shall be established and set there on its own base.

נָשִׁים יוֹצְאוֹת וְרוּחַ בְּכַנְפֵיהֶם וְלָהֵנָּה כְנָפַיִם כְּכַנְפֵי הַחֲסִידָה

the stork | the like of wings | wings | they for (had) | their in ;wings | the And (was) wind | came .out | women

10 וַתִּשֶּׂנָה אֶת־הָאֵיפָה בֵּין הָאָרֶץ וּבֵין הַשָּׁמָיִם׃ וָאֹמַר אֶל־

to | I Then said | the .heavens | and | the earth | between | the ephah | they And up lifted

הַמַּלְאָךְ הַדֹּבֵר בִּי אָנָה הֵמָּה מוֹלִכוֹת אֶת־הָאֵיפָה׃

the ?ephah | with | going | they | Where (are) | with ,me | was who speaking | the angel

11 וַיֹּאמֶר אֵלַי לִבְנוֹת־לָה בַיִת בְּאֶרֶץ שִׁנְעָר וְהוּכַן וְהֻנִּיחָה

set and | will it and fixed be | ;Shinar | the in of land | a house | for it | To build | ,me to | he And said

שָׁם עַל־מְכֻנָתָהּ׃

own its .place | on there

CAP. VI ו

CHAPTER 6

CHAPTER 6

[1] And I turned and lifted up my eyes and looked. And, behold, four chariots came from between two mountains. And the mountains (were) mountains of bronze. [2] Red horses (were) in the first chariot; and in the second chariot black horses; [3] and in the third chariot white horses; and in the fourth chariot dappled and speckled horses. [4] Then I answered and said to the angel who was talking with me, What (are) these, my lord? [5] And the angel answered and said to me, These (are) the four spirits of Heaven who go forth from standing before the Lord of all the earth. [6] The black horses which (are) in it go into the north country; and the white go after them; and the dappled ones go toward the south country. [7] And the speckled ones went out and sought to go, to walk to and fro in the earth. And he said, Go, walk to and fro in the earth. So they walked to and fro in the earth. [8] Then he cried out to me

1 וָאָשֻׁב וָאֶשָּׂא עֵינַי וָאֶרְאֶה וְהִנֵּה אַרְבַּע מַרְכָּבוֹת יֹצְאוֹת

were coming | chariots | four | and ,behold | and ;looked | my eyes | lifted up | And again

2 מִבֵּין שְׁנֵי הֶהָרִים וְהֶהָרִים הָרֵי נְחֹשֶׁת׃ בַּמֶּרְכָּבָה הָרִאשֹׁנָה

first | the With chariot | .bronze | moun- of tains | the And mountains | moun- .tains | two | from between

סוּסִים אֲדֻמִּים וּבַמֶּרְכָּבָה הַשֵּׁנִית סוּסִים שְׁחֹרִים׃

;black | horses | second | with and chariot the | ;red | (were) horses

3 וּבַמֶּרְכָּבָה הַשְּׁלִשִׁית סוּסִים לְבָנִים וּבַמֶּרְכָּבָה הָרְבִעִית

fourth | the with and chariot | ;white | horses | third | the with and chariot

4 סוּסִים בְּרֻדִּים אֲמֻצִּים׃ וָאַעַן וָאֹמַר אֶל־הַמַּלְאָךְ הַדֹּבֵר

was who speaking | the angel | to | said and | I Then answered | (and) .piebald | dappled | horses

5 בִּי מָה־אֵלֶּה אֲדֹנִי׃ וַיַּעַן הַמַּלְאָךְ וַיֹּאמֶר אֵלַי אֵלֶּה אַרְבַּע

four | the These (are) | to ,me | said and | angel the | Then answered | my ?lord | ,these | What (are) | with ,me

רֻחוֹת הַשָּׁמַיִם יוֹצְאוֹת מֵהִתְיַצֵּב עַל־אֲדוֹן כָּל־הָאָרֶץ׃

the ;earth | all | the of Lord | before | standing from | go who forth | the heavens | spirits of

6 אֲשֶׁר־בָּהּ הַסּוּסִים הַשְּׁחֹרִים יֹצְאִים אֶל־אֶרֶץ צָפוֹן

the ;north | country | into | forth go | black | horses the | with it | which (are)

וְהַלְּבָנִים יָצְאוּ אֶל־אַחֲרֵיהֶם וְהַבְּרֻדִּים יָצְאוּ אֶל־אֶרֶץ

a country | to | go forth | the and ones dappled | after ;them | into (north the) | go forth | the and white

7 הַתֵּימָן׃ וְהָאֲמֻצִּים יָצְאוּ וַיְבַקְשׁוּ לָלֶכֶת לְהִתְהַלֵּךְ בָּאָרֶץ

the in .earth | walk to fro and to | go to | sought and | went forth | the And piebald | the .south

8 וַיֹּאמֶר לְכוּ הִתְהַלְּכוּ בָּאָרֶץ וַתִּתְהַלַּכְנָה בָּאָרֶץ׃ וַיַּזְעֵק

he Then out cried | the in .earth | walked they So fro and to | the in .earth | to walk fro and | ,Go | he And ,said

and spoke to me, saying, Behold, these who go toward the north country have caused My Spirit to rest in the north country.

[9] And the word of Jehovah was to me saying, [10] Take from Heldai, from Tobijah and from Jedaiah, from the exiles, who have come from Babylon; and in that day you go and enter the house of Josiah the son of Zephaniah; [11] yea, take silver and gold and make crowns; and set (it) on the head of Joshua the son of Jehozadak, the high priest. [12] And speak to him, saying, Thus says Jehovah of hosts, saying, Behold! The Man whose name is THE BRANCH! And He shall grow up out of His place, and He shall build the temple of Jehovah. [13] Even He shall build the temple of Jehovah. And He shall bear the majesty and shall sit and rule on His throne; and He shall be a priest on His throne; and the counsel of peace shall be between them both. [14] And the crowns shall be for a memorial in the temple of Jehovah to Helem, and to Tobijah, and to Jedaiah, and to Hen the son of Zephaniah. [15] And the distant ones shall come and build in the temple of Jehovah, and you shall know that Jehovah of hosts has sent me to you. And (this) shall come to pass if you will completely obey the voice of Jehovah your God.

אֹתִי וַיְדַבֵּר אֵלַי לֵאמֹר רְאֵה הַיּוֹצְאִים אֶל־אֶרֶץ צָפוֹן הֵנִיחוּ
set have the country to who those ,See ,saying ,me to and to
rest at north forth go spoke me

9 אֶת־רוּחִי בְּאֶרֶץ צָפוֹן׃ וַיְהִי דְבַר־יְהוָה אֵלַי לֵאמֹר׃
,saying to Jehovah the And the in My
,me of word was .north country Spirit

10 לָקוֹחַ מֵאֵת הַגּוֹלָה מֵחֶלְדַּי וּמֵאֵת טוֹבִיָּה וּמֵאֵת יְדַעְיָה
,Jedaiah and ,Tobijah from from the from Take
from ,Heldai ,exiles

וּבָאתָ אַתָּה בַּיּוֹם הַהוּא וּבָאתָ בֵּית יֹאשִׁיָּה בֶן־צְפַנְיָה
Zepha- the Josiah the and that day in you go and
,niah of son of house enter

11 אֲשֶׁר־בָּאוּ מִבָּבֶל׃ וְלָקַחְתָּ כֶסֶף־וְזָהָב וְעָשִׂיתָ עֲטָרוֹת
;crowns and and silver take and from have who
make gold ;Babylon come

12 וְשַׂמְתָּ בְּרֹאשׁ יְהוֹשֻׁעַ בֶּן־יְהוֹצָדָק הַכֹּהֵן הַגָּדוֹל׃ וְאָמַרְתָּ
speak And .high the Jehosadak the Joshua the on set and
priest of son of head (it)

אֵלָיו לֵאמֹר כֹּה אָמַר יְהוָה צְבָאוֹת לֵאמֹר הִנֵּה־אִישׁ צֶמַח
BRANCH A !Behold ,saying ,hosts Jehovah says Thus ,saying ,him to
(is) ,man of

13 שְׁמוֹ וּמִתַּחְתָּיו יִצְמָח וּבָנָה אֶת־הֵיכַל יְהוָה׃ וְהוּא יִבְנֶה
shall Even .Jehovah the He and will He from And His
build He of temple build will ,sprout place His .name

אֶת־הֵיכַל יְהוָה וְהוּא־יִשָּׂא הוֹד וְיָשַׁב וּמָשַׁל עַל־כִּסְאוֹ וְהָיָה
He and His on rule and shall and the shall and ,Jehovah the
be shall ;throne sit majesty bear He of temple

14 כֹהֵן עַל־כִּסְאוֹ וַעֲצַת שָׁלוֹם תִּהְיֶה בֵּין שְׁנֵיהֶם׃ וְהָעֲטָרֹת
the And two the between shall peace the and His on a
crowns .them of be of counsel ;throne priest

תִּהְיֶה לְחֵלֶם וּלְטוֹבִיָּה וְלִידַעְיָה וּלְחֵן בֶּן־צְפַנְיָה לְזִכָּרוֹן
a for Zephaniah the to and to and to and to shall
reminder of son Hen ,Jedaiah ,Tobijah ,Helem be

15 בְּהֵיכַל יְהוָה׃ וּרְחוֹקִים ׀ יָבֹאוּ וּבָנוּ בְּהֵיכַל יְהוָה וִידַעְתֶּם
you and ,Jehovah the in and shall the And .Jehovah the in
know shall of temple build come ones distant of temple

כִּי־יְהוָה צְבָאוֹת שְׁלָחַנִי אֲלֵיכֶם וְהָיָה אִם־שָׁמוֹעַ תִּשְׁמְעוּן
obey you diligently if it And .you to sent has hosts Jeho- that
,be will me of vah

בְּקוֹל יְהוָה אֱלֹהֵיכֶם׃
.God your Jehovah the
of voice

CAP. VII ז

CHAPTER 7

1 וַיְהִי בִּשְׁנַת אַרְבַּע לְדָרְיָוֶשׁ הַמֶּלֶךְ הָיָה דְבַר־יְהוָה אֶל־
to Jehovah the came ,king the Darius of fourth the in it And
of word year was

2 זְכַרְיָה בְּאַרְבָּעָה לַחֹדֶשׁ הַתְּשִׁעִי בְּכִסְלֵו׃ וַיִּשְׁלַח בֵּית־
Beth- had Now .Chislev in ,ninth the month of the in Zechariah
sent fourth

CHAPTER 7

[1] And in the fourth year of King Darius, the word of Jehovah was to Zechariah in the fourth of the ninth month, in Chislev: [2] Now had sent Sherezer

and Regem-melech and his men to Beth-el to seek the favor of the face of Jehovah, [3] to speak to the priests who (belong) to the house of Jehovah of hosts, and to the prophets, saying, Should I weep in the fifth month, separating myself, as I have done these many years?

[4] Then was the word of Jehovah of hosts to me, saying, [5] Speak to all the people of the land, and to the priests, saying, When you fasted and mourned in the fifth and seventh (months), even those seventy years, did you truly fast to Me, (even) to Me? [6] And when you ate, and when you drank, was it not for those eating, and for those drinking? [7] Are not (these) the words which Jehovah has proclaimed by the former prophets, when Jerusalem was inhabited and prosperous with her cities all around her; and the Negev and the Shephelah were inhabited?

[8] And the word of Jehovah was to Zechariah, saying, [9] Thus speaks Jehovah of hosts, saying, Judge true judgment and practice kindness and pity, (each) man with his brother. [10] And do not oppress the widow or the fatherless, the stranger, or the poor. And do not devise the evil of a man (against) his brother in your heart. [11] But they refused to listen and gave a stubborn shoulder and made their ears heavy against hearing. [12] Yes, they made their hearts adamant against hearing the law and the words which Jehovah of hosts has sent by His Spirit by the former prophets. Therefore great wrath came from Jehovah of hosts.

אֶל שַׂרְאֶצֶר וְרֶגֶם מֶלֶךְ וַאֲנָשָׁיו לְחַלּוֹת אֶת־פְּנֵי יְהוָה׃
,Jehovah the the seek to his and melech and Sherezer el
of face of favor men Regem-

3 לֵאמֹר אֶל־הַכֹּהֲנִים אֲשֶׁר לְבֵית־יְהוָה צְבָאוֹת וְאֶל־הַנְּבִיאִים
the and ,hosts Jehovah the to who the to to
,prophets to of of house (belong) priests speak

לֵאמֹר הַאֶבְכֶּה בַּחֹדֶשׁ הַחֲמִשִׁי הִנָּזֵר כַּאֲשֶׁר עָשִׂיתִי זֶה
these have I as consecrating ,fifth the in I Should ,saying
done myself month weep

4 כַּמֶּה שָׁנִים׃ וַיְהִי דְּבַר־יְהוָה צְבָאוֹת אֵלַי לֵאמֹר׃
,saying ,me to hosts Jehovah the And ?years many
of of word came

5 אֱמֹר אֶל־כָּל־עַם הָאָרֶץ וְאֶל־הַכֹּהֲנִים לֵאמֹר כִּי־צַמְתֶּם
you When ,saying the and the the all to Speak
fasted ,priests to ,land of people

וְסָפוֹד בַּחֲמִישִׁי וּבַשְּׁבִיעִי וְזֶה שִׁבְעִים שָׁנָה הֲצוֹם צַמְתֻּנִי
you did truly ,years seventy even seventh and the in and
,Me for fast those ,(months) fifth mourned

6 אָנִי׃ וְכִי תֹאכְלוּ וְכִי תִשְׁתּוּ הֲלוֹא אַתֶּם הָאֹכְלִים וְאַתֶּם
for and those (for) (it was) you and ate you And (just)
,you ;eating ,you not ,drank when when ?Me

7 הַשֹּׁתִים׃ הֲלוֹא אֶת־הַדְּבָרִים אֲשֶׁר קָרָא יְהוָה בְּיַד
by Jehovah pro- which the (these) (Are) those
claimed words not ?drinking

הַנְּבִיאִים הָרִאשֹׁנִים בִּהְיוֹת יְרוּשָׁלִַם יֹשֶׁבֶת וּשְׁלֵוָה וְעָרֶיהָ
her with and inhabited Jerusalem was when ,former the
cities prosperous prophets

8 סְבִיבֹתֶיהָ וְהַנֶּגֶב וְהַשְּׁפֵלָה יֹשֵׁב׃ וַיְהִי דְּבַר־יְהוָה
Jehovah the And in- were the and the and around all
of word was ?habited Shephelah Negev ,her

9 אֶל־זְכַרְיָה לֵאמֹר׃ כֹּה אָמַר יְהוָה צְבָאוֹת לֵאמֹר מִשְׁפַּט
judgment ,saying ,hosts Jehovah says Thus ,saying ,Zechariah to
of

10 אֱמֶת שְׁפֹטוּ וְחֶסֶד וְרַחֲמִים עֲשׂוּ אִישׁ אֶת־אָחִיו׃ וְאַלְמָנָה
the And his with (each) practice and and Judge true
widow .brother man compassion kindness

וְיָתוֹם גֵּר וְעָנִי אַל־תַּעֲשֹׁקוּ וְרָעַת אִישׁ אָחִיו אַל־תַּחְשְׁבוּ
do not his man a the And do not the or the the or
devise brother (against) of evil .oppress ,poor ,alien ,orphan

11 בִּלְבַבְכֶם׃ וַיְמָאֲנוּ לְהַקְשִׁיב וַיִּתְּנוּ כָתֵף סֹרָרֶת וְאָזְנֵיהֶם
their and stubborn a gave and to they But your in
ears shoulder listen refused .heart

12 הִכְבִּידוּ מִשְּׁמוֹעַ׃ וְלִבָּם שָׂמוּ שָׁמִיר מִשְּׁמוֹעַ אֶת־הַתּוֹרָה
law the from adamant they their And from made they
hearing made heart .hearing heavy

וְאֶת־הַדְּבָרִים אֲשֶׁר שָׁלַח יְהוָה צְבָאוֹת בְּרוּחוֹ בְּיַד
by through hosts Jehovah has which the and
Spirit His of sent words

הַנְּבִיאִים הָרִאשֹׁנִים וַיְהִי קֶצֶף גָּדוֹל מֵאֵת יְהוָה צְבָאוֹת׃
.hosts Jehovah from great wrath Thus .former the
of came prophets

[13] And it will be, as He called, and they did not listen, so they called and I did not listen, says Jehovah of hosts. [14] But I stormed them away among all the nations whom they knew not. So the land is wasted behind them, from passing through and from returning, for they made the land of desire a waste.

13 וַיְהִי כַאֲשֶׁר־קָרָא וְלֹא שָׁמֵעוּ כֵּן יִקְרְאוּ וְלֹא אֶשְׁמָע אָמַר

says did I and they so they and He just it And
,listen not called listened not called as be will

14 יְהוָה צְבָאוֹת׃ וְאֵסָעֲרֵם עַל כָּל־הַגּוֹיִם אֲשֶׁר לֹא־יְדָעוּם

did they not whom the all on I And .hosts Jehovah
.them know nations away them stormed of

וְהָאָרֶץ נָשַׁמָּה אַחֲרֵיהֶם מֵעֹבֵר וּמִשָּׁב וַיָּשִׂימוּ אֶרֶץ

the they for from and from behind is the So
of land made ,returning passing them desolated land

חֶמְדָּה לְשַׁמָּה׃

.waste a desire

CAP. VIII ח

CHAPTER 8

CHAPTER 8

[1] And was the word of Jehovah of hosts, saying, [2] Thus says Jehovah of hosts: I was jealous for Zion (with) great jealousy, and I was jealous for her (with) great wrath. [3] Thus says Jehovah: I have returned to Zion and will dwell in the midst of Jerusalem. And Jerusalem shall be called a city of truth, and the mountain of Jehovah of hosts the holy mountain. [4] Thus says Jehovah of hosts: There shall yet be old men and old women sitting in the streets of Jerusalem, and (each) man (with) his staff in his hand because of (their) many days. [5] And the streets of the city shall be full of boys and girls playing in its streets. [6] Thus says Jehovah of hosts: If it is marvelous in the eyes of the remnant of this people in those days, will it also be marvelous in My eyes, says Jehovah of hosts? [7] Thus says Jehovah of hosts: Behold, I will save My people from the east country and from the setting sun country. [8] And I will bring them, and they shall live in the midst of Jerusalem. And they shall be My people, and I will be their God, in

1 וַיְהִי דְּבַר־יְהוָה צְבָאוֹת לֵאמֹר׃ כֹּה אָמַר יְהוָה צְבָאוֹת
2

:hosts Jehovah says Thus ,saying ,hosts Jehovah the And
of of of word came

קִנֵּאתִי לְצִיּוֹן קִנְאָה גְדוֹלָה וְחֵמָה גְדוֹלָה קִנֵּאתִי לָהּ׃

for was I great (with) and great (with) for was I
.her jealous wrath jealousy Zion jealous

3 כֹּה אָמַר יְהוָה שַׁבְתִּי אֶל־צִיּוֹן וְשָׁכַנְתִּי בְּתוֹךְ יְרוּשָׁלָםִ

.Jerusalem the in will and Zion to have I :Jehovah says Thus
of midst dwell returned

וְנִקְרְאָה יְרוּשָׁלַםִ עִיר הָאֱמֶת וְהַר־יְהוָה צְבָאוֹת הַר

moun- ,hosts Jehovah the and ,truth city a Jerusalem shall And
tain of mountain of called be

4 הַקֹּדֶשׁ׃ כֹּה אָמַר יְהוָה צְבָאוֹת עֹד יֵשְׁבוּ זְקֵנִים

Old will again :hosts Jehovah says Thus .holy the
men sit of

וּזְקֵנוֹת בִּרְחֹבוֹת יְרוּשָׁלָםִ וְאִישׁ מִשְׁעַנְתּוֹ בְּיָדוֹ מֵרֹב יָמִים׃

.days from his in his (with) a and ,Jerusalem the in old and
many the ,hand staff man of plazas women

5 וּרְחֹבוֹת הָעִיר יִמָּלְאוּ יְלָדִים וִילָדוֹת מְשַׂחֲקִים בִּרְחֹבֹתֶיהָ׃

:plazas its in playing girls and boys be shall the the And
of full city of plazas

6 כֹּה אָמַר יְהוָה צְבָאוֹת כִּי יִפָּלֵא בְּעֵינֵי שְׁאֵרִית

the the in is it If :hosts Jehovah says Thus
of remnant of eyes difficult of

הָעָם הַזֶּה בַּיָּמִים הָהֵם גַּם־בְּעֵינַי יִפָּלֵא נְאֻם יְהוָה צְבָאוֹת׃

?hosts Jehovah says it will My in also ,those days in this people
of ;difficult be eyes

7 כֹּה אָמַר יְהוָה צְבָאוֹת הִנְנִי מוֹשִׁיעַ אֶת־עַמִּי מֵאֶרֶץ

the from My save will ,Behold :hosts Jehovah says Thus
of land people I of

8 מִזְרָח וּמֵאֶרֶץ מְבוֹא הַשָּׁמֶשׁ׃ וְהֵבֵאתִי אֹתָם וְשָׁכְנוּ בְּתוֹךְ

the in they and ,them will I .sun the from and the
of midst live shall bring will setting of land the rising

יְרוּשָׁלָםִ וְהָיוּ־לִי לְעָם וַאֲנִי אֶהְיֶה לָהֶם לֵאלֹהִים בֶּאֱמֶת

truth in ,God for to be will and a for will they And .Jerusalem
them I ,people Me to be

truth and in righteousness.
[9] Thus says Jehovah of hosts: Let your hands be strong, you who hear in these days these words by the mouth of the prophets, that in the day the house of Jehovah of hosts is laid, the temple (is) to be built.
[10] For before those days (there) was not wage for man, nor was a wage for animal; and there was no peace to him who went out or came in, from the adversary; for I sent every man, a man against his neighbor.
[11] But now I (will) not (be) to the remnant of this people as in the former days, says Jehovah of hosts.
[12] For there (shall be) peace (for) the seed; the vine shall give its fruit and the ground shall give its produce; and the heavens shall give their dew; and I will cause the remnant of this people to inherit all these. [13] And it shall be, as you were a curse among the nations, O house of Judah and house of Israel, so I will save you, and you shall be a blessing. Do not fear; let your hands be strong. [14] For thus says Jehovah of hosts: As I purposed to punish you when your fathers provoked Me to wrath, says Jehovah of hosts, and I did not repent,
[15] so again I have purposed in these days to do good to Jerusalem and the house of Judah: do not fear.

[16] These (are) the things that you shall do. (Let each) man speak the truth with his neighbor. Judge (with) truth and judgment (for) peace in your gates. [17] And let each devise no evil in your heart (against) his neighbor; and

9 ובצדקה׃ כה־אמר יהוה צבאות תחזקנה ידיכם
your be Let :hosts Jehovah says Thus in and
,hands strong of .righteousness

השמעים בימים האלה את הדברים האלה מפי הנביאים
the the from these words these days in who (you)
,prophets of mouth hear

10 אשר ביום יסד בית־יהוה צבאות ההיכל להבנות׃ כי
For .rebuild to the ,hosts' Jehovah house is the in that
temple of founded day

לפני הימים ההם שכר האדם לא נהיה ושכר הבהמה
animal wages or there not man wages those days before
for ,was for

איננה וליוצא ולבא אין־שלום מן־הצר ואשלח את־כל־
every I for the from ,peace not for or for and was
sent ;adversary coming him going him ,not

11 האדם איש ברעהו׃ ועתה לא כימים הראשנים אני
I former the as not But his against a ,man
(be will) days ,now .neighbor man

12 לשארית העם הזה נאם יהוה צבאות׃ כי־זרע השלום
(have will) the For .hosts Jehovah says ,this people the to
,peace seed of of remnant

הגפן תתן פריה והארץ תתן את־יבולה והשמים יתנו
will the and its will the and its will the
give heavens ;produce give land fruit give vine

טלם והנחלתי את־שארית העם הזה את־כל־אלה׃
these all this people the will I and their
.(things) of remnant inherit to cause ;dew

13 והיה כאשר הייתם קללה בגוים בית יהודה ובית
and Judah O the among curse a were you as it And
of house of house ,nations ,be shall

ישראל כן אושיע אתכם והייתם ברכה אל־תיראו
;fear Do not a you and ,you will I so ,Israel
.blessing be shall save

14 תחזקנה ידיכם׃ כי כה אמר יהוה צבאות כאשר
As :hosts Jehovah says thus For your be let
of .hands strong

זממתי להרע לכם בהקציף אבתיכם אתי אמר יהוה
Jehovah says ,Me your provoked when you harm to pur- I
of fathers wrath to posed

15 צבאות ולא נחמתי׃ כן שבתי זממתי בימים האלה
these days in have I again so did I and ,hosts
purposed ,repent not

16 להיטיב את־ירושלם ואת־בית יהודה אל־תיראו׃ אלה
These .fear do not ;Judah the and Jerusalem do to
(are) of house to good

הדברים אשר תעשו דברו אמת איש את־רעהו אמת
(with) his with (each) truth Let shall you that the
truth ;neighbor man speak .do things

17 ומשפט שלום שפטו בשעריכם׃ ואיש את־רעת רעהו
his the And your in judge (for) and
neighbor of harm each .gates peace justice

love no false oath. For all these I hate, says Jehovah.
[18] And the word of Jehovah of hosts was to me, saying, [19] Thus says Jehovah of hosts: The fast of the fourth (month), and the fast of the fifth, and the fast of the seventh, and the fast of the tenth shall become to the house of Judah for joy and gladness and cheerful feasts. Therefore love truth and peace. [20] Thus says Jehovah of hosts: There shall yet come people, and inhabitants of many cities; [21] and the inhabitants of one shall go to another, saying, Let us go at once to seek the favor of the face of Jehovah; and to seek Jehovah of hosts, I will go also. [22] And many peoples and strong nations shall come to seek Jehovah of hosts in Jerusalem, and to seek the favor of the face of Jehovah. [23] Thus says Jehovah of hosts: In those days ten men shall take hold, out of all languages of the nations, and will seize the skirt of a man, a Jew, saying, Let us go with you, for we have heard that God (is) with you.

אַל־תַּחְשְׁבוּ בִּלְבַבְכֶם וּשְׁבֻעַת שֶׁקֶר אַל־תֶּאֱהָבוּ כִּי אֶת־

For .love do not false a oath and your in let not
;heart devise

18 כָּל־אֵלֶּה אֲשֶׁר שָׂנֵאתִי נְאֻם־יְהוָה׃ וַיְהִי דְּבַר־יְהוָה

Jehovah the And .Jehovah says ,hate I these all
of of word was

19 צְבָאוֹת אֵלַי לֵאמֹר׃ כֹּה־אָמַר יְהוָה צְבָאוֹת צוֹם הָרְבִיעִי

fourth the The :hosts Jehovah says Thus ,saying ,me to hosts
,(month) of fast of

וְצוֹם הַחֲמִישִׁי וְצוֹם הַשְּׁבִיעִי וְצוֹם הָעֲשִׂירִי יִהְיֶה לְבֵית־

the to shall the the and the the and the the and
of house be tenth of fast ,seventh of fast ,fifth of fast

יְהוּדָה לְשָׂשׂוֹן וּלְשִׂמְחָה וּלְמֹעֲדִים טוֹבִים וְהָאֱמֶת וְהַשָּׁלוֹם

peace and Thus .cheerful for and for and joy for Judah
truth feasts gladness

20 אֱהָבוּ׃ כֹּה אָמַר יְהוָה צְבָאוֹת עֹד אֲשֶׁר יָבֹאוּ עַמִּים

peoples There again :hosts Jehovah says Thus .love
come shall of

21 וְיֹשְׁבֵי עָרִים רַבּוֹת׃ וְהָלְכוּ יֹשְׁבֵי אַחַת אֶל־אַחַת לֵאמֹר

,saying ,another to one resi- the will and ;many cities resi- and
(city) of dents go of dents

נֵלְכָה הָלוֹךְ לְחַלּוֹת אֶת־פְּנֵי יְהוָה וּלְבַקֵּשׁ אֶת־יְהוָה צְבָאוֹת

;hosts Jehovah to and ;Jehovah the the seek to at us Let
of seek of face of favor once go

22 אֵלְכָה גַּם־אָנִי׃ וּבָאוּ עַמִּים רַבִּים וְגוֹיִם עֲצוּמִים לְבַקֵּשׁ

seek to mighty and many peoples shall And .I also go will
nations come

אֶת־יְהוָה צְבָאוֹת בִּירוּשָׁלִָם וּלְחַלּוֹת אֶת־פְּנֵי יְהוָה׃

.Jehovah the seek to and in hosts Jehovah
of face of favor the ,Jerusalem of

23 כֹּה־אָמַר יְהוָה צְבָאוֹת בַּיָּמִים הָהֵמָּה אֲשֶׁר יַחֲזִיקוּ עֲשָׂרָה

ten take shall those days In :hosts Jehovah says Thus
hold of

אֲנָשִׁים מִכֹּל לְשֹׁנוֹת הַגּוֹיִם וְהֶחֱזִיקוּ בִּכְנַף אִישׁ יְהוּדִי

,Jew a ,man a the they and the languages of out ,men
of skirt seize will ,nations of all

לֵאמֹר נֵלְכָה עִמָּכֶם כִּי שָׁמַעְנוּ אֱלֹהִים עִמָּכֶם׃

.you with (is) God have we for with Let ,saying
that heard ,you go us

CAP. IX ט

CHAPTER 9

[1] The burden of the word of Jehovah against the land of Hadrach; and Damascus, its resting-place — when the eye of man, and all the tribes of Israel, (shall be) toward Jehovah — [2] and Hamath also borders on it; Tyre and Sidon, though very wise — [3] and Tyre shall build herself a fortress, and shall heap up silver like the dust, and fine

1 מַשָּׂא דְבַר־יְהוָה בְּאֶרֶץ חַדְרָךְ וְדַמֶּשֶׂק מְנֻחָתוֹ כִּי לַיהוָה

toward when rest- its and ;Hadrach against Jehovah the bur- The
Jehovah —place ing Damascus of land the of word of den

2 עֵין אָדָם וְכֹל שִׁבְטֵי יִשְׂרָאֵל׃ וְגַם־חֲמָת תִּגְבָּל־בָּהּ צֹר

Tyre ;it on borders Hamath and —Israel the all and man eye the
also of tribes (be shall) of

3 וְצִידוֹן כִּי חָכְמָה מְאֹד׃ וַתִּבֶן צֹר מָצוֹר לָהּ וַתִּצְבָּר־כֶּסֶף

silver shall and for for- a Tyre And .very (are they) though and
up pile herself .tress build shall wise ,Sidon

gold like the mud of the
streets; [4] behold, the
Lord will cast her out, and
He will strike her wealth in
the sea, and she shall be
consumed with fire —
[5] Ashkelon shall see and
fear; Gaza also shall writhe
in great pain, and Ekron, for
her hope will be ashamed;
and the king shall perish
from Gaza, and Ashkelon
shall not be inhabited.
[6] And a bastard shall
dwell in Ashdod, and I will
cut off the pride of the
Philistines. [7] And I will
take away his bloods out of
his mouth, and his idolatries
from between his teeth. But
the remnant, even he (shall
be) for our God. And he
shall be as a governor in
Judah, and Ekron, like a
Jebusite. [8] And I will
camp around My house be-
cause of an army, because
of him who passes by and
because of him who re-
turns; and no tyrant shall
pass through them any
more. For now I have seen
with My eyes.

[9] Rejoice greatly, O
daughter of Zion! Shout, O
daughter of Jerusalem! Behold! Your King comes to
you! He (is) righteous and
victorious; lowly and riding
on an ass, even on a colt, the
son of an ass. [10] And I
will cut off the chariot from
Ephraim, and the horse
from Jerusalem. And the
battle bow shall be cut off,
and He shall speak peace to
the nations. And His dominion (shall be) from sea to
sea, and from the River to
the ends of the earth.
[11] Also you, by the
blood of your covenant I
have freed your prisoners
out of the pit; no water is in
it. [12] Turn to the stronghold, O prisoners of hope!
Even today I declare I will
return to you double.
[13] When I have bent
Judah for Me, as a bow I
filled (it) with Ephraim, and
I will stir up your sons, O
Zion, against your sons, O
Greece, and make you as
the sword of a mighty man;
[14] then Jehovah shall be
seen over them, and His
arrow shall go out like
lightning; and the Lord

4 כעפר וחרוץ כטיט חוצות: הנה אדני יורשנה והכה
He and expel will the ,behold the the like and like
strike will ,her Lord ;streets of mud gold ,dust

5 בים חילה והיא באש תאכל: תרא אשקלון ותירא ועזה
Gaza and Ashkelon see will be will with and her the in
also ;fear .devoured fire she ,wealth sea

ותחיל מאד ועקרון כי־הביש מבטה ואבד מלך מעזה
from the will and her be will for and ,great writhe shall
,Gaza king perish ;hope ashamed Ekron pain in

6 ואשקלון לא תשב: וישב ממזר באשדוד והכרתי גאון
pride will I and ,Ashdod in a will And be will not and
off cut bastard dwell .inhabited Ashkelon

7 פלשתים: והסרתי דמיו מפיו ושקציו מבין שניו ונשאר
the And his from his and his from his will I And the
,remnant .teeth between abominations mouth bloods away take .Philistines

גם־הוא לאלהינו והיה כאלף ביהודה ועקרון כיבוסי:
a like and ,Judah in a as he And our for he even
.Jebusite Ekron chief be shall .God (be will)

8 וחניתי לביתי מצבה מעבר ומשב ולא־יעבר עליהם עוד
again them shall not and from and the from an from My will I And
pass ,returner the passer ,army house about camp

9 נגש כי־עתה ראיתי בעיני: גילי מאד בת־ציון
!Zion O ,greatly Rejoice My with have I now For an
of daughter .eyes seen .oppressor

הריעי בת־ירושלם הנה מלכך יבוא לך צדיק ונושע
and righteous to is Your !Behold !Jerusalem O ,Shout
victorious !you coming King of daughter

10 הוא עני ורכב על־חמור ועל־עיר בן־אתנות: והכרתי־
will I And she- a the a even ,ass an on and humble He
off cut .ass of son ,colt on riding ;(is)

רכב מאפרים וסוס מירושלם ונכרתה קשת מלחמה
war bow the shall And from the and from the
of off cut be .Jerusalem horse ,Ephraim chariot

ודבר שלום לגוים ומשלו מים עד־ים ומנהר עד־אפסי־
the to from and ,sea to (be will) His And the to peace He and
of ends River the sea from dominion .nations speak shall

11 ארץ: גם־את בדם־בריתך שלחתי אסיריך מבור אין
not the from your have I your the by ,you Also the
is ;pit prisoners freed covenant of blood .earth

12 מים בו: שובו לבצרון אסירי התקוה גם־היום מגיד
I today Even !hope the pris- O the to Turn .it in water
declare of oners ,stronghold

13 משנה אשיב לך: כי־דרכתי לי יהודה קשת מלאתי
filled I a (as) Judah for have I For to will I double
with (it) ,bow Me bent .you restore

אפרים ועוררתי בניך ציון על־בניך יון ושמתיך כחרב
the as make and O your against O your will I and ,Ephraim
of sword you ,Greece ,sons ,Zion ,sons up stir

14 גבור: ויהוה עליהם יראה ויצא כברק חצו ואדני יהוה
Jehovah the and His light- as shall and will over then mighty a
Lord ;arrow ning out go ,appear them Jehovah ;man

Jehovah shall blow the ram's horn and shall go out with tempests of the south. [15] Jehovah of hosts shall defend them. And they shall devour and trample on sling stones. Yea, they shall drink and be boisterous as with wine. And they shall be full like a bowl, like the corners of the altar. [16] And Jehovah their God shall save them in that day as the flock of His people; for (they are as) stones of a crown, lifted up as a banner over His land. [17] For how great (is) its goodness, and how great its beauty! Grain shall make the young men flourish, and new wine the virgins.

15 בַּשּׁוֹפָר יִתְקָע וְהָלַךְ בְּסַעֲרוֹת תֵּימָן׃ יְהֹוָה צְבָאוֹת יָגֵן

will hosts Jehovah the the with shall and shall ram's the
protect of .south of windstorms forth go blow horn

עֲלֵיהֶם וְאָכְלוּ וְכָבְשׁוּ אַבְנֵי־קֶלַע וְשָׁתוּ וְהָמוּ כְּמוֹ־יָיִן

.wine as be and they And the and they And .them
with boisterous drink shall .sling of stones trample devour shall

16 וּמָלְאוּ כַּמִּזְרָק כְּזָוִיּוֹת מִזְבֵּחַ׃ וְהוֹשִׁיעָם יְהֹוָה אֱלֹהֵיהֶם

their Jehovah will And the the like a as they And
God them save .altar of corners ,bowl full be will

בַּיּוֹם הַהוּא כְּצֹאן עַמּוֹ כִּי אַבְנֵי־נֵזֶר מִתְנוֹסְסוֹת עַל־

over as up lifted (as are they) for His the as that day in
banner a crown a of stones ;people of flock

17 אַדְמָתוֹ׃ כִּי מַה־טּוּבוֹ וּמַה־יָפְיוֹ דָּגָן בַּחוּרִים וְתִירוֹשׁ

new and young the Grain its and its how For .land His
wine men !beauty goodness (great)

יְנוֹבֵב בְּתֻלוֹת׃

the make shall
.virgins flourish

CAP. X י

CHAPTER 10

1 שַׁאֲלוּ מֵיְהֹוָה מָטָר בְּעֵת מַלְקוֹשׁ יְהֹוָה עֹשֶׂה חֲזִיזִים

thunder shall Jehovah latter the the in rain from Ask
,bolts make .rain of time Jehovah

2 וּמְטַר־גֶּשֶׁם יִתֵּן לָהֶם לְאִישׁ עֵשֶׂב בַּשָּׂדֶה׃ כִּי הַתְּרָפִים

family the For the in grass (each) to to He showers and
idols .field man ,them gives rain of

דִּבְּרוּ־אָוֶן וְהַקּוֹסְמִים חָזוּ שֶׁקֶר וַחֲלֹמוֹת הַשָּׁוְא יְדַבֵּרוּ

have false and ,lie a have the and ,iniquity speak
.told dreams seen diviners

הֶבֶל יְנַחֵמוּן עַל־כֵּן נָסְעוּ כְמוֹ־צֹאן יַעֲנוּ כִּי־אֵין רֹעֶה׃

.shepherd not for they ;flock a like they Therefore they in
is ,afflicted are wandered .comfort vain

3 עַל־הָרֹעִים חָרָה אַפִּי וְעַל־הָעַתּוּדִים אֶפְקוֹד כִּי־פָקַד יְהֹוָה

Jehovah has For will I the and My is the against
of visited .punish he-goats and —anger kindled shepherds

צְבָאוֹת אֶת־עֶדְרוֹ אֶת־בֵּית יְהוּדָה וְשָׂם אוֹתָם כְּסוּס הוֹדוֹ

His as them and ,Judah His His hosts
splendid horse made of house ,flock

4 בַּמִּלְחָמָה׃ מִמֶּנּוּ פִנָּה מִמֶּנּוּ יָתֵד מִמֶּנּוּ קֶשֶׁת מִלְחָמָה

,battle the from the from cor- the From .battle in
of bow Him ,nail Him ;nerstone Him

5 מִמֶּנּוּ יֵצֵא כָל־נוֹגֵשׂ יַחְדָּו׃ וְהָיוּ כְגִבֹּרִים בּוֹסִים בְּטִיט

mud the who mighty like they And .together ruler every came from
of trample ones be shall out Him

חוּצוֹת בַּמִּלְחָמָה וְנִלְחֲמוּ כִּי יְהֹוָה עִמָּם וְהֹבִישׁוּ רֹכְבֵי

riders shall they and with Jehovah because they And the in the
of ashamed make ,them (is) fight shall .battle streets

6 סוּסִים׃ וְגִבַּרְתִּי אֶת־בֵּית יְהוּדָה וְאֶת־בֵּית יוֹסֵף אוֹשִׁיעַ

will I Joseph the and ,Judah the will I And horses
,save of house of house strenghten

CHAPTER 10

[1] Ask rain from Jehovah in the time of the latter rain. Jehovah shall make storm clouds, and He gives them showers of rain, grass to everyone in the field. [2] For the family idols speak vanity, and the diviners have seen a lie and have told false dreams. They comfort in vain. Therefore they wandered like a flock. They were troubled because there was no shepherd. [3] My anger is kindled against the shepherds — and I punished the he-goats. For Jehovah of hosts has visited His flock, the house of Judah, and made them as His magnificent horse in battle. [4] Out of him came the cornerstone; out of him the nail, out of him the battle bow, out of him every ruler together. [5] And they shall be like mighty ones who trample down the mud of the streets in the battle. And they shall fight because Jehovah (is) with them, and they shall make the riders of horses ashamed. [6] And I will strengthen the house of Judah, and I will save the

house of Joseph, and I will bring them again, for I have compassion on them. And they shall be as though I had not cast them off; for I (am) Jehovah their God, and I will answer them. [7] And Ephraim shall be like a mighty one, and their heart shall rejoice as (through) wine. Yes, their sons shall see and be glad; their heart shall rejoice in Jehovah. [8] I will whistle for them and gather them; for I have redeemed them. And they shall multiply as they have multiplied. [9] And I will sow them among the peoples, and they shall remember Me in far countries; and they shall live with their sons and return. [10] And I will bring them again out of the land of Egypt, and gather them out of Assyria. And I will bring them into the land of Gilead and Lebanon; for shall not be found (room) for them. [11] And he shall pass through the sea of distress and strike the waves in the sea; and all the depths in the Nile shall dry up. And the pride of Assyria shall be brought down, and the scepter of Egypt shall go away. [12] And I will strengthen them in Jehovah; and they shall walk up and down in His name, says Jehovah.

CHAPTER 11

[1] Open your doors, O Lebanon, so that the fire may devour your cedars. [2] Howl, fir-tree, for the cedar has fallen; because the mighty are stripped. Howl, O oaks of Bashan; for the inaccessible forest has come down.

[3] A voice of the wailing of the shepherds; for their glory is destroyed; a voice of the roaring of young lions; for the pride of Jordan is destroyed. [4] For thus says Jehovah my God: Feed the flock of the slaughter; [5] those who buy them kill them and hold themselves not guilty. And those who sell them say, Blessed (be) Jehovah, for I am rich; and their own

וְהוֹשְׁבוֹתִים כִּי רִחַמְתִּים וְהָיוּ כַּאֲשֶׁר לֹא־זְנַחְתִּים כִּי
for had I not though as they And pity have I for will I and
them rejected be shall .them on ,back them bring

7 אֲנִי יְהוָה אֱלֹהֵיהֶם וְאֶעֱנֵם׃ וְהָיוּ כְגִבּוֹר אֶפְרַיִם וְשָׂמַח
shall and ,Ephraim a like shall And will I and their Jehovah I
rejoice man mighty be .them answer ,God (am)

לִבָּם כְּמוֹ־יָיִן וּבְנֵיהֶם יִרְאוּ וְשָׂמֵחוּ יָגֵל לִבָּם בַּיהוָה׃
.Jehovah in their shall be and shall their And .wine as their
heart rejoice ;glad see sons (in) heart

8 אֶשְׁרְקָה לָהֶם וַאֲקַבְּצֵם כִּי פְדִיתִים וְרָבוּ כְּמוֹ רָבוּ׃
were they as they And re- have I for gather and for shall I
.many many be will .them deemed ;them them whistle

9 וְאֶזְרָעֵם בָּעַמִּים וּבַמֶּרְחַקִּים יִזְכְּרוּנִי וְחָיוּ אֶת־בְּנֵיהֶם
their with they and shall they the in and the among will I And
sons live shall ;Me remember distances ,peoples them sow

10 וָשָׁבוּ׃ וַהֲשֵׁבוֹתִים מֵאֶרֶץ מִצְרַיִם וּמֵאַשּׁוּר אֲקַבְּצֵם וְאֶל־
And will I from and ,Egypt the from will I And and
to .them gather Assyria of land back them bring .return

11 אֶרֶץ גִּלְעָד וּלְבָנוֹן אֲבִיאֵם וְלֹא יִמָּצֵא לָהֶם׃ וְעָבַר בַּיָּם
the by He And for (room) be shall and will I and Gilead the
of sea pass will .them found not ;them bring Lebanon of land

צָרָה וְהִכָּה בַיָּם גַּלִּים וְהֹבִישׁוּ כֹּל מְצוּלוֹת יְאֹר וְהוּרַד
be will And the the all shall and the the in shall and dis-
humbled .Nile of depths up dry ;waves sea strike ,tress

12 גְּאוֹן אַשּׁוּר וְשֵׁבֶט מִצְרַיִם יָסוּר׃ וְגִבַּרְתִּים בַּיהוָה וּבִשְׁמוֹ
His in and in will I And shall Egypt the and ,Assyria the
name ;Jehovah them strengthen .depart of scepter of pride

יִתְהַלָּכוּ נְאֻם יְהוָה׃
.Jehovah says will they
,walk

CAP. XI יא

CHAPTER 11

1
2 פְּתַח לְבָנוֹן דְּלָתֶיךָ וְתֹאכַל אֵשׁ בַּאֲרָזֶיךָ׃ הֵילֵל בְּרוֹשׁ
O ,Howl your the that so your O ,Open
,juniper .cedars fire devour may ,doors ,Lebanon

כִּי־נָפַל אֶרֶז אֲשֶׁר אַדִּרִים שֻׁדָּדוּ הֵילִילוּ אַלּוֹנֵי בָשָׁן כִּי
for ;Bashan O ,Howl been have majestic the because the has for
of oaks .destroyed (trees) ;cedar fallen

3 יָרַד יַעַר הַבָּצוֹר׃ קוֹל יִלְלַת הָרֹעִים כִּי שֻׁדְּדָה אַדַּרְתָּם
their is for the the voice A .inaccesible the come has
;splendor destroyed ;shepherds of wail of forest down

4 קוֹל שַׁאֲגַת כְּפִירִים כִּי שֻׁדַּד גְּאוֹן הַיַּרְדֵּן׃ כֹּה אָמַר
says Thus .Jordan the is for ;lions young the voice a
of pride destroyed of roaring of

5 יְהוָה אֱלֹהָי רְעֵה אֶת־צֹאן הַהֲרֵגָה׃ אֲשֶׁר קֹנֵיהֶן יַהַרְגֻן
kill buy who Those the the Feed my Jehovah
them them .slaughter of flock :God

וְלֹא יֶאְשָׁמוּ וּמֹכְרֵיהֶן יֹאמַר בָּרוּךְ יְהוָה וַאעְשִׁר וְרֹעֵיהֶם
their and I for ,Jehovah Blessed ,say who those And held are and
shepherds ;rich am be them sell .guilty not

shepherds do not pity them. [6] For I will never again pity the inhabitants of the land, says Jehovah. But, lo, I will make fall the men, each one into his neighbor's hand and into the hand of his king. And they shall strike the land, and I will not deliver out of their hand. [7] And I fed the flock of slaughter, the truly poor of the flock. And I took two staffs for Myself: the one I called Kindness; and the other I called Union. And I fed the flock. [8] I also cut off three shepherds in one month. And My soul despised them, and their soul also detested Me. [9] Then I said, I will not feed you; that which dies, let it die; and that which is to be cut off, let it be cut off; and let the rest eat, each one the flesh of her neighbor.

[10] And I took My staff Kindness and broke it apart, to break My covenant which I had cut with all the peoples. [11] And it was broken in that day; and so the poor of the flock who were watching Me knew that it (was) the word of Jehovah. [12] And I said to them, If (it is) good in your eyes, give My price; and if not, let it go. So they weighed My price, thirty (pieces of) silver. [13] And Jehovah said to Me. Throw it to the potter, the magnificent price at which I was valued by them. And I took the thirty (pieces of) silver and threw it to the potter in the house of Jehovah. [14] Then I broke My second staff apart, Union, that I might break the brotherhood between Judah and Israel.

6 לֹא יַחְמוֹל עֲלֵיהֶן׃ כִּי לֹא אֶחְמוֹל עוֹד עַל־יֹשְׁבֵי הָאָרֶץ
the the upon again will I not For upon have do not
,land of inhabitants pity have ,them

נְאֻם־יְהוָה וְהִנֵּה אָנֹכִי מַמְצִיא אֶת־הָאָדָם אִישׁ בְּיַד־רֵעֵהוּ
his into each the make will I But .Jehovah says
neighbor's hand man ,men fall ,lo

7 וּבְיַד מַלְכּוֹ וְכִתְּתוּ אֶת־הָאָרֶץ וְלֹא אַצִּיל מִיָּדָם׃ וָאֶרְעֶה
I So of out will I and the they and his into and
fed .hand their deliver not ,land beat will ;king's hand

אֶת־צֹאן הַהֲרֵגָה לָכֵן עֲנִיֵּי הַצֹּאן וָאֶקַּח־לִי שְׁנֵי מַקְלוֹת
:staffs two for I And the the even the the
Myself took .flock of poor ,slaughter of flock

לְאַחַד קָרָאתִי נֹעַם וּלְאַחַד קָרָאתִי חֹבְלִים וָאֶרְעֶה אֶת־
I And .Union called I the and Kind- called I one the
fed other ,ness

8 הַצֹּאן׃ וָאַכְחִד אֶת־שְׁלֹשֶׁת הָרֹעִים בְּיֶרַח אֶחָד וַתִּקְצַר
was And .one in shepherds three I And the
impatient month destroyed .flock

9 נַפְשִׁי בָּהֶם וְגַם־נַפְשָׁם בָּחֲלָה בִי׃ וָאֹמַר לֹא אֶרְעֶה
will I not I Then '.Me detested their and with My
feed ,said soul also ,them soul

אֶתְכֶם הַמֵּתָה תָמוּת וְהַנִּכְחֶדֶת תִּכָּחֵד וְהַנִּשְׁאָרוֹת תֹּאכַלְנָה
them let who those and be it let to is what and it let is What .you
eat left are .destroyed destroyed be ;die ,die to

10 אִשָּׁה אֶת־בְּשַׂר רְעוּתָהּ׃ וָאֶקַּח אֶת־מַקְלִי אֶת־נֹעַם וָאֶגְדַּע י
broke and ,Kindness My I And her the each
pieces in staff took .neighbor of flesh woman

אֹתוֹ לְהָפֵיר אֶת־בְּרִיתִי אֲשֶׁר כָּרַתִּי אֶת־כָּל־הָעַמִּים׃
the all with had I which My break to ,it
.peoples cut covenant

11 וַתֻּפַר בַּיּוֹם הַהוּא וַיֵּדְעוּ כֵן עֲנִיֵּי הַצֹּאן הַשֹּׁמְרִים אֹתִי כִּי
that Me were who the the so and ;that day in it And
watching flock of poor knew broken was

12 דְבַר־יְהוָה הוּא׃ וָאֹמַר אֲלֵיהֶם אִם־טוֹב בְּעֵינֵיכֶם הָבוּ
give your in good If ,them to I And it Jehovah the
,eyes (is it) said .(was) of word

שְׂכָרִי וְאִם־לֹא ׀ חֲדָלוּ וַיִּשְׁקְלוּ אֶת־שְׂכָרִי שְׁלֹשִׁים כָּסֶף׃
.silver thirty My they So it let ,not but My
(of pieces) ,wages weighed .go if ,wages

13 וַיֹּאמֶר יְהוָה אֵלַי הַשְׁלִיכֵהוּ אֶל־הַיּוֹצֵר אֶדֶר הַיְקָר אֲשֶׁר
at price the the to it Throw to Jehovah And
which splendid ,potter ,Me said

יָקַרְתִּי מֵעֲלֵיהֶם וָאֶקְחָה שְׁלֹשִׁים הַכֶּסֶף וָאַשְׁלִיךְ אֹתוֹ
it threw and silver thirty the I And .them by was I
(of pieces) took valued

14 בֵּית יְהוָה אֶל־הַיּוֹצֵר׃ וָאֶגְדַּע אֶת־מַקְלִי הַשֵּׁנִי אֵת
,second My broke I Then the to Jehovah the in
staff pieces in .potter of house

הַחֹבְלִים לְהָפֵר אֶת־הָאַחֲוָה בֵּין יְהוּדָה וּבֵין יִשְׂרָאֵל׃
.Israel and Judah between the break to ,Union
brotherhood

[15] And Jehovah said to me, Take to yourself yet the instruments of a foolish shepherd. [16] For, lo, I will raise up a shepherd in the land; he shall not visit those who are cut off, nor seek the young one, nor heal that which is broken, nor feed that which stands. But he shall eat the flesh of the fat and tear their hooks in pieces. [17] Woe to the worthless shepherd who abandons the flock! The sword (shall be) on his arm and on his right eye; his arm shall be completely dried up, and his right eye shall be completely darkened.

15 וַיֹּאמֶר יְהוָה אֵלָי עוֹד קַח לְךָ כְּלִי רֹעֶה אֱוִלִי׃
16 כִּי הִנֵּה־

,lo ,For .foolish shep- a tools to Take again ,me to Jehovah And
herd's yourself said

אָנֹכִי מֵקִים רֹעֶה בָּאָרֶץ הַנִּכְחָדוֹת לֹא־יִפְקֹד הַנַּעַר לֹא־

not the will he not going those the in a will I
young ,for care ruin to ;land shepherd praise

יְבַקֵּשׁ וְהַנִּשְׁבֶּרֶת לֹא יְרַפֵּא הַנִּצָּבָה לֹא יְכַלְכֵּל וּבְשַׂר

the but will he not which that will he not which that and will he
of flesh ,sustain stands ,heal broken is ,seek

17 הַבְּרִיאָה יֹאכַל וּפַרְסֵיהֶן יְפָרֵק׃ הוֹי רֹעִי הָאֱלִיל עֹזְבִי

who worthless the Woe shall he their and shall he fat the
abandons shepherd to .off tear hoofs ,eat

הַצֹּאן חֶרֶב עַל־זְרוֹעוֹ וְעַל־עֵין יְמִינוֹ זְרֹעוֹ יָבוֹשׁ תִּיבָשׁ וְעֵין

and be shall totally his his eye and his (be shall) The the
eye ,withered arm ;right against arm against sword !flock

יְמִינוֹ כָּהֹה תִכְהֶה׃

be shall totally his
.darkened right

CAP. XII יב

CHAPTER 12

[1] The burden of the word of Jehovah for Israel, says Jehovah, who stretches forth the heavens and lays the foundation of the earth, and forms the spirit of man within him. [2] Behold, I will make Jerusalem a cup of trembling to all the people all around, and it shall also be against Judah in the siege against Jerusalem.

[3] And in that day I will make Jerusalem a burdensome stone for all the peoples; all who lift it shall be cut in pieces, and all the nations of the earth will be gathered together against it. [4] In that day, says Jehovah, I will strike every horse with terror and his rider with madness. And I will open My eyes on the house of Judah, and I will strike every horse of the peoples with blindness. [5] And the leaders of Judah shall say in their heart, The inhabitants of Jerusalem (shall be) my strength in Jenovah of hosts their God.

[6] In that day I will make the leaders of Judah like a hearth of fire among the wood, and like a torch

1 מַשָּׂא דְבַר־יְהוָה עַל־יִשְׂרָאֵל נְאֻם־יְהוָה נֹטֶה שָׁמַיִם וְיֹסֵד

and hea- the who ,Jehovah says ,Israel for Jehovah the bur- The
founds ,vens spreads of word of den

2 אֶרֶץ וְיֹצֵר רוּחַ־אָדָם בְּקִרְבּוֹ׃ הִנֵּה אָנֹכִי שָׂם אֶת־יְרוּשָׁלִַם

Jerusalem will I ,Behold his in man the and the
make .midst of spirit forms ,earth

סַף־רַעַל לְכָל־הָעַמִּים סָבִיב וְגַם עַל־יְהוּדָה יִהְיֶה בַמָּצוֹר

the in shall it Judah against and all the to reeling a
siege be also ,around peoples all of cup

3 עַל־יְרוּשָׁלִָם׃ וְהָיָה בַיּוֹם־הַהוּא אָשִׂים אֶת־יְרוּשָׁלִַם אֶבֶן

a Jerusalem will I that day in it And .Jerusalem against
stone make ,be will

מַעֲמָסָה לְכָל־הָעַמִּים כָּל־עֹמְסֶיהָ שָׂרוֹט יִשָּׂרֵטוּ וְנֶאֶסְפוּ

be will and be will severely lift who all the all for heavy
gathered ,lacerated it ;peoples

4 עָלֶיהָ כֹּל גּוֹיֵי הָאָרֶץ׃ בַּיּוֹם הַהוּא נְאֻם־יְהוָה אַכֶּה כָל־

every will I ,Jehovah says ,that day In the the all against
strike earth of nations it

סוּס בַּתִּמָּהוֹן וְרֹכְבוֹ בַּשִּׁגָּעוֹן וְעַל־בֵּית יְהוּדָה אֶפְקַח אֶת־

will I Judah the And with its and with horse
open of house on .madness rider ,panic

5 עֵינַי וְכֹל סוּס הָעַמִּים אַכֶּה בַּעִוָּרוֹן׃ וְאָמְרוּ אַלֻּפֵי יְהוּדָה

Judah the shall And with will I the horse and My
of leaders say .blindness strike peoples of every ,eyes

בְּלִבָּם אַמְצָה לִי יֹשְׁבֵי יְרוּשָׁלִַם בַּיהוָה צְבָאוֹת אֱלֹהֵיהֶם׃

their hosts through Jerusalem The me to (be shall) their in
.God of Jehovah of dwellers strength ,heart

6 בַּיּוֹם הַהוּא אָשִׂים אֶת־אַלֻּפֵי יְהוּדָה כְּכִיּוֹר אֵשׁ בְּעֵצִים

the among fire a like Judah the will I that day In
,wood of hearth of leaders make

of fire in a sheaf. And they shall devour all the peoples all around, on the right hand and on the left. And Jerusalem shall be inhabited again in her place, in Jerusalem. [7] Jehovah also shall save the tents of Judah first, so that the glory of the house of David and the glory of the inhabitants of Jerusalem may not be magnified above Judah. [8] In that day Jehovah shall defend around the inhabitants of Jerusalem. And it will be, he who is feeble among them in that day (shall be) like David; and the house of David (shall be) like God, as the Angel of Jehovah before them.

[9] And it shall be, in that day I will seek to destroy all the nations that come against Jerusalem. [10] And I will pour on the house of David, and on the inhabitants of Jerusalem, the spirit of grace and of prayers. And they shall look on Me whom they have pierced, and they shall mourn for Him, as one mourns for an only (son), and shall be bitter over Him, as one that is in bitterness over the firstborn. [11] In that day shall be great the mourning in Jerusalem, like the mourning of Hadad-rimmon in the valley of Megiddo. [12] And the land shall mourn, each family apart; the family of the house of David apart, and their wives apart; the family of the house of Nathan apart, and their wives apart; [13] the family of the house of Levi apart, and their wives apart; the family of Shimei apart, and their wives apart; [14] all the families who remain, each family apart and their wives apart.

וּכְלַפִּיד אֵשׁ בְּעָמִיר וְאָכְלוּ עַל־יָמִין וְעַל־שְׂמֹאול אֶת־
left the and the on they And among fire like and
hand on hand right devour shall .grain cut of torch a

כָּל־הָעַמִּים סָבִיב וְיָשְׁבָה יְרוּשָׁלַםִ עוֹד תַּחְתֶּיהָ בִּירוּשָׁלָםִ׃
in her in again Jerusalem And all the all
.Jerusalem ,place dwells .around peoples

7 וְהוֹשִׁיעַ יְהוָה אֶת־אָהֳלֵי יְהוּדָה בָּרִאשֹׁנָה לְמַעַן לֹא־תִגְדַּל
be may not that so ,first Judah the Jehovah And
magnified of tents save shall

תִּפְאֶרֶת בֵּית־דָּוִיד וְתִפְאֶרֶת יֹשֵׁב יְרוּשָׁלַםִ עַל־יְהוּדָה׃
.Judah above Jerusalem in- the the and David the glory the
of habitants of glory of house of

8 בַּיּוֹם הַהוּא יָגֵן יְהוָה בְּעַד יוֹשֵׁב יְרוּשָׁלַםִ וְהָיָה הַנִּכְשָׁל
who he it And .Jerusalem the around Jehovah shall that In
feeble is ,be will of inhabitants protect day

בָּהֶם בַּיּוֹם הַהוּא כְּדָוִיד וּבֵית דָּוִיד כֵּאלֹהִים כְּמַלְאַךְ
the like (be shall) David the and (be shall) that day in among
of Angel ,God like of house ;David like them

9 יְהוָה לִפְנֵיהֶם׃ וְהָיָה בַּיּוֹם הַהוּא אֲבַקֵּשׁ לְהַשְׁמִיד אֶת־
destroy to will I that day in it And before Jehovah
seek ,be shall ‹them

10 כָּל־הַגּוֹיִם הַבָּאִים עַל־יְרוּשָׁלָםִ׃ וְשָׁפַכְתִּי עַל־בֵּית
the on will I And .Jerusalem against that the all
of house out pour come nations

דָּוִיד וְעַל ׀ יוֹשֵׁב יְרוּשָׁלַםִ רוּחַ חֵן וְתַחֲנוּנִים וְהִבִּיטוּ אֵלַי
on they And and grace the ,Jerusalem in- the and ,David
Me look shall .prayers of Spirit of habitants on

אֵת אֲשֶׁר־דָּקָרוּ וְסָפְדוּ עָלָיו כְּמִסְפֵּד עַל־הַיָּחִיד וְהָמֵר
will and only an for one as for they and have they whom
bitter be ,son mourns ,Him mourn shall ,pierced

11 עָלָיו כְּהָמֵר עַל־הַבְּכוֹר׃ בַּיּוֹם הַהוּא יִגְדַּל הַמִּסְפֵּד
the be will that day In the over the like over
mourning great .firstborn bitterness Him

12 בִּירוּשָׁלַםִ כְּמִסְפַּד הֲדַדְרִמּוֹן בְּבִקְעַת מְגִדּוֹן׃ וְסָפְדָה
shall And .Megiddo the in Hadad-rimmon the like in
mourn of valley of mourning ,Jerusalem

הָאָרֶץ מִשְׁפָּחוֹת מִשְׁפָּחוֹת לְבָד מִשְׁפַּחַת בֵּית־דָּוִיד
David the family the ;alone families families the
of house of (by) ,land

לְבָד וּנְשֵׁיהֶם לְבָד מִשְׁפַּחַת בֵּית־נָתָן לְבָד וּנְשֵׁיהֶם לְבָד׃
;alone their and ,alone Nathan the family the ;alone their and ,alone
wives of house of wives

13 מִשְׁפַּחַת בֵּית־לֵוִי לְבָד וּנְשֵׁיהֶם לְבָד מִשְׁפַּחַת הַשִּׁמְעִי
Shimei family the ;alone their and ,alone Levi the family the
of wives of house of

14 לְבָד וּנְשֵׁיהֶם לְבָד׃ כֹּל הַמִּשְׁפָּחוֹת הַנִּשְׁאָרוֹת מִשְׁפָּחֹת
family are who families the all ;alone their and ,alone
left wives

מִשְׁפָּחֹת לְבָד וּנְשֵׁיהֶם לְבָד׃
.alone their and ,alone family (by)
wives

CAP. XIII יג

CHAPTER 13

CHAPTER 13

[1] In that day a fountain shall be opened to the house of David and to the inhabitants of Jerusalem for sin and for impurity.

[2] And it shall be, in that day, says Jehovah of hosts, I will cut off the names of the idols out of the land, and they shall be remembered no more. And I also will cause the prophets and the unclean spirit to pass out of the land. [3] And it shall be, when any shall prophesy again, his father and his mother who brought him forth shall say to him then, You shall not live; for you speak lies in the name of Jehovah. And his father and his mother who brought him forth shall thrust him through when he prophesies. [4] And it shall be, in that day the prophets shall be ashamed, each one of his vision, when he prophesies; and they shall not wear a hairy garment to deceive. [5] But he shall say, I am not a prophet; I (am) a man, I (am) a tiller of the ground; for man caused me to buy from my youth. [6] And (one) shall say to him, What (are) these wounds between your hands? Then he shall answer, (Those) with which I was struck (in) the house of my friends.

[7] Awake, O sword, against My Shepherd, and against the Man (who is) My companion, says Jehovah of hosts; strike the Shepherd, and the sheep will be scattered. And I will turn My hand on the little ones. [8] And it shall be, in all the land, says Jehovah, two parts shall be cut off; they shall die; but the third shall be left in it. [9] And I will bring the third part through the fire, and will refine them as silver is refined, and will try them as gold is tried. They shall call

1 בַּיּוֹם הַהוּא יִהְיֶה מָקוֹר נִפְתָּח לְבֵית דָּוִיד וּלְיֹשְׁבֵי יְרוּשָׁלָ͏ִם

Jerusalem the to and David the to opened a be shall that In
of inhabitants of house fountain day

2 לְחַטַּאת וּלְנִדָּה: וְהָיָה בַיּוֹם הַהוּא נְאֻם ׀ יְהוָה צְבָאוֹת

,hosts Jehovah says ,that day in it And for and sin for
of ,be shall .impurity

אַכְרִית אֶת־שְׁמוֹת הָעֲצַבִּים מִן־הָאָרֶץ וְלֹא יִזָּכְרוּ עוֹד

.again be will they and the from idols the the will I
recalled not ,land of names off cut

וְגַם אֶת־הַנְּבִיאִים וְאֶת־רוּחַ הַטֻּמְאָה אַעֲבִיר מִן־הָאָרֶץ:

the from unclean the and prophets the And
.land pass to cause spirit also

3 וְהָיָה כִּי־יִנָּבֵא אִישׁ עוֹד וְאָמְרוּ אֵלָיו אָבִיו וְאִמּוֹ יֹלְדָיו

gave who his and his to shall then ,again a shall when it And
,birth him mother father him say man prophesy ,be shall

לֹא תִחְיֶה כִּי שֶׁקֶר דִּבַּרְתָּ בְּשֵׁם יְהוָה וּדְקָרֻהוּ אָבִיהוּ

his shall And .Jehovah the in speak you lies for shall you not
father him pierce of name ;live

4 וְאִמּוֹ יֹלְדָיו בְּהִנָּבְאוֹ: וְהָיָה ׀ בַּיּוֹם הַהוּא יֵבֹשׁוּ הַנְּבִיאִים

the be shall that day in it And he when gave who his and
,prophets ashamed ,be shall .prophesies birth him mother

אִישׁ מֵחֶזְיֹנוֹ בְּהִנָּבְאֹתוֹ וְלֹא יִלְבְּשׁוּ אַדֶּרֶת שֵׂעָר לְמַעַן

order in hairy a shall they and his of (each) man
to garment wear not ;prophesies vision

5 כַּחֵשׁ: וְאָמַר לֹא נָבִיא אָנֹכִי אִישׁ עֹבֵד אֲדָמָה אָנֹכִי

;(am) I the tiller a ,man a ;(am) I a not he But .deceive
ground of prophet ,say shall

6 כִּי־אָדָם הִקְנַנִי מִנְּעוּרָי: וְאָמַר אֵלָיו מָה הַמַּכּוֹת הָאֵלֶּה

these wounds What ,him to (one) And my from me caused a for
(are) say shall .youth buy to man

7 בֵּין יָדֶיךָ וְאָמַר אֲשֶׁר הֻכֵּיתִי בֵּית מְאַהֲבָי: חֶרֶב

O who those the (in) was I with (Those) he And your be-
sword .me love of house struck which ,say shall ?hands tween

עוּרִי עַל־רֹעִי וְעַל־גֶּבֶר עֲמִיתִי נְאֻם יְהוָה צְבָאוֹת הַךְ

strike ;hosts Jehovah says My the and My against awake
of ,Associate ,Man against ,Shepherd

אֶת־הָרֹעֶה וּתְפוּצֶיןָ הַצֹּאן וַהֲשִׁבֹתִי יָדִי עַל־הַצֹּעֲרִים:

little the against My will I And the be will and the
.ones hand turn .sheep scattered Shepherd

8 וְהָיָה בְכָל־הָאָרֶץ נְאֻם־יְהוָה פִּי־שְׁנַיִם בָּהּ יִכָּרְתוּ יִגְוָעוּ

(and) be shall it in two parts ,Jehovah says the all in it And
,perish off cut ,land ,be shall

9 וְהַשְּׁלִשִׁית יִוָּתֶר בָּהּ: וְהֵבֵאתִי אֶת־הַשְּׁלִשִׁית בָּאֵשׁ

through third the will I And .it in be shall the but
,fire the (part) bring left third

וּצְרַפְתִּים כִּצְרֹף אֶת־הַכֶּסֶף וּבְחַנְתִּים כִּבְחֹן אֶת־הַזָּהָב

.gold is as test and ,silver is as will and
tested them refined them refine

on My name and I will answer them. I will say, It (is) My people; and he shall say, Jehovah (is) my God.

CHAPTER 14

[1] Behold, the day of Jehovah comes, and your spoil shall be divided among you. [2] For I will gather all the nations against Jerusalem to battle. And the city shall be captured, and the houses plundered, and the women ravished. And half the city shall go into captivity, and the rest of the people shall not be cut off from the city. [3] Then Jehovah shall go out and fight against those nations, like the day He fought in the day of battle.

[4] And His feet shall stand in that day on the Mount of Olives, which (is) before Jerusalem on the east, and the Mount of Olives shall divide from its middle from the east and to the west, a very great valley. And half of the mountain shall move toward the north, and half of it toward the south. [5] And you shall flee to the valley of My mountains, for the valley of the mountains shall reach to Azal. And you shall flee as you fled from before the earthquake in the days of Uzziah king of Judah. And Jehovah my God shall come, (and) all the saints with You. [6] And it will be in that day, that there shall not be light; the glorious ones shall congeal. [7] And it will be one day which shall be known to Jehovah; not day, and not night, but it will be, at evening time, there will be light. [8] And it shall be, in that day, living waters shall go out from Jerusalem; half of them (shall go) toward the eastern sea, and half of

הוּא יִקְרָא בִשְׁמִי וַאֲנִי אֶעֱנֶה אֹתוֹ אָמַרְתִּי עַמִּי הוּא וְהוּא
and he | it (is) | My people | will I say | ;them | will answer | I and | My on ,name | will call | They

יֹאמַר יְהוָה אֱלֹהָי׃
.God my | Jehovah (is) | shall ,say

CAP. XIV יד

CHAPTER 14

1 2 הִנֵּה יוֹם־בָּא לַיהוָה וְחֻלַּק שְׁלָלֵךְ בְּקִרְבֵּךְ׃ וְאָסַפְתִּי
will I And gather | your in .midst | your spoil | shall and divided be | of ,Jehovah | is coming | the ,Behold day

אֶת־כָּל־הַגּוֹיִם ׀ אֶל־יְרוּשָׁלַםִ לַמִּלְחָמָה וְנִלְכְּדָה הָעִיר
the city | be shall And captured | .battle to | Jerusalem | against | the nations | all

וְנָשַׁסּוּ הַבָּתִּים וְהַנָּשִׁים תִּשָּׁגַלְנָה וְיָצָא חֲצִי הָעִיר בַּגּוֹלָה
into ,exile | the city | half shall And go | .ravished | the and women | the ,houses | and plundered

3 וְיֶתֶר הָעָם לֹא יִכָּרֵת מִן־הָעִיר׃ וְיָצָא יְהוָה וְנִלְחַם בַּגּוֹיִם
against nations | and fight | Jehovah | shall Then out go | the .city | from | be shall off cut | not | the people | the and of rest

4 הָהֵם כְּיוֹם הִלָּחֲמוֹ בְּיוֹם קְרָב׃ וְעָמְדוּ רַגְלָיו בַּיּוֹם־הַהוּא
that | day in | His feet | shall And stand | .battle | the in of day | He fought | the like day | ,those

עַל־הַר הַזֵּיתִים אֲשֶׁר עַל־פְּנֵי יְרוּשָׁלַםִ מִקֶּדֶם וְנִבְקַע הַר
the of Mount | shall and split | the on ;east | Jerusalem | front in of | which (is) | ,Olives | the of Mount | on

הַזֵּיתִים מֵחֶצְיוֹ מִזְרָחָה וָיָמָּה גֵּיא גְּדוֹלָה מְאֹד וּמָשׁ חֲצִי
half of | will And move | .very | great | a valley | to even ,west the | the from east | its from middle | Olives

5 הָהָר צָפוֹנָה וְחֶצְיוֹ־נֶגְבָּה׃ וְנַסְתֶּם גֵּיא־הָרַי כִּי־יַגִּיעַ גֵּי
the of valley | shall reach | for ;mountains | of valley my | the to | you And flee shall | south- .ward | half and it of | ,northward | the mountain

הָרִים אֶל־אָצַל וְנַסְתֶּם כַּאֲשֶׁר נַסְתֶּם מִפְּנֵי הָרַעַשׁ בִּימֵי
the in of days | the earthquake | from before | fled you | as | you And flee shall | .Azal | to | the mountains

עֻזִּיָּה מֶלֶךְ־יְהוּדָה וּבָא יְהוָה אֱלֹהַי כָּל־קְדֹשִׁים עִמָּךְ׃
with .you | holy the ones | (and) all | my ,God | Jehovah | shall And come | .Judah | king of | Uzziah

6 וְהָיָה בַּיּוֹם הַהוּא לֹא־יִהְיֶה אוֹר יְקָרוֹת יְקִפָּאוֹן׃
will .shrink | glorious the ones | ;light | there be shall | not | ,that | day in | it And be shall

7 וְהָיָה יוֹם־אֶחָד הוּא יִוָּדַע לַיהוָה לֹא־יוֹם וְלֹא־לַיְלָה וְהָיָה
it but be will | ,night | and not | day | not | to ;Jehovah | shall known be | which | one | day | it And be will

8 לְעֵת־עֶרֶב יִהְיֶה־אוֹר׃ וְהָיָה ׀ בַּיּוֹם הַהוּא יֵצְאוּ מַיִם־
waters | shall out go | that | day in | it And be will | .light | there be will | ,evening | the at of time

חַיִּים מִירוּשָׁלַםִ חֶצְיָם אֶל־הַיָּם הַקַּדְמוֹנִי וְחֶצְיָם אֶל־הַיָּם
the sea | to | half and them of | ,eastern | the sea | to | half them of | from ;Jerusalem | living

them toward the western sea; in summer and in winter it shall be. [9] And Jehovah shall be king over all the earth; in that day there shall be one Jehovah, and His name one. [10] All the land shall be turned as a plain from Geba to Rimmon south of Jerusalem. And it shall rise and dwell in its place, from Benjamin's gate to the place of the first gate, to the Corner Gate, and (from) the Tower of Hananeel to the king's winepresses. [11] And they shall live in it. And there shall not again be a curse, but Jerusalem shall live safely.

[12] And this shall be the plague with which Jehovah will strike all the peoples who have fought against Jerusalem. His flesh shall rot while he stands on his feet, and his eyes shall rot in their sockets and his tongue shall rot in their mouth. [13] And it shall be, in that day a great panic of Jehovah shall be among them; and they shall each one lay hold on the hand of his neighbor, and his hand shall rise up against the hand of his neighbor. [14] And Judah also shall fight at Jerusalem. And the wealth of all the nations all around shall be gathered together, gold and silver and clothing, very much. [15] And so shall be the plague of the horse, the mule, the camel, and the ass, and all the beasts which shall be in those camps, like this plague.

[16] And it shall be, everyone who is left from all the nations which came up against Jerusalem shall go up from year to year to worship the King, Jehovah of hosts, and to keep the feast of tabernacles. [17] And it shall be, whoever will not go up from the

9 הָאַחֲרוֹן בַּקַּיִץ וּבָחֹרֶף יִהְיֶה׃ וְהָיָה יְהוָה לְמֶלֶךְ עַל־
over king Jehovah And shall it in and in ;western
be shall .be winter summer

כָּל־הָאָרֶץ בַּיּוֹם הַהוּא יִהְיֶה יְהוָה אֶחָד וּשְׁמוֹ אֶחָד׃
.one His and ,one Jehovah there that day in the all
name be shall ;earth

10 יִסּוֹב כָּל־הָאָרֶץ כָּעֲרָבָה מִגֶּבַע לְרִמּוֹן נֶגֶב יְרוּשָׁלִָם
.Jerusalem south to from a like the All be will
of Rimmon Geba plain land turned

וְרָאֲמָה וְיָשְׁבָה תַחְתֶּיהָ לְמִשַּׁעַר בִּנְיָמִן עַד־מְקוֹם שַׁעַר
the the to Benjamin's from her in and it And
gate of place gate ,place dwell rise will

הָרִאשׁוֹן עַד־שַׁעַר הַפִּנִּים וּמִגְדַּל חֲנַנְאֵל עַד יִקְבֵי הַמֶּלֶךְ׃
the wine to Hananeel from and ,Corner the to ,first
.king's presses of tower the Gate

11 וְיָשְׁבוּ בָהּ וְחֵרֶם לֹא יִהְיֶה־עוֹד וְיָשְׁבָה יְרוּשָׁלִַם לָבֶטַח׃
.safely Jerusalem shall but ,again shall not a And in they And
dwell be curse .it dwell shall

12 וְזֹאת ׀ תִּהְיֶה הַמַּגֵּפָה אֲשֶׁר יִגֹּף יְהוָה אֶת־כָּל־
all Jehovah will (with) the be shall And
strike which plague this

הָעַמִּים אֲשֶׁר צָבְאוּ עַל־יְרוּשָׁלִָם הָמֵק ׀ בְּשָׂרוֹ וְהוּא עֹמֵד
is while his will He .Jerusalem against have who the
standing he flesh rot make fought peoples

עַל־רַגְלָיו וְעֵינָיו תִּמַּקְנָה בְחֹרֵיהֶן וּלְשׁוֹנוֹ תִּמַּק בְּפִיהֶם׃
their in will his and their in rot will his and his on
.mouth rot tongue ;sockets eyes ,feet

13 וְהָיָה בַּיּוֹם הַהוּא תִּהְיֶה מְהוּמַת־יְהוָה רַבָּה בָּהֶם וְהֶחֱזִיקוּ
they and among great Jehovah a be shall that day in it And
seize shall ;them of panic ,be shall

14 אִישׁ יַד רֵעֵהוּ וְעָלְתָה יָדוֹ עַל־יַד רֵעֵהוּ׃ וְגַם־יְהוּדָה
Judah And his the against his will and his hand (each)
also .neighbor of hand hand up rise ,neighbor's man

תִּלָּחֵם בִּירוּשָׁלִָם וְאֻסַּף חֵיל כָּל־הַגּוֹיִם סָבִיב זָהָב וָכֶסֶף
and gold surround- the all the shall And at shall
silver ,ing nations of wealth gathered be .Jerusalem fight

15 וּבְגָדִים לָרֹב מְאֹד׃ וְכֵן תִּהְיֶה מַגֵּפַת הַסּוּס הַפֶּרֶד
the the the be shall And .very much and
,mule ,horse of plague so clothing

הַגָּמָל וְהַחֲמוֹר וְכָל־הַבְּהֵמָה אֲשֶׁר יִהְיֶה בַּמַּחֲנוֹת הָהֵמָּה
,those camps in shall which the and the and the
be cattle all ,ass ,camel

16 כַּמַּגֵּפָה הַזֹּאת׃ וְהָיָה כָּל־הַנּוֹתָר מִכָּל־הַגּוֹיִם
the from is who every- it And .this like
nations all left one ,be shall plague

הַבָּאִים עַל־יְרוּשָׁלִָם וְעָלוּ מִדֵּי שָׁנָה בְשָׁנָה לְהִשְׁתַּחֲוֹת
worship to year to year from shall Jerusalem against which
up go up came

17 לְמֶלֶךְ יְהוָה צְבָאוֹת וְלָחֹג אֶת־חַג הַסֻּכּוֹת׃ וְהָיָה אֲשֶׁר
who- it And .booths the to and ,hosts Jehovah the
ever ,be shall of feast keep of ,King

families of the earth to Jerusalem to worship the King, Jehovah of hosts, even on them shall be no rain. [18] And if the family of Egypt does not go up, nor come in, then (the rain) shall not be on them; (but) the plague with which Jehovah shall strike the nations who do not come up to keep the feast of tabernacles. [19] This shall be Egypt's offense and the offense of all nations who do not come up to keep the feast of tabernacles.

[20] In that day there shall be on the bells of the horses, HOLY TO JEHOVAH. And the pots in Jehovah's house shall be like the bowls before the altar. [21] And every pot in Jerusalem and in Judah shall be holy to Jehovah of hosts. And all those who sacrifice shall come and take of them and boil in them. And in that day there shall not be a trader in the house of Jehovah of hosts any more.

לֹא־יַעֲלֶה מֵאֵת מִשְׁפְּחוֹת הָאָרֶץ אֶל־יְרוּשָׁלִַם לְהִשְׁתַּחֲוֺת
worship to Jerusalem to the earth families the of from will up go not

18 לְמֶלֶךְ יְהוָה צְבָאוֹת וְלֹא עֲלֵיהֶם יִהְיֶה הַגָּשֶׁם׃ וְאִם־
if And .rain the be shall them on even not ,hosts of Jehovah the ,King

מִשְׁפַּחַת מִצְרַיִם לֹא־תַעֲלֶה וְלֹא בָאָה וְלֹא עֲלֵיהֶם תִּהְיֶה
be will ;(rain) them on then not does ,enter and not go does ,up not Egypt family the of

הַמַּגֵּפָה אֲשֶׁר יִגֹּף יְהוָה אֶת־הַגּוֹיִם אֲשֶׁר לֹא יַעֲלוּ לָחֹג
to keep do up not come who the nations Jehovah will strike (with) which (same) the plague

19 אֶת־חַג הַסֻּכּוֹת׃ זֹאת תִּהְיֶה חַטַּאת מִצְרַיִם וְחַטַּאת כָּל־
all the and of offense Egypt's offense be shall This .booths the of feast

20 הַגּוֹיִם אֲשֶׁר לֹא יַעֲלוּ לָחֹג אֶת־חַג הַסֻּכּוֹת׃ בַּיּוֹם הַהוּא
that day In .booths the of feast keep to do up not come who nations

יִהְיֶה עַל־מְצִלּוֹת הַסּוּס קֹדֶשׁ לַיהוָה וְהָיָה הַסִּירוֹת
pots the And be shall TO .JEHOVAH HOLY the ,horses bells the of on there be shall

21 בְּבֵית יְהוָה כַּמִּזְרָקִים לִפְנֵי הַמִּזְבֵּחַ׃ וְהָיָה כָּל־סִיר
pot every And be shall .altar the before bowls the like Jehovah the in of house

בִּירוּשָׁלִַם וּבִיהוּדָה קֹדֶשׁ לַיהוָה צְבָאוֹת וּבָאוּ כָּל־
all shall And come .hosts to of Jehovah holy in and Judah in Jerusalem

הַזֹּבְחִים וְלָקְחוּ מֵהֶם וּבִשְּׁלוּ בָהֶם וְלֹא־יִהְיֶה כְנַעֲנִי עוֹד
again trader a there be shall And not .them in boil and of them and take who those sacrifice

בְּבֵית־יְהוָה צְבָאוֹת בַּיּוֹם הַהוּא׃
.that day in hosts of Jehovah the in of house

מ ל א כ י

LIBER MALACHIAE

CAPUT. I א

CHAPTER 1

[1] The burden of the word of Jehovah to Israel by Malachi: [2] I have loved you, says Jehovah; but you say, In what way have You loved us? Was not Esau Jacob's brother? states Jehovah. Yet I loved Jacob, [3] and I have hated Esau, and have wasted his mountains and his inheritance for the jackals of the desert. [4] If Edom says, We are beaten down, but we will return and build the ruined places. Thus says Jehovah of hosts: They shall build, but I will throw down. And they shall call them the region of wickedness, and the people (with) whom Jehovah is indignant until forever. [5] And you shall see, and you shall say, Jehovah will be magnified beyond Israel's border.

[6] A son honors (his) father, and a servant his master. If then I (am) a father, where (is) My honor? and if I (am) a master, where (is) My fear? says Jehovah of hosts to you, O priests who despise My name. But you say, In what (way) have we despised Your name? [7] You are offering defiled food on My altar, and you say, In what have we defiled You? In your saying, The table of Jehovah, it (is) to be despised. [8] And if you offer the blind for sacrifice, is it not evil? And if you offer the lame and the sick, is it not evil? Bring it now to your governor. Will he accept you or lift up your

1 2 מַשָּׂא דְבַר־יְהוָה אֶל־יִשְׂרָאֵל בְּיַד מַלְאָכִי׃ אָהַבְתִּי אֶתְכֶם

,you have I :Malachi the by Israel to Jehovah the bur- The
loved of hand of word of den

אָמַר יְהוָה וַאֲמַרְתֶּם בַּמָּה אֲהַבְתָּנוּ הֲלוֹא־אָח עֵשָׂו

Esau brother (Was) You have what In you but ;Jehovah says
not ?us loved (way) ,say

3 לְיַעֲקֹב נְאֻם־יְהוָה וָאֹהַב אֶת־יַעֲקֹב׃ וְאֶת־עֵשָׂו שָׂנֵאתִי

have I Esau and ,Jacob I Yet .Jehovah states to
,hated loved ?Jacob

4 וָאָשִׂים אֶת־הָרָיו שְׁמָמָה וְאֶת־נַחֲלָתוֹ לְתַנּוֹת מִדְבָּר׃ כִּי־

If wil- the the for his and deso- a his have and
.derness of jackals inheritance lation mountains made

תֹאמַר אֱדוֹם רֻשַּׁשְׁנוּ וְנָשׁוּב וְנִבְנֶה חֳרָבוֹת כֹּה אָמַר יְהוָה

Jehovah says thus ruined the and we but are We ,Edom says
;places build return will ,down beaten

צְבָאוֹת הֵמָּה יִבְנוּ וַאֲנִי אֶהֱרוֹס וְקָרְאוּ לָהֶם גְּבוּל רִשְׁעָה

wicked- the them they And tear will but shall They :hosts
,ness of region call shall .down I ,build

5 וְהָעָם אֲשֶׁר־זָעַם יְהוָה עַד־עוֹלָם׃ וְעֵינֵיכֶם תִּרְאֶינָה וְאַתֶּם

and ,see shall your And .forever till Jehovah is (with) the and
you eyes indignant whom people

6 תֹּאמְרוּ יִגְדַּל יְהוָה מֵעַל לִגְבוּל יִשְׂרָאֵל׃ בֵּן יְכַבֵּד אָב

(his) honors A .Israel the to above Jehovah be May shall
father son of border magnified ,say

וְעֶבֶד אֲדֹנָיו וְאִם־אָב אָנִי אַיֵּה כְבוֹדִי וְאִם־אֲדוֹנִים אָנִי

I master a And My where I a now his a and
,(am) if ?honor (is) ,(am) father if ;master servant

אַיֵּה מוֹרָאִי אָמַר ׀ יְהוָה צְבָאוֹת לָכֶם הַכֹּהֲנִים בּוֹזֵי שְׁמִי

My de- ,priests O ,you to hosts Jehovah says My where
?name of spisers of ?fear (is)

7 וַאֲמַרְתֶּם בַּמֶּה בָזִינוּ אֶת־שְׁמֶךָ׃ מַגִּישִׁים עַל־מִזְבְּחִי לֶחֶם

food My on (are You) Your we have what In you But
altar presenting ?name despised (way) ,say

מְגֹאָל וַאֲמַרְתֶּם בַּמֶּה גֵאַלְנוּךָ בֶּאֱמָרְכֶם שֻׁלְחַן יְהוָה

Jehovah The your In we have what In you and ,defiled
of table ,saying ?You defiled (way) ,say

8 נִבְזֶה הוּא׃ וְכִי־תַגִּשׁוּן עִוֵּר לִזְבֹּחַ אֵין רָע וְכִי תַגִּישׁוּ

you And ?evil it is for the you And .(is) it despic-
present if not ,sacrifice blind present if able

פִּסֵּחַ וְחֹלֶה אֵין רָע הַקְרִיבֵהוּ נָא לְפֶחָתֶךָ הֲיִרְצְךָ אוֹ

or he Will your to now it Bring ?evil it is the and the
you accept .governor not ,sick lame

face, says Jehovah of hosts?
[9] And now entreat the face of God, that He will be gracious to us. This has been by your hands; will He lift up your faces, says Jehovah of hosts? [10] Who (is) even among you that will shut the doors, and you not kindle (fire on) My altar in vain! No delight is to Me in you, says Jehovah of hosts. I will not be pleased with a food offering from you. [11] For from the east to the west, My name (shall be) great among the nations, and everywhere incense shall be offered to My name; and a pure food offering. For My name (shall be) great among the nations, says Jehovah of hosts.

[12] But you are profaning it when you say, The table of the Lord, it (is) polluted; and its fruit, His food, is to be despised. [13] You also have said, Behold, what weariness! And you have puffed at it, says Jehovah of hosts. And you bring plunder, and the lame, and the sick; and you bring the meal offering. Should I accept it from your hand, says Jehovah? [14] But cursed (be) a deceiver, and there is in his flock a male, yet he vows (it), but is sacrificing to the Lord a blemished thing. For I (am) a great king, says Jehovah of hosts; and My name (is) feared among the nations!

9 הִשָּׂא פָנֶיךָ אָמַר יְהוָה צְבָאוֹת׃ וְעַתָּה חַלּוּ־נָא פְנֵי־אֵל
God the now Entreat And .hosts Jehovah says your he will
of face ,now of ?face up lift

וִיחָנֵנוּ מִיֶּדְכֶם הָיְתָה זֹּאת הֲיִשָּׂא מִכֶּם פָּנִים אָמַר יְהוָה
Jehovah says ?faces from He will ;this has your By He that
of you up lift been hands .us favor

10 צְבָאוֹת׃ מִי גַם־בָּכֶם וְיִסְגֹּר דְּלָתַיִם וְלֹא־תָאִירוּ מִזְבְּחִי
My (on) you and ,doors the and among even Who .hosts
altar (fire) kindle not shut would you (is)

חִנָּם אֵין־לִי חֵפֶץ בָּכֶם אָמַר יְהוָה צְבָאוֹת וּמִנְחָה לֹא־
not food a And .hosts Jehovah says ,you in delight to Nor in
offering of Me is .vain

11 אֶרְצֶה מִיֶּדְכֶם׃ כִּי מִמִּזְרַח־שֶׁמֶשׁ וְעַד־מְבוֹאוֹ גָּדוֹל
great going its and sun the the from For your from will I
in of rising .hand accept

שְׁמִי בַּגּוֹיִם וּבְכָל־מָקוֹם מֻקְטָר מֻגָּשׁ לִשְׁמִי וּמִנְחָה
food and My to be shall incense place in and among name My
offering ,name presented every ,nations the (be shall)

12 טְהוֹרָה כִּי־גָדוֹל שְׁמִי בַּגּוֹיִם אָמַר יְהוָה צְבָאוֹת׃ וְאַתֶּם
But .hosts Jehovah says the among My great for ;pure a
you of ,nations name (be shall)

מְחַלְּלִים אוֹתוֹ בֶּאֱמָרְכֶם שֻׁלְחַן אֲדֹנָי מְגֹאָל הוּא וְנִיבוֹ
its and ,(is) defiled the The you when ,it (are)
fruit Lord of table ,say profaning

13 נִבְזֶה אָכְלוֹ׃ וַאֲמַרְתֶּם הִנֵּה מַתְּלָאָה וְהִפַּחְתֶּם אוֹתוֹ
,it have you And what ,Behold you And His de- is
at sniffed !weariness ,said have .food spicable

אָמַר יְהוָה צְבָאוֹת וַהֲבֵאתֶם גָּזוּל וְאֶת־הַפִּסֵּחַ וְאֶת־
and the and the you And .hosts Jehovah says
lame stolen bring of

הַחוֹלֶה וַהֲבֵאתֶם אֶת־הַמִּנְחָה הַאֶרְצֶה אוֹתָהּ מִיֶּדְכֶם
your from it I Should meal the you and the
?hand accept .offering bring ,sick

14 אָמַר יְהוָה׃ וְאָרוּר נוֹכֵל וְיֵשׁ בְּעֶדְרוֹ זָכָר וְנֹדֵר וְזֹבֵחַ
sac- but he and a his in and a (be) But .Jehovah says
rifices ,(it) vows ,male flock is there ,deceiver cursed

מָשְׁחָת לַאדֹנָי כִּי מֶלֶךְ גָּדוֹל אָנִי אָמַר יְהוָה צְבָאוֹת
;hosts Jehovah says I great king a For the to blem- a
of ,(am) .Lord (one) ished

וּשְׁמִי נוֹרָא בַגּוֹיִם׃
the among (is) My and
.nations feared name

CAP. II ב

CHAPTER 2

CHAPTER 2

[1] And now, O priests, this command (is) to you. [2] If you will not hear, and if you will not set on (your) heart to give glory to My name, says Jehovah of

1-2 וְעַתָּה אֲלֵיכֶם הַמִּצְוָה הַזֹּאת הַכֹּהֲנִים׃ אִם־לֹא תִשְׁמְעוּ
will you not If .priests O ,this command you to And
,hear (is) now

וְאִם־לֹא תָשִׂימוּ עַל־לֵב לָתֵת כָּבוֹד לִשְׁמִי אָמַר יְהוָה
Jehovah says My to glory give to heart upon will you not and
of ,name set if

hosts, then I will send the curse on you, and I will curse your blessings. And indeed, I have cursed it, because you (are) not setting (it) on (your) heart. [3] Behold, I (am) rebuking your seed and I will spread dung on your faces, the dung of your solemn feasts; and one will bear you to it. [4] And you shall know that I have sent this commandment to you to be My covenant with Levi, says Jehovah of hosts. [5] My covenant with him was life and peace, and I gave them to him (for) fear, and he did fear Me and from before My name he is put in awe. [6] He spoke the true law, and no iniquity was found in his lips. In peace and in uprightness He walked with Me, and he turned many from iniquity. [7] For the priest's lips shall keep knowledge, and they should seek the law at his mouth; for he (is) the messenger of Jehovah of hosts. [8] But you have turned out of the way; you have caused many to stumble at the law. You have corrupted the covenant of Levi, says Jehovah of hosts. [9] So I have also made you despised and low to all the people, just as you have not kept My ways but have lifted up faces in the law. [10] Is there not one father to us all? (Has) not one God created us? Why do we act deceitfully, each one against his brother, to profane the covenant of our fathers?

[11] Judah has dealt treacherously, and a hateful thing has been committed in Israel and in Jerusalem; for Judah has profaned the holy (place) of Jehovah which He loves, and has married the daughter of a strange god. [12] Jehovah will cut off the man who

צבאות ושלחתי בכם את־המארה וארותי את־ברכותיכם
your I and the you on I then ,hosts
;blessings curse will ,curse send will

3 וגם ארותיה כי אינכם שמים על־לב: הנני גער לכם
you to (am) Behold .heart on (are) you because have I and
rebuking I (your) setting not ,it cursed indeed

את־הזרע וזריתי פרש על־פניכם פרש חגיכם ונשא
one and your the your on dung I and ,seed the
lift will ,feasts of dung ,faces spread will

4 אתכם אליו: וידעתם כי שלחתי אליכם את המצוה
command you to have I that you And .it to you
sent know shall

5 הזאת להיות בריתי את־לוי אמר יהוה צבאות: בריתי ׀
My .hosts Jehovah says ,Levi with My be to this
covenant of covenant

היתה אתו החיים והשלום ואתנם־לו מורא וייראני
he and (for) to I and ,peace and life with was
,Me feared ;fear him them gave him

6 ומפני שמי נחת הוא: תורת אמת היתה בפיהו ועולה
and his in was truth The .he put is My from and
iniquity ,mouth of law awe in name before

לא־נמצא בשפתיו בשלום ובמישור הלך אתי ורבים
many and with he in and peace In his on was not
,Me walked uprightness .lips found

7 השיב מעון: כי־שפתי כהן ישמרו־דעת ותורה יבקשו
should they the and know- should the lips the For from he
seek law ,ledge guard priest of .iniquity turned

8 מפיהו כי מלאך יהוה־צבאות הוא: ואתם סרתם מן־
from have you But .(is) he hosts Jehovah the for his from
turned of of messenger ;mouth

הדרך הכשלתם רבים בתורה שחתם ברית הלוי אמר
says !Levi cove- the have you the at many made have you the
of nant corrupted ;law stumble ;way

9 יהוה צבאות: וגם־אני נתתי אתכם נבזים ושפלים לכל־
all to and despised you have I And .hosts Jehovah
abased made also of

העם כפי אשר אינכם שמרים את־דרכי ונשאים פנים
faces (are) but My (are) not you because the
up lifting ,ways keeping people

10 בתורה: הלוא אב אחד לכלנו הלוא אל אחד בראנו
created one God (Has) us to one father not Is the in
?us not ?all there .law

11 מדוע נבגד איש באחיו לחלל ברית אבתינו: בגדה
acted has our cove- the to his with (each) act we do Why
deceitfully ?fathers of nant profane ,brother man deceitfully

יהודה ותועבה נעשתה בישראל ובירושלם כי ׀ חלל
has for in and Israel in been has an and ,Judah
profaned ;Jerusalem done abomination

12 יהודה קדש יהוה אשר אהב ובעל בת־אל נכר: יכרת
cut May .foreign a daughter and He which Jehovah the Judah
off god's married ,loves of holy,

does it, stirring and answering out of the tents of Jacob, and offering a food offering to Jehovah of hosts. [13] And this (is) a second (thing) you have done; covering the altar of Jehovah (with) tears, (with) weeping, and (with) crying out, for not is any facing toward the food offering still, or taking (it with) good will from your hand.

[14] Yet you say, On what (cause)? Because Jehovah has been witness between you and the wife of your youth, against whom you have dealt deceitfully, and she (is) your companion and your covenant wife. [15] And did He not make one? And He had the vestige of the Spirit? And what (of) the one? He was seeking a seed of God. So guard your spirit, and do not deal deceitfully against the wife of your youth. [16] Jehovah, the God of Israel, says, He hates sending away, and he (who) has covered his garments (with) violence, says Jehovah of hosts. Because of this, guard your spirit, and do not act deceitfully.

[17] You have wearied Jehovah with your words. Yet you say, In what have we wearied Him? When you say, Every evildoer (is) good in the eyes of Jehovah, and He delights in them; or, Where (is) the God of justice?

יְהוָה לָאִישׁ אֲשֶׁר יַעֲשֶׂנָּה עֵר וְעֹנֶה מֵאָהֳלֵי יַעֲקֹב וּמַגִּישׁ
pre- or Jacob the from an- and stirring —it does who the Jehovah
senting of tents —swering man

13 מִנְחָה לַיהוָה צְבָאוֹת׃ וְזֹאת שֵׁנִית תַּעֲשׂוּ כַּסּוֹת דִּמְעָה
(with) (you) :do you a this And .hosts to food a
tears cover second (is) of Jehovah offering

אֶת־מִזְבַּח יְהוָה בְּכִי וַאֲנָקָה מֵאֵין עוֹד פְּנוֹת אֶל־הַמִּנְחָה
food the toward (any) yet from and (with) ,Jehovah the
offering facing being not ;groaning weeping of altar

14 וְלָקַחַת רָצוֹן מִיֶּדְכֶם׃ וַאֲמַרְתֶּם עַל־מָה עַל כִּי־יְהוָה
Jehovah On what On you Yet your from (with) and
that ?(cause) ,say .hand delight taking

הֵעִיד בֵּינְךָ וּבֵין ׀ אֵשֶׁת נְעוּרֶיךָ אֲשֶׁר אַתָּה בָּגַדְתָּה בָּהּ
;against dealt have you whom your the and between been has
deceitfully ,youth of wife you witness

15 וְהִיא חֲבֶרְתְּךָ וְאֵשֶׁת בְּרִיתֶךָ׃ וְלֹא־אֶחָד עָשָׂה וּשְׁאָר רוּחַ
the a And He did one But your the and com- your and
Spirit of vestige ?make not .covenant of wife panion (is) she

לוֹ וּמָה הָאֶחָד מְבַקֵּשׁ זֶרַע אֱלֹהִים וְנִשְׁמַרְתֶּם בְּרוּחֲכֶם
,spirit your guard And .God seed a was He ?one the And to (is)
of seeking (of) what .him

16 וּבְאֵשֶׁת נְעוּרֶיךָ אַל־יִבְגֹּד׃ כִּי־שָׂנֵא שַׁלַּח אָמַר יְהוָה
,Jehovah says sending hates He deal not your with and
,away deceitfully youth of wife the

אֱלֹהֵי יִשְׂרָאֵל וְכִסָּה חָמָס עַל־לְבוּשׁוֹ אָמַר יְהוָה צְבָאוֹת
.hosts Jehovah says his on (with) to and ,Israel the
of ,garment violence cover of God

17 וְנִשְׁמַרְתֶּם בְּרוּחֲכֶם וְלֹא תִבְגֹּדוּ׃ הוֹגַעְתֶּם יְהוָה
Jehovah have You act do and your guard And
wearied .deceitfully not spirit

בְּדִבְרֵיכֶם וַאֲמַרְתֶּם בַּמָּה הוֹגַעְנוּ בֶּאֱמָרְכֶם כָּל־עֹשֵׂה
doer Every you When we have what In you Yet your with
of ,say ?Him wearied (way) ,say .words

רָע טוֹב ׀ בְּעֵינֵי יְהוָה וּבָהֶם הוּא חָפֵץ אוֹ אַיֵּה אֱלֹהֵי
the Where ,or ;delights He in and ,Jehovah the in (is) evil
of God (is) them of eyes good

הַמִּשְׁפָּט׃
?justice

CAP. III ג

CHAPTER 3

[1] Behold, I (am) sending My messenger, and he shall prepare the way before Me. And the Lord, whom you seek, shall suddenly come to His temple, even the Angel of the Covenant, in whom you delight. Behold, He comes, says Jehovah of hosts. [2] But who can endure the day of

CHAPTER 3

1 הִנְנִי שֹׁלֵחַ מַלְאָכִי וּפִנָּה־דֶרֶךְ לְפָנָי וּפִתְאֹם יָבוֹא אֶל־
to shall And before the he and mes- My (am) ,Behold
come suddenly .Me way clear will ,senger sending I

הֵיכָלוֹ הָאָדוֹן ׀ אֲשֶׁר־אַתֶּם מְבַקְשִׁים וּמַלְאַךְ הַבְּרִית אֲשֶׁר
(in) the the even (are) you whom the His
whom ,covenant of Angel ,seeking Lord ,temple

2 אַתֶּם חֲפֵצִים הִנֵּה־בָא אָמַר יְהוָה צְבָאוֹת׃ וּמִי מְכַלְכֵּל
can But .hosts Jehovah says He ,Behold (are) you
endure who of ,comes .delighting

His coming? And who will stand when He appears? For He (is) like a refiner's fire, and like fullers' soap. [3] And He shall sit as a refiner and purifier of silver; and He shall purify the sons of Levi, and purge them as gold and as silver, that they may be offerers to Jehovah of a food offering in righteousness. [4] Then the food offering of Judah and Jerusalem shall be pleasing to Jehovah, as (in) the days of old and as (in) former years. [5] And I will come near to you for judgment; and I will be a swift witness against the sorcerers, and against the adulterers, and against false swearers, and against those who extort from a worker (his) wages, (and) the widow and the orphan, and those who turn the stranger aside; and who do not fear Me, says Jehovah of hosts. [6] For I (am) Jehovah, (I) change not; therefore you sons of Jacob are not destroyed.

[7] From the days of your fathers, you have turned aside from My statutes and have not observed (them). Return to Me, and I will return to you, says Jehovah of hosts. But you say, In what (way) shall we return?

[8] Will a man rob God? Yet you have robbed Me. But you say, In what have we robbed You? In the tithe and the offering! [9] You are cursed with a curse; for you (are) robbing Me, the nation all of it. [10] Bring all the tithe into the storehouse, so that there may be food in My house. And test Me now with this, says Jehovah of hosts, whether I will not open the windows of the heavens for you and pour out for you a blessing, until there is no sufficiency. [11] And I will rebuke the devourer for you, and he shall not destroy against you the fruit of your

אֶת־יוֹם בּוֹאוֹ וּמִי הָעֹמֵד בְּהֵרָאוֹתוֹ כִּי־הוּא כְּאֵשׁ מְצָרֵף
a like He For His at (be will) And His the
refiner's fire (is) ?appearing standing who ?coming of day

3 וּכְבֹרִית מְכַבְּסִים׃ וְיָשַׁב מְצָרֵף וּמְטַהֵר כֶּסֶף וְטִהַר אֶת־
He and ;silver pur- and a (as) He And .fuller's like and
purify shall of ifier refiner sit shall soap

בְּנֵי־לֵוִי וְזִקַּק אֹתָם כַּזָּהָב וְכַכָּסֶף וְהָיוּ לַיהוָה מַגִּישֵׁי מִנְחָה
offerings presenters to they that like and like them and ,Levi the
of Jehovah be may ,silver gold purge of sons

4 בִּצְדָקָה׃ וְעָרְבָה לַיהוָה מִנְחַת יְהוּדָה וִירוּשָׁלִָם כִּימֵי
(in) as and Judah food the to shall Then righ- in
of days ,Jerusalem of offering Jehovah pleasing be .teousness

5 עוֹלָם וּכְשָׁנִים קַדְמֹנִיֹּת׃ וְקָרַבְתִּי אֲלֵיכֶם לַמִּשְׁפָּט וְהָיִיתִי ׀
I and for you to will I And .former (in) as and old
be will ;judgment near draw years

עֵד מְמַהֵר בַּמְכַשְּׁפִים וּבַמְנָאֲפִים וּבַנִּשְׁבָּעִים לַשָּׁקֶר
a to against and against and the against swift a
,lie swearing those adulterers the sorcerers witness

וּבְעֹשְׁקֵי שְׂכַר־שָׂכִיר אַלְמָנָה וְיָתוֹם וּמַטֵּי־גֵר וְלֹא יְרֵאוּנִי
fearing and turning and the and the hired the hire against and
,Me not ,alien the away ,orphan widow ,laborer's of extorters

6 אָמַר יְהוָה צְבָאוֹת׃ כִּי אֲנִי יְהוָה לֹא שָׁנִיתִי וְאַתֶּם בְּנֵי־
sons and do not Jehovah I For .hosts Jehovah says
of you ;change of

7 יַעֲקֹב לֹא כְלִיתֶם׃ לְמִימֵי אֲבֹתֵיכֶם סַרְתֶּם מֵחֻקַּי וְלֹא
and My from have you your the From come have not Jacob
not statutes turned ,fathers of days .end an to

שְׁמַרְתֶּם שׁוּבוּ אֵלַי וְאָשׁוּבָה אֲלֵיכֶם אָמַר יְהוָה צְבָאוֹת
.hosts Jehovah says ,you to I and to Return kept have
of return will ,Me .(them)

8 וַאֲמַרְתֶּם בַּמֶּה נָשׁוּב׃ הֲיִקְבַּע אָדָם אֱלֹהִים כִּי אַתֶּם
you Yet ?God man a rob Will we shall what In you But
?return (way) ,say

קֹבְעִים אֹתִי וַאֲמַרְתֶּם בַּמֶּה קְבַעֲנוּךָ הַמַּעֲשֵׂר וְהַתְּרוּמָה׃
the and the (In) we have what In you But .Me (are)
!offering tithe ?You robbed (way) ,say robbing

9
10 בַּמְּאֵרָה אַתֶּם נֵאָרִים וְאֹתִי אַתֶּם קֹבְעִים הַגּוֹי כֻּלּוֹ׃ הָבִיאוּ
Bring of all the (are) you for being you a With
.it ,nation robbing Me ;cursed (are) curse

אֶת־כָּל־הַמַּעֲשֵׂר אֶל־בֵּית הָאוֹצָר וִיהִי טֶרֶף בְּבֵיתִי וּבְחָנוּנִי
And My in food that stored the into the all
Me test .house be may goods of house tithe

נָא בָּזֹאת אָמַר יְהוָה צְבָאוֹת אִם־לֹא אֶפְתַּח לָכֶם אֵת
for will I not if ,hosts Jehovah says in now
you open of ,this

11 אֲרֻבּוֹת הַשָּׁמַיִם וַהֲרִיקֹתִי לָכֶם בְּרָכָה עַד־בְּלִי־דָי׃ וְגָעַרְתִּי
will I And suffi- not until a for pour and the win- the
rebuke .ciency (is) blessing you out heavens of dows

לָכֶם בָּאֹכֵל וְלֹא־יַשְׁחִת לָכֶם אֶת־פְּרִי הָאֲדָמָה וְלֹא־
and the the against shall he and the for
not ,ground of fruit you destroy not devourer you

ground, nor shall your vine miscarry against you in the field, says Jehovah of hosts. [12] And all nations shall call you blessed; for you shall be a delightful land, says Jehovah of hosts.

[13] Your words have been strong against Me, says Jehovah. Yet you say, What have we spoken together against You? [14] You have said, (It is) vain to serve God. And, What profit (is it) that we have kept His charge, and that we have walked as mourners before Jehovah of hosts? [15] And now we call the arrogant happy. Not only those who work wickedness are exalted, also they test God, and escape.

[16] Then those who feared Jehovah spoke together, each one to his neighbor. And Jehovah listened and heard; and a book of remembrance was written before Him for those who feared Jehovah, and those esteeming His name. [17] And they shall be Mine, says Jehovah of hosts, for the day that I will make up My treasure. And I will spare them as a man spares his own son who serves him. [18] Then you shall again see the (difference) between the righteous and the wicked, between him who serves God and him who does not serve Him.

CHAPTER 4

[1] For, behold, the day is coming, burning like an oven; and all the proud, and every wicked doer, shall be stubble. And the coming day will set them ablaze, says Jehovah of hosts, which will not leave to them root or branches.

[2] But to you who fear My name, the Sun of righteousness shall rise, and healing on His wings. And you shall go forth and frisk like calves of the stall. [3] And you shall trample the wicked, for they shall be ashes under the soles of

12 תְשַׁכֵּל לָכֶם הַגֶּפֶן בַּשָּׂדֶה אָמַר יְהוָה צְבָאוֹת׃ וְאִשְּׁרוּ
shall And .hosts Jehovah says the in the against will
blessed call of ,field vine you miscarry

אֶתְכֶם כָּל־הַגּוֹיִם כִּי־תִהְיוּ אַתֶּם אֶרֶץ חֵפֶץ אָמַר יְהוָה
Jehovah says ,delight a you be shall for the all you
of of land ;nations

13 צְבָאוֹת׃ חָזְקוּ עָלַי דִּבְרֵיכֶם אָמַר יְהוָה וַאֲמַרְתֶּם
you Yet .Jehovah says your against been Have .hosts
,say ,words Me strong

14 מַה־נִּדְבַּרְנוּ עָלֶיךָ׃ אֲמַרְתֶּם שָׁוְא עֲבֹד אֱלֹהִים וּמַה־
and ,God serve To (is) have You against we have What
what vanity ,said ?You together spoken

בֶּצַע כִּי שָׁמַרְנוּ מִשְׁמַרְתּוֹ וְכִי הָלַכְנוּ קְדֹרַנִּית מִפְּנֵי יְהוָה
Jehovah before as have we and His have we that unjust
of mourners walked that ,charge kept profit

15 צְבָאוֹת׃ וְעַתָּה אֲנַחְנוּ מְאַשְּׁרִים זֵדִים גַּם־נִבְנוּ עֹשֵׂי
doers are Not the calling (are) we And ?hosts
of up built only arrogant blessed now

16 רִשְׁעָה גַּם בָּחֲנוּ אֱלֹהִים וַיִּמָּלֵטוּ׃ אָז נִדְבְּרוּ יִרְאֵי יְהוָה
Jehovah the spoke Then and God they also wicked-
of fearers together .escape test ,ness

אִישׁ אֶל־רֵעֵהוּ וַיַּקְשֵׁב יְהוָה וַיִּשְׁמָע וַיִּכָּתֵב סֵפֶר זִכָּרוֹן
remem- book a was and and Jehovah gave and his to (each)
brance of written ;heard attention ,neighbor man

17 לְפָנָיו לְיִרְאֵי יְהוָה וּלְחֹשְׁבֵי שְׁמוֹ׃ וְהָיוּ לִי אָמַר יְהוָה
Jehovah says to they And His those for and Jehovah the for before
of ,Me be shall .name esteeming of fearers Him

צְבָאוֹת לַיּוֹם אֲשֶׁר אֲנִי עֹשֶׂה סְגֻלָּה וְחָמַלְתִּי עֲלֵיהֶם
them on will I and (My) make will I that the for ,hosts
pity have ;treasure up day

18 כַּאֲשֶׁר יַחְמֹל אִישׁ עַל־בְּנוֹ הָעֹבֵד אֹתוֹ׃ וְשַׁבְתֶּם וּרְאִיתֶם
see and you And .him serving his on man a has as
return shall son pity

19 בֵּין צַדִּיק לְרָשָׁע בֵּין עֹבֵד אֱלֹהִים לַאֲשֶׁר לֹא עֲבָדוֹ׃ כִּי
For serving not him and God him be- the and the between
.Him serving tween ,wicked righteous

הִנֵּה הַיּוֹם בָּא בֹּעֵר כַּתַּנּוּר וְהָיוּ כָל־זֵדִים וְכָל־עֹשֵׂה
of doer and the all will and a like burning is the ,behold
every ,arrogant be ;fire-pot ,coming day

רִשְׁעָה קַשׁ וְלִהַט אֹתָם הַיּוֹם הַבָּא אָמַר יְהוָה צְבָאוֹת
,hosts Jehovah says ,coming the them will And .chaff wicked-
of day ablaze set ness

20 אֲשֶׁר לֹא־יַעֲזֹב לָהֶם שֹׁרֶשׁ וְעָנָף׃ וְזָרְחָה לָכֶם יִרְאֵי שְׁמִי
My fearing for shall And or root to will not which
name you rise .branches them leave

שֶׁמֶשׁ צְדָקָה וּמַרְפֵּא בִּכְנָפֶיהָ וִיצָאתֶם וּפִשְׁתֶּם כְּעֶגְלֵי
like frisk and you And His on and righteousness the
of calves out go shall .wings healing of Sun

21 מַרְבֵּק׃ וְעַסּוֹתֶם רְשָׁעִים כִּי־יִהְיוּ אֵפֶר תַּחַת כַּפּוֹת
the under ashes they for the you And .stall
of soles be shall ,wicked trample shall

your feet in the day which I (am) preparing, says Jehovah of hosts.

[4] Remember the law of My servant Moses, which I commanded him in Horeb for all Israel, the statutes and judgments.

[5] Behold, I (am) sending you Elijah the prophet before the coming of the great and dreadful day of Jehovah. [6] And he shall turn the heart of the fathers to the sons, and the heart of the sons to their fathers, lest I come and strike the earth (with) utter destruction.

---

22 רַגְלֵיכֶם בַּיּוֹם אֲשֶׁר אֲנִי עֹשֶׂה אָמַר יְהוָה צְבָאוֹת׃ זִכְרוּ

Remember .hosts Jehovah says (am) I which the in feet your
of ,preparing day

23 תּוֹרַת מֹשֶׁה עַבְדִּי אֲשֶׁר צִוִּיתִי אוֹתוֹ בְחֹרֵב עַל־כָּל־יִשְׂרָאֵל

,Israel all for in him I which My Moses the
Horeb commanded ,servant of Law

24 חֻקִּים וּמִשְׁפָּטִים׃ הִנֵּה אָנֹכִי שֹׁלֵחַ לָכֶם אֵת אֵלִיָּה הַנָּבִיא

the Elijah to (am) I ,Behold the and the
prophet you sending .judgments statutes

לִפְנֵי בּוֹא יוֹם יְהוָה הַגָּדוֹל וְהַנּוֹרָא׃ וְהֵשִׁיב לֵב־אָבוֹת

of heart the he And the and the Jehovah day the before
fathers the turn shall .fearful great of of coming

עַל־בָּנִים וְלֵב בָּנִים עַל־אֲבוֹתָם פֶּן־אָבוֹא וְהִכֵּיתִי אֶת־

strike and I lest their to the the and the to
come ,fathers sons of heart ,sons

הָאָרֶץ חֵרֶם׃ ע״כ

utter (with) the
.destruction land